The
Green Bible

N R S V
New Revised Standard Version

HarperOne
An Imprint of HarperCollinsPublishers

Canticle of the Creatures

Saint Francis of Assisi

Most High, all-powerful, good Lord,
    Yours are the praises, the glory, and the honor, and all blessing,
To You alone, Most High, do they belong,
    and no human is worthy to mention Your name.
Praised be You, my Lord, with all Your creatures,
    especially Sir Brother Sun,
    Who is the day and through whom You give us light.
And he is beautiful and radiant with great splendor;
    and bears a likeness of You, Most High One.
Praised be You, my Lord, through Sister Moon and the stars,
    in heaven You formed them clear and precious and beautiful.
Praised be You, my Lord, through Brother Wind,
    and through the air, cloudy and serene, and every kind of weather,
    through whom You give sustenance to Your creatures.
Praised be You, my Lord through Sister Water,
    who is very useful and humble and precious and chaste.
Praised be You, my Lord, through Brother Fire,
    through whom You light the night,
    and he is beautiful and playful and robust and strong.
Praised be You, my Lord, through our Sister Mother Earth,
    who sustains and governs us,
    and who produces various fruit with colored flowers and herbs.

Praised be You, my Lord, through those who give pardon for Your love,
    and bear infirmity and tribulation.
    Blessed are those who endure in peace
for by You, Most High, shall they be crowned.

Praised be You, my Lord, through our Sister Bodily Death,
    From whom no one living can escape.
    Woe to those who die in mortal sin.
    Blessed are those whom death will find in Your most holy will,
for the second death shall do them no harm.

Praise and bless my Lord and give Him thanks
    and serve Him with great humility.

Texts from *Francis of Assisi: Early Documents,* Vol. 1, *The Saint;* Vol. 2, *The Founder;* Vol. 3, *The Prophet.*
Used with permission. Copyright 1999, 2000, 2001, Franciscan Institute of St. Bonaventure, New York.
Published by New City Press, 202 Cardinal Rd., Hyde Park, NY 12538 (www.newcitypress.com).

The Clearing Rests in Song and Shade

Wendell Berry

The clearing rests in song and shade.
It is a creature made
By old light held in soil and leaf,
By human joy and grief,
By human work,
Fidelity of sight and stroke,
By rain, by water on
The parent stone.

We join our work to Heaven's gift,
Our hope to what is left,
That field and woods at last agree
In an economy
Of widest worth.
High Heaven's Kingdom come on earth.
Imagine Paradise.
O dust, arise!

Contents

Contents

Abbreviations

The following abbreviations are used for the books of the Bible:

THE OLD TESTAMENT

Genesis	Gen	2 Chronicles	2 Chr	Daniel	Dan
Exodus	Ex	Ezra	Ezra	Hosea	Hos
Leviticus	Lev	Nehemiah	Neh	Joel	Joel
Numbers	Num	Esther	Esth	Amos	Am
Deuteronomy	Deut	Job	Job	Obadiah	Ob
Joshua	Josh	Psalms	Ps	Jonah	Jon
Judges	Judg	Proverbs	Prov	Micah	Mic
Ruth	Ruth	Ecclesiastes	Eccl	Nahum	Nah
1 Samuel	1 Sam	Song of Solomon	Song	Habakkuk	Hab
2 Samuel	2 Sam	Isaiah	Isa	Zephaniah	Zeph
1 Kings	1 Kings	Jeremiah	Jer	Haggai	Hag
2 Kings	2 Kings	Lamentations	Lam	Zechariah	Zech
1 Chronicles	1 Chr	Ezekiel	Ezek	Malachi	Mal

THE NEW TESTAMENT

Matthew	Mt	Ephesians	Eph	Hebrews	Heb
Mark	Mk	Philippians	Phil	James	Jas
Luke	Lk	Colossians	Col	1 Peter	1 Pet
John	Jn	1 Thessalonians	1 Thess	2 Peter	2 Pet
Acts of the Apostles	Acts	2 Thessalonians	2 Thess	1 John	1 Jn
Romans	Rom	1 Timothy	1 Tim	2 John	2 Jn
1 Corinthians	1 Cor	2 Timothy	2 Tim	3 John	3 Jn
2 Corinthians	2 Cor	Titus	Titus	Jude	Jude
Galatians	Gal	Philemon	Philem	Revelation	Rev

In the notes to the books of the Old Testament, the following abbreviations are used:

Ant. ....*Josephus, Antiquities of the Jews*

Aram ....Aramaic

Ch, chs...Chapter, chapters

Cn............................Correction; made where the text has suffered in transmission and the versions provide no satisfactory restoration but where the Standard Bible Committee agrees with the judgment of competent scholars as to the most probable reconstruction of the original text.

Gk ....Septuagint, Greek version of the Old Testament

Heb ....Hebrew of the consonantal Masoretic Text of the Old Testament

Josephus ....Flavius Josephus (Jewish historian, about A.D. 37 to about 95)

Macc..The book(s) of the Maccabees

Ms(s) ....Manuscript(s)

MT ....The Hebrew of the pointed Masoretic Text of the Old Testament

OL..Old Latin

Q Ms(s).............................Manuscript(s) found at Qumran by the Dead Sea

Sam ....Samaritan Hebrew text of the Old Testament

Syr ....Syriac Version of the Old Testament

Syr H.................................Syriac Version of Origen's Hexapla

Tg ....Targum

Vg.............................Vulgate, Latin Version of the Old Testament

Editors, Advisory Board, and Contributors

Project Editors
Michael G. Maudlin and Marlene Baer

Managing Editor
John R. Kohlenberger III

Production Editor
Alison Petersen

Advisory Board

Gordon Aeschliman, President, Target Earth International

Sally Bingham, Founder and President, The Regeneration Project; Chair, Episcopal Diocesan Commission for the Environment

Steven Bouma-Prediger, Professor, Hope College, author of *For the Beauty of the Earth*

Cassandra Carmichael, Program Director, National Council of Churches Eco-Justice Program

Ellen F. Davis, Professor of Bible and Practical Theology, Duke Divinity School, author of *Scripture, Culture, and Agriculture*

Carol J. Dempsey, O.P., Professor of Theology, University of Portland; Coeditor of *Earth, Wind, and Fire: Biblical and Theological Perspectives on Creation*

Calvin B. DeWitt, President, Academy of Evangelical Scientists and Ethicists; Professor, University of Wisconsin–Madison

Rich Dixon, Co-Director, A Rocha, Santa Barbara

Walter Grazer, Former Director, Environmental Justice Program,
United States Conference of Catholic Bishops

James Jones, Bishop of Liverpool, author of *Jesus and the Earth*

Fred Krueger, Executive Director, Religious Campaign for Forest Conservation

Daniel Misleh, Executive Director, Catholic Coalition on Climate Change

Lowell (Rusty) Pritchard, Ph.D., Editor, *Creation Care* magazine;
National Outreach Director, Evangelical Environmental Network

Tri Robinson, Pastor and Founder, Let's Tend the Garden
Environmental Stewardship Ministries, Vineyard Boise

Rosemary Radford Ruether, Emerita Professor, Graduate Theological Union,
Professor, Claremont Graduate University

J. Matthew Sleeth, M.D., Executive Director, Blessed Earth;
author of *Serve God, Save the Planet*

Paul de Vries, Ph.D., President, New York Divinity School; Founder,
Center for Applied Christian Ethics (Wheaton College)

Keith Douglass Warner, O.F.M., Religious Studies Department
Santa Clara University

Loren Wilkinson, Professor, Regent College; author of *Caring for Creation in
Your Own Backyard;* Editor, *Earthkeeping: Christian Stewardship of Creation*

Contributors

Gordon Aeschliman has served as president of Target Earth International (targetearth.org) since 1992. Aeschliman is also the founding editor of *Green Cross* magazine, a founding board member of the Evangelical Environmental Network, and coauthor of *Everybody Wants to Change the World.*

Carla Barnhill [The Green Bible Trail Guide] served as editor of the *Teen Devotional Bible* (Zondervan) and has written devotional materials for several other Bible projects. She is the author of *The Myth of the Perfect Mother* and the editor of *A Year with Dietrich Bonhoeffer.*

Ellen Bernstein (ellenbernstein.org) founded Shomrei Adamah, Keepers of the Earth, the first national Jewish environmental organization, in 1988. She is author of *The Splendor of Creation: A Biblical Ecology* and editor of *Ecology and the Jewish Spirit.* She teaches courses on the Bible as ecological literature at Hebrew College.

Wendell Berry is a conservationist, naturalist, farmer, and author of more than forty books of poetry, fiction, and essays, including *The Gift of the Good Land*. He has been honored with the Ingersoll Foundation's T. S. Eliot Award, the Aiken Taylor Award for Poetry, and the John Hay Award.

Ellen F. Davis is professor of Bible and practical theology at Duke Divinity School. She is the author of eight books, including *Scripture, Culture, and Agriculture: An Agrarian Reading of the Bible, Getting Involved with God: Rediscovering the Old Testament*, and *Who Are You, My Daughter?: Reading Ruth through Image and Text*.

Calvin B. DeWitt is professor of environmental studies at the University of Wisconsin–Madison, former president of Au Sable Institute, and president of the Academy of Evangelical Scientists and Ethicists. His books include *Earth-Wise, Caring for Creation*, and *The Environment and the Christian*.

Saint Francis of Assisi (1182–1226) shaped the spirituality of early thirteenth-century Europe as a Roman Catholic friar and founder of the Franciscans. He lived out a radical commitment to the gospel message of poverty and is known as the patron saint of those who promote environmental concern.

Pope John Paul II (1920–2005), born Karol Józef Wojtyła in Poland, took the name John Paul II upon his October 1978 election to the papacy, when he solemnly inaugurated his ministry as the 263rd successor to the apostle Peter, one of the longest in the history of the church, lasting nearly twenty-seven years.

James Jones has been Bishop of Liverpool since 1998. He writes and lectures widely on environmental and faith issues and has set up Faiths4Change, which engages local people in the transformation of their local environment. He is the author of several books, including *Jesus and the Earth,* chairman of Wycliffe Hall at the University of Oxford, and copresident of Liverpool Hope University.

Fred Krueger [The Green Subject Index] is the national coordinator for the Religious Campaign for Forest Conservation and the executive director for the Orthodox Fellowship of the Transfiguration. He previously has served as a founder and first executive director for both the North American Conference on Christianity and Ecology (NACCE) and the GREEN Cross.

Brian McLaren (brianmclaren.net) served as a pastor for twenty-four years in the Washington, D.C., area. He now works as an author, speaker, and activist.

A founding member of emergentvillage.com, he also serves as board chair for Sojourners. His books include *Everything Must Change, A Generous Orthodoxy,* and *A New Kind of Christian.*

J. Matthew Sleeth, a former emergency-medicine doctor, is a leading national speaker on faith and the environment and author of *Serve God, Save the Planet.* Sleeth serves as the executive director of Blessed Earth and is the Visiting Scholar of Creation Care at Houghton College.

Barbara Brown Taylor is an adjunct professor of Christian spirituality at Columbia Theological Seminary, a frequent guest preacher and teacher at churches and universities, an editor-at-large for *Christian Century,* and the author of *Leaving Church.*

Paul de Vries is president of New York Divinity School, a board member of the National Association of Evangelicals, lead author of four books in applied ethics, including the *Manufacturer's Manual,* on green scriptures. He founded the Center for Applied Christian Ethics (Wheaton College), the Office of Volunteer Community Service (University of Virginia), and an affordable housing network.

N.T. Wright is one of the world's top biblical scholars and the Bishop of Durham for the Church of England. He taught New Testament studies for twenty years at Cambridge, McGill, and Oxford Universities. Among his many published works are *Surprised by Hope, Simply Christian, The Challenge of Jesus,* and *The Resurrection of the Son of God.*

Foreword

Archbishop Desmond Tutu

I would not know how to be human, how to think as a human being, how to walk as a human being, how to talk or how to eat as a human being except by learning from other human beings. I learn to be human by associating with other human beings. We are thus, according to the Bible, made for family. We're made for community, we're made for togetherness, we're made for friendship. We're made to live in a delicate network of interdependence, for we are made for complementarity. I have gifts you don't have. And you have gifts that I don't have. Thus we are made different so that we can know our need of one another. And this is a fundamental law of our being.

All kinds of things go horribly wrong when we flout this law—when we don't ensure that God's children everywhere have a supply of clean water, a safe environment, a decent home, a full stomach. We could do that if we remembered that we are created to be members of one family, the human family, God's family.

We must act now and wake up to our moral obligations. The poor and vulnerable are members of God's family and are the most severely affected by droughts, high temperatures, the flooding of coastal cities, and more severe and unpredictable weather events resulting from climate change. We, who should have been responsible stewards preserving our vulnerable, fragile planet home, have been wantonly wasteful through our reckless consumerism, devouring irreplaceable natural resources. We need to be accountable to God's family. Once we start living in a way that is people-friendly to all of God's family, we will also be environment-friendly.

As you read *The Green Bible* starting in Genesis, you will see that after God created birds, fish, and animals he created humans to be his viceroys and to act "compassionately and gently" toward all forms of life. The future of our fragile, beautiful planet home is in our hands. As God's family, we are stewards of God's creation. We can be wantonly irresponsible, or we can be caring and compassionate. God says, "I have set before you life and death.... Choose life" (Deut. 30:19).

At the center of Christian faith and the Bible is the Cross. Jesus is described as our peace, the One who has broken down the wall of partition. He says of his ascent to the cross, "And I, when I am lifted up from the earth, will draw all people to myself" (John 12:32). As if in this cosmic embrace, Jesus would wish to enfold all that God has created, the entire universe, into unity. His supreme work is to reconcile us to God and to one another and, indeed, to reconcile us to all of God's creation. It is possible to have a new kind of world, a world where there will be more compassion, more gentleness, more caring, more laughter, more joy for all of God's creation, because that is God's dream. And God says, "Help me, help me, help me realize my dream."

Thank you.

Preface

Is God green? Did Jesus have anything to say about the environment? What is my role as a Christian in caring for the earth? People are starting to ask these questions as we confront a new situation unique to our history—are we killing our planet? And for Christians, the Bible is a natural place to look for answers, since it promises to be God's Word to us and for us.

What is surprising are the answers people are finding. Our role in creation's care may be a new question unique to our place in history, but the Bible turns out to be amazingly relevant. In fact, it is almost as if it were waiting for this moment to speak to us. With over a thousand references to the earth and caring for creation in the Bible, the message is clear: all in God's creation—nature, animals, humanity—are inextricably linked to one another. As God cares for all of creation, so too we cannot love one dimension without caring for the others. We are called to care for all God has made.

Developed by scholars and practitioners, *The Green Bible* encourages you to see God's vision for creation and helps you engage in the work of healing and sustaining it. *The Green Bible* includes the following features.

Green-Letter Edition

Many Bibles, called "red-letter editions," have Jesus' direct statements printed in red. We have adapted this practice to introduce the "green-letter edition." In it we highlight the rich and varied ways the books of the Bible speak directly to how we should think and act as we confront the environmental crisis facing our planet. As you read the Scriptures, you will see that passages speaking directly to the project's core mission are printed in green. Great care was taken in selecting the highlighted passages. Many more passages could easily have been chosen, but the strongest and most direct passages were selected based on how well they demonstrate:

- how God and Jesus interact with, care for, and are intimately involved with all of creation

- how all the elements of creation—land, water, air, plants, animals, humans—are interdependent

- how nature responds to God

- how we are called to care for creation

The Green Subject Index

Located in the back of the Bible, The Green Subject Index is available for use in further study. It includes listings of Bible passages that cover such topics as *animals, caring for your neighbor, land,* and *water.* Each verse listed in this subject index is highlighted in green in the biblical text.

The Green Bible Trail Guide

The Green Bible Trail Guide is a series of Bible studies on the main themes of creation care and God's role in creation. It is meant to lead you through a selection of Bible passages that touch on six green themes appearing throughout the biblical narrative. You can use this guide for your own personal study or gather a group of friends and work through these readings together.

Essays

Essays from respected conservationists and theologians highlight important themes related to God's care of creation and show how to read the Bible through a "green lens." Cumulatively, the essays lay out an excellent and broad vision for the central calling on Christian lives to care for God's creation.

Where Do You Go from Here?

A resource guide provides ideas as well as organizations to partner with as you take steps toward caring for creation.

Introduction: The Power of a Green God

J. Matthew Sleeth, M.D.

The Green Bible, which you hold in your hands, is an answer to prayer. It has been an amazing journey to arrive at this place. But before I get ahead of myself, let me first share my story and how I got here.

One February break, at the turn of the millennium, our family left the gray winter of northern New England and headed to an island off the coast of Florida for vacation. On the second day, our children, Clark and Emma, wore themselves out playing in the surf, building sand castles, and catching chameleons. The kids went to bed early, and my wife, Nancy, and I found ourselves alone.

We sat on the porch watching the sun set and the stars rise. The island on which we stayed had no cars or roads. The cares of the world were an ocean away, and the sights and sounds of nature lulled us to peace. Time slowed. The nebula in the constellation Orion shone clearly. In that relaxed moment, surrounded by palm trees murmuring in the wind, Nancy asked me a question that was to change my life forever.

"What," she queried, "is the biggest problem facing the world?"

Despite, or because of, the peaceful surroundings, I considered her question in earnest. The contenders for humankind's greatest problem are many—war, terrorism, poverty, disease, starvation, and, at the root of everything, selfishness. I considered the choices and said, "The world is dying."

My answer did not come from abstract sources. Many changes had already taken place in my life and are now readily apparent to anyone with eyes to see. The last of the majestic chestnut trees near my childhood home are now extinct. There are no chestnuts on Chestnut Lane, no elms on Elm Street, no caribou in Caribou, Maine, and no buffalo in Buffalo, New York. Multiple states have had to change their official tree, animal, or flower because of extinctions.

I grew up in the Mid-Atlantic area. In just a single generation, the fields that supported three hundred years of inhabitants have all been replanted with houses. The flocks of birds that migrated for hours over our backyard in spring and fall are gone. The snow fences that road crews put up every October are no longer needed because it rarely snows now.

These changes in the health of the planet are mirrored in humans. A few months before vacation, I had admitted three women to the hospital. All three were in their thirties, all three had breast cancer, and all three died. It is not easy to tell a man with one child on his hip and another in hand that he is on his own. There is only one response: to hug and cry with him.

Later, I wondered about the lifetime risk of breast cancer, so I went and looked it up. When I started medicine, one in nineteen women in America got breast cancer. When I saw the three women with breast cancer, the same updated medical text said it was one in nine. Now a few years later, it is one in seven. There is currently a pandemic of cancers, and the most dramatic increases have been in young people. Similarly, there have been increases in asthma, autoimmune diseases, autism, and other maladies, which many believe have direct environmental links. No one can suppose that these trends in nature and in us can continue unchanged and everything will turn out all right.

"What will you do about it?" Nancy wanted to know, that night in Florida.

I had no answer.

When we returned home, my journey began. On the surface, our life looked good. I had a job as an emergency-room physician and was chief of the medical staff at a picturesque hospital. We had the traditional nuclear family, complete with son and daughter. I drove a fast car with a teak dashboard, and when I got home, I pushed a button and one of the two garage doors opened automatically.

Yet we had no spiritual anchor, no particular religious worldview. Nancy and I grew up in different faith backgrounds. She had been raised in a conservative Jewish home. I had been raised in a Protestant home, but it "hadn't taken." Other than to see someone wed or memorialized, I'd not been inside a church in twenty-five years. I believed that good science and reasoning could resolve all of life's problems.

My search for environmental answers paralleled a new faith journey. It began to be apparent to me that there was something more. So much of what makes up the human experience cannot be measured by micrometer. How does one quantify justice, love, peace, or beauty? How does one explain evil?

So I began reading through the world's sacred texts. There are many truths to be found on the pages of the Bhagavad-Gita, the Qur'an, and the Ramayana. But I did not find the answers I sought. One day, sitting in the waiting room of the hospital, I picked up a copy of the Bible. I began reading the book of Matthew. It changed everything. I found answers.

I learned that the compelling truth of the Scriptures is not to be proven by archaeological, scientific, or theological theorems. The power of the Bible is most evident in its ability to change lives. It can transform a wealthy Italian playboy into a saint (Saint Francis of Assisi). By its amazing grace, it can transform a debauching, murderous slave trader into a humble abolitionist (John Newton). It can transfigure prostitutes into women of virtue, cowards into rocks of the church, and the proud into the meek.

When I read the Gospels and thought about the world's environmental problems, I found answers. Matthew 7:1 struck me as particularly compelling: "Do not judge, so that you may not be judged. For with the judgment you make you will be judged, and the measure you give will be the measure you get." How often, in all walks of life, do we judge others by a standard different from the one we use to measure our own shortcomings?

When I applied these words of Christ to myself, I did not like what I found. I was concerned about pollution and the death of the world, but what about our family's part in it?

So we took an accounting. Our family added up all the energy we used and the trash and pollution we made. This exercise is called ecologic footprinting. We found our family was average for the United States. Although this was better than most doctors or people in our neighborhood, it was a poor showing compared to the rest of the world. On average, consumption by Americans is double that of our British counterparts, and multiple times more than our African, Chinese, or Indian brothers and sisters.

After telling us not to judge others, Christ instructs us to clean up our own act. He understands that the surest excuse for us not to do the right thing is our innate ability to spot flaws in others. We are instructed to get the two-by-four out of our own eye before we worry about the speck of sawdust in our neighbor's eye.

After we measured our energy usage, our family took Christ at his word and set about changing. First, my job, paycheck, and doctor-sized house went. As I told the hospital board when I resigned as chief of staff, I felt called to "serve God and save the planet"—with an unpaid, undefined job and a financial leap of faith. We moved to a home the exact height, width, and depth of our old garage. Don't feel sorry for us—we had a doctor-sized garage. We found that one set of couches served us fine; two of our other sofas helped young couples starting out. Without multiple televisions, stereos, alarm clocks, garage openers, a clothes dryer, and incandescent bulbs, we were able to cut our electric bill to one-tenth the national average.

Our family also began to distinguish between our wants and our needs. We stopped defining ourselves by what we did and began to concentrate on what we were becoming. First I, then Clark, then Nancy, and finally Emma became followers of Christ.

We began attending a church and small faith group, which helped us learn about giving of ourselves, our time, and our resources. Through the positive examples of our mentors, we learned an essential law of any faith life: complacency is the greatest obstacle to spiritual growth.

One morning at church, I was talking about my environmental concerns with a friend. Eventually he asked, "You're not one of those tree huggers, are you?"

I went home and questioned myself. Being "born again" had changed my worldview. I no longer watched the same movies, listened to the same music, or traveled in the same social circles. I felt a deep conviction to care for the environment—yet I knew no one at church who shared my views. I was aware of the standard biblical proof texts supporting creation care but, as Shakespeare once wrote, "The devil can cite Scripture for his own purpose." Much harm has been done in the past by taking one or two lines from the Bible and building an entire theology on them. Was the call to care for creation one of those instances? Was my church right in remaining silent on creation care?

The good news is that the Christian faith is not based upon trends, but is instead founded on a book—the Bible. We turn to it when a child is born, a couple marries, and a loved one dies. I turned to it to answer my question. I began reading the Bible from cover to cover, underlining verses every time they told of care for creation, God revealed through nature, or God interacting with creation.

What my reading of the Bible disclosed is that creation care is at the very core of our Christian walk. Take, for example, the biblical view of trees. The Bible begins with a tree—the Tree of Life. It is the symbol of the Lord. This is why throughout history many Bibles have featured an etching or drawing of a tree on the opening page.

From Genesis to Revelation, I discovered a trail of green trees as well as vines, bushes, branches, and leaves. "And the LORD God planted a garden in Eden, in the east; and there he put the man whom he had formed. Out of the ground the LORD God made to grow every tree that is pleasant to the sight and good for food, the tree of life also in the midst of the garden, and the tree of knowledge of good and evil" (Genesis 2:8–9).

In the first chapters of Genesis we see a relationship that will continue throughout the pages of history: God, humans, and trees. In Genesis, we learn that trees have a purpose beyond prosaic utilitarianism. They are "pleasant to the sight." Because we are created in God's image, we share this aesthetic standard. Trees are beautiful—it is a biblical truth. Trees are also the source of oxygen. No trees means no oxygen, and no life for humans. The Tree of Life in Genesis is indeed aptly named. We breathe in the wind, and that wind is made of multiple, ethereal realities.

Alpha is the first letter of the Greek alphabet, and *omega* is the last. If something is an alpha or an omega in the Bible, it is worth paying attention to. This is the case with trees. We have encountered the alpha of trees—the Tree of Life—in Genesis. What of the Omega tree? In the last chapter, on the last page of the Bible, we again encounter the Tree of Life: "Then the angel showed me the river of the water of life, bright as crystal, flowing from the throne of God and of the Lamb through the middle of the street of the city. On either side of the river is the tree of life with its twelve kinds of fruit, producing its fruit each month; and the leaves of the tree are for the healing of the nations" (Revelation 22:1–2).

Talmudic writings about the Tree of Life state that it is so large it would take five hundred years to climb. Imagine the proportions of this tree based upon its height. We are also told that the tree is so large it drinks from the mighty River of Life. In its shade, all the nations will be healed. We will be able to live together in peace as brothers and sisters. God does not merely tolerate trees. He puts one at the center of heaven.

The Tree of Life forms the bookends of the Scriptures; trees, together with branches, vines, leaves, and bushes, punctuate a thousand passages in the Bible. Noah is handed an olive branch (Genesis 8:11). Abraham meets angels and the Lord while sitting in the shade of oaks (18:1). Isaac's life is spared by a ram caught in branches (22:13). Joseph is described as a fruitful tree (49:22). Moses hears God in a bush (Exodus 3:4), parts the sea with a stick (14:16), and makes the waters of Marah drinkable with a piece of bark (15:25).

In Judges, the trees speak for themselves, debating leadership. We hear from an olive tree, a fig tree, and a grapevine. The brambles threaten the cedars of Lebanon (Judges 9:7–15). The prophetess Deborah holds court under a palm tree (4:5).

Trees intertwine with the lives of kings, princes, and prophets. David seeks safety in the forest of Hereth (1 Samuel 22:5). As a blessing, God gave Solomon the knowledge of all botany—from the tall cedars to the tiniest hyssop (1 Kings 4:33). An oak branch catches vain Absalom by his long tresses (2 Samuel 18:9), and Elijah succumbs to despair under a broom tree (1 Kings 19:4). God's symbol is the longest lived of flora and fauna. As Job laments, "For there is hope for a tree, if it is cut down, that it will sprout again, and that its shoots will not cease" (14:7).

What of you and me? What if we find favor in the eyes of the Lord? Then we will be "like trees planted by streams of water" (Psalm 1:3). Wisdom too is "a tree of life to those who lay hold of her" (Proverbs 3:18).

Jonah went to Nineveh in the mouth of a whale. He prophesied and preached, and all repented. Then he had a tantrum under the shade of a tree (4:6). God taught Jonah a gentle lesson when that tree died. God cares for everyone, even the innocent animals of Nineveh (4:11). You and I, as well as Jonah, should care too.

Considering the importance of trees to us, and to God, it is not by chance that the most important event in the Bible is framed by trees. Jesus is one of only two named carpenters in the Bible. He spent the thirty years preceding his ministry working with wood. He describes the kingdom of heaven as a mustard seed that grows into a tree where birds can nest (Mark 4:31–32). He is the true vine and describes his followers as fruit-bearing orchards. Palm leaves are spread before him. In the end, he will stretch out his strong, calloused carpenter's hands and die on a tree.

When Jesus of Nazareth arose from his grave, the first person to see him was Mary of Magdala. It is no accident that at first she mistook him for the gardener. Jesus is the gardener, arisen to redeem all of creation.

Christ the gardener has returned. This is the good news. God's plan for the redemption of the earth is no less bold or powerful than his original, creative one. The difference is that, although we were not part of his original creative team, we are invited to be on the redemptive one. Caring for creation is not a new theology; rather, it has simply been forgotten.

A study of Scripture and thousands of years of writings by theologians and saints reveals a cohesive singularity of thought regarding believers' responsibility. We are to follow God's first instruction to humanity. We are to "serve and protect" the earth (Genesis 2:15; NRSV: "till it and keep it"). Reading through the Bible with creation care in mind revealed that my spiritual and environmental journeys were not disparate or mutually exclusive; they were one and mutually supportive.

In the past several years, I have been blessed by opportunities to preach and teach about creation care all across America. I have spoken at graduate schools and with elementary-aged students. I've talked with secular and religious audiences. I've spoken in churches with tens of thousands and one where only one person showed up.

I have heard every kind of objection and rationalization for not protecting our earthly ark of life. Most of the arguments boil down to selfishness. I have met those who would bet the futures of their grandchildren on wishful thinking that the earth will end tomorrow; however, I've met none willing to bet their 401Ks on such end-times thinking.

Years of practice in emergency medicine taught me the truth of Christ's words: death can come swiftly and when we least expect it. We should all be living as if we knew with 100 percent certainty that this was our last year on earth. The followers of Christ are to concern themselves with others. Further, we are to look out for those who cannot care for themselves. By definition, our responsibility includes the next generation.

None of Christ's teachings offers better instruction on how to care for all of God's creation than the parable of the Good Samaritan. In the Gospel of Luke, Christ is asked point-blank, "What must I do to inherit eternal life?"

The answer sums up all of Scripture and may be the most instructive passage regarding the world's environmental problems: "You shall love the Lord your God with all your heart, and with all your soul, and with all your strength, and with all your mind; and your neighbor as yourself" (10:27).

The questioner then asks, "Who is my neighbor?"

Christ tells of a Jewish man who, going down from Jerusalem to Jericho, falls into the hands of robbers who strip him, beat him, and leave him "half dead." Jesus then tells of a priest from the mugged man's own religious group who walks by, but offers no assistance. A second religious man comes along, a Levite. He sees the hurt man, but crosses to the other side of the road, also offering no help.

Finally, a Samaritan comes along, traveling on a donkey. He is from a wealthier socioeconomic class, riding rather than walking. He is also a Samaritan, from a group of people despised by the Jews, and vice versa. But the Samaritan is moved by compassion. He gets off his donkey and begins making bandages, using his own oil and wine to help the man. He then puts the mugged man on his donkey and pays for care at an inn, the equivalent of a hospital in that day. Finally, he agrees to pick up the bill for any additional care.

As an ER physician, I saw a total of some thirty thousand patients in my career. Only once did someone come in and pay the hospital bill for a stranger.

Christ closes the parable by asking who showed mercy to the mugged man. The scribe must answer, "The Samaritan." But the answer is more: it is an instruction in how to have eternal life.

The parable demonstrates a continuum of compassion. The priest represents those of us who refuse to take any responsibility for environmental problems. We close our eyes and walk on by. The second passerby, the Levite, is like most of us. He sees the problem, then says: "I should get back to Jerusalem and raise awareness. Maybe I'll blog on the problem of highway muggings or send a letter off to the Roman centurion about beefing up patrols and installing better streetlights." Like the Levite, we see the hardship caused by environmental problems, particularly for the poorest among us. Our hearts are moved to compassion, but we do little, if anything, to help. Only the Samaritan, the one who is least likely to view the mugged man as his neighbor, takes action.

What does this parable teach us about how we should approach environmental problems today?

- To have any lasting effect, our hearts must be moved by compassion.
- We may find it dangerous.
- We may have to use our own resources.
- It may be inconvenient.
- It may be expensive.
- We may be ridiculed.
- We will have to take ongoing responsibility.
- Everyone is our neighbor, including people across the globe and future generations.

All of these lessons apply directly to our environmental problems today. However, I believe that the most important lesson of the Good Samaritan—the one that can separate us from the priest and Levite—is that we must "get off our donkey" before we can become part of the solution. The future will not be saved by our good intentions. It will be made better, or worse, only by our actions.

We show our love for the Lord by loving our neighbors. Every time our family buys anything or takes any action, we now ask two questions: Will this help me love God? Will this help me love my neighbor? The answer always leads us to right action.

If we take shorter showers, car pool, or plant a tree, no one will necessarily notice or thank us. But if these things are done as an act to serve the Lord and to protect our neighbors, then we will have grown as loving, spiritual beings.

My journey from that island in Florida has taught me a life-changing lesson: each and every one of us must be the change that Christ wishes to see in the world. It is my prayer that the readers of *The Green Bible* will begin in earnest the work of protecting and serving God's beautiful creation.

Reading the Bible through a Green Lens

Calvin B. DeWitt

The Bible is hardly a minor contributor on writings about caring for creation. In fact, the Bible turns out to be a powerful ecological handbook on how to live rightly on earth.

Since God creates and sustains all of creation, we should expect the Bible to call us to bring honor to what is God's—after all, God repeatedly calls his creation "good" (Genesis 1:4, 10, 12, 18, 21, 25, 31). Moreover, since the Bible professes Jesus Christ as the one through whom *all things* are reconciled to God (Colossians 1:20), we should expect the Bible to decry creation's destruction, to call for its restoration, and to look forward to its being made right again.

The Bible presents a serious call to take care of the creation God has given us. But often we just don't do many of the things we know we should do. In many cases, there are reasons for this. It's important to identify the stumbling blocks that may prevent us from taking action as well as any major pitfalls we'll want to avoid, so that we don't get swallowed up along the path of creation stewardship. Having done this, we will be ready to put our beliefs into practice.

Stumbling Blocks to Creation's Care

There are quite a number of troublesome stumbling blocks in the way of creation-keeping discipleship that we have invented ourselves or have been devised by our friends or enemies. Here are some common ones along with comments that may help us in removing or avoiding these obstacles.

This world is not my home; I'm just passing through. (Translation: Since we're headed for heaven anyway, why take care of creation?) Although it's true that people who believe in Jesus Christ receive the gift of everlasting life, everlasting life in

Christ includes the here-and-now. Just as we take care of our teeth, our hair, our bodies, our possessions—clothes, automobiles, homes, and so on—as Christians under the rule of the kingdom of heaven, so we take care of God's earth as part of God's rule today. The world we live in is much more enduring than ourselves or our possessions. So shouldn't the care of creation also be a part of our here-and-now concern?

There are too many worldly people out there doing environmental things. (Translation: If people who don't share my beliefs in God are working to save the earth, I know it can't be right for me.) In Isaiah 45:1–6 we read that unbelieving Cyrus the Persian was anointed to do God's work. Often if God's people are unwilling or unable to do God's work, God sees to it that the work gets done anyway. So if there are some worldly people out there doing God's work, let's be glad for the help and not use this fact to excuse ourselves from our God-given task as stewards of God's creation.

I don't want to be an extremist or alarmist. (Translation: I want to be considered normal and not some kind of prophet of gloom and doom.) Gloom and doom are not necessary components of the message about caring for creation. Frightening ourselves into action is far less preferable than caring for creation out of gratitude and love for God. As for being called an alarmist, is it wrong to sound the fire alarm when a building is burning? In many cases today it may be necessary to sound the alarm.

I believe God gave us the job to do what we want with creation. (Translation: I think the Bible says we have the right to destroy things that get in our way; that's what dominion is all about.) Many people have pointed to Genesis 1:28 to show that they have the license to do whatever they please with creation (i.e., air pollution, the loss of animal species). But dominion as outright oppression is not advocated or condoned by Scripture. First, Genesis 1:28 gave the blessing and mandate to people *before the fall into sin.* Second, this passage must be understood not in isolation, but in the context of the rest of the Bible, which shows that dominion means responsible stewardship. God gave humans a special role and responsibility as stewards of his creation. Having dominion over creation is an important aspect of being made in God's image, as we reflect his presence on the earth. Part of our human dignity is tied to God's entrusting us with stewardship over creation. When God gave humans dominion over creation, the intent was not for us to destroy creation, but to preserve and care for it so it could benefit all people and creatures for generations to come.

People are more important than the environment. (Translation: We should care more about people than saving species of plants and animals.) We often hear this rationalization for not saving living species threatened with extinction. But again we must ask, "What does the Bible teach?" Recall the account of the flood in Genesis 6–9. Who perishes? Who is saved? Are species less important than individual people? At the very least, care for living species cannot be disregarded because of the importance of people. Christ's redemption covers all creation, not just humans.

I disagree with what some environmentalists and scientists say will happen. (Translation: If I work to care and heal the environment, I will be supporting people I strongly disagree with.) The first thing to say is that doing what is right and what God calls us to do should not carry a litmus test for who is allowed to do it. Plus, we need to recognize that there are concerted efforts to promote doubt and uncertainty whenever it helps maintain sinful structures and institutions. Just as the tobacco industry is able to promote confusion and distrust of cancer research despite extensive evidence showing that smoking produces lung cancer and other health concerns, similar efforts have been used to discredit the science of climatology and its findings on global climate change. Promoters of doubt about the findings of climatology and environmental science have become experts in playing on the fears and apprehensions of the public. A major strategy for discrediting this science is to seek any contrary opinions, dress them up in scientific garb, and put them on display and in debate with the findings of science.

Now What Must We Do about Creation?

Our ultimate purpose is to honor God as creator in such a way that Christian environmental stewardship is part and parcel of everything we do. Our goal is to make tending the garden of creation, in all its aspects, an unquestioned and all-pervasive part of our service to each other, to our community, to God's world. The framework for our response can follow these three steps.

Awareness

In a time when so much calls for our attention—international affairs, local politics, our work or schooling, family needs, church commitments, and other busyness—we might only barely notice the natural and environmental aspects of creation in our surroundings. We must consciously make ourselves aware of what is happening in God's creation.

Awareness involves seeing, naming, identifying, and locating different parts of God's creation. It means taking off blinders that we or society may put on us to keep us focused on our pursuits in life. It means providing ourselves with enough quiet, reflection, and learning time that we can notice and identify a tree or mountain, bird or river.

Appreciation

From awareness comes appreciation; we cannot appreciate something we are unaware of. At the very least, appreciation means tolerating what we are aware of. We may tolerate, for example, worms and hyenas. But appreciation can also involve respect. We certainly respect a large bear, but we can also develop respect for a lowly worm as we learn of its critical importance to the rest of creation. We can move, as well, from toleration to respect to valuing. The earth and everything in it has value because God made it so. As we become aware of the order of creation, we will see God's valuing of all his works.

Stewardship

Appreciation needs to lead to stewardship. Stewardship takes us beyond appreciation to restoration. We now work for the restoration of what has been degraded in the past.

Beyond restoration, stewardship means serving. As we understand that God through creation is in so many ways serving us, we grow to willingly return this service with our own. This service includes loving, caring, and keeping what God has given us to hold in trust. Our service in creation will eventually involve entrusting others with what we have served, kept, and restored.

Biblical Principles for Creation Care

So keeping in mind that many people today yearn to restore the integrity of creation, it can be helpful to read the Scriptures afresh, searching for their ecological insights on how rightly to live on the earth. The following eight biblical principles will help disclose the Bible's powerful environmental message.

The Earthkeeping Principle

As the Lord keeps and sustains us, so we must keep and sustain our Lord's creation.

Genesis 2:15 conveys a marvelous teaching. Adam is expected by God to *serve* the garden and to *keep* it. God expected Adam and his descendants to meet the needs of the garden of creation so that it would persist and flourish.

God also expected Adam and his descendants to *keep* the garden. The word for *keep* (*shamar*) is sometimes translated "guard," "safeguard," "take care of," or "look after." *Shamar* indicates a loving, caring, sustaining kind of keeping. In the blessing of Aaron in Numbers 6:24, "The LORD bless you and keep you," the word for "keep" is the Hebrew word *shamar*. When we invoke God's blessing to *keep* us, we are not asking that God would keep us in a kind of preserved, inactive state. Instead, we are calling on God to keep us in all of our vitality, with all our energy and beauty. The keeping we expect of God when we invoke this ancient blessing is one that nurtures all of our life-fulfilling relationships—with family, neighbors, and friends; with the land, air, and water of the earth; and of course with God.

So too with our keeping of God's creation. Our relationship to creation must be a loving, caring, keeping relationship. When we fulfill God's mandate to *keep* the creation, we make sure that the creatures and other living things under our care are maintained so that they can flourish. They must remain connected with members of the same species, with the many other species with which they interact, and with the soil, air, and water they depend on.

As God *keeps* people, so God's people should *keep* his creation.

The Fruitfulness Principle

We should enjoy but not destroy creation's fruitfulness.

God's blessing of fruitfulness is for the whole creation. In Genesis, God declares, "Let the waters bring forth swarms of living creatures, and let birds fly above the earth across the dome of the sky" (1:20). And God blesses these creatures with fruitfulness: "Be fruitful and multiply and fill the waters in the seas, and let birds multiply on the earth" (1:22). God also says, "Let the earth bring forth living creatures of every kind: cattle and creeping things and wild animals of the earth of every kind" (1:24).

God's creation reflects God's fruitful work, giving to land and life what satisfies and sustains it. Psalm 104:10–13 expresses this beautifully:

> You make springs gush forth in the valleys; they flow between the hills, giving drink to every wild animal; the wild asses quench their thirst. By the streams the birds of the air have their habitation; they sing among the branches. From your lofty abode you water the mountains; the earth is satisfied with the fruit of your work.

As God's fruitful work brings fruit to creation, so should ours. As God provides for all his creatures, so should we who are created to reflect God's image. As Noah cared for God's creatures when they were threatened with extinction, so should we. In Noah's time a flood of water covered the land. In our time floods of people in many places sprawl across the land, often displacing God's other creatures, limiting *their* potential to fulfill their blessing and God's command to be fruitful. To those who would allow a human flood across the land at the expense of all other creatures, the prophet Isaiah warns, "Ah, you who join house to house, who add field to field, until there is room for no one but you, and you are left to live alone in the midst of the land" (5:8).

So although we are expected to enjoy creation and its many fruits, we may not destroy the *fruitfulness* that creation's fullness depends on. Like Noah, we must preserve and care for God's many species whose interactions and relationships with each other and with land and water make up the fabric of the biosphere. We must let the profound admonition of Ezekiel 34:18 echo in our minds: "Is it not enough for you to feed on the good pasture, but you must tread down with your feet the rest of your pasture? When you drink of clear water, must you foul the rest with your feet?"

The Sabbath Principle

We must provide for creation's Sabbath rests.

In Exodus 20 and Deuteronomy 5, God commands us to set aside one day in seven as a day of rest for people and for animals. This Sabbath day is given to help us all get "off the treadmill," to protect us all from the hazards of continuous work, to help us pull our lives together again. It's a time to worship the Lord and enjoy the fruits of his creation, a time for rest and restoration. In Exodus 23:12, God commands, "Six days you shall do your work, but on the seventh day you shall rest, so that your ox and your donkey may have relief, and your homeborn slave and the resident alien may be refreshed."

The same chapter in Scripture says that the land also must have its time of Sabbath rest. Nothing in all creation must be relentlessly pressed. "For six years you shall sow your land and gather in its yield; but the seventh year you shall let it rest and lie fallow, so that the poor of your people may eat; and what they leave the wild animals may eat. You shall do the same with your vineyard, and with your olive orchard" (Exodus 23:10–11).

Does this command create a problem for people? Leviticus 25:20–21 says, "Should you ask, 'What shall we eat in the seventh year, if we may not sow or gather in our crop?'" God's answer: "I will order my blessing for you in the sixth year, so that it will yield a crop for three years."

God was instructing people not to worry, but to practice his law so that the land would be *fruitful.* "If you follow my statutes and keep my commandments and observe them faithfully, I will give you your rains in their season, and the land shall yield its produce, and the trees of the field shall yield their fruit" (Leviticus 26:3–4).

In the New Testament, Jesus clearly defines for us the meaning of Sabbath in our lives: the Sabbath is made for those who are served by it—not the other way around (Mark 2:27). The Sabbath is made for people and, through them, for all the rest of God's creation. The Sabbath year is given to protect the land from relentless exploitation, to help it rejuvenate, to give it a time of rest and restoration.

This Sabbath is not merely a legalistic requirement; it's a profound principle. That's why in some farming communities the land is allowed to rest every *second* year, because that is what it needs. The Sabbath is made for the land—not the land for the Sabbath. The Sabbath law is therefore not restricted to agriculture, but applies to all of creation. It affects our use of water and air, as we discharge our exhaust, smoke, sewage, and other things we "throw away." God speaks strongly on this issue:

> But if you will not obey me, and do not observe all these commandments, if you spurn my statutes, and abhor my ordinances...and you break my covenant...your land shall be a desolation, and your cities a waste. Then the land shall enjoy its sabbath years as long as it lies desolate...then the land shall rest, and enjoy its sabbath years. As long as it lies desolate, it shall have the rest it did not have on your sabbaths when you were living on it. (Leviticus 26:14–15, 33–35)

These are harsh words from the holy Creator who is concerned for his creation. But God's promises of blessing are equally powerful for all who will listen:

> If you refrain from trampling the sabbath, from pursuing your own interests on my holy day...then you shall take delight in the LORD, and I will make you ride upon the heights of the earth. (Isaiah 58:13–14)

The Discipleship Principle

We must be disciples of Jesus Christ—the Creator, Sustainer, and Reconciler of all things.

No question about it—the Bible calls us to be disciples, or *followers after* someone. But we are not to be disciples of the first Adam, who neglected to serve (*'abad*) and keep (*shamar*) the creation. We must not follow those who choose to go their own way and do their own thing.

Instead, the Bible tells us, we must be disciples of "the last Adam," Jesus Christ (1 Corinthians 15:45). In John 3:16 the New Testament teaches that God loved the world so much that he gave his only Son—to bring true life, to make things right again. "For as all die in Adam, so all will be made alive in Christ" (1 Corinthians 15:22).

All who follow Jesus follow the example of the one who makes all things new, the one who makes all things right again (Revelation 21:5). Colossians 1:20 puts it this way: "God was pleased to reconcile to himself all things, whether on earth or in heaven, by making peace through the blood of his cross."

Who is this Christ we are to follow? He is the one *in whom* and *for whom* all things were created (Colossians. 1:16). He is the one *through whom* God made the universe and *through whom* God redeems his people (John 1:3; Colossians 1:16, 20; Hebrews 1:3).

God reaches out sacrificially to make things right again. Jesus Christ, the final Adam, undoes the damage done by the first Adam and his followers. While Adam's followers bring death and degradation, Christ brings life and restoration (Romans 5:12–17). The children of God work as followers and disciples of the final Adam. People who are happy being Christ's servant-stewards are the people for whom the whole creation is eagerly looking (8:19).

We must, then, be disciples of Jesus Christ. We walk in the footsteps of the one who reconciles all things. We are disciples of the last Adam, not the first. We work to reconcile all things to God in Christ.

The Kingdom Priority Principle

We must seek first the kingdom of God.

Our culture today proclaims, "Seek first a job (money, success), and all other things will be yours as well." It is tempting to yield to this message and to follow people whose highest priority is to gather up immense material gains. But Jesus advises us to seek first the kingdom of God and God's rightness; then everything else we need will be given to us as well (Matthew 6:33).

Personal happiness, joy, and fulfillment are not what we seek first of all in life. Instead, we seek the kingdom of God and strive to sustain and renew God's creation. In seeking God's kingdom, we discover that happiness and joy are *by-products* of our stewardship; fulfillment comes as a *result* of seeking the kingdom.

Who will inherit this kingdom? Those who seek it as their first priority. Its inheritance is not for people who arrogantly exploit their neighbors, the land, and earth's creatures for all they are worth. Nor is the inheritance for those who carelessly and knowingly destroy the earth. Seeking God's kingdom first is our calling, our vocation. We affirm this calling whenever we pray as Jesus taught us: "Our Father in heaven, hallowed be your name. Your kingdom come. Your will be done, *on earth…*" (Matthew 6:9–10).

The Contentment Principle

We must seek true contentment.

The fruitful and beautiful creation did not satisfy our first parents and succeeding generations. Even though God promised not to forsake or leave them, people chose to go their own way—grasping more and more from creation for selfish advancement. In our day we feel the effects of this relentless pressing of land and life to produce more. This relentless pressing is what is so seriously degrading God's creation today. Our prayer should be that of Psalm 119:36: "Turn my heart to your decrees, and not to selfish gain."

If accumulating the goods of creation is selfish gain, then what is godly gain?

Godly gain is doing the work God would have us do in the world. In 1 Timothy 6:6 we learn that "there is great gain in godliness combined with contentment." Contentment means aiming to have the things that will sustain us while not pressing beyond that. An Amish saying based on this passage goes like this: "To desire to be rich is to desire to have more than what we need to be content."

Why is it important not to pass the point of contentment? In the words of 1 Timothy 6:11, by not passing this point we can "pursue righteousness, godliness, faith, love, endurance, gentleness." Hebrews 13:5 puts it this way: "Keep your lives free from the love of money, and be content with what you have; for he has said, 'I will never leave you or forsake you.'"

Being content helps preserve creation's integrity. All the things we use, all the things we make, everything we manipulate, everything we accumulate derives from creation itself. If we learn to seek godly contentment as our great gain, we will demand less from the land. We will leave room for God's other creatures. We will be responsible stewards, caretakers, keepers of creation. We will regularly allow creation to heal itself and perpetuate its fruitfulness, to the glory and praise of its Maker.

The Praxis Principle
We must practice what we believe.

Scripture admonishes us to act on what we know is right. Merely knowing God's requirements for stewardship is not enough. Merely believing in God is not enough, for Scripture tells us that even demons believe in God (James 2:19). We must practice God's requirements, or they do no good.

The failure of God's people to act on what they know is right is well-documented—and challenged—in the pages of Scripture:

> They come to you as people come, and they sit before you as my people, and they hear your words, but they will not obey them. For flattery is on their lips, but their heart is set on their gain. To them you are like a singer of love songs, one who has a beautiful voice and plays well on an instrument; they hear what you say, but they will not do it. (Ezekiel 33:31–32)

> Why do you call me "Lord, Lord," and do not do what I tell you? (Luke 6:46)

Studying the Bible to learn God's requirements for creation care brings us directly to the question, *Now what must we do?* The challenge before us now is to move forward and put what we know and believe into practice.

The Conservation Principle

We must return creation's service to us with service of our own.

This principle encircles all the others. The root meaning of the word *conserve* is *con + serve,* which means "to serve with."

As we considered the earthkeeping principle, we noted from Genesis 2:15 that Adam was expected to *serve* the creation and to *keep* it. The Hebrew word *'abad* ("serve") in this passage occurs 290 times in the Old Testament, and it is most often translated as "serve"—as in Joshua 24:15: "Choose this day whom you will serve.... As for me and my household, we will serve the LORD." The various Bible translations of *'abad* in Genesis 2:15—"serve," "till," "dress," and "work"—relate to worthy service. God calls us to give the garden of creation our caring service.

We already know from experience that this garden serves us. It serves us with good food, beauty, herbs, fiber, medicine, pleasant microclimates, continual soil-making, nutrient processing, and seed production. The garden and the larger biosphere provide what ecologists call "ecosystem services" such as water purification by evaporation and percolation, moderation of flood peaks and drought flows by river-system wetlands, development of soils from the weathering of rocks, and moderation of local climates by nearby bodies of water. Yet Genesis addresses *our* service to the garden. The garden's service *to us* is implicit; service *from us* to the garden is explicit.

Like Adam, we are expected to return the service of the garden with service of our own. This is a reciprocal service, a "service with." This reciprocal service defines an engaging relationship between garden and gardener, between the biosphere and its safeguarding stewards.

So we can call this "never taking from creation without returning service of our own." Our love of our Creator God, God's love of the creation, and our imaging this love of God—all join together to commission us as *con-servers* of creation. As *conservers,* we follow the example of the second Adam—Jesus Christ (see 1 Corinthians 15:22, 45).

Adapted from Calvin B. DeWitt, *Earth-Wise: A Biblical Response to Environmental Issues,* 2nd ed., copyright © 2007 by Faith Alive Christian Resources, 2850 Kalamazoo Ave. SE, Grand Rapids, MI 49560; 1-800-333-8300; www.FaithAliveResources.org. Used by permission.

Peace with God the Creator, Peace with All of Creation

Message of His Holiness Pope John Paul II for the Celebration of the World Day of Peace January 1, 1990, Vatican City

Introduction

1. In our day, there is a growing awareness that world peace is threatened not only by the arms race, regional conflicts and continued injustices among peoples and nations, but also by a lack of *due respect for nature*, by the plundering of natural resources and by a progressive decline in the quality of life. The sense of precariousness and insecurity that such a situation engenders is a seedbed for collective selfishness, disregard for others and dishonesty.

Faced with the widespread destruction of the environment, people everywhere are coming to understand that we cannot continue to use the goods of the earth as we have in the past. The public in general as well as political leaders are concerned about this problem, and experts from a wide range of disciplines are studying its causes. Moreover, a new *ecological awareness* is beginning to emerge which, rather than being downplayed, ought to be encouraged to develop into concrete programmes and initiatives.

2. Many ethical values, fundamental to the development of a *peaceful society*, are particularly relevant to the ecological question. The fact that many challenges facing the world today are interdependent confirms the need for carefully coordinated solutions based on a morally coherent world view.

For Christians, such a world view is grounded in religious convictions drawn from Revelation. That is why I should like to begin this Message with a reflection on the biblical account of creation. I would hope that even those who do not share these same beliefs will find in these pages a common ground for reflection and action.

I. "And God saw that it was good"

3. In the Book of Genesis, where we find God's first self-revelation to humanity (*Gen* 1—3), there is a recurring refrain: *"And God saw that it was good"*. After creating the heavens, the sea, the earth and all it contains, God created man and woman. At this point the refrain changes markedly: "And God saw everything that he had made, and behold, *it was very good* (*Gen* 1:31). God entrusted the whole of creation to the man and woman, and only then—as we read—could he rest "from all his work" (*Gen* 2:3).

Adam and Eve's call to share in the unfolding of God's plan of creation brought into play those abilities and gifts which distinguish the human being from all other creatures. At the same time, their call established a fixed relationship between mankind and the rest of creation. Made in the image and likeness of God, Adam and Eve were to have exercised their dominion over the earth (*Gen* 1:28) with wisdom and love. Instead, they destroyed the existing harmony *by deliberately going against the Creator's plan*, that is, by choosing to sin. This resulted not only in man's alienation from himself, in death and fratricide, but also in the earth's "rebellion" against him (cf. *Gen* 3:17–19; 4:12). All of creation became subject to futility, waiting in a mysterious way to be set free and to obtain a glorious liberty together with all the children of God (cf. *Rom* 8:20–21).

4. Christians believe that the Death and Resurrection of Christ accomplished the work of reconciling humanity to the Father, who "was pleased...through (Christ) to reconcile to himself *all things*, whether on earth or in heaven, making peace by the blood of his cross" (*Col* 1:19–20). Creation was thus made new (cf. *Rev* 21:5). Once subjected to the bondage of sin and decay (cf. *Rom* 8:21), it has now received new life while "we wait for new heavens and a new earth in which righteousness dwells" (2 *Pt* 3:13). Thus, the Father "has made known to us in all wisdom and insight the mystery...which he set forth in Christ as a plan for the fulness of time, to unite *all things* in him, all things in heaven and things on earth" (*Eph* 1:9–10).

5. These biblical considerations help us to understand better *the relationship between human activity and the whole of creation*. When man turns his back on the Creator's plan, he provokes a disorder which has inevitable repercussions on the rest of the created order. If man is not at peace with God, then earth itself cannot be at peace: "Therefore the land mourns and all who dwell in it languish, and also the beasts of the field and the birds of the air and even the fish of the sea are taken away" (*Hos* 4:3).

The profound sense that the earth is "suffering" is also shared by those who do not profess our faith in God. Indeed, the increasing devastation of the world of nature is apparent to all. It results from the behaviour of people who show a callous disregard for the hidden, yet perceivable requirements of the order and harmony which govern nature itself.

People are asking anxiously if it is still possible to remedy the damage which has been done. Clearly, an adequate solution cannot be found merely in a better management or a more rational use of the earth's resources, as important as these may be. Rather, we must go to the source of the problem and face in its entirety that profound moral crisis *of which the destruction of the environment is only one troubling aspect.*

II. The ecological crisis: a moral problem

6. Certain elements of today's ecological crisis reveal its moral character. First among these is the *indiscriminate* application of advances in science and technology. Many recent discoveries have brought undeniable benefits to humanity. Indeed, they demonstrate the nobility of the human vocation to participate *responsibly* in God's creative action in the world. Unfortunately, it is now clear that the application of these discoveries in the fields of industry and agriculture have produced harmful long-term effects. This has led to the painful realization that *we cannot interfere in one area of the ecosystem without paying due attention both to the consequences of such interference in other areas and to the well-being of future generations.*

The gradual depletion of the ozone layer and the related "greenhouse effect"has now reached crisis proportions as a consequence of industrial growth, massive urban concentrations and vastly increased energy needs. Industrial waste, the burning of fossil fuels, unrestricted deforestation, the use of certain types of herbicides, coolants and propellants: all of these are known to harm the atmosphere and environment. The resulting meteorological and atmospheric changes range from damage to health to the possible future submersion of low-lying lands.

While in some cases the damage already done may well be irreversible, in many other cases it can still be halted. It is necessary, however, that the entire human community—individuals, States and international bodies—take seriously the responsibility that is theirs.

7. The most profound and serious indication of the moral implications underlying the ecological problem is the lack of *respect for life* evident in many of the patterns of environmental pollution. Often, the interests of production prevail over concern for the dignity of workers, while economic interests take priority over the good of individuals and even entire peoples. In these cases, pollution or environmental destruction is the result of an unnatural and reductionist vision which at times leads to a genuine contempt for man.

On another level, delicate ecological balances are upset by the uncontrolled destruction of animal and plant life or by a reckless exploitation of natural resources. It should be pointed out that all of this, even if carried out in the name of progress and well-being, is ultimately to mankind's disadvantage.

Finally, we can only look with deep concern at the enormous possibilities of biological research. We are not yet in a position to assess the biological disturbance that could result from indiscriminate genetic manipulation and from the unscrupulous development of new forms of plant and animal life, to say nothing of unacceptable experimentation regarding the origins of human life itself. It is evident to all that in any area as delicate as this, indifference to fundamental ethical norms, or their rejection, would lead mankind to the very threshold of self-destruction.

Respect for life, and above all for the dignity of the human person, is the ultimate guiding norm for any sound economic, industrial or scientific progress.

The complexity of the ecological question is evident to all. There are, however, certain underlying principles, which, while respecting the legitimate autonomy and the specific competence of those involved, can direct research towards adequate and lasting solutions. These principles are essential to the building of a peaceful society; *no peaceful society can afford to neglect either respect for life or the fact that there is an integrity to creation.*

III. In search of a solution

8. Theology, philosophy and science all speak of a harmonious universe, of a "cosmos" endowed with its own integrity, its own internal, dynamic balance. *This order must be respected.* The human race is called to explore this order, to examine it with due care and to make use of it while safeguarding its integrity.

On the other hand, the earth is ultimately *a common heritage, the fruits of which are for the benefit of all.* In the words of the Second Vatican Council, "God destined the earth and all it contains for the use of every individual and all peoples" (*Gaudium et Spes*, 69). This has direct consequences for the problem at hand. It is manifestly unjust that a privileged few should continue to accumulate excess goods, squandering available resources, while masses of people are living in conditions of misery at the very lowest level of subsistence. Today, the dramatic threat of ecological breakdown is teaching us the extent to which greed and selfishness—both individual and collective—are contrary to the order of creation, an order which is characterized by mutual interdependence.

9. The concepts of an ordered universe and a common heritage both point to the necessity of a *more internationally coordinated approach to the management of the earth's goods.* In many cases the effects of ecological problems transcend the borders of individual States; hence their solution cannot be found solely on the national level.

Recently there have been some promising steps towards such international action, yet the existing mechanisms and bodies are clearly not adequate for the development of a comprehensive plan of action. Political obstacles, forms of exaggerated nationalism and economic interests—to mention only a few factors—impede international cooperation and long-term effective action.

The need for joint action on the international level *does not lessen the responsibility of each individual State.* Not only should each State join with others in implementing internationally accepted standards, but it should also make or facilitate necessary socio-economic adjustments within its own borders, giving special attention to the most vulnerable sectors of society. The State should also actively endeavour within its own territory to prevent destruction of the atmosphere and biosphere, by carefully monitoring, among other things, the impact of new technological or scientific advances. The State also has the responsibility of ensuring that its citizens are not exposed to dangerous pollutants or toxic wastes. *The right to a safe environment* is ever more insistently presented today as a right that must be included in an updated Charter of Human Rights.

IV. The urgent need for a new solidarity

10. The ecological crisis reveals the *urgent moral need for a new solidarity*, especially in relations between the developing nations and those that are highly industrialized. States must increasingly share responsibility, in complimentary ways, for the promotion of a natural and social environment that is both peaceful and healthy. The newly industrialized States cannot, for example, be asked to apply restrictive environmental standards to their emerging industries unless the industrialized States first apply them within their own boundaries. At the same time, countries in the process of industrialization are not morally free to repeat the errors made in the past by others, and recklessly continue to damage the environment through industrial pollutants, radical deforestation or unlimited exploitation of non-renewable resources. In this context, there is urgent need to find a solution to the treatment and disposal of toxic wastes.

No plan or organization, however, will be able to effect the necessary changes unless world leaders are truly convinced of the absolute need for this new solidarity, which is demanded of them by the ecological crisis and which is essential for peace. *This need presents new opportunities for strengthening cooperative and peaceful relations among States.*

11. It must also be said that the proper ecological balance will not be found without *directly addressing the structural forms of poverty* that exist throughout the world. Rural poverty and unjust land distribution in many countries, for example, have led to subsistence farming and to the exhaustion of the soil. Once their land yields

no more, many farmers move on to clear new land, thus accelerating uncontrolled deforestation, or they settle in urban centres which lack the infrastructure to receive them. Likewise, some heavily indebted countries are destroying their natural heritage, at the price of irreparable ecological imbalances, in order to develop new products for export. In the face of such situations it would be wrong to assign responsibility to the poor alone for the negative environmental consequences of their actions. Rather, the poor, to whom the earth is entrusted no less than to others, must be enabled to find a way out of their poverty. This will require a courageous reform of structures, as well as new ways of relating among peoples and States.

12. But there is another dangerous menace which threatens us, namely *war*. Unfortunately, modern science already has the capacity to change the environment for hostile purposes. Alterations of this kind over the long term could have unforeseeable and still more serious consequences. Despite the international agreements which prohibit chemical, bacteriological and biological warfare, the fact is that laboratory research continues to develop new offensive weapons capable of altering the balance of nature.

Today, any form of war on a global scale would lead to incalculable ecological damage. But even local or regional wars, however limited, not only destroy human life and social structures, but also damage the land, ruining crops and vegetation as well as poisoning the soil and water. The survivors of war are forced to begin a new life in very difficult environmental conditions, which in turn create situations of extreme social unrest, with further negative consequences for the environment.

13. Modern society will find no solution to the ecological problem unless it *takes a serious look at its life style*. In many parts of the world society is given to instant gratification and consumerism while remaining indifferent to the damage which these cause. As I have already stated, the seriousness of the ecological issue lays bare the depth of man's moral crisis. If an appreciation of the value of the human person and of human life is lacking, we will also lose interest in others and in the earth itself. Simplicity, moderation and discipline, as well as a spirit of sacrifice, must become a part of everyday life, lest all suffer the negative consequences of the careless habits of a few.

An education in ecological responsibility is urgent: responsibility for oneself, for others, and for the earth. This education cannot be rooted in mere sentiment or empty wishes. Its purpose cannot be ideological or political. It must not be based on a rejection of the modern world or a vague desire to return to some "paradise lost". Instead, a true education in responsibility entails a genuine conversion in ways of thought and behaviour. Churches and religious bodies, non-governmental and governmental organizations, indeed all members of society, have a precise role to play in such education. The first educator, however, is the family, where the child learns to respect his neighbour and to love nature.

14. *Finally, the aesthetic value of creation cannot be overlooked.* Our very contact with nature has a deep restorative power; contemplation of its magnificence imparts peace and serenity. The Bible speaks again and again of the goodness and beauty of creation, which is called to glorify God (cf. *Gen* 1:4ff; *Ps* 8:2; 104:1ff; *Wis* 13:3-5; *Sir* 39:16, 33; 43:1, 9). More difficult perhaps, but no less profound, is the contemplation of the works of human ingenuity. Even cities can have a beauty all their own, one that ought to motivate people to care for their surroundings. Good urban planning is an important part of environmental protection, and respect for the natural contours of the land is an indispensable prerequisite for ecologically sound development. The relationship between a good aesthetic education and the maintenance of a healthy environment cannot be overlooked.

V. The ecological crisis: a common responsibility

15. Today the ecological crisis has assumed such proportions as to be *the responsibility of everyone*. As I have pointed out, its various aspects demonstrate the need for concerted efforts aimed at establishing the duties and obligations that belong to individuals, peoples, States and the international community. This not only goes hand in hand with efforts to build true peace, but also confirms and reinforces those efforts in a concrete way. When the ecological crisis is set within the broader context of *the search for peace* within society, we can understand better the importance of giving attention to what the earth and its atmosphere are telling us: namely, that there is an order in the universe which must be respected, and that the human person, endowed with the capability of choosing freely, has a grave responsibility to preserve this order for the well-being of future generations. I wish to repeat that *the ecological crisis is a moral issue.*

Even men and women without any particular religious conviction, but with an acute sense of their responsibilities for the common good, recognize their obligation to contribute to the restoration of a healthy environment. All the more should men and women who believe in God the Creator, and who are thus convinced that there is a well-defined unity and order in the world, feel called to address the problem. Christians, in particular, realize that their responsibility within creation and their duty towards nature and the Creator are an essential part of their faith. As a result, they are conscious of a vast field of ecumenical and interreligious cooperation opening up before them.

16. At the conclusion of this Message, I should like to address directly my brothers and sisters in the Catholic Church, in order to remind them of their serious obligation to care for all of creation. The commitment of believers to a healthy

environment for everyone stems directly from their belief in God the Creator, from their recognition of the effects of original and personal sin, and from the certainty of having been redeemed by Christ. Respect for life and for the dignity of the human person extends also to the rest of creation, which is called to join man in praising God (cf. *Ps* 148:96).

In 1979, I proclaimed Saint Francis of Assisi as the heavenly Patron of those who promote ecology (cf. Apostolic Letter *Inter Sanctos: AAS* 71 [1979], 1509f.). He offers Christians an example of genuine and deep respect for the integrity of creation. As a friend of the poor who was loved by God's creatures, Saint Francis invited all of creation—animals, plants, natural forces, even Brother Sun and Sister Moon—to give honour and praise to the Lord. The poor man of Assisi gives us striking witness that when we are at peace with God we are better able to devote ourselves to building up that peace with all creation which is inseparable from peace among all peoples.

It is my hope that the inspiration of Saint Francis will help us to keep ever alive a sense of "fraternity" with all those good and beautiful things which Almighty God has created. And may he remind us of our serious obligation to respect and watch over them with care, in light of that greater and higher fraternity that exists within the human family.

Why I Am Green

Brian McLaren

I magine that right now you are standing with me, thigh-deep in muck. Clad in hip waders, we're slogging through a spring-fed bog in northern Maryland. We're surrounded by tussock sedge, alder, jewelweed, skunk cabbage, and swamp rose. The June sun is hot, I'm sweaty, I've got six mosquito bites on the back of my neck, and my forearms are scratched and itchy from thorns of various sizes. And I'm having a great time. I'm glad to have your company here in this beautiful place.

I've done this for a couple of days almost every spring for the last dozen years. I'm out here as a volunteer with the Department of Natural Resources to do wildlife surveys. In particular we're looking for the rarest turtle in North America, *glyptemys muhlenbergii*, the little four-inch bog turtle. In the 1970s, it was found in more than four hundred sites in our little state. In the 1990s, we could only find it in about half those sites. The other sites had been ditched, drained, bulldozed, polluted, invaded by nonnative plants, raided by collectors, bisected by roads for turtle-smashing cars, or otherwise made uninhabitable for these little creatures.

While my fellow volunteers and I are out here in the bogs, we also keep alert for other rare species: butterflies, birds, wildflowers, insects, amphibians. Our efforts help wildlife biologists keep track of how certain "indicator species" are doing; their status tells us how fast and how much the environment is suffering from human interference. Occasionally, there's good news too—when we stop mine runoff from poisoning creeks and rivers, when suburban homes stop shocking downstream ecosystems with runoff from lawn pesticides and fertilizers, when sewage treatment facilities find ways to stop raw sewage from overflowing into waterways after rainstorms.

When I meet professional wildlife biologists and other volunteers, they're surprised that a Christian pastor would be out here doing this sort of thing on his day off. They're not used to seeing mud-smeared pastors groping around in bog muck for turtles. I know what they're thinking: *Christians are part of the problem, not part of the solution.*

Too often my environmentally concerned friends are right. Too often we put the gospel of Jesus through the strainer of consumerist capitalism and retain only the thin broth that this modern-day Caesar lets pass through. We often display a reactionary tendency to be against whatever "liberals" are for. These nongreen shoots are sourced by deeper theological roots of environmental disinterest. Fortunately, other root systems are spreading beneath the surface, and signs of an environmental spring are breaking through the formerly barren soil.

People who are sensitive to creation know that creation is in constant flux. Continents drift, ocean currents wobble, climates warm and cool, magnetic poles flip-flop, and bogs like this one gradually give way to wet meadows and then various kinds of forests. There's a natural succession out here under the June sun, and I think there's a kind of natural succession going on theologically for many Christians as well. Let me mention six elements of this theological succession.

The standard, stagnant theology of creation/fall is giving way to a more vigorous theology of continual creation.

For much of Western Christianity, the doctrine of creation (a biblical term) has been eaten alive by the doctrine of the fall (not a biblical term). In other words, creation's downfall resulting from human sin has eclipsed its original glow as God's handiwork, radiant with God's glory. Make no mistake. Human sin is awful and reprehensible beyond words, and the whole earthly creation suffers because of it. But if, due to an exaggerated doctrine of the fall, God's creation loses its sacredness as God's beloved artwork, we have magnified human sin beyond sane bounds—and in fact added to its sad effects.

As a result, in many circles, about the only time the word *creation* comes up these days is before *versus evolution*. The God-affirmed goodness of creation, the beauty of creation, its priceless preciousness and meaning as God's own handiwork—these values are seldom heard. Instead, more discouraging words are heard—about the ruin of creation via an "ontological fall," a concept that conveniently seems to degrade God's inherently valuable handiwork into humanity's bargain resources for profitable exploitation. It's far easier to put a price tag on a fallen creation than on a still sacred one.

Many of us have grown uneasy with this understanding of "the fall" (and with it, an exaggerated understanding of the doctrine of "original sin"). So we are looking to the Eastern Orthodox tradition and to emerging narrative theologies in which creation is still seen as sacred, "good," "very good," and, in fact, ongoing.

When one is careful to not lose the enduring glory and continuity of creation, when one takes human sin seriously enough but no more seriously than one should, later elements in the biblical narrative (election, redemption, revelation, salvation, eschaton) are themselves understood and integrated as glorious new unfoldings of continuing creation. Creation may have been swallowed alive by a runaway, exaggerated understanding of "the fall," but, like Jonah, it's crawling back up the beach.

Seen this way, creation is revalued (i.e., redeemed) and made sacred again. It isn't relegated to the "seconds" bin at the factory as merchandise that has been ruined and devalued by an ontological accident, now marketed for a cut-rate, fire-sale price to the first industrialist who comes along with cash. No, in this view, these little bog turtles we're looking for today are priceless treasures, original creations of the greatest Artist in (and beyond) history—even though they are deemed precisely worthless to someone who would want to build an interstate highway through this bog. Even this black muck squishing out between my fingers is precious, for it represents the natural recycling of organic matter of who-knows-how-many hundreds of years, decomposed leaves and grasses that now nurture the tussock sedge, the skunk cabbage, and all that depend on them.

If you see our world this way, you can't help becoming a Saint Francis, a brother to the whip-poor-will, a sister to the meadow vole, a friend of trees, hailing your fellow creatures in God's world in a spirit of good cheer and good, clean fun. G. K. Chesterton wisely noted how a Franciscan view of creation avoids both the profaning of creation so common in the West and the divinization of creation so common in the East:

> The essence of all pantheism, evolutionism, and modern cosmic religion is really in this proposition: that Nature is our mother.... The main point of Christianity was this: that Nature is not our mother: Nature is our sister. We can be proud of her beauty, since we have the same father, but she has no authority over us; we have to admire, but not to imitate. This gives to the typically Christian pleasure in this earth a strange touch of lightness that is almost frivolity.... Nature is not solemn to Francis of Assisi or George Herbert. To St. Francis, Nature is a sister, and even a younger sister: a little, dancing sister, to be laughed at as well as loved. (*Orthodoxy*, 120)

Follow Saint Francis and Chesterton, and you won't sell your little sister; you will seek to enjoy her, cherish her, protect her, and encourage her to become all she can be.

The eschatology of abandonment is being succeeded by an engaging gospel of the kingdom.

Evangelical-dispensational "left-behind" eschatology (the doctrine of last things or end times that expects the world to be destroyed in just over seven years or one thousand and seven years, depending on the fine print) makes perfect sense in the modern world. Understandably, Christians in the power centers of modernity (England in the 1800s, the United States in the 1900s) saw nothing ahead in the secular story of industrial modernity—nothing but spiritual decline and global destruction. Their only hope? A skyhook second coming, wrapping up the whole of creation in an empty candy wrapper and throwing it in the cosmic Dumpster so God can finally bring our souls to heaven, beyond time, beyond messy matter, beyond this creation entirely. There is virtually no continuity between this creation and the new heavenly creation in this model; this creation is erased like a mistake, discarded like a nonrecyclable milk carton. Why care for creation? Why get sentimental about a container that's served its purpose and is about to be discarded into the cosmic trash compactor of nothingness?

This pop evangelical eschatology made an understandable but serious mistake: it wrongly assumed that modernity was all there was or ever would be, while it rightly assessed how hopeless the future would be if modernity-without-end was indeed upon us. Just as the early Christians could not imagine the gospel outlasting the Roman Empire (unless they got the point of the apocalypse of John), nineteenth- and twentieth-century evangelicals couldn't imagine the gospel outlasting modernity, the empire of scientism, consumerism, and individualism. This eschatology, or expectation regarding the end of the world, has been recently popularized through the *Left Behind* series of novels.

For pop evangelical eschatology to proliferate, it had to ignore or, better, reinterpret much written by the Old Testament prophets. Prophetic visions of reconciliation and shalom *within* history (metaphorically conveyed via lions and lambs, children and serpents, swords and plowshares, spears and pruning hooks) had to be pushed *beyond* history, either into a spiritualized heaven or a millennial middle ground—a posthistoric time zone between history and eternity, so to speak. They also had to marginalize Jesus, with all his talk of the kingdom of God coming on earth, being among us now, and being accessible today.

But now, as more and more of us celebrate Jesus as master teacher as well as Savior, we are struck by the present hope of the "kingdom of God" that is so central in Jesus' message. In this kingdom, Jesus said, sparrows matter. Lilies of the field matter. Yes, people matter even more, but it's not a matter of either/or; it's a matter of degree in a realm where everything that is good matters—where everything God made matters, including that damselfly darting back and forth up above us and the little pickerel frog peering out from the ferns over there.

Increased concern for the poor and oppressed leads to increased concern for all of creation.

God sent Jesus into the world with a saving love, and Jesus sends us with a similar saving love—love for the fatherless and widows, the poor and forgotten to be sure, but also for all God's little creatures who suffer from the same selfish greed and arrogance that oppress vulnerable humans. The same forces that hurt widows and orphans, minorities and women, children and the elderly also hurt the songbirds and trout, the ferns and old-growth forests: greed, impatience, selfishness, arrogance, hurry, anger, competition, irreverence—plus a theology that cares for souls but neglects bodies, that focuses on eternity in heaven but abandons history on earth. When greed and consumerism are exposed, when arrogance and irreverence are unplugged, when hurry and selfishness are named and repented of, when the sacred-secular rift in our thinking is healed, the world and all it contains (widows, orphans, trees, soil) are revalued and made sacred again.

So, as the old system of church as chaplain/baptizer/servant-of-state-and-commerce gives way to a new prophetic role, the poor and forgotten benefit, and so do all living things. One realizes that the spirit of Saint Francis and the spirit of Mother Teresa are one and the same: the Spirit of Jesus, to whom the poor and sick and the sparrows and salamanders are all precious, each in a unique way.

There is a succession in our understanding of ownership.

If a strain of liberal Christianity was once tempted to become the civil religion of socialism (which reverences state ownership), then certainly conservative Christianity has become the happy mistress of capitalism (which enshrines private ownership). No wonder, then, that many Christians defend private ownership and private enterprise as vigorously as a line in the creeds.

At this moment some are asking, "What's wrong with that?" So I ask, "Can we imagine other understandings of ownership that acknowledge, whatever land records say, that *the earth is the Lord's, and all it contains*? Can we imagine an economy based on stewardship rather than exclusive ownership?"

For increasing numbers of us who consider ourselves postliberal and postconservative, "sacred" words such as *private* (meaning personal and individual), *ownership* (meaning autonomous personal and individual control), and *enterprise* (meaning autonomous, personal, individual control over projects that use God's world for our purposes) seem to fly in the face of kingdom values like *communal* (meaning seeing beyond the individual to the community), *fellowship* (which means sharing, holding in common with the community, not grasping as "Mine!"), and *mission* (meaning our participation in God's projects in God's world for God's purposes).

I must admit that, apart from a miracle, I see no human power capable of standing up to the expanding empire of global consumerism. But as a Christian, miracles aren't out of the question for me. It is very possible that a biblical stewardship that celebrates *God's* ultimate ownership could someday fuel a new grace-based economy—just as private ownership currently fuels our greed-based consumerist economy (or as government ownership fuels a control-based socialist economy).

An economy of stewardship doesn't see every majestic mountain as a potential site for strip-mining operations. Nor does it view forests as board feet of marketable lumber. Nor does it assess this spring-fed emergent wetland (once properly drained and bulldozed) as a lucrative site for a "housing development" (an unfitting term if there ever was one, since bulldozers and pavement *un-develop* in hours what it took God's creation centuries to *develop*).

We see everything as God's—from the spring peepers singing in the pool to my right to the aluminum used to manufacture the beer can floating by the cattails to my left. For us, whatever we "own" is really entrusted to us by God, borrowed and reverently used by us for a time, after which we must let go one way or another—either through giving and sharing or through dying and releasing our former possessions to others. Even the molecules that make up our bodies are on loan to us. One day we will give them all back, rendering an account of how we have used them through time—time also being a precious gift of which we have been made stewards.

There is a succession from local/national to global/local.

Modern Protestant Christianity has focused on the local church and the national church. Even when it was involved in "world mission," it often simply expanded its national church structures to other locales, in a kind of spiritual colonialism. But now, many factors lead Christians of all types to become less nationalistic and more global in their thinking.

These factors include the global reach (and domination) of the Euro-American economy and military, the global impact of terrorism, and the global dimensions of ecological threats such as global warming, soil depletion, and air and water pollution. Smokestacks in Japan can kill orcas in Puget Sound; smokestacks in Ohio can kill yellow perch in the Adirondacks; runoff from farms in Pennsylvania can bury oysters in Chesapeake Bay; the pet trade in the United States can deplete rare parrots in New Guinea.

This move from local/national to global/local helps us see the world in more creaturely terms and in more spiritual terms. Creatures live more essentially in local watersheds than nations. Creatures live in ecological habitats, not just political states. Lines on maps between nations and states are, in a sense, human fictions, changing fashions, revealing some truths but obscuring others, facilitating justice in some ways but frustrating it in others.

The more we root ourselves in our local environment, the more we honor our status as creatures. The more we remember that we are part of one planet, the more we acknowledge where God has situated us. The ecological problems we face will require nation-states to address them, no doubt, but the nation-states will have to take themselves less seriously while taking local environments and their interconnection in our integral, holistic (holonic) planetary system more seriously.[1]

A new understanding of neighborliness is replacing an old sense of rugged (a.k.a. selfish) individualism.

Clearly, if our thinking extends beyond "me, myself, and I" to our neighbors (human and nonhuman) as the gospel teaches us, we will realize that our neighbors downstream suffer from our water pollution, downwind from our air pollution, and downhill from our erosion. And when we consider our neighbors in time as well as space, we start thinking differently about our children, grandchildren, and more distant descendants. What toxins are we sending downstream in time to poison them?

What kind of world do we want to bequeath to those downstream from us in time? Do we want to deprive our grandchildren of seeing elephants and tigers and hummingbirds in the wild (consoling ourselves that zoos will keep a few caged ones alive, and museums will have dusty stuffed ones)? Do we want to leave them a world even less in balance than our world today? Is that neighborly? The more we as Christians follow Jesus by thinking in terms of our duty to our neighbors "downstream" in space and time, the more we will take our stewardship of creation seriously.

What exactly will we *do* differently in this emerging theological habitat, this new stage in the spiritual forest succession? That remains to be seen. But for starters, we will see differently and care differently and value differently. If those differences catch on widely among Christians, with Christianity being the largest religion in the world, there are bound to be good effects in our world.

Ultimately, those effects will have to go beyond the important but limited conservation actions of individuals (recycling, reusing, abstaining, etc.). The effects of caring will have to change our systems—transportation systems that depend on fossil fuels and that divide and devastate our nonhuman neighbors' habitats,

---

[1] For more on holonic and integral thinking, see Ken Wilber's *A Theory of Everything* (Boston: Shambala, 2001).

housing systems that maximize human impact through suburban sprawl, farming systems that rape rather than steward land, advertising systems that make us want more stuff that we don't need and that will soon fill even more square miles with rotting, rusting trash.

Even our family systems will need reconsideration. For example, we may realize that the nuclear family (of so much Christian focus) and "subatomic family" (i.e., the nuclear family further split by divorce) both require (and waste) more resources than the truly traditional family—the extended or "molecular" one. Could extended families and intentional households ever make a comeback? If they do, it will be good news for all of creation—including humans.

Those systemic changes may be a hundred years out (please, God, not that long), but if our theology doesn't change our level of caring soon, they may be a thousand and seven years out, and that will surely be too late. Just caring is a good start. That's a real start. Who knows where it could lead?

Volunteering at my watershed (which, again, is the environmental address that matters more than nation, state, or zip code) is one small way to express my care for creation. My care flows from my generously orthodox identity: a creature who wants to care generously for other creatures because I am made in the image of a Creator who cares generously for us all. I hope you'll find your own ways to express care too, whatever your environmental address.

Creation Theology: A Jewish Perspective

Ellen Bernstein

I have a problem. Every time I bring up the term *creation theology*—or even just *creation*—with my highly educated friends and colleagues (scholars and rabbis), even my husband, they all squirm uncomfortably in their seats. But creation theology isn't creationism, the belief that the world was created by God in seven days. Creation theology is interested in the nature of nature, the nature of humanity, and the interplay of the two. It understands God as the continual, creative presence in the world rather than the triumphal, redemptive presence bound to the Israelites. Finally, although creation theology derives from the Bible's two creation accounts, it is in no way limited to these accounts.[1] Rather, the ecological language of the creation accounts helps us discern the ecological vision alive throughout the Hebrew Bible (what Christians call the Old Testament). And I believe that creation theology can be profoundly helpful to us today, particularly in light of the environmental crisis.

Creation, at least in Judaism, is an ongoing process, not a one-time event. The Jewish prayer book reminds us, "Who renews daily the creation…" Life is an unfolding, evolving process. God does not just originate the world; God sustains the world. God is the being of the world or, to use a more ecological metaphor, the ground of our being.

Although creation theology is commonly discussed, I have not found an adequate definition or framework for its application. I believe that naming creation

---

[1] Although creation theology derives from the creation stories in particular, it not bound to them; rather, creation theology and its abiding sense of place, space, and deep time infuse the corpus of biblical literature. There are several other creation texts, including Prov. 8:22–31; Pss. 8; 104.

theology as a legitimate category of thought and interest may help expand our conversation on environment, spirituality, outreach, and interfaith matters.

The Ten Commandments of Creation Theology

Generally the high point of Jewish faith is thought to be the moment when God revealed the law to Moses. But according to some of the ancient rabbis, creation was God's *first* revelation, and inscribed in the creation itself is another dimension of God's law. Unlike Sinai's law, which is explicit, creation's law in Genesis 1–2 is implicit. So we begin with a literary reading of these texts to see what we can learn about God and God's relation to the world, and about nature and human nature.

1. God as Creator

The first face of God we encounter in the Bible is God as Creator. God appears as the wind (Heb. *ruach elohim*), significantly not as the warrior who wrests creation out of chaos.[2] The nature of the creator God is a gentle pulsing, enlivening energy. The rabbis said that it was as if God were like a mother eagle hovering over the fledglings in her nest. Then God's wind or breath crystallized into sound and God spoke the world into being.

In the creation stories, God is artist, potter, farmer, clothes designer, arborist, and provider. God is generative and generous, blessing the animals and people with multitudes, feeding every last one. God is constantly in relationship with the creatures, engaged with the habitats in cocreation, engaged with Adam in naming the creatures.

Outside of Eden, the creator God is the God of the harvest, God of the animals, God of the weather, and God of each person. The creator God is the one that the biblical ancestors encountered in so many natural settings, whether it's in an oak tree at Mamre, a burning bush, a stone pillow, a cloud, or a mountain. The biblical characters were no different from many of us today who tend to find God more easily outside of our day-to-day lives in the stillness and quiet of nature.

2. Goodness

According to the first creation story, everything that was created—light, the sky and water, earth, grasses and fruit trees, sun and stars, days and years, fish, sea monsters and birds, crawly creatures and wild animals, men and women[3]—is good and has value. This value cannot be determined by any human measure; rather, nature has essential value simply because it exists. It was created by God. Being itself

---

[2] This is the view of the Creator found in the older creation accounts in Ps. 74:12–17.

[3] Human beings are (very) good.

is related to godliness. This respect for "all that is" is a clear principle of creation theology.

3. Beauty

The creatures, in all their diverse forms, colors, and textures, are also beautiful. In his commentary on Genesis 1, Rashi's son Rashbam translated *tov,* which is normally rendered "good," as "beautiful." In other words, on (almost) every day, God sees creation—seas, lands, vegetation, swimmers, flyers, and walkers—as beautiful. "Beautiful" conveys a very different feeling than "good."

The experience of creation's beauty can engage us more deeply in the world. Creation's aromatic scents, exotic colors, and rhythmical sounds can stimulate our senses and trigger a full-bodied connection to the world. The experience of beauty can attract, and it can inspire and motivate.

Seeing the whole world as beautiful requires a change in us. We must become open and vulnerable if we are to experience the fullness of beauty. Beauty is an important part of a creation theology; it bids us to give up our self-centeredness and teaches us to care.

4. Habitat: A Sense of Place

God's very first actions involve dividing up the *tohu v vohu* (Heb., unformed matter) to shape the inhabitable and generative spaces of water, air, and earth. Only when the habitats are formed can fish, birds, and animals emerge, each relative to its specific habitat. In the second story, God starts with soil and water, makes a man, and then breathes air into him to give him life.

In both accounts, habitat (air, water, earth) matters. Place matters. *Place* and *habitat* are words from two different domains—culture and biology—that refer to the same thing: the physical environment in which a creature (inhabitant) makes its home. Without habitat, without a home providing food, shelter, and air, no creature can exist.

5. Fruitfulness and Sustainability

Creation, as understood in Genesis 1, provides a vision of a healthy world that is not only able to generate multitudes, but is also able to sustain and diversify itself. The biblical author is preoccupied with establishing a world that will continue *on its own* into perpetuity (with no help from people). This theme of fruitfulness is evident in Genesis 1:11–12, as the Hebrew root *zra,* or "seed," is used six times in two verses. (In the NRSV, the verb form of *zra* is translated as "yielding.") The repetition of the phrase "of every kind" (Genesis 1:11, 12, 21, 24, 25), which translates literally as either "after its kind" or "after their kind," and the explicit blessing for fertility in Genesis 1:22 and 1:28 also speak to the Bible's abiding interest in sustainability. The ending of Genesis 2:3, which in the NRSV is translated "(God) had done in creation" is literally translated "God created to make"—in other words, make more of itself—providing further indication for God's primary concern with the creation's ability to sustain itself into the future.

6. Interdependence, Relationship, and Community

In Genesis 1, God depends on the habitats and unnamed others to help God create. On day three, the text states, "Let *the earth* put forth vegetation," as opposed to "Let there be vegetation" (1:11). On day six, God addresses some unknown being(s), saying, "Let *us* make humankind in our image, according to *our* likeness" (1:26). There is a sense of cocreation.

And although all the creations are deemed "good," only everything altogether, the *interdependent* world completed on day six, is understood as *very* good and is the only one referred to as *the* day. "God saw *everything* that He had made, and indeed, it was very good. And there was evening and there was morning, *the* sixth day" (1:31).

An interdependent universe is by nature a relational one. Creation theology understands the intimate relationship between earth, humans, and animals. God creates *adam* (humans) from *adamah* (soil). Both humans and animals are made of soil, cut from the same cloth. Both fall in the same category of *nephesh chaya,* "living souls."

Furthermore, in the effort to find a suitable partner for Adam, God fashions all the animals from the soil and brings them before him. Adam recognizes the essence of each creature and names it accordingly. We name what we care about. That God offers the animals as potential partners and that Adam names each one are both expressions of the close relationship that exists between the human creature and the rest of the creatures. In naming the creatures, Adam binds himself to them; he now has a stake in the creation.

7. Language

The language we choose to describe our world matters, because language reflects our perceptions and reactions. Through language, we make sense of the world. The language of the creation stories is colorful and lyrical. Genesis 1 uses highly cadenced, rhythmic language to express a sense of the eternal; the language infuses the creation with dignity, even regality. On the other hand, the gripping narrative of Genesis 2 is profoundly compelling in its simplicity, physicality, color, and directness.

With all this attention to language, creation theology teaches that throughout the Bible the allusions to land, water, and air; fish, birds, and beasts; barrenness and fertility; and famine, rain, and food are not meaningless or empty. According to the rabbis, there are no extra words in the Bible; biblical language is not arbitrary. The biblical author would not have wasted words on nature, were it not significant. Indeed, it is impossible to tell the biblical story without the language of creation and the ideas it represents.

If we pay attention to language, we find in the creation accounts a profound sense of place. A sense of place is simultaneously an environmental principle, a literary principle, and a religious principle.

8. Boundaries

In the first creation story, earth, water, and air are created through the act of dividing or the establishment of boundaries. Boundaries ensure integrity and protect that which is bounded off.

People have difficulties respecting boundaries and limits, and herein lies a primary reason for today's environmental crisis. Like Adam and Eve, we always are craving something more. The boundaries inscribed in the creation are a regular reminder that the observance and practice of "limits" is essential to a healthy and sustainable world.

In the second creation story, the earth is cursed when Adam and Eve cross God's boundary, grabbing from the tree that was not theirs. Once the earth was rich, healthy, and bountiful, but now it would yield only thorns and thistles. Once people plucked low-hanging fruits whenever they felt hungry, but now they must toil their lives away in the heat of the sun to bring forth grains from the soil to make bread to eat.

There is no such thing as running "away" or throwing anything "away" in an interconnected universe. What goes around, whether it is a physical pollutant or a spiritual one, ultimately comes around. This is the character of the creator God's world.

9. Humanity's Place: Dominion and Service

In the first creation account, humanity is granted dominion over the world. Although there is much dispute about the meaning of *dominion,* I stand firmly with those who argue that it's our job to act as God's deputies on earth, and it is our honor—indeed our blessing—and our privilege to ensure the continuity and unfolding of creation on God's behalf. God, after all, not humans, owns the land and all its inhabitants.

In the second creation story, humanity is called to "work" and "guard" the garden (Genesis 2:15; NRSV: "till" and "keep"). Yet the Hebrew verb *la-avod,* usually translated "to work," also means "to serve" in a religious sense and is often used in situations of service to God. The Hebrew word *lishmor,* often translated "to guard," also means "to keep" or "to observe" in a religious sense, as in observing Shabbat, the Sabbath. Humanity's place, then, is to serve and observe the garden of the world, and we can understand this service as a religious endeavor.

From my perspective, many environmentalists mistakenly read the Bible's blessing of human dominion in anthropocentric terms and see it as the bane of our existence and the root of all environmental problems. In fact, creation theology offers an elegant environmental ethic: it balances human dominion and human service with an entirely creation-centric view of the world—that is Shabbat.

10. Shabbat: Time Out

Each individual creature is deemed *good* and everything together is pronounced *very good,* but the whole of creation at rest on Shabbat is called *holy.* A day of utter rest and peace, a day apart, Shabbat offers a profound and necessary respite for humans and all of creation.

A day of rest built into the fabric of the week can be a profound environmental practice. The idea of "one day off a week" has been promoted by environmentalists who believe that if we "fast" from driving and using electrical appliances once a week, we will naturally learn to cultivate a greater respect for creation. This "time out" will help us to live more environmentally sustainable lives. These environmentalists are unaware that the twenty-five-hundred-year-old convention of Shabbat is the answer they are seeking.

On Shabbat we, along with all the other creatures, are called to recognize our creatureliness, our earthliness; we are to refrain from our use of nature and simply rest in creation, content in the deep peace of an interdependent universe (that does not rely on people). The workweek encourages an active stance in the world, but Shabbat is reserved for simply "being" and celebrating the delight of creation.

Creation's Language

Creation theology expounds a series of ecological principles, but speaks in a poetic and redolent language to communicate them. As a people rooted in language and story, we must reflect on how our story might provide us the language and perspectives to help us cope with today's mushrooming environmental ills.

The language of creation has multiple valences; it simultaneously speaks to nature, creativity, and humility, and herein lie its power and strength. It teaches morals without moralizing and without preaching. It values the artistry and beauty of the world as well as its boundaries.

People today are seeking refuge from the pervasive idols of constant grasping, the need to push ahead, the obsession with progress and the future, the belief that more is better, and the conflating of success with wealth and status. The language and values of creation can offer a sanctuary to those who are aching to stop and simply be, to appreciate the ordinary—to reap the fruit of the day-to-day. Creation values are consistent with a spiritual practice that is interested in a sense of interiority and spaciousness—that seeks to experience life moment to moment.

Creation theology is inherently generative and hopeful. It implies that the way to address the environmental problems and other problems of our world is through our own creativity. It speaks the universal language of sand, stars, earth, and heaven. It provides a common language by which we can express our deepest yearnings, communicate across cultures and beliefs, and work together on the most pressing issues of our day.

© Ellen Bernstein

Knowing Our Place on Earth:
Learning Environmental Responsibility from the Old Testament
Ellen F. Davis

My argument is simple. The Old Testament offers indispensable insight into the sources of our current environmental crisis as well as guidance toward wiser and more faithful ways of relating to God's creation. On the face of it, the idea that the Bible has anything to teach us about environmental responsibility seems absurd on two grounds. First, the study of the environment, ecology, is a modern science, barely a couple of generations old. The environmental crisis we face is largely a by-product of the technological changes of the last century. How can an ancient text speak to these matters? Second, doesn't the Bible offer *spiritual* guidance? Our problems require sophisticated scientific solutions. How can the Bible help us today?

Those objections are important, because they indicate our society's "commonsense" tendency to separate the physical world from the spiritual realm. Yet the Bible's own perspective is both material *and* spiritual, for God is the creator of everything that is. Therefore the environmental crisis must be seen as a profound religious crisis; it is a massive disordering of our relationship with the God who created heaven and earth. Beginning in Genesis, the Old Testament shows, in image after image, the exquisite design of God's creation. Thus it invites us to accept the privileged and responsible status of *creatures* in the world that God has made.

Learning to Be Creatures

Learning to be creatures may be the most important work we have to do. The loudest and most authoritative voices in our culture, including the advertising industry, have persuaded us that we are autonomous beings, powerful and smart enough to bend the world to meet our present desires. But the perspective of the Bible is radically different, and ultimately more hopeful for all God's creatures. All of us are "the work of [God's] hands" (Ps. 138:8). God has formed the world not as chaos, but "to be inhabited," as the prophet Isaiah declares (45:18). There is a place on earth for every living thing.

However, the art of being responsible creatures is now nearly lost among us,[1] and so "the whole creation has been groaning," as the apostle Paul (who was himself steeped in the Old Testament) writes in Romans 8:22. It "waits with eager longing for the revealing of the children of God" (8:19). "The children of God" are not angels, but simply ordinary human beings, created in God's image (Genesis 1:26–27). The whole created world is longing for *us* to become fully human.

What it means to be fully human is the subject of the first few chapters of Genesis. In the first instance, it means recognizing that the earth is neither a platform for human activity nor a repository of resources to be mined for our convenience. Far from being inert, the earth is living and responsive to God; it generates life, putting forth vegetation in response to God's command (Genesis. 1:11). Likewise, the "swarming" creatures of sea and sky produce offspring at God's word. The great blessing, "Be fruitful and multiply," is spoken to fish and birds on the fifth day (1:22)—before humans have even appeared and received the very same blessing (1:28). From God's perspective, creation is surely *not* all about us.

It is a sad irony that fish and birds, those creatures whose fertility was first blessed by God, are now among the most endangered species on the planet. We have fallen short of God's intention that we should enact our resemblance to God through the exercise of benevolent dominion over the creatures. Instead, through our greed we have turned into a curse God's blessing of fruitfulness for the non-human creatures. From the perspective of the creation story, then, our truly *human* work lies still ahead of us.

Life from the Soil

Being fully human means also understanding our unbreakable bond with the land, the material base of life. One cannot go more than a few chapters in the Old Testament without seeing some vivid reference to land and its importance for humanity, beginning with the image of *adam* (Heb., "man, humankind") formed from *adamah* ("soil") in Genesis 2:7. That wordplay suggests a kind of familial

[1] See Rowan Williams, "On Being Creatures," in *On Christian Theology* (Oxford: Blackwell, 2000), 63–78.

connection; it is a subtle yet powerful reminder that the life of a people comes from its land.

We belong to the fertile earth more than it can ever belong to us. Because we have no life apart from the health of soil and water, we must care for it as one would care for a beloved family member. And so that first "genealogical" statement is followed quickly by a vocational one: "The LORD God took the man (*adam*) and put him in the garden of Eden to *till* it and *keep* it" (Genesis 2:15). Those words could equally be translated, "...to *serve* it and *observe* (or *preserve*) it." Being fully human begins with a careful, nurturing attention to the fertile earth. Land care itself is a primary religious obligation.

All this was well known to the ancient Israelites, since the vast majority of them were farmers. And if one looks at the land of Israel through a farmer's eyes, it is easy to see why that point should be made already in the second chapter of the Bible. The Israelites occupied a fragile ecological niche, the uplands of Canaan (later Judah and Israel), much of which is marginal for agriculture. So they had little enough land to feed their own population, and none at all to misuse. Thin topsoil, periodic droughts, heavy winter rains, and strong winds meant that the Israelites were always contending with the threats of erosion and desertification. Moreover, those mountain slopes and small valleys constitute one of the world's most varied agricultural landscapes. With patterns of wind, rain, and sun that change drastically over a small area, the country is hard to farm well and easy to ruin.

In order to "serve and preserve" the arable land, each farm family had to know its own small plot of land intimately and perpetuate that knowledge through the generations. Young farmers, women and men alike, acquired from their elders crucial skills and very particular local knowledge. The interconnectedness of people and land, of natural systems and human communities, over a long period of time may well be the chief "family value" reflected in the Old Testament. "Honor your father and mother" are among the best known words in the Bible, yet few of us are aware that the Fifth Commandment continues: "...so that your days may be long *and that it may go well for you on the fertile-soil* (adamah) *that the LORD your God is giving you*" (Deut. 5:16, my own translation). Being fully human means honoring those who preceded us by living within the natural limits of the world, caring for the soil, and living wisely on the earth that they have bequeathed to us.

Our Suffering Earth

The Old Testament's abiding concern for the health of the soil may seem completely irrelevant to us today. In the United States, less than 1 percent of the population consists of full-time farmers. But every one of us eats, and so we all depend directly on the health of soil, even if we never think about it. Those who eat in

North America depend on the health of soil not only on the Great Plains, but also in Brazil, Indonesia, Central America, and other places they have never seen. And most have no idea that the effects of our agricultural practices—the largest of all human industries—are catastrophic in every part of the world. Half our forests have been destroyed, a great part of them for industrial-scale agriculture. As for the soil on which human life depends, erosion rates outpace replacement rates by thirteen times, on average.[2] Agriculture is the largest user of freshwater, and many rivers of all sizes have been tapped so drastically that they no longer reach their mouths. Runoff from nitrogen fertilizer has produced the huge dead zone at the mouth of the Mississippi as well as countless others, less notorious, around the globe. We are literally consuming our planet, taking our food in a way that violates its natural systems.

In this situation, it is instructive to notice that the first human sin, as the Bible represents it, is an eating violation. God sets a limit, and the humans choose to override it. God responds with a question both indignant and incredulous: "Have you eaten from the tree of which I commanded you not to eat?" (Genesis 3:11). The immediate result of this first violation is that the ground itself is "cursed" (3:17). It sprouts "thorns and thistles," a clear sign of fragile land that has been mistreated. A group of young farmers with whom I studied this passage opened my eyes to what any ordinary Israelite would have seen in it. They said, "It's obvious: when humans are disconnected from God, the soil will be the first to suffer." They had no theological training, and yet they immediately saw something my urbanized students and I had missed about the meaning of the cursed soil. Beginning here and continuing throughout the Old Testament, land degradation (e.g., Lev. 26:18–20; Deut. 28:15–18) is a sure sign that humans have turned away from God. Conversely, the flourishing of the land (e.g., Lev. 26:3–6, 10; Deut. 28:2–5, 11–12; Isaiah 35; Psalms 65; 72) marks a return to God. In short, the Old Testament represents the condition of the land as the single best index of human responsiveness to God.

It would be overly literal to interpret every natural disaster, every drought or crop failure, as a sign of God's judgment. But the Bible uses stories and evocative language to express profound truths about the order of creation. The truth we should not miss in these passages is that *adam* and *adamah*, humanity and fertile soil, are bound together; there can be no long-term flourishing of the one without the other. As the young farmers saw, human dysfunction evidences itself in the natural order.

---

[2] Brian Halweil, "Where Have All the Farmers Gone?" *World Watch* (September/October 2000): 12–28.

Covenant and the Earth Community

The covenant made at Sinai between God and Israel forms the basis for life in the land that God has promised to the people. Exodus, Leviticus, and Deuteronomy develop Israel's earthy vision for responsible life in community. Here it is rare to read more than a few verses without being reminded of the concrete conditions, the limitations and difficulties, of life in an agrarian community. So what does one do if a neighbor's ox falls on the road, or if a farmer has an ox that is known to be dangerous and yet does nothing to restrain it? (See Deut. 22:4; Exodus 21:28–36.) How often should the fields be left fallow? (See Exod. 23:10–11.) What about the poor in the community, who have no land? How will they get food and gainful employment? (See Lev. 19:9–10; Deut. 23:24–25; 24:19–22.)

Many of us find this part of the Bible boring, because we do not know how to read it. The point is that Israel knows nothing of religious obligation or spiritual experience that is abstracted from the daily business of living responsibly in community with others. The strength of covenant relationship evidences itself "on the ground," as we say, in concrete practices: caring for neighbors and outsiders ("sojourners"), caring for the earth and sharing its bounty, caring also for the domestic animals upon whom we depend, while not exploiting the wild creatures. Obedience to God means remembering that the land itself and all the life it yields are gifts— not outright gifts, but given in trust, placed in our hands *on the condition* that we use each good thing wisely and gratefully. Otherwise, as Israel knew well, all that God has given can be lost.

At Sinai, Israel commits itself to *covenant relationship* with God. God's own covenant history goes back to the days after the flood, to a commitment made to Noah and his descendants and through them to "every living creature that is with you, for all future generations" (Gen. 9:12). Thus the covenant commitment puts us permanently in the same boat with every other vulnerable creature. It draws us into God's own commitment to the well-being of "all flesh that is on the earth" (9:17).

The Perspective of the Prophets

The prophets of the Old Testament look at human behavior in relation to creation from the perspective of God's covenant commitments, made through Noah and later at Sinai. Their perspective is profoundly realistic and at the same time visionary as it stretches from creation to the end of the world. The Bible does not assume that the world as we know it will endure forever, but nonetheless we are answerable for what is now in our hands. The notion that we can knowingly act in ways that severely damage the created order and *not* be judged harshly for it stands in direct opposition to the message of many strands of biblical tradition, especially the prophetic books (from Isaiah to Malachi).

The prophets challenge us to see human conduct and the world as a whole as God must see it. "I looked on the earth, and lo, it was waste and void," Jeremiah says (4:23), echoing the opening words of Genesis. His vision traces a step-by-step dismantling of the created order. First the light disappears, then the mountains shake loose from their foundations. Humans and birds disappear from sight, and then comes the anguished conclusion:

> I looked, and lo, the fruitful land was a desert,
> and all its cities were laid in ruins
> before the LORD, before his fierce anger. (4:26)

In a similar vision of total wreckage, Isaiah sees that the world "languishes and withers":

> The earth lies polluted
> under its inhabitants,
> for they have transgressed laws,
> violated the statutes,
> broken the everlasting covenant.
> Therefore a curse devours the earth,
> and its inhabitants suffer for their guilt. (24:5–6)

In their own historical contexts, both prophets were addressing what we would call national crises: economic injustice, failures of political and religious leadership, false worship. Probably none of us would see in such evils a *direct* threat to the physical integrity of the planet. Yet Isaiah and Jeremiah insisted upon a truth we have too long overlooked: the moral order of the world cannot be neatly separated from its physical order. Their descriptions of the undoing of creation and covenant are more than metaphors for trauma; they express the insight that human sin strikes fundamentally at the integrity of creation. Perhaps only now can we appreciate the full import of these prophetic visions, twenty-six centuries or more after they were recorded.

Intimacy with Our Place on Earth

In and from the land they knew so well, the Israelites learned about God. Indeed, intimacy with land may be the single most important *religious* difference between the biblical writers and ourselves, for so many of us have been formed by an urbanized culture that treats the earth as an abstraction and therefore imagines that God has only "spiritual" concerns.

Learning any form of intimacy is heart-work, best practiced on a daily basis. Certainly this is true of intimacy with God and the things of God. For guidance in that work, Jews and Christians have traditionally looked to the Psalms, 150 poem-prayers, each of which speaks to a moment or facet of our life with God. The Psalms celebrate the world as the work of God's hands; they mourn its brokenness as the result of human sin. Although many of them witness to the reality of profound despair (e.g., Pss. 88; 130), the book as a whole tends toward hope—more explicitly, toward praise. The Hebrew name for the book of Psalms is *Tehilim,* "Praises." These prayers aim at restoring all creation to its proper function of praising God:

> My mouth will speak the praise of the LORD,
> and *all flesh* will bless his holy name forever and ever. (Ps. 145:21)

"All flesh" is a subtle allusion to God's covenant through Noah with the earth and all its creatures, the "everlasting covenant" that humans have subsequently violated (Isa. 24:5). Now the psalmist commits to praying and singing the world back to God.

Psalm 65 gives a detailed picture of God the farmer and humble caretaker of the earth. The One who (literally) "set" the mountains on their foundations now gives exquisite attention to "setting" the grain in abundance (vv. 6, 9). God waters the furrows, smoothes the ridges, "melts" the sun-baked soil with showers, "blesses its growth" (v. 10). And the earth responds eagerly to God's loving care:

> ...your wagon tracks overflow with richness.
> The pastures of the wilderness overflow,
> the hills gird themselves with joy,
> the meadows clothe themselves with flocks,
> the valleys deck themselves with grain,
> they shout and sing together for joy. (vv. 11–13)

What an astonishing picture of God's care for the world. The Creator of heaven and earth viewed as a hardworking but gratified farmer, hot and dirty no doubt, driving home a wagonload of grain. Certainly such a surprising image of God has something vital to say to us who are formed in God's image. In a word, the psalm has power to *humble* those who read and pray it, to root us in the soil on which all life depends. The psalm is an icon, a powerful and holy image of the God-given, exacting, and ultimately joyful work of earth care. God does it, and so must we.

Jesus: Savior of the Earth

James Jones

U p until I began to seriously study the issue, if you had asked me what Jesus had to say about the earth or what could be found in the Gospels to help formulate an environmental ethic, I would have thought, "Precious little." However, all that has changed. I have read the Gospels again and again in light of those questions, and I am still reading. I am determined to read out of the text and not into it. I find myself unearthing things in the Gospels that persuade me that Jesus not only was "earthed," but also saw his mission as none other than the earthing of heaven. "Your will be done on earth as it is in heaven" was the logical sequitur of his prayer for the coming of the kingdom.

My search for evidence of the connectedness of Jesus to the earth begins in the stormiest of waters, with the furious debates over what Jesus meant when he called himself the "Son of Man." It is the only title that he uses of himself. He affirms acclamations that he is the Son of God, Lord, and God and cautiously acknowledges that he is the Christ, the Messiah. Yet when it comes to describing himself, he exclusively uses the phrase "Son of Man."

In a conversation, a chief rabbi reminded me that in Hebrew the phrase "Son of Man" is *ben adam,* "son of Adam," and Adam is the one hewn from the earth, *adamah* in Hebrew. I returned to the Gospel text with a new eagerness. Searching for evidence of a connectedness between Jesus and the earth, I took special notice of those episodes in which he called himself the "Son of Man" and wondered whether I would find there any echoes of Adam or *adamah,* the earth. Every time I came across a "Son of Man" saying I wrote down the verse and marked it in red. Then a remarkable question intruded upon my thinking. It felt like an intrusion, for it seemed to come out of the blue, or at least at an angle to my linear thought processes at the time. "Are there any occasions when Jesus calls himself the Son of Man and in the same breath or in the same context talks about the earth?" There are! As I read through the Gospels again, I wrote down all references to the earth and marked them in green.

I discovered, to my surprise, that there are at least seven occasions where the green and red marks appear together, where we come across the earth mentioned in the same context as the Son of Man. I was genuinely excited by this discovery and read the Gospels, especially these seven passages, with all the eagerness of a new convert. Here they are (the italics are mine):

1. "The *Son of Man* has authority on *earth* to forgive sins" (Matthew 9:6; also Mark 2:10; Luke 5:24).
2. "The *Son of Man* will be in the heart of the *earth*" (Matthew 12:40).
3. "The sign of the *Son of Man* will appear in heaven, and then all the tribes of the *earth* will mourn" (Matthew 24:30).
4. "[God] will quickly grant justice to them. And yet, when the *Son of Man* comes, will he find faith on *earth*?" (Luke 18:8).
5. "For it will come upon all who live on the face of the whole *earth*. Be alert at all times, praying that you may have the strength...to stand before the *Son of Man*" (Luke 21:35–36).
6. "The hour has come for the *Son of Man* to be glorified. Very truly, I tell you, unless a grain of wheat falls into the *earth* and dies, it remains just a single grain" (John 12:23–24).
7. "I, when I am lifted up from the *earth,* will draw all people to myself."... "How can you say that the *Son of Man* must be lifted up?" (John 12:32–34).

(See also Matthew 16:13–19; Mark 14:35–41; Luke 12:39–51; John 3:11–15.)

Every theologian I have talked to has urged me to be cautious about the significance of this and about assuming that Jesus would have been conscious of the Adam/*adamah* root of the designation "Son of Man." What is clear is that this is the only title, if it is that, that he uses of himself. And if it has its roots in Old Testament usage, is it Daniel or Ezekiel or Genesis or the Psalms that is being evoked? However debatable that question is, what is indisputable is that Paul clearly saw a defining relationship between Jesus and Adam (Romans 5; 1 Corinthians 15). But was this ever in the mind of Jesus or even the writers of the Gospels? And if so, is it to be found in his unique self-reference as Son of Man, a title that Paul never uses of him?

Of the passages in the Gospels where the Son of Man and the earth are explicitly mentioned together, let us look at three, one each from Luke, Matthew, and John.

Authority on Earth

The text of the Lukan passage, 5:24, occurs in all three synoptic Gospels. It is the story of the forgiving and healing of a man paralyzed and incapable of walking. Having absolved him, Jesus says to him and his critics, "The Son of Man has authority on earth to forgive sins."

Each synoptic Gospel account includes the reference to the earth. Why "on earth"? What is added to the meaning of his authority to forgive by stating explicitly that it was "on earth"? Many avenues of inquiry are opened up by this question. By suggesting one in particular I am not suggesting the closing down of others. If the title "Son of Man" had any allusion to Adam, to *adamah* and the earth, one avenue of inquiry would lead us to the opening chapters of Genesis. The context of this saying of Jesus is the forgiving of the paralyzed man, "Son, your sins are forgiven." Once in Genesis the topic of sin takes us directly to the disobedience of the first Adam, the sin, and its consequences. But is there any mention of the earth in the story of Adam's falling into sin? There is, of course. The result of his sin is that the earth is cursed. Adam, who was hewn from the earth and called to serve the earth (Genesis 7:7, 15), finds that his sin wreaks havoc on the earth: "Cursed is the ground because of you" (3:17).

The only way the earth can be relieved of its curse is through the forgiveness, healing, and restoration of Adam's successors. It is not only Christian, Muslim, and Jewish theologians who would concur with this view. Countless environmentalists, pressure groups, and lobbyists would testify to the truth that the wholeness of the earth and the future of the planet depend upon the repentance and restoration to wholeness of the human family. You don't have to believe in God to believe the biblical adage "You reap what you sow." The earth bears the wounds of human sinfulness. "The whole creation has been groaning," says Paul, clinging to the "hope that the creation itself will be set free from its bondage to decay" (Romans 8:21–22).

The future wholeness of the earth and the whole of creation according to Paul are bound up with the destiny of the children of God. A redeemed humanity is central to that vision. Key to that redemption is God's forgiveness. In short, how can the earth be freed from the curse of human sinfulness? Only through God's appointing and anointing a successor to Adam to have "authority *on earth* to forgive sins." This is clearly how Luke saw Jesus. This Jesus who is "the Son of Man [who] has authority on earth to forgive sins" undoes the earth-damaging work of Adam. Luke is in no doubt that the person and work of Jesus are related to the first Adam. He may not articulate it with the eloquence of Paul in Romans 5 and 1 Corinthians 15. Yet two chapters earlier, in the climax of his genealogy of Jesus, Luke unequivocally states that this Son of Man who has authority on earth to forgive sins in chapter 5 is descended directly from none other than the "son of Adam," i.e., "son of the one hewn from the earth." "Jesus was about thirty years old when he began his *work*. He was the son of Joseph…son of Enos, son of Seth, son of Adam, son of God" (Luke 3:23–38).

In the Heart of the Earth

Let us turn to Matthew for the second time that the Son of Man and the earth appear in the same context.

Forgiveness presupposes judgment. The authority of the Son of Man to forgive sins on earth assumes that the earth and its people are under some form of divine judgment. This is a theological idea that is out of fashion in many church circles, although it is embedded in the popular imagination along with the question, "Well, if there is a God, why doesn't he do something about the state of the world?" This is an expectation that God will discern between good and bad, divide the people, and act against people and things that are evil. Herein lies an aspiration for a God of justice to judge! I have often said that if we press the question and the hope for God to act in such a way, who, do we imagine, would be left? Such a longing for justice leaves us hoping for mercy. We look to God, therefore, to be both Judge and Savior.

This notion that the earth and its people live under some experience of judgment is strongly felt by environmental lobbyists who daily point to the result of abusive human exploitation of the planet and to the ecological crisis now upon us. "Crisis" comes from the Greek word for "judgment." When the media broadcast the headline "Environmental Crisis," they are declaring to the world a truth greater than we realize. We are reaping what we sow. This is the crisis, the judgment. "Do not be deceived," wrote Paul, "God is not mocked, for you reap whatever you sow" (Galatians 6:7).

It is in the context of judgment that we come to the next passage in which we find Jesus speaking of himself as "Son of Man" and in the same breath talking about the earth: "For just as Jonah was three days and three nights in the belly of the sea monster, so for three days and three nights the Son of Man will be in the heart of the earth" (Matthew 12:40). This reference to his death and burial yields many possible comparisons with Jonah's experience. For the purpose of this book I confine myself to the significance of laying the Son of Man, son of Adam, "in the heart of the earth" by simply posing the question, "What happened to the earth when he died?" The earth quaked (Matthew 27:51). What happened when God raised him from the earth? The earth quaked again (Matthew 28:2). Prior to his placement in the earth and upon his raising from the earth, there were great earthquakes.

I have to confess that when preaching about the crucifixion I have seldom spoken of the earthquake, preferring to concentrate on the other phenomenon, the tearing of the temple curtain from top to bottom. I have overlooked the fact that in the Passion narrative the earth speaks as powerfully as the curtain. As the son of the one hewn from the earth is laid in the heart of the earth, there is a seismic response from the earth's heart. Is this a voice in the chorus of the collective groaning of the whole of creation that Paul writes about in Romans 8:22? The earth, God's creation, is longing for liberation from the curse in Genesis and somehow knows that its own freedom "from the bondage of decay" is inextricably bound up with "the children of God" and "their redemption" and "their freedom," and that comes about through the death and resurrection of Christ Jesus, "who has set us free" and in whom there is "now no condemnation" (Romans 8:1–2).

Staying with the motif of judgment, it cannot escape consideration that Jonah's sojourn in the belly of a whale was a direct result of his disobedience and his determination "to flee from the presence of the LORD" (Jonah 1:10). Like Adam and Eve, who first "hid themselves from the presence of the LORD" (Genesis 3:8) after the fateful act of disobedience when they ate of the tree in the middle of the garden of Eden, so Jonah found himself under the judgment of God. The judgment on Adam was to "return to the ground…and to the dust" (Genesis 3:19). When, therefore, Jesus says that the son of Adam will, like Jonah judged in the belly of a whale, be laid in the heart of the earth, are there echoes here of the judgment of the first Adam, who was sentenced to return to the earth?

The second Adam, the Son of Man, retraces the steps of the first Adam and tastes vicariously the wages of sin—not just death, exclusion from the presence of God, but the return to earth, whence the human family came. The question is therefore raised: as the Son of Man is laid in the heart of the earth after the manner of Adam and Jonah, is there a hint here of God's judgment being visited on Jesus vicariously as he takes upon himself the sins of the cosmos that desecrate the earth? Whatever construction is to be put on the story, the truth is that the earth did not stay silent as it witnessed the Son of Man's death and resurrection.

There are two other instances of earthquakes in the Gospel of Matthew. The first is in the catalog of cataclysmic events that will preface "the birth pangs" of the end of the age (Matthew 24:3, 8). "For nation will rise against nation, and kingdom against kingdom, and there will be famines and earthquakes in various places: all this is but the beginning of the birth pangs" (Matthew 24:7–8).

The language of labor pains in the Gospel here is of a piece with the word and image that Paul uses in Romans 8:22 of the whole of creation being in labor. The earth quakes as the whole of creation goes into labor to give birth to the reality of the new earth and the new heavens as prophesied in Isaiah 65. Central to these eschatological events on earth, according to Jesus in the same chapter in Matthew, is none other than "the Son of Man" (Matthew 24:27–31). Without going into the detail of this apocalyptic passage, the point to make is that Jesus, the Son of Man, seems especially conscious of his relationship with the earth, and the earth seems vigorously vocal as the mission of the Son of Man unfolds. Indeed, in Matthew 19:28–29 Jesus sees the "Son of Man" as central to "the renewal of all things." The Greek word for "renewal" here is *palingenesis*—"the birth again"—of all things. Jesus said to them, "Truly I tell you, at the renewal of all things, when the Son of Man is seated on the throne of his glory, you who have followed me...will inherit eternal life."

The first earthquake in Matthew's Gospel is hidden from view by the way it is translated. It is in Matthew 8 (the four earthquakes in Matthew's Gospel are in 8:23–27; 24:7–8; 27:51–54; and 28:2). Jesus has spoken poignantly of how he, the Son of Man, has nowhere to lay his head. The foxes have holes (in the earth) and the birds of heaven their nests, but he is pillowless. After getting into a boat on the Sea of Galilee, he falls asleep. And there is a storm; actually it's more than a storm—it's an earthquake. In Greek the word here is *seismos*. This is what accounts for the boat being swamped by a great wave. When Jesus then silences the sea and the wind, the disciples are amazed and question, "What sort of person is this?" The earth, which gave birth to Adam, now raises the question as to the identity of Jesus, the son of Adam, at the outset of his mission. And what is that mission? To do God's will on earth as it is done in heaven. It is his prayer and ours. His mission and ours. The earthing of heaven. This is the mission of God. Little wonder the earth quakes as that mission unfolds through the unique ministry of the son of Adam.

Lifted Up from the Earth

Turning to the Gospel of John, we are arrested by the declaration: "All things came into being through him, and without him not one thing came into being" (1:3). This is a confessional statement about the Word, who is Jesus. This is echoed through the primary chapters of Colossians, Ephesians, and Hebrews. Colossians 1:16: "For in him all things in heaven and on earth were created, things visible and invisible.... All things have been created through him and for him." Never has so much theology hung on two such small prepositions, "through" and "for"!

It is these creedal statements that lead to a high view of creation. It is the gift of Christ. Respect and reverence for the earth follow, as they do for the whole of the created order contained in that small "all." This distinctively Christian insight ought to shape and form the Christian attitude toward the environment. Creation does not exist for the human family, but for Christ. The earth is here for us to delight in, to manage, to serve, but its center is inhabited by Christ alone and not us. It is a blasphemy to usurp Christ's place. When critics of Christian attitudes toward the environment have lambasted us for elevating ourselves over the rest of creation and exploiting it by our own devices and for our own desires, they have been right to challenge such anthropocentrism. The Bible dethrones such ambitions and affirms the centrality of Christ not just to salvation, but also to creation.

In John 12:32–34 we find a third combination of the Son of Man and the earth: "'And I, when I am lifted up from the earth, will draw all people [all things] to myself.' He said this to indicate the kind of death he was to die. The crowd answered...'How can you say that the Son of Man must be lifted up?'" Here again the Son of Man is found in the same context as the earth and is cast in the role of the one who will draw all to himself. Echoes again of Colossians: "And through him God was pleased to reconcile to himself all things, whether on earth or in heaven, by making peace through the blood of the cross" (1:20). The Son of Man's ministry is one of connectedness with the earth. Jesus self-consciously sees himself on a mission through which he should lose nothing of what has been given to him. "I have come down from heaven [to earth], not to do my own will, but the will of him who sent me. And this is the will of him who sent me, that I should lose nothing of all that he has given me" (John 6:38–39). Jesus has the whole cosmos in his sights, not just individual souls who want to escape earth and bag a place elsewhere. The earth is within God's cosmic purposes.

The mission of the Son of Man is the renewing of all things. Jesus comes to the earth as the Son of Man urging us to pray for the coming of God's kingdom, which is the doing of God's will on earth as it is done in heaven. Whatever the relationship between the Son of Man and the earth, the clear message of the Gospels is that the earth is the arena of the mission of Jesus.

Jesus Is Coming—Plant a Tree!

Dr. N.T. Wright, Bishop of Durham

My aim is always to allow Scripture itself to enter into dialogue with the issues of our time, including those issues considered as "biblical," and to critique them when they are themselves in fact less than fully in accordance with Scripture. And it is my judgment that the broad sweep of Western theology has been sub-biblical in its approach to the potent combination of end-time discussions and the environment.

We declare, in the Nicene Creed, that Jesus Christ "will come again in glory to judge the living and the dead, and his kingdom shall have no end." But neither mainline Catholic nor mainline Protestant theology has explored very much what exactly we mean by all that. Instead, we have embraced the belief that the ultimate destiny of God's people is "heaven," seen as somewhere detached from "earth." So, the aim of Christianity as a whole, and of conversion, justification, sanctification, and salvation itself, is seen in terms of leaving "earth" behind and going "home" to a place called "heaven."

So powerful is this belief in a great deal of popular preaching, liturgy, and hymns that it comes as a shock to many people to be told that this is simply not how the earliest Christians saw things. For early Christians, the resurrection of Jesus launched God's new creation upon the world, beginning the fulfillment of the prayer that Jesus taught his followers in which God's kingdom would come "on earth as in heaven" and anticipating the "new heavens and new earth" promised by Isaiah and promised again in the New Testament. From this point of view, to borrow a friend's shrewd book title, heaven is undoubtedly important, but it's not the end of the world. Early Christians were not very interested, as our world has been interested, in what happens to people immediately after they die. Instead, they were extremely interested in a topic many Western Christians today have forgotten about altogether, namely, the final new creation, new heavens and new earth joined together, and the resurrection of the body, which will create new human beings to live in that new world.

The question of how you think about the ultimate future has an obvious and direct impact on how you think about the task of the church in the present time and how it relates to the current state of the environment. To put it crudely and at the risk of caricaturing, if you suppose that the present world of space, time, and matter is a thoroughly bad thing, then the task is to escape from this world yourself and enable as many others to do so as possible. If you go that route, you will end up, most likely, in some form of gnosticism; and the one thing gnostics have no interest in is improving the lot of human beings or the state of the physical universe in the present time. Why wallpaper the house if it's going to be knocked down tomorrow?

At the opposite end of the spectrum, some theologians have been so impressed with the presence and activity of God within the present world that they have supposed God wants simply to go on working at it, to go on improving it, until eventually it becomes the perfect place he has in mind. Therefore, the task of Christians is to work at programs of social and cultural improvement, including care for the natural environment, so that God's kingdom will come on earth and the present world attains the result God ultimately intends.

As I said, these are of course caricatures, but they do exist in reality here and there. Those who incline toward one or the other regularly sustain their end of the spectrum by pointing out the folly of those who live at the other end. It won't surprise you to know that I want to take a position at neither extreme. However, I don't just want to occupy a kind of middle ground, but rather the high ground of a biblical eschatology, the doctrine of God's ultimate future, which transcends altogether the kind of "either/or" such a spectrum might indicate.

But before I get down to business, let me illustrate just a little. I first ran into the problem I'm addressing today when I went to do a weekend of lectures in Thunder Bay, Ontario, in the early 1980s. I was working in Montreal at the time and was asked to talk about Jesus in his historical context, which I'd been lecturing about and which eventually turned into my book *Jesus and the Victory of God*. But to my surprise, the main question people had in mind was not the meaning of the parables, or of the cross, or the incarnation itself, but questions of ecology and the environment. Some people in the church had been saying that there was no point in worrying about the trees and acid rain, the rivers and lakes and water pollution, or climate change in relation to crops and harvests, because Jesus was coming back soon and Armageddon would destroy the present world. Not only was there no point in being concerned about the state of the ecosystem; it was actually unspiritual to do so, a form of worldliness that constituted a distraction from the real task of the gospel, which was the saving and nurturing of souls for a spiritual eternity. I can't now remember what sort of answers I gave to these questions, but they have stayed with me and are part of the backdrop for the present environmental crisis.

Our Responsibility in the World

Where, then, do we go to articulate the rich and deep New Testament eschatology that will help us make sense of Christian responsibility in the present world? One place above all, a chapter that towers above most others and without which I personally would be quite lost within my worldview: Romans 8.

Romans 8 is so rich and dense, so full of comfort and challenge, that it's easy to get lost and fail to see both the forest for the trees and, in some cases, some particular trees because of the forest. I'll begin with the key passage, verses 18–27, and I shall then pull the camera back a bit, widen the angle as it were, so we can see the larger narrative within which this forms the great climax.

That last point itself may well be controversial. As a lifelong student of Romans and of commentaries on it, I am impressed by—and depressed by—the strength of the tradition that has effectively marginalized these verses. On the face of it, purely in terms of the flow of Paul's argument, verses 18–27 must be counted the rhetorical climax of this, the central section of Paul's longest and most intricately argued letter. And yet, as I say, preachers, commentators, and theologians in the Western tradition, both Catholic and Protestant, have almost routinely regarded this section as something of a distraction. We know that Romans is basically "about" how individuals get saved and find their way to heaven at last, having been justified by faith and led by the Spirit into a life of holiness. So our eyes skip over the rather difficult language in verses 19–23, the heart of the passage, and go on from the call of holiness in verses 13–17 to the assurance of salvation in verses 28–30, relishing the matchless coda in verses 31–39 and forgetting the awkward bit in the middle. But, as usual when we do this kind of thing with Paul, we lose something absolutely vital, and in this case something that calls into question an entire worldview.

Paul is talking about the glory he says is to be revealed "to us" (v. 18). What he means by that is instantly explained and unpacked in the next few verses. The whole creation, the entire cosmos, is on tiptoe with expectation for God's glory to be revealed to his children. "Glory" is not simply a kind of luminescence, as though the point of salvation were that we would eventually shine like electric lightbulbs. "Glory" means, among other things, rule and power and authority. As other writers (notably Saint John the Divine) make clear, part of the point of God's saving of his people is that they are destined not merely to enjoy a relaxing endless vacation in a place called "heaven," but that they are designed to be God's stewards, ruling over the whole creation with healing and restorative justice and love.

Verses 20–21 make this plain. The whole creation has become, by God's decree, a place of corruption and deterioration both moral and physical. We often think of the universe of space, time, and matter as automatically corruptible, but Paul insists this was not the Creator's original intention. As always, when he's dealing with the ultimate future, Paul goes back to Genesis 1–3, so that his eschatology is rooted in a strong view of creation as God's good handiwork. Then comes the great statement of the ultimate future in verse 21: the creation itself will be set free from the slavery that consists in corruption, set free to obtain the freedom from slavery that will be its lot when God's children are glorified. Many translations obscure this, implying a generalized freedom and glory that is shared equally by the redeemed and by creation, but this is not what Paul says and certainly not what he means. What he means in verses 18–19 is that when God's redeemed people are finally rescued and we are given our resurrection bodies, then we will be set in "glory" and, as God's image-bearing children, have sovereign rule over the whole creation. Then, God's project will be where it was supposed to be going right at the start when God created humankind in his own image, to be fruitful and to look after the garden. When humans are put right, creation will be put right. That is the ultimate point, the glorious full sweep of Paul's doctrine of salvation through Jesus Christ.

Our Responsibility in the Present Time

Paul's critique of his fellow Jews is that they had failed to see that the reason God called them in the first place was so that, through them, he could rescue the whole human race. They were right to regard their call as nonnegotiable, but wrong to think it was only about them all along. The same thing seems to have happened in today's Christian readings of Paul. We have been right to think that Paul is vitally concerned with the salvation of human beings, the redeeming death of Jesus, justification by grace through faith, and so on. But we have been wrong to suppose that the only purpose of this was the salvation of humans, as it were away from the world, away from the whole created order. As Israel was in God's purposes vis-à-vis the whole human race, so are humans vis-à-vis the whole created order. That's how it has been since Genesis 1–2, and that's how, according to Paul, God intends it to be at the last.

And that is why, in the passage that follows, Paul describes the concentric circles of "groaning": the world groaning in travail, like a woman in labor awaiting the birth of the child; the church groaning with inexpressible sighs, longing for the resurrection of the body; and the most remarkable thing of all, the Spirit groaning within us in ways too deep for articulate speech (v. 26). I have written elsewhere about the way in which this is no accidental or incidental reference to prayer and the work of the Spirit. The whole point is that when we pray we are not mere distant or feeble petitioners. We are starting to take up our responsibility as God's image-bearing human beings, sharing God's rule over creation. Because we ourselves are weak and corrupted in our unresurrected state, the exercise of this "glory" is always mysterious and even painful as we find ourselves in prayer at the heart of the pain of the world and yet discover God's Spirit groaning within us. That is a key part of our calling in the present time and very relevant to today's topic: that we should take responsibility in the present time in prayer, even if it can't come to articulate speech for God's world as it groans in travail.

And underneath that responsibility there is of course the analysis of God's world, of the whole creation. We are not to regard the created order as random or to see its present disarray as somehow its own fault, but to understand it in terms of an initially good creation now radically spoiled but awaiting redemption. There is nothing wrong with space, time, and matter themselves; what is wrong is what's happened to this good creation. It is enslaved; and what slaves need is redemption.

The Redemption of the Earth

That theme, of slaves being redeemed, provides the clue that will help us glimpse and grasp the larger picture Paul has been developing for the last few chapters in Romans. That picture ought to frame our conversations about a Christian view of the whole created order in the future and in the present. Paul was far more aware of the story of creation, and also of the Exodus—the time when the Creator God went down to Egypt to rescue his people from slavery and lead them home through the wilderness to their promised land, guiding them to that inheritance by his own personal presence. Among the key stages of this divine work are the crossing of the Red Sea, bringing the people through the water out of slavery and into freedom, and the arrival at Mount Sinai for the giving of the law. All this happened as the long fulfillment of the promises God made to Abraham in Genesis 15, the chapter in which he established his covenant with him and his family, requiring Abraham to believe that God was indeed the creator and life-giver, the one who gives life to the dead and calls into existence things that are nonexistent. This aspect of God's character, his promise-keeping covenant faithfulness, by which he will put his world to rights, can be summed up in a single phrase: God's righteousness.

And with that, working back step by step from the language of Romans 8:18–27, we realize that we have been describing the whole theme of the Letter to the Romans. Romans is not just about me, my sin, and my salvation, though to be sure it certainly is about those too. It is about the way in which the Creator God keeps the covenant he made with Abraham by providing an exodus to beat all exoduses.

Now watch and see how this works out in the detail of Romans and realize what a powerful emphasis this places on the God-given human responsibility for creation. Having announced and explored his main theme of God's righteousness in chapters 1–3, Paul grounds it in Romans 4 by expounding the promises of God to Abraham and the faith by which Abraham grasped those promises. Summarizing these promises, Paul declares that God's promise to Abraham was that he would inherit the *world*. Paul, in company with some other Jewish thinkers of the time, looks beyond the temporary and limited reach of a territorially restricted promise to God's ultimate intention. The whole world, he is declaring, is now God's holy land. This then sets the scene for the story of the great, ultimate exodus—the exodus of the human race and, with it, of all creation.

Paul begins with Adam in Romans 5, in slavery to sin with his descendants. Then, in chapter 6, he describes how they come through the water from slavery to freedom, through baptism into Christ's death and resurrection. This brings them naturally to Mount Sinai and the giving of the law. But now it becomes clear that the law, although it's God's holy and righteous law, can only and must only condemn them. Like Israel in the wilderness, they are destined to perish because of their disobedience, were it not for the fresh act of grace by which God rescues them. What the law could not do, because it was weak through the flesh, God has done in the death of Jesus Christ and in the power and presence of the Spirit.

Romans 8 thus comes up in three dimensions. Paul's emphasis on the indwelling of the Spirit in verses 1–11 corresponds directly to the way in which, as the children of Israel were on their way through the wilderness, God dwelt in their midst in the pillar of cloud and fire. The result, as in Jewish theology, is the rebuilding of the Temple or tabernacle, which in the terms of Romans 8 means neither more nor less than the resurrection of the body (vv. 9–11).

This brings us to the crucial passage, Romans 8:12–17. Here Paul speaks of Christians being "led by the Spirit" and so refusing the opportunity to go back again into slavery and fear (vv. 12, 15), like the Israelites in the wilderness fantasizing about going back to Egypt and being told instead to go on, led by the presence of God in their midst. That presence assures them, again just like with the Israelites, that they are God's children. "Israel is my firstborn son," the great slogan of the Exodus 4:22, is answered here by "(we) have received a spirit of adoption. When we cry, 'Abba! Father!'" (Rom. 8:15). Thus it is that same Spirit that bears witness with our spirit that we are God's children and therefore also his "heirs" (8:17), those who will receive the promised inheritance (cf. Gal. 4:1–7; Eph. 1:14).

Our Inheritance: Heaven or Holy Land?

But what is the "inheritance"? Here centuries of the Western Christian tradition have given the emphatic, though often implicit, reply: "heaven." Heaven is our home, our inheritance. We have reread the story of the Exodus in those terms, with the crossing of the Jordan symbolizing the bodily death that will bring us to heaven itself, the "Canaan" for which we long. But this, as you will realize, is the whole point I've taken so long to get to. *This is precisely not what Paul says.* What he says would have been clear, had not the whole Western tradition been determined to look the other way at the crucial point. The inheritance is not "heaven." Nor is it, of course, Palestine, a small geographical strip in the Middle East. The inheritance is the whole renewed, restored creation. I will say it again: *the whole world is now God's holy land.* That is how Paul's retold Exodus narrative makes full and complete sense. And that, I suggest, is the ground plan for a fully biblical and fully Christian view of creation and of our responsibility toward it.

Let me just take this one step farther before turning to my second major topic, that of the second coming itself. Even granted the reading of Romans I have offered you, it might still be possible for someone to say: "Well, maybe one day God will renew the whole created order. That will be marvelous. I look forward to sharing in it with my resurrection body. But I don't have that resurrection body yet, so what can I hope to do to help creation in its present state of groaning? And isn't it a bit presumptuous to think there's anything I can do, if in fact God will eventually do it all himself? Shouldn't we just wait until then?"

Well, there might be some logic to that. But the whole point of the Christian gospel is that, with the resurrection of Jesus and the gift of the Spirit, God's future has come forward to meet us in the present. What God intends to do at the last has already broken into the world the way it is. (That, indeed, is the really dramatic point about Easter: not that God has simply done an extraordinary miracle on Jesus' behalf, but that with Jesus, new creation has already begun, and Jesus' followers are invited not only to benefit from it, but to share in the new project it unleashes.) We are not in the position of first-century Jews, waiting for the great eschatological event. We are with the early Christians, celebrating the fact that part one of that great event has already happened in the resurrection of Jesus and the outpouring of the Spirit, and looking forward eagerly to part two when what began at Easter and Pentecost will at last be completed.

We Are God's Agents of Renewal

With Easter and Pentecost, the remaking of God's creation of space, time, and matter has already begun. One of the primary places where that is to be seen and known is in Christian holiness. It is not a matter of certain rules and regulations being observed, but a matter of Christians taking proper human responsibility for a bit of the created order, their own bodies, and working at making them reflect the image of God as they were meant to (see Rom. 8:29). Bearing God's image doesn't just mean sorting yourself out, but reflecting that image into the creation in wise stewardship, the renewal of human life to which we are called in Romans 8:12–17. It's no surprise that Romans 8 does indeed issue Christian responsibility for creation not only in the future, but also in the present.

Look at it like this. What if a friend came to you and said, "I'm having real trouble resisting temptation, and I'm always falling helplessly into sin. But it doesn't really matter, because one day God will give me a new body that won't be capable of sinning, so why shouldn't I wait for that?"

I hope you would respond by saying, "But God has *already* begun that ultimate, final work of new creation. By baptism and faith, you have left behind the old order of sin and death, and by God's Spirit within you you have God's own resurrection power to enable you, even in the present, to resist sin and live as a fully human being at last. You must therefore live, in the present, as far as possible as you are going to live ultimately in the future."

So now apply that to Christian care for God's good creation. One day God will renew the whole created order, and according to Romans 8 he will do it by setting over it, as he always intended, his own image-bearing creatures. They will reflect God's glory into his world and bring God's saving justice to bear, putting the world to rights and making the desert blossom like the rose. And if we are already in Christ, already indwelt by the Spirit, we cannot say we shall wait until God does it in the end. We must be God's agents in bringing, at the very least, signs of that renewal in the present time. And that must mean that we are called in the present time to search out how the present, groaning creation can be set free from its bondage to decay and experience the freedom that comes when the children of God are glorified. In Christ and by the Spirit, we already are. To deny a Christian passion for environmental work, for putting the world to rights insofar as we can right now, is to deny the goodness of creation, on the one hand, or the power of God in the resurrection and the Spirit, on the other, or quite possibly both.

The "Second Coming"

"Jesus is coming, so plant a tree!" The reason that statement is counterintuitive to the point of being funny is that for a great many Christians who devoutly believe in the second coming of Jesus, the second coming *is* the point. The whole world as we know it is done away with, and Jesus snatches his own people up to heaven to live there with him forever. And if that's what's going to happen, why would you plant a tree? Why oil the wheels of a car that's about to be driven over a cliff?

But is that what the second coming's all about? We shall look in a moment at one of the key passages in which many Christians have discovered that sort of doctrine, and I shall suggest that it has been sorely misunderstood. But first, let me sketch very briefly one or two points of central importance in the New Testament that strongly hint that if we read the second coming like that, we are missing the point. In Ephesians 1:10 Paul declares that God's purpose from all eternity was to sum up all things in Christ, things in heaven and things on earth. Colossians 1:15–20, one of the most astonishing Christian poems ever written, declares that all things were created and reconciled through and for Christ. Neither Ephesians nor Colossians gives any support to the idea that a major part of the created order is destined to be thrown into the trash can, while redeemed humans are going to live forever somewhere else entirely. Indeed, in Colossians 3 we get a hint of a different way altogether of looking at what is commonly called the "second coming." The Greek term often rendered "reveal" (NRSV) can also be translated "appear." Paul says, "For you have died, and your life is hidden with Christ in God. When Christ who is your life appears, then you also will be revealed with him in glory" (Col. 3:3–4).

Think about the meaning of "appear" for a moment. When we talk of Jesus "coming," we make it sound as though he is presently a long way away, as though, in order to "come," he would have to make a massive journey from a far distance. But "appear" is different. As we find in many passages of the New Testament, Jesus is not far away; he is in heaven. *Heaven is not a place up in the sky—it is God's dimension of what we think of as ordinary reality.* This is one of the most fundamental things to grasp about the biblical structure of the universe, and it is the failure to grasp it that leaves many Christians puzzled about how to put together the biblical picture of the end times of God's ultimate future.

The point is that Jesus is presently in God's dimension, heaven. Heaven is not a place within our space-time continuum, but a different sphere of reality that overlaps and interlocks with our sphere in numerous though always mysterious ways. It is as though there is a great invisible curtain hanging across a room, disguising the fact that there is another space back there that can be integrated with the space in front, our space. One day the curtain will be pulled back, and the two spaces or spheres will be joined forever, and of course Jesus himself will be the central figure. Now at that point you could say that he had "come," in the sense that we hadn't been aware of him and then we were. But Colossians speaks of his "appearing," and so does 1 John 3:2, where it is written, "What we do know is this: when he is revealed, we will be like him, for we will see him as he is."

The picture of the Son of Man "coming on the clouds" in Mark 13:26 demands to be read in light of the biblical passage quoted from Daniel 7:13. In Daniel, the "one like a son of man" is ascending, not descending. He is "coming" up to God, not "coming" back to earth from heaven. I have therefore argued, in line with several other scholars, that these passages are not at all about the "second coming" of Jesus, but rather about his vindication after suffering. I therefore leave them aside from this discussion—not because I don't believe in the second coming, but because I don't believe these passages teach it.

But the second coming itself is presupposed or asserted all over the place in the New Testament. Not so often, however, is it integrated with the picture we have seen in Romans 8 of the whole creation being renewed and with the new creation being born from the womb of the old. Various passages attempt something like this. In 1 Corinthians 15, Paul sketches an extraordinary picture of the coming end-times scenario with a great battle between good and evil, a battle that God wins through the victory of Jesus Christ. The whole point of the chapter is that God is going to remake the whole creation. Once again, Genesis 1–3 are very close up in Paul's mind. His focus on the bodily resurrection takes place within the larger scenario in which God will win the victory over all the forces of corruption and decay, with the final enemy being death itself. This victory will be the moment of Jesus' "royal appearing." So here in 1 Corinthians, we have the final victory and renewal, the resurrection of the dead, and the royal appearing of Jesus all together.

Something similar could be said of Revelation 21, though here it is, remarkably, the church, not Jesus, that comes down from heaven. Indeed, Revelation 21 has rightly been hailed as the ultimate rejection of all attempts to rethink salvation in terms of an escape to heaven from earth. On the contrary, the bride of Christ has been waiting in heaven all along and now appears on earth to be married to the bridegroom. Like those in Romans 8 and 1 Corinthians 15, this is a remarkable picture of continuity and discontinuity. On the one hand, the new creation is genuinely new, to the point where the text says that the first heaven and the first earth had passed away. On the other hand, there is clearly strong continuity between the two worlds, since part of the task of God in the new world is to wipe away all tears from all eyes. This is a mystery to which we shall return.

Before I come to the most contested passage, let me say a word about those passages, such as 1 Peter, that speak of a salvation being "reserved in heaven for you." The point again is that heaven is God's space, where God keeps his purposes ready and waiting against the day when it's the right time to bring them out onto the stage of the earth. If I get home late and my wife leaves me a message saying, "Your dinner is in the oven," that doesn't mean she expects me to get into the oven to eat my dinner. It means it's ready and waiting and when the time comes I can get it out and eat it at the table in the ordinary way. Our problem here (compounded by the radical misreading of the phrase "kingdom of heaven" to mean a place called "heaven" to which God's people go after their death, rather than the reign of heaven) is that centuries of people who have supposed that the name of the Christian game was simply to "go to heaven when you die" have left the church. Often, very devout churchgoers regard the present world as essentially evil and believe the purpose of salvation is to escape it. Not so. The Jesus who taught us to pray "Thy kingdom come on earth as in heaven" also declared that all authority in heaven *and on earth* had been given to him. Luke's account of the Ascension and what follows indicates well enough that the point of Jesus being in heaven is that he is now enthroned as Lord of the world, not that he has gone far away and is merely waiting for us to follow him.

That brings me to two lines that are always quoted in this connection. In John 14:2–3, Jesus says there are many dwelling places in his Father's house and that he's going to prepare a place for his followers. Now, the Greek word for "dwelling places" here is *monai,* the plural of *monē.* If you look up *monē* in a Greek lexicon, you'll find that it doesn't mean "dwelling place" as in "a home where you go and live forever," but rather a lodging house, a place to stay a while, rest, and be refreshed until it's time to continue on your journey. What Jesus is apparently saying is that between death and resurrection there is a place prepared, a place of light and peace and rest, where we can wait in the presence of Jesus until the final day. That too is what Paul means in Philippians 1:23 when he talks about being "with Christ, which is far better." So, again, when Jesus says to the brigand in Luke 23:43, "Today you will be with me in Paradise," he isn't talking about the ultimate resurrection life. After all, even Jesus didn't go straight to that, but was well and truly dead and buried and then raised bodily three days later. Where was he in between? *Paradise* is a Persian word for a beautiful garden and was already a term in use to denote the place where the dead go to be looked after and refreshed until the time of resurrection.

Now to the key passage in 1 Thessalonians 4, where generations have taken Paul's wonderful mixed metaphors as though they were meant literally. In chapter 4, writing to a situation where some in the church had died, Paul has five things to say about what will happen at the end. First, when the last day comes, we shall be together with those who have died in the Lord. Second, the Christian dead will be raised to new bodily life, and the Christian living will be transformed. Third, this will be a great act of vindication, especially for those Christians who have suffered for the faith. Fourth, this will all happen when Jesus is revealed as king and lord of the whole world. Fifth, when this happens, the reappearance of Jesus will be like Moses coming down Mount Sinai with the law to judge the people.

Now suppose you're Paul. You're good at mixing your metaphors, and you try to say all those things all at once, knowing perfectly well that heaven is not a location within our space-time universe, but rather a different kind of space that intersects with ours in complex and interesting ways. How are you going to create this effect?

Well, you might try to say that Jesus' appearing from heaven will be like Moses reappearing from the cloudy mountaintop after the divine trumpet blast. Or you might try to put that together with the image from Daniel about the Son of Man "coming on the clouds." Or you might try to indicate that Jesus' reappearing was like Caesar's "coming" to a town or city, or perhaps returning to Rome after some great victory, and the citizens going out to meet him in order to escort him into the city. And if you are Paul, trying to say all those things at once, you might well write something like this: "The Lord himself, with a cry of command, with the archangel's call and with the sound of God's trumpet, will descend from heaven, and the dead in Christ will rise first. Then we who are alive, who are left, will be caught up in the clouds together with them to meet the Lord in the air; and so we will be with the Lord forever. Therefore encourage one another with these words" (1 Thess. 4:16–18). And Paul would not think for a moment that a whole school of theology would try to combine those into a single literal picture.

Now I hope you see the point I'm making. It isn't a matter simply of deconstructing the massive "left behind" theology, though we must do that if we are to think biblically. We must focus on one element in particular. The Greek word *parousia,* "royal appearing," was regularly used to describe Caesar's "coming" or "royal appearing" when visiting a city or when returning home to Rome. And what happened at such a *parousia* was that the leading citizens would go out to meet him. But when the citizens went out to meet Caesar, they didn't stay out there in the countryside or have a picnic out in the fields and then bid him farewell. They went out *to escort their lord into their city.*

In other words, Paul's picture must not be pressed into the nonbiblical image of the second coming according to which Jesus is "coming back to take us home," swooping down, scooping up his people, and zooming off back to heaven with them, away from the wicked earth forever. As Revelation makes clear in several passages, the point is that Jesus will reign on the earth. At his royal appearing, his faithful ones will go to meet him in order to escort him back into the world, which is rightfully his and which he comes to claim—to judge and to rule with healing and wise sovereignty. "When Christ shall come," we sing in a favorite hymn, "with shout of acclamation, and take me home, what joy shall fill my heart." What we ought to sing is, "When Christ shall come, with shout of acclamation, *and heal his world,* what joy shall fill my heart." In the New Testament the second coming is not the point at which Jesus snatches people up, away from the earth, to live forever with him somewhere else. The second coming is the point at which he returns to reign not in heaven, merely, but upon the earth. After all, the risen Jesus in Matthew 28:18 declares, "All authority in heaven and on earth has been given to me," and makes that the basis for his commission to his disciples.

What, then, of the frequently quoted line "My kingdom is not from this world" (John 18:36)? Jesus' kingdom is not *from* this world. It doesn't originate in the present world order. If it did, as he goes on to say, his followers would use violence. But there is no question in John's Gospel that Jesus' kingdom is *for* this world. It comes from heaven but is destined for earth, or rather for the new heavens and new earth spoken of elsewhere in the New Testament. That is why, as the Judean leaders declare, if Pilate lets him go, he is no friend of Caesar.

God's New Creation

It is very striking how the earliest Christians clung on, as indeed did the mainstream rabbis of the period, to the twin doctrines of creation and judgment: God made the world and made it good, and one day he will come and sort it all out. Take away the goodness of creation, and you have a judgment in which the world is thrown away as garbage, leaving us sitting on a disembodied cloud playing disembodied harps. Take away judgment, and you have this world rumbling forward with no hope. Put creation and judgment together, and you get new heavens and new earth, created not *ex nihilo,* but *ex vetere,* not out of nothing, but out of the old one, the existing one. And the model for that is of course the resurrection of Jesus himself, who didn't leave his body behind in the tomb and grow a new one, but whose body, dead and buried, was raised to life three days later and recognized by the marks of the nails and the spear. Easter is the beginning of God's new creation. We don't have to wait. It has already burst in. And the whole point of John 20–21 is that we who believe in Jesus are to become, in the power of his Spirit, not only beneficiaries of that new creation, but also agents.

I end with an extraordinary verse. "Therefore, my beloved, be steadfast, immovable, always excelling in the work of the Lord, because you know that in the Lord your labor is not in vain" (1 Cor. 15:58). Now what is that exhortation doing at the end of a chapter on resurrection? If we were to take the normal Western view of life after death, a long chapter on resurrection might end up with something like: "Therefore, my beloved, lift up your heads and wait for the wonderful hope that is coming to you eventually." But for Paul, as is clear throughout 1 Corinthians, *the resurrection means that what you do in the present matters into God's future.*

The resurrection, God's recreation of his wonderful world, which has begun with the resurrection of Jesus and continues mysteriously as God's people live in the risen Christ and in the power of his Spirit, means that what we do in Christ and by the Spirit in the present is not wasted. It will last, and be enhanced, in God's new world. I have no idea what precisely this means. I do not know how the painting an artist paints today in prayer and wisdom will find a place in God's new world. I don't know what musical instruments we shall have to play, though I'm sure Bach's music will be there. I don't know how my planting a tree today will relate to the wonderful trees that will be in God's recreated world. I don't know how my work for justice for the poor and for remission of global debts will reappear in that new world.

But I know that God's new world of justice and joy, of hope for the whole earth, was launched when Jesus came out of the tomb on Easter morning. I know he calls me and you to live in him and by the power of his Spirit to be new-creation people here and now, bringing signs and symbols of the kingdom to birth on earth as in heaven. The resurrection of Jesus and the gift of the Spirit mean that we are called to bring real and effective signs of God's renewed creation to birth even in the midst of the present age. Not to do so is at best to put ourselves in the position of those Second Temple Jews who believed they had to wait passively for God to act—when God *has* acted in Jesus to inaugurate his kingdom on earth as in heaven. At worst, not to bring works and signs of renewal to birth within God's creation is to collude with the forces of sin and death themselves.

This doesn't mean that we are called to build the kingdom by our own efforts or even with the help of the Spirit. The final kingdom, when it comes, will always remain the free gift of God, a massive act of grace and new creation. But we are called to build *for* the kingdom. Like craftsmen working on a great cathedral, we have been given instructions about the particular stone we are to spend our lives carving, without knowing or being able to guess where it will take its place within the grand eventual design. What we are assured, by the words of Paul and by the fact of Jesus' resurrection as the launch of that new creation, is that the work we thus do *is not in vain*. That says it all. That is the mandate we need for every act of justice and mercy, every environmental program, every effort to reflect God's wise, stewardly image into his creation.

In the new creation the ancient human mandate to look after the garden is dramatically reaffirmed. The resurrection of Jesus is the reaffirmation of the goodness of creation, and the gift of the Spirit is there to make us the fully human beings we were supposed to be, precisely so that we can fulfill that mandate at last. What are we waiting for? Jesus is coming. Let's go and plant those trees.

The Dominion of Love

Barbara Brown Taylor

I f birds could write books, then their story of creation would no doubt read
quite differently from ours. Sea creatures would probably still arrive on day
five in the bird book of creation—pelicans would insist on that—plus, it makes
sense to work your way up from the depths of the sea to the vaults of the heavens, filling creation with creatures as you draw nearer and nearer to God. By that
reasoning, land creatures would come next—mice, chipmunks, goats, humans,
camels—things like that—earthbound creatures that could not get off the ground
for more than a second or two without coming right back down again—hard—on
all those *feet*.

Bats were good in the air. Mountain goats were so-so, but humans, well ... It
was really kind of pitiful watching them try to fly—jumping off rocks, flapping
their arms. Sometimes when they slept you could see their limbs twitching, as if
they were dreaming of flight. None of this was their fault, of course. Bird mothers taught their children never to make fun of land creatures. "God made them
that way," the mothers said, "the same way God made you. Now go outside and
fly."

But day six! That was the day everyone got excited about when the book of
creation was read in Bird Church—the day God created birds in the divine image.
Male and female God created them: sparrows, ravens, wood ducks, and hoopoes;
whooping cranes, turtledoves, mockingbirds, and indigo buntings. They were all
different and they were all alike, with two eyes, one beak, and those two marvelous
wings—their daily assurance that they were made in the image of the Creator.

"Guard me as the apple of the eye; hide me in the shadow of your wings," they
read in the book of Psalms (17:8). "Be merciful to me, O God, be merciful to me,

for in you my soul takes refuge; in the shadow of your wings I will take refuge, until the destroying storms pass by" (57:1). "How precious is your steadfast love, O God! All people may take refuge in the shadow of your wings" (36:7).

Made in God's image, the birds were glad to do what they could—waking people up in the morning with sweet songs, thrilling human children with their aerobatics, and pretending to like the gummy white bread the children fed them down by the lake. Sometimes, under special orders from God, they made some bread deliveries of their own in the wilderness. A few of the birds even volunteered to become food themselves, when a bunch of humans got lost in the desert and did some really unbearable groaning about how hungry they were. The quail gave their lives—but really, what else are you going to do, when you are the only creatures in all of creation made in the image of God? You love as God loves, right? You love *what* God loves, because that is what your life is for.

I cannot tell you how many times I read the first chapter of Genesis before I noticed something new on day six. For years and years I thought that we humans had day six all to ourselves—you know, the pinnacle of the story—God's last, best word in the utterance of creation. With all lesser creatures out of the way, the sixth day finally arrived.

God ordered a kettledrum roll, cleared the divine throat, and said, "Let us make *humankind* in our image, according to our likeness"—*Yes, yes, here we are at last!*—"and let them have dominion"—*Oh, yes! Do let us have that! I have always wanted dominion!*—"over the fish of the sea, and over the birds of the air, and over the cattle, and over all the wild animals of the earth, and over every creeping thing that creeps upon the earth" (Gen. 1:26). *Over the whole ranch! As far as the eye can see! This really is a wonderful book, don't you think?*

Then I noticed for the first time that day six does not start there. Day six starts two verses earlier, with the creation of land animals—cattle, to be exact. The text does not mention any other animals by name *except* cattle—twice, in fact, along with unspecified creeping things and wild animals.

So now all of a sudden I do not have day six to myself anymore. I am sharing it with *cows,* for God's sake, which I do not have anything against except that they seem incredibly stupid, they slobber a lot, and basically all they do is eat grass. Couldn't God have started day six with—oh, I don't know—*snow leopards?* Or maybe *antelope?*

I understand that cows were probably very valuable in the ancient world—like buffalo for Native Americans—one single animal that provided milk, meat, hide, and even dung for the fire. Cows are sacred in India, after all. Cows rank higher there than most humans. And then there is the book of Jonah, with the best last line in the whole Bible: "And should not I spare Nineveh, that great city, wherein are more than sixscore thousand persons that cannot discern between their right hand and their left hand; and also much cattle?" (4:11, KJV).

Still, this new information is a real comedown—a reminder that although God may have made human beings for special purposes, we were not made of any more special stuff than the rest of creation. We were made on the same day as cows and creeping things and wild animals of every kind. God gave us dominion, it is true, but God did not pronounce us better than anything else God had made. "God saw everything that he had made, and indeed, it was very good. And there was evening and there was morning, the sixth day" (Genesis 1:31).

In 1967, a historian named Lynn White wrote an article for *Science* magazine in which he charged that the roots of the ecological crisis are essentially religious. The problems derive from Christian tradition in particular, he said, which has taught people to view themselves as "superior to nature, contemptuous of it, willing to use it for our slightest whim."[1]

The Christian ethicist James Gustafson, who recognizes what White describes, calls this "despotism"—one of the historical ways that people of faith have interpreted their divine right to dominion over the earth. In this view, you do not have to ask a tree before you bulldoze it for a subdivision. You just knock it down, push it into a pile with the corpses of other trees, and set it on fire. Then you are free to scrape the clear-cut earth free of green moss, tiny wild iris, unsuspecting toads, and a couple of thousand years' worth of topsoil before calling the pavers to come cover your artwork with steaming asphalt. Oh, and if the mountain laurel block your view of the river, just turn the dozer on them too. The next time the river floods, the banks will collapse without those living roots. The river will silt up eventually, until you can push a sharp stick three feet straight down in the sandy bottom without ever hitting what used to be the riverbed. But what the heck, if the trout die, you can still buy some at the grocery store already cleaned and boned for just a few dollars a pound. You are Lord over this playground, after all—God *said* so, right? It is all for you.

A lot has happened since 1967—so much that I do not hear many Christians sounding like despots anymore. The word I hear more often these days is "stewards." We are stewards of God's creation—not masters ourselves, but divine employees, entrusted with caring for the vineyard until the master comes home. In this view, you can still build your subdivision, but you are going to save all the trees you can, planting two for every one you cut down, and covering the rudely exposed topsoil with wheat straw so that it does not blow away. Why will you go to all this trouble, which will certainly cost you more money than despotism would? You will

---

[1] James M. Gustafson, *A Sense of the Divine* (Cleveland, OH: Pilgrim Press, 1994), 87.

do it because the earth is not your possession. Like the talents in Matthew's parable, these natural resources are all on loan to you, and you will be held accountable for what you have done with them when the loan comes due.

There is a fair amount of threat in this view, which can keep the motivation for stewardship in the neighborhood of fear. There is also that problematic phrase "natural resources." "As stewards of creation, we are called to protect our natural resources," I hear people say, which also protects the sense that nature exists primarily for our use. We do not defend earth, wind, and water because they are worthy of defending. We defend them because we need them to live. If we do not take care of them now, they will not be here later—and we will be on our way to Mars.

I can think of at least two more biblical models for dominion, however, especially if you understand the word to mean being in relationship to creation in the same way God is in relationship to creation. In 1923, the Jesuit priest Teilhard de Chardin celebrated a "Mass over the World" right in the middle of a desert in China. With his hands in the air, he offered the whole cosmos back to God. Doing so, he embodied his deep conviction that human beings exist neither to rule the world nor to use it up, but to bless its elements the same way we bless bread and wine—offering the fruits of God's body back to God, with humble and hearty thanks for all our lives.[2]

Maybe you have to be Catholic to warm up to an image like that, but I think even the most frills-free Protestant—or, for that matter, any sixth-day creature at all—can get something from Carl Sagan's view of creation. He was a scientist, of course, so he used the longer time frame, but here is what he said. If we could squeeze the creation of the cosmos into a single year, then the big bang happened on January 1. The sun and the planets came into existence on September 10. Human beings arrived on the scene at ten minutes before midnight on December 31.[3]

Yet it is in us, at this late date, that the universe has become conscious. We are the first creatures to articulate the motion of the planets. We are the first to discern the commonality of all life. For those of us who believe God is the source from which we all arose, we are the first creatures to say so out loud. God may well prefer the sound of spring peepers, but I have to believe there was joy in heaven when the first human being looked at the sky and said, "Thank you for all this."[4]

Saint Francis, of course, did not say it. He sang it, composing songs to Brother Sun and Sister Moon:

[2] Ian Bradley, *God Is Green* (New York: Doubleday, Image Books, 1990), 104.
[3] Carl Sagan, *Dragons of Eden* (New York: Random House, 1977), 13–17.
[4] Barbara Brown Taylor, *The Luminous Web* (Boston: Cowley, 2000), 42–43.

All creatures of our God and King,
lift up your voices, let us sing:
Alleluia, Alleluia!
Bright burning sun with golden beams,
pale silver moon that gently gleams,
O praise him, O praise him,
Alleluia, alleluia, alleluia!

For Francis, being human meant being in communion with all creation. Cows? *Sure!* Sparrows? *Of course!* Clouds? *Why not?* I do not think Francis got the distinction between "animate" and "inanimate" any better than he got the distinction between princes and lepers. Life was life for him, and God was love. To be made in God's image meant to be made in the image of love. Once, when he was too sick to preach, Francis simply stood up in front of his congregation and regarded them with love. "Preach the gospel always," he said, once he got his voice back. "If necessary, use words."

I think I know where he learned that. You have heard it too, haven't you? "You have heard that it was said, 'You shall love your neighbor and hate your enemy.' But I say to you, Love your enemies and pray for those who persecute you, so that you may be children of your Father in heaven" (Matthew 5:43–45).

Wait, wait, wait a minute. How does that work? Well, there is one sun in heaven that shines on everyone and everything. See, no matter what genus or species they are, no matter how good or bad they smell, no matter what they have done or left undone, they all get sun. In the same way, when the rain comes down, everyone and everything gets refreshed—those who deserve it right along with those who do not. That is just the way God is with God's creatures. If they are here, God made them, and if God made them, God loves them.

Sure, some of them give God headaches and others break God's heart, but we humans do not get to make distinctions. Unlike cows, we are here to preside over the dominion of love. Made in the divine image, we are here to love as God loves. "Be perfect, therefore, as your heavenly Father is perfect" (Matthew 5:48).

Wait, wait, wait a minute. How does that work? Well, you know how it feels under the shadow of those wings, right? Perfect. So move over. Make room, because there is a whole creation seeking refuge, and you, you are the spitting image of the One who gives life to all.

Amen.

Loving the Earth Is Loving the Poor

Gordon Aeschliman

Serving God's creation and doing justice for the poor are inseparable missions in today's world. Said another way, to hurt the earth is to hurt the poor; to serve the earth is to serve the poor. It shouldn't be surprising that creation and justice are inextricably linked. Creation (the environment) is the opening story of our faith tradition. Human beings are called to the sacred duty of caring for creation. That care is not a light responsibility. Genesis 2:15 calls us to "keep" the garden. That word *keep* is the same notion as the one in the lovely blessing in the Old Testament in which we pray, "The LORD bless you and keep you" (Num. 6:24). In the manner that God keeps us we are to keep creation.

Just as keeping God's creation sits within the original mission given to humans, compassion and justice for the poor sit at the core of our faith tradition. The Scriptures are plentiful regarding God's love for those who are poor. In the earlier biblical texts in which God is giving Israelites instructions on how to live faithfully, they are told as agrarian people not to go through their fields twice to reap the harvest, but instead to leave the second harvest for the poor. Not only is this command given to seed farmers, but to those who produce olives, grapes, and oil as well. "You shall not strip your vineyard bare, or gather the fallen grapes of your vineyard; you shall leave them for the poor and the alien: I am the LORD your God" (Lev. 19:10). In what would seem an extreme requirement in today's market economy, God instructs the faithful to leave their land fallow on every seventh year for the benefit of the poor. "The seventh year you shall let it rest and lie fallow, so that the poor of your people may eat.... You shall do the same with your vineyard, and with your olive orchard" (Exod. 23:11).

The prophet Isaiah suggests that the true form of spiritual worship is to "share your bread with the hungry, and bring the homeless poor into your house; when you see the naked, to cover them" (58:7). This idea is echoed by Jesus, who tells his followers that he knows who true believers are by what they have done for those who are hungry, naked, thirsty, sick, and in prison (Matt. 25:31–46). God even makes the idea of compassion for the poor personal: "Whoever is kind to the poor lends to the LORD, and will be repaid in full" (Prov. 19:17). Imagine, God sits in our debt if we are kind to those who are poor.

Creation Bears the Burden of the Twenty-First Century

Two modern realities make the combination of care of the earth and justice for the poor particularly salient today. First, the world population is expanding exponentially. My grandparents were born into a world where the total human population was less than the current population of China alone. Today the world population is equal to six of those Chinas. And my grandparents were born into a world of few flushing toilets, no shopping malls, no credit cards, very few cars, no jet engines, no electronic household appliances or computer games.

Second, our modern lifestyle of consumption puts a heavy burden on the earth. In contrast, Grandpa and Grandma recycled everything. The United States, for example, constitutes roughly 4 percent of the global population, but it consumes almost one-third of the world's resources to support modern convenience and expectations. What that means is we are living outside the capability of our own land to support us. Even worse, we are taking from others to bolster our way of life. We go to another's valley, well, river, forest, mine, and even sky to supply our high level of consumption. Our high level of consumption also means a high level of waste—from all the effluence from manufacturing and packaging to the toys that last for barely a year and the clothes that quickly go out of fashion. The United States produces more than a quarter of the world's greenhouse gases and is responsible for more than 30 percent of the garbage, toxins, and other kinds of waste that make it into the earth's rivers, lakes, oceans, and landfills.[1]

And here's the harsh reality for the poor: it's usually their resources we are capturing to support our lifestyle, and their land, rivers, and lakes where we are dumping our waste. Quite literally, the poorest of the earth live on wealthy people's garbage. In the United States, close to 85 percent of all toxic landfills are in neighborhoods comprised of people of lower economic means and people of color. Native American reservations often agree to accept landfill waste as a means to increase their income, sometimes with life-threatening consequences.

For example, the Spokane Indians in Washington State agreed to create a landfill for the Dawn Mining Company, which meant that they would receive waste from

---

[1] Environmental Defense Fund, United Nations Environmental Program, National Wildlife Federation.

thirteen of its sites throughout the United States. What they did not realize was they were accepting dangerous toxic tailings from gold and silver mines, waste that brought harm to both their environment and their bodies. For the Dawn Mining Company, this was a good economic transaction: it was able to bypass federal requirements for toxic waste management by going to a poor community on a reservation.

West Africa has often been the dumping ground for toxic waste from the United States, although the local communities were not aware of the dangerous nature of the substances they agreed to "store" for a lucrative fee. At times the environmental group Greenpeace has been able to warn villages and towns that they were literally trading their children's health and the health of their land for a commercial payoff.[2]

Being a Voice for the Poor of the Earth

"Who speaks for the poor?" is a perfectly good question. The Scriptures instruct: "Speak out for those who cannot speak, for the rights of all the destitute. Speak out, judge righteously, defend the rights of the poor and needy" (Prov. 31:8–9). The poor of the earth too often bear the burdens of our Western lifestyle. The age-old biblical tradition is pretty clear about where we are supposed to stand in this modern travesty.

If we are wealthy, there is the sense that we live above the land. Our water comes from faucets for showering and bathing, from bottles for drinking. Our food comes from grocery stores; our fuel, from pumps on any number of street corners; our heat, air conditioning, lights, and power, from little switches on the walls. We don't look to see if there is water in the well, to see if our goat has enough milk to share with us, to see if there are enough trees left to provide us warmth through another bitterly cold winter, to see if the rain has brought enough moisture for our crops (unless we are part of the small percentage of Americans who farm for business).

In the wealthy West we live what is called a "phantom" lifestyle. Rather than relying on the earth around us, we almost invisibly (like a phantom) rely on the earth of others. If we run out of vegetables, we import them from another country. If we need more electricity, we import it from another state or river or region. The same is true for water, minerals, fruit, and meat. If we need more petroleum, we import it from abroad. Very often we lose our innocence in the capturing of those resources. We take land that belongs to another group of people; we invade countries; we destroy rain forests. The true cost of living the modern lifestyle is

---

[2]The statistics and stories in these paragraphs are from numerous reports generated by the World Bank, United Nations Development Program, United Nations Environmental Program, Environmental Development Fund, World Wide Fund, Greenpeace, and the Environmental Protection Agency.

not measured by what we pay at the cash register. Rather, it is measured by what we have done to other people's rivers, valleys, oceans, and land. And, more precisely, what we have done to the poor.

It would probably surprise us to know how regularly the poor show up in our daily routines, even in something as simple as a glass of orange juice at breakfast. While working on some poverty issues in Belize, my team and I at Target Earth were confronted with intestinal illnesses and rashes affecting Mayan kids in a little village of six hundred people. These Mayans used to live in the rain forest for thousands of years, but had been kicked out in the early 1990s when their ancestral land was sold to a large orange producer. (The Mayans never kept title to land; they didn't believe you could personally own it.) These six hundred people are what we call "environmental refugees," the real poor of the earth and the "least of these" shut off from God's creation. While investigating the source of the illnesses these kids had, we discovered that there were toxins in the river they were using for drinking water and washing. As it turns out, when the rain forest where they used to live was cut down to grow oranges, pesticides and fungicides leeched into the river. Not only were these people kicked off their land, but they were poisoned by the cultivation of the crops that replaced their rain forest. The oranges that were produced were converted to concentrate that showed up in orange juice throughout the United States. One could say that the true price of a glass of orange juice is the rain forest, the river, and the home of the Mayan community in Belize. And they are the ones paying the price, while those who are wealthy enjoy the nourishment of the orange juice.

The biblical notion of compassion is a demanding concept. It does not allow for an arrogant disposition toward those who are "have-nots." Scripture pushes into the arena of justice. To do justice is to correct the systems that unfairly harm the poor. It's not enough to hand out turkey baskets at Thanksgiving or presents at Christmas (both of which are lovely compassionate traditions), but God's followers are called to ensure justice on behalf of the poor. "The righteous know the rights of the poor; the wicked have no such understanding" (Prov. 29:7). "Give justice to the weak and the orphan; maintain the right of the lowly and the destitute" (Ps. 82:3). "I know that the LORD maintains the cause of the needy, and executes justice for the poor" (Ps. 140:12). The mistreatment of the poor is seen as callous and coldhearted. But, to make clear God's disdain for this behavior, harming the poor is put on par with sexual immorality. "They who trample the head of the poor into the dust of the earth, and push the afflicted out of the way; father and son go into the same girl, so that my holy name is profaned" (Am. 2:7). It's "personal" against God to harm the poor. "Those who oppress the poor insult their Maker" (Prov. 14:31).

Poverty Is a Severe Reality Today

In today's modern times, one out of every three people lives on less than $2 per day—2.4 billion people total.[3] That's impossible to comprehend. If a third of the world cannot afford one cup of Starbucks a day, that should matter to Christians. Not because we care about the Starbucks part, but rather because the integrity of our faith hangs on what we do about those whom Jesus referred to as "the least of these" (Matt. 25:40).

The poor always live on the margins of God's creation. They do not have the luxury of living above God's handiwork as we seem to. In our romantic bond to the modern lifestyle and the promise of pleasure that comes through wealth and technology, we have lost our moorings as people of faith. We trample the earth and the poor with a kind of disregard that in earlier days would cause one to blush and feel a healthy kind of shame. Culturally, it used to be a shared Christian value to live in moderation, to avoid excess, to share our resources with those less fortunate rather than to hoard them for a flagrant display of wealth.

Within our faith community we now have preachers who specifically call the faithful to pursue wealth and prosperity as their right; we have economists who equate consumption and the free-market system with Christianity—as if God designed or endorses a free-for-all grab of the earth. We even celebrate the economics of monopoly, "winner-takes-all" living. The game of Monopoly teaches us to take control of all properties, all lands, and, if we modernized it, all rivers, lakes, and oceans. The problem for Christians is that you cannot win at Monopoly, because the poor lose.

The cultural preoccupation with wealth and its temporal benefits is not founded in the faith tradition. Indeed, that preoccupation is as dangerous to our spirituality as it is to the bodies of the poor. It certainly is not in sync with the character and call of the Creator. Our wholesale destruction of God's creation in the pursuit of our self-defined good life is certainly a curious contrast to the biblical notion of the character of Christians—temperate, self-controlled, compassionate, satisfied, not coveting, not stealing, not harming those who have little.

It should seem normal to those of faith that the Creator is the one who is the most concerned with the poor of the earth. All of us were created fearfully and wonderfully in our mother's womb. Each person is an act of personal creation. Thousands of years ago, even before the presage of a booming world population and a no-holds-barred cultural pursuit of wealth, God articulated the call to be kind to the earth and to the poor who depend upon the earth "When the poor and needy seek water, and there is none, and their tongue is parched with thirst, I the LORD will answer them, I the God of Israel will not forsake them" (Isa.

---

[3] The World Bank, United Nations Development Program.

41:17). If it's not too mundane for God to worry about where the poor will get water and food, neither should it be too mundane for us. By God's original intent, all creation was to flourish. All the beasts of the earth, all flying things, all people were instructed to multiply and fill the whole earth. The vision of the garden back then was a place of nurture and goodwill for all its members. All of it was perfect. Neither God's character nor mission has altered since those founding days of our good earth.

The Church Can Be a Positive Agent of Change

But there is hope. Throughout the world, I have seen Christians and churches who have found effective and simple ways to serve both the earth and the poor. Through *advocacy* churches are speaking up for the rights of indigenous peoples and the poor whose land, rivers, and forests are being taken away by corporations, governments, and the wealthy. They are opposing the construction of toxic waste sites, landfills, or toxic manufacturing plants near the homes of the poor or near the land and rivers that impact the poor. Christians have gathered annually in Washington, D.C., through the efforts of the Religious Campaign for Forest Conservation, Target Earth, and the Evangelical Environmental Network, among others, to lobby directly with members of Congress on these issues. Because of their joint public campaign, these groups have halted the government's intention to squash the Endangered Species Act.

Through *protection* churches are helping to fund the purchase of rain-forest or other sensitive lands. This is one way to protect endangered species, indigenous peoples, rivers, and lakes all in one action. Through the Eden Conservancy Project, for example, thousands of acres of rain forest have been set aside in the Mayan foothills of Belize, protecting a major biological corridor for endangered species. All of that land was purchased through donations by various Christian groups, and the land has been set aside in a permanent environmental trust.

Floods and hurricanes usually affect the poor more than any other group. That's because the poor usually can only afford to live on land that is more vulnerable (steep hillsides, floodplains, and coastal zones that are affected by tsunamis). One way the church has served the earth and the poor is through *restoration*—replanting ruined crops, establishing nurseries (for new vegetable and fruit seedlings to replace what was ruined), and relocating communities to safer lands.

Becoming free of the "American dream" is no easy task, but it can happen on many levels. The first thing to do is to evaluate our *personal consumption* and to become free of the idea that our worth and fulfillment are wrapped up in the pursuit of "stuff" and status symbols. (It's hard to imagine Jesus preaching a life of getting all the goods we want or of seeking the approval of the cultural establishment.) The less we consume, the less we are taking from the earth of the poor, from the rivers of the poor, from the future of the poor. The less we consume, the less garbage we are dumping into the rivers and backyards of the poor. Developing an ethic of consumption that meets our needs while also defending God's creation and delivering justice for the poor is the frontline biblical work for Christians today.

We are promised that one day there will be no more tears. God will wipe them all away. We are promised a new heaven and a new earth. In this new heaven and earth there will be no more pain (Revelation 21:1–4). That's a world without thirst, without hunger. But that day will not be our doing. What we have is now. And so we reverently keep God's earth. And we seek justice for the poor of God's earth. Nothing less suits our faith, nothing less honors the Creator. And in today's modern world, nothing less makes sense.

When asked what he'd do if he knew God were coming back tomorrow, the theologian Martin Luther responded that he'd plant a tree. There's something wonderfully pure and hopeful about that response. He understood that tending God's good earth was itself a high act of spiritual worship, an act of faith that honored the possession of the Lord. If it's true that to hurt the earth is to hurt the poor, it is also true that being kind to the earth is being kind to the poor. Every time we save another acre of rain forest, clean up another river, recycle another bottle, say no to another frivolous purchase, we are serving God's creation and we are serving the poor.

Teachings on Creation through the Ages

Edited by J. Matthew Sleeth, M.D.

The gathering of this collection of historical quotes was both inspiring and sobering. Inspiring because so many over the years have spoken about the need to care for creation, including a vast number of theologians and believers. Sobering because of our refusal to heed these, and the Bible's, instructions and wisdom. Inspiring because of the unity of thought by those who lived in vastly different times, places, and circumstances. Sobering because of the magnitude of the consequences of our consumerism for future generations if we do not align our actions with God's mandate to be humble and meek.

In his parting words, Jesus tells his disciples, "Go into all the world and proclaim the good news to the whole creation" (Mark 16:15). What follows is a collection of writings on that great commissioning.

I believe in God, the Father almighty, creator of heaven and earth.

The Apostles' Creed (first century)

Let us turn our eyes to the Father and Creator of the universe, and consider... the total absence of any friction that marks the ordering of His whole creation.

Clement of Rome (ca. 37–101), *Letter to the Corinthians* 1:19

The initial step for a soul to come to knowledge of God is contemplation of nature.

Irenaeus (120–202)

The sending of rain is an event greater than the giving of the Torah. The Torah was a joy for Israel only, but rain gives joy to the entire world, including animals and birds.

Midrash Psalms 117 (second century)

Nature is schoolmistress, the soul the pupil; and whatever one has taught or the other has learned has come from God—the Teacher of the teacher.

Tertullian (160–ca. 230), *De Testimonio Animae*

Whoever destroys anything that could be useful to others breaks the law of *bal tashchit,* "Do not waste."

Babylonian Talmud, *Kodashim* 32a (second or third century)

While the sage, Honi, was walking along a road, he saw a man planting a carob tree. Honi asked him, "How long will it take for this tree to bear fruit?"

"Seventy years," replied the man.

Honi then asked, "Are you so healthy a man that you expect to live that length of time and eat its fruit?"

The man answered, "I found a fruitful world because my ancestors planted it for me. Likewise I am planting for my children."

Babylonian Talmud, *Taanit* 23a (second or third century)

By the greatness and the beauty of the creatures, proportionately the Maker of them is seen.

Athanasius (297–373), *Against the Heathen* 45:1–2

I want creation to penetrate you with so much admiration that wherever you go, the least plant may bring you the clear remembrance of the Creator.... One blade of grass or one speck of dust is enough to occupy your entire mind in beholding the art with which it has been made.

Basil the Great (329–79), *Hexaemeron,* Homily V,
"The Germination of the Earth"

The world has been created for everyone's use, but you few rich are trying to keep it for yourselves. For not merely the possession of the earth, but the very sky, the air, and the sea are claimed for the use of the rich few.... The earth belongs to all, not just to the rich.

Ambrose of Milan (340–97), *De Nabuthe* 3

There is nothing that has been created without some reason, even if human nature is incapable of knowing precisely the reason for them all.

John Chrysostom (ca. 354–407), *Homilies on Genesis* 7.14

Even though you may think them superfluous in this world, creatures such as flies, bugs, and gnats have their allotted task in the scheme of creation.

Genesis Rabbah 10:7 (third–fifth centuries)

Without earth, there is no rain, and without rain, the earth cannot endure, and without either, humans cannot exist.

Genesis Rabbah 13:3 (third–fifth centuries)

Even if you are old, you must plant. Just as you found trees planted by others, you must plant them for your children.

Midrash Tanchuma, Kodashim 8 (fourth–fifth centuries)

Some people, in order to discover God, read books. But there is a great book: the very appearance of created things. Look above you! Look below you! Read it. God, whom you want to discover, never wrote that book with ink. Instead, He set before your eyes the things that He had made. Can you ask for a louder voice than that?

Augustine (354–430), *De Civitate Dei,* Book 16

We should remain within the limits imposed by our basic needs and strive with all our power not to exceed them. Once we are carried beyond these limits in our desire for the pleasures of life, there is no criterion to check our onward movement, since no bounds can be set to that which exceeds the necessary.

Nilus of Ancyra (407–94), *Ascetic Discourses,* vol. 1, *Philokalia*

If a dead man is raised to life, all men spring up in astonishment. Yet every day one that had no being is born, and no man wonders, though it is plain to all, without doubt, that it is a greater thing for that to be created which was without being than for that which had being to be restored. Because the dry rod of Aaron budded, all men were in astonishment; every day a tree is produced from the dry earth…and no man wonders…. Five thousand men were filled with five loaves;… every day the grains of seed that are sown are multiplied in a fullness of ears, and no man wonders. All…wondered to see water once turned into wine. Every day the earth's moisture, being drawn into the root of the vine, is turned by the grape into wine, and no man wonders. Full of wonder then are all the things which men never think to wonder at, because...they are by habit become dull to the consideration of them.

Pope Gregory the Great (540–604)

How can a person of flesh and blood follow God?... God, from the very beginning of creation, was occupied before all else with planting, as it is written, "And first of all, the Eternal God planted a Garden in Eden." Therefore...occupy yourselves first and foremost with planting.

Leviticus Rabbah 25:3 (fifth–seventh centuries)

"See my works, how fine and excellent they are! All that I created, I created for you. Reflect on this, and do not corrupt or desolate my world; for if you do, there will be no one to repair it after you."

Ecclesiastes Rabbah 7:13 (sixth–eighth centuries)

Poor innocent little creatures, if you were reasoning beings and could speak, you would curse us. For we are the cause of your death, and what have you done to deserve it?

Isaac the Syrian (late seventh century)

The whole earth is a living icon of the face of God.

John of Damascus (675–749), *Treatise*

I do not worship matter. I worship the Creator of matter who became matter for my sake, who willed to take His abode in matter, who worked out my salvation through matter.... Because of this I salute all remaining matter with reverence, because God has filled it with his grace and power. Through it my salvation has come to me.

John of Damascus, *On the Divine Images* 1:16

Christ wears "two shoes" in the world: Scripture and nature. Both are necessary to understand the Lord, and at no stage can creation be seen as a separation of things from God.

John Scotus Eriugena (810–77)

"They shall take dominion (*v'yirdu*)." The Hebrew connotes both "dominion" (derived from *radah*) and "descent" (derived from *yarad*): when humanity is worthy, we have dominion over the animal kingdom; when we are not, we descend below the level of animals and the animals rule over us.

Rashi (1040–1105)

Wherever I turn my eyes, around on Earth or to the heavens
I see You in the field of stars
I see You in the yield of the land
In every breath and sound, a blade of grass, a simple flower,
An echo of Your holy Name.

Abraham ibn Ezra (1092–1167)

We shall awaken from our dullness and rise vigorously toward justice. If we fall in love with creation deeper and deeper, we will respond to its endangerment with passion.

Hildegard of Bingen (1098–1179)

The quality of urban air compared to the air in the deserts and the forests is like thick and turbulent water compared to pure and light water. In the cities with their tall buildings and narrow roads, the pollution that comes from their residents, their waste makes their entire air reeking and thick although no one is aware of it.

Maimonides (1135–1204)

If you have men who will exclude any of God's creatures from the shelter of compassion and pity, you will have men who will deal likewise with their fellow men.

All creatures of our God and King, lift up your voice and with us sing....
O brother wind, air, clouds, and rain, by which all creatures ye sustain...
O sister water, flowing clear, make music for thy Lord to hear....
Dear mother earth, who day by day unfoldest blessings on our day...
O praise ye! Alleluia!

Francis of Assisi (1181–1226)

Any error about creation also leads to an error about God.

Thomas Aquinas (1225–74), *Summa Contra Gentiles* 11.3

If I spend enough time with the tiniest creature—even a caterpillar—I would never have to prepare a sermon. So full of God is every creature.

Meister Eckhart (ca. 1260–ca. 1327), *Sermons*

Let a man fear, above all, me, his God, and so much the gentler will he become toward my creatures and animals, on whom, on account of me, their Creator, he ought to have compassion.

Birgitta (1303–73), *Revelations*

I saw three properties in the world: the first is that God made it. The second is that God loveth it. The third is that God keepeth it. But what beheld I therein? Verily the Maker, the Keeper, the Lover.

Julian of Norwich (1342–1423), Revelations of Divine Love

I [God] did not intend my creatures to make themselves servants and slaves to the world's pleasures. They owe their first love to me. Everything else they should love and possess, as I told you, not as if they owned it, but as something lent them.

Catherine of Siena (1347–80), The Dialogue

If thy heart were right, then every creature would be a mirror of life and a book of holy doctrine. There is no creature so small and abject, but it reflects the goodness of God.

Thomas à Kempis (1380–1471), The Imitation of Christ

God writes the Gospel not in the Bible alone, but also on trees, and in the flowers and clouds and stars.

Martin Luther (1483–1546)

The creation is quite like a spacious and splendid house, provided and filled with the most exquisite and the most abundant furnishings. Everything in it tells us of God.

John Calvin (1509–64), Institutes 1:14

Let everyone regard himself as the steward of God in all things which he possesses. Then he will neither conduct himself dissolutely, nor corrupt by abuse those things which God requires to be preserved.

John Calvin, Commentary on Genesis

If we learn to love the earth, we will find labyrinths, gardens, fountains, and precious jewels! A whole new world will open itself to us. We will discover what it means to be truly alive.

Teresa of Avila (1515–82)

All the creatures—not the higher creatures alone, but also the lower, according to that which each of them has received in itself from God—each one raises its voice in testimony to that which God is,… each one after its manner exalts God, since it has God in itself.

John of the Cross (1542–91)

We give you thanks, most gracious God, for the beauty of the earth and sky and sea; for the richness of mountains, plains, and rivers; for the songs of birds and the loveliness of flowers. We praise you for these good gifts and pray that we may safeguard them for our posterity. Grant that we may continue to grow in our grateful enjoyment of your abundant creation, to the honor and glory of your name, now and forever.

The Book of Common Prayer (1549)

Open your eyes, and behold, the whole world is full of God.

Jacob Boehme (1575–1624), *The Way to Christ*

Thou art in small things great, not small in any.... For thou art infinite in one and all.

George Herbert (1593–1633), "Providence"

Praise God, from whom all blessings flow; praise him, all creatures here below.... Praise God, the source of all our gifts.

Thomas Ken (1637–1711)

It would go a long way to caution and direct people in their use of the world that they were better studied and known in the creation of it. For how could man find the confidence to abuse it, while they should see the Great Creator stare them in the face, in all and every part thereof?

William Penn (1644–1718), *Fruits of Solitude*

Chrysostom, I remember, mentions a twofold book of God: the book of the creatures, and the book of the scriptures: God having taught us first of all by his works, did it afterwards, by his Words. We will now for a while read the former of these books; 'twill help us in reading the latter. They will admirably assist one another.

Cotton Mather (1663–1728), *The Twofold Book of God*

There's not a plant or flower below but makes Thy glories known,
And clouds arise, and tempests blow by order from Thy throne;
While all that borrows life from Thee is ever in Thy care;
And everywhere that we can be, Thou, God art present there.

Isaac Watts (1674–1748), *Divine and Moral Songs for Children*

All created things are living in the hand of God. The senses see only the action of the creatures, but faith sees in everything the action of God.

> Jean Pierre de Caussade (1675–1751), *Abandonment to Divine Providence*

All that is sweet, delightful, and amiable in this world, in the serenity of the air, the fineness of seasons, the joy of light, the melody of sounds, the beauty of colors, the fragrancy of smells, the splendor of precious stones, is nothing else but Heaven breaking through the veil of this world.

> William Law (1686–1761), *Rules for Living a Holy Life*

All are but parts of one stupendous whole,
Whose body Nature is, and God the soul.

> Alexander Pope (1688–1744), *An Essay on Man*

I believe in my heart that faith in Jesus Christ can and will lead us beyond an exclusive concern for the well-being of other human beings to the broader concern for the well-being of the birds in our backyards, the fish in our rivers, and every living creature on the face of the earth.

> John Wesley (1701–91)

When we behold the light and brightness of the sun, the golden edges of an evening cloud, or the beauteous rainbow, we behold the adumbrations of His glory and goodness, and in the blue sky, of his mildness and gentleness.

> Jonathan Edwards (1703–58), *Reflections of God's Glory*

The produce of the earth is a gift from our gracious Creator to the inhabitants, and to impoverish the earth now to support outward greatness appears to be an injury to the succeeding age.

> John Woolman (1720–72)

Men will become poor because they will not have a love for trees.... If you don't love trees, you don't love God.

> Nikephoros of Chios (1750–1821), *A Lack of Trees Brings Poverty*

All abuse and waste of God's creatures are spoil and robbery on the property of the Creator.

> Adam Clarke (1762–1832)

The world is too much with us; late and soon,
Getting and spending, we lay waste our powers:
Little we see in Nature that is ours.
  William Wordsworth (1770–1850), "The World Is Too Much with Us"

Master of the Universe,
Grant me the ability to be alone;
May it be my custom to go outdoors each day
among the trees and grass—among all growing things—
and there may I be alone, and enter into prayer,
to talk with the one to whom I belong.
          Nachman of Bratslav (1772–1810)

Beauty is but the sensible image of the infinite. Like truth and justice, it lives within us; like virtue and the moral law, it is a companion of the soul.
          George Bancroft (1800–1891)

All that I have ever seen teaches me to trust the Creator for all that I have not seen.

         Ralph Waldo Emerson (1803–82)

Earth is crammed with Heaven.
And every bush aflame with God.
But only those who see take off their shoes.
      Elizabeth Barrett Browning (1806–61)

And nature, the old nurse, took
 The child upon her knee,
Saying, "Here is a story book
 My Father hath writ for thee.
Come, wander with me," she said,
 "In regions yet untrod,
And read what is still unread
 in the manuscripts of God."
     Henry Wadsworth Longfellow (1807–82),
      "The Fiftieth Birthday of Agassiz"

Flowers may beckon toward us, but they speak toward heaven and God.
  Henry Ward Beecher (1813–87), *Proverbs from Plymouth Pulpit*

There are crowds who trample a flower into the dust without thinking once that they have one of the sweetest thoughts of God under their heel.

J. G. Holland (1819–81), *Gold-Foil: Hammered from Popular Proverbs*

Love all of God's creation, the whole of it and every grain of sand. Love every leaf, every ray of God's light! Love the animals, love the plants, love everything.

Fyodor Dostoyevsky (1821–81), *The Brothers Karamazov*

If it were not for the outside world, we should have no inside world to understand things by. Least of all could we understand God without these millions of sights and sounds and scents and motions weaving their endless harmonies. They come out of His heart to let us know a little of what is in it.

George MacDonald (1824–1905), *The Highlander's Last Song*

Ten thousand leaves on every tree, and each a miracle to me; and yet there be "men" who question God!

Joaquin Miller (1837–1913)

I wish you could come here and rest a year in the simple unmingled love-fountains of God. You would return with fresh truth gathered and absorbed from pines and waterfalls and deep-singing winds, and you would find that they all sang of fountain love just as did Jesus Christ.

John Muir (1838–1914), *My First Summer in the Sierras*

When a group of people are sailing in a boat, none of them has a right to bore a hole under his own seat.

Israel Meir ha-Kohen (1838–1933)

Give me fellowship with the beast and bird. Let me enter into sympathy with their hunger, their thirst, their weariness, their cold, their frequent homelessness. Let me give their wants a place in my prayers.... Let me be to them what Thou hast been to me—a protector, a Providence.

George Matheson (1842–1906)

The world is charged with the grandeur of God.
    It will flame out, like shining from shook foil;
    It gathers to a greatness, like the ooze of oil
Crushed. Why do men then now not reck his rod?
Generations have trod, have trod, have trod;

And all is seared with trade; bleared, smeared with toil;
   And wears man's smudge and shares man's smell: the soil
Is bare now, nor can foot feel, being shod.

And for all this, nature is never spent;
   There lives the dearest freshness deep down things;
And though the last lights off the black West went
   Oh, morning, at the brown brink eastward, springs—
Because the Holy Ghost over the bent
   World broods with warm breast and with ah! bright wings.
                 Gerard Manly Hopkins (1844–89), "God's Grandeur"

This is my Father's world: He shines in all that's fair;
In the rustling grass I hear Him pass, He speaks to me everywhere.
              Maltbie D. Babock (1858–1901), "This Is My Father's World"

Man has been endowed with reason, with the power to create, so that he can add
to what's been given. But up to now he hasn't been a creator, only a destroyer. Forests keep disappearing, rivers dry up, wild life's become extinct, the climates ruined,
and the land grows poorer and uglier every day.
                          Anton Chekhov (1860–1904), *Uncle Vanya*

Reading about nature is fine, but if a person walks in the woods and listens
carefully, he can learn more than what is in books, for they speak with the voice
of God.

I love to think of nature as an unlimited broadcasting station through which
God speaks to us every hour, if we will only tune in.
                          George Washington Carver (ca. 1864–1943)

Jesus set before me the book of nature. I understood how all the flowers He has
created are beautiful, how the splendor of the rose and whiteness of the lily do not
take away the perfume of the little violet or the delightful simplicity of the daisy.

With enraptured gaze we beheld the white moon rising quietly behind the tall
trees, the silvery rays it was casting upon sleeping nature, the bright stars twinkling
in the deep skies, the light breath of the evening breeze making the snowy clouds
float easily along; all this raised our souls to heaven.
                                    Thérèse of Lisieux (1873–97)

In the created world around us we see the Eternal Artist, Eternal Love at work.

Evelyn Underwood (1875–1941)

The harvested fields bathed in the autumn mists speak of God and his goodness far more vividly than any human lips.

Albert Schweitzer (1875–1965), *Reverence for Life*

When you defile the pleasant streams and the wild bird's abiding place, you massacre a million dreams and cast your spittle in God's face.

John Drinkwater (1882–1937)

I am I plus my surroundings, and if I do not preserve the latter, I do not preserve myself.

José Ortega y Gasset (1883–1955), *Meditations on Quixote*

A wrong attitude toward nature implies, somewhere, a wrong attitude toward God.

T.S. Elliot (1888–1965), *The Idea of a Christian Society*

A society in which consumption has to be artificially stimulated in order to keep production going is a society founded on trash and waste, and such a society is a house built upon sand.

Dorothy Sayers (1893–1957)

It can thus rightly be asked if, in spite of all his conquests, man is not turning back against himself the results of his activity. Having rationally endeavored to control nature, is he not now becoming the slave of the objects he makes?

Pope Paul VI (1897–1978)

What we call Man's power over Nature turns out to be a power exercised by some men over other men with Nature as an instrument.

Because God created the natural—invented it out of His love and artistry—it demands our reverence.

Nature never taught me that there exists a God of glory and infinite majesty. I had to learn that in other ways. But nature gave the word *glory* a meaning for me. I still do not know where else I could have found one.

C.S. Lewis (1898–1963)

I would feel more optimistic about a bright future for man if he spent less time proving that he can outwit Nature and more time tasting her sweetness and respecting her seniority.

E.B. White (1899–1985), Essays of E. B. White

God is not identified with the world, for he made it; but God is not separated from His world, either. For he made it.

Joseph Sittler (1904–87)

After all, I don't see why I am always asking for private, individual, selfish miracles when every year there are miracles like white dogwood.

Anne Morrow Lindbergh (1906–2001)

The beauty of the world is Christ's tender smile for us coming through matter.

Simone Weil (1909–43)

We need to find God, but we cannot find him in noise or in excitement. See how nature, the trees, the flowers, the grass grow in deep silence. See how the stars, the moon, and the sun all move in silence.

Mother Teresa (1910–97)

We are to exercise our dominion over these things, not as though entitled to exploit them, but as things borrowed or held in trust.... Man's dominion is under God's Dominion, and in God's Domain.

If I am going to be in the right relationship with God, I should treat the things he has made in the same way he treats them.

Francis Schaeffer (1912–84), Pollution and the Death of Man

One has to be alone, under the sky, before everything falls into place and one finds his own place in the midst of it all.

Thomas Merton (1915–68), Conjectures of a Guilty Bystander

The growing possibility of our destroying ourselves and the world with our own neglect and excess is tragic and very real.

Billy Graham (1918–), Approaching Hoofbeats

To drive to extinction something He has created is wrong. He has a purpose for everything.... We Christians have a responsibility to take the lead in caring for the earth.

Billy Graham, *Detroit Free Press*

When man turns his back on the Creator's plan, he provokes a disorder which has inevitable repercussions on the rest of the created order. If man is not at peace with God, then earth itself cannot be at peace.

The seriousness of ecological degradation lays bare the depth of man's moral crisis.... Simplicity, moderation, and discipline as well as the spirit of sacrifice must become a part of everyday life.

Pope John Paul II (1920–2005), *Peace with God the Creator, Peace with All of Creation*

Around the world, we can see the results of exploitation which destroys much without taking future generations into account. Today, all men have a duty to show themselves worthy of the mission given them by the Creator by ensuring the safe-keeping of that creation.

Pope John Paul II, press conference, Antannanarivo, Malagasy Republic

Christians will want to be in the vanguard in favoring ways of life that decisively break with the exhausting and joyless frenzy of consumerism.

Pope John Paul II, speech at Yankee Stadium

Did God make the world? Does he sustain it? Has he committed its resources to our care? His personal concern for his own creation should be sufficient to inspire us to be equally concerned.

John R.W. Stott (1921–), *Under the Bright Wings*

God intends...our care of creation to reflect our love for the Creator.

John R.W. Stott, *The Care of Creation*

The maternal sea is polluted, the heavens are rent, the forests are being de-stroyed and the desert areas are increasing. We must protect creation. Better yet, we must embellish it, render it spiritual, transfigure it. But nothing will be done unless there is a general conversion of men's minds and hearts.

Patriarch Ignatius IV of Antioch (1921–), *A Theology of Creation*

If nature is not transfigured, she becomes disfigured.
> Patriarch Ignatius IV of Antioch, *The Responsibility of Christians*

Once we repossess a sense of our own holiness, we will recover the sense of the holiness of the world.... Only in this way will we once again become aware that our destiny and the destiny of nature are one and the same.
> Philip Sherrard (1922–95), *Human Image, World Image*

I see skies of blue and clouds of white
The bright blessed day, the dark sacred night
And I think to myself, what a wonderful world.
> Bob Thiele (1922–96) and George David Weiss (1921–),
> "What a Wonderful World," recorded by Louis Armstrong (1901–70)

The chariot of human development has gained momentum but seems to be running amok without a charioteer. We know that consumerism is bad, but what can we do except go on consuming more and more? We know that the gap between the rich and the poor is widening, but what can we do except live with our guilt and lend an occasional hand to the poor?
> Paulos Mar Gregorios (1924–97), *The Human Presence:*
> *Ecological Spirituality in the Age of the Spirit*

Through His spirits God himself is present in His creation. The whole creation is a fabric woven and shot through by the efficacies of the Spirit.
> Jürgen Moltmann (1926–)

The family needs a home, a fit environment in which to develop its proper relationships. For the human family, this home is the earth, the environment that God the Creator has given us to inhabit with creativity and responsibility. We need to care for the environment: it has been entrusted to men and women to be protected and cultivated with responsible freedom, with the good of all as a constant guiding criterion.
> Pope Benedict XVI (1927–), 2007 World Day of Peace message

The best remedy for those who are afraid, lonely or unhappy is to go outside, somewhere where they can be quiet, alone with the heavens, nature and God. Because only then does one feel that all is as it should be and that God wishes to see people happy, amidst the simple beauty of nature.... I firmly believe that nature brings solace in all troubles.
> Anne Frank (1929–45), *Diary*

We must work passionately and indefatigably to bridge the gulf between our scientific progress and our moral progress. One of the great problems of mankind is that we suffer from a poverty of the spirit which stands in glaring contrast to our scientific and technological abundance. The richer we have become materially, the poorer we have become morally and spiritually.

Martin Luther King Jr. (1929–68)

The first law of our being is that we are set in a delicate network of interdependence with our fellow human beings and with the rest of God's creation.

Desmond Tutu (1931–), God Has a Dream

The same God who commanded us to love one another also commands us to work and take care of the garden. Here, humans find that God has delegated to them authority and responsibility to protect and preserve what we do not own, what belongs to God. God did not abdicate ownership. Rather, God appointed a steward, a caretaker. Justice demands that the steward faithfully execute the assigned responsibility.

George D. McKinney, Jr. (1931–)

Our predicament now, I believe, requires us to learn to read and understand the Bible in the light of the present fact of Creation.

Wendell Berry (1934–) Sex, Economy, Freedom, and Community

The Bible makes clear a basic truth that we self-centered humans find difficult to accept, namely, that the natural universe was not created primarily for us. There is no doubt that God wants us to enjoy it and even use its resources to optimize a good life for ourselves. But the ultimate purpose of creation is worship. Nature and all living things were created to glorify God.

Tony Campolo (1935–), Carpe Diem

Right after Moses had delivered the Ten Commandments, he received instructions to build an altar of unhewn stone "for if thou lift up thy tool upon it, thou hast polluted it."... I don't think such a scripture means we are never to shape the earth with our art or science, but that the scientist and the artist must remain subordinate to the larger Creation. The chances of disrupting nature's patterns, upon which we are dependent, are greatly reduced if we assume this modest posture.

Wes Jackson (1936–), Altars of Unhewn Stone

How we treat the earth and all of creation defines the relationship that each of us has with God.... To commit a crime against the natural world is a sin. For humans to cause species to become extinct and to destroy the biological diversity of God's creation...for humans to degrade the integrity of Earth by causing changes in its climate, by stripping the Earth of its natural forests, or destroying its wetlands...for humans to injure other humans with disease...for humans to contaminate the Earth's waters, its land, its air, and its life, with poisonous substances, these things are sins.

Ecumenical Patriarch Bartholomew (1940–),
Remarks at the Symposium on Religion,
Science and the Environment, Santa Barbara, California

In a time of ecological emergency, the church can offer to the world a hope that is rooted in the power of God to bring new life into all that has been created. Wesley Granberg-Michaelson (1945–), *Ecology and Life*

We cannot be all that God wants us to be without caring about the earth. Rick Warren (1954–), author of *The Purpose Driven Life*

To the Reader

This preface is addressed to you by the Committee of translators, who wish to explain, as briefly as possible, the origin and character of our work. The publication of our revision is yet another step in the long, continual process of making the Bible available in the form of the English language that is most widely current in our day. To summarize in a single sentence: the New Revised Standard Version of the Bible is an authorized revision of the Revised Standard Version, published in 1952, which was a revision of the American Standard Version, published in 1901, which, in turn, embodied earlier revisions of the King James Version, published in 1611.

In the course of time, the King James Version came to be regarded as "the Authorized Version." With good reason it has been termed "the noblest monument of English prose," and it has entered, as no other book has, into the making of the personal character and the public institutions of the English-speaking peoples. We owe to it an incalculable debt.

Yet the King James Version has serious defects. By the middle of the nineteenth century, the development of biblical studies and the discovery of many biblical manuscripts more ancient than those on which the King James Version was based made it apparent that these defects were so many as to call for revision. The task was begun, by authority of the Church of England, in 1870. The (British) Revised Version of the Bible was published in 1881–1885; and the American Standard Version, its variant embodying the preferences of the American scholars associated with the work, was published, as was mentioned above, in 1901. In 1928 the copyright of the latter was acquired by the International Council of Religious Education and thus passed into the ownership of the Churches of the United States and Canada that were associated in this Council through their boards of education and publication.

The Council appointed a committee of scholars to have charge of the text of the American Standard Version and to undertake inquiry concerning the need for further revision. After studying the questions whether or not revision should be undertaken, and if so, what its nature and extent should be, in 1937 the Council authorized a revision. The scholars who served as members of the Committee worked in two sections, one dealing with the Old Testament and one with the New Testament. In 1946 the Revised Standard Version of the New Testament was published. The publication of the Revised Standard Version of the Bible, containing the Old and New Testaments, took place on September 30, 1952. A translation of the *Apocryphal/Deuterocanonical Books of the Old Testament* followed in 1957. In 1977 this collection was issued in an expanded edition, containing three additional texts received by Eastern Orthodox communions (3 and 4 Maccabees and Psalm 151). Thereafter the Revised Standard Version gained the distinction of being officially authorized for use by all major Christian churches: Protestant, Anglican, Roman Catholic, and Eastern Orthodox.

The Revised Standard Version Bible Committee is a continuing body, comprising about thirty members, both men and women. Ecumenical in representation, it includes scholars affiliated with various Protestant denominations, as well as several Roman Catholic members, an Eastern Orthodox member, and a Jewish member who serves in the Old Testament section. For a period of time the Committee included several members from Canada and from England.

Because no translation of the Bible is perfect or is acceptable to all groups of readers, and because discoveries of older manuscripts and further investigation of linguistic features of the text continue to become available, renderings of the Bible have proliferated. During the years following the publication of the Revised Standard Version, twenty-six other English translations and revisions of the Bible were produced by committees and by individual scholars—not to mention twenty-five other translations and revisions of the New Testament alone. One of the latter was the second edition of the RSV New Testament, issued in 1971, twenty-five years after its initial publication.

Following the publication of the RSV Old Testament in 1952, significant advances were made in the discovery and interpretation of documents in Semitic languages related to Hebrew. In addition to the information that had become available in the late 1940s from the Dead Sea texts of Isaiah and Habakkuk, subsequent acquisitions from the same area brought to light many other early copies of all the books of the Hebrew Scriptures (except Esther), though most of these copies are fragmentary. During the same period early Greek manuscript copies of books of the New Testament also became available.

In order to take these discoveries into account, along with recent studies of documents in Semitic languages related to Hebrew, in 1974 the Policies Committee of the Revised Standard Version, which is a standing committee of the National Council of the Churches of Christ in the U.S.A., authorized the preparation of a revision of the entire RSV Bible.

For the Old Testament the Committee has made use of the *Biblia Hebraica Stuttgartensia* (1977; ed. sec. emendata, 1983). This is an edition of the Hebrew and Aramaic text as current early in the Christian era and fixed by Jewish scholars (the "Masoretes") of the sixth to the ninth centuries. The vowel signs, which were added by the Masoretes, are accepted in the main, but where a more probable and convincing reading can be obtained by assuming different vowels, this has been done. No notes are given in such cases, because the vowel points are less ancient and reliable than the consonants. When an alternative reading given by the Masoretes is translated in a footnote, this is identified by the words "Another reading is."

Departures from the consonantal text of the best manuscripts have been made only where it seems clear that errors in copying had been made before the text was standardized. Most of the corrections adopted are based on the ancient versions (translations into Greek, Aramaic, Syriac, and Latin), which were made prior to the time of the work of the Masoretes and which therefore may reflect earlier forms of the Hebrew text. In such instances a footnote specifies the version or versions from which the correction has been derived and also gives a translation of the Masoretic Text. Where it was deemed appropriate to do so, information is supplied in footnotes from subsidiary Jewish traditions concerning other textual readings (the *Tiqqune Sopherim,* "emendations of the scribes"). These are identified in the footnotes as "Ancient Heb tradition."

Occasionally it is evident that the text has suffered in transmission and that none of the versions provides a satisfactory restoration. Here we can only follow the best judgment of competent scholars as to the most probable reconstruction of the original text. Such reconstructions are indicated in footnotes by the abbreviation Cn ("Correction"), and a translation of the Masoretic Text is added.

For the Apocryphal/Deuterocanonical Books of the Old Testament the Committee has made use of a number of texts. For most of these books the basic Greek text from which the present translation was made is the edition of the Septuagint prepared by Alfred Rahlfs and published by the Württemberg Bible Society (Stuttgart, 1935). For several of the books the more recently published individual volumes of the Göttingen Septuagint project were utilized. For the book of Tobit it was decided to follow the form of the Greek text found in codex Sinaiticus (supported as it is by evidence from Qumran); where this text is defective, it was supplemented and corrected by other Greek manuscripts. For the three Additions to Daniel (namely, Susanna, the Prayer of Azariah and the Song of the Three Jews, and Bel and the Dragon) the Committee continued to use the Greek version attributed to Theodotion (the so-called "Theodotion-Daniel"). In translating Ecclesiasticus (Sirach), while constant reference was made to the Hebrew fragments of a large portion of this book (those discovered at Qumran and Masada as well as those recovered from the Cairo Geniza), the Committee generally followed the Greek text (including verse numbers) published by Joseph Ziegler in the Göttingen Septuagint (1965). But in many places the Committee has translated the Hebrew text when this provides a reading that is clearly superior to the Greek; the Syriac and Latin versions were also consulted throughout and occasionally adopted. The basic text adopted in rendering 2 Esdras is the Latin version given in *Biblia Sacra,* edited by Robert Weber (Stuttgart, 1971). This was supplemented by consulting the Latin text as edited by R.L. Bensly (1895) and by Bruno Violet (1910), as well as by taking into account the several Oriental versions of 2 Esdras, namely, the Syriac, Ethiopic, Arabic (two forms, referred to as Arabic 1 and Arabic 2), Armenian, and Georgian versions. Finally, since the Additions to the Book of Esther are disjointed and quite unintelligible as they stand in most editions of the Apocrypha, we have provided them with their original context by translating the whole of the Greek version of Esther from Robert Hanhart's Göttingen edition (1983).

For the New Testament the Committee has based its work on the most recent edition of *The Greek New Testament,* prepared by an interconfessional and international committee and published by the United Bible Societies (1966; 3rd ed. corrected, 1983; information concerning changes to be introduced into the critical apparatus of the forthcoming fourth edition was available to the Committee). As in that edition, double brackets are used to enclose a few passages that are generally regarded to be later additions to the text, but which we have retained because of their evident antiquity and their importance in the textual tradition. Only in very rare instances have we replaced the text or the punctuation of the Bible Societies' edition by an alternative that seemed to us to be superior. Here and there in the footnotes the phrase, "Other ancient authorities read," identifies alternative readings preserved by Greek manuscripts and early versions. In both Testaments, alternative renderings of the text are indicated by the word "Or."

As for the style of English adopted for the present revision, among the mandates given to the Committee in 1980 by the Division of Education and Ministry of the National Council of Churches of Christ (which now holds the copyright of the RSV Bible) was the directive to continue in the tradition of the King James Bible, but to introduce such changes as are warranted on the basis of accuracy, clarity, euphony, and current English usage. Within the constraints set by the original texts and by the mandates of the Division, the Committee has followed the maxim, "As literal as possible, as free as necessary." As a consequence, the New Revised

Standard Version (NRSV) remains essentially a literal translation. Paraphrastic renderings have been adopted only sparingly, and then chiefly to compensate for a deficiency in the English language—the lack of a common gender third person singular pronoun.

During the almost half a century since the publication of the RSV, many in the churches have become sensitive to the danger of linguistic sexism arising from the inherent bias of the English language toward the masculine gender, a bias that in the case of the Bible has often restricted or obscured the meaning of the original text. The mandates from the Division specified that, in references to men and women, masculine-oriented language should be eliminated as far as this can be done without altering passages that reflect the historical situation of ancient patriarchal culture. As can be appreciated, more than once the Committee found that the several mandates stood in tension and even in conflict. The various concerns had to be balanced case by case in order to provide a faithful and acceptable rendering without using contrived English. Only very occasionally has the pronoun "he" or "him" been retained in passages where the reference may have been to a woman as well as to a man; for example, in several legal texts in Leviticus and Deuteronomy. In such instances of formal, legal language, the options of either putting the passage in the plural or of introducing additional nouns to avoid masculine pronouns in English seemed to the Committee to obscure the historic structure and literary character of the original. In the vast majority of cases, however, inclusiveness has been attained by simple rephrasing or by introducing plural forms when this does not distort the meaning of the passage. Of course, in narrative and in parable no attempt was made to generalize the sex of individual persons.

Another aspect of style will be detected by readers who compare the more stately English rendering of the Old Testament with the less formal rendering adopted for the New Testament. For example, the traditional distinction between *shall* and *will* in English has been retained in the Old Testament as appropriate in rendering a document that embodies what may be termed the classic form of Hebrew, while in the New Testament the abandonment of such distinctions in the usage of the future tense in English reflects the more colloquial nature of the *koine* Greek used by most New Testament authors except when they are quoting the Old Testament.

Careful readers will notice that here and there in the Old Testament the word LORD (or in certain cases GOD) is printed in capital letters. This represents the traditional manner in English versions of rendering the Divine Name, the "Tetragrammaton" (see the notes on Exodus 3:14, 15), following the precedent of the ancient Greek and Latin translators and the long established practice in the reading of the Hebrew Scriptures in the synagogue. While it is almost if not quite certain that the Name was originally pronounced "Yahweh," this pronunciation was not indicated when the Masoretes added vowel sounds to the consonantal Hebrew text. To the four consonants YHWH of the Name, which had come to be regarded as too sacred to be pronounced, they attached vowel signs indicating that in its place should be read the Hebrew word *Adonai,* meaning "Lord" (or *Elohim,* meaning "God"). Ancient Greek translators employed the word *Kyrios* ("Lord") for the Name. The Vulgate likewise used the Latin word *Dominus* ("Lord"). The form "Jehovah" is of late medieval origin; it is a combination of the consonants of the Divine Name and the vowels attached to it by the Masoretes but belonging to an entirely different word. Although the American Standard Version (1901) had used "Jehovah" to render the Tetragrammaton (the sound of Y being represented by J and the sound of W by V, as in Latin), for two reasons the Committees that produced the RSV and the NRSV returned to the more familiar usage of the King James Version. (1) The word "Jehovah" does not accurately represent any form of the Name ever used in Hebrew. (2) The use of any proper name for the one and only God, as though there were other gods from whom the true God had to be distinguished, began to be discontinued in Judaism before the Christian era and is inappropriate for the universal faith of the Christian Church.

It will be seen that in the Psalms and in other prayers addressed to God the archaic second person singular pronouns *(thee, thou, thine)* and verb forms *(art, hast, hadst)* are no longer used. Although some readers may regret this change, it should be pointed out that in the original languages neither the Old Testament nor the New makes any linguistic distinction between addressing a human being and addressing the Deity. Furthermore, in the tradition of the King James Version one will not expect to find the use of capital letters for pronouns that refer to the Deity—such capitalization is an unnecessary innovation that has only recently been introduced into a few English translations of the Bible. Finally, we have left to the discretion of the licensed publishers such matters as section headings, cross-references, and clues to the pronunciation of proper names.

This new version seeks to preserve all that is best in the English Bible as it has been known and used through the years. It is intended for use in public reading and congregational worship, as well as in private study, instruction, and meditation. We have resisted the temptation to introduce terms and phrases that merely reflect current moods, and have tried to put the message of the Scriptures in simple, enduring words and expressions that are worthy to stand in the great tradition of the King James Bible and its predecessors.

In traditional Judaism and Christianity, the Bible has been more than a historical document to be preserved or a classic of literature to be cherished and admired; it is recognized as the unique record of God's dealings with people over the ages. The Old Testament sets forth the call of a special people to enter into covenant relation with the God of justice and steadfast love and to bring God's law to the nations. The New Testament records the life and work of Jesus Christ, the one in whom "the Word became flesh," as well as describes the rise and spread of the early Christian Church. The Bible carries its full message, not to those who regard it simply as a noble literary heritage of the past or who wish to use it to enhance political purposes and advance otherwise desirable goals, but to all persons and communities who read it so that they may discern and understand what God is saying to them. That message must not be disguised in phrases that are no longer clear, or hidden under words that have changed or lost their meaning; it must be presented in language that is direct and plain and meaningful to people today. It is the hope and prayer of the translators that this version of the Bible may continue to hold a large place in congregational life and to speak to all readers, young and old alike, helping them to understand and believe and respond to its message.

For the Committee,
BRUCE M. METZGER

The
Old Testament

GENESIS

Six Days of Creation and the Sabbath

1 In the beginning when God created*a* the heavens and the earth, ²the earth was a formless void and darkness covered the face of the deep, while a wind from God*b* swept over the face of the waters. ³Then God said, "Let there be light"; and there was light. ⁴And God saw that the light was good; and God separated the light from the darkness. ⁵God called the light Day, and the darkness he called Night. And there was evening and there was morning, the first day.

6 And God said, "Let there be a dome in the midst of the waters, and let it separate the waters from the waters." ⁷So God made the dome and separated the waters that were under the dome from the waters that were above the dome. And it was so. ⁸God called the dome Sky. And there was evening and there was morning, the second day.

9 And God said, "Let the waters under the sky be gathered together into one place, and let the dry land appear." And it was so. ¹⁰God called the dry land Earth, and the waters that were gathered together he called Seas. And God saw that it was good. ¹¹Then God said, "Let the earth put forth vegetation: plants yielding seed, and fruit trees of every kind on earth that bear fruit with the seed in it." And it was so. ¹²The earth brought forth vegetation: plants yielding seed of every kind, and trees of every kind bearing fruit with the seed in it. And God saw that it was good. ¹³And there was evening and there was morning, the third day.

14 And God said, "Let there be lights in the dome of the sky to separate the day from the night; and let them be for signs and for seasons and for days and years, ¹⁵and let them be lights in the dome of the sky to give light upon the earth." And it was so. ¹⁶God made the two great lights—the greater light to rule the day and the lesser light to rule the night—and the stars. ¹⁷God set them in the dome of the sky to give light upon the earth, ¹⁸to rule over the day and over the night, and to separate the light from the darkness. And God saw that it was good. ¹⁹And there was evening and there was morning, the fourth day.

20 And God said, "Let the waters bring forth swarms of living creatures, and let birds fly above the earth across the dome of the sky." ²¹So God created the great sea monsters and every living creature that moves, of every kind, with which the waters swarm, and every winged bird of every kind. And God saw that it was good. ²²God blessed them, saying, "Be fruitful and multiply and fill the waters in the seas, and let birds multiply on the earth." ²³And there was evening and there was morning, the fifth day.

24 And God said, "Let the earth bring forth living creatures of every kind: cattle and creeping things and wild animals of the earth of every kind." And it was so. ²⁵God made the wild animals of the earth of every kind, and the cattle of every kind, and everything that creeps upon the ground of every kind. And God saw that it was good.

26 Then God said, "Let us make humankind*c* in our image, according to our likeness; and let them have dominion over the fish of the sea, and over the birds of the air, and over the cattle, and over all the wild animals of the earth,*d* and over every creeping thing that creeps upon the earth."

27 So God created humankind*c* in his
        image,
     in the image of God he created
        them;*e*
     male and female he created them.

²⁸God blessed them, and God said to them, "Be fruitful and multiply, and fill the earth and subdue it; and have dominion over the fish of the sea and over the birds of the air and over every living thing that moves upon the earth." ²⁹God said, "See, I have given you every plant yielding seed that is upon the face of all the earth, and every tree with seed in its

---

a Or *when God began to create* or *In the beginning God created*   *b* Or *while the spirit of God* or *while a mighty wind*
c Heb *adam*   *d* Syr: Heb *and over all the earth*   *e* Heb *him*

fruit; you shall have them for food. ³⁰And to every beast of the earth, and to every bird of the air, and to everything that creeps on the earth, everything that has the breath of life, I have given every green plant for food." And it was so. ³¹God saw everything that he had made, and indeed, it was very good. And there was evening and there was morning, the sixth · day.

2 Thus the heavens and the earth were finished, and all their multitude. ²And on the seventh day God finished the work that he had done, and he rested on the seventh day from all the work that he had done. ³So God blessed the seventh day and hallowed it, because on it God rested from all the work that he had done in creation.

4 These are the generations of the heavens and the earth when they were created.

Another Account of the Creation

In the day that the LORD*a* God made the earth and the heavens, ⁵when no plant of the field was yet in the earth and no herb of the field had yet sprung up—for the LORD God had not caused it to rain upon the earth, and there was no one to till the ground; ⁶but a stream would rise from the earth, and water the whole face of the ground— ⁷then the LORD God formed man from the dust of the ground,*b* and breathed into his nostrils the breath of life; and the man became a living being. ⁸And the LORD God planted a garden in Eden, in the east; and there he put the man whom he had formed. ⁹Out of the ground the LORD God made to grow every tree that is pleasant to the sight and good for food, the tree of life also in the midst of the garden, and the tree of the knowledge of good and evil.

10 A river flows out of Eden to water the garden, and from there it divides and becomes four branches. ¹¹The name of the first is Pishon; it is the one that flows around the whole land of Havilah, where there is gold; ¹²and the gold of that land is good; bdellium and onyx stone are there. ¹³The name of the second

river is Gihon; it is the one that flows around the whole land of Cush. ¹⁴The name of the third river is Tigris, which flows east of Assyria. And the fourth river is the Euphrates.

15 The LORD God took the man and put him in the garden of Eden to till it and keep it. ¹⁶And the LORD God commanded the man, "You may freely eat of every tree of the garden; ¹⁷but of the tree of the knowledge of good and evil you shall not eat, for in the day that you eat of it you shall die."

18 Then the LORD God said, "It is not good that the man should be alone; I will make him a helper as his partner." ¹⁹So out of the ground the LORD God formed every animal of the field and every bird of the air, and brought them to the man to see what he would call them; and whatever the man called every living creature, that was its name. ²⁰The man gave names to all cattle, and to the birds of the air, and to every animal of the field; but for the man*c* there was not found a helper as his partner. ²¹So the LORD God caused a deep sleep to fall upon the man, and he slept; then he took one of his ribs and closed up its place with flesh. ²²And the rib that the LORD God had taken from the man he made into a woman and brought her to the man. ²³Then the man said,

"This at last is bone of my bones
    and flesh of my flesh;
this one shall be called Woman,*d*
    for out of Man*e* this one was taken."

²⁴Therefore a man leaves his father and his mother and clings to his wife, and they become one flesh. ²⁵And the man and his wife were both naked, and were not ashamed.

The First Sin and Its Punishment

3 Now the serpent was more crafty than any other wild animal that the LORD God had made. He said to the woman, "Did God say, 'You shall not eat from any tree in the garden'?" ²The woman said to the serpent, "We may eat of the fruit of the trees in the garden; ³but God said, 'You shall not eat of the fruit

---

a Heb YHWH, as in other places where "LORD" is spelled with capital letters (see also Exod 3.14-15 with notes).
b Or *formed a man* (Heb *adam*) *of dust from the ground* (Heb *adamah*)   *c* Or *for Adam*   *d* Heb *ishshah*   *e* Heb *ish*

of the tree that is in the middle of the garden, nor shall you touch it, or you shall die.'" 4But the serpent said to the woman, "You will not die; 5for God knows that when you eat of it your eyes will be opened, and you will be like God,*a* knowing good and evil." 6So when the woman saw that the tree was good for food, and that it was a delight to the eyes, and that the tree was to be desired to make one wise, she took of its fruit and ate; and she also gave some to her husband, who was with her, and he ate. 7Then the eyes of both were opened, and they knew that they were naked; and they sewed fig leaves together and made loincloths for themselves.

8 They heard the sound of the LORD God walking in the garden at the time of the evening breeze, and the man and his wife hid themselves from the presence of the LORD God among the trees of the garden. 9But the LORD God called to the man, and said to him, "Where are you?" 10He said, "I heard the sound of you in the garden, and I was afraid, because I was naked; and I hid myself." 11He said, "Who told you that you were naked? Have you eaten from the tree of which I commanded you not to eat?" 12The man said, "The woman whom you gave to be with me, she gave me fruit from the tree, and I ate." 13Then the LORD God said to the woman, "What is this that you have done?" The woman said, "The serpent tricked me, and I ate." 14The LORD God said to the serpent,

"Because you have done this,
    cursed are you among all animals
    and among all wild creatures;
    upon your belly you shall go,
    and dust you shall eat
    all the days of your life.
15   I will put enmity between you and the
        woman,
    and between your offspring and hers;
    he will strike your head,
    and you will strike your heel."

16To the woman he said,

"I will greatly increase your pangs in
    childbearing;
    in pain you shall bring forth children,
yet your desire shall be for your
    husband,
    and he shall rule over you."

17And to the man *b* he said,

"Because you have listened to the voice
    of your wife,
    and have eaten of the tree
about which I commanded you,
    'You shall not eat of it,'
cursed is the ground because of you;
    in toil you shall eat of it all the days
        of your life;
18   thorns and thistles it shall bring forth
        for you;
    and you shall eat the plants of the
        field.
19   By the sweat of your face
        you shall eat bread
    until you return to the ground,
        for out of it you were taken;
    you are dust,
        and to dust you shall return."

20 The man named his wife Eve,*c* because she was the mother of all living. 21And the LORD God made garments of skins for the man*d* and for his wife, and clothed them.

22 Then the LORD God said, "See, the man has become like one of us, knowing good and evil; and now, he might reach out his hand and take also from the tree of life, and eat, and live forever"— 23therefore the LORD God sent him forth from the garden of Eden, to till the ground from which he was taken. 24He drove out the man; and at the east of the garden of Eden he placed the cherubim, and a sword flaming and turning to guard the way to the tree of life.

Cain Murders Abel

4 Now the man knew his wife Eve, and she conceived and bore Cain, saying, "I have produced*e* a man with the help of the LORD." 2Next she bore his brother Abel. Now Abel

---

a Or *gods*   *b* Or *to Adam*   *c* In Heb *Eve* resembles the word for *living*   *d* Or *for Adam*   *e* The verb in Heb resembles the word for *Cain* was a keeper of sheep, and Cain a tiller of the ground. ³In the course of time Cain brought to the LORD an offering of the fruit of the ground, ⁴and Abel for his part brought of the firstlings of his flock, their fat portions. And the LORD had regard for Abel and his offering, ⁵but for Cain and his offering he had no regard. So Cain was very angry, and his countenance fell. ⁶The LORD said to Cain, "Why are you angry, and why has your countenance fallen? ⁷If you do well, will you not be accepted? And if you do not do well, sin is lurking at the door; its desire is for you, but you must master it."

8 Cain said to his brother Abel, "Let us go out to the field."ᵃ And when they were in the field, Cain rose up against his brother Abel, and killed him. ⁹Then the LORD said to Cain, "Where is your brother Abel?" He said, "I do not know; am I my brother's keeper?" ¹⁰And the LORD said, "What have you done? Listen; your brother's blood is crying out to me from the ground! ¹¹And now you are cursed from the ground, which has opened its mouth to receive your brother's blood from your hand. ¹²When you till the ground, it will no longer yield to you its strength; you will be a fugitive and a wanderer on the earth." ¹³Cain said to the LORD, "My punishment is greater than I can bear! ¹⁴Today you have driven me away from the soil, and I shall be hidden from your face; I shall be a fugitive and a wanderer on the earth, and anyone who meets me may kill me." ¹⁵Then the LORD said to him, "Not so!ᵇ Whoever kills Cain will suffer a sevenfold vengeance." And the LORD put a mark on Cain, so that no one who came upon him would kill him. ¹⁶Then Cain went away from the presence of the LORD, and settled in the land of Nod,ᶜ east of Eden.

Beginnings of Civilization

17 Cain knew his wife, and she conceived and bore Enoch; and he built a city, and named it Enoch after his son Enoch. ¹⁸To Enoch was born Irad; and Irad was the father of Mehujael, and Mehujael the father of Methushael,

and Methushael the father of Lamech. ¹⁹Lamech took two wives; the name of the one was Adah, and the name of the other Zillah. ²⁰Adah bore Jabal; he was the ancestor of those who live in tents and have livestock. ²¹His brother's name was Jubal; he was the ancestor of all those who play the lyre and pipe. ²²Zillah bore Tubal-cain, who made all kinds of bronze and iron tools. The sister of Tubal-cain was Naamah.

23 Lamech said to his wives:
"Adah and Zillah, hear my voice;
   you wives of Lamech, listen to what I say:
I have killed a man for wounding me,
   a young man for striking me.
24 If Cain is avenged sevenfold,
   truly Lamech seventy-sevenfold."

25 Adam knew his wife again, and she bore a son and named him Seth, for she said, "God has appointedᵈ for me another child instead of Abel, because Cain killed him." ²⁶To Seth also a son was born, and he named him Enosh. At that time people began to invoke the name of the LORD.

Adam's Descendants to Noah and His Sons

5 This is the list of the descendants of Adam. When God created humankind,ᵉ he made themᶠ in the likeness of God. ²Male and female he created them, and he blessed them and named them "Humankind"ᵉ when they were created.

3 When Adam had lived one hundred thirty years, he became the father of a son in his likeness, according to his image, and named him Seth. ⁴The days of Adam after he became the father of Seth were eight hundred years; and he had other sons and daughters. ⁵Thus all the days that Adam lived were nine hundred thirty years; and he died.

6 When Seth had lived one hundred five years, he became the father of Enosh. ⁷Seth lived after the birth of Enosh eight hundred seven years, and had other sons and daughters.

ᵃ Sam Gk Syr Compare Vg: MT lacks *Let us go out to the field*   ᵇ Gk Syr Vg: Heb *Therefore*   ᶜ That is *Wandering*
ᵈ The verb in Heb resembles the word for *Seth*   ᵉ Heb *adam*   ᶠ Heb *him*

8Thus all the days of Seth were nine hundred twelve years; and he died.

9 When Enosh had lived ninety years, he became the father of Kenan. 10Enosh lived after the birth of Kenan eight hundred fifteen years, and had other sons and daughters. 11Thus all the days of Enosh were nine hundred five years; and he died.

12 When Kenan had lived seventy years, he became the father of Mahalalel. 13Kenan lived after the birth of Mahalalel eight hundred and forty years, and had other sons and daughters. 14Thus all the days of Kenan were nine hundred and ten years; and he died.

15 When Mahalalel had lived sixty-five years, he became the father of Jared. 16Mahalalel lived after the birth of Jared eight hundred thirty years, and had other sons and daughters. 17Thus all the days of Mahalalel were eight hundred ninety-five years; and he died.

18 When Jared had lived one hundred sixty-two years he became the father of Enoch. 19Jared lived after the birth of Enoch eight hundred years, and had other sons and daughters. 20Thus all the days of Jared were nine hundred sixty-two years; and he died.

21 When Enoch had lived sixty-five years, he became the father of Methuselah. 22Enoch walked with God after the birth of Methuselah three hundred years, and had other sons and daughters. 23Thus all the days of Enoch were three hundred sixty-five years. 24Enoch walked with God; then he was no more, because God took him.

25 When Methuselah had lived one hundred eighty-seven years, he became the father of Lamech. 26Methuselah lived after the birth of Lamech seven hundred eighty-two years, and had other sons and daughters. 27Thus all the days of Methuselah were nine hundred sixty-nine years; and he died.

28 When Lamech had lived one hundred eighty-two years, he became the father of a son; 29he named him Noah, saying, "Out of the ground that the LORD has cursed this one shall bring us relief from our work and from the toil of our hands." 30Lamech lived after the birth of Noah five hundred ninety-five years, and had other sons and daughters. 31Thus all the days of Lamech were seven hundred seventy-seven years; and he died.

32 After Noah was five hundred years old, Noah became the father of Shem, Ham, and Japheth.

The Wickedness of Humankind

6 When people began to multiply on the face of the ground, and daughters were born to them, 2the sons of God saw that they were fair; and they took wives for themselves of all that they chose. 3Then the LORD said, "My spirit shall not abide*a* in mortals forever, for they are flesh; their days shall be one hundred twenty years." 4The Nephilim were on the earth in those days—and also afterward—when the sons of God went in to the daughters of humans, who bore children to them. These were the heroes that were of old, warriors of renown.

5 The LORD saw that the wickedness of humankind was great in the earth, and that every inclination of the thoughts of their hearts was only evil continually. 6And the LORD was sorry that he had made humankind on the earth, and it grieved him to his heart. 7So the LORD said, "I will blot out from the earth the human beings I have created—people together with animals and creeping things and birds of the air, for I am sorry that I have made them." 8But Noah found favor in the sight of the LORD.

Noah Pleases God

9 These are the descendants of Noah. Noah was a righteous man, blameless in his generation; Noah walked with God. 10And Noah had three sons, Shem, Ham, and Japheth.

11 Now the earth was corrupt in God's sight, and the earth was filled with violence. 12And God saw that the earth was corrupt; for all flesh had corrupted its ways upon the earth.

a Meaning of Heb uncertain

13And God said to Noah, "I have determined to make an end of all flesh, for the earth is filled with violence because of them; now I am going to destroy them along with the earth. 14Make yourself an ark of cypress*a* wood; make rooms in the ark, and cover it inside and out with pitch. 15This is how you are to make it: the length of the ark three hundred cubits, its width fifty cubits, and its height thirty cubits. 16Make a roof*b* for the ark, and finish it to a cubit above; and put the door of the ark in its side; make it with lower, second, and third decks. 17For my part, I am going to bring a flood of waters on the earth, to destroy from under heaven all flesh in which is the breath of life; everything that is on the earth shall die. 18But I will establish my covenant with you; and you shall come into the ark, you, your sons, your wife, and your sons' wives with you. 19And of every living thing, of all flesh, you shall bring two of every kind into the ark, to keep them alive with you; they shall be male and female. 20Of the birds according to their kinds, and of the animals according to their kinds, of every creeping thing of the ground according to its kind, two of every kind shall come in to you, to keep them alive. 21Also take with you every kind of food that is eaten, and store it up; and it shall serve as food for you and for them." 22Noah did this; he did all that God commanded him.

The Great Flood

7 Then the LORD said to Noah, "Go into the ark, you and all your household, for I have seen that you alone are righteous before me in this generation. 2Take with you seven pairs of all clean animals, the male and its mate; and a pair of the animals that are not clean, the male and its mate; 3and seven pairs of the birds of the air also, male and female, to keep their kind alive on the face of all the earth. 4For in seven days I will send rain on the earth for forty days and forty nights; and every living thing that I have made I will blot out

from the face of the ground." 5And Noah did all that the LORD had commanded him.

6 Noah was six hundred years old when the flood of waters came on the earth. 7And Noah with his sons and his wife and his sons' wives went into the ark to escape the waters of the flood. 8Of clean animals, and of animals that are not clean, and of birds, and of everything that creeps on the ground, 9two and two, male and female, went into the ark with Noah, as God had commanded Noah. 10And after seven days the waters of the flood came on the earth.

11 In the six hundredth year of Noah's life, in the second month, on the seventeenth day of the month, on that day all the fountains of the great deep burst forth, and the windows of the heavens were opened. 12The rain fell on the earth forty days and forty nights. 13On the very same day Noah with his sons, Shem and Ham and Japheth, and Noah's wife and the three wives of his sons entered the ark, 14they and every wild animal of every kind, and all domestic animals of every kind, and every creeping thing that creeps on the earth, and every bird of every kind—every bird, every winged creature. 15They went into the ark with Noah, two and two of all flesh in which there was the breath of life. 16And those that entered, male and female of all flesh, went in as God had commanded him; and the LORD shut him in.

17 The flood continued forty days on the earth; and the waters increased, and bore up the ark, and it rose high above the earth. 18The waters swelled and increased greatly on the earth; and the ark floated on the face of the waters. 19The waters swelled so mightily on the earth that all the high mountains under the whole heaven were covered; 20the waters swelled above the mountains, covering them fifteen cubits deep. 21And all flesh died that moved on the earth, birds, domestic animals, wild animals, all swarming creatures that swarm on the earth, and all human beings; 22everything on dry land in whose nostrils was the breath of life died. 23He blotted out every living thing that

a Meaning of Heb uncertain　　*b* Or *window*

was on the face of the ground, human beings and animals and creeping things and birds of the air; they were blotted out from the earth. Only Noah was left, and those that were with him in the ark. 24And the waters swelled on the earth for one hundred fifty days.

The Flood Subsides

8 But God remembered Noah and all the wild animals and all the domestic animals that were with him in the ark. And God made a wind blow over the earth, and the waters subsided; 2the fountains of the deep and the windows of the heavens were closed, the rain from the heavens was restrained, 3and the waters gradually receded from the earth. At the end of one hundred fifty days the waters had abated; 4and in the seventh month, on the seventeenth day of the month, the ark came to rest on the mountains of Ararat. 5The waters continued to abate until the tenth month; in the tenth month, on the first day of the month, the tops of the mountains appeared.

6 At the end of forty days Noah opened the window of the ark that he had made 7and sent out the raven; and it went to and fro until the waters were dried up from the earth. 8Then he sent out the dove from him, to see if the waters had subsided from the face of the ground; 9but the dove found no place to set its foot, and it returned to him to the ark, for the waters were still on the face of the whole earth. So he put out his hand and took it and brought it into the ark with him. 10He waited another seven days, and again he sent out the dove from the ark; 11and the dove came back to him in the evening, and there in its beak was a freshly plucked olive leaf; so Noah knew that the waters had subsided from the earth. 12Then he waited another seven days, and sent out the dove; and it did not return to him any more.

13 In the six hundred first year, in the first month, on the first day of the month, the waters were dried up from the earth; and Noah removed the covering of the ark, and looked, and saw that the face of the ground was drying. 14In the second month, on the twenty-sev-enth day of the month, the earth was dry. 15Then God said to Noah, 16"Go out of the ark, you and your wife, and your sons and your sons' wives with you. 17Bring out with you every living thing that is with you of all flesh— birds and animals and every creeping thing that creeps on the earth—so that they may abound on the earth, and be fruitful and multiply on the earth." 18So Noah went out with his sons and his wife and his sons' wives. 19And every animal, every creeping thing, and every bird, everything that moves on the earth, went out of the ark by families.

God's Promise to Noah

20 Then Noah built an altar to the LORD, and took of every clean animal and of every clean bird, and offered burnt offerings on the altar. 21And when the LORD smelled the pleasing odor, the LORD said in his heart, "I will never again curse the ground because of humankind, for the inclination of the human heart is evil from youth; nor will I ever again destroy every living creature as I have done.
22   As long as the earth endures,
     seedtime and harvest, cold and heat,
     summer and winter, day and night,
     shall not cease."

The Covenant with Noah

9 God blessed Noah and his sons, and said to them, "Be fruitful and multiply, and fill the earth. 2The fear and dread of you shall rest on every animal of the earth, and on every bird of the air, on everything that creeps on the ground, and on all the fish of the sea; into your hand they are delivered. 3Every moving thing that lives shall be food for you; and just as I gave you the green plants, I give you everything. 4Only, you shall not eat flesh with its life, that is, its blood. 5For your own lifeblood I will surely require a reckoning: from every animal I will require it and from human beings, each one for the blood of another, I will require a reckoning for human life.
6   Whoever sheds the blood of a human,
     by a human shall that person's blood
     be shed;

for in his own image
God made humankind.

7And you, be fruitful and multiply, abound on the earth and multiply in it."

8 Then God said to Noah and to his sons with him, 9"As for me, I am establishing my covenant with you and your descendants after you, 10and with every living creature that is with you, the birds, the domestic animals, and every animal of the earth with you, as many as came out of the ark.*a* 11I establish my covenant with you, that never again shall all flesh be cut off by the waters of a flood, and never again shall there be a flood to destroy the earth." 12God said, "This is the sign of the covenant that I make between me and you and every living creature that is with you, for all future generations: 13I have set my bow in the clouds, and it shall be a sign of the covenant between me and the earth. 14When I bring clouds over the earth and the bow is seen in the clouds, 15I will remember my covenant that is between me and you and every living creature of all flesh; and the waters shall never again become a flood to destroy all flesh. 16When the bow is in the clouds, I will see it and remember the everlasting covenant between God and every living creature of all flesh that is on the earth." 17God said to Noah, "This is the sign of the covenant that I have established between me and all flesh that is on the earth."

Noah and His Sons

18 The sons of Noah who went out of the ark were Shem, Ham, and Japheth. Ham was the father of Canaan. 19These three were the sons of Noah; and from these the whole earth was peopled.

20 Noah, a man of the soil, was the first to plant a vineyard. 21He drank some of the wine and became drunk, and he lay uncovered in his tent. 22And Ham, the father of Canaan, saw the nakedness of his father, and told his two brothers outside. 23Then Shem and Japheth took a garment, laid it on both their shoulders, and walked backward and covered the nakedness of their father; their faces were turned away, and they did not see their father's nakedness. 24When Noah awoke from his wine and knew what his youngest son had done to him, 25he said,

"Cursed be Canaan;
lowest of slaves shall he be to his
brothers."
26He also said,

"Blessed by the LORD my God be Shem;
and let Canaan be his slave.
27 May God make space for*b* Japheth,
and let him live in the tents of Shem;
and let Canaan be his slave."

28 After the flood Noah lived three hundred fifty years. 29All the days of Noah were nine hundred fifty years; and he died.

Nations Descended from Noah

10 These are the descendants of Noah's sons, Shem, Ham, and Japheth; children were born to them after the flood.

2 The descendants of Japheth: Gomer, Magog, Madai, Javan, Tubal, Meshech, and Tiras. 3The descendants of Gomer: Ashkenaz, Riphath, and Togarmah. 4The descendants of Javan: Elishah, Tarshish, Kittim, and Rodanim.*c* 5From these the coastland peoples spread. These are the descendants of Japheth*d* in their lands, with their own language, by their families, in their nations.

6 The descendants of Ham: Cush, Egypt, Put, and Canaan. 7The descendants of Cush: Seba, Havilah, Sabtah, Raamah, and Sabteca. The descendants of Raamah: Sheba and Dedan. 8Cush became the father of Nimrod; he was the first on earth to become a mighty warrior. 9He was a mighty hunter before the LORD; therefore it is said, "Like Nimrod a mighty hunter before the LORD." 10The beginning of his kingdom was Babel, Erech, and Accad, all of them in the land of Shinar. 11From that land he went into Assyria, and built Nineveh, Rehoboth-ir, Calah, and 12Resen between Nineveh and Calah; that is the

---

a Gk: Heb adds *every animal of the earth*   *b* Heb *yapht*, a play on *Japheth*   *c* Heb Mss Sam Gk See 1 Chr 1.7: MT *Dodanim*   *d* Compare verses 20, 31. Heb lacks *These are the descendants of Japheth* great city. [13]Egypt became the father of Ludim, Anamim, Lehabim, Naphtuhim, [14]Pathrusim, Casluhim, and Caphtorim, from which the Philistines come.[a]

21 To Shem also, the father of all the children of Eber, the elder brother of Japheth, children were born. [22]The descendants of Shem: Elam, Asshur, Arpachshad, Lud, and Aram. [23]The descendants of Aram: Uz, Hul, Gether, and Mash. [24]Arpachshad became the father of Shelah; and Shelah became the father of Eber. [25]To Eber were born two sons: the name of the one was Peleg,[b] for in his days the earth was divided, and his brother's name was Joktan. [26]Joktan became the father of Almodad, Sheleph, Hazarmaveth, Jerah, [27]Hadoram, Uzal, Diklah, [28]Obal, Abimael, Sheba, [29]Ophir, Havilah, and Jobab; all these were the descendants of Joktan. [30]The territory in which they lived extended from Mesha in the direction of Sephar, the hill country of the east. [31]These are the descendants of Shem, by their families, their languages, their lands, and their nations.

15 Canaan became the father of Sidon his firstborn, and Heth, [16]and the Jebusites, the Amorites, the Girgashites, [17]the Hivites, the Arkites, the Sinites, [18]the Arvadites, the Zemarites, and the Hamathites. Afterward the families of the Canaanites spread abroad. [19]And the territory of the Canaanites extended from Sidon, in the direction of Gerar, as far as Gaza, and in the direction of Sodom, Gomorrah, Admah, and Zeboiim, as far as Lasha. [20]These are the descendants of Ham, by their families, their languages, their lands, and their nations.

32 These are the families of Noah's sons, according to their genealogies, in their nations; and from these the nations spread abroad on the earth after the flood.

The Tower of Babel

11 Now the whole earth had one language and the same words. [2]And as they migrated from the east,[c] they came upon a plain in the land of Shinar and settled there. [3]And they said to one another, "Come, let us make bricks, and burn them thoroughly." And they had brick for stone, and bitumen for mortar. [4]Then they said, "Come, let us build ourselves a city, and a tower with its top in the heavens, and let us make a name for ourselves; otherwise we shall be scattered abroad upon the face of the whole earth." [5]The LORD came down to see the city and the tower, which mortals had built. [6]And the LORD said, "Look, they are one people, and they have all one language; and this is only the beginning of what they will do; nothing that they propose to do will now be impossible for them. [7]Come, let us go down, and confuse their language there, so that they will not understand one another's speech." [8]So the LORD scattered them abroad from there over the face of all the earth, and they left off building the city. [9]Therefore it was called Babel, because there the LORD confused[d] the language of all the earth; and from there the LORD scattered them abroad over the face of all the earth.

Descendants of Shem

10 These are the descendants of Shem. When Shem was one hundred years old, he became the father of Arpachshad two years after the flood; [11]and Shem lived after the birth of Arpachshad five hundred years, and had other sons and daughters.

12 When Arpachshad had lived thirty-five years, he became the father of Shelah; [13]and Arpachshad lived after the birth of Shelah four hundred three years, and had other sons and daughters.

14 When Shelah had lived thirty years, he became the father of Eber; [15]and Shelah lived after the birth of Eber four hundred three years, and had other sons and daughters.

16 When Eber had lived thirty-four years, he became the father of Peleg; [17]and Eber lived after the birth of Peleg four hundred thirty years, and had other sons and daughters.

18 When Peleg had lived thirty years, he be-

a Cn: Heb *Casluhim, from which the Philistines come, and Caphtorim*   b That is *Division*   c Or *migrated eastward*
d Heb *balal*, meaning *to confuse*

came the father of Reu; [19]and Peleg lived after the birth of Reu two hundred nine years, and had other sons and daughters.

20 When Reu had lived thirty-two years, he became the father of Serug; [21]and Reu lived after the birth of Serug two hundred seven years, and had other sons and daughters.

22 When Serug had lived thirty years, he became the father of Nahor; [23]and Serug lived after the birth of Nahor two hundred years, and had other sons and daughters.

24 When Nahor had lived twenty-nine years, he became the father of Terah; [25]and Nahor lived after the birth of Terah one hundred nineteen years, and had other sons and daughters.

26 When Terah had lived seventy years, he became the father of Abram, Nahor, and Haran.

Descendants of Terah

27 Now these are the descendants of Terah. Terah was the father of Abram, Nahor, and Haran; and Haran was the father of Lot. [28]Haran died before his father Terah in the land of his birth, in Ur of the Chaldeans. [29]Abram and Nahor took wives; the name of Abram's wife was Sarai, and the name of Nahor's wife was Milcah. She was the daughter of Haran the father of Milcah and Iscah. [30]Now Sarai was barren; she had no child.

31 Terah took his son Abram and his grandson Lot son of Haran, and his daughter-in-law Sarai, his son Abram's wife, and they went out together from Ur of the Chaldeans to go into the land of Canaan; but when they came to Haran, they settled there. [32]The days of Terah were two hundred five years; and Terah died in Haran.

The Call of Abram

12 Now the LORD said to Abram, "Go from your country and your kindred and your father's house to the land that I will show you. [2]I will make of you a great nation, and I will bless you, and make your name great, so that you will be a blessing. [3]I will bless those who bless you, and the one who curses you I will curse; and in you all the families of the earth shall be blessed."[a]

4 So Abram went, as the LORD had told him; and Lot went with him. Abram was seventy-five years old when he departed from Haran. [5]Abram took his wife Sarai and his brother's son Lot, and all the possessions that they had gathered, and the persons whom they had acquired in Haran; and they set forth to go to the land of Canaan. When they had come to the land of Canaan, [6]Abram passed through the land to the place at Shechem, to the oak[b] of Moreh. At that time the Canaanites were in the land. [7]Then the LORD appeared to Abram, and said, "To your offspring[c] I will give this land." So he built there an altar to the LORD, who had appeared to him. [8]From there he moved on to the hill country on the east of Bethel, and pitched his tent, with Bethel on the west and Ai on the east; and there he built an altar to the LORD and invoked the name of the LORD. [9]And Abram journeyed on by stages toward the Negeb.

Abram and Sarai in Egypt

10 Now there was a famine in the land. So Abram went down to Egypt to reside there as an alien, for the famine was severe in the land. [11]When he was about to enter Egypt, he said to his wife Sarai, "I know well that you are a woman beautiful in appearance; [12]and when the Egyptians see you, they will say, 'This is his wife'; then they will kill me, but they will let you live. [13]Say you are my sister, so that it may go well with me because of you, and that my life may be spared on your account." [14]When Abram entered Egypt the Egyptians saw that the woman was very beautiful. [15]When the officials of Pharaoh saw her, they praised her to Pharaoh. And the woman was taken into Pharaoh's house. [16]And for her sake he dealt well with Abram; and he had sheep, oxen, male donkeys, male and female slaves, female donkeys, and camels.

a Or *by you all the families of the earth shall bless themselves*   *b* Or *terebinth*   *c* Heb *seed*

17 But the LORD afflicted Pharaoh and his house with great plagues because of Sarai, Abram's wife. 18So Pharaoh called Abram, and said, "What is this you have done to me? Why did you not tell me that she was your wife? 19Why did you say, 'She is my sister,' so that I took her for my wife? Now then, here is your wife, take her, and be gone." 20And Pharaoh gave his men orders concerning him; and they set him on the way, with his wife and all that he had.

Abram and Lot Separate

13 So Abram went up from Egypt, he and his wife, and all that he had, and Lot with him, into the Negeb.

2 Now Abram was very rich in livestock, in silver, and in gold. 3He journeyed on by stages from the Negeb as far as Bethel, to the place where his tent had been at the beginning, between Bethel and Ai, 4to the place where he had made an altar at the first; and there Abram called on the name of the LORD. 5Now Lot, who went with Abram, also had flocks and herds and tents, 6so that the land could not support both of them living together; for their possessions were so great that they could not live together, 7and there was strife between the herders of Abram's livestock and the herders of Lot's livestock. At that time the Canaanites and the Perizzites lived in the land.

8 Then Abram said to Lot, "Let there be no strife between you and me, and between your herders and my herders; for we are kindred. 9Is not the whole land before you? Separate yourself from me. If you take the left hand, then I will go to the right; or if you take the right hand, then I will go to the left." 10Lot looked about him, and saw that the plain of the Jordan was well watered everywhere like the garden of the LORD, like the land of Egypt, in the direction of Zoar; this was before the LORD had destroyed Sodom and Gomorrah. 11So Lot chose for himself all the plain of the Jordan, and Lot journeyed eastward; thus they separated from each other.

12Abram settled in the land of Canaan, while Lot settled among the cities of the Plain and moved his tent as far as Sodom. 13Now the people of Sodom were wicked, great sinners against the LORD.

14 The LORD said to Abram, after Lot had separated from him, "Raise your eyes now, and look from the place where you are, northward and southward and eastward and westward; 15for all the land that you see I will give to you and to your offspring*a* forever. 16I will make your offspring like the dust of the earth; so that if one can count the dust of the earth, your offspring also can be counted. 17Rise up, walk through the length and the breadth of the land, for I will give it to you." 18So Abram moved his tent, and came and settled by the oaks*b* of Mamre, which are at Hebron; and there he built an altar to the LORD.

Lot's Captivity and Rescue

14 In the days of King Amraphel of Shinar, King Arioch of Ellasar, King Chedorlaomer of Elam, and King Tidal of Goiim, 2these kings made war with King Bera of Sodom, King Birsha of Gomorrah, King Shinab of Admah, King Shemeber of Zeboiim, and the king of Bela (that is, Zoar). 3All these joined forces in the Valley of Siddim (that is, the Dead Sea).*c* 4Twelve years they had served Chedorlaomer, but in the thirteenth year they rebelled. 5In the fourteenth year Chedorlaomer and the kings who were with him came and subdued the Rephaim in Ashteroth-karnaim, the Zuzim in Ham, the Emim in Shaveh-kiriathaim, 6and the Horites in the hill country of Seir as far as El-paran on the edge of the wilderness; 7then they turned back and came to En-mishpat (that is, Kadesh), and subdued all the country of the Amalekites, and also the Amorites who lived in Hazazon-tamar. 8Then the king of Sodom, the king of Gomorrah, the king of Admah, the king of Zeboiim, and the king of Bela (that is, Zoar) went out, and they joined battle in the Valley of Siddim 9with King Chedorlaomer of Elam,

a Heb *seed*   *b* Or *terebinths*   *c* Heb *Salt Sea*

King Tidal of Goiim, King Amraphel of Shinar, and King Arioch of Ellasar, four kings against five. 10Now the Valley of Siddim was full of bitumen pits; and as the kings of Sodom and Gomorrah fled, some fell into them, and the rest fled to the hill country. 11So the enemy took all the goods of Sodom and Gomorrah, and all their provisions, and went their way; 12they also took Lot, the son of Abram's brother, who lived in Sodom, and his goods, and departed.

13 Then one who had escaped came and told Abram the Hebrew, who was living by the oaks*a* of Mamre the Amorite, brother of Eshcol and of Aner; these were allies of Abram. 14When Abram heard that his nephew had been taken captive, he led forth his trained men, born in his house, three hundred eighteen of them, and went in pursuit as far as Dan. 15He divided his forces against them by night, he and his servants, and routed them and pursued them to Hobah, north of Damascus. 16Then he brought back all the goods, and also brought back his nephew Lot with his goods, and the women and the people.

Abram Blessed by Melchizedek

17 After his return from the defeat of Chedorlaomer and the kings who were with him, the king of Sodom went out to meet him at the Valley of Shaveh (that is, the King's Valley). 18And King Melchizedek of Salem brought out bread and wine; he was priest of God Most High.*b* 19He blessed him and said,

"Blessed be Abram by God Most High,*b*
    maker of heaven and earth;
20   and blessed be God Most High,*b*
    who has delivered your enemies into
        your hand!"

And Abram gave him one-tenth of everything. 21Then the king of Sodom said to Abram, "Give me the persons, but take the goods for yourself." 22But Abram said to the king of Sodom, "I have sworn to the LORD, God Most High,*b* maker of heaven and earth, 23that I would not take a thread or a sandal-thong or anything that is yours, so that you might not say, 'I have made Abram rich.' 24I will take nothing but what the young men have eaten, and the share of the men who went with me—Aner, Eshcol, and Mamre. Let them take their share."

God's Covenant with Abram

15 After these things the word of the LORD came to Abram in a vision, "Do not be afraid, Abram, I am your shield; your reward shall be very great." 2But Abram said, "O Lord GOD, what will you give me, for I continue childless, and the heir of my house is Eliezer of Damascus?"*c* 3And Abram said, "You have given me no offspring, and so a slave born in my house is to be my heir." 4But the word of the LORD came to him, "This man shall not be your heir; no one but your very own issue shall be your heir." 5He brought him outside and said, "Look toward heaven and count the stars, if you are able to count them." Then he said to him, "So shall your descendants be." 6And he believed the LORD; and the LORD*d* reckoned it to him as righteousness.

7 Then he said to him, "I am the LORD who brought you from Ur of the Chaldeans, to give you this land to possess." 8But he said, "O Lord GOD, how am I to know that I shall possess it?" 9He said to him, "Bring me a heifer three years old, a female goat three years old, a ram three years old, a turtledove, and a young pigeon." 10He brought him all these and cut them in two, laying each half over against the other; but he did not cut the birds in two. 11And when birds of prey came down on the carcasses, Abram drove them away.

12 As the sun was going down, a deep sleep fell upon Abram, and a deep and terrifying darkness descended upon him. 13Then the LORD*d* said to Abram, "Know this for certain, that your offspring shall be aliens in a land that is not theirs, and shall be slaves there, and they shall be oppressed for four hundred years; 14but I will bring judgment on the nation that they serve, and afterward they shall come out

a Or *terebinths*   *b* Heb *El Elyon*   *c* Meaning of Heb uncertain   *d* Heb *he* with great possessions. [15]As for yourself, you shall go to your ancestors in peace; you shall be buried in a good old age. [16]And they shall come back here in the fourth generation; for the iniquity of the Amorites is not yet complete."

17 When the sun had gone down and it was dark, a smoking fire pot and a flaming torch passed between these pieces. [18]On that day the LORD made a covenant with Abram, saying, "To your descendants I give this land, from the river of Egypt to the great river, the river Euphrates, [19]the land of the Kenites, the Kenizzites, the Kadmonites, [20]the Hittites, the Perizzites, the Rephaim, [21]the Amorites, the Canaanites, the Girgashites, and the Jebusites."

The Birth of Ishmael

16 Now Sarai, Abram's wife, bore him no children. She had an Egyptian slave-girl whose name was Hagar, [2]and Sarai said to Abram, "You see that the LORD has prevented me from bearing children; go in to my slave-girl; it may be that I shall obtain children by her." And Abram listened to the voice of Sarai. [3]So, after Abram had lived ten years in the land of Canaan, Sarai, Abram's wife, took Hagar the Egyptian, her slave-girl, and gave her to her husband Abram as a wife. [4]He went in to Hagar, and she conceived; and when she saw that she had conceived, she looked with contempt on her mistress. [5]Then Sarai said to Abram, "May the wrong done to me be on you! I gave my slave-girl to your embrace, and when she saw that she had conceived, she looked on me with contempt. May the LORD judge between you and me!" [6]But Abram said to Sarai, "Your slave-girl is in your power; do to her as you please." Then Sarai dealt harshly with her, and she ran away from her.

7 The angel of the LORD found her by a spring of water in the wilderness, the spring on the way to Shur. [8]And he said, "Hagar, slave-girl of Sarai, where have you come from and where are you going?" She said, "I am running away from my mistress Sarai." [9]The angel of the LORD said to her, "Return to your mistress, and submit to her." [10]The angel of the LORD also said to her, "I will so greatly multiply your offspring that they cannot be counted for multitude." [11]And the angel of the LORD said to her,

"Now you have conceived and shall bear
    a son;
  you shall call him Ishmael,[a]
    for the LORD has given heed to your
    affliction.
[12] He shall be a wild ass of a man,
    with his hand against everyone,
    and everyone's hand against him;
  and he shall live at odds with all his kin."

[13]So she named the LORD who spoke to her, "You are El-roi";[b] for she said, "Have I really seen God and remained alive after seeing him?"[c] [14]Therefore the well was called Beer-lahai-roi;[d] it lies between Kadesh and Bered.

15 Hagar bore Abram a son; and Abram named his son, whom Hagar bore, Ishmael. [16]Abram was eighty-six years old when Hagar bore him[e] Ishmael.

The Sign of the Covenant

17 When Abram was ninety-nine years old, the LORD appeared to Abram, and said to him, "I am God Almighty;[f] walk before me, and be blameless. [2]And I will make my covenant between me and you, and will make you exceedingly numerous." [3]Then Abram fell on his face; and God said to him, [4]"As for me, this is my covenant with you: You shall be the ancestor of a multitude of nations. [5]No longer shall your name be Abram,[g] but your name shall be Abraham;[h] for I have made you the ancestor of a multitude of nations. [6]I will make you exceedingly fruitful; and I will make nations of you, and kings shall come from you. [7]I will establish my covenant between me and you, and your offspring after you throughout their generations, for an everlasting covenant, to be God to you and to

a That is God hears   b Perhaps God of seeing or God who sees   c Meaning of Heb uncertain   d That is the Well of the Living One who sees me   e Heb Abram   f Traditional rendering of Heb El Shaddai   g That is exalted ancestor   h Here taken to mean ancestor of a multitude your offspring[a] after you. 8And I will give to you, and to your offspring after you, the land where you are now an alien, all the land of Canaan, for a perpetual holding; and I will be their God."

9 God said to Abraham, "As for you, you shall keep my covenant, you and your offspring after you throughout their generations. 10This is my covenant, which you shall keep, between me and you and your offspring after you: Every male among you shall be circumcised. 11You shall circumcise the flesh of your foreskins, and it shall be a sign of the covenant between me and you. 12Throughout your generations every male among you shall be circumcised when he is eight days old, including the slave born in your house and the one bought with your money from any foreigner who is not of your offspring. 13Both the slave born in your house and the one bought with your money must be circumcised. So shall my covenant be in your flesh an everlasting covenant. 14Any uncircumcised male who is not circumcised in the flesh of his foreskin shall be cut off from his people; he has broken my covenant."

15 God said to Abraham, "As for Sarai your wife, you shall not call her Sarai, but Sarah shall be her name. 16I will bless her, and moreover I will give you a son by her. I will bless her, and she shall give rise to nations; kings of peoples shall come from her." 17Then Abraham fell on his face and laughed, and said to himself, "Can a child be born to a man who is a hundred years old? Can Sarah, who is ninety years old, bear a child?" 18And Abraham said to God, "O that Ishmael might live in your sight!" 19God said, "No, but your wife Sarah shall bear you a son, and you shall name him Isaac.[b] I will establish my covenant with him as an everlasting covenant for his offspring after him. 20As for Ishmael, I have heard you; I will bless him and make him fruitful and exceedingly numerous; he shall be the father of twelve princes, and I will make him a great nation. 21But my covenant I will establish with Isaac, whom Sarah shall bear to you at this season next year." 22And when he had finished talking with him, God went up from Abraham.

23 Then Abraham took his son Ishmael and all the slaves born in his house or bought with his money, every male among the men of Abraham's house, and he circumcised the flesh of their foreskins that very day, as God had said to him. 24Abraham was ninety-nine years old when he was circumcised in the flesh of his foreskin. 25And his son Ishmael was thirteen years old when he was circumcised in the flesh of his foreskin. 26That very day Abraham and his son Ishmael were circumcised; 27and all the men of his house, slaves born in the house and those bought with money from a foreigner, were circumcised with him.

A Son Promised to Abraham and Sarah

18 The LORD appeared to Abraham[c] by the oaks[d] of Mamre, as he sat at the entrance of his tent in the heat of the day. 2He looked up and saw three men standing near him. When he saw them, he ran from the tent entrance to meet them, and bowed down to the ground. 3He said, "My lord, if I find favor with you, do not pass by your servant. 4Let a little water be brought, and wash your feet, and rest yourselves under the tree. 5Let me bring a little bread, that you may refresh yourselves, and after that you may pass on—since you have come to your servant." So they said, "Do as you have said." 6And Abraham hastened into the tent to Sarah, and said, "Make ready quickly three measures[e] of choice flour, knead it, and make cakes." 7Abraham ran to the herd, and took a calf, tender and good, and gave it to the servant, who hastened to prepare it. 8Then he took curds and milk and the calf that he had prepared, and set it before them; and he stood by them under the tree while they ate.

9 They said to him, "Where is your wife Sarah?" And he said, "There, in the tent." 10Then one said, "I will surely return to you in due season, and your wife Sarah shall have a

---

a Heb seed   b That is he laughs   c Heb him   d Or terebinths   e Heb seahs son." And Sarah was listening at the tent entrance behind him. [11]Now Abraham and Sarah were old, advanced in age; it had ceased to be with Sarah after the manner of women. [12]So Sarah laughed to herself, saying, "After I have grown old, and my husband is old, shall I have pleasure?" [13]The LORD said to Abraham, "Why did Sarah laugh, and say, 'Shall I indeed bear a child, now that I am old?' [14]Is anything too wonderful for the LORD? At the set time I will return to you, in due season, and Sarah shall have a son." [15]But Sarah denied, saying, "I did not laugh"; for she was afraid. He said, "Oh yes, you did laugh."

Judgment Pronounced on Sodom

16 Then the men set out from there, and they looked toward Sodom; and Abraham went with them to set them on their way. [17]The LORD said, "Shall I hide from Abraham what I am about to do, [18]seeing that Abraham shall become a great and mighty nation, and all the nations of the earth shall be blessed in him?[a] [19]No, for I have chosen[b] him, that he may charge his children and his household after him to keep the way of the LORD by doing righteousness and justice; so that the LORD may bring about for Abraham what he has promised him." [20]Then the LORD said, "How great is the outcry against Sodom and Gomorrah and how very grave their sin! [21]I must go down and see whether they have done altogether according to the outcry that has come to me; and if not, I will know."

22 So the men turned from there, and went toward Sodom, while Abraham remained standing before the LORD.[c] [23]Then Abraham came near and said, "Will you indeed sweep away the righteous with the wicked? [24]Suppose there are fifty righteous within the city; will you then sweep away the place and not forgive it for the fifty righteous who are in it? [25]Far be it from you to do such a thing, to slay the righteous with the wicked, so that the righteous fare as the wicked! Far be that from you! Shall not the Judge of all the earth do what is

just?" [26]And the LORD said, "If I find at Sodom fifty righteous in the city, I will forgive the whole place for their sake." [27]Abraham answered, "Let me take it upon myself to speak to the Lord, I who am but dust and ashes. [28]Suppose five of the fifty righteous are lacking? Will you destroy the whole city for lack of five?" And he said, "I will not destroy it if I find forty-five there." [29]Again he spoke to him, "Suppose forty are found there." He answered, "For the sake of forty I will not do it." [30]Then he said, "Oh do not let the Lord be angry if I speak. Suppose thirty are found there." He answered, "I will not do it, if I find thirty there." [31]He said, "Let me take it upon myself to speak to the Lord. Suppose twenty found there." He answered, "For the sake of twenty I will not destroy it." [32]Then he said, "Oh do not let the Lord be angry if I speak just once more. Suppose ten are found there." He answered, "For the sake of ten I will not destroy it." [33]And the LORD went his way, when he had finished speaking to Abraham; and Abraham returned to his place.

The Depravity of Sodom

19 The two angels came to Sodom in the evening, and Lot was sitting in the gateway of Sodom. When Lot saw them, he rose to meet them, and bowed down with his face to the ground. [2]He said, "Please, my lords, turn aside to your servant's house and spend the night, and wash your feet; then you can rise early and go on your way." They said, "No; we will spend the night in the square." [3]But he urged them strongly; so they turned aside to him and entered his house; and he made them a feast, and baked unleavened bread, and they ate. [4]But before they lay down, the men of the city, the men of Sodom, both young and old, all the people to the last man, surrounded the house; [5]and they called to Lot, "Where are the men who came to you tonight? Bring them out to us, so that we may know them." [6]Lot went out of the door to the men, shut the door after him, [7]and said, "I beg you, my brothers,

---

a Or and all the nations of the earth shall bless themselves by him while the LORD remained standing before Abraham   b Heb known   c Another ancient tradition reads do not act so wickedly. [8]Look, I have two daughters who have not known a man; let me bring them out to you, and do to them as you please; only do nothing to these men, for they have come under the shelter of my roof." [9]But they replied, "Stand back!" And they said, "This fellow came here as an alien, and he would play the judge! Now we will deal worse with you than with them." Then they pressed hard against the man Lot, and came near the door to break it down. [10]But the men inside reached out their hands and brought Lot into the house with them, and shut the door. [11]And they struck with blindness the men who were at the door of the house, both small and great, so that they were unable to find the door.

Sodom and Gomorrah Destroyed

12 Then the men said to Lot, "Have you anyone else here? Sons-in-law, sons, daughters, or anyone you have in the city—bring them out of the place. [13]For we are about to destroy this place, because the outcry against its people has become great before the LORD, and the LORD has sent us to destroy it." [14]So Lot went out and said to his sons-in-law, who were to marry his daughters, "Up, get out of this place; for the LORD is about to destroy the city." But he seemed to his sons-in-law to be jesting. 15 When morning dawned, the angels urged Lot, saying, "Get up, take your wife and your two daughters who are here, or else you will be consumed in the punishment of the city." [16]But he lingered; so the men seized him and his wife and his two daughters by the hand, the LORD being merciful to him, and they brought him out and left him outside the city. [17]When they had brought them outside, they[a] said, "Flee for your life; do not look back or stop anywhere in the Plain; flee to the hills, or else you will be consumed." [18]And Lot said to them, "Oh, no, my lords; [19]your servant has found favor with you, and you have shown me great kindness in saving my life; but I cannot flee to the hills, for fear the

disaster will overtake me and I die. [20]Look, that city is near enough to flee to, and it is a little one. Let me escape there—is it not a little one?—and my life will be saved!" [21]He said to him, "Very well, I grant you this favor too, and will not overthrow the city of which you have spoken. [22]Hurry, escape there, for I can do nothing until you arrive there." Therefore the city was called Zoar.[b] [23]The sun had risen on the earth when Lot came to Zoar.

24 Then the LORD rained on Sodom and Gomorrah sulfur and fire from the LORD out of heaven; [25]and he overthrew those cities, and all the Plain, and all the inhabitants of the cities, and what grew on the ground. [26]But Lot's wife, behind him, looked back, and she became a pillar of salt.

27 Abraham went early in the morning to the place where he had stood before the LORD; [28]and he looked down toward Sodom and Gomorrah and toward all the land of the Plain and saw the smoke of the land going up like the smoke of a furnace.

29 So it was that, when God destroyed the cities of the Plain, God remembered Abraham, and sent Lot out of the midst of the overthrow, when he overthrew the cities in which Lot had settled.

The Shameful Origin of Moab and Ammon

30 Now Lot went up out of Zoar and settled in the hills with his two daughters, for he was afraid to stay in Zoar; so he lived in a cave with his two daughters. [31]And the firstborn said to the younger, "Our father is old, and there is not a man on earth to come in to us after the manner of all the world. [32]Come, let us make our father drink wine, and we will lie with him, so that we may preserve offspring through our father." [33]So they made their father drink wine that night; and the firstborn went in, and lay with her father; he did not know when she lay down or when she rose. [34]On the next day, the firstborn said to the younger, "Look, I lay last night with my father; let us make him drink wine tonight also;

---

a Gk Syr Vg: Heb *he*   *b* That is *Little*

then you go in and lie with him, so that we may preserve offspring through our father." 35So they made their father drink wine that night also; and the younger rose, and lay with him; and he did not know when she lay down or when she rose. 36Thus both the daughters of Lot became pregnant by their father. 37The firstborn bore a son, and named him Moab; he is the ancestor of the Moabites to this day. 38The younger also bore a son and named him Ben-ammi; he is the ancestor of the Ammonites to this day.

Abraham and Sarah at Gerar

20 From there Abraham journeyed toward the region of the Negeb, and settled between Kadesh and Shur. While residing in Gerar as an alien, 2Abraham said of his wife Sarah, "She is my sister." And King Abimelech of Gerar sent and took Sarah. 3But God came to Abimelech in a dream by night, and said to him, "You are about to die because of the woman whom you have taken; for she is a married woman." 4Now Abimelech had not approached her; so he said, "Lord, will you destroy an innocent people? 5Did he not himself say to me, 'She is my sister'? And she herself said, 'He is my brother.' I did this in the integrity of my heart and the innocence of my hands." 6Then God said to him in the dream, "Yes, I know that you did this in the integrity of your heart; furthermore it was I who kept you from sinning against me. Therefore I did not let you touch her. 7Now then, return the man's wife; for he is a prophet, and he will pray for you and you shall live. But if you do not restore her, know that you shall surely die, you and all that are yours."

8 So Abimelech rose early in the morning, and called all his servants and told them all these things; and the men were very much afraid. 9Then Abimelech called Abraham, and said to him, "What have you done to us? How have I sinned against you, that you have brought such great guilt on me and my kingdom? You have done things to me that ought not to be done." 10And Abimelech said to Abraham, "What were you thinking of, that

you did this thing?" 11Abraham said, "I did it because I thought, There is no fear of God at all in this place, and they will kill me because of my wife. 12Besides, she is indeed my sister, the daughter of my father but not the daughter of my mother; and she became my wife. 13And when God caused me to wander from my father's house, I said to her, 'This is the kindness you must do me: at every place to which we come, say of me, He is my brother.'" 14Then Abimelech took sheep and oxen, and male and female slaves, and gave them to Abraham, and restored his wife Sarah to him. 15Abimelech said, "My land is before you; settle where it pleases you." 16To Sarah he said, "Look, I have given your brother a thousand pieces of silver; it is your exoneration before all who are with you; you are completely vindicated." 17Then Abraham prayed to God; and God healed Abimelech, and also healed his wife and female slaves so that they bore children. 18For the LORD had closed fast all the wombs of the house of Abimelech because of Sarah, Abraham's wife.

The Birth of Isaac

21 The LORD dealt with Sarah as he had said, and the LORD did for Sarah as he had promised. 2Sarah conceived and bore Abraham a son in his old age, at the time of which God had spoken to him. 3Abraham gave the name Isaac to his son whom Sarah bore him. 4And Abraham circumcised his son Isaac when he was eight days old, as God had commanded him. 5Abraham was a hundred years old when his son Isaac was born to him. 6Now Sarah said, "God has brought laughter for me; everyone who hears will laugh with me." 7And she said, "Who would ever have said to Abraham that Sarah would nurse children? Yet I have borne him a son in his old age."

Hagar and Ishmael Sent Away

8 The child grew, and was weaned; and Abraham made a great feast on the day that Isaac was weaned. 9But Sarah saw the son of Hagar the Egyptian, whom she had borne to

Abraham, playing with her son Isaac.*a* 10So she said to Abraham, "Cast out this slave woman with her son; for the son of this slave woman shall not inherit along with my son Isaac." 11The matter was very distressing to Abraham on account of his son. 12But God said to Abraham, "Do not be distressed because of the boy and because of your slave woman; whatever Sarah says to you, do as she tells you, for it is through Isaac that offspring shall be named for you. 13As for the son of the slave woman, I will make a nation of him also, because he is your offspring." 14So Abraham rose early in the morning, and took bread and a skin of water, and gave it to Hagar, putting it on her shoulder, along with the child, and sent her away. And she departed, and wandered about in the wilderness of Beer-sheba.

15 When the water in the skin was gone, she cast the child under one of the bushes. 16Then she went and sat down opposite him a good way off, about the distance of a bowshot; for she said, "Do not let me look on the death of the child." And as she sat opposite him, she lifted up her voice and wept. 17And God heard the voice of the boy; and the angel of God called to Hagar from heaven, and said to her, "What troubles you, Hagar? Do not be afraid; for God has heard the voice of the boy where he is. 18Come, lift up the boy and hold him fast with your hand, for I will make a great nation of him." 19Then God opened her eyes and she saw a well of water. She went, and filled the skin with water, and gave the boy a drink.

20 God was with the boy, and he grew up; he lived in the wilderness, and became an expert with the bow. 21He lived in the wilderness of Paran; and his mother got a wife for him from the land of Egypt.

Abraham and Abimelech Make a Covenant

22 At that time Abimelech, with Phicol the commander of his army, said to Abraham, "God is with you in all that you do; 23now therefore swear to me here by God that you will not deal falsely with me or with my offspring or with my posterity, but as I have dealt loyally with you, you will deal with me and with the land where you have resided as an alien." 24And Abraham said, "I swear it."

25 When Abraham complained to Abimelech about a well of water that Abimelech's servants had seized, 26Abimelech said, "I do not know who has done this; you did not tell me, and I have not heard of it until today." 27So Abraham took sheep and oxen and gave them to Abimelech, and the two men made a covenant. 28Abraham set apart seven ewe lambs of the flock. 29And Abimelech said to Abraham, "What is the meaning of these seven ewe lambs that you have set apart?" 30He said, "These seven ewe lambs you shall accept from my hand, in order that you may be a witness for me that I dug this well." 31Therefore that place was called Beer-sheba;*b* because there both of them swore an oath. 32When they had made a covenant at Beer-sheba, Abimelech, with Phicol the commander of his army, left and returned to the land of the Philistines. 33Abraham*c* planted a tamarisk tree in Beer-sheba, and called there on the name of the LORD, the Everlasting God.*d* 34And Abraham resided as an alien many days in the land of the Philistines.

The Command to Sacrifice Isaac

22 After these things God tested Abraham. He said to him, "Abraham!" And he said, "Here I am." 2He said, "Take your son, your only son Isaac, whom you love, and go to the land of Moriah, and offer him there as a burnt offering on one of the mountains that I shall show you." 3So Abraham rose early in the morning, saddled his donkey, and took two of his young men with him, and his son Isaac; he cut the wood for the burnt offering, and set out and went to the place in the distance that God had shown him. 4On the third day Abraham looked up and saw the place far away. 5Then Abraham said to his young men, "Stay here with the donkey; the boy and I will

---

a Gk Vg: Heb lacks *with her son Isaac*   *b* That is *Well of seven* or *Well of the oath*   *c* Heb He   *d* Or *the LORD,*
El Olam

go over there; we will worship, and then we will come back to you." 6Abraham took the wood of the burnt offering and laid it on his son Isaac, and he himself carried the fire and the knife. So the two of them walked on together. 7Isaac said to his father Abraham, "Father!" And he said, "Here I am, my son." He said, "The fire and the wood are here, but where is the lamb for a burnt offering?" 8Abraham said, "God himself will provide the lamb for a burnt offering, my son." So the two of them walked on together.

9 When they came to the place that God had shown him, Abraham built an altar there and laid the wood in order. He bound his son Isaac, and laid him on the altar, on top of the wood. 10Then Abraham reached out his hand and took the knife to kill*a* his son. 11But the angel of the LORD called to him from heaven, and said, "Abraham, Abraham!" And he said, "Here I am." 12He said, "Do not lay your hand on the boy or do anything to him; for now I know that you fear God, since you have not withheld your son, your only son, from me." 13And Abraham looked up and saw a ram, caught in a thicket by its horns. Abraham went and took the ram and offered it up as a burnt offering instead of his son. 14So Abraham called that place "The LORD will provide";*b* as it is said to this day, "On the mount of the LORD it shall be provided."*c*

15 The angel of the LORD called to Abraham a second time from heaven, 16and said, "By myself I have sworn, says the LORD: Because you have done this, and have not withheld your son, your only son, 17I will indeed bless you, and I will make your offspring as numerous as the stars of heaven and as the sand that is on the seashore. And your offspring shall possess the gate of their enemies, 18and by your offspring shall all the nations of the earth gain blessing for themselves, because you have obeyed my voice." 19So Abraham returned to his young men, and they arose and went together to Beer-sheba; and Abraham lived at Beer-sheba.

The Children of Nahor

20 Now after these things it was told Abraham, "Milcah also has borne children, to your brother Nahor: 21Uz the firstborn, Buz his brother, Kemuel the father of Aram, 22Chesed, Hazo, Pildash, Jidlaph, and Bethuel." 23Bethuel became the father of Rebekah. These eight Milcah bore to Nahor, Abraham's brother. 24Moreover, his concubine, whose name was Reumah, bore Tebah, Gaham, Tahash, and Maacah.

Sarah's Death and Burial

23 Sarah lived one hundred twenty-seven years; this was the length of Sarah's life. 2And Sarah died at Kiriath-arba (that is, Hebron) in the land of Canaan; and Abraham went in to mourn for Sarah and to weep for her. 3Abraham rose up from beside his dead, and said to the Hittites, 4"I am a stranger and an alien residing among you; give me property among you for a burying place, so that I may bury my dead out of my sight." 5The Hittites answered Abraham, 6"Hear us, my lord; you are a mighty prince among us. Bury your dead in the choicest of our burial places; none of us will withhold from you any burial ground for burying your dead." 7Abraham rose and bowed to the Hittites, the people of the land. 8He said to them, "If you are willing that I should bury my dead out of my sight, hear me, and entreat for me Ephron son of Zohar, 9so that he may give me the cave of Machpelah, which he owns; it is at the end of his field. For the full price let him give it to me in your presence as a possession for a burying place." 10Now Ephron was sitting among the Hittites; and Ephron the Hittite answered Abraham in the hearing of the Hittites, of all who went in at the gate of his city, 11"No, my lord, hear me; I give you the field, and I give you the cave that is in it; in the presence of my people I give it to you; bury your dead." 12Then Abraham bowed down before the people of the land. 13He said to Ephron in the hearing of the people of the land, "If you only will lis-

a Or *to slaughter*   *b* Or *will see*; Heb traditionally transliterated *Jehovah Jireh*   *c* Or *he shall be seen* ten to me! I will give the price of the field; accept it from me, so that I may bury my dead there." [14]Ephron answered Abraham, [15]"My lord, listen to me; a piece of land worth four hundred shekels of silver—what is that between you and me? Bury your dead." [16]Abraham agreed with Ephron; and Abraham weighed out for Ephron the silver that he had named in the hearing of the Hittites, four hundred shekels of silver, according to the weights current among the merchants.

17 So the field of Ephron in Machpelah, which was to the east of Mamre, the field with the cave that was in it and all the trees that were in the field, throughout its whole area, passed [18]to Abraham as a possession in the presence of the Hittites, in the presence of all who went in at the gate of his city. [19]After this, Abraham buried Sarah his wife in the cave of the field of Machpelah facing Mamre (that is, Hebron) in the land of Canaan. [20]The field and the cave that is in it passed from the Hittites into Abraham's possession as a burying place.

The Marriage of Isaac and Rebekah

24 Now Abraham was old, well advanced in years; and the LORD had blessed Abraham in all things. [2]Abraham said to his servant, the oldest of his house, who had charge of all that he had, "Put your hand under my thigh [3]and I will make you swear by the LORD, the God of heaven and earth, that you will not get a wife for my son from the daughters of the Canaanites, among whom I live, [4]but will go to my country and to my kindred and get a wife for my son Isaac." [5]The servant said to him, "Perhaps the woman may not be willing to follow me to this land; must I then take your son back to the land from which you came?" [6]Abraham said to him, "See to it that you do not take my son back there. [7]The LORD, the God of heaven, who took me from my father's house and from the land of my birth, and who spoke to me and swore to me, 'To your offspring I will give this land,' he will send his angel before you, and you shall take a wife for my son from there. [8]But if the woman is not willing to follow you, then you will be free from this oath of mine; only you must not take my son back there." [9]So the servant put his hand under the thigh of Abraham his master and swore to him concerning this matter.

10 Then the servant took ten of his master's camels and departed, taking all kinds of choice gifts from his master; and he set out and went to Aram-naharaim, to the city of Nahor. [11]He made the camels kneel down outside the city by the well of water; it was toward evening, the time when women go out to draw water. [12]And he said, "O LORD, God of my master Abraham, please grant me success today and show steadfast love to my master Abraham. [13]I am standing here by the spring of water, and the daughters of the townspeople are coming out to draw water. [14]Let the girl to whom I shall say, 'Please offer your jar that I may drink,' and who shall say, 'Drink, and I will water your camels'—let her be the one whom you have appointed for your servant Isaac. By this I shall know that you have shown steadfast love to my master."

15 Before he had finished speaking, there was Rebekah, who was born to Bethuel son of Milcah, the wife of Nahor, Abraham's brother, coming out with her water jar on her shoulder. [16]The girl was very fair to look upon, a virgin, whom no man had known. She went down to the spring, filled her jar, and came up. [17]Then the servant ran to meet her and said, "Please let me sip a little water from your jar." [18]"Drink, my lord," she said, and quickly lowered her jar upon her hand and gave him a drink. [19]When she had finished giving him a drink, she said, "I will draw for your camels also, until they have finished drinking." [20]So she quickly emptied her jar into the trough and ran again to the well to draw, and she drew for all his camels. [21]The man gazed at her in silence to learn whether or not the LORD had made his journey successful.

22 When the camels had finished drinking, the man took a gold nose-ring weighing a half shekel, and two bracelets for her arms weighing ten gold shekels, [23]and said, "Tell me whose daughter you are. Is there room in your

father's house for us to spend the night?" ²⁴She said to him, "I am the daughter of Bethuel son of Milcah, whom she bore to Nahor." ²⁵She added, "We have plenty of straw and fodder and a place to spend the night." ²⁶The man bowed his head and worshiped the LORD ²⁷and said, "Blessed be the LORD, the God of my master Abraham, who has not forsaken his steadfast love and his faithfulness toward my master. As for me, the LORD has led me on the way to the house of my master's kin."

28 Then the girl ran and told her mother's household about these things. ²⁹Rebekah had a brother whose name was Laban; and Laban ran out to the man, to the spring. ³⁰As soon as he had seen the nose-ring, and the bracelets on his sister's arms, and when he heard the words of his sister Rebekah, "Thus the man spoke to me," he went to the man; and there he was, standing by the camels at the spring. ³¹He said, "Come in, O blessed of the LORD. Why do you stand outside when I have prepared the house and a place for the camels?" ³²So the man came into the house; and Laban unloaded the camels, and gave him straw and fodder for the camels, and water to wash his feet and the feet of the men who were with him. ³³Then food was set before him to eat; but he said, "I will not eat until I have told my errand." He said, "Speak on."

34 So he said, "I am Abraham's servant. ³⁵The LORD has greatly blessed my master, and he has become wealthy; he has given him flocks and herds, silver and gold, male and female slaves, camels and donkeys. ³⁶And Sarah my master's wife bore a son to my master when she was old; and he has given him all that he has. ³⁷My master made me swear, saying, 'You shall not take a wife for my son from the daughters of the Canaanites, in whose land I live; ³⁸but you shall go to my father's house, to my kindred, and get a wife for my son.' ³⁹I said to my master, 'Perhaps the woman will not follow me.' ⁴⁰But he said to me, 'The LORD, before whom I walk, will send his angel with you and make your way successful. You shall get a wife for my son from my kindred, from

my father's house. ⁴¹Then you will be free from my oath, when you come to my kindred; even if they will not give her to you, you will be free from my oath.'

42 "I came today to the spring, and said, 'O LORD, the God of my master Abraham, if now you will only make successful the way I am going! ⁴³I am standing here by the spring of water; let the young woman who comes out to draw, to whom I shall say, "Please give me a little water from your jar to drink," ⁴⁴and who will say to me, "Drink, and I will draw for your camels also"—let her be the woman whom the LORD has appointed for my master's son.'

45 "Before I had finished speaking in my heart, there was Rebekah coming out with her water jar on her shoulder; and she went down to the spring, and drew. I said to her, 'Please let me drink.' ⁴⁶She quickly let down her jar from her shoulder, and said, 'Drink, and I will also water your camels.' So I drank, and she also watered the camels. ⁴⁷Then I asked her, 'Whose daughter are you?' She said, 'The daughter of Bethuel, Nahor's son, whom Milcah bore to him.' So I put the ring on her nose, and the bracelets on her arms. ⁴⁸Then I bowed my head and worshiped the LORD, and blessed the LORD, the God of my master Abraham, who had led me by the right way to obtain the daughter of my master's kinsman for his son. ⁴⁹Now then, if you will deal loyally and truly with my master, tell me; and if not, tell me, so that I may turn either to the right hand or to the left."

50 Then Laban and Bethuel answered, "The thing comes from the LORD; we cannot speak to you anything bad or good. ⁵¹Look, Rebekah is before you, take her and go, and let her be the wife of your master's son, as the LORD has spoken."

52 When Abraham's servant heard their words, he bowed himself to the ground before the LORD. ⁵³And the servant brought out jewelry of silver and of gold, and garments, and gave them to Rebekah; he also gave to her brother and to her mother costly ornaments. ⁵⁴Then he and the men who were with him ate

and drank, and they spent the night there. When they rose in the morning, he said, "Send me back to my master." 55Her brother and her mother said, "Let the girl remain with us a while, at least ten days; after that she may go." 56But he said to them, "Do not delay me, since the LORD has made my journey successful; let me go that I may go to my master." 57They said, "We will call the girl, and ask her." 58And they called Rebekah, and said to her, "Will you go with this man?" She said, "I will." 59So they sent away their sister Rebekah and her nurse along with Abraham's servant and his men. 60And they blessed Rebekah and said to her,

"May you, our sister, become
    thousands of myriads;
may your offspring gain possession
    of the gates of their foes."

61Then Rebekah and her maids rose up, mounted the camels, and followed the man; thus the servant took Rebekah, and went his way.

62 Now Isaac had come from *a* Beer-lahai-roi, and was settled in the Negeb. 63Isaac went out in the evening to walk *b* in the field; and looking up, he saw camels coming. 64And Rebekah looked up, and when she saw Isaac, she slipped quickly from the camel, 65and said to the servant, "Who is the man over there, walking in the field to meet us?" The servant said, "It is my master." So she took her veil and covered herself. 66And the servant told Isaac all the things that he had done. 67Then Isaac brought her into his mother Sarah's tent. He took Rebekah, and she became his wife; and he loved her. So Isaac was comforted after his mother's death.

Abraham Marries Keturah

25 Abraham took another wife, whose name was Keturah. 2She bore him Zimran, Jokshan, Medan, Midian, Ishbak, and Shuah. 3Jokshan was the father of Sheba and Dedan. The sons of Dedan were Asshurim, Letushim, and Leummim. 4The sons of Mid-

ian were Ephah, Epher, Hanoch, Abida, and Eldaah. All these were the children of Keturah. 5Abraham gave all he had to Isaac. 6But to the sons of his concubines Abraham gave gifts, while he was still living, and he sent them away from his son Isaac, eastward to the east country.

The Death of Abraham

7 This is the length of Abraham's life, one hundred seventy-five years. 8Abraham breathed his last and died in a good old age, an old man and full of years, and was gathered to his people. 9His sons Isaac and Ishmael buried him in the cave of Machpelah, in the field of Ephron son of Zohar the Hittite, east of Mamre, 10the field that Abraham purchased from the Hittites. There Abraham was buried, with his wife Sarah. 11After the death of Abraham God blessed his son Isaac. And Isaac settled at Beer-lahai-roi.

Ishmael's Descendants

12 These are the descendants of Ishmael, Abraham's son, whom Hagar the Egyptian, Sarah's slave-girl, bore to Abraham. 13These are the names of the sons of Ishmael, named in the order of their birth: Nebaioth, the first-born of Ishmael; and Kedar, Adbeel, Mibsam, 14Mishma, Dumah, Massa, 15Hadad, Tema, Jetur, Naphish, and Kedemah. 16These are the sons of Ishmael and these are their names, by their villages and by their encampments, twelve princes according to their tribes. 17(This is the length of the life of Ishmael, one hundred thirty-seven years; he breathed his last and died, and was gathered to his people.) 18They settled from Havilah to Shur, which is opposite Egypt in the direction of Assyria; he settled down *c* alongside of *d* all his people.

The Birth and Youth of Esau and Jacob

19 These are the descendants of Isaac, Abraham's son: Abraham was the father of Isaac, 20and Isaac was forty years old when he married Rebekah, daughter of Bethuel the Ar-

a Syr Tg: Heb *from coming to*   *b* Meaning of Heb word is uncertain   *c* Heb *he fell*   *d* Or *down in opposition to* amean of Paddan-aram, sister of Laban the Aramean. 21Isaac prayed to the LORD for his wife, because she was barren; and the LORD granted his prayer, and his wife Rebekah conceived. 22The children struggled together within her; and she said, "If it is to be this way, why do I live?"*a* So she went to inquire of the LORD. 23And the LORD said to her,

"Two nations are in your womb,
　　and two peoples born of you shall be
　　　　divided;
　the one shall be stronger than the other,
　　the elder shall serve the younger."

24When her time to give birth was at hand, there were twins in her womb. 25The first came out red, all his body like a hairy mantle; so they named him Esau. 26Afterward his brother came out, with his hand gripping Esau's heel; so he was named Jacob.*b* Isaac was sixty years old when she bore them.

27 When the boys grew up, Esau was a skillful hunter, a man of the field, while Jacob was a quiet man, living in tents. 28Isaac loved Esau, because he was fond of game; but Rebekah loved Jacob.

Esau Sells His Birthright

29 Once when Jacob was cooking a stew, Esau came in from the field, and he was famished. 30Esau said to Jacob, "Let me eat some of that red stuff, for I am famished!" (Therefore he was called Edom.*c*) 31Jacob said, "First sell me your birthright." 32Esau said, "I am about to die; of what use is a birthright to me?" 33Jacob said, "Swear to me first."*d* So he swore to him, and sold his birthright to Jacob. 34Then Jacob gave Esau bread and lentil stew, and he ate and drank, and rose and went his way. Thus Esau despised his birthright.

Isaac and Abimelech

26 Now there was a famine in the land, besides the former famine that had occurred in the days of Abraham. And Isaac went to Gerar, to King Abimelech of the Philistines. 2The LORD appeared to Isaac*e* and said, "Do not go down to Egypt; settle in the land that I shall show you. 3Reside in this land as an alien, and I will be with you, and will bless you; for to you and to your descendants I will give all these lands, and I will fulfill the oath that I swore to your father Abraham. 4I will make your offspring as numerous as the stars of heaven, and will give to your offspring all these lands; and all the nations of the earth shall gain blessing for themselves through your offspring, 5because Abraham obeyed my voice and kept my charge, my commandments, my statutes, and my laws."

6 So Isaac settled in Gerar. 7When the men of the place asked him about his wife, he said, "She is my sister"; for he was afraid to say, "My wife," thinking, "or else the men of the place might kill me for the sake of Rebekah, because she is attractive in appearance." 8When Isaac had been there a long time, King Abimelech of the Philistines looked out of a window and saw him fondling his wife Rebekah. 9So Abimelech called for Isaac, and said, "So she is your wife! Why then did you say, 'She is my sister'?" Isaac said to him, "Because I thought I might die because of her." 10Abimelech said, "What is this you have done to us? One of the people might easily have lain with your wife, and you would have brought guilt upon us." 11So Abimelech warned all the people, saying, "Whoever touches this man or his wife shall be put to death."

12 Isaac sowed seed in that land, and in the same year reaped a hundredfold. The LORD blessed him, 13and the man became rich; he prospered more and more until he became very wealthy. 14He had possessions of flocks and herds, and a great household, so that the Philistines envied him. 15(Now the Philistines had stopped up and filled with earth all the wells that his father's servants had dug in the days of his father Abraham.) 16And Abimelech said to Isaac, "Go away from us; you have become too powerful for us."

17 So Isaac departed from there and camped in the valley of Gerar and settled

a Syr: Meaning of Heb uncertain　　*b* That is *He takes by the heel* or *He supplants*　　*c* That is *Red*　　*d* Heb *today*
e Heb *him*

there. ¹⁸Isaac dug again the wells of water that had been dug in the days of his father Abraham; for the Philistines had stopped them up after the death of Abraham; and he gave them the names that his father had given them. ¹⁹But when Isaac's servants dug in the valley and found there a well of spring water, ²⁰the herders of Gerar quarreled with Isaac's herders, saying, "The water is ours." So he called the well Esek,ᵃ because they contended with him. ²¹Then they dug another well, and they quarreled over that one also; so he called it Sitnah.ᵇ ²²He moved from there and dug another well, and they did not quarrel over it; so he called it Rehoboth,ᶜ saying, "Now the LORD has made room for us, and we shall be fruitful in the land."

23 From there he went up to Beer-sheba. ²⁴And that very night the LORD appeared to him and said, "I am the God of your father Abraham; do not be afraid, for I am with you and will bless you and make your offspring numerous for my servant Abraham's sake." ²⁵So he built an altar there, called on the name of the LORD, and pitched his tent there. And there Isaac's servants dug a well.

26 Then Abimelech went to him from Gerar, with Ahuzzath his adviser and Phicol the commander of his army. ²⁷Isaac said to them, "Why have you come to me, seeing that you hate me and have sent me away from you?" ²⁸They said, "We see plainly that the LORD has been with you; so we say, let there be an oath between you and us, and let us make a covenant with you ²⁹so that you will do us no harm, just as we have not touched you and have done to you nothing but good and have sent you away in peace. You are now the blessed of the LORD." ³⁰So he made them a feast, and they ate and drank. ³¹In the morning they rose early and exchanged oaths; Isaac set them on their way, and they departed from him in peace. ³²That same day Isaac's servants came and told him about the well that they had dug, and said to him, "We have found water!" ³³He called it Shibah;ᵈ therefore

the name of the city is Beer-shebaᵉ to this day.

Esau's Hittite Wives

34 When Esau was forty years old, he married Judith daughter of Beeri the Hittite, and Basemath daughter of Elon the Hittite; ³⁵and they made life bitter for Isaac and Rebekah.

Isaac Blesses Jacob

27 When Isaac was old and his eyes were dim so that he could not see, he called his elder son Esau and said to him, "My son"; and he answered, "Here I am." ²He said, "See, I am old; I do not know the day of my death. ³Now then, take your weapons, your quiver and your bow, and go out to the field, and hunt game for me. ⁴Then prepare for me savory food, such as I like, and bring it to me to eat, so that I may bless you before I die."

5 Now Rebekah was listening when Isaac spoke to his son Esau. So when Esau went to the field to hunt for game and bring it, ⁶Rebekah said to her son Jacob, "I heard your father say to your brother Esau, ⁷'Bring me game, and prepare for me savory food to eat, that I may bless you before the LORD before I die.' ⁸Now therefore, my son, obey my word as I command you. ⁹Go to the flock, and get me two choice kids, so that I may prepare from them savory food for your father, such as he likes; ¹⁰and you shall take it to your father to eat, so that he may bless you before he dies." ¹¹But Jacob said to his mother Rebekah, "Look, my brother Esau is a hairy man, and I am a man of smooth skin. ¹²Perhaps my father will feel me, and I shall seem to be mocking him, and bring a curse on myself and not a blessing." ¹³His mother said to him, "Let your curse be on me, my son; only obey my word, and go, get them for me." ¹⁴So he went and got them and brought them to his mother; and his mother prepared savory food, such as his father loved. ¹⁵Then Rebekah took the best garments of her elder son Esau, which were with her in the house, and put them on her younger

---

ᵃ That is *Contention*   ᵇ That is *Enmity*   ᶜ That is *Broad places* or *Room*   ᵈ A word resembling the word for *oath*
ᵉ That is *Well of the oath* or *Well of seven*

son Jacob; [16]and she put the skins of the kids on his hands and on the smooth part of his neck. [17]Then she handed the savory food, and the bread that she had prepared, to her son Jacob.

18 So he went in to his father, and said, "My father"; and he said, "Here I am; who are you, my son?" [19]Jacob said to his father, "I am Esau your firstborn. I have done as you told me; now sit up and eat of my game, so that you may bless me." [20]But Isaac said to his son, "How is it that you have found it so quickly, my son?" He answered, "Because the LORD your God granted me success." [21]Then Isaac said to Jacob, "Come near, that I may feel you, my son, to know whether you are really my son Esau or not." [22]So Jacob went up to his father Isaac, who felt him and said, "The voice is Jacob's voice, but the hands are the hands of Esau." [23]He did not recognize him, because his hands were hairy like his brother Esau's hands; so he blessed him. [24]He said, "Are you really my son Esau?" He answered, "I am." [25]Then he said, "Bring it to me, that I may eat of my son's game and bless you." So he brought it to him, and he ate; and he brought him wine, and he drank. [26]Then his father Isaac said to him, "Come near and kiss me, my son." [27]So he came near and kissed him; and he smelled the smell of his garments, and blessed him, and said,

"Ah, the smell of my son
    is like the smell of a field that the
        LORD has blessed.
[28] May God give you of the dew of
        heaven,
    and of the fatness of the earth,
    and plenty of grain and wine.
[29] Let peoples serve you,
    and nations bow down to you.
Be lord over your brothers,
    and may your mother's sons bow
        down to you.
Cursed be everyone who curses you,
    and blessed be everyone who blesses
        you!"

Esau's Lost Blessing

30 As soon as Isaac had finished blessing Jacob, when Jacob had scarcely gone out from the presence of his father Isaac, his brother Esau came in from his hunting. [31]He also prepared savory food, and brought it to his father. And he said to his father, "Let my father sit up and eat of his son's game, so that you may bless me." [32]His father Isaac said to him, "Who are you?" He answered, "I am your firstborn son, Esau." [33]Then Isaac trembled violently, and said, "Who was it then that hunted game and brought it to me, and I ate it all[a] before you came, and I have blessed him?—yes, and blessed he shall be!" [34]When Esau heard his father's words, he cried out with an exceedingly great and bitter cry, and said to his father, "Bless me, me also, father!" [35]But he said, "Your brother came deceitfully, and he has taken away your blessing." [36]Esau said, "Is he not rightly named Jacob?[b] For he has supplanted me these two times. He took away my birthright; and look, now he has taken away my blessing." Then he said, "Have you not reserved a blessing for me?" [37]Isaac answered Esau, "I have already made him your lord, and I have given him all his brothers as servants, and with grain and wine I have sustained him. What then can I do for you, my son?" [38]Esau said to his father, "Have you only one blessing, father? Bless me, me also, father!" And Esau lifted up his voice and wept.

39 Then his father Isaac answered him:

"See, away from[c] the fatness of the
        earth shall your home be,
    and away from[d] the dew of heaven
        on high.
[40] By your sword you shall live,
    and you shall serve your brother;
but when you break loose,[e]
    you shall break his yoke from your
        neck."

Jacob Escapes Esau's Fury

41 Now Esau hated Jacob because of the blessing with which his father had blessed

---

a Cn: Heb of all   b That is He supplants or He takes by the heel   c Or See, of   d Or and of   e Meaning of Heb uncertain him, and Esau said to himself, "The days of mourning for my father are approaching; then I will kill my brother Jacob." 42But the words of her elder son Esau were told to Rebekah; so she sent and called her younger son Jacob and said to him, "Your brother Esau is consoling himself by planning to kill you. 43Now therefore, my son, obey my voice; flee at once to my brother Laban in Haran, 44and stay with him a while, until your brother's fury turns away— 45until your brother's anger against you turns away, and he forgets what you have done to him; then I will send, and bring you back from there. Why should I lose both of you in one day?"

46 Then Rebekah said to Isaac, "I am weary of my life because of the Hittite women. If Jacob marries one of the Hittite women such as these, one of the women of the land, what good will my life be to me?"

28 Then Isaac called Jacob and blessed him, and charged him, "You shall not marry one of the Canaanite women. 2Go at once to Paddan-aram to the house of Bethuel, your mother's father; and take as wife from there one of the daughters of Laban, your mother's brother. 3May God Almightya bless you and make you fruitful and numerous, that you may become a company of peoples. 4May he give to you the blessing of Abraham, to you and to your offspring with you, so that you may take possession of the land where you now live as an alien—land that God gave to Abraham." 5Thus Isaac sent Jacob away; and he went to Paddan-aram, to Laban son of Bethuel the Aramean, the brother of Rebekah, Jacob's and Esau's mother.

Esau Marries Ishmael's Daughter

6 Now Esau saw that Isaac had blessed Jacob and sent him away to Paddan-aram to take a wife from there, and that as he blessed him he charged him, "You shall not marry one of the Canaanite women," 7and that Jacob had obeyed his father and his mother and gone to Paddan-aram. 8So when Esau saw that the Canaanite women did not please his father Isaac, 9Esau went to Ishmael and took Mahalath daughter of Abraham's son Ishmael, and sister of Nebaioth, to be his wife in addition to the wives he had.

Jacob's Dream at Bethel

10 Jacob left Beer-sheba and went toward Haran. 11He came to a certain place and stayed there for the night, because the sun had set. Taking one of the stones of the place, he put it under his head and lay down in that place. 12And he dreamed that there was a ladderb set up on the earth, the top of it reaching to heaven; and the angels of God were ascending and descending on it. 13And the LORD stood beside himc and said, "I am the LORD, the God of Abraham your father and the God of Isaac; the land on which you lie I will give to you and to your offspring; 14and your offspring shall be like the dust of the earth, and you shall spread abroad to the west and to the east and to the north and to the south; and all the families of the earth shall be blessedd in you and in your offspring. 15Know that I am with you and will keep you wherever you go, and will bring you back to this land; for I will not leave you until I have done what I have promised you." 16Then Jacob woke from his sleep and said, "Surely the LORD is in this place—and I did not know it!" 17And he was afraid, and said, "How awesome is this place! This is none other than the house of God, and this is the gate of heaven."

18 So Jacob rose early in the morning, and he took the stone that he had put under his head and set it up for a pillar and poured oil on the top of it. 19He called that place Bethel;e but the name of the city was Luz at the first. 20Then Jacob made a vow, saying, "If God will be with me, and will keep me in this way that I go, and will give me bread to eat and clothing to wear, 21so that I come again to my father's house in peace, then the LORD shall be my God, 22and this stone, which I have set up for a pillar, shall be God's house; and of all that you give me I will surely give one-tenth to you."

---

a Traditional rendering of Heb El Shaddai   b Or stairway or ramp   c Or stood above it   d Or shall bless themselves   e That is House of God

Jacob Meets Rachel

29

Then Jacob went on his journey, and came to the land of the people of the east. ²As he looked, he saw a well in the field and three flocks of sheep lying there beside it; for out of that well the flocks were watered. The stone on the well's mouth was large, ³and when all the flocks were gathered there, the shepherds would roll the stone from the mouth of the well, and water the sheep, and put the stone back in its place on the mouth of the well.

4 Jacob said to them, "My brothers, where do you come from?" They said, "We are from Haran." ⁵He said to them, "Do you know Laban son of Nahor?" They said, "We do." ⁶He said to them, "Is it well with him?" "Yes," they replied, "and here is his daughter Rachel, coming with the sheep." ⁷He said, "Look, it is still broad daylight; it is not time for the animals to be gathered together. Water the sheep, and go, pasture them." ⁸But they said, "We cannot until all the flocks are gathered together, and the stone is rolled from the mouth of the well; then we water the sheep."

9 While he was still speaking with them, Rachel came with her father's sheep; for she kept them. ¹⁰Now when Jacob saw Rachel, the daughter of his mother's brother Laban, and the sheep of his mother's brother Laban, Jacob went up and rolled the stone from the well's mouth, and watered the flock of his mother's brother Laban. ¹¹Then Jacob kissed Rachel, and wept aloud. ¹²And Jacob told Rachel that he was her father's kinsman, and that he was Rebekah's son; and she ran and told her father.

13 When Laban heard the news about his sister's son Jacob, he ran to meet him; he embraced him and kissed him, and brought him to his house. Jacob*ᵃ* told Laban all these things, ¹⁴and Laban said to him, "Surely you are my bone and my flesh!" And he stayed with him a month.

Jacob Marries Laban's Daughters

15 Then Laban said to Jacob, "Because you are my kinsman, should you therefore serve me for nothing? Tell me, what shall your wages be?" ¹⁶Now Laban had two daughters; the name of the elder was Leah, and the name of the younger was Rachel. ¹⁷Leah's eyes were lovely,*ᵇ* and Rachel was graceful and beautiful. ¹⁸Jacob loved Rachel; so he said, "I will serve you seven years for your younger daughter Rachel." ¹⁹Laban said, "It is better that I give her to you than that I should give her to any other man; stay with me." ²⁰So Jacob served seven years for Rachel, and they seemed to him but a few days because of the love he had for her.

21 Then Jacob said to Laban, "Give me my wife that I may go in to her, for my time is completed." ²²So Laban gathered together all the people of the place, and made a feast. ²³But in the evening he took his daughter Leah and brought her to Jacob; and he went in to her. ²⁴(Laban gave his maid Zilpah to his daughter Leah to be her maid.) ²⁵When morning came, it was Leah! And Jacob said to Laban, "What is this you have done to me? Did I not serve with you for Rachel? Why then have you deceived me?" ²⁶Laban said, "This is not done in our country—giving the younger before the firstborn. ²⁷Complete the week of this one, and we will give you the other also in return for serving me another seven years." ²⁸Jacob did so, and completed her week; then Laban gave him his daughter Rachel as a wife. ²⁹(Laban gave his maid Bilhah to his daughter Rachel to be her maid.) ³⁰So Jacob went in to Rachel also, and he loved Rachel more than Leah. He served Laban*ᶜ* for another seven years.

31 When the Lord saw that Leah was unloved, he opened her womb; but Rachel was barren. ³²Leah conceived and bore a son, and she named him Reuben;*ᵈ* for she said, "Because the Lord has looked on my affliction; surely now my husband will love me." ³³She conceived again and bore a son, and

---

a Heb *He*   *b* Meaning of Heb uncertain   *c* Heb *him*   *d* That is *See, a son* said, "Because the LORD has heard*a* that I am hated, he has given me this son also"; and she named him Simeon. 34Again she conceived and bore a son, and said, "Now this time my husband will be joined*b* to me, because I have borne him three sons"; therefore he was named Levi. 35She conceived again and bore a son, and said, "This time I will praise*c* the LORD"; therefore she named him Judah; then she ceased bearing.

30 When Rachel saw that she bore Jacob no children, she envied her sister; and she said to Jacob, "Give me children, or I shall die!" 2Jacob became very angry with Rachel and said, "Am I in the place of God, who has withheld from you the fruit of the womb?" 3Then she said, "Here is my maid Bilhah; go in to her, that she may bear upon my knees and that I too may have children through her." 4So she gave him her maid Bilhah as a wife; and Jacob went in to her. 5And Bilhah conceived and bore Jacob a son. 6Then Rachel said, "God has judged me, and has also heard my voice and given me a son"; therefore she named him Dan.*d* 7Rachel's maid Bilhah conceived again and bore Jacob a second son. 8Then Rachel said, "With mighty wrestlings I have wrestled*e* with my sister, and have prevailed"; so she named him Naphtali.

9 When Leah saw that she had ceased bearing children, she took her maid Zilpah and gave her to Jacob as a wife. 10Then Leah's maid Zilpah bore Jacob a son. 11And Leah said, "Good fortune!" so she named him Gad.*f* 12Leah's maid Zilpah bore Jacob a second son. 13And Leah said, "Happy am I! For the women will call me happy"; so she named him Asher.*g*

14 In the days of wheat harvest Reuben went and found mandrakes in the field, and brought them to his mother Leah. Then Rachel said to Leah, "Please give me some of your son's mandrakes." 15But she said to her, "Is it a small matter that you have taken away my husband? Would you take away my son's mandrakes also?" Rachel said, "Then he may lie with you tonight for your son's mandrakes."

16When Jacob came from the field in the evening, Leah went out to meet him, and said, "You must come in to me; for I have hired you with my son's mandrakes." So he lay with her that night. 17And God heeded Leah, and she conceived and bore Jacob a fifth son. 18Leah said, "God has given me my hire*b* because I gave my maid to my husband"; so she named him Issachar. 19And Leah conceived again, and she bore Jacob a sixth son. 20Then Leah said, "God has endowed me with a good dowry; now my husband will honor*i* me, because I have borne him six sons"; so she named him Zebulun. 21Afterwards she bore a daughter, and named her Dinah.

22 Then God remembered Rachel, and God heeded her and opened her womb. 23She conceived and bore a son, and said, "God has taken away my reproach"; 24and she named him Joseph,*j* saying, "May the LORD add to me another son!"

Jacob Prospers at Laban's Expense

25 When Rachel had borne Joseph, Jacob said to Laban, "Send me away, that I may go to my own home and country. 26Give me my wives and my children for whom I have served you, and let me go; for you know very well the service I have given you." 27But Laban said to him, "If you will allow me to say so, I have learned by divination that the LORD has blessed me because of you; 28name your wages, and I will give it." 29Jacob said to him, "You yourself know how I have served you, and how your cattle have fared with me. 30For you had little before I came, and it has increased abundantly; and the LORD has blessed you wherever I turned. But now when shall I provide for my own household also?" 31He said, "What shall I give you?" Jacob said, "You shall not give me anything; if you will do this for me, I will again feed your flock and keep it: 32let me pass through all your flock today, removing from it every speckled and spotted sheep and every black lamb, and the spotted and speckled among the goats; and such shall be my wages.

a Heb *shama*   *b* Heb *lawah*   *c* Heb *hodah*   *d* That is *He judged*   *e* Heb *niphtal*   *f* That is *Fortune*   *g* That is *Happy*   *h* Heb *sakar*   *i* Heb *zabal*   *j* That is *He adds*

[33]So my honesty will answer for me later, when you come to look into my wages with you. Every one that is not speckled and spotted among the goats and black among the lambs, if found with me, shall be counted stolen." [34]Laban said, "Good! Let it be as you have said." [35]But that day Laban removed the male goats that were striped and spotted, and all the female goats that were speckled and spotted, every one that had white on it, and every lamb that was black, and put them in charge of his sons; [36]and he set a distance of three days' journey between himself and Jacob, while Jacob was pasturing the rest of Laban's flock.

[37] Then Jacob took fresh rods of poplar and almond and plane, and peeled white streaks in them, exposing the white of the rods. [38]He set the rods that he had peeled in front of the flocks in the troughs, that is, the watering places, where the flocks came to drink. And since they bred when they came to drink, [39]the flocks bred in front of the rods, and so the flocks produced young that were striped, speckled, and spotted. [40]Jacob separated the lambs, and set the faces of the flocks toward the striped and the completely black animals in the flock of Laban; and he put his own droves apart, and did not put them with Laban's flock. [41]Whenever the stronger of the flock were breeding, Jacob laid the rods in the troughs before the eyes of the flock, that they might breed among the rods, [42]but for the feebler of the flock he did not lay them there; so the feebler were Laban's, and the stronger Jacob's. [43]Thus the man grew exceedingly rich, and had large flocks, and male and female slaves, and camels and donkeys.

Jacob Flees with Family and Flocks

31 Now Jacob heard that the sons of Laban were saying, "Jacob has taken all that was our father's; he has gained all this wealth from what belonged to our father." [2]And Jacob saw that Laban did not regard him as favorably as he did before. [3]Then the LORD said to Jacob, "Return to the land of your ancestors and to your kindred, and I will be with you." [4]So Jacob sent and called Rachel and Leah into the field where his flock was, [5]and said to them, "I see that your father does not regard me as favorably as he did before. But the God of my father has been with me. [6]You know that I have served your father with all my strength; [7]yet your father has cheated me and changed my wages ten times, but God did not permit him to harm me. [8]If he said, 'The speckled shall be your wages,' then all the flock bore speckled; and if he said, 'The striped shall be your wages,' then all the flock bore striped. [9]Thus God has taken away the livestock of your father, and given them to me.

[10] "During the mating of the flock I once had a dream in which I looked up and saw that the male goats that leaped upon the flock were striped, speckled, and mottled. [11]Then the angel of God said to me in the dream, 'Jacob,' and I said, 'Here I am!' [12]And he said, 'Look up and see that all the goats that leap on the flock are striped, speckled, and mottled; for I have seen all that Laban is doing to you. [13]I am the God of Bethel,[a] where you anointed a pillar and made a vow to me. Now leave this land at once and return to the land of your birth.'" [14]Then Rachel and Leah answered him, "Is there any portion or inheritance left to us in our father's house? [15]Are we not regarded by him as foreigners? For he has sold us, and he has been using up the money given for us. [16]All the property that God has taken away from our father belongs to us and to our children; now then, do whatever God has said to you."

[17] So Jacob arose, and set his children and his wives on camels; [18]and he drove away all his livestock, all the property that he had gained, the livestock in his possession that he had acquired in Paddan-aram, to go to his father Isaac in the land of Canaan.

[19] Now Laban had gone to shear his sheep, and Rachel stole her father's household gods. [20]And Jacob deceived Laban the Aramean, in that he did not tell him that he intended to flee.

a Cn: Meaning of Heb uncertain

21So he fled with all that he had; starting out he crossed the Euphrates,*a* and set his face toward the hill country of Gilead.

Laban Overtakes Jacob

22 On the third day Laban was told that Jacob had fled. 23So he took his kinsfolk with him and pursued him for seven days until he caught up with him in the hill country of Gilead. 24But God came to Laban the Aramean in a dream by night, and said to him, "Take heed that you say not a word to Jacob, either good or bad."

25 Laban overtook Jacob. Now Jacob had pitched his tent in the hill country, and Laban with his kinsfolk camped in the hill country of Gilead. 26Laban said to Jacob, "What have you done? You have deceived me, and carried away my daughters like captives of the sword. 27Why did you flee secretly and deceive me and not tell me? I would have sent you away with mirth and songs, with tambourine and lyre. 28And why did you not permit me to kiss my sons and my daughters farewell? What you have done is foolish. 29It is in my power to do you harm; but the God of your father spoke to me last night, saying, 'Take heed that you speak to Jacob neither good nor bad.' 30Even though you had to go because you longed greatly for your father's house, why did you steal my gods?" 31Jacob answered Laban, "Because I was afraid, for I thought that you would take your daughters from me by force. 32But anyone with whom you find your gods shall not live. In the presence of our kinsfolk, point out what I have that is yours, and take it." Now Jacob did not know that Rachel had stolen the gods.*b*

33 So Laban went into Jacob's tent, and into Leah's tent, and into the tent of the two maids, but he did not find them. And he went out of Leah's tent, and entered Rachel's. 34Now Rachel had taken the household gods and put them in the camel's saddle, and sat on them. Laban felt all about in the tent, but did not find them. 35And she said to her father, "Let not my lord be angry that I cannot rise before you, for the way of women is upon me." So he searched, but did not find the household gods.

36 Then Jacob became angry, and upbraided Laban. Jacob said to Laban, "What is my offense? What is my sin, that you have hotly pursued me? 37Although you have felt about through all my goods, what have you found of all your household goods? Set it here before my kinsfolk and your kinsfolk, so that they may decide between us two. 38These twenty years I have been with you; your ewes and your female goats have not miscarried, and I have not eaten the rams of your flocks. 39That which was torn by wild beasts I did not bring to you; I bore the loss of it myself; of my hand you required it, whether stolen by day or stolen by night. 40It was like this with me: by day the heat consumed me, and the cold by night, and my sleep fled from my eyes. 41These twenty years I have been in your house; I served you fourteen years for your two daughters, and six years for your flock, and you have changed my wages ten times. 42If the God of my father, the God of Abraham and the Fear*c* of Isaac, had not been on my side, surely now you would have sent me away empty-handed. God saw my affliction and the labor of my hands, and rebuked you last night."

Laban and Jacob Make a Covenant

43 Then Laban answered and said to Jacob, "The daughters are my daughters, the children are my children, the flocks are my flocks, and all that you see is mine. But what can I do today about these daughters of mine, or about their children whom they have borne? 44Come now, let us make a covenant, you and I; and let it be a witness between you and me." 45So Jacob took a stone, and set it up as a pillar. 46And Jacob said to his kinsfolk, "Gather stones," and they took stones, and made a heap; and they ate there by the heap. 47Laban called it Jegar-sahadutha:*d* but Jacob called it Galeed.*e* 48Laban said, "This heap is a witness between you and me today." Therefore he called it Galeed, 49and the pillar*f* Mizpah,*g* for

---

a Heb *the river*   *b* Heb *them*   *c* Meaning of Heb uncertain   *d* In Aramaic *The heap of witness*   *e* In Hebrew *The heap of witness*   *f* Compare Sam: MT lacks *the pillar*   *g* That is *Watchpost* he said, "The LORD watch between you and me, when we are absent one from the other. 50If you ill-treat my daughters, or if you take wives in addition to my daughters, though no one else is with us, remember that God is witness between you and me."

51 Then Laban said to Jacob, "See this heap and see the pillar, which I have set between you and me. 52This heap is a witness, and the pillar is a witness, that I will not pass beyond this heap to you, and you will not pass beyond this heap and this pillar to me, for harm. 53May the God of Abraham and the God of Nahor"—the God of their father— "judge between us." So Jacob swore by the Fear*a* of his father Isaac, 54and Jacob offered a sacrifice on the height and called his kinsfolk to eat bread; and they ate bread and tarried all night in the hill country.

55*b* Early in the morning Laban rose up, and kissed his grandchildren and his daughters and blessed them; then he departed and returned home.

32 Jacob went on his way and the angels of God met him; 2and when Jacob saw them he said, "This is God's camp!" So he called that place Mahanaim.*c*

Jacob Sends Presents to Appease Esau

3 Jacob sent messengers before him to his brother Esau in the land of Seir, the country of Edom, 4instructing them, "Thus you shall say to my lord Esau: Thus says your servant Jacob, 'I have lived with Laban as an alien, and stayed until now; 5and I have oxen, donkeys, flocks, male and female slaves; and I have sent to tell my lord, in order that I may find favor in your sight.'"

6 The messengers returned to Jacob, saying, "We came to your brother Esau, and he is coming to meet you, and four hundred men are with him." 7Then Jacob was greatly afraid and distressed; and he divided the people that were with him, and the flocks and herds and camels, into two companies, 8thinking, "If Esau comes to the one company and destroys it, then the company that is left will escape."

9 And Jacob said, "O God of my father Abraham and God of my father Isaac, O LORD who said to me, 'Return to your country and to your kindred, and I will do you good,' 10I am not worthy of the least of all the steadfast love and all the faithfulness that you have shown to your servant, for with only my staff I crossed this Jordan; and now I have become two companies. 11Deliver me, please, from the hand of my brother, from the hand of Esau, for I am afraid of him; he may come and kill us all, the mothers with the children. 12Yet you have said, 'I will surely do you good, and make your offspring as the sand of the sea, which cannot be counted because of their number.'"

13 So he spent that night there, and from what he had with him he took a present for his brother Esau, 14two hundred female goats and twenty male goats, two hundred ewes and twenty rams, 15thirty milch camels and their colts, forty cows and ten bulls, twenty female donkeys and ten male donkeys. 16These he delivered into the hand of his servants, every drove by itself, and said to his servants, "Pass on ahead of me, and put a space between drove and drove." 17He instructed the foremost, "When Esau my brother meets you, and asks you, 'To whom do you belong? Where are you going? And whose are these ahead of you?' 18then you shall say, 'They belong to your servant Jacob; they are a present sent to my lord Esau; and moreover he is behind us.'" 19He likewise instructed the second and the third and all who followed the droves, "You shall say the same thing to Esau when you meet him, 20and you shall say, 'Moreover your servant Jacob is behind us.'" For he thought, "I may appease him with the present that goes ahead of me, and afterwards I shall see his face; perhaps he will accept me." 21So the present passed on ahead of him; and he himself spent that night in the camp.

a Meaning of Heb uncertain   *b* Ch 32.1 in Heb   *c* Here taken to mean *Two camps*

Jacob Wrestles at Peniel

22 The same night he got up and took his two wives, his two maids, and his eleven children, and crossed the ford of the Jabbok. 23He took them and sent them across the stream, and likewise everything that he had. 24Jacob was left alone; and a man wrestled with him until daybreak. 25When the man saw that he did not prevail against Jacob, he struck him on the hip socket; and Jacob's hip was put out of joint as he wrestled with him. 26Then he said, "Let me go, for the day is breaking." But Jacob said, "I will not let you go, unless you bless me." 27So he said to him, "What is your name?" And he said, "Jacob." 28Then the man*a* said, "You shall no longer be called Jacob, but Israel,*b* for you have striven with God and with humans,*c* and have prevailed." 29Then Jacob asked him, "Please tell me your name." But he said, "Why is it that you ask my name?" And there he blessed him. 30So Jacob called the place Peniel,*d* saying, "For I have seen God face to face, and yet my life is preserved." 31The sun rose upon him as he passed Penuel, limping because of his hip. 32Therefore to this day the Israelites do not eat the thigh muscle that is on the hip socket, because he struck Jacob on the hip socket at the thigh muscle.

Jacob and Esau Meet

33 Now Jacob looked up and saw Esau coming, and four hundred men with him. So he divided the children among Leah and Rachel and the two maids. 2He put the maids with their children in front, then Leah with her children, and Rachel and Joseph last of all. 3He himself went on ahead of them, bowing himself to the ground seven times, until he came near his brother.

4 But Esau ran to meet him, and embraced him, and fell on his neck and kissed him, and they wept. 5When Esau looked up and saw the women and children, he said, "Who are these with you?" Jacob said, "The children whom God has graciously given your servant." 6Then the maids drew near, they and their children, and bowed down; 7Leah likewise and her children drew near and bowed down; and finally Joseph and Rachel drew near, and they bowed down. 8Esau said, "What do you mean by all this company that I met?" Jacob answered, "To find favor with my lord." 9But Esau said, "I have enough, my brother; keep what you have for yourself." 10Jacob said, "No, please; if I find favor with you, then accept my present from my hand; for truly to see your face is like seeing the face of God—since you have received me with such favor. 11Please accept my gift that is brought to you, because God has dealt graciously with me, and because I have everything I want." So he urged him, and he took it.

12 Then Esau said, "Let us journey on our way, and I will go alongside you." 13But Jacob said to him, "My lord knows that the children are frail and that the flocks and herds, which are nursing, are a care to me; and if they are overdriven for one day, all the flocks will die. 14Let my lord pass on ahead of his servant, and I will lead on slowly, according to the pace of the cattle that are before me and according to the pace of the children, until I come to my lord in Seir."

15 So Esau said, "Let me leave with you some of the people who are with me." But he said, "Why should my lord be so kind to me?" 16So Esau returned that day on his way to Seir. 17But Jacob journeyed to Succoth,*e* and built himself a house, and made booths for his cattle; therefore the place is called Succoth.

Jacob Reaches Shechem

18 Jacob came safely to the city of Shechem, which is in the land of Canaan, on his way from Paddan-aram; and he camped before the city. 19And from the sons of Hamor, Shechem's father, he bought for one hundred pieces of money*f* the plot of land on which he had pitched his tent. 20There he erected an altar and called it El-Elohe-Israel.*g*

---

a Heb *he*   *b* That is *The one who strives with God* or *God strives*   *c* Or *with divine and human beings*   *d* That is *The face of God*   *e* That is *Booths*   *f* Heb *one hundred qesitah*   *g* That is *God, the God of Israel*

The Rape of Dinah

34 Now Dinah the daughter of Leah, whom she had borne to Jacob, went out to visit the women of the region. [2]When Shechem son of Hamor the Hivite, prince of the region, saw her, he seized her and lay with her by force. [3]And his soul was drawn to Dinah daughter of Jacob; he loved the girl, and spoke tenderly to her. [4]So Shechem spoke to his father Hamor, saying, "Get me this girl to be my wife."

5 Now Jacob heard that Shechem[a] had defiled his daughter Dinah; but his sons were with his cattle in the field, so Jacob held his peace until they came. [6]And Hamor the father of Shechem went out to Jacob to speak with him, [7]just as the sons of Jacob came in from the field. When they heard of it, the men were indignant and very angry, because he had committed an outrage in Israel by lying with Jacob's daughter, for such a thing ought not to be done.

8 But Hamor spoke with them, saying, "The heart of my son Shechem longs for your daughter; please give her to him in marriage. [9]Make marriages with us; give your daughters to us, and take our daughters for yourselves. [10]You shall live with us; and the land shall be open to you; live and trade in it, and get property in it." [11]Shechem also said to her father and to her brothers, "Let me find favor with you, and whatever you say to me I will give. [12]Put the marriage present and gift as high as you like, and I will give whatever you ask me; only give me the girl to be my wife."

13 The sons of Jacob answered Shechem and his father Hamor deceitfully, because he had defiled their sister Dinah. [14]They said to them, "We cannot do this thing, to give our sister to one who is uncircumcised, for that would be a disgrace to us. [15]Only on this condition will we consent to you: that you will become as we are and every male among you be circumcised. [16]Then we will give our daughters to you, and we will take your daughters for ourselves, and we will live among you and become one people. [17]But if you will not listen to us and be circumcised, then we will take our daughter and be gone."

18 Their words pleased Hamor and Hamor's son Shechem. [19]And the young man did not delay to do the thing, because he was delighted with Jacob's daughter. Now he was the most honored of all his family. [20]So Hamor and his son Shechem came to the gate of their city and spoke to the men of their city, saying, [21]"These people are friendly with us; let them live in the land and trade in it, for the land is large enough for them; let us take their daughters in marriage, and let us give them our daughters. [22]Only on this condition will they agree to live among us, to become one people: that every male among us be circumcised as they are circumcised. [23]Will not their livestock, their property, and all their animals be ours? Only let us agree with them, and they will live among us." [24]And all who went out of the city gate heeded Hamor and his son Shechem; and every male was circumcised, all who went out of the gate of his city.

Dinah's Brothers Avenge Their Sister

25 On the third day, when they were still in pain, two of the sons of Jacob, Simeon and Levi, Dinah's brothers, took their swords and came against the city unawares, and killed all the males. [26]They killed Hamor and his son Shechem with the sword, and took Dinah out of Shechem's house, and went away. [27]And the other sons of Jacob came upon the slain, and plundered the city, because their sister had been defiled. [28]They took their flocks and their herds, their donkeys, and whatever was in the city and in the field. [29]All their wealth, all their little ones and their wives, all that was in the houses, they captured and made their prey. [30]Then Jacob said to Simeon and Levi, "You have brought trouble on me by making me odious to the inhabitants of the land, the Canaanites and the Perizzites; my numbers are few, and if they gather themselves against me and attack me, I shall be destroyed, both I and my household." [31]But they said, "Should our sister be treated like a whore?"

a Heb *he*

Jacob Returns to Bethel

35 God said to Jacob, "Arise, go up to Bethel, and settle there. Make an altar there to the God who appeared to you when you fled from your brother Esau." ²So Jacob said to his household and to all who were with him, "Put away the foreign gods that are among you, and purify yourselves, and change your clothes; ³then come, let us go up to Bethel, that I may make an altar there to the God who answered me in the day of my distress and has been with me wherever I have gone." ⁴So they gave to Jacob all the foreign gods that they had, and the rings that were in their ears; and Jacob hid them under the oak that was near Shechem.

5 As they journeyed, a terror from God fell upon the cities all around them, so that no one pursued them. ⁶Jacob came to Luz (that is, Bethel), which is in the land of Canaan, he and all the people who were with him, ⁷and there he built an altar and called the place El-bethel,ᵃ because it was there that God had revealed himself to him when he fled from his brother. ⁸And Deborah, Rebekah's nurse, died, and she was buried under an oak below Bethel. So it was called Allon-bacuth.ᵇ

9 God appeared to Jacob again when he came from Paddan-aram, and he blessed him. ¹⁰God said to him, "Your name is Jacob; no longer shall you be called Jacob, but Israel shall be your name." So he was called Israel. ¹¹God said to him, "I am God Almighty:ᶜ be fruitful and multiply; a nation and a company of nations shall come from you, and kings shall spring from you. ¹²The land that I gave to Abraham and Isaac I will give to you, and I will give the land to your offspring after you." ¹³Then God went up from him at the place where he had spoken with him. ¹⁴Jacob set up a pillar in the place where he had spoken with him, a pillar of stone; and he poured out a drink offering on it, and poured oil on it. ¹⁵So Jacob called the place where God had spoken with him Bethel.

The Birth of Benjamin and the Death of Rachel

16 Then they journeyed from Bethel; and when they were still some distance from Ephrath, Rachel was in childbirth, and she had hard labor. ¹⁷When she was in her hard labor, the midwife said to her, "Do not be afraid; for now you will have another son." ¹⁸As her soul was departing (for she died), she named him Ben-oni;ᵈ but his father called him Benjamin.ᵉ ¹⁹So Rachel died, and she was buried on the way to Ephrath (that is, Bethlehem), ²⁰and Jacob set up a pillar at her grave; it is the pillar of Rachel's tomb, which is there to this day. ²¹Israel journeyed on, and pitched his tent beyond the tower of Eder.

22 While Israel lived in that land, Reuben went and lay with Bilhah his father's concubine; and Israel heard of it.

Now the sons of Jacob were twelve. ²³The sons of Leah: Reuben (Jacob's firstborn), Simeon, Levi, Judah, Issachar, and Zebulun. ²⁴The sons of Rachel: Joseph and Benjamin. ²⁵The sons of Bilhah, Rachel's maid: Dan and Naphtali. ²⁶The sons of Zilpah, Leah's maid: Gad and Asher. These were the sons of Jacob who were born to him in Paddan-aram.

The Death of Isaac

27 Jacob came to his father Isaac at Mamre, or Kiriath-arba (that is, Hebron), where Abraham and Isaac had resided as aliens. ²⁸Now the days of Isaac were one hundred eighty years. ²⁹And Isaac breathed his last; he died and was gathered to his people, old and full of days; and his sons Esau and Jacob buried him.

Esau's Descendants

36 These are the descendants of Esau (that is, Edom). ²Esau took his wives from the Canaanites: Adah daughter of Elon the Hittite, Oholibamah daughter of Anah sonᶠ of Zibeon the Hivite, ³and Basemath, Ishmael's daughter, sister of Nebaioth. ⁴Adah bore Eliphaz to Esau; Basemath bore Reuel; ⁵and Oholibamah bore Jeush, Jalam, and Ko-

---

ᵃ That is *God of Bethel*   ᵇ That is *Oak of weeping*   ᶜ Traditional rendering of Heb *El Shaddai*   ᵈ That is *Son of my sorrow*   ᵉ That is *Son of the right hand* or *Son of the South*   ᶠ Sam Gk Syr: Heb *daughter* rah. These are the sons of Esau who were born to him in the land of Canaan.

6 Then Esau took his wives, his sons, his daughters, and all the members of his household, his cattle, all his livestock, and all the property he had acquired in the land of Canaan; and he moved to a land some distance from his brother Jacob. 7For their possessions were too great for them to live together; the land where they were staying could not support them because of their livestock. 8So Esau settled in the hill country of Seir; Esau is Edom.

9 These are the descendants of Esau, ancestor of the Edomites, in the hill country of Seir. 10These are the names of Esau's sons: Eliphaz son of Adah the wife of Esau; Reuel, the son of Esau's wife Basemath. 11The sons of Eliphaz were Teman, Omar, Zepho, Gatam, and Kenaz. 12(Timna was a concubine of Eliphaz, Esau's son; she bore Amalek to Eliphaz.) These were the sons of Adah, Esau's wife. 13These were the sons of Reuel: Nahath, Zerah, Shammah, and Mizzah. These were the sons of Esau's wife, Basemath. 14These were the sons of Esau's wife Oholibamah, daughter of Anah son*a* of Zibeon: she bore to Esau Jeush, Jalam, and Korah.

Clans and Kings of Edom

15 These are the clans*b* of the sons of Esau. The sons of Eliphaz the firstborn of Esau: the clans*b* Teman, Omar, Zepho, Kenaz, 16Korah, Gatam, and Amalek; these are the clans*b* of Eliphaz in the land of Edom; they are the sons of Adah. 17These are the sons of Esau's son Reuel: the clans*b* Nahath, Zerah, Shammah, and Mizzah; these are the clans*b* of Reuel in the land of Edom; they are the sons of Esau's wife Basemath. 18These are the sons of Esau's wife Oholibamah: the clans*b* Jeush, Jalam, and Korah; these are the clans*b* born of Esau's wife Oholibamah, the daughter of Anah. 19These are the sons of Esau (that is, Edom), and these are their clans.*b*

20 These are the sons of Seir the Horite, the inhabitants of the land: Lotan, Shobal,

Zibeon, Anah, 21Dishon, Ezer, and Dishan; these are the clans*b* of the Horites, the sons of Seir in the land of Edom. 22The sons of Lotan were Hori and Heman; and Lotan's sister was Timna. 23These are the sons of Shobal: Alvan, Manahath, Ebal, Shepho, and Onam. 24These are the sons of Zibeon: Aiah and Anah; he is the Anah who found the springs*c* in the wilderness, as he pastured the donkeys of his father Zibeon. 25These are the children of Anah: Dishon and Oholibamah daughter of Anah. 26These are the sons of Dishon: Hemdan, Eshban, Ithran, and Cheran. 27These are the sons of Ezer: Bilhan, Zaavan, and Akan. 28These are the sons of Dishan: Uz and Aran. 29These are the clans*b* of the Horites: the clans*b* Lotan, Shobal, Zibeon, Anah, 30Dishon, Ezer, and Dishan; these are the clans*b* of the Horites, clan by clan*d* in the land of Seir.

31 These are the kings who reigned in the land of Edom, before any king reigned over the Israelites. 32Bela son of Beor reigned in Edom, the name of his city being Dinhabah. 33Bela died, and Jobab son of Zerah of Bozrah succeeded him as king. 34Jobab died, and Husham of the land of the Temanites succeeded him as king. 35Husham died, and Hadad son of Bedad, who defeated Midian in the country of Moab, succeeded him as king, the name of his city being Avith. 36Hadad died, and Samlah of Masrekah succeeded him as king. 37Samlah died, and Shaul of Rehoboth on the Euphrates succeeded him as king. 38Shaul died, and Baal-hanan son of Achbor succeeded him as king. 39Baal-hanan son of Achbor died, and Hadar succeeded him as king, the name of his city being Pau; his wife's name was Mehetabel, the daughter of Matred, daughter of Me-zahab.

40 These are the names of the clans*b* of Esau, according to their families and their localities by their names: the clans*b* Timna, Alvah, Jetheth, 41Oholibamah, Elah, Pinon, 42Kenaz, Teman, Mibzar, 43Magdiel, and Iram; these are the clans*b* of Edom (that is, Esau, the father of Edom), according to their settlements in the land that they held.

a Gk Syr: Heb *daughter*   *b* Or *chiefs*   *c* Meaning of Heb uncertain   *d* Or *chief by chief*

Joseph Dreams of Greatness

37 Jacob settled in the land where his father had lived as an alien, the land of Canaan. ²This is the story of the family of Jacob.

Joseph, being seventeen years old, was shepherding the flock with his brothers; he was a helper to the sons of Bilhah and Zilpah, his father's wives; and Joseph brought a bad report of them to their father. ³Now Israel loved Joseph more than any other of his children, because he was the son of his old age; and he had made him a long robe with sleeves.*a* ⁴But when his brothers saw that their father loved him more than all his brothers, they hated him, and could not speak peaceably to him.

5 Once Joseph had a dream, and when he told it to his brothers, they hated him even more. ⁶He said to them, "Listen to this dream that I dreamed. ⁷There we were, binding sheaves in the field. Suddenly my sheaf rose and stood upright; then your sheaves gathered around it, and bowed down to my sheaf." ⁸His brothers said to him, "Are you indeed to reign over us? Are you indeed to have dominion over us?" So they hated him even more because of his dreams and his words.

9 He had another dream, and told it to his brothers, saying, "Look, I have had another dream: the sun, the moon, and eleven stars were bowing down to me." ¹⁰But when he told it to his father and to his brothers, his father rebuked him, and said to him, "What kind of dream is this that you have had? Shall we indeed come, I and your mother and your brothers, and bow to the ground before you?" ¹¹So his brothers were jealous of him, but his father kept the matter in mind.

Joseph Is Sold by His Brothers

12 Now his brothers went to pasture their father's flock near Shechem. ¹³And Israel said to Joseph, "Are not your brothers pasturing the flock at Shechem? Come, I will send you to them." He answered, "Here I am." ¹⁴So he said to him, "Go now, see if it is well with your brothers and with the flock; and bring word back to me." So he sent him from the valley of Hebron.

He came to Shechem, ¹⁵and a man found him wandering in the fields; the man asked him, "What are you seeking?" ¹⁶"I am seeking my brothers," he said; "tell me, please, where they are pasturing the flock." ¹⁷The man said, "They have gone away, for I heard them say, 'Let us go to Dothan.' " So Joseph went after his brothers, and found them at Dothan. ¹⁸They saw him from a distance, and before he came near to them, they conspired to kill him. ¹⁹They said to one another, "Here comes this dreamer. ²⁰Come now, let us kill him and throw him into one of the pits; then we shall say that a wild animal has devoured him, and we shall see what will become of his dreams." ²¹But when Reuben heard it, he delivered him out of their hands, saying, "Let us not take his life." ²²Reuben said to them, "Shed no blood; throw him into this pit here in the wilderness, but lay no hand on him"—that he might rescue him out of their hand and restore him to his father. ²³So when Joseph came to his brothers, they stripped him of his robe, the long robe with sleeves*b* that he wore; ²⁴and they took him and threw him into a pit. The pit was empty; there was no water in it.

25 Then they sat down to eat; and looking up they saw a caravan of Ishmaelites coming from Gilead, with their camels carrying gum, balm, and resin, on their way to carry it down to Egypt. ²⁶Then Judah said to his brothers, "What profit is it if we kill our brother and conceal his blood? ²⁷Come, let us sell him to the Ishmaelites, and not lay our hands on him, for he is our brother, our own flesh." And his brothers agreed. ²⁸When some Midianite traders passed by, they drew Joseph up, lifting him out of the pit, and sold him to the Ishmaelites for twenty pieces of silver. And they took Joseph to Egypt.

29 When Reuben returned to the pit and saw that Joseph was not in the pit, he tore his clothes. ³⁰He returned to his brothers, and

---

a Traditional rendering (compare Gk): *a coat of many colors*; meaning of Heb uncertain   *b* See note on 37.3

said, "The boy is gone; and I, where can I turn?" ³¹Then they took Joseph's robe, slaughtered a goat, and dipped the robe in the blood. ³²They had the long robe with sleeves *a* taken to their father, and they said, "This we have found; see now whether it is your son's robe or not." ³³He recognized it, and said, "It is my son's robe! A wild animal has devoured him; Joseph is without doubt torn to pieces." ³⁴Then Jacob tore his garments, and put sackcloth on his loins, and mourned for his son many days. ³⁵All his sons and all his daughters sought to comfort him; but he refused to be comforted, and said, "No, I shall go down to Sheol to my son, mourning." Thus his father bewailed him. ³⁶Meanwhile the Midianites had sold him in Egypt to Potiphar, one of Pharaoh's officials, the captain of the guard.

Judah and Tamar

38 It happened at that time that Judah went down from his brothers and settled near a certain Adullamite whose name was Hirah. ²There Judah saw the daughter of a certain Canaanite whose name was Shua; he married her and went in to her. ³She conceived and bore a son; and he named him Er. ⁴Again she conceived and bore a son whom she named Onan. ⁵Yet again she bore a son, and she named him Shelah. She *b* was in Chezib when she bore him. ⁶Judah took a wife for Er his firstborn; her name was Tamar. ⁷But Er, Judah's firstborn, was wicked in the sight of the LORD, and the LORD put him to death. ⁸Then Judah said to Onan, "Go in to your brother's wife and perform the duty of a brother-in-law to her; raise up offspring for your brother." ⁹But since Onan knew that the offspring would not be his, he spilled his semen on the ground whenever he went in to his brother's wife, so that he would not give offspring to his brother. ¹⁰What he did was displeasing in the sight of the LORD, and he put him to death also. ¹¹Then Judah said to his daughter-in-law Tamar, "Remain a widow in your father's house until my son Shelah grows up"—for he

feared that he too would die, like his brothers. So Tamar went to live in her father's house.

12 In course of time the wife of Judah, Shua's daughter, died; when Judah's time of mourning was over, *c* he went up to Timnah to his sheepshearers, he and his friend Hirah the Adullamite. ¹³When Tamar was told, "Your father-in-law is going up to Timnah to shear his sheep," ¹⁴she put off her widow's garments, put on a veil, wrapped herself up, and sat down at the entrance to Enaim, which is on the road to Timnah. She saw that Shelah was grown up, yet she had not been given to him in marriage. ¹⁵When Judah saw her, he thought her to be a prostitute, for she had covered her face. ¹⁶He went over to her at the roadside, and said, "Come, let me come in to you," for he did not know that she was his daughter-in-law. She said, "What will you give me, that you may come in to me?" ¹⁷He answered, "I will send you a kid from the flock." And she said, "Only if you give me a pledge, until you send it." ¹⁸He said, "What pledge shall I give you?" She replied, "Your signet and your cord, and the staff that is in your hand." So he gave them to her, and went in to her, and she conceived by him. ¹⁹Then she got up and went away, and taking off her veil she put on the garments of her widowhood.

20 When Judah sent the kid by his friend the Adullamite, to recover the pledge from the woman, he could not find her. ²¹He asked the townspeople, "Where is the temple prostitute who was at Enaim by the wayside?" But they said, "No prostitute has been here." ²²So he returned to Judah, and said, "I have not found her; moreover the townspeople said, 'No prostitute has been here.'" ²³Judah replied, "Let her keep the things as her own, otherwise we will be laughed at; you see, I sent this kid, and you could not find her."

24 About three months later Judah was told, "Your daughter-in-law Tamar has played the whore; moreover she is pregnant as a result of whoredom." And Judah said, "Bring her out, and let her be burned." ²⁵As she was

---

a See note on 37.3   *b* Gk: Heb *He*   *c* Heb *when Judah was comforted* being brought out, she sent word to her father-in-law, "It was the owner of these who made me pregnant." And she said, "Take note, please, whose these are, the signet and the cord and the staff." 26Then Judah acknowledged them and said, "She is more in the right than I, since I did not give her to my son Shelah." And he did not lie with her again.

27 When the time of her delivery came, there were twins in her womb. 28While she was in labor, one put out a hand; and the midwife took and bound on his hand a crimson thread, saying, "This one came out first." 29But just then he drew back his hand, and out came his brother; and she said, "What a breach you have made for yourself!" Therefore he was named Perez. *a* 30Afterward his brother came out with the crimson thread on his hand; and he was named Zerah. *b*

Joseph and Potiphar's Wife

39 Now Joseph was taken down to Egypt, and Potiphar, an officer of Pharaoh, the captain of the guard, an Egyptian, bought him from the Ishmaelites who had brought him down there. 2The LORD was with Joseph, and he became a successful man; he was in the house of his Egyptian master. 3His master saw that the LORD was with him, and that the LORD caused all that he did to prosper in his hands. 4So Joseph found favor in his sight and attended him; he made him overseer of his house and put him in charge of all that he had. 5From the time that he made him overseer in his house and over all that he had, the LORD blessed the Egyptian's house for Joseph's sake; the blessing of the LORD was on all that he had, in house and field. 6So he left all that he had in Joseph's charge; and, with him there, he had no concern for anything but the food that he ate.

Now Joseph was handsome and good-looking. 7And after a time his master's wife cast her eyes on Joseph and said, "Lie with me." 8But he refused and said to his master's wife, "Look, with me here, my master has no concern about anything in the house, and he has put everything that he has in my hand. 9He is not greater in this house than I am, nor has he kept back anything from me except yourself, because you are his wife. How then could I do this great wickedness, and sin against God?" 10And although she spoke to Joseph day after day, he would not consent to lie beside her or to be with her. 11One day, however, when he went into the house to do his work, and while no one else was in the house, 12she caught hold of his garment, saying, "Lie with me!" But he left his garment in her hand, and fled and ran outside. 13When she saw that he had left his garment in her hand and had fled outside, 14she called out to the members of her household and said to them, "See, my husband *c* has brought among us a Hebrew to insult us! He came in to me to lie with me, and I cried out with a loud voice; 15and when he heard me raise my voice and cry out, he left his garment beside me, and fled outside." 16Then she kept his garment by her until his master came home, 17and she told him the same story, saying, "The Hebrew servant, whom you have brought among us, came in to me to insult me; 18but as soon as I raised my voice and cried out, he left his garment beside me, and fled outside."

19 When his master heard the words that his wife spoke to him, saying, "This is the way your servant treated me," he became enraged. 20And Joseph's master took him and put him into the prison, the place where the king's prisoners were confined; he remained there in prison. 21But the LORD was with Joseph and showed him steadfast love; he gave him favor in the sight of the chief jailer. 22The chief jailer committed to Joseph's care all the prisoners who were in the prison, and whatever was done there, he was the one who did it. 23The chief jailer paid no heed to anything that was in Joseph's care, because the LORD was with him; and whatever he did, the LORD made it prosper.

a That is *A breach*   *b* That is *Brightness*; perhaps alluding to the crimson thread   *c* Heb *he*

The Dreams of Two Prisoners

40

Some time after this, the cupbearer of the king of Egypt and his baker offended their lord the king of Egypt. 2Pharaoh was angry with his two officers, the chief cupbearer and the chief baker, 3and he put them in custody in the house of the captain of the guard, in the prison where Joseph was confined. 4The captain of the guard charged Joseph with them, and he waited on them; and they continued for some time in custody. 5One night they both dreamed—the cupbearer and the baker of the king of Egypt, who were confined in the prison—each his own dream, and each dream with its own meaning. 6When Joseph came to them in the morning, he saw that they were troubled. 7So he asked Pharaoh's officers, who were with him in custody in his master's house, "Why are your faces downcast today?" 8They said to him, "We have had dreams, and there is no one to interpret them." And Joseph said to them, "Do not interpretations belong to God? Please tell them to me."

9 So the chief cupbearer told his dream to Joseph, and said to him, "In my dream there was a vine before me, 10and on the vine there were three branches. As soon as it budded, its blossoms came out and the clusters ripened into grapes. 11Pharaoh's cup was in my hand; and I took the grapes and pressed them into Pharaoh's cup, and placed the cup in Pharaoh's hand." 12Then Joseph said to him, "This is its interpretation: the three branches are three days; 13within three days Pharaoh will lift up your head and restore you to your office; and you shall place Pharaoh's cup in his hand, just as you used to do when you were his cupbearer. 14But remember me when it is well with you; please do me the kindness to make mention of me to Pharaoh, and so get me out of this place. 15For in fact I was stolen out of the land of the Hebrews; and here also I have done nothing that they should have put me into the dungeon."

16 When the chief baker saw that the interpretation was favorable, he said to Joseph, "I also had a dream: there were three cake baskets on my head, 17and in the uppermost basket there were all sorts of baked food for Pharaoh, but the birds were eating it out of the basket on my head." 18And Joseph answered, "This is its interpretation: the three baskets are three days; 19within three days Pharaoh will lift up your head—from you!—and hang you on a pole; and the birds will eat the flesh from you."

20 On the third day, which was Pharaoh's birthday, he made a feast for all his servants, and lifted up the head of the chief cupbearer and the head of the chief baker among his servants. 21He restored the chief cupbearer to his cupbearing, and he placed the cup in Pharaoh's hand; 22but the chief baker he hanged, just as Joseph had interpreted to them. 23Yet the chief cupbearer did not remember Joseph, but forgot him.

Joseph Interprets Pharaoh's Dream

41

After two whole years, Pharaoh dreamed that he was standing by the Nile, 2and there came up out of the Nile seven sleek and fat cows, and they grazed in the reed grass. 3Then seven other cows, ugly and thin, came up out of the Nile after them, and stood by the other cows on the bank of the Nile. 4The ugly and thin cows ate up the seven sleek and fat cows. And Pharaoh awoke. 5Then he fell asleep and dreamed a second time; seven ears of grain, plump and good, were growing on one stalk. 6Then seven ears, thin and blighted by the east wind, sprouted after them. 7The thin ears swallowed up the seven plump and full ears. Pharaoh awoke, and it was a dream. 8In the morning his spirit was troubled; so he sent and called for all the magicians of Egypt and all its wise men. Pharaoh told them his dreams, but there was no one who could interpret them to Pharaoh.

9 Then the chief cupbearer said to Pharaoh, "I remember my faults today. 10Once Pharaoh was angry with his servants, and put me and the chief baker in custody in the house of the captain of the guard. 11We dreamed on the same night, he and I, each having a dream with its own meaning. 12A young Hebrew was there with us, a servant of the captain of the

guard. When we told him, he interpreted our dreams to us, giving an interpretation to each according to his dream. ¹³As he interpreted to us, so it turned out; I was restored to my office, and the baker was hanged."

14 Then Pharaoh sent for Joseph, and he was hurriedly brought out of the dungeon. When he had shaved himself and changed his clothes, he came in before Pharaoh. ¹⁵And Pharaoh said to Joseph, "I have had a dream, and there is no one who can interpret it. I have heard it said of you that when you hear a dream you can interpret it." ¹⁶Joseph answered Pharaoh, "It is not I; God will give Pharaoh a favorable answer." ¹⁷Then Pharaoh said to Joseph, "In my dream I was standing on the banks of the Nile; ¹⁸and seven cows, fat and sleek, came up out of the Nile and fed in the reed grass. ¹⁹Then seven other cows came up after them, poor, very ugly, and thin. Never had I seen such ugly ones in all the land of Egypt. ²⁰The thin and ugly cows ate up the first seven fat cows, ²¹but when they had eaten them no one would have known that they had done so, for they were still as ugly as before. Then I awoke. ²²I fell asleep a second time*a* and I saw in my dream seven ears of grain, full and good, growing on one stalk, ²³and seven ears, withered, thin, and blighted by the east wind, sprouting after them; ²⁴and the thin ears swallowed up the seven good ears. But when I told it to the magicians, there was no one who could explain it to me."

25 Then Joseph said to Pharaoh, "Pharaoh's dreams are one and the same; God has revealed to Pharaoh what he is about to do. ²⁶The seven good cows are seven years, and the seven good ears are seven years; the dreams are one. ²⁷The seven lean and ugly cows that came up after them are seven years, as are the seven empty ears blighted by the east wind. They are seven years of famine. ²⁸It is as I told Pharaoh; God has shown to Pharaoh what he is about to do. ²⁹There will come seven years of great plenty throughout all the land of Egypt. ³⁰After them there will arise seven years of famine,

and all the plenty will be forgotten in the land of Egypt; the famine will consume the land. ³¹The plenty will no longer be known in the land because of the famine that will follow, for it will be very grievous. ³²And the doubling of Pharaoh's dream means that the thing is fixed by God, and God will shortly bring it about. ³³Now therefore let Pharaoh select a man who is discerning and wise, and set him over the land of Egypt. ³⁴Let Pharaoh proceed to appoint overseers over the land, and take one-fifth of the produce of the land of Egypt during the seven plenteous years. ³⁵Let them gather all the food of these good years that are coming, and lay up grain under the authority of Pharaoh for food in the cities, and let them keep it. ³⁶That food shall be a reserve for the land against the seven years of famine that are to befall the land of Egypt, so that the land may not perish through the famine."

Joseph's Rise to Power

37 The proposal pleased Pharaoh and all his servants. ³⁸Pharaoh said to his servants, "Can we find anyone else like this—one in whom is the spirit of God?" ³⁹So Pharaoh said to Joseph, "Since God has shown you all this, there is no one so discerning and wise as you. ⁴⁰You shall be over my house, and all my people shall order themselves as you command; only with regard to the throne will I be greater than you." ⁴¹And Pharaoh said to Joseph, "See, I have set you over all the land of Egypt." ⁴²Removing his signet ring from his hand, Pharaoh put it on Joseph's hand; he arrayed him in garments of fine linen, and put a gold chain around his neck. ⁴³He had him ride in the chariot of his second-in-command; and they cried out in front of him, "Bow the knee!"*b* Thus he set him over all the land of Egypt. ⁴⁴Moreover Pharaoh said to Joseph, "I am Pharaoh, and without your consent no one shall lift up hand or foot in all the land of Egypt." ⁴⁵Pharaoh gave Joseph the name Zaphenath-paneah; and he gave him Asenath daughter of Potiphera, priest of On, as his

---

a Gk Syr Vg: Heb lacks *I fell asleep a second time*   *b Abrek*, apparently an Egyptian word similar in sound to the Hebrew word meaning *to kneel* wife. Thus Joseph gained authority over the land of Egypt.

46 Joseph was thirty years old when he entered the service of Pharaoh king of Egypt. And Joseph went out from the presence of Pharaoh, and went through all the land of Egypt. 47During the seven plenteous years the earth produced abundantly. 48He gathered up all the food of the seven years when there was plenty*a* in the land of Egypt, and stored up food in the cities; he stored up in every city the food from the fields around it. 49So Joseph stored up grain in such abundance—like the sand of the sea—that he stopped measuring it; it was beyond measure.

50 Before the years of famine came, Joseph had two sons, whom Asenath daughter of Potiphera, priest of On, bore to him. 51Joseph named the firstborn Manasseh,*b* "For," he said, "God has made me forget all my hardship and all my father's house." 52The second he named Ephraim,*c* "For God has made me fruitful in the land of my misfortunes."

53 The seven years of plenty that prevailed in the land of Egypt came to an end; 54and the seven years of famine began to come, just as Joseph had said. There was famine in every country, but throughout the land of Egypt there was bread. 55When all the land of Egypt was famished, the people cried to Pharaoh for bread. Pharaoh said to all the Egyptians, "Go to Joseph; what he says to you, do." 56And since the famine had spread over all the land, Joseph opened all the storehouses,*d* and sold to the Egyptians, for the famine was severe in the land of Egypt. 57Moreover, all the world came to Joseph in Egypt to buy grain, because the famine became severe throughout the world.

Joseph's Brothers Go to Egypt

42 When Jacob learned that there was grain in Egypt, he said to his sons, "Why do you keep looking at one another? 2I have heard," he said, "that there is grain in Egypt; go down and buy grain for us there,

that we may live and not die." 3So ten of Joseph's brothers went down to buy grain in Egypt. 4But Jacob did not send Joseph's brother Benjamin with his brothers, for he feared that harm might come to him. 5Thus the sons of Israel were among the other people who came to buy grain, for the famine had reached the land of Canaan.

6 Now Joseph was governor over the land; it was he who sold to all the people of the land. And Joseph's brothers came and bowed themselves before him with their faces to the ground. 7When Joseph saw his brothers, he recognized them, but he treated them like strangers and spoke harshly to them. "Where do you come from?" he said. They said, "From the land of Canaan, to buy food." 8Although Joseph had recognized his brothers, they did not recognize him. 9Joseph also remembered the dreams that he had dreamed about them. He said to them, "You are spies; you have come to see the nakedness of the land!" 10They said to him, "No, my lord; your servants have come to buy food. 11We are all sons of one man; we are honest men; your servants have never been spies." 12But he said to them, "No, you have come to see the nakedness of the land!" 13They said, "We, your servants, are twelve brothers, the sons of a certain man in the land of Canaan; the youngest, however, is now with our father, and one is no more." 14But Joseph said to them, "It is just as I have said to you; you are spies! 15Here is how you shall be tested: as Pharaoh lives, you shall not leave this place unless your youngest brother comes here! 16Let one of you go and bring your brother, while the rest of you remain in prison, in order that your words may be tested, whether there is truth in you; or else, as Pharaoh lives, surely you are spies." 17And he put them all together in prison for three days.

18 On the third day Joseph said to them, "Do this and you will live, for I fear God: 19if you are honest men, let one of your brothers stay here where you are imprisoned. The rest

a Sam Gk: MT *the seven years that were*   *b* That is *Making to forget*   *c* From a Hebrew word meaning *to be fruitful*
d Gk Vg Compare Syr: Heb *opened all that was in* (or, *among*) *them*

of you shall go and carry grain for the famine of your households, [20]and bring your youngest brother to me. Thus your words will be verified, and you shall not die." And they agreed to do so. [21]They said to one another, "Alas, we are paying the penalty for what we did to our brother; we saw his anguish when he pleaded with us, but we would not listen. That is why this anguish has come upon us." [22]Then Reuben answered them, "Did I not tell you not to wrong the boy? But you would not listen. So now there comes a reckoning for his blood." [23]They did not know that Joseph understood them, since he spoke with them through an interpreter. [24]He turned away from them and wept; then he returned and spoke to them. And he picked out Simeon and had him bound before their eyes. [25]Joseph then gave orders to fill their bags with grain, to return every man's money to his sack, and to give them provisions for their journey. This was done for them.

Joseph's Brothers Return to Canaan

26 They loaded their donkeys with their grain, and departed. [27]When one of them opened his sack to give his donkey fodder at the lodging place, he saw his money at the top of the sack. [28]He said to his brothers, "My money has been put back; here it is in my sack!" At this they lost heart and turned trembling to one another, saying, "What is this that God has done to us?"

29 When they came to their father Jacob in the land of Canaan, they told him all that had happened to them, saying, [30]"The man, the lord of the land, spoke harshly to us, and charged us with spying on the land. [31]But we said to him, 'We are honest men, we are not spies. [32]We are twelve brothers, sons of our father; one is no more, and the youngest is now with our father in the land of Canaan.' [33]Then the man, the lord of the land, said to us, 'By this I shall know that you are honest men: leave one of your brothers with me, take grain for the famine of your households, and go your way. [34]Bring your youngest brother to me, and I shall know that you are not spies but

honest men. Then I will release your brother to you, and you may trade in the land.'"

35 As they were emptying their sacks, there in each one's sack was his bag of money. When they and their father saw their bundles of money, they were dismayed. [36]And their father Jacob said to them, "I am the one you have bereaved of children: Joseph is no more, and Simeon is no more, and now you would take Benjamin. All this has happened to me!" [37]Then Reuben said to his father, "You may kill my two sons if I do not bring him back to you. Put him in my hands, and I will bring him back to you." [38]But he said, "My son shall not go down with you, for his brother is dead, and he alone is left. If harm should come to him on the journey that you are to make, you would bring down my gray hairs with sorrow to Sheol."

The Brothers Come Again, Bringing Benjamin

43 Now the famine was severe in the land. [2]And when they had eaten up the grain that they had brought from Egypt, their father said to them, "Go again, buy us a little more food." [3]But Judah said to him, "The man solemnly warned us, saying, 'You shall not see my face unless your brother is with you.' [4]If you will send our brother with us, we will go down and buy you food; [5]but if you will not send him, we will not go down, for the man said to us, 'You shall not see my face, unless your brother is with you.'" [6]Israel said, "Why did you treat me so badly as to tell the man that you had another brother?" [7]They replied, "The man questioned us carefully about ourselves and our kindred, saying, 'Is your father still alive? Have you another brother?' What we told him was in answer to these questions. Could we in any way know that he would say, 'Bring your brother down'?" [8]Then Judah said to his father Israel, "Send the boy with me, and let us be on our way, so that we may live and not die—you and we and also our little ones. [9]I myself will be surety for him; you can hold me accountable for him. If I do not bring him back to you and set him before you, then let me bear the blame forever. [10]If we had

not delayed, we would now have returned twice."

11 Then their father Israel said to them, "If it must be so, then do this: take some of the choice fruits of the land in your bags, and carry them down as a present to the man—a little balm and a little honey, gum, resin, pistachio nuts, and almonds. 12Take double the money with you. Carry back with you the money that was returned in the top of your sacks; perhaps it was an oversight. 13Take your brother also, and be on your way again to the man; 14may God Almighty*a* grant you mercy before the man, so that he may send back your other brother and Benjamin. As for me, if I am bereaved of my children, I am bereaved." 15So the men took the present, and they took double the money with them, as well as Benjamin. Then they went on their way down to Egypt, and stood before Joseph.

16 When Joseph saw Benjamin with them, he said to the steward of his house, "Bring the men into the house, and slaughter an animal and make ready, for the men are to dine with me at noon." 17The man did as Joseph said, and brought the men to Joseph's house. 18Now the men were afraid because they were brought to Joseph's house, and they said, "It is because of the money, replaced in our sacks the first time, that we have been brought in, so that he may have an opportunity to fall upon us, to make slaves of us and take our donkeys." 19So they went up to the steward of Joseph's house and spoke with him at the entrance to the house. 20They said, "Oh, my lord, we came down the first time to buy food; 21and when we came to the lodging place we opened our sacks, and there was each one's money in the top of his sack, our money in full weight. So we have brought it back with us. 22Moreover we have brought down with us additional money to buy food. We do not know who put our money in our sacks." 23He replied, "Rest assured, do not be afraid; your God and the God of your father must have put treasure in your sacks for you; I received your money."

Then he brought Simeon out to them. 24When the steward*b* had brought the men into Joseph's house, and given them water, and they had washed their feet, and when he had given their donkeys fodder, 25they made the present ready for Joseph's coming at noon, for they had heard that they would dine there.

26 When Joseph came home, they brought him the present that they had carried into the house, and bowed to the ground before him. 27He inquired about their welfare, and said, "Is your father well, the old man of whom you spoke? Is he still alive?" 28They said, "Your servant our father is well; he is still alive." And they bowed their heads and did obeisance. 29Then he looked up and saw his brother Benjamin, his mother's son, and said, "Is this your youngest brother, of whom you spoke to me? God be gracious to you, my son!" 30With that, Joseph hurried out, because he was overcome with affection for his brother, and he was about to weep. So he went into a private room and wept there. 31Then he washed his face and came out; and controlling himself he said, "Serve the meal." 32They served him by himself, and them by themselves, and the Egyptians who ate with him by themselves, because the Egyptians could not eat with the Hebrews, for that is an abomination to the Egyptians. 33When they were seated before him, the firstborn according to his birthright and the youngest according to his youth, the men looked at one another in amazement. 34Portions were taken to them from Joseph's table, but Benjamin's portion was five times as much as any of theirs. So they drank and were merry with him.

Joseph Detains Benjamin

44 Then he commanded the steward of his house, "Fill the men's sacks with food, as much as they can carry, and put each man's money in the top of his sack. 2Put my cup, the silver cup, in the top of the sack of the youngest, with his money for the grain." And he did as Joseph told him. 3As soon as the

---

a Traditional rendering of Heb *El Shaddai*   *b* Heb *the man* morning was light, the men were sent away with their donkeys. 4When they had gone only a short distance from the city, Joseph said to his steward, "Go, follow after the men; and when you overtake them, say to them, 'Why have you returned evil for good? Why have you stolen my silver cup?a 5Is it not from this that my lord drinks? Does he not indeed use it for divination? You have done wrong in doing this.'"

6 When he overtook them, he repeated these words to them. 7They said to him, "Why does my lord speak such words as these? Far be it from your servants that they should do such a thing! 8Look, the money that we found at the top of our sacks, we brought back to you from the land of Canaan; why then would we steal silver or gold from your lord's house? 9Should it be found with any one of your servants, let him die; moreover the rest of us will become my lord's slaves." 10He said, "Even so; in accordance with your words, let it be: he with whom it is found shall become my slave, but the rest of you shall go free." 11Then each one quickly lowered his sack to the ground, and each opened his sack. 12He searched, beginning with the eldest and ending with the youngest; and the cup was found in Benjamin's sack. 13At this they tore their clothes. Then each one loaded his donkey, and they returned to the city.

14 Judah and his brothers came to Joseph's house while he was still there; and they fell to the ground before him. 15Joseph said to them, "What deed is this that you have done? Do you not know that one such as I can practice divination?" 16And Judah said, "What can we say to my lord? What can we speak? How can we clear ourselves? God has found out the guilt of your servants; here we are then, my lord's slaves, both we and also the one in whose possession the cup has been found." 17But he said, "Far be it from me that I should do so! Only the one in whose possession the cup was found shall be my slave; but as for you, go up in peace to your father."

Judah Pleads for Benjamin's Release

18 Then Judah stepped up to him and said, "O my lord, let your servant please speak a word in my lord's ears, and do not be angry with your servant; for you are like Pharaoh himself. 19My lord asked his servants, saying, 'Have you a father or a brother?' 20And we said to my lord, 'We have a father, an old man, and a young brother, the child of his old age. His brother is dead; he alone is left of his mother's children, and his father loves him.' 21Then you said to your servants, 'Bring him down to me, so that I may set my eyes on him.' 22We said to my lord, 'The boy cannot leave his father, for if he should leave his father, his father would die.' 23Then you said to your servants, 'Unless your youngest brother comes down with you, you shall see my face no more.' 24When we went back to your servant my father we told him the words of my lord. 25And when our father said, 'Go again, buy us a little food,' 26we said, 'We cannot go down. Only if our youngest brother goes with us, will we go down; for we cannot see the man's face unless our youngest brother is with us.' 27Then your servant my father said to us, 'You know that my wife bore me two sons; 28one left me, and I said, Surely he has been torn to pieces; and I have never seen him since. 29If you take this one also from me, and harm comes to him, you will bring down my gray hairs in sorrow to Sheol.' 30Now therefore, when I come to your servant my father and the boy is not with us, then, as his life is bound up in the boy's life, 31when he sees that the boy is not with us, he will die; and your servants will bring down the gray hairs of your servant our father with sorrow to Sheol. 32For your servant became surety for the boy to my father, saying, 'If I do not bring him back to you, then I will bear the blame in the sight of my father all my life.' 33Now therefore, please let your servant remain as a slave to my lord in place of the boy; and let the boy go back with his brothers. 34For how can I go back to my father if the boy is not with me? I fear to see the suffering that would come upon my father."

a Gk Compare Vg: Heb lacks *Why have you stolen my silver cup?*

Joseph Reveals Himself to His Brothers

45

Then Joseph could no longer control himself before all those who stood by him, and he cried out, "Send everyone away from me." So no one stayed with him when Joseph made himself known to his brothers. ²And he wept so loudly that the Egyptians heard it, and the household of Pharaoh heard it. ³Joseph said to his brothers, "I am Joseph. Is my father still alive?" But his brothers could not answer him, so dismayed were they at his presence.

4 Then Joseph said to his brothers, "Come closer to me." And they came closer. He said, "I am your brother, Joseph, whom you sold into Egypt. ⁵And now do not be distressed, or angry with yourselves, because you sold me here; for God sent me before you to preserve life. ⁶For the famine has been in the land these two years; and there are five more years in which there will be neither plowing nor harvest. ⁷God sent me before you to preserve for you a remnant on earth, and to keep alive for you many survivors. ⁸So it was not you who sent me here, but God; he has made me a father to Pharaoh, and lord of all his house and ruler over all the land of Egypt. ⁹Hurry and go up to my father and say to him, 'Thus says your son Joseph, God has made me lord of all Egypt; come down to me, do not delay. ¹⁰You shall settle in the land of Goshen, and you shall be near me, you and your children and your children's children, as well as your flocks, your herds, and all that you have. ¹¹I will provide for you there—since there are five more years of famine to come—so that you and your household, and all that you have, will not come to poverty.' ¹²And now your eyes and the eyes of my brother Benjamin see that it is my own mouth that speaks to you. ¹³You must tell my father how greatly I am honored in Egypt, and all that you have seen. Hurry and bring my father down here." ¹⁴Then he fell upon his brother Benjamin's neck and wept, while Benjamin wept upon his neck. ¹⁵And he kissed all

his brothers and wept upon them; and after that his brothers talked with him.

16 When the report was heard in Pharaoh's house, "Joseph's brothers have come," Pharaoh and his servants were pleased. ¹⁷Pharaoh said to Joseph, "Say to your brothers, 'Do this: load your animals and go back to the land of Canaan. ¹⁸Take your father and your households and come to me, so that I may give you the best of the land of Egypt, and you may enjoy the fat of the land.' ¹⁹You are further charged to say, 'Do this: take wagons from the land of Egypt for your little ones and for your wives, and bring your father, and come. ²⁰Give no thought to your possessions, for the best of all the land of Egypt is yours.' "

21 The sons of Israel did so. Joseph gave them wagons according to the instruction of Pharaoh, and he gave them provisions for the journey. ²²To each one of them he gave a set of garments; but to Benjamin he gave three hundred pieces of silver and five sets of garments. ²³To his father he sent the following: ten donkeys loaded with the good things of Egypt, and ten female donkeys loaded with grain, bread, and provision for his father on the journey. ²⁴Then he sent his brothers on their way, and as they were leaving he said to them, "Do not quarrel*ᵃ* along the way."

25 So they went up out of Egypt and came to their father Jacob in the land of Canaan. ²⁶And they told him, "Joseph is still alive! He is even ruler over all the land of Egypt." He was stunned; he could not believe them. ²⁷But when they told him all the words of Joseph that he had said to them, and when he saw the wagons that Joseph had sent to carry him, the spirit of their father Jacob revived. ²⁸Israel said, "Enough! My son Joseph is still alive. I must go and see him before I die."

Jacob Brings His Whole Family to Egypt

46

When Israel set out on his journey with all that he had and came to Beersheba, he offered sacrifices to the God of his father Isaac. ²God spoke to Israel in visions of

a Or *be agitated*

the night, and said, "Jacob, Jacob." And he said, "Here I am." [3]Then he said, "I am God,[a] the God of your father; do not be afraid to go down to Egypt, for I will make of you a great nation there. [4]I myself will go down with you to Egypt, and I will also bring you up again; and Joseph's own hand shall close your eyes."

5 Then Jacob set out from Beer-sheba; and the sons of Israel carried their father Jacob, their little ones, and their wives, in the wagons that Pharaoh had sent to carry him. [6]They also took their livestock and the goods that they had acquired in the land of Canaan, and they came into Egypt, Jacob and all his offspring with him, [7]his sons, and his sons' sons with him, his daughters, and his sons' daughters; all his offspring he brought with him into Egypt.

8 Now these are the names of the Israelites, Jacob and his offspring, who came to Egypt. Reuben, Jacob's firstborn, [9]and the children of Reuben: Hanoch, Pallu, Hezron, and Carmi. [10]The children of Simeon: Jemuel, Jamin, Ohad, Jachin, Zohar, and Shaul,[b] the son of a Canaanite woman. [11]The children of Levi: Gershon, Kohath, and Merari. [12]The children of Judah: Er, Onan, Shelah, Perez, and Zerah (but Er and Onan died in the land of Canaan); and the children of Perez were Hezron and Hamul. [13]The children of Issachar: Tola, Puvah, Jashub,[c] and Shimron. [14]The children of Zebulun: Sered, Elon, and Jahleel [15](these are the sons of Leah, whom she bore to Jacob in Paddan-aram, together with his daughter Dinah; in all his sons and his daughters numbered thirty-three). [16]The children of Gad: Ziphion, Haggi, Shuni, Ezbon, Eri, Arodi, and Areli. [17]The children of Asher: Imnah, Ishvah, Ishvi, Beriah, and their sister Serah. The children of Beriah: Heber and Malchiel [18](these are the children of Zilpah, whom Laban gave to his daughter Leah; and these she bore to Jacob—sixteen persons). [19]The children of Jacob's wife Rachel: Joseph and Benjamin. [20]To Joseph in the land of Egypt were born Manasseh and Ephraim, whom Asenath daughter of Potiphera, priest of On, bore to him. [21]The children of Benjamin: Bela, Becher, Ashbel, Gera, Naaman, Ehi, Rosh, Muppim, Huppim, and Ard [22](these are the children of Rachel, who were born to Jacob—fourteen persons in all). [23]The children of Dan: Hashum.[d] [24]The children of Naphtali: Jahzeel, Guni, Jezer, and Shillem [25](these are the children of Bilhah, whom Laban gave to his daughter Rachel, and these she bore to Jacob—seven persons in all). [26]All the persons belonging to Jacob who came into Egypt, who were his own offspring, not including the wives of his sons, were sixty-six persons in all. [27]The children of Joseph, who were born to him in Egypt, were two; all the persons of the house of Jacob who came into Egypt were seventy.

Jacob Settles in Goshen

28 Israel[e] sent Judah ahead to Joseph to lead the way before him into Goshen. When they came to the land of Goshen, [29]Joseph made ready his chariot and went up to meet his father Israel in Goshen. He presented himself to him, fell on his neck, and wept on his neck a good while. [30]Israel said to Joseph, "I can die now, having seen for myself that you are still alive." [31]Joseph said to his brothers and to his father's household, "I will go up and tell Pharaoh, and will say to him, 'My brothers and my father's household, who were in the land of Canaan, have come to me. [32]The men are shepherds, for they have been keepers of livestock; and they have brought their flocks, and their herds, and all that they have.' [33]When Pharaoh calls you, and says, 'What is your occupation?' [34]you shall say, 'Your servants have been keepers of livestock from our youth even until now, both we and our ancestors'—in order that you may settle in the land of Goshen, because all shepherds are abhorrent to the Egyptians."

47 So Joseph went and told Pharaoh, "My father and my brothers, with their flocks and herds and all that they possess,

---

[a] Heb *the God*   [b] Or *Saul*   [c] Compare Sam Gk Num 26.24; 1 Chr 7.1: MT *Iob*   [d] Gk: Heb *Hushim*
[e] Heb *He*

have come from the land of Canaan; they are now in the land of Goshen." 2From among his brothers he took five men and presented them to Pharaoh. 3Pharaoh said to his brothers, "What is your occupation?" And they said to Pharaoh, "Your servants are shepherds, as our ancestors were." 4They said to Pharaoh, "We have come to reside as aliens in the land; for there is no pasture for your servants' flocks because the famine is severe in the land of Canaan. Now, we ask you, let your servants settle in the land of Goshen." 5Then Pharaoh said to Joseph, "Your father and your brothers have come to you. 6The land of Egypt is before you; settle your father and your brothers in the best part of the land; let them live in the land of Goshen; and if you know that there are capable men among them, put them in charge of my livestock."

7 Then Joseph brought in his father Jacob, and presented him before Pharaoh, and Jacob blessed Pharaoh. 8Pharaoh said to Jacob, "How many are the years of your life?" 9Jacob said to Pharaoh, "The years of my earthly sojourn are one hundred thirty; few and hard have been the years of my life. They do not compare with the years of the life of my ancestors during their long sojourn." 10Then Jacob blessed Pharaoh, and went out from the presence of Pharaoh. 11Joseph settled his father and his brothers, and granted them a holding in the land of Egypt, in the best part of the land, in the land of Rameses, as Pharaoh had instructed. 12And Joseph provided his father, his brothers, and all his father's household with food, according to the number of their dependents.

The Famine in Egypt

13 Now there was no food in all the land, for the famine was very severe. The land of Egypt and the land of Canaan languished because of the famine. 14Joseph collected all the money to be found in the land of Egypt and in the land of Canaan, in exchange for the grain that they bought; and Joseph brought the money into Pharaoh's house. 15When the money from the land of Egypt and from the land of Canaan was spent, all the Egyptians came to Joseph, and said, "Give us food! Why should we die before your eyes? For our money is gone." 16And Joseph answered, "Give me your livestock, and I will give you food in exchange for your livestock, if your money is gone." 17So they brought their livestock to Joseph; and Joseph gave them food in exchange for the horses, the flocks, the herds, and the donkeys. That year he supplied them with food in exchange for all their livestock. 18When that year was ended, they came to him the following year, and said to him, "We can not hide from my lord that our money is all spent; and the herds of cattle are my lord's. There is nothing left in the sight of my lord but our bodies and our lands. 19Shall we die before your eyes, both we and our land? Buy us and our land in exchange for food. We with our land will become slaves to Pharaoh; just give us seed, so that we may live and not die, and that the land may not become desolate."

20 So Joseph bought all the land of Egypt for Pharaoh. All the Egyptians sold their fields, because the famine was severe upon them; and the land became Pharaoh's. 21As for the people, he made slaves of them*a* from one end of Egypt to the other. 22Only the land of the priests he did not buy; for the priests had a fixed allowance from Pharaoh, and lived on the allowance that Pharaoh gave them; therefore they did not sell their land. 23Then Joseph said to the people, "Now that I have this day bought you and your land for Pharaoh, here is seed for you; sow the land. 24And at the harvests you shall give one-fifth to Pharaoh, and four-fifths shall be your own, as seed for the field and as food for yourselves and your households, and as food for your little ones." 25They said, "You have saved our lives; may it please my lord, we will be slaves to Pharaoh." 26So Joseph made it a statute concerning the land of Egypt, and it stands to this day, that

---

a Sam Gk Compare Vg: MT *He removed them to the cities*

Pharaoh should have the fifth. The land of the priests alone did not become Pharaoh's.

The Last Days of Jacob

27 Thus Israel settled in the land of Egypt, in the region of Goshen; and they gained possessions in it, and were fruitful and multiplied exceedingly. 28Jacob lived in the land of Egypt seventeen years; so the days of Jacob, the years of his life, were one hundred forty-seven years.

29 When the time of Israel's death drew near, he called his son Joseph and said to him, "If I have found favor with you, put your hand under my thigh and promise to deal loyally and truly with me. Do not bury me in Egypt. 30When I lie down with my ancestors, carry me out of Egypt and bury me in their burial place." He answered, "I will do as you have said." 31And he said, "Swear to me"; and he swore to him. Then Israel bowed himself on the head of his bed.

Jacob Blesses Joseph's Sons

48 After this Joseph was told, "Your father is ill." So he took with him his two sons, Manasseh and Ephraim. 2When Jacob was told, "Your son Joseph has come to you," he*a* summoned his strength and sat up in bed. 3And Jacob said to Joseph, "God Almighty*b* appeared to me at Luz in the land of Canaan, and he blessed me, 4and said to me, 'I am going to make you fruitful and increase your numbers; I will make of you a company of peoples, and will give this land to your offspring after you for a perpetual holding.' 5Therefore your two sons, who were born to you in the land of Egypt before I came to you in Egypt, are now mine; Ephraim and Manasseh shall be mine, just as Reuben and Simeon are. 6As for the offspring born to you after them, they shall be yours. They shall be recorded under the names of their brothers with regard to their inheritance. 7For when I came from Paddan, Rachel, alas, died in the land of Canaan on the way, while there was still some distance to go to Ephrath; and I buried her there on the way to Ephrath" (that is, Bethlehem).

8 When Israel saw Joseph's sons, he said, "Who are these?" 9Joseph said to his father, "They are my sons, whom God has given me here." And he said, "Bring them to me, please, that I may bless them." 10Now the eyes of Israel were dim with age, and he could not see well. So Joseph brought them near him; and he kissed them and embraced them. 11Israel said to Joseph, "I did not expect to see your face; and here God has let me see your children also." 12Then Joseph removed them from his father's knees,*c* and he bowed himself with his face to the earth. 13Joseph took them both, Ephraim in his right hand toward Israel's left, and Manasseh in his left hand toward Israel's right, and brought them near him. 14But Israel stretched out his right hand and laid it on the head of Ephraim, who was the younger, and his left hand on the head of Manasseh, crossing his hands, for Manasseh was the firstborn. 15He blessed Joseph, and said,

> "The God before whom my ancestors
> Abraham and Isaac walked,
> the God who has been my shepherd all
> my life to this day,
> 16 the angel who has redeemed me from all
> harm, bless the boys;
> and in them let my name be
> perpetuated, and the name of
> my ancestors Abraham and
> Isaac;
> and let them grow into a multitude on
> the earth."

17 When Joseph saw that his father laid his right hand on the head of Ephraim, it displeased him; so he took his father's hand, to remove it from Ephraim's head to Manasseh's head. 18Joseph said to his father, "Not so, my father! Since this one is the firstborn, put your right hand on his head." 19But his father refused, and said, "I know, my son, I know; he also shall become a people, and he also shall be great. Nevertheless his younger brother shall be greater than he, and his offspring shall

---

a Heb *Israel*   *b* Traditional rendering of Heb *El Shaddai*   *c* Heb *from his knees* become a multitude of nations." ²⁰So he blessed them that day, saying,

> "By you*ᵃ* Israel will invoke blessings,
> saying,
> 'God make you*ᵃ* like Ephraim and like
> Manasseh.' "

So he put Ephraim ahead of Manasseh. ²¹Then Israel said to Joseph, "I am about to die, but God will be with you and will bring you again to the land of your ancestors. ²²I now give to you one portion*ᵇ* more than to your brothers, the portion*ᵇ* that I took from the hand of the Amorites with my sword and with my bow."

Jacob's Last Words to His Sons

49 Then Jacob called his sons, and said: "Gather around, that I may tell you what will happen to you in days to come.

2 Assemble and hear, O sons of Jacob;
> listen to Israel your father.

3 Reuben, you are my firstborn,
> my might and the first fruits of my
> vigor,
> excelling in rank and excelling in power.
4 Unstable as water, you shall no longer
> excel
> because you went up onto your
> father's bed;
> then you defiled it—you*ᶜ* went up
> onto my couch!

5 Simeon and Levi are brothers;
> weapons of violence are their swords.
6 May I never come into their council;
> may I not be joined to their
> company—
> for in their anger they killed men,
> and at their whim they hamstrung
> oxen.
7 Cursed be their anger, for it is fierce,
> and their wrath, for it is cruel!
> I will divide them in Jacob,
> and scatter them in Israel.

8 Judah, your brothers shall praise you;
> your hand shall be on the neck of
> your enemies;
> your father's sons shall bow down
> before you.
9 Judah is a lion's whelp;
> from the prey, my son, you have gone
> up.
> He crouches down, he stretches out like
> a lion,
> like a lioness—who dares rouse him
> up?
10 The scepter shall not depart from Judah,
> nor the ruler's staff from between his
> feet,
> until tribute comes to him;*ᵈ*
> and the obedience of the peoples is
> his.
11 Binding his foal to the vine
> and his donkey's colt to the choice
> vine,
> he washes his garments in wine
> and his robe in the blood of grapes;
12 his eyes are darker than wine,
> and his teeth whiter than milk.

13 Zebulun shall settle at the shore of the
> sea;
> he shall be a haven for ships,
> and his border shall be at Sidon.

14 Issachar is a strong donkey,
> lying down between the sheepfolds;
15 he saw that a resting place was good,
> and that the land was pleasant;
> so he bowed his shoulder to the burden,
> and became a slave at forced labor.

16 Dan shall judge his people
> as one of the tribes of Israel.
17 Dan shall be a snake by the roadside,
> a viper along the path,
> that bites the horse's heels
> so that its rider falls backward.

---

a you here is singular in Heb   *b* Or *mountain slope* (Heb *shekem*, a play on the name of the town and district of Shechem)   *c* Gk Syr Tg: Heb *he*   *d* Or *until Shiloh comes* or *until he comes to Shiloh* or (with Syr) *until he comes to whom it belongs*

18 I wait for your salvation, O LORD.

19 Gad shall be raided by raiders,
    but he shall raid at their heels.

20 Asher's*a* food shall be rich,
    and he shall provide royal delicacies.

21 Naphtali is a doe let loose
    that bears lovely fawns.*b*

22 Joseph is a fruitful bough,
    a fruitful bough by a spring;
    his branches run over the wall.*c*

23 The archers fiercely attacked him;
    they shot at him and pressed him
        hard.

24 Yet his bow remained taut,
    and his arms*d* were made agile
    by the hands of the Mighty One of
        Jacob,
    by the name of the Shepherd, the
        Rock of Israel,

25 by the God of your father, who will
        help you,
    by the Almighty*e* who will bless you
    with blessings of heaven above,
    blessings of the deep that lies beneath,
    blessings of the breasts and of the
        womb.

26 The blessings of your father
    are stronger than the blessings of the
        eternal mountains,
    the bounties*f* of the everlasting hills;
    may they be on the head of Joseph,
    on the brow of him who was set
        apart from his brothers.

27 Benjamin is a ravenous wolf,
    in the morning devouring the prey,
    and at evening dividing the spoil."

28 All these are the twelve tribes of Israel,
and this is what their father said to them when
he blessed them, blessing each one of them
with a suitable blessing.

Jacob's Death and Burial

29 Then he charged them, saying to them,
"I am about to be gathered to my people.
Bury me with my ancestors—in the cave in the
field of Ephron the Hittite, 30in the cave in the
field at Machpelah, near Mamre, in the land of
Canaan, in the field that Abraham bought
from Ephron the Hittite as a burial site.
31There Abraham and his wife Sarah were
buried; there Isaac and his wife Rebekah were
buried; and there I buried Leah— 32the field
and the cave that is in it were purchased from
the Hittites." 33When Jacob ended his charge
to his sons, he drew up his feet into the bed,
breathed his last, and was gathered to his people.

50 Then Joseph threw himself on his father's face and wept over him and
kissed him. 2Joseph commanded the physicians in his service to embalm his father. So the
physicians embalmed Israel; 3they spent forty
days in doing this, for that is the time required
for embalming. And the Egyptians wept for
him seventy days.

4 When the days of weeping for him were
past, Joseph addressed the household of Pharaoh, "If now I have found favor with you,
please speak to Pharaoh as follows: 5My father
made me swear an oath; he said, 'I am about
to die. In the tomb that I hewed out for myself in the land of Canaan, there you shall
bury me.' Now therefore let me go up, so that
I may bury my father; then I will return."
6Pharaoh answered, "Go up, and bury your father, as he made you swear to do."

7 So Joseph went up to bury his father.
With him went up all the servants of Pharaoh,
the elders of his household, and all the elders
of the land of Egypt, 8as well as all the household of Joseph, his brothers, and his father's
household. Only their children, their flocks,
and their herds were left in the land of Goshen. 9Both chariots and charioteers went up
with him. It was a very great company. 10When
they came to the threshing floor of Atad,
which is beyond the Jordan, they held there a

---

a Gk Vg Syr: Heb *From Asher*   *b* Or *that gives beautiful words*   *c* Meaning of Heb uncertain   *d* Heb *the arms of
his hands*   *e* Traditional rendering of Heb *Shaddai*   *f* Cn Compare Gk: Heb *of my progenitors to the boundaries*

very great and sorrowful lamentation; and he observed a time of mourning for his father seven days. [11]When the Canaanite inhabitants of the land saw the mourning on the threshing floor of Atad, they said, "This is a grievous mourning on the part of the Egyptians." Therefore the place was named Abel-mizraim;[a] it is beyond the Jordan. [12]Thus his sons did for him as he had instructed them. [13]They carried him to the land of Canaan and buried him in the cave of the field at Machpelah, the field near Mamre, which Abraham bought as a burial site from Ephron the Hittite. [14]After he had buried his father, Joseph returned to Egypt with his brothers and all who had gone up with him to bury his father.

Joseph Forgives His Brothers

[15] Realizing that their father was dead, Joseph's brothers said, "What if Joseph still bears a grudge against us and pays us back in full for all the wrong that we did to him?" [16]So they approached[b] Joseph, saying, "Your father gave this instruction before he died, [17]'Say to Joseph: I beg you, forgive the crime of your brothers and the wrong they did in harming you.' Now therefore please forgive the crime of the servants of the God of your father." Joseph wept when they spoke to him. [18]Then his brothers also wept,[c] fell down before him, and said, "We are here as your slaves." [19]But Joseph said to them, "Do not be afraid! Am I in the place of God? [20]Even though you intended to do harm to me, God intended it for good, in order to preserve a numerous people, as he is doing today. [21]So have no fear; I myself will provide for you and your little ones." In this way he reassured them, speaking kindly to them.

Joseph's Last Days and Death

[22] So Joseph remained in Egypt, he and his father's household; and Joseph lived one hundred ten years. [23]Joseph saw Ephraim's children of the third generation; the children of Machir son of Manasseh were also born on Joseph's knees.

[24] Then Joseph said to his brothers, "I am about to die; but God will surely come to you, and bring you up out of this land to the land that he swore to Abraham, to Isaac, and to Jacob." [25]So Joseph made the Israelites swear, saying, "When God comes to you, you shall carry up my bones from here." [26]And Joseph died, being one hundred ten years old; he was embalmed and placed in a coffin in Egypt.

---

a That is *mourning* (or *meadow*) *of Egypt*   *b* Gk Syr: Heb *they commanded*   *c* Cn: Heb *also came*

EXODUS

1 These are the names of the sons of Israel who came to Egypt with Jacob, each with his household: [2]Reuben, Simeon, Levi, and Judah, [3]Issachar, Zebulun, and Benjamin, [4]Dan and Naphtali, Gad and Asher. [5]The total number of people born to Jacob was seventy. Joseph was already in Egypt. [6]Then Joseph died, and all his brothers, and that whole generation. [7]But the Israelites were fruitful and prolific; they multiplied and grew exceedingly strong, so that the land was filled with them.

The Israelites Are Oppressed

8 Now a new king arose over Egypt, who did not know Joseph. [9]He said to his people, "Look, the Israelite people are more numerous and more powerful than we. [10]Come, let us deal shrewdly with them, or they will increase and, in the event of war, join our enemies and fight against us and escape from the land." [11]Therefore they set taskmasters over them to oppress them with forced labor. They built supply cities, Pithom and Rameses, for Pharaoh. [12]But the more they were oppressed, the more they multiplied and spread, so that the Egyptians came to dread the Israelites. [13]The Egyptians became ruthless in imposing tasks on the Israelites, [14]and made their lives bitter with hard service in mortar and brick and in every kind of field labor. They were ruthless in all the tasks that they imposed on them.

15 The king of Egypt said to the Hebrew midwives, one of whom was named Shiphrah and the other Puah, [16]"When you act as midwives to the Hebrew women, and see them on the birthstool, if it is a boy, kill him; but if it is a girl, she shall live." [17]But the midwives feared God; they did not do as the king of Egypt commanded them, but they let the boys live. [18]So the king of Egypt summoned the midwives and said to them, "Why have you done this, and allowed the boys to live?" [19]The midwives said to Pharaoh, "Because the Hebrew women are not like the Egyptian women; for

they are vigorous and give birth before the midwife comes to them." [20]So God dealt well with the midwives; and the people multiplied and became very strong. [21]And because the midwives feared God, he gave them families. [22]Then Pharaoh commanded all his people, "Every boy that is born to the Hebrews[a] you shall throw into the Nile, but you shall let every girl live."

Birth and Youth of Moses

2 Now a man from the house of Levi went and married a Levite woman. [2]The woman conceived and bore a son; and when she saw that he was a fine baby, she hid him three months. [3]When she could hide him no longer she got a papyrus basket for him, and plastered it with bitumen and pitch; she put the child in it and placed it among the reeds on the bank of the river. [4]His sister stood at a distance, to see what would happen to him.

5 The daughter of Pharaoh came down to bathe at the river, while her attendants walked beside the river. She saw the basket among the reeds and sent her maid to bring it. [6]When she opened it, she saw the child. He was crying, and she took pity on him. "This must be one of the Hebrews' children," she said. [7]Then his sister said to Pharaoh's daughter, "Shall I go and get you a nurse from the Hebrew women to nurse the child for you?" [8]Pharaoh's daughter said to her, "Yes." So the girl went and called the child's mother. [9]Pharaoh's daughter said to her, "Take this child and nurse it for me, and I will give you your wages." So the woman took the child and nursed it. [10]When the child grew up, she brought him to Pharaoh's daughter, and she took him as her son. She named him Moses,[b] "because," she said, "I drew him out[c] of the water."

Moses Flees to Midian

11 One day, after Moses had grown up, he went out to his people and saw their forced la-

---

a Sam Gk Tg: Heb lacks *to the Hebrews*   *b* Heb *Mosheh*   *c* Heb *mashah* bor. He saw an Egyptian beating a Hebrew, one of his kinsfolk. [12]He looked this way and that, and seeing no one he killed the Egyptian and hid him in the sand. [13]When he went out the next day, he saw two Hebrews fighting; and he said to the one who was in the wrong, "Why do you strike your fellow Hebrew?" [14]He answered, "Who made you a ruler and judge over us? Do you mean to kill me as you killed the Egyptian?" Then Moses was afraid and thought, "Surely the thing is known." [15]When Pharaoh heard of it, he sought to kill Moses.

But Moses fled from Pharaoh. He settled in the land of Midian, and sat down by a well. [16]The priest of Midian had seven daughters. They came to draw water, and filled the troughs to water their father's flock. [17]But some shepherds came and drove them away. Moses got up and came to their defense and watered their flock. [18]When they returned to their father Reuel, he said, "How is it that you have come back so soon today?" [19]They said, "An Egyptian helped us against the shepherds; he even drew water for us and watered the flock." [20]He said to his daughters, "Where is he? Why did you leave the man? Invite him to break bread." [21]Moses agreed to stay with the man, and he gave Moses his daughter Zipporah in marriage. [22]She bore a son, and he named him Gershom; for he said, "I have been an alien[a] residing in a foreign land."

[23] After a long time the king of Egypt died. The Israelites groaned under their slavery, and cried out. Out of the slavery their cry for help rose up to God. [24]God heard their groaning, and God remembered his covenant with Abraham, Isaac, and Jacob. [25]God looked upon the Israelites, and God took notice of them.

Moses at the Burning Bush

3 Moses was keeping the flock of his father-in-law Jethro, the priest of Midian; he led his flock beyond the wilderness, and came to Horeb, the mountain of God. [2]There the angel of the LORD appeared to him in a flame of fire out of a bush; he looked, and the bush was blazing, yet it was not consumed. [3]Then Moses said, "I must turn aside and look at this great sight, and see why the bush is not burned up." [4]When the LORD saw that he had turned aside to see, God called to him out of the bush, "Moses, Moses!" And he said, "Here I am." [5]Then he said, "Come no closer! Remove the sandals from your feet, for the place on which you are standing is holy ground." [6]He said further, "I am the God of your father, the God of Abraham, the God of Isaac, and the God of Jacob." And Moses hid his face, for he was afraid to look at God.

[7] Then the LORD said, "I have observed the misery of my people who are in Egypt; I have heard their cry on account of their taskmasters. Indeed, I know their sufferings, [8]and I have come down to deliver them from the Egyptians, and to bring them up out of that land to a good and broad land, a land flowing with milk and honey, to the country of the Canaanites, the Hittites, the Amorites, the Perizzites, the Hivites, and the Jebusites. [9]The cry of the Israelites has now come to me; I have also seen how the Egyptians oppress them. [10]So come, I will send you to Pharaoh to bring my people, the Israelites, out of Egypt." [11]But Moses said to God, "Who am I that I should go to Pharaoh, and bring the Israelites out of Egypt?" [12]He said, "I will be with you; and this shall be the sign for you that it is I who sent you: when you have brought the people out of Egypt, you shall worship God on this mountain."

The Divine Name Revealed

[13] But Moses said to God, "If I come to the Israelites and say to them, 'The God of your ancestors has sent me to you,' and they ask me, 'What is his name?' what shall I say to them?" [14]God said to Moses, "I AM WHO I AM."[b] He said further, "Thus you shall say to the Israelites, 'I AM has sent me to you.'" [15]God also said to Moses, "Thus you shall say to the Israelites, 'The LORD,[c] the God of your ancestors, the God of Abraham, the God of

---

a Heb *ger*   *b* Or *I AM WHAT I AM* or *I WILL BE WHAT I WILL BE*   *c* The word "LORD" when spelled with capital letters stands for the divine name, *YHWH*, which is here connected with the verb *hayah*, "to be"

Isaac, and the God of Jacob, has sent me to you':

This is my name forever,
and this my title for all generations.

16Go and assemble the elders of Israel, and say to them, 'The LORD, the God of your ancestors, the God of Abraham, of Isaac, and of Jacob, has appeared to me, saying: I have given heed to you and to what has been done to you in Egypt. 17I declare that I will bring you up out of the misery of Egypt, to the land of the Canaanites, the Hittites, the Amorites, the Perizzites, the Hivites, and the Jebusites, a land flowing with milk and honey.' 18They will listen to your voice; and you and the elders of Israel shall go to the king of Egypt and say to him, 'The LORD, the God of the Hebrews, has met with us; let us now go a three days' journey into the wilderness, so that we may sacrifice to the LORD our God.' 19I know, however, that the king of Egypt will not let you go unless compelled by a mighty hand. *a* 20So I will stretch out my hand and strike Egypt with all my wonders that I will perform in it; after that he will let you go. 21I will bring this people into such favor with the Egyptians that, when you go, you will not go empty-handed; 22each woman shall ask her neighbor and any woman living in the neighbor's house for jewelry of silver and of gold, and clothing, and you shall put them on your sons and on your daughters; and so you shall plunder the Egyptians."

Moses' Miraculous Power

4 Then Moses answered, "But suppose they do not believe me or listen to me, but say, 'The LORD did not appear to you.' " 2The LORD said to him, "What is that in your hand?" He said, "A staff." 3And he said, "Throw it on the ground." So he threw the staff on the ground, and it became a snake; and Moses drew back from it. 4Then the LORD said to Moses, "Reach out your hand, and seize it by the tail"—so he reached out his hand and grasped it, and it became a staff in his hand— 5"so that they may believe that the LORD, the God of their an-

cestors, the God of Abraham, the God of Isaac, and the God of Jacob, has appeared to you."

6 Again, the LORD said to him, "Put your hand inside your cloak." He put his hand into his cloak; and when he took it out, his hand was leprous, *b* as white as snow. 7Then God said, "Put your hand back into your cloak"—so he put his hand back into his cloak, and when he took it out, it was restored like the rest of his body— 8"If they will not believe you or heed the first sign, they may believe the second sign. 9If they will not believe even these two signs or heed you, you shall take some water from the Nile and pour it on the dry ground; and the water that you shall take from the Nile will become blood on the dry ground."

10 But Moses said to the LORD, "O my Lord, I have never been eloquent, neither in the past nor even now that you have spoken to your servant; but I am slow of speech and slow of tongue." 11Then the LORD said to him, "Who gives speech to mortals? Who makes them mute or deaf, seeing or blind? Is it not I, the LORD? 12Now go, and I will be with your mouth and teach you what you are to speak." 13But he said, "O my Lord, please send someone else." 14Then the anger of the LORD was kindled against Moses and he said, "What of your brother Aaron the Levite? I know that he can speak fluently; even now he is coming out to meet you, and when he sees you his heart will be glad. 15You shall speak to him and put the words in his mouth; and I will be with your mouth and with his mouth, and will teach you what you shall do. 16He indeed shall speak for you to the people; he shall serve as a mouth for you, and you shall serve as God for him. 17Take in your hand this staff, with which you shall perform the signs."

Moses Returns to Egypt

18 Moses went back to his father-in-law Jethro and said to him, "Please let me go back to my kindred in Egypt and see whether they are still living." And Jethro said to Moses, "Go

---

a Gk Vg: Heb *no, not by a mighty hand*   *b* A term for several skin diseases; precise meaning uncertain in peace." [19]The LORD said to Moses in Midian, "Go back to Egypt; for all those who were seeking your life are dead." [20]So Moses took his wife and his sons, put them on a donkey, and went back to the land of Egypt; and Moses carried the staff of God in his hand.

21 And the LORD said to Moses, "When you go back to Egypt, see that you perform before Pharaoh all the wonders that I have put in your power; but I will harden his heart, so that he will not let the people go. [22]Then you shall say to Pharaoh, 'Thus says the LORD: Israel is my firstborn son. [23]I said to you, "Let my son go that he may worship me." But you refused to let him go; now I will kill your firstborn son.'"

24 On the way, at a place where they spent the night, the LORD met him and tried to kill him. [25]But Zipporah took a flint and cut off her son's foreskin, and touched Moses'[a] feet with it, and said, "Truly you are a bridegroom of blood to me!" [26]So he let him alone. It was then she said, "A bridegroom of blood by circumcision."

27 The LORD said to Aaron, "Go into the wilderness to meet Moses." So he went; and he met him at the mountain of God and kissed him. [28]Moses told Aaron all the words of the LORD with which he had sent him, and all the signs with which he had charged him. [29]Then Moses and Aaron went and assembled all the elders of the Israelites. [30]Aaron spoke all the words that the LORD had spoken to Moses, and performed the signs in the sight of the people. [31]The people believed; and when they heard that the LORD had given heed to the Israelites and that he had seen their misery, they bowed down and worshiped.

Bricks without Straw

5 Afterward Moses and Aaron went to Pharaoh and said, "Thus says the LORD, the God of Israel, 'Let my people go, so that they may celebrate a festival to me in the wilderness.'" [2]But Pharaoh said, "Who is the LORD, that I should heed him and let Israel go? I do not know the LORD, and I will not let Israel go."

[3]Then they said, "The God of the Hebrews has revealed himself to us; let us go a three days' journey into the wilderness to sacrifice to the LORD our God, or he will fall upon us with pestilence or sword." [4]But the king of Egypt said to them, "Moses and Aaron, why are you taking the people away from their work? Get to your labors!" [5]Pharaoh continued, "Now they are more numerous than the people of the land[b] and yet you want them to stop working!" [6]That same day Pharaoh commanded the taskmasters of the people, as well as their supervisors, [7]"You shall no longer give the people straw to make bricks, as before; let them go and gather straw for themselves. [8]But you shall require of them the same quantity of bricks as they have made previously; do not diminish it, for they are lazy; that is why they cry, 'Let us go and offer sacrifice to our God.' [9]Let heavier work be laid on them; then they will labor at it and pay no attention to deceptive words."

10 So the taskmasters and the supervisors of the people went out and said to the people, "Thus says Pharaoh, 'I will not give you straw. [11]Go and get straw yourselves, wherever you can find it; but your work will not be lessened in the least.'" [12]So the people scattered throughout the land of Egypt, to gather stubble for straw. [13]The taskmasters were urgent, saying, "Complete your work, the same daily assignment as when you were given straw." [14]And the supervisors of the Israelites, whom Pharaoh's taskmasters had set over them, were beaten, and were asked, "Why did you not finish the required quantity of bricks yesterday and today, as you did before?"

15 Then the Israelite supervisors came to Pharaoh and cried, "Why do you treat your servants like this? [16]No straw is given to your servants, yet they say to us, 'Make bricks!' Look how your servants are beaten! You are unjust to your own people."[c] [17]He said, "You are lazy, lazy; that is why you say, 'Let us go and sacrifice to the LORD.' [18]Go now, and work; for no straw shall be given you, but you shall still deliver the same number of bricks." [19]The Isra-

---

a Heb *his*   b Sam: Heb *The people of the land are now many people*   c Gk Compare Syr Vg: Heb *beaten; and the sin of your* elite supervisors saw that they were in trouble when they were told, "You shall not lessen your daily number of bricks." 20As they left Pharaoh, they came upon Moses and Aaron who were waiting to meet them. 21They said to them, "The LORD look upon you and judge! You have brought us into bad odor with Pharaoh and his officials, and have put a sword in their hand to kill us."

22 Then Moses turned again to the LORD and said, "O LORD, why have you mistreated this people? Why did you ever send me? 23Since I first came to Pharaoh to speak in your name, he has mistreated this people, and you have done nothing at all to deliver your people."

Israel's Deliverance Assured

6 Then the LORD said to Moses, "Now you shall see what I will do to Pharaoh: Indeed, by a mighty hand he will let them go; by a mighty hand he will drive them out of his land."

2 God also spoke to Moses and said to him: "I am the LORD. 3I appeared to Abraham, Isaac, and Jacob as God Almighty,*a* but by my name 'The LORD'*b* I did not make myself known to them. 4I also established my covenant with them, to give them the land of Canaan, the land in which they resided as aliens. 5I have also heard the groaning of the Israelites whom the Egyptians are holding as slaves, and I have remembered my covenant. 6Say therefore to the Israelites, 'I am the LORD, and I will free you from the burdens of the Egyptians and deliver you from slavery to them. I will redeem you with an outstretched arm and with mighty acts of judgment. 7I will take you as my people, and I will be your God. You shall know that I am the LORD your God, who has freed you from the burdens of the Egyptians. 8I will bring you into the land that I swore to give to Abraham, Isaac, and Jacob; I will give it to you for a possession. I am the LORD.' " 9Moses told this to the Israelites; but they would not listen to Moses, because of their broken spirit and their cruel slavery.

10 Then the LORD spoke to Moses, 11"Go and tell Pharaoh king of Egypt to let the Israelites go out of his land." 12But Moses spoke to the LORD, "The Israelites have not listened to me; how then shall Pharaoh listen to me, poor speaker that I am?"*c* 13Thus the LORD spoke to Moses and Aaron, and gave them orders regarding the Israelites and Pharaoh king of Egypt, charging them to free the Israelites from the land of Egypt.

The Genealogy of Moses and Aaron

14 The following are the heads of their ancestral houses: the sons of Reuben, the firstborn of Israel: Hanoch, Pallu, Hezron, and Carmi; these are the families of Reuben. 15The sons of Simeon: Jemuel, Jamin, Ohad, Jachin, Zohar, and Shaul,*d* the son of a Canaanite woman; these are the families of Simeon. 16The following are the names of the sons of Levi according to their genealogies: Gershon,*e* Kohath, and Merari, and the length of Levi's life was one hundred thirty-seven years. 17The sons of Gershon:*e* Libni and Shimei, by their families. 18The sons of Kohath: Amram, Izhar, Hebron, and Uzziel, and the length of Kohath's life was one hundred thirty-three years. 19The sons of Merari: Mahli and Mushi. These are the families of the Levites according to their genealogies. 20Amram married Jochebed his father's sister and she bore him Aaron and Moses, and the length of Amram's life was one hundred thirty-seven years. 21The sons of Izhar: Korah, Nepheg, and Zichri. 22The sons of Uzziel: Mishael, Elzaphan, and Sithri. 23Aaron married Elisheba, daughter of Amminadab and sister of Nahshon, and she bore him Nadab, Abihu, Eleazar, and Ithamar. 24The sons of Korah: Assir, Elkanah, and Abiasaph; these are the families of the Korahites. 25Aaron's son Eleazar married one of the daughters of Putiel, and she bore him Phinehas. These are the heads of the ancestral houses of the Levites by their families.

26 It was this same Aaron and Moses to whom the LORD said, "Bring the Israelites out

---

a Traditional rendering of Heb *El Shaddai*   *b* Heb *YHWH*; see note at 3.15   *c* Heb *me? I am uncircumcised of lips*   *d* Or *Saul*   *e* Also spelled *Gershom*; see 2.22

of the land of Egypt, company by company."
²⁷It was they who spoke to Pharaoh king of
Egypt to bring the Israelites out of Egypt, the
same Moses and Aaron.

Moses and Aaron Obey God's Commands

28 On the day when the LORD spoke to
Moses in the land of Egypt, ²⁹he said to him,
"I am the LORD; tell Pharaoh king of Egypt all
that I am speaking to you." ³⁰But Moses said
in the LORD's presence, "Since I am a poor
speaker,ᵃ why would Pharaoh listen to me?"
7 The LORD said to Moses, "See, I have
made you like God to Pharaoh, and your
brother Aaron shall be your prophet. ²You
shall speak all that I command you, and your
brother Aaron shall tell Pharaoh to let the Israelites go out of his land. ³But I will harden
Pharaoh's heart, and I will multiply my signs
and wonders in the land of Egypt. ⁴When
Pharaoh does not listen to you, I will lay my
hand upon Egypt and bring my people the Israelites, company by company, out of the land
of Egypt by great acts of judgment. ⁵The
Egyptians shall know that I am the LORD,
when I stretch out my hand against Egypt and
bring the Israelites out from among them."
⁶Moses and Aaron did so; they did just as the
LORD commanded them. ⁷Moses was eighty
years old and Aaron eighty-three when they
spoke to Pharaoh.

Aaron's Miraculous Rod

8 The LORD said to Moses and Aaron,
⁹"When Pharaoh says to you, 'Perform a wonder,' then you shall say to Aaron, 'Take your
staff and throw it down before Pharaoh, and
it will become a snake.'" ¹⁰So Moses and Aaron went to Pharaoh and did as the LORD had
commanded; Aaron threw down his staff before Pharaoh and his officials, and it became a
snake. ¹¹Then Pharaoh summoned the wise
men and the sorcerers; and they also, the magicians of Egypt, did the same by their secret
arts. ¹²Each one threw down his staff, and they
became snakes; but Aaron's staff swallowed

up theirs. ¹³Still Pharaoh's heart was hardened,
and he would not listen to them, as the LORD
had said.

The First Plague: Water Turned to Blood

14 Then the LORD said to Moses, "Pharaoh's heart is hardened; he refuses to let the
people go. ¹⁵Go to Pharaoh in the morning, as
he is going out to the water; stand by at the river bank to meet him, and take in your hand the
staff that was turned into a snake. ¹⁶Say to him,
'The LORD, the God of the Hebrews, sent me
to you to say, "Let my people go, so that they
may worship me in the wilderness." But until
now you have not listened. ¹⁷Thus says the
LORD, "By this you shall know that I am the
LORD." See, with the staff that is in my hand I
will strike the water that is in the Nile, and it shall
be turned to blood. ¹⁸The fish in the river shall
die, the river itself shall stink, and the Egyptians
shall be unable to drink water from the Nile.'"
¹⁹The LORD said to Moses, "Say to Aaron, 'Take
your staff and stretch out your hand over the waters of Egypt—over its rivers, its canals, and its
ponds, and all its pools of water—so that they
may become blood; and there shall be blood
throughout the whole land of Egypt, even in
vessels of wood and in vessels of stone.'"

20 Moses and Aaron did just as the LORD
commanded. In the sight of Pharaoh and of
his officials he lifted up the staff and struck the
water in the river, and all the water in the river
was turned into blood, ²¹and the fish in the river died. The river stank so that the Egyptians
could not drink its water, and there was blood
throughout the whole land of Egypt. ²²But
the magicians of Egypt did the same by their
secret arts; so Pharaoh's heart remained hardened, and he would not listen to them, as the
LORD had said. ²³Pharaoh turned and went
into his house, and he did not take even this to
heart. ²⁴And all the Egyptians had to dig along
the Nile for water to drink, for they could not
drink the water of the river.

25 Seven days passed after the LORD had
struck the Nile.

ᵃ Heb *am uncircumcised of lips*; see 6.12

The Second Plague: Frogs

8 [a] Then the LORD said to Moses, "Go to Pharaoh and say to him, 'Thus says the LORD: Let my people go, so that they may worship me. [2] If you refuse to let them go, I will plague your whole country with frogs. [3] The river shall swarm with frogs; they shall come up into your palace, into your bedchamber and your bed, and into the houses of your officials and of your people, [b] and into your ovens and your kneading bowls. [4] The frogs shall come up on you and on your people and on all your officials.' " [5] [c] And the LORD said to Moses, "Say to Aaron, 'Stretch out your hand with your staff over the rivers, the canals, and the pools, and make frogs come up on the land of Egypt.' " [6] So Aaron stretched out his hand over the waters of Egypt; and the frogs came up and covered the land of Egypt. **[7] But the magicians did the same by their secret arts, and brought frogs up on the land of Egypt.**

[8] Then Pharaoh called Moses and Aaron, and said, "Pray to the LORD to take away the frogs from me and my people, and I will let the people go to sacrifice to the LORD." [9] Moses said to Pharaoh, "Kindly tell me when I am to pray for you and for your officials and for your people, that the frogs may be removed from you and your houses and be left only in the Nile." [10] And he said, "Tomorrow." Moses said, "As you say! So that you may know that there is no one like the LORD our God, [11] the frogs shall leave you and your houses and your officials and your people; they shall be left only in the Nile." [12] Then Moses and Aaron went out from Pharaoh; and Moses cried out to the LORD concerning the frogs that he had brought upon Pharaoh. [d] [13] And the LORD did as Moses requested: the frogs died in the houses, the courtyards, and the fields. [14] And they gathered them together in heaps, and the land stank. [15] But when Pharaoh saw that there was a respite, he hardened his heart, and would not listen to them, just as the LORD had said.

The Third Plague: Gnats

[16] Then the LORD said to Moses, "Say to Aaron, 'Stretch out your staff and strike the dust of the earth, so that it may become gnats throughout the whole land of Egypt.' " [17] And they did so; Aaron stretched out his hand with his staff and struck the dust of the earth, and gnats came on humans and animals alike; all the dust of the earth turned into gnats throughout the whole land of Egypt. **[18] The magicians tried to produce gnats by their secret arts, but they could not. There were gnats on both humans and animals. [19] And the magicians said to Pharaoh, "This is the finger of God!"** But Pharaoh's heart was hardened, and he would not listen to them, just as the LORD had said.

The Fourth Plague: Flies

[20] Then the LORD said to Moses, "Rise early in the morning and present yourself before Pharaoh, as he goes out to the water, and say to him, 'Thus says the LORD: Let my people go, so that they may worship me. [21] For if you will not let my people go, I will send swarms of flies on you, your officials, and your people, and into your houses; and the houses of the Egyptians shall be filled with swarms of flies; so also the land where they live. [22] But on that day I will set apart the land of Goshen, where my people live, so that no swarms of flies shall be there, that you may know that I the LORD am in this land. [23] Thus I will make a distinction [e] between my people and your people. This sign shall appear tomorrow.' " [24] The LORD did so, and great swarms of flies came into the house of Pharaoh and into his officials' houses; in all of Egypt the land was ruined because of the flies.

[25] Then Pharaoh summoned Moses and Aaron, and said, "Go, sacrifice to your God within the land." [26] But Moses said, "It would not be right to do so; for the sacrifices that we offer to the LORD our God are offensive to the Egyptians. If we offer in the sight of the Egyptians sacrifices that are offensive to them, will they not stone us? [27] We must go a three days'

---

[a] Ch 7.26 in Heb   [b] Gk: Heb *upon your people*   [c] Ch 8.1 in Heb   [d] Or *frogs, as he had agreed with Pharaoh*
[e] Gk Vg: Heb *will set redemption*

journey into the wilderness and sacrifice to the LORD our God as he commands us." 28So Pharaoh said, "I will let you go to sacrifice to the LORD your God in the wilderness, provided you do not go very far away. Pray for me." 29Then Moses said, "As soon as I leave you, I will pray to the LORD that the swarms of flies may depart tomorrow from Pharaoh, from his officials, and from his people; only do not let Pharaoh again deal falsely by not letting the people go to sacrifice to the LORD."

30 So Moses went out from Pharaoh and prayed to the LORD. 31And the LORD did as Moses asked: he removed the swarms of flies from Pharaoh, from his officials, and from his people; not one remained. 32But Pharaoh hardened his heart this time also, and would not let the people go.

The Fifth Plague: Livestock Diseased

9 Then the LORD said to Moses, "Go to Pharaoh, and say to him, 'Thus says the LORD, the God of the Hebrews: Let my people go, so that they may worship me. 2For if you refuse to let them go and still hold them, 3the hand of the LORD will strike with a deadly pestilence your livestock in the field: the horses, the donkeys, the camels, the herds, and the flocks. 4But the LORD will make a distinction between the livestock of Israel and the livestock of Egypt, so that nothing shall die of all that belongs to the Israelites.' " 5The LORD set a time, saying, "Tomorrow the LORD will do this thing in the land." 6And on the next day the LORD did so; all the livestock of the Egyptians died, but of the livestock of the Israelites not one died. 7Pharaoh inquired and found that not one of the livestock of the Israelites was dead. But the heart of Pharaoh was hardened, and he would not let the people go.

The Sixth Plague: Boils

8 Then the LORD said to Moses and Aaron, "Take handfuls of soot from the kiln, and let Moses throw it in the air in the sight of Pharaoh. 9It shall become fine dust all over the land of Egypt, and shall cause festering boils on humans and animals throughout the whole land of Egypt." 10So they took soot from the kiln, and stood before Pharaoh, and Moses threw it in the air, and it caused festering boils on humans and animals. 11The magicians could not stand before Moses because of the boils, for the boils afflicted the magicians as well as all the Egyptians. 12But the LORD hardened the heart of Pharaoh, and he would not listen to them, just as the LORD had spoken to Moses.

The Seventh Plague: Thunder and Hail

13 Then the LORD said to Moses, "Rise up early in the morning and present yourself before Pharaoh, and say to him, 'Thus says the LORD, the God of the Hebrews: Let my people go, so that they may worship me. 14For this time I will send all my plagues upon you yourself, and upon your officials, and upon your people, so that you may know that there is no one like me in all the earth. 15For by now I could have stretched out my hand and struck you and your people with pestilence, and you would have been cut off from the earth. 16But this is why I have let you live: to show you my power, and to make my name resound through all the earth. 17You are still exalting yourself against my people, and will not let them go. 18Tomorrow at this time I will cause the heaviest hail to fall that has ever fallen in Egypt from the day it was founded until now. 19Send, therefore, and have your livestock and everything that you have in the open field brought to a secure place; every human or animal that is in the open field and is not brought under shelter will die when the hail comes down upon them.' " 20Those officials of Pharaoh who feared the word of the LORD hurried their slaves and livestock off to a secure place. 21Those who did not regard the word of the LORD left their slaves and livestock in the open field.

22 The LORD said to Moses, "Stretch out your hand toward heaven so that hail may fall on the whole land of Egypt, on humans and animals and all the plants of the field in the land of Egypt." 23Then Moses stretched out his staff toward heaven, and the LORD sent thunder and hail, and fire came down on the earth.

And the LORD rained hail on the land of Egypt; ²⁴there was hail with fire flashing continually in the midst of it, such heavy hail as had never fallen in all the land of Egypt since it became a nation. ²⁵The hail struck down everything that was in the open field throughout all the land of Egypt, both human and animal; the hail also struck down all the plants of the field, and shattered every tree in the field. ²⁶Only in the land of Goshen, where the Israelites were, there was no hail.

27 Then Pharaoh summoned Moses and Aaron, and said to them, "This time I have sinned; the LORD is in the right, and I and my people are in the wrong. ²⁸Pray to the LORD! Enough of God's thunder and hail! I will let you go; you need stay no longer." ²⁹Moses said to him, "As soon as I have gone out of the city, I will stretch out my hands to the LORD; the thunder will cease, and there will be no more hail, so that you may know that the earth is the LORD's. ³⁰But as for you and your officials, I know that you do not yet fear the LORD God." ³¹(Now the flax and the barley were ruined, for the barley was in the ear and the flax was in bud. ³²But the wheat and the spelt were not ruined, for they are late in coming up.) ³³So Moses left Pharaoh, went out of the city, and stretched out his hands to the LORD; then the thunder and the hail ceased, and the rain no longer poured down on the earth. ³⁴But when Pharaoh saw that the rain and the hail and the thunder had ceased, he sinned once more and hardened his heart, he and his officials. ³⁵So the heart of Pharaoh was hardened, and he would not let the Israelites go, just as the LORD had spoken through Moses.

The Eighth Plague: Locusts

10 Then the LORD said to Moses, "Go to Pharaoh; for I have hardened his heart and the heart of his officials, in order that I may show these signs of mine among them, ²and that you may tell your children and grandchildren how I have made fools of the Egyptians and what signs I have done among them—so that you may know that I am the LORD."

3 So Moses and Aaron went to Pharaoh, and said to him, "Thus says the LORD, the God of the Hebrews, 'How long will you refuse to humble yourself before me? Let my people go, so that they may worship me. ⁴For if you refuse to let my people go, tomorrow I will bring locusts into your country. ⁵They shall cover the surface of the land, so that no one will be able to see the land. They shall devour the last remnant left you after the hail, and they shall devour every tree of yours that grows in the field. ⁶They shall fill your houses, and the houses of all your officials and of all the Egyptians—something that neither your parents nor your grandparents have seen, from the day they came on earth to this day.' " Then he turned and went out from Pharaoh.

7 Pharaoh's officials said to him, "How long shall this fellow be a snare to us? Let the people go, so that they may worship the LORD their God; do you not yet understand that Egypt is ruined?" ⁸So Moses and Aaron were brought back to Pharaoh, and he said to them, "Go, worship the LORD your God! But which ones are to go?" ⁹Moses said, "We will go with our young and our old; we will go with our sons and daughters and with our flocks and herds, because we have the LORD's festival to celebrate." ¹⁰He said to them, "The LORD indeed will be with you, if ever I let your little ones go with you! Plainly, you have some evil purpose in mind. ¹¹No, never! Your men may go and worship the LORD, for that is what you are asking." And they were driven out from Pharaoh's presence.

12 Then the LORD said to Moses, "Stretch out your hand over the land of Egypt, so that the locusts may come upon it and eat every plant in the land, all that the hail has left." ¹³So Moses stretched out his staff over the land of Egypt, and the LORD brought an east wind upon the land all that day and all that night; when morning came, the east wind had brought the locusts. ¹⁴The locusts came upon all the land of Egypt and settled on the whole country of Egypt, such a dense swarm of locusts as had never been before, nor ever shall be again. ¹⁵They covered the surface of the whole land, so that the land was black; and

they ate all the plants in the land and all the fruit of the trees that the hail had left; nothing green was left, no tree, no plant in the field, in all the land of Egypt. ¹⁶Pharaoh hurriedly summoned Moses and Aaron and said, "I have sinned against the LORD your God, and against you. ¹⁷Do forgive my sin just this once, and pray to the LORD your God that at the least he remove this deadly thing from me." ¹⁸So he went out from Pharaoh and prayed to the LORD. ¹⁹The LORD changed the wind into a very strong west wind, which lifted the locusts and drove them into the Red Sea;*a* not a single locust was left in all the country of Egypt. ²⁰But the LORD hardened Pharaoh's heart, and he would not let the Israelites go.

The Ninth Plague: Darkness

²¹ Then the LORD said to Moses, "Stretch out your hand toward heaven so that there may be darkness over the land of Egypt, a darkness that can be felt." ²²So Moses stretched out his hand toward heaven, and there was dense darkness in all the land of Egypt for three days. ²³People could not see one another, and for three days they could not move from where they were; but all the Israelites had light where they lived. ²⁴Then Pharaoh summoned Moses, and said, "Go, worship the LORD. Only your flocks and your herds shall remain behind. Even your children may go with you." ²⁵But Moses said, "You must also let us have sacrifices and burnt offerings to sacrifice to the LORD our God. ²⁶Our livestock also must go with us; not a hoof shall be left behind, for we must choose some of them for the worship of the LORD our God, and we will not know what to use to worship the LORD until we arrive there." ²⁷But the LORD hardened Pharaoh's heart, and he was unwilling to let them go. ²⁸Then Pharaoh said to him, "Get away from me! Take care that you do not see my face again, for on the day you see my face you shall die." ²⁹Moses said, "Just as you say! I will never see your face again."

a Or Sea of Reeds

Warning of the Final Plague

11 The LORD said to Moses, "I will bring one more plague upon Pharaoh and upon Egypt; afterwards he will let you go from here; indeed, when he lets you go, he will drive you away. ²Tell the people that every man is to ask his neighbor and every woman is to ask her neighbor for objects of silver and gold." ³The LORD gave the people favor in the sight of the Egyptians. Moreover, Moses himself was a man of great importance in the land of Egypt, in the sight of Pharaoh's officials and in the sight of the people.

4 Moses said, "Thus says the LORD: About midnight I will go out through Egypt. ⁵Every firstborn in the land of Egypt shall die, from the firstborn of Pharaoh who sits on his throne to the firstborn of the female slave who is behind the handmill, and all the firstborn of the livestock. ⁶Then there will be a loud cry throughout the whole land of Egypt, such as has never been or will ever be again. ⁷But not a dog shall growl at any of the Israelites—not at people, not at animals—so that you may know that the LORD makes a distinction between Egypt and Israel. ⁸Then all these officials of yours shall come down to me, and bow low to me, saying, 'Leave us, you and all the people who follow you.' After that I will leave." And in hot anger he left Pharaoh.

9 The LORD said to Moses, "Pharaoh will not listen to you, in order that my wonders may be multiplied in the land of Egypt." ¹⁰Moses and Aaron performed all these wonders before Pharaoh; but the LORD hardened Pharaoh's heart, and he did not let the people of Israel go out of his land.

The First Passover Instituted

12 The LORD said to Moses and Aaron in the land of Egypt: ²This month shall mark for you the beginning of months; it shall be the first month of the year for you. ³Tell the whole congregation of Israel that on the tenth of this month they are to take a lamb for each family, a lamb for each household. ⁴If a household is too small for a whole lamb, it shall join its closest neighbor in obtaining one; the lamb shall be divided in proportion to the number of people who eat of it. 5Your lamb shall be without blemish, a year-old male; you may take it from the sheep or from the goats. 6You shall keep it until the fourteenth day of this month; then the whole assembled congregation of Israel shall slaughter it at twilight. 7They shall take some of the blood and put it on the two doorposts and the lintel of the houses in which they eat it. 8They shall eat the lamb that same night; they shall eat it roasted over the fire with unleavened bread and bitter herbs. 9Do not eat any of it raw or boiled in water, but roasted over the fire, with its head, legs, and inner organs. 10You shall let none of it remain until the morning; anything that remains until the morning you shall burn. 11This is how you shall eat it: your loins girded, your sandals on your feet, and your staff in your hand; and you shall eat it hurriedly. It is the passover of the LORD. 12For I will pass through the land of Egypt that night, and I will strike down every firstborn in the land of Egypt, both human beings and animals; on all the gods of Egypt I will execute judgments: I am the LORD. 13The blood shall be a sign for you on the houses where you live: when I see the blood, I will pass over you, and no plague shall destroy you when I strike the land of Egypt.

14 This day shall be a day of remembrance for you. You shall celebrate it as a festival to the LORD; throughout your generations you shall observe it as a perpetual ordinance. 15Seven days you shall eat unleavened bread; on the first day you shall remove leaven from your houses, for whoever eats leavened bread from the first day until the seventh day shall be cut off from Israel. 16On the first day you shall hold a solemn assembly, and on the seventh day a solemn assembly; no work shall be done on those days; only what everyone must eat, that alone may be prepared by you. 17You shall observe the festival of unleavened bread, for on this very day I brought your companies out of the land of Egypt: you shall observe this day throughout your generations as a perpetual ordinance. 18In the first month, from the evening of the fourteenth day until the evening of the twenty-first day, you shall eat unleavened bread. 19For seven days no leaven shall be found in your houses; for whoever eats what is leavened shall be cut off from the congregation of Israel, whether an alien or a native of the land. 20You shall eat nothing leavened; in all your settlements you shall eat unleavened bread.

21 Then Moses called all the elders of Israel and said to them, "Go, select lambs for your families, and slaughter the passover lamb. 22Take a bunch of hyssop, dip it in the blood that is in the basin, and touch the lintel and the two doorposts with the blood in the basin. None of you shall go outside the door of your house until morning. 23For the LORD will pass through to strike down the Egyptians; when he sees the blood on the lintel and on the two doorposts, the LORD will pass over that door and will not allow the destroyer to enter your houses to strike you down. 24You shall observe this rite as a perpetual ordinance for you and your children. 25When you come to the land that the LORD will give you, as he has promised, you shall keep this observance. 26And when your children ask you, 'What do you mean by this observance?' 27you shall say, 'It is the passover sacrifice to the LORD, for he passed over the houses of the Israelites in Egypt, when he struck down the Egyptians but spared our houses.'" And the people bowed down and worshiped.

28 The Israelites went and did just as the LORD had commanded Moses and Aaron.

The Tenth Plague: Death of the Firstborn

29 At midnight the LORD struck down all the firstborn in the land of Egypt, from the firstborn of Pharaoh who sat on his throne to the firstborn of the prisoner who was in the dungeon, and all the firstborn of the livestock. 30Pharaoh arose in the night, he and all his officials and all the Egyptians; and there was a loud cry in Egypt, for there was not a house without someone dead. 31Then he summoned Moses and Aaron in the night, and said, "Rise up, go away from my people, both you and the

Israelites! Go, worship the LORD, as you said. ³²Take your flocks and your herds, as you said, and be gone. And bring a blessing on me too!"

The Exodus: From Rameses to Succoth

33 The Egyptians urged the people to hasten their departure from the land, for they said, "We shall all be dead." ³⁴So the people took their dough before it was leavened, with their kneading bowls wrapped up in their cloaks on their shoulders. ³⁵The Israelites had done as Moses told them; they had asked the Egyptians for jewelry of silver and gold, and for clothing, ³⁶and the LORD had given the people favor in the sight of the Egyptians, so that they let them have what they asked. And so they plundered the Egyptians.

37 The Israelites journeyed from Rameses to Succoth, about six hundred thousand men on foot, besides children. ³⁸A mixed crowd also went up with them, and livestock in great numbers, both flocks and herds. ³⁹They baked unleavened cakes of the dough that they had brought out of Egypt; it was not leavened, because they were driven out of Egypt and could not wait, nor had they prepared any provisions for themselves.

40 The time that the Israelites had lived in Egypt was four hundred thirty years. ⁴¹At the end of four hundred thirty years, on that very day, all the companies of the LORD went out from the land of Egypt. ⁴²That was for the LORD a night of vigil, to bring them out of the land of Egypt. That same night is a vigil to be kept for the LORD by all the Israelites throughout their generations.

Directions for the Passover

43 The LORD said to Moses and Aaron: This is the ordinance for the passover: no foreigner shall eat of it, ⁴⁴but any slave who has been purchased may eat of it after he has been circumcised; ⁴⁵no bound or hired servant may eat of it. ⁴⁶It shall be eaten in one house; you shall not take any of the animal outside the house, and you shall not break any of its bones. ⁴⁷The whole congregation of Israel shall celebrate it. ⁴⁸If an alien who resides with you

wants to celebrate the passover to the LORD, all his males shall be circumcised; then he may draw near to celebrate it; he shall be regarded as a native of the land. But no uncircumcised person shall eat of it; ⁴⁹there shall be one law for the native and for the alien who resides among you.

50 All the Israelites did just as the LORD had commanded Moses and Aaron. ⁵¹That very day the LORD brought the Israelites out of the land of Egypt, company by company.

13 The LORD said to Moses: ²Consecrate to me all the firstborn; whatever is the first to open the womb among the Israelites, of human beings and animals, is mine.

The Festival of Unleavened Bread

3 Moses said to the people, "Remember this day on which you came out of Egypt, out of the house of slavery, because the LORD brought you out from there by strength of hand; no leavened bread shall be eaten. ⁴Today, in the month of Abib, you are going out. ⁵When the LORD brings you into the land of the Canaanites, the Hittites, the Amorites, the Hivites, and the Jebusites, which he swore to your ancestors to give you, a land flowing with milk and honey, you shall keep this observance in this month. ⁶Seven days you shall eat unleavened bread, and on the seventh day there shall be a festival to the LORD. ⁷Unleavened bread shall be eaten for seven days; no leavened bread shall be seen in your possession, and no leaven shall be seen among you in all your territory. ⁸You shall tell your child on that day, 'It is because of what the LORD did for me when I came out of Egypt.' ⁹It shall serve for you as a sign on your hand and as a reminder on your forehead, so that the teaching of the LORD may be on your lips; for with a strong hand the LORD brought you out of Egypt. ¹⁰You shall keep this ordinance at its proper time from year to year.

The Consecration of the Firstborn

11 "When the LORD has brought you into the land of the Canaanites, as he swore to you and your ancestors, and has given it to you,

12you shall set apart to the LORD all that first opens the womb. All the firstborn of your livestock that are males shall be the LORD's. 13But every firstborn donkey you shall redeem with a sheep; if you do not redeem it, you must break its neck. Every firstborn male among your children you shall redeem. 14When in the future your child asks you, 'What does this mean?' you shall answer, 'By strength of hand the LORD brought us out of Egypt, from the house of slavery. 15When Pharaoh stubbornly refused to let us go, the LORD killed all the firstborn in the land of Egypt, from human firstborn to the firstborn of animals. Therefore I sacrifice to the LORD every male that first opens the womb, but every firstborn of my sons I redeem.' 16It shall serve as a sign on your hand and as an emblem*a* on your forehead that by strength of hand the LORD brought us out of Egypt."

The Pillars of Cloud and Fire

17 When Pharaoh let the people go, God did not lead them by way of the land of the Philistines, although that was nearer; for God thought, "If the people face war, they may change their minds and return to Egypt." 18So God led the people by the roundabout way of the wilderness toward the Red Sea.*b* The Israelites went up out of the land of Egypt prepared for battle. 19And Moses took with him the bones of Joseph who had required a solemn oath of the Israelites, saying, "God will surely take notice of you, and then you must carry my bones with you from here." 20They set out from Succoth, and camped at Etham, on the edge of the wilderness. 21The LORD went in front of them in a pillar of cloud by day, to lead them along the way, and in a pillar of fire by night, to give them light, so that they might travel by day and by night. 22Neither the pillar of cloud by day nor the pillar of fire by night left its place in front of the people.

Crossing the Red Sea

14 Then the LORD said to Moses: 2Tell the Israelites to turn back and camp in front of Pi-hahiroth, between Migdol and the sea, in front of Baal-zephon; you shall camp opposite it, by the sea. 3Pharaoh will say of the Israelites, "They are wandering aimlessly in the land; the wilderness has closed in on them." 4I will harden Pharaoh's heart, and he will pursue them, so that I will gain glory for myself over Pharaoh and all his army; and the Egyptians shall know that I am the LORD. And they did so.

5 When the king of Egypt was told that the people had fled, the minds of Pharaoh and his officials were changed toward the people, and they said, "What have we done, letting Israel leave our service?" 6So he had his chariot made ready, and took his army with him; 7he took six hundred picked chariots and all the other chariots of Egypt with officers over all of them. 8The LORD hardened the heart of Pharaoh king of Egypt and he pursued the Israelites, who were going out boldly. 9The Egyptians pursued them, all Pharaoh's horses and chariots, his chariot drivers and his army; they overtook them camped by the sea, by Pi-hahiroth, in front of Baal-zephon.

10 As Pharaoh drew near, the Israelites looked back, and there were the Egyptians advancing on them. In great fear the Israelites cried out to the LORD. 11They said to Moses, "Was it because there were no graves in Egypt that you have taken us away to die in the wilderness? What have you done to us, bringing us out of Egypt? 12Is this not the very thing we told you in Egypt, 'Let us alone and let us serve the Egyptians'? For it would have been better for us to serve the Egyptians than to die in the wilderness." 13But Moses said to the people, "Do not be afraid, stand firm, and see the deliverance that the LORD will accomplish for you today; for the Egyptians whom you see today you shall never see again. 14The LORD will fight for you, and you have only to keep still."

15 Then the LORD said to Moses, "Why

---

a Or *as a frontlet*; meaning of Heb uncertain   *b* Or *Sea of Reeds* do you cry out to me? Tell the Israelites to go forward. ¹⁶But you lift up your staff, and stretch out your hand over the sea and divide it, that the Israelites may go into the sea on dry ground. ¹⁷Then I will harden the hearts of the Egyptians so that they will go in after them; and so I will gain glory for myself over Pharaoh and all his army, his chariots, and his chariot drivers. ¹⁸And the Egyptians shall know that I am the LORD, when I have gained glory for myself over Pharaoh, his chariots, and his chariot drivers."

19 The angel of God who was going before the Israelite army moved and went behind them; and the pillar of cloud moved from in front of them and took its place behind them. ²⁰It came between the army of Egypt and the army of Israel. And so the cloud was there with the darkness, and it lit up the night; one did not come near the other all night.

21 Then Moses stretched out his hand over the sea. The LORD drove the sea back by a strong east wind all night, and turned the sea into dry land; and the waters were divided. ²²The Israelites went into the sea on dry ground, the waters forming a wall for them on their right and on their left. ²³The Egyptians pursued, and went into the sea after them, all of Pharaoh's horses, chariots, and chariot drivers. ²⁴At the morning watch the LORD in the pillar of fire and cloud looked down upon the Egyptian army, and threw the Egyptian army into panic. ²⁵He clogged*ᵃ* their chariot wheels so that they turned with difficulty. The Egyptians said, "Let us flee from the Israelites, for the LORD is fighting for them against Egypt."

The Pursuers Drowned

26 Then the LORD said to Moses, "Stretch out your hand over the sea, so that the water may come back upon the Egyptians, upon their chariots and chariot drivers." ²⁷So Moses stretched out his hand over the sea, and at dawn the sea returned to its normal depth. As the Egyptians fled before it, the LORD tossed the Egyptians into the sea. ²⁸The waters re-turned and covered the chariots and the chariot drivers, the entire army of Pharaoh that had followed them into the sea; not one of them remained. ²⁹But the Israelites walked on dry ground through the sea, the waters forming a wall for them on their right and on their left.

30 Thus the LORD saved Israel that day from the Egyptians; and Israel saw the Egyptians dead on the seashore. ³¹Israel saw the great work that the LORD did against the Egyptians. So the people feared the LORD and believed in the LORD and in his servant Moses.

The Song of Moses

15 Then Moses and the Israelites sang this song to the LORD:

"I will sing to the LORD, for he has
    triumphed gloriously;
  horse and rider he has thrown into the
    sea.
2 The LORD is my strength and my might,*ᵇ*
    and he has become my salvation;
  this is my God, and I will praise him,
    my father's God, and I will exalt him.
3 The LORD is a warrior;
    the LORD is his name.

4 "Pharaoh's chariots and his army he cast
    into the sea;
  his picked officers were sunk in the
    Red Sea.*ᶜ*
5 The floods covered them;
    they went down into the depths like a
    stone.
6 Your right hand, O LORD, glorious in
    power—
  your right hand, O LORD, shattered
    the enemy.
7 In the greatness of your majesty you
    overthrew your adversaries;
  you sent out your fury, it consumed
    them like stubble.
8 At the blast of your nostrils the waters
    piled up,
  the floods stood up in a heap;

---

a Sam Gk Syr: MT *removed*   *b* Or *song*   *c* Or *Sea of Reeds*

the deeps congealed in the heart of
the sea.

9   The enemy said, 'I will pursue, I will
overtake,
I will divide the spoil, my desire shall
have its fill of them.
I will draw my sword, my hand shall
destroy them.'

10   You blew with your wind, the sea
covered them;
they sank like lead in the mighty
waters.

11   "Who is like you, O LORD, among the
gods?
Who is like you, majestic in holiness,
awesome in splendor, doing wonders?

12   You stretched out your right hand,
the earth swallowed them.

13   "In your steadfast love you led the
people whom you redeemed;
you guided them by your strength to
your holy abode.

14   The peoples heard, they trembled;
pangs seized the inhabitants of
Philistia.

15   Then the chiefs of Edom were
dismayed;
trembling seized the leaders of Moab;
all the inhabitants of Canaan melted
away.

16   Terror and dread fell upon them;
by the might of your arm, they
became still as a stone
until your people, O LORD, passed by,
until the people whom you acquired
passed by.

17   You brought them in and planted them
on the mountain of your own
possession,
the place, O LORD, that you made
your abode,
the sanctuary, O LORD, that your
hands have established.

18   The LORD will reign forever and ever."

19   When the horses of Pharaoh with his
chariots and his chariot drivers went into the
sea, the LORD brought back the waters of the
sea upon them; but the Israelites walked
through the sea on dry ground.

The Song of Miriam

20   Then the prophet Miriam, Aaron's sister,
took a tambourine in her hand; and all the
women went out after her with tambourines
and with dancing. 21 And Miriam sang to them:
"Sing to the LORD, for he has triumphed
gloriously;
horse and rider he has thrown into the
sea."

Bitter Water Made Sweet

22   Then Moses ordered Israel to set out
from the Red Sea,ᵃ and they went into the
wilderness of Shur. They went three days in the
wilderness and found no water. 23 When they
came to Marah, they could not drink the water
of Marah because it was bitter. That is why it
was called Marah.ᵇ 24 And the people complained against Moses, saying, "What shall we
drink?" 25 He cried out to the LORD; and the
LORD showed him a piece of wood;ᶜ he threw
it into the water, and the water became sweet.

There the LORDᵈ made for them a statute
and an ordinance and there he put them to the
test. 26 He said, "If you will listen carefully to the
voice of the LORD your God, and do what is
right in his sight, and give heed to his commandments and keep all his statutes, I will not
bring upon you any of the diseases that I
brought upon the Egyptians; for I am the
LORD who heals you."

27   Then they came to Elim, where there
were twelve springs of water and seventy palm
trees; and they camped there by the water.

Bread from Heaven

16   The whole congregation of the Israelites set out from Elim; and Israel came
to the wilderness of Sin, which is between
Elim and Sinai, on the fifteenth day of the

---

a Or *Sea of Reeds*   *b* That is *Bitterness*   *c* Or *a tree*   *d* Heb *he* second month after they had departed from the land of Egypt. ²The whole congregation of the Israelites complained against Moses and Aaron in the wilderness. ³The Israelites said to them, "If only we had died by the hand of the LORD in the land of Egypt, when we sat by the fleshpots and ate our fill of bread; for you have brought us out into this wilderness to kill this whole assembly with hunger."

4 Then the LORD said to Moses, "I am going to rain bread from heaven for you, and each day the people shall go out and gather enough for that day. In that way I will test them, whether they will follow my instruction or not. ⁵On the sixth day, when they prepare what they bring in, it will be twice as much as they gather on other days." ⁶So Moses and Aaron said to all the Israelites, "In the evening you shall know that it was the LORD who brought you out of the land of Egypt, ⁷and in the morning you shall see the glory of the LORD, because he has heard your complaining against the LORD. For what are we, that you complain against us?" ⁸And Moses said, "When the LORD gives you meat to eat in the evening and your fill of bread in the morning, because the LORD has heard the complaining that you utter against him—what are we? Your complaining is not against us but against the LORD."

9 Then Moses said to Aaron, "Say to the whole congregation of the Israelites, 'Draw near to the LORD, for he has heard your complaining.'" ¹⁰And as Aaron spoke to the whole congregation of the Israelites, they looked toward the wilderness, and the glory of the LORD appeared in the cloud. ¹¹The LORD spoke to Moses and said, ¹²"I have heard the complaining of the Israelites; say to them, 'At twilight you shall eat meat, and in the morning you shall have your fill of bread; then you shall know that I am the LORD your God.'"

13 In the evening quails came up and covered the camp; and in the morning there was a layer of dew around the camp. ¹⁴When the layer of dew lifted, there on the surface of the wilderness was a fine flaky substance, as fine as frost on the ground. ¹⁵When the Israelites saw it, they said to one another, "What is it?"ᵃ For they did not know what it was. Moses said to them, "It is the bread that the LORD has given you to eat. ¹⁶This is what the LORD has commanded: 'Gather as much of it as each of you needs, an omer to a person according to the number of persons, all providing for those in their own tents.'" ¹⁷The Israelites did so, some gathering more, some less. ¹⁸But when they measured it with an omer, those who gathered much had nothing over, and those who gathered little had no shortage; they gathered as much as each of them needed. ¹⁹And Moses said to them, "Let no one leave any of it over until morning." ²⁰But they did not listen to Moses; some left part of it until morning, and it bred worms and became foul. And Moses was angry with them. ²¹Morning by morning they gathered it, as much as each needed; but when the sun grew hot, it melted.

22 On the sixth day they gathered twice as much food, two omers apiece. When all the leaders of the congregation came and told Moses, ²³he said to them, "This is what the LORD has commanded: 'Tomorrow is a day of solemn rest, a holy sabbath to the LORD; bake what you want to bake and boil what you want to boil, and all that is left over put aside to be kept until morning.'" ²⁴So they put it aside until morning, as Moses commanded them; and it did not become foul, and there were no worms in it. ²⁵Moses said, "Eat it today, for today is a sabbath to the LORD; today you will not find it in the field. ²⁶Six days you shall gather it; but on the seventh day, which is a sabbath, there will be none."

27 On the seventh day some of the people went out to gather, and they found none. ²⁸The LORD said to Moses, "How long will you refuse to keep my commandments and instructions? ²⁹See! The LORD has given you the sabbath, therefore on the sixth day he gives you food for two days; each of you stay where you are; do not leave your place on the seventh day." ³⁰So the people rested on the seventh day.

---

a Or *"It is manna"* (Heb *man hu*, see verse 31)

31 The house of Israel called it manna; it was like coriander seed, white, and the taste of it was like wafers made with honey. 32Moses said, "This is what the LORD has commanded: 'Let an omer of it be kept throughout your generations, in order that they may see the food with which I fed you in the wilderness, when I brought you out of the land of Egypt.'" 33And Moses said to Aaron, "Take a jar, and put an omer of manna in it, and place it before the LORD, to be kept throughout your generations." 34As the LORD commanded Moses, so Aaron placed it before the covenant,ᵃ for safekeeping. 35The Israelites ate manna forty years, until they came to a habitable land; they ate manna, until they came to the border of the land of Canaan. 36An omer is a tenth of an ephah.

Water from the Rock

17 From the wilderness of Sin the whole congregation of the Israelites journeyed by stages, as the LORD commanded. They camped at Rephidim, but there was no water for the people to drink. 2The people quarreled with Moses, and said, "Give us water to drink." Moses said to them, "Why do you quarrel with me? Why do you test the LORD?" 3But the people thirsted there for water; and the people complained against Moses and said, "Why did you bring us out of Egypt, to kill us and our children and livestock with thirst?" 4So Moses cried out to the LORD, "What shall I do with this people? They are almost ready to stone me." 5The LORD said to Moses, "Go on ahead of the people, and take some of the elders of Israel with you; take in your hand the staff with which you struck the Nile, and go. 6I will be standing there in front of you on the rock at Horeb. Strike the rock, and water will come out of it, so that the people may drink." Moses did so, in the sight of the elders of Israel. 7He called the place Massahᵇ and Meribah,ᶜ because the Israelites quarreled and tested the LORD, saying, "Is the LORD among us or not?"

Amalek Attacks Israel and Is Defeated

8 Then Amalek came and fought with Israel at Rephidim. 9Moses said to Joshua, "Choose some men for us and go out, fight with Amalek. Tomorrow I will stand on the top of the hill with the staff of God in my hand." 10So Joshua did as Moses told him, and fought with Amalek, while Moses, Aaron, and Hur went up to the top of the hill. 11Whenever Moses held up his hand, Israel prevailed; and whenever he lowered his hand, Amalek prevailed. 12But Moses' hands grew weary; so they took a stone and put it under him, and he sat on it. Aaron and Hur held up his hands, one on one side, and the other on the other side; so his hands were steady until the sun set. 13And Joshua defeated Amalek and his people with the sword.

14 Then the LORD said to Moses, "Write this as a reminder in a book and recite it in the hearing of Joshua: I will utterly blot out the remembrance of Amalek from under heaven." 15And Moses built an altar and called it, The LORD is my banner. 16He said, "A hand upon the banner of the LORD!ᵈ The LORD will have war with Amalek from generation to generation."

Jethro's Advice

18 Jethro, the priest of Midian, Moses' father-in-law, heard of all that God had done for Moses and for his people Israel, how the LORD had brought Israel out of Egypt. 2After Moses had sent away his wife Zipporah, his father-in-law Jethro took her back, 3along with her two sons. The name of the one was Gershom (for he said, "I have been an alienᵉ in a foreign land"), 4and the name of the other, Eliezerᶠ (for he said, "The God of my father was my help, and delivered me from the sword of Pharaoh"). 5Jethro, Moses' father-in-law, came into the wilderness where Moses was encamped at the mountain of God, bringing Moses' sons and wife to him. 6He sent word to Moses, "I, your father-in-law Jethro, am coming to you, with your wife and her two sons." 7Moses went out to meet his father-in-law; he

---

ᵃ Or *treaty* or *testimony*; Heb *eduth*   ᵇ That is *Test*   ᶜ That is *Quarrel*   ᵈ Cn: Meaning of Heb uncertain   ᵉ Heb *ger*   ᶠ Heb *Eli*, my God; *ezer*, help bowed down and kissed him; each asked after the other's welfare, and they went into the tent. [8]Then Moses told his father-in-law all that the LORD had done to Pharaoh and to the Egyptians for Israel's sake, all the hardship that had beset them on the way, and how the LORD had delivered them. [9]Jethro rejoiced for all the good that the LORD had done to Israel, in delivering them from the Egyptians.

10 Jethro said, "Blessed be the LORD, who has delivered you from the Egyptians and from Pharaoh. [11]Now I know that the LORD is greater than all gods, because he delivered the people from the Egyptians,[a] when they dealt arrogantly with them." [12]And Jethro, Moses' father-in-law, brought a burnt offering and sacrifices to God; and Aaron came with all the elders of Israel to eat bread with Moses' father-in-law in the presence of God.

13 The next day Moses sat as judge for the people, while the people stood around him from morning until evening. [14]When Moses' father-in-law saw all that he was doing for the people, he said, "What is this that you are doing for the people? Why do you sit alone, while all the people stand around you from morning until evening?" [15]Moses said to his father-in-law, "Because the people come to me to inquire of God. [16]When they have a dispute, they come to me and I decide between one person and another, and I make known to them the statutes and instructions of God." [17]Moses' father-in-law said to him, "What you are doing is not good. [18]You will surely wear yourself out, both you and these people with you. For the task is too heavy for you; you cannot do it alone. [19]Now listen to me. I will give you counsel, and God be with you! You should represent the people before God, and you should bring their cases before God; [20]teach them the statutes and instructions and make known to them the way they are to go and the things they are to do. [21]You should also look for able men among all the people, men who fear God, are trustworthy, and hate dishonest gain; set such men over them as officers over thousands,

hundreds, fifties, and tens. [22]Let them sit as judges for the people at all times; let them bring every important case to you, but decide every minor case themselves. So it will be easier for you, and they will bear the burden with you. [23]If you do this, and God so commands you, then you will be able to endure, and all these people will go to their home in peace."

24 So Moses listened to his father-in-law and did all that he had said. [25]Moses chose able men from all Israel and appointed them as heads over the people, as officers over thousands, hundreds, fifties, and tens. [26]And they judged the people at all times; hard cases they brought to Moses, but any minor case they decided themselves. [27]Then Moses let his father-in-law depart, and he went off to his own country.

The Israelites Reach Mount Sinai

19 On the third new moon after the Israelites had gone out of the land of Egypt, on that very day, they came into the wilderness of Sinai. [2]They had journeyed from Rephidim, entered the wilderness of Sinai, and camped in the wilderness; Israel camped there in front of the mountain. [3]Then Moses went up to God; the LORD called to him from the mountain, saying, "Thus you shall say to the house of Jacob, and tell the Israelites: [4]You have seen what I did to the Egyptians, and how I bore you on eagles' wings and brought you to myself. [5]Now therefore, if you obey my voice and keep my covenant, you shall be my treasured possession out of all the peoples. Indeed, the whole earth is mine, [6]but you shall be for me a priestly kingdom and a holy nation. These are the words that you shall speak to the Israelites."

7 So Moses came, summoned the elders of the people, and set before them all these words that the LORD had commanded him. [8]The people all answered as one: "Everything that the LORD has spoken we will do." Moses reported the words of the people to the LORD. [9]Then the LORD said to Moses, "I am going to come to you in a dense cloud, in order that the peo-

---

[a] The clause *because . . . Egyptians* has been transposed from verse 10

ple may hear when I speak with you and so trust you ever after."

The People Consecrated

When Moses had told the words of the people to the LORD, 10the LORD said to Moses: "Go to the people and consecrate them today and tomorrow. Have them wash their clothes 11and prepare for the third day, because on the third day the LORD will come down upon Mount Sinai in the sight of all the people. 12You shall set limits for the people all around, saying, 'Be careful not to go up the mountain or to touch the edge of it. Any who touch the mountain shall be put to death. 13No hand shall touch them, but they shall be stoned or shot with arrows;*a* whether animal or human being, they shall not live.' When the trumpet sounds a long blast, they may go up on the mountain." 14So Moses went down from the mountain to the people. He consecrated the people, and they washed their clothes. 15And he said to the people, "Prepare for the third day; do not go near a woman."

16 On the morning of the third day there was thunder and lightning, as well as a thick cloud on the mountain, and a blast of a trumpet so loud that all the people who were in the camp trembled. 17Moses brought the people out of the camp to meet God. They took their stand at the foot of the mountain. 18Now Mount Sinai was wrapped in smoke, because the LORD had descended upon it in fire; the smoke went up like the smoke of a kiln, while the whole mountain shook violently. 19As the blast of the trumpet grew louder and louder, Moses would speak and God would answer him in thunder. 20When the LORD descended upon Mount Sinai, to the top of the mountain, the LORD summoned Moses to the top of the mountain, and Moses went up. 21Then the LORD said to Moses, "Go down and warn the people not to break through to the LORD to look; otherwise many of them will perish. 22Even the priests who approach the LORD must consecrate themselves or the LORD will

break out against them." 23Moses said to the LORD, "The people are not permitted to come up to Mount Sinai; for you yourself warned us, saying, 'Set limits around the mountain and keep it holy.'" 24The LORD said to him, "Go down, and come up bringing Aaron with you; but do not let either the priests or the people break through to come up to the LORD; otherwise he will break out against them." 25So Moses went down to the people and told them.

The Ten Commandments

20 Then God spoke all these words:
2 I am the LORD your God, who brought you out of the land of Egypt, out of the house of slavery; 3you shall have no other gods before*b* me.

4 You shall not make for yourself an idol, whether in the form of anything that is in heaven above, or that is on the earth beneath, or that is in the water under the earth. 5You shall not bow down to them or worship them; for I the LORD your God am a jealous God, punishing children for the iniquity of parents, to the third and the fourth generation of those who reject me, 6but showing steadfast love to the thousandth generation*c* of those who love me and keep my commandments.

7 You shall not make wrongful use of the name of the LORD your God, for the LORD will not acquit anyone who misuses his name.

8 Remember the sabbath day, and keep it holy. 9Six days you shall labor and do all your work. 10But the seventh day is a sabbath to the LORD your God; you shall not do any work—you, your son or your daughter, your male or female slave, your livestock, or the alien resident in your towns. 11For in six days the LORD made heaven and earth, the sea, and all that is in them, but rested the seventh day; therefore the LORD blessed the sabbath day and consecrated it.

12 Honor your father and your mother, so that your days may be long in the land that the LORD your God is giving you.

a Heb lacks *with arrows*   *b* Or *besides*   *c* Or *to thousands*

13 You shall not murder. *a*

14 You shall not commit adultery.

15 You shall not steal.

16 You shall not bear false witness against your neighbor.

17 You shall not covet your neighbor's house; you shall not covet your neighbor's wife, or male or female slave, or ox, or donkey, or anything that belongs to your neighbor.

18 When all the people witnessed the thunder and lightning, the sound of the trumpet, and the mountain smoking, they were afraid *b* and trembled and stood at a distance, 19and said to Moses, "You speak to us, and we will listen; but do not let God speak to us, or we will die." 20Moses said to the people, "Do not be afraid; for God has come only to test you and to put the fear of him upon you so that you do not sin." 21Then the people stood at a distance, while Moses drew near to the thick darkness where God was.

The Law concerning the Altar

22 The LORD said to Moses: Thus you shall say to the Israelites: "You have seen for yourselves that I spoke with you from heaven. 23You shall not make gods of silver alongside me, nor shall you make for yourselves gods of gold. 24You need make for me only an altar of earth and sacrifice on it your burnt offerings and your offerings of well-being, your sheep and your oxen; in every place where I cause my name to be remembered I will come to you and bless you. 25But if you make for me an altar of stone, do not build it of hewn stones; for if you use a chisel upon it you profane it. 26You shall not go up by steps to my altar, so that your nakedness may not be exposed on it."

The Law concerning Slaves

21 These are the ordinances that you shall set before them:

2 When you buy a male Hebrew slave, he shall serve six years, but in the seventh he shall go out a free person, without debt. 3If he comes in single, he shall go out single; if he comes in married, then his wife shall go out with him. 4If his master gives him a wife and she bears him sons or daughters, the wife and her children shall be her master's and he shall go out alone. 5But if the slave declares, "I love my master, my wife, and my children; I will not go out a free person," 6then his master shall bring him before God. *c* He shall be brought to the door or the doorpost; and his master shall pierce his ear with an awl; and he shall serve him for life.

7 When a man sells his daughter as a slave, she shall not go out as the male slaves do. 8If she does not please her master, who designated her for himself, then he shall let her be redeemed; he shall have no right to sell her to a foreign people, since he has dealt unfairly with her. 9If he designates her for his son, he shall deal with her as with a daughter. 10If he takes another wife to himself, he shall not diminish the food, clothing, or marital rights of the first wife. *d* 11And if he does not do these three things for her, she shall go out without debt, without payment of money.

The Law concerning Violence

12 Whoever strikes a person mortally shall be put to death. 13If it was not premeditated, but came about by an act of God, then I will appoint for you a place to which the killer may flee. 14But if someone willfully attacks and kills another by treachery, you shall take the killer from my altar for execution.

15 Whoever strikes father or mother shall be put to death.

16 Whoever kidnaps a person, whether that person has been sold or is still held in possession, shall be put to death.

17 Whoever curses father or mother shall be put to death.

18 When individuals quarrel and one strikes the other with a stone or fist so that the injured party, though not dead, is confined to bed, 19but recovers and walks around outside with the help of a staff, then the assailant shall be free of liability, except to pay for the loss of time, and to arrange for full recovery.

a Or *kill*   *b* Sam Gk Syr Vg: MT *they saw*   *c* Or *to the judges*   *d* Heb *of her*

20 When a slaveowner strikes a male or female slave with a rod and the slave dies immediately, the owner shall be punished. 21But if the slave survives a day or two, there is no punishment; for the slave is the owner's property.

22 When people who are fighting injure a pregnant woman so that there is a miscarriage, and yet no further harm follows, the one responsible shall be fined what the woman's husband demands, paying as much as the judges determine. 23If any harm follows, then you shall give life for life, 24eye for eye, tooth for tooth, hand for hand, foot for foot, 25burn for burn, wound for wound, stripe for stripe.

26 When a slaveowner strikes the eye of a male or female slave, destroying it, the owner shall let the slave go, a free person, to compensate for the eye. 27If the owner knocks out a tooth of a male or female slave, the slave shall be let go, a free person, to compensate for the tooth.

Laws concerning Property

28 When an ox gores a man or a woman to death, the ox shall be stoned, and its flesh shall not be eaten; but the owner of the ox shall not be liable. 29If the ox has been accustomed to gore in the past, and its owner has been warned but has not restrained it, and it kills a man or a woman, the ox shall be stoned, and its owner also shall be put to death. 30If a ransom is imposed on the owner, then the owner shall pay whatever is imposed for the redemption of the victim's life. 31If it gores a boy or a girl, the owner shall be dealt with according to this same rule. 32If the ox gores a male or female slave, the owner shall pay to the slaveowner thirty shekels of silver, and the ox shall be stoned.

33 If someone leaves a pit open, or digs a pit and does not cover it, and an ox or a donkey falls into it, 34the owner of the pit shall make restitution, giving money to its owner, but keeping the dead animal.

35 If someone's ox hurts the ox of another, so that it dies, then they shall sell the live ox and divide the price of it; and the dead animal they shall also divide. 36But if it was known that the ox was accustomed to gore in the past, and its owner has not restrained it, the owner shall restore ox for ox, but keep the dead animal.

Laws of Restitution

22 *a* When someone steals an ox or a sheep, and slaughters it or sells it, the thief shall pay five oxen for an ox, and four sheep for a sheep. *b* The thief shall make restitution, but if unable to do so, shall be sold for the theft. 4When the animal, whether ox or donkey or sheep, is found alive in the thief's possession, the thief shall pay double.

2*c* If a thief is found breaking in, and is beaten to death, no bloodguilt is incurred; 3but if it happens after sunrise, bloodguilt is incurred.

5 When someone causes a field or vineyard to be grazed over, or lets livestock loose to graze in someone else's field, restitution shall be made from the best in the owner's field or vineyard.

6 When fire breaks out and catches in thorns so that the stacked grain or the standing grain or the field is consumed, the one who started the fire shall make full restitution.

7 When someone delivers to a neighbor money or goods for safekeeping, and they are stolen from the neighbor's house, then the thief, if caught, shall pay double. 8If the thief is not caught, the owner of the house shall be brought before God,*d* to determine whether or not the owner had laid hands on the neighbor's goods.

9 In any case of disputed ownership involving ox, donkey, sheep, clothing, or any other loss, of which one party says, "This is mine," the case of both parties shall come before God;*d* the one whom God condemns*e* shall pay double to the other.

10 When someone delivers to another a donkey, ox, sheep, or any other animal for safekeeping, and it dies or is injured or is carried off,

---

a Ch 21.37 in Heb   *b* Verses 2, 3, and 4 rearranged thus: 3b, 4, 2, 3a   *c* Ch 22.1 in Heb   *d* Or *before the judges*
e Or *the judges condemn*

without anyone seeing it, [11] an oath before the LORD shall decide between the two of them that the one has not laid hands on the property of the other; the owner shall accept the oath, and no restitution shall be made. [12] But if it was stolen, restitution shall be made to its owner. [13] If it was mangled by beasts, let it be brought as evidence; restitution shall not be made for the mangled remains.

14 When someone borrows an animal from another and it is injured or dies, the owner not being present, full restitution shall be made. [15] If the owner was present, there shall be no restitution; if it was hired, only the hiring fee is due.

Social and Religious Laws

16 When a man seduces a virgin who is not engaged to be married, and lies with her, he shall give the bride-price for her and make her his wife. [17] But if her father refuses to give her to him, he shall pay an amount equal to the bride-price for virgins.

18 You shall not permit a female sorcerer to live.

19 Whoever lies with an animal shall be put to death.

20 Whoever sacrifices to any god, other than the LORD alone, shall be devoted to destruction.

21 You shall not wrong or oppress a resident alien, for you were aliens in the land of Egypt. [22] You shall not abuse any widow or orphan. [23] If you do abuse them, when they cry out to me, I will surely heed their cry; [24] my wrath will burn, and I will kill you with the sword, and your wives shall become widows and your children orphans.

25 If you lend money to my people, to the poor among you, you shall not deal with them as a creditor; you shall not exact interest from them. [26] If you take your neighbor's cloak in pawn, you shall restore it before the sun goes down; [27] for it may be your neighbor's only clothing to use as cover; in what else shall that person sleep? And if your neighbor cries out to me, I will listen, for I am compassionate.

28 You shall not revile God, or curse a leader of your people.

29 You shall not delay to make offerings from the fullness of your harvest and from the outflow of your presses. [a]

The firstborn of your sons you shall give to me. [30] You shall do the same with your oxen and with your sheep: seven days it shall remain with its mother; on the eighth day you shall give it to me.

31 You shall be people consecrated to me; therefore you shall not eat any meat that is mangled by beasts in the field; you shall throw it to the dogs.

Justice for All

23 You shall not spread a false report. You shall not join hands with the wicked to act as a malicious witness. [2] You shall not follow a majority in wrongdoing; when you bear witness in a lawsuit, you shall not side with the majority so as to pervert justice; [3] nor shall you be partial to the poor in a lawsuit.

4 When you come upon your enemy's ox or donkey going astray, you shall bring it back.

5 When you see the donkey of one who hates you lying under its burden and you would hold back from setting it free, you must help to set it free. [a]

6 You shall not pervert the justice due to your poor in their lawsuits. [7] Keep far from a false charge, and do not kill the innocent and those in the right, for I will not acquit the guilty. [8] You shall take no bribe, for a bribe blinds the officials, and subverts the cause of those who are in the right.

9 You shall not oppress a resident alien; you know the heart of an alien, for you were aliens in the land of Egypt.

Sabbatical Year and Sabbath

10 For six years you shall sow your land and gather in its yield; [11] but the seventh year you shall let it rest and lie fallow, so that the poor of your people may eat; and what they leave the wild animals may eat. You shall do the

---

a Meaning of Heb uncertain

same with your vineyard, and with your olive orchard.

12 Six days you shall do your work, but on the seventh day you shall rest, so that your ox and your donkey may have relief, and your homeborn slave and the resident alien may be refreshed. 13Be attentive to all that I have said to you. Do not invoke the names of other gods; do not let them be heard on your lips.

The Annual Festivals

14 Three times in the year you shall hold a festival for me. 15You shall observe the festival of unleavened bread; as I commanded you, you shall eat unleavened bread for seven days at the appointed time in the month of Abib, for in it you came out of Egypt.

No one shall appear before me empty-handed.

16 You shall observe the festival of harvest, of the first fruits of your labor, of what you sow in the field. You shall observe the festival of ingathering at the end of the year, when you gather in from the field the fruit of your labor. 17Three times in the year all your males shall appear before the Lord GOD.

18 You shall not offer the blood of my sacrifice with anything leavened, or let the fat of my festival remain until the morning.

19 The choicest of the first fruits of your ground you shall bring into the house of the LORD your God.

You shall not boil a kid in its mother's milk.

The Conquest of Canaan Promised

20 I am going to send an angel in front of you, to guard you on the way and to bring you to the place that I have prepared. 21Be attentive to him and listen to his voice; do not rebel against him, for he will not pardon your transgression; for my name is in him.

22 But if you listen attentively to his voice and do all that I say, then I will be an enemy to your enemies and a foe to your foes.

23 When my angel goes in front of you, and brings you to the Amorites, the Hittites, the

Perizzites, the Canaanites, the Hivites, and the Jebusites, and I blot them out, 24you shall not bow down to their gods, or worship them, or follow their practices, but you shall utterly demolish them and break their pillars in pieces. 25You shall worship the LORD your God, and I*a* will bless your bread and your water; and I will take sickness away from among you. 26No one shall miscarry or be barren in your land; I will fulfill the number of your days. 27I will send my terror in front of you, and will throw into confusion all the people against whom you shall come, and I will make all your enemies turn their backs to you. 28And I will send the pestilence*b* in front of you, which shall drive out the Hivites, the Canaanites, and the Hittites from before you. 29I will not drive them out from before you in one year, or the land would become desolate and the wild animals would multiply against you. 30Little by little I will drive them out from before you, until you have increased and possess the land. 31I will set your borders from the Red Sea*c* to the sea of the Philistines, and from the wilderness to the Euphrates; for I will hand over to you the inhabitants of the land, and you shall drive them out before you. 32You shall make no covenant with them and their gods. 33They shall not live in your land, or they will make you sin against me; for if you worship their gods, it will surely be a snare to you.

The Blood of the Covenant

24 Then he said to Moses, "Come up to the LORD, you and Aaron, Nadab, and Abihu, and seventy of the elders of Israel, and worship at a distance. 2Moses alone shall come near the LORD; but the others shall not come near, and the people shall not come up with him."

3 Moses came and told the people all the words of the LORD and all the ordinances; and all the people answered with one voice, and said, "All the words that the LORD has spoken we will do." 4And Moses wrote down all the words of the LORD. He rose early in the morn-

---

a Gk Vg: Heb *he*   *b* Or *hornets*: Meaning of Heb uncertain   *c* Or *Sea of Reeds* ing, and built an altar at the foot of the mountain, and set up twelve pillars, corresponding to the twelve tribes of Israel. 5He sent young men of the people of Israel, who offered burnt offerings and sacrificed oxen as offerings of well-being to the LORD. 6Moses took half of the blood and put it in basins, and half of the blood he dashed against the altar. 7Then he took the book of the covenant, and read it in the hearing of the people; and they said, "All that the LORD has spoken we will do, and we will be obedient." 8Moses took the blood and dashed it on the people, and said, "See the blood of the covenant that the LORD has made with you in accordance with all these words."

On the Mountain with God

9 Then Moses and Aaron, Nadab, and Abihu, and seventy of the elders of Israel went up, 10and they saw the God of Israel. Under his feet there was something like a pavement of sapphire stone, like the very heaven for clearness. 11Godᵃ did not lay his hand on the chief men of the people of Israel; also they beheld God, and they ate and drank.

12 The LORD said to Moses, "Come up to me on the mountain, and wait there; and I will give you the tablets of stone, with the law and the commandment, which I have written for their instruction." 13So Moses set out with his assistant Joshua, and Moses went up into the mountain of God. 14To the elders he had said, "Wait here for us, until we come to you again; for Aaron and Hur are with you; whoever has a dispute may go to them."

15 Then Moses went up on the mountain, and the cloud covered the mountain. 16The glory of the LORD settled on Mount Sinai, and the cloud covered it for six days; on the seventh day he called to Moses out of the cloud. 17Now the appearance of the glory of the LORD was like a devouring fire on the top of the mountain in the sight of the people of Israel. 18Moses entered the cloud, and went up on the mountain. Moses was on the mountain for forty days and forty nights.

Offerings for the Tabernacle

25 The LORD said to Moses: 2Tell the Israelites to take for me an offering; from all whose hearts prompt them to give you shall receive the offering for me. 3This is the offering that you shall receive from them: gold, silver, and bronze, 4blue, purple, and crimson yarns and fine linen, goats' hair, 5tanned rams' skins, fine leather,ᵇ acacia wood, 6oil for the lamps, spices for the anointing oil and for the fragrant incense, 7onyx stones and gems to be set in the ephod and for the breastpiece. 8And have them make me a sanctuary, so that I may dwell among them. 9In accordance with all that I show you concerning the pattern of the tabernacle and of all its furniture, so you shall make it.

The Ark of the Covenant

10 They shall make an ark of acacia wood; it shall be two and a half cubits long, a cubit and a half wide, and a cubit and a half high. 11You shall overlay it with pure gold, inside and outside you shall overlay it, and you shall make a molding of gold upon it all around. 12You shall cast four rings of gold for it and put them on its four feet, two rings on the one side of it, and two rings on the other side. 13You shall make poles of acacia wood, and overlay them with gold. 14And you shall put the poles into the rings on the sides of the ark, by which to carry the ark. 15The poles shall remain in the rings of the ark; they shall not be taken from it. 16You shall put into the ark the covenantᶜ that I shall give you.

17 Then you shall make a mercy seatᵈ of pure gold; two cubits and a half shall be its length, and a cubit and a half its width. 18You shall make two cherubim of gold; you shall make them of hammered work, at the two ends of the mercy seat.ᵉ 19Make one cherub at the one end, and one cherub at the other; of one piece with the mercy seatᵉ you shall make the cherubim at its two ends. 20The cherubim shall spread out their wings above, overshadowing the mercy seatᵉ with their wings. They

---

a Heb *He*　　*b* Meaning of Heb uncertain　　*c* Or *treaty*, or *testimony*; Heb *eduth*　　*d* Or *a cover*　　*e* Or *the cover* shall face one to another; the faces of the cherubim shall be turned toward the mercy seat. *a* ²¹You shall put the mercy seat *a* on the top of the ark; and in the ark you shall put the covenant *b* that I shall give you. ²²There I will meet with you, and from above the mercy seat, *a* from between the two cherubim that are on the ark of the covenant, *b* I will deliver to you all my commands for the Israelites.

The Table for the Bread of the Presence

23 You shall make a table of acacia wood, two cubits long, one cubit wide, and a cubit and a half high. ²⁴You shall overlay it with pure gold, and make a molding of gold around it. ²⁵You shall make around it a rim a handbreadth wide, and a molding of gold around the rim. ²⁶You shall make for it four rings of gold, and fasten the rings to the four corners at its four legs. ²⁷The rings that hold the poles used for carrying the table shall be close to the rim. ²⁸You shall make the poles of acacia wood, and overlay them with gold, and the table shall be carried with these. ²⁹You shall make its plates and dishes for incense, and its flagons and bowls with which to pour drink offerings; you shall make them of pure gold. ³⁰And you shall set the bread of the Presence on the table before me always.

The Lampstand

31 You shall make a lampstand of pure gold. The base and the shaft of the lampstand shall be made of hammered work; its cups, its calyxes, and its petals shall be of one piece with it; ³²and there shall be six branches going out of its sides, three branches of the lampstand out of one side of it and three branches of the lampstand out of the other side of it; ³³three cups shaped like almond blossoms, each with calyx and petals, on one branch, and three cups shaped like almond blossoms, each with calyx and petals, on the other branch—so for the six branches going out of the lampstand. ³⁴On the lampstand itself there shall be four cups shaped like almond blossoms, each with its calyxes and petals. ³⁵There shall be a calyx of one piece with it under the first pair of branches, a calyx of one piece with it under the next pair of branches, and a calyx of one piece with it under the last pair of branches—so for the six branches that go out of the lampstand. ³⁶Their calyxes and their branches shall be of one piece with it, the whole of it one hammered piece of pure gold. ³⁷You shall make the seven lamps for it; and the lamps shall be set up so as to give light on the space in front of it. ³⁸Its snuffers and trays shall be of pure gold. ³⁹It, and all these utensils, shall be made from a talent of pure gold. ⁴⁰And see that you make them according to the pattern for them, which is being shown you on the mountain.

The Tabernacle

26 Moreover you shall make the tabernacle with ten curtains of fine twisted linen, and blue, purple, and crimson yarns; you shall make them with cherubim skillfully worked into them. ²The length of each curtain shall be twenty-eight cubits, and the width of each curtain four cubits; all the curtains shall be of the same size. ³Five curtains shall be joined to one another; and the other five curtains shall be joined to one another. ⁴You shall make loops of blue on the edge of the outermost curtain in the first set; and likewise you shall make loops on the edge of the outermost curtain in the second set. ⁵You shall make fifty loops on the one curtain, and you shall make fifty loops on the edge of the curtain that is in the second set; the loops shall be opposite one another. ⁶You shall make fifty clasps of gold, and join the curtains to one another with the clasps, so that the tabernacle may be one whole.

7 You shall also make curtains of goats' hair for a tent over the tabernacle; you shall make eleven curtains. ⁸The length of each curtain shall be thirty cubits, and the width of each curtain four cubits; the eleven curtains shall be of the same size. ⁹You shall join five curtains by themselves, and six curtains by themselves, and the sixth curtain you shall dou-

---

a Or *the cover*   *b* Or *treaty*, or *testimony*; Heb *eduth* ble over at the front of the tent. ¹⁰You shall make fifty loops on the edge of the curtain that is outermost in one set, and fifty loops on the edge of the curtain that is outermost in the second set.

11 You shall make fifty clasps of bronze, and put the clasps into the loops, and join the tent together, so that it may be one whole. ¹²The part that remains of the curtains of the tent, the half curtain that remains, shall hang over the back of the tabernacle. ¹³The cubit on the one side, and the cubit on the other side, of what remains in the length of the curtains of the tent, shall hang over the sides of the tabernacle, on this side and that side, to cover it. ¹⁴You shall make for the tent a covering of tanned rams' skins and an outer covering of fine leather. *a*

The Framework

15 You shall make upright frames of acacia wood for the tabernacle. ¹⁶Ten cubits shall be the length of a frame, and a cubit and a half the width of each frame. ¹⁷There shall be two pegs in each frame to fit the frames together; you shall make these for all the frames of the tabernacle. ¹⁸You shall make the frames for the tabernacle: twenty frames for the south side; ¹⁹and you shall make forty bases of silver under the twenty frames, two bases under the first frame for its two pegs, and two bases under the next frame for its two pegs; ²⁰and for the second side of the tabernacle, on the north side twenty frames, ²¹and their forty bases of silver, two bases under the first frame, and two bases under the next frame; ²²and for the rear of the tabernacle westward you shall make six frames. ²³You shall make two frames for corners of the tabernacle in the rear; ²⁴they shall be separate beneath, but joined at the top, at the first ring; it shall be the same with both of them; they shall form the two corners. ²⁵And so there shall be eight frames, with their bases of silver, sixteen bases; two bases under the first frame, and two bases under the next frame.

26 You shall make bars of acacia wood, five for the frames of the one side of the tabernacle, ²⁷and five bars for the frames of the other side of the tabernacle, and five bars for the frames of the side of the tabernacle at the rear westward. ²⁸The middle bar, halfway up the frames, shall pass through from end to end. ²⁹You shall overlay the frames with gold, and shall make their rings of gold to hold the bars; and you shall overlay the bars with gold. ³⁰Then you shall erect the tabernacle according to the plan for it that you were shown on the mountain.

The Curtain

31 You shall make a curtain of blue, purple, and crimson yarns, and of fine twisted linen; it shall be made with cherubim skillfully worked into it. ³²You shall hang it on four pillars of acacia overlaid with gold, which have hooks of gold and rest on four bases of silver. ³³You shall hang the curtain under the clasps, and bring the ark of the covenant *b* in there, within the curtain; and the curtain shall separate for you the holy place from the most holy. ³⁴You shall put the mercy seat *c* on the ark of the covenant *a* in the most holy place. ³⁵You shall set the table outside the curtain, and the lampstand on the south side of the tabernacle opposite the table; and you shall put the table on the north side.

36 You shall make a screen for the entrance of the tent, of blue, purple, and crimson yarns, and of fine twisted linen, embroidered with needlework. ³⁷You shall make for the screen five pillars of acacia, and overlay them with gold; their hooks shall be of gold, and you shall cast five bases of bronze for them.

The Altar of Burnt Offering

27 You shall make the altar of acacia wood, five cubits long and five cubits wide; the altar shall be square, and it shall be three cubits high. ²You shall make horns for it on its four corners; its horns shall be of one piece with it, and you shall overlay it with bronze. ³You shall make pots for it to receive

---

a Meaning of Heb uncertain   *b* Or *treaty*, or *testimony*; Heb *eduth*   *c* Or *the cover* its ashes, and shovels and basins and forks and firepans; you shall make all its utensils of bronze. 4You shall also make for it a grating, a network of bronze; and on the net you shall make four bronze rings at its four corners. 5You shall set it under the ledge of the altar so that the net shall extend halfway down the altar. 6You shall make poles for the altar, poles of acacia wood, and overlay them with bronze; 7the poles shall be put through the rings, so that the poles shall be on the two sides of the altar when it is carried. 8You shall make it hollow, with boards. They shall be made just as you were shown on the mountain.

The Court and Its Hangings

9 You shall make the court of the tabernacle. On the south side the court shall have hangings of fine twisted linen one hundred cubits long for that side; 10its twenty pillars and their twenty bases shall be of bronze, but the hooks of the pillars and their bands shall be of silver. 11Likewise for its length on the north side there shall be hangings one hundred cubits long, their pillars twenty and their bases twenty, of bronze, but the hooks of the pillars and their bands shall be of silver. 12For the width of the court on the west side there shall be fifty cubits of hangings, with ten pillars and ten bases. 13The width of the court on the front to the east shall be fifty cubits. 14There shall be fifteen cubits of hangings on the one side, with three pillars and three bases. 15There shall be fifteen cubits of hangings on the other side, with three pillars and three bases. 16For the gate of the court there shall be a screen twenty cubits long, of blue, purple, and crimson yarns, and of fine twisted linen, embroidered with needlework; it shall have four pillars and with them four bases. 17All the pillars around the court shall be banded with silver; their hooks shall be of silver, and their bases of bronze. 18The length of the court shall be one hundred cubits, the width fifty, and the height five cubits, with hangings of fine twisted linen and bases of bronze. 19All the utensils of the tabernacle for every use, and all its pegs and all the pegs of the court, shall be of bronze.

The Oil for the Lamp

20 You shall further command the Israelites to bring you pure oil of beaten olives for the light, so that a lamp may be set up to burn regularly. 21In the tent of meeting, outside the curtain that is before the covenant,[a] Aaron and his sons shall tend it from evening to morning before the LORD. It shall be a perpetual ordinance to be observed throughout their generations by the Israelites.

Vestments for the Priesthood

28 Then bring near to you your brother Aaron, and his sons with him, from among the Israelites, to serve me as priests— Aaron and Aaron's sons, Nadab and Abihu, Eleazar and Ithamar. 2You shall make sacred vestments for the glorious adornment of your brother Aaron. 3And you shall speak to all who have ability, whom I have endowed with skill, that they make Aaron's vestments to consecrate him for my priesthood. 4These are the vestments that they shall make: a breastpiece, an ephod, a robe, a checkered tunic, a turban, and a sash. When they make these sacred vestments for your brother Aaron and his sons to serve me as priests, 5they shall use gold, blue, purple, and crimson yarns, and fine linen.

The Ephod

6 They shall make the ephod of gold, of blue, purple, and crimson yarns, and of fine twisted linen, skillfully worked. 7It shall have two shoulder-pieces attached to its two edges, so that it may be joined together. 8The decorated band on it shall be of the same workmanship and materials, of gold, of blue, purple, and crimson yarns, and of fine twisted linen. 9You shall take two onyx stones, and engrave on them the names of the sons of Israel, 10six of their names on the one stone, and the names of the remaining six on the other stone, in the order of their birth. 11As a gem-

a Or *treaty*, or *testimony*; Heb *eduth*

cutter engraves signets, so you shall engrave the two stones with the names of the sons of Israel; you shall mount them in settings of gold filigree. 12You shall set the two stones on the shoulder-pieces of the ephod, as stones of remembrance for the sons of Israel; and Aaron shall bear their names before the LORD on his two shoulders for remembrance. 13You shall make settings of gold filigree, 14and two chains of pure gold, twisted like cords; and you shall attach the corded chains to the settings.

The Breastplate

15 You shall make a breastpiece of judgment, in skilled work; you shall make it in the style of the ephod; of gold, of blue and purple and crimson yarns, and of fine twisted linen you shall make it. 16It shall be square and doubled, a span in length and a span in width. 17You shall set in it four rows of stones. A row of carnelian,*a* chrysolite, and emerald shall be the first row; 18and the second row a turquoise, a sapphire,*b* and a moonstone; 19and the third row a jacinth, an agate, and an amethyst; 20and the fourth row a beryl, an onyx, and a jasper; they shall be set in gold filigree. 21There shall be twelve stones with names corresponding to the names of the sons of Israel; they shall be like signets, each engraved with its name, for the twelve tribes. 22You shall make for the breastpiece chains of pure gold, twisted like cords; 23and you shall make for the breastpiece two rings of gold, and put the two rings on the two edges of the breastpiece. 24You shall put the two cords of gold in the two rings at the edges of the breastpiece; 25the two ends of the two cords you shall attach to the two settings, and so attach it in front to the shoulder-pieces of the ephod. 26You shall make two rings of gold, and put them at the two ends of the breastpiece, on its inside edge next to the ephod. 27You shall make two rings of gold, and attach them in front to the lower part of the two shoulder-pieces of the ephod, at its joining above the decorated band of the ephod. 28The breastpiece shall be bound by its rings to the rings of the ephod with a blue cord, so that it may lie on the decorated band of the ephod, and so that the breastpiece shall not come loose from the ephod. 29So Aaron shall bear the names of the sons of Israel in the breastpiece of judgment on his heart when he goes into the holy place, for a continual remembrance before the LORD. 30In the breastpiece of judgment you shall put the Urim and the Thummim, and they shall be on Aaron's heart when he goes in before the LORD; thus Aaron shall bear the judgment of the Israelites on his heart before the LORD continually.

Other Priestly Vestments

31 You shall make the robe of the ephod all of blue. 32It shall have an opening for the head in the middle of it, with a woven binding around the opening, like the opening in a coat of mail,*c* so that it may not be torn. 33On its lower hem you shall make pomegranates of blue, purple, and crimson yarns, all around the lower hem, with bells of gold between them all around— 34a golden bell and a pomegranate alternating all around the lower hem of the robe. 35Aaron shall wear it when he ministers, and its sound shall be heard when he goes into the holy place before the LORD, and when he comes out, so that he may not die.

36 You shall make a rosette of pure gold, and engrave on it, like the engraving of a signet, "Holy to the LORD." 37You shall fasten it on the turban with a blue cord; it shall be on the front of the turban. 38It shall be on Aaron's forehead, and Aaron shall take on himself any guilt incurred in the holy offering that the Israelites consecrate as their sacred donations; it shall always be on his forehead, in order that they may find favor before the LORD.

39 You shall make the checkered tunic of fine linen, and you shall make a turban of fine linen, and you shall make a sash embroidered with needlework.

40 For Aaron's sons you shall make tunics and sashes and headdresses; you shall make them for their glorious adornment. 41You shall

---

a The identity of several of these stones is uncertain　　*b* Or *lapis lazuli*　　*c* Meaning of Heb uncertain put them on your brother Aaron, and on his sons with him, and shall anoint them and ordain them and consecrate them, so that they may serve me as priests. 42You shall make for them linen undergarments to cover their naked flesh; they shall reach from the hips to the thighs; 43Aaron and his sons shall wear them when they go into the tent of meeting, or when they come near the altar to minister in the holy place; or they will bring guilt on themselves and die. This shall be a perpetual ordinance for him and for his descendants after him.

The Ordination of the Priests

29 Now this is what you shall do to them to consecrate them, so that they may serve me as priests. Take one young bull and two rams without blemish, 2and unleavened bread, unleavened cakes mixed with oil, and unleavened wafers spread with oil. You shall make them of choice wheat flour. 3You shall put them in one basket and bring them in the basket, and bring the bull and the two rams. 4You shall bring Aaron and his sons to the entrance of the tent of meeting, and wash them with water. 5Then you shall take the vestments, and put on Aaron the tunic and the robe of the ephod, and the ephod, and the breastpiece, and gird him with the decorated band of the ephod; 6and you shall set the turban on his head, and put the holy diadem on the turban. 7You shall take the anointing oil, and pour it on his head and anoint him. 8Then you shall bring his sons, and put tunics on them, 9and you shall gird them with sashes a and tie headdresses on them; and the priesthood shall be theirs by a perpetual ordinance. You shall then ordain Aaron and his sons.

10 You shall bring the bull in front of the tent of meeting. Aaron and his sons shall lay their hands on the head of the bull, 11and you shall slaughter the bull before the LORD, at the entrance of the tent of meeting, 12and shall take some of the blood of the bull and put it on the horns of the altar with your finger, and all the rest of the blood you shall pour out at the base of the altar. 13You shall take all the fat that covers the entrails, and the appendage of the liver, and the two kidneys with the fat that is on them, and turn them into smoke on the altar. 14But the flesh of the bull, and its skin, and its dung, you shall burn with fire outside the camp; it is a sin offering.

15 Then you shall take one of the rams, and Aaron and his sons shall lay their hands on the head of the ram, 16and you shall slaughter the ram, and shall take its blood and dash it against all sides of the altar. 17Then you shall cut the ram into its parts, and wash its entrails and its legs, and put them with its parts and its head, 18and turn the whole ram into smoke on the altar; it is a burnt offering to the LORD; it is a pleasing odor, an offering by fire to the LORD.

19 You shall take the other ram; and Aaron and his sons shall lay their hands on the head of the ram, 20and you shall slaughter the ram, and take some of its blood and put it on the lobe of Aaron's right ear and on the lobes of the right ears of his sons, and on the thumbs of their right hands, and on the big toes of their right feet, and dash the rest of the blood against all sides of the altar. 21Then you shall take some of the blood that is on the altar, and some of the anointing oil, and sprinkle it on Aaron and his vestments and on his sons and his sons' vestments with him; then he and his vestments shall be holy, as well as his sons and his sons' vestments.

22 You shall also take the fat of the ram, the fat tail, the fat that covers the entrails, the appendage of the liver, the two kidneys with the fat that is on them, and the right thigh (for it is a ram of ordination), 23and one loaf of bread, one cake of bread made with oil, and one wafer, out of the basket of unleavened bread that is before the LORD; 24and you shall place all these on the palms of Aaron and on the palms of his sons, and raise them as an elevation offering before the LORD. 25Then you shall take them from their hands, and turn them into smoke on the altar on top of the

a Gk: Heb sashes, Aaron and his sons

burnt offering of pleasing odor before the LORD; it is an offering by fire to the LORD.

26 You shall take the breast of the ram of Aaron's ordination and raise it as an elevation offering before the LORD; and it shall be your portion. ²⁷You shall consecrate the breast that was raised as an elevation offering and the thigh that was raised as an elevation offering from the ram of ordination, from that which belonged to Aaron and his sons. ²⁸These things shall be a perpetual ordinance for Aaron and his sons from the Israelites, for this is an offering; and it shall be an offering by the Israelites from their sacrifice of offerings of well-being, their offering to the LORD.

29 The sacred vestments of Aaron shall be passed on to his sons after him; they shall be anointed in them and ordained in them. ³⁰The son who is priest in his place shall wear them seven days, when he comes into the tent of meeting to minister in the holy place.

31 You shall take the ram of ordination, and boil its flesh in a holy place; ³²and Aaron and his sons shall eat the flesh of the ram and the bread that is in the basket, at the entrance of the tent of meeting. ³³They themselves shall eat the food by which atonement is made, to ordain and consecrate them, but no one else shall eat of them, because they are holy. ³⁴If any of the flesh for the ordination, or of the bread, remains until the morning, then you shall burn the remainder with fire; it shall not be eaten, because it is holy.

35 Thus you shall do to Aaron and to his sons, just as I have commanded you; through seven days you shall ordain them. ³⁶Also every day you shall offer a bull as a sin offering for atonement. Also you shall offer a sin offering for the altar, when you make atonement for it, and shall anoint it, to consecrate it. ³⁷Seven days you shall make atonement for the altar, and consecrate it, and the altar shall be most holy; whatever touches the altar shall become holy.

The Daily Offerings

38 Now this is what you shall offer on the altar: two lambs a year old regularly each day. ³⁹One lamb you shall offer in the morning, and the other lamb you shall offer in the evening; ⁴⁰and with the first lamb one-tenth of a measure of choice flour mixed with one-fourth of a hin of beaten oil, and one-fourth of a hin of wine for a drink offering. ⁴¹And the other lamb you shall offer in the evening, and shall offer with it a grain offering and its drink offering, as in the morning, for a pleasing odor, an offering by fire to the LORD. ⁴²It shall be a regular burnt offering throughout your generations at the entrance of the tent of meeting before the LORD, where I will meet with you, to speak to you there. ⁴³I will meet with the Israelites there, and it shall be sanctified by my glory; ⁴⁴I will consecrate the tent of meeting and the altar; Aaron also and his sons I will consecrate, to serve me as priests. ⁴⁵I will dwell among the Israelites, and I will be their God. ⁴⁶And they shall know that I am the LORD their God, who brought them out of the land of Egypt that I might dwell among them; I am the LORD their God.

The Altar of Incense

30 You shall make an altar on which to offer incense; you shall make it of acacia wood. ²It shall be one cubit long, and one cubit wide; it shall be square, and shall be two cubits high; its horns shall be of one piece with it. ³You shall overlay it with pure gold, its top, and its sides all around and its horns; and you shall make for it a molding of gold all around. ⁴And you shall make two golden rings for it; under its molding on two opposite sides of it you shall make them, and they shall hold the poles with which to carry it. ⁵You shall make the poles of acacia wood, and overlay them with gold. ⁶You shall place it in front of the curtain that is above the ark of the covenant,ᵃ in front of the mercy seatᵇ that is over the covenant,ᵃ where I will meet with you. ⁷Aaron shall offer fragrant incense on it; every morn-

---

a Or *treaty,* or *testimony;* Heb *eduth*   *b* Or *the cover* ing when he dresses the lamps he shall offer it, [8]and when Aaron sets up the lamps in the evening, he shall offer it, a regular incense offering before the LORD throughout your generations. [9]You shall not offer unholy incense on it, or a burnt offering, or a grain offering; and you shall not pour a drink offering on it. [10]Once a year Aaron shall perform the rite of atonement on its horns. Throughout your generations he shall perform the atonement for it once a year with the blood of the atoning sin offering. It is most holy to the LORD.

The Half Shekel for the Sanctuary

11 The LORD spoke to Moses: [12]When you take a census of the Israelites to register them, at registration all of them shall give a ransom for their lives to the LORD, so that no plague may come upon them for being registered. [13]This is what each one who is registered shall give: half a shekel according to the shekel of the sanctuary (the shekel is twenty gerahs), half a shekel as an offering to the LORD. [14]Each one who is registered, from twenty years old and upward, shall give the LORD's offering. [15]The rich shall not give more, and the poor shall not give less, than the half shekel, when you bring this offering to the LORD to make atonement for your lives. [16]You shall take the atonement money from the Israelites and shall designate it for the service of the tent of meeting; before the LORD it will be a reminder to the Israelites of the ransom given for your lives.

The Bronze Basin

17 The LORD spoke to Moses: [18]You shall make a bronze basin with a bronze stand for washing. You shall put it between the tent of meeting and the altar, and you shall put water in it; [19]with the water[a] Aaron and his sons shall wash their hands and their feet. [20]When they go into the tent of meeting, or when they come near the altar to minister, to make an offering by fire to the LORD, they shall wash with water, so that they may not die. [21]They shall wash their hands and their feet, so that they may

not die: it shall be a perpetual ordinance for them, for him and for his descendants throughout their generations.

The Anointing Oil and Incense

22 The LORD spoke to Moses: [23]Take the finest spices: of liquid myrrh five hundred shekels, and of sweet-smelling cinnamon half as much, that is, two hundred fifty, and two hundred fifty of aromatic cane, [24]and five hundred of cassia—measured by the sanctuary shekel—and a hin of olive oil; [25]and you shall make of these a sacred anointing oil blended as by the perfumer; it shall be a holy anointing oil. [26]With it you shall anoint the tent of meeting and the ark of the covenant,[b] [27]and the table and all its utensils, and the lampstand and its utensils, and the altar of incense, [28]and the altar of burnt offering with all its utensils, and the basin with its stand; [29]you shall consecrate them, so that they may be most holy; whatever touches them will become holy. [30]You shall anoint Aaron and his sons, and consecrate them, in order that they may serve me as priests. [31]You shall say to the Israelites, "This shall be my holy anointing oil throughout your generations. [32]It shall not be used in any ordinary anointing of the body, and you shall make no other like it in composition; it is holy, and it shall be holy to you. [33]Whoever compounds any like it or whoever puts any of it on an unqualified person shall be cut off from the people."

34 The LORD said to Moses: Take sweet spices, stacte, and onycha, and galbanum, sweet spices with pure frankincense (an equal part of each), [35]and make an incense blended as by the perfumer, seasoned with salt, pure and holy; [36]and you shall beat some of it into powder, and put part of it before the covenant[b] in the tent of meeting where I shall meet with you; it shall be for you most holy. [37]When you make incense according to this composition, you shall not make it for yourselves; it shall be regarded by you as holy to the LORD. [38]Whoever makes any like it to use as perfume shall be cut off from the people.

---

a Heb *it*   *b* Or *treaty*, or *testimony*; Heb *eduth*

Bezalel and Oholiab

31 The LORD spoke to Moses: [2]See, I have called by name Bezalel son of Uri son of Hur, of the tribe of Judah: [3]and I have filled him with divine spirit,[a] with ability, intelligence, and knowledge in every kind of craft, [4]to devise artistic designs, to work in gold, silver, and bronze, [5]in cutting stones for setting, and in carving wood, in every kind of craft. [6]Moreover, I have appointed with him Oholiab son of Ahisamach, of the tribe of Dan; and I have given skill to all the skillful, so that they may make all that I have commanded you: [7]the tent of meeting, and the ark of the covenant,[b] and the mercy seat[c] that is on it, and all the furnishings of the tent, [8]the table and its utensils, and the pure lampstand with all its utensils, and the altar of incense, [9]and the altar of burnt offering with all its utensils, and the basin with its stand, [10]and the finely worked vestments, the holy vestments for the priest Aaron and the vestments of his sons, for their service as priests, [11]and the anointing oil and the fragrant incense for the holy place. They shall do just as I have commanded you.

The Sabbath Law

12 The LORD said to Moses: [13]You yourself are to speak to the Israelites: "You shall keep my sabbaths, for this is a sign between me and you throughout your generations, given in order that you may know that I, the LORD, sanctify you. [14]You shall keep the sabbath, because it is holy for you; everyone who profanes it shall be put to death; whoever does any work on it shall be cut off from among the people. [15]Six days shall work be done, but the seventh day is a sabbath of solemn rest, holy to the LORD; whoever does any work on the sabbath day shall be put to death. [16]Therefore the Israelites shall keep the sabbath, observing the sabbath throughout their generations, as a perpetual covenant. [17]It is a sign forever between me and the people of Israel that in six days the LORD made heaven and earth, and on the seventh day he rested, and was refreshed."

The Two Tablets of the Covenant

18 When God[d] finished speaking with Moses on Mount Sinai, he gave him the two tablets of the covenant,[b] tablets of stone, written with the finger of God.

The Golden Calf

32 When the people saw that Moses delayed to come down from the mountain, the people gathered around Aaron, and said to him, "Come, make gods for us, who shall go before us; as for this Moses, the man who brought us up out of the land of Egypt, we do not know what has become of him." [2]Aaron said to them, "Take off the gold rings that are on the ears of your wives, your sons, and your daughters, and bring them to me." [3]So all the people took off the gold rings from their ears, and brought them to Aaron. [4]He took the gold from them, formed it in a mold,[e] and cast an image of a calf; and they said, "These are your gods, O Israel, who brought you up out of the land of Egypt!" [5]When Aaron saw this, he built an altar before it; and Aaron made proclamation and said, "Tomorrow shall be a festival to the LORD." [6]They rose early the next day, and offered burnt offerings and brought sacrifices of well-being; and the people sat down to eat and drink, and rose up to revel.

7 The LORD said to Moses, "Go down at once! Your people, whom you brought up out of the land of Egypt, have acted perversely; [8]they have been quick to turn aside from the way that I commanded them; they have cast for themselves an image of a calf, and have worshiped it and sacrificed to it, and said, 'These are your gods, O Israel, who brought you up out of the land of Egypt!' " [9]The LORD said to Moses, "I have seen this people, how stiffnecked they are. [10]Now let me alone, so that my wrath may burn hot against them and I may consume them; and of you I will make a great nation."

11 But Moses implored the LORD his God, and said, "O LORD, why does your wrath burn

---

a Or with the spirit of God   b Or treaty, or testimony; Heb eduth   c Or the cover   d Heb he   e Or fashioned it with a graving tool; Meaning of Heb uncertain hot against your people, whom you brought out of the land of Egypt with great power and with a mighty hand? 12Why should the Egyptians say, 'It was with evil intent that he brought them out to kill them in the mountains, and to consume them from the face of the earth'? Turn from your fierce wrath; change your mind and do not bring disaster on your people. 13Remember Abraham, Isaac, and Israel, your servants, how you swore to them by your own self, saying to them, 'I will multiply your descendants like the stars of heaven, and all this land that I have promised I will give to your descendants, and they shall inherit it forever.'" 14And the LORD changed his mind about the disaster that he planned to bring on his people.

15 Then Moses turned and went down from the mountain, carrying the two tablets of the covenant*a* in his hands, tablets that were written on both sides, written on the front and on the back. 16The tablets were the work of God, and the writing was the writing of God, engraved upon the tablets. 17When Joshua heard the noise of the people as they shouted, he said to Moses, "There is a noise of war in the camp." 18But he said,

"It is not the sound made by victors,
    or the sound made by losers;
it is the sound of revelers that I hear."
19As soon as he came near the camp and saw the calf and the dancing, Moses' anger burned hot, and he threw the tablets from his hands and broke them at the foot of the mountain. 20He took the calf that they had made, burned it with fire, ground it to powder, scattered it on the water, and made the Israelites drink it.

21 Moses said to Aaron, "What did this people do to you that you have brought so great a sin upon them?" 22And Aaron said, "Do not let the anger of my lord burn hot; you know the people, that they are bent on evil. 23They said to me, 'Make us gods, who shall go before us; as for this Moses, the man who brought us up out of the land of Egypt, we do not know what has become of him.' 24So I said to them, 'Whoever has gold, take it off'; so they

gave it to me, and I threw it into the fire, and out came this calf!"

25 When Moses saw that the people were running wild (for Aaron had let them run wild, to the derision of their enemies), 26then Moses stood in the gate of the camp, and said, "Who is on the LORD's side? Come to me!" And all the sons of Levi gathered around him. 27He said to them, "Thus says the LORD, the God of Israel, 'Put your sword on your side, each of you! Go back and forth from gate to gate throughout the camp, and each of you kill your brother, your friend, and your neighbor.'" 28The sons of Levi did as Moses commanded, and about three thousand of the people fell on that day. 29Moses said, "Today you have ordained yourselves*b* for the service of the LORD, each one at the cost of a son or a brother, and so have brought a blessing on yourselves this day."

30 On the next day Moses said to the people, "You have sinned a great sin. But now I will go up to the LORD; perhaps I can make atonement for your sin." 31So Moses returned to the LORD and said, "Alas, this people has sinned a great sin; they have made for themselves gods of gold. 32But now, if you will only forgive their sin—but if not, blot me out of the book that you have written." 33But the LORD said to Moses, "Whoever has sinned against me I will blot out of my book. 34But now go, lead the people to the place about which I have spoken to you; see, my angel shall go in front of you. Nevertheless, when the day comes for punishment, I will punish them for their sin."

35 Then the LORD sent a plague on the people, because they made the calf—the one that Aaron made.

The Command to Leave Sinai

33 The LORD said to Moses, "Go, leave this place, you and the people whom you have brought up out of the land of Egypt, and go to the land of which I swore to Abraham, Isaac, and Jacob, saying, 'To your descendants I will give it.' 2I will send an angel be-

a Or *treaty*, or *testimony*; Heb *eduth*   *b* Gk Vg Compare Tg: Heb *Today ordain yourselves* fore you, and I will drive out the Canaanites, the Amorites, the Hittites, the Perizzites, the Hivites, and the Jebusites. ³Go up to a land flowing with milk and honey; but I will not go up among you, or I would consume you on the way, for you are a stiff-necked people."

4 When the people heard these harsh words, they mourned, and no one put on ornaments. ⁵For the LORD had said to Moses, "Say to the Israelites, 'You are a stiff-necked people; if for a single moment I should go up among you, I would consume you. So now take off your ornaments, and I will decide what to do to you.'" ⁶Therefore the Israelites stripped themselves of their ornaments, from Mount Horeb onward.

The Tent outside the Camp

7 Now Moses used to take the tent and pitch it outside the camp, far off from the camp; he called it the tent of meeting. And everyone who sought the LORD would go out to the tent of meeting, which was outside the camp. ⁸Whenever Moses went out to the tent, all the people would rise and stand, each of them, at the entrance of their tents and watch Moses until he had gone into the tent. ⁹When Moses entered the tent, the pillar of cloud would descend and stand at the entrance of the tent, and the LORD would speak with Moses. ¹⁰When all the people saw the pillar of cloud standing at the entrance of the tent, all the people would rise and bow down, all of them, at the entrance of their tent. ¹¹Thus the LORD used to speak to Moses face to face, as one speaks to a friend. Then he would return to the camp; but his young assistant, Joshua son of Nun, would not leave the tent.

Moses' Intercession

12 Moses said to the LORD, "See, you have said to me, 'Bring up this people'; but you have not let me know whom you will send with me. Yet you have said, 'I know you by name, and you have also found favor in my sight.' ¹³Now if I have found favor in your sight, show me

your ways, so that I may know you and find favor in your sight. Consider too that this nation is your people." ¹⁴He said, "My presence will go with you, and I will give you rest." ¹⁵And he said to him, "If your presence will not go, do not carry us up from here. ¹⁶For how shall it be known that I have found favor in your sight, I and your people, unless you go with us? In this way, we shall be distinct, I and your people, from every people on the face of the earth."

17 The LORD said to Moses, "I will do the very thing that you have asked; for you have found favor in my sight, and I know you by name." ¹⁸Moses said, "Show me your glory, I pray." ¹⁹And he said, "I will make all my goodness pass before you, and will proclaim before you the name, 'The LORD';ᵃ and I will be gracious to whom I will be gracious, and will show mercy on whom I will show mercy. ²⁰But," he said, "you cannot see my face; for no one shall see me and live." ²¹And the LORD continued, "See, there is a place by me where you shall stand on the rock; ²²and while my glory passes by I will put you in a cleft of the rock, and I will cover you with my hand until I have passed by; ²³then I will take away my hand, and you shall see my back; but my face shall not be seen."

Moses Makes New Tablets

34 The LORD said to Moses, "Cut two tablets of stone like the former ones, and I will write on the tablets the words that were on the former tablets, which you broke. ²Be ready in the morning, and come up in the morning to Mount Sinai and present yourself there to me, on the top of the mountain. ³No one shall come up with you, and do not let anyone be seen throughout all the mountain; and do not let flocks or herds graze in front of that mountain." ⁴So Moses cut two tablets of stone like the former ones; and he rose early in the morning and went up on Mount Sinai, as the LORD had commanded him, and took in his hand the two tablets of stone. ⁵The LORD descended in the cloud and stood with him there,

---

ᵃ Heb YHWH; see note at 3.15

and proclaimed the name, "The LORD." *a* 6The LORD passed before him, and proclaimed,

"The LORD, the LORD,
a God merciful and gracious,
slow to anger,
and abounding in steadfast love and
faithfulness,
7   keeping steadfast love for the
thousandth generation, *b*
forgiving iniquity and transgression and
sin,
yet by no means clearing the guilty,
but visiting the iniquity of the parents
upon the children
and the children's children,
to the third and the fourth generation."

8And Moses quickly bowed his head toward the earth, and worshiped. 9He said, "If now I have found favor in your sight, O Lord, I pray, let the Lord go with us. Although this is a stiff-necked people, pardon our iniquity and our sin, and take us for your inheritance."

The Covenant Renewed

10 He said: I hereby make a covenant. Before all your people I will perform marvels, such as have not been performed in all the earth or in any nation; and all the people among whom you live shall see the work of the LORD; for it is an awesome thing that I will do with you.

11 Observe what I command you today. See, I will drive out before you the Amorites, the Canaanites, the Hittites, the Perizzites, the Hivites, and the Jebusites. 12Take care not to make a covenant with the inhabitants of the land to which you are going, or it will become a snare among you. 13You shall tear down their altars, break their pillars, and cut down their sacred poles *c* 14(for you shall worship no other god, because the LORD, whose name is Jealous, is a jealous God). 15You shall not make a covenant with the inhabitants of the land, for when they prostitute themselves to their gods and sacrifice to their gods, someone among them will invite you, and you will eat of the sac-

rifice. 16And you will take wives from among their daughters for your sons, and their daughters who prostitute themselves to their gods will make your sons also prostitute themselves to their gods.

17 You shall not make cast idols.

18 You shall keep the festival of unleavened bread. Seven days you shall eat unleavened bread, as I commanded you, at the time appointed in the month of Abib; for in the month of Abib you came out from Egypt.

19 All that first opens the womb is mine, all your male *d* livestock, the firstborn of cow and sheep. 20The firstborn of a donkey you shall redeem with a lamb, or if you will not redeem it you shall break its neck. All the firstborn of your sons you shall redeem.

No one shall appear before me empty-handed.

21 Six days you shall work, but on the seventh day you shall rest; even in plowing time and in harvest time you shall rest. 22You shall observe the festival of weeks, the first fruits of wheat harvest, and the festival of ingathering at the turn of the year. 23Three times in the year all your males shall appear before the LORD God, the God of Israel. 24For I will cast out nations before you, and enlarge your borders; no one shall covet your land when you go up to appear before the LORD your God three times in the year.

25 You shall not offer the blood of my sacrifice with leaven, and the sacrifice of the festival of the passover shall not be left until the morning.

26 The best of the first fruits of your ground you shall bring to the house of the LORD your God.

You shall not boil a kid in its mother's milk.

27 The LORD said to Moses: Write these words; in accordance with these words I have made a covenant with you and with Israel. 28He was there with the LORD forty days and forty nights; he neither ate bread nor drank water. And he wrote on the tablets the words of the covenant, the ten commandments. *e*

a Heb *YHWH*; see note at 3.15   *b* Or *for thousands*   *c* Heb *Asherim*   *d* Gk Theodotion Vg Tg: Meaning of Heb uncertain   *e* Heb *words*

The Shining Face of Moses

29 Moses came down from Mount Sinai. As he came down from the mountain with the two tablets of the covenant*a* in his hand, Moses did not know that the skin of his face shone because he had been talking with God. ³⁰When Aaron and all the Israelites saw Moses, the skin of his face was shining, and they were afraid to come near him. ³¹But Moses called to them; and Aaron and all the leaders of the congregation returned to him, and Moses spoke with them. ³²Afterward all the Israelites came near, and he gave them in commandment all that the LORD had spoken with him on Mount Sinai. ³³When Moses had finished speaking with them, he put a veil on his face; ³⁴but whenever Moses went in before the LORD to speak with him, he would take the veil off, until he came out; and when he came out, and told the Israelites what he had been commanded, ³⁵the Israelites would see the face of Moses, that the skin of his face was shining; and Moses would put the veil on his face again, until he went in to speak with him.

Sabbath Regulations

35 Moses assembled all the congregation of the Israelites and said to them: These are the things that the LORD has commanded you to do: 2 Six days shall work be done, but on the seventh day you shall have a holy sabbath of solemn rest to the LORD; whoever does any work on it shall be put to death. ³You shall kindle no fire in all your dwellings on the sabbath day.

Preparations for Making the Tabernacle

4 Moses said to all the congregation of the Israelites: This is the thing that the LORD has commanded: ⁵Take from among you an offering to the LORD; let whoever is of a generous heart bring the LORD's offering: gold, silver, and bronze; ⁶blue, purple, and crimson yarns, and fine linen; goats' hair, ⁷tanned rams' skins, and fine leather;*b* acacia wood, ⁸oil for the light, spices for the anointing oil and for the fragrant incense, ⁹and onyx stones and gems to be set in the ephod and the breastpiece.

10 All who are skillful among you shall come and make all that the LORD has commanded: the tabernacle, ¹¹its tent and its covering, its clasps and its frames, its bars, its pillars, and its bases; ¹²the ark with its poles, the mercy seat,*c* and the curtain for the screen; ¹³the table with its poles and all its utensils, and the bread of the Presence; ¹⁴the lampstand also for the light, with its utensils and its lamps, and the oil for the light; ¹⁵and the altar of incense, with its poles, and the anointing oil and the fragrant incense, and the screen for the entrance, the entrance of the tabernacle; ¹⁶the altar of burnt offering, with its grating of bronze, its poles, and all its utensils, the basin with its stand; ¹⁷the hangings of the court, its pillars and its bases, and the screen for the gate of the court; ¹⁸the pegs of the tabernacle and the pegs of the court, and their cords; ¹⁹the finely worked vestments for ministering in the holy place, the holy vestments for the priest Aaron, and the vestments of his sons, for their service as priests.

Offerings for the Tabernacle

20 Then all the congregation of the Israelites withdrew from the presence of Moses. ²¹And they came, everyone whose heart was stirred, and everyone whose spirit was willing, and brought the LORD's offering to be used for the tent of meeting, and for all its service, and for the sacred vestments. ²²So they came, both men and women; all who were of a willing heart brought brooches and earrings and signet rings and pendants, all sorts of gold objects, everyone bringing an offering of gold to the LORD. ²³And everyone who possessed blue or purple or crimson yarn or fine linen or goats' hair or tanned rams' skins or fine leather,*b* brought them. ²⁴Everyone who could make an offering of silver or bronze brought it as the LORD's offering; and everyone who possessed acacia wood of any use in the work, brought it.

---

a Or *treaty*, or *testimony*; Heb *eduth*　　*b* Meaning of Heb uncertain　　*c* Or *the cover*

25All the skillful women spun with their hands, and brought what they had spun in blue and purple and crimson yarns and fine linen; 26all the women whose hearts moved them to use their skill spun the goats' hair. 27And the leaders brought onyx stones and gems to be set in the ephod and the breastpiece, 28and spices and oil for the light, and for the anointing oil, and for the fragrant incense. 29All the Israelite men and women whose hearts made them willing to bring anything for the work that the LORD had commanded by Moses to be done, brought it as a freewill offering to the LORD.

Bezalel and Oholiab

30 Then Moses said to the Israelites: See, the LORD has called by name Bezalel son of Uri son of Hur, of the tribe of Judah; 31he has filled him with divine spirit,a with skill, intelligence, and knowledge in every kind of craft, 32to devise artistic designs, to work in gold, silver, and bronze, 33in cutting stones for setting, and in carving wood, in every kind of craft. 34And he has inspired him to teach, both him and Oholiab son of Ahisamach, of the tribe of Dan. 35He has filled them with skill to do every kind of work done by an artisan or by a designer or by an embroiderer in blue, purple, and crimson yarns, and in fine linen, or by a weaver—by any sort of artisan or skilled designer.

36 Bezalel and Oholiab and every skillful one to whom the LORD has given skill and understanding to know how to do any work in the construction of the sanctuary shall work in accordance with all that the LORD has commanded.

2 Moses then called Bezalel and Oholiab and every skillful one to whom the LORD had given skill, everyone whose heart was stirred to come to do the work; 3and they received from Moses all the freewill offerings that the Israelites had brought for doing the work on the sanctuary. They still kept bringing him freewill offerings every morning, 4so that all the artisans who were doing every sort of task on the sanctuary came, each from the task being per-

formed, 5and said to Moses, "The people are bringing much more than enough for doing the work that the LORD has commanded us to do." 6So Moses gave command, and word was proclaimed throughout the camp: "No man or woman is to make anything else as an offering for the sanctuary." So the people were restrained from bringing; 7for what they had already brought was more than enough to do all the work.

Construction of the Tabernacle

8 All those with skill among the workers made the tabernacle with ten curtains; they were made of fine twisted linen, and blue, purple, and crimson yarns, with cherubim skillfully worked into them. 9The length of each curtain was twenty-eight cubits, and the width of each curtain four cubits; all the curtains were of the same size.

10 He joined five curtains to one another, and the other five curtains he joined to one another. 11He made loops of blue on the edge of the outermost curtain of the first set; likewise he made them on the edge of the outermost curtain of the second set; 12he made fifty loops on the one curtain, and he made fifty loops on the edge of the curtain that was in the second set; the loops were opposite one another. 13And he made fifty clasps of gold, and joined the curtains one to the other with clasps; so the tabernacle was one whole.

14 He also made curtains of goats' hair for a tent over the tabernacle; he made eleven curtains. 15The length of each curtain was thirty cubits, and the width of each curtain four cubits; the eleven curtains were of the same size. 16He joined five curtains by themselves, and six curtains by themselves. 17He made fifty loops on the edge of the outermost curtain of the one set, and fifty loops on the edge of the other connecting curtain. 18He made fifty clasps of bronze to join the tent together so that it might be one whole. 19And he made for the tent a covering of tanned rams' skins and an outer covering of fine leather.b

a Or the spirit of God   b Meaning of Heb uncertain

20 Then he made the upright frames for the tabernacle of acacia wood. ²¹Ten cubits was the length of a frame, and a cubit and a half the width of each frame. ²²Each frame had two pegs for fitting together; he did this for all the frames of the tabernacle. ²³The frames for the tabernacle he made in this way: twenty frames for the south side; ²⁴and he made forty bases of silver under the twenty frames, two bases under the first frame for its two pegs, and two bases under the next frame for its two pegs. ²⁵For the second side of the tabernacle, on the north side, he made twenty frames ²⁶and their forty bases of silver, two bases under the first frame and two bases under the next frame. ²⁷For the rear of the tabernacle westward he made six frames. ²⁸He made two frames for corners of the tabernacle in the rear. ²⁹They were separate beneath, but joined at the top, at the first ring; he made two of them in this way, for the two corners. ³⁰There were eight frames with their bases of silver: sixteen bases, under every frame two bases.

31 He made bars of acacia wood, five for the frames of the one side of the tabernacle, ³²and five bars for the frames of the other side of the tabernacle, and five bars for the frames of the tabernacle at the rear westward. ³³He made the middle bar to pass through from end to end halfway up the frames. ³⁴And he overlaid the frames with gold, and made rings of gold for them to hold the bars, and overlaid the bars with gold.

35 He made the curtain of blue, purple, and crimson yarns, and fine twisted linen, with cherubim skillfully worked into it. ³⁶For it he made four pillars of acacia, and overlaid them with gold; their hooks were of gold, and he cast for them four bases of silver. ³⁷He also made a screen for the entrance to the tent, of blue, purple, and crimson yarns, and fine twisted linen, embroidered with needlework; ³⁸and its five pillars with their hooks. He overlaid their capitals and their bases with gold, but their five bases were of bronze.

Making the Ark of the Covenant

37 Bezalel made the ark of acacia wood; it was two and a half cubits long, a cubit and a half wide, and a cubit and a half high. ²He overlaid it with pure gold inside and outside, and made a molding of gold around it. ³He cast for it four rings of gold for its four feet, two rings on its one side and two rings on its other side. ⁴He made poles of acacia wood, and overlaid them with gold, ⁵and put the poles into the rings on the sides of the ark, to carry the ark. ⁶He made a mercy seat*a* of pure gold; two cubits and a half was its length, and a cubit and a half its width. ⁷He made two cherubim of hammered gold; at the two ends of the mercy seat*b* he made them, ⁸one cherub at the one end, and one cherub at the other end; of one piece with the mercy seat*b* he made the cherubim at its two ends. ⁹The cherubim spread out their wings above, overshadowing the mercy seat*b* with their wings. They faced one another; the faces of the cherubim were turned toward the mercy seat.*b*

Making the Table for the Bread of the Presence

10 He also made the table of acacia wood, two cubits long, one cubit wide, and a cubit and a half high. ¹¹He overlaid it with pure gold, and made a molding of gold around it. ¹²He made around it a rim a handbreadth wide, and made a molding of gold around the rim. ¹³He cast for it four rings of gold, and fastened the rings to the four corners at its four legs. ¹⁴The rings that held the poles used for carrying the table were close to the rim. ¹⁵He made the poles of acacia wood to carry the table, and overlaid them with gold. ¹⁶And he made the vessels of pure gold that were to be on the table, its plates and dishes for incense, and its bowls and flagons with which to pour drink offerings.

Making the Lampstand

17 He also made the lampstand of pure gold. The base and the shaft of the lampstand were made of hammered work; its cups, its calyxes, and its petals were of one piece with

---

a Or *a cover*   *b* Or *the cover*

it. 18There were six branches going out of its sides, three branches of the lampstand out of one side of it and three branches of the lampstand out of the other side of it; 19three cups shaped like almond blossoms, each with calyx and petals, on one branch, and three cups shaped like almond blossoms, each with calyx and petals, on the other branch—so for the six branches going out of the lampstand. 20On the lampstand itself there were four cups shaped like almond blossoms, each with its calyxes and petals. 21There was a calyx of one piece with it under the first pair of branches, a calyx of one piece with it under the next pair of branches, and a calyx of one piece with it under the last pair of branches. 22Their calyxes and their branches were of one piece with it, the whole of it one hammered piece of pure gold. 23He made its seven lamps and its snuffers and its trays of pure gold. 24He made it and all its utensils of a talent of pure gold.

Making the Altar of Incense

25 He made the altar of incense of acacia wood, one cubit long, and one cubit wide; it was square, and was two cubits high; its horns were of one piece with it. 26He overlaid it with pure gold, its top, and its sides all around, and its horns; and he made for it a molding of gold all around, 27and made two golden rings for it under its molding, on two opposite sides of it, to hold the poles with which to carry it. 28And he made the poles of acacia wood, and overlaid them with gold.

Making the Anointing Oil and the Incense

29 He made the holy anointing oil also, and the pure fragrant incense, blended as by the perfumer.

Making the Altar of Burnt Offering

38 He made the altar of burnt offering also of acacia wood; it was five cubits long, and five cubits wide; it was square, and three cubits high. 2He made horns for it on its four corners; its horns were of one piece with it, and he overlaid it with bronze. 3He made all the utensils of the altar, the pots, the shovels, the basins, the forks, and the firepans: all its utensils he made of bronze. 4He made for the altar a grating, a network of bronze, under its ledge, extending halfway down. 5He cast four rings on the four corners of the bronze grating to hold the poles; 6he made the poles of acacia wood, and overlaid them with bronze. 7And he put the poles through the rings on the sides of the altar, to carry it with them; he made it hollow, with boards.

8 He made the basin of bronze with its stand of bronze, from the mirrors of the women who served at the entrance to the tent of meeting.

Making the Court of the Tabernacle

9 He made the court; for the south side the hangings of the court were of fine twisted linen, one hundred cubits long; 10its twenty pillars and their twenty bases were of bronze, but the hooks of the pillars and their bands were of silver. 11For the north side there were hangings one hundred cubits long; its twenty pillars and their twenty bases were of bronze, but the hooks of the pillars and their bands were of silver. 12For the west side there were hangings fifty cubits long, with ten pillars and ten bases; the hooks of the pillars and their bands were of silver. 13And for the front to the east, fifty cubits. 14The hangings for one side of the gate were fifteen cubits, with three pillars and three bases. 15And so for the other side; on each side of the gate of the court were hangings of fifteen cubits, with three pillars and three bases. 16All the hangings around the court were of fine twisted linen. 17The bases for the pillars were of bronze, but the hooks of the pillars and their bands were of silver; the overlaying of their capitals was also of silver, and all the pillars of the court were banded with silver. 18The screen for the entrance to the court was embroidered with needlework in blue, purple, and crimson yarns and fine twisted linen. It was twenty cubits long and, along the width of it, five cubits high, corresponding to the hangings of the court. 19There were four pillars; their four bases were of bronze, their hooks of silver, and the overlaying of their

capitals and their bands of silver. ²⁰All the pegs for the tabernacle and for the court all around were of bronze.

Materials of the Tabernacle

21 These are the records of the tabernacle, the tabernacle of the covenant,ᵃ which were drawn up at the commandment of Moses, the work of the Levites being under the direction of Ithamar son of the priest Aaron. ²²Bezalel son of Uri son of Hur, of the tribe of Judah, made all that the LORD commanded Moses; ²³and with him was Oholiab son of Ahisamach, of the tribe of Dan, engraver, designer, and embroiderer in blue, purple, and crimson yarns, and in fine linen.

24 All the gold that was used for the work, in all the construction of the sanctuary, the gold from the offering, was twenty-nine talents and seven hundred thirty shekels, measured by the sanctuary shekel. ²⁵The silver from those of the congregation who were counted was one hundred talents and one thousand seven hundred seventy-five shekels, measured by the sanctuary shekel; ²⁶a beka a head (that is, half a shekel, measured by the sanctuary shekel), for everyone who was counted in the census, from twenty years old and upward, for six hundred three thousand, five hundred fifty men. ²⁷The hundred talents of silver were for casting the bases of the sanctuary, and the bases of the curtain; one hundred bases for the hundred talents, a talent for a base. ²⁸Of the thousand seven hundred seventy-five shekels he made hooks for the pillars, and overlaid their capitals and made bands for them. ²⁹The bronze that was contributed was seventy talents, and two thousand four hundred shekels; ³⁰with it he made the bases for the entrance of the tent of meeting, the bronze altar and the bronze grating for it and all the utensils of the altar, ³¹the bases all around the court, and the bases of the gate of the court, all the pegs of the tabernacle, and all the pegs around the court.

Making the Vestments for the Priesthood

39 Of the blue, purple, and crimson yarns they made finely worked vestments, for ministering in the holy place; they made the sacred vestments for Aaron; as the LORD had commanded Moses.

2 He made the ephod of gold, of blue, purple, and crimson yarns, and of fine twisted linen. ³Gold leaf was hammered out and cut into threads to work into the blue, purple, and crimson yarns and into the fine twisted linen, in skilled design. ⁴They made for the ephod shoulder-pieces, joined to it at its two edges. ⁵The decorated band on it was of the same materials and workmanship, of gold, of blue, purple, and crimson yarns, and of fine twisted linen; as the LORD had commanded Moses.

6 The onyx stones were prepared, enclosed in settings of gold filigree and engraved like the engravings of a signet, according to the names of the sons of Israel. ⁷He set them on the shoulder-pieces of the ephod, to be stones of remembrance for the sons of Israel; as the LORD had commanded Moses.

8 He made the breastpiece, in skilled work, like the work of the ephod, of gold, of blue, purple, and crimson yarns, and of fine twisted linen. ⁹It was square; the breastpiece was made double, a span in length and a span in width when doubled. ¹⁰They set in it four rows of stones. A row of carnelian,ᵇ chrysolite, and emerald was the first row; ¹¹and the second row, a turquoise, a sapphire,ᶜ and a moonstone; ¹²and the third row, a jacinth, an agate, and an amethyst; ¹³and the fourth row, a beryl, an onyx, and a jasper; they were enclosed in settings of gold filigree. ¹⁴There were twelve stones with names corresponding to the names of the sons of Israel; they were like signets, each engraved with its name, for the twelve tribes. ¹⁵They made on the breastpiece chains of pure gold, twisted like cords; ¹⁶and they made two settings of gold filigree and two gold rings, and put the two rings on the two edges of the breastpiece; ¹⁷and they put the two cords of gold in the two rings at the edges of

---

a Or *treaty,* or *testimony;* Heb *eduth*   *b* The identification of several of these stones is uncertain   *c* Or *lapis lazuli* the breastpiece. [18]Two ends of the two cords they had attached to the two settings of filigree; in this way they attached it in front to the shoulder-pieces of the ephod. [19]Then they made two rings of gold, and put them at the two ends of the breastpiece, on its inside edge next to the ephod. [20]They made two rings of gold, and attached them in front to the lower part of the two shoulder-pieces of the ephod, at its joining above the decorated band of the ephod. [21]They bound the breastpiece by its rings to the rings of the ephod with a blue cord, so that it should lie on the decorated band of the ephod, and that the breastpiece should not come loose from the ephod; as the LORD had commanded Moses.

22 He also made the robe of the ephod woven all of blue yarn; [23]and the opening of the robe in the middle of it was like the opening in a coat of mail,[a] with a binding around the opening, so that it might not be torn. [24]On the lower hem of the robe they made pomegranates of blue, purple, and crimson yarns, and of fine twisted linen. [25]They also made bells of pure gold, and put the bells between the pomegranates on the lower hem of the robe all around, between the pomegranates; [26]a bell and a pomegranate, a bell and a pomegranate all around on the lower hem of the robe for ministering; as the LORD had commanded Moses.

27 They also made the tunics, woven of fine linen, for Aaron and his sons, [28]and the turban of fine linen, and the headdresses of fine linen, and the linen undergarments of fine twisted linen, [29]and the sash of fine twisted linen, and of blue, purple, and crimson yarns, embroidered with needlework; as the LORD had commanded Moses.

30 They made the rosette of the holy diadem of pure gold, and wrote on it an inscription, like the engraving of a signet, "Holy to the LORD." [31]They tied to it a blue cord, to fasten it on the turban above; as the LORD had commanded Moses.

The Work Completed

32 In this way all the work of the tabernacle of the tent of meeting was finished; the Israelites had done everything just as the LORD had commanded Moses. [33]Then they brought the tabernacle to Moses, the tent and all its utensils, its hooks, its frames, its bars, its pillars, and its bases; [34]the covering of tanned rams' skins and the covering of fine leather,[a] and the curtain for the screen; [35]the ark of the covenant[b] with its poles and the mercy seat;[c] [36]the table with all its utensils, and the bread of the Presence; [37]the pure lampstand with its lamps set on it and all its utensils, and the oil for the light; [38]the golden altar, the anointing oil and the fragrant incense, and the screen for the entrance of the tent; [39]the bronze altar, and its grating of bronze, its poles, and all its utensils; the basin with its stand; [40]the hangings of the court, its pillars, and its bases, and the screen for the gate of the court, its cords, and its pegs; and all the utensils for the service of the tabernacle, for the tent of meeting; [41]the finely worked vestments for ministering in the holy place, the sacred vestments for the priest Aaron, and the vestments of his sons to serve as priests. [42]The Israelites had done all of the work just as the LORD had commanded Moses. [43]When Moses saw that they had done all the work just as the LORD had commanded, he blessed them.

The Tabernacle Erected and Its Equipment Installed

40 The LORD spoke to Moses: [2]On the first day of the first month you shall set up the tabernacle of the tent of meeting. [3]You shall put in it the ark of the covenant,[b] and you shall screen the ark with the curtain. [4]You shall bring in the table, and arrange its setting; and you shall bring in the lampstand, and set up its lamps. [5]You shall put the golden altar for incense before the ark of the covenant,[b] and set up the screen for the entrance of the tabernacle. [6]You shall set the altar of burnt offering before the entrance of the tabernacle of the tent

---

a Meaning of Heb uncertain   b Or treaty, or testimony; Heb eduth   c Or the cover of meeting, [7]and place the basin between the tent of meeting and the altar, and put water in it. [8]You shall set up the court all around, and hang up the screen for the gate of the court. [9]Then you shall take the anointing oil, and anoint the tabernacle and all that is in it, and consecrate it and all its furniture, so that it shall become holy. [10]You shall also anoint the altar of burnt offering and all its utensils, and consecrate the altar, so that the altar shall be most holy. [11]You shall also anoint the basin with its stand, and consecrate it. [12]Then you shall bring Aaron and his sons to the entrance of the tent of meeting, and shall wash them with water, [13]and put on Aaron the sacred vestments, and you shall anoint him and consecrate him, so that he may serve me as priest. [14]You shall bring his sons also and put tunics on them, [15]and anoint them, as you anointed their father, that they may serve me as priests: and their anointing shall admit them to a perpetual priesthood throughout all generations to come.

16 Moses did everything just as the LORD had commanded him. [17]In the first month in the second year, on the first day of the month, the tabernacle was set up. [18]Moses set up the tabernacle; he laid its bases, and set up its frames, and put in its poles, and raised up its pillars; [19]and he spread the tent over the tabernacle, and put the covering of the tent over it; as the LORD had commanded Moses. [20]He took the covenant[a] and put it into the ark, and put the poles on the ark, and set the mercy seat[b] above the ark; [21]and he brought the ark into tabernacle, and set up the curtain for screening, and screened the ark of the covenant;[a] as the LORD had commanded Moses. [22]He put the table in the tent of meeting, on the north side of the tabernacle, outside the curtain, [23]and set the bread in order on it before the LORD; as the

LORD had commanded Moses. [24]He put the lampstand in the tent of meeting, opposite the table on the south side of the tabernacle, [25]and set up the lamps before the LORD; as the LORD had commanded Moses. [26]He put the golden altar in the tent of meeting before the curtain, [27]and offered fragrant incense on it; as the LORD had commanded Moses. [28]He also put in place the screen for the entrance of the tabernacle. [29]He set the altar of burnt offering at the entrance of the tabernacle of the tent of meeting, and offered on it the burnt offering and the grain offering as the LORD had commanded Moses. [30]He set the basin between the tent of meeting and the altar, and put water in it for washing, [31]with which Moses and Aaron and his sons washed their hands and their feet. [32]When they went into the tent of meeting, and when they approached the altar, they washed; as the LORD had commanded Moses. [33]He set up the court around the tabernacle and the altar, and put up the screen at the gate of the court. So Moses finished the work.

The Cloud and the Glory

34 Then the cloud covered the tent of meeting, and the glory of the LORD filled the tabernacle. [35]Moses was not able to enter the tent of meeting because the cloud settled upon it, and the glory of the LORD filled the tabernacle. [36]Whenever the cloud was taken up from the tabernacle, the Israelites would set out on each stage of their journey; [37]but if the cloud was not taken up, then they did not set out until the day that it was taken up. [38]For the cloud of the LORD was on the tabernacle by day, and fire was in the cloud[c] by night, before the eyes of all the house of Israel at each stage of their journey.

a Or treaty, or testimony; Heb eduth   b Or the cover   c Heb it

LEVITICUS

The Burnt Offering

1 The LORD summoned Moses and spoke to him from the tent of meeting, saying: 2Speak to the people of Israel and say to them: When any of you bring an offering of livestock to the LORD, you shall bring your offering from the herd or from the flock.

3 If the offering is a burnt offering from the herd, you shall offer a male without blemish; you shall bring it to the entrance of the tent of meeting, for acceptance in your behalf before the LORD. 4You shall lay your hand on the head of the burnt offering, and it shall be acceptable in your behalf as atonement for you. 5The bull shall be slaughtered before the LORD; and Aaron's sons the priests shall offer the blood, dashing the blood against all sides of the altar that is at the entrance of the tent of meeting. 6The burnt offering shall be flayed and cut up into its parts. 7The sons of the priest Aaron shall put fire on the altar and arrange wood on the fire. 8Aaron's sons the priests shall arrange the parts, with the head and the suet, on the wood that is on the fire on the altar; 9but its entrails and its legs shall be washed with water. Then the priest shall turn the whole into smoke on the altar as a burnt offering, an offering by fire of pleasing odor to the LORD.

10 If your gift for a burnt offering is from the flock, from the sheep or goats, your offering shall be a male without blemish. 11It shall be slaughtered on the north side of the altar before the LORD, and Aaron's sons the priests shall dash its blood against all sides of the altar. 12It shall be cut up into its parts, with its head and its suet, and the priest shall arrange them on the wood that is on the fire on the altar; 13but the entrails and the legs shall be washed with water. Then the priest shall offer the whole and turn it into smoke on the altar; it is a burnt offering, an offering by fire of pleasing odor to the LORD.

14 If your offering to the LORD is a burnt offering of birds, you shall choose your offer-ing from turtledoves or pigeons. 15The priest shall bring it to the altar and wring off its head, and turn it into smoke on the altar; and its blood shall be drained out against the side of the altar. 16He shall remove its crop with its contents *a* and throw it at the east side of the altar, in the place for ashes. 17He shall tear it open by its wings without severing it. Then the priest shall turn it into smoke on the altar, on the wood that is on the fire; it is a burnt offering, an offering by fire of pleasing odor to the LORD.

Grain Offerings

2 When anyone presents a grain offering to the LORD, the offering shall be of choice flour; the worshiper shall pour oil on it, and put frankincense on it, 2and bring it to Aaron's sons the priests. After taking from it a handful of the choice flour and oil, with all its frankincense, the priest shall turn this token portion into smoke on the altar, an offering by fire of pleasing odor to the LORD. 3And what is left of the grain offering shall be for Aaron and his sons, a most holy part of the offerings by fire to the LORD.

4 When you present a grain offering baked in the oven, it shall be of choice flour: unleavened cakes mixed with oil, or unleavened wafers spread with oil. 5If your offering is grain prepared on a griddle, it shall be of choice flour mixed with oil, unleavened; 6break it in pieces, and pour oil on it; it is a grain offering. 7If your offering is grain prepared in a pan, it shall be made of choice flour in oil. 8You shall bring to the LORD the grain offering that is prepared in any of these ways; and when it is presented to the priest, he shall take it to the altar. 9The priest shall remove from the grain offering its token portion and turn this into smoke on the altar, an offering by fire of pleasing odor to the LORD. 10And what is left of the grain offering shall be for Aaron and his sons; it is a most holy part of the offerings by fire to the LORD.

a Meaning of Heb uncertain

11 No grain offering that you bring to the LORD shall be made with leaven, for you must not turn any leaven or honey into smoke as an offering by fire to the LORD. 12You may bring them to the LORD as an offering of choice products, but they shall not be offered on the altar for a pleasing odor. 13You shall not omit from your grain offerings the salt of the covenant with your God; with all your offerings you shall offer salt.

14 If you bring a grain offering of first fruits to the LORD, you shall bring as the grain offering of your first fruits coarse new grain from fresh ears, parched with fire. 15You shall add oil to it and lay frankincense on it; it is a grain offering. 16And the priest shall turn a token portion of it into smoke—some of the coarse grain and oil with all its frankincense; it is an offering by fire to the LORD.

Offerings of Well-Being

3 If the offering is a sacrifice of well-being, if you offer an animal of the herd, whether male or female, you shall offer one without blemish before the LORD. 2You shall lay your hand on the head of the offering and slaughter it at the entrance of the tent of meeting; and Aaron's sons the priests shall dash the blood against all sides of the altar. 3You shall offer from the sacrifice of well-being, as an offering by fire to the LORD, the fat that covers the entrails and all the fat that is around the entrails; 4the two kidneys with the fat that is on them at the loins, and the appendage of the liver, which he shall remove with the kidneys. 5Then Aaron's sons shall turn these into smoke on the altar, with the burnt offering that is on the wood on the fire, as an offering by fire of pleasing odor to the LORD.

6 If your offering for a sacrifice of well-being to the LORD is from the flock, male or female, you shall offer one without blemish. 7If you present a sheep as your offering, you shall bring it before the LORD 8and lay your hand on the head of the offering. It shall be slaughtered before the tent of meeting, and Aaron's sons shall dash its blood against all sides of the altar. 9You shall present its fat from the sacrifice of well-being, as an offering by fire to the LORD: the whole broad tail, which shall be removed close to the backbone, the fat that covers the entrails, and all the fat that is around the entrails; 10the two kidneys with the fat that is on them at the loins, and the appendage of the liver, which you shall remove with the kidneys. 11Then the priest shall turn these into smoke on the altar as a food offering by fire to the LORD.

12 If your offering is a goat, you shall bring it before the LORD 13and lay your hand on its head; it shall be slaughtered before the tent of meeting; and the sons of Aaron shall dash its blood against all sides of the altar. 14You shall present as your offering from it, as an offering by fire to the LORD, the fat that covers the entrails, and all the fat that is around the entrails; 15the two kidneys with the fat that is on them at the loins, and the appendage of the liver, which you shall remove with the kidneys. 16Then the priest shall turn these into smoke on the altar as a food offering by fire for a pleasing odor.

All fat is the LORD's. 17It shall be a perpetual statute throughout your generations, in all your settlements: you must not eat any fat or any blood.

Sin Offerings

4 The LORD spoke to Moses, saying, 2Speak to the people of Israel, saying: When anyone sins unintentionally in any of the LORD's commandments about things not to be done, and does any one of them:

3 If it is the anointed priest who sins, thus bringing guilt on the people, he shall offer for the sin that he has committed a bull of the herd without blemish as a sin offering to the LORD. 4He shall bring the bull to the entrance of the tent of meeting before the LORD and lay his hand on the head of the bull; the bull shall be slaughtered before the LORD. 5The anointed priest shall take some of the blood of the bull and bring it into the tent of meeting. 6The priest shall dip his finger in the blood and sprinkle some of the blood seven times before the LORD in front of the curtain of the sanctuary. 7The priest shall put some of the blood

on the horns of the altar of fragrant incense that is in the tent of meeting before the LORD; and the rest of the blood of the bull he shall pour out at the base of the altar of burnt offering, which is at the entrance of the tent of meeting. 8 He shall remove all the fat from the bull of sin offering: the fat that covers the entrails and all the fat that is around the entrails; 9 the two kidneys with the fat that is on them at the loins; and the appendage of the liver, which he shall remove with the kidneys, 10 just as these are removed from the ox of the sacrifice of well-being. The priest shall turn them into smoke upon the altar of burnt offering. 11 But the skin of the bull and all its flesh, as well as its head, its legs, its entrails, and its dung— 12 all the rest of the bull—he shall carry out to a clean place outside the camp, to the ash heap, and shall burn it on a wood fire; at the ash heap it shall be burned.

13 If the whole congregation of Israel errs unintentionally and the matter escapes the notice of the assembly, and they do any one of the things that by the LORD's commandments ought not to be done and incur guilt; 14 when the sin that they have committed becomes known, the assembly shall offer a bull of the herd for a sin offering and bring it before the tent of meeting. 15 The elders of the congregation shall lay their hands on the head of the bull before the LORD, and the bull shall be slaughtered before the LORD. 16 The anointed priest shall bring some of the blood of the bull into the tent of meeting, 17 and the priest shall dip his finger in the blood and sprinkle it seven times before the LORD, in front of the curtain. 18 He shall put some of the blood on the horns of the altar that is before the LORD in the tent of meeting; and the rest of the blood he shall pour out at the base of the altar of burnt offering that is at the entrance of the tent of meeting. 19 He shall remove all its fat and turn it into smoke on the altar. 20 He shall do with the bull just as is done with the bull of sin offering; he shall do the same with this. The priest shall make atonement for them, and they shall be forgiven. 21 He shall carry the bull outside the camp, and burn it as he burned the first bull; it is the sin offering for the assembly.

22 When a ruler sins, doing unintentionally any one of all the things that by commandments of the LORD his God ought not to be done and incurs guilt, 23 once the sin that he has committed is made known to him, he shall bring as his offering a male goat without blemish. 24 He shall lay his hand on the head of the goat; it shall be slaughtered at the spot where the burnt offering is slaughtered before the LORD; it is a sin offering. 25 The priest shall take some of the blood of the sin offering with his finger and put it on the horns of the altar of burnt offering, and pour out the rest of its blood at the base of the altar of burnt offering. 26 All its fat he shall turn into smoke on the altar, like the fat of the sacrifice of well-being. Thus the priest shall make atonement on his behalf for his sin, and he shall be forgiven.

27 If anyone of the ordinary people among you sins unintentionally in doing any one of the things that by the LORD's commandments ought not to be done and incurs guilt, 28 when the sin that you have committed is made known to you, you shall bring a female goat without blemish as your offering, for the sin that you have committed. 29 You shall lay your hand on the head of the sin offering; and the sin offering shall be slaughtered at the place of the burnt offering. 30 The priest shall take some of its blood with his finger and put it on the horns of the altar of burnt offering, and he shall pour out the rest of its blood at the base of the altar. 31 He shall remove all its fat, as the fat is removed from the offering of well-being, and the priest shall turn it into smoke on the altar for a pleasing odor to the LORD. Thus the priest shall make atonement on your behalf, and you shall be forgiven.

32 If the offering you bring as a sin offering is a sheep, you shall bring a female without blemish. 33 You shall lay your hand on the head of the sin offering; and it shall be slaughtered as a sin offering at the spot where the burnt offering is slaughtered. 34 The priest shall take some of the blood of the sin offering with his finger and put it on the horns of the altar of

burnt offering, and pour out the rest of its blood at the base of the altar. 35You shall remove all its fat, as the fat of the sheep is removed from the sacrifice of well-being, and the priest shall turn it into smoke on the altar, with the offerings by fire to the LORD. Thus the priest shall make atonement on your behalf for the sin that you have committed, and you shall be forgiven.

5 When any of you sin in that you have heard a public adjuration to testify and—though able to testify as one who has seen or learned of the matter—do not speak up, you are subject to punishment. 2Or when any of you touch any unclean thing—whether the carcass of an unclean beast or the carcass of unclean livestock or the carcass of an unclean swarming thing—and are unaware of it, you have become unclean, and are guilty. 3Or when you touch human uncleanness—any uncleanness by which one can become unclean—and are unaware of it, when you come to know it, you shall be guilty. 4Or when any of you utter aloud a rash oath for a bad or a good purpose, whatever people utter in an oath, and are unaware of it, when you come to know it, you shall in any of these be guilty. 5When you realize your guilt in any of these, you shall confess the sin that you have committed. 6And you shall bring to the LORD, as your penalty for the sin that you have committed, a female from the flock, a sheep or a goat, as a sin offering; and the priest shall make atonement on your behalf for your sin.

7 But if you cannot afford a sheep, you shall bring to the LORD, as your penalty for the sin that you have committed, two turtledoves or two pigeons, one for a sin offering and the other for a burnt offering. 8You shall bring them to the priest, who shall offer first the one for the sin offering, wringing its head at the nape without severing it. 9He shall sprinkle some of the blood of the sin offering on the side of the altar, while the rest of the blood shall be drained out at the base of the altar; it is a sin offering. 10And the second he shall of-

fer for a burnt offering according to the regulation. Thus the priest shall make atonement on your behalf for the sin that you have committed, and you shall be forgiven.

11 But if you cannot afford two turtledoves or two pigeons, you shall bring as your offering for the sin that you have committed one-tenth of an ephah of choice flour for a sin offering; you shall not put oil on it or lay frankincense on it, for it is a sin offering. 12You shall bring it to the priest, and the priest shall scoop up a handful of it as its memorial portion, and turn this into smoke on the altar, with the offerings by fire to the LORD; it is a sin offering. 13Thus the priest shall make atonement on your behalf for whichever of these sins you have committed, and you shall be forgiven. Like the grain offering, the rest shall be for the priest.

Offerings with Restitution

14 The LORD spoke to Moses, saying: 15When any of you commit a trespass and sin unintentionally in any of the holy things of the LORD, you shall bring, as your guilt offering to the LORD, a ram without blemish from the flock, convertible into silver by the sanctuary shekel; it is a guilt offering. 16And you shall make restitution for the holy thing in which you were remiss, and shall add one-fifth to it and give it to the priest. The priest shall make atonement on your behalf with the ram of the guilt offering, and you shall be forgiven.

17 If any of you sin without knowing it, doing any of the things that by the LORD's commandments ought not to be done, you have incurred guilt, and are subject to punishment. 18You shall bring to the priest a ram without blemish from the flock, or the equivalent, as a guilt offering; and the priest shall make atonement on your behalf for the error that you committed unintentionally, and you shall be forgiven. 19It is a guilt offering; you have incurred guilt before the LORD.

6 *a* The LORD spoke to Moses, saying: 2When any of you sin and commit a trespass

a Ch 5.20 in Heb

against the LORD by deceiving a neighbor in a matter of a deposit or a pledge, or by robbery, or if you have defrauded a neighbor, ³or have found something lost and lied about it—if you swear falsely regarding any of the various things that one may do and sin thereby— ⁴when you have sinned and realize your guilt, and would restore what you took by robbery or by fraud or the deposit that was committed to you, or the lost thing that you found, ⁵or anything else about which you have sworn falsely, you shall repay the principal amount and shall add one-fifth to it. You shall pay it to its owner when you realize your guilt. ⁶And you shall bring to the priest, as your guilt offering to the LORD, a ram without blemish from the flock, or its equivalent, for a guilt offering. ⁷The priest shall make atonement on your behalf before the LORD, and you shall be forgiven for any of the things that one may do and incur guilt thereby.

Instructions concerning Sacrifices

8ᵃ The LORD spoke to Moses, saying: ⁹Command Aaron and his sons, saying: This is the ritual of the burnt offering. The burnt offering itself shall remain on the hearth upon the altar all night until the morning, while the fire on the altar shall be kept burning. ¹⁰The priest shall put on his linen vestments after putting on his linen undergarments next to his body; and he shall take up the ashes to which the fire has reduced the burnt offering on the altar, and place them beside the altar. ¹¹Then he shall take off his vestments and put on other garments, and carry the ashes out to a clean place outside the camp. ¹²The fire on the altar shall be kept burning; it shall not go out. Every morning the priest shall add wood to it, lay out the burnt offering on it, and turn into smoke the fat pieces of the offerings of well-being. ¹³A perpetual fire shall be kept burning on the altar; it shall not go out.

14 This is the ritual of the grain offering: The sons of Aaron shall offer it before the LORD, in front of the altar. ¹⁵They shall take from it a handful of the choice flour and oil of the grain offering, with all the frankincense that is on the offering, and they shall turn its memorial portion into smoke on the altar as a pleasing odor to the LORD. ¹⁶Aaron and his sons shall eat what is left of it; it shall be eaten as unleavened cakes in a holy place; in the court of the tent of meeting they shall eat it. ¹⁷It shall not be baked with leaven. I have given it as their portion of my offerings by fire; it is most holy, like the sin offering and the guilt offering. ¹⁸Every male among the descendants of Aaron shall eat of it, as their perpetual due throughout your generations, from the LORD's offerings by fire; anything that touches them shall become holy.

19 The LORD spoke to Moses, saying: ²⁰This is the offering that Aaron and his sons shall offer to the LORD on the day when he is anointed: one-tenth of an ephah of choice flour as a regular offering, half of it in the morning and half in the evening. ²¹It shall be made with oil on a griddle; you shall bring it well soaked, as a grain offering of bakedᵇ pieces, and you shall present it as a pleasing odor to the LORD. ²²And so the priest, anointed from among Aaron's descendants as a successor, shall prepare it; it is the LORD's—a perpetual due—to be turned entirely into smoke. ²³Every grain offering of a priest shall be wholly burned; it shall not be eaten.

24 The LORD spoke to Moses, saying: ²⁵Speak to Aaron and his sons, saying: This is the ritual of the sin offering. The sin offering shall be slaughtered before the LORD at the spot where the burnt offering is slaughtered; it is most holy. ²⁶The priest who offers it as a sin offering shall eat of it; it shall be eaten in a holy place, in the court of the tent of meeting. ²⁷Whatever touches its flesh shall become holy; and when any of its blood is spattered on a garment, you shall wash the bespattered part in a holy place. ²⁸An earthen vessel in which it was boiled shall be broken; but if it is boiled in a bronze vessel, that shall be scoured and rinsed in water. ²⁹Every male among the priests shall eat of it; it is most holy. ³⁰But no sin offering shall be eaten from which any blood is brought

---

a Ch 6.1 in Heb   b Meaning of Heb uncertain

into the tent of meeting for atonement in the holy place; it shall be burned with fire.

7 This is the ritual of the guilt offering. It is most holy; [2]at the spot where the burnt offering is slaughtered, they shall slaughter the guilt offering, and its blood shall be dashed against all sides of the altar. [3]All its fat shall be offered: the broad tail, the fat that covers the entrails, [4]the two kidneys with the fat that is on them at the loins, and the appendage of the liver, which shall be removed with the kidneys. [5]The priest shall turn them into smoke on the altar as an offering by fire to the LORD; it is a guilt offering. [6]Every male among the priests shall eat of it; it shall be eaten in a holy place; it is most holy.

7 The guilt offering is like the sin offering, there is the same ritual for them; the priest who makes atonement with it shall have it. [8]So, too, the priest who offers anyone's burnt offering shall keep the skin of the burnt offering that he has offered. [9]And every grain offering baked in the oven, and all that is prepared in a pan or on a griddle, shall belong to the priest who offers it. [10]But every other grain offering, mixed with oil or dry, shall belong to all the sons of Aaron equally.

Further Instructions

11 This is the ritual of the sacrifice of the offering of well-being that one may offer to the LORD. [12]If you offer it for thanksgiving, you shall offer with the thank offering unleavened cakes mixed with oil, unleavened wafers spread with oil, and cakes of choice flour well soaked in oil. [13]With your thanksgiving sacrifice of well-being you shall bring your offering with cakes of leavened bread. [14]From this you shall offer one cake from each offering, as a gift to the LORD; it shall belong to the priest who dashes the blood of the offering of well-being. [15]And the flesh of your thanksgiving sacrifice of well-being shall be eaten on the day it is offered; you shall not leave any of it until morning. [16]But if the sacrifice you offer is a votive offering or a freewill offering, it shall be eaten on the day that you offer your sacrifice, and what is left of it shall be eaten the next day;

[17]but what is left of the flesh of the sacrifice shall be burned up on the third day. [18]If any of the flesh of your sacrifice of well-being is eaten on the third day, it shall not be acceptable, nor shall it be credited to the one who offers it; it shall be an abomination, and the one who eats of it shall incur guilt.

19 Flesh that touches any unclean thing shall not be eaten; it shall be burned up. As for other flesh, all who are clean may eat such flesh. [20]But those who eat flesh from the LORD's sacrifice of well-being while in a state of uncleanness shall be cut off from their kin. [21]When any one of you touches any unclean thing—human uncleanness or an unclean animal or any unclean creature—and then eats flesh from the LORD's sacrifice of well-being, you shall be cut off from your kin.

22 The LORD spoke to Moses, saying: [23]Speak to the people of Israel, saying: You shall eat no fat of ox or sheep or goat. [24]The fat of an animal that died or was torn by wild animals may be put to any other use, but you must not eat it. [25]If any one of you eats the fat from an animal of which an offering by fire may be made to the LORD, you who eat it shall be cut off from your kin. [26]You must not eat any blood whatever, either of bird or of animal, in any of your settlements. [27]Any one of you who eats any blood shall be cut off from your kin.

28 The LORD spoke to Moses, saying: [29]Speak to the people of Israel, saying: Any one of you who would offer to the LORD your sacrifice of well-being must yourself bring to the LORD your offering from your sacrifice of well-being. [30]Your own hands shall bring the LORD's offering by fire; you shall bring the fat with the breast, so that the breast may be raised as an elevation offering before the LORD. [31]The priest shall turn the fat into smoke on the altar, but the breast shall belong to Aaron and his sons. [32]And the right thigh from your sacrifices of well-being you shall give to the priest as an offering; [33]the one among the sons of Aaron who offers the blood and fat of the offering of well-being shall have the right thigh for a portion. [34]For I have taken the breast of the ele-

vation offering, and the thigh that is offered, from the people of Israel, from their sacrifices of well-being, and have given them to Aaron the priest and to his sons, as a perpetual due from the people of Israel. 35This is the portion allotted to Aaron and to his sons from the offerings made by fire to the LORD, once they have been brought forward to serve the LORD as priests; 36these the LORD commanded to be given them, when he anointed them, as a perpetual due from the people of Israel throughout their generations.

37 This is the ritual of the burnt offering, the grain offering, the sin offering, the guilt offering, the offering of ordination, and the sacrifice of well-being, 38which the LORD commanded Moses on Mount Sinai, when he commanded the people of Israel to bring their offerings to the LORD, in the wilderness of Sinai.

The Rites of Ordination

8 The LORD spoke to Moses, saying: 2Take Aaron and his sons with him, the vestments, the anointing oil, the bull of sin offering, the two rams, and the basket of unleavened bread; 3and assemble the whole congregation at the entrance of the tent of meeting. 4And Moses did as the LORD commanded him. When the congregation was assembled at the entrance of the tent of meeting, 5Moses said to the congregation, "This is what the LORD has commanded to be done."

6 Then Moses brought Aaron and his sons forward, and washed them with water. 7He put the tunic on him, fastened the sash around him, clothed him with the robe, and put the ephod on him. He then put the decorated band of the ephod around him, tying the ephod to him with it. 8He placed the breastpiece on him, and in the breastpiece he put the Urim and the Thummim. 9And he set the turban on his head, and on the turban, in front, he set the golden ornament, the holy crown, as the LORD commanded Moses.

10 Then Moses took the anointing oil and anointed the tabernacle and all that was in it, and consecrated them. 11He sprinkled some of it on the altar seven times, and anointed the al-

tar and all its utensils, and the basin and its base, to consecrate them. 12He poured some of the anointing oil on Aaron's head and anointed him, to consecrate him. 13And Moses brought forward Aaron's sons, and clothed them with tunics, and fastened sashes around them, and tied headdresses on them, as the LORD commanded Moses.

14 He led forward the bull of sin offering; and Aaron and his sons laid their hands upon the head of the bull of sin offering, 15and it was slaughtered. Moses took the blood and with his finger put some on each of the horns of the altar, purifying the altar; then he poured out the blood at the base of the altar. Thus he consecrated it, to make atonement for it. 16Moses took all the fat that was around the entrails, and the appendage of the liver, and the two kidneys with their fat, and turned them into smoke on the altar. 17But the bull itself, its skin and flesh and its dung, he burned with fire outside the camp, as the LORD commanded Moses.

18 Then he brought forward the ram of burnt offering. Aaron and his sons laid their hands on the head of the ram, 19and it was slaughtered. Moses dashed the blood against all sides of the altar. 20The ram was cut into its parts, and Moses turned into smoke the head and the parts and the suet. 21And after the entrails and the legs were washed with water, Moses turned into smoke the whole ram on the altar; it was a burnt offering for a pleasing odor, an offering by fire to the LORD, as the LORD commanded Moses.

22 Then he brought forward the second ram, the ram of ordination. Aaron and his sons laid their hands on the head of the ram, 23and it was slaughtered. Moses took some of its blood and put it on the lobe of Aaron's right ear and on the thumb of his right hand and on the big toe of his right foot. 24After Aaron's sons were brought forward, Moses put some of the blood on the lobes of their right ears and on the thumbs of their right hands and on the big toes of their right feet; and Moses dashed the rest of the blood against all sides of the altar. 25He took the fat—the broad tail, all the fat that was around the entrails, the ap-

pendage of the liver, and the two kidneys with their fat—and the right thigh. 26From the basket of unleavened bread that was before the LORD, he took one cake of unleavened bread, one cake of bread with oil, and one wafer, and placed them on the fat and on the right thigh. 27He placed all these on the palms of Aaron and on the palms of his sons, and raised them as an elevation offering before the LORD. 28Then Moses took them from their hands and turned them into smoke on the altar with the burnt offering. This was an ordination offering for a pleasing odor, an offering by fire to the LORD. 29Moses took the breast and raised it as an elevation offering before the LORD; it was Moses' portion of the ram of ordination, as the LORD commanded Moses.

30 Then Moses took some of the anointing oil and some of the blood that was on the altar and sprinkled them on Aaron and his vestments, and also on his sons and their vestments. Thus he consecrated Aaron and his vestments, and also his sons and their vestments.

31 And Moses said to Aaron and his sons, "Boil the flesh at the entrance of the tent of meeting, and eat it there with the bread that is in the basket of ordination offerings, as I was commanded, 'Aaron and his sons shall eat it'; 32and what remains of the flesh and the bread you shall burn with fire. 33You shall not go outside the entrance of the tent of meeting for seven days, until the day when your period of ordination is completed. For it will take seven days to ordain you; 34as has been done today, the LORD has commanded to be done to make atonement for you. 35You shall remain at the entrance of the tent of meeting day and night for seven days, keeping the LORD's charge so that you do not die; for so I am commanded." 36Aaron and his sons did all the things that the LORD commanded through Moses.

Aaron's Priesthood Inaugurated

9 On the eighth day Moses summoned Aaron and his sons and the elders of Israel. 2He said to Aaron, "Take a bull calf for a sin offering and a ram for a burnt offering, without blemish, and offer them before the LORD. 3And say to the people of Israel, 'Take a male goat for a sin offering; a calf and a lamb, yearlings without blemish, for a burnt offering; 4and an ox and a ram for an offering of well-being to sacrifice before the LORD; and a grain offering mixed with oil. For today the LORD will appear to you.' " 5They brought what Moses commanded to the front of the tent of meeting; and the whole congregation drew near and stood before the LORD. 6And Moses said, "This is the thing that the LORD commanded you to do, so that the glory of the LORD may appear to you." 7Then Moses said to Aaron, "Draw near to the altar and sacrifice your sin offering and your burnt offering, and make atonement for yourself and for the people; and sacrifice the offering of the people, and make atonement for them; as the LORD has commanded."

8 Aaron drew near to the altar, and slaughtered the calf of the sin offering, which was for himself. 9The sons of Aaron presented the blood to him, and he dipped his finger in the blood and put it on the horns of the altar; and the rest of the blood he poured out at the base of the altar. 10But the fat, the kidneys, and the appendage of the liver from the sin offering he turned into smoke on the altar, as the LORD commanded Moses; 11and the flesh and the skin he burned with fire outside the camp.

12 Then he slaughtered the burnt offering. Aaron's sons brought him the blood, and he dashed it against all sides of the altar. 13And they brought him the burnt offering piece by piece, and the head, which he turned into smoke on the altar. 14He washed the entrails and the legs and, with the burnt offering, turned them into smoke on the altar.

15 Next he presented the people's offering. He took the goat of the sin offering that was for the people, and slaughtered it, and presented it as a sin offering like the first one. 16He presented the burnt offering, and sacrificed it according to regulation. 17He presented the grain offering, and, taking a handful of it, he turned it into smoke on the altar, in addition to the burnt offering of the morning.

18 He slaughtered the ox and the ram as a sacrifice of well-being for the people. Aaron's sons brought him the blood, which he dashed against all sides of the altar, 19and the fat of the ox and of the ram—the broad tail, the fat that covers the entrails, the two kidneys and the fat on them,*a* and the appendage of the liver. 20They first laid the fat on the breasts, and the fat was turned into smoke on the altar; 21and the breasts and the right thigh Aaron raised as an elevation offering before the LORD, as Moses had commanded.

22 Aaron lifted his hands toward the people and blessed them; and he came down after sacrificing the sin offering, the burnt offering, and the offering of well-being. 23Moses and Aaron entered the tent of meeting, and then came out and blessed the people; and the glory of the LORD appeared to all the people. 24Fire came out from the LORD and consumed the burnt offering and the fat on the altar; and when all the people saw it, they shouted and fell on their faces.

Nadab and Abihu

10 Now Aaron's sons, Nadab and Abihu, each took his censer, put fire in it, and laid incense on it; and they offered unholy fire before the LORD, such as he had not commanded them. 2And fire came out from the presence of the LORD and consumed them, and they died before the LORD. 3Then Moses said to Aaron, "This is what the LORD meant when he said,

'Through those who are near me
   I will show myself holy,
and before all the people
   I will be glorified.'"
And Aaron was silent.

4 Moses summoned Mishael and Elzaphan, sons of Uzziel the uncle of Aaron, and said to them, "Come forward, and carry your kinsmen away from the front of the sanctuary to a place outside the camp." 5They came forward and carried them by their tunics out of the camp, as Moses had ordered. 6And Moses

said to Aaron and to his sons Eleazar and Ithamar, "Do not dishevel your hair, and do not tear your vestments, or you will die and wrath will strike all the congregation; but your kindred, the whole house of Israel, may mourn the burning that the LORD has sent. 7You shall not go outside the entrance of the tent of meeting, or you will die; for the anointing oil of the LORD is on you." And they did as Moses had ordered.

8 And the LORD spoke to Aaron: 9Drink no wine or strong drink, neither you nor your sons, when you enter the tent of meeting, that you may not die; it is a statute forever throughout your generations. 10You are to distinguish between the holy and the common, and between the unclean and the clean; 11and you are to teach the people of Israel all the statutes that the LORD has spoken to them through Moses.

12 Moses spoke to Aaron and to his remaining sons, Eleazar and Ithamar: Take the grain offering that is left from the LORD's offerings by fire, and eat it unleavened beside the altar, for it is most holy; 13you shall eat it in a holy place, because it is your due and your sons' due, from the offerings by fire to the LORD; for so I am commanded. 14But the breast that is elevated and the thigh that is raised, you and your sons and daughters as well may eat in any clean place; for they have been assigned to you and your children from the sacrifices of the offerings of well-being of the people of Israel. 15The thigh that is raised and the breast that is elevated they shall bring, together with the offerings by fire of the fat, to raise for an elevation offering before the LORD; they are to be your due and that of your children forever, as the LORD has commanded.

16 Then Moses made inquiry about the goat of the sin offering, and—it had already been burned! He was angry with Eleazar and Ithamar, Aaron's remaining sons, and said, 17"Why did you not eat the sin offering in the sacred area? For it is most holy, and God*b* has given it to you that you may remove the guilt of the congregation, to make atonement on

---

a Gk: Heb *the broad tail, and that which covers, and the kidneys*   *b* Heb *he* their behalf before the LORD. [18]Its blood was not brought into the inner part of the sanctuary. You should certainly have eaten it in the sanctuary, as I commanded." [19]And Aaron spoke to Moses, "See, today they offered their sin offering and their burnt offering before the LORD; and yet such things as these have befallen me! If I had eaten the sin offering today, would it have been agreeable to the LORD?" [20]And when Moses heard that, he agreed.

Clean and Unclean Foods

11 The LORD spoke to Moses and Aaron, saying to them: [2]Speak to the people of Israel, saying:

From among all the land animals, these are the creatures that you may eat. [3]Any animal that has divided hoofs and is cleft-footed and chews the cud—such you may eat. [4]But among those that chew the cud or have divided hoofs, you shall not eat the following: the camel, for even though it chews the cud, it does not have divided hoofs; it is unclean for you. [5]The rock badger, for even though it chews the cud, it does not have divided hoofs; it is unclean for you. [6]The hare, for even though it chews the cud, it does not have divided hoofs; it is unclean for you. [7]The pig, for even though it has divided hoofs and is cleft-footed, it does not chew the cud; it is unclean for you. [8]Of their flesh you shall not eat, and their carcasses you shall not touch; they are unclean for you.

9 These you may eat, of all that are in the waters. Everything in the waters that has fins and scales, whether in the seas or in the streams—such you may eat. [10]But anything in the seas or the streams that does not have fins and scales, of the swarming creatures in the waters and among all the other living creatures that are in the waters—they are detestable to you [11]and detestable they shall remain. Of their flesh you shall not eat, and their carcasses you shall regard as detestable. [12]Everything in the waters that does not have fins and scales is detestable to you.

13 These you shall regard as detestable among the birds. They shall not be eaten; they are an abomination: the eagle, the vulture, the osprey, [14]the buzzard, the kite of any kind; [15]every raven of any kind; [16]the ostrich, the nighthawk, the sea gull, the hawk of any kind; [17]the little owl, the cormorant, the great owl, [18]the water hen, the desert owl,[a] the carrion vulture, [19]the stork, the heron of any kind, the hoopoe, and the bat.[b]

20 All winged insects that walk upon all fours are detestable to you. [21]But among the winged insects that walk on all fours you may eat those that have jointed legs above their feet, with which to leap on the ground. [22]Of them you may eat: the locust according to its kind, the bald locust according to its kind, the cricket according to its kind, and the grasshopper according to its kind. [23]But all other winged insects that have four feet are detestable to you.

Unclean Animals

24 By these you shall become unclean; whoever touches the carcass of any of them shall be unclean until the evening, [25]and whoever carries any part of the carcass of any of them shall wash his clothes and be unclean until evening. [26]Every animal that has divided hoofs but is not cleft-footed or does not chew the cud is unclean for you; everyone who touches one of them shall be unclean. [27]All that walk on their paws, among the animals that walk on all fours, are unclean for you; whoever touches the carcass of any of them shall be unclean until the evening, [28]and the one who carries the carcass shall wash his clothes and be unclean until the evening; they are unclean for you.

29 These are unclean for you among the creatures that swarm upon the earth: the weasel, the mouse, the great lizard according to its kind, [30]the gecko, the land crocodile, the lizard, the sand lizard, and the chameleon. [31]These are unclean for you among all that swarm; whoever touches one of them when they are dead shall be unclean until the evening. [32]And anything upon which any of them falls when they are dead shall be unclean, whether

---

a Or *pelican*   *b* Identification of several of the birds in verses 13-19 is uncertain an article of wood or cloth or skin or sacking, any article that is used for any purpose; it shall be dipped into water, and it shall be unclean until the evening, and then it shall be clean. 33And if any of them falls into any earthen vessel, all that is in it shall be unclean, and you shall break the vessel. 34Any food that could be eaten shall be unclean if water from any such vessel comes upon it; and any liquid that could be drunk shall be unclean if it was in any such vessel. 35Everything on which any part of the carcass falls shall be unclean; whether an oven or stove, it shall be broken in pieces; they are unclean, and shall remain unclean for you. 36But a spring or a cistern holding water shall be clean, while whatever touches the carcass in it shall be unclean. 37If any part of their carcass falls upon any seed set aside for sowing, it is clean; 38but if water is put on the seed and any part of their carcass falls on it, it is unclean for you.

39 If an animal of which you may eat dies, anyone who touches its carcass shall be unclean until the evening. 40Those who eat of its carcass shall wash their clothes and be unclean until the evening; and those who carry the carcass shall wash their clothes and be unclean until the evening.

41 All creatures that swarm upon the earth are detestable; they shall not be eaten. 42Whatever moves on its belly, and whatever moves on all fours, or whatever has many feet, all the creatures that swarm upon the earth, you shall not eat; for they are detestable. 43You shall not make yourselves detestable with any creature that swarms; you shall not defile yourselves with them, and so become unclean. 44For I am the LORD your God; sanctify yourselves therefore, and be holy, for I am holy. You shall not defile yourselves with any swarming creature that moves on the earth. 45For I am the LORD who brought you up from the land of Egypt, to be your God; you shall be holy, for I am holy.

46 This is the law pertaining to land animal and bird and every living creature that moves through the waters and every creature that swarms upon the earth, 47to make a distinction between the unclean and the clean, and between the living creature that may be eaten and the living creature that may not be eaten.

Purification of Women after Childbirth

12 The LORD spoke to Moses, saying: 2Speak to the people of Israel, saying:

If a woman conceives and bears a male child, she shall be ceremonially unclean seven days; as at the time of her menstruation, she shall be unclean. 3On the eighth day the flesh of his foreskin shall be circumcised. 4Her time of blood purification shall be thirty-three days; she shall not touch any holy thing, or come into the sanctuary, until the days of her purification are completed. 5If she bears a female child, she shall be unclean two weeks, as in her menstruation; her time of blood purification shall be sixty-six days.

6 When the days of her purification are completed, whether for a son or for a daughter, she shall bring to the priest at the entrance of the tent of meeting a lamb in its first year for a burnt offering, and a pigeon or a turtledove for a sin offering. 7He shall offer it before the LORD, and make atonement on her behalf; then she shall be clean from her flow of blood. This is the law for her who bears a child, male or female. 8If she cannot afford a sheep, she shall take two turtledoves or two pigeons, one for a burnt offering and the other for a sin offering; and the priest shall make atonement on her behalf, and she shall be clean.

Leprosy, Varieties and Symptoms

13 The LORD spoke to Moses and Aaron, saying:

2 When a person has on the skin of his body a swelling or an eruption or a spot, and it turns into a leprous[a] disease on the skin of his body, he shall be brought to Aaron the priest or to one of his sons the priests. 3The priest shall examine the disease on the skin of his body, and if the hair in the diseased area has turned white and the disease appears to be deeper than the skin of his body, it is a leprous[a]

---

[a] A term for several skin diseases; precise meaning uncertain

disease; after the priest has examined him he shall pronounce him ceremonially unclean. [4]But if the spot is white in the skin of his body, and appears no deeper than the skin, and the hair in it has not turned white, the priest shall confine the diseased person for seven days. [5]The priest shall examine him on the seventh day, and if he sees that the disease is checked and the disease has not spread in the skin, then the priest shall confine him seven days more. [6]The priest shall examine him again on the seventh day, and if the disease has abated and the disease has not spread in the skin, the priest shall pronounce him clean; it is only an eruption; and he shall wash his clothes, and be clean. [7]But if the eruption spreads in the skin after he has shown himself to the priest for his cleansing, he shall appear again before the priest. [8]The priest shall make an examination, and if the eruption has spread in the skin, the priest shall pronounce him unclean; it is a leprous[a] disease.

9 When a person contracts a leprous[a] disease, he shall be brought to the priest. [10]The priest shall make an examination, and if there is a white swelling in the skin that has turned the hair white, and there is quick raw flesh in the swelling, [11]it is a chronic leprous[a] disease in the skin of his body. The priest shall pronounce him unclean; he shall not confine him, for he is unclean. [12]But if the disease breaks out in the skin, so that it covers all the skin of the diseased person from head to foot, so far as the priest can see, [13]then the priest shall make an examination, and if the disease has covered all his body, he shall pronounce him clean of the disease; since it has all turned white, he is clean. [14]But if raw flesh ever appears on him, he shall be unclean; [15]the priest shall examine the raw flesh and pronounce him unclean. Raw flesh is unclean, for it is a leprous[a] disease. [16]But if the raw flesh again turns white, he shall come to the priest; [17]the priest shall examine him, and if the disease has turned white, the priest shall pronounce the diseased person clean. He is clean.

18 When there is on the skin of one's body a boil that has healed, [19]and in the place of the boil there appears a white swelling or a reddish-white spot, it shall be shown to the priest. [20]The priest shall make an examination, and if it appears deeper than the skin and its hair has turned white, the priest shall pronounce him unclean; this is a leprous[a] disease, broken out in the boil. [21]But if the priest examines it and the hair on it is not white, nor is it deeper than the skin but has abated, the priest shall confine him seven days. [22]If it spreads in the skin, the priest shall pronounce him unclean; it is diseased. [23]But if the spot remains in one place and does not spread, it is the scar of the boil; the priest shall pronounce him clean.

24 Or, when the body has a burn on the skin and the raw flesh of the burn becomes a spot, reddish-white or white, [25]the priest shall examine it. If the hair in the spot has turned white and it appears deeper than the skin, it is a leprous[a] disease; it has broken out in the burn, and the priest shall pronounce him unclean. This is a leprous[a] disease. [26]But if the priest examines it and the hair in the spot is not white, and it is no deeper than the skin but has abated, the priest shall confine him seven days. [27]The priest shall examine him the seventh day; if it is spreading in the skin, the priest shall pronounce him unclean. This is a leprous[a] disease. [28]But if the spot remains in one place and does not spread in the skin but has abated, it is a swelling from the burn, and the priest shall pronounce him clean; for it is the scar of the burn.

29 When a man or woman has a disease on the head or in the beard, [30]the priest shall examine the disease. If it appears deeper than the skin and the hair in it is yellow and thin, the priest shall pronounce him unclean; it is an itch, a leprous[a] disease of the head or the beard. [31]If the priest examines the itching disease, and it appears no deeper than the skin and there is no black hair in it, the priest shall confine the person with the itching disease for seven days. [32]On the seventh day the priest shall examine the itch; if the itch has not

---

[a] A term for several skin diseases; precise meaning uncertain

spread, and there is no yellow hair in it, and the itch appears to be no deeper than the skin, 33he shall shave, but the itch he shall not shave. The priest shall confine the person with the itch for seven days more. 34On the seventh day the priest shall examine the itch; if the itch has not spread in the skin and it appears to be no deeper than the skin, the priest shall pronounce him clean. He shall wash his clothes and be clean. 35But if the itch spreads in the skin after he was pronounced clean, 36the priest shall examine him. If the itch has spread in the skin, the priest need not seek for the yellow hair; he is unclean. 37But if in his eyes the itch is checked, and black hair has grown in it, the itch is healed, he is clean; and the priest shall pronounce him clean.

38 When a man or a woman has spots on the skin of the body, white spots, 39the priest shall make an examination, and if the spots on the skin of the body are of a dull white, it is a rash that has broken out on the skin; he is clean.

40 If anyone loses the hair from his head, he is bald but he is clean. 41If he loses the hair from his forehead and temples, he has baldness of the forehead but he is clean. 42But if there is on the bald head or the bald forehead a reddish-white diseased spot, it is a leprous*a* disease breaking out on his bald head or his bald forehead. 43The priest shall examine him; if the diseased swelling is reddish-white on his bald head or on his bald forehead, which resembles a leprous*a* disease in the skin of the body, 44he is leprous,*a* he is unclean. The priest shall pronounce him unclean; the disease is on his head.

45 The person who has the leprous*a* disease shall wear torn clothes and let the hair of his head be disheveled; and he shall cover his upper lip and cry out, "Unclean, unclean." 46He shall remain unclean as long as he has the disease; he is unclean. He shall live alone; his dwelling shall be outside the camp.

47 Concerning clothing: when a leprous*a* disease appears in it, in woolen or linen cloth, 48in warp or woof of linen or wool, or in a skin or in anything made of skin, 49if the disease shows greenish or reddish in the garment, whether in warp or woof or in skin or in anything made of skin, it is a leprous*a* disease and shall be shown to the priest. 50The priest shall examine the disease, and put the diseased article aside for seven days. 51He shall examine the disease on the seventh day. If the disease has spread in the cloth, in warp or woof, or in the skin, whatever be the use of the skin, this is a spreading leprous*a* disease; it is unclean. 52He shall burn the clothing, whether diseased in warp or woof, woolen or linen, or anything of skin, for it is a spreading leprous*a* disease; it shall be burned in fire.

53 If the priest makes an examination, and the disease has not spread in the clothing, in warp or woof or in anything of skin, 54the priest shall command them to wash the article in which the disease appears, and he shall put it aside seven days more. 55The priest shall examine the diseased article after it has been washed. If the diseased spot has not changed color, though the disease has not spread, it is unclean; you shall burn it in fire, whether the leprous*a* spot is on the inside or on the outside.

56 If the priest makes an examination, and the disease has abated after it is washed, he shall tear the spot out of the cloth, in warp or woof, or out of skin. 57If it appears again in the garment, in warp or woof, or in anything of skin, it is spreading; you shall burn with fire that in which the disease appears. 58But the cloth, warp or woof, or anything of skin from which the disease disappears when you have washed it, shall then be washed a second time, and it shall be clean.

59 This is the ritual for a leprous*a* disease in a cloth of wool or linen, either in warp or woof, or in anything of skin, to decide whether it is clean or unclean.

Purification of Lepers and Leprous Houses

14 The LORD spoke to Moses, saying: 2This shall be the ritual for the leprous*a* person at the time of his cleansing:

He shall be brought to the priest; 3the priest

---

a A term for several skin diseases; precise meaning uncertain

shall go out of the camp, and the priest shall make an examination. If the disease is healed in the leprous*a* person, 4the priest shall command that two living clean birds and cedarwood and crimson yarn and hyssop be brought for the one who is to be cleansed. 5The priest shall command that one of the birds be slaughtered over fresh water in an earthen vessel. 6He shall take the living bird with the cedarwood and the crimson yarn and the hyssop, and dip them and the living bird in the blood of the bird that was slaughtered over the fresh water. 7He shall sprinkle it seven times upon the one who is to be cleansed of the leprous*a* disease; then he shall pronounce him clean, and he shall let the living bird go into the open field. 8The one who is to be cleansed shall wash his clothes, and shave off all his hair, and bathe himself in water, and he shall be clean. After that he shall come into the camp, but shall live outside his tent seven days. 9On the seventh day he shall shave all his hair: of head, beard, eyebrows; he shall shave all his hair. Then he shall wash his clothes, and bathe his body in water, and he shall be clean.

10 On the eighth day he shall take two male lambs without blemish, and one ewe lamb in its first year without blemish, and a grain offering of three-tenths of an ephah of choice flour mixed with oil, and one log*b* of oil. 11The priest who cleanses shall set the person to be cleansed, along with these things, before the LORD, at the entrance of the tent of meeting. 12The priest shall take one of the lambs, and offer it as a guilt offering, along with the log*b* of oil, and raise them as an elevation offering before the LORD. 13He shall slaughter the lamb in the place where the sin offering and the burnt offering are slaughtered in the holy place; for the guilt offering, like the sin offering, belongs to the priest: it is most holy. 14The priest shall take some of the blood of the guilt offering and put it on the lobe of the right ear of the one to be cleansed, and on the thumb of the right hand, and on the big toe of the right foot. 15The priest shall take some of the log*b*

of oil and pour it into the palm of his own left hand, 16and dip his right finger in the oil that is in his left hand and sprinkle some oil with his finger seven times before the LORD. 17Some of the oil that remains in his hand the priest shall put on the lobe of the right ear of the one to be cleansed, and on the thumb of the right hand, and on the big toe of the right foot, on top of the blood of the guilt offering. 18The rest of the oil that is in the priest's hand he shall put on the head of the one to be cleansed. Then the priest shall make atonement on his behalf before the LORD: 19the priest shall offer the sin offering, to make atonement for the one to be cleansed from his uncleanness. Afterward he shall slaughter the burnt offering; 20and the priest shall offer the burnt offering and the grain offering on the altar. Thus the priest shall make atonement on his behalf and he shall be clean.

21 But if he is poor and cannot afford so much, he shall take one male lamb for a guilt offering to be elevated, to make atonement on his behalf, and one-tenth of an ephah of choice flour mixed with oil for a grain offering and a log*b* of oil; 22also two turtledoves or two pigeons, such as he can afford, one for a sin offering and the other for a burnt offering. 23On the eighth day he shall bring them for his cleansing to the priest, to the entrance of the tent of meeting, before the LORD; 24and the priest shall take the lamb of the guilt offering and the log*b* of oil, and the priest shall raise them as an elevation offering before the LORD. 25The priest shall slaughter the lamb of the guilt offering and shall take some of the blood of the guilt offering, and put it on the lobe of the right ear of the one to be cleansed, and on the thumb of the right hand, and on the big toe of the right foot. 26The priest shall pour some of the oil into the palm of his own left hand, 27and shall sprinkle with his right finger some of the oil that is in his left hand seven times before the LORD. 28The priest shall put some of the oil that is in his hand on the lobe of the right ear of the one to be cleansed, and on the

---

a A term for several skin diseases; precise meaning uncertain   *b* A liquid measure thumb of the right hand, and the big toe of the right foot, where the blood of the guilt offering was placed. 29The rest of the oil that is in the priest's hand he shall put on the head of the one to be cleansed, to make atonement on his behalf before the LORD. 30And he shall offer, of the turtledoves or pigeons such as he can afford, 31one*a* for a sin offering and the other for a burnt offering, along with a grain offering; and the priest shall make atonement before the LORD on behalf of the one being cleansed. 32This is the ritual for the one who has a leprous*b* disease, who cannot afford the offerings for his cleansing.

33 The LORD spoke to Moses and Aaron, saying:

34 When you come into the land of Canaan, which I give you for a possession, and I put a leprous*b* disease in a house in the land of your possession, 35the owner of the house shall come and tell the priest, saying, "There seems to me to be some sort of disease in my house." 36The priest shall command that they empty the house before the priest goes to examine the disease, or all that is in the house will become unclean; and afterward the priest shall go in to inspect the house. 37He shall examine the disease; if the disease is in the walls of the house with greenish or reddish spots, and if it appears to be deeper than the surface, 38the priest shall go outside to the door of the house and shut up the house seven days. 39The priest shall come again on the seventh day and make an inspection; if the disease has spread in the walls of the house, 40the priest shall command that the stones in which the disease appears be taken out and thrown into an unclean place outside the city. 41He shall have the inside of the house scraped thoroughly, and the plaster that is scraped off shall be dumped in an unclean place outside the city. 42They shall take other stones and put them in the place of those stones, and take other plaster and plaster the house.

43 If the disease breaks out again in the house, after he has taken out the stones and scraped the house and plastered it, 44the priest shall go and make inspection; if the disease has spread in the house, it is a spreading leprous*b* disease in the house; it is unclean. 45He shall have the house torn down, its stones and timber and all the plaster of the house, and taken outside the city to an unclean place. 46All who enter the house while it is shut up shall be unclean until the evening; 47and all who sleep in the house shall wash their clothes; and all who eat in the house shall wash their clothes.

48 If the priest comes and makes an inspection, and the disease has not spread in the house after the house was plastered, the priest shall pronounce the house clean; the disease is healed. 49For the cleansing of the house he shall take two birds, with cedarwood and crimson yarn and hyssop, 50and shall slaughter one of the birds over fresh water in an earthen vessel, 51and shall take the cedarwood and the hyssop and the crimson yarn, along with the living bird, and dip them in the blood of the slaughtered bird and the fresh water, and sprinkle the house seven times. 52Thus he shall cleanse the house with the blood of the bird, and with the fresh water, and with the living bird, and with the cedarwood and hyssop and crimson yarn; 53and he shall let the living bird go out of the city into the open field; so he shall make atonement for the house, and it shall be clean.

54 This is the ritual for any leprous*b* disease: for an itch, 55for leprous*b* diseases in clothing and houses, 56and for a swelling or an eruption or a spot, 57to determine when it is unclean and when it is clean. This is the ritual for leprous*b* diseases.

Concerning Bodily Discharges

15 The LORD spoke to Moses and Aaron, saying: 2Speak to the people of Israel and say to them:

When any man has a discharge from his member,*c* his discharge makes him ceremonially unclean. 3The uncleanness of his discharge is this: whether his member*c* flows with his

---

a Gk Syr: Heb *afford,* *31such as he can afford,* one   *b* A term for several skin diseases; precise meaning uncertain
c Heb *flesh*

discharge, or his member*a* is stopped from discharging, it is uncleanness for him. ⁴Every bed on which the one with the discharge lies shall be unclean; and everything on which he sits shall be unclean. ⁵Anyone who touches his bed shall wash his clothes, and bathe in water, and be unclean until the evening. ⁶All who sit on anything on which the one with the discharge has sat shall wash their clothes, and bathe in water, and be unclean until the evening. ⁷All who touch the body of the one with the discharge shall wash their clothes, and bathe in water, and be unclean until the evening. ⁸If the one with the discharge spits on persons who are clean, then they shall wash their clothes, and bathe in water, and be unclean until the evening. ⁹Any saddle on which the one with the discharge rides shall be unclean. ¹⁰All who touch anything that was under him shall be unclean until the evening, and all who carry such a thing shall wash their clothes, and bathe in water, and be unclean until the evening. ¹¹All those whom the one with the discharge touches without his having rinsed his hands in water shall wash their clothes, and bathe in water, and be unclean until the evening. ¹²Any earthen vessel that the one with the discharge touches shall be broken; and every vessel of wood shall be rinsed in water.

13 When the one with a discharge is cleansed of his discharge, he shall count seven days for his cleansing; he shall wash his clothes and bathe his body in fresh water, and he shall be clean. ¹⁴On the eighth day he shall take two turtledoves or two pigeons and come before the LORD to the entrance of the tent of meeting and give them to the priest. ¹⁵The priest shall offer them, one for a sin offering and the other for a burnt offering; and the priest shall make atonement on his behalf before the LORD for his discharge.

16 If a man has an emission of semen, he shall bathe his whole body in water, and be unclean until the evening. ¹⁷Everything made of cloth or of skin on which the semen falls shall be washed with water, and be unclean until the evening. ¹⁸If a man lies with a woman and has an emission of semen, both of them shall bathe in water, and be unclean until the evening.

19 When a woman has a discharge of blood that is her regular discharge from her body, she shall be in her impurity for seven days, and whoever touches her shall be unclean until the evening. ²⁰Everything upon which she lies during her impurity shall be unclean; everything also upon which she sits shall be unclean. ²¹Whoever touches her bed shall wash his clothes, and bathe in water, and be unclean until the evening. ²²Whoever touches anything upon which she sits shall wash his clothes, and bathe in water, and be unclean until the evening; ²³whether it is the bed or anything upon which she sits, when he touches it he shall be unclean until the evening. ²⁴If any man lies with her, and her impurity falls on him, he shall be unclean seven days; and every bed on which he lies shall be unclean.

25 If a woman has a discharge of blood for many days, not at the time of her impurity, or if she has a discharge beyond the time of her impurity, all the days of the discharge she shall continue in uncleanness; as in the days of her impurity, she shall be unclean. ²⁶Every bed on which she lies during all the days of her discharge shall be treated as the bed of her impurity; and everything on which she sits shall be unclean, as in the uncleanness of her impurity. ²⁷Whoever touches these things shall be unclean, and shall wash his clothes, and bathe in water, and be unclean until the evening. ²⁸If she is cleansed of her discharge, she shall count seven days, and after that she shall be clean. ²⁹On the eighth day she shall take two turtledoves or two pigeons and bring them to the priest at the entrance of the tent of meeting. ³⁰The priest shall offer one for a sin offering and the other for a burnt offering; and the priest shall make atonement on her behalf before the LORD for her unclean discharge.

31 Thus you shall keep the people of Israel separate from their uncleanness, so that they

a Heb *flesh*

do not die in their uncleanness by defiling my tabernacle that is in their midst.

32 This is the ritual for those who have a discharge: for him who has an emission of semen, becoming unclean thereby, 33for her who is in the infirmity of her period, for anyone, male or female, who has a discharge, and for the man who lies with a woman who is unclean.

The Day of Atonement

16 The LORD spoke to Moses after the death of the two sons of Aaron, when they drew near before the LORD and died. 2The LORD said to Moses:

Tell your brother Aaron not to come just at any time into the sanctuary inside the curtain before the mercy seat*a* that is upon the ark, or he will die; for I appear in the cloud upon the mercy seat.*a* 3Thus shall Aaron come into the holy place: with a young bull for a sin offering and a ram for a burnt offering. 4He shall put on the holy linen tunic, and shall have the linen undergarments next to his body, fasten the linen sash, and wear the linen turban; these are the holy vestments. He shall bathe his body in water, and then put them on. 5He shall take from the congregation of the people of Israel two male goats for a sin offering, and one ram for a burnt offering.

6 Aaron shall offer the bull as a sin offering for himself, and shall make atonement for himself and for his house. 7He shall take the two goats and set them before the LORD at the entrance of the tent of meeting; 8and Aaron shall cast lots on the two goats, one lot for the LORD and the other lot for Azazel.*b* 9Aaron shall present the goat on which the lot fell for the LORD, and offer it as a sin offering; 10but the goat on which the lot fell for Azazel*b* shall be presented alive before the LORD to make atonement over it, that it may be sent away into the wilderness to Azazel.*b*

11 Aaron shall present the bull as a sin offering for himself, and shall make atonement for himself and for his house; he shall slaughter the bull as a sin offering for himself. 12He

shall take a censer full of coals of fire from the altar before the LORD, and two handfuls of crushed sweet incense, and he shall bring it inside the curtain 13and put the incense on the fire before the LORD, that the cloud of the incense may cover the mercy seat*a* that is upon the covenant,*c* or he will die. 14He shall take some of the blood of the bull, and sprinkle it with his finger on the front of the mercy seat,*a* and before the mercy seat*a* he shall sprinkle the blood with his finger seven times.

15 He shall slaughter the goat of the sin offering that is for the people and bring its blood inside the curtain, and do with its blood as he did with the blood of the bull, sprinkling it upon the mercy seat*a* and before the mercy seat.*a* 16Thus he shall make atonement for the sanctuary, because of the uncleannesses of the people of Israel, and because of their transgressions, all their sins; and so he shall do for the tent of meeting, which remains with them in the midst of their uncleannesses. 17No one shall be in the tent of meeting from the time he enters to make atonement in the sanctuary until he comes out and has made atonement for himself and for his house and for all the assembly of Israel. 18Then he shall go out to the altar that is before the LORD and make atonement on its behalf, and shall take some of the blood of the bull and of the blood of the goat, and put it on each of the horns of the altar. 19He shall sprinkle some of the blood on it with his finger seven times, and cleanse it and hallow it from the uncleannesses of the people of Israel.

20 When he has finished atoning for the holy place and the tent of meeting and the altar, he shall present the live goat. 21Then Aaron shall lay both his hands on the head of the live goat, and confess over it all the iniquities of the people of Israel, and all their transgressions, all their sins, putting them on the head of the goat, and sending it away into the wilderness by means of someone designated for the task.*d* 22The goat shall bear on itself all their in-

---

a Or *the cover*   *b* Traditionally rendered *a scapegoat*   *c* Or *treaty*, or *testament*; Heb *eduth*   *d* Meaning of Heb uncertain iquities to a barren region; and the goat shall be set free in the wilderness.

23 Then Aaron shall enter the tent of meeting, and shall take off the linen vestments that he put on when he went into the holy place, and shall leave them there. 24He shall bathe his body in water in a holy place, and put on his vestments; then he shall come out and offer his burnt offering and the burnt offering of the people, making atonement for himself and for the people. 25The fat of the sin offering he shall turn into smoke on the altar. 26The one who sets the goat free for Azazel*a* shall wash his clothes and bathe his body in water, and afterward may come into the camp. 27The bull of the sin offering and the goat of the sin offering, whose blood was brought in to make atonement in the holy place, shall be taken outside the camp; their skin and their flesh and their dung shall be consumed in fire. 28The one who burns them shall wash his clothes and bathe his body in water, and afterward may come into the camp.

29 This shall be a statute to you forever: In the seventh month, on the tenth day of the month, you shall deny yourselves,*b* and shall do no work, neither the citizen nor the alien who resides among you. 30For on this day atonement shall be made for you, to cleanse you; from all your sins you shall be clean before the LORD. 31It is a sabbath of complete rest to you, and you shall deny yourselves;*b* it is a statute forever. 32The priest who is anointed and consecrated as priest in his father's place shall make atonement, wearing the linen vestments, the holy vestments. 33He shall make atonement for the sanctuary, and he shall make atonement for the tent of meeting and for the altar, and he shall make atonement for the priests and for all the people of the assembly. 34This shall be an everlasting statute for you, to make atonement for the people of Israel once in the year for all their sins. And Moses did as the LORD had commanded him.

The Slaughtering of Animals

17 The LORD spoke to Moses: 2 Speak to Aaron and his sons and to all the people of Israel and say to them: This is what the LORD has commanded. 3If anyone of the house of Israel slaughters an ox or a lamb or a goat in the camp, or slaughters it outside the camp, 4and does not bring it to the entrance of the tent of meeting, to present it as an offering to the LORD before the tabernacle of the LORD, he shall be held guilty of bloodshed; he has shed blood, and he shall be cut off from the people. 5This is in order that the people of Israel may bring their sacrifices that they offer in the open field, that they may bring them to the LORD, to the priest at the entrance of the tent of meeting, and offer them as sacrifices of well-being to the LORD. 6The priest shall dash the blood against the altar of the LORD at the entrance of the tent of meeting, and turn the fat into smoke as a pleasing odor to the LORD, 7so that they may no longer offer their sacrifices for goat-demons, to whom they prostitute themselves. This shall be a statute forever to them throughout their generations.

8 And say to them further: Anyone of the house of Israel or of the aliens who reside among them who offers a burnt offering or sacrifice, 9and does not bring it to the entrance of the tent of meeting, to sacrifice it to the LORD, shall be cut off from the people.

Eating Blood Prohibited

10 If anyone of the house of Israel or of the aliens who reside among them eats any blood, I will set my face against that person who eats blood, and will cut that person off from the people. 11For the life of the flesh is in the blood; and I have given it to you for making atonement for your lives on the altar; for, as life, it is the blood that makes atonement. 12Therefore I have said to the people of Israel: No person among you shall eat blood, nor shall any alien who resides among you eat blood. 13And anyone of the people of Israel,

---

a Traditionally rendered *a scapegoat*   *b* Or *shall fast* or of the aliens who reside among them, who hunts down an animal or bird that may be eaten shall pour out its blood and cover it with earth.

14 For the life of every creature—its blood is its life; therefore I have said to the people of Israel: You shall not eat the blood of any creature, for the life of every creature is its blood; whoever eats it shall be cut off. 15All persons, citizens or aliens, who eat what dies of itself or what has been torn by wild animals, shall wash their clothes, and bathe themselves in water, and be unclean until the evening; then they shall be clean. 16But if they do not wash themselves or bathe their body, they shall bear their guilt.

Sexual Relations

18 The LORD spoke to Moses, saying: 2 Speak to the people of Israel and say to them: I am the LORD your God. 3You shall not do as they do in the land of Egypt, where you lived, and you shall not do as they do in the land of Canaan, to which I am bringing you. You shall not follow their statutes. 4My ordinances you shall observe and my statutes you shall keep, following them: I am the LORD your God. 5You shall keep my statutes and my ordinances; by doing so one shall live: I am the LORD.

6 None of you shall approach anyone near of kin to uncover nakedness: I am the LORD. 7You shall not uncover the nakedness of your father, which is the nakedness of your mother; she is your mother, you shall not uncover her nakedness. 8You shall not uncover the nakedness of your father's wife; it is the nakedness of your father. 9You shall not uncover the nakedness of your sister, your father's daughter or your mother's daughter, whether born at home or born abroad. 10You shall not uncover the nakedness of your son's daughter or of your daughter's daughter, for their nakedness is your own nakedness. 11You shall not uncover the nakedness of your father's wife's daughter, begotten by your father, since she is your sister.

12You shall not uncover the nakedness of your father's sister; she is your father's flesh. 13You shall not uncover the nakedness of your mother's sister, for she is your mother's flesh. 14You shall not uncover the nakedness of your father's brother, that is, you shall not approach his wife; she is your aunt. 15You shall not uncover the nakedness of your daughter-in-law: she is your son's wife; you shall not uncover her nakedness. 16You shall not uncover the nakedness of your brother's wife; it is your brother's nakedness. 17You shall not uncover the nakedness of a woman and her daughter, and you shall not take*a* her son's daughter or her daughter's daughter to uncover her nakedness; they are your*b* flesh; it is depravity. 18And you shall not take*a* a woman as a rival to her sister, uncovering her nakedness while her sister is still alive.

19 You shall not approach a woman to uncover her nakedness while she is in her menstrual uncleanness. 20You shall not have sexual relations with your kinsman's wife, and defile yourself with her. 21You shall not give any of your offspring to sacrifice them*c* to Molech, and so profane the name of your God: I am the LORD. 22You shall not lie with a male as with a woman; it is an abomination. 23You shall not have sexual relations with any animal and defile yourself with it, nor shall any woman give herself to an animal to have sexual relations with it: it is perversion.

24 Do not defile yourselves in any of these ways, for by all these practices the nations I am casting out before you have defiled themselves. 25Thus the land became defiled; and I punished it for its iniquity, and the land vomited out its inhabitants. 26But you shall keep my statutes and my ordinances and commit none of these abominations, either the citizen or the alien who resides among you 27(for the inhabitants of the land, who were before you, committed all of these abominations, and the land became defiled); 28otherwise the land will vomit you out for defiling it, as it vomited out the nation that was before you. 29For whoever commits any of these abominations shall be cut off

---

a Or *marry*   *b* Gk: Heb lacks *your*   *c* Heb *to pass them over* from their people. ³⁰So keep my charge not to commit any of these abominations that were done before you, and not to defile yourselves by them: I am the LORD your God.

Ritual and Moral Holiness

19 The LORD spoke to Moses, saying: 2 Speak to all the congregation of the people of Israel and say to them: You shall be holy, for I the LORD your God am holy. ³You shall each revere your mother and father, and you shall keep my sabbaths: I am the LORD your God. ⁴Do not turn to idols or make cast images for yourselves: I am the LORD your God.

5 When you offer a sacrifice of well-being to the LORD, offer it in such a way that it is acceptable in your behalf. ⁶It shall be eaten on the same day you offer it, or on the next day; and anything left over until the third day shall be consumed in fire. ⁷If it is eaten at all on the third day, it is an abomination; it will not be acceptable. ⁸All who eat it shall be subject to punishment, because they have profaned what is holy to the LORD; and any such person shall be cut off from the people.

9 When you reap the harvest of your land, you shall not reap to the very edges of your field, or gather the gleanings of your harvest. ¹⁰You shall not strip your vineyard bare, or gather the fallen grapes of your vineyard; you shall leave them for the poor and the alien: I am the LORD your God.

11 You shall not steal; you shall not deal falsely; and you shall not lie to one another. ¹²And you shall not swear falsely by my name, profaning the name of your God: I am the LORD.

13 You shall not defraud your neighbor; you shall not steal; and you shall not keep for yourself the wages of a laborer until morning. ¹⁴You shall not revile the deaf or put a stumbling block before the blind; you shall fear your God: I am the LORD.

15 You shall not render an unjust judgment; you shall not be partial to the poor or defer to the great: with justice you shall judge your neighbor. ¹⁶You shall not go around as a slanderer*a* among your people, and you shall not profit by the blood*b* of your neighbor: I am the LORD.

17 You shall not hate in your heart anyone of your kin; you shall reprove your neighbor, or you will incur guilt yourself. ¹⁸You shall not take vengeance or bear a grudge against any of your people, but you shall love your neighbor as yourself: I am the LORD.

19 You shall keep my statutes. You shall not let your animals breed with a different kind; you shall not sow your field with two kinds of seed; nor shall you put on a garment made of two different materials.

20 If a man has sexual relations with a woman who is a slave, designated for another man but not ransomed or given her freedom, an inquiry shall be held. They shall not be put to death, since she has not been freed; ²¹but he shall bring a guilt offering for himself to the LORD, at the entrance of the tent of meeting, a ram as guilt offering. ²²And the priest shall make atonement for him with the ram of guilt offering before the LORD for his sin that he committed; and the sin he committed shall be forgiven him.

23 When you come into the land and plant all kinds of trees for food, then you shall regard their fruit as forbidden;*c* three years it shall be forbidden*d* to you, it must not be eaten. ²⁴In the fourth year all their fruit shall be set apart for rejoicing in the LORD. ²⁵But in the fifth year you may eat of their fruit, that their yield may be increased for you: I am the LORD your God.

26 You shall not eat anything with its blood. You shall not practice augury or witchcraft. ²⁷You shall not round off the hair on your temples or mar the edges of your beard. ²⁸You shall not make any gashes in your flesh for the dead or tattoo any marks upon you: I am the LORD.

29 Do not profane your daughter by making her a prostitute, that the land not become prostituted and full of depravity. ³⁰You shall keep my sabbaths and reverence my sanctuary: I am the LORD.

---

a Meaning of Heb uncertain   *b* Heb *stand against the blood*   *c* Heb *as their uncircumcision*   *d* Heb *uncircumcision*

31 Do not turn to mediums or wizards; do not seek them out, to be defiled by them: I am the LORD your God.

32 You shall rise before the aged, and defer to the old; and you shall fear your God: I am the LORD.

33 When an alien resides with you in your land, you shall not oppress the alien. 34The alien who resides with you shall be to you as the citizen among you; you shall love the alien as yourself, for you were aliens in the land of Egypt: I am the LORD your God.

35 You shall not cheat in measuring length, weight, or quantity. 36You shall have honest balances, honest weights, an honest ephah, and an honest hin: I am the LORD your God, who brought you out of the land of Egypt. 37You shall keep all my statutes and all my ordinances, and observe them: I am the LORD.

Penalties for Violations of Holiness

20 The LORD spoke to Moses, saying: 2Say further to the people of Israel:

Any of the people of Israel, or of the aliens who reside in Israel, who give any of their offspring to Molech shall be put to death; the people of the land shall stone them to death. 3I myself will set my face against them, and will cut them off from the people, because they have given of their offspring to Molech, defiling my sanctuary and profaning my holy name. 4And if the people of the land should ever close their eyes to them, when they give of their offspring to Molech, and do not put them to death, 5I myself will set my face against them and against their family, and will cut them off from among their people, them and all who follow them in prostituting themselves to Molech.

6 If any turn to mediums and wizards, prostituting themselves to them, I will set my face against them, and will cut them off from the people. 7Consecrate yourselves therefore, and be holy; for I am the LORD your God. 8Keep my statutes, and observe them; I am the LORD; I sanctify you. 9All who curse father or moth-

er shall be put to death; having cursed father or mother, their blood is upon them.

10 If a man commits adultery with the wife of*a* his neighbor, both the adulterer and the adulteress shall be put to death. 11The man who lies with his father's wife has uncovered his father's nakedness; both of them shall be put to death; their blood is upon them. 12If a man lies with his daughter-in-law, both of them shall be put to death; they have committed perversion, their blood is upon them. 13If a man lies with a male as with a woman, both of them have committed an abomination; they shall be put to death; their blood is upon them. 14If a man takes a wife and her mother also, it is depravity; they shall be burned to death, both he and they, that there may be no depravity among you. 15If a man has sexual relations with an animal, he shall be put to death; and you shall kill the animal. 16If a woman approaches any animal and has sexual relations with it, you shall kill the woman and the animal; they shall be put to death, their blood is upon them.

17 If a man takes his sister, a daughter of his father or a daughter of his mother, and sees her nakedness, and she sees his nakedness, it is a disgrace, and they shall be cut off in the sight of their people; he has uncovered his sister's nakedness, he shall be subject to punishment. 18If a man lies with a woman having her sickness and uncovers her nakedness, he has laid bare her flow and she has laid bare her flow of blood; both of them shall be cut off from their people. 19You shall not uncover the nakedness of your mother's sister or of your father's sister, for that is to lay bare one's own flesh; they shall be subject to punishment. 20If a man lies with his uncle's wife, he has uncovered his uncle's nakedness; they shall be subject to punishment; they shall die childless. 21If a man takes his brother's wife, it is impurity; he has uncovered his brother's nakedness; they shall be childless.

22 You shall keep all my statutes and all my ordinances, and observe them, so that the land to which I bring you to settle in may not

---

a Heb repeats *if a man commits adultery with the wife of* vomit you out. 23You shall not follow the practices of the nation that I am driving out before you. Because they did all these things, I abhorred them. 24But I have said to you: You shall inherit their land, and I will give it to you to possess, a land flowing with milk and honey. I am the LORD your God; I have separated you from the peoples. 25You shall therefore make a distinction between the clean animal and the unclean, and between the unclean bird and the clean; you shall not bring abomination on yourselves by animal or by bird or by anything with which the ground teems, which I have set apart for you to hold unclean. 26You shall be holy to me; for I the LORD am holy, and I have separated you from the other peoples to be mine.

27 A man or a woman who is a medium or a wizard shall be put to death; they shall be stoned to death, their blood is upon them.

The Holiness of Priests

21 The LORD said to Moses: Speak to the priests, the sons of Aaron, and say to them:

No one shall defile himself for a dead person among his relatives, 2except for his nearest kin: his mother, his father, his son, his daughter, his brother; 3likewise, for a virgin sister, close to him because she has had no husband, he may defile himself for her. 4But he shall not defile himself as a husband among his people and so profane himself. 5They shall not make bald spots upon their heads, or shave off the edges of their beards, or make any gashes in their flesh. 6They shall be holy to their God, and not profane the name of their God; for they offer the LORD's offerings by fire, the food of their God; therefore they shall be holy. 7They shall not marry a prostitute or a woman who has been defiled; neither shall they marry a woman divorced from her husband. For they are holy to their God, 8and you shall treat them as holy, since they offer the food of your God; they shall be holy to you, for I the LORD, I who sanctify you, am holy. 9When the daughter of a priest profanes herself through prostitution, she profanes her father; she shall be burned to death.

10 The priest who is exalted above his fellows, on whose head the anointing oil has been poured and who has been consecrated to wear the vestments, shall not dishevel his hair, nor tear his vestments. 11He shall not go where there is a dead body; he shall not defile himself even for his father or mother. 12He shall not go outside the sanctuary and thus profane the sanctuary of his God; for the consecration of the anointing oil of his God is upon him: I am the LORD. 13He shall marry only a woman who is a virgin. 14A widow, or a divorced woman, or a woman who has been defiled, a prostitute, these he shall not marry. He shall marry a virgin of his own kin, 15that he may not profane his offspring among his kin; for I am the LORD; I sanctify him.

16 The LORD spoke to Moses, saying: 17Speak to Aaron and say: No one of your offspring throughout their generations who has a blemish may approach to offer the food of his God. 18For no one who has a blemish shall draw near, one who is blind or lame, or one who has a mutilated face or a limb too long, 19or one who has a broken foot or a broken hand, 20or a hunchback, or a dwarf, or a man with a blemish in his eyes or an itching disease or scabs or crushed testicles. 21No descendant of Aaron the priest who has a blemish shall come near to offer the LORD's offerings by fire; since he has a blemish, he shall not come near to offer the food of his God. 22He may eat the food of his God, of the most holy as well as of the holy. 23But he shall not come near the curtain or approach the altar, because he has a blemish, that he may not profane my sanctuaries; for I am the LORD; I sanctify them. 24Thus Moses spoke to Aaron and to his sons and to all the people of Israel.

The Use of Holy Offerings

22 The LORD spoke to Moses, saying: 2Direct Aaron and his sons to deal carefully with the sacred donations of the people of Israel, which they dedicate to me, so that they may not profane my holy name; I am the LORD. 3Say to them: If anyone among all your offspring throughout your generations comes near the sacred donations, which the people of

Israel dedicate to the LORD, while he is in a state of uncleanness, that person shall be cut off from my presence: I am the LORD. 4No one of Aaron's offspring who has a leprous*a* disease or suffers a discharge may eat of the sacred donations until he is clean. Whoever touches anything made unclean by a corpse or a man who has had an emission of semen, 5and whoever touches any swarming thing by which he may be made unclean or any human being by whom he may be made unclean—whatever his uncleanness may be— 6the person who touches any such shall be unclean until evening and shall not eat of the sacred donations unless he has washed his body in water. 7When the sun sets he shall be clean; and afterward he may eat of the sacred donations, for they are his food. 8That which died or was torn by wild animals he shall not eat, becoming unclean by it: I am the LORD. 9They shall keep my charge, so that they may not incur guilt and die in the sanctuary*b* for having profaned it: I am the LORD; I sanctify them.

10 No lay person shall eat of the sacred donations. No bound or hired servant of the priest shall eat of the sacred donations; 11but if a priest acquires anyone by purchase, the person may eat of them; and those that are born in his house may eat of his food. 12If a priest's daughter marries a layman, she shall not eat of the offering of the sacred donations; 13but if a priest's daughter is widowed or divorced, without offspring, and returns to her father's house, as in her youth, she may eat of her father's food. No lay person shall eat of it. 14If a man eats of the sacred donation unintentionally, he shall add one-fifth of its value to it, and give the sacred donation to the priest. 15No one shall profane the sacred donations of the people of Israel, which they offer to the LORD, 16causing them to bear guilt requiring a guilt offering, by eating their sacred donations: for I am the LORD; I sanctify them.

Acceptable Offerings

17 The LORD spoke to Moses, saying: 18Speak to Aaron and his sons and all the people of Israel and say to them: When anyone of the house of Israel or of the aliens residing in Israel presents an offering, whether in payment of a vow or as a freewill offering that is offered to the LORD as a burnt offering, 19to be acceptable in your behalf it shall be a male without blemish, of the cattle or the sheep or the goats. 20You shall not offer anything that has a blemish, for it will not be acceptable in your behalf.

21 When anyone offers a sacrifice of well-being to the LORD, in fulfillment of a vow or as a freewill offering, from the herd or from the flock, to be acceptable it must be perfect; there shall be no blemish in it. 22Anything blind, or injured, or maimed, or having a discharge or an itch or scabs—these you shall not offer to the LORD or put any of them on the altar as offerings by fire to the LORD. 23An ox or a lamb that has a limb too long or too short you may present for a freewill offering; but it will not be accepted for a vow. 24Any animal that has its testicles bruised or crushed or torn or cut, you shall not offer to the LORD; such you shall not do within your land, 25nor shall you accept any such animals from a foreigner to offer as food to your God; since they are mutilated, with a blemish in them, they shall not be accepted in your behalf.

26 The LORD spoke to Moses, saying: 27When an ox or a sheep or a goat is born, it shall remain seven days with its mother, and from the eighth day on it shall be acceptable as the LORD's offering by fire. 28But you shall not slaughter, from the herd or the flock, an animal with its young on the same day. 29When you sacrifice a thanksgiving offering to the LORD, you shall sacrifice it so that it may be acceptable in your behalf. 30It shall be eaten on the same day; you shall not leave any of it until morning: I am the LORD.

31 Thus you shall keep my commandments and observe them: I am the LORD. 32You shall not profane my holy name, that I may be sanctified among the people of Israel: I am the

---

a A term for several skin diseases; precise meaning uncertain   *b* Vg: Heb *incur guilt for it and die in it*

LORD; I sanctify you, ³³I who brought you out of the land of Egypt to be your God: I am the LORD.

Appointed Festivals

23 The LORD spoke to Moses, saying: ²Speak to the people of Israel and say to them: These are the appointed festivals of the LORD that you shall proclaim as holy convocations, my appointed festivals.

The Sabbath, Passover, and Unleavened Bread

3 Six days shall work be done; but the seventh day is a sabbath of complete rest, a holy convocation; you shall do no work: it is a sabbath to the LORD throughout your settlements.

4 These are the appointed festivals of the LORD, the holy convocations, which you shall celebrate at the time appointed for them. ⁵In the first month, on the fourteenth day of the month, at twilight,^a there shall be a passover offering to the LORD, ⁶and on the fifteenth day of the same month is the festival of unleavened bread to the LORD; seven days you shall eat unleavened bread. ⁷On the first day you shall have a holy convocation; you shall not work at your occupations. ⁸For seven days you shall present the LORD's offerings by fire; on the seventh day there shall be a holy convocation: you shall not work at your occupations.

The Offering of First Fruits

9 The LORD spoke to Moses: ¹⁰Speak to the people of Israel and say to them: When you enter the land that I am giving you and you reap its harvest, you shall bring the sheaf of the first fruits of your harvest to the priest. ¹¹He shall raise the sheaf before the LORD, that you may find acceptance; on the day after the sabbath the priest shall raise it. ¹²On the day when you raise the sheaf, you shall offer a lamb a year old, without blemish, as a burnt offering to the LORD. ¹³And the grain offering with it shall be two-tenths of an ephah of choice flour mixed with oil, an offering by fire of pleasing odor to the LORD; and the drink offering with it shall

be of wine, one-fourth of a hin. ¹⁴You shall eat no bread or parched grain or fresh ears until that very day, until you have brought the offering of your God: it is a statute forever throughout your generations in all your settlements.

The Festival of Weeks

15 And from the day after the sabbath, from the day on which you bring the sheaf of the elevation offering, you shall count off seven weeks; they shall be complete. ¹⁶You shall count until the day after the seventh sabbath, fifty days; then you shall present an offering of new grain to the LORD. ¹⁷You shall bring from your settlements two loaves of bread as an elevation offering, each made of two-tenths of an ephah; they shall be of choice flour, baked with leaven, as first fruits to the LORD. ¹⁸You shall present with the bread seven lambs a year old without blemish, one young bull, and two rams; they shall be a burnt offering to the LORD, along with their grain offering and their drink offerings, an offering by fire of pleasing odor to the LORD. ¹⁹You shall also offer one male goat for a sin offering, and two male lambs a year old as a sacrifice of well-being. ²⁰The priest shall raise them with the bread of the first fruits as an elevation offering before the LORD, together with the two lambs; they shall be holy to the LORD for the priest. ²¹On that same day you shall make proclamation; you shall hold a holy convocation; you shall not work at your occupations. This is a statute forever in all your settlements throughout your generations.

22 When you reap the harvest of your land, you shall not reap to the very edges of your field, or gather the gleanings of your harvest; you shall leave them for the poor and for the alien: I am the LORD your God.

The Festival of Trumpets

23 The LORD spoke to Moses, saying: ²⁴Speak to the people of Israel, saying: In the seventh month, on the first day of the month,

a Heb *between the two evenings*

you shall observe a day of complete rest, a holy convocation commemorated with trumpet blasts. 25You shall not work at your occupations; and you shall present the LORD's offering by fire.

The Day of Atonement

26 The LORD spoke to Moses, saying: 27Now, the tenth day of this seventh month is the day of atonement; it shall be a holy convocation for you: you shall deny yourselves*a* and present the LORD's offering by fire; 28and you shall do no work during that entire day; for it is a day of atonement, to make atonement on your behalf before the LORD your God. 29For anyone who does not practice self-denial*b* during that entire day shall be cut off from the people. 30And anyone who does any work during that entire day, such a one I will destroy from the midst of the people. 31You shall do no work: it is a statute forever throughout your generations in all your settlements. 32It shall be to you a sabbath of complete rest, and you shall deny yourselves;*a* on the ninth day of the month at evening, from evening to evening you shall keep your sabbath.

The Festival of Booths

33 The LORD spoke to Moses, saying: 34Speak to the people of Israel, saying: On the fifteenth day of this seventh month, and lasting seven days, there shall be the festival of booths*c* to the LORD. 35The first day shall be a holy convocation; you shall not work at your occupations. 36Seven days you shall present the LORD's offerings by fire; on the eighth day you shall observe a holy convocation and present the LORD's offerings by fire; it is a solemn assembly; you shall not work at your occupations.

37 These are the appointed festivals of the LORD, which you shall celebrate as times of holy convocation, for presenting to the LORD offerings by fire—burnt offerings and grain offerings, sacrifices and drink offerings, each on its proper day— 38apart from the sabbaths of

the LORD, and apart from your gifts, and apart from all your votive offerings, and apart from all your freewill offerings, which you give to the LORD.

39 Now, the fifteenth day of the seventh month, when you have gathered in the produce of the land, you shall keep the festival of the LORD, lasting seven days; a complete rest on the first day, and a complete rest on the eighth day. 40On the first day you shall take the fruit of majestic*d* trees, branches of palm trees, boughs of leafy trees, and willows of the brook; and you shall rejoice before the LORD your God for seven days. 41You shall keep it as a festival to the LORD seven days in the year; you shall keep it in the seventh month as a statute forever throughout your generations. 42You shall live in booths for seven days; all that are citizens in Israel shall live in booths, 43so that your generations may know that I made the people of Israel live in booths when I brought them out of the land of Egypt: I am the LORD your God.

44 Thus Moses declared to the people of Israel the appointed festivals of the LORD.

The Lamp

24 The LORD spoke to Moses, saying: 2Command the people of Israel to bring you pure oil of beaten olives for the lamp, that a light may be kept burning regularly. 3Aaron shall set it up in the tent of meeting, outside the curtain of the covenant,*e* to burn from evening to morning before the LORD regularly; it shall be a statute forever throughout your generations. 4He shall set up the lamps on the lampstand of pure gold*f* before the LORD regularly.

The Bread for the Tabernacle

5 You shall take choice flour, and bake twelve loaves of it; two-tenths of an ephah shall be in each loaf. 6You shall place them in two rows, six in a row, on the table of pure gold.*g* 7You shall put pure frankincense with each row, to be a token offering for the bread, as an offering by fire to the LORD. 8Every sab-

---

a Or *shall fast*   *b* Or *does not fast*   *c* Or *tabernacles*: Heb *succoth*   *d* Meaning of Heb uncertain   *e* Or *treaty*, or *testament*; Heb *eduth*   *f* Heb *pure lampstand*   *g* Heb *pure table* bath day Aaron shall set them in order before the LORD regularly as a commitment of the people of Israel, as a covenant forever. ⁹They shall be for Aaron and his descendants, who shall eat them in a holy place, for they are most holy portions for him from the offerings by fire to the LORD, a perpetual due.

Blasphemy and Its Punishment

10 A man whose mother was an Israelite and whose father was an Egyptian came out among the people of Israel; and the Israelite woman's son and a certain Israelite began fighting in the camp. ¹¹The Israelite woman's son blasphemed the Name in a curse. And they brought him to Moses—now his mother's name was Shelomith, daughter of Dibri, of the tribe of Dan— ¹²and they put him in custody, until the decision of the LORD should be made clear to them.

13 The LORD said to Moses, saying: ¹⁴Take the blasphemer outside the camp; and let all who were within hearing lay their hands on his head, and let the whole congregation stone him. ¹⁵And speak to the people of Israel, saying: Anyone who curses God shall bear the sin. ¹⁶One who blasphemes the name of the LORD shall be put to death; the whole congregation shall stone the blasphemer. Aliens as well as citizens, when they blaspheme the Name, shall be put to death. ¹⁷Anyone who kills a human being shall be put to death. ¹⁸Anyone who kills an animal shall make restitution for it, life for life. ¹⁹Anyone who maims another shall suffer the same injury in return: ²⁰fracture for fracture, eye for eye, tooth for tooth; the injury inflicted is the injury to be suffered. ²¹One who kills an animal shall make restitution for it; but one who kills a human being shall be put to death. ²²You shall have one law for the alien and for the citizen: for I am the LORD your God. ²³Moses spoke thus to the people of Israel; and they took the blasphemer outside the camp, and stoned him to death. The people of Israel did as the LORD had commanded Moses.

The Sabbatical Year

25 The LORD spoke to Moses on Mount Sinai, saying: ²Speak to the people of Israel and say to them: When you enter the land that I am giving you, the land shall observe a sabbath for the LORD. ³Six years you shall sow your field, and six years you shall prune your vineyard, and gather in their yield; ⁴but in the seventh year there shall be a sabbath of complete rest for the land, a sabbath for the LORD: you shall not sow your field or prune your vineyard. ⁵You shall not reap the aftergrowth of your harvest or gather the grapes of your unpruned vine: it shall be a year of complete rest for the land. ⁶You may eat what the land yields during its sabbath—you, your male and female slaves, your hired and your bound laborers who live with you; ⁷for your livestock also, and for the wild animals in your land all its yield shall be for food.

The Year of Jubilee

8 You shall count off seven weeks*a* of years, seven times seven years, so that the period of seven weeks of years gives forty-nine years. ⁹Then you shall have the trumpet sounded loud; on the tenth day of the seventh month—on the day of atonement—you shall have the trumpet sounded throughout all your land. ¹⁰And you shall hallow the fiftieth year and you shall proclaim liberty throughout the land to all its inhabitants. It shall be a jubilee for you: you shall return, every one of you, to your property and every one of you to your family. ¹¹That fiftieth year shall be a jubilee for you: you shall not sow, or reap the aftergrowth, or harvest the unpruned vines. ¹²For it is a jubilee; it shall be holy to you: you shall eat only what the field itself produces.

13 In this year of jubilee you shall return, every one of you, to your property. ¹⁴When you make a sale to your neighbor or buy from your neighbor, you shall not cheat one another. ¹⁵When you buy from your neighbor, you shall pay only for the number of years since the jubilee; the seller shall charge you only for the re-

a Or *sabbaths*

maining crop years. 16If the years are more, you shall increase the price, and if the years are fewer, you shall diminish the price; for it is a certain number of harvests that are being sold to you. 17You shall not cheat one another, but you shall fear your God; for I am the LORD your God.

18 You shall observe my statutes and faithfully keep my ordinances, so that you may live on the land securely. 19The land will yield its fruit, and you will eat your fill and live on it securely. 20Should you ask, "What shall we eat in the seventh year, if we may not sow or gather in our crop?" 21I will order my blessing for you in the sixth year, so that it will yield a crop for three years. 22When you sow in the eighth year, you will be eating from the old crop; until the ninth year, when its produce comes in, you shall eat the old. 23The land shall not be sold in perpetuity, for the land is mine; with me you are but aliens and tenants. 24Throughout the land that you hold, you shall provide for the redemption of the land.

25 If anyone of your kin falls into difficulty and sells a piece of property, then the next of kin shall come and redeem what the relative has sold. 26If the person has no one to redeem it, but then prospers and finds sufficient means to do so, 27the years since its sale shall be computed and the difference shall be refunded to the person to whom it was sold, and the property shall be returned. 28But if there are not sufficient means to recover it, what was sold shall remain with the purchaser until the year of jubilee; in the jubilee it shall be released, and the property shall be returned.

29 If anyone sells a dwelling house in a walled city, it may be redeemed until a year has elapsed since its sale; the right of redemption shall be one year. 30If it is not redeemed before a full year has elapsed, a house that is in a walled city shall pass in perpetuity to the purchaser, throughout the generations; it shall not be released in the jubilee. 31But houses in villages that have no walls around them shall be classed as open country; they may be redeemed, and they shall be released in the jubilee. 32As for the cities of the Levites, the Levites shall forever have the right of redemption of the houses in the cities belonging to them. 33Such property as may be redeemed from the Levites—houses sold in a city belonging to them—shall be released in the jubilee; because the houses in the cities of the Levites are their possession among the people of Israel. 34But the open land around their cities may not be sold; for that is their possession for all time.

35 If any of your kin fall into difficulty and become dependent on you,*a* you shall support them; they shall live with you as though resident aliens. 36Do not take interest in advance or otherwise make a profit from them, but fear your God; let them live with you. 37You shall not lend them your money at interest taken in advance, or provide them food at a profit. 38I am the LORD your God, who brought you out of the land of Egypt, to give you the land of Canaan, to be your God.

39 If any who are dependent on you become so impoverished that they sell themselves to you, you shall not make them serve as slaves. 40They shall remain with you as hired or bound laborers. They shall serve with you until the year of the jubilee. 41Then they and their children with them shall be free from your authority; they shall go back to their own family and return to their ancestral property. 42For they are my servants, whom I brought out of the land of Egypt; they shall not be sold as slaves are sold. 43You shall not rule over them with harshness, but shall fear your God. 44As for the male and female slaves whom you may have, it is from the nations around you that you may acquire male and female slaves. 45You may also acquire them from among the aliens residing with you, and from their families that are with you, who have been born in your land; and they may be your property. 46You may keep them as a possession for your children after you, for them to inherit as property. These you may treat as slaves, but as for your fellow Israelites, no one shall rule over the other with harshness.

a Meaning of Heb uncertain

47 If resident aliens among you prosper, and if any of your kin fall into difficulty with one of them and sell themselves to an alien, or to a branch of the alien's family, 48after they have sold themselves they shall have the right of redemption; one of their brothers may redeem them, 49or their uncle or their uncle's son may redeem them, or anyone of their family who is of their own flesh may redeem them; or if they prosper they may redeem themselves. 50They shall compute with the purchaser the total from the year when they sold themselves to the alien until the jubilee year; the price of the sale shall be applied to the number of years: the time they were with the owner shall be rated as the time of a hired laborer. 51If many years remain, they shall pay for their redemption in proportion to the purchase price; 52and if few years remain until the jubilee year, they shall compute thus: according to the years involved they shall make payment for their redemption. 53As a laborer hired by the year they shall be under the alien's authority, who shall not, however, rule with harshness over them in your sight. 54And if they have not been redeemed in any of these ways, they and their children with them shall go free in the jubilee year. 55For to me the people of Israel are servants; they are my servants whom I brought out from the land of Egypt: I am the LORD your God.

Rewards for Obedience

26 You shall make for yourselves no idols and erect no carved images or pillars, and you shall not place figured stones in your land, to worship at them; for I am the LORD your God. 2You shall keep my sabbaths and reverence my sanctuary: I am the LORD.

3 If you follow my statutes and keep my commandments and observe them faithfully, 4I will give you your rains in their season, and the land shall yield its produce, and the trees of the field shall yield their fruit. 5Your threshing shall overtake the vintage, and the vintage shall overtake the sowing; you shall eat your bread to the full, and live securely in your land. 6And I will grant peace in the land, and you shall lie down, and no one shall make you afraid; I will remove dangerous animals from the land, and no sword shall go through your land. 7You shall give chase to your enemies, and they shall fall before you by the sword. 8Five of you shall give chase to a hundred, and a hundred of you shall give chase to ten thousand; your enemies shall fall before you by the sword. 9I will look with favor upon you and make you fruitful and multiply you; and I will maintain my covenant with you. 10You shall eat old grain long stored, and you shall have to clear out the old to make way for the new. 11I will place my dwelling in your midst, and I shall not abhor you. 12And I will walk among you, and will be your God, and you shall be my people. 13I am the LORD your God who brought you out of the land of Egypt, to be their slaves no more; I have broken the bars of your yoke and made you walk erect.

Penalties for Disobedience

14 But if you will not obey me, and do not observe all these commandments, 15if you spurn my statutes, and abhor my ordinances, so that you will not observe all my commandments, and you break my covenant, 16I in turn will do this to you: I will bring terror on you; consumption and fever that waste the eyes and cause life to pine away. You shall sow your seed in vain, for your enemies shall eat it. 17I will set my face against you, and you shall be struck down by your enemies; your foes shall rule over you, and you shall flee though no one pursues you. 18And if in spite of this you will not obey me, I will continue to punish you sevenfold for your sins. 19I will break your proud glory, and I will make your sky like iron and your earth like copper. 20Your strength shall be spent to no purpose: your land shall not yield its produce, and the trees of the land shall not yield their fruit.

21 If you continue hostile to me, and will not obey me, I will continue to plague you sevenfold for your sins. 22I will let loose wild animals against you, and they shall bereave you of your children and destroy your livestock; they shall make you few in number, and your roads shall be deserted.

23 If in spite of these punishments you

have not turned back to me, but continue hostile to me, [24]then I too will continue hostile to you: I myself will strike you sevenfold for your sins. [25]I will bring the sword against you, executing vengeance for the covenant; and if you withdraw within your cities, I will send pestilence among you, and you shall be delivered into enemy hands. [26]When I break your staff of bread, ten women shall bake your bread in a single oven, and they shall dole out your bread by weight; and though you eat, you shall not be satisfied.

[27] But if, despite this, you disobey me, and continue hostile to me, [28]I will continue hostile to you in fury; I in turn will punish you myself sevenfold for your sins. [29]You shall eat the flesh of your sons, and you shall eat the flesh of your daughters. [30]I will destroy your high places and cut down your incense altars; I will heap your carcasses on the carcasses of your idols. I will abhor you. [31]I will lay your cities waste, will make your sanctuaries desolate, and I will not smell your pleasing odors. [32]I will devastate the land, so that your enemies who come to settle in it shall be appalled at it. [33]And you I will scatter among the nations, and I will unsheathe the sword against you; your land shall be a desolation, and your cities a waste.

[34] Then the land shall enjoy*a* its sabbath years as long as it lies desolate, while you are in the land of your enemies; then the land shall rest, and enjoy*a* its sabbath years. [35]As long as it lies desolate, it shall have the rest it did not have on your sabbaths when you were living on it. [36]And as for those of you who survive, I will send faintness into their hearts in the lands of their enemies; the sound of a driven leaf shall put them to flight, and they shall flee as one flees from the sword, and they shall fall though no one pursues. [37]They shall stumble over one another, as if to escape a sword, though no one pursues; and you shall have no power to stand against your enemies. [38]You shall perish among the nations, and the land of your enemies shall devour you. [39]And those of you who survive shall languish in the land of your enemies because of their iniquities; also they shall languish because of the iniquities of their ancestors.

[40] But if they confess their iniquity and the iniquity of their ancestors, in that they committed treachery against me and, moreover, that they continued hostile to me— [41]so that I, in turn, continued hostile to them and brought them into the land of their enemies; if then their uncircumcised heart is humbled and they make amends for their iniquity, [42]then will I remember my covenant with Jacob; I will remember also my covenant with Isaac and also my covenant with Abraham, and I will remember the land. [43]For the land shall be deserted by them, and enjoy*a* its sabbath years by lying desolate without them, while they shall make amends for their iniquity, because they dared to spurn my ordinances, and they abhorred my statutes. [44]Yet for all that, when they are in the land of their enemies, I will not spurn them, or abhor them so as to destroy them utterly and break my covenant with them; for I am the LORD their God; [45]but I will remember in their favor the covenant with their ancestors whom I brought out of the land of Egypt in the sight of the nations, to be their God: I am the LORD.

[46] These are the statutes and ordinances and laws that the LORD established between himself and the people of Israel on Mount Sinai through Moses.

Votive Offerings

27 The LORD spoke to Moses, saying: [2]Speak to the people of Israel and say to them: When a person makes an explicit vow to the LORD concerning the equivalent for a human being, [3]the equivalent for a male shall be: from twenty to sixty years of age the equivalent shall be fifty shekels of silver by the sanctuary shekel. [4]If the person is a female, the equivalent is thirty shekels. [5]If the age is from five to twenty years of age, the equivalent is twenty shekels for a male and ten shekels for a female. [6]If the age is from one month to five

a Or *make up for*

years, the equivalent for a male is five shekels of silver, and for a female the equivalent is three shekels of silver. 7And if the person is sixty years old or over, then the equivalent for a male is fifteen shekels, and for a female ten shekels. 8If any cannot afford the equivalent, they shall be brought before the priest and the priest shall assess them; the priest shall assess them according to what each one making a vow can afford.

9 If it concerns an animal that may be brought as an offering to the LORD, any such that may be given to the LORD shall be holy. 10Another shall not be exchanged or substituted for it, either good for bad or bad for good; and if one animal is substituted for another, both that one and its substitute shall be holy. 11If it concerns any unclean animal that may not be brought as an offering to the LORD, the animal shall be presented before the priest. 12The priest shall assess it: whether good or bad, according to the assessment of the priest, so it shall be. 13But if it is to be redeemed, one-fifth must be added to the assessment.

14 If a person consecrates a house to the LORD, the priest shall assess it: whether good or bad, as the priest assesses it, so it shall stand. 15And if the one who consecrates the house wishes to redeem it, one-fifth shall be added to its assessed value, and it shall revert to the original owner.

16 If a person consecrates to the LORD any inherited landholding, its assessment shall be in accordance with its seed requirements: fifty shekels of silver to a homer of barley seed. 17If the person consecrates the field as of the year of jubilee, that assessment shall stand; 18but if the field is consecrated after the jubilee, the priest shall compute the price for it according to the years that remain until the year of jubilee, and the assessment shall be reduced. 19And if the one who consecrates the field wishes to redeem it, then one-fifth shall be added to its assessed value, and it shall revert to the original

owner; 20but if the field is not redeemed, or if it has been sold to someone else, it shall no longer be redeemable. 21But when the field is released in the jubilee, it shall be holy to the LORD as a devoted field; it becomes the priest's holding. 22If someone consecrates to the LORD a field that has been purchased, which is not a part of the inherited landholding, 23the priest shall compute for it the proportionate assessment up to the year of jubilee, and the assessment shall be paid as of that day, a sacred donation to the LORD. 24In the year of jubilee the field shall return to the one from whom it was bought, whose holding the land is. 25All assessments shall be by the sanctuary shekel: twenty gerahs shall make a shekel.

26 A firstling of animals, however, which as a firstling belongs to the LORD, cannot be consecrated by anyone; whether ox or sheep, it is the LORD's. 27If it is an unclean animal, it shall be ransomed at its assessment, with one-fifth added; if it is not redeemed, it shall be sold at its assessment.

28 Nothing that a person owns that has been devoted to destruction for the LORD, be it human or animal, or inherited landholding, may be sold or redeemed; every devoted thing is most holy to the LORD. 29No human beings who have been devoted to destruction can be ransomed; they shall be put to death.

30 All tithes from the land, whether the seed from the ground or the fruit from the tree, are the LORD's; they are holy to the LORD. 31If persons wish to redeem any of their tithes, they must add one-fifth to them. 32All tithes of herd and flock, every tenth one that passes under the shepherd's staff, shall be holy to the LORD. 33Let no one inquire whether it is good or bad, or make substitution for it; if one makes substitution for it, then both it and the substitute shall be holy and cannot be redeemed.

34 These are the commandments that the LORD gave to Moses for the people of Israel on Mount Sinai.

NUMBERS

The First Census of Israel

1 The LORD spoke to Moses in the wilderness of Sinai, in the tent of meeting, on the first day of the second month, in the second year after they had come out of the land of Egypt, saying: ²Take a census of the whole congregation of Israelites, in their clans, by ancestral houses, according to the number of names, every male individually; ³from twenty years old and upward, everyone in Israel able to go to war. You and Aaron shall enroll them, company by company. ⁴A man from each tribe shall be with you, each man the head of his ancestral house. ⁵These are the names of the men who shall assist you:

From Reuben, Elizur son of Shedeur.
6 From Simeon, Shelumiel son of
      Zurishaddai.
7 From Judah, Nahshon son of
      Amminadab.
8 From Issachar, Nethanel son of Zuar.
9 From Zebulun, Eliab son of Helon.
10 From the sons of Joseph:
   from Ephraim, Elishama son of
      Ammihud;
   from Manasseh, Gamaliel son of
      Pedahzur.
11 From Benjamin, Abidan son of Gideoni.
12 From Dan, Ahiezer son of
      Ammishaddai.
13 From Asher, Pagiel son of Ochran.
14 From Gad, Eliasaph son of Deuel.
15 From Naphtali, Ahira son of Enan.

¹⁶These were the ones chosen from the congregation, the leaders of their ancestral tribes, the heads of the divisions of Israel.

17 Moses and Aaron took these men who had been designated by name, ¹⁸and on the first day of the second month they assembled the whole congregation together. They registered themselves in their clans, by their ancestral houses, according to the number of names from twenty years old and upward, individually, ¹⁹as the LORD commanded Moses. So he enrolled them in the wilderness of Sinai.

20 The descendants of Reuben, Israel's firstborn, their lineage, in their clans, by their ancestral houses, according to the number of names, individually, every male from twenty years old and upward, everyone able to go to war: ²¹those enrolled of the tribe of Reuben were forty-six thousand five hundred.

22 The descendants of Simeon, their lineage, in their clans, by their ancestral houses, those of them that were numbered, according to the number of names, individually, every male from twenty years old and upward, everyone able to go to war: ²³those enrolled of the tribe of Simeon were fifty-nine thousand three hundred.

24 The descendants of Gad, their lineage, in their clans, by their ancestral houses, according to the number of the names, from twenty years old and upward, everyone able to go to war: ²⁵those enrolled of the tribe of Gad were forty-five thousand six hundred fifty.

26 The descendants of Judah, their lineage, in their clans, by their ancestral houses, according to the number of names, from twenty years old and upward, everyone able to go to war: ²⁷those enrolled of the tribe of Judah were seventy-four thousand six hundred.

28 The descendants of Issachar, their lineage, in their clans, by their ancestral houses, according to the number of names, from twenty years old and upward, everyone able to go to war: ²⁹those enrolled of the tribe of Issachar were fifty-four thousand four hundred.

30 The descendants of Zebulun, their lineage, in their clans, by their ancestral houses, according to the number of names, from twenty years old and upward, everyone able to go to war: ³¹those enrolled of the tribe of Zebulun were fifty-seven thousand four hundred.

32 The descendants of Joseph, namely, the descendants of Ephraim, their lineage, in their clans, by their ancestral houses, according to the number of names, from twenty years old and upward, everyone able to go to war: ³³those enrolled of the tribe of Ephraim were forty thousand five hundred.

34 The descendants of Manasseh, their lin-

eage, in their clans, by their ancestral houses, according to the number of names, from twenty years old and upward, everyone able to go to war: ³⁵those enrolled of the tribe of Manasseh were thirty-two thousand two hundred.

36 The descendants of Benjamin, their lineage, in their clans, by their ancestral houses, according to the number of names, from twenty years old and upward, everyone able to go to war: ³⁷those enrolled of the tribe of Benjamin were thirty-five thousand four hundred.

38 The descendants of Dan, their lineage, in their clans, by their ancestral houses, according to the number of names, from twenty years old and upward, everyone able to go to war: ³⁹those enrolled of the tribe of Dan were sixty-two thousand seven hundred.

40 The descendants of Asher, their lineage, in their clans, by their ancestral houses, according to the number of names, from twenty years old and upward, everyone able to go to war: ⁴¹those enrolled of the tribe of Asher were forty-one thousand five hundred.

42 The descendants of Naphtali, their lineage, in their clans, by their ancestral houses, according to the number of names, from twenty years old and upward, everyone able to go to war: ⁴³those enrolled of the tribe of Naphtali were fifty-three thousand four hundred.

44 These are those who were enrolled, whom Moses and Aaron enrolled with the help of the leaders of Israel, twelve men, each representing his ancestral house. ⁴⁵So the whole number of the Israelites, by their ancestral houses, from twenty years old and upward, everyone able to go to war in Israel— ⁴⁶their whole number was six hundred three thousand five hundred fifty. ⁴⁷The Levites, however, were not numbered by their ancestral tribe along with them.

48 The LORD had said to Moses: ⁴⁹Only the tribe of Levi you shall not enroll, and you shall not take a census of them with the other Israelites. ⁵⁰Rather you shall appoint the Levites over the tabernacle of the covenant,ᵃ and over all its equipment, and over all that belongs to

it; they are to carry the tabernacle and all its equipment, and they shall tend it, and shall camp around the tabernacle. ⁵¹When the tabernacle is to set out, the Levites shall take it down; and when the tabernacle is to be pitched, the Levites shall set it up. And any outsider who comes near shall be put to death. ⁵²The other Israelites shall camp in their respective regimental camps, by companies; ⁵³but the Levites shall camp around the tabernacle of the covenant,ᵃ that there may be no wrath on the congregation of the Israelites; and the Levites shall perform the guard duty of the tabernacle of the covenant.ᵃ ⁵⁴The Israelites did so; they did just as the LORD commanded Moses.

The Order of Encampment and Marching

2 The LORD spoke to Moses and Aaron, saying: ²The Israelites shall camp each in their respective regiments, under ensigns by their ancestral houses; they shall camp facing the tent of meeting on every side. ³Those to camp on the east side toward the sunrise shall be of the regimental encampment of Judah by companies. The leader of the people of Judah shall be Nahshon son of Amminadab, ⁴with a company as enrolled of seventy-four thousand six hundred. ⁵Those to camp next to him shall be the tribe of Issachar. The leader of the Issacharites shall be Nethanel son of Zuar, ⁶with a company as enrolled of fifty-four thousand four hundred. ⁷Then the tribe of Zebulun: The leader of the Zebulunites shall be Eliab son of Helon, ⁸with a company as enrolled of fifty-seven thousand four hundred. ⁹The total enrollment of the camp of Judah, by companies, is one hundred eighty-six thousand four hundred. They shall set out first on the march.

10 On the south side shall be the regimental encampment of Reuben by companies. The leader of the Reubenites shall be Elizur son of Shedeur, ¹¹with a company as enrolled of forty-six thousand five hundred. ¹²And those to camp next to him shall be the tribe of Simeon. The leader of the Simeonites shall be Shelumiel son of Zurishaddai, ¹³with a company as en-

---

ᵃ Or *treaty*, or *testimony*; Heb *eduth*

rolled of fifty-nine thousand three hundred. 14Then the tribe of Gad: The leader of the Gadites shall be Eliasaph son of Reuel, 15with a company as enrolled of forty-five thousand six hundred fifty. 16The total enrollment of the camp of Reuben, by companies, is one hundred fifty-one thousand four hundred fifty. They shall set out second.

17 The tent of meeting, with the camp of the Levites, shall set out in the center of the camps; they shall set out just as they camp, each in position, by their regiments.

18 On the west side shall be the regimental encampment of Ephraim by companies. The leader of the people of Ephraim shall be Elishama son of Ammihud, 19with a company as enrolled of forty thousand five hundred. 20Next to him shall be the tribe of Manasseh. The leader of the people of Manasseh shall be Gamaliel son of Pedahzur, 21with a company as enrolled of thirty-two thousand two hundred. 22Then the tribe of Benjamin: The leader of the Benjaminites shall be Abidan son of Gideoni, 23with a company as enrolled of thirty-five thousand four hundred. 24The total enrollment of the camp of Ephraim, by companies, is one hundred eight thousand one hundred. They shall set out third on the march.

25 On the north side shall be the regimental encampment of Dan by companies. The leader of the Danites shall be Ahiezer son of Ammishaddai, 26with a company as enrolled of sixty-two thousand seven hundred. 27Those to camp next to him shall be the tribe of Asher. The leader of the Asherites shall be Pagiel son of Ochran, 28with a company as enrolled of forty-one thousand five hundred. 29Then the tribe of Naphtali: The leader of the Naphtalites shall be Ahira son of Enan, 30with a company as enrolled of fifty-three thousand four hundred. 31The total enrollment of the camp of Dan is one hundred fifty-seven thousand six hundred. They shall set out last, by companies.*a*

32 This was the enrollment of the Israelites by their ancestral houses; the total enrollment

in the camps by their companies was six hundred three thousand five hundred fifty. 33Just as the LORD had commanded Moses, the Levites were not enrolled among the other Israelites.

34 The Israelites did just as the LORD had commanded Moses: They camped by regiments, and they set out the same way, everyone by clans, according to ancestral houses.

The Sons of Aaron

3 This is the lineage of Aaron and Moses at the time when the LORD spoke with Moses on Mount Sinai. 2These are the names of the sons of Aaron: Nadab the firstborn, and Abihu, Eleazar, and Ithamar; 3these are the names of the sons of Aaron, the anointed priests, whom he ordained to minister as priests. 4Nadab and Abihu died before the LORD when they offered unholy fire before the LORD in the wilderness of Sinai, and they had no children. Eleazar and Ithamar served as priests in the lifetime of their father Aaron.

The Duties of the Levites

5 Then the LORD spoke to Moses, saying: 6Bring the tribe of Levi near, and set them before Aaron the priest, so that they may assist him. 7They shall perform duties for him and for the whole congregation in front of the tent of meeting, doing service at the tabernacle; 8they shall be in charge of all the furnishings of the tent of meeting, and attend to the duties for the Israelites as they do service at the tabernacle. 9You shall give the Levites to Aaron and his descendants; they are unreservedly given to him from among the Israelites. 10But you shall make a register of Aaron and his descendants; it is they who shall attend to the priesthood, and any outsider who comes near shall be put to death.

11 Then the LORD spoke to Moses, saying: 12I hereby accept the Levites from among the Israelites as substitutes for all the firstborn that open the womb among the Israelites. The Levites shall be mine, 13for all the firstborn are mine; when I killed all the firstborn in the land of Egypt, I consecrated for my own all the first-

a Compare verses 9, 16, 24: Heb *by their regiments*

born in Israel, both human and animal; they shall be mine. I am the LORD.

A Census of the Levites

14 Then the LORD spoke to Moses in the wilderness of Sinai, saying: [15]Enroll the Levites by ancestral houses and by clans. You shall enroll every male from a month old and upward. [16]So Moses enrolled them according to the word of the LORD, as he was commanded. [17]The following were the sons of Levi, by their names: Gershon, Kohath, and Merari. [18]These are the names of the sons of Gershon by their clans: Libni and Shimei. [19]The sons of Kohath by their clans: Amram, Izhar, Hebron, and Uzziel. [20]The sons of Merari by their clans: Mahli and Mushi. These are the clans of the Levites, by their ancestral houses.

21 To Gershon belonged the clan of the Libnites and the clan of the Shimeites; these were the clans of the Gershonites. [22]Their enrollment, counting all the males from a month old and upward, was seven thousand five hundred. [23]The clans of the Gershonites were to camp behind the tabernacle on the west, [24]with Eliasaph son of Lael as head of the ancestral house of the Gershonites. [25]The responsibility of the sons of Gershon in the tent of meeting was to be the tabernacle, the tent with its covering, the screen for the entrance of the tent of meeting, [26]the hangings of the court, the screen for the entrance of the court that is around the tabernacle and the altar, and its cords—all the service pertaining to these.

27 To Kohath belonged the clan of the Amramites, the clan of the Izharites, the clan of the Hebronites, and the clan of the Uzzielites; these are the clans of the Kohathites. [28]Counting all the males, from a month old and upward, there were eight thousand six hundred, attending to the duties of the sanctuary. [29]The clans of the Kohathites were to camp on the south side of the tabernacle, [30]with Elizaphan son of Uzziel as head of the ancestral house of the clans of the Kohathites. [31]Their responsibility was to be the ark, the table, the lampstand, the altars, the vessels of the sanctuary with which the priests minister, and the screen—all the service pertaining to these. [32]Eleazar son of Aaron the priest was to be chief over the leaders of the Levites, and to have oversight of those who had charge of the sanctuary.

33 To Merari belonged the clan of the Mahlites and the clan of the Mushites: these are the clans of Merari. [34]Their enrollment, counting all the males from a month old and upward, was six thousand two hundred. [35]The head of the ancestral house of the clans of Merari was Zuriel son of Abihail; they were to camp on the north side of the tabernacle. [36]The responsibility assigned to the sons of Merari was to be the frames of the tabernacle, the bars, the pillars, the bases, and all their accessories—all the service pertaining to these; [37]also the pillars of the court all around, with their bases and pegs and cords.

38 Those who were to camp in front of the tabernacle on the east—in front of the tent of meeting toward the east—were Moses and Aaron and Aaron's sons, having charge of the rites within the sanctuary, whatever had to be done for the Israelites; and any outsider who came near was to be put to death. [39]The total enrollment of the Levites whom Moses and Aaron enrolled at the commandment of the LORD, by their clans, all the males from a month old and upward, was twenty-two thousand.

The Redemption of the Firstborn

40 Then the LORD said to Moses: Enroll all the firstborn males of the Israelites, from a month old and upward, and count their names. [41]But you shall accept the Levites for me—I am the LORD—as substitutes for all the firstborn among the Israelites, and the livestock of the Levites as substitutes for all the firstborn among the livestock of the Israelites. [42]So Moses enrolled all the firstborn among the Israelites, as the LORD commanded him. [43]The total enrollment, all the firstborn males from a month old and upward, counting the number of names, was twenty-two thousand two hundred seventy-three.

44 Then the LORD spoke to Moses, saying:

45Accept the Levites as substitutes for all the firstborn among the Israelites, and the livestock of the Levites as substitutes for their livestock; and the Levites shall be mine. I am the LORD. 46As the price of redemption of the two hundred seventy-three of the firstborn of the Israelites, over and above the number of the Levites, 47you shall accept five shekels apiece, reckoning by the shekel of the sanctuary, a shekel of twenty gerahs. 48Give to Aaron and his sons the money by which the excess number of them is redeemed. 49So Moses took the redemption money from those who were over and above those redeemed by the Levites; 50from the firstborn of the Israelites he took the money, one thousand three hundred sixty-five shekels, reckoned by the shekel of the sanctuary; 51and Moses gave the redemption money to Aaron and his sons, according to the word of the LORD, as the LORD had commanded Moses.

The Kohathites

4 The LORD spoke to Moses and Aaron, saying: 2Take a census of the Kohathites separate from the other Levites, by their clans and their ancestral houses, 3from thirty years old up to fifty years old, all who qualify to do work relating to the tent of meeting. 4The service of the Kohathites relating to the tent of meeting concerns the most holy things.

5 When the camp is to set out, Aaron and his sons shall go in and take down the screening curtain, and cover the ark of the covenant*a* with it; 6then they shall put on it a covering of fine leather,*b* and spread over that a cloth all of blue, and shall put its poles in place. 7Over the table of the bread of the Presence they shall spread a blue cloth, and put on it the plates, the dishes for incense, the bowls, and the flagons for the drink offering; the regular bread also shall be on it; 8then they shall spread over them a crimson cloth, and cover it with a covering of fine leather,*b* and shall put its poles in place. 9They shall take a blue cloth, and cover the lampstand for the light, with its lamps, its

snuffers, its trays, and all the vessels for oil with which it is supplied; 10and they shall put it with all its utensils in a covering of fine leather,*b* and put it on the carrying frame. 11Over the golden altar they shall spread a blue cloth, and cover it with a covering of fine leather,*b* and shall put its poles in place; 12and they shall take all the utensils of the service that are used in the sanctuary, and put them in a blue cloth, and cover them with a covering of fine leather,*b* and put them on the carrying frame. 13They shall take away the ashes from the altar, and spread a purple cloth over it; 14and they shall put on it all the utensils of the altar, which are used for the service there, the firepans, the forks, the shovels, and the basins, all the utensils of the altar; and they shall spread on it a covering of fine leather,*b* and shall put its poles in place. 15When Aaron and his sons have finished covering the sanctuary and all the furnishings of the sanctuary, as the camp sets out, after that the Kohathites shall come to carry these, but they must not touch the holy things, or they will die. These are the things of the tent of meeting that the Kohathites are to carry.

16 Eleazar son of Aaron the priest shall have charge of the oil for the light, the fragrant incense, the regular grain offering, and the anointing oil, the oversight of all the tabernacle and all that is in it, in the sanctuary and in its utensils.

17 Then the LORD spoke to Moses and Aaron, saying: 18You must not let the tribe of the clans of the Kohathites be destroyed from among the Levites. 19This is how you must deal with them in order that they may live and not die when they come near to the most holy things: Aaron and his sons shall go in and assign each to a particular task or burden. 20But the Kohathites*c* must not go in to look on the holy things even for a moment; otherwise they will die.

The Gershonites and Merarites

21 Then the LORD spoke to Moses, saying: 22Take a census of the Gershonites also, by

---

a Or *treaty*, or *testimony*; Heb *eduth*   *b* Meaning of Heb uncertain   *c* Heb *they* their ancestral houses and by their clans; 23from thirty years old up to fifty years old you shall enroll them, all who qualify to do work in the tent of meeting. 24This is the service of the clans of the Gershonites, in serving and bearing burdens: 25They shall carry the curtains of the tabernacle, and the tent of meeting with its covering, and the outer covering of fine leather*a* that is on top of it, and the screen for the entrance of the tent of meeting, 26and the hangings of the court, and the screen for the entrance of the gate of the court that is around the tabernacle and the altar, and their cords, and all the equipment for their service; and they shall do all that needs to be done with regard to them. 27All the service of the Gershonites shall be at the command of Aaron and his sons, in all that they are to carry, and in all that they have to do; and you shall assign to their charge all that they are to carry. 28This is the service of the clans of the Gershonites relating to the tent of meeting, and their responsibilities are to be under the oversight of Ithamar son of Aaron the priest.

29 As for the Merarites, you shall enroll them by their clans and their ancestral houses; 30from thirty years old up to fifty years old you shall enroll them, everyone who qualifies to do the work of the tent of meeting. 31This is what they are charged to carry, as the whole of their service in the tent of meeting: the frames of the tabernacle, with its bars, pillars, and bases, 32and the pillars of the court all around with their bases, pegs, and cords, with all their equipment and all their related service; and you shall assign by name the objects that they are required to carry. 33This is the service of the clans of the Merarites, the whole of their service relating to the tent of meeting, under the hand of Ithamar son of Aaron the priest.

Census of the Levites

34 So Moses and Aaron and the leaders of the congregation enrolled the Kohathites, by their clans and their ancestral houses, 35from thirty years old up to fifty years old, everyone who qualified for work relating to the tent of meeting; 36and their enrollment by clans was two thousand seven hundred fifty. 37This was the enrollment of the clans of the Kohathites, all who served at the tent of meeting, whom Moses and Aaron enrolled according to the commandment of the LORD by Moses.

38 The enrollment of the Gershonites, by their clans and their ancestral houses, 39from thirty years old up to fifty years old, everyone who qualified for work relating to the tent of meeting— 40their enrollment by their clans and their ancestral houses was two thousand six hundred thirty. 41This was the enrollment of the clans of the Gershonites, all who served at the tent of meeting, whom Moses and Aaron enrolled according to the commandment of the LORD.

42 The enrollment of the clans of the Merarites, by their clans and their ancestral houses, 43from thirty years old up to fifty years old, everyone who qualified for work relating to the tent of meeting— 44their enrollment by their clans was three thousand two hundred. 45This is the enrollment of the clans of the Merarites, whom Moses and Aaron enrolled according to the commandment of the LORD by Moses.

46 All those who were enrolled of the Levites, whom Moses and Aaron and the leaders of Israel enrolled, by their clans and their ancestral houses, 47from thirty years old up to fifty years old, everyone who qualified to do the work of service and the work of bearing burdens relating to the tent of meeting, 48their enrollment was eight thousand five hundred eighty. 49According to the commandment of the LORD through Moses they were appointed to their several tasks of serving or carrying; thus they were enrolled by him, as the LORD commanded Moses.

Unclean Persons

5 The LORD spoke to Moses, saying: 2Command the Israelites to put out of the camp

---

a Meaning of Heb uncertain

everyone who is leprous,*a* or has a discharge, and everyone who is unclean through contact with a corpse; ³you shall put out both male and female, putting them outside the camp; they must not defile their camp, where I dwell among them. ⁴The Israelites did so, putting them outside the camp; as the LORD had spoken to Moses, so the Israelites did.

Confession and Restitution

5 The LORD spoke to Moses, saying: ⁶Speak to the Israelites: When a man or a woman wrongs another, breaking faith with the LORD, that person incurs guilt ⁷and shall confess the sin that has been committed. The person shall make full restitution for the wrong, adding one-fifth to it, and giving it to the one who was wronged. ⁸If the injured party has no next of kin to whom restitution may be made for the wrong, the restitution for wrong shall go to the LORD for the priest, in addition to the ram of atonement with which atonement is made for the guilty party. ⁹Among all the sacred donations of the Israelites, every gift that they bring to the priest shall be his. ¹⁰The sacred donations of all are their own; whatever anyone gives to the priest shall be his.

Concerning an Unfaithful Wife

11 The LORD spoke to Moses, saying: ¹²Speak to the Israelites and say to them: If any man's wife goes astray and is unfaithful to him, ¹³if a man has had intercourse with her but it is hidden from her husband, so that she is undetected though she has defiled herself, and there is no witness against her since she was not caught in the act; ¹⁴if a spirit of jealousy comes on him, and he is jealous of his wife who has defiled herself; or if a spirit of jealousy comes on him, and he is jealous of his wife, though she has not defiled herself; ¹⁵then the man shall bring his wife to the priest. And he shall bring the offering required for her, one-tenth of an ephah of barley flour. He shall pour no oil on it and put no frankincense on it, for it is a grain offering of jealousy, a grain offering of

remembrance, bringing iniquity to remembrance.

16 Then the priest shall bring her near, and set her before the LORD; ¹⁷the priest shall take holy water in an earthen vessel, and take some of the dust that is on the floor of the tabernacle and put it into the water. ¹⁸The priest shall set the woman before the LORD, dishevel the woman's hair, and place in her hands the grain offering of remembrance, which is the grain offering of jealousy. In his own hand the priest shall have the water of bitterness that brings the curse. ¹⁹Then the priest shall make her take an oath, saying, "If no man has lain with you, if you have not turned aside to uncleanness while under your husband's authority, be immune to this water of bitterness that brings the curse. ²⁰But if you have gone astray while under your husband's authority, if you have defiled yourself and some man other than your husband has had intercourse with you," ²¹—let the priest make the woman take the oath of the curse and say to the woman—"the LORD make you an execration and an oath among your people, when the LORD makes your uterus drop, your womb discharge; ²²now may this water that brings the curse enter your bowels and make your womb discharge, your uterus drop!" And the woman shall say, "Amen. Amen."

23 Then the priest shall put these curses in writing, and wash them off into the water of bitterness. ²⁴He shall make the woman drink the water of bitterness that brings the curse, and the water that brings the curse shall enter her and cause bitter pain. ²⁵The priest shall take the grain offering of jealousy out of the woman's hand, and shall elevate the grain offering before the LORD and bring it to the altar; ²⁶and the priest shall take a handful of the grain offering, as its memorial portion, and turn it into smoke on the altar, and afterward shall make the woman drink the water. ²⁷When he has made her drink the water, then, if she has defiled herself and has been unfaithful to her husband, the water that brings the curse shall enter into her and cause bitter pain, and

---

a A term for several skin diseases; precise meaning uncertain

her womb shall discharge, her uterus drop, and the woman shall become an execration among her people. 28But if the woman has not defiled herself and is clean, then she shall be immune and be able to conceive children.

29 This is the law in cases of jealousy, when a wife, while under her husband's authority, goes astray and defiles herself, 30or when a spirit of jealousy comes on a man and he is jealous of his wife; then he shall set the woman before the LORD, and the priest shall apply this entire law to her. 31The man shall be free from iniquity, but the woman shall bear her iniquity.

The Nazirites

6 The LORD spoke to Moses, saying: 2Speak to the Israelites and say to them: When either men or women make a special vow, the vow of a nazirite,*a* to separate themselves to the LORD, 3they shall separate themselves from wine and strong drink; they shall drink no wine vinegar or other vinegar, and shall not drink any grape juice or eat grapes, fresh or dried. 4All their days as nazirites*b* they shall eat nothing that is produced by the grapevine, not even the seeds or the skins.

5 All the days of their nazirite vow no razor shall come upon the head; until the time is completed for which they separate themselves to the LORD, they shall be holy; they shall let the locks of the head grow long.

6 All the days that they separate themselves to the LORD they shall not go near a corpse. 7Even if their father or mother, brother or sister, should die, they may not defile themselves; because their consecration to God is upon the head. 8All their days as nazirites*b* they are holy to the LORD.

9 If someone dies very suddenly nearby, defiling the consecrated head, then they shall shave the head on the day of their cleansing; on the seventh day they shall shave it. 10On the eighth day they shall bring two turtledoves or two young pigeons to the priest at the entrance of the tent of meeting, 11and the priest shall offer one as a sin offering and the other as a burnt offering, and make atonement for them, because they incurred guilt by reason of the corpse. They shall sanctify the head that same day, 12and separate themselves to the LORD for their days as nazirites,*b* and bring a male lamb a year old as a guilt offering. The former time shall be void, because the consecrated head was defiled.

13 This is the law for the nazirites*b* when the time of their consecration has been completed: they shall be brought to the entrance of the tent of meeting, 14and they shall offer their gift to the LORD, one male lamb a year old without blemish as a burnt offering, one ewe lamb a year old without blemish as a sin offering, one ram without blemish as an offering of well-being, 15and a basket of unleavened bread, cakes of choice flour mixed with oil and unleavened wafers spread with oil, with their grain offering and their drink offerings. 16The priest shall present them before the LORD and offer their sin offering and burnt offering, 17and shall offer the ram as a sacrifice of well-being to the LORD, with the basket of unleavened bread; the priest also shall make the accompanying grain offering and drink offering. 18Then the nazirites*b* shall shave the consecrated head at the entrance of the tent of meeting, and shall take the hair from the consecrated head and put it on the fire under the sacrifice of well-being. 19The priest shall take the shoulder of the ram, when it is boiled, and one unleavened cake out of the basket, and one unleavened wafer, and shall put them in the palms of the nazirites,*b* after they have shaved the consecrated head. 20Then the priest shall elevate them as an elevation offering before the LORD; they are a holy portion for the priest, together with the breast that is elevated and the thigh that is offered. After that the nazirites*b* may drink wine.

21 This is the law for the nazirites*b* who take a vow. Their offering to the LORD must be in accordance with the nazirite*a* vow, apart from what else they can afford. In accordance with whatever vow they take, so they shall do, following the law for their consecration.

---

a That is *one separated* or *one consecrated*   *b* That is *those separated* or *those consecrated*

The Priestly Benediction

22 The LORD spoke to Moses, saying: 23Speak to Aaron and his sons, saying, Thus you shall bless the Israelites: You shall say to them,

24   The LORD bless you and keep you;

25   the LORD make his face to shine upon
            you, and be gracious to you;

26   the LORD lift up his countenance upon
            you, and give you peace.

27 So they shall put my name on the Israelites, and I will bless them.

Offerings of the Leaders

7 On the day when Moses had finished setting up the tabernacle, and had anointed and consecrated it with all its furnishings, and had anointed and consecrated the altar with all its utensils, 2the leaders of Israel, heads of their ancestral houses, the leaders of the tribes, who were over those who were enrolled, made offerings. 3They brought their offerings before the LORD, six covered wagons and twelve oxen, a wagon for every two of the leaders, and for each one an ox; they presented them before the tabernacle. 4Then the LORD said to Moses: 5Accept these from them, that they may be used in doing the service of the tent of meeting, and give them to the Levites, to each according to his service. 6So Moses took the wagons and the oxen, and gave them to the Levites. 7Two wagons and four oxen he gave to the Gershonites, according to their service; 8and four wagons and eight oxen he gave to the Merarites, according to their service, under the direction of Ithamar son of Aaron the priest. 9But to the Kohathites he gave none, because they were charged with the care of the holy things that had to be carried on the shoulders.

10 The leaders also presented offerings for the dedication of the altar at the time when it was anointed; the leaders presented their offering before the altar. 11The LORD said to Moses: They shall present their offerings, one leader each day, for the dedication of the altar. 12 The one who presented his offering the first day was Nahshon son of Amminadab, of the tribe of Judah; 13his offering was one silver plate weighing one hundred thirty shekels, one silver basin weighing seventy shekels, according to the shekel of the sanctuary, both of them full of choice flour mixed with oil for a grain offering; 14one golden dish weighing ten shekels, full of incense; 15one young bull, one ram, one male lamb a year old, for a burnt offering; 16one male goat for a sin offering; 17and for the sacrifice of well-being, two oxen, five rams, five male goats, and five male lambs a year old. This was the offering of Nahshon son of Amminadab.

18 On the second day Nethanel son of Zuar, the leader of Issachar, presented an offering; 19he presented for his offering one silver plate weighing one hundred thirty shekels, one silver basin weighing seventy shekels, according to the shekel of the sanctuary, both of them full of choice flour mixed with oil for a grain offering; 20one golden dish weighing ten shekels, full of incense; 21one young bull, one ram, one male lamb a year old, as a burnt offering; 22one male goat as a sin offering; 23and for the sacrifice of well-being, two oxen, five rams, five male goats, and five male lambs a year old. This was the offering of Nethanel son of Zuar.

24 On the third day Eliab son of Helon, the leader of the Zebulunites: 25his offering was one silver plate weighing one hundred thirty shekels, one silver basin weighing seventy shekels, according to the shekel of the sanctuary, both of them full of choice flour mixed with oil for a grain offering; 26one golden dish weighing ten shekels, full of incense; 27one young bull, one ram, one male lamb a year old, for a burnt offering; 28one male goat for a sin offering; 29and for the sacrifice of well-being, two oxen, five rams, five male goats, and five male lambs a year old. This was the offering of Eliab son of Helon.

30 On the fourth day Elizur son of Shedeur, the leader of the Reubenites: 31his offering was one silver plate weighing one hundred thirty shekels, one silver basin weighing seventy shekels, according to the shekel of the sanctuary, both of them full of choice flour mixed with oil for a grain offering; 32one golden dish

weighing ten shekels, full of incense; 33one young bull, one ram, one male lamb a year old, for a burnt offering; 34one male goat for a sin offering; 35and for the sacrifice of well-being, two oxen, five rams, five male goats, and five male lambs a year old. This was the offering of Elizur son of Shedeur.

36 On the fifth day Shelumiel son of Zurishaddai, the leader of the Simeonites: 37his offering was one silver plate weighing one hundred thirty shekels, one silver basin weighing seventy shekels, according to the shekel of the sanctuary, both of them full of choice flour mixed with oil for a grain offering; 38one golden dish weighing ten shekels, full of incense; 39one young bull, one ram, one male lamb a year old, for a burnt offering; 40one male goat for a sin offering; 41and for the sacrifice of well-being, two oxen, five rams, five male goats, and five male lambs a year old. This was the offering of Shelumiel son of Zurishaddai.

42 On the sixth day Eliasaph son of Deuel, the leader of the Gadites: 43his offering was one silver plate weighing one hundred thirty shekels, one silver basin weighing seventy shekels, according to the shekel of the sanctuary, both of them full of choice flour mixed with oil for a grain offering; 44one golden dish weighing ten shekels, full of incense; 45one young bull, one ram, one male lamb a year old, for a burnt offering; 46one male goat for a sin offering; 47and for the sacrifice of well-being, two oxen, five rams, five male goats, and five male lambs a year old. This was the offering of Eliasaph son of Deuel.

48 On the seventh day Elishama son of Ammihud, the leader of the Ephraimites: 49his offering was one silver plate weighing one hundred thirty shekels, one silver basin weighing seventy shekels, according to the shekel of the sanctuary, both of them full of choice flour mixed with oil for a grain offering; 50one golden dish weighing ten shekels, full of incense; 51one young bull, one ram, one male lamb a year old, for a burnt offering; 52one male goat for a sin offering; 53and for the sacrifice of well-being, two oxen, five rams, five male goats,

and five male lambs a year old. This was the offering of Elishama son of Ammihud.

54 On the eighth day Gamaliel son of Pedahzur, the leader of the Manassites: 55his offering was one silver plate weighing one hundred thirty shekels, one silver basin weighing seventy shekels, according to the shekel of the sanctuary, both of them full of choice flour mixed with oil for a grain offering; 56one golden dish weighing ten shekels, full of incense; 57one young bull, one ram, one male lamb a year old, for a burnt offering; 58one male goat for a sin offering; 59and for the sacrifice of well-being, two oxen, five rams, five male goats, and five male lambs a year old. This was the offering of Gamaliel son of Pedahzur.

60 On the ninth day Abidan son of Gideoni, the leader of the Benjaminites: 61his offering was one silver plate weighing one hundred thirty shekels, one silver basin weighing seventy shekels, according to the shekel of the sanctuary, both of them full of choice flour mixed with oil for a grain offering; 62one golden dish weighing ten shekels, full of incense; 63one young bull, one ram, one male lamb a year old, for a burnt offering; 64one male goat for a sin offering; 65and for the sacrifice of well-being, two oxen, five rams, five male goats, and five male lambs a year old. This was the offering of Abidan son of Gideoni.

66 On the tenth day Ahiezer son of Ammishaddai, the leader of the Danites: 67his offering was one silver plate weighing one hundred thirty shekels, one silver basin weighing seventy shekels, according to the shekel of the sanctuary, both of them full of choice flour mixed with oil for a grain offering; 68one golden dish weighing ten shekels, full of incense; 69one young bull, one ram, one male lamb a year old, for a burnt offering; 70one male goat for a sin offering; 71and for the sacrifice of well-being, two oxen, five rams, five male goats, and five male lambs a year old. This was the offering of Ahiezer son of Ammishaddai.

72 On the eleventh day Pagiel son of Ochran, the leader of the Asherites: 73his offering was one silver plate weighing one hundred thirty shekels, one silver basin weighing

seventy shekels, according to the shekel of the sanctuary, both of them full of choice flour mixed with oil for a grain offering; [74]one golden dish weighing ten shekels, full of incense; [75]one young bull, one ram, one male lamb a year old, for a burnt offering; [76]one male goat for a sin offering; [77]and for the sacrifice of well-being, two oxen, five rams, five male goats, and five male lambs a year old. This was the offering of Pagiel son of Ochran.

[78] On the twelfth day Ahira son of Enan, the leader of the Naphtalites: [79]his offering was one silver plate weighing one hundred thirty shekels, one silver basin weighing seventy shekels, according to the shekel of the sanctuary, both of them full of choice flour mixed with oil for a grain offering; [80]one golden dish weighing ten shekels, full of incense; [81]one young bull, one ram, one male lamb a year old, for a burnt offering; [82]one male goat for a sin offering; [83]and for the sacrifice of well-being, two oxen, five rams, five male goats, and five male lambs a year old. This was the offering of Ahira son of Enan.

[84] This was the dedication offering for the altar, at the time when it was anointed, from the leaders of Israel: twelve silver plates, twelve silver basins, twelve golden dishes, [85]each silver plate weighing one hundred thirty shekels and each basin seventy, all the silver of the vessels two thousand four hundred shekels according to the shekel of the sanctuary, [86]the twelve golden dishes, full of incense, weighing ten shekels apiece according to the shekel of the sanctuary, all the gold of the dishes being one hundred twenty shekels; [87]all the livestock for the burnt offering twelve bulls, twelve rams, twelve male lambs a year old, with their grain offering; and twelve male goats for a sin offering; [88]and all the livestock for the sacrifice of well-being twenty-four bulls, the rams sixty, the male goats sixty, the male lambs a year old sixty. This was the dedication offering for the altar, after it was anointed.

[89] When Moses went into the tent of meeting to speak with the LORD,[a] he would hear the voice speaking to him from above the mercy seat[b] that was on the ark of the covenant[c] from between the two cherubim; thus it spoke to him.

The Seven Lamps

8 The LORD spoke to Moses, saying: [2]Speak to Aaron and say to him: When you set up the lamps, the seven lamps shall give light in front of the lampstand. [3]Aaron did so; he set up its lamps to give light in front of the lampstand, as the LORD had commanded Moses. [4]Now this was how the lampstand was made, out of hammered work of gold. From its base to its flowers, it was hammered work; according to the pattern that the LORD had shown Moses, so he made the lampstand.

Consecration and Service of the Levites

[5] The LORD spoke to Moses, saying: [6]Take the Levites from among the Israelites and cleanse them. [7]Thus you shall do to them, to cleanse them: sprinkle the water of purification on them, have them shave their whole body with a razor and wash their clothes, and so cleanse themselves. [8]Then let them take a young bull and its grain offering of choice flour mixed with oil, and you shall take another young bull for a sin offering. [9]You shall bring the Levites before the tent of meeting, and assemble the whole congregation of the Israelites. [10]When you bring the Levites before the LORD, the Israelites shall lay their hands on the Levites, [11]and Aaron shall present the Levites before the LORD as an elevation offering from the Israelites, that they may do the service of the LORD. [12]The Levites shall lay their hands on the heads of the bulls, and he shall offer the one for a sin offering and the other for a burnt offering to the LORD, to make atonement for the Levites. [13]Then you shall have the Levites stand before Aaron and his sons, and you shall present them as an elevation offering to the LORD.

[14] Thus you shall separate the Levites from among the other Israelites, and the Levites shall be mine. [15]Thereafter the Levites may go

a Heb him   b Or the cover   c Or treaty, or testimony; Heb eduth in to do service at the tent of meeting, once you have cleansed them and presented them as an elevation offering. [16]For they are unreservedly given to me from among the Israelites; I have taken them for myself, in place of all that open the womb, the firstborn of all the Israelites. [17]For all the firstborn among the Israelites are mine, both human and animal. On the day that I struck down all the firstborn in the land of Egypt I consecrated them for myself, [18]but I have taken the Levites in place of all the firstborn among the Israelites. [19]Moreover, I have given the Levites as a gift to Aaron and his sons from among the Israelites, to do the service for the Israelites at the tent of meeting, and to make atonement for the Israelites, in order that there may be no plague among the Israelites for coming too close to the sanctuary.

20 Moses and Aaron and the whole congregation of the Israelites did with the Levites accordingly; the Israelites did with the Levites just as the LORD had commanded Moses concerning them. [21]The Levites purified themselves from sin and washed their clothes; then Aaron presented them as an elevation offering before the LORD, and Aaron made atonement for them to cleanse them. [22]Thereafter the Levites went in to do their service in the tent of meeting in attendance on Aaron and his sons. As the LORD had commanded Moses concerning the Levites, so they did with them.

23 The LORD spoke to Moses, saying: [24]This applies to the Levites: from twenty-five years old and upward they shall begin to do duty in the service of the tent of meeting; [25]and from the age of fifty years they shall retire from the duty of the service and serve no more. [26]They may assist their brothers in the tent of meeting in carrying out their duties, but they shall perform no service. Thus you shall do with the Levites in assigning their duties.

The Passover at Sinai

9 The LORD spoke to Moses in the wilderness of Sinai, in the first month of the second year after they had come out of the land of Egypt, saying: [2]Let the Israelites keep the passover at its appointed time. [3]On the fourteenth day of this month, at twilight,[a] you shall keep it at its appointed time; according to all its statutes and all its regulations you shall keep it. [4]So Moses told the Israelites that they should keep the passover. [5]They kept the passover in the first month, on the fourteenth day of the month, at twilight,[a] in the wilderness of Sinai. Just as the LORD had commanded Moses, so the Israelites did. [6]Now there were certain people who were unclean through touching a corpse, so that they could not keep the passover on that day. They came before Moses and Aaron on that day, [7]and said to him, "Although we are unclean through touching a corpse, why must we be kept from presenting the LORD's offering at its appointed time among the Israelites?" [8]Moses spoke to them, "Wait, so that I may hear what the LORD will command concerning you."

9 The LORD spoke to Moses, saying: [10]Speak to the Israelites, saying: Anyone of you or your descendants who is unclean through touching a corpse, or is away on a journey, shall still keep the passover to the LORD. [11]In the second month on the fourteenth day, at twilight,[a] they shall keep it; they shall eat it with unleavened bread and bitter herbs. [12]They shall leave none of it until morning, nor break a bone of it; according to all the statute for the passover they shall keep it. [13]But anyone who is clean and is not on a journey, and yet refrains from keeping the passover, shall be cut off from the people for not presenting the LORD's offering at its appointed time; such a one shall bear the consequences for the sin. [14]Any alien residing among you who wishes to keep the passover to the LORD shall do so according to the statute of the passover and according to its regulation; you shall have one statute for both the resident alien and the native.

The Cloud and the Fire

15 On the day the tabernacle was set up, the

_a_ Heb _between the two evenings_

cloud covered the tabernacle, the tent of the covenant;[a] and from evening until morning it was over the tabernacle, having the appearance of fire. 16It was always so: the cloud covered it by day[b] and the appearance of fire by night. 17Whenever the cloud lifted from over the tent, then the Israelites would set out; and in the place where the cloud settled down, there the Israelites would camp. 18At the command of the LORD the Israelites would set out, and at the command of the LORD they would camp. As long as the cloud rested over the tabernacle, they would remain in camp. 19Even when the cloud continued over the tabernacle many days, the Israelites would keep the charge of the LORD, and would not set out. 20Sometimes the cloud would remain a few days over the tabernacle, and according to the command of the LORD they would remain in camp; then according to the command of the LORD they would set out. 21Sometimes the cloud would remain from evening until morning; and when the cloud lifted in the morning, they would set out, or if it continued for a day and a night, when the cloud lifted they would set out. 22Whether it was two days, or a month, or a longer time, that the cloud continued over the tabernacle, resting upon it, the Israelites would remain in camp and would not set out; but when it lifted they would set out. 23At the command of the LORD they would camp, and at the command of the LORD they would set out. They kept the charge of the LORD, at the command of the LORD by Moses.

The Silver Trumpets

10 The LORD spoke to Moses, saying: 2Make two silver trumpets; you shall make them of hammered work; and you shall use them for summoning the congregation, and for breaking camp. 3When both are blown, the whole congregation shall assemble before you at the entrance of the tent of meeting. 4But if only one is blown, then the leaders, the heads of the tribes of Israel, shall assemble before you. 5When you blow an alarm, the camps on the east side shall set out; 6when you blow a second alarm, the camps on the south side shall set out. An alarm is to be blown whenever they are to set out. 7But when the assembly is to be gathered, you shall blow, but you shall not sound an alarm. 8The sons of Aaron, the priests, shall blow the trumpets; this shall be a perpetual institution for you throughout your generations. 9When you go to war in your land against the adversary who oppresses you, you shall sound an alarm with the trumpets, so that you may be remembered before the LORD your God and be saved from your enemies. 10Also on your days of rejoicing, at your appointed festivals, and at the beginnings of your months, you shall blow the trumpets over your burnt offerings and over your sacrifices of well-being; they shall serve as a reminder on your behalf before the LORD your God: I am the LORD your God.

Departure from Sinai

11 In the second year, in the second month, on the twentieth day of the month, the cloud lifted from over the tabernacle of the covenant.[a] 12Then the Israelites set out by stages from the wilderness of Sinai, and the cloud settled down in the wilderness of Paran. 13They set out for the first time at the command of the LORD by Moses. 14The standard of the camp of Judah set out first, company by company, and over the whole company was Nahshon son of Amminadab. 15Over the company of the tribe of Issachar was Nethanel son of Zuar; 16and over the company of the tribe of Zebulun was Eliab son of Helon.

17 Then the tabernacle was taken down, and the Gershonites and the Merarites, who carried the tabernacle, set out. 18Next the standard of the camp of Reuben set out, company by company; and over the whole company was Elizur son of Shedeur. 19Over the company of the tribe of Simeon was Shelumiel son of Zurishaddai, 20and over the company of the tribe of Gad was Eliasaph son of Deuel.

21 Then the Kohathites, who carried the

---

a Or *treaty*, or *testimony*; Heb *eduth*   *b* Gk Syr Vg: Heb lacks *by day* holy things, set out; and the tabernacle was set up before their arrival. 22Next the standard of the Ephraimite camp set out, company by company, and over the whole company was Elishama son of Ammihud. 23Over the company of the tribe of Manasseh was Gamaliel son of Pedahzur, 24and over the company of the tribe of Benjamin was Abidan son of Gideoni.

25 Then the standard of the camp of Dan, acting as the rear guard of all the camps, set out, company by company, and over the whole company was Ahiezer son of Ammishaddai. 26Over the company of the tribe of Asher was Pagiel son of Ochran, 27and over the company of the tribe of Naphtali was Ahira son of Enan. 28This was the order of march of the Israelites, company by company, when they set out.

29 Moses said to Hobab son of Reuel the Midianite, Moses' father-in-law, "We are setting out for the place of which the LORD said, 'I will give it to you'; come with us, and we will treat you well; for the LORD has promised good to Israel." 30But he said to him, "I will not go, but I will go back to my own land and to my kindred." 31He said, "Do not leave us, for you know where we should camp in the wilderness, and you will serve as eyes for us. 32Moreover, if you go with us, whatever good the LORD does for us, the same we will do for you."

33 So they set out from the mount of the LORD three days' journey with the ark of the covenant of the LORD going before them three days' journey, to seek out a resting place for them, 34the cloud of the LORD being over them by day when they set out from the camp.

35 Whenever the ark set out, Moses would say,

"Arise, O LORD, let your enemies be
    scattered,
    and your foes flee before you."
36And whenever it came to rest, he would say,
"Return, O LORD of the ten thousand
    thousands of Israel." a

Complaining in the Desert

11 Now when the people complained in the hearing of the LORD about their misfortunes, the LORD heard it and his anger was kindled. Then the fire of the LORD burned against them, and consumed some outlying parts of the camp. 2But the people cried out to Moses; and Moses prayed to the LORD, and the fire abated. 3So that place was called Taberah, b because the fire of the LORD burned against them.

4 The rabble among them had a strong craving; and the Israelites also wept again, and said, "If only we had meat to eat! 5We remember the fish we used to eat in Egypt for nothing, the cucumbers, the melons, the leeks, the onions, and the garlic; 6but now our strength is dried up, and there is nothing at all but this manna to look at."

7 Now the manna was like coriander seed, and its color was like the color of gum resin. 8The people went around and gathered it, ground it in mills or beat it in mortars, then boiled it in pots and made cakes of it; and the taste of it was like the taste of cakes baked with oil. 9When the dew fell on the camp in the night, the manna would fall with it.

10 Moses heard the people weeping throughout their families, all at the entrances of their tents. Then the LORD became very angry, and Moses was displeased. 11So Moses said to the LORD, "Why have you treated your servant so badly? Why have I not found favor in your sight, that you lay the burden of all this people on me? 12Did I conceive all this people? Did I give birth to them, that you should say to me, 'Carry them in your bosom, as a nurse carries a sucking child, to the land that you promised on oath to their ancestors'? 13Where am I to get meat to give to all this people? For they come weeping to me and say, 'Give us meat to eat!' 14I am not able to carry all this people alone, for they are too heavy for me. 15If this is the way you are going to treat me, put me to death at once—if I have found favor in your sight—and do not let me see my misery."

a Meaning of Heb uncertain   b That is *Burning*

The Seventy Elders

16 So the LORD said to Moses, "Gather for me seventy of the elders of Israel, whom you know to be the elders of the people and officers over them; bring them to the tent of meeting, and have them take their place there with you. ¹⁷I will come down and talk with you there; and I will take some of the spirit that is on you and put it on them; and they shall bear the burden of the people along with you so that you will not bear it all by yourself. ¹⁸And say to the people: Consecrate yourselves for tomorrow, and you shall eat meat; for you have wailed in the hearing of the LORD, saying, 'If only we had meat to eat! Surely it was better for us in Egypt.' Therefore the LORD will give you meat, and you shall eat. ¹⁹You shall eat not only one day, or two days, or five days, or ten days, or twenty days, ²⁰but for a whole month—until it comes out of your nostrils and becomes loathsome to you—because you have rejected the LORD who is among you, and have wailed before him, saying, 'Why did we ever leave Egypt?' " ²¹But Moses said, "The people I am with number six hundred thousand on foot; and you say, 'I will give them meat, that they may eat for a whole month'! ²²Are there enough flocks and herds to slaughter for them? Are there enough fish in the sea to catch for them?" ²³The LORD said to Moses, "Is the LORD's power limited?ᵃ Now you shall see whether my word will come true for you or not."

24 So Moses went out and told the people the words of the LORD; and he gathered seventy elders of the people, and placed them all around the tent. ²⁵Then the LORD came down in the cloud and spoke to him, and took some of the spirit that was on him and put it on the seventy elders; and when the spirit rested upon them, they prophesied. But they did not do so again.

26 Two men remained in the camp, one named Eldad, and the other named Medad, and the spirit rested on them; they were among those registered, but they had not gone out to the tent, and so they prophesied in the camp. ²⁷And a young man ran and told Moses, "Eldad and Medad are prophesying in the camp." ²⁸And Joshua son of Nun, the assistant of Moses, one of his chosen men,ᵇ said, "My lord Moses, stop them!" ²⁹But Moses said to him, "Are you jealous for my sake? Would that all the LORD's people were prophets, and that the LORD would put his spirit on them!" ³⁰And Moses and the elders of Israel returned to the camp.

The Quails

31 Then a wind went out from the LORD, and it brought quails from the sea and let them fall beside the camp, about a day's journey on this side and a day's journey on the other side, all around the camp, about two cubits deep on the ground. ³²So the people worked all that day and night and all the next day, gathering the quails; the least anyone gathered was ten homers; and they spread them out for themselves all around the camp. ³³But while the meat was still between their teeth, before it was consumed, the anger of the LORD was kindled against the people, and the LORD struck the people with a very great plague. ³⁴So that place was called Kibroth-hattaavah,ᶜ because there they buried the people who had the craving. ³⁵From Kibroth-hattaavah the people journeyed to Hazeroth.

Aaron and Miriam Jealous of Moses

12 While they were at Hazeroth, Miriam and Aaron spoke against Moses because of the Cushite woman whom he had married (for he had indeed married a Cushite woman); ²and they said, "Has the LORD spoken only through Moses? Has he not spoken through us also?" And the LORD heard it. ³Now the man Moses was very humble,ᵈ more so than anyone else on the face of the earth. ⁴Suddenly the LORD said to Moses, Aaron, and Miriam, "Come out, you three, to the tent of meeting." So the three of them came out. ⁵Then the LORD came down in a pillar of

---

a Heb LORD's *hand too short?*   *b* Or *of Moses from his youth*   *c* That is *Graves of craving*   *d* Or *devout* cloud, and stood at the entrance of the tent, and called Aaron and Miriam; and they both came forward. 6And he said, "Hear my words:

When there are prophets among you,
I the LORD make myself known to
them in visions;
I speak to them in dreams.
7 Not so with my servant Moses;
he is entrusted with all my house.
8 With him I speak face to face— clearly,
not in riddles;
and he beholds the form of the LORD.

Why then were you not afraid to speak against my servant Moses?" 9And the anger of the LORD was kindled against them, and he departed.

10 When the cloud went away from over the tent, Miriam had become leprous,a as white as snow. And Aaron turned towards Miriam and saw that she was leprous. 11Then Aaron said to Moses, "Oh, my lord, do not punish usb for a sin that we have so foolishly committed. 12Do not let her be like one stillborn, whose flesh is half consumed when it comes out of its mother's womb." 13And Moses cried to the LORD, "O God, please heal her." 14But the LORD said to Moses, "If her father had but spit in her face, would she not bear her shame for seven days? Let her be shut out of the camp for seven days, and after that she may be brought in again." 15So Miriam was shut out of the camp for seven days; and the people did not set out on the march until Miriam had been brought in again. 16After that the people set out from Hazeroth, and camped in the wilderness of Paran.

Spies Sent into Canaan

13 The LORD said to Moses, 2"Send men to spy out the land of Canaan, which I am giving to the Israelites; from each of their ancestral tribes you shall send a man, every one a leader among them." 3So Moses sent them from the wilderness of Paran, according to the command of the LORD, all of them leading men among the Israelites. 4These were

their names: From the tribe of Reuben, Shammua son of Zaccur; 5from the tribe of Simeon, Shaphat son of Hori; 6from the tribe of Judah, Caleb son of Jephunneh; 7from the tribe of Issachar, Igal son of Joseph; 8from the tribe of Ephraim, Hoshea son of Nun; 9from the tribe of Benjamin, Palti son of Raphu; 10from the tribe of Zebulun, Gaddiel son of Sodi; 11from the tribe of Joseph (that is, from the tribe of Manasseh), Gaddi son of Susi; 12from the tribe of Dan, Ammiel son of Gemalli; 13from the tribe of Asher, Sethur son of Michael; 14from the tribe of Naphtali, Nahbi son of Vophsi; 15from the tribe of Gad, Geuel son of Machi. 16These were the names of the men whom Moses sent to spy out the land. And Moses changed the name of Hoshea son of Nun to Joshua.

17 Moses sent them to spy out the land of Canaan, and said to them, "Go up there into the Negeb, and go up into the hill country, 18and see what the land is like, and whether the people who live in it are strong or weak, whether they are few or many, 19and whether the land they live in is good or bad, and whether the towns that they live in are unwalled or fortified, 20and whether the land is rich or poor, and whether there are trees in it or not. Be bold, and bring some of the fruit of the land." Now it was the season of the first ripe grapes.

21 So they went up and spied out the land from the wilderness of Zin to Rehob, near Lebo-hamath. 22They went up into the Negeb, and came to Hebron; and Ahiman, Sheshai, and Talmai, the Anakites, were there. (Hebron was built seven years before Zoan in Egypt.) 23And they came to the Wadi Eshcol, and cut down from there a branch with a single cluster of grapes, and they carried it on a pole between two of them. They also brought some pomegranates and figs. 24That place was called the Wadi Eshcol,c because of the cluster that the Israelites cut down from there.

The Report of the Spies

25 At the end of forty days they returned

---

a A term for several skin diseases; precise meaning uncertain   b Heb *do not lay sin upon us*   c That is *Cluster* from spying out the land. 26And they came to Moses and Aaron and to all the congregation of the Israelites in the wilderness of Paran, at Kadesh; they brought back word to them and to all the congregation, and showed them the fruit of the land. 27And they told him, "We came to the land to which you sent us; it flows with milk and honey, and this is its fruit. 28Yet the people who live in the land are strong, and the towns are fortified and very large; and besides, we saw the descendants of Anak there. 29The Amalekites live in the land of the Negeb; the Hittites, the Jebusites, and the Amorites live in the hill country; and the Canaanites live by the sea, and along the Jordan."

30 But Caleb quieted the people before Moses, and said, "Let us go up at once and occupy it, for we are well able to overcome it." 31Then the men who had gone up with him said, "We are not able to go up against this people, for they are stronger than we." 32So they brought to the Israelites an unfavorable report of the land that they had spied out, saying, "The land that we have gone through as spies is a land that devours its inhabitants; and all the people that we saw in it are of great size. 33There we saw the Nephilim (the Anakites come from the Nephilim); and to ourselves we seemed like grasshoppers, and so we seemed to them."

The People Rebel

14 Then all the congregation raised a loud cry, and the people wept that night. 2And all the Israelites complained against Moses and Aaron; the whole congregation said to them, "Would that we had died in the land of Egypt! Or would that we had died in this wilderness! 3Why is the LORD bringing us into this land to fall by the sword? Our wives and our little ones will become booty; would it not be better for us to go back to Egypt?" 4So they said to one another, "Let us choose a captain, and go back to Egypt."

5 Then Moses and Aaron fell on their faces before all the assembly of the congregation of the Israelites. 6And Joshua son of Nun and Caleb son of Jephunneh, who were among those who had spied out the land, tore their clothes 7and said to all the congregation of the Israelites, "The land that we went through as spies is an exceedingly good land. 8If the LORD is pleased with us, he will bring us into this land and give it to us, a land that flows with milk and honey. 9Only, do not rebel against the LORD; and do not fear the people of the land, for they are no more than bread for us; their protection is removed from them, and the LORD is with us; do not fear them." 10But the whole congregation threatened to stone them.

Then the glory of the LORD appeared at the tent of meeting to all the Israelites. 11And the LORD said to Moses, "How long will this people despise me? And how long will they refuse to believe in me, in spite of all the signs that I have done among them? 12I will strike them with pestilence and disinherit them, and I will make of you a nation greater and mightier than they."

Moses Intercedes for the People

13 But Moses said to the LORD, "Then the Egyptians will hear of it, for in your might you brought up this people from among them, 14and they will tell the inhabitants of this land. They have heard that you, O LORD, are in the midst of this people; for you, O LORD, are seen face to face, and your cloud stands over them and you go in front of them, in a pillar of cloud by day and in a pillar of fire by night. 15Now if you kill this people all at one time, then the nations who have heard about you will say, 16'It is because the LORD was not able to bring this people into the land he swore to give them that he has slaughtered them in the wilderness.' 17And now, therefore, let the power of the LORD be great in the way that you promised when you spoke, saying,

18   'The LORD is slow to anger,
          and abounding in steadfast love,
          forgiving iniquity and transgression,
          but by no means clearing the guilty,
          visiting the iniquity of the parents
             upon the children
          to the third and the fourth generation.'

19Forgive the iniquity of this people according

to the greatness of your steadfast love, just as you have pardoned this people, from Egypt even until now."

20 Then the LORD said, "I do forgive, just as you have asked; 21nevertheless—as I live, and as all the earth shall be filled with the glory of the LORD— 22none of the people who have seen my glory and the signs that I did in Egypt and in the wilderness, and yet have tested me these ten times and have not obeyed my voice, 23shall see the land that I swore to give to their ancestors; none of those who despised me shall see it. 24But my servant Caleb, because he has a different spirit and has followed me wholeheartedly, I will bring into the land into which he went, and his descendants shall possess it. 25Now, since the Amalekites and the Canaanites live in the valleys, turn tomorrow and set out for the wilderness by the way to the Red Sea."a

An Attempted Invasion is Repulsed

26 And the LORD spoke to Moses and to Aaron, saying: 27How long shall this wicked congregation complain against me? I have heard the complaints of the Israelites, which they complain against me. 28Say to them, "As I live," says the LORD, "I will do to you the very things I heard you say: 29your dead bodies shall fall in this very wilderness; and of all your number, included in the census, from twenty years old and upward, who have complained against me, 30not one of you shall come into the land in which I swore to settle you, except Caleb son of Jephunneh and Joshua son of Nun. 31But your little ones, who you said would become booty, I will bring in, and they shall know the land that you have despised. 32But as for you, your dead bodies shall fall in this wilderness. 33And your children shall be shepherds in the wilderness for forty years, and shall suffer for your faithlessness, until the last of your dead bodies lies in the wilderness. 34According to the number of the days in which you spied out the land, forty days, for every day a year, you shall bear your iniquity,

forty years, and you shall know my displeasure." 35I the LORD have spoken; surely I will do thus to all this wicked congregation gathered together against me: in this wilderness they shall come to a full end, and there they shall die.

36 And the men whom Moses sent to spy out the land, who returned and made all the congregation complain against him by bringing a bad report about the land— 37the men who brought an unfavorable report about the land died by a plague before the LORD. 38But Joshua son of Nun and Caleb son of Jephunneh alone remained alive, of those men who went to spy out the land.

39 When Moses told these words to all the Israelites, the people mourned greatly. 40They rose early in the morning and went up to the heights of the hill country, saying, "Here we are. We will go up to the place that the LORD has promised, for we have sinned." 41But Moses said, "Why do you continue to transgress the command of the LORD? That will not succeed. 42Do not go up, for the LORD is not with you; do not let yourselves be struck down before your enemies. 43For the Amalekites and the Canaanites will confront you there, and you shall fall by the sword; because you have turned back from following the LORD, the LORD will not be with you." 44But they presumed to go up to the heights of the hill country, even though the ark of the covenant of the LORD, and Moses, had not left the camp. 45Then the Amalekites and the Canaanites who lived in that hill country came down and defeated them, pursuing them as far as Hormah.

Various Offerings

15 The LORD spoke to Moses, saying: 2Speak to the Israelites and say to them: When you come into the land you are to inhabit, which I am giving you, 3and you make an offering by fire to the LORD from the herd or from the flock—whether a burnt offering or a sacrifice, to fulfill a vow or as a freewill offering or at your appointed festivals—to make a pleasing odor for the LORD, 4then whoever

a Or Sea of Reeds

presents such an offering to the LORD shall present also a grain offering, one-tenth of an ephah of choice flour, mixed with one-fourth of a hin of oil. 5Moreover, you shall offer one-fourth of a hin of wine as a drink offering with the burnt offering or the sacrifice, for each lamb. 6For a ram, you shall offer a grain offering, two-tenths of an ephah of choice flour mixed with one-third of a hin of oil; 7and as a drink offering you shall offer one-third of a hin of wine, a pleasing odor to the LORD. 8When you offer a bull as a burnt offering or a sacrifice, to fulfill a vow or as an offering of well-being to the LORD, 9then you shall present with the bull a grain offering, three-tenths of an ephah of choice flour, mixed with half a hin of oil, 10and you shall present as a drink offering half a hin of wine, as an offering by fire, a pleasing odor to the LORD.

11 Thus it shall be done for each ox or ram, or for each of the male lambs or the kids. 12According to the number that you offer, so you shall do with each and every one. 13Every native Israelite shall do these things in this way, in presenting an offering by fire, a pleasing odor to the LORD. 14An alien who lives with you, or who takes up permanent residence among you, and wishes to offer an offering by fire, a pleasing odor to the LORD, shall do as you do. 15As for the assembly, there shall be for both you and the resident alien a single statute, a perpetual statute throughout your generations; you and the alien shall be alike before the LORD. 16You and the alien who resides with you shall have the same law and the same ordinance.

17 The LORD spoke to Moses, saying: 18Speak to the Israelites and say to them: After you come into the land to which I am bringing you, 19whenever you eat of the bread of the land, you shall present a donation to the LORD. 20From your first batch of dough you shall present a loaf as a donation; you shall present it just as you present a donation from the threshing floor. 21Throughout your generations you shall give to the LORD a donation from the first of your batch of dough.

22 But if you unintentionally fail to observe all these commandments that the LORD has spoken to Moses— 23everything that the LORD has commanded you by Moses, from the day the LORD gave commandment and thereafter, throughout your generations— 24then if it was done unintentionally without the knowledge of the congregation, the whole congregation shall offer one young bull for a burnt offering, a pleasing odor to the LORD, together with its grain offering and its drink offering, according to the ordinance, and one male goat for a sin offering. 25The priest shall make atonement for all the congregation of the Israelites, and they shall be forgiven; it was unintentional, and they have brought their offering, an offering by fire to the LORD, and their sin offering before the LORD, for their error. 26All the congregation of the Israelites shall be forgiven, as well as the aliens residing among them, because the whole people was involved in the error.

27 An individual who sins unintentionally shall present a female goat a year old for a sin offering. 28And the priest shall make atonement before the LORD for the one who commits an error, when it is unintentional, to make atonement for the person, who then shall be forgiven. 29For both the native among the Israelites and the alien residing among them— you shall have the same law for anyone who acts in error. 30But whoever acts high-handedly, whether a native or an alien, affronts the LORD, and shall be cut off from among the people. 31Because of having despised the word of the LORD and broken his commandment, such a person shall be utterly cut off and bear the guilt.

Penalty for Violating the Sabbath

32 When the Israelites were in the wilderness, they found a man gathering sticks on the sabbath day. 33Those who found him gathering sticks brought him to Moses, Aaron, and to the whole congregation. 34They put him in custody, because it was not clear what should be done to him. 35Then the LORD said to Moses, "The man shall be put to death; all the congregation shall stone him outside the camp."

36The whole congregation brought him outside the camp and stoned him to death, just as the LORD had commanded Moses.

Fringes on Garments

37 The LORD said to Moses: 38Speak to the Israelites, and tell them to make fringes on the corners of their garments throughout their generations and to put a blue cord on the fringe at each corner. 39You have the fringe so that, when you see it, you will remember all the commandments of the LORD and do them, and not follow the lust of your own heart and your own eyes. 40So you shall remember and do all my commandments, and you shall be holy to your God. 41I am the LORD your God, who brought you out of the land of Egypt, to be your God: I am the LORD your God.

Revolt of Korah, Dathan, and Abiram

16 Now Korah son of Izhar son of Kohath son of Levi, along with Dathan and Abiram sons of Eliab, and On son of Peleth—descendants of Reuben—took 2two hundred fifty Israelite men, leaders of the congregation, chosen from the assembly, well-known men,*a* and they confronted Moses. 3They assembled against Moses and against Aaron, and said to them, "You have gone too far! All the congregation are holy, every one of them, and the LORD is among them. So why then do you exalt yourselves above the assembly of the LORD?" 4When Moses heard it, he fell on his face. 5Then he said to Korah and all his company, "In the morning the LORD will make known who is his, and who is holy, and who will be allowed to approach him; the one whom he will choose he will allow to approach him. 6Do this: take censers, Korah and all your*b* company, 7and tomorrow put fire in them, and lay incense on them before the LORD; and the man whom the LORD chooses shall be the holy one. You Levites have gone too far!" 8Then Moses said to Korah, "Hear now, you Levites! 9Is it too little for you that the God of Israel has separated you from the congregation of Isra-

el, to allow you to approach him in order to perform the duties of the LORD's tabernacle, and to stand before the congregation and serve them? 10He has allowed you to approach him, and all your brother Levites with you; yet you seek the priesthood as well! 11Therefore you and all your company have gathered together against the LORD. What is Aaron that you rail against him?"

12 Moses sent for Dathan and Abiram sons of Eliab; but they said, "We will not come! 13Is it too little that you have brought us up out of a land flowing with milk and honey to kill us in the wilderness, that you must also lord it over us? 14It is clear you have not brought us into a land flowing with milk and honey, or given us an inheritance of fields and vineyards. Would you put out the eyes of these men? We will not come!"

15 Moses was very angry and said to the LORD, "Pay no attention to their offering. I have not taken one donkey from them, and I have not harmed any one of them." 16And Moses said to Korah, "As for you and all your company, be present tomorrow before the LORD, you and they and Aaron; 17and let each one of you take his censer, and put incense on it, and each one of you present his censer before the LORD, two hundred fifty censers; you also, and Aaron, each his censer." 18So each man took his censer, and they put fire in the censers and laid incense on them, and they stood at the entrance of the tent of meeting with Moses and Aaron. 19Then Korah assembled the whole congregation against them at the entrance of the tent of meeting. And the glory of the LORD appeared to the whole congregation.

20 Then the LORD spoke to Moses and to Aaron, saying: 21Separate yourselves from this congregation, so that I may consume them in a moment. 22They fell on their faces, and said, "O God, the God of the spirits of all flesh, shall one person sin and you become angry with the whole congregation?"

23 And the LORD spoke to Moses, saying:

a Cn: Heb *and they confronted Moses, and two hundred fifty men . . . well-known men*   *b* Heb *his*

24Say to the congregation: Get away from the dwellings of Korah, Dathan, and Abiram. 25So Moses got up and went to Dathan and Abiram; the elders of Israel followed him. 26He said to the congregation, "Turn away from the tents of these wicked men, and touch nothing of theirs, or you will be swept away for all their sins." 27So they got away from the dwellings of Korah, Dathan, and Abiram; and Dathan and Abiram came out and stood at the entrance of their tents, together with their wives, their children, and their little ones. 28And Moses said, "This is how you shall know that the LORD has sent me to do all these works; it has not been of my own accord: 29If these people die a natural death, or if a natural fate comes on them, then the LORD has not sent me. 30But if the LORD creates something new, and the ground opens its mouth and swallows them up, with all that belongs to them, and they go down alive into Sheol, then you shall know that these men have despised the LORD."

31 As soon as he finished speaking all these words, the ground under them was split apart. 32The earth opened its mouth and swallowed them up, along with their households—everyone who belonged to Korah and all their goods. 33So they with all that belonged to them went down alive into Sheol; the earth closed over them, and they perished from the midst of the assembly. 34All Israel around them fled at their outcry, for they said, "The earth will swallow us too!" 35And fire came out from the LORD and consumed the two hundred fifty men offering the incense.

36a Then the LORD spoke to Moses, saying: 37Tell Eleazar son of Aaron the priest to take the censers out of the blaze; then scatter the fire far and wide. 38For the censers of these sinners have become holy at the cost of their lives. Make them into hammered plates as a covering for the altar, for they presented them before the LORD and they became holy. Thus they shall be a sign to the Israelites. 39So Eleazar the priest took the bronze censers that had been presented by those who were burned; and they

were hammered out as a covering for the altar— 40a reminder to the Israelites that no outsider, who is not of the descendants of Aaron, shall approach to offer incense before the LORD, so as not to become like Korah and his company—just as the LORD had said to him through Moses.

41 On the next day, however, the whole congregation of the Israelites rebelled against Moses and against Aaron, saying, "You have killed the people of the LORD." 42And when the congregation had assembled against them, Moses and Aaron turned toward the tent of meeting; the cloud had covered it and the glory of the LORD appeared. 43Then Moses and Aaron came to the front of the tent of meeting, 44and the LORD spoke to Moses, saying, 45"Get away from this congregation, so that I may consume them in a moment." And they fell on their faces. 46Moses said to Aaron, "Take your censer, put fire on it from the altar and lay incense on it, and carry it quickly to the congregation and make atonement for them. For wrath has gone out from the LORD; the plague has begun." 47So Aaron took it as Moses had ordered, and ran into the middle of the assembly, where the plague had already begun among the people. He put on the incense, and made atonement for the people. 48He stood between the dead and the living; and the plague was stopped. 49Those who died by the plague were fourteen thousand seven hundred, besides those who died in the affair of Korah. 50When the plague was stopped, Aaron returned to Moses at the entrance of the tent of meeting.

The Budding of Aaron's Rod

17 b The LORD spoke to Moses, saying: 2Speak to the Israelites, and get twelve staffs from them, one for each ancestral house, from all the leaders of their ancestral houses. Write each man's name on his staff, 3and write Aaron's name on the staff of Levi. For there shall be one staff for the head of each ancestral house. 4Place them in the tent of meeting

a Ch 17.1 in Heb   b Ch 17.16 in Heb

before the covenant,*a* where I meet with you. 5And the staff of the man whom I choose shall sprout; thus I will put a stop to the complaints of the Israelites that they continually make against you. 6Moses spoke to the Israelites; and all their leaders gave him staffs, one for each leader, according to their ancestral houses, twelve staffs; and the staff of Aaron was among theirs. 7So Moses placed the staffs before the LORD in the tent of the covenant.*a*

8 When Moses went into the tent of the covenant*a* on the next day, the staff of Aaron for the house of Levi had sprouted. It put forth buds, produced blossoms, and bore ripe almonds. 9Then Moses brought out all the staffs from before the LORD to all the Israelites; and they looked, and each man took his staff. 10And the LORD said to Moses, "Put back the staff of Aaron before the covenant,*a* to be kept as a warning to rebels, so that you may make an end of their complaints against me, or else they will die." 11Moses did so; just as the LORD commanded him, so he did.

12 The Israelites said to Moses, "We are perishing; we are lost, all of us are lost! 13Everyone who approaches the tabernacle of the LORD will die. Are we all to perish?"

Responsibility of Priests and Levites

18 The LORD said to Aaron: You and your sons and your ancestral house with you shall bear responsibility for offenses connected with the sanctuary, while you and your sons alone shall bear responsibility for offenses connected with the priesthood. 2So bring with you also your brothers of the tribe of Levi, your ancestral tribe, in order that they may be joined to you, and serve you while you and your sons with you are in front of the tent of the covenant.*a* 3They shall perform duties for you and for the whole tent. But they must not approach either the utensils of the sanctuary or the altar, otherwise both they and you will die. 4They are attached to you in order to perform the duties of the tent of meeting, for all the service of the tent; no outsider shall approach you. 5You

yourselves shall perform the duties of the sanctuary and the duties of the altar, so that wrath may never again come upon the Israelites. 6It is I who now take your brother Levites from among the Israelites; they are now yours as a gift, dedicated to the LORD, to perform the service of the tent of meeting. 7But you and your sons with you shall diligently perform your priestly duties in all that concerns the altar and the area behind the curtain. I give your priesthood as a gift;*b* any outsider who approaches shall be put to death.

The Priests' Portion

8 The LORD spoke to Aaron: I have given you charge of the offerings made to me, all the holy gifts of the Israelites; I have given them to you and your sons as a priestly portion due you in perpetuity. 9This shall be yours from the most holy things, reserved from the fire: every offering of theirs that they render to me as a most holy thing, whether grain offering, sin offering, or guilt offering, shall belong to you and your sons. 10As a most holy thing you shall eat it; every male may eat it; it shall be holy to you. 11This also is yours: I have given to you, together with your sons and daughters, as a perpetual due, whatever is set aside from the gifts of all the elevation offerings of the Israelites; everyone who is clean in your house may eat them. 12All the best of the oil and all the best of the wine and of the grain, the choice produce that they give to the LORD, I have given to you. 13The first fruits of all that is in their land, which they bring to the LORD, shall be yours; everyone who is clean in your house may eat of it. 14Every devoted thing in Israel shall be yours. 15The first issue of the womb of all creatures, human and animal, which is offered to the LORD, shall be yours; but the firstborn of human beings you shall redeem, and the firstborn of unclean animals you shall redeem. 16Their redemption price, reckoned from one month of age, you shall fix at five shekels of silver, according to the shekel of the sanctuary (that is, twenty gerahs). 17But the firstborn

a Or *treaty,* or *testimony;* Heb *eduth*   *b* Heb *as a service of gift* of a cow, or the firstborn of a sheep, or the firstborn of a goat, you shall not redeem; they are holy. You shall dash their blood on the altar, and shall turn their fat into smoke as an offering by fire for a pleasing odor to the LORD; 18but their flesh shall be yours, just as the breast that is elevated and as the right thigh are yours. 19All the holy offerings that the Israelites present to the LORD I have given to you, together with your sons and daughters, as a perpetual due; it is a covenant of salt forever before the LORD for you and your descendants as well. 20Then the LORD said to Aaron: You shall have no allotment in their land, nor shall you have any share among them; I am your share and your possession among the Israelites.

21 To the Levites I have given every tithe in Israel for a possession in return for the service that they perform, the service in the tent of meeting. 22From now on the Israelites shall no longer approach the tent of meeting, or else they will incur guilt and die. 23But the Levites shall perform the service of the tent of meeting, and they shall bear responsibility for their own offenses; it shall be a perpetual statute throughout your generations. But among the Israelites they shall have no allotment, 24because I have given to the Levites as their portion the tithe of the Israelites, which they set apart as an offering to the LORD. Therefore I have said of them that they shall have no allotment among the Israelites.

25 Then the LORD spoke to Moses, saying: 26You shall speak to the Levites, saying: When you receive from the Israelites the tithe that I have given you from them for your portion, you shall set apart an offering from it to the LORD, a tithe of the tithe. 27It shall be reckoned to you as your gift, the same as the grain of the threshing floor and the fullness of the wine press. 28Thus you also shall set apart an offering to the LORD from all the tithes that you receive from the Israelites; and from them you shall give the LORD's offering to the priest Aaron. 29Out of all the gifts to you, you shall set apart every offering due to the LORD; the best of all of

them is the part to be consecrated. 30Say also to them: When you have set apart the best of it, then the rest shall be reckoned to the Levites as produce of the threshing floor, and as produce of the wine press. 31You may eat it in any place, you and your households; for it is your payment for your service in the tent of meeting. 32You shall incur no guilt by reason of it, when you have offered the best of it. But you shall not profane the holy gifts of the Israelites, on pain of death.

Ceremony of the Red Heifer

19 The LORD spoke to Moses and Aaron, saying: 2This is a statute of the law that the LORD has commanded: Tell the Israelites to bring you a red heifer without defect, in which there is no blemish and on which no yoke has been laid. 3You shall give it to the priest Eleazar, and it shall be taken outside the camp and slaughtered in his presence. 4The priest Eleazar shall take some of its blood with his finger and sprinkle it seven times towards the front of the tent of meeting. 5Then the heifer shall be burned in his sight; its skin, its flesh, and its blood, with its dung, shall be burned. 6The priest shall take cedarwood, hyssop, and crimson material, and throw them into the fire in which the heifer is burning. 7Then the priest shall wash his clothes and bathe his body in water, and afterwards he may come into the camp; but the priest shall remain unclean until evening. 8The one who burns the heifer*a* shall wash his clothes in water and bathe his body in water; he shall remain unclean until evening. 9Then someone who is clean shall gather up the ashes of the heifer, and deposit them outside the camp in a clean place; and they shall be kept for the congregation of the Israelites for the water for cleansing. It is a purification offering. 10The one who gathers the ashes of the heifer shall wash his clothes and be unclean until evening.

This shall be a perpetual statute for the Israelites and for the alien residing among them. 11Those who touch the dead body of any hu-

a Heb *it*

man being shall be unclean seven days. 12They shall purify themselves with the water on the third day and on the seventh day, and so be clean; but if they do not purify themselves on the third day and on the seventh day, they will not become clean. 13All who touch a corpse, the body of a human being who has died, and do not purify themselves, defile the tabernacle of the LORD; such persons shall be cut off from Israel. Since water for cleansing was not dashed on them, they remain unclean; their uncleanness is still on them.

14 This is the law when someone dies in a tent: everyone who comes into the tent, and everyone who is in the tent, shall be unclean seven days. 15And every open vessel with no cover fastened on it is unclean. 16Whoever in the open field touches one who has been killed by a sword, or who has died naturally,*a* or a human bone, or a grave, shall be unclean seven days. 17For the unclean they shall take some ashes of the burnt purification offering, and running water shall be added in a vessel; 18then a clean person shall take hyssop, dip it in the water, and sprinkle it on the tent, on all the furnishings, on the persons who were there, and on whoever touched the bone, the slain, the corpse, or the grave. 19The clean person shall sprinkle the unclean ones on the third day and on the seventh day, thus purifying them on the seventh day. Then they shall wash their clothes and bathe themselves in water, and at evening they shall be clean. 20Any who are unclean but do not purify themselves, those persons shall be cut off from the assembly, for they have defiled the sanctuary of the LORD. Since the water for cleansing has not been dashed on them, they are unclean.

21 It shall be a perpetual statute for them. The one who sprinkles the water for cleansing shall wash his clothes, and whoever touches the water for cleansing shall be unclean until evening. 22Whatever the unclean person touches shall be unclean, and anyone who touches it shall be unclean until evening.

The Waters of Meribah

20 The Israelites, the whole congregation, came into the wilderness of Zin in the first month, and the people stayed in Kadesh. Miriam died there, and was buried there.

2 Now there was no water for the congregation; so they gathered together against Moses and against Aaron. 3The people quarreled with Moses and said, "Would that we had died when our kindred died before the LORD! 4Why have you brought the assembly of the LORD into this wilderness for us and our livestock to die here? 5Why have you brought us up out of Egypt, to bring us to this wretched place? It is no place for grain, or figs, or vines, or pomegranates; and there is no water to drink." 6Then Moses and Aaron went away from the assembly to the entrance of the tent of meeting; they fell on their faces, and the glory of the LORD appeared to them. 7The LORD spoke to Moses, saying: 8Take the staff, and assemble the congregation, you and your brother Aaron, and command the rock before their eyes to yield its water. Thus you shall bring water out of the rock for them; thus you shall provide drink for the congregation and their livestock.

9 So Moses took the staff from before the LORD, as he had commanded him. 10Moses and Aaron gathered the assembly together before the rock, and he said to them, "Listen, you rebels, shall we bring water for you out of this rock?" 11Then Moses lifted up his hand and struck the rock twice with his staff; water came out abundantly, and the congregation and their livestock drank. 12But the LORD said to Moses and Aaron, "Because you did not trust in me, to show my holiness before the eyes of the Israelites, therefore you shall not bring this assembly into the land that I have given them." 13These are the waters of Meribah,*b* where the people of Israel quarreled with the LORD, and by which he showed his holiness.

Passage through Edom Refused

14 Moses sent messengers from Kadesh to the king of Edom, "Thus says your broth-

---

a Heb lacks *naturally*   *b* That is *Quarrel*

er Israel: You know all the adversity that has befallen us: 15how our ancestors went down to Egypt, and we lived in Egypt a long time; and the Egyptians oppressed us and our ancestors; 16and when we cried to the LORD, he heard our voice, and sent an angel and brought us out of Egypt; and here we are in Kadesh, a town on the edge of your territory. 17Now let us pass through your land. We will not pass through field or vineyard, or drink water from any well; we will go along the King's Highway, not turning aside to the right hand or to the left until we have passed through your territory."

18 But Edom said to him, "You shall not pass through, or we will come out with the sword against you." 19The Israelites said to him, "We will stay on the highway; and if we drink of your water, we and our livestock, then we will pay for it. It is only a small matter; just let us pass through on foot." 20But he said, "You shall not pass through." And Edom came out against them with a large force, heavily armed. 21Thus Edom refused to give Israel passage through their territory; so Israel turned away from them.

The Death of Aaron

22 They set out from Kadesh, and the Israelites, the whole congregation, came to Mount Hor. 23Then the LORD said to Moses and Aaron at Mount Hor, on the border of the land of Edom, 24"Let Aaron be gathered to his people. For he shall not enter the land that I have given to the Israelites, because you rebelled against my command at the waters of Meribah. 25Take Aaron and his son Eleazar, and bring them up Mount Hor; 26strip Aaron of his vestments, and put them on his son Eleazar. But Aaron shall be gathered to his people,a and shall die there." 27Moses did as the LORD had commanded; they went up Mount Hor in the sight of the whole congregation. 28Moses stripped Aaron of his vestments, and put them on his son Eleazar; and Aaron died there on the top of the mountain. Moses and Eleazar came down from the mountain.

29When all the congregation saw that Aaron had died, all the house of Israel mourned for Aaron thirty days.

The Bronze Serpent

21 When the Canaanite, the king of Arad, who lived in the Negeb, heard that Israel was coming by the way of Atharim, he fought against Israel and took some of them captive. 2Then Israel made a vow to the LORD and said, "If you will indeed give this people into our hands, then we will utterly destroy their towns." 3The LORD listened to the voice of Israel, and handed over the Canaanites; and they utterly destroyed them and their towns; so the place was called Hormah.b

4 From Mount Hor they set out by the way to the Red Sea,c to go around the land of Edom; but the people became impatient on the way. 5The people spoke against God and against Moses, "Why have you brought us up out of Egypt to die in the wilderness? For there is no food and no water, and we detest this miserable food." 6Then the LORD sent poisonousd serpents among the people, and they bit the people, so that many Israelites died. 7The people came to Moses and said, "We have sinned by speaking against the LORD and against you; pray to the LORD to take away the serpents from us." So Moses prayed for the people. 8And the LORD said to Moses, "Make a poisonouse serpent, and set it on a pole; and everyone who is bitten shall look at it and live." 9So Moses made a serpent of bronze, and put it upon a pole; and whenever a serpent bit someone, that person would look at the serpent of bronze and live.

The Journey to Moab

10 The Israelites set out, and camped in Oboth. 11They set out from Oboth, and camped at Iye-abarim, in the wilderness bordering Moab toward the sunrise. 12From there they set out, and camped in the Wadi Zered. 13From there they set out, and camped on the other side of the Arnon, inf the wilderness

a Heb lacks to his people   b Heb Destruction   c Or Sea of Reeds   d Or fiery; Heb seraphim   e Or fiery; Heb seraph   f Gk: Heb which is in that extends from the boundary of the Amorites; for the Arnon is the boundary of Moab, between Moab and the Amorites. 14Wherefore it is said in the Book of the Wars of the LORD,

"Waheb in Suphah and the wadis.
The Arnon 15and the slopes of the wadis
that extend to the seat of Ar,
and lie along the border of Moab." *a*

16 From there they continued to Beer;*b* that is the well of which the LORD said to Moses, "Gather the people together, and I will give them water." 17Then Israel sang this song:
"Spring up, O well!—Sing to it!—
18 the well that the leaders sank,
that the nobles of the people dug,
with the scepter, with the staff."

From the wilderness to Mattanah, 19from Mattanah to Nahaliel, from Nahaliel to Bamoth, 20and from Bamoth to the valley lying in the region of Moab by the top of Pisgah that overlooks the wasteland.*c*

King Sihon Defeated

21 Then Israel sent messengers to King Sihon of the Amorites, saying, 22"Let me pass through your land; we will not turn aside into field or vineyard; we will not drink the water of any well; we will go by the King's Highway until we have passed through your territory." 23But Sihon would not allow Israel to pass through his territory. Sihon gathered all his people together, and went out against Israel to the wilderness; he came to Jahaz, and fought against Israel. 24Israel put him to the sword, and took possession of his land from the Arnon to the Jabbok, as far as to the Ammonites; for the boundary of the Ammonites was strong. 25Israel took all these towns, and Israel settled in all the towns of the Amorites, in Heshbon, and in all its villages. 26For Heshbon was the city of King Sihon of the Amorites, who had fought against the former king of Moab and captured all his land as far as the Arnon. 27Therefore the ballad singers say,

"Come to Heshbon, let it be built;

let the city of Sihon be established.
28 For fire came out from Heshbon,
flame from the city of Sihon.
It devoured Ar of Moab,
and swallowed up*d* the heights of the Arnon.
29 Woe to you, O Moab!
You are undone, O people of Chemosh!
He has made his sons fugitives,
and his daughters captives,
to an Amorite king, Sihon.
30 So their posterity perished
from Heshbon*e* to Dibon,
and we laid waste until fire spread to Medeba."*f*

31 Thus Israel settled in the land of the Amorites. 32Moses sent to spy out Jazer; and they captured its villages, and dispossessed the Amorites who were there.

King Og Defeated

33 Then they turned and went up the road to Bashan; and King Og of Bashan came out against them, he and all his people, to battle at Edrei. 34But the LORD said to Moses, "Do not be afraid of him; for I have given him into your hand, with all his people, and all his land. You shall do to him as you did to King Sihon of the Amorites, who ruled in Heshbon." 35So they killed him, his sons, and all his people, until there was no survivor left; and they took possession of his land.

Balak Summons Balaam to Curse Israel

22 The Israelites set out, and camped in the plains of Moab across the Jordan from Jericho. 2Now Balak son of Zippor saw all that Israel had done to the Amorites. 3Moab was in great dread of the people, because they were so numerous; Moab was overcome with fear of the people of Israel. 4And Moab said to the elders of Midian, "This horde will now lick up all that is around us, as an ox licks up the grass of the field." Now Balak son of Zippor was king of Moab at that time. 5He sent mes-

---

a Meaning of Heb uncertain   *b* That is *Well*   *c* Or *Jeshimon*   *d* Gk: Heb *and the lords of*   *e* Gk: Heb *we have shot at them; Heshbon has perished*   *f* Compare Sam Gk: Meaning of MT uncertain sengers to Balaam son of Beor at Pethor, which is on the Euphrates, in the land of Amaw,*a* to summon him, saying, "A people has come out of Egypt; they have spread over the face of the earth, and they have settled next to me. 6Come now, curse this people for me, since they are stronger than I; perhaps I shall be able to defeat them and drive them from the land; for I know that whomever you bless is blessed, and whomever you curse is cursed."

7 So the elders of Moab and the elders of Midian departed with the fees for divination in their hand; and they came to Balaam, and gave him Balak's message. 8He said to them, "Stay here tonight, and I will bring back word to you, just as the LORD speaks to me"; so the officials of Moab stayed with Balaam. 9God came to Balaam and said, "Who are these men with you?" 10Balaam said to God, "King Balak son of Zippor of Moab, has sent me this message: 11'A people has come out of Egypt and has spread over the face of the earth; now come, curse them for me; perhaps I shall be able to fight against them and drive them out.'" 12God said to Balaam, "You shall not go with them; you shall not curse the people, for they are blessed." 13So Balaam rose in the morning, and said to the officials of Balak, "Go to your own land, for the LORD has refused to let me go with you." 14So the officials of Moab rose and went to Balak, and said, "Balaam refuses to come with us."

15 Once again Balak sent officials, more numerous and more distinguished than these. 16They came to Balaam and said to him, "Thus says Balak son of Zippor: 'Do not let anything hinder you from coming to me; 17for I will surely do you great honor, and whatever you say to me I will do; come, curse this people for me.'" 18But Balaam replied to the servants of Balak, "Although Balak were to give me his house full of silver and gold, I could not go beyond the command of the LORD my God, to do less or more. 19You remain here, as the others did, so that I may learn what more the LORD may say to me." 20That night God

came to Balaam and said to him, "If the men have come to summon you, get up and go with them; but do only what I tell you to do." 21So Balaam got up in the morning, saddled his donkey, and went with the officials of Moab.

Balaam, the Donkey, and the Angel

22 God's anger was kindled because he was going, and the angel of the LORD took his stand in the road as his adversary. Now he was riding on the donkey, and his two servants were with him. 23The donkey saw the angel of the LORD standing in the road, with a drawn sword in his hand; so the donkey turned off the road, and went into the field; and Balaam struck the donkey, to turn it back onto the road. 24Then the angel of the LORD stood in a narrow path between the vineyards, with a wall on either side. 25When the donkey saw the angel of the LORD, it scraped against the wall, and scraped Balaam's foot against the wall; so he struck it again. 26Then the angel of the LORD went ahead, and stood in a narrow place, where there was no way to turn either to the right or to the left. 27When the donkey saw the angel of the LORD, it lay down under Balaam; and Balaam's anger was kindled, and he struck the donkey with his staff. 28Then the LORD opened the mouth of the donkey, and it said to Balaam, "What have I done to you, that you have struck me these three times?" 29Balaam said to the donkey, "Because you have made a fool of me! I wish I had a sword in my hand! I would kill you right now!" 30But the donkey said to Balaam, "Am I not your donkey, which you have ridden all your life to this day? Have I been in the habit of treating you this way?" And he said, "No."

31 Then the LORD opened the eyes of Balaam, and he saw the angel of the LORD standing in the road, with his drawn sword in his hand; and he bowed down, falling on his face. 32The angel of the LORD said to him, "Why have you struck your donkey these three times? I have come out as an adversary, because your way is perverse*b* before me. 33The donkey saw

a Or *land of his kinsfolk*   *b* Meaning of Heb uncertain me, and turned away from me these three times. If it had not turned away from me, surely just now I would have killed you and let it live." 34Then Balaam said to the angel of the LORD, "I have sinned, for I did not know that you were standing in the road to oppose me. Now therefore, if it is displeasing to you, I will return home." 35The angel of the LORD said to Balaam, "Go with the men; but speak only what I tell you to speak." So Balaam went on with the officials of Balak.

36 When Balak heard that Balaam had come, he went out to meet him at Ir-moab, on the boundary formed by the Arnon, at the farthest point of the boundary. 37Balak said to Balaam, "Did I not send to summon you? Why did you not come to me? Am I not able to honor you?" 38Balaam said to Balak, "I have come to you now, but do I have power to say just anything? The word God puts in my mouth, that is what I must say." 39Then Balaam went with Balak, and they came to Kiriath-huzoth. 40Balak sacrificed oxen and sheep, and sent them to Balaam and to the officials who were with him.

Balaam's First Oracle

41 On the next day Balak took Balaam and brought him up to Bamoth-baal; and from there he could see part of the people of Israel.*a* **23** 1Then Balaam said to Balak, "Build me seven altars here, and prepare seven bulls and seven rams for me." 2Balak did as Balaam had said; and Balak and Balaam offered a bull and a ram on each altar. 3Then Balaam said to Balak, "Stay here beside your burnt offerings while I go aside. Perhaps the LORD will come to meet me. Whatever he shows me I will tell you." And he went to a bare height.

4 Then God met Balaam; and Balaam said to him, "I have arranged the seven altars, and have offered a bull and a ram on each altar." 5The LORD put a word in Balaam's mouth, and said, "Return to Balak, and this is what you must say." 6So he returned to Balak,*b* who was standing beside his burnt offerings with all the officials of Moab. 7Then Balaam*c* uttered his oracle, saying:

"Balak has brought me from Aram,
　　the king of Moab from the eastern
　　　　mountains:
'Come, curse Jacob for me;
　　Come, denounce Israel!'
8　How can I curse whom God has not
　　　　cursed?
　　How can I denounce those whom the
　　　　LORD has not denounced?
9　For from the top of the crags I see him,
　　from the hills I behold him.
　　Here is a people living alone,
　　　　and not reckoning itself among the
　　　　　　nations!
10　Who can count the dust of Jacob,
　　　　or number the dust-cloud*d* of Israel?
　　Let me die the death of the upright,
　　　　and let my end be like his!"

11 Then Balak said to Balaam, "What have you done to me? I brought you to curse my enemies, but now you have done nothing but bless them." 12He answered, "Must I not take care to say what the LORD puts into my mouth?"

Balaam's Second Oracle

13 So Balak said to him, "Come with me to another place from which you may see them; you shall see only part of them, and shall not see them all; then curse them for me from there." 14So he took him to the field of Zophim, to the top of Pisgah. He built seven altars, and offered a bull and a ram on each altar. 15Balaam said to Balak, "Stand here beside your burnt offerings, while I meet the LORD over there." 16The LORD met Balaam, put a word into his mouth, and said, "Return to Balak, and this is what you shall say." 17When he came to him, he was standing beside his burnt offerings with the officials of Moab. Balak said to him, "What has the LORD said?" 18Then Balaam uttered his oracle, saying:

"Rise, Balak, and hear;
　　listen to me, O son of Zippor:

---

a Heb lacks *of Israel*　　*b* Heb *him*　　*c* Heb *he*　　*d* Or *fourth part*

19 God is not a human being, that he
       should lie,
    or a mortal, that he should change his
       mind.
    Has he promised, and will he not do it?
    Has he spoken, and will he not fulfill
       it?

20 See, I received a command to bless;
    he has blessed, and I cannot revoke it.

21 He has not beheld misfortune in Jacob;
    nor has he seen trouble in Israel.
    The LORD their God is with them,
       acclaimed as a king among them.

22 God, who brings them out of Egypt,
    is like the horns of a wild ox for them.

23 Surely there is no enchantment against
       Jacob,
    no divination against Israel;
    now it shall be said of Jacob and Israel,
    'See what God has done!'

24 Look, a people rising up like a lioness,
    and rousing itself like a lion!
    It does not lie down until it has eaten the
       prey
    and drunk the blood of the slain."

25 Then Balak said to Balaam, "Do not curse them at all, and do not bless them at all." 26But Balaam answered Balak, "Did I not tell you, 'Whatever the LORD says, that is what I must do'?"

27 So Balak said to Balaam, "Come now, I will take you to another place; perhaps it will please God that you may curse them for me from there." 28So Balak took Balaam to the top of Peor, which overlooks the wasteland. a 29Balaam said to Balak, "Build me seven altars here, and prepare seven bulls and seven rams for me." 30So Balak did as Balaam had said, and offered a bull and a ram on each altar.

Balaam's Third Oracle

24 Now Balaam saw that it pleased the LORD to bless Israel, so he did not go, as at other times, to look for omens, but set his face toward the wilderness. 2Balaam looked up and saw Israel camping tribe by tribe. Then the spirit of God came upon him, 3and he uttered his oracle, saying:

    "The oracle of Balaam son of Beor,
       the oracle of the man whose eye is
          clear, b

4   the oracle of one who hears the words
          of God,
       who sees the vision of the Almighty, c
       who falls down, but with eyes
          uncovered:

5   how fair are your tents, O Jacob,
       your encampments, O Israel!

6   Like palm groves that stretch far away,
       like gardens beside a river,
    like aloes that the LORD has planted,
       like cedar trees beside the waters.

7   Water shall flow from his buckets,
       and his seed shall have abundant
          water,
    his king shall be higher than Agag,
       and his kingdom shall be exalted.

8   God who brings him out of Egypt,
       is like the horns of a wild ox for him;
    he shall devour the nations that are his
          foes
       and break their bones.
    He shall strike with his arrows. d

9   He crouched, he lay down like a lion,
       and like a lioness; who will rouse him
          up?
    Blessed is everyone who blesses you,
       and cursed is everyone who curses
          you."

10 Then Balak's anger was kindled against Balaam, and he struck his hands together. Balak said to Balaam, "I summoned you to curse my enemies, but instead you have blessed them these three times. 11Now be off with you! Go home! I said, 'I will reward you richly,' but the LORD has denied you any reward." 12And Balaam said to Balak, "Did I not tell your messengers whom you sent to me, 13'If Balak should give me his house full of silver and gold, I would not be able to go beyond the word of the LORD, to do either good or bad of my own will; what the LORD says, that is what

a Or overlooks Jeshimon   b Or closed or open   c Traditional rendering of Heb Shaddai   d Meaning of Heb uncertain

I will say'? ¹⁴So now, I am going to my people; let me advise you what this people will do to your people in days to come."

Balaam's Fourth Oracle

15 So he uttered his oracle, saying:
"The oracle of Balaam son of Beor,
  the oracle of the man whose eye is
    clear,^a
¹⁶ the oracle of one who hears the words
    of God,
  and knows the knowledge of the
    Most High,^b
who sees the vision of the Almighty,^c
  who falls down, but with his eyes
    uncovered:
¹⁷ I see him, but not now;
  I behold him, but not near—
a star shall come out of Jacob,
  and a scepter shall rise out of Israel;
it shall crush the borderlands^d of Moab,
  and the territory^e of all the Shethites.
¹⁸ Edom will become a possession,
  Seir a possession of its enemies,^f
  while Israel does valiantly.
¹⁹ One out of Jacob shall rule,
  and destroy the survivors of Ir."

20 Then he looked on Amalek, and uttered his oracle, saying:
"First among the nations was Amalek,
  but its end is to perish forever."

21 Then he looked on the Kenite, and uttered his oracle, saying:
"Enduring is your dwelling place,
  and your nest is set in the rock;
²² yet Kain is destined for burning.
  How long shall Asshur take you away
    captive?"

23 Again he uttered his oracle, saying:
"Alas, who shall live when God does
  this?
²⁴ But ships shall come from Kittim
and shall afflict Asshur and Eber;
  and he also shall perish forever."

25 Then Balaam got up and went back to his place, and Balak also went his way.

Worship of Baal of Peor

25 While Israel was staying at Shittim, the people began to have sexual relations with the women of Moab. ²These invited the people to the sacrifices of their gods, and the people ate and bowed down to their gods. ³Thus Israel yoked itself to the Baal of Peor, and the LORD's anger was kindled against Israel. ⁴The LORD said to Moses, "Take all the chiefs of the people, and impale them in the sun before the LORD, in order that the fierce anger of the LORD may turn away from Israel." ⁵And Moses said to the judges of Israel, "Each of you shall kill any of your people who have yoked themselves to the Baal of Peor."

6 Just then one of the Israelites came and brought a Midianite woman into his family, in the sight of Moses and in the sight of the whole congregation of the Israelites, while they were weeping at the entrance of the tent of meeting. ⁷When Phinehas son of Eleazar, son of Aaron the priest, saw it, he got up and left the congregation. Taking a spear in his hand, ⁸he went after the Israelite man into the tent, and pierced the two of them, the Israelite and the woman, through the belly. So the plague was stopped among the people of Israel. ⁹Nevertheless those that died by the plague were twenty-four thousand.

10 The LORD spoke to Moses, saying: ¹¹"Phinehas son of Eleazar, son of Aaron the priest, has turned back my wrath from the Israelites by manifesting such zeal among them on my behalf that in my jealousy I did not consume the Israelites. ¹²Therefore say, 'I hereby grant him my covenant of peace. ¹³It shall be for him and for his descendants after him a covenant of perpetual priesthood, because he was zealous for his God, and made atonement for the Israelites.' "

14 The name of the slain Israelite man, who was killed with the Midianite woman, was Zimri son of Salu, head of an ancestral house belonging to the Simeonites. ¹⁵The name of the Midianite woman who was killed was Cozbi

---

a Or *closed* or *open*   *b* Or *of Elyon*   *c* Traditional rendering of Heb *Shaddai*   *d* Or *forehead*   *e* Some Mss read *skull*   *f* Heb *Seir, its enemies, a possession* daughter of Zur, who was the head of a clan, an ancestral house in Midian.

16 The LORD said to Moses, 17"Harass the Midianites, and defeat them; 18for they have harassed you by the trickery with which they deceived you in the affair of Peor, and in the affair of Cozbi, the daughter of a leader of Midian, their sister; she was killed on the day of the plague that resulted from Peor."

A Census of the New Generation

26 After the plague the LORD said to Moses and to Eleazar son of Aaron the priest, 2"Take a census of the whole congregation of the Israelites, from twenty years old and upward, by their ancestral houses, everyone in Israel able to go to war." 3Moses and Eleazar the priest spoke with them in the plains of Moab by the Jordan opposite Jericho, saying, 4"Take a census of the people,*a* from twenty years old and upward," as the LORD commanded Moses.

The Israelites, who came out of the land of Egypt, were:

5 Reuben, the firstborn of Israel. The descendants of Reuben: of Hanoch, the clan of the Hanochites; of Pallu, the clan of the Palluites; 6of Hezron, the clan of the Hezronites; of Carmi, the clan of the Carmites. 7These are the clans of the Reubenites; the number of those enrolled was forty-three thousand seven hundred thirty. 8And the descendants of Pallu: Eliab. 9The descendants of Eliab: Nemuel, Dathan, and Abiram. These are the same Dathan and Abiram, chosen from the congregation, who rebelled against Moses and Aaron in the company of Korah, when they rebelled against the LORD, 10and the earth opened its mouth and swallowed them up along with Korah, when that company died, when the fire devoured two hundred fifty men; and they became a warning. 11Notwithstanding, the sons of Korah did not die.

12 The descendants of Simeon by their clans: of Nemuel, the clan of the Nemuelites; of Jamin, the clan of the Jaminites; of Jachin,

the clan of the Jachinites; 13of Zerah, the clan of the Zerahites; of Shaul, the clan of the Shaulites.*b* 14These are the clans of the Simeonites, twenty-two thousand two hundred.

15 The children of Gad by their clans: of Zephon, the clan of the Zephonites; of Haggi, the clan of the Haggites; of Shuni, the clan of the Shunites; 16of Ozni, the clan of the Oznites; of Eri, the clan of the Erites; 17of Arod, the clan of the Arodites; of Areli, the clan of the Arelites. 18These are the clans of the Gadites: the number of those enrolled was forty thousand five hundred.

19 The sons of Judah: Er and Onan; Er and Onan died in the land of Canaan. 20The descendants of Judah by their clans were: of Shelah, the clan of the Shelanites; of Perez, the clan of the Perezites; of Zerah, the clan of the Zerahites. 21The descendants of Perez were: of Hezron, the clan of the Hezronites; of Hamul, the clan of the Hamulites. 22These are the clans of Judah: the number of those enrolled was seventy-six thousand five hundred.

23 The descendants of Issachar by their clans: of Tola, the clan of the Tolaites; of Puvah, the clan of the Punites; 24of Jashub, the clan of the Jashubites; of Shimron, the clan of the Shimronites. 25These are the clans of Issachar: sixty-four thousand three hundred enrolled.

26 The descendants of Zebulun by their clans: of Sered, the clan of the Seredites; of Elon, the clan of the Elonites; of Jahleel, the clan of the Jahleelites. 27These are the clans of the Zebulunites; the number of those enrolled was sixty thousand five hundred.

28 The sons of Joseph by their clans: Manasseh and Ephraim. 29The descendants of Manasseh: of Machir, the clan of the Machirites; and Machir was the father of Gilead; of Gilead, the clan of the Gileadites. 30These are the descendants of Gilead: of Iezer, the clan of the Iezerites; of Helek, the clan of the Helekites; 31and of Asriel, the clan of the Asrielites; and of Shechem, the clan of the Shechemites; 32and of Shemida, the clan of

---

a Heb lacks *take a census of the people*: Compare verse 2   *b* Or *Saul . . . Saulites* the Shemidaites; and of Hepher, the clan of the Hepherites. ³³Now Zelophehad son of Hepher had no sons, but daughters: and the names of the daughters of Zelophehad were Mahlah, Noah, Hoglah, Milcah, and Tirzah. ³⁴These are the clans of Manasseh; the number of those enrolled was fifty-two thousand seven hundred.

35 These are the descendants of Ephraim according to their clans: of Shuthelah, the clan of the Shuthelahites; of Becher, the clan of the Becherites; of Tahan, the clan of the Tahanites. ³⁶And these are the descendants of Shuthelah: of Eran, the clan of the Eranites. ³⁷These are the clans of the Ephraimites: the number of those enrolled was thirty-two thousand five hundred. These are the descendants of Joseph by their clans.

38 The descendants of Benjamin by their clans: of Bela, the clan of the Belaites; of Ashbel, the clan of the Ashbelites; of Ahiram, the clan of the Ahiramites; ³⁹of Shephupham, the clan of the Shuphamites; of Hupham, the clan of the Huphamites. ⁴⁰And the sons of Bela were Ard and Naaman: of Ard, the clan of the Ardites; of Naaman, the clan of the Naamites. ⁴¹These are the descendants of Benjamin by their clans; the number of those enrolled was forty-five thousand six hundred.

42 These are the descendants of Dan by their clans: of Shuham, the clan of the Shuhamites. These are the clans of Dan by their clans. ⁴³All the clans of the Shuhamites: sixty-four thousand four hundred enrolled.

44 The descendants of Asher by their families: of Imnah, the clan of the Imnites; of Ishvi, the clan of the Ishvites; of Beriah, the clan of the Beriites. ⁴⁵Of the descendants of Beriah: of Heber, the clan of the Heberites; of Malchiel, the clan of the Malchielites. ⁴⁶And the name of the daughter of Asher was Serah. ⁴⁷These are the clans of the Asherites: the number of those enrolled was fifty-three thousand four hundred.

48 The descendants of Naphtali by their clans: of Jahzeel, the clan of the Jahzeelites; of Guni, the clan of the Gunites; ⁴⁹of Jezer, the clan of the Jezerites; of Shillem, the clan of the Shillemites. ⁵⁰These are the Naphtalites *a* by their clans: the number of those enrolled was forty-five thousand four hundred.

51 This was the number of the Israelites enrolled: six hundred and one thousand seven hundred thirty.

52 The LORD spoke to Moses, saying: ⁵³To these the land shall be apportioned for inheritance according to the number of names. ⁵⁴To a large tribe you shall give a large inheritance, and to a small tribe you shall give a small inheritance; every tribe shall be given its inheritance according to its enrollment. ⁵⁵But the land shall be apportioned by lot; according to the names of their ancestral tribes they shall inherit. ⁵⁶Their inheritance shall be apportioned according to lot between the larger and the smaller.

57 This is the enrollment of the Levites by their clans: of Gershon, the clan of the Gershonites; of Kohath, the clan of the Kohathites; of Merari, the clan of the Merarites. ⁵⁸These are the clans of Levi: the clan of the Libnites, the clan of the Hebronites, the clan of the Mahlites, the clan of the Mushites, the clan of the Korahites. Now Kohath was the father of Amram. ⁵⁹The name of Amram's wife was Jochebed daughter of Levi, who was born to Levi in Egypt; and she bore to Amram: Aaron, Moses, and their sister Miriam. ⁶⁰To Aaron were born Nadab, Abihu, Eleazar, and Ithamar. ⁶¹But Nadab and Abihu died when they offered unholy fire before the LORD. ⁶²The number of those enrolled was twenty-three thousand, every male one month old and upward; for they were not enrolled among the Israelites because there was no allotment given to them among the Israelites.

63 These were those enrolled by Moses and Eleazar the priest, who enrolled the Israelites in the plains of Moab by the Jordan opposite Jericho. ⁶⁴Among these there was not one of those enrolled by Moses and Aaron the priest, who had enrolled the Israelites in the

a Heb *clans of Naphtali*

wilderness of Sinai. ⁶⁵For the LORD had said of them, "They shall die in the wilderness." Not one of them was left, except Caleb son of Jephunneh and Joshua son of Nun.

The Daughters of Zelophehad

27 Then the daughters of Zelophehad came forward. Zelophehad was son of Hepher son of Gilead son of Machir son of Manasseh son of Joseph, a member of the Manassite clans. The names of his daughters were: Mahlah, Noah, Hoglah, Milcah, and Tirzah. ²They stood before Moses, Eleazar the priest, the leaders, and all the congregation, at the entrance of the tent of meeting, and they said, ³"Our father died in the wilderness; he was not among the company of those who gathered themselves together against the LORD in the company of Korah, but died for his own sin; and he had no sons. ⁴Why should the name of our father be taken away from his clan because he had no son? Give to us a possession among our father's brothers."

5 Moses brought their case before the LORD. ⁶And the LORD spoke to Moses, saying: ⁷The daughters of Zelophehad are right in what they are saying; you shall indeed let them possess an inheritance among their father's brothers and pass the inheritance of their father on to them. ⁸You shall also say to the Israelites, "If a man dies, and has no son, then you shall pass his inheritance on to his daughter. ⁹If he has no daughter, then you shall give his inheritance to his brothers. ¹⁰If he has no brothers, then you shall give his inheritance to his father's brothers. ¹¹And if his father has no brothers, then you shall give his inheritance to the nearest kinsman of his clan, and he shall possess it. It shall be for the Israelites a statute and ordinance, as the LORD commanded Moses."

Joshua Appointed Moses' Successor

12 The LORD said to Moses, "Go up this mountain of the Abarim range, and see the land that I have given to the Israelites. ¹³When

you have seen it, you also shall be gathered to your people, as your brother Aaron was, ¹⁴because you rebelled against my word in the wilderness of Zin when the congregation quarreled with me. *ᵃ* You did not show my holiness before their eyes at the waters." (These are the waters of Meribath-kadesh in the wilderness of Zin.) ¹⁵Moses spoke to the LORD, saying, ¹⁶"Let the LORD, the God of the spirits of all flesh, appoint someone over the congregation ¹⁷who shall go out before them and come in before them, who shall lead them out and bring them in, so that the congregation of the LORD may not be like sheep without a shepherd." ¹⁸So the LORD said to Moses, "Take Joshua son of Nun, a man in whom is the spirit, and lay your hand upon him; ¹⁹have him stand before Eleazar the priest and all the congregation, and commission him in their sight. ²⁰You shall give him some of your authority, so that all the congregation of the Israelites may obey. ²¹But he shall stand before Eleazar the priest, who shall inquire for him by the decision of the Urim before the LORD; at his word they shall go out, and at his word they shall come in, both he and all the Israelites with him, the whole congregation." ²²So Moses did as the LORD commanded him. He took Joshua and had him stand before Eleazar the priest and the whole congregation; ²³he laid his hands on him and commissioned him—as the LORD had directed through Moses.

Daily Offerings

28 The LORD spoke to Moses, saying: ²Command the Israelites, and say to them: My offering, the food for my offerings by fire, my pleasing odor, you shall take care to offer to me at its appointed time. ³And you shall say to them, This is the offering by fire that you shall offer to the LORD: two male lambs a year old without blemish, daily, as a regular offering. ⁴One lamb you shall offer in the morning, and the other lamb you shall offer at twilight; *ᵇ* ⁵also one-tenth of an ephah of choice flour for a grain offering, mixed with one-

a Heb lacks *with me*   *b* Heb *between the two evenings* fourth of a hin of beaten oil. [6]It is a regular burnt offering, ordained at Mount Sinai for a pleasing odor, an offering by fire to the LORD. [7]Its drink offering shall be one-fourth of a hin for each lamb; in the sanctuary you shall pour out a drink offering of strong drink to the LORD. [8]The other lamb you shall offer at twilight[a] with a grain offering and a drink offering like the one in the morning; you shall offer it as an offering by fire, a pleasing odor to the LORD.

Sabbath Offerings

9 On the sabbath day: two male lambs a year old without blemish, and two-tenths of an ephah of choice flour for a grain offering, mixed with oil, and its drink offering— [10]this is the burnt offering for every sabbath, in addition to the regular burnt offering and its drink offering.

Monthly Offerings

11 At the beginnings of your months you shall offer a burnt offering to the LORD: two young bulls, one ram, seven male lambs a year old without blemish; [12]also three-tenths of an ephah of choice flour for a grain offering, mixed with oil, for each bull; and two-tenths of choice flour for a grain offering, mixed with oil, for the one ram; [13]and one-tenth of choice flour mixed with oil as a grain offering for every lamb—a burnt offering of pleasing odor, an offering by fire to the LORD. [14]Their drink offerings shall be half a hin of wine for a bull, one-third of a hin for a ram, and one-fourth of a hin for a lamb. This is the burnt offering of every month throughout the months of the year. [15]And there shall be one male goat for a sin offering to the LORD; it shall be offered in addition to the regular burnt offering and its drink offering.

Offerings at Passover

16 On the fourteenth day of the first month there shall be a passover offering to the LORD. [17]And on the fifteenth day of this month is a festival; seven days shall unleavened bread be eaten. [18]On the first day there shall be a holy convocation. You shall not work at your occupations. [19]You shall offer an offering by fire, a burnt offering to the LORD: two young bulls, one ram, and seven male lambs a year old; see that they are without blemish. [20]Their grain offering shall be of choice flour mixed with oil: three-tenths of an ephah shall you offer for a bull, and two-tenths for a ram; [21]one-tenth shall you offer for each of the seven lambs; [22]also one male goat for a sin offering, to make atonement for you. [23]You shall offer these in addition to the burnt offering of the morning, which belongs to the regular burnt offering. [24]In the same way you shall offer daily, for seven days, the food of an offering by fire, a pleasing odor to the LORD; it shall be offered in addition to the regular burnt offering and its drink offering. [25]And on the seventh day you shall have a holy convocation; you shall not work at your occupations.

Offerings at the Festival of Weeks

26 On the day of the first fruits, when you offer a grain offering of new grain to the LORD at your festival of weeks, you shall have a holy convocation; you shall not work at your occupations. [27]You shall offer a burnt offering, a pleasing odor to the LORD: two young bulls, one ram, seven male lambs a year old. [28]Their grain offering shall be of choice flour mixed with oil, three-tenths of an ephah for each bull, two-tenths for one ram, [29]one-tenth for each of the seven lambs; [30]with one male goat, to make atonement for you. [31]In addition to the regular burnt offering with its grain offering, you shall offer them and their drink offering. They shall be without blemish.

Offerings at the Festival of Trumpets

29 On the first day of the seventh month you shall have a holy convocation; you shall not work at your occupations. It is a day for you to blow the trumpets, [2]and you shall offer a burnt offering, a pleasing odor to the

---

a Heb *between the two evenings*

LORD: one young bull, one ram, seven male lambs a year old without blemish. ³Their grain offering shall be of choice flour mixed with oil, three-tenths of one ephah for the bull, two-tenths for the ram, ⁴and one-tenth for each of the seven lambs; ⁵with one male goat for a sin offering, to make atonement for you. ⁶These are in addition to the burnt offering of the new moon and its grain offering, and the regular burnt offering and its grain offering, and their drink offerings, according to the ordinance for them, a pleasing odor, an offering by fire to the LORD.

Offerings on the Day of Atonement

7 On the tenth day of this seventh month you shall have a holy convocation, and deny yourselves;ᵃ you shall do no work. ⁸You shall offer a burnt offering to the LORD, a pleasing odor: one young bull, one ram, seven male lambs a year old. They shall be without blemish. ⁹Their grain offering shall be of choice flour mixed with oil, three-tenths of an ephah for the bull, two-tenths for the one ram, ¹⁰one-tenth for each of the seven lambs; ¹¹with one male goat for a sin offering, in addition to the sin offering of atonement, and the regular burnt offering and its grain offering, and their drink offerings.

Offerings at the Festival of Booths

12 On the fifteenth day of the seventh month you shall have a holy convocation; you shall not work at your occupations. You shall celebrate a festival to the LORD seven days. ¹³You shall offer a burnt offering, an offering by fire, a pleasing odor to the LORD: thirteen young bulls, two rams, fourteen male lambs a year old. They shall be without blemish. ¹⁴Their grain offering shall be of choice flour mixed with oil, three-tenths of an ephah for each of the thirteen bulls, two-tenths for each of the two rams, ¹⁵and one-tenth for each of the fourteen lambs; ¹⁶also one male goat for a sin offering, in addition to the regular burnt offering, its grain offering and its drink offering.

17 On the second day: twelve young bulls, two rams, fourteen male lambs a year old without blemish, ¹⁸with the grain offering and the drink offerings for the bulls, for the rams, and for the lambs, as prescribed in accordance with their number; ¹⁹also one male goat for a sin offering, in addition to the regular burnt offering and its grain offering, and their drink offerings.

20 On the third day: eleven bulls, two rams, fourteen male lambs a year old without blemish, ²¹with the grain offering and the drink offerings for the bulls, for the rams, and for the lambs, as prescribed in accordance with their number; ²²also one male goat for a sin offering, in addition to the regular burnt offering and its grain offering and its drink offering.

23 On the fourth day: ten bulls, two rams, fourteen male lambs a year old without blemish, ²⁴with the grain offering and the drink offerings for the bulls, for the rams, and for the lambs, as prescribed in accordance with their number; ²⁵also one male goat for a sin offering, in addition to the regular burnt offering, its grain offering and its drink offering.

26 On the fifth day: nine bulls, two rams, fourteen male lambs a year old without blemish, ²⁷with the grain offering and the drink offerings for the bulls, for the rams, and for the lambs, as prescribed in accordance with their number; ²⁸also one male goat for a sin offering, in addition to the regular burnt offering and its grain offering and its drink offering.

29 On the sixth day: eight bulls, two rams, fourteen male lambs a year old without blemish, ³⁰with the grain offering and the drink offerings for the bulls, for the rams, and for the lambs, as prescribed in accordance with their number; ³¹also one male goat for a sin offering, in addition to the regular burnt offering, its grain offering, and its drink offerings.

32 On the seventh day: seven bulls, two rams, fourteen male lambs a year old without blemish, ³³with the grain offering and the drink offerings for the bulls, for the rams, and for the lambs, as prescribed in accordance with their number; ³⁴also one male goat for a sin offering,

ᵃ Or *and fast*

besides the regular burnt offering, its grain offering, and its drink offering.

35 On the eighth day you shall have a solemn assembly; you shall not work at your occupations. 36You shall offer a burnt offering, an offering by fire, a pleasing odor to the LORD: one bull, one ram, seven male lambs a year old without blemish, 37and the grain offering and the drink offerings for the bull, for the ram, and for the lambs, as prescribed in accordance with their number; 38also one male goat for a sin offering, in addition to the regular burnt offering and its grain offering and its drink offering.

39 These you shall offer to the LORD at your appointed festivals, in addition to your votive offerings and your freewill offerings, as your burnt offerings, your grain offerings, your drink offerings, and your offerings of well-being.

40ᵃ So Moses told the Israelites everything just as the LORD had commanded Moses.

Vows Made by Women

30 Then Moses said to the heads of the tribes of the Israelites: This is what the LORD has commanded. 2When a man makes a vow to the LORD, or swears an oath to bind himself by a pledge, he shall not break his word; he shall do according to all that proceeds out of his mouth.

3 When a woman makes a vow to the LORD, or binds herself by a pledge, while within her father's house, in her youth, 4and her father hears of her vow or her pledge by which she has bound herself, and says nothing to her; then all her vows shall stand, and any pledge by which she has bound herself shall stand. 5But if her father expresses disapproval to her at the time that he hears of it, no vow of hers, and no pledge by which she has bound herself, shall stand; and the LORD will forgive her, because her father had expressed to her his disapproval.

6 If she marries, while obligated by her vows or any thoughtless utterance of her lips by which she has bound herself, 7and her husband hears of it and says nothing to her at the time that he hears, then her vows shall stand, and her pledges by which she has bound herself shall stand. 8But if, at the time that her husband hears of it, he expresses disapproval to her, then he shall nullify the vow by which she was obligated, or the thoughtless utterance of her lips, by which she bound herself; and the LORD will forgive her. 9(But every vow of a widow or of a divorced woman, by which she has bound herself, shall be binding upon her.) 10And if she made a vow in her husband's house, or bound herself by a pledge with an oath, 11and her husband heard it and said nothing to her, and did not express disapproval to her, then all her vows shall stand, and any pledge by which she bound herself shall stand. 12But if her husband nullifies them at the time that he hears them, then whatever proceeds out of her lips concerning her vows, or concerning her pledge of herself, shall not stand. Her husband has nullified them, and the LORD will forgive her. 13Any vow or any binding oath to deny herself,ᵇ her husband may allow to stand, or her husband may nullify. 14But if her husband says nothing to her from day to day,ᶜ then he validates all her vows, or all her pledges, by which she is obligated; he has validated them, because he said nothing to her at the time that he heard of them. 15But if he nullifies them some time after he has heard of them, then he shall bear her guilt.

16 These are the statutes that the LORD commanded Moses concerning a husband and his wife, and a father and his daughter while she is still young and in her father's house.

War against Midian

31 The LORD spoke to Moses, saying, 2"Avenge the Israelites on the Midianites; afterward you shall be gathered to your people." 3So Moses said to the people, "Arm some of your number for the war, so that they may go against Midian, to execute the LORD's vengeance on Midian. 4You shall send a thousand from each of the tribes of Israel to the

---

a Ch 30.1 in Heb   b Or to fast   c Or from that day to the next war." ⁵So out of the thousands of Israel, a thousand from each tribe were conscripted, twelve thousand armed for battle. ⁶Moses sent them to the war, a thousand from each tribe, along with Phinehas son of Eleazar the priest,ᵃ with the vessels of the sanctuary and the trumpets for sounding the alarm in his hand. ⁷They did battle against Midian, as the LORD had commanded Moses, and killed every male. ⁸They killed the kings of Midian: Evi, Rekem, Zur, Hur, and Reba, the five kings of Midian, in addition to others who were slain by them; and they also killed Balaam son of Beor with the sword. ⁹The Israelites took the women of Midian and their little ones captive; and they took all their cattle, their flocks, and all their goods as booty. ¹⁰All their towns where they had settled, and all their encampments, they burned, ¹¹but they took all the spoil and all the booty, both people and animals. ¹²Then they brought the captives and the booty and the spoil to Moses, to Eleazar the priest, and to the congregation of the Israelites, at the camp on the plains of Moab by the Jordan at Jericho.

Return from the War

13 Moses, Eleazar the priest, and all the leaders of the congregation went to meet them outside the camp. ¹⁴Moses became angry with the officers of the army, the commanders of thousands and the commanders of hundreds, who had come from service in the war. ¹⁵Moses said to them, "Have you allowed all the women to live? ¹⁶These women here, on Balaam's advice, made the Israelites act treacherously against the LORD in the affair of Peor, so that the plague came among the congregation of the LORD. ¹⁷Now therefore, kill every male among the little ones, and kill every woman who has known a man by sleeping with him. ¹⁸But all the young girls who have not known a man by sleeping with him, keep alive for yourselves. ¹⁹Camp outside the camp seven days; whoever of you has killed any person or touched a corpse, purify yourselves and your captives on the third and on the seventh day.

²⁰You shall purify every garment, every article of skin, everything made of goats' hair, and every article of wood."

21 Eleazar the priest said to the troops who had gone to battle: "This is the statute of the law that the LORD has commanded Moses: ²²gold, silver, bronze, iron, tin, and lead— ²³everything that can withstand fire, shall be passed through fire, and it shall be clean. Nevertheless it shall also be purified with the water for purification; and whatever cannot withstand fire, shall be passed through the water. ²⁴You must wash your clothes on the seventh day, and you shall be clean; afterward you may come into the camp."

Disposition of Captives and Booty

25 The LORD spoke to Moses, saying, ²⁶"You and Eleazar the priest and the heads of the ancestral houses of the congregation make an inventory of the booty captured, both human and animal. ²⁷Divide the booty into two parts, between the warriors who went out to battle and all the congregation. ²⁸From the share of the warriors who went out to battle, set aside as tribute for the LORD, one item out of every five hundred, whether persons, oxen, donkeys, sheep, or goats. ²⁹Take it from their half and give it to Eleazar the priest as an offering to the LORD. ³⁰But from the Israelites' half you shall take one out of every fifty, whether persons, oxen, donkeys, sheep, or goats—all the animals—and give them to the Levites who have charge of the tabernacle of the LORD."

31 Then Moses and Eleazar the priest did as the LORD had commanded Moses:

32 The booty remaining from the spoil that the troops had taken totaled six hundred seventy-five thousand sheep, ³³seventy-two thousand oxen, ³⁴sixty-one thousand donkeys, ³⁵and thirty-two thousand persons in all, women who had not known a man by sleeping with him.

36 The half-share, the portion of those who had gone out to war, was in number three hundred thirty-seven thousand five hundred

a Gk: Heb adds *to the war*

sheep and goats, 37and the LORD's tribute of sheep and goats was six hundred seventy-five. 38The oxen were thirty-six thousand, of which the LORD's tribute was seventy-two. 39The donkeys were thirty thousand five hundred, of which the LORD's tribute was sixty-one. 40The persons were sixteen thousand, of which LORD's tribute was thirty-two persons. 41Moses gave the tribute, the offering for the LORD, to Eleazar the priest, as the LORD had commanded Moses.

42 As for the Israelites' half, which Moses separated from that of the troops, 43the congregation's half was three hundred thirty-seven thousand five hundred sheep and goats, 44thirty-six thousand oxen, 45thirty thousand five hundred donkeys, 46and sixteen thousand persons. 47From the Israelites' half Moses took one of every fifty, both of persons and of animals, and gave them to the Levites who had charge of the tabernacle of the LORD; as the LORD had commanded Moses.

48 Then the officers who were over the thousands of the army, the commanders of thousands and the commanders of hundreds, approached Moses, 49and said to Moses, "Your servants have counted the warriors who are under our command, and not one of us is missing. 50And we have brought the LORD's offering, what each of us found, articles of gold, armlets and bracelets, signet rings, earrings, and pendants, to make atonement for ourselves before the LORD." 51Moses and Eleazar the priest received the gold from them, all in the form of crafted articles. 52And all the gold of the offering that they offered to the LORD, from the commanders of thousands and the commanders of hundreds, was sixteen thousand seven hundred fifty shekels. 53(The troops had all taken plunder for themselves.) 54So Moses and Eleazar the priest received the gold from the commanders of thousands and of hundreds, and brought it into the tent of meeting as a memorial for the Israelites before the LORD.

Conquest and Division of Transjordan

32 Now the Reubenites and the Gadites owned a very great number of cattle. When they saw that the land of Jazer and the land of Gilead was a good place for cattle, 2the Gadites and the Reubenites came and spoke to Moses, to Eleazar the priest, and to the leaders of the congregation, saying, 3"Ataroth, Dibon, Jazer, Nimrah, Heshbon, Elealeh, Sebam, Nebo, and Beon— 4the land that the LORD subdued before the congregation of Israel—is a land for cattle; and your servants have cattle." 5They continued, "If we have found favor in your sight, let this land be given to your servants for a possession; do not make us cross the Jordan."

6 But Moses said to the Gadites and to the Reubenites, "Shall your brothers go to war while you sit here? 7Why will you discourage the hearts of the Israelites from going over into the land that the LORD has given them? 8Your fathers did this, when I sent them from Kadesh-barnea to see the land. 9When they went up to the Wadi Eshcol and saw the land, they discouraged the hearts of the Israelites from going into the land that the LORD had given them. 10The LORD's anger was kindled on that day and he swore, saying, 11'Surely none of the people who came up out of Egypt, from twenty years old and upward, shall see the land that I swore to give to Abraham, to Isaac, and to Jacob, because they have not unreservedly followed me— 12none except Caleb son of Jephunneh the Kenizzite and Joshua son of Nun, for they have unreservedly followed the LORD.' 13And the LORD's anger was kindled against Israel, and he made them wander in the wilderness for forty years, until all the generation that had done evil in the sight of the LORD had disappeared. 14And now you, a brood of sinners, have risen in place of your fathers, to increase the LORD's fierce anger against Israel! 15If you turn away from following him, he will again abandon them in the wilderness; and you will destroy all this people."

16 Then they came up to him and said, "We will build sheepfolds here for our flocks, and towns for our little ones, 17but we will take

up arms as a vanguard*a* before the Israelites, until we have brought them to their place. Meanwhile our little ones will stay in the fortified towns because of the inhabitants of the land. 18We will not return to our homes until all the Israelites have obtained their inheritance. 19We will not inherit with them on the other side of the Jordan and beyond, because our inheritance has come to us on this side of the Jordan to the east."

20 So Moses said to them, "If you do this—if you take up arms to go before the LORD for the war, 21and all those of you who bear arms cross the Jordan before the LORD, until he has driven out his enemies from before him 22and the land is subdued before the LORD—then after that you may return and be free of obligation to the LORD and to Israel, and this land shall be your possession before the LORD. 23But if you do not do this, you have sinned against the LORD; and be sure your sin will find you out. 24Build towns for your little ones, and folds for your flocks; but do what you have promised."

25 Then the Gadites and the Reubenites said to Moses, "Your servants will do as my lord commands. 26Our little ones, our wives, our flocks, and all our livestock shall remain there in the towns of Gilead; 27but your servants will cross over, everyone armed for war, to do battle for the LORD, just as my lord orders."

28 So Moses gave command concerning them to Eleazar the priest, to Joshua son of Nun, and to the heads of the ancestral houses of the Israelite tribes. 29And Moses said to them, "If the Gadites and the Reubenites, everyone armed for battle before the LORD, will cross over the Jordan with you and the land shall be subdued before you, then you shall give them the land of Gilead for a possession; 30but if they will not cross over with you armed, they shall have possessions among you in the land of Canaan." 31The Gadites and the Reubenites answered, "As the LORD has spoken to your servants, so we will do. 32We will cross over armed before the LORD into the land of Canaan, but the possession of our inheritance shall remain with us on this side of*b* the Jordan."

33 Moses gave to them—to the Gadites and to the Reubenites and to the half-tribe of Manasseh son of Joseph—the kingdom of King Sihon of the Amorites and the kingdom of King Og of Bashan, the land and its towns, with the territories of the surrounding towns. 34And the Gadites rebuilt Dibon, Ataroth, Aroer, 35Atroth-shophan, Jazer, Jogbehah, 36Beth-nimrah, and Beth-haran, fortified cities, and folds for sheep. 37And the Reubenites rebuilt Heshbon, Elealeh, Kiriathaim, 38Nebo, and Baal-meon (some names being changed), and Sibmah; and they gave names to the towns that they rebuilt. 39The descendants of Machir son of Manasseh went to Gilead, captured it, and dispossessed the Amorites who were there; 40so Moses gave Gilead to Machir son of Manasseh, and he settled there. 41Jair son of Manasseh went and captured their villages, and renamed them Havvoth-jair.*c* 42And Nobah went and captured Kenath and its villages, and renamed it Nobah after himself.

The Stages of Israel's Journey from Egypt

33 These are the stages by which the Israelites went out of the land of Egypt in military formation under the leadership of Moses and Aaron. 2Moses wrote down their starting points, stage by stage, by command of the LORD; and these are their stages according to their starting places. 3They set out from Rameses in the first month, on the fifteenth day of the first month; on the day after the passover the Israelites went out boldly in the sight of all the Egyptians, 4while the Egyptians were burying all their firstborn, whom the LORD had struck down among them. The LORD executed judgments even against their gods.

5 So the Israelites set out from Rameses, and camped at Succoth. 6They set out from Succoth, and camped at Etham, which is on the edge of the wilderness. 7They set out from

a Cn: Heb *hurrying*   *b* Heb *beyond*   *c* That is *the villages of Jair*

Etham, and turned back to Pi-hahiroth, which faces Baal-zephon; and they camped before Migdol. 8They set out from Pi-hahiroth, passed through the sea into the wilderness, went a three days' journey in the wilderness of Etham, and camped at Marah. 9They set out from Marah and came to Elim; at Elim there were twelve springs of water and seventy palm trees, and they camped there. 10They set out from Elim and camped by the Red Sea.*a* 11They set out from the Red Sea*a* and camped in the wilderness of Sin. 12They set out from the wilderness of Sin and camped at Dophkah. 13They set out from Dophkah and camped at Alush. 14They set out from Alush and camped at Rephidim, where there was no water for the people to drink. 15They set out from Rephidim and camped in the wilderness of Sinai. 16They set out from the wilderness of Sinai and camped at Kibroth-hattaavah. 17They set out from Kibroth-hattaavah and camped at Hazeroth. 18They set out from Hazeroth and camped at Rithmah. 19They set out from Rithmah and camped at Rimmon-perez. 20They set out from Rimmon-perez and camped at Libnah. 21They set out from Libnah and camped at Rissah. 22They set out from Rissah and camped at Kehelathah. 23They set out from Kehelathah and camped at Mount Shepher. 24They set out from Mount Shepher and camped at Haradah. 25They set out from Haradah and camped at Makheloth. 26They set out from Makheloth and camped at Tahath. 27They set out from Tahath and camped at Terah. 28They set out from Terah and camped at Mithkah. 29They set out from Mithkah and camped at Hashmonah. 30They set out from Hashmonah and camped at Moseroth. 31They set out from Moseroth and camped at Bene-jaakan. 32They set out from Bene-jaakan and camped at Hor-haggidgad. 33They set out from Hor-haggidgad and camped at Jotbathah. 34They set out from Jotbathah and camped at Abronah. 35They set out from Abronah and camped at Ezion-geber. 36They set out from Ezion-geber and camped

in the wilderness of Zin (that is, Kadesh). 37They set out from Kadesh and camped at Mount Hor, on the edge of the land of Edom.

38 Aaron the priest went up Mount Hor at the command of the LORD and died there in the fortieth year after the Israelites had come out of the land of Egypt, on the first day of the fifth month. 39Aaron was one hundred twenty-three years old when he died on Mount Hor.

40 The Canaanite, the king of Arad, who lived in the Negeb in the land of Canaan, heard of the coming of the Israelites.

41 They set out from Mount Hor and camped at Zalmonah. 42They set out from Zalmonah and camped at Punon. 43They set out from Punon and camped at Oboth. 44They set out from Oboth and camped at Iye-abarim, in the territory of Moab. 45They set out from Iyim and camped at Dibon-gad. 46They set out from Dibon-gad and camped at Almon-diblathaim. 47They set out from Almon-diblathaim and camped in the mountains of Abarim, before Nebo. 48They set out from the mountains of Abarim and camped in the plains of Moab by the Jordan at Jericho; 49they camped by the Jordan from Beth-jeshimoth as far as Abel-shittim in the plains of Moab.

Directions for the Conquest of Canaan

50 In the plains of Moab by the Jordan at Jericho, the LORD spoke to Moses, saying: 51Speak to the Israelites, and say to them: When you cross over the Jordan into the land of Canaan, 52you shall drive out all the inhabitants of the land from before you, destroy all their figured stones, destroy all their cast images, and demolish all their high places. 53You shall take possession of the land and settle in it, for I have given you the land to possess. 54You shall apportion the land by lot according to your clans; to a large one you shall give a large inheritance, and to a small one you shall give a small inheritance; the inheritance shall belong to the person on whom the lot falls; according to your ancestral tribes you shall inherit. 55But if you do not drive out the inhabitants of the land

a Or *Sea of Reeds*

from before you, then those whom you let remain shall be as barbs in your eyes and thorns in your sides; they shall trouble you in the land where you are settling. 56And I will do to you as I thought to do to them.

The Boundaries of the Land

34 The LORD spoke to Moses, saying: 2Command the Israelites, and say to them: When you enter the land of Canaan (this is the land that shall fall to you for an inheritance, the land of Canaan, defined by its boundaries), 3your south sector shall extend from the wilderness of Zin along the side of Edom. Your southern boundary shall begin from the end of the Dead Sea*a* on the east; 4your boundary shall turn south of the ascent of Akrabbim, and cross to Zin, and its outer limit shall be south of Kadesh-barnea; then it shall go on to Hazar-addar, and cross to Azmon; 5the boundary shall turn from Azmon to the Wadi of Egypt, and its termination shall be at the Sea.

6 For the western boundary, you shall have the Great Sea and its*b* coast; this shall be your western boundary.

7 This shall be your northern boundary: from the Great Sea you shall mark out your line to Mount Hor; 8from Mount Hor you shall mark it out to Lebo-hamath, and the outer limit of the boundary shall be at Zedad; 9then the boundary shall extend to Ziphron, and its end shall be at Hazar-enan; this shall be your northern boundary.

10 You shall mark out your eastern boundary from Hazar-enan to Shepham; 11and the boundary shall continue down from Shepham to Riblah on the east side of Ain; and the boundary shall go down, and reach the eastern slope of the sea of Chinnereth; 12and the boundary shall go down to the Jordan, and its end shall be at the Dead Sea.*a* This shall be your land with its boundaries all around.

13 Moses commanded the Israelites, saying: This is the land that you shall inherit by lot, which the LORD has commanded to give to the nine tribes and to the half-tribe; 14for the tribe of the Reubenites by their ancestral houses and the tribe of the Gadites by their ancestral houses have taken their inheritance, and also the half-tribe of Manasseh; 15the two tribes and the half-tribe have taken their inheritance beyond the Jordan at Jericho eastward, toward the sunrise.

Tribal Leaders

16 The LORD spoke to Moses, saying: 17These are the names of the men who shall apportion the land to you for inheritance: the priest Eleazar and Joshua son of Nun. 18You shall take one leader of every tribe to apportion the land for inheritance. 19These are the names of the men: Of the tribe of Judah, Caleb son of Jephunneh. 20Of the tribe of the Simeonites, Shemuel son of Ammihud. 21Of the tribe of Benjamin, Elidad son of Chislon. 22Of the tribe of the Danites a leader, Bukki son of Jogli. 23Of the Josephites: of the tribe of the Manassites a leader, Hanniel son of Ephod, 24and of the tribe of the Ephraimites a leader, Kemuel son of Shiphtan. 25Of the tribe of the Zebulunites a leader, Eli-zaphan son of Parnach. 26Of the tribe of the Issacharites a leader, Paltiel son of Azzan. 27And of the tribe of the Asherites a leader, Ahihud son of Shelomi. 28Of the tribe of the Naphtalites a leader, Pedahel son of Ammihud. 29These were the ones whom the LORD commanded to apportion the inheritance for the Israelites in the land of Canaan.

Cities for the Levites

35 In the plains of Moab by the Jordan at Jericho, the LORD spoke to Moses, saying: 2Command the Israelites to give, from the inheritance that they possess, towns for the Levites to live in; you shall also give to the Levites pasture lands surrounding the towns. 3The towns shall be theirs to live in, and their pasture lands shall be for their cattle, for their livestock, and for all their animals. 4The pasture lands of the towns, which you shall give to the

---

a Heb *Salt Sea*   *b* Syr: Heb lacks *its*

Levites, shall reach from the wall of the town outward a thousand cubits all around. 5You shall measure, outside the town, for the east side two thousand cubits, for the south side two thousand cubits, for the west side two thousand cubits, and for the north side two thousand cubits, with the town in the middle; this shall belong to them as pasture land for their towns.

6 The towns that you give to the Levites shall include the six cities of refuge, where you shall permit a slayer to flee, and in addition to them you shall give forty-two towns. 7The towns that you give to the Levites shall total forty-eight, with their pasture lands. 8And as for the towns that you shall give from the possession of the Israelites, from the larger tribes you shall take many, and from the smaller tribes you shall take few; each, in proportion to the inheritance that it obtains, shall give of its towns to the Levites.

Cities of Refuge

9 The LORD spoke to Moses, saying: 10Speak to the Israelites, and say to them: When you cross the Jordan into the land of Canaan, 11then you shall select cities to be cities of refuge for you, so that a slayer who kills a person without intent may flee there. 12The cities shall be for you a refuge from the avenger, so that the slayer may not die until there is a trial before the congregation.

13 The cities that you designate shall be six cities of refuge for you: 14you shall designate three cities beyond the Jordan, and three cities in the land of Canaan, to be cities of refuge. 15These six cities shall serve as refuge for the Israelites, for the resident or transient alien among them, so that anyone who kills a person without intent may flee there.

Concerning Murder and Blood Revenge

16 But anyone who strikes another with an iron object, and death ensues, is a murderer; the murderer shall be put to death. 17Or anyone who strikes another with a stone in hand that could cause death, and death ensues, is a mur-

derer; the murderer shall be put to death. 18Or anyone who strikes another with a weapon of wood in hand that could cause death, and death ensues, is a murderer; the murderer shall be put to death. 19The avenger of blood is the one who shall put the murderer to death; when they meet, the avenger of blood shall execute the sentence. 20Likewise, if someone pushes another from hatred, or hurls something at another, lying in wait, and death ensues, 21or in enmity strikes another with the hand, and death ensues, then the one who struck the blow shall be put to death; that person is a murderer; the avenger of blood shall put the murderer to death, when they meet.

22 But if someone pushes another suddenly without enmity, or hurls any object without lying in wait, 23or, while handling any stone that could cause death, unintentionally*a* drops it on another and death ensues, though they were not enemies, and no harm was intended, 24then the congregation shall judge between the slayer and the avenger of blood, in accordance with these ordinances; 25and the congregation shall rescue the slayer from the avenger of blood. Then the congregation shall send the slayer back to the original city of refuge. The slayer shall live in it until the death of the high priest who was anointed with the holy oil. 26But if the slayer shall at any time go outside the bounds of the original city of refuge, 27and is found by the avenger of blood outside the bounds of the city of refuge, and is killed by the avenger, no bloodguilt shall be incurred. 28For the slayer must remain in the city of refuge until the death of the high priest; but after the death of the high priest the slayer may return home.

29 These things shall be a statute and ordinance for you throughout your generations wherever you live.

30 If anyone kills another, the murderer shall be put to death on the evidence of witnesses; but no one shall be put to death on the testimony of a single witness. 31Moreover you shall accept no ransom for the life of a mur-

---

a Heb *without seeing*

derer who is subject to the death penalty; a murderer must be put to death. ³²Nor shall you accept ransom for one who has fled to a city of refuge, enabling the fugitive to return to live in the land before the death of the high priest. ³³You shall not pollute the land in which you live; for blood pollutes the land, and no expiation can be made for the land, for the blood that is shed in it, except by the blood of the one who shed it. ³⁴You shall not defile the land in which you live, in which I also dwell; for I the LORD dwell among the Israelites.

Marriage of Female Heirs

36 The heads of the ancestral houses of the clans of the descendants of Gilead son of Machir son of Manasseh, of the Josephite clans, came forward and spoke in the presence of Moses and the leaders, the heads of the ancestral houses of the Israelites; ²they said, "The LORD commanded my lord to give the land for inheritance by lot to the Israelites; and my lord was commanded by the LORD to give the inheritance of our brother Zelophehad to his daughters. ³But if they are married into another Israelite tribe, then their inheritance will be taken from the inheritance of our ancestors and added to the inheritance of the tribe into which they marry; so it will be taken away from the allotted portion of our inheritance. ⁴And when the jubilee of the Israelites comes, then their inheritance will be added to the inheritance of the tribe into which they have married; and their inheritance will be taken from the inheritance of our ancestral tribe."

5 Then Moses commanded the Israelites according to the word of the LORD, saying, "The descendants of the tribe of Joseph are right in what they are saying. ⁶This is what the LORD commands concerning the daughters of Zelophehad, 'Let them marry whom they think best; only it must be into a clan of their father's tribe that they are married, ⁷so that no inheritance of the Israelites shall be transferred from one tribe to another; for all Israelites shall retain the inheritance of their ancestral tribes. ⁸Every daughter who possesses an inheritance in any tribe of the Israelites shall marry one from the clan of her father's tribe, so that all Israelites may continue to possess their ancestral inheritance. ⁹No inheritance shall be transferred from one tribe to another; for each of the tribes of the Israelites shall retain its own inheritance.' "

10 The daughters of Zelophehad did as the LORD had commanded Moses. ¹¹Mahlah, Tirzah, Hoglah, Milcah, and Noah, the daughters of Zelophehad, married sons of their father's brothers. ¹²They were married into the clans of the descendants of Manasseh son of Joseph, and their inheritance remained in the tribe of their father's clan.

13 These are the commandments and the ordinances that the LORD commanded through Moses to the Israelites in the plains of Moab by the Jordan at Jericho.

DEUTERONOMY

Events at Horeb Recalled

1 These are the words that Moses spoke to all Israel beyond the Jordan—in the wilderness, on the plain opposite Suph, between Paran and Tophel, Laban, Hazeroth, and Di-zahab. ²(By the way of Mount Seir it takes eleven days to reach Kadesh-barnea from Horeb.) ³In the fortieth year, on the first day of the eleventh month, Moses spoke to the Israelites just as the LORD had commanded him to speak to them. ⁴This was after he had defeated King Sihon of the Amorites, who reigned in Heshbon, and King Og of Bashan, who reigned in Ashtaroth and *a* in Edrei. ⁵Beyond the Jordan in the land of Moab, Moses undertook to expound this law as follows:

6 The LORD our God spoke to us at Horeb, saying, "You have stayed long enough at this mountain. ⁷Resume your journey, and go into the hill country of the Amorites as well as into the neighboring regions—the Arabah, the hill country, the Shephelah, the Negeb, and the seacoast—the land of the Canaanites and the Lebanon, as far as the great river, the river Euphrates. ⁸See, I have set the land before you; go in and take possession of the land that I *b* swore to your ancestors, to Abraham, to Isaac, and to Jacob, to give to them and to their descendants after them."

Appointment of Tribal Leaders

9 At that time I said to you, "I am unable by myself to bear you. ¹⁰The LORD your God has multiplied you, so that today you are as numerous as the stars of heaven. ¹¹May the LORD, the God of your ancestors, increase you a thousand times more and bless you, as he has promised you! ¹²But how can I bear the heavy burden of your disputes all by myself? ¹³Choose for each of your tribes individuals who are wise, discerning, and reputable to be your leaders." ¹⁴You answered me, "The plan you have proposed is a good one." ¹⁵So I took the leaders of your tribes, wise and reputable individuals, and installed them as leaders over you, commanders of thousands, commanders of hundreds, commanders of fifties, commanders of tens, and officials, throughout your tribes. ¹⁶I charged your judges at that time: "Give the members of your community a fair hearing, and judge rightly between one person and another, whether citizen or resident alien. ¹⁷You must not be partial in judging: hear out the small and the great alike; you shall not be intimidated by anyone, for the judgment is God's. Any case that is too hard for you, bring to me, and I will hear it." ¹⁸So I charged you at that time with all the things that you should do.

Israel's Refusal to Enter the Land

19 Then, just as the LORD our God had ordered us, we set out from Horeb and went through all that great and terrible wilderness that you saw, on the way to the hill country of the Amorites, until we reached Kadesh-barnea. ²⁰I said to you, "You have reached the hill country of the Amorites, which the LORD our God is giving us. ²¹See, the LORD your God has given the land to you; go up, take possession, as the LORD, the God of your ancestors, has promised you; do not fear or be dismayed."

22 All of you came to me and said, "Let us send men ahead of us to explore the land for us and bring back a report to us regarding the route by which we should go up and the cities we will come to." ²³The plan seemed good to me, and I selected twelve of you, one from each tribe. ²⁴They set out and went up into the hill country, and when they reached the Valley of Eshcol they spied it out ²⁵and gathered some of the land's produce, which they brought down to us. They brought back a report to us, and said, "It is a good land that the LORD our God is giving us."

26 But you were unwilling to go up. You rebelled against the command of the LORD your God; ²⁷you grumbled in your tents and said, "It

---

a Gk Syr Vg Compare Josh 12.4: Heb lacks *and*   *b* Sam Gk: MT *the* LORD is because the LORD hates us that he has brought us out of the land of Egypt, to hand us over to the Amorites to destroy us. 28Where are we headed? Our kindred have made our hearts melt by reporting, 'The people are stronger and taller than we; the cities are large and fortified up to heaven! We actually saw there the offspring of the Anakim!' " 29I said to you, "Have no dread or fear of them. 30The LORD your God, who goes before you, is the one who will fight for you, just as he did for you in Egypt before your very eyes, 31and in the wilderness, where you saw how the LORD your God carried you, just as one carries a child, all the way that you traveled until you reached this place. 32But in spite of this, you have no trust in the LORD your God, 33who goes before you on the way to seek out a place for you to camp, in fire by night, and in the cloud by day, to show you the route you should take."

The Penalty for Israel's Rebellion

34 When the LORD heard your words, he was wrathful and swore: 35"Not one of these—not one of this evil generation—shall see the good land that I swore to give to your ancestors, 36except Caleb son of Jephunneh. He shall see it, and to him and to his descendants I will give the land on which he set foot, because of his complete fidelity to the LORD." 37Even with me the LORD was angry on your account, saying, "You also shall not enter there. 38Joshua son of Nun, your assistant, shall enter there; encourage him, for he is the one who will secure Israel's possession of it. 39And as for your little ones, who you thought would become booty, your children, who today do not yet know right from wrong, they shall enter there; to them I will give it, and they shall take possession of it. 40But as for you, journey back into the wilderness, in the direction of the Red Sea." *a*

41 You answered me, "We have sinned against the LORD! We are ready to go up and fight, just as the LORD our God commanded us." So all of you strapped on your battle gear, and thought it easy to go up into the hill country. 42The LORD said to me, "Say to them, 'Do not go up and do not fight, for I am not in the midst of you; otherwise you will be defeated by your enemies.' " 43Although I told you, you would not listen. You rebelled against the command of the LORD and presumptuously went up into the hill country. 44The Amorites who lived in that hill country then came out against you and chased you as bees do. They beat you down in Seir as far as Hormah. 45When you returned and wept before the LORD, the LORD would neither heed your voice nor pay you any attention.

The Desert Years

46 After you had stayed at Kadesh as many days as you did, 1we journeyed back into the wilderness, in the direction of the Red Sea,*a* as the LORD had told me and skirted Mount Seir for many days. 2Then the LORD said to me: 3"You have been skirting this hill country long enough. Head north, 4and charge the people as follows: You are about to pass through the territory of your kindred, the descendants of Esau, who live in Seir. They will be afraid of you, so, be very careful 5not to engage in battle with them, for I will not give you even so much as a foot's length of their land, since I have given Mount Seir to Esau as a possession. 6You shall purchase food from them for money, so that you may eat; and you shall also buy water from them for money, so that you may drink. 7Surely the LORD your God has blessed you in all your undertakings; he knows your going through this great wilderness. These forty years the LORD your God has been with you; you have lacked nothing." 8So we passed by our kin, the descendants of Esau who live in Seir, leaving behind the route of the Arabah, and leaving behind Elath and Eziongeber.

When we had headed out along the route of the wilderness of Moab, 9the LORD said to me: "Do not harass Moab or engage them in battle, for I will not give you any of its land as

a Or *Sea of Reeds*

a possession, since I have given Ar as a possession to the descendants of Lot." 10(The Emim—a large and numerous people, as tall as the Anakim—had formerly inhabited it. 11Like the Anakim, they are usually reckoned as Rephaim, though the Moabites call them Emim. 12Moreover, the Horim had formerly inhabited Seir, but the descendants of Esau dispossessed them, destroying them and settling in their place, as Israel has done in the land that the LORD gave them as a possession.) 13"Now then, proceed to cross over the Wadi Zered."

So we crossed over the Wadi Zered. 14And the length of time we had traveled from Kadesh-barnea until we crossed the Wadi Zered was thirty-eight years, until the entire generation of warriors had perished from the camp, as the LORD had sworn concerning them. 15Indeed, the LORD's own hand was against them, to root them out from the camp, until all had perished.

16 Just as soon as all the warriors had died off from among the people, 17the LORD spoke to me, saying, 18"Today you are going to cross the boundary of Moab at Ar. 19When you approach the frontier of the Ammonites, do not harass them or engage them in battle, for I will not give the land of the Ammonites to you as a possession, because I have given it to the descendants of Lot." 20(It also is usually reckoned as a land of Rephaim. Rephaim formerly inhabited it, though the Ammonites call them Zamzummim, 21a strong and numerous people, as tall as the Anakim. But the LORD destroyed them from before the Ammonites so that they could dispossess them and settle in their place. 22He did the same for the descendants of Esau, who live in Seir, by destroying the Horim before them so that they could dispossess them and settle in their place even to this day. 23As for the Avvim, who had lived in settlements in the vicinity of Gaza, the Caphtorim, who came from Caphtor, destroyed them and settled in their place.) 24"Proceed on your journey and cross the Wadi Arnon. See, I have handed over to you King Sihon the Amorite of Heshbon, and his land. Begin to take possession by engaging him in battle. 25This day I will begin to put the dread and fear of you upon the peoples everywhere under heaven; when they hear report of you, they will tremble and be in anguish because of you."

Defeat of King Sihon

26 So I sent messengers from the wilderness of Kedemoth to King Sihon of Heshbon with the following terms of peace: 27"If you let me pass through your land, I will travel only along the road; I will turn aside neither to the right nor to the left. 28You shall sell me food for money, so that I may eat, and supply me water for money, so that I may drink. Only allow me to pass through on foot— 29just as the descendants of Esau who live in Seir have done for me and likewise the Moabites who live in Ar—until I cross the Jordan into the land that the LORD our God is giving us." 30But King Sihon of Heshbon was not willing to let us pass through, for the LORD your God had hardened his spirit and made his heart defiant in order to hand him over to you, as he has now done.

31 The LORD said to me, "See, I have begun to give Sihon and his land over to you. Begin now to take possession of his land." 32So when Sihon came out against us, he and all his people for battle at Jahaz, 33the LORD our God gave him over to us; and we struck him down, along with his offspring and all his people. 34At that time we captured all his towns, and in each town we utterly destroyed men, women, and children. We left not a single survivor. 35Only the livestock we kept as spoil for ourselves, as well as the plunder of the towns that we had captured. 36From Aroer on the edge of the Wadi Arnon (including the town that is in the wadi itself) as far as Gilead, there was no citadel too high for us. The LORD our God gave everything to us. 37You did not encroach, however, on the land of the Ammonites, avoiding the whole upper region of the Wadi Jabbok as well as the towns of the hill country, just as[a] the LORD our God had charged.

a Gk Tg: Heb *and all*

Defeat of King Og

3 When we headed up the road to Bashan, King Og of Bashan came out against us, he and all his people, for battle at Edrei. ²The LORD said to me, "Do not fear him, for I have handed him over to you, along with his people and his land. Do to him as you did to King Sihon of the Amorites, who reigned in Heshbon." ³So the LORD our God also handed over to us King Og of Bashan and all his people. We struck him down until not a single survivor was left. ⁴At that time we captured all his towns; there was no citadel that we did not take from them—sixty towns, the whole region of Argob, the kingdom of Og in Bashan. ⁵All these were fortress towns with high walls, double gates, and bars, besides a great many villages. ⁶And we utterly destroyed them, as we had done to King Sihon of Heshbon, in each city utterly destroying men, women, and children. ⁷But all the livestock and the plunder of the towns we kept as spoil for ourselves.

8 So at that time we took from the two kings of the Amorites the land beyond the Jordan, from the Wadi Arnon to Mount Hermon ⁹(the Sidonians call Hermon Sirion, while the Amorites call it Senir), ¹⁰all the towns of the tableland, the whole of Gilead, and all of Bashan, as far as Salecah and Edrei, towns of Og's kingdom in Bashan. ¹¹(Now only King Og of Bashan was left of the remnant of the Rephaim. In fact his bed, an iron bed, can still be seen in Rabbah of the Ammonites. By the common cubit it is nine cubits long and four cubits wide.) ¹²As for the land that we took possession of at that time, I gave to the Reubenites and Gadites the territory north of Aroer,ᵃ that is on the edge of the Wadi Arnon, as well as half the hill country of Gilead with its towns, ¹³and I gave to the half-tribe of Manasseh the rest of Gilead and all of Bashan, Og's kingdom. (The whole region of Argob: all that portion of Bashan used to be called a land of Rephaim; ¹⁴Jair the Manassite acquired the whole region of Argob as far as the border of the Geshurites and the Maacathites,

and he named them—that is, Bashan—after himself, Havvoth-jair,ᵇ as it is to this day.) ¹⁵To Machir I gave Gilead. ¹⁶And to the Reubenites and the Gadites I gave the territory from Gilead as far as the Wadi Arnon, with the middle of the wadi as a boundary, and up to the Jabbok, the wadi being boundary of the Ammonites; ¹⁷the Arabah also, with the Jordan and its banks, from Chinnereth down to the sea of the Arabah, the Dead Sea,ᶜ with the lower slopes of Pisgah on the east.

18 At that time, I charged you as follows: "Although the LORD your God has given you this land to occupy, all your troops shall cross over armed as the vanguard of your Israelite kin. ¹⁹Only your wives, your children, and your livestock—I know that you have much livestock—shall stay behind in the towns that I have given to you. ²⁰When the LORD gives rest to your kindred, as to you, and they too have occupied the land that the LORD your God is giving them beyond the Jordan, then each of you may return to the property that I have given to you." ²¹And I charged Joshua as well at that time, saying: "Your own eyes have seen everything that the LORD your God has done to these two kings; so the LORD will do to all the kingdoms into which you are about to cross. ²²Do not fear them, for it is the LORD your God who fights for you."

Moses Views Canaan from Pisgah

23 At that time, too, I entreated the LORD, saying: ²⁴"O Lord GOD, you have only begun to show your servant your greatness and your might; what god in heaven or on earth can perform deeds and mighty acts like yours! ²⁵Let me cross over to see the good land beyond the Jordan, that good hill country and the Lebanon." ²⁶But the LORD was angry with me on your account and would not heed me. The LORD said to me, "Enough from you! Never speak to me of this matter again! ²⁷Go up to the top of Pisgah and look around you to the west, to the north, to the south, and to the east. Look well, for you shall not cross over this Jor-

---

ᵃ Heb *territory from Aroer*   ᵇ That is *Settlement of Jair*   ᶜ Heb *Salt Sea* dan. [28]But charge Joshua, and encourage and strengthen him, because it is he who shall cross over at the head of this people and who shall secure their possession of the land that you will see." [29]So we remained in the valley opposite Beth-peor.

Moses Commands Obedience

4 So now, Israel, give heed to the statutes and ordinances that I am teaching you to observe, so that you may live to enter and occupy the land that the LORD, the God of your ancestors, is giving you. [2]You must neither add anything to what I command you nor take away anything from it, but keep the commandments of the LORD your God with which I am charging you. [3]You have seen for yourselves what the LORD did with regard to the Baal of Peor—how the LORD your God destroyed from among you everyone who followed the Baal of Peor, [4]while those of you who held fast to the LORD your God are all alive today.

[5] See, just as the LORD my God has charged me, I now teach you statutes and ordinances for you to observe in the land that you are about to enter and occupy. [6]You must observe them diligently, for this will show your wisdom and discernment to the peoples, who, when they hear all these statutes, will say, "Surely this great nation is a wise and discerning people!" [7]For what other great nation has a god so near to it as the LORD our God is whenever we call to him? [8]And what other great nation has statutes and ordinances as just as this entire law that I am setting before you today?

[9] But take care and watch yourselves closely, so as neither to forget the things that your eyes have seen nor to let them slip from your mind all the days of your life; make them known to your children and your children's children— [10]how you once stood before the LORD your God at Horeb, when the LORD said to me, "Assemble the people for me, and I will let them hear my words, so that they may learn to fear me as long as they live on the earth, and may teach their children so"; [11]you approached and stood at the foot of the mountain while the mountain was blazing up to the very heavens, shrouded in dark clouds. [12]Then the LORD spoke to you out of the fire. You heard the sound of words but saw no form; there was only a voice. [13]He declared to you his covenant, which he charged you to observe, that is, the ten commandments;[a] and he wrote them on two stone tablets. [14]And the LORD charged me at that time to teach you statutes and ordinances for you to observe in the land that you are about to cross into and occupy.

[15] Since you saw no form when the LORD spoke to you at Horeb out of the fire, take care and watch yourselves closely, [16]so that you do not act corruptly by making an idol for yourselves, in the form of any figure—the likeness of male or female, [17]the likeness of any animal that is on the earth, the likeness of any winged bird that flies in the air, [18]the likeness of anything that creeps on the ground, the likeness of any fish that is in the water under the earth. [19]And when you look up to the heavens and see the sun, the moon, and the stars, all the host of heaven, do not be led astray and bow down to them and serve them, things that the LORD your God has allotted to all the peoples everywhere under heaven. [20]But the LORD has taken you and brought you out of the iron-smelter, out of Egypt, to become a people of his very own possession, as you are now.

[21] The LORD was angry with me because of you, and he vowed that I should not cross the Jordan and that I should not enter the good land that the LORD your God is giving for your possession. [22]For I am going to die in this land without crossing over the Jordan, but you are going to cross over to take possession of that good land. [23]So be careful not to forget the covenant that the LORD your God made with you, and not to make for yourselves an idol in the form of anything that the LORD your God has forbidden you. [24]For the LORD your God is a devouring fire, a jealous God.

a Heb *the ten words*

25. When you have had children and children's children, and become complacent in the land, if you act corruptly by making an idol in the form of anything, thus doing what is evil in the sight of the LORD your God, and provoking him to anger, 26I call heaven and earth to witness against you today that you will soon utterly perish from the land that you are crossing the Jordan to occupy; you will not live long on it, but will be utterly destroyed. 27The LORD will scatter you among the peoples; only a few of you will be left among the nations where the LORD will lead you. 28There you will serve other gods made by human hands, objects of wood and stone that neither see, nor hear, nor eat, nor smell. 29From there you will seek the LORD your God, and you will find him if you search after him with all your heart and soul. 30In your distress, when all these things have happened to you in time to come, you will return to the LORD your God and heed him. 31Because the LORD your God is a merciful God, he will neither abandon you nor destroy you; he will not forget the covenant with your ancestors that he swore to them.

32 For ask now about former ages, long before your own, ever since the day that God created human beings on the earth; ask from one end of heaven to the other: has anything so great as this ever happened or has its like ever been heard of? 33Has any people ever heard the voice of a god speaking out of a fire, as you have heard, and lived? 34Or has any god ever attempted to go and take a nation for himself from the midst of another nation, by trials, by signs and wonders, by war, by a mighty hand and an outstretched arm, and by terrifying displays of power, as the LORD your God did for you in Egypt before your very eyes? 35To you it was shown so that you would acknowledge that the LORD is God; there is no other besides him. 36From heaven he made you hear his voice to discipline you. On earth he showed you his great fire, while you heard his words coming out of the fire. 37And because he loved your ancestors, he chose their descendants after them. He brought you out of Egypt with his own presence, by his great power, 38driving out before you nations greater and mightier than yourselves, to bring you in, giving you their land for a possession, as it is still today. 39So acknowledge today and take to heart that the LORD is God in heaven above and on the earth beneath; there is no other. 40Keep his statutes and his commandments, which I am commanding you today for your own well-being and that of your descendants after you, so that you may long remain in the land that the LORD your God is giving you for all time.

Cities of Refuge East of the Jordan

41 Then Moses set apart on the east side of the Jordan three cities 42to which a homicide could flee, someone who unintentionally kills another person, the two not having been at enmity before; the homicide could flee to one of these cities and live: 43Bezer in the wilderness on the tableland belonging to the Reubenites, Ramoth in Gilead belonging to the Gadites, and Golan in Bashan belonging to the Manassites.

Transition to the Second Address

44 This is the law that Moses set before the Israelites. 45These are the decrees and the statutes and ordinances that Moses spoke to the Israelites when they had come out of Egypt, 46beyond the Jordan in the valley opposite Beth-peor, in the land of King Sihon of the Amorites, who reigned at Heshbon, whom Moses and the Israelites defeated when they came out of Egypt. 47They occupied his land and the land of King Og of Bashan, the two kings of the Amorites on the eastern side of the Jordan: 48from Aroer, which is on the edge of the Wadi Arnon, as far as Mount Sirion*a* (that is, Hermon), 49together with all the Arabah on the east side of the Jordan as far as the Sea of the Arabah, under the slopes of Pisgah.

a Syr: Heb *Sion*

The Ten Commandments

5 Moses convened all Israel, and said to them:

Hear, O Israel, the statutes and ordinances that I am addressing to you today; you shall learn them and observe them diligently. [2]The LORD our God made a covenant with us at Horeb. [3]Not with our ancestors did the LORD make this covenant, but with us, who are all of us here alive today. [4]The LORD spoke with you face to face at the mountain, out of the fire. [5](At that time I was standing between the LORD and you to declare to you the words[a] of the LORD; for you were afraid because of the fire and did not go up the mountain.) And he said:

6 I am the LORD your God, who brought you out of the land of Egypt, out of the house of slavery; [7]you shall have no other gods before[b] me.

8 You shall not make for yourself an idol, whether in the form of anything that is in heaven above, or that is on the earth beneath, or that is in the water under the earth. [9]You shall not bow down to them or worship them; for I the LORD your God am a jealous God, punishing children for the iniquity of parents, to the third and fourth generation of those who reject me, [10]but showing steadfast love to the thousandth generation[c] of those who love me and keep my commandments.

11 You shall not make wrongful use of the name of the LORD your God, for the LORD will not acquit anyone who misuses his name.

12 Observe the sabbath day and keep it holy, as the LORD your God commanded you. [13]Six days you shall labor and do all your work. [14]But the seventh day is a sabbath to the LORD your God; you shall not do any work—you, or your son or your daughter, or your male or female slave, or your ox or your donkey, or any of your livestock, or the resident alien in your towns, so that your male and female slave may rest as well as you. [15]Remember that you were a slave in the land of Egypt, and the LORD your God brought you out from there with a mighty hand and an outstretched arm; therefore the LORD your God commanded you to keep the sabbath day.

16 Honor your father and your mother, as the LORD your God commanded you, so that your days may be long and that it may go well with you in the land that the LORD your God is giving you.

17 You shall not murder.[d]

18 Neither shall you commit adultery.

19 Neither shall you steal.

20 Neither shall you bear false witness against your neighbor.

21 Neither shall you covet your neighbor's wife.

Neither shall you desire your neighbor's house, or field, or male or female slave, or ox, or donkey, or anything that belongs to your neighbor.

Moses the Mediator of God's Will

22 These words the LORD spoke with a loud voice to your whole assembly at the mountain, out of the fire, the cloud, and the thick darkness, and he added no more. He wrote them on two stone tablets, and gave them to me. [23]When you heard the voice out of the darkness, while the mountain was burning with fire, you approached me, all the heads of your tribes and your elders; [24]and you said, "Look, the LORD our God has shown us his glory and greatness, and we have heard his voice out of the fire. Today we have seen that God may speak to someone and the person may still live. [25]So now why should we die? For this great fire will consume us; if we hear the voice of the LORD our God any longer, we shall die. [26]For who is there of all flesh that has heard the voice of the living God speaking out of fire, as we have, and remained alive? [27]Go near, you yourself, and hear all that the LORD our God will say. Then tell us everything that the LORD our God tells you, and we will listen and do it."

28 The LORD heard your words when you spoke to me, and the LORD said to me: "I

---

a Q Mss Sam Gk Syr Vg Tg: MT *word*   b Or *besides*   c Or *to thousands*   d Or *kill* have heard the words of this people, which they have spoken to you; they are right in all that they have spoken. ²⁹If only they had such a mind as this, to fear me and to keep all my commandments always, so that it might go well with them and with their children forever! ³⁰Go say to them, 'Return to your tents.' ³¹But you, stand here by me, and I will tell you all the commandments, the statutes and the ordinances, that you shall teach them, so that they may do them in the land that I am giving them to possess." ³²You must therefore be careful to do as the LORD your God has commanded you; you shall not turn to the right or to the left. ³³You must follow exactly the path that the LORD your God has commanded you, so that you may live, and that it may go well with you, and that you may live long in the land that you are to possess.

The Great Commandment

6 Now this is the commandment—the statutes and the ordinances—that the LORD your God charged me to teach you to observe in the land that you are about to cross into and occupy, ²so that you and your children and your children's children may fear the LORD your God all the days of your life, and keep all his decrees and his commandments that I am commanding you, so that your days may be long. ³Hear therefore, O Israel, and observe them diligently, so that it may go well with you, and so that you may multiply greatly in a land flowing with milk and honey, as the LORD, the God of your ancestors, has promised you.

4 Hear, O Israel: The LORD is our God, the LORD alone.^a ⁵You shall love the LORD your God with all your heart, and with all your soul, and with all your might. ⁶Keep these words that I am commanding you today in your heart. ⁷Recite them to your children and talk about them when you are at home and when you are away, when you lie down and when you rise. ⁸Bind them as a sign on your hand, fix them as an emblem^b on your forehead, ⁹and write

them on the doorposts of your house and on your gates.

Caution against Disobedience

10 When the LORD your God has brought you into the land that he swore to your ancestors, to Abraham, to Isaac, and to Jacob, to give you—a land with fine, large cities that you did not build, ¹¹houses filled with all sorts of goods that you did not fill, hewn cisterns that you did not hew, vineyards and olive groves that you did not plant—and when you have eaten your fill, ¹²take care that you do not forget the LORD, who brought you out of the land of Egypt, out of the house of slavery. ¹³The LORD your God you shall fear; him you shall serve, and by his name alone you shall swear. ¹⁴Do not follow other gods, any of the gods of the peoples who are all around you, ¹⁵because the LORD your God, who is present with you, is a jealous God. The anger of the LORD your God would be kindled against you and he would destroy you from the face of the earth.

16 Do not put the LORD your God to the test, as you tested him at Massah. ¹⁷You must diligently keep the commandments of the LORD your God, and his decrees, and his statutes that he has commanded you. ¹⁸Do what is right and good in the sight of the LORD, so that it may go well with you, and so that you may go in and occupy the good land that the LORD swore to your ancestors to give you, ¹⁹thrusting out all your enemies from before you, as the LORD has promised.

20 When your children ask you in time to come, "What is the meaning of the decrees and the statutes and the ordinances that the LORD our God has commanded you?" ²¹then you shall say to your children, "We were Pharaoh's slaves in Egypt, but the LORD brought us out of Egypt with a mighty hand. ²²The LORD displayed before our eyes great and awesome signs and wonders against Egypt, against Pharaoh and all his household. ²³He brought us out from there in order to bring us in, to give us the land that he promised on oath to our an-

---

a Or *The LORD our God is one LORD,* or *The LORD our God, the LORD is one,* or *The LORD is our God, the LORD is one*
b Or *as a frontlet*

cestors. ²⁴Then the LORD commanded us to observe all these statutes, to fear the LORD our God, for our lasting good, so as to keep us alive, as is now the case. ²⁵If we diligently observe this entire commandment before the LORD our God, as he has commanded us, we will be in the right."

A Chosen People

7 When the LORD your God brings you into the land that you are about to enter and occupy, and he clears away many nations before you—the Hittites, the Girgashites, the Amorites, the Canaanites, the Perizzites, the Hivites, and the Jebusites, seven nations mightier and more numerous than you— ²and when the LORD your God gives them over to you and you defeat them, then you must utterly destroy them. Make no covenant with them and show them no mercy. ³Do not intermarry with them, giving your daughters to their sons or taking their daughters for your sons, ⁴for that would turn away your children from following me, to serve other gods. Then the anger of the LORD would be kindled against you, and he would destroy you quickly. ⁵But this is how you must deal with them: break down their altars, smash their pillars, hew down their sacred poles,ᵃ and burn their idols with fire. ⁶For you are a people holy to the LORD your God; the LORD your God has chosen you out of all the peoples on earth to be his people, his treasured possession.

7 It was not because you were more numerous than any other people that the LORD set his heart on you and chose you—for you were the fewest of all peoples. ⁸It was because the LORD loved you and kept the oath that he swore to your ancestors, that the LORD has brought you out with a mighty hand, and redeemed you from the house of slavery, from the hand of Pharaoh king of Egypt. ⁹Know therefore that the LORD your God is God, the faithful God who maintains covenant loyalty with those who love him and keep his commandments, to a thousand generations, ¹⁰and

who repays in their own person those who reject him. He does not delay but repays in their own person those who reject him. ¹¹Therefore, observe diligently the commandment—the statutes and the ordinances—that I am commanding you today.

Blessings for Obedience

12 If you heed these ordinances, by diligently observing them, the LORD your God will maintain with you the covenant loyalty that he swore to your ancestors; ¹³he will love you, bless you, and multiply you; he will bless the fruit of your womb and the fruit of your ground, your grain and your wine and your oil, the increase of your cattle and the issue of your flock, in the land that he swore to your ancestors to give you. ¹⁴You shall be the most blessed of peoples, with neither sterility nor barrenness among you or your livestock. ¹⁵The LORD will turn away from you every illness; all the dread diseases of Egypt that you experienced, he will not inflict on you, but he will lay them on all who hate you. ¹⁶You shall devour all the peoples that the LORD your God is giving over to you, showing them no pity; you shall not serve their gods, for that would be a snare to you.

17 If you say to yourself, "These nations are more numerous than I; how can I dispossess them?" ¹⁸do not be afraid of them. Just remember what the LORD your God did to Pharaoh and to all Egypt, ¹⁹the great trials that your eyes saw, the signs and wonders, the mighty hand and the outstretched arm by which the LORD your God brought you out. The LORD your God will do the same to all the peoples of whom you are afraid. ²⁰Moreover, the LORD your God will send the pestilenceᵇ against them, until even the survivors and the fugitives are destroyed. ²¹Have no dread of them, for the LORD your God, who is present with you, is a great and awesome God. ²²The LORD your God will clear away these nations before you little by little; you will not be able to make a quick end of them, otherwise the wild animals

---

ᵃ Heb *Asherim*   ᵇ Or *hornets*. Meaning of Heb uncertain

would become too numerous for you. ²³But the LORD your God will give them over to you, and throw them into great panic, until they are destroyed. ²⁴He will hand their kings over to you and you shall blot out their name from under heaven; no one will be able to stand against you, until you have destroyed them. ²⁵The images of their gods you shall burn with fire. Do not covet the silver or the gold that is on them and take it for yourself, because you could be ensnared by it; for it is abhorrent to the LORD your God. ²⁶Do not bring an abhorrent thing into your house, or you will be set apart for destruction like it. You must utterly detest and abhor it, for it is set apart for destruction.

A Warning Not to Forget God in Prosperity

8 This entire commandment that I command you today you must diligently observe, so that you may live and increase, and go in and occupy the land that the LORD promised on oath to your ancestors. ²Remember the long way that the LORD your God has led you these forty years in the wilderness, in order to humble you, testing you to know what was in your heart, whether or not you would keep his commandments. ³He humbled you by letting you hunger, then by feeding you with manna, with which neither you nor your ancestors were acquainted, in order to make you understand that one does not live by bread alone, but by every word that comes from the mouth of the LORD. ᵃ ⁴The clothes on your back did not wear out and your feet did not swell these forty years. ⁵Know then in your heart that as a parent disciplines a child so the LORD your God disciplines you. ⁶Therefore keep the commandments of the LORD your God, by walking in his ways and by fearing him. ⁷For the LORD your God is bringing you into a good land, a land with flowing streams, with springs and underground waters welling up in valleys and hills, ⁸a land of wheat and barley, of vines and fig trees and pomegranates, a land of olive trees and honey, ⁹a land where you may eat bread without scarcity, where you will lack

nothing, a land whose stones are iron and from whose hills you may mine copper. ¹⁰You shall eat your fill and bless the LORD your God for the good land that he has given you.

11 Take care that you do not forget the LORD your God, by failing to keep his commandments, his ordinances, and his statutes, which I am commanding you today. ¹²When you have eaten your fill and have built fine houses and live in them, ¹³and when your herds and flocks have multiplied, and your silver and gold is multiplied, and all that you have is multiplied, ¹⁴then do not exalt yourself, forgetting the LORD your God, who brought you out of the land of Egypt, out of the house of slavery, ¹⁵who led you through the great and terrible wilderness, an arid wasteland with poisonous ᵇ snakes and scorpions. He made water flow for you from flint rock, ¹⁶and fed you in the wilderness with manna that your ancestors did not know, to humble you and to test you, and in the end to do you good. ¹⁷Do not say to yourself, "My power and the might of my own hand have gotten me this wealth." ¹⁸But remember the LORD your God, for it is he who gives you power to get wealth, so that he may confirm his covenant that he swore to your ancestors, as he is doing today. ¹⁹If you do forget the LORD your God and follow other gods to serve and worship them, I solemnly warn you today that you shall surely perish. ²⁰Like the nations that the LORD is destroying before you, so shall you perish, because you would not obey the voice of the LORD your God.

The Consequences of Rebelling against God

9 Hear, O Israel! You are about to cross the Jordan today, to go in and dispossess nations larger and mightier than you, great cities, fortified to the heavens, ²a strong and tall people, the offspring of the Anakim, whom you know. You have heard it said of them, "Who can stand up to the Anakim?" ³Know then today that the LORD your God is the one who crosses over before you as a devouring fire; he will defeat them and subdue them be-

---

a Or *by anything that the LORD decrees*   *b* Or *fiery*; Heb *seraph* fore you, so that you may dispossess and destroy them quickly, as the LORD has promised you.

4 When the LORD your God thrusts them out before you, do not say to yourself, "It is because of my righteousness that the LORD has brought me in to occupy this land"; it is rather because of the wickedness of these nations that the LORD is dispossessing them before you. ⁵It is not because of your righteousness or the uprightness of your heart that you are going in to occupy their land; but because of the wickedness of these nations the LORD your God is dispossessing them before you, in order to fulfill the promise that the LORD made on oath to your ancestors, to Abraham, to Isaac, and to Jacob.

6 Know, then, that the LORD your God is not giving you this good land to occupy because of your righteousness; for you are a stubborn people. ⁷Remember and do not forget how you provoked the LORD your God to wrath in the wilderness; you have been rebellious against the LORD from the day you came out of the land of Egypt until you came to this place.

8 Even at Horeb you provoked the LORD to wrath, and the LORD was so angry with you that he was ready to destroy you. ⁹When I went up the mountain to receive the stone tablets, the tablets of the covenant that the LORD made with you, I remained on the mountain forty days and forty nights; I neither ate bread nor drank water. ¹⁰And the LORD gave me the two stone tablets written with the finger of God; on them were all the words that the LORD had spoken to you at the mountain out of the fire on the day of the assembly. ¹¹At the end of forty days and forty nights the LORD gave me the two stone tablets, the tablets of the covenant. ¹²Then the LORD said to me, "Get up, go down quickly from here, for your people whom you have brought from Egypt have acted corruptly. They have been quick to turn from the way that I commanded them; they have cast an image for themselves." ¹³Furthermore the LORD said to me, "I have seen that this people is indeed a stubborn people. ¹⁴Let me alone that I may destroy them and blot out their name from under heaven; and I will make of you a nation mightier and more numerous than they."

15 So I turned and went down from the mountain, while the mountain was ablaze; the two tablets of the covenant were in my two hands. ¹⁶Then I saw that you had indeed sinned against the LORD your God, by casting for yourselves an image of a calf; you had been quick to turn from the way that the LORD had commanded you. ¹⁷So I took hold of the two tablets and flung them from my two hands, smashing them before your eyes. ¹⁸Then I lay prostrate before the LORD as before, forty days and forty nights; I neither ate bread nor drank water, because of all the sin you had committed, provoking the LORD by doing what was evil in his sight. ¹⁹For I was afraid that the anger that the LORD bore against you was so fierce that he would destroy you. But the LORD listened to me that time also. ²⁰The LORD was so angry with Aaron that he was ready to destroy him, but I interceded also on behalf of Aaron at that same time. ²¹Then I took the sinful thing you had made, the calf, and burned it with fire and crushed it, grinding it thoroughly, until it was reduced to dust; and I threw the dust of it into the stream that runs down the mountain.

22 At Taberah also, and at Massah, and at Kibroth-hattaavah, you provoked the LORD to wrath. ²³And when the LORD sent you from Kadesh-barnea, saying, "Go up and occupy the land that I have given you," you rebelled against the command of the LORD your God, neither trusting him nor obeying him. ²⁴You have been rebellious against the LORD as long as he has*a* known you.

25 Throughout the forty days and forty nights that I lay prostrate before the LORD when the LORD intended to destroy you, ²⁶I prayed to the LORD and said, "Lord GOD, do not destroy the people who are your very own

a Sam Gk: MT I have

possession, whom you redeemed in your greatness, whom you brought out of Egypt with a mighty hand. 27Remember your servants, Abraham, Isaac, and Jacob; pay no attention to the stubbornness of this people, their wickedness and their sin, 28otherwise the land from which you have brought us might say, 'Because the LORD was not able to bring them into the land that he promised them, and because he hated them, he has brought them out to let them die in the wilderness.' 29For they are the people of your very own possession, whom you brought out by your great power and by your outstretched arm."

The Second Pair of Tablets

10 At that time the LORD said to me, "Carve out two tablets of stone like the former ones, and come up to me on the mountain, and make an ark of wood. 2I will write on the tablets the words that were on the former tablets, which you smashed, and you shall put them in the ark." 3So I made an ark of acacia wood, cut two tablets of stone like the former ones, and went up the mountain with the two tablets in my hand. 4Then he wrote on the tablets the same words as before, the ten commandments*a* that the LORD had spoken to you on the mountain out of the fire on the day of the assembly; and the LORD gave them to me. 5So I turned and came down from the mountain, and put the tablets in the ark that I had made; and there they are, as the LORD commanded me.

6 (The Israelites journeyed from Beeroth-bene-jaakan*b* to Moserah. There Aaron died, and there he was buried; his son Eleazar succeeded him as priest. 7From there they journeyed to Gudgodah, and from Gudgodah to Jotbathah, a land with flowing streams. 8At that time the LORD set apart the tribe of Levi to carry the ark of the covenant of the LORD, to stand before the LORD to minister to him, and to bless in his name, to this day. 9Therefore Levi has no allotment or inheritance with

his kindred; the LORD is his inheritance, as the LORD your God promised him.)

10 I stayed on the mountain forty days and forty nights, as I had done the first time. And once again the LORD listened to me. The LORD was unwilling to destroy you. 11The LORD said to me, "Get up, go on your journey at the head of the people, that they may go in and occupy the land that I swore to their ancestors to give them."

The Essence of the Law

12 So now, O Israel, what does the LORD your God require of you? Only to fear the LORD your God, to walk in all his ways, to love him, to serve the LORD your God with all your heart and with all your soul, 13and to keep the commandments of the LORD your God*c* and his decrees that I am commanding you today, for your own well-being. 14Although heaven and the heaven of heavens belong to the LORD your God, the earth with all that is in it, 15yet the LORD set his heart in love on your ancestors alone and chose you, their descendants after them, out of all the peoples, as it is today. 16Circumcise, then, the foreskin of your heart, and do not be stubborn any longer. 17For the LORD your God is God of gods and Lord of lords, the great God, mighty and awesome, who is not partial and takes no bribe, 18who executes justice for the orphan and the widow, and who loves the strangers, providing them food and clothing. 19You shall also love the stranger, for you were strangers in the land of Egypt. 20You shall fear the LORD your God; him alone you shall worship; to him you shall hold fast, and by his name you shall swear. 21He is your praise; he is your God, who has done for you these great and awesome things that your own eyes have seen. 22Your ancestors went down to Egypt seventy persons; and now the LORD your God has made you as numerous as the stars in heaven.

---

a Heb *the ten words*   *b* Or *the wells of the Bene-jaakan*   *c* Q Ms Gk Syr: MT lacks *your God*

Rewards for Obedience

11 You shall love the LORD your God, therefore, and keep his charge, his decrees, his ordinances, and his commandments always. 2Remember today that it was not your children (who have not known or seen the discipline of the LORD your God), but it is you who must acknowledge his greatness, his mighty hand and his outstretched arm, 3his signs and his deeds that he did in Egypt to Pharaoh, the king of Egypt, and to all his land; 4what he did to the Egyptian army, to their horses and chariots, how he made the water of the Red Sea*a* flow over them as they pursued you, so that the LORD has destroyed them to this day; 5what he did to you in the wilderness, until you came to this place; 6and what he did to Dathan and Abiram, sons of Eliab son of Reuben, how in the midst of all Israel the earth opened its mouth and swallowed them up, along with their households, their tents, and every living being in their company; 7for it is your own eyes that have seen every great deed that the LORD did.

8 Keep, then, this entire commandment that I am commanding you today, so that you may have strength to go in and occupy the land that you are crossing over to occupy, 9and so that you may live long in the land that the LORD swore to your ancestors to give them and to their descendants, a land flowing with milk and honey. 10For the land that you are about to enter to occupy is not like the land of Egypt, from which you have come, where you sow your seed and irrigate by foot like a vegetable garden. 11But the land that you are crossing over to occupy is a land of hills and valleys, watered by rain from the sky, 12a land that the LORD your God looks after. The eyes of the LORD your God are always on it, from the beginning of the year to the end of the year.

13 If you will only heed his every commandment*b* that I am commanding you today—loving the LORD your God, and serving him with all your heart and with all your soul—

14then he*c* will give the rain for your land in its season, the early rain and the later rain, and you will gather in your grain, your wine, and your oil; 15and he*c* will give grass in your fields for your livestock, and you will eat your fill. 16Take care, or you will be seduced into turning away, serving other gods and worshiping them, 17for then the anger of the LORD will be kindled against you and he will shut up the heavens, so that there will be no rain and the land will yield no fruit; then you will perish quickly off the good land that the LORD is giving you.

18 You shall put these words of mine in your heart and soul, and you shall bind them as a sign on your hand, and fix them as an emblem*d* on your forehead. 19Teach them to your children, talking about them when you are at home and when you are away, when you lie down and when you rise. 20Write them on the doorposts of your house and on your gates, 21so that your days and the days of your children may be multiplied in the land that the LORD swore to your ancestors to give them, as long as the heavens are above the earth.

22 If you will diligently observe this entire commandment that I am commanding you, loving the LORD your God, walking in all his ways, and holding fast to him, 23then the LORD will drive out all these nations before you, and you will dispossess nations larger and mightier than yourselves. 24Every place on which you set foot shall be yours; your territory shall extend from the wilderness to the Lebanon and from the River, the river Euphrates, to the Western Sea. 25No one will be able to stand against you; the LORD your God will put the fear and dread of you on all the land on which you set foot, as he promised you.

26 See, I am setting before you today a blessing and a curse: 27the blessing, if you obey the commandments of the LORD your God that I am commanding you today; 28and the curse, if you do not obey the commandments of the LORD your God, but turn from the way that I am commanding you today, to follow other gods that you have not known.

a Or *Sea of Reeds*   *b* Compare Gk: Heb *my commandments*   *c* Sam Gk Vg: MT *I*   *d* Or *as a frontlet*

29 When the LORD your God has brought you into the land that you are entering to occupy, you shall set the blessing on Mount Gerizim and the curse on Mount Ebal. 30As you know, they are beyond the Jordan, some distance to the west, in the land of the Canaanites who live in the Arabah, opposite Gilgal, beside the oak*a* of Moreh.

31 When you cross the Jordan to go in to occupy the land that the LORD your God is giving you, and when you occupy it and live in it, 32you must diligently observe all the statutes and ordinances that I am setting before you today.

Pagan Shrines to Be Destroyed

12 These are the statutes and ordinances that you must diligently observe in the land that the LORD, the God of your ancestors, has given you to occupy all the days that you live on the earth.

2 You must demolish completely all the places where the nations whom you are about to dispossess served their gods, on the mountain heights, on the hills, and under every leafy tree. 3Break down their altars, smash their pillars, burn their sacred poles*b* with fire, and hew down the idols of their gods, and thus blot out their name from their places. 4You shall not worship the LORD your God in such ways. 5But you shall seek the place that the LORD your God will choose out of all your tribes as his habitation to put his name there. You shall go there, 6bringing there your burnt offerings and your sacrifices, your tithes and your donations, your votive gifts, your freewill offerings, and the firstlings of your herds and flocks. 7And you shall eat there in the presence of the LORD your God, you and your households together, rejoicing in all the undertakings in which the LORD your God has blessed you.

8 You shall not act as we are acting here today, all of us according to our own desires, 9for you have not yet come into the rest and the possession that the LORD your God is giving you. 10When you cross over the Jordan and live in the land that the LORD your God is allotting to you, and when he gives you rest from your enemies all around so that you live in safety, 11then you shall bring everything that I command you to the place that the LORD your God will choose as a dwelling for his name: your burnt offerings and your sacrifices, your tithes and your donations, and all your choice votive gifts that you vow to the LORD. 12And you shall rejoice before the LORD your God, you together with your sons and your daughters, your male and female slaves, and the Levites who reside in your towns (since they have no allotment or inheritance with you).

A Prescribed Place of Worship

13 Take care that you do not offer your burnt offerings at any place you happen to see. 14But only at the place that the LORD will choose in one of your tribes—there you shall offer your burnt offerings and there you shall do everything I command you.

15 Yet whenever you desire you may slaughter and eat meat within any of your towns, according to the blessing that the LORD your God has given you; the unclean and the clean may eat of it, as they would of gazelle or deer. 16The blood, however, you must not eat; you shall pour it out on the ground like water. 17Nor may you eat within your towns the tithe of your grain, your wine, and your oil, the firstlings of your herds and your flocks, any of your votive gifts that you vow, your freewill offerings, or your donations; 18these you shall eat in the presence of the LORD your God at the place that the LORD your God will choose, you together with your son and your daughter, your male and female slaves, and the Levites resident in your towns, rejoicing in the presence of the LORD your God in all your undertakings. 19Take care that you do not neglect the Levite as long as you live in your land.

20 When the LORD your God enlarges your territory, as he has promised you, and you say, "I am going to eat some meat," because you wish to eat meat, you may eat meat whenever

a Gk Syr: Compare Gen 12.6; Heb *oaks* or *terebinths*   *b* Heb *Asherim* you have the desire. ²¹If the place where the LORD your God will choose to put his name is too far from you, and you slaughter as I have commanded you any of your herd or flock that the LORD has given you, then you may eat within your towns whenever you desire. ²²Indeed, just as gazelle or deer is eaten, so you may eat it; the unclean and the clean alike may eat it. ²³Only be sure that you do not eat the blood; for the blood is the life, and you shall not eat the life with the meat. ²⁴Do not eat it; you shall pour it out on the ground like water. ²⁵Do not eat it, so that all may go well with you and your children after you, because you do what is right in the sight of the LORD. ²⁶But the sacred donations that are due from you, and your votive gifts, you shall bring to the place that the LORD will choose. ²⁷You shall present your burnt offerings, both the meat and the blood, on the altar of the LORD your God; the blood of your other sacrifices shall be poured out beside[a] the altar of the LORD your God, but the meat you may eat.

28 Be careful to obey all these words that I command you today,[b] so that it may go well with you and with your children after you forever, because you will be doing what is good and right in the sight of the LORD your God.

Warning against Idolatry

29 When the LORD your God has cut off before you the nations whom you are about to enter to dispossess them, when you have dispossessed them and live in their land, ³⁰take care that you are not snared into imitating them, after they have been destroyed before you: do not inquire concerning their gods, saying, "How did these nations worship their gods? I also want to do the same." ³¹You must not do the same for the LORD your God, because every abhorrent thing that the LORD hates they have done for their gods. They would even burn their sons and their daughters in the fire to their gods. ³²[c] You must diligently observe everything that I command you; do not add to it or take anything from it.

13

^dIf prophets or those who divine by dreams appear among you and promise you omens or portents, ²and the omens or the portents declared by them take place, and they say, "Let us follow other gods" (whom you have not known) "and let us serve them," ³you must not heed the words of those prophets or those who divine by dreams; for the LORD your God is testing you, to know whether you indeed love the LORD your God with all your heart and soul. ⁴The LORD your God you shall follow, him alone you shall fear, his commandments you shall keep, his voice you shall obey, him you shall serve, and to him you shall hold fast. ⁵But those prophets or those who divine by dreams shall be put to death for having spoken treason against the LORD your God—who brought you out of the land of Egypt and redeemed you from the house of slavery—to turn you from the way in which the LORD your God commanded you to walk. So you shall purge the evil from your midst.

6 If anyone secretly entices you—even if it is your brother, your father's son or[e] your mother's son, or your own son or daughter, or the wife you embrace, or your most intimate friend—saying, "Let us go worship other gods," whom neither you nor your ancestors have known, ⁷any of the gods of the peoples that are around you, whether near you or far away from you, from one end of the earth to the other, ⁸you must not yield to or heed any such persons. Show them no pity or compassion and do not shield them. ⁹But you shall surely kill them; your own hand shall be first against them to execute them, and afterwards the hand of all the people. ¹⁰Stone them to death for trying to turn you away from the LORD your God, who brought you out of the land of Egypt, out of the house of slavery. ¹¹Then all Israel shall hear and be afraid, and never again do any such wickedness.

12 If you hear it said about one of the towns that the LORD your God is giving you to live in, ¹³that scoundrels from among you

---

a Or *on*   *b* Gk Sam Syr: MT lacks *today*   *c* Ch 13.1 in Heb   *d* Ch 13.2 in Heb   *e* Sam Gk Compare Tg: MT lacks *your father's son or* have gone out and led the inhabitants of the town astray, saying, "Let us go and worship other gods," whom you have not known, 14then you shall inquire and make a thorough investigation. If the charge is established that such an abhorrent thing has been done among you, 15you shall put the inhabitants of that town to the sword, utterly destroying it and everything in it—even putting its livestock to the sword. 16All of its spoil you shall gather into its public square; then burn the town and all its spoil with fire, as a whole burnt offering to the LORD your God. It shall remain a perpetual ruin, never to be rebuilt. 17Do not let anything devoted to destruction stick to your hand, so that the LORD may turn from his fierce anger and show you compassion, and in his compassion multiply you, as he swore to your ancestors, 18if you obey the voice of the LORD your God by keeping all his commandments that I am commanding you today, doing what is right in the sight of the LORD your God.

Pagan Practices Forbidden

14 You are children of the LORD your God. You must not lacerate yourselves or shave your forelocks for the dead. 2For you are a people holy to the LORD your God; it is you the LORD has chosen out of all the peoples on earth to be his people, his treasured possession.

Clean and Unclean Foods

3 You shall not eat any abhorrent thing. 4These are the animals you may eat: the ox, the sheep, the goat, 5the deer, the gazelle, the roebuck, the wild goat, the ibex, the antelope, and the mountain-sheep. 6Any animal that divides the hoof and has the hoof cleft in two, and chews the cud, among the animals, you may eat. 7Yet of those that chew the cud or have the hoof cleft you shall not eat these: the camel, the hare, and the rock badger, because they chew the cud but do not divide the hoof; they are unclean for you. 8And the pig, because it divides the hoof but does not chew the cud, is unclean for you. You shall not eat their meat, and you shall not touch their carcasses.

9 Of all that live in water you may eat these: whatever has fins and scales you may eat. 10And whatever does not have fins and scales you shall not eat; it is unclean for you.

11 You may eat any clean birds. 12But these are the ones that you shall not eat: the eagle, the vulture, the osprey, 13the buzzard, the kite of any kind; 14every raven of any kind; 15the ostrich, the nighthawk, the sea gull, the hawk of any kind; 16the little owl and the great owl, the water hen 17and the desert owl, *a* the carrion vulture and the cormorant, 18the stork, the heron of any kind; the hoopoe and the bat. *b* 19And all winged insects are unclean for you; they shall not be eaten. 20You may eat any clean winged creature.

21 You shall not eat anything that dies of itself; you may give it to aliens residing in your towns for them to eat, or you may sell it to a foreigner. For you are a people holy to the LORD your God.

You shall not boil a kid in its mother's milk.

Regulations concerning Tithes

22 Set apart a tithe of all the yield of your seed that is brought in yearly from the field. 23In the presence of the LORD your God, in the place that he will choose as a dwelling for his name, you shall eat the tithe of your grain, your wine, and your oil, as well as the firstlings of your herd and flock, so that you may learn to fear the LORD your God always. 24But if, when the LORD your God has blessed you, the distance is so great that you are unable to transport it, because the place where the LORD your God will choose to set his name is too far away from you, 25then you may turn it into money. With the money secure in hand, go to the place that the LORD your God will choose; 26spend the money for whatever you wish—oxen, sheep, wine, strong drink, or whatever you desire. And you shall eat there in the presence of the LORD your God, you and your

a Or *pelican*   *b* Identification of several of the birds in verses 12-18 is uncertain household rejoicing together. 27As for the Levites resident in your towns, do not neglect them, because they have no allotment or inheritance with you.

28 Every third year you shall bring out the full tithe of your produce for that year, and store it within your towns; 29the Levites, because they have no allotment or inheritance with you, as well as the resident aliens, the orphans, and the widows in your towns, may come and eat their fill so that the LORD your God may bless you in all the work that you undertake.

Laws concerning the Sabbatical Year

15 Every seventh year you shall grant a remission of debts. 2And this is the manner of the remission: every creditor shall remit the claim that is held against a neighbor, not exacting it of a neighbor who is a member of the community, because the LORD's remission has been proclaimed. 3Of a foreigner you may exact it, but you must remit your claim on whatever any member of your community owes you. 4There will, however, be no one in need among you, because the LORD is sure to bless you in the land that the LORD your God is giving you as a possession to occupy, 5if only you will obey the LORD your God by diligently observing this entire commandment that I command you today. 6When the LORD your God has blessed you, as he promised you, you will lend to many nations, but you will not borrow; you will rule over many nations, but they will not rule over you.

7 If there is among you anyone in need, a member of your community in any of your towns within the land that the LORD your God is giving you, do not be hard-hearted or tight-fisted toward your needy neighbor. 8You should rather open your hand, willingly lending enough to meet the need, whatever it may be. 9Be careful that you do not entertain a mean thought, thinking, "The seventh year, the year of remission, is near," and therefore view your needy neighbor with hostility and give

nothing; your neighbor might cry to the LORD against you, and you would incur guilt. 10Give liberally and be ungrudging when you do so, for on this account the LORD your God will bless you in all your work and in all that you undertake. 11Since there will never cease to be some in need on the earth, I therefore command you, "Open your hand to the poor and needy neighbor in your land."

12 If a member of your community, whether a Hebrew man or a Hebrew woman, is sold*a* to you and works for you six years, in the seventh year you shall set that person free. 13And when you send a male slave*b* out from you a free person, you shall not send him out empty-handed. 14Provide liberally out of your flock, your threshing floor, and your wine press, thus giving to him some of the bounty with which the LORD your God has blessed you. 15Remember that you were a slave in the land of Egypt, and the LORD your God redeemed you; for this reason I lay this command upon you today. 16But if he says to you, "I will not go out from you," because he loves you and your household, since he is well off with you, 17then you shall take an awl and thrust it through his earlobe into the door, and he shall be your slave*c* forever.

You shall do the same with regard to your female slave.*d*

18 Do not consider it a hardship when you send them out from you free persons, because for six years they have given you services worth the wages of hired laborers; and the LORD your God will bless you in all that you do.

The Firstborn of Livestock

19 Every firstling male born of your herd and flock you shall consecrate to the LORD your God; you shall not do work with your firstling ox nor shear the firstling of your flock. 20You shall eat it, you together with your household, in the presence of the LORD your God year by year at the place that the LORD will choose. 21But if it has any defect—any serious defect, such as lameness or blindness—

---

a Or *sells himself or herself*   *b* Heb *him*   *c* Or *bondman*   *d* Or *bondwoman* you shall not sacrifice it to the LORD your God; 22within your towns you may eat it, the unclean and the clean alike, as you would a gazelle or deer. 23Its blood, however, you must not eat; you shall pour it out on the ground like water.

The Passover Reviewed

16 Observe the month *a* of Abib by keeping the passover to the LORD your God, for in the month of Abib the LORD your God brought you out of Egypt by night. 2You shall offer the passover sacrifice to the LORD your God, from the flock and the herd, at the place that the LORD will choose as a dwelling for his name. 3You must not eat with it anything leavened. For seven days you shall eat unleavened bread with it—the bread of affliction—because you came out of the land of Egypt in great haste, so that all the days of your life you may remember the day of your departure from the land of Egypt. 4No leaven shall be seen with you in all your territory for seven days; and none of the meat of what you slaughter on the evening of the first day shall remain until morning. 5You are not permitted to offer the passover sacrifice within any of your towns that the LORD your God is giving you. 6But at the place that the LORD your God will choose as a dwelling for his name, only there shall you offer the passover sacrifice, in the evening at sunset, the time of day when you departed from Egypt. 7You shall cook it and eat it at the place that the LORD your God will choose; the next morning you may go back to your tents. 8For six days you shall continue to eat unleavened bread, and on the seventh day there shall be a solemn assembly for the LORD your God, when you shall do no work.

The Festival of Weeks Reviewed

9 You shall count seven weeks; begin to count the seven weeks from the time the sickle is first put to the standing grain. 10Then you shall keep the festival of weeks to the LORD your God, contributing a freewill offering in proportion to the blessing that you have received from the LORD your God. 11Rejoice before the LORD your God—you and your sons and your daughters, your male and female slaves, the Levites resident in your towns, as well as the strangers, the orphans, and the widows who are among you—at the place that the LORD your God will choose as a dwelling for his name. 12Remember that you were a slave in Egypt, and diligently observe these statutes.

The Festival of Booths Reviewed

13 You shall keep the festival of booths *b* for seven days, when you have gathered in the produce from your threshing floor and your wine press. 14Rejoice during your festival, you and your sons and your daughters, your male and female slaves, as well as the Levites, the strangers, the orphans, and the widows resident in your towns. 15Seven days you shall keep the festival to the LORD your God at the place that the LORD will choose; for the LORD your God will bless you in all your produce and in all your undertakings, and you shall surely celebrate.

16 Three times a year all your males shall appear before the LORD your God at the place that he will choose: at the festival of unleavened bread, at the festival of weeks, and at the festival of booths. *b* They shall not appear before the LORD empty-handed; 17all shall give as they are able, according to the blessing of the LORD your God that he has given you.

Municipal Judges and Officers

18 You shall appoint judges and officials throughout your tribes, in all your towns that the LORD your God is giving you, and they shall render just decisions for the people. 19You must not distort justice; you must not show partiality; and you must not accept bribes, for a bribe blinds the eyes of the wise and subverts the cause of those who are in the right. 20Justice, and only justice, you shall pursue, so that

a Or *new moon*   *b* Or *tabernacles*; Heb *succoth*

you may live and occupy the land that the LORD your God is giving you.

Forbidden Forms of Worship

21 You shall not plant any tree as a sacred pole[a] beside the altar that you make for the LORD your God; 22nor shall you set up a stone pillar—things that the LORD your God hates. 17 You must not sacrifice to the LORD your God an ox or a sheep that has a defect, anything seriously wrong; for that is abhorrent to the LORD your God.

2 If there is found among you, in one of your towns that the LORD your God is giving you, a man or woman who does what is evil in the sight of the LORD your God, and transgresses his covenant 3by going to serve other gods and worshiping them—whether the sun or the moon or any of the host of heaven, which I have forbidden— 4and if it is reported to you or you hear of it, and you make a thorough inquiry, and the charge is proved true that such an abhorrent thing has occurred in Israel, 5then you shall bring out to your gates that man or that woman who has committed this crime and you shall stone the man or woman to death. 6On the evidence of two or three witnesses the death sentence shall be executed; a person must not be put to death on the evidence of only one witness. 7The hands of the witnesses shall be the first raised against the person to execute the death penalty, and afterward the hands of all the people. So you shall purge the evil from your midst.

Legal Decisions by Priests and Judges

8 If a judicial decision is too difficult for you to make between one kind of bloodshed and another, one kind of legal right and another, or one kind of assault and another—any such matters of dispute in your towns—then you shall immediately go up to the place that the LORD your God will choose, 9where you shall consult with the levitical priests and the judge who is in office in those days; they shall announce to you the decision in the case.

10Carry out exactly the decision that they announce to you from the place that the LORD will choose, diligently observing everything they instruct you. 11You must carry out fully the law that they interpret for you or the ruling that they announce to you; do not turn aside from the decision that they announce to you, either to the right or to the left. 12As for anyone who presumes to disobey the priest appointed to minister there to the LORD your God, or the judge, that person shall die. So you shall purge the evil from Israel. 13All the people will hear and be afraid, and will not act presumptuously again.

Limitations of Royal Authority

14 When you have come into the land that the LORD your God is giving you, and have taken possession of it and settled in it, and you say, "I will set a king over me, like all the nations that are around me," 15you may indeed set over you a king whom the LORD your God will choose. One of your own community you may set as king over you; you are not permitted to put a foreigner over you, who is not of your own community. 16Even so, he must not acquire many horses for himself, or return the people to Egypt in order to acquire more horses, since the LORD has said to you, "You must never return that way again." 17And he must not acquire many wives for himself, or else his heart will turn away; also silver and gold he must not acquire in great quantity for himself. 18When he has taken the throne of his kingdom, he shall have a copy of this law written for him in the presence of the levitical priests. 19It shall remain with him and he shall read in it all the days of his life, so that he may learn to fear the LORD his God, diligently observing all the words of this law and these statutes, 20neither exalting himself above other members of the community nor turning aside from the commandment, either to the right or to the left, so that he and his descendants may reign long over his kingdom in Israel.

a Heb *Asherah*

Privileges of Priests and Levites

18 The levitical priests, the whole tribe of Levi, shall have no allotment or inheritance within Israel. They may eat the sacrifices that are the LORD's portion*a* 2but they shall have no inheritance among the other members of the community; the LORD is their inheritance, as he promised them.

3 This shall be the priests' due from the people, from those offering a sacrifice, whether an ox or a sheep: they shall give to the priest the shoulder, the two jowls, and the stomach. 4The first fruits of your grain, your wine, and your oil, as well as the first of the fleece of your sheep, you shall give him. 5For the LORD your God has chosen Levi*b* out of all your tribes, to stand and minister in the name of the LORD, him and his sons for all time.

6 If a Levite leaves any of your towns, from wherever he has been residing in Israel, and comes to the place that the LORD will choose (and he may come whenever he wishes), 7then he may minister in the name of the LORD his God, like all his fellow-Levites who stand to minister there before the LORD. 8They shall have equal portions to eat, even though they have income from the sale of family possessions.*a*

Child-Sacrifice, Divination, and Magic Prohibited

9 When you come into the land that the LORD your God is giving you, you must not learn to imitate the abhorrent practices of those nations. 10No one shall be found among you who makes a son or daughter pass through fire, or who practices divination, or is a soothsayer, or an augur, or a sorcerer, 11or one who casts spells, or who consults ghosts or spirits, or who seeks oracles from the dead. 12For whoever does these things is abhorrent to the LORD; it is because of such abhorrent practices that the LORD your God is driving them out before you. 13You must remain completely loyal to the LORD your God. 14Although these nations that you are about to dispossess do give heed to soothsayers and diviners, as for you, the LORD your God does not permit you to do so.

A New Prophet Like Moses

15 The LORD your God will raise up for you a prophet*c* like me from among your own people; you shall heed such a prophet.*d* 16This is what you requested of the LORD your God at Horeb on the day of the assembly when you said: "If I hear the voice of the LORD my God any more, or ever again see this great fire, I will die." 17Then the LORD replied to me: "They are right in what they have said. 18I will raise up for them a prophet*c* like you from among their own people; I will put my words in the mouth of the prophet,*e* who shall speak to them everything that I command. 19Anyone who does not heed the words that the prophet*f* shall speak in my name, I myself will hold accountable. 20But any prophet who speaks in the name of other gods, or who presumes to speak in my name a word that I have not commanded the prophet to speak—that prophet shall die." 21You may say to yourself, "How can we recognize a word that the LORD has not spoken?" 22If a prophet speaks in the name of the LORD but the thing does not take place or prove true, it is a word that the LORD has not spoken. The prophet has spoken it presumptuously; do not be frightened by it.

Laws concerning the Cities of Refuge

19 When the LORD your God has cut off the nations whose land the LORD your God is giving you, and you have dispossessed them and settled in their towns and in their houses, 2you shall set apart three cities in the land that the LORD your God is giving you to possess. 3You shall calculate the distances*g* and divide into three regions the land that the LORD your God gives you as a possession, so that any homicide can flee to one of them.

4 Now this is the case of a homicide who might flee there and live, that is, someone who has killed another person unintentionally when

---

a Meaning of Heb uncertain   *b* Heb *him*   *c* Or *prophets*   *d* Or *such prophets*   *e* Or *mouths of the prophets*
f Heb *he*   *g* Or *prepare roads to them*

the two had not been at enmity before: 5Suppose someone goes into the forest with another to cut wood, and when one of them swings the ax to cut down a tree, the head slips from the handle and strikes the other person who then dies; the killer may flee to one of these cities and live. 6But if the distance is too great, the avenger of blood in hot anger might pursue and overtake and put the killer to death, although a death sentence was not deserved, since the two had not been at enmity before. 7Therefore I command you: You shall set apart three cities.

8 If the LORD your God enlarges your territory, as he swore to your ancestors—and he will give you all the land that he promised your ancestors to give you, 9provided you diligently observe this entire commandment that I command you today, by loving the LORD your God and walking always in his ways—then you shall add three more cities to these three, 10so that the blood of an innocent person may not be shed in the land that the LORD your God is giving you as an inheritance, thereby bringing bloodguilt upon you.

11 But if someone at enmity with another lies in wait and attacks and takes the life of that person, and flees into one of these cities, 12then the elders of the killer's city shall send to have the culprit taken from there and handed over to the avenger of blood to be put to death. 13Show no pity; you shall purge the guilt of innocent blood from Israel, so that it may go well with you.

Property Boundaries

14 You must not move your neighbor's boundary marker, set up by former generations, on the property that will be allotted to you in the land that the LORD your God is giving you to possess.

Law concerning Witnesses

15 A single witness shall not suffice to convict a person of any crime or wrongdoing in connection with any offense that may be committed. Only on the evidence of two or three witnesses shall a charge be sustained. 16If a malicious witness comes forward to accuse someone of wrongdoing, 17then both parties to the dispute shall appear before the LORD, before the priests and the judges who are in office in those days, 18and the judges shall make a thorough inquiry. If the witness is a false witness, having testified falsely against another, 19then you shall do to the false witness just as the false witness had meant to do to the other. So you shall purge the evil from your midst. 20The rest shall hear and be afraid, and a crime such as this shall never again be committed among you. 21Show no pity: life for life, eye for eye, tooth for tooth, hand for hand, foot for foot.

Rules of Warfare

20 When you go out to war against your enemies, and see horses and chariots, an army larger than your own, you shall not be afraid of them; for the LORD your God is with you, who brought you up from the land of Egypt. 2Before you engage in battle, the priest shall come forward and speak to the troops, 3and shall say to them: "Hear, O Israel! Today you are drawing near to do battle against your enemies. Do not lose heart, or be afraid, or panic, or be in dread of them; 4for it is the LORD your God who goes with you, to fight for you against your enemies, to give you victory." 5Then the officials shall address the troops, saying, "Has anyone built a new house but not dedicated it? He should go back to his house, or he might die in the battle and another dedicate it. 6Has anyone planted a vineyard but not yet enjoyed its fruit? He should go back to his house, or he might die in the battle and another be first to enjoy its fruit. 7Has anyone become engaged to a woman but not yet married her? He should go back to his house, or he might die in the battle and another marry her." 8The officials shall continue to address the troops, saying, "Is anyone afraid or disheartened? He should go back to his house, or he might cause the heart of his comrades to melt like his own." 9When the officials have finished addressing the troops, then the commanders shall take charge of them.

10 When you draw near to a town to fight against it, offer it terms of peace. 11If it accepts your terms of peace and surrenders to you, then all the people in it shall serve you at forced labor. 12If it does not submit to you peacefully, but makes war against you, then you shall besiege it; 13and when the LORD your God gives it into your hand, you shall put all its males to the sword. 14You may, however, take as your booty the women, the children, livestock, and everything else in the town, all its spoil. You may enjoy the spoil of your enemies, which the LORD your God has given you. 15Thus you shall treat all the towns that are very far from you, which are not towns of the nations here. 16But as for the towns of these peoples that the LORD your God is giving you as an inheritance, you must not let anything that breathes remain alive. 17You shall annihilate them—the Hittites and the Amorites, the Canaanites and the Perizzites, the Hivites and the Jebusites—just as the LORD your God has commanded, 18so that they may not teach you to do all the abhorrent things that they do for their gods, and you thus sin against the LORD your God.

19 If you besiege a town for a long time, making war against it in order to take it, you must not destroy its trees by wielding an ax against them. Although you may take food from them, you must not cut them down. Are trees in the field human beings that they should come under siege from you? 20You may destroy only the trees that you know do not produce food; you may cut them down for use in building siegeworks against the town that makes war with you, until it falls.

Law concerning Murder by Persons Unknown

21 If, in the land that the LORD your God is giving you to possess, a body is found lying in open country, and it is not known who struck the person down, 2then your elders and your judges shall come out to measure the distances to the towns that are near the body. 3The elders of the town nearest the body shall take a heifer that has never been worked, one that has not pulled in the yoke; 4the elders of that town shall bring the heifer down to a wadi with running water, which is neither plowed nor sown, and shall break the heifer's neck there in the wadi. 5Then the priests, the sons of Levi, shall come forward, for the LORD your God has chosen them to minister to him and to pronounce blessings in the name of the LORD, and by their decision all cases of dispute and assault shall be settled. 6All the elders of that town nearest the body shall wash their hands over the heifer whose neck was broken in the wadi, 7and they shall declare: "Our hands did not shed this blood, nor were we witnesses to it. 8Absolve, O LORD, your people Israel, whom you redeemed; do not let the guilt of innocent blood remain in the midst of your people Israel." Then they will be absolved of bloodguilt. 9So you shall purge the guilt of innocent blood from your midst, because you must do what is right in the sight of the LORD.

Female Captives

10 When you go out to war against your enemies, and the LORD your God hands them over to you and you take them captive, 11suppose you see among the captives a beautiful woman whom you desire and want to marry, 12and so you bring her home to your house: she shall shave her head, pare her nails, 13discard her captive's garb, and shall remain in your house a full month, mourning for her father and mother; after that you may go in to her and be her husband, and she shall be your wife. 14But if you are not satisfied with her, you shall let her go free and not sell her for money. You must not treat her as a slave, since you have dishonored her.

The Right of the Firstborn

15 If a man has two wives, one of them loved and the other disliked, and if both the loved and the disliked have borne him sons, the firstborn being the son of the one who is disliked, 16then on the day when he wills his possessions to his sons, he is not permitted to treat the son of the loved as the firstborn in preference to the son of the disliked, who is the

firstborn. [17]He must acknowledge as firstborn the son of the one who is disliked, giving him a double portion[a] of all that he has; since he is the first issue of his virility, the right of the firstborn is his.

Rebellious Children

18 If someone has a stubborn and rebellious son who will not obey his father and mother, who does not heed them when they discipline him, [19]then his father and his mother shall take hold of him and bring him out to the elders of his town at the gate of that place. [20]They shall say to the elders of his town, "This son of ours is stubborn and rebellious. He will not obey us. He is a glutton and a drunkard." [21]Then all the men of the town shall stone him to death. So you shall purge the evil from your midst; and all Israel will hear, and be afraid.

Miscellaneous Laws

22 When someone is convicted of a crime punishable by death and is executed, and you hang him on a tree, [23]his corpse must not remain all night upon the tree; you shall bury him that same day, for anyone hung on a tree is under God's curse. You must not defile the land that the LORD your God is giving you for possession.

22 You shall not watch your neighbor's ox or sheep straying away and ignore them; you shall take them back to their owner. [2]If the owner does not reside near you or you do not know who the owner is, you shall bring it to your own house, and it shall remain with you until the owner claims it; then you shall return it. [3]You shall do the same with a neighbor's donkey; you shall do the same with a neighbor's garment; and you shall do the same with anything else that your neighbor loses and you find. You may not withhold your help.

4 You shall not see your neighbor's donkey or ox fallen on the road and ignore it; you shall help to lift it up.

5 A woman shall not wear a man's apparel, nor shall a man put on a woman's garment; for whoever does such things is abhorrent to the LORD your God.

6 If you come on a bird's nest, in any tree or on the ground, with fledglings or eggs, with the mother sitting on the fledglings or on the eggs, you shall not take the mother with the young. [7]Let the mother go, taking only the young for yourself, in order that it may go well with you and you may live long.

8 When you build a new house, you shall make a parapet for your roof; otherwise you might have bloodguilt on your house, if anyone should fall from it.

9 You shall not sow your vineyard with a second kind of seed, or the whole yield will have to be forfeited, both the crop that you have sown and the yield of the vineyard itself.

10 You shall not plow with an ox and a donkey yoked together.

11 You shall not wear clothes made of wool and linen woven together.

12 You shall make tassels on the four corners of the cloak with which you cover yourself.

Laws concerning Sexual Relations

13 Suppose a man marries a woman, but after going in to her, he dislikes her [14]and makes up charges against her, slandering her by saying, "I married this woman; but when I lay with her, I did not find evidence of her virginity." [15]The father of the young woman and her mother shall then submit the evidence of the young woman's virginity to the elders of the city at the gate. [16]The father of the young woman shall say to the elders: "I gave my daughter in marriage to this man but he dislikes her; [17]now he has made up charges against her, saying, 'I did not find evidence of your daughter's virginity.' But here is the evidence of my daughter's virginity." Then they shall spread out the cloth before the elders of the town. [18]The elders of that town shall take the man and punish him; [19]they shall fine him one hun-

a Heb two-thirds

dred shekels of silver (which they shall give to the young woman's father) because he has slandered a virgin of Israel. She shall remain his wife; he shall not be permitted to divorce her as long as he lives.

20 If, however, this charge is true, that evidence of the young woman's virginity was not found, 21then they shall bring the young woman out to the entrance of her father's house and the men of her town shall stone her to death, because she committed a disgraceful act in Israel by prostituting herself in her father's house. So you shall purge the evil from your midst.

22 If a man is caught lying with the wife of another man, both of them shall die, the man who lay with the woman as well as the woman. So you shall purge the evil from Israel.

23 If there is a young woman, a virgin already engaged to be married, and a man meets her in the town and lies with her, 24you shall bring both of them to the gate of that town and stone them to death, the young woman because she did not cry for help in the town and the man because he violated his neighbor's wife. So you shall purge the evil from your midst.

25 But if the man meets the engaged woman in the open country, and the man seizes her and lies with her, then only the man who lay with her shall die. 26You shall do nothing to the young woman; the young woman has not committed an offense punishable by death, because this case is like that of someone who attacks and murders a neighbor. 27Since he found her in the open country, the engaged woman may have cried for help, but there was no one to rescue her.

28 If a man meets a virgin who is not engaged, and seizes her and lies with her, and they are caught in the act, 29the man who lay with her shall give fifty shekels of silver to the young woman's father, and she shall become his wife. Because he violated her he shall not be permitted to divorce her as long as he lives.

30 a A man shall not marry his father's wife, thereby violating his father's rights. b

Those Excluded from the Assembly

23 No one whose testicles are crushed or whose penis is cut off shall be admitted to the assembly of the LORD.

2 Those born of an illicit union shall not be admitted to the assembly of the LORD. Even to the tenth generation, none of their descendants shall be admitted to the assembly of the LORD.

3 No Ammonite or Moabite shall be admitted to the assembly of the LORD. Even to the tenth generation, none of their descendants shall be admitted to the assembly of the LORD, 4because they did not meet you with food and water on your journey out of Egypt, and because they hired against you Balaam son of Beor, from Pethor of Mesopotamia, to curse you. 5(Yet the LORD your God refused to heed Balaam; the LORD your God turned the curse into a blessing for you, because the LORD your God loved you.) 6You shall never promote their welfare or their prosperity as long as you live.

7 You shall not abhor any of the Edomites, for they are your kin. You shall not abhor any of the Egyptians, because you were an alien residing in their land. 8The children of the third generation that are born to them may be admitted to the assembly of the LORD.

Sanitary, Ritual, and Humanitarian Precepts

9 When you are encamped against your enemies you shall guard against any impropriety.

10 If one of you becomes unclean because of a nocturnal emission, then he shall go outside the camp; he must not come within the camp. 11When evening comes, he shall wash himself with water, and when the sun has set, he may come back into the camp.

12 You shall have a designated area outside the camp to which you shall go. 13With your utensils you shall have a trowel; when you re-

a Ch 23.1 in Heb   b Heb uncovering his father's skirt

lieve yourself outside, you shall dig a hole with it and then cover up your excrement. 14Because the LORD your God travels along with your camp, to save you and to hand over your enemies to you, therefore your camp must be holy, so that he may not see anything indecent among you and turn away from you.

15 Slaves who have escaped to you from their owners shall not be given back to them. 16They shall reside with you, in your midst, in any place they choose in any one of your towns, wherever they please; you shall not oppress them.

17 None of the daughters of Israel shall be a temple prostitute; none of the sons of Israel shall be a temple prostitute. 18You shall not bring the fee of a prostitute or the wages of a male prostitute*a* into the house of the LORD your God in payment for any vow, for both of these are abhorrent to the LORD your God.

19 You shall not charge interest on loans to another Israelite, interest on money, interest on provisions, interest on anything that is lent. 20On loans to a foreigner you may charge interest, but on loans to another Israelite you may not charge interest, so that the LORD your God may bless you in all your undertakings in the land that you are about to enter and possess.

21 If you make a vow to the LORD your God, do not postpone fulfilling it; for the LORD your God will surely require it of you, and you would incur guilt. 22But if you refrain from vowing, you will not incur guilt. 23Whatever your lips utter you must diligently perform, just as you have freely vowed to the LORD your God with your own mouth.

24 If you go into your neighbor's vineyard, you may eat your fill of grapes, as many as you wish, but you shall not put any in a container.

25 If you go into your neighbor's standing grain, you may pluck the ears with your hand, but you shall not put a sickle to your neighbor's standing grain.

Laws concerning Marriage and Divorce

24 Suppose a man enters into marriage with a woman, but she does not please him because he finds something objectionable about her, and so he writes her a certificate of divorce, puts it in her hand, and sends her out of his house; she then leaves his house 2and goes off to become another man's wife. 3Then suppose the second man dislikes her, writes her a bill of divorce, puts it in her hand, and sends her out of his house (or the second man who married her dies); 4her first husband, who sent her away, is not permitted to take her again to be his wife after she has been defiled; for that would be abhorrent to the LORD, and you shall not bring guilt on the land that the LORD your God is giving you as a possession.

Miscellaneous Laws

5 When a man is newly married, he shall not go out with the army or be charged with any related duty. He shall be free at home one year, to be happy with the wife whom he has married.

6 No one shall take a mill or an upper millstone in pledge, for that would be taking a life in pledge.

7 If someone is caught kidnaping another Israelite, enslaving or selling the Israelite, then that kidnaper shall die. So you shall purge the evil from your midst.

8 Guard against an outbreak of a leprous*b* skin disease by being very careful; you shall carefully observe whatever the levitical priests instruct you, just as I have commanded them. 9Remember what the LORD your God did to Miriam on your journey out of Egypt.

10 When you make your neighbor a loan of any kind, you shall not go into the house to take the pledge. 11You shall wait outside, while the person to whom you are making the loan brings the pledge out to you. 12If the person is poor, you shall not sleep in the garment given you as*c* the pledge. 13You shall give the pledge back by sunset, so that your neighbor

---

a Heb *a dog*   *b* A term for several skin diseases; precise meaning uncertain   *c* Heb lacks *the garment given you as* may sleep in the cloak and bless you; and it will be to your credit before the LORD your God.

14 You shall not withhold the wages of poor and needy laborers, whether other Israelites or aliens who reside in your land in one of your towns. 15You shall pay them their wages daily before sunset, because they are poor and their livelihood depends on them; otherwise they might cry to the LORD against you, and you would incur guilt.

16 Parents shall not be put to death for their children, nor shall children be put to death for their parents; only for their own crimes may persons be put to death.

17 You shall not deprive a resident alien or an orphan of justice; you shall not take a widow's garment in pledge. 18Remember that you were a slave in Egypt and the LORD your God redeemed you from there; therefore I command you to do this.

19 When you reap your harvest in your field and forget a sheaf in the field, you shall not go back to get it; it shall be left for the alien, the orphan, and the widow, so that the LORD your God may bless you in all your undertakings. 20When you beat your olive trees, do not strip what is left; it shall be for the alien, the orphan, and the widow.

21 When you gather the grapes of your vineyard, do not glean what is left; it shall be for the alien, the orphan, and the widow. 22Remember that you were a slave in the land of Egypt; therefore I am commanding you to do this.

25 Suppose two persons have a dispute and enter into litigation, and the judges decide between them, declaring one to be in the right and the other to be in the wrong. 2If the one in the wrong deserves to be flogged, the judge shall make that person lie down and be beaten in his presence with the number of lashes proportionate to the offense. 3Forty lashes may be given but not more; if more lashes than these are given, your neighbor will be degraded in your sight.

4 You shall not muzzle an ox while it is treading out the grain.

Levirate Marriage

5 When brothers reside together, and one of them dies and has no son, the wife of the deceased shall not be married outside the family to a stranger. Her husband's brother shall go in to her, taking her in marriage, and performing the duty of a husband's brother to her, 6and the firstborn whom she bears shall succeed to the name of the deceased brother, so that his name may not be blotted out of Israel. 7But if the man has no desire to marry his brother's widow, then his brother's widow shall go up to the elders at the gate and say, "My husband's brother refuses to perpetuate his brother's name in Israel; he will not perform the duty of a husband's brother to me." 8Then the elders of his town shall summon him and speak to him. If he persists, saying, "I have no desire to marry her," 9then his brother's wife shall go up to him in the presence of the elders, pull his sandal off his foot, spit in his face, and declare, "This is what is done to the man who does not build up his brother's house." 10Throughout Israel his family shall be known as "the house of him whose sandal was pulled off."

Various Commands

11 If men get into a fight with one another, and the wife of one intervenes to rescue her husband from the grip of his opponent by reaching out and seizing his genitals, 12you shall cut off her hand; show no pity.

13 You shall not have in your bag two kinds of weights, large and small. 14You shall not have in your house two kinds of measures, large and small. 15You shall have only a full and honest weight; you shall have only a full and honest measure, so that your days may be long in the land that the LORD your God is giving you. 16For all who do such things, all who act dishonestly, are abhorrent to the LORD your God.

17 Remember what Amalek did to you on your journey out of Egypt, 18how he attacked you on the way, when you were faint and weary, and struck down all who lagged behind you; he did not fear God. 19Therefore when the LORD

your God has given you rest from all your enemies on every hand, in the land that the LORD your God is giving you as an inheritance to possess, you shall blot out the remembrance of Amalek from under heaven; do not forget.

First Fruits and Tithes

26 When you have come into the land that the LORD your God is giving you as an inheritance to possess, and you possess it, and settle in it, ²you shall take some of the first of all the fruit of the ground, which you harvest from the land that the LORD your God is giving you, and you shall put it in a basket and go to the place that the LORD your God will choose as a dwelling for his name. ³You shall go to the priest who is in office at that time, and say to him, "Today I declare to the LORD your God that I have come into the land that the LORD swore to our ancestors to give us." ⁴When the priest takes the basket from your hand and sets it down before the altar of the LORD your God, ⁵you shall make this response before the LORD your God: "A wandering Aramean was my ancestor; he went down into Egypt and lived there as an alien, few in number, and there he became a great nation, mighty and populous. ⁶When the Egyptians treated us harshly and afflicted us, by imposing hard labor on us, ⁷we cried to the LORD, the God of our ancestors; the LORD heard our voice and saw our affliction, our toil, and our oppression. ⁸The LORD brought us out of Egypt with a mighty hand and an outstretched arm, with a terrifying display of power, and with signs and wonders; ⁹and he brought us into this place and gave us this land, a land flowing with milk and honey. ¹⁰So now I bring the first of the fruit of the ground that you, O LORD, have given me." You shall set it down before the LORD your God and bow down before the LORD your God. ¹¹Then you, together with the Levites and the aliens who reside among you, shall celebrate with all the bounty that the LORD your God has given to you and to your house.

12 When you have finished paying all the tithe of your produce in the third year (which is the year of the tithe), giving it to the Levites, the aliens, the orphans, and the widows, so that they may eat their fill within your towns, ¹³then you shall say before the LORD your God: "I have removed the sacred portion from the house, and I have given it to the Levites, the resident aliens, the orphans, and the widows, in accordance with your entire commandment that you commanded me; I have neither transgressed nor forgotten any of your commandments: ¹⁴I have not eaten of it while in mourning; I have not removed any of it while I was unclean; and I have not offered any of it to the dead. I have obeyed the LORD my God, doing just as you commanded me. ¹⁵Look down from your holy habitation, from heaven, and bless your people Israel and the ground that you have given us, as you swore to our ancestors—a land flowing with milk and honey."

Concluding Exhortation

16 This very day the LORD your God is commanding you to observe these statutes and ordinances; so observe them diligently with all your heart and with all your soul. ¹⁷Today you have obtained the LORD's agreement: to be your God; and for you to walk in his ways, to keep his statutes, his commandments, and his ordinances, and to obey him. ¹⁸Today the LORD has obtained your agreement: to be his treasured people, as he promised you, and to keep his commandments; ¹⁹for him to set you high above all nations that he has made, in praise and in fame and in honor; and for you to be a people holy to the LORD your God, as he promised.

The Inscribed Stones and Altar on Mount Ebal

27 Then Moses and the elders of Israel charged all the people as follows: Keep the entire commandment that I am commanding you today. ²On the day that you cross over the Jordan into the land that the LORD your God is giving you, you shall set up large stones and cover them with plaster. ³You shall write on them all the words of this law when you have crossed over, to enter the land that

the LORD your God is giving you, a land flowing with milk and honey, as the LORD, the God of your ancestors, promised you. ⁴So when you have crossed over the Jordan, you shall set up these stones, about which I am commanding you today, on Mount Ebal, and you shall cover them with plaster. ⁵And you shall build an altar there to the LORD your God, an altar of stones on which you have not used an iron tool. ⁶You must build the altar of the LORD your God of unhewn ᵃ stones. Then offer up burnt offerings on it to the LORD your God, ⁷make sacrifices of well-being, and eat them there, rejoicing before the LORD your God. ⁸You shall write on the stones all the words of this law very clearly.

9 Then Moses and the levitical priests spoke to all Israel, saying: Keep silence and hear, O Israel! This very day you have become the people of the LORD your God. ¹⁰Therefore obey the LORD your God, observing his commandments and his statutes that I am commanding you today.

Twelve Curses

11 The same day Moses charged the people as follows: ¹²When you have crossed over the Jordan, these shall stand on Mount Gerizim for the blessing of the people: Simeon, Levi, Judah, Issachar, Joseph, and Benjamin. ¹³And these shall stand on Mount Ebal for the curse: Reuben, Gad, Asher, Zebulun, Dan, and Naphtali. ¹⁴Then the Levites shall declare in a loud voice to all the Israelites:

15 "Cursed be anyone who makes an idol or casts an image, anything abhorrent to the LORD, the work of an artisan, and sets it up in secret." All the people shall respond, saying, "Amen!"

16 "Cursed be anyone who dishonors father or mother." All the people shall say, "Amen!"

17 "Cursed be anyone who moves a neighbor's boundary marker." All the people shall say, "Amen!"

18 "Cursed be anyone who misleads a blind person on the road." All the people shall say, "Amen!"

19 "Cursed be anyone who deprives the alien, the orphan, and the widow of justice." All the people shall say, "Amen!"

20 "Cursed be anyone who lies with his father's wife, because he has violated his father's rights." ᵇ All the people shall say, "Amen!"

21 "Cursed be anyone who lies with any animal." All the people shall say, "Amen!"

22 "Cursed be anyone who lies with his sister, whether the daughter of his father or the daughter of his mother." All the people shall say, "Amen!"

23 "Cursed be anyone who lies with his mother-in-law." All the people shall say, "Amen!"

24 "Cursed be anyone who strikes down a neighbor in secret." All the people shall say, "Amen!"

25 "Cursed be anyone who takes a bribe to shed innocent blood." All the people shall say, "Amen!"

26 "Cursed be anyone who does not uphold the words of this law by observing them." All the people shall say, "Amen!"

Blessings for Obedience

28 If you will only obey the LORD your God, by diligently observing all his commandments that I am commanding you today, the LORD your God will set you high above all the nations of the earth; ²all these blessings shall come upon you and overtake you, if you obey the LORD your God:

3 Blessed shall you be in the city, and blessed shall you be in the field.

4 Blessed shall be the fruit of your womb, the fruit of your ground, and the fruit of your livestock, both the increase of your cattle and the issue of your flock.

5 Blessed shall be your basket and your kneading bowl.

6 Blessed shall you be when you come in, and blessed shall you be when you go out.

7 The LORD will cause your enemies who

---

a Heb *whole*   *b* Heb *uncovered his father's skirt*

rise against you to be defeated before you; they shall come out against you one way, and flee before you seven ways. ⁸The LORD will command the blessing upon you in your barns, and in all that you undertake; he will bless you in the land that the LORD your God is giving you. ⁹The LORD will establish you as his holy people, as he has sworn to you, if you keep the commandments of the LORD your God and walk in his ways. ¹⁰All the peoples of the earth shall see that you are called by the name of the LORD, and they shall be afraid of you. ¹¹The LORD will make you abound in prosperity, in the fruit of your womb, in the fruit of your livestock, and in the fruit of your ground in the land that the LORD swore to your ancestors to give you. ¹²The LORD will open for you his rich storehouse, the heavens, to give the rain of your land in its season and to bless all your undertakings. You will lend to many nations, but you will not borrow. ¹³The LORD will make you the head, and not the tail; you shall be only at the top, and not at the bottom—if you obey the commandments of the LORD your God, which I am commanding you today, by diligently observing them, ¹⁴and if you do not turn aside from any of the words that I am commanding you today, either to the right or to the left, following other gods to serve them.

Warnings against Disobedience

15 But if you will not obey the LORD your God by diligently observing all his commandments and decrees, which I am commanding you today, then all these curses shall come upon you and overtake you:

16 Cursed shall you be in the city, and cursed shall you be in the field.

17 Cursed shall be your basket and your kneading bowl.

18 Cursed shall be the fruit of your womb, the fruit of your ground, the increase of your cattle and the issue of your flock.

19 Cursed shall you be when you come in, and cursed shall you be when you go out.

20 The LORD will send upon you disaster, panic, and frustration in everything you attempt to do, until you are destroyed and per-

ish quickly, on account of the evil of your deeds, because you have forsaken me. ²¹The LORD will make the pestilence cling to you until it has consumed you off the land that you are entering to possess. ²²The LORD will afflict you with consumption, fever, inflammation, with fiery heat and drought, and with blight and mildew; they shall pursue you until you perish. ²³The sky over your head shall be bronze, and the earth under you iron. ²⁴The LORD will change the rain of your land into powder, and only dust shall come down upon you from the sky until you are destroyed.

25 The LORD will cause you to be defeated before your enemies; you shall go out against them one way and flee before them seven ways. You shall become an object of horror to all the kingdoms of the earth. ²⁶Your corpses shall be food for every bird of the air and animal of the earth, and there shall be no one to frighten them away. ²⁷The LORD will afflict you with the boils of Egypt, with ulcers, scurvy, and itch, of which you cannot be healed. ²⁸The LORD will afflict you with madness, blindness, and confusion of mind; ²⁹you shall grope about at noon as blind people grope in darkness, but you shall be unable to find your way; and you shall be continually abused and robbed, without anyone to help. ³⁰You shall become engaged to a woman, but another man shall lie with her. You shall build a house, but not live in it. You shall plant a vineyard, but not enjoy its fruit. ³¹Your ox shall be butchered before your eyes, but you shall not eat of it. Your donkey shall be stolen in front of you, and shall not be restored to you. Your sheep shall be given to your enemies, without anyone to help you. ³²Your sons and daughters shall be given to another people, while you look on; you will strain your eyes looking for them all day but be powerless to do anything. ³³A people whom you do not know shall eat up the fruit of your ground and of all your labors; you shall be continually abused and crushed, ³⁴and driven mad by the sight that your eyes shall see. ³⁵The LORD will strike you on the knees and on the legs with grievous boils of which you cannot be healed, from the

sole of your foot to the crown of your head. [36]The LORD will bring you, and the king whom you set over you, to a nation that neither you nor your ancestors have known, where you shall serve other gods, of wood and stone. [37]You shall become an object of horror, a proverb, and a byword among all the peoples where the LORD will lead you.

38 You shall carry much seed into the field but shall gather little in, for the locust shall consume it. [39]You shall plant vineyards and dress them, but you shall neither drink the wine nor gather the grapes, for the worm shall eat them. [40]You shall have olive trees throughout all your territory, but you shall not anoint yourself with the oil, for your olives shall drop off. [41]You shall have sons and daughters, but they shall not remain yours, for they shall go into captivity. [42]All your trees and the fruit of your ground the cicada shall take over. [43]Aliens residing among you shall ascend above you higher and higher, while you shall descend lower and lower. [44]They shall lend to you but you shall not lend to them; they shall be the head and you shall be the tail.

45 All these curses shall come upon you, pursuing and overtaking you until you are destroyed, because you did not obey the LORD your God, by observing the commandments and the decrees that he commanded you. [46]They shall be among you and your descendants as a sign and a portent forever.

47 Because you did not serve the LORD your God joyfully and with gladness of heart for the abundance of everything, [48]therefore you shall serve your enemies whom the LORD will send against you, in hunger and thirst, in nakedness and lack of everything. He will put an iron yoke on your neck until he has destroyed you. [49]The LORD will bring a nation from far away, from the end of the earth, to swoop down on you like an eagle, a nation whose language you do not understand, [50]a grim-faced nation showing no respect to the old or favor to the young. [51]It shall consume the fruit of your livestock and the fruit of your ground until you are destroyed, leaving you neither grain, wine, and oil, nor the increase of your cattle and the issue of your flock, until it has made you perish. [52]It shall besiege you in all your towns until your high and fortified walls, in which you trusted, come down throughout your land; it shall besiege you in all your towns throughout the land that the LORD your God has given you. [53]In the desperate straits to which the enemy siege reduces you, you will eat the fruit of your womb, the flesh of your own sons and daughters whom the LORD your God has given you. [54]Even the most refined and gentle of men among you will begrudge food to his own brother, to the wife whom he embraces, and to the last of his remaining children, [55]giving to none of them any of the flesh of his children whom he is eating, because nothing else remains to him, in the desperate straits to which the enemy siege will reduce you in all your towns. [56]She who is the most refined and gentle among you, so gentle and refined that she does not venture to set the sole of her foot on the ground, will begrudge food to the husband whom she embraces, to her own son, and to her own daughter, [57]begrudging even the afterbirth that comes out from between her thighs, and the children that she bears, because she is eating them in secret for lack of anything else, in the desperate straits to which the enemy siege will reduce you in your towns.

58 If you do not diligently observe all the words of this law that are written in this book, fearing this glorious and awesome name, the LORD your God, [59]then the LORD will overwhelm both you and your offspring with severe and lasting afflictions and grievous and lasting maladies. [60]He will bring back upon you all the diseases of Egypt, of which you were in dread, and they shall cling to you. [61]Every other malady and affliction, even though not recorded in the book of this law, the LORD will inflict on you until you are destroyed. [62]Although once you were as numerous as the stars in heaven, you shall be left few in number, because you did not obey the LORD your God. [63]And just as the LORD took delight in making you prosperous and numerous, so the LORD will take delight in bringing you to

ruin and destruction; you shall be plucked off the land that you are entering to possess. 64The LORD will scatter you among all peoples, from one end of the earth to the other; and there you shall serve other gods, of wood and stone, which neither you nor your ancestors have known. 65Among those nations you shall find no ease, no resting place for the sole of your foot. There the LORD will give you a trembling heart, failing eyes, and a languishing spirit. 66Your life shall hang in doubt before you; night and day you shall be in dread, with no assurance of your life. 67In the morning you shall say, "If only it were evening!" and at evening you shall say, "If only it were morning!"—because of the dread that your heart shall feel and the sights that your eyes shall see. 68The LORD will bring you back in ships to Egypt, by a route that I promised you would never see again; and there you shall offer yourselves for sale to your enemies as male and female slaves, but there will be no buyer.

29 *a* These are the words of the covenant that the LORD commanded Moses to make with the Israelites in the land of Moab, in addition to the covenant that he had made with them at Horeb.

The Covenant Renewed in Moab

2*b* Moses summoned all Israel and said to them: You have seen all that the LORD did before your eyes in the land of Egypt, to Pharaoh and to all his servants and to all his land, 3the great trials that your eyes saw, the signs, and those great wonders. 4But to this day the LORD has not given you a mind to understand, or eyes to see, or ears to hear. 5I have led you forty years in the wilderness. The clothes on your back have not worn out, and the sandals on your feet have not worn out; 6you have not eaten bread, and you have not drunk wine or strong drink—so that you may know that I am the LORD your God. 7When you came to this place, King Sihon of Heshbon and King Og of Bashan came out against us for battle, but we defeated them. 8We took their land

and gave it as an inheritance to the Reubenites, the Gadites, and the half-tribe of Manasseh. 9Therefore diligently observe the words of this covenant, in order that you may succeed*c* in everything that you do.

10 You stand assembled today, all of you, before the LORD your God—the leaders of your tribes,*d* your elders, and your officials, all the men of Israel, 11your children, your women, and the aliens who are in your camp, both those who cut your wood and those who draw your water— 12to enter into the covenant of the LORD your God, sworn by an oath, which the LORD your God is making with you today; 13in order that he may establish you today as his people, and that he may be your God, as he promised you and as he swore to your ancestors, to Abraham, to Isaac, and to Jacob. 14I am making this covenant, sworn by an oath, not only with you who stand here with us today before the LORD our God, 15but also with those who are not here with us today. 16You know how we lived in the land of Egypt, and how we came through the midst of the nations through which you passed. 17You have seen their detestable things, the filthy idols of wood and stone, of silver and gold, that were among them. 18It may be that there is among you a man or woman, or a family or tribe, whose heart is already turning away from the LORD our God to serve the gods of those nations. It may be that there is among you a root sprouting poisonous and bitter growth. 19All who hear the words of this oath and bless themselves, thinking in their hearts, "We are safe even though we go our own stubborn ways" (thus bringing disaster on moist and dry alike)*e*— 20the LORD will be unwilling to pardon them, for the LORD's anger and passion will smoke against them. All the curses written in this book will descend on them, and the LORD will blot out their names from under heaven. 21The LORD will single them out from all the tribes of Israel for calamity, in accordance with all the curses of the covenant written in this book of the law.

---

a Ch 28.69 in Heb   *b* Ch 29.1 in Heb   *c* Or *deal wisely* Heb uncertain   *d* Gk Syr: Heb *your leaders, your tribes*   *e* Meaning of Heb uncertain

22The next generation, your children who rise up after you, as well as the foreigner who comes from a distant country, will see the devastation of that land and the afflictions with which the LORD has afflicted it— 23all its soil burned out by sulfur and salt, nothing planted, nothing sprouting, unable to support any vegetation, like the destruction of Sodom and Gomorrah, Admah and Zeboiim, which the LORD destroyed in his fierce anger— 24they and indeed all the nations will wonder, "Why has the LORD done thus to this land? What caused this great display of anger?" 25They will conclude, "It is because they abandoned the covenant of the LORD, the God of their ancestors, which he made with them when he brought them out of the land of Egypt. 26They turned and served other gods, worshiping them, gods whom they had not known and whom he had not allotted to them; 27so the anger of the LORD was kindled against that land, bringing on it every curse written in this book. 28The LORD uprooted them from their land in anger, fury, and great wrath, and cast them into another land, as is now the case." 29The secret things belong to the LORD our God, but the revealed things belong to us and to our children forever, to observe all the words of this law.

God's Fidelity Assured

30 When all these things have happened to you, the blessings and the curses that I have set before you, if you call them to mind among all the nations where the LORD your God has driven you, 2and return to the LORD your God, and you and your children obey him with all your heart and with all your soul, just as I am commanding you today, 3then the LORD your God will restore your fortunes and have compassion on you, gathering you again from all the peoples among whom the LORD your God has scattered you. 4Even if you are exiled to the ends of the world,a from there the LORD your God will gather you, and from there he will bring you back.

5The LORD your God will bring you into the land that your ancestors possessed, and you will possess it; he will make you more prosperous and numerous than your ancestors.

6 Moreover, the LORD your God will circumcise your heart and the heart of your descendants, so that you will love the LORD your God with all your heart and with all your soul, in order that you may live. 7The LORD your God will put all these curses on your enemies and on the adversaries who took advantage of you. 8Then you shall again obey the LORD, observing all his commandments that I am commanding you today, 9and the LORD your God will make you abundantly prosperous in all your undertakings, in the fruit of your body, in the fruit of your livestock, and in the fruit of your soil. For the LORD will again take delight in prospering you, just as he delighted in prospering your ancestors, 10when you obey the LORD your God by observing his commandments and decrees that are written in this book of the law, because you turn to the LORD your God with all your heart and with all your soul.

Exhortation to Choose Life

11 Surely, this commandment that I am commanding you today is not too hard for you, nor is it too far away. 12It is not in heaven, that you should say, "Who will go up to heaven for us, and get it for us so that we may hear it and observe it?" 13Neither is it beyond the sea, that you should say, "Who will cross to the other side of the sea for us, and get it for us so that we may hear it and observe it?" 14No, the word is very near to you; it is in your mouth and in your heart for you to observe.

15 See, I have set before you today life and prosperity, death and adversity. 16If you obey the commandments of the LORD your Godb that I am commanding you today, by loving the LORD your God, walking in his ways, and observing his commandments, decrees, and ordinances, then you shall live and become nu-

---

a Heb of heaven   b Gk: Heb lacks If you obey the commandments of the LORD your God merous, and the LORD your God will bless you in the land that you are entering to possess. 17But if your heart turns away and you do not hear, but are led astray to bow down to other gods and serve them, 18I declare to you today that you shall perish; you shall not live long in the land that you are crossing the Jordan to enter and possess. 19I call heaven and earth to witness against you today that I have set before you life and death, blessings and curses. Choose life so that you and your descendants may live, 20loving the LORD your God, obeying him, and holding fast to him; for that means life to you and length of days, so that you may live in the land that the LORD swore to give to your ancestors, to Abraham, to Isaac, and to Jacob.

Joshua Becomes Moses' Successor

31 When Moses had finished speaking all*a* these words to all Israel, 2he said to them: "I am now one hundred twenty years old. I am no longer able to get about, and the LORD has told me, 'You shall not cross over this Jordan.' 3The LORD your God himself will cross over before you. He will destroy these nations before you, and you shall dispossess them. Joshua also will cross over before you, as the LORD promised. 4The LORD will do to them as he did to Sihon and Og, the kings of the Amorites, and to their land, when he destroyed them. 5The LORD will give them over to you and you shall deal with them in full accord with the command that I have given to you. 6Be strong and bold; have no fear or dread of them, because it is the LORD your God who goes with you; he will not fail you or forsake you."

7 Then Moses summoned Joshua and said to him in the sight of all Israel: "Be strong and bold, for you are the one who will go with this people into the land that the LORD has sworn to their ancestors to give them; and you will put them in possession of it. 8It is the LORD who goes before you. He will be with you; he will

not fail you or forsake you. Do not fear or be dismayed."

The Law to Be Read Every Seventh Year

9 Then Moses wrote down this law, and gave it to the priests, the sons of Levi, who carried the ark of the covenant of the LORD, and to all the elders of Israel. 10Moses commanded them: "Every seventh year, in the scheduled year of remission, during the festival of booths,*b* 11when all Israel comes to appear before the LORD your God at the place that he will choose, you shall read this law before all Israel in their hearing. 12Assemble the people—men, women, and children, as well as the aliens residing in your towns—so that they may hear and learn to fear the LORD your God and to observe diligently all the words of this law, 13and so that their children, who have not known it, may hear and learn to fear the LORD your God, as long as you live in the land that you are crossing over the Jordan to possess."

Moses and Joshua Receive God's Charge

14 The LORD said to Moses, "Your time to die is near; call Joshua and present yourselves in the tent of meeting, so that I may commission him." So Moses and Joshua went and presented themselves in the tent of meeting, 15and the LORD appeared at the tent in a pillar of cloud; the pillar of cloud stood at the entrance to the tent.

16 The LORD said to Moses, "Soon you will lie down with your ancestors. Then this people will begin to prostitute themselves to the foreign gods in their midst, the gods of the land into which they are going; they will forsake me, breaking my covenant that I have made with them. 17My anger will be kindled against them in that day. I will forsake them and hide my face from them; they will become easy prey, and many terrible troubles will come upon them. In that day they will say, 'Have not these troubles come upon us because our God is not in our midst?' 18On that day I will surely hide my face on account of all

a Q Ms Gk: MT *Moses went and spoke*　　*b* Or *tabernacles*; Heb *succoth* the evil they have done by turning to other gods. ¹⁹Now therefore write this song, and teach it to the Israelites; put it in their mouths, in order that this song may be a witness for me against the Israelites. ²⁰For when I have brought them into the land flowing with milk and honey, which I promised on oath to their ancestors, and they have eaten their fill and grown fat, they will turn to other gods and serve them, despising me and breaking my covenant. ²¹And when many terrible troubles come upon them, this song will confront them as a witness, because it will not be lost from the mouths of their descendants. For I know what they are inclined to do even now, before I have brought them into the land that I promised them on oath." ²²That very day Moses wrote this song and taught it to the Israelites.

23 Then the LORD commissioned Joshua son of Nun and said, "Be strong and bold, for you shall bring the Israelites into the land that I promised them; I will be with you."

24 When Moses had finished writing down in a book the words of this law to the very end, ²⁵Moses commanded the Levites who carried the ark of the covenant of the LORD, saying, ²⁶"Take this book of the law and put it beside the ark of the covenant of the LORD your God; let it remain there as a witness against you. ²⁷For I know well how rebellious and stubborn you are. If you already have been so rebellious toward the LORD while I am still alive among you, how much more after my death! ²⁸Assemble to me all the elders of your tribes and your officials, so that I may recite these words in their hearing and call heaven and earth to witness against them. ²⁹For I know that after my death you will surely act corruptly, turning aside from the way that I have commanded you. In time to come trouble will befall you, because you will do what is evil in the sight of the LORD, provoking him to anger through the work of your hands."

The Song of Moses

30 Then Moses recited the words of this song, to the very end, in the hearing of the whole assembly of Israel:

32 Give ear, O heavens, and I will
speak;
let the earth hear the words of my
mouth.
2 May my teaching drop like the rain,
my speech condense like the dew;
like gentle rain on grass,
like showers on new growth.
3 For I will proclaim the name of the
LORD;
ascribe greatness to our God!

4 The Rock, his work is perfect,
and all his ways are just.
A faithful God, without deceit,
just and upright is he;
5 yet his degenerate children have dealt
falsely with him, ᵃ
a perverse and crooked generation.
6 Do you thus repay the LORD,
O foolish and senseless people?
Is not he your father, who created you,
who made you and established you?
7 Remember the days of old,
consider the years long past;
ask your father, and he will inform you;
your elders, and they will tell you.
8 When the Most High ᵇ apportioned the
nations,
when he divided humankind,
he fixed the boundaries of the peoples
according to the number of the
gods; ᶜ
9 the LORD's own portion was his people,
Jacob his allotted share.

10 He sustained ᵈ him in a desert land,
in a howling wilderness waste;
he shielded him, cared for him,
guarded him as the apple of his eye.
11 As an eagle stirs up its nest,
and hovers over its young;
as it spreads its wings, takes them up,
and bears them aloft on its pinions,

ᵃ Meaning of Heb uncertain   ᵇ Traditional rendering of Heb *Elyon*   ᶜ Q Ms Compare Gk Tg: MT *the Israelites*
ᵈ Sam Gk Compare Tg: MT *found*

12 the LORD alone guided him;
 no foreign god was with him.
13 He set him atop the heights of the land,
 and fed him with*a* produce of the
 field;
 he nursed him with honey from the
 crags,
 with oil from flinty rock;
14 curds from the herd, and milk from the
 flock,
 with fat of lambs and rams;
 Bashan bulls and goats,
 together with the choicest wheat—
 you drank fine wine from the blood
 of grapes.
15 Jacob ate his fill;*b*
 Jeshurun grew fat, and kicked.
 You grew fat, bloated, and gorged!
 He abandoned God who made him,
 and scoffed at the Rock of his
 salvation.
16 They made him jealous with strange gods,
 with abhorrent things they provoked
 him.
17 They sacrificed to demons, not God,
 to deities they had never known,
 to new ones recently arrived,
 whom your ancestors had not feared.
18 You were unmindful of the Rock that
 bore you;*c*
 you forgot the God who gave you
 birth.

19 The LORD saw it, and was jealous;*d*
 he spurned*e* his sons and daughters.
20 He said: I will hide my face from them,
 I will see what their end will be;
 for they are a perverse generation,
 children in whom there is no
 faithfulness.
21 They made me jealous with what is no
 god,
 provoked me with their idols.
 So I will make them jealous with what is
 no people,
 provoke them with a foolish nation.

22 For a fire is kindled by my anger,
 and burns to the depths of Sheol;
 it devours the earth and its increase,
 and sets on fire the foundations of
 the mountains.
23 I will heap disasters upon them,
 spend my arrows against them:
24 wasting hunger,
 burning consumption,
 bitter pestilence.
 The teeth of beasts I will send against
 them,
 with venom of things crawling in the
 dust.
25 In the street the sword shall bereave,
 and in the chambers terror,
 for young man and woman alike,
 nursing child and old gray head.
26 I thought to scatter them*f*
 and blot out the memory of them
 from humankind;
27 but I feared provocation by the enemy,
 for their adversaries might
 misunderstand
 and say, "Our hand is triumphant;
 it was not the LORD who did all this."

28 They are a nation void of sense;
 there is no understanding in them.
29 If they were wise, they would
 understand this;
 they would discern what the end
 would be.
30 How could one have routed a thousand,
 and two put a myriad to flight,
 unless their Rock had sold them,
 the LORD had given them up?
31 Indeed their rock is not like our Rock;
 our enemies are fools.*f*
32 Their vine comes from the vinestock of
 Sodom,
 from the vineyards of Gomorrah;
 their grapes are grapes of poison,
 their clusters are bitter;
33 their wine is the poison of serpents,
 the cruel venom of asps.

---

a Sam Gk Syr Tg: MT *he ate*   *b* Q Mss Sam Gk: MT lacks *Jacob ate his fill*   *c* Or *that begot you*   *d* Q Mss Gk:
MT lacks *was jealous*   *e* Cn: Heb *he spurned because of provocation*   *f* Gk: Meaning of Heb uncertain

34 Is not this laid up in store with me,
    sealed up in my treasuries?
35 Vengeance is mine, and recompense,
    for the time when their foot shall slip;
because the day of their calamity is at
    hand,
    their doom comes swiftly.

36 Indeed the LORD will vindicate his
    people,
    have compassion on his servants,
when he sees that their power is gone,
    neither bond nor free remaining.
37 Then he will say: Where are their gods,
    the rock in which they took refuge,
38 who ate the fat of their sacrifices,
    and drank the wine of their libations?
Let them rise up and help you,
    let them be your protection!

39 See now that I, even I, am he;
    there is no god besides me.
I kill and I make alive;
    I wound and I heal;
    and no one can deliver from my hand.
40 For I lift up my hand to heaven,
    and swear: As I live forever,
41 when I whet my flashing sword,
    and my hand takes hold on judgment;
I will take vengeance on my adversaries,
    and will repay those who hate me.
42 I will make my arrows drunk with
    blood,
    and my sword shall devour flesh—
with the blood of the slain and the
    captives,
    from the long-haired enemy.

43 Praise, O heavens,*a* his people,
    worship him, all you gods!*b*
For he will avenge the blood of his
    children,*c*
    and take vengeance on his
    adversaries;

he will repay those who hate him,*b*
    and cleanse the land for his people.*d*

44 Moses came and recited all the words of this song in the hearing of the people, he and Joshua*e* son of Nun. 45When Moses had finished reciting all these words to all Israel, 46he said to them: "Take to heart all the words that I am giving in witness against you today; give them as a command to your children, so that they may diligently observe all the words of this law. 47This is no trifling matter for you, but rather your very life; through it you may live long in the land that you are crossing over the Jordan to possess."

Moses' Death Foretold

48 On that very day the LORD addressed Moses as follows: 49"Ascend this mountain of the Abarim, Mount Nebo, which is in the land of Moab, across from Jericho, and view the land of Canaan, which I am giving to the Israelites for a possession; 50you shall die there on the mountain that you ascend and shall be gathered to your kin, as your brother Aaron died on Mount Hor and was gathered to his kin; 51because both of you broke faith with me among the Israelites at the waters of Meribath-kadesh in the wilderness of Zin, by failing to maintain my holiness among the Israelites. 52Although you may view the land from a distance, you shall not enter it—the land that I am giving to the Israelites."

Moses' Final Blessing on Israel

33 This is the blessing with which Moses, the man of God, blessed the Israelites before his death. 2He said:
    The LORD came from Sinai,
    and dawned from Seir upon us;*f*
    he shone forth from Mount Paran.
    With him were myriads of holy ones;*g*
    at his right, a host of his own.*b*
3   Indeed, O favorite among*i* peoples,
    all his holy ones were in your charge;

---

a Q Ms Gk: MT *nations*   *b* Q Ms Gk: MT lacks this line   *c* Q Ms Gk: MT *his servants*   *d* Q Ms Sam Gk Vg: MT *his land his people*   *e* Sam Gk Syr Vg: MT *Hoshea*   *f* Gk Syr Vg Compare Tg: Heb *upon them*
g Cn Compare Gk Sam Syr Vg: MT *He came from Ribeboth-kodesh,*   *h* Cn Compare Gk: meaning of Heb uncertain
i Or *O lover of the*

they marched at your heels,
accepted direction from you.
4 Moses charged us with the law,
as a possession for the assembly of
Jacob.
5 There arose a king in Jeshurun,
when the leaders of the people
assembled—
the united tribes of Israel.

6 May Reuben live, and not die out,
even though his numbers are few.

7 And this he said of Judah:
O LORD, give heed to Judah,
and bring him to his people;
strengthen his hands for him,*a*
and be a help against his adversaries.

8 And of Levi he said:
Give to Levi*b* your Thummim,
and your Urim to your loyal one,
whom you tested at Massah,
with whom you contended at the
waters of Meribah;
9 who said of his father and mother,
"I regard them not";
he ignored his kin,
and did not acknowledge his children.
For they observed your word,
and kept your covenant.
10 They teach Jacob your ordinances,
and Israel your law;
they place incense before you,
and whole burnt offerings on your
altar.
11 Bless, O LORD, his substance,
and accept the work of his hands;
crush the loins of his adversaries,
of those that hate him, so that they
do not rise again.

12 Of Benjamin he said:
The beloved of the LORD rests in
safety—

the High God*c* surrounds him all day
long—
the beloved*d* rests between his
shoulders.

13 And of Joseph he said:
Blessed by the LORD be his land,
with the choice gifts of heaven above,
and of the deep that lies beneath;
14 with the choice fruits of the sun,
and the rich yield of the months;
15 with the finest produce of the ancient
mountains,
and the abundance of the everlasting
hills;
16 with the choice gifts of the earth and its
fullness,
and the favor of the one who dwells
on Sinai.*e*
Let these come on the head of Joseph,
on the brow of the prince among his
brothers.
17 A firstborn*f* bull—majesty is his!
His horns are the horns of a wild ox;
with them he gores the peoples,
driving them to*g* the ends of the
earth;
such are the myriads of Ephraim,
such the thousands of Manasseh.

18 And of Zebulun he said:
Rejoice, Zebulun, in your going out;
and Issachar, in your tents.
19 They call peoples to the mountain;
there they offer the right sacrifices;
for they suck the affluence of the seas
and the hidden treasures of the sand.

20 And of Gad he said:
Blessed be the enlargement of Gad!
Gad lives like a lion;
he tears at arm and scalp.
21 He chose the best for himself,
for there a commander's allotment
was reserved;
he came at the head of the people,

---

a Cn: Heb *with his hands he contended*   *b* Q Ms Gk: MT lacks *Give to Levi*   *c* Heb *above him*   *d* Heb *he*
e Cn: Heb *in the bush*   *f* Q Ms Gk Syr Vg: MT *His firstborn*   *g* Cn: Heb *the peoples, together*

he executed the justice of the LORD,
and his ordinances for Israel.

22And of Dan he said:
Dan is a lion's whelp
that leaps forth from Bashan.

23And of Naphtali he said:
O Naphtali, sated with favor,
full of the blessing of the LORD,
possess the west and the south.

24And of Asher he said:
Most blessed of sons be Asher;
may he be the favorite of his
brothers,
and may he dip his foot in oil.
25 Your bars are iron and bronze;
and as your days, so is your strength.

26 There is none like God, O Jeshurun,
who rides through the heavens to
your help,
majestic through the skies.
27 He subdues the ancient gods,*a*
shatters*b* the forces of old;*c*
he drove out the enemy before you,
and said, "Destroy!"
28 So Israel lives in safety,
untroubled is Jacob's abode*d*
in a land of grain and wine,
where the heavens drop down dew.
29 Happy are you, O Israel! Who is like
you,
a people saved by the LORD,
the shield of your help,
and the sword of your triumph!
Your enemies shall come fawning to
you,
and you shall tread on their backs.

Moses Dies and Is Buried in the Land of Moab

34 Then Moses went up from the plains of Moab to Mount Nebo, to the top of Pisgah, which is opposite Jericho, and the LORD showed him the whole land: Gilead as far as Dan, 2all Naphtali, the land of Ephraim and Manasseh, all the land of Judah as far as the Western Sea, 3the Negeb, and the Plain—that is, the valley of Jericho, the city of palm trees—as far as Zoar. 4The LORD said to him, "This is the land of which I swore to Abraham, to Isaac, and to Jacob, saying, 'I will give it to your descendants'; I have let you see it with your eyes, but you shall not cross over there." 5Then Moses, the servant of the LORD, died there in the land of Moab, at the LORD's command. 6He was buried in a valley in the land of Moab, opposite Beth-peor, but no one knows his burial place to this day. 7Moses was one hundred twenty years old when he died; his sight was unimpaired and his vigor had not abated. 8The Israelites wept for Moses in the plains of Moab thirty days; then the period of mourning for Moses was ended.

9 Joshua son of Nun was full of the spirit of wisdom, because Moses had laid his hands on him; and the Israelites obeyed him, doing as the LORD had commanded Moses.

10 Never since has there arisen a prophet in Israel like Moses, whom the LORD knew face to face. 11He was unequaled for all the signs and wonders that the LORD sent him to perform in the land of Egypt, against Pharaoh and all his servants and his entire land, 12and for all the mighty deeds and all the terrifying displays of power that Moses performed in the sight of all Israel.

---

a Or *The eternal God is a dwelling place*   *b* Cn: Heb *from underneath*   *c* Or *the everlasting arms*   *d* Or *fountain*

JOSHUA

God's Commission to Joshua

1 After the death of Moses the servant of the LORD, the LORD spoke to Joshua son of Nun, Moses' assistant, saying, 2"My servant Moses is dead. Now proceed to cross the Jordan, you and all this people, into the land that I am giving to them, to the Israelites. 3Every place that the sole of your foot will tread upon I have given to you, as I promised to Moses. 4From the wilderness and the Lebanon as far as the great river, the river Euphrates, all the land of the Hittites, to the Great Sea in the west shall be your territory. 5No one shall be able to stand against you all the days of your life. As I was with Moses, so I will be with you; I will not fail you or forsake you. 6Be strong and courageous; for you shall put this people in possession of the land that I swore to their ancestors to give them. 7Only be strong and very courageous, being careful to act in accordance with all the law that my servant Moses commanded you; do not turn from it to the right hand or to the left, so that you may be successful wherever you go. 8This book of the law shall not depart out of your mouth; you shall meditate on it day and night, so that you may be careful to act in accordance with all that is written in it. For then you shall make your way prosperous, and then you shall be successful. 9I hereby command you: Be strong and courageous; do not be frightened or dismayed, for the LORD your God is with you wherever you go."

Preparations for the Invasion

10 Then Joshua commanded the officers of the people, 11"Pass through the camp, and command the people: 'Prepare your provisions; for in three days you are to cross over the Jordan, to go in to take possession of the land that the LORD your God gives you to possess.'"

12 To the Reubenites, the Gadites, and the half-tribe of Manasseh Joshua said, 13"Remember the word that Moses the servant of the LORD commanded you, saying, 'The LORD your God is providing you a place of rest, and will give you this land.' 14Your wives, your little ones, and your livestock shall remain in the land that Moses gave you beyond the Jordan. But all the warriors among you shall cross over armed before your kindred and shall help them, 15until the LORD gives rest to your kindred as well as to you, and they too take possession of the land that the LORD your God is giving them. Then you shall return to your own land and take possession of it, the land that Moses the servant of the LORD gave you beyond the Jordan to the east."

16 They answered Joshua: "All that you have commanded us we will do, and wherever you send us we will go. 17Just as we obeyed Moses in all things, so we will obey you. Only may the LORD your God be with you, as he was with Moses! 18Whoever rebels against your orders and disobeys your words, whatever you command, shall be put to death. Only be strong and courageous."

Spies Sent to Jericho

2 Then Joshua son of Nun sent two men secretly from Shittim as spies, saying, "Go, view the land, especially Jericho." So they went, and entered the house of a prostitute whose name was Rahab, and spent the night there. 2The king of Jericho was told, "Some Israelites have come here tonight to search out the land." 3Then the king of Jericho sent orders to Rahab, "Bring out the men who have come to you, who entered your house, for they have come only to search out the whole land." 4But the woman took the two men and hid them. Then she said, "True, the men came to me, but I did not know where they came from. 5And when it was time to close the gate at dark, the men went out. Where the men went I do not know. Pursue them quickly, for you can overtake them." 6She had, however, brought them up to the roof and hidden them with the stalks of flax that she had laid out on the roof. 7So the men pursued them on the way to the Jordan as far as the fords. As soon as the pursuers had gone out, the gate was shut.

8 Before they went to sleep, she came up to them on the roof ⁹and said to the men: "I know that the LORD has given you the land, and that dread of you has fallen on us, and that all the inhabitants of the land melt in fear before you. ¹⁰For we have heard how the LORD dried up the water of the Red Sea*ᵃ* before you when you came out of Egypt, and what you did to the two kings of the Amorites that were beyond the Jordan, to Sihon and Og, whom you utterly destroyed. ¹¹As soon as we heard it, our hearts melted, and there was no courage left in any of us because of you. The LORD your God is indeed God in heaven above and on earth below. ¹²Now then, since I have dealt kindly with you, swear to me by the LORD that you in turn will deal kindly with my family. Give me a sign of good faith ¹³that you will spare my father and mother, my brothers and sisters, and all who belong to them, and deliver our lives from death." ¹⁴The men said to her, "Our life for yours! If you do not tell this business of ours, then we will deal kindly and faithfully with you when the LORD gives us the land."

15 Then she let them down by a rope through the window, for her house was on the outer side of the city wall and she resided within the wall itself. ¹⁶She said to them, "Go toward the hill country, so that the pursuers may not come upon you. Hide yourselves there three days, until the pursuers have returned; then afterward you may go your way." ¹⁷The men said to her, "We will be released from this oath that you have made us swear to you ¹⁸if we invade the land and you do not tie this crimson cord in the window through which you let us down, and you do not gather into your house your father and mother, your brothers, and all your family. ¹⁹If any of you go out of the doors of your house into the street, they shall be responsible for their own death, and we shall be innocent; but if a hand is laid upon any who are with you in the house, we shall bear the

responsibility for their death. ²⁰But if you tell this business of ours, then we shall be released from this oath that you made us swear to you." ²¹She said, "According to your words, so be it." She sent them away and they departed. Then she tied the crimson cord in the window.

22 They departed and went into the hill country and stayed there three days, until the pursuers returned. The pursuers had searched all along the way and found nothing. ²³Then the two men came down again from the hill country. They crossed over, came to Joshua son of Nun, and told him all that had happened to them. ²⁴They said to Joshua, "Truly the LORD has given all the land into our hands; moreover all the inhabitants of the land melt in fear before us."

Israel Crosses the Jordan

3 Early in the morning Joshua rose and set out from Shittim with all the Israelites, and they came to the Jordan. They camped there before crossing over. ²At the end of three days the officers went through the camp ³and commanded the people, "When you see the ark of the covenant of the LORD your God being carried by the levitical priests, then you shall set out from your place. Follow it, ⁴so that you may know the way you should go, for you have not passed this way before. Yet there shall be a space between you and it, a distance of about two thousand cubits; do not come any nearer to it." ⁵Then Joshua said to the people, "Sanctify yourselves; for tomorrow the LORD will do wonders among you." ⁶To the priests Joshua said, "Take up the ark of the covenant, and pass on in front of the people." So they took up the ark of the covenant and went in front of the people.

7 The LORD said to Joshua, "This day I will begin to exalt you in the sight of all Israel, so that they may know that I will be with you as I was with Moses. ⁸You are the one who shall command the priests who bear the ark of the covenant, 'When you come to the edge of the waters of the Jordan, you shall stand still in the

a Or Sea of Reeds

Jordan.' " ⁹Joshua then said to the Israelites, "Draw near and hear the words of the LORD your God." ¹⁰Joshua said, "By this you shall know that among you is the living God who without fail will drive out from before you the Canaanites, Hittites, Hivites, Perizzites, Girgashites, Amorites, and Jebusites: ¹¹the ark of the covenant of the Lord of all the earth is going to pass before you into the Jordan. ¹²So now select twelve men from the tribes of Israel, one from each tribe. ¹³When the soles of the feet of the priests who bear the ark of the LORD, the Lord of all the earth, rest in the waters of the Jordan, the waters of the Jordan flowing from above shall be cut off; they shall stand in a single heap."

14 When the people set out from their tents to cross over the Jordan, the priests bearing the ark of the covenant were in front of the people. ¹⁵Now the Jordan overflows all its banks throughout the time of harvest. So when those who bore the ark had come to the Jordan, and the feet of the priests bearing the ark were dipped in the edge of the water, ¹⁶the waters flowing from above stood still, rising up in a single heap far off at Adam, the city that is beside Zarethan, while those flowing toward the sea of the Arabah, the Dead Sea,ᵃ were wholly cut off. Then the people crossed over opposite Jericho. ¹⁷While all Israel were crossing over on dry ground, the priests who bore the ark of the covenant of the LORD stood on dry ground in the middle of the Jordan, until the entire nation finished crossing over the Jordan.

Twelve Stones Set Up at Gilgal

4 When the entire nation had finished crossing over the Jordan, the LORD said to Joshua: ²"Select twelve men from the people, one from each tribe, ³and command them, 'Take twelve stones from here out of the middle of the Jordan, from the place where the priests' feet stood, carry them over with you, and lay them down in the place where you camp tonight.' " ⁴Then Joshua summoned the twelve

men from the Israelites, whom he had appointed, one from each tribe. ⁵Joshua said to them, "Pass on before the ark of the LORD your God into the middle of the Jordan, and each of you take up a stone on his shoulder, one for each of the tribes of the Israelites, ⁶so that this may be a sign among you. When your children ask in time to come, 'What do those stones mean to you?' ⁷then you shall tell them that the waters of the Jordan were cut off in front of the ark of the covenant of the LORD. When it crossed over the Jordan, the waters of the Jordan were cut off. So these stones shall be to the Israelites a memorial forever."

8 The Israelites did as Joshua commanded. They took up twelve stones out of the middle of the Jordan, according to the number of the tribes of the Israelites, as the LORD told Joshua, carried them over with them to the place where they camped, and laid them down there. ⁹(Joshua set up twelve stones in the middle of the Jordan, in the place where the feet of the priests bearing the ark of the covenant had stood; and they are there to this day.)

10 The priests who bore the ark remained standing in the middle of the Jordan, until everything was finished that the LORD commanded Joshua to tell the people, according to all that Moses had commanded Joshua. The people crossed over in haste. ¹¹As soon as all the people had finished crossing over, the ark of the LORD, and the priests, crossed over in front of the people. ¹²The Reubenites, the Gadites, and the half-tribe of Manasseh crossed over armed before the Israelites, as Moses had ordered them. ¹³About forty thousand armed for war crossed over before the LORD to the plains of Jericho for battle.

14 On that day the LORD exalted Joshua in the sight of all Israel; and they stood in awe of him, as they had stood in awe of Moses, all the days of his life.

15 The LORD said to Joshua, ¹⁶"Command the priests who bear the ark of the covenant,ᵇ to come up out of the Jordan." ¹⁷Joshua therefore commanded the priests, "Come up out of

---

a Heb *Salt Sea*　　*b* Or *treaty,* or *testimony;* Heb *eduth* the Jordan." ¹⁸When the priests bearing the ark of the covenant of the LORD came up from the middle of the Jordan, and the soles of the priests' feet touched dry ground, the waters of the Jordan returned to their place and overflowed all its banks, as before.

19 The people came up out of the Jordan on the tenth day of the first month, and they camped in Gilgal on the east border of Jericho. ²⁰Those twelve stones, which they had taken out of the Jordan, Joshua set up in Gilgal, ²¹saying to the Israelites, "When your children ask their parents in time to come, 'What do these stones mean?' ²²then you shall let your children know, 'Israel crossed over the Jordan here on dry ground.' ²³For the LORD your God dried up the waters of the Jordan for you until you crossed over, as the LORD your God did to the Red Sea,ᵃ which he dried up for us until we crossed over, ²⁴so that all the peoples of the earth may know that the hand of the LORD is mighty, and so that you may fear the LORD your God forever."

The New Generation Circumcised

5 When all the kings of the Amorites beyond the Jordan to the west, and all the kings of the Canaanites by the sea, heard that the LORD had dried up the waters of the Jordan for the Israelites until they had crossed over, their hearts melted, and there was no longer any spirit in them, because of the Israelites.

2 At that time the LORD said to Joshua, "Make flint knives and circumcise the Israelites a second time." ³So Joshua made flint knives, and circumcised the Israelites at Gibeath-haaraloth.ᵇ ⁴This is the reason why Joshua circumcised them: all the males of the people who came out of Egypt, all the warriors, had died during the journey through the wilderness after they had come out of Egypt. ⁵Although all the people who came out had been circumcised, yet all the people born on the journey through the wilderness after they had come out of Egypt had not been circumcised. ⁶For

the Israelites traveled forty years in the wilderness, until all the nation, the warriors who came out of Egypt, perished, not having listened to the voice of the LORD. To them the LORD swore that he would not let them see the land that he had sworn to their ancestors to give us, a land flowing with milk and honey. ⁷So it was their children, whom he raised up in their place, that Joshua circumcised; for they were uncircumcised, because they had not been circumcised on the way.

8 When the circumcising of all the nation was done, they remained in their places in the camp until they were healed. ⁹The LORD said to Joshua, "Today I have rolled away from you the disgrace of Egypt." And so that place is called Gilgalᶜ to this day.

The Passover at Gilgal

10 While the Israelites were camped in Gilgal they kept the passover in the evening on the fourteenth day of the month in the plains of Jericho. ¹¹On the day after the passover, on that very day, they ate the produce of the land, unleavened cakes and parched grain. ¹²The manna ceased on the day they ate the produce of the land, and the Israelites no longer had manna; they ate the crops of the land of Canaan that year.

Joshua's Vision

13 Once when Joshua was by Jericho, he looked up and saw a man standing before him with a drawn sword in his hand. Joshua went to him and said to him, "Are you one of us, or one of our adversaries?" ¹⁴He replied, "Neither; but as commander of the army of the LORD I have now come." And Joshua fell on his face to the earth and worshiped, and he said to him, "What do you command your servant, my lord?" ¹⁵The commander of the army of the LORD said to Joshua, "Remove the sandals from your feet, for the place where you stand is holy." And Joshua did so.

ᵃ Or *Sea of Reeds*   ᵇ That is *the Hill of the Foreskins*   ᶜ Related to Heb *galal* to roll

Jericho Taken and Destroyed

6 Now Jericho was shut up inside and out because of the Israelites; no one came out and no one went in. ²The LORD said to Joshua, "See, I have handed Jericho over to you, along with its king and soldiers. ³You shall march around the city, all the warriors circling the city once. Thus you shall do for six days, ⁴with seven priests bearing seven trumpets of rams' horns before the ark. On the seventh day you shall march around the city seven times, the priests blowing the trumpets. ⁵When they make a long blast with the ram's horn, as soon as you hear the sound of the trumpet, then all the people shall shout with a great shout; and the wall of the city will fall down flat, and all the people shall charge straight ahead." ⁶So Joshua son of Nun summoned the priests and said to them, "Take up the ark of the covenant, and have seven priests carry seven trumpets of rams' horns in front of the ark of the LORD." ⁷To the people he said, "Go forward and march around the city; have the armed men pass on before the ark of the LORD."

8 As Joshua had commanded the people, the seven priests carrying the seven trumpets of rams' horns before the LORD went forward, blowing the trumpets, with the ark of the covenant of the LORD following them. ⁹And the armed men went before the priests who blew the trumpets; the rear guard came after the ark, while the trumpets blew continually. ¹⁰To the people Joshua gave this command: "You shall not shout or let your voice be heard, nor shall you utter a word, until the day I tell you to shout. Then you shall shout." ¹¹So the ark of the LORD went around the city, circling it once; and they came into the camp, and spent the night in the camp.

12 Then Joshua rose early in the morning, and the priests took up the ark of the LORD. ¹³The seven priests carrying the seven trumpets of rams' horns before the ark of the LORD passed on, blowing the trumpets continually. The armed men went before them, and the rear guard came after the ark of the LORD, while the

trumpets blew continually. ¹⁴On the second day they marched around the city once and then returned to the camp. They did this for six days.

15 On the seventh day they rose early, at dawn, and marched around the city in the same manner seven times. It was only on that day that they marched around the city seven times. ¹⁶And at the seventh time, when the priests had blown the trumpets, Joshua said to the people, "Shout! For the LORD has given you the city. ¹⁷The city and all that is in it shall be devoted to the LORD for destruction. Only Rahab the prostitute and all who are with her in her house shall live because she hid the messengers we sent. ¹⁸As for you, keep away from the things devoted to destruction, so as not to covet*a* and take any of the devoted things and make the camp of Israel an object for destruction, bringing trouble upon it. ¹⁹But all silver and gold, and vessels of bronze and iron, are sacred to the LORD; they shall go into the treasury of the LORD." ²⁰So the people shouted, and the trumpets were blown. As soon as the people heard the sound of the trumpets, they raised a great shout, and the wall fell down flat; so the people charged straight ahead into the city and captured it. ²¹Then they devoted to destruction by the edge of the sword all in the city, both men and women, young and old, oxen, sheep, and donkeys.

22 Joshua said to the two men who had spied out the land, "Go into the prostitute's house, and bring the woman out of it and all who belong to her, as you swore to her." ²³So the young men who had been spies went in and brought Rahab out, along with her father, her mother, her brothers, and all who belonged to her—they brought all her kindred out—and set them outside the camp of Israel. ²⁴They burned down the city, and everything in it; only the silver and gold, and the vessels of bronze and iron, they put into the treasury of the house of the LORD. ²⁵But Rahab the prostitute, with her family and all who belonged to her, Joshua spared. Her family*b* has lived in Israel

---

a Gk: Heb *devote to destruction* Compare 7.21   *b* Heb *She* ever since. For she hid the messengers whom Joshua sent to spy out Jericho.

26 Joshua then pronounced this oath, saying,

"Cursed before the LORD be anyone
who tries
to build this city—this Jericho!
At the cost of his firstborn he shall lay
its foundation,
and at the cost of his youngest he
shall set up its gates!"

27 So the LORD was with Joshua; and his fame was in all the land.

The Sin of Achan and Its Punishment

7 But the Israelites broke faith in regard to the devoted things: Achan son of Carmi son of Zabdi son of Zerah, of the tribe of Judah, took some of the devoted things; and the anger of the LORD burned against the Israelites.

2 Joshua sent men from Jericho to Ai, which is near Beth-aven, east of Bethel, and said to them, "Go up and spy out the land." And the men went up and spied out Ai. 3Then they returned to Joshua and said to him, "Not all the people need go up; about two or three thousand men should go up and attack Ai. Since they are so few, do not make the whole people toil up there." 4So about three thousand of the people went up there; and they fled before the men of Ai. 5The men of Ai killed about thirty-six of them, chasing them from outside the gate as far as Shebarim and killing them on the slope. The hearts of the people melted and turned to water.

6 Then Joshua tore his clothes, and fell to the ground on his face before the ark of the LORD until the evening, he and the elders of Israel; and they put dust on their heads. 7Joshua said, "Ah, Lord GOD! Why have you brought this people across the Jordan at all, to hand us over to the Amorites so as to destroy us? Would that we had been content to settle beyond the Jordan! 8O Lord, what can I say, now that Israel has turned their backs to their enemies!

9The Canaanites and all the inhabitants of the land will hear of it, and surround us, and cut off our name from the earth. Then what will you do for your great name?"

10 The LORD said to Joshua, "Stand up! Why have you fallen upon your face? 11Israel has sinned; they have transgressed my covenant that I imposed on them. They have taken some of the devoted things; they have stolen, they have acted deceitfully, and they have put them among their own belongings. 12Therefore the Israelites are unable to stand before their enemies; they turn their backs to their enemies, because they have become a thing devoted for destruction themselves. I will be with you no more, unless you destroy the devoted things from among you. 13Proceed to sanctify the people, and say, 'Sanctify yourselves for tomorrow; for thus says the LORD, the God of Israel, "There are devoted things among you, O Israel; you will be unable to stand before your enemies until you take away the devoted things from among you." 14In the morning therefore you shall come forward tribe by tribe. The tribe that the LORD takes shall come near by clans, the clan that the LORD takes shall come near by households, and the household that the LORD takes shall come near one by one. 15And the one who is taken as having the devoted things shall be burned with fire, together with all that he has, for having transgressed the covenant of the LORD, and for having done an outrageous thing in Israel.'"

16 So Joshua rose early in the morning, and brought Israel near tribe by tribe, and the tribe of Judah was taken. 17He brought near the clans of Judah, and the clan of the Zerahites was taken; and he brought near the clan of the Zerahites, family by family,*a* and Zabdi was taken. 18And he brought near his household one by one, and Achan son of Carmi son of Zabdi son of Zerah, of the tribe of Judah, was taken. 19Then Joshua said to Achan, "My son, give glory to the LORD God of Israel and make confession to him. Tell me now what

---

a Mss Syr: MT *man by man*

you have done; do not hide it from me." ²⁰And Achan answered Joshua, "It is true; I am the one who sinned against the LORD God of Israel. This is what I did: ²¹when I saw among the spoil a beautiful mantle from Shinar, and two hundred shekels of silver, and a bar of gold weighing fifty shekels, then I coveted them and took them. They now lie hidden in the ground inside my tent, with the silver underneath."

22 So Joshua sent messengers, and they ran to the tent; and there it was, hidden in his tent with the silver underneath. ²³They took them out of the tent and brought them to Joshua and all the Israelites; and they spread them out before the LORD. ²⁴Then Joshua and all Israel with him took Achan son of Zerah, with the silver, the mantle, and the bar of gold, with his sons and daughters, with his oxen, donkeys, and sheep, and his tent and all that he had; and they brought them up to the Valley of Achor. ²⁵Joshua said, "Why did you bring trouble on us? The LORD is bringing trouble on you today." And all Israel stoned him to death; they burned them with fire, cast stones on them, ²⁶and raised over him a great heap of stones that remains to this day. Then the LORD turned from his burning anger. Therefore that place to this day is called the Valley of Achor. ^a

Ai Captured by a Stratagem and Destroyed

8 Then the LORD said to Joshua, "Do not fear or be dismayed; take all the fighting men with you, and go up now to Ai. See, I have handed over to you the king of Ai with his people, his city, and his land. ²You shall do to Ai and its king as you did to Jericho and its king; only its spoil and its livestock you may take as booty for yourselves. Set an ambush against the city, behind it."

3 So Joshua and all the fighting men set out to go up against Ai. Joshua chose thirty thousand warriors and sent them out by night ⁴with the command, "You shall lie in ambush against the city, behind it; do not go very far from the city, but all of you stay alert. ⁵I and all

the people who are with me will approach the city. When they come out against us, as before, we shall flee from them. ⁶They will come out after us until we have drawn them away from the city; for they will say, 'They are fleeing from us, as before.' While we flee from them, ⁷you shall rise up from the ambush and seize the city; for the LORD your God will give it into your hand. ⁸And when you have taken the city, you shall set the city on fire, doing as the LORD has ordered; see, I have commanded you." ⁹So Joshua sent them out; and they went to the place of ambush, and lay between Bethel and Ai, to the west of Ai; but Joshua spent that night in the camp. ^b

10 In the morning Joshua rose early and mustered the people, and went up, with the elders of Israel, before the people to Ai. ¹¹All the fighting men who were with him went up, and drew near before the city, and camped on the north side of Ai, with a ravine between them and Ai. ¹²Taking about five thousand men, he set them in ambush between Bethel and Ai, to the west of the city. ¹³So they stationed the forces, the main encampment that was north of the city and its rear guard west of the city. But Joshua spent that night in the valley. ¹⁴When the king of Ai saw this, he and all his people, the inhabitants of the city, hurried out early in the morning to the meeting place facing the Arabah to meet Israel in battle; but he did not know that there was an ambush against him behind the city. ¹⁵And Joshua and all Israel made a pretense of being beaten before them, and fled in the direction of the wilderness. ¹⁶So all the people who were in the city were called together to pursue them, and as they pursued Joshua they were drawn away from the city. ¹⁷There was not a man left in Ai or Bethel who did not go out after Israel; they left the city open, and pursued Israel.

18 Then the LORD said to Joshua, "Stretch out the sword that is in your hand toward Ai; for I will give it into your hand." And Joshua stretched out the sword that was in his hand toward the city. ¹⁹As soon as he stretched out his

---

a That is *Trouble*   *b* Heb *among the people*

hand, the troops in ambush rose quickly out of their place and rushed forward. They entered the city, took it, and at once set the city on fire. ²⁰So when the men of Ai looked back, the smoke of the city was rising to the sky. They had no power to flee this way or that, for the people who fled to the wilderness turned back against the pursuers. ²¹When Joshua and all Israel saw that the ambush had taken the city and that the smoke of the city was rising, then they turned back and struck down the men of Ai. ²²And the others came out from the city against them; so they were surrounded by Israelites, some on one side, and some on the other; and Israel struck them down until no one was left who survived or escaped. ²³But the king of Ai was taken alive and brought to Joshua.

24 When Israel had finished slaughtering all the inhabitants of Ai in the open wilderness where they pursued them, and when all of them to the very last had fallen by the edge of the sword, all Israel returned to Ai, and attacked it with the edge of the sword. ²⁵The total of those who fell that day, both men and women, was twelve thousand—all the people of Ai. ²⁶For Joshua did not draw back his hand, with which he stretched out the sword, until he had utterly destroyed all the inhabitants of Ai. ²⁷Only the livestock and the spoil of that city Israel took as their booty, according to the word of the LORD that he had issued to Joshua. ²⁸So Joshua burned Ai, and made it forever a heap of ruins, as it is to this day. ²⁹And he hanged the king of Ai on a tree until evening; and at sunset Joshua commanded, and they took his body down from the tree, threw it down at the entrance of the gate of the city, and raised over it a great heap of stones, which stands there to this day.

Joshua Renews the Covenant

30 Then Joshua built on Mount Ebal an altar to the LORD, the God of Israel, ³¹just as Moses the servant of the LORD had commanded the Israelites, as it is written in the book of the law of Moses, "an altar of unhewn *ᵃ* stones, on which no iron tool has been used"; and they offered on it burnt offerings to the LORD, and sacrificed offerings of well-being. ³²And there, in the presence of the Israelites, Joshua *ᵇ* wrote on the stones a copy of the law of Moses, which he had written. ³³All Israel, alien as well as citizen, with their elders and officers and their judges, stood on opposite sides of the ark in front of the levitical priests who carried the ark of the covenant of the LORD, half of them in front of Mount Gerizim and half of them in front of Mount Ebal, as Moses the servant of the LORD had commanded at the first, that they should bless the people of Israel. ³⁴And afterward he read all the words of the law, blessings and curses, according to all that is written in the book of the law. ³⁵There was not a word of all that Moses commanded that Joshua did not read before all the assembly of Israel, and the women, and the little ones, and the aliens who resided among them.

The Gibeonites Save Themselves by Trickery

9 Now when all the kings who were beyond the Jordan in the hill country and in the lowland all along the coast of the Great Sea toward Lebanon—the Hittites, the Amorites, the Canaanites, the Perizzites, the Hivites, and the Jebusites—heard of this, ²they gathered together with one accord to fight Joshua and Israel.

3 But when the inhabitants of Gibeon heard what Joshua had done to Jericho and to Ai, ⁴they on their part acted with cunning: they went and prepared provisions, *ᶜ* and took worn-out sacks for their donkeys, and wineskins, worn-out and torn and mended, ⁵with worn-out, patched sandals on their feet, and worn-out clothes; and all their provisions were dry and moldy. ⁶They went to Joshua in the camp at Gilgal, and said to him and to the Israelites, "We have come from a far country; so now make a treaty with us." ⁷But the Israelites said to the Hivites, "Perhaps you live among us;

a Heb *whole*   *b* Heb *he*   *c* Cn: Meaning of Heb uncertain then how can we make a treaty with you?" [8]They said to Joshua, "We are your servants." And Joshua said to them, "Who are you? And where do you come from?" [9]They said to him, "Your servants have come from a very far country, because of the name of the LORD your God; for we have heard a report of him, of all that he did in Egypt, [10]and of all that he did to the two kings of the Amorites who were beyond the Jordan, King Sihon of Heshbon, and King Og of Bashan who lived in Ashtaroth. [11]So our elders and all the inhabitants of our country said to us, 'Take provisions in your hand for the journey; go to meet them, and say to them, "We are your servants; come now, make a treaty with us." ' [12]Here is our bread; it was still warm when we took it from our houses as our food for the journey, on the day we set out to come to you, but now, see, it is dry and moldy; [13]these wineskins were new when we filled them, and see, they are burst; and these garments and sandals of ours are worn out from the very long journey." [14]So the leaders[a] partook of their provisions, and did not ask direction from the LORD. [15]And Joshua made peace with them, guaranteeing their lives by a treaty; and the leaders of the congregation swore an oath to them.

16 But when three days had passed after they had made a treaty with them, they heard that they were their neighbors and were living among them. [17]So the Israelites set out and reached their cities on the third day. Now their cities were Gibeon, Chephirah, Beeroth, and Kiriath-jearim. [18]But the Israelites did not attack them, because the leaders of the congregation had sworn to them by the LORD, the God of Israel. Then all the congregation murmured against the leaders. [19]But all the leaders said to all the congregation, "We have sworn to them by the LORD, the God of Israel, and now we must not touch them. [20]This is what we will do to them: We will let them live, so that wrath may not come upon us, because of the oath that we swore to them." [21]The leaders said to them, "Let them live." So they became hewers of wood and drawers of water for all the congregation, as the leaders had decided concerning them.

22 Joshua summoned them, and said to them, "Why did you deceive us, saying, 'We are very far from you,' while in fact you are living among us? [23]Now therefore you are cursed, and some of you shall always be slaves, hewers of wood and drawers of water for the house of my God." [24]They answered Joshua, "Because it was told to your servants for a certainty that the LORD your God had commanded his servant Moses to give you all the land, and to destroy all the inhabitants of the land before you; so we were in great fear for our lives because of you, and did this thing. [25]And now we are in your hand: do as it seems good and right in your sight to do to us." [26]This is what he did for them: he saved them from the Israelites; and they did not kill them. [27]But on that day Joshua made them hewers of wood and drawers of water for the congregation and for the altar of the LORD, to continue to this day, in the place that he should choose.

The Sun Stands Still

10 When King Adoni-zedek of Jerusalem heard how Joshua had taken Ai, and had utterly destroyed it, doing to Ai and its king as he had done to Jericho and its king, and how the inhabitants of Gibeon had made peace with Israel and were among them, [2]he[b] became greatly frightened, because Gibeon was a large city, like one of the royal cities, and was larger than Ai, and all its men were warriors. [3]So King Adoni-zedek of Jerusalem sent a message to King Hoham of Hebron, to King Piram of Jarmuth, to King Japhia of Lachish, and to King Debir of Eglon, saying, [4]"Come up and help me, and let us attack Gibeon; for it has made peace with Joshua and with the Israelites." [5]Then the five kings of the Amorites— the king of Jerusalem, the king of Hebron, the king of Jarmuth, the king of Lachish, and the king of Eglon—gathered their forces, and

[a] Gk: Heb men   [b] Heb they

went up with all their armies and camped against Gibeon, and made war against it.

6 And the Gibeonites sent to Joshua at the camp in Gilgal, saying, "Do not abandon your servants; come up to us quickly, and save us, and help us; for all the kings of the Amorites who live in the hill country are gathered against us." 7So Joshua went up from Gilgal, he and all the fighting force with him, all the mighty warriors. 8The LORD said to Joshua, "Do not fear them, for I have handed them over to you; not one of them shall stand before you." 9So Joshua came upon them suddenly, having marched up all night from Gilgal. 10And the LORD threw them into a panic before Israel, who inflicted a great slaughter on them at Gibeon, chased them by the way of the ascent of Beth-horon, and struck them down as far as Azekah and Makkedah. 11As they fled before Israel, while they were going down the slope of Beth-horon, the LORD threw down huge stones from heaven on them as far as Azekah, and they died; there were more who died because of the hailstones than the Israelites killed with the sword.

12 On the day when the LORD gave the Amorites over to the Israelites, Joshua spoke to the LORD; and he said in the sight of Israel,

"Sun, stand still at Gibeon,
   and Moon, in the valley of Aijalon."
13 And the sun stood still, and the moon
     stopped,
   until the nation took vengeance on
     their enemies.

Is this not written in the Book of Jashar? The sun stopped in midheaven, and did not hurry to set for about a whole day. 14There has been no day like it before or since, when the LORD heeded a human voice; for the LORD fought for Israel.

15 Then Joshua returned, and all Israel with him, to the camp at Gilgal.

Five Kings Defeated

16 Meanwhile, these five kings fled and hid themselves in the cave at Makkedah. 17And it was told Joshua, "The five kings have been found, hidden in the cave at Makkedah." 18Joshua said, "Roll large stones against the mouth of the cave, and set men by it to guard them; 19but do not stay there yourselves; pursue your enemies, and attack them from the rear. Do not let them enter their towns, for the LORD your God has given them into your hand." 20When Joshua and the Israelites had finished inflicting a very great slaughter on them, until they were wiped out, and when the survivors had entered into the fortified towns, 21all the people returned safe to Joshua in the camp at Makkedah; no one dared to speak*a* against any of the Israelites.

22 Then Joshua said, "Open the mouth of the cave, and bring those five kings out to me from the cave." 23They did so, and brought the five kings out to him from the cave, the king of Jerusalem, the king of Hebron, the king of Jarmuth, the king of Lachish, and the king of Eglon. 24When they brought the kings out to Joshua, Joshua summoned all the Israelites, and said to the chiefs of the warriors who had gone with him, "Come near, put your feet on the necks of these kings." Then they came near and put their feet on their necks. 25And Joshua said to them, "Do not be afraid or dismayed; be strong and courageous; for thus the LORD will do to all the enemies against whom you fight." 26Afterward Joshua struck them down and put them to death, and he hung them on five trees. And they hung on the trees until evening. 27At sunset Joshua commanded, and they took them down from the trees and threw them into the cave where they had hidden themselves; they set large stones against the mouth of the cave, which remain to this very day.

28 Joshua took Makkedah on that day, and struck it and its king with the edge of the sword; he utterly destroyed every person in it; he left no one remaining. And he did to the king of Makkedah as he had done to the king of Jericho.

29 Then Joshua passed on from Makkedah, and all Israel with him, to Libnah, and

a Heb *moved his tongue*

fought against Libnah. [30]The LORD gave it also and its king into the hand of Israel; and he struck it with the edge of the sword, and every person in it; he left no one remaining in it; and he did to its king as he had done to the king of Jericho.

31 Next Joshua passed on from Libnah, and all Israel with him, to Lachish, and laid siege to it, and assaulted it. [32]The LORD gave Lachish into the hand of Israel, and he took it on the second day, and struck it with the edge of the sword, and every person in it, as he had done to Libnah.

33 Then King Horam of Gezer came up to help Lachish; and Joshua struck him and his people, leaving him no survivors.

34 From Lachish Joshua passed on with all Israel to Eglon; and they laid siege to it, and assaulted it; [35]and they took it that day, and struck it with the edge of the sword; and every person in it he utterly destroyed that day, as he had done to Lachish.

36 Then Joshua went up with all Israel from Eglon to Hebron; they assaulted it, [37]and took it, and struck it with the edge of the sword, and its king and its towns, and every person in it; he left no one remaining, just as he had done to Eglon, and utterly destroyed it with every person in it.

38 Then Joshua, with all Israel, turned back to Debir and assaulted it, [39]and he took it with its king and all its towns; they struck them with the edge of the sword, and utterly destroyed every person in it; he left no one remaining; just as he had done to Hebron, and, as he had done to Libnah and its king, so he did to Debir and its king.

40 So Joshua defeated the whole land, the hill country and the Negeb and the lowland and the slopes, and all their kings; he left no one remaining, but utterly destroyed all that breathed, as the LORD God of Israel commanded. [41]And Joshua defeated them from Kadesh-barnea to Gaza, and all the country of Goshen, as far as Gibeon. [42]Joshua took all these kings and their land at one time, because the LORD God of Israel fought for Israel. [43]Then Joshua returned, and all Israel with him, to the camp at Gilgal.

The United Kings of Northern Canaan Defeated

11 When King Jabin of Hazor heard of this, he sent to King Jobab of Madon, to the king of Shimron, to the king of Achshaph, [2]and to the kings who were in the northern hill country, and in the Arabah south of Chinneroth, and in the lowland, and in Naphoth-dor on the west, [3]to the Canaanites in the east and the west, the Amorites, the Hittites, the Perizzites, and the Jebusites in the hill country, and the Hivites under Hermon in the land of Mizpah. [4]They came out, with all their troops, a great army, in number like the sand on the seashore, with very many horses and chariots. [5]All these kings joined their forces, and came and camped together at the waters of Merom, to fight with Israel.

6 And the LORD said to Joshua, "Do not be afraid of them, for tomorrow at this time I will hand over all of them, slain, to Israel; you shall hamstring their horses, and burn their chariots with fire." [7]So Joshua came suddenly upon them with all his fighting force, by the waters of Merom, and fell upon them. [8]And the LORD handed them over to Israel, who attacked them and chased them as far as Great Sidon and Misrephoth-maim, and eastward as far as the valley of Mizpeh. They struck them down, until they had left no one remaining. [9]And Joshua did to them as the LORD commanded him; he hamstrung their horses, and burned their chariots with fire.

10 Joshua turned back at that time, and took Hazor, and struck its king down with the sword. Before that time Hazor was the head of all those kingdoms. [11]And they put to the sword all who were in it, utterly destroying them; there was no one left who breathed, and he burned Hazor with fire. [12]And all the towns of those kings, and all their kings, Joshua took, and struck them with the edge of the sword, utterly destroying them, as Moses the servant of the LORD had commanded. [13]But Israel burned none of the towns that stood on mounds except Hazor, which Joshua did burn. [14]All the spoil of these towns, and the livestock, the Israelites took for their booty; but all the people

they struck down with the edge of the sword, until they had destroyed them, and they did not leave any who breathed. 15As the LORD had commanded his servant Moses, so Moses commanded Joshua, and so Joshua did; he left nothing undone of all that the LORD had commanded Moses.

Summary of Joshua's Conquests

16 So Joshua took all that land: the hill country and all the Negeb and all the land of Goshen and the lowland and the Arabah and the hill country of Israel and its lowland, 17from Mount Halak, which rises toward Seir, as far as Baal-gad in the valley of Lebanon below Mount Hermon. He took all their kings, struck them down, and put them to death. 18Joshua made war a long time with all those kings. 19There was not a town that made peace with the Israelites, except the Hivites, the inhabitants of Gibeon; all were taken in battle. 20For it was the LORD's doing to harden their hearts so that they would come against Israel in battle, in order that they might be utterly destroyed, and might receive no mercy, but be exterminated, just as the LORD had commanded Moses.

21 At that time Joshua came and wiped out the Anakim from the hill country, from Hebron, from Debir, from Anab, and from all the hill country of Judah, and from all the hill country of Israel; Joshua utterly destroyed them with their towns. 22None of the Anakim was left in the land of the Israelites; some remained only in Gaza, in Gath, and in Ashdod. 23So Joshua took the whole land, according to all that the LORD had spoken to Moses; and Joshua gave it for an inheritance to Israel according to their tribal allotments. And the land had rest from war.

The Kings Conquered by Moses

12 Now these are the kings of the land, whom the Israelites defeated, whose land they occupied beyond the Jordan toward the east, from the Wadi Arnon to Mount Hermon, with all the Arabah eastward: 2King Sihon of the Amorites who lived at Heshbon, and ruled from Aroer, which is on the edge of the Wadi Arnon, and from the middle of the valley as far as the river Jabbok, the boundary of the Ammonites, that is, half of Gilead, 3and the Arabah to the Sea of Chinneroth eastward, and in the direction of Beth-jeshimoth, to the sea of the Arabah, the Dead Sea,*a* southward to the foot of the slopes of Pisgah; 4and King Og*b* of Bashan, one of the last of the Rephaim, who lived at Ashtaroth and at Edrei 5and ruled over Mount Hermon and Salecah and all Bashan to the boundary of the Geshurites and the Maacathites, and over half of Gilead to the boundary of King Sihon of Heshbon. 6Moses, the servant of the LORD, and the Israelites defeated them; and Moses the servant of the LORD gave their land for a possession to the Reubenites and the Gadites and the half-tribe of Manasseh.

The Kings Conquered by Joshua

7 The following are the kings of the land whom Joshua and the Israelites defeated on the west side of the Jordan, from Baal-gad in the valley of Lebanon to Mount Halak, that rises toward Seir (and Joshua gave their land to the tribes of Israel as a possession according to their allotments, 8in the hill country, in the lowland, in the Arabah, in the slopes, in the wilderness, and in the Negeb, the land of the Hittites, Amorites, Canaanites, Perizzites, Hivites, and Jebusites):

9	the king of Jericho	one
	the king of Ai, which is next to Bethel	one
10	the king of Jerusalem	one
	the king of Hebron	one
11	the king of Jarmuth	one
	the king of Lachish	one
12	the king of Eglon	one
	the king of Gezer	one
13	the king of Debir	one
	the king of Geder	one
14	the king of Hormah	one
	the king of Arad	one

---

a Heb *Salt Sea*   *b* Gk: Heb *the boundary of King Og*

15 the king of Libnah	one
the king of Adullam	one
16 the king of Makkedah	one
the king of Bethel	one
17 the king of Tappuah	one
the king of Hepher	one
18 the king of Aphek	one
the king of Lasharon	one
19 the king of Madon	one
the king of Hazor	one
20 the king of Shimron-meron	one
the king of Achshaph	one
21 the king of Taanach	one
the king of Megiddo	one
22 the king of Kedesh	one
the king of Jokneam in Carmel	one
23 the king of Dor in Naphath-dor	one
the king of Goiim in Galilee,a	one
24 the king of Tirzah	one

thirty-one kings in all.

The Parts of Canaan Still Unconquered

13 Now Joshua was old and advanced in years; and the LORD said to him, "You are old and advanced in years, and very much of the land still remains to be possessed. 2This is the land that still remains: all the regions of the Philistines, and all those of the Geshurites 3(from the Shihor, which is east of Egypt, northward to the boundary of Ekron, it is reckoned as Canaanite; there are five rulers of the Philistines, those of Gaza, Ashdod, Ashkelon, Gath, and Ekron), and those of the Avvim 4in the south; all the land of the Canaanites, and Mearah that belongs to the Sidonians, to Aphek, to the boundary of the Amorites, 5and the land of the Gebalites, and all Lebanon, toward the east, from Baal-gad below Mount Hermon to Lebo-hamath, 6all the inhabitants of the hill country from Lebanon to Misrephoth-maim, even all the Sidonians. I will myself drive them out from before the Israelites; only allot the land to Israel for an inheritance, as I have commanded you. 7Now therefore divide this land for an inheritance to the nine tribes and the half-tribe of Manasseh."

The Territory East of the Jordan

8 With the other half-tribe of Manassehb the Reubenites and the Gadites received their inheritance, which Moses gave them, beyond the Jordan eastward, as Moses the servant of the LORD gave them: 9from Aroer, which is on the edge of the Wadi Arnon, and the town that is in the middle of the valley, and all the tableland fromc Medeba as far as Dibon; 10and all the cities of King Sihon of the Amorites, who reigned in Heshbon, as far as the boundary of the Ammonites; 11and Gilead, and the region of the Geshurites and Maacathites, and all Mount Hermon, and all Bashan to Salecah; 12all the kingdom of Og in Bashan, who reigned in Ashtaroth and in Edrei (he alone was left of the survivors of the Rephaim); these Moses had defeated and driven out. 13Yet the Israelites did not drive out the Geshurites or the Maacathites; but Geshur and Maacath live within Israel to this day.

14 To the tribe of Levi alone Moses gave no inheritance; the offerings by fire to the LORD God of Israel are their inheritance, as he said to them.

The Territory of Reuben

15 Moses gave an inheritance to the tribe of the Reubenites according to their clans. 16Their territory was from Aroer, which is on the edge of the Wadi Arnon, and the town that is in the middle of the valley, and all the tableland by Medeba; 17with Heshbon, and all its towns that are in the tableland; Dibon, and Bamoth-baal, and Beth-baal-meon, 18and Jahaz, and Kedemoth, and Mephaath, 19and Kiriathaim, and Sibmah, and Zereth-shahar on the hill of the valley, 20and Beth-peor, and the slopes of Pisgah, and Beth-jeshimoth, 21that is, all the towns of the tableland, and all the kingdom of King Sihon of the Amorites, who reigned in Heshbon, whom Moses defeated with the leaders of Midian, Evi and Rekem and Zur and Hur and Reba, as princes of Sihon, who lived in the land. 22Along with the rest of those they put to death, the Israelites also put to the sword

a Gk: Heb Gilgal　　b Cn: Heb With it　　c Compare Gk: Heb lacks from

Balaam son of Beor, who practiced divination. 23And the border of the Reubenites was the Jordan and its banks. This was the inheritance of the Reubenites according to their families with their towns and villages.

The Territory of Gad

24 Moses gave an inheritance also to the tribe of the Gadites, according to their families. 25Their territory was Jazer, and all the towns of Gilead, and half the land of the Ammonites, to Aroer, which is east of Rabbah, 26and from Heshbon to Ramath-mizpeh and Betonim, and from Mahanaim to the territory of Debir,*a* 27and in the valley Beth-haram, Beth-nimrah, Succoth, and Zaphon, the rest of the kingdom of King Sihon of Heshbon, the Jordan and its banks, as far as the lower end of the Sea of Chinnereth, eastward beyond the Jordan. 28This is the inheritance of the Gadites according to their clans, with their towns and villages.

The Territory of the Half-Tribe of Manasseh (East)

29 Moses gave an inheritance to the half-tribe of Manasseh; it was allotted to the half-tribe of the Manassites according to their families. 30Their territory extended from Mahanaim, through all Bashan, the whole kingdom of King Og of Bashan, and all the settlements of Jair, which are in Bashan, sixty towns, 31and half of Gilead, and Ashtaroth, and Edrei, the towns of the kingdom of Og in Bashan; these were allotted to the people of Machir son of Manasseh according to their clans—for half the Machirites.

32 These are the inheritances that Moses distributed in the plains of Moab, beyond the Jordan east of Jericho. 33But to the tribe of Levi Moses gave no inheritance; the LORD God of Israel is their inheritance, as he said to them.

The Distribution of Territory West of the Jordan

14 These are the inheritances that the Israelites received in the land of Canaan, which the priest Eleazar, and Joshua son of Nun, and the heads of the families of the tribes of the Israelites distributed to them. 2Their inheritance was by lot, as the LORD had commanded Moses for the nine and one-half tribes. 3For Moses had given an inheritance to the two and one-half tribes beyond the Jordan; but to the Levites he gave no inheritance among them. 4For the people of Joseph were two tribes, Manasseh and Ephraim; and no portion was given to the Levites in the land, but only towns to live in, with their pasture lands for their flocks and herds. 5The Israelites did as the LORD commanded Moses; they allotted the land.

Hebron Allotted to Caleb

6 Then the people of Judah came to Joshua at Gilgal; and Caleb son of Jephunneh the Kenizzite said to him, "You know what the LORD said to Moses the man of God in Kadesh-barnea concerning you and me. 7I was forty years old when Moses the servant of the LORD sent me from Kadesh-barnea to spy out the land; and I brought him an honest report. 8But my companions who went up with me made the heart of the people melt; yet I wholeheartedly followed the LORD my God. 9And Moses swore on that day, saying, 'Surely the land on which your foot has trodden shall be an inheritance for you and your children forever, because you have wholeheartedly followed the LORD my God.' 10And now, as you see, the LORD has kept me alive, as he said, these forty-five years since the time that the LORD spoke this word to Moses, while Israel was journeying through the wilderness; and here I am today, eighty-five years old. 11I am still as strong today as I was on the day that Moses sent me; my strength now is as my strength was then, for war, and for going and coming. 12So now give me this hill country of which the

a Gk Syr Vg: Heb *Lidebir*

LORD spoke on that day; for you heard on that day how the Anakim were there, with great fortified cities; it may be that the LORD will be with me, and I shall drive them out, as the LORD said."

13 Then Joshua blessed him, and gave Hebron to Caleb son of Jephunneh for an inheritance. ¹⁴So Hebron became the inheritance of Caleb son of Jephunneh the Kenizzite to this day, because he wholeheartedly followed the LORD, the God of Israel. ¹⁵Now the name of Hebron formerly was Kiriath-arba;ᵃ this Arba wasᵇ the greatest man among the Anakim. And the land had rest from war.

The Territory of Judah

15 The lot for the tribe of the people of Judah according to their families reached southward to the boundary of Edom, to the wilderness of Zin at the farthest south. ²And their south boundary ran from the end of the Dead Sea,ᶜ from the bay that faces southward; ³it goes out southward of the ascent of Akrabbim, passes along to Zin, and goes up south of Kadesh-barnea, along by Hezron, up to Addar, makes a turn to Karka, ⁴passes along to Azmon, goes out by the Wadi of Egypt, and comes to its end at the sea. This shall be your south boundary. ⁵And the east boundary is the Dead Sea,ᶜ to the mouth of the Jordan. And the boundary on the north side runs from the bay of the sea at the mouth of the Jordan; ⁶and the boundary goes up to Beth-hoglah, and passes along north of Beth-arabah; and the boundary goes up to the Stone of Bohan, Reuben's son; ⁷and the boundary goes up to Debir from the Valley of Achor, and so northward, turning toward Gilgal, which is opposite the ascent of Adummim, which is on the south side of the valley; and the boundary passes along to the waters of En-shemesh, and ends at En-rogel; ⁸then the boundary goes up by the valley of the son of Hinnom at the southern slope of the Jebusites (that is, Jerusalem); and the boundary goes up to the top of the mountain that lies over against the valley of Hinnom, on the west,

at the northern end of the valley of Rephaim; ⁹then the boundary extends from the top of the mountain to the spring of the Waters of Nephtoah, and from there to the towns of Mount Ephron; then the boundary bends around to Baalah (that is, Kiriath-jearim); ¹⁰and the boundary circles west of Baalah to Mount Seir, passes along to the northern slope of Mount Jearim (that is, Chesalon), and goes down to Beth-shemesh, and passes along by Timnah; ¹¹the boundary goes out to the slope of the hill north of Ekron, then the boundary bends around to Shikkeron, and passes along to Mount Baalah, and goes out to Jabneel; then the boundary comes to an end at the sea. ¹²And the west boundary was the Mediterranean with its coast. This is the boundary surrounding the people of Judah according to their families.

Caleb Occupies His Portion

13 According to the commandment of the LORD to Joshua, he gave to Caleb son of Jephunneh a portion among the people of Judah, Kiriath-arba,ᵃ that is, Hebron (Arba was the father of Anak). ¹⁴And Caleb drove out from there the three sons of Anak: Sheshai, Ahiman, and Talmai, the descendants of Anak. ¹⁵From there he went up against the inhabitants of Debir; now the name of Debir formerly was Kiriath-sepher. ¹⁶And Caleb said, "Whoever attacks Kiriath-sepher and takes it, to him I will give my daughter Achsah as wife." ¹⁷Othniel son of Kenaz, the brother of Caleb, took it; and he gave him his daughter Achsah as wife. ¹⁸When she came to him, she urged him to ask her father for a field. As she dismounted from her donkey, Caleb said to her, "What do you wish?" ¹⁹She said to him, "Give me a present; since you have set me in the land of the Negeb, give me springs of water as well." So Caleb gave her the upper springs and the lower springs.

The Towns of Judah

20 This is the inheritance of the tribe of the people of Judah according to their families. ²¹The towns belonging to the tribe of the peo-

---

ᵃ That is *the city of Arba*   ᵇ Heb lacks *this Arba was*   ᶜ Heb *Salt Sea* ple of Judah in the extreme south, toward the boundary of Edom, were Kabzeel, Eder, Jagur, 22Kinah, Dimonah, Adadah, 23Kedesh, Hazor, Ithnan, 24Ziph, Telem, Bealoth, 25Hazor-hadattah, Kerioth-hezron (that is, Hazor), 26Amam, Shema, Moladah, 27Hazar-gaddah, Heshmon, Beth-pelet, 28Hazar-shual, Beer-sheba, Biziothiah, 29Baalah, Iim, Ezem, 30Eltolad, Chesil, Hormah, 31Ziklag, Madmannah, Sansannah, 32Lebaoth, Shilhim, Ain, and Rimmon: in all, twenty-nine towns, with their villages.

33 And in the lowland, Eshtaol, Zorah, Ashnah, 34Zanoah, En-gannim, Tappuah, Enam, 35Jarmuth, Adullam, Socoh, Azekah, 36Shaaraim, Adithaim, Gederah, Gederothaim: fourteen towns with their villages.

37 Zenan, Hadashah, Migdal-gad, 38Dilan, Mizpeh, Jokthe-el, 39Lachish, Bozkath, Eglon, 40Cabbon, Lahmam, Chitlish, 41Gederoth, Beth-dagon, Naamah, and Makkedah: sixteen towns with their villages.

42 Libnah, Ether, Ashan, 43Iphtah, Ashnah, Nezib, 44Keilah, Achzib, and Mareshah: nine towns with their villages.

45 Ekron, with its dependencies and its villages; 46from Ekron to the sea, all that were near Ashdod, with their villages.

47 Ashdod, its towns and its villages; Gaza, its towns and its villages; to the Wadi of Egypt, and the Great Sea with its coast.

48 And in the hill country, Shamir, Jattir, Socoh, 49Dannah, Kiriath-sannah (that is, Debir), 50Anab, Eshtemoh, Anim, 51Goshen, Holon, and Giloh: eleven towns with their villages.

52 Arab, Dumah, Eshan, 53Janim, Bethtappuah, Aphekah, 54Humtah, Kiriath-arba (that is, Hebron), and Zior: nine towns with their villages.

55 Maon, Carmel, Ziph, Juttah, 56Jezreel, Jokdeam, Zanoah, 57Kain, Gibeah, and Timnah: ten towns with their villages.

58 Halhul, Beth-zur, Gedor, 59Maarath, Beth-anoth, and Eltekon: six towns with their villages.

60 Kiriath-baal (that is, Kiriath-jearim) and Rabbah: two towns with their villages.

61 In the wilderness, Beth-arabah, Middin, Secacah, 62Nibshan, the City of Salt, and Engedi: six towns with their villages.

63 But the people of Judah could not drive out the Jebusites, the inhabitants of Jerusalem; so the Jebusites live with the people of Judah in Jerusalem to this day.

The Territory of Ephraim

16 The allotment of the Josephites went from the Jordan by Jericho, east of the waters of Jericho, into the wilderness, going up from Jericho into the hill country to Bethel; 2then going from Bethel to Luz, it passes along to Ataroth, the territory of the Archites; 3then it goes down westward to the territory of the Japhletites, as far as the territory of Lower Beth-horon, then to Gezer, and it ends at the sea.

4 The Josephites—Manasseh and Ephraim—received their inheritance.

5 The territory of the Ephraimites by their families was as follows: the boundary of their inheritance on the east was Ataroth-addar as far as Upper Beth-horon, 6and the boundary goes from there to the sea; on the north is Michmethath; then on the east the boundary makes a turn toward Taanath-shiloh, and passes along beyond it on the east to Janoah, 7then it goes down from Janoah to Ataroth and to Naarah, and touches Jericho, ending at the Jordan. 8From Tappuah the boundary goes westward to the Wadi Kanah, and ends at the sea. Such is the inheritance of the tribe of the Ephraimites by their families, 9together with the towns that were set apart for the Ephraimites within the inheritance of the Manassites, all those towns with their villages. 10They did not, however, drive out the Canaanites who lived in Gezer: so the Canaanites have lived within Ephraim to this day but have been made to do forced labor.

The Other Half-Tribe of Manasseh (West)

17 Then allotment was made to the tribe of Manasseh, for he was the firstborn of Joseph. To Machir the firstborn of Manasseh, the father of Gilead, were allotted Gilead

and Bashan, because he was a warrior. ²And allotments were made to the rest of the tribe of Manasseh, by their families, Abiezer, Helek, Asriel, Shechem, Hepher, and Shemida; these were the male descendants of Manasseh son of Joseph, by their families.

3 Now Zelophehad son of Hepher son of Gilead son of Machir son of Manasseh had no sons, but only daughters; and these are the names of his daughters: Mahlah, Noah, Hoglah, Milcah, and Tirzah. ⁴They came before the priest Eleazar and Joshua son of Nun and the leaders, and said, "The LORD commanded Moses to give us an inheritance along with our male kin." So according to the commandment of the LORD he gave them an inheritance among the kinsmen of their father. ⁵Thus there fell to Manasseh ten portions, besides the land of Gilead and Bashan, which is on the other side of the Jordan, ⁶because the daughters of Manasseh received an inheritance along with his sons. The land of Gilead was allotted to the rest of the Manassites.

7 The territory of Manasseh reached from Asher to Michmethath, which is east of Shechem; then the boundary goes along southward to the inhabitants of En-tappuah. ⁸The land of Tappuah belonged to Manasseh, but the town of Tappuah on the boundary of Manasseh belonged to the Ephraimites. ⁹Then the boundary went down to the Wadi Kanah. The towns here, to the south of the wadi, among the towns of Manasseh, belong to Ephraim. Then the boundary of Manasseh goes along the north side of the wadi and ends at the sea. ¹⁰The land to the south is Ephraim's and that to the north is Manasseh's, with the sea forming its boundary; on the north Asher is reached, and on the east Issachar. ¹¹Within Issachar and Asher, Manasseh had Beth-shean and its villages, Ibleam and its villages, the inhabitants of Dor and its villages, the inhabitants of En-dor and its villages, the inhabitants of Taanach and its villages, and the inhabitants of Megiddo and its villages (the third is Naphath).ᵃ ¹²Yet the Manassites could not take possession of those towns; but the Canaanites continued to live in that land. ¹³But when the Israelites grew strong, they put the Canaanites to forced labor, but did not utterly drive them out.

The Tribe of Joseph Protests

14 The tribe of Joseph spoke to Joshua, saying, "Why have you given me but one lot and one portion as an inheritance, since we are a numerous people, whom all along the LORD has blessed?" ¹⁵And Joshua said to them, "If you are a numerous people, go up to the forest, and clear ground there for yourselves in the land of the Perizzites and the Rephaim, since the hill country of Ephraim is too narrow for you." ¹⁶The tribe of Joseph said, "The hill country is not enough for us; yet all the Canaanites who live in the plain have chariots of iron, both those in Beth-shean and its villages and those in the Valley of Jezreel." ¹⁷Then Joshua said to the house of Joseph, to Ephraim and Manasseh, "You are indeed a numerous people, and have great power; you shall not have one lot only, ¹⁸but the hill country shall be yours, for though it is a forest, you shall clear it and possess it to its farthest borders; for you shall drive out the Canaanites, though they have chariots of iron, and though they are strong."

The Territories of the Remaining Tribes

18 Then the whole congregation of the Israelites assembled at Shiloh, and set up the tent of meeting there. The land lay subdued before them.

2 There remained among the Israelites seven tribes whose inheritance had not yet been apportioned. ³So Joshua said to the Israelites, "How long will you be slack about going in and taking possession of the land that the LORD, the God of your ancestors, has given you? ⁴Provide three men from each tribe, and I will send them out that they may begin to go throughout the land, writing a description of it with a view to their inheritances. Then come back to me. ⁵They shall divide it into seven por-

ᵃ Meaning of Heb uncertain

tions, Judah continuing in its territory on the south, and the house of Joseph in their territory on the north. 6You shall describe the land in seven divisions and bring the description here to me; and I will cast lots for you here before the LORD our God. 7The Levites have no portion among you, for the priesthood of the LORD is their heritage; and Gad and Reuben and the half-tribe of Manasseh have received their inheritance beyond the Jordan eastward, which Moses the servant of the LORD gave them."

8 So the men started on their way; and Joshua charged those who went to write the description of the land, saying, "Go throughout the land and write a description of it, and come back to me; and I will cast lots for you here before the LORD in Shiloh." 9So the men went and traversed the land and set down in a book a description of it by towns in seven divisions; then they came back to Joshua in the camp at Shiloh, 10and Joshua cast lots for them in Shiloh before the LORD; and there Joshua apportioned the land to the Israelites, to each a portion.

The Territory of Benjamin

11 The lot of the tribe of Benjamin according to its families came up, and the territory allotted to it fell between the tribe of Judah and the tribe of Joseph. 12On the north side their boundary began at the Jordan; then the boundary goes up to the slope of Jericho on the north, then up through the hill country westward; and it ends at the wilderness of Beth-aven. 13From there the boundary passes along southward in the direction of Luz, to the slope of Luz (that is, Bethel), then the boundary goes down to Ataroth-addar, on the mountain that lies south of Lower Beth-horon. 14Then the boundary goes in another direction, turning on the western side southward from the mountain that lies to the south, opposite Beth-horon, and it ends at Kiriath-baal (that is, Kiriath-jearim), a town belonging to the tribe of Judah. This forms the western side. 15The

southern side begins at the outskirts of Kiriath-jearim; and the boundary goes from there to Ephron,a to the spring of the Waters of Nephtoah; 16then the boundary goes down to the border of the mountain that overlooks the valley of the son of Hinnom, which is at the north end of the valley of Rephaim; and it then goes down the valley of Hinnom, south of the slope of the Jebusites, and downward to En-rogel; 17then it bends in a northerly direction going on to En-shemesh, and from there goes to Geliloth, which is opposite the ascent of Adummim; then it goes down to the Stone of Bohan, Reuben's son; 18and passing on to the north of the slope of Beth-arabahb it goes down to the Arabah; 19then the boundary passes on to the north of the slope of Beth-hoglah; and the boundary ends at the northern bay of the Dead Sea,c at the south end of the Jordan: this is the southern border. 20The Jordan forms its boundary on the eastern side. This is the inheritance of the tribe of Benjamin, according to its families, boundary by boundary all around.

21 Now the towns of the tribe of Benjamin according to their families were Jericho, Beth-hoglah, Emek-keziz, 22Beth-arabah, Zemaraim, Bethel, 23Avvim, Parah, Ophrah, 24Chephar-ammoni, Ophni, and Geba—twelve towns with their villages: 25Gibeon, Ramah, Beeroth, 26Mizpeh, Chephirah, Mozah, 27Rekem, Irpeel, Taralah, 28Zela, Haeleph, Jebusd (that is, Jerusalem), Gibeahe and Kiriath-jearimf—fourteen towns with their villages. This is the inheritance of the tribe of Benjamin according to its families.

The Territory of Simeon

19 The second lot came out for Simeon, for the tribe of Simeon, according to its families; its inheritance lay within the inheritance of the tribe of Judah. 2It had for its inheritance Beer-sheba, Sheba, Moladah, 3Hazar-shual, Balah, Ezem, 4Eltolad, Bethul, Hormah, 5Ziklag, Beth-marcaboth, Hazar-susah, 6Beth-lebaoth, and Sharuhen—thirteen towns

---

a Cn See 15.9. Heb westward   b Gk: Heb to the slope over against the Arabah   c Heb Salt Sea   d Gk Syr Vg: Heb the Jebusite   e Heb Gibeath   f Gk: Heb Kiriath with their villages; 7Ain, Rimmon, Ether, and Ashan—four towns with their villages; 8together with all the villages all around these towns as far as Baalath-beer, Ramah of the Negeb. This was the inheritance of the tribe of Simeon according to its families. 9The inheritance of the tribe of Simeon formed part of the territory of Judah; because the portion of the tribe of Judah was too large for them, the tribe of Simeon obtained an inheritance within their inheritance.

The Territory of Zebulun

10 The third lot came up for the tribe of Zebulun, according to its families. The boundary of its inheritance reached as far as Sarid; 11then its boundary goes up westward, and on to Maralah, and touches Dabbesheth, then the wadi that is east of Jokneam; 12from Sarid it goes in the other direction eastward toward the sunrise to the boundary of Chisloth-tabor; from there it goes to Daberath, then up to Japhia; 13from there it passes along on the east toward the sunrise to Gath-hepher, to Eth-kazin, and going on to Rimmon it bends toward Neah; 14then on the north the boundary makes a turn to Hannathon, and it ends at the valley of Iphtah-el; 15and Kattath, Nahalal, Shimron, Idalah, and Bethlehem—twelve towns with their villages. 16This is the inheritance of the tribe of Zebulun, according to its families—these towns with their villages.

The Territory of Issachar

17 The fourth lot came out for Issachar, for the tribe of Issachar, according to its families. 18Its territory included Jezreel, Chesulloth, Shunem, 19Hapharaim, Shion, Anaharath, 20Rabbith, Kishion, Ebez, 21Remeth, En-gannim, En-haddah, Beth-pazzez; 22the boundary also touches Tabor, Shahazumah, and Beth-shemesh, and its boundary ends at the Jordan—sixteen towns with their villages. 23This is the inheritance of the tribe of Issachar, according to its families—the towns with their villages.

The Territory of Asher

24 The fifth lot came out for the tribe of Asher according to its families. 25Its boundary included Helkath, Hali, Beten, Achshaph, 26Allammelech, Amad, and Mishal; on the west it touches Carmel and Shihor-libnath, 27then it turns eastward, goes to Beth-dagon, and touches Zebulun and the valley of Iphtah-el northward to Beth-emek and Neiel; then it continues in the north to Cabul, 28Ebron, Rehob, Hammon, Kanah, as far as Great Sidon; 29then the boundary turns to Ramah, reaching to the fortified city of Tyre; then the boundary turns to Hosah, and it ends at the sea; Mahalab,a Achzib, 30Ummah, Aphek, and Rehob—twenty-two towns with their villages. 31This is the inheritance of the tribe of Asher according to its families—these towns with their villages.

The Territory of Naphtali

32 The sixth lot came out for the tribe of Naphtali, for the tribe of Naphtali, according to its families. 33And its boundary ran from Heleph, from the oak in Zaanannim, and Adaminekeb, and Jabneel, as far as Lakkum; and it ended at the Jordan; 34then the boundary turns westward to Aznoth-tabor, and goes from there to Hukkok, touching Zebulun at the south, and Asher on the west, and Judah on the east at the Jordan. 35The fortified towns are Ziddim, Zer, Hammath, Rakkath, Chinnereth, 36Adamah, Ramah, Hazor, 37Kedesh, Edrei, En-hazor, 38Iron, Migdal-el, Horem, Beth-anath, and Beth-shemesh—nineteen towns with their villages. 39This is the inheritance of the tribe of Naphtali according to its families—the towns with their villages.

The Territory of Dan

40 The seventh lot came out for the tribe of Dan, according to its families. 41The territory of its inheritance included Zorah, Eshtaol, Irshemesh, 42Shaalabbin, Aijalon, Ithlah, 43Elon, Timnah, Ekron, 44Eltekeh, Gibbethon, Baalath, 45Jehud, Bene-berak, Gath-rimmon, 46Me-jar-

a Cn Compare Gk: Heb Mehebel

kon, and Rakkon at the border opposite Joppa. ⁴⁷When the territory of the Danites was lost to them, the Danites went up and fought against Leshem, and after capturing it and putting it to the sword, they took possession of it and settled in it, calling Leshem, Dan, after their ancestor Dan. ⁴⁸This is the inheritance of the tribe of Dan, according to their families— these towns with their villages.

Joshua's Inheritance

49 When they had finished distributing the several territories of the land as inheritances, the Israelites gave an inheritance among them to Joshua son of Nun. ⁵⁰By command of the LORD they gave him the town that he asked for, Timnath-serah in the hill country of Ephraim; he rebuilt the town, and settled in it.

51 These are the inheritances that the priest Eleazar and Joshua son of Nun and the heads of the families of the tribes of the Israelites distributed by lot at Shiloh before the LORD, at the entrance of the tent of meeting. So they finished dividing the land.

The Cities of Refuge

20 Then the LORD spoke to Joshua, saying, ²"Say to the Israelites, 'Appoint the cities of refuge, of which I spoke to you through Moses, ³so that anyone who kills a person without intent or by mistake may flee there; they shall be for you a refuge from the avenger of blood. ⁴The slayer shall flee to one of these cities and shall stand at the entrance of the gate of the city, and explain the case to the elders of that city; then the fugitive shall be taken into the city, and given a place, and shall remain with them. ⁵And if the avenger of blood is in pursuit, they shall not give up the slayer, because the neighbor was killed by mistake, there having been no enmity between them before. ⁶The slayer shall remain in that city until there is a trial before the congregation, until the death of the one who is high priest at the time: then the slayer may return home, to the town in which the deed was done.'"

7 So they set apart Kedesh in Galilee in the hill country of Naphtali, and Shechem in the hill country of Ephraim, and Kiriath-arba (that is, Hebron) in the hill country of Judah. ⁸And beyond the Jordan east of Jericho, they appointed Bezer in the wilderness on the tableland, from the tribe of Reuben, and Ramoth in Gilead, from the tribe of Gad, and Golan in Bashan, from the tribe of Manasseh. ⁹These were the cities designated for all the Israelites, and for the aliens residing among them, that anyone who killed a person without intent could flee there, so as not to die by the hand of the avenger of blood, until there was a trial before the congregation.

Cities Allotted to the Levites

21 Then the heads of the families of the Levites came to the priest Eleazar and to Joshua son of Nun and to the heads of families of the tribes of the Israelites; ²they said to them at Shiloh in the land of Canaan, "The LORD commanded through Moses that we be given towns to live in, along with their pasture lands for our livestock." ³So by command of the LORD the Israelites gave to the Levites the following towns and pasture lands out of their inheritance.

4 The lot came out for the families of the Kohathites. So those Levites who were descendants of Aaron the priest received by lot thirteen towns from the tribes of Judah, Simeon, and Benjamin.

5 The rest of the Kohathites received by lot ten towns from the families of the tribe of Ephraim, from the tribe of Dan, and the half-tribe of Manasseh.

6 The Gershonites received by lot thirteen towns from the families of the tribe of Issachar, from the tribe of Asher, from the tribe of Naphtali, and from the half-tribe of Manasseh in Bashan.

7 The Merarites according to their families received twelve towns from the tribe of Reuben, the tribe of Gad, and the tribe of Zebulun.

8 These towns and their pasture lands the Israelites gave by lot to the Levites, as the LORD had commanded through Moses.

9 Out of the tribe of Judah and the tribe of

Simeon they gave the following towns mentioned by name, 10which went to the descendants of Aaron, one of the families of the Kohathites who belonged to the Levites, since the lot fell to them first. 11They gave them Kiriath-arba (Arba being the father of Anak), that is Hebron, in the hill country of Judah, along with the pasture lands around it. 12But the fields of the town and its villages had been given to Caleb son of Jephunneh as his holding.

13 To the descendants of Aaron the priest they gave Hebron, the city of refuge for the slayer, with its pasture lands, Libnah with its pasture lands, 14Jattir with its pasture lands, Eshtemoa with its pasture lands, 15Holon with its pasture lands, Debir with its pasture lands, 16Ain with its pasture lands, Juttah with its pasture lands, and Beth-shemesh with its pasture lands—nine towns out of these two tribes. 17Out of the tribe of Benjamin: Gibeon with its pasture lands, Geba with its pasture lands, 18Anathoth with its pasture lands, and Almon with its pasture lands—four towns. 19The towns of the descendants of Aaron—the priests—were thirteen in all, with their pasture lands.

20 As to the rest of the Kohathites belonging to the Kohathite families of the Levites, the towns allotted to them were out of the tribe of Ephraim. 21To them were given Shechem, the city of refuge for the slayer, with its pasture lands in the hill country of Ephraim, Gezer with its pasture lands, 22Kibzaim with its pasture lands, and Beth-horon with its pasture lands—four towns. 23Out of the tribe of Dan: Elteke with its pasture lands, Gibbethon with its pasture lands, 24Aijalon with its pasture lands, Gath-rimmon with its pasture lands—four towns. 25Out of the half-tribe of Manasseh: Taanach with its pasture lands, and Gath-rimmon with its pasture lands—two towns. 26The towns of the families of the rest of the Kohathites were ten in all, with their pasture lands.

27 To the Gershonites, one of the families of the Levites, were given out of the half-tribe of Manasseh, Golan in Bashan with its pasture lands, the city of refuge for the slayer, and Beeshterah with its pasture lands—two towns. 28Out of the tribe of Issachar: Kishion with its pasture lands, Daberath with its pasture lands, 29Jarmuth with its pasture lands, En-gannim with its pasture lands—four towns. 30Out of the tribe of Asher: Mishal with its pasture lands, Abdon with its pasture lands, 31Helkath with its pasture lands, and Rehob with its pasture lands—four towns. 32Out of the tribe of Naphtali: Kedesh in Galilee with its pasture lands, the city of refuge for the slayer, Hammoth-dor with its pasture lands, and Kartan with its pasture lands—three towns. 33The towns of the several families of the Gershonites were in all thirteen, with their pasture lands.

34 To the rest of the Levites—the Merarite families—were given out of the tribe of Zebulun: Jokneam with its pasture lands, Kartah with its pasture lands, 35Dimnah with its pasture lands, Nahalal with its pasture lands—four towns. 36Out of the tribe of Reuben: Bezer with its pasture lands, Jahzah with its pasture lands, 37Kedemoth with its pasture lands, and Mephaath with its pasture lands—four towns. 38Out of the tribe of Gad: Ramoth in Gilead with its pasture lands, the city of refuge for the slayer, Mahanaim with its pasture lands, 39Heshbon with its pasture lands, Jazer with its pasture lands—four towns in all. 40As for the towns of the several Merarite families, that is, the remainder of the families of the Levites, those allotted to them were twelve in all.

41 The towns of the Levites within the holdings of the Israelites were in all forty-eight towns with their pasture lands. 42Each of these towns had its pasture lands around it; so it was with all these towns.

43 Thus the LORD gave to Israel all the land that he swore to their ancestors that he would give them; and having taken possession of it, they settled there. 44And the LORD gave them rest on every side just as he had sworn to their ancestors; not one of all their enemies had withstood them, for the LORD had given all their enemies into their hands. 45Not one of all the good promises that the LORD had made to the house of Israel had failed; all came to pass.

The Eastern Tribes Return to Their Territory

22 Then Joshua summoned the Reubenites, the Gadites, and the half-tribe of Manasseh, ²and said to them, "You have observed all that Moses the servant of the LORD commanded you, and have obeyed me in all that I have commanded you; ³you have not forsaken your kindred these many days, down to this day, but have been careful to keep the charge of the LORD your God. ⁴And now the LORD your God has given rest to your kindred, as he promised them; therefore turn and go to your tents in the land where your possession lies, which Moses the servant of the LORD gave you on the other side of the Jordan. ⁵Take good care to observe the commandment and instruction that Moses the servant of the LORD commanded you, to love the LORD your God, to walk in all his ways, to keep his commandments, and to hold fast to him, and to serve him with all your heart and with all your soul." ⁶So Joshua blessed them and sent them away, and they went to their tents.

7 Now to the one half of the tribe of Manasseh Moses had given a possession in Bashan; but to the other half Joshua had given a possession beside their fellow Israelites in the land west of the Jordan. And when Joshua sent them away to their tents and blessed them, ⁸he said to them, "Go back to your tents with much wealth, and with very much livestock, with silver, gold, bronze, and iron, and with a great quantity of clothing; divide the spoil of your enemies with your kindred." ⁹So the Reubenites and the Gadites and the half-tribe of Manasseh returned home, parting from the Israelites at Shiloh, which is in the land of Canaan, to go to the land of Gilead, their own land of which they had taken possession by command of the LORD through Moses.

A Memorial Altar East of the Jordan

10 When they came to the region*ᵃ* near the Jordan that lies in the land of Canaan, the Reubenites and the Gadites and the half-tribe of Manasseh built there an altar by the Jordan, an altar of great size. ¹¹The Israelites heard that the Reubenites and the Gadites and the half-tribe of Manasseh had built an altar at the frontier of the land of Canaan, in the region*ᵃ* near the Jordan, on the side that belongs to the Israelites. ¹²And when the people of Israel heard of it, the whole assembly of the Israelites gathered at Shiloh, to make war against them.

13 Then the Israelites sent the priest Phinehas son of Eleazar to the Reubenites and the Gadites and the half-tribe of Manasseh, in the land of Gilead, ¹⁴and with him ten chiefs, one from each of the tribal families of Israel, every one of them the head of a family among the clans of Israel. ¹⁵They came to the Reubenites, the Gadites, and the half-tribe of Manasseh, in the land of Gilead, and they said to them, ¹⁶"Thus says the whole congregation of the LORD, 'What is this treachery that you have committed against the God of Israel in turning away today from following the LORD, by building yourselves an altar today in rebellion against the LORD? ¹⁷Have we not had enough of the sin at Peor from which even yet we have not cleansed ourselves, and for which a plague came upon the congregation of the LORD, ¹⁸that you must turn away today from following the LORD! If you rebel against the LORD today, he will be angry with the whole congregation of Israel tomorrow. ¹⁹But now, if your land is unclean, cross over into the LORD's land where the LORD's tabernacle now stands, and take for yourselves a possession among us; only do not rebel against the LORD, or rebel against us*ᵇ* by building yourselves an altar other than the altar of the LORD our God. ²⁰Did not Achan son of Zerah break faith in the matter of the devoted things, and wrath fell upon all the congregation of Israel? And he did not perish alone for his iniquity!'"

21 Then the Reubenites, the Gadites, and the half-tribe of Manasseh said in answer to the heads of the families of Israel, ²²"The LORD, God of gods! The LORD, God of gods! He knows; and let Israel itself know! If it was in rebellion or in breach of faith toward the LORD,

---

a Or *to Geliloth*   *b* Or *make rebels of us*

do not spare us today [23]for building an altar to turn away from following the LORD; or if we did so to offer burnt offerings or grain offerings or offerings of well-being on it, may the LORD himself take vengeance. [24]No! We did it from fear that in time to come your children might say to our children, 'What have you to do with the LORD, the God of Israel? [25]For the LORD has made the Jordan a boundary between us and you, you Reubenites and Gadites; you have no portion in the LORD.' So your children might make our children cease to worship the LORD. [26]Therefore we said, 'Let us now build an altar, not for burnt offering, nor for sacrifice, [27]but to be a witness between us and you, and between the generations after us, that we do perform the service of the LORD in his presence with our burnt offerings and sacrifices and offerings of well-being; so that your children may never say to our children in time to come, "You have no portion in the LORD."' [28]And we thought, If this should be said to us or to our descendants in time to come, we could say, 'Look at this copy of the altar of the LORD, which our ancestors made, not for burnt offerings, nor for sacrifice, but to be a witness between us and you.' [29]Far be it from us that we should rebel against the LORD, and turn away this day from following the LORD by building an altar for burnt offering, grain offering, or sacrifice, other than the altar of the LORD our God that stands before his tabernacle!"

30 When the priest Phinehas and the chiefs of the congregation, the heads of the families of Israel who were with him, heard the words that the Reubenites and the Gadites and the Manassites spoke, they were satisfied. [31]The priest Phinehas son of Eleazar said to the Reubenites and the Gadites and the Manassites, "Today we know that the LORD is among us, because you have not committed this treachery against the LORD; now you have saved the Israelites from the hand of the LORD."

32 Then the priest Phinehas son of Eleazar and the chiefs returned from the Reubenites and the Gadites in the land of Gilead to the land of Canaan, to the Israelites, and brought back word to them. [33]The report pleased the Israelites; and the Israelites blessed God and spoke no more of making war against them, to destroy the land where the Reubenites and the Gadites were settled. [34]The Reubenites and the Gadites called the altar Witness;[a] "For," said they, "it is a witness between us that the LORD is God."

Joshua Exhorts the People

23 A long time afterward, when the LORD had given rest to Israel from all their enemies all around, and Joshua was old and well advanced in years, [2]Joshua summoned all Israel, their elders and heads, their judges and officers, and said to them, "I am now old and well advanced in years; [3]and you have seen all that the LORD your God has done to all these nations for your sake, for it is the LORD your God who has fought for you. [4]I have allotted to you as an inheritance for your tribes those nations that remain, along with all the nations that I have already cut off, from the Jordan to the Great Sea in the west. [5]The LORD your God will push them back before you, and drive them out of your sight; and you shall possess their land, as the LORD your God promised you. [6]Therefore be very steadfast to observe and do all that is written in the book of the law of Moses, turning aside from it neither to the right nor to the left, [7]so that you may not be mixed with these nations left here among you, or make mention of the names of their gods, or swear by them, or serve them, or bow yourselves down to them, [8]but hold fast to the LORD your God, as you have done to this day. [9]For the LORD has driven out before you great and strong nations; and as for you, no one has been able to withstand you to this day. [10]One of you puts to flight a thousand, since it is the LORD your God who fights for you, as he promised you. [11]Be very careful, therefore, to love the LORD your God. [12]For if you turn back, and join the survivors of these nations left here among you, and intermarry with them,

a Cn Compare Syr: Heb lacks *Witness*

so that you marry their women and they yours, 13know assuredly that the LORD your God will not continue to drive out these nations before you; but they shall be a snare and a trap for you, a scourge on your sides, and thorns in your eyes, until you perish from this good land that the LORD your God has given you.

14 "And now I am about to go the way of all the earth, and you know in your hearts and souls, all of you, that not one thing has failed of all the good things that the LORD your God promised concerning you; all have come to pass for you, not one of them has failed. 15But just as all the good things that the LORD your God promised concerning you have been fulfilled for you, so the LORD will bring upon you all the bad things, until he has destroyed you from this good land that the LORD your God has given you. 16If you transgress the covenant of the LORD your God, which he enjoined on you, and go and serve other gods and bow down to them, then the anger of the LORD will be kindled against you, and you shall perish quickly from the good land that he has given to you."

The Tribes Renew the Covenant

24 Then Joshua gathered all the tribes of Israel to Shechem, and summoned the elders, the heads, the judges, and the officers of Israel; and they presented themselves before God. 2And Joshua said to all the people, "Thus says the LORD, the God of Israel: Long ago your ancestors—Terah and his sons Abraham and Nahor—lived beyond the Euphrates and served other gods. 3Then I took your father Abraham from beyond the River and led him through all the land of Canaan and made his offspring many. I gave him Isaac; 4and to Isaac I gave Jacob and Esau. I gave Esau the hill country of Seir to possess, but Jacob and his children went down to Egypt. 5Then I sent Moses and Aaron, and I plagued Egypt with what I did in its midst; and afterwards I brought you out. 6When I brought your ancestors out of Egypt, you came to the sea; and the Egyp-

tians pursued your ancestors with chariots and horsemen to the Red Sea.*a* 7When they cried out to the LORD, he put darkness between you and the Egyptians, and made the sea come upon them and cover them; and your eyes saw what I did to Egypt. Afterwards you lived in the wilderness a long time. 8Then I brought you to the land of the Amorites, who lived on the other side of the Jordan; they fought with you, and I handed them over to you, and you took possession of their land, and I destroyed them before you. 9Then King Balak son of Zippor of Moab, set out to fight against Israel. He sent and invited Balaam son of Beor to curse you, 10but I would not listen to Balaam; therefore he blessed you; so I rescued you out of his hand. 11When you went over the Jordan and came to Jericho, the citizens of Jericho fought against you, and also the Amorites, the Perizzites, the Canaanites, the Hittites, the Girgashites, the Hivites, and the Jebusites; and I handed them over to you. 12I sent the hornet*b* ahead of you, which drove out before you the two kings of the Amorites; it was not by your sword or by your bow. 13I gave you a land on which you had not labored, and towns that you had not built, and you live in them; you eat the fruit of vineyards and oliveyards that you did not plant.

14 "Now therefore revere the LORD, and serve him in sincerity and in faithfulness; put away the gods that your ancestors served beyond the River and in Egypt, and serve the LORD. 15Now if you are unwilling to serve the LORD, choose this day whom you will serve, whether the gods your ancestors served in the region beyond the River or the gods of the Amorites in whose land you are living; but as for me and my household, we will serve the LORD."

16 Then the people answered, "Far be it from us that we should forsake the LORD to serve other gods; 17for it is the LORD our God who brought us and our ancestors up from the land of Egypt, out of the house of slavery, and who did those great signs in our sight. He pro-

a Or *Sea of Reeds*   *b* Meaning of Heb uncertain

tected us along all the way that we went, and among all the peoples through whom we passed; 18and the LORD drove out before us all the peoples, the Amorites who lived in the land. Therefore we also will serve the LORD, for he is our God."

19 But Joshua said to the people, "You cannot serve the LORD, for he is a holy God. He is a jealous God; he will not forgive your transgressions or your sins. 20If you forsake the LORD and serve foreign gods, then he will turn and do you harm, and consume you, after having done you good." 21And the people said to Joshua, "No, we will serve the LORD!" 22Then Joshua said to the people, "You are witnesses against yourselves that you have chosen the LORD, to serve him." And they said, "We are witnesses." 23He said, "Then put away the foreign gods that are among you, and incline your hearts to the LORD, the God of Israel." 24The people said to Joshua, "The LORD our God we will serve, and him we will obey." 25So Joshua made a covenant with the people that day, and made statutes and ordinances for them at Shechem. 26Joshua wrote these words in the book of the law of God; and he took a large stone, and set it up there under the oak in the sanctuary of the LORD. 27Joshua said to all the people, "See, this stone shall be a witness against us; for it has heard all the words of the LORD that he spoke to us; therefore it shall be a witness against you, if you deal falsely with your God." 28So Joshua sent the people away to their inheritances.

Death of Joshua and Eleazar

29 After these things Joshua son of Nun, the servant of the LORD, died, being one hundred ten years old. 30They buried him in his own inheritance at Timnath-serah, which is in the hill country of Ephraim, north of Mount Gaash.

31 Israel served the LORD all the days of Joshua, and all the days of the elders who outlived Joshua and had known all the work that the LORD did for Israel.

32 The bones of Joseph, which the Israelites had brought up from Egypt, were buried at Shechem, in the portion of ground that Jacob had bought from the children of Hamor, the father of Shechem, for one hundred pieces of money;a it became an inheritance of the descendants of Joseph.

33 Eleazar son of Aaron died; and they buried him at Gibeah, the town of his son Phinehas, which had been given him in the hill country of Ephraim.

a Heb one hundred qesitah

JUDGES

Israel's Failure to Complete the Conquest of Canaan

1 After the death of Joshua, the Israelites inquired of the LORD, "Who shall go up first for us against the Canaanites, to fight against them?" 2The LORD said, "Judah shall go up. I hereby give the land into his hand." 3Judah said to his brother Simeon, "Come up with me into the territory allotted to me, that we may fight against the Canaanites; then I too will go with you into the territory allotted to you." So Simeon went with him. 4Then Judah went up and the LORD gave the Canaanites and the Perizzites into their hand; and they defeated ten thousand of them at Bezek. 5They came upon Adoni-bezek at Bezek, and fought against him, and defeated the Canaanites and the Perizzites. 6Adoni-bezek fled; but they pursued him, and caught him, and cut off his thumbs and big toes. 7Adoni-bezek said, "Seventy kings with their thumbs and big toes cut off used to pick up scraps under my table; as I have done, so God has paid me back." They brought him to Jerusalem, and he died there.

8 Then the people of Judah fought against Jerusalem and took it. They put it to the sword and set the city on fire. 9Afterward the people of Judah went down to fight against the Canaanites who lived in the hill country, in the Negeb, and in the lowland. 10Judah went against the Canaanites who lived in Hebron (the name of Hebron was formerly Kiriath-arba); and they defeated Sheshai and Ahiman and Talmai.

11 From there they went against the inhabitants of Debir (the name of Debir was formerly Kiriath-sepher). 12Then Caleb said, "Whoever attacks Kiriath-sepher and takes it, I will give him my daughter Achsah as wife." 13And Othniel son of Kenaz, Caleb's younger brother, took it; and he gave him his daughter Achsah as wife. 14When she came to him, she urged him to ask her father for a field. As she dismounted from her donkey, Caleb said to her, "What do you wish?" 15She said to him, "Give me a present;

since you have set me in the land of the Negeb, give me also Gulloth-mayim." *a* So Caleb gave her Upper Gulloth and Lower Gulloth.

16 The descendants of Hobab *b* the Kenite, Moses' father-in-law, went up with the people of Judah from the city of palms into the wilderness of Judah, which lies in the Negeb near Arad. Then they went and settled with the Amalekites. *c* 17Judah went with his brother Simeon, and they defeated the Canaanites who inhabited Zephath, and devoted it to destruction. So the city was called Hormah. 18Judah took Gaza with its territory, Ashkelon with its territory, and Ekron with its territory. 19The LORD was with Judah, and he took possession of the hill country, but could not drive out the inhabitants of the plain, because they had chariots of iron. 20Hebron was given to Caleb, as Moses had said; and he drove out from it the three sons of Anak. 21But the Benjaminites did not drive out the Jebusites who lived in Jerusalem; so the Jebusites have lived in Jerusalem among the Benjaminites to this day.

22 The house of Joseph also went up against Bethel; and the LORD was with them. 23The house of Joseph sent out spies to Bethel (the name of the city was formerly Luz). 24When the spies saw a man coming out of the city, they said to him, "Show us the way into the city, and we will deal kindly with you." 25So he showed them the way into the city; and they put the city to the sword, but they let the man and all his family go. 26So the man went to the land of the Hittites and built a city, and named it Luz; that is its name to this day.

27 Manasseh did not drive out the inhabitants of Beth-shean and its villages, or Taanach and its villages, or the inhabitants of Dor and its villages, or the inhabitants of Ibleam and its villages, or the inhabitants of Megiddo and its villages; but the Canaanites continued to live in that land. 28When Israel grew strong, they put the Canaanites to forced labor, but did not in fact drive them out.

a That is *Basins of Water*   *b* Gk: Heb lacks *Hobab*   *c* See 1 Sam 15.6: Heb *people*

29 And Ephraim did not drive out the Canaanites who lived in Gezer; but the Canaanites lived among them in Gezer.

30 Zebulun did not drive out the inhabitants of Kitron, or the inhabitants of Nahalol; but the Canaanites lived among them, and became subject to forced labor.

31 Asher did not drive out the inhabitants of Acco, or the inhabitants of Sidon, or of Ahlab, or of Achzib, or of Helbah, or of Aphik, or of Rehob; 32but the Asherites lived among the Canaanites, the inhabitants of the land; for they did not drive them out.

33 Naphtali did not drive out the inhabitants of Beth-shemesh, or the inhabitants of Beth-anath, but lived among the Canaanites, the inhabitants of the land; nevertheless the inhabitants of Beth-shemesh and of Beth-anath became subject to forced labor for them.

34 The Amorites pressed the Danites back into the hill country; they did not allow them to come down to the plain. 35The Amorites continued to live in Har-heres, in Aijalon, and in Shaalbim, but the hand of the house of Joseph rested heavily on them, and they became subject to forced labor. 36The border of the Amorites ran from the ascent of Akrabbim, from Sela and upward.

Israel's Disobedience

2 Now the angel of the LORD went up from Gilgal to Bochim, and said, "I brought you up from Egypt, and brought you into the land that I had promised to your ancestors. I said, 'I will never break my covenant with you. 2For your part, do not make a covenant with the inhabitants of this land; tear down their altars.' But you have not obeyed my command. See what you have done! 3So now I say, I will not drive them out before you; but they shall become adversaries*a* to you, and their gods shall be a snare to you." 4When the angel of the LORD spoke these words to all the Israelites, the people lifted up their voices and wept. 5So they named that place Bochim,*b* and there they sacrificed to the LORD.

Death of Joshua

6 When Joshua dismissed the people, the Israelites all went to their own inheritances to take possession of the land. 7The people worshiped the LORD all the days of Joshua, and all the days of the elders who outlived Joshua, who had seen all the great work that the LORD had done for Israel. 8Joshua son of Nun, the servant of the LORD, died at the age of one hundred ten years. 9So they buried him within the bounds of his inheritance in Timnath-heres, in the hill country of Ephraim, north of Mount Gaash. 10Moreover, that whole generation was gathered to their ancestors, and another generation grew up after them, who did not know the LORD or the work that he had done for Israel.

Israel's Unfaithfulness

11 Then the Israelites did what was evil in the sight of the LORD and worshiped the Baals; 12and they abandoned the LORD, the God of their ancestors, who had brought them out of the land of Egypt; they followed other gods, from among the gods of the peoples who were all around them, and bowed down to them; and they provoked the LORD to anger. 13They abandoned the LORD, and worshiped Baal and the Astartes. 14So the anger of the LORD was kindled against Israel, and he gave them over to plunderers who plundered them, and he sold them into the power of their enemies all around, so that they could no longer withstand their enemies. 15Whenever they marched out, the hand of the LORD was against them to bring misfortune, as the LORD had warned them and sworn to them; and they were in great distress.

16 Then the LORD raised up judges, who delivered them out of the power of those who plundered them. 17Yet they did not listen even to their judges; for they lusted after other gods and bowed down to them. They soon turned aside from the way in which their ancestors had walked, who had obeyed the commandments of the LORD; they did not follow their example. 18Whenever the LORD raised up judges

a OL Vg Compare Gk: Heb *sides*   *b* That is *Weepers*

for them, the LORD was with the judge, and he delivered them from the hand of their enemies all the days of the judge; for the LORD would be moved to pity by their groaning because of those who persecuted and oppressed them. 19But whenever the judge died, they would relapse and behave worse than their ancestors, following other gods, worshiping them and bowing down to them. They would not drop any of their practices or their stubborn ways. 20So the anger of the LORD was kindled against Israel; and he said, "Because this people have transgressed my covenant that I commanded their ancestors, and have not obeyed my voice, 21I will no longer drive out before them any of the nations that Joshua left when he died." 22In order to test Israel, whether or not they would take care to walk in the way of the LORD as their ancestors did, 23the LORD had left those nations, not driving them out at once, and had not handed them over to Joshua.

Nations Remaining in the Land

3 Now these are the nations that the LORD left to test all those in Israel who had no experience of any war in Canaan 2(it was only that successive generations of Israelites might know war, to teach those who had no experience of it before): 3the five lords of the Philistines, and all the Canaanites, and the Sidonians, and the Hivites who lived on Mount Lebanon, from Mount Baal-hermon as far as Lebo-hamath. 4They were for the testing of Israel, to know whether Israel would obey the commandments of the LORD, which he commanded their ancestors by Moses. 5So the Israelites lived among the Canaanites, the Hittites, the Amorites, the Perizzites, the Hivites, and the Jebusites; 6and they took their daughters as wives for themselves, and their own daughters they gave to their sons; and they worshiped their gods.

Othniel

7 The Israelites did what was evil in the sight of the LORD, forgetting the LORD their God, and worshiping the Baals and the Ashe-

rahs. 8Therefore the anger of the LORD was kindled against Israel, and he sold them into the hand of King Cushan-rishathaim of Aram-naharaim; and the Israelites served Cushan-rishathaim eight years. 9But when the Israelites cried out to the LORD, the LORD raised up a deliverer for the Israelites, who delivered them, Othniel son of Kenaz, Caleb's younger brother. 10The spirit of the LORD came upon him, and he judged Israel; he went out to war, and the LORD gave King Cushan-rishathaim of Aram into his hand; and his hand prevailed over Cushan-rishathaim. 11So the land had rest forty years. Then Othniel son of Kenaz died.

Ehud

12 The Israelites again did what was evil in the sight of the LORD; and the LORD strengthened King Eglon of Moab against Israel, because they had done what was evil in the sight of the LORD. 13In alliance with the Ammonites and the Amalekites, he went and defeated Israel; and they took possession of the city of palms. 14So the Israelites served King Eglon of Moab eighteen years.

15 But when the Israelites cried out to the LORD, the LORD raised up for them a deliverer, Ehud son of Gera, the Benjaminite, a left-handed man. The Israelites sent tribute by him to King Eglon of Moab. 16Ehud made for himself a sword with two edges, a cubit in length; and he fastened it on his right thigh under his clothes. 17Then he presented the tribute to King Eglon of Moab. Now Eglon was a very fat man. 18When Ehud had finished presenting the tribute, he sent the people who carried the tribute on their way. 19But he himself turned back at the sculptured stones near Gilgal, and said, "I have a secret message for you, O king." So the king said,a "Silence!" and all his attendants went out from his presence. 20Ehud came to him, while he was sitting alone in his cool roof chamber, and said, "I have a message from God for you." So he rose from his seat. 21Then Ehud reached with his left hand, took the sword from his right thigh, and thrust it into

a Heb he said

Eglon's*a* belly; 22the hilt also went in after the blade, and the fat closed over the blade, for he did not draw the sword out of his belly; and the dirt came out.*b* 23Then Ehud went out into the vestibule,*c* and closed the doors of the roof chamber on him, and locked them.

24 After he had gone, the servants came. When they saw that the doors of the roof chamber were locked, they thought, "He must be relieving himself*d* in the cool chamber." 25So they waited until they were embarrassed. When he still did not open the doors of the roof chamber, they took the key and opened them. There was their lord lying dead on the floor.

26 Ehud escaped while they delayed, and passed beyond the sculptured stones, and escaped to Seirah. 27When he arrived, he sounded the trumpet in the hill country of Ephraim; and the Israelites went down with him from the hill country, having him at their head. 28He said to them, "Follow after me; for the LORD has given your enemies the Moabites into your hand." So they went down after him, and seized the fords of the Jordan against the Moabites, and allowed no one to cross over. 29At that time they killed about ten thousand of the Moabites, all strong, able-bodied men; no one escaped. 30So Moab was subdued that day under the hand of Israel. And the land had rest eighty years.

Shamgar

31 After him came Shamgar son of Anath, who killed six hundred of the Philistines with an oxgoad. He too delivered Israel.

Deborah and Barak

4 The Israelites again did what was evil in the sight of the LORD, after Ehud died. 2So the LORD sold them into the hand of King Jabin of Canaan, who reigned in Hazor; the commander of his army was Sisera, who lived in Harosheth-ha-goiim. 3Then the Israelites cried out to the LORD for help; for he had nine hundred chariots of iron, and had oppressed the Israelites cruelly twenty years.

4 At that time Deborah, a prophetess, wife of Lappidoth, was judging Israel. 5She used to sit under the palm of Deborah between Ramah and Bethel in the hill country of Ephraim; and the Israelites came up to her for judgment. 6She sent and summoned Barak son of Abinoam from Kedesh in Naphtali, and said to him, "The LORD, the God of Israel, commands you, 'Go, take position at Mount Tabor, bringing ten thousand from the tribe of Naphtali and the tribe of Zebulun. 7I will draw out Sisera, the general of Jabin's army, to meet you by the Wadi Kishon with his chariots and his troops; and I will give him into your hand.'" 8Barak said to her, "If you will go with me, I will go; but if you will not go with me, I will not go." 9And she said, "I will surely go with you; nevertheless, the road on which you are going will not lead to your glory, for the LORD will sell Sisera into the hand of a woman." Then Deborah got up and went with Barak to Kedesh. 10Barak summoned Zebulun and Naphtali to Kedesh; and ten thousand warriors went up behind him; and Deborah went up with him.

11 Now Heber the Kenite had separated from the other Kenites,*e* that is, the descendants of Hobab the father-in-law of Moses, and had encamped as far away as Elon-bezaanannim, which is near Kedesh.

12 When Sisera was told that Barak son of Abinoam had gone up to Mount Tabor, 13Sisera called out all his chariots, nine hundred chariots of iron, and all the troops who were with him, from Harosheth-ha-goiim to the Wadi Kishon. 14Then Deborah said to Barak, "Up! For this is the day on which the LORD has given Sisera into your hand. The LORD is indeed going out before you." So Barak went down from Mount Tabor with ten thousand warriors following him. 15And the LORD threw Sisera and all his chariots and all his army into a panic/*f* before Barak; Sisera got down from his chariot and fled away on foot, 16while Barak pursued the chariots and the army to Harosheth-ha-goiim. All the army of Sisera fell by the sword; no one was left.

17 Now Sisera had fled away on foot to

the tent of Jael wife of Heber the Kenite; for there was peace between King Jabin of Hazor and the clan of Heber the Kenite. 18Jael came out to meet Sisera, and said to him, "Turn aside, my lord, turn aside to me; have no fear." So he turned aside to her into the tent, and she covered him with a rug. 19Then he said to her, "Please give me a little water to drink; for I am thirsty." So she opened a skin of milk and gave him a drink and covered him. 20He said to her, "Stand at the entrance of the tent, and if anybody comes and asks you, 'Is anyone here?' say, 'No.'" 21But Jael wife of Heber took a tent peg, and took a hammer in her hand, and went softly to him and drove the peg into his temple, until it went down into the ground—he was lying fast asleep from weariness—and he died. 22Then, as Barak came in pursuit of Sisera, Jael went out to meet him, and said to him, "Come, and I will show you the man whom you are seeking." So he went into her tent; and there was Sisera lying dead, with the tent peg in his temple.

23 So on that day God subdued King Jabin of Canaan before the Israelites. 24Then the hand of the Israelites bore harder and harder on King Jabin of Canaan, until they destroyed King Jabin of Canaan.

The Song of Deborah

5 Then Deborah and Barak son of Abinoam sang on that day, saying:

2 "When locks are long in Israel,
when the people offer themselves
willingly—
bless*a* the LORD!

3 "Hear, O kings; give ear, O princes;
to the LORD I will sing,
I will make melody to the LORD, the
God of Israel.

4 "LORD, when you went out from Seir,
when you marched from the region of
Edom,
the earth trembled,

and the heavens poured,
the clouds indeed poured water.

5 The mountains quaked before the LORD,
the One of Sinai,
before the LORD, the God of Israel.

6 "In the days of Shamgar son of Anath,
in the days of Jael, caravans ceased
and travelers kept to the byways.

7 The peasantry prospered in Israel,
they grew fat on plunder,
because you arose, Deborah,
arose as a mother in Israel.

8 When new gods were chosen,
then war was in the gates.
Was shield or spear to be seen
among forty thousand in Israel?

9 My heart goes out to the commanders of
Israel
who offered themselves willingly
among the people.
Bless the LORD.

10 "Tell of it, you who ride on white
donkeys,
you who sit on rich carpets*b*
and you who walk by the way.

11 To the sound of musicians*b* at the
watering places,
there they repeat the triumphs of the
LORD,
the triumphs of his peasantry in
Israel.

"Then down to the gates marched the
people of the LORD.

12 "Awake, awake, Deborah!
Awake, awake, utter a song!
Arise, Barak, lead away your captives,
O son of Abinoam.

13 Then down marched the remnant of the
noble;
the people of the LORD marched
down for him*c* against the
mighty.

a Or You who offer yourselves willingly among the people, bless   *b* Meaning of Heb uncertain   *c* Gk: Heb me

14   From Ephraim they set out*a* into the
      valley,*b*
    following you, Benjamin, with your
      kin;
  from Machir marched down the
      commanders,
    and from Zebulun those who bear the
      marshal's staff;
15 the chiefs of Issachar came with
      Deborah,
    and Issachar faithful to Barak;
    into the valley they rushed out at his
      heels.
  Among the clans of Reuben
    there were great searchings of heart.
16 Why did you tarry among the
      sheepfolds,
    to hear the piping for the flocks?
  Among the clans of Reuben
    there were great searchings of heart.
17 Gilead stayed beyond the Jordan;
    and Dan, why did he abide with the
      ships?
  Asher sat still at the coast of the sea,
    settling down by his landings.*c*
18 Zebulun is a people that scorned death;
    Naphtali too, on the heights of the
      field.

19 "The kings came, they fought;
    then fought the kings of Canaan,
  at Taanach, by the waters of Megiddo;
    they got no spoils of silver.
20 The stars fought from heaven,
    from their courses they fought against
      Sisera.
21 The torrent Kishon swept them away,
    the onrushing torrent, the torrent
      Kishon.
  March on, my soul, with might!

22 "Then loud beat the horses' hoofs
    with the galloping, galloping of his
      steeds.

23 "Curse Meroz, says the angel of the
      LORD,
    curse bitterly its inhabitants,
  because they did not come to the help of
      the LORD,
    to the help of the LORD against the
      mighty.

24 "Most blessed of women be Jael,
    the wife of Heber the Kenite,
    of tent-dwelling women most blessed.
25 He asked water and she gave him milk,
    she brought him curds in a lordly bowl.
26 She put her hand to the tent peg
    and her right hand to the workmen's
      mallet;
  she struck Sisera a blow,
    she crushed his head,
    she shattered and pierced his temple.
27 He sank, he fell,
    he lay still at her feet;
  at her feet he sank, he fell;
    where he sank, there he fell dead.

28 "Out of the window she peered,
    the mother of Sisera gazed*c* through
      the lattice:
  'Why is his chariot so long in coming?
    Why tarry the hoofbeats of his
      chariots?'
29 Her wisest ladies make answer,
    indeed, she answers the question
      herself:
30 'Are they not finding and dividing the
      spoil?—
    A girl or two for every man;
  spoil of dyed stuffs for Sisera,
    spoil of dyed stuffs embroidered,
    two pieces of dyed work embroidered
      for my neck as spoil?'

31 "So perish all your enemies, O LORD!
    But may your friends be like the sun
      as it rises in its might."

And the land had rest forty years.

---

a Cn: Heb *From Ephraim their root*   *b* Gk: Heb *in Amalek*   *c* Gk Compare Tg: Heb *exclaimed*

The Midianite Oppression

6 The Israelites did what was evil in the sight of the LORD, and the LORD gave them into the hand of Midian seven years. ²The hand of Midian prevailed over Israel; and because of Midian the Israelites provided for themselves hiding places in the mountains, caves and strongholds. ³For whenever the Israelites put in seed, the Midianites and the Amalekites and the people of the east would come up against them. ⁴They would encamp against them and destroy the produce of the land, as far as the neighborhood of Gaza, and leave no sustenance in Israel, and no sheep or ox or donkey. ⁵For they and their livestock would come up, and they would even bring their tents, as thick as locusts; neither they nor their camels could be counted; so they wasted the land as they came in. ⁶Thus Israel was greatly impoverished because of Midian; and the Israelites cried out to the LORD for help.

7 When the Israelites cried to the LORD on account of the Midianites, ⁸the LORD sent a prophet to the Israelites; and he said to them, "Thus says the LORD, the God of Israel: I led you up from Egypt, and brought you out of the house of slavery; ⁹and I delivered you from the hand of the Egyptians, and from the hand of all who oppressed you, and drove them out before you, and gave you their land; ¹⁰and I said to you, 'I am the LORD your God; you shall not pay reverence to the gods of the Amorites, in whose land you live.' But you have not given heed to my voice."

The Call of Gideon

11 Now the angel of the LORD came and sat under the oak at Ophrah, which belonged to Joash the Abiezrite, as his son Gideon was beating out wheat in the wine press, to hide it from the Midianites. ¹²The angel of the LORD appeared to him and said to him, "The LORD is with you, you mighty warrior." ¹³Gideon answered him, "But sir, if the LORD is with us, why then has all this happened to us? And where are all his wonderful deeds that our ancestors re-

counted to us, saying, 'Did not the LORD bring us up from Egypt?' But now the LORD has cast us off, and given us into the hand of Midian." ¹⁴Then the LORD turned to him and said, "Go in this might of yours and deliver Israel from the hand of Midian; I hereby commission you." ¹⁵He responded, "But sir, how can I deliver Israel? My clan is the weakest in Manasseh, and I am the least in my family." ¹⁶The LORD said to him, "But I will be with you, and you shall strike down the Midianites, every one of them." ¹⁷Then he said to him, "If now I have found favor with you, then show me a sign that it is you who speak with me. ¹⁸Do not depart from here until I come to you, and bring out my present, and set it before you." And he said, "I will stay until you return."

19 So Gideon went into his house and prepared a kid, and unleavened cakes from an ephah of flour; the meat he put in a basket, and the broth he put in a pot, and brought them to him under the oak and presented them. ²⁰The angel of God said to him, "Take the meat and the unleavened cakes, and put them on this rock, and pour out the broth." And he did so. ²¹Then the angel of the LORD reached out the tip of the staff that was in his hand, and touched the meat and the unleavened cakes; and fire sprang up from the rock and consumed the meat and the unleavened cakes; and the angel of the LORD vanished from his sight. ²²Then Gideon perceived that it was the angel of the LORD; and Gideon said, "Help me, Lord GOD! For I have seen the angel of the LORD face to face." ²³But the LORD said to him, "Peace be to you; do not fear, you shall not die." ²⁴Then Gideon built an altar there to the LORD, and called it, The LORD is peace. To this day it still stands at Ophrah, which belongs to the Abiezrites.

25 That night the LORD said to him, "Take your father's bull, the second bull seven years old, and pull down the altar of Baal that belongs to your father, and cut down the sacred pole*a* that is beside it; ²⁶and build an altar to the LORD your God on the top of the stronghold

a Heb *Asherah*

here, in proper order; then take the second bull, and offer it as a burnt offering with the wood of the sacred pole*a* that you shall cut down." 27So Gideon took ten of his servants, and did as the LORD had told him; but because he was too afraid of his family and the townspeople to do it by day, he did it by night.

Gideon Destroys the Altar of Baal

28 When the townspeople rose early in the morning, the altar of Baal was broken down, and the sacred pole*a* beside it was cut down, and the second bull was offered on the altar that had been built. 29So they said to one another, "Who has done this?" After searching and inquiring, they were told, "Gideon son of Joash did it." 30Then the townspeople said to Joash, "Bring out your son, so that he may die, for he has pulled down the altar of Baal and cut down the sacred pole*a* beside it." 31But Joash said to all who were arrayed against him, "Will you contend for Baal? Or will you defend his cause? Whoever contends for him shall be put to death by morning. If he is a god, let him contend for himself, because his altar has been pulled down." 32Therefore on that day Gideon*b* was called Jerubbaal, that is to say, "Let Baal contend against him," because he pulled down his altar.

33 Then all the Midianites and the Amalekites and the people of the east came together, and crossing the Jordan they encamped in the Valley of Jezreel. 34But the spirit of the LORD took possession of Gideon; and he sounded the trumpet, and the Abiezrites were called out to follow him. 35He sent messengers throughout all Manasseh, and they too were called out to follow him. He also sent messengers to Asher, Zebulun, and Naphtali, and they went up to meet them.

The Sign of the Fleece

36 Then Gideon said to God, "In order to see whether you will deliver Israel by my hand, as you have said, 37I am going to lay a fleece of wool on the threshing floor; if there is dew on the fleece alone, and it is dry on all the ground, then I shall know that you will deliver Israel by my hand, as you have said." 38And it was so. When he rose early next morning and squeezed the fleece, he wrung enough dew from the fleece to fill a bowl with water. 39Then Gideon said to God, "Do not let your anger burn against me, let me speak one more time; let me, please, make trial with the fleece just once more; let it be dry only on the fleece, and on all the ground let there be dew." 40And God did so that night. It was dry on the fleece only, and on all the ground there was dew.

Gideon Surprises and Routs the Midianites

7 Then Jerubbaal (that is, Gideon) and all the troops that were with him rose early and encamped beside the spring of Harod; and the camp of Midian was north of them, below*c* the hill of Moreh, in the valley.

2 The LORD said to Gideon, "The troops with you are too many for me to give the Midianites into their hand. Israel would only take the credit away from me, saying, 'My own hand has delivered me.' 3Now therefore proclaim this in the hearing of the troops, 'Whoever is fearful and trembling, let him return home.' " Thus Gideon sifted them out;*d* twenty-two thousand returned, and ten thousand remained.

4 Then the LORD said to Gideon, "The troops are still too many; take them down to the water and I will sift them out for you there. When I say, 'This one shall go with you,' he shall go with you; and when I say, 'This one shall not go with you,' he shall not go." 5So he brought the troops down to the water; and the LORD said to Gideon, "All those who lap the water with their tongues, as a dog laps, you shall put to one side; all those who kneel down to drink, putting their hands to their mouths,*e* you shall put to the other side." 6The number of those that lapped was three hundred; but all the rest of the troops knelt down to drink water. 7Then the LORD said to Gideon, "With the three hundred that lapped I will deliver you, and give the Midianites into your hand. Let

a Heb *Asherah*   *b* Heb *he*   *c* Heb *from*   *d* Cn: Heb *home, and depart from Mount Gilead' "*   *e* Heb *places the words putting their hands to their mouths after the word lapped in verse 6* all the others go to their homes." [8]So he took the jars of the troops from their hands,[a] and their trumpets; and he sent all the rest of Israel back to their own tents, but retained the three hundred. The camp of Midian was below him in the valley.

9 That same night the LORD said to him, "Get up, attack the camp; for I have given it into your hand. [10]But if you fear to attack, go down to the camp with your servant Purah; [11]and you shall hear what they say, and afterward your hands shall be strengthened to attack the camp." Then he went down with his servant Purah to the outposts of the armed men that were in the camp. [12]The Midianites and the Amalekites and all the people of the east lay along the valley as thick as locusts; and their camels were without number, countless as the sand on the seashore. [13]When Gideon arrived, there was a man telling a dream to his comrade; and he said, "I had a dream, and in it a cake of barley bread tumbled into the camp of Midian, and came to the tent, and struck it so that it fell; it turned upside down, and the tent collapsed." [14]And his comrade answered, "This is no other than the sword of Gideon son of Joash, a man of Israel; into his hand God has given Midian and all the army."

15 When Gideon heard the telling of the dream and its interpretation, he worshiped; and he returned to the camp of Israel, and said, "Get up; for the LORD has given the army of Midian into your hand." [16]After he divided the three hundred men into three companies, and put trumpets into the hands of all of them, and empty jars, with torches inside the jars, [17]he said to them, "Look at me, and do the same; when I come to the outskirts of the camp, do as I do. [18]When I blow the trumpet, I and all who are with me, then you also blow the trumpets around the whole camp, and shout, 'For the LORD and for Gideon!' "

19 So Gideon and the hundred who were with him came to the outskirts of the camp at the beginning of the middle watch, when they had just set the watch; and they blew the trum-

pets and smashed the jars that were in their hands. [20]So the three companies blew the trumpets and broke the jars, holding in their left hands the torches, and in their right hands the trumpets to blow; and they cried, "A sword for the LORD and for Gideon!" [21]Every man stood in his place all around the camp, and all the men in camp ran; they cried out and fled. [22]When they blew the three hundred trumpets, the LORD set every man's sword against his fellow and against all the army; and the army fled as far as Beth-shittah toward Zererah,[b] as far as the border of Abel-meholah, by Tabbath. [23]And the men of Israel were called out from Naphtali and from Asher and from all Manasseh, and they pursued after the Midianites.

24 Then Gideon sent messengers throughout all the hill country of Ephraim, saying, "Come down against the Midianites and seize the waters against them, as far as Beth-barah, and also the Jordan." So all the men of Ephraim were called out, and they seized the waters as far as Beth-barah, and also the Jordan. [25]They captured the two captains of Midian, Oreb and Zeeb; they killed Oreb at the rock of Oreb, and Zeeb they killed at the wine press of Zeeb, as they pursued the Midianites. They brought the heads of Oreb and Zeeb to Gideon beyond the Jordan.

Gideon's Triumph and Vengeance

8 Then the Ephraimites said to him, "What have you done to us, not to call us when you went to fight against the Midianites?" And they upbraided him violently. [2]So he said to them, "What have I done now in comparison with you? Is not the gleaning of the grapes of Ephraim better than the vintage of Abiezer? [3]God has given into your hands the captains of Midian, Oreb and Zeeb; what have I been able to do in comparison with you?" When he said this, their anger against him subsided.

4 Then Gideon came to the Jordan and crossed over, he and the three hundred who were with him, exhausted and famished.[c] [5]So he said to the people of Succoth, "Please give

a Cn: Heb *So the people took provisions in their hands*　　b Another reading is *Zeredah*　　c Gk: Heb *pursuing* some loaves of bread to my followers, for they are exhausted, and I am pursuing Zebah and Zalmunna, the kings of Midian." 6But the officials of Succoth said, "Do you already have in your possession the hands of Zebah and Zalmunna, that we should give bread to your army?" 7Gideon replied, "Well then, when the LORD has given Zebah and Zalmunna into my hand, I will trample your flesh on the thorns of the wilderness and on briers." 8From there he went up to Penuel, and made the same request of them; and the people of Penuel answered him as the people of Succoth had answered. 9So he said to the people of Penuel, "When I come back victorious, I will break down this tower."

10 Now Zebah and Zalmunna were in Karkor with their army, about fifteen thousand men, all who were left of all the army of the people of the east; for one hundred twenty thousand men bearing arms had fallen. 11So Gideon went up by the caravan route east of Nobah and Jogbehah, and attacked the army; for the army was off its guard. 12Zebah and Zalmunna fled; and he pursued them and took the two kings of Midian, Zebah and Zalmunna, and threw all the army into a panic.

13 When Gideon son of Joash returned from the battle by the ascent of Heres, 14he caught a young man, one of the people of Succoth, and questioned him; and he listed for him the officials and elders of Succoth, seventy-seven people. 15Then he came to the people of Succoth, and said, "Here are Zebah and Zalmunna, about whom you taunted me, saying, 'Do you already have in your possession the hands of Zebah and Zalmunna, that we should give bread to your troops who are exhausted?' " 16So he took the elders of the city and he took thorns of the wilderness and briers and with them he trampled*a* the people of Succoth. 17He also broke down the tower of Penuel, and killed the men of the city.

18 Then he said to Zebah and Zalmunna, "What about the men whom you killed at Tabor?" They answered, "As you are, so were

they, every one of them; they resembled the sons of a king." 19And he replied, "They were my brothers, the sons of my mother; as the LORD lives, if you had saved them alive, I would not kill you." 20So he said to Jether his firstborn, "Go kill them!" But the boy did not draw his sword, for he was afraid, because he was still a boy. 21Then Zebah and Zalmunna said, "You come and kill us; for as the man is, so is his strength." So Gideon proceeded to kill Zebah and Zalmunna; and he took the crescents that were on the necks of their camels.

Gideon's Idolatry

22 Then the Israelites said to Gideon, "Rule over us, you and your son and your grandson also; for you have delivered us out of the hand of Midian." 23Gideon said to them, "I will not rule over you, and my son will not rule over you; the LORD will rule over you." 24Then Gideon said to them, "Let me make a request of you; each of you give me an earring he has taken as booty." (For the enemy *b* had golden earrings, because they were Ishmaelites.) 25"We will willingly give them," they answered. So they spread a garment, and each threw into it an earring he had taken as booty. 26The weight of the golden earrings that he requested was one thousand seven hundred shekels of gold (apart from the crescents and the pendants and the purple garments worn by the kings of Midian, and the collars that were on the necks of their camels). 27Gideon made an ephod of it and put it in his town, in Ophrah; and all Israel prostituted themselves to it there, and it became a snare to Gideon and to his family. 28So Midian was subdued before the Israelites, and they lifted up their heads no more. So the land had rest forty years in the days of Gideon.

Death of Gideon

29 Jerubbaal son of Joash went to live in his own house. 30Now Gideon had seventy sons, his own offspring, for he had many wives. 31His concubine who was in Shechem also bore him a son, and he named him Abimelech.

---

a With verse 7, Compare Gk: Heb *he taught*   *b* Heb *they*

32Then Gideon son of Joash died at a good old age, and was buried in the tomb of his father Joash at Ophrah of the Abiezrites.

33 As soon as Gideon died, the Israelites relapsed and prostituted themselves with the Baals, making Baal-berith their god. 34The Israelites did not remember the LORD their God, who had rescued them from the hand of all their enemies on every side; 35and they did not exhibit loyalty to the house of Jerubbaal (that is, Gideon) in return for all the good that he had done to Israel.

Abimelech Attempts to Establish a Monarchy

9 Now Abimelech son of Jerubbaal went to Shechem to his mother's kinsfolk and said to them and to the whole clan of his mother's family, 2"Say in the hearing of all the lords of Shechem, 'Which is better for you, that all seventy of the sons of Jerubbaal rule over you, or that one rule over you?' Remember also that I am your bone and your flesh." 3So his mother's kinsfolk spoke all these words on his behalf in the hearing of all the lords of Shechem; and their hearts inclined to follow Abimelech, for they said, "He is our brother." 4They gave him seventy pieces of silver out of the temple of Baal-berith with which Abimelech hired worthless and reckless fellows, who followed him. 5He went to his father's house at Ophrah, and killed his brothers the sons of Jerubbaal, seventy men, on one stone; but Jotham, the youngest son of Jerubbaal, survived, for he hid himself. 6Then all the lords of Shechem and all Beth-millo came together, and they went and made Abimelech king, by the oak of the pillar*a* at Shechem.

The Parable of the Trees

7 When it was told to Jotham, he went and stood on the top of Mount Gerizim, and cried aloud and said to them, "Listen to me, you lords of Shechem, so that God may listen to you.

8   The trees once went out
           to anoint a king over themselves.

So they said to the olive tree,
           'Reign over us.'
9   The olive tree answered them,
           'Shall I stop producing my rich oil
               by which gods and mortals are
                   honored,
               and go to sway over the trees?'
10   Then the trees said to the fig tree,
           'You come and reign over us.'
11   But the fig tree answered them,
           'Shall I stop producing my sweetness
               and my delicious fruit,
               and go to sway over the trees?'
12   Then the trees said to the vine,
           'You come and reign over us.'
13   But the vine said to them,
           'Shall I stop producing my wine
               that cheers gods and mortals,
               and go to sway over the trees?'
14   So all the trees said to the bramble,
           'You come and reign over us.'
15   And the bramble said to the trees,
           'If in good faith you are anointing me
               king over you,
               then come and take refuge in my
                   shade;
               but if not, let fire come out of the
                   bramble
               and devour the cedars of Lebanon.'

16 "Now therefore, if you acted in good faith and honor when you made Abimelech king, and if you have dealt well with Jerubbaal and his house, and have done to him as his actions deserved— 17for my father fought for you, and risked his life, and rescued you from the hand of Midian; 18but you have risen up against my father's house this day, and have killed his sons, seventy men on one stone, and have made Abimelech, the son of his slave woman, king over the lords of Shechem, because he is your kinsman— 19if, I say, you have acted in good faith and honor with Jerubbaal and with his house this day, then rejoice in Abimelech, and let him also rejoice in you; 20but if not, let fire come out from Abimelech, and devour the lords of Shechem, and Beth-

a Cn: Meaning of Heb uncertain

millo; and let fire come out from the lords of Shechem, and from Beth-millo, and devour Abimelech." 21Then Jotham ran away and fled, going to Beer, where he remained for fear of his brother Abimelech.

The Downfall of Abimelech

22 Abimelech ruled over Israel three years. 23But God sent an evil spirit between Abimelech and the lords of Shechem; and the lords of Shechem dealt treacherously with Abimelech. 24This happened so that the violence done to the seventy sons of Jerubbaal might be avenged[a] and their blood be laid on their brother Abimelech, who killed them, and on the lords of Shechem, who strengthened his hands to kill his brothers. 25So, out of hostility to him, the lords of Shechem set ambushes on the mountain tops. They robbed all who passed by them along that way; and it was reported to Abimelech.

26 When Gaal son of Ebed moved into Shechem with his kinsfolk, the lords of Shechem put confidence in him. 27They went out into the field and gathered the grapes from their vineyards, trod them, and celebrated. Then they went into the temple of their god, ate and drank, and ridiculed Abimelech. 28Gaal son of Ebed said, "Who is Abimelech, and who are we of Shechem, that we should serve him? Did not the son of Jerubbaal and Zebul his officer serve the men of Hamor father of Shechem? Why then should we serve him? 29If only this people were under my command! Then I would remove Abimelech; I would say[b] to him, 'Increase your army, and come out.' "

30 When Zebul the ruler of the city heard the words of Gaal son of Ebed, his anger was kindled. 31He sent messengers to Abimelech at Arumah,[c] saying, "Look, Gaal son of Ebed and his kinsfolk have come to Shechem, and they are stirring up[d] the city against you. 32Now therefore, go by night, you and the troops that are with you, and lie in wait in the fields. 33Then early in the morning, as soon as the sun rises, get up and rush on the city; and when he and the troops that are with him come out against you, you may deal with them as best you can."

34 So Abimelech and all the troops with him got up by night and lay in wait against Shechem in four companies. 35When Gaal son of Ebed went out and stood in the entrance of the gate of the city, Abimelech and the troops with him rose from the ambush. 36And when Gaal saw them, he said to Zebul, "Look, people are coming down from the mountain tops!" And Zebul said to him, "The shadows on the mountains look like people to you." 37Gaal spoke again and said, "Look, people are coming down from Tabbur-erez, and one company is coming from the direction of Elon-meonenim."[e] 38Then Zebul said to him, "Where is your boast[f] now, you who said, 'Who is Abimelech, that we should serve him?' Are not these the troops you made light of? Go out now and fight with them." 39So Gaal went out at the head of the lords of Shechem, and fought with Abimelech. 40Abimelech chased him, and he fled before him. Many fell wounded, up to the entrance of the gate. 41So Abimelech resided at Arumah; and Zebul drove out Gaal and his kinsfolk, so that they could not live on at Shechem.

42 On the following day the people went out into the fields. When Abimelech was told, 43he took his troops and divided them into three companies, and lay in wait in the fields. When he looked and saw the people coming out of the city, he rose against them and killed them. 44Abimelech and the company that was[g] with him rushed forward and stood at the entrance of the gate of the city, while the two companies rushed on all who were in the fields and killed them. 45Abimelech fought against the city all that day; he took the city, and killed the people that were in it; and he razed the city and sowed it with salt.

46 When all the lords of the Tower of Shechem heard of it, they entered the stronghold of the temple of El-berith. 47Abimelech was told that all the lords of the Tower of Shechem were gathered together. 48So Abimelech went up to Mount Zalmon, he and all the troops that

a Heb *might come*   b Gk: Heb *and he said*   c Cn See 9.41. Heb *Tormah*   d Cn: Heb *are besieging*   e That is Diviners' Oak   f Heb *mouth*   g Vg and some Gk Mss: Heb *companies that were*

were with him. Abimelech took an ax in his hand, cut down a bundle of brushwood, and took it up and laid it on his shoulder. Then he said to the troops with him, "What you have seen me do, do quickly, as I have done." 49So every one of the troops cut down a bundle and following Abimelech put it against the stronghold, and they set the stronghold on fire over them, so that all the people of the Tower of Shechem also died, about a thousand men and women.

50 Then Abimelech went to Thebez, and encamped against Thebez, and took it. 51But there was a strong tower within the city, and all the men and women and all the lords of the city fled to it and shut themselves in; and they went to the roof of the tower. 52Abimelech came to the tower, and fought against it, and came near to the entrance of the tower to burn it with fire. 53But a certain woman threw an upper millstone on Abimelech's head, and crushed his skull. 54Immediately he called to the young man who carried his armor and said to him, "Draw your sword and kill me, so people will not say about me, 'A woman killed him.'" So the young man thrust him through, and he died. 55When the Israelites saw that Abimelech was dead, they all went home. 56Thus God repaid Abimelech for the crime he committed against his father in killing his seventy brothers; 57and God also made all the wickedness of the people of Shechem fall back on their heads, and on them came the curse of Jotham son of Jerubbaal.

Tola and Jair

10 After Abimelech, Tola son of Puah son of Dodo, a man of Issachar, who lived at Shamir in the hill country of Ephraim, rose to deliver Israel. 2He judged Israel twenty-three years. Then he died, and was buried at Shamir.

3 After him came Jair the Gileadite, who judged Israel twenty-two years. 4He had thirty sons who rode on thirty donkeys; and they had thirty towns, which are in the land of Gilead, and are called Havvoth-jair to this day. 5Jair died, and was buried in Kamon.

Oppression by the Ammonites

6 The Israelites again did what was evil in the sight of the LORD, worshiping the Baals and the Astartes, the gods of Aram, the gods of Sidon, the gods of Moab, the gods of the Ammonites, and the gods of the Philistines. Thus they abandoned the LORD, and did not worship him. 7So the anger of the LORD was kindled against Israel, and he sold them into the hand of the Philistines and into the hand of the Ammonites, 8and they crushed and oppressed the Israelites that year. For eighteen years they oppressed all the Israelites that were beyond the Jordan in the land of the Amorites, which is in Gilead. 9The Ammonites also crossed the Jordan to fight against Judah and against Benjamin and against the house of Ephraim; so that Israel was greatly distressed.

10 So the Israelites cried to the LORD, saying, "We have sinned against you, because we have abandoned our God and have worshiped the Baals." 11And the LORD said to the Israelites, "Did I not deliver you*a* from the Egyptians and from the Amorites, from the Ammonites and from the Philistines? 12The Sidonians also, and the Amalekites, and the Maonites, oppressed you; and you cried to me, and I delivered you out of their hand. 13Yet you have abandoned me and worshiped other gods; therefore I will deliver you no more. 14Go and cry to the gods whom you have chosen; let them deliver you in the time of your distress." 15And the Israelites said to the LORD, "We have sinned; do to us whatever seems good to you; but deliver us this day!" 16So they put away the foreign gods from among them and worshiped the LORD; and he could no longer bear to see Israel suffer.

17 Then the Ammonites were called to arms, and they encamped in Gilead; and the Israelites came together, and they encamped at Mizpah. 18The commanders of the people of Gilead said to one another, "Who will begin the fight against the Ammonites? He shall be head over all the inhabitants of Gilead."

a Heb lacks *Did I not deliver you*

Jephthah

11

Now Jephthah the Gileadite, the son of a prostitute, was a mighty warrior. Gilead was the father of Jephthah. ²Gilead's wife also bore him sons; and when his wife's sons grew up, they drove Jephthah away, saying to him, "You shall not inherit anything in our father's house; for you are the son of another woman." ³Then Jephthah fled from his brothers and lived in the land of Tob. Outlaws collected around Jephthah and went raiding with him.

4 After a time the Ammonites made war against Israel. ⁵And when the Ammonites made war against Israel, the elders of Gilead went to bring Jephthah from the land of Tob. ⁶They said to Jephthah, "Come and be our commander, so that we may fight with the Ammonites." ⁷But Jephthah said to the elders of Gilead, "Are you not the very ones who rejected me and drove me out of my father's house? So why do you come to me now when you are in trouble?" ⁸The elders of Gilead said to Jephthah, "Nevertheless, we have now turned back to you, so that you may go with us and fight with the Ammonites, and become head over us, over all the inhabitants of Gilead." ⁹Jephthah said to the elders of Gilead, "If you bring me home again to fight with the Ammonites, and the LORD gives them over to me, I will be your head." ¹⁰And the elders of Gilead said to Jephthah, "The LORD will be witness between us; we will surely do as you say." ¹¹So Jephthah went with the elders of Gilead, and the people made him head and commander over them; and Jephthah spoke all his words before the LORD at Mizpah.

12 Then Jephthah sent messengers to the king of the Ammonites and said, "What is there between you and me, that you have come to me to fight against my land?" ¹³The king of the Ammonites answered the messengers of Jephthah, "Because Israel, on coming from Egypt, took away my land from the Arnon to the Jabbok and to the Jordan; now therefore restore it peaceably." ¹⁴Once again Jephthah sent messengers to the king of the Ammonites ¹⁵and said to him: "Thus says Jephthah: Israel did not take away the land of Moab or the land of the Ammonites, ¹⁶but when they came up from Egypt, Israel went through the wilderness to the Red Sea*ᵃ* and came to Kadesh. ¹⁷Israel then sent messengers to the king of Edom, saying, 'Let us pass through your land'; but the king of Edom would not listen. They also sent to the king of Moab, but he would not consent. So Israel remained at Kadesh. ¹⁸Then they journeyed through the wilderness, went around the land of Edom and the land of Moab, arrived on the east side of the land of Moab, and camped on the other side of the Arnon. They did not enter the territory of Moab, for the Arnon was the boundary of Moab. ¹⁹Israel then sent messengers to King Sihon of the Amorites, king of Heshbon; and Israel said to him, 'Let us pass through your land to our country.' ²⁰But Sihon did not trust Israel to pass through his territory; so Sihon gathered all his people together, and encamped at Jahaz, and fought with Israel. ²¹Then the LORD, the God of Israel, gave Sihon and all his people into the hand of Israel, and they defeated them; so Israel occupied all the land of the Amorites, who inhabited that country. ²²They occupied all the territory of the Amorites from the Arnon to the Jabbok and from the wilderness to the Jordan. ²³So now the LORD, the God of Israel, has conquered the Amorites for the benefit of his people Israel. Do you intend to take their place? ²⁴Should you not possess what your god Chemosh gives you to possess? And should we not be the ones to possess everything that the LORD our God has conquered for our benefit? ²⁵Now are you any better than King Balak son of Zippor of Moab? Did he ever enter into conflict with Israel, or did he ever go to war with them? ²⁶While Israel lived in Heshbon and its villages, and in Aroer and its villages, and in all the towns that are along the Arnon, three hundred years, why did you not recover them within that time? ²⁷It is not I who have sinned against you, but you are the

a Or Sea of Reeds

one who does me wrong by making war on me. Let the LORD, who is judge, decide today for the Israelites or for the Ammonites." 28But the king of the Ammonites did not heed the message that Jephthah sent him.

Jephthah's Vow

29 Then the spirit of the LORD came upon Jephthah, and he passed through Gilead and Manasseh. He passed on to Mizpah of Gilead, and from Mizpah of Gilead he passed on to the Ammonites. 30And Jephthah made a vow to the LORD, and said, "If you will give the Ammonites into my hand, 31then whoever comes out of the doors of my house to meet me, when I return victorious from the Ammonites, shall be the LORD's, to be offered up by me as a burnt offering." 32So Jephthah crossed over to the Ammonites to fight against them; and the LORD gave them into his hand. 33He inflicted a massive defeat on them from Aroer to the neighborhood of Minnith, twenty towns, and as far as Abel-keramim. So the Ammonites were subdued before the people of Israel.

Jephthah's Daughter

34 Then Jephthah came to his home at Mizpah; and there was his daughter coming out to meet him with timbrels and with dancing. She was his only child; he had no son or daughter except her. 35When he saw her, he tore his clothes, and said, "Alas, my daughter! You have brought me very low; you have become the cause of great trouble to me. For I have opened my mouth to the LORD, and I cannot take back my vow." 36She said to him, "My father, if you have opened your mouth to the LORD, do to me according to what has gone out of your mouth, now that the LORD has given you vengeance against your enemies, the Ammonites." 37And she said to her father, "Let this thing be done for me: Grant me two months, so that I may go and wander*a* on the mountains, and bewail my virginity, my companions and I." 38"Go," he said and sent her away for two months. So she departed, she and her companions, and bewailed her virginity on the mountains. 39At the end of two months, she returned to her father, who did with her according to the vow he had made. She had never slept with a man. So there arose an Israelite custom that 40for four days every year the daughters of Israel would go out to lament the daughter of Jephthah the Gileadite.

Intertribal Dissension

12 The men of Ephraim were called to arms, and they crossed to Zaphon and said to Jephthah, "Why did you cross over to fight against the Ammonites, and did not call us to go with you? We will burn your house down over you!" 2Jephthah said to them, "My people and I were engaged in conflict with the Ammonites who oppressed us*b* severely. But when I called you, you did not deliver me from their hand. 3When I saw that you would not deliver me, I took my life in my hand, and crossed over against the Ammonites, and the LORD gave them into my hand. Why then have you come up to me this day, to fight against me?" 4Then Jephthah gathered all the men of Gilead and fought with Ephraim; and the men of Gilead defeated Ephraim, because they said, "You are fugitives from Ephraim, you Gileadites—in the heart of Ephraim and Manasseh."*c* 5Then the Gileadites took the fords of the Jordan against the Ephraimites. Whenever one of the fugitives of Ephraim said, "Let me go over," the men of Gilead would say to him, "Are you an Ephraimite?" When he said, "No," 6they said to him, "Then say Shibboleth," and he said, "Sibboleth," for he could not pronounce it right. Then they seized him and killed him at the fords of the Jordan. Forty-two thousand of the Ephraimites fell at that time.

7 Jephthah judged Israel six years. Then Jephthah the Gileadite died, and was buried in his town in Gilead.*d*

Ibzan, Elon, and Abdon

8 After him Ibzan of Bethlehem judged Israel. 9He had thirty sons. He gave his thirty

---

a Cn: Heb *go down*   *b* Gk OL, Syr H: Heb lacks *who oppressed us*   *c* Meaning of Heb uncertain: Gk omits *because . . . Manasseh*   *d* Gk: Heb *in the towns of Gilead* daughters in marriage outside his clan and brought in thirty young women from outside for his sons. He judged Israel seven years. ¹⁰Then Ibzan died, and was buried at Bethlehem.

11 After him Elon the Zebulunite judged Israel; and he judged Israel ten years. ¹²Then Elon the Zebulunite died, and was buried at Aijalon in the land of Zebulun.

13 After him Abdon son of Hillel the Pirathonite judged Israel. ¹⁴He had forty sons and thirty grandsons, who rode on seventy donkeys; he judged Israel eight years. ¹⁵Then Abdon son of Hillel the Pirathonite died, and was buried at Pirathon in the land of Ephraim, in the hill country of the Amalekites.

The Birth of Samson

13 The Israelites again did what was evil in the sight of the LORD, and the LORD gave them into the hand of the Philistines forty years.

2 There was a certain man of Zorah, of the tribe of the Danites, whose name was Manoah. His wife was barren, having borne no children. ³And the angel of the LORD appeared to the woman and said to her, "Although you are barren, having borne no children, you shall conceive and bear a son. ⁴Now be careful not to drink wine or strong drink, or to eat anything unclean, ⁵for you shall conceive and bear a son. No razor is to come on his head, for the boy shall be a nazirite*ᵃ* to God from birth. It is he who shall begin to deliver Israel from the hand of the Philistines." ⁶Then the woman came and told her husband, "A man of God came to me, and his appearance was like that of an angel*ᵇ* of God, most awe-inspiring; I did not ask him where he came from, and he did not tell me his name; ⁷but he said to me, 'You shall conceive and bear a son. So then drink no wine or strong drink, and eat nothing unclean, for the boy shall be a nazirite*ᵃ* to God from birth to the day of his death.'"

8 Then Manoah entreated the LORD, and said, "O LORD, I pray, let the man of God

whom you sent come to us again and teach us what we are to do concerning the boy who will be born." ⁹God listened to Manoah, and the angel of God came again to the woman as she sat in the field; but her husband Manoah was not with her. ¹⁰So the woman ran quickly and told her husband, "The man who came to me the other day has appeared to me." ¹¹Manoah got up and followed his wife, and came to the man and said to him, "Are you the man who spoke to this woman?" And he said, "I am." ¹²Then Manoah said, "Now when your words come true, what is to be the boy's rule of life; what is he to do?" ¹³The angel of the LORD said to Manoah, "Let the woman give heed to all that I said to her. ¹⁴She may not eat of anything that comes from the vine. She is not to drink wine or strong drink, or eat any unclean thing. She is to observe everything that I commanded her."

15 Manoah said to the angel of the LORD, "Allow us to detain you, and prepare a kid for you." ¹⁶The angel of the LORD said to Manoah, "If you detain me, I will not eat your food; but if you want to prepare a burnt offering, then offer it to the LORD." (For Manoah did not know that he was the angel of the LORD.) ¹⁷Then Manoah said to the angel of the LORD, "What is your name, so that we may honor you when your words come true?" ¹⁸But the angel of the LORD said to him, "Why do you ask my name? It is too wonderful."

19 So Manoah took the kid with the grain offering, and offered it on the rock to the LORD, to him who works*ᶜ* wonders.*ᵈ* ²⁰When the flame went up toward heaven from the altar, the angel of the LORD ascended in the flame of the altar while Manoah and his wife looked on; and they fell on their faces to the ground. ²¹The angel of the LORD did not appear again to Manoah and his wife. Then Manoah realized that it was the angel of the LORD. ²²And Manoah said to his wife, "We shall surely die, for we have seen God." ²³But his wife said to him, "If the LORD had meant to kill us, he would not have accepted a burnt offering

---

ᵃ That is *one separated* or *one consecrated*   *ᵇ* Or *the angel and his wife looked on*   *ᶜ* Gk Vg: Heb *and working*   *ᵈ* Heb *wonders, while Manoah* and a grain offering at our hands, or shown us all these things, or now announced to us such things as these."

24 The woman bore a son, and named him Samson. The boy grew, and the LORD blessed him. 25The spirit of the LORD began to stir him in Mahaneh-dan, between Zorah and Eshtaol.

Samson's Marriage

14 Once Samson went down to Timnah, and at Timnah he saw a Philistine woman. 2Then he came up, and told his father and mother, "I saw a Philistine woman at Timnah; now get her for me as my wife." 3But his father and mother said to him, "Is there not a woman among your kin, or among all our*a* people, that you must go to take a wife from the uncircumcised Philistines?" But Samson said to his father, "Get her for me, because she pleases me." 4His father and mother did not know that this was from the LORD; for he was seeking a pretext to act against the Philistines. At that time the Philistines had dominion over Israel.

5 Then Samson went down with his father and mother to Timnah. When he came to the vineyards of Timnah, suddenly a young lion roared at him. 6The spirit of the LORD rushed on him, and he tore the lion apart barehanded as one might tear apart a kid. But he did not tell his father or his mother what he had done. 7Then he went down and talked with the woman, and she pleased Samson. 8After a while he returned to marry her, and he turned aside to see the carcass of the lion, and there was a swarm of bees in the body of the lion, and honey. 9He scraped it out into his hands, and went on, eating as he went. When he came to his father and mother, he gave some to them, and they ate it. But he did not tell them that he had taken the honey from the carcass of the lion.

10 His father went down to the woman, and Samson made a feast there as the young men were accustomed to do. 11When the people saw him, they brought thirty companions to be with him. 12Samson said to them, "Let me now put a riddle to you. If you can explain it to me within the seven days of the feast, and find it out, then I will give you thirty linen garments and thirty festal garments. 13But if you cannot explain it to me, then you shall give me thirty linen garments and thirty festal garments." So they said to him, "Ask your riddle; let us hear it." 14He said to them,

> "Out of the eater came something to
> eat.
> Out of the strong came something
> sweet."

But for three days they could not explain the riddle.

15 On the fourth*b* day they said to Samson's wife, "Coax your husband to explain the riddle to us, or we will burn you and your father's house with fire. Have you invited us here to impoverish us?" 16So Samson's wife wept before him, saying, "You hate me; you do not really love me. You have asked a riddle of my people, but you have not explained it to me." He said to her, "Look, I have not told my father or my mother. Why should I tell you?" 17She wept before him the seven days that their feast lasted; and because she nagged him, on the seventh day he told her. Then she explained the riddle to her people. 18The men of the town said to him on the seventh day before the sun went down,

> "What is sweeter than honey?
> What is stronger than a lion?"

And he said to them,

> "If you had not plowed with my heifer,
> you would not have found out my
> riddle."

19Then the spirit of the LORD rushed on him, and he went down to Ashkelon. He killed thirty men of the town, took their spoil, and gave the festal garments to those who had explained the riddle. In hot anger he went back to his father's house. 20And Samson's wife was given to his companion, who had been his best man.

a Cn: Heb *my*   *b* Gk Syr: Heb *seventh*

Samson Defeats the Philistines

15 After a while, at the time of the wheat harvest, Samson went to visit his wife, bringing along a kid. He said, "I want to go into my wife's room." But her father would not allow him to go in. 2Her father said, "I was sure that you had rejected her; so I gave her to your companion. Is not her younger sister prettier than she? Why not take her instead?" 3Samson said to them, "This time, when I do mischief to the Philistines, I will be without blame." 4So Samson went and caught three hundred foxes, and took some torches; and he turned the foxes*a* tail to tail, and put a torch between each pair of tails. 5When he had set fire to the torches, he let the foxes go into the standing grain of the Philistines, and burned up the shocks and the standing grain, as well as the vineyards and*b* olive groves. 6Then the Philistines asked, "Who has done this?" And they said, "Samson, the son-in-law of the Timnite, because he has taken Samson's wife and given her to his companion." So the Philistines came up, and burned her and her father. 7Samson said to them, "If this is what you do, I swear I will not stop until I have taken revenge on you." 8He struck them down hip and thigh with great slaughter; and he went down and stayed in the cleft of the rock of Etam.

9 Then the Philistines came up and encamped in Judah, and made a raid on Lehi. 10The men of Judah said, "Why have you come up against us?" They said, "We have come up to bind Samson, to do to him as he did to us." 11Then three thousand men of Judah went down to the cleft of the rock of Etam, and they said to Samson, "Do you not know that the Philistines are rulers over us? What then have you done to us?" He replied, "As they did to me, so I have done to them." 12They said to him, "We have come down to bind you, so that we may give you into the hands of the Philistines." Samson answered them, "Swear to me that you yourselves will not attack me." 13They said to him, "No, we will only bind you and give you into their hands; we will not

kill you." So they bound him with two new ropes, and brought him up from the rock.

14 When he came to Lehi, the Philistines came shouting to meet him; and the spirit of the LORD rushed on him, and the ropes that were on his arms became like flax that has caught fire, and his bonds melted off his hands. 15Then he found a fresh jawbone of a donkey, reached down and took it, and with it he killed a thousand men. 16And Samson said,

"With the jawbone of a donkey,
    heaps upon heaps,
with the jawbone of a donkey
    I have slain a thousand men."

17When he had finished speaking, he threw away the jawbone; and that place was called Ra-math-lehi.*c*

18 By then he was very thirsty, and he called on the LORD, saying, "You have granted this great victory by the hand of your servant. Am I now to die of thirst, and fall into the hands of the uncircumcised?" 19So God split open the hollow place that is at Lehi, and water came from it. When he drank, his spirit returned, and he revived. Therefore it was named En-hakko-re,*d* which is at Lehi to this day. 20And he judged Israel in the days of the Philistines twenty years.

Samson and Delilah

16 Once Samson went to Gaza, where he saw a prostitute and went in to her. 2The Gazites were told,*e* "Samson has come here." So they circled around and lay in wait for him all night at the city gate. They kept quiet all night, thinking, "Let us wait until the light of the morning; then we will kill him." 3But Samson lay only until midnight. Then at midnight he rose up, took hold of the doors of the city gate and the two posts, pulled them up, bar and all, put them on his shoulders, and carried them to the top of the hill that is in front of Hebron.

4 After this he fell in love with a woman in the valley of Sorek, whose name was Delilah. 5The lords of the Philistines came to her and said to her, "Coax him, and find out what makes his strength so great, and how we may

overpower him, so that we may bind him in order to subdue him; and we will each give you eleven hundred pieces of silver." [6]So Delilah said to Samson, "Please tell me what makes your strength so great, and how you could be bound, so that one could subdue you." [7]Samson said to her, "If they bind me with seven fresh bowstrings that are not dried out, then I shall become weak, and be like anyone else." [8]Then the lords of the Philistines brought her seven fresh bowstrings that had not dried out, and she bound him with them. [9]While men were lying in wait in an inner chamber, she said to him, "The Philistines are upon you, Samson!" But he snapped the bowstrings, as a strand of fiber snaps when it touches the fire. So the secret of his strength was not known.

10 Then Delilah said to Samson, "You have mocked me and told me lies; please tell me how you could be bound." [11]He said to her, "If they bind me with new ropes that have not been used, then I shall become weak, and be like anyone else." [12]So Delilah took new ropes and bound him with them, and said to him, "The Philistines are upon you, Samson!" (The men lying in wait were in an inner chamber.) But he snapped the ropes off his arms like a thread.

13 Then Delilah said to Samson, "Until now you have mocked me and told me lies; tell me how you could be bound." He said to her, "If you weave the seven locks of my head with the web and make it tight with the pin, then I shall become weak, and be like anyone else." [14]So while he slept, Delilah took the seven locks of his head and wove them into the web,[a] and made them tight with the pin. Then she said to him, "The Philistines are upon you, Samson!" But he awoke from his sleep, and pulled away the pin, the loom, and the web.

15 Then she said to him, "How can you say, 'I love you,' when your heart is not with me? You have mocked me three times now and have not told me what makes your strength so great." [16]Finally, after she had nagged him with her words day after day, and pestered him, he was tired to death. [17]So he told her his whole se-

cret, and said to her, "A razor has never come upon my head; for I have been a nazirite[b] to God from my mother's womb. If my head were shaved, then my strength would leave me; I would become weak, and be like anyone else."

18 When Delilah realized that he had told her his whole secret, she sent and called the lords of the Philistines, saying, "This time come up, for he has told his whole secret to me." Then the lords of the Philistines came up to her, and brought the money in their hands. [19]She let him fall asleep on her lap; and she called a man, and had him shave off the seven locks of his head. He began to weaken,[c] and his strength left him. [20]Then she said, "The Philistines are upon you, Samson!" When he awoke from his sleep, he thought, "I will go out as at other times, and shake myself free." But he did not know that the LORD had left him. [21]So the Philistines seized him and gouged out his eyes. They brought him down to Gaza and bound him with bronze shackles; and he ground at the mill in the prison. [22]But the hair of his head began to grow again after it had been shaved.

Samson's Death

23 Now the lords of the Philistines gathered to offer a great sacrifice to their god Dagon, and to rejoice; for they said, "Our god has given Samson our enemy into our hand." [24]When the people saw him, they praised their god; for they said, "Our god has given our enemy into our hand, the ravager of our country, who has killed many of us." [25]And when their hearts were merry, they said, "Call Samson, and let him entertain us." So they called Samson out of the prison, and he performed for them. They made him stand between the pillars; [26]and Samson said to the attendant who held him by the hand, "Let me feel the pillars on which the house rests, so that I may lean against them." [27]Now the house was full of men and women; all the lords of the Philistines were there, and on the roof there were about three thousand men and women, who looked on while Samson performed.

a Compare Gk: in verses 13-14, Heb lacks *and make it tight . . . into the web*   *b* That is *one separated* or *one consecrated*
c Gk: Heb *She began to torment him*

28 Then Samson called to the LORD and said, "Lord GOD, remember me and strengthen me only this once, O God, so that with this one act of revenge I may pay back the Philistines for my two eyes."*a* 29 And Samson grasped the two middle pillars on which the house rested, and he leaned his weight against them, his right hand on the one and his left hand on the other. 30 Then Samson said, "Let me die with the Philistines." He strained with all his might; and the house fell on the lords and all the people who were in it. So those he killed at his death were more than those he had killed during his life. 31 Then his brothers and all his family came down and took him and brought him up and buried him between Zorah and Eshtaol in the tomb of his father Manoah. He had judged Israel twenty years.

Micah and the Levite

17 There was a man in the hill country of Ephraim whose name was Micah. 2 He said to his mother, "The eleven hundred pieces of silver that were taken from you, about which you uttered a curse, and even spoke it in my hearing,—that silver is in my possession; I took it; but now I will return it to you."*b* And his mother said, "May my son be blessed by the LORD!" 3 Then he returned the eleven hundred pieces of silver to his mother; and his mother said, "I consecrate the silver to the LORD from my hand for my son, to make an idol of cast metal." 4 So when he returned the money to his mother, his mother took two hundred pieces of silver, and gave it to the silversmith, who made it into an idol of cast metal; and it was in the house of Micah. 5 This man Micah had a shrine, and he made an ephod and teraphim, and installed one of his sons, who became his priest. 6 In those days there was no king in Israel; all the people did what was right in their own eyes.

7 Now there was a young man of Bethlehem in Judah, of the clan of Judah. He was a Levite residing there. 8 This man left the town of Bethlehem in Judah, to live wherever he could find a place. He came to the house of Micah in the hill country of Ephraim to carry on his work.*c* 9 Micah said to him, "From where do you come?" He replied, "I am a Levite of Bethlehem in Judah, and I am going to live wherever I can find a place." 10 Then Micah said to him, "Stay with me, and be to me a father and a priest, and I will give you ten pieces of silver a year, a set of clothes, and your living."*d* 11 The Levite agreed to stay with the man; and the young man became to him like one of his sons. 12 So Micah installed the Levite, and the young man became his priest, and was in the house of Micah. 13 Then Micah said, "Now I know that the LORD will prosper me, because the Levite has become my priest."

The Migration of Dan

18 In those days there was no king in Israel. And in those days the tribe of the Danites was seeking for itself a territory to live in; for until then no territory among the tribes of Israel had been allotted to them. 2 So the Danites sent five valiant men from the whole number of their clan, from Zorah and from Eshtaol, to spy out the land and to explore it; and they said to them, "Go, explore the land." When they came to the hill country of Ephraim, to the house of Micah, they stayed there. 3 While they were at Micah's house, they recognized the voice of the young Levite; so they went over and asked him, "Who brought you here? What are you doing in this place? What is your business here?" 4 He said to them, "Micah did such and such for me, and he hired me, and I have become his priest." 5 Then they said to him, "Inquire of God that we may know whether the mission we are undertaking will succeed." 6 The priest replied, "Go in peace. The mission you are on is under the eye of the LORD."

7 The five men went on, and when they came to Laish, they observed the people who were there living securely, after the manner of the Sidonians, quiet and unsuspecting, lacking*e* nothing on earth, and possessing wealth.*f*

a Or *so that I may be avenged upon the Philistines for one of my two eyes*   *b* The words *but now I will return it to you* are transposed from the end of verse 3 in Heb   *c* Or *Ephraim, continuing his journey*   *d* Heb *living, and the Levite went*   *e* Cn Compare 18.10: Meaning of Heb uncertain   *f* Meaning of Heb uncertain

Furthermore, they were far from the Sidonians and had no dealings with Aram. *a* 8When they came to their kinsfolk at Zorah and Eshtaol, they said to them, "What do you report?" 9They said, "Come, let us go up against them; for we have seen the land, and it is very good. Will you do nothing? Do not be slow to go, but enter in and possess the land. 10When you go, you will come to an unsuspecting people. The land is broad—God has indeed given it into your hands—a place where there is no lack of anything on earth."

11 Six hundred men of the Danite clan, armed with weapons of war, set out from Zorah and Eshtaol, 12and went up and encamped at Kiriath-jearim in Judah. On this account that place is called Mahaneh-dan *b* to this day; it is west of Kiriath-jearim. 13From there they passed on to the hill country of Ephraim, and came to the house of Micah.

14 Then the five men who had gone to spy out the land (that is, Laish) said to their comrades, "Do you know that in these buildings there are an ephod, teraphim, and an idol of cast metal? Now therefore consider what you will do." 15So they turned in that direction and came to the house of the young Levite, at the home of Micah, and greeted him. 16While the six hundred men of the Danites, armed with their weapons of war, stood by the entrance of the gate, 17the five men who had gone to spy out the land proceeded to enter and take the idol of cast metal, the ephod, and the teraphim. *c* The priest was standing by the entrance of the gate with the six hundred men armed with weapons of war. 18When the men went into Micah's house and took the idol of cast metal, the ephod, and the teraphim, the priest said to them, "What are you doing?" 19They said to him, "Keep quiet! Put your hand over your mouth, and come with us, and be to us a father and a priest. Is it better for you to be priest to the house of one person, or to be priest to a tribe and clan in Israel?" 20Then the priest accepted the offer. He took the ephod,

the teraphim, and the idol, and went along with the people.

21 So they resumed their journey, putting the little ones, the livestock, and the goods in front of them. 22When they were some distance from the home of Micah, the men who were in the houses near Micah's house were called out, and they overtook the Danites. 23They shouted to the Danites, who turned around and said to Micah, "What is the matter that you come with such a company?" 24He replied, "You take my gods that I made, and the priest, and go away, and what have I left? How then can you ask me, 'What is the matter?'" 25And the Danites said to him, "You had better not let your voice be heard among us or else hot-tempered fellows will attack you, and you will lose your life and the lives of your household." 26Then the Danites went their way. When Micah saw that they were too strong for him, he turned and went back to his home.

The Danites Settle in Laish

27 The Danites, having taken what Micah had made, and the priest who belonged to him, came to Laish, to a people quiet and unsuspecting, put them to the sword, and burned down the city. 28There was no deliverer, because it was far from Sidon and they had no dealings with Aram. *d* It was in the valley that belongs to Beth-rehob. They rebuilt the city, and lived in it. 29They named the city Dan, after their ancestor Dan, who was born to Israel; but the name of the city was formerly Laish. 30Then the Danites set up the idol for themselves. Jonathan son of Gershom, son of Moses, *e* and his sons were priests to the tribe of the Danites until the time the land went into captivity. 31So they maintained as their own Micah's idol that he had made, as long as the house of God was at Shiloh.

The Levite's Concubine

19 In those days, when there was no king in Israel, a certain Levite, residing in the remote parts of the hill country of Ephra-

---

a Symmachus: Heb *with anyone*   *b* That is *Camp of Dan*   *c* Compare 17.4, 5; 18.14: Heb *teraphim and the cast metal*   *d* Cn Compare verse 7: Heb *with anyone*   *e* Another reading is *son of Manasseh* im, took to himself a concubine from Bethlehem in Judah. ²But his concubine became angry with*a* him, and she went away from him to her father's house at Bethlehem in Judah, and was there some four months. ³Then her husband set out after her, to speak tenderly to her and bring her back. He had with him his servant and a couple of donkeys. When he reached*b* her father's house, the girl's father saw him and came with joy to meet him. ⁴His father-in-law, the girl's father, made him stay, and he remained with him three days; so they ate and drank, and he*c* stayed there. ⁵On the fourth day they got up early in the morning, and he prepared to go; but the girl's father said to his son-in-law, "Fortify yourself with a bit of food, and after that you may go." ⁶So the two men sat and ate and drank together; and the girl's father said to the man, "Why not spend the night and enjoy yourself?" ⁷When the man got up to go, his father-in-law kept urging him until he spent the night there again. ⁸On the fifth day he got up early in the morning to leave; and the girl's father said, "Fortify yourself." So they lingered*d* until the day declined, and the two of them ate and drank.*e* ⁹When the man with his concubine and his servant got up to leave, his father-in-law, the girl's father, said to him, "Look, the day has worn on until it is almost evening. Spend the night. See, the day has drawn to a close. Spend the night here and enjoy yourself. Tomorrow you can get up early in the morning for your journey, and go home."

10 But the man would not spend the night; he got up and departed, and arrived opposite Jebus (that is, Jerusalem). He had with him a couple of saddled donkeys, and his concubine was with him. ¹¹When they were near Jebus, the day was far spent, and the servant said to his master, "Come now, let us turn aside to this city of the Jebusites, and spend the night in it." ¹²But his master said to him, "We will not turn aside into a city of foreigners, who do not belong to the people of Israel; but we will continue on to Gibeah." ¹³Then he said to his servant, "Come, let us try to reach one of these places, and spend the night at Gibeah or at Ramah." ¹⁴So they passed on and went their way; and the sun went down on them near Gibeah, which belongs to Benjamin. ¹⁵They turned aside there, to go in and spend the night at Gibeah. He went in and sat down in the open square of the city, but no one took them in to spend the night.

16 Then at evening there was an old man coming from his work in the field. The man was from the hill country of Ephraim, and he was residing in Gibeah. (The people of the place were Benjaminites.) ¹⁷When the old man looked up and saw the wayfarer in the open square of the city, he said, "Where are you going and where do you come from?" ¹⁸He answered him, "We are passing from Bethlehem in Judah to the remote parts of the hill country of Ephraim, from which I come. I went to Bethlehem in Judah; and I am going to my home.*f* Nobody has offered to take me in. ¹⁹We your servants have straw and fodder for our donkeys, with bread and wine for me and the woman and the young man along with us. We need nothing more." ²⁰The old man said, "Peace be to you. I will care for all your wants; only do not spend the night in the square." ²¹So he brought him into his house, and fed the donkeys; they washed their feet, and ate and drank.

Gibeah's Crime

22 While they were enjoying themselves, the men of the city, a perverse lot, surrounded the house, and started pounding on the door. They said to the old man, the master of the house, "Bring out the man who came into your house, so that we may have intercourse with him." ²³And the man, the master of the house, went out to them and said to them, "No, my brothers, do not act so wickedly. Since this man is my guest, do not do this vile thing. ²⁴Here are my virgin daughter and his concubine; let me bring them out now. Ravish them and do whatever you want to them; but against this man do not do such a vile thing." ²⁵But the men would not listen to him. So the man seized

---

a Gk OL: Heb *prostituted herself against*   *b* Gk: Heb *she brought him to*   *c* Compare verse 7 and Gk: Heb *they*
d Cn: Heb *Linger*   *e* Gk: Heb lacks *and drank*   *f* Gk Compare 19.29. Heb *to the house of the LORD*

his concubine, and put her out to them. They wantonly raped her, and abused her all through the night until the morning. And as the dawn began to break, they let her go. 26As morning appeared, the woman came and fell down at the door of the man's house where her master was, until it was light.

27 In the morning her master got up, opened the doors of the house, and when he went out to go on his way, there was his concubine lying at the door of the house, with her hands on the threshold. 28"Get up," he said to her, "we are going." But there was no answer. Then he put her on the donkey; and the man set out for his home. 29When he had entered his house, he took a knife, and grasping his concubine he cut her into twelve pieces, limb by limb, and sent her throughout all the territory of Israel. 30Then he commanded the men whom he sent, saying, "Thus shall you say to all the Israelites, 'Has such a thing ever happened*a* since the day that the Israelites came up from the land of Egypt until this day? Consider it, take counsel, and speak out.' "

The Other Tribes Attack Benjamin

20 Then all the Israelites came out, from Dan to Beer-sheba, including the land of Gilead, and the congregation assembled in one body before the LORD at Mizpah. 2The chiefs of all the people, of all the tribes of Israel, presented themselves in the assembly of the people of God, four hundred thousand foot-soldiers bearing arms. 3(Now the Benjaminites heard that the people of Israel had gone up to Mizpah.) And the Israelites said, "Tell us, how did this criminal act come about?" 4The Levite, the husband of the woman who was murdered, answered, "I came to Gibeah that belongs to Benjamin, I and my concubine, to spend the night. 5The lords of Gibeah rose up against me, and surrounded the house at night. They intended to kill me, and they raped my concubine until she died. 6Then I took my concubine and cut her into pieces, and sent her throughout the whole extent of Is-

rael's territory; for they have committed a vile outrage in Israel. 7So now, you Israelites, all of you, give your advice and counsel here."

8 All the people got up as one, saying, "We will not any of us go to our tents, nor will any of us return to our houses. 9But now this is what we will do to Gibeah: we will go up*b* against it by lot. 10We will take ten men of a hundred throughout all the tribes of Israel, and a hundred of a thousand, and a thousand of ten thousand, to bring provisions for the troops, who are going to repay*c* Gibeah of Benjamin for all the disgrace that they have done in Israel." 11So all the men of Israel gathered against the city, united as one.

12 The tribes of Israel sent men through all the tribe of Benjamin, saying, "What crime is this that has been committed among you? 13Now then, hand over those scoundrels in Gibeah, so that we may put them to death, and purge the evil from Israel." But the Benjaminites would not listen to their kinsfolk, the Israelites. 14The Benjaminites came together out of the towns to Gibeah, to go out to battle against the Israelites. 15On that day the Benjaminites mustered twenty-six thousand armed men from their towns, besides the inhabitants of Gibeah. 16Of all this force, there were seven hundred picked men who were left-handed; every one could sling a stone at a hair, and not miss. 17And the Israelites, apart from Benjamin, mustered four hundred thousand armed men, all of them warriors.

18 The Israelites proceeded to go up to Bethel, where they inquired of God, "Which of us shall go up first to battle against the Benjaminites?" And the LORD answered, "Judah shall go up first."

19 Then the Israelites got up in the morning, and encamped against Gibeah. 20The Israelites went out to battle against Benjamin; and the Israelites drew up the battle line against them at Gibeah. 21The Benjaminites came out of Gibeah, and struck down on that day twenty-two thousand of the Israelites. 23*d* The Israelites went up and wept before the LORD

---

a Compare Gk: Heb *30And all who saw it said, "Such a thing has not happened or been seen*   *b* Gk: Heb lacks *we will go up*   *c* Compare Gk: Meaning of Heb uncertain   *d* Verses 22 and 23 are transposed until the evening; and they inquired of the LORD, "Shall we again draw near to battle against our kinsfolk the Benjaminites?" And the LORD said, "Go up against them." 22The Israelites took courage, and again formed the battle line in the same place where they had formed it on the first day.

24 So the Israelites advanced against the Benjaminites the second day. 25Benjamin moved out against them from Gibeah the second day, and struck down eighteen thousand of the Israelites, all of them armed men. 26Then all the Israelites, the whole army, went back to Bethel and wept, sitting there before the LORD; they fasted that day until evening. Then they offered burnt offerings and sacrifices of well-being before the LORD. 27And the Israelites inquired of the LORD (for the ark of the covenant of God was there in those days, 28and Phinehas son of Eleazar, son of Aaron, ministered before it in those days), saying, "Shall we go out once more to battle against our kinsfolk the Benjaminites, or shall we desist?" The LORD answered, "Go up, for tomorrow I will give them into your hand."

29 So Israel stationed men in ambush around Gibeah. 30Then the Israelites went up against the Benjaminites on the third day, and set themselves in array against Gibeah, as before. 31When the Benjaminites went out against the army, they were drawn away from the city. As before they began to inflict casualties on the troops, along the main roads, one of which goes up to Bethel and the other to Gibeah, as well as in the open country, killing about thirty men of Israel. 32The Benjaminites thought, "They are being routed before us, as previously." But the Israelites said, "Let us retreat and draw them away from the city toward the roads." 33The main body of the Israelites drew back its battle line to Baal-tamar, while those Israelites who were in ambush rushed out of their place west*a* of Geba. 34There came against Gibeah ten thousand picked men out of all Israel, and the battle was fierce. But the Ben-

jaminites did not realize that disaster was close upon them.

35 The LORD defeated Benjamin before Israel; and the Israelites destroyed twenty-five thousand one hundred men of Benjamin that day, all of them armed.

36 Then the Benjaminites saw that they were defeated. *b*

The Israelites gave ground to Benjamin, because they trusted to the troops in ambush that they had stationed against Gibeah. 37The troops in ambush rushed quickly upon Gibeah. Then they put the whole city to the sword. 38Now the agreement between the main body of Israel and the men in ambush was that when they sent up a cloud of smoke out of the city 39the main body of Israel should turn in battle. But Benjamin had begun to inflict casualties on the Israelites, killing about thirty of them; so they thought, "Surely they are defeated before us, as in the first battle." 40But when the cloud, a column of smoke, began to rise out of the city, the Benjaminites looked behind them—and there was the whole city going up in smoke toward the sky! 41Then the main body of Israel turned, and the Benjaminites were dismayed, for they saw that disaster was close upon them. 42Therefore they turned away from the Israelites in the direction of the wilderness; but the battle overtook them, and those who came out of the city*c* were slaughtering them in between. *d* 43Cutting down*e* the Benjaminites, they pursued them from Nohah*f* and trod them down as far as a place east of Gibeah. 44Eighteen thousand Benjaminites fell, all of them courageous fighters. 45When they turned and fled toward the wilderness to the rock of Rimmon, five thousand of them were cut down on the main roads, and they were pursued as far as Gidom, and two thousand of them were slain. 46So all who fell that day of Benjamin were twenty-five thousand arms-bearing men, all of them courageous fighters. 47But six hundred turned and fled toward the wilderness to the rock of Rimmon,

a Gk Vg: Heb *in the plain*   *b* This sentence is continued by verse 45.   *c* Compare Vg and some Gk Mss: Heb *cities*   *d* Compare Syr: Meaning of Heb uncertain   *e* Gk: Heb *Surrounding*   *f* Gk: Heb *pursued them at their resting place* and remained at the rock of Rimmon for four months. 48Meanwhile, the Israelites turned back against the Benjaminites, and put them to the sword—the city, the people, the animals, and all that remained. Also the remaining towns they set on fire.

The Benjaminites Saved from Extinction

21 Now the Israelites had sworn at Mizpah, "No one of us shall give his daughter in marriage to Benjamin." 2And the people came to Bethel, and sat there until evening before God, and they lifted up their voices and wept bitterly. 3They said, "O LORD, the God of Israel, why has it come to pass that today there should be one tribe lacking in Israel?" 4On the next day, the people got up early, and built an altar there, and offered burnt offerings and sacrifices of well-being. 5Then the Israelites said, "Which of all the tribes of Israel did not come up in the assembly to the LORD?" For a solemn oath had been taken concerning whoever did not come up to the LORD to Mizpah, saying, "That one shall be put to death." 6But the Israelites had compassion for Benjamin their kin, and said, "One tribe is cut off from Israel this day. 7What shall we do for wives for those who are left, since we have sworn by the LORD that we will not give them any of our daughters as wives?"

8 Then they said, "Is there anyone from the tribes of Israel who did not come up to the LORD to Mizpah?" It turned out that no one from Jabesh-gilead had come to the camp, to the assembly. 9For when the roll was called among the people, not one of the inhabitants of Jabesh-gilead was there. 10So the congregation sent twelve thousand soldiers there and commanded them, "Go, put the inhabitants of Jabesh-gilead to the sword, including the women and the little ones. 11This is what you shall do; every male and every woman that has lain with a male you shall devote to destruction." 12And they found among the inhabitants of Jabesh-gilead four hundred young virgins who had never slept with a man and brought them to the camp at Shiloh, which is in the land of Canaan.

13 Then the whole congregation sent word to the Benjaminites who were at the rock of Rimmon, and proclaimed peace to them. 14Benjamin returned at that time; and they gave them the women whom they had saved alive of the women of Jabesh-gilead; but they did not suffice for them.

15 The people had compassion on Benjamin because the LORD had made a breach in the tribes of Israel. 16So the elders of the congregation said, "What shall we do for wives for those who are left, since there are no women left in Benjamin?" 17And they said, "There must be heirs for the survivors of Benjamin, in order that a tribe may not be blotted out from Israel. 18Yet we cannot give any of our daughters to them as wives." For the Israelites had sworn, "Cursed be anyone who gives a wife to Benjamin." 19So they said, "Look, the yearly festival of the LORD is taking place at Shiloh, which is north of Bethel, on the east of the highway that goes up from Bethel to Shechem, and south of Lebonah." 20And they instructed the Benjaminites, saying, "Go and lie in wait in the vineyards, 21and watch; when the young women of Shiloh come out to dance in the dances, then come out of the vineyards and each of you carry off a wife for himself from the young women of Shiloh, and go to the land of Benjamin. 22Then if their fathers or their brothers come to complain to us, we will say to them, 'Be generous and allow us to have them; because we did not capture in battle a wife for each man. But neither did you incur guilt by giving your daughters to them.'" 23The Benjaminites did so; they took wives for each of them from the dancers whom they abducted. Then they went and returned to their territory, and rebuilt the towns, and lived in them. 24So the Israelites departed from there at that time by tribes and families, and they went out from there to their own territories.

25 In those days there was no king in Israel; all the people did what was right in their own eyes.

RUTH

Elimelech's Family Goes to Moab

1 In the days when the judges ruled, there was a famine in the land, and a certain man of Bethlehem in Judah went to live in the country of Moab, he and his wife and two sons. ²The name of the man was Elimelech and the name of his wife Naomi, and the names of his two sons were Mahlon and Chilion; they were Ephrathites from Bethlehem in Judah. They went into the country of Moab and remained there. ³But Elimelech, the husband of Naomi, died, and she was left with her two sons. ⁴These took Moabite wives; the name of the one was Orpah and the name of the other Ruth. When they had lived there about ten years, ⁵both Mahlon and Chilion also died, so that the woman was left without her two sons and her husband.

Naomi and Her Moabite Daughters-in-Law

6 Then she started to return with her daughters-in-law from the country of Moab, for she had heard in the country of Moab that the LORD had considered his people and given them food. ⁷So she set out from the place where she had been living, she and her two daughters-in-law, and they went on their way to go back to the land of Judah. ⁸But Naomi said to her two daughters-in-law, "Go back each of you to your mother's house. May the LORD deal kindly with you, as you have dealt with the dead and with me. ⁹The LORD grant that you may find security, each of you in the house of your husband." Then she kissed them, and they wept aloud. ¹⁰They said to her, "No, we will return with you to your people." ¹¹But Naomi said, "Turn back, my daughters, why will you go with me? Do I still have sons in my womb that they may become your husbands? ¹²Turn back, my daughters, go your way, for I am too old to have a husband. Even if I thought there was hope for me, even if I should have a husband tonight and bear sons, ¹³would you then wait until they were grown?

Would you then refrain from marrying? No, my daughters, it has been far more bitter for me than for you, because the hand of the LORD has turned against me." ¹⁴Then they wept aloud again. Orpah kissed her mother-in-law, but Ruth clung to her.

15 So she said, "See, your sister-in-law has gone back to her people and to her gods; return after your sister-in-law." ¹⁶But Ruth said,

"Do not press me to leave you
      or to turn back from following you!
Where you go, I will go;
      where you lodge, I will lodge;
your people shall be my people,
      and your God my God.
17   Where you die, I will die—
      there will I be buried.
May the LORD do thus and so to me,
      and more as well,
if even death parts me from you!"

¹⁸When Naomi saw that she was determined to go with her, she said no more to her.

19 So the two of them went on until they came to Bethlehem. When they came to Bethlehem, the whole town was stirred because of them; and the women said, "Is this Naomi?" ²⁰She said to them,

"Call me no longer Naomi,ᵃ
      call me Mara,ᵇ
for the Almightyᶜ has dealt bitterly
      with me.
21   I went away full,
      but the LORD has brought me back
            empty;
why call me Naomi
      when the LORD has dealt harshly
            withᵈ me,
      and the Almightyᶜ has brought
            calamity upon me?"

22 So Naomi returned together with Ruth the Moabite, her daughter-in-law, who came back with her from the country of Moab. They came to Bethlehem at the beginning of the barley harvest.

---

a That is *Pleasant*   b That is *Bitter*   c Traditional rendering of Heb *Shaddai*   d Or *has testified against*

Ruth Meets Boaz

2 Now Naomi had a kinsman on her husband's side, a prominent rich man, of the family of Elimelech, whose name was Boaz. 2And Ruth the Moabite said to Naomi, "Let me go to the field and glean among the ears of grain, behind someone in whose sight I may find favor." She said to her, "Go, my daughter." 3So she went. She came and gleaned in the field behind the reapers. As it happened, she came to the part of the field belonging to Boaz, who was of the family of Elimelech. 4Just then Boaz came from Bethlehem. He said to the reapers, "The LORD be with you." They answered, "The LORD bless you." 5Then Boaz said to his servant who was in charge of the reapers, "To whom does this young woman belong?" 6The servant who was in charge of the reapers answered, "She is the Moabite who came back with Naomi from the country of Moab. 7She said, 'Please, let me glean and gather among the sheaves behind the reapers.' So she came, and she has been on her feet from early this morning until now, without resting even for a moment."[a]

8 Then Boaz said to Ruth, "Now listen, my daughter, do not go to glean in another field or leave this one, but keep close to my young women. 9Keep your eyes on the field that is being reaped, and follow behind them. I have ordered the young men not to bother you. If you get thirsty, go to the vessels and drink from what the young men have drawn." 10Then she fell prostrate, with her face to the ground, and said to him, "Why have I found favor in your sight, that you should take notice of me, when I am a foreigner?" 11But Boaz answered her, "All that you have done for your mother-in-law since the death of your husband has been fully told me, and how you left your father and mother and your native land and came to a people that you did not know before. 12May the LORD reward you for your deeds, and may you have a full reward from the LORD, the God of Israel, under whose wings you have come for refuge!" 13Then she said, "May I continue to find favor in your sight, my lord, for you have comforted me and spoken kindly to your servant, even though I am not one of your servants."

14 At mealtime Boaz said to her, "Come here, and eat some of this bread, and dip your morsel in the sour wine." So she sat beside the reapers, and he heaped up for her some parched grain. She ate until she was satisfied, and she had some left over. 15When she got up to glean, Boaz instructed his young men, "Let her glean even among the standing sheaves, and do not reproach her. 16You must also pull out some handfuls for her from the bundles, and leave them for her to glean, and do not rebuke her."

17 So she gleaned in the field until evening. Then she beat out what she had gleaned, and it was about an ephah of barley. 18She picked it up and came into the town, and her mother-in-law saw how much she had gleaned. Then she took out and gave her what was left over after she herself had been satisfied. 19Her mother-in-law said to her, "Where did you glean today? And where have you worked? Blessed be the man who took notice of you." So she told her mother-in-law with whom she had worked, and said, "The name of the man with whom I worked today is Boaz." 20Then Naomi said to her daughter-in-law, "Blessed be he by the LORD, whose kindness has not forsaken the living or the dead!" Naomi also said to her, "The man is a relative of ours, one of our nearest kin."[b] 21Then Ruth the Moabite said, "He even said to me, 'Stay close by my servants, until they have finished all my harvest.'" 22Naomi said to Ruth, her daughter-in-law, "It is better, my daughter, that you go out with his young women, otherwise you might be bothered in another field." 23So she stayed close to the young women of Boaz, gleaning until the end of the barley and wheat harvests; and she lived with her mother-in-law.

a Compare Gk Vg: Meaning of Heb uncertain   *b* Or *one with the right to redeem*

Ruth and Boaz at the Threshing Floor

3 Naomi her mother-in-law said to her, "My daughter, I need to seek some security for you, so that it may be well with you. 2Now here is our kinsman Boaz, with whose young women you have been working. See, he is winnowing barley tonight at the threshing floor. 3Now wash and anoint yourself, and put on your best clothes and go down to the threshing floor; but do not make yourself known to the man until he has finished eating and drinking. 4When he lies down, observe the place where he lies; then, go and uncover his feet and lie down; and he will tell you what to do." 5She said to her, "All that you tell me I will do."

6 So she went down to the threshing floor and did just as her mother-in-law had instructed her. 7When Boaz had eaten and drunk, and he was in a contented mood, he went to lie down at the end of the heap of grain. Then she came stealthily and uncovered his feet, and lay down. 8At midnight the man was startled, and turned over, and there, lying at his feet, was a woman! 9He said, "Who are you?" And she answered, "I am Ruth, your servant; spread your cloak over your servant, for you are next-of-kin."a 10He said, "May you be blessed by the LORD, my daughter; this last instance of your loyalty is better than the first; you have not gone after young men, whether poor or rich. 11And now, my daughter, do not be afraid, I will do for you all that you ask, for all the assembly of my people know that you are a worthy woman. 12But now, though it is true that I am a near kinsman, there is another kinsman more closely related than I. 13Remain this night, and in the morning, if he will act as next-of-kina for you, good; let him do it. If he is not willing to act as next-of-kina for you, then, as the LORD lives, I will act as next-of-kina for you. Lie down until the morning."

14 So she lay at his feet until morning, but got up before one person could recognize another; for he said, "It must not be known that the woman came to the threshing floor." 15Then he said, "Bring the cloak you are wearing and hold it out." So she held it, and he measured out six measures of barley, and put it on her back; then he went into the city. 16She came to her mother-in-law, who said, "How did things go with you,b my daughter?" Then she told her all that the man had done for her, 17saying, "He gave me these six measures of barley, for he said, 'Do not go back to your mother-in-law empty-handed.'" 18She replied, "Wait, my daughter, until you learn how the matter turns out, for the man will not rest, but will settle the matter today."

The Marriage of Boaz and Ruth

4 No sooner had Boaz gone up to the gate and sat down there than the next-of-kin,a of whom Boaz had spoken, came passing by. So Boaz said, "Come over, friend; sit down here." And he went over and sat down. 2Then Boaz took ten men of the elders of the city, and said, "Sit down here"; so they sat down. 3He then said to the next-of-kin,a "Naomi, who has come back from the country of Moab, is selling the parcel of land that belonged to our kinsman Elimelech. 4So I thought I would tell you of it, and say: Buy it in the presence of those sitting here, and in the presence of the elders of my people. If you will redeem it, redeem it; but if you will not, tell me, so that I may know; for there is no one prior to you to redeem it, and I come after you." So he said, "I will redeem it." 5Then Boaz said, "The day you acquire the field from the hand of Naomi, you are also acquiring Ruthc the Moabite, the widow of the dead man, to maintain the dead man's name on his inheritance." 6At this, the next-of-kina said, "I cannot redeem it for myself without damaging my own inheritance. Take my right of redemption yourself, for I cannot redeem it."

7 Now this was the custom in former times in Israel concerning redeeming and exchanging: to confirm a transaction, the one took off a sandal and gave it to the other; this was the manner of attesting in Israel. 8So

a Or *one with the right to redeem*   b Or *"Who are you,*   c OL Vg: Heb *from the hand of Naomi and from Ruth* when the next-of-kin*a* said to Boaz, "Acquire it for yourself," he took off his sandal. 9Then Boaz said to the elders and all the people, "Today you are witnesses that I have acquired from the hand of Naomi all that belonged to Elimelech and all that belonged to Chilion and Mahlon. 10I have also acquired Ruth the Moabite, the wife of Mahlon, to be my wife, to maintain the dead man's name on his inheritance, in order that the name of the dead may not be cut off from his kindred and from the gate of his native place; today you are witnesses." 11Then all the people who were at the gate, along with the elders, said, "We are witnesses. May the LORD make the woman who is coming into your house like Rachel and Leah, who together built up the house of Israel. May you produce children in Ephrathah and bestow a name in Bethlehem; 12and, through the children that the LORD will give you by this young woman, may your house be like the house of Perez, whom Tamar bore to Judah."

The Genealogy of David

13 So Boaz took Ruth and she became his wife. When they came together, the LORD made her conceive, and she bore a son. 14Then the women said to Naomi, "Blessed be the LORD, who has not left you this day without next-of-kin;*a* and may his name be renowned in Israel! 15He shall be to you a restorer of life and a nourisher of your old age; for your daughter-in-law who loves you, who is more to you than seven sons, has borne him." 16Then Naomi took the child and laid him in her bosom, and became his nurse. 17The women of the neighborhood gave him a name, saying, "A son has been born to Naomi." They named him Obed; he became the father of Jesse, the father of David.

18 Now these are the descendants of Perez: Perez became the father of Hezron, 19Hezron of Ram, Ram of Amminadab, 20Amminadab of Nahshon, Nahshon of Salmon, 21Salmon of Boaz, Boaz of Obed, 22Obed of Jesse, and Jesse of David.

a Or one with the right to redeem

1 SAMUEL

Samuel's Birth and Dedication

1 There was a certain man of Ramathaim, a Zuphite[a] from the hill country of Ephraim, whose name was Elkanah son of Jeroham son of Elihu son of Tohu son of Zuph, an Ephraimite. 2He had two wives; the name of the one was Hannah, and the name of the other Peninnah. Peninnah had children, but Hannah had no children.

3 Now this man used to go up year by year from his town to worship and to sacrifice to the LORD of hosts at Shiloh, where the two sons of Eli, Hophni and Phinehas, were priests of the LORD. 4On the day when Elkanah sacrificed, he would give portions to his wife Peninnah and to all her sons and daughters; 5but to Hannah he gave a double portion,[b] because he loved her, though the LORD had closed her womb. 6Her rival used to provoke her severely, to irritate her, because the LORD had closed her womb. 7So it went on year by year; as often as she went up to the house of the LORD, she used to provoke her. Therefore Hannah wept and would not eat. 8Her husband Elkanah said to her, "Hannah, why do you weep? Why do you not eat? Why is your heart sad? Am I not more to you than ten sons?"

9 After they had eaten and drunk at Shiloh, Hannah rose and presented herself before the LORD.[c] Now Eli the priest was sitting on the seat beside the doorpost of the temple of the LORD. 10She was deeply distressed and prayed to the LORD, and wept bitterly. 11She made this vow: "O LORD of hosts, if only you will look on the misery of your servant, and remember me, and not forget your servant, but will give to your servant a male child, then I will set him before you as a nazirite[d] until the day of his death. He shall drink neither wine nor intoxicants,[e] and no razor shall touch his head."

12 As she continued praying before the LORD, Eli observed her mouth. 13Hannah was praying silently; only her lips moved, but her voice was not heard; therefore Eli thought she was drunk. 14So Eli said to her, "How long will you make a drunken spectacle of yourself? Put away your wine." 15But Hannah answered, "No, my lord, I am a woman deeply troubled; I have drunk neither wine nor strong drink, but I have been pouring out my soul before the LORD. 16Do not regard your servant as a worthless woman, for I have been speaking out of my great anxiety and vexation all this time." 17Then Eli answered, "Go in peace; the God of Israel grant the petition you have made to him." 18And she said, "Let your servant find favor in your sight." Then the woman went to her quarters,[f] ate and drank with her husband,[g] and her countenance was sad no longer.[h]

19 They rose early in the morning and worshiped before the LORD; then they went back to their house at Ramah. Elkanah knew his wife Hannah, and the LORD remembered her. 20In due time Hannah conceived and bore a son. She named him Samuel, for she said, "I have asked him of the LORD."

21 The man Elkanah and all his household went up to offer to the LORD the yearly sacrifice, and to pay his vow. 22But Hannah did not go up, for she said to her husband, "As soon as the child is weaned, I will bring him, that he may appear in the presence of the LORD, and remain there forever; I will offer him as a nazirite[d] for all time."[i] 23Her husband Elkanah said to her, "Do what seems best to you, wait until you have weaned him; only— may the LORD establish his word."[j] So the woman remained and nursed her son, until she weaned him. 24When she had weaned him, she took him up with her, along with a three-year-old bull,[k] an ephah of flour, and a skin of wine. She brought him to the house of the

---

a Compare Gk and 1 Chr 6.35-36: Heb *Ramathaim-zophim* b Syr: Meaning of Heb uncertain c Gk: Heb lacks *and presented herself before the LORD* d That is *one separated* or *one consecrated* e Cn Compare Gk Q Ms 1.22: MT *then I will give him to the LORD all the days of his life* f Gk: Heb *went her way* g Gk: Heb lacks *and drank with her husband* h Gk: Meaning of Heb uncertain i Cn Compare Q Ms: MT lacks *I will offer him as a nazirite for all time* j MT: Q Ms Gk Compare Syr *that which goes out of your mouth* k Q Ms Gk Syr: MT *three bulls*

LORD at Shiloh; and the child was young. 25Then they slaughtered the bull, and they brought the child to Eli. 26And she said, "Oh, my lord! As you live, my lord, I am the woman who was standing here in your presence, praying to the LORD. 27For this child I prayed; and the LORD has granted me the petition that I made to him. 28Therefore I have lent him to the LORD; as long as he lives, he is given to the LORD."

She left him there for^a the LORD.

Hannah's Prayer

2 Hannah prayed and said,
"My heart exults in the LORD;
   my strength is exalted in my God.^b
My mouth derides my enemies,
   because I rejoice in my^c victory.

2   "There is no Holy One like the LORD,
   no one besides you;
   there is no Rock like our God.
3   Talk no more so very proudly,
   let not arrogance come from your
     mouth;
   for the LORD is a God of knowledge,
   and by him actions are weighed.
4   The bows of the mighty are broken,
   but the feeble gird on strength.
5   Those who were full have hired
     themselves out for bread,
   but those who were hungry are fat
     with spoil.
The barren has borne seven,
   but she who has many children is
     forlorn.
6   The LORD kills and brings to life;
   he brings down to Sheol and raises
     up.
7   The LORD makes poor and makes rich;
   he brings low, he also exalts.
8   He raises up the poor from the dust;
   he lifts the needy from the ash heap,
to make them sit with princes
   and inherit a seat of honor.^d

For the pillars of the earth are the
   LORD's,
   and on them he has set the world.

9   "He will guard the feet of his faithful
     ones,
   but the wicked shall be cut off in
     darkness;
   for not by might does one prevail.
10   The LORD! His adversaries shall be
     shattered;
   the Most High^e will thunder in
     heaven.
The LORD will judge the ends of the
     earth;
   he will give strength to his king,
   and exalt the power of his anointed."

Eli's Wicked Sons

11 Then Elkanah went home to Ramah, while the boy remained to minister to the LORD, in the presence of the priest Eli.

12 Now the sons of Eli were scoundrels; they had no regard for the LORD 13or for the duties of the priests to the people. When anyone offered sacrifice, the priest's servant would come, while the meat was boiling, with a three-pronged fork in his hand, 14and he would thrust it into the pan, or kettle, or caldron, or pot; all that the fork brought up the priest would take for himself.^f This is what they did at Shiloh to all the Israelites who came there. 15Moreover, before the fat was burned, the priest's servant would come and say to the one who was sacrificing, "Give meat for the priest to roast; for he will not accept boiled meat from you, but only raw." 16And if the man said to him, "Let them burn the fat first, and then take whatever you wish," he would say, "No, you must give it now; if not, I will take it by force." 17Thus the sin of the young men was very great in the sight of the LORD; for they treated the offerings of the LORD with contempt.

The Child Samuel at Shiloh

18 Samuel was ministering before the LORD, a boy wearing a linen ephod. 19His mother used to make for him a little robe and take it to him each year, when she went up with her husband to offer the yearly sacrifice. 20Then Eli would bless Elkanah and his wife, and say, "May the LORD repay*a* you with children by this woman for the gift that she made to*b* the LORD"; and then they would return to their home.

21 And*c* the LORD took note of Hannah; she conceived and bore three sons and two daughters. And the boy Samuel grew up in the presence of the LORD.

Prophecy against Eli's Household

22 Now Eli was very old. He heard all that his sons were doing to all Israel, and how they lay with the women who served at the entrance to the tent of meeting. 23He said to them, "Why do you do such things? For I hear of your evil dealings from all these people. 24No, my sons; it is not a good report that I hear the people of the LORD spreading abroad. 25If one person sins against another, someone can intercede for the sinner with the LORD;*d* but if someone sins against the LORD, who can make intercession?" But they would not listen to the voice of their father; for it was the will of the LORD to kill them.

26 Now the boy Samuel continued to grow both in stature and in favor with the LORD and with the people.

27 A man of God came to Eli and said to him, "Thus the LORD has said, 'I revealed*e* myself to the family of your ancestor in Egypt when they were slaves*f* to the house of Pharaoh. 28I chose him out of all the tribes of Israel to be my priest, to go up to my altar, to offer incense, to wear an ephod before me; and I gave to the family of your ancestor all my offerings by fire from the people of Israel. 29Why then look with greedy eyes*g* at my sacrifices

and my offerings that I commanded, and honor your sons more than me by fattening yourselves on the choicest parts of every offering of my people Israel?' 30Therefore the LORD the God of Israel declares: 'I promised that your family and the family of your ancestor should go in and out before me forever'; but now the LORD declares: 'Far be it from me; for those who honor me I will honor, and those who despise me shall be treated with contempt. 31See, a time is coming when I will cut off your strength and the strength of your ancestor's family, so that no one in your family will live to old age. 32Then in distress you will look with greedy eye*h* on all the prosperity that shall be bestowed upon Israel; and no one in your family shall ever live to old age. 33The only one of you whom I shall not cut off from my altar shall be spared to weep out his*i* eyes and grieve his*j* heart; all the members of your household shall die by the sword.*k* 34The fate of your two sons, Hophni and Phinehas, shall be the sign to you—both of them shall die on the same day. 35I will raise up for myself a faithful priest, who shall do according to what is in my heart and in my mind. I will build him a sure house, and he shall go in and out before my anointed one forever. 36Everyone who is left in your family shall come to implore him for a piece of silver or a loaf of bread, and shall say, Please put me in one of the priest's places, that I may eat a morsel of bread.' "

Samuel's Calling and Prophetic Activity

3 Now the boy Samuel was ministering to the LORD under Eli. The word of the LORD was rare in those days; visions were not widespread.

2 At that time Eli, whose eyesight had begun to grow dim so that he could not see, was lying down in his room; 3the lamp of God had not yet gone out, and Samuel was lying down in the temple of the LORD, where the ark of

---

a Q Ms Gk: MT *give*   *b* Q Ms Gk: MT *for the petition that she asked of*   *c* Q Ms Gk: MT *When*   *d* Gk Compare Q Ms: MT *another, God will mediate for him*   *e* Gk Tg Syr: Heb *Did I reveal*   *f* Q Ms Gk: MT lacks *slaves*   *g* Q Ms Gk: MT *then kick*   *h* Q Ms Gk: MT *will kick*   *i* Q Ms Gk: MT *your*   *j* Q Ms Gk: Heb *your*   *k* Q Ms See Gk: MT *die like mortals*

God was. 4Then the LORD called, "Samuel! Samuel!"*a* and he said, "Here I am!" 5and ran to Eli, and said, "Here I am, for you called me." But he said, "I did not call; lie down again." So he went and lay down. 6The LORD called again, "Samuel!" Samuel got up and went to Eli, and said, "Here I am, for you called me." But he said, "I did not call, my son; lie down again." 7Now Samuel did not yet know the LORD, and the word of the LORD had not yet been revealed to him. 8The LORD called Samuel again, a third time. And he got up and went to Eli, and said, "Here I am, for you called me." Then Eli perceived that the LORD was calling the boy. 9Therefore Eli said to Samuel, "Go, lie down; and if he calls you, you shall say, 'Speak, LORD, for your servant is listening.' " So Samuel went and lay down in his place.

10 Now the LORD came and stood there, calling as before, "Samuel! Samuel!" And Samuel said, "Speak, for your servant is listening." 11Then the LORD said to Samuel, "See, I am about to do something in Israel that will make both ears of anyone who hears of it tingle. 12On that day I will fulfill against Eli all that I have spoken concerning his house, from beginning to end. 13For I have told him that I am about to punish his house forever, for the iniquity that he knew, because his sons were blaspheming God,*b* and he did not restrain them. 14Therefore I swear to the house of Eli that the iniquity of Eli's house shall not be expiated by sacrifice or offering forever."

15 Samuel lay there until morning; then he opened the doors of the house of the LORD. Samuel was afraid to tell the vision to Eli. 16But Eli called Samuel and said, "Samuel, my son." He said, "Here I am." 17Eli said, "What was it that he told you? Do not hide it from me. May God do so to you and more also, if you hide anything from me of all that he told you." 18So Samuel told him everything and hid nothing from him. Then he said, "It is the LORD; let him do what seems good to him."

19 As Samuel grew up, the LORD was with him and let none of his words fall to the ground. 20And all Israel from Dan to Beer-sheba knew that Samuel was a trustworthy prophet of the LORD. 21The LORD continued to appear at Shiloh, for the LORD revealed himself to Samuel at Shiloh by the word of the LORD. 1And the word of Samuel came to all Israel.

The Ark of God Captured

In those days the Philistines mustered for war against Israel,*c* and Israel went out to battle against them;*d* they encamped at Ebenezer, and the Philistines encamped at Aphek. 2The Philistines drew up in line against Israel, and when the battle was joined,*e* Israel was defeated by the Philistines, who killed about four thousand men on the field of battle. 3When the troops came to the camp, the elders of Israel said, "Why has the LORD put us to rout today before the Philistines? Let us bring the ark of the covenant of the LORD here from Shiloh, so that he may come among us and save us from the power of our enemies." 4So the people sent to Shiloh, and brought from there the ark of the covenant of the LORD of hosts, who is enthroned on the cherubim. The two sons of Eli, Hophni and Phinehas, were there with the ark of the covenant of God.

5 When the ark of the covenant of the LORD came into the camp, all Israel gave a mighty shout, so that the earth resounded. 6When the Philistines heard the noise of the shouting, they said, "What does this great shouting in the camp of the Hebrews mean?" When they learned that the ark of the LORD had come to the camp, 7the Philistines were afraid; for they said, "Gods have*f* come into the camp." They also said, "Woe to us! For nothing like this has happened before. 8Woe to us! Who can deliver us from the power of these mighty gods? These are the gods who struck the Egyptians with every sort of plague in the wilderness. 9Take courage, and be men,

a Q Ms Gk See 3.10: MT *the LORD called Samuel*   *b* Another reading is *for themselves*   *c* Gk: Heb lacks *In those days the Philistines mustered for war against Israel*   *d* Gk: Heb *against the Philistines*   *e* Meaning of Heb uncertain   *f* Or *A god has*

O Philistines, in order not to become slaves to the Hebrews as they have been to you; be men and fight."

10 So the Philistines fought; Israel was defeated, and they fled, everyone to his home. There was a very great slaughter, for there fell of Israel thirty thousand foot soldiers. ¹¹The ark of God was captured; and the two sons of Eli, Hophni and Phinehas, died.

Death of Eli

12 A man of Benjamin ran from the battle line, and came to Shiloh the same day, with his clothes torn and with earth upon his head. ¹³When he arrived, Eli was sitting upon his seat by the road watching, for his heart trembled for the ark of God. When the man came into the city and told the news, all the city cried out. ¹⁴When Eli heard the sound of the outcry, he said, "What is this uproar?" Then the man came quickly and told Eli. ¹⁵Now Eli was ninety-eight years old and his eyes were set, so that he could not see. ¹⁶The man said to Eli, "I have just come from the battle; I fled from the battle today." He said, "How did it go, my son?" ¹⁷The messenger replied, "Israel has fled before the Philistines, and there has also been a great slaughter among the troops; your two sons also, Hophni and Phinehas, are dead, and the ark of God has been captured." ¹⁸When he mentioned the ark of God, Eli*ᵃ* fell over backward from his seat by the side of the gate; and his neck was broken and he died, for he was an old man, and heavy. He had judged Israel forty years.

19 Now his daughter-in-law, the wife of Phinehas, was pregnant, about to give birth. When she heard the news that the ark of God was captured, and that her father-in-law and her husband were dead, she bowed and gave birth; for her labor pains overwhelmed her. ²⁰As she was about to die, the women attending her said to her, "Do not be afraid, for you have borne a son." But she did not answer or give heed. ²¹She named the child Ichabod, meaning, "The glory has departed from Isra-

el," because the ark of God had been captured and because of her father-in-law and her husband. ²²She said, "The glory has departed from Israel, for the ark of God has been captured."

The Philistines and the Ark

5 When the Philistines captured the ark of God, they brought it from Ebenezer to Ashdod; ²then the Philistines took the ark of God and brought it into the house of Dagon and placed it beside Dagon. ³When the people of Ashdod rose early the next day, there was Dagon, fallen on his face to the ground before the ark of the LORD. So they took Dagon and put him back in his place. ⁴But when they rose early on the next morning, Dagon had fallen on his face to the ground before the ark of the LORD, and the head of Dagon and both his hands were lying cut off upon the threshold; only the trunk ofᵇ Dagon was left to him. ⁵This is why the priests of Dagon and all who enter the house of Dagon do not step on the threshold of Dagon in Ashdod to this day.

6 The hand of the LORD was heavy upon the people of Ashdod, and he terrified and struck them with tumors, both in Ashdod and in its territory. ⁷And when the inhabitants of Ashdod saw how things were, they said, "The ark of the God of Israel must not remain with us; for his hand is heavy on us and on our god Dagon." ⁸So they sent and gathered together all the lords of the Philistines, and said, "What shall we do with the ark of the God of Israel?" The inhabitants of Gath replied, "Let the ark of God be moved on to us."ᶜ So they moved the ark of the God of Israel to Gath.ᵈ ⁹But after they had brought it to Gath,ᵈ the hand of the LORD was against the city, causing a very great panic; he struck the inhabitants of the city, both young and old, so that tumors broke out on them. ¹⁰So they sent the ark of the God of Israelᵉ to Ekron. But when the ark of God came to Ekron, the people of Ekron cried out, "Whyᶠ have they brought around to

---

a Heb *he*　　*b* Heb lacks *the trunk of*　　*c* Gk Compare Q Ms: MT *They answered, "Let the ark of the God of Israel be brought around to Gath."*　　*d* Gk: Heb lacks *to Gath*　　*e* Q Ms Gk: MT lacks *of Israel*　　*f* Q Ms Gk: MT lacks *Why* us*a* the ark of the God of Israel to kill us*a* and our*b* people?" 11They sent therefore and gathered together all the lords of the Philistines, and said, "Send away the ark of the God of Israel, and let it return to its own place, that it may not kill us and our people." For there was a deathly panic*c* throughout the whole city. The hand of God was very heavy there; 12those who did not die were stricken with tumors, and the cry of the city went up to heaven.

The Ark Returned to Israel

6 The ark of the LORD was in the country of the Philistines seven months. 2Then the Philistines called for the priests and the diviners and said, "What shall we do with the ark of the LORD? Tell us what we should send with it to its place." 3They said, "If you send away the ark of the God of Israel, do not send it empty, but by all means return him a guilt offering. Then you will be healed and will be ransomed;*d* will not his hand then turn from you?" 4And they said, "What is the guilt offering that we shall return to him?" They answered, "Five gold tumors and five gold mice, according to the number of the lords of the Philistines; for the same plague was upon all of you and upon your lords. 5So you must make images of your tumors and images of your mice that ravage the land, and give glory to the God of Israel; perhaps he will lighten his hand on you and your gods and your land. 6Why should you harden your hearts as the Egyptians and Pharaoh hardened their hearts? After he had made fools of them, did they not let the people go, and they departed? 7Now then, get ready a new cart and two milch cows that have never borne a yoke, and yoke the cows to the cart, but take their calves home, away from them. 8Take the ark of the LORD and place it on the cart, and put in a box at its side the figures of gold, which you are returning to him as a guilt offering. Then send it off, and let it go its way. 9And watch; if it goes up on the way

to its own land, to Beth-shemesh, then it is he who has done us this great harm; but if not, then we shall know that it is not his hand that struck us; it happened to us by chance."

10 The men did so; they took two milch cows and yoked them to the cart, and shut up their calves at home. 11They put the ark of the LORD on the cart, and the box with the gold mice and the images of their tumors. 12The cows went straight in the direction of Beth-shemesh along one highway, lowing as they went; they turned neither to the right nor to the left, and the lords of the Philistines went after them as far as the border of Beth-shemesh.

13 Now the people of Beth-shemesh were reaping their wheat harvest in the valley. When they looked up and saw the ark, they went with rejoicing to meet it.*e* 14The cart came into the field of Joshua of Beth-shemesh, and stopped there. A large stone was there; so they split up the wood of the cart and offered the cows as a burnt offering to the LORD. 15The Levites took down the ark of the LORD and the box that was beside it, in which were the gold objects, and set them upon the large stone. Then the people of Beth-shemesh offered burnt offerings and presented sacrifices on that day to the LORD. 16When the five lords of the Philistines saw it, they returned that day to Ekron.

17 These are the gold tumors, which the Philistines returned as a guilt offering to the LORD: one for Ashdod, one for Gaza, one for Ashkelon, one for Gath, one for Ekron; 18also the gold mice, according to the number of all the cities of the Philistines belonging to the five lords, both fortified cities and unwalled villages. The great stone, beside which they set down the ark of the LORD, is a witness to this day in the field of Joshua of Beth-shemesh.

The Ark at Kiriath-jearim

19 The descendants of Jeconiah did not rejoice with the people of Beth-shemesh when they greeted*f* the ark of the LORD; and he killed seventy men of them.*g* The people

---

a Heb *me*   *b* Heb *my*   *c* Q Ms reads *a panic from the* LORD   *d* Q Ms Gk: MT *and it will be known to you*
e Gk: Heb *rejoiced to see it*   *f* Gk: Heb *And he killed some of the people of Beth-shemesh, because they looked into*
g Heb *killed seventy men, fifty thousand men*

mourned because the LORD had made a great slaughter among the people. 20Then the people of Beth-shemesh said, "Who is able to stand before the LORD, this holy God? To whom shall he go so that we may be rid of him?" 21So they sent messengers to the inhabitants of Kiriath-jearim, saying, "The Philistines have returned the ark of the LORD. 7 Come down and take it up to you." 1And the people of Kiriath-jearim came and took up the ark of the LORD, and brought it to the house of Abinadab on the hill. They consecrated his son, Eleazar, to have charge of the ark of the LORD.

2 From the day that the ark was lodged at Kiriath-jearim, a long time passed, some twenty years, and all the house of Israel lamented*a* after the LORD.

Samuel as Judge

3 Then Samuel said to all the house of Israel, "If you are returning to the LORD with all your heart, then put away the foreign gods and the Astartes from among you. Direct your heart to the LORD, and serve him only, and he will deliver you out of the hand of the Philistines." 4So Israel put away the Baals and the Astartes, and they served the LORD only.

5 Then Samuel said, "Gather all Israel at Mizpah, and I will pray to the LORD for you." 6So they gathered at Mizpah, and drew water and poured it out before the LORD. They fasted that day, and said, "We have sinned against the LORD." And Samuel judged the people of Israel at Mizpah.

7 When the Philistines heard that the people of Israel had gathered at Mizpah, the lords of the Philistines went up against Israel. And when the people of Israel heard of it they were afraid of the Philistines. 8The people of Israel said to Samuel, "Do not cease to cry out to the LORD our God for us, and pray that he may save us from the hand of the Philistines." 9So Samuel took a sucking lamb and offered it as a whole burnt offering to the LORD; Samuel cried out to the LORD for Israel, and the

LORD answered him. 10As Samuel was offering up the burnt offering, the Philistines drew near to attack Israel; but the LORD thundered with a mighty voice that day against the Philistines and threw them into confusion; and they were routed before Israel. 11And the men of Israel went out of Mizpah and pursued the Philistines, and struck them down as far as beyond Beth-car.

12 Then Samuel took a stone and set it up between Mizpah and Jeshanah,*b* and named it Ebenezer;*c* for he said, "Thus far the LORD has helped us." 13So the Philistines were subdued and did not again enter the territory of Israel; the hand of the LORD was against the Philistines all the days of Samuel. 14The towns that the Philistines had taken from Israel were restored to Israel, from Ekron to Gath; and Israel recovered their territory from the hand of the Philistines. There was peace also between Israel and the Amorites.

15 Samuel judged Israel all the days of his life. 16He went on a circuit year by year to Bethel, Gilgal, and Mizpah; and he judged Israel in all these places. 17Then he would come back to Ramah, for his home was there; he administered justice there to Israel, and built there an altar to the LORD.

Israel Demands a King

8 When Samuel became old, he made his sons judges over Israel. 2The name of his firstborn son was Joel, and the name of his second, Abijah; they were judges in Beer-sheba. 3Yet his sons did not follow in his ways, but turned aside after gain; they took bribes and perverted justice.

4 Then all the elders of Israel gathered together and came to Samuel at Ramah, 5and said to him, "You are old and your sons do not follow in your ways; appoint for us, then, a king to govern us, like other nations." 6But the thing displeased Samuel when they said, "Give us a king to govern us." Samuel prayed to the LORD, 7and the LORD said to Samuel, "Listen to the voice of the people in all that they say

---

a Meaning of Heb uncertain   *b* Gk Syr: Heb *Shen*   *c* That is *Stone of Help* to you; for they have not rejected you, but they have rejected me from being king over them. ⁸Just as they have done to me,ᵃ from the day I brought them up out of Egypt to this day, forsaking me and serving other gods, so also they are doing to you. ⁹Now then, listen to their voice; only—you shall solemnly warn them, and show them the ways of the king who shall reign over them."

10 So Samuel reported all the words of the LORD to the people who were asking him for a king. ¹¹He said, "These will be the ways of the king who will reign over you: he will take your sons and appoint them to his chariots and to be his horsemen, and to run before his chariots; ¹²and he will appoint for himself commanders of thousands and commanders of fifties, and some to plow his ground and to reap his harvest, and to make his implements of war and the equipment of his chariots. ¹³He will take your daughters to be perfumers and cooks and bakers. ¹⁴He will take the best of your fields and vineyards and olive orchards and give them to his courtiers. ¹⁵He will take one-tenth of your grain and of your vineyards and give it to his officers and his courtiers. ¹⁶He will take your male and female slaves, and the best of your cattleᵇ and donkeys, and put them to his work. ¹⁷He will take one-tenth of your flocks, and you shall be his slaves. ¹⁸And in that day you will cry out because of your king, whom you have chosen for yourselves; but the LORD will not answer you in that day."

Israel's Request for a King Granted

19 But the people refused to listen to the voice of Samuel; they said, "No! but we are determined to have a king over us, ²⁰so that we also may be like other nations, and that our king may govern us and go out before us and fight our battles." ²¹When Samuel had heard all the words of the people, he repeated them in the ears of the LORD. ²²The LORD said to Samuel, "Listen to their voice and set a king

over them." Samuel then said to the people of Israel, "Each of you return home."

Saul Chosen to Be King

9 There was a man of Benjamin whose name was Kish son of Abiel son of Zeror son of Becorath son of Aphiah, a Benjaminite, a man of wealth. ²He had a son whose name was Saul, a handsome young man. There was not a man among the people of Israel more handsome than he; he stood head and shoulders above everyone else.

3 Now the donkeys of Kish, Saul's father, had strayed. So Kish said to his son Saul, "Take one of the boys with you; go and look for the donkeys." ⁴He passed through the hill country of Ephraim and passed through the land of Shalishah, but they did not find them. And they passed through the land of Shaalim, but they were not there. Then he passed through the land of Benjamin, but they did not find them.

5 When they came to the land of Zuph, Saul said to the boy who was with him, "Let us turn back, or my father will stop worrying about the donkeys and worry about us." ⁶But he said to him, "There is a man of God in this town; he is a man held in honor. Whatever he says always comes true. Let us go there now; perhaps he will tell us about the journey on which we have set out." ⁷Then Saul replied to the boy, "But if we go, what can we bring the man? For the bread in our sacks is gone, and there is no present to bring to the man of God. What have we?" ⁸The boy answered Saul again, "Here, I have with me a quarter shekel of silver; I will give it to the man of God, to tell us our way." ⁹(Formerly in Israel, anyone who went to inquire of God would say, "Come, let us go to the seer"; for the one who is now called a prophet was formerly called a seer.) ¹⁰Saul said to the boy, "Good; come, let us go." So they went to the town where the man of God was.

11 As they went up the hill to the town, they met some girls coming out to draw water,

ᵃ Gk: Heb lacks *to me*   ᵇ Gk: Heb *young men*

and said to them, "Is the seer here?" 12They answered, "Yes, there he is just ahead of you. Hurry; he has come just now to the town, because the people have a sacrifice today at the shrine. 13As soon as you enter the town, you will find him, before he goes up to the shrine to eat. For the people will not eat until he comes, since he must bless the sacrifice; afterward those eat who are invited. Now go up, for you will meet him immediately." 14So they went up to the town. As they were entering the town, they saw Samuel coming out toward them on his way up to the shrine.

15 Now the day before Saul came, the LORD had revealed to Samuel: 16"Tomorrow about this time I will send to you a man from the land of Benjamin, and you shall anoint him to be ruler over my people Israel. He shall save my people from the hand of the Philistines; for I have seen the suffering of*a* my people, because their outcry has come to me." 17When Samuel saw Saul, the LORD told him, "Here is the man of whom I spoke to you. He it is who shall rule over my people." 18Then Saul approached Samuel inside the gate, and said, "Tell me, please, where is the house of the seer?" 19Samuel answered Saul, "I am the seer; go up before me to the shrine, for today you shall eat with me, and in the morning I will let you go and will tell you all that is on your mind. 20As for your donkeys that were lost three days ago, give no further thought to them, for they have been found. And on whom is all Israel's desire fixed, if not on you and on all your ancestral house?" 21Saul answered, "I am only a Benjaminite, from the least of the tribes of Israel, and my family is the humblest of all the families of the tribe of Benjamin. Why then have you spoken to me in this way?"

22 Then Samuel took Saul and his servant-boy and brought them into the hall, and gave them a place at the head of those who had been invited, of whom there were about thirty. 23And Samuel said to the cook, "Bring the portion I gave you, the one I asked you to put aside." 24The cook took up the thigh and what went with it*b* and set them before Saul. Samuel said, "See, what was kept is set before you. Eat; for it is set*c* before you at the appointed time, so that you might eat with the guests."*d*

So Saul ate with Samuel that day. 25When they came down from the shrine into the town, a bed was spread for Saul*e* on the roof, and he lay down to sleep.*f* 26Then at the break of dawn*g* Samuel called to Saul upon the roof, "Get up, so that I may send you on your way." Saul got up, and both he and Samuel went out into the street.

Samuel Anoints Saul

27 As they were going down to the outskirts of the town, Samuel said to Saul, "Tell the boy to go on before us, and when he has passed on, stop here yourself for a while, that I may make known to you the word of God."

10 1Samuel took a vial of oil and poured it on his head, and kissed him; he said, "The LORD has anointed you ruler over his people Israel. You shall reign over the people of the LORD and you will save them from the hand of their enemies all around. Now this shall be the sign to you that the LORD has anointed you ruler*b* over his heritage: 2When you depart from me today you will meet two men by Rachel's tomb in the territory of Benjamin at Zelzah; they will say to you, 'The donkeys that you went to seek are found, and now your father has stopped worrying about them and is worrying about you, saying: What shall I do about my son?' 3Then you shall go on from there further and come to the oak of Tabor; three men going up to God at Bethel will meet you there, one carrying three kids, another carrying three loaves of bread, and another carrying a skin of wine. 4They will greet you and give you two loaves of bread, which you

---

a Gk: Heb lacks *the suffering of*   *b* Meaning of Heb uncertain   *c* Q Ms Gk: MT *it was kept*   *d* Cn: Heb *it was kept for you, saying, I have invited the people*   *e* Gk: Heb *and he spoke with Saul*   *f* Gk: Heb lacks *and he lay down to sleep*   *g* Gk: Heb *and they arose early and at break of dawn*   *h* Gk: Heb lacks *over his people Israel. You shall . . . anointed you ruler* shall accept from them. 5After that you shall come to Gibeath-elohim,*a* at the place where the Philistine garrison is; there, as you come to the town, you will meet a band of prophets coming down from the shrine with harp, tambourine, flute, and lyre playing in front of them; they will be in a prophetic frenzy. 6Then the spirit of the LORD will possess you, and you will be in a prophetic frenzy along with them and be turned into a different person. 7Now when these signs meet you, do whatever you see fit to do, for God is with you. 8And you shall go down to Gilgal ahead of me; then I will come down to you to present burnt offerings and offer sacrifices of well-being. Seven days you shall wait, until I come to you and show you what you shall do."

Saul Prophesies

9 As he turned away to leave Samuel, God gave him another heart; and all these signs were fulfilled that day. 10When they were going from there*b* to Gibeah,*c* a band of prophets met him; and the spirit of God possessed him, and he fell into a prophetic frenzy along with them. 11When all who knew him before saw how he prophesied with the prophets, the people said to one another, "What has come over the son of Kish? Is Saul also among the prophets?" 12A man of the place answered, "And who is their father?" Therefore it became a proverb, "Is Saul also among the prophets?" 13When his prophetic frenzy had ended, he went home.*d*

14 Saul's uncle said to him and to the boy, "Where did you go?" And he replied, "To seek the donkeys; and when we saw they were not to be found, we went to Samuel." 15Saul's uncle said, "Tell me what Samuel said to you." 16Saul said to his uncle, "He told us that the donkeys had been found." But about the matter of the kingship, of which Samuel had spoken, he did not tell him anything.

Saul Proclaimed King

17 Samuel summoned the people to the LORD at Mizpah 18and said to them,*e* "Thus says the LORD, the God of Israel, 'I brought up Israel out of Egypt, and I rescued you from the hand of the Egyptians and from the hand of all the kingdoms that were oppressing you.' 19But today you have rejected your God, who saves you from all your calamities and your distresses; and you have said, 'No! but set a king over us.' Now therefore present yourselves before the LORD by your tribes and by your clans."

20 Then Samuel brought all the tribes of Israel near, and the tribe of Benjamin was taken by lot. 21He brought the tribe of Benjamin near by its families, and the family of the Matrites was taken by lot. Finally he brought the family of the Matrites near man by man,*f* and Saul the son of Kish was taken by lot. But when they sought him, he could not be found. 22So they inquired again of the LORD, "Did the man come here?"*g* and the LORD said, "See, he has hidden himself among the baggage." 23Then they ran and brought him from there. When he took his stand among the people, he was head and shoulders taller than any of them. 24Samuel said to all the people, "Do you see the one whom the LORD has chosen? There is no one like him among all the people." And all the people shouted, "Long live the king!"

25 Samuel told the people the rights and duties of the kingship; and he wrote them in a book and laid it up before the LORD. Then Samuel sent all the people back to their homes. 26Saul also went to his home at Gibeah, and with him went warriors whose hearts God had touched. 27But some worthless fellows said, "How can this man save us?" They despised him and brought him no present. But he held his peace.

Now Nahash, king of the Ammonites, had been grievously oppressing the Gadites and the Reubenites. He would gouge out the right eye of each of them and would not grant Israel a deliverer. No one was left of the Israelites across the Jordan whose right eye Nahash,

---

a Or *the Hill of God*   *b* Gk: Heb *they came there*   *c* Or *the hill*   *d* Cn: Heb *he came to the shrine*   *e* Heb *to the people of Israel*   *f* Gk: Heb lacks *Finally . . . man by man*   *g* Gk: Heb *Is there yet a man to come here?*

king of the Ammonites, had not gouged out. But there were seven thousand men who had escaped from the Ammonites and had entered Jabesh-gilead. *a*

Saul Defeats the Ammonites

11 About a month later, *b* Nahash the Ammonite went up and besieged Jabesh-gilead; and all the men of Jabesh said to Nahash, "Make a treaty with us, and we will serve you." 2But Nahash the Ammonite said to them, "On this condition I will make a treaty with you, namely that I gouge out everyone's right eye, and thus put disgrace upon all Israel." 3The elders of Jabesh said to him, "Give us seven days' respite that we may send messengers through all the territory of Israel. Then, if there is no one to save us, we will give ourselves up to you." 4When the messengers came to Gibeah of Saul, they reported the matter in the hearing of the people; and all the people wept aloud.

5 Now Saul was coming from the field behind the oxen; and Saul said, "What is the matter with the people, that they are weeping?" So they told him the message from the inhabitants of Jabesh. 6And the spirit of God came upon Saul in power when he heard these words, and his anger was greatly kindled. 7He took a yoke of oxen, and cut them in pieces and sent them throughout all the territory of Israel by messengers, saying, "Whoever does not come out after Saul and Samuel, so shall it be done to his oxen!" Then the dread of the LORD fell upon the people, and they came out as one. 8When he mustered them at Bezek, those from Israel were three hundred thousand, and those from Judah seventy*c* thousand. 9They said to the messengers who had come, "Thus shall you say to the inhabitants of Jabesh-gilead: 'Tomorrow, by the time the sun is hot, you shall have deliverance.' " When the messengers came and told the inhabitants of Jabesh, they rejoiced. 10So the inhabitants of Jabesh said, "Tomorrow we will give ourselves up to you, and you may do to us whatever seems good to you." 11The next day Saul put the people in three companies. At the morning watch they came into the camp and cut down the Ammonites until the heat of the day; and those who survived were scattered, so that no two of them were left together.

12 The people said to Samuel, "Who is it that said, 'Shall Saul reign over us?' Give them to us so that we may put them to death." 13But Saul said, "No one shall be put to death this day, for today the LORD has brought deliverance to Israel."

14 Samuel said to the people, "Come, let us go to Gilgal and there renew the kingship." 15So all the people went to Gilgal, and there they made Saul king before the LORD in Gilgal. There they sacrificed offerings of well-being before the LORD, and there Saul and all the Israelites rejoiced greatly.

Samuel's Farewell Address

12 Samuel said to all Israel, "I have listened to you in all that you have said to me, and have set a king over you. 2See, it is the king who leads you now; I am old and gray, but my sons are with you. I have led you from my youth until this day. 3Here I am; testify against me before the LORD and before his anointed. Whose ox have I taken? Or whose donkey have I taken? Or whom have I defrauded? Whom have I oppressed? Or from whose hand have I taken a bribe to blind my eyes with it? Testify against me*d* and I will restore it to you." 4They said, "You have not defrauded us or oppressed us or taken anything from the hand of anyone." 5He said to them, "The LORD is witness against you, and his anointed is witness this day, that you have not found anything in my hand." And they said, "He is witness."

6 Samuel said to the people, "The LORD is witness, who*e* appointed Moses and Aaron and brought your ancestors up out of the land of Egypt. 7Now therefore take your stand, so

---

a Q Ms Compare Josephus, *Antiquities* VI.v.1 (68-71): MT lacks *Now Nahash . . . entered Jabesh-gilead.*   *b* Q Ms Gk: MT lacks *About a month later*   *c* Q Ms Gk: MT *thirty*   *d* Gk: Heb lacks *Testify against me*   *e* Gk: Heb lacks *is witness, who* that I may enter into judgment with you before the LORD, and I will declare to you[a] all the saving deeds of the LORD that he performed for you and for your ancestors. [8]When Jacob went into Egypt and the Egyptians oppressed them,[b] then your ancestors cried to the LORD and the LORD sent Moses and Aaron, who brought forth your ancestors out of Egypt, and settled them in this place. [9]But they forgot the LORD their God; and he sold them into the hand of Sisera, commander of the army of King Jabin of[c] Hazor, and into the hand of the Philistines, and into the hand of the king of Moab; and they fought against them. [10]Then they cried to the LORD, and said, 'We have sinned, because we have forsaken the LORD, and have served the Baals and the Astartes; but now rescue us out of the hand of our enemies, and we will serve you.' [11]And the LORD sent Jerubbaal and Barak,[d] and Jephthah, and Samson,[e] and rescued you out of the hand of your enemies on every side; and you lived in safety. [12]But when you saw that King Nahash of the Ammonites came against you, you said to me, 'No, but a king shall reign over us,' though the LORD your God was your king. [13]See, here is the king whom you have chosen, for whom you have asked; see, the LORD has set a king over you. [14]If you will fear the LORD and serve him and heed his voice and not rebel against the commandment of the LORD, and if both you and the king who reigns over you will follow the LORD your God, it will be well; [15]but if you will not heed the voice of the LORD, but rebel against the commandment of the LORD, then the hand of the LORD will be against you and your king.[f] [16]Now therefore take your stand and see this great thing that the LORD will do before your eyes. [17]Is it not the wheat harvest today? I will call upon the LORD, that he may send thunder and rain; and you shall know and see that the wickedness that you have done in the sight of the LORD is great in demanding a king for yourselves." [18]So Samuel called upon the LORD, and the LORD sent thunder and rain that day; and all the people greatly feared the LORD and Samuel.

19 All the people said to Samuel, "Pray to the LORD your God for your servants, so that we may not die; for we have added to all our sins the evil of demanding a king for ourselves." [20]And Samuel said to the people, "Do not be afraid; you have done all this evil, yet do not turn aside from following the LORD, but serve the LORD with all your heart; [21]and do not turn aside after useless things that cannot profit or save, for they are useless. [22]For the LORD will not cast away his people, for his great name's sake, because it has pleased the LORD to make you a people for himself. [23]Moreover as for me, far be it from me that I should sin against the LORD by ceasing to pray for you; and I will instruct you in the good and the right way. [24]Only fear the LORD, and serve him faithfully with all your heart; for consider what great things he has done for you. [25]But if you still do wickedly, you shall be swept away, both you and your king."

Saul's Unlawful Sacrifice

13 Saul was . . .[g] years old when he began to reign; and he reigned . . . and two[h] years over Israel.

2 Saul chose three thousand out of Israel; two thousand were with Saul in Michmash and the hill country of Bethel, and a thousand were with Jonathan in Gibeah of Benjamin; the rest of the people he sent home to their tents. [3]Jonathan defeated the garrison of the Philistines that was at Geba; and the Philistines heard of it. And Saul blew the trumpet throughout all the land, saying, "Let the Hebrews hear!" [4]When all Israel heard that Saul had defeated the garrison of the Philistines, and also that Israel had become odious to the Philistines, the people were called out to join Saul at Gilgal.

5 The Philistines mustered to fight with

---

a Gk: Heb lacks *and I will declare to you*　　*b* Gk: Heb lacks *and the Egyptians oppressed them*　　*c* Gk: Heb lacks *King Jabin of*　　*d* Gk Syr: Heb *Bedan*　　*e* Gk: Heb *Samuel*　　*f* Gk: Heb *and your ancestors*　　*g* The number is lacking in the Heb text (the verse is lacking in the Septuagint).　　*h* *Two* is not the entire number; something has dropped out.

Israel, thirty thousand chariots, and six thousand horsemen, and troops like the sand on the seashore in multitude; they came up and encamped at Michmash, to the east of Beth-aven. 6When the Israelites saw that they were in distress (for the troops were hard pressed), the people hid themselves in caves and in holes and in rocks and in tombs and in cisterns. 7Some Hebrews crossed the Jordan to the land of Gad and Gilead. Saul was still at Gilgal, and all the people followed him trembling.

8 He waited seven days, the time appointed by Samuel; but Samuel did not come to Gilgal, and the people began to slip away from Saul. *a* 9So Saul said, "Bring the burnt offering here to me, and the offerings of well-being." And he offered the burnt offering. 10As soon as he had finished offering the burnt offering, Samuel arrived; and Saul went out to meet him and salute him. 11Samuel said, "What have you done?" Saul replied, "When I saw that the people were slipping away from me, and that you did not come within the days appointed, and that the Philistines were mustering at Michmash, 12I said, 'Now the Philistines will come down upon me at Gilgal, and I have not entreated the favor of the LORD'; so I forced myself, and offered the burnt offering." 13Samuel said to Saul, "You have done foolishly; you have not kept the commandment of the LORD your God, which he commanded you. The LORD would have established your kingdom over Israel forever, 14but now your kingdom will not continue; the LORD has sought out a man after his own heart; and the LORD has appointed him to be ruler over his people, because you have not kept what the LORD commanded you." 15And Samuel left and went on his way from Gilgal. *b* The rest of the people followed Saul to join the army; they went up from Gilgal toward Gibeah of Benjamin. *c*

Preparations for Battle

Saul counted the people who were present with him, about six hundred men. 16Saul, his son Jonathan, and the people who were present with them stayed in Geba of Benjamin; but the Philistines encamped at Michmash. 17And raiders came out of the camp of the Philistines in three companies; one company turned toward Ophrah, to the land of Shual, 18another company turned toward Beth-horon, and another company turned toward the mountain *d* that looks down upon the valley of Zeboim toward the wilderness.

19 Now there was no smith to be found throughout all the land of Israel; for the Philistines said, "The Hebrews must not make swords or spears for themselves"; 20so all the Israelites went down to the Philistines to sharpen their plowshares, mattocks, axes, or sickles; *e* 21The charge was two-thirds of a shekel *f* for the plowshares and for the mattocks, and one-third of a shekel for sharpening the axes and for setting the goads. *g* 22So on the day of the battle neither sword nor spear was to be found in the possession of any of the people with Saul and Jonathan; but Saul and his son Jonathan had them.

Jonathan Surprises and Routs the Philistines

23 Now a garrison of the Philistines had gone out to the pass of Michmash. 14 1One day Jonathan son of Saul said to the young man who carried his armor, "Come, let us go over to the Philistine garrison on the other side." But he did not tell his father. 2Saul was staying in the outskirts of Gibeah under the pomegranate tree that is at Migron; the troops that were with him were about six hundred men, 3along with Ahijah son of Ahitub, Ichabod's brother, son of Phinehas son of Eli, the priest of the LORD in Shiloh, carrying an ephod. Now the people did not know that Jonathan had gone. 4In the pass, *b* by which Jonathan tried to go over to the Philistine garrison, there was a rocky crag on one side and a rocky crag on the other; the name of the one was Bozez, and the name of the other Seneh.

---

a Heb *him*   *b* Gk: Heb *went up from Gilgal to Gibeah of Benjamin*   *c* Gk: Heb lacks *The rest . . . of Benjamin*
d Cn Compare Gk: Heb *toward the border*   *e* Gk: Heb *plowshare*   *f* Heb *was a pim*   *g* Cn: Meaning of Heb uncertain   *h* Heb *Between the passes*

5One crag rose on the north in front of Michmash, and the other on the south in front of Geba.

6 Jonathan said to the young man who carried his armor, "Come, let us go over to the garrison of these uncircumcised; it may be that the LORD will act for us; for nothing can hinder the LORD from saving by many or by few." 7His armor-bearer said to him, "Do all that your mind inclines to.*a* I am with you; as your mind is, so is mine."*b* 8Then Saul said, "Now we will cross over to those men and will show ourselves to them. 9If they say to us, 'Wait until we come to you,' then we will stand still in our place, and we will not go up to them. 10But if they say, 'Come up to us,' then we will go up; for the LORD has given them into our hand. That will be the sign for us." 11So both of them showed themselves to the garrison of the Philistines; and the Philistines said, "Look, Hebrews are coming out of the holes where they have hidden themselves." 12The men of the garrison hailed Jonathan and his armor-bearer, saying, "Come up to us, and we will show you something." Jonathan said to his armor-bearer, "Come up after me; for the LORD has given them into the hand of Israel." 13Then Jonathan climbed up on his hands and feet, with his armor-bearer following after him. The Philistines*c* fell before Jonathan, and his armor-bearer, coming after him, killed them. 14In that first slaughter Jonathan and his armor-bearer killed about twenty men within an area about half a furrow long in an acre*d* of land. 15There was a panic in the camp, in the field, and among all the people; the garrison and even the raiders trembled; the earth quaked; and it became a very great panic.

16 Saul's lookouts in Gibeah of Benjamin were watching as the multitude was surging back and forth.*e* 17Then Saul said to the troops that were with him, "Call the roll and see who has gone from us." When they had called the roll, Jonathan and his armor-bearer were not there. 18Saul said to Ahijah, "Bring the ark*f* of God here." For at that time the ark*f* of God

went with the Israelites. 19While Saul was talking to the priest, the tumult in the camp of the Philistines increased more and more; and Saul said to the priest, "Withdraw your hand." 20Then Saul and all the people who were with him rallied and went into the battle; and every sword was against the other, so that there was very great confusion. 21Now the Hebrews who previously had been with the Philistines and had gone up with them into the camp turned and joined the Israelites who were with Saul and Jonathan. 22Likewise, when all the Israelites who had gone into hiding in the hill country of Ephraim heard that the Philistines were fleeing, they too followed closely after them in the battle. 23So the LORD gave Israel the victory that day.

The battle passed beyond Beth-aven, and the troops with Saul numbered altogether about ten thousand men. The battle spread out over the hill country of Ephraim.

Saul's Rash Oath

24 Now Saul committed a very rash act on that day.*g* He had laid an oath on the troops, saying, "Cursed be anyone who eats food before it is evening and I have been avenged on my enemies." So none of the troops tasted food. 25All the troops*b* came upon a honeycomb; and there was honey on the ground. 26When the troops came upon the honeycomb, the honey was dripping out; but they did not put their hands to their mouths, for they feared the oath. 27But Jonathan had not heard his father charge the troops with the oath; so he extended the staff that was in his hand, and dipped the tip of it in the honeycomb, and put his hand to his mouth; and his eyes brightened. 28Then one of the soldiers said, "Your father strictly charged the troops with an oath, saying, 'Cursed be anyone who eats food this day.' And so the troops are faint." 29Then Jonathan said, "My father has troubled the land; see how my eyes have brightened because I tasted a little of this honey. 30How much better if today the troops had eaten freely of the

---

a Gk: Heb *Do all that is in your mind. Turn*   *b* Gk: Heb lacks *so is mine*   *c* Heb *They*   *d* Heb *yoke*   *e* Gk: Heb *they went and there*   *f* Gk *the ephod*   *g* Gk: Heb *The Israelites were distressed that day*   *h* Heb *land* spoil taken from their enemies; for now the slaughter among the Philistines has not been great."

31 After they had struck down the Philistines that day from Michmash to Aijalon, the troops were very faint; ³²so the troops flew upon the spoil, and took sheep and oxen and calves, and slaughtered them on the ground; and the troops ate them with the blood. ³³Then it was reported to Saul, "Look, the troops are sinning against the LORD by eating with the blood." And he said, "You have dealt treacherously; roll a large stone before me here."ᵃ ³⁴Saul said, "Disperse yourselves among the troops, and say to them, 'Let all bring their oxen or their sheep, and slaughter them here, and eat; and do not sin against the LORD by eating with the blood.'" So all of the troops brought their oxen with them that night, and slaughtered them there. ³⁵And Saul built an altar to the LORD; it was the first altar that he built to the LORD.

Jonathan in Danger of Death

36 Then Saul said, "Let us go down after the Philistines by night and despoil them until the morning light; let us not leave one of them." They said, "Do whatever seems good to you." But the priest said, "Let us draw near to God here." ³⁷So Saul inquired of God, "Shall I go down after the Philistines? Will you give them into the hand of Israel?" But he did not answer him that day. ³⁸Saul said, "Come here, all you leaders of the people; and let us find out how this sin has arisen today. ³⁹For as the LORD lives who saves Israel, even if it is in my son Jonathan, he shall surely die!" But there was no one among all the people who answered him. ⁴⁰He said to all Israel, "You shall be on one side, and I and my son Jonathan will be on the other side." The people said to Saul, "Do what seems good to you." ⁴¹Then Saul said, "O LORD God of Israel, why have you not answered your servant today? If this guilt is in me or in my son Jonathan, O LORD God of Israel, give Urim; but

if this guilt is in your people Israel,ᵇ give Thummim." And Jonathan and Saul were indicated by the lot, but the people were cleared. ⁴²Then Saul said, "Cast the lot between me and my son Jonathan." And Jonathan was taken.

43 Then Saul said to Jonathan, "Tell me what you have done." Jonathan told him, "I tasted a little honey with the tip of the staff that was in my hand; here I am, I will die." ⁴⁴Saul said, "God do so to me and more also; you shall surely die, Jonathan!" ⁴⁵Then the people said to Saul, "Shall Jonathan die, who has accomplished this great victory in Israel? Far from it! As the LORD lives, not one hair of his head shall fall to the ground; for he has worked with God today." So the people ransomed Jonathan, and he did not die. ⁴⁶Then Saul withdrew from pursuing the Philistines; and the Philistines went to their own place.

Saul's Continuing Wars

47 When Saul had taken the kingship over Israel, he fought against all his enemies on every side—against Moab, against the Ammonites, against Edom, against the kings of Zobah, and against the Philistines; wherever he turned he routed them. ⁴⁸He did valiantly, and struck down the Amalekites, and rescued Israel out of the hands of those who plundered them.

49 Now the sons of Saul were Jonathan, Ishvi, and Malchishua; and the names of his two daughters were these: the name of the firstborn was Merab, and the name of the younger, Michal. ⁵⁰The name of Saul's wife was Ahinoam daughter of Ahimaaz. And the name of the commander of his army was Abner son of Ner, Saul's uncle; ⁵¹Kish was the father of Saul, and Ner the father of Abner was the son of Abiel.

52 There was hard fighting against the Philistines all the days of Saul; and when Saul saw any strong or valiant warrior, he took him into his service.

ᵃ Gk: Heb *me this day*   ᵇ Vg Compare Gk: Heb ⁴¹*Saul said to the LORD, the God of Israel*

Saul Defeats the Amalekites but Spares Their King

15 Samuel said to Saul, "The LORD sent me to anoint you king over his people Israel; now therefore listen to the words of the LORD. 2Thus says the LORD of hosts, 'I will punish the Amalekites for what they did in opposing the Israelites when they came up out of Egypt. 3Now go and attack Amalek, and utterly destroy all that they have; do not spare them, but kill both man and woman, child and infant, ox and sheep, camel and donkey.'"

4 So Saul summoned the people, and numbered them in Telaim, two hundred thousand foot soldiers, and ten thousand soldiers of Judah. 5Saul came to the city of the Amalekites and lay in wait in the valley. 6Saul said to the Kenites, "Go! Leave! Withdraw from among the Amalekites, or I will destroy you with them; for you showed kindness to all the people of Israel when they came up out of Egypt." So the Kenites withdrew from the Amalekites. 7Saul defeated the Amalekites, from Havilah as far as Shur, which is east of Egypt. 8He took King Agag of the Amalekites alive, but utterly destroyed all the people with the edge of the sword. 9Saul and the people spared Agag, and the best of the sheep and of the cattle and of the fatlings, and the lambs, and all that was valuable, and would not utterly destroy them; all that was despised and worthless they utterly destroyed.

Saul Rejected as King

10 The word of the LORD came to Samuel: 11"I regret that I made Saul king, for he has turned back from following me, and has not carried out my commands." Samuel was angry; and he cried out to the LORD all night. 12Samuel rose early in the morning to meet Saul, and Samuel was told, "Saul went to Carmel, where he set up a monument for himself, and on returning he passed on down to Gilgal." 13When Samuel came to Saul, Saul said to him, "May you be blessed by the LORD; I have carried out the command of the LORD." 14But Samuel said, "What then is this bleating of sheep in my ears, and the lowing of cattle that I hear?"

15Saul said, "They have brought them from the Amalekites; for the people spared the best of the sheep and the cattle, to sacrifice to the LORD your God; but the rest we have utterly destroyed." 16Then Samuel said to Saul, "Stop! I will tell you what the LORD said to me last night." He replied, "Speak."

17 Samuel said, "Though you are little in your own eyes, are you not the head of the tribes of Israel? The LORD anointed you king over Israel. 18And the LORD sent you on a mission, and said, 'Go, utterly destroy the sinners, the Amalekites, and fight against them until they are consumed.' 19Why then did you not obey the voice of the LORD? Why did you swoop down on the spoil, and do what was evil in the sight of the LORD?" 20Saul said to Samuel, "I have obeyed the voice of the LORD, I have gone on the mission on which the LORD sent me, I have brought Agag the king of Amalek, and I have utterly destroyed the Amalekites. 21But from the spoil the people took sheep and cattle, the best of the things devoted to destruction, to sacrifice to the LORD your God in Gilgal." 22And Samuel said,

"Has the LORD as great delight in burnt
        offerings and sacrifices,
    as in obedience to the voice of the
        LORD?
Surely, to obey is better than sacrifice,
    and to heed than the fat of rams.
23 For rebellion is no less a sin than
        divination,
    and stubbornness is like iniquity and
        idolatry.
Because you have rejected the word of
        the LORD,
    he has also rejected you from being
        king."

24 Saul said to Samuel, "I have sinned; for I have transgressed the commandment of the LORD and your words, because I feared the people and obeyed their voice. 25Now therefore, I pray, pardon my sin, and return with me, so that I may worship the LORD." 26Samuel said to Saul, "I will not return with you; for you have rejected the word of the LORD, and the LORD has rejected you from being king over Is-

rael." ²⁷As Samuel turned to go away, Saul caught hold of the hem of his robe, and it tore. ²⁸And Samuel said to him, "The LORD has torn the kingdom of Israel from you this very day, and has given it to a neighbor of yours, who is better than you. ²⁹Moreover the Glory of Israel will not recant*a* or change his mind; for he is not a mortal, that he should change his mind." ³⁰Then Saul*b* said, "I have sinned; yet honor me now before the elders of my people and before Israel, and return with me, so that I may worship the LORD your God." ³¹So Samuel turned back after Saul; and Saul worshiped the LORD.

32 Then Samuel said, "Bring Agag king of the Amalekites here to me." And Agag came to him haltingly.*c* Agag said, "Surely this is the bitterness of death."*d* ³³But Samuel said,

"As your sword has made women
          childless,
    so your mother shall be childless
          among women."

And Samuel hewed Agag in pieces before the LORD in Gilgal.

34 Then Samuel went to Ramah; and Saul went up to his house in Gibeah of Saul. ³⁵Samuel did not see Saul again until the day of his death, but Samuel grieved over Saul. And the LORD was sorry that he had made Saul king over Israel.

David Anointed as King

16 The LORD said to Samuel, "How long will you grieve over Saul? I have rejected him from being king over Israel. Fill your horn with oil and set out; I will send you to Jesse the Bethlehemite, for I have provided for myself a king among his sons." ²Samuel said, "How can I go? If Saul hears of it, he will kill me." And the LORD said, "Take a heifer with you, and say, 'I have come to sacrifice to the LORD.' ³Invite Jesse to the sacrifice, and I will show you what you shall do; and you shall anoint for me the one whom I name to you." ⁴Samuel did what the LORD commanded, and came to Bethlehem. The elders of the city

came to meet him trembling, and said, "Do you come peaceably?" ⁵He said, "Peaceably; I have come to sacrifice to the LORD; sanctify yourselves and come with me to the sacrifice." And he sanctified Jesse and his sons and invited them to the sacrifice.

6 When they came, he looked on Eliab and thought, "Surely the LORD's anointed is now before the LORD."*e* ⁷But the LORD said to Samuel, "Do not look on his appearance or on the height of his stature, because I have rejected him; for the LORD does not see as mortals see; they look on the outward appearance, but the LORD looks on the heart." ⁸Then Jesse called Abinadab, and made him pass before Samuel. He said, "Neither has the LORD chosen this one." ⁹Then Jesse made Shammah pass by. And he said, "Neither has the LORD chosen this one." ¹⁰Jesse made seven of his sons pass before Samuel, and Samuel said to Jesse, "The LORD has not chosen any of these." ¹¹Samuel said to Jesse, "Are all your sons here?" And he said, "There remains yet the youngest, but he is keeping the sheep." And Samuel said to Jesse, "Send and bring him; for we will not sit down until he comes here." ¹²He sent and brought him in. Now he was ruddy, and had beautiful eyes, and was handsome. The LORD said, "Rise and anoint him; for this is the one." ¹³Then Samuel took the horn of oil, and anointed him in the presence of his brothers; and the spirit of the LORD came mightily upon David from that day forward. Samuel then set out and went to Ramah.

David Plays the Lyre for Saul

14 Now the spirit of the LORD departed from Saul, and an evil spirit from the LORD tormented him. ¹⁵And Saul's servants said to him, "See now, an evil spirit from God is tormenting you. ¹⁶Let our lord now command the servants who attend you to look for someone who is skillful in playing the lyre; and when the evil spirit from God is upon you, he will play it, and you will feel better." ¹⁷So Saul said to his

---

a Q Ms Gk: MT *deceive*   *b* Heb *he*   *c* Cn Compare Gk: Meaning of Heb uncertain   *d* Q Ms Gk: MT *Surely the bitterness of death is past*   *e* Heb *him* servants, "Provide for me someone who can play well, and bring him to me." ¹⁸One of the young men answered, "I have seen a son of Jesse the Bethlehemite who is skillful in playing, a man of valor, a warrior, prudent in speech, and a man of good presence; and the LORD is with him." ¹⁹So Saul sent messengers to Jesse, and said, "Send me your son David who is with the sheep." ²⁰Jesse took a donkey loaded with bread, a skin of wine, and a kid, and sent them by his son David to Saul. ²¹And David came to Saul, and entered his service. Saul loved him greatly, and he became his armor-bearer. ²²Saul sent to Jesse, saying, "Let David remain in my service, for he has found favor in my sight." ²³And whenever the evil spirit from God came upon Saul, David took the lyre and played it with his hand, and Saul would be relieved and feel better, and the evil spirit would depart from him.

David and Goliath

17 Now the Philistines gathered their armies for battle; they were gathered at Socoh, which belongs to Judah, and encamped between Socoh and Azekah, in Ephes-dammim. ²Saul and the Israelites gathered and encamped in the valley of Elah, and formed ranks against the Philistines. ³The Philistines stood on the mountain on the one side, and Israel stood on the mountain on the other side, with a valley between them. ⁴And there came out from the camp of the Philistines a champion named Goliath, of Gath, whose height was six *a* cubits and a span. ⁵He had a helmet of bronze on his head, and he was armed with a coat of mail; the weight of the coat was five thousand shekels of bronze. ⁶He had greaves of bronze on his legs and a javelin of bronze slung between his shoulders. ⁷The shaft of his spear was like a weaver's beam, and his spear's head weighed six hundred shekels of iron; and his shield-bearer went before him. ⁸He stood and shouted to the ranks of Israel, "Why have you come out to draw up for battle? Am I not a Philistine, and are you not ser-

vants of Saul? Choose a man for yourselves, and let him come down to me. ⁹If he is able to fight with me and kill me, then we will be your servants; but if I prevail against him and kill him, then you shall be our servants and serve us." ¹⁰And the Philistine said, "Today I defy the ranks of Israel! Give me a man, that we may fight together." ¹¹When Saul and all Israel heard these words of the Philistine, they were dismayed and greatly afraid.

12 Now David was the son of an Ephrathite of Bethlehem in Judah, named Jesse, who had eight sons. In the days of Saul the man was already old and advanced in years. *b* ¹³The three eldest sons of Jesse had followed Saul to the battle; the names of his three sons who went to the battle were Eliab the firstborn, and next to him Abinadab, and the third Shammah. ¹⁴David was the youngest; the three eldest followed Saul, ¹⁵but David went back and forth from Saul to feed his father's sheep at Bethlehem. ¹⁶For forty days the Philistine came forward and took his stand, morning and evening.

17 Jesse said to his son David, "Take for your brothers an ephah of this parched grain and these ten loaves, and carry them quickly to the camp to your brothers; ¹⁸also take these ten cheeses to the commander of their thousand. See how your brothers fare, and bring some token from them."

19 Now Saul, and they, and all the men of Israel, were in the valley of Elah, fighting with the Philistines. ²⁰David rose early in the morning, left the sheep with a keeper, took the provisions, and went as Jesse had commanded him. He came to the encampment as the army was going forth to the battle line, shouting the war cry. ²¹Israel and the Philistines drew up for battle, army against army. ²²David left the things in charge of the keeper of the baggage, ran to the ranks, and went and greeted his brothers. ²³As he talked with them, the champion, the Philistine of Gath, Goliath by name, came up out of the ranks of the Philistines,

a MT: Q Ms Gk *four*   *b* Gk Syr: Heb *among men*

and spoke the same words as before. And David heard him.

24 All the Israelites, when they saw the man, fled from him and were very much afraid. 25The Israelites said, "Have you seen this man who has come up? Surely he has come up to defy Israel. The king will greatly enrich the man who kills him, and will give him his daughter and make his family free in Israel." 26David said to the men who stood by him, "What shall be done for the man who kills this Philistine, and takes away the reproach from Israel? For who is this uncircumcised Philistine that he should defy the armies of the living God?" 27The people answered him in the same way, "So shall it be done for the man who kills him."

28 His eldest brother Eliab heard him talking to the men; and Eliab's anger was kindled against David. He said, "Why have you come down? With whom have you left those few sheep in the wilderness? I know your presumption and the evil of your heart; for you have come down just to see the battle." 29David said, "What have I done now? It was only a question." 30He turned away from him toward another and spoke in the same way; and the people answered him again as before.

31 When the words that David spoke were heard, they repeated them before Saul; and he sent for him. 32David said to Saul, "Let no one's heart fail because of him; your servant will go and fight with this Philistine." 33Saul said to David, "You are not able to go against this Philistine to fight with him; for you are just a boy, and he has been a warrior from his youth." 34But David said to Saul, "Your servant used to keep sheep for his father; and whenever a lion or a bear came, and took a lamb from the flock, 35I went after it and struck it down, rescuing the lamb from its mouth; and if it turned against me, I would catch it by the jaw, strike it down, and kill it. 36Your servant has killed both lions and bears; and this uncircumcised Philistine shall be like one of them, since he has defied the armies of the living God." 37David said, "The LORD, who saved me from the paw of the lion and from

the paw of the bear, will save me from the hand of this Philistine." So Saul said to David, "Go, and may the LORD be with you!"

38 Saul clothed David with his armor; he put a bronze helmet on his head and clothed him with a coat of mail. 39David strapped Saul's sword over the armor, and he tried in vain to walk, for he was not used to them. Then David said to Saul, "I cannot walk with these; for I am not used to them." So David removed them. 40Then he took his staff in his hand, and chose five smooth stones from the wadi, and put them in his shepherd's bag, in the pouch; his sling was in his hand, and he drew near to the Philistine.

41 The Philistine came on and drew near to David, with his shield-bearer in front of him. 42When the Philistine looked and saw David, he disdained him, for he was only a youth, ruddy and handsome in appearance. 43The Philistine said to David, "Am I a dog, that you come to me with sticks?" And the Philistine cursed David by his gods. 44The Philistine said to David, "Come to me, and I will give your flesh to the birds of the air and to the wild animals of the field." 45But David said to the Philistine, "You come to me with sword and spear and javelin; but I come to you in the name of the LORD of hosts, the God of the armies of Israel, whom you have defied. 46This very day the LORD will deliver you into my hand, and I will strike you down and cut off your head; and I will give the dead bodies of the Philistine army this very day to the birds of the air and to the wild animals of the earth, so that all the earth may know that there is a God in Israel, 47and that all this assembly may know that the LORD does not save by sword and spear; for the battle is the LORD's and he will give you into our hand."

48 When the Philistine drew nearer to meet David, David ran quickly toward the battle line to meet the Philistine. 49David put his hand in his bag, took out a stone, slung it, and struck the Philistine on his forehead; the stone sank into his forehead, and he fell face down on the ground.

50 So David prevailed over the Philistine

with a sling and a stone, striking down the Philistine and killing him; there was no sword in David's hand. ⁵¹Then David ran and stood over the Philistine; he grasped his sword, drew it out of its sheath, and killed him; then he cut off his head with it.

When the Philistines saw that their champion was dead, they fled. ⁵²The troops of Israel and Judah rose up with a shout and pursued the Philistines as far as Gath *a* and the gates of Ekron, so that the wounded Philistines fell on the way from Shaaraim as far as Gath and Ekron. ⁵³The Israelites came back from chasing the Philistines, and they plundered their camp. ⁵⁴David took the head of the Philistine and brought it to Jerusalem; but he put his armor in his tent.

55 When Saul saw David go out against the Philistine, he said to Abner, the commander of the army, "Abner, whose son is this young man?" Abner said, "As your soul lives, O king, I do not know." ⁵⁶The king said, "Inquire whose son the stripling is." ⁵⁷On David's return from killing the Philistine, Abner took him and brought him before Saul, with the head of the Philistine in his hand. ⁵⁸Saul said to him, "Whose son are you, young man?" And David answered, "I am the son of your servant Jesse the Bethlehemite."

Jonathan's Covenant with David

18 When David *b* had finished speaking to Saul, the soul of Jonathan was bound to the soul of David, and Jonathan loved him as his own soul. ²Saul took him that day and would not let him return to his father's house. ³Then Jonathan made a covenant with David, because he loved him as his own soul. ⁴Jonathan stripped himself of the robe that he was wearing, and gave it to David, and his armor, and even his sword and his bow and his belt. ⁵David went out and was successful wherever Saul sent him; as a result, Saul set him over the army. And all the people, even the servants of Saul, approved.

6 As they were coming home, when David returned from killing the Philistine, the women came out of all the towns of Israel, singing and dancing, to meet King Saul, with tambourines, with songs of joy, and with musical instruments. *c* ⁷And the women sang to one another as they made merry,

"Saul has killed his thousands,
    and David his ten thousands."
⁸Saul was very angry, for this saying displeased him. He said, "They have ascribed to David ten thousands, and to me they have ascribed thousands; what more can he have but the kingdom?" ⁹So Saul eyed David from that day on.

Saul Tries to Kill David

10 The next day an evil spirit from God rushed upon Saul, and he raved within his house, while David was playing the lyre, as he did day by day. Saul had his spear in his hand; ¹¹and Saul threw the spear, for he thought, "I will pin David to the wall." But David eluded him twice.

12 Saul was afraid of David, because the LORD was with him but had departed from Saul. ¹³So Saul removed him from his presence, and made him a commander of a thousand; and David marched out and came in, leading the army. ¹⁴David had success in all his undertakings; for the LORD was with him. ¹⁵When Saul saw that he had great success, he stood in awe of him. ¹⁶But all Israel and Judah loved David; for it was he who marched out and came in leading them.

David Marries Michal

17 Then Saul said to David, "Here is my elder daughter Merab; I will give her to you as a wife; only be valiant for me and fight the LORD's battles." For Saul thought, "I will not raise a hand against him; let the Philistines deal with him." ¹⁸David said to Saul, "Who am I and who are my kinsfolk, my father's family in Israel, that I should be son-in-law to the king?" ¹⁹But at the time when Saul's daughter Merab should have been given to David, she was given to Adriel the Meholathite as a wife.

a Gk Syr: Heb *Gai*   *b* Heb *he*   *c* Or *triangles,* or *three-stringed instruments*

20 Now Saul's daughter Michal loved David. Saul was told, and the thing pleased him. ²¹Saul thought, "Let me give her to him that she may be a snare for him and that the hand of the Philistines may be against him." Therefore Saul said to David a second time,ᵃ "You shall now be my son-in-law." ²²Saul commanded his servants, "Speak to David in private and say, 'See, the king is delighted with you, and all his servants love you; now then, become the king's son-in-law.' " ²³So Saul's servants reported these words to David in private. And David said, "Does it seem to you a little thing to become the king's son-in-law, seeing that I am a poor man and of no repute?" ²⁴The servants of Saul told him, "This is what David said." ²⁵Then Saul said, "Thus shall you say to David, 'The king desires no marriage present except a hundred foreskins of the Philistines, that he may be avenged on the king's enemies.' " Now Saul planned to make David fall by the hand of the Philistines. ²⁶When his servants told David these words, David was well pleased to be the king's son-in-law. Before the time had expired, ²⁷David rose and went, along with his men, and killed one hundredᵇ of the Philistines; and David brought their foreskins, which were given in full number to the king, that he might become the king's son-in-law. Saul gave him his daughter Michal as a wife. ²⁸But when Saul realized that the LORD was with David, and that Saul's daughter Michal loved him, ²⁹Saul was still more afraid of David. So Saul was David's enemy from that time forward.

30 Then the commanders of the Philistines came out to battle; and as often as they came out, David had more success than all the servants of Saul, so that his fame became very great.

Jonathan Intercedes for David

19 Saul spoke with his son Jonathan and with all his servants about killing David. But Saul's son Jonathan took great delight in David. ²Jonathan told David, "My father Saul is trying to kill you; therefore be on guard tomorrow morning; stay in a secret place and hide yourself. ³I will go out and stand beside my father in the field where you are, and I will speak to my father about you; if I learn anything I will tell you." ⁴Jonathan spoke well of David to his father Saul, saying to him, "The king should not sin against his servant David, because he has not sinned against you, and because his deeds have been of good service to you; ⁵for he took his life in his hand when he attacked the Philistine, and the LORD brought about a great victory for all Israel. You saw it, and rejoiced; why then will you sin against an innocent person by killing David without cause?" ⁶Saul heeded the voice of Jonathan; Saul swore, "As the LORD lives, he shall not be put to death." ⁷So Jonathan called David and related all these things to him. Jonathan then brought David to Saul, and he was in his presence as before.

Michal Helps David Escape from Saul

8 Again there was war, and David went out to fight the Philistines. He launched a heavy attack on them, so that they fled before him. ⁹Then an evil spirit from the LORD came upon Saul, as he sat in his house with his spear in his hand, while David was playing music. ¹⁰Saul sought to pin David to the wall with the spear; but he eluded Saul, so that he struck the spear into the wall. David fled and escaped that night.

11 Saul sent messengers to David's house to keep watch over him, planning to kill him in the morning. David's wife Michal told him, "If you do not save your life tonight, tomorrow you will be killed." ¹²So Michal let David down through the window; he fled away and escaped. ¹³Michal took an idolᶜ and laid it on the bed; she put a netᵈ of goats' hair on its head, and covered it with the clothes. ¹⁴When Saul sent messengers to take David, she said, "He is sick." ¹⁵Then Saul sent the messengers to see David for themselves. He said, "Bring him up to me in the bed, that I may kill him."

a Heb *by two*   b Gk Compare 2 Sam 3.14: Heb *two hundred*   c Heb *took the teraphim*   d Meaning of Heb uncertain

16When the messengers came in, the idol*a* was in the bed, with the covering*b* of goats' hair on its head. 17Saul said to Michal, "Why have you deceived me like this, and let my enemy go, so that he has escaped?" Michal answered Saul, "He said to me, 'Let me go; why should I kill you?' "

David Joins Samuel in Ramah

18 Now David fled and escaped; he came to Samuel at Ramah, and told him all that Saul had done to him. He and Samuel went and settled at Naioth. 19Saul was told, "David is at Naioth in Ramah." 20Then Saul sent messengers to take David. When they saw the company of the prophets in a frenzy, with Samuel standing in charge of*b* them, the spirit of God came upon the messengers of Saul, and they also fell into a prophetic frenzy. 21When Saul was told, he sent other messengers, and they also fell into a frenzy. Saul sent messengers again the third time, and they also fell into a frenzy. 22Then he himself went to Ramah. He came to the great well that is in Secu;*c* he asked, "Where are Samuel and David?" And someone said, "They are at Naioth in Ramah." 23He went there, toward Naioth in Ramah; and the spirit of God came upon him. As he was going, he fell into a prophetic frenzy, until he came to Naioth in Ramah. 24He too stripped off his clothes, and he too fell into a frenzy before Samuel. He lay naked all that day and all that night. Therefore it is said, "Is Saul also among the prophets?"

The Friendship of David and Jonathan

20 David fled from Naioth in Ramah. He came before Jonathan and said, "What have I done? What is my guilt? And what is my sin against your father that he is trying to take my life?" 2He said to him, "Far from it! You shall not die. My father does nothing either great or small without disclosing it to me; and why should my father hide this from me? Never!" 3But David also swore, "Your father knows well that you like me; and

he thinks, 'Do not let Jonathan know this, or he will be grieved.' But truly, as the LORD lives and as you yourself live, there is but a step between me and death." 4Then Jonathan said to David, "Whatever you say, I will do for you." 5David said to Jonathan, "Tomorrow is the new moon, and I should not fail to sit with the king at the meal; but let me go, so that I may hide in the field until the third evening. 6If your father misses me at all, then say, 'David earnestly asked leave of me to run to Bethlehem his city; for there is a yearly sacrifice there for all the family.' 7If he says, 'Good!' it will be well with your servant; but if he is angry, then know that evil has been determined by him. 8Therefore deal kindly with your servant, for you have brought your servant into a sacred covenant*d* with you. But if there is guilt in me, kill me yourself; why should you bring me to your father?" 9Jonathan said, "Far be it from you! If I knew that it was decided by my father that evil should come upon you, would I not tell you?" 10Then David said to Jonathan, "Who will tell me if your father answers you harshly?" 11Jonathan replied to David, "Come, let us go out into the field." So they both went out into the field.

12 Jonathan said to David, "By the LORD, the God of Israel! When I have sounded out my father, about this time tomorrow, or on the third day, if he is well disposed toward David, shall I not then send and disclose it to you? 13But if my father intends to do you harm, the LORD do so to Jonathan, and more also, if I do not disclose it to you, and send you away, so that you may go in safety. May the LORD be with you, as he has been with my father. 14If I am still alive, show me the faithful love of the LORD; but if I die,*b* 15never cut off your faithful love from my house, even if the LORD were to cut off every one of the enemies of David from the face of the earth." 16Thus Jonathan made a covenant with the house of David, saying, "May the LORD seek out the enemies of David." 17Jonathan made David

---

a Heb *the teraphim*   *b* Meaning of Heb uncertain   *c* Gk reads *to the well of the threshing floor on the bare height*
d Heb *a covenant of the* LORD

swear again by his love for him; for he loved him as he loved his own life.

18 Jonathan said to him, "Tomorrow is the new moon; you will be missed, because your place will be empty. ¹⁹On the day after tomorrow, you shall go a long way down; go to the place where you hid yourself earlier, and remain beside the stone there.ᵃ ²⁰I will shoot three arrows to the side of it, as though I shot at a mark. ²¹Then I will send the boy, saying, 'Go, find the arrows.' If I say to the boy, 'Look, the arrows are on this side of you, collect them,' then you are to come, for, as the LORD lives, it is safe for you and there is no danger. ²²But if I say to the young man, 'Look, the arrows are beyond you,' then go; for the LORD has sent you away. ²³As for the matter about which you and I have spoken, the LORD is witnessᵇ between you and me forever."

24 So David hid himself in the field. When the new moon came, the king sat at the feast to eat. ²⁵The king sat upon his seat, as at other times, upon the seat by the wall. Jonathan stood, while Abner sat by Saul's side; but David's place was empty.

26 Saul did not say anything that day; for he thought, "Something has befallen him; he is not clean, surely he is not clean." ²⁷But on the second day, the day after the new moon, David's place was empty. And Saul said to his son Jonathan, "Why has the son of Jesse not come to the feast, either yesterday or today?" ²⁸Jonathan answered Saul, "David earnestly asked leave of me to go to Bethlehem; ²⁹he said, 'Let me go; for our family is holding a sacrifice in the city, and my brother has commanded me to be there. So now, if I have found favor in your sight, let me get away, and see my brothers.' For this reason he has not come to the king's table."

30 Then Saul's anger was kindled against Jonathan. He said to him, "You son of a perverse, rebellious woman! Do I not know that you have chosen the son of Jesse to your own shame, and to the shame of your mother's nakedness? ³¹For as long as the son of Jesse

lives upon the earth, neither you nor your kingdom shall be established. Now send and bring him to me, for he shall surely die." ³²Then Jonathan answered his father Saul, "Why should he be put to death? What has he done?" ³³But Saul threw his spear at him to strike him; so Jonathan knew that it was the decision of his father to put David to death. ³⁴Jonathan rose from the table in fierce anger and ate no food on the second day of the month, for he was grieved for David, and because his father had disgraced him.

35 In the morning Jonathan went out into the field to the appointment with David, and with him was a little boy. ³⁶He said to the boy, "Run and find the arrows that I shoot." As the boy ran, he shot an arrow beyond him. ³⁷When the boy came to the place where Jonathan's arrow had fallen, Jonathan called after the boy and said, "Is the arrow not beyond you?" ³⁸Jonathan called after the boy, "Hurry, be quick, do not linger." So Jonathan's boy gathered up the arrows and came to his master. ³⁹But the boy knew nothing; only Jonathan and David knew the arrangement. ⁴⁰Jonathan gave his weapons to the boy and said to him, "Go and carry them to the city." ⁴¹As soon as the boy had gone, David rose from beside the stone heapᶜ and prostrated himself with his face to the ground. He bowed three times, and they kissed each other, and wept with each other; David wept the more.ᵈ ⁴²Then Jonathan said to David, "Go in peace, since both of us have sworn in the name of the LORD, saying, 'The LORD shall be between me and you, and between my descendants and your descendants, forever.'" He got up and left; and Jonathan went into the city.ᵉ

David and the Holy Bread

21 ᶠDavid came to Nob to the priest Ahimelech. Ahimelech came trembling to meet David, and said to him, "Why are you alone, and no one with you?" ²David said to the priest Ahimelech, "The king has charged me with a matter, and said to me, 'No one

---

ᵃ Meaning of Heb uncertain   ᵇ Gk: Heb lacks *witness*   ᶜ Gk: Heb *from beside the south*   ᵈ Vg: Meaning of Heb uncertain   ᵉ This sentence is 21.1 in Heb   ᶠ Ch 21.2 in Heb must know anything of the matter about which I send you, and with which I have charged you.' I have made an appointment*ᵃ* with the young men for such and such a place. ³Now then, what have you at hand? Give me five loaves of bread, or whatever is here." ⁴The priest answered David, "I have no ordinary bread at hand, only holy bread—provided that the young men have kept themselves from women." ⁵David answered the priest, "Indeed women have been kept from us as always when I go on an expedition; the vessels of the young men are holy even when it is a common journey; how much more today will their vessels be holy?" ⁶So the priest gave him the holy bread; for there was no bread there except the bread of the Presence, which is removed from before the LORD, to be replaced by hot bread on the day it is taken away.

7 Now a certain man of the servants of Saul was there that day, detained before the LORD; his name was Doeg the Edomite, the chief of Saul's shepherds.

8 David said to Ahimelech, "Is there no spear or sword here with you? I did not bring my sword or my weapons with me, because the king's business required haste." ⁹The priest said, "The sword of Goliath the Philistine, whom you killed in the valley of Elah, is here wrapped in a cloth behind the ephod; if you will take that, take it, for there is none here except that one." David said, "There is none like it; give it to me."

David Flees to Gath

10 David rose and fled that day from Saul; he went to King Achish of Gath. ¹¹The servants of Achish said to him, "Is this not David the king of the land? Did they not sing to one another of him in dances,

'Saul has killed his thousands,
    and David his ten thousands'?"

¹²David took these words to heart and was very much afraid of King Achish of Gath. ¹³So he changed his behavior before them; he pretended to be mad when in their presence.*ᵇ*

He scratched marks on the doors of the gate, and let his spittle run down his beard. ¹⁴Achish said to his servants, "Look, you see the man is mad; why then have you brought him to me? ¹⁵Do I lack madmen, that you have brought this fellow to play the madman in my presence? Shall this fellow come into my house?"

David and His Followers at Adullam

22 David left there and escaped to the cave of Adullam; when his brothers and all his father's house heard of it, they went down there to him. ²Everyone who was in distress, and everyone who was in debt, and everyone who was discontented gathered to him; and he became captain over them. Those who were with him numbered about four hundred.

3 David went from there to Mizpeh of Moab. He said to the king of Moab, "Please let my father and mother come*ᶜ* to you, until I know what God will do for me." ⁴He left them with the king of Moab, and they stayed with him all the time that David was in the stronghold. ⁵Then the prophet Gad said to David, "Do not remain in the stronghold; leave, and go into the land of Judah." So David left, and went into the forest of Hereth.

Saul Slaughters the Priests at Nob

6 Saul heard that David and those who were with him had been located. Saul was sitting at Gibeah, under the tamarisk tree on the height, with his spear in his hand, and all his servants were standing around him. ⁷Saul said to his servants who stood around him, "Hear now, you Benjaminites; will the son of Jesse give every one of you fields and vineyards, will he make you all commanders of thousands and commanders of hundreds? ⁸Is that why all of you have conspired against me? No one discloses to me when my son makes a league with the son of Jesse, none of you is sorry for me or discloses to me that my son has stirred up my servant against me, to lie in wait, as he is doing today." ⁹Doeg the Edomite,

a Q Ms Vg Compare Gk: Meaning of MT uncertain   *b* Heb *in their hands*   *c* Syr Vg: Heb *come out* who was in charge of Saul's servants, answered, "I saw the son of Jesse coming to Nob, to Ahimelech son of Ahitub; 10he inquired of the LORD for him, gave him provisions, and gave him the sword of Goliath the Philistine."

11 The king sent for the priest Ahimelech son of Ahitub and for all his father's house, the priests who were at Nob; and all of them came to the king. 12Saul said, "Listen now, son of Ahitub." He answered, "Here I am, my lord." 13Saul said to him, "Why have you conspired against me, you and the son of Jesse, by giving him bread and a sword, and by inquiring of God for him, so that he has risen against me, to lie in wait, as he is doing today?"

14 Then Ahimelech answered the king, "Who among all your servants is so faithful as David? He is the king's son-in-law, and is quicka to do your bidding, and is honored in your house. 15Is today the first time that I have inquired of God for him? By no means! Do not let the king impute anything to his servant or to any member of my father's house; for your servant has known nothing of all this, much or little." 16The king said, "You shall surely die, Ahimelech, you and all your father's house." 17The king said to the guard who stood around him, "Turn and kill the priests of the LORD, because their hand also is with David; they knew that he fled, and did not disclose it to me." But the servants of the king would not raise their hand to attack the priests of the LORD. 18Then the king said to Doeg, "You, Doeg, turn and attack the priests." Doeg the Edomite turned and attacked the priests; on that day he killed eighty-five who wore the linen ephod. 19Nob, the city of the priests, he put to the sword; men and women, children and infants, oxen, donkeys, and sheep, he put to the sword.

20 But one of the sons of Ahimelech son of Ahitub, named Abiathar, escaped and fled after David. 21Abiathar told David that Saul had killed the priests of the LORD. 22David said to Abiathar, "I knew on that day, when Doeg the Edomite was there, that he would surely tell Saul. I am responsibleb for the lives of all your father's house. 23Stay with me, and do not be afraid; for the one who seeks my life seeks your life; you will be safe with me."

David Saves the City of Keilah

23 Now they told David, "The Philistines are fighting against Keilah, and are robbing the threshing floors." 2David inquired of the LORD, "Shall I go and attack these Philistines?" The LORD said to David, "Go and attack the Philistines and save Keilah." 3But David's men said to him, "Look, we are afraid here in Judah; how much more then if we go to Keilah against the armies of the Philistines?" 4Then David inquired of the LORD again. The LORD answered him, "Yes, go down to Keilah; for I will give the Philistines into your hand." 5So David and his men went to Keilah, fought with the Philistines, brought away their livestock, and dealt them a heavy defeat. Thus David rescued the inhabitants of Keilah.

6 When Abiathar son of Ahimelech fled to David at Keilah, he came down with an ephod in his hand. 7Now it was told Saul that David had come to Keilah. And Saul said, "God has givenc him into my hand; for he has shut himself in by entering a town that has gates and bars." 8Saul summoned all the people to war, to go down to Keilah, to besiege David and his men. 9When David learned that Saul was plotting evil against him, he said to the priest Abiathar, "Bring the ephod here." 10David said, "O LORD, the God of Israel, your servant has heard that Saul seeks to come to Keilah, to destroy the city on my account. 11And now, willd Saul come down as your servant has heard? O LORD, the God of Israel, I beseech you, tell your servant." The LORD said, "He will come down." 12Then David said, "Will the men of Keilah surrender me and my men into the hand of Saul?" The LORD said, "They will surrender you." 13Then David and his men, who were about six hundred, set out and left

---

a Heb *and turns aside*   b Gk Vg: Meaning of Heb uncertain   c Gk Tg: Heb *made a stranger of*   d Q Ms Compare Gk: MT *Will the men of Keilah surrender me into his hand? Will*

Keilah; they wandered wherever they could go. When Saul was told that David had escaped from Keilah, he gave up the expedition. ¹⁴David remained in the strongholds in the wilderness, in the hill country of the Wilderness of Ziph. Saul sought him every day, but the LORD*a* did not give him into his hand.

David Eludes Saul in the Wilderness

15 David was in the Wilderness of Ziph at Horesh when he learned that*b* Saul had come out to seek his life. ¹⁶Saul's son Jonathan set out and came to David at Horesh; there he strengthened his hand through the LORD.*c* ¹⁷He said to him, "Do not be afraid; for the hand of my father Saul shall not find you; you shall be king over Israel, and I shall be second to you; my father Saul also knows that this is so." ¹⁸Then the two of them made a covenant before the LORD; David remained at Horesh, and Jonathan went home.

19 Then some Ziphites went up to Saul at Gibeah and said, "David is hiding among us in the strongholds of Horesh, on the hill of Hachilah, which is south of Jeshimon. ²⁰Now, O king, whenever you wish to come down, do so; and our part will be to surrender him into the king's hand." ²¹Saul said, "May you be blessed by the LORD for showing me compassion! ²²Go and make sure once more; find out exactly where he is, and who has seen him there; for I am told that he is very cunning. ²³Look around and learn all the hiding places where he lurks, and come back to me with sure information. Then I will go with you; and if he is in the land, I will search him out among all the thousands of Judah." ²⁴So they set out and went to Ziph ahead of Saul.

David and his men were in the wilderness of Maon, in the Arabah to the south of Jeshimon. ²⁵Saul and his men went to search for him. When David was told, he went down to the rock and stayed in the wilderness of Maon. When Saul heard that, he pursued David into the wilderness of Maon. ²⁶Saul went on one side of the mountain, and David and his men

on the other side of the mountain. David was hurrying to get away from Saul, while Saul and his men were closing in on David and his men to capture them. ²⁷Then a messenger came to Saul, saying, "Hurry and come; for the Philistines have made a raid on the land." ²⁸So Saul stopped pursuing David, and went against the Philistines; therefore that place was called the Rock of Escape.*d* ²⁹*e* David then went up from there, and lived in the strongholds of En-gedi.

David Spares Saul's Life

24 When Saul returned from following the Philistines, he was told, "David is in the wilderness of En-gedi." ²Then Saul took three thousand chosen men out of all Israel, and went to look for David and his men in the direction of the Rocks of the Wild Goats. ³He came to the sheepfolds beside the road, where there was a cave; and Saul went in to relieve himself.*f* Now David and his men were sitting in the innermost parts of the cave. ⁴The men of David said to him, "Here is the day of which the LORD said to you, 'I will give your enemy into your hand, and you shall do to him as it seems good to you.'" Then David went and stealthily cut off a corner of Saul's cloak. ⁵Afterward David was stricken to the heart because he had cut off a corner of Saul's cloak. ⁶He said to his men, "The LORD forbid that I should do this thing to my lord, the LORD's anointed, to raise my hand against him; for he is the LORD's anointed." ⁷So David scolded his men severely and did not permit them to attack Saul. Then Saul got up and left the cave, and went on his way.

8 Afterwards David also rose up and went out of the cave and called after Saul, "My lord the king!" When Saul looked behind him, David bowed with his face to the ground, and did obeisance. ⁹David said to Saul, "Why do you listen to the words of those who say, 'David seeks to do you harm'? ¹⁰This very day your eyes have seen how the LORD gave you into my hand in the cave; and some urged me to kill

---

a Q Ms Gk: MT *God*   *b* Or *saw that*   *c* Compare Q Ms Gk: MT *God*   *d* Or *Rock of Division*; meaning of Heb uncertain   *e* Ch 24.1 in Heb   *f* Heb *to cover his feet* you, but I spared[a] you. I said, 'I will not raise my hand against my lord; for he is the LORD's anointed.' 11See, my father, see the corner of your cloak in my hand; for by the fact that I cut off the corner of your cloak, and did not kill you, you may know for certain that there is no wrong or treason in my hands. I have not sinned against you, though you are hunting me to take my life. 12May the LORD judge between me and you! May the LORD avenge me on you; but my hand shall not be against you. 13As the ancient proverb says, 'Out of the wicked comes forth wickedness'; but my hand shall not be against you. 14Against whom has the king of Israel come out? Whom do you pursue? A dead dog? A single flea? 15May the LORD therefore be judge, and give sentence between me and you. May he see to it, and plead my cause, and vindicate me against you."

16 When David had finished speaking these words to Saul, Saul said, "Is this your voice, my son David?" Saul lifted up his voice and wept. 17He said to David, "You are more righteous than I; for you have repaid me good, whereas I have repaid you evil. 18Today you have explained how you have dealt well with me, in that you did not kill me when the LORD put me into your hands. 19For who has ever found an enemy, and sent the enemy safely away? So may the LORD reward you with good for what you have done to me this day. 20Now I know that you shall surely be king, and that the kingdom of Israel shall be established in your hand. 21Swear to me therefore by the LORD that you will not cut off my descendants after me, and that you will not wipe out my name from my father's house." 22So David swore this to Saul. Then Saul went home; but David and his men went up to the stronghold.

Death of Samuel

25 Now Samuel died; and all Israel assembled and mourned for him. They buried him at his home in Ramah.

Then David got up and went down to the wilderness of Paran.

David and the Wife of Nabal

2 There was a man in Maon, whose property was in Carmel. The man was very rich; he had three thousand sheep and a thousand goats. He was shearing his sheep in Carmel. 3Now the name of the man was Nabal, and the name of his wife Abigail. The woman was clever and beautiful, but the man was surly and mean; he was a Calebite. 4David heard in the wilderness that Nabal was shearing his sheep. 5So David sent ten young men; and David said to the young men, "Go up to Carmel, and go to Nabal, and greet him in my name. 6Thus you shall salute him: 'Peace be to you, and peace be to your house, and peace be to all that you have. 7I hear that you have shearers; now your shepherds have been with us, and we did them no harm, and they missed nothing, all the time they were in Carmel. 8Ask your young men, and they will tell you. Therefore let my young men find favor in your sight; for we have come on a feast day. Please give whatever you have at hand to your servants and to your son David.' "

9 When David's young men came, they said all this to Nabal in the name of David; and then they waited. 10But Nabal answered David's servants, "Who is David? Who is the son of Jesse? There are many servants today who are breaking away from their masters. 11Shall I take my bread and my water and the meat that I have butchered for my shearers, and give it to men who come from I do not know where?" 12So David's young men turned away, and came back and told him all this. 13David said to his men, "Every man strap on his sword!" And every one of them strapped on his sword; David also strapped on his sword; and about four hundred men went up after David, while two hundred remained with the baggage.

14 But one of the young men told Abigail, Nabal's wife, "David sent messengers out of the wilderness to salute our master; and he shouted insults at them. 15Yet the men were very good to us, and we suffered no harm, and

we never missed anything when we were in the fields, as long as we were with them; 16they were a wall to us both by night and by day, all the while we were with them keeping the sheep. 17Now therefore know this and consider what you should do; for evil has been decided against our master and against all his house; he is so ill-natured that no one can speak to him."

18 Then Abigail hurried and took two hundred loaves, two skins of wine, five sheep ready dressed, five measures of parched grain, one hundred clusters of raisins, and two hundred cakes of figs. She loaded them on donkeys 19and said to her young men, "Go on ahead of me; I am coming after you." But she did not tell her husband Nabal. 20As she rode on the donkey and came down under cover of the mountain, David and his men came down toward her; and she met them. 21Now David had said, "Surely it was in vain that I protected all that this fellow has in the wilderness, so that nothing was missed of all that belonged to him; but he has returned me evil for good. 22God do so to David*a* and more also, if by morning I leave so much as one male of all who belong to him."

23 When Abigail saw David, she hurried and alighted from the donkey, and fell before David on her face, bowing to the ground. 24She fell at his feet and said, "Upon me alone, my lord, be the guilt; please let your servant speak in your ears, and hear the words of your servant. 25My lord, do not take seriously this ill-natured fellow, Nabal; for as his name is, so is he; Nabal*b* is his name, and folly is with him; but I, your servant, did not see the young men of my lord, whom you sent.

26 "Now then, my lord, as the LORD lives, and as you yourself live, since the LORD has restrained you from bloodguilt and from taking vengeance with your own hand, now let your enemies and those who seek to do evil to my lord be like Nabal. 27And now let this present that your servant has brought to my lord be given to the young men who follow my lord.

28Please forgive the trespass of your servant; for the LORD will certainly make my lord a sure house, because my lord is fighting the battles of the LORD; and evil shall not be found in you so long as you live. 29If anyone should rise up to pursue you and to seek your life, the life of my lord shall be bound in the bundle of the living under the care of the LORD your God; but the lives of your enemies he shall sling out as from the hollow of a sling. 30When the LORD has done to my lord according to all the good that he has spoken concerning you, and has appointed you prince over Israel, 31my lord shall have no cause of grief, or pangs of conscience, for having shed blood without cause or for having saved himself. And when the LORD has dealt well with my lord, then remember your servant."

32 David said to Abigail, "Blessed be the LORD, the God of Israel, who sent you to meet me today! 33Blessed be your good sense, and blessed be you, who have kept me today from bloodguilt and from avenging myself by my own hand! 34For as surely as the LORD the God of Israel lives, who has restrained me from hurting you, unless you had hurried and come to meet me, truly by morning there would not have been left to Nabal so much as one male." 35Then David received from her hand what she had brought him; he said to her, "Go up to your house in peace; see, I have heeded your voice, and I have granted your petition."

36 Abigail came to Nabal; he was holding a feast in his house, like the feast of a king. Nabal's heart was merry within him, for he was very drunk; so she told him nothing at all until the morning light. 37In the morning, when the wine had gone out of Nabal, his wife told him these things, and his heart died within him; he became like a stone. 38About ten days later the LORD struck Nabal, and he died.

39 When David heard that Nabal was dead, he said, "Blessed be the LORD who has judged the case of Nabal's insult to me, and has kept back his servant from evil; the LORD has re-

---

a Gk Compare Syr: Heb *the enemies of David*   *b* That is *Fool* turned the evildoing of Nabal upon his own head." Then David sent and wooed Abigail, to make her his wife. ⁴⁰When David's servants came to Abigail at Carmel, they said to her, "David has sent us to you to take you to him as his wife." ⁴¹She rose and bowed down, with her face to the ground, and said, "Your servant is a slave to wash the feet of the servants of my lord." ⁴²Abigail got up hurriedly and rode away on a donkey; her five maids attended her. She went after the messengers of David and became his wife.

43 David also married Ahinoam of Jezreel; both of them became his wives. ⁴⁴Saul had given his daughter Michal, David's wife, to Palti son of Laish, who was from Gallim.

David Spares Saul's Life a Second Time

26 Then the Ziphites came to Saul at Gibeah, saying, "David is in hiding on the hill of Hachilah, which is opposite Jeshimon."ᵃ ²So Saul rose and went down to the Wilderness of Ziph, with three thousand chosen men of Israel, to seek David in the Wilderness of Ziph. ³Saul encamped on the hill of Hachilah, which is opposite Jeshimonᵃ beside the road. But David remained in the wilderness. When he learned that Saul had come after him into the wilderness, ⁴David sent out spies, and learned that Saul had indeed arrived. ⁵Then David set out and came to the place where Saul had encamped; and David saw the place where Saul lay, with Abner son of Ner, the commander of his army. Saul was lying within the encampment, while the army was encamped around him.

6 Then David said to Ahimelech the Hittite, and to Joab's brother Abishai son of Zeruiah, "Who will go down with me into the camp to Saul?" Abishai said, "I will go down with you." ⁷So David and Abishai went to the army by night; there Saul lay sleeping within the encampment, with his spear stuck in the ground at his head; and Abner and the army lay around him. ⁸Abishai said to David, "God has given your enemy into your hand today;

now therefore let me pin him to the ground with one stroke of the spear; I will not strike him twice." ⁹But David said to Abishai, "Do not destroy him; for who can raise his hand against the LORD's anointed, and be guiltless?" ¹⁰David said, "As the LORD lives, the LORD will strike him down; or his day will come to die; or he will go down into battle and perish. ¹¹The LORD forbid that I should raise my hand against the LORD's anointed; but now take the spear that is at his head, and the water jar, and let us go." ¹²So David took the spear that was at Saul's head and the water jar, and they went away. No one saw it, or knew it, nor did anyone awake; for they were all asleep, because a deep sleep from the LORD had fallen upon them.

13 Then David went over to the other side, and stood on top of a hill far away, with a great distance between them. ¹⁴David called to the army and to Abner son of Ner, saying, "Abner! Will you not answer?" Then Abner replied, "Who are you that calls to the king?" ¹⁵David said to Abner, "Are you not a man? Who is like you in Israel? Why then have you not kept watch over your lord the king? For one of the people came in to destroy your lord the king. ¹⁶This thing that you have done is not good. As the LORD lives, you deserve to die, because you have not kept watch over your lord, the LORD's anointed. See now, where is the king's spear, or the water jar that was at his head?"

17 Saul recognized David's voice, and said, "Is this your voice, my son David?" David said, "It is my voice, my lord, O king." ¹⁸And he added, "Why does my lord pursue his servant? For what have I done? What guilt is on my hands? ¹⁹Now therefore let my lord the king hear the words of his servant. If it is the LORD who has stirred you up against me, may he accept an offering; but if it is mortals, may they be cursed before the LORD, for they have driven me out today from my share in the heritage of the LORD, saying, 'Go, serve other gods.' ²⁰Now therefore, do not let my blood

ᵃ Or *opposite the wasteland*

fall to the ground, away from the presence of the LORD; for the king of Israel has come out to seek a single flea, like one who hunts a partridge in the mountains."

21 Then Saul said, "I have done wrong; come back, my son David, for I will never harm you again, because my life was precious in your sight today; I have been a fool, and have made a great mistake." 22David replied, "Here is the spear, O king! Let one of the young men come over and get it. 23The LORD rewards everyone for his righteousness and his faithfulness; for the LORD gave you into my hand today, but I would not raise my hand against the LORD's anointed. 24As your life was precious today in my sight, so may my life be precious in the sight of the LORD, and may he rescue me from all tribulation." 25Then Saul said to David, "Blessed be you, my son David! You will do many things and will succeed in them." So David went his way, and Saul returned to his place.

David Serves King Achish of Gath

27 David said in his heart, "I shall now perish one day by the hand of Saul; there is nothing better for me than to escape to the land of the Philistines; then Saul will despair of seeking me any longer within the borders of Israel, and I shall escape out of his hand." 2So David set out and went over, he and the six hundred men who were with him, to King Achish son of Maoch of Gath. 3David stayed with Achish at Gath, he and his troops, every man with his household, and David with his two wives, Ahinoam of Jezreel, and Abigail of Carmel, Nabal's widow. 4When Saul was told that David had fled to Gath, he no longer sought for him.

5 Then David said to Achish, "If I have found favor in your sight, let a place be given me in one of the country towns, so that I may live there; for why should your servant live in the royal city with you?" 6So that day Achish gave him Ziklag; therefore Ziklag has belonged to the kings of Judah to this day. 7The length

of time that David lived in the country of the Philistines was one year and four months.

8 Now David and his men went up and made raids on the Geshurites, the Girzites, and the Amalekites; for these were the landed settlements from Telam*a* on the way to Shur and on to the land of Egypt. 9David struck the land, leaving neither man nor woman alive, but took away the sheep, the oxen, the donkeys, the camels, and the clothing, and came back to Achish. 10When Achish asked, "Against whom*b* have you made a raid today?" David would say, "Against the Negeb of Judah," or "Against the Negeb of the Jerahmeelites," or, "Against the Negeb of the Kenites." 11David left neither man nor woman alive to be brought back to Gath, thinking, "They might tell about us, and say, 'David has done so and so.' " Such was his practice all the time he lived in the country of the Philistines. 12Achish trusted David, thinking, "He has made himself utterly abhorrent to his people Israel; therefore he shall always be my servant."

28 In those days the Philistines gathered their forces for war, to fight against Israel. Achish said to David, "You know, of course, that you and your men are to go out with me in the army." 2David said to Achish, "Very well, then you shall know what your servant can do." Achish said to David, "Very well, I will make you my bodyguard for life."

Saul Consults a Medium

3 Now Samuel had died, and all Israel had mourned for him and buried him in Ramah, his own city. Saul had expelled the mediums and the wizards from the land. 4The Philistines assembled, and came and encamped at Shunem. Saul gathered all Israel, and they encamped at Gilboa. 5When Saul saw the army of the Philistines, he was afraid, and his heart trembled greatly. 6When Saul inquired of the LORD, the LORD did not answer him, not by dreams, or by Urim, or by prophets. 7Then Saul said to his servants, "Seek out for me a

---

a Compare Gk 15.4: Heb *from of old*   *b* Q Ms Gk Vg: MT lacks *whom* woman who is a medium, so that I may go to her and inquire of her." His servants said to him, "There is a medium at Endor."

8 So Saul disguised himself and put on other clothes and went there, he and two men with him. They came to the woman by night. And he said, "Consult a spirit for me, and bring up for me the one whom I name to you." [9]The woman said to him, "Surely you know what Saul has done, how he has cut off the mediums and the wizards from the land. Why then are you laying a snare for my life to bring about my death?" [10]But Saul swore to her by the LORD, "As the LORD lives, no punishment shall come upon you for this thing." [11]Then the woman said, "Whom shall I bring up for you?" He answered, "Bring up Samuel for me." [12]When the woman saw Samuel, she cried out with a loud voice; and the woman said to Saul, "Why have you deceived me? You are Saul!" [13]The king said to her, "Have no fear; what do you see?" The woman said to Saul, "I see a divine being[a] coming up out of the ground." [14]He said to her, "What is his appearance?" She said, "An old man is coming up; he is wrapped in a robe." So Saul knew that it was Samuel, and he bowed with his face to the ground, and did obeisance.

15 Then Samuel said to Saul, "Why have you disturbed me by bringing me up?" Saul answered, "I am in great distress, for the Philistines are warring against me, and God has turned away from me and answers me no more, either by prophets or by dreams; so I have summoned you to tell me what I should do." [16]Samuel said, "Why then do you ask me, since the LORD has turned from you and become your enemy? [17]The LORD has done to you just as he spoke by me; for the LORD has torn the kingdom out of your hand, and given it to your neighbor, David. [18]Because you did not obey the voice of the LORD, and did not carry out his fierce wrath against Amalek, therefore the LORD has done this thing to you today. [19]Moreover the LORD will give Israel along with you into the hands of the Philis-

tines; and tomorrow you and your sons shall be with me; the LORD will also give the army of Israel into the hands of the Philistines."

20 Immediately Saul fell full length on the ground, filled with fear because of the words of Samuel; and there was no strength in him, for he had eaten nothing all day and all night. [21]The woman came to Saul, and when she saw that he was terrified, she said to him, "Your servant has listened to you; I have taken my life in my hand, and have listened to what you have said to me. [22]Now therefore, you also listen to your servant; let me set a morsel of bread before you. Eat, that you may have strength when you go on your way." [23]He refused, and said, "I will not eat." But his servants, together with the woman, urged him; and he listened to their words. So he got up from the ground and sat on the bed. [24]Now the woman had a fatted calf in the house. She quickly slaughtered it, and she took flour, kneaded it, and baked unleavened cakes. [25]She put them before Saul and his servants, and they ate. Then they rose and went away that night.

The Philistines Reject David

29 Now the Philistines gathered all their forces at Aphek, while the Israelites were encamped by the fountain that is in Jezreel. [2]As the lords of the Philistines were passing on by hundreds and by thousands, and David and his men were passing on in the rear with Achish, [3]the commanders of the Philistines said, "What are these Hebrews doing here?" Achish said to the commanders of the Philistines, "Is this not David, the servant of King Saul of Israel, who has been with me now for days and years? Since he deserted to me I have found no fault in him to this day." [4]But the commanders of the Philistines were angry with him; and the commanders of the Philistines said to him, "Send the man back, so that he may return to the place that you have assigned to him; he shall not go down with us to battle, or else he may become an adversary

_a_ Or _a god_; or _gods_

to us in the battle. For how could this fellow reconcile himself to his lord? Would it not be with the heads of the men here? ⁵Is this not David, of whom they sing to one another in dances,

'Saul has killed his thousands,
and David his ten thousands'?"

6 Then Achish called David and said to him, "As the LORD lives, you have been honest, and to me it seems right that you should march out and in with me in the campaign; for I have found nothing wrong in you from the day of your coming to me until today. Nevertheless the lords do not approve of you. ⁷So go back now; and go peaceably; do nothing to displease the lords of the Philistines." ⁸David said to Achish, "But what have I done? What have you found in your servant from the day I entered your service until now, that I should not go and fight against the enemies of my lord the king?" ⁹Achish replied to David, "I know that you are as blameless in my sight as an angel of God; nevertheless, the commanders of the Philistines have said, 'He shall not go up with us to the battle.' ¹⁰Now then rise early in the morning, you and the servants of your lord who came with you, and go to the place that I appointed for you. As for the evil report, do not take it to heart, for you have done well before me.ᵃ Start early in the morning, and leave as soon as you have light." ¹¹So David set out with his men early in the morning, to return to the land of the Philistines. But the Philistines went up to Jezreel.

David Avenges the Destruction of Ziklag

30 Now when David and his men came to Ziklag on the third day, the Amalekites had made a raid on the Negeb and on Ziklag. They had attacked Ziklag, burned it down, ²and taken captive the women and allᵇ who were in it, both small and great; they killed none of them, but carried them off, and went their way. ³When David and his men came to the city, they found it burned down, and their wives and sons and daughters taken

captive. ⁴Then David and the people who were with him raised their voices and wept, until they had no more strength to weep. ⁵David's two wives also had been taken captive, Ahinoam of Jezreel, and Abigail the widow of Nabal of Carmel. ⁶David was in great danger; for the people spoke of stoning him, because all the people were bitter in spirit for their sons and daughters. But David strengthened himself in the LORD his God.

7 David said to the priest Abiathar son of Ahimelech, "Bring me the ephod." So Abiathar brought the ephod to David. ⁸David inquired of the LORD, "Shall I pursue this band? Shall I overtake them?" He answered him, "Pursue; for you shall surely overtake and shall surely rescue." ⁹So David set out, he and the six hundred men who were with him. They came to the Wadi Besor, where those stayed who were left behind. ¹⁰But David went on with the pursuit, he and four hundred men; two hundred stayed behind, too exhausted to cross the Wadi Besor.

11 In the open country they found an Egyptian, and brought him to David. They gave him bread and he ate; they gave him water to drink; ¹²they also gave him a piece of fig cake and two clusters of raisins. When he had eaten, his spirit revived; for he had not eaten bread or drunk water for three days and three nights. ¹³Then David said to him, "To whom do you belong? Where are you from?" He said, "I am a young man of Egypt, servant to an Amalekite. My master left me behind because I fell sick three days ago. ¹⁴We had made a raid on the Negeb of the Cherethites and on that which belongs to Judah and on the Negeb of Caleb; and we burned Ziklag down." ¹⁵David said to him, "Will you take me down to this raiding party?" He said, "Swear to me by God that you will not kill me, or hand me over to my master, and I will take you down to them."

16 When he had taken him down, they were spread out all over the ground, eating and drinking and dancing, because of the great amount of spoil they had taken from the land

---

ᵃ Gk: Heb lacks *and go to the place . . . done well before me*   ᵇ Gk: Heb lacks *and all* of the Philistines and from the land of Judah. ¹⁷David attacked them from twilight until the evening of the next day. Not one of them escaped, except four hundred young men, who mounted camels and fled. ¹⁸David recovered all that the Amalekites had taken; and David rescued his two wives. ¹⁹Nothing was missing, whether small or great, sons or daughters, spoil or anything that had been taken; David brought back everything. ²⁰David also captured all the flocks and herds, which were driven ahead of the other cattle; people said, "This is David's spoil."

21 Then David came to the two hundred men who had been too exhausted to follow David, and who had been left at the Wadi Besor. They went out to meet David and to meet the people who were with him. When David drew near to the people he saluted them. ²²Then all the corrupt and worthless fellows among the men who had gone with David said, "Because they did not go with us, we will not give them any of the spoil that we have recovered, except that each man may take his wife and children, and leave." ²³But David said, "You shall not do so, my brothers, with what the LORD has given us; he has preserved us and handed over to us the raiding party that attacked us. ²⁴Who would listen to you in this matter? For the share of the one who goes down into the battle shall be the same as the share of the one who stays by the baggage; they shall share alike." ²⁵From that day forward he made it a statute and an ordinance for Israel; it continues to the present day.

26 When David came to Ziklag, he sent part of the spoil to his friends, the elders of Judah, saying, "Here is a present for you from the spoil of the enemies of the LORD"; ²⁷it was for those in Bethel, in Ramoth of the Negeb, in Jattir, ²⁸in Aroer, in Siphmoth, in Eshtemoa, ²⁹in Racal, in the towns of the Jerahmeelites, in the towns of the Kenites, ³⁰in Hormah, in Bor-ashan, in Athach, ³¹in Hebron, all the places where David and his men had roamed.

The Death of Saul and His Sons

31 Now the Philistines fought against Israel; and the men of Israel fled before the Philistines, and many fell*a* on Mount Gilboa. ²The Philistines overtook Saul and his sons; and the Philistines killed Jonathan and Abinadab and Malchishua, the sons of Saul. ³The battle pressed hard upon Saul; the archers found him, and he was badly wounded by them. ⁴Then Saul said to his armor-bearer, "Draw your sword and thrust me through with it, so that these uncircumcised may not come and thrust me through, and make sport of me." But his armor-bearer was unwilling; for he was terrified. So Saul took his own sword and fell upon it. ⁵When his armor-bearer saw that Saul was dead, he also fell upon his sword and died with him. ⁶So Saul and his three sons and his armor-bearer and all his men died together on the same day. ⁷When the men of Israel who were on the other side of the valley and those beyond the Jordan saw that the men of Israel had fled and that Saul and his sons were dead, they forsook their towns and fled; and the Philistines came and occupied them.

8 The next day, when the Philistines came to strip the dead, they found Saul and his three sons fallen on Mount Gilboa. ⁹They cut off his head, stripped off his armor, and sent messengers throughout the land of the Philistines to carry the good news to the houses of their idols and to the people. ¹⁰They put his armor in the temple of Astarte;*b* and they fastened his body to the wall of Beth-shan. ¹¹But when the inhabitants of Jabesh-gilead heard what the Philistines had done to Saul, ¹²all the valiant men set out, traveled all night long, and took the body of Saul and the bodies of his sons from the wall of Beth-shan. They came to Jabesh and burned them there. ¹³Then they took their bones and buried them under the tamarisk tree in Jabesh, and fasted seven days.

a Heb *and they fell slain*   *b* Heb plural

2 SAMUEL

David Mourns for Saul and Jonathan

1 After the death of Saul, when David had returned from defeating the Amalekites, David remained two days in Ziklag. ²On the third day, a man came from Saul's camp, with his clothes torn and dirt on his head. When he came to David, he fell to the ground and did obeisance. ³David said to him, "Where have you come from?" He said to him, "I have escaped from the camp of Israel." ⁴David said to him, "How did things go? Tell me!" He answered, "The army fled from the battle, but also many of the army fell and died; and Saul and his son Jonathan also died." ⁵Then David asked the young man who was reporting to him, "How do you know that Saul and his son Jonathan died?" ⁶The young man reporting to him said, "I happened to be on Mount Gilboa; and there was Saul leaning on his spear, while the chariots and the horsemen drew close to him. ⁷When he looked behind him, he saw me, and called to me. I answered, 'Here sir.' ⁸And he said to me, 'Who are you?' I answered him, 'I am an Amalekite.' ⁹He said to me, 'Come, stand over me and kill me; for convulsions have seized me, and yet my life still lingers.' ¹⁰So I stood over him, and killed him, for I knew that he could not live after he had fallen. I took the crown that was on his head and the armlet that was on his arm, and I have brought them here to my lord."

11 Then David took hold of his clothes and tore them; and all the men who were with him did the same. ¹²They mourned and wept, and fasted until evening for Saul and for his son Jonathan, and for the army of the LORD and for the house of Israel, because they had fallen by the sword. ¹³David said to the young man who had reported to him, "Where do you come from?" He answered, "I am the son of a resident alien, an Amalekite." ¹⁴David said to him, "Were you not afraid to lift your hand to destroy the LORD's anointed?" ¹⁵Then David called one of the young men and said, "Come here and strike him down." So he struck him down and he died. ¹⁶David said to him, "Your blood be on your head; for your own mouth has testified against you, saying, 'I have killed the LORD's anointed.'"

17 David intoned this lamentation over Saul and his son Jonathan. ¹⁸(He ordered that The Song of the Bow*a* be taught to the people of Judah; it is written in the Book of Jashar.) He said:

19 Your glory, O Israel, lies slain upon your
          high places!
      How the mighty have fallen!
20 Tell it not in Gath,
          proclaim it not in the streets of
              Ashkelon;
      or the daughters of the Philistines will
              rejoice,
          the daughters of the uncircumcised
              will exult.

21 You mountains of Gilboa,
          let there be no dew or rain upon you,
          nor bounteous fields!*b*
      For there the shield of the mighty was
              defiled,
          the shield of Saul, anointed with oil
              no more.

22 From the blood of the slain,
          from the fat of the mighty,
      the bow of Jonathan did not turn back,
          nor the sword of Saul return empty.

23 Saul and Jonathan, beloved and lovely!
      In life and in death they were not
              divided;
      they were swifter than eagles,
          they were stronger than lions.

24 O daughters of Israel, weep over Saul,
          who clothed you with crimson, in
              luxury,
          who put ornaments of gold on your
              apparel.

---

a Heb *that The Bow*   *b* Meaning of Heb uncertain

²⁵ How the mighty have fallen
    in the midst of the battle!

Jonathan lies slain upon your high places.
²⁶   I am distressed for you, my brother
        Jonathan;
    greatly beloved were you to me;
    your love to me was wonderful,
    passing the love of women.

²⁷ How the mighty have fallen,
    and the weapons of war perished!

David Anointed King of Judah

2 After this David inquired of the LORD, "Shall I go up into any of the cities of Judah?" The LORD said to him, "Go up." David said, "To which shall I go up?" He said, "To Hebron." ²So David went up there, along with his two wives, Ahinoam of Jezreel, and Abigail the widow of Nabal of Carmel. ³David brought up the men who were with him, every one with his household; and they settled in the towns of Hebron. ⁴Then the people of Judah came, and there they anointed David king over the house of Judah.

When they told David, "It was the people of Jabesh-gilead who buried Saul," ⁵David sent messengers to the people of Jabesh-gilead, and said to them, "May you be blessed by the LORD, because you showed this loyalty to Saul your lord, and buried him! ⁶Now may the LORD show steadfast love and faithfulness to you! And I too will reward you because you have done this thing. ⁷Therefore let your hands be strong, and be valiant; for Saul your lord is dead, and the house of Judah has anointed me king over them."

Ishbaal King of Israel

8 But Abner son of Ner, commander of Saul's army, had taken Ishbaal^a son of Saul, and brought him over to Mahanaim. ⁹He made him king over Gilead, the Ashurites, Jezreel, Ephraim, Benjamin, and over all Israel. ¹⁰Ishbaal,^a Saul's son, was forty years old when he began to reign over Israel, and he reigned two years. But the house of Judah followed David. ¹¹The time that David was king in Hebron over the house of Judah was seven years and six months.

The Battle of Gibeon

12 Abner son of Ner, and the servants of Ishbaal^a son of Saul, went out from Mahanaim to Gibeon. ¹³Joab son of Zeruiah, and the servants of David, went out and met them at the pool of Gibeon. One group sat on one side of the pool, while the other sat on the other side of the pool. ¹⁴Abner said to Joab, "Let the young men come forward and have a contest before us." Joab said, "Let them come forward." ¹⁵So they came forward and were counted as they passed by, twelve for Benjamin and Ishbaal^a son of Saul, and twelve of the servants of David. ¹⁶Each grasped his opponent by the head, and thrust his sword in his opponent's side; so they fell down together. Therefore that place was called Helkath-hazzurim,^b which is at Gibeon. ¹⁷The battle was very fierce that day; and Abner and the men of Israel were beaten by the servants of David.

18 The three sons of Zeruiah were there, Joab, Abishai, and Asahel. Now Asahel was as swift of foot as a wild gazelle. ¹⁹Asahel pursued Abner, turning neither to the right nor to the left as he followed him. ²⁰Then Abner looked back and said, "Is it you, Asahel?" He answered, "Yes, it is." ²¹Abner said to him, "Turn to your right or to your left, and seize one of the young men, and take his spoil." But Asahel would not turn away from following him. ²²Abner said again to Asahel, "Turn away from following me; why should I strike you to the ground? How then could I show my face to your brother Joab?" ²³But he refused to turn away. So Abner struck him in the stomach with the butt of his spear, so that the spear came out at his back. He fell there, and died where he lay. And all those who came to the place where Asahel had fallen and died, stood still.

24 But Joab and Abishai pursued Abner. As

---

a Gk Compare 1 Chr 8.33; 9.39: Heb *Ish-bosheth,* "man of shame"   *b* That is *Field of Sword-edges* the sun was going down they came to the hill of Ammah, which lies before Giah on the way to the wilderness of Gibeon. 25The Benjaminites rallied around Abner and formed a single band; they took their stand on the top of a hill. 26Then Abner called to Joab, "Is the sword to keep devouring forever? Do you not know that the end will be bitter? How long will it be before you order your people to turn from the pursuit of their kinsmen?" 27Joab said, "As God lives, if you had not spoken, the people would have continued to pursue their kinsmen, not stopping until morning." 28Joab sounded the trumpet and all the people stopped; they no longer pursued Israel or engaged in battle any further.

29 Abner and his men traveled all that night through the Arabah; they crossed the Jordan, and, marching the whole forenoon,*a* they came to Mahanaim. 30Joab returned from the pursuit of Abner; and when he had gathered all the people together, there were missing of David's servants nineteen men besides Asahel. 31But the servants of David had killed of Benjamin three hundred sixty of Abner's men. 32They took up Asahel and buried him in the tomb of his father, which was at Bethlehem. Joab and his men marched all night, and the day broke upon them at Hebron.

Abner Defects to David

3 There was a long war between the house of Saul and the house of David; David grew stronger and stronger, while the house of Saul became weaker and weaker.

2 Sons were born to David at Hebron: his firstborn was Amnon, of Ahinoam of Jezreel; 3his second, Chileab, of Abigail the widow of Nabal of Carmel; the third, Absalom son of Maacah, daughter of King Talmai of Geshur; 4the fourth, Adonijah son of Haggith; the fifth, Shephatiah son of Abital; 5and the sixth, Ithream, of David's wife Eglah. These were born to David in Hebron.

6 While there was war between the house of Saul and the house of David, Abner was making himself strong in the house of Saul. 7Now Saul had a concubine whose name was Rizpah daughter of Aiah. And Ishbaal*b* said to Abner, "Why have you gone in to my father's concubine?" 8The words of Ishbaal*c* made Abner very angry; he said, "Am I a dog's head for Judah? Today I keep showing loyalty to the house of your father Saul, to his brothers, and to his friends, and have not given you into the hand of David; and yet you charge me now with a crime concerning this woman. 9So may God do to Abner and so may he add to it! For just what the LORD has sworn to David, that will I accomplish for him, 10to transfer the kingdom from the house of Saul, and set up the throne of David over Israel and over Judah, from Dan to Beer-sheba." 11And Ishbaal*b* could not answer Abner another word, because he feared him.

12 Abner sent messengers to David at Hebron,*d* saying, "To whom does the land belong? Make your covenant with me, and I will give you my support to bring all Israel over to you." 13He said, "Good; I will make a covenant with you. But one thing I require of you: you shall never appear in my presence unless you bring Saul's daughter Michal when you come to see me." 14Then David sent messengers to Saul's son Ishbaal,*e* saying, "Give me my wife Michal, to whom I became engaged at the price of one hundred foreskins of the Philistines." 15Ishbaal*e* sent and took her from her husband Paltiel the son of Laish. 16But her husband went with her, weeping as he walked behind her all the way to Bahurim. Then Abner said to him, "Go back home!" So he went back.

17 Abner sent word to the elders of Israel, saying, "For some time past you have been seeking David as king over you. 18Now then bring it about; for the LORD has promised David: Through my servant David I will save my people Israel from the hand of the Philistines, and from all their enemies." 19Abner also spoke directly to the Benjaminites; then Abner went

a Meaning of Heb uncertain   *b* Heb *And he*   *c* Gk Compare 1 Chr 8.33; 9.39: Heb *Ish-bosheth*, "man of shame"   *d* Gk: Heb *where he was*   *e* Heb *Ish-bosheth* to tell David at Hebron all that Israel and the whole house of Benjamin were ready to do.

20 When Abner came with twenty men to David at Hebron, David made a feast for Abner and the men who were with him. 21 Abner said to David, "Let me go and rally all Israel to my lord the king, in order that they may make a covenant with you, and that you may reign over all that your heart desires." So David dismissed Abner, and he went away in peace.

Abner Is Killed by Joab

22 Just then the servants of David arrived with Joab from a raid, bringing much spoil with them. But Abner was not with David at Hebron, for David*a* had dismissed him, and he had gone away in peace. 23 When Joab and all the army that was with him came, it was told Joab, "Abner son of Ner came to the king, and he has dismissed him, and he has gone away in peace." 24 Then Joab went to the king and said, "What have you done? Abner came to you; why did you dismiss him, so that he got away? 25 You know that Abner son of Ner came to deceive you, and to learn your comings and goings and to learn all that you are doing."

26 When Joab came out from David's presence, he sent messengers after Abner, and they brought him back from the cistern of Sirah; but David did not know about it. 27 When Abner returned to Hebron, Joab took him aside in the gateway to speak with him privately, and there he stabbed him in the stomach. So he died for shedding*b* the blood of Asahel, Joab's*c* brother. 28 Afterward, when David heard of it, he said, "I and my kingdom are forever guiltless before the LORD for the blood of Abner son of Ner. 29 May the guilt*d* fall on the head of Joab, and on all his father's house; and may the house of Joab never be without one who has a discharge, or who is leprous,*e* or who holds a spindle, or who falls by the sword, or who lacks food!" 30 So Joab and his brother Abishai murdered Abner because he had killed their brother Asahel in the battle at Gibeon.

31 Then David said to Joab and to all the people who were with him, "Tear your clothes, and put on sackcloth, and mourn over Abner." And King David followed the bier. 32 They buried Abner at Hebron. The king lifted up his voice and wept at the grave of Abner, and all the people wept. 33 The king lamented for Abner, saying,

"Should Abner die as a fool dies?
34   Your hands were not bound,
     your feet were not fettered;
   as one falls before the wicked
     you have fallen."

And all the people wept over him again. 35 Then all the people came to persuade David to eat something while it was still day; but David swore, saying, "So may God do to me, and more, if I taste bread or anything else before the sun goes down!" 36 All the people took notice of it, and it pleased them; just as everything the king did pleased all the people. 37 So all the people and all Israel understood that day that the king had no part in the killing of Abner son of Ner. 38 And the king said to his servants, "Do you not know that a prince and a great man has fallen this day in Israel? 39 Today I am powerless, even though anointed king; these men, the sons of Zeruiah, are too violent for me. The LORD pay back the one who does wickedly in accordance with his wickedness!"

Ishbaal Assassinated

4 When Saul's son Ishbaal*f* heard that Abner had died at Hebron, his courage failed, and all Israel was dismayed. 2 Saul's son had two captains of raiding bands; the name of the one was Baanah, and the name of the other Rechab. They were sons of Rimmon a Benjaminite from Beeroth—for Beeroth is considered to belong to Benjamin. 3 (Now the people of Beeroth had fled to Gittaim and are there as resident aliens to this day).

4 Saul's son Jonathan had a son who was crippled in his feet. He was five years old when the news about Saul and Jonathan came from Jezreel. His nurse picked him up and fled; and,

---

a Heb *he*   *b* Heb lacks *shedding*   *c* Heb *his*   *d* Heb *May it*   *e* A term for several skin diseases; precise meaning uncertain   *f* Heb lacks *Ishbaal* in her haste to flee, it happened that he fell and became lame. His name was Mephibosheth.ᵃ

5 Now the sons of Rimmon the Beerothite, Rechab and Baanah, set out, and about the heat of the day they came to the house of Ishbaal,ᵇ while he was taking his noonday rest. ⁶They came inside the house as though to take wheat, and they struck him in the stomach; then Rechab and his brother Baanah escaped.ᶜ ⁷Now they had come into the house while he was lying on his couch in his bedchamber; they attacked him, killed him, and beheaded him. Then they took his head and traveled by way of the Arabah all night long. ⁸They brought the head of Ishbaalᵇ to David at Hebron and said to the king, "Here is the head of Ishbaal,ᵇ son of Saul, your enemy, who sought your life; the LORD has avenged my lord the king this day on Saul and on his offspring."

9 David answered Rechab and his brother Baanah, the sons of Rimmon the Beerothite, "As the LORD lives, who has redeemed my life out of every adversity, ¹⁰when the one who told me, 'See, Saul is dead,' thought he was bringing good news, I seized him and killed him at Ziklag—this was the reward I gave him for his news. ¹¹How much more then, when wicked men have killed a righteous man on his bed in his own house! And now shall I not require his blood at your hand, and destroy you from the earth?" ¹²So David commanded the young men, and they killed them; they cut off their hands and feet, and hung their bodies beside the pool at Hebron. But the head of Ishbaalᵇ they took and buried in the tomb of Abner at Hebron.

David Anointed King of All Israel

5 Then all the tribes of Israel came to David at Hebron, and said, "Look, we are your bone and flesh. ²For some time, while Saul was king over us, it was you who led out Israel and brought it in. The LORD said to you: It is you who shall be shepherd of my people Israel, you who shall be ruler over Israel." ³So all the elders of Israel came to the king at Hebron; and King David made a covenant with them at Hebron before the LORD, and they anointed David king over Israel. ⁴David was thirty years old when he began to reign, and he reigned forty years. ⁵At Hebron he reigned over Judah seven years and six months; and at Jerusalem he reigned over all Israel and Judah thirty-three years.

Jerusalem Made Capital of the United Kingdom

6 The king and his men marched to Jerusalem against the Jebusites, the inhabitants of the land, who said to David, "You will not come in here, even the blind and the lame will turn you back"—thinking, "David cannot come in here." ⁷Nevertheless David took the stronghold of Zion, which is now the city of David. ⁸David had said on that day, "Whoever would strike down the Jebusites, let him get up the water shaft to attack the lame and the blind, those whom David hates."ᵈ Therefore it is said, "The blind and the lame shall not come into the house." ⁹David occupied the stronghold, and named it the city of David. David built the city all around from the Millo inward. ¹⁰And David became greater and greater, for the LORD, the God of hosts, was with him.

11 King Hiram of Tyre sent messengers to David, along with cedar trees, and carpenters and masons who built David a house. ¹²David then perceived that the LORD had established him king over Israel, and that he had exalted his kingdom for the sake of his people Israel.

13 In Jerusalem, after he came from Hebron, David took more concubines and wives; and more sons and daughters were born to David. ¹⁴These are the names of those who were born to him in Jerusalem: Shammua, Shobab, Nathan, Solomon, ¹⁵Ibhar, Elishua, Nepheg, Japhia, ¹⁶Elishama, Eliada, and Eliphelet.

Philistine Attack Repulsed

17 When the Philistines heard that David had been anointed king over Israel, all the Phi-

---

ᵃ In 1 Chr 8.34 and 9.40, *Merib-baal* reading is *those who hate David*   ᵇ Heb *Ish-bosheth*   ᶜ Meaning of Heb of verse 6 uncertain   ᵈ Another listines went up in search of David; but David heard about it and went down to the stronghold. ¹⁸Now the Philistines had come and spread out in the valley of Rephaim. ¹⁹David inquired of the LORD, "Shall I go up against the Philistines? Will you give them into my hand?" The LORD said to David, "Go up; for I will certainly give the Philistines into your hand." ²⁰So David came to Baal-perazim, and David defeated them there. He said, "The LORD has burst forth against*a* my enemies before me, like a bursting flood." Therefore that place is called Baal-perazim. *b* ²¹The Philistines abandoned their idols there, and David and his men carried them away.

22 Once again the Philistines came up, and were spread out in the valley of Rephaim. ²³When David inquired of the LORD, he said, "You shall not go up; go around to their rear, and come upon them opposite the balsam trees. ²⁴When you hear the sound of marching in the tops of the balsam trees, then be on the alert; for then the LORD has gone out before you to strike down the army of the Philistines." ²⁵David did just as the LORD had commanded him; and he struck down the Philistines from Geba all the way to Gezer.

David Brings the Ark to Jerusalem

6 David again gathered all the chosen men of Israel, thirty thousand. ²David and all the people with him set out and went from Baale-judah, to bring up from there the ark of God, which is called by the name of the LORD of hosts who is enthroned on the cherubim. ³They carried the ark of God on a new cart, and brought it out of the house of Abinadab, which was on the hill. Uzzah and Ahio,*c* the sons of Abinadab, were driving the new cart ⁴with the ark of God;*d* and Ahio*e* went in front of the ark. ⁵David and all the house of Israel were dancing before the LORD with all their might, with songs*e* and lyres and harps and tambourines and castanets and cymbals.

6 When they came to the threshing floor of Nacon, Uzzah reached out his hand to the ark of God and took hold of it, for the oxen shook it. ⁷The anger of the LORD was kindled against Uzzah; and God struck him there because he reached out his hand to the ark;*f* and he died there beside the ark of God. ⁸David was angry because the LORD had burst forth with an outburst upon Uzzah; so that place is called Perez-uzzah,*g* to this day. ⁹David was afraid of the LORD that day; he said, "How can the ark of the LORD come into my care?" ¹⁰So David was unwilling to take the ark of the LORD into his care in the city of David; instead David took it to the house of Obed-edom the Gittite. ¹¹The ark of the LORD remained in the house of Obed-edom the Gittite three months; and the LORD blessed Obed-edom and all his household.

12 It was told King David, "The LORD has blessed the household of Obed-edom and all that belongs to him, because of the ark of God." So David went and brought up the ark of God from the house of Obed-edom to the city of David with rejoicing; ¹³and when those who bore the ark of the LORD had gone six paces, he sacrificed an ox and a fatling. ¹⁴David danced before the LORD with all his might; David was girded with a linen ephod. ¹⁵So David and all the house of Israel brought up the ark of the LORD with shouting, and with the sound of the trumpet.

16 As the ark of the LORD came into the city of David, Michal daughter of Saul looked out of the window, and saw King David leaping and dancing before the LORD; and she despised him in her heart.

17 They brought in the ark of the LORD, and set it in its place, inside the tent that David had pitched for it; and David offered burnt offerings and offerings of well-being before the LORD. ¹⁸When David had finished offering the burnt offerings and the offerings of well-being, he blessed the people in the name of the LORD of hosts, ¹⁹and distributed food among all the people, the whole multitude of Israel,

---

a Heb *paraz*   *b* That is *Lord of Bursting Forth*   *c* Or *and his brother*   *d* Compare Gk: Heb *and brought it out of the house of Abinadab, which was on the hill with the ark of God*   *e* Q Ms Gk 1 Chr 13.8: Heb *fir trees*   *f* 1 Chr 13.10 Compare Q Ms: Meaning of Heb uncertain   *g* That is *Bursting Out Against Uzzah* both men and women, to each a cake of bread, a portion of meat, *a* and a cake of raisins. Then all the people went back to their homes.

20 David returned to bless his household. But Michal the daughter of Saul came out to meet David, and said, "How the king of Israel honored himself today, uncovering himself today before the eyes of his servants' maids, as any vulgar fellow might shamelessly uncover himself!" 21 David said to Michal, "It was before the LORD, who chose me in place of your father and all his household, to appoint me as prince over Israel, the people of the LORD, that I have danced before the LORD. 22 I will make myself yet more contemptible than this, and I will be abased in my own eyes; but by the maids of whom you have spoken, by them I shall be held in honor." 23 And Michal the daughter of Saul had no child to the day of her death.

God's Covenant with David

7 Now when the king was settled in his house, and the LORD had given him rest from all his enemies around him, 2 the king said to the prophet Nathan, "See now, I am living in a house of cedar, but the ark of God stays in a tent." 3 Nathan said to the king, "Go, do all that you have in mind; for the LORD is with you."

4 But that same night the word of the LORD came to Nathan: 5 Go and tell my servant David: Thus says the LORD: Are you the one to build me a house to live in? 6 I have not lived in a house since the day I brought up the people of Israel from Egypt to this day, but I have been moving about in a tent and a tabernacle. 7 Wherever I have moved about among all the people of Israel, did I ever speak a word with any of the tribal leaders *b* of Israel, whom I commanded to shepherd my people Israel, saying, "Why have you not built me a house of cedar?" 8 Now therefore thus you shall say to my servant David: Thus says the LORD of hosts: I took you from the pasture, from following the sheep to be prince over my people Israel; 9 and I have

been with you wherever you went, and have cut off all your enemies from before you; and I will make for you a great name, like the name of the great ones of the earth. 10 And I will appoint a place for my people Israel and will plant them, so that they may live in their own place, and be disturbed no more; and evildoers shall afflict them no more, as formerly, 11 from the time that I appointed judges over my people Israel; and I will give you rest from all your enemies. Moreover the LORD declares to you that the LORD will make you a house. 12 When your days are fulfilled and you lie down with your ancestors, I will raise up your offspring after you, who shall come forth from your body, and I will establish his kingdom. 13 He shall build a house for my name, and I will establish the throne of his kingdom forever. 14 I will be a father to him, and he shall be a son to me. When he commits iniquity, I will punish him with a rod such as mortals use, with blows inflicted by human beings. 15 But I will not take *c* my steadfast love from him, as I took it from Saul, whom I put away from before you. 16 Your house and your kingdom shall be made sure forever before me; *d* your throne shall be established forever. 17 In accordance with all these words and with all this vision, Nathan spoke to David.

David's Prayer

18 Then King David went in and sat before the LORD, and said, "Who am I, O Lord GOD, and what is my house, that you have brought me thus far? 19 And yet this was a small thing in your eyes, O Lord GOD; you have spoken also of your servant's house for a great while to come. May this be instruction for the people, *e* O Lord GOD! 20 And what more can David say to you? For you know your servant, O Lord GOD! 21 Because of your promise, and according to your own heart, you have wrought all this greatness, so that your servant may know it. 22 Therefore you are great, O LORD God; for there is no one like you, and there is no God besides you, according to all that we have heard with our ears. 23 Who is like your people, like Israel? Is there

---

a Vg: Meaning of Heb uncertain   *b* Or *any of the tribes*   *c* Gk Syr Vg 1 Chr 17.13: Heb *shall not depart*
d Gk Heb Mss: MT *before you*; Compare 2 Sam 7.26, 29   *e* Meaning of Heb uncertain

another*a* nation on earth whose God went to redeem it as a people, and to make a name for himself, doing great and awesome things for them,*b* by driving out*c* before his people nations and their gods?*d* ²⁴And you established your people Israel for yourself to be your people forever; and you, O LORD, became their God. ²⁵And now, O LORD God, as for the word that you have spoken concerning your servant and concerning his house, confirm it forever; do as you have promised. ²⁶Thus your name will be magnified forever in the saying, 'The LORD of hosts is God over Israel'; and the house of your servant David will be established before you. ²⁷For you, O LORD of hosts, the God of Israel, have made this revelation to your servant, saying, 'I will build you a house'; therefore your servant has found courage to pray this prayer to you. ²⁸And now, O Lord GOD, you are God, and your words are true, and you have promised this good thing to your servant; ²⁹now therefore may it please you to bless the house of your servant, so that it may continue forever before you; for you, O Lord GOD, have spoken, and with your blessing shall the house of your servant be blessed forever."

David's Wars

8 Some time afterward, David attacked the Philistines and subdued them; David took Metheg-ammah out of the hand of the Philistines.

2 He also defeated the Moabites and, making them lie down on the ground, measured them off with a cord; he measured two lengths of cord for those who were to be put to death, and one length*e* for those who were to be spared. And the Moabites became servants to David and brought tribute.

3 David also struck down King Hadadezer son of Rehob of Zobah, as he went to restore his monument*f* at the river Euphrates. ⁴David took from him one thousand seven hundred horsemen, and twenty thousand foot soldiers. David hamstrung all the chariot horses, but

left enough for a hundred chariots. ⁵When the Arameans of Damascus came to help King Hadadezer of Zobah, David killed twenty-two thousand men of the Arameans. ⁶Then David put garrisons among the Arameans of Damascus; and the Arameans became servants to David and brought tribute. The LORD gave victory to David wherever he went. ⁷David took the gold shields that were carried by the servants of Hadadezer, and brought them to Jerusalem. ⁸From Betah and from Berothai, towns of Hadadezer, King David took a great amount of bronze.

9 When King Toi of Hamath heard that David had defeated the whole army of Hadadezer, ¹⁰Toi sent his son Joram to King David, to greet him and to congratulate him because he had fought against Hadadezer and defeated him. Now Hadadezer had often been at war with Toi. Joram brought with him articles of silver, gold, and bronze; ¹¹these also King David dedicated to the LORD, together with the silver and gold that he dedicated from all the nations he subdued, ¹²from Edom, Moab, the Ammonites, the Philistines, Amalek, and from the spoil of King Hadadezer son of Rehob of Zobah.

13 David won a name for himself. When he returned, he killed eighteen thousand Edomites*g* in the Valley of Salt. ¹⁴He put garrisons in Edom; throughout all Edom he put garrisons, and all the Edomites became David's servants. And the LORD gave victory to David wherever he went.

David's Officers

15 So David reigned over all Israel; and David administered justice and equity to all his people. ¹⁶Joab son of Zeruiah was over the army; Jehoshaphat son of Ahilud was recorder; ¹⁷Zadok son of Ahitub and Ahimelech son of Abiathar were priests; Seraiah was secretary; ¹⁸Benaiah son of Jehoiada was over*h* the Cherethites and the Pelethites; and David's sons were priests.

---

a Gk: Heb *one*   *b* Heb *you*   *c* Gk 1 Chr 17.21: Heb *for your land*   *d* Cn: Heb *before your people, whom you redeemed for yourself from Egypt, nations and its gods*   *e* Heb *one full length*   *f* Compare 1 Sam 15.12 and 2 Sam 18.18
g Gk: Heb *returned from striking down eighteen thousand Arameans*   *h* Syr Tg Vg 20.23; 1 Chr 18.17: Heb lacks *was over*

David's Kindness to Mephibosheth

9 David asked, "Is there still anyone left of the house of Saul to whom I may show kindness for Jonathan's sake?" [2]Now there was a servant of the house of Saul whose name was Ziba, and he was summoned to David. The king said to him, "Are you Ziba?" And he said, "At your service!" [3]The king said, "Is there anyone remaining of the house of Saul to whom I may show the kindness of God?" Ziba said to the king, "There remains a son of Jonathan; he is crippled in his feet." [4]The king said to him, "Where is he?" Ziba said to the king, "He is in the house of Machir son of Ammiel, at Lo-debar." [5]Then King David sent and brought him from the house of Machir son of Ammiel, at Lo-debar. [6]Mephibosheth[a] son of Jonathan son of Saul came to David, and fell on his face and did obeisance. David said, "Mephibosheth!"[a] He answered, "I am your servant." [7]David said to him, "Do not be afraid, for I will show you kindness for the sake of your father Jonathan; I will restore to you all the land of your grandfather Saul, and you yourself shall eat at my table always." [8]He did obeisance and said, "What is your servant, that you should look upon a dead dog such as I?"

9 Then the king summoned Saul's servant Ziba, and said to him, "All that belonged to Saul and to all his house I have given to your master's grandson. [10]You and your sons and your servants shall till the land for him, and shall bring in the produce, so that your master's grandson may have food to eat; but your master's grandson Mephibosheth[a] shall always eat at my table." Now Ziba had fifteen sons and twenty servants. [11]Then Ziba said to the king, "According to all that my lord the king commands his servant, so your servant will do." Mephibosheth[a] ate at David's[b] table, like one of the king's sons. [12]Mephibosheth[a] had a young son whose name was Mica. And all who lived in Ziba's house became Mephibosheth's[c] servants. [13]Mephibosheth[a] lived in Jerusalem, for

he always ate at the king's table. Now he was lame in both his feet.

The Ammonites and Arameans Are Defeated

10 Some time afterward, the king of the Ammonites died, and his son Hanun succeeded him. [2]David said, "I will deal loyally with Hanun son of Nahash, just as his father dealt loyally with me." So David sent envoys to console him concerning his father. When David's envoys came into the land of the Ammonites, [3]the princes of the Ammonites said to their lord Hanun, "Do you really think that David is honoring your father just because he has sent messengers with condolences to you? Has not David sent his envoys to you to search the city, to spy it out, and to overthrow it?" [4]So Hanun seized David's envoys, shaved off half the beard of each, cut off their garments in the middle at their hips, and sent them away. [5]When David was told, he sent to meet them, for the men were greatly ashamed. The king said, "Remain at Jericho until your beards have grown, and then return."

6 When the Ammonites saw that they had become odious to David, the Ammonites sent and hired the Arameans of Beth-rehob and the Arameans of Zobah, twenty thousand foot soldiers, as well as the king of Maacah, one thousand men, and the men of Tob, twelve thousand men. [7]When David heard of it, he sent Joab and all the army with the warriors. [8]The Ammonites came out and drew up in battle array at the entrance of the gate; but the Arameans of Zobah and of Rehob, and the men of Tob and Maacah, were by themselves in the open country.

9 When Joab saw that the battle was set against him both in front and in the rear, he chose some of the picked men of Israel, and arrayed them against the Arameans; [10]the rest of his men he put in the charge of his brother Abishai, and he arrayed them against the Ammonites. [11]He said, "If the Arameans are too strong for me, then you shall help me; but if the Ammonites are too strong for you, then

a Or *Merib-baal*: See 4.4 note   *b* Gk: Heb *my*   *c* Or *Merib-baal's*: See 4.4 note

I will come and help you. 12Be strong, and let us be courageous for the sake of our people, and for the cities of our God; and may the LORD do what seems good to him." 13So Joab and the people who were with him moved forward into battle against the Arameans; and they fled before him. 14When the Ammonites saw that the Arameans fled, they likewise fled before Abishai, and entered the city. Then Joab returned from fighting against the Ammonites, and came to Jerusalem.

15 But when the Arameans saw that they had been defeated by Israel, they gathered themselves together. 16Hadadezer sent and brought out the Arameans who were beyond the Euphrates; and they came to Helam, with Shobach the commander of the army of Hadadezer at their head. 17When it was told David, he gathered all Israel together, and crossed the Jordan, and came to Helam. The Arameans arrayed themselves against David and fought with him. 18The Arameans fled before Israel; and David killed of the Arameans seven hundred chariot teams, and forty thousand horsemen,*a* and wounded Shobach the commander of their army, so that he died there. 19When all the kings who were servants of Hadadezer saw that they had been defeated by Israel, they made peace with Israel, and became subject to them. So the Arameans were afraid to help the Ammonites any more.

David Commits Adultery with Bathsheba

11 In the spring of the year, the time when kings go out to battle, David sent Joab with his officers and all Israel with him; they ravaged the Ammonites, and besieged Rabbah. But David remained at Jerusalem.

2 It happened, late one afternoon, when David rose from his couch and was walking about on the roof of the king's house, that he saw from the roof a woman bathing; the woman was very beautiful. 3David sent someone to inquire about the woman. It was reported, "This is Bathsheba daughter of Eliam, the wife of Uriah the Hittite." 4So David sent messengers to get her, and she came to him, and he lay with her. (Now she was purifying herself after her period.) Then she returned to her house. 5The woman conceived; and she sent and told David, "I am pregnant."

6 So David sent word to Joab, "Send me Uriah the Hittite." And Joab sent Uriah to David. 7When Uriah came to him, David asked how Joab and the people fared, and how the war was going. 8Then David said to Uriah, "Go down to your house, and wash your feet." Uriah went out of the king's house, and there followed him a present from the king. 9But Uriah slept at the entrance of the king's house with all the servants of his lord, and did not go down to his house. 10When they told David, "Uriah did not go down to his house," David said to Uriah, "You have just come from a journey. Why did you not go down to your house?" 11Uriah said to David, "The ark and Israel and Judah remain in booths;*b* and my lord Joab and the servants of my lord are camping in the open field; shall I then go to my house, to eat and to drink, and to lie with my wife? As you live, and as your soul lives, I will not do such a thing." 12Then David said to Uriah, "Remain here today also, and tomorrow I will send you back." So Uriah remained in Jerusalem that day. On the next day, 13David invited him to eat and drink in his presence and made him drunk; and in the evening he went out to lie on his couch with the servants of his lord, but he did not go down to his house.

David Has Uriah Killed

14 In the morning David wrote a letter to Joab, and sent it by the hand of Uriah. 15In the letter he wrote, "Set Uriah in the forefront of the hardest fighting, and then draw back from him, so that he may be struck down and die." 16As Joab was besieging the city, he assigned Uriah to the place where he knew there were valiant warriors. 17The men of the city came out and fought with Joab; and some of the servants of David among the people fell. Uriah

---

a 1 Chr 19.18 and some Gk Mss read *foot soldiers*   *b* Or *at Succoth* the Hittite was killed as well. 18Then Joab sent and told David all the news about the fighting; 19and he instructed the messenger, "When you have finished telling the king all the news about the fighting, 20then, if the king's anger rises, and if he says to you, 'Why did you go so near the city to fight? Did you not know that they would shoot from the wall? 21Who killed Abimelech son of Jerubbaal?*a* Did not a woman throw an upper millstone on him from the wall, so that he died at Thebez? Why did you go so near the wall?' then you shall say, 'Your servant Uriah the Hittite is dead too.'"

22 So the messenger went, and came and told David all that Joab had sent him to tell. 23The messenger said to David, "The men gained an advantage over us, and came out against us in the field; but we drove them back to the entrance of the gate. 24Then the archers shot at your servants from the wall; some of the king's servants are dead; and your servant Uriah the Hittite is dead also." 25David said to the messenger, "Thus you shall say to Joab, 'Do not let this matter trouble you, for the sword devours now one and now another; press your attack on the city, and overthrow it.' And encourage him."

26 When the wife of Uriah heard that her husband was dead, she made lamentation for him. 27When the mourning was over, David sent and brought her to his house, and she became his wife, and bore him a son.

Nathan Condemns David

12 But the thing that David had done displeased the LORD, 1and the LORD sent Nathan to David. He came to him, and said to him, "There were two men in a certain city, the one rich and the other poor. 2The rich man had very many flocks and herds; 3but the poor man had nothing but one little ewe lamb, which he had bought. He brought it up, and it grew up with him and with his children; it used to eat of his meager fare, and drink from his cup, and lie in his bosom, and it was like a daughter to him. 4Now there came a traveler to the rich man, and he was loath to take one of his own flock or herd to prepare for the wayfarer who had come to him, but he took the poor man's lamb, and prepared that for the guest who had come to him." 5Then David's anger was greatly kindled against the man. He said to Nathan, "As the LORD lives, the man who has done this deserves to die; 6he shall restore the lamb fourfold, because he did this thing, and because he had no pity."

7 Nathan said to David, "You are the man! Thus says the LORD, the God of Israel: I anointed you king over Israel, and I rescued you from the hand of Saul; 8I gave you your master's house, and your master's wives into your bosom, and gave you the house of Israel and of Judah; and if that had been too little, I would have added as much more. 9Why have you despised the word of the LORD, to do what is evil in his sight? You have struck down Uriah the Hittite with the sword, and have taken his wife to be your wife, and have killed him with the sword of the Ammonites. 10Now therefore the sword shall never depart from your house, for you have despised me, and have taken the wife of Uriah the Hittite to be your wife. 11Thus says the LORD: I will raise up trouble against you from within your own house; and I will take your wives before your eyes, and give them to your neighbor, and he shall lie with your wives in the sight of this very sun. 12For you did it secretly; but I will do this thing before all Israel, and before the sun." 13David said to Nathan, "I have sinned against the LORD." Nathan said to David, "Now the LORD has put away your sin; you shall not die. 14Nevertheless, because by this deed you have utterly scorned the LORD,*b* the child that is born to you shall die." 15Then Nathan went to his house.

Bathsheba's Child Dies

The LORD struck the child that Uriah's wife bore to David, and it became very ill. 16David therefore pleaded with God for the child; David fasted, and went in and lay all night on the

---

a Gk Syr Judg 7.1: Heb *Jerubbesheth*   *b* Ancient scribal tradition: Compare 1 Sam 25.22 note: Heb *scorned the enemies of the LORD* ground. [17]The elders of his house stood beside him, urging him to rise from the ground; but he would not, nor did he eat food with them. [18]On the seventh day the child died. And the servants of David were afraid to tell him that the child was dead; for they said, "While the child was still alive, we spoke to him, and he did not listen to us; how then can we tell him the child is dead? He may do himself some harm." [19]But when David saw that his servants were whispering together, he perceived that the child was dead; and David said to his servants, "Is the child dead?" They said, "He is dead."

20 Then David rose from the ground, washed, anointed himself, and changed his clothes. He went into the house of the LORD, and worshiped; he then went to his own house; and when he asked, they set food before him and he ate. [21]Then his servants said to him, "What is this thing that you have done? You fasted and wept for the child while it was alive; but when the child died, you rose and ate food." [22]He said, "While the child was still alive, I fasted and wept; for I said, 'Who knows? The LORD may be gracious to me, and the child may live.' [23]But now he is dead; why should I fast? Can I bring him back again? I shall go to him, but he will not return to me."

Solomon Is Born

24 Then David consoled his wife Bathsheba, and went to her, and lay with her; and she bore a son, and he named him Solomon. The LORD loved him, [25]and sent a message by the prophet Nathan; so he named him Jedidiah,[a] because of the LORD.

The Ammonites Crushed

26 Now Joab fought against Rabbah of the Ammonites, and took the royal city. [27]Joab sent messengers to David, and said, "I have fought against Rabbah; moreover, I have taken the water city. [28]Now, then, gather the rest of the people together, and encamp against the city, and take it; or I myself will take the city, and it will be called by my name." [29]So David gath-

ered all the people together and went to Rabbah, and fought against it and took it. [30]He took the crown of Milcom[b] from his head; the weight of it was a talent of gold, and in it was a precious stone; and it was placed on David's head. He also brought forth the spoil of the city, a very great amount. [31]He brought out the people who were in it, and set them to work with saws and iron picks and iron axes, or sent them to the brickworks. Thus he did to all the cities of the Ammonites. Then David and all the people returned to Jerusalem.

Amnon and Tamar

13 Some time passed. David's son Absalom had a beautiful sister whose name was Tamar; and David's son Amnon fell in love with her. [2]Amnon was so tormented that he made himself ill because of his sister Tamar, for she was a virgin and it seemed impossible to Amnon to do anything to her. [3]But Amnon had a friend whose name was Jonadab, the son of David's brother Shimeah; and Jonadab was a very crafty man. [4]He said to him, "O son of the king, why are you so haggard morning after morning? Will you not tell me?" Amnon said to him, "I love Tamar, my brother Absalom's sister." [5]Jonadab said to him, "Lie down on your bed, and pretend to be ill; and when your father comes to see you, say to him, 'Let my sister Tamar come and give me something to eat, and prepare the food in my sight, so that I may see it and eat it from her hand.' " [6]So Amnon lay down, and pretended to be ill; and when the king came to see him, Amnon said to the king, "Please let my sister Tamar come and make a couple of cakes in my sight, so that I may eat from her hand."

7 Then David sent home to Tamar, saying, "Go to your brother Amnon's house, and prepare food for him." [8]So Tamar went to her brother Amnon's house, where he was lying down. She took dough, kneaded it, made cakes in his sight, and baked the cakes. [9]Then she took the pan and set them[c] out before him, but he refused to eat. Amnon said, "Send out

---

a That is *Beloved of the* LORD   *b* Gk See 1 Kings 11.5, 33: Heb *their kings*   *c* Heb *and poured* everyone from me." So everyone went out from him. [10]Then Amnon said to Tamar, "Bring the food into the chamber, so that I may eat from your hand." So Tamar took the cakes she had made, and brought them into the chamber to Amnon her brother. [11]But when she brought them near him to eat, he took hold of her, and said to her, "Come, lie with me, my sister." [12]She answered him, "No, my brother, do not force me; for such a thing is not done in Israel; do not do anything so vile! [13]As for me, where could I carry my shame? And as for you, you would be as one of the scoundrels in Israel. Now therefore, I beg you, speak to the king; for he will not withhold me from you." [14]But he would not listen to her; and being stronger than she, he forced her and lay with her.

15 Then Amnon was seized with a very great loathing for her; indeed, his loathing was even greater than the lust he had felt for her. Amnon said to her, "Get out!" [16]But she said to him, "No, my brother;[a] for this wrong in sending me away is greater than the other that you did to me." But he would not listen to her. [17]He called the young man who served him and said, "Put this woman out of my presence, and bolt the door after her." [18](Now she was wearing a long robe with sleeves; for this is how the virgin daughters of the king were clothed in earlier times.[b]) So his servant put her out, and bolted the door after her. [19]But Tamar put ashes on her head, and tore the long robe that she was wearing; she put her hand on her head, and went away, crying aloud as she went.

20 Her brother Absalom said to her, "Has Amnon your brother been with you? Be quiet for now, my sister; he is your brother; do not take this to heart." So Tamar remained, a desolate woman, in her brother Absalom's house. [21]When King David heard of all these things, he became very angry, but he would not punish his son Amnon, because he loved him, for he was his firstborn.[c] [22]But Absalom spoke to Amnon neither good nor bad; for Absalom

hated Amnon, because he had raped his sister Tamar.

Absalom Avenges the Violation of His Sister

23 After two full years Absalom had sheepshearers at Baal-hazor, which is near Ephraim, and Absalom invited all the king's sons. [24]Absalom came to the king, and said, "Your servant has sheepshearers; will the king and his servants please go with your servant?" [25]But the king said to Absalom, "No, my son, let us not all go, or else we will be burdensome to you." He pressed him, but he would not go but gave him his blessing. [26]Then Absalom said, "If not, please let my brother Amnon go with us." The king said to him, "Why should he go with you?" [27]But Absalom pressed him until he let Amnon and all the king's sons go with him. Absalom made a feast like a king's feast.[d] [28]Then Absalom commanded his servants, "Watch when Amnon's heart is merry with wine, and when I say to you, 'Strike Amnon,' then kill him. Do not be afraid; have I not myself commanded you? Be courageous and valiant." [29]So the servants of Absalom did to Amnon as Absalom had commanded. Then all the king's sons rose, and each mounted his mule and fled.

30 While they were on the way, the report came to David that Absalom had killed all the king's sons, and not one of them was left. [31]The king rose, tore his garments, and lay on the ground; and all his servants who were standing by tore their garments. [32]But Jonadab, the son of David's brother Shimeah, said, "Let not my lord suppose that they have killed all the young men the king's sons; Amnon alone is dead. This has been determined by Absalom from the day Amnon[e] raped his sister Tamar. [33]Now therefore, do not let my lord the king take it to heart, as if all the king's sons were dead; for Amnon alone is dead."

34 But Absalom fled. When the young man who kept watch looked up, he saw many people coming from the Horonaim road[f] by the

---

a Cn Compare Gk Vg: Meaning of Heb uncertain   b Cn: Heb were clothed in robes   c Q Ms Gk: MT lacks but he would not punish . . . firstborn   d Gk Compare Q Ms: MT lacks Absalom made a feast like a king's feast   e Heb he   f Cn Compare Gk: Heb the road behind him side of the mountain. ³⁵Jonadab said to the king, "See, the king's sons have come; as your servant said, so it has come about." ³⁶As soon as he had finished speaking, the king's sons arrived, and raised their voices and wept; and the king and all his servants also wept very bitterly.

37 But Absalom fled, and went to Talmai son of Ammihud, king of Geshur. David mourned for his son day after day. ³⁸Absalom, having fled to Geshur, stayed there three years. ³⁹And the heart of*ᵃ* the king went out, yearning for Absalom; for he was now consoled over the death of Amnon.

Absalom Returns to Jerusalem

14 Now Joab son of Zeruiah perceived that the king's mind was on Absalom. ²Joab sent to Tekoa and brought from there a wise woman. He said to her, "Pretend to be a mourner; put on mourning garments, do not anoint yourself with oil, but behave like a woman who has been mourning many days for the dead. ³Go to the king and speak to him as follows." And Joab put the words into her mouth.

4 When the woman of Tekoa came to the king, she fell on her face to the ground and did obeisance, and said, "Help, O king!" ⁵The king asked her, "What is your trouble?" She answered, "Alas, I am a widow; my husband is dead. ⁶Your servant had two sons, and they fought with one another in the field; there was no one to part them, and one struck the other and killed him. ⁷Now the whole family has risen against your servant. They say, 'Give up the man who struck his brother, so that we may kill him for the life of his brother whom he murdered, even if we destroy the heir as well.' Thus they would quench my one remaining ember, and leave to my husband neither name nor remnant on the face of the earth."

8 Then the king said to the woman, "Go to your house, and I will give orders concerning you." ⁹The woman of Tekoa said to the king, "On me be the guilt, my lord the king, and on my father's house; let the king and his throne be guiltless." ¹⁰The king said, "If anyone says anything to you, bring him to me, and he shall never touch you again." ¹¹Then she said, "Please, may the king keep the Lᴏʀᴅ your God in mind, so that the avenger of blood may kill no more, and my son not be destroyed." He said, "As the Lᴏʀᴅ lives, not one hair of your son shall fall to the ground."

12 Then the woman said, "Please let your servant speak a word to my lord the king." He said, "Speak." ¹³The woman said, "Why then have you planned such a thing against the people of God? For in giving this decision the king convicts himself, inasmuch as the king does not bring his banished one home again. ¹⁴We must all die; we are like water spilled on the ground, which cannot be gathered up. But God will not take away a life; he will devise plans so as not to keep an outcast banished forever from his presence.*ᵇ* ¹⁵Now I have come to say this to my lord the king because the people have made me afraid; your servant thought, 'I will speak to the king; it may be that the king will perform the request of his servant. ¹⁶For the king will hear, and deliver his servant from the hand of the man who would cut both me and my son off from the heritage of God.' ¹⁷Your servant thought, 'The word of my lord the king will set me at rest'; for my lord the king is like the angel of God, discerning good and evil. The Lᴏʀᴅ your God be with you!"

18 Then the king answered the woman, "Do not withhold from me anything I ask you." The woman said, "Let my lord the king speak." ¹⁹The king said, "Is the hand of Joab with you in all this?" The woman answered and said, "As surely as you live, my lord the king, one cannot turn right or left from anything that my lord the king has said. For it was your servant Joab who commanded me; it was he who put all these words into the mouth of your servant. ²⁰In order to change the course of affairs your servant Joab did this. But my lord has wisdom like the wisdom of the angel

---

a Q Ms Gk: MT *And David*   *b* Meaning of Heb uncertain of God to know all things that are on the earth."

21 Then the king said to Joab, "Very well, I grant this; go, bring back the young man Absalom." ²²Joab prostrated himself with his face to the ground and did obeisance, and blessed the king; and Joab said, "Today your servant knows that I have found favor in your sight, my lord the king, in that the king has granted the request of his servant." ²³So Joab set off, went to Geshur, and brought Absalom to Jerusalem. ²⁴The king said, "Let him go to his own house; he is not to come into my presence." So Absalom went to his own house, and did not come into the king's presence.

David Forgives Absalom

25 Now in all Israel there was no one to be praised so much for his beauty as Absalom; from the sole of his foot to the crown of his head there was no blemish in him. ²⁶When he cut the hair of his head (for at the end of every year he used to cut it; when it was heavy on him, he cut it), he weighed the hair of his head, two hundred shekels by the king's weight. ²⁷There were born to Absalom three sons, and one daughter whose name was Tamar; she was a beautiful woman.

28 So Absalom lived two full years in Jerusalem, without coming into the king's presence. ²⁹Then Absalom sent for Joab to send him to the king; but Joab would not come to him. He sent a second time, but Joab would not come. ³⁰Then he said to his servants, "Look, Joab's field is next to mine, and he has barley there; go and set it on fire." So Absalom's servants set the field on fire. ³¹Then Joab rose and went to Absalom at his house, and said to him, "Why have your servants set my field on fire?" ³²Absalom answered Joab, "Look, I sent word to you: Come here, that I may send you to the king with the question, 'Why have I come from Geshur? It would be better for me to be there still.' Now let me go into the king's presence; if there is guilt in me, let him kill me!" ³³Then Joab went to the king and told him; and he

summoned Absalom. So he came to the king and prostrated himself with his face to the ground before the king; and the king kissed Absalom.

Absalom Usurps the Throne

15 After this Absalom got himself a chariot and horses, and fifty men to run ahead of him. ²Absalom used to rise early and stand beside the road into the gate; and when anyone brought a suit before the king for judgment, Absalom would call out and say, "From what city are you?" When the person said, "Your servant is of such and such a tribe in Israel," ³Absalom would say, "See, your claims are good and right; but there is no one deputed by the king to hear you." ⁴Absalom said moreover, "If only I were judge in the land! Then all who had a suit or cause might come to me, and I would give them justice." ⁵Whenever people came near to do obeisance to him, he would put out his hand and take hold of them, and kiss them. ⁶Thus Absalom did to every Israelite who came to the king for judgment; so Absalom stole the hearts of the people of Israel.

7 At the end of four*ᵃ* years Absalom said to the king, "Please let me go to Hebron and pay the vow that I have made to the LORD. ⁸For your servant made a vow while I lived at Geshur in Aram: If the LORD will indeed bring me back to Jerusalem, then I will worship the LORD in Hebron."*ᵇ* ⁹The king said to him, "Go in peace." So he got up, and went to Hebron. ¹⁰But Absalom sent secret messengers throughout all the tribes of Israel, saying, "As soon as you hear the sound of the trumpet, then shout: Absalom has become king at Hebron!" ¹¹Two hundred men from Jerusalem went with Absalom; they were invited guests, and they went in their innocence, knowing nothing of the matter. ¹²While Absalom was offering the sacrifices, he sent for*ᶜ* Ahithophel the Gilonite, David's counselor, from his city Giloh. The conspiracy grew in strength, and the people with Absalom kept increasing.

a Gk Syr: Heb *forty*   *b* Gk Mss: Heb lacks *in Hebron*   *c* Or *he sent*

David Flees from Jerusalem

13 A messenger came to David, saying, "The hearts of the Israelites have gone after Absalom." 14Then David said to all his officials who were with him at Jerusalem, "Get up! Let us flee, or there will be no escape for us from Absalom. Hurry, or he will soon overtake us, and bring disaster down upon us, and attack the city with the edge of the sword." 15The king's officials said to the king, "Your servants are ready to do whatever our lord the king decides." 16So the king left, followed by all his household, except ten concubines whom he left behind to look after the house. 17The king left, followed by all the people; and they stopped at the last house. 18All his officials passed by him; and all the Cherethites, and all the Pelethites, and all the six hundred Gittites who had followed him from Gath, passed on before the king.

19 Then the king said to Ittai the Gittite, "Why are you also coming with us? Go back, and stay with the king; for you are a foreigner, and also an exile from your home. 20You came only yesterday, and shall I today make you wander about with us, while I go wherever I can? Go back, and take your kinsfolk with you; and may the LORD show*a* steadfast love and faithfulness to you." 21But Ittai answered the king, "As the LORD lives, and as my lord the king lives, wherever my lord the king may be, whether for death or for life, there also your servant will be." 22David said to Ittai, "Go then, march on." So Ittai the Gittite marched on, with all his men and all the little ones who were with him. 23The whole country wept aloud as all the people passed by; the king crossed the Wadi Kidron, and all the people moved on toward the wilderness.

24 Abiathar came up, and Zadok also, with all the Levites, carrying the ark of the covenant of God. They set down the ark of God, until the people had all passed out of the city. 25Then the king said to Zadok, "Carry the ark of God back into the city. If I find favor in the eyes of the LORD, he will bring me back and let me see both it and the place where it stays. 26But if he says, 'I take no pleasure in you,' here I am, let him do to me what seems good to him." 27The king also said to the priest Zadok, "Look,*b* go back to the city in peace, you and Abiathar,*c* with your two sons, Ahimaaz your son, and Jonathan son of Abiathar. 28See, I will wait at the fords of the wilderness until word comes from you to inform me." 29So Zadok and Abiathar carried the ark of God back to Jerusalem, and they remained there.

30 But David went up the ascent of the Mount of Olives, weeping as he went, with his head covered and walking barefoot; and all the people who were with him covered their heads and went up, weeping as they went. 31David was told that Ahithophel was among the conspirators with Absalom. And David said, "O LORD, I pray you, turn the counsel of Ahithophel into foolishness."

Hushai Becomes David's Spy

32 When David came to the summit, where God was worshiped, Hushai the Archite came to meet him with his coat torn and earth on his head. 33David said to him, "If you go on with me, you will be a burden to me. 34But if you return to the city and say to Absalom, 'I will be your servant, O king; as I have been your father's servant in time past, so now I will be your servant,' then you will defeat for me the counsel of Ahithophel. 35The priests Zadok and Abiathar will be with you there. So whatever you hear from the king's house, tell it to the priests Zadok and Abiathar. 36Their two sons are with them there, Zadok's son Ahimaaz and Abiathar's son Jonathan; and by them you shall report to me everything you hear." 37So Hushai, David's friend, came into the city, just as Absalom was entering Jerusalem.

David's Adversaries

16 When David had passed a little beyond the summit, Ziba the servant of Mephibosheth*d* met him, with a couple of donkeys saddled, carrying two hundred loaves of

---

a Gk Compare 2.6: Heb lacks *may the LORD show*   *b* Gk: Heb *Are you a seer* or *Do you see?*   *c* Cn: Heb lacks *and Abiathar*   *d* Or *Merib-baal*: See 4.4 note bread, one hundred bunches of raisins, one hundred of summer fruits, and one skin of wine. ²The king said to Ziba, "Why have you brought these?" Ziba answered, "The donkeys are for the king's household to ride, the bread and summer fruit for the young men to eat, and the wine is for those to drink who faint in the wilderness." ³The king said, "And where is your master's son?" Ziba said to the king, "He remains in Jerusalem; for he said, 'Today the house of Israel will give me back my grandfather's kingdom.' " ⁴Then the king said to Ziba, "All that belonged to Mephibosheth*a* is now yours." Ziba said, "I do obeisance; let me find favor in your sight, my lord the king."

Shimei Curses David

5 When King David came to Bahurim, a man of the family of the house of Saul came out whose name was Shimei son of Gera; he came out cursing. ⁶He threw stones at David and at all the servants of King David; now all the people and all the warriors were on his right and on his left. ⁷Shimei shouted while he cursed, "Out! Out! Murderer! Scoundrel! ⁸The LORD has avenged on all of you the blood of the house of Saul, in whose place you have reigned; and the LORD has given the kingdom into the hand of your son Absalom. See, disaster has overtaken you; for you are a man of blood."

9 Then Abishai son of Zeruiah said to the king, "Why should this dead dog curse my lord the king? Let me go over and take off his head." ¹⁰But the king said, "What have I to do with you, you sons of Zeruiah? If he is cursing because the LORD has said to him, 'Curse David,' who then shall say, 'Why have you done so?' " ¹¹David said to Abishai and to all his servants, "My own son seeks my life; how much more now may this Benjaminite! Let him alone, and let him curse; for the LORD has bidden him. ¹²It may be that the LORD will look on my distress,*b* and the LORD will repay me with good for this cursing of me today." ¹³So David and his men went on the road, while Shimei went along on the hillside opposite him and cursed as he went, throwing stones and flinging dust at him. ¹⁴The king and all the people who were with him arrived weary at the Jordan;*c* and there he refreshed himself.

The Counsel of Ahithophel

15 Now Absalom and all the Israelites*d* came to Jerusalem; Ahithophel was with him. ¹⁶When Hushai the Archite, David's friend, came to Absalom, Hushai said to Absalom, "Long live the king! Long live the king!" ¹⁷Absalom said to Hushai, "Is this your loyalty to your friend? Why did you not go with your friend?" ¹⁸Hushai said to Absalom, "No; but the one whom the LORD and this people and all the Israelites have chosen, his I will be, and with him I will remain. ¹⁹Moreover, whom should I serve? Should it not be his son? Just as I have served your father, so I will serve you."

20 Then Absalom said to Ahithophel, "Give us your counsel; what shall we do?" ²¹Ahithophel said to Absalom, "Go in to your father's concubines, the ones he has left to look after the house; and all Israel will hear that you have made yourself odious to your father, and the hands of all who are with you will be strengthened." ²²So they pitched a tent for Absalom upon the roof; and Absalom went in to his father's concubines in the sight of all Israel. ²³Now in those days the counsel that Ahithophel gave was as if one consulted the oracle*e* of God; so all the counsel of Ahithophel was esteemed, both by David and by Absalom.

17 Moreover Ahithophel said to Absalom, "Let me choose twelve thousand men, and I will set out and pursue David tonight. ²I will come upon him while he is weary and discouraged, and throw him into a panic; and all the people who are with him will flee. I will strike down only the king, ³and I will bring all the people back to you as a bride comes home to her husband. You seek the life of only one man,*f* and all the people will be at

---

a Or *Merib-baal*: See 4.4 note   *b* Gk Vg: Heb *iniquity*   *c* Gk: Heb lacks *at the Jordan*   *d* Gk: Heb *all the people, the men of Israel*   *e* Heb *word*   *f* Gk: Heb *like the return of the whole (is) the man whom you seek* peace." ⁴The advice pleased Absalom and all the elders of Israel.

The Counsel of Hushai

5 Then Absalom said, "Call Hushai the Archite also, and let us hear too what he has to say." ⁶When Hushai came to Absalom, Absalom said to him, "This is what Ahithophel has said; shall we do as he advises? If not, you tell us." ⁷Then Hushai said to Absalom, "This time the counsel that Ahithophel has given is not good." ⁸Hushai continued, "You know that your father and his men are warriors, and that they are enraged, like a bear robbed of her cubs in the field. Besides, your father is expert in war; he will not spend the night with the troops. ⁹Even now he has hidden himself in one of the pits, or in some other place. And when some of our troops*ᵃ* fall at the first attack, whoever hears it will say, 'There has been a slaughter among the troops who follow Absalom.' ¹⁰Then even the valiant warrior, whose heart is like the heart of a lion, will utterly melt with fear; for all Israel knows that your father is a warrior, and that those who are with him are valiant warriors. ¹¹But my counsel is that all Israel be gathered to you, from Dan to Beersheba, like the sand by the sea for multitude, and that you go to battle in person. ¹²So we shall come upon him in whatever place he may be found, and we shall light on him as the dew falls on the ground; and he will not survive, nor will any of those with him. ¹³If he withdraws into a city, then all Israel will bring ropes to that city, and we shall drag it into the valley, until not even a pebble is to be found there." ¹⁴Absalom and all the men of Israel said, "The counsel of Hushai the Archite is better than the counsel of Ahithophel." For the LORD had ordained to defeat the good counsel of Ahithophel, so that the LORD might bring ruin on Absalom.

Hushai Warns David to Escape

15 Then Hushai said to the priests Zadok and Abiathar, "Thus and so did Ahithophel counsel Absalom and the elders of Israel; and thus and so I have counseled. ¹⁶Therefore send quickly and tell David, 'Do not lodge tonight at the fords of the wilderness, but by all means cross over; otherwise the king and all the people who are with him will be swallowed up.' " ¹⁷Jonathan and Ahimaaz were waiting at En-rogel; a servant-girl used to go and tell them, and they would go and tell King David; for they could not risk being seen entering the city. ¹⁸But a boy saw them, and told Absalom; so both of them went away quickly, and came to the house of a man at Bahurim, who had a well in his courtyard; and they went down into it. ¹⁹The man's wife took a covering, stretched it over the well's mouth, and spread out grain on it; and nothing was known of it. ²⁰When Absalom's servants came to the woman at the house, they said, "Where are Ahimaaz and Jonathan?" The woman said to them, "They have crossed over the brook*ᵇ* of water." And when they had searched and could not find them, they returned to Jerusalem.

21 After they had gone, the men came up out of the well, and went and told King David. They said to David, "Go and cross the water quickly; for thus and so has Ahithophel counseled against you." ²²So David and all the people who were with him set out and crossed the Jordan; by daybreak not one was left who had not crossed the Jordan.

23 When Ahithophel saw that his counsel was not followed, he saddled his donkey and went off home to his own city. He set his house in order, and hanged himself; he died and was buried in the tomb of his father.

24 Then David came to Mahanaim, while Absalom crossed the Jordan with all the men of Israel. ²⁵Now Absalom had set Amasa over the army in the place of Joab. Amasa was the son of a man named Ithra the Ishmaelite,*ᶜ* who had married Abigal daughter of Nahash, sister of Zeruiah, Joab's mother. ²⁶The Israelites and Absalom encamped in the land of Gilead.

27 When David came to Mahanaim, Shobi son of Nahash from Rabbah of the Am-

---

a Gk Mss: Heb *some of them*   *b* Meaning of Heb uncertain   *c* 1 Chr 2.17: Heb *Israelite* monites, and Machir son of Ammiel from Lo-debar, and Barzillai the Gileadite from Rogelim, 28brought beds, basins, and earthen vessels, wheat, barley, meal, parched grain, beans and lentils,*a* 29honey and curds, sheep, and cheese from the herd, for David and the people with him to eat; for they said, "The troops are hungry and weary and thirsty in the wilderness."

The Defeat and Death of Absalom

18 Then David mustered the men who were with him, and set over them commanders of thousands and commanders of hundreds. 2And David divided the army into three groups:*b* one third under the command of Joab, one third under the command of Abishai son of Zeruiah, Joab's brother, and one third under the command of Ittai the Gittite. The king said to the men, "I myself will also go out with you." 3But the men said, "You shall not go out. For if we flee, they will not care about us. If half of us die, they will not care about us. But you are worth ten thousand of us;*c* therefore it is better that you send us help from the city." 4The king said to them, "Whatever seems best to you I will do." So the king stood at the side of the gate, while all the army marched out by hundreds and by thousands. 5The king ordered Joab and Abishai and Ittai, saying, "Deal gently for my sake with the young man Absalom." And all the people heard when the king gave orders to all the commanders concerning Absalom.

6 So the army went out into the field against Israel; and the battle was fought in the forest of Ephraim. 7The men of Israel were defeated there by the servants of David, and the slaughter there was great on that day, twenty thousand men. 8The battle spread over the face of all the country; and the forest claimed more victims that day than the sword.

9 Absalom happened to meet the servants of David. Absalom was riding on his mule, and the mule went under the thick branches of a great oak. His head caught fast in the oak, and he was left hanging*d* between heaven and earth, while the mule that was under him went on. 10A man saw it, and told Joab, "I saw Absalom hanging in an oak." 11Joab said to the man who told him, "What, you saw him! Why then did you not strike him there to the ground? I would have been glad to give you ten pieces of silver and a belt." 12But the man said to Joab, "Even if I felt in my hand the weight of a thousand pieces of silver, I would not raise my hand against the king's son; for in our hearing the king commanded you and Abishai and Ittai, saying: For my sake protect the young man Absalom! 13On the other hand, if I had dealt treacherously against his life*e* (and there is nothing hidden from the king), then you yourself would have stood aloof." 14Joab said, "I will not waste time like this with you." He took three spears in his hand, and thrust them into the heart of Absalom, while he was still alive in the oak. 15And ten young men, Joab's armor-bearers, surrounded Absalom and struck him, and killed him.

16 Then Joab sounded the trumpet, and the troops came back from pursuing Israel, for Joab restrained the troops. 17They took Absalom, threw him into a great pit in the forest, and raised over him a very great heap of stones. Meanwhile all the Israelites fled to their homes. 18Now Absalom in his lifetime had taken and set up for himself a pillar that is in the King's Valley, for he said, "I have no son to keep my name in remembrance"; he called the pillar by his own name. It is called Absalom's Monument to this day.

David Hears of Absalom's Death

19 Then Ahimaaz son of Zadok said, "Let me run, and carry tidings to the king that the LORD has delivered him from the power of his enemies." 20Joab said to him, "You are not to carry tidings today; you may carry tidings another day, but today you shall not do so, because the king's son is dead." 21Then Joab said to a Cushite, "Go, tell the king what you have seen." The Cushite bowed before Joab, and ran. 22Then Ahimaaz son of Zadok said again

a Heb *and lentils and parched grain*   *b* Gk: Heb *sent forth the army*   *c* Gk Vg Symmachus: Heb *for now there are ten thousand such as we*   *d* Gk Syr Tg: Heb *was put*   *e* Another reading is *at the risk of my life* to Joab, "Come what may, let me also run after the Cushite." And Joab said, "Why will you run, my son, seeing that you have no reward[a] for the tidings?" 23"Come what may," he said, "I will run." So he said to him, "Run." Then Ahimaaz ran by the way of the Plain, and outran the Cushite.

24 Now David was sitting between the two gates. The sentinel went up to the roof of the gate by the wall, and when he looked up, he saw a man running alone. 25The sentinel shouted and told the king. The king said, "If he is alone, there are tidings in his mouth." He kept coming, and drew near. 26Then the sentinel saw another man running; and the sentinel called to the gatekeeper and said, "See, another man running alone!" The king said, "He also is bringing tidings." 27The sentinel said, "I think the running of the first one is like the running of Ahimaaz son of Zadok." The king said, "He is a good man, and comes with good tidings."

28 Then Ahimaaz cried out to the king, "All is well!" He prostrated himself before the king with his face to the ground, and said, "Blessed be the LORD your God, who has delivered up the men who raised their hand against my lord the king." 29The king said, "Is it well with the young man Absalom?" Ahimaaz answered, "When Joab sent your servant,[b] I saw a great tumult, but I do not know what it was." 30The king said, "Turn aside, and stand here." So he turned aside, and stood still.

31 Then the Cushite came; and the Cushite said, "Good tidings for my lord the king! For the LORD has vindicated you this day, delivering you from the power of all who rose up against you." 32The king said to the Cushite, "Is it well with the young man Absalom?" The Cushite answered, "May the enemies of my lord the king, and all who rise up to do you harm, be like that young man."

David Mourns for Absalom

33[c]The king was deeply moved, and went up to the chamber over the gate, and wept; and

as he went, he said, "O my son Absalom, my son, my son Absalom! Would I had died instead of you, O Absalom, my son, my son!"

19 It was told Joab, "The king is weeping and mourning for Absalom." 2So the victory that day was turned into mourning for all the troops; for the troops heard that day, "The king is grieving for his son." 3The troops stole into the city that day as soldiers steal in who are ashamed when they flee in battle. 4The king covered his face, and the king cried with a loud voice, "O my son Absalom, O Absalom, my son, my son!" 5Then Joab came into the house to the king, and said, "Today you have covered with shame the faces of all your officers who have saved your life today, and the lives of your sons and your daughters, and the lives of your wives and your concubines, 6for love of those who hate you and for hatred of those who love you. You have made it clear today that commanders and officers are nothing to you; for I perceive that if Absalom were alive and all of us were dead today, then you would be pleased. 7So go out at once and speak kindly to your servants; for I swear by the LORD, if you do not go, not a man will stay with you this night; and this will be worse for you than any disaster that has come upon you from your youth until now." 8Then the king got up and took his seat in the gate. The troops were all told, "See, the king is sitting in the gate"; and all the troops came before the king.

David Recalled to Jerusalem

Meanwhile, all the Israelites had fled to their homes. 9All the people were disputing throughout all the tribes of Israel, saying, "The king delivered us from the hand of our enemies, and saved us from the hand of the Philistines; and now he has fled out of the land because of Absalom. 10But Absalom, whom we anointed over us, is dead in battle. Now therefore why do you say nothing about bringing the king back?"

11 King David sent this message to the priests Zadok and Abiathar, "Say to the elders

a Meaning of Heb uncertain   b Heb the king's servant, your servant   c Ch 19.1 in Heb of Judah, 'Why should you be the last to bring the king back to his house? The talk of all Israel has come to the king.[a] 12You are my kin, you are my bone and my flesh; why then should you be the last to bring back the king?' 13And say to Amasa, 'Are you not my bone and my flesh? So may God do to me, and more, if you are not the commander of my army from now on, in place of Joab.' " 14Amasa[b] swayed the hearts of all the people of Judah as one, and they sent word to the king, "Return, both you and all your servants." 15So the king came back to the Jordan; and Judah came to Gilgal to meet the king and to bring him over the Jordan.

16 Shimei son of Gera, the Benjaminite, from Bahurim, hurried to come down with the people of Judah to meet King David; 17with him were a thousand people from Benjamin. And Ziba, the servant of the house of Saul, with his fifteen sons and his twenty servants, rushed down to the Jordan ahead of the king, 18while the crossing was taking place,[c] to bring over the king's household, and to do his pleasure.

David's Mercy to Shimei

Shimei son of Gera fell down before the king, as he was about to cross the Jordan, 19and said to the king, "May my lord not hold me guilty or remember how your servant did wrong on the day my lord the king left Jerusalem; may the king not bear it in mind. 20For your servant knows that I have sinned; therefore, see, I have come this day, the first of all the house of Joseph to come down to meet my lord the king." 21Abishai son of Zeruiah answered, "Shall not Shimei be put to death for this, because he cursed the LORD's anointed?" 22But David said, "What have I to do with you, you sons of Zeruiah, that you should today become an adversary to me? Shall anyone be put to death in Israel this day? For do I not know that I am this day king over Israel?" 23The king said to Shimei, "You shall not die." And the king gave him his oath.

David and Mephibosheth Meet

24 Mephibosheth[d] grandson of Saul came down to meet the king; he had not taken care of his feet, or trimmed his beard, or washed his clothes, from the day the king left until the day he came back in safety. 25When he came from Jerusalem to meet the king, the king said to him, "Why did you not go with me, Mephibosheth?"[d] 26He answered, "My lord, O king, my servant deceived me; for your servant said to him, 'Saddle a donkey for me,[e] so that I may ride on it and go with the king.' For your servant is lame. 27He has slandered your servant to my lord the king. But my lord the king is like the angel of God; do therefore what seems good to you. 28For all my father's house were doomed to death before my lord the king; but you set your servant among those who eat at your table. What further right have I, then, to appeal to the king?" 29The king said to him, "Why speak any more of your affairs? I have decided: you and Ziba shall divide the land." 30Mephibosheth[d] said to the king, "Let him take it all, since my lord the king has arrived home safely."

David's Kindness to Barzillai

31 Now Barzillai the Gileadite had come down from Rogelim; he went on with the king to the Jordan, to escort him over the Jordan. 32Barzillai was a very aged man, eighty years old. He had provided the king with food while he stayed at Mahanaim, for he was a very wealthy man. 33The king said to Barzillai, "Come over with me, and I will provide for you in Jerusalem at my side." 34But Barzillai said to the king, "How many years have I still to live, that I should go up with the king to Jerusalem? 35Today I am eighty years old; can I discern what is pleasant and what is not? Can your servant taste what he eats or what he drinks? Can I still listen to the voice of singing men and singing women? Why then should your servant be an added burden to my lord the king? 36Your servant will go a little way over the Jordan with the king. Why should the king recompense me

a Gk: Heb to the king, to his house   b Heb He   c Cn: Heb the ford crossed   d Or Merib-baal: See 4.4 note
e Gk Syr Vg: Heb said, 'I will saddle a donkey for myself

with such a reward? 37Please let your servant return, so that I may die in my own town, near the graves of my father and my mother. But here is your servant Chimham; let him go over with my lord the king; and do for him whatever seems good to you." 38The king answered, "Chimham shall go over with me, and I will do for him whatever seems good to you; and all that you desire of me I will do for you." 39Then all the people crossed over the Jordan, and the king crossed over; the king kissed Barzillai and blessed him, and he returned to his own home. 40The king went on to Gilgal, and Chimham went on with him; all the people of Judah, and also half the people of Israel, brought the king on his way.

41 Then all the people of Israel came to the king, and said to him, "Why have our kindred the people of Judah stolen you away, and brought the king and his household over the Jordan, and all David's men with him?" 42All the people of Judah answered the people of Israel, "Because the king is near of kin to us. Why then are you angry over this matter? Have we eaten at all at the king's expense? Or has he given us any gift?" 43But the people of Israel answered the people of Judah, "We have ten shares in the king, and in David also we have more than you. Why then did you despise us? Were we not the first to speak of bringing back our king?" But the words of the people of Judah were fiercer than the words of the people of Israel.

The Rebellion of Sheba

20 Now a scoundrel named Sheba son of Bichri, a Benjaminite, happened to be there. He sounded the trumpet and cried out,

"We have no portion in David,
    no share in the son of Jesse!
Everyone to your tents, O Israel!"

2So all the people of Israel withdrew from David and followed Sheba son of Bichri; but the people of Judah followed their king steadfastly from the Jordan to Jerusalem.

3 David came to his house at Jerusalem; and the king took the ten concubines whom he had left to look after the house, and put them in a house under guard, and provided for them, but did not go in to them. So they were shut up until the day of their death, living as if in widowhood.

4 Then the king said to Amasa, "Call the men of Judah together to me within three days, and be here yourself." 5So Amasa went to summon Judah; but he delayed beyond the set time that had been appointed him. 6David said to Abishai, "Now Sheba son of Bichri will do us more harm than Absalom; take your lord's servants and pursue him, or he will find fortified cities for himself, and escape from us." 7Joab's men went out after him, along with the Cherethites, the Pelethites, and all the warriors; they went out from Jerusalem to pursue Sheba son of Bichri. 8When they were at the large stone that is in Gibeon, Amasa came to meet them. Now Joab was wearing a soldier's garment and over it was a belt with a sword in its sheath fastened at his waist; as he went forward it fell out. 9Joab said to Amasa, "Is it well with you, my brother?" And Joab took Amasa by the beard with his right hand to kiss him. 10But Amasa did not notice the sword in Joab's hand; Joab struck him in the belly so that his entrails poured out on the ground, and he died. He did not strike a second blow.

Then Joab and his brother Abishai pursued Sheba son of Bichri. 11And one of Joab's men took his stand by Amasa, and said, "Whoever favors Joab, and whoever is for David, let him follow Joab." 12Amasa lay wallowing in his blood on the highway, and the man saw that all the people were stopping. Since he saw that all who came by him were stopping, he carried Amasa from the highway into a field, and threw a garment over him. 13Once he was removed from the highway, all the people went on after Joab to pursue Sheba son of Bichri.

14 Sheba*a* passed through all the tribes of Israel to Abel of Beth-maacah;*b* and all the Bichrites*c* assembled, and followed him inside. 15Joab's forces*d* came and besieged him in Abel

a Heb He   *b* Compare 20.15: Heb *and Beth-maacah*   *c* Compare Gk Vg: Heb *Berites*   *d* Heb *They* of Beth-maacah; they threw up a siege ramp against the city, and it stood against the rampart. Joab's forces were battering the wall to break it down. ¹⁶Then a wise woman called from the city, "Listen! Listen! Tell Joab, 'Come here, I want to speak to you.'" ¹⁷He came near her; and the woman said, "Are you Joab?" He answered, "I am." Then she said to him, "Listen to the words of your servant." He answered, "I am listening." ¹⁸Then she said, "They used to say in the old days, 'Let them inquire at Abel'; and so they would settle a matter. ¹⁹I am one of those who are peaceable and faithful in Israel; you seek to destroy a city that is a mother in Israel; why will you swallow up the heritage of the LORD?" ²⁰Joab answered, "Far be it from me, far be it, that I should swallow up or destroy! ²¹That is not the case! But a man of the hill country of Ephraim, called Sheba son of Bichri, has lifted up his hand against King David; give him up alone, and I will withdraw from the city." The woman said to Joab, "His head shall be thrown over the wall to you." ²²Then the woman went to all the people with her wise plan. And they cut off the head of Sheba son of Bichri, and threw it out to Joab. So he blew the trumpet, and they dispersed from the city, and all went to their homes, while Joab returned to Jerusalem to the king.

23 Now Joab was in command of all the army of Israel;*ᵃ* Benaiah son of Jehoiada was in command of the Cherethites and the Pelethites; ²⁴Adoram was in charge of the forced labor; Jehoshaphat son of Ahilud was the recorder; ²⁵Sheva was secretary; Zadok and Abiathar were priests; ²⁶and Ira the Jairite was also David's priest.

David Avenges the Gibeonites

21 Now there was a famine in the days of David for three years, year after year; and David inquired of the LORD. The LORD said, "There is bloodguilt on Saul and on his house, because he put the Gibeonites to death." ²So the king called the Gibeonites and spoke to them. (Now the Gibeonites were not of the people of Israel, but of the remnant of the Amorites; although the people of Israel had sworn to spare them, Saul had tried to wipe them out in his zeal for the people of Israel and Judah.) ³David said to the Gibeonites, "What shall I do for you? How shall I make expiation, that you may bless the heritage of the LORD?" ⁴The Gibeonites said to him, "It is not a matter of silver or gold between us and Saul or his house; neither is it for us to put anyone to death in Israel." He said, "What do you say that I should do for you?" ⁵They said to the king, "The man who consumed us and planned to destroy us, so that we should have no place in all the territory of Israel— ⁶let seven of his sons be handed over to us, and we will impale them before the LORD at Gibeon on the mountain of the LORD."*ᵇ* The king said, "I will hand them over."

7 But the king spared Mephibosheth,*ᶜ* the son of Saul's son Jonathan, because of the oath of the LORD that was between them, between David and Jonathan son of Saul. ⁸The king took the two sons of Rizpah daughter of Aiah, whom she bore to Saul, Armoni and Mephibosheth;*ᶜ* and the five sons of Merab*ᵈ* daughter of Saul, whom she bore to Adriel son of Barzillai the Meholathite; ⁹he gave them into the hands of the Gibeonites, and they impaled them on the mountain before the LORD. The seven of them perished together. They were put to death in the first days of harvest, at the beginning of barley harvest.

10 Then Rizpah the daughter of Aiah took sackcloth, and spread it on a rock for herself, from the beginning of harvest until rain fell on them from the heavens; she did not allow the birds of the air to come on the bodies*ᵉ* by day, or the wild animals by night. ¹¹When David was told what Rizpah daughter of Aiah, the concubine of Saul, had done, ¹²David went and took the bones of Saul and the bones of his son Jonathan from the people of Jabesh-gilead, who had stolen them from the public square of Beth-shan, where the Philistines had hung them up, on the day the Philistines killed Saul

---

a Cn: Heb *Joab to all the army, Israel*   *b* Cn Compare Gk and 21.9: Heb *at Gibeah of Saul, the chosen of the* LORD
c Or *Merib-baal.* See 4.4 note   *d* Two Heb Mss Syr Compare Gk: MT *Michal*   *e* Heb *them*

on Gilboa. 13He brought up from there the bones of Saul and the bones of his son Jonathan; and they gathered the bones of those who had been impaled. 14They buried the bones of Saul and of his son Jonathan in the land of Benjamin in Zela, in the tomb of his father Kish; they did all that the king commanded. After that, God heeded supplications for the land.

Exploits of David's Men

15 The Philistines went to war again with Israel, and David went down together with his servants. They fought against the Philistines, and David grew weary. 16Ishbi-benob, one of the descendants of the giants, whose spear weighed three hundred shekels of bronze, and who was fitted out with new weapons, *a* said he would kill David. 17But Abishai son of Zeruiah came to his aid, and attacked the Philistine and killed him. Then David's men swore to him, "You shall not go out with us to battle any longer, so that you do not quench the lamp of Israel."

18 After this a battle took place with the Philistines, at Gob; then Sibbecai the Hushathite killed Saph, who was one of the descendants of the giants. 19Then there was another battle with the Philistines at Gob; and Elhanan son of Jaare-oregim, the Bethlehemite, killed Goliath the Gittite, the shaft of whose spear was like a weaver's beam. 20There was again war at Gath, where there was a man of great size, who had six fingers on each hand, and six toes on each foot, twenty-four in number; he too was descended from the giants. 21When he taunted Israel, Jonathan son of David's brother Shimei, killed him. 22These four were descended from the giants in Gath; they fell by the hands of David and his servants.

David's Song of Thanksgiving

22 David spoke to the LORD the words of this song on the day when the LORD delivered him from the hand of all his enemies, and from the hand of Saul. 2He said:

The LORD is my rock, my fortress, and
        my deliverer,
3   my God, my rock, in whom I take
        refuge,
my shield and the horn of my salvation,
    my stronghold and my refuge,
    my savior; you save me from violence.
4   I call upon the LORD, who is worthy to
        be praised,
    and I am saved from my enemies.

5   For the waves of death encompassed
        me,
    the torrents of perdition assailed me;
6   the cords of Sheol entangled me,
    the snares of death confronted me.

7   In my distress I called upon the LORD;
        to my God I called.
From his temple he heard my voice,
    and my cry came to his ears.

8   Then the earth reeled and rocked;
    the foundations of the heavens
        trembled
    and quaked, because he was angry.
9   Smoke went up from his nostrils,
    and devouring fire from his mouth;
    glowing coals flamed forth from him.
10 He bowed the heavens, and came down;
    thick darkness was under his feet.
11 He rode on a cherub, and flew;
    he was seen upon the wings of the
        wind.
12 He made darkness around him a canopy,
    thick clouds, a gathering of water.
13 Out of the brightness before him
    coals of fire flamed forth.
14 The LORD thundered from heaven;
    the Most High uttered his voice.
15 He sent out arrows, and scattered them
    —lightning, and routed them.
16 Then the channels of the sea were seen,
    the foundations of the world were laid
        bare
at the rebuke of the LORD,

a Heb *was belted anew*

at the blast of the breath of his
nostrils.

17 He reached from on high, he took me,
he drew me out of mighty waters.
18 He delivered me from my strong enemy,
from those who hated me;
for they were too mighty for me.
19 They came upon me in the day of my
calamity,
but the LORD was my stay.
20 He brought me out into a broad place;
he delivered me, because he delighted
in me.

21 The LORD rewarded me according to my
righteousness;
according to the cleanness of my
hands he recompensed me.
22 For I have kept the ways of the LORD,
and have not wickedly departed from
my God.
23 For all his ordinances were before me,
and from his statutes I did not turn
aside.
24 I was blameless before him,
and I kept myself from guilt.
25 Therefore the LORD has recompensed
me according to my
righteousness,
according to my cleanness in his sight.

26 With the loyal you show yourself loyal;
with the blameless you show yourself
blameless;
27 with the pure you show yourself pure,
and with the crooked you show
yourself perverse.
28 You deliver a humble people,
but your eyes are upon the haughty to
bring them down.
29 Indeed, you are my lamp, O LORD,
the LORD lightens my darkness.
30 By you I can crush a troop,
and by my God I can leap over a wall.
31 This God—his way is perfect;

the promise of the LORD proves true;
he is a shield for all who take refuge in
him.

32 For who is God, but the LORD?
And who is a rock, except our God?
33 The God who has girded me with
strength*a*
has opened wide my path.*b*
34 He made my*c* feet like the feet of deer,
and set me secure on the heights.
35 He trains my hands for war,
so that my arms can bend a bow of
bronze.
36 You have given me the shield of your
salvation,
and your help*d* has made me great.
37 You have made me stride freely,
and my feet do not slip;
38 I pursued my enemies and destroyed
them,
and did not turn back until they were
consumed.
39 I consumed them; I struck them down,
so that they did not rise;
they fell under my feet.
40 For you girded me with strength for the
battle;
you made my assailants sink under me.
41 You made my enemies turn their backs
to me,
those who hated me, and I destroyed
them.
42 They looked, but there was no one to
save them;
they cried to the LORD, but he did not
answer them.
43 I beat them fine like the dust of the
earth,
I crushed them and stamped them
down like the mire of the streets.

44 You delivered me from strife with the
peoples;*e*
you kept me as the head of the
nations;

---

a Q Ms Gk Syr Vg Compare Ps 18.32: MT *God is my strong refuge*   *b* Meaning of Heb uncertain   *c* Another
reading is *his*   *d* Q Ms: MT *your answering*   *e* Gk: Heb *from strife with my people*

people whom I had not known served
   me.
45 Foreigners came cringing to me;
   as soon as they heard of me, they
      obeyed me.
46 Foreigners lost heart,
   and came trembling out of their
      strongholds.

47 The LORD lives! Blessed be my rock,
   and exalted be my God, the rock of
      my salvation,
48 the God who gave me vengeance
   and brought down peoples under me,
49 who brought me out from my enemies;
   you exalted me above my adversaries,
   you delivered me from the violent.

50 For this I will extol you, O LORD, among
      the nations,
   and sing praises to your name.
51 He is a tower of salvation for his king,
   and shows steadfast love to his
      anointed,
   to David and his descendants forever.

The Last Words of David

23 Now these are the last words of David:
   The oracle of David, son of Jesse,
   the oracle of the man whom God
      exalted,*a*
the anointed of the God of Jacob,
   the favorite of the Strong One of
      Israel:

2 The spirit of the LORD speaks through
      me,
   his word is upon my tongue.
3 The God of Israel has spoken,
   the Rock of Israel has said to me:
One who rules over people justly,
   ruling in the fear of God,
4 is like the light of morning,
   like the sun rising on a cloudless
      morning,

gleaming from the rain on the grassy
   land.

5 Is not my house like this with God?
For he has made with me an
   everlasting covenant,
   ordered in all things and secure.
Will he not cause to prosper
   all my help and my desire?
6 But the godless are*b* all like thorns that
   are thrown away;
   for they cannot be picked up with the
      hand;
7 to touch them one uses an iron bar
   or the shaft of a spear.
   And they are entirely consumed in fire
      on the spot.*c*

David's Mighty Men

8 These are the names of the warriors whom David had: Josheb-basshebeth a Tahchemonite; he was chief of the Three;*d* he wielded his spear*e* against eight hundred whom he killed at one time.

9 Next to him among the three warriors was Eleazar son of Dodo son of Ahohi. He was with David when they defied the Philistines who were gathered there for battle. The Israelites withdrew, 10but he stood his ground. He struck down the Philistines until his arm grew weary, though his hand clung to the sword. The LORD brought about a great victory that day. Then the people came back to him—but only to strip the dead.

11 Next to him was Shammah son of Agee, the Hararite. The Philistines gathered together at Lehi, where there was a plot of ground full of lentils; and the army fled from the Philistines. 12But he took his stand in the middle of the plot, defended it, and killed the Philistines; and the LORD brought about a great victory.

13 Towards the beginning of harvest three of the thirty*f* chiefs went down to join David at the cave of Adullam, while a band of Philistines was encamped in the valley of Rephaim. 14David was then in the stronghold; and the

---

a Q Ms: MT *who was raised on high*   *b* Heb *But worthlessness*   *c* Heb *in sitting*   *d* Gk Vg Compare 1 Chr 11.11:
Meaning of Heb uncertain   *e* 1 Chr 11.11: Meaning of Heb uncertain   *f* Heb adds *head*

garrison of the Philistines was then at Bethlehem. [15]David said longingly, "O that someone would give me water to drink from the well of Bethlehem that is by the gate!" [16]Then the three warriors broke through the camp of the Philistines, drew water from the well of Bethlehem that was by the gate, and brought it to David. But he would not drink of it; he poured it out to the LORD, [17]for he said, "The LORD forbid that I should do this. Can I drink the blood of the men who went at the risk of their lives?" Therefore he would not drink it. The three warriors did these things.

18 Now Abishai son of Zeruiah, the brother of Joab, was chief of the Thirty.*a* With his spear he fought against three hundred men and killed them, and won a name beside the Three. [19]He was the most renowned of the Thirty,*b* and became their commander; but he did not attain to the Three.

20 Benaiah son of Jehoiada was a valiant warrior*c* from Kabzeel, a doer of great deeds; he struck down two sons of Ariel*d* of Moab. He also went down and killed a lion in a pit on a day when snow had fallen. [21]And he killed an Egyptian, a handsome man. The Egyptian had a spear in his hand; but Benaiah went against him with a staff, snatched the spear out of the Egyptian's hand, and killed him with his own spear. [22]Such were the things Benaiah son of Jehoiada did, and won a name beside the three warriors. [23]He was renowned among the Thirty, but he did not attain to the Three. And David put him in charge of his bodyguard.

24 Among the Thirty were Asahel brother of Joab; Elhanan son of Dodo of Bethlehem; [25]Shammah of Harod; Elika of Harod; [26]Helez the Paltite; Ira son of Ikkesh of Tekoa; [27]Abiezer of Anathoth; Mebunnai the Hushathite; [28]Zalmon the Ahohite; Maharai of Netophah; [29]Heleb son of Baanah of Netophah; Ittai son of Ribai of Gibeah of the Benjaminites; [30]Benaiah of Pirathon; Hiddai of the torrents of Gaash; [31]Abi-albon the Ar-

bathite; Azmaveth of Bahurim; [32]Eliahba of Shaalbon; the sons of Jashen: Jonathan [33]son of*e* Shammah the Hararite; Ahiam son of Sharar the Hararite; [34]Eliphelet son of Ahasbai of Maacah; Eliam son of Ahithophel the Gilonite; [35]Hezro*f* of Carmel; Paarai the Arbite; [36]Igal son of Nathan of Zobah; Bani the Gadite; [37]Zelek the Ammonite; Naharai of Beeroth, the armor-bearer of Joab son of Zeruiah; [38]Ira the Ithrite; Gareb the Ithrite; [39]Uriah the Hittite—thirty-seven in all.

David's Census of Israel and Judah

24 Again the anger of the LORD was kindled against Israel, and he incited David against them, saying, "Go, count the people of Israel and Judah." [2]So the king said to Joab and the commanders of the army,*g* who were with him, "Go through all the tribes of Israel, from Dan to Beer-sheba, and take a census of the people, so that I may know how many there are." [3]But Joab said to the king, "May the LORD your God increase the number of the people a hundredfold, while the eyes of my lord the king can still see it! But why does my lord the king want to do this?" [4]But the king's word prevailed against Joab and the commanders of the army. So Joab and the commanders of the army went out from the presence of the king to take a census of the people of Israel. [5]They crossed the Jordan, and began from*b* Aroer and from the city that is in the middle of the valley, toward Gad and on to Jazer. [6]Then they came to Gilead, and to Kadesh in the land of the Hittites;*i* and they came to Dan, and from Dan*j* they went around to Sidon, [7]and came to the fortress of Tyre and to all the cities of the Hivites and Canaanites; and they went out to the Negeb of Judah at Beer-sheba. [8]So when they had gone through all the land, they came back to Jerusalem at the end of nine months and twenty days. [9]Joab reported to the king the number of those who had been recorded: in Israel there were eight

---

a Two Heb Mss Syr: MT *Three*   b Syr Compare 1 Chr 11.25: Heb *Was he the most renowned of the Three?*
c Another reading is *the son of Ish-hai*   d Gk: Heb lacks *sons of*   e Gk: Heb lacks *son of*   f Another reading is *Hezrai*   g 1 Chr 21.2 Gk: Heb *to Joab the commander of the army*   h Gk Mss: Heb *encamped in Aroer south of*
i Gk: Heb *to the land of Tahtim-hodshi*   j Cn Compare Gk: Heb *they came to Dan-jaan and*

hundred thousand soldiers able to draw the sword, and those of Judah were five hundred thousand.

Judgment on David's Sin

10 But afterward, David was stricken to the heart because he had numbered the people. David said to the LORD, "I have sinned greatly in what I have done. But now, O LORD, I pray you, take away the guilt of your servant; for I have done very foolishly." 11When David rose in the morning, the word of the LORD came to the prophet Gad, David's seer, saying, 12"Go and say to David: Thus says the LORD: Three things I offer[a] you; choose one of them, and I will do it to you." 13So Gad came to David and told him; he asked him, "Shall three[b] years of famine come to you on your land? Or will you flee three months before your foes while they pursue you? Or shall there be three days' pestilence in your land? Now consider, and decide what answer I shall return to the one who sent me." 14Then David said to Gad, "I am in great distress; let us fall into the hand of the LORD, for his mercy is great; but let me not fall into human hands."

15 So the LORD sent a pestilence on Israel from that morning until the appointed time; and seventy thousand of the people died, from Dan to Beer-sheba. 16But when the angel stretched out his hand toward Jerusalem to destroy it, the LORD relented concerning the evil, and said to the angel who was bringing destruction among the people, "It is enough; now stay your hand." The angel of the LORD was then by the threshing floor of Araunah the Jebusite. 17When David saw the angel who was destroying the people, he said to the LORD, "I alone have sinned, and I alone have done wickedly; but these sheep, what have they done? Let your hand, I pray, be against me and against my father's house."

David's Altar on the Threshing Floor

18 That day Gad came to David and said to him, "Go up and erect an altar to the LORD on the threshing floor of Araunah the Jebusite." 19Following Gad's instructions, David went up, as the LORD had commanded. 20When Araunah looked down, he saw the king and his servants coming toward him; and Araunah went out and prostrated himself before the king with his face to the ground. 21Araunah said, "Why has my lord the king come to his servant?" David said, "To buy the threshing floor from you in order to build an altar to the LORD, so that the plague may be averted from the people." 22Then Araunah said to David, "Let my lord the king take and offer up what seems good to him; here are the oxen for the burnt offering, and the threshing sledges and the yokes of the oxen for the wood. 23All this, O king, Araunah gives to the king." And Araunah said to the king, "May the LORD your God respond favorably to you."

24 But the king said to Araunah, "No, but I will buy them from you for a price; I will not offer burnt offerings to the LORD my God that cost me nothing." So David bought the threshing floor and the oxen for fifty shekels of silver. 25David built there an altar to the LORD, and offered burnt offerings and offerings of well-being. So the LORD answered his supplication for the land, and the plague was averted from Israel.

---

a Or *hold over*   *b* 1 Chr 21.12 Gk: Heb *seven*

1 KINGS

The Struggle for the Succession

1 King David was old and advanced in years; and although they covered him with clothes, he could not get warm. ²So his servants said to him, "Let a young virgin be sought for my lord the king, and let her wait on the king, and be his attendant; let her lie in your bosom, so that my lord the king may be warm." ³So they searched for a beautiful girl throughout all the territory of Israel, and found Abishag the Shunammite, and brought her to the king. ⁴The girl was very beautiful. She became the king's attendant and served him, but the king did not know her sexually.

5 Now Adonijah son of Haggith exalted himself, saying, "I will be king"; he prepared for himself chariots and horsemen, and fifty men to run before him. ⁶His father had never at any time displeased him by asking, "Why have you done thus and so?" He was also a very handsome man, and he was born next after Absalom. ⁷He conferred with Joab son of Zeruiah and with the priest Abiathar, and they supported Adonijah. ⁸But the priest Zadok, and Benaiah son of Jehoiada, and the prophet Nathan, and Shimei, and Rei, and David's own warriors did not side with Adonijah.

9 Adonijah sacrificed sheep, oxen, and fatted cattle by the stone Zoheleth, which is beside En-rogel, and he invited all his brothers, the king's sons, and all the royal officials of Judah, ¹⁰but he did not invite the prophet Nathan or Benaiah or the warriors or his brother Solomon.

11 Then Nathan said to Bathsheba, Solomon's mother, "Have you not heard that Adonijah son of Haggith has become king and our lord David does not know it? ¹²Now therefore come, let me give you advice, so that you may save your own life and the life of your son Solomon. ¹³Go in at once to King David, and say to him, 'Did you not, my lord the king, swear to your servant, saying: Your son Solomon shall succeed me as king, and he shall sit on my throne? Why then is Adonijah king?' ¹⁴Then while you are still there speaking with the king, I will come in after you and confirm your words."

15 So Bathsheba went to the king in his room. The king was very old; Abishag the Shunammite was attending the king. ¹⁶Bathsheba bowed and did obeisance to the king, and the king said, "What do you wish?" ¹⁷She said to him, "My lord, you swore to your servant by the LORD your God, saying: Your son Solomon shall succeed me as king, and he shall sit on my throne. ¹⁸But now suddenly Adonijah has become king, though you, my lord the king, do not know it. ¹⁹He has sacrificed oxen, fatted cattle, and sheep in abundance, and has invited all the children of the king, the priest Abiathar, and Joab the commander of the army; but your servant Solomon he has not invited. ²⁰But you, my lord the king—the eyes of all Israel are on you to tell them who shall sit on the throne of my lord the king after him. ²¹Otherwise it will come to pass, when my lord the king sleeps with his ancestors, that my son Solomon and I will be counted offenders."

22 While she was still speaking with the king, the prophet Nathan came in. ²³The king was told, "Here is the prophet Nathan." When he came in before the king, he did obeisance to the king, with his face to the ground. ²⁴Nathan said, "My lord the king, have you said, 'Adonijah shall succeed me as king, and he shall sit on my throne'? ²⁵For today he has gone down and has sacrificed oxen, fatted cattle, and sheep in abundance, and has invited all the king's children, Joab the commander*a* of the army, and the priest Abiathar, who are now eating and drinking before him, and saying, 'Long live King Adonijah!' ²⁶But he did not invite me, your servant, and the priest Zadok, and Benaiah son of Jehoiada, and your servant Solomon. ²⁷Has this thing been brought about by my lord the king and you

---

a Gk: Heb *the commanders*

have not let your servants know who should sit on the throne of my lord the king after him?"

The Accession of Solomon

28 King David answered, "Summon Bathsheba to me." So she came into the king's presence, and stood before the king. 29The king swore, saying, "As the LORD lives, who has saved my life from every adversity, 30as I swore to you by the LORD, the God of Israel, 'Your son Solomon shall succeed me as king, and he shall sit on my throne in my place,' so will I do this day." 31Then Bathsheba bowed with her face to the ground, and did obeisance to the king, and said, "May my lord King David live forever!"

32 King David said, "Summon to me the priest Zadok, the prophet Nathan, and Benaiah son of Jehoiada." When they came before the king, 33the king said to them, "Take with you the servants of your lord, and have my son Solomon ride on my own mule, and bring him down to Gihon. 34There let the priest Zadok and the prophet Nathan anoint him king over Israel; then blow the trumpet, and say, 'Long live King Solomon!' 35You shall go up following him. Let him enter and sit on my throne; he shall be king in my place; for I have appointed him to be ruler over Israel and over Judah." 36Benaiah son of Jehoiada answered the king, "Amen! May the LORD, the God of my lord the king, so ordain. 37As the LORD has been with my lord the king, so may he be with Solomon, and make his throne greater than the throne of my lord King David."

38 So the priest Zadok, the prophet Nathan, and Benaiah son of Jehoiada, and the Cherethites and the Pelethites, went down and had Solomon ride on King David's mule, and led him to Gihon. 39There the priest Zadok took the horn of oil from the tent and anointed Solomon. Then they blew the trumpet, and all the people said, "Long live King Solomon!" 40And all the people went up following him,

playing on pipes and rejoicing with great joy, so that the earth quaked at their noise.

41 Adonijah and all the guests who were with him heard it as they finished feasting. When Joab heard the sound of the trumpet, he said, "Why is the city in an uproar?" 42While he was still speaking, Jonathan son of the priest Abiathar arrived. Adonijah said, "Come in, for you are a worthy man and surely you bring good news." 43Jonathan answered Adonijah, "No, for our lord King David has made Solomon king; 44the king has sent with him the priest Zadok, the prophet Nathan, and Benaiah son of Jehoiada, and the Cherethites and the Pelethites; and they had him ride on the king's mule; 45the priest Zadok and the prophet Nathan have anointed him king at Gihon; and they have gone up from there rejoicing, so that the city is in an uproar. This is the noise that you heard. 46Solomon now sits on the royal throne. 47Moreover the king's servants came to congratulate our lord King David, saying, 'May God make the name of Solomon more famous than yours, and make his throne greater than your throne.' The king bowed in worship on the bed 48and went on to pray thus, 'Blessed be the LORD, the God of Israel, who today has granted one of my offspring*a* to sit on my throne and permitted me to witness it.'"

49 Then all the guests of Adonijah got up trembling and went their own ways. 50Adonijah, fearing Solomon, got up and went to grasp the horns of the altar. 51Solomon was informed, "Adonijah is afraid of King Solomon; see, he has laid hold of the horns of the altar, saying, 'Let King Solomon swear to me first that he will not kill his servant with the sword.'" 52So Solomon responded, "If he proves to be a worthy man, not one of his hairs shall fall to the ground; but if wickedness is found in him, he shall die." 53Then King Solomon sent to have him brought down from the altar. He came to do obeisance to King Solomon; and Solomon said to him, "Go home."

a Gk: Heb *one*

David's Instruction to Solomon

2 When David's time to die drew near, he charged his son Solomon, saying: [2]"I am about to go the way of all the earth. Be strong, be courageous, [3]and keep the charge of the LORD your God, walking in his ways and keeping his statutes, his commandments, his ordinances, and his testimonies, as it is written in the law of Moses, so that you may prosper in all that you do and wherever you turn. [4]Then the LORD will establish his word that he spoke concerning me: 'If your heirs take heed to their way, to walk before me in faithfulness with all their heart and with all their soul, there shall not fail you a successor on the throne of Israel.'

5 "Moreover you know also what Joab son of Zeruiah did to me, how he dealt with the two commanders of the armies of Israel, Abner son of Ner, and Amasa son of Jether, whom he murdered, retaliating in time of peace for blood that had been shed in war, and putting the blood of war on the belt around his waist, and on the sandals on his feet. [6]Act therefore according to your wisdom, but do not let his gray head go down to Sheol in peace. [7]Deal loyally, however, with the sons of Barzillai the Gileadite, and let them be among those who eat at your table; for with such loyalty they met me when I fled from your brother Absalom. [8]There is also with you Shimei son of Gera, the Benjaminite from Bahurim, who cursed me with a terrible curse on the day when I went to Mahanaim; but when he came down to meet me at the Jordan, I swore to him by the LORD, 'I will not put you to death with the sword.' [9]Therefore do not hold him guiltless, for you are a wise man; you will know what you ought to do to him, and you must bring his gray head down with blood to Sheol."

Death of David

10 Then David slept with his ancestors, and was buried in the city of David. [11]The time that David reigned over Israel was forty years; he reigned seven years in Hebron, and thirty-three years in Jerusalem. [12]So Solomon sat on the throne of his father David; and his kingdom was firmly established.

Solomon Consolidates His Reign

13 Then Adonijah son of Haggith came to Bathsheba, Solomon's mother. She asked, "Do you come peaceably?" He said, "Peaceably." [14]Then he said, "May I have a word with you?" She said, "Go on." [15]He said, "You know that the kingdom was mine, and that all Israel expected me to reign; however, the kingdom has turned about and become my brother's, for it was his from the LORD. [16]And now I have one request to make of you; do not refuse me." She said to him, "Go on." [17]He said, "Please ask King Solomon—he will not refuse you—to give me Abishag the Shunammite as my wife." [18]Bathsheba said, "Very well; I will speak to the king on your behalf."

19 So Bathsheba went to King Solomon, to speak to him on behalf of Adonijah. The king rose to meet her, and bowed down to her; then he sat on his throne, and had a throne brought for the king's mother, and she sat on his right. [20]Then she said, "I have one small request to make of you; do not refuse me." And the king said to her, "Make your request, my mother; for I will not refuse you." [21]She said, "Let Abishag the Shunammite be given to your brother Adonijah as his wife." [22]King Solomon answered his mother, "And why do you ask Abishag the Shunammite for Adonijah? Ask for him the kingdom as well! For he is my elder brother; ask not only for him but also for the priest Abiathar and for Joab son of Zeruiah!" [23]Then King Solomon swore by the LORD, "So may God do to me, and more also, for Adonijah has devised this scheme at the risk of his life! [24]Now therefore as the LORD lives, who has established me and placed me on the throne of my father David, and who has made me a house as he promised, today Adonijah shall be put to death." [25]So King Solomon sent Benaiah son of Jehoiada; he struck him down, and he died.

26 The king said to the priest Abiathar, "Go to Anathoth, to your estate; for you deserve death. But I will not at this time put you

to death, because you carried the ark of the Lord GOD before my father David, and because you shared in all the hardships my father endured." 27So Solomon banished Abiathar from being priest to the LORD, thus fulfilling the word of the LORD that he had spoken concerning the house of Eli in Shiloh.

28 When the news came to Joab—for Joab had supported Adonijah though he had not supported Absalom—Joab fled to the tent of the LORD and grasped the horns of the altar. 29When it was told King Solomon, "Joab has fled to the tent of the LORD and now is beside the altar," Solomon sent Benaiah son of Jehoiada, saying, "Go, strike him down." 30So Benaiah came to the tent of the LORD and said to him, "The king commands, 'Come out.'" But he said, "No, I will die here." Then Benaiah brought the king word again, saying, "Thus said Joab, and thus he answered me." 31The king replied to him, "Do as he has said, strike him down and bury him; and thus take away from me and from my father's house the guilt for the blood that Joab shed without cause. 32The LORD will bring back his bloody deeds on his own head, because, without the knowledge of my father David, he attacked and killed with the sword two men more righteous and better than himself, Abner son of Ner, commander of the army of Israel, and Amasa son of Jether, commander of the army of Judah. 33So shall their blood come back on the head of Joab and on the head of his descendants forever; but to David, and to his descendants, and to his house, and to his throne, there shall be peace from the LORD forevermore." 34Then Benaiah son of Jehoiada went up and struck him down and killed him; and he was buried at his own house near the wilderness. 35The king put Benaiah son of Jehoiada over the army in his place, and the king put the priest Zadok in the place of Abiathar.

36 Then the king sent and summoned Shimei, and said to him, "Build yourself a house in Jerusalem, and live there, and do not go out from there to any place whatever. 37For on the day you go out, and cross the Wadi Kidron, know for certain that you shall die; your blood shall be on your own head." 38And Shimei said to the king, "The sentence is fair; as my lord the king has said, so will your servant do." So Shimei lived in Jerusalem many days.

39 But it happened at the end of three years that two of Shimei's slaves ran away to King Achish son of Maacah of Gath. When it was told Shimei, "Your slaves are in Gath," 40Shimei arose and saddled a donkey, and went to Achish in Gath, to search for his slaves; Shimei went and brought his slaves from Gath. 41When Solomon was told that Shimei had gone from Jerusalem to Gath and returned, 42the king sent and summoned Shimei, and said to him, "Did I not make you swear by the LORD, and solemnly adjure you, saying, 'Know for certain that on the day you go out and go to any place whatever, you shall die'? And you said to me, 'The sentence is fair; I accept.' 43Why then have you not kept your oath to the LORD and the commandment with which I charged you?" 44The king also said to Shimei, "You know in your own heart all the evil that you did to my father David; so the LORD will bring back your evil on your own head. 45But King Solomon shall be blessed, and the throne of David shall be established before the LORD forever." 46Then the king commanded Benaiah son of Jehoiada; and he went out and struck him down, and he died.

So the kingdom was established in the hand of Solomon.

Solomon's Prayer for Wisdom

3 Solomon made a marriage alliance with Pharaoh king of Egypt; he took Pharaoh's daughter and brought her into the city of David, until he had finished building his own house and the house of the LORD and the wall around Jerusalem. 2The people were sacrificing at the high places, however, because no house had yet been built for the name of the LORD.

3 Solomon loved the LORD, walking in the statutes of his father David; only, he sacrificed and offered incense at the high places. 4The king went to Gibeon to sacrifice there,

for that was the principal high place; Solomon used to offer a thousand burnt offerings on that altar. 5At Gibeon the LORD appeared to Solomon in a dream by night; and God said, "Ask what I should give you." 6And Solomon said, "You have shown great and steadfast love to your servant my father David, because he walked before you in faithfulness, in righteousness, and in uprightness of heart toward you; and you have kept for him this great and steadfast love, and have given him a son to sit on his throne today. 7And now, O LORD my God, you have made your servant king in place of my father David, although I am only a little child; I do not know how to go out or come in. 8And your servant is in the midst of the people whom you have chosen, a great people, so numerous they cannot be numbered or counted. 9Give your servant therefore an understanding mind to govern your people, able to discern between good and evil; for who can govern this your great people?"

10 It pleased the Lord that Solomon had asked this. 11God said to him, "Because you have asked this, and have not asked for yourself long life or riches, or for the life of your enemies, but have asked for yourself understanding to discern what is right, 12I now do according to your word. Indeed I give you a wise and discerning mind; no one like you has been before you and no one like you shall arise after you. 13I give you also what you have not asked, both riches and honor all your life; no other king shall compare with you. 14If you will walk in my ways, keeping my statutes and my commandments, as your father David walked, then I will lengthen your life."

15 Then Solomon awoke; it had been a dream. He came to Jerusalem where he stood before the ark of the covenant of the LORD. He offered up burnt offerings and offerings of well-being, and provided a feast for all his servants.

Solomon's Wisdom in Judgment

16 Later, two women who were prostitutes came to the king and stood before him. 17The one woman said, "Please, my lord, this woman and I live in the same house; and I gave birth while she was in the house. 18Then on the third day after I gave birth, this woman also gave birth. We were together; there was no one else with us in the house, only the two of us were in the house. 19Then this woman's son died in the night, because she lay on him. 20She got up in the middle of the night and took my son from beside me while your servant slept. She laid him at her breast, and laid her dead son at my breast. 21When I rose in the morning to nurse my son, I saw that he was dead; but when I looked at him closely in the morning, clearly it was not the son I had borne." 22But the other woman said, "No, the living son is mine, and the dead son is yours." The first said, "No, the dead son is yours, and the living son is mine." So they argued before the king.

23 Then the king said, "The one says, 'This is my son that is alive, and your son is dead'; while the other says, 'Not so! Your son is dead, and my son is the living one.' " 24So the king said, "Bring me a sword," and they brought a sword before the king. 25The king said, "Divide the living boy in two; then give half to the one, and half to the other." 26But the woman whose son was alive said to the king—because compassion for her son burned within her— "Please, my lord, give her the living boy; certainly do not kill him!" The other said, "It shall be neither mine nor yours; divide it." 27Then the king responded: "Give the first woman the living boy; do not kill him. She is his mother." 28All Israel heard of the judgment that the king had rendered; and they stood in awe of the king, because they perceived that the wisdom of God was in him, to execute justice.

Solomon's Administrative Officers

4 King Solomon was king over all Israel, 2and these were his high officials: Azariah son of Zadok was the priest; 3Elihoreph and Ahijah sons of Shisha were secretaries; Jehoshaphat son of Ahilud was recorder; 4Benaiah son of Jehoiada was in command of the army; Zadok and Abiathar were priests;

5Azariah son of Nathan was over the officials; Zabud son of Nathan was priest and king's friend; 6Ahishar was in charge of the palace; and Adoniram son of Abda was in charge of the forced labor.

7 Solomon had twelve officials over all Israel, who provided food for the king and his household; each one had to make provision for one month in the year. 8These were their names: Ben-hur, in the hill country of Ephraim; 9Ben-deker, in Makaz, Shaalbim, Beth-shemesh, and Elon-beth-hanan; 10Ben-hesed, in Arubboth (to him belonged Socoh and all the land of Hepher); 11Ben-abinadab, in all Naphath-dor (he had Taphath, Solomon's daughter, as his wife); 12Baana son of Ahilud, in Taanach, Megiddo, and all Beth-shean, which is beside Zarethan below Jezreel, and from Beth-shean to Abel-meholah, as far as the other side of Jokmeam; 13Ben-geber, in Ramoth-gilead (he had the villages of Jair son of Manasseh, which are in Gilead, and he had the region of Argob, which is in Bashan, sixty great cities with walls and bronze bars); 14Ahinadab son of Iddo, in Mahanaim; 15Ahimaaz, in Naphtali (he had taken Basemath, Solomon's daughter, as his wife); 16Baana son of Hushai, in Asher and Bealoth; 17Jehoshaphat son of Paruah, in Issachar; 18Shimei son of Ela, in Benjamin; 19Geber son of Uri, in the land of Gilead, the country of King Sihon of the Amorites and of King Og of Bashan. And there was one official in the land of Judah.

Magnificence of Solomon's Rule

20 Judah and Israel were as numerous as the sand by the sea; they ate and drank and were happy. 21 a Solomon was sovereign over all the kingdoms from the Euphrates to the land of the Philistines, even to the border of Egypt; they brought tribute and served Solomon all the days of his life.

22 Solomon's provision for one day was thirty cors of choice flour, and sixty cors of meal, 23ten fat oxen, and twenty pasture-fed cattle, one hundred sheep, besides deer, gazelles, roebucks, and fatted fowl. 24For he had dominion over all the region west of the Euphrates from Tiphsah to Gaza, over all the kings west of the Euphrates; and he had peace on all sides. 25During Solomon's lifetime Judah and Israel lived in safety, from Dan even to Beer-sheba, all of them under their vines and fig trees. 26Solomon also had forty thousand stalls of horses for his chariots, and twelve thousand horsemen. 27Those officials supplied provisions for King Solomon and for all who came to King Solomon's table, each one in his month; they let nothing be lacking. 28They also brought to the required place barley and straw for the horses and swift steeds, each according to his charge.

Fame of Solomon's Wisdom

29 God gave Solomon very great wisdom, discernment, and breadth of understanding as vast as the sand on the seashore, 30so that Solomon's wisdom surpassed the wisdom of all the people of the east, and all the wisdom of Egypt. 31He was wiser than anyone else, wiser than Ethan the Ezrahite, and Heman, Calcol, and Darda, children of Mahol; his fame spread throughout all the surrounding nations. 32He composed three thousand proverbs, and his songs numbered a thousand and five. 33He would speak of trees, from the cedar that is in the Lebanon to the hyssop that grows in the wall; he would speak of animals, and birds, and reptiles, and fish. 34People came from all the nations to hear the wisdom of Solomon; they came from all the kings of the earth who had heard of his wisdom.

Preparations and Materials for the Temple

5b Now King Hiram of Tyre sent his servants to Solomon, when he heard that they had anointed him king in place of his father; for Hiram had always been a friend to David. 2Solomon sent word to Hiram, saying, 3"You know that my father David could not build a house for the name of the LORD his God because of the warfare with which his en-

a Ch 5.1 in Heb   b Ch 5.15 in Heb

emies surrounded him, until the LORD put them under the soles of his feet.*ᵃ 4But now the LORD my God has given me rest on every side; there is neither adversary nor misfortune. 5So I intend to build a house for the name of the LORD my God, as the LORD said to my father David, 'Your son, whom I will set on your throne in your place, shall build the house for my name.' 6Therefore command that cedars from the Lebanon be cut for me. My servants will join your servants, and I will give you whatever wages you set for your servants; for you know that there is no one among us who knows how to cut timber like the Sidonians."

7 When Hiram heard the words of Solomon, he rejoiced greatly, and said, "Blessed be the LORD today, who has given to David a wise son to be over this great people." 8Hiram sent word to Solomon, "I have heard the message that you have sent to me; I will fulfill all your needs in the matter of cedar and cypress timber. 9My servants shall bring it down to the sea from the Lebanon; I will make it into rafts to go by sea to the place you indicate. I will have them broken up there for you to take away. And you shall meet my needs by providing food for my household." 10So Hiram supplied Solomon's every need for timber of cedar and cypress. 11Solomon in turn gave Hiram twenty thousand cors of wheat as food for his household, and twenty cors of fine oil. Solomon gave this to Hiram year by year. 12So the LORD gave Solomon wisdom, as he promised him. There was peace between Hiram and Solomon; and the two of them made a treaty.

13 King Solomon conscripted forced labor out of all Israel; the levy numbered thirty thousand men. 14He sent them to the Lebanon, ten thousand a month in shifts; they would be a month in the Lebanon and two months at home; Adoniram was in charge of the forced labor. 15Solomon also had seventy thousand laborers and eighty thousand stonecutters in the hill country, 16besides Solomon's

three thousand three hundred supervisors who were over the work, having charge of the people who did the work. 17At the king's command, they quarried out great, costly stones in order to lay the foundation of the house with dressed stones. 18So Solomon's builders and Hiram's builders and the Gebalites did the stonecutting and prepared the timber and the stone to build the house.

Solomon Builds the Temple

6 In the four hundred eightieth year after the Israelites came out of the land of Egypt, in the fourth year of Solomon's reign over Israel, in the month of Ziv, which is the second month, he began to build the house of the LORD. 2The house that King Solomon built for the LORD was sixty cubits long, twenty cubits wide, and thirty cubits high. 3The vestibule in front of the nave of the house was twenty cubits wide, across the width of the house. Its depth was ten cubits in front of the house. 4For the house he made windows with recessed frames.ᵇ 5He also built a structure against the wall of the house, running around the walls of the house, both the nave and the inner sanctuary; and he made side chambers all around. 6The lowest storyᶜ was five cubits wide, the middle one was six cubits wide, and the third was seven cubits wide; for around the outside of the house he made offsets on the wall in order that the supporting beams should not be inserted into the walls of the house.

7 The house was built with stone finished at the quarry, so that neither hammer nor ax nor any tool of iron was heard in the temple while it was being built.

8 The entrance for the middle story was on the south side of the house: one went up by winding stairs to the middle story, and from the middle story to the third. 9So he built the house, and finished it; he roofed the house with beams and planks of cedar. 10He built the structure against the whole house, each storyᵈ five cubits high, and it was joined to the house with timbers of cedar.

---

a Gk Tg Vg: Heb *my feet* or *his feet*   *b* Gk: Meaning of Heb uncertain   *c* Gk: Heb *structure*   *d* Heb lacks *each story*

11 Now the word of the LORD came to Solomon, 12"Concerning this house that you are building, if you will walk in my statutes, obey my ordinances, and keep all my commandments by walking in them, then I will establish my promise with you, which I made to your father David. 13I will dwell among the children of Israel, and will not forsake my people Israel."

14 So Solomon built the house, and finished it. 15He lined the walls of the house on the inside with boards of cedar; from the floor of the house to the rafters of the ceiling, he covered them on the inside with wood; and he covered the floor of the house with boards of cypress. 16He built twenty cubits of the rear of the house with boards of cedar from the floor to the rafters, and he built this within as an inner sanctuary, as the most holy place. 17The house, that is, the nave in front of the inner sanctuary, was forty cubits long. 18The cedar within the house had carvings of gourds and open flowers; all was cedar, no stone was seen. 19The inner sanctuary he prepared in the innermost part of the house, to set there the ark of the covenant of the LORD. 20The interior of the inner sanctuary was twenty cubits long, twenty cubits wide, and twenty cubits high; he overlaid it with pure gold. He also overlaid the altar with cedar. *a* 21Solomon overlaid the inside of the house with pure gold, then he drew chains of gold across, in front of the inner sanctuary, and overlaid it with gold. 22Next he overlaid the whole house with gold, in order that the whole house might be perfect; even the whole altar that belonged to the inner sanctuary he overlaid with gold.

The Furnishings of the Temple

23 In the inner sanctuary he made two cherubim of olivewood, each ten cubits high. 24Five cubits was the length of one wing of the cherub, and five cubits the length of the other wing of the cherub; it was ten cubits from the tip of one wing to the tip of the other. 25The other cherub also measured ten cubits; both cherubim had the same measure and the same form. 26The height of one cherub was ten cubits, and so was that of the other cherub. 27He put the cherubim in the innermost part of the house; the wings of the cherubim were spread out so that a wing of one was touching the one wall, and a wing of the other cherub was touching the other wall; their other wings toward the center of the house were touching wing to wing. 28He also overlaid the cherubim with gold.

29 He carved the walls of the house all around about with carved engravings of cherubim, palm trees, and open flowers, in the inner and outer rooms. 30The floor of the house he overlaid with gold, in the inner and outer rooms.

31 For the entrance to the inner sanctuary he made doors of olivewood; the lintel and the doorposts were five-sided. *a* 32He covered the two doors of olivewood with carvings of cherubim, palm trees, and open flowers; he overlaid them with gold, and spread gold on the cherubim and on the palm trees.

33 So also he made for the entrance to the nave doorposts of olivewood, four-sided each, 34and two doors of cypress wood; the two leaves of the one door were folding, and the two leaves of the other door were folding. 35He carved cherubim, palm trees, and open flowers, overlaying them with gold evenly applied upon the carved work. 36He built the inner court with three courses of dressed stone to one course of cedar beams.

37 In the fourth year the foundation of the house of the LORD was laid, in the month of Ziv. 38In the eleventh year, in the month of Bul, which is the eighth month, the house was finished in all its parts, and according to all its specifications. He was seven years in building it.

Solomon's Palace and Other Buildings

7 Solomon was building his own house thirteen years, and he finished his entire house.

a Meaning of Heb uncertain

2 He built the House of the Forest of the Lebanon one hundred cubits long, fifty cubits wide, and thirty cubits high, built on four rows of cedar pillars, with cedar beams on the pillars. ³It was roofed with cedar on the forty-five rafters, fifteen in each row, which were on the pillars. ⁴There were window frames in the three rows, facing each other in the three rows. ⁵All the doorways and doorposts had four-sided frames, opposite, facing each other in the three rows.

6 He made the Hall of Pillars fifty cubits long and thirty cubits wide. There was a porch in front with pillars, and a canopy in front of them.

7 He made the Hall of the Throne where he was to pronounce judgment, the Hall of Justice, covered with cedar from floor to floor.

8 His own house where he would reside, in the other court back of the hall, was of the same construction. Solomon also made a house like this hall for Pharaoh's daughter, whom he had taken in marriage.

9 All these were made of costly stones, cut according to measure, sawed with saws, back and front, from the foundation to the coping, and from outside to the great court. ¹⁰The foundation was of costly stones, huge stones, stones of eight and ten cubits. ¹¹There were costly stones above, cut to measure, and cedarwood. ¹²The great court had three courses of dressed stone to one layer of cedar beams all around; so had the inner court of the house of the LORD, and the vestibule of the house.

Products of Hiram the Bronzeworker

13 Now King Solomon invited and received Hiram from Tyre. ¹⁴He was the son of a widow of the tribe of Naphtali, whose father, a man of Tyre, had been an artisan in bronze; he was full of skill, intelligence, and knowledge in working bronze. He came to King Solomon, and did all his work.

15 He cast two pillars of bronze. Eighteen cubits was the height of the one, and a cord of twelve cubits would encircle it; the second pillar was the same. ᵃ ¹⁶He also made two capitals of molten bronze, to set on the tops of the pillars; the height of the one capital was five cubits, and the height of the other capital was five cubits. ¹⁷There were nets of checker work with wreaths of chain work for the capitals on the tops of the pillars; seven ᵇ for the one capital, and seven ᵇ for the other capital. ¹⁸He made the columns with two rows around each latticework to cover the capitals that were above the pomegranates; he did the same with the other capital. ¹⁹Now the capitals that were on the tops of the pillars in the vestibule were of lily-work, four cubits high. ²⁰The capitals were on the two pillars and also above the rounded projection that was beside the latticework; there were two hundred pomegranates in rows all around; and so with the other capital. ²¹He set up the pillars at the vestibule of the temple; he set up the pillar on the south and called it Jachin; and he set up the pillar on the north and called it Boaz. ²²On the tops of the pillars was lily-work. Thus the work of the pillars was finished.

23 Then he made the molten sea; it was round, ten cubits from brim to brim, and five cubits high. A line of thirty cubits would encircle it completely. ²⁴Under its brim were panels all around it, each of ten cubits, surrounding the sea; there were two rows of panels, cast when it was cast. ²⁵It stood on twelve oxen, three facing north, three facing west, three facing south, and three facing east; the sea was set on them. The hindquarters of each were toward the inside. ²⁶Its thickness was a handbreadth; its brim was made like the brim of a cup, like the flower of a lily; it held two thousand baths. ᶜ

27 He also made the ten stands of bronze; each stand was four cubits long, four cubits wide, and three cubits high. ²⁸This was the construction of the stands: they had borders; the borders were within the frames; ²⁹on the borders that were set in the frames were lions, oxen, and cherubim. On the frames, both above and below the lions and oxen, there

---

ᵃ Cn: Heb *and a cord of twelve cubits encircled the second pillar*; Compare Jer 52.21   ᵇ Heb: Gk *a net*   ᶜ A Heb measure of volume were wreaths of beveled work. ³⁰Each stand had four bronze wheels and axles of bronze; at the four corners were supports for a basin. The supports were cast with wreaths at the side of each. ³¹Its opening was within the crown whose height was one cubit; its opening was round, as a pedestal is made; it was a cubit and a half wide. At its opening there were carvings; its borders were four-sided, not round. ³²The four wheels were underneath the borders; the axles of the wheels were in the stands; and the height of a wheel was a cubit and a half. ³³The wheels were made like a chariot wheel; their axles, their rims, their spokes, and their hubs were all cast. ³⁴There were four supports at the four corners of each stand; the supports were of one piece with the stands. ³⁵On the top of the stand there was a round band half a cubit high; on the top of the stand, its stays and its borders were of one piece with it. ³⁶On the surfaces of its stays and on its borders he carved cherubim, lions, and palm trees, where each had space, with wreaths all around. ³⁷In this way he made the ten stands; all of them were cast alike, with the same size and the same form.

38 He made ten basins of bronze; each basin held forty baths,ᵃ each basin measured four cubits; there was a basin for each of the ten stands. ³⁹He set five of the stands on the south side of the house, and five on the north side of the house; he set the sea on the southeast corner of the house.

40 Hiram also made the pots, the shovels, and the basins. So Hiram finished all the work that he did for King Solomon on the house of the LORD: ⁴¹the two pillars, the two bowls of the capitals that were on the tops of the pillars, the two latticeworks to cover the two bowls of the capitals that were on the tops of the pillars; ⁴²the four hundred pomegranates for the two latticeworks, two rows of pomegranates for each latticework, to cover the two bowls of the capitals that were on the pillars; ⁴³the ten stands, the ten basins on the stands; ⁴⁴the one sea, and the twelve oxen underneath the sea.

ᵃ A Heb measure of volume

45 The pots, the shovels, and the basins, all these vessels that Hiram made for King Solomon for the house of the LORD were of burnished bronze. ⁴⁶In the plain of the Jordan the king cast them, in the clay ground between Succoth and Zarethan. ⁴⁷Solomon left all the vessels unweighed, because there were so many of them; the weight of the bronze was not determined.

48 So Solomon made all the vessels that were in the house of the LORD: the golden altar, the golden table for the bread of the Presence, ⁴⁹the lampstands of pure gold, five on the south side and five on the north, in front of the inner sanctuary; the flowers, the lamps, and the tongs, of gold; ⁵⁰the cups, snuffers, basins, dishes for incense, and firepans, of pure gold; the sockets for the doors of the innermost part of the house, the most holy place, and for the doors of the nave of the temple, of gold.

51 Thus all the work that King Solomon did on the house of the LORD was finished. Solomon brought in the things that his father David had dedicated, the silver, the gold, and the vessels, and stored them in the treasuries of the house of the LORD.

Dedication of the Temple

8 Then Solomon assembled the elders of Israel and all the heads of the tribes, the leaders of the ancestral houses of the Israelites, before King Solomon in Jerusalem, to bring up the ark of the covenant of the LORD out of the city of David, which is Zion. ²All the people of Israel assembled to King Solomon at the festival in the month Ethanim, which is the seventh month. ³And all the elders of Israel came, and the priests carried the ark. ⁴So they brought up the ark of the LORD, the tent of meeting, and all the holy vessels that were in the tent; the priests and the Levites brought them up. ⁵King Solomon and all the congregation of Israel, who had assembled before him, were with him before the ark, sacrificing so many sheep and oxen that they

could not be counted or numbered. 6Then the priests brought the ark of the covenant of the LORD to its place, in the inner sanctuary of the house, in the most holy place, underneath the wings of the cherubim. 7For the cherubim spread out their wings over the place of the ark, so that the cherubim made a covering above the ark and its poles. 8The poles were so long that the ends of the poles were seen from the holy place in front of the inner sanctuary; but they could not be seen from outside; they are there to this day. 9There was nothing in the ark except the two tablets of stone that Moses had placed there at Horeb, where the LORD made a covenant with the Israelites, when they came out of the land of Egypt. 10And when the priests came out of the holy place, a cloud filled the house of the LORD, 11so that the priests could not stand to minister because of the cloud; for the glory of the LORD filled the house of the LORD.

12 Then Solomon said,

"The LORD has said that he would dwell
in thick darkness.
13   I have built you an exalted house,
a place for you to dwell in forever."

Solomon's Speech

14 Then the king turned around and blessed all the assembly of Israel, while all the assembly of Israel stood. 15He said, "Blessed be the LORD, the God of Israel, who with his hand has fulfilled what he promised with his mouth to my father David, saying, 16'Since the day that I brought my people Israel out of Egypt, I have not chosen a city from any of the tribes of Israel in which to build a house, that my name might be there; but I chose David to be over my people Israel.' 17My father David had it in mind to build a house for the name of the LORD, the God of Israel. 18But the LORD said to my father David, 'You did well to consider building a house for my name; 19nevertheless you shall not build the house, but your son who shall be born to you shall build the house for my name.' 20Now the LORD has upheld the promise that he made; for I have risen in the place of my father Da-

vid; I sit on the throne of Israel, as the LORD promised, and have built the house for the name of the LORD, the God of Israel. 21There I have provided a place for the ark, in which is the covenant of the LORD that he made with our ancestors when he brought them out of the land of Egypt."

Solomon's Prayer of Dedication

22 Then Solomon stood before the altar of the LORD in the presence of all the assembly of Israel, and spread out his hands to heaven. 23He said, "O LORD, God of Israel, there is no God like you in heaven above or on earth beneath, keeping covenant and steadfast love for your servants who walk before you with all their heart, 24the covenant that you kept for your servant my father David as you declared to him; you promised with your mouth and have this day fulfilled with your hand. 25Therefore, O LORD, God of Israel, keep for your servant my father David that which you promised him, saying, 'There shall never fail you a successor before me to sit on the throne of Israel, if only your children look to their way, to walk before me as you have walked before me.' 26Therefore, O God of Israel, let your word be confirmed, which you promised to your servant my father David.

27 "But will God indeed dwell on the earth? Even heaven and the highest heaven cannot contain you, much less this house that I have built! 28Regard your servant's prayer and his plea, O LORD my God, heeding the cry and the prayer that your servant prays to you today; 29that your eyes may be open night and day toward this house, the place of which you said, 'My name shall be there,' that you may heed the prayer that your servant prays toward this place. 30Hear the plea of your servant and of your people Israel when they pray toward this place; O hear in heaven your dwelling place; heed and forgive.

31 "If someone sins against a neighbor and is given an oath to swear, and comes and swears before your altar in this house, 32then hear in heaven, and act, and judge your servants, condemning the guilty by bringing their

conduct on their own head, and vindicating the righteous by rewarding them according to their righteousness.

33 "When your people Israel, having sinned against you, are defeated before an enemy but turn again to you, confess your name, pray and plead with you in this house, 34then hear in heaven, forgive the sin of your people Israel, and bring them again to the land that you gave to their ancestors.

35 "When heaven is shut up and there is no rain because they have sinned against you, and then they pray toward this place, confess your name, and turn from their sin, because you punish*a* them, 36then hear in heaven, and forgive the sin of your servants, your people Israel, when you teach them the good way in which they should walk; and grant rain on your land, which you have given to your people as an inheritance.

37 "If there is famine in the land, if there is plague, blight, mildew, locust, or caterpillar; if their enemy besieges them in any*b* of their cities; whatever plague, whatever sickness there is; 38whatever prayer, whatever plea there is from any individual or from all your people Israel, all knowing the afflictions of their own hearts so that they stretch out their hands toward this house; 39then hear in heaven your dwelling place, forgive, act, and render to all whose hearts you know—according to all their ways, for only you know what is in every human heart— 40so that they may fear you all the days that they live in the land that you gave to our ancestors.

41 "Likewise when a foreigner, who is not of your people Israel, comes from a distant land because of your name 42—for they shall hear of your great name, your mighty hand, and your outstretched arm—when a foreigner comes and prays toward this house, 43then hear in heaven your dwelling place, and do according to all that the foreigner calls to you, so that all the peoples of the earth may know your name and fear you, as do your people Israel, and so that they may know that your

name has been invoked on this house that I have built.

44 "If your people go out to battle against their enemy, by whatever way you shall send them, and they pray to the LORD toward the city that you have chosen and the house that I have built for your name, 45then hear in heaven their prayer and their plea, and maintain their cause.

46 "If they sin against you—for there is no one who does not sin—and you are angry with them and give them to an enemy, so that they are carried away captive to the land of the enemy, far off or near; 47yet if they come to their senses in the land to which they have been taken captive, and repent, and plead with you in the land of their captors, saying, 'We have sinned, and have done wrong; we have acted wickedly'; 48if they repent with all their heart and soul in the land of their enemies, who took them captive, and pray to you toward their land, which you gave to their ancestors, the city that you have chosen, and the house that I have built for your name; 49then hear in heaven your dwelling place their prayer and their plea, maintain their cause 50and forgive your people who have sinned against you, and all their transgressions that they have committed against you; and grant them compassion in the sight of their captors, so that they may have compassion on them 51(for they are your people and heritage, which you brought out of Egypt, from the midst of the iron-smelter). 52Let your eyes be open to the plea of your servant, and to the plea of your people Israel, listening to them whenever they call to you. 53For you have separated them from among all the peoples of the earth, to be your heritage, just as you promised through Moses, your servant, when you brought our ancestors out of Egypt, O Lord GOD."

Solomon Blesses the Assembly

54 Now when Solomon finished offering all this prayer and this plea to the LORD, he arose from facing the altar of the LORD, where

---

a Or *when you answer*   *b* Gk Syr: Heb *in the land*

he had knelt with hands outstretched toward heaven; [55]he stood and blessed all the assembly of Israel with a loud voice:

56 "Blessed be the LORD, who has given rest to his people Israel according to all that he promised; not one word has failed of all his good promise, which he spoke through his servant Moses. [57]The LORD our God be with us, as he was with our ancestors; may he not leave us or abandon us, [58]but incline our hearts to him, to walk in all his ways, and to keep his commandments, his statutes, and his ordinances, which he commanded our ancestors. [59]Let these words of mine, with which I pleaded before the LORD, be near to the LORD our God day and night, and may he maintain the cause of his servant and the cause of his people Israel, as each day requires; [60]so that all the peoples of the earth may know that the LORD is God; there is no other. [61]Therefore devote yourselves completely to the LORD our God, walking in his statutes and keeping his commandments, as at this day."

Solomon Offers Sacrifices

62 Then the king, and all Israel with him, offered sacrifice before the LORD. [63]Solomon offered as sacrifices of well-being to the LORD twenty-two thousand oxen and one hundred twenty thousand sheep. So the king and all the people of Israel dedicated the house of the LORD. [64]The same day the king consecrated the middle of the court that was in front of the house of the LORD; for there he offered the burnt offerings and the grain offerings and the fat pieces of the sacrifices of well-being, because the bronze altar that was before the LORD was too small to receive the burnt offerings and the grain offerings and the fat pieces of the sacrifices of well-being.

65 So Solomon held the festival at that time, and all Israel with him—a great assembly, people from Lebo-hamath to the Wadi of Egypt—before the LORD our God, seven days.[a] [66]On the eighth day he sent the people away; and they blessed the king, and went to

their tents, joyful and in good spirits because of all the goodness that the LORD had shown to his servant David and to his people Israel.

God Appears Again to Solomon

9 When Solomon had finished building the house of the LORD and the king's house and all that Solomon desired to build, [2]the LORD appeared to Solomon a second time, as he had appeared to him at Gibeon. [3]The LORD said to him, "I have heard your prayer and your plea, which you made before me; I have consecrated this house that you have built, and put my name there forever; my eyes and my heart will be there for all time. [4]As for you, if you will walk before me, as David your father walked, with integrity of heart and uprightness, doing according to all that I have commanded you, and keeping my statutes and my ordinances, [5]then I will establish your royal throne over Israel forever, as I promised your father David, saying, 'There shall not fail you a successor on the throne of Israel.'

6 "If you turn aside from following me, you or your children, and do not keep my commandments and my statutes that I have set before you, but go and serve other gods and worship them, [7]then I will cut Israel off from the land that I have given them; and the house that I have consecrated for my name I will cast out of my sight; and Israel will become a proverb and a taunt among all peoples. [8]This house will become a heap of ruins;[b] everyone passing by it will be astonished, and will hiss; and they will say, 'Why has the LORD done such a thing to this land and to this house?' [9]Then they will say, 'Because they have forsaken the LORD their God, who brought their ancestors out of the land of Egypt, and embraced other gods, worshiping them and serving them; therefore the LORD has brought this disaster upon them.' "

10 At the end of twenty years, in which Solomon had built the two houses, the house of the LORD and the king's house, [11]King Hiram of Tyre having supplied Solomon with

---

a Compare Gk: Heb *seven days and seven days, fourteen days*   *b* Syr Old Latin: Heb *will become high* cedar and cypress timber and gold, as much as he desired, King Solomon gave to Hiram twenty cities in the land of Galilee. 12But when Hiram came from Tyre to see the cities that Solomon had given him, they did not please him. 13Therefore he said, "What kind of cities are these that you have given me, my brother?" So they are called the land of Cabul*a* to this day. 14But Hiram had sent to the king one hundred twenty talents of gold.

Other Acts of Solomon

15 This is the account of the forced labor that King Solomon conscripted to build the house of the LORD and his own house, the Millo and the wall of Jerusalem, Hazor, Megiddo, Gezer 16(Pharaoh king of Egypt had gone up and captured Gezer and burned it down, had killed the Canaanites who lived in the city, and had given it as dowry to his daughter, Solomon's wife; 17so Solomon rebuilt Gezer), Lower Beth-horon, 18Baalath, Tamar in the wilderness, within the land, 19as well as all of Solomon's storage cities, the cities for his chariots, the cities for his cavalry, and whatever Solomon desired to build, in Jerusalem, in Lebanon, and in all the land of his dominion. 20All the people who were left of the Amorites, the Hittites, the Perizzites, the Hivites, and the Jebusites, who were not of the people of Israel— 21their descendants who were still left in the land, whom the Israelites were unable to destroy completely—these Solomon conscripted for slave labor, and so they are to this day. 22But of the Israelites Solomon made no slaves; they were the soldiers, they were his officials, his commanders, his captains, and the commanders of his chariotry and cavalry.

23 These were the chief officers who were over Solomon's work: five hundred fifty, who had charge of the people who carried on the work.

24 But Pharaoh's daughter went up from the city of David to her own house that Solomon had built for her; then he built the Millo.

25 Three times a year Solomon used to offer up burnt offerings and sacrifices of well-being on the altar that he built for the LORD, offering incense*b* before the LORD. So he completed the house.

Solomon's Commercial Activity

26 King Solomon built a fleet of ships at Ezion-geber, which is near Eloth on the shore of the Red Sea,*c* in the land of Edom. 27Hiram sent his servants with the fleet, sailors who were familiar with the sea, together with the servants of Solomon. 28They went to Ophir, and imported from there four hundred twenty talents of gold, which they delivered to King Solomon.

Visit of the Queen of Sheba

10 When the queen of Sheba heard of the fame of Solomon (fame due to*d* the name of the LORD), she came to test him with hard questions. 2She came to Jerusalem with a very great retinue, with camels bearing spices, and very much gold, and precious stones; and when she came to Solomon, she told him all that was on her mind. 3Solomon answered all her questions; there was nothing hidden from the king that he could not explain to her. 4When the queen of Sheba had observed all the wisdom of Solomon, the house that he had built, 5the food of his table, the seating of his officials, and the attendance of his servants, their clothing, his valets, and his burnt offerings that he offered at the house of the LORD, there was no more spirit in her.

6 So she said to the king, "The report was true that I heard in my own land of your accomplishments and of your wisdom, 7but I did not believe the reports until I came and my own eyes had seen it. Not even half had been told me; your wisdom and prosperity far surpass the report that I had heard. 8Happy are your wives!*e* Happy are these your servants, who continually attend you and hear your wisdom! 9Blessed be the LORD your God, who has delighted in you and set you on the throne

---

a Perhaps meaning *a land good for nothing*   *b* Gk: Heb *offering incense with it that was*   *c* Or *Sea of Reeds*
d Meaning of Heb uncertain   *e* Gk Syr: Heb *men*

of Israel! Because the LORD loved Israel forever, he has made you king to execute justice and righteousness." 10Then she gave the king one hundred twenty talents of gold, a great quantity of spices, and precious stones; never again did spices come in such quantity as that which the queen of Sheba gave to King Solomon.

11 Moreover, the fleet of Hiram, which carried gold from Ophir, brought from Ophir a great quantity of almug wood and precious stones. 12From the almug wood the king made supports for the house of the LORD, and for the king's house, lyres also and harps for the singers; no such almug wood has come or been seen to this day.

13 Meanwhile King Solomon gave to the queen of Sheba every desire that she expressed, as well as what he gave her out of Solomon's royal bounty. Then she returned to her own land, with her servants.

14 The weight of gold that came to Solomon in one year was six hundred sixty-six talents of gold, 15besides that which came from the traders and from the business of the merchants, and from all the kings of Arabia and the governors of the land. 16King Solomon made two hundred large shields of beaten gold; six hundred shekels of gold went into each large shield. 17He made three hundred shields of beaten gold; three minas of gold went into each shield; and the king put them in the House of the Forest of Lebanon. 18The king also made a great ivory throne, and overlaid it with the finest gold. 19The throne had six steps. The top of the throne was rounded in the back, and on each side of the seat were arm rests and two lions standing beside the arm rests, 20while twelve lions were standing, one on each end of a step on the six steps. Nothing like it was ever made in any kingdom. 21All King Solomon's drinking vessels were of gold, and all the vessels of the House of the Forest of Lebanon were of pure gold; none were of silver—it was not considered as anything in the days of Solomon. 22For the king had a fleet of ships of Tarshish at sea with the fleet of Hiram. Once every three years the fleet of ships of Tarshish used to come bringing gold, silver, ivory, apes, and peacocks.*a*

23 Thus King Solomon excelled all the kings of the earth in riches and in wisdom. 24The whole earth sought the presence of Solomon to hear his wisdom, which God had put into his mind. 25Every one of them brought a present, objects of silver and gold, garments, weaponry, spices, horses, and mules, so much year by year.

26 Solomon gathered together chariots and horses; he had fourteen hundred chariots and twelve thousand horses, which he stationed in the chariot cities and with the king in Jerusalem. 27The king made silver as common in Jerusalem as stones, and he made cedars as numerous as the sycamores of the Shephelah. 28Solomon's import of horses was from Egypt and Kue, and the king's traders received them from Kue at a price. 29A chariot could be imported from Egypt for six hundred shekels of silver, and a horse for one hundred fifty; so through the king's traders they were exported to all the kings of the Hittites and the kings of Aram.

Solomon's Errors

11 King Solomon loved many foreign women along with the daughter of Pharaoh: Moabite, Ammonite, Edomite, Sidonian, and Hittite women, 2from the nations concerning which the LORD had said to the Israelites, "You shall not enter into marriage with them, neither shall they with you; for they will surely incline your heart to follow their gods"; Solomon clung to these in love. 3Among his wives were seven hundred princesses and three hundred concubines; and his wives turned away his heart. 4For when Solomon was old, his wives turned away his heart after other gods; and his heart was not true to the LORD his God, as was the heart of his father David. 5For Solomon followed Astarte the goddess of the Sidonians, and Milcom the

a Or *baboons*

abomination of the Ammonites. 6So Solomon did what was evil in the sight of the LORD, and did not completely follow the LORD, as his father David had done. 7Then Solomon built a high place for Chemosh the abomination of Moab, and for Molech the abomination of the Ammonites, on the mountain east of Jerusalem. 8He did the same for all his foreign wives, who offered incense and sacrificed to their gods.

9 Then the LORD was angry with Solomon, because his heart had turned away from the LORD, the God of Israel, who had appeared to him twice, 10and had commanded him concerning this matter, that he should not follow other gods; but he did not observe what the LORD commanded. 11Therefore the LORD said to Solomon, "Since this has been your mind and you have not kept my covenant and my statutes that I have commanded you, I will surely tear the kingdom from you and give it to your servant. 12Yet for the sake of your father David I will not do it in your lifetime; I will tear it out of the hand of your son. 13I will not, however, tear away the entire kingdom; I will give one tribe to your son, for the sake of my servant David and for the sake of Jerusalem, which I have chosen."

Adversaries of Solomon

14 Then the LORD raised up an adversary against Solomon, Hadad the Edomite; he was of the royal house in Edom. 15For when David was in Edom, and Joab the commander of the army went up to bury the dead, he killed every male in Edom 16(for Joab and all Israel remained there six months, until he had eliminated every male in Edom); 17but Hadad fled to Egypt with some Edomites who were servants of his father. He was a young boy at that time. 18They set out from Midian and came to Paran; they took people with them from Paran and came to Egypt, to Pharaoh king of Egypt, who gave him a house, assigned him an allowance of food, and gave him land. 19Hadad found great favor in the sight of Pharaoh, so

that he gave him his sister-in-law for a wife, the sister of Queen Tahpenes. 20The sister of Tahpenes gave birth by him to his son Genubath, whom Tahpenes weaned in Pharaoh's house; Genubath was in Pharaoh's house among the children of Pharaoh. 21When Hadad heard in Egypt that David slept with his ancestors and that Joab the commander of the army was dead, Hadad said to Pharaoh, "Let me depart, that I may go to my own country." 22But Pharaoh said to him, "What do you lack with me that you now seek to go to your own country?" And he said, "No, do let me go."

23 God raised up another adversary against Solomon,[a] Rezon son of Eliada, who had fled from his master, King Hadadezer of Zobah. 24He gathered followers around him and became leader of a marauding band, after the slaughter by David; they went to Damascus, settled there, and made him king in Damascus. 25He was an adversary of Israel all the days of Solomon, making trouble as Hadad did; he despised Israel and reigned over Aram.

Jeroboam's Rebellion

26 Jeroboam son of Nebat, an Ephraimite of Zeredah, a servant of Solomon, whose mother's name was Zeruah, a widow, rebelled against the king. 27The following was the reason he rebelled against the king. Solomon built the Millo, and closed up the gap in the wall[b] of the city of his father David. 28The man Jeroboam was very able, and when Solomon saw that the young man was industrious he gave him charge over all the forced labor of the house of Joseph. 29About that time, when Jeroboam was leaving Jerusalem, the prophet Ahijah the Shilonite found him on the road. Ahijah had clothed himself with a new garment. The two of them were alone in the open country 30when Ahijah laid hold of the new garment he was wearing and tore it into twelve pieces. 31He then said to Jeroboam: Take for yourself ten pieces; for thus says the LORD, the God of Israel, "See, I am about to tear the kingdom from the hand of Solomon,

_a_ Heb _him_   _b_ Heb lacks _in the wall_

and will give you ten tribes. 32One tribe will remain his, for the sake of my servant David and for the sake of Jerusalem, the city that I have chosen out of all the tribes of Israel. 33This is because he has*a* forsaken me, worshiped Astarte the goddess of the Sidonians, Chemosh the god of Moab, and Milcom the god of the Ammonites, and has*a* not walked in my ways, doing what is right in my sight and keeping my statutes and my ordinances, as his father David did. 34Nevertheless I will not take the whole kingdom away from him but will make him ruler all the days of his life, for the sake of my servant David whom I chose and who did keep my commandments and my statutes; 35but I will take the kingdom away from his son and give it to you—that is, the ten tribes. 36Yet to his son I will give one tribe, so that my servant David may always have a lamp before me in Jerusalem, the city where I have chosen to put my name. 37I will take you, and you shall reign over all that your soul desires; you shall be king over Israel. 38If you will listen to all that I command you, walk in my ways, and do what is right in my sight by keeping my statutes and my commandments, as David my servant did, I will be with you, and will build you an enduring house, as I built for David, and I will give Israel to you. 39For this reason I will punish the descendants of David, but not forever." 40Solomon sought therefore to kill Jeroboam; but Jeroboam promptly fled to Egypt, to King Shishak of Egypt, and remained in Egypt until the death of Solomon.

Death of Solomon

41 Now the rest of the acts of Solomon, all that he did as well as his wisdom, are they not written in the Book of the Acts of Solomon? 42The time that Solomon reigned in Jerusalem over all Israel was forty years. 43Solomon slept with his ancestors and was buried in the city of his father David; and his son Rehoboam succeeded him.

The Northern Tribes Secede

12 Rehoboam went to Shechem, for all Israel had come to Shechem to make him king. 2When Jeroboam son of Nebat heard of it (for he was still in Egypt, where he had fled from King Solomon), then Jeroboam returned from*b* Egypt. 3And they sent and called him; and Jeroboam and all the assembly of Israel came and said to Rehoboam, 4"Your father made our yoke heavy. Now therefore lighten the hard service of your father and his heavy yoke that he placed on us, and we will serve you." 5He said to them, "Go away for three days, then come again to me." So the people went away.

6 Then King Rehoboam took counsel with the older men who had attended his father Solomon while he was still alive, saying, "How do you advise me to answer this people?" 7They answered him, "If you will be a servant to this people today and serve them, and speak good words to them when you answer them, then they will be your servants forever." 8But he disregarded the advice that the older men gave him, and consulted with the young men who had grown up with him and now attended him. 9He said to them, "What do you advise that we answer this people who have said to me, 'Lighten the yoke that your father put on us'?" 10The young men who had grown up with him said to him, "Thus you should say to this people who spoke to you, 'Your father made our yoke heavy, but you must lighten it for us'; thus you should say to them, 'My little finger is thicker than my father's loins. 11Now, whereas my father laid on you a heavy yoke, I will add to your yoke. My father disciplined you with whips, but I will discipline you with scorpions.'"

12 So Jeroboam and all the people came to Rehoboam the third day, as the king had said, "Come to me again the third day." 13The king answered the people harshly. He disregarded the advice that the older men had given him 14and spoke to them according to the advice of the young men, "My father made your yoke

a Gk Syr Vg: Heb *they have*   *b* Gk Vg Compare 2 Chr 10.2: Heb *lived in* heavy, but I will add to your yoke; my father disciplined you with whips, but I will discipline you with scorpions." 15So the king did not listen to the people, because it was a turn of affairs brought about by the LORD that he might fulfill his word, which the LORD had spoken by Ahijah the Shilonite to Jeroboam son of Nebat.

16 When all Israel saw that the king would not listen to them, the people answered the king,

"What share do we have in David?
    We have no inheritance in the son of Jesse.
To your tents, O Israel!
    Look now to your own house,
        O David."

So Israel went away to their tents. 17But Rehoboam reigned over the Israelites who were living in the towns of Judah. 18When King Rehoboam sent Adoram, who was taskmaster over the forced labor, all Israel stoned him to death. King Rehoboam then hurriedly mounted his chariot to flee to Jerusalem. 19So Israel has been in rebellion against the house of David to this day.

First Dynasty: Jeroboam Reigns over Israel

20 When all Israel heard that Jeroboam had returned, they sent and called him to the assembly and made him king over all Israel. There was no one who followed the house of David, except the tribe of Judah alone.

21 When Rehoboam came to Jerusalem, he assembled all the house of Judah and the tribe of Benjamin, one hundred eighty thousand chosen troops to fight against the house of Israel, to restore the kingdom to Rehoboam son of Solomon. 22But the word of God came to Shemaiah the man of God: 23Say to King Rehoboam of Judah, son of Solomon, and to all the house of Judah and Benjamin, and to the rest of the people, 24"Thus says the LORD, You shall not go up or fight against your kindred the people of Israel. Let everyone go home, for this thing is from me." So they

heeded the word of the LORD and went home again, according to the word of the LORD.

Jeroboam's Golden Calves

25 Then Jeroboam built Shechem in the hill country of Ephraim, and resided there; he went out from there and built Penuel. 26Then Jeroboam said to himself, "Now the kingdom may well revert to the house of David. 27If this people continues to go up to offer sacrifices in the house of the LORD at Jerusalem, the heart of this people will turn again to their master, King Rehoboam of Judah; they will kill me and return to King Rehoboam of Judah." 28So the king took counsel, and made two calves of gold. He said to the people,*a* "You have gone up to Jerusalem long enough. Here are your gods, O Israel, who brought you up out of the land of Egypt." 29He set one in Bethel, and the other he put in Dan. 30And this thing became a sin, for the people went to worship before the one at Bethel and before the other as far as Dan.*b* 31He also made houses*c* on high places, and appointed priests from among all the people, who were not Levites. 32Jeroboam appointed a festival on the fifteenth day of the eighth month like the festival that was in Judah, and he offered sacrifices on the altar; so he did in Bethel, sacrificing to the calves that he had made. And he placed in Bethel the priests of the high places that he had made. 33He went up to the altar that he had made in Bethel on the fifteenth day in the eighth month, in the month that he alone had devised; he appointed a festival for the people of Israel, and he went up to the altar to offer incense.

A Man of God from Judah

13 While Jeroboam was standing by the altar to offer incense, a man of God came out of Judah by the word of the LORD to Bethel 2and proclaimed against the altar by the word of the LORD, and said, "O altar, altar, thus says the LORD: 'A son shall be born to the house of David, Josiah by name; and he

---

a Gk: Heb *to them*   *b* Compare Gk: Heb *went to the one as far as Dan*   *c* Gk Vg Compare 13.32: Heb *a house* shall sacrifice on you the priests of the high places who offer incense on you, and human bones shall be burned on you.'" ³He gave a sign the same day, saying, "This is the sign that the LORD has spoken: 'The altar shall be torn down, and the ashes that are on it shall be poured out.'" ⁴When the king heard what the man of God cried out against the altar at Bethel, Jeroboam stretched out his hand from the altar, saying, "Seize him!" But the hand that he stretched out against him withered so that he could not draw it back to himself. ⁵The altar also was torn down, and the ashes poured out from the altar, according to the sign that the man of God had given by the word of the LORD. ⁶The king said to the man of God, "Entreat now the favor of the LORD your God, and pray for me, so that my hand may be restored to me." So the man of God entreated the LORD; and the king's hand was restored to him, and became as it was before. ⁷Then the king said to the man of God, "Come home with me and dine, and I will give you a gift." ⁸But the man of God said to the king, "If you give me half your kingdom, I will not go in with you; nor will I eat food or drink water in this place. ⁹For thus I was commanded by the word of the LORD: You shall not eat food, or drink water, or return by the way that you came." ¹⁰So he went another way, and did not return by the way that he had come to Bethel.

11 Now there lived an old prophet in Bethel. One of his sons came and told him all that the man of God had done that day in Bethel; the words also that he had spoken to the king, they told to their father. ¹²Their father said to them, "Which way did he go?" And his sons showed him the way that the man of God who came from Judah had gone. ¹³Then he said to his sons, "Saddle a donkey for me." So they saddled a donkey for him, and he mounted it. ¹⁴He went after the man of God, and found him sitting under an oak tree. He said to him, "Are you the man of God who came from Judah?" He answered, "I am." ¹⁵Then he

said to him, "Come home with me and eat some food." ¹⁶But he said, "I cannot return with you, or go in with you; nor will I eat food or drink water with you in this place; ¹⁷for it was said to me by the word of the LORD: You shall not eat food or drink water there, or return by the way that you came." ¹⁸Then the other*a* said to him, "I also am a prophet as you are, and an angel spoke to me by the word of the LORD: Bring him back with you into your house so that he may eat food and drink water." But he was deceiving him. ¹⁹Then the man of God*a* went back with him, and ate food and drank water in his house.

20 As they were sitting at the table, the word of the LORD came to the prophet who had brought him back; ²¹and he proclaimed to the man of God who came from Judah, "Thus says the LORD: Because you have disobeyed the word of the LORD, and have not kept the commandment that the LORD your God commanded you, ²²but have come back and have eaten food and drunk water in the place of which he said to you, 'Eat no food, and drink no water,' your body shall not come to your ancestral tomb." ²³After the man of God*a* had eaten food and had drunk, they saddled for him a donkey belonging to the prophet who had brought him back. ²⁴Then as he went away, a lion met him on the road and killed him. His body was thrown in the road, and the donkey stood beside it; the lion also stood beside the body. ²⁵People passed by and saw the body thrown in the road, with the lion standing by the body. And they came and told it in the town where the old prophet lived.

26 When the prophet who had brought him back from the way heard of it, he said, "It is the man of God who disobeyed the word of the LORD; therefore the LORD has given him to the lion, which has torn him and killed him according to the word that the LORD spoke to him." ²⁷Then he said to his sons, "Saddle a donkey for me." So they saddled one, ²⁸and he went and found the body thrown in the road, with the donkey and the lion standing beside

a Heb *he*

the body. The lion had not eaten the body or attacked the donkey. ²⁹The prophet took up the body of the man of God, laid it on the donkey, and brought it back to the city,ᵃ to mourn and to bury him. ³⁰He laid the body in his own grave; and they mourned over him, saying, "Alas, my brother!" ³¹After he had buried him, he said to his sons, "When I die, bury me in the grave in which the man of God is buried; lay my bones beside his bones. ³²For the saying that he proclaimed by the word of the LORD against the altar in Bethel, and against all the houses of the high places that are in the cities of Samaria, shall surely come to pass."

33 Even after this event Jeroboam did not turn from his evil way, but made priests for the high places again from among all the people; any who wanted to be priests he consecrated for the high places. ³⁴This matter became sin to the house of Jeroboam, so as to cut it off and to destroy it from the face of the earth.

Judgment on the House of Jeroboam

14 At that time Abijah son of Jeroboam fell sick. ²Jeroboam said to his wife, "Go, disguise yourself, so that it will not be known that you are the wife of Jeroboam, and go to Shiloh; for the prophet Ahijah is there, who said of me that I should be king over this people. ³Take with you ten loaves, some cakes, and a jar of honey, and go to him; he will tell you what shall happen to the child."

4 Jeroboam's wife did so; she set out and went to Shiloh, and came to the house of Ahijah. Now Ahijah could not see, for his eyes were dim because of his age. ⁵But the LORD said to Ahijah, "The wife of Jeroboam is coming to inquire of you concerning her son; for he is sick. Thus and thus you shall say to her."

When she came, she pretended to be another woman. ⁶But when Ahijah heard the sound of her feet, as she came in at the door, he said, "Come in, wife of Jeroboam; why do you pretend to be another? For I am charged with heavy tidings for you. ⁷Go, tell Jeroboam,

'Thus says the LORD, the God of Israel: Because I exalted you from among the people, made you leader over my people Israel, ⁸and tore the kingdom away from the house of David to give it to you; yet you have not been like my servant David, who kept my commandments and followed me with all his heart, doing only that which was right in my sight, ⁹but you have done evil above all those who were before you and have gone and made for yourself other gods, and cast images, provoking me to anger, and have thrust me behind your back; ¹⁰therefore, I will bring evil upon the house of Jeroboam. I will cut off from Jeroboam every male, both bond and free in Israel, and will consume the house of Jeroboam, just as one burns up dung until it is all gone. ¹¹Anyone belonging to Jeroboam who dies in the city, the dogs shall eat; and anyone who dies in the open country, the birds of the air shall eat; for the LORD has spoken.' ¹²Therefore set out, go to your house. When your feet enter the city, the child shall die. ¹³All Israel shall mourn for him and bury him; for he alone of Jeroboam's family shall come to the grave, because in him there is found something pleasing to the LORD, the God of Israel, in the house of Jeroboam. ¹⁴Moreover the LORD will raise up for himself a king over Israel, who shall cut off the house of Jeroboam today, even right now!ᵇ

15 "The LORD will strike Israel, as a reed is shaken in the water; he will root up Israel out of this good land that he gave to their ancestors, and scatter them beyond the Euphrates, because they have made their sacred poles,ᶜ provoking the LORD to anger. ¹⁶He will give Israel up because of the sins of Jeroboam, which he sinned and which he caused Israel to commit."

17 Then Jeroboam's wife got up and went away, and she came to Tirzah. As she came to the threshold of the house, the child died. ¹⁸All Israel buried him and mourned for him, according to the word of the LORD, which he spoke by his servant the prophet Ahijah.

ᵃ Gk: Heb *he came to the town of the old prophet*   ᵇ Meaning of Heb uncertain   ᶜ Heb *Asherim*

Death of Jeroboam

19 Now the rest of the acts of Jeroboam, how he warred and how he reigned, are written in the Book of the Annals of the Kings of Israel. 20The time that Jeroboam reigned was twenty-two years; then he slept with his ancestors, and his son Nadab succeeded him.

Rehoboam Reigns over Judah

21 Now Rehoboam son of Solomon reigned in Judah. Rehoboam was forty-one years old when he began to reign, and he reigned seventeen years in Jerusalem, the city that the LORD had chosen out of all the tribes of Israel, to put his name there. His mother's name was Naamah the Ammonite. 22Judah did what was evil in the sight of the LORD; they provoked him to jealousy with their sins that they committed, more than all that their ancestors had done. 23For they also built for themselves high places, pillars, and sacred poles*a* on every high hill and under every green tree; 24there were also male temple prostitutes in the land. They committed all the abominations of the nations that the LORD drove out before the people of Israel.

25 In the fifth year of King Rehoboam, King Shishak of Egypt came up against Jerusalem; 26he took away the treasures of the house of the LORD and the treasures of the king's house; he took everything. He also took away all the shields of gold that Solomon had made; 27so King Rehoboam made shields of bronze instead, and committed them to the hands of the officers of the guard, who kept the door of the king's house. 28As often as the king went into the house of the LORD, the guard carried them and brought them back to the guardroom.

29 Now the rest of the acts of Rehoboam, and all that he did, are they not written in the Book of the Annals of the Kings of Judah? 30There was war between Rehoboam and Jeroboam continually. 31Rehoboam slept with his ancestors and was buried with his ancestors in the city of David. His mother's name was Na-amah the Ammonite. His son Abijam succeeded him.

Abijam Reigns over Judah: Idolatry and War

15 Now in the eighteenth year of King Jeroboam son of Nebat, Abijam began to reign over Judah. 2He reigned for three years in Jerusalem. His mother's name was Maacah daughter of Abishalom. 3He committed all the sins that his father did before him; his heart was not true to the LORD his God, like the heart of his father David. 4Nevertheless for David's sake the LORD his God gave him a lamp in Jerusalem, setting up his son after him, and establishing Jerusalem; 5because David did what was right in the sight of the LORD, and did not turn aside from anything that he commanded him all the days of his life, except in the matter of Uriah the Hittite. 6The war begun between Rehoboam and Jeroboam continued all the days of his life. 7The rest of the acts of Abijam, and all that he did, are they not written in the Book of the Annals of the Kings of Judah? There was war between Abijam and Jeroboam. 8Abijam slept with his ancestors, and they buried him in the city of David. Then his son Asa succeeded him.

Asa Reigns over Judah

9 In the twentieth year of King Jeroboam of Israel, Asa began to reign over Judah; 10he reigned forty-one years in Jerusalem. His mother's name was Maacah daughter of Abishalom. 11Asa did what was right in the sight of the LORD, as his father David had done. 12He put away the male temple prostitutes out of the land, and removed all the idols that his ancestors had made. 13He also removed his mother Maacah from being queen mother, because she had made an abominable image for Asherah; Asa cut down her image and burned it at the Wadi Kidron. 14But the high places were not taken away. Nevertheless the heart of Asa was true to the LORD all his days. 15He brought into the house of the LORD

the votive gifts of his father and his own votive gifts—silver, gold, and utensils.

Alliance with Aram against Israel

16 There was war between Asa and King Baasha of Israel all their days. ¹⁷King Baasha of Israel went up against Judah, and built Ramah, to prevent anyone from going out or coming in to King Asa of Judah. ¹⁸Then Asa took all the silver and the gold that were left in the treasures of the house of the LORD and the treasures of the king's house, and gave them into the hands of his servants. King Asa sent them to King Ben-hadad son of Tabrimmon son of Hezion of Aram, who resided in Damascus, saying, ¹⁹"Let there be an alliance between me and you, like that between my father and your father: I am sending you a present of silver and gold; go, break your alliance with King Baasha of Israel, so that he may withdraw from me." ²⁰Ben-hadad listened to King Asa, and sent the commanders of his armies against the cities of Israel. He conquered Ijon, Dan, Abel-beth-maacah, and all Chinneroth, with all the land of Naphtali. ²¹When Baasha heard of it, he stopped building Ramah and lived in Tirzah. ²²Then King Asa made a proclamation to all Judah, none was exempt: they carried away the stones of Ramah and its timber, with which Baasha had been building; with them King Asa built Geba of Benjamin and Mizpah. ²³Now the rest of all the acts of Asa, all his power, all that he did, and the cities that he built, are they not written in the Book of the Annals of the Kings of Judah? But in his old age he was diseased in his feet. ²⁴Then Asa slept with his ancestors, and was buried with his ancestors in the city of his father David; his son Jehoshaphat succeeded him.

Nadab Reigns over Israel

25 Nadab son of Jeroboam began to reign over Israel in the second year of King Asa of Judah; he reigned over Israel two years. ²⁶He did what was evil in the sight of the LORD, walking in the way of his ancestor and in the sin that he caused Israel to commit.

27 Baasha son of Ahijah, of the house of Issachar, conspired against him; and Baasha struck him down at Gibbethon, which belonged to the Philistines; for Nadab and all Israel were laying siege to Gibbethon. ²⁸So Baasha killed Nadab^a in the third year of King Asa of Judah, and succeeded him. ²⁹As soon as he was king, he killed all the house of Jeroboam; he left to the house of Jeroboam not one that breathed, until he had destroyed it, according to the word of the LORD that he spoke by his servant Ahijah the Shilonite— ³⁰because of the sins of Jeroboam that he committed and that he caused Israel to commit, and because of the anger to which he provoked the LORD, the God of Israel.

31 Now the rest of the acts of Nadab, and all that he did, are they not written in the Book of the Annals of the Kings of Israel? ³²There was war between Asa and King Baasha of Israel all their days.

Second Dynasty: Baasha Reigns over Israel

33 In the third year of King Asa of Judah, Baasha son of Ahijah began to reign over all Israel at Tirzah; he reigned twenty-four years. ³⁴He did what was evil in the sight of the LORD, walking in the way of Jeroboam and in the sin that he caused Israel to commit.

16 The word of the LORD came to Jehu son of Hanani against Baasha, saying, ²"Since I exalted you out of the dust and made you leader over my people Israel, and you have walked in the way of Jeroboam, and have caused my people Israel to sin, provoking me to anger with their sins, ³therefore, I will consume Baasha and his house, and I will make your house like the house of Jeroboam son of Nebat. ⁴Anyone belonging to Baasha who dies in the city the dogs shall eat; and anyone of his who dies in the field the birds of the air shall eat."

5 Now the rest of the acts of Baasha, what he did, and his power, are they not written in

a Heb *him*

the Book of the Annals of the Kings of Israel? 6Baasha slept with his ancestors, and was buried at Tirzah; and his son Elah succeeded him. 7Moreover the word of the LORD came by the prophet Jehu son of Hanani against Baasha and his house, both because of all the evil that he did in the sight of the LORD, provoking him to anger with the work of his hands, in being like the house of Jeroboam, and also because he destroyed it.

Elah Reigns over Israel

8 In the twenty-sixth year of King Asa of Judah, Elah son of Baasha began to reign over Israel in Tirzah; he reigned two years. 9But his servant Zimri, commander of half his chariots, conspired against him. When he was at Tirzah, drinking himself drunk in the house of Arza, who was in charge of the palace at Tirzah, 10Zimri came in and struck him down and killed him, in the twenty-seventh year of King Asa of Judah, and succeeded him.

11 When he began to reign, as soon as he had seated himself on his throne, he killed all the house of Baasha; he did not leave him a single male of his kindred or his friends. 12Thus Zimri destroyed all the house of Baasha, according to the word of the LORD, which he spoke against Baasha by the prophet Jehu— 13because of all the sins of Baasha and the sins of his son Elah that they committed, and that they caused Israel to commit, provoking the LORD God of Israel to anger with their idols. 14Now the rest of the acts of Elah, and all that he did, are they not written in the Book of the Annals of the Kings of Israel?

Third Dynasty: Zimri Reigns over Israel

15 In the twenty-seventh year of King Asa of Judah, Zimri reigned seven days in Tirzah. Now the troops were encamped against Gibbethon, which belonged to the Philistines, 16and the troops who were encamped heard it said, "Zimri has conspired, and he has killed the king"; therefore all Israel made Omri, the commander of the army, king over Israel that day in the camp. 17So Omri went up from Gibbethon, and all Israel with him, and they besieged Tirzah. 18When Zimri saw that the city was taken, he went into the citadel of the king's house; he burned down the king's house over himself with fire, and died— 19because of the sins that he committed, doing evil in the sight of the LORD, walking in the way of Jeroboam, and for the sin that he committed, causing Israel to sin. 20Now the rest of the acts of Zimri, and the conspiracy that he made, are they not written in the Book of the Annals of the Kings of Israel?

Fourth Dynasty: Omri Reigns over Israel

21 Then the people of Israel were divided into two parts; half of the people followed Tibni son of Ginath, to make him king, and half followed Omri. 22But the people who followed Omri overcame the people who followed Tibni son of Ginath; so Tibni died, and Omri became king. 23In the thirty-first year of King Asa of Judah, Omri began to reign over Israel; he reigned for twelve years, six of them in Tirzah.

Samaria the New Capital

24 He bought the hill of Samaria from Shemer for two talents of silver; he fortified the hill, and called the city that he built, Samaria, after the name of Shemer, the owner of the hill.

25 Omri did what was evil in the sight of the LORD; he did more evil than all who were before him. 26For he walked in all the way of Jeroboam son of Nebat, and in the sins that he caused Israel to commit, provoking the LORD, the God of Israel, to anger by their idols. 27Now the rest of the acts of Omri that he did, and the power that he showed, are they not written in the Book of the Annals of the Kings of Israel? 28Omri slept with his ancestors, and was buried in Samaria; his son Ahab succeeded him.

Ahab Reigns over Israel

29 In the thirty-eighth year of King Asa of Judah, Ahab son of Omri began to reign over Israel; Ahab son of Omri reigned over Israel in Samaria twenty-two years. 30Ahab son of

Omri did evil in the sight of the LORD more than all who were before him.

Ahab Marries Jezebel and Worships Baal

31 And as if it had been a light thing for him to walk in the sins of Jeroboam son of Nebat, he took as his wife Jezebel daughter of King Ethbaal of the Sidonians, and went and served Baal, and worshiped him. 32He erected an altar for Baal in the house of Baal, which he built in Samaria. 33Ahab also made a sacred pole.*a* Ahab did more to provoke the anger of the LORD, the God of Israel, than had all the kings of Israel who were before him. 34In his days Hiel of Bethel built Jericho; he laid its foundation at the cost of Abiram his first-born, and set up its gates at the cost of his youngest son Segub, according to the word of the LORD, which he spoke by Joshua son of Nun.

Elijah Predicts a Drought

17 Now Elijah the Tishbite, of Tishbe*b* in Gilead, said to Ahab, "As the LORD the God of Israel lives, before whom I stand, there shall be neither dew nor rain these years, except by my word." 2The word of the LORD came to him, saying, 3"Go from here and turn eastward, and hide yourself by the Wadi Cherith, which is east of the Jordan. 4You shall drink from the wadi, and I have commanded the ravens to feed you there." 5So he went and did according to the word of the LORD; he went and lived by the Wadi Cherith, which is east of the Jordan. 6The ravens brought him bread and meat in the morning, and bread and meat in the evening; and he drank from the wadi. 7But after a while the wadi dried up, because there was no rain in the land.

The Widow of Zarephath

8 Then the word of the LORD came to him, saying, 9"Go now to Zarephath, which belongs to Sidon, and live there; for I have commanded a widow there to feed you." 10So he set out and went to Zarephath. When he came to the gate of the town, a widow was there gathering sticks; he called to her and said, "Bring me a little water in a vessel, so that I may drink." 11As she was going to bring it, he called to her and said, "Bring me a morsel of bread in your hand." 12But she said, "As the LORD your God lives, I have nothing baked, only a handful of meal in a jar, and a little oil in a jug; I am now gathering a couple of sticks, so that I may go home and prepare it for myself and my son, that we may eat it, and die." 13Elijah said to her, "Do not be afraid; go and do as you have said; but first make me a little cake of it and bring it to me, and afterwards make something for yourself and your son. 14For thus says the LORD the God of Israel: The jar of meal will not be emptied and the jug of oil will not fail until the day that the LORD sends rain on the earth." 15She went and did as Elijah said, so that she as well as he and her household ate for many days. 16The jar of meal was not emptied, neither did the jug of oil fail, according to the word of the LORD that he spoke by Elijah.

Elijah Revives the Widow's Son

17 After this the son of the woman, the mistress of the house, became ill; his illness was so severe that there was no breath left in him. 18She then said to Elijah, "What have you against me, O man of God? You have come to me to bring my sin to remembrance, and to cause the death of my son!" 19But he said to her, "Give me your son." He took him from her bosom, carried him up into the upper chamber where he was lodging, and laid him on his own bed. 20He cried out to the LORD, "O LORD my God, have you brought calamity even upon the widow with whom I am staying, by killing her son?" 21Then he stretched himself upon the child three times, and cried out to the LORD, "O LORD my God, let this child's life come into him again." 22The LORD listened to the voice of Elijah; the life of the child came into him again, and he revived.

a Heb *Asherah*   *b* Gk: Heb *of the settlers*

23Elijah took the child, brought him down from the upper chamber into the house, and gave him to his mother; then Elijah said, "See, your son is alive." 24So the woman said to Elijah, "Now I know that you are a man of God, and that the word of the LORD in your mouth is truth."

Elijah's Message to Ahab

18 After many days the word of the LORD came to Elijah, in the third year of the drought,*a* saying, "Go, present yourself to Ahab; I will send rain on the earth." 2So Elijah went to present himself to Ahab. The famine was severe in Samaria. 3Ahab summoned Obadiah, who was in charge of the palace. (Now Obadiah revered the LORD greatly; 4when Jezebel was killing off the prophets of the LORD, Obadiah took a hundred prophets, hid them fifty to a cave, and provided them with bread and water.) 5Then Ahab said to Obadiah, "Go through the land to all the springs of water and to all the wadis; perhaps we may find grass to keep the horses and mules alive, and not lose some of the animals." 6So they divided the land between them to pass through it; Ahab went in one direction by himself, and Obadiah went in another direction by himself.

7 As Obadiah was on the way, Elijah met him; Obadiah recognized him, fell on his face, and said, "Is it you, my lord Elijah?" 8He answered him, "It is I. Go, tell your lord that Elijah is here." 9And he said, "How have I sinned, that you would hand your servant over to Ahab, to kill me? 10As the LORD your God lives, there is no nation or kingdom to which my lord has not sent to seek you; and when they would say, 'He is not here,' he would require an oath of the kingdom or nation, that they had not found you. 11But now you say, 'Go, tell your lord that Elijah is here.' 12As soon as I have gone from you, the spirit of the LORD will carry you I know not where; so, when I come and tell Ahab and he cannot find you, he will kill me, although I your ser-vant have revered the LORD from my youth. 13Has it not been told my lord what I did when Jezebel killed the prophets of the LORD, how I hid a hundred of the LORD's prophets fifty to a cave, and provided them with bread and water? 14Yet now you say, 'Go, tell your lord that Elijah is here'; he will surely kill me." 15Elijah said, "As the LORD of hosts lives, before whom I stand, I will surely show myself to him today." 16So Obadiah went to meet Ahab, and told him; and Ahab went to meet Elijah.

17 When Ahab saw Elijah, Ahab said to him, "Is it you, you troubler of Israel?" 18He answered, "I have not troubled Israel; but you have, and your father's house, because you have forsaken the commandments of the LORD and followed the Baals. 19Now therefore have all Israel assemble for me at Mount Carmel, with the four hundred fifty prophets of Baal and the four hundred prophets of Asherah, who eat at Jezebel's table."

Elijah's Triumph over the Priests of Baal

20 So Ahab sent to all the Israelites, and assembled the prophets at Mount Carmel. 21Elijah then came near to all the people, and said, "How long will you go limping with two different opinions? If the LORD is God, follow him; but if Baal, then follow him." The people did not answer him a word. 22Then Elijah said to the people, "I, even I only, am left a prophet of the LORD; but Baal's prophets number four hundred fifty. 23Let two bulls be given to us; let them choose one bull for themselves, cut it in pieces, and lay it on the wood, but put no fire to it; I will prepare the other bull and lay it on the wood, but put no fire to it. 24Then you call on the name of your god and I will call on the name of the LORD; the god who answers by fire is indeed God." All the people answered, "Well spoken!" 25Then Elijah said to the prophets of Baal, "Choose for yourselves one bull and prepare it first, for you are many; then call on the name of your god, but put no fire to it." 26So they took

a Heb lacks *of the drought*

the bull that was given them, prepared it, and called on the name of Baal from morning until noon, crying, "O Baal, answer us!" But there was no voice, and no answer. They limped about the altar that they had made. ²⁷At noon Elijah mocked them, saying, "Cry aloud! Surely he is a god; either he is meditating, or he has wandered away, or he is on a journey, or perhaps he is asleep and must be awakened." ²⁸Then they cried aloud and, as was their custom, they cut themselves with swords and lances until the blood gushed out over them. ²⁹As midday passed, they raved on until the time of the offering of the oblation, but there was no voice, no answer, and no response.

30 Then Elijah said to all the people, "Come closer to me"; and all the people came closer to him. First he repaired the altar of the LORD that had been thrown down; ³¹Elijah took twelve stones, according to the number of the tribes of the sons of Jacob, to whom the word of the LORD came, saying, "Israel shall be your name"; ³²with the stones he built an altar in the name of the LORD. Then he made a trench around the altar, large enough to contain two measures of seed. ³³Next he put the wood in order, cut the bull in pieces, and laid it on the wood. He said, "Fill four jars with water and pour it on the burnt offering and on the wood." ³⁴Then he said, "Do it a second time"; and they did it a second time. Again he said, "Do it a third time"; and they did it a third time, ³⁵so that the water ran all around the altar, and filled the trench also with water.

36 At the time of the offering of the oblation, the prophet Elijah came near and said, "O LORD, God of Abraham, Isaac, and Israel, let it be known this day that you are God in Israel, that I am your servant, and that I have done all these things at your bidding. ³⁷Answer me, O LORD, answer me, so that this people may know that you, O LORD, are God, and that you have turned their hearts back." ³⁸Then the fire of the LORD fell and consumed the burnt offering, the wood, the stones, and the dust, and even licked up the water that was in

the trench. ³⁹When all the people saw it, they fell on their faces and said, "The LORD indeed is God; the LORD indeed is God." ⁴⁰Elijah said to them, "Seize the prophets of Baal; do not let one of them escape." Then they seized them; and Elijah brought them down to the Wadi Kishon, and killed them there.

The Drought Ends

41 Elijah said to Ahab, "Go up, eat and drink; for there is a sound of rushing rain." ⁴²So Ahab went up to eat and to drink. Elijah went up to the top of Carmel; there he bowed himself down upon the earth and put his face between his knees. ⁴³He said to his servant, "Go up now, look toward the sea." He went up and looked, and said, "There is nothing." Then he said, "Go again seven times." ⁴⁴At the seventh time he said, "Look, a little cloud no bigger than a person's hand is rising out of the sea." Then he said, "Go say to Ahab, 'Harness your chariot and go down before the rain stops you.' " ⁴⁵In a little while the heavens grew black with clouds and wind; there was a heavy rain. Ahab rode off and went to Jezreel. ⁴⁶But the hand of the LORD was on Elijah; he girded up his loins and ran in front of Ahab to the entrance of Jezreel.

Elijah Flees from Jezebel

19 Ahab told Jezebel all that Elijah had done, and how he had killed all the prophets with the sword. ²Then Jezebel sent a messenger to Elijah, saying, "So may the gods do to me, and more also, if I do not make your life like the life of one of them by this time tomorrow." ³Then he was afraid; he got up and fled for his life, and came to Beer-sheba, which belongs to Judah; he left his servant there.

4 But he himself went a day's journey into the wilderness, and came and sat down under a solitary broom tree. He asked that he might die: "It is enough; now, O LORD, take away my life, for I am no better than my ancestors." ⁵Then he lay down under the broom tree and fell asleep. Suddenly an angel touched him and said to him, "Get up and eat." ⁶He looked,

and there at his head was a cake baked on hot stones, and a jar of water. He ate and drank, and lay down again. ⁷The angel of the LORD came a second time, touched him, and said, "Get up and eat, otherwise the journey will be too much for you." ⁸He got up, and ate and drank; then he went in the strength of that food forty days and forty nights to Horeb the mount of God. ⁹At that place he came to a cave, and spent the night there.

Then the word of the LORD came to him, saying, "What are you doing here, Elijah?" ¹⁰He answered, "I have been very zealous for the LORD, the God of hosts; for the Israelites have forsaken your covenant, thrown down your altars, and killed your prophets with the sword. I alone am left, and they are seeking my life, to take it away."

Elijah Meets God at Horeb

11 He said, "Go out and stand on the mountain before the LORD, for the LORD is about to pass by." Now there was a great wind, so strong that it was splitting mountains and breaking rocks in pieces before the LORD, but the LORD was not in the wind; and after the wind an earthquake, but the LORD was not in the earthquake; ¹²and after the earthquake a fire, but the LORD was not in the fire; and after the fire a sound of sheer silence. ¹³When Elijah heard it, he wrapped his face in his mantle and went out and stood at the entrance of the cave. Then there came a voice to him that said, "What are you doing here, Elijah?" ¹⁴He answered, "I have been very zealous for the LORD, the God of hosts; for the Israelites have forsaken your covenant, thrown down your altars, and killed your prophets with the sword. I alone am left, and they are seeking my life, to take it away." ¹⁵Then the LORD said to him, "Go, return on your way to the wilderness of Damascus; when you arrive, you shall anoint Hazael as king over Aram. ¹⁶Also you shall anoint Jehu son of Nimshi as king over Israel; and you shall anoint Elisha son of Shaphat of Abel-meholah as prophet in your

place. ¹⁷Whoever escapes from the sword of Hazael, Jehu shall kill; and whoever escapes from the sword of Jehu, Elisha shall kill. ¹⁸Yet I will leave seven thousand in Israel, all the knees that have not bowed to Baal, and every mouth that has not kissed him."

Elisha Becomes Elijah's Disciple

19 So he set out from there, and found Elisha son of Shaphat, who was plowing. There were twelve yoke of oxen ahead of him, and he was with the twelfth. Elijah passed by him and threw his mantle over him. ²⁰He left the oxen, ran after Elijah, and said, "Let me kiss my father and my mother, and then I will follow you." Then Elijah*ᵃ* said to him, "Go back again; for what have I done to you?" ²¹He returned from following him, took the yoke of oxen, and slaughtered them; using the equipment from the oxen, he boiled their flesh, and gave it to the people, and they ate. Then he set out and followed Elijah, and became his servant.

Ahab's Wars with the Arameans

20 King Ben-hadad of Aram gathered all his army together; thirty-two kings were with him, along with horses and chariots. He marched against Samaria, laid siege to it, and attacked it. ²Then he sent messengers into the city to King Ahab of Israel, and said to him: "Thus says Ben-hadad: ³Your silver and gold are mine; your fairest wives and children also are mine." ⁴The king of Israel answered, "As you say, my lord, O king, I am yours, and all that I have." ⁵The messengers came again and said: "Thus says Ben-hadad: I sent to you, saying, 'Deliver to me your silver and gold, your wives and children'; ⁶nevertheless I will send my servants to you tomorrow about this time, and they shall search your house and the houses of your servants, and lay hands on whatever pleases them,*ᵇ* and take it away."

7 Then the king of Israel called all the elders of the land, and said, "Look now! See how this man is seeking trouble; for he sent to

---

a Heb *he*   *b* Gk Syr Vg: Heb *you*

me for my wives, my children, my silver, and my gold; and I did not refuse him." ⁸Then all the elders and all the people said to him, "Do not listen or consent." ⁹So he said to the messengers of Ben-hadad, "Tell my lord the king: All that you first demanded of your servant I will do; but this thing I cannot do." The messengers left and brought him word again. ¹⁰Ben-hadad sent to him and said, "The gods do so to me, and more also, if the dust of Samaria will provide a handful for each of the people who follow me." ¹¹The king of Israel answered, "Tell him: One who puts on armor should not brag like one who takes it off." ¹²When Ben-hadad heard this message—now he had been drinking with the kings in the booths—he said to his men, "Take your positions!" And they took their positions against the city.

Prophetic Opposition to Ahab

13 Then a certain prophet came up to King Ahab of Israel and said, "Thus says the LORD, Have you seen all this great multitude? Look, I will give it into your hand today; and you shall know that I am the LORD." ¹⁴Ahab said, "By whom?" He said, "Thus says the LORD, By the young men who serve the district governors." Then he said, "Who shall begin the battle?" He answered, "You." ¹⁵Then he mustered the young men who served the district governors, two hundred thirty-two; after them he mustered all the people of Israel, seven thousand.

16 They went out at noon, while Ben-hadad was drinking himself drunk in the booths, he and the thirty-two kings allied with him. ¹⁷The young men who served the district governors went out first. Ben-hadad had sent out scouts,ᵃ and they reported to him, "Men have come out from Samaria." ¹⁸He said, "If they have come out for peace, take them alive; if they have come out for war, take them alive." 19 But these had already come out of the city: the young men who served the district governors, and the army that followed them. ²⁰Each killed his man; the Arameans fled and

Israel pursued them, but King Ben-hadad of Aram escaped on a horse with the cavalry. ²¹The king of Israel went out, attacked the horses and chariots, and defeated the Arameans with a great slaughter.

22 Then the prophet approached the king of Israel and said to him, "Come, strengthen yourself, and consider well what you have to do; for in the spring the king of Aram will come up against you."

The Arameans Are Defeated

23 The servants of the king of Aram said to him, "Their gods are gods of the hills, and so they were stronger than we; but let us fight against them in the plain, and surely we shall be stronger than they. ²⁴Also do this: remove the kings, each from his post, and put commanders in place of them; ²⁵and muster an army like the army that you have lost, horse for horse, and chariot for chariot; then we will fight against them in the plain, and surely we shall be stronger than they." He heeded their voice, and did so.

26 In the spring Ben-hadad mustered the Arameans and went up to Aphek to fight against Israel. ²⁷After the Israelites had been mustered and provisioned, they went out to engage them; the people of Israel encamped opposite them like two little flocks of goats, while the Arameans filled the country. ²⁸A man of God approached and said to the king of Israel, "Thus says the LORD: Because the Arameans have said, 'The LORD is a god of the hills but he is not a god of the valleys,' therefore I will give all this great multitude into your hand, and you shall know that I am the LORD." ²⁹They encamped opposite one another seven days. Then on the seventh day the battle began; the Israelites killed one hundred thousand Aramean foot soldiers in one day. ³⁰The rest fled into the city of Aphek; and the wall fell on twenty-seven thousand men that were left.

Ben-hadad also fled, and entered the city to hide. ³¹His servants said to him, "Look, we

ᵃ Heb lacks *scouts*

have heard that the kings of the house of Israel are merciful kings; let us put sackcloth around our waists and ropes on our heads, and go out to the king of Israel; perhaps he will spare your life." ³²So they tied sackcloth around their waists, put ropes on their heads, went to the king of Israel, and said, "Your servant Ben-hadad says, 'Please let me live.' " And he said, "Is he still alive? He is my brother." ³³Now the men were watching for an omen; they quickly took it up from him and said, "Yes, Ben-hadad is your brother." Then he said, "Go and bring him." So Ben-hadad came out to him; and he had him come up into the chariot. ³⁴Ben-hadad*ᵃ* said to him, "I will restore the towns that my father took from your father; and you may establish bazaars for yourself in Damascus, as my father did in Samaria." The king of Israel responded,*ᵇ* "I will let you go on those terms." So he made a treaty with him and let him go.

A Prophet Condemns Ahab

35 At the command of the LORD a certain member of a company of prophets*ᶜ* said to another, "Strike me!" But the man refused to strike him. ³⁶Then he said to him, "Because you have not obeyed the voice of the LORD, as soon as you have left me, a lion will kill you." And when he had left him, a lion met him and killed him. ³⁷Then he found another man and said, "Strike me!" So the man hit him, striking and wounding him. ³⁸Then the prophet departed, and waited for the king along the road, disguising himself with a bandage over his eyes. ³⁹As the king passed by, he cried to the king and said, "Your servant went out into the thick of the battle; then a soldier turned and brought a man to me, and said, 'Guard this man; if he is missing, your life shall be given for his life, or else you shall pay a talent of silver.' ⁴⁰While your servant was busy here and there, he was gone." The king of Israel said to him, "So shall your judgment be; you yourself have decided it." ⁴¹Then he quickly took the bandage away from his eyes. The king of Is-

rael recognized him as one of the prophets. ⁴²Then he said to him, "Thus says the LORD, 'Because you have let the man go whom I had devoted to destruction, therefore your life shall be for his life, and your people for his people.' " ⁴³The king of Israel set out toward home, resentful and sullen, and came to Samaria.

Naboth's Vineyard

21 Later the following events took place: Naboth the Jezreelite had a vineyard in Jezreel, beside the palace of King Ahab of Samaria. ²And Ahab said to Naboth, "Give me your vineyard, so that I may have it for a vegetable garden, because it is near my house; I will give you a better vineyard for it; or, if it seems good to you, I will give you its value in money." ³But Naboth said to Ahab, "The LORD forbid that I should give you my ancestral inheritance." ⁴Ahab went home resentful and sullen because of what Naboth the Jezreelite had said to him; for he had said, "I will not give you my ancestral inheritance." He lay down on his bed, turned away his face, and would not eat.

5 His wife Jezebel came to him and said, "Why are you so depressed that you will not eat?" ⁶He said to her, "Because I spoke to Naboth the Jezreelite and said to him, 'Give me your vineyard for money; or else, if you prefer, I will give you another vineyard for it'; but he answered, 'I will not give you my vineyard.' " ⁷His wife Jezebel said to him, "Do you now govern Israel? Get up, eat some food, and be cheerful; I will give you the vineyard of Naboth the Jezreelite."

8 So she wrote letters in Ahab's name and sealed them with his seal; she sent the letters to the elders and the nobles who lived with Naboth in his city. ⁹She wrote in the letters, "Proclaim a fast, and seat Naboth at the head of the assembly; ¹⁰seat two scoundrels opposite him, and have them bring a charge against him, saying, 'You have cursed God and the king.' Then take him out, and stone him to death."

---

a Heb *He*   *b* Heb lacks *The king of Israel responded*   *c* Heb *of the sons of the prophets*

11The men of his city, the elders and the nobles who lived in his city, did as Jezebel had sent word to them. Just as it was written in the letters that she had sent to them, 12they proclaimed a fast and seated Naboth at the head of the assembly. 13The two scoundrels came in and sat opposite him; and the scoundrels brought a charge against Naboth, in the presence of the people, saying, "Naboth cursed God and the king." So they took him outside the city, and stoned him to death. 14Then they sent to Jezebel, saying, "Naboth has been stoned; he is dead."

15 As soon as Jezebel heard that Naboth had been stoned and was dead, Jezebel said to Ahab, "Go, take possession of the vineyard of Naboth the Jezreelite, which he refused to give you for money; for Naboth is not alive, but dead." 16As soon as Ahab heard that Naboth was dead, Ahab set out to go down to the vineyard of Naboth the Jezreelite, to take possession of it.

Elijah Pronounces God's Sentence

17 Then the word of the LORD came to Elijah the Tishbite, saying: 18Go down to meet King Ahab of Israel, who rules*a* in Samaria; he is now in the vineyard of Naboth, where he has gone to take possession. 19You shall say to him, "Thus says the LORD: Have you killed, and also taken possession?" You shall say to him, "Thus says the LORD: In the place where dogs licked up the blood of Naboth, dogs will also lick up your blood."

20 Ahab said to Elijah, "Have you found me, O my enemy?" He answered, "I have found you. Because you have sold yourself to do what is evil in the sight of the LORD, 21I will bring disaster on you; I will consume you, and will cut off from Ahab every male, bond or free, in Israel; 22and I will make your house like the house of Jeroboam son of Nebat, and like the house of Baasha son of Ahijah, because you have provoked me to anger and have caused Israel to sin. 23Also concerning Jezebel the LORD said, 'The dogs shall eat Jez-

ebel within the bounds of Jezreel.' 24Anyone belonging to Ahab who dies in the city the dogs shall eat; and anyone of his who dies in the open country the birds of the air shall eat."

25 (Indeed, there was no one like Ahab, who sold himself to do what was evil in the sight of the LORD, urged on by his wife Jezebel. 26He acted most abominably in going after idols, as the Amorites had done, whom the LORD drove out before the Israelites.)

27 When Ahab heard those words, he tore his clothes and put sackcloth over his bare flesh; he fasted, lay in the sackcloth, and went about dejectedly. 28Then the word of the LORD came to Elijah the Tishbite: 29"Have you seen how Ahab has humbled himself before me? Because he has humbled himself before me, I will not bring the disaster in his days; but in his son's days I will bring the disaster on his house."

Joint Campaign with Judah against Aram

22 For three years Aram and Israel continued without war. 2But in the third year King Jehoshaphat of Judah came down to the king of Israel. 3The king of Israel said to his servants, "Do you know that Ramoth-gilead belongs to us, yet we are doing nothing to take it out of the hand of the king of Aram?" 4He said to Jehoshaphat, "Will you go with me to battle at Ramoth-gilead?" Jehoshaphat replied to the king of Israel, "I am as you are; my people are your people, my horses are your horses."

5 But Jehoshaphat also said to the king of Israel, "Inquire first for the word of the LORD." 6Then the king of Israel gathered the prophets together, about four hundred of them, and said to them, "Shall I go to battle against Ramoth-gilead, or shall I refrain?" They said, "Go up; for the LORD will give it into the hand of the king." 7But Jehoshaphat said, "Is there no other prophet of the LORD here of whom we may inquire?" 8The king of Israel said to Jehoshaphat, "There is still one other

a Heb *who is*

by whom we may inquire of the LORD, Micaiah son of Imlah; but I hate him, for he never prophesies anything favorable about me, but only disaster." Jehoshaphat said, "Let the king not say such a thing." 9Then the king of Israel summoned an officer and said, "Bring quickly Micaiah son of Imlah." 10Now the king of Israel and King Jehoshaphat of Judah were sitting on their thrones, arrayed in their robes, at the threshing floor at the entrance of the gate of Samaria; and all the prophets were prophesying before them. 11Zedekiah son of Chenaanah made for himself horns of iron, and he said, "Thus says the LORD: With these you shall gore the Arameans until they are destroyed." 12All the prophets were prophesying the same and saying, "Go up to Ramoth-gilead and triumph; the LORD will give it into the hand of the king."

Micaiah Predicts Failure

13 The messenger who had gone to summon Micaiah said to him, "Look, the words of the prophets with one accord are favorable to the king; let your word be like the word of one of them, and speak favorably." 14But Micaiah said, "As the LORD lives, whatever the LORD says to me, that I will speak."

15 When he had come to the king, the king said to him, "Micaiah, shall we go to Ramoth-gilead to battle, or shall we refrain?" He answered him, "Go up and triumph; the LORD will give it into the hand of the king." 16But the king said to him, "How many times must I make you swear to tell me nothing but the truth in the name of the LORD?" 17Then Micaiah[a] said, "I saw all Israel scattered on the mountains, like sheep that have no shepherd; and the LORD said, 'These have no master; let each one go home in peace.'" 18The king of Israel said to Jehoshaphat, "Did I not tell you that he would not prophesy anything favorable about me, but only disaster?"

19 Then Micaiah[a] said, "Therefore hear the word of the LORD: I saw the LORD sitting on his throne, with all the host of heaven

standing beside him to the right and to the left of him. 20And the LORD said, 'Who will entice Ahab, so that he may go up and fall at Ramoth-gilead?' Then one said one thing, and another said another, 21until a spirit came forward and stood before the LORD, saying, 'I will entice him.' 22'How?' the LORD asked him. He replied, 'I will go out and be a lying spirit in the mouth of all his prophets.' Then the LORD[a] said, 'You are to entice him, and you shall succeed; go out and do it.' 23So you see, the LORD has put a lying spirit in the mouth of all these your prophets; the LORD has decreed disaster for you."

24 Then Zedekiah son of Chenaanah came up to Micaiah, slapped him on the cheek, and said, "Which way did the spirit of the LORD pass from me to speak to you?" 25Micaiah replied, "You will find out on that day when you go in to hide in an inner chamber." 26The king of Israel then ordered, "Take Micaiah, and return him to Amon the governor of the city and to Joash the king's son, 27and say, 'Thus says the king: Put this fellow in prison, and feed him on reduced rations of bread and water until I come in peace.'" 28Micaiah said, "If you return in peace, the LORD has not spoken by me." And he said, "Hear, you peoples, all of you!"

Defeat and Death of Ahab

29 So the king of Israel and King Jehoshaphat of Judah went up to Ramoth-gilead. 30The king of Israel said to Jehoshaphat, "I will disguise myself and go into battle, but you wear your robes." So the king of Israel disguised himself and went into battle. 31Now the king of Aram had commanded the thirty-two captains of his chariots, "Fight with no one small or great, but only with the king of Israel." 32When the captains of the chariots saw Jehoshaphat, they said, "It is surely the king of Israel." So they turned to fight against him; and Jehoshaphat cried out. 33When the captains of the chariots saw that it was not the king of Israel, they turned back from pursuing him.

a Heb *he*

³⁴But a certain man drew his bow and unknowingly struck the king of Israel between the scale armor and the breastplate; so he said to the driver of his chariot, "Turn around, and carry me out of the battle, for I am wounded." ³⁵The battle grew hot that day, and the king was propped up in his chariot facing the Arameans, until at evening he died; the blood from the wound had flowed into the bottom of the chariot. ³⁶Then about sunset a shout went through the army, "Every man to his city, and every man to his country!"

37 So the king died, and was brought to Samaria; they buried the king in Samaria. ³⁸They washed the chariot by the pool of Samaria; the dogs licked up his blood, and the prostitutes washed themselves in it,*a* according to the word of the LORD that he had spoken. ³⁹Now the rest of the acts of Ahab, and all that he did, and the ivory house that he built, and all the cities that he built, are they not written in the Book of the Annals of the Kings of Israel? ⁴⁰So Ahab slept with his ancestors; and his son Ahaziah succeeded him.

Jehoshaphat Reigns over Judah

41 Jehoshaphat son of Asa began to reign over Judah in the fourth year of King Ahab of Israel. ⁴²Jehoshaphat was thirty-five years old when he began to reign, and he reigned twenty-five years in Jerusalem. His mother's name was Azubah daughter of Shilhi. ⁴³He walked in all the way of his father Asa; he did not turn aside from it, doing what was right in the sight of the LORD; yet the high places were not taken away, and the people still sacrificed and offered incense on the high places. ⁴⁴Jehoshaphat also made peace with the king of Israel.

45 Now the rest of the acts of Jehoshaphat, and his power that he showed, and how he waged war, are they not written in the Book of the Annals of the Kings of Judah? ⁴⁶The remnant of the male temple prostitutes who were still in the land in the days of his father Asa, he exterminated.

47 There was no king in Edom; a deputy was king. ⁴⁸Jehoshaphat made ships of the Tarshish type to go to Ophir for gold; but they did not go, for the ships were wrecked at Ezion-geber. ⁴⁹Then Ahaziah son of Ahab said to Jehoshaphat, "Let my servants go with your servants in the ships," but Jehoshaphat was not willing. ⁵⁰Jehoshaphat slept with his ancestors and was buried with his ancestors in the city of his father David; his son Jehoram succeeded him.

Ahaziah Reigns over Israel

51 Ahaziah son of Ahab began to reign over Israel in Samaria in the seventeenth year of King Jehoshaphat of Judah; he reigned two years over Israel. ⁵²He did what was evil in the sight of the LORD, and walked in the way of his father and mother, and in the way of Jeroboam son of Nebat, who caused Israel to sin. ⁵³He served Baal and worshiped him; he provoked the LORD, the God of Israel, to anger, just as his father had done.

a Heb lacks *in it*

2 KINGS

Elijah Denounces Ahaziah

1 After the death of Ahab, Moab rebelled against Israel.

2 Ahaziah had fallen through the lattice in his upper chamber in Samaria, and lay injured; so he sent messengers, telling them, "Go, inquire of Baal-zebub, the god of Ekron, whether I shall recover from this injury." [3]But the angel of the LORD said to Elijah the Tishbite, "Get up, go to meet the messengers of the king of Samaria, and say to them, 'Is it because there is no God in Israel that you are going to inquire of Baal-zebub, the god of Ekron?' [4]Now therefore thus says the LORD, 'You shall not leave the bed to which you have gone, but you shall surely die.' " So Elijah went.

5 The messengers returned to the king, who said to them, "Why have you returned?" [6]They answered him, "There came a man to meet us, who said to us, 'Go back to the king who sent you, and say to him: Thus says the LORD: Is it because there is no God in Israel that you are sending to inquire of Baal-zebub, the god of Ekron? Therefore you shall not leave the bed to which you have gone, but shall surely die.' " [7]He said to them, "What sort of man was he who came to meet you and told you these things?" [8]They answered him, "A hairy man, with a leather belt around his waist." He said, "It is Elijah the Tishbite."

9 Then the king sent to him a captain of fifty with his fifty men. He went up to Elijah, who was sitting on the top of a hill, and said to him, "O man of God, the king says, 'Come down.' " [10]But Elijah answered the captain of fifty, "If I am a man of God, let fire come down from heaven and consume you and your fifty." Then fire came down from heaven, and consumed him and his fifty.

11 Again the king sent to him another captain of fifty with his fifty. He went up[a] and said to him, "O man of God, this is the king's order: Come down quickly!" [12]But Elijah answered them, "If I am a man of God, let fire come down from heaven and consume you and your fifty." Then the fire of God came down from heaven and consumed him and his fifty.

13 Again the king sent the captain of a third fifty with his fifty. So the third captain of fifty went up, and came and fell on his knees before Elijah, and entreated him, "O man of God, please let my life, and the life of these fifty servants of yours, be precious in your sight. [14]Look, fire came down from heaven and consumed the two former captains of fifty men with their fifties; but now let my life be precious in your sight." [15]Then the angel of the LORD said to Elijah, "Go down with him; do not be afraid of him." So he set out and went down with him to the king, [16]and said to him, "Thus says the LORD: Because you have sent messengers to inquire of Baal-zebub, the god of Ekron,—is it because there is no God in Israel to inquire of his word?—therefore you shall not leave the bed to which you have gone, but you shall surely die."

Death of Ahaziah

17 So he died according to the word of the LORD that Elijah had spoken. His brother,[b] Jehoram succeeded him as king in the second year of King Jehoram son of Jehoshaphat of Judah, because Ahaziah had no son. [18]Now the rest of the acts of Ahaziah that he did, are they not written in the Book of the Annals of the Kings of Israel?

Elijah Ascends to Heaven

2 Now when the LORD was about to take Elijah up to heaven by a whirlwind, Elijah and Elisha were on their way from Gilgal. [2]Elijah said to Elisha, "Stay here; for the LORD has sent me as far as Bethel." But Elisha said, "As the LORD lives, and as you yourself live, I will not leave you." So they went down to Bethel. [3]The company of prophets[c] who were in Bethel came out to Elisha, and said to him, "Do you

---

a Gk Compare verses 9, 13: Heb *He answered*   *b* Gk Syr: Heb lacks *His brother*   *c* Heb *sons of the prophets* know that today the LORD will take your master away from you?" And he said, "Yes, I know; keep silent."

4 Elijah said to him, "Elisha, stay here; for the LORD has sent me to Jericho." But he said, "As the LORD lives, and as you yourself live, I will not leave you." So they came to Jericho. [5]The company of prophets[a] who were at Jericho drew near to Elisha, and said to him, "Do you know that today the LORD will take your master away from you?" And he answered, "Yes, I know; be silent."

6 Then Elijah said to him, "Stay here; for the LORD has sent me to the Jordan." But he said, "As the LORD lives, and as you yourself live, I will not leave you." So the two of them went on. [7]Fifty men of the company of prophets[a] also went, and stood at some distance from them, as they both were standing by the Jordan. [8]Then Elijah took his mantle and rolled it up, and struck the water; the water was parted to the one side and to the other, until the two of them crossed on dry ground.

9 When they had crossed, Elijah said to Elisha, "Tell me what I may do for you, before I am taken from you." Elisha said, "Please let me inherit a double share of your spirit." [10]He responded, "You have asked a hard thing; yet, if you see me as I am being taken from you, it will be granted you; if not, it will not." [11]As they continued walking and talking, a chariot of fire and horses of fire separated the two of them, and Elijah ascended in a whirlwind into heaven. [12]Elisha kept watching and crying out, "Father, father! The chariots of Israel and its horsemen!" But when he could no longer see him, he grasped his own clothes and tore them in two pieces.

Elisha Succeeds Elijah

13 He picked up the mantle of Elijah that had fallen from him, and went back and stood on the bank of the Jordan. [14]He took the mantle of Elijah that had fallen from him, and struck the water, saying, "Where is the LORD, the God of Elijah?" When he had struck the water, the water was parted to the one side and to the other, and Elisha went over.

15 When the company of prophets[a] who were at Jericho saw him at a distance, they declared, "The spirit of Elijah rests on Elisha." They came to meet him and bowed to the ground before him. [16]They said to him, "See now, we have fifty strong men among your servants; please let them go and seek your master; it may be that the spirit of the LORD has caught him up and thrown him down on some mountain or into some valley." He responded, "No, do not send them." [17]But when they urged him until he was ashamed, he said, "Send them." So they sent fifty men who searched for three days but did not find him. [18]When they came back to him (he had remained at Jericho), he said to them, "Did I not say to you, Do not go?"

Elisha Performs Miracles

19 Now the people of the city said to Elisha, "The location of this city is good, as my lord sees; but the water is bad, and the land is unfruitful." [20]He said, "Bring me a new bowl, and put salt in it." So they brought it to him. [21]Then he went to the spring of water and threw the salt into it, and said, "Thus says the LORD, I have made this water wholesome; from now on neither death nor miscarriage shall come from it." [22]So the water has been wholesome to this day, according to the word that Elisha spoke.

23 He went up from there to Bethel; and while he was going up on the way, some small boys came out of the city and jeered at him, saying, "Go away, baldhead! Go away, baldhead!" [24]When he turned around and saw them, he cursed them in the name of the LORD. Then two she-bears came out of the woods and mauled forty-two of the boys. [25]From there he went on to Mount Carmel, and then returned to Samaria.

Jehoram Reigns over Israel

3 In the eighteenth year of King Jehoshaphat of Judah, Jehoram son of Ahab be-

---

a Heb *sons of the prophets*

came king over Israel in Samaria; he reigned twelve years. 2He did what was evil in the sight of the LORD, though not like his father and mother, for he removed the pillar of Baal that his father had made. 3Nevertheless he clung to the sin of Jeroboam son of Nebat, which he caused Israel to commit; he did not depart from it.

War with Moab

4 Now King Mesha of Moab was a sheep breeder, who used to deliver to the king of Israel one hundred thousand lambs, and the wool of one hundred thousand rams. 5But when Ahab died, the king of Moab rebelled against the king of Israel. 6So King Jehoram marched out of Samaria at that time and mustered all Israel. 7As he went he sent word to King Jehoshaphat of Judah, "The king of Moab has rebelled against me; will you go with me to battle against Moab?" He answered, "I will; I am with you, my people are your people, my horses are your horses." 8Then he asked, "By which way shall we march?" Jehoram answered, "By the way of the wilderness of Edom."

9 So the king of Israel, the king of Judah, and the king of Edom set out; and when they had made a roundabout march of seven days, there was no water for the army or for the animals that were with them. 10Then the king of Israel said, "Alas! The LORD has summoned us, three kings, only to be handed over to Moab." 11But Jehoshaphat said, "Is there no prophet of the LORD here, through whom we may inquire of the LORD?" Then one of the servants of the king of Israel answered, "Elisha son of Shaphat, who used to pour water on the hands of Elijah, is here." 12Jehoshaphat said, "The word of the LORD is with him." So the king of Israel and Jehoshaphat and the king of Edom went down to him.

13 Elisha said to the king of Israel, "What have I to do with you? Go to your father's prophets or to your mother's." But the king of Israel said to him, "No; it is the LORD who has summoned us, three kings, only to be handed

over to Moab." 14Elisha said, "As the LORD of hosts lives, whom I serve, were it not that I have regard for King Jehoshaphat of Judah, I would give you neither a look nor a glance. 15But get me a musician." And then, while the musician was playing, the power of the LORD came on him. 16And he said, "Thus says the LORD, 'I will make this wadi full of pools.' 17For thus says the LORD, 'You shall see neither wind nor rain; but the wadi shall be filled with water, so that you shall drink, you, your cattle, and your animals.' 18This is only a trifle in the sight of the LORD, for he will also hand Moab over to you. 19You shall conquer every fortified city and every choice city; every good tree you shall fell, all springs of water you shall stop up, and every good piece of land you shall ruin with stones." 20The next day, about the time of the morning offering, suddenly water began to flow from the direction of Edom, until the country was filled with water.

21 When all the Moabites heard that the kings had come up to fight against them, all who were able to put on armor, from the youngest to the oldest, were called out and were drawn up at the frontier. 22When they rose early in the morning, and the sun shone upon the water, the Moabites saw the water opposite them as red as blood. 23They said, "This is blood; the kings must have fought together, and killed one another. Now then, Moab, to the spoil!" 24But when they came to the camp of Israel, the Israelites rose up and attacked the Moabites, who fled before them; as they entered Moab they continued the attack.*a* 25The cities they overturned, and on every good piece of land everyone threw a stone, until it was covered; every spring of water they stopped up, and every good tree they felled. Only at Kir-hareseth did the stone walls remain, until the slingers surrounded and attacked it. 26When the king of Moab saw that the battle was going against him, he took with him seven hundred swordsmen to break through, opposite the king of Edom; but they could not. 27Then he took his firstborn son who was to succeed

a Compare Gk Syr: Meaning of Heb uncertain

him, and offered him as a burnt offering on the wall. And great wrath came upon Israel, so they withdrew from him and returned to their own land.

Elisha and the Widow's Oil

4 Now the wife of a member of the company of prophets*a* cried to Elisha, "Your servant my husband is dead; and you know that your servant feared the LORD, but a creditor has come to take my two children as slaves." 2Elisha said to her, "What shall I do for you? Tell me, what do you have in the house?" She answered, "Your servant has nothing in the house, except a jar of oil." 3He said, "Go outside, borrow vessels from all your neighbors, empty vessels and not just a few. 4Then go in, and shut the door behind you and your children, and start pouring into all these vessels; when each is full, set it aside." 5So she left him and shut the door behind her and her children; they kept bringing vessels to her, and she kept pouring. 6When the vessels were full, she said to her son, "Bring me another vessel." But he said to her, "There are no more." Then the oil stopped flowing. 7She came and told the man of God, and he said, "Go sell the oil and pay your debts, and you and your children can live on the rest."

Elisha Raises the Shunammite's Son

8 One day Elisha was passing through Shunem, where a wealthy woman lived, who urged him to have a meal. So whenever he passed that way, he would stop there for a meal. 9She said to her husband, "Look, I am sure that this man who regularly passes our way is a holy man of God. 10Let us make a small roof chamber with walls, and put there for him a bed, a table, a chair, and a lamp, so that he can stay there whenever he comes to us."

11 One day when he came there, he went up to the chamber and lay down there. 12He said to his servant Gehazi, "Call the Shunammite woman." When he had called her, she stood before him. 13He said to him, "Say to her,

Since you have taken all this trouble for us, what may be done for you? Would you have a word spoken on your behalf to the king or to the commander of the army?" She answered, "I live among my own people." 14He said, "What then may be done for her?" Gehazi answered, "Well, she has no son, and her husband is old." 15He said, "Call her." When he had called her, she stood at the door. 16He said, "At this season, in due time, you shall embrace a son." She replied, "No, my lord, O man of God; do not deceive your servant."

17 The woman conceived and bore a son at that season, in due time, as Elisha had declared to her.

18 When the child was older, he went out one day to his father among the reapers. 19He complained to his father, "Oh, my head, my head!" The father said to his servant, "Carry him to his mother." 20He carried him and brought him to his mother; the child sat on her lap until noon, and he died. 21She went up and laid him on the bed of the man of God, closed the door on him, and left. 22Then she called to her husband, and said, "Send me one of the servants and one of the donkeys, so that I may quickly go to the man of God and come back again." 23He said, "Why go to him today? It is neither new moon nor sabbath." She said, "It will be all right." 24Then she saddled the donkey and said to her servant, "Urge the animal on; do not hold back for me unless I tell you." 25So she set out, and came to the man of God at Mount Carmel.

When the man of God saw her coming, he said to Gehazi his servant, "Look, there is the Shunammite woman; 26run at once to meet her, and say to her, Are you all right? Is your husband all right? Is the child all right?" She answered, "It is all right." 27When she came to the man of God at the mountain, she caught hold of his feet. Gehazi approached to push her away. But the man of God said, "Let her alone, for she is in bitter distress; the LORD has hidden it from me and has not told me." 28Then she said, "Did I ask my lord for a son? Did I

---

a Heb *the sons of the prophets*

not say, Do not mislead me?" [29]He said to Gehazi, "Gird up your loins, and take my staff in your hand, and go. If you meet anyone, give no greeting, and if anyone greets you, do not answer; and lay my staff on the face of the child." [30]Then the mother of the child said, "As the LORD lives, and as you yourself live, I will not leave without you." So he rose up and followed her. [31]Gehazi went on ahead and laid the staff on the face of the child, but there was no sound or sign of life. He came back to meet him and told him, "The child has not awakened."

[32] When Elisha came into the house, he saw the child lying dead on his bed. [33]So he went in and closed the door on the two of them, and prayed to the LORD. [34]Then he got up on the bed[a] and lay upon the child, putting his mouth upon his mouth, his eyes upon his eyes, and his hands upon his hands; and while he lay bent over him, the flesh of the child became warm. [35]He got down, walked once to and fro in the room, then got up again and bent over him; the child sneezed seven times, and the child opened his eyes. [36]Elisha[b] summoned Gehazi and said, "Call the Shunammite woman." So he called her. When she came to him, he said, "Take your son." [37]She came and fell at his feet, bowing to the ground; then she took her son and left.

Elisha Purifies the Pot of Stew

[38] When Elisha returned to Gilgal, there was a famine in the land. As the company of prophets was[c] sitting before him, he said to his servant, "Put the large pot on, and make some stew for the company of prophets."[d] [39]One of them went out into the field to gather herbs; he found a wild vine and gathered from it a lapful of wild gourds, and came and cut them up into the pot of stew, not knowing what they were. [40]They served some for the men to eat. But while they were eating the stew, they cried out, "O man of God, there is death in the pot!" They could not eat it. [41]He said, "Then bring some flour." He threw it into the pot, and

said, "Serve the people and let them eat." And there was nothing harmful in the pot.

Elisha Feeds One Hundred Men

[42] A man came from Baal-shalishah, bringing food from the first fruits to the man of God: twenty loaves of barley and fresh ears of grain in his sack. Elisha said, "Give it to the people and let them eat." [43]But his servant said, "How can I set this before a hundred people?" So he repeated, "Give it to the people and let them eat, for thus says the LORD, 'They shall eat and have some left.'" [44]He set it before them, they ate, and had some left, according to the word of the LORD.

The Healing of Naaman

5 Naaman, commander of the army of the king of Aram, was a great man and in high favor with his master, because by him the LORD had given victory to Aram. The man, though a mighty warrior, suffered from leprosy.[e] [2]Now the Arameans on one of their raids had taken a young girl captive from the land of Israel, and she served Naaman's wife. [3]She said to her mistress, "If only my lord were with the prophet who is in Samaria! He would cure him of his leprosy."[e] [4]So Naaman[b] went in and told his lord just what the girl from the land of Israel had said. [5]And the king of Aram said, "Go then, and I will send along a letter to the king of Israel."

He went, taking with him ten talents of silver, six thousand shekels of gold, and ten sets of garments. [6]He brought the letter to the king of Israel, which read, "When this letter reaches you, know that I have sent to you my servant Naaman, that you may cure him of his leprosy."[e] [7]When the king of Israel read the letter, he tore his clothes and said, "Am I God, to give death or life, that this man sends word to me to cure a man of his leprosy?[e] Just look and see how he is trying to pick a quarrel with me."

[8] But when Elisha the man of God heard that the king of Israel had torn his clothes, he sent a message to the king, "Why have you

---

a Heb lacks *on the bed*   b Heb *he*   c Heb *sons of the prophets were*   d Heb *sons of the prophets*   e A term for several skin diseases; precise meaning uncertain torn your clothes? Let him come to me, that he may learn that there is a prophet in Israel." ⁹So Naaman came with his horses and chariots, and halted at the entrance of Elisha's house. ¹⁰Elisha sent a messenger to him, saying, "Go, wash in the Jordan seven times, and your flesh shall be restored and you shall be clean." ¹¹But Naaman became angry and went away, saying, "I thought that for me he would surely come out, and stand and call on the name of the LORD his God, and would wave his hand over the spot, and cure the leprosy!ᵃ ¹²Are not Abanaᵇ and Pharpar, the rivers of Damascus, better than all the waters of Israel? Could I not wash in them, and be clean?" He turned and went away in a rage. ¹³But his servants approached and said to him, "Father, if the prophet had commanded you to do something difficult, would you not have done it? How much more, when all he said to you was, 'Wash, and be clean'?" ¹⁴So he went down and immersed himself seven times in the Jordan, according to the word of the man of God; his flesh was restored like the flesh of a young boy, and he was clean.

15 Then he returned to the man of God, he and all his company; he came and stood before him and said, "Now I know that there is no God in all the earth except in Israel; please accept a present from your servant." ¹⁶But he said, "As the LORD lives, whom I serve, I will accept nothing!" He urged him to accept, but he refused. ¹⁷Then Naaman said, "If not, please let two mule-loads of earth be given to your servant; for your servant will no longer offer burnt offering or sacrifice to any god except the LORD. ¹⁸But may the LORD pardon your servant on one count: when my master goes into the house of Rimmon to worship there, leaning on my arm, and I bow down in the house of Rimmon, when I do bow down in the house of Rimmon, may the LORD pardon your servant on this one count." ¹⁹He said to him, "Go in peace."

Gehazi's Greed

But when Naaman had gone from him a short distance, ²⁰Gehazi, the servant of Elisha the man of God, thought, "My master has let that Aramean Naaman off too lightly by not accepting from him what he offered. As the LORD lives, I will run after him and get something out of him." ²¹So Gehazi went after Naaman. When Naaman saw someone running after him, he jumped down from the chariot to meet him and said, "Is everything all right?" ²²He replied, "Yes, but my master has sent me to say, 'Two members of a company of prophetsᶜ have just come to me from the hill country of Ephraim; please give them a talent of silver and two changes of clothing.'" ²³Naaman said, "Please accept two talents." He urged him, and tied up two talents of silver in two bags, with two changes of clothing, and gave them to two of his servants, who carried them in front of Gehazi.ᵈ ²⁴When he came to the citadel, he took the bagsᵉ from them, and stored them inside; he dismissed the men, and they left.

25 He went in and stood before his master; and Elisha said to him, "Where have you been, Gehazi?" He answered, "Your servant has not gone anywhere at all." ²⁶But he said to him, "Did I not go with you in spirit when someone left his chariot to meet you? Is this a time to accept money and to accept clothing, olive orchards and vineyards, sheep and oxen, and male and female slaves? ²⁷Therefore the leprosyᵃ of Naaman shall cling to you, and to your descendants forever." So he left his presence leprous,ᵃ as white as snow.

The Miracle of the Ax Head

6 Now the company of prophetsᶜ said to Elisha, "As you see, the place where we live under your charge is too small for us. ²Let us go to the Jordan, and let us collect logs there, one for each of us, and build a place there for us to live." He answered, "Do so." ³Then one of them said, "Please come with your servants." And he answered, "I will." ⁴So he went

---

ᵃ A term for several skin diseases; precise meaning uncertain   ᵇ Another reading is *Amana*   ᶜ Heb *sons of the prophets*   ᵈ Heb *him*   ᵉ Heb lacks *the bags* with them. When they came to the Jordan, they cut down trees. 5But as one was felling a log, his ax head fell into the water; he cried out, "Alas, master! It was borrowed." 6Then the man of God said, "Where did it fall?" When he showed him the place, he cut off a stick, and threw it in there, and made the iron float. 7He said, "Pick it up." So he reached out his hand and took it.

The Aramean Attack Is Thwarted

8 Once when the king of Aram was at war with Israel, he took counsel with his officers. He said, "At such and such a place shall be my camp." 9But the man of God sent word to the king of Israel, "Take care not to pass this place, because the Arameans are going down there." 10The king of Israel sent word to the place of which the man of God spoke. More than once or twice he warned such a place*a* so that it was on the alert.

11 The mind of the king of Aram was greatly perturbed because of this; he called his officers and said to them, "Now tell me who among us sides with the king of Israel?" 12Then one of his officers said, "No one, my lord king. It is Elisha, the prophet in Israel, who tells the king of Israel the words that you speak in your bedchamber." 13He said, "Go and find where he is; I will send and seize him." He was told, "He is in Dothan." 14So he sent horses and chariots there and a great army; they came by night, and surrounded the city.

15 When an attendant of the man of God rose early in the morning and went out, an army with horses and chariots was all around the city. His servant said, "Alas, master! What shall we do?" 16He replied, "Do not be afraid, for there are more with us than there are with them." 17Then Elisha prayed: "O LORD, please open his eyes that he may see." So the LORD opened the eyes of the servant, and he saw; the mountain was full of horses and chariots of fire all around Elisha. 18When the Arameans*b* came down against him, Elisha prayed to the LORD, and said, "Strike this people, please, with blind-

ness." So he struck them with blindness as Elisha had asked. 19Elisha said to them, "This is not the way, and this is not the city; follow me, and I will bring you to the man whom you seek." And he led them to Samaria.

20 As soon as they entered Samaria, Elisha said, "O LORD, open the eyes of these men so that they may see." The LORD opened their eyes, and they saw that they were inside Samaria. 21When the king of Israel saw them he said to Elisha, "Father, shall I kill them? Shall I kill them?" 22He answered, "No! Did you capture with your sword and your bow those whom you want to kill? Set food and water before them so that they may eat and drink; and let them go to their master." 23So he prepared for them a great feast; after they ate and drank, he sent them on their way, and they went to their master. And the Arameans no longer came raiding into the land of Israel.

Ben-hadad's Siege of Samaria

24 Some time later King Ben-hadad of Aram mustered his entire army; he marched against Samaria and laid siege to it. 25As the siege continued, famine in Samaria became so great that a donkey's head was sold for eighty shekels of silver, and one-fourth of a kab of dove's dung for five shekels of silver. 26Now as the king of Israel was walking on the city wall, a woman cried out to him, "Help, my lord king!" 27He said, "No! Let the LORD help you. How can I help you? From the threshing floor or from the wine press?" 28But then the king asked her, "What is your complaint?" She answered, "This woman said to me, 'Give up your son; we will eat him today, and we will eat my son tomorrow.' 29So we cooked my son and ate him. The next day I said to her, 'Give up your son and we will eat him.' But she has hidden her son." 30When the king heard the words of the woman he tore his clothes— now since he was walking on the city wall, the people could see that he had sackcloth on his body underneath— 31and he said, "So may God do to me, and more, if the head of Eli-

a Heb *warned it*   *b* Heb *they*

sha son of Shaphat stays on his shoulders today." [32]So he dispatched a man from his presence.

Now Elisha was sitting in his house, and the elders were sitting with him. Before the messenger arrived, Elisha said to the elders, "Are you aware that this murderer has sent someone to take off my head? When the messenger comes, see that you shut the door and hold it closed against him. Is not the sound of his master's feet behind him?" [33]While he was still speaking with them, the king[a] came down to him and said, "This trouble is from the LORD! 7 Why should I hope in the LORD any longer?" [1]But Elisha said, "Hear the word of the LORD: thus says the LORD, Tomorrow about this time a measure of choice meal shall be sold for a shekel, and two measures of barley for a shekel, at the gate of Samaria." [2]Then the captain on whose hand the king leaned said to the man of God, "Even if the LORD were to make windows in the sky, could such a thing happen?" But he said, "You shall see it with your own eyes, but you shall not eat from it."

The Arameans Flee

3 Now there were four leprous[b] men outside the city gate, who said to one another, "Why should we sit here until we die? [4]If we say, 'Let us enter the city,' the famine is in the city, and we shall die there; but if we sit here, we shall also die. Therefore, let us desert to the Aramean camp; if they spare our lives, we shall live; and if they kill us, we shall but die." [5]So they arose at twilight to go to the Aramean camp; but when they came to the edge of the Aramean camp, there was no one there at all. [6]For the Lord had caused the Aramean army to hear the sound of chariots, and of horses, the sound of a great army, so that they said to one another, "The king of Israel has hired the kings of the Hittites and the kings of Egypt to fight against us." [7]So they fled away in the twilight and abandoned their tents, their horses, and their donkeys leaving the camp just as it was, and fled for their lives. [8]When these leprous[b] men had come to the edge of the camp, they went into a tent, ate and drank, carried off silver, gold, and clothing, and went and hid them. Then they came back, entered another tent, carried off things from it, and went and hid them.

9 Then they said to one another, "What we are doing is wrong. This is a day of good news; if we are silent and wait until the morning light, we will be found guilty; therefore let us go and tell the king's household." [10]So they came and called to the gatekeepers of the city, and told them, "We went to the Aramean camp, but there was no one to be seen or heard there, nothing but the horses tied, the donkeys tied, and the tents as they were." [11]Then the gatekeepers called out and proclaimed it to the king's household. [12]The king got up in the night, and said to his servants, "I will tell you what the Arameans have prepared against us. They know that we are starving; so they have left the camp to hide themselves in the open country, thinking, 'When they come out of the city, we shall take them alive and get into the city.'" [13]One of his servants said, "Let some men take five of the remaining horses, since those left here will suffer the fate of the whole multitude of Israel that have perished already;[c] let us send and find out." [14]So they took two mounted men, and the king sent them after the Aramean army, saying, "Go and find out." [15]So they went after them as far as the Jordan; the whole way was littered with garments and equipment that the Arameans had thrown away in their haste. So the messengers returned, and told the king.

16 Then the people went out, and plundered the camp of the Arameans. So a measure of choice meal was sold for a shekel, and two measures of barley for a shekel, according to the word of the LORD. [17]Now the king had appointed the captain on whose hand he leaned to have charge of the gate; the people trampled him to death in the gate, just as the man of God had said when the king came down to

---

a See 7.2: Heb *messenger*　　*b* A term for several skin diseases; precise meaning uncertain　　*c* Compare Gk Syr Vg: Meaning of Heb uncertain him. ¹⁸For when the man of God had said to the king, "Two measures of barley shall be sold for a shekel, and a measure of choice meal for a shekel, about this time tomorrow in the gate of Samaria," ¹⁹the captain had answered the man of God, "Even if the LORD were to make windows in the sky, could such a thing happen?" And he had answered, "You shall see it with your own eyes, but you shall not eat from it." ²⁰It did indeed happen to him; the people trampled him to death in the gate.

The Shunammite Woman's Land Restored

8 Now Elisha had said to the woman whose son he had restored to life, "Get up and go with your household, and settle wherever you can; for the LORD has called for a famine, and it will come on the land for seven years." ²So the woman got up and did according to the word of the man of God; she went with her household and settled in the land of the Philistines seven years. ³At the end of the seven years, when the woman returned from the land of the Philistines, she set out to appeal to the king for her house and her land. ⁴Now the king was talking with Gehazi the servant of the man of God, saying, "Tell me all the great things that Elisha has done." ⁵While he was telling the king how Elisha had restored a dead person to life, the woman whose son he had restored to life appealed to the king for her house and her land. Gehazi said, "My lord king, here is the woman, and here is her son whom Elisha restored to life." ⁶When the king questioned the woman, she told him. So the king appointed an official for her, saying, "Restore all that was hers, together with all the revenue of the fields from the day that she left the land until now."

Death of Ben-hadad

7 Elisha went to Damascus while King Ben-hadad of Aram was ill. When it was told him, "The man of God has come here," ⁸the king said to Hazael, "Take a present with you and go to meet the man of God. Inquire of the LORD through him, whether I shall recover from this illness." ⁹So Hazael went to meet him, taking a present with him, all kinds of goods of Damascus, forty camel loads. When he entered and stood before him, he said, "Your son King Ben-hadad of Aram has sent me to you, saying, 'Shall I recover from this illness?' " ¹⁰Elisha said to him, "Go, say to him, 'You shall certainly recover'; but the LORD has shown me that he shall certainly die." ¹¹He fixed his gaze and stared at him, until he was ashamed. Then the man of God wept. ¹²Hazael asked, "Why does my lord weep?" He answered, "Because I know the evil that you will do to the people of Israel; you will set their fortresses on fire, you will kill their young men with the sword, dash in pieces their little ones, and rip up their pregnant women." ¹³Hazael said, "What is your servant, who is a mere dog, that he should do this great thing?" Elisha answered, "The LORD has shown me that you are to be king over Aram." ¹⁴Then he left Elisha, and went to his master Ben-hadad,ᵃ who said to him, "What did Elisha say to you?" And he answered, "He told me that you would certainly recover." ¹⁵But the next day he took the bed-cover and dipped it in water and spread it over the king's face, until he died. And Hazael succeeded him.

Jehoram Reigns over Judah

16 In the fifth year of King Joram son of Ahab of Israel,ᵇ Jehoram son of King Jehoshaphat of Judah began to reign. ¹⁷He was thirty-two years old when he became king, and he reigned eight years in Jerusalem. ¹⁸He walked in the way of the kings of Israel, as the house of Ahab had done, for the daughter of Ahab was his wife. He did what was evil in the sight of the LORD. ¹⁹Yet the LORD would not destroy Judah, for the sake of his servant David, since he had promised to give a lamp to him and to his descendants forever.

20 In his days Edom revolted against the rule of Judah, and set up a king of their own. ²¹Then Joram crossed over to Zair with all his chariots. He set out by night and attacked the

---

a Heb lacks *Ben-hadad*   *b* Gk Syr: Heb adds *Jehoshaphat being king of Judah,*

Edomites and their chariot commanders who had surrounded him;*a* but his army fled home. 22So Edom has been in revolt against the rule of Judah to this day. Libnah also revolted at the same time. 23Now the rest of the acts of Joram, and all that he did, are they not written in the Book of the Annals of the Kings of Judah? 24So Joram slept with his ancestors, and was buried with them in the city of David; his son Ahaziah succeeded him.

Ahaziah Reigns over Judah

25 In the twelfth year of King Joram son of Ahab of Israel, Ahaziah son of King Jehoram of Judah began to reign. 26Ahaziah was twenty-two years old when he began to reign; he reigned one year in Jerusalem. His mother's name was Athaliah, a granddaughter of King Omri of Israel. 27He also walked in the way of the house of Ahab, doing what was evil in the sight of the LORD, as the house of Ahab had done, for he was son-in-law to the house of Ahab.

28 He went with Joram son of Ahab to wage war against King Hazael of Aram at Ramoth-gilead, where the Arameans wounded Joram. 29King Joram returned to be healed in Jezreel of the wounds that the Arameans had inflicted on him at Ramah, when he fought against King Hazael of Aram. King Ahaziah son of Jehoram of Judah went down to see Joram son of Ahab in Jezreel, because he was wounded.

Anointing of Jehu

9 Then the prophet Elisha called a member of the company of prophets*b* and said to him, "Gird up your loins; take this flask of oil in your hand, and go to Ramoth-gilead. 2When you arrive, look there for Jehu son of Jehoshaphat, son of Nimshi; go in and get him to leave his companions, and take him into an inner chamber. 3Then take the flask of oil, pour it on his head, and say, 'Thus says the LORD: I anoint you king over Israel.' Then open the door and flee; do not linger."

4 So the young man, the young prophet, went to Ramoth-gilead. 5He arrived while the commanders of the army were in council, and he announced, "I have a message for you, commander." "For which one of us?" asked Jehu. "For you, commander." 6So Jehu*c* got up and went inside; the young man poured the oil on his head, saying to him, "Thus says the LORD the God of Israel: I anoint you king over the people of the LORD, over Israel. 7You shall strike down the house of your master Ahab, so that I may avenge on Jezebel the blood of my servants the prophets, and the blood of all the servants of the LORD. 8For the whole house of Ahab shall perish; I will cut off from Ahab every male, bond or free, in Israel. 9I will make the house of Ahab like the house of Jeroboam son of Nebat, and like the house of Baasha son of Ahijah. 10The dogs shall eat Jezebel in the territory of Jezreel, and no one shall bury her." Then he opened the door and fled.

11 When Jehu came back to his master's officers, they said to him, "Is everything all right? Why did that madman come to you?" He answered them, "You know the sort and how they babble." 12They said, "Liar! Come on, tell us!" So he said, "This is just what he said to me: 'Thus says the LORD, I anoint you king over Israel.'" 13Then hurriedly they all took their cloaks and spread them for him on the bare*a* steps; and they blew the trumpet, and proclaimed, "Jehu is king."

Joram of Israel Killed

14 Thus Jehu son of Jehoshaphat son of Nimshi conspired against Joram. Joram with all Israel had been on guard at Ramoth-gilead against King Hazael of Aram; 15but King Joram had returned to be healed in Jezreel of the wounds that the Arameans had inflicted on him, when he fought against King Hazael of Aram. So Jehu said, "If this is your wish, then let no one slip out of the city to go and tell the news in Jezreel." 16Then Jehu mounted his chariot and went to Jezreel, where Joram was

lying ill. King Ahaziah of Judah had come down to visit Joram.

17 In Jezreel, the sentinel standing on the tower spied the company of Jehu arriving, and said, "I see a company." Joram said, "Take a horseman; send him to meet them, and let him say, 'Is it peace?'" 18So the horseman went to meet him; he said, "Thus says the king, 'Is it peace?'" Jehu responded, "What have you to do with peace? Fall in behind me." The sentinel reported, saying, "The messenger reached them, but he is not coming back." 19Then he sent out a second horseman, who came to them and said, "Thus says the king, 'Is it peace?'" Jehu answered, "What have you to do with peace? Fall in behind me." 20Again the sentinel reported, "He reached them, but he is not coming back. It looks like the driving of Jehu son of Nimshi; for he drives like a maniac."

21 Joram said, "Get ready." And they got his chariot ready. Then King Joram of Israel and King Ahaziah of Judah set out, each in his chariot, and went to meet Jehu; they met him at the property of Naboth the Jezreelite. 22When Joram saw Jehu, he said, "Is it peace, Jehu?" He answered, "What peace can there be, so long as the many whoredoms and sorceries of your mother Jezebel continue?" 23Then Joram reined about and fled, saying to Ahaziah, "Treason, Ahaziah!" 24Jehu drew his bow with all his strength, and shot Joram between the shoulders, so that the arrow pierced his heart; and he sank in his chariot. 25Jehu said to his aide Bidkar, "Lift him out, and throw him on the plot of ground belonging to Naboth the Jezreelite; for remember, when you and I rode side by side behind his father Ahab how the LORD uttered this oracle against him: 26'For the blood of Naboth and for the blood of his children that I saw yesterday, says the LORD, I swear I will repay you on this very plot of ground.' Now therefore lift him out and throw him on the plot of ground, in accordance with the word of the LORD."

Ahaziah of Judah Killed

27 When King Ahaziah of Judah saw this, he fled in the direction of Beth-haggan. Jehu pursued him, saying, "Shoot him also!" And they shot him*a* in the chariot at the ascent to Gur, which is by Ibleam. Then he fled to Megiddo, and died there. 28His officers carried him in a chariot to Jerusalem, and buried him in his tomb with his ancestors in the city of David.

29 In the eleventh year of Joram son of Ahab, Ahaziah began to reign over Judah.

Jezebel's Violent Death

30 When Jehu came to Jezreel, Jezebel heard of it; she painted her eyes, and adorned her head, and looked out of the window. 31As Jehu entered the gate, she said, "Is it peace, Zimri, murderer of your master?" 32He looked up to the window and said, "Who is on my side? Who?" Two or three eunuchs looked out at him. 33He said, "Throw her down." So they threw her down; some of her blood spattered on the wall and on the horses, which trampled on her. 34Then he went in and ate and drank; he said, "See to that cursed woman and bury her; for she is a king's daughter." 35But when they went to bury her, they found no more of her than the skull and the feet and the palms of her hands. 36When they came back and told him, he said, "This is the word of the LORD, which he spoke by his servant Elijah the Tishbite, 'In the territory of Jezreel the dogs shall eat the flesh of Jezebel; 37the corpse of Jezebel shall be like dung on the field in the territory of Jezreel, so that no one can say, This is Jezebel.'"

Massacre of Ahab's Descendants

10 Now Ahab had seventy sons in Samaria. So Jehu wrote letters and sent them to Samaria, to the rulers of Jezreel,*b* to the elders, and to the guardians of the sons of*c* Ahab, saying, 2"Since your master's sons are with you and you have at your disposal chariots and horses, a fortified city, and weapons,

---

a Syr Vg Compare Gk: Heb lacks *and they shot him*   *b* Or *of the city*; Vg Compare Gk   *c* Gk: Heb lacks *of the sons of*

³select the son of your master who is the best qualified, set him on his father's throne, and fight for your master's house." ⁴But they were utterly terrified and said, "Look, two kings could not withstand him; how then can we stand?" ⁵So the steward of the palace, and the governor of the city, along with the elders and the guardians, sent word to Jehu: "We are your servants; we will do anything you say. We will not make anyone king; do whatever you think right." ⁶Then he wrote them a second letter, saying, "If you are on my side, and if you are ready to obey me, take the heads of your master's sons and come to me at Jezreel tomorrow at this time." Now the king's sons, seventy persons, were with the leaders of the city, who were charged with their upbringing. ⁷When the letter reached them, they took the king's sons and killed them, seventy persons; they put their heads in baskets and sent them to him at Jezreel. ⁸When the messenger came and told him, "They have brought the heads of the king's sons," he said, "Lay them in two heaps at the entrance of the gate until the morning." ⁹Then in the morning when he went out, he stood and said to all the people, "You are innocent. It was I who conspired against my master and killed him; but who struck down all these? ¹⁰Know then that there shall fall to the earth nothing of the word of the LORD, which the LORD spoke concerning the house of Ahab; for the LORD has done what he said through his servant Elijah." ¹¹So Jehu killed all who were left of the house of Ahab in Jezreel, all his leaders, close friends, and priests, until he left him no survivor.

12 Then he set out and went to Samaria. On the way, when he was at Beth-eked of the Shepherds, ¹³Jehu met relatives of King Ahaziah of Judah and said, "Who are you?" They answered, "We are kin of Ahaziah; we have come down to visit the royal princes and the sons of the queen mother." ¹⁴He said, "Take them alive." They took them alive, and slaughtered them at the pit of Beth-eked, forty-two in all; he spared none of them.

15 When he left there, he met Jehonadab son of Rechab coming to meet him; he greeted him, and said to him, "Is your heart as true to mine as mine is to yours?"ᵃ Jehonadab answered, "It is." Jehu said,ᵇ "If it is, give me your hand." So he gave him his hand. Jehu took him up with him into the chariot. ¹⁶He said, "Come with me, and see my zeal for the LORD." So heᶜ had him ride in his chariot. ¹⁷When he came to Samaria, he killed all who were left to Ahab in Samaria, until he had wiped them out, according to the word of the LORD that he spoke to Elijah.

Slaughter of Worshipers of Baal

18 Then Jehu assembled all the people and said to them, "Ahab offered Baal small service; but Jehu will offer much more. ¹⁹Now therefore summon to me all the prophets of Baal, all his worshipers, and all his priests; let none be missing, for I have a great sacrifice to offer to Baal; whoever is missing shall not live." But Jehu was acting with cunning in order to destroy the worshipers of Baal. ²⁰Jehu decreed, "Sanctify a solemn assembly for Baal." So they proclaimed it. ²¹Jehu sent word throughout all Israel; all the worshipers of Baal came, so that there was no one left who did not come. They entered the temple of Baal, until the temple of Baal was filled from wall to wall. ²²He said to the keeper of the wardrobe, "Bring out the vestments for all the worshipers of Baal." So he brought out the vestments for them. ²³Then Jehu entered the temple of Baal with Jehonadab son of Rechab; he said to the worshipers of Baal, "Search and see that there is no worshiper of the LORD here among you, but only worshipers of Baal." ²⁴Then they proceeded to offer sacrifices and burnt offerings.

Now Jehu had stationed eighty men outside, saying, "Whoever allows any of those to escape whom I deliver into your hands shall forfeit his life." ²⁵As soon as he had finished presenting the burnt offering, Jehu said to the guards and to the officers, "Come in and kill them; let no one escape." So they put them to

---

a Gk: Heb *Is it right with your heart, as my heart is with your heart?*   *b* Gk: Heb lacks *Jehu said*   *c* Gk Syr Tg: Heb *they* the sword. The guards and the officers threw them out, and then went into the citadel of the temple of Baal. 26They brought out the pillar*a* that was in the temple of Baal, and burned it. 27Then they demolished the pillar of Baal, and destroyed the temple of Baal, and made it a latrine to this day.

28 Thus Jehu wiped out Baal from Israel. 29But Jehu did not turn aside from the sins of Jeroboam son of Nebat, which he caused Israel to commit—the golden calves that were in Bethel and in Dan. 30The LORD said to Jehu, "Because you have done well in carrying out what I consider right, and in accordance with all that was in my heart have dealt with the house of Ahab, your sons of the fourth generation shall sit on the throne of Israel." 31But Jehu was not careful to follow the law of the LORD the God of Israel with all his heart; he did not turn from the sins of Jeroboam, which he caused Israel to commit.

Death of Jehu

32 In those days the LORD began to trim off parts of Israel. Hazael defeated them throughout the territory of Israel: 33from the Jordan eastward, all the land of Gilead, the Gadites, the Reubenites, and the Manassites, from Aroer, which is by the Wadi Arnon, that is, Gilead and Bashan. 34Now the rest of the acts of Jehu, all that he did, and all his power, are they not written in the Book of the Annals of the Kings of Israel? 35So Jehu slept with his ancestors, and they buried him in Samaria. His son Jehoahaz succeeded him. 36The time that Jehu reigned over Israel in Samaria was twenty-eight years.

Athaliah Reigns over Judah

11 Now when Athaliah, Ahaziah's mother, saw that her son was dead, she set about to destroy all the royal family. 2But Jehosheba, King Joram's daughter, Ahaziah's sister, took Joash son of Ahaziah, and stole him away from among the king's children who were about to be killed; she put*b* him and his nurse in a bedroom. Thus she*c* hid him from Atha-

liah, so that he was not killed; 3he remained with her six years, hidden in the house of the LORD, while Athaliah reigned over the land.

Jehoiada Anoints the Child Joash

4 But in the seventh year Jehoiada summoned the captains of the Carites and of the guards and had them come to him in the house of the LORD. He made a covenant with them and put them under oath in the house of the LORD; then he showed them the king's son. 5He commanded them, "This is what you are to do: one-third of you, those who go off duty on the sabbath and guard the king's house 6(another third being at the gate Sur and a third at the gate behind the guards), shall guard the palace; 7and your two divisions that come on duty in force on the sabbath and guard the house of the LORD*d* 8shall surround the king, each with weapons in hand; and whoever approaches the ranks is to be killed. Be with the king in his comings and goings."

9 The captains did according to all that the priest Jehoiada commanded; each brought his men who were to go off duty on the sabbath, with those who were to come on duty on the sabbath, and came to the priest Jehoiada. 10The priest delivered to the captains the spears and shields that had been King David's, which were in the house of the LORD; 11the guards stood, every man with his weapons in his hand, from the south side of the house to the north side of the house, around the altar and the house, to guard the king on every side. 12Then he brought out the king's son, put the crown on him, and gave him the covenant;*e* they proclaimed him king, and anointed him; they clapped their hands and shouted, "Long live the king!"

Death of Athaliah

13 When Athaliah heard the noise of the guard and of the people, she went into the house of the LORD to the people; 14when she looked, there was the king standing by the pillar, according to custom, with the captains and

a Gk Vg Syr Tg: Heb *pillars*   *b* With 2 Chr 22.11: Heb lacks *she put*   *c* Gk Syr Vg Compare 2 Chr 22.11: Heb *they*   *d* Heb *the LORD to the king*   *e* Or *treaty* or *testimony*; Heb *eduth* the trumpeters beside the king, and all the people of the land rejoicing and blowing trumpets. Athaliah tore her clothes and cried, "Treason! Treason!" [15]Then the priest Jehoiada commanded the captains who were set over the army, "Bring her out between the ranks, and kill with the sword anyone who follows her." For the priest said, "Let her not be killed in the house of the LORD." [16]So they laid hands on her; she went through the horses' entrance to the king's house, and there she was put to death.

17 Jehoiada made a covenant between the LORD and the king and people, that they should be the LORD's people; also between the king and the people. [18]Then all the people of the land went to the house of Baal, and tore it down; his altars and his images they broke in pieces, and they killed Mattan, the priest of Baal, before the altars. The priest posted guards over the house of the LORD. [19]He took the captains, the Carites, the guards, and all the people of the land; then they brought the king down from the house of the LORD, marching through the gate of the guards to the king's house. He took his seat on the throne of the kings. [20]So all the people of the land rejoiced; and the city was quiet after Athaliah had been killed with the sword at the king's house.

21 [a] Jehoash [b] was seven years old when he began to reign.

The Temple Repaired

12 In the seventh year of Jehu, Jehoash began to reign; he reigned forty years in Jerusalem. His mother's name was Zibiah of Beer-sheba. [2]Jehoash did what was right in the sight of the LORD all his days, because the priest Jehoiada instructed him. [3]Nevertheless the high places were not taken away; the people continued to sacrifice and make offerings on the high places.

4 Jehoash said to the priests, "All the money offered as sacred donations that is brought into the house of the LORD, the money for which each person is assessed—the money

from the assessment of persons—and the money from the voluntary offerings brought into the house of the LORD, [5]let the priests receive from each of the donors; and let them repair the house wherever any need of repairs is discovered." [6]But by the twenty-third year of King Jehoash the priests had made no repairs on the house. [7]Therefore King Jehoash summoned the priest Jehoiada with the other priests and said to them, "Why are you not repairing the house? Now therefore do not accept any more money from your donors but hand it over for the repair of the house." [8]So the priests agreed that they would neither accept more money from the people nor repair the house.

9 Then the priest Jehoiada took a chest, made a hole in its lid, and set it beside the altar on the right side as one entered the house of the LORD; the priests who guarded the threshold put in it all the money that was brought into the house of the LORD. [10]Whenever they saw that there was a great deal of money in the chest, the king's secretary and the high priest went up, counted the money that was found in the house of the LORD, and tied it up in bags. [11]They would give the money that was weighed out into the hands of the workers who had the oversight of the house of the LORD; then they paid it out to the carpenters and the builders who worked on the house of the LORD, [12]to the masons and the stonecutters, as well as to buy timber and quarried stone for making repairs on the house of the LORD, as well as for any outlay for repairs of the house. [13]But for the house of the LORD no basins of silver, snuffers, bowls, trumpets, or any vessels of gold, or of silver, were made from the money that was brought into the house of the LORD, [14]for that was given to the workers who were repairing the house of the LORD with it. [15]They did not ask an accounting from those into whose hand they delivered the money to pay out to the workers, for they dealt honestly. [16]The money from the guilt offerings and the money from the sin offerings was not brought

---

a Ch 12.1 in Heb   *b* Another spelling is *Joash*; see verse 19 into the house of the LORD; it belonged to the priests.

Hazael Threatens Jerusalem

17 At that time King Hazael of Aram went up, fought against Gath, and took it. But when Hazael set his face to go up against Jerusalem, 18King Jehoash of Judah took all the votive gifts that Jehoshaphat, Jehoram, and Ahaziah, his ancestors, the kings of Judah, had dedicated, as well as his own votive gifts, all the gold that was found in the treasuries of the house of the LORD and of the king's house, and sent these to King Hazael of Aram. Then Hazael withdrew from Jerusalem.

Death of Joash

19 Now the rest of the acts of Joash, and all that he did, are they not written in the Book of the Annals of the Kings of Judah? 20His servants arose, devised a conspiracy, and killed Joash in the house of Millo, on the way that goes down to Silla. 21It was Jozacar son of Shimeath and Jehozabad son of Shomer, his servants, who struck him down, so that he died. He was buried with his ancestors in the city of David; then his son Amaziah succeeded him.

Jehoahaz Reigns over Israel

13 In the twenty-third year of King Joash son of Ahaziah of Judah, Jehoahaz son of Jehu began to reign over Israel in Samaria; he reigned seventeen years. 2He did what was evil in the sight of the LORD, and followed the sins of Jeroboam son of Nebat, which he caused Israel to sin; he did not depart from them. 3The anger of the LORD was kindled against Israel, so that he gave them repeatedly into the hand of King Hazael of Aram, then into the hand of Ben-hadad son of Hazael. 4But Jehoahaz entreated the LORD, and the LORD heeded him; for he saw the oppression of Israel, how the king of Aram oppressed them. 5Therefore the LORD gave Israel a savior, so that they escaped from the hand

of the Arameans; and the people of Israel lived in their homes as formerly. 6Nevertheless they did not depart from the sins of the house of Jeroboam, which he caused Israel to sin, but walked*a* in them; the sacred pole*b* also remained in Samaria. 7So Jehoahaz was left with an army of not more than fifty horsemen, ten chariots and ten thousand footmen; for the king of Aram had destroyed them and made them like the dust at threshing. 8Now the rest of the acts of Jehoahaz and all that he did, including his might, are they not written in the Book of the Annals of the Kings of Israel? 9So Jehoahaz slept with his ancestors, and they buried him in Samaria; then his son Joash succeeded him.

Jehoash Reigns over Israel

10 In the thirty-seventh year of King Joash of Judah, Jehoash son of Jehoahaz began to reign over Israel in Samaria; he reigned sixteen years. 11He also did what was evil in the sight of the LORD; he did not depart from all the sins of Jeroboam son of Nebat, which he caused Israel to sin, but he walked in them. 12Now the rest of the acts of Joash, and all that he did, as well as the might with which he fought against King Amaziah of Judah, are they not written in the Book of the Annals of the Kings of Israel? 13So Joash slept with his ancestors, and Jeroboam sat upon his throne; Joash was buried in Samaria with the kings of Israel.

Death of Elisha

14 Now when Elisha had fallen sick with the illness of which he was to die, King Joash of Israel went down to him, and wept before him, crying, "My father, my father! The chariots of Israel and its horsemen!" 15Elisha said to him, "Take a bow and arrows"; so he took a bow and arrows. 16Then he said to the king of Israel, "Draw the bow"; and he drew it. Elisha laid his hands on the king's hands. 17Then he said, "Open the window eastward"; and he opened it. Elisha said, "Shoot"; and he shot. Then he said, "The LORD's arrow of vic-

a Gk Syr Tg Vg: Heb *he walked*   *b* Heb *Asherah*

tory, the arrow of victory over Aram! For you shall fight the Arameans in Aphek until you have made an end of them." ¹⁸He continued, "Take the arrows"; and he took them. He said to the king of Israel, "Strike the ground with them"; he struck three times, and stopped. ¹⁹Then the man of God was angry with him, and said, "You should have struck five or six times; then you would have struck down Aram until you had made an end of it, but now you will strike down Aram only three times."

20 So Elisha died, and they buried him. Now bands of Moabites used to invade the land in the spring of the year. ²¹As a man was being buried, a marauding band was seen and the man was thrown into the grave of Elisha; as soon as the man touched the bones of Elisha, he came to life and stood on his feet.

Israel Recaptures Cities from Aram

22 Now King Hazael of Aram oppressed Israel all the days of Jehoahaz. ²³But the LORD was gracious to them and had compassion on them; he turned toward them, because of his covenant with Abraham, Isaac, and Jacob, and would not destroy them; nor has he banished them from his presence until now.

24 When King Hazael of Aram died, his son Ben-hadad succeeded him. ²⁵Then Jehoash son of Jehoahaz took again from Ben-hadad son of Hazael the towns that he had taken from his father Jehoahaz in war. Three times Joash defeated him and recovered the towns of Israel.

Amaziah Reigns over Judah

14 In the second year of King Joash son of Joahaz of Israel, King Amaziah son of Joash of Judah, began to reign. ²He was twenty-five years old when he began to reign, and he reigned twenty-nine years in Jerusalem. His mother's name was Jehoaddin of Jerusalem. ³He did what was right in the sight of the LORD, yet not like his ancestor David; in all things he did as his father Joash had done. ⁴But the high places were not removed; the people still sacrificed and made offerings on the high places. ⁵As soon as the royal power was

firmly in his hand he killed his servants who had murdered his father the king. ⁶But he did not put to death the children of the murderers; according to what is written in the book of the law of Moses, where the LORD commanded, "The parents shall not be put to death for the children, or the children be put to death for the parents; but all shall be put to death for their own sins."

7 He killed ten thousand Edomites in the Valley of Salt and took Sela by storm; he called it Jokthe-el, which is its name to this day.

8 Then Amaziah sent messengers to King Jehoash son of Jehoahaz, son of Jehu, of Israel, saying, "Come, let us look one another in the face." ⁹King Jehoash of Israel sent word to King Amaziah of Judah, "A thornbush on Lebanon sent to a cedar on Lebanon, saying, 'Give your daughter to my son for a wife'; but a wild animal of Lebanon passed by and trampled down the thornbush. ¹⁰You have indeed defeated Edom, and your heart has lifted you up. Be content with your glory, and stay at home; for why should you provoke trouble so that you fall, you and Judah with you?"

11 But Amaziah would not listen. So King Jehoash of Israel went up; he and King Amaziah of Judah faced one another in battle at Beth-shemesh, which belongs to Judah. ¹²Judah was defeated by Israel; everyone fled home. ¹³King Jehoash of Israel captured King Amaziah of Judah son of Jehoash, son of Ahaziah, at Beth-shemesh; he came to Jerusalem, and broke down the wall of Jerusalem from the Ephraim Gate to the Corner Gate, a distance of four hundred cubits. ¹⁴He seized all the gold and silver, and all the vessels that were found in the house of the LORD and in the treasuries of the king's house, as well as hostages; then he returned to Samaria.

15 Now the rest of the acts that Jehoash did, his might, and how he fought with King Amaziah of Judah, are they not written in the Book of the Annals of the Kings of Israel? ¹⁶Jehoash slept with his ancestors, and was buried in Samaria with the kings of Israel; then his son Jeroboam succeeded him.

17 King Amaziah son of Joash of Judah

lived fifteen years after the death of King Jehoash son of Jehoahaz of Israel. 18Now the rest of the deeds of Amaziah, are they not written in the Book of the Annals of the Kings of Judah? 19They made a conspiracy against him in Jerusalem, and he fled to Lachish. But they sent after him to Lachish, and killed him there. 20They brought him on horses; he was buried in Jerusalem with his ancestors in the city of David. 21All the people of Judah took Azariah, who was sixteen years old, and made him king to succeed his father Amaziah. 22He rebuilt Elath and restored it to Judah, after King Amaziah*a* slept with his ancestors.

Jeroboam II Reigns over Israel

23 In the fifteenth year of King Amaziah son of Joash of Judah, King Jeroboam son of Joash of Israel began to reign in Samaria; he reigned forty-one years. 24He did what was evil in the sight of the LORD; he did not depart from all the sins of Jeroboam son of Nebat, which he caused Israel to sin. 25He restored the border of Israel from Lebo-hamath as far as the Sea of the Arabah, according to the word of the LORD, the God of Israel, which he spoke by his servant Jonah son of Amittai, the prophet, who was from Gath-hepher. 26For the LORD saw that the distress of Israel was very bitter; there was no one left, bond or free, and no one to help Israel. 27But the LORD had not said that he would blot out the name of Israel from under heaven, so he saved them by the hand of Jeroboam son of Joash.

28 Now the rest of the acts of Jeroboam, and all that he did, and his might, how he fought, and how he recovered for Israel Damascus and Hamath, which had belonged to Judah, are they not written in the Book of Annals of the Kings of Israel? 29Jeroboam slept with his ancestors, the kings of Israel; his son Zechariah succeeded him.

Azariah Reigns over Judah

15 In the twenty-seventh year of King Jeroboam of Israel King Azariah son of Amaziah of Judah began to reign. 2He was sixteen years old when he began to reign, and he reigned fifty-two years in Jerusalem. His mother's name was Jecoliah of Jerusalem. 3He did what was right in the sight of the LORD, just as his father Amaziah had done. 4Nevertheless the high places were not taken away; the people still sacrificed and made offerings on the high places. 5The LORD struck the king, so that he was leprous*b* to the day of his death, and lived in a separate house. Jotham the king's son was in charge of the palace, governing the people of the land. 6Now the rest of the acts of Azariah, and all that he did, are they not written in the Book of the Annals of the Kings of Judah? 7Azariah slept with his ancestors; they buried him with his ancestors in the city of David; his son Jotham succeeded him.

Zechariah Reigns over Israel

8 In the thirty-eighth year of King Azariah of Judah, Zechariah son of Jeroboam reigned over Israel in Samaria six months. 9He did what was evil in the sight of the LORD, as his ancestors had done. He did not depart from the sins of Jeroboam son of Nebat, which he caused Israel to sin. 10Shallum son of Jabesh conspired against him, and struck him down in public and killed him, and reigned in place of him. 11Now the rest of the deeds of Zechariah are written in the Book of the Annals of the Kings of Israel. 12This was the promise of the LORD that he gave to Jehu, "Your sons shall sit on the throne of Israel to the fourth generation." And so it happened.

Shallum Reigns over Israel

13 Shallum son of Jabesh began to reign in the thirty-ninth year of King Uzziah of Judah; he reigned one month in Samaria. 14Then Menahem son of Gadi came up from Tirzah and came to Samaria; he struck down Shallum son of Jabesh in Samaria and killed him; he reigned in place of him. 15Now the rest of the deeds of Shallum, including the conspiracy that he made, are written in the Book of the

---

a Heb *the king*   *b* A term for several skin diseases; precise meaning uncertain

Annals of the Kings of Israel. 16At that time Menahem sacked Tiphsah, all who were in it and its territory from Tirzah on; because they did not open it to him, he sacked it. He ripped open all the pregnant women in it.

Menahem Reigns over Israel

17 In the thirty-ninth year of King Azariah of Judah, Menahem son of Gadi began to reign over Israel; he reigned ten years in Samaria. 18He did what was evil in the sight of the LORD; he did not depart all his days from any of the sins of Jeroboam son of Nebat, which he caused Israel to sin. 19King Pul of Assyria came against the land; Menahem gave Pul a thousand talents of silver, so that he might help him confirm his hold on the royal power. 20Menahem exacted the money from Israel, that is, from all the wealthy, fifty shekels of silver from each one, to give to the king of Assyria. So the king of Assyria turned back, and did not stay there in the land. 21Now the rest of the deeds of Menahem, and all that he did, are they not written in the Book of the Annals of the Kings of Israel? 22Menahem slept with his ancestors, and his son Pekahiah succeeded him.

Pekahiah Reigns over Israel

23 In the fiftieth year of King Azariah of Judah, Pekahiah son of Menahem began to reign over Israel in Samaria; he reigned two years. 24He did what was evil in the sight of the LORD; he did not turn away from the sins of Jeroboam son of Nebat, which he caused Israel to sin. 25Pekah son of Remaliah, his captain, conspired against him with fifty of the Gileadites, and attacked him in Samaria, in the citadel of the palace along with Argob and Arieh; he killed him, and reigned in place of him. 26Now the rest of the deeds of Pekahiah, and all that he did, are written in the Book of the Annals of the Kings of Israel.

Pekah Reigns over Israel

27 In the fifty-second year of King Azariah of Judah, Pekah son of Remaliah began to reign over Israel in Samaria; he reigned twen-

ty years. 28He did what was evil in the sight of the LORD; he did not depart from the sins of Jeroboam son of Nebat, which he caused Israel to sin.

29 In the days of King Pekah of Israel, King Tiglath-pileser of Assyria came and captured Ijon, Abel-beth-maacah, Janoah, Kedesh, Hazor, Gilead, and Galilee, all the land of Naphtali; and he carried the people captive to Assyria. 30Then Hoshea son of Elah made a conspiracy against Pekah son of Remaliah, attacked him, and killed him; he reigned in place of him, in the twentieth year of Jotham son of Uzziah. 31Now the rest of the acts of Pekah, and all that he did, are written in the Book of the Annals of the Kings of Israel.

Jotham Reigns over Judah

32 In the second year of King Pekah son of Remaliah of Israel, King Jotham son of Uzziah of Judah began to reign. 33He was twenty-five years old when he began to reign and reigned sixteen years in Jerusalem. His mother's name was Jerusha daughter of Zadok. 34He did what was right in the sight of the LORD, just as his father Uzziah had done. 35Nevertheless the high places were not removed; the people still sacrificed and made offerings on the high places. He built the upper gate of the house of the LORD. 36Now the rest of the acts of Jotham, and all that he did, are they not written in the Book of the Annals of the Kings of Judah? 37In those days the LORD began to send King Rezin of Aram and Pekah son of Remaliah against Judah. 38Jotham slept with his ancestors, and was buried with his ancestors in the city of David, his ancestor; his son Ahaz succeeded him.

Ahaz Reigns over Judah

16 In the seventeenth year of Pekah son of Remaliah, King Ahaz son of Jotham of Judah began to reign. 2Ahaz was twenty years old when he began to reign; he reigned sixteen years in Jerusalem. He did not do what was right in the sight of the LORD his God, as his ancestor David had done, 3but he walked in the way of the kings of Israel. He even made

his son pass through fire, according to the abominable practices of the nations whom the LORD drove out before the people of Israel. 4He sacrificed and made offerings on the high places, on the hills, and under every green tree.

5 Then King Rezin of Aram and King Pekah son of Remaliah of Israel came up to wage war on Jerusalem; they besieged Ahaz but could not conquer him. 6At that time the king of Edom*a* recovered Elath for Edom,*b* and drove the Judeans from Elath; and the Edomites came to Elath, where they live to this day. 7Ahaz sent messengers to King Tiglath-pileser of Assyria, saying, "I am your servant and your son. Come up, and rescue me from the hand of the king of Aram and from the hand of the king of Israel, who are attacking me." 8Ahaz also took the silver and gold found in the house of the LORD and in the treasures of the king's house, and sent a present to the king of Assyria. 9The king of Assyria listened to him; the king of Assyria marched up against Damascus, and took it, carrying its people captive to Kir; then he killed Rezin.

10 When King Ahaz went to Damascus to meet King Tiglath-pileser of Assyria, he saw the altar that was at Damascus. King Ahaz sent to the priest Uriah a model of the altar, and its pattern, exact in all its details. 11The priest Uriah built the altar; in accordance with all that King Ahaz had sent from Damascus, just so did the priest Uriah build it, before King Ahaz arrived from Damascus. 12When the king came from Damascus, the king viewed the altar. Then the king drew near to the altar, went up on it, 13and offered his burnt offering and his grain offering, poured his drink offering, and dashed the blood of his offerings of well-being against the altar. 14The bronze altar that was before the LORD he removed from the front of the house, from the place between his altar and the house of the LORD, and put it on the north side of his altar. 15King Ahaz commanded the priest Uriah, saying, "Upon the great altar offer the morning burnt offering, and the evening grain offering, and the king's

burnt offering, and his grain offering, with the burnt offering of all the people of the land, their grain offering, and their drink offering; then dash against it all the blood of the burnt offering, and all the blood of the sacrifice; but the bronze altar shall be for me to inquire by." 16The priest Uriah did everything that King Ahaz commanded.

17 Then King Ahaz cut off the frames of the stands, and removed the laver from them; he removed the sea from the bronze oxen that were under it, and put it on a pediment of stone. 18The covered portal for use on the sabbath that had been built inside the palace, and the outer entrance for the king he removed from*c* the house of the LORD. He did this because of the king of Assyria. 19Now the rest of the acts of Ahaz that he did, are they not written in the Book of the Annals of the Kings of Judah? 20Ahaz slept with his ancestors, and was buried with his ancestors in the city of David; his son Hezekiah succeeded him.

Hoshea Reigns over Israel

17 In the twelfth year of King Ahaz of Judah, Hoshea son of Elah began to reign in Samaria over Israel; he reigned nine years. 2He did what was evil in the sight of the LORD, yet not like the kings of Israel who were before him. 3King Shalmaneser of Assyria came up against him; Hoshea became his vassal, and paid him tribute. 4But the king of Assyria found treachery in Hoshea; for he had sent messengers to King So of Egypt, and offered no tribute to the king of Assyria, as he had done year by year; therefore the king of Assyria confined him and imprisoned him.

Israel Carried Captive to Assyria

5 Then the king of Assyria invaded all the land and came to Samaria; for three years he besieged it. 6In the ninth year of Hoshea the king of Assyria captured Samaria; he carried the Israelites away to Assyria. He placed them in Halah, on the Habor, the river of Gozan, and in the cities of the Medes.

a Cn: Heb *King Rezin of Aram*   *b* Cn: Heb *Aram*   *c* Cn: Heb lacks *from*

7 This occurred because the people of Israel had sinned against the LORD their God, who had brought them up out of the land of Egypt from under the hand of Pharaoh king of Egypt. They had worshiped other gods 8and walked in the customs of the nations whom the LORD drove out before the people of Israel, and in the customs that the kings of Israel had introduced.*a* 9The people of Israel secretly did things that were not right against the LORD their God. They built for themselves high places at all their towns, from watchtower to fortified city; 10they set up for themselves pillars and sacred poles*b* on every high hill and under every green tree; 11there they made offerings on all the high places, as the nations did whom the LORD carried away before them. They did wicked things, provoking the LORD to anger; 12they served idols, of which the LORD had said to them, "You shall not do this." 13Yet the LORD warned Israel and Judah by every prophet and every seer, saying, "Turn from your evil ways and keep my commandments and my statutes, in accordance with all the law that I commanded your ancestors and that I sent to you by my servants the prophets." 14They would not listen but were stubborn, as their ancestors had been, who did not believe in the LORD their God. 15They despised his statutes, and his covenant that he made with their ancestors, and the warnings that he gave them. They went after false idols and became false; they followed the nations that were around them, concerning whom the LORD had commanded them that they should not do as they did. 16They rejected all the commandments of the LORD their God and made for themselves cast images of two calves; they made a sacred pole,*c* worshiped all the host of heaven, and served Baal. 17They made their sons and their daughters pass through fire; they used divination and augury; and they sold themselves to do evil in the sight of the LORD, provoking him to anger. 18Therefore the LORD was very angry with Israel and removed them

out of his sight; none was left but the tribe of Judah alone.

19 Judah also did not keep the commandments of the LORD their God but walked in the customs that Israel had introduced. 20The LORD rejected all the descendants of Israel; he punished them and gave them into the hand of plunderers, until he had banished them from his presence.

21 When he had torn Israel from the house of David, they made Jeroboam son of Nebat king. Jeroboam drove Israel from following the LORD and made them commit great sin. 22The people of Israel continued in all the sins that Jeroboam committed; they did not depart from them 23until the LORD removed Israel out of his sight, as he had foretold through all his servants the prophets. So Israel was exiled from their own land to Assyria until this day.

Assyria Resettles Samaria

24 The king of Assyria brought people from Babylon, Cuthah, Avva, Hamath, and Sepharvaim, and placed them in the cities of Samaria in place of the people of Israel; they took possession of Samaria, and settled in its cities. 25When they first settled there, they did not worship the LORD; therefore the LORD sent lions among them, which killed some of them. 26So the king of Assyria was told, "The nations that you have carried away and placed in the cities of Samaria do not know the law of the god of the land; therefore he has sent lions among them; they are killing them, because they do not know the law of the god of the land." 27Then the king of Assyria commanded, "Send there one of the priests whom you carried away from there; let him*d* go and live there, and teach them the law of the god of the land." 28So one of the priests whom they had carried away from Samaria came and lived in Bethel; he taught them how they should worship the LORD.

29 But every nation still made gods of its own and put them in the shrines of the high places that the people of Samaria had made,

a Meaning of Heb uncertain　　*b* Heb *Asherim*　　*c* Heb *Asherah*　　*d* Syr Vg: Heb *them* every nation in the cities in which they lived; ³⁰the people of Babylon made Succoth-be-noth, the people of Cuth made Nergal, the people of Hamath made Ashima; ³¹the Avvites made Nibhaz and Tartak; the Sepharvites burned their children in the fire to Adramme-lech and Anammelech, the gods of Sephar-vaim. ³²They also worshiped the LORD and appointed from among themselves all sorts of people as priests of the high places, who sac-rificed for them in the shrines of the high places. ³³So they worshiped the LORD but also served their own gods, after the manner of the nations from among whom they had been carried away. ³⁴To this day they continue to practice their former customs.

They do not worship the LORD and they do not follow the statutes or the ordinances or the law or the commandment that the LORD com-manded the children of Jacob, whom he named Israel. ³⁵The LORD had made a covenant with them and commanded them, "You shall not worship other gods or bow yourselves to them or serve them or sacrifice to them, ³⁶but you shall worship the LORD, who brought you out of the land of Egypt with great power and with an outstretched arm; you shall bow yourselves to him, and to him you shall sacrifice. ³⁷The statutes and the ordinances and the law and the commandment that he wrote for you, you shall always be careful to observe. You shall not worship other gods; ³⁸you shall not forget the covenant that I have made with you. You shall not worship other gods, ³⁹but you shall worship the LORD your God; he will deliver you out of the hand of all your enemies." ⁴⁰They would not listen, however, but they continued to prac-tice their former custom.

41 So these nations worshiped the LORD, but also served their carved images; to this day their children and their children's children con-tinue to do as their ancestors did.

Hezekiah's Reign over Judah

18 In the third year of King Hoshea son of Elah of Israel, Hezekiah son of King Ahaz of Judah began to reign. ²He was twenty-five years old when he began to reign; he reigned twenty-nine years in Jerusalem. His mother's name was Abi daughter of Zechari-ah. ³He did what was right in the sight of the LORD just as his ancestor David had done. ⁴He removed the high places, broke down the pil-lars, and cut down the sacred pole.ᵃ He broke in pieces the bronze serpent that Moses had made, for until those days the people of Isra-el had made offerings to it; it was called Ne-hushtan. ⁵He trusted in the LORD the God of Israel; so that there was no one like him among all the kings of Judah after him, or among those who were before him. ⁶For he held fast to the LORD; he did not depart from following him but kept the commandments that the LORD commanded Moses. ⁷The LORD was with him; wherever he went, he prospered. He rebelled against the king of Assyria and would not serve him. ⁸He attacked the Philistines as far as Gaza and its territory, from watchtower to fortified city.

9 In the fourth year of King Hezekiah, which was the seventh year of King Hoshea son of Elah of Israel, King Shalmaneser of As-syria came up against Samaria, besieged it, ¹⁰and at the end of three years, took it. In the sixth year of Hezekiah, which was the ninth year of King Hoshea of Israel, Samaria was taken. ¹¹The king of Assyria carried the Isra-elites away to Assyria, settled them in Halah, on the Habor, the river of Gozan, and in the cit-ies of the Medes, ¹²because they did not obey the voice of the LORD their God but trans-gressed his covenant—all that Moses the ser-vant of the LORD had commanded; they nei-ther listened nor obeyed.

Sennacherib Invades Judah

13 In the fourteenth year of King Hezeki-ah, King Sennacherib of Assyria came up against all the fortified cities of Judah and cap-tured them. ¹⁴King Hezekiah of Judah sent to the king of Assyria at Lachish, saying, "I have done wrong; withdraw from me; whatever you

a Heb *Asherah*

impose on me I will bear." The king of Assyria demanded of King Hezekiah of Judah three hundred talents of silver and thirty talents of gold. 15Hezekiah gave him all the silver that was found in the house of the LORD and in the treasuries of the king's house. 16At that time Hezekiah stripped the gold from the doors of the temple of the LORD, and from the doorposts that King Hezekiah of Judah had overlaid and gave it to the king of Assyria. 17The king of Assyria sent the Tartan, the Rabsaris, and the Rabshakeh with a great army from Lachish to King Hezekiah at Jerusalem. They went up and came to Jerusalem. When they arrived, they came and stood by the conduit of the upper pool, which is on the highway to the Fuller's Field. 18When they called for the king, there came out to them Eliakim son of Hilkiah, who was in charge of the palace, and Shebnah the secretary, and Joah son of Asaph, the recorder.

19 The Rabshakeh said to them, "Say to Hezekiah: Thus says the great king, the king of Assyria: On what do you base this confidence of yours? 20Do you think that mere words are strategy and power for war? On whom do you now rely, that you have rebelled against me? 21See, you are relying now on Egypt, that broken reed of a staff, which will pierce the hand of anyone who leans on it. Such is Pharaoh king of Egypt to all who rely on him. 22But if you say to me, 'We rely on the LORD our God,' is it not he whose high places and altars Hezekiah has removed, saying to Judah and to Jerusalem, 'You shall worship before this altar in Jerusalem'? 23Come now, make a wager with my master the king of Assyria: I will give you two thousand horses, if you are able on your part to set riders on them. 24How then can you repulse a single captain among the least of my master's servants, when you rely on Egypt for chariots and for horsemen? 25Moreover, is it without the LORD that I have come up against this place to destroy it? The LORD said to me, Go up against this land, and destroy it."

26 Then Eliakim son of Hilkiah, and Shebnah, and Joah said to the Rabshakeh, "Please speak to your servants in the Aramaic language, for we understand it; do not speak to us in the language of Judah within the hearing of the people who are on the wall." 27But the Rabshakeh said to them, "Has my master sent me to speak these words to your master and to you, and not to the people sitting on the wall, who are doomed with you to eat their own dung and to drink their own urine?"

28 Then the Rabshakeh stood and called out in a loud voice in the language of Judah, "Hear the word of the great king, the king of Assyria! 29Thus says the king: 'Do not let Hezekiah deceive you, for he will not be able to deliver you out of my hand. 30Do not let Hezekiah make you rely on the LORD by saying, The LORD will surely deliver us, and this city will not be given into the hand of the king of Assyria.' 31Do not listen to Hezekiah; for thus says the king of Assyria: 'Make your peace with me and come out to me; then every one of you will eat from your own vine and your own fig tree, and drink water from your own cistern, 32until I come and take you away to a land like your own land, a land of grain and wine, a land of bread and vineyards, a land of olive oil and honey, that you may live and not die. Do not listen to Hezekiah when he misleads you by saying, The LORD will deliver us. 33Has any of the gods of the nations ever delivered its land out of the hand of the king of Assyria? 34Where are the gods of Hamath and Arpad? Where are the gods of Sepharvaim, Hena, and Ivvah? Have they delivered Samaria out of my hand? 35Who among all the gods of the countries have delivered their countries out of my hand, that the LORD should deliver Jerusalem out of my hand?'"

36 But the people were silent and answered him not a word, for the king's command was, "Do not answer him." 37Then Eliakim son of Hilkiah, who was in charge of the palace, and Shebna the secretary, and Joah son of Asaph, the recorder, came to Hezekiah with their clothes torn and told him the words of the Rabshakeh.

Hezekiah Consults Isaiah

19 When King Hezekiah heard it, he tore his clothes, covered himself with sackcloth, and went into the house of the LORD. ²And he sent Eliakim, who was in charge of the palace, and Shebna the secretary, and the senior priests, covered with sackcloth, to the prophet Isaiah son of Amoz. ³They said to him, "Thus says Hezekiah, This day is a day of distress, of rebuke, and of disgrace; children have come to the birth, and there is no strength to bring them forth. ⁴It may be that the LORD your God heard all the words of the Rabshakeh, whom his master the king of Assyria has sent to mock the living God, and will rebuke the words that the LORD your God has heard; therefore lift up your prayer for the remnant that is left." ⁵When the servants of King Hezekiah came to Isaiah, ⁶Isaiah said to them, "Say to your master, 'Thus says the LORD: Do not be afraid because of the words that you have heard, with which the servants of the king of Assyria have reviled me. ⁷I myself will put a spirit in him, so that he shall hear a rumor and return to his own land; I will cause him to fall by the sword in his own land.'"

Sennacherib's Threat

8 The Rabshakeh returned, and found the king of Assyria fighting against Libnah; for he had heard that the king had left Lachish. ⁹When the king*a* heard concerning King Tirhakah of Ethiopia,*b* "See, he has set out to fight against you," he sent messengers again to Hezekiah, saying, ¹⁰"Thus shall you speak to King Hezekiah of Judah: Do not let your God on whom you rely deceive you by promising that Jerusalem will not be given into the hand of the king of Assyria. ¹¹See, you have heard what the kings of Assyria have done to all lands, destroying them utterly. Shall you be delivered? ¹²Have the gods of the nations delivered them, the nations that my predecessors destroyed, Gozan, Haran, Rezeph, and the people of Eden who were in Telassar? ¹³Where is the king of Hamath, the king of Arpad, the king

of the city of Sepharvaim, the king of Hena, or the king of Ivvah?"

Hezekiah's Prayer

14 Hezekiah received the letter from the hand of the messengers and read it; then Hezekiah went up to the house of the LORD and spread it before the LORD. ¹⁵And Hezekiah prayed before the LORD, and said: "O LORD the God of Israel, who are enthroned above the cherubim, you are God, you alone, of all the kingdoms of the earth; you have made heaven and earth. ¹⁶Incline your ear, O LORD, and hear; open your eyes, O LORD, and see; hear the words of Sennacherib, which he has sent to mock the living God. ¹⁷Truly, O LORD, the kings of Assyria have laid waste the nations and their lands, ¹⁸and have hurled their gods into the fire, though they were no gods but the work of human hands—wood and stone—and so they were destroyed. ¹⁹So now, O LORD our God, save us, I pray you, from his hand, so that all the kingdoms of the earth may know that you, O LORD, are God alone."

20 Then Isaiah son of Amoz sent to Hezekiah, saying, "Thus says the LORD, the God of Israel: I have heard your prayer to me about King Sennacherib of Assyria. ²¹This is the word that the LORD has spoken concerning him:

> She despises you, she scorns you—
>   virgin daughter Zion;
> she tosses her head—behind your back,
>   daughter Jerusalem.

22 "Whom have you mocked and reviled?
>   Against whom have you raised your
>   voice
> and haughtily lifted your eyes?
>   Against the Holy One of Israel!
23 By your messengers you have mocked
>   the Lord,
>   and you have said, 'With my many
>   chariots
> I have gone up the heights of the
>   mountains,

a Heb he   b Or Nubia; Heb Cush

to the far recesses of Lebanon;
I felled its tallest cedars,
    its choicest cypresses;
I entered its farthest retreat,
    its densest forest.
24 I dug wells
    and drank foreign waters,
I dried up with the sole of my foot
    all the streams of Egypt.'

25 "Have you not heard
    that I determined it long ago?
I planned from days of old
    what now I bring to pass,
that you should make fortified cities
    crash into heaps of ruins,
26 while their inhabitants, shorn of
        strength,
    are dismayed and confounded;
they have become like plants of the field
    and like tender grass,
like grass on the housetops,
    blighted before it is grown.

27 "But I know your rising[a] and your
        sitting,
    your going out and coming in,
    and your raging against me.
28 Because you have raged against me
    and your arrogance has come to my
        ears,
I will put my hook in your nose
    and my bit in your mouth;
I will turn you back on the way
    by which you came.

29 "And this shall be the sign for you: This year you shall eat what grows of itself, and in the second year what springs from that; then in the third year sow, reap, plant vineyards, and eat their fruit. 30The surviving remnant of the house of Judah shall again take root downward, and bear fruit upward; 31for from Jerusalem a remnant shall go out, and from Mount Zion a band of survivors. The zeal of the LORD of hosts will do this.

32 "Therefore thus says the LORD concerning the king of Assyria: He shall not come into this city, shoot an arrow there, come before it with a shield, or cast up a siege ramp against it. 33By the way that he came, by the same he shall return; he shall not come into this city, says the LORD. 34For I will defend this city to save it, for my own sake and for the sake of my servant David."

Sennacherib's Defeat and Death

35 That very night the angel of the LORD set out and struck down one hundred eighty-five thousand in the camp of the Assyrians; when morning dawned, they were all dead bodies. 36Then King Sennacherib of Assyria left, went home, and lived at Nineveh. 37As he was worshiping in the house of his god Nisroch, his sons Adrammelech and Sharezer killed him with the sword, and they escaped into the land of Ararat. His son Esar-haddon succeeded him.

Hezekiah's Illness

20 In those days Hezekiah became sick and was at the point of death. The prophet Isaiah son of Amoz came to him, and said to him, "Thus says the LORD: Set your house in order, for you shall die; you shall not recover." 2Then Hezekiah turned his face to the wall and prayed to the LORD: 3"Remember now, O LORD, I implore you, how I have walked before you in faithfulness with a whole heart, and have done what is good in your sight." Hezekiah wept bitterly. 4Before Isaiah had gone out of the middle court, the word of the LORD came to him: 5"Turn back, and say to Hezekiah prince of my people, Thus says the LORD, the God of your ancestor David: I have heard your prayer, I have seen your tears; indeed, I will heal you; on the third day you shall go up to the house of the LORD. 6I will add fifteen years to your life. I will deliver you and this city out of the hand of the king of Assyria; I will defend this city for my own sake and for my servant David's sake." 7Then Isaiah said,

---

a Gk Compare Isa 37.27 Q Ms: MT lacks *rising*

"Bring a lump of figs. Let them take it and apply it to the boil, so that he may recover."

8 Hezekiah said to Isaiah, "What shall be the sign that the LORD will heal me, and that I shall go up to the house of the LORD on the third day?" ⁹Isaiah said, "This is the sign to you from the LORD, that the LORD will do the thing that he has promised: the shadow has now advanced ten intervals; shall it retreat ten intervals?" ¹⁰Hezekiah answered, "It is normal for the shadow to lengthen ten intervals; rather let the shadow retreat ten intervals." ¹¹The prophet Isaiah cried to the LORD; and he brought the shadow back the ten intervals, by which the sun*a* had declined on the dial of Ahaz.

Envoys from Babylon

12 At that time King Merodach-baladan son of Baladan of Babylon sent envoys with letters and a present to Hezekiah, for he had heard that Hezekiah had been sick. ¹³Hezekiah welcomed them;*b* he showed them all his treasure house, the silver, the gold, the spices, the precious oil, his armory, all that was found in his storehouses; there was nothing in his house or in all his realm that Hezekiah did not show them. ¹⁴Then the prophet Isaiah came to King Hezekiah, and said to him, "What did these men say? From where did they come to you?" Hezekiah answered, "They have come from a far country, from Babylon." ¹⁵He said, "What have they seen in your house?" Hezekiah answered, "They have seen all that is in my house; there is nothing in my storehouses that I did not show them."

16 Then Isaiah said to Hezekiah, "Hear the word of the LORD: ¹⁷Days are coming when all that is in your house, and that which your ancestors have stored up until this day, shall be carried to Babylon; nothing shall be left, says the LORD. ¹⁸Some of your own sons who are born to you shall be taken away; they shall be eunuchs in the palace of the king of Babylon." ¹⁹Then Hezekiah said to Isaiah, "The word of the LORD that you have spoken is good." For

he thought, "Why not, if there will be peace and security in my days?"

Death of Hezekiah

20 The rest of the deeds of Hezekiah, all his power, how he made the pool and the conduit and brought water into the city, are they not written in the Book of the Annals of the Kings of Judah? ²¹Hezekiah slept with his ancestors; and his son Manasseh succeeded him.

Manasseh Reigns over Judah

21 Manasseh was twelve years old when he began to reign; he reigned fifty-five years in Jerusalem. His mother's name was Hephzibah. ²He did what was evil in the sight of the LORD, following the abominable practices of the nations that the LORD drove out before the people of Israel. ³For he rebuilt the high places that his father Hezekiah had destroyed; he erected altars for Baal, made a sacred pole,*c* as King Ahab of Israel had done, worshiped all the host of heaven, and served them. ⁴He built altars in the house of the LORD, of which the LORD had said, "In Jerusalem I will put my name." ⁵He built altars for all the host of heaven in the two courts of the house of the LORD. ⁶He made his son pass through fire; he practiced soothsaying and augury, and dealt with mediums and with wizards. He did much evil in the sight of the LORD, provoking him to anger. ⁷The carved image of Asherah that he had made he set in the house of which the LORD said to David and to his son Solomon, "In this house, and in Jerusalem, which I have chosen out of all the tribes of Israel, I will put my name forever; ⁸I will not cause the feet of Israel to wander any more out of the land that I gave to their ancestors, if only they will be careful to do according to all that I have commanded them, and according to all the law that my servant Moses commanded them." ⁹But they did not listen; Manasseh misled them to do more evil than the nations had done that the LORD destroyed before the people of Israel.

a Syr See Isa 38.8 and Tg: Heb *it*   *b* Gk Vg Syr: Heb *When Hezekiah heard about them*   *c* Heb *Asherah*

10 The LORD said by his servants the prophets, 11"Because King Manasseh of Judah has committed these abominations, has done things more wicked than all that the Amorites did, who were before him, and has caused Judah also to sin with his idols; 12therefore thus says the LORD, the God of Israel, I am bringing upon Jerusalem and Judah such evil that the ears of everyone who hears of it will tingle. 13I will stretch over Jerusalem the measuring line for Samaria, and the plummet for the house of Ahab; I will wipe Jerusalem as one wipes a dish, wiping it and turning it upside down. 14I will cast off the remnant of my heritage, and give them into the hand of their enemies; they shall become a prey and a spoil to all their enemies, 15because they have done what is evil in my sight and have provoked me to anger, since the day their ancestors came out of Egypt, even to this day."

16 Moreover Manasseh shed very much innocent blood, until he had filled Jerusalem from one end to another, besides the sin that he caused Judah to sin so that they did what was evil in the sight of the LORD.

17 Now the rest of the acts of Manasseh, all that he did, and the sin that he committed, are they not written in the Book of the Annals of the Kings of Judah? 18Manasseh slept with his ancestors, and was buried in the garden of his house, in the garden of Uzza. His son Amon succeeded him.

Amon Reigns over Judah

19 Amon was twenty-two years old when he began to reign; he reigned two years in Jerusalem. His mother's name was Meshullemeth daughter of Haruz of Jotbah. 20He did what was evil in the sight of the LORD, as his father Manasseh had done. 21He walked in all the way in which his father walked, served the idols that his father served, and worshiped them; 22he abandoned the LORD, the God of his ancestors, and did not walk in the way of the LORD. 23The servants of Amon conspired against him, and killed the king in his house. 24But the people of the land killed all those who had conspired against King Amon, and

the people of the land made his son Josiah king in place of him. 25Now the rest of the acts of Amon that he did, are they not written in the Book of the Annals of the Kings of Judah? 26He was buried in his tomb in the garden of Uzza; then his son Josiah succeeded him.

Josiah Reigns over Judah

22 Josiah was eight years old when he began to reign; he reigned thirty-one years in Jerusalem. His mother's name was Jedidah daughter of Adaiah of Bozkath. 2He did what was right in the sight of the LORD, and walked in all the way of his father David; he did not turn aside to the right or to the left.

Hilkiah Finds the Book of the Law

3 In the eighteenth year of King Josiah, the king sent Shaphan son of Azaliah, son of Meshullam, the secretary, to the house of the LORD, saying, 4"Go up to the high priest Hilkiah, and have him count the entire sum of the money that has been brought into the house of the LORD, which the keepers of the threshold have collected from the people; 5let it be given into the hand of the workers who have the oversight of the house of the LORD; let them give it to the workers who are at the house of the LORD, repairing the house, 6that is, to the carpenters, to the builders, to the masons; and let them use it to buy timber and quarried stone to repair the house. 7But no accounting shall be asked from them for the money that is delivered into their hand, for they deal honestly."

8 The high priest Hilkiah said to Shaphan the secretary, "I have found the book of the law in the house of the LORD." When Hilkiah gave the book to Shaphan, he read it. 9Then Shaphan the secretary came to the king, and reported to the king, "Your servants have emptied out the money that was found in the house, and have delivered it into the hand of the workers who have oversight of the house of the LORD." 10Shaphan the secretary informed the king, "The priest Hilkiah has given me a book." Shaphan then read it aloud to the king.

11 When the king heard the words of the

book of the law, he tore his clothes. 12Then the king commanded the priest Hilkiah, Ahikam son of Shaphan, Achbor son of Micaiah, Shaphan the secretary, and the king's servant Asaiah, saying, 13"Go, inquire of the LORD for me, for the people, and for all Judah, concerning the words of this book that has been found; for great is the wrath of the LORD that is kindled against us, because our ancestors did not obey the words of this book, to do according to all that is written concerning us."

14 So the priest Hilkiah, Ahikam, Achbor, Shaphan, and Asaiah went to the prophetess Huldah the wife of Shallum son of Tikvah, son of Harhas, keeper of the wardrobe; she resided in Jerusalem in the Second Quarter, where they consulted her. 15She declared to them, "Thus says the LORD, the God of Israel: Tell the man who sent you to me, 16Thus says the LORD, I will indeed bring disaster on this place and on its inhabitants—all the words of the book that the king of Judah has read. 17Because they have abandoned me and have made offerings to other gods, so that they have provoked me to anger with all the work of their hands, therefore my wrath will be kindled against this place, and it will not be quenched. 18But as to the king of Judah, who sent you to inquire of the LORD, thus shall you say to him, Thus says the LORD, the God of Israel: Regarding the words that you have heard, 19because your heart was penitent, and you humbled yourself before the LORD, when you heard how I spoke against this place, and against its inhabitants, that they should become a desolation and a curse, and because you have torn your clothes and wept before me, I also have heard you, says the LORD. 20Therefore, I will gather you to your ancestors, and you shall be gathered to your grave in peace; your eyes shall not see all the disaster that I will bring on this place." They took the message back to the king.

Josiah's Reformation

23 Then the king directed that all the elders of Judah and Jerusalem should be gathered to him. 2The king went up to the house of the LORD, and with him went all the people of Judah, all the inhabitants of Jerusalem, the priests, the prophets, and all the people, both small and great; he read in their hearing all the words of the book of the covenant that had been found in the house of the LORD. 3The king stood by the pillar and made a covenant before the LORD, to follow the LORD, keeping his commandments, his decrees, and his statutes, with all his heart and all his soul, to perform the words of this covenant that were written in this book. All the people joined in the covenant.

4 The king commanded the high priest Hilkiah, the priests of the second order, and the guardians of the threshold, to bring out of the temple of the LORD all the vessels made for Baal, for Asherah, and for all the host of heaven; he burned them outside Jerusalem in the fields of the Kidron, and carried their ashes to Bethel. 5He deposed the idolatrous priests whom the kings of Judah had ordained to make offerings in the high places at the cities of Judah and around Jerusalem; those also who made offerings to Baal, to the sun, the moon, the constellations, and all the host of the heavens. 6He brought out the image of*a* Asherah from the house of the LORD, outside Jerusalem, to the Wadi Kidron, burned it at the Wadi Kidron, beat it to dust and threw the dust of it upon the graves of the common people. 7He broke down the houses of the male temple prostitutes that were in the house of the LORD, where the women did weaving for Asherah. 8He brought all the priests out of the towns of Judah, and defiled the high places where the priests had made offerings, from Geba to Beer-sheba; he broke down the high places of the gates that were at the entrance of the gate of Joshua the governor of the city, which were on the left at the gate of the city. 9The priests of the high places, however, did not come up to the altar of the LORD in Jerusalem, but ate unleavened bread among their kindred. 10He defiled Topheth, which is in the

a Heb lacks *image of*

valley of Ben-hinnom, so that no one would make a son or a daughter pass through fire as an offering to Molech. [11]He removed the horses that the kings of Judah had dedicated to the sun, at the entrance to the house of the LORD, by the chamber of the eunuch Nathan-melech, which was in the precincts;[a] then he burned the chariots of the sun with fire. [12]The altars on the roof of the upper chamber of Ahaz, which the kings of Judah had made, and the altars that Manasseh had made in the two courts of the house of the LORD, he pulled down from there and broke in pieces, and threw the rubble into the Wadi Kidron. [13]The king defiled the high places that were east of Jerusalem, to the south of the Mount of Destruction, which King Solomon of Israel had built for Astarte the abomination of the Sidonians, for Chemosh the abomination of Moab, and for Milcom the abomination of the Ammonites. [14]He broke the pillars in pieces, cut down the sacred poles,[b] and covered the sites with human bones.

15 Moreover, the altar at Bethel, the high place erected by Jeroboam son of Nebat, who caused Israel to sin—he pulled down that altar along with the high place. He burned the high place, crushing it to dust; he also burned the sacred pole.[c] [16]As Josiah turned, he saw the tombs there on the mount; and he sent and took the bones out of the tombs, and burned them on the altar, and defiled it, according to the word of the LORD that the man of God proclaimed,[d] when Jeroboam stood by the altar at the festival; he turned and looked up at the tomb of the man of God who had predicted these things. [17]Then he said, "What is that monument that I see?" The people of the city told him, "It is the tomb of the man of God who came from Judah and predicted these things that you have done against the altar at Bethel." [18]He said, "Let him rest; let no one move his bones." So they let his bones alone, with the bones of the prophet who came out of Samaria. [19]Moreover, Josiah removed all the shrines of the high places that were in the towns of Samaria, which kings of Israel had made, provoking the LORD to anger; he did to them just as he had done at Bethel. [20]He slaughtered on the altars all the priests of the high places who were there, and burned human bones on them. Then he returned to Jerusalem.

The Passover Celebrated

21 The king commanded all the people, "Keep the passover to the LORD your God as prescribed in this book of the covenant." [22]No such passover had been kept since the days of the judges who judged Israel, even during all the days of the kings of Israel and of the kings of Judah; [23]but in the eighteenth year of King Josiah this passover was kept to the LORD in Jerusalem.

24 Moreover Josiah put away the mediums, wizards, teraphim,[e] idols, and all the abominations that were seen in the land of Judah and in Jerusalem, so that he established the words of the law that were written in the book that the priest Hilkiah had found in the house of the LORD. [25]Before him there was no king like him, who turned to the LORD with all his heart, with all his soul, and with all his might, according to all the law of Moses; nor did any like him arise after him.

26 Still the LORD did not turn from the fierceness of his great wrath, by which his anger was kindled against Judah, because of all the provocations with which Manasseh had provoked him. [27]The LORD said, "I will remove Judah also out of my sight, as I have removed Israel; and I will reject this city that I have chosen, Jerusalem, and the house of which I said, My name shall be there."

Josiah Dies in Battle

28 Now the rest of the acts of Josiah, and all that he did, are they not written in the Book of the Annals of the Kings of Judah? [29]In his days Pharaoh Neco king of Egypt went up to the king of Assyria to the river Euphrates. King Josiah went to meet him; but when Pharaoh Neco met him at Megiddo, he killed him.

---

a Meaning of Heb uncertain   *b* Heb *Asherim*   *c* Heb *Asherah*   *d* Gk: Heb *proclaimed, who had predicted these things*   *e* Or *household gods*

[30]His servants carried him dead in a chariot from Megiddo, brought him to Jerusalem, and buried him in his own tomb. The people of the land took Jehoahaz son of Josiah, anointed him, and made him king in place of his father.

Reign and Captivity of Jehoahaz

31 Jehoahaz was twenty-three years old when he began to reign; he reigned three months in Jerusalem. His mother's name was Hamutal daughter of Jeremiah of Libnah. [32]He did what was evil in the sight of the LORD, just as his ancestors had done. [33]Pharaoh Neco confined him at Riblah in the land of Hamath, so that he might not reign in Jerusalem, and imposed tribute on the land of one hundred talents of silver and a talent of gold. [34]Pharaoh Neco made Eliakim son of Josiah king in place of his father Josiah, and changed his name to Jehoiakim. But he took Jehoahaz away; he came to Egypt, and died there. [35]Jehoiakim gave the silver and the gold to Pharaoh, but he taxed the land in order to meet Pharaoh's demand for money. He exacted the silver and the gold from the people of the land, from all according to their assessment, to give it to Pharaoh Neco.

Jehoiakim Reigns over Judah

36 Jehoiakim was twenty-five years old when he began to reign; he reigned eleven years in Jerusalem. His mother's name was Zebidah daughter of Pedaiah of Rumah. [37]He did what was evil in the sight of the LORD, just as all his ancestors had done.

Judah Overrun by Enemies

24 In his days King Nebuchadnezzar of Babylon came up; Jehoiakim became his servant for three years; then he turned and rebelled against him. [2]The LORD sent against him bands of the Chaldeans, bands of the Arameans, bands of the Moabites, and bands of the Ammonites; he sent them against Judah to destroy it, according to the word of the LORD that he spoke by his servants the prophets. [3]Surely this came upon Judah at the command of the LORD, to remove them out of his sight, for the sins of Manasseh, for all that he had committed, [4]and also for the innocent blood that he had shed; for he filled Jerusalem with innocent blood, and the LORD was not willing to pardon. [5]Now the rest of the deeds of Jehoiakim, and all that he did, are they not written in the Book of the Annals of the Kings of Judah? [6]So Jehoiakim slept with his ancestors; then his son Jehoiachin succeeded him. [7]The king of Egypt did not come again out of his land, for the king of Babylon had taken over all that belonged to the king of Egypt from the Wadi of Egypt to the River Euphrates.

Reign and Captivity of Jehoiachin

8 Jehoiachin was eighteen years old when he began to reign; he reigned three months in Jerusalem. His mother's name was Nehushta daughter of Elnathan of Jerusalem. [9]He did what was evil in the sight of the LORD, just as his father had done.

10 At that time the servants of King Nebuchadnezzar of Babylon came up to Jerusalem, and the city was besieged. [11]King Nebuchadnezzar of Babylon came to the city, while his servants were besieging it; [12]King Jehoiachin of Judah gave himself up to the king of Babylon, himself, his mother, his servants, his officers, and his palace officials. The king of Babylon took him prisoner in the eighth year of his reign.

Capture of Jerusalem

13 He carried off all the treasures of the house of the LORD, and the treasures of the king's house; he cut in pieces all the vessels of gold in the temple of the LORD, which King Solomon of Israel had made, all this as the LORD had foretold. [14]He carried away all Jerusalem, all the officials, all the warriors, ten thousand captives, all the artisans and the smiths; no one remained, except the poorest people of the land. [15]He carried away Jehoiachin to Babylon; the king's mother, the king's wives, his officials, and the elite of the land, he took into captivity from Jerusalem to Babylon. [16]The king of Babylon brought captive to Babylon all the men of valor, seven thousand, the artisans and the smiths, one thousand, all of them strong

and fit for war. [17]The king of Babylon made Mattaniah, Jehoiachin's uncle, king in his place, and changed his name to Zedekiah.

Zedekiah Reigns over Judah

18 Zedekiah was twenty-one years old when he began to reign; he reigned eleven years in Jerusalem. His mother's name was Hamutal daughter of Jeremiah of Libnah. [19]He did what was evil in the sight of the LORD, just as Jehoiakim had done. [20]Indeed, Jerusalem and Judah so angered the LORD that he expelled them from his presence.

The Fall and Captivity of Judah

Zedekiah rebelled against the king of Babylon. [1]And in the ninth year of his reign, in the tenth month, on the tenth day of the month, King Nebuchadnezzar of Babylon came with all his army against Jerusalem, and laid siege to it; they built siegeworks against it all around. [2]So the city was besieged until the eleventh year of King Zedekiah. [3]On the ninth day of the fourth month the famine became so severe in the city that there was no food for the people of the land. [4]Then a breach was made in the city wall;[a] the king with all the soldiers fled[b] by night by the way of the gate between the two walls, by the king's garden, though the Chaldeans were all around the city. They went in the direction of the Arabah. [5]But the army of the Chaldeans pursued the king, and overtook him in the plains of Jericho; all his army was scattered, deserting him. [6]Then they captured the king and brought him up to the king of Babylon at Riblah, who passed sentence on him. [7]They slaughtered the sons of Zedekiah before his eyes, then put out the eyes of Zedekiah; they bound him in fetters and took him to Babylon.

8 In the fifth month, on the seventh day of the month—which was the nineteenth year of King Nebuchadnezzar, king of Babylon—Nebuzaradan, the captain of the bodyguard, a servant of the king of Babylon, came to Jerusalem. [9]He burned the house of the LORD, the king's house, and all the houses of Jerusalem; every great house he burned down. [10]All the army of the Chaldeans who were with the captain of the guard broke down the walls around Jerusalem. [11]Nebuzaradan the captain of the guard carried into exile the rest of the people who were left in the city and the deserters who had defected to the king of Babylon—all the rest of the population. [12]But the captain of the guard left some of the poorest people of the land to be vinedressers and tillers of the soil.

13 The bronze pillars that were in the house of the LORD, as well as the stands and the bronze sea that were in the house of the LORD, the Chaldeans broke in pieces, and carried the bronze to Babylon. [14]They took away the pots, the shovels, the snuffers, the dishes for incense, and all the bronze vessels used in the temple service, [15]as well as the firepans and the basins. What was made of gold the captain of the guard took away for the gold, and what was made of silver, for the silver. [16]As for the two pillars, the one sea, and the stands, which Solomon had made for the house of the LORD, the bronze of all these vessels was beyond weighing. [17]The height of the one pillar was eighteen cubits, and on it was a bronze capital; the height of the capital was three cubits; latticework and pomegranates, all of bronze, were on the capital all around. The second pillar had the same, with the latticework.

18 The captain of the guard took the chief priest Seraiah, the second priest Zephaniah, and the three guardians of the threshold; [19]from the city he took an officer who had been in command of the soldiers, and five men of the king's council who were found in the city; the secretary who was the commander of the army who mustered the people of the land; and sixty men of the people of the land who were found in the city. [20]Nebuzaradan the captain of the guard took them, and brought them to the king of Babylon at Riblah. [21]The king of Babylon struck them down and put them to death at Riblah in the land of

---

a Heb lacks *wall*   *b* Gk Compare Jer 39.4; 52.7: Heb lacks *the king* and lacks *fled*

Hamath. So Judah went into exile out of its land.

Gedaliah Made Governor of Judah

22 He appointed Gedaliah son of Ahikam son of Shaphan as governor over the people who remained in the land of Judah, whom King Nebuchadnezzar of Babylon had left. 23Now when all the captains of the forces and their men heard that the king of Babylon had appointed Gedaliah as governor, they came with their men to Gedaliah at Mizpah, namely, Ishmael son of Nethaniah, Johanan son of Kareah, Seraiah son of Tanhumeth the Netophathite, and Jaazaniah son of the Maacathite. 24Gedaliah swore to them and their men, saying, "Do not be afraid because of the Chaldean officials; live in the land, serve the king of Babylon, and it shall be well with you." 25But in the seventh month, Ishmael son of Nethaniah son of Elishama, of the royal family, came with ten men; they struck down Gedaliah so that he died, along with the Judeans and Chaldeans who were with him at Mizpah. 26Then all the people, high and low,*a* and the captains of the forces set out and went to Egypt; for they were afraid of the Chaldeans.

Jehoiachin Released from Prison

27 In the thirty-seventh year of the exile of King Jehoiachin of Judah, in the twelfth month, on the twenty-seventh day of the month, King Evil-merodach of Babylon, in the year that he began to reign, released King Jehoiachin of Judah from prison; 28he spoke kindly to him, and gave him a seat above the other seats of the kings who were with him in Babylon. 29So Jehoiachin put aside his prison clothes. Every day of his life he dined regularly in the king's presence. 30For his allowance, a regular allowance was given him by the king, a portion every day, as long as he lived.

---

a Or *young and old*

1 CHRONICLES

From Adam to Abraham

1 Adam, Seth, Enosh; [2]Kenan, Mahalalel, Jared; [3]Enoch, Methuselah, Lamech; [4]Noah, Shem, Ham, and Japheth.

5 The descendants of Japheth: Gomer, Magog, Madai, Javan, Tubal, Meshech, and Tiras. [6]The descendants of Gomer: Ashkenaz, Diphath,*a* and Togarmah. [7]The descendants of Javan: Elishah, Tarshish, Kittim, and Rodanim.*b*

8 The descendants of Ham: Cush, Egypt, Put, and Canaan. [9]The descendants of Cush: Seba, Havilah, Sabta, Raama, and Sabteca. The descendants of Raamah: Sheba and Dedan. [10]Cush became the father of Nimrod; he was the first to be a mighty one on the earth.

11 Egypt became the father of Ludim, Anamim, Lehabim, Naphtuhim, [12]Pathrusim, Casluhim, and Caphtorim, from whom the Philistines come.*c*

13 Canaan became the father of Sidon his firstborn, and Heth, [14]and the Jebusites, the Amorites, the Girgashites, [15]the Hivites, the Arkites, the Sinites, [16]the Arvadites, the Zemarites, and the Hamathites.

17 The descendants of Shem: Elam, Asshur, Arpachshad, Lud, Aram, Uz, Hul, Gether, and Meshech.*d* [18]Arpachshad became the father of Shelah; and Shelah became the father of Eber. [19]To Eber were born two sons: the name of the one was Peleg (for in his days the earth was divided), and the name of his brother Joktan. [20]Joktan became the father of Almodad, Sheleph, Hazarmaveth, Jerah, [21]Hadoram, Uzal, Diklah, [22]Ebal, Abimael, Sheba, [23]Ophir, Havilah, and Jobab; all these were the descendants of Joktan.

24 Shem, Arpachshad, Shelah; [25]Eber, Peleg, Reu; [26]Serug, Nahor, Terah; [27]Abram, that is, Abraham.

From Abraham to Jacob

28 The sons of Abraham: Isaac and Ishmael. [29]These are their genealogies: the firstborn of Ishmael, Nebaioth; and Kedar, Adbeel, Mibsam, [30]Mishma, Dumah, Massa, Hadad, Tema, [31]Jetur, Naphish, and Kedemah. These are the sons of Ishmael. [32]The sons of Keturah, Abraham's concubine: she bore Zimran, Jokshan, Medan, Midian, Ishbak, and Shuah. The sons of Jokshan: Sheba and Dedan. [33]The sons of Midian: Ephah, Epher, Hanoch, Abida, and Eldaah. All these were the descendants of Keturah.

34 Abraham became the father of Isaac. The sons of Isaac: Esau and Israel. [35]The sons of Esau: Eliphaz, Reuel, Jeush, Jalam, and Korah. [36]The sons of Eliphaz: Teman, Omar, Zephi, Gatam, Kenaz, Timna, and Amalek. [37]The sons of Reuel: Nahath, Zerah, Shammah, and Mizzah.

38 The sons of Seir: Lotan, Shobal, Zibeon, Anah, Dishon, Ezer, and Dishan. [39]The sons of Lotan: Hori and Homam; and Lotan's sister was Timna. [40]The sons of Shobal: Alian, Manahath, Ebal, Shephi, and Onam. The sons of Zibeon: Aiah and Anah. [41]The sons of Anah: Dishon. The sons of Dishon: Hamran, Eshban, Ithran, and Cheran. [42]The sons of Ezer: Bilhan, Zaavan, and Jaakan.*e* The sons of Dishan:*f* Uz and Aran.

43 These are the kings who reigned in the land of Edom before any king reigned over the Israelites: Bela son of Beor, whose city was called Dinhabah. [44]When Bela died, Jobab son of Zerah of Bozrah succeeded him. [45]When Jobab died, Husham of the land of the Temanites succeeded him. [46]When Husham died, Hadad son of Bedad, who defeated Midian in the country of Moab, succeeded him; and the name of his city was Avith. [47]When Hadad died, Samlah of Masrekah succeeded him. [48]When Samlah died, Shaul*g* of Rehoboth on the Euphrates succeeded him. [49]When Shaul*g* died, Baal-hanan son of Achbor succeeded him. [50]When Baal-hanan died, Hadad succeeded him; the name of his city was Pai, and

---

a Gen 10.3 *Ripath*; See Gk Vg   *b* Gen 10.4 *Dodanim*, See Syr Vg   *c* Heb *Casluhim, from which the Philistines come,*
Caphtorim; See Am 9.7, Jer 47.4   *d* *Mash* in Gen 10.23   *e* Or *and Akan*; See Gen 36.27   *f* See 1.38: Heb
Dishon   *g* Or *Saul*

his wife's name Mehetabel daughter of Matred, daughter of Me-zahab. ⁵¹And Hadad died.

The clans*a* of Edom were: clans*a* Timna, Aliah,*b* Jetheth, ⁵²Oholibamah, Elah, Pinon, ⁵³Kenaz, Teman, Mibzar, ⁵⁴Magdiel, and Iram; these are the clans*a* of Edom.

The Sons of Israel and the Descendants of Judah

2 These are the sons of Israel: Reuben, Simeon, Levi, Judah, Issachar, Zebulun, ²Dan, Joseph, Benjamin, Naphtali, Gad, and Asher. ³The sons of Judah: Er, Onan, and Shelah; these three the Canaanite woman Bath-shua bore to him. Now Er, Judah's firstborn, was wicked in the sight of the LORD, and he put him to death. ⁴His daughter-in-law Tamar also bore him Perez and Zerah. Judah had five sons in all.

5 The sons of Perez: Hezron and Hamul. ⁶The sons of Zerah: Zimri, Ethan, Heman, Calcol, and Dara,*c* five in all. ⁷The sons of Carmi: Achar, the troubler of Israel, who transgressed in the matter of the devoted thing; ⁸and Ethan's son was Azariah.

9 The sons of Hezron, who were born to him: Jerahmeel, Ram, and Chelubai. ¹⁰Ram became the father of Amminadab, and Amminadab became the father of Nahshon, prince of the sons of Judah. ¹¹Nahshon became the father of Salma, Salma of Boaz, ¹²Boaz of Obed, Obed of Jesse. ¹³Jesse became the father of Eliab his firstborn, Abinadab the second, Shimea the third, ¹⁴Nethanel the fourth, Raddai the fifth, ¹⁵Ozem the sixth, David the seventh; ¹⁶and their sisters were Zeruiah and Abigail. The sons of Zeruiah: Abishai, Joab, and Asahel, three. ¹⁷Abigail bore Amasa, and the father of Amasa was Jether the Ishmaelite.

18 Caleb son of Hezron had children by his wife Azubah, and by Jerioth; these were her sons: Jesher, Shobab, and Ardon. ¹⁹When Azubah died, Caleb married Ephrath, who bore him Hur. ²⁰Hur became the father of Uri, and Uri became the father of Bezalel.

21 Afterward Hezron went in to the daughter of Machir father of Gilead, whom he married when he was sixty years old; and she bore him Segub; ²²and Segub became the father of Jair, who had twenty-three towns in the land of Gilead. ²³But Geshur and Aram took from them Havvoth-jair, Kenath and its villages, sixty towns. All these were descendants of Machir, father of Gilead. ²⁴After the death of Hezron, in Caleb-ephrathah, Abijah wife of Hezron bore him Ashhur, father of Tekoa.

25 The sons of Jerahmeel, the firstborn of Hezron: Ram his firstborn, Bunah, Oren, Ozem, and Ahijah. ²⁶Jerahmeel also had another wife, whose name was Atarah; she was the mother of Onam. ²⁷The sons of Ram, the firstborn of Jerahmeel: Maaz, Jamin, and Eker. ²⁸The sons of Onam: Shammai and Jada. The sons of Shammai: Nadab and Abishur. ²⁹The name of Abishur's wife was Abihail, and she bore him Ahban and Molid. ³⁰The sons of Nadab: Seled and Appaim; and Seled died childless. ³¹The son*d* of Appaim: Ishi. The son*d* of Ishi: Sheshan. The son*d* of Sheshan: Ahlai. ³²The sons of Jada, Shammai's brother: Jether and Jonathan; and Jether died childless. ³³The sons of Jonathan: Peleth and Zaza. These were the descendants of Jerahmeel. ³⁴Now Sheshan had no sons, only daughters; but Sheshan had an Egyptian slave, whose name was Jarha. ³⁵So Sheshan gave his daughter in marriage to his slave Jarha; and she bore him Attai. ³⁶Attai became the father of Nathan, and Nathan of Zabad. ³⁷Zabad became the father of Ephlal, and Ephlal of Obed. ³⁸Obed became the father of Jehu, and Jehu of Azariah. ³⁹Azariah became the father of Helez, and Helez of Eleasah. ⁴⁰Eleasah became the father of Sismai, and Sismai of Shallum. ⁴¹Shallum became the father of Jekamiah, and Jekamiah of Elishama.

42 The sons of Caleb brother of Jerahmeel: Mesha*e* his firstborn, who was father of Ziph. The sons of Mareshah father of Hebron. ⁴³The sons of Hebron: Korah, Tappuah, Rekem, and Shema. ⁴⁴Shema became father of Raham, father of Jorkeam; and Rekem be-

a Or *chiefs*   *b* Or *Alvah*; See Gen 36.40   *c* Or *Darda*; Compare Syr Tg some Gk Mss; See 1 Kings 4.31
d Heb *sons*   *e* Gk reads *Mareshah*

came the father of Shammai. ⁴⁵The son of Shammai: Maon; and Maon was the father of Beth-zur. ⁴⁶Ephah also, Caleb's concubine, bore Haran, Moza, and Gazez; and Haran became the father of Gazez. ⁴⁷The sons of Jahdai: Regem, Jotham, Geshan, Pelet, Ephah, and Shaaph. ⁴⁸Maacah, Caleb's concubine, bore Sheber and Tirhanah. ⁴⁹She also bore Shaaph father of Madmannah, Sheva father of Machbenah and father of Gibea; and the daughter of Caleb was Achsah. ⁵⁰These were the descendants of Caleb.

The sons[a] of Hur the firstborn of Ephrathah: Shobal father of Kiriath-jearim, ⁵¹Salma father of Bethlehem, and Hareph father of Beth-gader. ⁵²Shobal father of Kiriath-jearim had other sons: Haroeh, half of the Menuhoth. ⁵³And the families of Kiriath-jearim: the Ithrites, the Puthites, the Shumathites, and the Mishraites; from these came the Zorathites and the Eshtaolites. ⁵⁴The sons of Salma: Bethlehem, the Netophathites, Atroth-beth-joab, and half of the Manahathites, the Zorites. ⁵⁵The families also of the scribes that lived at Jabez: the Tirathites, the Shimeathites, and the Sucathites. These are the Kenites who came from Hammath, father of the house of Rechab.

Descendants of David and Solomon

3 These are the sons of David who were born to him in Hebron: the firstborn Amnon, by Ahinoam the Jezreelite; the second Daniel, by Abigail the Carmelite; ²the third Absalom, son of Maacah, daughter of King Talmai of Geshur; the fourth Adonijah, son of Haggith; ³the fifth Shephatiah, by Abital; the sixth Ithream, by his wife Eglah; ⁴six were born to him in Hebron, where he reigned for seven years and six months. And he reigned thirty-three years in Jerusalem. ⁵These were born to him in Jerusalem: Shimea, Shobab, Nathan, and Solomon, four by Bath-shua, daughter of Ammiel; ⁶then Ibhar, Elishama, Eliphelet, ⁷Nogah, Nepheg, Japhia, ⁸Elishama, Eliada, and Eliphelet, nine. ⁹All these were

David's sons, besides the sons of the concubines; and Tamar was their sister.

10 The descendants of Solomon: Rehoboam, Abijah his son, Asa his son, Jehoshaphat his son, ¹¹Joram his son, Ahaziah his son, Joash his son, ¹²Amaziah his son, Azariah his son, Jotham his son, ¹³Ahaz his son, Hezekiah his son, Manasseh his son, ¹⁴Amon his son, Josiah his son. ¹⁵The sons of Josiah: Johanan the firstborn, the second Jehoiakim, the third Zedekiah, the fourth Shallum. ¹⁶The descendants of Jehoiakim: Jeconiah his son, Zedekiah his son; ¹⁷and the sons of Jeconiah, the captive: Shealtiel his son, ¹⁸Malchiram, Pedaiah, Shenazzar, Jekamiah, Hoshama, and Nedabiah; ¹⁹The sons of Pedaiah: Zerubbabel and Shimei; and the sons of Zerubbabel: Meshullam and Hananiah, and Shelomith was their sister; ²⁰and Hashubah, Ohel, Berechiah, Hasadiah, and Jushab-hesed, five. ²¹The sons of Hananiah: Pelatiah and Jeshaiah, his son[b] Rephaiah, his son[b] Arnan, his son[b] Obadiah, his son[b] Shecaniah. ²²The son[c] of Shecaniah: Shemaiah. And the sons of Shemaiah: Hattush, Igal, Bariah, Neariah, and Shaphat, six. ²³The sons of Neariah: Elioenai, Hizkiah, and Azrikam, three. ²⁴The sons of Elioenai: Hodaviah, Eliashib, Pelaiah, Akkub, Johanan, Delaiah, and Anani, seven.

Descendants of Judah

4 The sons of Judah: Perez, Hezron, Carmi, Hur, and Shobal. ²Reaiah son of Shobal became the father of Jahath, and Jahath became the father of Ahumai and Lahad. These were the families of the Zorathites. ³These were the sons[d] of Etam: Jezreel, Ishma, and Idbash; and the name of their sister was Hazzelelponi, ⁴and Penuel was the father of Gedor, and Ezer the father of Hushah. These were the sons of Hur, the firstborn of Ephrathah, the father of Bethlehem. ⁵Ashhur father of Tekoa had two wives, Helah and Naarah; ⁶Naarah bore him Ahuzzam, Hepher, Temeni, and Haahashtari.[e] These were the sons of Naarah. ⁷The sons of Helah: Zereth, Izhar,[f] and Ethnan. ⁸Koz became the father of Anub, Zobe-

---

a Gk Vg: Heb *son*   b Gk Compare Syr Vg: Heb *sons of*   c Heb *sons*   d Gk Compare Vg: Heb *the father*
e Or *Ahashtari*   f Another reading is *Zohar*

bah, and the families of Aharhel son of Harum. ⁹Jabez was honored more than his brothers; and his mother named him Jabez, saying, "Because I bore him in pain." ¹⁰Jabez called on the God of Israel, saying, "Oh that you would bless me and enlarge my border, and that your hand might be with me, and that you would keep me from hurt and harm!" And God granted what he asked. ¹¹Chelub the brother of Shuhah became the father of Mehir, who was the father of Eshton. ¹²Eshton became the father of Beth-rapha, Paseah, and Tehinnah the father of Ir-nahash. These are the men of Recah. ¹³The sons of Kenaz: Othniel and Seraiah; and the sons of Othniel: Hathath and Meonothai.ᵃ ¹⁴Meonothai became the father of Ophrah; and Seraiah became the father of Joab father of Ge-harashim,ᵇ so-called because they were artisans. ¹⁵The sons of Caleb son of Jephunneh: Iru, Elah, and Naam; and the sonᶜ of Elah: Kenaz. ¹⁶The sons of Jehallelel: Ziph, Ziphah, Tiria, and Asarel. ¹⁷The sons of Ezrah: Jether, Mered, Epher, and Jalon. These are the sons of Bithiah, daughter of Pharaoh, whom Mered married;ᵈ and she conceived and boreᵉ Miriam, Shammai, and Ishbah father of Eshtemoa. ¹⁸And his Judean wife bore Jered father of Gedor, Heber father of Soco, and Jekuthiel father of Zanoah. ¹⁹The sons of the wife of Hodiah, the sister of Naham, were the fathers of Keilah the Garmite and Eshtemoa the Maacathite. ²⁰The sons of Shimon: Amnon, Rinnah, Benhanan, and Tilon. The sons of Ishi: Zoheth and Ben-zoheth. ²¹The sons of Shelah son of Judah: Er father of Lecah, Laadah father of Mareshah, and the families of the guild of linen workers at Beth-ashbea; ²²and Jokim, and the men of Cozeba, and Joash, and Saraph, who married into Moab but returned to Lehemᶠ (now the recordsᵍ are ancient). ²³These were the potters and inhabitants of Netaim and Gederah; they lived there with the king in his service.

Descendants of Simeon

24 The sons of Simeon: Nemuel, Jamin, Jarib, Zerah, Shaul;ᵇ ²⁵Shallum was his son, Mibsam his son, Mishma his son. ²⁶The sons of Mishma: Hammuel his son, Zaccur his son, Shimei his son. ²⁷Shimei had sixteen sons and six daughters; but his brothers did not have many children, nor did all their family multiply like the Judeans. ²⁸They lived in Beer-sheba, Moladah, Hazar-shual, ²⁹Bilhah, Ezem, Tolad, ³⁰Bethuel, Hormah, Ziklag, ³¹Beth-marcaboth, Hazar-susim, Beth-biri, and Shaaraim. These were their towns until David became king. ³²And their villages were Etam, Ain, Rimmon, Tochen, and Ashan, five towns, ³³along with all their villages that were around these towns as far as Baal. These were their settlements. And they kept a genealogical record.

34 Meshobab, Jamlech, Joshah son of Amaziah, ³⁵Joel, Jehu son of Joshibiah son of Seraiah son of Asiel, ³⁶Elioenai, Jaakobah, Jeshohaiah, Asaiah, Adiel, Jesimiel, Benaiah, ³⁷Ziza son of Shiphi son of Allon son of Jedaiah son of Shimri son of Shemaiah— ³⁸these mentioned by name were leaders in their families, and their clans increased greatly. ³⁹They journeyed to the entrance of Gedor, to the east side of the valley, to seek pasture for their flocks, ⁴⁰where they found rich, good pasture, and the land was very broad, quiet, and peaceful; for the former inhabitants there belonged to Ham. ⁴¹These, registered by name, came in the days of King Hezekiah of Judah, and attacked their tents and the Meunim who were found there, and exterminated them to this day, and settled in their place, because there was pasture there for their flocks. ⁴²And some of them, five hundred men of the Simeonites, went to Mount Seir, having as their leaders Pelatiah, Neariah, Rephaiah, and Uzziel, sons of Ishi; ⁴³they destroyed the remnant of the Amalekites that had escaped, and they have lived there to this day.

Descendants of Reuben

5 The sons of Reuben the firstborn of Israel. (He was the firstborn, but because he

---

ᵃ Gk Vg: Heb lacks *and Meonothai*   ᵇ That is *Valley of artisans*   ᶜ Heb *sons*   ᵈ The clause: *These are . . . married* is transposed from verse 18   ᵉ Heb lacks *and bore*   ᶠ Vg Compare Gk: Heb *and Jashubi-lahem*   ᵍ Or *matters*
ᵇ Or *Saul*

defiled his father's bed his birthright was given to the sons of Joseph son of Israel, so that he is not enrolled in the genealogy according to the birthright; ²though Judah became prominent among his brothers and a ruler came from him, yet the birthright belonged to Joseph.) ³The sons of Reuben, the firstborn of Israel: Hanoch, Pallu, Hezron, and Carmi. ⁴The sons of Joel: Shemaiah his son, Gog his son, Shimei his son, ⁵Micah his son, Reaiah his son, Baal his son, ⁶Beerah his son, whom King Tilgath-pilneser of Assyria carried away into exile; he was a chieftain of the Reubenites. ⁷And his kindred by their families, when the genealogy of their generations was reckoned: the chief, Jeiel, and Zechariah, ⁸and Bela son of Azaz, son of Shema, son of Joel, who lived in Aroer, as far as Nebo and Baal-meon. ⁹He also lived to the east as far as the beginning of the desert this side of the Euphrates, because their cattle had multiplied in the land of Gilead. ¹⁰And in the days of Saul they made war on the Hagrites, who fell by their hand; and they lived in their tents throughout all the region east of Gilead.

Descendants of Gad

11 The sons of Gad lived beside them in the land of Bashan as far as Salecah: ¹²Joel the chief, Shapham the second, Janai, and Shaphat in Bashan. ¹³And their kindred according to their clans: Michael, Meshullam, Sheba, Jorai, Jacan, Zia, and Eber, seven. ¹⁴These were the sons of Abihail son of Huri, son of Jaroah, son of Gilead, son of Michael, son of Jeshishai, son of Jahdo, son of Buz; ¹⁵Ahi son of Abdiel, son of Guni, was chief in their clan; ¹⁶and they lived in Gilead, in Bashan and in its towns, and in all the pasture lands of Sharon to their limits. ¹⁷All of these were enrolled by genealogies in the days of King Jotham of Judah, and in the days of King Jeroboam of Israel.

18 The Reubenites, the Gadites, and the half-tribe of Manasseh had valiant warriors, who carried shield and sword, and drew the bow, expert in war, forty-four thousand seven hundred sixty, ready for service. ¹⁹They made war on the Hagrites, Jetur, Naphish, and Nodab; ²⁰and when they received help against them, the Hagrites and all who were with them were given into their hands, for they cried to God in the battle, and he granted their entreaty because they trusted in him. ²¹They captured their livestock: fifty thousand of their camels, two hundred fifty thousand sheep, two thousand donkeys, and one hundred thousand captives. ²²Many fell slain, because the war was of God. And they lived in their territory until the exile.

The Half-Tribe of Manasseh

23 The members of the half-tribe of Manasseh lived in the land; they were very numerous from Bashan to Baal-hermon, Senir, and Mount Hermon. ²⁴These were the heads of their clans: Epher,ᵃ Ishi, Eliel, Azriel, Jeremiah, Hodaviah, and Jahdiel, mighty warriors, famous men, heads of their clans. ²⁵But they transgressed against the God of their ancestors, and prostituted themselves to the gods of the peoples of the land, whom God had destroyed before them. ²⁶So the God of Israel stirred up the spirit of King Pul of Assyria, the spirit of King Tilgath-pilneser of Assyria, and he carried them away, namely, the Reubenites, the Gadites, and the half-tribe of Manasseh, and brought them to Halah, Habor, Hara, and the river Gozan, to this day.

Descendants of Levi

6ᵇ The sons of Levi: Gershom,ᶜ Kohath, and Merari. ²The sons of Kohath: Amram, Izhar, Hebron, and Uzziel. ³The children of Amram: Aaron, Moses, and Miriam. The sons of Aaron: Nadab, Abihu, Eleazar, and Ithamar. ⁴Eleazar became the father of Phinehas, Phinehas of Abishua, ⁵Abishua of Bukki, Bukki of Uzzi, ⁶Uzzi of Zerahiah, Zerahiah of Meraioth, ⁷Meraioth of Amariah, Amariah of Ahitub, ⁸Ahitub of Zadok, Zadok of Ahimaaz, ⁹Ahimaaz of Azariah, Azariah of Johanan, ¹⁰and Johanan of Azariah (it was he who served as priest in the house that Solomon built in Jeru-

---

a Gk Vg: Heb *and Epher*   *b* Ch 5.27 in Heb   *c* Heb *Gershon*, variant of *Gershom*; See 6.16

salem). [11]Azariah became the father of Amariah, Amariah of Ahitub, [12]Ahitub of Zadok, Zadok of Shallum, [13]Shallum of Hilkiah, Hilkiah of Azariah, [14]Azariah of Seraiah, Seraiah of Jehozadak; [15]and Jehozadak went into exile when the LORD sent Judah and Jerusalem into exile by the hand of Nebuchadnezzar.

[16][a] The sons of Levi: Gershom, Kohath, and Merari. [17]These are the names of the sons of Gershom: Libni and Shimei. [18]The sons of Kohath: Amram, Izhar, Hebron, and Uzziel. [19]The sons of Merari: Mahli and Mushi. These are the clans of the Levites according to their ancestry. [20]Of Gershom: Libni his son, Jahath his son, Zimmah his son, [21]Joah his son, Iddo his son, Zerah his son, Jeatherai his son. [22]The sons of Kohath: Amminadab his son, Korah his son, Assir his son, [23]Elkanah his son, Ebiasaph his son, Assir his son, [24]Tahath his son, Uriel his son, Uzziah his son, and Shaul his son. [25]The sons of Elkanah: Amasai and Ahimoth, [26]Elkanah his son, Zophai his son, Nahath his son, [27]Eliab his son, Jeroham his son, Elkanah his son. [28]The sons of Samuel: Joel[b] his firstborn, the second Abijah.[c] [29]The sons of Merari: Mahli, Libni his son, Shimei his son, Uzzah his son, [30]Shimea his son, Haggiah his son, and Asaiah his son.

Musicians Appointed by David

31 These are the men whom David put in charge of the service of song in the house of the LORD, after the ark came to rest there. [32]They ministered with song before the tabernacle of the tent of meeting, until Solomon had built the house of the LORD in Jerusalem; and they performed their service in due order. [33]These are the men who served; and their sons were: Of the Kohathites: Heman, the singer, son of Joel, son of Samuel, [34]son of Elkanah, son of Jeroham, son of Eliel, son of Toah, [35]son of Zuph, son of Elkanah, son of Mahath, son of Amasai, [36]son of Elkanah, son of Joel, son of Azariah, son of Zephaniah, [37]son of Tahath, son of Assir, son of Ebiasaph, son of Korah, [38]son of Izhar, son of Kohath, son of Levi, son of Israel; [39]and his brother Asaph, who stood on his right, namely, Asaph son of Berechiah, son of Shimea, [40]son of Michael, son of Baaseiah, son of Malchijah, [41]son of Ethni, son of Zerah, son of Adaiah, [42]son of Ethan, son of Zimmah, son of Shimei, [43]son of Jahath, son of Gershom, son of Levi. [44]On the left were their kindred the sons of Merari: Ethan son of Kishi, son of Abdi, son of Malluch, [45]son of Hashabiah, son of Amaziah, son of Hilkiah, [46]son of Amzi, son of Bani, son of Shemer, [47]son of Mahli, son of Mushi, son of Merari, son of Levi; [48]and their kindred the Levites were appointed for all the service of the tabernacle of the house of God.

49 But Aaron and his sons made offerings on the altar of burnt offering and on the altar of incense, doing all the work of the most holy place, to make atonement for Israel, according to all that Moses the servant of God had commanded. [50]These are the sons of Aaron: Eleazar his son, Phinehas his son, Abishua his son, [51]Bukki his son, Uzzi his son, Zerahiah his son, [52]Meraioth his son, Amariah his son, Ahitub his son, [53]Zadok his son, Ahimaaz his son.

Settlements of the Levites

54 These are their dwelling places according to their settlements within their borders: to the sons of Aaron of the families of Kohathites— for the lot fell to them first— [55]to them they gave Hebron in the land of Judah and its surrounding pasture lands, [56]but the fields of the city and its villages they gave to Caleb son of Jephunneh. [57]To the sons of Aaron they gave the cities of refuge: Hebron, Libnah with its pasture lands, Jattir, Eshtemoa with its pasture lands, [58]Hilen[d] with its pasture lands, Debir with its pasture lands, [59]Ashan with its pasture lands, and Beth-shemesh with its pasture lands. [60]From the tribe of Benjamin, Geba with its pasture lands, Alemeth with its pasture lands, and Anathoth with its pasture lands. All their towns throughout their families were thirteen.

61 To the rest of the Kohathites were giv-

---

a Ch 6.1 in Heb   b Gk Syr Compare verse 33 and 1 Sam 8.2: Heb lacks *Joel*   c Heb reads *Vashni, and Abijah* for *the second Abijah*, taking *the second* as a proper name   d Other readings *Hilez, Holon*; See Josh 21.15

en by lot out of the family of the tribe, out of the half-tribe, the half of Manasseh, ten towns. ⁶²To the Gershomites according to their families were allotted thirteen towns out of the tribes of Issachar, Asher, Naphtali, and Manasseh in Bashan. ⁶³To the Merarites according to their families were allotted twelve towns out of the tribes of Reuben, Gad, and Zebulun. ⁶⁴So the people of Israel gave the Levites the towns with their pasture lands. ⁶⁵They also gave them by lot out of the tribes of Judah, Simeon, and Benjamin these towns that are mentioned by name.

66 And some of the families of the sons of Kohath had towns of their territory out of the tribe of Ephraim. ⁶⁷They were given the cities of refuge: Shechem with its pasture lands in the hill country of Ephraim, Gezer with its pasture lands, ⁶⁸Jokmeam with its pasture lands, Beth-horon with its pasture lands, ⁶⁹Aijalon with its pasture lands, Gath-rimmon with its pasture lands; ⁷⁰and out of the half-tribe of Manasseh, Aner with its pasture lands, and Bileam with its pasture lands, for the rest of the families of the Kohathites.

71 To the Gershomites: out of the half-tribe of Manasseh: Golan in Bashan with its pasture lands and Ashtaroth with its pasture lands; ⁷²and out of the tribe of Issachar: Kedesh with its pasture lands, Daberath ͣ with its pasture lands, ⁷³Ramoth with its pasture lands, and Anem with its pasture lands; ⁷⁴out of the tribe of Asher: Mashal with its pasture lands, Abdon with its pasture lands, ⁷⁵Hukok with its pasture lands, and Rehob with its pasture lands; ⁷⁶and out of the tribe of Naphtali: Kedesh in Galilee with its pasture lands, Hammon with its pasture lands, and Kiriathaim with its pasture lands. ⁷⁷To the rest of the Merarites out of the tribe of Zebulun: Rimmono with its pasture lands, Tabor with its pasture lands, ⁷⁸and across the Jordan from Jericho, on the east side of the Jordan, out of the tribe of Reuben: Bezer in the steppe with its pasture lands, Jahzah with its pasture lands, ⁷⁹Kedemoth with its pasture lands, and Mephaath with its pasture

lands; ⁸⁰and out of the tribe of Gad: Ramoth in Gilead with its pasture lands, Mahanaim with its pasture lands, ⁸¹Heshbon with its pasture lands, and Jazer with its pasture lands.

Descendants of Issachar

7 The sons ͪ of Issachar: Tola, Puah, Jashub, and Shimron, four. ²The sons of Tola: Uzzi, Rephaiah, Jeriel, Jahmai, Ibsam, and Shemuel, heads of their ancestral houses, namely of Tola, mighty warriors of their generations, their number in the days of David being twenty-two thousand six hundred. ³The son ͨ of Uzzi: Izrahiah. And the sons of Izrahiah: Michael, Obadiah, Joel, and Isshiah, five, all of them chiefs; ⁴and along with them, by their generations, according to their ancestral houses, were units of the fighting force, thirty-six thousand, for they had many wives and sons. ⁵Their kindred belonging to all the families of Issachar were in all eighty-seven thousand mighty warriors, enrolled by genealogy.

Descendants of Benjamin

6 The sons of Benjamin: Bela, Becher, and Jediael, three. ⁷The sons of Bela: Ezbon, Uzzi, Uzziel, Jerimoth, and Iri, five, heads of ancestral houses, mighty warriors; and their enrollment by genealogies was twenty-two thousand thirty-four. ⁸The sons of Becher: Zemirah, Joash, Eliezer, Elioenai, Omri, Jeremoth, Abijah, Anathoth, and Alemeth. All these were the sons of Becher; ⁹and their enrollment by genealogies, according to their generations, as heads of their ancestral houses, mighty warriors, was twenty thousand two hundred. ¹⁰The sons of Jediael: Bilhan. And the sons of Bilhan: Jeush, Benjamin, Ehud, Chenaanah, Zethan, Tarshish, and Ahishahar. ¹¹All these were the sons of Jediael according to the heads of their ancestral houses, mighty warriors, seventeen thousand two hundred, ready for service in war. ¹²And Shuppim and Huppim were the sons of Ir, Hushim the son ͨ of Aher.

---

a Or *Dobrath*   *b* Syr Compare Vg: Heb *And to the sons*   *c* Heb *sons*

Descendants of Naphtali

13 The descendants of Naphtali: Jahziel, Guni, Jezer, and Shallum, the descendants of Bilhah.

Descendants of Manasseh

14 The sons of Manasseh: Asriel, whom his Aramean concubine bore; she bore Machir the father of Gilead. 15And Machir took a wife for Huppim and for Shuppim. The name of his sister was Maacah. And the name of the second was Zelophehad; and Zelophehad had daughters. 16Maacah the wife of Machir bore a son, and she named him Peresh; the name of his brother was Sheresh; and his sons were Ulam and Rekem. 17The son*a* of Ulam: Bedan. These were the sons of Gilead son of Machir, son of Manasseh. 18And his sister Hammolecheth bore Ishhod, Abiezer, and Mahlah. 19The sons of Shemida were Ahian, Shechem, Likhi, and Aniam.

Descendants of Ephraim

20 The sons of Ephraim: Shuthelah, and Bered his son, Tahath his son, Eleadah his son, Tahath his son, 21Zabad his son, Shuthelah his son, and Ezer and Elead. Now the people of Gath, who were born in the land, killed them, because they came down to raid their cattle. 22And their father Ephraim mourned many days, and his brothers came to comfort him. 23Ephraim*b* went in to his wife, and she conceived and bore a son; and he named him Beriah, because disaster*c* had befallen his house. 24His daughter was Sheerah, who built both Lower and Upper Beth-horon, and Uzzensheerah. 25Rephah was his son, Resheph his son, Telah his son, Tahan his son, 26Ladan his son, Ammihud his son, Elishama his son, 27Nun*d* his son, Joshua his son. 28Their possessions and settlements were Bethel and its towns, and eastward Naaran, and westward Gezer and its towns, Shechem and its towns, as far as Ayyah and its towns; 29also along the borders of the Manassites, Beth-shean and its towns, Taanach and its towns, Megiddo and its towns, Dor and its towns. In these lived the sons of Joseph son of Israel.

Descendants of Asher

30 The sons of Asher: Imnah, Ishvah, Ishvi, Beriah, and their sister Serah. 31The sons of Beriah: Heber and Malchiel, who was the father of Birzaith. 32Heber became the father of Japhlet, Shomer, Hotham, and their sister Shua. 33The sons of Japhlet: Pasach, Bimhal, and Ashvath. These are the sons of Japhlet. 34The sons of Shemer: Ahi, Rohgah, Hubbah, and Aram. 35The sons of Helem*e* his brother: Zophah, Imna, Shelesh, and Amal. 36The sons of Zophah: Suah, Harnepher, Shual, Beri, Imrah, 37Bezer, Hod, Shamma, Shilshah, Ithran, and Beera. 38The sons of Jether: Jephunneh, Pispa, and Ara. 39The sons of Ulla: Arah, Hanniel, and Rizia. 40All of these were men of Asher, heads of ancestral houses, select mighty warriors, chief of the princes. Their number enrolled by genealogies, for service in war, was twenty-six thousand men.

Descendants of Benjamin

8 Benjamin became the father of Bela his firstborn, Ashbel the second, Aharah the third, 2Nohah the fourth, and Rapha the fifth. 3And Bela had sons: Addar, Gera, Abihud,*f* 4Abishua, Naaman, Ahoah, 5Gera, Shephuphan, and Huram. 6These are the sons of Ehud (they were heads of ancestral houses of the inhabitants of Geba, and they were carried into exile to Manahath): 7Naaman,*g* Ahijah, and Gera, that is, Heglam,*h* who became the father of Uzza and Ahihud. 8And Shaharaim had sons in the country of Moab after he had sent away his wives Hushim and Baara. 9He had sons by his wife Hodesh: Jobab, Zibia, Mesha, Malcam, 10Jeuz, Sachia, and Mirmah. These were his sons, heads of ancestral houses. 11He also had sons by Hushim: Abitub and Elpaal. 12The sons of Elpaal: Eber, Misham, and Shemed, who built Ono and Lod with its towns, 13and Beriah and Shema (they were heads of ancestral houses of the inhabitants of Aija-

a Heb *sons*   *b* Heb *He*   *c* Heb *beraah*   *d* Here spelled *Non*; see Ex 33.11   *e* Or *Hotham*; see 7.32
f Or *father of Ehud*; see 8.6   *g* Heb *and Naaman*   *h* Or *he carried them into exile*

lon, who put to flight the inhabitants of Gath); [14]and Ahio, Shashak, and Jeremoth. [15]Zebadiah, Arad, Eder, [16]Michael, Ishpah, and Joha were sons of Beriah. [17]Zebadiah, Meshullam, Hizki, Heber, [18]Ishmerai, Izliah, and Jobab were the sons of Elpaal. [19]Jakim, Zichri, Zabdi, [20]Elienai, Zillethai, Eliel, [21]Adaiah, Beraiah, and Shimrath were the sons of Shimei. [22]Ishpan, Eber, Eliel, [23]Abdon, Zichri, Hanan, [24]Hananiah, Elam, Anthothijah, [25]Iphdeiah, and Penuel were the sons of Shashak. [26]Shamsherai, Shehariah, Athaliah, [27]Jaareshiah, Elijah, and Zichri were the sons of Jeroham. [28]These were the heads of ancestral houses, according to their generations, chiefs. These lived in Jerusalem.

[29] Jeiel[a] the father of Gibeon lived in Gibeon, and the name of his wife was Maacah. [30]His firstborn son: Abdon, then Zur, Kish, Baal,[b] Nadab, [31]Gedor, Ahio, Zecher, [32]and Mikloth, who became the father of Shimeah. Now these also lived opposite their kindred in Jerusalem, with their kindred. [33]Ner became the father of Kish, Kish of Saul,[c] Saul[c] of Jonathan, Malchishua, Abinadab, and Esh-baal; [34]and the son of Jonathan was Merib-baal; and Merib-baal became the father of Micah. [35]The sons of Micah: Pithon, Melech, Tarea, and Ahaz. [36]Ahaz became the father of Jehoaddah; and Jehoaddah became the father of Alemeth, Azmaveth, and Zimri; Zimri became the father of Moza. [37]Moza became the father of Binea; Raphah was his son, Eleasah his son, Azel his son. [38]Azel had six sons, and these are their names: Azrikam, Bocheru, Ishmael, Sheariah, Obadiah, and Hanan; all these were the sons of Azel. [39]The sons of his brother Eshek: Ulam his firstborn, Jeush the second, and Eliphelet the third. [40]The sons of Ulam were mighty warriors, archers, having many children and grandchildren, one hundred fifty. All these were Benjaminites.

9 So all Israel was enrolled by genealogies; and these are written in the Book of the Kings of Israel. And Judah was taken into exile in Babylon because of their unfaithfulness.

[2]Now the first to live again in their possessions in their towns were Israelites, priests, Levites, and temple servants.

Inhabitants of Jerusalem after the Exile

3 And some of the people of Judah, Benjamin, Ephraim, and Manasseh lived in Jerusalem: [4]Uthai son of Ammihud, son of Omri, son of Imri, son of Bani, from the sons of Perez son of Judah. [5]And of the Shilonites: Asaiah the firstborn, and his sons. [6]Of the sons of Zerah: Jeuel and their kin, six hundred ninety. [7]Of the Benjaminites: Sallu son of Meshullam, son of Hodaviah, son of Hassenuah, [8]Ibneiah son of Jeroham, Elah son of Uzzi, son of Michri, and Meshullam son of Shephatiah, son of Reuel, son of Ibnijah; [9]and their kindred according to their generations, nine hundred fifty-six. All these were heads of families according to their ancestral houses.

Priestly Families

10 Of the priests: Jedaiah, Jehoiarib, Jachin, [11]and Azariah son of Hilkiah, son of Meshullam, son of Zadok, son of Meraioth, son of Ahitub, the chief officer of the house of God; [12]and Adaiah son of Jeroham, son of Pashhur, son of Malchijah, and Maasai son of Adiel, son of Jahzerah, son of Meshullam, son of Meshillemith, son of Immer; [13]besides their kindred, heads of their ancestral houses, one thousand seven hundred sixty, qualified for the work of the service of the house of God.

Levitical Families

14 Of the Levites: Shemaiah son of Hasshub, son of Azrikam, son of Hashabiah, of the sons of Merari; [15]and Bakbakkar, Heresh, Galal, and Mattaniah son of Mica, son of Zichri, son of Asaph; [16]and Obadiah son of Shemaiah, son of Galal, son of Jeduthun, and Berechiah son of Asa, son of Elkanah, who lived in the villages of the Netophathites.

17 The gatekeepers were: Shallum, Akkub, Talmon, Ahiman; and their kindred Shallum was the chief, [18]stationed previously in the

---

a Compare 9.35: Heb lacks *Jeiel*   *b* Gk Ms adds *Ner*; Compare 8.33 and 9.36   *c* Or *Shaul* king's gate on the east side. These were the gatekeepers of the camp of the Levites. [19]Shallum son of Kore, son of Ebiasaph, son of Korah, and his kindred of his ancestral house, the Korahites, were in charge of the work of the service, guardians of the thresholds of the tent, as their ancestors had been in charge of the camp of the LORD, guardians of the entrance. [20]And Phinehas son of Eleazar was chief over them in former times; the LORD was with him. [21]Zechariah son of Meshelemiah was gatekeeper at the entrance of the tent of meeting. [22]All these, who were chosen as gatekeepers at the thresholds, were two hundred twelve. They were enrolled by genealogies in their villages. David and the seer Samuel established them in their office of trust. [23]So they and their descendants were in charge of the gates of the house of the LORD, that is, the house of the tent, as guards. [24]The gatekeepers were on the four sides, east, west, north, and south; [25]and their kindred who were in their villages were obliged to come in every seven days, in turn, to be with them; [26]for the four chief gatekeepers, who were Levites, were in charge of the chambers and the treasures of the house of God. [27]And they would spend the night near the house of God; for on them lay the duty of watching, and they had charge of opening it every morning.

28 Some of them had charge of the utensils of service, for they were required to count them when they were brought in and taken out. [29]Others of them were appointed over the furniture, and over all the holy utensils, also over the choice flour, the wine, the oil, the incense, and the spices. [30]Others, of the sons of the priests, prepared the mixing of the spices, [31]and Mattithiah, one of the Levites, the firstborn of Shallum the Korahite, was in charge of making the flat cakes. [32]Also some of their kindred of the Kohathites had charge of the rows of bread, to prepare them for each sabbath.

33 Now these are the singers, the heads of ancestral houses of the Levites, living in the chambers of the temple free from other service, for they were on duty day and night. [34]These were heads of ancestral houses of the Levites, according to their generations; these leaders lived in Jerusalem.

The Family of King Saul

35 In Gibeon lived the father of Gibeon, Jeiel, and the name of his wife was Maacah. [36]His firstborn son was Abdon, then Zur, Kish, Baal, Ner, Nadab, [37]Gedor, Ahio, Zechariah, and Mikloth; [38]and Mikloth became the father of Shimeam; and these also lived opposite their kindred in Jerusalem, with their kindred. [39]Ner became the father of Kish, Kish of Saul, Saul of Jonathan, Malchishua, Abinadab, and Eshbaal; [40]and the son of Jonathan was Merib-baal; and Merib-baal became the father of Micah. [41]The sons of Micah: Pithon, Melech, Tahrea, and Ahaz;[a] [42]and Ahaz became the father of Jarah, and Jarah of Alemeth, Azmaveth, and Zimri; and Zimri became the father of Moza. [43]Moza became the father of Binea; and Rephaiah was his son, Eleasah his son, Azel his son. [44]Azel had six sons, and these are their names: Azrikam, Bocheru, Ishmael, Sheariah, Obadiah, and Hanan; these were the sons of Azel.

Death of Saul and His Sons

10 Now the Philistines fought against Israel; and the men of Israel fled before the Philistines, and fell slain on Mount Gilboa. [2]The Philistines overtook Saul and his sons; and the Philistines killed Jonathan and Abinadab and Malchishua, sons of Saul. [3]The battle pressed hard on Saul; and the archers found him, and he was wounded by the archers. [4]Then Saul said to his armor-bearer, "Draw your sword, and thrust me through with it, so that these uncircumcised may not come and make sport of me." But his armor-bearer was unwilling, for he was terrified. So Saul took his own sword and fell on it. [5]When his armor-bearer saw that Saul was dead, he also fell on his sword and died. [6]Thus Saul died; he and his

---

a Compare 8.35: Heb lacks and Ahaz

three sons and all his house died together. [7]When all the men of Israel who were in the valley saw that the army[a] had fled and that Saul and his sons were dead, they abandoned their towns and fled; and the Philistines came and occupied them.

8 The next day when the Philistines came to strip the dead, they found Saul and his sons fallen on Mount Gilboa. [9]They stripped him and took his head and his armor, and sent messengers throughout the land of the Philistines to carry the good news to their idols and to the people. [10]They put his armor in the temple of their gods, and fastened his head in the temple of Dagon. [11]But when all Jabesh-gilead heard everything that the Philistines had done to Saul, [12]all the valiant warriors got up and took away the body of Saul and the bodies of his sons, and brought them to Jabesh. Then they buried their bones under the oak in Jabesh, and fasted seven days.

13 So Saul died for his unfaithfulness; he was unfaithful to the LORD in that he did not keep the command of the LORD; moreover, he had consulted a medium, seeking guidance, [14]and did not seek guidance from the LORD. Therefore the LORD[b] put him to death and turned the kingdom over to David son of Jesse.

David Anointed King of All Israel

11 Then all Israel gathered together to David at Hebron and said, "See, we are your bone and flesh. [2]For some time now, even while Saul was king, it was you who commanded the army of Israel. The LORD your God said to you: It is you who shall be shepherd of my people Israel, you who shall be ruler over my people Israel." [3]So all the elders of Israel came to the king at Hebron, and David made a covenant with them at Hebron before the LORD. And they anointed David king over Israel, according to the word of the LORD by Samuel.

Jerusalem Captured

4 David and all Israel marched to Jerusalem, that is Jebus, where the Jebusites were, the inhabitants of the land. [5]The inhabitants of Jebus said to David, "You will not come in here." Nevertheless David took the stronghold of Zion, now the city of David. [6]David had said, "Whoever attacks the Jebusites first shall be chief and commander." And Joab son of Zeruiah went up first, so he became chief. [7]David resided in the stronghold; therefore it was called the city of David. [8]He built the city all around, from the Millo in complete circuit; and Joab repaired the rest of the city. [9]And David became greater and greater, for the LORD of hosts was with him.

David's Mighty Men and Their Exploits

10 Now these are the chiefs of David's warriors, who gave him strong support in his kingdom, together with all Israel, to make him king, according to the word of the LORD concerning Israel. [11]This is an account of David's mighty warriors: Jashobeam, son of Hachmoni,[c] was chief of the Three;[d] he wielded his spear against three hundred whom he killed at one time.

12 And next to him among the three warriors was Eleazar son of Dodo, the Ahohite. [13]He was with David at Pas-dammim when the Philistines were gathered there for battle. There was a plot of ground full of barley. Now the people had fled from the Philistines, [14]but he and David took their stand in the middle of the plot, defended it, and killed the Philistines; and the LORD saved them by a great victory.

15 Three of the thirty chiefs went down to the rock to David at the cave of Adullam, while the army of Philistines was encamped in the valley of Rephaim. [16]David was then in the stronghold; and the garrison of the Philistines was then at Bethlehem. [17]David said longingly, "O that someone would give me water to drink from the well of Bethlehem that is by the gate!" [18]Then the Three broke through the camp of the Philistines, and drew water from the well of Bethlehem that was by the gate, and they brought it to David. But David would

a Heb *they*   *b* Heb *he*   *c* Or *a Hachmonite*   *d* Compare 2 Sam 23.8: Heb *Thirty* or *captains* not drink of it; he poured it out to the LORD, [19]and said, "My God forbid that I should do this. Can I drink the blood of these men? For at the risk of their lives they brought it." Therefore he would not drink it. The three warriors did these things.

20 Now Abishai,[a] the brother of Joab, was chief of the Thirty.[b] With his spear he fought against three hundred and killed them, and won a name beside the Three. [21]He was the most renowned[c] of the Thirty,[b] and became their commander; but he did not attain to the Three.

22 Benaiah son of Jehoiada was a valiant man[d] of Kabzeel, a doer of great deeds; he struck down two sons of[e] Ariel of Moab. He also went down and killed a lion in a pit on a day when snow had fallen. [23]And he killed an Egyptian, a man of great stature, five cubits tall. The Egyptian had in his hand a spear like a weaver's beam; but Benaiah went against him with a staff, snatched the spear out of the Egyptian's hand, and killed him with his own spear. [24]Such were the things Benaiah son of Jehoiada did, and he won a name beside the three warriors. [25]He was renowned among Thirty, but he did not attain to the Three. And David put him in charge of his bodyguard.

26 The warriors of the armies were Asahel brother of Joab, Elhanan son of Dodo of Bethlehem, [27]Shammoth of Harod,[f] Helez the Pelonite, [28]Ira son of Ikkesh of Tekoa, Abiezer of Anathoth, [29]Sibbecai the Hushathite, Ilai the Ahohite, [30]Maharai of Netophah, Heled son of Baanah of Netophah, [31]Ithai son of Ribai of Gibeah of the Benjaminites, Benaiah of Pirathon, [32]Hurai of the wadis of Gaash, Abiel the Arbathite, [33]Azmaveth of Baharum, Eliahba of Shaalbon, [34]Hashem[g] the Gizonite, Jonathan son of Shagee the Hararite, [35]Ahiam son of Sachar the Hararite, Eliphal son of Ur, [36]Hepher the Mecherathite, Ahijah the Pelonite, [37]Hezro of Carmel, Naarai son of Ezbai, [38]Joel the brother of Nathan, Mibhar son of Hagri, [39]Zelek the Ammonite, Naharai of Beeroth,

the armor-bearer of Joab son of Zeruiah, [40]Ira the Ithrite, Gareb the Ithrite, [41]Uriah the Hittite, Zabad son of Ahlai, [42]Adina son of Shiza the Reubenite, a leader of the Reubenites, and thirty with him, [43]Hanan son of Maacah, and Joshaphat the Mithnite, [44]Uzzia the Ashterathite, Shama and Jeiel sons of Hotham the Aroerite, [45]Jediael son of Shimri, and his brother Joha the Tizite, [46]Eliel the Mahavite, and Jeribai and Joshaviah sons of Elnaam, and Ithmah the Moabite, [47]Eliel, and Obed, and Jaasiel the Mezobaite.

David's Followers in the Wilderness

12 The following are those who came to David at Ziklag, while he could not move about freely because of Saul son of Kish; they were among the mighty warriors who helped him in war. [2]They were archers, and could shoot arrows and sling stones with either the right hand or the left; they were Benjaminites, Saul's kindred. [3]The chief was Ahiezer, then Joash, both sons of Shemaah of Gibeah; also Jeziel and Pelet sons of Azmaveth; Beracah, Jehu of Anathoth, [4]Ishmaiah of Gibeon, a warrior among the Thirty and a leader over the Thirty; Jeremiah,[h] Jahaziel, Johanan, Jozabad of Gederah, [5]Eluzai,[i] Jerimoth, Bealiah, Shemariah, Shephatiah the Haruphite; [6]Elkanah, Isshiah, Azarel, Joezer, and Jashobeam, the Korahites; [7]and Joelah and Zebadiah, sons of Jeroham of Gedor.

8 From the Gadites there went over to David at the stronghold in the wilderness mighty and experienced warriors, expert with shield and spear, whose faces were like the faces of lions, and who were swift as gazelles on the mountains: [9]Ezer the chief, Obadiah second, Eliab third, [10]Mishmannah fourth, Jeremiah fifth, [11]Attai sixth, Eliel seventh, [12]Johanan eighth, Elzabad ninth, [13]Jeremiah tenth, Machbannai eleventh. [14]These Gadites were officers of the army, the least equal to a hundred and the greatest to a thousand. [15]These are the men who crossed the Jordan in the first

month, when it was overflowing all its banks, and put to flight all those in the valleys, to the east and to the west.

16 Some Benjaminites and Judahites came to the stronghold to David. [17]David went out to meet them and said to them, "If you have come to me in friendship, to help me, then my heart will be knit to you; but if you have come to betray me to my adversaries, though my hands have done no wrong, then may the God of our ancestors see and give judgment." [18]Then the spirit came upon Amasai, chief of the Thirty, and he said,

"We are yours, O David;
    and with you, O son of Jesse!
Peace, peace to you,
    and peace to the one who helps you!
    For your God is the one who helps
        you."

Then David received them, and made them officers of his troops.

19 Some of the Manassites deserted to David when he came with the Philistines for the battle against Saul. (Yet he did not help them, for the rulers of the Philistines took counsel and sent him away, saying, "He will desert to his master Saul at the cost of our heads.") [20]As he went to Ziklag these Manassites deserted to him: Adnah, Jozabad, Jediael, Michael, Jozabad, Elihu, and Zillethai, chiefs of the thousands in Manasseh. [21]They helped David against the band of raiders,[a] for they were all warriors and commanders in the army. [22]Indeed from day to day people kept coming to David to help him, until there was a great army, like an army of God.

David's Army at Hebron

23 These are the numbers of the divisions of the armed troops who came to David in Hebron to turn the kingdom of Saul over to him, according to the word of the LORD. [24]The people of Judah bearing shield and spear numbered six thousand eight hundred armed troops.

[25]Of the Simeonites, mighty warriors, seven thousand one hundred. [26]Of the Levites four thousand six hundred. [27]Jehoiada, leader of the house of Aaron, and with him three thousand seven hundred. [28]Zadok, a young warrior, and twenty-two commanders from his own ancestral house. [29]Of the Benjaminites, the kindred of Saul, three thousand, of whom the majority had continued to keep their allegiance to the house of Saul. [30]Of the Ephraimites, twenty thousand eight hundred, mighty warriors, notables in their ancestral houses. [31]Of the half-tribe of Manasseh, eighteen thousand, who were expressly named to come and make David king. [32]Of Issachar, those who had understanding of the times, to know what Israel ought to do, two hundred chiefs, and all their kindred under their command. [33]Of Zebulun, fifty thousand seasoned troops, equipped for battle with all the weapons of war, to help David[b] with singleness of purpose. [34]Of Naphtali, a thousand commanders, with whom there were thirty-seven thousand armed with shield and spear. [35]Of the Danites, twenty-eight thousand six hundred equipped for battle. [36]Of Asher, forty thousand seasoned troops ready for battle. [37]Of the Reubenites and Gadites and the half-tribe of Manasseh from beyond the Jordan, one hundred twenty thousand armed with all the weapons of war.

38 All these, warriors arrayed in battle order, came to Hebron with full intent to make David king over all Israel; likewise all the rest of Israel were of a single mind to make David king. [39]They were there with David for three days, eating and drinking, for their kindred had provided for them. [40]And also their neighbors, from as far away as Issachar and Zebulun and Naphtali, came bringing food on donkeys, camels, mules, and oxen—abundant provisions of meal, cakes of figs, clusters of raisins, wine, oil, oxen, and sheep, for there was joy in Israel.

The Ark Brought from Kiriath-jearim

13 David consulted with the commanders of the thousands and of the hundreds,

---

a Or *as officers of his troops*   *b* Gk: Heb lacks *David* with every leader. ²David said to the whole assembly of Israel, "If it seems good to you, and if it is the will of the LORD our God, let us send abroad to our kindred who remain in all the land of Israel, including the priests and Levites in the cities that have pasture lands, that they may come together to us. ³Then let us bring again the ark of our God to us; for we did not turn to it in the days of Saul." ⁴The whole assembly agreed to do so, for the thing pleased all the people.

5 So David assembled all Israel from the Shihor of Egypt to Lebo-hamath, to bring the ark of God from Kiriath-jearim. ⁶And David and all Israel went up to Baalah, that is, to Kiriath-jearim, which belongs to Judah, to bring up from there the ark of God, the LORD, who is enthroned on the cherubim, which is called by his*a* name. ⁷They carried the ark of God on a new cart, from the house of Abinadab, and Uzzah and Ahio*b* were driving the cart. ⁸David and all Israel were dancing before God with all their might, with song and lyres and harps and tambourines and cymbals and trumpets.

9 When they came to the threshing floor of Chidon, Uzzah put out his hand to hold the ark, for the oxen shook it. ¹⁰The anger of the LORD was kindled against Uzzah; he struck him down because he put out his hand to the ark; and he died there before God. ¹¹David was angry because the LORD had burst out against Uzzah; so that place is called Perez-uzzah*c* to this day. ¹²David was afraid of God that day; he said, "How can I bring the ark of God into my care?" ¹³So David did not take the ark into his care into the city of David; he took it instead to the house of Obed-edom the Gittite. ¹⁴The ark of God remained with the household of Obed-edom in his house three months, and the LORD blessed the household of Obed-edom and all that he had.

David Established at Jerusalem

14 King Hiram of Tyre sent messengers to David, along with cedar logs, and masons and carpenters to build a house for him. ²David then perceived that the LORD had established him as king over Israel, and that his kingdom was highly exalted for the sake of his people Israel.

3 David took more wives in Jerusalem, and David became the father of more sons and daughters. ⁴These are the names of the children whom he had in Jerusalem: Shammua, Shobab, and Nathan; Solomon, ⁵Ibhar, Elishua, and Elpelet; ⁶Nogah, Nepheg, and Japhia; ⁷Elishama, Beeliada, and Eliphelet.

Defeat of the Philistines

8 When the Philistines heard that David had been anointed king over all Israel, all the Philistines went up in search of David; and David heard of it and went out against them. ⁹Now the Philistines had come and made a raid in the valley of Rephaim. ¹⁰David inquired of God, "Shall I go up against the Philistines? Will you give them into my hand?" The LORD said to him, "Go up, and I will give them into your hand." ¹¹So he went up to Baal-perazim, and David defeated them there. David said, "God has burst out*d* against my enemies by my hand, like a bursting flood." Therefore that place is called Baal-perazim.*e* ¹²They abandoned their gods there, and at David's command they were burned.

13 Once again the Philistines made a raid in the valley. ¹⁴When David again inquired of God, God said to him, "You shall not go up after them; go around and come on them opposite the balsam trees. ¹⁵When you hear the sound of marching in the tops of the balsam trees, then go out to battle; for God has gone out before you to strike down the army of the Philistines." ¹⁶David did as God had commanded him, and they struck down the Philistine army from Gibeon to Gezer. ¹⁷The fame of David went out into all lands, and the LORD brought the fear of him on all nations.

The Ark Brought to Jerusalem

15 David*f* built houses for himself in the city of David, and he prepared a place

---

a Heb lacks *his*   *b* Or *and his brother*   *c* That is *Bursting Out Against Uzzah*   *d* Heb *paraz*   *e* That is *Lord of Bursting Out*   *f* Heb *He* for the ark of God and pitched a tent for it. [2]Then David commanded that no one but the Levites were to carry the ark of God, for the LORD had chosen them to carry the ark of the LORD and to minister to him forever. [3]David assembled all Israel in Jerusalem to bring up the ark of the LORD to its place, which he had prepared for it. [4]Then David gathered together the descendants of Aaron and the Levites: [5]of the sons of Kohath, Uriel the chief, with one hundred twenty of his kindred; [6]of the sons of Merari, Asaiah the chief, with two hundred twenty of his kindred; [7]of the sons of Gershom, Joel the chief, with one hundred thirty of his kindred; [8]of the sons of Elizaphan, Shemaiah the chief, with two hundred of his kindred; [9]of the sons of Hebron, Eliel the chief, with eighty of his kindred; [10]of the sons of Uzziel, Amminadab the chief, with one hundred twelve of his kindred.

11 David summoned the priests Zadok and Abiathar, and the Levites Uriel, Asaiah, Joel, Shemaiah, Eliel, and Amminadab. [12]He said to them, "You are the heads of families of the Levites; sanctify yourselves, you and your kindred, so that you may bring up the ark of the LORD, the God of Israel, to the place that I have prepared for it. [13]Because you did not carry it the first time,[a] the LORD our God burst out against us, because we did not give it proper care." [14]So the priests and the Levites sanctified themselves to bring up the ark of the LORD, the God of Israel. [15]And the Levites carried the ark of God on their shoulders with the poles, as Moses had commanded according to the word of the LORD.

16 David also commanded the chiefs of the Levites to appoint their kindred as the singers to play on musical instruments, on harps and lyres and cymbals, to raise loud sounds of joy. [17]So the Levites appointed Heman son of Joel; and of his kindred Asaph son of Berechiah; and of the sons of Merari, their kindred, Ethan son of Kushaiah; [18]and with them their kindred of the second order, Zechariah, Jaaziel, Shemiramoth, Jehiel, Unni, Eliab, Benaiah, Maaseiah,

Mattithiah, Eliphelehu, and Mikneiah, and the gatekeepers Obed-edom and Jeiel. [19]The singers Heman, Asaph, and Ethan were to sound bronze cymbals; [20]Zechariah, Aziel, Shemiramoth, Jehiel, Unni, Eliab, Maaseiah, and Benaiah were to play harps according to Alamoth; [21]but Mattithiah, Eliphelehu, Mikneiah, Obed-edom, Jeiel, and Azaziah were to lead with lyres according to the Sheminith. [22]Chenaniah, leader of the Levites in music, was to direct the music, for he understood it. [23]Berechiah and Elkanah were to be gatekeepers for the ark. [24]Shebaniah, Joshaphat, Nethanel, Amasai, Zechariah, Benaiah, and Eliezer, the priests, were to blow the trumpets before the ark of God. Obed-edom and Jehiah also were to be gatekeepers for the ark.

25 So David and the elders of Israel, and the commanders of the thousands, went to bring up the ark of the covenant of the LORD from the house of Obed-edom with rejoicing. [26]And because God helped the Levites who were carrying the ark of the covenant of the LORD, they sacrificed seven bulls and seven rams. [27]David was clothed with a robe of fine linen, as also were all the Levites who were carrying the ark, and the singers, and Chenaniah the leader of the music of the singers; and David wore a linen ephod. [28]So all Israel brought up the ark of the covenant of the LORD with shouting, to the sound of the horn, trumpets, and cymbals, and made loud music on harps and lyres.

29 As the ark of the covenant of the LORD came to the city of David, Michal daughter of Saul looked out of the window, and saw King David leaping and dancing; and she despised him in her heart.

The Ark Placed in the Tent

16 They brought in the ark of God, and set it inside the tent that David had pitched for it; and they offered burnt offerings and offerings of well-being before God. [2]When David had finished offering the burnt offerings and the offerings of well-being, he blessed the

---

a Meaning of Heb uncertain

people in the name of the LORD; ³and he distributed to every person in Israel—man and woman alike—to each a loaf of bread, a portion of meat,ᵃ and a cake of raisins.

4 He appointed certain of the Levites as ministers before the ark of the LORD, to invoke, to thank, and to praise the LORD, the God of Israel. ⁵Asaph was the chief, and second to him Zechariah, Jeiel, Shemiramoth, Jehiel, Mattithiah, Eliab, Benaiah, Obed-edom, and Jeiel, with harps and lyres; Asaph was to sound the cymbals, ⁶and the priests Benaiah and Jahaziel were to blow trumpets regularly, before the ark of the covenant of God.

David's Psalm of Thanksgiving

7 Then on that day David first appointed the singing of praises to the LORD by Asaph and his kindred.

8 O give thanks to the LORD, call on his
      name,
   make known his deeds among the
      peoples.
9 Sing to him, sing praises to him,
   tell of all his wonderful works.
10 Glory in his holy name;
   let the hearts of those who seek the
      LORD rejoice.
11 Seek the LORD and his strength,
   seek his presence continually.
12 Remember the wonderful works he has
      done,
   his miracles, and the judgments he
      uttered,
13 O offspring of his servant Israel,ᵇ
   children of Jacob, his chosen ones.

14 He is the LORD our God;
   his judgments are in all the earth.
15 Remember his covenant forever,
   the word that he commanded, for a
      thousand generations,
16 the covenant that he made with
      Abraham,
   his sworn promise to Isaac,

17 which he confirmed to Jacob as a statute,
   to Israel as an everlasting covenant,
18 saying, "To you I will give the land of
      Canaan
   as your portion for an inheritance."

19 When they were few in number,
   of little account, and strangers in the
      land,ᶜ
20 wandering from nation to nation,
   from one kingdom to another people,
21 he allowed no one to oppress them;
   he rebuked kings on their account,
22 saying, "Do not touch my anointed ones;
   do my prophets no harm."

23 Sing to the LORD, all the earth.
   Tell of his salvation from day to day.
24 Declare his glory among the nations,
   his marvelous works among all the
      peoples.
25 For great is the LORD, and greatly to be
      praised;
   he is to be revered above all gods.
26 For all the gods of the peoples are idols,
   but the LORD made the heavens.
27 Honor and majesty are before him;
   strength and joy are in his place.

28 Ascribe to the LORD, O families of the
      peoples,
   ascribe to the LORD glory and strength.
29 Ascribe to the LORD the glory due his
      name;
   bring an offering, and come before
      him.
   Worship the LORD in holy splendor;
30   tremble before him, all the earth.
   The world is firmly established; it shall
      never be moved.
31 Let the heavens be glad, and let the earth
      rejoice,
   and let them say among the nations,
      "The LORD is king!"
32 Let the sea roar, and all that fills it;
   let the field exult, and everything in it.

ᵃ Compare Gk Syr Vg: Meaning of Heb uncertain   ᵇ Another reading is *Abraham* (compare Ps 105.6)
ᶜ Heb *in it*

33   Then shall the trees of the forest sing
            for joy
      before the LORD, for he comes to
            judge the earth.
34   O give thanks to the LORD, for he is
            good;
      for his steadfast love endures forever.

35 Say also:
      "Save us, O God of our salvation,
            and gather and rescue us from among
                  the nations,
      that we may give thanks to your holy
                  name,
            and glory in your praise.
36   Blessed be the LORD, the God of Israel,
            from everlasting to everlasting."
Then all the people said "Amen!" and praised
the LORD.

Regular Worship Maintained

37   David left Asaph and his kinsfolk there
before the ark of the covenant of the LORD to
minister regularly before the ark as each day required, 38and also Obed-edom and his*a* sixty-
eight kinsfolk; while Obed-edom son of Jeduthun and Hosah were to be gatekeepers. 39And
he left the priest Zadok and his kindred the
priests before the tabernacle of the LORD in the
high place that was at Gibeon, 40to offer burnt
offerings to the LORD on the altar of burnt offering regularly, morning and evening, according to all that is written in the law of the LORD
that he commanded Israel. 41With them were
Heman and Jeduthun, and the rest of those
chosen and expressly named to render thanks
to the LORD, for his steadfast love endures
forever. 42Heman and Jeduthun had with them
trumpets and cymbals for the music, and instruments for sacred song. The sons of Jeduthun were appointed to the gate.

43   Then all the people departed to their
homes, and David went home to bless his
household.

God's Covenant with David

17 Now when David settled in his house,
David said to the prophet Nathan, "I
am living in a house of cedar, but the ark of the
covenant of the LORD is under a tent." 2Nathan
said to David, "Do all that you have in mind,
for God is with you."

3   But that same night the word of the LORD
came to Nathan, saying: 4Go and tell my servant David: Thus says the LORD: You shall not
build me a house to live in. 5For I have not lived
in a house since the day I brought out Israel to
this very day, but I have lived in a tent and a
tabernacle.*b* 6Wherever I have moved about
among all Israel, did I ever speak a word with
any of the judges of Israel, whom I commanded to shepherd my people, saying, Why
have you not built me a house of cedar? 7Now
therefore thus you shall say to my servant David: Thus says the LORD of hosts: I took you
from the pasture, from following the sheep, to
be ruler over my people Israel; 8and I have
been with you wherever you went, and have cut
off all your enemies before you; and I will
make for you a name, like the name of the
great ones of the earth. 9I will appoint a place
for my people Israel, and will plant them, so
that they may live in their own place, and be disturbed no more; and evildoers shall wear them
down no more, as they did formerly, 10from the
time that I appointed judges over my people Israel; and I will subdue all your enemies.

Moreover I declare to you that the LORD will
build you a house. 11When your days are fulfilled to go to be with your ancestors, I will raise
up your offspring after you, one of your own
sons, and I will establish his kingdom. 12He
shall build a house for me, and I will establish
his throne forever. 13I will be a father to him,
and he shall be a son to me. I will not take my
steadfast love from him, as I took it from him
who was before you, 14but I will confirm him
in my house and in my kingdom forever, and
his throne shall be established forever. 15In accordance with all these words and all this vision,
Nathan spoke to David.

a Gk Syr Vg: Heb *their*   b Gk 2 Sam 7.6: Heb *but I have been from tent to tent and from tabernacle*

David's Prayer

16 Then King David went in and sat before the LORD, and said, "Who am I, O LORD God, and what is my house, that you have brought me thus far? 17And even this was a small thing in your sight, O God; you have also spoken of your servant's house for a great while to come. You regard me as someone of high rank,*a* O LORD God! 18And what more can David say to you for honoring your servant? You know your servant. 19For your servant's sake, O LORD, and according to your own heart, you have done all these great deeds, making known all these great things. 20There is no one like you, O LORD, and there is no God besides you, according to all that we have heard with our ears. 21Who is like your people Israel, one nation on the earth whom God went to redeem to be his people, making for yourself a name for great and terrible things, in driving out nations before your people whom you redeemed from Egypt? 22And you made your people Israel to be your people forever; and you, O LORD, became their God.

23 "And now, O LORD, as for the word that you have spoken concerning your servant and concerning his house, let it be established forever, and do as you have promised. 24Thus your name will be established and magnified forever in the saying, 'The LORD of hosts, the God of Israel, is Israel's God'; and the house of your servant David will be established in your presence. 25For you, my God, have revealed to your servant that you will build a house for him; therefore your servant has found it possible to pray before you. 26And now, O LORD, you are God, and you have promised this good thing to your servant; 27therefore may it please you to bless the house of your servant, that it may continue forever before you. For you, O LORD, have blessed and are blessed*b* forever."

David's Kingdom Established and Extended

18 Some time afterward, David attacked the Philistines and subdued them; he took Gath and its villages from the Philistines.

2 He defeated Moab, and the Moabites became subject to David and brought tribute.

3 David also struck down King Hadadezer of Zobah, toward Hamath,*a* as he went to set up a monument at the river Euphrates. 4David took from him one thousand chariots, seven thousand cavalry, and twenty thousand foot soldiers. David hamstrung all the chariot horses, but left one hundred of them. 5When the Arameans of Damascus came to help King Hadadezer of Zobah, David killed twenty-two thousand Arameans. 6Then David put garrisons*c* in Aram of Damascus; and the Arameans became subject to David, and brought tribute. The LORD gave victory to David wherever he went. 7David took the gold shields that were carried by the servants of Hadadezer, and brought them to Jerusalem. 8From Tibhath and from Cun, cities of Hadadezer, David took a vast quantity of bronze; with it Solomon made the bronze sea and the pillars and the vessels of bronze.

9 When King Tou of Hamath heard that David had defeated the whole army of King Hadadezer of Zobah, 10he sent his son Hadoram to King David, to greet him and to congratulate him, because he had fought against Hadadezer and defeated him. Now Hadadezer had often been at war with Tou. He sent all sorts of articles of gold, of silver, and of bronze; 11these also King David dedicated to the LORD, together with the silver and gold that he had carried off from all the nations, from Edom, Moab, the Ammonites, the Philistines, and Amalek.

12 Abishai son of Zeruiah killed eighteen thousand Edomites in the Valley of Salt. 13He put garrisons in Edom; and all the Edomites became subject to David. And the LORD gave victory to David wherever he went.

a Meaning of Heb uncertain   *b* Or *and it is blessed*   *c* Gk Vg 2 Sam 8.6 Compare Syr: Heb lacks *garrisons*

David's Administration

14 So David reigned over all Israel; and he administered justice and equity to all his people. 15Joab son of Zeruiah was over the army; Jehoshaphat son of Ahilud was recorder; 16Zadok son of Ahitub and Ahimelech son of Abiathar were priests; Shavsha was secretary; 17Benaiah son of Jehoiada was over the Cherethites and the Pelethites; and David's sons were the chief officials in the service of the king.

Defeat of the Ammonites and Arameans

19 Some time afterward, King Nahash of the Ammonites died, and his son succeeded him. 2David said, "I will deal loyally with Hanun son of Nahash, for his father dealt loyally with me." So David sent messengers to console him concerning his father. When David's servants came to Hanun in the land of the Ammonites, to console him, 3the officials of the Ammonites said to Hanun, "Do you think, because David has sent consolers to you, that he is honoring your father? Have not his servants come to you to search and to overthrow and to spy out the land?" 4So Hanun seized David's servants, shaved them, cut off their garments in the middle at their hips, and sent them away; 5and they departed. When David was told about the men, he sent messengers to them, for they felt greatly humiliated. The king said, "Remain at Jericho until your beards have grown, and then return."

6 When the Ammonites saw that they had made themselves odious to David, Hanun and the Ammonites sent a thousand talents of silver to hire chariots and cavalry from Mesopotamia, from Aram-maacah and from Zobah. 7They hired thirty-two thousand chariots and the king of Maacah with his army, who came and camped before Medeba. And the Ammonites were mustered from their cities and came to battle. 8When David heard of it, he sent Joab and all the army of the warriors. 9The Ammonites came out and drew up in battle array at the entrance of the city, and the kings who had come were by themselves in the open country.

10 When Joab saw that the line of battle was set against him both in front and in the rear, he chose some of the picked men of Israel and arrayed them against the Arameans; 11the rest of his troops he put in the charge of his brother Abishai, and they were arrayed against the Ammonites. 12He said, "If the Arameans are too strong for me, then you shall help me; but if the Ammonites are too strong for you, then I will help you. 13Be strong, and let us be courageous for our people and for the cities of our God; and may the LORD do what seems good to him." 14So Joab and the troops who were with him advanced toward the Arameans for battle; and they fled before him. 15When the Ammonites saw that the Arameans fled, they likewise fled before Abishai, Joab's brother, and entered the city. Then Joab came to Jerusalem.

16 But when the Arameans saw that they had been defeated by Israel, they sent messengers and brought out the Arameans who were beyond the Euphrates, with Shophach the commander of the army of Hadadezer at their head. 17When David was informed, he gathered all Israel together, crossed the Jordan, came to them, and drew up his forces against them. When David set the battle in array against the Arameans, they fought with him. 18The Arameans fled before Israel; and David killed seven thousand Aramean charioteers and forty thousand foot soldiers, and also killed Shophach the commander of their army. 19When the servants of Hadadezer saw that they had been defeated by Israel, they made peace with David, and became subject to him. So the Arameans were not willing to help the Ammonites any more.

Siege and Capture of Rabbah

20 In the spring of the year, the time when kings go out to battle, Joab led out the army, ravaged the country of the Ammonites, and came and besieged Rabbah. But David remained at Jerusalem. Joab attacked Rabbah, and overthrew it. 2David took the crown of Milcom[a] from his head; he found

a Gk Vg See 1 Kings 11.5, 33: MT of their king

that it weighed a talent of gold, and in it was a precious stone; and it was placed on David's head. He also brought out the booty of the city, a very great amount. ³He brought out the people who were in it, and set them to work*a* with saws and iron picks and axes. *b* Thus David did to all the cities of the Ammonites. Then David and all the people returned to Jerusalem.

Exploits against the Philistines

4 After this, war broke out with the Philistines at Gezer; then Sibbecai the Hushathite killed Sippai, who was one of the descendants of the giants; and the Philistines were subdued. ⁵Again there was war with the Philistines; and Elhanan son of Jair killed Lahmi the brother of Goliath the Gittite, the shaft of whose spear was like a weaver's beam. ⁶Again there was war at Gath, where there was a man of great size, who had six fingers on each hand, and six toes on each foot, twenty-four in number; he also was descended from the giants. ⁷When he taunted Israel, Jonathan son of Shimea, David's brother, killed him. ⁸These were descended from the giants in Gath; they fell by the hand of David and his servants.

The Census and Plague

21 Satan stood up against Israel, and incited David to count the people of Israel. ²So David said to Joab and the commanders of the army, "Go, number Israel, from Beer-sheba to Dan, and bring me a report, so that I may know their number." ³But Joab said, "May the LORD increase the number of his people a hundredfold! Are they not, my lord the king, all of them my lord's servants? Why then should my lord require this? Why should he bring guilt on Israel?" ⁴But the king's word prevailed against Joab. So Joab departed and went throughout all Israel, and came back to Jerusalem. ⁵Joab gave the total count of the people to David. In all Israel there were one million one hundred thousand men who drew the sword, and in Judah four hundred seventy thousand who drew the sword. ⁶But he did not include

Levi and Benjamin in the numbering, for the king's command was abhorrent to Joab.

7 But God was displeased with this thing, and he struck Israel. ⁸David said to God, "I have sinned greatly in that I have done this thing. But now, I pray you, take away the guilt of your servant; for I have done very foolishly." ⁹The LORD spoke to Gad, David's seer, saying, ¹⁰"Go and say to David, 'Thus says the LORD: Three things I offer you; choose one of them, so that I may do it to you.'" ¹¹So Gad came to David and said to him, "Thus says the LORD, 'Take your choice: ¹²either three years of famine; or three months of devastation by your foes, while the sword of your enemies overtakes you; or three days of the sword of the LORD, pestilence on the land, and the angel of the LORD destroying throughout all the territory of Israel.' Now decide what answer I shall return to the one who sent me." ¹³Then David said to Gad, "I am in great distress; let me fall into the hand of the LORD, for his mercy is very great; but let me not fall into human hands."

14 So the LORD sent a pestilence on Israel; and seventy thousand persons fell in Israel. ¹⁵And God sent an angel to Jerusalem to destroy it; but when he was about to destroy it, the LORD took note and relented concerning the calamity; he said to the destroying angel, "Enough! Stay your hand." The angel of the LORD was then standing by the threshing floor of Ornan the Jebusite. ¹⁶David looked up and saw the angel of the LORD standing between earth and heaven, and in his hand a drawn sword stretched out over Jerusalem. Then David and the elders, clothed in sackcloth, fell on their faces. ¹⁷And David said to God, "Was it not I who gave the command to count the people? It is I who have sinned and done very wickedly. But these sheep, what have they done? Let your hand, I pray, O LORD my God, be against me and against my father's house; but do not let your people be plagued!"

David's Altar and Sacrifice

18 Then the angel of the LORD com-

---

a Compare 2 Sam 12.31: Heb *and he sawed*   *b* Compare 2 Sam 12.31: Heb *saws* manded Gad to tell David that he should go up and erect an altar to the LORD on the threshing floor of Ornan the Jebusite. [19]So David went up following Gad's instructions, which he had spoken in the name of the LORD. [20]Ornan turned and saw the angel; and while his four sons who were with him hid themselves, Ornan continued to thresh wheat. [21]As David came to Ornan, Ornan looked and saw David; he went out from the threshing floor, and did obeisance to David with his face to the ground. [22]David said to Ornan, "Give me the site of the threshing floor that I may build on it an altar to the LORD—give it to me at its full price—so that the plague may be averted from the people." [23]Then Ornan said to David, "Take it; and let my lord the king do what seems good to him; see, I present the oxen for burnt offerings, and the threshing sledges for the wood, and the wheat for a grain offering. I give it all." [24]But King David said to Ornan, "No; I will buy them for the full price. I will not take for the LORD what is yours, nor offer burnt offerings that cost me nothing." [25]So David paid Ornan six hundred shekels of gold by weight for the site. [26]David built there an altar to the LORD and presented burnt offerings and offerings of well-being. He called upon the LORD, and he answered him with fire from heaven on the altar of burnt offering. [27]Then the LORD commanded the angel, and he put his sword back into its sheath.

The Place Chosen for the Temple

[28] At that time, when David saw that the LORD had answered him at the threshing floor of Ornan the Jebusite, he made his sacrifices there. [29]For the tabernacle of the LORD, which Moses had made in the wilderness, and the altar of burnt offering were at that time in the high place at Gibeon; [30]but David could not go before it to inquire of God, for he was afraid of the sword of the angel of the LORD. **22** [1]Then David said, "Here shall be the house of the LORD God and here the altar of burnt offering for Israel."

David Prepares to Build the Temple

2 David gave orders to gather together the aliens who were residing in the land of Israel, and he set stonecutters to prepare dressed stones for building the house of God. [3]David also provided great stores of iron for nails for the doors of the gates and for clamps, as well as bronze in quantities beyond weighing, [4]and cedar logs without number—for the Sidonians and Tyrians brought great quantities of cedar to David. [5]For David said, "My son Solomon is young and inexperienced, and the house that is to be built for the LORD must be exceedingly magnificent, famous and glorified throughout all lands; I will therefore make preparation for it." So David provided materials in great quantity before his death.

David's Charge to Solomon and the Leaders

6 Then he called for his son Solomon and charged him to build a house for the LORD, the God of Israel. [7]David said to Solomon, "My son, I had planned to build a house to the name of the LORD my God. [8]But the word of the LORD came to me, saying, 'You have shed much blood and have waged great wars; you shall not build a house to my name, because you have shed so much blood in my sight on the earth. [9]See, a son shall be born to you; he shall be a man of peace. I will give him peace from all his enemies on every side; for his name shall be Solomon,*a* and I will give peace*b* and quiet to Israel in his days. [10]He shall build a house for my name. He shall be a son to me, and I will be a father to him, and I will establish his royal throne in Israel forever.' [11]Now, my son, the LORD be with you, so that you may succeed in building the house of the LORD your God, as he has spoken concerning you. [12]Only, may the LORD grant you discretion and understanding, so that when he gives you charge over Israel you may keep the law of the LORD your God. [13]Then you will prosper if you are careful to observe the statutes and the ordinances that the LORD commanded Moses for Israel. Be strong and of good courage. Do not be afraid or dis-

a Heb *Shelomoh*   *b* Heb *shalom*

mayed. [14]With great pains I have provided for the house of the LORD one hundred thousand talents of gold, one million talents of silver, and bronze and iron beyond weighing, for there is so much of it; timber and stone too I have provided. To these you must add more. [15]You have an abundance of workers: stonecutters, masons, carpenters, and all kinds of artisans without number, skilled in working [16]gold, silver, bronze, and iron. Now begin the work, and the LORD be with you."

17 David also commanded all the leaders of Israel to help his son Solomon, saying, [18]"Is not the LORD your God with you? Has he not given you peace on every side? For he has delivered the inhabitants of the land into my hand; and the land is subdued before the LORD and his people. [19]Now set your mind and heart to seek the LORD your God. Go and build the sanctuary of the LORD God so that the ark of the covenant of the LORD and the holy vessels of God may be brought into a house built for the name of the LORD."

Families of the Levites and Their Functions

23 When David was old and full of days, he made his son Solomon king over Israel.

2 David assembled all the leaders of Israel and the priests and the Levites. [3]The Levites, thirty years old and upward, were counted, and the total was thirty-eight thousand. [4]"Twenty-four thousand of these," David said, "shall have charge of the work in the house of the LORD, six thousand shall be officers and judges, [5]four thousand gatekeepers, and four thousand shall offer praises to the LORD with the instruments that I have made for praise." [6]And David organized them in divisions corresponding to the sons of Levi: Gershon,*a* Kohath, and Merari.

7 The sons of Gershon*b* were Ladan and Shimei. [8]The sons of Ladan: Jehiel the chief, Zetham, and Joel, three. [9]The sons of Shimei: Shelomoth, Haziel, and Haran, three. These were the heads of families of Ladan. [10]And the sons of Shimei: Jahath, Zina, Jeush, and Beriah. These four were the sons of Shimei. [11]Jahath was the chief, and Zizah the second; but Jeush and Beriah did not have many sons, so they were enrolled as a single family.

12 The sons of Kohath: Amram, Izhar, Hebron, and Uzziel, four. [13]The sons of Amram: Aaron and Moses. Aaron was set apart to consecrate the most holy things, so that he and his sons forever should make offerings before the LORD, and minister to him and pronounce blessings in his name forever; [14]but as for Moses the man of God, his sons were to be reckoned among the tribe of Levi. [15]The sons of Moses: Gershom and Eliezer. [16]The sons of Gershom: Shebuel the chief. [17]The sons of Eliezer: Rehabiah the chief; Eliezer had no other sons, but the sons of Rehabiah were very numerous. [18]The sons of Izhar: Shelomith the chief. [19]The sons of Hebron: Jeriah the chief, Amariah the second, Jahaziel the third, and Jekameam the fourth. [20]The sons of Uzziel: Micah the chief and Isshiah the second.

21 The sons of Merari: Mahli and Mushi. The sons of Mahli: Eleazar and Kish. [22]Eleazar died having no sons, but only daughters; their kindred, the sons of Kish, married them. [23]The sons of Mushi: Mahli, Eder, and Jeremoth, three.

24 These were the sons of Levi by their ancestral houses, the heads of families as they were enrolled according to the number of the names of the individuals from twenty years old and upward who were to do the work for the service of the house of the LORD. [25]For David said, "The LORD, the God of Israel, has given rest to his people; and he resides in Jerusalem forever. [26]And so the Levites no longer need to carry the tabernacle or any of the things for its service"— [27]for according to the last words of David these were the number of the Levites from twenty years old and upward— [28]"but their duty shall be to assist the descendants of Aaron for the service of the house of the LORD, having the care of the courts and the chambers, the cleansing of all that is holy, and

---

a Or *Gershom*; See 1 Chr 6.1, note, and 23.15   *b* Vg Compare Gk Syr: Heb *to the Gershonite* any work for the service of the house of God; [29]to assist also with the rows of bread, the choice flour for the grain offering, the wafers of unleavened bread, the baked offering, the offering mixed with oil, and all measures of quantity or size. [30]And they shall stand every morning, thanking and praising the LORD, and likewise at evening, [31]and whenever burnt offerings are offered to the LORD on sabbaths, new moons, and appointed festivals, according to the number required of them, regularly before the LORD. [32]Thus they shall keep charge of the tent of meeting and the sanctuary, and shall attend the descendants of Aaron, their kindred, for the service of the house of the LORD."

Divisions of the Priests

24 The divisions of the descendants of Aaron were these. The sons of Aaron: Nadab, Abihu, Eleazar, and Ithamar. [2]But Nadab and Abihu died before their father, and had no sons; so Eleazar and Ithamar became the priests. [3]Along with Zadok of the sons of Eleazar, and Ahimelech of the sons of Ithamar, David organized them according to the appointed duties in their service. [4]Since more chief men were found among the sons of Eleazar than among the sons of Ithamar, they organized them under sixteen heads of ancestral houses of the sons of Eleazar, and eight of the sons of Ithamar. [5]They organized them by lot, all alike, for there were officers of the sanctuary and officers of God among both the sons of Eleazar and the sons of Ithamar. [6]The scribe Shemaiah son of Nethanel, a Levite, recorded them in the presence of the king, and the officers, and Zadok the priest, and Ahimelech son of Abiathar, and the heads of ancestral houses of the priests and of the Levites; one ancestral house being chosen for Eleazar and one chosen for Ithamar.

[7] The first lot fell to Jehoiarib, the second to Jedaiah, [8]the third to Harim, the fourth to Seorim, [9]the fifth to Malchijah, the sixth to Mijamin, [10]the seventh to Hakkoz, the eighth to Abijah, [11]the ninth to Jeshua, the tenth to Sheca-

niah, [12]the eleventh to Eliashib, the twelfth to Jakim, [13]the thirteenth to Huppah, the fourteenth to Jeshebeab, [14]the fifteenth to Bilgah, the sixteenth to Immer, [15]the seventeenth to Hezir, the eighteenth to Happizzez, [16]the nineteenth to Pethahiah, the twentieth to Jehezkel, [17]the twenty-first to Jachin, the twenty-second to Gamul, [18]the twenty-third to Delaiah, the twenty-fourth to Maaziah. [19]These had as their appointed duty in their service to enter the house of the LORD according to the procedure established for them by their ancestor Aaron, as the LORD God of Israel had commanded him.

Other Levites

[20] And of the rest of the sons of Levi: of the sons of Amram, Shubael; of the sons of Shubael, Jehdeiah. [21]Of Rehabiah: of the sons of Rehabiah, Isshiah the chief. [22]Of the Izharites, Shelomoth; of the sons of Shelomoth, Jahath. [23]The sons of Hebron:*a* Jeriah the chief,*b* Amariah the second, Jahaziel the third, Jekameam the fourth. [24]The sons of Uzziel, Micah; of the sons of Micah, Shamir. [25]The brother of Micah, Isshiah; of the sons of Isshiah, Zechariah. [26]The sons of Merari: Mahli and Mushi. The sons of Jaaziah: Beno.*c* [27]The sons of Merari: of Jaaziah, Beno,*c* Shoham, Zaccur, and Ibri. [28]Of Mahli: Eleazar, who had no sons. [29]Of Kish, the sons of Kish: Jerahmeel. [30]The sons of Mushi: Mahli, Eder, and Jerimoth. These were the sons of the Levites according to their ancestral houses. [31]These also cast lots corresponding to their kindred, the descendants of Aaron, in the presence of King David, Zadok, Ahimelech, and the heads of ancestral houses of the priests and of the Levites, the chief as well as the youngest brother.

The Temple Musicians

25 David and the officers of the army also set apart for the service the sons of Asaph, and of Heman, and of Jeduthun, who should prophesy with lyres, harps, and cymbals. The list of those who did the work and of their duties was: [2]Of the sons of Asaph:

---

a See 23.19: Heb lacks *Hebron*   *b* See 23.19: Heb lacks *the chief*   *c* Or *his son*: Meaning of Heb uncertain

Zaccur, Joseph, Nethaniah, and Asarelah, sons of Asaph, under the direction of Asaph, who prophesied under the direction of the king. [3]Of Jeduthun, the sons of Jeduthun: Gedaliah, Zeri, Jeshaiah, Shimei,[a] Hashabiah, and Mattithiah, six, under the direction of their father Jeduthun, who prophesied with the lyre in thanksgiving and praise to the LORD. [4]Of Heman, the sons of Heman: Bukkiah, Mattaniah, Uzziel, Shebuel, and Jerimoth, Hananiah, Hanani, Eliathah, Giddalti, and Romamti-ezer, Joshbekashah, Mallothi, Hothir, Mahazioth. [5]All these were the sons of Heman the king's seer, according to the promise of God to exalt him; for God had given Heman fourteen sons and three daughters. [6]They were all under the direction of their father for the music in the house of the LORD with cymbals, harps, and lyres for the service of the house of God. Asaph, Jeduthun, and Heman were under the order of the king. [7]They and their kindred, who were trained in singing to the LORD, all of whom were skillful, numbered two hundred eighty-eight. [8]And they cast lots for their duties, small and great, teacher and pupil alike.

[9] The first lot fell for Asaph to Joseph; the second to Gedaliah, to him and his brothers and his sons, twelve; [10]the third to Zaccur, his sons and his brothers, twelve; [11]the fourth to Izri, his sons and his brothers, twelve; [12]the fifth to Nethaniah, his sons and his brothers, twelve; [13]the sixth to Bukkiah, his sons and his brothers, twelve; [14]the seventh to Jesarelah,[b] his sons and his brothers, twelve; [15]the eighth to Jeshaiah, his sons and his brothers, twelve; [16]the ninth to Mattaniah, his sons and his brothers, twelve; [17]the tenth to Shimei, his sons and his brothers, twelve; [18]the eleventh to Azarel, his sons and his brothers, twelve; [19]the twelfth to Hashabiah, his sons and his brothers, twelve; [20]to the thirteenth, Shubael, his sons and his brothers, twelve; [21]to the fourteenth, Mattithiah, his sons and his brothers, twelve; [22]to the fifteenth, to Jeremoth, his sons and his brothers, twelve; [23]to the sixteenth, to Hananiah, his sons and his brothers, twelve; [24]to the seven-

teenth, to Joshbekashah, his sons and his brothers, twelve; [25]to the eighteenth, to Hanani, his sons and his brothers, twelve; [26]to the nineteenth, to Mallothi, his sons and his brothers, twelve; [27]to the twentieth, to Eliathah, his sons and his brothers, twelve; [28]to the twenty-first, to Hothir, his sons and his brothers, twelve; [29]to the twenty-second, to Giddalti, his sons and his brothers, twelve; [30]to the twenty-third, to Mahazioth, his sons and his brothers, twelve; [31]to the twenty-fourth, to Romamti-ezer, his sons and his brothers, twelve.

The Gatekeepers

26 As for the divisions of the gatekeepers: of the Korahites, Meshelemiah son of Kore, of the sons of Asaph. [2]Meshelemiah had sons: Zechariah the firstborn, Jediael the second, Zebadiah the third, Jathniel the fourth, [3]Elam the fifth, Jehohanan the sixth, Eliehoenai the seventh. [4]Obed-edom had sons: Shemaiah the firstborn, Jehozabad the second, Joah the third, Sachar the fourth, Nethanel the fifth, [5]Ammiel the sixth, Issachar the seventh, Peullethai the eighth; for God blessed him. [6]Also to his son Shemaiah sons were born who exercised authority in their ancestral houses, for they were men of great ability. [7]The sons of Shemaiah: Othni, Rephael, Obed, and Elzabad, whose brothers were able men, Elihu and Semachiah. [8]All these, sons of Obed-edom with their sons and brothers, were able men qualified for the service; sixty-two of Obed-edom. [9]Meshelemiah had sons and brothers, able men, eighteen. [10]Hosah, of the sons of Merari, had sons: Shimri the chief (for though he was not the firstborn, his father made him chief), [11]Hilkiah the second, Tebaliah the third, Zechariah the fourth: all the sons and brothers of Hosah totaled thirteen.

[12] These divisions of the gatekeepers, corresponding to their leaders, had duties, just as their kindred did, ministering in the house of the LORD; [13]and they cast lots by ancestral houses, small and great alike, for their gates. [14]The lot for the east fell to Shelemiah. They

cast lots also for his son Zechariah, a prudent counselor, and his lot came out for the north. 15Obed-edom's came out for the south, and to his sons was allotted the storehouse. 16For Shuppim and Hosah it came out for the west, at the gate of Shallecheth on the ascending road. Guard corresponded to guard. 17On the east there were six Levites each day,*a* on the north four each day, on the south four each day, as well as two and two at the storehouse; 18and for the colonnade*b* on the west there were four at the road and two at the colonnade.*b* 19These were the divisions of the gatekeepers among the Korahites and the sons of Merari.

The Treasurers, Officers, and Judges

20 And of the Levites, Ahijah had charge of the treasuries of the house of God and the treasuries of the dedicated gifts. 21The sons of Ladan, the sons of the Gershonites belonging to Ladan, the heads of families belonging to Ladan the Gershonite: Jehieli.*c*

22 The sons of Jehieli, Zetham and his brother Joel, were in charge of the treasuries of the house of the LORD. 23Of the Amramites, the Izharites, the Hebronites, and the Uzzielites: 24Shebuel son of Gershom, son of Moses, was chief officer in charge of the treasuries. 25His brothers: from Eliezer were his son Rehabiah, his son Jeshaiah, his son Joram, his son Zichri, and his son Shelomoth. 26This Shelomoth and his brothers were in charge of all the treasuries of the dedicated gifts that King David, and the heads of families, and the officers of the thousands and the hundreds, and the commanders of the army, had dedicated. 27From booty won in battles they dedicated gifts for the maintenance of the house of the LORD. 28Also all that Samuel the seer, and Saul son of Kish, and Abner son of Ner, and Joab son of Zeruiah had dedicated—all dedicated gifts were in the care of Shelomoth*d* and his brothers.

29 Of the Izharites, Chenaniah and his sons were appointed to outside duties for Israel, as officers and judges. 30Of the Hebronites, Hashabiah and his brothers, one thousand seven hundred men of ability, had the oversight of Israel west of the Jordan for all the work of the LORD and for the service of the king. 31Of the Hebronites, Jerijah was chief of the Hebronites. (In the fortieth year of David's reign search was made, of whatever genealogy or family, and men of great ability among them were found at Jazer in Gilead.) 32King David appointed him and his brothers, two thousand seven hundred men of ability, heads of families, to have the oversight of the Reubenites, the Gadites, and the half-tribe of the Manassites for everything pertaining to God and for the affairs of the king.

The Military Divisions

27 This is the list of the people of Israel, the heads of families, the commanders of the thousands and the hundreds, and their officers who served the king in all matters concerning the divisions that came and went, month after month throughout the year, each division numbering twenty-four thousand:

2 Jashobeam son of Zabdiel was in charge of the first division in the first month; in his division were twenty-four thousand. 3He was a descendant of Perez, and was chief of all the commanders of the army for the first month. 4Dodai the Ahohite was in charge of the division of the second month; Mikloth was the chief officer of his division. In his division were twenty-four thousand. 5The third commander, for the third month, was Benaiah son of the priest Jehoiada, as chief; in his division were twenty-four thousand. 6This is the Benaiah who was a mighty man of the Thirty and in command of the Thirty; his son Ammizabad was in charge of his division.*e* 7Asahel brother of Joab was fourth, for the fourth month, and his son Zebadiah after him; in his division were twenty-four thousand. 8The fifth commander, for the fifth month, was Shamhuth, the Izrahite; in his division were twenty-four thousand. 9Sixth, for the sixth month, was Ira son of Ikkesh the Tekoite; in his division were twenty-four thousand. 10Seventh, for the sev-

---

a Gk: Heb lacks *each day*   *b* Heb *parbar*: meaning uncertain   *c* The Hebrew text of verse 21 is confused   *d* Gk Compare 26.28: Heb *Shelomith*   *e* Gk Vg: Heb *Ammizabad was his division* enth month, was Helez the Pelonite, of the Ephraimites; in his division were twenty-four thousand. 11 Eighth, for the eighth month, was Sibbecai the Hushathite, of the Zerahites; in his division were twenty-four thousand. 12 Ninth, for the ninth month, was Abiezer of Anathoth, a Benjaminite; in his division were twenty-four thousand. 13 Tenth, for the tenth month, was Maharai of Netophah, of the Zerahites; in his division were twenty-four thousand. 14 Eleventh, for the eleventh month, was Benaiah of Pirathon, of the Ephraimites; in his division were twenty-four thousand. 15 Twelfth, for the twelfth month, was Heldai the Netophathite, of Othniel; in his division were twenty-four thousand.

Leaders of Tribes

16 Over the tribes of Israel, for the Reubenites, Eliezer son of Zichri was chief officer; for the Simeonites, Shephatiah son of Maacah; 17 for Levi, Hashabiah son of Kemuel; for Aaron, Zadok; 18 for Judah, Elihu, one of David's brothers; for Issachar, Omri son of Michael; 19 for Zebulun, Ishmaiah son of Obadiah; for Naphtali, Jerimoth son of Azriel; 20 for the Ephraimites, Hoshea son of Azaziah; for the half-tribe of Manasseh, Joel son of Pedaiah; 21 for the half-tribe of Manasseh in Gilead, Iddo son of Zechariah; for Benjamin, Jaasiel son of Abner; 22 for Dan, Azarel son of Jeroham. These were the leaders of the tribes of Israel. 23 David did not count those below twenty years of age, for the LORD had promised to make Israel as numerous as the stars of heaven. 24 Joab son of Zeruiah began to count them, but did not finish; yet wrath came upon Israel for this, and the number was not entered into the account of the Annals of King David.

Other Civic Officials

25 Over the king's treasuries was Azmaveth son of Adiel. Over the treasuries in the country, in the cities, in the villages and in the towers, was Jonathan son of Uzziah. 26 Over those who did the work of the field, tilling the soil, was Ezri son of Chelub. 27 Over the vineyards was Shimei the Ramathite. Over the pro-

duce of the vineyards for the wine cellars was Zabdi the Shiphmite. 28 Over the olive and sycamore trees in the Shephelah was Baal-hanan the Gederite. Over the stores of oil was Joash. 29 Over the herds that pastured in Sharon was Shitrai the Sharonite. Over the herds in the valleys was Shaphat son of Adlai. 30 Over the camels was Obil the Ishmaelite. Over the donkeys was Jehdeiah the Meronothite. Over the flocks was Jaziz the Hagrite. 31 All these were stewards of King David's property.

32 Jonathan, David's uncle, was a counselor, being a man of understanding and a scribe; Jehiel son of Hachmoni attended the king's sons. 33 Ahithophel was the king's counselor, and Hushai the Archite was the king's friend. 34 After Ahithophel came Jehoiada son of Benaiah, and Abiathar. Joab was commander of the king's army.

Solomon Instructed to Build the Temple

28 David assembled at Jerusalem all the officials of Israel, the officials of the tribes, the officers of the divisions that served the king, the commanders of the thousands, the commanders of the hundreds, the stewards of all the property and cattle of the king and his sons, together with the palace officials, the mighty warriors, and all the warriors. 2 Then King David rose to his feet and said: "Hear me, my brothers and my people. I had planned to build a house of rest for the ark of the covenant of the LORD, for the footstool of our God; and I made preparations for building. 3 But God said to me, 'You shall not build a house for my name, for you are a warrior and have shed blood.' 4 Yet the LORD God of Israel chose me from all my ancestral house to be king over Israel forever; for he chose Judah as leader, and in the house of Judah my father's house, and among my father's sons he took delight in making me king over all Israel. 5 And of all my sons, for the LORD has given me many, he has chosen my son Solomon to sit upon the throne of the kingdom of the LORD over Israel. 6 He said to me, 'It is your son Solomon who shall build my house and my courts, for I have chosen him to be a son to me, and I will be a father to

him. 7I will establish his kingdom forever if he continues resolute in keeping my commandments and my ordinances, as he is today.' 8Now therefore in the sight of all Israel, the assembly of the LORD, and in the hearing of our God, observe and search out all the commandments of the LORD your God; that you may possess this good land, and leave it for an inheritance to your children after you forever.

9 "And you, my son Solomon, know the God of your father, and serve him with single mind and willing heart; for the LORD searches every mind, and understands every plan and thought. If you seek him, he will be found by you; but if you forsake him, he will abandon you forever. 10Take heed now, for the LORD has chosen you to build a house as the sanctuary; be strong, and act."

11 Then David gave his son Solomon the plan of the vestibule of the temple, and of its houses, its treasuries, its upper rooms, and its inner chambers, and of the room for the mercy seat;*a* 12and the plan of all that he had in mind: for the courts of the house of the LORD, all the surrounding chambers, the treasuries of the house of God, and the treasuries for dedicated gifts; 13for the divisions of the priests and of the Levites, and all the work of the service in the house of the LORD; for all the vessels for the service in the house of the LORD, 14the weight of gold for all golden vessels for each service, the weight of silver vessels for each service, 15the weight of the golden lampstands and their lamps, the weight of gold for each lampstand and its lamps, the weight of silver for a lampstand and its lamps, according to the use of each in the service, 16the weight of gold for each table for the rows of bread, the silver for the silver tables, 17and pure gold for the forks, the basins, and the cups; for the golden bowls and the weight of each; for the silver bowls and the weight of each; 18for the altar of incense made of refined gold, and its weight; also his plan for the golden chariot of the cherubim that spread their wings and covered the ark of the covenant of the LORD.

19 "All this, in writing at the LORD's direction, he made clear to me—the plan of all the works."

20 David said further to his son Solomon, "Be strong and of good courage, and act. Do not be afraid or dismayed; for the LORD God, my God, is with you. He will not fail you or forsake you, until all the work for the service of the house of the LORD is finished. 21Here are the divisions of the priests and the Levites for all the service of the house of God; and with you in all the work will be every volunteer who has skill for any kind of service; also the officers and all the people will be wholly at your command."

Offerings for Building the Temple

29 King David said to the whole assembly, "My son Solomon, whom alone God has chosen, is young and inexperienced, and the work is great; for the temple*b* will not be for mortals but for the LORD God. 2So I have provided for the house of my God, so far as I was able, the gold for the things of gold, the silver for the things of silver, and the bronze for the things of bronze, the iron for the things of iron, and wood for the things of wood, besides great quantities of onyx and stones for setting, antimony, colored stones, all sorts of precious stones, and marble in abundance. 3Moreover, in addition to all that I have provided for the holy house, I have a treasure of my own of gold and silver, and because of my devotion to the house of my God I give it to the house of my God: 4three thousand talents of gold, of the gold of Ophir, and seven thousand talents of refined silver, for overlaying the walls of the house, 5and for all the work to be done by artisans, gold for the things of gold and silver for the things of silver. Who then will offer willingly, consecrating themselves today to the LORD?"

6 Then the leaders of ancestral houses made their freewill offerings, as did also the leaders of the tribes, the commanders of the thousands and of the hundreds, and the offi-

---

a Or *the cover*   *b* Heb *fortress*

cers over the king's work. [7]They gave for the service of the house of God five thousand talents and ten thousand darics of gold, ten thousand talents of silver, eighteen thousand talents of bronze, and one hundred thousand talents of iron. [8]Whoever had precious stones gave them to the treasury of the house of the LORD, into the care of Jehiel the Gershonite. [9]Then the people rejoiced because these had given willingly, for with single mind they had offered freely to the LORD; King David also rejoiced greatly.

David's Praise to God

10 Then David blessed the LORD in the presence of all the assembly; David said: "Blessed are you, O LORD, the God of our ancestor Israel, forever and ever. [11]Yours, O LORD, are the greatness, the power, the glory, the victory, and the majesty; for all that is in the heavens and on the earth is yours; yours is the kingdom, O LORD, and you are exalted as head above all. [12]Riches and honor come from you, and you rule over all. In your hand are power and might; and it is in your hand to make great and to give strength to all. [13]And now, our God, we give thanks to you and praise your glorious name.

14 "But who am I, and what is my people, that we should be able to make this freewill offering? For all things come from you, and of your own have we given you. [15]For we are aliens and transients before you, as were all our ancestors; our days on the earth are like a shadow, and there is no hope. [16]O LORD our God, all this abundance that we have provided for building you a house for your holy name comes from your hand and is all your own. [17]I know, my God, that you search the heart, and take pleasure in uprightness; in the uprightness of my heart I have freely offered all these things, and now I have seen your people, who are present here, offering freely and joyously to you. [18]O LORD, the God of Abraham, Isaac, and Israel, our ancestors, keep forever such purposes and thoughts in the hearts of your people, and direct their hearts toward you. [19]Grant to my son Solomon that with single mind he may keep your commandments, your decrees, and your statutes, performing all of them, and that he may build the temple[a] for which I have made provision."

20 Then David said to the whole assembly, "Bless the LORD your God." And all the assembly blessed the LORD, the God of their ancestors, and bowed their heads and prostrated themselves before the LORD and the king. [21]On the next day they offered sacrifices and burnt offerings to the LORD, a thousand bulls, a thousand rams, and a thousand lambs, with their libations, and sacrifices in abundance for all Israel; [22]and they ate and drank before the LORD on that day with great joy.

Solomon Anointed King

They made David's son Solomon king a second time; they anointed him as the LORD's prince, and Zadok as priest. [23]Then Solomon sat on the throne of the LORD, succeeding his father David as king; he prospered, and all Israel obeyed him. [24]All the leaders and the mighty warriors, and also all the sons of King David, pledged their allegiance to King Solomon. [25]The LORD highly exalted Solomon in the sight of all Israel, and bestowed upon him such royal majesty as had not been on any king before him in Israel.

Summary of David's Reign

26 Thus David son of Jesse reigned over all Israel. [27]The period that he reigned over Israel was forty years; he reigned seven years in Hebron, and thirty-three years in Jerusalem. [28]He died in a good old age, full of days, riches, and honor; and his son Solomon succeeded him. [29]Now the acts of King David, from first to last, are written in the records of the seer Samuel, and in the records of the prophet Nathan, and in the records of the seer Gad, [30]with accounts of all his rule and his might and of the events that befell him and Israel and all the kingdoms of the earth.

a Heb *fortress*

2 CHRONICLES

Solomon Requests Wisdom

1 Solomon son of David established himself in his kingdom; the LORD his God was with him and made him exceedingly great.

2 Solomon summoned all Israel, the commanders of the thousands and of the hundreds, the judges, and all the leaders of all Israel, the heads of families. ³Then Solomon, and the whole assembly with him, went to the high place that was at Gibeon; for God's tent of meeting, which Moses the servant of the LORD had made in the wilderness, was there. ⁴(But David had brought the ark of God up from Kiriath-jearim to the place that David had prepared for it; for he had pitched a tent for it in Jerusalem.) ⁵Moreover the bronze altar that Bezalel son of Uri, son of Hur, had made, was there in front of the tabernacle of the LORD. And Solomon and the assembly inquired at it. ⁶Solomon went up there to the bronze altar before the LORD, which was at the tent of meeting, and offered a thousand burnt offerings on it.

7 That night God appeared to Solomon, and said to him, "Ask what I should give you." ⁸Solomon said to God, "You have shown great and steadfast love to my father David, and have made me succeed him as king. ⁹O LORD God, let your promise to my father David now be fulfilled, for you have made me king over a people as numerous as the dust of the earth. ¹⁰Give me now wisdom and knowledge to go out and come in before this people, for who can rule this great people of yours?" ¹¹God answered Solomon, "Because this was in your heart, and you have not asked for possessions, wealth, honor, or the life of those who hate you, and have not even asked for long life, but have asked for wisdom and knowledge for yourself that you may rule my people over whom I have made you king, ¹²wisdom and knowledge are granted to you. I will also give you riches, possessions, and honor, such as none of the kings had who were before you,

and none after you shall have the like." ¹³So Solomon came from*a* the high place at Gibeon, from the tent of meeting, to Jerusalem. And he reigned over Israel.

Solomon's Military and Commercial Activity

14 Solomon gathered together chariots and horses; he had fourteen hundred chariots and twelve thousand horses, which he stationed in the chariot cities and with the king in Jerusalem. ¹⁵The king made silver and gold as common in Jerusalem as stone, and he made cedar as plentiful as the sycamore of the Shephelah. ¹⁶Solomon's horses were imported from Egypt and Kue; the king's traders received them from Kue at the prevailing price. ¹⁷They imported from Egypt, and then exported, a chariot for six hundred shekels of silver, and a horse for one hundred fifty; so through them these were exported to all the kings of the Hittites and the kings of Aram.

Preparations for Building the Temple

2 *b*Solomon decided to build a temple for the name of the LORD, and a royal palace for himself. 2 *c*Solomon conscripted seventy thousand laborers and eighty thousand stonecutters in the hill country, with three thousand six hundred to oversee them.

Alliance with Huram of Tyre

3 Solomon sent word to King Huram of Tyre: "Once you dealt with my father David and sent him cedar to build himself a house to live in. ⁴I am now about to build a house for the name of the LORD my God and dedicate it to him for offering fragrant incense before him, and for the regular offering of the rows of bread, and for burnt offerings morning and evening, on the sabbaths and the new moons and the appointed festivals of the LORD our God, as ordained forever for Israel. ⁵The house that I am about to build will be great, for our God is greater than other gods. ⁶But who is

a Gk Vg: Heb *to*   *b* Ch 1.18 in Heb   *c* Ch 2.1 in Heb able to build him a house, since heaven, even highest heaven, cannot contain him? Who am I to build a house for him, except as a place to make offerings before him? 7So now send me an artisan skilled to work in gold, silver, bronze, and iron, and in purple, crimson, and blue fabrics, trained also in engraving, to join the skilled workers who are with me in Judah and Jerusalem, whom my father David provided. 8Send me also cedar, cypress, and algum timber from Lebanon, for I know that your servants are skilled in cutting Lebanon timber. My servants will work with your servants 9to prepare timber for me in abundance, for the house I am about to build will be great and wonderful. 10I will provide for your servants, those who cut the timber, twenty thousand cors of crushed wheat, twenty thousand cors of barley, twenty thousand baths*a* of wine, and twenty thousand baths of oil."

11 Then King Huram of Tyre answered in a letter that he sent to Solomon, "Because the LORD loves his people he has made you king over them." 12Huram also said, "Blessed be the LORD God of Israel, who made heaven and earth, who has given King David a wise son, endowed with discretion and understanding, who will build a temple for the LORD, and a royal palace for himself.

13 "I have dispatched Huram-abi, a skilled artisan, endowed with understanding, 14the son of one of the Danite women, his father a Tyrian. He is trained to work in gold, silver, bronze, iron, stone, and wood, and in purple, blue, and crimson fabrics and fine linen, and to do all sorts of engraving and execute any design that may be assigned him, with your artisans, the artisans of my lord, your father David. 15Now, as for the wheat, barley, oil, and wine, of which my lord has spoken, let him send them to his servants. 16We will cut whatever timber you need from Lebanon, and bring it to you as rafts by sea to Joppa; you will take it up to Jerusalem."

17 Then Solomon took a census of all the aliens who were residing in the land of Israel, after the census that his father David had taken; and there were found to be one hundred fifty-three thousand six hundred. 18Seventy thousand of them he assigned as laborers, eighty thousand as stonecutters in the hill country, and three thousand six hundred as overseers to make the people work.

Solomon Builds the Temple

3 Solomon began to build the house of the LORD in Jerusalem on Mount Moriah, where the LORD had appeared to his father David, at the place that David had designated, on the threshing floor of Ornan the Jebusite. 2He began to build on the second day of the second month of the fourth year of his reign. 3These are Solomon's measurements*b* for building the house of God: the length, in cubits of the old standard, was sixty cubits, and the width twenty cubits. 4The vestibule in front of the nave of the house was twenty cubits long, across the width of the house;*c* and its height was one hundred twenty cubits. He overlaid it on the inside with pure gold. 5The nave he lined with cypress, covered it with fine gold, and made palms and chains on it. 6He adorned the house with settings of precious stones. The gold was gold from Parvaim. 7So he lined the house with gold—its beams, its thresholds, its walls, and its doors; and he carved cherubim on the walls.

8 He made the most holy place; its length, corresponding to the width of the house, was twenty cubits, and its width was twenty cubits; he overlaid it with six hundred talents of fine gold. 9The weight of the nails was fifty shekels of gold. He overlaid the upper chambers with gold.

10 In the most holy place he made two carved cherubim and overlaid*d* them with gold. 11The wings of the cherubim together extended twenty cubits: one wing of the one, five cubits long, touched the wall of the house, and its other wing, five cubits long, touched the wing of the other cherub; 12and of this cherub, one wing, five cubits long, touched the wall of the house, and the other wing, also five cu-

---

a A Hebrew measure of volume   *b* Syr: Heb *foundations*   *c* Compare 1 Kings 6.3: Meaning of Heb uncertain
d Heb *they overlaid*

bits long, was joined to the wing of the first cherub. 13The wings of these cherubim extended twenty cubits; the cherubim*a* stood on their feet, facing the nave. 14And Solomon*b* made the curtain of blue and purple and crimson fabrics and fine linen, and worked cherubim into it.

15 In front of the house he made two pillars thirty-five cubits high, with a capital of five cubits on the top of each. 16He made encircling*c* chains and put them on the tops of the pillars; and he made one hundred pomegranates, and put them on the chains. 17He set up the pillars in front of the temple, one on the right, the other on the left; the one on the right he called Jachin, and the one on the left, Boaz.

Furnishings of the Temple

4 He made an altar of bronze, twenty cubits long, twenty cubits wide, and ten cubits high. 2Then he made the molten sea; it was round, ten cubits from rim to rim, and five cubits high. A line of thirty cubits would encircle it completely. 3Under it were panels all around, each of ten cubits, surrounding the sea; there were two rows of panels, cast when it was cast. 4It stood on twelve oxen, three facing north, three facing west, three facing south, and three facing east; the sea was set on them. The hindquarters of each were toward the inside. 5Its thickness was a handbreadth; its rim was made like the rim of a cup, like the flower of a lily; it held three thousand baths.*d* 6He also made ten basins in which to wash, and set five on the right side, and five on the left. In these they were to rinse what was used for the burnt offering. The sea was for the priests to wash in.

7 He made ten golden lampstands as prescribed, and set them in the temple, five on the south side and five on the north. 8He also made ten tables and placed them in the temple, five on the right side and five on the left. And he made one hundred basins of gold. 9He made the court of the priests, and the great court, and doors for the court; he overlaid

their doors with bronze. 10He set the sea at the southeast corner of the house.

11 And Huram made the pots, the shovels, and the basins. Thus Huram finished the work that he did for King Solomon on the house of God: 12the two pillars, the bowls, and the two capitals on the top of the pillars; and the two latticeworks to cover the two bowls of the capitals that were on the top of the pillars; 13the four hundred pomegranates for the two latticeworks, two rows of pomegranates for each latticework, to cover the two bowls of the capitals that were on the pillars. 14He made the stands, the basins on the stands, 15the one sea, and the twelve oxen underneath it. 16The pots, the shovels, the forks, and all the equipment for these Huram-abi made of burnished bronze for King Solomon for the house of the LORD. 17In the plain of the Jordan the king cast them, in the clay ground between Succoth and Zeredah. 18Solomon made all these things in great quantities, so that the weight of the bronze was not determined.

19 So Solomon made all the things that were in the house of God: the golden altar, the tables for the bread of the Presence, 20the lampstands and their lamps of pure gold to burn before the inner sanctuary, as prescribed; 21the flowers, the lamps, and the tongs, of purest gold; 22the snuffers, basins, ladles, and firepans, of pure gold. As for the entrance to the temple: the inner doors to the most holy place and the doors of the nave of the temple were of gold.

5 Thus all the work that Solomon did for the house of the LORD was finished. Solomon brought in the things that his father David had dedicated, and stored the silver, the gold, and all the vessels in the treasuries of the house of God.

The Ark Brought into the Temple

2 Then Solomon assembled the elders of Israel and all the heads of the tribes, the leaders of the ancestral houses of the people of Israel, in Jerusalem, to bring up the ark of the cov-

---

a Heb *they*   *b* Heb *he*   *c* Cn: Heb *in the inner sanctuary*   *d* A Hebrew measure of volume enant of the LORD out of the city of David, which is Zion. ³And all the Israelites assembled before the king at the festival that is in the seventh month. ⁴And all the elders of Israel came, and the Levites carried the ark. ⁵So they brought up the ark, the tent of meeting, and all the holy vessels that were in the tent; the priests and the Levites brought them up. ⁶King Solomon and all the congregation of Israel, who had assembled before him, were before the ark, sacrificing so many sheep and oxen that they could not be numbered or counted. ⁷Then the priests brought the ark of the covenant of the LORD to its place, in the inner sanctuary of the house, in the most holy place, underneath the wings of the cherubim. ⁸For the cherubim spread out their wings over the place of the ark, so that the cherubim made a covering above the ark and its poles. ⁹The poles were so long that the ends of the poles were seen from the holy place in front of the inner sanctuary; but they could not be seen from outside; they are there to this day. ¹⁰There was nothing in the ark except the two tablets that Moses put there at Horeb, where the LORD made a covenant*a* with the people of Israel after they came out of Egypt.

11 Now when the priests came out of the holy place (for all the priests who were present had sanctified themselves, without regard to their divisions), ¹²all the levitical singers, Asaph, Heman, and Jeduthun, their sons and kindred, arrayed in fine linen, with cymbals, harps, and lyres, stood east of the altar with one hundred twenty priests who were trumpeters. ¹³It was the duty of the trumpeters and singers to make themselves heard in unison in praise and thanksgiving to the LORD, and when the song was raised, with trumpets and cymbals and other musical instruments, in praise to the LORD,

"For he is good,
    for his steadfast love endures forever,"

the house, the house of the LORD, was filled with a cloud, ¹⁴so that the priests could not stand to minister because of the cloud; for the glory of the LORD filled the house of God.

Dedication of the Temple

6 Then Solomon said, "The LORD has said that he would reside in thick darkness. ²I have built you an exalted house, a place for you to reside in forever."

3 Then the king turned around and blessed all the assembly of Israel, while all the assembly of Israel stood. ⁴And he said, "Blessed be the LORD, the God of Israel, who with his hand has fulfilled what he promised with his mouth to my father David, saying, ⁵'Since the day that I brought my people out of the land of Egypt, I have not chosen a city from any of the tribes of Israel in which to build a house, so that my name might be there, and I chose no one as ruler over my people Israel; ⁶but I have chosen Jerusalem in order that my name may be there, and I have chosen David to be over my people Israel.' ⁷My father David had it in mind to build a house for the name of the LORD, the God of Israel. ⁸But the LORD said to my father David, 'You did well to consider building a house for my name; ⁹nevertheless you shall not build the house, but your son who shall be born to you shall build the house for my name.' ¹⁰Now the LORD has fulfilled his promise that he made; for I have succeeded my father David, and sit on the throne of Israel, as the LORD promised, and have built the house for the name of the LORD, the God of Israel. ¹¹There I have set the ark, in which is the covenant of the LORD that he made with the people of Israel."

Solomon's Prayer of Dedication

12 Then Solomon*b* stood before the altar of the LORD in the presence of the whole assembly of Israel, and spread out his hands. ¹³Solomon had made a bronze platform five cubits long, five cubits wide, and three cubits high, and had set it in the court; and he stood on it. Then he knelt on his knees in the presence of the whole assembly of Israel, and spread out his hands toward heaven. ¹⁴He said, "O LORD, God of Israel, there is no God like you, in heaven or on earth, keeping covenant

---

a Heb lacks *a covenant*   *b* Heb *he*

in steadfast love with your servants who walk before you with all their heart— [15]you who have kept for your servant, my father David, what you promised to him. Indeed, you promised with your mouth and this day have fulfilled with your hand. [16]Therefore, O LORD, God of Israel, keep for your servant, my father David, that which you promised him, saying, 'There shall never fail you a successor before me to sit on the throne of Israel, if only your children keep to their way, to walk in my law as you have walked before me.' [17]Therefore, O LORD, God of Israel, let your word be confirmed, which you promised to your servant David.

18 "But will God indeed reside with mortals on earth? Even heaven and the highest heaven cannot contain you, how much less this house that I have built! [19]Regard your servant's prayer and his plea, O LORD my God, heeding the cry and the prayer that your servant prays to you. [20]May your eyes be open day and night toward this house, the place where you promised to set your name, and may you heed the prayer that your servant prays toward this place. [21]And hear the plea of your servant and of your people Israel, when they pray toward this place; may you hear from heaven your dwelling place; hear and forgive.

22 "If someone sins against another and is required to take an oath and comes and swears before your altar in this house, [23]may you hear from heaven, and act, and judge your servants, repaying the guilty by bringing their conduct on their own head, and vindicating those who are in the right by rewarding them in accordance with their righteousness.

24 "When your people Israel, having sinned against you, are defeated before an enemy but turn again to you, confess your name, pray and plead with you in this house, [25]may you hear from heaven, and forgive the sin of your people Israel, and bring them again to the land that you gave to them and to their ancestors.

26 "When heaven is shut up and there is no rain because they have sinned against you, and then they pray toward this place, confess your name, and turn from their sin, because you punish them, [27]may you hear in heaven, forgive the sin of your servants, your people Israel, when you teach them the good way in which they should walk; and send down rain upon your land, which you have given to your people as an inheritance.

28 "If there is famine in the land, if there is plague, blight, mildew, locust, or caterpillar; if their enemies besiege them in any of the settlements of the lands; whatever suffering, whatever sickness there is; [29]whatever prayer, whatever plea from any individual or from all your people Israel, all knowing their own suffering and their own sorrows so that they stretch out their hands toward this house; [30]may you hear from heaven, your dwelling place, forgive, and render to all whose heart you know, according to all their ways, for only you know the human heart. [31]Thus may they fear you and walk in your ways all the days that they live in the land that you gave to our ancestors.

32 "Likewise when foreigners, who are not of your people Israel, come from a distant land because of your great name, and your mighty hand, and your outstretched arm, when they come and pray toward this house, [33]may you hear from heaven your dwelling place, and do whatever the foreigners ask of you, in order that all the peoples of the earth may know your name and fear you, as do your people Israel, and that they may know that your name has been invoked on this house that I have built.

34 "If your people go out to battle against their enemies, by whatever way you shall send them, and they pray to you toward this city that you have chosen and the house that I have built for your name, [35]then hear from heaven their prayer and their plea, and maintain their cause.

36 "If they sin against you—for there is no one who does not sin—and you are angry with them and give them to an enemy, so that they are carried away captive to a land far or near; [37]then if they come to their senses in the land to which they have been taken captive, and repent, and plead with you in the land of their captivity, saying, 'We have sinned, and have done wrong; we have acted wickedly'; [38]if they

repent with all their heart and soul in the land of their captivity, to which they were taken captive, and pray toward their land, which you gave to their ancestors, the city that you have chosen, and the house that I have built for your name, ³⁹then hear from heaven your dwelling place their prayer and their pleas, maintain their cause and forgive your people who have sinned against you. ⁴⁰Now, O my God, let your eyes be open and your ears attentive to prayer from this place.

⁴¹ "Now rise up, O LORD God, and go to
         your resting place,
     you and the ark of your might.
 Let your priests, O LORD God, be
         clothed with salvation,
     and let your faithful rejoice in your
         goodness.
⁴² O LORD God, do not reject your
         anointed one.
     Remember your steadfast love for
         your servant David."

Solomon Dedicates the Temple

7 When Solomon had ended his prayer, fire came down from heaven and consumed the burnt offering and the sacrifices; and the glory of the LORD filled the temple. ²The priests could not enter the house of the LORD, because the glory of the LORD filled the LORD's house. ³When all the people of Israel saw the fire come down and the glory of the LORD on the temple, they bowed down on the pavement with their faces to the ground, and worshiped and gave thanks to the LORD, saying,

     "For he is good,
         for his steadfast love endures forever."

4 Then the king and all the people offered sacrifice before the LORD. ⁵King Solomon offered as a sacrifice twenty-two thousand oxen and one hundred twenty thousand sheep. So the king and all the people dedicated the house of God. ⁶The priests stood at their posts; the Levites also, with the instruments for music to the LORD that King David had made for giving thanks to the LORD—for his steadfast love endures forever—whenever David offered

praises by their ministry. Opposite them the priests sounded trumpets; and all Israel stood.

7 Solomon consecrated the middle of the court that was in front of the house of the LORD; for there he offered the burnt offerings and the fat of the offerings of well-being because the bronze altar Solomon had made could not hold the burnt offering and the grain offering and the fat parts.

8 At that time Solomon held the festival for seven days, and all Israel with him, a very great congregation, from Lebo-hamath to the Wadi of Egypt. ⁹On the eighth day they held a solemn assembly; for they had observed the dedication of the altar seven days and the festival seven days. ¹⁰On the twenty-third day of the seventh month he sent the people away to their homes, joyful and in good spirits because of the goodness that the LORD had shown to David and to Solomon and to his people Israel.

11 Thus Solomon finished the house of the LORD and the king's house; all that Solomon had planned to do in the house of the LORD and in his own house he successfully accomplished.

God's Second Appearance to Solomon

12 Then the LORD appeared to Solomon in the night and said to him: "I have heard your prayer, and have chosen this place for myself as a house of sacrifice. ¹³When I shut up the heavens so that there is no rain, or command the locust to devour the land, or send pestilence among my people, ¹⁴if my people who are called by my name humble themselves, pray, seek my face, and turn from their wicked ways, then I will hear from heaven, and will forgive their sin and heal their land. ¹⁵Now my eyes will be open and my ears attentive to the prayer that is made in this place. ¹⁶For now I have chosen and consecrated this house so that my name may be there forever; my eyes and my heart will be there for all time. ¹⁷As for you, if you walk before me, as your father David walked, doing according to all that I have commanded you and keeping my statutes and my ordinances, ¹⁸then I will establish your royal throne, as I

made covenant with your father David saying, 'You shall never lack a successor to rule over Israel.'

19 "But if you*a* turn aside and forsake my statutes and my commandments that I have set before you, and go and serve other gods and worship them, 20then I will pluck you*b* up from the land that I have given you;*b* and this house, which I have consecrated for my name, I will cast out of my sight, and will make it a proverb and a byword among all peoples. 21And regarding this house, now exalted, everyone passing by will be astonished, and say, 'Why has the LORD done such a thing to this land and to this house?' 22Then they will say, 'Because they abandoned the LORD the God of their ancestors who brought them out of the land of Egypt, and they adopted other gods, and worshiped them and served them; therefore he has brought all this calamity upon them.'"

Various Activities of Solomon

8 At the end of twenty years, during which Solomon had built the house of the LORD and his own house, 2Solomon rebuilt the cities that Huram had given to him, and settled the people of Israel in them.

3 Solomon went to Hamath-zobah, and captured it. 4He built Tadmor in the wilderness and all the storage towns that he built in Hamath. 5He also built Upper Beth-horon and Lower Beth-horon, fortified cities, with walls, gates, and bars, 6and Baalath, as well as all Solomon's storage towns, and all the towns for his chariots, the towns for his cavalry, and whatever Solomon desired to build, in Jerusalem, in Lebanon, and in all the land of his dominion. 7All the people who were left of the Hittites, the Amorites, the Perizzites, the Hivites, and the Jebusites, who were not of Israel, 8from their descendants who were still left in the land, whom the people of Israel had not destroyed—these Solomon conscripted for forced labor, as is still the case today. 9But of the people of Israel Solomon made no slaves for his work; they were soldiers, and his officers,

the commanders of his chariotry and cavalry. 10These were the chief officers of King Solomon, two hundred fifty of them, who exercised authority over the people.

11 Solomon brought Pharaoh's daughter from the city of David to the house that he had built for her, for he said, "My wife shall not live in the house of King David of Israel, for the places to which the ark of the LORD has come are holy."

12 Then Solomon offered up burnt offerings to the LORD on the altar of the LORD that he had built in front of the vestibule, 13as the duty of each day required, offering according to the commandment of Moses for the sabbaths, the new moons, and the three annual festivals—the festival of unleavened bread, the festival of weeks, and the festival of booths. 14According to the ordinance of his father David, he appointed the divisions of the priests for their service, and the Levites for their offices of praise and ministry alongside the priests as the duty of each day required, and the gatekeepers in their divisions for the several gates; for so David the man of God had commanded. 15They did not turn away from what the king had commanded the priests and Levites regarding anything at all, or regarding the treasuries.

16 Thus all the work of Solomon was accomplished from*c* the day the foundation of the house of the LORD was laid until the house of the LORD was finished completely.

17 Then Solomon went to Ezion-geber and Eloth on the shore of the sea, in the land of Edom. 18Huram sent him, in the care of his servants, ships and servants familiar with the sea. They went to Ophir, together with the servants of Solomon, and imported from there four hundred fifty talents of gold and brought it to King Solomon.

Visit of the Queen of Sheba

9 When the queen of Sheba heard of the fame of Solomon, she came to Jerusalem to test him with hard questions, having a very

---

a The word *you* in this verse is plural   *b* Heb *them*   *c* Gk Syr Vg: Heb *to* great retinue and camels bearing spices and very much gold and precious stones. When she came to Solomon, she discussed with him all that was on her mind. ²Solomon answered all her questions; there was nothing hidden from Solomon that he could not explain to her. ³When the queen of Sheba had observed the wisdom of Solomon, the house that he had built, ⁴the food of his table, the seating of his officials, and the attendance of his servants, and their clothing, his valets, and their clothing, and his burnt offerings*a* that he offered at the house of the LORD, there was no more spirit left in her.

5 So she said to the king, "The report was true that I heard in my own land of your accomplishments and of your wisdom, ⁶but I did not believe the*b* reports until I came and my own eyes saw it. Not even half of the greatness of your wisdom had been told to me; you far surpass the report that I had heard. ⁷Happy are your people! Happy are these your servants, who continually attend you and hear your wisdom! ⁸Blessed be the LORD your God, who has delighted in you and set you on his throne as king for the LORD your God. Because your God loved Israel and would establish them forever, he has made you king over them, that you may execute justice and righteousness." ⁹Then she gave the king one hundred twenty talents of gold, a very great quantity of spices, and precious stones: there were no spices such as those that the queen of Sheba gave to King Solomon.

10 Moreover the servants of Huram and the servants of Solomon who brought gold from Ophir brought algum wood and precious stones. ¹¹From the algum wood, the king made steps*c* for the house of the LORD and for the king's house, lyres also and harps for the singers; there never was seen the like of them before in the land of Judah.

12 Meanwhile King Solomon granted the queen of Sheba every desire that she expressed, well beyond what she had brought to the king.

Then she returned to her own land, with her servants.

Solomon's Great Wealth

13 The weight of gold that came to Solomon in one year was six hundred sixty-six talents of gold, ¹⁴besides that which the traders and merchants brought; and all the kings of Arabia and the governors of the land brought gold and silver to Solomon. ¹⁵King Solomon made two hundred large shields of beaten gold; six hundred shekels of beaten gold went into each large shield. ¹⁶He made three hundred shields of beaten gold; three hundred shekels of gold went into each shield; and the king put them in the House of the Forest of Lebanon. ¹⁷The king also made a great ivory throne, and overlaid it with pure gold. ¹⁸The throne had six steps and a footstool of gold, which were attached to the throne, and on each side of the seat were arm rests and two lions standing beside the arm rests, ¹⁹while twelve lions were standing, one on each end of a step on the six steps. The like of it was never made in any kingdom. ²⁰All King Solomon's drinking vessels were of gold, and all the vessels of the House of the Forest of Lebanon were of pure gold; silver was not considered as anything in the days of Solomon. ²¹For the king's ships went to Tarshish with the servants of Huram; once every three years the ships of Tarshish used to come bringing gold, silver, ivory, apes, and peacocks.*d*

22 Thus King Solomon excelled all the kings of the earth in riches and in wisdom. ²³All the kings of the earth sought the presence of Solomon to hear his wisdom, which God had put into his mind. ²⁴Every one of them brought a present, objects of silver and gold, garments, weaponry, spices, horses, and mules, so much year by year. ²⁵Solomon had four thousand stalls for horses and chariots, and twelve thousand horses, which he stationed in the chariot cities and with the king in Jerusalem. ²⁶He ruled over all the kings from the Euphrates to the land of the Philistines, and to the

---

a Gk Syr Vg 1 Kings 10.5: Heb *ascent*   *b* Heb *their*   *c* Gk Vg: Meaning of Heb uncertain   *d* Or *baboons* border of Egypt. 27The king made silver as common in Jerusalem as stone, and cedar as plentiful as the sycamore of the Shephelah. 28Horses were imported for Solomon from Egypt and from all lands.

Death of Solomon

29 Now the rest of the acts of Solomon, from first to last, are they not written in the history of the prophet Nathan, and in the prophecy of Ahijah the Shilonite, and in the visions of the seer Iddo concerning Jeroboam son of Nebat? 30Solomon reigned in Jerusalem over all Israel forty years. 31Solomon slept with his ancestors and was buried in the city of his father David; and his son Rehoboam succeeded him.

The Revolt against Rehoboam

10 Rehoboam went to Shechem, for all Israel had come to Shechem to make him king. 2When Jeroboam son of Nebat heard of it (for he was in Egypt, where he had fled from King Solomon), then Jeroboam returned from Egypt. 3They sent and called him; and Jeroboam and all Israel came and said to Rehoboam, 4"Your father made our yoke heavy. Now therefore lighten the hard service of your father and his heavy yoke that he placed on us, and we will serve you." 5He said to them, "Come to me again in three days." So the people went away.

6 Then King Rehoboam took counsel with the older men who had attended his father Solomon while he was still alive, saying, "How do you advise me to answer this people?" 7They answered him, "If you will be kind to this people and please them, and speak good words to them, then they will be your servants forever." 8But he rejected the advice that the older men gave him, and consulted the young men who had grown up with him and now attended him. 9He said to them, "What do you advise that we answer this people who have said to me, 'Lighten the yoke that your father put on us'?" 10The young men who had grown up with him said to him, "Thus should you speak to the people who said to you, 'Your father made our yoke heavy, but you must lighten it

for us'; tell them, 'My little finger is thicker than my father's loins. 11Now, whereas my father laid on you a heavy yoke, I will add to your yoke. My father disciplined you with whips, but I will discipline you with scorpions.'"

12 So Jeroboam and all the people came to Rehoboam the third day, as the king had said, "Come to me again the third day." 13The king answered them harshly. King Rehoboam rejected the advice of the older men; 14he spoke to them in accordance with the advice of the young men, "My father made your yoke heavy, but I will add to it; my father disciplined you with whips, but I will discipline you with scorpions." 15So the king did not listen to the people, because it was a turn of affairs brought about by God so that the LORD might fulfill his word, which he had spoken by Ahijah the Shilonite to Jeroboam son of Nebat.

16 When all Israel saw that the king would not listen to them, the people answered the king,

"What share do we have in David?
　We have no inheritance in the son of
　　Jesse.
Each of you to your tents, O Israel!
　Look now to your own house,
　　O David."

So all Israel departed to their tents. 17But Rehoboam reigned over the people of Israel who were living in the cities of Judah. 18When King Rehoboam sent Hadoram, who was taskmaster over the forced labor, the people of Israel stoned him to death. King Rehoboam hurriedly mounted his chariot to flee to Jerusalem. 19So Israel has been in rebellion against the house of David to this day.

Judah and Benjamin Fortified

11 When Rehoboam came to Jerusalem, he assembled one hundred eighty thousand chosen troops of the house of Judah and Benjamin to fight against Israel, to restore the kingdom to Rehoboam. 2But the word of the LORD came to Shemaiah the man of God: 3Say to King Rehoboam of Judah, son of Solomon, and to all Israel in Judah and Benjamin, 4"Thus says the LORD: You shall not go up or

fight against your kindred. Let everyone return home, for this thing is from me." So they heeded the word of the LORD and turned back from the expedition against Jeroboam.

5 Rehoboam resided in Jerusalem, and he built cities for defense in Judah. [6]He built up Bethlehem, Etam, Tekoa, [7]Beth-zur, Soco, Adullam, [8]Gath, Mareshah, Ziph, [9]Adoraim, Lachish, Azekah, [10]Zorah, Aijalon, and Hebron, fortified cities that are in Judah and in Benjamin. [11]He made the fortresses strong, and put commanders in them, and stores of food, oil, and wine. [12]He also put large shields and spears in all the cities, and made them very strong. So he held Judah and Benjamin.

Priests and Levites Support Rehoboam

13 The priests and the Levites who were in all Israel presented themselves to him from all their territories. [14]The Levites had left their common lands and their holdings and had come to Judah and Jerusalem, because Jeroboam and his sons had prevented them from serving as priests of the LORD, [15]and had appointed his own priests for the high places, and for the goat-demons, and for the calves that he had made. [16]Those who had set their hearts to seek the LORD God of Israel came after them from all the tribes of Israel to Jerusalem to sacrifice to the LORD, the God of their ancestors. [17]They strengthened the kingdom of Judah, and for three years they made Rehoboam son of Solomon secure, for they walked for three years in the way of David and Solomon.

Rehoboam's Marriages

18 Rehoboam took as his wife Mahalath daughter of Jerimoth son of David, and of Abihail daughter of Eliab son of Jesse. [19]She bore him sons: Jeush, Shemariah, and Zaham. [20]After her he took Maacah daughter of Absalom, who bore him Abijah, Attai, Ziza, and Shelomith. [21]Rehoboam loved Maacah daughter of Absalom more than all his other wives and concubines (he took eighteen wives and sixty concubines, and became the father of twenty-eight sons and sixty daughters). [22]Rehoboam appointed Abijah son of Maacah as chief prince among his brothers, for he intended to make him king. [23]He dealt wisely, and distributed some of his sons through all the districts of Judah and Benjamin, in all the fortified cities; he gave them abundant provisions, and found many wives for them.

Egypt Attacks Judah

12 When the rule of Rehoboam was established and he grew strong, he abandoned the law of the LORD, he and all Israel with him. [2]In the fifth year of King Rehoboam, because they had been unfaithful to the LORD, King Shishak of Egypt came up against Jerusalem [3]with twelve hundred chariots and sixty thousand cavalry. A countless army came with him from Egypt—Libyans, Sukkiim, and Ethiopians.[a] [4]He took the fortified cities of Judah and came as far as Jerusalem. [5]Then the prophet Shemaiah came to Rehoboam and to the officers of Judah, who had gathered at Jerusalem because of Shishak, and said to them, "Thus says the LORD: You abandoned me, so I have abandoned you to the hand of Shishak." [6]Then the officers of Israel and the king humbled themselves and said, "The LORD is in the right." [7]When the LORD saw that they humbled themselves, the word of the LORD came to Shemaiah, saying: "They have humbled themselves; I will not destroy them, but I will grant them some deliverance, and my wrath shall not be poured out on Jerusalem by the hand of Shishak. [8]Nevertheless they shall be his servants, so that they may know the difference between serving me and serving the kingdoms of other lands."

9 So King Shishak of Egypt came up against Jerusalem; he took away the treasures of the house of the LORD and the treasures of the king's house; he took everything. He also took away the shields of gold that Solomon had made; [10]but King Rehoboam made in place of them shields of bronze, and committed them to the hands of the officers of the guard,

a Or Nubians; Heb Cushites

who kept the door of the king's house. [11]Whenever the king went into the house of the LORD, the guard would come along bearing them, and would then bring them back to the guardroom. [12]Because he humbled himself the wrath of the LORD turned from him, so as not to destroy them completely; moreover, conditions were good in Judah.

Death of Rehoboam

13 So King Rehoboam established himself in Jerusalem and reigned. Rehoboam was forty-one years old when he began to reign; he reigned seventeen years in Jerusalem, the city that the LORD had chosen out of all the tribes of Israel to put his name there. His mother's name was Naamah the Ammonite. [14]He did evil, for he did not set his heart to seek the LORD.

15 Now the acts of Rehoboam, from first to last, are they not written in the records of the prophet Shemaiah and of the seer Iddo, recorded by genealogy? There were continual wars between Rehoboam and Jeroboam. [16]Rehoboam slept with his ancestors and was buried in the city of David; and his son Abijah succeeded him.

Abijah Reigns over Judah

13 In the eighteenth year of King Jeroboam, Abijah began to reign over Judah. [2]He reigned for three years in Jerusalem. His mother's name was Micaiah daughter of Uriel of Gibeah.

Now there was war between Abijah and Jeroboam. [3]Abijah engaged in battle, having an army of valiant warriors, four hundred thousand picked men; and Jeroboam drew up his line of battle against him with eight hundred thousand picked mighty warriors. [4]Then Abijah stood on the slope of Mount Zemaraim that is in the hill country of Ephraim, and said, "Listen to me, Jeroboam and all Israel! [5]Do you not know that the LORD God of Israel gave the kingship over Israel forever to David and his sons by a covenant of salt? [6]Yet Jeroboam son

of Nebat, a servant of Solomon son of David, rose up and rebelled against his lord; [7]and certain worthless scoundrels gathered around him and defied Rehoboam son of Solomon, when Rehoboam was young and irresolute and could not withstand them.

8 "And now you think that you can withstand the kingdom of the LORD in the hand of the sons of David, because you are a great multitude and have with you the golden calves that Jeroboam made as gods for you. [9]Have you not driven out the priests of the LORD, the descendants of Aaron, and the Levites, and made priests for yourselves like the peoples of other lands? Whoever comes to be consecrated with a young bull or seven rams becomes a priest of what are no gods. [10]But as for us, the LORD is our God, and we have not abandoned him. We have priests ministering to the LORD who are descendants of Aaron, and Levites for their service. [11]They offer to the LORD every morning and every evening burnt offerings and fragrant incense, set out the rows of bread on the table of pure gold, and care for the golden lampstand so that its lamps may burn every evening; for we keep the charge of the LORD our God, but you have abandoned him. [12]See, God is with us at our head, and his priests have their battle trumpets to sound the call to battle against you. O Israelites, do not fight against the LORD, the God of your ancestors; for you cannot succeed."

13 Jeroboam had sent an ambush around to come on them from behind; thus his troops[a] were in front of Judah, and the ambush was behind them. [14]When Judah turned, the battle was in front of them and behind them. They cried out to the LORD, and the priests blew the trumpets. [15]Then the people of Judah raised the battle shout. And when the people of Judah shouted, God defeated Jeroboam and all Israel before Abijah and Judah. [16]The Israelites fled before Judah, and God gave them into their hands. [17]Abijah and his army defeated them with great slaughter; five hundred thousand picked men of Israel fell slain. [18]Thus the Israelites were

a Heb *they*

subdued at that time, and the people of Judah prevailed, because they relied on the LORD, the God of their ancestors. 19Abijah pursued Jeroboam, and took cities from him: Bethel with its villages and Jeshanah with its villages and Ephron*a* with its villages. 20Jeroboam did not recover his power in the days of Abijah; the LORD struck him down, and he died. 21But Abijah grew strong. He took fourteen wives, and became the father of twenty-two sons and sixteen daughters. 22The rest of the acts of Abijah, his behavior and his deeds, are written in the story of the prophet Iddo.

Asa Reigns

14 *b* So Abijah slept with his ancestors, and they buried him in the city of David. His son Asa succeeded him. In his days the land had rest for ten years. 2*c* Asa did what was good and right in the sight of the LORD his God. 3He took away the foreign altars and the high places, broke down the pillars, hewed down the sacred poles,*d* 4and commanded Judah to seek the LORD, the God of their ancestors, and to keep the law and the commandment. 5He also removed from all the cities of Judah the high places and the incense altars. And the kingdom had rest under him. 6He built fortified cities in Judah while the land had rest. He had no war in those years, for the LORD gave him peace. 7He said to Judah, "Let us build these cities, and surround them with walls and towers, gates and bars; the land is still ours because we have sought the LORD our God; we have sought him, and he has given us peace on every side." So they built and prospered. 8Asa had an army of three hundred thousand from Judah, armed with large shields and spears, and two hundred eighty thousand troops from Benjamin who carried shields and drew bows; all these were mighty warriors.

Ethiopian Invasion Repulsed

9 Zerah the Ethiopian*e* came out against them with an army of a million men and three hundred chariots, and came as far as Mareshah. 10Asa went out to meet him, and they drew up their lines of battle in the valley of Zephathah at Mareshah. 11Asa cried to the LORD his God, "O LORD, there is no difference for you between helping the mighty and the weak. Help us, O LORD our God, for we rely on you, and in your name we have come against this multitude. O LORD, you are our God; let no mortal prevail against you." 12So the LORD defeated the Ethiopians*f* before Asa and before Judah, and the Ethiopians*f* fled. 13Asa and the army with him pursued them as far as Gerar, and the Ethiopians*f* fell until no one remained alive; for they were broken before the LORD and his army. The people of Judah*g* carried away a great quantity of booty. 14They defeated all the cities around Gerar, for the fear of the LORD was on them. They plundered all the cities; for there was much plunder in them. 15They also attacked the tents of those who had livestock,*h* and carried away sheep and goats in abundance, and camels. Then they returned to Jerusalem.

15 The spirit of God came upon Azariah son of Oded. 2He went out to meet Asa and said to him, "Hear me, Asa, and all Judah and Benjamin: The LORD is with you, while you are with him. If you seek him, he will be found by you, but if you abandon him, he will abandon you. 3For a long time Israel was without the true God, and without a teaching priest, and without law; 4but when in their distress they turned to the LORD, the God of Israel, and sought him, he was found by them. 5In those times it was not safe for anyone to go or come, for great disturbances afflicted all the inhabitants of the lands. 6They were broken in pieces, nation against nation and city against city, for God troubled them with every sort of distress. 7But you, take courage! Do not let your hands be weak, for your work shall be rewarded."

8 When Asa heard these words, the prophecy of Azariah son of Oded,*i* he took courage, and put away the abominable idols from all

---

a Another reading is *Ephrain*   *b* Ch 13.23 in Heb   *c* Ch 14.1 in Heb   *d* Heb *Asherim*   *e* Or *Nubian*; Heb *Cushite*   *f* Or *Nubians*; Heb *Cushites*   *g* Heb *They*   *h* Meaning of Heb uncertain   *i* Compare Syr Vg: Heb *the prophecy, the prophet Obed* the land of Judah and Benjamin and from the towns that he had taken in the hill country of Ephraim. He repaired the altar of the LORD that was in front of the vestibule of the house of the LORD.*a* 9He gathered all Judah and Benjamin, and those from Ephraim, Manasseh, and Simeon who were residing as aliens with them, for great numbers had deserted to him from Israel when they saw that the LORD his God was with him. 10They were gathered at Jerusalem in the third month of the fifteenth year of the reign of Asa. 11They sacrificed to the LORD on that day, from the booty that they had brought, seven hundred oxen and seven thousand sheep. 12They entered into a covenant to seek the LORD, the God of their ancestors, with all their heart and with all their soul. 13Whoever would not seek the LORD, the God of Israel, should be put to death, whether young or old, man or woman. 14They took an oath to the LORD with a loud voice, and with shouting, and with trumpets, and with horns. 15All Judah rejoiced over the oath; for they had sworn with all their heart, and had sought him with their whole desire, and he was found by them, and the LORD gave them rest all around.

16 King Asa even removed his mother Maacah from being queen mother because she had made an abominable image for Asherah. Asa cut down her image, crushed it, and burned it at the Wadi Kidron. 17But the high places were not taken out of Israel. Nevertheless the heart of Asa was true all his days. 18He brought into the house of God the votive gifts of his father and his own votive gifts—silver, gold, and utensils. 19And there was no more war until the thirty-fifth year of the reign of Asa.

Alliance with Aram Condemned

16 In the thirty-sixth year of the reign of Asa, King Baasha of Israel went up against Judah, and built Ramah, to prevent anyone from going out or coming into the territory of*b* King Asa of Judah. 2Then Asa took silver and gold from the treasures of the house of the LORD and the king's house, and sent them to King Ben-hadad of Aram, who resided in Damascus, saying, 3"Let there be an alliance between me and you, like that between my father and your father; I am sending to you silver and gold; go, break your alliance with King Baasha of Israel, so that he may withdraw from me." 4Ben-hadad listened to King Asa, and sent the commanders of his armies against the cities of Israel. They conquered Ijon, Dan, Abel-maim, and all the store-cities of Naphtali. 5When Baasha heard of it, he stopped building Ramah, and let his work cease. 6Then King Asa brought all Judah, and they carried away the stones of Ramah and its timber, with which Baasha had been building, and with them he built up Geba and Mizpah.

7 At that time the seer Hanani came to King Asa of Judah, and said to him, "Because you relied on the king of Aram, and did not rely on the LORD your God, the army of the king of Aram has escaped you. 8Were not the Ethiopians*c* and the Libyans a huge army with exceedingly many chariots and cavalry? Yet because you relied on the LORD, he gave them into your hand. 9For the eyes of the LORD range throughout the entire earth, to strengthen those whose heart is true to him. You have done foolishly in this; for from now on you will have wars." 10Then Asa was angry with the seer, and put him in the stocks, in prison, for he was in a rage with him because of this. And Asa inflicted cruelties on some of the people at the same time.

Asa's Disease and Death

11 The acts of Asa, from first to last, are written in the Book of the Kings of Judah and Israel. 12In the thirty-ninth year of his reign Asa was diseased in his feet, and his disease became severe; yet even in his disease he did not seek the LORD, but sought help from physicians. 13Then Asa slept with his ancestors, dying in the forty-first year of his reign. 14They buried him in the tomb that he had hewn out for himself in the city of David. They laid him

---

a Heb *the vestibule of the* LORD   *b* Heb lacks *the territory of*   *c* Or *Nubians*; Heb *Cushites* on a bier that had been filled with various kinds of spices prepared by the perfumer's art; and they made a very great fire in his honor.

Jehoshaphat's Reign

17 His son Jehoshaphat succeeded him, and strengthened himself against Israel. 2He placed forces in all the fortified cities of Judah, and set garrisons in the land of Judah, and in the cities of Ephraim that his father Asa had taken. 3The LORD was with Jehoshaphat, because he walked in the earlier ways of his father;*a* he did not seek the Baals, 4but sought the God of his father and walked in his commandments, and not according to the ways of Israel. 5Therefore the LORD established the kingdom in his hand. All Judah brought tribute to Jehoshaphat, and he had great riches and honor. 6His heart was courageous in the ways of the LORD; and furthermore he removed the high places and the sacred poles*b* from Judah.

7 In the third year of his reign he sent his officials, Ben-hail, Obadiah, Zechariah, Nethanel, and Micaiah, to teach in the cities of Judah. 8With them were the Levites, Shemaiah, Nethaniah, Zebadiah, Asahel, Shemiramoth, Jehonathan, Adonijah, Tobijah, and Tob-adonijah; and with these Levites, the priests Elishama and Jehoram. 9They taught in Judah, having the book of the law of the LORD with them; they went around through all the cities of Judah and taught among the people.

10 The fear of the LORD fell on all the kingdoms of the lands around Judah, and they did not make war against Jehoshaphat. 11Some of the Philistines brought Jehoshaphat presents, and silver for tribute; and the Arabs also brought him seven thousand seven hundred rams and seven thousand seven hundred male goats. 12Jehoshaphat grew steadily greater. He built fortresses and storage cities in Judah. 13He carried out great works in the cities of Judah. He had soldiers, mighty warriors, in Jerusalem. 14This was the muster of them by ancestral houses: Of Judah, the commanders of the thousands: Adnah the commander, with three hundred thousand mighty warriors, 15and next to him Jehohanan the commander, with two hundred eighty thousand, 16and next to him Amasiah son of Zichri, a volunteer for the service of the LORD, with two hundred thousand mighty warriors. 17Of Benjamin: Eliada, a mighty warrior, with two hundred thousand armed with bow and shield, 18and next to him Jehozabad with one hundred eighty thousand armed for war. 19These were in the service of the king, besides those whom the king had placed in the fortified cities throughout all Judah.

Micaiah Predicts Failure

18 Now Jehoshaphat had great riches and honor; and he made a marriage alliance with Ahab. 2After some years he went down to Ahab in Samaria. Ahab slaughtered an abundance of sheep and oxen for him and for the people who were with him, and induced him to go up against Ramoth-gilead. 3King Ahab of Israel said to King Jehoshaphat of Judah, "Will you go with me to Ramoth-gilead?" He answered him, "I am with you, my people are your people. We will be with you in the war."

4 But Jehoshaphat also said to the king of Israel, "Inquire first for the word of the LORD." 5Then the king of Israel gathered the prophets together, four hundred of them, and said to them, "Shall we go to battle against Ramoth-gilead, or shall I refrain?" They said, "Go up; for God will give it into the hand of the king." 6But Jehoshaphat said, "Is there no other prophet of the LORD here of whom we may inquire?" 7The king of Israel said to Jehoshaphat, "There is still one other by whom we may inquire of the LORD, Micaiah son of Imlah; but I hate him, for he never prophesies anything favorable about me, but only disaster." Jehoshaphat said, "Let the king not say such a thing." 8Then the king of Israel summoned an officer and said, "Bring quickly Micaiah son of Imlah." 9Now the king of Israel and King Jehoshaphat of Judah were sitting on their thrones, ar-

a Another reading is *his father David*   *b* Heb *Asherim* rayed in their robes; and they were sitting at the threshing floor at the entrance of the gate of Samaria; and all the prophets were prophesying before them. [10]Zedekiah son of Chenaanah made for himself horns of iron, and he said, "Thus says the LORD: With these you shall gore the Arameans until they are destroyed." [11]All the prophets were prophesying the same and saying, "Go up to Ramoth-gilead and triumph; the LORD will give it into the hand of the king."

12 The messenger who had gone to summon Micaiah said to him, "Look, the words of the prophets with one accord are favorable to the king; let your word be like the word of one of them, and speak favorably." [13]But Micaiah said, "As the LORD lives, whatever my God says, that I will speak."

14 When he had come to the king, the king said to him, "Micaiah, shall we go to Ramoth-gilead to battle, or shall I refrain?" He answered, "Go up and triumph; they will be given into your hand." [15]But the king said to him, "How many times must I make you swear to tell me nothing but the truth in the name of the LORD?" [16]Then Micaiah[a] said, "I saw all Israel scattered on the mountains, like sheep without a shepherd; and the LORD said, 'These have no master; let each one go home in peace.'" [17]The king of Israel said to Jehoshaphat, "Did I not tell you that he would not prophesy anything favorable about me, but only disaster?"

18 Then Micaiah[a] said, "Therefore hear the word of the LORD: I saw the LORD sitting on his throne, with all the host of heaven standing to the right and to the left of him. [19]And the LORD said, 'Who will entice King Ahab of Israel, so that he may go up and fall at Ramoth-gilead?' Then one said one thing, and another said another, [20]until a spirit came forward and stood before the LORD, saying, 'I will entice him.' The LORD asked him, 'How?' [21]He replied, 'I will go out and be a lying spirit in the mouth of all his prophets.' Then the LORD[a] said, 'You are to entice him, and you

shall succeed; go out and do it.' [22]So you see, the LORD has put a lying spirit in the mouth of these your prophets; the LORD has decreed disaster for you."

23 Then Zedekiah son of Chenaanah came up to Micaiah, slapped him on the cheek, and said, "Which way did the spirit of the LORD pass from me to speak to you?" [24]Micaiah replied, "You will find out on that day when you go in to hide in an inner chamber." [25]The king of Israel then ordered, "Take Micaiah, and return him to Amon the governor of the city and to Joash the king's son; [26]and say, 'Thus says the king: Put this fellow in prison, and feed him on reduced rations of bread and water until I return in peace.'" [27]Micaiah said, "If you return in peace, the LORD has not spoken by me." And he said, "Hear, you peoples, all of you!"

Defeat and Death of Ahab

28 So the king of Israel and King Jehoshaphat of Judah went up to Ramoth-gilead. [29]The king of Israel said to Jehoshaphat, "I will disguise myself and go into battle, but you wear your robes." So the king of Israel disguised himself, and they went into battle. [30]Now the king of Aram had commanded the captains of his chariots, "Fight with no one small or great, but only with the king of Israel." [31]When the captains of the chariots saw Jehoshaphat, they said, "It is the king of Israel." So they turned to fight against him; and Jehoshaphat cried out, and the LORD helped him. God drew them away from him, [32]for when the captains of the chariots saw that it was not the king of Israel, they turned back from pursuing him. [33]But a certain man drew his bow and unknowingly struck the king of Israel between the scale armor and the breastplate; so he said to the driver of his chariot, "Turn around, and carry me out of the battle, for I am wounded." [34]The battle grew hot that day, and the king of Israel propped himself up in his chariot facing the Arameans until evening; then at sunset he died.

a Heb he

19 King Jehoshaphat of Judah returned in safety to his house in Jerusalem. ²Jehu son of Hanani the seer went out to meet him and said to King Jehoshaphat, "Should you help the wicked and love those who hate the LORD? Because of this, wrath has gone out against you from the LORD. ³Nevertheless, some good is found in you, for you destroyed the sacred poles*a* out of the land, and have set your heart to seek God."

The Reforms of Jehoshaphat

4 Jehoshaphat resided at Jerusalem; then he went out again among the people, from Beer-sheba to the hill country of Ephraim, and brought them back to the LORD, the God of their ancestors. ⁵He appointed judges in the land in all the fortified cities of Judah, city by city, ⁶and said to the judges, "Consider what you are doing, for you judge not on behalf of human beings but on the LORD's behalf; he is with you in giving judgment. ⁷Now, let the fear of the LORD be upon you; take care what you do, for there is no perversion of justice with the LORD our God, or partiality, or taking of bribes."

8 Moreover in Jerusalem Jehoshaphat appointed certain Levites and priests and heads of families of Israel, to give judgment for the LORD and to decide disputed cases. They had their seat at Jerusalem. ⁹He charged them: "This is how you shall act: in the fear of the LORD, in faithfulness, and with your whole heart; ¹⁰whenever a case comes to you from your kindred who live in their cities, concerning bloodshed, law or commandment, statutes or ordinances, then you shall instruct them, so that they may not incur guilt before the LORD and wrath may not come on you and your kindred. Do so, and you will not incur guilt. ¹¹See, Amariah the chief priest is over you in all matters of the LORD; and Zebadiah son of Ishmael, the governor of the house of Judah, in all the king's matters; and the Levites will serve you as officers. Deal courageously, and may the LORD be with the good!"

Invasion from the East

20 After this the Moabites and Ammonites, and with them some of the Meunites,*b* came against Jehoshaphat for battle. ²Messengers*c* came and told Jehoshaphat, "A great multitude is coming against you from Edom,*d* from beyond the sea; already they are at Hazazon-tamar" (that is, En-gedi). ³Jehoshaphat was afraid; he set himself to seek the LORD, and proclaimed a fast throughout all Judah. ⁴Judah assembled to seek help from the LORD; from all the towns of Judah they came to seek the LORD.

Jehoshaphat's Prayer and Victory

5 Jehoshaphat stood in the assembly of Judah and Jerusalem, in the house of the LORD, before the new court, ⁶and said, "O LORD, God of our ancestors, are you not God in heaven? Do you not rule over all the kingdoms of the nations? In your hand are power and might, so that no one is able to withstand you. ⁷Did you not, O our God, drive out the inhabitants of this land before your people Israel, and give it forever to the descendants of your friend Abraham? ⁸They have lived in it, and in it have built you a sanctuary for your name, saying, ⁹'If disaster comes upon us, the sword, judgment,*e* or pestilence, or famine, we will stand before this house, and before you, for your name is in this house, and cry to you in our distress, and you will hear and save.' ¹⁰See now, the people of Ammon, Moab, and Mount Seir, whom you would not let Israel invade when they came from the land of Egypt, and whom they avoided and did not destroy— ¹¹they reward us by coming to drive us out of your possession that you have given us to inherit. ¹²O our God, will you not execute judgment upon them? For we are powerless against this great multitude that is coming against us. We do not know what to do, but our eyes are on you."

13 Meanwhile all Judah stood before the LORD, with their little ones, their wives, and their children. ¹⁴Then the spirit of the LORD came upon Jahaziel son of Zechariah, son of

---

a Heb *Asheroth*   *b* Compare 26.7: Heb *Ammonites*   *c* Heb *They*   *d* One Ms: MT *Aram*   *e* Or *the sword of judgment*

Benaiah, son of Jeiel, son of Mattaniah, a Levite of the sons of Asaph, in the middle of the assembly. ¹⁵He said, "Listen, all Judah and inhabitants of Jerusalem, and King Jehoshaphat: Thus says the LORD to you: 'Do not fear or be dismayed at this great multitude; for the battle is not yours but God's. ¹⁶Tomorrow go down against them; they will come up by the ascent of Ziz; you will find them at the end of the valley, before the wilderness of Jeruel. ¹⁷This battle is not for you to fight; take your position, stand still, and see the victory of the LORD on your behalf, O Judah and Jerusalem.' Do not fear or be dismayed; tomorrow go out against them, and the LORD will be with you."

18 Then Jehoshaphat bowed down with his face to the ground, and all Judah and the inhabitants of Jerusalem fell down before the LORD, worshiping the LORD. ¹⁹And the Levites, of the Kohathites and the Korahites, stood up to praise the LORD, the God of Israel, with a very loud voice.

20 They rose early in the morning and went out into the wilderness of Tekoa; and as they went out, Jehoshaphat stood and said, "Listen to me, O Judah and inhabitants of Jerusalem! Believe in the LORD your God and you will be established; believe his prophets." ²¹When he had taken counsel with the people, he appointed those who were to sing to the LORD and praise him in holy splendor, as they went before the army, saying,

"Give thanks to the LORD,
    for his steadfast love endures forever."

²²As they began to sing and praise, the LORD set an ambush against the Ammonites, Moab, and Mount Seir, who had come against Judah, so that they were routed. ²³For the Ammonites and Moab attacked the inhabitants of Mount Seir, destroying them utterly; and when they had made an end of the inhabitants of Seir, they all helped to destroy one another.

24 When Judah came to the watchtower of the wilderness, they looked toward the multitude; they were corpses lying on the ground; no one had escaped. ²⁵When Jehoshaphat and his people came to take the booty from them, they found livestock*ª* in great numbers, goods, clothing, and precious things, which they took for themselves until they could carry no more. They spent three days taking the booty, because of its abundance. ²⁶On the fourth day they assembled in the Valley of Beracah, for there they blessed the LORD; therefore that place has been called the Valley of Beracah*ᵇ* to this day. ²⁷Then all the people of Judah and Jerusalem, with Jehoshaphat at their head, returned to Jerusalem with joy, for the LORD had enabled them to rejoice over their enemies. ²⁸They came to Jerusalem, with harps and lyres and trumpets, to the house of the LORD. ²⁹The fear of God came on all the kingdoms of the countries when they heard that the LORD had fought against the enemies of Israel. ³⁰And the realm of Jehoshaphat was quiet, for his God gave him rest all around.

The End of Jehoshaphat's Reign

31 So Jehoshaphat reigned over Judah. He was thirty-five years old when he began to reign; he reigned twenty-five years in Jerusalem. His mother's name was Azubah daughter of Shilhi. ³²He walked in the way of his father Asa and did not turn aside from it, doing what was right in the sight of the LORD. ³³Yet the high places were not removed; the people had not yet set their hearts upon the God of their ancestors.

34 Now the rest of the acts of Jehoshaphat, from first to last, are written in the Annals of Jehu son of Hanani, which are recorded in the Book of the Kings of Israel.

35 After this King Jehoshaphat of Judah joined with King Ahaziah of Israel, who did wickedly. ³⁶He joined him in building ships to go to Tarshish; they built the ships in Ezion-geber. ³⁷Then Eliezer son of Dodavahu of Mareshah prophesied against Jehoshaphat, saying, "Because you have joined with Ahaziah, the LORD will destroy what you have made." And the ships were wrecked and were not able to go to Tarshish.

a Gk: Heb *among them*   *b* That is *Blessing*

Jehoram's Reign

21 Jehoshaphat slept with his ancestors and was buried with his ancestors in the city of David; his son Jehoram succeeded him. ²He had brothers, the sons of Jehoshaphat: Azariah, Jehiel, Zechariah, Azariah, Michael, and Shephatiah; all these were the sons of King Jehoshaphat of Judah.*ᵃ* ³Their father gave them many gifts, of silver, gold, and valuable possessions, together with fortified cities in Judah; but he gave the kingdom to Jehoram, because he was the firstborn. ⁴When Jehoram had ascended the throne of his father and was established, he put all his brothers to the sword, and also some of the officials of Israel. ⁵Jehoram was thirty-two years old when he began to reign; he reigned eight years in Jerusalem. ⁶He walked in the way of the kings of Israel, as the house of Ahab had done; for the daughter of Ahab was his wife. He did what was evil in the sight of the LORD. ⁷Yet the LORD would not destroy the house of David because of the covenant that he had made with David, and since he had promised to give a lamp to him and to his descendants forever.

Revolt of Edom

8 In his days Edom revolted against the rule of Judah and set up a king of their own. ⁹Then Jehoram crossed over with his commanders and all his chariots. He set out by night and attacked the Edomites, who had surrounded him and his chariot commanders. ¹⁰So Edom has been in revolt against the rule of Judah to this day. At that time Libnah also revolted against his rule, because he had forsaken the LORD, the God of his ancestors.

Elijah's Letter

11 Moreover he made high places in the hill country of Judah, and led the inhabitants of Jerusalem into unfaithfulness, and made Judah go astray. ¹²A letter came to him from the prophet Elijah, saying: "Thus says the LORD, the God of your father David: Because you have not walked in the ways of your father Jehoshaphat or in the ways of King Asa of Judah, ¹³but have walked in the way of the kings of Israel, and have led Judah and the inhabitants of Jerusalem into unfaithfulness, as the house of Ahab led Israel into unfaithfulness, and because you also have killed your brothers, members of your father's house, who were better than yourself, ¹⁴see, the LORD will bring a great plague on your people, your children, your wives, and all your possessions, ¹⁵and you yourself will have a severe sickness with a disease of your bowels, until your bowels come out, day after day, because of the disease."

16 The LORD aroused against Jehoram the anger of the Philistines and of the Arabs who are near the Ethiopians.*ᵇ* ¹⁷They came up against Judah, invaded it, and carried away all the possessions they found that belonged to the king's house, along with his sons and his wives, so that no son was left to him except Jehoahaz, his youngest son.

Disease and Death of Jehoram

18 After all this the LORD struck him in his bowels with an incurable disease. ¹⁹In course of time, at the end of two years, his bowels came out because of the disease, and he died in great agony. His people made no fire in his honor, like the fires made for his ancestors. ²⁰He was thirty-two years old when he began to reign; he reigned eight years in Jerusalem. He departed with no one's regret. They buried him in the city of David, but not in the tombs of the kings.

Ahaziah's Reign

22 The inhabitants of Jerusalem made his youngest son Ahaziah king as his successor; for the troops who came with the Arabs to the camp had killed all the older sons. So Ahaziah son of Jehoram reigned as king of Judah. ²Ahaziah was forty-two years old when he began to reign; he reigned one year in Jerusalem. His mother's name was Athaliah, a granddaughter of Omri. ³He also walked in the ways of the house of Ahab, for his mother was his counselor in doing wickedly. ⁴He did what

a Gk Syr: Heb *Israel*   *b* Or *Nubians*; Heb *Cushites* was evil in the sight of the LORD, as the house of Ahab had done; for after the death of his father they were his counselors, to his ruin. 5He even followed their advice, and went with Jehoram son of King Ahab of Israel to make war against King Hazael of Aram at Ramoth-gilead. The Arameans wounded Joram, 6and he returned to be healed in Jezreel of the wounds that he had received at Ramah, when he fought King Hazael of Aram. And Ahaziah son of King Jehoram of Judah went down to see Joram son of Ahab in Jezreel, because he was sick.

7 But it was ordained by God that the downfall of Ahaziah should come about through his going to visit Joram. For when he came there he went out with Jehoram to meet Jehu son of Nimshi, whom the LORD had anointed to destroy the house of Ahab. 8When Jehu was executing judgment on the house of Ahab, he met the officials of Judah and the sons of Ahaziah's brothers, who attended Ahaziah, and he killed them. 9He searched for Ahaziah, who was captured while hiding in Samaria and was brought to Jehu, and put to death. They buried him, for they said, "He is the grandson of Jehoshaphat, who sought the LORD with all his heart." And the house of Ahaziah had no one able to rule the kingdom.

Athaliah Seizes the Throne

10 Now when Athaliah, Ahaziah's mother, saw that her son was dead, she set about to destroy all the royal family of the house of Judah. 11But Jehoshabeath, the king's daughter, took Joash son of Ahaziah, and stole him away from among the king's children who were about to be killed; she put him and his nurse in a bedroom. Thus Jehoshabeath, daughter of King Jehoram and wife of the priest Jehoiada—because she was a sister of Ahaziah—hid him from Athaliah, so that she did not kill him; 12he remained with them six years, hidden in the house of God, while Athaliah reigned over the land.

23 But in the seventh year Jehoiada took courage, and entered into a compact with the commanders of the hundreds, Azariah son of Jeroham, Ishmael son of Jehohanan, Azariah son of Obed, Maaseiah son of Adaiah, and Elishaphat son of Zichri. 2They went around through Judah and gathered the Levites from all the towns of Judah, and the heads of families of Israel, and they came to Jerusalem. 3Then the whole assembly made a covenant with the king in the house of God. Jehoiada a said to them, "Here is the king's son! Let him reign, as the LORD promised concerning the sons of David. 4This is what you are to do: one-third of you, priests and Levites, who come on duty on the sabbath, shall be gatekeepers, 5one-third shall be at the king's house, and one-third at the Gate of the Foundation; and all the people shall be in the courts of the house of the LORD. 6Do not let anyone enter the house of the LORD except the priests and ministering Levites; they may enter, for they are holy, but all the other b people shall observe the instructions of the LORD. 7The Levites shall surround the king, each with his weapons in his hand; and whoever enters the house shall be killed. Stay with the king in his comings and goings."

Joash Crowned King

8 The Levites and all Judah did according to all that the priest Jehoiada commanded; each brought his men, who were to come on duty on the sabbath, with those who were to go off duty on the sabbath; for the priest Jehoiada did not dismiss the divisions. 9The priest Jehoiada delivered to the captains the spears and the large and small shields that had been King David's, which were in the house of God; 10and he set all the people as a guard for the king, everyone with weapon in hand, from the south side of the house to the north side of the house, around the altar and the house. 11Then he brought out the king's son, put the crown on him, and gave him the covenant;c they proclaimed him king, and Jehoiada and his sons

---

a Heb He   b Heb lacks other   c Or treaty, or testimony; Heb eduth anointed him; and they shouted, "Long live the king!"

Athaliah Murdered

12 When Athaliah heard the noise of the people running and praising the king, she went into the house of the LORD to the people; 13and when she looked, there was the king standing by his pillar at the entrance, and the captains and the trumpeters beside the king, and all the people of the land rejoicing and blowing trumpets, and the singers with their musical instruments leading in the celebration. Athaliah tore her clothes, and cried, "Treason! Treason!" 14Then the priest Jehoiada brought out the captains who were set over the army, saying to them, "Bring her out between the ranks; anyone who follows her is to be put to the sword." For the priest said, "Do not put her to death in the house of the LORD." 15So they laid hands on her; she went into the entrance of the Horse Gate of the king's house, and there they put her to death.

16 Jehoiada made a covenant between himself and all the people and the king that they should be the LORD's people. 17Then all the people went to the house of Baal, and tore it down; his altars and his images they broke in pieces, and they killed Mattan, the priest of Baal, in front of the altars. 18Jehoiada assigned the care of the house of the LORD to the levitical priests whom David had organized to be in charge of the house of the LORD, to offer burnt offerings to the LORD, as it is written in the law of Moses, with rejoicing and with singing, according to the order of David. 19He stationed the gatekeepers at the gates of the house of the LORD so that no one should enter who was in any way unclean. 20And he took the captains, the nobles, the governors of the people, and all the people of the land, and they brought the king down from the house of the LORD, marching through the upper gate to the king's house. They set the king on the royal throne. 21So all the people of the land rejoiced, and the city was quiet after Athaliah had been killed with the sword.

Joash Repairs the Temple

24 Joash was seven years old when he began to reign; he reigned forty years in Jerusalem; his mother's name was Zibiah of Beer-sheba. 2Joash did what was right in the sight of the LORD all the days of the priest Jehoiada. 3Jehoiada got two wives for him, and he became the father of sons and daughters.

4 Some time afterward Joash decided to restore the house of the LORD. 5He assembled the priests and the Levites and said to them, "Go out to the cities of Judah and gather money from all Israel to repair the house of your God, year by year; and see that you act quickly." But the Levites did not act quickly. 6So the king summoned Jehoiada the chief, and said to him, "Why have you not required the Levites to bring in from Judah and Jerusalem the tax levied by Moses, the servant of the LORD, on ᵃ the congregation of Israel for the tent of the covenant?" ᵇ 7For the children of Athaliah, that wicked woman, had broken into the house of God, and had even used all the dedicated things of the house of the LORD for the Baals.

8 So the king gave command, and they made a chest, and set it outside the gate of the house of the LORD. 9A proclamation was made throughout Judah and Jerusalem to bring in for the LORD the tax that Moses the servant of God laid on Israel in the wilderness. 10All the leaders and all the people rejoiced and brought their tax and dropped it into the chest until it was full. 11Whenever the chest was brought to the king's officers by the Levites, when they saw that there was a large amount of money in it, the king's secretary and the officer of the chief priest would come and empty the chest and take it and return it to its place. So they did day after day, and collected money in abundance. 12The king and Jehoiada gave it to those who had charge of the work of the house of the LORD, and they hired masons and carpenters to restore the house of the LORD, and also work-

<hr>

a Compare Vg: Heb *and*   b Or *treaty*, or *testimony*; Heb *eduth* ers in iron and bronze to repair the house of the LORD. 13So those who were engaged in the work labored, and the repairing went forward at their hands, and they restored the house of God to its proper condition and strengthened it. 14When they had finished, they brought the rest of the money to the king and Jehoiada, and with it were made utensils for the house of the LORD, utensils for the service and for the burnt offerings, and ladles, and vessels of gold and silver. They offered burnt offerings in the house of the LORD regularly all the days of Jehoiada.

Apostasy of Joash

15 But Jehoiada grew old and full of days, and died; he was one hundred thirty years old at his death. 16And they buried him in the city of David among the kings, because he had done good in Israel, and for God and his house.

17 Now after the death of Jehoiada the officials of Judah came and did obeisance to the king; then the king listened to them. 18They abandoned the house of the LORD, the God of their ancestors, and served the sacred poles*a* and the idols. And wrath came upon Judah and Jerusalem for this guilt of theirs. 19Yet he sent prophets among them to bring them back to the LORD; they testified against them, but they would not listen.

20 Then the spirit of God took possession of*b* Zechariah son of the priest Jehoiada; he stood above the people and said to them, "Thus says God: Why do you transgress the commandments of the LORD, so that you cannot prosper? Because you have forsaken the LORD, he has also forsaken you." 21But they conspired against him, and by command of the king they stoned him to death in the court of the house of the LORD. 22King Joash did not remember the kindness that Jehoiada, Zechariah's father, had shown him, but killed his son. As he was dying, he said, "May the LORD see and avenge!"

Death of Joash

23 At the end of the year the army of Aram came up against Joash. They came to Judah and Jerusalem, and destroyed all the officials of the people from among them, and sent all the booty they took to the king of Damascus. 24Although the army of Aram had come with few men, the LORD delivered into their hand a very great army, because they had abandoned the LORD, the God of their ancestors. Thus they executed judgment on Joash.

25 When they had withdrawn, leaving him severely wounded, his servants conspired against him because of the blood of the son*c* of the priest Jehoiada, and they killed him on his bed. So he died; and they buried him in the city of David, but they did not bury him in the tombs of the kings. 26Those who conspired against him were Zabad son of Shimeath the Ammonite, and Jehozabad son of Shimrith the Moabite. 27Accounts of his sons, and of the many oracles against him, and of the rebuilding*d* of the house of God are written in the Commentary on the Book of the Kings. And his son Amaziah succeeded him.

Reign of Amaziah

25 Amaziah was twenty-five years old when he began to reign, and he reigned twenty-nine years in Jerusalem. His mother's name was Jehoaddan of Jerusalem. 2He did what was right in the sight of the LORD, yet not with a true heart. 3As soon as the royal power was firmly in his hand he killed his servants who had murdered his father the king. 4But he did not put their children to death, according to what is written in the law, in the book of Moses, where the LORD commanded, "The parents shall not be put to death for the children, or the children be put to death for the parents; but all shall be put to death for their own sins."

Slaughter of the Edomites

5 Amaziah assembled the people of Judah, and set them by ancestral houses under commanders of the thousands and of the hun-

---

a Heb *Asherim*   *b* Heb *clothed itself with*   *c* Gk Vg: Heb *sons*   *d* Heb *founding* dreds for all Judah and Benjamin. He mustered those twenty years old and upward, and found that they were three hundred thousand picked troops fit for war, able to handle spear and shield. [6]He also hired one hundred thousand mighty warriors from Israel for one hundred talents of silver. [7]But a man of God came to him and said, "O king, do not let the army of Israel go with you, for the LORD is not with Israel—all these Ephraimites. [8]Rather, go by yourself and act; be strong in battle, or God will fling you down before the enemy; for God has power to help or to overthrow." [9]Amaziah said to the man of God, "But what shall we do about the hundred talents that I have given to the army of Israel?" The man of God answered, "The LORD is able to give you much more than this." [10]Then Amaziah discharged the army that had come to him from Ephraim, letting them go home again. But they became very angry with Judah, and returned home in fierce anger.

11 Amaziah took courage, and led out his people; he went to the Valley of Salt, and struck down ten thousand men of Seir. [12]The people of Judah captured another ten thousand alive, took them to the top of Sela, and threw them down from the top of Sela, so that all of them were dashed to pieces. [13]But the men of the army whom Amaziah sent back, not letting them go with him to battle, fell on the cities of Judah from Samaria to Beth-horon; they killed three thousand people in them, and took much booty.

14 Now after Amaziah came from the slaughter of the Edomites, he brought the gods of the people of Seir, set them up as his gods, and worshiped them, making offerings to them. [15]The LORD was angry with Amaziah and sent to him a prophet, who said to him, "Why have you resorted to a people's gods who could not deliver their own people from your hand?" [16]But as he was speaking the king[a] said to him, "Have we made you a royal counselor? Stop! Why should you be put to death?" So the prophet stopped, but said, "I know that

God has determined to destroy you, because you have done this and have not listened to my advice."

Israel Defeats Judah

17 Then King Amaziah of Judah took counsel and sent to King Joash son of Jehoahaz son of Jehu of Israel, saying, "Come, let us look one another in the face." [18]King Joash of Israel sent word to King Amaziah of Judah, "A thornbush on Lebanon sent to a cedar on Lebanon, saying, 'Give your daughter to my son for a wife'; but a wild animal of Lebanon passed by and trampled down the thornbush. [19]You say, 'See, I have defeated Edom,' and your heart has lifted you up in boastfulness. Now stay at home; why should you provoke trouble so that you fall, you and Judah with you?"

20 But Amaziah would not listen—it was God's doing, in order to hand them over, because they had sought the gods of Edom. [21]So King Joash of Israel went up; he and King Amaziah of Judah faced one another in battle at Beth-shemesh, which belongs to Judah. [22]Judah was defeated by Israel; everyone fled home. [23]King Joash of Israel captured King Amaziah of Judah, son of Joash, son of Ahaziah, at Beth-shemesh; he brought him to Jerusalem, and broke down the wall of Jerusalem from the Ephraim Gate to the Corner Gate, a distance of four hundred cubits. [24]He seized all the gold and silver, and all the vessels that were found in the house of God, and Obed-edom with them; he seized also the treasuries of the king's house, also hostages; then he returned to Samaria.

Death of Amaziah

25 King Amaziah son of Joash of Judah, lived fifteen years after the death of King Joash son of Jehoahaz of Israel. [26]Now the rest of the deeds of Amaziah, from first to last, are they not written in the Book of the Kings of Judah and Israel? [27]From the time that Amaziah turned away from the LORD they made a conspiracy against him in Jerusalem, and he fled

a Heb he

to Lachish. But they sent after him to Lachish, and killed him there. 28They brought him back on horses; he was buried with his ancestors in the city of David.

Reign of Uzziah

26 Then all the people of Judah took Uzziah, who was sixteen years old, and made him king to succeed his father Amaziah. 2He rebuilt Eloth and restored it to Judah, after the king slept with his ancestors. 3Uzziah was sixteen years old when he began to reign, and he reigned fifty-two years in Jerusalem. His mother's name was Jecoliah of Jerusalem. 4He did what was right in the sight of the LORD, just as his father Amaziah had done. 5He set himself to seek God in the days of Zechariah, who instructed him in the fear of God; and as long as he sought the LORD, God made him prosper.

6 He went out and made war against the Philistines, and broke down the wall of Gath and the wall of Jabneh and the wall of Ashdod; he built cities in the territory of Ashdod and elsewhere among the Philistines. 7God helped him against the Philistines, against the Arabs who lived in Gur-baal, and against the Meunites. 8The Ammonites paid tribute to Uzziah, and his fame spread even to the border of Egypt, for he became very strong. 9Moreover Uzziah built towers in Jerusalem at the Corner Gate, at the Valley Gate, and at the Angle, and fortified them. 10He built towers in the wilderness and hewed out many cisterns, for he had large herds, both in the Shephelah and in the plain, and he had farmers and vinedressers in the hills and in the fertile lands, for he loved the soil. 11Moreover Uzziah had an army of soldiers, fit for war, in divisions according to the numbers in the muster made by the secretary Jeiel and the officer Maaseiah, under the direction of Hananiah, one of the king's commanders. 12The whole number of the heads of ancestral houses of mighty warriors was two thousand six hundred. 13Under their command was an army of three hundred seven thousand

five hundred, who could make war with mighty power, to help the king against the enemy. 14Uzziah provided for all the army the shields, spears, helmets, coats of mail, bows, and stones for slinging. 15In Jerusalem he set up machines, invented by skilled workers, on the towers and the corners for shooting arrows and large stones. And his fame spread far, for he was marvelously helped until he became strong.

Pride and Apostasy

16 But when he had become strong he grew proud, to his destruction. For he was false to the LORD his God, and entered the temple of the LORD to make offering on the altar of incense. 17But the priest Azariah went in after him, with eighty priests of the LORD who were men of valor; 18they withstood King Uzziah, and said to him, "It is not for you, Uzziah, to make offering to the LORD, but for the priests the descendants of Aaron, who are consecrated to make offering. Go out of the sanctuary; for you have done wrong, and it will bring you no honor from the LORD God." 19Then Uzziah was angry. Now he had a censer in his hand to make offering, and when he became angry with the priests a leprous*a* disease broke out on his forehead, in the presence of the priests in the house of the LORD, by the altar of incense. 20When the chief priest Azariah, and all the priests, looked at him, he was leprous*a* in his forehead. They hurried him out, and he himself hurried to get out, because the LORD had struck him. 21King Uzziah was leprous*a* to the day of his death, and being leprous*a* lived in a separate house, for he was excluded from the house of the LORD. His son Jotham was in charge of the palace of the king, governing the people of the land.

22 Now the rest of the acts of Uzziah, from first to last, the prophet Isaiah son of Amoz wrote. 23Uzziah slept with his ancestors; they buried him near his ancestors in the burial field that belonged to the kings, for they said, "He is leprous."*a* His son Jotham succeeded him.

---

a A term for several skin diseases; precise meaning uncertain

Reign of Jotham

27 Jotham was twenty-five years old when he began to reign; he reigned sixteen years in Jerusalem. His mother's name was Jerushah daughter of Zadok. 2He did what was right in the sight of the LORD just as his father Uzziah had done—only he did not invade the temple of the LORD. But the people still followed corrupt practices. 3He built the upper gate of the house of the LORD, and did extensive building on the wall of Ophel. 4Moreover he built cities in the hill country of Judah, and forts and towers on the wooded hills. 5He fought with the king of the Ammonites and prevailed against them. The Ammonites gave him that year one hundred talents of silver, ten thousand cors of wheat and ten thousand of barley. The Ammonites paid him the same amount in the second and the third years. 6So Jotham became strong because he ordered his ways before the LORD his God. 7Now the rest of the acts of Jotham, and all his wars and his ways, are written in the Book of the Kings of Israel and Judah. 8He was twenty-five years old when he began to reign; he reigned sixteen years in Jerusalem. 9Jotham slept with his ancestors, and they buried him in the city of David; and his son Ahaz succeeded him.

Reign of Ahaz

28 Ahaz was twenty years old when he began to reign; he reigned sixteen years in Jerusalem. He did not do what was right in the sight of the LORD, as his ancestor David had done, 2but he walked in the ways of the kings of Israel. He even made cast images for the Baals; 3and he made offerings in the valley of the son of Hinnom, and made his sons pass through fire, according to the abominable practices of the nations whom the LORD drove out before the people of Israel. 4He sacrificed and made offerings on the high places, on the hills, and under every green tree.

Aram and Israel Defeat Judah

5 Therefore the LORD his God gave him into the hand of the king of Aram, who defeated him and took captive a great number of his people and brought them to Damascus. He was also given into the hand of the king of Israel, who defeated him with great slaughter. 6Pekah son of Remaliah killed one hundred twenty thousand in Judah in one day, all of them valiant warriors, because they had abandoned the LORD, the God of their ancestors. 7And Zichri, a mighty warrior of Ephraim, killed the king's son Maaseiah, Azrikam the commander of the palace, and Elkanah the next in authority to the king.

Intervention of Oded

8 The people of Israel took captive two hundred thousand of their kin, women, sons, and daughters; they also took much booty from them and brought the booty to Samaria. 9But a prophet of the LORD was there, whose name was Oded; he went out to meet the army that came to Samaria, and said to them, "Because the LORD, the God of your ancestors, was angry with Judah, he gave them into your hand, but you have killed them in a rage that has reached up to heaven. 10Now you intend to subjugate the people of Judah and Jerusalem, male and female, as your slaves. But what have you except sins against the LORD your God? 11Now hear me, and send back the captives whom you have taken from your kindred, for the fierce wrath of the LORD is upon you." 12Moreover, certain chiefs of the Ephraimites, Azariah son of Johanan, Berechiah son of Meshillemoth, Jehizkiah son of Shallum, and Amasa son of Hadlai, stood up against those who were coming from the war, 13and said to them, "You shall not bring the captives in here, for you propose to bring on us guilt against the LORD in addition to our present sins and guilt. For our guilt is already great, and there is fierce wrath against Israel." 14So the warriors left the captives and the booty before the officials and all the assembly. 15Then those who were mentioned by name got up and took the captives, and with the booty they clothed all that were naked among them; they clothed them, gave them sandals, provided them with food and drink, and anointed them; and carrying all the feeble among them on donkeys, they brought

them to their kindred at Jericho, the city of palm trees. Then they returned to Samaria.

Assyria Refuses to Help Judah

16 At that time King Ahaz sent to the king[a] of Assyria for help. 17For the Edomites had again invaded and defeated Judah, and carried away captives. 18And the Philistines had made raids on the cities in the Shephelah and the Negeb of Judah, and had taken Beth-shemesh, Aijalon, Gederoth, Soco with its villages, Timnah with its villages, and Gimzo with its villages; and they settled there. 19For the LORD brought Judah low because of King Ahaz of Israel, for he had behaved without restraint in Judah and had been faithless to the LORD. 20So King Tilgath-pilneser of Assyria came against him, and oppressed him instead of strengthening him. 21For Ahaz plundered the house of the LORD and the houses of the king and of the officials, and gave tribute to the king of Assyria; but it did not help him.

Apostasy and Death of Ahaz

22 In the time of his distress he became yet more faithless to the LORD—this same King Ahaz. 23For he sacrificed to the gods of Damascus, which had defeated him, and said, "Because the gods of the kings of Aram helped them, I will sacrifice to them so that they may help me." But they were the ruin of him, and of all Israel. 24Ahaz gathered together the utensils of the house of God, and cut in pieces the utensils of the house of God. He shut up the doors of the house of the LORD and made himself altars in every corner of Jerusalem. 25In every city of Judah he made high places to make offerings to other gods, provoking to anger the LORD, the God of his ancestors. 26Now the rest of his acts and all his ways, from first to last, are written in the Book of the Kings of Judah and Israel. 27Ahaz slept with his ancestors, and they buried him in the city, in Jerusalem; but they did not bring him into the tombs of the kings of Israel. His son Hezekiah succeeded him.

Reign of Hezekiah

29 Hezekiah began to reign when he was twenty-five years old; he reigned twenty-nine years in Jerusalem. His mother's name was Abijah daughter of Zechariah. 2He did what was right in the sight of the LORD, just as his ancestor David had done.

The Temple Cleansed

3 In the first year of his reign, in the first month, he opened the doors of the house of the LORD and repaired them. 4He brought in the priests and the Levites and assembled them in the square on the east. 5He said to them, "Listen to me, Levites! Sanctify yourselves, and sanctify the house of the LORD, the God of your ancestors, and carry out the filth from the holy place. 6For our ancestors have been unfaithful and have done what was evil in the sight of the LORD our God; they have forsaken him, and have turned away their faces from the dwelling of the LORD, and turned their backs. 7They also shut the doors of the vestibule and put out the lamps, and have not offered incense or made burnt offerings in the holy place to the God of Israel. 8Therefore the wrath of the LORD came upon Judah and Jerusalem, and he has made them an object of horror, of astonishment, and of hissing, as you see with your own eyes. 9Our fathers have fallen by the sword and our sons and our daughters and our wives are in captivity for this. 10Now it is in my heart to make a covenant with the LORD, the God of Israel, so that his fierce anger may turn away from us. 11My sons, do not now be negligent, for the LORD has chosen you to stand in his presence to minister to him, and to be his ministers and make offerings to him."

12 Then the Levites arose, Mahath son of Amasai, and Joel son of Azariah, of the sons of the Kohathites; and of the sons of Merari, Kish son of Abdi, and Azariah son of Jehallelel; and of the Gershonites, Joah son of Zimmah, and Eden son of Joah; 13and of the sons of Elizaphan, Shimri and Jeuel; and of the

---

a Gk Syr Vg Compare 2 Kings 16.7: Heb *kings*

sons of Asaph, Zechariah and Mattaniah; 14and of the sons of Heman, Jehuel and Shimei; and of the sons of Jeduthun, Shemaiah and Uzziel. 15They gathered their brothers, sanctified themselves, and went in as the king had commanded, by the words of the LORD, to cleanse the house of the LORD. 16The priests went into the inner part of the house of the LORD to cleanse it, and they brought out all the unclean things that they found in the temple of the LORD into the court of the house of the LORD; and the Levites took them and carried them out to the Wadi Kidron. 17They began to sanctify on the first day of the first month, and on the eighth day of the month they came to the vestibule of the LORD; then for eight days they sanctified the house of the LORD, and on the sixteenth day of the first month they finished. 18Then they went inside to King Hezekiah and said, "We have cleansed all the house of the LORD, the altar of burnt offering and all its utensils, and the table for the rows of bread and all its utensils. 19All the utensils that King Ahaz repudiated during his reign when he was faithless, we have made ready and sanctified; see, they are in front of the altar of the LORD."

Temple Worship Restored

20 Then King Hezekiah rose early, assembled the officials of the city, and went up to the house of the LORD. 21They brought seven bulls, seven rams, seven lambs, and seven male goats for a sin offering for the kingdom and for the sanctuary and for Judah. He commanded the priests the descendants of Aaron to offer them on the altar of the LORD. 22So they slaughtered the bulls, and the priests received the blood and dashed it against the altar; they slaughtered the rams and their blood was dashed against the altar; they also slaughtered the lambs and their blood was dashed against the altar. 23Then the male goats for the sin offering were brought to the king and the assembly; they laid their hands on them, 24and the priests slaughtered them and made a sin offering with their blood at the altar, to make atone-ment for all Israel. For the king commanded that the burnt offering and the sin offering should be made for all Israel.

25 He stationed the Levites in the house of the LORD with cymbals, harps, and lyres, according to the commandment of David and of Gad the king's seer and of the prophet Nathan, for the commandment was from the LORD through his prophets. 26The Levites stood with the instruments of David, and the priests with the trumpets. 27Then Hezekiah commanded that the burnt offering be offered on the altar. When the burnt offering began, the song to the LORD began also, and the trumpets, accompanied by the instruments of King David of Israel. 28The whole assembly worshiped, the singers sang, and the trumpeters sounded; all this continued until the burnt offering was finished. 29When the offering was finished, the king and all who were present with him bowed down and worshiped. 30King Hezekiah and the officials commanded the Levites to sing praises to the LORD with the words of David and of the seer Asaph. They sang praises with gladness, and they bowed down and worshiped.

31 Then Hezekiah said, "You have now consecrated yourselves to the LORD; come near, bring sacrifices and thank offerings to the house of the LORD." The assembly brought sacrifices and thank offerings; and all who were of a willing heart brought burnt offerings. 32The number of the burnt offerings that the assembly brought was seventy bulls, one hundred rams, and two hundred lambs; all these were for a burnt offering to the LORD. 33The consecrated offerings were six hundred bulls and three thousand sheep. 34But the priests were too few and could not skin all the burnt offerings, so, until other priests had sanctified themselves, their kindred, the Levites, helped them until the work was finished—for the Levites were more conscientious[a] than the priests in sanctifying themselves. 35Besides the great number of burnt offerings there was the fat of the offerings of well-being, and there were the drink offerings for the burnt offerings. Thus the

a Heb *upright in heart*

service of the house of the LORD was restored. ³⁶And Hezekiah and all the people rejoiced because of what God had done for the people; for the thing had come about suddenly.

The Great Passover

30 Hezekiah sent word to all Israel and Judah, and wrote letters also to Ephraim and Manasseh, that they should come to the house of the LORD at Jerusalem, to keep the passover to the LORD the God of Israel. ²For the king and his officials and all the assembly in Jerusalem had taken counsel to keep the passover in the second month ³(for they could not keep it at its proper time because the priests had not sanctified themselves in sufficient number, nor had the people assembled in Jerusalem). ⁴The plan seemed right to the king and all the assembly. ⁵So they decreed to make a proclamation throughout all Israel, from Beersheba to Dan, that the people should come and keep the passover to the LORD the God of Israel, at Jerusalem; for they had not kept it in great numbers as prescribed. ⁶So couriers went throughout all Israel and Judah with letters from the king and his officials, as the king had commanded, saying, "O people of Israel, return to the LORD, the God of Abraham, Isaac, and Israel, so that he may turn again to the remnant of you who have escaped from the hand of the kings of Assyria. ⁷Do not be like your ancestors and your kindred, who were faithless to the LORD God of their ancestors, so that he made them a desolation, as you see. ⁸Do not now be stiff-necked as your ancestors were, but yield yourselves to the LORD and come to his sanctuary, which he has sanctified forever, and serve the LORD your God, so that his fierce anger may turn away from you. ⁹For as you return to the LORD, your kindred and your children will find compassion with their captors, and return to this land. For the LORD your God is gracious and merciful, and will not turn away his face from you, if you return to him."

10 So the couriers went from city to city through the country of Ephraim and Manasseh, and as far as Zebulun; but they laughed them to scorn, and mocked them. ¹¹Only a few from Asher, Manasseh, and Zebulun humbled themselves and came to Jerusalem. ¹²The hand of God was also on Judah to give them one heart to do what the king and the officials commanded by the word of the LORD.

13 Many people came together in Jerusalem to keep the festival of unleavened bread in the second month, a very large assembly. ¹⁴They set to work and removed the altars that were in Jerusalem, and all the altars for offering incense they took away and threw into the Wadi Kidron. ¹⁵They slaughtered the passover lamb on the fourteenth day of the second month. The priests and the Levites were ashamed, and they sanctified themselves and brought burnt offerings into the house of the LORD. ¹⁶They took their accustomed posts according to the law of Moses the man of God; the priests dashed the blood that they received*a* from the hands of the Levites. ¹⁷For there were many in the assembly who had not sanctified themselves; therefore the Levites had to slaughter the passover lamb for everyone who was not clean, to make it holy to the LORD. ¹⁸For a multitude of the people, many of them from Ephraim, Manasseh, Issachar, and Zebulun, had not cleansed themselves, yet they ate the passover otherwise than as prescribed. But Hezekiah prayed for them, saying, "The good LORD pardon all ¹⁹who set their hearts to seek God, the LORD the God of their ancestors, even though not in accordance with the sanctuary's rules of cleanness." ²⁰The LORD heard Hezekiah, and healed the people. ²¹The people of Israel who were present at Jerusalem kept the festival of unleavened bread seven days with great gladness; and the Levites and the priests praised the LORD day by day, accompanied by loud instruments for the LORD. ²²Hezekiah spoke encouragingly to all the Levites who showed good skill in the service of the LORD. So the people ate the food of the festival for seven days, sacrificing offerings of well-being and giving thanks to the LORD the God of their ancestors.

a Heb lacks *that they received*

23 Then the whole assembly agreed together to keep the festival for another seven days; so they kept it for another seven days with gladness. 24For King Hezekiah of Judah gave the assembly a thousand bulls and seven thousand sheep for offerings, and the officials gave the assembly a thousand bulls and ten thousand sheep. The priests sanctified themselves in great numbers. 25The whole assembly of Judah, the priests and the Levites, and the whole assembly that came out of Israel, and the resident aliens who came out of the land of Israel, and the resident aliens who lived in Judah, rejoiced. 26There was great joy in Jerusalem, for since the time of Solomon son of King David of Israel there had been nothing like this in Jerusalem. 27Then the priests and the Levites stood up and blessed the people, and their voice was heard; their prayer came to his holy dwelling in heaven.

Pagan Shrines Destroyed

31 Now when all this was finished, all Israel who were present went out to the cities of Judah and broke down the pillars, hewed down the sacred poles,*a* and pulled down the high places and the altars throughout all Judah and Benjamin, and in Ephraim and Manasseh, until they had destroyed them all. Then all the people of Israel returned to their cities, all to their individual properties.

2 Hezekiah appointed the divisions of the priests and of the Levites, division by division, everyone according to his service, the priests and the Levites, for burnt offerings and offerings of well-being, to minister in the gates of the camp of the LORD and to give thanks and praise. 3The contribution of the king from his own possessions was for the burnt offerings: the burnt offerings of morning and evening, and the burnt offerings for the sabbaths, the new moons, and the appointed festivals, as it is written in the law of the LORD. 4He commanded the people who lived in Jerusalem to give the portion due to the priests and the Levites, so that they might devote themselves to the law of the LORD. 5As soon as the word spread, the people of Israel gave in abundance the first fruits of grain, wine, oil, honey, and of all the produce of the field; and they brought in abundantly the tithe of everything. 6The people of Israel and Judah who lived in the cities of Judah also brought in the tithe of cattle and sheep, and the tithe of the dedicated things that had been consecrated to the LORD their God, and laid them in heaps. 7In the third month they began to pile up the heaps, and finished them in the seventh month. 8When Hezekiah and the officials came and saw the heaps, they blessed the LORD and his people Israel. 9Hezekiah questioned the priests and the Levites about the heaps. 10The chief priest Azariah, who was of the house of Zadok, answered him, "Since they began to bring the contributions into the house of the LORD, we have had enough to eat and have plenty to spare; for the LORD has blessed his people, so that we have this great supply left over."

Reorganization of Priests and Levites

11 Then Hezekiah commanded them to prepare store-chambers in the house of the LORD; and they prepared them. 12Faithfully they brought in the contributions, the tithes and the dedicated things. The chief officer in charge of them was Conaniah the Levite, with his brother Shimei as second; 13while Jehiel, Azaziah, Nahath, Asahel, Jerimoth, Jozabad, Eliel, Ismachiah, Mahath, and Benaiah were overseers assisting Conaniah and his brother Shimei, by the appointment of King Hezekiah and of Azariah the chief officer of the house of God. 14Kore son of Imnah the Levite, keeper of the east gate, was in charge of the freewill offerings to God, to apportion the contribution reserved for the LORD and the most holy offerings. 15Eden, Miniamin, Jeshua, Shemaiah, Amariah, and Shecaniah were faithfully assisting him in the cities of the priests, to distribute the portions to their kindred, old and young alike, by divisions, 16except those enrolled by genealogy, males from three years old and up-

a Heb *Asherim*

wards, all who entered the house of the LORD as the duty of each day required, for their service according to their offices, by their divisions. ¹⁷The enrollment of the priests was according to their ancestral houses; that of the Levites from twenty years old and upwards was according to their offices, by their divisions. ¹⁸The priests were enrolled with all their little children, their wives, their sons, and their daughters, the whole multitude; for they were faithful in keeping themselves holy. ¹⁹And for the descendants of Aaron, the priests, who were in the fields of common land belonging to their towns, town by town, the people designated by name were to distribute portions to every male among the priests and to everyone among the Levites who was enrolled.

20 Hezekiah did this throughout all Judah; he did what was good and right and faithful before the LORD his God. ²¹And every work that he undertook in the service of the house of God, and in accordance with the law and the commandments, to seek his God, he did with all his heart; and he prospered.

Sennacherib's Invasion

32 After these things and these acts of faithfulness, King Sennacherib of Assyria came and invaded Judah and encamped against the fortified cities, thinking to win them for himself. ²When Hezekiah saw that Sennacherib had come and intended to fight against Jerusalem, ³he planned with his officers and his warriors to stop the flow of the springs that were outside the city; and they helped him. ⁴A great many people were gathered, and they stopped all the springs and the wadi that flowed through the land, saying, "Why should the Assyrian kings come and find water in abundance?" ⁵Hezekiah*a* set to work resolutely and built up the entire wall that was broken down, and raised towers on it,*b* and outside it he built another wall; he also strengthened the Millo in the city of David, and made weapons and shields in abundance. ⁶He appointed combat commanders over the people, and gathered

them together to him in the square at the gate of the city and spoke encouragingly to them, saying, ⁷"Be strong and of good courage. Do not be afraid or dismayed before the king of Assyria and all the horde that is with him; for there is one greater with us than with him. ⁸With him is an arm of flesh; but with us is the LORD our God, to help us and to fight our battles." The people were encouraged by the words of King Hezekiah of Judah.

9 After this, while King Sennacherib of Assyria was at Lachish with all his forces, he sent his servants to Jerusalem to King Hezekiah of Judah and to all the people of Judah that were in Jerusalem, saying, ¹⁰"Thus says King Sennacherib of Assyria: On what are you relying, that you undergo the siege of Jerusalem? ¹¹Is not Hezekiah misleading you, handing you over to die by famine and by thirst, when he tells you, 'The LORD our God will save us from the hand of the king of Assyria'? ¹²Was it not this same Hezekiah who took away his high places and his altars and commanded Judah and Jerusalem, saying, 'Before one altar you shall worship, and upon it you shall make your offerings'? ¹³Do you not know what I and my ancestors have done to all the peoples of other lands? Were the gods of the nations of those lands at all able to save their lands out of my hand? ¹⁴Who among all the gods of those nations that my ancestors utterly destroyed was able to save his people from my hand, that your God should be able to save you from my hand? ¹⁵Now therefore do not let Hezekiah deceive you or mislead you in this fashion, and do not believe him, for no god of any nation or kingdom has been able to save his people from my hand or from the hand of my ancestors. How much less will your God save you out of my hand!"

16 His servants said still more against the Lord GOD and against his servant Hezekiah. ¹⁷He also wrote letters to throw contempt on the LORD the God of Israel and to speak against him, saying, "Just as the gods of the nations in other lands did not rescue their people

---

a Heb He   *b* Vg: Heb *and raised on the towers*

from my hands, so the God of Hezekiah will not rescue his people from my hand." [18]They shouted it with a loud voice in the language of Judah to the people of Jerusalem who were on the wall, to frighten and terrify them, in order that they might take the city. [19]They spoke of the God of Jerusalem as if he were like the gods of the peoples of the earth, which are the work of human hands.

Sennacherib's Defeat and Death

20 Then King Hezekiah and the prophet Isaiah son of Amoz prayed because of this and cried to heaven. [21]And the LORD sent an angel who cut off all the mighty warriors and commanders and officers in the camp of the king of Assyria. So he returned in disgrace to his own land. When he came into the house of his god, some of his own sons struck him down there with the sword. [22]So the LORD saved Hezekiah and the inhabitants of Jerusalem from the hand of King Sennacherib of Assyria and from the hand of all his enemies; he gave them rest[a] on every side. [23]Many brought gifts to the LORD in Jerusalem and precious things to King Hezekiah of Judah, so that he was exalted in the sight of all nations from that time onward.

Hezekiah's Sickness

24 In those days Hezekiah became sick and was at the point of death. He prayed to the LORD, and he answered him and gave him a sign. [25]But Hezekiah did not respond according to the benefit done to him, for his heart was proud. Therefore wrath came upon him and upon Judah and Jerusalem. [26]Then Hezekiah humbled himself for the pride of his heart, both he and the inhabitants of Jerusalem, so that the wrath of the LORD did not come upon them in the days of Hezekiah.

Hezekiah's Prosperity and Achievements

27 Hezekiah had very great riches and honor; and he made for himself treasuries for silver, for gold, for precious stones, for spices, for shields, and for all kinds of costly objects; [28]storehouses also for the yield of grain, wine, and oil; and stalls for all kinds of cattle, and sheepfolds.[b] [29]He likewise provided cities for himself, and flocks and herds in abundance; for God had given him very great possessions. [30]This same Hezekiah closed the upper outlet of the waters of Gihon and directed them down to the west side of the city of David. Hezekiah prospered in all his works. [31]So also in the matter of the envoys of the officials of Babylon, who had been sent to him to inquire about the sign that had been done in the land, God left him to himself, in order to test him and to know all that was in his heart.

32 Now the rest of the acts of Hezekiah, and his good deeds, are written in the vision of the prophet Isaiah son of Amoz in the Book of the Kings of Judah and Israel. [33]Hezekiah slept with his ancestors, and they buried him on the ascent to the tombs of the descendants of David; and all Judah and the inhabitants of Jerusalem did him honor at his death. His son Manasseh succeeded him.

Reign of Manasseh

33 Manasseh was twelve years old when he began to reign; he reigned fifty-five years in Jerusalem. [2]He did what was evil in the sight of the LORD, according to the abominable practices of the nations whom the LORD drove out before the people of Israel. [3]For he rebuilt the high places that his father Hezekiah had pulled down, and erected altars to the Baals, made sacred poles,[c] worshiped all the host of heaven, and served them. [4]He built altars in the house of the LORD, of which the LORD had said, "In Jerusalem shall my name be forever." [5]He built altars for all the host of heaven in the two courts of the house of the LORD. [6]He made his son pass through fire in the valley of the son of Hinnom, practiced soothsaying and augury and sorcery, and dealt with mediums and with wizards. He did much evil in the sight of the LORD, provoking him to anger. [7]The carved image of the idol that he

---

a Gk Vg: Heb *guided them*   b Gk Vg: Heb *flocks for folds*   c Heb *Asheroth* had made he set in the house of God, of which God said to David and to his son Solomon, "In this house, and in Jerusalem, which I have chosen out of all the tribes of Israel, I will put my name forever; [8]I will never again remove the feet of Israel from the land that I appointed for your ancestors, if only they will be careful to do all that I have commanded them, all the law, the statutes, and the ordinances given through Moses." [9]Manasseh misled Judah and the inhabitants of Jerusalem, so that they did more evil than the nations whom the LORD had destroyed before the people of Israel.

Manasseh Restored after Repentance

10 The LORD spoke to Manasseh and to his people, but they gave no heed. [11]Therefore the LORD brought against them the commanders of the army of the king of Assyria, who took Manasseh captive in manacles, bound him with fetters, and brought him to Babylon. [12]While he was in distress he entreated the favor of the LORD his God and humbled himself greatly before the God of his ancestors. [13]He prayed to him, and God received his entreaty, heard his plea, and restored him again to Jerusalem and to his kingdom. Then Manasseh knew that the LORD indeed was God.

14 Afterward he built an outer wall for the city of David west of Gihon, in the valley, reaching the entrance at the Fish Gate; he carried it around Ophel, and raised it to a very great height. He also put commanders of the army in all the fortified cities in Judah. [15]He took away the foreign gods and the idol from the house of the LORD, and all the altars that he had built on the mountain of the house of the LORD and in Jerusalem, and he threw them out of the city. [16]He also restored the altar of the LORD and offered on it sacrifices of well-being and of thanksgiving; and he commanded Judah to serve the LORD the God of Israel. [17]The people, however, still sacrificed at the high places, but only to the LORD their God.

Death of Manasseh

18 Now the rest of the acts of Manasseh, his prayer to his God, and the words of the seers who spoke to him in the name of the LORD God of Israel, these are in the Annals of the Kings of Israel. [19]His prayer, and how God received his entreaty, all his sin and his faithlessness, the sites on which he built high places and set up the sacred poles[a] and the images, before he humbled himself, these are written in the records of the seers. [b] [20]So Manasseh slept with his ancestors, and they buried him in his house. His son Amon succeeded him.

Amon's Reign and Death

21 Amon was twenty-two years old when he began to reign; he reigned two years in Jerusalem. [22]He did what was evil in the sight of the LORD, as his father Manasseh had done. Amon sacrificed to all the images that his father Manasseh had made, and served them. [23]He did not humble himself before the LORD, as his father Manasseh had humbled himself, but this Amon incurred more and more guilt. [24]His servants conspired against him and killed him in his house. [25]But the people of the land killed all those who had conspired against King Amon; and the people of the land made his son Josiah king to succeed him.

Reign of Josiah

34 Josiah was eight years old when he began to reign; he reigned thirty-one years in Jerusalem. [2]He did what was right in the sight of the LORD, and walked in the ways of his ancestor David; he did not turn aside to the right or to the left. [3]For in the eighth year of his reign, while he was still a boy, he began to seek the God of his ancestor David, and in the twelfth year he began to purge Judah and Jerusalem of the high places, the sacred poles,[a] and the carved and the cast images. [4]In his presence they pulled down the altars of the Baals; he demolished the incense altars that stood above them. He broke down the sacred poles[a] and the carved and the cast images; he made

a Heb *Asherim*   b One Ms Gk: MT *of Hozai*

dust of them and scattered it over the graves of those who had sacrificed to them. ⁵He also burned the bones of the priests on their altars, and purged Judah and Jerusalem. ⁶In the towns of Manasseh, Ephraim, and Simeon, and as far as Naphtali, in their ruins*a* all around, ⁷he broke down the altars, beat the sacred poles*b* and the images into powder, and demolished all the incense altars throughout all the land of Israel. Then he returned to Jerusalem.

Discovery of the Book of the Law

8 In the eighteenth year of his reign, when he had purged the land and the house, he sent Shaphan son of Azaliah, Maaseiah the governor of the city, and Joah son of Joahaz, the recorder, to repair the house of the LORD his God. ⁹They came to the high priest Hilkiah and delivered the money that had been brought into the house of God, which the Levites, the keepers of the threshold, had collected from Manasseh and Ephraim and from all the remnant of Israel and from all Judah and Benjamin and from the inhabitants of Jerusalem. ¹⁰They delivered it to the workers who had the oversight of the house of the LORD, and the workers who were working in the house of the LORD gave it for repairing and restoring the house. ¹¹They gave it to the carpenters and the builders to buy quarried stone, and timber for binders, and beams for the buildings that the kings of Judah had let go to ruin. ¹²The people did the work faithfully. Over them were appointed the Levites Jahath and Obadiah, of the sons of Merari, along with Zechariah and Meshullam, of the sons of the Kohathites, to have oversight. Other Levites, all skillful with instruments of music, ¹³were over the burden bearers and directed all who did work in every kind of service; and some of the Levites were scribes, and officials, and gatekeepers.

14 While they were bringing out the money that had been brought into the house of the LORD, the priest Hilkiah found the book of the law of the LORD given through Moses. ¹⁵Hilkiah said to the secretary Shaphan, "I have found the book of the law in the house of the LORD"; and Hilkiah gave the book to Shaphan. ¹⁶Shaphan brought the book to the king, and further reported to the king, "All that was committed to your servants they are doing. ¹⁷They have emptied out the money that was found in the house of the LORD and have delivered it into the hand of the overseers and the workers." ¹⁸The secretary Shaphan informed the king, "The priest Hilkiah has given me a book." Shaphan then read it aloud to the king.

19 When the king heard the words of the law he tore his clothes. ²⁰Then the king commanded Hilkiah, Ahikam son of Shaphan, Abdon son of Micah, the secretary Shaphan, and the king's servant Asaiah: ²¹"Go, inquire of the LORD for me and for those who are left in Israel and in Judah, concerning the words of the book that has been found; for the wrath of the LORD that is poured out on us is great, because our ancestors did not keep the word of the LORD, to act in accordance with all that is written in this book."

The Prophet Huldah Consulted

22 So Hilkiah and those whom the king had sent went to the prophet Huldah, the wife of Shallum son of Tokhath son of Hasrah, keeper of the wardrobe (who lived in Jerusalem in the Second Quarter) and spoke to her to that effect. ²³She declared to them, "Thus says the LORD, the God of Israel: Tell the man who sent you to me, ²⁴Thus says the LORD: I will indeed bring disaster upon this place and upon its inhabitants, all the curses that are written in the book that was read before the king of Judah. ²⁵Because they have forsaken me and have made offerings to other gods, so that they have provoked me to anger with all the works of their hands, my wrath will be poured out on this place and will not be quenched. ²⁶But as to the king of Judah, who sent you to inquire of the LORD, thus shall you say to him: Thus says the LORD, the God of Israel: Regarding the words that you have heard, ²⁷because your heart was penitent and you humbled

a Meaning of Heb uncertain   *b* Heb *Asherim*

yourself before God when you heard his words against this place and its inhabitants, and you have humbled yourself before me, and have torn your clothes and wept before me, I also have heard you, says the LORD. ²⁸I will gather you to your ancestors and you shall be gathered to your grave in peace; your eyes shall not see all the disaster that I will bring on this place and its inhabitants." They took the message back to the king.

The Covenant Renewed

29 Then the king sent word and gathered together all the elders of Judah and Jerusalem. ³⁰The king went up to the house of the LORD, with all the people of Judah, the inhabitants of Jerusalem, the priests and the Levites, all the people both great and small; he read in their hearing all the words of the book of the covenant that had been found in the house of the LORD. ³¹The king stood in his place and made a covenant before the LORD, to follow the LORD, keeping his commandments, his decrees, and his statutes, with all his heart and all his soul, to perform the words of the covenant that were written in this book. ³²Then he made all who were present in Jerusalem and in Benjamin pledge themselves to it. And the inhabitants of Jerusalem acted according to the covenant of God, the God of their ancestors. ³³Josiah took away all the abominations from all the territory that belonged to the people of Israel, and made all who were in Israel worship the LORD their God. All his days they did not turn away from following the LORD the God of their ancestors.

Celebration of the Passover

35 Josiah kept a passover to the LORD in Jerusalem; they slaughtered the passover lamb on the fourteenth day of the first month. ²He appointed the priests to their offices and encouraged them in the service of the house of the LORD. ³He said to the Levites who taught all Israel and who were holy to the LORD, "Put the holy ark in the house that Sol-omon son of David, king of Israel, built; you need no longer carry it on your shoulders. Now serve the LORD your God and his people Israel. ⁴Make preparations by your ancestral houses by your divisions, following the written directions of King David of Israel and the written directions of his son Solomon. ⁵Take position in the holy place according to the groupings of the ancestral houses of your kindred the people, and let there be Levites for each division of an ancestral house.ᵃ ⁶Slaughter the passover lamb, sanctify yourselves, and on behalf of your kindred make preparations, acting according to the word of the LORD by Moses."

7 Then Josiah contributed to the people, as passover offerings for all that were present, lambs and kids from the flock to the number of thirty thousand, and three thousand bulls; these were from the king's possessions. ⁸His officials contributed willingly to the people, to the priests, and to the Levites. Hilkiah, Zechariah, and Jehiel, the chief officers of the house of God, gave to the priests for the passover offerings two thousand six hundred lambs and kids and three hundred bulls. ⁹Conaniah also, and his brothers Shemaiah and Nethanel, and Hashabiah and Jeiel and Jozabad, the chiefs of the Levites, gave to the Levites for the passover offerings five thousand lambs and kids and five hundred bulls.

10 When the service had been prepared for, the priests stood in their place, and the Levites in their divisions according to the king's command. ¹¹They slaughtered the passover lamb, and the priests dashed the blood that they receivedᵇ from them, while the Levites did the skinning. ¹²They set aside the burnt offerings so that they might distribute them according to the groupings of the ancestral houses of the people, to offer to the LORD, as it is written in the book of Moses. And they did the same with the bulls. ¹³They roasted the passover lamb with fire according to the ordinance; and they boiled the holy offerings in pots, in caldrons, and in pans, and carried them quickly to all the people. ¹⁴Afterward they made

---

a Meaning of Heb uncertain   *b* Heb lacks *that they received* preparations for themselves and for the priests, because the priests the descendants of Aaron were occupied in offering the burnt offerings and the fat parts until night; so the Levites made preparations for themselves and for the priests, the descendants of Aaron. ¹⁵The singers, the descendants of Asaph, were in their place according to the command of David, and Asaph, and Heman, and the king's seer Jeduthun. The gatekeepers were at each gate; they did not need to interrupt their service, for their kindred the Levites made preparations for them.

16 So all the service of the LORD was prepared that day, to keep the passover and to offer burnt offerings on the altar of the LORD, according to the command of King Josiah. ¹⁷The people of Israel who were present kept the passover at that time, and the festival of unleavened bread seven days. ¹⁸No passover like it had been kept in Israel since the days of the prophet Samuel; none of the kings of Israel had kept such a passover as was kept by Josiah, by the priests and the Levites, by all Judah and Israel who were present, and by the inhabitants of Jerusalem. ¹⁹In the eighteenth year of the reign of Josiah this passover was kept.

Defeat by Pharaoh Neco and Death of Josiah

20 After all this, when Josiah had set the temple in order, King Neco of Egypt went up to fight at Carchemish on the Euphrates, and Josiah went out against him. ²¹But Neco*a* sent envoys to him, saying, "What have I to do with you, king of Judah? I am not coming against you today, but against the house with which I am at war; and God has commanded me to hurry. Cease opposing God, who is with me, so that he will not destroy you." ²²But Josiah would not turn away from him, but disguised himself in order to fight with him. He did not listen to the words of Neco from the mouth of God, but joined battle in the plain of Megiddo. ²³The archers shot King Josiah; and the king said to his servants, "Take me away, for I am badly wounded." ²⁴So his servants took him out of the chariot and carried him in his second chariot*b* and brought him to Jerusalem. There he died, and was buried in the tombs of his ancestors. All Judah and Jerusalem mourned for Josiah. ²⁵Jeremiah also uttered a lament for Josiah, and all the singing men and singing women have spoken of Josiah in their laments to this day. They made these a custom in Israel; they are recorded in the Laments. ²⁶Now the rest of the acts of Josiah and his faithful deeds in accordance with what is written in the law of the LORD, ²⁷and his acts, first and last, are written in the Book of the Kings of Israel and Judah.

Reign of Jehoahaz

36 The people of the land took Jehoahaz son of Josiah and made him king to succeed his father in Jerusalem. ²Jehoahaz was twenty-three years old when he began to reign; he reigned three months in Jerusalem. ³Then the king of Egypt deposed him in Jerusalem and laid on the land a tribute of one hundred talents of silver and one talent of gold. ⁴The king of Egypt made his brother Eliakim king over Judah and Jerusalem, and changed his name to Jehoiakim; but Neco took his brother Jehoahaz and carried him to Egypt.

Reign and Captivity of Jehoiakim

5 Jehoiakim was twenty-five years old when he began to reign; he reigned eleven years in Jerusalem. He did what was evil in the sight of the LORD his God. ⁶Against him King Nebuchadnezzar of Babylon came up, and bound him with fetters to take him to Babylon. ⁷Nebuchadnezzar also carried some of the vessels of the house of the LORD to Babylon and put them in his palace in Babylon. ⁸Now the rest of the acts of Jehoiakim, and the abominations that he did, and what was found against him, are written in the Book of the Kings of Israel and Judah; and his son Jehoiachin succeeded him.

a Heb *he*   *b* Or *the chariot of his deputy*

Reign and Captivity of Jehoiachin

9 Jehoiachin was eight years old when he began to reign; he reigned three months and ten days in Jerusalem. He did what was evil in the sight of the LORD. [10]In the spring of the year King Nebuchadnezzar sent and brought him to Babylon, along with the precious vessels of the house of the LORD, and made his brother Zedekiah king over Judah and Jerusalem.

Reign of Zedekiah

11 Zedekiah was twenty-one years old when he began to reign; he reigned eleven years in Jerusalem. [12]He did what was evil in the sight of the LORD his God. He did not humble himself before the prophet Jeremiah who spoke from the mouth of the LORD. [13]He also rebelled against King Nebuchadnezzar, who had made him swear by God; he stiffened his neck and hardened his heart against turning to the LORD, the God of Israel. [14]All the leading priests and the people also were exceedingly unfaithful, following all the abominations of the nations; and they polluted the house of the LORD that he had consecrated in Jerusalem.

The Fall of Jerusalem

15 The LORD, the God of their ancestors, sent persistently to them by his messengers, because he had compassion on his people and on his dwelling place; [16]but they kept mocking the messengers of God, despising his words, and scoffing at his prophets, until the wrath of the LORD against his people became so great that there was no remedy.

17 Therefore he brought up against them the king of the Chaldeans, who killed their youths with the sword in the house of their sanctuary, and had no compassion on young man or young woman, the aged or the feeble; he gave them all into his hand. [18]All the vessels of the house of God, large and small, and the treasures of the house of the LORD, and the treasures of the king and of his officials, all these he brought to Babylon. [19]They burned the house of God, broke down the wall of Jerusalem, burned all its palaces with fire, and destroyed all its precious vessels. [20]He took into exile in Babylon those who had escaped from the sword, and they became servants to him and to his sons until the establishment of the kingdom of Persia, [21]to fulfill the word of the LORD by the mouth of Jeremiah, until the land had made up for its sabbaths. All the days that it lay desolate it kept sabbath, to fulfill seventy years.

Cyrus Proclaims Liberty for the Exiles

22 In the first year of King Cyrus of Persia, in fulfillment of the word of the LORD spoken by Jeremiah, the LORD stirred up the spirit of King Cyrus of Persia so that he sent a herald throughout all his kingdom and also declared in a written edict: [23]"Thus says King Cyrus of Persia: The LORD, the God of heaven, has given me all the kingdoms of the earth, and he has charged me to build him a house at Jerusalem, which is in Judah. Whoever is among you of all his people, may the LORD his God be with him! Let him go up."

EZRA

End of the Babylonian Captivity

1 In the first year of King Cyrus of Persia, in order that the word of the LORD by the mouth of Jeremiah might be accomplished, the LORD stirred up the spirit of King Cyrus of Persia so that he sent a herald throughout all his kingdom, and also in a written edict declared:

2 "Thus says King Cyrus of Persia: The LORD, the God of heaven, has given me all the kingdoms of the earth, and he has charged me to build him a house at Jerusalem in Judah. ³Any of those among you who are of his people—may their God be with them!—are now permitted to go up to Jerusalem in Judah, and rebuild the house of the LORD, the God of Israel—he is the God who is in Jerusalem; ⁴and let all survivors, in whatever place they reside, be assisted by the people of their place with silver and gold, with goods and with animals, besides freewill offerings for the house of God in Jerusalem."

5 The heads of the families of Judah and Benjamin, and the priests and the Levites—everyone whose spirit God had stirred—got ready to go up and rebuild the house of the LORD in Jerusalem. ⁶All their neighbors aided them with silver vessels, with gold, with goods, with animals, and with valuable gifts, besides all that was freely offered. ⁷King Cyrus himself brought out the vessels of the house of the LORD that Nebuchadnezzar had carried away from Jerusalem and placed in the house of his gods. ⁸King Cyrus of Persia had them released into the charge of Mithredath the treasurer, who counted them out to Sheshbazzar the prince of Judah. ⁹And this was the inventory: gold basins, thirty; silver basins, one thousand; knives, *a* twenty-nine; ¹⁰gold bowls, thirty; other silver bowls, four hundred ten; other vessels, one thousand; ¹¹the total of the gold and silver vessels was five thousand four hundred. All these Sheshbazzar brought up, when the exiles were brought up from Babylonia to Jerusalem.

List of the Returned Exiles

2 Now these were the people of the province who came from those captive exiles whom King Nebuchadnezzar of Babylon had carried captive to Babylonia; they returned to Jerusalem and Judah, all to their own towns. ²They came with Zerubbabel, Jeshua, Nehemiah, Seraiah, Reelaiah, Mordecai, Bilshan, Mispar, Bigvai, Rehum, and Baanah.

The number of the Israelite people: ³the descendants of Parosh, two thousand one hundred seventy-two. ⁴Of Shephatiah, three hundred seventy-two. ⁵Of Arah, seven hundred seventy-five. ⁶Of Pahath-moab, namely the descendants of Jeshua and Joab, two thousand eight hundred twelve. ⁷Of Elam, one thousand two hundred fifty-four. ⁸Of Zattu, nine hundred forty-five. ⁹Of Zaccai, seven hundred sixty. ¹⁰Of Bani, six hundred forty-two. ¹¹Of Bebai, six hundred twenty-three. ¹²Of Azgad, one thousand two hundred twenty-two. ¹³Of Adonikam, six hundred sixty-six. ¹⁴Of Bigvai, two thousand fifty-six. ¹⁵Of Adin, four hundred fifty-four. ¹⁶Of Ater, namely of Hezekiah, ninety-eight. ¹⁷Of Bezai, three hundred twenty-three. ¹⁸Of Jorah, one hundred twelve. ¹⁹Of Hashum, two hundred twenty-three. ²⁰Of Gibbar, ninety-five. ²¹Of Bethlehem, one hundred twenty-three. ²²The people of Netophah, fifty-six. ²³Of Anathoth, one hundred twenty-eight. ²⁴The descendants of Azmaveth, forty-two. ²⁵Of Kiriatharim, Chephirah, and Beeroth, seven hundred forty-three. ²⁶Of Ramah and Geba, six hundred twenty-one. ²⁷The people of Michmas, one hundred twenty-two. ²⁸Of Bethel and Ai, two hundred twenty-three. ²⁹The descendants of Nebo, fifty-two. ³⁰Of Magbish, one hundred fifty-six. ³¹Of the other Elam, one thousand two hundred fifty-four. ³²Of Harim, three hundred twenty. ³³Of Lod, Hadid, and Ono, seven hundred twenty-five. ³⁴Of Jericho, three hundred forty-five. ³⁵Of Senaah, three thousand six hundred thirty.

a Vg: Meaning of Heb uncertain

36 The priests: the descendants of Jedaiah, of the house of Jeshua, nine hundred seventy-three. ³⁷Of Immer, one thousand fifty-two. ³⁸Of Pashhur, one thousand two hundred forty-seven. ³⁹Of Harim, one thousand seventeen.

40 The Levites: the descendants of Jeshua and Kadmiel, of the descendants of Hodaviah, seventy-four. ⁴¹The singers: the descendants of Asaph, one hundred twenty-eight. ⁴²The descendants of the gatekeepers: of Shallum, of Ater, of Talmon, of Akkub, of Hatita, and of Shobai, in all one hundred thirty-nine.

43 The temple servants: the descendants of Ziha, Hasupha, Tabbaoth, ⁴⁴Keros, Siaha, Padon, ⁴⁵Lebanah, Hagabah, Akkub, ⁴⁶Hagab, Shamlai, Hanan, ⁴⁷Giddel, Gahar, Reaiah, ⁴⁸Rezin, Nekoda, Gazzam, ⁴⁹Uzza, Paseah, Besai, ⁵⁰Asnah, Meunim, Nephisim, ⁵¹Bakbuk, Hakupha, Harhur, ⁵²Bazluth, Mehida, Harsha, ⁵³Barkos, Sisera, Temah, ⁵⁴Neziah, and Hatipha.

55 The descendants of Solomon's servants: Sotai, Hassophereth, Peruda, ⁵⁶Jaalah, Darkon, Giddel, ⁵⁷Shephatiah, Hattil, Pochereth-hazzebaim, and Ami.

58 All the temple servants and the descendants of Solomon's servants were three hundred ninety-two.

59 The following were those who came up from Tel-melah, Tel-harsha, Cherub, Addan, and Immer, though they could not prove their families or their descent, whether they belonged to Israel: ⁶⁰the descendants of Delaiah, Tobiah, and Nekoda, six hundred fifty-two. ⁶¹Also, of the descendants of the priests: the descendants of Habaiah, Hakkoz, and Barzillai (who had married one of the daughters of Barzillai the Gileadite, and was called by their name). ⁶²These looked for their entries in the genealogical records, but they were not found there, and so they were excluded from the priesthood as unclean; ⁶³the governor told them that they were not to partake of the most holy food, until there should be a priest to consult Urim and Thummim.

64 The whole assembly together was forty-two thousand three hundred sixty, ⁶⁵besides their male and female servants, of whom there were seven thousand three hundred thirty-seven; and they had two hundred male and female singers. ⁶⁶They had seven hundred thirty-six horses, two hundred forty-five mules, ⁶⁷four hundred thirty-five camels, and six thousand seven hundred twenty donkeys.

68 As soon as they came to the house of the LORD in Jerusalem, some of the heads of families made freewill offerings for the house of God, to erect it on its site. ⁶⁹According to their resources they gave to the building fund sixty-one thousand darics of gold, five thousand minas of silver, and one hundred priestly robes.

70 The priests, the Levites, and some of the people lived in Jerusalem and its vicinity;ᵃ and the singers, the gatekeepers, and the temple servants lived in their towns, and all Israel in their towns.

Worship Restored at Jerusalem

3 When the seventh month came, and the Israelites were in the towns, the people gathered together in Jerusalem. ²Then Jeshua son of Jozadak, with his fellow priests, and Zerubbabel son of Shealtiel with his kin set out to build the altar of the God of Israel, to offer burnt offerings on it, as prescribed in the law of Moses the man of God. ³They set up the altar on its foundation, because they were in dread of the neighboring peoples, and they offered burnt offerings upon it to the LORD, morning and evening. ⁴And they kept the festival of booths,ᵇ as prescribed, and offered the daily burnt offerings by number according to the ordinance, as required for each day, ⁵and after that the regular burnt offerings, the offerings at the new moon and at all the sacred festivals of the LORD, and the offerings of everyone who made a freewill offering to the LORD. ⁶From the first day of the seventh

_a_ 1 Esdras 5.46: Heb lacks _lived in Jerusalem and its vicinity_   _b_ Or _tabernacles_; Heb _succoth_ month they began to offer burnt offerings to the LORD. But the foundation of the temple of the LORD was not yet laid. 7So they gave money to the masons and the carpenters, and food, drink, and oil to the Sidonians and the Tyrians to bring cedar trees from Lebanon to the sea, to Joppa, according to the grant that they had from King Cyrus of Persia.

Foundation Laid for the Temple

8 In the second year after their arrival at the house of God at Jerusalem, in the second month, Zerubbabel son of Shealtiel and Jeshua son of Jozadak made a beginning, together with the rest of their people, the priests and the Levites and all who had come to Jerusalem from the captivity. They appointed the Levites, from twenty years old and upward, to have the oversight of the work on the house of the LORD. 9And Jeshua with his sons and his kin, and Kadmiel and his sons, Binnui and Hodaviah*a* along with the sons of Henadad, the Levites, their sons and kin, together took charge of the workers in the house of God.

10 When the builders laid the foundation of the temple of the LORD, the priests in their vestments were stationed to praise the LORD with trumpets, and the Levites, the sons of Asaph, with cymbals, according to the directions of King David of Israel; 11and they sang responsively, praising and giving thanks to the LORD,

"For he is good,
for his steadfast love endures forever
toward Israel."

And all the people responded with a great shout when they praised the LORD, because the foundation of the house of the LORD was laid. 12But many of the priests and Levites and heads of families, old people who had seen the first house on its foundations, wept with a loud voice when they saw this house, though many shouted aloud for joy, 13so that the people could not distinguish the sound of the joyful shout from the sound of the people's weeping, for the people shouted so loudly that the sound was heard far away.

Resistance to Rebuilding the Temple

4 When the adversaries of Judah and Benjamin heard that the returned exiles were building a temple to the LORD, the God of Israel, 2they approached Zerubbabel and the heads of families and said to them, "Let us build with you, for we worship your God as you do, and we have been sacrificing to him ever since the days of King Esar-haddon of Assyria who brought us here." 3But Zerubbabel, Jeshua, and the rest of the heads of families in Israel said to them, "You shall have no part with us in building a house to our God; but we alone will build to the LORD, the God of Israel, as King Cyrus of Persia has commanded us."

4 Then the people of the land discouraged the people of Judah, and made them afraid to build, 5and they bribed officials to frustrate their plan throughout the reign of King Cyrus of Persia and until the reign of King Darius of Persia.

Rebuilding of Jerusalem Opposed

6 In the reign of Ahasuerus, in his accession year, they wrote an accusation against the inhabitants of Judah and Jerusalem.

7 And in the days of Artaxerxes, Bishlam and Mithredath and Tabeel and the rest of their associates wrote to King Artaxerxes of Persia; the letter was written in Aramaic and translated.*b* 8Rehum the royal deputy and Shimshai the scribe wrote a letter against Jerusalem to King Artaxerxes as follows 9(then Rehum the royal deputy, Shimshai the scribe, and the rest of their associates, the judges, the envoys, the officials, the Persians, the people of Erech, the Babylonians, the people of Susa, that is, the Elamites, 10and the rest of the nations whom the great and noble Osnappar deported and settled in the cities of Samaria and in the rest of the province Beyond the River wrote—and

a Compare 2.40; Neh 7.43; 1 Esdras 5.58: Heb *sons of Judah*   *b* Heb adds *in Aramaic,* indicating that 4.8–6.18 is in Aramaic. Another interpretation is *The letter was written in the Aramaic script and set forth in the Aramaic language* now [11]this is a copy of the letter that they sent):

"To King Artaxerxes: Your servants, the people of the province Beyond the River, send greeting. And now [12]may it be known to the king that the Jews who came up from you to us have gone to Jerusalem. They are rebuilding that rebellious and wicked city; they are finishing the walls and repairing the foundations. [13]Now may it be known to the king that, if this city is rebuilt and the walls finished, they will not pay tribute, custom, or toll, and the royal revenue will be reduced. [14]Now because we share the salt of the palace and it is not fitting for us to witness the king's dishonor, therefore we send and inform the king, [15]so that a search may be made in the annals of your ancestors. You will discover in the annals that this is a rebellious city, hurtful to kings and provinces, and that sedition was stirred up in it from long ago. On that account this city was laid waste. [16]We make known to the king that, if this city is rebuilt and its walls finished, you will then have no possession in the province Beyond the River."

[17] The king sent an answer: "To Rehum the royal deputy and Shimshai the scribe and the rest of their associates who live in Samaria and in the rest of the province Beyond the River, greeting. And now [18]the letter that you sent to us has been read in translation before me. [19]So I made a decree, and someone searched and discovered that this city has risen against kings from long ago, and that rebellion and sedition have been made in it. [20]Jerusalem has had mighty kings who ruled over the whole province Beyond the River, to whom tribute, custom, and toll were paid. [21]Therefore issue an order that these people be made to cease, and that this city not be rebuilt, until I make a decree. [22]Moreover, take care not to be slack in this matter; why should damage grow to the hurt of the king?"

[23] Then when the copy of King Artaxerxes' letter was read before Rehum and the scribe Shimshai and their associates, they hurried to the Jews in Jerusalem and by force and power made them cease. [24]At that time the work on the house of God in Jerusalem stopped and was discontinued until the second year of the reign of King Darius of Persia.

Restoration of the Temple Resumed

5 Now the prophets, Haggai[a] and Zechariah son of Iddo, prophesied to the Jews who were in Judah and Jerusalem, in the name of the God of Israel who was over them. [2]Then Zerubbabel son of Shealtiel and Jeshua son of Jozadak set out to rebuild the house of God in Jerusalem; and with them were the prophets of God, helping them.

[3] At the same time Tattenai the governor of the province Beyond the River and Shethar-bozenai and their associates came to them and spoke to them thus, "Who gave you a decree to build this house and to finish this structure?" [4]They[b] also asked them this, "What are the names of the men who are building this building?" [5]But the eye of their God was upon the elders of the Jews, and they did not stop them until a report reached Darius and then answer was returned by letter in reply to it.

[6] The copy of the letter that Tattenai the governor of the province Beyond the River and Shethar-bozenai and his associates the envoys who were in the province Beyond the River sent to King Darius; [7]they sent him a report, in which was written as follows: "To Darius the king, all peace! [8]May it be known to the king that we went to the province of Judah, to the house of the great God. It is being built of hewn stone, and timber is laid in the walls; this work is being done diligently and prospers in their hands. [9]Then we spoke to those elders and asked them, 'Who gave you a decree to build this house and to finish this structure?' [10]We also asked them their names, for your information, so that we might write down the names of the men at their head. [11]This was their reply to us: 'We are the servants of the God of heaven and earth, and we are rebuilding the house that was built many years ago, which a

a Aram adds *the prophet*   *b* Gk Syr: Aram *We*

great king of Israel built and finished. [12]But because our ancestors had angered the God of heaven, he gave them into the hand of King Nebuchadnezzar of Babylon, the Chaldean, who destroyed this house and carried away the people to Babylonia. [13]However, King Cyrus of Babylon, in the first year of his reign, made a decree that this house of God should be rebuilt. [14]Moreover, the gold and silver vessels of the house of God, which Nebuchadnezzar had taken out of the temple in Jerusalem and had brought into the temple of Babylon, these King Cyrus took out of the temple of Babylon, and they were delivered to a man named Sheshbazzar, whom he had made governor. [15]He said to him, "Take these vessels; go and put them in the temple in Jerusalem, and let the house of God be rebuilt on its site." [16]Then this Sheshbazzar came and laid the foundations of the house of God in Jerusalem; and from that time until now it has been under construction, and it is not yet finished.' [17]And now, if it seems good to the king, have a search made in the royal archives there in Babylon, to see whether a decree was issued by King Cyrus for the rebuilding of this house of God in Jerusalem. Let the king send us his pleasure in this matter."

The Decree of Darius

6 Then King Darius made a decree, and they searched the archives where the documents were stored in Babylon. [2]But it was in Ecbatana, the capital in the province of Media, that a scroll was found on which this was written: "A record. [3]In the first year of his reign, King Cyrus issued a decree: Concerning the house of God at Jerusalem, let the house be rebuilt, the place where sacrifices are offered and burnt offerings are brought;*a* its height shall be sixty cubits and its width sixty cubits, [4]with three courses of hewn stones and one course of timber; let the cost be paid from the royal treasury. [5]Moreover, let the gold and silver vessels of the house of God, which Nebuchadnezzar took out of the temple in Jerusalem

and brought to Babylon, be restored and brought back to the temple in Jerusalem, each to its place; you shall put them in the house of God."

6 "Now you, Tattenai, governor of the province Beyond the River, Shethar-bozenai, and you, their associates, the envoys in the province Beyond the River, keep away; [7]let the work on this house of God alone; let the governor of the Jews and the elders of the Jews rebuild this house of God on its site. [8]Moreover I make a decree regarding what you shall do for these elders of the Jews for the rebuilding of this house of God: the cost is to be paid to these people, in full and without delay, from the royal revenue, the tribute of the province Beyond the River. [9]Whatever is needed—young bulls, rams, or sheep for burnt offerings to the God of heaven, wheat, salt, wine, or oil, as the priests in Jerusalem require—let that be given to them day by day without fail, [10]so that they may offer pleasing sacrifices to the God of heaven, and pray for the life of the king and his children. [11]Furthermore I decree that if anyone alters this edict, a beam shall be pulled out of the house of the perpetrator, who then shall be impaled on it. The house shall be made a dunghill. [12]May the God who has established his name there overthrow any king or people that shall put forth a hand to alter this, or to destroy this house of God in Jerusalem. I, Darius, make a decree; let it be done with all diligence."

Completion and Dedication of the Temple

13 Then, according to the word sent by King Darius, Tattenai, the governor of the province Beyond the River, Shethar-bozenai, and their associates did with all diligence what King Darius had ordered. [14]So the elders of the Jews built and prospered, through the prophesying of the prophet Haggai and Zechariah son of Iddo. They finished their building by command of the God of Israel and by decree of Cyrus, Darius, and King Artaxerxes of Persia; [15]and this house was finished on the third

a Meaning of Aram uncertain

day of the month of Adar, in the sixth year of the reign of King Darius.

16 The people of Israel, the priests and the Levites, and the rest of the returned exiles, celebrated the dedication of this house of God with joy. 17They offered at the dedication of this house of God one hundred bulls, two hundred rams, four hundred lambs, and as a sin offering for all Israel, twelve male goats, according to the number of the tribes of Israel. 18Then they set the priests in their divisions and the Levites in their courses for the service of God at Jerusalem, as it is written in the book of Moses.

The Passover Celebrated

19 On the fourteenth day of the first month the returned exiles kept the passover. 20For both the priests and the Levites had purified themselves; all of them were clean. So they killed the passover lamb for all the returned exiles, for their fellow priests, and for themselves. 21It was eaten by the people of Israel who had returned from exile, and also by all who had joined them and separated themselves from the pollutions of the nations of the land to worship the LORD, the God of Israel. 22With joy they celebrated the festival of unleavened bread seven days; for the LORD had made them joyful, and had turned the heart of the king of Assyria to them, so that he aided them in the work on the house of God, the God of Israel.

The Coming and Work of Ezra

7 After this, in the reign of King Artaxerxes of Persia, Ezra son of Seraiah, son of Azariah, son of Hilkiah, 2son of Shallum, son of Zadok, son of Ahitub, 3son of Amariah, son of Azariah, son of Meraioth, 4son of Zerahiah, son of Uzzi, son of Bukki, 5son of Abishua, son of Phinehas, son of Eleazar, son of the chief priest Aaron— 6this Ezra went up from Babylonia. He was a scribe skilled in the law of Moses that the LORD the God of Israel had given; and the king granted him all that

he asked, for the hand of the LORD his God was upon him.

7 Some of the people of Israel, and some of the priests and Levites, the singers and gatekeepers, and the temple servants also went up to Jerusalem, in the seventh year of King Artaxerxes. 8They came to Jerusalem in the fifth month, which was in the seventh year of the king. 9On the first day of the first month the journey up from Babylon was begun, and on the first day of the fifth month he came to Jerusalem, for the gracious hand of his God was upon him. 10For Ezra had set his heart to study the law of the LORD, and to do it, and to teach the statutes and ordinances in Israel.

The Letter of Artaxerxes to Ezra

11 This is a copy of the letter that King Artaxerxes gave to the priest Ezra, the scribe, a scholar of the text of the commandments of the LORD and his statutes for Israel: 12"Artaxerxes, king of kings, to the priest Ezra, the scribe of the law of the God of heaven: Peace.[a] And now 13I decree that any of the people of Israel or their priests or Levites in my kingdom who freely offers to go to Jerusalem may go with you. 14For you are sent by the king and his seven counselors to make inquiries about Judah and Jerusalem according to the law of your God, which is in your hand, 15and also to convey the silver and gold that the king and his counselors have freely offered to the God of Israel, whose dwelling is in Jerusalem, 16with all the silver and gold that you shall find in the whole province of Babylonia, and with the freewill offerings of the people and the priests, given willingly for the house of their God in Jerusalem. 17With this money, then, you shall with all diligence buy bulls, rams, and lambs, and their grain offerings and their drink offerings, and you shall offer them on the altar of the house of your God in Jerusalem. 18Whatever seems good to you and your colleagues to do with the rest of the silver and gold, you may do, according to the will of your God. 19The vessels that have been given you for the service

a Syr Vg 1 Esdras 8.9: Aram Perfect

of the house of your God, you shall deliver before the God of Jerusalem. 20And whatever else is required for the house of your God, which you are responsible for providing, you may provide out of the king's treasury.

21 "I, King Artaxerxes, decree to all the treasurers in the province Beyond the River: Whatever the priest Ezra, the scribe of the law of the God of heaven, requires of you, let it be done with all diligence, 22up to one hundred talents of silver, one hundred cors of wheat, one hundred baths*a* of wine, one hundred baths*a* of oil, and unlimited salt. 23Whatever is commanded by the God of heaven, let it be done with zeal for the house of the God of heaven, or wrath will come upon the realm of the king and his heirs. 24We also notify you that it shall not be lawful to impose tribute, custom, or toll on any of the priests, the Levites, the singers, the doorkeepers, the temple servants, or other servants of this house of God.

25 "And you, Ezra, according to the God-given wisdom you possess, appoint magistrates and judges who may judge all the people in the province Beyond the River who know the laws of your God; and you shall teach those who do not know them. 26All who will not obey the law of your God and the law of the king, let judgment be strictly executed on them, whether for death or for banishment or for confiscation of their goods or for imprisonment."

27 Blessed be the LORD, the God of our ancestors, who put such a thing as this into the heart of the king to glorify the house of the LORD in Jerusalem, 28and who extended to me steadfast love before the king and his counselors, and before all the king's mighty officers. I took courage, for the hand of the LORD my God was upon me, and I gathered leaders from Israel to go up with me.

Heads of Families Who Returned with Ezra

8 These are their family heads, and this is the genealogy of those who went up with me from Babylonia, in the reign of King Artaxerxes: 2Of the descendants of Phinehas, Ger-

shom. Of Ithamar, Daniel. Of David, Hattush, 3of the descendants of Shecaniah. Of Parosh, Zechariah, with whom were registered one hundred fifty males. 4Of the descendants of Pahath-moab, Eliehoenai son of Zerahiah, and with him two hundred males. 5Of the descendants of Zattu,*b* Shecaniah son of Jahaziel, and with him three hundred males. 6Of the descendants of Adin, Ebed son of Jonathan, and with him fifty males. 7Of the descendants of Elam, Jeshaiah son of Athaliah, and with him seventy males. 8Of the descendants of Shephatiah, Zebadiah son of Michael, and with him eighty males. 9Of the descendants of Joab, Obadiah son of Jehiel, and with him two hundred eighteen males. 10Of the descendants of Bani,*c* Shelomith son of Josiphiah, and with him one hundred sixty males. 11Of the descendants of Bebai, Zechariah son of Bebai, and with him twenty-eight males. 12Of the descendants of Azgad, Johanan son of Hakkatan, and with him one hundred ten males. 13Of the descendants of Adonikam, those who came later, their names being Eliphelet, Jeuel, and Shemaiah, and with them sixty males. 14Of the descendants of Bigvai, Uthai and Zaccur, and with them seventy males.

Servants for the Temple

15 I gathered them by the river that runs to Ahava, and there we camped three days. As I reviewed the people and the priests, I found there none of the descendants of Levi. 16Then I sent for Eliezer, Ariel, Shemaiah, Elnathan, Jarib, Elnathan, Nathan, Zechariah, and Meshullam, who were leaders, and for Joiarib and Elnathan, who were wise, 17and sent them to Iddo, the leader at the place called Casiphia, telling them what to say to Iddo and his colleagues the temple servants at Casiphia, namely, to send us ministers for the house of our God. 18Since the gracious hand of our God was upon us, they brought us a man of discretion, of the descendants of Mahli son of Levi son of Israel, namely Sherebiah, with his sons and kin, eighteen; 19also Hashabiah and

---

a A Heb measure of volume   *b* Gk 1 Esdras 8.32: Heb lacks *of Zattu*   *c* Gk 1 Esdras 8.36: Heb lacks *Bani*

with him Jeshaiah of the descendants of Merari, with his kin and their sons, twenty; [20]be-
sides two hundred twenty of the temple servants, whom David and his officials had set
apart to attend the Levites. These were all mentioned by name.

Fasting and Prayer for Protection

21 Then I proclaimed a fast there, at the river Ahava, that we might deny ourselves[a] before
our God, to seek from him a safe journey for
ourselves, our children, and all our possessions.
[22]For I was ashamed to ask the king for a band
of soldiers and cavalry to protect us against the
enemy on our way, since we had told the king
that the hand of our God is gracious to all who
seek him, but his power and his wrath are
against all who forsake him. [23]So we fasted
and petitioned our God for this, and he listened
to our entreaty.

Gifts for the Temple

24 Then I set apart twelve of the leading
priests: Sherebiah, Hashabiah, and ten of their
kin with them. [25]And I weighed out to them the
silver and the gold and the vessels, the offering
for the house of our God that the king, his
counselors, his lords, and all Israel there present
had offered; [26]I weighed out into their hand six
hundred fifty talents of silver, and one hundred
silver vessels worth . . . talents,[b] and one hundred talents of gold, [27]twenty gold bowls worth
a thousand darics, and two vessels of fine polished bronze as precious as gold. [28]And I said
to them, "You are holy to the LORD, and the
vessels are holy; and the silver and the gold are
a freewill offering to the LORD, the God of
your ancestors. [29]Guard them and keep them
until you weigh them before the chief priests
and the Levites and the heads of families in Israel at Jerusalem, within the chambers of the
house of the LORD." [30]So the priests and the
Levites took over the silver, the gold, and the
vessels as they were weighed out, to bring them
to Jerusalem, to the house of our God.

The Return to Jerusalem

31 Then we left the river Ahava on the
twelfth day of the first month, to go to Jerusalem; the hand of our God was upon us, and
he delivered us from the hand of the enemy
and from ambushes along the way. [32]We came
to Jerusalem and remained there three days.
[33]On the fourth day, within the house of our
God, the silver, the gold, and the vessels were
weighed into the hands of the priest Meremoth son of Uriah, and with him was Eleazar
son of Phinehas, and with them were the Levites, Jozabad son of Jeshua and Noadiah son
of Binnui. [34]The total was counted and
weighed, and the weight of everything was
recorded.

35 At that time those who had come from
captivity, the returned exiles, offered burnt offerings to the God of Israel, twelve bulls for all
Israel, ninety-six rams, seventy-seven lambs,
and as a sin offering twelve male goats; all this
was a burnt offering to the LORD. [36]They also
delivered the king's commissions to the king's
satraps and to the governors of the province
Beyond the River; and they supported the people and the house of God.

Denunciation of Mixed Marriages

9 After these things had been done, the officials approached me and said, "The people of Israel, the priests, and the Levites have
not separated themselves from the peoples of
the lands with their abominations, from the
Canaanites, the Hittites, the Perizzites, the Jebusites, the Ammonites, the Moabites, the Egyptians, and the Amorites. [2]For they have taken
some of their daughters as wives for themselves and for their sons. Thus the holy seed has
mixed itself with the peoples of the lands, and
in this faithlessness the officials and leaders
have led the way." [3]When I heard this, I tore my
garment and my mantle, and pulled hair from
my head and beard, and sat appalled. [4]Then all
who trembled at the words of the God of Israel, because of the faithlessness of the re-

---

a Or *might fast*   *b* The number of talents is lacking turned exiles, gathered around me while I sat appalled until the evening sacrifice.

Ezra's Prayer

5 At the evening sacrifice I got up from my fasting, with my garments and my mantle torn, and fell on my knees, spread out my hands to the LORD my God, ⁶and said,

"O my God, I am too ashamed and embarrassed to lift my face to you, my God, for our iniquities have risen higher than our heads, and our guilt has mounted up to the heavens. ⁷From the days of our ancestors to this day we have been deep in guilt, and for our iniquities we, our kings, and our priests have been handed over to the kings of the lands, to the sword, to captivity, to plundering, and to utter shame, as is now the case. ⁸But now for a brief moment favor has been shown by the LORD our God, who has left us a remnant, and given us a stake in his holy place, in order that he^a may brighten our eyes and grant us a little sustenance in our slavery. ⁹For we are slaves; yet our God has not forsaken us in our slavery, but has extended to us his steadfast love before the kings of Persia, to give us new life to set up the house of our God, to repair its ruins, and to give us a wall in Judea and Jerusalem.

10 "And now, our God, what shall we say after this? For we have forsaken your commandments, ¹¹which you commanded by your servants the prophets, saying, 'The land that you are entering to possess is a land unclean with the pollutions of the peoples of the lands, with their abominations. They have filled it from end to end with their uncleanness. ¹²Therefore do not give your daughters to their sons, neither take their daughters for your sons, and never seek their peace or prosperity, so that you may be strong and eat the good of the land and leave it for an inheritance to your children forever.' ¹³After all that has come upon us for our evil deeds and for our great guilt, seeing that you, our God, have punished us less than our iniquities deserved and have given us such a remnant as this, ¹⁴shall we

break your commandments again and intermarry with the peoples who practice these abominations? Would you not be angry with us until you destroy us without remnant or survivor? ¹⁵O LORD, God of Israel, you are just, but we have escaped as a remnant, as is now the case. Here we are before you in our guilt, though no one can face you because of this."

The People's Response

10 While Ezra prayed and made confession, weeping and throwing himself down before the house of God, a very great assembly of men, women, and children gathered to him out of Israel; the people also wept bitterly. ²Shecaniah son of Jehiel, of the descendants of Elam, addressed Ezra, saying, "We have broken faith with our God and have married foreign women from the peoples of the land, but even now there is hope for Israel in spite of this. ³So now let us make a covenant with our God to send away all these wives and their children, according to the counsel of my lord and of those who tremble at the commandment of our God; and let it be done according to the law. ⁴Take action, for it is your duty, and we are with you; be strong, and do it." ⁵Then Ezra stood up and made the leading priests, the Levites, and all Israel swear that they would do as had been said. So they swore.

Foreign Wives and Their Children Rejected

6 Then Ezra withdrew from before the house of God, and went to the chamber of Jehohanan son of Eliashib, where he spent the night.^b He did not eat bread or drink water, for he was mourning over the faithlessness of the exiles. ⁷They made a proclamation throughout Judah and Jerusalem to all the returned exiles that they should assemble at Jerusalem, ⁸and that if any did not come within three days, by order of the officials and the elders all their property should be forfeited, and they themselves banned from the congregation of the exiles.

9 Then all the people of Judah and Benja-

---

a Heb *our God*   b 1 Esdras 9.2: Heb *where he went*

min assembled at Jerusalem within the three days; it was the ninth month, on the twentieth day of the month. All the people sat in the open square before the house of God, trembling because of this matter and because of the heavy rain. 10Then Ezra the priest stood up and said to them, "You have trespassed and married foreign women, and so increased the guilt of Israel. 11Now make confession to the LORD the God of your ancestors, and do his will; separate yourselves from the peoples of the land and from the foreign wives." 12Then all the assembly answered with a loud voice, "It is so; we must do as you have said. 13But the people are many, and it is a time of heavy rain; we cannot stand in the open. Nor is this a task for one day or for two, for many of us have transgressed in this matter. 14Let our officials represent the whole assembly, and let all in our towns who have taken foreign wives come at appointed times, and with them the elders and judges of every town, until the fierce wrath of our God on this account is averted from us." 15Only Jonathan son of Asahel and Jahzeiah son of Tikvah opposed this, and Meshullam and Shabbethai the Levites supported them.

16 Then the returned exiles did so. Ezra the priest selected men,*a* heads of families, according to their families, each of them designated by name. On the first day of the tenth month they sat down to examine the matter. 17By the first day of the first month they had come to the end of all the men who had married foreign women.

18 There were found of the descendants of the priests who had married foreign women, of the descendants of Jeshua son of Jozadak and his brothers: Maaseiah, Eliezer, Jarib, and Gedaliah. 19They pledged themselves to send away their wives, and their guilt offering was a ram

of the flock for their guilt. 20Of the descendants of Immer: Hanani and Zebadiah. 21Of the descendants of Harim: Maaseiah, Elijah, Shemaiah, Jehiel, and Uzziah. 22Of the descendants of Pashhur: Elioenai, Maaseiah, Ishmael, Nethanel, Jozabad, and Elasah.

23 Of the Levites: Jozabad, Shimei, Kelaiah (that is, Kelita), Pethahiah, Judah, and Eliezer. 24Of the singers: Eliashib. Of the gatekeepers: Shallum, Telem, and Uri.

25 And of Israel: of the descendants of Parosh: Ramiah, Izziah, Malchijah, Mijamin, Eleazar, Hashabiah,*b* and Benaiah. 26Of the descendants of Elam: Mattaniah, Zechariah, Jehiel, Abdi, Jeremoth, and Elijah. 27Of the descendants of Zattu: Elioenai, Eliashib, Mattaniah, Jeremoth, Zabad, and Aziza. 28Of the descendants of Bebai: Jehohanan, Hananiah, Zabbai, and Athlai. 29Of the descendants of Bani: Meshullam, Malluch, Adaiah, Jashub, Sheal, and Jeremoth. 30Of the descendants of Pahath-moab: Adna, Chelal, Benaiah, Maaseiah, Mattaniah, Bezalel, Binnui, and Manasseh. 31Of the descendants of Harim: Eliezer, Isshijah, Malchijah, Shemaiah, Shimeon, 32Benjamin, Malluch, and Shemariah. 33Of the descendants of Hashum: Mattenai, Mattattah, Zabad, Eliphelet, Jeremai, Manasseh, and Shimei. 34Of the descendants of Bani: Maadai, Amram, Uel, 35Benaiah, Bedeiah, Cheluhi, 36Vaniah, Meremoth, Eliashib, 37Mattaniah, Mattenai, and Jaasu. 38Of the descendants of Binnui:*c* Shimei, 39Shelemiah, Nathan, Adaiah, 40Machnadebai, Shashai, Sharai, 41Azarel, Shelemiah, Shemariah, 42Shallum, Amariah, and Joseph. 43Of the descendants of Nebo: Jeiel, Mattithiah, Zabad, Zebina, Jaddai, Joel, and Benaiah. 44All these had married foreign women, and they sent them away with their children.*d*

---

a 1 Esdras 9.16: Syr: Heb *And there were selected Ezra, Binnui*   *d* 1 Esdras 9.36; meaning of Heb uncertain   *b* 1 Esdras 9.26 Gk: Heb *Malchijah*   *c* Gk: Heb *Bani,*

NEHEMIAH

Nehemiah Prays for His People

1 The words of Nehemiah son of Hacaliah. In the month of Chislev, in the twentieth year, while I was in Susa the capital, ²one of my brothers, Hanani, came with certain men from Judah; and I asked them about the Jews that survived, those who had escaped the captivity, and about Jerusalem. ³They replied, "The survivors there in the province who escaped captivity are in great trouble and shame; the wall of Jerusalem is broken down, and its gates have been destroyed by fire."

4 When I heard these words I sat down and wept, and mourned for days, fasting and praying before the God of heaven. ⁵I said, "O LORD God of heaven, the great and awesome God who keeps covenant and steadfast love with those who love him and keep his commandments; ⁶let your ear be attentive and your eyes open to hear the prayer of your servant that I now pray before you day and night for your servants, the people of Israel, confessing the sins of the people of Israel, which we have sinned against you. Both I and my family have sinned. ⁷We have offended you deeply, failing to keep the commandments, the statutes, and the ordinances that you commanded your servant Moses. ⁸Remember the word that you commanded your servant Moses, 'If you are unfaithful, I will scatter you among the peoples; ⁹but if you return to me and keep my commandments and do them, though your outcasts are under the farthest skies, I will gather them from there and bring them to the place at which I have chosen to establish my name.' ¹⁰They are your servants and your people, whom you redeemed by your great power and your strong hand. ¹¹O Lord, let your ear be attentive to the prayer of your servant, and to the prayer of your servants who delight in revering your name. Give success to your servant today, and grant him mercy in the sight of this man!"

At the time, I was cupbearer to the king.

Nehemiah Sent to Judah

2 In the month of Nisan, in the twentieth year of King Artaxerxes, when wine was served him, I carried the wine and gave it to the king. Now, I had never been sad in his presence before. ²So the king said to me, "Why is your face sad, since you are not sick? This can only be sadness of the heart." Then I was very much afraid. ³I said to the king, "May the king live forever! Why should my face not be sad, when the city, the place of my ancestors' graves, lies waste, and its gates have been destroyed by fire?" ⁴Then the king said to me, "What do you request?" So I prayed to the God of heaven. ⁵Then I said to the king, "If it pleases the king, and if your servant has found favor with you, I ask that you send me to Judah, to the city of my ancestors' graves, so that I may rebuild it." ⁶The king said to me (the queen also was sitting beside him), "How long will you be gone, and when will you return?" So it pleased the king to send me, and I set him a date. ⁷Then I said to the king, "If it pleases the king, let letters be given me to the governors of the province Beyond the River, that they may grant me passage until I arrive in Judah; ⁸and a letter to Asaph, the keeper of the king's forest, directing him to give me timber to make beams for the gates of the temple fortress, and for the wall of the city, and for the house that I shall occupy." And the king granted me what I asked, for the gracious hand of my God was upon me.

9 Then I came to the governors of the province Beyond the River, and gave them the king's letters. Now the king had sent officers of the army and cavalry with me. ¹⁰When Sanballat the Horonite and Tobiah the Ammonite official heard this, it displeased them greatly that someone had come to seek the welfare of the people of Israel.

Nehemiah's Inspection of the Walls

11 So I came to Jerusalem and was there for three days. ¹²Then I got up during the night, I and a few men with me; I told no one what my God had put into my heart to do for Jerusalem.

The only animal I took was the animal I rode. [13]I went out by night by the Valley Gate past the Dragon's Spring and to the Dung Gate, and I inspected the walls of Jerusalem that had been broken down and its gates that had been destroyed by fire. [14]Then I went on to the Fountain Gate and to the King's Pool; but there was no place for the animal I was riding to continue. [15]So I went up by way of the valley by night and inspected the wall. Then I turned back and entered by the Valley Gate, and so returned. [16]The officials did not know where I had gone or what I was doing; I had not yet told the Jews, the priests, the nobles, the officials, and the rest that were to do the work.

Decision to Restore the Walls

17 Then I said to them, "You see the trouble we are in, how Jerusalem lies in ruins with its gates burned. Come, let us rebuild the wall of Jerusalem, so that we may no longer suffer disgrace." [18]I told them that the hand of my God had been gracious upon me, and also the words that the king had spoken to me. Then they said, "Let us start building!" So they committed themselves to the common good. [19]But when Sanballat the Horonite and Tobiah the Ammonite official, and Geshem the Arab heard of it, they mocked and ridiculed us, saying, "What is this that you are doing? Are you rebelling against the king?" [20]Then I replied to them, "The God of heaven is the one who will give us success, and we his servants are going to start building; but you have no share or claim or historic right in Jerusalem."

Organization of the Work

3 Then the high priest Eliashib set to work with his fellow priests and rebuilt the Sheep Gate. They consecrated it and set up its doors; they consecrated it as far as the Tower of the Hundred and as far as the Tower of Hananel. [2]And the men of Jericho built next to him. And next to them[a] Zaccur son of Imri built.

3 The sons of Hassenaah built the Fish Gate; they laid its beams and set up its doors, its bolts, and its bars. [4]Next to them Meremoth son of Uriah son of Hakkoz made repairs. Next to them Meshullam son of Berechiah son of Meshezabel made repairs. Next to them Zadok son of Baana made repairs. [5]Next to them the Tekoites made repairs; but their nobles would not put their shoulders to the work of their Lord.[b]

6 Joiada son of Paseah and Meshullam son of Besodeiah repaired the Old Gate; they laid its beams and set up its doors, its bolts, and its bars. [7]Next to them repairs were made by Melatiah the Gibeonite and Jadon the Meronothite—the men of Gibeon and of Mizpah—who were under the jurisdiction of[c] the governor of the province Beyond the River. [8]Next to them Uzziel son of Harhaiah, one of the goldsmiths, made repairs. Next to him Hananiah, one of the perfumers, made repairs; and they restored Jerusalem as far as the Broad Wall. [9]Next to them Rephaiah son of Hur, ruler of half the district of[d] Jerusalem, made repairs. [10]Next to them Jedaiah son of Harumaph made repairs opposite his house; and next to him Hattush son of Hashabneiah made repairs. [11]Malchijah son of Harim and Hasshub son of Pahath-moab repaired another section and the Tower of the Ovens. [12]Next to him Shallum son of Hallohesh, ruler of half the district of[d] Jerusalem, made repairs, he and his daughters.

13 Hanun and the inhabitants of Zanoah repaired the Valley Gate; they rebuilt it and set up its doors, its bolts, and its bars, and repaired a thousand cubits of the wall, as far as the Dung Gate.

14 Malchijah son of Rechab, ruler of the district of[e] Beth-haccherem, repaired the Dung Gate; he rebuilt it and set up its doors, its bolts, and its bars.

15 And Shallum son of Col-hozeh, ruler of the district of[e] Mizpah, repaired the Fountain Gate; he rebuilt it and covered it and set up its doors, its bolts, and its bars; and he built the wall of the Pool of Shelah of the king's garden,

---

a Heb *him*   *b* Or *lords*   *c* Meaning of Heb uncertain   *d* Or *supervisor of half the portion assigned to*
e Or *supervisor of the portion assigned to*

as far as the stairs that go down from the City of David. 16After him Nehemiah son of Azbuk, ruler of half the district of*a* Beth-zur, repaired from a point opposite the graves of David, as far as the artificial pool and the house of the warriors. 17After him the Levites made repairs: Rehum son of Bani; next to him Hashabiah, ruler of half the district of*a* Keilah, made repairs for his district. 18After him their kin made repairs: Binnui,*b* son of Henadad, ruler of half the district of*a* Keilah; 19next to him Ezer son of Jeshua, ruler*c* of Mizpah, repaired another section opposite the ascent to the armory at the Angle. 20After him Baruch son of Zabbai repaired another section from the Angle to the door of the house of the high priest Eliashib. 21After him Meremoth son of Uriah son of Hakkoz repaired another section from the door of the house of Eliashib to the end of the house of Eliashib. 22After him the priests, the men of the surrounding area, made repairs. 23After them Benjamin and Hasshub made repairs opposite their house. After them Azariah son of Maaseiah son of Ananiah made repairs beside his own house. 24After him Binnui son of Henadad repaired another section, from the house of Azariah to the Angle and to the corner. 25Palal son of Uzai repaired opposite the Angle and the tower projecting from the upper house of the king at the court of the guard. After him Pedaiah son of Parosh 26and the temple servants living*d* on Ophel made repairs up to a point opposite the Water Gate on the east and the projecting tower. 27After him the Tekoites repaired another section opposite the great projecting tower as far as the wall of Ophel.

28 Above the Horse Gate the priests made repairs, each one opposite his own house. 29After them Zadok son of Immer made repairs opposite his own house. After him Shemaiah son of Shecaniah, the keeper of the East Gate, made repairs. 30After him Hananiah son of Shelemiah and Hanun sixth son of Zalaph repaired another section. After him Meshullam son of Berechiah made repairs opposite his living quarters. 31After him Malchijah, one of the goldsmiths, made repairs as far as the house of the temple servants and of the merchants, opposite the Muster Gate,*e* and to the upper room of the corner. 32And between the upper room of the corner and the Sheep Gate the goldsmiths and the merchants made repairs.

Hostile Plots Thwarted

4*f* Now when Sanballat heard that we were building the wall, he was angry and greatly enraged, and he mocked the Jews. 2He said in the presence of his associates and of the army of Samaria, "What are these feeble Jews doing? Will they restore things? Will they sacrifice? Will they finish it in a day? Will they revive the stones out of the heaps of rubbish— and burned ones at that?" 3Tobiah the Ammonite was beside him, and he said, "That stone wall they are building—any fox going up on it would break it down!" 4Hear, O our God, for we are despised; turn their taunt back on their own heads, and give them over as plunder in a land of captivity. 5Do not cover their guilt, and do not let their sin be blotted out from your sight; for they have hurled insults in the face of the builders.

6 So we rebuilt the wall, and all the wall was joined together to half its height; for the people had a mind to work.

7*g* But when Sanballat and Tobiah and the Arabs and the Ammonites and the Ashdodites heard that the repairing of the walls of Jerusalem was going forward and the gaps were beginning to be closed, they were very angry, 8and all plotted together to come and fight against Jerusalem and to cause confusion in it. 9So we prayed to our God, and set a guard as a protection against them day and night.

10 But Judah said, "The strength of the burden bearers is failing, and there is too much rubbish so that we are unable to work on the wall." 11And our enemies said, "They will not know or see anything before we come upon them and kill them and stop the work." 12When the Jews who lived near them came, they said

a Or *supervisor of half the portion assigned to*   *b* Gk Syr Compare verse 24, 10.9: Heb *Bavvai*   *c* Or *supervisor*
d Cn: Heb *were living*   *e* Or *Hammiphkad Gate*   *f* Ch 3.33 in Heb   *g* Ch 4.1 in Heb

to us ten times, "From all the places where they live*a* they will come up against us."*b* 13So in the lowest parts of the space behind the wall, in open places, I stationed the people according to their families,*c* with their swords, their spears, and their bows. 14After I looked these things over, I stood up and said to the nobles and the officials and the rest of the people, "Do not be afraid of them. Remember the LORD, who is great and awesome, and fight for your kin, your sons, your daughters, your wives, and your homes."

15 When our enemies heard that their plot was known to us, and that God had frustrated it, we all returned to the wall, each to his work. 16From that day on, half of my servants worked on construction, and half held the spears, shields, bows, and body-armor; and the leaders posted themselves behind the whole house of Judah, 17who were building the wall. The burden bearers carried their loads in such a way that each labored on the work with one hand and with the other held a weapon. 18And each of the builders had his sword strapped at his side while he built. The man who sounded the trumpet was beside me. 19And I said to the nobles, the officials, and the rest of the people, "The work is great and widely spread out, and we are separated far from one another on the wall. 20Rally to us wherever you hear the sound of the trumpet. Our God will fight for us."

21 So we labored at the work, and half of them held the spears from break of dawn until the stars came out. 22I also said to the people at that time, "Let every man and his servant pass the night inside Jerusalem, so that they may be a guard for us by night and may labor by day." 23So neither I nor my brothers nor my servants nor the men of the guard who followed me ever took off our clothes; each kept his weapon in his right hand.*d*

Nehemiah Deals with Oppression

5 Now there was a great outcry of the people and of their wives against their Jewish kin. 2For there were those who said, "With

our sons and our daughters, we are many; we must get grain, so that we may eat and stay alive." 3There were also those who said, "We are having to pledge our fields, our vineyards, and our houses in order to get grain during the famine." 4And there were those who said, "We are having to borrow money on our fields and vineyards to pay the king's tax. 5Now our flesh is the same as that of our kindred; our children are the same as their children; and yet we are forcing our sons and daughters to be slaves, and some of our daughters have been ravished; we are powerless, and our fields and vineyards now belong to others."

6 I was very angry when I heard their outcry and these complaints. 7After thinking it over, I brought charges against the nobles and the officials; I said to them, "You are all taking interest from your own people." And I called a great assembly to deal with them, 8and said to them, "As far as we were able, we have bought back our Jewish kindred who had been sold to other nations; but now you are selling your own kin, who must then be bought back by us!" They were silent, and could not find a word to say. 9So I said, "The thing that you are doing is not good. Should you not walk in the fear of our God, to prevent the taunts of the nations our enemies? 10Moreover I and my brothers and my servants are lending them money and grain. Let us stop this taking of interest. 11Restore to them, this very day, their fields, their vineyards, their olive orchards, and their houses, and the interest on money, grain, wine, and oil that you have been exacting from them." 12Then they said, "We will restore everything and demand nothing more from them. We will do as you say." And I called the priests, and made them take an oath to do as they had promised. 13I also shook out the fold of my garment and said, "So may God shake out everyone from house and from property who does not perform this promise. Thus may they be shaken out and emptied." And all the assembly said, "Amen," and praised the LORD. And the people did as they had promised.

---

a Cn: Heb *you return*   *b* Compare Gk Syr: Meaning of Heb uncertain   *c* Meaning of Heb uncertain
d Cn: Heb *each his weapon the water*

The Generosity of Nehemiah

14 Moreover from the time that I was appointed to be their governor in the land of Judah, from the twentieth year to the thirty-second year of King Artaxerxes, twelve years, neither I nor my brothers ate the food allowance of the governor. 15The former governors who were before me laid heavy burdens on the people, and took food and wine from them, besides forty shekels of silver. Even their servants lorded it over the people. But I did not do so, because of the fear of God. 16Indeed, I devoted myself to the work on this wall, and acquired no land; and all my servants were gathered there for the work. 17Moreover there were at my table one hundred fifty people, Jews and officials, besides those who came to us from the nations around us. 18Now that which was prepared for one day was one ox and six choice sheep; also fowls were prepared for me, and every ten days skins of wine in abundance; yet with all this I did not demand the food allowance of the governor, because of the heavy burden of labor on the people. 19Remember for my good, O my God, all that I have done for this people.

Intrigues of Enemies Foiled

6 Now when it was reported to Sanballat and Tobiah and to Geshem the Arab and to the rest of our enemies that I had built the wall and that there was no gap left in it (though up to that time I had not set up the doors in the gates), 2Sanballat and Geshem sent to me, saying, "Come and let us meet together in one of the villages in the plain of Ono." But they intended to do me harm. 3So I sent messengers to them, saying, "I am doing a great work and I cannot come down. Why should the work stop while I leave it to come down to you?" 4They sent to me four times in this way, and I answered them in the same manner. 5In the same way Sanballat for the fifth time sent his servant to me with an open letter in his hand. 6In it was written, "It is reported among the nations—and Geshem*a* also says it—that you

and the Jews intend to rebel; that is why you are building the wall; and according to this report you wish to become their king. 7You have also set up prophets to proclaim in Jerusalem concerning you, 'There is a king in Judah!' And now it will be reported to the king according to these words. So come, therefore, and let us confer together." 8Then I sent to him, saying, "No such things as you say have been done; you are inventing them out of your own mind" 9—for they all wanted to frighten us, thinking, "Their hands will drop from the work, and it will not be done." But now, O God, strengthen my hands.

10 One day when I went into the house of Shemaiah son of Delaiah son of Mehetabel, who was confined to his house, he said, "Let us meet together in the house of God, within the temple, and let us close the doors of the temple, for they are coming to kill you; indeed, tonight they are coming to kill you." 11But I said, "Should a man like me run away? Would a man like me go into the temple to save his life? I will not go in!" 12Then I perceived and saw that God had not sent him at all, but he had pronounced the prophecy against me because Tobiah and Sanballat had hired him. 13He was hired for this purpose, to intimidate me and make me sin by acting in this way, and so they could give me a bad name, in order to taunt me. 14Remember Tobiah and Sanballat, O my God, according to these things that they did, and also the prophetess Noadiah and the rest of the prophets who wanted to make me afraid.

The Wall Completed

15 So the wall was finished on the twenty-fifth day of the month Elul, in fifty-two days. 16And when all our enemies heard of it, all the nations around us were afraid*b* and fell greatly in their own esteem; for they perceived that this work had been accomplished with the help of our God. 17Moreover in those days the nobles of Judah sent many letters to Tobiah, and Tobiah's letters came to them. 18For many in Judah were bound by oath to him, be-

a Heb *Gashmu*   *b* Another reading is *saw*

cause he was the son-in-law of Shecaniah son of Arah: and his son Jehohanan had married the daughter of Meshullam son of Berechiah. ¹⁹Also they spoke of his good deeds in my presence, and reported my words to him. And Tobiah sent letters to intimidate me.

7 Now when the wall had been built and I had set up the doors, and the gatekeepers, the singers, and the Levites had been appointed, ²I gave my brother Hanani charge over Jerusalem, along with Hananiah the commander of the citadel—for he was a faithful man and feared God more than many. ³And I said to them, "The gates of Jerusalem are not to be opened until the sun is hot; while the gatekeepers *a* are still standing guard, let them shut and bar the doors. Appoint guards from among the inhabitants of Jerusalem, some at their watch posts, and others before their own houses." ⁴The city was wide and large, but the people within it were few and no houses had been built.

Lists of the Returned Exiles

5 Then my God put it into my mind to assemble the nobles and the officials and the people to be enrolled by genealogy. And I found the book of the genealogy of those who were the first to come back, and I found the following written in it:

6 These are the people of the province who came up out of the captivity of those exiles whom King Nebuchadnezzar of Babylon had carried into exile; they returned to Jerusalem and Judah, each to his town. ⁷They came with Zerubbabel, Jeshua, Nehemiah, Azariah, Raamiah, Nahamani, Mordecai, Bilshan, Mispereth, Bigvai, Nehum, Baanah.

The number of the Israelite people: ⁸the descendants of Parosh, two thousand one hundred seventy-two. ⁹Of Shephatiah, three hundred seventy-two. ¹⁰Of Arah, six hundred fifty-two. ¹¹Of Pahath-moab, namely the descendants of Jeshua and Joab, two thousand eight hundred eighteen. ¹²Of Elam, one thousand two hundred fifty-four. ¹³Of Zattu, eight hundred forty-five. ¹⁴Of Zaccai, seven hundred sixty. ¹⁵Of Binnui, six hundred forty-eight. ¹⁶Of Bebai, six hundred twenty-eight. ¹⁷Of Azgad, two thousand three hundred twenty-two. ¹⁸Of Adonikam, six hundred sixty-seven. ¹⁹Of Bigvai, two thousand sixty-seven. ²⁰Of Adin, six hundred fifty-five. ²¹Of Ater, namely of Hezekiah, ninety-eight. ²²Of Hashum, three hundred twenty-eight. ²³Of Bezai, three hundred twenty-four. ²⁴Of Hariph, one hundred twelve. ²⁵Of Gibeon, ninety-five. ²⁶The people of Bethlehem and Netophah, one hundred eighty-eight. ²⁷Of Anathoth, one hundred twenty-eight. ²⁸Of Beth-azmaveth, forty-two. ²⁹Of Kiriath-jearim, Chephirah, and Beeroth, seven hundred forty-three. ³⁰Of Ramah and Geba, six hundred twenty-one. ³¹Of Michmas, one hundred twenty-two. ³²Of Bethel and Ai, one hundred twenty-three. ³³Of the other Nebo, fifty-two. ³⁴The descendants of the other Elam, one thousand two hundred fifty-four. ³⁵Of Harim, three hundred twenty. ³⁶Of Jericho, three hundred forty-five. ³⁷Of Lod, Hadid, and Ono, seven hundred twenty-one. ³⁸Of Senaah, three thousand nine hundred thirty.

39 The priests: the descendants of Jedaiah, namely the house of Jeshua, nine hundred seventy-three. ⁴⁰Of Immer, one thousand fifty-two. ⁴¹Of Pashhur, one thousand two hundred forty-seven. ⁴²Of Harim, one thousand seventeen.

43 The Levites: the descendants of Jeshua, namely of Kadmiel of the descendants of Hodevah, seventy-four. ⁴⁴The singers: the descendants of Asaph, one hundred forty-eight. ⁴⁵The gatekeepers: the descendants of Shallum, of Ater, of Talmon, of Akkub, of Hatita, of Shobai, one hundred thirty-eight.

46 The temple servants: the descendants of Ziha, of Hasupha, of Tabbaoth, ⁴⁷of Keros, of Sia, of Padon, ⁴⁸of Lebana, of Hagaba, of Shalmai, ⁴⁹of Hanan, of Giddel, of Gahar, ⁵⁰of Reaiah, of Rezin, of Nekoda, ⁵¹of Gazzam, of Uzza, of Paseah, ⁵²of Besai, of Meunim, of Nephushesim, ⁵³of Bakbuk, of

a Heb *while they*

Hakupha, of Harhur, [54]of Bazlith, of Mehida, of Harsha, [55]of Barkos, of Sisera, of Temah, [56]of Neziah, of Hatipha.

57 The descendants of Solomon's servants: of Sotai, of Sophereth, of Perida, [58]of Jaala, of Darkon, of Giddel, [59]of Shephatiah, of Hattil, of Pochereth-hazzebaim, of Amon.

60 All the temple servants and the descendants of Solomon's servants were three hundred ninety-two.

61 The following were those who came up from Tel-melah, Tel-harsha, Cherub, Addon, and Immer, but they could not prove their ancestral houses or their descent, whether they belonged to Israel: [62]the descendants of Delaiah, of Tobiah, of Nekoda, six hundred forty-two. [63]Also, of the priests: the descendants of Hobaiah, of Hakkoz, of Barzillai (who had married one of the daughters of Barzillai the Gileadite and was called by their name). [64]These sought their registration among those enrolled in the genealogies, but it was not found there, so they were excluded from the priesthood as unclean; [65]the governor told them that they were not to partake of the most holy food, until a priest with Urim and Thummim should come.

66 The whole assembly together was forty-two thousand three hundred sixty, [67]besides their male and female slaves, of whom there were seven thousand three hundred thirty-seven; and they had two hundred forty-five singers, male and female. [68]They had seven hundred thirty-six horses, two hundred forty-five mules,[a] [69]four hundred thirty-five camels, and six thousand seven hundred twenty donkeys.

70 Now some of the heads of ancestral houses contributed to the work. The governor gave to the treasury one thousand darics of gold, fifty basins, and five hundred thirty priestly robes. [71]And some of the heads of ancestral houses gave into the building fund twenty thousand darics of gold and two thousand two hundred minas of silver. [72]And what the rest of the people gave was twenty thousand dar-

ics of gold, two thousand minas of silver, and sixty-seven priestly robes.

73 So the priests, the Levites, the gatekeepers, the singers, some of the people, the temple servants, and all Israel settled in their towns.

Ezra Summons the People to Obey the Law

When the seventh month came—the people of Israel being settled in their towns— [1]all the people gathered together into the square before the Water Gate. They told the scribe Ezra to bring the book of the law of Moses, which the LORD had given to Israel. [2]Accordingly, the priest Ezra brought the law before the assembly, both men and women and all who could hear with understanding. This was on the first day of the seventh month. [3]He read from it facing the square before the Water Gate from early morning until midday, in the presence of the men and the women and those who could understand; and the ears of all the people were attentive to the book of the law. [4]The scribe Ezra stood on a wooden platform that had been made for the purpose; and beside him stood Mattithiah, Shema, Anaiah, Uriah, Hilkiah, and Maaseiah on his right hand; and Pedaiah, Mishael, Malchijah, Hashum, Hash-baddanah, Zechariah, and Meshullam on his left hand. [5]And Ezra opened the book in the sight of all the people, for he was standing above all the people; and when he opened it, all the people stood up. [6]Then Ezra blessed the LORD, the great God, and all the people answered, "Amen, Amen," lifting up their hands. Then they bowed their heads and worshiped the LORD with their faces to the ground. [7]Also Jeshua, Bani, Sherebiah, Jamin, Akkub, Shabbethai, Hodiah, Maaseiah, Kelita, Azariah, Jozabad, Hanan, Pelaiah, the Levites,[b] helped the people to understand the law, while the people remained in their places. [8]So they read from the book, from the law of God, with interpretation. They gave the sense, so that the people understood the reading.

9 And Nehemiah, who was the governor,

a Ezra 2.66 and the margins of some Hebrew Mss: MT lacks *They had . . . forty-five mules*   *b* 1 Esdras 9.48 Vg: Heb *and the Levites* and Ezra the priest and scribe, and the Levites who taught the people said to all the people, "This day is holy to the LORD your God; do not mourn or weep." For all the people wept when they heard the words of the law. 10Then he said to them, "Go your way, eat the fat and drink sweet wine and send portions of them to those for whom nothing is prepared, for this day is holy to our LORD; and do not be grieved, for the joy of the LORD is your strength." 11So the Levites stilled all the people, saying, "Be quiet, for this day is holy; do not be grieved." 12And all the people went their way to eat and drink and to send portions and to make great rejoicing, because they had understood the words that were declared to them.

The Festival of Booths Celebrated

13 On the second day the heads of ancestral houses of all the people, with the priests and the Levites, came together to the scribe Ezra in order to study the words of the law. 14And they found it written in the law, which the LORD had commanded by Moses, that the people of Israel should live in booths*a* during the festival of the seventh month, 15and that they should publish and proclaim in all their towns and in Jerusalem as follows, "Go out to the hills and bring branches of olive, wild olive, myrtle, palm, and other leafy trees to make booths,*a* as it is written." 16So the people went out and brought them, and made booths*a* for themselves, each on the roofs of their houses, and in their courts and in the courts of the house of God, and in the square at the Water Gate and in the square at the Gate of Ephraim. 17And all the assembly of those who had returned from the captivity made booths*a* and lived in them; for from the days of Jeshua son of Nun to that day the people of Israel had not done so. And there was very great rejoicing. 18And day by day, from the first day to the last day, he read from the book of the law of God. They kept the festival seven days; and on the eighth day there was a solemn assembly, according to the ordinance.

National Confession

9 Now on the twenty-fourth day of this month the people of Israel were assembled with fasting and in sackcloth, and with earth on their heads.*b* 2Then those of Israelite descent separated themselves from all foreigners, and stood and confessed their sins and the iniquities of their ancestors. 3They stood up in their place and read from the book of the law of the LORD their God for a fourth part of the day, and for another fourth they made confession and worshiped the LORD their God. 4Then Jeshua, Bani, Kadmiel, Shebaniah, Bunni, Sherebiah, Bani, and Chenani stood on the stairs of the Levites and cried out with a loud voice to the LORD their God. 5Then the Levites, Jeshua, Kadmiel, Bani, Hashabneiah, Sherebiah, Hodiah, Shebaniah, and Pethahiah, said, "Stand up and bless the LORD your God from everlasting to everlasting. Blessed be your glorious name, which is exalted above all blessing and praise."

6 And Ezra said:*c* "You are the LORD, you alone; you have made heaven, the heaven of heavens, with all their host, the earth and all that is on it, the seas and all that is in them. To all of them you give life, and the host of heaven worships you. 7You are the LORD, the God who chose Abram and brought him out of Ur of the Chaldeans and gave him the name Abraham; 8and you found his heart faithful before you, and made with him a covenant to give to his descendants the land of the Canaanite, the Hittite, the Amorite, the Perizzite, the Jebusite, and the Girgashite; and you have fulfilled your promise, for you are righteous.

9 "And you saw the distress of our ancestors in Egypt and heard their cry at the Red Sea.*d* 10You performed signs and wonders against Pharaoh and all his servants and all the people of his land, for you knew that they acted insolently against our ancestors. You made a name for yourself, which remains to this day. 11And you divided the sea before them, so that they passed through the sea on dry land, but you threw their pursuers into the depths, like

---

a Or *tabernacles*; Heb *succoth*   *b* Heb *on them*   *c* Gk: Heb lacks *And Ezra said*   *d* Or *Sea of Reeds* a stone into mighty waters. [12]Moreover, you led them by day with a pillar of cloud, and by night with a pillar of fire, to give them light on the way in which they should go. [13]You came down also upon Mount Sinai, and spoke with them from heaven, and gave them right ordinances and true laws, good statutes and commandments, [14]and you made known your holy sabbath to them and gave them commandments and statutes and a law through your servant Moses. [15]For their hunger you gave them bread from heaven, and for their thirst you brought water for them out of the rock, and you told them to go in to possess the land that you swore to give them.

16 "But they and our ancestors acted presumptuously and stiffened their necks and did not obey your commandments; [17]they refused to obey, and were not mindful of the wonders that you performed among them; but they stiffened their necks and determined to return to their slavery in Egypt. But you are a God ready to forgive, gracious and merciful, slow to anger and abounding in steadfast love, and you did not forsake them. [18]Even when they had cast an image of a calf for themselves and said, 'This is your God who brought you up out of Egypt,' and had committed great blasphemies, [19]you in your great mercies did not forsake them in the wilderness; the pillar of cloud that led them in the way did not leave them by day, nor the pillar of fire by night that gave them light on the way by which they should go. [20]You gave your good spirit to instruct them, and did not withhold your manna from their mouths, and gave them water for their thirst. [21]Forty years you sustained them in the wilderness so that they lacked nothing; their clothes did not wear out and their feet did not swell. [22]And you gave them kingdoms and peoples, and allotted to them every corner,[a] so they took possession of the land of King Sihon of Heshbon and the land of King Og of Bashan. [23]You multiplied their descendants like the stars of heaven, and brought them into the land that you had told their ancestors to enter

and possess. [24]So the descendants went in and possessed the land, and you subdued before them the inhabitants of the land, the Canaanites, and gave them into their hands, with their kings and the peoples of the land, to do with them as they pleased. [25]And they captured fortress cities and a rich land, and took possession of houses filled with all sorts of goods, hewn cisterns, vineyards, olive orchards, and fruit trees in abundance; so they ate, and were filled and became fat, and delighted themselves in your great goodness.

26 "Nevertheless they were disobedient and rebelled against you and cast your law behind their backs and killed your prophets, who had warned them in order to turn them back to you, and they committed great blasphemies. [27]Therefore you gave them into the hands of their enemies, who made them suffer. Then in the time of their suffering they cried out to you and you heard them from heaven, and according to your great mercies you gave them saviors who saved them from the hands of their enemies. [28]But after they had rest, they again did evil before you, and you abandoned them to the hands of their enemies, so that they had dominion over them; yet when they turned and cried to you, you heard from heaven, and many times you rescued them according to your mercies. [29]And you warned them in order to turn them back to your law. Yet they acted presumptuously and did not obey your commandments, but sinned against your ordinances, by the observance of which a person shall live. They turned a stubborn shoulder and stiffened their neck and would not obey. [30]Many years you were patient with them, and warned them by your spirit through your prophets; yet they would not listen. Therefore you handed them over to the peoples of the lands. [31]Nevertheless, in your great mercies you did not make an end of them or forsake them, for you are a gracious and merciful God.

32 "Now therefore, our God—the great and mighty and awesome God, keeping covenant and steadfast love—do not treat lightly

---

a Meaning of Heb uncertain

all the hardship that has come upon us, upon our kings, our officials, our priests, our prophets, our ancestors, and all your people, since the time of the kings of Assyria until today. 33You have been just in all that has come upon us, for you have dealt faithfully and we have acted wickedly; 34our kings, our officials, our priests, and our ancestors have not kept your law or heeded the commandments and the warnings that you gave them. 35Even in their own kingdom, and in the great goodness you bestowed on them, and in the large and rich land that you set before them, they did not serve you and did not turn from their wicked works. 36Here we are, slaves to this day—slaves in the land that you gave to our ancestors to enjoy its fruit and its good gifts. 37Its rich yield goes to the kings whom you have set over us because of our sins; they have power also over our bodies and over our livestock at their pleasure, and we are in great distress."

Those Who Signed the Covenant

38*a* Because of all this we make a firm agreement in writing, and on that sealed document are inscribed the names of our officials, our Levites, and our priests.

10*b* Upon the sealed document are the names of Nehemiah the governor, son of Hacaliah, and Zedekiah; 2Seraiah, Azariah, Jeremiah, 3Pashhur, Amariah, Malchijah, 4Hattush, Shebaniah, Malluch, 5Harim, Meremoth, Obadiah, 6Daniel, Ginnethon, Baruch, 7Meshullam, Abijah, Mijamin, 8Maaziah, Bilgai, Shemaiah; these are the priests. 9And the Levites: Jeshua son of Azaniah, Binnui of the sons of Henadad, Kadmiel; 10and their associates, Shebaniah, Hodiah, Kelita, Pelaiah, Hanan, 11Mica, Rehob, Hashabiah, 12Zaccur, Sherebiah, Shebaniah, 13Hodiah, Bani, Beninu. 14The leaders of the people: Parosh, Pahathmoab, Elam, Zattu, Bani, 15Bunni, Azgad, Bebai, 16Adonijah, Bigvai, Adin, 17Ater, Hezekiah, Azzur, 18Hodiah, Hashum, Bezai, 19Hariph, Anathoth, Nebai, 20Magpiash, Meshullam, Hezir, 21Meshezabel, Zadok, Jaddua, 22Pelatiah,

Hanan, Anaiah, 23Hoshea, Hananiah, Hasshub, 24Hallohesh, Pilha, Shobek, 25Rehum, Hashabnah, Maaseiah, 26Ahiah, Hanan, Anan, 27Malluch, Harim, and Baanah.

Summary of the Covenant

28 The rest of the people, the priests, the Levites, the gatekeepers, the singers, the temple servants, and all who have separated themselves from the peoples of the lands to adhere to the law of God, their wives, their sons, their daughters, all who have knowledge and understanding, 29join with their kin, their nobles, and enter into a curse and an oath to walk in God's law, which was given by Moses the servant of God, and to observe and do all the commandments of the LORD our Lord and his ordinances and his statutes. 30We will not give our daughters to the peoples of the land or take their daughters for our sons; 31and if the peoples of the land bring in merchandise or any grain on the sabbath day to sell, we will not buy it from them on the sabbath or on a holy day; and we will forego the crops of the seventh year and the exaction of every debt.

32 We also lay on ourselves the obligation to charge ourselves yearly one-third of a shekel for the service of the house of our God: 33for the rows of bread, the regular grain offering, the regular burnt offering, the sabbaths, the new moons, the appointed festivals, the sacred donations, and the sin offerings to make atonement for Israel, and for all the work of the house of our God. 34We have also cast lots among the priests, the Levites, and the people, for the wood offering, to bring it into the house of our God, by ancestral houses, at appointed times, year by year, to burn on the altar of the LORD our God, as it is written in the law. 35We obligate ourselves to bring the first fruits of our soil and the first fruits of all fruit of every tree, year by year, to the house of the LORD; 36also to bring to the house of our God, to the priests who minister in the house of our God, the firstborn of our sons and of our livestock, as it is written in the law, and the firstlings of

a Ch 10.1 in Heb   *b* Ch 10.2 in Heb

our herds and of our flocks; [37]and to bring the first of our dough, and our contributions, the fruit of every tree, the wine and the oil, to the priests, to the chambers of the house of our God; and to bring to the Levites the tithes from our soil, for it is the Levites who collect the tithes in all our rural towns. [38]And the priest, the descendant of Aaron, shall be with the Levites when the Levites receive the tithes; and the Levites shall bring up a tithe of the tithes to the house of our God, to the chambers of the storehouse. [39]For the people of Israel and the sons of Levi shall bring the contribution of grain, wine, and oil to the storerooms where the vessels of the sanctuary are, and where the priests that minister, and the gatekeepers and the singers are. We will not neglect the house of our God.

Population of the City Increased

11 Now the leaders of the people lived in Jerusalem; and the rest of the people cast lots to bring one out of ten to live in the holy city Jerusalem, while nine-tenths remained in the other towns. [2]And the people blessed all those who willingly offered to live in Jerusalem.

[3] These are the leaders of the province who lived in Jerusalem; but in the towns of Judah all lived on their property in their towns: Israel, the priests, the Levites, the temple servants, and the descendants of Solomon's servants. [4]And in Jerusalem lived some of the Judahites and of the Benjaminites. Of the Judahites: Athaiah son of Uzziah son of Zechariah son of Amariah son of Shephatiah son of Mahalalel, of the descendants of Perez; [5]and Maaseiah son of Baruch son of Col-hozeh son of Hazaiah son of Adaiah son of Joiarib son of Zechariah son of the Shilonite. [6]All the descendants of Perez who lived in Jerusalem were four hundred sixty-eight valiant warriors.

[7] And these are the Benjaminites: Sallu son of Meshullam son of Joed son of Pedaiah son of Kolaiah son of Maaseiah son of Ithiel son of Jeshaiah. [8]And his brothers*a* Gabbai, Sallai: nine hundred twenty-eight. [9]Joel son of Zichri

was their overseer; and Judah son of Hassenuah was second in charge of the city.

[10] Of the priests: Jedaiah son of Joiarib, Jachin, [11]Seraiah son of Hilkiah son of Meshullam son of Zadok son of Meraioth son of Ahitub, officer of the house of God, [12]and their associates who did the work of the house, eight hundred twenty-two; and Adaiah son of Jeroham son of Pelaliah son of Amzi son of Zechariah son of Pashhur son of Malchijah, [13]and his associates, heads of ancestral houses, two hundred forty-two; and Amashsai son of Azarel son of Ahzai son of Meshillemoth son of Immer, [14]and their associates, valiant warriors, one hundred twenty-eight; their overseer was Zabdiel son of Haggedolim.

[15] And of the Levites: Shemaiah son of Hasshub son of Azrikam son of Hashabiah son of Bunni; [16]and Shabbethai and Jozabad, of the leaders of the Levites, who were over the outside work of the house of God; [17]and Mattaniah son of Mica son of Zabdi son of Asaph, who was the leader to begin the thanksgiving in prayer, and Bakbukiah, the second among his associates; and Abda son of Shammua son of Galal son of Jeduthun. [18]All the Levites in the holy city were two hundred eighty-four.

[19] The gatekeepers, Akkub, Talmon and their associates, who kept watch at the gates, were one hundred seventy-two. [20]And the rest of Israel, and of the priests and the Levites, were in all the towns of Judah, all of them in their inheritance. [21]But the temple servants lived on Ophel; and Ziha and Gishpa were over the temple servants.

[22] The overseer of the Levites in Jerusalem was Uzzi son of Bani son of Hashabiah son of Mattaniah son of Mica, of the descendants of Asaph, the singers, in charge of the work of the house of God. [23]For there was a command from the king concerning them, and a settled provision for the singers, as was required every day. [24]And Pethahiah son of Meshezabel, of the descendants of Zerah son of Judah, was at the king's hand in all matters concerning the people.

a Gk Mss: Heb *And after him*

Villages outside Jerusalem

25 And as for the villages, with their fields, some of the people of Judah lived in Kiriath-arba and its villages, and in Dibon and its villages, and in Jekabzeel and its villages, 26and in Jeshua and in Moladah and Beth-pelet, 27in Hazar-shual, in Beer-sheba and its villages, 28in Ziklag, in Meconah and its villages, 29in En-rimmon, in Zorah, in Jarmuth, 30Zanoah, Adullam, and their villages, Lachish and its fields, and Azekah and its villages. So they camped from Beer-sheba to the valley of Hinnom. 31The people of Benjamin also lived from Geba onward, at Michmash, Aija, Bethel and its villages, 32Anathoth, Nob, Ananiah, 33Hazor, Ramah, Gittaim, 34Hadid, Zeboim, Neballat, 35Lod, and Ono, the valley of artisans. 36And certain divisions of the Levites in Judah were joined to Benjamin.

A List of Priests and Levites

12 These are the priests and the Levites who came up with Zerubbabel son of Shealtiel, and Jeshua: Seraiah, Jeremiah, Ezra, 2Amariah, Malluch, Hattush, 3Shecaniah, Rehum, Meremoth, 4Iddo, Ginnethoi, Abijah, 5Mijamin, Maadiah, Bilgah, 6Shemaiah, Joiarib, Jedaiah, 7Sallu, Amok, Hilkiah, Jedaiah. These were the leaders of the priests and of their associates in the days of Jeshua.

8 And the Levites: Jeshua, Binnui, Kadmiel, Sherebiah, Judah, and Mattaniah, who with his associates was in charge of the songs of thanksgiving. 9And Bakbukiah and Unno their associates stood opposite them in the service. 10Jeshua was the father of Joiakim, Joiakim the father of Eliashib, Eliashib the father of Joiada, 11Joiada the father of Jonathan, and Jonathan the father of Jaddua.

12 In the days of Joiakim the priests, heads of ancestral houses, were: of Seraiah, Meraiah; of Jeremiah, Hananiah; 13of Ezra, Meshullam; of Amariah, Jehohanan; 14of Malluchi, Jonathan; of Shebaniah, Joseph; 15of Harim, Adna; of Meraioth, Helkai; 16of Iddo, Zechariah; of Ginnethon, Meshullam; 17of Abijah, Zichri; of Miniamin, of Moadiah, Piltai; 18of Bilgah, Shammua; of Shemaiah, Jehonathan; 19of Joi-

arib, Mattenai; of Jedaiah, Uzzi; 20of Sallai, Kallai; of Amok, Eber; 21of Hilkiah, Hashabiah; of Jedaiah, Nethanel.

22 As for the Levites, in the days of Eliashib, Joiada, Johanan, and Jaddua, there were recorded the heads of ancestral houses; also the priests until the reign of Darius the Persian. 23The Levites, heads of ancestral houses, were recorded in the Book of the Annals until the days of Johanan son of Eliashib. 24And the leaders of the Levites: Hashabiah, Sherebiah, and Jeshua son of Kadmiel, with their associates over against them, to praise and to give thanks, according to the commandment of David the man of God, section opposite to section. 25Mattaniah, Bakbukiah, Obadiah, Meshullam, Talmon, and Akkub were gatekeepers standing guard at the storehouses of the gates. 26These were in the days of Joiakim son of Jeshua son of Jozadak, and in the days of the governor Nehemiah and of the priest Ezra, the scribe.

Dedication of the City Wall

27 Now at the dedication of the wall of Jerusalem they sought out the Levites in all their places, to bring them to Jerusalem to celebrate the dedication with rejoicing, with thanksgivings and with singing, with cymbals, harps, and lyres. 28The companies of the singers gathered together from the circuit around Jerusalem and from the villages of the Netophathites; 29also from Beth-gilgal and from the region of Geba and Azmaveth; for the singers had built for themselves villages around Jerusalem. 30And the priests and the Levites purified themselves; and they purified the people and the gates and the wall.

31 Then I brought the leaders of Judah up onto the wall, and appointed two great companies that gave thanks and went in procession. One went to the right on the wall to the Dung Gate; 32and after them went Hoshaiah and half the officials of Judah, 33and Azariah, Ezra, Meshullam, 34Judah, Benjamin, Shemaiah, and Jeremiah, 35and some of the young priests with trumpets: Zechariah son of Jonathan son of Shemaiah son of Mattaniah son of Micaiah son

of Zaccur son of Asaph; [36]and his kindred, Shemaiah, Azarel, Milalai, Gilalai, Maai, Nethanel, Judah, and Hanani, with the musical instruments of David the man of God; and the scribe Ezra went in front of them. [37]At the Fountain Gate, in front of them, they went straight up by the stairs of the city of David, at the ascent of the wall, above the house of David, to the Water Gate on the east.

38 The other company of those who gave thanks went to the left,[a] and I followed them with half of the people on the wall, above the Tower of the Ovens, to the Broad Wall, [39]and above the Gate of Ephraim, and by the Old Gate, and by the Fish Gate and the Tower of Hananel and the Tower of the Hundred, to the Sheep Gate; and they came to a halt at the Gate of the Guard. [40]So both companies of those who gave thanks stood in the house of God, and I and half of the officials with me; [41]and the priests Eliakim, Maaseiah, Miniamin, Micaiah, Elioenai, Zechariah, and Hananiah, with trumpets; [42]and Maaseiah, Shemaiah, Eleazar, Uzzi, Jehohanan, Malchijah, Elam, and Ezer. And the singers sang with Jezrahiah as their leader. [43]They offered great sacrifices that day and rejoiced, for God had made them rejoice with great joy; the women and children also rejoiced. The joy of Jerusalem was heard far away.

Temple Responsibilities

44 On that day men were appointed over the chambers for the stores, the contributions, the first fruits, and the tithes, to gather into them the portions required by the law for the priests and for the Levites from the fields belonging to the towns; for Judah rejoiced over the priests and the Levites who ministered. [45]They performed the service of their God and the service of purification, as did the singers and the gatekeepers, according to the command of David and his son Solomon. [46]For in the days of David and Asaph long ago there was a leader of the singers, and there were songs of praise and thanksgiving to God.

[47]In the days of Zerubbabel and in the days of Nehemiah all Israel gave the daily portions for the singers and the gatekeepers. They set apart that which was for the Levites; and the Levites set apart that which was for the descendants of Aaron.

Foreigners Separated from Israel

13 On that day they read from the book of Moses in the hearing of the people; and in it was found written that no Ammonite or Moabite should ever enter the assembly of God, [2]because they did not meet the Israelites with bread and water, but hired Balaam against them to curse them—yet our God turned the curse into a blessing. [3]When the people heard the law, they separated from Israel all those of foreign descent.

The Reforms of Nehemiah

4 Now before this, the priest Eliashib, who was appointed over the chambers of the house of our God, and who was related to Tobiah, [5]prepared for Tobiah a large room where they had previously put the grain offering, the frankincense, the vessels, and the tithes of grain, wine, and oil, which were given by commandment to the Levites, singers, and gatekeepers, and the contributions for the priests. [6]While this was taking place I was not in Jerusalem, for in the thirty-second year of King Artaxerxes of Babylon I went to the king. After some time I asked leave of the king [7]and returned to Jerusalem. I then discovered the wrong that Eliashib had done on behalf of Tobiah, preparing a room for him in the courts of the house of God. [8]And I was very angry, and I threw all the household furniture of Tobiah out of the room. [9]Then I gave orders and they cleansed the chambers, and I brought back the vessels of the house of God, with the grain offering and the frankincense.

10 I also found out that the portions of the Levites had not been given to them; so that the Levites and the singers, who had conducted the service, had gone back to their

a Cn: Heb *opposite*

fields. [11]So I remonstrated with the officials and said, "Why is the house of God forsaken?" And I gathered them together and set them in their stations. [12]Then all Judah brought the tithe of the grain, wine, and oil into the storehouses. [13]And I appointed as treasurers over the storehouses the priest Shelemiah, the scribe Zadok, and Pedaiah of the Levites, and as their assistant Hanan son of Zaccur son of Mattaniah, for they were considered faithful; and their duty was to distribute to their associates. [14]Remember me, O my God, concerning this, and do not wipe out my good deeds that I have done for the house of my God and for his service.

Sabbath Reforms Begun

15 In those days I saw in Judah people treading wine presses on the sabbath, and bringing in heaps of grain and loading them on donkeys; and also wine, grapes, figs, and all kinds of burdens, which they brought into Jerusalem on the sabbath day; and I warned them at that time against selling food. [16]Tyrians also, who lived in the city, brought in fish and all kinds of merchandise and sold them on the sabbath to the people of Judah, and in Jerusalem. [17]Then I remonstrated with the nobles of Judah and said to them, "What is this evil thing that you are doing, profaning the sabbath day? [18]Did not your ancestors act in this way, and did not our God bring all this disaster on us and on this city? Yet you bring more wrath on Israel by profaning the sabbath."

19 When it began to be dark at the gates of Jerusalem before the sabbath, I commanded that the doors should be shut and gave orders that they should not be opened until after the sabbath. And I set some of my servants over the gates, to prevent any burden from being brought in on the sabbath day. [20]Then the merchants and sellers of all kinds of merchandise spent the night outside Jerusalem once or twice. [21]But I warned them and said to them, "Why do you spend the night in front of the wall? If you do so again, I will lay hands on you." From that time on they did not come on the sabbath. [22]And I commanded the Levites that they should purify themselves and come and guard the gates, to keep the sabbath day holy. Remember this also in my favor, O my God, and spare me according to the greatness of your steadfast love.

Mixed Marriages Condemned

23 In those days also I saw Jews who had married women of Ashdod, Ammon, and Moab; [24]and half of their children spoke the language of Ashdod, and they could not speak the language of Judah, but spoke the language of various peoples. [25]And I contended with them and cursed them and beat some of them and pulled out their hair; and I made them take an oath in the name of God, saying, "You shall not give your daughters to their sons, or take their daughters for your sons or for yourselves. [26]Did not King Solomon of Israel sin on account of such women? Among the many nations there was no king like him, and he was beloved by his God, and God made him king over all Israel; nevertheless, foreign women made even him to sin. [27]Shall we then listen to you and do all this great evil and act treacherously against our God by marrying foreign women?"

28 And one of the sons of Jehoiada, son of the high priest Eliashib, was the son-in-law of Sanballat the Horonite; I chased him away from me. [29]Remember them, O my God, because they have defiled the priesthood, the covenant of the priests and the Levites.

30 Thus I cleansed them from everything foreign, and I established the duties of the priests and Levites, each in his work; [31]and I provided for the wood offering, at appointed times, and for the first fruits. Remember me, O my God, for good.

ESTHER

King Ahasuerus Deposes Queen Vashti

1 This happened in the days of Ahasuerus, the same Ahasuerus who ruled over one hundred twenty-seven provinces from India to Ethiopia.*ᵃ* ²In those days when King Ahasuerus sat on his royal throne in the citadel of Susa, ³in the third year of his reign, he gave a banquet for all his officials and ministers. The army of Persia and Media and the nobles and governors of the provinces were present, ⁴while he displayed the great wealth of his kingdom and the splendor and pomp of his majesty for many days, one hundred eighty days in all.

5 When these days were completed, the king gave for all the people present in the citadel of Susa, both great and small, a banquet lasting for seven days, in the court of the garden of the king's palace. ⁶There were white cotton curtains and blue hangings tied with cords of fine linen and purple to silver rings *ᵇ* and marble pillars. There were couches of gold and silver on a mosaic pavement of porphyry, marble, mother-of-pearl, and colored stones. ⁷Drinks were served in golden goblets, goblets of different kinds, and the royal wine was lavished according to the bounty of the king. ⁸Drinking was by flagons, without restraint; for the king had given orders to all the officials of his palace to do as each one desired. ⁹Furthermore, Queen Vashti gave a banquet for the women in the palace of King Ahasuerus.

10 On the seventh day, when the king was merry with wine, he commanded Mehuman, Biztha, Harbona, Bigtha and Abagtha, Zethar and Carkas, the seven eunuchs who attended him, ¹¹to bring Queen Vashti before the king, wearing the royal crown, in order to show the peoples and the officials her beauty; for she was fair to behold. ¹²But Queen Vashti refused to come at the king's command conveyed by the eunuchs. At this the king was enraged, and his anger burned within him.

13 Then the king consulted the sages who knew the laws *ᶜ* (for this was the king's procedure toward all who were versed in law and custom, ¹⁴and those next to him were Carshena, Shethar, Admatha, Tarshish, Meres, Marsena, and Memucan, the seven officials of Persia and Media, who had access to the king, and sat first in the kingdom): ¹⁵"According to the law, what is to be done to Queen Vashti because she has not performed the command of King Ahasuerus conveyed by the eunuchs?" ¹⁶Then Memucan said in the presence of the king and the officials, "Not only has Queen Vashti done wrong to the king, but also to all the officials and all the peoples who are in all the provinces of King Ahasuerus. ¹⁷For this deed of the queen will be made known to all women, causing them to look with contempt on their husbands, since they will say, 'King Ahasuerus commanded Queen Vashti to be brought before him, and she did not come.' ¹⁸This very day the noble ladies of Persia and Media who have heard of the queen's behavior will rebel against*ᵈ* the king's officials, and there will be no end of contempt and wrath! ¹⁹If it pleases the king, let a royal order go out from him, and let it be written among the laws of the Persians and the Medes so that it may not be altered, that Vashti is never again to come before King Ahasuerus; and let the king give her royal position to another who is better than she. ²⁰So when the decree made by the king is proclaimed throughout all his kingdom, vast as it is, all women will give honor to their husbands, high and low alike."

21 This advice pleased the king and the officials, and the king did as Memucan proposed; ²²he sent letters to all the royal provinces, to every province in its own script and to every people in its own language, declaring that every man should be master in his own house. *ᵉ*

---

a Or *Nubia*; Heb *Cush*   *b* Or *rods*   *c* Cn: Heb *times*   *d* Cn: Heb *will tell*   *e* Heb adds *and speak according to the language of his people*

Esther Becomes Queen

2 After these things, when the anger of King Ahasuerus had abated, he remembered Vashti and what she had done and what had been decreed against her. ²Then the king's servants who attended him said, "Let beautiful young virgins be sought out for the king. ³And let the king appoint commissioners in all the provinces of his kingdom to gather all the beautiful young virgins to the harem in the citadel of Susa under custody of Hegai, the king's eunuch, who is in charge of the women; let their cosmetic treatments be given them. ⁴And let the girl who pleases the king be queen instead of Vashti." This pleased the king, and he did so.

5 Now there was a Jew in the citadel of Susa whose name was Mordecai son of Jair son of Shimei son of Kish, a Benjaminite. ⁶Kish*a* had been carried away from Jerusalem among the captives carried away with King Jeconiah of Judah, whom King Nebuchadnezzar of Babylon had carried away. ⁷Mordecai*b* had brought up Hadassah, that is Esther, his cousin, for she had neither father nor mother; the girl was fair and beautiful, and when her father and her mother died, Mordecai adopted her as his own daughter. ⁸So when the king's order and his edict were proclaimed, and when many young women were gathered in the citadel of Susa in custody of Hegai, Esther also was taken into the king's palace and put in custody of Hegai, who had charge of the women. ⁹The girl pleased him and won his favor, and he quickly provided her with her cosmetic treatments and her portion of food, and with seven chosen maids from the king's palace, and advanced her and her maids to the best place in the harem. ¹⁰Esther did not reveal her people or kindred, for Mordecai had charged her not to tell. ¹¹Every day Mordecai would walk around in front of the court of the harem, to learn how Esther was and how she fared.

12 The turn came for each girl to go in to King Ahasuerus, after being twelve months un-

der the regulations for the women, since this was the regular period of their cosmetic treatment, six months with oil of myrrh and six months with perfumes and cosmetics for women. ¹³When the girl went in to the king she was given whatever she asked for to take with her from the harem to the king's palace. ¹⁴In the evening she went in; then in the morning she came back to the second harem in custody of Shaashgaz, the king's eunuch, who was in charge of the concubines; she did not go in to the king again, unless the king delighted in her and she was summoned by name.

15 When the turn came for Esther daughter of Abihail the uncle of Mordecai, who had adopted her as his own daughter, to go in to the king, she asked for nothing except what Hegai the king's eunuch, who had charge of the women, advised. Now Esther was admired by all who saw her. ¹⁶When Esther was taken to King Ahasuerus in his royal palace in the tenth month, which is the month of Tebeth, in the seventh year of his reign, ¹⁷the king loved Esther more than all the other women; of all the virgins she won his favor and devotion, so that he set the royal crown on her head and made her queen instead of Vashti. ¹⁸Then the king gave a great banquet to all his officials and ministers—"Esther's banquet." He also granted a holiday*c* to the provinces, and gave gifts with royal liberality.

Mordecai Discovers a Plot

19 When the virgins were being gathered together,*d* Mordecai was sitting at the king's gate. ²⁰Now Esther had not revealed her kindred or her people, as Mordecai had charged her; for Esther obeyed Mordecai just as when she was brought up by him. ²¹In those days, while Mordecai was sitting at the king's gate, Bigthan and Teresh, two of the king's eunuchs, who guarded the threshold, became angry and conspired to assassinate*e* King Ahasuerus. ²²But the matter came to the knowledge of Mordecai, and he told it to Queen Esther, and Esther told the king in the name of Mordecai.

---

a Heb *a Benjaminite* ⁶*who*   *b* Heb *He*   *c* Or *an amnesty*   *d* Heb adds *a second time*   *e* Heb *to lay hands on*

23When the affair was investigated and found to be so, both the men were hanged on the gallows. It was recorded in the book of the annals in the presence of the king.

Haman Undertakes to Destroy the Jews

3 After these things King Ahasuerus promoted Haman son of Hammedatha the Agagite, and advanced him and set his seat above all the officials who were with him. 2And all the king's servants who were at the king's gate bowed down and did obeisance to Haman; for the king had so commanded concerning him. But Mordecai did not bow down or do obeisance. 3Then the king's servants who were at the king's gate said to Mordecai, "Why do you disobey the king's command?" 4When they spoke to him day after day and he would not listen to them, they told Haman, in order to see whether Mordecai's words would avail; for he had told them that he was a Jew. 5When Haman saw that Mordecai did not bow down or do obeisance to him, Haman was infuriated. 6But he thought it beneath him to lay hands on Mordecai alone. So, having been told who Mordecai's people were, Haman plotted to destroy all the Jews, the people of Mordecai, throughout the whole kingdom of Ahasuerus.

7 In the first month, which is the month of Nisan, in the twelfth year of King Ahasuerus, they cast Pur—which means "the lot"—before Haman for the day and for the month, and the lot fell on the thirteenth day*a* of the twelfth month, which is the month of Adar. 8Then Haman said to King Ahasuerus, "There is a certain people scattered and separated among the peoples in all the provinces of your kingdom; their laws are different from those of every other people, and they do not keep the king's laws, so that it is not appropriate for the king to tolerate them. 9If it pleases the king, let a decree be issued for their destruction, and I will pay ten thousand talents of silver into the hands of those who have charge of the king's business, so that they may put it into the king's

treasuries." 10So the king took his signet ring from his hand and gave it to Haman son of Hammedatha the Agagite, the enemy of the Jews. 11The king said to Haman, "The money is given to you, and the people as well, to do with them as it seems good to you."

12 Then the king's secretaries were summoned on the thirteenth day of the first month, and an edict, according to all that Haman commanded, was written to the king's satraps and to the governors over all the provinces and to the officials of all the peoples, to every province in its own script and every people in its own language; it was written in the name of King Ahasuerus and sealed with the king's ring. 13Letters were sent by couriers to all the king's provinces, giving orders to destroy, to kill, and to annihilate all Jews, young and old, women and children, in one day, the thirteenth day of the twelfth month, which is the month of Adar, and to plunder their goods. 14A copy of the document was to be issued as a decree in every province by proclamation, calling on all the peoples to be ready for that day. 15The couriers went quickly by order of the king, and the decree was issued in the citadel of Susa. The king and Haman sat down to drink; but the city of Susa was thrown into confusion.

Esther Agrees to Help the Jews

4 When Mordecai learned all that had been done, Mordecai tore his clothes and put on sackcloth and ashes, and went through the city, wailing with a loud and bitter cry; 2he went up to the entrance of the king's gate, for no one might enter the king's gate clothed with sackcloth. 3In every province, wherever the king's command and his decree came, there was great mourning among the Jews, with fasting and weeping and lamenting, and most of them lay in sackcloth and ashes.

4 When Esther's maids and her eunuchs came and told her, the queen was deeply distressed; she sent garments to clothe Mordecai, so that he might take off his sackcloth; but he would not accept them. 5Then Esther called

a Cn Compare Gk and verse 13 below: Heb *the twelfth month* for Hathach, one of the king's eunuchs, who had been appointed to attend her, and ordered him to go to Mordecai to learn what was happening and why. 6Hathach went out to Mordecai in the open square of the city in front of the king's gate, 7and Mordecai told him all that had happened to him, and the exact sum of money that Haman had promised to pay into the king's treasuries for the destruction of the Jews. 8Mordecai also gave him a copy of the written decree issued in Susa for their destruction, that he might show it to Esther, explain it to her, and charge her to go to the king to make supplication to him and entreat him for her people.

9 Hathach went and told Esther what Mordecai had said. 10Then Esther spoke to Hathach and gave him a message for Mordecai, saying, 11"All the king's servants and the people of the king's provinces know that if any man or woman goes to the king inside the inner court without being called, there is but one law—all alike are to be put to death. Only if the king holds out the golden scepter to someone, may that person live. I myself have not been called to come in to the king for thirty days." 12When they told Mordecai what Esther had said, 13Mordecai told them to reply to Esther, "Do not think that in the king's palace you will escape any more than all the other Jews. 14For if you keep silence at such a time as this, relief and deliverance will rise for the Jews from another quarter, but you and your father's family will perish. Who knows? Perhaps you have come to royal dignity for just such a time as this." 15Then Esther said in reply to Mordecai, 16"Go, gather all the Jews to be found in Susa, and hold a fast on my behalf, and neither eat nor drink for three days, night or day. I and my maids will also fast as you do. After that I will go to the king, though it is against the law; and if I perish, I perish." 17Mordecai then went away and did everything as Esther had ordered him.

Esther's Banquet

5 On the third day Esther put on her royal robes and stood in the inner court of the king's palace, opposite the king's hall. The king was sitting on his royal throne inside the palace opposite the entrance to the palace. 2As soon as the king saw Queen Esther standing in the court, she won his favor and he held out to her the golden scepter that was in his hand. Then Esther approached and touched the top of the scepter. 3The king said to her, "What is it, Queen Esther? What is your request? It shall be given you, even to the half of my kingdom." 4Then Esther said, "If it pleases the king, let the king and Haman come today to a banquet that I have prepared for the king." 5Then the king said, "Bring Haman quickly, so that we may do as Esther desires." So the king and Haman came to the banquet that Esther had prepared. 6While they were drinking wine, the king said to Esther, "What is your petition? It shall be granted you. And what is your request? Even to the half of my kingdom, it shall be fulfilled." 7Then Esther said, "This is my petition and request: 8If I have won the king's favor, and if it pleases the king to grant my petition and fulfill my request, let the king and Haman come tomorrow to the banquet that I will prepare for them, and then I will do as the king has said."

Haman Plans to Have Mordecai Hanged

9 Haman went out that day happy and in good spirits. But when Haman saw Mordecai in the king's gate, and observed that he neither rose nor trembled before him, he was infuriated with Mordecai; 10nevertheless Haman restrained himself and went home. Then he sent and called for his friends and his wife Zeresh, 11and Haman recounted to them the splendor of his riches, the number of his sons, all the promotions with which the king had honored him, and how he had advanced him above the officials and the ministers of the king. 12Haman added, "Even Queen Esther let no one but myself come with the king to the banquet that she prepared. Tomorrow also I am invited by her, together with the king. 13Yet all this does me no good so long as I see the Jew Mordecai sitting at the king's gate." 14Then his wife Zeresh and all his friends said to him,

"Let a gallows fifty cubits high be made, and in the morning tell the king to have Mordecai hanged on it; then go with the king to the banquet in good spirits." This advice pleased Haman, and he had the gallows made.

The King Honors Mordecai

6 On that night the king could not sleep, and he gave orders to bring the book of records, the annals, and they were read to the king. 2It was found written how Mordecai had told about Bigthana and Teresh, two of the king's eunuchs, who guarded the threshold, and who had conspired to assassinate[a] King Ahasuerus. 3Then the king said, "What honor or distinction has been bestowed on Mordecai for this?" The king's servants who attended him said, "Nothing has been done for him." 4The king said, "Who is in the court?" Now Haman had just entered the outer court of the king's palace to speak to the king about having Mordecai hanged on the gallows that he had prepared for him. 5So the king's servants told him, "Haman is there, standing in the court." The king said, "Let him come in." 6So Haman came in, and the king said to him, "What shall be done for the man whom the king wishes to honor?" Haman said to himself, "Whom would the king wish to honor more than me?" 7So Haman said to the king, "For the man whom the king wishes to honor, 8let royal robes be brought, which the king has worn, and a horse that the king has ridden, with a royal crown on its head. 9Let the robes and the horse be handed over to one of the king's most noble officials; let him[b] robe the man whom the king wishes to honor, and let him[b] conduct the man on horseback through the open square of the city, proclaiming before him: 'Thus shall it be done for the man whom the king wishes to honor.' " 10Then the king said to Haman, "Quickly, take the robes and the horse, as you have said, and do so to the Jew Mordecai who sits at the king's gate. Leave out nothing that you have mentioned." 11So Haman took the robes and the horse and robed Mordecai and led him riding through the open square of the city, proclaiming, "Thus shall it be done for the man whom the king wishes to honor."

12 Then Mordecai returned to the king's gate, but Haman hurried to his house, mourning and with his head covered. 13When Haman told his wife Zeresh and all his friends everything that had happened to him, his advisers and his wife Zeresh said to him, "If Mordecai, before whom your downfall has begun, is of the Jewish people, you will not prevail against him, but will surely fall before him."

Haman's Downfall and Mordecai's Advancement

14 While they were still talking with him, the king's eunuchs arrived and hurried Haman off 7 to the banquet that Esther had prepared. 1So the king and Haman went in to feast with Queen Esther. 2On the second day, as they were drinking wine, the king again said to Esther, "What is your petition, Queen Esther? It shall be granted you. And what is your request? Even to the half of my kingdom, it shall be fulfilled." 3Then Queen Esther answered, "If I have won your favor, O king, and if it pleases the king, let my life be given me—that is my petition—and the lives of my people— that is my request. 4For we have been sold, I and my people, to be destroyed, to be killed, and to be annihilated. If we had been sold merely as slaves, men and women, I would have held my peace; but no enemy can compensate for this damage to the king."[c] 5Then King Ahasuerus said to Queen Esther, "Who is he, and where is he, who has presumed to do this?" 6Esther said, "A foe and enemy, this wicked Haman!" Then Haman was terrified before the king and the queen. 7The king rose from the feast in wrath and went into the palace garden, but Haman stayed to beg his life from Queen Esther, for he saw that the king had determined to destroy him. 8When the king returned from the palace garden to the banquet hall, Haman had thrown himself on

a Heb to lay hands on   b Heb them   c Meaning of Heb uncertain the couch where Esther was reclining; and the king said, "Will he even assault the queen in my presence, in my own house?" As the words left the mouth of the king, they covered Haman's face. 9Then Harbona, one of the eunuchs in attendance on the king, said, "Look, the very gallows that Haman has prepared for Mordecai, whose word saved the king, stands at Haman's house, fifty cubits high." And the king said, "Hang him on that." 10So they hanged Haman on the gallows that he had prepared for Mordecai. Then the anger of the king abated.

Esther Saves the Jews

8 On that day King Ahasuerus gave to Queen Esther the house of Haman, the enemy of the Jews; and Mordecai came before the king, for Esther had told what he was to her. 2Then the king took off his signet ring, which he had taken from Haman, and gave it to Mordecai. So Esther set Mordecai over the house of Haman.

3 Then Esther spoke again to the king; she fell at his feet, weeping and pleading with him to avert the evil design of Haman the Agagite and the plot that he had devised against the Jews. 4The king held out the golden scepter to Esther, 5and Esther rose and stood before the king. She said, "If it pleases the king, and if I have won his favor, and if the thing seems right before the king, and I have his approval, let an order be written to revoke the letters devised by Haman son of Hammedatha the Agagite, which he wrote giving orders to destroy the Jews who are in all the provinces of the king. 6For how can I bear to see the calamity that is coming on my people? Or how can I bear to see the destruction of my kindred?" 7Then King Ahasuerus said to Queen Esther and to the Jew Mordecai, "See, I have given Esther the house of Haman, and they have hanged him on the gallows, because he plotted to lay hands on the Jews. 8You may write as you please with regard to the Jews, in the name of the king, and seal it with the king's ring; for an edict written in the name of the king and sealed with the king's ring cannot be revoked."

9 The king's secretaries were summoned at that time, in the third month, which is the month of Sivan, on the twenty-third day; and an edict was written, according to all that Mordecai commanded, to the Jews and to the satraps and the governors and the officials of the provinces from India to Ethiopia,[a] one hundred twenty-seven provinces, to every province in its own script and to every people in its own language, and also to the Jews in their script and their language. 10He wrote letters in the name of King Ahasuerus, sealed them with the king's ring, and sent them by mounted couriers riding on fast steeds bred from the royal herd.[b] 11By these letters the king allowed the Jews who were in every city to assemble and defend their lives, to destroy, to kill, and to annihilate any armed force of any people or province that might attack them, with their children and women, and to plunder their goods 12on a single day throughout all the provinces of King Ahasuerus, on the thirteenth day of the twelfth month, which is the month of Adar. 13A copy of the writ was to be issued as a decree in every province and published to all peoples, and the Jews were to be ready on that day to take revenge on their enemies. 14So the couriers, mounted on their swift royal steeds, hurried out, urged by the king's command. The decree was issued in the citadel of Susa.

15 Then Mordecai went out from the presence of the king, wearing royal robes of blue and white, with a great golden crown and a mantle of fine linen and purple, while the city of Susa shouted and rejoiced. 16For the Jews there was light and gladness, joy and honor. 17In every province and in every city, wherever the king's command and his edict came, there was gladness and joy among the Jews, a festival and a holiday. Furthermore, many of the peoples of the country professed to be Jews, because the fear of the Jews had fallen upon them.

a Or Nubia; Heb Cush   b Meaning of Heb uncertain

Destruction of the Enemies of the Jews

9 Now in the twelfth month, which is the month of Adar, on the thirteenth day, when the king's command and edict were about to be executed, on the very day when the enemies of the Jews hoped to gain power over them, but which had been changed to a day when the Jews would gain power over their foes, 2the Jews gathered in their cities throughout all the provinces of King Ahasuerus to lay hands on those who had sought their ruin; and no one could withstand them, because the fear of them had fallen upon all peoples. 3All the officials of the provinces, the satraps and the governors, and the royal officials were supporting the Jews, because the fear of Mordecai had fallen upon them. 4For Mordecai was powerful in the king's house, and his fame spread throughout all the provinces as the man Mordecai grew more and more powerful. 5So the Jews struck down all their enemies with the sword, slaughtering, and destroying them, and did as they pleased to those who hated them. 6In the citadel of Susa the Jews killed and destroyed five hundred people. 7They killed Parshandatha, Dalphon, Aspatha, 8Poratha, Adalia, Aridatha, 9Parmashta, Arisai, Aridai, Vaizatha, 10the ten sons of Haman son of Hammedatha, the enemy of the Jews; but they did not touch the plunder.

11 That very day the number of those killed in the citadel of Susa was reported to the king. 12The king said to Queen Esther, "In the citadel of Susa the Jews have killed five hundred people and also the ten sons of Haman. What have they done in the rest of the king's provinces? Now what is your petition? It shall be granted you. And what further is your request? It shall be fulfilled." 13Esther said, "If it pleases the king, let the Jews who are in Susa be allowed tomorrow also to do according to this day's edict, and let the ten sons of Haman be hanged on the gallows." 14So the king commanded this to be done; a decree was issued in Susa, and the ten sons of Haman were hanged. 15The Jews who were in Susa gathered also on the fourteenth day of the month of Adar and they killed three hundred

persons in Susa; but they did not touch the plunder.

16 Now the other Jews who were in the king's provinces also gathered to defend their lives, and gained relief from their enemies, and killed seventy-five thousand of those who hated them; but they laid no hands on the plunder. 17This was on the thirteenth day of the month of Adar, and on the fourteenth day they rested and made that a day of feasting and gladness.

The Feast of Purim Inaugurated

18 But the Jews who were in Susa gathered on the thirteenth day and on the fourteenth, and rested on the fifteenth day, making that a day of feasting and gladness. 19Therefore the Jews of the villages, who live in the open towns, hold the fourteenth day of the month of Adar as a day for gladness and feasting, a holiday on which they send gifts of food to one another.

20 Mordecai recorded these things, and sent letters to all the Jews who were in all the provinces of King Ahasuerus, both near and far, 21enjoining them that they should keep the fourteenth day of the month Adar and also the fifteenth day of the same month, year by year, 22as the days on which the Jews gained relief from their enemies, and as the month that had been turned for them from sorrow into gladness and from mourning into a holiday; that they should make them days of feasting and gladness, days for sending gifts of food to one another and presents to the poor. 23So the Jews adopted as a custom what they had begun to do, as Mordecai had written to them.

24 Haman son of Hammedatha the Agagite, the enemy of all the Jews, had plotted against the Jews to destroy them, and had cast Pur—that is "the lot"—to crush and destroy them; 25but when Esther came before the king, he gave orders in writing that the wicked plot that he had devised against the Jews should come upon his own head, and that he and his sons should be hanged on the gallows. 26Therefore these days are called Purim, from the word Pur. Thus because of all that

was written in this letter, and of what they had faced in this matter, and of what had happened to them, ²⁷the Jews established and accepted as a custom for themselves and their descendants and all who joined them, that without fail they would continue to observe these two days every year, as it was written and at the time appointed. ²⁸These days should be remembered and kept throughout every generation, in every family, province, and city; and these days of Purim should never fall into disuse among the Jews, nor should the commemoration of these days cease among their descendants.

29 Queen Esther daughter of Abihail, along with the Jew Mordecai, gave full written authority, confirming this second letter about Purim. ³⁰Letters were sent wishing peace and security to all the Jews, to the one hundred twenty-seven provinces of the kingdom of Ahasuerus, ³¹and giving orders that these days of Purim should be observed at their appointed seasons, as the Jew Mordecai and Queen Esther enjoined on the Jews, just as they had laid down for themselves and for their descendants regulations concerning their fasts and their lamentations. ³²The command of Queen Esther fixed these practices of Purim, and it was recorded in writing.

10 King Ahasuerus laid tribute on the land and on the islands of the sea. ²All the acts of his power and might, and the full account of the high honor of Mordecai, to which the king advanced him, are they not written in the annals of the kings of Media and Persia? ³For Mordecai the Jew was next in rank to King Ahasuerus, and he was powerful among the Jews and popular with his many kindred, for he sought the good of his people and interceded for the welfare of all his descendants.

JOB

Job and His Family

1 There was once a man in the land of Uz whose name was Job. That man was blameless and upright, one who feared God and turned away from evil. ²There were born to him seven sons and three daughters. ³He had seven thousand sheep, three thousand camels, five hundred yoke of oxen, five hundred donkeys, and very many servants; so that this man was the greatest of all the people of the east. ⁴His sons used to go and hold feasts in one another's houses in turn; and they would send and invite their three sisters to eat and drink with them. ⁵And when the feast days had run their course, Job would send and sanctify them, and he would rise early in the morning and offer burnt offerings according to the number of them all; for Job said, "It may be that my children have sinned, and cursed God in their hearts." This is what Job always did.

Attack on Job's Character

6 One day the heavenly beings[a] came to present themselves before the LORD, and Satan[b] also came among them. ⁷The LORD said to Satan,[b] "Where have you come from?" Satan[b] answered the LORD, "From going to and fro on the earth, and from walking up and down on it." ⁸The LORD said to Satan,[b] "Have you considered my servant Job? There is no one like him on the earth, a blameless and upright man who fears God and turns away from evil." ⁹Then Satan[b] answered the LORD, "Does Job fear God for nothing? ¹⁰Have you not put a fence around him and his house and all that he has, on every side? You have blessed the work of his hands, and his possessions have increased in the land. ¹¹But stretch out your hand now, and touch all that he has, and he will curse you to your face." ¹²The LORD said to Satan,[b] "Very well, all that he has is in your power; only do not stretch out your hand against him!" So Satan[b] went out from the presence of the LORD.

Job Loses Property and Children

13 One day when his sons and daughters were eating and drinking wine in the eldest brother's house, ¹⁴a messenger came to Job and said, "The oxen were plowing and the donkeys were feeding beside them, ¹⁵and the Sabeans fell on them and carried them off, and killed the servants with the edge of the sword; I alone have escaped to tell you." ¹⁶While he was still speaking, another came and said, "The fire of God fell from heaven and burned up the sheep and the servants, and consumed them; I alone have escaped to tell you." ¹⁷While he was still speaking, another came and said, "The Chaldeans formed three columns, made a raid on the camels and carried them off, and killed the servants with the edge of the sword; I alone have escaped to tell you." ¹⁸While he was still speaking, another came and said, "Your sons and daughters were eating and drinking wine in their eldest brother's house, ¹⁹and suddenly a great wind came across the desert, struck the four corners of the house, and it fell on the young people, and they are dead; I alone have escaped to tell you."

20 Then Job arose, tore his robe, shaved his head, and fell on the ground and worshiped. ²¹He said, "Naked I came from my mother's womb, and naked shall I return there; the LORD gave, and the LORD has taken away; blessed be the name of the LORD."

22 In all this Job did not sin or charge God with wrongdoing.

Attack on Job's Health

2 One day the heavenly beings[a] came to present themselves before the LORD, and Satan[b] also came among them to present himself before the LORD. ²The LORD said to Satan,[b] "Where have you come from?" Satan[b] answered the LORD, "From going to and fro on the earth, and from walking up and down on it." ³The LORD said to Satan,[b] "Have you considered my servant Job? There is no one like

---

a Heb *sons of God*   *b* Or *the Accuser*, Heb *ha-satan* him on the earth, a blameless and upright man who fears God and turns away from evil. He still persists in his integrity, although you incited me against him, to destroy him for no reason." ⁴Then Satan*ᵃ* answered the LORD, "Skin for skin! All that people have they will give to save their lives.*ᵇ* ⁵But stretch out your hand now and touch his bone and his flesh, and he will curse you to your face." ⁶The LORD said to Satan,*ᵃ* "Very well, he is in your power; only spare his life."

7 So Satan*ᵃ* went out from the presence of the LORD, and inflicted loathsome sores on Job from the sole of his foot to the crown of his head. ⁸Job*ᶜ* took a potsherd with which to scrape himself, and sat among the ashes.

9 Then his wife said to him, "Do you still persist in your integrity? Curse*ᵈ* God, and die." ¹⁰But he said to her, "You speak as any foolish woman would speak. Shall we receive the good at the hand of God, and not receive the bad?" In all this Job did not sin with his lips.

Job's Three Friends

11 Now when Job's three friends heard of all these troubles that had come upon him, each of them set out from his home—Eliphaz the Temanite, Bildad the Shuhite, and Zophar the Naamathite. They met together to go and console and comfort him. ¹²When they saw him from a distance, they did not recognize him, and they raised their voices and wept aloud; they tore their robes and threw dust in the air upon their heads. ¹³They sat with him on the ground seven days and seven nights, and no one spoke a word to him, for they saw that his suffering was very great.

Job Curses the Day He Was Born

3 After this Job opened his mouth and cursed the day of his birth. ²Job said:
3   "Let the day perish in which I was born,
      and the night that said,
      'A man-child is conceived.'
4   Let that day be darkness!
      May God above not seek it,

or light shine on it.
5   Let gloom and deep darkness claim it.
      Let clouds settle upon it;
      let the blackness of the day terrify it.
6   That night—let thick darkness seize it!
      let it not rejoice among the days of
         the year;
      let it not come into the number of the
         months.
7   Yes, let that night be barren;
      let no joyful cry be heard*ᵉ* in it.
8   Let those curse it who curse the Sea,*ᶠ*
      those who are skilled to rouse up
         Leviathan.
9   Let the stars of its dawn be dark;
      let it hope for light, but have none;
      may it not see the eyelids of the
         morning—
10 because it did not shut the doors of my
         mother's womb,
      and hide trouble from my eyes.

11 "Why did I not die at birth,
      come forth from the womb and
         expire?
12 Why were there knees to receive me,
      or breasts for me to suck?
13 Now I would be lying down and quiet;
      I would be asleep; then I would be at
         rest
14 with kings and counselors of the earth
      who rebuild ruins for themselves,
15 or with princes who have gold,
      who fill their houses with silver.
16 Or why was I not buried like a stillborn
         child,
      like an infant that never sees the light?
17 There the wicked cease from troubling,
      and there the weary are at rest.
18 There the prisoners are at ease together;
      they do not hear the voice of the
         taskmaster.
19 The small and the great are there,
      and the slaves are free from their
         masters.

a Or *the Accuser,* Heb *ha-satan*   *b* Or *All that the man has he will give for his life*   *c* Heb *He*   *d* Heb *Bless*
e Heb *come*   *f* Cn: Heb *day*

20 "Why is light given to one in misery,
and life to the bitter in soul,

21 who long for death, but it does not
come,
and dig for it more than for hidden
treasures;

22 who rejoice exceedingly,
and are glad when they find the grave?

23 Why is light given to one who cannot see
the way,
whom God has fenced in?

24 For my sighing comes like*a* my bread,
and my groanings are poured out like
water.

25 Truly the thing that I fear comes upon
me,
and what I dread befalls me.

26 I am not at ease, nor am I quiet;
I have no rest; but trouble comes."

Eliphaz Speaks: Job Has Sinned

4 Then Eliphaz the Temanite answered:
2 "If one ventures a word with you, will
you be offended?
But who can keep from speaking?

3 See, you have instructed many;
you have strengthened the weak
hands.

4 Your words have supported those who
were stumbling,
and you have made firm the feeble
knees.

5 But now it has come to you, and you are
impatient;
it touches you, and you are dismayed.

6 Is not your fear of God your confidence,
and the integrity of your ways your
hope?

7 "Think now, who that was innocent ever
perished?
Or where were the upright cut off?

8 As I have seen, those who plow iniquity
and sow trouble reap the same.

9 By the breath of God they perish,

and by the blast of his anger they are
consumed.

10 The roar of the lion, the voice of the
fierce lion,
and the teeth of the young lions are
broken.

11 The strong lion perishes for lack of prey,
and the whelps of the lioness are
scattered.

12 "Now a word came stealing to me,
my ear received the whisper of it.

13 Amid thoughts from visions of the
night,
when deep sleep falls on mortals,

14 dread came upon me, and trembling,
which made all my bones shake.

15 A spirit glided past my face;
the hair of my flesh bristled.

16 It stood still,
but I could not discern its appearance.
A form was before my eyes;
there was silence, then I heard a voice:

17 'Can mortals be righteous before*b* God?
Can human beings be pure before*b*
their Maker?

18 Even in his servants he puts no trust,
and his angels he charges with error;

19 how much more those who live in
houses of clay,
whose foundation is in the dust,
who are crushed like a moth.

20 Between morning and evening they are
destroyed;
they perish forever without any
regarding it.

21 Their tent-cord is plucked up within
them,
and they die devoid of wisdom.'

Job Is Corrected by God

5 "Call now; is there anyone who will
answer you?
To which of the holy ones will you turn?

2 Surely vexation kills the fool,
and jealousy slays the simple.

a Heb *before*   *b* Or *more than*

3   I have seen fools taking root,
     but suddenly I cursed their dwelling.
4   Their children are far from safety,
     they are crushed in the gate,
     and there is no one to deliver them.
5   The hungry eat their harvest,
     and they take it even out of the
        thorns;*a*
     and the thirsty*b* pant after their wealth.
6   For misery does not come from the
        earth,
     nor does trouble sprout from the
        ground;
7   but human beings are born to trouble
     just as sparks*c* fly upward.

8   "As for me, I would seek God,
     and to God I would commit my cause.
9   He does great things and unsearchable,
     marvelous things without number.
10   He gives rain on the earth
     and sends waters on the fields;
11   he sets on high those who are lowly,
     and those who mourn are lifted to
        safety.
12   He frustrates the devices of the crafty,
     so that their hands achieve no success.
13   He takes the wise in their own craftiness;
     and the schemes of the wily are
        brought to a quick end.
14   They meet with darkness in the daytime,
     and grope at noonday as in the night.
15   But he saves the needy from the sword
        of their mouth,
     from the hand of the mighty.
16   So the poor have hope,
     and injustice shuts its mouth.

17   "How happy is the one whom God
        reproves;
     therefore do not despise the discipline
        of the Almighty.*d*
18   For he wounds, but he binds up;
     he strikes, but his hands heal.
19   He will deliver you from six troubles;
     in seven no harm shall touch you.

20   In famine he will redeem you from
        death,
     and in war from the power of the
        sword.
21   You shall be hidden from the scourge of
        the tongue,
     and shall not fear destruction when it
        comes.
22   At destruction and famine you shall
        laugh,
     and shall not fear the wild animals of
        the earth.
23   For you shall be in league with the stones
        of the field,
     and the wild animals shall be at peace
        with you.
24   You shall know that your tent is safe,
     you shall inspect your fold and miss
        nothing.
25   You shall know that your descendants
        will be many,
     and your offspring like the grass of
        the earth.
26   You shall come to your grave in ripe old
        age,
     as a shock of grain comes up to the
        threshing floor in its season.
27   See, we have searched this out; it is true.
     Hear, and know it for yourself."

Job Replies: My Complaint Is Just

6   Then Job answered:
2   "O that my vexation were weighed,
     and all my calamity laid in the
        balances!
3   For then it would be heavier than the
        sand of the sea;
     therefore my words have been rash.
4   For the arrows of the Almighty*d* are in
        me;
     my spirit drinks their poison;
     the terrors of God are arrayed against
        me.
5   Does the wild ass bray over its grass,
     or the ox low over its fodder?

---

a Meaning of Heb uncertain   *b* Aquila Symmachus Syr Vg: Heb *snare*   *c* Or *birds*; Heb *sons of Resheph*
d Traditional rendering of Heb *Shaddai*

6 Can that which is tasteless be eaten
        without salt,
      or is there any flavor in the juice of
        mallows?*a*

7 My appetite refuses to touch them;
      they are like food that is loathsome to
        me.*a*

8 "O that I might have my request,
      and that God would grant my desire;

9 that it would please God to crush me,
      that he would let loose his hand and
        cut me off!

10 This would be my consolation;
      I would even exult*a* in unrelenting
        pain;
      for I have not denied the words of the
        Holy One.

11 What is my strength, that I should wait?
      And what is my end, that I should be
        patient?

12 Is my strength the strength of stones,
      or is my flesh bronze?

13 In truth I have no help in me,
      and any resource is driven from me.

14 "Those who withhold*b* kindness from a
        friend
      forsake the fear of the Almighty.*c*

15 My companions are treacherous like a
        torrent-bed,
      like freshets that pass away,

16 that run dark with ice,
      turbid with melting snow.

17 In time of heat they disappear;
      when it is hot, they vanish from their
        place.

18 The caravans turn aside from their
        course;
      they go up into the waste, and perish.

19 The caravans of Tema look,
      the travelers of Sheba hope.

20 They are disappointed because they were
        confident;
      they come there and are confounded.

21 Such you have now become to me;*d*

      you see my calamity, and are afraid.

22 Have I said, 'Make me a gift'?
      Or, 'From your wealth offer a bribe
        for me'?

23 Or, 'Save me from an opponent's hand'?
      Or, 'Ransom me from the hand of
        oppressors'?

24 "Teach me, and I will be silent;
      make me understand how I have gone
        wrong.

25 How forceful are honest words!
      But your reproof, what does it
        reprove?

26 Do you think that you can reprove
        words,
      as if the speech of the desperate were
        wind?

27 You would even cast lots over the
        orphan,
      and bargain over your friend.

28 "But now, be pleased to look at me;
      for I will not lie to your face.

29 Turn, I pray, let no wrong be done.
      Turn now, my vindication is at stake.

30 Is there any wrong on my tongue?
      Cannot my taste discern calamity?

Job: My Suffering Is without End

7 "Do not human beings have a hard
        service on earth,
      and are not their days like the days of
        a laborer?

2 Like a slave who longs for the shadow,
      and like laborers who look for their
        wages,

3 so I am allotted months of emptiness,
      and nights of misery are apportioned
        to me.

4 When I lie down I say, 'When shall I
        rise?'
      But the night is long,
      and I am full of tossing until dawn.

5 My flesh is clothed with worms and dirt;

a Meaning of Heb uncertain   *b* Syr Vg Compare Tg: Meaning of Heb uncertain   *c* Traditional rendering of Heb *Shaddai*   *d* Cn Compare Gk Syr: Meaning of Heb uncertain

my skin hardens, then breaks out
        again.
6   My days are swifter than a weaver's
        shuttle,
     and come to their end without hope. *a*

7   "Remember that my life is a breath;
        my eye will never again see good.
8   The eye that beholds me will see me no
        more;
        while your eyes are upon me, I shall
            be gone.
9   As the cloud fades and vanishes,
        so those who go down to Sheol do
            not come up;
10   they return no more to their houses,
        nor do their places know them any
            more.

11   "Therefore I will not restrain my mouth;
     I will speak in the anguish of my
        spirit;
     I will complain in the bitterness of my
        soul.
12   Am I the Sea, or the Dragon,
        that you set a guard over me?
13   When I say, 'My bed will comfort me,
        my couch will ease my complaint,'
14   then you scare me with dreams
        and terrify me with visions,
15   so that I would choose strangling
        and death rather than this body.
16   I loathe my life; I would not live forever.
        Let me alone, for my days are a
            breath.
17   What are human beings, that you make
        so much of them,
        that you set your mind on them,
18   visit them every morning,
        test them every moment?
19   Will you not look away from me for a
        while,
        let me alone until I swallow my spittle?
20   If I sin, what do I do to you, you
        watcher of humanity?
     Why have you made me your target?

Why have I become a burden to you?
21   Why do you not pardon my
        transgression
     and take away my iniquity?
     For now I shall lie in the earth;
        you will seek me, but I shall not be."

Bildad Speaks: Job Should Repent

8   Then Bildad the Shuhite answered:
2   "How long will you say these things,
        and the words of your mouth be a
            great wind?
3   Does God pervert justice?
        Or does the Almighty *b* pervert the
            right?
4   If your children sinned against him,
        he delivered them into the power of
            their transgression.
5   If you will seek God
        and make supplication to the
            Almighty, *b*
6   if you are pure and upright,
        surely then he will rouse himself for
            you
        and restore to you your rightful place.
7   Though your beginning was small,
        your latter days will be very great.

8   "For inquire now of bygone generations,
        and consider what their ancestors
            have found;
9   for we are but of yesterday, and we
        know nothing,
        for our days on earth are but a
            shadow.
10   Will they not teach you and tell you
        and utter words out of their
            understanding?

11   "Can papyrus grow where there is no
        marsh?
        Can reeds flourish where there is no
            water?
12   While yet in flower and not cut down,
        they wither before any other plant.

---

a Or *as the thread runs out*   *b* Traditional rendering of Heb *Shaddai*

13 Such are the paths of all who forget
        God;
    the hope of the godless shall perish.
14 Their confidence is gossamer,
    a spider's house their trust.
15 If one leans against its house, it will not
        stand;
    if one lays hold of it, it will not
        endure.
16 The wicked thrive*a* before the sun,
    and their shoots spread over the
        garden.
17 Their roots twine around the stoneheap;
    they live among the rocks.*b*
18 If they are destroyed from their place,
    then it will deny them, saying, 'I have
        never seen you.'
19 See, these are their happy ways,*c*
    and out of the earth still others will
        spring.

20 "See, God will not reject a blameless
        person,
    nor take the hand of evildoers.
21 He will yet fill your mouth with laughter,
    and your lips with shouts of joy.
22 Those who hate you will be clothed with
        shame,
    and the tent of the wicked will be no
        more."

Job Replies: There Is No Mediator

9 Then Job answered:
2 "Indeed I know that this is so;
    but how can a mortal be just before
        God?
3 If one wished to contend with him,
    one could not answer him once in a
        thousand.
4 He is wise in heart, and mighty in
        strength
    —who has resisted him, and
        succeeded?—
5 he who removes mountains, and they do
        not know it,
    when he overturns them in his anger;

6 who shakes the earth out of its place,
    and its pillars tremble;
7 who commands the sun, and it does not
        rise;
    who seals up the stars;
8 who alone stretched out the heavens
    and trampled the waves of the Sea;*d*
9 who made the Bear and Orion,
    the Pleiades and the chambers of the
        south;
10 who does great things beyond
        understanding,
    and marvelous things without
        number.
11 Look, he passes by me, and I do not see
        him;
    he moves on, but I do not perceive
        him.
12 He snatches away; who can stop him?
    Who will say to him, 'What are you
        doing?'

13 "God will not turn back his anger;
    the helpers of Rahab bowed beneath
        him.
14 How then can I answer him,
    choosing my words with him?
15 Though I am innocent, I cannot answer
        him;
    I must appeal for mercy to my
        accuser.*e*
16 If I summoned him and he answered
        me,
    I do not believe that he would listen to
        my voice.
17 For he crushes me with a tempest,
    and multiplies my wounds without
        cause;
18 he will not let me get my breath,
    but fills me with bitterness.
19 If it is a contest of strength, he is the
        strong one!
    If it is a matter of justice, who can
        summon him?*f*
20 Though I am innocent, my own mouth
        would condemn me;

---

a Heb *He thrives*   *b* Gk Vg: Meaning of Heb uncertain   *c* Meaning of Heb uncertain   *d* Or *trampled the back
of the sea dragon*   *e* Or *for my right*   *f* Compare Gk: Heb *me*

though I am blameless, he would
  prove me perverse.
21 I am blameless; I do not know myself;
  I loathe my life.
22 It is all one; therefore I say,
  he destroys both the blameless and
    the wicked.
23 When disaster brings sudden death,
  he mocks at the calamity*a* of the
    innocent.
24 The earth is given into the hand of the
    wicked;
  he covers the eyes of its judges—
  if it is not he, who then is it?

25 "My days are swifter than a runner;
  they flee away, they see no good.
26 They go by like skiffs of reed,
  like an eagle swooping on the prey.
27 If I say, 'I will forget my complaint;
  I will put off my sad countenance and
    be of good cheer,'
28 I become afraid of all my suffering,
  for I know you will not hold me
    innocent.
29 I shall be condemned;
  why then do I labor in vain?
30 If I wash myself with soap
  and cleanse my hands with lye,
31 yet you will plunge me into filth,
  and my own clothes will abhor me.
32 For he is not a mortal, as I am, that I
    might answer him,
  that we should come to trial together.
33 There is no umpire*b* between us,
  who might lay his hand on us both.
34 If he would take his rod away from me,
  and not let dread of him terrify me,
35 then I would speak without fear of him,
  for I know I am not what I am
    thought to be.*c*

Job: I Loathe My Life

10 "I loathe my life;
  I will give free utterance to my
    complaint;

I will speak in the bitterness of my
    soul.
2 I will say to God, Do not condemn me;
  let me know why you contend against
    me.
3 Does it seem good to you to oppress,
  to despise the work of your hands
  and favor the schemes of the
    wicked?
4 Do you have eyes of flesh?
  Do you see as humans see?
5 Are your days like the days of
    mortals,
  or your years like human years,
6 that you seek out my iniquity
  and search for my sin,
7 although you know that I am not
    guilty,
  and there is no one to deliver out of
    your hand?
8 Your hands fashioned and made me;
  and now you turn and destroy me.*d*
9 Remember that you fashioned me like
    clay;
  and will you turn me to dust again?
10 Did you not pour me out like milk
  and curdle me like cheese?
11 You clothed me with skin and flesh,
  and knit me together with bones and
    sinews.
12 You have granted me life and steadfast
    love,
  and your care has preserved my
    spirit.
13 Yet these things you hid in your heart;
  I know that this was your purpose.
14 If I sin, you watch me,
  and do not acquit me of my iniquity.
15 If I am wicked, woe to me!
  If I am righteous, I cannot lift up my
    head,
  for I am filled with disgrace
  and look upon my affliction.
16 Bold as a lion you hunt me;
  you repeat your exploits against me.
17 You renew your witnesses against me,

---

a Meaning of Heb uncertain   *b* Another reading is *Would that there were an umpire*   *c* Cn: Heb *for I am not so in myself*   *d* Cn Compare Gk Syr: Heb *made me together all around, and you destroy me*

and increase your vexation toward me;
you bring fresh troops against me. *a*

18 "Why did you bring me forth from the
womb?
Would that I had died before any eye
had seen me,

19 and were as though I had not been,
carried from the womb to the grave.

20 Are not the days of my life few? *b*
Let me alone, that I may find a little
comfort *c*

21 before I go, never to return,
to the land of gloom and deep
darkness,

22 the land of gloom *d* and chaos,
where light is like darkness."

Zophar Speaks: Job's Guilt Deserves Punishment

11 Then Zophar the Naamathite answered:

2 "Should a multitude of words go
unanswered,
and should one full of talk be
vindicated?

3 Should your babble put others to silence,
and when you mock, shall no one
shame you?

4 For you say, 'My conduct *e* is pure,
and I am clean in God's *f* sight.'

5 But O that God would speak,
and open his lips to you,

6 and that he would tell you the secrets of
wisdom!
For wisdom is many-sided. *g*
Know then that God exacts of you less
than your guilt deserves.

7 "Can you find out the deep things of
God?
Can you find out the limit of the
Almighty? *h*

8 It is higher than heaven *i*—what can you
do?
Deeper than Sheol—what can you
know?

9 Its measure is longer than the earth,
and broader than the sea.

10 If he passes through, and imprisons,
and assembles for judgment, who can
hinder him?

11 For he knows those who are worthless;
when he sees iniquity, will he not
consider it?

12 But a stupid person will get
understanding,
when a wild ass is born human. *g*

13 "If you direct your heart rightly,
you will stretch out your hands toward
him.

14 If iniquity is in your hand, put it far
away,
and do not let wickedness reside in
your tents.

15 Surely then you will lift up your face
without blemish;
you will be secure, and will not fear.

16 You will forget your misery;
you will remember it as waters that
have passed away.

17 And your life will be brighter than the
noonday;
its darkness will be like the morning.

18 And you will have confidence, because
there is hope;
you will be protected *j* and take your
rest in safety.

19 You will lie down, and no one will make
you afraid;
many will entreat your favor.

20 But the eyes of the wicked will fail;
all way of escape will be lost to them,
and their hope is to breathe their last."

a Cn Compare Gk: Heb *toward me; changes and a troop are with me
Let him cease!* *c* Heb *that I may brighten up a little* *d* Heb *gloom as darkness, deep darkness* *e* Gk: Heb *teaching* *b* Cn Compare Gk Syr: Heb *Are not my days few?*
f Heb *your* *g* Meaning of Heb uncertain *h* Traditional rendering of Heb *Shaddai* *i* Heb *The heights of heaven* *j* Or *you will look around*

Job Replies: I Am a Laughingstock

12 Then Job answered:
2 "No doubt you are the people,
and wisdom will die with you.
3 But I have understanding as well as you;
I am not inferior to you.
Who does not know such things as
these?
4 I am a laughingstock to my friends;
I, who called upon God and he
answered me,
a just and blameless man, I am a
laughingstock.
5 Those at ease have contempt for
misfortune,*a*
but it is ready for those whose feet are
unstable.
6 The tents of robbers are at peace,
and those who provoke God are
secure,
who bring their god in their hands.*b*

7 "But ask the animals, and they will teach
you;
the birds of the air, and they will tell
you;
8 ask the plants of the earth,*c* and they will
teach you;
and the fish of the sea will declare to
you.
9 Who among all these does not know
that the hand of the LORD has done
this?
10 In his hand is the life of every living
thing
and the breath of every human being.
11 Does not the ear test words
as the palate tastes food?
12 Is wisdom with the aged,
and understanding in length of days?

13 "With God*d* are wisdom and strength;
he has counsel and understanding.
14 If he tears down, no one can rebuild;
if he shuts someone in, no one can
open up.

15 If he withholds the waters, they dry up;
if he sends them out, they overwhelm
the land.
16 With him are strength and wisdom;
the deceived and the deceiver are his.
17 He leads counselors away stripped,
and makes fools of judges.
18 He looses the sash of kings,
and binds a waistcloth on their loins.
19 He leads priests away stripped,
and overthrows the mighty.
20 He deprives of speech those who are
trusted,
and takes away the discernment of the
elders.
21 He pours contempt on princes,
and looses the belt of the strong.
22 He uncovers the deeps out of darkness,
and brings deep darkness to light.
23 He makes nations great, then destroys
them;
he enlarges nations, then leads them
away.
24 He strips understanding from the
leaders*e* of the earth,
and makes them wander in a pathless
waste.
25 They grope in the dark without light;
he makes them stagger like a
drunkard.

13 "Look, my eye has seen all this,
my ear has heard and understood it.
2 What you know, I also know;
I am not inferior to you.
3 But I would speak to the Almighty,*f*
and I desire to argue my case with
God.
4 As for you, you whitewash with lies;
all of you are worthless physicians.
5 If you would only keep silent,
that would be your wisdom!
6 Hear now my reasoning,
and listen to the pleadings of my lips.
7 Will you speak falsely for God,
and speak deceitfully for him?

---

a Meaning of Heb uncertain   *b* Or *whom God brought forth by his hand*; Meaning of Heb uncertain   *c* Or *speak to the earth*   *d* Heb *him*   *e* Heb adds *of the people*   *f* Traditional rendering of Heb *Shaddai*

8 Will you show partiality toward him,
    will you plead the case for God?
9 Will it be well with you when he searches
    you out?
    Or can you deceive him, as one
      person deceives another?
10 He will surely rebuke you
    if in secret you show partiality.
11 Will not his majesty terrify you,
    and the dread of him fall upon you?
12 Your maxims are proverbs of ashes,
    your defenses are defenses of clay.

13 "Let me have silence, and I will speak,
    and let come on me what may.
14 I will take my flesh in my teeth,
    and put my life in my hand.*a*
15 See, he will kill me; I have no hope;*b*
    but I will defend my ways to his face.
16 This will be my salvation,
    that the godless shall not come before
      him.
17 Listen carefully to my words,
    and let my declaration be in your ears.
18 I have indeed prepared my case;
    I know that I shall be vindicated.
19 Who is there that will contend with me?
    For then I would be silent and die.

Job's Despondent Prayer
20 Only grant two things to me,
    then I will not hide myself from your
      face:
21 withdraw your hand far from me,
    and do not let dread of you terrify me.
22 Then call, and I will answer;
    or let me speak, and you reply to me.
23 How many are my iniquities and my
      sins?
    Make me know my transgression and
      my sin.
24 Why do you hide your face,
    and count me as your enemy?
25 Will you frighten a windblown leaf
    and pursue dry chaff?
26 For you write bitter things against me,

and make me reap*c* the iniquities of
    my youth.
27 You put my feet in the stocks,
    and watch all my paths;
    you set a bound to the soles of my
      feet.
28 One wastes away like a rotten thing,
    like a garment that is moth-eaten.

14 "A mortal, born of woman, few of
    days and full of trouble,
2 comes up like a flower and withers,
    flees like a shadow and does not last.
3 Do you fix your eyes on such a one?
    Do you bring me into judgment with
      you?
4 Who can bring a clean thing out of an
      unclean?
    No one can.
5 Since their days are determined,
    and the number of their months is
      known to you,
    and you have appointed the bounds
      that they cannot pass,
6 look away from them, and desist,*d*
    that they may enjoy, like laborers, their
      days.

7 "For there is hope for a tree,
    if it is cut down, that it will sprout
      again,
    and that its shoots will not cease.
8 Though its root grows old in the earth,
    and its stump dies in the ground,
9 yet at the scent of water it will bud
    and put forth branches like a young
      plant.
10 But mortals die, and are laid low;
    humans expire, and where are they?
11 As waters fail from a lake,
    and a river wastes away and dries up,
12 so mortals lie down and do not rise
      again;
    until the heavens are no more, they
      will not awake
    or be roused out of their sleep.

---

a Gk: Heb *Why should I take . . . in my hand?*   *b* Or *Though he kill me, yet I will trust in him*   *c* Heb *inherit*
d Cn: Heb *that they may desist*

13 O that you would hide me in Sheol,
    that you would conceal me until your
        wrath is past,
    that you would appoint me a set time,
        and remember me!
14 If mortals die, will they live again?
    All the days of my service I would
        wait
    until my release should come.
15 You would call, and I would answer you;
    you would long for the work of your
        hands.
16 For then you would not*a* number my
        steps,
    you would not keep watch over my
        sin;
17 my transgression would be sealed up in a
        bag,
    and you would cover over my iniquity.

18 "But the mountain falls and crumbles
        away,
    and the rock is removed from its
        place;
19 the waters wear away the stones;
    the torrents wash away the soil of the
        earth;
    so you destroy the hope of mortals.
20 You prevail forever against them, and
        they pass away;
    you change their countenance, and
        send them away.
21 Their children come to honor, and they
        do not know it;
    they are brought low, and it goes
        unnoticed.
22 They feel only the pain of their own
        bodies,
    and mourn only for themselves."

Eliphaz Speaks: Job Undermines Religion

15 Then Eliphaz the Temanite answered:
2 "Should the wise answer with
        windy knowledge,
    and fill themselves with the east wind?
3 Should they argue in unprofitable talk,

or in words with which they can do no
        good?
4 But you are doing away with the fear of
        God,
    and hindering meditation before God.
5 For your iniquity teaches your mouth,
    and you choose the tongue of the
        crafty.
6 Your own mouth condemns you, and
        not I;
    your own lips testify against you.

7 "Are you the firstborn of the human
        race?
    Were you brought forth before the
        hills?
8 Have you listened in the council of
        God?
    And do you limit wisdom to yourself?
9 What do you know that we do not
        know?
    What do you understand that is not
        clear to us?
10 The gray-haired and the aged are on our
        side,
    those older than your father.
11 Are the consolations of God too small
        for you,
    or the word that deals gently with you?
12 Why does your heart carry you away,
    and why do your eyes flash,*b*
13 so that you turn your spirit against God,
    and let such words go out of your
        mouth?
14 What are mortals, that they can be clean?
    Or those born of woman, that they
        can be righteous?
15 God puts no trust even in his holy ones,
    and the heavens are not clean in his
        sight;
16 how much less one who is abominable
        and corrupt,
    one who drinks iniquity like water!

17 "I will show you; listen to me;
    what I have seen I will declare—

a Syr: Heb lacks *not*   *b* Meaning of Heb uncertain

18 what sages have told,
       and their ancestors have not hidden,
19 to whom alone the land was given,
       and no stranger passed among them.
20 The wicked writhe in pain all their days,
       through all the years that are laid up
          for the ruthless.
21 Terrifying sounds are in their ears;
       in prosperity the destroyer will come
          upon them.
22 They despair of returning from
          darkness,
       and they are destined for the sword.
23 They wander abroad for bread, saying,
          'Where is it?'
       They know that a day of darkness is
          ready at hand;
24 distress and anguish terrify them;
       they prevail against them, like a king
          prepared for battle.
25 Because they stretched out their hands
          against God,
       and bid defiance to the Almighty,*a*
26 running stubbornly against him
       with a thick-bossed shield;
27 because they have covered their faces
          with their fat,
       and gathered fat upon their loins,
28 they will live in desolate cities,
       in houses that no one should inhabit,
       houses destined to become heaps of
          ruins;
29 they will not be rich, and their wealth will
          not endure,
       nor will they strike root in the earth;*b*
30 they will not escape from darkness;
       the flame will dry up their shoots,
       and their blossom*c* will be swept
          away*d* by the wind.
31 Let them not trust in emptiness,
          deceiving themselves;
       for emptiness will be their
          recompense.
32 It will be paid in full before their time,
       and their branch will not be green.

33 They will shake off their unripe grape,
          like the vine,
       and cast off their blossoms, like the
          olive tree.
34 For the company of the godless is
          barren,
       and fire consumes the tents of bribery.
35 They conceive mischief and bring forth
          evil
       and their heart prepares deceit."

Job Reaffirms His Innocence

16 Then Job answered:
    2 "I have heard many such things;
       miserable comforters are you all.
3   Have windy words no limit?
       Or what provokes you that you keep
          on talking?
4   I also could talk as you do,
       if you were in my place;
       I could join words together against you,
       and shake my head at you.
5   I could encourage you with my mouth,
       and the solace of my lips would
          assuage your pain.

6   "If I speak, my pain is not assuaged,
       and if I forbear, how much of it
          leaves me?
7   Surely now God has worn me out;
       he has*e* made desolate all my company.
8   And he has*e* shriveled me up,
       which is a witness against me;
       my leanness has risen up against me,
       and it testifies to my face.
9   He has torn me in his wrath, and hated
          me;
       he has gnashed his teeth at me;
       my adversary sharpens his eyes against
          me.
10 They have gaped at me with their
          mouths;
       they have struck me insolently on the
          cheek;
       they mass themselves together against
          me.

---

a Traditional rendering of Heb *Shaddai*   *b* Vg: Meaning of Heb uncertain   *c* Gk: Heb *mouth*   *d* Cn: Heb *will
depart*   *e* Heb *you have*

11 God gives me up to the ungodly,
and casts me into the hands of the
wicked.
12 I was at ease, and he broke me in two;
he seized me by the neck and dashed
me to pieces;
he set me up as his target;
13   his archers surround me.
He slashes open my kidneys, and shows
no mercy;
he pours out my gall on the ground.
14 He bursts upon me again and again;
he rushes at me like a warrior.
15 I have sewed sackcloth upon my skin,
and have laid my strength in the dust.
16 My face is red with weeping,
and deep darkness is on my eyelids,
17 though there is no violence in my hands,
and my prayer is pure.

18 "O earth, do not cover my blood;
let my outcry find no resting place.
19 Even now, in fact, my witness is in
heaven,
and he that vouches for me is on high.
20 My friends scorn me;
my eye pours out tears to God,
21 that he would maintain the right of a
mortal with God,
as *a* one does for a neighbor.
22 For when a few years have come,
I shall go the way from which I shall
not return.

Job Prays for Relief

17 My spirit is broken, my days are
extinct,
the grave is ready for me.
2 Surely there are mockers around me,
and my eye dwells on their
provocation.

3 "Lay down a pledge for me with
yourself;
who is there that will give surety for
me?

4 Since you have closed their minds to
understanding,
therefore you will not let them
triumph.
5 Those who denounce friends for
reward—
the eyes of their children will fail.

6 "He has made me a byword of the
peoples,
and I am one before whom people
spit.
7 My eye has grown dim from grief,
and all my members are like a shadow.
8 The upright are appalled at this,
and the innocent stir themselves up
against the godless.
9 Yet the righteous hold to their way,
and they that have clean hands grow
stronger and stronger.
10 But you, come back now, all of you,
and I shall not find a sensible person
among you.
11 My days are past, my plans are broken
off,
the desires of my heart.
12 They make night into day;
'The light,' they say, 'is near to the
darkness.' *b*
13 If I look for Sheol as my house,
if I spread my couch in darkness,
14 if I say to the Pit, 'You are my father,'
and to the worm, 'My mother,' or 'My
sister,'
15 where then is my hope?
Who will see my hope?
16 Will it go down to the bars of Sheol?
Shall we descend together into the
dust?"

Bildad Speaks: God Punishes the Wicked

18 Then Bildad the Shuhite answered:
2 "How long will you hunt for words?
Consider, and then we shall speak.
3 Why are we counted as cattle?
Why are we stupid in your sight?

a Syr Vg Tg: Heb *and*   *b* Meaning of Heb uncertain

4 You who tear yourself in your anger—
  shall the earth be forsaken because of
    you,
  or the rock be removed out of its
    place?

5 "Surely the light of the wicked is put
    out,
  and the flame of their fire does not
    shine.
6 The light is dark in their tent,
  and the lamp above them is put out.
7 Their strong steps are shortened,
  and their own schemes throw them
    down.
8 For they are thrust into a net by their
    own feet,
  and they walk into a pitfall.
9 A trap seizes them by the heel;
  a snare lays hold of them.
10 A rope is hid for them in the ground,
  a trap for them in the path.
11 Terrors frighten them on every side,
  and chase them at their heels.
12 Their strength is consumed by hunger,[a]
  and calamity is ready for their
    stumbling.
13 By disease their skin is consumed,[b]
  the firstborn of Death consumes their
    limbs.
14 They are torn from the tent in which
    they trusted,
  and are brought to the king of terrors.
15 In their tents nothing remains;
  sulfur is scattered upon their
    habitations.
16 Their roots dry up beneath,
  and their branches wither above.
17 Their memory perishes from the earth,
  and they have no name in the street.
18 They are thrust from light into darkness,
  and driven out of the world.
19 They have no offspring or descendant
    among their people,
  and no survivor where they used to
    live.

20 They of the west are appalled at their
    fate,
  and horror seizes those of the east.
21 Surely such are the dwellings of the
    ungodly,
  such is the place of those who do not
    know God."

Job Replies: I Know That My Redeemer Lives

19 Then Job answered:
2 "How long will you torment me,
  and break me in pieces with words?
3 These ten times you have cast reproach
    upon me;
  are you not ashamed to wrong me?
4 And even if it is true that I have erred,
  my error remains with me.
5 If indeed you magnify yourselves against
    me,
  and make my humiliation an argument
    against me,
6 know then that God has put me in the
    wrong,
  and closed his net around me.
7 Even when I cry out, 'Violence!' I am
    not answered;
  I call aloud, but there is no justice.
8 He has walled up my way so that I
    cannot pass,
  and he has set darkness upon my
    paths.
9 He has stripped my glory from me,
  and taken the crown from my head.
10 He breaks me down on every side, and I
    am gone,
  he has uprooted my hope like a tree.
11 He has kindled his wrath against me,
  and counts me as his adversary.
12 His troops come on together;
  they have thrown up siegeworks[c]
    against me,
  and encamp around my tent.

13 "He has put my family far from me,
  and my acquaintances are wholly
    estranged from me.

---

a Or *Disaster is hungry for them*   *b* Cn: Heb *It consumes the limbs of his skin*   *c* Cn: Heb *their way*

14 My relatives and my close friends have
       failed me;
15   the guests in my house have forgotten
       me;
    my serving girls count me as a stranger;
       I have become an alien in their eyes.
16 I call to my servant, but he gives me no
       answer;
    I must myself plead with him.
17 My breath is repulsive to my wife;
    I am loathsome to my own family.
18 Even young children despise me;
    when I rise, they talk against me.
19 All my intimate friends abhor me,
       and those whom I loved have turned
       against me.
20 My bones cling to my skin and to my
       flesh,
    and I have escaped by the skin of my
       teeth.
21 Have pity on me, have pity on me,
       O you my friends,
    for the hand of God has touched me!
22 Why do you, like God, pursue me,
    never satisfied with my flesh?

23 "O that my words were written down!
    O that they were inscribed in a book!
24 O that with an iron pen and with lead
    they were engraved on a rock forever!
25 For I know that my Redeemer*a* lives,
       and that at the last he*b* will stand upon
       the earth;*c*
26 and after my skin has been thus
       destroyed,
    then in*d* my flesh I shall see God,*e*
27 whom I shall see on my side,*f*
    and my eyes shall behold, and not
       another.
    My heart faints within me!
28 If you say, 'How we will persecute him!'
    and, 'The root of the matter is found
       in him';
29 be afraid of the sword,
       for wrath brings the punishment of
       the sword,

so that you may know there is a
    judgment."

Zophar Speaks: Wickedness Receives Just Retribution

20 Then Zophar the Naamathite an-
       swered:
2   "Pay attention! My thoughts urge me to
       answer,
    because of the agitation within me.
3   I hear censure that insults me,
       and a spirit beyond my understanding
       answers me.
4   Do you not know this from of old,
       ever since mortals were placed on
       earth,
5   that the exulting of the wicked is short,
       and the joy of the godless is but for a
       moment?
6   Even though they mount up high as the
       heavens,
       and their head reaches to the clouds,
7   they will perish forever like their own
       dung;
       those who have seen them will say,
       'Where are they?'
8   They will fly away like a dream, and not
       be found;
       they will be chased away like a vision
       of the night.
9   The eye that saw them will see them no
       more,
       nor will their place behold them any
       longer.
10 Their children will seek the favor of the
       poor,
       and their hands will give back their
       wealth.
11 Their bodies, once full of youth,
       will lie down in the dust with them.

12 "Though wickedness is sweet in their
       mouth,
       though they hide it under their
       tongues,
13 though they are loath to let it go,

---

a Or *Vindicator*   *b* Or *that he the Last*   *c* Heb *dust*   *d* Or *without*   *e* Meaning of Heb of this verse uncertain
f Or *for myself*

and hold it in their mouths,

14 yet their food is turned in their
stomachs;
it is the venom of asps within them.

15 They swallow down riches and vomit
them up again;
God casts them out of their bellies.

16 They will suck the poison of asps;
the tongue of a viper will kill them.

17 They will not look on the rivers,
the streams flowing with honey and
curds.

18 They will give back the fruit of their toil,
and will not swallow it down;
from the profit of their trading
they will get no enjoyment.

19 For they have crushed and abandoned
the poor,
they have seized a house that they did
not build.

20 "They knew no quiet in their bellies;
in their greed they let nothing escape.

21 There was nothing left after they had
eaten;
therefore their prosperity will not
endure.

22 In full sufficiency they will be in distress;
all the force of misery will come upon
them.

23 To fill their belly to the full
God*a* will send his fierce anger into
them,
and rain it upon them as their food.*b*

24 They will flee from an iron weapon;
a bronze arrow will strike them
through.

25 It is drawn forth and comes out of their
body,
and the glittering point comes out of
their gall;
terrors come upon them.

26 Utter darkness is laid up for their
treasures;
a fire fanned by no one will devour
them;

what is left in their tent will be
consumed.

27 The heavens will reveal their iniquity,
and the earth will rise up against them.

28 The possessions of their house will be
carried away,
dragged off in the day of God's*c*
wrath.

29 This is the portion of the wicked from
God,
the heritage decreed for them by
God."

Job Replies: The Wicked Often Go Unpunished

21 Then Job answered:
2 "Listen carefully to my words,
and let this be your consolation.

3 Bear with me, and I will speak;
then after I have spoken, mock on.

4 As for me, is my complaint addressed to
mortals?
Why should I not be impatient?

5 Look at me, and be appalled,
and lay your hand upon your mouth.

6 When I think of it I am dismayed,
and shuddering seizes my flesh.

7 Why do the wicked live on,
reach old age, and grow mighty in
power?

8 Their children are established in their
presence,
and their offspring before their eyes.

9 Their houses are safe from fear,
and no rod of God is upon them.

10 Their bull breeds without fail;
their cow calves and never miscarries.

11 They send out their little ones like a
flock,
and their children dance around.

12 They sing to the tambourine and the
lyre,
and rejoice to the sound of the pipe.

13 They spend their days in prosperity,
and in peace they go down to Sheol.

14 They say to God, 'Leave us alone!
We do not desire to know your ways.

a Heb *he*   *b* Cn: Meaning of Heb uncertain   *c* Heb *his*

15 What is the Almighty,*a* that we should
　　serve him?
　　And what profit do we get if we pray
　　　to him?'

16 Is not their prosperity indeed their own
　　achievement?*b*
　　The plans of the wicked are
　　　repugnant to me.

17 "How often is the lamp of the wicked
　　put out?
　　How often does calamity come upon
　　　them?
　　How often does God*c* distribute pains
　　　in his anger?

18 How often are they like straw before the
　　wind,
　　and like chaff that the storm carries
　　　away?

19 You say, 'God stores up their iniquity for
　　their children.'
　　Let it be paid back to them, so that
　　　they may know it.

20 Let their own eyes see their destruction,
　　and let them drink of the wrath of the
　　　Almighty.*a*

21 For what do they care for their
　　household after them,
　　when the number of their months is
　　　cut off?

22 Will any teach God knowledge,
　　seeing that he judges those that are on
　　　high?

23 One dies in full prosperity,
　　being wholly at ease and secure,

24 his loins full of milk
　　and the marrow of his bones moist.

25 Another dies in bitterness of soul,
　　never having tasted of good.

26 They lie down alike in the dust,
　　and the worms cover them.

27 "Oh, I know your thoughts,
　　and your schemes to wrong me.

28 For you say, 'Where is the house of the
　　prince?

Where is the tent in which the wicked
　　lived?'

29 Have you not asked those who travel the
　　roads,
　　and do you not accept their testimony,

30 that the wicked are spared in the day of
　　calamity,
　　and are rescued in the day of wrath?

31 Who declares their way to their face,
　　and who repays them for what they
　　　have done?

32 When they are carried to the grave,
　　a watch is kept over their tomb.

33 The clods of the valley are sweet to
　　them;
　　everyone will follow after,
　　and those who went before are
　　　innumerable.

34 How then will you comfort me with
　　empty nothings?
　　There is nothing left of your answers
　　　but falsehood."

Eliphaz Speaks: Job's Wickedness Is Great

22 Then Eliphaz the Temanite answered:
2 "Can a mortal be of use to God?
　　Can even the wisest be of service to
　　　him?

3 Is it any pleasure to the Almighty*a* if you
　　are righteous,
　　or is it gain to him if you make your
　　　ways blameless?

4 Is it for your piety that he reproves you,
　　and enters into judgment with you?

5 Is not your wickedness great?
　　There is no end to your iniquities.

6 For you have exacted pledges from your
　　family for no reason,
　　and stripped the naked of their
　　　clothing.

7 You have given no water to the weary to
　　drink,
　　and you have withheld bread from the
　　　hungry.

8 The powerful possess the land,
　　and the favored live in it.

a Traditional rendering of Heb *Shaddai*　　　*b* Heb *in their hand*　　　*c* Heb *he*

9 You have sent widows away empty-
handed,
and the arms of the orphans you have
crushed.[a]

10 Therefore snares are around you,
and sudden terror overwhelms you,

11 or darkness so that you cannot see;
a flood of water covers you.

12 "Is not God high in the heavens?
See the highest stars, how lofty they
are!

13 Therefore you say, 'What does God
know?
Can he judge through the deep
darkness?

14 Thick clouds enwrap him, so that he
does not see,
and he walks on the dome of heaven.'

15 Will you keep to the old way
that the wicked have trod?

16 They were snatched away before their
time;
their foundation was washed away by
a flood.

17 They said to God, 'Leave us alone,'
and 'What can the Almighty[b] do to
us?'[c]

18 Yet he filled their houses with good
things—
but the plans of the wicked are
repugnant to me.

19 The righteous see it and are glad;
the innocent laugh them to scorn,

20 saying, 'Surely our adversaries are cut off,
and what they left, the fire has
consumed.'

21 "Agree with God,[d] and be at peace;
in this way good will come to you.

22 Receive instruction from his mouth,
and lay up his words in your heart.

23 If you return to the Almighty,[b] you will
be restored,
if you remove unrighteousness from
your tents,

24 if you treat gold like dust,
and gold of Ophir like the stones of
the torrent-bed,

25 and if the Almighty[b] is your gold
and your precious silver,

26 then you will delight yourself in the
Almighty,[b]
and lift up your face to God.

27 You will pray to him, and he will hear
you,
and you will pay your vows.

28 You will decide on a matter, and it will
be established for you,
and light will shine on your ways.

29 When others are humiliated, you say it is
pride;
for he saves the humble.

30 He will deliver even those who are guilty;
they will escape because of the
cleanness of your hands."[e]

Job Replies: My Complaint Is Bitter

23 Then Job answered:
2 "Today also my complaint is bitter;[f]
his[g] hand is heavy despite my
groaning.

3 Oh, that I knew where I might find him,
that I might come even to his
dwelling!

4 I would lay my case before him,
and fill my mouth with arguments.

5 I would learn what he would answer me,
and understand what he would say to
me.

6 Would he contend with me in the
greatness of his power?
No; but he would give heed to me.

7 There an upright person could reason
with him,
and I should be acquitted forever by
my judge.

8 "If I go forward, he is not there;
or backward, I cannot perceive him;

9 on the left he hides, and I cannot behold
him;

---

a Gk Syr Tg Vg: Heb *were crushed*   b Traditional rendering of Heb *Shaddai*   c Gk Syr: Heb *them*   d Heb *him*
e Meaning of Heb uncertain   f Syr Vg Tg: Heb *rebellious*   g Gk Syr: Heb *my*

I turn[a] to the right, but I cannot see
   him.
10 But he knows the way that I take;
   when he has tested me, I shall come
     out like gold.
11 My foot has held fast to his steps;
   I have kept his way and have not
     turned aside.
12 I have not departed from the
   commandment of his lips;
   I have treasured in[b] my bosom the
     words of his mouth.
13 But he stands alone and who can
   dissuade him?
   What he desires, that he does.
14 For he will complete what he appoints
   for me;
   and many such things are in his mind.
15 Therefore I am terrified at his presence;
   when I consider, I am in dread of
     him.
16 God has made my heart faint;
   the Almighty[c] has terrified me;
17 If only I could vanish in darkness,
   and thick darkness would cover my
     face![d]

Job Complains of Violence on the Earth

24 "Why are times not kept by the
     Almighty,[c]
   and why do those who know him
     never see his days?
2 The wicked[e] remove landmarks;
   they seize flocks and pasture them.
3 They drive away the donkey of the
   orphan;
   they take the widow's ox for a pledge.
4 They thrust the needy off the road;
   the poor of the earth all hide
     themselves.
5 Like wild asses in the desert
   they go out to their toil,
  scavenging in the wasteland
  food for their young.
6 They reap in a field not their own

and they glean in the vineyard of the
   wicked.
7 They lie all night naked, without
   clothing,
   and have no covering in the cold.
8 They are wet with the rain of the
   mountains,
   and cling to the rock for want of
     shelter.
9 "There are those who snatch the orphan
   child from the breast,
   and take as a pledge the infant of the
     poor.
10 They go about naked, without clothing;
   though hungry, they carry the sheaves;
11 between their terraces[f] they press out oil;
   they tread the wine presses, but suffer
     thirst.
12 From the city the dying groan,
   and the throat of the wounded cries
     for help;
   yet God pays no attention to their
     prayer.

13 "There are those who rebel against the
   light,
   who are not acquainted with its ways,
   and do not stay in its paths.
14 The murderer rises at dusk
   to kill the poor and needy,
   and in the night is like a thief.
15 The eye of the adulterer also waits for
   the twilight,
   saying, 'No eye will see me';
   and he disguises his face.
16 In the dark they dig through houses;
   by day they shut themselves up;
   they do not know the light.
17 For deep darkness is morning to all of
   them;
   for they are friends with the terrors of
     deep darkness.

18 "Swift are they on the face of the waters;
   their portion in the land is cursed;

---

a Syr Vg: Heb *he turns*   b Gk Vg: Heb *from*   c Traditional rendering of Heb *Shaddai*   d Or *But I am not destroyed by the darkness; he has concealed the thick darkness from me*   e Gk: Heb *they*   f Meaning of Heb uncertain

no treader turns toward their
vineyards.

19 Drought and heat snatch away the snow
waters;
so does Sheol those who have sinned.

20 The womb forgets them;
the worm finds them sweet;
they are no longer remembered;
so wickedness is broken like a tree.

21 "They harm*a* the childless woman,
and do no good to the widow.

22 Yet God*b* prolongs the life of the mighty
by his power;
they rise up when they despair of life.

23 He gives them security, and they are
supported;
his eyes are upon their ways.

24 They are exalted a little while, and then
are gone;
they wither and fade like the mallow;*c*
they are cut off like the heads of
grain.

25 If it is not so, who will prove me a liar,
and show that there is nothing in what
I say?"

Bildad Speaks: How Can a Mortal Be Righteous Before God?

25 Then Bildad the Shuhite answered:
2 "Dominion and fear are with God;*d*
he makes peace in his high heaven.

3 Is there any number to his armies?
Upon whom does his light not arise?

4 How then can a mortal be righteous
before God?
How can one born of woman be
pure?

5 If even the moon is not bright
and the stars are not pure in his sight,

6 how much less a mortal, who is a
maggot,
and a human being, who is a worm!"

Job Replies: God's Majesty Is Unsearchable

26 Then Job answered:
2 "How you have helped one who has
no power!
How you have assisted the arm that
has no strength!

3 How you have counseled one who has
no wisdom,
and given much good advice!

4 With whose help have you uttered
words,
and whose spirit has come forth from
you?

5 The shades below tremble,
the waters and their inhabitants.

6 Sheol is naked before God,
and Abaddon has no covering.

7 He stretches out Zaphon*e* over the void,
and hangs the earth upon nothing.

8 He binds up the waters in his thick
clouds,
and the cloud is not torn open by
them.

9 He covers the face of the full moon,
and spreads over it his cloud.

10 He has described a circle on the face of
the waters,
at the boundary between light and
darkness.

11 The pillars of heaven tremble,
and are astounded at his rebuke.

12 By his power he stilled the Sea;
by his understanding he struck down
Rahab.

13 By his wind the heavens were made fair;
his hand pierced the fleeing serpent.

14 These are indeed but the outskirts of his
ways;
and how small a whisper do we hear
of him!
But the thunder of his power who can
understand?"

Job Maintains His Integrity

27 Job again took up his discourse and
said:

a Gk Tg: Heb *feed on* or *associate with*   *b* Heb *he*   *c* Gk: Heb *like all others*   *d* Heb *him*   *e* Or *the North*

2 "As God lives, who has taken away my
right,
and the Almighty,*a* who has made my
soul bitter,
3 as long as my breath is in me
and the spirit of God is in my nostrils,
4 my lips will not speak falsehood,
and my tongue will not utter deceit.
5 Far be it from me to say that you are
right;
until I die I will not put away my
integrity from me.
6 I hold fast my righteousness, and will not
let it go;
my heart does not reproach me for
any of my days.

7 "May my enemy be like the wicked,
and may my opponent be like the
unrighteous.
8 For what is the hope of the godless
when God cuts them off,
when God takes away their lives?
9 Will God hear their cry
when trouble comes upon them?
10 Will they take delight in the Almighty?*a*
Will they call upon God at all times?
11 I will teach you concerning the hand of
God;
that which is with the Almighty*a* I will
not conceal.
12 All of you have seen it yourselves;
why then have you become altogether
vain?

13 "This is the portion of the wicked with
God,
and the heritage that oppressors
receive from the Almighty:*a*
14 If their children are multiplied, it is for
the sword;
and their offspring have not enough
to eat.
15 Those who survive them the pestilence
buries,

and their widows make no
lamentation.
16 Though they heap up silver like dust,
and pile up clothing like clay—
17 they may pile it up, but the just will wear
it,
and the innocent will divide the silver.
18 They build their houses like nests,
like booths made by sentinels of the
vineyard.
19 They go to bed with wealth, but will do
so no more;
they open their eyes, and it is gone.
20 Terrors overtake them like a flood;
in the night a whirlwind carries them
off.
21 The east wind lifts them up and they are
gone;
it sweeps them out of their place.
22 It*b* hurls at them without pity;
they flee from its*c* power in headlong
flight.
23 It*b* claps its*c* hands at them,
and hisses at them from its*c* place.

Interlude: Where Wisdom Is Found

28 "Surely there is a mine for silver,
and a place for gold to be refined.
2 Iron is taken out of the earth,
and copper is smelted from ore.
3 Miners put*d* an end to darkness,
and search out to the farthest bound
the ore in gloom and deep darkness.
4 They open shafts in a valley away from
human habitation;
they are forgotten by travelers,
they sway suspended, remote from
people.
5 As for the earth, out of it comes bread;
but underneath it is turned up as by
fire.
6 Its stones are the place of sapphires,*e*
and its dust contains gold.

7 "That path no bird of prey knows,
and the falcon's eye has not seen it.

---

a Traditional rendering of Heb *Shaddai*   *b* Or *He* (that is God)   *c* Or *his*   *d* Heb *He puts*
e Or *lapis lazuli*

8 The proud wild animals have not
        trodden it;
    the lion has not passed over it.

9 "They put their hand to the flinty rock,
        and overturn mountains by the roots.
10 They cut out channels in the rocks,
        and their eyes see every precious thing.
11 The sources of the rivers they probe;*a*
        hidden things they bring to light.

12 "But where shall wisdom be found?
        And where is the place of
            understanding?
13 Mortals do not know the way to it,*b*
        and it is not found in the land of the
            living.
14 The deep says, 'It is not in me,'
        and the sea says, 'It is not with me.'
15 It cannot be gotten for gold,
        and silver cannot be weighed out as its
            price.
16 It cannot be valued in the gold of Ophir,
        in precious onyx or sapphire.*c*
17 Gold and glass cannot equal it,
        nor can it be exchanged for jewels of
            fine gold.
18 No mention shall be made of coral or of
        crystal;
    the price of wisdom is above pearls.
19 The chrysolite of Ethiopia*d* cannot
        compare with it,
    nor can it be valued in pure gold.

20 "Where then does wisdom come from?
        And where is the place of
            understanding?
21 It is hidden from the eyes of all living,
        and concealed from the birds of the
            air.
22 Abaddon and Death say,
        'We have heard a rumor of it with our
            ears.'

23 "God understands the way to it,
        and he knows its place.

24 For he looks to the ends of the earth,
        and sees everything under the
            heavens.
25 When he gave to the wind its weight,
        and apportioned out the waters by
            measure;
26 when he made a decree for the rain,
        and a way for the thunderbolt;
27 then he saw it and declared it;
        he established it, and searched it out.
28 And he said to humankind,
        'Truly, the fear of the Lord, that is
            wisdom;
    and to depart from evil is
        understanding.' "

Job Finishes His Defense

29 Job again took up his discourse and
    said:
2 "O that I were as in the months of old,
        as in the days when God watched over
            me;
3 when his lamp shone over my head,
        and by his light I walked through
            darkness;
4 when I was in my prime,
        when the friendship of God was upon
            my tent;
5 when the Almighty*e* was still with me,
        when my children were around me;
6 when my steps were washed with milk,
        and the rock poured out for me
            streams of oil!
7 When I went out to the gate of the city,
        when I took my seat in the square,
8 the young men saw me and withdrew,
        and the aged rose up and stood;
9 the nobles refrained from talking,
        and laid their hands on their mouths;
10 the voices of princes were hushed,
        and their tongues stuck to the roof of
            their mouths.
11 When the ear heard, it commended me,
        and when the eye saw, it approved;
12 because I delivered the poor who cried,
        and the orphan who had no helper.

a Gk Vg: Heb *bind*   *b* Gk: Heb *its price*   *c* Or *lapis lazuli*   *d* Or *Nubia*; Heb *Cush*   *e* Traditional rendering of
Heb *Shaddai*

13 The blessing of the wretched came upon
     me,
   and I caused the widow's heart to sing
     for joy.
14 I put on righteousness, and it clothed
     me;
   my justice was like a robe and a
     turban.
15 I was eyes to the blind,
   and feet to the lame.
16 I was a father to the needy,
   and I championed the cause of the
     stranger.
17 I broke the fangs of the unrighteous,
   and made them drop their prey from
     their teeth.
18 Then I thought, 'I shall die in my nest,
   and I shall multiply my days like the
     phoenix;ᵃ
19 my roots spread out to the waters,
   with the dew all night on my
     branches;
20 my glory was fresh with me,
   and my bow ever new in my hand.'

21 "They listened to me, and waited,
   and kept silence for my counsel.
22 After I spoke they did not speak again,
   and my word dropped upon them like
     dew.ᵇ
23 They waited for me as for the rain;
   they opened their mouths as for the
     spring rain.
24 I smiled on them when they had no
     confidence;
   and the light of my countenance they
     did not extinguish.ᶜ
25 I chose their way, and sat as chief,
   and I lived like a king among his
     troops,
   like one who comforts mourners.

30 "But now they make sport of me,
   those who are younger than I,
   whose fathers I would have disdained
   to set with the dogs of my flock.

2 What could I gain from the strength of
     their hands?
   All their vigor is gone.
3 Through want and hard hunger
   they gnaw the dry and desolate
     ground,
4 they pick mallow and the leaves of
     bushes,
   and to warm themselves the roots of
     broom.
5 They are driven out from society;
   people shout after them as after a
     thief.
6 In the gullies of wadis they must live,
   in holes in the ground, and in the
     rocks.
7 Among the bushes they bray;
   under the nettles they huddle together.
8 A senseless, disreputable brood,
   they have been whipped out of the
     land.

9 "And now they mock me in song;
   I am a byword to them.
10 They abhor me, they keep aloof from
     me;
   they do not hesitate to spit at the sight
     of me.
11 Because God has loosed my bowstring
   and humbled me,
   they have cast off restraint in my
     presence.
12 On my right hand the rabble rise up;
   they send me sprawling,
   and build roads for my ruin.
13 They break up my path,
   they promote my calamity;
   no one restrainsᵈ them.
14 As through a wide breach they come;
   amid the crash they roll on.
15 Terrors are turned upon me;
   my honor is pursued as by the wind,
   and my prosperity has passed away
   like a cloud.

---

a Or *like sand*   *b* Heb lacks *like dew*   *c* Meaning of Heb uncertain   *d* Cn: Heb *helps*

16 "And now my soul is poured out within
        me;
      days of affliction have taken hold of
        me.
17 The night racks my bones,
      and the pain that gnaws me takes no
        rest.
18 With violence he seizes my garment;*a*
      he grasps me by*b* the collar of my
        tunic.
19 He has cast me into the mire,
      and I have become like dust and
        ashes.
20 I cry to you and you do not answer me;
      I stand, and you merely look at me.
21 You have turned cruel to me;
      with the might of your hand you
        persecute me.
22 You lift me up on the wind, you make
        me ride on it,
      and you toss me about in the roar of
        the storm.
23 I know that you will bring me to death,
      and to the house appointed for all
        living.

24 "Surely one does not turn against the
        needy,*c*
      when in disaster they cry for help.*d*
25 Did I not weep for those whose day was
        hard?
      Was not my soul grieved for the poor?
26 But when I looked for good, evil came;
      and when I waited for light, darkness
        came.
27 My inward parts are in turmoil, and are
        never still;
      days of affliction come to meet me.
28 I go about in sunless gloom;
      I stand up in the assembly and cry for
        help.
29 I am a brother of jackals,
      and a companion of ostriches.
30 My skin turns black and falls from me,
      and my bones burn with heat.
31 My lyre is turned to mourning,

      and my pipe to the voice of those
        who weep.

31 "I have made a covenant with my
        eyes;
      how then could I look upon a virgin?
2 What would be my portion from God
        above,
      and my heritage from the Almighty*e*
        on high?
3 Does not calamity befall the unrighteous,
      and disaster the workers of iniquity?
4 Does he not see my ways,
      and number all my steps?

5 "If I have walked with falsehood,
      and my foot has hurried to deceit—
6 let me be weighed in a just balance,
      and let God know my integrity!—
7 if my step has turned aside from the
        way,
      and my heart has followed my eyes,
      and if any spot has clung to my
        hands;
8 then let me sow, and another eat;
      and let what grows for me be rooted
        out.

9 "If my heart has been enticed by a
        woman,
      and I have lain in wait at my
        neighbor's door;
10 then let my wife grind for another,
      and let other men kneel over her.
11 For that would be a heinous crime;
      that would be a criminal offense;
12 for that would be a fire consuming down
        to Abaddon,
      and it would burn to the root all my
        harvest.

13 "If I have rejected the cause of my male
        or female slaves,
      when they brought a complaint
        against me;
14 what then shall I do when God rises up?

---

a Gk: Heb *my garment is disfigured*   *b* Heb *like*   *c* Heb *ruin*   *d* Cn: Meaning of Heb uncertain   *e* Traditional
rendering of Heb *Shaddai*

When he makes inquiry, what shall I
    answer him?
15 Did not he who made me in the womb
    make them?
    And did not one fashion us in the
        womb?

16 "If I have withheld anything that the
    poor desired,
    or have caused the eyes of the widow
        to fail,
17 or have eaten my morsel alone,
    and the orphan has not eaten from
        it—
18 for from my youth I reared the orphan*a*
    like a father,
    and from my mother's womb I guided
        the widow*b*—
19 if I have seen anyone perish for lack of
    clothing,
    or a poor person without covering,
20 whose loins have not blessed me,
    and who was not warmed with the
        fleece of my sheep;
21 if I have raised my hand against the
    orphan,
    because I saw I had supporters at the
        gate;
22 then let my shoulder blade fall from my
    shoulder,
    and let my arm be broken from its
        socket.
23 For I was in terror of calamity from
    God,
    and I could not have faced his majesty.

24 "If I have made gold my trust,
    or called fine gold my confidence;
25 if I have rejoiced because my wealth was
    great,
    or because my hand had gotten much;
26 if I have looked at the sun*c* when it
    shone,
    or the moon moving in splendor,
27 and my heart has been secretly enticed,
    and my mouth has kissed my hand;

28 this also would be an iniquity to be
    punished by the judges,
    for I should have been false to God
        above.

29 "If I have rejoiced at the ruin of those
    who hated me,
    or exulted when evil overtook them—
30 I have not let my mouth sin
    by asking for their lives with a curse—
31 if those of my tent ever said,
    'O that we might be sated with his
        flesh!'*d*—
32 the stranger has not lodged in the street;
    I have opened my doors to the
        traveler—
33 if I have concealed my transgressions as
    others do,*e*
    by hiding my iniquity in my bosom,
34 because I stood in great fear of the
    multitude,
    and the contempt of families terrified
        me,
    so that I kept silence, and did not go
        out of doors—
35 O that I had one to hear me!
    (Here is my signature! Let the
        Almighty*f* answer me!)
    O that I had the indictment written by
        my adversary!
36 Surely I would carry it on my shoulder;
    I would bind it on me like a crown;
37 I would give him an account of all my
    steps;
    like a prince I would approach him.

38 "If my land has cried out against me,
    and its furrows have wept together;
39 if I have eaten its yield without payment,
    and caused the death of its owners;
40 let thorns grow instead of wheat,
    and foul weeds instead of barley."

The words of Job are ended.

---

a Heb *him*   *b* Heb *her*   *c* Heb *the light*   *d* Meaning of Heb uncertain   *e* Or *as Adam did*   *f* Traditional
rendering of Heb *Shaddai*

Elihu Rebukes Job's Friends

32 So these three men ceased to answer Job, because he was righteous in his own eyes. 2Then Elihu son of Barachel the Buzite, of the family of Ram, became angry. He was angry at Job because he justified himself rather than God; 3he was angry also at Job's three friends because they had found no answer, though they had declared Job to be in the wrong.^a [a] 4Now Elihu had waited to speak to Job, because they were older than he. 5But when Elihu saw that there was no answer in the mouths of these three men, he became angry.

6 Elihu son of Barachel the Buzite answered:

"I am young in years,
  and you are aged;
therefore I was timid and afraid
  to declare my opinion to you.
7 I said, 'Let days speak,
  and many years teach wisdom.'
8 But truly it is the spirit in a mortal,
  the breath of the Almighty,[b] that
    makes for understanding.
9 It is not the old[c] that are wise,
  nor the aged that understand what is
    right.
10 Therefore I say, 'Listen to me;
  let me also declare my opinion.'

11 "See, I waited for your words,
  I listened for your wise sayings,
  while you searched out what to say.
12 I gave you my attention,
  but there was in fact no one that
    confuted Job,
  no one among you that answered his
    words.
13 Yet do not say, 'We have found wisdom;
  God may vanquish him, not a human.'
14 He has not directed his words against
    me,
  and I will not answer him with your
    speeches.

15 "They are dismayed, they answer no
    more;
  they have not a word to say.
16 And am I to wait, because they do not
    speak,
  because they stand there, and answer
    no more?
17 I also will give my answer;
  I also will declare my opinion.
18 For I am full of words;
  the spirit within me constrains me.
19 My heart is indeed like wine that has no
    vent;
  like new wineskins, it is ready to burst.
20 I must speak, so that I may find relief;
  I must open my lips and answer.
21 I will not show partiality to any person
  or use flattery toward anyone.
22 For I do not know how to flatter—
  or my Maker would soon put an end
    to me!

Elihu Rebukes Job

33 "But now, hear my speech, O Job,
  and listen to all my words.
2 See, I open my mouth;
  the tongue in my mouth speaks.
3 My words declare the uprightness of my
    heart,
  and what my lips know they speak
    sincerely.
4 The spirit of God has made me,
  and the breath of the Almighty[b] gives
    me life.
5 Answer me, if you can;
  set your words in order before me;
    take your stand.
6 See, before God I am as you are;
  I too was formed from a piece of clay.
7 No fear of me need terrify you;
  my pressure will not be heavy on you.

8 "Surely, you have spoken in my hearing,
  and I have heard the sound of your
    words.

---

a Another ancient tradition reads *answer, and had put God in the wrong*   *b* Traditional rendering of Heb *Shaddai*
c Gk Syr Vg: Heb *many*

9 You say, 'I am clean, without
      transgression;
   I am pure, and there is no iniquity in
      me.
10 Look, he finds occasions against me,
   he counts me as his enemy;
11 he puts my feet in the stocks,
   and watches all my paths.'

12 "But in this you are not right. I will
      answer you:
   God is greater than any mortal.
13 Why do you contend against him,
   saying, 'He will answer none of my*a*
      words'?
14 For God speaks in one way,
   and in two, though people do not
      perceive it.
15 In a dream, in a vision of the night,
   when deep sleep falls on mortals,
   while they slumber on their beds,
16 then he opens their ears,
   and terrifies them with warnings,
17 that he may turn them aside from their
      deeds,
   and keep them from pride,
18 to spare their souls from the Pit,
   their lives from traversing the River.
19 They are also chastened with pain upon
      their beds,
   and with continual strife in their
      bones,
20 so that their lives loathe bread,
   and their appetites dainty food.
21 Their flesh is so wasted away that it
      cannot be seen;
   and their bones, once invisible, now
      stick out.
22 Their souls draw near the Pit,
   and their lives to those who bring
      death.
23 Then, if there should be for one of
      them an angel,
   a mediator, one of a thousand,
   one who declares a person upright,

24 and he is gracious to that person, and
      says,
   'Deliver him from going down into
      the Pit;
   I have found a ransom;
25 let his flesh become fresh with youth;
   let him return to the days of his
      youthful vigor';
26 then he prays to God, and is accepted by
      him,
   he comes into his presence with joy,
   and God*b* repays him for his
      righteousness.
27 That person sings to others and says,
   'I sinned, and perverted what was right,
   and it was not paid back to me.
28 He has redeemed my soul from going
      down to the Pit,
   and my life shall see the light.'

29 "God indeed does all these things,
   twice, three times, with mortals,
30 to bring back their souls from the Pit,
   so that they may see the light of life.*c*
31 Pay heed, Job, listen to me;
   be silent, and I will speak.
32 If you have anything to say, answer me;
   speak, for I desire to justify you.
33 If not, listen to me;
   be silent, and I will teach you
      wisdom."

Elihu Proclaims God's Justice

34 Then Elihu continued and said:
2 "Hear my words, you wise men,
   and give ear to me, you who know;
3 for the ear tests words
   as the palate tastes food.
4 Let us choose what is right;
   let us determine among ourselves
      what is good.
5 For Job has said, 'I am innocent,
   and God has taken away my right;
6 in spite of being right I am counted a
      liar;

a Compare Gk: Heb *his*   *b* Heb *he*   *c* Syr: Heb *to be lighted with the light of life*

my wound is incurable, though I am
    without transgression.'

7   Who is there like Job,
        who drinks up scoffing like water,

8   who goes in company with evildoers
        and walks with the wicked?

9   For he has said, 'It profits one nothing
        to take delight in God.'

10 "Therefore, hear me, you who have
        sense,
            far be it from God that he should do
                wickedness,
            and from the Almighty*a* that he
                should do wrong.

11 For according to their deeds he will
        repay them,
            and according to their ways he will
                make it befall them.

12 Of a truth, God will not do wickedly,
        and the Almighty*a* will not pervert
            justice.

13 Who gave him charge over the earth
        and who laid on him*b* the whole
            world?

14 If he should take back his spirit*c* to
        himself,
            and gather to himself his breath,

15 all flesh would perish together,
        and all mortals return to dust.

16 "If you have understanding, hear this;
        listen to what I say.

17 Shall one who hates justice govern?
        Will you condemn one who is
            righteous and mighty,

18 who says to a king, 'You scoundrel!'
        and to princes, 'You wicked men!';

19 who shows no partiality to nobles,
        nor regards the rich more than the
            poor,
        for they are all the work of his hands?

20 In a moment they die;
        at midnight the people are shaken and
            pass away,

and the mighty are taken away by no
    human hand.

21 "For his eyes are upon the ways of
        mortals,
            and he sees all their steps.

22 There is no gloom or deep darkness
        where evildoers may hide themselves.

23 For he has not appointed a time*d* for
        anyone
            to go before God in judgment.

24 He shatters the mighty without
        investigation,
            and sets others in their place.

25 Thus, knowing their works,
        he overturns them in the night, and
            they are crushed.

26 He strikes them for their wickedness
        while others look on,

27 because they turned aside from
        following him,
            and had no regard for any of his ways,

28 so that they caused the cry of the poor
        to come to him,
            and he heard the cry of the
                afflicted—

29 When he is quiet, who can condemn?
        When he hides his face, who can
            behold him,
        whether it be a nation or an
            individual?—

30 so that the godless should not reign,
        or those who ensnare the people.

31 "For has anyone said to God,
        'I have endured punishment; I will not
            offend any more;

32 teach me what I do not see;
        if I have done iniquity, I will do it no
            more'?

33 Will he then pay back to suit you,
        because you reject it?
    For you must choose, and not I;
        therefore declare what you know.*e*

34 Those who have sense will say to me,
        and the wise who hear me will say,

---

a Traditional rendering of Heb *Shaddai*   *b* Heb lacks *on him*   *c* Heb *his heart his spirit*   *d* Cn: Heb *yet*
e Meaning of Heb of verses 29-33 uncertain

35 'Job speaks without knowledge,
    his words are without insight.'
36 Would that Job were tried to the limit,
    because his answers are those of the
        wicked.
37 For he adds rebellion to his sin;
    he claps his hands among us,
    and multiplies his words against God."

Elihu Condemns Self-Righteousness

35 Elihu continued and said:
2"Do you think this to be just?
    You say, 'I am in the right before
        God.'
3 If you ask, 'What advantage have I?
    How am I better off than if I had
        sinned?'
4 I will answer you
    and your friends with you.
5 Look at the heavens and see;
    observe the clouds, which are higher
        than you.
6 If you have sinned, what do you
        accomplish against him?
    And if your transgressions are
        multiplied, what do you do to
        him?
7 If you are righteous, what do you give to
        him;
    or what does he receive from your
        hand?
8 Your wickedness affects others like you,
    and your righteousness, other human
        beings.

9 "Because of the multitude of
        oppressions people cry out;
    they call for help because of the arm
        of the mighty.
10 But no one says, 'Where is God my
        Maker,
    who gives strength in the night,
11 who teaches us more than the animals of
        the earth,
    and makes us wiser than the birds of
        the air?'

12 There they cry out, but he does not
        answer,
    because of the pride of evildoers.
13 Surely God does not hear an empty cry,
    nor does the Almighty*a* regard it.
14 How much less when you say that you
        do not see him,
    that the case is before him, and you
        are waiting for him!
15 And now, because his anger does not
        punish,
    and he does not greatly heed
        transgression,*b*
16 Job opens his mouth in empty talk,
    he multiplies words without
        knowledge."

Elihu Exalts God's Goodness

36 Elihu continued and said:
2"Bear with me a little, and I will
        show you,
    for I have yet something to say on
        God's behalf.
3 I will bring my knowledge from far away,
    and ascribe righteousness to my
        Maker.
4 For truly my words are not false;
    one who is perfect in knowledge is
        with you.

5 "Surely God is mighty and does not
        despise any;
    he is mighty in strength of
        understanding.
6 He does not keep the wicked alive,
    but gives the afflicted their right.
7 He does not withdraw his eyes from the
        righteous,
    but with kings on the throne
    he sets them forever, and they are
        exalted.
8 And if they are bound in fetters
    and caught in the cords of affliction,
9 then he declares to them their work
    and their transgressions, that they are
        behaving arrogantly.

a Traditional rendering of Heb *Shaddai*   *b* Theodotion Symmachus Compare Vg: Meaning of Heb uncertain

10 He opens their ears to instruction,
  and commands that they return from
    iniquity.
11 If they listen, and serve him,
  they complete their days in prosperity,
    and their years in pleasantness.
12 But if they do not listen, they shall
    perish by the sword,
  and die without knowledge.

13 "The godless in heart cherish anger;
  they do not cry for help when he
    binds them.
14 They die in their youth,
  and their life ends in shame. *a*
15 He delivers the afflicted by their
    affliction,
  and opens their ear by adversity.
16 He also allured you out of distress
  into a broad place where there was no
    constraint,
  and what was set on your table was
    full of fatness.

17 "But you are obsessed with the case of
    the wicked;
  judgment and justice seize you.
18 Beware that wrath does not entice you
    into scoffing,
  and do not let the greatness of the
    ransom turn you aside.
19 Will your cry avail to keep you from
    distress,
  or will all the force of your strength?
20 Do not long for the night,
  when peoples are cut off in their
    place.
21 Beware! Do not turn to iniquity;
  because of that you have been tried by
    affliction.
22 See, God is exalted in his power;
  who is a teacher like him?
23 Who has prescribed for him his way,
  or who can say, 'You have done
    wrong'?

Elihu Proclaims God's Majesty

24 "Remember to extol his work,
  of which mortals have sung.
25 All people have looked on it;
  everyone watches it from far away.
26 Surely God is great, and we do not know
    him;
  the number of his years is
    unsearchable.
27 For he draws up the drops of water;
  he distills *b* his mist in rain,
28 which the skies pour down
  and drop upon mortals abundantly.
29 Can anyone understand the spreading of
    the clouds,
  the thunderings of his pavilion?
30 See, he scatters his lightning around him
  and covers the roots of the sea.
31 For by these he governs peoples;
  he gives food in abundance.
32 He covers his hands with the lightning,
  and commands it to strike the mark.
33 Its crashing *c* tells about him;
  he is jealous *c* with anger against
    iniquity.

37 "At this also my heart trembles,
  and leaps out of its place.
2 Listen, listen to the thunder of his voice
  and the rumbling that comes from his
    mouth.
3 Under the whole heaven he lets it loose,
  and his lightning to the corners of the
    earth.
4 After it his voice roars;
  he thunders with his majestic voice
  and he does not restrain the
    lightnings *d* when his voice is
    heard.
5 God thunders wondrously with his
    voice;
  he does great things that we cannot
    comprehend.
6 For to the snow he says, 'Fall on the
    earth';

a Heb *ends among the temple prostitutes*   *b* Cn: Heb *they distill*   *c* Meaning of Heb uncertain   *d* Heb *them*

and the shower of rain, his heavy
    shower of rain,

7 serves as a sign on everyone's hand,
    so that all whom he has made may
      know it.*

8 Then the animals go into their lairs
    and remain in their dens.

9 From its chamber comes the whirlwind,
    and cold from the scattering winds.

10 By the breath of God ice is given,
    and the broad waters are frozen fast.

11 He loads the thick cloud with moisture;
    the clouds scatter his lightning.

12 They turn round and round by his
      guidance,
    to accomplish all that he commands
      them
    on the face of the habitable world.

13 Whether for correction, or for his land,
    or for love, he causes it to happen.

14 "Hear this, O Job;
    stop and consider the wondrous
      works of God.

15 Do you know how God lays his
      command upon them,
    and causes the lightning of his cloud
      to shine?

16 Do you know the balancings of the
      clouds,
    the wondrous works of the one
      whose knowledge is perfect,

17 you whose garments are hot
    when the earth is still because of the
      south wind?

18 Can you, like him, spread out the skies,
    hard as a molten mirror?

19 Teach us what we shall say to him;
    we cannot draw up our case because
      of darkness.

20 Should he be told that I want to speak?
    Did anyone ever wish to be swallowed
      up?

21 Now, no one can look on the light
    when it is bright in the skies,

when the wind has passed and cleared
    them.

22 Out of the north comes golden
      splendor;
    around God is awesome majesty.

23 The Almighty*—we cannot find him;
    he is great in power and justice,
    and abundant righteousness he will
      not violate.

24 Therefore mortals fear him;
    he does not regard any who are wise
      in their own conceit."

The LORD Answers Job

38 Then the LORD answered Job out of
the whirlwind:

2 "Who is this that darkens counsel by
      words without knowledge?

3 Gird up your loins like a man,
    I will question you, and you shall
      declare to me.

4 "Where were you when I laid the
      foundation of the earth?
    Tell me, if you have understanding.

5 Who determined its measurements—
      surely you know!
    Or who stretched the line upon it?

6 On what were its bases sunk,
    or who laid its cornerstone

7 when the morning stars sang together
    and all the heavenly beings* shouted
      for joy?

8 "Or who shut in the sea with doors
    when it burst out from the womb?—

9 when I made the clouds its garment,
    and thick darkness its swaddling band,

10 and prescribed bounds for it,
    and set bars and doors,

11 and said, 'Thus far shall you come, and
      no farther,
    and here shall your proud waves be
      stopped'?

---

a Meaning of Heb of verse 7 uncertain   *b* Traditional rendering of Heb *Shaddai*   *c* Heb *sons of God*

12 "Have you commanded the morning
        since your days began,
    and caused the dawn to know its
        place,
13 so that it might take hold of the skirts of
        the earth,
    and the wicked be shaken out of it?
14 It is changed like clay under the seal,
    and it is dyed*a* like a garment.
15 Light is withheld from the wicked,
    and their uplifted arm is broken.

16 "Have you entered into the springs of
        the sea,
    or walked in the recesses of the deep?
17 Have the gates of death been revealed to
        you,
    or have you seen the gates of deep
        darkness?
18 Have you comprehended the expanse of
        the earth?
    Declare, if you know all this.

19 "Where is the way to the dwelling of
        light,
    and where is the place of darkness,
20 that you may take it to its territory
    and that you may discern the paths to
        its home?
21 Surely you know, for you were born
        then,
    and the number of your days is great!

22 "Have you entered the storehouses of
        the snow,
    or have you seen the storehouses of
        the hail,
23 which I have reserved for the time of
        trouble,
    for the day of battle and war?
24 What is the way to the place where the
        light is distributed,
    or where the east wind is scattered
        upon the earth?

25 "Who has cut a channel for the torrents
        of rain,
    and a way for the thunderbolt,
26 to bring rain on a land where no one
        lives,
    on the desert, which is empty of
        human life,
27 to satisfy the waste and desolate land,
    and to make the ground put forth
        grass?

28 "Has the rain a father,
    or who has begotten the drops of
        dew?
29 From whose womb did the ice come
        forth,
    and who has given birth to the
        hoarfrost of heaven?
30 The waters become hard like stone,
    and the face of the deep is frozen.

31 "Can you bind the chains of the
        Pleiades,
    or loose the cords of Orion?
32 Can you lead forth the Mazzaroth in
        their season,
    or can you guide the Bear with its
        children?
33 Do you know the ordinances of the
        heavens?
    Can you establish their rule on the
        earth?

34 "Can you lift up your voice to the clouds,
    so that a flood of waters may cover
        you?
35 Can you send forth lightnings, so that
        they may go
    and say to you, 'Here we are'?
36 Who has put wisdom in the inward
        parts,*b*
    or given understanding to the mind?*b*
37 Who has the wisdom to number the
        clouds?
    Or who can tilt the waterskins of the
        heavens,

a Cn: Heb *and they stand forth*   *b* Meaning of Heb uncertain

38 when the dust runs into a mass
   and the clods cling together?

39 "Can you hunt the prey for the lion,
   or satisfy the appetite of the young
      lions,
40 when they crouch in their dens,
   or lie in wait in their covert?
41 Who provides for the raven its prey,
   when its young ones cry to God,
   and wander about for lack of food?

39
"Do you know when the mountain
      goats give birth?
   Do you observe the calving of the
      deer?
2 Can you number the months that they
      fulfill,
   and do you know the time when they
      give birth,
3 when they crouch to give birth to their
      offspring,
   and are delivered of their young?
4 Their young ones become strong, they
      grow up in the open;
   they go forth, and do not return to
      them.

5 "Who has let the wild ass go free?
   Who has loosed the bonds of the
      swift ass,
6 to which I have given the steppe for its
      home,
   the salt land for its dwelling place?
7 It scorns the tumult of the city;
   it does not hear the shouts of the
      driver.
8 It ranges the mountains as its pasture,
   and it searches after every green thing.

9 "Is the wild ox willing to serve you?
   Will it spend the night at your crib?
10 Can you tie it in the furrow with ropes,
   or will it harrow the valleys after you?
11 Will you depend on it because its
      strength is great,

and will you hand over your labor to
   it?
12 Do you have faith in it that it will return,
   and bring your grain to your threshing
      floor? *a*

13 "The ostrich's wings flap wildly,
   though its pinions lack plumage. *b*
14 For it leaves its eggs to the earth,
   and lets them be warmed on the
      ground,
15 forgetting that a foot may crush them,
   and that a wild animal may trample
      them.
16 It deals cruelly with its young, as if they
      were not its own;
   though its labor should be in vain, yet
      it has no fear;
17 because God has made it forget wisdom,
   and given it no share in understanding.
18 When it spreads its plumes aloft, *b*
   it laughs at the horse and its rider.

19 "Do you give the horse its might?
   Do you clothe its neck with mane?
20 Do you make it leap like the locust?
   Its majestic snorting is terrible.
21 It paws *c* violently, exults mightily;
   it goes out to meet the weapons.
22 It laughs at fear, and is not dismayed;
   it does not turn back from the sword.
23 Upon it rattle the quiver,
   the flashing spear, and the javelin.
24 With fierceness and rage it swallows the
      ground;
   it cannot stand still at the sound of
      the trumpet.
25 When the trumpet sounds, it says 'Aha!'
   From a distance it smells the battle,
   the thunder of the captains, and the
      shouting.

26 "Is it by your wisdom that the hawk
      soars,
   and spreads its wings toward the
      south?

---

a Heb *your grain and your threshing floor*   *b* Meaning of Heb uncertain   *c* Gk Syr Vg: Heb *they dig*

27 Is it at your command that the eagle
         mounts up
     and makes its nest on high?
28 It lives on the rock and makes its home
     in the fastness of the rocky crag.
29 From there it spies the prey;
     its eyes see it from far away.
30 Its young ones suck up blood;
     and where the slain are, there it is."

40 And the LORD said to Job:
2 "Shall a faultfinder contend with the
     Almighty?ᵃ
     Anyone who argues with God must
         respond."

Job's Response to God

3 Then Job answered the LORD:
4 "See, I am of small account; what shall I
         answer you?
     I lay my hand on my mouth.
5 I have spoken once, and I will not
         answer;
     twice, but will proceed no further."

God's Challenge to Job

6 Then the LORD answered Job out of the
whirlwind:
7 "Gird up your loins like a man;
     I will question you, and you declare to
         me.
8 Will you even put me in the wrong?
     Will you condemn me that you may
         be justified?
9 Have you an arm like God,
     and can you thunder with a voice like
         his?

10 "Deck yourself with majesty and dignity;
     clothe yourself with glory and
         splendor.
11 Pour out the overflowings of your anger,
     and look on all who are proud, and
         abase them.
12 Look on all who are proud, and bring
     them low;

tread down the wicked where they
     stand.
13 Hide them all in the dust together;
     bind their faces in the world below.ᵇ
14 Then I will also acknowledge to you
     that your own right hand can give you
         victory.

15 "Look at Behemoth,
     which I made just as I made you;
     it eats grass like an ox.
16 Its strength is in its loins,
     and its power in the muscles of its
         belly.
17 It makes its tail stiff like a cedar;
     the sinews of its thighs are knit
         together.
18 Its bones are tubes of bronze,
     its limbs like bars of iron.

19 "It is the first of the great acts of
         God—
     only its Maker can approach it with
         the sword.
20 For the mountains yield food for it
     where all the wild animals play.
21 Under the lotus plants it lies,
     in the covert of the reeds and in the
         marsh.
22 The lotus trees cover it for shade;
     the willows of the wadi surround it.
23 Even if the river is turbulent, it is not
         frightened;
     it is confident though Jordan rushes
         against its mouth.
24 Can one take it with hooksᶜ
     or pierce its nose with a snare?

41 ᵈ "Can you draw out Leviathanᵉ with a
         fishhook,
     or press down its tongue with a cord?
2 Can you put a rope in its nose,
     or pierce its jaw with a hook?
3 Will it make many supplications to you?
     Will it speak soft words to you?
4 Will it make a covenant with you

ᵃ Traditional rendering of Heb *Shaddai*   ᵇ Heb *the hidden place*   ᶜ Cn: Heb *in his eyes*   ᵈ Ch 40.25 in Heb
ᵉ Or *the crocodile*

to be taken as your servant forever?

5 Will you play with it as with a bird,
     or will you put it on leash for your
       girls?

6 Will traders bargain over it?
     Will they divide it up among the
       merchants?

7 Can you fill its skin with harpoons,
     or its head with fishing spears?

8 Lay hands on it;
     think of the battle; you will not do it
       again!

9 *a* Any hope of capturing it *b* will be
       disappointed;
     were not even the gods *c* overwhelmed
       at the sight of it?

10 No one is so fierce as to dare to stir it up.
      Who can stand before it? *d*

11 Who can confront it *d* and be safe? *e*
      —under the whole heaven, who? *f*

12 "I will not keep silence concerning its
        limbs,
      or its mighty strength, or its splendid
        frame.

13 Who can strip off its outer garment?
      Who can penetrate its double coat of
        mail? *g*

14 Who can open the doors of its face?
      There is terror all around its teeth.

15 Its back *h* is made of shields in rows,
      shut up closely as with a seal.

16 One is so near to another
      that no air can come between them.

17 They are joined one to another;
      they clasp each other and cannot be
        separated.

18 Its sneezes flash forth light,
      and its eyes are like the eyelids of the
        dawn.

19 From its mouth go flaming torches;
      sparks of fire leap out.

20 Out of its nostrils comes smoke,
      as from a boiling pot and burning
        rushes.

21 Its breath kindles coals,

and a flame comes out of its mouth.

22 In its neck abides strength,
      and terror dances before it.

23 The folds of its flesh cling together;
      it is firmly cast and immovable.

24 Its heart is as hard as stone,
      as hard as the lower millstone.

25 When it raises itself up the gods are
        afraid;
      at the crashing they are beside
        themselves.

26 Though the sword reaches it, it does not
        avail,
      nor does the spear, the dart, or the
        javelin.

27 It counts iron as straw,
      and bronze as rotten wood.

28 The arrow cannot make it flee;
      slingstones, for it, are turned to chaff.

29 Clubs are counted as chaff;
      it laughs at the rattle of javelins.

30 Its underparts are like sharp potsherds;
      it spreads itself like a threshing sledge
        on the mire.

31 It makes the deep boil like a pot;
      it makes the sea like a pot of
        ointment.

32 It leaves a shining wake behind it;
      one would think the deep to be
        white-haired.

33 On earth it has no equal,
      a creature without fear.

34 It surveys everything that is lofty;
      it is king over all that are proud."

Job Is Humbled and Satisfied

42 Then Job answered the Lord:
2 "I know that you can do all things,
      and that no purpose of yours can be
        thwarted.

3 'Who is this that hides counsel without
        knowledge?'
      Therefore I have uttered what I did not
        understand,
      things too wonderful for me, which I
        did not know.

---

a Ch 41.1 in Heb   *b* Heb *of it*   *c* Cn Compare Symmachus Syr: Heb *one is*   *d* Heb *me*   *e* Gk: Heb *that I
shall repay*   *f* Heb *to me*   *g* Gk: Heb *bridle*   *h* Cn Compare Gk Vg: Heb *pride*

4 'Hear, and I will speak;
  I will question you, and you declare to
    me.'
5 I had heard of you by the hearing of the
    ear,
  but now my eye sees you;
6 therefore I despise myself,
    and repent in dust and ashes."

Job's Friends Are Humiliated

7 After the LORD had spoken these words to Job, the LORD said to Eliphaz the Temanite: "My wrath is kindled against you and against your two friends; for you have not spoken of me what is right, as my servant Job has. 8Now therefore take seven bulls and seven rams, and go to my servant Job, and offer up for yourselves a burnt offering; and my servant Job shall pray for you, for I will accept his prayer not to deal with you according to your folly; for you have not spoken of me what is right, as my servant Job has done." 9So Eliphaz the Temanite and Bildad the Shuhite and Zophar the Naamathite went and did what the LORD had told them; and the LORD accepted Job's prayer.

Job's Fortunes Are Restored Twofold

10 And the LORD restored the fortunes of Job when he had prayed for his friends; and the LORD gave Job twice as much as he had before. 11Then there came to him all his brothers and sisters and all who had known him before, and they ate bread with him in his house; they showed him sympathy and comforted him for all the evil that the LORD had brought upon him; and each of them gave him a piece of money*a* and a gold ring. 12The LORD blessed the latter days of Job more than his beginning; and he had fourteen thousand sheep, six thousand camels, a thousand yoke of oxen, and a thousand donkeys. 13He also had seven sons and three daughters. 14He named the first Jemimah, the second Keziah, and the third Keren-happuch. 15In all the land there were no women so beautiful as Job's daughters; and their father gave them an inheritance along with their brothers. 16After this Job lived one hundred and forty years, and saw his children, and his children's children, four generations. 17And Job died, old and full of days.

a Heb *a qesitah*

THE PSALMS

BOOK I

(Psalms 1–41)

Psalm 1

The Two Ways

1 Happy are those
   who do not follow the advice of the
     wicked,
   or take the path that sinners tread,
   or sit in the seat of scoffers;
2 but their delight is in the law of the
     LORD,
   and on his law they meditate day and
     night.
3 They are like trees
   planted by streams of water,
   which yield their fruit in its season,
   and their leaves do not wither.
   In all that they do, they prosper.

4 The wicked are not so,
   but are like chaff that the wind drives
     away.
5 Therefore the wicked will not stand in
     the judgment,
   nor sinners in the congregation of
     the righteous;
6 for the LORD watches over the way of
     the righteous,
   but the way of the wicked will perish.

Psalm 2

God's Promise to His Anointed

1 Why do the nations conspire,
   and the peoples plot in vain?
2 The kings of the earth set themselves,
   and the rulers take counsel together,
   against the LORD and his anointed,
     saying,
3 "Let us burst their bonds asunder,
   and cast their cords from us."

4 He who sits in the heavens laughs;
   the LORD has them in derision.
5 Then he will speak to them in his wrath,
   and terrify them in his fury, saying,
6 "I have set my king on Zion, my holy
     hill."

7 I will tell of the decree of the LORD:
   He said to me, "You are my son;
   today I have begotten you.
8 Ask of me, and I will make the nations
     your heritage,
   and the ends of the earth your
     possession.
9 You shall break them with a rod of
     iron,
   and dash them in pieces like a potter's
     vessel."

10 Now therefore, O kings, be wise;
    be warned, O rulers of the earth.
11 Serve the LORD with fear,
    with trembling 12kiss his feet, *a*
   or he will be angry, and you will perish
     in the way;
   for his wrath is quickly kindled.

   Happy are all who take refuge in him.

Psalm 3

Trust in God under Adversity

A Psalm of David, when he fled from his
     son Absalom.

1 O LORD, how many are my foes!
   Many are rising against me;
2 many are saying to me,
   "There is no help for you *b* in God."
                                    Selah

3 But you, O LORD, are a shield around
     me,
   my glory, and the one who lifts up my
     head.

---

a Cn: Meaning of Heb of verses 11b and 12a is uncertain   *b* Syr: Heb *him*

4 I cry aloud to the LORD,
   and he answers me from his holy hill.
                   Selah

5 I lie down and sleep;
   I wake again, for the LORD sustains me.
6 I am not afraid of ten thousands of
      people
   who have set themselves against me
      all around.

7 Rise up, O LORD!
   Deliver me, O my God!
   For you strike all my enemies on the
      cheek;
   you break the teeth of the wicked.

8 Deliverance belongs to the LORD;
   may your blessing be on your people!
                   Selah

Psalm 4

Confident Plea for Deliverance from Enemies

To the leader: with stringed instruments.
A Psalm of David.

1 Answer me when I call, O God of my
      right!
   You gave me room when I was in
      distress.
   Be gracious to me, and hear my
      prayer.

2 How long, you people, shall my honor
      suffer shame?
   How long will you love vain words,
      and seek after lies?   *Selah*
3 But know that the LORD has set apart
      the faithful for himself;
   the LORD hears when I call to him.

4 When you are disturbed,*a* do not sin;
   ponder it on your beds, and be silent.
                   Selah
5 Offer right sacrifices,
   and put your trust in the LORD.

6 There are many who say, "O that we
      might see some good!
   Let the light of your face shine on us,
      O LORD!"
7 You have put gladness in my heart
   more than when their grain and wine
      abound.

8 I will both lie down and sleep in peace;
   for you alone, O LORD, make me lie
      down in safety.

Psalm 5

Trust in God for Deliverance from Enemies

To the leader: for the flutes. A Psalm
of David.

1 Give ear to my words, O LORD;
   give heed to my sighing.
2 Listen to the sound of my cry,
   my King and my God,
   for to you I pray.
3 O LORD, in the morning you hear my
      voice;
   in the morning I plead my case to
      you, and watch.

4 For you are not a God who delights in
      wickedness;
   evil will not sojourn with you.
5 The boastful will not stand before your
      eyes;
   you hate all evildoers.
6 You destroy those who speak lies;
   the LORD abhors the bloodthirsty and
      deceitful.

7 But I, through the abundance of your
      steadfast love,
   will enter your house,
   I will bow down toward your holy
      temple
   in awe of you.
8 Lead me, O LORD, in your righteousness
   because of my enemies;
   make your way straight before me.

a Or *are angry*

9 For there is no truth in their mouths;
    their hearts are destruction;
  their throats are open graves;
    they flatter with their tongues.
10 Make them bear their guilt, O God;
    let them fall by their own counsels;
  because of their many transgressions
    cast them out,
    for they have rebelled against you.

11 But let all who take refuge in you
    rejoice;
    let them ever sing for joy.
  Spread your protection over them,
    so that those who love your name
    may exult in you.
12 For you bless the righteous, O LORD;
    you cover them with favor as with a
    shield.

Psalm 6

Prayer for Recovery from Grave Illness

To the leader: with stringed instruments;
according to The Sheminith. A Psalm
of David.

1 O LORD, do not rebuke me in your
    anger,
    or discipline me in your wrath.
2 Be gracious to me, O LORD, for I am
    languishing;
  O LORD, heal me, for my bones are
    shaking with terror.
3 My soul also is struck with terror,
    while you, O LORD—how long?

4 Turn, O LORD, save my life;
    deliver me for the sake of your
    steadfast love.
5 For in death there is no remembrance of
    you;
    in Sheol who can give you praise?

6 I am weary with my moaning;
    every night I flood my bed with tears;
    I drench my couch with my weeping.

7 My eyes waste away because of grief;
    they grow weak because of all my
    foes.

8 Depart from me, all you workers of evil,
    for the LORD has heard the sound of
    my weeping.
9 The LORD has heard my supplication;
    the LORD accepts my prayer.
10 All my enemies shall be ashamed and
    struck with terror;
  they shall turn back, and in a moment
    be put to shame.

Psalm 7

Plea for Help against Persecutors

A Shiggaion of David, which he sang to
the LORD concerning Cush, a
Benjaminite.

1 O LORD my God, in you I take refuge;
    save me from all my pursuers, and
    deliver me,
2 or like a lion they will tear me apart;
    they will drag me away, with no one
    to rescue.

3 O LORD my God, if I have done this,
    if there is wrong in my hands,
4 if I have repaid my ally with harm
    or plundered my foe without cause,
5 then let the enemy pursue and overtake
    me,
    trample my life to the ground,
    and lay my soul in the dust.   *Selah*

6 Rise up, O LORD, in your anger;
    lift yourself up against the fury of my
    enemies;
  awake, O my God;*a* you have
    appointed a judgment.
7 Let the assembly of the peoples be
    gathered around you,
    and over it take your seat*b* on high.
8 The LORD judges the peoples;

a Or *awake for me*   *b* Cn: Heb *return*

judge me, O LORD, according to my
  righteousness
  and according to the integrity that is
    in me.

9 O let the evil of the wicked come to an
    end,
    but establish the righteous,
  you who test the minds and hearts,
    O righteous God.
10 God is my shield,
    who saves the upright in heart.
11 God is a righteous judge,
    and a God who has indignation every
      day.

12 If one does not repent, God*a* will whet
    his sword;
    he has bent and strung his bow;
13 he has prepared his deadly weapons,
    making his arrows fiery shafts.
14 See how they conceive evil,
    and are pregnant with mischief,
    and bring forth lies.
15 They make a pit, digging it out,
    and fall into the hole that they have
      made.
16 Their mischief returns upon their own
      heads,
    and on their own heads their violence
      descends.

17 I will give to the LORD the thanks due to
    his righteousness,
    and sing praise to the name of the
      LORD, the Most High.

Psalm 8

Divine Majesty and Human Dignity

To the leader: according to The Gittith.
A Psalm of David.

1 O LORD, our Sovereign,
    how majestic is your name in all the
      earth!

You have set your glory above the
    heavens.
2 Out of the mouths of babes and
      infants
  you have founded a bulwark because of
      your foes,
    to silence the enemy and the
      avenger.

3 When I look at your heavens, the work
    of your fingers,
    the moon and the stars that you have
      established;
4 what are human beings that you are
    mindful of them,
    mortals*b* that you care for them?

5 Yet you have made them a little lower
    than God,*c*
    and crowned them with glory and
      honor.
6 You have given them dominion over the
    works of your hands;
    you have put all things under their
      feet,
7 all sheep and oxen,
    and also the beasts of the field,
8 the birds of the air, and the fish of the
      sea,
    whatever passes along the paths of
      the seas.

9 O LORD, our Sovereign,
    how majestic is your name in all the
      earth!

Psalm 9

God's Power and Justice

To the leader: according to Muth-labben.
A Psalm of David.

1 I will give thanks to the LORD with my
      whole heart;
    I will tell of all your wonderful deeds.
2 I will be glad and exult in you;

a Heb *he*   *b* Heb *ben adam*, lit. *son of man*   *c* Or *than the divine beings* or *angels*: Heb *elohim*

I will sing praise to your name,
   O Most High.

3 When my enemies turned back,
   they stumbled and perished before
    you.
4 For you have maintained my just cause;
   you have sat on the throne giving
    righteous judgment.

5 You have rebuked the nations, you have
   destroyed the wicked;
   you have blotted out their name
    forever and ever.
6 The enemies have vanished in
   everlasting ruins;
   their cities you have rooted out;
   the very memory of them has
    perished.

7 But the LORD sits enthroned forever,
   he has established his throne for
    judgment.
8 He judges the world with righteousness;
   he judges the peoples with equity.

9 The LORD is a stronghold for the
   oppressed,
   a stronghold in times of trouble.
10 And those who know your name put
   their trust in you,
   for you, O LORD, have not forsaken
    those who seek you.

11 Sing praises to the LORD, who dwells in
   Zion.
   Declare his deeds among the peoples.
12 For he who avenges blood is mindful of
   them;
   he does not forget the cry of the
    afflicted.

13 Be gracious to me, O LORD.
   See what I suffer from those who
    hate me;
   you are the one who lifts me up from
    the gates of death,
14 so that I may recount all your praises,

and, in the gates of daughter Zion,
   rejoice in your deliverance.

15 The nations have sunk in the pit that
   they made;
   in the net that they hid has their own
    foot been caught.
16 The LORD has made himself known, he
   has executed judgment;
   the wicked are snared in the work of
    their own hands.   *Higgaion. Selah*

17 The wicked shall depart to Sheol,
   all the nations that forget God.

18 For the needy shall not always be
   forgotten,
   nor the hope of the poor perish
    forever.

19 Rise up, O LORD! Do not let mortals
   prevail;
   let the nations be judged before you.
20 Put them in fear, O LORD;
   let the nations know that they are
    only human.   *Selah*

Psalm 10

Prayer for Deliverance from Enemies

1 Why, O LORD, do you stand far off?
   Why do you hide yourself in times of
    trouble?
2 In arrogance the wicked persecute the
   poor—
   let them be caught in the schemes
    they have devised.

3 For the wicked boast of the desires of
   their heart,
   those greedy for gain curse and
    renounce the LORD.
4 In the pride of their countenance the
   wicked say, "God will not seek it
    out";
   all their thoughts are, "There is no
    God."

5 Their ways prosper at all times;
  your judgments are on high, out of
      their sight;
  as for their foes, they scoff at them.
6 They think in their heart, "We shall not
      be moved;
  throughout all generations we shall
      not meet adversity."

7 Their mouths are filled with cursing and
      deceit and oppression;
  under their tongues are mischief and
      iniquity.
8 They sit in ambush in the villages;
  in hiding places they murder the
      innocent.

  Their eyes stealthily watch for the
      helpless;
9 they lurk in secret like a lion in its
      covert;
  they lurk that they may seize the poor;
  they seize the poor and drag them off
      in their net.

10 They stoop, they crouch,
   and the helpless fall by their might.
11 They think in their heart, "God has
       forgotten,
   he has hidden his face, he will never
       see it."

12 Rise up, O LORD; O God, lift up your
       hand;
   do not forget the oppressed.
13 Why do the wicked renounce God,
   and say in their hearts, "You will not
       call us to account"?

14 But you do see! Indeed you note trouble
       and grief,
   that you may take it into your hands;
   the helpless commit themselves to you;
   you have been the helper of the
       orphan.

15 Break the arm of the wicked and
       evildoers;
   seek out their wickedness until you
       find none.
16 The LORD is king forever and ever;
   the nations shall perish from his land.

17 O LORD, you will hear the desire of the
       meek;
   you will strengthen their heart, you
       will incline your ear
18 to do justice for the orphan and the
       oppressed,
   so that those from earth may strike
       terror no more. *a*

Psalm 11

Song of Trust in God

To the leader. Of David.

1 In the LORD I take refuge; how can you
       say to me,
   "Flee like a bird to the mountains; *b*
2 for look, the wicked bend the bow,
   they have fitted their arrow to the
       string,
   to shoot in the dark at the upright in
       heart.
3 If the foundations are destroyed,
   what can the righteous do?"

4 The LORD is in his holy temple;
   the LORD's throne is in heaven.
   His eyes behold, his gaze examines
       humankind.
5 The LORD tests the righteous and the
       wicked,
   and his soul hates the lover of
       violence.
6 On the wicked he will rain coals of fire
       and sulfur;
   a scorching wind shall be the portion
       of their cup.
7 For the LORD is righteous;
   he loves righteous deeds;
   the upright shall behold his face.

a Meaning of Heb uncertain   *b* Gk Syr Jerome Tg: Heb *flee to your mountain, O bird*

Psalm 12

Plea for Help in Evil Times

To the leader: according to The
Sheminith. A Psalm of David.

1   Help, O LORD, for there is no longer
            anyone who is godly;
        the faithful have disappeared from
            humankind.
2   They utter lies to each other;
        with flattering lips and a double heart
            they speak.

3   May the LORD cut off all flattering lips,
        the tongue that makes great boasts,
4   those who say, "With our tongues we
            will prevail;
        our lips are our own—who is our
            master?"

5   "Because the poor are despoiled,
            because the needy groan,
        I will now rise up," says the LORD;
        "I will place them in the safety for
            which they long."
6   The promises of the LORD are promises
            that are pure,
        silver refined in a furnace on the
            ground,
        purified seven times.

7   You, O LORD, will protect us;
        you will guard us from this generation
            forever.
8   On every side the wicked prowl,
        as vileness is exalted among
            humankind.

Psalm 13

Prayer for Deliverance from Enemies

To the leader. A Psalm of David.

1   How long, O LORD? Will you forget me
            forever?

How long will you hide your face
            from me?
2   How long must I bear pain[a] in my soul,
        and have sorrow in my heart all day
            long?
How long shall my enemy be exalted
            over me?

3   Consider and answer me, O LORD my
            God!
        Give light to my eyes, or I will sleep
            the sleep of death,
4   and my enemy will say, "I have
            prevailed";
        my foes will rejoice because I am
            shaken.

5   But I trusted in your steadfast love;
        my heart shall rejoice in your
            salvation.
6   I will sing to the LORD,
        because he has dealt bountifully with
            me.

Psalm 14

Denunciation of Godlessness

To the leader. Of David.

1   Fools say in their hearts, "There is no
            God."
        They are corrupt, they do abominable
            deeds;
        there is no one who does good.

2   The LORD looks down from heaven on
            humankind
        to see if there are any who are wise,
        who seek after God.

3   They have all gone astray, they are all
            alike perverse;
        there is no one who does good,
        no, not one.

4   Have they no knowledge, all the
            evildoers

a Syr: Heb *hold counsels*

who eat up my people as they eat
 bread,
 and do not call upon the LORD?

5 There they shall be in great terror,
 for God is with the company of the
  righteous.
6 You would confound the plans of the
  poor,
 but the LORD is their refuge.

7 O that deliverance for Israel would
  come from Zion!
 When the LORD restores the fortunes
  of his people,
 Jacob will rejoice; Israel will be glad.

Psalm 15

Who Shall Abide in God's Sanctuary?

A Psalm of David.

1 O LORD, who may abide in your tent?
 Who may dwell on your holy hill?

2 Those who walk blamelessly, and do
  what is right,
 and speak the truth from their heart;
3 who do not slander with their tongue,
 and do no evil to their friends,
 nor take up a reproach against their
  neighbors;
4 in whose eyes the wicked are despised,
 but who honor those who fear the
  LORD;
 who stand by their oath even to their
  hurt;
5 who do not lend money at interest,
 and do not take a bribe against the
  innocent.

Those who do these things shall never
 be moved.

Psalm 16

Song of Trust and Security in God

A Miktam of David.

1 Protect me, O God, for in you I take
 refuge.
2 I say to the LORD, "You are my Lord;
 I have no good apart from you."*a*

3 As for the holy ones in the land, they are
  the noble,
 in whom is all my delight.

4 Those who choose another god multiply
  their sorrows;*b*
 their drink offerings of blood I will
  not pour out
 or take their names upon my lips.

5 The LORD is my chosen portion and my
  cup;
 you hold my lot.
6 The boundary lines have fallen for me in
  pleasant places;
 I have a goodly heritage.

7 I bless the LORD who gives me counsel;
 in the night also my heart instructs
  me.
8 I keep the LORD always before me;
 because he is at my right hand, I shall
  not be moved.

9 Therefore my heart is glad, and my soul
  rejoices;
 my body also rests secure.
10 For you do not give me up to Sheol,
 or let your faithful one see the Pit.

11 You show me the path of life.
 In your presence there is fullness of
  joy;
 in your right hand are pleasures
  forevermore.

a Jerome Tg: Meaning of Heb uncertain *b* Cn: Meaning of Heb uncertain

Psalm 17

Prayer for Deliverance from Persecutors

A Prayer of David.

1 Hear a just cause, O LORD; attend to my
    cry;
    give ear to my prayer from lips free of
    deceit.

2 From you let my vindication come;
    let your eyes see the right.

3 If you try my heart, if you visit me by
    night,
    if you test me, you will find no
    wickedness in me;
    my mouth does not transgress.

4 As for what others do, by the word of
    your lips
    I have avoided the ways of the
    violent.

5 My steps have held fast to your paths;
    my feet have not slipped.

6 I call upon you, for you will answer me,
    O God;
    incline your ear to me, hear my words.

7 Wondrously show your steadfast love,
    O savior of those who seek refuge
    from their adversaries at your right
    hand.

8 Guard me as the apple of the eye;
    hide me in the shadow of your wings,

9 from the wicked who despoil me,
    my deadly enemies who surround me.

10 They close their hearts to pity;
    with their mouths they speak
    arrogantly.

11 They track me down;*a* now they
    surround me;
    they set their eyes to cast me to the
    ground.

12 They are like a lion eager to tear,
    like a young lion lurking in ambush.

13 Rise up, O LORD, confront them,
    overthrow them!
    By your sword deliver my life from
    the wicked,

14 from mortals—by your hand, O LORD—
    from mortals whose portion in life is
    in this world.
    May their bellies be filled with what you
    have stored up for them;
    may their children have more than
    enough;
    may they leave something over to
    their little ones.

15 As for me, I shall behold your face in
    righteousness;
    when I awake I shall be satisfied,
    beholding your likeness.

Psalm 18

Royal Thanksgiving for Victory

To the leader. A Psalm of David the
servant of the LORD, who addressed the
words of this song to the LORD on the
day when the LORD delivered him from
the hand of all his enemies, and from the
hand of Saul. He said:

1 I love you, O LORD, my strength.

2 The LORD is my rock, my fortress, and
    my deliverer,
    my God, my rock in whom I take
    refuge,
    my shield, and the horn of my
    salvation, my stronghold.

3 I call upon the LORD, who is worthy to
    be praised,
    so I shall be saved from my enemies.

4 The cords of death encompassed me;
    the torrents of perdition assailed me;

5 the cords of Sheol entangled me;
    the snares of death confronted me.

6 In my distress I called upon the LORD;
    to my God I cried for help.

---

a One Ms Compare Syr: MT *Our steps*

From his temple he heard my voice,
and my cry to him reached his ears.

7 Then the earth reeled and rocked;
the foundations also of the
mountains trembled
and quaked, because he was angry.

8 Smoke went up from his nostrils,
and devouring fire from his mouth;
glowing coals flamed forth from him.

9 He bowed the heavens, and came down;
thick darkness was under his feet.

10 He rode on a cherub, and flew;
he came swiftly upon the wings of
the wind.

11 He made darkness his covering around
him,
his canopy thick clouds dark with
water.

12 Out of the brightness before him
there broke through his clouds
hailstones and coals of fire.

13 The LORD also thundered in the
heavens,
and the Most High uttered his voice. *a*

14 And he sent out his arrows, and
scattered them;
he flashed forth lightnings, and
routed them.

15 Then the channels of the sea were seen,
and the foundations of the world
were laid bare
at your rebuke, O LORD,
at the blast of the breath of your
nostrils.

16 He reached down from on high, he took
me;
he drew me out of mighty waters.

17 He delivered me from my strong enemy,
and from those who hated me;
for they were too mighty for me.

18 They confronted me in the day of my
calamity;
but the LORD was my support.

19 He brought me out into a broad place;

he delivered me, because he delighted
in me.

20 The LORD rewarded me according to
my righteousness;
according to the cleanness of my
hands he recompensed me.

21 For I have kept the ways of the LORD,
and have not wickedly departed from
my God.

22 For all his ordinances were before me,
and his statutes I did not put away
from me.

23 I was blameless before him,
and I kept myself from guilt.

24 Therefore the LORD has recompensed
me according to my
righteousness,
according to the cleanness of my
hands in his sight.

25 With the loyal you show yourself loyal;
with the blameless you show yourself
blameless;

26 with the pure you show yourself pure;
and with the crooked you show
yourself perverse.

27 For you deliver a humble people,
but the haughty eyes you bring down.

28 It is you who light my lamp;
the LORD, my God, lights up my
darkness.

29 By you I can crush a troop,
and by my God I can leap over a wall.

30 This God—his way is perfect;
the promise of the LORD proves true;
he is a shield for all who take refuge
in him.

31 For who is God except the LORD?
And who is a rock besides our
God?—

32 the God who girded me with strength,
and made my way safe.

33 He made my feet like the feet of a deer,
and set me secure on the heights.

a Gk See 2 Sam 22.14: Heb adds *hailstones and coals of fire*

34 He trains my hands for war,
> so that my arms can bend a bow of
> bronze.
35 You have given me the shield of your
> salvation,
> and your right hand has supported
> me;
> your help*a* has made me great.
36 You gave me a wide place for my steps
> under me,
> and my feet did not slip.
37 I pursued my enemies and overtook
> them;
> and did not turn back until they were
> consumed.
38 I struck them down, so that they were
> not able to rise;
> they fell under my feet.
39 For you girded me with strength for the
> battle;
> you made my assailants sink under
> me.
40 You made my enemies turn their backs
> to me,
> and those who hated me I destroyed.
41 They cried for help, but there was no
> one to save them;
> they cried to the LORD, but he did not
> answer them.
42 I beat them fine, like dust before the
> wind;
> I cast them out like the mire of the
> streets.

43 You delivered me from strife with the
> peoples;*b*
> you made me head of the nations;
> people whom I had not known
> served me.
44 As soon as they heard of me they
> obeyed me;
> foreigners came cringing to me.
45 Foreigners lost heart,
> and came trembling out of their
> strongholds.

46 The LORD lives! Blessed be my rock,
> and exalted be the God of my
> salvation,
47 the God who gave me vengeance
> and subdued peoples under me;
48 who delivered me from my enemies;
> indeed, you exalted me above my
> adversaries;
> you delivered me from the violent.

49 For this I will extol you, O LORD,
> among the nations,
> and sing praises to your name.
50 Great triumphs he gives to his king,
> and shows steadfast love to his
> anointed,
> to David and his descendants forever.

Psalm 19

God's Glory in Creation and the Law

To the leader. A Psalm of David.

1 The heavens are telling the glory of
> God;
> and the firmament*c* proclaims his
> handiwork.
2 Day to day pours forth speech,
> and night to night declares
> knowledge.
3 There is no speech, nor are there words;
> their voice is not heard;
4 yet their voice*d* goes out through all the
> earth,
> and their words to the end of the
> world.

> In the heavens*e* he has set a tent for the
> sun,
5 which comes out like a bridegroom
> from his wedding canopy,
> and like a strong man runs its course
> with joy.
6 Its rising is from the end of the heavens,
> and its circuit to the end of them;
> and nothing is hid from its heat.

---

a Or *gentleness*   *b* Gk Tg: Heb *people*   *c* Or *dome*   *d* Gk Jerome Compare Syr: Heb *line*   *e* Heb *In them*

7   The law of the LORD is perfect,
        reviving the soul;
    the decrees of the LORD are sure,
        making wise the simple;
8   the precepts of the LORD are right,
        rejoicing the heart;
    the commandment of the LORD is clear,
        enlightening the eyes;
9   the fear of the LORD is pure,
        enduring forever;
    the ordinances of the LORD are true
        and righteous altogether.
10 More to be desired are they than gold,
        even much fine gold;
    sweeter also than honey,
        and drippings of the honeycomb.

11 Moreover by them is your servant
        warned;
    in keeping them there is great reward.
12 But who can detect their errors?
        Clear me from hidden faults.
13 Keep back your servant also from the
        insolent;[a]
    do not let them have dominion over
        me.
    Then I shall be blameless,
        and innocent of great transgression.

14 Let the words of my mouth and the
        meditation of my heart
    be acceptable to you,
        O LORD, my rock and my redeemer.

Psalm 20

Prayer for Victory

To the leader. A Psalm of David.

1   The LORD answer you in the day of
        trouble!
    The name of the God of Jacob
        protect you!
2   May he send you help from the
        sanctuary,
        and give you support from Zion.
3   May he remember all your offerings,
    and regard with favor your burnt
        sacrifices.   *Selah*

4   May he grant you your heart's desire,
        and fulfill all your plans.
5   May we shout for joy over your victory,
        and in the name of our God set up
            our banners.
    May the LORD fulfill all your petitions.

6   Now I know that the LORD will help his
        anointed;
    he will answer him from his holy
        heaven
    with mighty victories by his right
        hand.
7   Some take pride in chariots, and some in
        horses,
    but our pride is in the name of the
        LORD our God.
8   They will collapse and fall,
        but we shall rise and stand upright.

9   Give victory to the king, O LORD;
        answer us when we call.[b]

Psalm 21

Thanksgiving for Victory

To the leader. A Psalm of David.

1   In your strength the king rejoices,
        O LORD,
    and in your help how greatly he
        exults!
2   You have given him his heart's desire,
        and have not withheld the request of
            his lips.   *Selah*
3   For you meet him with rich blessings;
        you set a crown of fine gold on his
            head.
4   He asked you for life; you gave it to
        him—
    length of days forever and ever.
5   His glory is great through your help;
        splendor and majesty you bestow on
            him.

---

a Or *from proud thoughts*   *b* Gk: Heb *give victory, O* LORD; *let the King answer us when we call*

6 You bestow on him blessings forever;
      you make him glad with the joy of
         your presence.
7 For the king trusts in the LORD,
      and through the steadfast love of the
         Most High he shall not be
            moved.

8 Your hand will find out all your enemies;
      your right hand will find out those
         who hate you.
9 You will make them like a fiery furnace
      when you appear.
   The LORD will swallow them up in his
      wrath,
      and fire will consume them.
10 You will destroy their offspring from the
      earth,
      and their children from among
         humankind.
11 If they plan evil against you,
      if they devise mischief, they will not
         succeed.
12 For you will put them to flight;
      you will aim at their faces with your
         bows.

13 Be exalted, O LORD, in your strength!
      We will sing and praise your power.

Psalm 22

*Plea for Deliverance from Suffering and
Hostility*

To the leader: according to The Deer of
   the Dawn. A Psalm of David.

1 My God, my God, why have you
      forsaken me?
   Why are you so far from helping me,
      from the words of my groaning?
2 O my God, I cry by day, but you do not
      answer;
      and by night, but find no rest.

3 Yet you are holy,
      enthroned on the praises of Israel.

4 In you our ancestors trusted;
      they trusted, and you delivered them.
5 To you they cried, and were saved;
      in you they trusted, and were not put
         to shame.

6 But I am a worm, and not human;
      scorned by others, and despised by
         the people.
7 All who see me mock at me;
      they make mouths at me, they shake
         their heads;
8 "Commit your cause to the LORD; let
      him deliver—
      let him rescue the one in whom he
         delights!"

9 Yet it was you who took me from the
      womb;
      you kept me safe on my mother's
         breast.
10 On you I was cast from my birth,
      and since my mother bore me you
         have been my God.
11 Do not be far from me,
      for trouble is near
      and there is no one to help.

12 Many bulls encircle me,
      strong bulls of Bashan surround me;
13 they open wide their mouths at me,
      like a ravening and roaring lion.

14 I am poured out like water,
      and all my bones are out of joint;
   my heart is like wax;
      it is melted within my breast;
15 my mouth[a] is dried up like a potsherd,
      and my tongue sticks to my jaws;
      you lay me in the dust of death.

16 For dogs are all around me;
      a company of evildoers encircles me.
   My hands and feet have shriveled;[b]
17 I can count all my bones.
      They stare and gloat over me;

a Cn: Heb *strength*   b Meaning of Heb uncertain

18 they divide my clothes among
    themselves,
    and for my clothing they cast lots.

19 But you, O LORD, do not be far away!
    O my help, come quickly to my aid!
20 Deliver my soul from the sword,
    my life*a* from the power of the dog!
21 Save me from the mouth of the lion!

    From the horns of the wild oxen you
      have rescued*b* me.
22 I will tell of your name to my brothers
    and sisters;*c*
    in the midst of the congregation I
      will praise you:
23 You who fear the LORD, praise him!
    All you offspring of Jacob, glorify
      him;
    stand in awe of him, all you offspring
      of Israel!
24 For he did not despise or abhor
    the affliction of the afflicted;
    he did not hide his face from me,*d*
    but heard when I*e* cried to him.

25 From you comes my praise in the great
    congregation;
    my vows I will pay before those who
      fear him.
26 The poor*f* shall eat and be satisfied;
    those who seek him shall praise the
      LORD.
    May your hearts live forever!

27 All the ends of the earth shall
      remember
    and turn to the LORD;
    and all the families of the nations
    shall worship before him.*g*
28 For dominion belongs to the LORD,
    and he rules over the nations.

29 To him,*b* indeed, shall all who sleep in*i*
    the earth bow down;
    before him shall bow all who go
      down to the dust,
    and I shall live for him.*j*
30 Posterity will serve him;
    future generations will be told about
      the Lord,
31 and*k* proclaim his deliverance to a
    people yet unborn,
    saying that he has done it.

Psalm 23

The Divine Shepherd

A Psalm of David.

1 The LORD is my shepherd, I shall not
    want.
2 He makes me lie down in green
    pastures;
    he leads me beside still waters;*l*
3 he restores my soul.*m*
    He leads me in right paths*n*
    for his name's sake.

4 Even though I walk through the darkest
    valley,*o*
    I fear no evil;
    for you are with me;
    your rod and your staff—
    they comfort me.

5 You prepare a table before me
    in the presence of my enemies;
    you anoint my head with oil;
    my cup overflows.
6 Surely*p* goodness and mercy*q* shall
    follow me
    all the days of my life,
    and I shall dwell in the house of the
      LORD
    my whole life long.*r*

---

a Heb *my only one*   *b* Heb *answered*   *c* Or *kindred*   *d* Heb *him*   *e* Heb *he*   *f* Or *afflicted*   *g* Gk Syr Jerome:
Heb *you*   *h* Cn: Heb *They have eaten and*   *i* Cn: Heb *all the fat ones*   *j* Compare Gk Syr Vg: Heb *and he who
cannot keep himself alive*   *k* Compare Gk: Heb *it will be told about the Lord to the generation,* 31*they will come and*
l Heb *waters of rest*   *m* Or *life*   *n* Or *paths of righteousness*   *o* Or *the valley of the shadow of death*   *p* Or *Only*
q Or *kindness*   *r* Heb *for length of days*

Psalm 24

Entrance into the Temple

Of David. A Psalm.

1 The earth is the LORD's and all that is
in it,
  the world, and those who live in it;
2 for he has founded it on the seas,
  and established it on the rivers.

3 Who shall ascend the hill of the LORD?
  And who shall stand in his holy place?
4 Those who have clean hands and pure
hearts,
  who do not lift up their souls to what
is false,
  and do not swear deceitfully.
5 They will receive blessing from the
LORD,
  and vindication from the God of
their salvation.
6 Such is the company of those who seek
him,
  who seek the face of the God of
Jacob.*a*   *Selah*

7 Lift up your heads, O gates!
  and be lifted up, O ancient doors!
  that the King of glory may come in.
8 Who is the King of glory?
  The LORD, strong and mighty,
  the LORD, mighty in battle.
9 Lift up your heads, O gates!
  and be lifted up, O ancient doors!
  that the King of glory may come in.
10 Who is this King of glory?
  The LORD of hosts,
  he is the King of glory.   *Selah*

Psalm 25

Prayer for Guidance and for Deliverance

Of David.

1 To you, O LORD, I lift up my soul.
2 O my God, in you I trust;

do not let me be put to shame;
  do not let my enemies exult over me.
3 Do not let those who wait for you be
  put to shame;
  let them be ashamed who are
wantonly treacherous.

4 Make me to know your ways, O LORD;
  teach me your paths.
5 Lead me in your truth, and teach me,
  for you are the God of my salvation;
  for you I wait all day long.

6 Be mindful of your mercy, O LORD, and
  of your steadfast love,
  for they have been from of old.
7 Do not remember the sins of my youth
  or my transgressions;
  according to your steadfast love
remember me,
  for your goodness' sake, O LORD!

8 Good and upright is the LORD;
  therefore he instructs sinners in the
way.
9 He leads the humble in what is right,
  and teaches the humble his way.
10 All the paths of the LORD are steadfast
love and faithfulness,
  for those who keep his covenant and
his decrees.

11 For your name's sake, O LORD,
  pardon my guilt, for it is great.
12 Who are they that fear the LORD?
  He will teach them the way that they
should choose.

13 They will abide in prosperity,
  and their children shall possess the
land.
14 The friendship of the LORD is for those
who fear him,
  and he makes his covenant known to
them.
15 My eyes are ever toward the LORD,

---

a Gk Syr: Heb *your face, O Jacob*

for he will pluck my feet out of the
    net.

16 Turn to me and be gracious to me,
    for I am lonely and afflicted.
17 Relieve the troubles of my heart,
    and bring me*a* out of my distress.
18 Consider my affliction and my trouble,
    and forgive all my sins.

19 Consider how many are my foes,
    and with what violent hatred they
      hate me.
20 O guard my life, and deliver me;
    do not let me be put to shame, for I
      take refuge in you.
21 May integrity and uprightness preserve
    me,
    for I wait for you.

22 Redeem Israel, O God,
    out of all its troubles.

Psalm 26

Plea for Justice and Declaration of Righteousness

Of David.

1 Vindicate me, O LORD,
    for I have walked in my integrity,
    and I have trusted in the LORD
      without wavering.
2 Prove me, O LORD, and try me;
    test my heart and mind.
3 For your steadfast love is before my eyes,
    and I walk in faithfulness to you.*b*

4 I do not sit with the worthless,
    nor do I consort with hypocrites;
5 I hate the company of evildoers,
    and will not sit with the wicked.

6 I wash my hands in innocence,
    and go around your altar, O LORD,
7 singing aloud a song of thanksgiving,
    and telling all your wondrous deeds.

8 O LORD, I love the house in which you
    dwell,
    and the place where your glory abides.
9 Do not sweep me away with sinners,
    nor my life with the bloodthirsty,
10 those in whose hands are evil devices,
    and whose right hands are full of
      bribes.

11 But as for me, I walk in my integrity;
    redeem me, and be gracious to me.
12 My foot stands on level ground;
    in the great congregation I will bless
      the LORD.

Psalm 27

Triumphant Song of Confidence

Of David.

1 The LORD is my light and my salvation;
    whom shall I fear?
    The LORD is the stronghold*c* of my life;
    of whom shall I be afraid?

2 When evildoers assail me
    to devour my flesh—
    my adversaries and foes—
    they shall stumble and fall.

3 Though an army encamp against me,
    my heart shall not fear;
    though war rise up against me,
    yet I will be confident.

4 One thing I asked of the LORD,
    that will I seek after:
    to live in the house of the LORD
    all the days of my life,
    to behold the beauty of the LORD,
    and to inquire in his temple.

5 For he will hide me in his shelter
    in the day of trouble;
    he will conceal me under the cover of
      his tent;
    he will set me high on a rock.

a Or *The troubles of my heart are enlarged; bring me*   *b* Or *in your faithfulness*   *c* Or *refuge*

6 Now my head is lifted up
  above my enemies all around me,
and I will offer in his tent
  sacrifices with shouts of joy;
I will sing and make melody to the
  LORD.

7 Hear, O LORD, when I cry aloud,
  be gracious to me and answer me!
8 "Come," my heart says, "seek his face!"
  Your face, LORD, do I seek.
9 Do not hide your face from me.

  Do not turn your servant away in anger,
  you who have been my help.
  Do not cast me off, do not forsake me,
  O God of my salvation!
10 If my father and mother forsake me,
  the LORD will take me up.

11 Teach me your way, O LORD,
  and lead me on a level path
  because of my enemies.
12 Do not give me up to the will of my
  adversaries,
  for false witnesses have risen against
  me,
  and they are breathing out violence.

13 I believe that I shall see the goodness of
  the LORD
  in the land of the living.
14 Wait for the LORD;
  be strong, and let your heart take
  courage;
  wait for the LORD!

Psalm 28

Prayer for Help and Thanksgiving for It

Of David.

1 To you, O LORD, I call;
  my rock, do not refuse to hear me,
for if you are silent to me,
  I shall be like those who go down to
  the Pit.

2 Hear the voice of my supplication,
  as I cry to you for help,
  as I lift up my hands
  toward your most holy sanctuary. *a*

3 Do not drag me away with the wicked,
  with those who are workers of evil,
who speak peace with their neighbors,
  while mischief is in their hearts.
4 Repay them according to their work,
  and according to the evil of their
  deeds;
repay them according to the work of
  their hands;
  render them their due reward.
5 Because they do not regard the works of
  the LORD,
  or the work of his hands,
he will break them down and build them
  up no more.

6 Blessed be the LORD,
  for he has heard the sound of my
  pleadings.
7 The LORD is my strength and my shield;
  in him my heart trusts;
so I am helped, and my heart exults,
  and with my song I give thanks to
  him.

8 The LORD is the strength of his people;
  he is the saving refuge of his
  anointed.
9 O save your people, and bless your
  heritage;
  be their shepherd, and carry them
  forever.

Psalm 29

The Voice of God in a Great Storm

A Psalm of David.

1 Ascribe to the LORD, O heavenly
  beings, *b*
  ascribe to the LORD glory and
  strength.

a Heb *your innermost sanctuary*   *b* Heb *sons of gods*

2 Ascribe to the LORD the glory of his
    name;
        worship the LORD in holy splendor.

3 The voice of the LORD is over the waters;
    the God of glory thunders,
    the LORD, over mighty waters.
4 The voice of the LORD is powerful;
    the voice of the LORD is full of
        majesty.

5 The voice of the LORD breaks the
        cedars;
    the LORD breaks the cedars of
        Lebanon.
6 He makes Lebanon skip like a calf,
    and Sirion like a young wild ox.

7 The voice of the LORD flashes forth
        flames of fire.
8 The voice of the LORD shakes the
        wilderness;
    the LORD shakes the wilderness of
        Kadesh.

9 The voice of the LORD causes the oaks
        to whirl, *a*
    and strips the forest bare;
    and in his temple all say, "Glory!"

10 The LORD sits enthroned over the flood;
    the LORD sits enthroned as king
        forever.
11 May the LORD give strength to his
        people!
    May the LORD bless his people with
        peace!

Psalm 30

Thanksgiving for Recovery from Grave Illness

    A Psalm. A Song at the dedication of the
        temple. Of David.

1 I will extol you, O LORD, for you have
        drawn me up,

and did not let my foes rejoice over
        me.
2 O LORD my God, I cried to you for
        help,
    and you have healed me.
3 O LORD, you brought up my soul from
        Sheol,
    restored me to life from among those
        gone down to the Pit. *b*

4 Sing praises to the LORD, O you his
        faithful ones,
    and give thanks to his holy name.
5 For his anger is but for a moment;
    his favor is for a lifetime.
Weeping may linger for the night,
    but joy comes with the morning.

6 As for me, I said in my prosperity,
    "I shall never be moved."
7 By your favor, O LORD,
    you had established me as a strong
        mountain;
you hid your face;
    I was dismayed.

8 To you, O LORD, I cried,
    and to the LORD I made
        supplication:
9 "What profit is there in my death,
    if I go down to the Pit?
Will the dust praise you?
    Will it tell of your faithfulness?
10 Hear, O LORD, and be gracious to me!
    O LORD, be my helper!"

11 You have turned my mourning into
        dancing;
    you have taken off my sackcloth
    and clothed me with joy,
12 so that my soul *c* may praise you and not
        be silent.
    O LORD my God, I will give thanks to
        you forever.

---

a Or *causes the deer to calve*   *b* Or *that I should not go down to the Pit*   *c* Heb *that glory*

Psalm 31

*Prayer and Praise for Deliverance
from Enemies*

To the leader. A Psalm of David.

1 In you, O LORD, I seek refuge;
    do not let me ever be put to shame;
    in your righteousness deliver me.
2 Incline your ear to me;
    rescue me speedily.
  Be a rock of refuge for me,
    a strong fortress to save me.

3 You are indeed my rock and my fortress;
    for your name's sake lead me and
      guide me,
4 take me out of the net that is hidden for
      me,
    for you are my refuge.
5 Into your hand I commit my spirit;
    you have redeemed me, O LORD,
      faithful God.

6 You hate*a* those who pay regard to
      worthless idols,
    but I trust in the LORD.
7 I will exult and rejoice in your steadfast
      love,
    because you have seen my affliction;
    you have taken heed of my adversities,
8 and have not delivered me into the hand
      of the enemy;
    you have set my feet in a broad place.

9 Be gracious to me, O LORD, for I am in
      distress;
    my eye wastes away from grief,
    my soul and body also.
10 For my life is spent with sorrow,
    and my years with sighing;
  my strength fails because of my misery,*b*
    and my bones waste away.

11 I am the scorn of all my adversaries,
    a horror*c* to my neighbors,

an object of dread to my acquaintances;
    those who see me in the street flee
      from me.
12 I have passed out of mind like one who
      is dead;
    I have become like a broken vessel.
13 For I hear the whispering of many—
    terror all around!—
  as they scheme together against me,
    as they plot to take my life.

14 But I trust in you, O LORD;
    I say, "You are my God."
15 My times are in your hand;
    deliver me from the hand of my
      enemies and persecutors.
16 Let your face shine upon your servant;
    save me in your steadfast love.
17 Do not let me be put to shame,
      O LORD,
    for I call on you;
  let the wicked be put to shame;
    let them go dumbfounded to Sheol.
18 Let the lying lips be stilled
    that speak insolently against the
      righteous
    with pride and contempt.

19 O how abundant is your goodness
    that you have laid up for those who
      fear you,
  and accomplished for those who take
      refuge in you,
    in the sight of everyone!
20 In the shelter of your presence you hide
      them
    from human plots;
  you hold them safe under your shelter
    from contentious tongues.

21 Blessed be the LORD,
    for he has wondrously shown his
      steadfast love to me
    when I was beset as a city under siege.
22 I had said in my alarm,
    "I am driven far*d* from your sight."

---

a One Heb Ms Gk Syr Jerome: MT *I hate*   *b* Gk Syr: Heb *my iniquity*   *c* Cn: Heb *exceedingly*   *d* Another
reading is *cut off*

But you heard my supplications
  when I cried out to you for help.

23 Love the LORD, all you his saints.
  The LORD preserves the faithful,
  but abundantly repays the one who
    acts haughtily.
24 Be strong, and let your heart take
    courage,
  all you who wait for the LORD.

Psalm 32

The Joy of Forgiveness

Of David. A Maskil.

1 Happy are those whose transgression is
    forgiven,
  whose sin is covered.
2 Happy are those to whom the LORD
    imputes no iniquity,
  and in whose spirit there is no deceit.

3 While I kept silence, my body wasted
    away
  through my groaning all day long.
4 For day and night your hand was heavy
    upon me;
  my strength was dried up *a* as by the
    heat of summer.   *Selah*

5 Then I acknowledged my sin to you,
  and I did not hide my iniquity;
  I said, "I will confess my transgressions
    to the LORD,"
  and you forgave the guilt of my sin.
          Selah

6 Therefore let all who are faithful
    offer prayer to you;
  at a time of distress, *b* the rush of
    mighty waters
  shall not reach them.
7 You are a hiding place for me;
  you preserve me from trouble;
  you surround me with glad cries of
    deliverance.   *Selah*

8 I will instruct you and teach you the way
    you should go;
  I will counsel you with my eye upon
    you.
9 Do not be like a horse or a mule,
    without understanding,
  whose temper must be curbed with
    bit and bridle,
  else it will not stay near you.

10 Many are the torments of the wicked,
  but steadfast love surrounds those
    who trust in the LORD.
11 Be glad in the LORD and rejoice,
    O righteous,
  and shout for joy, all you upright in
    heart.

Psalm 33

The Greatness and Goodness of God

1 Rejoice in the LORD, O you
    righteous.
  Praise befits the upright.
2 Praise the LORD with the lyre;
  make melody to him with the harp of
    ten strings.
3 Sing to him a new song;
  play skillfully on the strings, with loud
    shouts.

4 For the word of the LORD is upright,
  and all his work is done in
    faithfulness.
5 He loves righteousness and justice;
  the earth is full of the steadfast love
    of the LORD.

6 By the word of the LORD the heavens
    were made,
  and all their host by the breath of his
    mouth.
7 He gathered the waters of the sea as in a
    bottle;
  he put the deeps in storehouses.

a Meaning of Heb uncertain   *b* Cn: Heb *at a time of finding only*

8 Let all the earth fear the LORD;
   let all the inhabitants of the world
      stand in awe of him.
9 For he spoke, and it came to be;
   he commanded, and it stood firm.

10 The LORD brings the counsel of the
      nations to nothing;
   he frustrates the plans of the peoples.
11 The counsel of the LORD stands
      forever,
   the thoughts of his heart to all
      generations.
12 Happy is the nation whose God is the
      LORD,
   the people whom he has chosen as
      his heritage.

13 The LORD looks down from heaven;
   he sees all humankind.
14 From where he sits enthroned he
      watches
   all the inhabitants of the earth—
15 he who fashions the hearts of them all,
   and observes all their deeds.
16 A king is not saved by his great army;
   a warrior is not delivered by his great
      strength.
17 The war horse is a vain hope for victory,
   and by its great might it cannot save.

18 Truly the eye of the LORD is on those
      who fear him,
   on those who hope in his steadfast
      love,
19 to deliver their soul from death,
   and to keep them alive in famine.

20 Our soul waits for the LORD;
   he is our help and shield.
21 Our heart is glad in him,
   because we trust in his holy name.
22 Let your steadfast love, O LORD, be
      upon us,
   even as we hope in you.

a Gk Syr Jerome: Heb *their*

Psalm 34

Praise for Deliverance from Trouble

Of David, when he feigned madness
before Abimelech, so that he drove him
out, and he went away.

1 I will bless the LORD at all times;
   his praise shall continually be in my
      mouth.
2 My soul makes its boast in the LORD;
   let the humble hear and be glad.
3 O magnify the LORD with me,
   and let us exalt his name together.

4 I sought the LORD, and he answered me,
   and delivered me from all my fears.
5 Look to him, and be radiant;
   so your*a* faces shall never be
      ashamed.
6 This poor soul cried, and was heard by
      the LORD,
   and was saved from every trouble.
7 The angel of the LORD encamps
   around those who fear him, and
      delivers them.
8 O taste and see that the LORD is good;
   happy are those who take refuge in
      him.
9 O fear the LORD, you his holy ones,
   for those who fear him have no want.
10 The young lions suffer want and hunger,
   but those who seek the LORD lack no
      good thing.

11 Come, O children, listen to me;
   I will teach you the fear of the LORD.
12 Which of you desires life,
   and covets many days to enjoy good?
13 Keep your tongue from evil,
   and your lips from speaking deceit.
14 Depart from evil, and do good;
   seek peace, and pursue it.

15 The eyes of the LORD are on the
      righteous,
   and his ears are open to their cry.

16 The face of the LORD is against
        evildoers,
        to cut off the remembrance of them
            from the earth.
17 When the righteous cry for help, the
        LORD hears,
        and rescues them from all their
            troubles.
18 The LORD is near to the brokenhearted,
        and saves the crushed in spirit.

19 Many are the afflictions of the
        righteous,
        but the LORD rescues them from
            them all.
20 He keeps all their bones;
        not one of them will be broken.
21 Evil brings death to the wicked,
        and those who hate the righteous will
            be condemned.
22 The LORD redeems the life of his
        servants;
        none of those who take refuge in him
            will be condemned.

Psalm 35

Prayer for Deliverance from Enemies

Of David.

1 Contend, O LORD, with those who
        contend with me;
        fight against those who fight against
            me!
2 Take hold of shield and buckler,
        and rise up to help me!
3 Draw the spear and javelin
        against my pursuers;
    say to my soul,
        "I am your salvation."

4 Let them be put to shame and
        dishonor
    who seek after my life.
    Let them be turned back and
        confounded
    who devise evil against me.

5 Let them be like chaff before the wind,
        with the angel of the LORD driving
            them on.
6 Let their way be dark and slippery,
        with the angel of the LORD pursuing
            them.

7 For without cause they hid their net*a* for
        me;
        without cause they dug a pit*b* for my
            life.
8 Let ruin come on them unawares.
    And let the net that they hid ensnare
        them;
        let them fall in it—to their ruin.

9 Then my soul shall rejoice in the LORD,
        exulting in his deliverance.
10 All my bones shall say,
        "O LORD, who is like you?
    You deliver the weak
        from those too strong for them,
        the weak and needy from those who
            despoil them."

11 Malicious witnesses rise up;
        they ask me about things I do not
            know.
12 They repay me evil for good;
        my soul is forlorn.
13 But as for me, when they were sick,
        I wore sackcloth;
        I afflicted myself with fasting.
    I prayed with head bowed*c* on my
        bosom,
14   as though I grieved for a friend or a
            brother;
    I went about as one who laments for a
        mother,
        bowed down and in mourning.

15 But at my stumbling they gathered in
        glee,
        they gathered together against me;
    ruffians whom I did not know
        tore at me without ceasing;

---

a Heb *a pit, their net*   *b* The word *pit* is transposed from the preceding line   *c* Or *My prayer turned back*

16 they impiously mocked more and more,*a*
    gnashing at me with their teeth.

17 How long, O LORD, will you look on?
    Rescue me from their ravages,
    my life from the lions!
18 Then I will thank you in the great
        congregation;
    in the mighty throng I will praise you.

19 Do not let my treacherous enemies
        rejoice over me,
    or those who hate me without cause
        wink the eye.
20 For they do not speak peace,
    but they conceive deceitful words
    against those who are quiet in the
        land.
21 They open wide their mouths against
        me;
    they say, "Aha, Aha,
    our eyes have seen it."

22 You have seen, O LORD; do not be
        silent!
    O Lord, do not be far from me!
23 Wake up! Bestir yourself for my defense,
    for my cause, my God and my Lord!
24 Vindicate me, O LORD, my God,
    according to your righteousness,
    and do not let them rejoice over me.
25 Do not let them say to themselves,
    "Aha, we have our heart's desire."
    Do not let them say, "We have
        swallowed you*b* up."

26 Let all those who rejoice at my calamity
    be put to shame and confusion;
    let those who exalt themselves against
        me
    be clothed with shame and dishonor.

27 Let those who desire my vindication
    shout for joy and be glad,
    and say evermore,
    "Great is the LORD,

who delights in the welfare of his
    servant."
28 Then my tongue shall tell of your
        righteousness
    and of your praise all day long.

Psalm 36

Human Wickedness and Divine Goodness

To the leader. Of David, the servant of
    the LORD.

1 Transgression speaks to the wicked
    deep in their hearts;
    there is no fear of God
    before their eyes.
2 For they flatter themselves in their own
        eyes
    that their iniquity cannot be found
        out and hated.
3 The words of their mouths are mischief
        and deceit;
    they have ceased to act wisely and do
        good.
4 They plot mischief while on their beds;
    they are set on a way that is not good;
    they do not reject evil.

5 Your steadfast love, O LORD, extends to
        the heavens,
    your faithfulness to the clouds.
6 Your righteousness is like the mighty
        mountains,
    your judgments are like the great deep;
    you save humans and animals alike,
        O LORD.

7 How precious is your steadfast love,
        O God!
    All people may take refuge in the
        shadow of your wings.
8 They feast on the abundance of your
        house,
    and you give them drink from the
        river of your delights.
9 For with you is the fountain of life;
    in your light we see light.

---

a Cn Compare Gk: Heb *like the profanest of mockers of a cake*   *b* Heb *him*

10 O continue your steadfast love to those
        who know you,
    and your salvation to the upright of
        heart!
11 Do not let the foot of the arrogant
        tread on me,
    or the hand of the wicked drive me
        away.
12 There the evildoers lie prostrate;
    they are thrust down, unable to rise.

Psalm 37

Exhortation to Patience and Trust

Of David.

1 Do not fret because of the wicked;
    do not be envious of wrongdoers,
2 for they will soon fade like the grass,
    and wither like the green herb.

3 Trust in the LORD, and do good;
    so you will live in the land, and enjoy
        security.
4 Take delight in the LORD,
    and he will give you the desires of
        your heart.

5 Commit your way to the LORD;
    trust in him, and he will act.
6 He will make your vindication shine like
        the light,
    and the justice of your cause like the
        noonday.

7 Be still before the LORD, and wait
        patiently for him;
    do not fret over those who prosper in
        their way,
    over those who carry out evil devices.

8 Refrain from anger, and forsake wrath.
    Do not fret—it leads only to evil.
9 For the wicked shall be cut off,
    but those who wait for the LORD shall
        inherit the land.

10 Yet a little while, and the wicked will be
        no more;
    though you look diligently for their
        place, they will not be there.
11 But the meek shall inherit the land,
    and delight themselves in abundant
        prosperity.

12 The wicked plot against the righteous,
    and gnash their teeth at them;
13 but the LORD laughs at the wicked,
    for he sees that their day is coming.

14 The wicked draw the sword and bend
        their bows
    to bring down the poor and needy,
    to kill those who walk uprightly;
15 their sword shall enter their own heart,
    and their bows shall be broken.

16 Better is a little that the righteous person
        has
    than the abundance of many wicked.
17 For the arms of the wicked shall be
        broken,
    but the LORD upholds the righteous.

18 The LORD knows the days of the
        blameless,
    and their heritage will abide forever;
19 they are not put to shame in evil times,
    in the days of famine they have
        abundance.

20 But the wicked perish,
    and the enemies of the LORD are like
        the glory of the pastures;
    they vanish—like smoke they vanish
        away.

21 The wicked borrow, and do not pay
        back,
    but the righteous are generous and
        keep giving;
22 for those blessed by the LORD shall
        inherit the land,
    but those cursed by him shall be cut
        off.

23 Our steps[a] are made firm by the LORD,
   when he delights in our[b] way;
24 though we stumble,[c] we[d] shall not fall
   headlong,
   for the LORD holds us[e] by the hand.

25 I have been young, and now am old,
   yet I have not seen the righteous
   forsaken
   or their children begging bread.
26 They are ever giving liberally and lending,
   and their children become a blessing.

27 Depart from evil, and do good;
   so you shall abide forever.
28 For the LORD loves justice;
   he will not forsake his faithful ones.

   The righteous shall be kept safe forever,
   but the children of the wicked shall
   be cut off.
29 The righteous shall inherit the land,
   and live in it forever.

30 The mouths of the righteous utter
   wisdom,
   and their tongues speak justice.
31 The law of their God is in their hearts;
   their steps do not slip.

32 The wicked watch for the righteous,
   and seek to kill them.
33 The LORD will not abandon them to
   their power,
   or let them be condemned when they
   are brought to trial.

34 Wait for the LORD, and keep to his way,
   and he will exalt you to inherit the
   land;
   you will look on the destruction of
   the wicked.

35 I have seen the wicked oppressing,
   and towering like a cedar of
   Lebanon.[f]

36 Again I[g] passed by, and they were no
   more;
   though I sought them, they could not
   be found.

37 Mark the blameless, and behold the
   upright,
   for there is posterity for the
   peaceable.
38 But transgressors shall be altogether
   destroyed;
   the posterity of the wicked shall be
   cut off.

39 The salvation of the righteous is from
   the LORD;
   he is their refuge in the time of
   trouble.
40 The LORD helps them and rescues them;
   he rescues them from the wicked, and
   saves them,
   because they take refuge in him.

Psalm 38

A Penitent Sufferer's Plea for Healing

A Psalm of David, for the memorial
offering.

1 O LORD, do not rebuke me in your
   anger,
   or discipline me in your wrath.
2 For your arrows have sunk into me,
   and your hand has come down on me.

3 There is no soundness in my flesh
   because of your indignation;
   there is no health in my bones
   because of my sin.
4 For my iniquities have gone over my
   head;
   they weigh like a burden too heavy
   for me.

5 My wounds grow foul and fester
   because of my foolishness;

a Heb *A man's steps*   *b* Heb *his*   *c* Heb *he stumbles*   *d* Heb *he*   *e* Heb *him*   *f* Gk: Meaning of Heb
uncertain   *g* Gk Syr Jerome: Heb *he*

6 I am utterly bowed down and prostrate;
      all day long I go around mourning.
7 For my loins are filled with burning,
      and there is no soundness in my flesh.
8 I am utterly spent and crushed;
      I groan because of the tumult of my
         heart.

9 O Lord, all my longing is known to you;
      my sighing is not hidden from you.
10 My heart throbs, my strength fails me;
      as for the light of my eyes—it also
         has gone from me.
11 My friends and companions stand aloof
         from my affliction,
      and my neighbors stand far off.

12 Those who seek my life lay their snares;
      those who seek to hurt me speak of
         ruin,
      and meditate treachery all day long.

13 But I am like the deaf, I do not hear;
      like the mute, who cannot speak.
14 Truly, I am like one who does not hear,
      and in whose mouth is no retort.

15 But it is for you, O Lord, that I wait;
      it is you, O Lord my God, who will
         answer.
16 For I pray, "Only do not let them rejoice
         over me,
      those who boast against me when my
         foot slips."

17 For I am ready to fall,
      and my pain is ever with me.
18 I confess my iniquity;
      I am sorry for my sin.
19 Those who are my foes without cause*a*
         are mighty,
      and many are those who hate me
         wrongfully.
20 Those who render me evil for good
      are my adversaries because I follow
         after good.

21 Do not forsake me, O Lord;
      O my God, do not be far from me;
22 make haste to help me,
      O Lord, my salvation.

Psalm 39

Prayer for Wisdom and Forgiveness

To the leader: to Jeduthun. A Psalm
         of David.

1 I said, "I will guard my ways
      that I may not sin with my tongue;
   I will keep a muzzle on my mouth
      as long as the wicked are in my
         presence."
2 I was silent and still;
      I held my peace to no avail;
   my distress grew worse,
3   my heart became hot within me.
   While I mused, the fire burned;
      then I spoke with my tongue:

4 "Lord, let me know my end,
      and what is the measure of my days;
      let me know how fleeting my life is.
5 You have made my days a few
         handbreadths,
      and my lifetime is as nothing in your
         sight.
   Surely everyone stands as a mere breath.
                                          Selah
6   Surely everyone goes about like a
         shadow.
   Surely for nothing they are in turmoil;
      they heap up, and do not know who
         will gather.

7 "And now, O Lord, what do I wait for?
      My hope is in you.
8 Deliver me from all my transgressions.
      Do not make me the scorn of the
         fool.
9 I am silent; I do not open my mouth,
      for it is you who have done it.
10 Remove your stroke from me;

a Q Ms: MT *my living foes*

I am worn down by the blows^a of
    your hand.

11 "You chastise mortals
    in punishment for sin,
consuming like a moth what is dear to
    them;
    surely everyone is a mere breath. *Selah*

12 "Hear my prayer, O LORD,
    and give ear to my cry;
    do not hold your peace at my tears.
For I am your passing guest,
    an alien, like all my forebears.
13 Turn your gaze away from me, that I
    may smile again,
    before I depart and am no more."

Psalm 40

*Thanksgiving for Deliverance and Prayer
for Help*

To the leader. Of David. A Psalm.

1 I waited patiently for the LORD;
    he inclined to me and heard my cry.
2 He drew me up from the desolate pit,^b
    out of the miry bog,
and set my feet upon a rock,
    making my steps secure.
3 He put a new song in my mouth,
    a song of praise to our God.
Many will see and fear,
    and put their trust in the LORD.

4 Happy are those who make
    the LORD their trust,
who do not turn to the proud,
    to those who go astray after false
    gods.
5 You have multiplied, O LORD my God,
    your wondrous deeds and your
    thoughts toward us;
    none can compare with you.
Were I to proclaim and tell of them,
    they would be more than can be
    counted.

6 Sacrifice and offering you do not desire,
    but you have given me an open ear.^c
Burnt offering and sin offering
    you have not required.
7 Then I said, "Here I am;
    in the scroll of the book it is written
    of me.^d
8 I delight to do your will, O my God;
    your law is within my heart."

9 I have told the glad news of deliverance
    in the great congregation;
see, I have not restrained my lips,
    as you know, O LORD.
10 I have not hidden your saving help
    within my heart,
I have spoken of your faithfulness
    and your salvation;
I have not concealed your steadfast love
    and your faithfulness
from the great congregation.

11 Do not, O LORD, withhold
    your mercy from me;
let your steadfast love and your
    faithfulness
    keep me safe forever.
12 For evils have encompassed me
    without number;
my iniquities have overtaken me,
    until I cannot see;
they are more than the hairs of my
    head,
    and my heart fails me.

13 Be pleased, O LORD, to deliver me;
    O LORD, make haste to help me.
14 Let all those be put to shame and
    confusion
    who seek to snatch away my life;
let those be turned back and brought to
    dishonor
    who desire my hurt.
15 Let those be appalled because of their
    shame
    who say to me, "Aha, Aha!"

a Heb *hostility*   *b* Cn: Heb *pit of tumult*   *c* Heb *ears you have dug for me*   *d* Meaning of Heb uncertain

16 But may all who seek you
    rejoice and be glad in you;
  may those who love your salvation
    say continually, "Great is the LORD!"
17 As for me, I am poor and needy,
    but the Lord takes thought for me.
  You are my help and my deliverer;
    do not delay, O my God.

Psalm 41

*Assurance of God's Help and a Plea
for Healing*

To the leader. A Psalm of David.

1 Happy are those who consider the
    poor;*a*
  the LORD delivers them in the day of
    trouble.
2 The LORD protects them and keeps
    them alive;
  they are called happy in the land.
  You do not give them up to the will
    of their enemies.
3 The LORD sustains them on their
    sickbed;
  in their illness you heal all their
    infirmities.*b*

4 As for me, I said, "O LORD, be gracious
    to me;
  heal me, for I have sinned against
    you."
5 My enemies wonder in malice
    when I will die, and my name perish.
6 And when they come to see me, they
    utter empty words,
  while their hearts gather mischief;
  when they go out, they tell it abroad.
7 All who hate me whisper together about
    me;
  they imagine the worst for me.

8 They think that a deadly thing has
    fastened on me,
  that I will not rise again from where I
    lie.

9 Even my bosom friend in whom I
    trusted,
  who ate of my bread, has lifted the
    heel against me.
10 But you, O LORD, be gracious to me,
    and raise me up, that I may repay
    them.

11 By this I know that you are pleased with
    me;
  because my enemy has not triumphed
    over me.
12 But you have upheld me because of my
    integrity,
  and set me in your presence forever.

13 Blessed be the LORD, the God of Israel,
  from everlasting to everlasting.
    Amen and Amen.

BOOK II

(Psalms 42–72)

Psalm 42

Longing for God and His Help in Distress

To the leader. A Maskil of the Korahites.

1 As a deer longs for flowing streams,
  so my soul longs for you, O God.
2 My soul thirsts for God,
  for the living God.
  When shall I come and behold
    the face of God?
3 My tears have been my food
  day and night,
  while people say to me continually,
    "Where is your God?"

4 These things I remember,
  as I pour out my soul:
  how I went with the throng,*c*
    and led them in procession to the
    house of God,
  with glad shouts and songs of
    thanksgiving,

a Or *weak*   *b* Heb *you change all his bed*   *c* Meaning of Heb uncertain a multitude keeping festival.

5 Why are you cast down, O my soul,
  and why are you disquieted within
    me?
  Hope in God; for I shall again praise
    him,
  my help ⁶and my God.

My soul is cast down within me;
  therefore I remember you
from the land of Jordan and of
    Hermon,
  from Mount Mizar.

7 Deep calls to deep
  at the thunder of your cataracts;
all your waves and your billows
  have gone over me.

8 By day the LORD commands his
    steadfast love,
  and at night his song is with me,
  a prayer to the God of my life.

9 I say to God, my rock,
  "Why have you forgotten me?
Why must I walk about mournfully
  because the enemy oppresses me?"

10 As with a deadly wound in my body,
  my adversaries taunt me,
while they say to me continually,
  "Where is your God?"

11 Why are you cast down, O my soul,
  and why are you disquieted within
    me?
  Hope in God; for I shall again praise
    him,
  my help and my God.

Psalm 43

Prayer to God in Time of Trouble

1 Vindicate me, O God, and defend my
    cause
  against an ungodly people;
from those who are deceitful and unjust
  deliver me!

2 For you are the God in whom I take
    refuge;
  why have you cast me off?
Why must I walk about mournfully
  because of the oppression of the
    enemy?

3 O send out your light and your truth;
  let them lead me;
let them bring me to your holy hill
  and to your dwelling.

4 Then I will go to the altar of God,
  to God my exceeding joy;
and I will praise you with the harp,
  O God, my God.

5 Why are you cast down, O my soul,
  and why are you disquieted within me?
Hope in God; for I shall again praise
    him,
  my help and my God.

Psalm 44

National Lament and Prayer for Help

To the leader. Of the Korahites.
A Maskil.

1 We have heard with our ears, O God,
  our ancestors have told us,
what deeds you performed in their days,
  in the days of old:

2 you with your own hand drove out the
    nations,
  but them you planted;
you afflicted the peoples,
  but them you set free;

3 for not by their own sword did they win
    the land,
  nor did their own arm give them
    victory;
but your right hand, and your arm,
  and the light of your countenance,
  for you delighted in them.

4 You are my King and my God;
  you command *a* victories for Jacob.

---

a Gk Syr: Heb *You are my King, O God; command*

5 Through you we push down our foes;
   through your name we tread down
      our assailants.
6 For not in my bow do I trust,
   nor can my sword save me.
7 But you have saved us from our foes,
   and have put to confusion those who
      hate us.
8 In God we have boasted continually,
   and we will give thanks to your name
      forever.   *Selah*

9 Yet you have rejected us and abased us,
   and have not gone out with our
      armies.
10 You made us turn back from the foe,
   and our enemies have gotten spoil.
11 You have made us like sheep for
      slaughter,
   and have scattered us among the
      nations.
12 You have sold your people for a trifle,
   demanding no high price for them.

13 You have made us the taunt of our
      neighbors,
   the derision and scorn of those
      around us.
14 You have made us a byword among the
      nations,
   a laughingstock*a* among the peoples.
15 All day long my disgrace is before me,
   and shame has covered my face
16 at the words of the taunters and revilers,
   at the sight of the enemy and the
      avenger.

17 All this has come upon us,
   yet we have not forgotten you,
   or been false to your covenant.
18 Our heart has not turned back,
   nor have our steps departed from
      your way,
19 yet you have broken us in the haunt of
      jackals,
   and covered us with deep darkness.

20 If we had forgotten the name of our
      God,
   or spread out our hands to a strange
      god,
21 would not God discover this?
   For he knows the secrets of the heart.
22 Because of you we are being killed all
      day long,
   and accounted as sheep for the
      slaughter.

23 Rouse yourself! Why do you sleep,
      O Lord?
   Awake, do not cast us off forever!
24 Why do you hide your face?
   Why do you forget our affliction and
      oppression?
25 For we sink down to the dust;
   our bodies cling to the ground.
26 Rise up, come to our help.
   Redeem us for the sake of your
      steadfast love.

Psalm 45

Ode for a Royal Wedding

To the leader: according to Lilies. Of the
   Korahites. A Maskil. A love song.

1 My heart overflows with a goodly
      theme;
   I address my verses to the king;
   my tongue is like the pen of a ready
      scribe.

2 You are the most handsome of men;
   grace is poured upon your lips;
   therefore God has blessed you
      forever.
3 Gird your sword on your thigh,
      O mighty one,
   in your glory and majesty.

4 In your majesty ride on victoriously
   for the cause of truth and to defend*b*
      the right;

a Heb *a shaking of the head*   *b* Cn: Heb *and the meekness of*

let your right hand teach you dread
     deeds.
5 Your arrows are sharp
     in the heart of the king's enemies;
     the peoples fall under you.

6 Your throne, O God,*a* endures forever
     and ever.
     Your royal scepter is a scepter of
        equity;
7 you love righteousness and hate
        wickedness.
Therefore God, your God, has anointed
        you
     with the oil of gladness beyond your
        companions;
8 your robes are all fragrant with myrrh
        and aloes and cassia.
From ivory palaces stringed instruments
        make you glad;
9 daughters of kings are among your
        ladies of honor;
     at your right hand stands the queen in
        gold of Ophir.

10 Hear, O daughter, consider and incline
        your ear;
     forget your people and your father's
        house,
11 and the king will desire your beauty.
Since he is your lord, bow to him;
12 the people*b* of Tyre will seek your
        favor with gifts,
     the richest of the people 13with all
        kinds of wealth.

The princess is decked in her chamber
        with gold-woven robes;*c*
14 in many-colored robes she is led to
        the king;
     behind her the virgins, her
        companions, follow.
15 With joy and gladness they are led along
     as they enter the palace of the king.

16 In the place of ancestors you, O king,*d*
        shall have sons;
     you will make them princes in all the
        earth.
17 I will cause your name to be celebrated
        in all generations;
     therefore the peoples will praise you
        forever and ever.

Psalm 46

God's Defense of His City and People

To the leader. Of the Korahites.
According to Alamoth. A Song.

1 God is our refuge and strength,
     a very present*e* help in trouble.
2 Therefore we will not fear, though the
        earth should change,
     though the mountains shake in the
        heart of the sea;
3 though its waters roar and foam,
     though the mountains tremble with
        its tumult.   *Selah*

4 There is a river whose streams make
        glad the city of God,
     the holy habitation of the Most High.
5 God is in the midst of the city;*f* it shall
        not be moved;
     God will help it when the morning
        dawns.
6 The nations are in an uproar, the
        kingdoms totter;
     he utters his voice, the earth melts.
7 The LORD of hosts is with us;
     the God of Jacob is our refuge.*g* *Selah*

8 Come, behold the works of the LORD;
     see what desolations he has brought
        on the earth.
9 He makes wars cease to the end of the
        earth;
     he breaks the bow, and shatters the
        spear;
     he burns the shields with fire.

---

a Or *Your throne is a throne of God, it*   *b* Heb *daughter*   *c* Or *people.* *13All glorious is the princess within, gold embroidery*
is her clothing   *d* Heb lacks *O king*   *e* Or *well proved*   *f* Heb *of it*   *g* Or *fortress*

10 "Be still, and know that I am God!
   I am exalted among the nations,
   I am exalted in the earth."
11 The LORD of hosts is with us;
   the God of Jacob is our refuge.*a* *Selah*

Psalm 47

God's Rule over the Nations

To the leader. Of the Korahites. A Psalm.

1 Clap your hands, all you peoples;
   shout to God with loud songs of joy.
2 For the LORD, the Most High, is
     awesome,
   a great king over all the earth.
3 He subdued peoples under us,
   and nations under our feet.
4 He chose our heritage for us,
   the pride of Jacob whom he loves.
                              Selah

5 God has gone up with a shout,
   the LORD with the sound of a
     trumpet.
6 Sing praises to God, sing praises;
   sing praises to our King, sing praises.
7 For God is the king of all the earth;
   sing praises with a psalm.*b*

8 God is king over the nations;
   God sits on his holy throne.
9 The princes of the peoples gather
   as the people of the God of
     Abraham.
   For the shields of the earth belong to
     God;
   he is highly exalted.

Psalm 48

The Glory and Strength of Zion

A Song. A Psalm of the Korahites.

1 Great is the LORD and greatly to be
     praised
   in the city of our God.

His holy mountain, 2beautiful in
     elevation,
   is the joy of all the earth,
Mount Zion, in the far north,
   the city of the great King.
3 Within its citadels God
   has shown himself a sure defense.

4 Then the kings assembled,
   they came on together.
5 As soon as they saw it, they were
     astounded;
   they were in panic, they took to flight;
6 trembling took hold of them there,
   pains as of a woman in labor,
7 as when an east wind shatters
   the ships of Tarshish.
8 As we have heard, so have we seen
   in the city of the LORD of hosts,
in the city of our God,
   which God establishes forever.   *Selah*

9 We ponder your steadfast love, O God,
   in the midst of your temple.
10 Your name, O God, like your praise,
   reaches to the ends of the earth.
   Your right hand is filled with victory.
11   Let Mount Zion be glad,
   let the towns*c* of Judah rejoice
   because of your judgments.

12 Walk about Zion, go all around it,
   count its towers,
13 consider well its ramparts;
   go through its citadels,
   that you may tell the next generation
14   that this is God,
   our God forever and ever.
   He will be our guide forever.

Psalm 49

The Folly of Trust in Riches

To the leader. Of the Korahites. A Psalm.

1 Hear this, all you peoples;
   give ear, all inhabitants of the world,

---

a Or *fortress*   *b* Heb *Maskil*   *c* Heb *daughters*

2 both low and high,
      rich and poor together.
3 My mouth shall speak wisdom;
      the meditation of my heart shall be
       understanding.
4 I will incline my ear to a proverb;
      I will solve my riddle to the music of
       the harp.

5 Why should I fear in times of trouble,
      when the iniquity of my persecutors
       surrounds me,
6 those who trust in their wealth
      and boast of the abundance of their
       riches?
7 Truly, no ransom avails for one's life,[a]
      there is no price one can give to God
       for it.
8 For the ransom of life is costly,
      and can never suffice,
9 that one should live on forever
      and never see the grave.[b]

10 When we look at the wise, they die;
       fool and dolt perish together
       and leave their wealth to others.
11 Their graves[c] are their homes forever,
       their dwelling places to all
        generations,
       though they named lands their own.
12 Mortals cannot abide in their pomp;
       they are like the animals that perish.

13 Such is the fate of the foolhardy,
       the end of those[d] who are pleased
        with their lot.   *Selah*
14 Like sheep they are appointed for Sheol;
       Death shall be their shepherd;
      straight to the grave they descend,[e]
       and their form shall waste away;
       Sheol shall be their home.[f]
15 But God will ransom my soul from the
        power of Sheol,
       for he will receive me.   *Selah*

16 Do not be afraid when some become
        rich,
       when the wealth of their houses
        increases.
17 For when they die they will carry
        nothing away;
       their wealth will not go down after
        them.
18 Though in their lifetime they count
        themselves happy
       —for you are praised when you do
        well for yourself—
19 they[g] will go to the company of their
        ancestors,
       who will never again see the light.
20 Mortals cannot abide in their pomp;
       they are like the animals that perish.

Psalm 50

The Acceptable Sacrifice

A Psalm of Asaph.

1 The mighty one, God the LORD,
      speaks and summons the earth
      from the rising of the sun to its
       setting.
2 Out of Zion, the perfection of beauty,
      God shines forth.

3 Our God comes and does not keep
       silence,
      before him is a devouring fire,
      and a mighty tempest all around him.
4 He calls to the heavens above
      and to the earth, that he may judge
       his people:
5 "Gather to me my faithful ones,
      who made a covenant with me by
       sacrifice!"
6 The heavens declare his righteousness,
      for God himself is judge.   *Selah*

7 "Hear, O my people, and I will speak,
      O Israel, I will testify against you.

---

a Another reading is *no one can ransom a brother*   *b* Heb *the pit*   *c* Gk Syr Compare Tg: Heb *their inward* (thought)
d Tg: Heb *after them*   *e* Cn: Heb *the upright shall have dominion over them in the morning*   *f* Meaning of Heb
uncertain   *g* Cn: Heb *you*

I am God, your God.

8 Not for your sacrifices do I rebuke you;
   your burnt offerings are continually
      before me.
9 I will not accept a bull from your house,
   or goats from your folds.
10 For every wild animal of the forest is
      mine,
   the cattle on a thousand hills.
11 I know all the birds of the air,*a*
   and all that moves in the field is mine.

12 "If I were hungry, I would not tell you,
   for the world and all that is in it is
      mine.
13 Do I eat the flesh of bulls,
   or drink the blood of goats?
14 Offer to God a sacrifice of
      thanksgiving,*b*
   and pay your vows to the Most High.
15 Call on me in the day of trouble;
   I will deliver you, and you shall glorify
      me."

16 But to the wicked God says:
   "What right have you to recite my
      statutes,
   or take my covenant on your lips?
17 For you hate discipline,
   and you cast my words behind you.
18 You make friends with a thief when you
      see one,
   and you keep company with
      adulterers.

19 "You give your mouth free rein for evil,
   and your tongue frames deceit.
20 You sit and speak against your kin;
   you slander your own mother's child.
21 These things you have done and I have
      been silent;
   you thought that I was one just like
      yourself.
   But now I rebuke you, and lay the
      charge before you.

22 "Mark this, then, you who forget God,
   or I will tear you apart, and there will
      be no one to deliver.
23 Those who bring thanksgiving as their
      sacrifice honor me;
   to those who go the right way*c*
   I will show the salvation of God."

Psalm 51

Prayer for Cleansing and Pardon

To the leader. A Psalm of David, when
the prophet Nathan came to him, after
he had gone in to Bathsheba.

1 Have mercy on me, O God,
   according to your steadfast love;
 according to your abundant mercy
   blot out my transgressions.
2 Wash me thoroughly from my iniquity,
   and cleanse me from my sin.

3 For I know my transgressions,
   and my sin is ever before me.
4 Against you, you alone, have I sinned,
   and done what is evil in your sight,
 so that you are justified in your sentence
   and blameless when you pass
      judgment.
5 Indeed, I was born guilty,
   a sinner when my mother conceived
      me.

6 You desire truth in the inward being;*d*
   therefore teach me wisdom in my
      secret heart.
7 Purge me with hyssop, and I shall be
      clean;
   wash me, and I shall be whiter than
      snow.
8 Let me hear joy and gladness;
   let the bones that you have crushed
      rejoice.
9 Hide your face from my sins,
   and blot out all my iniquities.

---

a Gk Syr Tg: Heb *mountains*   *b* Or *make thanksgiving your sacrifice to God*   *c* Heb *who set a way*   *d* Meaning of
Heb uncertain

10 Create in me a clean heart, O God,
     and put a new and right*a* spirit within
     me.
11 Do not cast me away from your
     presence,
     and do not take your holy spirit from
     me.
12 Restore to me the joy of your salvation,
     and sustain in me a willing*b* spirit.

13 Then I will teach transgressors your
     ways,
     and sinners will return to you.
14 Deliver me from bloodshed, O God,
     O God of my salvation,
     and my tongue will sing aloud of your
     deliverance.

15 O Lord, open my lips,
     and my mouth will declare your
     praise.
16 For you have no delight in sacrifice;
     if I were to give a burnt offering, you
     would not be pleased.
17 The sacrifice acceptable to God*c* is a
     broken spirit;
     a broken and contrite heart, O God,
     you will not despise.

18 Do good to Zion in your good pleasure;
     rebuild the walls of Jerusalem,
19 then you will delight in right sacrifices,
     in burnt offerings and whole burnt
     offerings;
     then bulls will be offered on your
     altar.

Psalm 52

Judgment on the Deceitful

To the leader. A Maskil of David, when
Doeg the Edomite came to Saul and said
to him, "David has come to the house of
Ahimelech."

1 Why do you boast, O mighty one,
of mischief done against the godly?*d*
All day long 2you are plotting
     destruction.
Your tongue is like a sharp razor,
     you worker of treachery.
3 You love evil more than good,
     and lying more than speaking the
     truth.   *Selah*
4 You love all words that devour,
     O deceitful tongue.

5 But God will break you down forever;
     he will snatch and tear you from your
     tent;
     he will uproot you from the land of
     the living.   *Selah*
6 The righteous will see, and fear,
     and will laugh at the evildoer,*e* saying,
7 "See the one who would not take
     refuge in God,
but trusted in abundant riches,
     and sought refuge in wealth!"*f*

8 But I am like a green olive tree
     in the house of God.
I trust in the steadfast love of God
     forever and ever.
9 I will thank you forever,
     because of what you have done.
In the presence of the faithful
     I will proclaim*g* your name, for it is
     good.

Psalm 53

Denunciation of Godlessness

To the leader: according to Mahalath.
A Maskil of David.

1 Fools say in their hearts, "There is no
     God."
They are corrupt, they commit
     abominable acts;
there is no one who does good.

---

a Or *steadfast*   *b* Or *generous*   *c* Or *My sacrifice, O God,*   *d* Cn Compare Syr: Heb *the kindness of God*
e Heb *him*   *f* Syr Tg: Heb *in his destruction*   *g* Cn: Heb *wait for*

2 God looks down from heaven on
        humankind
    to see if there are any who are wise,
    who seek after God.

3 They have all fallen away, they are all
        alike perverse;
    there is no one who does good,
    no, not one.

4 Have they no knowledge, those
        evildoers,
    who eat up my people as they eat
        bread,
    and do not call upon God?

5 There they shall be in great terror,
    in terror such as has not been.
    For God will scatter the bones of the
        ungodly;*a*
    they will be put to shame,*b* for God
        has rejected them.

6 O that deliverance for Israel would
        come from Zion!
    When God restores the fortunes of
        his people,
    Jacob will rejoice; Israel will be glad.

Psalm 54

Prayer for Vindication

To the leader: with stringed instruments.
A Maskil of David, when the Ziphites
went and told Saul, "David is in hiding
        among us."

1 Save me, O God, by your name,
    and vindicate me by your might.
2 Hear my prayer, O God;
    give ear to the words of my mouth.

3 For the insolent have risen against me,
    the ruthless seek my life;
    they do not set God before them. *Selah*

4 But surely, God is my helper;
    the Lord is the upholder of*c* my life.
5 He will repay my enemies for their evil.
    In your faithfulness, put an end to
        them.

6 With a freewill offering I will sacrifice to
        you;
    I will give thanks to your name,
    O LORD, for it is good.
7 For he has delivered me from every
        trouble,
    and my eye has looked in triumph on
        my enemies.

Psalm 55

Complaint about a Friend's Treachery

To the leader: with stringed instruments.
A Maskil of David.

1 Give ear to my prayer, O God;
    do not hide yourself from my
        supplication.
2 Attend to me, and answer me;
    I am troubled in my complaint.
I am distraught 3by the noise of the
        enemy,
    because of the clamor of the wicked.
For they bring*d* trouble upon me,
    and in anger they cherish enmity
        against me.

4 My heart is in anguish within me,
    the terrors of death have fallen upon
        me.
5 Fear and trembling come upon me,
    and horror overwhelms me.
6 And I say, "O that I had wings like a
        dove!
    I would fly away and be at rest;
7 truly, I would flee far away;
    I would lodge in the wilderness; *Selah*
8 I would hurry to find a shelter for
        myself
    from the raging wind and tempest."

---

a Cn Compare Gk Syr: Heb *him who encamps against you*   *b* Gk: Heb *you have put (them) to shame*   *c* Gk Syr
Jerome: Heb *is of those who uphold* or *is with those who uphold*   *d* Cn Compare Gk: Heb *they cause to totter*

9　Confuse, O Lord, confound their
　　　speech;
　　for I see violence and strife in the city.
10　Day and night they go around it
　　　on its walls,
　　and iniquity and trouble are within it;
11　ruin is in its midst;
　　oppression and fraud
　　　do not depart from its marketplace.

12　It is not enemies who taunt me—
　　　I could bear that;
　　it is not adversaries who deal insolently
　　　with me—
　　　I could hide from them.
13　But it is you, my equal,
　　my companion, my familiar friend,
14　with whom I kept pleasant company;
　　　we walked in the house of God with
　　　the throng.
15　Let death come upon them;
　　　let them go down alive to Sheol;
　　　for evil is in their homes and in their
　　　hearts.

16　But I call upon God,
　　and the LORD will save me.
17　Evening and morning and at noon
　　　I utter my complaint and moan,
　　and he will hear my voice.
18　He will redeem me unharmed
　　　from the battle that I wage,
　　for many are arrayed against me.
19　God, who is enthroned from of old,
　　　　　　　　　　　　　　　Selah
　　will hear, and will humble them—
　　because they do not change,
　　　and do not fear God.

20　My companion laid hands on a friend
　　　and violated a covenant with me*a*
21　with speech smoother than butter,
　　　but with a heart set on war;
　　with words that were softer than oil,
　　　but in fact were drawn swords.

22　Cast your burden*b* on the LORD,
　　　and he will sustain you;
　　he will never permit
　　　the righteous to be moved.

23　But you, O God, will cast them down
　　　into the lowest pit;
　　the bloodthirsty and treacherous
　　　shall not live out half their days.
　　But I will trust in you.

Psalm 56

Trust in God under Persecution

To the leader: according to The Dove on
Far-off Terebinths. Of David. A Miktam,
when the Philistines seized him in Gath.

1　Be gracious to me, O God, for people
　　　trample on me;
　　all day long foes oppress me;
2　my enemies trample on me all day long,
　　　for many fight against me.
　　O Most High, ³when I am afraid,
　　　I put my trust in you.
4　In God, whose word I praise,
　　　in God I trust; I am not afraid;
　　what can flesh do to me?

5　All day long they seek to injure my
　　　cause;
　　all their thoughts are against me for
　　　evil.
6　They stir up strife, they lurk,
　　　they watch my steps.
　　As they hoped to have my life,
7　so repay*c* them for their crime;
　　　in wrath cast down the peoples,
　　　O God!

8　You have kept count of my tossings;
　　　put my tears in your bottle.
　　Are they not in your record?
9　Then my enemies will retreat
　　　in the day when I call.
　　This I know, that*d* God is for me.
10　In God, whose word I praise,

---

a Heb lacks *with me*　　*b* Or *Cast what he has given you*　　*c* Cn: Heb *rescue*　　*d* Or *because*

in the LORD, whose word I praise,
11 in God I trust; I am not afraid.
      What can a mere mortal do to me?

12 My vows to you I must perform,
        O God;
      I will render thank offerings to you.
13 For you have delivered my soul from
        death,
      and my feet from falling,
    so that I may walk before God
      in the light of life.

Psalm 57

Praise and Assurance under Persecution

To the leader: Do Not Destroy. Of
David. A Miktam, when he fled from
Saul, in the cave.

1 Be merciful to me, O God, be merciful
        to me,
      for in you my soul takes refuge;
    in the shadow of your wings I will take
        refuge,
      until the destroying storms pass by.
2 I cry to God Most High,
      to God who fulfills his purpose for
        me.
3 He will send from heaven and save me,
      he will put to shame those who
        trample on me.   *Selah*
    God will send forth his steadfast love
      and his faithfulness.

4 I lie down among lions
      that greedily devour[a] human prey;
    their teeth are spears and arrows,
      their tongues sharp swords.

5 Be exalted, O God, above the heavens.
      Let your glory be over all the earth.

6 They set a net for my steps;
      my soul was bowed down.
    They dug a pit in my path,

but they have fallen into it
        themselves.   *Selah*
7 My heart is steadfast, O God,
      my heart is steadfast.
    I will sing and make melody.
8   Awake, my soul!
    Awake, O harp and lyre!
      I will awake the dawn.
9 I will give thanks to you, O Lord,
        among the peoples;
      I will sing praises to you among the
        nations.
10 For your steadfast love is as high as the
        heavens;
      your faithfulness extends to the
        clouds.

11 Be exalted, O God, above the heavens.
      Let your glory be over all the earth.

Psalm 58

Prayer for Vengeance

To the leader: Do Not Destroy. Of
David. A Miktam.

1 Do you indeed decree what is right, you
        gods?[b]
      Do you judge people fairly?
2 No, in your hearts you devise wrongs;
      your hands deal out violence on earth.

3 The wicked go astray from the womb;
      they err from their birth, speaking
        lies.
4 They have venom like the venom of a
        serpent,
      like the deaf adder that stops its ear,
5 so that it does not hear the voice of
        charmers
      or of the cunning enchanter.

6 O God, break the teeth in their mouths;
      tear out the fangs of the young lions,
        O LORD!
7 Let them vanish like water that runs
        away;

a Cn: Heb *are aflame for*   *b* Or *mighty lords*

like grass let them be trodden down[a]
and wither.

8 Let them be like the snail that dissolves
into slime;
like the untimely birth that never sees
the sun.

9 Sooner than your pots can feel the heat
of thorns,
whether green or ablaze, may he
sweep them away!

10 The righteous will rejoice when they see
vengeance done;
they will bathe their feet in the blood
of the wicked.

11 People will say, "Surely there is a reward
for the righteous;
surely there is a God who judges on
earth."

Psalm 59

Prayer for Deliverance from Enemies

To the leader: Do Not Destroy. Of
David. A Miktam, when Saul ordered his
house to be watched in order to kill him.

1 Deliver me from my enemies, O my
God;
protect me from those who rise up
against me.

2 Deliver me from those who work evil;
from the bloodthirsty save me.

3 Even now they lie in wait for my life;
the mighty stir up strife against me.
For no transgression or sin of mine,
O Lord,

4 for no fault of mine, they run and
make ready.

Rouse yourself, come to my help and
see!

5 You, Lord God of hosts, are God of
Israel.
Awake to punish all the nations;

spare none of those who
treacherously plot evil.   *Selah*

6 Each evening they come back,
howling like dogs
and prowling about the city.

7 There they are, bellowing with their
mouths,
with sharp words[b] on their lips—
for "Who," they think,[c] "will hear us?"

8 But you laugh at them, O Lord;
you hold all the nations in derision.

9 O my strength, I will watch for you;
for you, O God, are my fortress.

10 My God in his steadfast love will meet
me;
my God will let me look in triumph
on my enemies.

11 Do not kill them, or my people may
forget;
make them totter by your power, and
bring them down,
O Lord, our shield.

12 For the sin of their mouths, the words
of their lips,
let them be trapped in their pride.
For the cursing and lies that they utter,

13 consume them in wrath;
consume them until they are no more.
Then it will be known to the ends of
the earth
that God rules over Jacob.   *Selah*

14 Each evening they come back,
howling like dogs
and prowling about the city.

15 They roam about for food,
and growl if they do not get their fill.

16 But I will sing of your might;
I will sing aloud of your steadfast love
in the morning.
For you have been a fortress for me
and a refuge in the day of my distress.

a Cn: Meaning of Heb uncertain   b Heb *with swords*   c Heb lacks *they think*

17 O my strength, I will sing praises to you,
   for you, O God, are my fortress,
      the God who shows me steadfast
         love.

Psalm 60

Prayer for National Victory after Defeat

To the leader: according to the Lily of
the Covenant. A Miktam of David; for
instruction; when he struggled with
Aram-naharaim and with Aram-zobah,
and when Joab on his return killed twelve
thousand Edomites in the Valley of Salt.

1 O God, you have rejected us, broken
      our defenses;
   you have been angry; now restore
      us!
2 You have caused the land to quake; you
      have torn it open;
   repair the cracks in it, for it is
      tottering.
3 You have made your people suffer hard
      things;
   you have given us wine to drink that
      made us reel.

4 You have set up a banner for those who
      fear you,
   to rally to it out of bowshot.*a*   *Selah*
5 Give victory with your right hand, and
      answer us,*b*
   so that those whom you love may be
      rescued.

6 God has promised in his sanctuary:*c*
   "With exultation I will divide up
      Shechem,
   and portion out the Vale of Succoth.
7 Gilead is mine, and Manasseh is mine;
   Ephraim is my helmet;
      Judah is my scepter.
8 Moab is my washbasin;
   on Edom I hurl my shoe;
      over Philistia I shout in triumph."

9 Who will bring me to the fortified city?
   Who will lead me to Edom?
10 Have you not rejected us, O God?
   You do not go out, O God, with our
      armies.
11 O grant us help against the foe,
   for human help is worthless.
12 With God we shall do valiantly;
   it is he who will tread down our foes.

Psalm 61

Assurance of God's Protection

To the leader: with stringed instruments.
            Of David.

1 Hear my cry, O God;
   listen to my prayer.
2 From the end of the earth I call to you,
   when my heart is faint.

   Lead me to the rock
      that is higher than I;
3 for you are my refuge,
   a strong tower against the enemy.

4 Let me abide in your tent forever,
   find refuge under the shelter of your
      wings.   *Selah*
5 For you, O God, have heard my vows;
   you have given me the heritage of
      those who fear your name.

6 Prolong the life of the king;
   may his years endure to all
      generations!
7 May he be enthroned forever before
      God;
   appoint steadfast love and
      faithfulness to watch over him!

8 So I will always sing praises to your
      name,
   as I pay my vows day after day.

---

a Gk Syr Jerome: Heb *because of the truth*   *b* Another reading is *me*   *c* Or *by his holiness*

Psalm 62

Song of Trust in God Alone

To the leader: according to Jeduthun.
A Psalm of David.

1 For God alone my soul waits in silence;
     from him comes my salvation.
2 He alone is my rock and my salvation,
     my fortress; I shall never be shaken.

3 How long will you assail a person,
     will you batter your victim, all of you,
     as you would a leaning wall, a
          tottering fence?
4 Their only plan is to bring down a
          person of prominence.
     They take pleasure in falsehood;
   they bless with their mouths,
     but inwardly they curse.   *Selah*

5 For God alone my soul waits in silence,
     for my hope is from him.
6 He alone is my rock and my salvation,
     my fortress; I shall not be shaken.
7 On God rests my deliverance and my
          honor;
     my mighty rock, my refuge is in God.

8 Trust in him at all times, O people;
     pour out your heart before him;
   God is a refuge for us.   *Selah*

9 Those of low estate are but a breath,
     those of high estate are a delusion;
   in the balances they go up;
     they are together lighter than a breath.
10 Put no confidence in extortion,
     and set no vain hopes on robbery;
   if riches increase, do not set your
          heart on them.

11 Once God has spoken;
     twice have I heard this:
   that power belongs to God,
12   and steadfast love belongs to you,
          O Lord.

For you repay to all
     according to their work.

Psalm 63

Comfort and Assurance in God's Presence

A Psalm of David, when he was in the
     Wilderness of Judah.

1 O God, you are my God, I seek you,
     my soul thirsts for you;
   my flesh faints for you,
     as in a dry and weary land where
          there is no water.
2 So I have looked upon you in the
          sanctuary,
     beholding your power and glory.
3 Because your steadfast love is better
          than life,
     my lips will praise you.
4 So I will bless you as long as I live;
     I will lift up my hands and call on
          your name.

5 My soul is satisfied as with a rich feast,*a*
     and my mouth praises you with joyful
          lips
6 when I think of you on my bed,
     and meditate on you in the watches of
          the night;
7 for you have been my help,
     and in the shadow of your wings I
          sing for joy.
8 My soul clings to you;
     your right hand upholds me.

9 But those who seek to destroy my life
     shall go down into the depths of the
          earth;
10 they shall be given over to the power of
          the sword,
     they shall be prey for jackals.
11 But the king shall rejoice in God;
     all who swear by him shall exult,
   for the mouths of liars will be
          stopped.

a Heb *with fat and fatness*

Psalm 64

Prayer for Protection from Enemies

To the leader. A Psalm of David.

1 Hear my voice, O God, in my
    complaint;
    preserve my life from the dread
    enemy.
2 Hide me from the secret plots of the
    wicked,
    from the scheming of evildoers,
3 who whet their tongues like swords,
    who aim bitter words like arrows,
4 shooting from ambush at the blameless;
    they shoot suddenly and without fear.
5 They hold fast to their evil purpose;
    they talk of laying snares secretly,
    thinking, "Who can see us?"*a*
6 Who can search out our crimes?*b*
    We have thought out a cunningly
    conceived plot."
    For the human heart and mind are
    deep.

7 But God will shoot his arrow at them;
    they will be wounded suddenly.
8 Because of their tongue he will bring
    them to ruin;*c*
    all who see them will shake with
    horror.
9 Then everyone will fear;
    they will tell what God has brought
    about,
    and ponder what he has done.

10 Let the righteous rejoice in the LORD
    and take refuge in him.
    Let all the upright in heart glory.

Psalm 65

Thanksgiving for Earth's Bounty

To the leader. A Psalm of David. A Song.

1 Praise is due to you,
    O God, in Zion;
    and to you shall vows be performed,
2   O you who answer prayer!
    To you all flesh shall come.
3 When deeds of iniquity overwhelm us,
    you forgive our transgressions.
4 Happy are those whom you choose and
    bring near
    to live in your courts.
    We shall be satisfied with the goodness
    of your house,
    your holy temple.

5 By awesome deeds you answer us with
    deliverance,
    O God of our salvation;
    you are the hope of all the ends of the
    earth
    and of the farthest seas.
6 By your*d* strength you established the
    mountains;
    you are girded with might.
7 You silence the roaring of the seas,
    the roaring of their waves,
    the tumult of the peoples.
8 Those who live at earth's farthest
    bounds are awed by your signs;
    you make the gateways of the morning
    and the evening shout for joy.

9 You visit the earth and water it,
    you greatly enrich it;
    the river of God is full of water;
    you provide the people with grain,
    for so you have prepared it.
10 You water its furrows abundantly,
    settling its ridges,
    softening it with showers,
    and blessing its growth.
11 You crown the year with your bounty;
    your wagon tracks overflow with
    richness.
12 The pastures of the wilderness
    overflow,
    the hills gird themselves with joy,
13 the meadows clothe themselves with
    flocks,

a Syr: Heb *them*   *b* Cn: Heb *They search out crimes*
them   *d* Gk Jerome: Heb *his*   *c* Cn: Heb *They will bring him to ruin, their tongue being against*

the valleys deck themselves with
grain,
they shout and sing together for joy.

Psalm 66

Praise for God's Goodness to Israel

To the leader. A Song. A Psalm.

1 Make a joyful noise to God, all the
earth;
2 sing the glory of his name;
give to him glorious praise.
3 Say to God, "How awesome are your
deeds!
Because of your great power, your
enemies cringe before you.
4 All the earth worships you;
they sing praises to you,
sing praises to your name." *Selah*

5 Come and see what God has done:
he is awesome in his deeds among
mortals.
6 He turned the sea into dry land;
they passed through the river on foot.
There we rejoiced in him,
7 who rules by his might forever,
whose eyes keep watch on the nations—
let the rebellious not exalt themselves.
Selah

8 Bless our God, O peoples,
let the sound of his praise be heard,
9 who has kept us among the living,
and has not let our feet slip.
10 For you, O God, have tested us;
you have tried us as silver is tried.
11 You brought us into the net;
you laid burdens on our backs;
12 you let people ride over our heads;
we went through fire and through
water;
yet you have brought us out to a
spacious place.*a*

13 I will come into your house with burnt
offerings;
I will pay you my vows,
14 those that my lips uttered
and my mouth promised when I was
in trouble.
15 I will offer to you burnt offerings of
fatlings,
with the smoke of the sacrifice of
rams;
I will make an offering of bulls and
goats. *Selah*

16 Come and hear, all you who fear God,
and I will tell what he has done for
me.
17 I cried aloud to him,
and he was extolled with my tongue.
18 If I had cherished iniquity in my heart,
the Lord would not have listened.
19 But truly God has listened;
he has given heed to the words of my
prayer.

20 Blessed be God,
because he has not rejected my prayer
or removed his steadfast love from
me.

Psalm 67

The Nations Called to Praise God

To the leader: with stringed instruments.
A Psalm. A Song.

1 May God be gracious to us and bless us
and make his face to shine upon us,
Selah
2 that your way may be known upon
earth,
your saving power among all nations.
3 Let the peoples praise you, O God;
let all the peoples praise you.

4 Let the nations be glad and sing for joy,
for you judge the peoples with equity
and guide the nations upon earth. *Selah*

---

a Cn Compare Gk Syr Jerome Tg: Heb *to a saturation*

5 Let the peoples praise you, O God;
   let all the peoples praise you.

6 The earth has yielded its increase;
   God, our God, has blessed us.
7 May God continue to bless us;
   let all the ends of the earth revere
     him.

Psalm 68

Praise and Thanksgiving

To the leader. Of David. A Psalm.
     A Song.

1 Let God rise up, let his enemies be
     scattered;
   let those who hate him flee before
     him.
2 As smoke is driven away, so drive them
     away;
   as wax melts before the fire,
   let the wicked perish before God.
3 But let the righteous be joyful;
   let them exult before God;
   let them be jubilant with joy.

4 Sing to God, sing praises to his name;
   lift up a song to him who rides upon
     the clouds *a*—
   his name is the LORD—
   be exultant before him.

5 Father of orphans and protector of
     widows
   is God in his holy habitation.
6 God gives the desolate a home to live in;
   he leads out the prisoners to
     prosperity,
   but the rebellious live in a parched
     land.

7 O God, when you went out before your
     people,
   when you marched through the
     wilderness,   *Selah*

8 the earth quaked, the heavens poured
     down rain
   at the presence of God, the God of
     Sinai,
   at the presence of God, the God of
     Israel.
9 Rain in abundance, O God, you
     showered abroad;
   you restored your heritage when it
     languished;
10 your flock found a dwelling in it;
   in your goodness, O God, you
     provided for the needy.

11 The Lord gives the command;
   great is the company of those *b* who
     bore the tidings:
12 "The kings of the armies, they flee,
     they flee!"
   The women at home divide the spoil,
13   though they stay among the
     sheepfolds—
   the wings of a dove covered with silver,
   its pinions with green gold.
14 When the Almighty *c* scattered kings
     there,
   snow fell on Zalmon.

15 O mighty mountain, mountain of
     Bashan;
   O many-peaked mountain, mountain
     of Bashan!
16 Why do you look with envy, O many-
     peaked mountain,
   at the mount that God desired for his
     abode,
   where the LORD will reside forever?

17 With mighty chariotry, twice ten
     thousand,
   thousands upon thousands,
   the Lord came from Sinai into the
     holy place. *d*
18 You ascended the high mount,
   leading captives in your train
   and receiving gifts from people,

a Or *cast up a highway for him who rides through the deserts*   *b* Or *company of the women*   *c* Traditional rendering of
Heb *Shaddai*   *d* Cn: Heb *The Lord among them Sinai in the holy* (place)

even from those who rebel against the
    LORD God's abiding there.

19 Blessed be the Lord,
    who daily bears us up;
    God is our salvation.   *Selah*

20 Our God is a God of salvation,
    and to GOD, the Lord, belongs escape
      from death.

21 But God will shatter the heads of his
      enemies,
    the hairy crown of those who walk in
      their guilty ways.

22 The Lord said,
    "I will bring them back from Bashan,
    I will bring them back from the depths
      of the sea,

23 so that you may bathe*a* your feet in
      blood,
    so that the tongues of your dogs may
      have their share from the foe."

24 Your solemn processions are seen,*b*
    O God,
    the processions of my God, my King,
      into the sanctuary—

25 the singers in front, the musicians last,
    between them girls playing
      tambourines:

26 "Bless God in the great congregation,
    the LORD, O you who are of Israel's
      fountain!"

27 There is Benjamin, the least of them, in
      the lead,
    the princes of Judah in a body,
    the princes of Zebulun, the princes
      of Naphtali.

28 Summon your might, O God;
    show your strength, O God, as you
      have done for us before.

29 Because of your temple at Jerusalem
    kings bear gifts to you.

30 Rebuke the wild animals that live among
    the reeds,

the herd of bulls with the calves of
    the peoples.
Trample*c* under foot those who lust
    after tribute;
scatter the peoples who delight in war.*d*

31 Let bronze be brought from Egypt;
    let Ethiopia*e* hasten to stretch out its
      hands to God.

32 Sing to God, O kingdoms of the earth;
    sing praises to the Lord,   *Selah*

33 O rider in the heavens, the ancient
      heavens;
    listen, he sends out his voice, his
      mighty voice.

34 Ascribe power to God,
    whose majesty is over Israel;
    and whose power is in the skies.

35 Awesome is God in his*f* sanctuary,
    the God of Israel;
    he gives power and strength to his
      people.

Blessed be God!

Psalm 69

Prayer for Deliverance from Persecution

To the leader: according to Lilies.
Of David.

1 Save me, O God,
    for the waters have come up to my
      neck.

2 I sink in deep mire,
    where there is no foothold;
I have come into deep waters,
    and the flood sweeps over me.

3 I am weary with my crying;
    my throat is parched.
My eyes grow dim
    with waiting for my God.

4 More in number than the hairs of my
      head
    are those who hate me without cause;

---

a Gk Syr Tg: Heb *shatter*   *b* Or *have been seen*   *c* Cn: Heb *Trampling*   *d* Meaning of Heb of verse 30 is
uncertain   *e* Or *Nubia*; Heb *Cush*   *f* Gk: Heb *from your*

many are those who would destroy me,
    my enemies who accuse me falsely.
What I did not steal
    must I now restore?
5 O God, you know my folly;
    the wrongs I have done are not
    hidden from you.

6 Do not let those who hope in you be
    put to shame because of me,
  O Lord GOD of hosts;
do not let those who seek you be
    dishonored because of me,
  O God of Israel.
7 It is for your sake that I have borne
    reproach,
  that shame has covered my face.
8 I have become a stranger to my kindred,
  an alien to my mother's children.

9 It is zeal for your house that has
    consumed me;
  the insults of those who insult you
    have fallen on me.
10 When I humbled my soul with fasting,*a*
  they insulted me for doing so.
11 When I made sackcloth my clothing,
  I became a byword to them.
12 I am the subject of gossip for those
    who sit in the gate,
  and the drunkards make songs about
    me.

13 But as for me, my prayer is to you,
    O LORD.
  At an acceptable time, O God,
  in the abundance of your steadfast
    love, answer me.
  With your faithful help 14rescue me
    from sinking in the mire;
  let me be delivered from my enemies
    and from the deep waters.
15 Do not let the flood sweep over me,
    or the deep swallow me up,
    or the Pit close its mouth over me.

16 Answer me, O LORD, for your steadfast
    love is good;
  according to your abundant mercy,
    turn to me.
17 Do not hide your face from your
    servant,
  for I am in distress—make haste to
    answer me.
18 Draw near to me, redeem me,
  set me free because of my enemies.

19 You know the insults I receive,
  and my shame and dishonor;
  my foes are all known to you.
20 Insults have broken my heart,
  so that I am in despair.
I looked for pity, but there was none;
  and for comforters, but I found none.
21 They gave me poison for food,
  and for my thirst they gave me
    vinegar to drink.

22 Let their table be a trap for them,
  a snare for their allies.
23 Let their eyes be darkened so that they
    cannot see,
  and make their loins tremble
    continually.
24 Pour out your indignation upon them,
  and let your burning anger overtake
    them.
25 May their camp be a desolation;
  let no one live in their tents.
26 For they persecute those whom you
    have struck down,
  and those whom you have wounded,
    they attack still more.*b*
27 Add guilt to their guilt;
  may they have no acquittal from you.
28 Let them be blotted out of the book of
    the living;
  let them not be enrolled among the
    righteous.
29 But I am lowly and in pain;
  let your salvation, O God, protect me.

a Gk Syr: Heb *I wept, with fasting my soul*, or *I made my soul mourn with fasting*   *b* Gk Syr: Heb *recount the pain of*

30 I will praise the name of God with a
     song;
     I will magnify him with thanksgiving.
31 This will please the LORD more than an
     ox
     or a bull with horns and hoofs.
32 Let the oppressed see it and be glad;
     you who seek God, let your hearts
     revive.
33 For the LORD hears the needy,
     and does not despise his own that are
     in bonds.

34 Let heaven and earth praise him,
     the seas and everything that moves in
     them.
35 For God will save Zion
     and rebuild the cities of Judah;
   and his servants shall live*a* there and
     possess it;
36 the children of his servants shall
     inherit it,
     and those who love his name shall
     live in it.

Psalm 70

Prayer for Deliverance from Enemies

> To the leader. Of David, for the
> memorial offering.

1 Be pleased, O God, to deliver me.
     O LORD, make haste to help me!
2 Let those be put to shame and
     confusion
     who seek my life.
   Let those be turned back and brought to
     dishonor
     who desire to hurt me.
3 Let those who say, "Aha, Aha!"
     turn back because of their shame.

4 Let all who seek you
     rejoice and be glad in you.
   Let those who love your salvation
     say evermore, "God is great!"
5 But I am poor and needy;

hasten to me, O God!
You are my help and my deliverer;
     O LORD, do not delay!

Psalm 71

Prayer for Lifelong Protection and Help

1 In you, O LORD, I take refuge;
     let me never be put to shame.
2 In your righteousness deliver me and
     rescue me;
     incline your ear to me and save me.
3 Be to me a rock of refuge,
     a strong fortress,*b* to save me,
     for you are my rock and my fortress.

4 Rescue me, O my God, from the hand
     of the wicked,
     from the grasp of the unjust and
     cruel.
5 For you, O Lord, are my hope,
     my trust, O LORD, from my youth.
6 Upon you I have leaned from my birth;
     it was you who took me from my
     mother's womb.
   My praise is continually of you.

7 I have been like a portent to many,
     but you are my strong refuge.
8 My mouth is filled with your praise,
     and with your glory all day long.
9 Do not cast me off in the time of old
     age;
     do not forsake me when my strength
     is spent.
10 For my enemies speak concerning me,
     and those who watch for my life
     consult together.
11 They say, "Pursue and seize that person
     whom God has forsaken,
     for there is no one to deliver."

12 O God, do not be far from me;
     O my God, make haste to help me!
13 Let my accusers be put to shame and
     consumed;

---

a Syr: Heb *and they shall live*   *b* Gk Compare 31.3: Heb *to come continually you have commanded*

let those who seek to hurt me
    be covered with scorn and disgrace.
14 But I will hope continually,
    and will praise you yet more and
        more.
15 My mouth will tell of your righteous
        acts,
    of your deeds of salvation all day
        long,
    though their number is past my
        knowledge.
16 I will come praising the mighty deeds of
        the Lord GOD,
    I will praise your righteousness, yours
        alone.

17 O God, from my youth you have taught
        me,
    and I still proclaim your wondrous
        deeds.
18 So even to old age and gray hairs,
    O God, do not forsake me,
until I proclaim your might
    to all the generations to come. *a*
Your power 19and your righteousness,
    O God,
    reach the high heavens.

You who have done great things,
    O God, who is like you?
20 You who have made me see many
        troubles and calamities
    will revive me again;
from the depths of the earth
    you will bring me up again.
21 You will increase my honor,
    and comfort me once again.

22 I will also praise you with the harp
    for your faithfulness, O my God;
I will sing praises to you with the lyre,
    O Holy One of Israel.
23 My lips will shout for joy
    when I sing praises to you;
    my soul also, which you have rescued.

24 All day long my tongue will talk of your
        righteous help,
    for those who tried to do me harm
        have been put to shame, and
        disgraced.

Psalm 72

Prayer for Guidance and Support for the King

Of Solomon.

1 Give the king your justice, O God,
    and your righteousness to a king's son.
2 May he judge your people with
        righteousness,
    and your poor with justice.
3 May the mountains yield prosperity for
        the people,
    and the hills, in righteousness.
4 May he defend the cause of the poor of
        the people,
    give deliverance to the needy,
    and crush the oppressor.

5 May he live *b* while the sun endures,
    and as long as the moon, throughout
        all generations.
6 May he be like rain that falls on the
        mown grass,
    like showers that water the earth.
7 In his days may righteousness flourish
    and peace abound, until the moon is
        no more.

8 May he have dominion from sea to sea,
    and from the River to the ends of the
        earth.
9 May his foes *c* bow down before him,
    and his enemies lick the dust.
10 May the kings of Tarshish and of the
        isles
    render him tribute,
may the kings of Sheba and Seba
    bring gifts.
11 May all kings fall down before him,
    all nations give him service.

a Gk Compare Syr: Heb *to a generation, to all that come*   *b* Gk: Heb *may they fear you*   *c* Cn: Heb *those who live in the*
wilderness

12 For he delivers the needy when they call,
   the poor and those who have no
     helper.
13 He has pity on the weak and the needy,
   and saves the lives of the needy.
14 From oppression and violence he
     redeems their life;
   and precious is their blood in his
     sight.

15 Long may he live!
   May gold of Sheba be given to him.
  May prayer be made for him continually,
   and blessings invoked for him all day
     long.
16 May there be abundance of grain in the
     land;
   may it wave on the tops of the
     mountains;
   may its fruit be like Lebanon;
  and may people blossom in the cities
   like the grass of the field.
17 May his name endure forever,
   his fame continue as long as the sun.
  May all nations be blessed in him;[a]
   may they pronounce him happy.

18 Blessed be the LORD, the God of Israel,
   who alone does wondrous things.
19 Blessed be his glorious name forever;
   may his glory fill the whole earth.
     Amen and Amen.

20 The prayers of David son of Jesse are
   ended.

BOOK III

(Psalms 73–89)

Psalm 73

Plea for Relief from Oppressors

A Psalm of Asaph.

1 Truly God is good to the upright,[b]
   to those who are pure in heart.

2 But as for me, my feet had almost
     stumbled;
   my steps had nearly slipped.
3 For I was envious of the arrogant;
   I saw the prosperity of the wicked.

4 For they have no pain;
   their bodies are sound and sleek.
5 They are not in trouble as others are;
   they are not plagued like other people.
6 Therefore pride is their necklace;
   violence covers them like a garment.
7 Their eyes swell out with fatness;
   their hearts overflow with follies.
8 They scoff and speak with malice;
   loftily they threaten oppression.
9 They set their mouths against heaven,
   and their tongues range over the
     earth.

10 Therefore the people turn and praise
     them,[c]
   and find no fault in them.[d]
11 And they say, "How can God know?
   Is there knowledge in the Most
     High?"
12 Such are the wicked;
   always at ease, they increase in riches.
13 All in vain I have kept my heart clean
   and washed my hands in innocence.
14 For all day long I have been plagued,
   and am punished every morning.

15 If I had said, "I will talk on in this way,"
   I would have been untrue to the circle
     of your children.
16 But when I thought how to understand
     this,
   it seemed to me a wearisome task,
17 until I went into the sanctuary of God;
   then I perceived their end.
18 Truly you set them in slippery places;
   you make them fall to ruin.
19 How they are destroyed in a moment,
   swept away utterly by terrors!

---

a Or *bless themselves by him*   *b* Or *good to Israel*   *c* Cn: Heb *his people return here*   *d* Cn: Heb *abundant waters are drained by them*

20 They are *a* like a dream when one
  awakes;
  on awaking you despise their
   phantoms.

21 When my soul was embittered,
  when I was pricked in heart,
22 I was stupid and ignorant;
  I was like a brute beast toward you.
23 Nevertheless I am continually with you;
  you hold my right hand.
24 You guide me with your counsel,
  and afterward you will receive me
   with honor. *b*
25 Whom have I in heaven but you?
  And there is nothing on earth that I
   desire other than you.
26 My flesh and my heart may fail,
  but God is the strength *c* of my heart
   and my portion forever.

27 Indeed, those who are far from you will
  perish;
  you put an end to those who are false
   to you.
28 But for me it is good to be near God;
  I have made the Lord GOD my
   refuge,
  to tell of all your works.

Psalm 74

*Plea for Help in Time of National
Humiliation*

A Maskil of Asaph.

1 O God, why do you cast us off
  forever?
  Why does your anger smoke against
   the sheep of your pasture?
2 Remember your congregation, which
  you acquired long ago,
  which you redeemed to be the tribe
   of your heritage.
  Remember Mount Zion, where you
   came to dwell.

3 Direct your steps to the perpetual ruins;
  the enemy has destroyed everything in
   the sanctuary.

4 Your foes have roared within your holy
  place;
  they set up their emblems there.
5 At the upper entrance they hacked
  the wooden trellis with axes. *d*
6 And then, with hatchets and hammers,
  they smashed all its carved work.
7 They set your sanctuary on fire;
  they desecrated the dwelling place of
   your name,
  bringing it to the ground.
8 They said to themselves, "We will utterly
  subdue them";
  they burned all the meeting places of
   God in the land.

9 We do not see our emblems;
  there is no longer any prophet,
  and there is no one among us who
   knows how long.
10 How long, O God, is the foe to scoff?
  Is the enemy to revile your name
   forever?
11 Why do you hold back your hand;
  why do you keep your hand in *e* your
   bosom?

12 Yet God my King is from of old,
  working salvation in the earth.
13 You divided the sea by your might;
  you broke the heads of the dragons
   in the waters.
14 You crushed the heads of Leviathan;
  you gave him as food *f* for the
   creatures of the wilderness.
15 You cut openings for springs and
  torrents;
  you dried up ever-flowing streams.
16 Yours is the day, yours also the night;
  you established the luminaries *g* and
   the sun.

---

a Cn: Heb *Lord* *b* Or *to glory* *c* Heb *rock* *d* Cn Compare Gk Syr: Meaning of Heb uncertain *e* Cn: Heb
do you consume your right hand from *f* Heb *food for the people* *g* Or *moon*; Heb *light*

17 You have fixed all the bounds of the
earth;
   you made summer and winter.

18 Remember this, O LORD, how the
enemy scoffs,
   and an impious people reviles your
   name.
19 Do not deliver the soul of your dove to
the wild animals;
   do not forget the life of your poor
   forever.

20 Have regard for your*a* covenant,
   for the dark places of the land are full
   of the haunts of violence.
21 Do not let the downtrodden be put to
shame;
   let the poor and needy praise your
   name.
22 Rise up, O God, plead your cause;
   remember how the impious scoff at
   you all day long.
23 Do not forget the clamor of your foes,
   the uproar of your adversaries that
   goes up continually.

Psalm 75

Thanksgiving for God's Wondrous Deeds

To the leader: Do Not Destroy. A Psalm
of Asaph. A Song.

1 We give thanks to you, O God;
   we give thanks; your name is near.
People tell of your wondrous deeds.

2 At the set time that I appoint
   I will judge with equity.
3 When the earth totters, with all its
inhabitants,
   it is I who keep its pillars steady. *Selah*
4 I say to the boastful, "Do not boast,"
   and to the wicked, "Do not lift up
   your horn;
5 do not lift up your horn on high,
   or speak with insolent neck."

6 For not from the east or from the
west
   and not from the wilderness comes
   lifting up;
7 but it is God who executes judgment,
   putting down one and lifting up
   another.
8 For in the hand of the LORD there is a
cup
   with foaming wine, well mixed;
he will pour a draught from it,
   and all the wicked of the earth
   shall drain it down to the dregs.
9 But I will rejoice*b* forever;
   I will sing praises to the God of
   Jacob.

10 All the horns of the wicked I will cut
off,
   but the horns of the righteous shall
   be exalted.

Psalm 76

Israel's God—Judge of All the Earth

To the leader: with stringed instruments.
A Psalm of Asaph. A Song.

1 In Judah God is known,
   his name is great in Israel.
2 His abode has been established in
Salem,
   his dwelling place in Zion.
3 There he broke the flashing arrows,
   the shield, the sword, and the
   weapons of war. *Selah*

4 Glorious are you, more majestic
   than the everlasting mountains.*c*
5 The stouthearted were stripped of their
spoil;
   they sank into sleep;
none of the troops
   was able to lift a hand.
6 At your rebuke, O God of Jacob,
   both rider and horse lay stunned.

a Gk Syr: Heb *the*   *b* Gk: Heb *declare*   *c* Gk: Heb *the mountains of prey*

7 But you indeed are awesome!
  Who can stand before you
      when once your anger is roused?
8 From the heavens you uttered
      judgment;
  the earth feared and was still
9 when God rose up to establish
      judgment,
  to save all the oppressed of the earth.
                                    Selah

10 Human wrath serves only to praise you,
   when you bind the last bit of your*a*
      wrath around you.
11 Make vows to the LORD your God, and
      perform them;
   let all who are around him bring gifts
      to the one who is awesome,
12 who cuts off the spirit of princes,
   who inspires fear in the kings of the
      earth.

Psalm 77

God's Mighty Deeds Recalled

To the leader: according to Jeduthun. Of
Asaph. A Psalm.

1 I cry aloud to God,
   aloud to God, that he may hear me.
2 In the day of my trouble I seek the
      Lord;
   in the night my hand is stretched out
      without wearying;
   my soul refuses to be comforted.
3 I think of God, and I moan;
   I meditate, and my spirit faints.   *Selah*

4 You keep my eyelids from closing;
   I am so troubled that I cannot
      speak.
5 I consider the days of old,
   and remember the years of long
      ago.
6 I commune*b* with my heart in the
      night;
   I meditate and search my spirit:*c*

7 "Will the Lord spurn forever,
   and never again be favorable?
8 Has his steadfast love ceased
      forever?
   Are his promises at an end for all
      time?
9 Has God forgotten to be gracious?
   Has he in anger shut up his
      compassion?"   *Selah*
10 And I say, "It is my grief
   that the right hand of the Most High
      has changed."

11 I will call to mind the deeds of the
      LORD;
   I will remember your wonders of
      old.
12 I will meditate on all your work,
   and muse on your mighty deeds.
13 Your way, O God, is holy.
   What god is so great as our God?
14 You are the God who works wonders;
   you have displayed your might among
      the peoples.
15 With your strong arm you redeemed
      your people,
   the descendants of Jacob and Joseph.
                                    Selah

16 When the waters saw you, O God,
   when the waters saw you, they were
      afraid;
   the very deep trembled.
17 The clouds poured out water;
   the skies thundered;
   your arrows flashed on every side.
18 The crash of your thunder was in the
      whirlwind;
   your lightnings lit up the world;
   the earth trembled and shook.
19 Your way was through the sea,
   your path, through the mighty
      waters;
   yet your footprints were unseen.
20 You led your people like a flock
   by the hand of Moses and Aaron.

a Heb lacks *your*   *b* Gk Syr: Heb *My music*   *c* Syr Jerome: Heb *my spirit searches*

Psalm 78

God's Goodness and Israel's Ingratitude

A Maskil of Asaph.

1 Give ear, O my people, to my teaching;
  incline your ears to the words of my
    mouth.
2 I will open my mouth in a parable;
  I will utter dark sayings from of old,
3 things that we have heard and known,
  that our ancestors have told us.
4 We will not hide them from their
    children;
  we will tell to the coming generation
  the glorious deeds of the LORD, and his
    might,
  and the wonders that he has done.

5 He established a decree in Jacob,
  and appointed a law in Israel,
  which he commanded our ancestors
  to teach to their children;
6 that the next generation might know
    them,
  the children yet unborn,
  and rise up and tell them to their
    children,
7 so that they should set their hope in
    God,
  and not forget the works of God,
  but keep his commandments;
8 and that they should not be like their
    ancestors,
  a stubborn and rebellious generation,
  a generation whose heart was not
    steadfast,
  whose spirit was not faithful to God.

9 The Ephraimites, armed with*a* the bow,
  turned back on the day of battle.
10 They did not keep God's covenant,
  but refused to walk according to his
    law.
11 They forgot what he had done,
  and the miracles that he had shown
    them.

a Heb *armed with shooting*

12 In the sight of their ancestors he
    worked marvels
  in the land of Egypt, in the fields of
    Zoan.
13 He divided the sea and let them pass
    through it,
  and made the waters stand like a heap.
14 In the daytime he led them with a cloud,
  and all night long with a fiery light.
15 He split rocks open in the wilderness,
  and gave them drink abundantly as
    from the deep.
16 He made streams come out of the rock,
  and caused waters to flow down like
    rivers.

17 Yet they sinned still more against him,
  rebelling against the Most High in the
    desert.
18 They tested God in their heart
  by demanding the food they craved.
19 They spoke against God, saying,
  "Can God spread a table in the
    wilderness?
20 Even though he struck the rock so that
    water gushed out
  and torrents overflowed,
  can he also give bread,
  or provide meat for his people?"

21 Therefore, when the LORD heard, he
    was full of rage;
  a fire was kindled against Jacob,
  his anger mounted against Israel,
22 because they had no faith in God,
  and did not trust his saving power.
23 Yet he commanded the skies above,
  and opened the doors of heaven;
24 he rained down on them manna to eat,
  and gave them the grain of heaven.
25 Mortals ate of the bread of angels;
  he sent them food in abundance.
26 He caused the east wind to blow in the
    heavens,
  and by his power he led out the south
    wind;

27 he rained flesh upon them like dust,
    winged birds like the sand of the seas;
28 he let them fall within their camp,
    all around their dwellings.
29 And they ate and were well filled,
    for he gave them what they craved.
30 But before they had satisfied their
        craving,
    while the food was still in their
        mouths,
31 the anger of God rose against them
    and he killed the strongest of them,
    and laid low the flower of Israel.

32 In spite of all this they still sinned;
    they did not believe in his wonders.
33 So he made their days vanish like a
        breath,
    and their years in terror.
34 When he killed them, they sought for
        him;
    they repented and sought God
        earnestly.
35 They remembered that God was their
        rock,
    the Most High God their redeemer.
36 But they flattered him with their
        mouths;
    they lied to him with their tongues.
37 Their heart was not steadfast toward
        him;
    they were not true to his covenant.
38 Yet he, being compassionate,
    forgave their iniquity,
    and did not destroy them;
    often he restrained his anger,
    and did not stir up all his wrath.
39 He remembered that they were but
        flesh,
    a wind that passes and does not come
        again.
40 How often they rebelled against him in
        the wilderness
    and grieved him in the desert!
41 They tested God again and again,
    and provoked the Holy One of Israel.
42 They did not keep in mind his power,

    or the day when he redeemed them
        from the foe;
43 when he displayed his signs in Egypt,
    and his miracles in the fields of Zoan.
44 He turned their rivers to blood,
    so that they could not drink of their
        streams.
45 He sent among them swarms of flies,
    which devoured them,
    and frogs, which destroyed them.
46 He gave their crops to the caterpillar,
    and the fruit of their labor to the
        locust.
47 He destroyed their vines with hail,
    and their sycamores with frost.
48 He gave over their cattle to the hail,
    and their flocks to thunderbolts.
49 He let loose on them his fierce anger,
    wrath, indignation, and distress,
    a company of destroying angels.
50 He made a path for his anger;
    he did not spare them from death,
    but gave their lives over to the plague.
51 He struck all the firstborn in Egypt,
    the first issue of their strength in the
        tents of Ham.
52 Then he led out his people like sheep,
    and guided them in the wilderness
        like a flock.
53 He led them in safety, so that they were
        not afraid;
    but the sea overwhelmed their
        enemies.
54 And he brought them to his holy hill,
    to the mountain that his right hand
        had won.
55 He drove out nations before them;
    he apportioned them for a possession
    and settled the tribes of Israel in their
        tents.
56 Yet they tested the Most High God,
    and rebelled against him.
    They did not observe his decrees,
57 but turned away and were faithless like
        their ancestors;
    they twisted like a treacherous bow.

58 For they provoked him to anger with
their high places;
they moved him to jealousy with their
idols.
59 When God heard, he was full of
wrath,
and he utterly rejected Israel.
60 He abandoned his dwelling at Shiloh,
the tent where he dwelt among
mortals,
61 and delivered his power to captivity,
his glory to the hand of the foe.
62 He gave his people to the sword,
and vented his wrath on his
heritage.
63 Fire devoured their young men,
and their girls had no marriage
song.
64 Their priests fell by the sword,
and their widows made no
lamentation.
65 Then the Lord awoke as from sleep,
like a warrior shouting because of
wine.
66 He put his adversaries to rout;
he put them to everlasting disgrace.

67 He rejected the tent of Joseph,
he did not choose the tribe of
Ephraim;
68 but he chose the tribe of Judah,
Mount Zion, which he loves.
69 He built his sanctuary like the high
heavens,
like the earth, which he has founded
forever.
70 He chose his servant David,
and took him from the sheepfolds;
71 from tending the nursing ewes he
brought him
to be the shepherd of his people
Jacob,
of Israel, his inheritance.
72 With upright heart he tended them,
and guided them with skillful hand.

Psalm 79

Plea for Mercy for Jerusalem

A Psalm of Asaph.

1 O God, the nations have come into your
inheritance;
they have defiled your holy temple;
they have laid Jerusalem in ruins.
2 They have given the bodies of your
servants
to the birds of the air for food,
the flesh of your faithful to the wild
animals of the earth.
3 They have poured out their blood like
water
all around Jerusalem,
and there was no one to bury them.
4 We have become a taunt to our
neighbors,
mocked and derided by those around
us.

5 How long, O Lord? Will you be angry
forever?
Will your jealous wrath burn like fire?
6 Pour out your anger on the nations
that do not know you,
and on the kingdoms
that do not call on your name.
7 For they have devoured Jacob
and laid waste his habitation.

8 Do not remember against us the
iniquities of our ancestors;
let your compassion come speedily to
meet us,
for we are brought very low.
9 Help us, O God of our salvation,
for the glory of your name;
deliver us, and forgive our sins,
for your name's sake.
10 Why should the nations say,
"Where is their God?"
Let the avenging of the outpoured
blood of your servants
be known among the nations before
our eyes.

11 Let the groans of the prisoners come
        before you;
    according to your great power
        preserve those doomed to
        die.
12 Return sevenfold into the bosom of our
        neighbors
    the taunts with which they taunted
        you, O Lord!
13 Then we your people, the flock of your
        pasture,
    will give thanks to you forever;
    from generation to generation we will
        recount your praise.

Psalm 80

Prayer for Israel's Restoration

To the leader: on Lilies, a Covenant. Of
    Asaph. A Psalm.

1 Give ear, O Shepherd of Israel,
    you who lead Joseph like a flock!
   You who are enthroned upon the
        cherubim, shine forth
2   before Ephraim and Benjamin and
        Manasseh.
   Stir up your might,
    and come to save us!

3 Restore us, O God;
    let your face shine, that we may be
        saved.

4 O LORD God of hosts,
    how long will you be angry with your
        people's prayers?
5 You have fed them with the bread of
        tears,
    and given them tears to drink in full
        measure.
6 You make us the scorn *a* of our
        neighbors;
    our enemies laugh among
        themselves.

7 Restore us, O God of hosts;
    let your face shine, that we may be
        saved.

8 You brought a vine out of Egypt;
    you drove out the nations and planted
        it.
9 You cleared the ground for it;
    it took deep root and filled the
        land.
10 The mountains were covered with its
        shade,
    the mighty cedars with its
        branches;
11 it sent out its branches to the sea,
    and its shoots to the River.
12 Why then have you broken down its
        walls,
    so that all who pass along the way
        pluck its fruit?
13 The boar from the forest ravages it,
    and all that move in the field feed
        on it.

14 Turn again, O God of hosts;
    look down from heaven, and see;
   have regard for this vine,
15   the stock that your right hand
        planted. *b*
16 They have burned it with fire, they have
        cut it down; *c*
    may they perish at the rebuke of your
        countenance.
17 But let your hand be upon the one at
        your right hand,
    the one whom you made strong for
        yourself.
18 Then we will never turn back from
        you;
    give us life, and we will call on your
        name.

19 Restore us, O LORD God of hosts;
    let your face shine, that we may be
        saved.

a Syr: Heb *strife*   *b* Heb adds from verse 17 *and upon the one whom you made strong for yourself*   *c* Cn: Heb *it is cut down*

Psalm 81

God's Appeal to Stubborn Israel

To the leader: according to The Gittith.
Of Asaph.

1 Sing aloud to God our strength;
   shout for joy to the God of Jacob.
2 Raise a song, sound the tambourine,
   the sweet lyre with the harp.
3 Blow the trumpet at the new moon,
   at the full moon, on our festal day.
4 For it is a statute for Israel,
   an ordinance of the God of Jacob.
5 He made it a decree in Joseph,
   when he went out over*a* the land of
   Egypt.

I hear a voice I had not known:
6 "I relieved your*b* shoulder of the
   burden;
   your*b* hands were freed from the
   basket.
7 In distress you called, and I rescued you;
   I answered you in the secret place of
   thunder;
   I tested you at the waters of Meribah.
                                        Selah
8 Hear, O my people, while I admonish
   you;
   O Israel, if you would but listen to
   me!
9 There shall be no strange god among
   you;
   you shall not bow down to a foreign
   god.
10 I am the LORD your God,
   who brought you up out of the land
   of Egypt.
   Open your mouth wide and I will
   fill it.

11 "But my people did not listen to my
   voice;
   Israel would not submit to me.
12 So I gave them over to their stubborn
   hearts,
   to follow their own counsels.
13 O that my people would listen to me,
   that Israel would walk in my ways!
14 Then I would quickly subdue their
   enemies,
   and turn my hand against their foes.
15 Those who hate the LORD would cringe
   before him,
   and their doom would last forever.
16 I would feed you*c* with the finest of the
   wheat,
   and with honey from the rock I
   would satisfy you."

Psalm 82

A Plea for Justice

A Psalm of Asaph.

1 God has taken his place in the divine
   council;
   in the midst of the gods he holds
   judgment:
2 "How long will you judge unjustly
   and show partiality to the wicked?
                                        Selah
3 Give justice to the weak and the orphan;
   maintain the right of the lowly and
   the destitute.
4 Rescue the weak and the needy;
   deliver them from the hand of the
   wicked."

5 They have neither knowledge nor
   understanding,
   they walk around in darkness;
   all the foundations of the earth are
   shaken.

6 I say, "You are gods,
   children of the Most High, all of you;
7 nevertheless, you shall die like mortals,
   and fall like any prince."*d*

8 Rise up, O God, judge the earth;
   for all the nations belong to you!

a Or *against*   *b* Heb *his*   *c* Cn Compare verse 16b: Heb *he would feed him*   *d* Or *fall as one man, O princes*

Psalm 83

Prayer for Judgment on Israel's Foes

A Song. A Psalm of Asaph.

1 O God, do not keep silence;
    do not hold your peace or be still,
        O God!
2 Even now your enemies are in tumult;
    those who hate you have raised their
        heads.
3 They lay crafty plans against your
        people;
    they consult together against those
        you protect.
4 They say, "Come, let us wipe them out
        as a nation;
    let the name of Israel be remembered
        no more."
5 They conspire with one accord;
    against you they make a covenant—
6 the tents of Edom and the Ishmaelites,
    Moab and the Hagrites,
7 Gebal and Ammon and Amalek,
    Philistia with the inhabitants of Tyre;
8 Assyria also has joined them;
    they are the strong arm of the
        children of Lot.   *Selah*

9 Do to them as you did to Midian,
    as to Sisera and Jabin at the Wadi
        Kishon,
10 who were destroyed at En-dor,
    who became dung for the ground.
11 Make their nobles like Oreb and Zeeb,
    all their princes like Zebah and
        Zalmunna,
12 who said, "Let us take the pastures of
        God
    for our own possession."

13 O my God, make them like whirling
        dust,*a*
    like chaff before the wind.
14 As fire consumes the forest,
    as the flame sets the mountains
        ablaze,

15 so pursue them with your tempest
    and terrify them with your hurricane.
16 Fill their faces with shame,
    so that they may seek your name,
        O LORD.
17 Let them be put to shame and dismayed
        forever;
    let them perish in disgrace.
18 Let them know that you alone,
    whose name is the LORD,
    are the Most High over all the earth.

Psalm 84

The Joy of Worship in the Temple

To the leader: according to The Gittith.
    Of the Korahites. A Psalm.

1 How lovely is your dwelling place,
    O LORD of hosts!
2 My soul longs, indeed it faints
    for the courts of the LORD;
my heart and my flesh sing for joy
    to the living God.

3 Even the sparrow finds a home,
    and the swallow a nest for herself,
    where she may lay her young,
at your altars, O LORD of hosts,
    my King and my God.
4 Happy are those who live in your house,
    ever singing your praise.   *Selah*

5 Happy are those whose strength is in
        you,
    in whose heart are the highways to
        Zion.*b*
6 As they go through the valley of Baca
    they make it a place of springs;
    the early rain also covers it with pools.
7 They go from strength to strength;
    the God of gods will be seen in Zion.

8 O LORD God of hosts, hear my prayer;
    give ear, O God of Jacob!   *Selah*
9 Behold our shield, O God;
    look on the face of your anointed.

a Or *a tumbleweed*   *b* Heb lacks *to Zion*

10 For a day in your courts is better
      than a thousand elsewhere.
   I would rather be a doorkeeper in the
         house of my God
      than live in the tents of wickedness.
11 For the LORD God is a sun and shield;
      he bestows favor and honor.
   No good thing does the LORD withhold
      from those who walk uprightly.
12 O LORD of hosts,
      happy is everyone who trusts in you.

Psalm 85

Prayer for the Restoration of God's Favor

To the leader. Of the Korahites. A Psalm.

1 LORD, you were favorable to your
         land;
      you restored the fortunes of Jacob.
2 You forgave the iniquity of your people;
      you pardoned all their sin.   *Selah*
3 You withdrew all your wrath;
      you turned from your hot anger.

4 Restore us again, O God of our
         salvation,
      and put away your indignation toward
         us.
5 Will you be angry with us forever?
      Will you prolong your anger to all
         generations?
6 Will you not revive us again,
      so that your people may rejoice in
         you?
7 Show us your steadfast love, O LORD,
      and grant us your salvation.

8 Let me hear what God the LORD will
         speak,
      for he will speak peace to his people,
      to his faithful, to those who turn to
         him in their hearts. *a*
9 Surely his salvation is at hand for those
         who fear him,
      that his glory may dwell in our land.

10 Steadfast love and faithfulness will meet;
      righteousness and peace will kiss each
         other.
11 Faithfulness will spring up from the
         ground,
      and righteousness will look down
         from the sky.
12 The LORD will give what is good,
      and our land will yield its increase.
13 Righteousness will go before him,
      and will make a path for his steps.

Psalm 86

Supplication for Help against Enemies

A Prayer of David.

1 Incline your ear, O LORD, and answer
         me,
      for I am poor and needy.
2 Preserve my life, for I am devoted to
         you;
      save your servant who trusts in you.
   You are my God; 3be gracious to me,
         O Lord,
      for to you do I cry all day long.
4 Gladden the soul of your servant,
      for to you, O Lord, I lift up my soul.
5 For you, O Lord, are good and
         forgiving,
      abounding in steadfast love to all who
         call on you.
6 Give ear, O LORD, to my prayer;
      listen to my cry of supplication.
7 In the day of my trouble I call on you,
      for you will answer me.

8 There is none like you among the gods,
         O Lord,
      nor are there any works like yours.
9 All the nations you have made shall
         come
      and bow down before you, O Lord,
      and shall glorify your name.
10 For you are great and do wondrous
         things;
      you alone are God.

---

a Gk: Heb *but let them not turn back to folly*

11 Teach me your way, O LORD,
  that I may walk in your truth;
  give me an undivided heart to revere
   your name.
12 I give thanks to you, O Lord my God,
  with my whole heart,
  and I will glorify your name forever.
13 For great is your steadfast love toward
   me;
  you have delivered my soul from the
   depths of Sheol.

14 O God, the insolent rise up against
   me;
  a band of ruffians seeks my life,
  and they do not set you before them.
15 But you, O Lord, are a God merciful
   and gracious,
  slow to anger and abounding in
   steadfast love and faithfulness.
16 Turn to me and be gracious to me;
  give your strength to your servant;
  save the child of your serving girl.
17 Show me a sign of your favor,
  so that those who hate me may see it
   and be put to shame,
  because you, LORD, have helped me
   and comforted me.

Psalm 87

The Joy of Living in Zion

Of the Korahites. A Psalm. A Song.

1 On the holy mount stands the city he
   founded;
2 the LORD loves the gates of Zion
  more than all the dwellings of Jacob.
3 Glorious things are spoken of you,
  O city of God.   *Selah*

4 Among those who know me I mention
   Rahab and Babylon;
  Philistia too, and Tyre, with
   Ethiopia*ᵃ*—
  "This one was born there," they say.

5 And of Zion it shall be said,
  "This one and that one were born in
   it";
  for the Most High himself will
   establish it.
6 The LORD records, as he registers the
   peoples,
  "This one was born there." *Selah*

7 Singers and dancers alike say,
  "All my springs are in you."

Psalm 88

Prayer for Help in Despondency

A Song. A Psalm of the Korahites. To
the leader: according to Mahalath
Leannoth. A Maskil of Heman the
Ezrahite.

1 O LORD, God of my salvation,
  when, at night, I cry out in your
   presence,
2 let my prayer come before you;
  incline your ear to my cry.

3 For my soul is full of troubles,
  and my life draws near to Sheol.
4 I am counted among those who go
   down to the Pit;
  I am like those who have no help,
5 like those forsaken among the dead,
  like the slain that lie in the grave,
  like those whom you remember no
   more,
  for they are cut off from your hand.
6 You have put me in the depths of the
   Pit,
  in the regions dark and deep.
7 Your wrath lies heavy upon me,
  and you overwhelm me with all your
   waves.   *Selah*

8 You have caused my companions to
   shun me;
  you have made me a thing of horror
   to them.

a Or *Nubia*; Heb *Cush*

I am shut in so that I cannot escape;
9   my eye grows dim through sorrow.
Every day I call on you, O LORD;
I spread out my hands to you.
10 Do you work wonders for the dead?
Do the shades rise up to praise you?
                                    Selah

11 Is your steadfast love declared in the
grave,
or your faithfulness in Abaddon?
12 Are your wonders known in the
darkness,
or your saving help in the land of
forgetfulness?

13 But I, O LORD, cry out to you;
in the morning my prayer comes
before you.
14 O LORD, why do you cast me off?
Why do you hide your face from me?
15 Wretched and close to death from my
youth up,
I suffer your terrors; I am desperate. *a*
16 Your wrath has swept over me;
your dread assaults destroy me.
17 They surround me like a flood all day
long;
from all sides they close in on me.
18 You have caused friend and neighbor to
shun me;
my companions are in darkness.

Psalm 89

God's Covenant with David

A Maskil of Ethan the Ezrahite.

1   I will sing of your steadfast love,
O LORD, *b* forever;
with my mouth I will proclaim your
faithfulness to all generations.
2   I declare that your steadfast love is
established forever;
your faithfulness is as firm as the
heavens.

3   You said, "I have made a covenant with
my chosen one,
I have sworn to my servant David:
4   'I will establish your descendants
forever,
and build your throne for all
generations.'"   *Selah*

5   Let the heavens praise your wonders,
O LORD,
your faithfulness in the assembly of
the holy ones.
6   For who in the skies can be compared
to the LORD?
Who among the heavenly beings is
like the LORD,
7   a God feared in the council of the holy
ones,
great and awesome *c* above all that are
around him?
8   O LORD God of hosts,
who is as mighty as you, O LORD?
Your faithfulness surrounds you.
9   You rule the raging of the sea;
when its waves rise, you still them.
10 You crushed Rahab like a carcass;
you scattered your enemies with your
mighty arm.
11 The heavens are yours, the earth also is
yours;
the world and all that is in it—you
have founded them.
12 The north and the south *d*—you created
them;
Tabor and Hermon joyously praise
your name.
13 You have a mighty arm;
strong is your hand, high your right
hand.
14 Righteousness and justice are the
foundation of your throne;
steadfast love and faithfulness go
before you.
15 Happy are the people who know the
festal shout,

a Meaning of Heb uncertain   b Gk: Heb *the steadfast love of the* LORD   c Gk Syr: Heb *greatly awesome*
d Or *Zaphon and Yamin*

who walk, O LORD, in the light of
    your countenance;

16 they exult in your name all day long,
    and extol*a* your righteousness.

17 For you are the glory of their strength;
    by your favor our horn is exalted.

18 For our shield belongs to the LORD,
    our king to the Holy One of Israel.

19 Then you spoke in a vision to your
    faithful one, and said:
    "I have set the crown*b* on one who is
    mighty,
    I have exalted one chosen from the
    people.

20 I have found my servant David;
    with my holy oil I have anointed him;

21 my hand shall always remain with him;
    my arm also shall strengthen him.

22 The enemy shall not outwit him,
    the wicked shall not humble him.

23 I will crush his foes before him
    and strike down those who hate him.

24 My faithfulness and steadfast love shall
    be with him;
    and in my name his horn shall be
    exalted.

25 I will set his hand on the sea
    and his right hand on the rivers.

26 He shall cry to me, 'You are my Father,
    my God, and the Rock of my
    salvation!'

27 I will make him the firstborn,
    the highest of the kings of the earth.

28 Forever I will keep my steadfast love for
    him,
    and my covenant with him will stand
    firm.

29 I will establish his line forever,
    and his throne as long as the heavens
    endure.

30 If his children forsake my law
    and do not walk according to my
    ordinances,

31 if they violate my statutes
    and do not keep my commandments,

32 then I will punish their transgression
    with the rod
    and their iniquity with scourges;

33 but I will not remove from him my
    steadfast love,
    or be false to my faithfulness.

34 I will not violate my covenant,
    or alter the word that went forth from
    my lips.

35 Once and for all I have sworn by my
    holiness;
    I will not lie to David.

36 His line shall continue forever,
    and his throne endure before me like
    the sun.

37 It shall be established forever like the
    moon,
    an enduring witness in the skies." *Selah*

38 But now you have spurned and rejected
    him;
    you are full of wrath against your
    anointed.

39 You have renounced the covenant with
    your servant;
    you have defiled his crown in the
    dust.

40 You have broken through all his walls;
    you have laid his strongholds in ruins.

41 All who pass by plunder him;
    he has become the scorn of his
    neighbors.

42 You have exalted the right hand of his
    foes;
    you have made all his enemies rejoice.

43 Moreover, you have turned back the
    edge of his sword,
    and you have not supported him in
    battle.

44 You have removed the scepter from his
    hand,*c*
    and hurled his throne to the ground.

45 You have cut short the days of his
    youth;
    you have covered him with shame.
                  Selah

---

a Cn: Heb *are exalted in*   *b* Cn: Heb *help*   *c* Cn: Heb *removed his cleanness*

46 How long, O LORD? Will you hide
         yourself forever?
     How long will your wrath burn like
         fire?
47 Remember how short my time is—*a*
     for what vanity you have created all
         mortals!
48 Who can live and never see death?
     Who can escape the power of Sheol?
                                              Selah

49 Lord, where is your steadfast love of
         old,
     which by your faithfulness you swore
         to David?
50 Remember, O Lord, how your servant is
         taunted;
     how I bear in my bosom the insults
         of the peoples,*b*
51 with which your enemies taunt,
         O LORD,
     with which they taunted the footsteps
         of your anointed.

52 Blessed be the LORD forever.
     Amen and Amen.

BOOK IV

(Psalms 90–106)

Psalm 90

God's Eternity and Human Frailty

A Prayer of Moses, the man of God.

1 Lord, you have been our dwelling place*c*
     in all generations.
2 Before the mountains were brought
         forth,
     or ever you had formed the earth and
         the world,
     from everlasting to everlasting you are
         God.

3 You turn us*d* back to dust,
     and say, "Turn back, you mortals."

4 For a thousand years in your sight
     are like yesterday when it is past,
     or like a watch in the night.

5 You sweep them away; they are like a
         dream,
     like grass that is renewed in the
         morning;
6 in the morning it flourishes and is
         renewed;
     in the evening it fades and withers.

7 For we are consumed by your anger;
     by your wrath we are overwhelmed.
8 You have set our iniquities before you,
     our secret sins in the light of your
         countenance.

9 For all our days pass away under your
         wrath;
     our years come to an end*e* like a sigh.
10 The days of our life are seventy years,
     or perhaps eighty, if we are strong;
even then their span*f* is only toil and
         trouble;
     they are soon gone, and we fly away.

11 Who considers the power of your
         anger?
     Your wrath is as great as the fear that
         is due you.
12 So teach us to count our days
     that we may gain a wise heart.

13 Turn, O LORD! How long?
     Have compassion on your servants!
14 Satisfy us in the morning with your
         steadfast love,
     so that we may rejoice and be glad all
         our days.
15 Make us glad as many days as you have
         afflicted us,
     and as many years as we have seen
         evil.
16 Let your work be manifest to your
         servants,

---

a Meaning of Heb uncertain   *b* Cn: Heb *bosom all of many peoples*   *c* Another reading is *our refuge*
d Heb *humankind*   *e* Syr: Heb *we bring our years to an end*   *f* Cn Compare Gk Syr Jerome Tg: Heb *pride*

and your glorious power to their
    children.
17 Let the favor of the Lord our God be
    upon us,
    and prosper for us the work of our
      hands—
    O prosper the work of our hands!

Psalm 91

Assurance of God's Protection

1 You who live in the shelter of the Most
    High,
    who abide in the shadow of the
      Almighty,*a*
2 will say to the LORD, "My refuge and my
    fortress;
    my God, in whom I trust."
3 For he will deliver you from the snare of
    the fowler
    and from the deadly pestilence;
4 he will cover you with his pinions,
    and under his wings you will find
      refuge;
    his faithfulness is a shield and buckler.
5 You will not fear the terror of the night,
    or the arrow that flies by day,
6 or the pestilence that stalks in darkness,
    or the destruction that wastes at
      noonday.

7 A thousand may fall at your side,
    ten thousand at your right hand,
    but it will not come near you.
8 You will only look with your eyes
    and see the punishment of the
      wicked.

9 Because you have made the LORD your
    refuge,*b*
    the Most High your dwelling place,
10 no evil shall befall you,
    no scourge come near your tent.

11 For he will command his angels
    concerning you

to guard you in all your ways.
12 On their hands they will bear you up,
    so that you will not dash your foot
      against a stone.
13 You will tread on the lion and the adder,
    the young lion and the serpent you
      will trample under foot.

14 Those who love me, I will deliver;
    I will protect those who know my
      name.
15 When they call to me, I will answer
    them;
    I will be with them in trouble,
    I will rescue them and honor them.
16 With long life I will satisfy them,
    and show them my salvation.

Psalm 92

Thanksgiving for Vindication

A Psalm. A Song for the Sabbath Day.

1 It is good to give thanks to the LORD,
    to sing praises to your name, O Most
      High;
2 to declare your steadfast love in the
    morning,
    and your faithfulness by night,
3 to the music of the lute and the harp,
    to the melody of the lyre.
4 For you, O LORD, have made me glad by
    your work;
    at the works of your hands I sing for
      joy.

5 How great are your works, O LORD!
    Your thoughts are very deep!
6 The dullard cannot know,
    the stupid cannot understand this:
7 though the wicked sprout like grass
    and all evildoers flourish,
    they are doomed to destruction forever,
8 but you, O LORD, are on high forever.
9 For your enemies, O LORD,
    for your enemies shall perish;
    all evildoers shall be scattered.

---

a Traditional rendering of Heb *Shaddai*   *b* Cn: Heb *Because you, LORD, are my refuge; you have made*

10 But you have exalted my horn like that
        of the wild ox;
    you have poured over me*a* fresh oil.
11 My eyes have seen the downfall of my
        enemies;
    my ears have heard the doom of my
        evil assailants.

12 The righteous flourish like the palm
        tree,
    and grow like a cedar in Lebanon.
13 They are planted in the house of the
        LORD;
    they flourish in the courts of our
        God.
14 In old age they still produce fruit;
    they are always green and full of sap,
15 showing that the LORD is upright;
    he is my rock, and there is no
        unrighteousness in him.

Psalm 93

The Majesty of God's Rule

1 The LORD is king, he is robed in
        majesty;
    the LORD is robed, he is girded with
        strength.
    He has established the world; it shall
        never be moved;
2   your throne is established from of
        old;
    you are from everlasting.

3 The floods have lifted up, O LORD,
    the floods have lifted up their voice;
    the floods lift up their roaring.
4 More majestic than the thunders of
        mighty waters,
    more majestic than the waves*b* of the
        sea,
    majestic on high is the LORD!

5 Your decrees are very sure;
    holiness befits your house,
    O LORD, forevermore.

Psalm 94

God the Avenger of the Righteous

1 O LORD, you God of vengeance,
    you God of vengeance, shine forth!
2 Rise up, O judge of the earth;
    give to the proud what they
        deserve!
3 O LORD, how long shall the wicked,
    how long shall the wicked exult?

4 They pour out their arrogant words;
    all the evildoers boast.
5 They crush your people, O LORD,
    and afflict your heritage.
6 They kill the widow and the stranger,
    they murder the orphan,
7 and they say, "The LORD does not see;
    the God of Jacob does not perceive."

8 Understand, O dullest of the people;
    fools, when will you be wise?
9 He who planted the ear, does he not
        hear?
    He who formed the eye, does he not
        see?
10 He who disciplines the nations,
    he who teaches knowledge to
        humankind,
    does he not chastise?
11   The LORD knows our thoughts,*c*
    that they are but an empty breath.

12 Happy are those whom you discipline,
        O LORD,
    and whom you teach out of your law,
13 giving them respite from days of
        trouble,
    until a pit is dug for the wicked.
14 For the LORD will not forsake his
        people;
    he will not abandon his heritage;
15 for justice will return to the righteous,
    and all the upright in heart will
        follow it.

---

a Syr: Meaning of Heb uncertain   *b* Cn: Heb *majestic are the waves*   *c* Heb *the thoughts of humankind*

16 Who rises up for me against the wicked?
    Who stands up for me against
      evildoers?
17 If the LORD had not been my help,
    my soul would soon have lived in the
      land of silence.
18 When I thought, "My foot is slipping,"
    your steadfast love, O LORD, held me
      up.
19 When the cares of my heart are many,
    your consolations cheer my soul.
20 Can wicked rulers be allied with you,
    those who contrive mischief by
      statute?
21 They band together against the life of
      the righteous,
    and condemn the innocent to death.
22 But the LORD has become my
      stronghold,
    and my God the rock of my refuge.
23 He will repay them for their iniquity
    and wipe them out for their
      wickedness;
    the LORD our God will wipe them
      out.

Psalm 95

A Call to Worship and Obedience

1 O come, let us sing to the LORD;
    let us make a joyful noise to the rock
      of our salvation!
2 Let us come into his presence with
      thanksgiving;
    let us make a joyful noise to him with
      songs of praise!
3 For the LORD is a great God,
    and a great King above all gods.
4 In his hand are the depths of the earth;
    the heights of the mountains are his
      also.
5 The sea is his, for he made it,
    and the dry land, which his hands
      have formed.

6 O come, let us worship and bow down,
    let us kneel before the LORD, our
      Maker!

7 For he is our God,
    and we are the people of his pasture,
    and the sheep of his hand.

O that today you would listen to his
      voice!
8 Do not harden your hearts, as at
      Meribah,
    as on the day at Massah in the
      wilderness,
9 when your ancestors tested me,
    and put me to the proof, though they
      had seen my work.
10 For forty years I loathed that
      generation
    and said, "They are a people whose
      hearts go astray,
    and they do not regard my ways."
11 Therefore in my anger I swore,
    "They shall not enter my rest."

Psalm 96

Praise to God Who Comes in Judgment

1 O sing to the LORD a new song;
    sing to the LORD, all the earth.
2 Sing to the LORD, bless his name;
    tell of his salvation from day to day.
3 Declare his glory among the nations,
    his marvelous works among all the
      peoples.
4 For great is the LORD, and greatly to be
      praised;
    he is to be revered above all gods.
5 For all the gods of the peoples are idols,
    but the LORD made the heavens.
6 Honor and majesty are before him;
    strength and beauty are in his
      sanctuary.

7 Ascribe to the LORD, O families of the
      peoples,
    ascribe to the LORD glory and
      strength.
8 Ascribe to the LORD the glory due his
      name;
    bring an offering, and come into his
      courts.

9   Worship the LORD in holy splendor;
     tremble before him, all the earth.

10   Say among the nations, "The LORD is
     king!
     The world is firmly established; it
       shall never be moved.
     He will judge the peoples with
       equity."
11   Let the heavens be glad, and let the
       earth rejoice;
     let the sea roar, and all that fills it;
12   let the field exult, and everything in it.
     Then shall all the trees of the forest sing
       for joy
13   before the LORD; for he is coming,
     for he is coming to judge the earth.
     He will judge the world with
       righteousness,
     and the peoples with his truth.

Psalm 97

The Glory of God's Reign

1   The LORD is king! Let the earth rejoice;
     let the many coastlands be glad!
2   Clouds and thick darkness are all around
       him;
     righteousness and justice are the
       foundation of his throne.
3   Fire goes before him,
     and consumes his adversaries on
       every side.
4   His lightnings light up the world;
     the earth sees and trembles.
5   The mountains melt like wax before the
       LORD,
     before the Lord of all the earth.

6   The heavens proclaim his righteousness;
     and all the peoples behold his glory.
7   All worshipers of images are put to
       shame,
     those who make their boast in
       worthless idols;
     all gods bow down before him.

8   Zion hears and is glad,
     and the towns*a* of Judah rejoice,
     because of your judgments, O God.
9   For you, O LORD, are most high over all
       the earth;
     you are exalted far above all gods.

10   The LORD loves those who hate*b* evil;
     he guards the lives of his faithful;
     he rescues them from the hand of the
       wicked.
11   Light dawns*c* for the righteous,
     and joy for the upright in heart.
12   Rejoice in the LORD, O you righteous,
     and give thanks to his holy name!

Psalm 98

Praise the Judge of the World

A Psalm.

1   O sing to the LORD a new song,
     for he has done marvelous things.
     His right hand and his holy arm
       have gotten him victory.
2   The LORD has made known his
       victory;
     he has revealed his vindication in the
       sight of the nations.
3   He has remembered his steadfast love
       and faithfulness
     to the house of Israel.
     All the ends of the earth have seen
       the victory of our God.

4   Make a joyful noise to the LORD, all the
       earth;
     break forth into joyous song and sing
       praises.
5   Sing praises to the LORD with the lyre,
     with the lyre and the sound of
       melody.
6   With trumpets and the sound of the
       horn
     make a joyful noise before the King,
       the LORD.

---

a Heb *daughters*   *b* Cn: Heb *You who love the LORD hate*   *c* Gk Syr Jerome: Heb *is sown*

7 Let the sea roar, and all that fills it;
 the world and those who live in it.
8 Let the floods clap their hands;
 let the hills sing together for joy
9 at the presence of the LORD, for he is
  coming
 to judge the earth.
He will judge the world with
  righteousness,
 and the peoples with equity.

Psalm 99

Praise to God for His Holiness

1 The LORD is king; let the peoples
  tremble!
 He sits enthroned upon the
  cherubim; let the earth quake!
2 The LORD is great in Zion;
 he is exalted over all the peoples.
3 Let them praise your great and awesome
  name.
 Holy is he!
4 Mighty King,*a* lover of justice,
 you have established equity;
you have executed justice
 and righteousness in Jacob.
5 Extol the LORD our God;
 worship at his footstool.
 Holy is he!

6 Moses and Aaron were among his
  priests,
 Samuel also was among those who
  called on his name.
 They cried to the LORD, and he
  answered them.
7 He spoke to them in the pillar of
  cloud;
 they kept his decrees,
 and the statutes that he gave them.

8 O LORD our God, you answered them;
 you were a forgiving God to them,
 but an avenger of their wrongdoings.
9 Extol the LORD our God,

and worship at his holy mountain;
 for the LORD our God is holy.

Psalm 100

All Lands Summoned to Praise God

A Psalm of thanksgiving.

1 Make a joyful noise to the LORD, all the
  earth.
2   Worship the LORD with gladness;
 come into his presence with singing.

3 Know that the LORD is God.
 It is he that made us, and we are his;*b*
 we are his people, and the sheep of
  his pasture.

4 Enter his gates with thanksgiving,
 and his courts with praise.
 Give thanks to him, bless his name.

5 For the LORD is good;
 his steadfast love endures forever,
 and his faithfulness to all generations.

Psalm 101

A Sovereign's Pledge of Integrity and Justice

Of David. A Psalm.

1 I will sing of loyalty and of justice;
 to you, O LORD, I will sing.
2 I will study the way that is blameless.
 When shall I attain it?

 I will walk with integrity of heart
  within my house;
3 I will not set before my eyes
 anything that is base.

 I hate the work of those who fall away;
 it shall not cling to me.
4 Perverseness of heart shall be far from
  me;
 I will know nothing of evil.

---

a Cn: Heb *And a king's strength* *b* Another reading is *and not we ourselves*

5 One who secretly slanders a neighbor
   I will destroy.
   A haughty look and an arrogant heart
   I will not tolerate.

6 I will look with favor on the faithful in
      the land,
   so that they may live with me;
   whoever walks in the way that is
      blameless
   shall minister to me.

7 No one who practices deceit
   shall remain in my house;
   no one who utters lies
   shall continue in my presence.

8 Morning by morning I will destroy
   all the wicked in the land,
   cutting off all evildoers
   from the city of the LORD.

Psalm 102

Prayer to the Eternal King for Help

A prayer of one afflicted, when faint and
   pleading before the LORD.

1 Hear my prayer, O LORD;
   let my cry come to you.
2 Do not hide your face from me
   in the day of my distress.
   Incline your ear to me;
   answer me speedily in the day when I
      call.

3 For my days pass away like smoke,
   and my bones burn like a furnace.
4 My heart is stricken and withered like
      grass;
   I am too wasted to eat my bread.
5 Because of my loud groaning
   my bones cling to my skin.
6 I am like an owl of the wilderness,
   like a little owl of the waste places.
7 I lie awake;
   I am like a lonely bird on the
      housetop.

8 All day long my enemies taunt me;
   those who deride me use my name
      for a curse.
9 For I eat ashes like bread,
   and mingle tears with my drink,
10 because of your indignation and anger;
   for you have lifted me up and thrown
      me aside.
11 My days are like an evening shadow;
   I wither away like grass.

12 But you, O LORD, are enthroned
      forever;
   your name endures to all generations.
13 You will rise up and have compassion
      on Zion,
   for it is time to favor it;
   the appointed time has come.
14 For your servants hold its stones dear,
   and have pity on its dust.
15 The nations will fear the name of the
      LORD,
   and all the kings of the earth your
      glory.
16 For the LORD will build up Zion;
   he will appear in his glory.
17 He will regard the prayer of the
      destitute,
   and will not despise their prayer.

18 Let this be recorded for a generation to
      come,
   so that a people yet unborn may
      praise the LORD:
19 that he looked down from his holy
      height,
   from heaven the LORD looked at the
      earth,
20 to hear the groans of the prisoners,
   to set free those who were doomed to
      die;
21 so that the name of the LORD may be
      declared in Zion,
   and his praise in Jerusalem,
22 when peoples gather together,
   and kingdoms, to worship the LORD.

23 He has broken my strength in
        midcourse;
    he has shortened my days.
24 "O my God," I say, "do not take me
        away
    at the midpoint of my life,
    you whose years endure
        throughout all generations."

25 Long ago you laid the foundation of the
        earth,
        and the heavens are the work of your
        hands.
26 They will perish, but you endure;
        they will all wear out like a garment.
    You change them like clothing, and they
        pass away;
27 but you are the same, and your years
        have no end.
28 The children of your servants shall live
        secure;
        their offspring shall be established in
        your presence.

Psalm 103

Thanksgiving for God's Goodness

Of David.

1 Bless the LORD, O my soul,
        and all that is within me,
        bless his holy name.
2 Bless the LORD, O my soul,
        and do not forget all his benefits—
3 who forgives all your iniquity,
        who heals all your diseases,
4 who redeems your life from the Pit,
        who crowns you with steadfast love
        and mercy,
5 who satisfies you with good as long as
        you live*a*
        so that your youth is renewed like the
        eagle's.

6 The LORD works vindication
        and justice for all who are oppressed.
7 He made known his ways to Moses,

a Meaning of Heb uncertain

his acts to the people of Israel.
8 The LORD is merciful and gracious,
        slow to anger and abounding in
        steadfast love.
9 He will not always accuse,
        nor will he keep his anger forever.
10 He does not deal with us according to
        our sins,
        nor repay us according to our
        iniquities.
11 For as the heavens are high above the
        earth,
        so great is his steadfast love toward
        those who fear him;
12 as far as the east is from the west,
        so far he removes our transgressions
        from us.
13 As a father has compassion for his
        children,
        so the LORD has compassion for
        those who fear him.
14 For he knows how we were made;
        he remembers that we are dust.

15 As for mortals, their days are like grass;
        they flourish like a flower of the field;
16 for the wind passes over it, and it is
        gone,
        and its place knows it no more.
17 But the steadfast love of the LORD is
            from everlasting to everlasting
        on those who fear him,
        and his righteousness to children's
        children,
18 to those who keep his covenant
        and remember to do his
        commandments.

19 The LORD has established his throne in
        the heavens,
        and his kingdom rules over all.
20 Bless the LORD, O you his angels,
        you mighty ones who do his bidding,
        obedient to his spoken word.
21 Bless the LORD, all his hosts,
        his ministers that do his will.

22 Bless the LORD, all his works,
   in all places of his dominion.
Bless the LORD, O my soul.

Psalm 104

God the Creator and Provider

1 Bless the LORD, O my soul.
   O LORD my God, you are very great.
You are clothed with honor and majesty,
2   wrapped in light as with a garment.
You stretch out the heavens like a tent,
3   you set the beams of your*a* chambers
     on the waters,
you make the clouds your*a* chariot,
   you ride on the wings of the wind,
4 you make the winds your*a* messengers,
   fire and flame your*a* ministers.

5 You set the earth on its foundations,
   so that it shall never be shaken.
6 You cover it with the deep as with a
    garment;
   the waters stood above the
    mountains.
7 At your rebuke they flee;
   at the sound of your thunder they
    take to flight.
8 They rose up to the mountains, ran
    down to the valleys
   to the place that you appointed for
    them.
9 You set a boundary that they may not
    pass,
   so that they might not again cover the
    earth.

10 You make springs gush forth in the
    valleys;
   they flow between the hills,
11 giving drink to every wild animal;
   the wild asses quench their thirst.
12 By the streams*b* the birds of the air have
    their habitation;
   they sing among the branches.

13 From your lofty abode you water the
    mountains;
   the earth is satisfied with the fruit of
    your work.

14 You cause the grass to grow for the
    cattle,
   and plants for people to use,*c*
to bring forth food from the earth,
15   and wine to gladden the human heart,
oil to make the face shine,
   and bread to strengthen the human
    heart.
16 The trees of the LORD are watered
    abundantly,
   the cedars of Lebanon that he planted.
17 In them the birds build their nests;
   the stork has its home in the fir trees.
18 The high mountains are for the wild
    goats;
   the rocks are a refuge for the coneys.
19 You have made the moon to mark the
    seasons;
   the sun knows its time for setting.
20 You make darkness, and it is night,
   when all the animals of the forest
    come creeping out.
21 The young lions roar for their prey,
   seeking their food from God.
22 When the sun rises, they withdraw
   and lie down in their dens.
23 People go out to their work
   and to their labor until the evening.

24 O LORD, how manifold are your works!
   In wisdom you have made them all;
   the earth is full of your creatures.
25 Yonder is the sea, great and wide,
   creeping things innumerable are there,
   living things both small and great.
26 There go the ships,
   and Leviathan that you formed to
    sport in it.

27 These all look to you
   to give them their food in due season;

a Heb *his*   *b* Heb *By them*   *c* Or *to cultivate*

28 when you give to them, they gather it
up;
   when you open your hand, they are
filled with good things.
29 When you hide your face, they are
dismayed;
   when you take away their breath, they
die
and return to their dust.
30 When you send forth your spirit,*a* they
are created;
   and you renew the face of the
ground.

31 May the glory of the LORD endure
forever;
   may the LORD rejoice in his works—
32 who looks on the earth and it trembles,
   who touches the mountains and they
smoke.
33 I will sing to the LORD as long as I live;
   I will sing praise to my God while I
have being.
34 May my meditation be pleasing to him,
   for I rejoice in the LORD.
35 Let sinners be consumed from the
earth,
   and let the wicked be no more.
Bless the LORD, O my soul.
Praise the LORD!

Psalm 105

God's Faithfulness to Israel

1 O give thanks to the LORD, call on his
name,
   make known his deeds among the
peoples.
2 Sing to him, sing praises to him;
   tell of all his wonderful works.
3 Glory in his holy name;
   let the hearts of those who seek the
LORD rejoice.
4 Seek the LORD and his strength;
   seek his presence continually.

5 Remember the wonderful works he has
done,
   his miracles, and the judgments he
has uttered,
6 O offspring of his servant Abraham,*b*
   children of Jacob, his chosen ones.

7 He is the LORD our God;
   his judgments are in all the earth.
8 He is mindful of his covenant forever,
   of the word that he commanded, for
a thousand generations,
9 the covenant that he made with
Abraham,
   his sworn promise to Isaac,
10 which he confirmed to Jacob as a
statute,
   to Israel as an everlasting covenant,
11 saying, "To you I will give the land of
Canaan
   as your portion for an inheritance."

12 When they were few in number,
   of little account, and strangers in it,
13 wandering from nation to nation,
   from one kingdom to another people,
14 he allowed no one to oppress them;
   he rebuked kings on their account,
15 saying, "Do not touch my anointed
ones;
   do my prophets no harm."

16 When he summoned famine against the
land,
   and broke every staff of bread,
17 he had sent a man ahead of them,
   Joseph, who was sold as a slave.
18 His feet were hurt with fetters,
   his neck was put in a collar of iron;
19 until what he had said came to pass,
   the word of the LORD kept testing
him.
20 The king sent and released him;
   the ruler of the peoples set him free.
21 He made him lord of his house,
   and ruler of all his possessions,

a Or *your breath*   *b* Another reading is *Israel* (compare 1 Chr 16.13)

22 to instruct*a* his officials at his pleasure,
　　and to teach his elders wisdom.

23 Then Israel came to Egypt;
　　Jacob lived as an alien in the land of
　　　Ham.
24 And the LORD made his people very
　　　fruitful,
　　and made them stronger than their
　　　foes,
25 whose hearts he then turned to hate his
　　　people,
　　to deal craftily with his servants.

26 He sent his servant Moses,
　　and Aaron whom he had chosen.
27 They performed his signs among them,
　　and miracles in the land of Ham.
28 He sent darkness, and made the land
　　　dark;
　　they rebelled*b* against his words.
29 He turned their waters into blood,
　　and caused their fish to die.
30 Their land swarmed with frogs,
　　even in the chambers of their kings.
31 He spoke, and there came swarms of
　　　flies,
　　and gnats throughout their country.
32 He gave them hail for rain,
　　and lightning that flashed through
　　　their land.
33 He struck their vines and fig trees,
　　and shattered the trees of their
　　　country.
34 He spoke, and the locusts came,
　　and young locusts without number;
35 they devoured all the vegetation in their
　　　land,
　　and ate up the fruit of their ground.
36 He struck down all the firstborn in their
　　　land,
　　the first issue of all their strength.

37 Then he brought Israel*c* out with silver
　　and gold,

and there was no one among their
　　tribes who stumbled.
38 Egypt was glad when they departed,
　　for dread of them had fallen upon it.
39 He spread a cloud for a covering,
　　and fire to give light by night.
40 They asked, and he brought quails,
　　and gave them food from heaven in
　　　abundance.
41 He opened the rock, and water gushed
　　　out;
　　it flowed through the desert like a
　　　river.
42 For he remembered his holy promise,
　　and Abraham, his servant.

43 So he brought his people out with joy,
　　his chosen ones with singing.
44 He gave them the lands of the nations,
　　and they took possession of the
　　　wealth of the peoples,
45 that they might keep his statutes
　　and observe his laws.
Praise the LORD!

Psalm 106

A Confession of Israel's Sins

1 Praise the LORD!
　　O give thanks to the LORD, for he is
　　　good;
　　for his steadfast love endures forever.
2 Who can utter the mighty doings of the
　　　LORD,
　　or declare all his praise?
3 Happy are those who observe justice,
　　who do righteousness at all times.

4 Remember me, O LORD, when you
　　　show favor to your people;
　　help me when you deliver them;
5 that I may see the prosperity of your
　　　chosen ones,
　　that I may rejoice in the gladness of
　　　your nation,
　　that I may glory in your heritage.

a Gk Syr Jerome: Heb *to bind*　　*b* Cn Compare Gk Syr: Heb *they did not rebel*　　*c* Heb *them*

6 Both we and our ancestors have sinned;
  we have committed iniquity, have
  done wickedly.
7 Our ancestors, when they were in
  Egypt,
  did not consider your wonderful
  works;
  they did not remember the abundance
  of your steadfast love,
  but rebelled against the Most High*a* at
  the Red Sea.*b*
8 Yet he saved them for his name's sake,
  so that he might make known his
  mighty power.
9 He rebuked the Red Sea,*b* and it became
  dry;
  he led them through the deep as
  through a desert.
10 So he saved them from the hand of the
  foe,
  and delivered them from the hand of
  the enemy.
11 The waters covered their adversaries;
  not one of them was left.
12 Then they believed his words;
  they sang his praise.

13 But they soon forgot his works;
  they did not wait for his counsel.
14 But they had a wanton craving in the
  wilderness,
  and put God to the test in the desert;
15 he gave them what they asked,
  but sent a wasting disease among
  them.

16 They were jealous of Moses in the
  camp,
  and of Aaron, the holy one of the
  LORD.
17 The earth opened and swallowed up
  Dathan,
  and covered the faction of Abiram.
18 Fire also broke out in their company;
  the flame burned up the wicked.

19 They made a calf at Horeb
  and worshiped a cast image.
20 They exchanged the glory of God*c*
  for the image of an ox that eats grass.
21 They forgot God, their Savior,
  who had done great things in Egypt,
22 wondrous works in the land of Ham,
  and awesome deeds by the Red Sea.*b*
23 Therefore he said he would destroy
  them—
  had not Moses, his chosen one,
  stood in the breach before him,
  to turn away his wrath from
  destroying them.

24 Then they despised the pleasant land,
  having no faith in his promise.
25 They grumbled in their tents,
  and did not obey the voice of the
  LORD.
26 Therefore he raised his hand and swore
  to them
  that he would make them fall in the
  wilderness,
27 and would disperse*d* their descendants
  among the nations,
  scattering them over the lands.

28 Then they attached themselves to the
  Baal of Peor,
  and ate sacrifices offered to the dead;
29 they provoked the LORD to anger with
  their deeds,
  and a plague broke out among them.
30 Then Phinehas stood up and interceded,
  and the plague was stopped.
31 And that has been reckoned to him as
  righteousness
  from generation to generation forever.

32 They angered the LORD*e* at the waters of
  Meribah,
  and it went ill with Moses on their
  account;
33 for they made his spirit bitter,
  and he spoke words that were rash.

a Cn Compare 78.17, 56: Heb *rebelled at the sea*   *b* Or *Sea of Reeds*   *c* Compare Gk Mss: Heb *exchanged their glory*
d Syr Compare Ezek 20.23: Heb *cause to fall*   *e* Heb *him*

34 They did not destroy the peoples,
　　as the LORD commanded them,
35 but they mingled with the nations
　　and learned to do as they did.
36 They served their idols,
　　which became a snare to them.
37 They sacrificed their sons
　　and their daughters to the demons;
38 they poured out innocent blood,
　　the blood of their sons and
　　　daughters,
　　whom they sacrificed to the idols of
　　　Canaan;
　　and the land was polluted with blood.
39 Thus they became unclean by their acts,
　　and prostituted themselves in their
　　　doings.

40 Then the anger of the LORD was
　　　kindled against his people,
　　and he abhorred his heritage;
41 he gave them into the hand of the
　　　nations,
　　so that those who hated them ruled
　　　over them.
42 Their enemies oppressed them,
　　and they were brought into subjection
　　　under their power.
43 Many times he delivered them,
　　but they were rebellious in their
　　　purposes,
　　and were brought low through their
　　　iniquity.
44 Nevertheless he regarded their distress
　　when he heard their cry.
45 For their sake he remembered his
　　　covenant,
　　and showed compassion according to
　　　the abundance of his steadfast
　　　love.
46 He caused them to be pitied
　　by all who held them captive.

47 Save us, O LORD our God,
　　and gather us from among the
　　　nations,

that we may give thanks to your holy
　　name
and glory in your praise.

48 Blessed be the LORD, the God of Israel,
　　from everlasting to everlasting.
　　And let all the people say, "Amen."
　　Praise the LORD!

BOOK V

(Psalms 107–150)

Psalm 107

*Thanksgiving for Deliverance from Many
Troubles*

1 O give thanks to the LORD, for he is
　　　good;
　　for his steadfast love endures forever.
2 Let the redeemed of the LORD say so,
　　those he redeemed from trouble
3 and gathered in from the lands,
　　from the east and from the west,
　　from the north and from the south.ᵃ

4 Some wandered in desert wastes,
　　finding no way to an inhabited town;
5 hungry and thirsty,
　　their soul fainted within them.
6 Then they cried to the LORD in their
　　　trouble,
　　and he delivered them from their
　　　distress;
7 he led them by a straight way,
　　until they reached an inhabited town.
8 Let them thank the LORD for his
　　　steadfast love,
　　for his wonderful works to
　　　humankind.
9 For he satisfies the thirsty,
　　and the hungry he fills with good
　　　things.

10 Some sat in darkness and in gloom,
　　prisoners in misery and in irons,

a Cn: Heb *sea*

11 for they had rebelled against the words
            of God,
        and spurned the counsel of the Most
            High.
12 Their hearts were bowed down with
            hard labor;
        they fell down, with no one to help.
13 Then they cried to the LORD in their
            trouble,
        and he saved them from their distress;
14 he brought them out of darkness and
            gloom,
        and broke their bonds asunder.
15 Let them thank the LORD for his
            steadfast love,
        for his wonderful works to
            humankind.
16 For he shatters the doors of bronze,
        and cuts in two the bars of iron.

17 Some were sick*a* through their sinful
            ways,
        and because of their iniquities
            endured affliction;
18 they loathed any kind of food,
        and they drew near to the gates of
            death.
19 Then they cried to the LORD in their
            trouble,
        and he saved them from their distress;
20 he sent out his word and healed them,
        and delivered them from destruction.
21 Let them thank the LORD for his
            steadfast love,
        for his wonderful works to
            humankind.
22 And let them offer thanksgiving
            sacrifices,
        and tell of his deeds with songs of
            joy.

23 Some went down to the sea in ships,
        doing business on the mighty waters;
24 they saw the deeds of the LORD,
        his wondrous works in the deep.

25 For he commanded and raised the
            stormy wind,
        which lifted up the waves of the sea.
26 They mounted up to heaven, they went
            down to the depths;
        their courage melted away in their
            calamity;
27 they reeled and staggered like drunkards,
        and were at their wits' end.
28 Then they cried to the LORD in their
            trouble,
        and he brought them out from their
            distress;
29 he made the storm be still,
        and the waves of the sea were
            hushed.
30 Then they were glad because they had
            quiet,
        and he brought them to their desired
            haven.
31 Let them thank the LORD for his
            steadfast love,
        for his wonderful works to
            humankind.
32 Let them extol him in the congregation
            of the people,
        and praise him in the assembly of the
            elders.

33 He turns rivers into a desert,
        springs of water into thirsty ground,
34 a fruitful land into a salty waste,
        because of the wickedness of its
            inhabitants.
35 He turns a desert into pools of water,
        a parched land into springs of water.
36 And there he lets the hungry live,
        and they establish a town to live in;
37 they sow fields, and plant vineyards,
        and get a fruitful yield.
38 By his blessing they multiply greatly,
        and he does not let their cattle
            decrease.

39 When they are diminished and brought
            low

a Cn: Heb *fools*

through oppression, trouble, and
sorrow,

40 he pours contempt on princes
and makes them wander in trackless
wastes;

41 but he raises up the needy out of
distress,
and makes their families like flocks.

42 The upright see it and are glad;
and all wickedness stops its mouth.

43 Let those who are wise give heed to
these things,
and consider the steadfast love of the
LORD.

Psalm 108

Praise and Prayer for Victory

A Song. A Psalm of David.

1 My heart is steadfast, O God, my heart
is steadfast;*a*
I will sing and make melody.
Awake, my soul!*b*

2 Awake, O harp and lyre!
I will awake the dawn.

3 I will give thanks to you, O LORD,
among the peoples,
and I will sing praises to you among
the nations.

4 For your steadfast love is higher than
the heavens,
and your faithfulness reaches to the
clouds.

5 Be exalted, O God, above the heavens,
and let your glory be over all the
earth.

6 Give victory with your right hand, and
answer me,
so that those whom you love may be
rescued.

7 God has promised in his sanctuary:*c*
"With exultation I will divide up
Shechem,

and portion out the Vale of Succoth.

8 Gilead is mine; Manasseh is mine;
Ephraim is my helmet;
Judah is my scepter.

9 Moab is my washbasin;
on Edom I hurl my shoe;
over Philistia I shout in triumph."

10 Who will bring me to the fortified city?
Who will lead me to Edom?

11 Have you not rejected us, O God?
You do not go out, O God, with our
armies.

12 O grant us help against the foe,
for human help is worthless.

13 With God we shall do valiantly;
it is he who will tread down our foes.

Psalm 109

Prayer for Vindication and Vengeance

To the leader. Of David. A Psalm.

1 Do not be silent, O God of my praise.

2 For wicked and deceitful mouths are
opened against me,
speaking against me with lying
tongues.

3 They beset me with words of hate,
and attack me without cause.

4 In return for my love they accuse me,
even while I make prayer for them.*d*

5 So they reward me evil for good,
and hatred for my love.

6 They say,*e* "Appoint a wicked man
against him;
let an accuser stand on his right.

7 When he is tried, let him be found
guilty;
let his prayer be counted as sin.

8 May his days be few;
may another seize his position.

9 May his children be orphans,
and his wife a widow.

10 May his children wander about and beg;

---

a Heb Mss Gk Syr: MT lacks *my heart is steadfast*   *b* Compare 57.8: Heb *also my soul*   *c* Or *by his holiness*
d Syr: Heb *I prayer*   *e* Heb lacks *They say*

may they be driven out of[a] the ruins
they inhabit.

11 May the creditor seize all that he has;
may strangers plunder the fruits of
his toil.

12 May there be no one to do him a
kindness,
nor anyone to pity his orphaned
children.

13 May his posterity be cut off;
may his name be blotted out in the
second generation.

14 May the iniquity of his father[b] be
remembered before the LORD,
and do not let the sin of his mother
be blotted out.

15 Let them be before the LORD
continually,
and may his[c] memory be cut off from
the earth.

16 For he did not remember to show
kindness,
but pursued the poor and needy
and the brokenhearted to their death.

17 He loved to curse; let curses come on
him.
He did not like blessing; may it be far
from him.

18 He clothed himself with cursing as his
coat,
may it soak into his body like water,
like oil into his bones.

19 May it be like a garment that he wraps
around himself,
like a belt that he wears every day."

20 May that be the reward of my accusers
from the LORD,
of those who speak evil against my
life.

21 But you, O LORD my Lord,
act on my behalf for your name's
sake;
because your steadfast love is good,
deliver me.

22 For I am poor and needy,

and my heart is pierced within me.

23 I am gone like a shadow at evening;
I am shaken off like a locust.

24 My knees are weak through fasting;
my body has become gaunt.

25 I am an object of scorn to my
accusers;
when they see me, they shake their
heads.

26 Help me, O LORD my God!
Save me according to your steadfast
love.

27 Let them know that this is your hand;
you, O LORD, have done it.

28 Let them curse, but you will bless.
Let my assailants be put to shame;[d]
may your servant be glad.

29 May my accusers be clothed with
dishonor;
may they be wrapped in their own
shame as in a mantle.

30 With my mouth I will give great thanks
to the LORD;
I will praise him in the midst of the
throng.

31 For he stands at the right hand of the
needy,
to save them from those who would
condemn them to death.

Psalm 110

Assurance of Victory for God's Priest-King

Of David. A Psalm.

1 The LORD says to my lord,
"Sit at my right hand
until I make your enemies your
footstool."

2 The LORD sends out from Zion
your mighty scepter.
Rule in the midst of your foes.

3 Your people will offer themselves
willingly
on the day you lead your forces

---

a Gk: Heb *and seek*   *b* Cn: Heb *fathers*   *c* Gk: Heb *their*   *d* Gk: Heb *They have risen up and have been put to shame*

on the holy mountains. *a*
From the womb of the morning,
    like dew, your youth *b* will come to
      you.
4 The LORD has sworn and will not
    change his mind,
    "You are a priest forever according to
      the order of Melchizedek." *c*

5 The Lord is at your right hand;
    he will shatter kings on the day of his
      wrath.
6 He will execute judgment among the
    nations,
    filling them with corpses;
  he will shatter heads
    over the wide earth.
7 He will drink from the stream by the
    path;
    therefore he will lift up his head.

Psalm 111

Praise for God's Wonderful Works

1 Praise the LORD!
  I will give thanks to the LORD with my
    whole heart,
    in the company of the upright, in the
      congregation.
2 Great are the works of the LORD,
    studied by all who delight in them.
3 Full of honor and majesty is his work,
    and his righteousness endures forever.
4 He has gained renown by his wonderful
    deeds;
    the LORD is gracious and merciful.
5 He provides food for those who fear
    him;
    he is ever mindful of his covenant.
6 He has shown his people the power of
    his works,
    in giving them the heritage of the
      nations.
7 The works of his hands are faithful and
    just;
    all his precepts are trustworthy.

8 They are established forever and ever,
    to be performed with faithfulness and
      uprightness.
9 He sent redemption to his people;
    he has commanded his covenant
      forever.
  Holy and awesome is his name.
10 The fear of the LORD is the beginning
    of wisdom;
    all those who practice it *d* have a good
      understanding.
  His praise endures forever.

Psalm 112

Blessings of the Righteous

1 Praise the LORD!
  Happy are those who fear the LORD,
  who greatly delight in his
    commandments.
2 Their descendants will be mighty in the
    land;
    the generation of the upright will be
      blessed.
3 Wealth and riches are in their houses,
    and their righteousness endures
      forever.
4 They rise in the darkness as a light for
    the upright;
    they are gracious, merciful, and
      righteous.
5 It is well with those who deal generously
    and lend,
    who conduct their affairs with justice.
6 For the righteous will never be moved;
    they will be remembered forever.
7 They are not afraid of evil tidings;
    their hearts are firm, secure in the
      LORD.
8 Their hearts are steady, they will not be
    afraid;
    in the end they will look in triumph
      on their foes.
9 They have distributed freely, they have
    given to the poor;
    their righteousness endures forever;

---

a Another reading is *in holy splendor*   *b* Cn: Heb *the dew of your youth*   *c* Or *forever, a rightful king by my edict*
d Gk Syr: Heb *them*

their horn is exalted in honor.
10 The wicked see it and are angry;
    they gnash their teeth and melt away;
    the desire of the wicked comes to
        nothing.

Psalm 113

God the Helper of the Needy

1 Praise the LORD!
  Praise, O servants of the LORD;
    praise the name of the LORD.

2 Blessed be the name of the LORD
    from this time on and forevermore.
3 From the rising of the sun to its setting
    the name of the LORD is to be praised.
4 The LORD is high above all nations,
    and his glory above the heavens.

5 Who is like the LORD our God,
    who is seated on high,
6 who looks far down
    on the heavens and the earth?
7 He raises the poor from the dust,
    and lifts the needy from the ash heap,
8 to make them sit with princes,
    with the princes of his people.
9 He gives the barren woman a home,
    making her the joyous mother of
        children.
  Praise the LORD!

Psalm 114

God's Wonders at the Exodus

1 When Israel went out from Egypt,
    the house of Jacob from a people of
        strange language,
2 Judah became God's*a* sanctuary,
    Israel his dominion.

3 The sea looked and fled;
    Jordan turned back.
4 The mountains skipped like rams,
    the hills like lambs.

5 Why is it, O sea, that you flee?
    O Jordan, that you turn back?
6 O mountains, that you skip like rams?
    O hills, like lambs?

7 Tremble, O earth, at the presence of the
        LORD,
    at the presence of the God of
        Jacob,
8 who turns the rock into a pool of
        water,
    the flint into a spring of water.

Psalm 115

The Impotence of Idols and the Greatness of God

1 Not to us, O LORD, not to us, but to
        your name give glory,
    for the sake of your steadfast love
        and your faithfulness.
2 Why should the nations say,
    "Where is their God?"

3 Our God is in the heavens;
    he does whatever he pleases.
4 Their idols are silver and gold,
    the work of human hands.
5 They have mouths, but do not speak;
    eyes, but do not see.
6 They have ears, but do not hear;
    noses, but do not smell.
7 They have hands, but do not feel;
    feet, but do not walk;
    they make no sound in their
        throats.
8 Those who make them are like them;
    so are all who trust in them.

9 O Israel, trust in the LORD!
    He is their help and their shield.
10 O house of Aaron, trust in the LORD!
    He is their help and their shield.
11 You who fear the LORD, trust in the
        LORD!
    He is their help and their shield.

a Heb *his*

12 The LORD has been mindful of us; he
    will bless us;
    he will bless the house of Israel;
    he will bless the house of Aaron;
13 he will bless those who fear the LORD,
    both small and great.

14 May the LORD give you increase,
    both you and your children.
15 May you be blessed by the LORD,
    who made heaven and earth.

16 The heavens are the LORD's heavens,
    but the earth he has given to human
    beings.
17 The dead do not praise the LORD,
    nor do any that go down into silence.
18 But we will bless the LORD
    from this time on and forevermore.
    Praise the LORD!

Psalm 116

Thanksgiving for Recovery from Illness

1 I love the LORD, because he has heard
    my voice and my supplications.
2 Because he inclined his ear to me,
    therefore I will call on him as long as
    I live.
3 The snares of death encompassed me;
    the pangs of Sheol laid hold on me;
    I suffered distress and anguish.
4 Then I called on the name of the LORD:
    "O LORD, I pray, save my life!"

5 Gracious is the LORD, and righteous;
    our God is merciful.
6 The LORD protects the simple;
    when I was brought low, he saved me.
7 Return, O my soul, to your rest,
    for the LORD has dealt bountifully
    with you.

8 For you have delivered my soul from
    death,
    my eyes from tears,
    my feet from stumbling.
9 I walk before the LORD

in the land of the living.
10 I kept my faith, even when I said,
    "I am greatly afflicted";
11 I said in my consternation,
    "Everyone is a liar."

12 What shall I return to the LORD
    for all his bounty to me?
13 I will lift up the cup of salvation
    and call on the name of the LORD,
14 I will pay my vows to the LORD
    in the presence of all his people.
15 Precious in the sight of the LORD
    is the death of his faithful ones.
16 O LORD, I am your servant;
    I am your servant, the child of your
    serving girl.
    You have loosed my bonds.
17 I will offer to you a thanksgiving
    sacrifice
    and call on the name of the LORD.
18 I will pay my vows to the LORD
    in the presence of all his people,
19 in the courts of the house of the LORD,
    in your midst, O Jerusalem.
    Praise the LORD!

Psalm 117

Universal Call to Worship

1 Praise the LORD, all you nations!
    Extol him, all you peoples!
2 For great is his steadfast love toward us,
    and the faithfulness of the LORD
    endures forever.
    Praise the LORD!

Psalm 118

A Song of Victory

1 O give thanks to the LORD, for he is
    good;
    his steadfast love endures forever!

2 Let Israel say,
    "His steadfast love endures forever."
3 Let the house of Aaron say,
    "His steadfast love endures forever."

4 Let those who fear the LORD say,
    "His steadfast love endures forever."

5 Out of my distress I called on the
        LORD;
    the LORD answered me and set me in
        a broad place.
6 With the LORD on my side I do not fear.
    What can mortals do to me?
7 The LORD is on my side to help me;
    I shall look in triumph on those who
        hate me.
8 It is better to take refuge in the LORD
    than to put confidence in mortals.
9 It is better to take refuge in the LORD
    than to put confidence in princes.

10 All nations surrounded me;
     in the name of the LORD I cut them
         off!
11 They surrounded me, surrounded me
         on every side;
     in the name of the LORD I cut them
         off!
12 They surrounded me like bees;
     they blazed*a* like a fire of thorns;
     in the name of the LORD I cut them
         off!
13 I was pushed hard,*b* so that I was falling,
     but the LORD helped me.
14 The LORD is my strength and my
         might;
     he has become my salvation.

15 There are glad songs of victory in the
         tents of the righteous:
     "The right hand of the LORD does
         valiantly;
16   the right hand of the LORD is exalted;
     the right hand of the LORD does
         valiantly."
17 I shall not die, but I shall live,
     and recount the deeds of the LORD.
18 The LORD has punished me severely,
     but he did not give me over to death.

19 Open to me the gates of righteousness,
     that I may enter through them
     and give thanks to the LORD.
20 This is the gate of the LORD;
     the righteous shall enter through it.
21 I thank you that you have answered me
     and have become my salvation.
22 The stone that the builders rejected
     has become the chief cornerstone.
23 This is the LORD's doing;
     it is marvelous in our eyes.
24 This is the day that the LORD has made;
     let us rejoice and be glad in it.*c*
25 Save us, we beseech you, O LORD!
     O LORD, we beseech you, give us
         success!

26 Blessed is the one who comes in the
         name of the LORD.*d*
     We bless you from the house of the
         LORD.
27 The LORD is God,
     and he has given us light.
     Bind the festal procession with
         branches,
     up to the horns of the altar.*e*

28 You are my God, and I will give thanks
         to you;
     you are my God, I will extol you.

29 O give thanks to the LORD, for he is
         good,
     for his steadfast love endures forever.

Psalm 119

The Glories of God's Law

1 Happy are those whose way is
         blameless,
     who walk in the law of the LORD.
2 Happy are those who keep his decrees,
     who seek him with their whole heart,
3 who also do no wrong,

---

a Gk: Heb *were extinguished*   b Gk Syr Jerome: Heb *You pushed me hard*   c Or *in him*   d Or *Blessed in the name of the LORD is the one who comes*   e Meaning of Heb uncertain but walk in his ways.

4 You have commanded your precepts
  to be kept diligently.

5 O that my ways may be steadfast
  in keeping your statutes!

6 Then I shall not be put to shame,
  having my eyes fixed on all your
  commandments.

7 I will praise you with an upright heart,
  when I learn your righteous
  ordinances.

8 I will observe your statutes;
  do not utterly forsake me.

9 How can young people keep their way
  pure?
  By guarding it according to your
  word.

10 With my whole heart I seek you;
  do not let me stray from your
  commandments.

11 I treasure your word in my heart,
  so that I may not sin against you.

12 Blessed are you, O LORD;
  teach me your statutes.

13 With my lips I declare
  all the ordinances of your mouth.

14 I delight in the way of your decrees
  as much as in all riches.

15 I will meditate on your precepts,
  and fix my eyes on your ways.

16 I will delight in your statutes;
  I will not forget your word.

17 Deal bountifully with your servant,
  so that I may live and observe your
  word.

18 Open my eyes, so that I may behold
  wondrous things out of your law.

19 I live as an alien in the land;
  do not hide your commandments
  from me.

20 My soul is consumed with longing
  for your ordinances at all times.

21 You rebuke the insolent, accursed ones,
  who wander from your
  commandments;

22 take away from me their scorn and
  contempt,
  for I have kept your decrees.

23 Even though princes sit plotting against
  me,
  your servant will meditate on your
  statutes.

24 Your decrees are my delight,
  they are my counselors.

25 My soul clings to the dust;
  revive me according to your word.

26 When I told of my ways, you answered
  me;
  teach me your statutes.

27 Make me understand the way of your
  precepts,
  and I will meditate on your wondrous
  works.

28 My soul melts away for sorrow;
  strengthen me according to your
  word.

29 Put false ways far from me;
  and graciously teach me your law.

30 I have chosen the way of faithfulness;
  I set your ordinances before me.

31 I cling to your decrees, O LORD;
  let me not be put to shame.

32 I run the way of your commandments,
  for you enlarge my understanding.

33 Teach me, O LORD, the way of your
  statutes,
  and I will observe it to the end.

34 Give me understanding, that I may keep
  your law
  and observe it with my whole heart.

35 Lead me in the path of your
  commandments,
  for I delight in it.

36 Turn my heart to your decrees,
  and not to selfish gain.

37 Turn my eyes from looking at vanities;
  give me life in your ways.

38 Confirm to your servant your promise,
  which is for those who fear you.

39 Turn away the disgrace that I dread,
  for your ordinances are good.

40 See, I have longed for your precepts;
   in your righteousness give me life.

41 Let your steadfast love come to me,
       O LORD,
   your salvation according to your
       promise.
42 Then I shall have an answer for those
       who taunt me,
   for I trust in your word.
43 Do not take the word of truth utterly
       out of my mouth,
   for my hope is in your ordinances.
44 I will keep your law continually,
   forever and ever.
45 I shall walk at liberty,
   for I have sought your precepts.
46 I will also speak of your decrees before
       kings,
   and shall not be put to shame;
47 I find my delight in your
       commandments,
   because I love them.
48 I revere your commandments, which I
       love,
   and I will meditate on your statutes.

49 Remember your word to your
       servant,
   in which you have made me hope.
50 This is my comfort in my distress,
   that your promise gives me life.
51 The arrogant utterly deride me,
   but I do not turn away from your law.
52 When I think of your ordinances from
       of old,
   I take comfort, O LORD.
53 Hot indignation seizes me because of
       the wicked,
   those who forsake your law.
54 Your statutes have been my songs
   wherever I make my home.
55 I remember your name in the night,
       O LORD,
   and keep your law.
56 This blessing has fallen to me,
   for I have kept your precepts.

57 The LORD is my portion;
   I promise to keep your words.
58 I implore your favor with all my heart;
   be gracious to me according to your
       promise.
59 When I think of your ways,
   I turn my feet to your decrees;
60 I hurry and do not delay
   to keep your commandments.
61 Though the cords of the wicked
       ensnare me,
   I do not forget your law.
62 At midnight I rise to praise you,
   because of your righteous ordinances.
63 I am a companion of all who fear you,
   of those who keep your precepts.
64 The earth, O LORD, is full of your
       steadfast love;
   teach me your statutes.

65 You have dealt well with your servant,
   O LORD, according to your word.
66 Teach me good judgment and
       knowledge,
   for I believe in your commandments.
67 Before I was humbled I went astray,
   but now I keep your word.
68 You are good and do good;
   teach me your statutes.
69 The arrogant smear me with lies,
   but with my whole heart I keep your
       precepts.
70 Their hearts are fat and gross,
   but I delight in your law.
71 It is good for me that I was humbled,
   so that I might learn your statutes.
72 The law of your mouth is better to me
   than thousands of gold and silver
       pieces.

73 Your hands have made and fashioned
       me;
   give me understanding that I may
       learn your commandments.
74 Those who fear you shall see me and
       rejoice,
   because I have hoped in your word.

75 I know, O LORD, that your judgments
　　　are right,
　　and that in faithfulness you have
　　　humbled me.
76 Let your steadfast love become my
　　　comfort
　　according to your promise to your
　　　servant.
77 Let your mercy come to me, that I may
　　　live;
　　for your law is my delight.
78 Let the arrogant be put to shame,
　　because they have subverted me with
　　　guile;
　　as for me, I will meditate on your
　　　precepts.
79 Let those who fear you turn to me,
　　so that they may know your decrees.
80 May my heart be blameless in your
　　　statutes,
　　so that I may not be put to shame.

81 My soul languishes for your salvation;
　　I hope in your word.
82 My eyes fail with watching for your
　　　promise;
　　I ask, "When will you comfort me?"
83 For I have become like a wineskin in the
　　　smoke,
　　yet I have not forgotten your statutes.
84 How long must your servant endure?
　　When will you judge those who
　　　persecute me?
85 The arrogant have dug pitfalls for me;
　　they flout your law.
86 All your commandments are enduring;
　　I am persecuted without cause; help
　　　me!
87 They have almost made an end of me
　　　on earth;
　　but I have not forsaken your precepts.
88 In your steadfast love spare my life,
　　so that I may keep the decrees of
　　　your mouth.

89 The LORD exists forever;
　　your word is firmly fixed in heaven.

90 Your faithfulness endures to all
　　　generations;
　　you have established the earth, and it
　　　stands fast.
91 By your appointment they stand today,
　　for all things are your servants.
92 If your law had not been my delight,
　　I would have perished in my misery.
93 I will never forget your precepts,
　　for by them you have given me life.
94 I am yours; save me,
　　for I have sought your precepts.
95 The wicked lie in wait to destroy me,
　　but I consider your decrees.
96 I have seen a limit to all perfection,
　　but your commandment is
　　　exceedingly broad.

97 Oh, how I love your law!
　　It is my meditation all day long.
98 Your commandment makes me wiser
　　　than my enemies,
　　for it is always with me.
99 I have more understanding than all my
　　　teachers,
　　for your decrees are my meditation.
100 I understand more than the aged,
　　for I keep your precepts.
101 I hold back my feet from every evil way,
　　in order to keep your word.
102 I do not turn away from your
　　　ordinances,
　　for you have taught me.
103 How sweet are your words to my taste,
　　sweeter than honey to my mouth!
104 Through your precepts I get
　　　understanding;
　　therefore I hate every false way.

105 Your word is a lamp to my feet
　　and a light to my path.
106 I have sworn an oath and confirmed it,
　　to observe your righteous ordinances.
107 I am severely afflicted;
　　give me life, O LORD, according to
　　　your word.
108 Accept my offerings of praise, O LORD,
　　and teach me your ordinances.

109 I hold my life in my hand continually,
     but I do not forget your law.
110 The wicked have laid a snare for me,
     but I do not stray from your precepts.
111 Your decrees are my heritage forever;
     they are the joy of my heart.
112 I incline my heart to perform your
          statutes
     forever, to the end.

113 I hate the double-minded,
     but I love your law.
114 You are my hiding place and my shield;
     I hope in your word.
115 Go away from me, you evildoers,
     that I may keep the commandments
          of my God.
116 Uphold me according to your promise,
          that I may live,
     and let me not be put to shame in my
          hope.
117 Hold me up, that I may be safe
     and have regard for your statutes
          continually.
118 You spurn all who go astray from your
          statutes;
     for their cunning is in vain.
119 All the wicked of the earth you count as
          dross;
     therefore I love your decrees.
120 My flesh trembles for fear of you,
     and I am afraid of your judgments.

121 I have done what is just and right;
     do not leave me to my oppressors.
122 Guarantee your servant's well-being;
     do not let the godless oppress me.
123 My eyes fail from watching for your
          salvation,
     and for the fulfillment of your
          righteous promise.
124 Deal with your servant according to
          your steadfast love,
     and teach me your statutes.
125 I am your servant; give me
          understanding,

     so that I may know your decrees.
126 It is time for the LORD to act,
     for your law has been broken.
127 Truly I love your commandments
     more than gold, more than fine gold.
128 Truly I direct my steps by all your
          precepts;*a*
     I hate every false way.

129 Your decrees are wonderful;
     therefore my soul keeps them.
130 The unfolding of your words gives light;
     it imparts understanding to the
          simple.
131 With open mouth I pant,
     because I long for your
          commandments.
132 Turn to me and be gracious to me,
     as is your custom toward those who
          love your name.
133 Keep my steps steady according to your
          promise,
     and never let iniquity have dominion
          over me.
134 Redeem me from human oppression,
     that I may keep your precepts.
135 Make your face shine upon your servant,
     and teach me your statutes.
136 My eyes shed streams of tears
     because your law is not kept.

137 You are righteous, O LORD,
     and your judgments are right.
138 You have appointed your decrees in
          righteousness
     and in all faithfulness.
139 My zeal consumes me
     because my foes forget your words.
140 Your promise is well tried,
     and your servant loves it.
141 I am small and despised,
     yet I do not forget your precepts.
142 Your righteousness is an everlasting
          righteousness,
     and your law is the truth.

a Gk Jerome: Meaning of Heb uncertain

143 Trouble and anguish have come upon
        me,
    but your commandments are my
        delight.
144 Your decrees are righteous forever;
    give me understanding that I may live.

145 With my whole heart I cry; answer me,
        O LORD.
    I will keep your statutes.
146 I cry to you; save me,
    that I may observe your decrees.
147 I rise before dawn and cry for help;
    I put my hope in your words.
148 My eyes are awake before each watch of
        the night,
    that I may meditate on your promise.
149 In your steadfast love hear my voice;
    O LORD, in your justice preserve my
        life.
150 Those who persecute me with evil
        purpose draw near;
    they are far from your law.
151 Yet you are near, O LORD,
    and all your commandments are true.
152 Long ago I learned from your decrees
    that you have established them
        forever.

153 Look on my misery and rescue me,
    for I do not forget your law.
154 Plead my cause and redeem me;
    give me life according to your
        promise.
155 Salvation is far from the wicked,
    for they do not seek your statutes.
156 Great is your mercy, O LORD;
    give me life according to your justice.
157 Many are my persecutors and my
        adversaries,
    yet I do not swerve from your
        decrees.
158 I look at the faithless with disgust,
    because they do not keep your
        commands.
159 Consider how I love your precepts;
    preserve my life according to your
        steadfast love.

160 The sum of your word is truth;
    and every one of your righteous
        ordinances endures forever.

161 Princes persecute me without cause,
    but my heart stands in awe of your
        words.
162 I rejoice at your word
    like one who finds great spoil.
163 I hate and abhor falsehood,
    but I love your law.
164 Seven times a day I praise you
    for your righteous ordinances.
165 Great peace have those who love your
        law;
    nothing can make them stumble.
166 I hope for your salvation, O LORD,
    and I fulfill your commandments.
167 My soul keeps your decrees;
    I love them exceedingly.
168 I keep your precepts and decrees,
    for all my ways are before you.

169 Let my cry come before you,
        O LORD;
    give me understanding according to
        your word.
170 Let my supplication come before you;
    deliver me according to your
        promise.
171 My lips will pour forth praise,
    because you teach me your statutes.
172 My tongue will sing of your promise,
    for all your commandments are
        right.
173 Let your hand be ready to help me,
    for I have chosen your precepts.
174 I long for your salvation, O LORD,
    and your law is my delight.
175 Let me live that I may praise you,
    and let your ordinances help me.
176 I have gone astray like a lost sheep; seek
        out your servant,
    for I do not forget your
        commandments.

Psalm 120

Prayer for Deliverance from Slanderers

A Song of Ascents.

1   In my distress I cry to the LORD,
        that he may answer me:
2   "Deliver me, O LORD,
        from lying lips,
        from a deceitful tongue."

3   What shall be given to you?
        And what more shall be done to you,
        you deceitful tongue?
4   A warrior's sharp arrows,
        with glowing coals of the broom tree!

5   Woe is me, that I am an alien in
            Meshech,
        that I must live among the tents of
            Kedar.
6   Too long have I had my dwelling
        among those who hate peace.
7   I am for peace;
        but when I speak,
        they are for war.

Psalm 121

Assurance of God's Protection

A Song of Ascents.

1   I lift up my eyes to the hills—
        from where will my help come?
2   My help comes from the LORD,
        who made heaven and earth.

3   He will not let your foot be moved;
        he who keeps you will not slumber.
4   He who keeps Israel
        will neither slumber nor sleep.

5   The LORD is your keeper;
        the LORD is your shade at your right
            hand.
6   The sun shall not strike you by day,
        nor the moon by night.

7   The LORD will keep you from all evil;
        he will keep your life.
8   The LORD will keep
        your going out and your coming in
        from this time on and forevermore.

Psalm 122

Song of Praise and Prayer for Jerusalem

A Song of Ascents. Of David.

1   I was glad when they said to me,
        "Let us go to the house of the
            LORD!"
2   Our feet are standing
        within your gates, O Jerusalem.

3   Jerusalem—built as a city
        that is bound firmly together.
4   To it the tribes go up,
        the tribes of the LORD,
    as was decreed for Israel,
        to give thanks to the name of the
            LORD.
5   For there the thrones for judgment were
            set up,
        the thrones of the house of David.

6   Pray for the peace of Jerusalem:
        "May they prosper who love you.
7   Peace be within your walls,
        and security within your towers."
8   For the sake of my relatives and friends
        I will say, "Peace be within you."
9   For the sake of the house of the LORD
            our God,
        I will seek your good.

Psalm 123

Supplication for Mercy

A Song of Ascents.

1   To you I lift up my eyes,
        O you who are enthroned in the
            heavens!
2   As the eyes of servants
        look to the hand of their master,
    as the eyes of a maid
        to the hand of her mistress,

so our eyes look to the LORD our
    God,
  until he has mercy upon us.

3 Have mercy upon us, O LORD, have
    mercy upon us,
  for we have had more than enough of
    contempt.
4 Our soul has had more than its fill
  of the scorn of those who are at
    ease,
  of the contempt of the proud.

Psalm 124

Thanksgiving for Israel's Deliverance

A Song of Ascents. Of David.

1 If it had not been the LORD who was on
    our side
    —let Israel now say—
2 if it had not been the LORD who was on
    our side,
  when our enemies attacked us,
3 then they would have swallowed us up
    alive,
  when their anger was kindled against
    us;
4 then the flood would have swept us
    away,
  the torrent would have gone over
    us;
5 then over us would have gone
  the raging waters.

6 Blessed be the LORD,
  who has not given us
  as prey to their teeth.
7 We have escaped like a bird
  from the snare of the fowlers;
  the snare is broken,
  and we have escaped.

8 Our help is in the name of the LORD,
  who made heaven and earth.

a Or *brought back those who returned to Zion*

Psalm 125

The Security of God's People

A Song of Ascents.

1 Those who trust in the LORD are like
    Mount Zion,
  which cannot be moved, but abides
    forever.
2 As the mountains surround Jerusalem,
  so the LORD surrounds his people,
  from this time on and forevermore.
3 For the scepter of wickedness shall not
    rest
  on the land allotted to the righteous,
  so that the righteous might not stretch
    out
  their hands to do wrong.
4 Do good, O LORD, to those who are
    good,
  and to those who are upright in their
    hearts.
5 But those who turn aside to their own
    crooked ways
  the LORD will lead away with
    evildoers.
  Peace be upon Israel!

Psalm 126

A Harvest of Joy

A Song of Ascents.

1 When the LORD restored the fortunes of
    Zion,*a*
  we were like those who dream.
2 Then our mouth was filled with
    laughter,
  and our tongue with shouts of joy;
  then it was said among the nations,
    "The LORD has done great things for
    them."
3 The LORD has done great things for us,
  and we rejoiced.

4 Restore our fortunes, O LORD,
  like the watercourses in the Negeb.

5 May those who sow in tears
   reap with shouts of joy.
6 Those who go out weeping,
   bearing the seed for sowing,
   shall come home with shouts of joy,
   carrying their sheaves.

Psalm 127

God's Blessings in the Home

A Song of Ascents. Of Solomon.

1 Unless the LORD builds the house,
   those who build it labor in vain.
   Unless the LORD guards the city,
   the guard keeps watch in vain.
2 It is in vain that you rise up early
   and go late to rest,
   eating the bread of anxious toil;
   for he gives sleep to his beloved.*a*

3 Sons are indeed a heritage from the
   LORD,
   the fruit of the womb a reward.
4 Like arrows in the hand of a warrior
   are the sons of one's youth.
5 Happy is the man who has
   his quiver full of them.
   He shall not be put to shame
   when he speaks with his enemies in
   the gate.

Psalm 128

The Happy Home of the Faithful

A Song of Ascents.

1 Happy is everyone who fears the
   LORD,
   who walks in his ways.
2 You shall eat the fruit of the labor of
   your hands;
   you shall be happy, and it shall go well
   with you.

3 Your wife will be like a fruitful vine
   within your house;

your children will be like olive shoots
   around your table.
4 Thus shall the man be blessed
   who fears the LORD.

5 The LORD bless you from Zion.
   May you see the prosperity of
   Jerusalem
   all the days of your life.
6 May you see your children's children.
   Peace be upon Israel!

Psalm 129

*Prayer for the Downfall of
Israel's Enemies*

A Song of Ascents.

1 "Often have they attacked me from my
   youth"
   —let Israel now say—
2 "often have they attacked me from my
   youth,
   yet they have not prevailed against
   me.
3 The plowers plowed on my back;
   they made their furrows long."
4 The LORD is righteous;
   he has cut the cords of the
   wicked.
5 May all who hate Zion
   be put to shame and turned
   backward.
6 Let them be like the grass on the
   housetops
   that withers before it grows up,
7 with which reapers do not fill their
   hands
   or binders of sheaves their arms,
8 while those who pass by do not say,
   "The blessing of the LORD be upon
   you!
   We bless you in the name of the
   LORD!"

a Or *for he provides for his beloved during sleep*

Psalm 130

Waiting for Divine Redemption

A Song of Ascents.

1 Out of the depths I cry to you,
     O LORD.
2   Lord, hear my voice!
Let your ears be attentive
     to the voice of my supplications!

3 If you, O LORD, should mark iniquities,
     Lord, who could stand?
4 But there is forgiveness with you,
     so that you may be revered.

5 I wait for the LORD, my soul waits,
     and in his word I hope;
6 my soul waits for the Lord
     more than those who watch for the
         morning,
     more than those who watch for the
         morning.

7 O Israel, hope in the LORD!
     For with the LORD there is steadfast
         love,
     and with him is great power to redeem.
8 It is he who will redeem Israel
     from all its iniquities.

Psalm 131

Song of Quiet Trust

A Song of Ascents. Of David.

1 O LORD, my heart is not lifted up,
     my eyes are not raised too high;
I do not occupy myself with things
     too great and too marvelous for me.
2 But I have calmed and quieted my soul,
     like a weaned child with its mother;
     my soul is like the weaned child that is
         with me.*a*

3 O Israel, hope in the LORD
     from this time on and forevermore.

a Or my soul within me is like a weaned child

Psalm 132

The Eternal Dwelling of God in Zion

A Song of Ascents.

1 O LORD, remember in David's favor
     all the hardships he endured;
2 how he swore to the LORD
     and vowed to the Mighty One of
         Jacob,
3 "I will not enter my house
     or get into my bed;
4 I will not give sleep to my eyes
     or slumber to my eyelids,
5 until I find a place for the LORD,
     a dwelling place for the Mighty One
         of Jacob."

6 We heard of it in Ephrathah;
     we found it in the fields of Jaar.
7 "Let us go to his dwelling place;
     let us worship at his footstool."

8 Rise up, O LORD, and go to your resting
         place,
     you and the ark of your might.
9 Let your priests be clothed with
         righteousness,
     and let your faithful shout for joy.
10 For your servant David's sake
     do not turn away the face of your
         anointed one.

11 The LORD swore to David a sure oath
     from which he will not turn back:
"One of the sons of your body
     I will set on your throne.
12 If your sons keep my covenant
     and my decrees that I shall teach
         them,
their sons also, forevermore,
     shall sit on your throne."

13 For the LORD has chosen Zion;
     he has desired it for his habitation:
14 "This is my resting place forever;
     here I will reside, for I have desired it.

15 I will abundantly bless its provisions;
    I will satisfy its poor with bread.
16 Its priests I will clothe with salvation,
    and its faithful will shout for joy.
17 There I will cause a horn to sprout up
      for David;
    I have prepared a lamp for my
      anointed one.
18 His enemies I will clothe with disgrace,
    but on him, his crown will gleam."

Psalm 133

The Blessedness of Unity

A Song of Ascents.

1 How very good and pleasant it is
    when kindred live together in unity!
2 It is like the precious oil on the head,
    running down upon the beard,
on the beard of Aaron,
    running down over the collar of his
      robes.
3 It is like the dew of Hermon,
    which falls on the mountains of Zion.
For there the LORD ordained his blessing,
    life forevermore.

Psalm 134

Praise in the Night

A Song of Ascents.

1 Come, bless the LORD, all you servants
      of the LORD,
    who stand by night in the house of
      the LORD!
2 Lift up your hands to the holy place,
    and bless the LORD.

3 May the LORD, maker of heaven and
      earth,
    bless you from Zion.

Psalm 135

Praise for God's Goodness and Might

1 Praise the LORD!
    Praise the name of the LORD;

    give praise, O servants of the LORD,
2 you that stand in the house of the
      LORD,
    in the courts of the house of our
      God.
3 Praise the LORD, for the LORD is good;
    sing to his name, for he is gracious.
4 For the LORD has chosen Jacob for
      himself,
    Israel as his own possession.

5 For I know that the LORD is great;
    our Lord is above all gods.
6 Whatever the LORD pleases he does,
    in heaven and on earth,
    in the seas and all deeps.
7 He it is who makes the clouds rise at the
      end of the earth;
    he makes lightnings for the rain
    and brings out the wind from his
      storehouses.

8 He it was who struck down the
      firstborn of Egypt,
    both human beings and animals;
9 he sent signs and wonders
    into your midst, O Egypt,
    against Pharaoh and all his servants.
10 He struck down many nations
    and killed mighty kings—
11 Sihon, king of the Amorites,
    and Og, king of Bashan,
    and all the kingdoms of Canaan—
12 and gave their land as a heritage,
    a heritage to his people Israel.

13 Your name, O LORD, endures forever,
    your renown, O LORD, throughout all
      ages.
14 For the LORD will vindicate his people,
    and have compassion on his servants.

15 The idols of the nations are silver and
      gold,
    the work of human hands.
16 They have mouths, but they do not
      speak;
    they have eyes, but they do not see;

17 they have ears, but they do not hear,
    and there is no breath in their
        mouths.
18 Those who make them
    and all who trust them
    shall become like them.

19 O house of Israel, bless the LORD!
    O house of Aaron, bless the LORD!
20 O house of Levi, bless the LORD!
    You that fear the LORD, bless the
        LORD!
21 Blessed be the LORD from Zion,
    he who resides in Jerusalem.
    Praise the LORD!

Psalm 136

God's Work in Creation and in History

1 O give thanks to the LORD, for he is
    good,
    for his steadfast love endures forever.
2 O give thanks to the God of gods,
    for his steadfast love endures forever.
3 O give thanks to the Lord of lords,
    for his steadfast love endures forever;

4 who alone does great wonders,
    for his steadfast love endures forever;
5 who by understanding made the
    heavens,
    for his steadfast love endures forever;
6 who spread out the earth on the waters,
    for his steadfast love endures forever;
7 who made the great lights,
    for his steadfast love endures forever;
8 the sun to rule over the day,
    for his steadfast love endures forever;
9 the moon and stars to rule over the
    night,
    for his steadfast love endures forever;

10 who struck Egypt through their
    firstborn,
    for his steadfast love endures forever;

11 and brought Israel out from among
    them,
    for his steadfast love endures forever;
12 with a strong hand and an outstretched
    arm,
    for his steadfast love endures forever;
13 who divided the Red Sea*a* in two,
    for his steadfast love endures forever;
14 and made Israel pass through the midst
    of it,
    for his steadfast love endures forever;
15 but overthrew Pharaoh and his army in
    the Red Sea,*a*
    for his steadfast love endures forever;
16 who led his people through the
    wilderness,
    for his steadfast love endures forever;
17 who struck down great kings,
    for his steadfast love endures forever;
18 and killed famous kings,
    for his steadfast love endures forever;
19 Sihon, king of the Amorites,
    for his steadfast love endures forever;
20 and Og, king of Bashan,
    for his steadfast love endures forever;
21 and gave their land as a heritage,
    for his steadfast love endures forever;
22 a heritage to his servant Israel,
    for his steadfast love endures forever.

23 It is he who remembered us in our low
    estate,
    for his steadfast love endures forever;
24 and rescued us from our foes,
    for his steadfast love endures forever;
25 who gives food to all flesh,
    for his steadfast love endures forever.

26 O give thanks to the God of heaven,
    for his steadfast love endures forever.

Psalm 137

Lament over the Destruction of Jerusalem

1 By the rivers of Babylon—
    there we sat down and there we wept

a Or Sea of Reeds

when we remembered Zion.

2 On the willows^a there
    we hung up our harps.

3 For there our captors
    asked us for songs,
and our tormentors asked for mirth,
       saying,
    "Sing us one of the songs of Zion!"

4 How could we sing the LORD's song
    in a foreign land?

5 If I forget you, O Jerusalem,
    let my right hand wither!

6 Let my tongue cling to the roof of my
       mouth,
    if I do not remember you,
if I do not set Jerusalem
    above my highest joy.

7 Remember, O LORD, against the
       Edomites
    the day of Jerusalem's fall,
how they said, "Tear it down! Tear it
       down!
    Down to its foundations!"

8 O daughter Babylon, you devastator!^b
    Happy shall they be who pay you
       back
    what you have done to us!

9 Happy shall they be who take your little
       ones
    and dash them against the rock!

Psalm 138

Thanksgiving and Praise

Of David.

1 I give you thanks, O LORD, with my
       whole heart;
    before the gods I sing your praise;

2 I bow down toward your holy temple
    and give thanks to your name for
       your steadfast love and your
       faithfulness;

for you have exalted your name and
       your word
    above everything.^c

3 On the day I called, you answered me,
    you increased my strength of soul.^d

4 All the kings of the earth shall praise
       you, O LORD,
    for they have heard the words of your
       mouth.

5 They shall sing of the ways of the
       LORD,
    for great is the glory of the LORD.

6 For though the LORD is high, he regards
       the lowly;
    but the haughty he perceives from far
       away.

7 Though I walk in the midst of trouble,
    you preserve me against the wrath of
       my enemies;
you stretch out your hand,
    and your right hand delivers me.

8 The LORD will fulfill his purpose for me;
    your steadfast love, O LORD, endures
       forever.
    Do not forsake the work of your
       hands.

Psalm 139

The Inescapable God

To the leader. Of David. A Psalm.

1 O LORD, you have searched me and
       known me.

2 You know when I sit down and when I
       rise up;
    you discern my thoughts from far
       away.

3 You search out my path and my lying
       down,
    and are acquainted with all my ways.

4 Even before a word is on my tongue,
    O LORD, you know it completely.

5 You hem me in, behind and before,

---

a Or *poplars*   *b* Or *you who are devastated*   *c* Cn: Heb *you have exalted your word above all your name*   *d* Syr
Compare Gk Tg: Heb *you made me arrogant in my soul with strength*

and lay your hand upon me.
6 Such knowledge is too wonderful for
    me;
    it is so high that I cannot attain it.

7 Where can I go from your spirit?
    Or where can I flee from your
        presence?
8 If I ascend to heaven, you are there;
    if I make my bed in Sheol, you are
        there.
9 If I take the wings of the morning
    and settle at the farthest limits of the
        sea,
10 even there your hand shall lead me,
    and your right hand shall hold me
        fast.
11 If I say, "Surely the darkness shall cover
    me,
    and the light around me become
        night,"
12 even the darkness is not dark to you;
    the night is as bright as the day,
    for darkness is as light to you.

13 For it was you who formed my inward
        parts;
    you knit me together in my mother's
        womb.
14 I praise you, for I am fearfully and
        wonderfully made.
    Wonderful are your works;
    that I know very well.
15 My frame was not hidden from you,
    when I was being made in secret,
        intricately woven in the depths of the
            earth.
16 Your eyes beheld my unformed
        substance.
    In your book were written
    all the days that were formed for me,
    when none of them as yet existed.
17 How weighty to me are your thoughts,
        O God!
    How vast is the sum of them!

18 I try to count them—they are more than
        the sand;
    I come to the end*a*—I am still with
        you.

19 O that you would kill the wicked,
        O God,
    and that the bloodthirsty would
        depart from me—
20 those who speak of you maliciously,
    and lift themselves up against you for
        evil!*b*
21 Do I not hate those who hate you,
        O LORD?
    And do I not loathe those who rise
        up against you?
22 I hate them with perfect hatred;
    I count them my enemies.
23 Search me, O God, and know my heart;
    test me and know my thoughts.
24 See if there is any wicked*c* way in me,
    and lead me in the way everlasting.*d*

Psalm 140

Prayer for Deliverance from Enemies

To the leader. A Psalm of David.

1 Deliver me, O LORD, from evildoers;
    protect me from those who are
        violent,
2 who plan evil things in their minds
    and stir up wars continually.
3 They make their tongue sharp as a
        snake's,
    and under their lips is the venom of
        vipers.   *Selah*

4 Guard me, O LORD, from the hands of
        the wicked;
    protect me from the violent
    who have planned my downfall.
5 The arrogant have hidden a trap for me,
    and with cords they have spread a
        net,*e*

a Or *I awake*   *b* Cn: Meaning of Heb uncertain   *c* Heb *hurtful*   *d* Or *the ancient way.* Compare Jer 6.16
e Or *they have spread cords as a net*

along the road they have set snares
    for me.   *Selah*

6 I say to the LORD, "You are my God;
    give ear, O LORD, to the voice of my
      supplications."
7 O LORD, my Lord, my strong deliverer,
    you have covered my head in the day
      of battle.
8 Do not grant, O LORD, the desires of
    the wicked;
    do not further their evil plot.*a*   *Selah*

9 Those who surround me lift up their
    heads;*b*
    let the mischief of their lips
      overwhelm them!
10 Let burning coals fall on them!
    Let them be flung into pits, no more
      to rise!
11 Do not let the slanderer be established
    in the land;
    let evil speedily hunt down the
      violent!

12 I know that the LORD maintains the
    cause of the needy,
    and executes justice for the poor.
13 Surely the righteous shall give thanks to
    your name;
    the upright shall live in your presence.

Psalm 141

Prayer for Preservation from Evil

A Psalm of David.

1 I call upon you, O LORD; come quickly
    to me;
    give ear to my voice when I call to
      you.
2 Let my prayer be counted as incense
    before you,
    and the lifting up of my hands as an
      evening sacrifice.

3 Set a guard over my mouth, O LORD;
    keep watch over the door of my
      lips.
4 Do not turn my heart to any evil,
    to busy myself with wicked deeds
  in company with those who work
    iniquity;
    do not let me eat of their delicacies.

5 Let the righteous strike me;
    let the faithful correct me.
  Never let the oil of the wicked anoint
    my head,*c*
    for my prayer is continually*d* against
      their wicked deeds.
6 When they are given over to those who
    shall condemn them,
    then they shall learn that my words
      were pleasant.
7 Like a rock that one breaks apart and
    shatters on the land,
    so shall their bones be strewn at the
      mouth of Sheol.*e*

8 But my eyes are turned toward you,
    O GOD, my Lord;
    in you I seek refuge; do not leave me
      defenseless.
9 Keep me from the trap that they have
    laid for me,
    and from the snares of evildoers.
10 Let the wicked fall into their own nets,
    while I alone escape.

Psalm 142

Prayer for Deliverance from Persecutors

A Maskil of David. When he was in the
cave. A Prayer.

1 With my voice I cry to the LORD;
    with my voice I make supplication to
      the LORD.
2 I pour out my complaint before him;
    I tell my trouble before him.

---

a Heb adds *they are exalted*   *b* Cn Compare Gk: Heb *those who surround me are uplifted in head*; Heb divides verses 8 and 9 differently   *c* Gk: Meaning of Heb uncertain   *d* Cn: Heb *for continually and my prayer*   *e* Meaning of Heb of verses 5-7 is uncertain

3 When my spirit is faint,
  you know my way.

In the path where I walk
  they have hidden a trap for me.
4 Look on my right hand and see—
  there is no one who takes notice of
    me;
no refuge remains to me;
  no one cares for me.

5 I cry to you, O LORD;
  I say, "You are my refuge,
  my portion in the land of the
    living."
6 Give heed to my cry,
  for I am brought very low.

Save me from my persecutors,
  for they are too strong for me.
7 Bring me out of prison,
  so that I may give thanks to your
    name.
The righteous will surround me,
  for you will deal bountifully with me.

Psalm 143

Prayer for Deliverance from Enemies

A Psalm of David.

1 Hear my prayer, O LORD;
  give ear to my supplications in your
    faithfulness;
  answer me in your righteousness.
2 Do not enter into judgment with your
    servant,
  for no one living is righteous before
    you.

3 For the enemy has pursued me,
  crushing my life to the ground,
  making me sit in darkness like those
    long dead.
4 Therefore my spirit faints within me;
  my heart within me is appalled.

5 I remember the days of old,
  I think about all your deeds,
  I meditate on the works of your
    hands.
6 I stretch out my hands to you;
  my soul thirsts for you like a parched
    land.   *Selah*

7 Answer me quickly, O LORD;
  my spirit fails.
Do not hide your face from me,
  or I shall be like those who go down
    to the Pit.
8 Let me hear of your steadfast love in the
    morning,
  for in you I put my trust.
Teach me the way I should go,
  for to you I lift up my soul.

9 Save me, O LORD, from my enemies;
  I have fled to you for refuge.*a*
10 Teach me to do your will,
  for you are my God.
Let your good spirit lead me
  on a level path.

11 For your name's sake, O LORD, preserve
    my life.
  In your righteousness bring me out of
    trouble.
12 In your steadfast love cut off my enemies,
  and destroy all my adversaries,
  for I am your servant.

Psalm 144

Prayer for National Deliverance and Security

Of David.

1 Blessed be the LORD, my rock,
  who trains my hands for war, and my
    fingers for battle;
2 my rock *b* and my fortress,
  my stronghold and my deliverer,
my shield, in whom I take refuge,
  who subdues the peoples *c* under me.

---

a One Heb Ms Gk: MT *to you I have hidden*   *b* With 18.2 and 2 Sam 22.2: Heb *my steadfast love*   *c* Heb Mss Syr
Aquila Jerome: MT *my people*

3 O LORD, what are human beings that
        you regard them,
     or mortals that you think of them?
4 They are like a breath;
     their days are like a passing shadow.

5 Bow your heavens, O LORD, and come
        down;
     touch the mountains so that they
        smoke.
6 Make the lightning flash and scatter
        them;
     send out your arrows and rout them.
7 Stretch out your hand from on high;
     set me free and rescue me from the
        mighty waters,
     from the hand of aliens,
8 whose mouths speak lies,
     and whose right hands are false.

9 I will sing a new song to you, O God;
     upon a ten-stringed harp I will play to
        you,
10 the one who gives victory to kings,
     who rescues his servant David.
11 Rescue me from the cruel sword,
     and deliver me from the hand of
        aliens,
     whose mouths speak lies,
        and whose right hands are false.

12 May our sons in their youth
     be like plants full grown,
     our daughters like corner pillars,
        cut for the building of a palace.
13 May our barns be filled,
     with produce of every kind;
     may our sheep increase by thousands,
        by tens of thousands in our fields,
14   and may our cattle be heavy with
        young.
     May there be no breach in the walls,[a] no
        exile,
     and no cry of distress in our streets.

15 Happy are the people to whom such
        blessings fall;
     happy are the people whose God is
        the LORD.

Psalm 145

The Greatness and the Goodness of God

Praise. Of David.

1 I will extol you, my God and King,
     and bless your name forever and ever.
2 Every day I will bless you,
     and praise your name forever and
        ever.
3 Great is the LORD, and greatly to be
        praised;
     his greatness is unsearchable.

4 One generation shall laud your works to
        another,
     and shall declare your mighty acts.
5 On the glorious splendor of your
        majesty,
     and on your wondrous works, I will
        meditate.
6 The might of your awesome deeds shall
        be proclaimed,
     and I will declare your greatness.
7 They shall celebrate the fame of your
        abundant goodness,
     and shall sing aloud of your
        righteousness.

8 The LORD is gracious and merciful,
     slow to anger and abounding in
        steadfast love.
9 The LORD is good to all,
     and his compassion is over all that he
        has made.

10 All your works shall give thanks to you,
        O LORD,
     and all your faithful shall bless you.
11 They shall speak of the glory of your
        kingdom,
     and tell of your power,

a Heb lacks *in the walls*

12 to make known to all people your*
      mighty deeds,
   and the glorious splendor of your*
      kingdom.
13 Your kingdom is an everlasting
      kingdom,
   and your dominion endures
      throughout all generations.

   The LORD is faithful in all his words,
      and gracious in all his deeds. *
14 The LORD upholds all who are falling,
      and raises up all who are bowed
      down.
15 The eyes of all look to you,
      and you give them their food in due
      season.
16 You open your hand,
      satisfying the desire of every living
      thing.
17 The LORD is just in all his ways,
      and kind in all his doings.
18 The LORD is near to all who call on him,
      to all who call on him in truth.
19 He fulfills the desire of all who fear
      him;
   he also hears their cry, and saves
      them.
20 The LORD watches over all who love
      him,
   but all the wicked he will destroy.

21 My mouth will speak the praise of the
      LORD,
   and all flesh will bless his holy name
      forever and ever.

Psalm 146

Praise for God's Help

1 Praise the LORD!
   Praise the LORD, O my soul!
2 I will praise the LORD as long as I live;
   I will sing praises to my God all my
      life long.

3 Do not put your trust in princes,
      in mortals, in whom there is no help.
4 When their breath departs, they return
      to the earth;
   on that very day their plans perish.

5 Happy are those whose help is the God
      of Jacob,
   whose hope is in the LORD their God,
6 who made heaven and earth,
      the sea, and all that is in them;
   who keeps faith forever;
7   who executes justice for the
      oppressed;
   who gives food to the hungry.

   The LORD sets the prisoners free;
8   the LORD opens the eyes of the blind.
   The LORD lifts up those who are bowed
      down;
   the LORD loves the righteous.
9   The LORD watches over the strangers;
   he upholds the orphan and the
      widow,
   but the way of the wicked he brings
      to ruin.

10 The LORD will reign forever,
   your God, O Zion, for all
      generations.
   Praise the LORD!

Psalm 147

Praise for God's Care for Jerusalem

1 Praise the LORD!
   How good it is to sing praises to our
      God;
   for he is gracious, and a song of
      praise is fitting.
2 The LORD builds up Jerusalem;
   he gathers the outcasts of Israel.
3 He heals the brokenhearted,
   and binds up their wounds.
4 He determines the number of the stars;
   he gives to all of them their names.

a Gk Jerome Syr: Heb *his*   *b* Heb *his*   *c* These two lines supplied by Q Ms Gk Syr

5 Great is our Lord, and abundant in
         power;
    his understanding is beyond measure.
6 The LORD lifts up the downtrodden;
    he casts the wicked to the ground.

7 Sing to the LORD with thanksgiving;
    make melody to our God on the lyre.
8 He covers the heavens with clouds,
    prepares rain for the earth,
    makes grass grow on the hills.
9 He gives to the animals their food,
    and to the young ravens when they
        cry.
10 His delight is not in the strength of the
        horse,
    nor his pleasure in the speed of a
        runner;*a*
11 but the LORD takes pleasure in those
        who fear him,
    in those who hope in his steadfast
        love.

12 Praise the LORD, O Jerusalem!
    Praise your God, O Zion!
13 For he strengthens the bars of your
        gates;
    he blesses your children within you.
14 He grants peace*b* within your borders;
    he fills you with the finest of wheat.
15 He sends out his command to the earth;
    his word runs swiftly.
16 He gives snow like wool;
    he scatters frost like ashes.
17 He hurls down hail like crumbs—
    who can stand before his cold?
18 He sends out his word, and melts them;
    he makes his wind blow, and the
        waters flow.
19 He declares his word to Jacob,
    his statutes and ordinances to Israel.
20 He has not dealt thus with any other
        nation;
    they do not know his ordinances.
    Praise the LORD!

Psalm 148

Praise for God's Universal Glory

1 Praise the LORD!
    Praise the LORD from the heavens;
    praise him in the heights!
2 Praise him, all his angels;
    praise him, all his host!

3 Praise him, sun and moon;
    praise him, all you shining stars!
4 Praise him, you highest heavens,
    and you waters above the heavens!

5 Let them praise the name of the LORD,
    for he commanded and they were
        created.
6 He established them forever and ever;
    he fixed their bounds, which cannot
        be passed.*c*

7 Praise the LORD from the earth,
    you sea monsters and all deeps,
8 fire and hail, snow and frost,
    stormy wind fulfilling his command!

9 Mountains and all hills,
    fruit trees and all cedars!
10 Wild animals and all cattle,
    creeping things and flying birds!

11 Kings of the earth and all peoples,
    princes and all rulers of the earth!
12 Young men and women alike,
    old and young together!

13 Let them praise the name of the LORD,
    for his name alone is exalted;
    his glory is above earth and heaven.
14 He has raised up a horn for his people,
    praise for all his faithful,
    for the people of Israel who are close
        to him.
    Praise the LORD!

a Heb *legs of a person*   *b* Or *prosperity*   *c* Or *he set a law that cannot pass away*

Psalm 149

Praise for God's Goodness to Israel

1 Praise the LORD!
Sing to the LORD a new song,
   his praise in the assembly of the
      faithful.
2 Let Israel be glad in its Maker;
   let the children of Zion rejoice in
      their King.
3 Let them praise his name with dancing,
   making melody to him with
      tambourine and lyre.
4 For the LORD takes pleasure in his
      people;
   he adorns the humble with victory.
5 Let the faithful exult in glory;
   let them sing for joy on their couches.
6 Let the high praises of God be in their
      throats
   and two-edged swords in their hands,
7 to execute vengeance on the nations
   and punishment on the peoples,
8 to bind their kings with fetters
   and their nobles with chains of iron,
9 to execute on them the judgment
      decreed.
   This is glory for all his faithful ones.
Praise the LORD!

Psalm 150

Praise for God's Surpassing Greatness

1 Praise the LORD!
Praise God in his sanctuary;
   praise him in his mighty firmament! *a*
2 Praise him for his mighty deeds;
   praise him according to his surpassing
      greatness!

3 Praise him with trumpet sound;
   praise him with lute and harp!
4 Praise him with tambourine and dance;
   praise him with strings and pipe!
5 Praise him with clanging cymbals;
   praise him with loud clashing
      cymbals!
6 Let everything that breathes praise the
      LORD!
   Praise the LORD!

a Or *dome*

PROVERBS

1 The proverbs of Solomon son of David,
king of Israel:

Prologue

2 For learning about wisdom and
        instruction,
    for understanding words of insight,
3 for gaining instruction in wise dealing,
    righteousness, justice, and equity;
4 to teach shrewdness to the simple,
    knowledge and prudence to the
        young—
5 let the wise also hear and gain in
        learning,
    and the discerning acquire skill,
6 to understand a proverb and a figure,
    the words of the wise and their
        riddles.

7 The fear of the LORD is the beginning of
        knowledge;
    fools despise wisdom and instruction.

Warnings against Evil Companions

8 Hear, my child, your father's instruction,
    and do not reject your mother's
        teaching;
9 for they are a fair garland for your head,
    and pendants for your neck.
10 My child, if sinners entice you,
    do not consent.
11 If they say, "Come with us, let us lie in
        wait for blood;
    let us wantonly ambush the innocent;
12 like Sheol let us swallow them alive
    and whole, like those who go down to
        the Pit.
13 We shall find all kinds of costly things;
    we shall fill our houses with booty.
14 Throw in your lot among us;
    we will all have one purse"—
15 my child, do not walk in their way,
    keep your foot from their paths;
16 for their feet run to evil,

and they hurry to shed blood.
17 For in vain is the net baited
    while the bird is looking on;
18 yet they lie in wait—to kill themselves!
    and set an ambush—for their own
        lives!
19 Such is the end*a* of all who are greedy
        for gain;
    it takes away the life of its possessors.

The Call of Wisdom

20 Wisdom cries out in the street;
    in the squares she raises her voice.
21 At the busiest corner she cries out;
    at the entrance of the city gates she
        speaks:
22 "How long, O simple ones, will you love
        being simple?
    How long will scoffers delight in their
        scoffing
    and fools hate knowledge?
23 Give heed to my reproof;
    I will pour out my thoughts to you;
    I will make my words known to you.
24 Because I have called and you refused,
    have stretched out my hand and no
        one heeded,
25 and because you have ignored all my
        counsel
    and would have none of my reproof,
26 I also will laugh at your calamity;
    I will mock when panic strikes you,
27 when panic strikes you like a storm,
    and your calamity comes like a
        whirlwind,
    when distress and anguish come upon
        you.
28 Then they will call upon me, but I will
        not answer;
    they will seek me diligently, but will
        not find me.
29 Because they hated knowledge
    and did not choose the fear of the
        LORD,

a Gk: Heb *are the ways*

30 would have none of my counsel,
      and despised all my reproof,
31 therefore they shall eat the fruit of their
         way
      and be sated with their own devices.
32 For waywardness kills the simple,
      and the complacency of fools
         destroys them;
33 but those who listen to me will be secure
      and will live at ease, without dread of
         disaster."

The Value of Wisdom

2 My child, if you accept my words
      and treasure up my commandments
         within you,
2 making your ear attentive to wisdom
      and inclining your heart to
         understanding;
3 if you indeed cry out for insight,
      and raise your voice for
         understanding;
4 if you seek it like silver,
      and search for it as for hidden
         treasures—
5 then you will understand the fear of the
         LORD
      and find the knowledge of God.
6 For the LORD gives wisdom;
      from his mouth come knowledge and
         understanding;
7 he stores up sound wisdom for the
         upright;
      he is a shield to those who walk
         blamelessly,
8 guarding the paths of justice
      and preserving the way of his faithful
         ones.
9 Then you will understand righteousness
      and justice
      and equity, every good path;
10 for wisdom will come into your heart,
      and knowledge will be pleasant to
         your soul;
11 prudence will watch over you;
      and understanding will guard you.

12 It will save you from the way of evil,
      from those who speak perversely,
13 who forsake the paths of uprightness
      to walk in the ways of darkness,
14 who rejoice in doing evil
      and delight in the perverseness of evil;
15 those whose paths are crooked,
      and who are devious in their ways.

16 You will be saved from the loose*a*
         woman,
      from the adulteress with her smooth
         words,
17 who forsakes the partner of her youth
      and forgets her sacred covenant;
18 for her way*b* leads down to death,
      and her paths to the shades;
19 those who go to her never come back,
      nor do they regain the paths of life.

20 Therefore walk in the way of the good,
      and keep to the paths of the just.
21 For the upright will abide in the land,
      and the innocent will remain in it;
22 but the wicked will be cut off from the
         land,
      and the treacherous will be rooted out
         of it.

Admonition to Trust and Honor God

3 My child, do not forget my teaching,
      but let your heart keep my
         commandments;
2 for length of days and years of life
      and abundant welfare they will give
         you.

3 Do not let loyalty and faithfulness
         forsake you;
      bind them around your neck,
      write them on the tablet of your heart.
4 So you will find favor and good repute
      in the sight of God and of people.

5 Trust in the LORD with all your heart,
      and do not rely on your own insight.

a Heb *strange*   *b* Cn: Heb *house*

6 In all your ways acknowledge him,
      and he will make straight your paths.
7 Do not be wise in your own eyes;
      fear the LORD, and turn away from
         evil.
8 It will be a healing for your flesh
      and a refreshment for your body.
9 Honor the LORD with your substance
      and with the first fruits of all your
         produce;
10 then your barns will be filled with plenty,
      and your vats will be bursting with
         wine.

11 My child, do not despise the LORD's
      discipline
      or be weary of his reproof,
12 for the LORD reproves the one he loves,
      as a father the son in whom he
         delights.

The True Wealth
13 Happy are those who find wisdom,
      and those who get understanding,
14 for her income is better than silver,
      and her revenue better than gold.
15 She is more precious than jewels,
      and nothing you desire can compare
         with her.
16 Long life is in her right hand;
      in her left hand are riches and honor.
17 Her ways are ways of pleasantness,
      and all her paths are peace.
18 She is a tree of life to those who lay hold
         of her;
      those who hold her fast are called
         happy.

God's Wisdom in Creation
19 The LORD by wisdom founded the earth;
      by understanding he established the
         heavens;
20 by his knowledge the deeps broke open,
      and the clouds drop down the dew.

The True Security
21 My child, do not let these escape from
         your sight:
      keep sound wisdom and prudence,
22 and they will be life for your soul
      and adornment for your neck.
23 Then you will walk on your way securely
      and your foot will not stumble.
24 If you sit down,*a* you will not be afraid;
      when you lie down, your sleep will be
         sweet.
25 Do not be afraid of sudden panic,
      or of the storm that strikes the
         wicked;
26 for the LORD will be your confidence
      and will keep your foot from being
         caught.

27 Do not withhold good from those to
         whom it is due,*b*
      when it is in your power to do it.
28 Do not say to your neighbor, "Go, and
         come again,
      tomorrow I will give it"—when you
         have it with you.
29 Do not plan harm against your neighbor
      who lives trustingly beside you.
30 Do not quarrel with anyone without
         cause,
      when no harm has been done to you.
31 Do not envy the violent
      and do not choose any of their ways;
32 for the perverse are an abomination to
         the LORD,
      but the upright are in his confidence.
33 The LORD's curse is on the house of the
         wicked,
      but he blesses the abode of the
         righteous.
34 Toward the scorners he is scornful,
      but to the humble he shows favor.
35 The wise will inherit honor,
      but stubborn fools, disgrace.

a Gk: Heb *lie down*   *b* Heb *from its owners*

Parental Advice

4 Listen, children, to a father's instruction,
and be attentive, that you may gain[a]
insight;

2 for I give you good precepts:
do not forsake my teaching.

3 When I was a son with my father,
tender, and my mother's favorite,

4 he taught me, and said to me,
"Let your heart hold fast my words;
keep my commandments, and live.

5 Get wisdom; get insight: do not forget,
nor turn away
from the words of my mouth.

6 Do not forsake her, and she will keep
you;
love her, and she will guard you.

7 The beginning of wisdom is this: Get
wisdom,
and whatever else you get, get insight.

8 Prize her highly, and she will exalt you;
she will honor you if you embrace
her.

9 She will place on your head a fair
garland;
she will bestow on you a beautiful
crown."

Admonition to Keep to the Right Path

10 Hear, my child, and accept my words,
that the years of your life may be
many.

11 I have taught you the way of wisdom;
I have led you in the paths of
uprightness.

12 When you walk, your step will not be
hampered;
and if you run, you will not stumble.

13 Keep hold of instruction; do not let go;
guard her, for she is your life.

14 Do not enter the path of the wicked,
and do not walk in the way of
evildoers.

15 Avoid it; do not go on it;
turn away from it and pass on.

16 For they cannot sleep unless they have
done wrong;
they are robbed of sleep unless they
have made someone stumble.

17 For they eat the bread of wickedness
and drink the wine of violence.

18 But the path of the righteous is like the
light of dawn,
which shines brighter and brighter
until full day.

19 The way of the wicked is like deep
darkness;
they do not know what they stumble
over.

20 My child, be attentive to my words;
incline your ear to my sayings.

21 Do not let them escape from your sight;
keep them within your heart.

22 For they are life to those who find them,
and healing to all their flesh.

23 Keep your heart with all vigilance,
for from it flow the springs of life.

24 Put away from you crooked speech,
and put devious talk far from you.

25 Let your eyes look directly forward,
and your gaze be straight before you.

26 Keep straight the path of your feet,
and all your ways will be sure.

27 Do not swerve to the right or to the left;
turn your foot away from evil.

Warning against Impurity and Infidelity

5 My child, be attentive to my wisdom;
incline your ear to my understanding,

2 so that you may hold on to prudence,
and your lips may guard knowledge.

3 For the lips of a loose[b] woman drip
honey,
and her speech is smoother than oil;

4 but in the end she is bitter as
wormwood,
sharp as a two-edged sword.

5 Her feet go down to death;
her steps follow the path to Sheol.

6 She does not keep straight to the path of
life;

---

a Heb *know*   *b* Heb *strange*

her ways wander, and she does not
    know it.

7 And now, my child,*a* listen to me,
    and do not depart from the words of
      my mouth.
8 Keep your way far from her,
    and do not go near the door of her
      house;
9 or you will give your honor to others,
    and your years to the merciless,
10 and strangers will take their fill of your
      wealth,
    and your labors will go to the house
      of an alien;
11 and at the end of your life you will
      groan,
    when your flesh and body are
      consumed,
12 and you say, "Oh, how I hated discipline,
    and my heart despised reproof!
13 I did not listen to the voice of my
      teachers
    or incline my ear to my instructors.
14 Now I am at the point of utter ruin
    in the public assembly."

15 Drink water from your own cistern,
    flowing water from your own well.
16 Should your springs be scattered abroad,
    streams of water in the streets?
17 Let them be for yourself alone,
    and not for sharing with strangers.
18 Let your fountain be blessed,
    and rejoice in the wife of your youth,
19 a lovely deer, a graceful doe.
    May her breasts satisfy you at all times;
    may you be intoxicated always by her
      love.
20 Why should you be intoxicated, my son,
    by another woman
    and embrace the bosom of an
      adulteress?
21 For human ways are under the eyes of
      the LORD,
    and he examines all their paths.

22 The iniquities of the wicked ensnare
      them,
    and they are caught in the toils of
      their sin.
23 They die for lack of discipline,
    and because of their great folly they
      are lost.

Practical Admonitions

6 My child, if you have given your pledge
    to your neighbor,
    if you have bound yourself to
      another,*b*
2 you are snared by the utterance of your
      lips,*c*
    caught by the words of your mouth.
3 So do this, my child, and save yourself,
    for you have come into your
      neighbor's power:
    go, hurry,*d* and plead with your
      neighbor.
4 Give your eyes no sleep
    and your eyelids no slumber;
5 save yourself like a gazelle from the
      hunter,*e*
    like a bird from the hand of the fowler.

6 Go to the ant, you lazybones;
    consider its ways, and be wise.
7 Without having any chief
    or officer or ruler,
8 it prepares its food in summer,
    and gathers its sustenance in harvest.
9 How long will you lie there,
    O lazybones?
    When will you rise from your sleep?
10 A little sleep, a little slumber,
    a little folding of the hands to rest,
11 and poverty will come upon you like a
      robber,
    and want, like an armed warrior.

12 A scoundrel and a villain
    goes around with crooked speech,
13 winking the eyes, shuffling the feet,
    pointing the fingers,

---

a Gk Vg: Heb *children*   *b* Or *a stranger*   *c* Cn Compare Gk Syr: Heb *the words of your mouth*   *d* Or *humble yourself*   *e* Cn: Heb *from the hand*

14 with perverted mind devising evil,
      continually sowing discord;
15 on such a one calamity will descend
      suddenly;
      in a moment, damage beyond repair.

16 There are six things that the LORD hates,
      seven that are an abomination to him:
17 haughty eyes, a lying tongue,
      and hands that shed innocent blood,
18 a heart that devises wicked plans,
      feet that hurry to run to evil,
19 a lying witness who testifies falsely,
      and one who sows discord in a family.

20 My child, keep your father's
      commandment,
      and do not forsake your mother's
      teaching.
21 Bind them upon your heart always;
      tie them around your neck.
22 When you walk, they*a* will lead you;
      when you lie down, they*a* will watch
      over you;
      and when you awake, they*a* will talk
      with you.
23 For the commandment is a lamp and the
      teaching a light,
      and the reproofs of discipline are the
      way of life,
24 to preserve you from the wife of
      another,*b*
      from the smooth tongue of the
      adulteress.
25 Do not desire her beauty in your heart,
      and do not let her capture you with
      her eyelashes;
26 for a prostitute's fee is only a loaf of
      bread,*c*
      but the wife of another stalks a man's
      very life.
27 Can fire be carried in the bosom
      without burning one's clothes?
28 Or can one walk on hot coals
      without scorching the feet?

29 So is he who sleeps with his neighbor's
      wife;
      no one who touches her will go
      unpunished.
30 Thieves are not despised who steal only
      to satisfy their appetite when they are
      hungry.
31 Yet if they are caught, they will pay
      sevenfold;
      they will forfeit all the goods of their
      house.
32 But he who commits adultery has no
      sense;
      he who does it destroys himself.
33 He will get wounds and dishonor,
      and his disgrace will not be wiped
      away.
34 For jealousy arouses a husband's fury,
      and he shows no restraint when he
      takes revenge.
35 He will accept no compensation,
      and refuses a bribe no matter how
      great.

The False Attractions of Adultery

7 My child, keep my words
      and store up my commandments with
      you;
2 keep my commandments and live,
      keep my teachings as the apple of
      your eye;
3 bind them on your fingers,
      write them on the tablet of your heart.
4 Say to wisdom, "You are my sister,"
      and call insight your intimate friend,
5 that they may keep you from the loose*d*
      woman,
      from the adulteress with her smooth
      words.

6 For at the window of my house
      I looked out through my lattice,
7 and I saw among the simple ones,
      I observed among the youths,
      a young man without sense,
8 passing along the street near her corner,

---

a Heb *it*   *b* Gk: MT *the evil woman*   *c* Cn Compare Gk Syr Vg Tg: Heb *for because of a harlot to a piece of bread*
d Heb *strange*

taking the road to her house

9 in the twilight, in the evening,
at the time of night and darkness.

10 Then a woman comes toward him,
decked out like a prostitute, wily of
heart.*a*

11 She is loud and wayward;
her feet do not stay at home;

12 now in the street, now in the squares,
and at every corner she lies in wait.

13 She seizes him and kisses him,
and with impudent face she says to
him:

14 "I had to offer sacrifices,
and today I have paid my vows;

15 so now I have come out to meet you,
to seek you eagerly, and I have found
you!

16 I have decked my couch with coverings,
colored spreads of Egyptian linen;

17 I have perfumed my bed with myrrh,
aloes, and cinnamon.

18 Come, let us take our fill of love until
morning;
let us delight ourselves with love.

19 For my husband is not at home;
he has gone on a long journey.

20 He took a bag of money with him;
he will not come home until full
moon."

21 With much seductive speech she
persuades him;
with her smooth talk she compels him.

22 Right away he follows her,
and goes like an ox to the slaughter,
or bounds like a stag toward the trap*b*

23 until an arrow pierces its entrails.
He is like a bird rushing into a snare,
not knowing that it will cost him his
life.

24 And now, my children, listen to me,
and be attentive to the words of my
mouth.

25 Do not let your hearts turn aside to her
ways;
do not stray into her paths.

26 For many are those she has laid low,
and numerous are her victims.

27 Her house is the way to Sheol,
going down to the chambers of death.

The Gifts of Wisdom

8 Does not wisdom call,
and does not understanding raise her
voice?

2 On the heights, beside the way,
at the crossroads she takes her stand;

3 beside the gates in front of the town,
at the entrance of the portals she cries
out:

4 "To you, O people, I call,
and my cry is to all that live.

5 O simple ones, learn prudence;
acquire intelligence, you who lack it.

6 Hear, for I will speak noble things,
and from my lips will come what is
right;

7 for my mouth will utter truth;
wickedness is an abomination to my
lips.

8 All the words of my mouth are
righteous;
there is nothing twisted or crooked in
them.

9 They are all straight to one who
understands
and right to those who find
knowledge.

10 Take my instruction instead of silver,
and knowledge rather than choice
gold;

11 for wisdom is better than jewels,
and all that you may desire cannot
compare with her.

12 I, wisdom, live with prudence,*a*
and I attain knowledge and discretion.

13 The fear of the LORD is hatred of evil.
Pride and arrogance and the way of evil
and perverted speech I hate.

---

a Meaning of Heb uncertain   *b* Cn Compare Gk: Meaning of Heb uncertain

14 I have good advice and sound wisdom;
    I have insight, I have strength.
15 By me kings reign,
    and rulers decree what is just;
16 by me rulers rule,
    and nobles, all who govern rightly.
17 I love those who love me,
    and those who seek me diligently find
      me.
18 Riches and honor are with me,
    enduring wealth and prosperity.
19 My fruit is better than gold, even fine
      gold,
    and my yield than choice silver.
20 I walk in the way of righteousness,
    along the paths of justice,
21 endowing with wealth those who love
      me,
    and filling their treasuries.

Wisdom's Part in Creation

22 The LORD created me at the beginning*a*
    of his work,*b*
    the first of his acts of long ago.
23 Ages ago I was set up,
    at the first, before the beginning of
      the earth.
24 When there were no depths I was
      brought forth,
    when there were no springs
      abounding with water.
25 Before the mountains had been shaped,
    before the hills, I was brought forth—
26 when he had not yet made earth and
      fields,*c*
    or the world's first bits of soil.
27 When he established the heavens, I was
      there,
    when he drew a circle on the face of
      the deep,
28 when he made firm the skies above,
    when he established the fountains of
      the deep,
29 when he assigned to the sea its limit,
    so that the waters might not
      transgress his command,

when he marked out the foundations of
    the earth,
30   then I was beside him, like a master
      worker;*d*
  and I was daily his*e* delight,
    rejoicing before him always,
31 rejoicing in his inhabited world
    and delighting in the human race.

32 "And now, my children, listen to me:
    happy are those who keep my ways.
33 Hear instruction and be wise,
    and do not neglect it.
34 Happy is the one who listens to me,
    watching daily at my gates,
    waiting beside my doors.
35 For whoever finds me finds life
    and obtains favor from the LORD;
36 but those who miss me injure
      themselves;
    all who hate me love death."

Wisdom's Feast

9 Wisdom has built her house,
    she has hewn her seven pillars.
2 She has slaughtered her animals, she has
      mixed her wine,
    she has also set her table.
3 She has sent out her servant-girls, she
      calls
    from the highest places in the town,
4 "You that are simple, turn in here!"
    To those without sense she says,
5 "Come, eat of my bread
    and drink of the wine I have mixed.
6 Lay aside immaturity,*f* and live,
    and walk in the way of insight."

General Maxims

7 Whoever corrects a scoffer wins abuse;
    whoever rebukes the wicked gets hurt.
8 A scoffer who is rebuked will only hate
      you;
    the wise, when rebuked, will love you.
9 Give instruction*g* to the wise, and they
    will become wiser still;

---

a Or *me as the beginning*   *b* Heb *way*   *c* Meaning of Heb uncertain   *d* Another reading is *little child*
e Gk: Heb lacks *his*   *f* Or *simpleness*   *g* Heb lacks *instruction*

teach the righteous and they will gain
in learning.

10 The fear of the LORD is the beginning of
wisdom,
and the knowledge of the Holy One
is insight.

11 For by me your days will be multiplied,
and years will be added to your life.

12 If you are wise, you are wise for yourself;
if you scoff, you alone will bear it.

Folly's Invitation and Promise

13 The foolish woman is loud;
she is ignorant and knows nothing.

14 She sits at the door of her house,
on a seat at the high places of the
town,

15 calling to those who pass by,
who are going straight on their way,

16 "You who are simple, turn in here!"
And to those without sense she says,

17 "Stolen water is sweet,
and bread eaten in secret is pleasant."

18 But they do not know that the dead*a* are
there,
that her guests are in the depths of
Sheol.

Wise Sayings of Solomon

10 The proverbs of Solomon.

A wise child makes a glad father,
but a foolish child is a mother's grief.

2 Treasures gained by wickedness do not
profit,
but righteousness delivers from death.

3 The LORD does not let the righteous go
hungry,
but he thwarts the craving of the
wicked.

4 A slack hand causes poverty,
but the hand of the diligent makes
rich.

5 A child who gathers in summer is
prudent,

but a child who sleeps in harvest
brings shame.

6 Blessings are on the head of the
righteous,
but the mouth of the wicked conceals
violence.

7 The memory of the righteous is a
blessing,
but the name of the wicked will rot.

8 The wise of heart will heed
commandments,
but a babbling fool will come to ruin.

9 Whoever walks in integrity walks
securely,
but whoever follows perverse ways
will be found out.

10 Whoever winks the eye causes trouble,
but the one who rebukes boldly makes
peace.*b*

11 The mouth of the righteous is a fountain
of life,
but the mouth of the wicked conceals
violence.

12 Hatred stirs up strife,
but love covers all offenses.

13 On the lips of one who has
understanding wisdom is found,
but a rod is for the back of one who
lacks sense.

14 The wise lay up knowledge,
but the babbling of a fool brings ruin
near.

15 The wealth of the rich is their fortress;
the poverty of the poor is their ruin.

16 The wage of the righteous leads to life,
the gain of the wicked to sin.

17 Whoever heeds instruction is on the
path to life,
but one who rejects a rebuke goes
astray.

18 Lying lips conceal hatred,
and whoever utters slander is a fool.

19 When words are many, transgression is
not lacking,
but the prudent are restrained in
speech.

a Heb *shades*　　*b* Gk: Heb *but a babbling fool will come to ruin*

20 The tongue of the righteous is choice
     silver;
     the mind of the wicked is of little
       worth.
21 The lips of the righteous feed many,
     but fools die for lack of sense.
22 The blessing of the LORD makes rich,
     and he adds no sorrow with it. *a*
23 Doing wrong is like sport to a fool,
     but wise conduct is pleasure to a
       person of understanding.
24 What the wicked dread will come upon
     them,
     but the desire of the righteous will be
       granted.
25 When the tempest passes, the wicked are
     no more,
     but the righteous are established
       forever.
26 Like vinegar to the teeth, and smoke to
     the eyes,
     so are the lazy to their employers.
27 The fear of the LORD prolongs life,
     but the years of the wicked will be
       short.
28 The hope of the righteous ends in
     gladness,
     but the expectation of the wicked
       comes to nothing.
29 The way of the LORD is a stronghold for
     the upright,
     but destruction for evildoers.
30 The righteous will never be removed,
     but the wicked will not remain in the
       land.
31 The mouth of the righteous brings forth
     wisdom,
     but the perverse tongue will be cut
       off.
32 The lips of the righteous know what is
     acceptable,
     but the mouth of the wicked what is
       perverse.

11 A false balance is an abomination to
     the LORD,
     but an accurate weight is his delight.

2 When pride comes, then comes disgrace;
     but wisdom is with the humble.
3 The integrity of the upright guides them,
     but the crookedness of the
       treacherous destroys them.
4 Riches do not profit in the day of wrath,
     but righteousness delivers from death.
5 The righteousness of the blameless
     keeps their ways straight,
     but the wicked fall by their own
       wickedness.
6 The righteousness of the upright saves
     them,
     but the treacherous are taken captive
       by their schemes.
7 When the wicked die, their hope
     perishes,
     and the expectation of the godless
       comes to nothing.
8 The righteous are delivered from
     trouble,
     and the wicked get into it instead.
9 With their mouths the godless would
     destroy their neighbors,
     but by knowledge the righteous are
       delivered.
10 When it goes well with the righteous, the
     city rejoices;
     and when the wicked perish, there is
       jubilation.
11 By the blessing of the upright a city is
     exalted,
     but it is overthrown by the mouth of
       the wicked.
12 Whoever belittles another lacks sense,
     but an intelligent person remains silent.
13 A gossip goes about telling secrets,
     but one who is trustworthy in spirit
       keeps a confidence.
14 Where there is no guidance, a nation *b*
     falls,
     but in an abundance of counselors
       there is safety.
15 To guarantee loans for a stranger brings
     trouble,
     but there is safety in refusing to do so.

---

a Or *and toil adds nothing to it*   *b* Or *an army*

16 A gracious woman gets honor,
  but she who hates virtue is covered
   with shame. *a*
 The timid become destitute, *b*
  but the aggressive gain riches.
17 Those who are kind reward themselves,
  but the cruel do themselves harm.
18 The wicked earn no real gain,
  but those who sow righteousness get a
   true reward.
19 Whoever is steadfast in righteousness
   will live,
  but whoever pursues evil will die.
20 Crooked minds are an abomination to
   the LORD,
  but those of blameless ways are his
   delight.
21 Be assured, the wicked will not go
   unpunished,
  but those who are righteous will
   escape.
22 Like a gold ring in a pig's snout
  is a beautiful woman without good
   sense.
23 The desire of the righteous ends only in
   good;
  the expectation of the wicked in
   wrath.
24 Some give freely, yet grow all the richer;
  others withhold what is due, and only
   suffer want.
25 A generous person will be enriched,
  and one who gives water will get
   water.
26 The people curse those who hold back
   grain,
  but a blessing is on the head of those
   who sell it.
27 Whoever diligently seeks good seeks
   favor,
  but evil comes to the one who
   searches for it.
28 Those who trust in their riches will
   wither, *c*
  but the righteous will flourish like
   green leaves.

29 Those who trouble their households will
   inherit wind,
  and the fool will be servant to the wise.
30 The fruit of the righteous is a tree of
   life,
  but violence *d* takes lives away.
31 If the righteous are repaid on earth,
  how much more the wicked and the
   sinner!

12 Whoever loves discipline loves
  knowledge,
  but those who hate to be rebuked are
   stupid.
2 The good obtain favor from the LORD,
  but those who devise evil he
   condemns.
3 No one finds security by wickedness,
  but the root of the righteous will
   never be moved.
4 A good wife is the crown of her
   husband,
  but she who brings shame is like
   rottenness in his bones.
5 The thoughts of the righteous are just;
  the advice of the wicked is
   treacherous.
6 The words of the wicked are a deadly
   ambush,
  but the speech of the upright delivers
   them.
7 The wicked are overthrown and are no
   more,
  but the house of the righteous will
   stand.
8 One is commended for good sense,
  but a perverse mind is despised.
9 Better to be despised and have a servant,
  than to be self-important and lack
   food.
10 The righteous know the needs of their
   animals,
  but the mercy of the wicked is cruel.
11 Those who till their land will have plenty
   of food,
  but those who follow worthless
   pursuits have no sense.

a Compare Gk Syr: Heb lacks *but she . . . shame* *b* Gk: Heb lacks *The timid . . . destitute* *c* Cn: Heb *fall*
d Cn Compare Gk Syr: Heb *a wise man*

12 The wicked covet the proceeds of
  wickedness,*a*
    but the root of the righteous bears
    fruit.
13 The evil are ensnared by the
    transgression of their lips,
    but the righteous escape from trouble.
14 From the fruit of the mouth one is filled
    with good things,
    and manual labor has its reward.
15 Fools think their own way is right,
    but the wise listen to advice.
16 Fools show their anger at once,
    but the prudent ignore an insult.
17 Whoever speaks the truth gives honest
    evidence,
    but a false witness speaks deceitfully.
18 Rash words are like sword thrusts,
    but the tongue of the wise brings
    healing.
19 Truthful lips endure forever,
    but a lying tongue lasts only a
    moment.
20 Deceit is in the mind of those who plan
    evil,
    but those who counsel peace have joy.
21 No harm happens to the righteous,
    but the wicked are filled with trouble.
22 Lying lips are an abomination to the
    LORD,
    but those who act faithfully are his
    delight.
23 One who is clever conceals knowledge,
    but the mind of a fool*b* broadcasts
    folly.
24 The hand of the diligent will rule,
    while the lazy will be put to forced
    labor.
25 Anxiety weighs down the human heart,
    but a good word cheers it up.
26 The righteous gives good advice to
    friends,*c*
    but the way of the wicked leads astray.
27 The lazy do not roast*d* their game,
    but the diligent obtain precious
    wealth.*d*

28 In the path of righteousness there is life,
    in walking its path there is no death.

13 A wise child loves discipline,*e*
    but a scoffer does not listen to
    rebuke.
2 From the fruit of their words good
    persons eat good things,
    but the desire of the treacherous is for
    wrongdoing.
3 Those who guard their mouths preserve
    their lives;
    those who open wide their lips come
    to ruin.
4 The appetite of the lazy craves, and gets
    nothing,
    while the appetite of the diligent is
    richly supplied.
5 The righteous hate falsehood,
    but the wicked act shamefully and
    disgracefully.
6 Righteousness guards one whose way is
    upright,
    but sin overthrows the wicked.
7 Some pretend to be rich, yet have
    nothing;
    others pretend to be poor, yet have
    great wealth.
8 Wealth is a ransom for a person's life,
    but the poor get no threats.
9 The light of the righteous rejoices,
    but the lamp of the wicked goes out.
10 By insolence the heedless make strife,
    but wisdom is with those who take
    advice.
11 Wealth hastily gotten*f* will dwindle,
    but those who gather little by little will
    increase it.
12 Hope deferred makes the heart sick,
    but a desire fulfilled is a tree of life.
13 Those who despise the word bring
    destruction on themselves,
    but those who respect the
    commandment will be rewarded.
14 The teaching of the wise is a fountain of
    life,

---

a Or *covet the catch of the wicked*   *b* Heb *the heart of fools*
uncertain   *e* Cn: Heb *A wise child the discipline of his father*   *c* Syr: Meaning of Heb uncertain   *d* Meaning of Heb
f Gk Vg: Heb *from vanity*

so that one may avoid the snares of
   death.

15 Good sense wins favor,
      but the way of the faithless is their
         ruin.*a*

16 The clever do all things intelligently,
      but the fool displays folly.

17 A bad messenger brings trouble,
      but a faithful envoy, healing.

18 Poverty and disgrace are for the one who
         ignores instruction,
      but one who heeds reproof is
         honored.

19 A desire realized is sweet to the soul,
      but to turn away from evil is an
         abomination to fools.

20 Whoever walks with the wise becomes
         wise,
      but the companion of fools suffers
         harm.

21 Misfortune pursues sinners,
      but prosperity rewards the righteous.

22 The good leave an inheritance to their
         children's children,
      but the sinner's wealth is laid up for
         the righteous.

23 The field of the poor may yield much
         food,
      but it is swept away through injustice.

24 Those who spare the rod hate their
         children,
      but those who love them are diligent
         to discipline them.

25 The righteous have enough to satisfy
         their appetite,
      but the belly of the wicked is empty.

14 The wise woman*b* builds her house,
      but the foolish tears it down with
         her own hands.

2 Those who walk uprightly fear the
      LORD,
      but one who is devious in conduct
         despises him.

3 The talk of fools is a rod for their
         backs,*c*
      but the lips of the wise preserve them.

4 Where there are no oxen, there is no
      grain;
      abundant crops come by the strength
         of the ox.

5 A faithful witness does not lie,
      but a false witness breathes out lies.

6 A scoffer seeks wisdom in vain,
      but knowledge is easy for one who
         understands.

7 Leave the presence of a fool,
      for there you do not find words of
         knowledge.

8 It is the wisdom of the clever to
         understand where they go,
      but the folly of fools misleads.

9 Fools mock at the guilt offering,*d*
      but the upright enjoy God's favor.

10 The heart knows its own bitterness,
      and no stranger shares its joy.

11 The house of the wicked is destroyed,
      but the tent of the upright flourishes.

12 There is a way that seems right to a
         person,
      but its end is the way to death.*e*

13 Even in laughter the heart is sad,
      and the end of joy is grief.

14 The perverse get what their ways
         deserve,
      and the good, what their deeds
         deserve.*f*

15 The simple believe everything,
      but the clever consider their steps.

16 The wise are cautious and turn away
         from evil,
      but the fool throws off restraint and is
         careless.

17 One who is quick-tempered acts
         foolishly,
      and the schemer is hated.

18 The simple are adorned with*g* folly,
      but the clever are crowned with
         knowledge.

19 The evil bow down before the good,
      the wicked at the gates of the
         righteous.

---

a Cn Compare Gk Syr Vg Tg: Heb *is enduring*   *b* Heb *Wisdom of women*   *c* Cn: Heb *a rod of pride*   *d* Meaning
of Heb uncertain   *e* Heb *ways of death*   *f* Cn: Heb *from upon him*   *g* Or *inherit*

20 The poor are disliked even by their
    neighbors,
    but the rich have many friends.

21 Those who despise their neighbors are
    sinners,
    but happy are those who are kind to
    the poor.

22 Do they not err that plan evil?
    Those who plan good find loyalty and
    faithfulness.

23 In all toil there is profit,
    but mere talk leads only to poverty.

24 The crown of the wise is their wisdom,*a*
    but folly is the garland*b* of fools.

25 A truthful witness saves lives,
    but one who utters lies is a betrayer.

26 In the fear of the LORD one has strong
    confidence,
    and one's children will have a refuge.

27 The fear of the LORD is a fountain of
    life,
    so that one may avoid the snares of
    death.

28 The glory of a king is a multitude of
    people;
    without people a prince is ruined.

29 Whoever is slow to anger has great
    understanding,
    but one who has a hasty temper exalts
    folly.

30 A tranquil mind gives life to the flesh,
    but passion makes the bones rot.

31 Those who oppress the poor insult their
    Maker,
    but those who are kind to the needy
    honor him.

32 The wicked are overthrown by their
    evildoing,
    but the righteous find a refuge in their
    integrity.*c*

33 Wisdom is at home in the mind of one
    who has understanding,
    but it is not*d* known in the heart of
    fools.

34 Righteousness exalts a nation,
    but sin is a reproach to any people.

35 A servant who deals wisely has the king's
    favor,
    but his wrath falls on one who acts
    shamefully.

15 A soft answer turns away wrath,
    but a harsh word stirs up anger.

2 The tongue of the wise dispenses
    knowledge,*e*
    but the mouths of fools pour out folly.

3 The eyes of the LORD are in every place,
    keeping watch on the evil and the
    good.

4 A gentle tongue is a tree of life,
    but perverseness in it breaks the spirit.

5 A fool despises a parent's instruction,
    but the one who heeds admonition is
    prudent.

6 In the house of the righteous there is
    much treasure,
    but trouble befalls the income of the
    wicked.

7 The lips of the wise spread knowledge;
    not so the minds of fools.

8 The sacrifice of the wicked is an
    abomination to the LORD,
    but the prayer of the upright is his
    delight.

9 The way of the wicked is an
    abomination to the LORD,
    but he loves the one who pursues
    righteousness.

10 There is severe discipline for one who
    forsakes the way,
    but one who hates a rebuke will die.

11 Sheol and Abaddon lie open before the
    LORD,
    how much more human hearts!

12 Scoffers do not like to be rebuked;
    they will not go to the wise.

13 A glad heart makes a cheerful
    countenance,
    but by sorrow of heart the spirit is
    broken.

14 The mind of one who has
    understanding seeks knowledge,
    but the mouths of fools feed on folly.

---

a Cn Compare Gk: Heb *riches*   *b* Cn: Heb *is the folly*   *c* Gk Syr: Heb *in their death*   *d* Gk Syr: Heb lacks *not*
e Cn: Heb *makes knowledge good*

15 All the days of the poor are hard,
    but a cheerful heart has a continual
      feast.
16 Better is a little with the fear of the
    LORD
    than great treasure and trouble with it.
17 Better is a dinner of vegetables where
    love is
    than a fatted ox and hatred with it.
18 Those who are hot-tempered stir up
    strife,
    but those who are slow to anger calm
      contention.
19 The way of the lazy is overgrown with
    thorns,
    but the path of the upright is a level
      highway.
20 A wise child makes a glad father,
    but the foolish despise their mothers.
21 Folly is a joy to one who has no sense,
    but a person of understanding walks
      straight ahead.
22 Without counsel, plans go wrong,
    but with many advisers they succeed.
23 To make an apt answer is a joy to
    anyone,
    and a word in season, how good it is!
24 For the wise the path of life leads
    upward,
    in order to avoid Sheol below.
25 The LORD tears down the house of the
    proud,
    but maintains the widow's boundaries.
26 Evil plans are an abomination to the
    LORD,
    but gracious words are pure.
27 Those who are greedy for unjust gain
    make trouble for their
      households,
    but those who hate bribes will live.
28 The mind of the righteous ponders how
    to answer,
    but the mouth of the wicked pours
      out evil.
29 The LORD is far from the wicked,
    but he hears the prayer of the
      righteous.
30 The light of the eyes rejoices the heart,
    and good news refreshes the body.
31 The ear that heeds wholesome
    admonition
    will lodge among the wise.
32 Those who ignore instruction despise
    themselves,
    but those who heed admonition gain
      understanding.
33 The fear of the LORD is instruction in
    wisdom,
    and humility goes before honor.

16 The plans of the mind belong to
    mortals,
    but the answer of the tongue is from
      the LORD.
2 All one's ways may be pure in one's own
    eyes,
    but the LORD weighs the spirit.
3 Commit your work to the LORD,
    and your plans will be established.
4 The LORD has made everything for its
    purpose,
    even the wicked for the day of
      trouble.
5 All those who are arrogant are an
    abomination to the LORD;
    be assured, they will not go
      unpunished.
6 By loyalty and faithfulness iniquity is
    atoned for,
    and by the fear of the LORD one
      avoids evil.
7 When the ways of people please the
    LORD,
    he causes even their enemies to be at
      peace with them.
8 Better is a little with righteousness
    than large income with injustice.
9 The human mind plans the way,
    but the LORD directs the steps.
10 Inspired decisions are on the lips of a
    king;
    his mouth does not sin in judgment.
11 Honest balances and scales are the
    LORD's;
    all the weights in the bag are his work.
12 It is an abomination to kings to do evil,

for the throne is established by
righteousness.

13 Righteous lips are the delight of a king,
and he loves those who speak what is
right.

14 A king's wrath is a messenger of death,
and whoever is wise will appease it.

15 In the light of a king's face there is life,
and his favor is like the clouds that
bring the spring rain.

16 How much better to get wisdom than
gold!
To get understanding is to be chosen
rather than silver.

17 The highway of the upright avoids evil;
those who guard their way preserve
their lives.

18 Pride goes before destruction,
and a haughty spirit before a fall.

19 It is better to be of a lowly spirit among
the poor
than to divide the spoil with the
proud.

20 Those who are attentive to a matter will
prosper,
and happy are those who trust in the
LORD.

21 The wise of heart is called perceptive,
and pleasant speech increases
persuasiveness.

22 Wisdom is a fountain of life to one who
has it,
but folly is the punishment of fools.

23 The mind of the wise makes their
speech judicious,
and adds persuasiveness to their lips.

24 Pleasant words are like a honeycomb,
sweetness to the soul and health to the
body.

25 Sometimes there is a way that seems to
be right,
but in the end it is the way to death.

26 The appetite of workers works for them;
their hunger urges them on.

27 Scoundrels concoct evil,

and their speech is like a scorching
fire.

28 A perverse person spreads strife,
and a whisperer separates close
friends.

29 The violent entice their neighbors,
and lead them in a way that is not
good.

30 One who winks the eyes plans *a* perverse
things;
one who compresses the lips brings
evil to pass.

31 Gray hair is a crown of glory;
it is gained in a righteous life.

32 One who is slow to anger is better than
the mighty,
and one whose temper is controlled
than one who captures a city.

33 The lot is cast into the lap,
but the decision is the LORD's alone.

17 Better is a dry morsel with quiet
than a house full of feasting with
strife.

2 A slave who deals wisely will rule over a
child who acts shamefully,
and will share the inheritance as one
of the family.

3 The crucible is for silver, and the furnace
is for gold,
but the LORD tests the heart.

4 An evildoer listens to wicked lips;
and a liar gives heed to a mischievous
tongue.

5 Those who mock the poor insult their
Maker;
those who are glad at calamity will not
go unpunished.

6 Grandchildren are the crown of the
aged,
and the glory of children is their
parents.

7 Fine speech is not becoming to a fool;
still less is false speech to a ruler. *b*

8 A bribe is like a magic stone in the eyes
of those who give it;
wherever they turn they prosper.

---

a Gk Syr Vg Tg: Heb *to plan*   *b* Or *a noble person*

9   One who forgives an affront fosters
        friendship,
        but one who dwells on disputes will
            alienate a friend.
10 A rebuke strikes deeper into a discerning
        person
        than a hundred blows into a fool.
11 Evil people seek only rebellion,
        but a cruel messenger will be sent
            against them.
12 Better to meet a she-bear robbed of its
        cubs
        than to confront a fool immersed in
            folly.
13 Evil will not depart from the house
        of one who returns evil for good.
14 The beginning of strife is like letting out
        water;
        so stop before the quarrel breaks out.
15 One who justifies the wicked and one
        who condemns the righteous
        are both alike an abomination to the
            LORD.
16 Why should fools have a price in hand
        to buy wisdom, when they have no
            mind to learn?
17 A friend loves at all times,
        and kinsfolk are born to share
            adversity.
18 It is senseless to give a pledge,
        to become surety for a neighbor.
19 One who loves transgression loves strife;
        one who builds a high threshold
            invites broken bones.
20 The crooked of mind do not prosper,
        and the perverse of tongue fall into
            calamity.
21 The one who begets a fool gets trouble;
        the parent of a fool has no joy.
22 A cheerful heart is a good medicine,
        but a downcast spirit dries up the
            bones.
23 The wicked accept a concealed bribe
        to pervert the ways of justice.
24 The discerning person looks to wisdom,

        but the eyes of a fool to the ends of
            the earth.
25 Foolish children are a grief to their
        father
        and bitterness to her who bore them.
26 To impose a fine on the innocent is not
        right,
        or to flog the noble for their integrity.
27 One who spares words is
        knowledgeable;
        one who is cool in spirit has
            understanding.
28 Even fools who keep silent are
        considered wise;
        when they close their lips, they are
            deemed intelligent.

18 The one who lives alone is self-
        indulgent,
        showing contempt for all who have
            sound judgment.*a*
2   A fool takes no pleasure in
        understanding,
        but only in expressing personal
            opinion.
3   When wickedness comes, contempt
        comes also;
        and with dishonor comes disgrace.
4   The words of the mouth are deep
        waters;
        the fountain of wisdom is a gushing
            stream.
5   It is not right to be partial to the guilty,
        or to subvert the innocent in
            judgment.
6   A fool's lips bring strife,
        and a fool's mouth invites a flogging.
7   The mouths of fools are their ruin,
        and their lips a snare to themselves.
8   The words of a whisperer are like
        delicious morsels;
        they go down into the inner parts of
            the body.
9   One who is slack in work
        is close kin to a vandal.
10 The name of the LORD is a strong tower;
        the righteous run into it and are safe.

a Meaning of Heb uncertain

11 The wealth of the rich is their strong
city;
in their imagination it is like a high
wall.
12 Before destruction one's heart is
haughty,
but humility goes before honor.
13 If one gives answer before hearing,
it is folly and shame.
14 The human spirit will endure sickness;
but a broken spirit—who can bear?
15 An intelligent mind acquires knowledge,
and the ear of the wise seeks
knowledge.
16 A gift opens doors;
it gives access to the great.
17 The one who first states a case seems
right,
until the other comes and cross-
examines.
18 Casting the lot puts an end to disputes
and decides between powerful
contenders.
19 An ally offended is stronger than a city;*a*
such quarreling is like the bars of a
castle.
20 From the fruit of the mouth one's
stomach is satisfied;
the yield of the lips brings satisfaction.
21 Death and life are in the power of the
tongue,
and those who love it will eat its fruits.
22 He who finds a wife finds a good thing,
and obtains favor from the LORD.
23 The poor use entreaties,
but the rich answer roughly.
24 Some*b* friends play at friendship*c*
but a true friend sticks closer than
one's nearest kin.

19 Better the poor walking in integrity
than one perverse of speech who
is a fool.
2 Desire without knowledge is not good,
and one who moves too hurriedly
misses the way.
3 One's own folly leads to ruin,

yet the heart rages against the LORD.
4 Wealth brings many friends,
but the poor are left friendless.
5 A false witness will not go unpunished,
and a liar will not escape.
6 Many seek the favor of the generous,
and everyone is a friend to a giver of
gifts.
7 If the poor are hated even by their kin,
how much more are they shunned by
their friends!
When they call after them, they are not
there.*d*
8 To get wisdom is to love oneself;
to keep understanding is to prosper.
9 A false witness will not go unpunished,
and the liar will perish.
10 It is not fitting for a fool to live in luxury,
much less for a slave to rule over
princes.
11 Those with good sense are slow to
anger,
and it is their glory to overlook an
offense.
12 A king's anger is like the growling of a
lion,
but his favor is like dew on the grass.
13 A stupid child is ruin to a father,
and a wife's quarreling is a continual
dripping of rain.
14 House and wealth are inherited from
parents,
but a prudent wife is from the LORD.
15 Laziness brings on deep sleep;
an idle person will suffer hunger.
16 Those who keep the commandment will
live;
those who are heedless of their ways
will die.
17 Whoever is kind to the poor lends to the
LORD,
and will be repaid in full.
18 Discipline your children while there is
hope;
do not set your heart on their
destruction.

---

a Gk Syr Vg Tg: Meaning of Heb uncertain   *b* Syr Tg: Heb *A man of*   *c* Cn Compare Syr Vg Tg: Meaning of
Heb uncertain   *d* Meaning of Heb uncertain

19 A violent tempered person will pay the
penalty;
if you effect a rescue, you will only
have to do it again.[a]

20 Listen to advice and accept instruction,
that you may gain wisdom for the
future.

21 The human mind may devise many
plans,
but it is the purpose of the LORD that
will be established.

22 What is desirable in a person is loyalty,
and it is better to be poor than a liar.

23 The fear of the LORD is life indeed;
filled with it one rests secure
and suffers no harm.

24 The lazy person buries a hand in the
dish,
and will not even bring it back to the
mouth.

25 Strike a scoffer, and the simple will learn
prudence;
reprove the intelligent, and they will
gain knowledge.

26 Those who do violence to their father
and chase away their mother
are children who cause shame and
bring reproach.

27 Cease straying, my child, from the words
of knowledge,
in order that you may hear instruction.

28 A worthless witness mocks at justice,
and the mouth of the wicked devours
iniquity.

29 Condemnation is ready for scoffers,
and flogging for the backs of fools.

20 Wine is a mocker, strong drink a
brawler,
and whoever is led astray by it is not
wise.

2 The dread anger of a king is like the
growling of a lion;
anyone who provokes him to anger
forfeits life itself.

3 It is honorable to refrain from strife,
but every fool is quick to quarrel.

4 The lazy person does not plow in
season;
harvest comes, and there is nothing to
be found.

5 The purposes in the human mind are
like deep water,
but the intelligent will draw them out.

6 Many proclaim themselves loyal,
but who can find one worthy of trust?

7 The righteous walk in integrity—
happy are the children who follow
them!

8 A king who sits on the throne of
judgment
winnows all evil with his eyes.

9 Who can say, "I have made my heart
clean;
I am pure from my sin"?

10 Diverse weights and diverse measures
are both alike an abomination to the
LORD.

11 Even children make themselves known
by their acts,
by whether what they do is pure and
right.

12 The hearing ear and the seeing eye—
the LORD has made them both.

13 Do not love sleep, or else you will come
to poverty;
open your eyes, and you will have
plenty of bread.

14 "Bad, bad," says the buyer,
then goes away and boasts.

15 There is gold, and abundance of costly
stones;
but the lips informed by knowledge
are a precious jewel.

16 Take the garment of one who has given
surety for a stranger;
seize the pledge given as surety for
foreigners.

17 Bread gained by deceit is sweet,
but afterward the mouth will be full of
gravel.

18 Plans are established by taking advice;
wage war by following wise guidance.

a Meaning of Heb uncertain

19 A gossip reveals secrets;
    therefore do not associate with a
      babbler.
20 If you curse father or mother,
    your lamp will go out in utter
      darkness.
21 An estate quickly acquired in the
      beginning
    will not be blessed in the end.
22 Do not say, "I will repay evil";
    wait for the LORD, and he will help
      you.
23 Differing weights are an abomination to
      the LORD,
    and false scales are not good.
24 All our steps are ordered by the LORD;
    how then can we understand our own
      ways?
25 It is a snare for one to say rashly, "It is
      holy,"
    and begin to reflect only after making
      a vow.
26 A wise king winnows the wicked,
    and drives the wheel over them.
27 The human spirit is the lamp of the
      LORD,
    searching every inmost part.
28 Loyalty and faithfulness preserve the
      king,
    and his throne is upheld by
      righteousness.*a*
29 The glory of youths is their strength,
    but the beauty of the aged is their
      gray hair.
30 Blows that wound cleanse away evil;
    beatings make clean the innermost
      parts.

21 The king's heart is a stream of water
    in the hand of the LORD;
    he turns it wherever he will.
2 All deeds are right in the sight of the
      doer,
    but the LORD weighs the heart.
3 To do righteousness and justice
    is more acceptable to the LORD than
      sacrifice.

4 Haughty eyes and a proud heart—
    the lamp of the wicked—are sin.
5 The plans of the diligent lead surely to
      abundance,
    but everyone who is hasty comes only
      to want.
6 The getting of treasures by a lying
      tongue
    is a fleeting vapor and a snare*b* of
      death.
7 The violence of the wicked will sweep
      them away,
    because they refuse to do what is just.
8 The way of the guilty is crooked,
    but the conduct of the pure is right.
9 It is better to live in a corner of the
      housetop
    than in a house shared with a
      contentious wife.
10 The souls of the wicked desire evil;
    their neighbors find no mercy in their
      eyes.
11 When a scoffer is punished, the simple
      become wiser;
    when the wise are instructed, they
      increase in knowledge.
12 The Righteous One observes the house
      of the wicked;
    he casts the wicked down to ruin.
13 If you close your ear to the cry of the
      poor,
    you will cry out and not be heard.
14 A gift in secret averts anger;
    and a concealed bribe in the bosom,
      strong wrath.
15 When justice is done, it is a joy to the
      righteous,
    but dismay to evildoers.
16 Whoever wanders from the way of
      understanding
    will rest in the assembly of the dead.
17 Whoever loves pleasure will suffer want;
    whoever loves wine and oil will not be
      rich.
18 The wicked is a ransom for the
      righteous,

a Gk: Heb *loyalty*   *b* Gk: Heb *seekers*

and the faithless for the upright.

19 It is better to live in a desert land
    than with a contentious and fretful
        wife.
20 Precious treasure remains*a* in the house
      of the wise,
    but the fool devours it.
21 Whoever pursues righteousness and
      kindness
    will find life*b* and honor.
22 One wise person went up against a city
      of warriors
    and brought down the stronghold in
      which they trusted.
23 To watch over mouth and tongue
    is to keep out of trouble.
24 The proud, haughty person, named
      "Scoffer,"
    acts with arrogant pride.
25 The craving of the lazy person is fatal,
    for lazy hands refuse to labor.
26 All day long the wicked covet,*c*
    but the righteous give and do not hold
      back.
27 The sacrifice of the wicked is an
      abomination;
    how much more when brought with
      evil intent.
28 A false witness will perish,
    but a good listener will testify
      successfully.
29 The wicked put on a bold face,
    but the upright give thought to*d* their
      ways.
30 No wisdom, no understanding, no
      counsel,
    can avail against the LORD.
31 The horse is made ready for the day of
      battle,
    but the victory belongs to the LORD.

22 A good name is to be chosen rather
    than great riches,
    and favor is better than silver or gold.
2 The rich and the poor have this in
      common:
    the LORD is the maker of them all.

3 The clever see danger and hide;
    but the simple go on, and suffer for it.
4 The reward for humility and fear of the
      LORD
    is riches and honor and life.
5 Thorns and snares are in the way of the
      perverse;
    the cautious will keep far from them.
6 Train children in the right way,
    and when old, they will not stray.
7 The rich rule over the poor,
    and the borrower is the slave of the
      lender.
8 Whoever sows injustice will reap
      calamity,
    and the rod of anger will fail.
9 Those who are generous are blessed,
    for they share their bread with the
      poor.
10 Drive out a scoffer, and strife goes out;
    quarreling and abuse will cease.
11 Those who love a pure heart and are
      gracious in speech
    will have the king as a friend.
12 The eyes of the LORD keep watch over
      knowledge,
    but he overthrows the words of the
      faithless.
13 The lazy person says, "There is a lion
      outside!
    I shall be killed in the streets!"
14 The mouth of a loose*e* woman is a deep
      pit;
    he with whom the LORD is angry falls
      into it.
15 Folly is bound up in the heart of a boy,
    but the rod of discipline drives it far
      away.
16 Oppressing the poor in order to enrich
      oneself,
    and giving to the rich, will lead only to
      loss.

Sayings of the Wise
17   The words of the wise:

---

a Gk: Heb *and oil*   *b* Gk: Heb *life and righteousness*   *c* Gk: Heb *all day long one covets covetously*   *d* Another
reading is *establish*   *e* Heb *strange*

Incline your ear and hear my words,^a
   and apply your mind to my teaching;
18 for it will be pleasant if you keep them
      within you,
   if all of them are ready on your lips.
19 So that your trust may be in the LORD,
   I have made them known to you
      today—yes, to you.
20 Have I not written for you thirty sayings
   of admonition and knowledge,
21 to show you what is right and true,
   so that you may give a true answer to
      those who sent you?

22 Do not rob the poor because they are
      poor,
   or crush the afflicted at the gate;
23 for the LORD pleads their cause
   and despoils of life those who despoil
      them.
24 Make no friends with those given to
      anger,
   and do not associate with hotheads,
25 or you may learn their ways
   and entangle yourself in a snare.
26 Do not be one of those who give
      pledges,
   who become surety for debts.
27 If you have nothing with which to pay,
   why should your bed be taken from
      under you?
28 Do not remove the ancient landmark
   that your ancestors set up.
29 Do you see those who are skillful in their
      work?
   They will serve kings;
   they will not serve common people.

23 When you sit down to eat with a
      ruler,
   observe carefully what^b is before you,
2 and put a knife to your throat
   if you have a big appetite.
3 Do not desire the ruler's^c delicacies,
   for they are deceptive food.
4 Do not wear yourself out to get rich;

   be wise enough to desist.
5 When your eyes light upon it, it is gone;
   for suddenly it takes wings to itself,
   flying like an eagle toward heaven.
6 Do not eat the bread of the stingy;
   do not desire their delicacies;
7 for like a hair in the throat, so are they.^d
   "Eat and drink!" they say to you;
   but they do not mean it.
8 You will vomit up the little you have
      eaten,
   and you will waste your pleasant
      words.
9 Do not speak in the hearing of a fool,
   who will only despise the wisdom of
      your words.
10 Do not remove an ancient landmark
   or encroach on the fields of orphans,
11 for their redeemer is strong;
   he will plead their cause against you.
12 Apply your mind to instruction
   and your ear to words of knowledge.
13 Do not withhold discipline from your
      children;
   if you beat them with a rod, they will
      not die.
14 If you beat them with the rod,
   you will save their lives from Sheol.
15 My child, if your heart is wise,
   my heart too will be glad.
16 My soul will rejoice
   when your lips speak what is right.
17 Do not let your heart envy sinners,
   but always continue in the fear of the
      LORD.
18 Surely there is a future,
   and your hope will not be cut off.

19 Hear, my child, and be wise,
   and direct your mind in the way.
20 Do not be among winebibbers,
   or among gluttonous eaters of meat;
21 for the drunkard and the glutton will
      come to poverty,
   and drowsiness will clothe them with
      rags.

---

a Cn Compare Gk: Heb *Incline your ear, and hear the words of the wise*   *b* Or *who*   *c* Heb *his*   *d* Meaning of Heb
uncertain

22 Listen to your father who begot you,
   and do not despise your mother when
      she is old.
23 Buy truth, and do not sell it;
   buy wisdom, instruction, and
      understanding.
24 The father of the righteous will greatly
      rejoice;
   he who begets a wise son will be glad
      in him.
25 Let your father and mother be glad;
   let her who bore you rejoice.

26 My child, give me your heart,
   and let your eyes observe*a* my ways.
27 For a prostitute is a deep pit;
   an adulteress*b* is a narrow well.
28 She lies in wait like a robber
   and increases the number of the
      faithless.

29 Who has woe? Who has sorrow?
   Who has strife? Who has
      complaining?
   Who has wounds without cause?
   Who has redness of eyes?
30 Those who linger late over wine,
   those who keep trying mixed wines.
31 Do not look at wine when it is red,
   when it sparkles in the cup
   and goes down smoothly.
32 At the last it bites like a serpent,
   and stings like an adder.
33 Your eyes will see strange things,
   and your mind utter perverse things.
34 You will be like one who lies down in the
      midst of the sea,
   like one who lies on the top of a
      mast.*c*
35 "They struck me," you will say,*d* "but I
      was not hurt;
   they beat me, but I did not feel it.
   When shall I awake?
   I will seek another drink."

24 Do not envy the wicked,
   nor desire to be with them;

2 for their minds devise violence,
   and their lips talk of mischief.

3 By wisdom a house is built,
   and by understanding it is established;
4 by knowledge the rooms are filled
   with all precious and pleasant riches.
5 Wise warriors are mightier than strong
      ones,*e*
   and those who have knowledge than
      those who have strength;
6 for by wise guidance you can wage your
      war,
   and in abundance of counselors there
      is victory.
7 Wisdom is too high for fools;
   in the gate they do not open their
      mouths.

8 Whoever plans to do evil
   will be called a mischief-maker.
9 The devising of folly is sin,
   and the scoffer is an abomination to
      all.

10 If you faint in the day of adversity,
   your strength being small;
11 if you hold back from rescuing those
      taken away to death,
   those who go staggering to the
      slaughter;
12 if you say, "Look, we did not know
      this"—
   does not he who weighs the heart
      perceive it?
   Does not he who keeps watch over your
      soul know it?
   And will he not repay all according to
      their deeds?

13 My child, eat honey, for it is good,
   and the drippings of the honeycomb
      are sweet to your taste.
14 Know that wisdom is such to your soul;
   if you find it, you will find a future,
   and your hope will not be cut off.

---

a Another reading is *delight in*   *b* Heb *an alien woman*   *c* Meaning of Heb uncertain   *d* Gk Syr Vg Tg: Heb
lacks *you will say*   *e* Gk Compare Syr Tg: Heb *A wise man is strength*

15 Do not lie in wait like an outlaw against
     the home of the righteous;
   do no violence to the place where the
     righteous live;
16 for though they fall seven times, they will
     rise again;
   but the wicked are overthrown by
     calamity.

17 Do not rejoice when your enemies fall,
   and do not let your heart be glad
     when they stumble,
18 or else the LORD will see it and be
     displeased,
   and turn away his anger from them.

19 Do not fret because of evildoers.
   Do not envy the wicked;
20 for the evil have no future;
   the lamp of the wicked will go out.

21 My child, fear the LORD and the king,
   and do not disobey either of them;*a*
22 for disaster comes from them suddenly,
   and who knows the ruin that both can
     bring?

Further Sayings of the Wise

23 These also are sayings of the wise:

Partiality in judging is not good.
24 Whoever says to the wicked, "You are
     innocent,"
   will be cursed by peoples, abhorred by
     nations;
25 but those who rebuke the wicked will
     have delight,
   and a good blessing will come upon
     them.
26 One who gives an honest answer
   gives a kiss on the lips.

27 Prepare your work outside,
   get everything ready for you in the
     field;
   and after that build your house.

a Gk: Heb do not associate with those who change

28 Do not be a witness against your
     neighbor without cause,
   and do not deceive with your lips.
29 Do not say, "I will do to others as they
     have done to me;
   I will pay them back for what they
     have done."

30 I passed by the field of one who was
     lazy,
   by the vineyard of a stupid person;
31 and see, it was all overgrown with thorns;
   the ground was covered with nettles,
   and its stone wall was broken down.
32 Then I saw and considered it;
   I looked and received instruction.
33 A little sleep, a little slumber,
   a little folding of the hands to rest,
34 and poverty will come upon you like a
     robber,
   and want, like an armed warrior.

Further Wise Sayings of Solomon

25 These are other proverbs of Solomon
   that the officials of King Hezekiah of
Judah copied.

2 It is the glory of God to conceal things,
   but the glory of kings is to search
     things out.
3 Like the heavens for height, like the
     earth for depth,
   so the mind of kings is unsearchable.
4 Take away the dross from the silver,
   and the smith has material for a vessel;
5 take away the wicked from the presence
     of the king,
   and his throne will be established in
     righteousness.
6 Do not put yourself forward in the
     king's presence
   or stand in the place of the great;
7 for it is better to be told, "Come up
     here,"
   than to be put lower in the presence
     of a noble.

What your eyes have seen
8   do not hastily bring into court;
for*a* what will you do in the end,
        when your neighbor puts you to
            shame?
9   Argue your case with your neighbor
        directly,
    and do not disclose another's secret;
10   or else someone who hears you will
        bring shame upon you,
    and your ill repute will have no end.

11   A word fitly spoken
        is like apples of gold in a setting of
            silver.
12   Like a gold ring or an ornament of gold
        is a wise rebuke to a listening ear.
13   Like the cold of snow in the time of
            harvest
        are faithful messengers to those who
            send them;
        they refresh the spirit of their masters.
14   Like clouds and wind without rain
        is one who boasts of a gift never
            given.
15   With patience a ruler may be persuaded,
        and a soft tongue can break bones.
16   If you have found honey, eat only
            enough for you,
        or else, having too much, you will
            vomit it.
17   Let your foot be seldom in your
            neighbor's house,
        otherwise the neighbor will become
            weary of you and hate you.
18   Like a war club, a sword, or a sharp
            arrow
        is one who bears false witness against
            a neighbor.
19   Like a bad tooth or a lame foot
        is trust in a faithless person in time of
            trouble.
20   Like vinegar on a wound*b*
        is one who sings songs to a heavy
            heart.

Like a moth in clothing or a worm in
            wood,
        sorrow gnaws at the human heart.*c*
21   If your enemies are hungry, give them
            bread to eat;
        and if they are thirsty, give them water
            to drink;
22   for you will heap coals of fire on their
            heads,
        and the LORD will reward you.
23   The north wind produces rain,
        and a backbiting tongue, angry looks.
24   It is better to live in a corner of the
            housetop
        than in a house shared with a
            contentious wife.
25   Like cold water to a thirsty soul,
        so is good news from a far country.
26   Like a muddied spring or a polluted
            fountain
        are the righteous who give way before
            the wicked.
27   It is not good to eat much honey,
        or to seek honor on top of honor.
28   Like a city breached, without walls,
        is one who lacks self-control.

26

Like snow in summer or rain in
            harvest,
        so honor is not fitting for a fool.
2   Like a sparrow in its flitting, like a
            swallow in its flying,
        an undeserved curse goes nowhere.
3   A whip for the horse, a bridle for the
            donkey,
        and a rod for the back of fools.
4   Do not answer fools according to their
            folly,
        or you will be a fool yourself.
5   Answer fools according to their folly,
        or they will be wise in their own eyes.
6   It is like cutting off one's foot and
            drinking down violence,
        to send a message by a fool.
7   The legs of a disabled person hang limp;
        so does a proverb in the mouth of a
            fool.

---

a Cn: Heb *or else*   *b* Gk: Heb *Like one who takes off a garment on a cold day, like vinegar on lye*   *c* Gk Syr Tg: Heb
lacks *Like a moth . . . human heart*

8 It is like binding a stone in a sling
   to give honor to a fool.

9 Like a thornbush brandished by the
      hand of a drunkard
   is a proverb in the mouth of a fool.

10 Like an archer who wounds everybody
   is one who hires a passing fool or
      drunkard. *a*

11 Like a dog that returns to its vomit
   is a fool who reverts to his folly.

12 Do you see persons wise in their own
      eyes?
   There is more hope for fools than for
      them.

13 The lazy person says, "There is a lion in
      the road!
   There is a lion in the streets!"

14 As a door turns on its hinges,
   so does a lazy person in bed.

15 The lazy person buries a hand in the
      dish,
   and is too tired to bring it back to the
      mouth.

16 The lazy person is wiser in self-esteem
   than seven who can answer discreetly.

17 Like somebody who takes a passing dog
      by the ears
   is one who meddles in the quarrel of
      another.

18 Like a maniac who shoots deadly
      firebrands and arrows,

19 so is one who deceives a neighbor
   and says, "I am only joking!"

20 For lack of wood the fire goes out,
   and where there is no whisperer,
      quarreling ceases.

21 As charcoal is to hot embers and wood
      to fire,
   so is a quarrelsome person for
      kindling strife.

22 The words of a whisperer are like
      delicious morsels;
   they go down into the inner parts of
      the body.

23 Like the glaze *b* covering an earthen
      vessel

are smooth *c* lips with an evil heart.

24 An enemy dissembles in speaking
   while harboring deceit within;

25 when an enemy speaks graciously, do not
      believe it,
   for there are seven abominations
      concealed within;

26 though hatred is covered with guile,
   the enemy's wickedness will be
      exposed in the assembly.

27 Whoever digs a pit will fall into it,
   and a stone will come back on the one
      who starts it rolling.

28 A lying tongue hates its victims,
   and a flattering mouth works ruin.

27 Do not boast about tomorrow,
   for you do not know what a day may
      bring.

2 Let another praise you, and not your
      own mouth—
   a stranger, and not your own lips.

3 A stone is heavy, and sand is weighty,
   but a fool's provocation is heavier
      than both.

4 Wrath is cruel, anger is overwhelming,
   but who is able to stand before
      jealousy?

5 Better is open rebuke
   than hidden love.

6 Well meant are the wounds a friend
      inflicts,
   but profuse are the kisses of an
      enemy.

7 The sated appetite spurns honey,
   but to a ravenous appetite even the
      bitter is sweet.

8 Like a bird that strays from its nest
   is one who strays from home.

9 Perfume and incense make the heart
      glad,
   but the soul is torn by trouble. *d*

10 Do not forsake your friend or the friend
      of your parent;
   do not go to the house of your
      kindred in the day of your
      calamity.

---

a Meaning of Heb uncertain   *b* Cn: Heb *silver of dross*
is better than one's own counsel   *c* Gk: Heb *burning*   *d* Gk: Heb *the sweetness of a friend*

Better is a neighbor who is nearby
   than kindred who are far away.

11 Be wise, my child, and make my heart
     glad,
   so that I may answer whoever
     reproaches me.

12 The clever see danger and hide;
   but the simple go on, and suffer for it.

13 Take the garment of one who has given
     surety for a stranger;
   seize the pledge given as surety for
     foreigners. *a*

14 Whoever blesses a neighbor with a loud
     voice,
   rising early in the morning,
   will be counted as cursing.

15 A continual dripping on a rainy day
   and a contentious wife are alike;

16 to restrain her is to restrain the wind
   or to grasp oil in the right hand. *b*

17 Iron sharpens iron,
   and one person sharpens the wits *c* of
     another.

18 Anyone who tends a fig tree will eat its
     fruit,
   and anyone who takes care of a
     master will be honored.

19 Just as water reflects the face,
   so one human heart reflects another.

20 Sheol and Abaddon are never satisfied,
   and human eyes are never satisfied.

21 The crucible is for silver, and the furnace
     is for gold,
   so a person is tested *d* by being praised.

22 Crush a fool in a mortar with a pestle
     along with crushed grain,
   but the folly will not be driven out.

23 Know well the condition of your flocks,
   and give attention to your herds;

24 for riches do not last forever,
   nor a crown for all generations.

25 When the grass is gone, and new growth
     appears,
   and the herbage of the mountains is
     gathered,

26 the lambs will provide your clothing,
   and the goats the price of a field;

27 there will be enough goats' milk for your
     food,
   for the food of your household
   and nourishment for your servant-
     girls.

28

The wicked flee when no one
     pursues,
   but the righteous are as bold as a lion.

2 When a land rebels
   it has many rulers;
but with an intelligent ruler
   there is lasting order. *b*

3 A ruler *e* who oppresses the poor
   is a beating rain that leaves no food.

4 Those who forsake the law praise the
     wicked,
   but those who keep the law struggle
     against them.

5 The evil do not understand justice,
   but those who seek the LORD
     understand it completely.

6 Better to be poor and walk in integrity
   than to be crooked in one's ways even
     though rich.

7 Those who keep the law are wise
     children,
   but companions of gluttons shame
     their parents.

8 One who augments wealth by exorbitant
     interest
   gathers it for another who is kind to
     the poor.

9 When one will not listen to the law,
   even one's prayers are an abomination.

10 Those who mislead the upright into evil
     ways
   will fall into pits of their own making,
   but the blameless will have a goodly
     inheritance.

11 The rich is wise in self-esteem,
   but an intelligent poor person sees
     through the pose.

12 When the righteous triumph, there is
     great glory,

a Vg and 20.16: Heb *for a foreign woman*   *b* Meaning of Heb uncertain   *c* Heb *face*   *d* Heb lacks *is tested*
e Cn: Heb *A poor person*

but when the wicked prevail, people
go into hiding.

13 No one who conceals transgressions will
prosper,
but one who confesses and forsakes
them will obtain mercy.

14 Happy is the one who is never without
fear,
but one who is hard-hearted will fall
into calamity.

15 Like a roaring lion or a charging bear
is a wicked ruler over a poor people.

16 A ruler who lacks understanding is a
cruel oppressor;
but one who hates unjust gain will
enjoy a long life.

17 If someone is burdened with the blood
of another,
let that killer be a fugitive until death;
let no one offer assistance.

18 One who walks in integrity will be safe,
but whoever follows crooked ways
will fall into the Pit.[a]

19 Anyone who tills the land will have
plenty of bread,
but one who follows worthless
pursuits will have plenty of
poverty.

20 The faithful will abound with blessings,
but one who is in a hurry to be rich
will not go unpunished.

21 To show partiality is not good—
yet for a piece of bread a person may
do wrong.

22 The miser is in a hurry to get rich
and does not know that loss is sure to
come.

23 Whoever rebukes a person will afterward
find more favor
than one who flatters with the tongue.

24 Anyone who robs father or mother
and says, "That is no crime,"
is partner to a thug.

25 The greedy person stirs up strife,
but whoever trusts in the LORD will be
enriched.

26 Those who trust in their own wits are
fools;
but those who walk in wisdom come
through safely.

27 Whoever gives to the poor will lack
nothing,
but one who turns a blind eye will get
many a curse.

28 When the wicked prevail, people go into
hiding;
but when they perish, the righteous
increase.

29 One who is often reproved, yet
remains stubborn,
will suddenly be broken beyond
healing.

2 When the righteous are in authority, the
people rejoice;
but when the wicked rule, the people
groan.

3 A child who loves wisdom makes a
parent glad,
but to keep company with prostitutes
is to squander one's substance.

4 By justice a king gives stability to the
land,
but one who makes heavy exactions
ruins it.

5 Whoever flatters a neighbor
is spreading a net for the neighbor's
feet.

6 In the transgression of the evil there is a
snare,
but the righteous sing and rejoice.

7 The righteous know the rights of the
poor;
the wicked have no such
understanding.

8 Scoffers set a city aflame,
but the wise turn away wrath.

9 If the wise go to law with fools,
there is ranting and ridicule without
relief.

10 The bloodthirsty hate the blameless,
and they seek the life of the upright.

11 A fool gives full vent to anger,

---

a Syr: Heb *fall all at once*

but the wise quietly holds it back.

12 If a ruler listens to falsehood,
all his officials will be wicked.

13 The poor and the oppressor have this in
common:
the LORD gives light to the eyes of
both.

14 If a king judges the poor with equity,
his throne will be established forever.

15 The rod and reproof give wisdom,
but a mother is disgraced by a
neglected child.

16 When the wicked are in authority,
transgression increases,
but the righteous will look upon their
downfall.

17 Discipline your children, and they will
give you rest;
they will give delight to your heart.

18 Where there is no prophecy, the people
cast off restraint,
but happy are those who keep the law.

19 By mere words servants are not
disciplined,
for though they understand, they will
not give heed.

20 Do you see someone who is hasty in
speech?
There is more hope for a fool than for
anyone like that.

21 A slave pampered from childhood
will come to a bad end. *a*

22 One given to anger stirs up strife,
and the hothead causes much
transgression.

23 A person's pride will bring humiliation,
but one who is lowly in spirit will
obtain honor.

24 To be a partner of a thief is to hate one's
own life;
one hears the victim's curse, but
discloses nothing. *b*

25 The fear of others *c* lays a snare,
but one who trusts in the LORD is
secure.

26 Many seek the favor of a ruler,

but it is from the LORD that one gets
justice.

27 The unjust are an abomination to the
righteous,
but the upright are an abomination to
the wicked.

Sayings of Agur

30 The words of Agur son of Jakeh. An
oracle.

Thus says the man: I am weary, O God,
I am weary, O God. How can I
prevail? *d*

2 Surely I am too stupid to be human;
I do not have human understanding.

3 I have not learned wisdom,
nor have I knowledge of the holy
ones. *e*

4 Who has ascended to heaven and come
down?
Who has gathered the wind in the
hollow of the hand?
Who has wrapped up the waters in a
garment?
Who has established all the ends of
the earth?
What is the person's name?
And what is the name of the person's
child?
Surely you know!

5 Every word of God proves true;
he is a shield to those who take refuge
in him.

6 Do not add to his words,
or else he will rebuke you, and you will
be found a liar.

7 Two things I ask of you;
do not deny them to me before I die:

8 Remove far from me falsehood and lying;
give me neither poverty nor riches;
feed me with the food that I need,

9 or I shall be full, and deny you,
and say, "Who is the LORD?"

---

a Vg: Meaning of Heb uncertain   *b* Meaning of Heb uncertain   *c* Or *human fear*   *d* Or *I am spent*. Meaning
of Heb uncertain   *e* Or *Holy One*

or I shall be poor, and steal,
   and profane the name of my God.

10 Do not slander a servant to a master,
   or the servant will curse you, and you
      will be held guilty.

11 There are those who curse their fathers
   and do not bless their mothers.
12 There are those who are pure in their
      own eyes
   yet are not cleansed of their filthiness.
13 There are those—how lofty are their
      eyes,
   how high their eyelids lift!—
14 there are those whose teeth are swords,
   whose teeth are knives,
   to devour the poor from off the earth,
   the needy from among mortals.

15 The leech*a* has two daughters;
   "Give, give," they cry.
Three things are never satisfied;
   four never say, "Enough":
16 Sheol, the barren womb,
   the earth ever thirsty for water,
   and the fire that never says,
      "Enough."*a*

17 The eye that mocks a father
   and scorns to obey a mother
will be pecked out by the ravens of the
      valley
   and eaten by the vultures.

18 Three things are too wonderful for me;
   four I do not understand:
19 the way of an eagle in the sky,
   the way of a snake on a rock,
the way of a ship on the high seas,
   and the way of a man with a girl.

20 This is the way of an adulteress:
   she eats, and wipes her mouth,
   and says, "I have done no wrong."

21 Under three things the earth trembles;
   under four it cannot bear up:
22 a slave when he becomes king,
   and a fool when glutted with food;
23 an unloved woman when she gets a
      husband,
   and a maid when she succeeds her
      mistress.

24 Four things on earth are small,
   yet they are exceedingly wise:
25 the ants are a people without strength,
   yet they provide their food in the
      summer;
26 the badgers are a people without power,
   yet they make their homes in the
      rocks;
27 the locusts have no king,
   yet all of them march in rank;
28 the lizard*b* can be grasped in the hand,
   yet it is found in kings' palaces.

29 Three things are stately in their stride;
   four are stately in their gait:
30 the lion, which is mightiest among wild
      animals
   and does not turn back before any;
31 the strutting rooster,*c* the he-goat,
   and a king striding before*d* his people.

32 If you have been foolish, exalting
      yourself,
   or if you have been devising evil,
   put your hand on your mouth.
33 For as pressing milk produces curds,
   and pressing the nose produces blood,
   so pressing anger produces strife.

The Teaching of King Lemuel's Mother

31 The words of King Lemuel. An oracle
   that his mother taught him:

2 No, my son! No, son of my womb!
   No, son of my vows!
3 Do not give your strength to women,
   your ways to those who destroy kings.

a Meaning of Heb uncertain   *b* Or *spider*   *c* Gk Syr Tg Compare Vg: Meaning of Heb uncertain

4   It is not for kings, O Lemuel,
        it is not for kings to drink wine,
        or for rulers to desire*a* strong drink;
5   or else they will drink and forget what
            has been decreed,
        and will pervert the rights of all the
            afflicted.
6   Give strong drink to one who is
            perishing,
        and wine to those in bitter distress;
7   let them drink and forget their poverty,
        and remember their misery no more.
8   Speak out for those who cannot speak,
        for the rights of all the destitute.*b*
9   Speak out, judge righteously,
        defend the rights of the poor and
            needy.

Ode to a Capable Wife

10 A capable wife who can find?
        She is far more precious than jewels.
11 The heart of her husband trusts in her,
        and he will have no lack of gain.
12 She does him good, and not harm,
        all the days of her life.
13 She seeks wool and flax,
        and works with willing hands.
14 She is like the ships of the merchant,
        she brings her food from far away.
15 She rises while it is still night
        and provides food for her household
        and tasks for her servant-girls.
16 She considers a field and buys it;
        with the fruit of her hands she plants
            a vineyard.
17 She girds herself with strength,
        and makes her arms strong.
18 She perceives that her merchandise is
            profitable.

Her lamp does not go out at night.
19 She puts her hands to the distaff,
        and her hands hold the spindle.
20 She opens her hand to the poor,
        and reaches out her hands to the
            needy.
21 She is not afraid for her household when
            it snows,
        for all her household are clothed in
            crimson.
22 She makes herself coverings;
        her clothing is fine linen and purple.
23 Her husband is known in the city gates,
        taking his seat among the elders of
            the land.
24 She makes linen garments and sells
            them;
        she supplies the merchant with sashes.
25 Strength and dignity are her clothing,
        and she laughs at the time to come.
26 She opens her mouth with wisdom,
        and the teaching of kindness is on her
            tongue.
27 She looks well to the ways of her
            household,
        and does not eat the bread of idleness.
28 Her children rise up and call her happy;
        her husband too, and he praises her:
29 "Many women have done excellently,
        but you surpass them all."
30 Charm is deceitful, and beauty is vain,
        but a woman who fears the LORD is to
            be praised.
31 Give her a share in the fruit of her
            hands,
        and let her works praise her in the city
            gates.

---

a Cn: Heb *where*   *b* Heb *all children of passing away*

ECCLESIASTES

Reflections of a Royal Philosopher

1 The words of the Teacher,[a] the son of David, king in Jerusalem.

2 Vanity of vanities, says the Teacher,[a]
vanity of vanities! All is vanity.

3 What do people gain from all the toil
at which they toil under the sun?

4 A generation goes, and a generation comes,
but the earth remains forever.

5 The sun rises and the sun goes down,
and hurries to the place where it rises.

6 The wind blows to the south,
and goes around to the north;
round and round goes the wind,
and on its circuits the wind returns.

7 All streams run to the sea,
but the sea is not full;
to the place where the streams flow,
there they continue to flow.

8 All things[b] are wearisome;
more than one can express;
the eye is not satisfied with seeing,
or the ear filled with hearing.

9 What has been is what will be,
and what has been done is what will be done;
there is nothing new under the sun.

10 Is there a thing of which it is said,
"See, this is new"?
It has already been,
in the ages before us.

11 The people of long ago are not remembered,
nor will there be any remembrance
of people yet to come
by those who come after them.

The Futility of Seeking Wisdom

12 I, the Teacher,[a] when king over Israel in Jerusalem, 13applied my mind to seek and to search out by wisdom all that is done under heaven; it is an unhappy business that God has given to human beings to be busy with. 14I saw all the deeds that are done under the sun; and see, all is vanity and a chasing after wind.[c]

15 What is crooked cannot be made straight,
and what is lacking cannot be counted.

16 I said to myself, "I have acquired great wisdom, surpassing all who were over Jerusalem before me; and my mind has had great experience of wisdom and knowledge." 17And I applied my mind to know wisdom and to know madness and folly. I perceived that this also is but a chasing after wind.[c]

18 For in much wisdom is much vexation,
and those who increase knowledge
increase sorrow.

The Futility of Self-Indulgence

2 I said to myself, "Come now, I will make a test of pleasure; enjoy yourself." But again, this also was vanity. 2I said of laughter, "It is mad," and of pleasure, "What use is it?" 3I searched with my mind how to cheer my body with wine—my mind still guiding me with wisdom—and how to lay hold on folly, until I might see what was good for mortals to do under heaven during the few days of their life. 4I made great works; I built houses and planted vineyards for myself; 5I made myself gardens and parks, and planted in them all kinds of fruit trees. 6I made myself pools from which to water the forest of growing trees. 7I bought male and female slaves, and had slaves who were born in my house; I also had great possessions of herds and flocks, more than any who had been before me in Jerusalem. 8I also gathered for myself silver and gold and the treasure of kings and of the provinces; I got singers, both men and women, and delights of the flesh, and many concubines.[d]

9 So I became great and surpassed all who were before me in Jerusalem; also my wisdom remained with me. 10Whatever my eyes desired I did not keep from them; I kept my

---

a Heb *Qoheleth*, traditionally rendered *Preacher*   b Or *words*   c Or *a feeding on wind*. See Hos 12.1   d Meaning
of Heb uncertain

heart from no pleasure, for my heart found pleasure in all my toil, and this was my reward for all my toil. [11]Then I considered all that my hands had done and the toil I had spent in doing it, and again, all was vanity and a chasing after wind,[a] and there was nothing to be gained under the sun.

Wisdom and Joy Given to One Who Pleases God

12 So I turned to consider wisdom and madness and folly; for what can the one do who comes after the king? Only what has already been done. [13]Then I saw that wisdom excels folly as light excels darkness.

[14] The wise have eyes in their head,
        but fools walk in darkness.

Yet I perceived that the same fate befalls all of them. [15]Then I said to myself, "What happens to the fool will happen to me also; why then have I been so very wise?" And I said to myself that this also is vanity. [16]For there is no enduring remembrance of the wise or of fools, seeing that in the days to come all will have been long forgotten. How can the wise die just like fools? [17]So I hated life, because what is done under the sun was grievous to me; for all is vanity and a chasing after wind.[a]

18 I hated all my toil in which I had toiled under the sun, seeing that I must leave it to those who come after me [19]—and who knows whether they will be wise or foolish? Yet they will be master of all for which I toiled and used my wisdom under the sun. This also is vanity. [20]So I turned and gave my heart up to despair concerning all the toil of my labors under the sun, [21]because sometimes one who has toiled with wisdom and knowledge and skill must leave all to be enjoyed by another who did not toil for it. This also is vanity and a great evil. [22]What do mortals get from all the toil and strain with which they toil under the sun? [23]For all their days are full of pain, and their work is a vexation; even at night their minds do not rest. This also is vanity.

24 There is nothing better for mortals than to eat and drink, and find enjoyment in their toil. This also, I saw, is from the hand of God; [25]for apart from him[b] who can eat or who can have enjoyment? [26]For to the one who pleases him God gives wisdom and knowledge and joy; but to the sinner he gives the work of gathering and heaping, only to give to one who pleases God. This also is vanity and a chasing after wind.[a]

Everything Has Its Time

3 For everything there is a season, and a time for every matter under heaven:
[2] a time to be born, and a time to die;
      a time to plant, and a time to pluck up
            what is planted;
[3] a time to kill, and a time to heal;
      a time to break down, and a time to
            build up;
[4] a time to weep, and a time to laugh;
      a time to mourn, and a time to dance;
[5] a time to throw away stones, and a time
            to gather stones together;
      a time to embrace, and a time to refrain
            from embracing;
[6] a time to seek, and a time to lose;
      a time to keep, and a time to throw away;
[7] a time to tear, and a time to sew;
      a time to keep silence, and a time to
            speak;
[8] a time to love, and a time to hate;
      a time for war, and a time for peace.

The God-Given Task

9 What gain have the workers from their toil? [10]I have seen the business that God has given to everyone to be busy with. [11]He has made everything suitable for its time; moreover he has put a sense of past and future into their minds, yet they cannot find out what God has done from the beginning to the end. [12]I know that there is nothing better for them than to be happy and enjoy themselves as long as they live; [13]moreover, it is God's gift that all should eat and drink and take pleasure in all their toil. [14]I know that whatever God does endures forever; nothing can be added to it, nor anything tak-

a Or *a feeding on wind.* See Hos 12.1   b Gk Syr: Heb *apart from me* en from it; God has done this, so that all should stand in awe before him. ¹⁵That which is, already has been; that which is to be, already is; and God seeks out what has gone by.*a*

Judgment and the Future Belong to God

16 Moreover I saw under the sun that in the place of justice, wickedness was there, and in the place of righteousness, wickedness was there as well. ¹⁷I said in my heart, God will judge the righteous and the wicked, for he has appointed a time for every matter, and for every work. ¹⁸I said in my heart with regard to human beings that God is testing them to show that they are but animals. ¹⁹For the fate of humans and the fate of animals is the same; as one dies, so dies the other. They all have the same breath, and humans have no advantage over the animals; for all is vanity. ²⁰All go to one place; all are from the dust, and all turn to dust again. ²¹Who knows whether the human spirit goes upward and the spirit of animals goes downward to the earth? ²²So I saw that there is nothing better than that all should enjoy their work, for that is their lot; who can bring them to see what will be after them?

4 Again I saw all the oppressions that are practiced under the sun. Look, the tears of the oppressed—with no one to comfort them! On the side of their oppressors there was power—with no one to comfort them. ²And I thought the dead, who have already died, more fortunate than the living, who are still alive; ³but better than both is the one who has not yet been, and has not seen the evil deeds that are done under the sun.

4 Then I saw that all toil and all skill in work come from one person's envy of another. This also is vanity and a chasing after wind.*b*

5   Fools fold their hands
     and consume their own flesh.
6   Better is a handful with quiet
     than two handfuls with toil,
     and a chasing after wind.*b*

7 Again, I saw vanity under the sun: ⁸the case of solitary individuals, without sons or

brothers; yet there is no end to all their toil, and their eyes are never satisfied with riches. "For whom am I toiling," they ask, "and depriving myself of pleasure?" This also is vanity and an unhappy business.

The Value of a Friend

9 Two are better than one, because they have a good reward for their toil. ¹⁰For if they fall, one will lift up the other; but woe to one who is alone and falls and does not have another to help. ¹¹Again, if two lie together, they keep warm; but how can one keep warm alone? ¹²And though one might prevail against another, two will withstand one. A threefold cord is not quickly broken.

13 Better is a poor but wise youth than an old but foolish king, who will no longer take advice. ¹⁴One can indeed come out of prison to reign, even though born poor in the kingdom. ¹⁵I saw all the living who, moving about under the sun, follow that*c* youth who replaced the king;*d* ¹⁶there was no end to all those people whom he led. Yet those who come later will not rejoice in him. Surely this also is vanity and a chasing after wind.*b*

Reverence, Humility, and Contentment

5 *e*Guard your steps when you go to the house of God; to draw near to listen is better than the sacrifice offered by fools; for they do not know how to keep from doing evil.*f* ²*g*Never be rash with your mouth, nor let your heart be quick to utter a word before God, for God is in heaven, and you upon earth; therefore let your words be few.

3 For dreams come with many cares, and a fool's voice with many words.

4 When you make a vow to God, do not delay fulfilling it; for he has no pleasure in fools. Fulfill what you vow. ⁵It is better that you should not vow than that you should vow and not fulfill it. ⁶Do not let your mouth lead you into sin, and do not say before the messenger that it was a mistake; why should God be an-

---

a Heb *what is pursued*   *b* Or *a feeding on wind.* See Hos 12.1   *c* Heb *the second*   *d* Heb *him*   *e* Ch 4.17 in Heb
f Cn: Heb *they do not know how to do evil*   *g* Ch 5.1 in Heb

gry at your words, and destroy the work of your hands?

7 With many dreams come vanities and a multitude of words;*a* but fear God.

8 If you see in a province the oppression of the poor and the violation of justice and right, do not be amazed at the matter; for the high official is watched by a higher, and there are yet higher ones over them. ⁹But all things considered, this is an advantage for a land: a king for a plowed field.*a*

10 The lover of money will not be satisfied with money; nor the lover of wealth, with gain. This also is vanity.

11 When goods increase, those who eat them increase; and what gain has their owner but to see them with his eyes?

12 Sweet is the sleep of laborers, whether they eat little or much; but the surfeit of the rich will not let them sleep.

13 There is a grievous ill that I have seen under the sun: riches were kept by their owners to their hurt, ¹⁴and those riches were lost in a bad venture; though they are parents of children, they have nothing in their hands. ¹⁵As they came from their mother's womb, so they shall go again, naked as they came; they shall take nothing for their toil, which they may carry away with their hands. ¹⁶This also is a grievous ill: just as they came, so shall they go; and what gain do they have from toiling for the wind? ¹⁷Besides, all their days they eat in darkness, in much vexation and sickness and resentment.

18 This is what I have seen to be good: it is fitting to eat and drink and find enjoyment in all the toil with which one toils under the sun the few days of the life God gives us; for this is our lot. ¹⁹Likewise all to whom God gives wealth and possessions and whom he enables to enjoy them, and to accept their lot and find enjoyment in their toil—this is the gift of God. ²⁰For they will scarcely brood over the days of their lives, because God keeps them occupied with the joy of their hearts.

The Frustration of Desires

6 There is an evil that I have seen under the sun, and it lies heavy upon humankind: ²those to whom God gives wealth, possessions, and honor, so that they lack nothing of all that they desire, yet God does not enable them to enjoy these things, but a stranger enjoys them. This is vanity; it is a grievous ill. ³A man may beget a hundred children, and live many years; but however many are the days of his years, if he does not enjoy life's good things, or has no burial, I say that a stillborn child is better off than he. ⁴For it comes into vanity and goes into darkness, and in darkness its name is covered; ⁵moreover it has not seen the sun or known anything; yet it finds rest rather than he. ⁶Even though he should live a thousand years twice over, yet enjoy no good—do not all go to one place?

7 All human toil is for the mouth, yet the appetite is not satisfied. ⁸For what advantage have the wise over fools? And what do the poor have who know how to conduct themselves before the living? ⁹Better is the sight of the eyes than the wandering of desire; this also is vanity and a chasing after wind.*b*

10 Whatever has come to be has already been named, and it is known what human beings are, and that they are not able to dispute with those who are stronger. ¹¹The more words, the more vanity, so how is one the better? ¹²For who knows what is good for mortals while they live the few days of their vain life, which they pass like a shadow? For who can tell them what will be after them under the sun?

A Disillusioned View of Life

7 A good name is better than precious
       ointment,
     and the day of death, than the day of
       birth.
2   It is better to go to the house of
       mourning
     than to go to the house of feasting;
     for this is the end of everyone,
       and the living will lay it to heart.

---

a Meaning of Heb uncertain   *b* Or *a feeding on wind.* See Hos 12.1

3 Sorrow is better than laughter,
　　for by sadness of countenance the
　　　heart is made glad.
4 The heart of the wise is in the house of
　　mourning;
　　but the heart of fools is in the house
　　　of mirth.
5 It is better to hear the rebuke of the wise
　　than to hear the song of fools.
6 For like the crackling of thorns under a
　　pot,
　　so is the laughter of fools;
　　this also is vanity.
7 Surely oppression makes the wise
　　foolish,
　　and a bribe corrupts the heart.
8 Better is the end of a thing than its
　　beginning;
　　the patient in spirit are better than the
　　　proud in spirit.
9 Do not be quick to anger,
　　for anger lodges in the bosom of
　　　fools.
10 Do not say, "Why were the former days
　　better than these?"
　　For it is not from wisdom that you ask
　　　this.
11 Wisdom is as good as an inheritance,
　　an advantage to those who see the
　　　sun.
12 For the protection of wisdom is like the
　　protection of money,
　　and the advantage of knowledge is
　　　that wisdom gives life to the one
　　　who possesses it.
13 Consider the work of God;
　　who can make straight what he has
　　　made crooked?

14 In the day of prosperity be joyful, and in
the day of adversity consider; God has made
the one as well as the other, so that mortals may
not find out anything that will come after them.

The Riddles of Life

15 In my vain life I have seen everything;
there are righteous people who perish in their
righteousness, and there are wicked people
who prolong their life in their evildoing. 16Do
not be too righteous, and do not act too wise;
why should you destroy yourself? 17Do not be
too wicked, and do not be a fool; why should
you die before your time? 18It is good that you
should take hold of the one, without letting go
of the other; for the one who fears God shall
succeed with both.

19 Wisdom gives strength to the wise more
than ten rulers that are in a city.

20 Surely there is no one on earth so righteous as to do good without ever sinning.

21 Do not give heed to everything that people say, or you may hear your servant cursing
you; 22your heart knows that many times you
have yourself cursed others.

23 All this I have tested by wisdom; I said,
"I will be wise," but it was far from me. 24That
which is, is far off, and deep, very deep; who
can find it out? 25I turned my mind to know
and to search out and to seek wisdom and the
sum of things, and to know that wickedness is
folly and that foolishness is madness. 26I found
more bitter than death the woman who is a
trap, whose heart is snares and nets, whose
hands are fetters; one who pleases God escapes her, but the sinner is taken by her. 27See,
this is what I found, says the Teacher,a adding
one thing to another to find the sum, 28which
my mind has sought repeatedly, but I have not
found. One man among a thousand I found,
but a woman among all these I have not found.
29See, this alone I found, that God made human beings straightforward, but they have devised many schemes.

Obey the King and Enjoy Yourself

8 Who is like the wise man?
　　And who knows the interpretation of
　　　a thing?
　　Wisdom makes one's face shine,
　　and the hardness of one's
　　　countenance is changed.

2 Keepb the king's command because of
your sacred oath. 3Do not be terrified; go from

a Qoheleth, traditionally rendered Preacher　　b Heb I keep

his presence, do not delay when the matter is unpleasant, for he does whatever he pleases. 4For the word of the king is powerful, and who can say to him, "What are you doing?" 5Whoever obeys a command will meet no harm, and the wise mind will know the time and way. 6For every matter has its time and way, although the troubles of mortals lie heavy upon them. 7Indeed, they do not know what is to be, for who can tell them how it will be? 8No one has power over the wind*a* to restrain the wind,*a* or power over the day of death; there is no discharge from the battle, nor does wickedness deliver those who practice it. 9All this I observed, applying my mind to all that is done under the sun, while one person exercises authority over another to the other's hurt.

God's Ways Are Inscrutable

10 Then I saw the wicked buried; they used to go in and out of the holy place, and were praised in the city where they had done such things.*b* This also is vanity. 11Because sentence against an evil deed is not executed speedily, the human heart is fully set to do evil. 12Though sinners do evil a hundred times and prolong their lives, yet I know that it will be well with those who fear God, because they stand in fear before him, 13but it will not be well with the wicked, neither will they prolong their days like a shadow, because they do not stand in fear before God.

14 There is a vanity that takes place on earth, that there are righteous people who are treated according to the conduct of the wicked, and there are wicked people who are treated according to the conduct of the righteous. I said that this also is vanity. 15So I commend enjoyment, for there is nothing better for people under the sun than to eat, and drink, and enjoy themselves, for this will go with them in their toil through the days of life that God gives them under the sun.

16 When I applied my mind to know wisdom, and to see the business that is done on earth, how one's eyes see sleep neither day nor night, 17then I saw all the work of God, that no one can find out what is happening under the sun. However much they may toil in seeking, they will not find it out; even though those who are wise claim to know, they cannot find it out.

Take Life as It Comes

9 All this I laid to heart, examining it all, how the righteous and the wise and their deeds are in the hand of God; whether it is love or hate one does not know. Everything that confronts them 2is vanity,*c* since the same fate comes to all, to the righteous and the wicked, to the good and the evil,*d* to the clean and the unclean, to those who sacrifice and those who do not sacrifice. As are the good, so are the sinners; those who swear are like those who shun an oath. 3This is an evil in all that happens under the sun, that the same fate comes to everyone. Moreover, the hearts of all are full of evil; madness is in their hearts while they live, and after that they go to the dead. 4But whoever is joined with all the living has hope, for a living dog is better than a dead lion. 5The living know that they will die, but the dead know nothing; they have no more reward, and even the memory of them is lost. 6Their love and their hate and their envy have already perished; never again will they have any share in all that happens under the sun.

7 Go, eat your bread with enjoyment, and drink your wine with a merry heart; for God has long ago approved what you do. 8Let your garments always be white; do not let oil be lacking on your head. 9Enjoy life with the wife whom you love, all the days of your vain life that are given you under the sun, because that is your portion in life and in your toil at which you toil under the sun. 10Whatever your hand finds to do, do with your might; for there is no work or thought or knowledge or wisdom in Sheol, to which you are going.

11 Again I saw that under the sun the race is not to the swift, nor the battle to the strong, nor bread to the wise, nor riches to the intelli-

a Or *breath*   *b* Meaning of Heb uncertain   *c* Syr Compare Gk: Heb *Everything that confronts them* 2*is everything*
d Gk Syr Vg: Heb lacks *and the evil*

gent, nor favor to the skillful; but time and chance happen to them all. ¹²For no one can anticipate the time of disaster. Like fish taken in a cruel net, and like birds caught in a snare, so mortals are snared at a time of calamity, when it suddenly falls upon them.

Wisdom Superior to Folly

13 I have also seen this example of wisdom under the sun, and it seemed great to me. ¹⁴There was a little city with few people in it. A great king came against it and besieged it, building great siegeworks against it. ¹⁵Now there was found in it a poor wise man, and he by his wisdom delivered the city. Yet no one remembered that poor man. ¹⁶So I said, "Wisdom is better than might; yet the poor man's wisdom is despised, and his words are not heeded."

¹⁷ The quiet words of the wise are more to be heeded
    than the shouting of a ruler among fools.
¹⁸ Wisdom is better than weapons of war,
    but one bungler destroys much good.

Miscellaneous Observations

10 Dead flies make the perfumer's ointment give off a foul odor;
    so a little folly outweighs wisdom and honor.
² The heart of the wise inclines to the right,
    but the heart of a fool to the left.
³ Even when fools walk on the road, they lack sense,
    and show to everyone that they are fools.
⁴ If the anger of the ruler rises against you, do not leave your post,
    for calmness will undo great offenses.

5 There is an evil that I have seen under the sun, as great an error as if it proceeded from the ruler: ⁶folly is set in many high places, and the rich sit in a low place. ⁷I have seen slaves on horseback, and princes walking on foot like slaves.

8 Whoever digs a pit will fall into it;
    and whoever breaks through a wall will be bitten by a snake.
9 Whoever quarries stones will be hurt by them;
    and whoever splits logs will be endangered by them.
10 If the iron is blunt, and one does not whet the edge,
    then more strength must be exerted;
    but wisdom helps one to succeed.
11 If the snake bites before it is charmed,
    there is no advantage in a charmer.

12 Words spoken by the wise bring them favor,
    but the lips of fools consume them.
13 The words of their mouths begin in foolishness,
    and their talk ends in wicked madness;
14 yet fools talk on and on.
    No one knows what is to happen,
    and who can tell anyone what the future holds?
15 The toil of fools wears them out,
    for they do not even know the way to town.

16 Alas for you, O land, when your king is a servant,[a]
    and your princes feast in the morning!
17 Happy are you, O land, when your king is a nobleman,
    and your princes feast at the proper time—
    for strength, and not for drunkenness!
18 Through sloth the roof sinks in,
    and through indolence the house leaks.
19 Feasts are made for laughter;
    wine gladdens life,
    and money meets every need.
20 Do not curse the king, even in your thoughts,
    or curse the rich, even in your bedroom;

a Or a child

for a bird of the air may carry your voice,
or some winged creature tell the
matter.

The Value of Diligence

11 Send out your bread upon the waters,
for after many days you will get it back.

2 Divide your means seven ways, or even
eight,
for you do not know what disaster
may happen on earth.

3 When clouds are full,
they empty rain on the earth;
whether a tree falls to the south or to the
north,
in the place where the tree falls, there
it will lie.

4 Whoever observes the wind will not sow;
and whoever regards the clouds will
not reap.

5 Just as you do not know how the breath
comes to the bones in the mother's womb, so
you do not know the work of God, who makes
everything.

6 In the morning sow your seed, and at
evening do not let your hands be idle; for you
do not know which will prosper, this or that, or
whether both alike will be good.

Youth and Old Age

7 Light is sweet, and it is pleasant for the
eyes to see the sun.

8 Even those who live many years should
rejoice in them all; yet let them remember that
the days of darkness will be many. All that
comes is vanity.

9 Rejoice, young man, while you are young,
and let your heart cheer you in the days of
your youth. Follow the inclination of your
heart and the desire of your eyes, but know that
for all these things God will bring you into
judgment.

10 Banish anxiety from your mind, and put
away pain from your body; for youth and the
dawn of life are vanity.

12 Remember your creator in the days of
your youth, before the days of trouble
come, and the years draw near when you will
say, "I have no pleasure in them"; 2before the
sun and the light and the moon and the stars
are darkened and the clouds return with[a] the
rain; 3in the day when the guards of the house
tremble, and the strong men are bent, and the
women who grind cease working because they
are few, and those who look through the windows see dimly; 4when the doors on the street
are shut, and the sound of the grinding is low,
and one rises up at the sound of a bird, and all
the daughters of song are brought low; 5when
one is afraid of heights, and terrors are in the
road; the almond tree blossoms, the grasshopper drags itself along[b] and desire fails; because
all must go to their eternal home, and the
mourners will go about the streets; 6before the
silver cord is snapped,[c] and the golden bowl is
broken, and the pitcher is broken at the fountain, and the wheel broken at the cistern, 7and
the dust returns to the earth as it was, and the
breath[d] returns to God who gave it. 8Vanity of
vanities, says the Teacher;[e] all is vanity.

Epilogue

9 Besides being wise, the Teacher[e] also
taught the people knowledge, weighing and
studying and arranging many proverbs. 10The
Teacher[e] sought to find pleasing words, and he
wrote words of truth plainly.

11 The sayings of the wise are like goads,
and like nails firmly fixed are the collected sayings that are given by one shepherd.[f] 12Of anything beyond these, my child, beware. Of making many books there is no end, and much
study is a weariness of the flesh.

13 The end of the matter; all has been
heard. Fear God, and keep his commandments;
for that is the whole duty of everyone. 14For
God will bring every deed into judgment, including[g] every secret thing, whether good or
evil.

---

a Or after; Heb 'ahar   b Or is a burden   c Syr Vg Compare Gk: Heb is removed   d Or the spirit   e Qoheleth,
traditionally rendered Preacher   f Meaning of Heb uncertain   g Or into the judgment on

THE
SONG OF SOLOMON

1

The Song of Songs, which is Solomon's.

Colloquy of Bride and Friends

2 Let him kiss me with the kisses of his
      mouth!
    For your love is better than wine,
3   your anointing oils are fragrant,
    your name is perfume poured out;
      therefore the maidens love you.
4 Draw me after you, let us make haste.
    The king has brought me into his
      chambers.
    We will exult and rejoice in you;
      we will extol your love more than wine;
    rightly do they love you.

5 I am black and beautiful,
      O daughters of Jerusalem,
    like the tents of Kedar,
      like the curtains of Solomon.
6 Do not gaze at me because I am dark,
      because the sun has gazed on me.
    My mother's sons were angry with me;
      they made me keeper of the
        vineyards,
      but my own vineyard I have not kept!
7 Tell me, you whom my soul loves,
      where you pasture your flock,
      where you make it lie down at noon;
    for why should I be like one who is
        veiled
      beside the flocks of your
        companions?

8 If you do not know,
      O fairest among women,
    follow the tracks of the flock,
      and pasture your kids
      beside the shepherds' tents.

Colloquy of Bridegroom, Friends, and Bride

9 I compare you, my love,
      to a mare among Pharaoh's chariots.
10 Your cheeks are comely with ornaments,

    your neck with strings of jewels.
11 We will make you ornaments of gold,
      studded with silver.

12 While the king was on his couch,
      my nard gave forth its fragrance.
13 My beloved is to me a bag of myrrh
      that lies between my breasts.
14 My beloved is to me a cluster of henna
        blossoms
      in the vineyards of En-gedi.

15 Ah, you are beautiful, my love;
      ah, you are beautiful;
      your eyes are doves.
16 Ah, you are beautiful, my beloved,
      truly lovely.
    Our couch is green;
17   the beams of our house are cedar,
      our rafters*a* are pine.

2

I am a rose*b* of Sharon,
  a lily of the valleys.

2 As a lily among brambles,
      so is my love among maidens.

3 As an apple tree among the trees of the
        wood,
      so is my beloved among young men.
    With great delight I sat in his shadow,
      and his fruit was sweet to my taste.
4 He brought me to the banqueting house,
      and his intention toward me was love.
5 Sustain me with raisins,
      refresh me with apples;
    for I am faint with love.
6 O that his left hand were under my head,
      and that his right hand embraced me!
7 I adjure you, O daughters of Jerusalem,
      by the gazelles or the wild does:
    do not stir up or awaken love
      until it is ready!

---

a Meaning of Heb uncertain   *b* Heb *crocus*

Springtime Rhapsody

8   The voice of my beloved!
      Look, he comes,
    leaping upon the mountains,
      bounding over the hills.
9   My beloved is like a gazelle
      or a young stag.
    Look, there he stands
      behind our wall,
    gazing in at the windows,
      looking through the lattice.
10 My beloved speaks and says to me:
    "Arise, my love, my fair one,
      and come away;
11 for now the winter is past,
      the rain is over and gone.
12 The flowers appear on the earth;
      the time of singing has come,
    and the voice of the turtledove
      is heard in our land.
13 The fig tree puts forth its figs,
      and the vines are in blossom;
      they give forth fragrance.
    Arise, my love, my fair one,
      and come away.
14 O my dove, in the clefts of the rock,
      in the covert of the cliff,
    let me see your face,
      let me hear your voice;
    for your voice is sweet,
      and your face is lovely.
15 Catch us the foxes,
      the little foxes,
    that ruin the vineyards—
      for our vineyards are in blossom."

16 My beloved is mine and I am his;
      he pastures his flock among the lilies.
17 Until the day breathes
      and the shadows flee,
    turn, my beloved, be like a gazelle
      or a young stag on the cleft
        mountains.*a*

Love's Dream

3   Upon my bed at night
      I sought him whom my soul loves;
    I sought him, but found him not;
      I called him, but he gave no answer.*b*
2   "I will rise now and go about the city,
      in the streets and in the squares;
    I will seek him whom my soul loves."
      I sought him, but found him not.
3   The sentinels found me,
      as they went about in the city.
    "Have you seen him whom my soul
        loves?"
4   Scarcely had I passed them,
      when I found him whom my soul
        loves.
    I held him, and would not let him go
      until I brought him into my mother's
        house,
      and into the chamber of her that
        conceived me.
5   I adjure you, O daughters of Jerusalem,
      by the gazelles or the wild does:
    do not stir up or awaken love
      until it is ready!

The Groom and His Party Approach

6   What is that coming up from the
        wilderness,
      like a column of smoke,
    perfumed with myrrh and frankincense,
      with all the fragrant powders of the
        merchant?
7   Look, it is the litter of Solomon!
    Around it are sixty mighty men
      of the mighty men of Israel,
8   all equipped with swords
      and expert in war,
    each with his sword at his thigh
      because of alarms by night.
9   King Solomon made himself a palanquin
      from the wood of Lebanon.
10 He made its posts of silver,
      its back of gold, its seat of purple;
    its interior was inlaid with love.*c*
      Daughters of Jerusalem,

---

a Or *on the mountains of Bether*; meaning of Heb uncertain   *b* Gk: Heb lacks this line   *c* Meaning of Heb
uncertain

11   come out.
Look, O daughters of Zion,
    at King Solomon,
    at the crown with which his mother
        crowned him
    on the day of his wedding,
    on the day of the gladness of his
        heart.

The Bride's Beauty Extolled

4   How beautiful you are, my love,
        how very beautiful!
    Your eyes are doves
        behind your veil.
    Your hair is like a flock of goats,
        moving down the slopes of Gilead.
2   Your teeth are like a flock of shorn ewes
        that have come up from the washing,
    all of which bear twins,
        and not one among them is bereaved.
3   Your lips are like a crimson thread,
        and your mouth is lovely.
    Your cheeks are like halves of a
        pomegranate
        behind your veil.
4   Your neck is like the tower of David,
        built in courses;
    on it hang a thousand bucklers,
        all of them shields of warriors.
5   Your two breasts are like two fawns,
        twins of a gazelle,
        that feed among the lilies.
6   Until the day breathes
        and the shadows flee,
    I will hasten to the mountain of myrrh
        and the hill of frankincense.
7   You are altogether beautiful, my love;
        there is no flaw in you.
8   Come with me from Lebanon, my bride;
        come with me from Lebanon.
    Depart*a* from the peak of Amana,
        from the peak of Senir and Hermon,
    from the dens of lions,
        from the mountains of leopards.

9   You have ravished my heart, my sister,
        my bride,
    you have ravished my heart with a
        glance of your eyes,
    with one jewel of your necklace.
10 How sweet is your love, my sister, my
        bride!
    how much better is your love than
        wine,
    and the fragrance of your oils than
        any spice!
11 Your lips distill nectar, my bride;
    honey and milk are under your
        tongue;
    the scent of your garments is like the
        scent of Lebanon.
12 A garden locked is my sister, my bride,
        a garden locked, a fountain sealed.
13 Your channel*b* is an orchard of
        pomegranates
    with all choicest fruits,
        henna with nard,
14 nard and saffron, calamus and
        cinnamon,
    with all trees of frankincense,
    myrrh and aloes,
        with all chief spices—
15 a garden fountain, a well of living water,
        and flowing streams from Lebanon.

16 Awake, O north wind,
        and come, O south wind!
    Blow upon my garden
        that its fragrance may be wafted
            abroad.
    Let my beloved come to his garden,
        and eat its choicest fruits.

5   I come to my garden, my sister, my
        bride;
    I gather my myrrh with my spice,
    I eat my honeycomb with my honey,
    I drink my wine with my milk.

    Eat, friends, drink,
        and be drunk with love.

a Or *Look*   *b* Meaning of Heb uncertain

Another Dream

2 I slept, but my heart was awake.
   Listen! my beloved is knocking.
   "Open to me, my sister, my love,
      my dove, my perfect one;
   for my head is wet with dew,
      my locks with the drops of the night."
3 I had put off my garment;
      how could I put it on again?
   I had bathed my feet;
      how could I soil them?
4 My beloved thrust his hand into the
         opening,
      and my inmost being yearned for him.
5 I arose to open to my beloved,
      and my hands dripped with myrrh,
   my fingers with liquid myrrh,
      upon the handles of the bolt.
6 I opened to my beloved,
      but my beloved had turned and was
         gone.
   My soul failed me when he spoke.
   I sought him, but did not find him;
      I called him, but he gave no answer.
7 Making their rounds in the city
      the sentinels found me;
   they beat me, they wounded me,
      they took away my mantle,
      those sentinels of the walls.
8 I adjure you, O daughters of Jerusalem,
      if you find my beloved,
   tell him this:
      I am faint with love.

Colloquy of Friends and Bride

9 What is your beloved more than another
         beloved,
      O fairest among women?
   What is your beloved more than another
         beloved,
      that you thus adjure us?

10 My beloved is all radiant and ruddy,
      distinguished among ten thousand.
11 His head is the finest gold;
      his locks are wavy,

black as a raven.
12 His eyes are like doves
      beside springs of water,
   bathed in milk,
      fitly set.*a*
13 His cheeks are like beds of spices,
      yielding fragrance.
   His lips are lilies,
      distilling liquid myrrh.
14 His arms are rounded gold,
      set with jewels.
   His body is ivory work,*a*
      encrusted with sapphires.*b*
15 His legs are alabaster columns,
      set upon bases of gold.
   His appearance is like Lebanon,
      choice as the cedars.
16 His speech is most sweet,
      and he is altogether desirable.
   This is my beloved and this is my friend,
      O daughters of Jerusalem.

6 Where has your beloved gone,
   O fairest among women?
   Which way has your beloved turned,
      that we may seek him with you?

2 My beloved has gone down to his
         garden,
      to the beds of spices,
   to pasture his flock in the gardens,
      and to gather lilies.
3 I am my beloved's and my beloved is
         mine;
      he pastures his flock among the lilies.

The Bride's Matchless Beauty

4 You are beautiful as Tirzah, my love,
      comely as Jerusalem,
      terrible as an army with banners.
5 Turn away your eyes from me,
      for they overwhelm me!
   Your hair is like a flock of goats,
      moving down the slopes of Gilead.
6 Your teeth are like a flock of ewes,
      that have come up from the washing;

a Meaning of Heb uncertain   *b* Heb *lapis lazuli*

all of them bear twins,
    and not one among them is bereaved.

7 Your cheeks are like halves of a
      pomegranate
    behind your veil.

8 There are sixty queens and eighty
      concubines,
    and maidens without number.

9 My dove, my perfect one, is the only
      one,
    the darling of her mother,
    flawless to her that bore her.
The maidens saw her and called her
    happy;
    the queens and concubines also, and
      they praised her.

10 "Who is this that looks forth like the
      dawn,
    fair as the moon, bright as the sun,
    terrible as an army with banners?"

11 I went down to the nut orchard,
    to look at the blossoms of the valley,
to see whether the vines had budded,
    whether the pomegranates were in
      bloom.

12 Before I was aware, my fancy set me
    in a chariot beside my prince.ᵃ

13 ᵇ Return, return, O Shulammite!
    Return, return, that we may look upon
      you.

Why should you look upon the
      Shulammite,
    as upon a dance before two armies?ᶜ

Expressions of Praise

7 How graceful are your feet in sandals,
    O queenly maiden!
Your rounded thighs are like jewels,
    the work of a master hand.

2 Your navel is a rounded bowl
    that never lacks mixed wine.
Your belly is a heap of wheat,
    encircled with lilies.

3 Your two breasts are like two fawns,
    twins of a gazelle.

4 Your neck is like an ivory tower.
Your eyes are pools in Heshbon,
    by the gate of Bath-rabbim.
Your nose is like a tower of Lebanon,
    overlooking Damascus.

5 Your head crowns you like Carmel,
    and your flowing locks are like purple;
    a king is held captive in the tresses.ᵃ

6 How fair and pleasant you are,
    O loved one, delectable maiden!ᵈ

7 You are statelyᵉ as a palm tree,
    and your breasts are like its clusters.

8 I say I will climb the palm tree
    and lay hold of its branches.
O may your breasts be like clusters of
      the vine,
    and the scent of your breath like
      apples,

9 and your kissesᶠ like the best wine
    that goes downᵍ smoothly,
    gliding over lips and teeth.ʰ

10 I am my beloved's,
    and his desire is for me.

11 Come, my beloved,
    let us go forth into the fields,
    and lodge in the villages;

12 let us go out early to the vineyards,
    and see whether the vines have
      budded,
whether the grape blossoms have
      opened
    and the pomegranates are in bloom.
There I will give you my love.

13 The mandrakes give forth fragrance,
    and over our doors are all choice
      fruits,
new as well as old,
    which I have laid up for you, O my
      beloved.

8 O that you were like a brother to me,
    who nursed at my mother's breast!
If I met you outside, I would kiss you,

ᵃ Cn: Meaning of Heb uncertain   ᵇ Ch 7.1 in Heb   ᶜ Or *dance of Mahanaim*   ᵈ Syr: Heb *in delights*
ᵉ Heb *This your stature is*   ᶠ Heb *palate*   ᵍ Heb *down for my lover*   ʰ Gk Syr Vg: Heb *lips of sleepers*

and no one would despise me.

2 I would lead you and bring you
    into the house of my mother,
    and into the chamber of the one who
        bore me. *a*
  I would give you spiced wine to drink,
    the juice of my pomegranates.
3 O that his left hand were under my head,
    and that his right hand embraced me!
4 I adjure you, O daughters of Jerusalem,
    do not stir up or awaken love
    until it is ready!

Homecoming

5 Who is that coming up from the
        wilderness,
    leaning upon her beloved?

  Under the apple tree I awakened you.
  There your mother was in labor with
        you;
    there she who bore you was in labor.

6 Set me as a seal upon your heart,
    as a seal upon your arm;
  for love is strong as death,
    passion fierce as the grave.
  Its flashes are flashes of fire,
    a raging flame.
7 Many waters cannot quench love,
    neither can floods drown it.
  If one offered for love
    all the wealth of one's house,
    it would be utterly scorned.

8 We have a little sister,
    and she has no breasts.
  What shall we do for our sister,
    on the day when she is spoken for?
9 If she is a wall,
    we will build upon her a battlement of
        silver;
  but if she is a door,
    we will enclose her with boards of
        cedar.
10 I was a wall,
    and my breasts were like towers;
  then I was in his eyes
    as one who brings *b* peace.
11 Solomon had a vineyard at Baal-hamon;
    he entrusted the vineyard to keepers;
    each one was to bring for its fruit a
        thousand pieces of silver.
12 My vineyard, my very own, is for myself;
    you, O Solomon, may have the
        thousand,
    and the keepers of the fruit two
        hundred!

13 O you who dwell in the gardens,
    my companions are listening for your
        voice;
    let me hear it.

14 Make haste, my beloved,
    and be like a gazelle
  or a young stag
    upon the mountains of spices!

---

a Gk Syr: Heb *my mother; she* (or *you*) *will teach me*   *b* Or *finds*

ISAIAH

1 The vision of Isaiah son of Amoz, which he saw concerning Judah and Jerusalem in the days of Uzziah, Jotham, Ahaz, and Hezekiah, kings of Judah.

The Wickedness of Judah

2 Hear, O heavens, and listen, O earth;
　　for the LORD has spoken:
　　I reared children and brought them up,
　　　but they have rebelled against me.
3 The ox knows its owner,
　　and the donkey its master's crib;
　　but Israel does not know,
　　　my people do not understand.

4 Ah, sinful nation,
　　people laden with iniquity,
　　offspring who do evil,
　　　children who deal corruptly,
　　who have forsaken the LORD,
　　　who have despised the Holy One of
　　　　Israel,
　　who are utterly estranged!

5 Why do you seek further beatings?
　　Why do you continue to rebel?
　　The whole head is sick,
　　　and the whole heart faint.
6 From the sole of the foot even to the
　　　head,
　　there is no soundness in it,
　　but bruises and sores
　　　and bleeding wounds;
　　they have not been drained, or bound
　　　up,
　　　or softened with oil.

7 Your country lies desolate,
　　your cities are burned with fire;
　　in your very presence
　　　aliens devour your land;
　　　it is desolate, as overthrown by
　　　　foreigners.
8 And daughter Zion is left
　　like a booth in a vineyard,
　　like a shelter in a cucumber field,
　　like a besieged city.
9 If the LORD of hosts
　　had not left us a few survivors,
　　we would have been like Sodom,
　　　and become like Gomorrah.

10 Hear the word of the LORD,
　　you rulers of Sodom!
　　Listen to the teaching of our God,
　　　you people of Gomorrah!
11 What to me is the multitude of your
　　　sacrifices?
　　　says the LORD;
　　I have had enough of burnt offerings of
　　　rams
　　　and the fat of fed beasts;
　　I do not delight in the blood of bulls,
　　　or of lambs, or of goats.

12 When you come to appear before me,^a
　　who asked this from your hand?
　　Trample my courts no more;
13 bringing offerings is futile;
　　incense is an abomination to me.
　　New moon and sabbath and calling of
　　　convocation—
　　I cannot endure solemn assemblies
　　　with iniquity.
14 Your new moons and your appointed
　　　festivals
　　my soul hates;
　　they have become a burden to me,
　　　I am weary of bearing them.
15 When you stretch out your hands,
　　I will hide my eyes from you;
　　even though you make many prayers,
　　　I will not listen;
　　your hands are full of blood.
16 Wash yourselves; make yourselves clean;
　　remove the evil of your doings
　　　from before my eyes;
　　cease to do evil,

a Or *see my face*

17 learn to do good;
seek justice,
   rescue the oppressed,
defend the orphan,
   plead for the widow.

18 Come now, let us argue it out,
   says the LORD:
though your sins are like scarlet,
   they shall be like snow;
though they are red like crimson,
   they shall become like wool.
19 If you are willing and obedient,
   you shall eat the good of the land;
20 but if you refuse and rebel,
   you shall be devoured by the sword;
   for the mouth of the LORD has
      spoken.

The Degenerate City

21 How the faithful city
   has become a whore!
   She that was full of justice,
righteousness lodged in her—
   but now murderers!
22 Your silver has become dross,
   your wine is mixed with water.
23 Your princes are rebels
   and companions of thieves.
Everyone loves a bribe
   and runs after gifts.
They do not defend the orphan,
   and the widow's cause does not come
      before them.

24 Therefore says the Sovereign, the LORD
   of hosts, the Mighty One of
      Israel:
Ah, I will pour out my wrath on my
      enemies,
   and avenge myself on my foes!
25 I will turn my hand against you;
   I will smelt away your dross as with
      lye
   and remove all your alloy.

26 And I will restore your judges as at the
      first,
   and your counselors as at the
      beginning.
Afterward you shall be called the city of
      righteousness,
   the faithful city.

27 Zion shall be redeemed by justice,
   and those in her who repent, by
      righteousness.
28 But rebels and sinners shall be destroyed
      together,
   and those who forsake the LORD shall
      be consumed.
29 For you shall be ashamed of the oaks
   in which you delighted;
and you shall blush for the gardens
   that you have chosen.
30 For you shall be like an oak
   whose leaf withers,
   and like a garden without water.
31 The strong shall become like tinder,
   and their work *a* like a spark;
they and their work shall burn together,
   with no one to quench them.

The Future House of God

2 The word that Isaiah son of Amoz saw
  concerning Judah and Jerusalem.

2 In days to come
   the mountain of the LORD's house
shall be established as the highest of the
      mountains,
   and shall be raised above the hills;
all the nations shall stream to it.
3   Many peoples shall come and say,
"Come, let us go up to the mountain of
      the LORD,
   to the house of the God of Jacob;
that he may teach us his ways
   and that we may walk in his paths."
For out of Zion shall go forth
      instruction,

a Or *its makers*

and the word of the LORD from
    Jerusalem.
4 He shall judge between the nations,
    and shall arbitrate for many peoples;
they shall beat their swords into
    plowshares,
    and their spears into pruning hooks;
nation shall not lift up sword against
    nation,
    neither shall they learn war any more.

Judgment Pronounced on Arrogance

5 O house of Jacob,
    come, let us walk
    in the light of the LORD!
6 For you have forsaken the ways of *a* your
    people,
    O house of Jacob.
Indeed they are full of diviners *b* from
    the east
    and of soothsayers like the Philistines,
    and they clasp hands with foreigners.
7 Their land is filled with silver and gold,
    and there is no end to their treasures;
their land is filled with horses,
    and there is no end to their chariots.
8 Their land is filled with idols;
    they bow down to the work of their
    hands,
    to what their own fingers have made.
9 And so people are humbled,
    and everyone is brought low—
    do not forgive them!
10 Enter into the rock,
    and hide in the dust
from the terror of the LORD,
    and from the glory of his majesty.
11 The haughty eyes of people shall be
    brought low,
    and the pride of everyone shall be
    humbled;
    and the LORD alone will be exalted on
    that day.
12 For the LORD of hosts has a day
    against all that is proud and lofty,
    against all that is lifted up and high; *c*

13 against all the cedars of Lebanon,
    lofty and lifted up;
    and against all the oaks of Bashan;
14 against all the high mountains,
    and against all the lofty hills;
15 against every high tower,
    and against every fortified wall;
16 against all the ships of Tarshish,
    and against all the beautiful craft. *d*
17 The haughtiness of people shall be
    humbled,
    and the pride of everyone shall be
    brought low;
    and the LORD alone will be exalted on
    that day.
18 The idols shall utterly pass away.
19 Enter the caves of the rocks
    and the holes of the ground,
from the terror of the LORD,
    and from the glory of his majesty,
    when he rises to terrify the earth.
20 On that day people will throw away
    to the moles and to the bats
their idols of silver and their idols of
    gold,
    which they made for themselves to
    worship,
21 to enter the caverns of the rocks
    and the clefts in the crags,
from the terror of the LORD,
    and from the glory of his majesty,
    when he rises to terrify the earth.
22 Turn away from mortals,
    who have only breath in their nostrils,
    for of what account are they?

3 For now the Sovereign, the LORD of
    hosts,
    is taking away from Jerusalem and
    from Judah
support and staff—
    all support of bread,
    and all support of water—
2 warrior and soldier,
    judge and prophet,
    diviner and elder,
3 captain of fifty

---

a Heb lacks *the ways of*   *b* Cn: Heb lacks *of diviners*   *c* Cn Compare Gk: Heb *low*   *d* Compare Gk: Meaning of
Heb uncertain

and dignitary,
counselor and skillful magician
and expert enchanter.
4 And I will make boys their princes,
and babes shall rule over them.
5 The people will be oppressed,
everyone by another
and everyone by a neighbor;
the youth will be insolent to the elder,
and the base to the honorable.

6 Someone will even seize a relative,
a member of the clan, saying,
"You have a cloak;
you shall be our leader,
and this heap of ruins
shall be under your rule."
7 But the other will cry out on that day,
saying,
"I will not be a healer;
in my house there is neither bread nor
cloak;
you shall not make me
leader of the people."
8 For Jerusalem has stumbled
and Judah has fallen,
because their speech and their deeds are
against the LORD,
defying his glorious presence.

9 The look on their faces bears witness
against them;
they proclaim their sin like Sodom,
they do not hide it.
Woe to them!
For they have brought evil on
themselves.
10 Tell the innocent how fortunate they are,
for they shall eat the fruit of their
labors.
11 Woe to the guilty! How unfortunate they
are,
for what their hands have done shall
be done to them.
12 My people—children are their
oppressors,

and women rule over them.
O my people, your leaders mislead you,
and confuse the course of your paths.

13 The LORD rises to argue his case;
he stands to judge the peoples.
14 The LORD enters into judgment
with the elders and princes of his
people:
It is you who have devoured the
vineyard;
the spoil of the poor is in your
houses.
15 What do you mean by crushing my
people,
by grinding the face of the poor? says
the Lord GOD of hosts.

16 The LORD said:
Because the daughters of Zion are
haughty
and walk with outstretched necks,
glancing wantonly with their eyes,
mincing along as they go,
tinkling with their feet;
17 the Lord will afflict with scabs
the heads of the daughters of Zion,
and the LORD will lay bare their secret
parts.

18 In that day the Lord will take away the
finery of the anklets, the headbands, and
the crescents; 19 the pendants, the bracelets,
and the scarfs; 20 the headdresses, the armlets,
the sashes, the perfume boxes, and the amulets;
21 the signet rings and nose rings; 22 the festal
robes, the mantles, the cloaks, and the hand-
bags; 23 the garments of gauze, the linen garments, the turbans, and the veils.
24 Instead of perfume there will be a
stench;
and instead of a sash, a rope;
and instead of well-set hair, baldness;
and instead of a rich robe, a binding
of sackcloth;
instead of beauty, shame. *a*

a Q Ms: MT lacks *shame*

25 Your men shall fall by the sword
        and your warriors in battle.
26 And her gates shall lament and mourn;
        ravaged, she shall sit upon the
            ground.
4   Seven women shall take hold of one man
        in that day, saying,
    "We will eat our own bread and wear
        our own clothes;
    just let us be called by your name;
        take away our disgrace."

The Future Glory of the Survivors in Zion

2 On that day the branch of the LORD shall
be beautiful and glorious, and the fruit of the
land shall be the pride and glory of the survivors of Israel. ³Whoever is left in Zion and
remains in Jerusalem will be called holy, everyone who has been recorded for life in Jerusalem, ⁴once the Lord has washed away the filth
of the daughters of Zion and cleansed the
bloodstains of Jerusalem from its midst by a
spirit of judgment and by a spirit of burning.
⁵Then the LORD will create over the whole site
of Mount Zion and over its places of assembly a cloud by day and smoke and the shining
of a flaming fire by night. Indeed over all the
glory there will be a canopy. ⁶It will serve as a
pavilion, a shade by day from the heat, and a
refuge and a shelter from the storm and rain.

The Song of the Unfruitful Vineyard

5   Let me sing for my beloved
        my love-song concerning his
            vineyard:
    My beloved had a vineyard
        on a very fertile hill.
2   He dug it and cleared it of stones,
        and planted it with choice vines;
    he built a watchtower in the midst of it,
        and hewed out a wine vat in it;
    he expected it to yield grapes,
        but it yielded wild grapes.

3   And now, inhabitants of Jerusalem
        and people of Judah,

judge between me
        and my vineyard.
4   What more was there to do for my
            vineyard
        that I have not done in it?
    When I expected it to yield grapes,
        why did it yield wild grapes?

5   And now I will tell you
        what I will do to my vineyard.
    I will remove its hedge,
        and it shall be devoured;
    I will break down its wall,
        and it shall be trampled down.
6   I will make it a waste;
        it shall not be pruned or hoed,
        and it shall be overgrown with briers
            and thorns;
    I will also command the clouds
        that they rain no rain upon it.

7   For the vineyard of the LORD of hosts
        is the house of Israel,
    and the people of Judah
        are his pleasant planting;
    he expected justice,
        but saw bloodshed;
    righteousness,
        but heard a cry!

Social Injustice Denounced

8   Ah, you who join house to house,
        who add field to field,
    until there is room for no one but you,
        and you are left to live alone
        in the midst of the land!
9   The LORD of hosts has sworn in my
            hearing:
    Surely many houses shall be desolate,
        large and beautiful houses, without
            inhabitant.
10 For ten acres of vineyard shall yield but
            one bath,
        and a homer of seed shall yield a
            mere ephah. ᵃ

a The Heb *bath, homer,* and *ephah* are measures of quantity

11 Ah, you who rise early in the morning
      in pursuit of strong drink,
   who linger in the evening
      to be inflamed by wine,
12 whose feasts consist of lyre and harp,
      tambourine and flute and wine,
   but who do not regard the deeds of the
      LORD,
      or see the work of his hands!
13 Therefore my people go into exile
      without knowledge;
   their nobles are dying of hunger,
      and their multitude is parched with
      thirst.

14 Therefore Sheol has enlarged its
      appetite
   and opened its mouth beyond
      measure;
   the nobility of Jerusalem^a and her
      multitude go down,
   her throng and all who exult in her.
15 People are bowed down, everyone is
      brought low,
   and the eyes of the haughty are
      humbled.
16 But the LORD of hosts is exalted by
      justice,
   and the Holy God shows himself
      holy by righteousness.
17 Then the lambs shall graze as in their
      pasture,
   fatlings and kids^b shall feed among
      the ruins.

18 Ah, you who drag iniquity along with
      cords of falsehood,
   who drag sin along as with cart ropes,
19 who say, "Let him make haste,
      let him speed his work
      that we may see it;
   let the plan of the Holy One of Israel
      hasten to fulfillment,
      that we may know it!"
20 Ah, you who call evil good
      and good evil,

who put darkness for light
   and light for darkness,
who put bitter for sweet
   and sweet for bitter!
21 Ah, you who are wise in your own eyes,
   and shrewd in your own sight!
22 Ah, you who are heroes in drinking wine
   and valiant at mixing drink,
23 who acquit the guilty for a bribe,
   and deprive the innocent of their
      rights!

Foreign Invasion Predicted
24 Therefore, as the tongue of fire devours
      the stubble,
   and as dry grass sinks down in the
      flame,
   so their root will become rotten,
      and their blossom go up like dust;
   for they have rejected the instruction of
      the LORD of hosts,
   and have despised the word of the
      Holy One of Israel.

25 Therefore the anger of the LORD was
      kindled against his people,
   and he stretched out his hand against
      them and struck them;
   the mountains quaked,
   and their corpses were like refuse
      in the streets.
   For all this his anger has not turned
      away,
      and his hand is stretched out still.

26 He will raise a signal for a nation far
      away,
   and whistle for a people at the ends
      of the earth;
   Here they come, swiftly, speedily!
27 None of them is weary, none stumbles,
      none slumbers or sleeps,
   not a loincloth is loose,
      not a sandal-thong broken;
28 their arrows are sharp,
      all their bows bent,

a Heb *her nobility*   *b* Cn Compare Gk: Heb *aliens*

their horses' hoofs seem like flint,
and their wheels like the whirlwind.

29 Their roaring is like a lion,
like young lions they roar;
they growl and seize their prey,
they carry it off, and no one can
rescue.

30 They will roar over it on that day,
like the roaring of the sea.
And if one look to the land—
only darkness and distress;
and the light grows dark with clouds.

A Vision of God in the Temple

6 In the year that King Uzziah died, I saw the Lord sitting on a throne, high and lofty; and the hem of his robe filled the temple. 2Seraphs were in attendance above him; each had six wings: with two they covered their faces, and with two they covered their feet, and with two they flew. 3And one called to another and said:

"Holy, holy, holy is the LORD of hosts;
the whole earth is full of his glory."

4The pivots*a* on the thresholds shook at the voices of those who called, and the house filled with smoke. 5And I said: "Woe is me! I am lost, for I am a man of unclean lips, and I live among a people of unclean lips; yet my eyes have seen the King, the LORD of hosts!"

6 Then one of the seraphs flew to me, holding a live coal that had been taken from the altar with a pair of tongs. 7The seraph*b* touched my mouth with it and said: "Now that this has touched your lips, your guilt has departed and your sin is blotted out." 8Then I heard the voice of the Lord saying, "Whom shall I send, and who will go for us?" And I said, "Here am I; send me!" 9And he said, "Go and say to this people:

'Keep listening, but do not comprehend;
keep looking, but do not understand.'

10 Make the mind of this people dull,
and stop their ears,
and shut their eyes,

so that they may not look with their
eyes,
and listen with their ears,
and comprehend with their minds,
and turn and be healed."

11 Then I said, "How long, O Lord?" And
he said:

"Until cities lie waste
without inhabitant,
and houses without people,
and the land is utterly desolate;

12 until the LORD sends everyone far away,
and vast is the emptiness in the midst
of the land.

13 Even if a tenth part remain in it,
it will be burned again,
like a terebinth or an oak
whose stump remains standing
when it is felled."*a*
The holy seed is its stump.

Isaiah Reassures King Ahaz

7 In the days of Ahaz son of Jotham son of Uzziah, king of Judah, King Rezin of Aram and King Pekah son of Remaliah of Israel went up to attack Jerusalem, but could not mount an attack against it. 2When the house of David heard that Aram had allied itself with Ephraim, the heart of Ahaz*c* and the heart of his people shook as the trees of the forest shake before the wind.

3 Then the LORD said to Isaiah, Go out to meet Ahaz, you and your son Shear-jashub,*d* at the end of the conduit of the upper pool on the highway to the Fuller's Field, 4and say to him, Take heed, be quiet, do not fear, and do not let your heart be faint because of these two smoldering stumps of firebrands, because of the fierce anger of Rezin and Aram and the son of Remaliah. 5Because Aram—with Ephraim and the son of Remaliah—has plotted evil against you, saying, 6Let us go up against Judah and cut off Jerusalem*e* and conquer it for ourselves and make the son of Tabeel king in it; 7therefore thus says the Lord GOD:

a Meaning of Heb uncertain   *b* Heb *He*   *c* Heb *his heart*   *d* That is *A remnant shall return*   *e* Heb *cut it off*

It shall not stand,
and it shall not come to pass.
8 For the head of Aram is Damascus,
and the head of Damascus is Rezin.
(Within sixty-five years Ephraim will be
shattered, no longer a people.)
9 The head of Ephraim is Samaria,
and the head of Samaria is the son of
Remaliah.
If you do not stand firm in faith,
you shall not stand at all.

Isaiah Gives Ahaz the Sign of Immanuel

10 Again the LORD spoke to Ahaz, saying,
11 Ask a sign of the LORD your God; let it be
deep as Sheol or high as heaven. 12 But Ahaz
said, I will not ask, and I will not put the LORD
to the test. 13 Then Isaiah *a* said: "Hear then,
O house of David! Is it too little for you to
weary mortals, that you weary my God also?
14 Therefore the Lord himself will give you a
sign. Look, the young woman *b* is with child
and shall bear a son, and shall name him Immanuel. *c* 15 He shall eat curds and honey by the
time he knows how to refuse the evil and
choose the good. 16 For before the child knows
how to refuse the evil and choose the good, the
land before whose two kings you are in dread
will be deserted. 17 The LORD will bring on
you and on your people and on your ancestral
house such days as have not come since the
day that Ephraim departed from Judah—the
king of Assyria."
18 On that day the LORD will whistle for the
fly that is at the sources of the streams of
Egypt, and for the bee that is in the land of Assyria. 19 And they will all come and settle in the
steep ravines, and in the clefts of the rocks, and
on all the thornbushes, and on all the pastures.
20 On that day the Lord will shave with a
razor hired beyond the River—with the king
of Assyria—the head and the hair of the feet,
and it will take off the beard as well.
21 On that day one will keep alive a young
cow and two sheep, 22 and will eat curds because of the abundance of milk that they give;

for everyone that is left in the land shall eat
curds and honey.
23 On that day every place where there
used to be a thousand vines, worth a thousand
shekels of silver, will become briers and thorns.
24 With bow and arrows one will go there, for
all the land will be briers and thorns; 25 and as
for all the hills that used to be hoed with a hoe,
you will not go there for fear of briers and
thorns; but they will become a place where cattle are let loose and where sheep tread.

Isaiah's Son a Sign of the Assyrian Invasion

8 Then the LORD said to me, Take a large
tablet and write on it in common characters, "Belonging to Maher-shalal-hash-baz," *d*
2 and have it attested *e* for me by reliable witnesses, the priest Uriah and Zechariah son of
Jeberechiah. 3 And I went to the prophetess,
and she conceived and bore a son. Then the
LORD said to me, Name him Maher-shalal-
hash-baz; 4 for before the child knows how to
call "My father" or "My mother," the wealth
of Damascus and the spoil of Samaria will be
carried away by the king of Assyria.
5 The LORD spoke to me again: 6 Because
this people has refused the waters of Shiloah
that flow gently, and melt in fear before *f* Rezin and the son of Remaliah; 7 therefore, the
Lord is bringing up against it the mighty flood
waters of the River, the king of Assyria and all
his glory; it will rise above all its channels and
overflow all its banks; 8 it will sweep on into Judah as a flood, and, pouring over, it will reach
up to the neck; and its outspread wings will fill
the breadth of your land, O Immanuel.

9 Band together, you peoples, and be
dismayed;
listen, all you far countries;
gird yourselves and be dismayed;
gird yourselves and be dismayed!
10 Take counsel together, but it shall be
brought to naught;
speak a word, but it will not stand,
for God is with us. *g*

---

a Heb *he*   *b* Gk *the virgin*   *c* That is *God is with us*   *d* That is *The spoil speeds, the prey hastens*   *e* Q Ms Gk Syr:
MT *and I caused to be attested*   *f* Cn: Meaning of Heb uncertain   *g* Heb *immanu el*

11 For the LORD spoke thus to me while his hand was strong upon me, and warned me not to walk in the way of this people, saying: 12Do not call conspiracy all that this people calls conspiracy, and do not fear what it fears, or be in dread. 13But the LORD of hosts, him you shall regard as holy; let him be your fear, and let him be your dread. 14He will become a sanctuary, a stone one strikes against; for both houses of Israel he will become a rock one stumbles over—a trap and a snare for the inhabitants of Jerusalem. 15And many among them shall stumble; they shall fall and be broken; they shall be snared and taken.

Disciples of Isaiah

16 Bind up the testimony, seal the teaching among my disciples. 17I will wait for the LORD, who is hiding his face from the house of Jacob, and I will hope in him. 18See, I and the children whom the LORD has given me are signs and portents in Israel from the LORD of hosts, who dwells on Mount Zion. 19Now if people say to you, "Consult the ghosts and the familiar spirits that chirp and mutter; should not a people consult their gods, the dead on behalf of the living, 20for teaching and for instruction?" surely, those who speak like this will have no dawn! 21They will pass through the land,*a* greatly distressed and hungry; when they are hungry, they will be enraged and will curse*b* their king and their gods. They will turn their faces upward, 22or they will look to the earth, but will see only distress and darkness, the gloom of anguish; and they will be thrust into thick darkness.*c*

The Righteous Reign of the Coming King

9*d* But there will be no gloom for those who were in anguish. In the former time he brought into contempt the land of Zebulun and the land of Naphtali, but in the latter time he will make glorious the way of the sea, the land beyond the Jordan, Galilee of the nations. 2*e* The people who walked in darkness have seen a great light;

those who lived in a land of deep
  darkness—
  on them light has shined.
3 You have multiplied the nation,
   you have increased its joy;
 they rejoice before you
   as with joy at the harvest,
   as people exult when dividing plunder.
4 For the yoke of their burden,
    and the bar across their shoulders,
    the rod of their oppressor,
    you have broken as on the day of
     Midian.
5 For all the boots of the tramping
      warriors
   and all the garments rolled in blood
    shall be burned as fuel for the fire.
6 For a child has been born for us,
    a son given to us;
  authority rests upon his shoulders;
   and he is named
   Wonderful Counselor, Mighty God,
    Everlasting Father, Prince of Peace.
7 His authority shall grow continually,
    and there shall be endless peace
  for the throne of David and his
     kingdom.
    He will establish and uphold it
  with justice and with righteousness
    from this time onward and
     forevermore.
  The zeal of the LORD of hosts will do
     this.

Judgment on Arrogance and Oppression

8 The Lord sent a word against Jacob,
    and it fell on Israel;
9 and all the people knew it—
    Ephraim and the inhabitants of
     Samaria—
    but in pride and arrogance of heart
     they said:
10 "The bricks have fallen,
    but we will build with dressed stones;
  the sycamores have been cut down,
    but we will put cedars in their place."

a Heb *it*   *b* Or *curse by*   *c* Meaning of Heb uncertain   *d* Ch 8.23 in Heb   *e* Ch 9.1 in Heb

11   So the LORD raised adversaries[a] against
them,
     and stirred up their enemies,
12   the Arameans on the east and the
Philistines on the west,
     and they devoured Israel with open
mouth.
   For all this his anger has not turned
away,
     his hand is stretched out still.

13   The people did not turn to him who
struck them,
     or seek the LORD of hosts.
14   So the LORD cut off from Israel head
and tail,
     palm branch and reed in one day—
15   elders and dignitaries are the head,
     and prophets who teach lies are the
tail;
16   for those who led this people led them
astray,
     and those who were led by them were
left in confusion.
17   That is why the Lord did not have pity
on[b] their young people,
     or compassion on their orphans and
widows;
   for everyone was godless and an
evildoer,
     and every mouth spoke folly.
   For all this his anger has not turned
away,
     his hand is stretched out still.

18   For wickedness burned like a fire,
     consuming briers and thorns;
   it kindled the thickets of the forest,
     and they swirled upward in a column
of smoke.
19   Through the wrath of the LORD of
hosts
     the land was burned,
   and the people became like fuel for the
fire;
     no one spared another.

20   They gorged on the right, but still were
hungry,
     and they devoured on the left, but
were not satisfied;
   they devoured the flesh of their own
kindred;[c]
21   Manasseh devoured Ephraim, and
Ephraim Manasseh,
     and together they were against Judah.
   For all this his anger has not turned
away,
     his hand is stretched out still.

10   Ah, you who make iniquitous
decrees,
     who write oppressive statutes,
2   to turn aside the needy from justice
     and to rob the poor of my people of
their right,
   that widows may be your spoil,
     and that you may make the orphans
your prey!
3   What will you do on the day of
punishment,
     in the calamity that will come from
far away?
   To whom will you flee for help,
     and where will you leave your wealth,
4   so as not to crouch among the prisoners
     or fall among the slain?
   For all this his anger has not turned away;
     his hand is stretched out still.

Arrogant Assyria Also Judged

5   Ah, Assyria, the rod of my anger—
     the club in their hands is my fury!
6   Against a godless nation I send him,
     and against the people of my wrath I
command him,
   to take spoil and seize plunder,
     and to tread them down like the mire
of the streets.
7   But this is not what he intends,
     nor does he have this in mind;
   but it is in his heart to destroy,
     and to cut off nations not a few.

a Cn: Heb *the adversaries of Rezin*   *b* Q Ms: MT *rejoice over*   *c* Or *arm*

8 For he says:
"Are not my commanders all kings?
9 Is not Calno like Carchemish?
　Is not Hamath like Arpad?
　Is not Samaria like Damascus?
10 As my hand has reached to the
　　　kingdoms of the idols
　whose images were greater than those
　　　of Jerusalem and Samaria,
11 shall I not do to Jerusalem and her idols
　　what I have done to Samaria and her
　　　images?"

12 When the Lord has finished all his work on Mount Zion and on Jerusalem, he[a] will punish the arrogant boasting of the king of Assyria and his haughty pride. 13For he says:
"By the strength of my hand I have
　　　done it,
　and by my wisdom, for I have
　　　understanding;
I have removed the boundaries of
　　　peoples,
　　and have plundered their treasures;
　　like a bull I have brought down those
　　　who sat on thrones.
14 My hand has found, like a nest,
　　the wealth of the peoples;
and as one gathers eggs that have been
　　　forsaken,
　　so I have gathered all the earth;
and there was none that moved a wing,
　　or opened its mouth, or chirped."

15 Shall the ax vaunt itself over the one
　　　who wields it,
　　or the saw magnify itself against the
　　　one who handles it?
As if a rod should raise the one who
　　　lifts it up,
　　or as if a staff should lift the one
　　　who is not wood!
16 Therefore the Sovereign, the LORD of
　　　hosts,
　　will send wasting sickness among his
　　　stout warriors,

and under his glory a burning will be
　　　kindled,
　　like the burning of fire.
17 The light of Israel will become a fire,
　　and his Holy One a flame;
and it will burn and devour
　　his thorns and briers in one day.
18 The glory of his forest and his fruitful
　　　land
　　the LORD will destroy, both soul and
　　　body,
　　and it will be as when an invalid
　　　wastes away.
19 The remnant of the trees of his forest
　　　will be so few
　　that a child can write them down.

The Repentant Remnant of Israel

20 On that day the remnant of Israel and the survivors of the house of Jacob will no more lean on the one who struck them, but will lean on the LORD, the Holy One of Israel, in truth. 21A remnant will return, the remnant of Jacob, to the mighty God. 22For though your people Israel were like the sand of the sea, only a remnant of them will return. Destruction is decreed, overflowing with righteousness. 23For the Lord GOD of hosts will make a full end, as decreed, in all the earth.[b]

24 Therefore thus says the Lord GOD of hosts: O my people, who live in Zion, do not be afraid of the Assyrians when they beat you with a rod and lift up their staff against you as the Egyptians did. 25For in a very little while my indignation will come to an end, and my anger will be directed to their destruction. 26The LORD of hosts will wield a whip against them, as when he struck Midian at the rock of Oreb; his staff will be over the sea, and he will lift it as he did in Egypt. 27On that day his burden will be removed from your shoulder, and his yoke will be destroyed from your neck.

He has gone up from Rimmon,[c]
28 　he has come to Aiath;
　he has passed through Migron,

---

a Heb I　　b Or land　　c Cn: Heb and his yoke from your neck, and a yoke will be destroyed because of fatness

at Michmash he stores his baggage;
29 they have crossed over the pass,
        at Geba they lodge for the night;
    Ramah trembles,
        Gibeah of Saul has fled.
30 Cry aloud, O daughter Gallim!
        Listen, O Laishah!
        Answer her, O Anathoth!
31 Madmenah is in flight,
        the inhabitants of Gebim flee for
            safety.
32 This very day he will halt at Nob,
        he will shake his fist
        at the mount of daughter Zion,
        the hill of Jerusalem.

33 Look, the Sovereign, the LORD of hosts,
        will lop the boughs with terrifying
            power;
    the tallest trees will be cut down,
        and the lofty will be brought low.
34 He will hack down the thickets of the
            forest with an ax,
        and Lebanon with its majestic trees[a]
            will fall.

The Peaceful Kingdom

11 A shoot shall come out from the
        stump of Jesse,
        and a branch shall grow out of his
            roots.
2   The spirit of the LORD shall rest on
        him,
        the spirit of wisdom and
            understanding,
        the spirit of counsel and might,
        the spirit of knowledge and the fear
            of the LORD.
3   His delight shall be in the fear of the
        LORD.

    He shall not judge by what his eyes see,
        or decide by what his ears hear;
4   but with righteousness he shall judge the
        poor,

and decide with equity for the meek
    of the earth;
he shall strike the earth with the rod of
    his mouth,
    and with the breath of his lips he
        shall kill the wicked.
5   Righteousness shall be the belt around
        his waist,
        and faithfulness the belt around his
            loins.

6   The wolf shall live with the lamb,
        the leopard shall lie down with the
            kid,
    the calf and the lion and the fatling
        together,
        and a little child shall lead them.
7   The cow and the bear shall graze,
        their young shall lie down together;
        and the lion shall eat straw like the ox.
8   The nursing child shall play over the
        hole of the asp,
        and the weaned child shall put its
            hand on the adder's den.
9   They will not hurt or destroy
        on all my holy mountain;
    for the earth will be full of the
        knowledge of the LORD
        as the waters cover the sea.

Return of the Remnant of Israel and Judah

10 On that day the root of Jesse shall stand
as a signal to the peoples; the nations shall inquire of him, and his dwelling shall be glorious.

11 On that day the Lord will extend his
hand yet a second time to recover the remnant
that is left of his people, from Assyria, from
Egypt, from Pathros, from Ethiopia,[b] from
Elam, from Shinar, from Hamath, and from
the coastlands of the sea.
12 He will raise a signal for the nations,
        and will assemble the outcasts of
            Israel,
    and gather the dispersed of Judah
        from the four corners of the earth.

a Cn Compare Gk Vg: Heb *with a majestic one*   b Or *Nubia*; Heb *Cush*

13 The jealousy of Ephraim shall depart,
    the hostility of Judah shall be cut off;
  Ephraim shall not be jealous of Judah,
    and Judah shall not be hostile towards
      Ephraim.
14 But they shall swoop down on the backs
    of the Philistines in the west,
  together they shall plunder the people
    of the east.
  They shall put forth their hand against
    Edom and Moab,
  and the Ammonites shall obey them.
15 And the LORD will utterly destroy
    the tongue of the sea of Egypt;
  and will wave his hand over the River
    with his scorching wind;
  and will split it into seven channels,
    and make a way to cross on foot;
16 so there shall be a highway from Assyria
    for the remnant that is left of his
      people,
  as there was for Israel
    when they came up from the land of
      Egypt.

Thanksgiving and Praise

12 You will say in that day:
  I will give thanks to you,
    O LORD,
  for though you were angry with me,
  your anger turned away,
    and you comforted me.

2 Surely God is my salvation;
  I will trust, and will not be afraid,
  for the LORD GOD*a* is my strength and
    my might;
  he has become my salvation.

3 With joy you will draw water from the
wells of salvation. 4And you will say in that day:
  Give thanks to the LORD,
    call on his name;
  make known his deeds among the
    nations;
    proclaim that his name is exalted.

5 Sing praises to the LORD, for he has
    done gloriously;
  let this be known*b* in all the earth.
6 Shout aloud and sing for joy, O royal*c*
    Zion,
  for great in your midst is the Holy
    One of Israel.

Proclamation against Babylon

13 The oracle concerning Babylon that
  Isaiah son of Amoz saw.

2 On a bare hill raise a signal,
    cry aloud to them;
  wave the hand for them to enter
    the gates of the nobles.
3 I myself have commanded my
    consecrated ones,
  have summoned my warriors, my
    proudly exulting ones,
  to execute my anger.

4 Listen, a tumult on the mountains
    as of a great multitude!
  Listen, an uproar of kingdoms,
    of nations gathering together!
  The LORD of hosts is mustering
    an army for battle.
5 They come from a distant land,
    from the end of the heavens,
  the LORD and the weapons of his
    indignation,
    to destroy the whole earth.

6 Wail, for the day of the LORD is near;
    it will come like destruction from the
      Almighty!*d*
7 Therefore all hands will be feeble,
    and every human heart will melt,
8   and they will be dismayed.
  Pangs and agony will seize them;
    they will be in anguish like a woman
    in labor.
  They will look aghast at one another;
    their faces will be aflame.
9 See, the day of the LORD comes,

---

a Heb *for Yah, the* LORD   *b* Or *this is made known*   *c* Or *O inhabitant of*   *d* Traditional rendering of Heb *Shaddai*

cruel, with wrath and fierce anger,
to make the earth a desolation,
    and to destroy its sinners from it.
10 For the stars of the heavens and their
            constellations
      will not give their light;
    the sun will be dark at its rising,
      and the moon will not shed its light.
11 I will punish the world for its evil,
      and the wicked for their iniquity;
    I will put an end to the pride of the
            arrogant,
      and lay low the insolence of tyrants.
12 I will make mortals more rare than fine
            gold,
      and humans than the gold of Ophir.
13 Therefore I will make the heavens
            tremble,
      and the earth will be shaken out of its
            place,
    at the wrath of the LORD of hosts
      in the day of his fierce anger.
14 Like a hunted gazelle,
      or like sheep with no one to gather
            them,
    all will turn to their own people,
      and all will flee to their own lands.
15 Whoever is found will be thrust
            through,
      and whoever is caught will fall by the
            sword.
16 Their infants will be dashed to pieces
            before their eyes;
    their houses will be plundered,
      and their wives ravished.
17 See, I am stirring up the Medes against
            them,
      who have no regard for silver
      and do not delight in gold.
18 Their bows will slaughter the young
            men;
      they will have no mercy on the fruit
            of the womb;
      their eyes will not pity children.
19 And Babylon, the glory of kingdoms,

the splendor and pride of the
            Chaldeans,
    will be like Sodom and Gomorrah
      when God overthrew them.
20 It will never be inhabited
      or lived in for all generations;
    Arabs will not pitch their tents there,
      shepherds will not make their flocks
            lie down there.
21 But wild animals will lie down there,
      and its houses will be full of howling
            creatures;
    there ostriches will live,
      and there goat-demons will dance.
22 Hyenas will cry in its towers,
      and jackals in the pleasant palaces;
    its time is close at hand,
      and its days will not be prolonged.

Restoration of Judah

14 But the LORD will have compassion on
Jacob and will again choose Israel, and
will set them in their own land; and aliens will
join them and attach themselves to the house
of Jacob. ²And the nations will take them and
bring them to their place, and the house of Israel will possess the nations *a* as male and female slaves in the LORD's land; they will take
captive those who were their captors, and rule
over those who oppressed them.

Downfall of the King of Babylon

3 When the LORD has given you rest from
your pain and turmoil and the hard service
with which you were made to serve, ⁴you will
take up this taunt against the king of Babylon:

    How the oppressor has ceased!
      How his insolence *b* has ceased!
5   The LORD has broken the staff of the
            wicked,
      the scepter of rulers,
6   that struck down the peoples in wrath
      with unceasing blows,
    that ruled the nations in anger
      with unrelenting persecution.

a Heb *them*   *b* Q Ms Compare Gk Syr Vg: Meaning of MT uncertain

7 The whole earth is at rest and quiet;
   they break forth into singing.
8 The cypresses exult over you,
   the cedars of Lebanon, saying,
   "Since you were laid low,
   no one comes to cut us down."
9 Sheol beneath is stirred up
   to meet you when you come;
it rouses the shades to greet you,
   all who were leaders of the earth;
it raises from their thrones
   all who were kings of the nations.
10 All of them will speak
   and say to you:
   "You too have become as weak as we!
   You have become like us!"
11 Your pomp is brought down to Sheol,
   and the sound of your harps;
maggots are the bed beneath you,
   and worms are your covering.

12 How you are fallen from heaven,
   O Day Star, son of Dawn!
How you are cut down to the ground,
   you who laid the nations low!
13 You said in your heart,
   "I will ascend to heaven;
I will raise my throne
   above the stars of God;
I will sit on the mount of assembly
   on the heights of Zaphon;[a]
14 I will ascend to the tops of the clouds,
   I will make myself like the Most
     High."
15 But you are brought down to Sheol,
   to the depths of the Pit.
16 Those who see you will stare at you,
   and ponder over you:
   "Is this the man who made the earth
     tremble,
   who shook kingdoms,
17 who made the world like a desert
   and overthrew its cities,
   who would not let his prisoners go
     home?"
18 All the kings of the nations lie in glory,

   each in his own tomb;
19 but you are cast out, away from your
     grave,
   like loathsome carrion,[b]
clothed with the dead, those pierced by
     the sword,
   who go down to the stones of the
     Pit,
   like a corpse trampled underfoot.
20 You will not be joined with them in
     burial,
   because you have destroyed your land,
   you have killed your people.

May the descendants of evildoers
   nevermore be named!
21 Prepare slaughter for his sons
   because of the guilt of their father.[c]
Let them never rise to possess the earth
   or cover the face of the world with
     cities.

22 I will rise up against them, says the
LORD of hosts, and will cut off from Babylon
name and remnant, offspring and posterity,
says the LORD. 23 And I will make it a possession of the hedgehog, and pools of water,
and I will sweep it with the broom of destruction, says the LORD of hosts.

An Oracle concerning Assyria

24 The LORD of hosts has sworn:
   As I have designed,
     so shall it be;
   and as I have planned,
     so shall it come to pass:
25 I will break the Assyrian in my land,
   and on my mountains trample him
     under foot;
his yoke shall be removed from them,
   and his burden from their shoulders.
26 This is the plan that is planned
   concerning the whole earth;
and this is the hand that is stretched out
   over all the nations.
27 For the LORD of hosts has planned,

a Or *assembly in the far north*   b Cn Compare Gk: Heb *like a loathed branch*   c Syr Compare Gk: Heb *fathers*

and who will annul it?
His hand is stretched out,
    and who will turn it back?

An Oracle concerning Philistia

28 In the year that King Ahaz died this oracle
came:

29 Do not rejoice, all you Philistines,
        that the rod that struck you is broken,
    for from the root of the snake will
            come forth an adder,
        and its fruit will be a flying fiery
            serpent.
30 The firstborn of the poor will graze,
        and the needy lie down in safety;
    but I will make your root die of
            famine,
        and your remnant I*a* will kill.
31 Wail, O gate; cry, O city;
        melt in fear, O Philistia, all of you!
    For smoke comes out of the north,
        and there is no straggler in its ranks.

32 What will one answer the messengers of
            the nation?
    "The LORD has founded Zion,
        and the needy among his people
        will find refuge in her."

An Oracle concerning Moab

15 An oracle concerning Moab.

    Because Ar is laid waste in a night,
        Moab is undone;
    because Kir is laid waste in a night,
        Moab is undone.
2 Dibon*b* has gone up to the temple,
        to the high places to weep;
    over Nebo and over Medeba
        Moab wails.
    On every head is baldness,
        every beard is shorn;
3 in the streets they bind on sackcloth;
        on the housetops and in the squares
        everyone wails and melts in tears.

4 Heshbon and Elealeh cry out,
        their voices are heard as far as Jahaz;
    therefore the loins of Moab quiver;*c*
        his soul trembles.
5 My heart cries out for Moab;
        his fugitives flee to Zoar,
        to Eglath-shelishiyah.
    For at the ascent of Luhith
        they go up weeping;
    on the road to Horonaim
        they raise a cry of destruction;
6 the waters of Nimrim
        are a desolation;
    the grass is withered, the new growth
            fails,
        the verdure is no more.
7 Therefore the abundance they have
            gained
        and what they have laid up
    they carry away
        over the Wadi of the Willows.
8 For a cry has gone
        around the land of Moab;
    the wailing reaches to Eglaim,
        the wailing reaches to Beer-elim.
9 For the waters of Dibon*d* are full of
            blood;
        yet I will bring upon Dibon*d* even
            more—
    a lion for those of Moab who escape,
        for the remnant of the land.

16 Send lambs
    to the ruler of the land,
    from Sela, by way of the desert,
        to the mount of daughter Zion.
2 Like fluttering birds,
        like scattered nestlings,
    so are the daughters of Moab
        at the fords of the Arnon.
3 "Give counsel,
        grant justice;
    make your shade like night
        at the height of noon;
    hide the outcasts,
        do not betray the fugitive;
4 let the outcasts of Moab

---

a Q Ms Vg: MT *he*   *b* Cn: Heb *the house and Dibon*   *c* Cn Compare Gk Syr: Heb *the armed men of Moab cry aloud*
d Q Ms Vg Compare Syr: MT *Dimon*

settle among you;
be a refuge to them
from the destroyer."

When the oppressor is no more,
and destruction has ceased,
and marauders have vanished from the
land,
5 then a throne shall be established in
steadfast love
in the tent of David,
and on it shall sit in faithfulness
a ruler who seeks justice
and is swift to do what is right.

6 We have heard of the pride of Moab
—how proud he is!—
of his arrogance, his pride, and his
insolence;
his boasts are false.
7 Therefore let Moab wail,
let everyone wail for Moab.
Mourn, utterly stricken,
for the raisin cakes of Kir-hareseth.

8 For the fields of Heshbon languish,
and the vines of Sibmah,
whose clusters once made drunk
the lords of the nations,
reached to Jazer
and strayed to the desert;
their shoots once spread abroad
and crossed over the sea.
9 Therefore I weep with the weeping of
Jazer
for the vines of Sibmah;
I drench you with my tears,
O Heshbon and Elealeh;
for the shout over your fruit harvest
and your grain harvest has ceased.
10 Joy and gladness are taken away
from the fruitful field;
and in the vineyards no songs are sung,
no shouts are raised;
no treader treads out wine in the
presses;

the vintage-shout is hushed.[a]
11 Therefore my heart throbs like a harp
for Moab,
and my very soul for Kir-heres.
12 When Moab presents himself, when he
wearies himself upon the high place, when he
comes to his sanctuary to pray, he will not
prevail.
13 This was the word that the LORD spoke
concerning Moab in the past. [14]But now the
LORD says, In three years, like the years of a
hired worker, the glory of Moab will be
brought into contempt, in spite of all its great
multitude; and those who survive will be very
few and feeble.

An Oracle concerning Damascus

17 An oracle concerning Damascus.

See, Damascus will cease to be a city,
and will become a heap of ruins.
2 Her towns will be deserted forever;[a]
they will be places for flocks,
which will lie down, and no one will
make them afraid.
3 The fortress will disappear from
Ephraim,
and the kingdom from Damascus;
and the remnant of Aram will be
like the glory of the children of
Israel,
says the LORD of hosts.

4 On that day
the glory of Jacob will be brought
low,
and the fat of his flesh will grow lean.
5 And it shall be as when reapers gather
standing grain
and their arms harvest the ears,
and as when one gleans the ears of grain
in the Valley of Rephaim.
6 Gleanings will be left in it,
as when an olive tree is beaten—
two or three berries
in the top of the highest bough,

a Gk: Heb *I have hushed*   b Cn Compare Gk: Heb *the cities of Aroer are deserted*

four or five
on the branches of a fruit tree,
says the LORD God of Israel.

7 On that day people will regard their Maker, and their eyes will look to the Holy One of Israel; [8]they will not have regard for the altars, the work of their hands, and they will not look to what their own fingers have made, either the sacred poles[a] or the altars of incense. 9 On that day their strong cities will be like the deserted places of the Hivites and the Amorites,[b] which they deserted because of the children of Israel, and there will be desolation.

10 For you have forgotten the God of your
        salvation,
    and have not remembered the Rock
        of your refuge;
    therefore, though you plant pleasant
        plants
    and set out slips of an alien god,
11 though you make them grow on the day
        that you plant them,
    and make them blossom in the
        morning that you sow;
    yet the harvest will flee away
    in a day of grief and incurable pain.

12 Ah, the thunder of many peoples,
        they thunder like the thundering of
        the sea!
    Ah, the roar of nations,
        they roar like the roaring of mighty
        waters!
13 The nations roar like the roaring of
        many waters,
    but he will rebuke them, and they will
        flee far away,
    chased like chaff on the mountains
        before the wind
    and whirling dust before the storm.
14 At evening time, lo, terror!
        Before morning, they are no more.
    This is the fate of those who despoil us,
    and the lot of those who plunder us.

An Oracle concerning Ethiopia

18 Ah, land of whirring wings
        beyond the rivers of Ethiopia,[c]
2   sending ambassadors by the Nile
        in vessels of papyrus on the waters!
    Go, you swift messengers,
        to a nation tall and smooth,
    to a people feared near and far,
        a nation mighty and conquering,
        whose land the rivers divide.

3   All you inhabitants of the world,
        you who live on the earth,
    when a signal is raised on the
            mountains, look!
        When a trumpet is blown, listen!
4   For thus the LORD said to me:
    I will quietly look from my dwelling
        like clear heat in sunshine,
        like a cloud of dew in the heat of
            harvest.
5   For before the harvest, when the
            blossom is over
        and the flower becomes a ripening
            grape,
    he will cut off the shoots with pruning
            hooks,
        and the spreading branches he will
            hew away.
6   They shall all be left
        to the birds of prey of the mountains
        and to the animals of the earth.
    And the birds of prey will summer on
            them,
        and all the animals of the earth will
            winter on them.

7 At that time gifts will be brought to the LORD of hosts from[d] a people tall and smooth, from a people feared near and far, a nation mighty and conquering, whose land the rivers divide, to Mount Zion, the place of the name of the LORD of hosts.

---

a Heb Asherim   b Cn Compare Gk: Heb places of the wood and the highest bough   c Or Nubia; Heb Cush
d Q Ms Gk Vg: MT of

An Oracle concerning Egypt

19

An oracle concerning Egypt.

See, the LORD is riding on a swift cloud
　　and comes to Egypt;
the idols of Egypt will tremble at his
　　presence,
　　and the heart of the Egyptians will
　　melt within them.
2　I will stir up Egyptians against
　　Egyptians,
　　and they will fight, one against the
　　other,
　　neighbor against neighbor,
　　city against city, kingdom against
　　kingdom;
3　the spirit of the Egyptians within them
　　　will be emptied out,
　　and I will confound their plans;
they will consult the idols and the spirits
　　of the dead
　　and the ghosts and the familiar spirits;
4　I will deliver the Egyptians
　　into the hand of a hard master;
a fierce king will rule over them,
　　says the Sovereign, the LORD of
　　hosts.

5　The waters of the Nile will be dried up,
　　and the river will be parched and dry;
6　its canals will become foul,
　　and the branches of Egypt's Nile will
　　diminish and dry up,
　　reeds and rushes will rot away.
7　There will be bare places by the Nile,
　　on the brink of the Nile;
and all that is sown by the Nile will dry
　　up,
　　be driven away, and be no more.
8　Those who fish will mourn;
　　all who cast hooks in the Nile will
　　lament,
　　and those who spread nets on the
　　water will languish.
9　The workers in flax will be in despair,

and the carders and those at the loom
　　will grow pale.
10　Its weavers will be dismayed,
　　and all who work for wages will be
　　grieved.

11　The princes of Zoan are utterly foolish;
　　the wise counselors of Pharaoh give
　　stupid counsel.
How can you say to Pharaoh,
　　"I am one of the sages,
　　a descendant of ancient kings"?
12　Where now are your sages?
　　Let them tell you and make known
　　what the LORD of hosts has planned
　　against Egypt.
13　The princes of Zoan have become fools,
　　and the princes of Memphis are
　　deluded;
those who are the cornerstones of its
　　tribes
　　have led Egypt astray.
14　The LORD has poured into them[a]
　　a spirit of confusion;
and they have made Egypt stagger in all
　　its doings
　　as a drunkard staggers around in
　　vomit.
15　Neither head nor tail, palm branch or
　　reed,
　　will be able to do anything for Egypt.

16 On that day the Egyptians will be like
women, and tremble with fear before the hand
that the LORD of hosts raises against them.
17 And the land of Judah will become a terror
to the Egyptians; everyone to whom it is mentioned will fear because of the plan that the
LORD of hosts is planning against them.

Egypt, Assyria, and Israel Blessed

18 On that day there will be five cities in the
land of Egypt that speak the language of Canaan and swear allegiance to the LORD of
hosts. One of these will be called the City of
the Sun.

a Gk Compare Tg: Heb *it*

19 On that day there will be an altar to the LORD in the center of the land of Egypt, and a pillar to the LORD at its border. 20It will be a sign and a witness to the LORD of hosts in the land of Egypt; when they cry to the LORD because of oppressors, he will send them a savior, and will defend and deliver them. 21The LORD will make himself known to the Egyptians; and the Egyptians will know the LORD on that day, and will worship with sacrifice and burnt offering, and they will make vows to the LORD and perform them. 22The LORD will strike Egypt, striking and healing; they will return to the LORD, and he will listen to their supplications and heal them.

23 On that day there will be a highway from Egypt to Assyria, and the Assyrian will come into Egypt, and the Egyptian into Assyria, and the Egyptians will worship with the Assyrians.

24 On that day Israel will be the third with Egypt and Assyria, a blessing in the midst of the earth, 25whom the LORD of hosts has blessed, saying, "Blessed be Egypt my people, and Assyria the work of my hands, and Israel my heritage."

Isaiah Dramatizes the Conquest of Egypt and Ethiopia

20 In the year that the commander-in-chief, who was sent by King Sargon of Assyria, came to Ashdod and fought against it and took it— 2at that time the LORD had spoken to Isaiah son of Amoz, saying, "Go, and loose the sackcloth from your loins and take your sandals off your feet," and he had done so, walking naked and barefoot. 3Then the LORD said, "Just as my servant Isaiah has walked naked and barefoot for three years as a sign and a portent against Egypt and Ethiopia,a 4so shall the king of Assyria lead away the Egyptians as captives and the Ethiopiansb as exiles, both the young and the old, naked and barefoot, with buttocks uncovered, to the shame of Egypt. 5And they shall be dismayed and confounded because of Ethiopiaa

their hope and of Egypt their boast. 6In that day the inhabitants of this coastland will say, 'See, this is what has happened to those in whom we hoped and to whom we fled for help and deliverance from the king of Assyria! And we, how shall we escape?'"

Oracles concerning Babylon, Edom, and Arabia

21 The oracle concerning the wilderness of the sea.

As whirlwinds in the Negeb sweep on,
    it comes from the desert,
    from a terrible land.
2   A stern vision is told to me;
    the betrayer betrays,
    and the destroyer destroys.
Go up, O Elam,
    lay siege, O Media;
all the sighing she has caused
    I bring to an end.
3   Therefore my loins are filled with
            anguish;
    pangs have seized me,
    like the pangs of a woman in labor;
I am bowed down so that I cannot hear,
    I am dismayed so that I cannot see.
4   My mind reels, horror has appalled me;
    the twilight I longed for
    has been turned for me into
            trembling.
5   They prepare the table,
    they spread the rugs,
    they eat, they drink.
Rise up, commanders,
    oil the shield!
6   For thus the Lord said to me:
"Go, post a lookout,
    let him announce what he sees.
7   When he sees riders, horsemen in pairs,
        riders on donkeys, riders on camels,
    let him listen diligently,
    very diligently."
8   Then the watcherc called out:
"Upon a watchtower I stand, O Lord,

a Or Nubia; Heb Cush   b Or Nubians; Heb Cushites   c Q Ms: MT a lion

continually by day,
and at my post I am stationed
throughout the night.

9 Look, there they come, riders,
horsemen in pairs!"
Then he responded,
"Fallen, fallen is Babylon;
and all the images of her gods
lie shattered on the ground."

10 O my threshed and winnowed one,
what I have heard from the LORD of
hosts,
the God of Israel, I announce to you.

11 The oracle concerning Dumah.

One is calling to me from Seir,
"Sentinel, what of the night?
Sentinel, what of the night?"
12 The sentinel says:
"Morning comes, and also the night.
If you will inquire, inquire;
come back again."

13 The oracle concerning the desert plain.

In the scrub of the desert plain you will
lodge,
O caravans of Dedanites.
14 Bring water to the thirsty,
meet the fugitive with bread,
O inhabitants of the land of Tema.
15 For they have fled from the swords,
from the drawn sword,
from the bent bow,
and from the stress of battle.

16 For thus the Lord said to me: Within a
year, according to the years of a hired worker, all the glory of Kedar will come to an end;
17and the remaining bows of Kedar's warriors
will be few; for the LORD, the God of Israel,
has spoken.

A Warning of Destruction of Jerusalem

22 The oracle concerning the valley of
vision.

What do you mean that you have gone
up,
all of you, to the housetops,
2 you that are full of shoutings,
tumultuous city, exultant town?
Your slain are not slain by the sword,
nor are they dead in battle.
3 Your rulers have all fled together;
they were captured without the use of
a bow. *a*
All of you who were found were
captured,
though they had fled far away. *b*
4 Therefore I said:
Look away from me,
let me weep bitter tears;
do not try to comfort me
for the destruction of my beloved
people.

5 For the Lord GOD of hosts has a day
of tumult and trampling and
confusion
in the valley of vision,
a battering down of walls
and a cry for help to the mountains.
6 Elam bore the quiver
with chariots and cavalry, *c*
and Kir uncovered the shield.
7 Your choicest valleys were full of
chariots,
and the cavalry took their stand at the
gates.
8 He has taken away the covering of
Judah.

On that day you looked to the weapons of
the House of the Forest, 9and you saw that
there were many breaches in the city of David,
and you collected the waters of the lower pool.
10You counted the houses of Jerusalem, and
you broke down the houses to fortify the wall.
11You made a reservoir between the two walls
for the water of the old pool. But you did not
look to him who did it, or have regard for
him who planned it long ago.

a Or *without their bows*   *b* Gk Syr Vg: Heb *fled from far away*   *c* Meaning of Heb uncertain

12   In that day the Lord GOD of hosts
       called to weeping and mourning,
       to baldness and putting on sackcloth;
13   but instead there was joy and festivity,
       killing oxen and slaughtering sheep,
       eating meat and drinking wine.
       "Let us eat and drink,
       for tomorrow we die."
14   The LORD of hosts has revealed himself
       in my ears:
       Surely this iniquity will not be forgiven
         you until you die,
       says the Lord GOD of hosts.

Denunciation of Self-Seeking Officials

15 Thus says the Lord GOD of hosts: Come, go to this steward, to Shebna, who is master of the household, and say to him: 16What right do you have here? Who are your relatives here, that you have cut out a tomb here for yourself, cutting a tomb on the height, and carving a habitation for yourself in the rock? 17The LORD is about to hurl you away violently, my fellow. He will seize firm hold on you, 18whirl you round and round, and throw you like a ball into a wide land; there you shall die, and there your splendid chariots shall lie, O you disgrace to your master's house! 19I will thrust you from your office, and you will be pulled down from your post.

20 On that day I will call my servant Eliakim son of Hilkiah, 21and will clothe him with your robe and bind your sash on him. I will commit your authority to his hand, and he shall be a father to the inhabitants of Jerusalem and to the house of Judah. 22I will place on his shoulder the key of the house of David; he shall open, and no one shall shut; he shall shut, and no one shall open. 23I will fasten him like a peg in a secure place, and he will become a throne of honor to his ancestral house. 24And they will hang on him the whole weight of his ancestral house, the offspring and issue, every small vessel, from the cups to all the flagons. 25On that day, says the LORD of hosts, the peg that was fastened in a secure

place will give way; it will be cut down and fall, and the load that was on it will perish, for the LORD has spoken.

An Oracle concerning Tyre

23   The oracle concerning Tyre.

     Wail, O ships of Tarshish,
       for your fortress is destroyed.ᵃ
     When they came in from Cyprus
       they learned of it.
2   Be still, O inhabitants of the coast,
       O merchants of Sidon,
     your messengers crossed over the seaᵇ
3   and were on the mighty waters;
     your revenue was the grain of Shihor,
       the harvest of the Nile;
       you were the merchant of the nations.
4   Be ashamed, O Sidon, for the sea has
         spoken,
     the fortress of the sea, saying:
     "I have neither labored nor given birth,
       I have neither reared young men
       nor brought up young women."
5   When the report comes to Egypt,
       they will be in anguish over the report
         about Tyre.
6   Cross over to Tarshish—
       wail, O inhabitants of the coast!
7   Is this your exultant city
       whose origin is from days of old,
     whose feet carried her
       to settle far away?
8   Who has planned this
       against Tyre, the bestower of crowns,
     whose merchants were princes,
       whose traders were the honored of
         the earth?
9   The LORD of hosts has planned it—
       to defile the pride of all glory,
       to shame all the honored of the earth.
10   Cross over to your own land,
       O ships ofᶜ Tarshish;
       this is a harborᵈ no more.
11   He has stretched out his hand over the
         sea,

ᵃ Cn Compare verse 14: Heb *for it is destroyed, without houses*   ᵇ Q Ms: MT *crossing over the sea, they replenished you*
ᶜ Cn Compare Gk: Heb *like the Nile, daughter*   ᵈ Cn: Heb *restraint*

he has shaken the kingdoms;
  the LORD has given command
      concerning Canaan
  to destroy its fortresses.

12   He said:
  You will exult no longer,
    O oppressed virgin daughter Sidon;
  rise, cross over to Cyprus—
    even there you will have no rest.

13 Look at the land of the Chaldeans! This is the people; it was not Assyria. They destined Tyre for wild animals. They erected their siege towers, they tore down her palaces, they made her a ruin. *a*

14   Wail, O ships of Tarshish,
    for your fortress is destroyed.

15From that day Tyre will be forgotten for seventy years, the lifetime of one king. At the end of seventy years, it will happen to Tyre as in the song about the prostitute:

16   Take a harp,
    go about the city,
    you forgotten prostitute!
  Make sweet melody,
    sing many songs,
    that you may be remembered.

17At the end of seventy years, the LORD will visit Tyre, and she will return to her trade, and will prostitute herself with all the kingdoms of the world on the face of the earth. 18Her merchandise and her wages will be dedicated to the LORD; her profits*b* will not be stored or hoarded, but her merchandise will supply abundant food and fine clothing for those who live in the presence of the LORD.

Impending Judgment on the Earth

24 Now the LORD is about to lay waste
    the earth and make it desolate,
  and he will twist its surface and
    scatter its inhabitants.

2   And it shall be, as with the people, so
    with the priest;
  as with the slave, so with his master;
  as with the maid, so with her mistress;

as with the buyer, so with the seller;
  as with the lender, so with the
    borrower;
  as with the creditor, so with the debtor.

3   The earth shall be utterly laid waste and
    utterly despoiled;
  for the LORD has spoken this word.

4   The earth dries up and withers,
    the world languishes and withers;
  the heavens languish together with
    the earth.

5   The earth lies polluted
    under its inhabitants;
  for they have transgressed laws,
    violated the statutes,
    broken the everlasting covenant.

6   Therefore a curse devours the earth,
    and its inhabitants suffer for their guilt;
  therefore the inhabitants of the earth
    dwindled,
    and few people are left.

7   The wine dries up,
    the vine languishes,
    all the merry-hearted sigh.

8   The mirth of the timbrels is stilled,
    the noise of the jubilant has ceased,
    the mirth of the lyre is stilled.

9   No longer do they drink wine with
    singing;
  strong drink is bitter to those who
    drink it.

10   The city of chaos is broken down,
    every house is shut up so that no one
    can enter.

11   There is an outcry in the streets for lack
    of wine;
  all joy has reached its eventide;
  the gladness of the earth is banished.

12   Desolation is left in the city,
    the gates are battered into ruins.

13   For thus it shall be on the earth
    and among the nations,
  as when an olive tree is beaten,
    as at the gleaning when the grape
    harvest is ended.

a Meaning of Heb uncertain   *b* Heb *it*

14 They lift up their voices, they sing for
          joy;
      they shout from the west over the
          majesty of the LORD.
15 Therefore in the east give glory to the
          LORD;
      in the coastlands of the sea glorify the
          name of the LORD, the God of
          Israel.
16 From the ends of the earth we hear
          songs of praise,
      of glory to the Righteous One.
   But I say, I pine away,
      I pine away. Woe is me!
   For the treacherous deal treacherously,
      the treacherous deal very
          treacherously.

17 Terror, and the pit, and the snare
      are upon you, O inhabitant of the
          earth!
18 Whoever flees at the sound of the
          terror
      shall fall into the pit;
   and whoever climbs out of the pit
      shall be caught in the snare.
   For the windows of heaven are opened,
      and the foundations of the earth
          tremble.
19 The earth is utterly broken,
      the earth is torn asunder,
      the earth is violently shaken.
20 The earth staggers like a drunkard,
      it sways like a hut;
   its transgression lies heavy upon it,
      and it falls, and will not rise again.

21 On that day the LORD will punish
      the host of heaven in heaven,
      and on earth the kings of the earth.
22 They will be gathered together
      like prisoners in a pit;
   they will be shut up in a prison,
      and after many days they will be
          punished.
23 Then the moon will be abashed,
      and the sun ashamed;
   for the LORD of hosts will reign

on Mount Zion and in Jerusalem,
   and before his elders he will manifest his
      glory.

Praise for Deliverance from Oppression

25 O LORD, you are my God;
      I will exalt you, I will praise your
          name;
   for you have done wonderful things,
      plans formed of old, faithful and
          sure.
2 For you have made the city a heap,
      the fortified city a ruin;
   the palace of aliens is a city no more,
      it will never be rebuilt.
3 Therefore strong peoples will glorify
          you;
      cities of ruthless nations will fear you.
4 For you have been a refuge to the poor,
      a refuge to the needy in their distress,
      a shelter from the rainstorm and a
          shade from the heat.
   When the blast of the ruthless was like a
          winter rainstorm,
5   the noise of aliens like heat in a dry
          place,
   you subdued the heat with the shade of
          clouds;
      the song of the ruthless was stilled.

6 On this mountain the LORD of hosts
          will make for all peoples
      a feast of rich food, a feast of
          well-aged wines,
      of rich food filled with marrow, of
          well-aged wines strained clear.
7 And he will destroy on this mountain
      the shroud that is cast over all
          peoples,
      the sheet that is spread over all
          nations;
8   he will swallow up death forever.
   Then the Lord GOD will wipe away the
      tears from all faces,
   and the disgrace of his people he will
      take away from all the earth,
      for the LORD has spoken.
9 It will be said on that day,

Lo, this is our God; we have waited
> for him, so that he might save us.
This is the LORD for whom we have
> waited;
let us be glad and rejoice in his
> salvation.
10 For the hand of the LORD will rest on
> this mountain.

The Moabites shall be trodden down in
> their place
as straw is trodden down in a dung-
> pit.
11 Though they spread out their hands in
> the midst of it,
as swimmers spread out their hands
> to swim,
their pride will be laid low despite the
> struggle*a* of their hands.
12 The high fortifications of his walls will
> be brought down,
laid low, cast to the ground, even to
> the dust.

Judah's Song of Victory

26 On that day this song will be sung in
the land of Judah:
We have a strong city;
> he sets up victory
> like walls and bulwarks.
2 Open the gates,
> so that the righteous nation that
> keeps faith
> may enter in.
3 Those of steadfast mind you keep in
> peace—
> in peace because they trust in you.
4 Trust in the LORD forever,
> for in the LORD GOD*b*
> you have an everlasting rock.
5 For he has brought low
> the inhabitants of the height;
> the lofty city he lays low.
He lays it low to the ground,
> casts it to the dust.
6 The foot tramples it,

the feet of the poor,
> the steps of the needy.

7 The way of the righteous is level;
> O Just One, you make smooth the
> path of the righteous.
8 In the path of your judgments,
> O LORD, we wait for you;
your name and your renown
> are the soul's desire.
9 My soul yearns for you in the night,
> my spirit within me earnestly seeks you.
For when your judgments are in the
> earth,
> the inhabitants of the world learn
> righteousness.
10 If favor is shown to the wicked,
> they do not learn righteousness;
in the land of uprightness they deal
> perversely
> and do not see the majesty of the
> LORD.
11 O LORD, your hand is lifted up,
> but they do not see it.
Let them see your zeal for your people,
> and be ashamed.
Let the fire for your adversaries
> consume them.
12 O LORD, you will ordain peace for us,
> for indeed, all that we have done, you
> have done for us.
13 O LORD our God,
> other lords besides you have ruled
> over us,
> but we acknowledge your name alone.
14 The dead do not live;
> shades do not rise—
because you have punished and
> destroyed them,
> and wiped out all memory of them.
15 But you have increased the nation,
> O LORD,
> you have increased the nation; you are
> glorified;
> you have enlarged all the borders of
> the land.

a Meaning of Heb uncertain   *b* Heb *in Yah, the* LORD

16 O LORD, in distress they sought you,
      they poured out a prayer*a*
    when your chastening was on them.
17 Like a woman with child,
      who writhes and cries out in her
          pangs
      when she is near her time,
    so were we because of you, O LORD;
18   we were with child, we writhed,
      but we gave birth only to wind.
    We have won no victories on earth,
      and no one is born to inhabit the
          world.
19 Your dead shall live, their corpses*b* shall
          rise.
      O dwellers in the dust, awake and sing
          for joy!
    For your dew is a radiant dew,
      and the earth will give birth to those
          long dead.*c*

20 Come, my people, enter your chambers,
      and shut your doors behind you;
    hide yourselves for a little while
      until the wrath is past.
21 For the LORD comes out from his place
      to punish the inhabitants of the earth
          for their iniquity;
    the earth will disclose the blood shed on
          it,
      and will no longer cover its slain.

Israel's Redemption

27 On that day the LORD with his cruel
    and great and strong sword will pun-
ish Leviathan the fleeing serpent, Leviathan the
twisting serpent, and he will kill the dragon that
is in the sea.

2 On that day:
    A pleasant vineyard, sing about it!
3   I, the LORD, am its keeper;
      every moment I water it.
    I guard it night and day
      so that no one can harm it;
4   I have no wrath.

  If it gives me thorns and briers,
    I will march to battle against it.
    I will burn it up.
5 Or else let it cling to me for protection,
    let it make peace with me,
    let it make peace with me.

6 In days to come*d* Jacob shall take root,
    Israel shall blossom and put forth
        shoots,
      and fill the whole world with fruit.

7 Has he struck them down as he struck
        down those who struck them?
    Or have they been killed as their
        killers were killed?
8 By expulsion,*a* by exile you struggled
        against them;
      with his fierce blast he removed them
        in the day of the east wind.
9 Therefore by this the guilt of Jacob will
        be expiated,
      and this will be the full fruit of the
        removal of his sin:
    when he makes all the stones of the
        altars
      like chalkstones crushed to pieces,
      no sacred poles*e* or incense altars will
        remain standing.
10 For the fortified city is solitary,
      a habitation deserted and forsaken,
        like the wilderness;
    the calves graze there,
      there they lie down, and strip its
        branches.
11 When its boughs are dry, they are
        broken;
      women come and make a fire of
        them.
    For this is a people without
        understanding;
      therefore he that made them will not
        have compassion on them,
      he that formed them will show them
        no favor.

a Meaning of Heb uncertain   *b* Cn Compare Syr Tg: Heb *my corpse*   *c* Heb *to the shades*   *d* Heb *Those to come*
e Heb *Asherim*

12 On that day the LORD will thresh from the channel of the Euphrates to the Wadi of Egypt, and you will be gathered one by one, O people of Israel. 13And on that day a great trumpet will be blown, and those who were lost in the land of Assyria and those who were driven out to the land of Egypt will come and worship the LORD on the holy mountain at Jerusalem.

Judgment on Corrupt Rulers, Priests, and Prophets

28 Ah, the proud garland of the drunkards of Ephraim,
and the fading flower of its glorious beauty,
which is on the head of those bloated with rich food, of those overcome with wine!

2 See, the Lord has one who is mighty and strong;
like a storm of hail, a destroying tempest,
like a storm of mighty, overflowing waters;
with his hand he will hurl them down to the earth.

3 Trampled under foot will be
the proud garland of the drunkards of Ephraim.

4 And the fading flower of its glorious beauty,
which is on the head of those bloated with rich food,
will be like a first-ripe fig before the summer;
whoever sees it, eats it up
as soon as it comes to hand.

5 In that day the LORD of hosts will be a garland of glory,
and a diadem of beauty, to the remnant of his people;

6 and a spirit of justice to the one who sits in judgment,

and strength to those who turn back the battle at the gate.

7 These also reel with wine
and stagger with strong drink;
the priest and the prophet reel with strong drink,
they are confused with wine,
they stagger with strong drink;
they err in vision,
they stumble in giving judgment.

8 All tables are covered with filthy vomit;
no place is clean.

9 "Whom will he teach knowledge,
and to whom will he explain the message?
Those who are weaned from milk,
those taken from the breast?

10 For it is precept upon precept, precept upon precept,
line upon line, line upon line,
here a little, there a little."a

11 Truly, with stammering lip
and with alien tongue
he will speak to this people,

12 to whom he has said,
"This is rest;
give rest to the weary;
and this is repose";
yet they would not hear.

13 Therefore the word of the LORD will be to them,
"Precept upon precept, precept upon precept,
line upon line, line upon line,
here a little, there a little;"a
in order that they may go, and fall backward,
and be broken, and snared, and taken.

14 Therefore hear the word of the LORD,
you scoffers
who rule this people in Jerusalem.

a Meaning of Heb of this verse uncertain

15 Because you have said, "We have made a
          covenant with death,
     and with Sheol we have an agreement;
   when the overwhelming scourge passes
          through
     it will not come to us;
   for we have made lies our refuge,
     and in falsehood we have taken
          shelter";
16 therefore thus says the Lord GOD,
   See, I am laying in Zion a foundation
          stone,
     a tested stone,
   a precious cornerstone, a sure
          foundation:
   "One who trusts will not panic."
17 And I will make justice the line,
     and righteousness the plummet;
   hail will sweep away the refuge of lies,
     and waters will overwhelm the shelter.

18 Then your covenant with death will be
          annulled,
     and your agreement with Sheol will
          not stand;
   when the overwhelming scourge passes
          through
     you will be beaten down by it.
19 As often as it passes through, it will take
          you;
     for morning by morning it will pass
          through,
       by day and by night;
   and it will be sheer terror to understand
          the message.
20 For the bed is too short to stretch
          oneself on it,
     and the covering too narrow to wrap
          oneself in it.
21 For the LORD will rise up as on Mount
          Perazim,
     he will rage as in the valley of Gibeon
   to do his deed—strange is his deed!—
     and to work his work—alien is his
          work!
22 Now therefore do not scoff,
     or your bonds will be made stronger;

for I have heard a decree of destruction
     from the Lord GOD of hosts upon
          the whole land.

23 Listen, and hear my voice;
     Pay attention, and hear my speech.
24 Do those who plow for sowing plow
          continually?
     Do they continually open and harrow
          their ground?
25 When they have leveled its surface,
     do they not scatter dill, sow cummin,
   and plant wheat in rows
     and barley in its proper place,
     and spelt as the border?
26 For they are well instructed;
     their God teaches them.

27 Dill is not threshed with a threshing
          sledge,
     nor is a cart wheel rolled over
          cummin;
   but dill is beaten out with a stick,
     and cummin with a rod.
28 Grain is crushed for bread,
     but one does not thresh it forever;
   one drives the cart wheel and horses
          over it,
     but does not pulverize it.
29 This also comes from the LORD of
          hosts;
     he is wonderful in counsel,
     and excellent in wisdom.

The Siege of Jerusalem

29 Ah, Ariel, Ariel,
     the city where David encamped!
   Add year to year;
     let the festivals run their round.
2 Yet I will distress Ariel,
     and there shall be moaning and
          lamentation,
     and Jerusalem*a* shall be to me like an
          Ariel.*b*
3 And like David*c* I will encamp against
          you;

a Heb *she*   b Probable meaning, *altar hearth*; compare Ezek 43.15   c Gk: Meaning of Heb uncertain

I will besiege you with towers
and raise siegeworks against you.
4 Then deep from the earth you shall
speak,
from low in the dust your words shall
come;
your voice shall come from the ground
like the voice of a ghost,
and your speech shall whisper out of
the dust.

5 But the multitude of your foes*a* shall be
like small dust,
and the multitude of tyrants like
flying chaff.
And in an instant, suddenly,
6 you will be visited by the LORD of
hosts
with thunder and earthquake and great
noise,
with whirlwind and tempest, and the
flame of a devouring fire.
7 And the multitude of all the nations that
fight against Ariel,
all that fight against her and her
stronghold, and who distress her,
shall be like a dream, a vision of the
night.
8 Just as when a hungry person dreams of
eating
and wakes up still hungry,
or a thirsty person dreams of drinking
and wakes up faint, still thirsty,
so shall the multitude of all the nations
be
that fight against Mount Zion.

9 Stupefy yourselves and be in a stupor,
blind yourselves and be blind!
Be drunk, but not from wine;
stagger, but not from strong drink!
10 For the LORD has poured out upon you
a spirit of deep sleep;
he has closed your eyes, you prophets,
and covered your heads, you seers.
11 The vision of all this has become for

a Cn: Heb strangers

you like the words of a sealed document. If it
is given to those who can read, with the command, "Read this," they say, "We cannot, for
it is sealed." 12And if it is given to those who
cannot read, saying, "Read this," they say, "We
cannot read."

13 The Lord said:
Because these people draw near with
their mouths
and honor me with their lips,
while their hearts are far from me,
and their worship of me is a human
commandment learned by rote;
14 so I will again do
amazing things with this people,
shocking and amazing.
The wisdom of their wise shall perish,
and the discernment of the
discerning shall be hidden.

15 Ha! You who hide a plan too deep for
the LORD,
whose deeds are in the dark,
and who say, "Who sees us? Who
knows us?"
16 You turn things upside down!
Shall the potter be regarded as the
clay?
Shall the thing made say of its maker,
"He did not make me";
or the thing formed say of the one who
formed it,
"He has no understanding"?

Hope for the Future
17 Shall not Lebanon in a very little while
become a fruitful field,
and the fruitful field be regarded as a
forest?
18 On that day the deaf shall hear
the words of a scroll,
and out of their gloom and darkness
the eyes of the blind shall see.
19 The meek shall obtain fresh joy in the
LORD,

and the neediest people shall exult in
   the Holy One of Israel.
20 For the tyrant shall be no more,
   and the scoffer shall cease to be;
   all those alert to do evil shall be cut
      off—
21 those who cause a person to lose a
      lawsuit,
   who set a trap for the arbiter in the
      gate,
   and without grounds deny justice to
      the one in the right.

22 Therefore thus says the LORD, who redeemed Abraham, concerning the house of Jacob:
   No longer shall Jacob be ashamed,
      no longer shall his face grow pale.
23 For when he sees his children,
      the work of my hands, in his midst,
      they will sanctify my name;
   they will sanctify the Holy One of
      Jacob,
   and will stand in awe of the God of
      Israel.
24 And those who err in spirit will come to
      understanding,
   and those who grumble will accept
      instruction.

The Futility of Reliance on Egypt

30 Oh, rebellious children, says the
      LORD,
   who carry out a plan, but not mine;
   who make an alliance, but against my
      will,
      adding sin to sin;
2 who set out to go down to Egypt
      without asking for my counsel,
   to take refuge in the protection of
      Pharaoh,
   and to seek shelter in the shadow of
      Egypt;
3 Therefore the protection of Pharaoh
      shall become your shame,

and the shelter in the shadow of
   Egypt your humiliation.
4 For though his officials are at Zoan
   and his envoys reach Hanes,
5 everyone comes to shame
      through a people that cannot profit
         them,
   that brings neither help nor profit,
      but shame and disgrace.

6 An oracle concerning the animals of the
Negeb.

   Through a land of trouble and distress,
      of lioness and roaring[a] lion,
      of viper and flying serpent,
   they carry their riches on the backs of
         donkeys,
      and their treasures on the humps of
         camels,
      to a people that cannot profit them.
7 For Egypt's help is worthless and empty,
      therefore I have called her,
      "Rahab who sits still."[b]

A Rebellious People

8 Go now, write it before them on a
      tablet,
   and inscribe it in a book,
   so that it may be for the time to come
      as a witness forever.
9 For they are a rebellious people,
      faithless children,
   children who will not hear
      the instruction of the LORD;
10 who say to the seers, "Do not see";
      and to the prophets, "Do not
         prophesy to us what is right;
   speak to us smooth things,
      prophesy illusions,
11 leave the way, turn aside from the path,
      let us hear no more about the Holy
         One of Israel."
12 Therefore thus says the Holy One of
      Israel:
   Because you reject this word,

a Cn: Heb *from them*   b Meaning of Heb uncertain

and put your trust in oppression and
    deceit,
and rely on them;
13   therefore this iniquity shall become for
    you
    like a break in a high wall, bulging
       out, and about to collapse,
    whose crash comes suddenly, in an
       instant;
14   its breaking is like that of a potter's
    vessel
    that is smashed so ruthlessly
   that among its fragments not a sherd is
    found
    for taking fire from the hearth,
    or dipping water out of the cistern.

15   For thus said the Lord GOD, the Holy
    One of Israel:
    In returning and rest you shall be saved;
    in quietness and in trust shall be your
       strength.
    But you refused 16and said,
    "No! We will flee upon horses"—
    therefore you shall flee!
    and, "We will ride upon swift steeds"—
    therefore your pursuers shall be swift!
17   A thousand shall flee at the threat of
    one,
    at the threat of five you shall flee,
   until you are left
    like a flagstaff on the top of a
       mountain,
    like a signal on a hill.

God's Promise to Zion

18   Therefore the LORD waits to be gracious
    to you;
    therefore he will rise up to show
       mercy to you.
    For the LORD is a God of justice;
    blessed are all those who wait for
       him.
19 Truly, O people in Zion, inhabitants of
Jerusalem, you shall weep no more. He will
surely be gracious to you at the sound of your

cry; when he hears it, he will answer you.
20Though the Lord may give you the bread of
adversity and the water of affliction, yet your
Teacher will not hide himself any more, but
your eyes shall see your Teacher. 21And when
you turn to the right or when you turn to the
left, your ears shall hear a word behind you, saying, "This is the way; walk in it." 22Then you will
defile your silver-covered idols and your gold-
plated images. You will scatter them like filthy
rags; you will say to them, "Away with you!"

23 He will give rain for the seed with which
you sow the ground, and grain, the produce of
the ground, which will be rich and plenteous.
On that day your cattle will graze in broad
pastures; 24and the oxen and donkeys that till
the ground will eat silage, which has been winnowed with shovel and fork. 25On every lofty
mountain and every high hill there will be
brooks running with water—on a day of the
great slaughter, when the towers fall. 26More-
over the light of the moon will be like the
light of the sun, and the light of the sun will
be sevenfold, like the light of seven days, on
the day when the LORD binds up the injuries
of his people, and heals the wounds inflicted
by his blow.

Judgment on Assyria

27   See, the name of the LORD comes from
    far away,
    burning with his anger, and in thick
       rising smoke;a
   his lips are full of indignation,
    and his tongue is like a devouring fire;
28   his breath is like an overflowing stream
    that reaches up to the neck—
   to sift the nations with the sieve of
       destruction,
    and to place on the jaws of the
       peoples a bridle that leads them
       astray.

29 You shall have a song as in the night
when a holy festival is kept; and gladness of
heart, as when one sets out to the sound of the

---

a Meaning of Heb uncertain

flute to go to the mountain of the LORD, to the
Rock of Israel. 30And the LORD will cause his
majestic voice to be heard and the descending
blow of his arm to be seen, in furious anger and
a flame of devouring fire, with a cloudburst and
tempest and hailstones. 31The Assyrian will be
terror-stricken at the voice of the LORD, when
he strikes with his rod. 32And every stroke of
the staff of punishment that the LORD lays
upon him will be to the sound of timbrels and
lyres; battling with brandished arm he will fight
with him. 33For his burning place*a* has long
been prepared; truly it is made ready for the
king,*b* its pyre made deep and wide, with fire and
wood in abundance; the breath of the LORD,
like a stream of sulfur, kindles it.

Alliance with Egypt Is Futile

31 Alas for those who go down to
      Egypt for help
   and who rely on horses,
who trust in chariots because they are
         many
   and in horsemen because they are
         very strong,
but do not look to the Holy One of Israel
   or consult the LORD!
2 Yet he too is wise and brings disaster;
      he does not call back his words,
   but will rise against the house of the
         evildoers,
      and against the helpers of those who
         work iniquity.
3 The Egyptians are human, and not God;
      their horses are flesh, and not spirit.
   When the LORD stretches out his hand,
      the helper will stumble, and the one
         helped will fall,
      and they will all perish together.

4 For thus the LORD said to me,
      As a lion or a young lion growls over its
         prey,
      and—when a band of shepherds is
         called out against it—
   is not terrified by their shouting

or daunted at their noise,
   so the LORD of hosts will come down
      to fight upon Mount Zion and upon
         its hill.
5 Like birds hovering overhead, so the
         LORD of hosts
      will protect Jerusalem;
   he will protect and deliver it,
      he will spare and rescue it.

6 Turn back to him whom you*c* have deeply
betrayed, O people of Israel. 7For on that day
all of you shall throw away your idols of silver
and idols of gold, which your hands have sin-
fully made for you.
8 "Then the Assyrian shall fall by a sword,
         not of mortals;
      and a sword, not of humans, shall
         devour him;
   he shall flee from the sword,
      and his young men shall be put to
         forced labor.
9 His rock shall pass away in terror,
      and his officers desert the standard in
         panic,"
   says the LORD, whose fire is in Zion,
      and whose furnace is in Jerusalem.

Government with Justice Predicted

32 See, a king will reign in
      righteousness,
   and princes will rule with justice.
2 Each will be like a hiding place from the
         wind,
      a covert from the tempest,
   like streams of water in a dry place,
      like the shade of a great rock in a
         weary land.
3 Then the eyes of those who have sight
         will not be closed,
      and the ears of those who have
         hearing will listen.
4 The minds of the rash will have good
         judgment,
      and the tongues of stammerers will
         speak readily and distinctly.

---

a Or *Topheth*   *b* Or *Molech*   *c* Heb *they*

5 A fool will no longer be called noble,
     nor a villain said to be honorable.
6 For fools speak folly,
     and their minds plot iniquity:
   to practice ungodliness,
     to utter error concerning the LORD,
   to leave the craving of the hungry
       unsatisfied,
     and to deprive the thirsty of drink.
7 The villainies of villains are evil;
     they devise wicked devices
   to ruin the poor with lying words,
     even when the plea of the needy is
       right.
8 But those who are noble plan noble
       things,
     and by noble things they stand.

Complacent Women Warned of Disaster

9 Rise up, you women who are at ease,
       hear my voice;
     you complacent daughters, listen to
       my speech.
10 In little more than a year
       you will shudder, you complacent
         ones;
     for the vintage will fail,
       the fruit harvest will not come.
11 Tremble, you women who are at ease,
       shudder, you complacent ones;
     strip, and make yourselves bare,
       and put sackcloth on your loins.
12 Beat your breasts for the pleasant fields,
       for the fruitful vine,
13 for the soil of my people
       growing up in thorns and briers;
     yes, for all the joyous houses
       in the jubilant city.
14 For the palace will be forsaken,
       the populous city deserted;
     the hill and the watchtower
       will become dens forever,
     the joy of wild asses,
       a pasture for flocks;
15 until a spirit from on high is poured out
       on us,

and the wilderness becomes a fruitful
     field,
   and the fruitful field is deemed a
     forest.

The Peace of God's Reign

16 Then justice will dwell in the wilderness,
     and righteousness abide in the fruitful
       field.
17 The effect of righteousness will be
       peace,
     and the result of righteousness,
       quietness and trust forever.
18 My people will abide in a peaceful
       habitation,
     in secure dwellings, and in quiet
       resting places.
19 The forest will disappear completely,*a*
     and the city will be utterly laid low.
20 Happy will you be who sow beside
       every stream,
     who let the ox and the donkey range
       freely.

A Prophecy of Deliverance from Foes

33 Ah, you destroyer,
     who yourself have not been
         destroyed;
   you treacherous one,
       with whom no one has dealt
         treacherously!
   When you have ceased to destroy,
       you will be destroyed;
   and when you have stopped dealing
         treacherously,
       you will be dealt with treacherously.

2 O LORD, be gracious to us; we wait for
       you.
     Be our arm every morning,
       our salvation in the time of trouble.
3 At the sound of tumult, peoples fled;
     before your majesty, nations scattered.
4 Spoil was gathered as the caterpillar
       gathers;
     as locusts leap, they leaped*b* upon it.

a Cn: Heb *And it will hail when the forest comes down*   *b* Meaning of Heb uncertain

5 The LORD is exalted, he dwells on high;
    he filled Zion with justice and
      righteousness;
6 he will be the stability of your times,
    abundance of salvation, wisdom, and
      knowledge;
  the fear of the LORD is Zion's
    treasure.ᵃ

7 Listen! the valiantᵇ cry in the streets;
    the envoys of peace weep bitterly.
8 The highways are deserted,
    travelers have quit the road.
  The treaty is broken,
    its oathsᶜ are despised,
    its obligationᵈ is disregarded.
9 The land mourns and languishes;
    Lebanon is confounded and withers
      away;
  Sharon is like a desert;
    and Bashan and Carmel shake off
      their leaves.

10 "Now I will arise," says the LORD,
    "now I will lift myself up;
    now I will be exalted.
11 You conceive chaff, you bring forth
      stubble;
    your breath is a fire that will consume
      you.
12 And the peoples will be as if burned to
      lime,
    like thorns cut down, that are burned
      in the fire."

13 Hear, you who are far away, what I have
      done;
    and you who are near, acknowledge
      my might.
14 The sinners in Zion are afraid;
    trembling has seized the godless:
  "Who among us can live with the
      devouring fire?
  Who among us can live with
    everlasting flames?"

15 Those who walk righteously and speak
      uprightly,
    who despise the gain of oppression,
  who wave away a bribe instead of
      accepting it,
    who stop their ears from hearing of
      bloodshed
    and shut their eyes from looking on
      evil,
16 they will live on the heights;
    their refuge will be the fortresses of
      rocks;
    their food will be supplied, their water
      assured.

The Land of the Majestic King

17 Your eyes will see the king in his beauty;
    they will behold a land that stretches
      far away.
18 Your mind will muse on the terror:
    "Where is the one who counted?
  Where is the one who weighed the
      tribute?
  Where is the one who counted the
      towers?"
19 No longer will you see the insolent
      people,
    the people of an obscure speech that
      you cannot comprehend,
    stammering in a language that you
      cannot understand.
20 Look on Zion, the city of our appointed
      festivals!
    Your eyes will see Jerusalem,
    a quiet habitation, an immovable tent,
  whose stakes will never be pulled up,
    and none of whose ropes will be
      broken.
21 But there the LORD in majesty will be
      for us
    a place of broad rivers and streams,
  where no galley with oars can go,
    nor stately ship can pass.
22 For the LORD is our judge, the LORD is
      our ruler,
    the LORD is our king; he will save us.

ᵃ Heb *his treasure*; meaning of Heb uncertain   ᵇ Meaning of Heb uncertain   ᶜ Q Ms: MT *cities*   ᵈ Or *everyone*

23 Your rigging hangs loose;
   it cannot hold the mast firm in its
      place,
   or keep the sail spread out.

Then prey and spoil in abundance will
   be divided;
   even the lame will fall to plundering.
24 And no inhabitant will say, "I am sick";
   the people who live there will be
      forgiven their iniquity.

Judgment on the Nations

34 Draw near, O nations, to hear;
   O peoples, give heed!
Let the earth hear, and all that fills it;
   the world, and all that comes from it.
2 For the LORD is enraged against all the
      nations,
   and furious against all their hordes;
   he has doomed them, has given them
      over for slaughter.
3 Their slain shall be cast out,
   and the stench of their corpses shall
      rise;
   the mountains shall flow with their
      blood.
4 All the host of heaven shall rot away,
   and the skies roll up like a scroll.
All their host shall wither
   like a leaf withering on a vine,
   or fruit withering on a fig tree.

5 When my sword has drunk its fill in the
      heavens,
   lo, it will descend upon Edom,
   upon the people I have doomed to
      judgment.
6 The LORD has a sword; it is sated with
      blood,
   it is gorged with fat,
   with the blood of lambs and goats,
   with the fat of the kidneys of rams.
For the LORD has a sacrifice in Bozrah,
   a great slaughter in the land of Edom.
7 Wild oxen shall fall with them,

and young steers with the mighty
      bulls.
Their land shall be soaked with blood,
   and their soil made rich with fat.

8 For the LORD has a day of vengeance,
   a year of vindication by Zion's cause. [a]
9 And the streams of Edom [b] shall be
      turned into pitch,
   and her soil into sulfur;
   her land shall become burning pitch.
10 Night and day it shall not be quenched;
   its smoke shall go up forever.
From generation to generation it shall
      lie waste;
   no one shall pass through it forever
      and ever.
11 But the hawk [c] and the hedgehog [c] shall
      possess it;
   the owl [c] and the raven shall live in it.
He shall stretch the line of confusion
      over it,
   and the plummet of chaos over [d] its
      nobles.
12 They shall name it No Kingdom There,
   and all its princes shall be nothing.
13 Thorns shall grow over its strongholds,
   nettles and thistles in its fortresses.
It shall be the haunt of jackals,
   an abode for ostriches.
14 Wildcats shall meet with hyenas,
   goat-demons shall call to each other;
there too Lilith shall repose,
   and find a place to rest.
15 There shall the owl nest
   and lay and hatch and brood in its
      shadow;
there too the buzzards shall gather,
   each one with its mate.
16 Seek and read from the book of the
      LORD:
   Not one of these shall be missing;
   none shall be without its mate.
For the mouth of the LORD has
      commanded,
   and his spirit has gathered them.

a Or of recompense by Zion's defender   b Heb her streams   c Identification uncertain   d Heb lacks over

17 He has cast the lot for them,
         his hand has portioned it out to them
              with the line;
     they shall possess it forever,
         from generation to generation they
              shall live in it.

The Return of the Redeemed to Zion

35 The wilderness and the dry land
         shall be glad,
     the desert shall rejoice and blossom;
     like the crocus ²it shall blossom
         abundantly,
     and rejoice with joy and singing.
     The glory of Lebanon shall be given to
         it,
         the majesty of Carmel and Sharon.
     They shall see the glory of the LORD,
         the majesty of our God.

3   Strengthen the weak hands,
         and make firm the feeble knees.
4   Say to those who are of a fearful heart,
         "Be strong, do not fear!
     Here is your God.
     He will come with vengeance,
     with terrible recompense.
     He will come and save you."

5   Then the eyes of the blind shall be
         opened,
         and the ears of the deaf unstopped;
6   then the lame shall leap like a deer,
         and the tongue of the speechless sing
              for joy.
     For waters shall break forth in the
         wilderness,
         and streams in the desert;
7   the burning sand shall become a pool,
         and the thirsty ground springs of
              water;
     the haunt of jackals shall become a
         swamp,ᵃ
         the grass shall become reeds and
              rushes.

8   A highway shall be there,
         and it shall be called the Holy Way;
     the unclean shall not travel on it,ᵇ
         but it shall be for God's people;ᶜ
         no traveler, not even fools, shall go
              astray.
9   No lion shall be there,
         nor shall any ravenous beast come up
              on it;
     they shall not be found there,
         but the redeemed shall walk there.
10 And the ransomed of the LORD shall
         return,
         and come to Zion with singing;
     everlasting joy shall be upon their heads;
         they shall obtain joy and gladness,
         and sorrow and sighing shall flee
              away.

Sennacherib Threatens Jerusalem

36 In the fourteenth year of King Hezekiah, King Sennacherib of Assyria came up against all the fortified cities of Judah and captured them. ²The king of Assyria sent the Rabshakeh from Lachish to King Hezekiah at Jerusalem, with a great army. He stood by the conduit of the upper pool on the highway to the Fuller's Field. ³And there came out to him Eliakim son of Hilkiah, who was in charge of the palace, and Shebna the secretary, and Joah son of Asaph, the recorder.

4 The Rabshakeh said to them, "Say to Hezekiah: Thus says the great king, the king of Assyria: On what do you base this confidence of yours? ⁵Do you think that mere words are strategy and power for war? On whom do you now rely, that you have rebelled against me? ⁶See, you are relying on Egypt, that broken reed of a staff, which will pierce the hand of anyone who leans on it. Such is Pharaoh king of Egypt to all who rely on him. ⁷But if you say to me, 'We rely on the LORD our God,' is it not he whose high places and altars Hezekiah has removed, saying to Judah and to Jerusalem, 'You shall worship before this altar'? ⁸Come now, make a wager with my master

a Cn: Heb *in the haunt of jackals is her resting place*   *b* Or *pass it by*   *c* Cn: Heb *for them* the king of Assyria: I will give you two thousand horses, if you are able on your part to set riders on them. 9How then can you repulse a single captain among the least of my master's servants, when you rely on Egypt for chariots and for horsemen? 10Moreover, is it without the LORD that I have come up against this land to destroy it? The LORD said to me, Go up against this land, and destroy it."

11 Then Eliakim, Shebna, and Joah said to the Rabshakeh, "Please speak to your servants in Aramaic, for we understand it; do not speak to us in the language of Judah within the hearing of the people who are on the wall." 12But the Rabshakeh said, "Has my master sent me to speak these words to your master and to you, and not to the people sitting on the wall, who are doomed with you to eat their own dung and drink their own urine?"

13 Then the Rabshakeh stood and called out in a loud voice in the language of Judah, "Hear the words of the great king, the king of Assyria! 14Thus says the king: 'Do not let Hezekiah deceive you, for he will not be able to deliver you. 15Do not let Hezekiah make you rely on the LORD by saying, The LORD will surely deliver us; this city will not be given into the hand of the king of Assyria.' 16Do not listen to Hezekiah; for thus says the king of Assyria: 'Make your peace with me and come out to me; then every one of you will eat from your own vine and your own fig tree and drink water from your own cistern, 17until I come and take you away to a land like your own land, a land of grain and wine, a land of bread and vineyards. 18Do not let Hezekiah mislead you by saying, The LORD will save us. Has any of the gods of the nations saved their land out of the hand of the king of Assyria? 19Where are the gods of Hamath and Arpad? Where are the gods of Sepharvaim? Have they delivered Samaria out of my hand? 20Who among all the gods of these countries have saved their countries out of my hand, that the LORD should save Jerusalem out of my hand?'"

21 But they were silent and answered him not a word, for the king's command was, "Do not answer him." 22Then Eliakim son of Hilkiah, who was in charge of the palace, and Shebna the secretary, and Joah son of Asaph, the recorder, came to Hezekiah with their clothes torn, and told him the words of the Rabshakeh.

Hezekiah Consults Isaiah

37 When King Hezekiah heard it, he tore his clothes, covered himself with sackcloth, and went into the house of the LORD. 2And he sent Eliakim, who was in charge of the palace, and Shebna the secretary, and the senior priests, covered with sackcloth, to the prophet Isaiah son of Amoz. 3They said to him, "Thus says Hezekiah, This day is a day of distress, of rebuke, and of disgrace; children have come to the birth, and there is no strength to bring them forth. 4It may be that the LORD your God heard the words of the Rabshakeh, whom his master the king of Assyria has sent to mock the living God, and will rebuke the words that the LORD your God has heard; therefore lift up your prayer for the remnant that is left."

5 When the servants of King Hezekiah came to Isaiah, 6Isaiah said to them, "Say to your master, 'Thus says the LORD: Do not be afraid because of the words that you have heard, with which the servants of the king of Assyria have reviled me. 7I myself will put a spirit in him, so that he shall hear a rumor, and return to his own land; I will cause him to fall by the sword in his own land.'"

8 The Rabshakeh returned, and found the king of Assyria fighting against Libnah; for he had heard that the king had left Lachish. 9Now the king*a* heard concerning King Tirhakah of Ethiopia,*b* "He has set out to fight against you." When he heard it, he sent messengers to Hezekiah, saying, 10"Thus shall you speak to King Hezekiah of Judah: Do not let your God on whom you rely deceive you by promising that Jerusalem will not be given into the hand of the king of Assyria. 11See, you have heard what the kings of Assyria have done to all

---

a Heb *he*   *b* Or *Nubia*; Heb *Cush*

lands, destroying them utterly. Shall you be delivered? [12]Have the gods of the nations delivered them, the nations that my predecessors destroyed, Gozan, Haran, Rezeph, and the people of Eden who were in Telassar? [13]Where is the king of Hamath, the king of Arpad, the king of the city of Sepharvaim, the king of Hena, or the king of Ivvah?"

Hezekiah's Prayer

14 Hezekiah received the letter from the hand of the messengers and read it; then Hezekiah went up to the house of the LORD and spread it before the LORD. [15]And Hezekiah prayed to the LORD, saying: [16]"O LORD of hosts, God of Israel, who are enthroned above the cherubim, you are God, you alone, of all the kingdoms of the earth; you have made heaven and earth. [17]Incline your ear, O LORD, and hear; open your eyes, O LORD, and see; hear all the words of Sennacherib, which he has sent to mock the living God. [18]Truly, O LORD, the kings of Assyria have laid waste all the nations and their lands, [19]and have hurled their gods into the fire, though they were no gods, but the work of human hands—wood and stone—and so they were destroyed. [20]So now, O LORD our God, save us from his hand, so that all the kingdoms of the earth may know that you alone are the LORD."

21 Then Isaiah son of Amoz sent to Hezekiah, saying: "Thus says the LORD, the God of Israel: Because you have prayed to me concerning King Sennacherib of Assyria, [22]this is the word that the LORD has spoken concerning him:

She despises you, she scorns you—
    virgin daughter Zion;
she tosses her head—behind your back,
    daughter Jerusalem.

23   "Whom have you mocked and reviled?
    Against whom have you raised your
        voice
    and haughtily lifted your eyes?
    Against the Holy One of Israel!

24   By your servants you have mocked the
        Lord,
    and you have said, 'With my many
        chariots
    I have gone up the heights of the
        mountains,
        to the far recesses of Lebanon;
    I felled its tallest cedars,
        its choicest cypresses;
    I came to its remotest height,
        its densest forest.
25   I dug wells
        and drank waters,
    I dried up with the sole of my foot
        all the streams of Egypt.'

26   "Have you not heard
        that I determined it long ago?
    I planned from days of old
        what now I bring to pass,
    that you should make fortified cities
        crash into heaps of ruins,
27   while their inhabitants, shorn of strength,
        are dismayed and confounded;
    they have become like plants of the field
        and like tender grass,
    like grass on the housetops,
        blighted[a] before it is grown.

28   "I know your rising up[b] and your sitting
        down,
    your going out and coming in,
        and your raging against me.
29   Because you have raged against me
        and your arrogance has come to my
            ears,
    I will put my hook in your nose
        and my bit in your mouth;
    I will turn you back on the way
        by which you came.

30 "And this shall be the sign for you: This year eat what grows of itself, and in the second year what springs from that; then in the third year sow, reap, plant vineyards, and eat their fruit. [31]The surviving remnant of the

---

a With 2 Kings 19.26: Heb *field*   *b* Q Ms Gk: MT lacks *your rising up* house of Judah shall again take root downward, and bear fruit upward; ³²for from Jerusalem a remnant shall go out, and from Mount Zion a band of survivors. The zeal of the LORD of hosts will do this.

33 "Therefore thus says the LORD concerning the king of Assyria: He shall not come into this city, shoot an arrow there, come before it with a shield, or cast up a siege ramp against it. ³⁴By the way that he came, by the same he shall return; he shall not come into this city, says the LORD. ³⁵For I will defend this city to save it, for my own sake and for the sake of my servant David."

Sennacherib's Defeat and Death

36 Then the angel of the LORD set out and struck down one hundred eighty-five thousand in the camp of the Assyrians; when morning dawned, they were all dead bodies. ³⁷Then King Sennacherib of Assyria left, went home, and lived at Nineveh. ³⁸As he was worshiping in the house of his god Nisroch, his sons Adrammelech and Sharezer killed him with the sword, and they escaped into the land of Ararat. His son Esar-haddon succeeded him.

Hezekiah's Illness

38 In those days Hezekiah became sick and was at the point of death. The prophet Isaiah son of Amoz came to him, and said to him, "Thus says the LORD: Set your house in order, for you shall die; you shall not recover." ²Then Hezekiah turned his face to the wall, and prayed to the LORD: ³"Remember now, O LORD, I implore you, how I have walked before you in faithfulness with a whole heart, and have done what is good in your sight." And Hezekiah wept bitterly.

4 Then the word of the LORD came to Isaiah: ⁵"Go and say to Hezekiah, Thus says the LORD, the God of your ancestor David: I have heard your prayer, I have seen your tears; I will add fifteen years to your life. ⁶I will deliver you and this city out of the hand of the king of Assyria, and defend this city.

7 "This is the sign to you from the LORD, that the LORD will do this thing that he has promised: ⁸See, I will make the shadow cast by the declining sun on the dial of Ahaz turn back ten steps." So the sun turned back on the dial the ten steps by which it had declined. ᵃ

9 A writing of King Hezekiah of Judah, after he had been sick and had recovered from his sickness:

10   I said: In the noontide of my days
      I must depart;
    I am consigned to the gates of Sheol
      for the rest of my years.
11   I said, I shall not see the LORD
      in the land of the living;
    I shall look upon mortals no more
      among the inhabitants of the world.
12   My dwelling is plucked up and removed
      from me
      like a shepherd's tent;
    like a weaver I have rolled up my life;
      he cuts me off from the loom;
    from day to night you bring me to an
      end;ᵃ
13   I cry for helpᵇ until morning;
    like a lion he breaks all my bones;
      from day to night you bring me to an
      end.ᵃ

14   Like a swallow or a craneᵃ I clamor,
      I moan like a dove.
    My eyes are weary with looking upward.
      O Lord, I am oppressed; be my
      security!
15   But what can I say? For he has spoken
      to me,
      and he himself has done it.
    All my sleep has fledᶜ
      because of the bitterness of my soul.

16   O Lord, by these things people live,
      and in all these is the life of my
      spirit.ᵃ
      Oh, restore me to health and make
      me live!

ᵃ Meaning of Heb uncertain   ᵇ Cn: Meaning of Heb uncertain   ᶜ Cn Compare Syr: Heb *I will walk slowly all my years*

17 Surely it was for my welfare
        that I had great bitterness;
    but you have held back*a* my life
        from the pit of destruction,
    for you have cast all my sins
        behind your back.
18 For Sheol cannot thank you,
        death cannot praise you;
    those who go down to the Pit cannot
            hope
        for your faithfulness.
19 The living, the living, they thank you,
        as I do this day;
    fathers make known to children
        your faithfulness.

20 The LORD will save me,
        and we will sing to stringed
            instruments*b*
    all the days of our lives,
        at the house of the LORD.

21 Now Isaiah had said, "Let them take a
lump of figs, and apply it to the boil, so that
he may recover." 22Hezekiah also had said,
"What is the sign that I shall go up to the
house of the LORD?"

Envoys from Babylon Welcomed

39 At that time King Merodach-baladan
son of Baladan of Babylon sent en-
voys with letters and a present to Hezekiah, for
he heard that he had been sick and had recovered. 2Hezekiah welcomed them; he
showed them his treasure house, the silver,
the gold, the spices, the precious oil, his whole
armory, all that was found in his storehouses.
There was nothing in his house or in all his
realm that Hezekiah did not show them. 3Then
the prophet Isaiah came to King Hezekiah
and said to him, "What did these men say?
From where did they come to you?" Hezekiah answered, "They have come to me from a
far country, from Babylon." 4He said, "What
have they seen in your house?" Hezekiah answered, "They have seen all that is in my house;

there is nothing in my storehouses that I did
not show them."

5 Then Isaiah said to Hezekiah, "Hear the
word of the LORD of hosts: 6Days are coming when all that is in your house, and that
which your ancestors have stored up until this
day, shall be carried to Babylon; nothing shall
be left, says the LORD. 7Some of your own
sons who are born to you shall be taken away;
they shall be eunuchs in the palace of the king
of Babylon." 8Then Hezekiah said to Isaiah,
"The word of the LORD that you have spoken
is good." For he thought, "There will be peace
and security in my days."

God's People Are Comforted

40 Comfort, O comfort my people,
        says your God.
2   Speak tenderly to Jerusalem,
        and cry to her
    that she has served her term,
        that her penalty is paid,
    that she has received from the LORD's
            hand
        double for all her sins.

3   A voice cries out:
    "In the wilderness prepare the way of
            the LORD,
        make straight in the desert a highway
            for our God.
4   Every valley shall be lifted up,
        and every mountain and hill be made
            low;
    the uneven ground shall become level,
        and the rough places a plain.
5   Then the glory of the LORD shall be
            revealed,
        and all people shall see it together,
        for the mouth of the LORD has
            spoken."

6   A voice says, "Cry out!"
        And I said, "What shall I cry?"
    All people are grass,

---

a Cn Compare Gk Vg: Heb *loved*   *b* Heb *my stringed instruments*

their constancy is like the flower of
    the field.

7 The grass withers, the flower fades,
    when the breath of the LORD blows
        upon it;
    surely the people are grass.

8 The grass withers, the flower fades;
    but the word of our God will stand
        forever.

9 Get you up to a high mountain,
    O Zion, herald of good tidings;*a*
lift up your voice with strength,
    O Jerusalem, herald of good tidings,*b*
      lift it up, do not fear;
say to the cities of Judah,
    "Here is your God!"

10 See, the Lord GOD comes with might,
    and his arm rules for him;
his reward is with him,
    and his recompense before him.

11 He will feed his flock like a shepherd;
    he will gather the lambs in his arms,
and carry them in his bosom,
    and gently lead the mother sheep.

12 Who has measured the waters in the
      hollow of his hand
    and marked off the heavens with a
      span,
enclosed the dust of the earth in a
      measure,
    and weighed the mountains in scales
    and the hills in a balance?

13 Who has directed the spirit of the
      LORD,
    or as his counselor has instructed
      him?

14 Whom did he consult for his
      enlightenment,
    and who taught him the path of
      justice?
Who taught him knowledge,
    and showed him the way of
      understanding?

15 Even the nations are like a drop from a
    bucket,

and are accounted as dust on the
    scales;
see, he takes up the isles like fine dust.

16 Lebanon would not provide fuel
    enough,
    nor are its animals enough for a burnt
      offering.

17 All the nations are as nothing before
      him;
    they are accounted by him as less than
      nothing and emptiness.

18 To whom then will you liken God,
    or what likeness compare with him?

19 An idol? —A workman casts it,
    and a goldsmith overlays it with gold,
    and casts for it silver chains.

20 As a gift one chooses mulberry wood*c*
    —wood that will not rot—
then seeks out a skilled artisan
    to set up an image that will not topple.

21 Have you not known? Have you not
      heard?
    Has it not been told you from the
      beginning?
    Have you not understood from the
      foundations of the earth?

22 It is he who sits above the circle of the
      earth,
    and its inhabitants are like
      grasshoppers;
who stretches out the heavens like a
      curtain,
    and spreads them like a tent to live in;

23 who brings princes to naught,
    and makes the rulers of the earth as
      nothing.

24 Scarcely are they planted, scarcely sown,
    scarcely has their stem taken root in
      the earth,
when he blows upon them, and they
      wither,
    and the tempest carries them off like
      stubble.

a Or *O herald of good tidings to Zion*   *b* Or *O herald of good tidings to Jerusalem*   *c* Meaning of Heb uncertain

25 To whom then will you compare me,
  or who is my equal? says the Holy
    One.
26 Lift up your eyes on high and see:
    Who created these?
  He who brings out their host and
      numbers them,
    calling them all by name;
  because he is great in strength,
    mighty in power,
      not one is missing.

27 Why do you say, O Jacob,
    and speak, O Israel,
  "My way is hidden from the LORD,
    and my right is disregarded by my
      God"?
28 Have you not known? Have you not
      heard?
  The LORD is the everlasting God,
    the Creator of the ends of the earth.
  He does not faint or grow weary;
    his understanding is unsearchable.
29 He gives power to the faint,
    and strengthens the powerless.
30 Even youths will faint and be weary,
    and the young will fall exhausted;
31 but those who wait for the LORD shall
      renew their strength,
    they shall mount up with wings like
      eagles,
  they shall run and not be weary,
    they shall walk and not faint.

Israel Assured of God's Help

41 Listen to me in silence,
    O coastlands;
  let the peoples renew their strength;
  let them approach, then let them speak;
    let us together draw near for
      judgment.

2 Who has roused a victor from the east,
    summoned him to his service?
  He delivers up nations to him,
    and tramples kings under foot;
  he makes them like dust with his sword,
    like driven stubble with his bow.

3 He pursues them and passes on safely,
    scarcely touching the path with his
      feet.
4 Who has performed and done this,
    calling the generations from the
      beginning?
  I, the LORD, am first,
    and will be with the last.
5 The coastlands have seen and are afraid,
    the ends of the earth tremble;
    they have drawn near and come.
6 Each one helps the other,
    saying to one another, "Take courage!"
7 The artisan encourages the goldsmith,
    and the one who smooths with the
      hammer encourages the one
        who strikes the anvil,
  saying of the soldering, "It is good";
    and they fasten it with nails so that it
      cannot be moved.
8 But you, Israel, my servant,
    Jacob, whom I have chosen,
    the offspring of Abraham, my friend;
9 you whom I took from the ends of the
      earth,
    and called from its farthest corners,
  saying to you, "You are my servant,
    I have chosen you and not cast you
      off";
10 do not fear, for I am with you,
    do not be afraid, for I am your God;
  I will strengthen you, I will help you,
    I will uphold you with my victorious
      right hand.

11 Yes, all who are incensed against you
    shall be ashamed and disgraced;
  those who strive against you
    shall be as nothing and shall perish.
12 You shall seek those who contend with
      you,
    but you shall not find them;
  those who war against you
    shall be as nothing at all.
13 For I, the LORD your God,
    hold your right hand;
  it is I who say to you, "Do not fear,
    I will help you."

14 Do not fear, you worm Jacob,
   you insect[a] Israel!
I will help you, says the LORD;
   your Redeemer is the Holy One of
      Israel.
15 Now, I will make of you a threshing
      sledge,
   sharp, new, and having teeth;
you shall thresh the mountains and
      crush them,
   and you shall make the hills like chaff.
16 You shall winnow them and the wind
      shall carry them away,
   and the tempest shall scatter them.
Then you shall rejoice in the LORD;
   in the Holy One of Israel you shall
      glory.

17 When the poor and needy seek water,
   and there is none,
   and their tongue is parched with
      thirst,
I the LORD will answer them,
   I the God of Israel will not forsake
      them.
18 I will open rivers on the bare heights,[b]
   and fountains in the midst of the
      valleys;
I will make the wilderness a pool of
      water,
   and the dry land springs of water.
19 I will put in the wilderness the cedar,
   the acacia, the myrtle, and the olive;
I will set in the desert the cypress,
   the plane and the pine together,
20 so that all may see and know,
   all may consider and understand,
that the hand of the LORD has done
      this,
   the Holy One of Israel has created it.

The Futility of Idols

21 Set forth your case, says the LORD;
   bring your proofs, says the King of
      Jacob.
22 Let them bring them, and tell us

what is to happen.
Tell us the former things, what they are,
   so that we may consider them,
and that we may know their outcome;
   or declare to us the things to come.
23 Tell us what is to come hereafter,
   that we may know that you are gods;
do good, or do harm,
   that we may be afraid and terrified.
24 You, indeed, are nothing
   and your work is nothing at all;
whoever chooses you is an
      abomination.

25 I stirred up one from the north, and he
      has come,
   from the rising of the sun he was
      summoned by name.[c]
He shall trample[d] on rulers as on mortar,
   as the potter treads clay.
26 Who declared it from the beginning, so
      that we might know,
   and beforehand, so that we might say,
      "He is right"?
There was no one who declared it, none
      who proclaimed,
   none who heard your words.
27 I first have declared it to Zion,[e]
   and I give to Jerusalem a herald of
      good tidings.
28 But when I look there is no one;
   among these there is no counselor
who, when I ask, gives an answer.
29 No, they are all a delusion;
   their works are nothing;
   their images are empty wind.

The Servant, a Light to the Nations

42 Here is my servant, whom I uphold,
   my chosen, in whom my soul
      delights;
I have put my spirit upon him;
   he will bring forth justice to the
      nations.
2 He will not cry or lift up his voice,
   or make it heard in the street;

a Syr: Heb *men of*   b Or *trails*   c Cn Compare Q Ms Gk: MT *and he shall call on my name*   d Cn: Heb *come*
e Cn: Heb *First to Zion—Behold, behold them*

3   a bruised reed he will not break,
         and a dimly burning wick he will not
              quench;
      he will faithfully bring forth justice.
4   He will not grow faint or be crushed
         until he has established justice in the
              earth;
      and the coastlands wait for his
         teaching.

5   Thus says God, the LORD,
      who created the heavens and
         stretched them out,
      who spread out the earth and what
         comes from it,
   who gives breath to the people upon it
      and spirit to those who walk in it:
6   I am the LORD, I have called you in
         righteousness,
      I have taken you by the hand and kept
         you;
   I have given you as a covenant to the
      people, *a*
      a light to the nations,
7   to open the eyes that are blind,
   to bring out the prisoners from the
      dungeon,
      from the prison those who sit in
         darkness.
8   I am the LORD, that is my name;
      my glory I give to no other,
      nor my praise to idols.
9   See, the former things have come to
         pass,
      and new things I now declare;
   before they spring forth,
      I tell you of them.

A Hymn of Praise
10   Sing to the LORD a new song,
         his praise from the end of the earth!
      Let the sea roar *b* and all that fills it,
         the coastlands and their inhabitants.
11   Let the desert and its towns lift up their
         voice,
      the villages that Kedar inhabits;

let the inhabitants of Sela sing for joy,
   let them shout from the tops of the
      mountains.
12   Let them give glory to the LORD,
      and declare his praise in the
         coastlands.
13   The LORD goes forth like a soldier,
      like a warrior he stirs up his fury;
   he cries out, he shouts aloud,
      he shows himself mighty against his
         foes.

14   For a long time I have held my peace,
      I have kept still and restrained myself;
   now I will cry out like a woman in labor,
      I will gasp and pant.
15   I will lay waste mountains and hills,
      and dry up all their herbage;
   I will turn the rivers into islands,
      and dry up the pools.
16   I will lead the blind
      by a road they do not know,
   by paths they have not known
      I will guide them.
   I will turn the darkness before them into
      light,
      the rough places into level ground.
   These are the things I will do,
      and I will not forsake them.
17   They shall be turned back and utterly
         put to shame—
      those who trust in carved images,
   who say to cast images,
      "You are our gods."

18   Listen, you that are deaf;
      and you that are blind, look up and see!
19   Who is blind but my servant,
      or deaf like my messenger whom I
         send?
   Who is blind like my dedicated one,
      or blind like the servant of the LORD?
20   He sees many things, but does *c* not
         observe them;
      his ears are open, but he does not
         hear.

---

a Meaning of Heb uncertain   *b* Cn Compare Ps 96.11; 98.7: Heb *Those who go down to the sea*   *c* Heb *You see many things but do*

Israel's Disobedience

21 The LORD was pleased, for the sake of
    his righteousness,
      to magnify his teaching and make it
        glorious.
22 But this is a people robbed and
        plundered,
    all of them are trapped in holes
    and hidden in prisons;
    they have become a prey with no one to
      rescue,
      a spoil with no one to say, "Restore!"
23 Who among you will give heed to this,
    who will attend and listen for the time
      to come?
24 Who gave up Jacob to the spoiler,
    and Israel to the robbers?
    Was it not the LORD, against whom we
      have sinned,
      in whose ways they would not walk,
      and whose law they would not obey?
25 So he poured upon him the heat of his
      anger
    and the fury of war;
    it set him on fire all around, but he did
      not understand;
    it burned him, but he did not take it
      to heart.

Restoration and Protection Promised

43 But now thus says the LORD,
    he who created you, O Jacob,
    he who formed you, O Israel:
Do not fear, for I have redeemed you;
    I have called you by name, you are
      mine.
2 When you pass through the waters, I
      will be with you;
    and through the rivers, they shall not
      overwhelm you;
    when you walk through fire you shall
      not be burned,
    and the flame shall not consume you.
3 For I am the LORD your God,
    the Holy One of Israel, your Savior.
I give Egypt as your ransom,

Ethiopia[a] and Seba in exchange for
    you.
4 Because you are precious in my sight,
    and honored, and I love you,
I give people in return for you,
    nations in exchange for your life.
5 Do not fear, for I am with you;
    I will bring your offspring from the
      east,
    and from the west I will gather you;
6 I will say to the north, "Give them up,"
    and to the south, "Do not withhold;
bring my sons from far away
    and my daughters from the end of
      the earth—
7 everyone who is called by my name,
    whom I created for my glory,
    whom I formed and made."

8 Bring forth the people who are blind,
      yet have eyes,
    who are deaf, yet have ears!
9 Let all the nations gather together,
    and let the peoples assemble.
Who among them declared this,
    and foretold to us the former things?
Let them bring their witnesses to justify
      them,
    and let them hear and say, "It is true."
10 You are my witnesses, says the LORD,
    and my servant whom I have chosen,
so that you may know and believe me
    and understand that I am he.
Before me no god was formed,
    nor shall there be any after me.
11 I, I am the LORD,
    and besides me there is no savior.
12 I declared and saved and proclaimed,
    when there was no strange god
      among you;
    and you are my witnesses, says the
      LORD.
13 I am God, and also henceforth I am He;
    there is no one who can deliver from
      my hand;
    I work and who can hinder it?

a Or Nubia; Heb Cush

14 Thus says the LORD,
  your Redeemer, the Holy One of
    Israel:
  For your sake I will send to Babylon
    and break down all the bars,
    and the shouting of the Chaldeans
      will be turned to lamentation. *a*

15 I am the LORD, your Holy One,
  the Creator of Israel, your King.

16 Thus says the LORD,
  who makes a way in the sea,
    a path in the mighty waters,

17 who brings out chariot and horse,
    army and warrior;
  they lie down, they cannot rise,
    they are extinguished, quenched like a
      wick:

18 Do not remember the former things,
  or consider the things of old.

19 I am about to do a new thing;
  now it springs forth, do you not
    perceive it?
  I will make a way in the wilderness
    and rivers in the desert.

20 The wild animals will honor me,
    the jackals and the ostriches;
  for I give water in the wilderness,
    rivers in the desert,
  to give drink to my chosen people,

21   the people whom I formed for myself
  so that they might declare my praise.

22 Yet you did not call upon me, O Jacob;
    but you have been weary of me,
      O Israel!

23 You have not brought me your sheep
      for burnt offerings,
    or honored me with your sacrifices.
  I have not burdened you with offerings,
    or wearied you with frankincense.

24 You have not bought me sweet cane
      with money,
    or satisfied me with the fat of your
      sacrifices.
  But you have burdened me with your
      sins;

you have wearied me with your
    iniquities.

25 I, I am He
  who blots out your transgressions for
    my own sake,
  and I will not remember your sins.

26 Accuse me, let us go to trial;
  set forth your case, so that you may
    be proved right.

27 Your first ancestor sinned,
  and your interpreters transgressed
    against me.

28 Therefore I profaned the princes of the
    sanctuary,
  I delivered Jacob to utter destruction,
  and Israel to reviling.

God's Blessing on Israel

44 But now hear, O Jacob my servant,
  Israel whom I have chosen!

2 Thus says the LORD who made you,
  who formed you in the womb and
    will help you:
  Do not fear, O Jacob my servant,
  Jeshurun whom I have chosen.

3 For I will pour water on the thirsty land,
  and streams on the dry ground;
  I will pour my spirit upon your
    descendants,
  and my blessing on your offspring.

4 They shall spring up like a green
    tamarisk,
  like willows by flowing streams.

5 This one will say, "I am the LORD's,"
  another will be called by the name of
    Jacob,
  yet another will write on the hand, "The
    LORD's,"
  and adopt the name of Israel.

6 Thus says the LORD, the King of Israel,
  and his Redeemer, the LORD of hosts:
  I am the first and I am the last;
  besides me there is no god.

7 Who is like me? Let them proclaim it,

a Meaning of Heb uncertain

let them declare and set it forth
   before me.
Who has announced from of old the
   things to come?*a*
Let them tell us*b* what is yet to be.
8 Do not fear, or be afraid;
   have I not told you from of old and
      declared it?
   You are my witnesses!
Is there any god besides me?
   There is no other rock; I know not
      one.

The Absurdity of Idol Worship

9 All who make idols are nothing, and the things they delight in do not profit; their witnesses neither see nor know. And so they will be put to shame. 10Who would fashion a god or cast an image that can do no good? 11Look, all its devotees shall be put to shame; the artisans too are merely human. Let them all assemble, let them stand up; they shall be terrified, they shall all be put to shame.

12 The ironsmith fashions it*c* and works it over the coals, shaping it with hammers, and forging it with his strong arm; he becomes hungry and his strength fails, he drinks no water and is faint. 13The carpenter stretches a line, marks it out with a stylus, fashions it with planes, and marks it with a compass; he makes it in human form, with human beauty, to be set up in a shrine. 14He cuts down cedars or chooses a holm tree or an oak and lets it grow strong among the trees of the forest. He plants a cedar and the rain nourishes it. 15Then it can be used as fuel. Part of it he takes and warms himself; he kindles a fire and bakes bread. Then he makes a god and worships it, makes it a carved image and bows down before it. 16Half of it he burns in the fire; over this half he roasts meat, eats it and is satisfied. He also warms himself and says, "Ah, I am warm, I can feel the fire!" 17The rest of it he makes into a god, his idol, bows down to it and worships it; he prays to it and says, "Save me, for you are my god!"

18 They do not know, nor do they comprehend; for their eyes are shut, so that they cannot see, and their minds as well, so that they cannot understand. 19No one considers, nor is there knowledge or discernment to say, "Half of it I burned in the fire; I also baked bread on its coals, I roasted meat and have eaten. Now shall I make the rest of it an abomination? Shall I fall down before a block of wood?" 20He feeds on ashes; a deluded mind has led him astray, and he cannot save himself or say, "Is not this thing in my right hand a fraud?"

Israel Is Not Forgotten

21 Remember these things, O Jacob,
   and Israel, for you are my servant;
I formed you, you are my servant;
   O Israel, you will not be forgotten by
      me.
22 I have swept away your transgressions
      like a cloud,
   and your sins like mist;
return to me, for I have redeemed you.

23 Sing, O heavens, for the LORD has done
      it;
   shout, O depths of the earth;
break forth into singing, O mountains,
   O forest, and every tree in it!
For the LORD has redeemed Jacob,
   and will be glorified in Israel.

24 Thus says the LORD, your Redeemer,
   who formed you in the womb:
I am the LORD, who made all things,
   who alone stretched out the heavens,
   who by myself spread out the earth;
25 who frustrates the omens of liars,
   and makes fools of diviners;
who turns back the wise,
   and makes their knowledge foolish;
26 who confirms the word of his servant,
   and fulfills the prediction of his
      messengers;
who says of Jerusalem, "It shall be
      inhabited,"

---

a Cn: Heb *from my placing an eternal people and things to come*   *b* Tg: Heb *them*   *c* Cn: Heb *an ax*

and of the cities of Judah, "They
    shall be rebuilt,
and I will raise up their ruins";
27 who says to the deep, "Be dry—
    I will dry up your rivers";
28 who says of Cyrus, "He is my shepherd,
    and he shall carry out all my
        purpose";
and who says of Jerusalem, "It shall be
    rebuilt,"
and of the temple, "Your foundation
    shall be laid."

Cyrus, God's Instrument

45 Thus says the LORD to his anointed,
    to Cyrus,
whose right hand I have grasped
to subdue nations before him
    and strip kings of their robes,
to open doors before him—
    and the gates shall not be closed:
2 I will go before you
    and level the mountains,*a*
I will break in pieces the doors of
    bronze
    and cut through the bars of iron,
3 I will give you the treasures of darkness
    and riches hidden in secret places,
so that you may know that it is I, the
    LORD,
the God of Israel, who call you by
    your name.
4 For the sake of my servant Jacob,
    and Israel my chosen,
I call you by your name,
    I surname you, though you do not
    know me.
5 I am the LORD, and there is no other;
    besides me there is no god.
I arm you, though you do not know
    me,
6 so that they may know, from the rising
    of the sun
and from the west, that there is no
    one besides me;
I am the LORD, and there is no other.

7 I form light and create darkness,
    I make weal and create woe;
    I the LORD do all these things.

8 Shower, O heavens, from above,
    and let the skies rain down
        righteousness;
let the earth open, that salvation may
    spring up,*b*
    and let it cause righteousness to
        sprout up also;
    I the LORD have created it.

9 Woe to you who strive with your Maker,
    earthen vessels with the potter!*c*
Does the clay say to the one who
    fashions it, "What are you
        making"?
    or "Your work has no handles"?
10 Woe to anyone who says to a father,
    "What are you begetting?"
    or to a woman, "With what are you in
        labor?"
11 Thus says the LORD,
    the Holy One of Israel, and its
        Maker:
Will you question me*d* about my
    children,
    or command me concerning the work
        of my hands?
12 I made the earth,
    and created humankind upon it;
it was my hands that stretched out the
    heavens,
    and I commanded all their host.
13 I have aroused Cyrus*e* in righteousness,
    and I will make all his paths straight;
he shall build my city
    and set my exiles free,
not for price or reward,
    says the LORD of hosts.
14 Thus says the LORD:
The wealth of Egypt and the
    merchandise of Ethiopia,*f*
    and the Sabeans, tall of stature,
shall come over to you and be yours,

---

a Q Ms Gk: MT *the swellings*   *b* Q Ms: MT *that they may bring forth salvation*   *c* Cn: Heb *with the potsherds*, or *with the potters*   *d* Cn: Heb *Ask me of things to come*   *e* Heb *him*   *f* Or *Nubia*; Heb *Cush*

they shall follow you;
they shall come over in chains and
    bow down to you.
They will make supplication to you,
    saying,
    "God is with you alone, and there is
        no other;
    there is no god besides him."

15 Truly, you are a God who hides himself,
    O God of Israel, the Savior.
16 All of them are put to shame and
        confounded,
    the makers of idols go in confusion
        together.
17 But Israel is saved by the LORD
        with everlasting salvation;
    you shall not be put to shame or
        confounded
    to all eternity.

18 For thus says the LORD,
    who created the heavens
        (he is God!),
    who formed the earth and made it
        (he established it;
    he did not create it a chaos,
        he formed it to be inhabited!):
    I am the LORD, and there is no other.
19 I did not speak in secret,
        in a land of darkness;
    I did not say to the offspring of Jacob,
        "Seek me in chaos."
    I the LORD speak the truth,
        I declare what is right.

Idols Cannot Save Babylon
20 Assemble yourselves and come together,
        draw near, you survivors of the
        nations!
    They have no knowledge—
        those who carry about their wooden
        idols,
    and keep on praying to a god
        that cannot save.
21 Declare and present your case;
        let them take counsel together!
    Who told this long ago?
        Who declared it of old?

Was it not I, the LORD?
    There is no other god besides me,
a righteous God and a Savior;
    there is no one besides me.

22 Turn to me and be saved,
        all the ends of the earth!
    For I am God, and there is no other.
23 By myself I have sworn,
        from my mouth has gone forth in
        righteousness
    a word that shall not return:
    "To me every knee shall bow,
        every tongue shall swear."

24 Only in the LORD, it shall be said of me,
        are righteousness and strength;
    all who were incensed against him
        shall come to him and be ashamed.
25 In the LORD all the offspring of Israel
        shall triumph and glory.

46 Bel bows down, Nebo stoops,
    their idols are on beasts and cattle;
these things you carry are loaded
    as burdens on weary animals.
2 They stoop, they bow down together;
    they cannot save the burden,
    but themselves go into captivity.

3 Listen to me, O house of Jacob,
    all the remnant of the house of
        Israel,
who have been borne by me from your
        birth,
    carried from the womb;
4 even to your old age I am he,
        even when you turn gray I will carry
        you.
    I have made, and I will bear;
        I will carry and will save.

5 To whom will you liken me and make
        me equal,
    and compare me, as though we were
        alike?
6 Those who lavish gold from the purse,
    and weigh out silver in the scales—

they hire a goldsmith, who makes it into
    a god;
    then they fall down and worship!
7 They lift it to their shoulders, they carry
    it,
    they set it in its place, and it stands
        there;
    it cannot move from its place.
    If one cries out to it, it does not answer
        or save anyone from trouble.

8 Remember this and consider,*a*
    recall it to mind, you transgressors,
9   remember the former things of old;
    for I am God, and there is no other;
    I am God, and there is no one like me,
10 declaring the end from the beginning
        and from ancient times things not yet
            done,
    saying, "My purpose shall stand,
        and I will fulfill my intention,"
11 calling a bird of prey from the east,
        the man for my purpose from a far
            country.
    I have spoken, and I will bring it to pass;
        I have planned, and I will do it.

12 Listen to me, you stubborn of heart,
        you who are far from deliverance:
13 I bring near my deliverance, it is not far
        off,
    and my salvation will not tarry;
    I will put salvation in Zion,
        for Israel my glory.

The Humiliation of Babylon
47 Come down and sit in the dust,
    virgin daughter Babylon!
    Sit on the ground without a throne,
        daughter Chaldea!
    For you shall no more be called
        tender and delicate.
2 Take the millstones and grind meal,
        remove your veil,
    strip off your robe, uncover your legs,
        pass through the rivers.

a Meaning of Heb uncertain

3 Your nakedness shall be uncovered,
        and your shame shall be seen.
    I will take vengeance,
        and I will spare no one.
4 Our Redeemer—the LORD of hosts is
        his name—
    is the Holy One of Israel.

5 Sit in silence, and go into darkness,
        daughter Chaldea!
    For you shall no more be called
        the mistress of kingdoms.
6 I was angry with my people,
        I profaned my heritage;
    I gave them into your hand,
        you showed them no mercy;
    on the aged you made your yoke
        exceedingly heavy.
7 You said, "I shall be mistress forever,"
        so that you did not lay these things to
            heart
        or remember their end.

8 Now therefore hear this, you lover of
        pleasures,
    who sit securely,
    who say in your heart,
        "I am, and there is no one besides
            me;
    I shall not sit as a widow
        or know the loss of children"—
9 both these things shall come upon you
        in a moment, in one day:
    the loss of children and widowhood
        shall come upon you in full measure,
    in spite of your many sorceries
        and the great power of your
            enchantments.

10 You felt secure in your wickedness;
        you said, "No one sees me."
    Your wisdom and your knowledge
        led you astray,
    and you said in your heart,
        "I am, and there is no one besides
            me."

11 But evil shall come upon you,
    which you cannot charm away;
disaster shall fall upon you,
    which you will not be able to ward
        off;
and ruin shall come on you suddenly,
    of which you know nothing.

12 Stand fast in your enchantments
    and your many sorceries,
with which you have labored from
        your youth;
perhaps you may be able to succeed,
    perhaps you may inspire terror.
13 You are wearied with your many
        consultations;
    let those who study*a* the heavens
stand up and save you,
    those who gaze at the stars,
and at each new moon predict
    what*b* shall befall you.

14 See, they are like stubble,
    the fire consumes them;
they cannot deliver themselves
    from the power of the flame.
No coal for warming oneself is this,
    no fire to sit before!
15 Such to you are those with whom you
        have labored,
who have trafficked with you from
        your youth;
they all wander about in their own
        paths;
    there is no one to save you.

God the Creator and Redeemer

48 Hear this, O house of Jacob,
    who are called by the name of Israel,
and who came forth from the loins*c*
    of Judah;
who swear by the name of the LORD,
    and invoke the God of Israel,
    but not in truth or right.
2 For they call themselves after the holy
        city,

and lean on the God of Israel;
    the LORD of hosts is his name.

3 The former things I declared long ago,
    they went out from my mouth and I
        made them known;
then suddenly I did them and they
        came to pass.
4 Because I know that you are obstinate,
    and your neck is an iron sinew
    and your forehead brass,
5 I declared them to you from long ago,
    before they came to pass I announced
        them to you,
so that you would not say, "My idol did
        them,
my carved image and my cast image
    commanded them."

6 You have heard; now see all this;
    and will you not declare it?
From this time forward I make you hear
        new things,
hidden things that you have not
        known.
7 They are created now, not long ago;
    before today you have never heard of
        them,
so that you could not say, "I already
        knew them."
8 You have never heard, you have never
        known,
from of old your ear has not been
        opened.
For I knew that you would deal very
        treacherously,
    and that from birth you were called a
        rebel.

9 For my name's sake I defer my anger,
    for the sake of my praise I restrain it
        for you,
so that I may not cut you off.
10 See, I have refined you, but not like*d*
        silver;

---

a Meaning of Heb uncertain   *b* Gk Syr Compare Vg: Heb *from what*   *c* Cn: Heb *waters*   *d* Cn: Heb *with*

I have tested you in the furnace of
    adversity.
11 For my own sake, for my own sake, I do
    it,
    for why should my name*a* be
      profaned?
    My glory I will not give to another.

12 Listen to me, O Jacob,
    and Israel, whom I called:
    I am He; I am the first,
    and I am the last.
13 My hand laid the foundation of the earth,
    and my right hand spread out the
      heavens;
    when I summon them,
      they stand at attention.

14 Assemble, all of you, and hear!
    Who among them has declared these
      things?
    The LORD loves him;
    he shall perform his purpose on
      Babylon,
    and his arm shall be against the
      Chaldeans.
15 I, even I, have spoken and called him,
    I have brought him, and he will
      prosper in his way.
16 Draw near to me, hear this!
    From the beginning I have not
      spoken in secret,
    from the time it came to be I have
      been there.
    And now the Lord GOD has sent me
      and his spirit.

17 Thus says the LORD,
    your Redeemer, the Holy One of
      Israel:
    I am the LORD your God,
    who teaches you for your own good,
    who leads you in the way you should
      go.
18 O that you had paid attention to my
    commandments!

Then your prosperity would have
    been like a river,
    and your success like the waves of the
      sea;
19 your offspring would have been like the
    sand,
    and your descendants like its grains;
    their name would never be cut off
      or destroyed from before me.

20 Go out from Babylon, flee from
      Chaldea,
    declare this with a shout of joy,
      proclaim it,
    send it forth to the end of the earth;
    say, "The LORD has redeemed his
      servant Jacob!"
21 They did not thirst when he led them
      through the deserts;
    he made water flow for them from
      the rock;
    he split open the rock and the water
      gushed out.

22 "There is no peace," says the LORD, "for
    the wicked."

The Servant's Mission

49 Listen to me, O coastlands,
    pay attention, you peoples from far
      away!
    The LORD called me before I was born,
    while I was in my mother's womb he
      named me.
2 He made my mouth like a sharp sword,
    in the shadow of his hand he hid me;
    he made me a polished arrow,
    in his quiver he hid me away.
3 And he said to me, "You are my servant,
    Israel, in whom I will be glorified."
4 But I said, "I have labored in vain,
    I have spent my strength for nothing
      and vanity;
    yet surely my cause is with the LORD,
    and my reward with my God."

a Gk Old Latin: Heb *for why should it*

5 And now the LORD says,
  who formed me in the womb to be
      his servant,
  to bring Jacob back to him,
      and that Israel might be gathered to
          him,
  for I am honored in the sight of the
      LORD,
      and my God has become my
          strength—
6 he says,
  "It is too light a thing that you should
      be my servant
      to raise up the tribes of Jacob
      and to restore the survivors of Israel;
  I will give you as a light to the nations,
      that my salvation may reach to the
          end of the earth."

7 Thus says the LORD,
  the Redeemer of Israel and his Holy
      One,
  to one deeply despised, abhorred by the
      nations,
      the slave of rulers,
  "Kings shall see and stand up,
      princes, and they shall prostrate
          themselves,
  because of the LORD, who is faithful,
      the Holy One of Israel, who has
          chosen you."

Zion's Children to Be Brought Home

8 Thus says the LORD:
  In a time of favor I have answered you,
      on a day of salvation I have helped
          you;
  I have kept you and given you
      as a covenant to the people,*a*
  to establish the land,
      to apportion the desolate heritages;
9 saying to the prisoners, "Come out,"
      to those who are in darkness, "Show
          yourselves."
  They shall feed along the ways,

on all the bare heights*b* shall be their
      pasture;
10 they shall not hunger or thirst,
      neither scorching wind nor sun shall
          strike them down,
  for he who has pity on them will lead
      them,
      and by springs of water will guide
          them.
11 And I will turn all my mountains into a
      road,
      and my highways shall be raised up.
12 Lo, these shall come from far away,
      and lo, these from the north and from
          the west,
      and these from the land of Syene.*c*

13 Sing for joy, O heavens, and exult,
      O earth;
  break forth, O mountains, into
      singing!
  For the LORD has comforted his people,
      and will have compassion on his
          suffering ones.

14 But Zion said, "The LORD has forsaken
      me,
      my Lord has forgotten me."
15 Can a woman forget her nursing child,
      or show no compassion for the child
          of her womb?
  Even these may forget,
      yet I will not forget you.
16 See, I have inscribed you on the palms
      of my hands;
      your walls are continually before me.
17 Your builders outdo your destroyers,*d*
      and those who laid you waste go away
          from you.
18 Lift up your eyes all around and see;
      they all gather, they come to you.
  As I live, says the LORD,
      you shall put all of them on like an
          ornament,
      and like a bride you shall bind them
          on.

---

a Meaning of Heb uncertain   *b* Or *the trails*   *c* Q Ms: MT *Sinim*   *d* Or *Your children come swiftly; your destroyers*

19 Surely your waste and your desolate
            places
        and your devastated land—
    surely now you will be too crowded for
            your inhabitants,
        and those who swallowed you up will
            be far away.
20 The children born in the time of your
            bereavement
        will yet say in your hearing:
    "The place is too crowded for me;
        make room for me to settle."

21 Then you will say in your heart,
        "Who has borne me these?
    I was bereaved and barren,
        exiled and put away—
        so who has reared these?
    I was left all alone—
        where then have these come from?"

22 Thus says the Lord GOD:
    I will soon lift up my hand to the
            nations,
        and raise my signal to the peoples;
    and they shall bring your sons in their
            bosom,
        and your daughters shall be carried on
            their shoulders.
23 Kings shall be your foster fathers,
        and their queens your nursing
            mothers.
    With their faces to the ground they shall
            bow down to you,
        and lick the dust of your feet.
    Then you will know that I am the LORD;
        those who wait for me shall not be
            put to shame.

24 Can the prey be taken from the mighty,
        or the captives of a tyrant[a] be
            rescued?
25 But thus says the LORD:
    Even the captives of the mighty shall be
            taken,
        and the prey of the tyrant be rescued;

for I will contend with those who
        contend with you,
    and I will save your children.
26 I will make your oppressors eat their
            own flesh,
        and they shall be drunk with their
            own blood as with wine.
    Then all flesh shall know
        that I am the LORD your Savior,
        and your Redeemer, the Mighty One
            of Jacob.

50 Thus says the LORD:
    Where is your mother's bill of
            divorce
        with which I put her away?
    Or which of my creditors is it
        to whom I have sold you?
    No, because of your sins you were sold,
        and for your transgressions your
            mother was put away.
2   Why was no one there when I came?
        Why did no one answer when I
            called?
    Is my hand shortened, that it cannot
            redeem?
        Or have I no power to deliver?
    By my rebuke I dry up the sea,
        I make the rivers a desert;
    their fish stink for lack of water,
        and die of thirst.[b]
3   I clothe the heavens with blackness,
        and make sackcloth their covering.

The Servant's Humiliation and Vindication
4   The Lord GOD has given me
        the tongue of a teacher,[c]
    that I may know how to sustain
        the weary with a word.
    Morning by morning he wakens—
        wakens my ear
    to listen as those who are taught.
5   The Lord GOD has opened my ear,
        and I was not rebellious,
        I did not turn backward.
6   I gave my back to those who struck me,

---

a Q Ms Syr Vg: MT *of a righteous person*   b Or *die on the thirsty ground*   c Cn: Heb *of those who are taught*

and my cheeks to those who pulled
out the beard;
I did not hide my face
from insult and spitting.

7   The Lord GOD helps me;
therefore I have not been disgraced;
therefore I have set my face like flint,
and I know that I shall not be put to
shame;
8   he who vindicates me is near.
Who will contend with me?
Let us stand up together.
Who are my adversaries?
Let them confront me.
9   It is the Lord GOD who helps me;
who will declare me guilty?
All of them will wear out like a garment;
the moth will eat them up.

10 Who among you fears the LORD
and obeys the voice of his servant,
who walks in darkness
and has no light,
yet trusts in the name of the LORD
and relies upon his God?
11 But all of you are kindlers of fire,
lighters of firebrands. *a*
Walk in the flame of your fire,
and among the brands that you have
kindled!
This is what you shall have from my
hand:
you shall lie down in torment.

Blessings in Store for God's People

51 Listen to me, you that pursue
righteousness,
you that seek the LORD.
Look to the rock from which you were
hewn,
and to the quarry from which you
were dug.
2   Look to Abraham your father
and to Sarah who bore you;
for he was but one when I called him,

but I blessed him and made him
many.
3   For the LORD will comfort Zion;
he will comfort all her waste places,
and will make her wilderness like Eden,
her desert like the garden of the
LORD;
joy and gladness will be found in her,
thanksgiving and the voice of song.

4   Listen to me, my people,
and give heed to me, my nation;
for a teaching will go out from me,
and my justice for a light to the
peoples.
5   I will bring near my deliverance swiftly,
my salvation has gone out
and my arms will rule the peoples;
the coastlands wait for me,
and for my arm they hope.
6   Lift up your eyes to the heavens,
and look at the earth beneath;
for the heavens will vanish like smoke,
the earth will wear out like a garment,
and those who live on it will die like
gnats; *b*
but my salvation will be forever,
and my deliverance will never be
ended.

7   Listen to me, you who know
righteousness,
you people who have my teaching in
your hearts;
do not fear the reproach of others,
and do not be dismayed when they
revile you.
8   For the moth will eat them up like a
garment,
and the worm will eat them like wool;
but my deliverance will be forever,
and my salvation to all generations.

9   Awake, awake, put on strength,
O arm of the LORD!
Awake, as in days of old,

---

a Syr: Heb *you gird yourselves with firebrands*   *b* Or *in like manner*

the generations of long ago!
Was it not you who cut Rahab in pieces,
    who pierced the dragon?
10 Was it not you who dried up the sea,
    the waters of the great deep;
who made the depths of the sea a way
    for the redeemed to cross over?
11 So the ransomed of the LORD shall
      return,
    and come to Zion with singing;
everlasting joy shall be upon their heads;
    they shall obtain joy and gladness,
    and sorrow and sighing shall flee
      away.

12 I, I am he who comforts you;
    why then are you afraid of a mere
      mortal who must die,
    a human being who fades like grass?
13 You have forgotten the LORD, your
      Maker,
    who stretched out the heavens
    and laid the foundations of the earth.
You fear continually all day long
    because of the fury of the oppressor,
who is bent on destruction.
    But where is the fury of the
      oppressor?
14 The oppressed shall speedily be
      released;
    they shall not die and go down to the
      Pit,
    nor shall they lack bread.
15 For I am the LORD your God,
    who stirs up the sea so that its waves
      roar—
    the LORD of hosts is his name.
16 I have put my words in your mouth,
    and hidden you in the shadow of my
      hand,
stretching out*a* the heavens
    and laying the foundations of the
      earth,
    and saying to Zion, "You are my
      people."

17 Rouse yourself, rouse yourself!
    Stand up, O Jerusalem,
you who have drunk at the hand of the
    LORD
    the cup of his wrath,
who have drunk to the dregs
    the bowl of staggering.
18 There is no one to guide her
    among all the children she has borne;
there is no one to take her by the hand
    among all the children she has
      brought up.
19 These two things have befallen you
    —who will grieve with you?—
devastation and destruction, famine and
      sword—
    who will comfort you?*b*
20 Your children have fainted,
    they lie at the head of every street
    like an antelope in a net;
they are full of the wrath of the LORD,
    the rebuke of your God.

21 Therefore hear this, you who are
      wounded,*c*
    who are drunk, but not with wine:
22 Thus says your Sovereign, the LORD,
    your God who pleads the cause of his
      people:
See, I have taken from your hand the
      cup of staggering;
you shall drink no more
    from the bowl of my wrath.
23 And I will put it into the hand of your
      tormentors,
    who have said to you,
    "Bow down, that we may walk on
      you";
and you have made your back like the
      ground
    and like the street for them to walk on.

Let Zion Rejoice

52 Awake, awake,
    put on your strength, O Zion!
Put on your beautiful garments,

---

a Syr: Heb *planting*   *b* Q Ms Gk Syr Vg: MT *how may I comfort you?*   *c* Or *humbled*

O Jerusalem, the holy city;
  for the uncircumcised and the unclean
    shall enter you no more.
2 Shake yourself from the dust, rise up,
    O captive *a* Jerusalem;
  loose the bonds from your neck,
    O captive daughter Zion!

3 For thus says the LORD: You were sold for nothing, and you shall be redeemed without money. 4For thus says the Lord GOD: Long ago, my people went down into Egypt to reside there as aliens; the Assyrian, too, has oppressed them without cause. 5Now therefore what am I doing here, says the LORD, seeing that my people are taken away without cause? Their rulers howl, says the LORD, and continually, all day long, my name is despised. 6Therefore my people shall know my name; therefore in that day they shall know that it is I who speak; here am I.

7 How beautiful upon the mountains
    are the feet of the messenger who
      announces peace,
  who brings good news,
    who announces salvation,
    who says to Zion, "Your God reigns."
8 Listen! Your sentinels lift up their
      voices,
  together they sing for joy;
  for in plain sight they see
    the return of the LORD to Zion.
9 Break forth together into singing,
    you ruins of Jerusalem;
  for the LORD has comforted his people,
    he has redeemed Jerusalem.
10 The LORD has bared his holy arm
    before the eyes of all the nations;
  and all the ends of the earth shall see
    the salvation of our God.

11 Depart, depart, go out from there!
    Touch no unclean thing;
  go out from the midst of it, purify
    yourselves,

you who carry the vessels of the
    LORD.
12 For you shall not go out in haste,
    and you shall not go in flight;
  for the LORD will go before you,
    and the God of Israel will be your
      rear guard.

The Suffering Servant
13 See, my servant shall prosper;
    he shall be exalted and lifted up,
    and shall be very high.
14 Just as there were many who were
      astonished at him *b*
  —so marred was his appearance,
      beyond human semblance,
  and his form beyond that of
      mortals—
15 so he shall startle *c* many nations;
    kings shall shut their mouths because
      of him;
  for that which had not been told them
    they shall see,
  and that which they had not heard
    they shall contemplate.

53 Who has believed what we have
    heard?
  And to whom has the arm of the
    LORD been revealed?
2 For he grew up before him like a young
      plant,
  and like a root out of dry ground;
  he had no form or majesty that we
    should look at him,
  nothing in his appearance that we
    should desire him.
3 He was despised and rejected by others;
    a man of suffering *d* and acquainted
      with infirmity;
  and as one from whom others hide their
    faces *e*
  he was despised, and we held him of
    no account.

4 Surely he has borne our infirmities
    and carried our diseases;

a Cn: Heb *rise up, sit*   b Syr Tg: Heb *you*   c Meaning of Heb uncertain   d Or *a man of sorrows*   e Or *as one who hides his face from us*

yet we accounted him stricken,
    struck down by God, and afflicted.
5 But he was wounded for our
        transgressions,
    crushed for our iniquities;
upon him was the punishment that
        made us whole,
    and by his bruises we are healed.
6 All we like sheep have gone astray;
    we have all turned to our own way,
and the LORD has laid on him
    the iniquity of us all.

7 He was oppressed, and he was afflicted,
    yet he did not open his mouth;
like a lamb that is led to the slaughter,
    and like a sheep that before its
        shearers is silent,
    so he did not open his mouth.
8 By a perversion of justice he was taken
        away.
    Who could have imagined his future?
For he was cut off from the land of the
        living,
    stricken for the transgression of my
        people.
9 They made his grave with the wicked
    and his tomb*a* with the rich,*b*
although he had done no violence,
    and there was no deceit in his mouth.

10 Yet it was the will of the LORD to crush
        him with pain.*c*
When you make his life an offering for
        sin,*d*
    he shall see his offspring, and shall
        prolong his days;
through him the will of the LORD shall
        prosper.
11   Out of his anguish he shall see light;*e*
he shall find satisfaction through his
        knowledge.
    The righteous one,*f* my servant, shall
        make many righteous,
    and he shall bear their iniquities.

12 Therefore I will allot him a portion with
        the great,
    and he shall divide the spoil with the
        strong;
because he poured out himself to death,
    and was numbered with the
        transgressors;
yet he bore the sin of many,
    and made intercession for the
        transgressors.

The Eternal Covenant of Peace

54 Sing, O barren one who did not bear;
    burst into song and shout,
    you who have not been in labor!
For the children of the desolate woman
        will be more
    than the children of her that is
        married, says the LORD.
2 Enlarge the site of your tent,
    and let the curtains of your
        habitations be stretched out;
do not hold back; lengthen your cords
    and strengthen your stakes.
3 For you will spread out to the right and
        to the left,
    and your descendants will possess the
        nations
    and will settle the desolate towns.

4 Do not fear, for you will not be
        ashamed;
    do not be discouraged, for you will
        not suffer disgrace;
for you will forget the shame of your
        youth,
    and the disgrace of your widowhood
        you will remember no more.
5 For your Maker is your husband,
    the LORD of hosts is his name;
    the Holy One of Israel is your
        Redeemer,
    the God of the whole earth he is
        called.
6 For the LORD has called you

---

a Q Ms: MT *and in his death*   *b* Cn: Heb *with a rich person*   *c* Or *by disease*; meaning of Heb uncertain
d Meaning of Heb uncertain   *e* Q Mss: MT lacks *light*   *f* Or *and he shall find satisfaction. Through his knowledge, the*
righteous one

like a wife forsaken and grieved in
    spirit,
like the wife of a man's youth when she
    is cast off,
    says your God.
7 For a brief moment I abandoned you,
    but with great compassion I will
      gather you.
8 In overflowing wrath for a moment
    I hid my face from you,
but with everlasting love I will have
    compassion on you,
    says the LORD, your Redeemer.

9 This is like the days of Noah to me:
    Just as I swore that the waters of
      Noah
    would never again go over the earth,
so I have sworn that I will not be angry
    with you
    and will not rebuke you.
10 For the mountains may depart
    and the hills be removed,
but my steadfast love shall not depart
    from you,
    and my covenant of peace shall not
      be removed,
    says the LORD, who has compassion
      on you.

11 O afflicted one, storm-tossed, and not
    comforted,
    I am about to set your stones in
      antimony,
    and lay your foundations with
      sapphires.*a*
12 I will make your pinnacles of rubies,
    your gates of jewels,
    and all your wall of precious stones.
13 All your children shall be taught by the
    LORD,
    and great shall be the prosperity of
      your children.
14 In righteousness you shall be
    established;

a Or *lapis lazuli*

you shall be far from oppression, for
    you shall not fear;
    and from terror, for it shall not come
      near you.
15 If anyone stirs up strife,
    it is not from me;
whoever stirs up strife with you
    shall fall because of you.
16 See it is I who have created the smith
    who blows the fire of coals,
    and produces a weapon fit for its
      purpose;
I have also created the ravager to
    destroy.
17 No weapon that is fashioned against
    you shall prosper,
    and you shall confute every tongue
      that rises against you in
      judgment.
This is the heritage of the servants of
    the LORD
    and their vindication from me, says
      the LORD.

An Invitation to Abundant Life

55 Ho, everyone who thirsts,
    come to the waters;
and you that have no money,
    come, buy and eat!
Come, buy wine and milk
    without money and without price.
2 Why do you spend your money for that
    which is not bread,
    and your labor for that which does
      not satisfy?
Listen carefully to me, and eat what is
    good,
    and delight yourselves in rich food.
3 Incline your ear, and come to me;
    listen, so that you may live.
I will make with you an everlasting
    covenant,
    my steadfast, sure love for David.
4 See, I made him a witness to the
    peoples,

a leader and commander for the
    peoples.
5 See, you shall call nations that you do
    not know,
    and nations that do not know you
      shall run to you,
because of the LORD your God, the
    Holy One of Israel,
    for he has glorified you.

6 Seek the LORD while he may be found,
    call upon him while he is near;
7 let the wicked forsake their way,
    and the unrighteous their thoughts;
let them return to the LORD, that he
      may have mercy on them,
    and to our God, for he will
      abundantly pardon.
8 For my thoughts are not your thoughts,
    nor are your ways my ways, says the
      LORD.
9 For as the heavens are higher than the
    earth,
    so are my ways higher than your ways
    and my thoughts than your thoughts.

10 For as the rain and the snow come
      down from heaven,
    and do not return there until they
      have watered the earth,
making it bring forth and sprout,
    giving seed to the sower and bread to
      the eater,
11 so shall my word be that goes out from
    my mouth;
    it shall not return to me empty,
but it shall accomplish that which I
    purpose,
    and succeed in the thing for which I
      sent it.

12 For you shall go out in joy,
    and be led back in peace;
the mountains and the hills before you
    shall burst into song,
    and all the trees of the field shall clap
      their hands.

13 Instead of the thorn shall come up the
    cypress;
    instead of the brier shall come up the
      myrtle;
and it shall be to the LORD for a
    memorial,
    for an everlasting sign that shall not
      be cut off.

The Covenant Extended to All Who Obey

56 Thus says the LORD:
Maintain justice, and do what is
    right,
for soon my salvation will come,
    and my deliverance be revealed.

2 Happy is the mortal who does this,
    the one who holds it fast,
who keeps the sabbath, not profaning it,
    and refrains from doing any evil.

3 Do not let the foreigner joined to the
      LORD say,
    "The LORD will surely separate me
      from his people";
and do not let the eunuch say,
    "I am just a dry tree."
4 For thus says the LORD:
To the eunuchs who keep my sabbaths,
    who choose the things that please me
    and hold fast my covenant,
5 I will give, in my house and within my
    walls,
    a monument and a name
    better than sons and daughters;
I will give them an everlasting name
    that shall not be cut off.

6 And the foreigners who join themselves
      to the LORD,
    to minister to him, to love the name
      of the LORD,
    and to be his servants,
all who keep the sabbath, and do not
      profane it,
    and hold fast my covenant—
7 these I will bring to my holy mountain,

and make them joyful in my house of
     prayer;
their burnt offerings and their sacrifices
     will be accepted on my altar;
for my house shall be called a house of
     prayer
     for all peoples.
8 Thus says the Lord GOD,
     who gathers the outcasts of Israel,
I will gather others to them
     besides those already gathered. *a*

The Corruption of Israel's Rulers
9 All you wild animals,
     all you wild animals in the forest,
          come to devour!
10 Israel's *b* sentinels are blind,
     they are all without knowledge;
they are all silent dogs
     that cannot bark;
dreaming, lying down,
     loving to slumber.
11 The dogs have a mighty appetite;
     they never have enough.
The shepherds also have no
          understanding;
     they have all turned to their own way,
     to their own gain, one and all.
12 "Come," they say, "let us *c* get wine;
     let us fill ourselves with strong drink.
And tomorrow will be like today,
     great beyond measure."

Israel's Futile Idolatry
57 The righteous perish,
     and no one takes it to heart;
the devout are taken away,
     while no one understands.
For the righteous are taken away from
          calamity,
2 and they enter into peace;
those who walk uprightly
     will rest on their couches.
3 But as for you, come here,
     you children of a sorceress,

you offspring of an adulterer and a
     whore. *d*
4 Whom are you mocking?
     Against whom do you open your
          mouth wide
     and stick out your tongue?
Are you not children of transgression,
     the offspring of deceit—
5 you that burn with lust among the oaks,
     under every green tree;
you that slaughter your children in the
          valleys,
     under the clefts of the rocks?
6 Among the smooth stones of the valley
          is your portion;
     they, they, are your lot;
to them you have poured out a drink
          offering,
     you have brought a grain offering.
     Shall I be appeased for these things?
7 Upon a high and lofty mountain
     you have set your bed,
     and there you went up to offer
          sacrifice.
8 Behind the door and the doorpost
     you have set up your symbol;
for, in deserting me, *e* you have
          uncovered your bed,
     you have gone up to it,
     you have made it wide;
and you have made a bargain for
          yourself with them,
     you have loved their bed,
     you have gazed on their nakedness. *f*
9 You journeyed to Molech *g* with oil,
     and multiplied your perfumes;
you sent your envoys far away,
     and sent down even to Sheol.
10 You grew weary from your many
          wanderings,
     but you did not say, "It is useless."
You found your desire rekindled,
     and so you did not weaken.

11 Whom did you dread and fear
     so that you lied,

---

a Heb *besides his gathered ones*   *b* Heb *His*   *c* Q Ms Syr Vg Tg: MT *me*   *d* Heb *an adulterer and she plays the whore*
e Meaning of Heb uncertain   *f* Or *their phallus*; Heb *the hand*   *g* Or *the king*

and did not remember me
  or give me a thought?
Have I not kept silent and closed my
    eyes,*a*
  and so you do not fear me?
12 I will concede your righteousness and
    your works,
  but they will not help you.
13 When you cry out, let your collection of
    idols deliver you!
  The wind will carry them off,
  a breath will take them away.
But whoever takes refuge in me shall
    possess the land
  and inherit my holy mountain.

A Promise of Help and Healing
14 It shall be said,
  "Build up, build up, prepare the way,
    remove every obstruction from my
    people's way."
15 For thus says the high and lofty one
  who inhabits eternity, whose name is
    Holy:
I dwell in the high and holy place,
  and also with those who are contrite
    and humble in spirit,
to revive the spirit of the humble,
  and to revive the heart of the
    contrite.
16 For I will not continually accuse,
  nor will I always be angry;
for then the spirits would grow faint
    before me,
  even the souls that I have made.
17 Because of their wicked covetousness I
    was angry;
  I struck them, I hid and was angry;
  but they kept turning back to their
    own ways.
18 I have seen their ways, but I will heal
    them;
  I will lead them and repay them with
    comfort,
  creating for their mourners the fruit
    of the lips.*b*

19 Peace, peace, to the far and the near,
    says the LORD;
  and I will heal them.
20 But the wicked are like the tossing sea
    that cannot keep still;
  its waters toss up mire and mud.
21 There is no peace, says my God, for the
    wicked.

False and True Worship
58 Shout out, do not hold back!
  Lift up your voice like a trumpet!
Announce to my people their rebellion,
  to the house of Jacob their sins.
2 Yet day after day they seek me
  and delight to know my ways,
as if they were a nation that practiced
    righteousness
  and did not forsake the ordinance of
    their God;
they ask of me righteous judgments,
  they delight to draw near to God.
3 "Why do we fast, but you do not see?
  Why humble ourselves, but you do
    not notice?"
Look, you serve your own interest on
    your fast day,
  and oppress all your workers.
4 Look, you fast only to quarrel and to
    fight
  and to strike with a wicked fist.
Such fasting as you do today
  will not make your voice heard on
    high.
5 Is such the fast that I choose,
  a day to humble oneself?
Is it to bow down the head like a bulrush,
  and to lie in sackcloth and ashes?
Will you call this a fast,
  a day acceptable to the LORD?

6 Is not this the fast that I choose:
  to loose the bonds of injustice,
  to undo the thongs of the yoke,
to let the oppressed go free,
  and to break every yoke?

a Gk Vg: Heb *silent even for a long time*   *b* Meaning of Heb uncertain

7 Is it not to share your bread with the
    hungry,
     and bring the homeless poor into
       your house;
    when you see the naked, to cover them,
     and not to hide yourself from your
       own kin?
8 Then your light shall break forth like the
    dawn,
     and your healing shall spring up
       quickly;
    your vindicator*a* shall go before you,
     the glory of the LORD shall be your
       rear guard.
9 Then you shall call, and the LORD will
    answer;
     you shall cry for help, and he will say,
       Here I am.

    If you remove the yoke from among
       you,
     the pointing of the finger, the
       speaking of evil,
10 if you offer your food to the hungry
     and satisfy the needs of the afflicted,
    then your light shall rise in the darkness
     and your gloom be like the noonday.
11 The LORD will guide you continually,
     and satisfy your needs in parched
       places,
     and make your bones strong;
    and you shall be like a watered garden,
     like a spring of water,
     whose waters never fail.
12 Your ancient ruins shall be rebuilt;
     you shall raise up the foundations of
       many generations;
    you shall be called the repairer of the
       breach,
     the restorer of streets to live in.

13 If you refrain from trampling the
       sabbath,
     from pursuing your own interests on
       my holy day;
    if you call the sabbath a delight

and the holy day of the LORD
    honorable;
if you honor it, not going your own
    ways,
 serving your own interests, or
   pursuing your own affairs;*b*
14 then you shall take delight in the LORD,
   and I will make you ride upon the
     heights of the earth;
 I will feed you with the heritage of your
   ancestor Jacob,
  for the mouth of the LORD has
    spoken.

Injustice and Oppression to Be Punished

59 See, the LORD's hand is not too
     short to save,
   nor his ear too dull to hear.
2 Rather, your iniquities have been
     barriers
   between you and your God,
 and your sins have hidden his face from
   you
  so that he does not hear.
3 For your hands are defiled with blood,
   and your fingers with iniquity;
 your lips have spoken lies,
   your tongue mutters wickedness.
4 No one brings suit justly,
   no one goes to law honestly;
 they rely on empty pleas, they speak lies,
   conceiving mischief and begetting
     iniquity.
5 They hatch adders' eggs,
   and weave the spider's web;
 whoever eats their eggs dies,
   and the crushed egg hatches out a
     viper.
6 Their webs cannot serve as clothing;
   they cannot cover themselves with
     what they make.
 Their works are works of iniquity,
   and deeds of violence are in their
     hands.
7 Their feet run to evil,
   and they rush to shed innocent blood;

a Or *vindication*   *b* Heb *or speaking words*

their thoughts are thoughts of iniquity,
　　desolation and destruction are in their
　　　highways.
8 The way of peace they do not know,
　　and there is no justice in their paths.
Their roads they have made crooked;
　　no one who walks in them knows
　　　peace.

9 Therefore justice is far from us,
　　and righteousness does not reach us;
we wait for light, and lo! there is
　　darkness;
　　and for brightness, but we walk in
　　　gloom.
10 We grope like the blind along a wall,
　　groping like those who have no eyes;
we stumble at noon as in the twilight,
　　among the vigorous*a* as though we
　　　were dead.
11 We all growl like bears;
　　like doves we moan mournfully.
We wait for justice, but there is none;
　　for salvation, but it is far from us.
12 For our transgressions before you are
　　many,
　　and our sins testify against us.
Our transgressions indeed are with us,
　　and we know our iniquities:
13 transgressing, and denying the LORD,
　　and turning away from following our
　　　God,
talking oppression and revolt,
　　conceiving lying words and uttering
　　　them from the heart.
14 Justice is turned back,
　　and righteousness stands at a
　　　distance;
for truth stumbles in the public square,
　　and uprightness cannot enter.
15 Truth is lacking,
　　and whoever turns from evil is
　　　despoiled.

The LORD saw it, and it displeased him
　　that there was no justice.

16 He saw that there was no one,
　　and was appalled that there was no
　　　one to intervene;
so his own arm brought him victory,
　　and his righteousness upheld him.
17 He put on righteousness like a
　　breastplate,
　　and a helmet of salvation on his head;
he put on garments of vengeance for
　　clothing,
　　and wrapped himself in fury as in a
　　　mantle.
18 According to their deeds, so will he
　　repay;
　　wrath to his adversaries, requital to
　　　his enemies;
　　to the coastlands he will render
　　　requital.
19 So those in the west shall fear the name
　　of the LORD,
　　and those in the east, his glory;
for he will come like a pent-up stream
　　that the wind of the LORD drives on.

20 And he will come to Zion as Redeemer,
　　to those in Jacob who turn from
　　　transgression, says the LORD.

21 And as for me, this is my covenant with them, says the LORD: my spirit that is upon you, and my words that I have put in your mouth, shall not depart out of your mouth, or out of the mouths of your children, or out of the mouths of your children's children, says the LORD, from now on and forever.

The Ingathering of the Dispersed

60 Arise, shine; for your light has come,
　　and the glory of the LORD has risen
　　　upon you.
2 For darkness shall cover the earth,
　　and thick darkness the peoples;
but the LORD will arise upon you,
　　and his glory will appear over you.
3 Nations shall come to your light,
　　and kings to the brightness of your
　　　dawn.

a Meaning of Heb uncertain

4 Lift up your eyes and look around;
 they all gather together, they come to
 you;
 your sons shall come from far away,
 and your daughters shall be carried on
 their nurses' arms.
5 Then you shall see and be radiant;
 your heart shall thrill and rejoice,[a]
 because the abundance of the sea shall
 be brought to you,
 the wealth of the nations shall come
 to you.
6 A multitude of camels shall cover you,
 the young camels of Midian and
 Ephah;
 all those from Sheba shall come.
 They shall bring gold and frankincense,
 and shall proclaim the praise of the
 LORD.
7 All the flocks of Kedar shall be
 gathered to you,
 the rams of Nebaioth shall minister
 to you;
 they shall be acceptable on my altar,
 and I will glorify my glorious house.

8 Who are these that fly like a cloud,
 and like doves to their windows?
9 For the coastlands shall wait for me,
 the ships of Tarshish first,
 to bring your children from far away,
 their silver and gold with them,
 for the name of the LORD your God,
 and for the Holy One of Israel,
 because he has glorified you.
10 Foreigners shall build up your walls,
 and their kings shall minister to you;
 for in my wrath I struck you down,
 but in my favor I have had mercy on
 you.
11 Your gates shall always be open;
 day and night they shall not be shut,
 so that nations shall bring you their
 wealth,
 with their kings led in procession.
12 For the nation and kingdom

that will not serve you shall perish;
 those nations shall be utterly laid
 waste.
13 The glory of Lebanon shall come to
 you,
 the cypress, the plane, and the pine,
 to beautify the place of my sanctuary;
 and I will glorify where my feet rest.
14 The descendants of those who
 oppressed you
 shall come bending low to you,
 and all who despised you
 shall bow down at your feet;
 they shall call you the City of the LORD,
 the Zion of the Holy One of Israel.
15 Whereas you have been forsaken and
 hated,
 with no one passing through,
 I will make you majestic forever,
 a joy from age to age.
16 You shall suck the milk of nations,
 you shall suck the breasts of kings;
 and you shall know that I, the LORD, am
 your Savior
 and your Redeemer, the Mighty One
 of Jacob.

17 Instead of bronze I will bring gold,
 instead of iron I will bring silver;
 instead of wood, bronze,
 instead of stones, iron.
 I will appoint Peace as your overseer
 and Righteousness as your taskmaster.
18 Violence shall no more be heard in your
 land,
 devastation or destruction within your
 borders;
 you shall call your walls Salvation,
 and your gates Praise.

God the Glory of Zion
19 The sun shall no longer be
 your light by day,
 nor for brightness shall the moon
 give light to you by night;[b]

---

a Heb *be enlarged*   *b* Q Ms Gk Old Latin Tg: MT lacks *by night*

but the LORD will be your everlasting
light,
and your God will be your glory.
20 Your sun shall no more go down,
or your moon withdraw itself;
for the LORD will be your everlasting
light,
and your days of mourning shall be
ended.
21 Your people shall all be righteous;
they shall possess the land forever.
They are the shoot that I planted, the
work of my hands,
so that I might be glorified.
22 The least of them shall become a clan,
and the smallest one a mighty nation;
I am the LORD;
in its time I will accomplish it quickly.

The Good News of Deliverance

61 The spirit of the Lord GOD is upon
me,
because the LORD has anointed me;
he has sent me to bring good news to
the oppressed,
to bind up the brokenhearted,
to proclaim liberty to the captives,
and release to the prisoners;
2 to proclaim the year of the LORD's
favor,
and the day of vengeance of our
God;
to comfort all who mourn;
3 to provide for those who mourn in
Zion—
to give them a garland instead of
ashes,
the oil of gladness instead of mourning,
the mantle of praise instead of a faint
spirit.
They will be called oaks of
righteousness,
the planting of the LORD, to display
his glory.
4 They shall build up the ancient ruins,

they shall raise up the former
devastations;
they shall repair the ruined cities,
the devastations of many generations.

5 Strangers shall stand and feed your
flocks,
foreigners shall till your land and
dress your vines;
6 but you shall be called priests of the
LORD,
you shall be named ministers of our
God;
you shall enjoy the wealth of the
nations,
and in their riches you shall glory.
7 Because their*a* shame was double,
and dishonor was proclaimed as their
lot,
therefore they shall possess a double
portion;
everlasting joy shall be theirs.

8 For I the LORD love justice,
I hate robbery and wrongdoing;*b*
I will faithfully give them their
recompense,
and I will make an everlasting
covenant with them.
9 Their descendants shall be known
among the nations,
and their offspring among the
peoples;
all who see them shall acknowledge
that they are a people whom the
LORD has blessed.
10 I will greatly rejoice in the LORD,
my whole being shall exult in my
God;
for he has clothed me with the garments
of salvation,
he has covered me with the robe of
righteousness,
as a bridegroom decks himself with a
garland,

a Heb *your*   b Or *robbery with a burnt offering*

and as a bride adorns herself with her
jewels.
11 For as the earth brings forth its shoots,
and as a garden causes what is sown
in it to spring up,
so the Lord GOD will cause
righteousness and praise
to spring up before all the nations.

The Vindication and Salvation of Zion

62 For Zion's sake I will not keep silent,
and for Jerusalem's sake I will not rest,
until her vindication shines out like the
dawn,
and her salvation like a burning torch.
2 The nations shall see your vindication,
and all the kings your glory;
and you shall be called by a new name
that the mouth of the LORD will give.
3 You shall be a crown of beauty in the
hand of the LORD,
and a royal diadem in the hand of
your God.
4 You shall no more be termed Forsaken,ᵃ
and your land shall no more be
termed Desolate;ᵇ
but you shall be called My Delight Is in
Her,ᶜ
and your land Married;ᵈ
for the LORD delights in you,
and your land shall be married.
5 For as a young man marries a young
woman,
so shall your builderᵉ marry you,
and as the bridegroom rejoices over the
bride,
so shall your God rejoice over you.
6 Upon your walls, O Jerusalem,
I have posted sentinels;
all day and all night
they shall never be silent.
You who remind the LORD,
take no rest,
7 and give him no rest
until he establishes Jerusalem

and makes it renowned throughout
the earth.
8 The LORD has sworn by his right hand
and by his mighty arm:
I will not again give your grain
to be food for your enemies,
and foreigners shall not drink the
wine
for which you have labored;
9 but those who garner it shall eat it
and praise the LORD,
and those who gather it shall drink it
in my holy courts.

10 Go through, go through the gates,
prepare the way for the people;
build up, build up the highway,
clear it of stones,
lift up an ensign over the peoples.
11 The LORD has proclaimed
to the end of the earth:
Say to daughter Zion,
"See, your salvation comes;
his reward is with him,
and his recompense before him."
12 They shall be called, "The Holy
People,
The Redeemed of the LORD";
and you shall be called, "Sought Out,
A City Not Forsaken."

Vengeance on Edom

63 "Who is this that comes from
Edom,
from Bozrah in garments stained
crimson?
Who is this so splendidly robed,
marching in his great might?"

"It is I, announcing vindication,
mighty to save."

2 "Why are your robes red,
and your garments like theirs who
tread the wine press?"

---

a Heb *Azubah*   *b* Heb *Shemamah*   *c* Heb *Hephzibah*   *d* Heb *Beulah*   *e* Cn: Heb *your sons*

3 "I have trodden the wine press alone,
  and from the peoples no one was
    with me;
  I trod them in my anger
  and trampled them in my wrath;
  their juice spattered on my garments,
  and stained all my robes.
4 For the day of vengeance was in my
    heart,
  and the year for my redeeming work
    had come.
5 I looked, but there was no helper;
  I stared, but there was no one to
    sustain me;
  so my own arm brought me victory,
  and my wrath sustained me.
6 I trampled down peoples in my anger,
  I crushed them in my wrath,
  and I poured out their lifeblood on
    the earth."

God's Mercy Remembered

7 I will recount the gracious deeds of the
    LORD,
  the praiseworthy acts of the LORD,
  because of all that the LORD has done
    for us,
  and the great favor to the house of
    Israel
  that he has shown them according to his
    mercy,
  according to the abundance of his
    steadfast love.
8 For he said, "Surely they are my people,
  children who will not deal falsely";
  and he became their savior
9   in all their distress.
  It was no messenger*a* or angel
  but his presence that saved them;*b*
  in his love and in his pity he redeemed
    them;
  he lifted them up and carried them all
    the days of old.

10 But they rebelled
  and grieved his holy spirit;

therefore he became their enemy;
  he himself fought against them.
11 Then they*c* remembered the days of old,
  of Moses his servant.*d*
  Where is the one who brought them up
    out of the sea
  with the shepherds of his flock?
  Where is the one who put within them
    his holy spirit,
12 who caused his glorious arm
  to march at the right hand of Moses,
  who divided the waters before them
  to make for himself an everlasting
    name,
13 who led them through the depths?
  Like a horse in the desert,
  they did not stumble.
14 Like cattle that go down into the valley,
  the spirit of the LORD gave them rest.
  Thus you led your people,
  to make for yourself a glorious name.

A Prayer of Penitence

15 Look down from heaven and see,
  from your holy and glorious
    habitation.
  Where are your zeal and your might?
  The yearning of your heart and your
    compassion?
  They are withheld from me.
16 For you are our father,
  though Abraham does not know us
  and Israel does not acknowledge us;
  you, O LORD, are our father;
  our Redeemer from of old is your
    name.
17 Why, O LORD, do you make us stray
    from your ways
  and harden our heart, so that we do
    not fear you?
  Turn back for the sake of your servants,
  for the sake of the tribes that are your
    heritage.
18 Your holy people took possession for a
    little while;

---

a Gk: Heb *anguish*   *b* Or *savior.* *9In all their distress he was distressed; the angel of his presence saved them;*   *c* Heb *he*
d Cn: Heb *his people*

but now our adversaries have
    trampled down your sanctuary.
19 We have long been like those whom you
    do not rule,
    like those not called by your name.

64 O that you would tear open the
    heavens and come down,
    so that the mountains would quake at
    your presence—
2*a* as when fire kindles brushwood
    and the fire causes water to boil—
    to make your name known to your
    adversaries,
    so that the nations might tremble at
    your presence!
3 When you did awesome deeds that we
    did not expect,
    you came down, the mountains
    quaked at your presence.
4 From ages past no one has heard,
    no ear has perceived,
    no eye has seen any God besides you,
    who works for those who wait for
    him.
5 You meet those who gladly do right,
    those who remember you in your
    ways.
    But you were angry, and we sinned;
    because you hid yourself we
    transgressed.*b*
6 We have all become like one who is
    unclean,
    and all our righteous deeds are like a
    filthy cloth.
    We all fade like a leaf,
    and our iniquities, like the wind, take
    us away.
7 There is no one who calls on your
    name,
    or attempts to take hold of you;
    for you have hidden your face from us,
    and have delivered*c* us into the hand
    of our iniquity.
8 Yet, O LORD, you are our Father;

we are the clay, and you are our
    potter;
    we are all the work of your hand.
9 Do not be exceedingly angry, O LORD,
    and do not remember iniquity
    forever.
    Now consider, we are all your people.
10 Your holy cities have become a
    wilderness,
    Zion has become a wilderness,
    Jerusalem a desolation.
11 Our holy and beautiful house,
    where our ancestors praised you,
    has been burned by fire,
    and all our pleasant places have
    become ruins.
12 After all this, will you restrain yourself,
    O LORD?
    Will you keep silent, and punish us so
    severely?

The Righteousness of God's Judgment

65 I was ready to be sought out by
    those who did not ask,
    to be found by those who did not
    seek me.
    I said, "Here I am, here I am,"
    to a nation that did not call on my
    name.
2 I held out my hands all day long
    to a rebellious people,
    who walk in a way that is not good,
    following their own devices;
3 a people who provoke me
    to my face continually,
    sacrificing in gardens
    and offering incense on bricks;
4 who sit inside tombs,
    and spend the night in secret places;
    who eat swine's flesh,
    with broth of abominable things in
    their vessels;
5 who say, "Keep to yourself,
    do not come near me, for I am too
    holy for you."
    These are a smoke in my nostrils,

---

a Ch 64.1 in Heb   *b* Meaning of Heb uncertain   *c* Gk Syr Old Latin Tg: Heb *melted* a fire that burns all day long.

6 See, it is written before me:
      I will not keep silent, but I will repay;
      I will indeed repay into their laps
7   their*a* iniquities and their*a* ancestors'
         iniquities together,
                    says the LORD;
      because they offered incense on the
         mountains
      and reviled me on the hills,
      I will measure into their laps
      full payment for their actions.

8 Thus says the LORD:
      As the wine is found in the cluster,
         and they say, "Do not destroy it,
         for there is a blessing in it,"
      so I will do for my servants' sake,
         and not destroy them all.
9 I will bring forth descendants*b* from
         Jacob,
      and from Judah inheritors*c* of my
         mountains;
      my chosen shall inherit it,
         and my servants shall settle there.
10 Sharon shall become a pasture for
         flocks,
      and the Valley of Achor a place for
         herds to lie down,
      for my people who have sought me.
11 But you who forsake the LORD,
      who forget my holy mountain,
      who set a table for Fortune
         and fill cups of mixed wine for
         Destiny;
12 I will destine you to the sword,
      and all of you shall bow down to the
         slaughter;
      because, when I called, you did not
         answer,
      when I spoke, you did not listen,
      but you did what was evil in my sight,
         and chose what I did not delight in.
13 Therefore thus says the Lord GOD:
      My servants shall eat,
         but you shall be hungry;
      my servants shall drink,

      but you shall be thirsty;
      my servants shall rejoice,
         but you shall be put to shame;
14   my servants shall sing for gladness of
         heart,
      but you shall cry out for pain of
         heart,
      and shall wail for anguish of spirit.
15 You shall leave your name to my chosen
         to use as a curse,
      and the Lord GOD will put you to
         death;
      but to his servants he will give a
         different name.
16 Then whoever invokes a blessing in the
         land
      shall bless by the God of faithfulness,
   and whoever takes an oath in the land
      shall swear by the God of
         faithfulness;
   because the former troubles are
         forgotten
      and are hidden from my sight.

The Glorious New Creation

17 For I am about to create new heavens
      and a new earth;
   the former things shall not be
         remembered
      or come to mind.
18 But be glad and rejoice forever
      in what I am creating;
   for I am about to create Jerusalem as a
         joy,
      and its people as a delight.
19 I will rejoice in Jerusalem,
      and delight in my people;
   no more shall the sound of weeping be
         heard in it,
      or the cry of distress.
20 No more shall there be in it
      an infant that lives but a few days,
      or an old person who does not live
         out a lifetime;
   for one who dies at a hundred years will
         be considered a youth,

---

a Gk Syr: Heb *your*   *b* Or *a descendant*   *c* Or *an inheritor*

and one who falls short of a hundred
    will be considered accursed.
21 They shall build houses and inhabit
    them;
    they shall plant vineyards and eat their
      fruit.
22 They shall not build and another
    inhabit;
    they shall not plant and another eat;
for like the days of a tree shall the days
    of my people be,
    and my chosen shall long enjoy the
      work of their hands.
23 They shall not labor in vain,
    or bear children for calamity;*a*
for they shall be offspring blessed by the
    LORD—
    and their descendants as well.
24 Before they call I will answer,
    while they are yet speaking I will hear.
25 The wolf and the lamb shall feed
    together,
    the lion shall eat straw like the ox;
    but the serpent—its food shall be
      dust!
They shall not hurt or destroy
    on all my holy mountain,
            says the LORD.

The Worship God Demands

66 Thus says the LORD:
Heaven is my throne
and the earth is my footstool;
what is the house that you would build
    for me,
    and what is my resting place?
2 All these things my hand has made,
    and so all these things are mine,*b*
           says the LORD.
But this is the one to whom I will look,
    to the humble and contrite in spirit,
    who trembles at my word.

3 Whoever slaughters an ox is like one
    who kills a human being;

whoever sacrifices a lamb, like one
    who breaks a dog's neck;
whoever presents a grain offering, like
    one who offers swine's blood;*c*
whoever makes a memorial offering
    of frankincense, like one who
    blesses an idol.
These have chosen their own ways,
    and in their abominations they take
      delight;
4 I also will choose to mock*d* them,
    and bring upon them what they fear;
because, when I called, no one
    answered,
    when I spoke, they did not listen;
but they did what was evil in my sight,
    and chose what did not please me.

The LORD Vindicates Zion

5 Hear the word of the LORD,
    you who tremble at his word:
Your own people who hate you
    and reject you for my name's sake
have said, "Let the LORD be glorified,
    so that we may see your joy";
    but it is they who shall be put to
      shame.

6 Listen, an uproar from the city!
    A voice from the temple!
The voice of the LORD,
    dealing retribution to his enemies!

7 Before she was in labor
    she gave birth;
before her pain came upon her
    she delivered a son.
8 Who has heard of such a thing?
    Who has seen such things?
Shall a land be born in one day?
    Shall a nation be delivered in one
      moment?
Yet as soon as Zion was in labor
    she delivered her children.
9 Shall I open the womb and not deliver?
    says the LORD;

---

a Or *sudden terror*   *b* Gk Syr: Heb *these things came to be*   *c* Meaning of Heb uncertain   *d* Or *to punish*

shall I, the one who delivers, shut the
    womb?
    says your God.

10 Rejoice with Jerusalem, and be glad for
    her,
      all you who love her;
    rejoice with her in joy,
      all you who mourn over her—
11 that you may nurse and be satisfied
      from her consoling breast;
    that you may drink deeply with delight
      from her glorious bosom.

12 For thus says the LORD:
    I will extend prosperity to her like a
      river,
      and the wealth of the nations like an
        overflowing stream;
    and you shall nurse and be carried on
      her arm,
      and dandled on her knees.
13 As a mother comforts her child,
      so I will comfort you;
      you shall be comforted in Jerusalem.

The Reign and Indignation of God
14 You shall see, and your heart shall
      rejoice;
    your bodies*a* shall flourish like the
      grass;
    and it shall be known that the hand of
      the LORD is with his servants,
      and his indignation is against his
      enemies.
15 For the LORD will come in fire,
    and his chariots like the whirlwind,
    to pay back his anger in fury,
    and his rebuke in flames of fire.
16 For by fire will the LORD execute
      judgment,
      and by his sword, on all flesh;
      and those slain by the LORD shall be
      many.

17 Those who sanctify and purify themselves to go into the gardens, following the one
in the center, eating the flesh of pigs, vermin,
and rodents, shall come to an end together,
says the LORD.

18 For I know*b* their works and their
thoughts, and I am*c* coming to gather all nations and tongues; and they shall come and
shall see my glory, 19and I will set a sign among
them. From them I will send survivors to the
nations, to Tarshish, Put,*d* and Lud—which
draw the bow—to Tubal and Javan, to the
coastlands far away that have not heard of my
fame or seen my glory; and they shall declare
my glory among the nations. 20They shall bring
all your kindred from all the nations as an offering to the LORD, on horses, and in chariots,
and in litters, and on mules, and on drome-
daries, to my holy mountain Jerusalem, says the
LORD, just as the Israelites bring a grain offering in a clean vessel to the house of the
LORD. 21And I will also take some of them as
priests and as Levites, says the LORD.

22 For as the new heavens and the new
      earth,
      which I will make,
    shall remain before me, says the LORD;
      so shall your descendants and your
        name remain.
23 From new moon to new moon,
      and from sabbath to sabbath,
    all flesh shall come to worship before
      me,
    says the LORD.

24 And they shall go out and look at the
dead bodies of the people who have rebelled
against me; for their worm shall not die, their
fire shall not be quenched, and they shall be an
abhorrence to all flesh.

---

a Heb *bones*   *b* Gk Syr: Heb lacks *know*   *c* Gk Syr Vg Tg: Heb *it is*   *d* Gk: Heb *Pul*

JEREMIAH

1 The words of Jeremiah son of Hilkiah, of the priests who were in Anathoth in the land of Benjamin, ²to whom the word of the LORD came in the days of King Josiah son of Amon of Judah, in the thirteenth year of his reign. ³It came also in the days of King Jehoiakim son of Josiah of Judah, and until the end of the eleventh year of King Zedekiah son of Josiah of Judah, until the captivity of Jerusalem in the fifth month.

Jeremiah's Call and Commission

4 Now the word of the LORD came to me saying,

5   "Before I formed you in the womb I
        knew you,
  and before you were born I consecrated
        you;
  I appointed you a prophet to the
        nations."

⁶Then I said, "Ah, Lord GOD! Truly I do not know how to speak, for I am only a boy." ⁷But the LORD said to me,

  "Do not say, 'I am only a boy';
  for you shall go to all to whom I send
        you,
  and you shall speak whatever I
        command you.
8   Do not be afraid of them,
  for I am with you to deliver you,
                 says the LORD."

⁹Then the LORD put out his hand and touched my mouth; and the LORD said to me,

  "Now I have put my words in your
        mouth.
10   See, today I appoint you over nations
        and over kingdoms,
  to pluck up and to pull down,
  to destroy and to overthrow,
  to build and to plant."

11 The word of the LORD came to me, saying, "Jeremiah, what do you see?" And I said, "I see a branch of an almond tree."ᵃ ¹²Then the LORD said to me, "You have seen well, for I am

watchingᵇ over my word to perform it." ¹³The word of the LORD came to me a second time, saying, "What do you see?" And I said, "I see a boiling pot, tilted away from the north."

14 Then the LORD said to me: Out of the north disaster shall break out on all the inhabitants of the land. ¹⁵For now I am calling all the tribes of the kingdoms of the north, says the LORD; and they shall come and all of them shall set their thrones at the entrance of the gates of Jerusalem, against all its surrounding walls and against all the cities of Judah. ¹⁶And I will utter my judgments against them, for all their wickedness in forsaking me; they have made offerings to other gods, and worshiped the works of their own hands. ¹⁷But you, gird up your loins; stand up and tell them everything that I command you. Do not break down before them, or I will break you before them. ¹⁸And I for my part have made you today a fortified city, an iron pillar, and a bronze wall, against the whole land—against the kings of Judah, its princes, its priests, and the people of the land. ¹⁹They will fight against you; but they shall not prevail against you, for I am with you, says the LORD, to deliver you.

God Pleads with Israel to Repent

2 The word of the LORD came to me, saying: ²Go and proclaim in the hearing of Jerusalem, Thus says the LORD:

  I remember the devotion of your youth,
    your love as a bride,
  how you followed me in the wilderness,
    in a land not sown.
3   Israel was holy to the LORD,
    the first fruits of his harvest.
  All who ate of it were held guilty;
    disaster came upon them,
             says the LORD.

4 Hear the word of the LORD, O house of Jacob, and all the families of the house of Israel. ⁵Thus says the LORD:

---

a Heb *shaqed*   *b* Heb *shoqed*

What wrong did your ancestors find in me
    that they went far from me,
and went after worthless things, and
    became worthless themselves?

6 They did not say, "Where is the LORD
    who brought us up from the land of
        Egypt,
who led us in the wilderness,
    in a land of deserts and pits,
in a land of drought and deep darkness,
    in a land that no one passes through,
    where no one lives?"

7 I brought you into a plentiful land
    to eat its fruits and its good things.
But when you entered you defiled my
        land,
    and made my heritage an
        abomination.

8 The priests did not say, "Where is the
        LORD?"
    Those who handle the law did not
        know me;
the rulers*a* transgressed against me;
    the prophets prophesied by Baal,
    and went after things that do not
        profit.

9 Therefore once more I accuse you,
            says the LORD,
    and I accuse your children's children.

10 Cross to the coasts of Cyprus and look,
    send to Kedar and examine with care;
    see if there has ever been such a thing.

11 Has a nation changed its gods,
    even though they are no gods?
But my people have changed their glory
    for something that does not profit.

12 Be appalled, O heavens, at this,
    be shocked, be utterly desolate,
            says the LORD,

13 for my people have committed two evils:
    they have forsaken me,
    the fountain of living water,
        and dug out cisterns for themselves,
    cracked cisterns
        that can hold no water.

14 Is Israel a slave? Is he a homeborn
        servant?
    Why then has he become plunder?

15 The lions have roared against him,
    they have roared loudly.
They have made his land a waste;
    his cities are in ruins, without
        inhabitant.

16 Moreover, the people of Memphis and
        Tahpanhes
    have broken the crown of your head.

17 Have you not brought this upon yourself
    by forsaking the LORD your God,
    while he led you in the way?

18 What then do you gain by going to
        Egypt,
    to drink the waters of the Nile?
Or what do you gain by going to Assyria,
    to drink the waters of the Euphrates?

19 Your wickedness will punish you,
    and your apostasies will convict you.
Know and see that it is evil and bitter
    for you to forsake the LORD your
        God;
    the fear of me is not in you,
            says the Lord GOD of hosts.

20 For long ago you broke your yoke
    and burst your bonds,
    and you said, "I will not serve!"
On every high hill
    and under every green tree
    you sprawled and played the whore.

21 Yet I planted you as a choice vine,
    from the purest stock.
How then did you turn degenerate
    and become a wild vine?

22 Though you wash yourself with lye
    and use much soap,
    the stain of your guilt is still before
        me,
            says the Lord GOD.

23 How can you say, "I am not defiled,
    I have not gone after the Baals"?
Look at your way in the valley;
    know what you have done—

---

a Heb *shepherds*

a restive young camel interlacing her
    tracks,
24   a wild ass at home in the wilderness,
in her heat sniffing the wind!
    Who can restrain her lust?
None who seek her need weary
    themselves;
    in her month they will find her.
25   Keep your feet from going unshod
    and your throat from thirst.
But you said, "It is hopeless,
    for I have loved strangers,
    and after them I will go."

26   As a thief is shamed when caught,
    so the house of Israel shall be
        shamed—
they, their kings, their officials,
    their priests, and their prophets,
27   who say to a tree, "You are my father,"
    and to a stone, "You gave me birth."
For they have turned their backs to me,
    and not their faces.
But in the time of their trouble they say,
    "Come and save us!"
28   But where are your gods
    that you made for yourself?
Let them come, if they can save you,
    in your time of trouble;
for you have as many gods
    as you have towns, O Judah.

29   Why do you complain against me?
    You have all rebelled against me,
          says the LORD.
30   In vain I have struck down your
    children;
    they accepted no correction.
Your own sword devoured your
    prophets
    like a ravening lion.
31   And you, O generation, behold the word
    of the LORD!*a*
Have I been a wilderness to Israel,
    or a land of thick darkness?

Why then do my people say, "We are
    free,
    we will come to you no more"?
32   Can a girl forget her ornaments,
    or a bride her attire?
Yet my people have forgotten me,
    days without number.

33   How well you direct your course
    to seek lovers!
So that even to wicked women
    you have taught your ways.
34   Also on your skirts is found
    the lifeblood of the innocent poor,
though you did not catch them breaking
    in.
    Yet in spite of all these things*a*
35   you say, "I am innocent;
    surely his anger has turned from me."
Now I am bringing you to judgment
    for saying, "I have not sinned."
36   How lightly you gad about,
    changing your ways!
You shall be put to shame by Egypt
    as you were put to shame by Assyria.
37   From there also you will come away
    with your hands on your head;
for the LORD has rejected those in whom
    you trust,
    and you will not prosper through
        them.

Unfaithful Israel

3   If*b* a man divorces his wife
    and she goes from him
and becomes another man's wife,
    will he return to her?
Would not such a land be greatly
    polluted?
You have played the whore with many
    lovers;
    and would you return to me?
          says the LORD.
2   Look up to the bare heights,*c* and see!
    Where have you not been lain with?

---

a Meaning of Heb uncertain   *b* Q Ms Gk Syr: MT *Saying, If*   *c* Or *the trails*

By the waysides you have sat waiting for
    lovers,
  like a nomad in the wilderness.
You have polluted the land
  with your whoring and wickedness.
3 Therefore the showers have been
    withheld,
  and the spring rain has not come;
yet you have the forehead of a whore,
  you refuse to be ashamed.
4 Have you not just now called to me,
  "My Father, you are the friend of my
    youth—
5 will he be angry forever,
  will he be indignant to the end?"
This is how you have spoken,
  but you have done all the evil that you
    could.

A Call to Repentance

6 The LORD said to me in the days of King
Josiah: Have you seen what she did, that faithless one, Israel, how she went up on every high
hill and under every green tree, and played the
whore there? 7And I thought, "After she has
done all this she will return to me"; but she did
not return, and her false sister Judah saw it.
8She*a* saw that for all the adulteries of that
faithless one, Israel, I had sent her away with a
decree of divorce; yet her false sister Judah did
not fear, but she too went and played the whore.
9Because she took her whoredom so lightly,
she polluted the land, committing adultery with
stone and tree. 10Yet for all this her false sister
Judah did not return to me with her whole
heart, but only in pretense, says the LORD.

11 Then the LORD said to me: Faithless Israel has shown herself less guilty than false Judah. 12Go, and proclaim these words toward
the north, and say:
  Return, faithless Israel,
             says the LORD.
  I will not look on you in anger,
    for I am merciful,
             says the LORD;
  I will not be angry forever.

13 Only acknowledge your guilt,
  that you have rebelled against the
    LORD your God,
and scattered your favors among
    strangers under every green tree,
and have not obeyed my voice,
             says the LORD.
14 Return, O faithless children,
             says the LORD,
  for I am your master;
I will take you, one from a city and two
    from a family,
  and I will bring you to Zion.

15 I will give you shepherds after my own
heart, who will feed you with knowledge and
understanding. 16And when you have multiplied and increased in the land, in those days,
says the LORD, they shall no longer say, "The
ark of the covenant of the LORD." It shall not
come to mind, or be remembered, or missed;
nor shall another one be made. 17At that time
Jerusalem shall be called the throne of the
LORD, and all nations shall gather to it, to the
presence of the LORD in Jerusalem, and they
shall no longer stubbornly follow their own evil
will. 18In those days the house of Judah shall
join the house of Israel, and together they shall
come from the land of the north to the land
that I gave your ancestors for a heritage.

19 I thought
  how I would set you among my
    children,
  and give you a pleasant land,
    the most beautiful heritage of all the
    nations.
And I thought you would call me, My
    Father,
  and would not turn from following
    me.
20 Instead, as a faithless wife leaves her
    husband,
  so you have been faithless to me,
    O house of Israel,
             says the LORD.

---

a Q Ms Gk Mss Syr: MT *I*

21 A voice on the bare heights*a* is heard,
   the plaintive weeping of Israel's
      children,
because they have perverted their way,
   they have forgotten the LORD their
      God:
22 Return, O faithless children,
   I will heal your faithlessness.

"Here we come to you;
   for you are the LORD our God.
23 Truly the hills are*b* a delusion,
   the orgies on the mountains.
Truly in the LORD our God
   is the salvation of Israel.

24 "But from our youth the shameful thing has devoured all for which our ancestors had labored, their flocks and their herds, their sons and their daughters. 25Let us lie down in our shame, and let our dishonor cover us; for we have sinned against the LORD our God, we and our ancestors, from our youth even to this day; and we have not obeyed the voice of the LORD our God."

4 If you return, O Israel,
               says the LORD,
   if you return to me,
   if you remove your abominations from
      my presence,
   and do not waver,
2 and if you swear, "As the LORD lives!"
   in truth, in justice, and in uprightness,
then nations shall be blessed*c* by him,
   and by him they shall boast.

3 For thus says the LORD to the people of Judah and to the inhabitants of Jerusalem:
Break up your fallow ground,
   and do not sow among thorns.
4 Circumcise yourselves to the LORD,
   remove the foreskin of your hearts,
   O people of Judah and inhabitants of
      Jerusalem,
or else my wrath will go forth like fire,
   and burn with no one to quench it,
   because of the evil of your doings.

Invasion and Desolation of Judah Threatened

5 Declare in Judah, and proclaim in Jerusalem, and say:
Blow the trumpet through the land;
   shout aloud*d* and say,
"Gather together, and let us go
   into the fortified cities!"
6 Raise a standard toward Zion,
   flee for safety, do not delay,
for I am bringing evil from the north,
   and a great destruction.
7 A lion has gone up from its thicket,
   a destroyer of nations has set out;
   he has gone out from his place
to make your land a waste;
   your cities will be ruins
   without inhabitant.
8 Because of this put on sackcloth,
   lament and wail:
"The fierce anger of the LORD
   has not turned away from us."

9On that day, says the LORD, courage shall fail the king and the officials; the priests shall be appalled and the prophets astounded. 10Then I said, "Ah, Lord GOD, how utterly you have deceived this people and Jerusalem, saying, 'It shall be well with you,' even while the sword is at the throat!"

11 At that time it will be said to this people and to Jerusalem: A hot wind comes from me out of the bare heights*a* in the desert toward my poor people, not to winnow or cleanse— 12a wind too strong for that. Now it is I who speak in judgment against them.
13 Look! He comes up like clouds,
   his chariots like the whirlwind;
   his horses are swifter than eagles—
   woe to us, for we are ruined!
14 O Jerusalem, wash your heart clean of
      wickedness
   so that you may be saved.
How long shall your evil schemes
   lodge within you?
15 For a voice declares from Dan

---

a Or *the trails*   *b* Gk Syr Vg: Heb *Truly from the hills is* Heb *shout, fill* (your hand)   *c* Or *shall bless themselves*   *d* Or *shout, take your weapons.*

and proclaims disaster from Mount
  Ephraim.
16 Tell the nations, "Here they are!"
  Proclaim against Jerusalem,
  "Besiegers come from a distant land;
    they shout against the cities of Judah.
17 They have closed in around her like
      watchers of a field,
  because she has rebelled against me,
                              says the LORD.
18 Your ways and your doings
    have brought this upon you.
  This is your doom; how bitter it is!
    It has reached your very heart."

Sorrow for a Doomed Nation

19 My anguish, my anguish! I writhe in pain!
    Oh, the walls of my heart!
  My heart is beating wildly;
    I cannot keep silent;
  for I*a* hear the sound of the trumpet,
    the alarm of war.
20 Disaster overtakes disaster,
    the whole land is laid waste.
  Suddenly my tents are destroyed,
    my curtains in a moment.
21 How long must I see the standard,
    and hear the sound of the trumpet?
22 "For my people are foolish,
    they do not know me;
  they are stupid children,
    they have no understanding.
  They are skilled in doing evil,
    but do not know how to do good."

23 I looked on the earth, and lo, it was
      waste and void;
    and to the heavens, and they had no
      light.
24 I looked on the mountains, and lo, they
      were quaking,
    and all the hills moved to and fro.
25 I looked, and lo, there was no one at all,
    and all the birds of the air had fled.
26 I looked, and lo, the fruitful land was a
      desert,

and all its cities were laid in ruins
    before the LORD, before his fierce
      anger.
27 For thus says the LORD: The whole land
  shall be a desolation; yet I will not make a full
  end.
28 Because of this the earth shall mourn,
    and the heavens above grow black;
  for I have spoken, I have purposed;
    I have not relented nor will I turn
      back.

29 At the noise of horseman and archer
    every town takes to flight;
  they enter thickets; they climb among
      rocks;
  all the towns are forsaken,
    and no one lives in them.
30 And you, O desolate one,
  what do you mean that you dress in
      crimson,
    that you deck yourself with
      ornaments of gold,
    that you enlarge your eyes with paint?
  In vain you beautify yourself.
    Your lovers despise you;
      they seek your life.
31 For I heard a cry as of a woman in labor,
    anguish as of one bringing forth her
      first child,
  the cry of daughter Zion gasping for
      breath,
    stretching out her hands,
  "Woe is me! I am fainting before killers!"

The Utter Corruption of God's People

5 Run to and fro through the streets of
    Jerusalem,
  look around and take note!
  Search its squares and see
    if you can find one person
  who acts justly
    and seeks truth—
  so that I may pardon Jerusalem.*b*
2 Although they say, "As the LORD lives,"
    yet they swear falsely.

---

a Another reading is *for you, O my soul,*   *b* Heb *it*

3 O LORD, do your eyes not look for
    truth?
   You have struck them,
     but they felt no anguish;
   you have consumed them,
     but they refused to take correction.
   They have made their faces harder than
     rock;
     they have refused to turn back.

4 Then I said, "These are only the poor,
     they have no sense;
   for they do not know the way of the
     LORD,
     the law of their God.
5 Let me go to the rich*a*
     and speak to them;
   surely they know the way of the LORD,
     the law of their God."
   But they all alike had broken the yoke,
     they had burst the bonds.

6 Therefore a lion from the forest shall kill
     them,
     a wolf from the desert shall destroy
     them.
   A leopard is watching against their cities;
     everyone who goes out of them shall
     be torn in pieces—
   because their transgressions are many,
     their apostasies are great.

7 How can I pardon you?
     Your children have forsaken me,
     and have sworn by those who are no
     gods.
   When I fed them to the full,
     they committed adultery
     and trooped to the houses of
     prostitutes.
8 They were well-fed lusty stallions,
     each neighing for his neighbor's wife.
9 Shall I not punish them for these things?
                 says the LORD;
   and shall I not bring retribution
     on a nation such as this?

10 Go up through her vine-rows and
     destroy,
     but do not make a full end;
   strip away her branches,
     for they are not the LORD's.
11 For the house of Israel and the house of
     Judah
     have been utterly faithless to me,
                 says the LORD.
12 They have spoken falsely of the LORD,
     and have said, "He will do nothing.
   No evil will come upon us,
     and we shall not see sword or famine."
13 The prophets are nothing but wind,
     for the word is not in them.
   Thus shall it be done to them!

14 Therefore thus says the LORD, the God
     of hosts:
   Because they*b* have spoken this word,
   I am now making my words in your
     mouth a fire,
     and this people wood, and the fire
     shall devour them.
15 I am going to bring upon you
     a nation from far away, O house of
     Israel,
                 says the LORD.
   It is an enduring nation,
     it is an ancient nation,
   a nation whose language you do not
     know,
     nor can you understand what they say.
16 Their quiver is like an open tomb;
     all of them are mighty warriors.
17 They shall eat up your harvest and your
     food;
     they shall eat up your sons and your
     daughters;
   they shall eat up your flocks and your
     herds;
     they shall eat up your vines and your
     fig trees;
   they shall destroy with the sword
     your fortified cities in which you trust.

a Or *the great*   *b* Heb *you*

18 But even in those days, says the LORD, I will not make a full end of you. ¹⁹And when your people say, "Why has the LORD our God done all these things to us?" you shall say to them, "As you have forsaken me and served foreign gods in your land, so you shall serve strangers in a land that is not yours."

20 Declare this in the house of Jacob,
      proclaim it in Judah:
21 Hear this, O foolish and senseless
            people,
      who have eyes, but do not see,
      who have ears, but do not hear.
22 Do you not fear me? says the LORD;
      Do you not tremble before me?
   I placed the sand as a boundary for the
            sea,
         a perpetual barrier that it cannot pass;
   though the waves toss, they cannot
            prevail,
         though they roar, they cannot pass
            over it.
23 But this people has a stubborn and
            rebellious heart;
         they have turned aside and gone away.
24 They do not say in their hearts,
      "Let us fear the LORD our God,
   who gives the rain in its season,
         the autumn rain and the spring rain,
   and keeps for us
         the weeks appointed for the harvest."
25 Your iniquities have turned these away,
         and your sins have deprived you of
            good.
26 For scoundrels are found among my
            people;
         they take over the goods of others.
   Like fowlers they set a trap;ᵃ
         they catch human beings.
27 Like a cage full of birds,
         their houses are full of treachery;
   therefore they have become great and
            rich,
28 they have grown fat and sleek.

They know no limits in deeds of
            wickedness;
      they do not judge with justice
the cause of the orphan, to make it
            prosper,
      and they do not defend the rights of
            the needy.
29 Shall I not punish them for these things?
                           says the LORD,
      and shall I not bring retribution
         on a nation such as this?

30 An appalling and horrible thing
      has happened in the land:
31 the prophets prophesy falsely,
      and the priests rule as the prophets
            direct;ᵇ
   my people love to have it so,
      but what will you do when the end
            comes?

The Imminence and Horror of the Invasion

6 Flee for safety, O children of Benjamin,
      from the midst of Jerusalem!
   Blow the trumpet in Tekoa,
      and raise a signal on Beth-haccherem;
   for evil looms out of the north,
      and great destruction.
2 I have likened daughter Zion
      to the loveliest pasture.ᶜ
3 Shepherds with their flocks shall come
            against her.
      They shall pitch their tents around
            her;
      they shall pasture, all in their places.
4 "Prepare war against her;
      up, and let us attack at noon!"
   "Woe to us, for the day declines,
      the shadows of evening lengthen!"
5 "Up, and let us attack by night,
      and destroy her palaces!"
6 For thus says the LORD of hosts:
   Cut down her trees;
      cast up a siege ramp against Jerusalem.
   This is the city that must be punished;ᵈ

a Meaning of Heb uncertain   b Or rule by their own authority   c Or I will destroy daughter Zion, the loveliest pasture
d Or the city of license

there is nothing but oppression within
　her.

7　As a well keeps its water fresh,
　　so she keeps fresh her wickedness;
　violence and destruction are heard
　　　within her;
　　sickness and wounds are ever before
　　　me.

8　Take warning, O Jerusalem,
　　or I shall turn from you in disgust,
　and make you a desolation,
　　an uninhabited land.

9　Thus says the LORD of hosts:
　Glean*a* thoroughly as a vine
　　the remnant of Israel;
　like a grape-gatherer, pass your hand
　　　again
　　over its branches.

10　To whom shall I speak and give
　　　warning,
　　that they may hear?
　See, their ears are closed,*b*
　　they cannot listen.
　The word of the LORD is to them an
　　　object of scorn;
　　they take no pleasure in it.

11　But I am full of the wrath of the LORD;
　　I am weary of holding it in.

　Pour it out on the children in the street,
　　and on the gatherings of young men
　　　as well;
　both husband and wife shall be taken,
　　the old folk and the very aged.

12　Their houses shall be turned over to
　　　others,
　　their fields and wives together;
　for I will stretch out my hand
　　against the inhabitants of the land,
　　　　　　　　　　　　　says the LORD.

13　For from the least to the greatest of
　　　them,
　　everyone is greedy for unjust gain;

and from prophet to priest,
　everyone deals falsely.

14　They have treated the wound of my
　　　people carelessly,
　　saying, "Peace, peace,"
　　when there is no peace.

15　They acted shamefully, they committed
　　　abomination;
　　yet they were not ashamed,
　　they did not know how to blush.
　Therefore they shall fall among those
　　　who fall;
　　at the time that I punish them, they
　　　shall be overthrown,
　　　　　　　　　　　　　says the LORD.

16　Thus says the LORD:
　Stand at the crossroads, and look,
　　and ask for the ancient paths,
　where the good way lies; and walk in it,
　　and find rest for your souls.
　But they said, "We will not walk in it."

17　Also I raised up sentinels for you:
　　"Give heed to the sound of the
　　　trumpet!"
　But they said, "We will not give heed."

18　Therefore hear, O nations,
　　and know, O congregation, what will
　　　happen to them.

19　Hear, O earth; I am going to bring
　　　disaster on this people,
　　the fruit of their schemes,
　because they have not given heed to my
　　　words;
　　and as for my teaching, they have
　　　rejected it.

20　Of what use to me is frankincense that
　　　comes from Sheba,
　　or sweet cane from a distant land?
　Your burnt offerings are not
　　　acceptable,
　　nor are your sacrifices pleasing
　　　to me.

21　Therefore thus says the LORD:
　See, I am laying before this people
　　stumbling blocks against which they
　　　shall stumble;

---

a Cn: Heb *They shall glean*　　*b* Heb *are uncircumcised*

parents and children together,
neighbor and friend shall perish.

22 Thus says the LORD:
See, a people is coming from the land of
the north,
a great nation is stirring from the
farthest parts of the earth.
23 They grasp the bow and the javelin,
they are cruel and have no mercy,
their sound is like the roaring sea;
they ride on horses,
equipped like a warrior for battle,
against you, O daughter Zion!

24 "We have heard news of them,
our hands fall helpless;
anguish has taken hold of us,
pain as of a woman in labor.
25 Do not go out into the field,
or walk on the road;
for the enemy has a sword,
terror is on every side."

26 O my poor people, put on sackcloth,
and roll in ashes;
make mourning as for an only child,
most bitter lamentation:
for suddenly the destroyer
will come upon us.

27 I have made you a tester and a refiner*a*
among my people
so that you may know and test their
ways.
28 They are all stubbornly rebellious,
going about with slanders;
they are bronze and iron,
all of them act corruptly.
29 The bellows blow fiercely,
the lead is consumed by the fire;
in vain the refining goes on,
for the wicked are not removed.
30 They are called "rejected silver,"
for the LORD has rejected them.

Jeremiah Proclaims God's Judgment on the Nation

7 The word that came to Jeremiah from the
LORD: [2]Stand in the gate of the LORD's
house, and proclaim there this word, and say,
Hear the word of the LORD, all you people of
Judah, you that enter these gates to worship the
LORD. [3]Thus says the LORD of hosts, the God
of Israel: Amend your ways and your doings,
and let me dwell with you*b* in this place. [4]Do
not trust in these deceptive words: "This is*c* the
temple of the LORD, the temple of the LORD,
the temple of the LORD."

5 For if you truly amend your ways and
your doings, if you truly act justly one with another, [6]if you do not oppress the alien, the orphan, and the widow, or shed innocent blood
in this place, and if you do not go after other
gods to your own hurt, [7]then I will dwell with
you in this place, in the land that I gave of old
to your ancestors forever and ever.

8 Here you are, trusting in deceptive words
to no avail. [9]Will you steal, murder, commit
adultery, swear falsely, make offerings to Baal,
and go after other gods that you have not
known, [10]and then come and stand before me
in this house, which is called by my name, and
say, "We are safe!"—only to go on doing all
these abominations? [11]Has this house, which is
called by my name, become a den of robbers
in your sight? You know, I too am watching,
says the LORD. [12]Go now to my place that was
in Shiloh, where I made my name dwell at first,
and see what I did to it for the wickedness of
my people Israel. [13]And now, because you have
done all these things, says the LORD, and when
I spoke to you persistently, you did not listen,
and when I called you, you did not answer,
[14]therefore I will do to the house that is called
by my name, in which you trust, and to the
place that I gave to you and to your ancestors,
just what I did to Shiloh. [15]And I will cast you
out of my sight, just as I cast out all your kinsfolk, all the offspring of Ephraim.

a Or *a fortress*   *b* Or *and I will let you dwell*   *c* Heb *They are*

The People's Disobedience

16 As for you, do not pray for this people, do not raise a cry or prayer on their behalf, and do not intercede with me, for I will not hear you. 17Do you not see what they are doing in the towns of Judah and in the streets of Jerusalem? 18The children gather wood, the fathers kindle fire, and the women knead dough, to make cakes for the queen of heaven; and they pour out drink offerings to other gods, to provoke me to anger. 19Is it I whom they provoke? says the LORD. Is it not themselves, to their own hurt? 20Therefore thus says the Lord GOD: My anger and my wrath shall be poured out on this place, on human beings and animals, on the trees of the field and the fruit of the ground; it will burn and not be quenched.

21 Thus says the LORD of hosts, the God of Israel: Add your burnt offerings to your sacrifices, and eat the flesh. 22For in the day that I brought your ancestors out of the land of Egypt, I did not speak to them or command them concerning burnt offerings and sacrifices. 23But this command I gave them, "Obey my voice, and I will be your God, and you shall be my people; and walk only in the way that I command you, so that it may be well with you." 24Yet they did not obey or incline their ear, but, in the stubbornness of their evil will, they walked in their own counsels, and looked backward rather than forward. 25From the day that your ancestors came out of the land of Egypt until this day, I have persistently sent all my servants the prophets to them, day after day; 26yet they did not listen to me, or pay attention, but they stiffened their necks. They did worse than their ancestors did.

27 So you shall speak all these words to them, but they will not listen to you. You shall call to them, but they will not answer you. 28You shall say to them: This is the nation that did not obey the voice of the LORD their God, and did not accept discipline; truth has perished; it is cut off from their lips.

29 Cut off your hair and throw it away;

raise a lamentation on the bare
  heights,*a*
for the LORD has rejected and forsaken
  the generation that provoked his
  wrath.

30 For the people of Judah have done evil in my sight, says the LORD; they have set their abominations in the house that is called by my name, defiling it. 31And they go on building the high place*b* of Topheth, which is in the valley of the son of Hinnom, to burn their sons and their daughters in the fire—which I did not command, nor did it come into my mind. 32Therefore, the days are surely coming, says the LORD, when it will no more be called Topheth, or the valley of the son of Hinnom, but the valley of Slaughter: for they will bury in Topheth until there is no more room. 33The corpses of this people will be food for the birds of the air, and for the animals of the earth; and no one will frighten them away. 34And I will bring to an end the sound of mirth and gladness, the voice of the bride and bridegroom in the cities of Judah and in the streets of Jerusalem; for the land shall become a waste.

8 At that time, says the LORD, the bones of the kings of Judah, the bones of its officials, the bones of the priests, the bones of the prophets, and the bones of the inhabitants of Jerusalem shall be brought out of their tombs; 2and they shall be spread before the sun and the moon and all the host of heaven, which they have loved and served, which they have followed, and which they have inquired of and worshiped; and they shall not be gathered or buried; they shall be like dung on the surface of the ground. 3Death shall be preferred to life by all the remnant that remains of this evil family in all the places where I have driven them, says the LORD of hosts.

The Blind Perversity of the Whole Nation

4   You shall say to them, Thus says the
        LORD:
     When people fall, do they not get up
        again?

a Or *the trails*   b Gk Tg: Heb *high places*

If they go astray, do they not turn
back?

5 Why then has this people*a* turned away
in perpetual backsliding?
They have held fast to deceit,
they have refused to return.

6 I have given heed and listened,
but they do not speak honestly;
no one repents of wickedness,
saying, "What have I done!"
All of them turn to their own course,
like a horse plunging headlong into
battle.

7 Even the stork in the heavens
knows its times;
and the turtledove, swallow, and crane*b*
observe the time of their coming;
but my people do not know
the ordinance of the LORD.

8 How can you say, "We are wise,
and the law of the LORD is with us,"
when, in fact, the false pen of the scribes
has made it into a lie?

9 The wise shall be put to shame,
they shall be dismayed and taken;
since they have rejected the word of the
LORD,
what wisdom is in them?

10 Therefore I will give their wives to
others
and their fields to conquerors,
because from the least to the greatest
everyone is greedy for unjust gain;
from prophet to priest
everyone deals falsely.

11 They have treated the wound of my
people carelessly,
saying, "Peace, peace,"
when there is no peace.

12 They acted shamefully, they committed
abomination;
yet they were not at all ashamed,
they did not know how to blush.
Therefore they shall fall among those
who fall;

at the time when I punish them, they
shall be overthrown,
says the LORD.

13 When I wanted to gather them, says the
LORD,
there are*c* no grapes on the vine,
nor figs on the fig tree;
even the leaves are withered,
and what I gave them has passed away
from them.*b*

14 Why do we sit still?
Gather together, let us go into the
fortified cities
and perish there;
for the LORD our God has doomed us to
perish,
and has given us poisoned water to
drink,
because we have sinned against the
LORD.

15 We look for peace, but find no good,
for a time of healing, but there is
terror instead.

16 The snorting of their horses is heard
from Dan;
at the sound of the neighing of their
stallions
the whole land quakes.
They come and devour the land and all
that fills it,
the city and those who live in it.

17 See, I am letting snakes loose among
you,
adders that cannot be charmed,
and they shall bite you,
says the LORD.

The Prophet Mourns for the People

18 My joy is gone, grief is upon me,
my heart is sick.

19 Hark, the cry of my poor people
from far and wide in the land:
"Is the LORD not in Zion?
Is her King not in her?"

---

a One Ms Gk: MT *this people, Jerusalem,*   *b* Meaning of Heb uncertain   *c* Or *I will make an end of them, says the*
LORD. *There are*

("Why have they provoked me to anger
with their images,
with their foreign idols?")

20 "The harvest is past, the summer is
ended,
and we are not saved."

21 For the hurt of my poor people I am
hurt,
I mourn, and dismay has taken hold
of me.

22 Is there no balm in Gilead?
Is there no physician there?
Why then has the health of my poor
people
not been restored?

9 *a* O that my head were a spring of water,
and my eyes a fountain of tears,
so that I might weep day and night
for the slain of my poor people!

2 *b* O that I had in the desert
a traveler's lodging place,
that I might leave my people
and go away from them!
For they are all adulterers,
a band of traitors.

3 They bend their tongues like bows;
they have grown strong in the land for
falsehood, and not for truth;
for they proceed from evil to evil,
and they do not know me, says the
LORD.

4 Beware of your neighbors,
and put no trust in any of your kin; *c*
for all your kin *d* are supplanters,
and every neighbor goes around like a
slanderer.

5 They all deceive their neighbors,
and no one speaks the truth;
they have taught their tongues to speak
lies;
they commit iniquity and are too
weary to repent. *e*

6 Oppression upon oppression, deceit *f*
upon deceit!
They refuse to know me, says the
LORD.

7 Therefore thus says the LORD of hosts:
I will now refine and test them,
for what else can I do with my sinful
people? *g*

8 Their tongue is a deadly arrow;
it speaks deceit through the mouth.
They all speak friendly words to their
neighbors,
but inwardly are planning to lay an
ambush.

9 Shall I not punish them for these things?
says the LORD;
and shall I not bring retribution
on a nation such as this?

10 Take up *b* weeping and wailing for the
mountains,
and a lamentation for the pastures of
the wilderness,
because they are laid waste so that no
one passes through,
and the lowing of cattle is not heard;
both the birds of the air and the animals
have fled and are gone.

11 I will make Jerusalem a heap of ruins,
a lair of jackals;
and I will make the towns of Judah a
desolation,
without inhabitant.

12 Who is wise enough to understand this? To whom has the mouth of the LORD spoken, so that they may declare it? Why is the land ruined and laid waste like a wilderness, so that no one passes through? 13 And the LORD says: Because they have forsaken my law that I set before them, and have not obeyed my voice, or walked in accordance with it, 14 but have stubbornly followed their own hearts and have gone after the Baals, as their ancestors taught

---

a Ch 8.23 in Heb   *b* Ch 9.1 in Heb   *c* Heb *in a brother*   *d* Heb *for every brother*   *e* Cn Compare Gk: Heb *they weary themselves with iniquity.* *6* *Your dwelling*   *f* Cn: Heb *Your dwelling in the midst of deceit*   *g* Or *my poor people*   *b* Gk Syr: Heb *I will take up* them. 15Therefore thus says the LORD of hosts, the God of Israel: I am feeding this people with wormwood, and giving them poisonous water to drink. 16I will scatter them among nations that neither they nor their ancestors have known; and I will send the sword after them, until I have consumed them.

The People Mourn in Judgment

17 Thus says the LORD of hosts:
Consider, and call for the mourning
women to come;
send for the skilled women to come;
18 let them quickly raise a dirge over us,
so that our eyes may run down with
tears,
and our eyelids flow with water.
19 For a sound of wailing is heard from
Zion:
"How we are ruined!
We are utterly shamed,
because we have left the land,
because they have cast down our
dwellings."

20 Hear, O women, the word of the LORD,
and let your ears receive the word of
his mouth;
teach to your daughters a dirge,
and each to her neighbor a lament.
21 "Death has come up into our windows,
it has entered our palaces,
to cut off the children from the streets
and the young men from the squares."
22 Speak! Thus says the LORD:
"Human corpses shall fall
like dung upon the open field,
like sheaves behind the reaper,
and no one shall gather them."

23 Thus says the LORD: Do not let the wise boast in their wisdom, do not let the mighty boast in their might, do not let the wealthy boast in their wealth; 24but let those who boast boast in this, that they understand and know me, that I am the LORD; I act with steadfast love, justice,

and righteousness in the earth, for in these things I delight, says the LORD.

25 The days are surely coming, says the LORD, when I will attend to all those who are circumcised only in the foreskin: 26Egypt, Judah, Edom, the Ammonites, Moab, and all those with shaven temples who live in the desert. For all these nations are uncircumcised, and all the house of Israel is uncircumcised in heart.

Idolatry Has Brought Ruin on Israel

10 Hear the word that the LORD speaks to you, O house of Israel. 2Thus says the LORD:
Do not learn the way of the nations,
or be dismayed at the signs of the
heavens;
for the nations are dismayed at them.
3 For the customs of the peoples are false:
a tree from the forest is cut down,
and worked with an ax by the hands
of an artisan;
4 people deck it with silver and gold;
they fasten it with hammer and nails
so that it cannot move.
5 Their idols*a* are like scarecrows in a
cucumber field,
and they cannot speak;
they have to be carried,
for they cannot walk.
Do not be afraid of them,
for they cannot do evil,
nor is it in them to do good.

6 There is none like you, O LORD;
you are great, and your name is great
in might.
7 Who would not fear you, O King of the
nations?
For that is your due;
among all the wise ones of the nations
and in all their kingdoms
there is no one like you.
8 They are both stupid and foolish;
the instruction given by idols
is no better than wood!*b*

---

a Heb *They*   *b* Meaning of Heb uncertain

9 Beaten silver is brought from Tarshish,
      and gold from Uphaz.
   They are the work of the artisan and of
         the hands of the goldsmith;
      their clothing is blue and purple;
      they are all the product of skilled
         workers.
10 But the LORD is the true God;
      he is the living God and the
         everlasting King.
   At his wrath the earth quakes,
      and the nations cannot endure his
         indignation.

11 Thus shall you say to them: The gods
who did not make the heavens and the earth
shall perish from the earth and from under
the heavens.[a]

12 It is he who made the earth by his power,
      who established the world by his
         wisdom,
      and by his understanding stretched
         out the heavens.
13 When he utters his voice, there is a
         tumult of waters in the heavens,
      and he makes the mist rise from the
         ends of the earth.
   He makes lightnings for the rain,
      and he brings out the wind from his
         storehouses.
14 Everyone is stupid and without
         knowledge;
      goldsmiths are all put to shame by
         their idols;
   for their images are false,
      and there is no breath in them.
15 They are worthless, a work of delusion;
      at the time of their punishment they
         shall perish.
16 Not like these is the LORD,[b] the portion
         of Jacob,
      for he is the one who formed all
         things,
      and Israel is the tribe of his inheritance;
      the LORD of hosts is his name.

The Coming Exile

17 Gather up your bundle from the ground,
      O you who live under siege!
18 For thus says the LORD:
   I am going to sling out the inhabitants of
         the land
         at this time,
   and I will bring distress on them,
      so that they shall feel it.

19 Woe is me because of my hurt!
      My wound is severe.
   But I said, "Truly this is my punishment,
         and I must bear it."
20 My tent is destroyed,
      and all my cords are broken;
   my children have gone from me,
      and they are no more;
   there is no one to spread my tent again,
      and to set up my curtains.
21 For the shepherds are stupid,
      and do not inquire of the LORD;
   therefore they have not prospered,
      and all their flock is scattered.

22 Hear, a noise! Listen, it is coming—
      a great commotion from the land of
         the north
   to make the cities of Judah a desolation,
      a lair of jackals.

23 I know, O LORD, that the way of human
         beings is not in their control,
      that mortals as they walk cannot direct
         their steps.
24 Correct me, O LORD, but in just
         measure;
      not in your anger, or you will bring me
         to nothing.

25 Pour out your wrath on the nations that
         do not know you,
      and on the peoples that do not call on
         your name;
   for they have devoured Jacob;

---

a This verse is in Aramaic   *b* Heb lacks *the* LORD

they have devoured him and
    consumed him,
and have laid waste his habitation.

Israel and Judah Have Broken the Covenant

11 The word that came to Jeremiah from the LORD: ²Hear the words of this covenant, and speak to the people of Judah and the inhabitants of Jerusalem. ³You shall say to them, Thus says the LORD, the God of Israel: Cursed be anyone who does not heed the words of this covenant, ⁴which I commanded your ancestors when I brought them out of the land of Egypt, from the iron-smelter, saying, Listen to my voice, and do all that I command you. So shall you be my people, and I will be your God, ⁵that I may perform the oath that I swore to your ancestors, to give them a land flowing with milk and honey, as at this day. Then I answered, "So be it, LORD."

6 And the LORD said to me: Proclaim all these words in the cities of Judah, and in the streets of Jerusalem: Hear the words of this covenant and do them. ⁷For I solemnly warned your ancestors when I brought them up out of the land of Egypt, warning them persistently, even to this day, saying, Obey my voice. ⁸Yet they did not obey or incline their ear, but everyone walked in the stubbornness of an evil will. So I brought upon them all the words of this covenant, which I commanded them to do, but they did not.

9 And the LORD said to me: Conspiracy exists among the people of Judah and the inhabitants of Jerusalem. ¹⁰They have turned back to the iniquities of their ancestors of old, who refused to heed my words; they have gone after other gods to serve them; the house of Israel and the house of Judah have broken the covenant that I made with their ancestors. ¹¹Therefore, thus says the LORD, assuredly I am going to bring disaster upon them that they cannot escape; though they cry out to me, I will not listen to them. ¹²Then the cities of Judah and the inhabitants of Jerusalem will go and cry out to the gods to whom they make offerings, but they will never save them in the time of their trouble. ¹³For your gods have become as many as your towns, O Judah; and as many as the streets of Jerusalem are the altars to shame you have set up, altars to make offerings to Baal.

14 As for you, do not pray for this people, or lift up a cry or prayer on their behalf, for I will not listen when they call to me in the time of their trouble. ¹⁵What right has my beloved in my house, when she has done vile deeds? Can vows*ᵃ* and sacrificial flesh avert your doom? Can you then exult? ¹⁶The LORD once called you, "A green olive tree, fair with goodly fruit"; but with the roar of a great tempest he will set fire to it, and its branches will be consumed. ¹⁷The LORD of hosts, who planted you, has pronounced evil against you, because of the evil that the house of Israel and the house of Judah have done, provoking me to anger by making offerings to Baal.

Jeremiah's Life Threatened

18 It was the LORD who made it known to
    me, and I knew;
    then you showed me their evil deeds.
19 But I was like a gentle lamb
    led to the slaughter.
And I did not know it was against me
    that they devised schemes, saying,
"Let us destroy the tree with its fruit,
    let us cut him off from the land of
        the living,
    so that his name will no longer be
        remembered!"
20 But you, O LORD of hosts, who judge
    righteously,
    who try the heart and the mind,
let me see your retribution upon them,
    for to you I have committed my cause.

21 Therefore thus says the LORD concerning the people of Anathoth, who seek your life, and say, "You shall not prophesy in the name of the LORD, or you will die by our hand"— ²²therefore thus says the LORD of hosts: I am going to punish them; the young men shall die by the sword; their sons and their daughters

a Gk: Heb *Can many*

shall die by famine; ²³and not even a remnant shall be left of them. For I will bring disaster upon the people of Anathoth, the year of their punishment.

Jeremiah Complains to God

12 You will be in the right, O LORD,
    when I lay charges against you;
    but let me put my case to you.
    Why does the way of the guilty prosper?
    Why do all who are treacherous
       thrive?

2 You plant them, and they take root;
    they grow and bring forth fruit;
    you are near in their mouths
    yet far from their hearts.

3 But you, O LORD, know me;
    You see me and test me—my heart is
       with you.
    Pull them out like sheep for the
       slaughter,
    and set them apart for the day of
       slaughter.

4 How long will the land mourn,
    and the grass of every field wither?
    For the wickedness of those who live in it
    the animals and the birds are swept
       away,
    and because people said, "He is blind
       to our ways." *a*

God Replies to Jeremiah

5 If you have raced with foot-runners and
       they have wearied you,
    how will you compete with horses?
    And if in a safe land you fall down,
    how will you fare in the thickets of
       the Jordan?

6 For even your kinsfolk and your own
       family,
    even they have dealt treacherously
       with you;
    they are in full cry after you;
    do not believe them,
    though they speak friendly words to
       you.

7 I have forsaken my house,
    I have abandoned my heritage;
    I have given the beloved of my heart
       into the hands of her enemies.

8 My heritage has become to me
    like a lion in the forest;
    she has lifted up her voice against me—
       therefore I hate her.

9 Is the hyena greedy *b* for my heritage at
       my command?
    Are the birds of prey all around her?
    Go, assemble all the wild animals;
       bring them to devour her.

10 Many shepherds have destroyed my
       vineyard,
    they have trampled down my portion,
    they have made my pleasant portion
       a desolate wilderness.

11 They have made it a desolation;
       desolate, it mourns to me.
    The whole land is made desolate,
    but no one lays it to heart.

12 Upon all the bare heights *c* in the desert
       spoilers have come;
    for the sword of the LORD devours
       from one end of the land to the other;
    no one shall be safe.

13 They have sown wheat and have reaped
       thorns,
    they have tired themselves out but
       profit nothing.
    They shall be ashamed of their *d* harvests
       because of the fierce anger of the
       LORD.

14 Thus says the LORD concerning all my evil neighbors who touch the heritage that I have given my people Israel to inherit: I am about to pluck them up from their land, and I will pluck up the house of Judah from among them. ¹⁵And after I have plucked them up, I will again have compassion on them, and I will bring them again to their heritage and to their land, every one of them. ¹⁶And then, if they will diligently learn the ways of my people, to swear by my name, "As the LORD lives," as

---

a Gk: Heb *to our future*   *b* Cn: Heb *Is the hyena, the bird of prey*   *c* Or *the trails*   *d* Heb *your* they taught my people to swear by Baal, then they shall be built up in the midst of my people. [17]But if any nation will not listen, then I will completely uproot it and destroy it, says the LORD.

The Linen Loincloth

13 Thus said the LORD to me, "Go and buy yourself a linen loincloth, and put it on your loins, but do not dip it in water." [2]So I bought a loincloth according to the word of the LORD, and put it on my loins. [3]And the word of the LORD came to me a second time, saying, [4]"Take the loincloth that you bought and are wearing, and go now to the Euphrates,[a] and hide it there in a cleft of the rock." [5]So I went, and hid it by the Euphrates,[b] as the LORD commanded me. [6]And after many days the LORD said to me, "Go now to the Euphrates,[a] and take from there the loincloth that I commanded you to hide there." [7]Then I went to the Euphrates,[a] and dug, and I took the loincloth from the place where I had hidden it. But now the loincloth was ruined; it was good for nothing.

8 Then the word of the LORD came to me: [9]Thus says the LORD: Just so I will ruin the pride of Judah and the great pride of Jerusalem. [10]This evil people, who refuse to hear my words, who stubbornly follow their own will and have gone after other gods to serve them and worship them, shall be like this loincloth, which is good for nothing. [11]For as the loincloth clings to one's loins, so I made the whole house of Israel and the whole house of Judah cling to me, says the LORD, in order that they might be for me a people, a name, a praise, and a glory. But they would not listen.

Symbol of the Wine-Jars

12 You shall speak to them this word: Thus says the LORD, the God of Israel: Every wine-jar should be filled with wine. And they will say to you, "Do you think we do not know that every wine-jar should be filled with wine?" [13]Then you shall say to them: Thus says the LORD: I am about to fill all the inhabitants of this land—the kings who sit on David's throne, the priests, the prophets, and all the inhabitants of Jerusalem—with drunkenness. [14]And I will dash them one against another, parents and children together, says the LORD. I will not pity or spare or have compassion when I destroy them.

Exile Threatened

15 Hear and give ear; do not be haughty,
    for the LORD has spoken.
16 Give glory to the LORD your God
    before he brings darkness,
and before your feet stumble
    on the mountains at twilight;
while you look for light,
    he turns it into gloom
    and makes it deep darkness.
17 But if you will not listen,
    my soul will weep in secret for your
      pride;
my eyes will weep bitterly and run down
    with tears,
    because the LORD's flock has been
      taken captive.

18 Say to the king and the queen mother:
    "Take a lowly seat,
for your beautiful crown
    has come down from your head."[c]
19 The towns of the Negeb are shut up
    with no one to open them;
all Judah is taken into exile,
    wholly taken into exile.

20 Lift up your eyes and see
    those who come from the north.
Where is the flock that was given you,
    your beautiful flock?
21 What will you say when they set as head
      over you
    those whom you have trained
    to be your allies?
Will not pangs take hold of you,
    like those of a woman in labor?

a Or to Parah; Heb perath   b Or by Parah; Heb perath   c Gk Syr Vg: Meaning of Heb uncertain

22 And if you say in your heart,
      "Why have these things come upon
         me?"
      it is for the greatness of your iniquity
         that your skirts are lifted up,
         and you are violated.
23 Can Ethiopians*a* change their skin
         or leopards their spots?
      Then also you can do good
         who are accustomed to do evil.
24 I will scatter you*b* like chaff
         driven by the wind from the desert.
25 This is your lot,
         the portion I have measured out to
            you, says the LORD,
      because you have forgotten me
         and trusted in lies.
26 I myself will lift up your skirts over your
            face,
         and your shame will be seen.
27 I have seen your abominations,
         your adulteries and neighings, your
            shameless prostitutions
         on the hills of the countryside.
      Woe to you, O Jerusalem!
         How long will it be
         before you are made clean?

The Great Drought

14 The word of the LORD that came to
      Jeremiah concerning the drought:
2 Judah mourns
      and her gates languish;
      they lie in gloom on the ground,
      and the cry of Jerusalem goes up.
3 Her nobles send their servants for water;
      they come to the cisterns,
   they find no water,
      they return with their vessels empty.
   They are ashamed and dismayed
      and cover their heads,
4 because the ground is cracked.
      Because there has been no rain on the
         land
      the farmers are dismayed;
         they cover their heads.

5 Even the doe in the field forsakes her
            newborn fawn
         because there is no grass.
6 The wild asses stand on the bare
            heights,*c*
         they pant for air like jackals;
      their eyes fail
         because there is no herbage.

7 Although our iniquities testify against us,
         act, O LORD, for your name's sake;
      our apostasies indeed are many,
         and we have sinned against you.
8 O hope of Israel,
         its savior in time of trouble,
      why should you be like a stranger in the
            land,
         like a traveler turning aside for the
            night?
9 Why should you be like someone
            confused,
         like a mighty warrior who cannot give
            help?
      Yet you, O LORD, are in the midst of us,
         and we are called by your name;
         do not forsake us!

10 Thus says the LORD concerning this
            people:
      Truly they have loved to wander,
         they have not restrained their feet;
      therefore the LORD does not accept
            them,
         now he will remember their iniquity
         and punish their sins.

11 The LORD said to me: Do not pray for
the welfare of this people. 12Although they
fast, I do not hear their cry, and although they
offer burnt offering and grain offering, I do not
accept them; but by the sword, by famine, and
by pestilence I consume them.

Denunciation of Lying Prophets

13 Then I said: "Ah, Lord GOD! Here are
the prophets saying to them, 'You shall not

a Or Nubians; Heb Cushites   *b* Heb them   *c* Or the trails see the sword, nor shall you have famine, but I will give you true peace in this place.'" ¹⁴And the LORD said to me: The prophets are prophesying lies in my name; I did not send them, nor did I command them or speak to them. They are prophesying to you a lying vision, worthless divination, and the deceit of their own minds. ¹⁵Therefore thus says the LORD concerning the prophets who prophesy in my name though I did not send them, and who say, "Sword and famine shall not come on this land": By sword and famine those prophets shall be consumed. ¹⁶And the people to whom they prophesy shall be thrown out into the streets of Jerusalem, victims of famine and sword. There shall be no one to bury them—themselves, their wives, their sons, and their daughters. For I will pour out their wickedness upon them.

17 You shall say to them this word:
  Let my eyes run down with tears night
      and day,
    and let them not cease,
  for the virgin daughter—my people—is
      struck down with a crushing
      blow,
    with a very grievous wound.
18 If I go out into the field,
    look—those killed by the sword!
  And if I enter the city,
    look—those sick with ᵃ famine!
  For both prophet and priest ply their
      trade throughout the land,
    and have no knowledge.

The People Plead for Mercy

19 Have you completely rejected Judah?
    Does your heart loathe Zion?
  Why have you struck us down
    so that there is no healing for us?
  We look for peace, but find no good;
    for a time of healing, but there is
      terror instead.
20 We acknowledge our wickedness,
      O LORD,
    the iniquity of our ancestors,

for we have sinned against you.
21 Do not spurn us, for your name's sake;
    do not dishonor your glorious throne;
  remember and do not break your
      covenant with us.
22 Can any idols of the nations bring rain?
    Or can the heavens give showers?
  Is it not you, O LORD our God?
    We set our hope on you,
  for it is you who do all this.

Punishment Is Inevitable

15 Then the LORD said to me: Though Moses and Samuel stood before me, yet my heart would not turn toward this people. Send them out of my sight, and let them go! ²And when they say to you, "Where shall we go?" you shall say to them: Thus says the LORD:
  Those destined for pestilence, to
      pestilence,
    and those destined for the sword, to
      the sword;
  those destined for famine, to famine,
    and those destined for captivity, to
      captivity.

³And I will appoint over them four kinds of destroyers, says the LORD: the sword to kill, the dogs to drag away, and the birds of the air and the wild animals of the earth to devour and destroy. ⁴I will make them a horror to all the kingdoms of the earth because of what King Manasseh son of Hezekiah of Judah did in Jerusalem.

5 Who will have pity on you, O Jerusalem,
    or who will bemoan you?
  Who will turn aside
    to ask about your welfare?
6 You have rejected me, says the LORD,
    you are going backward;
  so I have stretched out my hand against
      you and destroyed you—
    I am weary of relenting.
7 I have winnowed them with a
      winnowing fork

ᵃ Heb look—the sicknesses of

in the gates of the land;
I have bereaved them, I have destroyed
   my people;
   they did not turn from their ways.
8   Their widows became more numerous
    than the sand of the seas;
I have brought against the mothers of
   youths
   a destroyer at noonday;
I have made anguish and terror
   fall upon her suddenly.
9   She who bore seven has languished;
    she has swooned away;
her sun went down while it was yet day;
    she has been shamed and disgraced.
And the rest of them I will give to the
   sword
   before their enemies,
             says the LORD.

Jeremiah Complains Again and Is Reassured

10 Woe is me, my mother, that you ever bore me, a man of strife and contention to the whole land! I have not lent, nor have I borrowed, yet all of them curse me. 11The LORD said: Surely I have intervened in your life*a* for good, surely I have imposed enemies on you in a time of trouble and in a time of distress.*b* 12Can iron and bronze break iron from the north?

13 Your wealth and your treasures I will give as plunder, without price, for all your sins, throughout all your territory. 14I will make you serve your enemies in a land that you do not know, for in my anger a fire is kindled that shall burn forever.
15   O LORD, you know;
   remember me and visit me,
   and bring down retribution for me on
    my persecutors.
In your forbearance do not take me
   away;
   know that on your account I suffer
    insult.
16   Your words were found, and I ate them,
   and your words became to me a joy

and the delight of my heart;
   for I am called by your name,
    O LORD, God of hosts.
17   I did not sit in the company of
    merrymakers,
   nor did I rejoice;
under the weight of your hand I sat
   alone,
   for you had filled me with indignation.
18   Why is my pain unceasing,
   my wound incurable,
   refusing to be healed?
Truly, you are to me like a deceitful
   brook,
   like waters that fail.

19   Therefore thus says the LORD:
If you turn back, I will take you back,
   and you shall stand before me.
If you utter what is precious, and not
    what is worthless,
   you shall serve as my mouth.
It is they who will turn to you,
   not you who will turn to them.
20   And I will make you to this people
   a fortified wall of bronze;
they will fight against you,
   but they shall not prevail over you,
for I am with you
   to save you and deliver you,
             says the LORD.
21   I will deliver you out of the hand of the
    wicked,
   and redeem you from the grasp of the
    ruthless.

Jeremiah's Celibacy and Message

16 The word of the LORD came to me: 2You shall not take a wife, nor shall you have sons or daughters in this place. 3For thus says the LORD concerning the sons and daughters who are born in this place, and concerning the mothers who bear them and the fathers who beget them in this land: 4They shall die of deadly diseases. They shall not be lamented, nor shall they be buried; they shall

---

a Heb *intervened with you*   *b* Meaning of Heb uncertain become like dung on the surface of the ground. They shall perish by the sword and by famine, and their dead bodies shall become food for the birds of the air and for the wild animals of the earth.

5 For thus says the LORD: Do not enter the house of mourning, or go to lament, or bemoan them; for I have taken away my peace from this people, says the LORD, my steadfast love and mercy. 6Both great and small shall die in this land; they shall not be buried, and no one shall lament for them; there shall be no gashing, no shaving of the head for them. 7No one shall break bread*a* for the mourner, to offer comfort for the dead; nor shall anyone give them the cup of consolation to drink for their fathers or their mothers. 8You shall not go into the house of feasting to sit with them, to eat and drink. 9For thus says the LORD of hosts, the God of Israel: I am going to banish from this place, in your days and before your eyes, the voice of mirth and the voice of gladness, the voice of the bridegroom and the voice of the bride.

10 And when you tell this people all these words, and they say to you, "Why has the LORD pronounced all this great evil against us? What is our iniquity? What is the sin that we have committed against the LORD our God?" 11then you shall say to them: It is because your ancestors have forsaken me, says the LORD, and have gone after other gods and have served and worshiped them, and have forsaken me and have not kept my law; 12and because you have behaved worse than your ancestors, for here you are, every one of you, following your stubborn evil will, refusing to listen to me. 13Therefore I will hurl you out of this land into a land that neither you nor your ancestors have known, and there you shall serve other gods day and night, for I will show you no favor.

God Will Restore Israel

14 Therefore, the days are surely coming, says the LORD, when it shall no longer be said, "As the LORD lives who brought the people of Israel up out of the land of Egypt," 15but "As the LORD lives who brought the people of Israel up out of the land of the north and out of all the lands where he had driven them." For I will bring them back to their own land that I gave to their ancestors.

16 I am now sending for many fishermen, says the LORD, and they shall catch them; and afterward I will send for many hunters, and they shall hunt them from every mountain and every hill, and out of the clefts of the rocks. 17For my eyes are on all their ways; they are not hidden from my presence, nor is their iniquity concealed from my sight. 18And*b* I will doubly repay their iniquity and their sin, because they have polluted my land with the carcasses of their detestable idols, and have filled my inheritance with their abominations.

19   O LORD, my strength and my
        stronghold,
    my refuge in the day of trouble,
  to you shall the nations come
    from the ends of the earth and say:
  Our ancestors have inherited nothing
        but lies,
    worthless things in which there is no
        profit.
20   Can mortals make for themselves gods?
    Such are no gods!

21 "Therefore I am surely going to teach them, this time I am going to teach them my power and my might, and they shall know that my name is the LORD."

Judah's Sin and Punishment

17 The sin of Judah is written with an iron pen; with a diamond point it is engraved on the tablet of their hearts, and on the horns of their altars, 2while their children remember their altars and their sacred poles,*c* beside every green tree, and on the high hills, 3on the mountains in the open country. Your wealth and all your treasures I will give for spoil as the price of your sin*d* throughout all

---

a Two Mss Gk: MT *break for them*   *b* Gk: Heb *And first*   *c* Heb *Asherim*   *d* Cn: Heb *spoil your high places for sin* your territory. ⁴By your own act you shall lose the heritage that I gave you, and I will make you serve your enemies in a land that you do not know, for in my anger a fire is kindled*a* that shall burn forever.

5   Thus says the LORD:
    Cursed are those who trust in mere
        mortals
    and make mere flesh their strength,
        whose hearts turn away from the
        LORD.
6   They shall be like a shrub in the desert,
        and shall not see when relief comes.
    They shall live in the parched places of
        the wilderness,
    in an uninhabited salt land.

7   Blessed are those who trust in the LORD,
        whose trust is the LORD.
8   They shall be like a tree planted by water,
        sending out its roots by the stream.
    It shall not fear when heat comes,
        and its leaves shall stay green;
    in the year of drought it is not anxious,
        and it does not cease to bear fruit.

9   The heart is devious above all else;
        it is perverse—
    who can understand it?
10 I the LORD test the mind
        and search the heart,
    to give to all according to their ways,
        according to the fruit of their doings.

11 Like the partridge hatching what it did
        not lay,
    so are all who amass wealth unjustly;
    in mid-life it will leave them,
        and at their end they will prove to be
        fools.

12 O glorious throne, exalted from the
        beginning,
    shrine of our sanctuary!
13 O hope of Israel! O LORD!

All who forsake you shall be put to
    shame;
those who turn away from you*b* shall be
    recorded in the underworld,*c*
for they have forsaken the fountain of
    living water, the LORD.

Jeremiah Prays for Vindication
14 Heal me, O LORD, and I shall be healed;
    save me, and I shall be saved;
        for you are my praise.
15 See how they say to me,
    "Where is the word of the LORD?
        Let it come!"
16 But I have not run away from being a
        shepherd*d* in your service,
    nor have I desired the fatal day.
    You know what came from my lips;
        it was before your face.
17 Do not become a terror to me;
    you are my refuge in the day of
        disaster;
18 Let my persecutors be shamed,
        but do not let me be shamed;
    let them be dismayed,
        but do not let me be dismayed;
    bring on them the day of disaster;
        destroy them with double destruction!

Hallow the Sabbath Day
    19 Thus said the LORD to me: Go and stand in the People's Gate, by which the kings of Judah enter and by which they go out, and in all the gates of Jerusalem, ²⁰and say to them: Hear the word of the LORD, you kings of Judah, and all Judah, and all the inhabitants of Jerusalem, who enter by these gates. ²¹Thus says the LORD: For the sake of your lives, take care that you do not bear a burden on the sabbath day or bring it in by the gates of Jerusalem. ²²And do not carry a burden out of your houses on the sabbath or do any work, but keep the sabbath day holy, as I commanded your ancestors. ²³Yet they did not listen or incline their ear; they stiffened their necks and would not hear or receive instruction.

a Two Mss Theodotion: *you kindled*   *b* Heb *me*   *c* Or *in the earth*   *d* Meaning of Heb uncertain

24 But if you listen to me, says the LORD, and bring in no burden by the gates of this city on the sabbath day, but keep the sabbath day holy and do no work on it, 25then there shall enter by the gates of this city kings*a* who sit on the throne of David, riding in chariots and on horses, they and their officials, the people of Judah and the inhabitants of Jerusalem; and this city shall be inhabited forever. 26And people shall come from the towns of Judah and the places around Jerusalem, from the land of Benjamin, from the Shephelah, from the hill country, and from the Negeb, bringing burnt offerings and sacrifices, grain offerings and frankincense, and bringing thank offerings to the house of the LORD. 27But if you do not listen to me, to keep the sabbath day holy, and to carry in no burden through the gates of Jerusalem on the sabbath day, then I will kindle a fire in its gates; it shall devour the palaces of Jerusalem and shall not be quenched.

The Potter and the Clay

18 The word that came to Jeremiah from the LORD: 2"Come, go down to the potter's house, and there I will let you hear my words." 3So I went down to the potter's house, and there he was working at his wheel. 4The vessel he was making of clay was spoiled in the potter's hand, and he reworked it into another vessel, as seemed good to him.

5 Then the word of the LORD came to me: 6Can I not do with you, O house of Israel, just as this potter has done? says the LORD. Just like the clay in the potter's hand, so are you in my hand, O house of Israel. 7At one moment I may declare concerning a nation or a kingdom, that I will pluck up and break down and destroy it, 8but if that nation, concerning which I have spoken, turns from its evil, I will change my mind about the disaster that I intended to bring on it. 9And at another moment I may declare concerning a nation or a kingdom that I will build and plant it, 10but if it does evil in my sight, not listening to my voice, then I will change my mind about the good that I had in-

tended to do it. 11Now, therefore, say to the people of Judah and the inhabitants of Jerusalem: Thus says the LORD: Look, I am a potter shaping evil against you and devising a plan against you. Turn now, all of you from your evil way, and amend your ways and your doings.

Israel's Stubborn Idolatry

12 But they say, "It is no use! We will follow our own plans, and each of us will act according to the stubbornness of our evil will."

13 Therefore thus says the LORD:
    Ask among the nations:
        Who has heard the like of this?
    The virgin Israel has done
        a most horrible thing.
14 Does the snow of Lebanon leave
        the crags of Sirion?*b*
    Do the mountain*c* waters run dry,*d*
        the cold flowing streams?
15 But my people have forgotten me,
        they burn offerings to a delusion;
    they have stumbled*e* in their ways,
        in the ancient roads,
    and have gone into bypaths,
        not the highway,
16 making their land a horror,
        a thing to be hissed at forever.
    All who pass by it are horrified
        and shake their heads.
17 Like the wind from the east,
        I will scatter them before the enemy.
    I will show them my back, not my face,
        in the day of their calamity.

A Plot against Jeremiah

18 Then they said, "Come, let us make plots against Jeremiah—for instruction shall not perish from the priest, nor counsel from the wise, nor the word from the prophet. Come, let us bring charges against him,*f* and let us not heed any of his words."

19 Give heed to me, O LORD,
        and listen to what my adversaries say!

a Cn: Heb *kings and officials*   *b* Cn: Heb *of the field*   *c* Cn: Heb *foreign*   *d* Cn: Heb *Are . . . plucked up?*
e Gk Syr Vg: Heb *they made them stumble*   *f* Heb *strike him with the tongue*

20 Is evil a recompense for good?
    Yet they have dug a pit for my life.
    Remember how I stood before you
       to speak good for them,
       to turn away your wrath from them.
21 Therefore give their children over to
       famine;
    hurl them out to the power of the
       sword,
    let their wives become childless and
       widowed.
    May their men meet death by
       pestilence,
    their youths be slain by the sword in
       battle.
22 May a cry be heard from their houses,
    when you bring the marauder
       suddenly upon them!
    For they have dug a pit to catch me,
       and laid snares for my feet.
23 Yet you, O LORD, know
       all their plotting to kill me.
    Do not forgive their iniquity,
       do not blot out their sin from your
       sight.
    Let them be tripped up before you;
       deal with them while you are angry.

The Broken Earthenware Jug

19 Thus said the LORD: Go and buy a
     potter's earthenware jug. Take with
you*a* some of the elders of the people and
some of the senior priests, 2and go out to the
valley of the son of Hinnom at the entry of the
Potsherd Gate, and proclaim there the words
that I tell you. 3You shall say: Hear the word of
the LORD, O kings of Judah and inhabitants of
Jerusalem. Thus says the LORD of hosts, the
God of Israel: I am going to bring such disaster upon this place that the ears of everyone
who hears of it will tingle. 4Because the people have forsaken me, and have profaned this
place by making offerings in it to other gods
whom neither they nor their ancestors nor the
kings of Judah have known, and because they
have filled this place with the blood of the in-

nocent, 5and gone on building the high places
of Baal to burn their children in the fire as
burnt offerings to Baal, which I did not command or decree, nor did it enter my mind;
6therefore the days are surely coming, says the
LORD, when this place shall no more be called
Topheth, or the valley of the son of Hinnom,
but the valley of Slaughter. 7And in this place
I will make void the plans of Judah and Jerusalem, and will make them fall by the sword before their enemies, and by the hand of those
who seek their life. I will give their dead bodies for food to the birds of the air and to the
wild animals of the earth. 8And I will make this
city a horror, a thing to be hissed at; everyone
who passes by it will be horrified and will hiss
because of all its disasters. 9And I will make
them eat the flesh of their sons and the flesh
of their daughters, and all shall eat the flesh of
their neighbors in the siege, and in the distress
with which their enemies and those who seek
their life afflict them.

10 Then you shall break the jug in the sight
of those who go with you, 11and shall say to
them: Thus says the LORD of hosts: So will I
break this people and this city, as one breaks a
potter's vessel, so that it can never be mended.
In Topheth they shall bury until there is no
more room to bury. 12Thus will I do to this
place, says the LORD, and to its inhabitants,
making this city like Topheth. 13And the houses
of Jerusalem and the houses of the kings of Judah shall be defiled like the place of Topheth—
all the houses upon whose roofs offerings have
been made to the whole host of heaven, and
libations have been poured out to other gods.

14 When Jeremiah came from Topheth,
where the LORD had sent him to prophesy, he
stood in the court of the LORD's house and said
to all the people: 15Thus says the LORD of
hosts, the God of Israel: I am now bringing
upon this city and upon all its towns all the disaster that I have pronounced against it, because they have stiffened their necks, refusing
to hear my words.

a Syr Tg Compare Gk: Heb lacks *take with you*

Jeremiah Persecuted by Pashhur

20 Now the priest Pashhur son of Immer, who was chief officer in the house of the LORD, heard Jeremiah prophesying these things. ²Then Pashhur struck the prophet Jeremiah, and put him in the stocks that were in the upper Benjamin Gate of the house of the LORD. ³The next morning when Pashhur released Jeremiah from the stocks, Jeremiah said to him, The LORD has named you not Pashhur but "Terror-all-around." ⁴For thus says the LORD: I am making you a terror to yourself and to all your friends; and they shall fall by the sword of their enemies while you look on. And I will give all Judah into the hand of the king of Babylon; he shall carry them captive to Babylon, and shall kill them with the sword. ⁵I will give all the wealth of this city, all its gains, all its prized belongings, and all the treasures of the kings of Judah into the hand of their enemies, who shall plunder them, and seize them, and carry them to Babylon. ⁶And you, Pashhur, and all who live in your house, shall go into captivity, and to Babylon you shall go; there you shall die, and there you shall be buried, you and all your friends, to whom you have prophesied falsely.

Jeremiah Denounces His Persecutors

7 O LORD, you have enticed me,
    and I was enticed;
  you have overpowered me,
    and you have prevailed.
  I have become a laughingstock all day
      long;
    everyone mocks me.
8 For whenever I speak, I must cry out,
    I must shout, "Violence and
        destruction!"
  For the word of the LORD has become
      for me
    a reproach and derision all day long.
9 If I say, "I will not mention him,
    or speak any more in his name,"
  then within me there is something like a
      burning fire
    shut up in my bones;
  I am weary with holding it in,

  and I cannot.
10 For I hear many whispering:
    "Terror is all around!
  Denounce him! Let us denounce him!"
    All my close friends
    are watching for me to stumble.
  "Perhaps he can be enticed,
    and we can prevail against him,
    and take our revenge on him."
11 But the LORD is with me like a dread
        warrior;
    therefore my persecutors will stumble,
    and they will not prevail.
  They will be greatly shamed,
    for they will not succeed.
  Their eternal dishonor
    will never be forgotten.
12 O LORD of hosts, you test the righteous,
    you see the heart and the mind;
  let me see your retribution upon them,
    for to you I have committed my cause.

13 Sing to the LORD;
    praise the LORD!
  For he has delivered the life of the needy
    from the hands of evildoers.

14 Cursed be the day
    on which I was born!
  The day when my mother bore me,
    let it not be blessed!
15 Cursed be the man
    who brought the news to my father,
        saying,
  "A child is born to you, a son,"
    making him very glad.
16 Let that man be like the cities
    that the LORD overthrew without pity;
  let him hear a cry in the morning
    and an alarm at noon,
17 because he did not kill me in the womb;
    so my mother would have been my
        grave,
    and her womb forever great.
18 Why did I come forth from the womb
    to see toil and sorrow,
    and spend my days in shame?

Jerusalem Will Fall to Nebuchadrezzar

21 This is the word that came to Jeremiah from the LORD, when King Zedekiah sent to him Pashhur son of Malchiah and the priest Zephaniah son of Maaseiah, saying, 2"Please inquire of the LORD on our behalf, for King Nebuchadrezzar of Babylon is making war against us; perhaps the LORD will perform a wonderful deed for us, as he has often done, and will make him withdraw from us."

3 Then Jeremiah said to them: 4Thus you shall say to Zedekiah: Thus says the LORD, the God of Israel: I am going to turn back the weapons of war that are in your hands and with which you are fighting against the king of Babylon and against the Chaldeans who are besieging you outside the walls; and I will bring them together into the center of this city. 5I myself will fight against you with outstretched hand and mighty arm, in anger, in fury, and in great wrath. 6And I will strike down the inhabitants of this city, both human beings and animals; they shall die of a great pestilence. 7Afterward, says the LORD, I will give King Zedekiah of Judah, and his servants, and the people in this city—those who survive the pestilence, sword, and famine—into the hands of King Nebuchadrezzar of Babylon, into the hands of their enemies, into the hands of those who seek their lives. He shall strike them down with the edge of the sword; he shall not pity them, or spare them, or have compassion.

8 And to this people you shall say: Thus says the LORD: See, I am setting before you the way of life and the way of death. 9Those who stay in this city shall die by the sword, by famine, and by pestilence; but those who go out and surrender to the Chaldeans who are besieging you shall live and shall have their lives as a prize of war. 10For I have set my face against this city for evil and not for good, says the LORD: it shall be given into the hands of the king of Babylon, and he shall burn it with fire.

Message to the House of David

11 To the house of the king of Judah say:

Hear the word of the LORD, 12O house of David! Thus says the LORD:

> Execute justice in the morning,
> and deliver from the hand of the
> oppressor
> anyone who has been robbed,
> or else my wrath will go forth like fire,
> and burn, with no one to quench it,
> because of your evil doings.

13   See, I am against you, O inhabitant of
> the valley,
> O rock of the plain,
> says the LORD;
> you who say, "Who can come down
> against us,
> or who can enter our places of
> refuge?"
14   I will punish you according to the fruit
> of your doings,
> says the LORD;
> I will kindle a fire in its forest,
> and it shall devour all that is around it.

Exhortation to Repent

22 Thus says the LORD: Go down to the house of the king of Judah, and speak there this word, 2and say: Hear the word of the LORD, O King of Judah sitting on the throne of David—you, and your servants, and your people who enter these gates. 3Thus says the LORD: Act with justice and righteousness, and deliver from the hand of the oppressor anyone who has been robbed. And do no wrong or violence to the alien, the orphan, and the widow, or shed innocent blood in this place. 4For if you will indeed obey this word, then through the gates of this house shall enter kings who sit on the throne of David, riding in chariots and on horses, they, and their servants, and their people. 5But if you will not heed these words, I swear by myself, says the LORD, that this house shall become a desolation. 6For thus says the LORD concerning the house of the king of Judah:

> You are like Gilead to me,
> like the summit of Lebanon;
> but I swear that I will make you a desert,

an uninhabited city.*a*

7 I will prepare destroyers against you,
  all with their weapons;
    they shall cut down your choicest cedars
    and cast them into the fire.

8 And many nations will pass by this city, and all of them will say one to another, "Why has the LORD dealt in this way with that great city?" 9And they will answer, "Because they abandoned the covenant of the LORD their God, and worshiped other gods and served them."

10 Do not weep for him who is dead,
    nor bemoan him;
  weep rather for him who goes away,
    for he shall return no more
    to see his native land.

Message to the Sons of Josiah

11 For thus says the LORD concerning Shallum son of King Josiah of Judah, who succeeded his father Josiah, and who went away from this place: He shall return here no more, 12but in the place where they have carried him captive he shall die, and he shall never see this land again.

13 Woe to him who builds his house by
      unrighteousness,
    and his upper rooms by injustice;
  who makes his neighbors work for
      nothing,
    and does not give them their wages;
14 who says, "I will build myself a spacious
      house
    with large upper rooms,"
  and who cuts out windows for it,
    paneling it with cedar,
    and painting it with vermilion.
15 Are you a king
    because you compete in cedar?
  Did not your father eat and drink
    and do justice and righteousness?
    Then it was well with him.

16 He judged the cause of the poor and
      needy;
    then it was well.
  Is not this to know me?
    says the LORD.
17 But your eyes and heart
    are only on your dishonest gain,
  for shedding innocent blood,
    and for practicing oppression and
      violence.

18 Therefore thus says the LORD concerning King Jehoiakim son of Josiah of Judah:
  They shall not lament for him, saying,
    "Alas, my brother!" or "Alas, sister!"
  They shall not lament for him, saying,
    "Alas, lord!" or "Alas, his majesty!"
19 With the burial of a donkey he shall be
      buried—
    dragged off and thrown out beyond
      the gates of Jerusalem.

20 Go up to Lebanon, and cry out,
    and lift up your voice in Bashan;
  cry out from Abarim,
    for all your lovers are crushed.
21 I spoke to you in your prosperity,
    but you said, "I will not listen."
  This has been your way from your youth,
    for you have not obeyed my voice.
22 The wind shall shepherd all your
      shepherds,
    and your lovers shall go into captivity;
  then you will be ashamed and dismayed
    because of all your wickedness.
23 O inhabitant of Lebanon,
    nested among the cedars,
  how you will groan*b* when pangs come
      upon you,
    pain as of a woman in labor!

Judgment on Coniah (Jehoiachin)

24 As I live, says the LORD, even if King Coniah son of Jehoiakim of Judah were the signet ring on my right hand, even from there I would tear you off 25and give you into the hands of those who seek your life, into the

---

a Cn: Heb *uninhabited cities*   *b* Gk Vg Syr: Heb *will be pitied* hands of those of whom you are afraid, even into the hands of King Nebuchadrezzar of Babylon and into the hands of the Chaldeans. 26I will hurl you and the mother who bore you into another country, where you were not born, and there you shall die. 27But they shall not return to the land to which they long to return.

28 Is this man Coniah a despised broken
          pot,
      a vessel no one wants?
    Why are he and his offspring hurled out
      and cast away in a land that they do
          not know?
29 O land, land, land,
      hear the word of the LORD!
30 Thus says the LORD:
    Record this man as childless,
      a man who shall not succeed in his
          days;
    for none of his offspring shall succeed
      in sitting on the throne of David,
      and ruling again in Judah.

Restoration after Exile

23 Woe to the shepherds who destroy and scatter the sheep of my pasture! says the LORD. 2Therefore thus says the LORD, the God of Israel, concerning the shepherds who shepherd my people: It is you who have scattered my flock, and have driven them away, and you have not attended to them. So I will attend to you for your evil doings, says the LORD. 3Then I myself will gather the remnant of my flock out of all the lands where I have driven them, and I will bring them back to their fold, and they shall be fruitful and multiply. 4I will raise up shepherds over them who will shepherd them, and they shall not fear any longer, or be dismayed, nor shall any be missing, says the LORD.

The Righteous Branch of David

5 The days are surely coming, says the LORD, when I will raise up for David a righteous Branch, and he shall reign as king and deal wisely, and shall execute justice and righ-

teousness in the land. 6In his days Judah will be saved and Israel will live in safety. And this is the name by which he will be called: "The LORD is our righteousness."

7 Therefore, the days are surely coming, says the LORD, when it shall no longer be said, "As the LORD lives who brought the people of Israel up out of the land of Egypt," 8but "As the LORD lives who brought out and led the offspring of the house of Israel out of the land of the north and out of all the lands where hea had driven them." Then they shall live in their own land.

False Prophets of Hope Denounced

9 Concerning the prophets:
    My heart is crushed within me,
      all my bones shake;
    I have become like a drunkard,
      like one overcome by wine,
    because of the LORD
      and because of his holy words.
10 For the land is full of adulterers;
      because of the curse the land mourns,
      and the pastures of the wilderness are
          dried up.
    Their course has been evil,
      and their might is not right.
11 Both prophet and priest are ungodly;
      even in my house I have found their
          wickedness,
                              says the LORD.
12 Therefore their way shall be to them
      like slippery paths in the darkness,
      into which they shall be driven and
          fall;
    for I will bring disaster upon them
      in the year of their punishment,
                              says the LORD.
13 In the prophets of Samaria
      I saw a disgusting thing:
    they prophesied by Baal
      and led my people Israel astray.
14 But in the prophets of Jerusalem
      I have seen a more shocking thing:
    they commit adultery and walk in lies;

a Gk: Heb I

they strengthen the hands of
    evildoers,
so that no one turns from wickedness;
all of them have become like Sodom to
    me,
    and its inhabitants like Gomorrah.
15 Therefore thus says the LORD of hosts
    concerning the prophets:
"I am going to make them eat
    wormwood,
    and give them poisoned water to
    drink;
for from the prophets of Jerusalem
    ungodliness has spread throughout
    the land."

16 Thus says the LORD of hosts: Do not listen to the words of the prophets who prophesy to you; they are deluding you. They speak
visions of their own minds, not from the
mouth of the LORD. 17They keep saying to
those who despise the word of the LORD, "It
shall be well with you"; and to all who stubbornly follow their own stubborn hearts, they
say, "No calamity shall come upon you."

18   For who has stood in the council of the
    LORD
    so as to see and to hear his word?
    Who has given heed to his word so as
    to proclaim it?
19   Look, the storm of the LORD!
    Wrath has gone forth,
  a whirling tempest;
    it will burst upon the head of the
    wicked.
20   The anger of the LORD will not turn
    back
    until he has executed and
    accomplished
    the intents of his mind.
  In the latter days you will understand it
    clearly.

21   I did not send the prophets,
    yet they ran;

    I did not speak to them,
    yet they prophesied.
22   But if they had stood in my council,
    then they would have proclaimed my
    words to my people,
  and they would have turned them from
    their evil way,
    and from the evil of their doings.

23 Am I a God near by, says the LORD, and
not a God far off? 24Who can hide in secret
places so that I cannot see them? says the
LORD. Do I not fill heaven and earth? says the
LORD. 25I have heard what the prophets have
said who prophesy lies in my name, saying, "I
have dreamed, I have dreamed!" 26How long?
Will the hearts of the prophets ever turn
back—those who prophesy lies, and who
prophesy the deceit of their own heart? 27They
plan to make my people forget my name by
their dreams that they tell one another, just as
their ancestors forgot my name for Baal. 28Let
the prophet who has a dream tell the dream,
but let the one who has my word speak my
word faithfully. What has straw in common
with wheat? says the LORD. 29Is not my word
like fire, says the LORD, and like a hammer that
breaks a rock in pieces? 30See, therefore, I am
against the prophets, says the LORD, who steal
my words from one another. 31See, I am against
the prophets, says the LORD, who use their
own tongues and say, "Says the LORD." 32See,
I am against those who prophesy lying dreams,
says the LORD, and who tell them, and who lead
my people astray by their lies and their reck-
lessness, when I did not send them or appoint
them; so they do not profit this people at all,
says the LORD.

33 When this people, or a prophet, or a
priest asks you, "What is the burden of the
LORD?" you shall say to them, "You are the burden,a and I will cast you off, says the LORD."
34And as for the prophet, priest, or the people
who say, "The burden of the LORD," I will
punish them and their households. 35Thus shall
you say to one another, among yourselves,

a Gk Vg: Heb *What burden*

"What has the LORD answered?" or "What has the LORD spoken?" 36But "the burden of the LORD" you shall mention no more, for the burden is everyone's own word, and so you pervert the words of the living God, the LORD of hosts, our God. 37Thus you shall ask the prophet, "What has the LORD answered you?" or "What has the LORD spoken?" 38But if you say, "the burden of the LORD," thus says the LORD: Because you have said these words, "the burden of the LORD," when I sent to you, saying, You shall not say, "the burden of the LORD," 39therefore, I will surely lift you up*a* and cast you away from my presence, you and the city that I gave to you and your ancestors. 40And I will bring upon you everlasting disgrace and perpetual shame, which shall not be forgotten.

The Good and the Bad Figs

24 The LORD showed me two baskets of figs placed before the temple of the LORD. This was after King Nebuchadrezzar of Babylon had taken into exile from Jerusalem King Jeconiah son of Jehoiakim of Judah, together with the officials of Judah, the artisans, and the smiths, and had brought them to Babylon. 2One basket had very good figs, like first-ripe figs, but the other basket had very bad figs, so bad that they could not be eaten. 3And the LORD said to me, "What do you see, Jeremiah?" I said, "Figs, the good figs very good, and the bad figs very bad, so bad that they cannot be eaten."

4 Then the word of the LORD came to me: 5Thus says the LORD, the God of Israel: Like these good figs, so I will regard as good the exiles from Judah, whom I have sent away from this place to the land of the Chaldeans. 6I will set my eyes upon them for good, and I will bring them back to this land. I will build them up, and not tear them down; I will plant them, and not pluck them up. 7I will give them a heart to know that I am the LORD; and they shall be my people and I will be their God, for they shall return to me with their whole heart.

8 But thus says the LORD: Like the bad figs that are so bad they cannot be eaten, so will I treat King Zedekiah of Judah, his officials, the remnant of Jerusalem who remain in this land, and those who live in the land of Egypt. 9I will make them a horror, an evil thing, to all the kingdoms of the earth—a disgrace, a byword, a taunt, and a curse in all the places where I shall drive them. 10And I will send sword, famine, and pestilence upon them, until they are utterly destroyed from the land that I gave to them and their ancestors.

The Babylonian Captivity Foretold

25 The word that came to Jeremiah concerning all the people of Judah, in the fourth year of King Jehoiakim son of Josiah of Judah (that was the first year of King Nebuchadrezzar of Babylon), 2which the prophet Jeremiah spoke to all the people of Judah and all the inhabitants of Jerusalem: 3For twenty-three years, from the thirteenth year of King Josiah son of Amon of Judah, to this day, the word of the LORD has come to me, and I have spoken persistently to you, but you have not listened. 4And though the LORD persistently sent you all his servants the prophets, you have neither listened nor inclined your ears to hear 5when they said, "Turn now, every one of you, from your evil way and wicked doings, and you will remain upon the land that the LORD has given to you and your ancestors from of old and forever; 6do not go after other gods to serve and worship them, and do not provoke me to anger with the work of your hands. Then I will do you no harm." 7Yet you did not listen to me, says the LORD, and so you have provoked me to anger with the work of your hands to your own harm.

8 Therefore thus says the LORD of hosts: Because you have not obeyed my words, 9I am going to send for all the tribes of the north, says the LORD, even for King Nebuchadrezzar of Babylon, my servant, and I will bring them against this land and its inhabitants, and against all these nations around; I will utterly destroy them, and make them an object of horror and

---

a Heb Mss Gk Vg: MT *forget you*

of hissing, and an everlasting disgrace.*[a] 10And I will banish from them the sound of mirth and the sound of gladness, the voice of the bridegroom and the voice of the bride, the sound of the millstones and the light of the lamp. 11This whole land shall become a ruin and a waste, and these nations shall serve the king of Babylon seventy years. 12Then after seventy years are completed, I will punish the king of Babylon and that nation, the land of the Chaldeans, for their iniquity, says the LORD, making the land an everlasting waste. 13I will bring upon that land all the words that I have uttered against it, everything written in this book, which Jeremiah prophesied against all the nations. 14For many nations and great kings shall make slaves of them also; and I will repay them according to their deeds and the work of their hands.

The Cup of God's Wrath

15 For thus the LORD, the God of Israel, said to me: Take from my hand this cup of the wine of wrath, and make all the nations to whom I send you drink it. 16They shall drink and stagger and go out of their minds because of the sword that I am sending among them.

17 So I took the cup from the LORD's hand, and made all the nations to whom the LORD sent me drink it: 18Jerusalem and the towns of Judah, its kings and officials, to make them a desolation and a waste, an object of hissing and of cursing, as they are today; 19Pharaoh king of Egypt, his servants, his officials, and all his people; 20all the mixed people;[b] all the kings of the land of Uz; all the kings of the land of the Philistines—Ashkelon, Gaza, Ekron, and the remnant of Ashdod; 21Edom, Moab, and the Ammonites; 22all the kings of Tyre, all the kings of Sidon, and the kings of the coastland across the sea; 23Dedan, Tema, Buz, and all who have shaven temples; 24all the kings of Arabia and all the kings of the mixed peoples[b] that live in the desert; 25all the kings of Zimri, all the kings of Elam, and all the kings of Media; 26all the kings of the north, far and near, one after another, and all the kingdoms of the world that are on the face of the earth. And after them the king of Sheshach[c] shall drink.

27 Then you shall say to them, Thus says the LORD of hosts, the God of Israel: Drink, get drunk and vomit, fall and rise no more, because of the sword that I am sending among you.

28 And if they refuse to accept the cup from your hand to drink, then you shall say to them: Thus says the LORD of hosts: You must drink! 29See, I am beginning to bring disaster on the city that is called by my name, and how can you possibly avoid punishment? You shall not go unpunished, for I am summoning a sword against all the inhabitants of the earth, says the LORD of hosts.

30 You, therefore, shall prophesy against them all these words, and say to them:

The LORD will roar from on high,
   and from his holy habitation utter his
      voice;
he will roar mightily against his fold,
   and shout, like those who tread
      grapes,
against all the inhabitants of the earth.
31   The clamor will resound to the ends of
         the earth,
   for the LORD has an indictment
      against the nations;
he is entering into judgment with all
      flesh,
   and the guilty he will put to the sword,
                     says the LORD.

32   Thus says the LORD of hosts:
   See, disaster is spreading
      from nation to nation,
   and a great tempest is stirring
      from the farthest parts of the earth!

33 Those slain by the LORD on that day shall extend from one end of the earth to the other. They shall not be lamented, or gathered, or buried; they shall become dung on the surface of the ground.

34   Wail, you shepherds, and cry out;
      roll in ashes, you lords of the flock,

---

a Gk Compare Syr: Heb *and everlasting desolations*   *b* Meaning of Heb uncertain   *c* *Sheshach* is a cryptogram for *Babel*, Babylon

for the days of your slaughter have
    come—and your dispersions,*
and you shall fall like a choice vessel.
35 Flight shall fail the shepherds,
    and there shall be no escape for the
        lords of the flock.
36 Hark! the cry of the shepherds,
    and the wail of the lords of the flock!
For the LORD is despoiling their pasture,
37   and the peaceful folds are devastated,
    because of the fierce anger of the
        LORD.
38 Like a lion he has left his covert;
    for their land has become a waste
because of the cruel sword,
    and because of his fierce anger.

Jeremiah's Prophecies in the Temple

26 At the beginning of the reign of King Jehoiakim son of Josiah of Judah, this word came from the LORD: 2Thus says the LORD: Stand in the court of the LORD's house, and speak to all the cities of Judah that come to worship in the house of the LORD; speak to them all the words that I command you; do not hold back a word. 3It may be that they will listen, all of them, and will turn from their evil way, that I may change my mind about the disaster that I intend to bring on them because of their evil doings. 4You shall say to them: Thus says the LORD: If you will not listen to me, to walk in my law that I have set before you, 5and to heed the words of my servants the prophets whom I send to you urgently—though you have not heeded— 6then I will make this house like Shiloh, and I will make this city a curse for all the nations of the earth.

7 The priests and the prophets and all the people heard Jeremiah speaking these words in the house of the LORD. 8And when Jeremiah had finished speaking all that the LORD had commanded him to speak to all the people, then the priests and the prophets and all the people laid hold of him, saying, "You shall die! 9Why have you prophesied in the name of the LORD, saying, 'This house shall be like Shiloh, and this city shall be desolate, without inhabitant'?" And all the people gathered around Jeremiah in the house of the LORD.

10 When the officials of Judah heard these things, they came up from the king's house to the house of the LORD and took their seat in the entry of the New Gate of the house of the LORD. 11Then the priests and the prophets said to the officials and to all the people, "This man deserves the sentence of death because he has prophesied against this city, as you have heard with your own ears."

12 Then Jeremiah spoke to all the officials and all the people, saying, "It is the LORD who sent me to prophesy against this house and this city all the words you have heard. 13Now therefore amend your ways and your doings, and obey the voice of the LORD your God, and the LORD will change his mind about the disaster that he has pronounced against you. 14But as for me, here I am in your hands. Do with me as seems good and right to you. 15Only know for certain that if you put me to death, you will be bringing innocent blood upon yourselves and upon this city and its inhabitants, for in truth the LORD sent me to you to speak all these words in your ears."

16 Then the officials and all the people said to the priests and the prophets, "This man does not deserve the sentence of death, for he has spoken to us in the name of the LORD our God." 17And some of the elders of the land arose and said to all the assembled people, 18"Micah of Moresheth, who prophesied during the days of King Hezekiah of Judah, said to all the people of Judah: 'Thus says the LORD of hosts,

Zion shall be plowed as a field;
    Jerusalem shall become a heap of
        ruins,
    and the mountain of the house a
        wooded height.'
19Did King Hezekiah of Judah and all Judah actually put him to death? Did he not fear the LORD and entreat the favor of the LORD, and did not the LORD change his mind about the di-

---

a Meaning of Heb uncertain

saster that he had pronounced against them? But we are about to bring great disaster on ourselves!"

20 There was another man prophesying in the name of the LORD, Uriah son of Shemaiah from Kiriath-jearim. He prophesied against this city and against this land in words exactly like those of Jeremiah. 21And when King Jehoiakim, with all his warriors and all the officials, heard his words, the king sought to put him to death; but when Uriah heard of it, he was afraid and fled and escaped to Egypt. 22Then King Jehoiakim sent *a* Elnathan son of Achbor and men with him to Egypt, 23and they took Uriah from Egypt and brought him to King Jehoiakim, who struck him down with the sword and threw his dead body into the burial place of the common people.

24 But the hand of Ahikam son of Shaphan was with Jeremiah so that he was not given over into the hands of the people to be put to death.

The Sign of the Yoke

27 In the beginning of the reign of King Zedekiah *b* son of Josiah of Judah, this word came to Jeremiah from the LORD. 2Thus the LORD said to me: Make yourself a yoke of straps and bars, and put them on your neck. 3Send word *c* to the king of Edom, the king of Moab, the king of the Ammonites, the king of Tyre, and the king of Sidon by the hand of the envoys who have come to Jerusalem to King Zedekiah of Judah. 4Give them this charge for their masters: Thus says the LORD of hosts, the God of Israel: This is what you shall say to your masters: 5It is I who by my great power and my outstretched arm have made the earth, with the people and animals that are on the earth, and I give it to whomever I please. 6Now I have given all these lands into the hand of King Nebuchadnezzar of Babylon, my servant, and I have given him even the wild animals of the field to serve him. 7All the nations shall serve him and his son and his grandson, until the time of his own land comes; then

many nations and great kings shall make him their slave.

8 But if any nation or kingdom will not serve this king, Nebuchadnezzar of Babylon, and put its neck under the yoke of the king of Babylon, then I will punish that nation with the sword, with famine, and with pestilence, says the LORD, until I have completed its *d* destruction by his hand. 9You, therefore, must not listen to your prophets, your diviners, your dreamers, *e* your soothsayers, or your sorcerers, who are saying to you, "You shall not serve the king of Babylon." 10For they are prophesying a lie to you, with the result that you will be removed far from your land; I will drive you out, and you will perish. 11But any nation that will bring its neck under the yoke of the king of Babylon and serve him, I will leave on its own land, says the LORD, to till it and live there.

12 I spoke to King Zedekiah of Judah in the same way: Bring your necks under the yoke of the king of Babylon, and serve him and his people, and live. 13Why should you and your people die by the sword, by famine, and by pestilence, as the LORD has spoken concerning any nation that will not serve the king of Babylon? 14Do not listen to the words of the prophets who are telling you not to serve the king of Babylon, for they are prophesying a lie to you. 15I have not sent them, says the LORD, but they are prophesying falsely in my name, with the result that I will drive you out and you will perish, you and the prophets who are prophesying to you.

16 Then I spoke to the priests and to all this people, saying, Thus says the LORD: Do not listen to the words of your prophets who are prophesying to you, saying, "The vessels of the LORD's house will soon be brought back from Babylon," for they are prophesying a lie to you. 17Do not listen to them; serve the king of Babylon and live. Why should this city become a desolation? 18If indeed they are prophets, and if the word of the LORD is with them, then let them intercede with the LORD of hosts, that the vessels left in the house of the LORD,

a Heb adds *men to Egypt*   *b* Another reading is *Jehoiakim*   *c* Cn: Heb *send them*   *d* Heb *their*   *e* Gk Syr Vg: Heb *dreams* in the house of the king of Judah, and in Jerusalem may not go to Babylon. ¹⁹For thus says the LORD of hosts concerning the pillars, the sea, the stands, and the rest of the vessels that are left in this city, ²⁰which King Nebuchadnezzar of Babylon did not take away when he took into exile from Jerusalem to Babylon King Jeconiah son of Jehoiakim of Judah, and all the nobles of Judah and Jerusalem— ²¹thus says the LORD of hosts, the God of Israel, concerning the vessels left in the house of the LORD, in the house of the king of Judah, and in Jerusalem: ²²They shall be carried to Babylon, and there they shall stay, until the day when I give attention to them, says the LORD. Then I will bring them up and restore them to this place.

Hananiah Opposes Jeremiah and Dies

28 In that same year, at the beginning of the reign of King Zedekiah of Judah, in the fifth month of the fourth year, the prophet Hananiah son of Azzur, from Gibeon, spoke to me in the house of the LORD, in the presence of the priests and all the people, saying, ²"Thus says the LORD of hosts, the God of Israel: I have broken the yoke of the king of Babylon. ³Within two years I will bring back to this place all the vessels of the LORD's house, which King Nebuchadnezzar of Babylon took away from this place and carried to Babylon. ⁴I will also bring back to this place King Jeconiah son of Jehoiakim of Judah, and all the exiles from Judah who went to Babylon, says the LORD, for I will break the yoke of the king of Babylon."

5 Then the prophet Jeremiah spoke to the prophet Hananiah in the presence of the priests and all the people who were standing in the house of the LORD; ⁶and the prophet Jeremiah said, "Amen! May the LORD do so; may the LORD fulfill the words that you have prophesied, and bring back to this place from Babylon the vessels of the house of the LORD, and all the exiles. ⁷But listen now to this word that I speak in your hearing and in the hearing of all the people. ⁸The prophets who preceded you and me from ancient times prophesied war, famine, and pestilence against many countries and great kingdoms. ⁹As for the prophet who prophesies peace, when the word of that prophet comes true, then it will be known that the LORD has truly sent the prophet."

10 Then the prophet Hananiah took the yoke from the neck of the prophet Jeremiah, and broke it. ¹¹And Hananiah spoke in the presence of all the people, saying, "Thus says the LORD: This is how I will break the yoke of King Nebuchadnezzar of Babylon from the neck of all the nations within two years." At this, the prophet Jeremiah went his way.

12 Sometime after the prophet Hananiah had broken the yoke from the neck of the prophet Jeremiah, the word of the LORD came to Jeremiah: ¹³Go, tell Hananiah, Thus says the LORD: You have broken wooden bars only to forge iron bars in place of them! ¹⁴For thus says the LORD of hosts, the God of Israel: I have put an iron yoke on the neck of all these nations so that they may serve King Nebuchadnezzar of Babylon, and they shall indeed serve him; I have even given him the wild animals. ¹⁵And the prophet Jeremiah said to the prophet Hananiah, "Listen, Hananiah, the LORD has not sent you, and you made this people trust in a lie. ¹⁶Therefore thus says the LORD: I am going to send you off the face of the earth. Within this year you will be dead, because you have spoken rebellion against the LORD."

17 In that same year, in the seventh month, the prophet Hananiah died.

Jeremiah's Letter to the Exiles in Babylon

29 These are the words of the letter that the prophet Jeremiah sent from Jerusalem to the remaining elders among the exiles, and to the priests, the prophets, and all the people, whom Nebuchadnezzar had taken into exile from Jerusalem to Babylon. ²This was after King Jeconiah, and the queen mother, the court officials, the leaders of Judah and Jerusalem, the artisans, and the smiths had departed from Jerusalem. ³The letter was sent by the hand of Elasah son of Shaphan and Gemariah son of Hilkiah, whom King Zedekiah of Judah sent to Babylon to King Nebuchadnezzar of Babylon. It said: [4]Thus says the LORD of hosts, the God of Israel, to all the exiles whom I have sent into exile from Jerusalem to Babylon: [5]Build houses and live in them; plant gardens and eat what they produce. [6]Take wives and have sons and daughters; take wives for your sons, and give your daughters in marriage, that they may bear sons and daughters; multiply there, and do not decrease. [7]But seek the welfare of the city where I have sent you into exile, and pray to the LORD on its behalf, for in its welfare you will find your welfare. [8]For thus says the LORD of hosts, the God of Israel: Do not let the prophets and the diviners who are among you deceive you, and do not listen to the dreams that they dream,[a] [9]for it is a lie that they are prophesying to you in my name; I did not send them, says the LORD.

10 For thus says the LORD: Only when Babylon's seventy years are completed will I visit you, and I will fulfill to you my promise and bring you back to this place. [11]For surely I know the plans I have for you, says the LORD, plans for your welfare and not for harm, to give you a future with hope. [12]Then when you call upon me and come and pray to me, I will hear you. [13]When you search for me, you will find me; if you seek me with all your heart, [14]I will let you find me, says the LORD, and I will restore your fortunes and gather you from all the nations and all the places where I have driven you, says the LORD, and I will bring you back to the place from which I sent you into exile.

15 Because you have said, "The LORD has raised up prophets for us in Babylon,"— [16]Thus says the LORD concerning the king who sits on the throne of David, and concerning all the people who live in this city, your kinsfolk who did not go out with you into exile: [17]Thus says the LORD of hosts, I am going to let loose on them sword, famine, and pestilence, and I will make them like rotten figs that are so bad they cannot be eaten. [18]I will pursue them with the sword, with famine, and with pestilence, and will make them a horror to all the king-

doms of the earth, to be an object of cursing, and horror, and hissing, and a derision among all the nations where I have driven them, [19]because they did not heed my words, says the LORD, when I persistently sent to you my servants the prophets, but they[b] would not listen, says the LORD. [20]But now, all you exiles whom I sent away from Jerusalem to Babylon, hear the word of the LORD: [21]Thus says the LORD of hosts, the God of Israel, concerning Ahab son of Kolaiah and Zedekiah son of Maaseiah, who are prophesying a lie to you in my name: I am going to deliver them into the hand of King Nebuchadrezzar of Babylon, and he shall kill them before your eyes. [22]And on account of them this curse shall be used by all the exiles from Judah in Babylon: "The LORD make you like Zedekiah and Ahab, whom the king of Babylon roasted in the fire," [23]because they have perpetrated outrage in Israel and have committed adultery with their neighbors' wives, and have spoken in my name lying words that I did not command them; I am the one who knows and bears witness, says the LORD.

The Letter of Shemaiah

24 To Shemaiah of Nehelam you shall say: [25]Thus says the LORD of hosts, the God of Israel: In your own name you sent a letter to all the people who are in Jerusalem, and to the priest Zephaniah son of Maaseiah, and to all the priests, saying, [26]The LORD himself has made you priest instead of the priest Jehoiada, so that there may be officers in the house of the LORD to control any madman who plays the prophet, to put him in the stocks and the collar. [27]So now why have you not rebuked Jeremiah of Anathoth who plays the prophet for you? [28]For he has actually sent to us in Babylon, saying, "It will be a long time; build houses and live in them, and plant gardens and eat what they produce."

29 The priest Zephaniah read this letter in the hearing of the prophet Jeremiah. [30]Then the word of the LORD came to Jeremiah: [31]Send to all the exiles, saying, Thus says the

---

a Cn: Heb *your dreams that you cause to dream*   b Syr: Heb *you*

LORD concerning Shemaiah of Nehelam: Because Shemaiah has prophesied to you, though I did not send him, and has led you to trust in a lie, [32]therefore thus says the LORD: I am going to punish Shemaiah of Nehelam and his descendants; he shall not have anyone living among this people to see[a] the good that I am going to do to my people, says the LORD, for he has spoken rebellion against the LORD.

Restoration Promised for Israel and Judah

30 The word that came to Jeremiah from the LORD: [2]Thus says the LORD, the God of Israel: Write in a book all the words that I have spoken to you. [3]For the days are surely coming, says the LORD, when I will restore the fortunes of my people, Israel and Judah, says the LORD, and I will bring them back to the land that I gave to their ancestors and they shall take possession of it.

4 These are the words that the LORD spoke concerning Israel and Judah:

5   Thus says the LORD:
    We have heard a cry of panic,
      of terror, and no peace.
6   Ask now, and see,
      can a man bear a child?
    Why then do I see every man
      with his hands on his loins like a
        woman in labor?
    Why has every face turned pale?
7   Alas! that day is so great
      there is none like it;
    it is a time of distress for Jacob;
      yet he shall be rescued from it.

8 On that day, says the LORD of hosts, I will break the yoke from off his[b] neck, and I will burst his[b] bonds, and strangers shall no more make a servant of him. [9]But they shall serve the LORD their God and David their king, whom I will raise up for them.

10   But as for you, have no fear, my servant
      Jacob, says the LORD,
    and do not be dismayed, O Israel;
    for I am going to save you from far away,
    and your offspring from the land of
      their captivity.
    Jacob shall return and have quiet and
      ease,
    and no one shall make him afraid.
11   For I am with you, says the LORD, to
      save you;
    I will make an end of all the nations
      among which I scattered you,
      but of you I will not make an end.
    I will chastise you in just measure,
      and I will by no means leave you
       unpunished.

12   For thus says the LORD:
    Your hurt is incurable,
      your wound is grievous.
13   There is no one to uphold your cause,
      no medicine for your wound,
      no healing for you.
14   All your lovers have forgotten you;
      they care nothing for you;
    for I have dealt you the blow of an
      enemy,
      the punishment of a merciless foe,
    because your guilt is great,
      because your sins are so numerous.
15   Why do you cry out over your hurt?
      Your pain is incurable.
    Because your guilt is great,
      because your sins are so numerous,
      I have done these things to you.
16   Therefore all who devour you shall be
      devoured,
    and all your foes, every one of them,
      shall go into captivity;
    those who plunder you shall be
      plundered,
    and all who prey on you I will make a
      prey.
17   For I will restore health to you,
      and your wounds I will heal,
                     says the LORD,
    because they have called you an outcast:
      "It is Zion; no one cares for her!"

a Gk: Heb *and he shall not see*   b Cn: Heb *your*

18 Thus says the LORD:
   I am going to restore the fortunes of the
      tents of Jacob,
         and have compassion on his dwellings;
   the city shall be rebuilt upon its mound,
      and the citadel set on its rightful site.
19 Out of them shall come thanksgiving,
      and the sound of merrymakers.
   I will make them many, and they shall
         not be few;
      I will make them honored, and they
         shall not be disdained.
20 Their children shall be as of old,
      their congregation shall be established
         before me;
      and I will punish all who oppress
         them.
21 Their prince shall be one of their own,
      their ruler shall come from their
         midst;
   I will bring him near, and he shall
         approach me,
      for who would otherwise dare to
         approach me?
                              says the LORD.
22 And you shall be my people,
      and I will be your God.

23 Look, the storm of the LORD!
      Wrath has gone forth,
   a whirling*a* tempest;
      it will burst upon the head of the
         wicked.
24 The fierce anger of the LORD will not
         turn back
      until he has executed and
         accomplished
      the intents of his mind.
   In the latter days you will understand
         this.

The Joyful Return of the Exiles

31 At that time, says the LORD, I will be
   the God of all the families of Israel,
and they shall be my people.
2 Thus says the LORD:

The people who survived the sword
   found grace in the wilderness;
when Israel sought for rest,
3   the LORD appeared to him*b* from far
         away.*c*
I have loved you with an everlasting love;
   therefore I have continued my
      faithfulness to you.
4 Again I will build you, and you shall be
      built,
   O virgin Israel!
Again you shall take*d* your tambourines,
   and go forth in the dance of the
      merrymakers.
5 Again you shall plant vineyards
   on the mountains of Samaria;
the planters shall plant,
   and shall enjoy the fruit.
6 For there shall be a day when sentinels
      will call
   in the hill country of Ephraim:
"Come, let us go up to Zion,
   to the LORD our God."

7 For thus says the LORD:
Sing aloud with gladness for Jacob,
   and raise shouts for the chief of the
      nations;
proclaim, give praise, and say,
   "Save, O LORD, your people,
   the remnant of Israel."
8 See, I am going to bring them from the
      land of the north,
   and gather them from the farthest
      parts of the earth,
among them the blind and the lame,
   those with child and those in labor,
      together;
a great company, they shall return
   here.
9 With weeping they shall come,
   and with consolations*e* I will lead
      them back,
I will let them walk by brooks of water,
   in a straight path in which they shall
      not stumble;

---

a One Ms: Meaning of MT uncertain   *b* Gk: Heb *me*   *c* Or *to him long ago*   *d* Or *adorn yourself with*
e Gk Compare Vg Tg: Heb *supplications*

for I have become a father to Israel,
   and Ephraim is my firstborn.

10 Hear the word of the LORD, O nations,
   and declare it in the coastlands far away;
say, "He who scattered Israel will gather
      him,
   and will keep him as a shepherd a
      flock."
11 For the LORD has ransomed Jacob,
   and has redeemed him from hands
      too strong for him.
12 They shall come and sing aloud on the
      height of Zion,
   and they shall be radiant over the
      goodness of the LORD,
over the grain, the wine, and the oil,
   and over the young of the flock and
      the herd;
their life shall become like a watered
      garden,
   and they shall never languish again.
13 Then shall the young women rejoice in
      the dance,
   and the young men and the old shall
      be merry.
I will turn their mourning into joy,
   I will comfort them, and give them
      gladness for sorrow.
14 I will give the priests their fill of fatness,
   and my people shall be satisfied with
      my bounty,
                says the LORD.

15 Thus says the LORD:
A voice is heard in Ramah,
   lamentation and bitter weeping.
Rachel is weeping for her children;
   she refuses to be comforted for her
      children,
   because they are no more.
16 Thus says the LORD:
Keep your voice from weeping,
   and your eyes from tears;
for there is a reward for your work,
                says the LORD:

they shall come back from the land of
      the enemy;
17 there is hope for your future,
                says the LORD:
your children shall come back to their
      own country.

18 Indeed I heard Ephraim pleading:
"You disciplined me, and I took the
      discipline;
   I was like a calf untrained.
Bring me back, let me come back,
   for you are the LORD my God.
19 For after I had turned away I repented;
   and after I was discovered, I struck my
      thigh;
I was ashamed, and I was dismayed
   because I bore the disgrace of my
      youth."
20 Is Ephraim my dear son?
   Is he the child I delight in?
As often as I speak against him,
   I still remember him.
Therefore I am deeply moved for him;
   I will surely have mercy on him,
                says the LORD.

21 Set up road markers for yourself,
   make yourself signposts;
consider well the highway,
   the road by which you went.
Return, O virgin Israel,
   return to these your cities.
22 How long will you waver,
   O faithless daughter?
For the LORD has created a new thing on
      the earth:
   a woman encompasses *a* a man.

23 Thus says the LORD of hosts, the God
of Israel: Once more they shall use these words
in the land of Judah and in its towns when I restore their fortunes:
   "The LORD bless you, O abode of
      righteousness,
     O holy hill!"

---

a Meaning of Heb uncertain

24And Judah and all its towns shall live there together, and the farmers and those who wander*a* with their flocks.

25   I will satisfy the weary,
       and all who are faint I will replenish.

26 Thereupon I awoke and looked, and my sleep was pleasant to me.

Individual Retribution

27 The days are surely coming, says the LORD, when I will sow the house of Israel and the house of Judah with the seed of humans and the seed of animals. 28And just as I have watched over them to pluck up and break down, to overthrow, destroy, and bring evil, so I will watch over them to build and to plant, says the LORD. 29In those days they shall no longer say:

"The parents have eaten sour grapes,
    and the children's teeth are set on
        edge."

30But all shall die for their own sins; the teeth of everyone who eats sour grapes shall be set on edge.

A New Covenant

31 The days are surely coming, says the LORD, when I will make a new covenant with the house of Israel and the house of Judah. 32It will not be like the covenant that I made with their ancestors when I took them by the hand to bring them out of the land of Egypt—a covenant that they broke, though I was their husband,*b* says the LORD. 33But this is the covenant that I will make with the house of Israel after those days, says the LORD: I will put my law within them, and I will write it on their hearts; and I will be their God, and they shall be my people. 34No longer shall they teach one another, or say to each other, "Know the LORD," for they shall all know me, from the least of them to the greatest, says the LORD; for I will forgive their iniquity, and remember their sin no more.

35   Thus says the LORD,
       who gives the sun for light by day
and the fixed order of the moon and
    the stars for light by night,
who stirs up the sea so that its waves
    roar—
the LORD of hosts is his name:

36 If this fixed order were ever to cease
    from my presence, says the LORD,
then also the offspring of Israel would
    cease
    to be a nation before me forever.

37 Thus says the LORD:
    If the heavens above can be measured,
        and the foundations of the earth
            below can be explored,
    then I will reject all the offspring of
        Israel
    because of all they have done,
                    says the LORD.

Jerusalem to Be Enlarged

38 The days are surely coming, says the LORD, when the city shall be rebuilt for the LORD from the tower of Hananel to the Corner Gate. 39And the measuring line shall go out farther, straight to the hill Gareb, and shall then turn to Goah. 40The whole valley of the dead bodies and the ashes, and all the fields as far as the Wadi Kidron, to the corner of the Horse Gate toward the east, shall be sacred to the LORD. It shall never again be uprooted or overthrown.

Jeremiah Buys a Field During the Siege

32 The word that came to Jeremiah from the LORD in the tenth year of King Zedekiah of Judah, which was the eighteenth year of Nebuchadrezzar. 2At that time the army of the king of Babylon was besieging Jerusalem, and the prophet Jeremiah was confined in the court of the guard that was in the palace of the king of Judah, 3where King Zedekiah of Judah had confined him. Zedekiah had said, "Why do you prophesy and say: Thus says the LORD: I am going to give this city into the hand of the king of Babylon, and he shall

---

a Cn Compare Syr Vg Tg: Heb *and they shall wander*   *b* Or *master* take it; [4]King Zedekiah of Judah shall not escape out of the hands of the Chaldeans, but shall surely be given into the hands of the king of Babylon, and shall speak with him face to face and see him eye to eye; [5]and he shall take Zedekiah to Babylon, and there he shall remain until I attend to him, says the LORD; though you fight against the Chaldeans, you shall not succeed?"

6 Jeremiah said, The word of the LORD came to me: [7]Hanamel son of your uncle Shallum is going to come to you and say, "Buy my field that is at Anathoth, for the right of redemption by purchase is yours." [8]Then my cousin Hanamel came to me in the court of the guard, in accordance with the word of the LORD, and said to me, "Buy my field that is at Anathoth in the land of Benjamin, for the right of possession and redemption is yours; buy it for yourself." Then I knew that this was the word of the LORD.

9 And I bought the field at Anathoth from my cousin Hanamel, and weighed out the money to him, seventeen shekels of silver. [10]I signed the deed, sealed it, got witnesses, and weighed the money on scales. [11]Then I took the sealed deed of purchase, containing the terms and conditions, and the open copy; [12]and I gave the deed of purchase to Baruch son of Neriah son of Mahseiah, in the presence of my cousin Hanamel, in the presence of the witnesses who signed the deed of purchase, and in the presence of all the Judeans who were sitting in the court of the guard. [13]In their presence I charged Baruch, saying, [14]Thus says the LORD of hosts, the God of Israel: Take these deeds, both this sealed deed of purchase and this open deed, and put them in an earthenware jar, in order that they may last for a long time. [15]For thus says the LORD of hosts, the God of Israel: Houses and fields and vineyards shall again be bought in this land.

Jeremiah Prays for Understanding

16 After I had given the deed of purchase to Baruch son of Neriah, I prayed to the LORD,

saying: [17]Ah Lord GOD! It is you who made the heavens and the earth by your great power and by your outstretched arm! Nothing is too hard for you. [18]You show steadfast love to the thousandth generation,[a] but repay the guilt of parents into the laps of their children after them, O great and mighty God whose name is the LORD of hosts, [19]great in counsel and mighty in deed; whose eyes are open to all the ways of mortals, rewarding all according to their ways and according to the fruit of their doings. [20]You showed signs and wonders in the land of Egypt, and to this day in Israel and among all humankind, and have made yourself a name that continues to this very day. [21]You brought your people Israel out of the land of Egypt with signs and wonders, with a strong hand and outstretched arm, and with great terror; [22]and you gave them this land, which you swore to their ancestors to give them, a land flowing with milk and honey; [23]and they entered and took possession of it. But they did not obey your voice or follow your law; of all you commanded them to do, they did nothing. Therefore you have made all these disasters come upon them. [24]See, the siege ramps have been cast up against the city to take it, and the city, faced with sword, famine, and pestilence, has been given into the hands of the Chaldeans who are fighting against it. What you spoke has happened, as you yourself can see. [25]Yet you, O Lord GOD, have said to me, "Buy the field for money and get witnesses"—though the city has been given into the hands of the Chaldeans.

God's Assurance of the People's Return

26 The word of the LORD came to Jeremiah: [27]See, I am the LORD, the God of all flesh; is anything too hard for me? [28]Therefore, thus says the LORD: I am going to give this city into the hands of the Chaldeans and into the hand of King Nebuchadrezzar of Babylon, and he shall take it. [29]The Chaldeans who are fighting against this city shall come, set it on fire, and burn it, with the houses on whose roofs of-

a Or to thousands

ferings have been made to Baal and libations have been poured out to other gods, to provoke me to anger. ³⁰For the people of Israel and the people of Judah have done nothing but evil in my sight from their youth; the people of Israel have done nothing but provoke me to anger by the work of their hands, says the LORD. ³¹This city has aroused my anger and wrath, from the day it was built until this day, so that I will remove it from my sight ³²because of all the evil of the people of Israel and the people of Judah that they did to provoke me to anger—they, their kings and their officials, their priests and their prophets, the citizens of Judah and the inhabitants of Jerusalem. ³³They have turned their backs to me, not their faces; though I have taught them persistently, they would not listen and accept correction. ³⁴They set up their abominations in the house that bears my name, and defiled it. ³⁵They built the high places of Baal in the valley of the son of Hinnom, to offer up their sons and daughters to Molech, though I did not command them, nor did it enter my mind that they should do this abomination, causing Judah to sin.

36 Now therefore thus says the LORD, the God of Israel, concerning this city of which you say, "It is being given into the hand of the king of Babylon by the sword, by famine, and by pestilence": ³⁷See, I am going to gather them from all the lands to which I drove them in my anger and my wrath and in great indignation; I will bring them back to this place, and I will settle them in safety. ³⁸They shall be my people, and I will be their God. ³⁹I will give them one heart and one way, that they may fear me for all time, for their own good and the good of their children after them. ⁴⁰I will make an everlasting covenant with them, never to draw back from doing good to them; and I will put the fear of me in their hearts, so that they may not turn from me. ⁴¹I will rejoice in doing good to them, and I will plant them in this land in faithfulness, with all my heart and all my soul.

42 For thus says the LORD: Just as I have brought all this great disaster upon this people, so I will bring upon them all the good fortune that I now promise them. ⁴³Fields shall be bought in this land of which you are saying, It is a desolation, without human beings or animals; it has been given into the hands of the Chaldeans. ⁴⁴Fields shall be bought for money, and deeds shall be signed and sealed and witnessed, in the land of Benjamin, in the places around Jerusalem, and in the cities of Judah, of the hill country, of the Shephelah, and of the Negeb; for I will restore their fortunes, says the LORD.

Healing after Punishment

33 The word of the LORD came to Jeremiah a second time, while he was still confined in the court of the guard: ²Thus says the LORD who made the earth,ᵃ the LORD who formed it to establish it—the LORD is his name: ³Call to me and I will answer you, and will tell you great and hidden things that you have not known. ⁴For thus says the LORD, the God of Israel, concerning the houses of this city and the houses of the kings of Judah that were torn down to make a defense against the siege ramps and before the sword:ᵇ ⁵The Chaldeans are coming in to fightᶜ and to fill them with the dead bodies of those whom I shall strike down in my anger and my wrath, for I have hidden my face from this city because of all their wickedness. ⁶I am going to bring it recovery and healing; I will heal them and reveal to them abundanceᵇ of prosperity and security. ⁷I will restore the fortunes of Judah and the fortunes of Israel, and rebuild them as they were at first. ⁸I will cleanse them from all the guilt of their sin against me, and I will forgive all the guilt of their sin and rebellion against me. ⁹And this cityᵈ shall be to me a name of joy, a praise and a glory before all the nations of the earth who shall hear of all the good that I do for them; they shall fear and tremble because of all the good and all the prosperity I provide for it.

10 Thus says the LORD: In this place of which you say, "It is a waste without human be-

---

ᵃ Gk: Heb *it*   ᵇ Meaning of Heb uncertain   ᶜ Cn: Heb *They are coming in to fight against the Chaldeans*
ᵈ Heb *And it*

ings or animals," in the towns of Judah and the streets of Jerusalem that are desolate, without inhabitants, human or animal, there shall once more be heard [11]the voice of mirth and the voice of gladness, the voice of the bridegroom and the voice of the bride, the voices of those who sing, as they bring thank offerings to the house of the LORD:

"Give thanks to the LORD of hosts,
    for the LORD is good,
for his steadfast love endures forever!"
For I will restore the fortunes of the land as at first, says the LORD.

12 Thus says the LORD of hosts: In this place that is waste, without human beings or animals, and in all its towns there shall again be pasture for shepherds resting their flocks. [13]In the towns of the hill country, of the Shephelah, and of the Negeb, in the land of Benjamin, the places around Jerusalem, and in the towns of Judah, flocks shall again pass under the hands of the one who counts them, says the LORD.

The Righteous Branch and the Covenant with David

14 The days are surely coming, says the LORD, when I will fulfill the promise I made to the house of Israel and the house of Judah. [15]In those days and at that time I will cause a righteous Branch to spring up for David; and he shall execute justice and righteousness in the land. [16]In those days Judah will be saved and Jerusalem will live in safety. And this is the name by which it will be called: "The LORD is our righteousness."

17 For thus says the LORD: David shall never lack a man to sit on the throne of the house of Israel, [18]and the levitical priests shall never lack a man in my presence to offer burnt offerings, to make grain offerings, and to make sacrifices for all time.

19 The word of the LORD came to Jeremiah: [20]Thus says the LORD: If any of you could break my covenant with the day and my covenant with the night, so that day and night

would not come at their appointed time, [21]only then could my covenant with my servant David be broken, so that he would not have a son to reign on his throne, and my covenant with my ministers the Levites. [22]Just as the host of heaven cannot be numbered and the sands of the sea cannot be measured, so I will increase the offspring of my servant David, and the Levites who minister to me.

23 The word of the LORD came to Jeremiah: [24]Have you not observed how these people say, "The two families that the LORD chose have been rejected by him," and how they hold my people in such contempt that they no longer regard them as a nation? [25]Thus says the LORD: Only if I had not established my covenant with day and night and the ordinances of heaven and earth, [26]would I reject the offspring of Jacob and of my servant David and not choose any of his descendants as rulers over the offspring of Abraham, Isaac, and Jacob. For I will restore their fortunes, and will have mercy upon them.

Death in Captivity Predicted for Zedekiah

34 The word that came to Jeremiah from the LORD, when King Nebuchadrezzar of Babylon and all his army and all the kingdoms of the earth and all the peoples under his dominion were fighting against Jerusalem and all its cities: [2]Thus says the LORD, the God of Israel: Go and speak to King Zedekiah of Judah and say to him: Thus says the LORD: I am going to give this city into the hand of the king of Babylon, and he shall burn it with fire. [3]And you yourself shall not escape from his hand, but shall surely be captured and handed over to him; you shall see the king of Babylon eye to eye and speak with him face to face; and you shall go to Babylon. [4]Yet hear the word of the LORD, O King Zedekiah of Judah! Thus says the LORD concerning you: You shall not die by the sword; [5]you shall die in peace. And as spices were burned*a* for your ancestors, the earlier kings who preceded you, so they shall burn spices*b* for you and lament for you, say-

---

a Heb *as there was burning*   *b* Heb *shall burn*

ing, "Alas, lord!" For I have spoken the word, says the LORD.

6 Then the prophet Jeremiah spoke all these words to Zedekiah king of Judah, in Jerusalem, 7when the army of the king of Babylon was fighting against Jerusalem and against all the cities of Judah that were left, Lachish and Azekah; for these were the only fortified cities of Judah that remained.

Treacherous Treatment of Slaves

8 The word that came to Jeremiah from the LORD, after King Zedekiah had made a covenant with all the people in Jerusalem to make a proclamation of liberty to them— 9that all should set free their Hebrew slaves, male and female, so that no one should hold another Judean in slavery. 10And they obeyed, all the officials and all the people who had entered into the covenant that all would set free their slaves, male or female, so that they would not be enslaved again; they obeyed and set them free. 11But afterward they turned around and took back the male and female slaves they had set free, and brought them again into subjection as slaves. 12The word of the LORD came to Jeremiah from the LORD: 13Thus says the LORD, the God of Israel: I myself made a covenant with your ancestors when I brought them out of the land of Egypt, out of the house of slavery, saying, 14"Every seventh year each of you must set free any Hebrews who have been sold to you and have served you six years; you must set them free from your service." But your ancestors did not listen to me or incline their ears to me. 15You yourselves recently repented and did what was right in my sight by proclaiming liberty to one another, and you made a covenant before me in the house that is called by my name; 16but then you turned around and profaned my name when each of you took back your male and female slaves, whom you had set free according to their desire, and you brought them again into subjection to be your slaves. 17Therefore, thus says the LORD: You have not obeyed me by granting a release to your neighbors and friends; I am going to grant a release to you, says the LORD— a release to the sword, to pestilence, and to famine. I will make you a horror to all the kingdoms of the earth. 18And those who transgressed my covenant and did not keep the terms of the covenant that they made before me, I will make like*a* the calf when they cut it in two and passed between its parts: 19the officials of Judah, the officials of Jerusalem, the eunuchs, the priests, and all the people of the land who passed between the parts of the calf 20shall be handed over to their enemies and to those who seek their lives. Their corpses shall become food for the birds of the air and the wild animals of the earth. 21And as for King Zedekiah of Judah and his officials, I will hand them over to their enemies and to those who seek their lives, to the army of the king of Babylon, which has withdrawn from you. 22I am going to command, says the LORD, and will bring them back to this city; and they will fight against it, and take it, and burn it with fire. The towns of Judah I will make a desolation without inhabitant.

The Rechabites Commended

35 The word that came to Jeremiah from the LORD in the days of King Jehoiakim son of Josiah of Judah: 2Go to the house of the Rechabites, and speak with them, and bring them to the house of the LORD, into one of the chambers; then offer them wine to drink. 3So I took Jaazaniah son of Jeremiah son of Habazziniah, and his brothers, and all his sons, and the whole house of the Rechabites. 4I brought them to the house of the LORD into the chamber of the sons of Hanan son of Igdaliah, the man of God, which was near the chamber of the officials, above the chamber of Maaseiah son of Shallum, keeper of the threshold. 5Then I set before the Rechabites pitchers full of wine, and cups; and I said to them, "Have some wine." 6But they answered, "We will drink no wine, for our ancestor Jonadab son of Rechab commanded

a Cn: Heb lacks *like*

us, 'You shall never drink wine, neither you nor your children; [7]nor shall you ever build a house, or sow seed; nor shall you plant a vineyard, or even own one; but you shall live in tents all your days, that you may live many days in the land where you reside.' [8]We have obeyed the charge of our ancestor Jonadab son of Rechab in all that he commanded us, to drink no wine all our days, ourselves, our wives, our sons, or our daughters, [9]and not to build houses to live in. We have no vineyard or field or seed; [10]but we have lived in tents, and have obeyed and done all that our ancestor Jonadab commanded us. [11]But when King Nebuchadrezzar of Babylon came up against the land, we said, 'Come, and let us go to Jerusalem for fear of the army of the Chaldeans and the army of the Arameans.' That is why we are living in Jerusalem."

[12] Then the word of the LORD came to Jeremiah: [13]Thus says the LORD of hosts, the God of Israel: Go and say to the people of Judah and the inhabitants of Jerusalem, Can you not learn a lesson and obey my words? says the LORD. [14]The command has been carried out that Jonadab son of Rechab gave to his descendants to drink no wine; and they drink none to this day, for they have obeyed their ancestor's command. But I myself have spoken to you persistently, and you have not obeyed me. [15]I have sent to you all my servants the prophets, sending them persistently, saying, "Turn now every one of you from your evil way, and amend your doings, and do not go after other gods to serve them, and then you shall live in the land that I gave to you and your ancestors." But you did not incline your ear or obey me. [16]The descendants of Jonadab son of Rechab have carried out the command that their ancestor gave them, but this people has not obeyed me. [17]Therefore, thus says the LORD, the God of hosts, the God of Israel: I am going to bring on Judah and on all the inhabitants of Jerusalem every disaster that I have pronounced against them; because I have spoken to them and they have not listened, I have called to them and they have not answered.

[18] But to the house of the Rechabites Jeremiah said: Thus says the LORD of hosts, the God of Israel: Because you have obeyed the command of your ancestor Jonadab, and kept all his precepts, and done all that he commanded you, [19]therefore thus says the LORD of hosts, the God of Israel: Jonadab son of Rechab shall not lack a descendant to stand before me for all time.

The Scroll Read in the Temple

36 In the fourth year of King Jehoiakim son of Josiah of Judah, this word came to Jeremiah from the LORD: [2]Take a scroll and write on it all the words that I have spoken to you against Israel and Judah and all the nations, from the day I spoke to you, from the days of Josiah until today. [3]It may be that when the house of Judah hears of all the disasters that I intend to do to them, all of them may turn from their evil ways, so that I may forgive their iniquity and their sin.

[4] Then Jeremiah called Baruch son of Neriah, and Baruch wrote on a scroll at Jeremiah's dictation all the words of the LORD that he had spoken to him. [5]And Jeremiah ordered Baruch, saying, "I am prevented from entering the house of the LORD; [6]so you go yourself, and on a fast day in the hearing of the people in the LORD's house you shall read the words of the LORD from the scroll that you have written at my dictation. You shall read them also in the hearing of all the people of Judah who come up from their towns. [7]It may be that their plea will come before the LORD, and that all of them will turn from their evil ways, for great is the anger and wrath that the LORD has pronounced against this people." [8]And Baruch son of Neriah did all that the prophet Jeremiah ordered him about reading from the scroll the words of the LORD in the LORD's house.

[9] In the fifth year of King Jehoiakim son of Josiah of Judah, in the ninth month, all the people in Jerusalem and all the people who came from the towns of Judah to Jerusalem proclaimed a fast before the LORD. [10]Then, in the hearing of all the people, Baruch read the words of Jeremiah from the scroll, in the house

of the LORD, in the chamber of Gemariah son of Shaphan the secretary, which was in the upper court, at the entry of the New Gate of the LORD's house.

The Scroll Read in the Palace

11 When Micaiah son of Gemariah son of Shaphan heard all the words of the LORD from the scroll, 12he went down to the king's house, into the secretary's chamber; and all the officials were sitting there: Elishama the secretary, Delaiah son of Shemaiah, Elnathan son of Achbor, Gemariah son of Shaphan, Zedekiah son of Hananiah, and all the officials. 13And Micaiah told them all the words that he had heard, when Baruch read the scroll in the hearing of the people. 14Then all the officials sent Jehudi son of Nethaniah son of Shelemiah son of Cushi to say to Baruch, "Bring the scroll that you read in the hearing of the people, and come." So Baruch son of Neriah took the scroll in his hand and came to them. 15And they said to him, "Sit down and read it to us." So Baruch read it to them. 16When they heard all the words, they turned to one another in alarm, and said to Baruch, "We certainly must report all these words to the king." 17Then they questioned Baruch, "Tell us now, how did you write all these words? Was it at his dictation?" 18Baruch answered them, "He dictated all these words to me, and I wrote them with ink on the scroll." 19Then the officials said to Baruch, "Go and hide, you and Jeremiah, and let no one know where you are."

Jehoiakim Burns the Scroll

20 Leaving the scroll in the chamber of Elishama the secretary, they went to the court of the king; and they reported all the words to the king. 21Then the king sent Jehudi to get the scroll, and he took it from the chamber of Elishama the secretary; and Jehudi read it to the king and all the officials who stood beside the king. 22Now the king was sitting in his winter apartment (it was the ninth month), and there was a fire burning in the brazier before him.

23As Jehudi read three or four columns, the king*a* would cut them off with a penknife and throw them into the fire in the brazier, until the entire scroll was consumed in the fire that was in the brazier. 24Yet neither the king, nor any of his servants who heard all these words, was alarmed, nor did they tear their garments. 25Even when Elnathan and Delaiah and Gemariah urged the king not to burn the scroll, he would not listen to them. 26And the king commanded Jerahmeel the king's son and Seraiah son of Azriel and Shelemiah son of Abdeel to arrest the secretary Baruch and the prophet Jeremiah. But the LORD hid them.

Jeremiah Dictates Another

27 Now, after the king had burned the scroll with the words that Baruch wrote at Jeremiah's dictation, the word of the LORD came to Jeremiah: 28Take another scroll and write on it all the former words that were in the first scroll, which King Jehoiakim of Judah has burned. 29And concerning King Jehoiakim of Judah you shall say: Thus says the LORD, You have dared to burn this scroll, saying, Why have you written in it that the king of Babylon will certainly come and destroy this land, and will cut off from it human beings and animals? 30Therefore thus says the LORD concerning King Jehoiakim of Judah: He shall have no one to sit upon the throne of David, and his dead body shall be cast out to the heat by day and the frost by night. 31And I will punish him and his offspring and his servants for their iniquity; I will bring on them, and on the inhabitants of Jerusalem, and on the people of Judah, all the disasters with which I have threatened them—but they would not listen.

32 Then Jeremiah took another scroll and gave it to the secretary Baruch son of Neriah, who wrote on it at Jeremiah's dictation all the words of the scroll that King Jehoiakim of Judah had burned in the fire; and many similar words were added to them.

a Heb *he*

Zedekiah's Vain Hope

37 Zedekiah son of Josiah, whom King Nebuchadrezzar of Babylon made king in the land of Judah, succeeded Coniah son of Jehoiakim. ²But neither he nor his servants nor the people of the land listened to the words of the LORD that he spoke through the prophet Jeremiah.

3 King Zedekiah sent Jehucal son of Shelemiah and the priest Zephaniah son of Maaseiah to the prophet Jeremiah saying, "Please pray for us to the LORD our God." ⁴Now Jeremiah was still going in and out among the people, for he had not yet been put in prison. ⁵Meanwhile, the army of Pharaoh had come out of Egypt; and when the Chaldeans who were besieging Jerusalem heard news of them, they withdrew from Jerusalem.

6 Then the word of the LORD came to the prophet Jeremiah: ⁷Thus says the LORD, God of Israel: This is what the two of you shall say to the king of Judah, who sent you to me to inquire of me: Pharaoh's army, which set out to help you, is going to return to its own land, to Egypt. ⁸And the Chaldeans shall return and fight against this city; they shall take it and burn it with fire. ⁹Thus says the LORD: Do not deceive yourselves, saying, "The Chaldeans will surely go away from us," for they will not go away. ¹⁰Even if you defeated the whole army of Chaldeans who are fighting against you, and there remained of them only wounded men in their tents, they would rise up and burn this city with fire.

Jeremiah Is Imprisoned

11 Now when the Chaldean army had withdrawn from Jerusalem at the approach of Pharaoh's army, ¹²Jeremiah set out from Jerusalem to go to the land of Benjamin to receive his share of property*a* among the people there. ¹³When he reached the Benjamin Gate, a sentinel there named Irijah son of Shelemiah son of Hananiah arrested the prophet Jeremiah saying, "You are deserting to the Chaldeans." ¹⁴And Jeremiah said, "That is a lie; I am not de-

serting to the Chaldeans." But Irijah would not listen to him, and arrested Jeremiah and brought him to the officials. ¹⁵The officials were enraged at Jeremiah, and they beat him and imprisoned him in the house of the secretary Jonathan, for it had been made a prison. ¹⁶Thus Jeremiah was put in the cistern house, in the cells, and remained there many days.

17 Then King Zedekiah sent for him, and received him. The king questioned him secretly in his house, and said, "Is there any word from the LORD?" Jeremiah said, "There is!" Then he said, "You shall be handed over to the king of Babylon." ¹⁸Jeremiah also said to King Zedekiah, "What wrong have I done to you or your servants or this people, that you have put me in prison? ¹⁹Where are your prophets who prophesied to you, saying, 'The king of Babylon will not come against you and against this land'? ²⁰Now please hear me, my lord king: be good enough to listen to my plea, and do not send me back to the house of the secretary Jonathan to die there." ²¹So King Zedekiah gave orders, and they committed Jeremiah to the court of the guard; and a loaf of bread was given him daily from the bakers' street, until all the bread of the city was gone. So Jeremiah remained in the court of the guard.

Jeremiah in the Cistern

38 Now Shephatiah son of Mattan, Gedaliah son of Pashhur, Jucal son of Shelemiah, and Pashhur son of Malchiah heard the words that Jeremiah was saying to all the people, ²Thus says the LORD, Those who stay in this city shall die by the sword, by famine, and by pestilence; but those who go out to the Chaldeans shall live; they shall have their lives as a prize of war, and live. ³Thus says the LORD, This city shall surely be handed over to the army of the king of Babylon and be taken. ⁴Then the officials said to the king, "This man ought to be put to death, because he is discouraging the soldiers who are left in this city, and all the people, by speaking such words to them. For this man is not seeking the welfare

a Meaning of Heb uncertain

of this people, but their harm." 5King Zedekiah said, "Here he is; he is in your hands; for the king is powerless against you." 6So they took Jeremiah and threw him into the cistern of Malchiah, the king's son, which was in the court of the guard, letting Jeremiah down by ropes. Now there was no water in the cistern, but only mud, and Jeremiah sank in the mud.

Jeremiah Is Rescued by Ebed-melech

7 Ebed-melech the Ethiopian,*a* a eunuch in the king's house, heard that they had put Jeremiah into the cistern. The king happened to be sitting at the Benjamin Gate, 8So Ebed-melech left the king's house and spoke to the king, 9"My lord king, these men have acted wickedly in all they did to the prophet Jeremiah by throwing him into the cistern to die there of hunger, for there is no bread left in the city." 10Then the king commanded Ebed-melech the Ethiopian,*a* "Take three men with you from here, and pull the prophet Jeremiah up from the cistern before he dies." 11So Ebed-melech took the men with him and went to the house of the king, to a wardrobe of*b* the storehouse, and took from there old rags and worn-out clothes, which he let down to Jeremiah in the cistern by ropes. 12Then Ebed-melech the Ethiopian*a* said to Jeremiah, "Just put the rags and clothes between your armpits and the ropes." Jeremiah did so. 13Then they drew Jeremiah up by the ropes and pulled him out of the cistern. And Jeremiah remained in the court of the guard.

Zedekiah Consults Jeremiah Again

14 King Zedekiah sent for the prophet Jeremiah and received him at the third entrance of the temple of the LORD. The king said to Jeremiah, "I have something to ask you; do not hide anything from me." 15Jeremiah said to Zedekiah, "If I tell you, you will put me to death, will you not? And if I give you advice, you will not listen to me." 16So King Zedekiah swore an oath in secret to Jeremiah, "As the LORD lives, who gave us our lives, I will not put

you to death or hand you over to these men who seek your life."

17 Then Jeremiah said to Zedekiah, "Thus says the LORD, the God of hosts, the God of Israel, If you will only surrender to the officials of the king of Babylon, then your life shall be spared, and this city shall not be burned with fire, and you and your house shall live. 18But if you do not surrender to the officials of the king of Babylon, then this city shall be handed over to the Chaldeans, and they shall burn it with fire, and you yourself shall not escape from their hand." 19King Zedekiah said to Jeremiah, "I am afraid of the Judeans who have deserted to the Chaldeans, for I might be handed over to them and they would abuse me." 20Jeremiah said, "That will not happen. Just obey the voice of the LORD in what I say to you, and it shall go well with you, and your life shall be spared. 21But if you are determined not to surrender, this is what the LORD has shown me— 22a vision of all the women remaining in the house of the king of Judah being led out to the officials of the king of Babylon and saying,

'Your trusted friends have seduced you
    and have overcome you;
Now that your feet are stuck in the mud,
    they desert you.'

23All your wives and your children shall be led out to the Chaldeans, and you yourself shall not escape from their hand, but shall be seized by the king of Babylon; and this city shall be burned with fire."

24 Then Zedekiah said to Jeremiah, "Do not let anyone else know of this conversation, or you will die. 25If the officials should hear that I have spoken with you, and they should come and say to you, 'Just tell us what you said to the king; do not conceal it from us, or we will put you to death. What did the king say to you?' 26then you shall say to them, 'I was presenting my plea to the king not to send me back to the house of Jonathan to die there.'" 27All the officials did come to Jeremiah and questioned him; and he answered them in the very words the king had commanded. So they stopped

---

a Or *Nubian*; Heb *Cushite*   *b* Cn: Heb *to under*

questioning him, for the conversation had not been overheard. ²⁸And Jeremiah remained in the court of the guard until the day that Jerusalem was taken.

The Fall of Jerusalem

39 In the ninth year of King Zedekiah of Judah, in the tenth month, King Nebuchadrezzar of Babylon and all his army came against Jerusalem and besieged it; ²in the eleventh year of Zedekiah, in the fourth month, on the ninth day of the month, a breach was made in the city. ³When Jerusalem was taken,ᵃ all the officials of the king of Babylon came and sat in the middle gate: Nergal-sharezer, Samgar-nebo, Sarsechim the Rabsaris, Nergal-sharezer the Rabmag, with all the rest of the officials of the king of Babylon. ⁴When King Zedekiah of Judah and all the soldiers saw them, they fled, going out of the city at night by way of the king's garden through the gate between the two walls; and they went toward the Arabah. ⁵But the army of the Chaldeans pursued them, and overtook Zedekiah in the plains of Jericho; and when they had taken him, they brought him up to King Nebuchadrezzar of Babylon, at Riblah, in the land of Hamath; and he passed sentence on him. ⁶The king of Babylon slaughtered the sons of Zedekiah at Riblah before his eyes; also the king of Babylon slaughtered all the nobles of Judah. ⁷He put out the eyes of Zedekiah, and bound him in fetters to take him to Babylon. ⁸The Chaldeans burned the king's house and the houses of the people, and broke down the walls of Jerusalem. ⁹Then Nebuzaradan the captain of the guard exiled to Babylon the rest of the people who were left in the city, those who had deserted to him, and the people who remained. ¹⁰Nebuzaradan the captain of the guard left in the land of Judah some of the poor people who owned nothing, and gave them vineyards and fields at the same time.

Jeremiah, Set Free, Remembers Ebed-melech

11 King Nebuchadrezzar of Babylon gave command concerning Jeremiah through Nebuzaradan, the captain of the guard, saying, ¹²"Take him, look after him well and do him no harm, but deal with him as he may ask you." ¹³So Nebuzaradan the captain of the guard, Nebushazban the Rabsaris, Nergal-sharezer the Rabmag, and all the chief officers of the king of Babylon sent ¹⁴and took Jeremiah from the court of the guard. They entrusted him to Gedaliah son of Ahikam son of Shaphan to be brought home. So he stayed with his own people.

15 The word of the LORD came to Jeremiah while he was confined in the court of the guard: ¹⁶Go and say to Ebed-melech the Ethiopian:ᵇ Thus says the LORD of hosts, the God of Israel: I am going to fulfill my words against this city for evil and not for good, and they shall be accomplished in your presence on that day. ¹⁷But I will save you on that day, says the LORD, and you shall not be handed over to those whom you dread. ¹⁸For I will surely save you, and you shall not fall by the sword; but you shall have your life as a prize of war, because you have trusted in me, says the LORD.

Jeremiah with Gedaliah the Governor

40 The word that came to Jeremiah from the LORD after Nebuzaradan the captain of the guard had let him go from Ramah, when he took him bound in fetters along with all the captives of Jerusalem and Judah who were being exiled to Babylon. ²The captain of the guard took Jeremiah and said to him, "The LORD your God threatened this place with this disaster; ³and now the LORD has brought it about, and has done as he said, because all of you sinned against the LORD and did not obey his voice. Therefore this thing has come upon you. ⁴Now look, I have just released you today from the fetters on your hands. If you wish to come with me to Babylon, come, and I will take good care of you; but if you do not wish to come with me to Babylon, you need not come. See, the whole land is before you; go wherever you think it good and right to go. ⁵If you re-

---

ᵃ This clause has been transposed from 38.28   ᵇ Or *Nubian*; Heb *Cushite* main,*a* then return to Gedaliah son of Ahikam son of Shaphan, whom the king of Babylon appointed governor of the towns of Judah, and stay with him among the people; or go wherever you think it right to go." So the captain of the guard gave him an allowance of food and a present, and let him go. 6Then Jeremiah went to Gedaliah son of Ahikam at Mizpah, and stayed with him among the people who were left in the land.

7 When all the leaders of the forces in the open country and their troops heard that the king of Babylon had appointed Gedaliah son of Ahikam governor in the land, and had committed to him men, women, and children, those of the poorest of the land who had not been taken into exile to Babylon, 8they went to Gedaliah at Mizpah—Ishmael son of Nethaniah, Johanan son of Kareah, Seraiah son of Tanhumeth, the sons of Ephai the Netophathite, Jezaniah son of the Maacathite, they and their troops. 9Gedaliah son of Ahikam son of Shaphan swore to them and their troops, saying, "Do not be afraid to serve the Chaldeans. Stay in the land and serve the king of Babylon, and it shall go well with you. 10As for me, I am staying at Mizpah to represent you before the Chaldeans who come to us; but as for you, gather wine and summer fruits and oil, and store them in your vessels, and live in the towns that you have taken over." 11Likewise, when all the Judeans who were in Moab and among the Ammonites and in Edom and in other lands heard that the king of Babylon had left a remnant in Judah and had appointed Gedaliah son of Ahikam son of Shaphan as governor over them, 12then all the Judeans returned from all the places to which they had been scattered and came to the land of Judah, to Gedaliah at Mizpah; and they gathered wine and summer fruits in great abundance.

13 Now Johanan son of Kareah and all the leaders of the forces in the open country came to Gedaliah at Mizpah 14and said to him, "Are you at all aware that Baalis king of the Ammonites has sent Ishmael son of Nethaniah to

take your life?" But Gedaliah son of Ahikam would not believe them. 15Then Johanan son of Kareah spoke secretly to Gedaliah at Mizpah, "Please let me go and kill Ishmael son of Nethaniah, and no one else will know. Why should he take your life, so that all the Judeans who are gathered around you would be scattered, and the remnant of Judah would perish?" 16But Gedaliah son of Ahikam said to Johanan son of Kareah, "Do not do such a thing, for you are telling a lie about Ishmael."

Insurrection against Gedaliah

41 In the seventh month, Ishmael son of Nethaniah son of Elishama, of the royal family, one of the chief officers of the king, came with ten men to Gedaliah son of Ahikam, at Mizpah. As they ate bread together there at Mizpah, 2Ishmael son of Nethaniah and the ten men with him got up and struck down Gedaliah son of Ahikam son of Shaphan with the sword and killed him, because the king of Babylon had appointed him governor in the land. 3Ishmael also killed all the Judeans who were with Gedaliah at Mizpah, and the Chaldean soldiers who happened to be there.

4 On the day after the murder of Gedaliah, before anyone knew of it, 5eighty men arrived from Shechem and Shiloh and Samaria, with their beards shaved and their clothes torn, and their bodies gashed, bringing grain offerings and incense to present at the temple of the LORD. 6And Ishmael son of Nethaniah came out from Mizpah to meet them, weeping as he came. As he met them, he said to them, "Come to Gedaliah son of Ahikam." 7When they reached the middle of the city, Ishmael son of Nethaniah and the men with him slaughtered them, and threw them*a* into a cistern. 8But there were ten men among them who said to Ishmael, "Do not kill us, for we have stores of wheat, barley, oil, and honey hidden in the fields." So he refrained, and did not kill them along with their companions.

9 Now the cistern into which Ishmael had

---

a Syr: Meaning of Heb uncertain   *b* Syr: Heb lacks *and threw them*, compare verse 9 thrown all the bodies of the men whom he had struck down was the large cistern*a* that King Asa had made for defense against King Baasha of Israel; Ishmael son of Nethaniah filled that cistern with those whom he had killed. 10Then Ishmael took captive all the rest of the people who were in Mizpah, the king's daughters and all the people who were left at Mizpah, whom Nebuzaradan, the captain of the guard, had committed to Gedaliah son of Ahikam. Ishmael son of Nethaniah took them captive and set out to cross over to the Ammonites.

11 But when Johanan son of Kareah and all the leaders of the forces with him heard of all the crimes that Ishmael son of Nethaniah had done, 12they took all their men and went to fight against Ishmael son of Nethaniah. They came upon him at the great pool that is in Gibeon. 13And when all the people who were with Ishmael saw Johanan son of Kareah and all the leaders of the forces with him, they were glad. 14So all the people whom Ishmael had carried away captive from Mizpah turned around and came back, and went to Johanan son of Kareah. 15But Ishmael son of Nethaniah escaped from Johanan with eight men, and went to the Ammonites. 16Then Johanan son of Kareah and all the leaders of the forces with him took all the rest of the people whom Ishmael son of Nethaniah had carried away captive*b* from Mizpah after he had slain Gedaliah son of Ahikam—soldiers, women, children, and eunuchs, whom Johanan brought back from Gibeon.*c* 17And they set out, and stopped at Geruth Chimham near Bethlehem, intending to go to Egypt 18because of the Chaldeans; for they were afraid of them, because Ishmael son of Nethaniah had killed Gedaliah son of Ahikam, whom the king of Babylon had made governor over the land.

Jeremiah Advises Survivors Not to Migrate

42 Then all the commanders of the forces, and Johanan son of Kareah and Azariah*d* son of Hoshaiah, and all the people from the least to the greatest, approached 2the prophet Jeremiah and said, "Be good enough to listen to our plea, and pray to the LORD your God for us—for all this remnant. For there are only a few of us left out of many, as your eyes can see. 3Let the LORD your God show us where we should go and what we should do." 4The prophet Jeremiah said to them, "Very well: I am going to pray to the LORD your God as you request, and whatever the LORD answers you I will tell you; I will keep nothing back from you." 5They in their turn said to Jeremiah, "May the LORD be a true and faithful witness against us if we do not act according to everything that the LORD your God sends us through you. 6Whether it is good or bad, we will obey the voice of the LORD our God to whom we are sending you, in order that it may go well with us when we obey the voice of the LORD our God."

7 At the end of ten days the word of the LORD came to Jeremiah. 8Then he summoned Johanan son of Kareah and all the commanders of the forces who were with him, and all the people from the least to the greatest, 9and said to them, "Thus says the LORD, the God of Israel, to whom you sent me to present your plea before him: 10If you will only remain in this land, then I will build you up and not pull you down; I will plant you, and not pluck you up; for I am sorry for the disaster that I have brought upon you. 11Do not be afraid of the king of Babylon, as you have been; do not be afraid of him, says the LORD, for I am with you, to save you and to rescue you from his hand. 12I will grant you mercy, and he will have mercy on you and restore you to your native soil. 13But if you continue to say, 'We will not stay in this land,' thus disobeying the voice of the LORD your God 14and saying, 'No, we will go to the land of Egypt, where we shall not see war, or hear the sound of the trumpet, or be hungry for bread, and there we will stay,' 15then hear the word of the LORD, O remnant of Judah. Thus says the LORD of hosts, the God of Israel: If you are determined to enter Egypt and go to settle there, 16then the sword that you

---

a Gk: Heb *whom he had killed by the hand of Gedaliah*   *b* Cn: Heb *whom he recovered from Ishmael son of Nethaniah*
c Meaning of Heb uncertain   *d* Gk: Heb *Jezaniah*

fear shall overtake you there, in the land of Egypt; and the famine that you dread shall follow close after you into Egypt; and there you shall die. 17All the people who have determined to go to Egypt to settle there shall die by the sword, by famine, and by pestilence; they shall have no remnant or survivor from the disaster that I am bringing upon them.

18 "For thus says the LORD of hosts, the God of Israel: Just as my anger and my wrath were poured out on the inhabitants of Jerusalem, so my wrath will be poured out on you when you go to Egypt. You shall become an object of execration and horror, of cursing and ridicule. You shall see this place no more. 19The LORD has said to you, O remnant of Judah, Do not go to Egypt. Be well aware that I have warned you today 20that you have made a fatal mistake. For you yourselves sent me to the LORD your God, saying, 'Pray for us to the LORD our God, and whatever the LORD our God says, tell us and we will do it.' 21So I have told you today, but you have not obeyed the voice of the LORD your God in anything that he sent me to tell you. 22Be well aware, then, that you shall die by the sword, by famine, and by pestilence in the place where you desire to go and settle."

Taken to Egypt, Jeremiah Warns of Judgment

43 When Jeremiah finished speaking to all the people all these words of the LORD their God, with which the LORD their God had sent him to them, 2Azariah son of Hoshaiah and Johanan son of Kareah and all the other insolent men said to Jeremiah, "You are telling a lie. The LORD our God did not send you to say, 'Do not go to Egypt to settle there'; 3but Baruch son of Neriah is inciting you against us, to hand us over to the Chaldeans, in order that they may kill us or take us into exile in Babylon." 4So Johanan son of Kareah and all the commanders of the forces and all the people did not obey the voice of the LORD, to stay in the land of Judah. 5But Johanan son of Kareah and all the command-

ers of the forces took all the remnant of Judah who had returned to settle in the land of Judah from all the nations to which they had been driven— 6the men, the women, the children, the princesses, and everyone whom Nebuzaradan the captain of the guard had left with Gedaliah son of Ahikam son of Shaphan; also the prophet Jeremiah and Baruch son of Neriah. 7And they came into the land of Egypt, for they did not obey the voice of the LORD. And they arrived at Tahpanhes.

8 Then the word of the LORD came to Jeremiah in Tahpanhes: 9Take some large stones in your hands, and bury them in the clay pavement*a* that is at the entrance to Pharaoh's palace in Tahpanhes. Let the Judeans see you do it, 10and say to them, Thus says the LORD of hosts, the God of Israel: I am going to send and take my servant King Nebuchadrezzar of Babylon, and he*b* will set his throne above these stones that I have buried, and he will spread his royal canopy over them. 11He shall come and ravage the land of Egypt, giving

> those who are destined for pestilence, to
>   pestilence,
> and those who are destined for
>   captivity, to captivity,
> and those who are destined for the
>   sword, to the sword.

12He*c* shall kindle a fire in the temples of the gods of Egypt; and he shall burn them and carry them away captive; and he shall pick clean the land of Egypt, as a shepherd picks his cloak clean of vermin; and he shall depart from there safely. 13He shall break the obelisks of Heliopolis, which is in the land of Egypt; and the temples of the gods of Egypt he shall burn with fire.

Denunciation of Persistent Idolatry

44 The word that came to Jeremiah for all the Judeans living in the land of Egypt, at Migdol, at Tahpanhes, at Memphis, and in the land of Pathros, 2Thus says the LORD of hosts, the God of Israel: You yourselves have seen all the disaster that I have brought on Je-

---

a Meaning of Heb uncertain   *b* Gk Syr: Heb *I*   *c* Gk Syr Vg: Heb *I* rusalem and on all the towns of Judah. Look at them; today they are a desolation, without an inhabitant in them, ³because of the wickedness that they committed, provoking me to anger, in that they went to make offerings and serve other gods that they had not known, neither they, nor you, nor your ancestors. ⁴Yet I persistently sent to you all my servants the prophets, saying, "I beg you not to do this abominable thing that I hate!" ⁵But they did not listen or incline their ear, to turn from their wickedness and make no offerings to other gods. ⁶So my wrath and my anger were poured out and kindled in the towns of Judah and in the streets of Jerusalem; and they became a waste and a desolation, as they still are today. ⁷And now thus says the LORD God of hosts, the God of Israel: Why are you doing such great harm to yourselves, to cut off man and woman, child and infant, from the midst of Judah, leaving yourselves without a remnant? ⁸Why do you provoke me to anger with the works of your hands, making offerings to other gods in the land of Egypt where you have come to settle? Will you be cut off and become an object of cursing and ridicule among all the nations of the earth? ⁹Have you forgotten the crimes of your ancestors, of the kings of Judah, of their *a* wives, your own crimes and those of your wives, which they committed in the land of Judah and in the streets of Jerusalem? ¹⁰They have shown no contrition or fear to this day, nor have they walked in my law and my statutes that I set before you and before your ancestors.

11 Therefore thus says the LORD of hosts, the God of Israel: I am determined to bring disaster on you, to bring all Judah to an end. ¹²I will take the remnant of Judah who are determined to come to the land of Egypt to settle, and they shall perish, everyone; in the land of Egypt they shall fall; by the sword and by famine they shall perish; from the least to the greatest, they shall die by the sword and by famine; and they shall become an object of execration and horror, of cursing and ridicule. ¹³I will punish those who live in the land of Egypt, as I have punished Jerusalem, with the sword, with famine, and with pestilence, ¹⁴so that none of the remnant of Judah who have come to settle in the land of Egypt shall escape or survive or return to the land of Judah. Although they long to go back to live there, they shall not go back, except some fugitives.

15 Then all the men who were aware that their wives had been making offerings to other gods, and all the women who stood by, a great assembly, all the people who lived in Pathros in the land of Egypt, answered Jeremiah: ¹⁶"As for the word that you have spoken to us in the name of the LORD, we are not going to listen to you. ¹⁷Instead, we will do everything that we have vowed, make offerings to the queen of heaven and pour out libations to her, just as we and our ancestors, our kings and our officials, used to do in the towns of Judah and in the streets of Jerusalem. We used to have plenty of food, and prospered, and saw no misfortune. ¹⁸But from the time we stopped making offerings to the queen of heaven and pouring out libations to her, we have lacked everything and have perished by the sword and by famine." ¹⁹And the women said, *b* "Indeed we will go on making offerings to the queen of heaven and pouring out libations to her; do you think that we made cakes for her, marked with her image, and poured out libations to her without our husbands' being involved?"

20 Then Jeremiah said to all the people, men and women, all the people who were giving him this answer: ²¹"As for the offerings that you made in the towns of Judah and in the streets of Jerusalem, you and your ancestors, your kings and your officials, and the people of the land, did not the LORD remember them? Did it not come into his mind? ²²The LORD could no longer bear the sight of your evil doings, the abominations that you committed; therefore your land became a desolation and a waste and a curse, without inhabitant, as it is to this day. ²³It is because you burned offerings, and because you sinned against the LORD and did not obey the voice of the LORD or walk in

a Heb *his*   *b* Compare Syr: Heb lacks *And the women said* his law and in his statutes and in his decrees, that this disaster has befallen you, as is still evident today."

24 Jeremiah said to all the people and all the women, "Hear the word of the LORD, all you Judeans who are in the land of Egypt, 25Thus says the LORD of hosts, the God of Israel: You and your wives have accomplished in deeds what you declared in words, saying, 'We are determined to perform the vows that we have made, to make offerings to the queen of heaven and to pour out libations to her.' By all means, keep your vows and make your libations! 26Therefore hear the word of the LORD, all you Judeans who live in the land of Egypt: Lo, I swear by my great name, says the LORD, that my name shall no longer be pronounced on the lips of any of the people of Judah in all the land of Egypt, saying, 'As the Lord GOD lives.' 27I am going to watch over them for harm and not for good; all the people of Judah who are in the land of Egypt shall perish by the sword and by famine, until not one is left. 28And those who escape the sword shall return from the land of Egypt to the land of Judah, few in number; and all the remnant of Judah, who have come to the land of Egypt to settle, shall know whose words will stand, mine or theirs! 29This shall be the sign to you, says the LORD, that I am going to punish you in this place, in order that you may know that my words against you will surely be carried out: 30Thus says the LORD, I am going to give Pharaoh Hophra, king of Egypt, into the hands of his enemies, those who seek his life, just as I gave King Zedekiah of Judah into the hand of King Nebuchadrezzar of Babylon, his enemy who sought his life."

A Word of Comfort to Baruch

45 The word that the prophet Jeremiah spoke to Baruch son of Neriah, when he wrote these words in a scroll at the dictation of Jeremiah, in the fourth year of King Jehoiakim son of Josiah of Judah: 2Thus says the LORD, the God of Israel, to you, O Baruch: 3You said, "Woe is me! The LORD has added sorrow to my pain; I am weary with my groan-

ing, and I find no rest." 4Thus you shall say to him, "Thus says the LORD: I am going to break down what I have built, and pluck up what I have planted—that is, the whole land. 5And you, do you seek great things for yourself? Do not seek them; for I am going to bring disaster upon all flesh, says the LORD; but I will give you your life as a prize of war in every place to which you may go."

Judgment on Egypt

46 The word of the LORD that came to the prophet Jeremiah concerning the nations.

2 Concerning Egypt, about the army of Pharaoh Neco, king of Egypt, which was by the river Euphrates at Carchemish and which King Nebuchadrezzar of Babylon defeated in the fourth year of King Jehoiakim son of Josiah of Judah:

3   Prepare buckler and shield,
       and advance for battle!
4   Harness the horses;
       mount the steeds!
    Take your stations with your helmets,
       whet your lances,
       put on your coats of mail!
5   Why do I see them terrified?
       They have fallen back;
    their warriors are beaten down,
       and have fled in haste.
    They do not look back—
       terror is all around!
                           says the LORD.
6   The swift cannot flee away,
       nor can the warrior escape;
    in the north by the river Euphrates
       they have stumbled and fallen.

7   Who is this, rising like the Nile,
       like rivers whose waters surge?
8   Egypt rises like the Nile,
       like rivers whose waters surge.
    It said, Let me rise, let me cover the
           earth,
       let me destroy cities and their
           inhabitants.
9   Advance, O horses,

and dash madly, O chariots!
Let the warriors go forth:
    Ethiopia*a* and Put who carry the
      shield,
    the Ludim, who draw*b* the bow.

10 That day is the day of the Lord GOD of
      hosts,
    a day of retribution,
    to gain vindication from his foes.
The sword shall devour and be sated,
    and drink its fill of their blood.
For the Lord GOD of hosts holds a
      sacrifice
    in the land of the north by the river
      Euphrates.

11 Go up to Gilead, and take balm,
    O virgin daughter Egypt!
In vain you have used many medicines;
    there is no healing for you.

12 The nations have heard of your shame,
    and the earth is full of your cry;
for warrior has stumbled against warrior;
    both have fallen together.

Babylonia Will Strike Egypt

13 The word that the LORD spoke to the
prophet Jeremiah about the coming of King
Nebuchadrezzar of Babylon to attack the land
of Egypt:

14 Declare in Egypt, and proclaim in
      Migdol;
    proclaim in Memphis and Tahpanhes;
Say, "Take your stations and be ready,
    for the sword shall devour those
      around you."

15 Why has Apis fled?*c*
    Why did your bull not stand?
    —because the LORD thrust him down.

16 Your multitude stumbled*d* and fell,
    and one said to another,*e*
"Come, let us go back to our own
      people
and to the land of our birth,
    because of the destroying sword."

17 Give Pharaoh, king of Egypt, the name
    "Braggart who missed his chance."

18 As I live, says the King,
    whose name is the LORD of hosts,
one is coming
    like Tabor among the mountains,
    and like Carmel by the sea.

19 Pack your bags for exile,
    sheltered daughter Egypt!
For Memphis shall become a waste,
    a ruin, without inhabitant.

20 A beautiful heifer is Egypt—
    a gadfly from the north lights upon
      her.

21 Even her mercenaries in her midst
    are like fatted calves;
they too have turned and fled together,
    they did not stand;
for the day of their calamity has come
      upon them,
    the time of their punishment.

22 She makes a sound like a snake gliding
      away;
    for her enemies march in force,
and come against her with axes,
    like those who fell trees.

23 They shall cut down her forest,
              says the LORD,
    though it is impenetrable,
because they are more numerous
    than locusts;
    they are without number.

24 Daughter Egypt shall be put to shame;
    she shall be handed over to a people
      from the north.

25 The LORD of hosts, the God of Israel,
said: See, I am bringing punishment upon
Amon of Thebes, and Pharaoh, and Egypt
and her gods and her kings, upon Pharaoh and
those who trust in him. 26I will hand them
over to those who seek their life, to King Nebuchadrezzar of Babylon and his officers. Afterward Egypt shall be inhabited as in the days
of old, says the LORD.

---

a Or *Nubia*; Heb *Cush*   *b* Cn: Heb *who grasp, who draw*   *c* Gk: Heb *Why was it swept away*   *d* Gk: Meaning of
Heb uncertain   *e* Gk: Heb *and fell one to another and they said*

God Will Save Israel

27 But as for you, have no fear, my servant
      Jacob,
    and do not be dismayed, O Israel;
  for I am going to save you from far away,
    and your offspring from the land of
      their captivity.
  Jacob shall return and have quiet and
      ease,
    and no one shall make him afraid.
28 As for you, have no fear, my servant
      Jacob,
                    says the LORD,
    for I am with you.
  I will make an end of all the nations
    among which I have banished you,
    but I will not make an end of you!
  I will chastise you in just measure,
    and I will by no means leave you
      unpunished.

Judgment on the Philistines

47 The word of the LORD that came to
      the prophet Jeremiah concerning the
Philistines, before Pharaoh attacked Gaza:
2 Thus says the LORD:
  See, waters are rising out of the north
    and shall become an overflowing
      torrent;
  they shall overflow the land and all that
      fills it,
    the city and those who live in it.
  People shall cry out,
    and all the inhabitants of the land
      shall wail.
3 At the noise of the stamping of the
      hoofs of his stallions,
    at the clatter of his chariots, at the
      rumbling of their wheels,
  parents do not turn back for children,
    so feeble are their hands,
4 because of the day that is coming
      to destroy all the Philistines,
    to cut off from Tyre and Sidon
      every helper that remains.

For the LORD is destroying the
      Philistines,
    the remnant of the coastland of
      Caphtor.
5 Baldness has come upon Gaza,
    Ashkelon is silenced.
  O remnant of their power!ᵃ
    How long will you gash yourselves?
6 Ah, sword of the LORD!
    How long until you are quiet?
  Put yourself into your scabbard,
    rest and be still!
7 How can itᵇ be quiet,
    when the LORD has given it an order?
  Against Ashkelon and against the
      seashore—
    there he has appointed it.

Judgment on Moab

48 Concerning Moab.
Thus says the LORD of hosts, the God of Is-
rael:
  Alas for Nebo, it is laid waste!
    Kiriathaim is put to shame, it is taken;
  the fortress is put to shame and broken
      down;
2   the renown of Moab is no more.
  In Heshbon they planned evil against her:
    "Come, let us cut her off from being
      a nation!"
  You also, O Madmen, shall be brought
      to silence;ᶜ
    the sword shall pursue you.

3 Hark! a cry from Horonaim,
    "Desolation and great destruction!"
4 "Moab is destroyed!"
    her little ones cry out.
5 For at the ascent of Luhith
    they goᵈ up weeping bitterly;
  for at the descent of Horonaim
    they have heard the distressing cry of
      anguish.
6 Flee! Save yourselves!
    Be like a wild assᵉ in the desert!

---

a Gk: Heb *their valley*   b Gk Vg: Heb *you*   c The place-name *Madmen* sounds like the Hebrew verb *to be silent*
d Cn: Heb *he goes*   e Gk Aquila: Heb *like Aroer*

7 Surely, because you trusted in your
        strongholds[a] and your treasures,
    you also shall be taken;
    Chemosh shall go out into exile,
        with his priests and his attendants.
8 The destroyer shall come upon every
        town,
        and no town shall escape;
    the valley shall perish,
        and the plain shall be destroyed,
        as the LORD has spoken.

9 Set aside salt for Moab,
        for she will surely fall;
    her towns shall become a desolation,
        with no inhabitant in them.

10 Accursed is the one who is slack in doing the work of the LORD; and accursed is the
one who keeps back the sword from bloodshed.

11 Moab has been at ease from his youth,
        settled like wine[b] on its dregs;
    he has not been emptied from vessel to
        vessel,
        nor has he gone into exile;
    therefore his flavor has remained
        and his aroma is unspoiled.
12 Therefore, the time is surely coming,
says the LORD, when I shall send to him de-
canters to decant him, and empty his vessels,
and break his[c] jars in pieces. 13Then Moab shall
be ashamed of Chemosh, as the house of Israel was ashamed of Bethel, their confidence.

14 How can you say, "We are heroes
        and mighty warriors"?
15 The destroyer of Moab and his towns
        has come up,
    and the choicest of his young men
        have gone down to slaughter,
    says the King, whose name is the
        LORD of hosts.
16 The calamity of Moab is near at hand
        and his doom approaches swiftly.

17 Mourn over him, all you his neighbors,
        and all who know his name;
    say, "How the mighty scepter is broken,
        the glorious staff!"

18 Come down from glory,
        and sit on the parched ground,
        enthroned daughter Dibon!
    For the destroyer of Moab has come up
        against you;
        he has destroyed your strongholds.
19 Stand by the road and watch,
        you inhabitant of Aroer!
    Ask the man fleeing and the woman
        escaping;
        say, "What has happened?"
20 Moab is put to shame, for it is broken
        down;
        wail and cry!
    Tell it by the Arnon,
        that Moab is laid waste.

21 Judgment has come upon the tableland,
upon Holon, and Jahzah, and Mephaath, 22and
Dibon, and Nebo, and Beth-diblathaim, 23and
Kiriathaim, and Beth-gamul, and Beth-meon,
24and Kerioth, and Bozrah, and all the towns
of the land of Moab, far and near. 25The horn
of Moab is cut off, and his arm is broken, says
the LORD.

26 Make him drunk, because he magnified
himself against the LORD; let Moab wallow in
his vomit; he too shall become a laughingstock. 27Israel was a laughingstock for you,
though he was not caught among thieves; but
whenever you spoke of him you shook your
head!

28 Leave the towns, and live on the rock,
        O inhabitants of Moab!
    Be like the dove that nests
        on the sides of the mouth of a gorge.
29 We have heard of the pride of Moab—
        he is very proud—
    of his loftiness, his pride, and his
        arrogance,

a Gk: Heb works   b Heb lacks like wine   c Gk Aquila: Heb their

and the haughtiness of his heart.
30 I myself know his insolence, says the
LORD;
his boasts are false,
his deeds are false.
31 Therefore I wail for Moab;
I cry out for all Moab;
for the people of Kir-heres I mourn.
32 More than for Jazer I weep for you,
O vine of Sibmah!
Your branches crossed over the sea,
reached as far as Jazer;*a*
upon your summer fruits and your
vintage
the destroyer has fallen.
33 Gladness and joy have been taken away
from the fruitful land of Moab;
I have stopped the wine from the wine
presses;
no one treads them with shouts of
joy;
the shouting is not the shout of joy.

34 Heshbon and Elealeh cry out;*b* as far as
Jahaz they utter their voice, from Zoar to Horonaim and Eglath-shelishiyah. For even the
waters of Nimrim have become desolate.
35And I will bring to an end in Moab, says the
LORD, those who offer sacrifice at a high place
and make offerings to their gods. 36Therefore
my heart moans for Moab like a flute, and my
heart moans like a flute for the people of Kir-
heres; for the riches they gained have perished.
37 For every head is shaved and every beard
cut off; on all the hands there are gashes, and
on the loins sackcloth. 38On all the housetops
of Moab and in the squares there is nothing but
lamentation; for I have broken Moab like a
vessel that no one wants, says the LORD. 39How
it is broken! How they wail! How Moab has
turned its back in shame! So Moab has become
a derision and a horror to all his neighbors.
40 For thus says the LORD:
Look, he shall swoop down like an eagle,
and spread his wings against Moab;
41 the towns*c* shall be taken

and the strongholds seized.
The hearts of the warriors of Moab, on
that day,
shall be like the heart of a woman in
labor.
42 Moab shall be destroyed as a people,
because he magnified himself against
the LORD.
43 Terror, pit, and trap
are before you, O inhabitants of
Moab!
says the LORD.
44 Everyone who flees from the terror
shall fall into the pit,
and everyone who climbs out of the pit
shall be caught in the trap.
For I will bring these things*d* upon Moab
in the year of their punishment,
says the LORD.

45 In the shadow of Heshbon
fugitives stop exhausted;
for a fire has gone out from Heshbon,
a flame from the house of Sihon;
it has destroyed the forehead of Moab,
the scalp of the people of tumult.*e*
46 Woe to you, O Moab!
The people of Chemosh have
perished,
for your sons have been taken captive,
and your daughters into captivity.
47 Yet I will restore the fortunes of Moab
in the latter days, says the LORD.
Thus far is the judgment on Moab.

Judgment on the Ammonites

49 Concerning the Ammonites.

Thus says the LORD:
Has Israel no sons?
Has he no heir?
Why then has Milcom dispossessed Gad,
and his people settled in its towns?
2 Therefore, the time is surely coming,
says the LORD,
when I will sound the battle alarm

---

a Two Mss and Isa 16.8: MT *the sea of Jazer*   *b* Cn: Heb *From the cry of Heshbon to Elealeh*   *c* Or *Kerioth*
d Gk Syr: Heb *bring upon it*   *e* Or *of Shaon*

against Rabbah of the Ammonites;
it shall become a desolate mound,
　　and its villages shall be burned with
　　　　fire;
then Israel shall dispossess those who
　　dispossessed him,
　　says the LORD.

3　Wail, O Heshbon, for Ai is laid waste!
　　Cry out, O daughters*a* of Rabbah!
　Put on sackcloth,
　　lament, and slash yourselves with
　　　whips!*b*
　For Milcom shall go into exile,
　　with his priests and his attendants.
4　Why do you boast in your strength?
　　Your strength is ebbing,
　O faithless daughter.
　　You trusted in your treasures, saying,
　　"Who will attack me?"
5　I am going to bring terror upon you,
　　says the Lord GOD of hosts,
　　from all your neighbors,
　and you will be scattered, each headlong,
　　with no one to gather the fugitives.
6　But afterward I will restore the fortunes
of the Ammonites, says the LORD.

Judgment on Edom
7　Concerning Edom.

Thus says the LORD of hosts:
　Is there no longer wisdom in Teman?
　　Has counsel perished from the
　　　prudent?
　　Has their wisdom vanished?
8　Flee, turn back, get down low,
　　　inhabitants of Dedan!
　For I will bring the calamity of Esau
　　　upon him,
　　the time when I punish him.
9　If grape-gatherers came to you,
　　would they not leave gleanings?
　If thieves came by night,
　　even they would pillage only what they
　　　wanted.

10　But as for me, I have stripped Esau bare,
　　I have uncovered his hiding places,
　　　and he is not able to conceal himself.
　His offspring are destroyed, his kinsfolk
　　and his neighbors; and he is no more.
11　Leave your orphans, I will keep them
　　　alive;
　　and let your widows trust in me.

12　For thus says the LORD: If those who do not deserve to drink the cup still have to drink it, shall you be the one to go unpunished? You shall not go unpunished; you must drink it. 13For by myself I have sworn, says the LORD, that Bozrah shall become an object of horror and ridicule, a waste, and an object of cursing; and all her towns shall be perpetual wastes.

14　I have heard tidings from the LORD,
　　and a messenger has been sent among
　　　the nations:
　"Gather yourselves together and come
　　　against her,
　　and rise up for battle!"
15　For I will make you least among the
　　　nations,
　　despised by humankind.
16　The terror you inspire
　　and the pride of your heart have
　　　deceived you,
　you who live in the clefts of the rock,*c*
　　who hold the height of the hill.
　Although you make your nest as high as
　　　the eagle's,
　　from there I will bring you down,
　　　　　　　　　　says the LORD.

17　Edom shall become an object of horror; everyone who passes by it will be horrified and will hiss because of all its disasters. 18As when Sodom and Gomorrah and their neighbors were overthrown, says the LORD, no one shall live there, nor shall anyone settle in it. 19Like a lion coming up from the thickets of the Jordan against a perennial pasture, I will suddenly chase Edom*d* away from it; and I will appoint over it whomever I choose.*e* For who is like me? Who can summon me? Who is the shepherd who can stand before me? 20There-

a Or *villages*　　*b* Cn: Meaning of Heb uncertain　　*c* Or *of Sela*　　*d* Heb *him*　　*e* Or *and I will single out the choicest of his rams*: Meaning of Heb uncertain fore hear the plan that the LORD has made against Edom and the purposes that he has formed against the inhabitants of Teman: Surely the little ones of the flock shall be dragged away; surely their fold shall be appalled at their fate. 21 At the sound of their fall the earth shall tremble; the sound of their cry shall be heard at the Red Sea.*a* 22 Look, he shall mount up and swoop down like an eagle, and spread his wings against Bozrah, and the heart of the warriors of Edom in that day shall be like the heart of a woman in labor.

Judgment on Damascus

23 Concerning Damascus.

Hamath and Arpad are confounded,
  for they have heard bad news;
they melt in fear, they are troubled like
    the sea*b*
  that cannot be quiet.
24 Damascus has become feeble, she
    turned to flee,
  and panic seized her;
anguish and sorrows have taken hold of
    her,
  as of a woman in labor.
25 How the famous city is forsaken,*c*
  the joyful town!*d*
26 Therefore her young men shall fall in her
    squares,
    and all her soldiers shall be destroyed
    in that day,
        says the LORD of hosts.
27 And I will kindle a fire at the wall of
    Damascus,
    and it shall devour the strongholds of
    Ben-hadad.

Judgment on Kedar and Hazor

28 Concerning Kedar and the kingdoms of Hazor that King Nebuchadrezzar of Babylon defeated.

Thus says the LORD:
Rise up, advance against Kedar!

Destroy the people of the east!
29 Take their tents and their flocks,
  their curtains and all their goods;
carry off their camels for yourselves,
  and a cry shall go up: "Terror is all
    around!"
30 Flee, wander far away, hide in deep
    places,
  O inhabitants of Hazor!
           says the LORD.
For King Nebuchadrezzar of Babylon
  has made a plan against you
  and formed a purpose against you.

31 Rise up, advance against a nation at ease,
  that lives secure,
          says the LORD,
that has no gates or bars,
  that lives alone.
32 Their camels shall become booty,
  their herds of cattle a spoil.
I will scatter to every wind
  those who have shaven temples,
and I will bring calamity
  against them from every side,
         says the LORD.
33 Hazor shall become a lair of jackals,
  an everlasting waste;
no one shall live there,
  nor shall anyone settle in it.

Judgment on Elam

34 The word of the LORD that came to the prophet Jeremiah concerning Elam, at the beginning of the reign of King Zedekiah of Judah.

35 Thus says the LORD of hosts: I am going to break the bow of Elam, the mainstay of their might; 36 and I will bring upon Elam the four winds from the four quarters of heaven; and I will scatter them to all these winds, and there shall be no nation to which the exiles from Elam shall not come. 37 I will terrify Elam before their enemies, and before those who seek their life; I will bring disaster upon them, my fierce anger, says the LORD. I will send the

---

a Or *Sea of Reeds*   *b* Cn: Heb *there is trouble in the sea*   *c* Vg: Heb *is not forsaken*   *d* Syr Vg Tg: Heb *the town of my joy* sword after them, until I have consumed them; [38]and I will set my throne in Elam, and destroy their king and officials, says the LORD.

39 But in the latter days I will restore the fortunes of Elam, says the LORD.

Judgment on Babylon

50 The word that the LORD spoke concerning Babylon, concerning the land of the Chaldeans, by the prophet Jeremiah:

2   Declare among the nations and
            proclaim,
        set up a banner and proclaim,
        do not conceal it, say:
    Babylon is taken,
        Bel is put to shame,
        Merodach is dismayed.
    Her images are put to shame,
        her idols are dismayed.

3 For out of the north a nation has come up against her; it shall make her land a desolation, and no one shall live in it; both human beings and animals shall flee away.

4 In those days and in that time, says the LORD, the people of Israel shall come, they and the people of Judah together; they shall come weeping as they seek the LORD their God. [5]They shall ask the way to Zion, with faces turned toward it, and they shall come and join*a* themselves to the LORD by an everlasting covenant that will never be forgotten.

6 My people have been lost sheep; their shepherds have led them astray, turning them away on the mountains; from mountain to hill they have gone, they have forgotten their fold. [7]All who found them have devoured them, and their enemies have said, "We are not guilty, because they have sinned against the LORD, the true pasture, the LORD, the hope of their ancestors."

8 Flee from Babylon, and go out of the land of the Chaldeans, and be like male goats leading the flock. [9]For I am going to stir up and bring against Babylon a company of great nations from the land of the north; and they shall array themselves against her; from there she shall be taken. Their arrows are like the arrows of a skilled warrior who does not return empty-handed. [10]Chaldea shall be plundered; all who plunder her shall be sated, says the LORD.

11   Though you rejoice, though you exult,
        O plunderers of my heritage,
    though you frisk about like a heifer on
            the grass,
        and neigh like stallions,
12   your mother shall be utterly shamed,
        and she who bore you shall be
            disgraced.
    Lo, she shall be the last of the nations,
        a wilderness, dry land, and a desert.
13   Because of the wrath of the LORD she
            shall not be inhabited,
        but shall be an utter desolation;
    everyone who passes by Babylon shall be
            appalled
        and hiss because of all her wounds.
14   Take up your positions around Babylon,
        all you that bend the bow;
    shoot at her, spare no arrows,
        for she has sinned against the LORD.
15   Raise a shout against her from all sides,
        "She has surrendered;
    her bulwarks have fallen,
        her walls are thrown down."
    For this is the vengeance of the LORD:
        take vengeance on her,
        do to her as she has done.
16   Cut off from Babylon the sower,
        and the wielder of the sickle in time
            of harvest;
    because of the destroying sword
        all of them shall return to their own
            people,
        and all of them shall flee to their own
            land.

17 Israel is a hunted sheep driven away by lions. First the king of Assyria devoured it,

---

a Gk: Heb *toward it. Come! They shall join*

and now at the end King Nebuchadrezzar of Babylon has gnawed its bones. ¹⁸Therefore, thus says the LORD of hosts, the God of Israel: I am going to punish the king of Babylon and his land, as I punished the king of Assyria. ¹⁹I will restore Israel to its pasture, and it shall feed on Carmel and in Bashan, and on the hills of Ephraim and in Gilead its hunger shall be satisfied. ²⁰In those days and at that time, says the LORD, the iniquity of Israel shall be sought, and there shall be none; and the sins of Judah, and none shall be found; for I will pardon the remnant that I have spared.

21 Go up to the land of Merathaim;ᵃ
       go up against her,
    and attack the inhabitants of Pekodᵇ
       and utterly destroy the last of them,ᶜ
                        says the LORD;
       do all that I have commanded you.
22 The noise of battle is in the land,
       and great destruction!
23 How the hammer of the whole earth
       is cut down and broken!
    How Babylon has become
       a horror among the nations!
24 You set a snare for yourself and you
                    were caught, O Babylon,
       but you did not know it;
    you were discovered and seized,
       because you challenged the LORD.
25 The LORD has opened his armory,
       and brought out the weapons of his
                             wrath,
    for the Lord GOD of hosts has a task to
                     do
       in the land of the Chaldeans.
26 Come against her from every quarter;
       open her granaries;
    pile her up like heaps of grain, and
                    destroy her utterly;
       let nothing be left of her.
27 Kill all her bulls,
       let them go down to the slaughter.
    Alas for them, their day has come,
       the time of their punishment!

28 Listen! Fugitives and refugees from the land of Babylon are coming to declare in Zion the vengeance of the LORD our God, vengeance for his temple.

29 Summon archers against Babylon, all who bend the bow. Encamp all around her; let no one escape. Repay her according to her deeds; just as she has done, do to her—for she has arrogantly defied the LORD, the Holy One of Israel. ³⁰Therefore her young men shall fall in her squares, and all her soldiers shall be destroyed on that day, says the LORD.

31 I am against you, O arrogant one,
       says the Lord GOD of hosts;
    for your day has come,
       the time when I will punish you.
32 The arrogant one shall stumble and fall,
       with no one to raise him up,
    and I will kindle a fire in his cities,
       and it will devour everything around
                    him.

33 Thus says the LORD of hosts: The people of Israel are oppressed, and so too are the people of Judah; all their captors have held them fast and refuse to let them go. ³⁴Their Redeemer is strong; the LORD of hosts is his name. He will surely plead their cause, that he may give rest to the earth, but unrest to the inhabitants of Babylon.

35 A sword against the Chaldeans, says the
                    LORD,
       and against the inhabitants of
                    Babylon,
       and against her officials and her sages!
36 A sword against the diviners,
       so that they may become fools!
    A sword against her warriors,
       so that they may be destroyed!
37 A sword against herᵈ horses and against
                    herᵈ chariots,
       and against all the foreign troops in
                    her midst,

---

a Or *of Double Rebellion*   *b* Or *of Punishment*   *c* Tg: Heb *destroy after them*   *d* Cn: Heb *his*

so that they may become women!
A sword against all her treasures,
that they may be plundered!
38 A drought*a* against her waters,
that they may be dried up!
For it is a land of images,
and they go mad over idols.

39 Therefore wild animals shall live with
hyenas in Babylon,*b* and ostriches shall inhabit her; she shall never again be peopled, or inhabited for all generations. 40As when God
overthrew Sodom and Gomorrah and their
neighbors, says the LORD, so no one shall live
there, nor shall anyone settle in her.

41 Look, a people is coming from the
north;
a mighty nation and many kings
are stirring from the farthest parts of
the earth.
42 They wield bow and spear,
they are cruel and have no mercy.
The sound of them is like the roaring
sea;
they ride upon horses,
set in array as a warrior for battle,
against you, O daughter Babylon!

43 The king of Babylon heard news of
them,
and his hands fell helpless;
anguish seized him,
pain like that of a woman in labor.

44 Like a lion coming up from the thickets
of the Jordan against a perennial pasture, I will
suddenly chase them away from her; and I will
appoint over her whomever I choose.*c* For
who is like me? Who can summon me? Who
is the shepherd who can stand before me?
45Therefore hear the plan that the LORD has
made against Babylon, and the purposes that he
has formed against the land of the Chaldeans:
Surely the little ones of the flock shall be

dragged away; surely their*d* fold shall be appalled at their fate. 46At the sound of the capture of Babylon the earth shall tremble, and her
cry shall be heard among the nations.

51 Thus says the LORD:
I am going to stir up a destructive
wind*e*
against Babylon
and against the inhabitants of
Leb-qamai;*f*
2 and I will send winnowers to Babylon,
and they shall winnow her.
They shall empty her land
when they come against her from
every side
on the day of trouble.
3 Let not the archer bend his bow,
and let him not array himself in his
coat of mail.
Do not spare her young men;
utterly destroy her entire army.
4 They shall fall down slain in the land of
the Chaldeans,
and wounded in her streets.
5 Israel and Judah have not been forsaken
by their God, the LORD of hosts,
though their land is full of guilt
before the Holy One of Israel.

6 Flee from the midst of Babylon,
save your lives, each of you!
Do not perish because of her guilt,
for this is the time of the LORD's
vengeance;
he is repaying her what is due.
7 Babylon was a golden cup in the LORD's
hand,
making all the earth drunken;
the nations drank of her wine,
and so the nations went mad.
8 Suddenly Babylon has fallen and is
shattered;
wail for her!
Bring balm for her wound;

---

a Another reading is *A sword*   *b* Heb lacks *in Babylon*   *c* Or *and I will single out the choicest of her rams.* Meaning of
Heb uncertain   *d* Syr Gk Tg Compare 49.20: Heb lacks *their*   *e* Or *stir up the spirit of a destroyer*   *f* Leb-qamai is
a cryptogram for *Kasdim*, Chaldea

perhaps she may be healed.

9 We tried to heal Babylon,
but she could not be healed.
Forsake her, and let each of us go
to our own country;
for her judgment has reached up to
heaven
and has been lifted up even to the
skies.

10 The LORD has brought forth our
vindication;
come, let us declare in Zion
the work of the LORD our God.

11 Sharpen the arrows!
Fill the quivers!
The LORD has stirred up the spirit of the kings
of the Medes, because his purpose concerning
Babylon is to destroy it, for that is the
vengeance of the LORD, vengeance for his
temple.

12 Raise a standard against the walls of
Babylon;
make the watch strong;
post sentinels;
prepare the ambushes;
for the LORD has both planned and done
what he spoke concerning the
inhabitants of Babylon.

13 You who live by mighty waters,
rich in treasures,
your end has come,
the thread of your life is cut.

14 The LORD of hosts has sworn by
himself:
Surely I will fill you with troops like a
swarm of locusts,
and they shall raise a shout of victory
over you.

15 It is he who made the earth by his
power,
who established the world by his
wisdom,
and by his understanding stretched out
the heavens.

16 When he utters his voice there is a
tumult of waters in the heavens,
and he makes the mist rise from the
ends of the earth.
He makes lightnings for the rain,
and he brings out the wind from his
storehouses.

17 Everyone is stupid and without
knowledge;
goldsmiths are all put to shame by
their idols;
for their images are false,
and there is no breath in them.

18 They are worthless, a work of delusion;
at the time of their punishment they
shall perish.

19 Not like these is the LORD,[a] the portion
of Jacob,
for he is the one who formed all
things,
and Israel is the tribe of his inheritance;
the LORD of hosts is his name.

Israel the Creator's Instrument

20 You are my war club, my weapon of
battle:
with you I smash nations;
with you I destroy kingdoms;

21 with you I smash the horse and its rider;
with you I smash the chariot and the
charioteer;

22 with you I smash man and woman;
with you I smash the old man and the
boy;
with you I smash the young man and the
girl;

23 with you I smash shepherds and their
flocks;
with you I smash farmers and their
teams;
with you I smash governors and
deputies.

The Doom of Babylon

24 I will repay Babylon and all the inhabitants of Chaldea before your very eyes for all

a Heb lacks the LORD

the wrong that they have done in Zion, says the
LORD.

25 I am against you, O destroying
        mountain,
                    says the LORD,
    that destroys the whole earth;
  I will stretch out my hand against you,
    and roll you down from the crags,
    and make you a burned-out mountain.
26 No stone shall be taken from you for a
        corner
    and no stone for a foundation,
  but you shall be a perpetual waste,
    says the LORD.

27 Raise a standard in the land,
    blow the trumpet among the
        nations;
  prepare the nations for war against her,
    summon against her the kingdoms,
    Ararat, Minni, and Ashkenaz;
  appoint a marshal against her,
    bring up horses like bristling
        locusts.
28 Prepare the nations for war against her,
    the kings of the Medes, with their
        governors and deputies,
    and every land under their dominion.
29 The land trembles and writhes,
    for the LORD's purposes against
        Babylon stand,
  to make the land of Babylon a
        desolation,
    without inhabitant.
30 The warriors of Babylon have given up
        fighting,
    they remain in their strongholds;
  their strength has failed,
    they have become women;
  her buildings are set on fire,
    her bars are broken.
31 One runner runs to meet another,
    and one messenger to meet another,
  to tell the king of Babylon
    that his city is taken from end to end:
32 the fords have been seized,

the marshes have been burned with
        fire,
    and the soldiers are in panic.
33 For thus says the LORD of hosts, the
        God of Israel:
  Daughter Babylon is like a threshing
        floor
    at the time when it is trodden;
  yet a little while
    and the time of her harvest will come.

34 "King Nebuchadrezzar of Babylon has
        devoured me,
    he has crushed me;
  he has made me an empty vessel,
    he has swallowed me like a monster;
  he has filled his belly with my
        delicacies,
    he has spewed me out.
35 May my torn flesh be avenged on
        Babylon,"
    the inhabitants of Zion shall say.
  "May my blood be avenged on the
        inhabitants of Chaldea,"
    Jerusalem shall say.
36 Therefore thus says the LORD:
  I am going to defend your cause
    and take vengeance for you.
  I will dry up her sea
    and make her fountain dry;
37 and Babylon shall become a heap of
        ruins,
    a den of jackals,
  an object of horror and of hissing,
    without inhabitant.

38 Like lions they shall roar together;
    they shall growl like lions' whelps.
39 When they are inflamed, I will set out
        their drink
    and make them drunk, until they
        become merry
  and then sleep a perpetual sleep
    and never wake, says the LORD.
40 I will bring them down like lambs to the
        slaughter,
    like rams and goats.

41 How Sheshach^a is taken,
      the pride of the whole earth seized!
   How Babylon has become
      an object of horror among the
         nations!
42 The sea has risen over Babylon;
      she has been covered by its
         tumultuous waves.
43 Her cities have become an object of
         horror,
      a land of drought and a desert,
   a land in which no one lives,
      and through which no mortal passes.
44 I will punish Bel in Babylon,
      and make him disgorge what he has
         swallowed.
   The nations shall no longer stream to
         him;
      the wall of Babylon has fallen.

45 Come out of her, my people!
      Save your lives, each of you,
      from the fierce anger of the LORD!
46 Do not be fainthearted or fearful
      at the rumors heard in the land—
   one year one rumor comes,
      the next year another,
   rumors of violence in the land
      and of ruler against ruler.

47 Assuredly, the days are coming
      when I will punish the images of
         Babylon;
   her whole land shall be put to shame,
      and all her slain shall fall in her midst.
48 Then the heavens and the earth,
      and all that is in them,
   shall shout for joy over Babylon;
      for the destroyers shall come against
         them out of the north,
                        says the LORD.
49 Babylon must fall for the slain of Israel,
      as the slain of all the earth have fallen
         because of Babylon.

50 You survivors of the sword,

a Sheshach is a cryptogram for Babel, Babylon

   go, do not linger!
   Remember the LORD in a distant land,
      and let Jerusalem come into your
         mind:
51 We are put to shame, for we have heard
         insults;
      dishonor has covered our face,
   for aliens have come
      into the holy places of the LORD's
         house.

52 Therefore the time is surely coming, says
         the LORD,
      when I will punish her idols,
   and through all her land
      the wounded shall groan.
53 Though Babylon should mount up to
         heaven,
      and though she should fortify her
         strong height,
   from me destroyers would come upon
         her,
      says the LORD.

54 Listen!—a cry from Babylon!
      A great crashing from the land of the
         Chaldeans!
55 For the LORD is laying Babylon waste,
      and stilling her loud clamor.
   Their waves roar like mighty waters,
      the sound of their clamor resounds;
56 for a destroyer has come against her,
      against Babylon;
   her warriors are taken,
      their bows are broken;
   for the LORD is a God of recompense,
      he will repay in full.
57 I will make her officials and her sages
         drunk,
      also her governors, her deputies, and
         her warriors;
   they shall sleep a perpetual sleep and
         never wake,
      says the King, whose name is the
         LORD of hosts.

58 Thus says the LORD of hosts:
    The broad wall of Babylon
        shall be leveled to the ground,
    and her high gates
        shall be burned with fire.
    The peoples exhaust themselves for
            nothing,
        and the nations weary themselves only
            for fire.*a*

Jeremiah's Command to Seraiah

59 The word that the prophet Jeremiah
commanded Seraiah son of Neriah son of
Mahseiah, when he went with King Zedekiah
of Judah to Babylon, in the fourth year of his
reign. Seraiah was the quartermaster. 60Jere-
miah wrote in a *b* scroll all the disasters that
would come on Babylon, all these words that
are written concerning Babylon. 61And Jeremiah said to Seraiah: "When you come to Babylon, see that you read all these words, 62and say,
'O LORD, you yourself threatened to destroy
this place so that neither human beings nor animals shall live in it, and it shall be desolate forever.' 63When you finish reading this scroll, tie
a stone to it, and throw it into the middle of the
Euphrates, 64and say, 'Thus shall Babylon sink,
to rise no more, because of the disasters that
I am bringing on her.' "*c*

Thus far are the words of Jeremiah.

The Destruction of Jerusalem Reviewed

52 Zedekiah was twenty-one years old
    when he began to reign; he reigned
eleven years in Jerusalem. His mother's name
was Hamutal daughter of Jeremiah of Libnah.
2He did what was evil in the sight of the LORD,
just as Jehoiakim had done. 3Indeed, Jerusalem
and Judah so angered the LORD that he expelled
them from his presence.

Zedekiah rebelled against the king of Babylon. 4And in the ninth year of his reign, in the
tenth month, on the tenth day of the month,
King Nebuchadrezzar of Babylon came with
all his army against Jerusalem, and they laid
siege to it; they built siegeworks against it all

around. 5So the city was besieged until the
eleventh year of King Zedekiah. 6On the ninth
day of the fourth month the famine became so
severe in the city that there was no food for the
people of the land. 7Then a breach was made
in the city wall;*d* and all the soldiers fled and
went out from the city by night by the way of
the gate between the two walls, by the king's
garden, though the Chaldeans were all around
the city. They went in the direction of the Arabah. 8But the army of the Chaldeans pursued the king, and overtook Zedekiah in the
plains of Jericho; and all his army was scattered,
deserting him. 9Then they captured the king,
and brought him up to the king of Babylon at
Riblah in the land of Hamath, and he passed
sentence on him. 10The king of Babylon killed
the sons of Zedekiah before his eyes, and also
killed all the officers of Judah at Riblah. 11He
put out the eyes of Zedekiah, and bound him
in fetters, and the king of Babylon took him to
Babylon, and put him in prison until the day of
his death.

12 In the fifth month, on the tenth day of
the month—which was the nineteenth year of
King Nebuchadrezzar, king of Babylon—Nebuzaradan the captain of the bodyguard who
served the king of Babylon, entered Jerusalem. 13He burned the house of the LORD, the
king's house, and all the houses of Jerusalem;
every great house he burned down. 14All the
army of the Chaldeans, who were with the
captain of the guard, broke down all the walls
around Jerusalem. 15Nebuzaradan the captain
of the guard carried into exile some of the
poorest of the people and the rest of the people who were left in the city and the deserters
who had defected to the king of Babylon, together with the rest of the artisans. 16But Nebuzaradan the captain of the guard left some of
the poorest people of the land to be vinedressers and tillers of the soil.

17 The pillars of bronze that were in the
house of the LORD, and the stands and the
bronze sea that were in the house of the LORD,
the Chaldeans broke in pieces, and carried all

---

a Gk Syr Compare Hab 2.13: Heb *and the nations for fire, and they are weary*   *b* Or *one*   *c* Gk: Heb *on her. And they shall weary themselves*   *d* Heb lacks *wall* the bronze to Babylon. 18They took away the pots, the shovels, the snuffers, the basins, the ladles, and all the vessels of bronze used in the temple service. 19The captain of the guard took away the small bowls also, the firepans, the basins, the pots, the lampstands, the ladles, and the bowls for libation, both those of gold and those of silver. 20As for the two pillars, the one sea, the twelve bronze bulls that were under the sea, and the stands,*a* which King Solomon had made for the house of the LORD, the bronze of all these vessels was beyond weighing. 21As for the pillars, the height of the one pillar was eighteen cubits, its circumference was twelve cubits; it was hollow and its thickness was four fingers. 22Upon it was a capital of bronze; the height of the capital was five cubits; latticework and pomegranates, all of bronze, encircled the top of the capital. And the second pillar had the same, with pomegranates. 23There were ninety-six pomegranates on the sides; all the pomegranates encircling the latticework numbered one hundred.

24 The captain of the guard took the chief priest Seraiah, the second priest Zephaniah, and the three guardians of the threshold; 25and from the city he took an officer who had been in command of the soldiers, and seven men of the king's council who were found in the city; the secretary of the commander of the army who mustered the people of the land; and sixty men of the people of the land who were found inside the city. 26Then Nebuzaradan the captain of the guard took them, and brought them to the king of Babylon at Riblah. 27And the king of Babylon struck them down, and put them to death at Riblah in the land of Hamath. So Judah went into exile out of its land.

28 This is the number of the people whom Nebuchadrezzar took into exile: in the seventh year, three thousand twenty-three Judeans; 29in the eighteenth year of Nebuchadrezzar he took into exile from Jerusalem eight hundred thirty-two persons; 30in the twenty-third year of Nebuchadrezzar, Nebuzaradan the captain of the guard took into exile of the Judeans seven hundred forty-five persons; all the persons were four thousand six hundred.

Jehoiachin Favored in Captivity

31 In the thirty-seventh year of the exile of King Jehoiachin of Judah, in the twelfth month, on the twenty-fifth day of the month, King Evil-merodach of Babylon, in the year he began to reign, showed favor to King Jehoiachin of Judah and brought him out of prison; 32he spoke kindly to him, and gave him a seat above the seats of the other kings who were with him in Babylon. 33So Jehoiachin put aside his prison clothes, and every day of his life he dined regularly at the king's table. 34For his allowance, a regular daily allowance was given him by the king of Babylon, as long as he lived, up to the day of his death.

---

a Cn: Heb *that were under the stands*

LAMENTATIONS

The Deserted City

1 How lonely sits the city
  that once was full of people!
How like a widow she has become,
  she that was great among the nations!
She that was a princess among the
    provinces
  has become a vassal.

2 She weeps bitterly in the night,
  with tears on her cheeks;
among all her lovers
  she has no one to comfort her;
all her friends have dealt treacherously
    with her,
  they have become her enemies.

3 Judah has gone into exile with
    suffering
  and hard servitude;
she lives now among the nations,
  and finds no resting place;
her pursuers have all overtaken her
  in the midst of her distress.

4 The roads to Zion mourn,
  for no one comes to the festivals;
all her gates are desolate,
  her priests groan;
her young girls grieve,*a*
  and her lot is bitter.

5 Her foes have become the masters,
  her enemies prosper,
because the LORD has made her suffer
  for the multitude of her
    transgressions;
her children have gone away,
  captives before the foe.

6 From daughter Zion has departed
  all her majesty.
Her princes have become like stags
  that find no pasture;

they fled without strength
  before the pursuer.

7 Jerusalem remembers,
  in the days of her affliction and
    wandering,
all the precious things
  that were hers in days of old.
When her people fell into the hand of
    the foe,
  and there was no one to help her,
the foe looked on mocking
  over her downfall.

8 Jerusalem sinned grievously,
  so she has become a mockery;
all who honored her despise her,
  for they have seen her nakedness;
she herself groans,
  and turns her face away.

9 Her uncleanness was in her skirts;
  she took no thought of her future;
her downfall was appalling,
  with none to comfort her.
"O LORD, look at my affliction,
  for the enemy has triumphed!"

10 Enemies have stretched out their hands
  over all her precious things;
she has even seen the nations
  invade her sanctuary,
those whom you forbade
  to enter your congregation.

11 All her people groan
  as they search for bread;
they trade their treasures for food
  to revive their strength.
Look, O LORD, and see
  how worthless I have become.

12 Is it nothing to you,*a* all you who pass
    by?

a Meaning of Heb uncertain

Look and see
if there is any sorrow like my sorrow,
    which was brought upon me,
which the LORD inflicted
    on the day of his fierce anger.

13 From on high he sent fire;
    it went deep into my bones;
he spread a net for my feet;
    he turned me back;
he has left me stunned,
    faint all day long.

14 My transgressions were bound*a* into a
        yoke;
    by his hand they were fastened
        together;
they weigh on my neck,
    sapping my strength;
the Lord handed me over
    to those whom I cannot withstand.

15 The LORD has rejected
    all my warriors in the midst of me;
he proclaimed a time against me
    to crush my young men;
the Lord has trodden as in a wine press
    the virgin daughter Judah.

16 For these things I weep;
    my eyes flow with tears;
for a comforter is far from me,
    one to revive my courage;
my children are desolate,
    for the enemy has prevailed.

17 Zion stretches out her hands,
    but there is no one to comfort her;
the LORD has commanded against Jacob
    that his neighbors should become his
        foes;
Jerusalem has become
    a filthy thing among them.

18 The LORD is in the right,
    for I have rebelled against his word;

but hear, all you peoples,
    and behold my suffering;
my young women and young men
    have gone into captivity.

19 I called to my lovers
    but they deceived me;
my priests and elders
    perished in the city
while seeking food
    to revive their strength.

20 See, O LORD, how distressed I am;
    my stomach churns,
my heart is wrung within me,
    because I have been very rebellious.
In the street the sword bereaves;
    in the house it is like death.

21 They heard how I was groaning,
    with no one to comfort me.
All my enemies heard of my trouble;
    they are glad that you have done it.
Bring on the day you have announced,
    and let them be as I am.

22 Let all their evil doing come before you;
    and deal with them
as you have dealt with me
    because of all my transgressions;
for my groans are many
    and my heart is faint.

God's Warnings Fulfilled

2 How the Lord in his anger
    has humiliated*a* daughter Zion!
He has thrown down from heaven to
        earth
    the splendor of Israel;
he has not remembered his footstool
    in the day of his anger.

2 The Lord has destroyed without mercy
    all the dwellings of Jacob;
in his wrath he has broken down
    the strongholds of daughter Judah;

a Meaning of Heb uncertain

he has brought down to the ground in
    dishonor
  the kingdom and its rulers.

3 He has cut down in fierce anger
    all the might of Israel;
he has withdrawn his right hand from
    them
  in the face of the enemy;
he has burned like a flaming fire in
    Jacob,
  consuming all around.

4 He has bent his bow like an enemy,
    with his right hand set like a foe;
he has killed all in whom we took pride
    in the tent of daughter Zion;
he has poured out his fury like fire.

5 The Lord has become like an enemy;
    he has destroyed Israel.
He has destroyed all its palaces,
    laid in ruins its strongholds,
and multiplied in daughter Judah
  mourning and lamentation.

6 He has broken down his booth like a
    garden,
    he has destroyed his tabernacle;
the LORD has abolished in Zion
    festival and sabbath,
and in his fierce indignation has spurned
  king and priest.

7 The Lord has scorned his altar,
    disowned his sanctuary;
he has delivered into the hand of the
    enemy
    the walls of her palaces;
a clamor was raised in the house of the
    LORD
    as on a day of festival.

8 The LORD determined to lay in ruins
    the wall of daughter Zion;
he stretched the line;
    he did not withhold his hand from
    destroying;

he caused rampart and wall to lament;
  they languish together.

9 Her gates have sunk into the ground;
    he has ruined and broken her bars;
her king and princes are among the
    nations;
    guidance is no more,
and her prophets obtain
    no vision from the LORD.

10 The elders of daughter Zion
    sit on the ground in silence;
they have thrown dust on their heads
    and put on sackcloth;
the young girls of Jerusalem
    have bowed their heads to the ground.

11 My eyes are spent with weeping;
    my stomach churns;
my bile is poured out on the ground
    because of the destruction of my
    people,
because infants and babes faint
    in the streets of the city.

12 They cry to their mothers,
    "Where is bread and wine?"
as they faint like the wounded
    in the streets of the city,
as their life is poured out
    on their mothers' bosom.

13 What can I say for you, to what compare
    you,
    O daughter Jerusalem?
To what can I liken you, that I may
    comfort you,
    O virgin daughter Zion?
For vast as the sea is your ruin;
    who can heal you?

14 Your prophets have seen for you
    false and deceptive visions;
they have not exposed your iniquity
    to restore your fortunes,
but have seen oracles for you
    that are false and misleading.

15 All who pass along the way
    clap their hands at you;
they hiss and wag their heads
    at daughter Jerusalem;
"Is this the city that was called
    the perfection of beauty,
    the joy of all the earth?"

16 All your enemies
    open their mouths against you;
they hiss, they gnash their teeth,
    they cry: "We have devoured her!
Ah, this is the day we longed for;
    at last we have seen it!"

17 The LORD has done what he purposed,
    he has carried out his threat;
as he ordained long ago,
    he has demolished without pity;
he has made the enemy rejoice over
        you,
    and exalted the might of your foes.

18 Cry aloud*a* to the Lord!
    O wall of daughter Zion!
Let tears stream down like a torrent
    day and night!
Give yourself no rest,
    your eyes no respite!

19 Arise, cry out in the night,
    at the beginning of the watches!
Pour out your heart like water
    before the presence of the Lord!
Lift your hands to him
    for the lives of your children,
who faint for hunger
    at the head of every street.

20 Look, O LORD, and consider!
    To whom have you done this?
Should women eat their offspring,
    the children they have borne?
Should priest and prophet be killed
    in the sanctuary of the Lord?

21 The young and the old are lying
    on the ground in the streets;
my young women and my young men
    have fallen by the sword;
in the day of your anger you have killed
        them,
    slaughtering without mercy.

22 You invited my enemies from all around
    as if for a day of festival;
and on the day of the anger of the LORD
    no one escaped or survived;
those whom I bore and reared
    my enemy has destroyed.

God's Steadfast Love Endures

3 I am one who has seen affliction
    under the rod of God's*b* wrath;
2 he has driven and brought me
    into darkness without any light;
3 against me alone he turns his hand,
    again and again, all day long.

4 He has made my flesh and my skin waste
        away,
    and broken my bones;
5 he has besieged and enveloped me
    with bitterness and tribulation;
6 he has made me sit in darkness
    like the dead of long ago.

7 He has walled me about so that I cannot
        escape;
    he has put heavy chains on me;
8 though I call and cry for help,
    he shuts out my prayer;
9 he has blocked my ways with hewn stones,
    he has made my paths crooked.

10 He is a bear lying in wait for me,
    a lion in hiding;
11 he led me off my way and tore me to
        pieces;
    he has made me desolate;
12 he bent his bow and set me
    as a mark for his arrow.

a Cn: Heb *Their heart cried*   *b* Heb *his*

13 He shot into my vitals
   the arrows of his quiver;
14 I have become the laughingstock of all
      my people,
   the object of their taunt-songs all day
      long.
15 He has filled me with bitterness,
   he has sated me with wormwood.

16 He has made my teeth grind on gravel,
   and made me cower in ashes;
17 my soul is bereft of peace;
   I have forgotten what happiness is;
18 so I say, "Gone is my glory,
   and all that I had hoped for from the
      LORD."

19 The thought of my affliction and my
      homelessness
   is wormwood and gall!
20 My soul continually thinks of it
   and is bowed down within me.
21 But this I call to mind,
   and therefore I have hope:

22 The steadfast love of the LORD never
      ceases,*a*
   his mercies never come to an end;
23 they are new every morning;
   great is your faithfulness.
24 "The LORD is my portion," says my soul,
   "therefore I will hope in him."

25 The LORD is good to those who wait for
      him,
   to the soul that seeks him.
26 It is good that one should wait quietly
   for the salvation of the LORD.
27 It is good for one to bear
   the yoke in youth,
28 to sit alone in silence
   when the Lord has imposed it,
29 to put one's mouth to the dust
   (there may yet be hope),
30 to give one's cheek to the smiter,
   and be filled with insults.

31 For the Lord will not
   reject forever.
32 Although he causes grief, he will have
      compassion
   according to the abundance of his
      steadfast love;
33 for he does not willingly afflict
   or grieve anyone.

34 When all the prisoners of the land
   are crushed under foot,
35 when human rights are perverted
   in the presence of the Most High,
36 when one's case is subverted
   —does the Lord not see it?

37 Who can command and have it done,
   if the Lord has not ordained it?
38 Is it not from the mouth of the Most
      High
   that good and bad come?
39 Why should any who draw breath
      complain
   about the punishment of their sins?

40 Let us test and examine our ways,
   and return to the LORD.
41 Let us lift up our hearts as well as our
      hands
   to God in heaven.
42 We have transgressed and rebelled,
   and you have not forgiven.

43 You have wrapped yourself with anger
      and pursued us,
   killing without pity;
44 you have wrapped yourself with a cloud
   so that no prayer can pass through.
45 You have made us filth and rubbish
   among the peoples.

46 All our enemies
   have opened their mouths against us;
47 panic and pitfall have come upon us,
   devastation and destruction.
48 My eyes flow with rivers of tears

a Syr Tg: Heb LORD, *we are not cut off*

because of the destruction of my
   people.

49 My eyes will flow without ceasing,
      without respite,
50 until the LORD from heaven
      looks down and sees.
51 My eyes cause me grief
      at the fate of all the young women in
         my city.

52 Those who were my enemies without
         cause
      have hunted me like a bird;
53 they flung me alive into a pit
      and hurled stones on me;
54 water closed over my head;
      I said, "I am lost."

55 I called on your name, O LORD,
      from the depths of the pit;
56 you heard my plea, "Do not close your
         ear
      to my cry for help, but give me relief!"
57 You came near when I called on you;
      you said, "Do not fear!"

58 You have taken up my cause, O Lord,
      you have redeemed my life.
59 You have seen the wrong done to me,
         O LORD;
      judge my cause.
60 You have seen all their malice,
      all their plots against me.

61 You have heard their taunts, O LORD,
      all their plots against me.
62 The whispers and murmurs of my
         assailants
      are against me all day long.
63 Whether they sit or rise—see,
      I am the object of their taunt-songs.

64 Pay them back for their deeds, O LORD,
      according to the work of their hands!
65 Give them anguish of heart;

your curse be on them!
66 Pursue them in anger and destroy them
      from under the LORD's heavens.

The Punishment of Zion

4 How the gold has grown dim,
      how the pure gold is changed!
   The sacred stones lie scattered
      at the head of every street.

2 The precious children of Zion,
      worth their weight in fine gold—
   how they are reckoned as earthen pots,
      the work of a potter's hands!

3 Even the jackals offer the breast
      and nurse their young,
   but my people has become cruel,
      like the ostriches in the wilderness.

4 The tongue of the infant sticks
      to the roof of its mouth for thirst;
   the children beg for food,
      but no one gives them anything.

5 Those who feasted on delicacies
      perish in the streets;
   those who were brought up in purple
      cling to ash heaps.

6 For the chastisement*a* of my people has
         been greater
      than the punishment*b* of Sodom,
   which was overthrown in a moment,
      though no hand was laid on it.*c*

7 Her princes were purer than snow,
      whiter than milk;
   their bodies were more ruddy than coral,
      their hair*c* like sapphire.*d*

8 Now their visage is blacker than soot;
      they are not recognized in the streets.
   Their skin has shriveled on their bones;
      it has become as dry as wood.

a Or *iniquity*   *b* Or *sin*   *c* Meaning of Heb uncertain   *d* Or *lapis lazuli*

9 Happier were those pierced by the sword
   than those pierced by hunger,
whose life drains away, deprived
   of the produce of the field.

10 The hands of compassionate women
   have boiled their own children;
they became their food
   in the destruction of my people.

11 The LORD gave full vent to his wrath;
   he poured out his hot anger,
and kindled a fire in Zion
   that consumed its foundations.

12 The kings of the earth did not believe,
   nor did any of the inhabitants of the
      world,
that foe or enemy could enter
   the gates of Jerusalem.

13 It was for the sins of her prophets
   and the iniquities of her priests,
who shed the blood of the righteous
   in the midst of her.

14 Blindly they wandered through the
      streets,
   so defiled with blood
that no one was able
   to touch their garments.

15 "Away! Unclean!" people shouted at
      them;
   "Away! Away! Do not touch!"
So they became fugitives and
      wanderers;
   it was said among the nations,
   "They shall stay here no longer."

16 The LORD himself has scattered
      them,
   he will regard them no more;
no honor was shown to the priests,
   no favor to the elders.

17 Our eyes failed, ever watching
   vainly for help;

we were watching eagerly
   for a nation that could not save.

18 They dogged our steps
   so that we could not walk in our
      streets;
our end drew near; our days were
      numbered;
   for our end had come.

19 Our pursuers were swifter
   than the eagles in the heavens;
they chased us on the mountains,
   they lay in wait for us in the
      wilderness.

20 The LORD's anointed, the breath of our
      life,
   was taken in their pits—
the one of whom we said, "Under his
      shadow
   we shall live among the nations."

21 Rejoice and be glad, O daughter Edom,
   you that live in the land of Uz;
but to you also the cup shall pass;
   you shall become drunk and strip
      yourself bare.

22 The punishment of your iniquity,
   O daughter Zion, is
      accomplished,
   he will keep you in exile no longer;
but your iniquity, O daughter Edom, he
      will punish,
   he will uncover your sins.

A Plea for Mercy

5 Remember, O Lord, what has befallen
      us;
   look, and see our disgrace!
2 Our inheritance has been turned over to
      strangers,
   our homes to aliens.
3 We have become orphans, fatherless;
   our mothers are like widows.
4 We must pay for the water we drink;
   the wood we get must be bought.

5 With a yoke*a* on our necks we are hard
    driven;
  we are weary, we are given no rest.
6 We have made a pact with*b* Egypt and
    Assyria,
  to get enough bread.
7 Our ancestors sinned; they are no more,
  and we bear their iniquities.
8 Slaves rule over us;
  there is no one to deliver us from their
    hand.
9 We get our bread at the peril of our lives,
  because of the sword in the
    wilderness.
10 Our skin is black as an oven
  from the scorching heat of famine.
11 Women are raped in Zion,
  virgins in the towns of Judah.
12 Princes are hung up by their hands;
  no respect is shown to the elders.
13 Young men are compelled to grind,
  and boys stagger under loads of
    wood.
14 The old men have left the city gate,

the young men their music.
15 The joy of our hearts has ceased;
  our dancing has been turned to
    mourning.
16 The crown has fallen from our head;
  woe to us, for we have sinned!
17 Because of this our hearts are sick,
  because of these things our eyes have
    grown dim:
18 because of Mount Zion, which lies
    desolate;
  jackals prowl over it.

19 But you, O LORD, reign forever;
  your throne endures to all generations.
20 Why have you forgotten us completely?
  Why have you forsaken us these many
    days?
21 Restore us to yourself, O LORD, that we
    may be restored;
  renew our days as of old—
22 unless you have utterly rejected us,
  and are angry with us beyond
    measure.

a Symmachus: Heb lacks *With a yoke*   *b* Heb *have given the hand to*

EZEKIEL

The Vision of the Chariot

1 In the thirtieth year, in the fourth month, on the fifth day of the month, as I was among the exiles by the river Chebar, the heavens were opened, and I saw visions of God. 2On the fifth day of the month (it was the fifth year of the exile of King Jehoiachin), 3the word of the LORD came to the priest Ezekiel son of Buzi, in the land of the Chaldeans by the river Chebar; and the hand of the LORD was on him there.

4 As I looked, a stormy wind came out of the north: a great cloud with brightness around it and fire flashing forth continually, and in the middle of the fire, something like gleaming amber. 5In the middle of it was something like four living creatures. This was their appearance: they were of human form. 6Each had four faces, and each of them had four wings. 7Their legs were straight, and the soles of their feet were like the sole of a calf's foot; and they sparkled like burnished bronze. 8Under their wings on their four sides they had human hands. And the four had their faces and their wings thus: 9their wings touched one another; each of them moved straight ahead, without turning as they moved. 10As for the appearance of their faces: the four had the face of a human being, the face of a lion on the right side, the face of an ox on the left side, and the face of an eagle; 11such were their faces. Their wings were spread out above; each creature had two wings, each of which touched the wing of another, while two covered their bodies. 12Each moved straight ahead; wherever the spirit would go, they went, without turning as they went. 13In the middle of *a* the living creatures there was something that looked like burning coals of fire, like torches moving to and fro among the living creatures; the fire was bright, and lightning issued from the fire. 14The living creatures darted to and fro, like a flash of lightning.

15 As I looked at the living creatures, I saw a wheel on the earth beside the living crea-tures, one for each of the four of them. *b* 16As for the appearance of the wheels and their construction: their appearance was like the gleaming of beryl; and the four had the same form, their construction being something like a wheel within a wheel. 17When they moved, they moved in any of the four directions with-out veering as they moved. 18Their rims were tall and awesome, for the rims of all four were full of eyes all around. 19When the living crea-tures moved, the wheels moved beside them; and when the living creatures rose from the earth, the wheels rose. 20Wherever the spirit would go, they went, and the wheels rose along with them; for the spirit of the living creatures was in the wheels. 21When they moved, the others moved; when they stopped, the others stopped; and when they rose from the earth, the wheels rose along with them; for the spir-it of the living creatures was in the wheels.

22 Over the heads of the living creatures there was something like a dome, shining like crystal, *c* spread out above their heads. 23Under the dome their wings were stretched out straight, one toward another; and each of the creatures had two wings covering its body. 24When they moved, I heard the sound of their wings like the sound of mighty waters, like the thunder of the Almighty, *d* a sound of tumult like the sound of an army; when they stopped, they let down their wings. 25And there came a voice from above the dome over their heads; when they stopped, they let down their wings.

26 And above the dome over their heads there was something like a throne, in appear-ance like sapphire; *e* and seated above the like-ness of a throne was something that seemed like a human form. 27Upward from what ap-peared like the loins I saw something like gleaming amber, something that looked like fire enclosed all around; and downward from what looked like the loins I saw something that looked like fire, and there was a splendor all around. 28Like the bow in a cloud on a rainy

day, such was the appearance of the splendor all around. This was the appearance of the likeness of the glory of the LORD.

When I saw it, I fell on my face, and I heard the voice of someone speaking.

The Vision of the Scroll

2 He said to me: O mortal,[a] stand up on your feet, and I will speak with you. 2And when he spoke to me, a spirit entered into me and set me on my feet; and I heard him speaking to me. 3He said to me, Mortal, I am sending you to the people of Israel, to a nation[b] of rebels who have rebelled against me; they and their ancestors have transgressed against me to this very day. 4The descendants are impudent and stubborn. I am sending you to them, and you shall say to them, "Thus says the Lord GOD." 5Whether they hear or refuse to hear (for they are a rebellious house), they shall know that there has been a prophet among them. 6And you, O mortal, do not be afraid of them, and do not be afraid of their words, though briers and thorns surround you and you live among scorpions; do not be afraid of their words, and do not be dismayed at their looks, for they are a rebellious house. 7You shall speak my words to them, whether they hear or refuse to hear; for they are a rebellious house.

8 But you, mortal, hear what I say to you; do not be rebellious like that rebellious house; open your mouth and eat what I give you. 9I looked, and a hand was stretched out to me, and a written scroll was in it. 10He spread it before me; it had writing on the front and on the back, and written on it were words of lamentation and mourning and woe.

3 He said to me, O mortal, eat what is offered to you; eat this scroll, and go, speak to the house of Israel. 2So I opened my mouth, and he gave me the scroll to eat. 3He said to me, Mortal, eat this scroll that I give you and fill your stomach with it. Then I ate it; and in my mouth it was as sweet as honey.

4 He said to me: Mortal, go to the house of Israel and speak my very words to them. 5For you are not sent to a people of obscure speech and difficult language, but to the house of Israel— 6not to many peoples of obscure speech and difficult language, whose words you cannot understand. Surely, if I sent you to them, they would listen to you. 7But the house of Israel will not listen to you, for they are not willing to listen to me; because all the house of Israel have a hard forehead and a stubborn heart. 8See, I have made your face hard against their faces, and your forehead hard against their foreheads. 9Like the hardest stone, harder than flint, I have made your forehead; do not fear them or be dismayed at their looks, for they are a rebellious house. 10He said to me: Mortal, all my words that I shall speak to you receive in your heart and hear with your ears; 11then go to the exiles, to your people, and speak to them. Say to them, "Thus says the Lord GOD"; whether they hear or refuse to hear.

Ezekiel at the River Chebar

12 Then the spirit lifted me up, and as the glory of the LORD rose[c] from its place, I heard behind me the sound of loud rumbling; 13it was the sound of the wings of the living creatures brushing against one another, and the sound of the wheels beside them, that sounded like a loud rumbling. 14The spirit lifted me up and bore me away; I went in bitterness in the heat of my spirit, the hand of the LORD being strong upon me. 15I came to the exiles at Tel-abib, who lived by the river Chebar.[d] And I sat there among them, stunned, for seven days.

16 At the end of seven days, the word of the LORD came to me: 17Mortal, I have made you a sentinel for the house of Israel; whenever you hear a word from my mouth, you shall give them warning from me. 18If I say to the wicked, "You shall surely die," and you give them no warning, or speak to warn the wicked from their wicked way, in order to save their life, those wicked persons shall die for their iniqui-

---

a Or son of man; Heb ben adam (and so throughout the book when Ezekiel is addressed)   b Syr: Heb to nations
c Cn: Heb and blessed be the glory of the LORD   d Two Mss Syr: Heb Chebar, and to where they lived. Another reading is Chebar, and I sat where they sat

ty; but their blood I will require at your hand.
[19]But if you warn the wicked, and they do not
turn from their wickedness, or from their
wicked way, they shall die for their iniquity;
but you will have saved your life. [20]Again, if the
righteous turn from their righteousness and
commit iniquity, and I lay a stumbling block before them, they shall die; because you have not
warned them, they shall die for their sin, and
their righteous deeds that they have done shall
not be remembered; but their blood I will require at your hand. [21]If, however, you warn
the righteous not to sin, and they do not sin,
they shall surely live, because they took warning; and you will have saved your life.

Ezekiel Isolated and Silenced

[22] Then the hand of the LORD was upon
me there; and he said to me, Rise up, go out
into the valley, and there I will speak with you.
[23]So I rose up and went out into the valley; and
the glory of the LORD stood there, like the
glory that I had seen by the river Chebar; and
I fell on my face. [24]The spirit entered into me,
and set me on my feet; and he spoke with me
and said to me: Go, shut yourself inside your
house. [25]As for you, mortal, cords shall be
placed on you, and you shall be bound with
them, so that you cannot go out among the
people; [26]and I will make your tongue cling to
the roof of your mouth, so that you shall be
speechless and unable to reprove them; for
they are a rebellious house. [27]But when I speak
with you, I will open your mouth, and you
shall say to them, "Thus says the Lord GOD";
let those who will hear, hear; and let those who
refuse to hear, refuse; for they are a rebellious
house.

The Siege of Jerusalem Portrayed

4 And you, O mortal, take a brick and set it
before you. On it portray a city, Jerusalem;
[2]and put siegeworks against it, and build a siege
wall against it, and cast up a ramp against it; set
camps also against it, and plant battering rams
against it all around. [3]Then take an iron plate
and place it as an iron wall between you and the
city; set your face toward it, and let it be in a
state of siege, and press the siege against it. This
is a sign for the house of Israel.

4 Then lie on your left side, and place the
punishment of the house of Israel upon it;
you shall bear their punishment for the number of the days that you lie there. [5]For I assign
to you a number of days, three hundred ninety days, equal to the number of the years of
their punishment; and so you shall bear the
punishment of the house of Israel. [6]When
you have completed these, you shall lie down
a second time, but on your right side, and bear
the punishment of the house of Judah; forty
days I assign you, one day for each year. [7]You
shall set your face toward the siege of Jerusalem, and with your arm bared you shall prophesy against it. [8]See, I am putting cords on you
so that you cannot turn from one side to the
other until you have completed the days of
your siege.

9 And you, take wheat and barley, beans
and lentils, millet and spelt; put them into one
vessel, and make bread for yourself. During
the number of days that you lie on your side,
three hundred ninety days, you shall eat it.
[10]The food that you eat shall be twenty shekels
a day by weight; at fixed times you shall eat it.
[11]And you shall drink water by measure, one-
sixth of a hin; at fixed times you shall drink.
[12]You shall eat it as a barley-cake, baking it in
their sight on human dung. [13]The LORD said,
"Thus shall the people of Israel eat their bread,
unclean, among the nations to which I will drive them." [14]Then I said, "Ah Lord GOD! I
have never defiled myself; from my youth up
until now I have never eaten what died of itself or was torn by animals, nor has carrion
flesh come into my mouth." [15]Then he said to
me, "See, I will let you have cow's dung instead
of human dung, on which you may prepare
your bread."

16 Then he said to me, Mortal, I am going
to break the staff of bread in Jerusalem; they
shall eat bread by weight and with fearfulness;
and they shall drink water by measure and in
dismay. [17]Lacking bread and water, they will
look at one another in dismay, and waste away
under their punishment.

A Sword against Jerusalem

5 And you, O mortal, take a sharp sword; use it as a barber's razor and run it over your head and your beard; then take balances for weighing, and divide the hair. ²One third of the hair you shall burn in the fire inside the city, when the days of the siege are completed; one third you shall take and strike with the sword all around the city;*a* and one third you shall scatter to the wind, and I will unsheathe the sword after them. ³Then you shall take from these a small number, and bind them in the skirts of your robe. ⁴From these, again, you shall take some, throw them into the fire and burn them up; from there a fire will come out against all the house of Israel.

5 Thus says the Lord GOD: This is Jerusalem; I have set her in the center of the nations, with countries all around her. ⁶But she has rebelled against my ordinances and my statutes, becoming more wicked than the nations and the countries all around her, rejecting my ordinances and not following my statutes. ⁷Therefore thus says the Lord GOD: Because you are more turbulent than the nations that are all around you, and have not followed my statutes or kept my ordinances, but have acted according to the ordinances of the nations that are all around you; ⁸therefore thus says the Lord GOD: I, I myself, am coming against you; I will execute judgments among you in the sight of the nations. ⁹And because of all your abominations, I will do to you what I have never yet done, and the like of which I will never do again. ¹⁰Surely, parents shall eat their children in your midst, and children shall eat their parents; I will execute judgments on you, and any of you who survive I will scatter to every wind. ¹¹Therefore, as I live, says the Lord GOD, surely, because you have defiled my sanctuary with all your detestable things and with all your abominations—therefore I will cut you down;*b* my eye will not spare, and I will have no pity. ¹²One third of you shall die of pestilence or be consumed by famine among you; one third shall fall by the sword around you; and one third I will scatter to every wind and will unsheathe the sword after them.

13 My anger shall spend itself, and I will vent my fury on them and satisfy myself; and they shall know that I, the LORD, have spoken in my jealousy, when I spend my fury on them. ¹⁴Moreover I will make you a desolation and an object of mocking among the nations around you, in the sight of all that pass by. ¹⁵You shall be*c* a mockery and a taunt, a warning and a horror, to the nations around you, when I execute judgments on you in anger and fury, and with furious punishments—I, the LORD, have spoken— ¹⁶when I loose against you*d* my deadly arrows of famine, arrows for destruction, which I will let loose to destroy you, and when I bring more and more famine upon you, and break your staff of bread. ¹⁷I will send famine and wild animals against you, and they will rob you of your children; pestilence and bloodshed shall pass through you; and I will bring the sword upon you. I, the LORD, have spoken.

Judgment on Idolatrous Israel

6 The word of the LORD came to me: ²O mortal, set your face toward the mountains of Israel, and prophesy against them, ³and say, You mountains of Israel, hear the word of the Lord GOD! Thus says the Lord GOD to the mountains and the hills, to the ravines and the valleys: I, I myself will bring a sword upon you, and I will destroy your high places. ⁴Your altars shall become desolate, and your incense stands shall be broken; and I will throw down your slain in front of your idols. ⁵I will lay the corpses of the people of Israel in front of their idols; and I will scatter your bones around your altars. ⁶Wherever you live, your towns shall be waste and your high places ruined, so that your altars will be waste and ruined,*e* your idols broken and destroyed, your incense stands cut down, and your works wiped out. ⁷The slain shall fall in your midst; then you shall know that I am the LORD.

8 But I will spare some. Some of you shall escape the sword among the nations and be

scattered through the countries. ⁹Those of you who escape shall remember me among the nations where they are carried captive, how I was crushed by their wanton heart that turned away from me, and their wanton eyes that turned after their idols. Then they will be loathsome in their own sight for the evils that they have committed, for all their abominations. ¹⁰And they shall know that I am the LORD; I did not threaten in vain to bring this disaster upon them.

11 Thus says the Lord GOD: Clap your hands and stamp your foot, and say, Alas for all the vile abominations of the house of Israel! For they shall fall by the sword, by famine, and by pestilence. ¹²Those far off shall die of pestilence; those nearby shall fall by the sword; and any who are left and are spared shall die of famine. Thus I will spend my fury upon them. ¹³And you shall know that I am the LORD, when their slain lie among their idols around their altars, on every high hill, on all the mountain tops, under every green tree, and under every leafy oak, wherever they offered pleasing odor to all their idols. ¹⁴I will stretch out my hand against them, and make the land desolate and waste, throughout all their settlements, from the wilderness to Riblah.ᵃ Then they shall know that I am the LORD.

Impending Disaster

7 The word of the LORD came to me: ²You, O mortal, thus says the Lord GOD to the land of Israel:

An end! The end has come
    upon the four corners of the land.
3 Now the end is upon you,
    I will let loose my anger upon you;
I will judge you according to your ways,
    I will punish you for all your
        abominations.
4 My eye will not spare you, I will have no
        pity.
I will punish you for your ways,
    while your abominations are among
        you.

Then you shall know that I am the LORD.
5 Thus says the Lord GOD:
    Disaster after disaster! See, it comes.
6   An end has come, the end has come.
It has awakened against you; see, it
        comes!
7 Your doomᵇ has come to you,
    O inhabitant of the land.
The time has come, the day is near—
    of tumult, not of reveling on the
        mountains.
8 Soon now I will pour out my wrath
        upon you;
    I will spend my anger against you.
I will judge you according to your ways,
    and punish you for all your
        abominations.
9 My eye will not spare; I will have no pity.
    I will punish you according to your
        ways,
    while your abominations are among
        you.

Then you shall know that it is I the LORD who strike.
10   See, the day! See, it comes!
    Your doomᵇ has gone out.
The rod has blossomed, pride has
        budded.
11   Violence has grown into a rod of
        wickedness.
None of them shall remain,
    not their abundance, not their wealth;
    no pre-eminence among them.ᵇ
12   The time has come, the day draws near;
    let not the buyer rejoice, nor the seller
        mourn,
    for wrath is upon all their multitude.
¹³For the sellers shall not return to what has been sold as long as they remain alive. For the vision concerns all their multitude; it shall not be revoked. Because of their iniquity, they cannot maintain their lives.ᵇ
14   They have blown the horn and made
        everything ready;
    but no one goes to battle,

ᵃ Another reading is *Diblah*   ᵇ Meaning of Heb uncertain

for my wrath is upon all their
    multitude.
15 The sword is outside, pestilence and
    famine are inside;
    those in the field die by the sword;
    those in the city—famine and
      pestilence devour them.
16 If any survivors escape,
    they shall be found on the mountains
    like doves of the valleys,
    all of them moaning over their iniquity.
17 All hands shall grow feeble,
    all knees turn to water.
18 They shall put on sackcloth,
    horror shall cover them.
    Shame shall be on all faces,
    baldness on all their heads.
19 They shall fling their silver into the
      streets,
    their gold shall be treated as unclean.
Their silver and gold cannot save them on the
day of the wrath of the LORD. They shall not
satisfy their hunger or fill their stomachs with
it. For it was the stumbling block of their iniquity. 20From their*a* beautiful ornament, in
which they took pride, they made their abominable images, their detestable things; therefore I will make of it an unclean thing to them.
21 I will hand it over to strangers as booty,
    to the wicked of the earth as plunder;
    they shall profane it.
22 I will avert my face from them,
    so that they may profane my
      treasured*b* place;
    the violent shall enter it,
    they shall profane it.
23 Make a chain!*c*
    For the land is full of bloody crimes;
    the city is full of violence.
24 I will bring the worst of the nations
    to take possession of their houses.
    I will put an end to the arrogance of the
      strong,
    and their holy places shall be
      profaned.

25 When anguish comes, they will seek
      peace,
    but there shall be none.
26 Disaster comes upon disaster,
    rumor follows rumor;
    they shall keep seeking a vision from the
      prophet;
    instruction shall perish from the
      priest,
    and counsel from the elders.
27 The king shall mourn,
    the prince shall be wrapped in despair,
    and the hands of the people of the
      land shall tremble.
    According to their way I will deal with
      them;
    according to their own judgments I
      will judge them.
And they shall know that I am the LORD.

Abominations in the Temple

8 In the sixth year, in the sixth month, on the
fifth day of the month, as I sat in my
house, with the elders of Judah sitting before
me, the hand of the Lord GOD fell upon me
there. 2I looked, and there was a figure that
looked like a human being;*d* below what appeared to be its loins it was fire, and above the
loins it was like the appearance of brightness,
like gleaming amber. 3It stretched out the form
of a hand, and took me by a lock of my head;
and the spirit lifted me up between earth and
heaven, and brought me in visions of God to
Jerusalem, to the entrance of the gateway of
the inner court that faces north, to the seat of
the image of jealousy, which provokes to jealousy. 4And the glory of the God of Israel was
there, like the vision that I had seen in the valley.

5 Then God*e* said to me, "O mortal, lift up
your eyes now in the direction of the north."
So I lifted up my eyes toward the north, and
there, north of the altar gate, in the entrance,
was this image of jealousy. 6He said to me,
"Mortal, do you see what they are doing, the
great abominations that the house of Israel

---

a Syr Symmachus: Heb *its*   *b* Or *secret*   *c* Meaning of Heb uncertain   *d* Gk: Heb *like fire*   *e* Heb *he* are committing here, to drive me far from my sanctuary? Yet you will see still greater abominations."

7 And he brought me to the entrance of the court; I looked, and there was a hole in the wall. 8Then he said to me, "Mortal, dig through the wall"; and when I dug through the wall, there was an entrance. 9He said to me, "Go in, and see the vile abominations that they are committing here." 10So I went in and looked; there, portrayed on the wall all around, were all kinds of creeping things, and loathsome animals, and all the idols of the house of Israel. 11Before them stood seventy of the elders of the house of Israel, with Jaazaniah son of Shaphan standing among them. Each had his censer in his hand, and the fragrant cloud of incense was ascending. 12Then he said to me, "Mortal, have you seen what the elders of the house of Israel are doing in the dark, each in his room of images? For they say, 'The LORD does not see us, the LORD has forsaken the land.'" 13He said also to me, "You will see still greater abominations that they are committing."

14 Then he brought me to the entrance of the north gate of the house of the LORD; women were sitting there weeping for Tammuz. 15Then he said to me, "Have you seen this, O mortal? You will see still greater abominations than these."

16 And he brought me into the inner court of the house of the LORD; there, at the entrance of the temple of the LORD, between the porch and the altar, were about twenty-five men, with their backs to the temple of the LORD, and their faces toward the east, prostrating themselves to the sun toward the east. 17Then he said to me, "Have you seen this, O mortal? Is it not bad enough that the house of Judah commits the abominations done here? Must they fill the land with violence, and provoke my anger still further? See, they are putting the branch to their nose! 18Therefore I will act in wrath; my eye will not spare, nor will I have pity; and though they cry in my hearing with a loud voice, I will not listen to them."

The Slaughter of the Idolaters

9 Then he cried in my hearing with a loud voice, saying, "Draw near, you executioners of the city, each with his destroying weapon in his hand." 2And six men came from the direction of the upper gate, which faces north, each with his weapon for slaughter in his hand; among them was a man clothed in linen, with a writing case at his side. They went in and stood beside the bronze altar.

3 Now the glory of the God of Israel had gone up from the cherub on which it rested to the threshold of the house. The LORD called to the man clothed in linen, who had the writing case at his side; 4and said to him, "Go through the city, through Jerusalem, and put a mark on the foreheads of those who sigh and groan over all the abominations that are committed in it." 5To the others he said in my hearing, "Pass through the city after him, and kill; your eye shall not spare, and you shall show no pity. 6Cut down old men, young men and young women, little children and women, but touch no one who has the mark. And begin at my sanctuary." So they began with the elders who were in front of the house. 7Then he said to them, "Defile the house, and fill the courts with the slain. Go!" So they went out and killed in the city. 8While they were killing, and I was left alone, I fell prostrate on my face and cried out, "Ah Lord GOD! will you destroy all who remain of Israel as you pour out your wrath upon Jerusalem?" 9He said to me, "The guilt of the house of Israel and Judah is exceedingly great; the land is full of bloodshed and the city full of perversity; for they say, 'The LORD has forsaken the land, and the LORD does not see.' 10As for me, my eye will not spare, nor will I have pity, but I will bring down their deeds upon their heads."

11 Then the man clothed in linen, with the writing case at his side, brought back word, saying, "I have done as you commanded me."

God's Glory Leaves Jerusalem

10 Then I looked, and above the dome that was over the heads of the cherubim there appeared above them something like

a sapphire,*a* in form resembling a throne. ²He said to the man clothed in linen, "Go within the wheelwork underneath the cherubim; fill your hands with burning coals from among the cherubim, and scatter them over the city." He went in as I looked on. ³Now the cherubim were standing on the south side of the house when the man went in; and a cloud filled the inner court. ⁴Then the glory of the LORD rose up from the cherub to the threshold of the house; the house was filled with the cloud, and the court was full of the brightness of the glory of the LORD. ⁵The sound of the wings of the cherubim was heard as far as the outer court, like the voice of God Almighty*b* when he speaks.

6 When he commanded the man clothed in linen, "Take fire from within the wheelwork, from among the cherubim," he went in and stood beside a wheel. ⁷And a cherub stretched out his hand from among the cherubim to the fire that was among the cherubim, took some of it and put it into the hands of the man clothed in linen, who took it and went out. ⁸The cherubim appeared to have the form of a human hand under their wings.

9 I looked, and there were four wheels beside the cherubim, one beside each cherub; and the appearance of the wheels was like gleaming beryl. ¹⁰And as for their appearance, the four looked alike, something like a wheel within a wheel. ¹¹When they moved, they moved in any of the four directions without veering as they moved; but in whatever direction the front wheel faced, the others followed without veering as they moved. ¹²Their entire body, their rims, their spokes, their wings, and the wheels—the wheels of the four of them— were full of eyes all around. ¹³As for the wheels, they were called in my hearing "the wheelwork." ¹⁴Each one had four faces: the first face was that of the cherub, the second face was that of a human being, the third that of a lion, and the fourth that of an eagle.

15 The cherubim rose up. These were the living creatures that I saw by the river Chebar.

¹⁶When the cherubim moved, the wheels moved beside them; and when the cherubim lifted up their wings to rise up from the earth, the wheels at their side did not veer. ¹⁷When they stopped, the others stopped, and when they rose up, the others rose up with them; for the spirit of the living creatures was in them.

18 Then the glory of the LORD went out from the threshold of the house and stopped above the cherubim. ¹⁹The cherubim lifted up their wings and rose up from the earth in my sight as they went out with the wheels beside them. They stopped at the entrance of the east gate of the house of the LORD; and the glory of the God of Israel was above them.

20 These were the living creatures that I saw underneath the God of Israel by the river Chebar; and I knew that they were cherubim. ²¹Each had four faces, each four wings, and underneath their wings something like human hands. ²²As for what their faces were like, they were the same faces whose appearance I had seen by the river Chebar. Each one moved straight ahead.

Judgment on Wicked Counselors

11 The spirit lifted me up and brought me to the east gate of the house of the LORD, which faces east. There, at the entrance of the gateway, were twenty-five men; among them I saw Jaazaniah son of Azzur, and Pelatiah son of Benaiah, officials of the people. ²He said to me, "Mortal, these are the men who devise iniquity and who give wicked counsel in this city; ³they say, 'The time is not near to build houses; this city is the pot, and we are the meat.' ⁴Therefore prophesy against them; prophesy, O mortal."

5 Then the spirit of the LORD fell upon me, and he said to me, "Say, Thus says the LORD: This is what you think, O house of Israel; I know the things that come into your mind. ⁶You have killed many in this city, and have filled its streets with the slain. ⁷Therefore thus says the Lord GOD: The slain whom you have placed within it are the meat, and this

a Or *lapis lazuli*   *b* Traditional rendering of Heb *El Shaddai* city is the pot; but you shall be taken out of it. [8]You have feared the sword; and I will bring the sword upon you, says the Lord GOD. [9]I will take you out of it and give you over to the hands of foreigners, and execute judgments upon you. [10]You shall fall by the sword; I will judge you at the border of Israel. And you shall know that I am the LORD. [11]This city shall not be your pot, and you shall not be the meat inside it; I will judge you at the border of Israel. [12]Then you shall know that I am the LORD, whose statutes you have not followed, and whose ordinances you have not kept, but you have acted according to the ordinances of the nations that are around you."

13 Now, while I was prophesying, Pelatiah son of Benaiah died. Then I fell down on my face, cried with a loud voice, and said, "Ah Lord GOD! will you make a full end of the remnant of Israel?"

God Will Restore Israel

14 Then the word of the LORD came to me: [15]Mortal, your kinsfolk, your own kin, your fellow exiles,[a] the whole house of Israel, all of them, are those of whom the inhabitants of Jerusalem have said, "They have gone far from the LORD; to us this land is given for a possession." [16]Therefore say: Thus says the Lord GOD: Though I removed them far away among the nations, and though I scattered them among the countries, yet I have been a sanctuary to them for a little while[b] in the countries where they have gone. [17]Therefore say: Thus says the Lord GOD: I will gather you from the peoples, and assemble you out of the countries where you have been scattered, and I will give you the land of Israel. [18]When they come there, they will remove from it all its detestable things and all its abominations. [19]I will give them one[c] heart, and put a new spirit within them; I will remove the heart of stone from their flesh and give them a heart of flesh, [20]so that they may follow my statutes and keep my ordinances and obey them. Then they shall be my people, and I will be their God. [21]But as for

those whose heart goes after their detestable things and their abominations,[d] I will bring their deeds upon their own heads, says the Lord GOD.

22 Then the cherubim lifted up their wings, with the wheels beside them; and the glory of the God of Israel was above them. [23]And the glory of the LORD ascended from the middle of the city, and stopped on the mountain east of the city. [24]The spirit lifted me up and brought me in a vision by the spirit of God into Chaldea, to the exiles. Then the vision that I had seen left me. [25]And I told the exiles all the things that the LORD had shown me.

Judah's Captivity Portrayed

12 The word of the LORD came to me: [2]Mortal, you are living in the midst of a rebellious house, who have eyes to see but do not see, who have ears to hear but do not hear; [3]for they are a rebellious house. Therefore, mortal, prepare for yourself an exile's baggage, and go into exile by day in their sight; you shall go like an exile from your place to another place in their sight. Perhaps they will understand, though they are a rebellious house. [4]You shall bring out your baggage by day in their sight, as baggage for exile; and you shall go out yourself at evening in their sight, as those do who go into exile. [5]Dig through the wall in their sight, and carry the baggage through it. [6]In their sight you shall lift the baggage on your shoulder, and carry it out in the dark; you shall cover your face, so that you may not see the land; for I have made you a sign for the house of Israel.

7 I did just as I was commanded. I brought out my baggage by day, as baggage for exile, and in the evening I dug through the wall with my own hands; I brought it out in the dark, carrying it on my shoulder in their sight.

8 In the morning the word of the LORD came to me: [9]Mortal, has not the house of Israel, the rebellious house, said to you, "What are you doing?" [10]Say to them, "Thus says the Lord GOD: This oracle concerns the prince in

---

a Gk Syr: Heb *people of your kindred*   b Or *to some extent*   c Another reading is *a new*   d Cn: Heb *And to the*
heart of their detestable things and their abominations their heart goes

Jerusalem and all the house of Israel in it."
11Say, "I am a sign for you: as I have done, so
shall it be done to them; they shall go into exile, into captivity." 12And the prince who is
among them shall lift his baggage on his shoulder in the dark, and shall go out; he*a* shall dig
through the wall and carry it through; he shall
cover his face, so that he may not see the land
with his eyes. 13I will spread my net over him,
and he shall be caught in my snare; and I will
bring him to Babylon, the land of the
Chaldeans, yet he shall not see it; and he shall
die there. 14I will scatter to every wind all who
are around him, his helpers and all his troops;
and I will unsheathe the sword behind them.
15And they shall know that I am the LORD,
when I disperse them among the nations and
scatter them through the countries. 16But I will
let a few of them escape from the sword, from
famine and pestilence, so that they may tell of
all their abominations among the nations where
they go; then they shall know that I am the
LORD.

Judgment Not Postponed

17 The word of the LORD came to me:
18Mortal, eat your bread with quaking, and
drink your water with trembling and with fearfulness; 19and say to the people of the land,
Thus says the Lord GOD concerning the inhabitants of Jerusalem in the land of Israel:
They shall eat their bread with fearfulness, and
drink their water in dismay, because their land
shall be stripped of all it contains, on account
of the violence of all those who live in it.
20The inhabited cities shall be laid waste, and
the land shall become a desolation; and you
shall know that I am the LORD.

21 The word of the LORD came to me:
22Mortal, what is this proverb of yours about
the land of Israel, which says, "The days are
prolonged, and every vision comes to nothing"? 23Tell them therefore, "Thus says the
Lord GOD: I will put an end to this proverb,
and they shall use it no more as a proverb in Israel." But say to them, The days are near, and

the fulfillment of every vision. 24For there shall
no longer be any false vision or flattering divination within the house of Israel. 25But I the
LORD will speak the word that I speak, and it
will be fulfilled. It will no longer be delayed; but
in your days, O rebellious house, I will speak the
word and fulfill it, says the Lord GOD.

26 The word of the LORD came to me:
27Mortal, the house of Israel is saying, "The vision that he sees is for many years ahead; he
prophesies for distant times." 28Therefore say
to them, Thus says the Lord GOD: None of my
words will be delayed any longer, but the word
that I speak will be fulfilled, says the Lord
GOD.

False Prophets Condemned

13 The word of the LORD came to me:
2Mortal, prophesy against the prophets
of Israel who are prophesying; say to those
who prophesy out of their own imagination:
"Hear the word of the LORD!" 3Thus says the
Lord GOD, Alas for the senseless prophets
who follow their own spirit, and have seen
nothing! 4Your prophets have been like jackals
among ruins, O Israel. 5You have not gone up
into the breaches, or repaired a wall for the
house of Israel, so that it might stand in battle on the day of the LORD. 6They have envi-
sioned falsehood and lying divination; they say,
"Says the LORD," when the LORD has not sent
them, and yet they wait for the fulfillment of
their word! 7Have you not seen a false vision or
uttered a lying divination, when you have said,
"Says the LORD," even though I did not speak?

8 Therefore thus says the Lord GOD: Because you have uttered falsehood and envi-
sioned lies, I am against you, says the Lord
GOD. 9My hand will be against the prophets
who see false visions and utter lying divinations;
they shall not be in the council of my people,
nor be enrolled in the register of the house of
Israel, nor shall they enter the land of Israel;
and you shall know that I am the Lord GOD.
10Because, in truth, because they have misled
my people, saying, "Peace," when there is no

a Gk Syr: Heb *they*

peace; and because, when the people build a wall, these prophets*a* smear whitewash on it. [11]Say to those who smear whitewash on it that it shall fall. There will be a deluge of rain,*b* great hailstones will fall, and a stormy wind will break out. [12]When the wall falls, will it not be said to you, "Where is the whitewash you smeared on it?" [13]Therefore thus says the Lord GOD: In my wrath I will make a stormy wind break out, and in my anger there shall be a deluge of rain, and hailstones in wrath to destroy it. [14]I will break down the wall that you have smeared with whitewash, and bring it to the ground, so that its foundation will be laid bare; when it falls, you shall perish within it; and you shall know that I am the LORD. [15]Thus I will spend my wrath upon the wall, and upon those who have smeared it with whitewash; and I will say to you, The wall is no more, nor those who smeared it— [16]the prophets of Israel who prophesied concerning Jerusalem and saw visions of peace for it, when there was no peace, says the Lord GOD.

17 As for you, mortal, set your face against the daughters of your people, who prophesy out of their own imagination; prophesy against them [18]and say, Thus says the Lord GOD: Woe to the women who sew bands on all wrists, and make veils for the heads of persons of every height, in the hunt for human lives! Will you hunt down lives among my people, and maintain your own lives? [19]You have profaned me among my people for handfuls of barley and for pieces of bread, putting to death persons who should not die and keeping alive persons who should not live, by your lies to my people, who listen to lies.

20 Therefore thus says the Lord GOD: I am against your bands with which you hunt lives;*c* I will tear them from your arms, and let the lives go free, the lives that you hunt down like birds. [21]I will tear off your veils, and save my people from your hands; they shall no longer be prey in your hands; and you shall know that I am the LORD. [22]Because you have disheartened the righteous falsely, although I

have not disheartened them, and you have encouraged the wicked not to turn from their wicked way and save their lives; [23]therefore you shall no longer see false visions or practice divination; I will save my people from your hand. Then you will know that I am the LORD.

God's Judgments Justified

14 Certain elders of Israel came to me and sat down before me. [2]And the word of the LORD came to me: [3]Mortal, these men have taken their idols into their hearts, and placed their iniquity as a stumbling block before them; shall I let myself be consulted by them? [4]Therefore speak to them, and say to them, Thus says the Lord GOD: Any of those of the house of Israel who take their idols into their hearts and place their iniquity as a stumbling block before them, and yet come to the prophet—I the LORD will answer those who come with the multitude of their idols, [5]in order that I may take hold of the hearts of the house of Israel, all of whom are estranged from me through their idols.

6 Therefore say to the house of Israel, Thus says the Lord GOD: Repent and turn away from your idols; and turn away your faces from all your abominations. [7]For any of those of the house of Israel, or of the aliens who reside in Israel, who separate themselves from me, taking their idols into their hearts and placing their iniquity as a stumbling block before them, and yet come to a prophet to inquire of me by him, I the LORD will answer them myself. [8]I will set my face against them; I will make them a sign and a byword and cut them off from the midst of my people; and you shall know that I am the LORD.

9 If a prophet is deceived and speaks a word, I, the LORD, have deceived that prophet, and I will stretch out my hand against him, and will destroy him from the midst of my people Israel. [10]And they shall bear their punishment—the punishment of the inquirer and the punishment of the prophet shall be the same— [11]so that the house of Israel may no

a Heb *they*   *b* Heb *rain and you*   *c* Gk Syr: Heb *lives for birds* longer go astray from me, nor defile themselves any more with all their transgressions. Then they shall be my people, and I will be their God, says the Lord GOD.

12 The word of the LORD came to me: ¹³Mortal, when a land sins against me by acting faithlessly, and I stretch out my hand against it, and break its staff of bread and send famine upon it, and cut off from it human beings and animals, ¹⁴even if Noah, Daniel,ᵃ and Job, these three, were in it, they would save only their own lives by their righteousness, says the Lord GOD. ¹⁵If I send wild animals through the land to ravage it, so that it is made desolate, and no one may pass through because of the animals; ¹⁶even if these three men were in it, as I live, says the Lord GOD, they would save neither sons nor daughters; they alone would be saved, but the land would be desolate. ¹⁷Or if I bring a sword upon that land and say, "Let a sword pass through the land," and I cut off human beings and animals from it; ¹⁸though these three men were in it, as I live, says the Lord GOD, they would save neither sons nor daughters, but they alone would be saved. ¹⁹Or if I send a pestilence into that land, and pour out my wrath upon it with blood, to cut off humans and animals from it; ²⁰even if Noah, Daniel,ᵃ and Job were in it, as I live, says the Lord GOD, they would save neither son nor daughter; they would save only their own lives by their righteousness.

21 For thus says the Lord GOD: How much more when I send upon Jerusalem my four deadly acts of judgment, sword, famine, wild animals, and pestilence, to cut off humans and animals from it! ²²Yet, survivors shall be left in it, sons and daughters who will be brought out; they will come out to you. When you see their ways and their deeds, you will be consoled for the evil that I have brought upon Jerusalem, for all that I have brought upon it. ²³They shall console you, when you see their ways and their deeds; and you shall know that it was not without cause that I did all that I have done in it, says the Lord GOD.

The Useless Vine

15 The word of the LORD came to me: ²O mortal, how does the wood of
the vine surpass all other
wood—
the vine branch that is among the
trees of the forest?
3   Is wood taken from it to make anything?
Does one take a peg from it on which
to hang any object?
4   It is put in the fire for fuel;
when the fire has consumed both
ends of it
and the middle of it is charred,
is it useful for anything?
5   When it was whole it was used for
nothing;
how much less—when the fire has
consumed it,
and it is charred—
can it ever be used for anything!

6 Therefore thus says the Lord GOD: Like the wood of the vine among the trees of the forest, which I have given to the fire for fuel, so I will give up the inhabitants of Jerusalem. ⁷I will set my face against them; although they escape from the fire, the fire shall still consume them; and you shall know that I am the LORD, when I set my face against them. ⁸And I will make the land desolate, because they have acted faithlessly, says the Lord GOD.

God's Faithless Bride

16 The word of the LORD came to me: ²Mortal, make known to Jerusalem her abominations, ³and say, Thus says the Lord GOD to Jerusalem: Your origin and your birth were in the land of the Canaanites; your father was an Amorite, and your mother a Hittite. ⁴As for your birth, on the day you were born your navel cord was not cut, nor were you washed with water to cleanse you, nor rubbed with salt, nor wrapped in cloths. ⁵No eye pitied you, to do any of these things for you out of compassion for you; but you were thrown out

ᵃ Or, as otherwise read, *Danel*

in the open field, for you were abhorred on the day you were born.

6 I passed by you, and saw you flailing about in your blood. As you lay in your blood, I said to you, "Live! 7and grow up*a* like a plant of the field." You grew up and became tall and arrived at full womanhood;*b* your breasts were formed, and your hair had grown; yet you were naked and bare.

8 I passed by you again and looked on you; you were at the age for love. I spread the edge of my cloak over you, and covered your nakedness: I pledged myself to you and entered into a covenant with you, says the Lord GOD, and you became mine. 9Then I bathed you with water and washed off the blood from you, and anointed you with oil. 10I clothed you with embroidered cloth and with sandals of fine leather; I bound you in fine linen and covered you with rich fabric.*c* 11I adorned you with ornaments: I put bracelets on your arms, a chain on your neck, 12a ring on your nose, earrings in your ears, and a beautiful crown upon your head. 13You were adorned with gold and silver, while your clothing was of fine linen, rich fabric,*c* and embroidered cloth. You had choice flour and honey and oil for food. You grew exceedingly beautiful, fit to be a queen. 14Your fame spread among the nations on account of your beauty, for it was perfect because of my splendor that I had bestowed on you, says the Lord GOD.

15 But you trusted in your beauty, and played the whore because of your fame, and lavished your whorings on any passer-by.*d* 16You took some of your garments, and made for yourself colorful shrines, and on them played the whore; nothing like this has ever been or ever shall be.*c* 17You also took your beautiful jewels of my gold and my silver that I had given you, and made for yourself male images, and with them played the whore; 18and you took your embroidered garments to cover them, and set my oil and my incense before them. 19Also my bread that I gave you—I fed you with choice flour and oil and honey—you

set it before them as a pleasing odor; and so it was, says the Lord GOD. 20You took your sons and your daughters, whom you had borne to me, and these you sacrificed to them to be devoured. As if your whorings were not enough! 21You slaughtered my children and delivered them up as an offering to them. 22And in all your abominations and your whorings you did not remember the days of your youth, when you were naked and bare, flailing about in your blood.

23 After all your wickedness (woe, woe to you! says the Lord GOD), 24you built yourself a platform and made yourself a lofty place in every square; 25at the head of every street you built your lofty place and prostituted your beauty, offering yourself to every passer-by, and multiplying your whoring. 26You played the whore with the Egyptians, your lustful neighbors, multiplying your whoring, to provoke me to anger. 27Therefore I stretched out my hand against you, reduced your rations, and gave you up to the will of your enemies, the daughters of the Philistines, who were ashamed of your lewd behavior. 28You played the whore with the Assyrians, because you were insatiable; you played the whore with them, and still you were not satisfied. 29You multiplied your whoring with Chaldea, the land of merchants; and even with this you were not satisfied.

30 How sick is your heart, says the Lord GOD, that you did all these things, the deeds of a brazen whore; 31building your platform at the head of every street, and making your lofty place in every square! Yet you were not like a whore, because you scorned payment. 32Adulterous wife, who receives strangers instead of her husband! 33Gifts are given to all whores; but you gave your gifts to all your lovers, bribing them to come to you from all around for your whorings. 34So you were different from other women in your whorings: no one solicited you to play the whore; and you gave payment, while no payment was given to you; you were different.

35 Therefore, O whore, hear the word of

---

a Gk Syr: Heb *Live! I made you a myriad*   *b* Cn: Heb *ornament of ornaments*   *c* Meaning of Heb uncertain
d Heb adds *let it be his*

the LORD: [36]Thus says the Lord GOD, Because your lust was poured out and your nakedness uncovered in your whoring with your lovers, and because of all your abominable idols, and because of the blood of your children that you gave to them, [37]therefore, I will gather all your lovers, with whom you took pleasure, all those you loved and all those you hated; I will gather them against you from all around, and will uncover your nakedness to them, so that they may see all your nakedness. [38]I will judge you as women who commit adultery and shed blood are judged, and bring blood upon you in wrath and jealousy. [39]I will deliver you into their hands, and they shall throw down your platform and break down your lofty places; they shall strip you of your clothes and take your beautiful objects and leave you naked and bare. [40]They shall bring up a mob against you, and they shall stone you and cut you to pieces with their swords. [41]They shall burn your houses and execute judgments on you in the sight of many women; I will stop you from playing the whore, and you shall also make no more payments. [42]So I will satisfy my fury on you, and my jealousy shall turn away from you; I will be calm, and will be angry no longer. [43]Because you have not remembered the days of your youth, but have enraged me with all these things; therefore, I have returned your deeds upon your head, says the Lord GOD.

Have you not committed lewdness beyond all your abominations? [44]See, everyone who uses proverbs will use this proverb about you, "Like mother, like daughter." [45]You are the daughter of your mother, who loathed her husband and her children; and you are the sister of your sisters, who loathed their husbands and their children. Your mother was a Hittite and your father an Amorite. [46]Your elder sister is Samaria, who lived with her daughters to the north of you; and your younger sister, who lived to the south of you, is Sodom with her daughters. [47]You not only followed their ways, and acted according to their abominations; within a very little time you were more corrupt than they in all your ways. [48]As I live, says the Lord GOD, your sister Sodom and her daughters have not done as you and your daughters have done. [49]This was the guilt of your sister Sodom: she and her daughters had pride, excess of food, and prosperous ease, but did not aid the poor and needy. [50]They were haughty, and did abominable things before me; therefore I removed them when I saw it. [51]Samaria has not committed half your sins; you have committed more abominations than they, and have made your sisters appear righteous by all the abominations that you have committed. [52]Bear your disgrace, you also, for you have brought about for your sisters a more favorable judgment; because of your sins in which you acted more abominably than they, they are more in the right than you. So be ashamed, you also, and bear your disgrace, for you have made your sisters appear righteous.

53 I will restore their fortunes, the fortunes of Sodom and her daughters and the fortunes of Samaria and her daughters, and I will restore your own fortunes along with theirs, [54]in order that you may bear your disgrace and be ashamed of all that you have done, becoming a consolation to them. [55]As for your sisters, Sodom and her daughters shall return to their former state, Samaria and her daughters shall return to their former state, and you and your daughters shall return to your former state. [56]Was not your sister Sodom a byword in your mouth in the day of your pride, [57]before your wickedness was uncovered? Now you are a mockery to the daughters of Aram[a] and all her neighbors, and to the daughters of the Philistines, those all around who despise you. [58]You must bear the penalty of your lewdness and your abominations, says the LORD.

An Everlasting Covenant

59 Yes, thus says the Lord GOD: I will deal with you as you have done, you who have despised the oath, breaking the covenant; [60]yet I will remember my covenant with you in the days of your youth, and I will establish with you

---

a Another reading is *Edom*

an everlasting covenant. 61Then you will remember your ways, and be ashamed when I*a*
take your sisters, both your elder and your
younger, and give them to you as daughters, but
not on account of my*b* covenant with you. 62I
will establish my covenant with you, and you
shall know that I am the LORD, 63in order that
you may remember and be confounded, and
never open your mouth again because of your
shame, when I forgive you all that you have
done, says the Lord GOD.

The Two Eagles and the Vine

17 The word of the LORD came to me:
2O mortal, propound a riddle, and
speak an allegory to the house of Israel. 3Say:
Thus says the Lord GOD:

A great eagle, with great wings and long
        pinions,
    rich in plumage of many colors,
    came to the Lebanon.
He took the top of the cedar,
4   broke off its topmost shoot;
    he carried it to a land of trade,
    set it in a city of merchants.
5   Then he took a seed from the land,
        placed it in fertile soil;
    a plant*c* by abundant waters,
    he set it like a willow twig.
6   It sprouted and became a vine
        spreading out, but low;
    its branches turned toward him,
        its roots remained where it stood.
    So it became a vine;
        it brought forth branches,
        put forth foliage.

7   There was another great eagle,
        with great wings and much plumage.
    And see! This vine stretched out
        its roots toward him;
    it shot out its branches toward him,
        so that he might water it.
    From the bed where it was planted
8   it was transplanted
    to good soil by abundant waters,

so that it might produce branches
    and bear fruit
    and become a noble vine.
9Say: Thus says the Lord GOD:
    Will it prosper?
    Will he not pull up its roots,
        cause its fruit to rot*c* and wither,
        its fresh sprouting leaves to fade?
    No strong arm or mighty army will be
            needed
        to pull it from its roots.
10 When it is transplanted, will it thrive?
    When the east wind strikes it,
        will it not utterly wither,
        wither on the bed where it grew?

11 Then the word of the LORD came to me:
12Say now to the rebellious house: Do you not
know what these things mean? Tell them: The
king of Babylon came to Jerusalem, took its
king and its officials, and brought them back
with him to Babylon. 13He took one of the royal offspring and made a covenant with him,
putting him under oath (he had taken away
the chief men of the land), 14so that the kingdom might be humble and not lift itself up, and
that by keeping his covenant it might stand.
15But he rebelled against him by sending ambassadors to Egypt, in order that they might
give him horses and a large army. Will he succeed? Can one escape who does such things?
Can he break the covenant and yet escape?
16As I live, says the Lord GOD, surely in the
place where the king resides who made him
king, whose oath he despised, and whose covenant with him he broke—in Babylon he shall
die. 17Pharaoh with his mighty army and great
company will not help him in war, when ramps
are cast up and siege walls built to cut off many
lives. 18Because he despised the oath and broke
the covenant, because he gave his hand and yet
did all these things, he shall not escape. 19There-
fore thus says the Lord GOD: As I live, I will
surely return upon his head my oath that he despised, and my covenant that he broke. 20I will
spread my net over him, and he shall be caught
in my snare; I will bring him to Babylon and en-

a Syr: Heb *you*   *b* Heb lacks *my*   *c* Meaning of Heb uncertain ter into judgment with him there for the treason he has committed against me. 21All the pick*a* of his troops shall fall by the sword, and the survivors shall be scattered to every wind; and you shall know that I, the LORD, have spoken.

Israel Exalted at Last

22 Thus says the Lord GOD:
 I myself will take a sprig
  from the lofty top of a cedar;
  I will set it out.
 I will break off a tender one
  from the topmost of its young twigs;
 I myself will plant it
  on a high and lofty mountain.
23 On the mountain height of Israel
  I will plant it,
 in order that it may produce boughs and
   bear fruit,
  and become a noble cedar.
 Under it every kind of bird will live;
  in the shade of its branches will nest
  winged creatures of every kind.
24 All the trees of the field shall know
  that I am the LORD.
 I bring low the high tree,
  I make high the low tree;
 I dry up the green tree
  and make the dry tree flourish.
 I the LORD have spoken;
  I will accomplish it.

Individual Retribution

18 The word of the LORD came to me: 2What do you mean by repeating this proverb concerning the land of Israel, "The parents have eaten sour grapes, and the children's teeth are set on edge"? 3As I live, says the Lord GOD, this proverb shall no more be used by you in Israel. 4Know that all lives are mine; the life of the parent as well as the life of the child is mine: it is only the person who sins that shall die.

5 If a man is righteous and does what is lawful and right— 6if he does not eat upon the mountains or lift up his eyes to the idols of the house of Israel, does not defile his neighbor's wife or approach a woman during her menstrual period, 7does not oppress anyone, but restores to the debtor his pledge, commits no robbery, gives his bread to the hungry and covers the naked with a garment, 8does not take advance or accrued interest, withholds his hand from iniquity, executes true justice between contending parties, 9follows my statutes, and is careful to observe my ordinances, acting faithfully—such a one is righteous; he shall surely live, says the Lord GOD.

10 If he has a son who is violent, a shedder of blood, 11who does any of these things (though his father*b* does none of them), who eats upon the mountains, defiles his neighbor's wife, 12oppresses the poor and needy, commits robbery, does not restore the pledge, lifts up his eyes to the idols, commits abomination, 13takes advance or accrued interest; shall he then live? He shall not. He has done all these abominable things; he shall surely die; his blood shall be upon himself.

14 But if this man has a son who sees all the sins that his father has done, considers, and does not do likewise, 15who does not eat upon the mountains or lift up his eyes to the idols of the house of Israel, does not defile his neighbor's wife, 16does not wrong anyone, exacts no pledge, commits no robbery, but gives his bread to the hungry and covers the naked with a garment, 17withholds his hand from iniquity,*c* takes no advance or accrued interest, observes my ordinances, and follows my statutes; he shall not die for his father's iniquity; he shall surely live. 18As for his father, because he practiced extortion, robbed his brother, and did what is not good among his people, he dies for his iniquity.

19 Yet you say, "Why should not the son suffer for the iniquity of the father?" When the son has done what is lawful and right, and has been careful to observe all my statutes, he shall surely live. 20The person who sins shall die. A child shall not suffer for the iniquity of a par-

a Another reading is *fugitives*   *b* Heb *he*   *c* Gk: Heb *the poor* ent, nor a parent suffer for the iniquity of a child; the righteousness of the righteous shall be his own, and the wickedness of the wicked shall be his own.

21 But if the wicked turn away from all their sins that they have committed and keep all my statutes and do what is lawful and right, they shall surely live; they shall not die. 22None of the transgressions that they have committed shall be remembered against them; for the righteousness that they have done they shall live. 23Have I any pleasure in the death of the wicked, says the Lord GOD, and not rather that they should turn from their ways and live? 24But when the righteous turn away from their righteousness and commit iniquity and do the same abominable things that the wicked do, shall they live? None of the righteous deeds that they have done shall be remembered; for the treachery of which they are guilty and the sin they have committed, they shall die.

25 Yet you say, "The way of the Lord is unfair." Hear now, O house of Israel: Is my way unfair? Is it not your ways that are unfair? 26When the righteous turn away from their righteousness and commit iniquity, they shall die for it; for the iniquity that they have committed they shall die. 27Again, when the wicked turn away from the wickedness they have committed and do what is lawful and right, they shall save their life. 28Because they considered and turned away from all the transgressions that they had committed, they shall surely live; they shall not die. 29Yet the house of Israel says, "The way of the Lord is unfair." O house of Israel, are my ways unfair? Is it not your ways that are unfair?

30 Therefore I will judge you, O house of Israel, all of you according to your ways, says the Lord GOD. Repent and turn from all your transgressions; otherwise iniquity will be your ruin.[a] 31Cast away from you all the transgressions that you have committed against me, and get yourselves a new heart and a new spirit! Why will you die, O house of Israel? 32For I

have no pleasure in the death of anyone, says the Lord GOD. Turn, then, and live.

Israel Degraded

19 As for you, raise up a lamentation for the princes of Israel, 2and say:
What a lioness was your mother
   among lions!
She lay down among young lions,
   rearing her cubs.
3 She raised up one of her cubs;
   he became a young lion,
and he learned to catch prey;
   he devoured humans.
4 The nations sounded an alarm against
     him;
   he was caught in their pit;
and they brought him with hooks
   to the land of Egypt.
5 When she saw that she was thwarted,
   that her hope was lost,
she took another of her cubs
   and made him a young lion.
6 He prowled among the lions;
   he became a young lion,
and he learned to catch prey;
   he devoured people.
7 And he ravaged their strongholds,[b]
   and laid waste their towns;
the land was appalled, and all in it,
   at the sound of his roaring.
8 The nations set upon him
   from the provinces all around;
they spread their net over him;
   he was caught in their pit.
9 With hooks they put him in a cage,
   and brought him to the king of
     Babylon;
they brought him into custody,
so that his voice should be heard no
     more
   on the mountains of Israel.
10 Your mother was like a vine in a
     vineyard[c]
   transplanted by the water,
fruitful and full of branches

---

a Or *so that they shall not be a stumbling block of iniquity to you*   b Heb *his widows*   c Cn: Heb *in your blood* from abundant water.

11 Its strongest stem became
        a ruler's scepter;*a*
    it towered aloft
        among the thick boughs;
    it stood out in its height
        with its mass of branches.
12 But it was plucked up in fury,
        cast down to the ground;
    the east wind dried it up;
        its fruit was stripped off,
    its strong stem was withered;
        the fire consumed it.
13 Now it is transplanted into the
        wilderness,
        into a dry and thirsty land.
14 And fire has gone out from its stem,
        has consumed its branches and fruit,
    so that there remains in it no strong
        stem,
        no scepter for ruling.

This is a lamentation, and it is used as a
lamentation.

Israel's Continuing Rebellion

20 In the seventh year, in the fifth month,
on the tenth day of the month, certain
elders of Israel came to consult the LORD, and
sat down before me. 2And the word of the
LORD came to me: 3Mortal, speak to the elders
of Israel, and say to them: Thus says the Lord
GOD: Why are you coming? To consult me? As
I live, says the Lord GOD, I will not be consulted by you. 4Will you judge them, mortal, will
you judge them? Then let them know the
abominations of their ancestors, 5and say to
them: Thus says the Lord GOD: On the day
when I chose Israel, I swore to the offspring of
the house of Jacob—making myself known to
them in the land of Egypt—I swore to them,
saying, I am the LORD your God. 6On that day
I swore to them that I would bring them out of
the land of Egypt into a land that I had
searched out for them, a land flowing with
milk and honey, the most glorious of all lands.

7And I said to them, Cast away the detestable
things your eyes feast on, every one of you, and
do not defile yourselves with the idols of
Egypt; I am the LORD your God. 8But they rebelled against me and would not listen to me;
not one of them cast away the detestable things
their eyes feasted on, nor did they forsake the
idols of Egypt.

Then I thought I would pour out my wrath
upon them and spend my anger against them
in the midst of the land of Egypt. 9But I acted for the sake of my name, that it should not
be profaned in the sight of the nations among
whom they lived, in whose sight I made myself
known to them in bringing them out of the
land of Egypt. 10So I led them out of the land
of Egypt and brought them into the wilderness.
11I gave them my statutes and showed them my
ordinances, by whose observance everyone
shall live. 12Moreover I gave them my sabbaths, as a sign between me and them, so that
they might know that I the LORD sanctify them.
13But the house of Israel rebelled against me
in the wilderness; they did not observe my
statutes but rejected my ordinances, by whose
observance everyone shall live; and my sabbaths they greatly profaned.

Then I thought I would pour out my wrath
upon them in the wilderness, to make an end
of them. 14But I acted for the sake of my
name, so that it should not be profaned in the
sight of the nations, in whose sight I had
brought them out. 15Moreover I swore to them
in the wilderness that I would not bring them
into the land that I had given them, a land
flowing with milk and honey, the most glorious
of all lands, 16because they rejected my ordinances and did not observe my statutes, and
profaned my sabbaths; for their heart went after their idols. 17Nevertheless my eye spared
them, and I did not destroy them or make an
end of them in the wilderness.

18 I said to their children in the wilderness,
Do not follow the statutes of your parents,
nor observe their ordinances, nor defile yourselves with their idols. 19I the LORD am your

a Heb *Its strongest stems became rulers' scepters*

God; follow my statutes, and be careful to observe my ordinances, 20and hallow my sabbaths that they may be a sign between me and you, so that you may know that I the LORD am your God. 21But the children rebelled against me; they did not follow my statutes, and were not careful to observe my ordinances, by whose observance everyone shall live; they profaned my sabbaths.

Then I thought I would pour out my wrath upon them and spend my anger against them in the wilderness. 22But I withheld my hand, and acted for the sake of my name, so that it should not be profaned in the sight of the nations, in whose sight I had brought them out. 23Moreover I swore to them in the wilderness that I would scatter them among the nations and disperse them through the countries, 24because they had not executed my ordinances, but had rejected my statutes and profaned my sabbaths, and their eyes were set on their ancestors' idols. 25Moreover I gave them statutes that were not good and ordinances by which they could not live. 26I defiled them through their very gifts, in their offering up all their firstborn, in order that I might horrify them, so that they might know that I am the LORD.

27 Therefore, mortal, speak to the house of Israel and say to them, Thus says the Lord GOD: In this again your ancestors blasphemed me, by dealing treacherously with me. 28For when I had brought them into the land that I swore to give them, then wherever they saw any high hill or any leafy tree, there they offered their sacrifices and presented the provocation of their offering; there they sent up their pleasing odors, and there they poured out their drink offerings. 29(I said to them, What is the high place to which you go? So it is called Bamah*a* to this day.) 30Therefore say to the house of Israel, Thus says the Lord GOD: Will you defile yourselves after the manner of your ancestors and go astray after their detestable things? 31When you offer your gifts and make your children pass through the fire, you defile yourselves with all your idols to this day. And

shall I be consulted by you, O house of Israel? As I live, says the Lord GOD, I will not be consulted by you.

32 What is in your mind shall never happen—the thought, "Let us be like the nations, like the tribes of the countries, and worship wood and stone."

God Will Restore Israel

33 As I live, says the Lord GOD, surely with a mighty hand and an outstretched arm, and with wrath poured out, I will be king over you. 34I will bring you out from the peoples and gather you out of the countries where you are scattered, with a mighty hand and an outstretched arm, and with wrath poured out; 35and I will bring you into the wilderness of the peoples, and there I will enter into judgment with you face to face. 36As I entered into judgment with your ancestors in the wilderness of the land of Egypt, so I will enter into judgment with you, says the Lord GOD. 37I will make you pass under the staff, and will bring you within the bond of the covenant. 38I will purge out the rebels among you, and those who transgress against me; I will bring them out of the land where they reside as aliens, but they shall not enter the land of Israel. Then you shall know that I am the LORD.

39 As for you, O house of Israel, thus says the Lord GOD: Go serve your idols, every one of you now and hereafter, if you will not listen to me; but my holy name you shall no more profane with your gifts and your idols.

40 For on my holy mountain, the mountain height of Israel, says the Lord GOD, there all the house of Israel, all of them, shall serve me in the land; there I will accept them, and there I will require your contributions and the choicest of your gifts, with all your sacred things. 41As a pleasing odor I will accept you, when I bring you out from the peoples, and gather you out of the countries where you have been scattered; and I will manifest my holiness among you in the sight of the nations. 42You shall know that I am the LORD, when I bring

---

a That is *High Place*

you into the land of Israel, the country that I swore to give to your ancestors. ⁴³There you shall remember your ways and all the deeds by which you have polluted yourselves; and you shall loathe yourselves for all the evils that you have committed. ⁴⁴And you shall know that I am the LORD, when I deal with you for my name's sake, not according to your evil ways, or corrupt deeds, O house of Israel, says the Lord GOD.

A Prophecy against the Negeb

45 ª The word of the LORD came to me: ⁴⁶Mortal, set your face toward the south, preach against the south, and prophesy against the forest land in the Negeb; ⁴⁷say to the forest of the Negeb, Hear the word of the LORD: Thus says the Lord GOD, I will kindle a fire in you, and it shall devour every green tree in you and every dry tree; the blazing flame shall not be quenched, and all faces from south to north shall be scorched by it. ⁴⁸All flesh shall see that I the LORD have kindled it; it shall not be quenched. ⁴⁹Then I said, "Ah Lord GOD! they are saying of me, 'Is he not a maker of allegories?'"

The Drawn Sword of God

21 ᵇ The word of the LORD came to me: ²Mortal, set your face toward Jerusalem and preach against the sanctuaries; prophesy against the land of Israel ³and say to the land of Israel, Thus says the LORD: I am coming against you, and will draw my sword out of its sheath, and will cut off from you both righteous and wicked. ⁴Because I will cut off from you both righteous and wicked, therefore my sword shall go out of its sheath against all flesh from south to north; ⁵and all flesh shall know that I the LORD have drawn my sword out of its sheath; it shall not be sheathed again. ⁶Moan therefore, mortal; moan with breaking heart and bitter grief before their eyes. ⁷And when they say to you, "Why do you moan?" you shall say, "Because of the news that has come. Every heart will melt and all hands will

be feeble, every spirit will faint and all knees will turn to water. See, it comes and it will be fulfilled," says the Lord GOD.

8 And the word of the LORD came to me: ⁹Mortal, prophesy and say: Thus says the Lord; Say:

A sword, a sword is sharpened,
　　it is also polished;
10　it is sharpened for slaughter,
　　honed to flash like lightning!
　How can we make merry?
　　You have despised the rod,
　　and all discipline.ᶜ
11　The sword ᵈ is given to be polished,
　　to be grasped in the hand;
　it is sharpened, the sword is polished,
　　to be placed in the slayer's hand.
12　Cry and wail, O mortal,
　　for it is against my people;
　it is against all Israel's princes;
　　they are thrown to the sword,
　　together with my people.
　　Ah! Strike the thigh!
¹³For consider: What! If you despise the rod, will it not happen?ᶜ says the Lord GOD.
14　And you, mortal, prophesy;
　　strike hand to hand.
　Let the sword fall twice, thrice;
　　it is a sword for killing.
　A sword for great slaughter—
　　it surrounds them;
15　therefore hearts melt
　　and many stumble.
　At all their gates I have set
　　the pointᶜ of the sword.
　Ah! It is made for flashing,
　　it is polishedᵉ for slaughter.
16　Attack to the right!
　　Engage to the left!
　　—wherever your edge is directed.
17　I too will strike hand to hand,
　　I will satisfy my fury;
　　I the LORD have spoken.

18 The word of the LORD came to me: ¹⁹Mortal, mark out two roads for the sword of the king of Babylon to come; both of them

a Ch 21.1 in Heb   b Ch 21.6 in Heb   c Meaning of Heb uncertain   d Heb It   e Tg: Heb wrapped up shall issue from the same land. And make a signpost, make it for a fork in the road leading to a city; ²⁰mark out the road for the sword to come to Rabbah of the Ammonites or to Judah and to*a* Jerusalem the fortified. ²¹For the king of Babylon stands at the parting of the way, at the fork in the two roads, to use divination; he shakes the arrows, he consults the teraphim,*b* he inspects the liver. ²²Into his right hand comes the lot for Jerusalem, to set battering rams, to call out for slaughter, for raising the battle cry, to set battering rams against the gates, to cast up ramps, to build siege towers. ²³But to them it will seem like a false divination; they have sworn solemn oaths; but he brings their guilt to remembrance, bringing about their capture.

24 Therefore thus says the Lord GOD: Because you have brought your guilt to remembrance, in that your transgressions are uncovered, so that in all your deeds your sins appear—because you have come to remembrance, you shall be taken in hand.*c*

25 As for you, vile, wicked prince of Israel,
      you whose day has come,
      the time of final punishment,
26 thus says the Lord GOD:
      Remove the turban, take off the crown;
      things shall not remain as they are.
      Exalt that which is low,
      abase that which is high.
27 A ruin, a ruin, a ruin—
      I will make it!
      (Such has never occurred.)
      Until he comes whose right it is;
      to him I will give it.

28 As for you, mortal, prophesy, and say, Thus says the Lord GOD concerning the Ammonites, and concerning their reproach; say:
      A sword, a sword! Drawn for slaughter,
      polished to consume,*d* to flash like
         lightning.
29 Offering false visions for you,
      divining lies for you,
      they place you over the necks
      of the vile, wicked ones—

those whose day has come,
      the time of final punishment.
30 Return it to its sheath!
      In the place where you were created,
      in the land of your origin,
      I will judge you.
31 I will pour out my indignation upon you,
      with the fire of my wrath
      I will blow upon you.
      I will deliver you into brutish hands,
      those skillful to destroy.
32 You shall be fuel for the fire,
      your blood shall enter the earth;
      you shall be remembered no more,
      for I the LORD have spoken.

The Bloody City

22 The word of the LORD came to me: ²You, mortal, will you judge, will you judge the bloody city? Then declare to it all its abominable deeds. ³You shall say, Thus says the Lord GOD: A city! Shedding blood within itself; its time has come; making its idols, defiling itself. ⁴You have become guilty by the blood that you have shed, and defiled by the idols that you have made; you have brought your day near, the appointed time of your years has come. Therefore I have made you a disgrace before the nations, and a mockery to all the countries. ⁵Those who are near and those who are far from you will mock you, you infamous one, full of tumult.

6 The princes of Israel in you, everyone according to his power, have been bent on shedding blood. ⁷Father and mother are treated with contempt in you; the alien residing within you suffers extortion; the orphan and the widow are wronged in you. ⁸You have despised my holy things, and profaned my sabbaths. ⁹In you are those who slander to shed blood, those in you who eat upon the mountains, who commit lewdness in your midst. ¹⁰In you they uncover their fathers' nakedness; in you they violate women in their menstrual periods. ¹¹One commits abomination with his neighbor's wife; another lewdly defiles his

---

a Gk Syr: Heb *Judah in*   *b* Or *the household gods*   *c* Or *be taken captive*   *d* Cn: Heb *to contain* daughter-in-law; another in you defiles his sister, his father's daughter. [12]In you, they take bribes to shed blood; you take both advance interest and accrued interest, and make gain of your neighbors by extortion; and you have forgotten me, says the Lord GOD.

13 See, I strike my hands together at the dishonest gain you have made, and at the blood that has been shed within you. [14]Can your courage endure, or can your hands remain strong in the days when I shall deal with you? I the LORD have spoken, and I will do it. [15]I will scatter you among the nations and disperse you through the countries, and I will purge your filthiness out of you. [16]And I[a] shall be profaned through you in the sight of the nations; and you shall know that I am the LORD.

17 The word of the LORD came to me: [18]Mortal, the house of Israel has become dross to me; all of them, silver,[b] bronze, tin, iron, and lead. In the smelter they have become dross. [19]Therefore thus says the Lord GOD: Because you have all become dross, I will gather you into the midst of Jerusalem. [20]As one gathers silver, bronze, iron, lead, and tin into a smelter, to blow the fire upon them in order to melt them; so I will gather you in my anger and in my wrath, and I will put you in and melt you. [21]I will gather you and blow upon you with the fire of my wrath, and you shall be melted within it. [22]As silver is melted in a smelter, so you shall be melted in it; and you shall know that I the LORD have poured out my wrath upon you.

23 The word of the LORD came to me: [24]Mortal, say to it: You are a land that is not cleansed, not rained upon in the day of indignation. [25]Its princes[c] within it are like a roaring lion tearing the prey; they have devoured human lives; they have taken treasure and precious things; they have made many widows within it. [26]Its priests have done violence to my teaching and have profaned my holy things; they have made no distinction between the holy and the common, neither have they taught the difference between the unclean and the clean, and they have disregarded my sabbaths, so that I am profaned among them. [27]Its officials within it are like wolves tearing the prey, shedding blood, destroying lives to get dishonest gain. [28]Its prophets have smeared whitewash on their behalf, seeing false visions and divining lies for them, saying, "Thus says the Lord GOD," when the LORD has not spoken. [29]The people of the land have practiced extortion and committed robbery; they have oppressed the poor and needy, and have extorted from the alien without redress. [30]And I sought for anyone among them who would repair the wall and stand in the breach before me on behalf of the land, so that I would not destroy it; but I found no one. [31]Therefore I have poured out my indignation upon them; I have consumed them with the fire of my wrath; I have returned their conduct upon their heads, says the Lord GOD.

Oholah and Oholibah

23 The word of the LORD came to me: [2]Mortal, there were two women, the daughters of one mother; [3]they played the whore in Egypt; they played the whore in their youth; their breasts were caressed there, and their virgin bosoms were fondled. [4]Oholah was the name of the elder and Oholibah the name of her sister. They became mine, and they bore sons and daughters. As for their names, Oholah is Samaria, and Oholibah is Jerusalem.

5 Oholah played the whore while she was mine; she lusted after her lovers the Assyrians, warriors[d] [6]clothed in blue, governors and commanders, all of them handsome young men, mounted horsemen. [7]She bestowed her favors upon them, the choicest men of Assyria all of them; and she defiled herself with all the idols of everyone for whom she lusted. [8]She did not give up her whorings that she had practiced since Egypt; for in her youth men had lain with her and fondled her virgin bosom and poured out their lust upon her. [9]Therefore I delivered her into the hands of her lovers, into the hands of the Assyrians, for whom she lusted. [10]These uncovered her nakedness; they seized

a Gk Syr Vg: Heb you   b Transposed from the end of the verse; compare verse 20   c Gk: Heb indignation. [25]A conspiracy of its prophets   d Meaning of Heb uncertain her sons and her daughters; and they killed her with the sword. Judgment was executed upon her, and she became a byword among women.

11 Her sister Oholibah saw this, yet she was more corrupt than she in her lusting and in her whorings, which were worse than those of her sister. ¹²She lusted after the Assyrians, governors and commanders, warriors *a* clothed in full armor, mounted horsemen, all of them handsome young men. ¹³And I saw that she was defiled; they both took the same way. ¹⁴But she carried her whorings further; she saw male figures carved on the wall, images of the Chaldeans portrayed in vermilion, ¹⁵with belts around their waists, with flowing turbans on their heads, all of them looking like officers— a picture of Babylonians whose native land was Chaldea. ¹⁶When she saw them she lusted after them, and sent messengers to them in Chaldea. ¹⁷And the Babylonians came to her into the bed of love, and they defiled her with their lust; and after she defiled herself with them, she turned from them in disgust. ¹⁸When she carried on her whorings so openly and flaunted her nakedness, I turned in disgust from her, as I had turned from her sister. ¹⁹Yet she increased her whorings, remembering the days of her youth, when she played the whore in the land of Egypt ²⁰and lusted after her paramours there, whose members were like those of donkeys, and whose emission was like that of stallions. ²¹Thus you longed for the lewdness of your youth, when the Egyptians *b* fondled your bosom and caressed *c* your young breasts.

22 Therefore, O Oholibah, thus says the Lord GOD: I will rouse against you your lovers from whom you turned in disgust, and I will bring them against you from every side: ²³the Babylonians and all the Chaldeans, Pekod and Shoa and Koa, and all the Assyrians with them, handsome young men, governors and commanders all of them, officers and warriors, *d* all of them riding on horses. ²⁴They shall come against you from the north *e* with chariots and wagons and a host of peoples; they shall set

themselves against you on every side with buckler, shield, and helmet, and I will commit the judgment to them, and they shall judge you according to their ordinances. ²⁵I will direct my indignation against you, in order that they may deal with you in fury. They shall cut off your nose and your ears, and your survivors shall fall by the sword. They shall seize your sons and your daughters, and your survivors shall be devoured by fire. ²⁶They shall also strip you of your clothes and take away your fine jewels. ²⁷So I will put an end to your lewdness and your whoring brought from the land of Egypt; you shall not long for them, or remember Egypt any more. ²⁸For thus says the Lord GOD: I will deliver you into the hands of those whom you hate, into the hands of those from whom you turned in disgust; ²⁹and they shall deal with you in hatred, and take away all the fruit of your labor, and leave you naked and bare, and the nakedness of your whorings shall be exposed. Your lewdness and your whorings ³⁰have brought this upon you, because you played the whore with the nations, and polluted yourself with their idols. ³¹You have gone the way of your sister; therefore I will give her cup into your hand. ³²Thus says the Lord GOD:

You shall drink your sister's cup,
  deep and wide;
you shall be scorned and derided,
  it holds so much.
33 You shall be filled with drunkenness and
    sorrow.

A cup of horror and desolation
  is the cup of your sister Samaria;
34 you shall drink it and drain it out,
    and gnaw its sherds,
    and tear out your breasts;

for I have spoken, says the Lord GOD. ³⁵Therefore thus says the Lord GOD: Because you have forgotten me and cast me behind your back, therefore bear the consequences of your lewdness and whorings.

36 The LORD said to me: Mortal, will you judge Oholah and Oholibah? Then declare to them their abominable deeds. ³⁷For they have

---

a Meaning of Heb uncertain   *b* Two Mss: MT *from Egypt*   *c* Cn: Heb *for the sake of*   *d* Compare verses 6 and 12: Heb *officers and called ones*   *e* Gk: Meaning of Heb uncertain committed adultery, and blood is on their hands; with their idols they have committed adultery; and they have even offered up to them for food the children whom they had borne to me. 38Moreover this they have done to me: they have defiled my sanctuary on the same day and profaned my sabbaths. 39For when they had slaughtered their children for their idols, on the same day they came into my sanctuary to profane it. This is what they did in my house.

40 They even sent for men to come from far away, to whom a messenger was sent, and they came. For them you bathed yourself, painted your eyes, and decked yourself with ornaments; 41you sat on a stately couch, with a table spread before it on which you had placed my incense and my oil. 42The sound of a raucous multitude was around her, with many of the rabble brought in drunken from the wilderness; and they put bracelets on the arms[a] of the women, and beautiful crowns upon their heads.

43 Then I said, Ah, she is worn out with adulteries, but they carry on their sexual acts with her. 44For they have gone in to her, as one goes in to a whore. Thus they went in to Oholah and to Oholibah, wanton women. 45But righteous judges shall declare them guilty of adultery and of bloodshed; because they are adulteresses and blood is on their hands.

46 For thus says the Lord GOD: Bring up an assembly against them, and make them an object of terror and of plunder. 47The assembly shall stone them and with their swords they shall cut them down; they shall kill their sons and their daughters, and burn up their houses. 48Thus will I put an end to lewdness in the land, so that all women may take warning and not commit lewdness as you have done. 49They shall repay you for your lewdness, and you shall bear the penalty for your sinful idolatry; and you shall know that I am the Lord GOD.

The Boiling Pot

24 In the ninth year, in the tenth month, on the tenth day of the month, the word of the LORD came to me: 2Mortal, write down the name of this day, this very day. The king of Babylon has laid siege to Jerusalem this very day. 3And utter an allegory to the rebellious house and say to them, Thus says the Lord GOD:

> Set on the pot, set it on,
>   pour in water also;
4   put in it the pieces,
>   all the good pieces, the thigh and the
>   shoulder;
>   fill it with choice bones.
5   Take the choicest one of the flock,
>   pile the logs[b] under it;
>   boil its pieces,[c]
>   seethe[d] also its bones in it.

6 Therefore thus says the Lord GOD:
> Woe to the bloody city,
>   the pot whose rust is in it,
>   whose rust has not gone out of it!
> Empty it piece by piece,
>   making no choice at all.[e]
7   For the blood she shed is inside it;
>   she placed it on a bare rock;
> she did not pour it out on the ground,
>   to cover it with earth.
8   To rouse my wrath, to take vengeance,
>   I have placed the blood she shed
>   on a bare rock,
>   so that it may not be covered.
9Therefore thus says the Lord GOD:
> Woe to the bloody city!
>   I will even make the pile great.
10   Heap up the logs, kindle the fire;
>   boil the meat well, mix in the spices,
>   let the bones be burned.
11   Stand it empty upon the coals,
>   so that it may become hot, its copper
>   glow,
>   its filth melt in it, its rust be
>   consumed.
12   In vain I have wearied myself;[f]
>   its thick rust does not depart.
>   To the fire with its rust![g]

---

a Heb *hands*   b Compare verse 10: Heb *the bones*   c Two Mss: Heb *its boilings*   d Cn: Heb *its bones seethe*
e Heb *piece, no lot has fallen on it*   f Cn: Meaning of Heb uncertain   g Meaning of Heb uncertain

13 Yet, when I cleansed you in your filthy
    lewdness,
      you did not become clean from your
        filth;
    you shall not again be cleansed
      until I have satisfied my fury upon
        you.
14I the LORD have spoken; the time is coming,
I will act. I will not refrain, I will not spare, I will
not relent. According to your ways and your doings I will judge you, says the Lord GOD.

Ezekiel's Bereavement

15 The word of the LORD came to me:
16Mortal, with one blow I am about to take
away from you the delight of your eyes; yet you
shall not mourn or weep, nor shall your tears
run down. 17Sigh, but not aloud; make no
mourning for the dead. Bind on your turban,
and put your sandals on your feet; do not cover your upper lip or eat the bread of mourners.*a*
18So I spoke to the people in the morning, and
at evening my wife died. And on the next
morning I did as I was commanded.

19 Then the people said to me, "Will you
not tell us what these things mean for us, that
you are acting this way?" 20Then I said to them:
The word of the LORD came to me: 21Say to
the house of Israel, Thus says the Lord GOD:
I will profane my sanctuary, the pride of your
power, the delight of your eyes, and your heart's
desire; and your sons and your daughters whom
you left behind shall fall by the sword. 22And
you shall do as I have done; you shall not cover your upper lip or eat the bread of mourners.*a*
23Your turbans shall be on your heads and your
sandals on your feet; you shall not mourn or
weep, but you shall pine away in your iniquities
and groan to one another. 24Thus Ezekiel shall
be a sign to you; you shall do just as he has
done. When this comes, then you shall know
that I am the Lord GOD.

25 And you, mortal, on the day when I take
from them their stronghold, their joy and glory, the delight of their eyes and their heart's affection, and also*b* their sons and their daugh-

ters, 26on that day, one who has escaped will
come to you to report to you the news. 27On
that day your mouth shall be opened to the one
who has escaped, and you shall speak and no
longer be silent. So you shall be a sign to them;
and they shall know that I am the LORD.

Proclamation against Ammon

25 The word of the LORD came to me:
2Mortal, set your face toward the Ammonites and prophesy against them. 3Say to the
Ammonites, Hear the word of the Lord GOD:
Thus says the Lord GOD, Because you said,
"Aha!" over my sanctuary when it was profaned, and over the land of Israel when it was
made desolate, and over the house of Judah
when it went into exile; 4therefore I am handing you over to the people of the east for a possession. They shall set their encampments
among you and pitch their tents in your midst;
they shall eat your fruit, and they shall drink
your milk. 5I will make Rabbah a pasture for
camels and Ammon a fold for flocks. Then you
shall know that I am the LORD. 6For thus says
the Lord GOD: Because you have clapped your
hands and stamped your feet and rejoiced with
all the malice within you against the land of Israel, 7therefore I have stretched out my hand
against you, and will hand you over as plunder
to the nations. I will cut you off from the peoples and will make you perish out of the countries; I will destroy you. Then you shall know
that I am the LORD.

Proclamation against Moab

8 Thus says the Lord GOD: Because Moab*c*
said, The house of Judah is like all the other nations, 9therefore I will lay open the flank of
Moab from the towns*d* on its frontier, the glory of the country, Beth-jeshimoth, Baal-meon,
and Kiriathaim. 10I will give it along with Ammon to the people of the east as a possession.
Thus Ammon shall be remembered no more
among the nations, 11and I will execute judgments upon Moab. Then they shall know that
I am the LORD.

---

a Vg Tg: Heb *of men*   *b* Heb lacks *and also*   *c* Gk Old Latin: Heb *Moab and Seir*   *d* Heb *towns from its towns*

Proclamation against Edom

12 Thus says the Lord GOD: Because Edom acted revengefully against the house of Judah and has grievously offended in taking vengeance upon them, 13therefore thus says the Lord GOD, I will stretch out my hand against Edom, and cut off from it humans and animals, and I will make it desolate; from Teman even to Dedan they shall fall by the sword. 14I will lay my vengeance upon Edom by the hand of my people Israel; and they shall act in Edom according to my anger and according to my wrath; and they shall know my vengeance, says the Lord GOD.

Proclamation against Philistia

15 Thus says the Lord GOD: Because with unending hostilities the Philistines acted in vengeance, and with malice of heart took revenge in destruction; 16therefore thus says the Lord GOD, I will stretch out my hand against the Philistines, cut off the Cherethites, and destroy the rest of the seacoast. 17I will execute great vengeance on them with wrathful punishments. Then they shall know that I am the LORD, when I lay my vengeance on them.

Proclamation against Tyre

26 In the eleventh year, on the first day of the month, the word of the LORD came to me: 2Mortal, because Tyre said concerning Jerusalem,

"Aha, broken is the gateway of the
    peoples;
  it has swung open to me;
I shall be replenished,
  now that it is wasted,"

3therefore, thus says the Lord GOD:
  See, I am against you, O Tyre!
  I will hurl many nations against you,
    as the sea hurls its waves.
4 They shall destroy the walls of Tyre
    and break down its towers.
  I will scrape its soil from it
    and make it a bare rock.
5 It shall become, in the midst of the sea,
    a place for spreading nets.
I have spoken, says the Lord GOD.

It shall become plunder for the nations,
6   and its daughter-towns in the country
    shall be killed by the sword.
Then they shall know that I am the LORD.

7 For thus says the Lord GOD: I will bring against Tyre from the north King Nebuchadrezzar of Babylon, king of kings, together with horses, chariots, cavalry, and a great and powerful army.
8 Your daughter-towns in the country
    he shall put to the sword.
  He shall set up a siege wall against you,
    cast up a ramp against you,
    and raise a roof of shields against
      you.
9 He shall direct the shock of his battering
    rams against your walls
  and break down your towers with his
    axes.
10 His horses shall be so many
    that their dust shall cover you.
  At the noise of cavalry, wheels, and
    chariots
  your very walls shall shake,
  when he enters your gates
    like those entering a breached city.
11 With the hoofs of his horses
    he shall trample all your streets.
  He shall put your people to the sword,
    and your strong pillars shall fall to the
      ground.
12 They will plunder your riches
    and loot your merchandise;
  they shall break down your walls
    and destroy your fine houses.
  Your stones and timber and soil
    they shall cast into the water.
13 I will silence the music of your songs;
    the sound of your lyres shall be heard
      no more.
14 I will make you a bare rock;
    you shall be a place for spreading nets.
  You shall never again be rebuilt,
    for I the LORD have spoken,
    says the Lord GOD.

15 Thus says the Lord GOD to Tyre: Shall not the coastlands shake at the sound of your fall, when the wounded groan, when slaughter

goes on within you? [16]Then all the princes of the sea shall step down from their thrones; they shall remove their robes and strip off their embroidered garments. They shall clothe themselves with trembling, and shall sit on the ground; they shall tremble every moment, and be appalled at you. [17]And they shall raise a lamentation over you, and say to you:

How you have vanished[a] from the seas,
 O city renowned,
once mighty on the sea,
 you and your inhabitants,[b]
who imposed your[c] terror
 on all the mainland![d]
18 Now the coastlands tremble
 on the day of your fall;
the coastlands by the sea
 are dismayed at your passing.

19 For thus says the Lord GOD: When I make you a city laid waste, like cities that are not inhabited, when I bring up the deep over you, and the great waters cover you, [20]then I will thrust you down with those who descend into the Pit, to the people of long ago, and I will make you live in the world below, among primeval ruins, with those who go down to the Pit, so that you will not be inhabited or have a place[e] in the land of the living. [21]I will bring you to a dreadful end, and you shall be no more; though sought for, you will never be found again, says the Lord GOD.

Lamentation over Tyre

27 The word of the LORD came to me: [2]Now you, mortal, raise a lamentation over Tyre, [3]and say to Tyre, which sits at the entrance to the sea, merchant of the peoples on many coastlands, Thus says the Lord GOD:

O Tyre, you have said,
 "I am perfect in beauty."
4 Your borders are in the heart of the seas;
 your builders made perfect your
  beauty.
5 They made all your planks
 of fir trees from Senir;

they took a cedar from Lebanon
 to make a mast for you.
6 From oaks of Bashan
 they made your oars;
they made your deck of pines[f]
 from the coasts of Cyprus,
 inlaid with ivory.
7 Of fine embroidered linen from Egypt
 was your sail,
 serving as your ensign;
blue and purple from the coasts of
 Elishah
 was your awning.
8 The inhabitants of Sidon and Arvad
 were your rowers;
skilled men of Zemer[g] were within you,
 they were your pilots.
9 The elders of Gebal and its artisans were
  within you,
 caulking your seams;
all the ships of the sea with their
  mariners were within you,
 to barter for your wares.
10 Paras[h] and Lud and Put
 were in your army,
 your mighty warriors;
they hung shield and helmet in you;
 they gave you splendor.
11 Men of Arvad and Helech[i]
 were on your walls all around;
men of Gamad were at your towers.
They hung their quivers all around your
  walls;
 they made perfect your beauty.

12 Tarshish did business with you out of the abundance of your great wealth; silver, iron, tin, and lead they exchanged for your wares. [13]Javan, Tubal, and Meshech traded with you; they exchanged human beings and vessels of bronze for your merchandise. [14]Beth-togarmah exchanged for your wares horses, war horses, and mules. [15]The Rhodians[j] traded with you; many coastlands were your own special markets; they brought you in payment ivory tusks and ebony. [16]Edom[k] did business with

---

a Gk OL Aquila: Heb *have vanished, O inhabited one,* *b* Heb *it and its inhabitants* *c* Heb *their* *d* Cn: Heb *its inhabitants* *e* Gk: Heb *I will give beauty* *f* Or *boxwood* *g* Cn Compare Gen 10.18: Heb *your skilled men, O Tyre* *h* Or *Persia* *i* Or *and your army* *j* Gk: Heb *The Dedanites* *k* Another reading is *Aram* you because of your abundant goods; they exchanged for your wares turquoise, purple, embroidered work, fine linen, coral, and rubies. ¹⁷Judah and the land of Israel traded with you; they exchanged for your merchandise wheat from Minnith, millet,ᵃ honey, oil, and balm. ¹⁸Damascus traded with you for your abundant goods—because of your great wealth of every kind—wine of Helbon, and white wool. ¹⁹Vedan and Javan from Uzalᵃ entered into trade for your wares; wrought iron, cassia, and sweet cane were bartered for your merchandise. ²⁰Dedan traded with you in saddlecloths for riding. ²¹Arabia and all the princes of Kedar were your favored dealers in lambs, rams, and goats; in these they did business with you. ²²The merchants of Sheba and Raamah traded with you; they exchanged for your wares the best of all kinds of spices, and all precious stones, and gold. ²³Haran, Canneh, Eden, the merchants of Sheba, Asshur, and Chilmad traded with you. ²⁴These traded with you in choice garments, in clothes of blue and embroidered work, and in carpets of colored material, bound with cords and made secure; in these they traded with you.ᵇ ²⁵The ships of Tarshish traveled for you in your trade.

So you were filled and heavily laden
    in the heart of the seas.
²⁶ Your rowers have brought you
    into the high seas.
The east wind has wrecked you
    in the heart of the seas.
²⁷ Your riches, your wares, your
        merchandise,
    your mariners and your pilots,
your caulkers, your dealers in
        merchandise,
    and all your warriors within you,
with all the company
    that is with you,
sink into the heart of the seas
    on the day of your ruin.
²⁸ At the sound of the cry of your pilots
    the countryside shakes,
²⁹ and down from their ships

come all that handle the oar.
The mariners and all the pilots of the sea
    stand on the shore
³⁰ and wail aloud over you,
    and cry bitterly.
They throw dust on their heads
    and wallow in ashes;
³¹ they make themselves bald for you,
    and put on sackcloth,
and they weep over you in bitterness of
        soul,
    with bitter mourning.
³² In their wailing they raise a lamentation
        for you,
    and lament over you:
"Who was ever destroyedᶜ like Tyre
    in the midst of the sea?
³³ When your wares came from the seas,
    you satisfied many peoples;
with your abundant wealth and
        merchandise
    you enriched the kings of the earth.
³⁴ Now you are wrecked by the seas,
    in the depths of the waters;
your merchandise and all your crew
    have sunk with you.
³⁵ All the inhabitants of the coastlands
    are appalled at you;
and their kings are horribly afraid,
    their faces are convulsed.
³⁶ The merchants among the peoples hiss
        at you;
    you have come to a dreadful end
    and shall be no more forever."

Proclamation against the King of Tyre

28 The word of the LORD came to me: ²Mortal, say to the prince of Tyre, Thus says the Lord GOD:

Because your heart is proud
    and you have said, "I am a god;
I sit in the seat of the gods,
    in the heart of the seas,"
yet you are but a mortal, and no god,
    though you compare your mind
    with the mind of a god.

---

a Meaning of Heb uncertain   *b* Cn: Heb *in your market*   *c* Tg Vg: Heb *like silence*

3 You are indeed wiser than Daniel;*a*
no secret is hidden from you;
4 by your wisdom and your understanding
you have amassed wealth for yourself,
and have gathered gold and silver
into your treasuries.
5 By your great wisdom in trade
you have increased your wealth,
and your heart has become proud in
your wealth.
6 Therefore thus says the Lord GOD:
Because you compare your mind
with the mind of a god,
7 therefore, I will bring strangers against
you,
the most terrible of the nations;
they shall draw their swords against the
beauty of your wisdom
and defile your splendor.
8 They shall thrust you down to the Pit,
and you shall die a violent death
in the heart of the seas.
9 Will you still say, "I am a god,"
in the presence of those who kill you,
though you are but a mortal, and no god,
in the hands of those who wound
you?
10 You shall die the death of the
uncircumcised
by the hand of foreigners;
for I have spoken, says the Lord GOD.

Lamentation over the King of Tyre

11 Moreover the word of the LORD came
to me: 12Mortal, raise a lamentation over the
king of Tyre, and say to him, Thus says the
Lord GOD:
You were the signet of perfection,*b*
full of wisdom and perfect in beauty.
13 You were in Eden, the garden of God;
every precious stone was your
covering,
carnelian, chrysolite, and moonstone,
beryl, onyx, and jasper,
sapphire,*c* turquoise, and emerald;
and worked in gold were your settings

and your engravings.*b*
On the day that you were created
they were prepared.
14 With an anointed cherub as guardian I
placed you;*b*
you were on the holy mountain of
God;
you walked among the stones of fire.
15 You were blameless in your ways
from the day that you were created,
until iniquity was found in you.
16 In the abundance of your trade
you were filled with violence, and you
sinned;
so I cast you as a profane thing from the
mountain of God,
and the guardian cherub drove you
out
from among the stones of fire.
17 Your heart was proud because of your
beauty;
you corrupted your wisdom for the
sake of your splendor.
I cast you to the ground;
I exposed you before kings,
to feast their eyes on you.
18 By the multitude of your iniquities,
in the unrighteousness of your trade,
you profaned your sanctuaries.
So I brought out fire from within you;
it consumed you,
and I turned you to ashes on the earth
in the sight of all who saw you.
19 All who know you among the peoples
are appalled at you;
you have come to a dreadful end
and shall be no more forever.

Proclamation against Sidon

20 The word of the LORD came to me:
21Mortal, set your face toward Sidon, and
prophesy against it, 22and say, Thus says the
Lord GOD:
I am against you, O Sidon,
and I will gain glory in your midst.
They shall know that I am the LORD

a Or, as otherwise read, *Daniel*   *b* Meaning of Heb uncertain   *c* Or *lapis lazuli*

when I execute judgments in it,
and manifest my holiness in it;

23 for I will send pestilence into it,
and bloodshed into its streets;
and the dead shall fall in its midst,
by the sword that is against it on every
side.

And they shall know that I am the LORD.
24 The house of Israel shall no longer find
a pricking brier or a piercing thorn among all
their neighbors who have treated them with
contempt. And they shall know that I am the
Lord GOD.

Future Blessing for Israel

25 Thus says the Lord GOD: When I gather the house of Israel from the peoples among
whom they are scattered, and manifest my holiness in them in the sight of the nations, then
they shall settle on their own soil that I gave to
my servant Jacob. 26They shall live in safety in
it, and shall build houses and plant vineyards.
They shall live in safety, when I execute judgments upon all their neighbors who have treated them with contempt. And they shall know
that I am the LORD their God.

Proclamation against Egypt

29 In the tenth year, in the tenth month,
on the twelfth day of the month, the
word of the LORD came to me: 2Mortal, set
your face against Pharaoh king of Egypt, and
prophesy against him and against all Egypt;
3speak, and say, Thus says the Lord GOD:

I am against you,
Pharaoh king of Egypt,
the great dragon sprawling
in the midst of its channels,
saying, "My Nile is my own;
I made it for myself."

4 I will put hooks in your jaws,
and make the fish of your channels
stick to your scales.
I will draw you up from your channels,
with all the fish of your channels
sticking to your scales.

5 I will fling you into the wilderness,
you and all the fish of your channels;
you shall fall in the open field,
and not be gathered and buried.
To the animals of the earth and to the
birds of the air
I have given you as food.

6 Then all the inhabitants of Egypt shall
know
that I am the LORD

because you*a* were a staff of reed
to the house of Israel;

7 when they grasped you with the hand,
you broke,
and tore all their shoulders;
and when they leaned on you, you broke,
and made all their legs unsteady.*b*

8 Therefore, thus says the Lord GOD: I will
bring a sword upon you, and will cut off from
you human being and animal; 9and the land of
Egypt shall be a desolation and a waste. Then
they shall know that I am the LORD.

Because you*c* said, "The Nile is mine, and I
made it," 10therefore, I am against you, and
against your channels, and I will make the land
of Egypt an utter waste and desolation, from
Migdol to Syene, as far as the border of
Ethiopia.*d* 11No human foot shall pass through
it, and no animal foot shall pass through it; it
shall be uninhabited forty years. 12I will make the
land of Egypt a desolation among desolated
countries; and her cities shall be a desolation
forty years among cities that are laid waste. I will
scatter the Egyptians among the nations, and
disperse them among the countries.

13 Further, thus says the Lord GOD: At the
end of forty years I will gather the Egyptians
from the peoples among whom they were scattered; 14and I will restore the fortunes of Egypt,
and bring them back to the land of Pathros, the
land of their origin; and there they shall be a
lowly kingdom. 15It shall be the most lowly of
the kingdoms, and never again exalt itself above
the nations; and I will make them so small that
they will never again rule over the nations. 16The
Egyptians*e* shall never again be the reliance of

a Gk Syr Vg: Heb *they*   *b* Syr: Heb *stand*   *c* Gk Syr Vg: Heb *he*   *d* Or *Nubia;* Heb *Cush*   *e* Heb *It* the house of Israel; they will recall their iniquity, when they turned to them for aid. Then they shall know that I am the Lord GOD.

Babylonia Will Plunder Egypt

17 In the twenty-seventh year, in the first month, on the first day of the month, the word of the LORD came to me: [18]Mortal, King Nebuchadrezzar of Babylon made his army labor hard against Tyre; every head was made bald and every shoulder was rubbed bare; yet neither he nor his army got anything from Tyre to pay for the labor that he had expended against it. [19]Therefore thus says the Lord GOD: I will give the land of Egypt to King Nebuchadrezzar of Babylon; and he shall carry off its wealth and despoil it and plunder it; and it shall be the wages for his army. [20]I have given him the land of Egypt as his payment for which he labored, because they worked for me, says the Lord GOD.

21 On that day I will cause a horn to sprout up for the house of Israel, and I will open your lips among them. Then they shall know that I am the LORD.

Lamentation for Egypt

30 The word of the LORD came to me: [2]Mortal, prophesy, and say, Thus says the Lord GOD:
Wail, "Alas for the day!"
3   For a day is near,
    the day of the LORD is near;
  it will be a day of clouds,
    a time of doom[a] for the nations.
4   A sword shall come upon Egypt,
    and anguish shall be in Ethiopia,[b]
  when the slain fall in Egypt,
    and its wealth is carried away,
    and its foundations are torn down.
[5]Ethiopia,[b] and Put, and Lud, and all Arabia, and Libya,[c] and the people of the allied land[d] shall fall with them by the sword.

6   Thus says the LORD:
  Those who support Egypt shall fall,

    and its proud might shall come down;
  from Migdol to Syene
    they shall fall within it by the sword,
  says the Lord GOD.
7   They shall be desolated among other
    desolated countries,
  and their cities shall lie among cities
    laid waste.
8   Then they shall know that I am the
    LORD,
    when I have set fire to Egypt,
    and all who help it are broken.

9 On that day, messengers shall go out from me in ships to terrify the unsuspecting Ethiopians;[e] and anguish shall come upon them on the day of Egypt's doom;[f] for it is coming!

10   Thus says the Lord GOD:
  I will put an end to the hordes of Egypt,
    by the hand of King Nebuchadrezzar
      of Babylon.
11   He and his people with him, the most
    terrible of the nations,
    shall be brought in to destroy the land;
  and they shall draw their swords against
    Egypt,
    and fill the land with the slain.
12   I will dry up the channels,
    and will sell the land into the hand of
      evildoers;
  I will bring desolation upon the land and
    everything in it
    by the hand of foreigners;
  I the LORD have spoken.

13   Thus says the Lord GOD:
  I will destroy the idols
    and put an end to the images in
      Memphis;
  there shall no longer be a prince in the
    land of Egypt;
    so I will put fear in the land of Egypt.
14   I will make Pathros a desolation,
    and will set fire to Zoan,
    and will execute acts of judgment on
      Thebes.

---

a Heb lacks *of doom*   *b* Or *Nubia*; Heb *Cush*   *c* Compare Gk Syr Vg: Heb *Cub*   *d* Meaning of Heb uncertain
e Or *Nubians*; Heb *Cush*   *f* Heb *the day of Egypt*

15 I will pour my wrath upon Pelusium,
      the stronghold of Egypt,
      and cut off the hordes of Thebes.
16 I will set fire to Egypt;
      Pelusium shall be in great agony;
    Thebes shall be breached,
      and Memphis face adversaries by day.
17 The young men of On and of Pi-beseth
        shall fall by the sword;
      and the cities themselves*a* shall go into
        captivity.
18 At Tehaphnehes the day shall be dark,
      when I break there the dominion of
        Egypt,
    and its proud might shall come to an
        end;
      the city*b* shall be covered by a cloud,
      and its daughter-towns shall go into
        captivity.
19 Thus I will execute acts of judgment on
        Egypt.
      Then they shall know that I am the
        LORD.

Proclamation against Pharaoh

20 In the eleventh year, in the first month,
on the seventh day of the month, the word of
the LORD came to me: 21Mortal, I have broken
the arm of Pharaoh king of Egypt; it has not
been bound up for healing or wrapped with a
bandage, so that it may become strong to wield
the sword. 22Therefore thus says the Lord
GOD: I am against Pharaoh king of Egypt,
and will break his arms, both the strong arm
and the one that was broken; and I will make
the sword fall from his hand. 23I will scatter the
Egyptians among the nations, and disperse
them throughout the lands. 24I will strengthen
the arms of the king of Babylon, and put my
sword in his hand; but I will break the arms of
Pharaoh, and he will groan before him with the
groans of one mortally wounded. 25I will
strengthen the arms of the king of Babylon,
but the arms of Pharaoh shall fall. And they
shall know that I am the LORD, when I put my
sword into the hand of the king of Babylon.

He shall stretch it out against the land of Egypt,
26and I will scatter the Egyptians among the nations and disperse them throughout the countries. Then they shall know that I am the LORD.

The Lofty Cedar

31 In the eleventh year, in the third
    month, on the first day of the month,
the word of the LORD came to me: 2Mortal, say
to Pharaoh king of Egypt and to his hordes:
      Whom are you like in your greatness?
3   Consider Assyria, a cedar of Lebanon,
    with fair branches and forest shade,
      and of great height,
      its top among the clouds.*c*
4   The waters nourished it,
      the deep made it grow tall,
    making its rivers flow*d*
      around the place it was planted,
    sending forth its streams
      to all the trees of the field.
5   So it towered high
      above all the trees of the field;
    its boughs grew large
      and its branches long,
      from abundant water in its shoots.
6   All the birds of the air
      made their nests in its boughs;
    under its branches all the animals of the
        field
      gave birth to their young;
    and in its shade
      all great nations lived.
7   It was beautiful in its greatness,
      in the length of its branches;
    for its roots went down
      to abundant water.
8   The cedars in the garden of God could
        not rival it,
      nor the fir trees equal its boughs;
    the plane trees were as nothing
      compared with its branches;
    no tree in the garden of God
      was like it in beauty.
9   I made it beautiful
      with its mass of branches,

---

a Heb *and they*   *b* Heb *she*   *c* Gk: Heb *thick boughs*   *d* Gk: Heb *rivers going*

the envy of all the trees of Eden
　　that were in the garden of God.

10　Therefore thus says the Lord GOD: Because it *a* towered high and set its top among the clouds, *b* and its heart was proud of its height, [11]I gave it into the hand of the prince of the nations; he has dealt with it as its wickedness deserves. I have cast it out. [12]Foreigners from the most terrible of the nations have cut it down and left it. On the mountains and in all the valleys its branches have fallen, and its boughs lie broken in all the watercourses of the land; and all the peoples of the earth went away from its shade and left it.

13　On its fallen trunk settle
　　all the birds of the air,
　and among its boughs lodge
　　all the wild animals.

[14]All this is in order that no trees by the waters may grow to lofty height or set their tops among the clouds, *b* and that no trees that drink water may reach up to them in height.

For all of them are handed over to
　　death,
　　to the world below;
　along with all mortals,
　　with those who go down to the Pit.

15　Thus says the Lord GOD: On the day it went down to Sheol I closed the deep over it and covered it; I restrained its rivers, and its mighty waters were checked. I clothed Lebanon in gloom for it, and all the trees of the field fainted because of it. [16]I made the nations quake at the sound of its fall, when I cast it down to Sheol with those who go down to the Pit; and all the trees of Eden, the choice and best of Lebanon, all that were well watered, were consoled in the world below. [17]They also went down to Sheol with it, to those killed by the sword, along with its allies, *c* those who lived in its shade among the nations.

18　Which among the trees of Eden was like you in glory and in greatness? Now you shall be brought down with the trees of Eden to the world below; you shall lie among the uncircumcised, with those who are killed by the sword. This is Pharaoh and all his horde, says the Lord GOD.

Lamentation over Pharaoh and Egypt

32　In the twelfth year, in the twelfth month, on the first day of the month, the word of the LORD came to me: [2]Mortal, raise a lamentation over Pharaoh king of Egypt, and say to him:

You consider yourself a lion among the
　　nations,
　　but you are like a dragon in the seas;
　you thrash about in your streams,
　　trouble the water with your feet,
　　and foul your *d* streams.

3　Thus says the Lord GOD:
　In an assembly of many peoples
　　I will throw my net over you;
　　and I *e* will haul you up in my dragnet.

4　I will throw you on the ground,
　　on the open field I will fling you,
　and will cause all the birds of the air to
　　settle on you,
　　and I will let the wild animals of the
　　　whole earth gorge themselves
　　　with you.

5　I will strew your flesh on the mountains,
　　and fill the valleys with your carcass. *f*

6　I will drench the land with your flowing
　　blood
　　up to the mountains,
　　and the watercourses will be filled
　　　with you.

7　When I blot you out, I will cover the
　　heavens,
　　and make their stars dark;
　I will cover the sun with a cloud,
　　and the moon shall not give its light.

8　All the shining lights of the heavens
　　I will darken above you,
　　and put darkness on your land,
　　　　　says the Lord GOD.

9　I will trouble the hearts of many
　　peoples,
　　as I carry you captive *g* among the
　　　nations,

---

a Syr Vg: Heb *you*　　*b* Gk: Heb *thick boughs*　　*c* Heb *its arms*　　*d* Heb *their*　　*e* Gk Vg: Heb *they*
f Symmachus Syr Vg: Heb *your height*　　*g* Gk: Heb *bring your destruction*

into countries you have not known.

10 I will make many peoples appalled at
you;
their kings shall shudder because of
you.
When I brandish my sword before them,
they shall tremble every moment
for their lives, each one of them,
on the day of your downfall.

11 For thus says the Lord GOD:
The sword of the king of Babylon shall
come against you.

12 I will cause your hordes to fall
by the swords of mighty ones,
all of them most terrible among the
nations.
They shall bring to ruin the pride of
Egypt,
and all its hordes shall perish.

13 I will destroy all its livestock
from beside abundant waters;
and no human foot shall trouble them
any more,
nor shall the hoofs of cattle trouble
them.

14 Then I will make their waters clear,
and cause their streams to run like oil,
says the Lord GOD.

15 When I make the land of Egypt desolate
and when the land is stripped of all
that fills it,
when I strike down all who live in it,
then they shall know that I am the
LORD.

16 This is a lamentation; it shall be chanted.
The women of the nations shall chant
it.
Over Egypt and all its hordes they shall
chant it,
says the Lord GOD.

Dirge over Egypt

17 In the twelfth year, in the first month,*a*
on the fifteenth day of the month, the word of
the LORD came to me:

18 Mortal, wail over the hordes of Egypt,
and send them down,
with Egypt *b* and the daughters of
majestic nations,
to the world below,
with those who go down to the Pit.

19 "Whom do you surpass in beauty?
Go down! Be laid to rest with the
uncircumcised!"

20 They shall fall among those who are killed by
the sword. Egypt *c* has been handed over to
the sword; carry away both it and its hordes.
21 The mighty chiefs shall speak of them, with
their helpers, out of the midst of Sheol: "They
have come down, they lie still, the uncircumcised, killed by the sword."

22 Assyria is there, and all its company,
their graves all around it, all of them killed, fallen by the sword. 23 Their graves are set in the
uttermost parts of the Pit. Its company is all
around its grave, all of them killed, fallen by the
sword, who spread terror in the land of the living.

24 Elam is there, and all its hordes around
its grave; all of them killed, fallen by the sword,
who went down uncircumcised into the world
below, who spread terror in the land of the living. They bear their shame with those who go
down to the Pit. 25 They have made Elam *b* a bed
among the slain with all its hordes, their graves
all around it, all of them uncircumcised, killed
by the sword; for terror of them was spread in
the land of the living, and they bear their shame
with those who go down to the Pit; they are
placed among the slain.

26 Meshech and Tubal are there, and all
their multitude, their graves all around them, all
of them uncircumcised, killed by the sword; for
they spread terror in the land of the living.
27 And they do not lie with the fallen warriors
of long ago *d* who went down to Sheol with
their weapons of war, whose swords were laid
under their heads, and whose shields *e* are upon
their bones; for the terror of the warriors was
in the land of the living. 28 So you shall be broken and lie among the uncircumcised, with
those who are killed by the sword.

29 Edom is there, its kings and all its princes, who for all their might are laid with those who are killed by the sword; they lie with the uncircumcised, with those who go down to the Pit.

30 The princes of the north are there, all of them, and all the Sidonians, who have gone down in shame with the slain, for all the terror that they caused by their might; they lie uncircumcised with those who are killed by the sword, and bear their shame with those who go down to the Pit.

31 When Pharaoh sees them, he will be consoled for all his hordes—Pharaoh and all his army, killed by the sword, says the Lord GOD. 32For he*a* spread terror in the land of the living; therefore he shall be laid to rest among the uncircumcised, with those who are slain by the sword—Pharaoh and all his multitude, says the Lord GOD.

Ezekiel Israel's Sentry

33 The word of the LORD came to me: 2O Mortal, speak to your people and say to them, If I bring the sword upon a land, and the people of the land take one of their number as their sentinel; 3and if the sentinel sees the sword coming upon the land and blows the trumpet and warns the people; 4then if any who hear the sound of the trumpet do not take warning, and the sword comes and takes them away, their blood shall be upon their own heads. 5They heard the sound of the trumpet and did not take warning; their blood shall be upon themselves. But if they had taken warning, they would have saved their lives. 6But if the sentinel sees the sword coming and does not blow the trumpet, so that the people are not warned, and the sword comes and takes any of them, they are taken away in their iniquity, but their blood I will require at the sentinel's hand.

7 So you, mortal, I have made a sentinel for the house of Israel; whenever you hear a word from my mouth, you shall give them warning from me. 8If I say to the wicked, "O wicked ones, you shall surely die," and you do not speak to warn the wicked to turn from their ways, the wicked shall die in their iniquity, but their blood I will require at your hand. 9But if you warn the wicked to turn from their ways, and they do not turn from their ways, the wicked shall die in their iniquity, but you will have saved your life.

God's Justice and Mercy

10 Now you, mortal, say to the house of Israel, Thus you have said: "Our transgressions and our sins weigh upon us, and we waste away because of them; how then can we live?" 11Say to them, As I live, says the Lord GOD, I have no pleasure in the death of the wicked, but that the wicked turn from their ways and live; turn back, turn back from your evil ways; for why will you die, O house of Israel? 12And you, mortal, say to your people, The righteousness of the righteous shall not save them when they transgress; and as for the wickedness of the wicked, it shall not make them stumble when they turn from their wickedness; and the righteous shall not be able to live by their righteousness*b* when they sin. 13Though I say to the righteous that they shall surely live, yet if they trust in their righteousness and commit iniquity, none of their righteous deeds shall be remembered; but in the iniquity that they have committed they shall die. 14Again, though I say to the wicked, "You shall surely die," yet if they turn from their sin and do what is lawful and right— 15if the wicked restore the pledge, give back what they have taken by robbery, and walk in the statutes of life, committing no iniquity—they shall surely live, they shall not die. 16None of the sins that they have committed shall be remembered against them; they have done what is lawful and right, they shall surely live.

17 Yet your people say, "The way of the Lord is not just," when it is their own way that is not just. 18When the righteous turn from their righteousness, and commit iniquity, they shall die for it.*c* 19And when the wicked turn

a Cn: Heb *I*   *b* Heb *by it*   *c* Heb *them*

from their wickedness, and do what is lawful and right, they shall live by it.*a* 20Yet you say, "The way of the Lord is not just." O house of Israel, I will judge all of you according to your ways!

The Fall of Jerusalem

21 In the twelfth year of our exile, in the tenth month, on the fifth day of the month, someone who had escaped from Jerusalem came to me and said, "The city has fallen." 22Now the hand of the LORD had been upon me the evening before the fugitive came; but he had opened my mouth by the time the fugitive came to me in the morning; so my mouth was opened, and I was no longer unable to speak.

The Survivors in Judah

23 The word of the LORD came to me: 24Mortal, the inhabitants of these waste places in the land of Israel keep saying, "Abraham was only one man, yet he got possession of the land; but we are many; the land is surely given us to possess." 25Therefore say to them, Thus says the Lord GOD: You eat flesh with the blood, and lift up your eyes to your idols, and shed blood; shall you then possess the land? 26You depend on your swords, you commit abominations, and each of you defiles his neighbor's wife; shall you then possess the land? 27Say this to them, Thus says the Lord GOD: As I live, surely those who are in the waste places shall fall by the sword; and those who are in the open field I will give to the wild animals to be devoured; and those who are in strongholds and in caves shall die by pestilence. 28I will make the land a desolation and a waste, and its proud might shall come to an end; and the mountains of Israel shall be so desolate that no one will pass through. 29Then they shall know that I am the LORD, when I have made the land a desolation and a waste because of all their abominations that they have committed.

30 As for you, mortal, your people who talk together about you by the walls, and at the doors of the houses, say to one another, each to a neighbor, "Come and hear what the word is that comes from the LORD." 31They come to you as people come, and they sit before you as my people, and they hear your words, but they will not obey them. For flattery is on their lips, but their heart is set on their gain. 32To them you are like a singer of love songs,*b* one who has a beautiful voice and plays well on an instrument; they hear what you say, but they will not do it. 33When this comes—and come it will!—then they shall know that a prophet has been among them.

Israel's False Shepherds

34 The word of the LORD came to me: 2Mortal, prophesy against the shepherds of Israel: prophesy, and say to them—to the shepherds: Thus says the Lord GOD: Ah, you shepherds of Israel who have been feeding yourselves! Should not shepherds feed the sheep? 3You eat the fat, you clothe yourselves with the wool, you slaughter the fatlings; but you do not feed the sheep. 4You have not strengthened the weak, you have not healed the sick, you have not bound up the injured, you have not brought back the strayed, you have not sought the lost, but with force and harshness you have ruled them. 5So they were scattered, because there was no shepherd; and scattered, they became food for all the wild animals. 6My sheep were scattered, they wandered over all the mountains and on every high hill; my sheep were scattered over all the face of the earth, with no one to search or seek for them.

7 Therefore, you shepherds, hear the word of the LORD: 8As I live, says the Lord GOD, because my sheep have become a prey, and my sheep have become food for all the wild animals, since there was no shepherd; and because my shepherds have not searched for my sheep, but the shepherds have fed themselves, and have not fed my sheep; 9therefore, you shepherds, hear the word of the LORD: 10Thus says the Lord GOD, I am against the shepherds; and I will demand my sheep at their

a Heb *them*   *b* Cn: Heb *like a love song*

hand, and put a stop to their feeding the sheep; no longer shall the shepherds feed themselves. I will rescue my sheep from their mouths, so that they may not be food for them.

God, the True Shepherd

11 For thus says the Lord GOD: I myself will search for my sheep, and will seek them out. 12As shepherds seek out their flocks when they are among their scattered sheep, so I will seek out my sheep. I will rescue them from all the places to which they have been scattered on a day of clouds and thick darkness. 13I will bring them out from the peoples and gather them from the countries, and will bring them into their own land; and I will feed them on the mountains of Israel, by the watercourses, and in all the inhabited parts of the land. 14I will feed them with good pasture, and the mountain heights of Israel shall be their pasture; there they shall lie down in good grazing land, and they shall feed on rich pasture on the mountains of Israel. 15I myself will be the shepherd of my sheep, and I will make them lie down, says the Lord GOD. 16I will seek the lost, and I will bring back the strayed, and I will bind up the injured, and I will strengthen the weak, but the fat and the strong I will destroy. I will feed them with justice.

17 As for you, my flock, thus says the Lord GOD: I shall judge between sheep and sheep, between rams and goats: 18Is it not enough for you to feed on the good pasture, but you must tread down with your feet the rest of your pasture? When you drink of clear water, must you foul the rest with your feet? 19And must my sheep eat what you have trodden with your feet, and drink what you have fouled with your feet?

20 Therefore, thus says the Lord GOD to them: I myself will judge between the fat sheep and the lean sheep. 21Because you pushed with flank and shoulder, and butted at all the weak animals with your horns until you scattered them far and wide, 22I will save my flock, and

they shall no longer be ravaged; and I will judge between sheep and sheep.

23 I will set up over them one shepherd, my servant David, and he shall feed them: he shall feed them and be their shepherd. 24And I, the LORD, will be their God, and my servant David shall be prince among them; I, the LORD, have spoken.

25 I will make with them a covenant of peace and banish wild animals from the land, so that they may live in the wild and sleep in the woods securely. 26I will make them and the region around my hill a blessing; and I will send down the showers in their season; they shall be showers of blessing. 27The trees of the field shall yield their fruit, and the earth shall yield its increase. They shall be secure on their soil; and they shall know that I am the LORD, when I break the bars of their yoke, and save them from the hands of those who enslaved them. 28They shall no more be plunder for the nations, nor shall the animals of the land devour them; they shall live in safety, and no one shall make them afraid. 29I will provide for them a splendid vegetation so that they shall no more be consumed with hunger in the land, and no longer suffer the insults of the nations. 30They shall know that I, the LORD their God, am with them, and that they, the house of Israel, are my people, says the Lord GOD. 31You are my sheep, the sheep of my pasture*a* and I am your God, says the Lord GOD.

Judgment on Mount Seir

35 The word of the LORD came to me: 2Mortal, set your face against Mount Seir, and prophesy against it, 3and say to it, Thus says the Lord GOD:

I am against you, Mount Seir;
    I stretch out my hand against you
      to make you a desolation and a waste.
4   I lay your towns in ruins;
    you shall become a desolation,
    and you shall know that I am the
      LORD.
5Because you cherished an ancient enmity, and

---

a Gk OL: Heb *pasture, you are people*

gave over the people of Israel to the power of the sword at the time of their calamity, at the time of their final punishment; [6]therefore, as I live, says the Lord GOD, I will prepare you for blood, and blood shall pursue you; since you did not hate bloodshed, bloodshed shall pursue you. [7]I will make Mount Seir a waste and a desolation; and I will cut off from it all who come and go. [8]I will fill its mountains with the slain; on your hills and in your valleys and in all your watercourses those killed with the sword shall fall. [9]I will make you a perpetual desolation, and your cities shall never be inhabited. Then you shall know that I am the LORD.

10 Because you said, "These two nations and these two countries shall be mine, and we will take possession of them,"—although the LORD was there— [11]therefore, as I live, says the Lord GOD, I will deal with you according to the anger and envy that you showed because of your hatred against them; and I will make myself known among you,[a] when I judge you. [12]You shall know that I, the LORD, have heard all the abusive speech that you uttered against the mountains of Israel, saying, "They are laid desolate, they are given us to devour." [13]And you magnified yourselves against me with your mouth, and multiplied your words against me; I heard it. [14]Thus says the Lord GOD: As the whole earth rejoices, I will make you desolate. [15]As you rejoiced over the inheritance of the house of Israel, because it was desolate, so I will deal with you; you shall be desolate, Mount Seir, and all Edom, all of it. Then they shall know that I am the LORD.

Blessing on Israel

36 And you, mortal, prophesy to the mountains of Israel, and say: O mountains of Israel, hear the word of the LORD. [2]Thus says the Lord GOD: Because the enemy said of you, "Aha!" and, "The ancient heights have become our possession," [3]therefore prophesy, and say: Thus says the Lord GOD: Because they made you desolate indeed, and crushed you from all sides, so that you became the possession of the rest of the nations, and you became an object of gossip and slander among the people; [4]therefore, O mountains of Israel, hear the word of the Lord GOD: Thus says the Lord GOD to the mountains and the hills, the watercourses and the valleys, the desolate wastes and the deserted towns, which have become a source of plunder and an object of derision to the rest of the nations all around; [5]therefore thus says the Lord GOD: I am speaking in my hot jealousy against the rest of the nations, and against all Edom, who, with wholehearted joy and utter contempt, took my land as their possession, because of its pasture, to plunder it. [6]Therefore prophesy concerning the land of Israel, and say to the mountains and hills, to the watercourses and valleys, Thus says the Lord GOD: I am speaking in my jealous wrath, because you have suffered the insults of the nations; [7]therefore thus says the Lord GOD: I swear that the nations that are all around you shall themselves suffer insults.

8 But you, O mountains of Israel, shall shoot out your branches, and yield your fruit to my people Israel; for they shall soon come home. [9]See now, I am for you; I will turn to you, and you shall be tilled and sown; [10]and I will multiply your population, the whole house of Israel, all of it; the towns shall be inhabited and the waste places rebuilt; [11]and I will multiply human beings and animals upon you. They shall increase and be fruitful; and I will cause you to be inhabited as in your former times, and will do more good to you than ever before. Then you shall know that I am the LORD. [12]I will lead people upon you—my people Israel—and they shall possess you, and you shall be their inheritance. No longer shall you bereave them of children.

13 Thus says the Lord GOD: Because they say to you, "You devour people, and you bereave your nation of children," [14]therefore you shall no longer devour people and no longer bereave your nation of children, says the Lord GOD; [15]and no longer will I let you hear the in-

a Gk: Heb *them*

sults of the nations, no longer shall you bear the disgrace of the peoples; and no longer shall you cause your nation to stumble, says the Lord GOD.

The Renewal of Israel

16 The word of the LORD came to me: [17]Mortal, when the house of Israel lived on their own soil, they defiled it with their ways and their deeds; their conduct in my sight was like the uncleanness of a woman in her menstrual period. [18]So I poured out my wrath upon them for the blood that they had shed upon the land, and for the idols with which they had defiled it. [19]I scattered them among the nations, and they were dispersed through the countries; in accordance with their conduct and their deeds I judged them. [20]But when they came to the nations, wherever they came, they profaned my holy name, in that it was said of them, "These are the people of the LORD, and yet they had to go out of his land." [21]But I had concern for my holy name, which the house of Israel had profaned among the nations to which they came.

22 Therefore say to the house of Israel, Thus says the Lord GOD: It is not for your sake, O house of Israel, that I am about to act, but for the sake of my holy name, which you have profaned among the nations to which you came. [23]I will sanctify my great name, which has been profaned among the nations, and which you have profaned among them; and the nations shall know that I am the LORD, says the Lord GOD, when through you I display my holiness before their eyes. [24]I will take you from the nations, and gather you from all the countries, and bring you into your own land. [25]I will sprinkle clean water upon you, and you shall be clean from all your uncleannesses, and from all your idols I will cleanse you. [26]A new heart I will give you, and a new spirit I will put within you; and I will remove from your body the heart of stone and give you a heart of flesh. [27]I will put my spirit within you, and make you follow my statutes and be careful to observe my ordinances. [28]Then you shall live in the land that I gave to your ancestors; and you shall be my people, and I will be your God. [29]I will save you from all your uncleannesses, and I will summon the grain and make it abundant and lay no famine upon you. [30]I will make the fruit of the tree and the produce of the field abundant, so that you may never again suffer the disgrace of famine among the nations. [31]Then you shall remember your evil ways, and your dealings that were not good; and you shall loathe yourselves for your iniquities and your abominable deeds. [32]It is not for your sake that I will act, says the Lord GOD; let that be known to you. Be ashamed and dismayed for your ways, O house of Israel.

33 Thus says the Lord GOD: On the day that I cleanse you from all your iniquities, I will cause the towns to be inhabited, and the waste places shall be rebuilt. [34]The land that was desolate shall be tilled, instead of being the desolation that it was in the sight of all who passed by. [35]And they will say, "This land that was desolate has become like the garden of Eden; and the waste and desolate and ruined towns are now inhabited and fortified." [36]Then the nations that are left all around you shall know that I, the LORD, have rebuilt the ruined places, and replanted that which was desolate; I, the LORD, have spoken, and I will do it.

37 Thus says the Lord GOD: I will also let the house of Israel ask me to do this for them: to increase their population like a flock. [38]Like the flock for sacrifices,*a* like the flock at Jerusalem during her appointed festivals, so shall the ruined towns be filled with flocks of people. Then they shall know that I am the LORD.

The Valley of Dry Bones

37 The hand of the LORD came upon me, and he brought me out by the spirit of the LORD and set me down in the middle of a valley; it was full of bones. [2]He led me all around them; there were very many lying in the valley, and they were very dry. [3]He said to me, "Mortal, can these bones live?" I answered,

a Heb *flock of holy things*

"O Lord GOD, you know." [4]Then he said to me, "Prophesy to these bones, and say to them: O dry bones, hear the word of the LORD. [5]Thus says the Lord GOD to these bones: I will cause breath[a] to enter you, and you shall live. [6]I will lay sinews on you, and will cause flesh to come upon you, and cover you with skin, and put breath[a] in you, and you shall live; and you shall know that I am the LORD."

7 So I prophesied as I had been commanded; and as I prophesied, suddenly there was a noise, a rattling, and the bones came together, bone to its bone. [8]I looked, and there were sinews on them, and flesh had come upon them, and skin had covered them; but there was no breath in them. [9]Then he said to me, "Prophesy to the breath, prophesy, mortal, and say to the breath:[b] Thus says the Lord GOD: Come from the four winds, O breath,[b] and breathe upon these slain, that they may live." [10]I prophesied as he commanded me, and the breath came into them, and they lived, and stood on their feet, a vast multitude.

11 Then he said to me, "Mortal, these bones are the whole house of Israel. They say, 'Our bones are dried up, and our hope is lost; we are cut off completely.' [12]Therefore prophesy, and say to them, Thus says the Lord GOD: I am going to open your graves, and bring you up from your graves, O my people; and I will bring you back to the land of Israel. [13]And you shall know that I am the LORD, when I open your graves, and bring you up from your graves, O my people. [14]I will put my spirit within you, and you shall live, and I will place you on your own soil; then you shall know that I, the LORD, have spoken and will act, says the LORD.'"

The Two Sticks

15 The word of the LORD came to me: [16]Mortal, take a stick and write on it, "For Judah, and the Israelites associated with it"; then take another stick and write on it, "For Joseph (the stick of Ephraim) and all the house of Israel associated with it"; [17]and join them together into one stick, so that they may become one in your hand. [18]And when your people say to you, "Will you not show us what you mean by these?" [19]say to them, Thus says the Lord GOD: I am about to take the stick of Joseph (which is in the hand of Ephraim) and the tribes of Israel associated with it; and I will put the stick of Judah upon it,[c] and make them one stick, in order that they may be one in my hand. [20]When the sticks on which you write are in your hand before their eyes, [21]then say to them, Thus says the Lord GOD: I will take the people of Israel from the nations among which they have gone, and will gather them from every quarter, and bring them to their own land. [22]I will make them one nation in the land, on the mountains of Israel; and one king shall be king over them all. Never again shall they be two nations, and never again shall they be divided into two kingdoms. [23]They shall never again defile themselves with their idols and their detestable things, or with any of their transgressions. I will save them from all the apostasies into which they have fallen,[d] and will cleanse them. Then they shall be my people, and I will be their God.

24 My servant David shall be king over them; and they shall all have one shepherd. They shall follow my ordinances and be careful to observe my statutes. [25]They shall live in the land that I gave to my servant Jacob, in which your ancestors lived; they and their children and their children's children shall live there forever; and my servant David shall be their prince forever. [26]I will make a covenant of peace with them; it shall be an everlasting covenant with them; and I will bless[e] them and multiply them, and will set my sanctuary among them forevermore. [27]My dwelling place shall be with them; and I will be their God, and they shall be my people. [28]Then the nations shall know that I the LORD sanctify Israel, when my sanctuary is among them forevermore.

---

a Or *spirit*   *b* Or *wind* or *spirit*   *c* Heb *I will put them upon it*   *d* Another reading is *from all the settlements in which they have sinned*   *e* Tg: Heb *give*

Invasion by Gog

38 The word of the LORD came to me: [2]Mortal, set your face toward Gog, of the land of Magog, the chief prince of Meshech and Tubal. Prophesy against him [3]and say: Thus says the Lord GOD: I am against you, O Gog, chief prince of Meshech and Tubal; [4]I will turn you around and put hooks into your jaws, and I will lead you out with all your army, horses and horsemen, all of them clothed in full armor, a great company, all of them with shield and buckler, wielding swords. [5]Persia, Ethiopia,[a] and Put are with them, all of them with buckler and helmet; [6]Gomer and all its troops; Beth-togarmah from the remotest parts of the north with all its troops—many peoples are with you.

7 Be ready and keep ready, you and all the companies that are assembled around you, and hold yourselves in reserve for them. [8]After many days you shall be mustered; in the latter years you shall go against a land restored from war, a land where people were gathered from many nations on the mountains of Israel, which had long lain waste; its people were brought out from the nations and now are living in safety, all of them. [9]You shall advance, coming on like a storm; you shall be like a cloud covering the land, you and all your troops, and many peoples with you.

10 Thus says the Lord GOD: On that day thoughts will come into your mind, and you will devise an evil scheme. [11]You will say, "I will go up against the land of unwalled villages; I will fall upon the quiet people who live in safety, all of them living without walls, and having no bars or gates"; [12]to seize spoil and carry off plunder; to assail the waste places that are now inhabited, and the people who were gathered from the nations, who are acquiring cattle and goods, who live at the center[b] of the earth. [13]Sheba and Dedan and the merchants of Tarshish and all its young warriors[c] will say to you, "Have you come to seize spoil? Have you assembled your horde to carry off plunder, to carry away silver and gold, to take away cattle and goods, to seize a great amount of booty?"

14 Therefore, mortal, prophesy, and say to Gog: Thus says the Lord GOD: On that day when my people Israel are living securely, you will rouse yourself[d] [15]and come from your place out of the remotest parts of the north, you and many peoples with you, all of them riding on horses, a great horde, a mighty army; [16]you will come up against my people Israel, like a cloud covering the earth. In the latter days I will bring you against my land, so that the nations may know me, when through you, O Gog, I display my holiness before their eyes.

Judgment on Gog

17 Thus says the Lord GOD: Are you he of whom I spoke in former days by my servants the prophets of Israel, who in those days prophesied for years that I would bring you against them? [18]On that day, when Gog comes against the land of Israel, says the Lord GOD, my wrath shall be aroused. [19]For in my jealousy and in my blazing wrath I declare: On that day there shall be a great shaking in the land of Israel; [20]the fish of the sea, and the birds of the air, and the animals of the field, and all creeping things that creep on the ground, and all human beings that are on the face of the earth, shall quake at my presence, and the mountains shall be thrown down, and the cliffs shall fall, and every wall shall tumble to the ground. [21]I will summon the sword against Gog[e] in[f] all my mountains, says the Lord GOD; the swords of all will be against their comrades. [22]With pestilence and bloodshed I will enter into judgment with him; and I will pour down torrential rains and hailstones, fire and sulfur, upon him and his troops and the many peoples that are with him. [23]So I will display my greatness and my holiness and make myself known in the eyes of many nations. Then they shall know that I am the LORD.

a Or *Nubia*; Heb *Cush*   *b* Heb *navel*   *c* Heb *young lions*   *d* Gk: Heb *will you not know?*   *e* Heb *him*   *f* Heb *to* or *for*

Gog's Armies Destroyed

39 And you, mortal, prophesy against Gog, and say: Thus says the Lord GOD: I am against you, O Gog, chief prince of Meshech and Tubal! ²I will turn you around and drive you forward, and bring you up from the remotest parts of the north, and lead you against the mountains of Israel. ³I will strike your bow from your left hand, and will make your arrows drop out of your right hand. ⁴You shall fall on the mountains of Israel, you and all your troops and the peoples that are with you; I will give you to birds of prey of every kind and to the wild animals to be devoured. ⁵You shall fall in the open field; for I have spoken, says the Lord GOD. ⁶I will send fire on Magog and on those who live securely in the coastlands; and they shall know that I am the LORD.

7 My holy name I will make known among my people Israel; and I will not let my holy name be profaned any more; and the nations shall know that I am the LORD, the Holy One in Israel. ⁸It has come! It has happened, says Lord GOD. This is the day of which I have spoken.

9 Then those who live in the towns of Israel will go out and make fires of the weapons and burn them—bucklers and shields, bows and arrows, handpikes and spears—and they will make fires of them for seven years. ¹⁰They will not need to take wood out of the field or cut down any trees in the forests, for they will make their fires of the weapons; they will despoil those who despoiled them, and plunder those who plundered them, says the Lord GOD.

The Burial of Gog

11 On that day I will give to Gog a place for burial in Israel, the Valley of the Travelers*ᵃ* east of the sea; it shall block the path of the travelers, for there Gog and all his horde will be buried; it shall be called the Valley of Hamon-gog.*ᵇ* ¹²Seven months the house of Israel shall spend burying them, in order to cleanse the land. ¹³All the people of the land shall bury them; and it will bring them honor on the day

that I show my glory, says the Lord GOD. ¹⁴They will set apart men to pass through the land regularly and bury any invaders*ᶜ* who remain on the face of the land, so as to cleanse it; for seven months they shall make their search. ¹⁵As the searchers*ᶜ* pass through the land, anyone who sees a human bone shall set up a sign by it, until the buriers have buried it in the Valley of Hamon-gog.*ᵇ* ¹⁶(A city Hamonah*ᵈ* is there also.) Thus they shall cleanse the land.

17 As for you, mortal, thus says the Lord GOD: Speak to the birds of every kind and to all the wild animals: Assemble and come, gather from all around to the sacrificial feast that I am preparing for you, a great sacrificial feast on the mountains of Israel, and you shall eat flesh and drink blood. ¹⁸You shall eat the flesh of the mighty, and drink the blood of the princes of the earth—of rams, of lambs, and of goats, of bulls, all of them fatlings of Bashan. ¹⁹You shall eat fat until you are filled, and drink blood until you are drunk, at the sacrificial feast that I am preparing for you. ²⁰And you shall be filled at my table with horses and charioteers,*ᵉ* with warriors and all kinds of soldiers, says the Lord GOD.

Israel Restored to the Land

21 I will display my glory among the nations; and all the nations shall see my judgment that I have executed, and my hand that I have laid on them. ²²The house of Israel shall know that I am the LORD their God, from that day forward. ²³And the nations shall know that the house of Israel went into captivity for their iniquity, because they dealt treacherously with me. So I hid my face from them and gave them into the hand of their adversaries, and they all fell by the sword. ²⁴I dealt with them according to their uncleanness and their transgressions, and hid my face from them.

25 Therefore thus says the Lord GOD: Now I will restore the fortunes of Jacob, and have mercy on the whole house of Israel; and I will be jealous for my holy name. ²⁶They shall forget*ᶠ* their shame, and all the treach-

a Or *of the Abarim*   *b* That is, *the Horde of Gog*   *c* Heb *travelers*   *d* That is *The Horde*   *e* Heb *chariots*
f Another reading is *They shall bear*

ery they have practiced against me, when they live securely in their land with no one to make them afraid, 27when I have brought them back from the peoples and gathered them from their enemies' lands, and through them have displayed my holiness in the sight of many nations. 28Then they shall know that I am the LORD their God because I sent them into exile among the nations, and then gathered them into their own land. I will leave none of them behind; 29and I will never again hide my face from them, when I pour out my spirit upon the house of Israel, says the Lord GOD.

The Vision of the New Temple

40 In the twenty-fifth year of our exile, at the beginning of the year, on the tenth day of the month, in the fourteenth year after the city was struck down, on that very day, the hand of the LORD was upon me, and he brought me there. 2He brought me, in visions of God, to the land of Israel, and set me down upon a very high mountain, on which was a structure like a city to the south. 3When he brought me there, a man was there, whose appearance shone like bronze, with a linen cord and a measuring reed in his hand; and he was standing in the gateway. 4The man said to me, "Mortal, look closely and listen attentively, and set your mind upon all that I shall show you, for you were brought here in order that I might show it to you; declare all that you see to the house of Israel."

5 Now there was a wall all around the outside of the temple area. The length of the measuring reed in the man's hand was six long cubits, each being a cubit and a handbreadth in length; so he measured the thickness of the wall, one reed; and the height, one reed. 6Then he went into the gateway facing east, going up its steps, and measured the threshold of the gate, one reed deep.a There were 7recesses, and each recess was one reed wide and one reed deep; and the space between the recesses, five cubits; and the threshold of the gate by the

vestibule of the gate at the inner end was one reed deep. 8Then he measured the inner vestibule of the gateway, one cubit. 9Then he measured the vestibule of the gateway, eight cubits; and its pilasters, two cubits; and the vestibule of the gate was at the inner end. 10There were three recesses on either side of the east gate; the three were of the same size; and the pilasters on either side were of the same size. 11Then he measured the width of the opening of the gateway, ten cubits; and the width of the gateway, thirteen cubits. 12There was a barrier before the recesses, one cubit on either side; and the recesses were six cubits on either side. 13Then he measured the gate from the backb of the one recess to the backb of the other, a width of twenty-five cubits, from wall to wall.c 14He measuredd also the vestibule, twenty cubits; and the gate next to the pilaster on every side of the court.e 15From the front of the gate at the entrance to the end of the inner vestibule of the gate was fifty cubits. 16The recesses and their pilasters had windows, with shutterse on the inside of the gateway all around, and the vestibules also had windows on the inside all around; and on the pilasters were palm trees.

17 Then he brought me into the outer court; there were chambers there, and a pavement, all around the court; thirty chambers fronted on the pavement. 18The pavement ran along the side of the gates, corresponding to the length of the gates; this was the lower pavement. 19Then he measured the distance from the inner front off the lower gate to the outer front of the inner court, one hundred cubits.g

20 Then he measured the gate of the outer court that faced north—its depth and width. 21Its recesses, three on either side, and its pilasters and its vestibule were of the same size as those of the first gate; its depth was fifty cubits, and its width twenty-five cubits. 22Its windows, its vestibule, and its palm trees were of the same size as those of the gate that faced toward the east. Seven steps led up to it; and its

---

a Heb deep, and one threshold, one reed deep   b Gk: Heb roof   c Heb opening facing opening   d Heb made
e Meaning of Heb uncertain   f Compare Gk: Heb from before   g Heb adds the east and the north

vestibule was on the inside. *a* ²³Opposite the gate on the north, as on the east, was a gate to the inner court; he measured from gate to gate, one hundred cubits.

24 Then he led me toward the south, and there was a gate on the south; and he measured its pilasters and its vestibule; they had the same dimensions as the others. ²⁵There were windows all around in it and in its vestibule, like the windows of the others; its depth was fifty cubits, and its width twenty-five cubits. ²⁶There were seven steps leading up to it; its vestibule was on the inside. *a* It had palm trees on its pilasters, one on either side. ²⁷There was a gate on the south of the inner court; and he measured from gate to gate toward the south, one hundred cubits.

28 Then he brought me to the inner court by the south gate, and he measured the south gate; it was of the same dimensions as the others. ²⁹Its recesses, its pilasters, and its vestibule were of the same size as the others; and there were windows all around in it and in its vestibule; its depth was fifty cubits, and its width twenty-five cubits. ³⁰There were vestibules all around, twenty-five cubits deep and five cubits wide. ³¹Its vestibule faced the outer court, and palm trees were on its pilasters, and its stairway had eight steps.

32 Then he brought me to the inner court on the east side, and he measured the gate; it was of the same size as the others. ³³Its recesses, its pilasters, and its vestibule were of the same dimensions as the others; and there were windows all around in it and in its vestibule; its depth was fifty cubits, and its width twenty-five cubits. ³⁴Its vestibule faced the outer court, and it had palm trees on its pilasters, on either side; and its stairway had eight steps.

35 Then he brought me to the north gate, and he measured it; it had the same dimensions as the others. ³⁶Its recesses, its pilasters, and its vestibule were of the same size as the others; *b* and it had windows all around. Its depth was fifty cubits, and its width twenty-five cubits.

³⁷Its vestibule *c* faced the outer court, and it had palm trees on its pilasters, on either side; and its stairway had eight steps.

38 There was a chamber with its door in the vestibule of the gate, *d* where the burnt offering was to be washed. ³⁹And in the vestibule of the gate were two tables on either side, on which the burnt offering and the sin offering and the guilt offering were to be slaughtered. ⁴⁰On the outside of the vestibule *e* at the entrance of the north gate were two tables; and on the other side of the vestibule of the gate were two tables. ⁴¹Four tables were on the inside, and four tables on the outside of the side of the gate, eight tables, on which the sacrifices were to be slaughtered. ⁴²There were also four tables of hewn stone for the burnt offering, a cubit and a half long, and one cubit and a half wide, and one cubit high, on which the instruments were to be laid with which the burnt offerings and the sacrifices were slaughtered. ⁴³There were pegs, one handbreadth long, fastened all around the inside. And on the tables the flesh of the offering was to be laid.

44 On the outside of the inner gateway there were chambers for the singers in the inner court, one *f* at the side of the north gate facing south, the other at the side of the east gate facing north. ⁴⁵He said to me, "This chamber that faces south is for the priests who have charge of the temple, ⁴⁶and the chamber that faces north is for the priests who have charge of the altar; these are the descendants of Zadok, who alone among the descendants of Levi may come near to the LORD to minister to him." ⁴⁷He measured the court, one hundred cubits deep, and one hundred cubits wide, a square; and the altar was in front of the temple.

The Temple

48 Then he brought me to the vestibule of the temple and measured the pilasters of the vestibule, five cubits on either side; and the width of the gate was fourteen cubits; and the

a Gk: Heb *before them*   *b* One Ms: Compare verses 29 and 33: MT lacks *were of the same size as the others*
c Gk Vg Compare verses 26, 31, 34: Heb *pilasters*   *d* Cn: Heb *at the pilasters of the gates*   *e* Cn: Heb *to him who goes*
up   *f* Heb lacks *one*

sidewalls of the gate were three cubits[a] on either side. [49]The depth of the vestibule was twenty cubits, and the width twelve[b] cubits; ten steps led up[c] to it; and there were pillars beside the pilasters on either side.

41 Then he brought me to the nave, and measured the pilasters; on each side six cubits was the width of the pilasters.[d] [2]The width of the entrance was ten cubits; and the sidewalls of the entrance were five cubits on either side. He measured the length of the nave, forty cubits, and its width, twenty cubits. [3]Then he went into the inner room and measured the pilasters of the entrance, two cubits; and the width of the entrance, six cubits; and the sidewalls[e] of the entrance, seven cubits. [4]He measured the depth of the room, twenty cubits, and its width, twenty cubits, beyond the nave. And he said to me, This is the most holy place.

5 Then he measured the wall of the temple, six cubits thick; and the width of the side chambers, four cubits, all around the temple. [6]The side chambers were in three stories, one over another, thirty in each story. There were offsets[f] all around the wall of the temple to serve as supports for the side chambers, so that they should not be supported by the wall of the temple. [7]The passageway[g] of the side chambers widened from story to story; for the structure was supplied with a stairway all around the temple. For this reason the structure became wider from story to story. One ascended from the bottom story to the uppermost story by way of the middle one. [8]I saw also that the temple had a raised platform all around; the foundations of the side chambers measured a full reed of six long cubits. [9]The thickness of the outer wall of the side chambers was five cubits; and the free space between the side chambers of the temple [10]and the chambers of the court was a width of twenty cubits all around the temple on every side. [11]The side chambers opened onto the area left free, one door toward the north, and another door toward the south; and the width of the part that was left free was five cubits all around.

12 The building that was facing the temple yard on the west side was seventy cubits wide; and the wall of the building was five cubits thick all around, and its depth ninety cubits.

13 Then he measured the temple, one hundred cubits deep; and the yard and the building with its walls, one hundred cubits deep; [14]also the width of the east front of the temple and the yard, one hundred cubits.

15 Then he measured the depth of the building facing the yard at the west, together with its galleries[h] on either side, one hundred cubits.

The nave of the temple and the inner room and the outer[i] vestibule [16]were paneled,[j] and, all around, all three had windows with recessed[k] frames. Facing the threshold the temple was paneled with wood all around, from the floor up to the windows (now the windows were covered), [17]to the space above the door, even to the inner room, and on the outside. And on all the walls all around in the inner room and the nave there was a pattern.[l] [18]It was formed of cherubim and palm trees, a palm tree between cherub and cherub. Each cherub had two faces: [19]a human face turned toward the palm tree on the one side, and the face of a young lion turned toward the palm tree on the other side. They were carved on the whole temple all around; [20]from the floor to the area above the door, cherubim and palm trees were carved on the wall.[m]

21 The doorposts of the nave were square. In front of the holy place was something resembling [22]an altar of wood, three cubits high, two cubits long, and two cubits wide;[n] its corners, its base,[o] and its walls were of wood. He said to me, "This is the table that stands before the Lord." [23]The nave

---

a Gk: Heb *and the width of the gate was three cubits*   b Gk: Heb *eleven*   c Gk: Heb *and by steps that went up*
d Compare Gk: Heb *tent*   e Gk: Heb *width*   f Gk Compare 1 Kings 6.6: Heb *they entered*   g Cn: Heb *it was surrounded*   h Cn: Meaning of Heb uncertain   i Gk: Heb *of the court*   j Gk: Heb *the thresholds*
k Cn Compare Gk 1 Kings 6.4: Meaning of Heb uncertain   l Heb *measures*   m Cn Compare verse 25: Heb *and the wall*   n Gk: Heb lacks *two cubits wide*   o Gk: Heb *length*

and the holy place had each a double door. [24]The doors had two leaves apiece, two swinging leaves for each door. [25]On the doors of the nave were carved cherubim and palm trees, such as were carved on the walls; and there was a canopy of wood in front of the vestibule outside. [26]And there were recessed windows and palm trees on either side, on the sidewalls of the vestibule. [a]

The Holy Chambers and the Outer Wall

42 Then he led me out into the outer court, toward the north, and he brought me to the chambers that were opposite the temple yard and opposite the building on the north. [2]The length of the building that was on the north side[b] was[c] one hundred cubits, and the width fifty cubits. [3]Across the twenty cubits that belonged to the inner court, and facing the pavement that belonged to the outer court, the chambers rose[d] gallery[e] by gallery[e] in three stories. [4]In front of the chambers was a passage on the inner side, ten cubits wide and one hundred cubits deep,[f] and its[g] entrances were on the north. [5]Now the upper chambers were narrower, for the galleries[e] took more away from them than from the lower and middle chambers in the building. [6]For they were in three stories, and they had no pillars like the pillars of the outer[h] court; for this reason the upper chambers were set back from the ground more than the lower and the middle ones. [7]There was a wall outside parallel to the chambers, toward the outer court, opposite the chambers, fifty cubits long. [8]For the chambers on the outer court were fifty cubits long, while those opposite the temple were one hundred cubits long. [9]At the foot of these chambers ran a passage that one entered from the east in order to enter them from the outer court. [10]The width of the passage[i] was fixed by the wall of the court.

On the south[j] also, opposite the vacant area and opposite the building, there were chambers [11]with a passage in front of them; they were similar to the chambers on the north, of the same length and width, with the same exits[k] and arrangements and doors. [12]So the entrances of the chambers to the south were entered through the entrance at the head of the corresponding passage, from the east, along the matching wall. [e]

[13] Then he said to me, "The north chambers and the south chambers opposite the vacant area are the holy chambers, where the priests who approach the LORD shall eat the most holy offerings; there they shall deposit the most holy offerings—the grain offering, the sin offering, and the guilt offering—for the place is holy. [14]When the priests enter the holy place, they shall not go out of it into the outer court without laying there the vestments in which they minister, for these are holy; they shall put on other garments before they go near to the area open to the people."

[15] When he had finished measuring the interior of the temple area, he led me out by the gate that faces east, and measured the temple area all around. [16]He measured the east side with the measuring reed, five hundred cubits by the measuring reed. [17]Then he turned and measured[l] the north side, five hundred cubits by the measuring reed. [18]Then he turned and measured[l] the south side, five hundred cubits by the measuring reed. [19]Then he turned to the west side and measured, five hundred cubits by the measuring reed. [20]He measured it on the four sides. It had a wall around it, five hundred cubits long and five hundred cubits wide, to make a separation between the holy and the common.

The Divine Glory Returns to the Temple

43 Then he brought me to the gate, the gate facing east. [2]And there, the glory of the God of Israel was coming from the east; the sound was like the sound of mighty waters; and the earth shone with his glory.

a Cn: Heb vestibule. And the side chambers of the temple and the canopies   b Gk: Heb door   c Gk: Heb before the length   d Heb lacks the chambers rose   e Meaning of Heb uncertain   f Gk Syr: Heb a way of one cubit   g Heb their   h Gk: Heb lacks outer   i Heb lacks of the passage   j Gk: Heb east   k Heb and all their exits   l Gk: Heb measuring reed all around. He measured

3 The *a* vision I saw was like the vision that I had seen when he came to destroy the city, and *b* like the vision that I had seen by the river Chebar; and I fell upon my face. 4 As the glory of the LORD entered the temple by the gate facing east, 5 the spirit lifted me up, and brought me into the inner court; and the glory of the LORD filled the temple.

6 While the man was standing beside me, I heard someone speaking to me out of the temple. 7 He said to me: Mortal, this is the place of my throne and the place for the soles of my feet, where I will reside among the people of Israel forever. The house of Israel shall no more defile my holy name, neither they nor their kings, by their whoring, and by the corpses of their kings at their death. *c* 8 When they placed their threshold by my threshold and their doorposts beside my doorposts, with only a wall between me and them, they were defiling my holy name by their abominations that they committed; therefore I have consumed them in my anger. 9 Now let them put away their idolatry and the corpses of their kings far from me, and I will reside among them forever.

10 As for you, mortal, describe the temple to the house of Israel, and let them measure the pattern; and let them be ashamed of their iniquities. 11 When they are ashamed of all that they have done, make known to them the plan of the temple, its arrangement, its exits and its entrances, and its whole form—all its ordinances and its entire plan and all its laws; and write it down in their sight, so that they may observe and follow the entire plan and all its ordinances. 12 This is the law of the temple: the whole territory on the top of the mountain all around shall be most holy. This is the law of the temple.

The Altar

13 These are the dimensions of the altar by cubits (the cubit being one cubit and a handbreadth): its base shall be one cubit high, *d* and one cubit wide, with a rim of one span around its edge. This shall be the height of the altar:

14 From the base on the ground to the lower ledge, two cubits, with a width of one cubit; and from the smaller ledge to the larger ledge, four cubits, with a width of one cubit; 15 and the altar hearth, four cubits; and from the altar hearth projecting upward, four horns. 16 The altar hearth shall be square, twelve cubits long by twelve wide. 17 The ledge also shall be square, fourteen cubits long by fourteen wide, with a rim around it half a cubit wide, and its surrounding base, one cubit. Its steps shall face east.

18 Then he said to me: Mortal, thus says the Lord GOD: These are the ordinances for the altar: On the day when it is erected for offering burnt offerings upon it and for dashing blood against it, 19 you shall give to the levitical priests of the family of Zadok, who draw near to me to minister to me, says the Lord GOD, a bull for a sin offering. 20 And you shall take some of its blood, and put it on the four horns of the altar, and on the four corners of the ledge, and upon the rim all around; thus you shall purify it and make atonement for it. 21 You shall also take the bull of the sin offering, and it shall be burnt in the appointed place belonging to the temple, outside the sacred area.

22 On the second day you shall offer a male goat without blemish for a sin offering; and the altar shall be purified, as it was purified with the bull. 23 When you have finished purifying it, you shall offer a bull without blemish and a ram from the flock without blemish. 24 You shall present them before the LORD, and the priests shall throw salt on them and offer them up as a burnt offering to the LORD. 25 For seven days you shall provide daily a goat for a sin offering; also a bull and a ram from the flock, without blemish, shall be provided. 26 Seven days shall they make atonement for the altar and cleanse it, and so consecrate it. 27 When these days are over, then from the eighth day onward the priests shall offer upon the altar your burnt offerings and your offerings of well-being; and I will accept you, says the Lord GOD.

---

a Gk: Heb *Like the vision*   *b* Syr: Heb *and the visions*   *c* Or *on their high places*   *d* Gk: Heb lacks *high*

The Closed Gate

44 Then he brought me back to the outer gate of the sanctuary, which faces east; and it was shut. ²The LORD said to me: This gate shall remain shut; it shall not be opened, and no one shall enter by it; for the LORD, the God of Israel, has entered by it; therefore it shall remain shut. ³Only the prince, because he is a prince, may sit in it to eat food before the LORD; he shall enter by way of the vestibule of the gate, and shall go out by the same way.

Admission to the Temple

4 Then he brought me by way of the north gate to the front of the temple; and I looked, and lo! the glory of the LORD filled the temple of the LORD; and I fell upon my face. ⁵The LORD said to me: Mortal, mark well, look closely, and listen attentively to all that I shall tell you concerning all the ordinances of the temple of the LORD and all its laws; and mark well those who may be admitted to*a* the temple and all those who are to be excluded from the sanctuary. ⁶Say to the rebellious house,*b* to the house of Israel, Thus says the Lord GOD: O house of Israel, let there be an end to all your abominations ⁷in admitting foreigners, uncircumcised in heart and flesh, to be in my sanctuary, profaning my temple when you offer to me my food, the fat and the blood. You*c* have broken my covenant with all your abominations. ⁸And you have not kept charge of my sacred offerings; but you have appointed foreigners*d* to act for you in keeping my charge in my sanctuary.

9 Thus says the Lord GOD: No foreigner, uncircumcised in heart and flesh, of all the foreigners who are among the people of Israel, shall enter my sanctuary. ¹⁰But the Levites who went far from me, going astray from me after their idols when Israel went astray, shall bear their punishment. ¹¹They shall be ministers in my sanctuary, having oversight at the gates of the temple, and serving in the temple; they shall slaughter the burnt offering and the sacrifice for the people, and they shall attend on them and serve them. ¹²Because they ministered to them before their idols and made the house of Israel stumble into iniquity, therefore I have sworn concerning them, says the Lord GOD, that they shall bear their punishment. ¹³They shall not come near to me, to serve me as priest, nor come near any of my sacred offerings, the things that are most sacred; but they shall bear their shame, and the consequences of the abominations that they have committed. ¹⁴Yet I will appoint them to keep charge of the temple, to do all its chores, all that is to be done in it.

The Levitical Priests

15 But the levitical priests, the descendants of Zadok, who kept the charge of my sanctuary when the people of Israel went astray from me, shall come near to me to minister to me; and they shall attend me to offer me the fat and the blood, says the Lord GOD. ¹⁶It is they who shall enter my sanctuary, it is they who shall approach my table, to minister to me, and they shall keep my charge. ¹⁷When they enter the gates of the inner court, they shall wear linen vestments; they shall have nothing of wool on them, while they minister at the gates of the inner court, and within. ¹⁸They shall have linen turbans on their heads, and linen undergarments on their loins; they shall not bind themselves with anything that causes sweat. ¹⁹When they go out into the outer court to the people, they shall remove the vestments in which they have been ministering, and lay them in the holy chambers; and they shall put on other garments, so that they may not communicate holiness to the people with their vestments. ²⁰They shall not shave their heads or let their locks grow long; they shall only trim the hair of their heads. ²¹No priest shall drink wine when he enters the inner court. ²²They shall not marry a widow, or a divorced woman, but only a virgin of the stock of the house of Israel, or a widow who is the widow of a priest. ²³They shall teach my people the difference between

a Cn: Heb *the entrance of*   *b* Gk: Heb lacks *house*   *c* Gk Syr Vg: Heb *They*   *d* Heb lacks *foreigners* the holy and the common, and show them how to distinguish between the unclean and the clean. ²⁴In a controversy they shall act as judges, and they shall decide it according to my judgments. They shall keep my laws and my statutes regarding all my appointed festivals, and they shall keep my sabbaths holy. ²⁵They shall not defile themselves by going near to a dead person; for father or mother, however, and for son or daughter, and for brother or unmarried sister they may defile themselves. ²⁶After he has become clean, they shall count seven days for him. ²⁷On the day that he goes into the holy place, into the inner court, to minister in the holy place, he shall offer his sin offering, says the Lord God.

28 This shall be their inheritance: I am their inheritance; and you shall give them no holding in Israel; I am their holding. ²⁹They shall eat the grain offering, the sin offering, and the guilt offering; and every devoted thing in Israel shall be theirs. ³⁰The first of all the first fruits of all kinds, and every offering of all kinds from all your offerings, shall belong to the priests; you shall also give to the priests the first of your dough, in order that a blessing may rest on your house. ³¹The priests shall not eat of anything, whether bird or animal, that died of itself or was torn by animals.

The Holy District

45 When you allot the land as an inheritance, you shall set aside for the Lord a portion of the land as a holy district, twenty-five thousand cubits long and twenty^a thousand cubits wide; it shall be holy throughout its entire extent. ²Of this, a square plot of five hundred by five hundred cubits shall be for the sanctuary, with fifty cubits for an open space around it. ³In the holy district you shall measure off a section twenty-five thousand cubits long and ten thousand wide, in which shall be the sanctuary, the most holy place. ⁴It shall be a holy portion of the land; it shall be for the priests, who minister in the sanctuary and approach the Lord to minister to him; and it

shall be both a place for their houses and a holy place for the sanctuary. ⁵Another section, twenty-five thousand cubits long and ten thousand cubits wide, shall be for the Levites who minister at the temple, as their holding for cities to live in.^b

6 Alongside the portion set apart as the holy district you shall assign as a holding for the city an area five thousand cubits wide, and twenty-five thousand cubits long; it shall belong to the whole house of Israel.

7 And to the prince shall belong the land on both sides of the holy district and the holding of the city, alongside the holy district and the holding of the city, on the west and on the east, corresponding in length to one of the tribal portions, and extending from the western to the eastern boundary ⁸of the land. It is to be his property in Israel. And my princes shall no longer oppress my people; but they shall let the house of Israel have the land according to their tribes.

9 Thus says the Lord God: Enough, O princes of Israel! Put away violence and oppression, and do what is just and right. Cease your evictions of my people, says the Lord God.

Weights and Measures

10 You shall have honest balances, an honest ephah, and an honest bath.^c ¹¹The ephah and the bath shall be of the same measure, the bath containing one-tenth of a homer, and the ephah one-tenth of a homer; the homer shall be the standard measure. ¹²The shekel shall be twenty gerahs. Twenty shekels, twenty-five shekels, and fifteen shekels shall make a mina for you.

Offerings

13 This is the offering that you shall make: one-sixth of an ephah from each homer of wheat, and one-sixth of an ephah from each homer of barley, ¹⁴and as the fixed portion of oil,^d one-tenth of a bath from each cor (the cor,^e like the homer, contains ten baths); ¹⁵and

---

a Gk: Heb *ten*   *b* Gk: Heb *as their holding, twenty chambers*   *c* A Heb measure of volume   *d* Cn: Heb *oil, the bath the oil*   *e* Vg: Heb *homer* one sheep from every flock of two hundred, from the pastures of Israel. This is the offering for grain offerings, burnt offerings, and offerings of well-being, to make atonement for them, says the Lord GOD. 16All the people of the land shall join with the prince in Israel in making this offering. 17But this shall be the obligation of the prince regarding the burnt offerings, grain offerings, and drink offerings, at the festivals, the new moons, and the sabbaths, all the appointed festivals of the house of Israel: he shall provide the sin offerings, grain offerings, the burnt offerings, and the offerings of well-being, to make atonement for the house of Israel.

Festivals

18 Thus says the Lord GOD: In the first month, on the first day of the month, you shall take a young bull without blemish, and purify the sanctuary. 19The priest shall take some of the blood of the sin offering and put it on the doorposts of the temple, the four corners of the ledge of the altar, and the posts of the gate of the inner court. 20You shall do the same on the seventh day of the month for anyone who has sinned through error or ignorance; so you shall make atonement for the temple.

21 In the first month, on the fourteenth day of the month, you shall celebrate the festival of the passover, and for seven days unleavened bread shall be eaten. 22On that day the prince shall provide for himself and all the people of the land a young bull for a sin offering. 23And during the seven days of the festival he shall provide as a burnt offering to the LORD seven young bulls and seven rams without blemish, on each of the seven days; and a male goat daily for a sin offering. 24He shall provide as a grain offering an ephah for each bull, an ephah for each ram, and a hin of oil to each ephah. 25In the seventh month, on the fifteenth day of the month and for the seven days of the festival, he shall make the same provision for sin offerings, burnt offerings, and grain offerings, and for the oil.

Miscellaneous Regulations

46 Thus says the Lord GOD: The gate of the inner court that faces east shall remain closed on the six working days; but on the sabbath day it shall be opened and on the day of the new moon it shall be opened. 2The prince shall enter by the vestibule of the gate from outside, and shall take his stand by the post of the gate. The priests shall offer his burnt offering and his offerings of well-being, and he shall bow down at the threshold of the gate. Then he shall go out, but the gate shall not be closed until evening. 3The people of the land shall bow down at the entrance of that gate before the LORD on the sabbaths and on the new moons. 4The burnt offering that the prince offers to the LORD on the sabbath day shall be six lambs without blemish and a ram without blemish; 5and the grain offering with the ram shall be an ephah, and the grain offering with the lambs shall be as much as he wishes to give, together with a hin of oil to each ephah. 6On the day of the new moon he shall offer a young bull without blemish, and six lambs and a ram, which shall be without blemish; 7as a grain offering he shall provide an ephah with the bull and an ephah with the ram, and with the lambs as much as he wishes, together with a hin of oil to each ephah. 8When the prince enters, he shall come in by the vestibule of the gate, and he shall go out by the same way.

9 When the people of the land come before the LORD at the appointed festivals, whoever enters by the north gate to worship shall go out by the south gate; and whoever enters by the south gate shall go out by the north gate: they shall not return by way of the gate by which they entered, but shall go out straight ahead. 10When they come in, the prince shall come in with them; and when they go out, he shall go out.

11 At the festivals and the appointed seasons the grain offering with a young bull shall be an ephah, and with a ram an ephah, and with the lambs as much as one wishes to give, together with a hin of oil to an ephah. 12When the prince provides a freewill offering, either a burnt offering or offerings of well-being as a

freewill offering to the LORD, the gate facing east shall be opened for him; and he shall offer his burnt offering or his offerings of well-being as he does on the sabbath day. Then he shall go out, and after he has gone out the gate shall be closed.

13 He shall provide a lamb, a yearling, without blemish, for a burnt offering to the LORD daily; morning by morning he shall provide it. [14]And he shall provide a grain offering with it morning by morning regularly, one-sixth of an ephah, and one-third of a hin of oil to moisten the choice flour, as a grain offering to the LORD; this is the ordinance for all time. [15]Thus the lamb and the grain offering and the oil shall be provided, morning by morning, as a regular burnt offering.

16 Thus says the Lord GOD: If the prince makes a gift to any of his sons out of his inheritance,[a] it shall belong to his sons, it is their holding by inheritance. [17]But if he makes a gift out of his inheritance to one of his servants, it shall be his to the year of liberty; then it shall revert to the prince; only his sons may keep a gift from his inheritance. [18]The prince shall not take any of the inheritance of the people, thrusting them out of their holding; he shall give his sons their inheritance out of his own holding, so that none of my people shall be dispossessed of their holding.

19 Then he brought me through the entrance, which was at the side of the gate, to the north row of the holy chambers for the priests; and there I saw a place at the extreme western end of them. [20]He said to me, "This is the place where the priests shall boil the guilt offering and the sin offering, and where they shall bake the grain offering, in order not to bring them out into the outer court and so communicate holiness to the people."

21 Then he brought me out to the outer court, and led me past the four corners of the court; and in each corner of the court there was a court— [22]in the four corners of the court were small[b] courts, forty cubits long and thirty wide; the four were of the same size. [23]On the inside, around each of the four courts[c] was a row of masonry, with hearths made at the bottom of the rows all around. [24]Then he said to me, "These are the kitchens where those who serve at the temple shall boil the sacrifices of the people."

Water Flowing from the Temple

47 Then he brought me back to the entrance of the temple; there, water was flowing from below the threshold of the temple toward the east (for the temple faced east); and the water was flowing down from below the south end of the threshold of the temple, south of the altar. [2]Then he brought me out by way of the north gate, and led me around on the outside to the outer gate that faces toward the east;[d] and the water was coming out on the south side.

3 Going on eastward with a cord in his hand, the man measured one thousand cubits, and then led me through the water; and it was ankle-deep. [4]Again he measured one thousand, and led me through the water; and it was knee-deep. Again he measured one thousand, and led me through the water; and it was up to the waist. [5]Again he measured one thousand, and it was a river that I could not cross, for the water had risen; it was deep enough to swim in, a river that could not be crossed. [6]He said to me, "Mortal, have you seen this?"

Then he led me back along the bank of the river. [7]As I came back, I saw on the bank of the river a great many trees on the one side and on the other. [8]He said to me, "This water flows toward the eastern region and goes down into the Arabah; and when it enters the sea, the sea of stagnant waters, the water will become fresh. [9]Wherever the river goes,[e] every living creature that swarms will live, and there will be very many fish, once these waters reach there. It will become fresh; and everything will live where the river goes. [10]People will stand fishing beside the sea[f] from En-gedi to En-eglaim; it will be a place for the spreading of nets; its fish will be of a great many kinds, like the fish of the

---

a Gk: Heb *it is his inheritance*   b Gk Syr Vg: Meaning of Heb uncertain   c Heb *the four of them*   d Meaning of Heb uncertain   e Gk Syr Vg Tg: Heb *the two rivers go*   f Heb *it*

Great Sea. [11]But its swamps and marshes will not become fresh; they are to be left for salt. [12]On the banks, on both sides of the river, there will grow all kinds of trees for food. Their leaves will not wither nor their fruit fail, but they will bear fresh fruit every month, because the water for them flows from the sanctuary. Their fruit will be for food, and their leaves for healing."

The New Boundaries of the Land

13 Thus says the Lord GOD: These are the boundaries by which you shall divide the land for inheritance among the twelve tribes of Israel. Joseph shall have two portions. [14]You shall divide it equally; I swore to give it to your ancestors, and this land shall fall to you as your inheritance.

15 This shall be the boundary of the land: On the north side, from the Great Sea by way of Hethlon to Lebo-hamath, and on to Zedad,[a] [16]Berothah, Sibraim (which lies between the border of Damascus and the border of Hamath), as far as Hazer-hatticon, which is on the border of Hauran. [17]So the boundary shall run from the sea to Hazar-enon, which is north of the border of Damascus, with the border of Hamath to the north.[b] This shall be the north side.

18 On the east side, between Hauran and Damascus; along the Jordan between Gilead and the land of Israel; to the eastern sea and as far as Tamar.[c] This shall be the east side.

19 On the south side, it shall run from Tamar as far as the waters of Meribath-kadesh, from there along the Wadi of Egypt[d] to the Great Sea. This shall be the south side.

20 On the west side, the Great Sea shall be the boundary to a point opposite Lebo-hamath. This shall be the west side.

21 So you shall divide this land among you according to the tribes of Israel. [22]You shall allot it as an inheritance for yourselves and for the aliens who reside among you and have begotten children among you. They shall be to you as citizens of Israel; with you they shall be allotted an inheritance among the tribes of Israel. [23]In whatever tribe aliens reside, there you shall assign them their inheritance, says the Lord GOD.

The Tribal Portions

48 These are the names of the tribes: Beginning at the northern border, on the Hethlon road,[e] from Lebo-hamath, as far as Hazar-enon (which is on the border of Damascus, with Hamath to the north), and[f] extending from the east side to the west,[g] Dan, one portion. [2]Adjoining the territory of Dan, from the east side to the west, Asher, one portion. [3]Adjoining the territory of Asher, from the east side to the west, Naphtali, one portion. [4]Adjoining the territory of Naphtali, from the east side to the west, Manasseh, one portion. [5]Adjoining the territory of Manasseh, from the east side to the west, Ephraim, one portion. [6]Adjoining the territory of Ephraim, from the east side to the west, Reuben, one portion. [7]Adjoining the territory of Reuben, from the east side to the west, Judah, one portion.

8 Adjoining the territory of Judah, from the east side to the west, shall be the portion that you shall set apart, twenty-five thousand cubits in width, and in length equal to one of the tribal portions, from the east side to the west, with the sanctuary in the middle of it. [9]The portion that you shall set apart for the LORD shall be twenty-five thousand cubits in length, and twenty[h] thousand in width. [10]These shall be the allotments of the holy portion: the priests shall have an allotment measuring twenty-five thousand cubits on the northern side, ten thousand cubits in width on the western side, ten thousand in width on the eastern side, and twenty-five thousand in length on the southern side, with the sanctuary of the LORD in the middle of it. [11]This shall be for the consecrated priests, the descendants[i] of Zadok,

---

a Gk: Heb *Lebo-zedad*, [16]*Hamath*   b Meaning of Heb uncertain   c Compare Syr: Heb *you shall measure*
d Heb lacks *of Egypt*   e Compare 47.15: Heb *by the side of the way*   f Cn: Heb *and they shall be his*
g Gk Compare verses 2-8: Heb *the east side the west*   h Compare 45.1: Heb *ten*   i One Ms Gk: Heb *of the descendants*

who kept my charge, who did not go astray when the people of Israel went astray, as the Levites did. 12It shall belong to them as a special portion from the holy portion of the land, a most holy place, adjoining the territory of the Levites. 13Alongside the territory of the priests, the Levites shall have an allotment twenty-five thousand cubits in length and ten thousand in width. The whole length shall be twenty-five thousand cubits and the width twenty*a* thousand. 14They shall not sell or exchange any of it; they shall not transfer this choice portion of the land, for it is holy to the LORD.

15 The remainder, five thousand cubits in width and twenty-five thousand in length, shall be for ordinary use for the city, for dwellings and for open country. In the middle of it shall be the city; 16and these shall be its dimensions: the north side four thousand five hundred cubits, the south side four thousand five hundred, the east side four thousand five hundred, and the west side four thousand five hundred. 17The city shall have open land: on the north two hundred fifty cubits, on the south two hundred fifty, on the east two hundred fifty, on the west two hundred fifty. 18The remainder of the length alongside the holy portion shall be ten thousand cubits to the east, and ten thousand to the west, and it shall be alongside the holy portion. Its produce shall be food for the workers of the city. 19The workers of the city, from all the tribes of Israel, shall cultivate it. 20The whole portion that you shall set apart shall be twenty-five thousand cubits square, that is, the holy portion together with the property of the city.

21 What remains on both sides of the holy portion and of the property of the city shall belong to the prince. Extending from the twenty-five thousand cubits of the holy portion to the east border, and westward from the twenty-five thousand cubits to the west border, parallel to the tribal portions, it shall belong to the prince. The holy portion with the sanctuary of the temple in the middle of it, 22and the property of the Levites and of the city, shall be in the middle of that which belongs to the prince. The portion of the prince shall lie between the territory of Judah and the territory of Benjamin.

23 As for the rest of the tribes: from the east side to the west, Benjamin, one portion. 24Adjoining the territory of Benjamin, from the east side to the west, Simeon, one portion. 25Adjoining the territory of Simeon, from the east side to the west, Issachar, one portion. 26Adjoining the territory of Issachar, from the east side to the west, Zebulun, one portion. 27Adjoining the territory of Zebulun, from the east side to the west, Gad, one portion. 28And adjoining the territory of Gad to the south, the boundary shall run from Tamar to the waters of Meribath-kadesh, from there along the Wadi of Egypt*b* to the Great Sea. 29This is the land that you shall allot as an inheritance among the tribes of Israel, and these are their portions, says the Lord GOD.

30 These shall be the exits of the city: On the north side, which is to be four thousand five hundred cubits by measure, 31three gates, the gate of Reuben, the gate of Judah, and the gate of Levi, the gates of the city being named after the tribes of Israel. 32On the east side, which is to be four thousand five hundred cubits, three gates, the gate of Joseph, the gate of Benjamin, and the gate of Dan. 33On the south side, which is to be four thousand five hundred cubits by measure, three gates, the gate of Simeon, the gate of Issachar, and the gate of Zebulun. 34On the west side, which is to be four thousand five hundred cubits, three gates,*c* the gate of Gad, the gate of Asher, and the gate of Naphtali. 35The circumference of the city shall be eighteen thousand cubits. And the name of the city from that time on shall be, The LORD is There.

---

a Gk: Heb *ten*   *b* Heb lacks *of Egypt*   *c* One Ms Gk Syr: MT *their gates three*

DANIEL

Four Young Israelites at the Babylonian Court

1 In the third year of the reign of King Jehoiakim of Judah, King Nebuchadnezzar of Babylon came to Jerusalem and besieged it. ²The Lord let King Jehoiakim of Judah fall into his power, as well as some of the vessels of the house of God. These he brought to the land of Shinar,ᵃ and placed the vessels in the treasury of his gods.

3 Then the king commanded his palace master Ashpenaz to bring some of the Israelites of the royal family and of the nobility, ⁴young men without physical defect and handsome, versed in every branch of wisdom, endowed with knowledge and insight, and competent to serve in the king's palace; they were to be taught the literature and language of the Chaldeans. ⁵The king assigned them a daily portion of the royal rations of food and wine. They were to be educated for three years, so that at the end of that time they could be stationed in the king's court. ⁶Among them were Daniel, Hananiah, Mishael, and Azariah, from the tribe of Judah. ⁷The palace master gave them other names: Daniel he called Belteshazzar, Hananiah he called Shadrach, Mishael he called Meshach, and Azariah he called Abednego.

8 But Daniel resolved that he would not defile himself with the royal rations of food and wine; so he asked the palace master to allow him not to defile himself. ⁹Now God allowed Daniel to receive favor and compassion from the palace master. ¹⁰The palace master said to Daniel, "I am afraid of my lord the king; he has appointed your food and your drink. If he should see you in poorer condition than the other young men of your own age, you would endanger my head with the king." ¹¹Then Daniel asked the guard whom the palace master had appointed over Daniel, Hananiah, Mishael, and Azariah: ¹²"Please test your servants for ten days. Let us be given vegetables to eat and water to drink. ¹³You can then compare our appearance with the appearance of the young men who eat the royal rations, and deal with your servants according to what you observe." ¹⁴So he agreed to this proposal and tested them for ten days. ¹⁵At the end of ten days it was observed that they appeared better and fatter than all the young men who had been eating the royal rations. ¹⁶So the guard continued to withdraw their royal rations and the wine they were to drink, and gave them vegetables. ¹⁷To these four young men God gave knowledge and skill in every aspect of literature and wisdom; Daniel also had insight into all visions and dreams.

18 At the end of the time that the king had set for them to be brought in, the palace master brought them into the presence of Nebuchadnezzar, ¹⁹and the king spoke with them. And among them all, no one was found to compare with Daniel, Hananiah, Mishael, and Azariah; therefore they were stationed in the king's court. ²⁰In every matter of wisdom and understanding concerning which the king inquired of them, he found them ten times better than all the magicians and enchanters in his whole kingdom. ²¹And Daniel continued there until the first year of King Cyrus.

Nebuchadnezzar's Dream

2 In the second year of Nebuchadnezzar's reign, Nebuchadnezzar dreamed such dreams that his spirit was troubled and his sleep left him. ²So the king commanded that the magicians, the enchanters, the sorcerers, and the Chaldeans be summoned to tell the king his dreams. When they came in and stood before the king, ³he said to them, "I have had such a dream that my spirit is troubled by the desire to understand it." ⁴The Chaldeans said to the king (in Aramaic),ᵇ "O king, live forever! Tell your servants the dream, and we will reveal the interpretation." ⁵The king answered the Chaldeans, "This is a public decree: if you do not tell me both the dream and its interpretation, you shall be torn limb from limb, and

your houses shall be laid in ruins. ⁶But if you do tell me the dream and its interpretation, you shall receive from me gifts and rewards and great honor. Therefore tell me the dream and its interpretation." ⁷They answered a second time, "Let the king first tell his servants the dream, then we can give its interpretation." ⁸The king answered, "I know with certainty that you are trying to gain time, because you see I have firmly decreed: ⁹if you do not tell me the dream, there is but one verdict for you. You have agreed to speak lying and misleading words to me until things take a turn. Therefore, tell me the dream, and I shall know that you can give me its interpretation." ¹⁰The Chaldeans answered the king, "There is no one on earth who can reveal what the king demands! In fact no king, however great and powerful, has ever asked such a thing of any magician or enchanter or Chaldean. ¹¹The thing that the king is asking is too difficult, and no one can reveal it to the king except the gods, whose dwelling is not with mortals."

12 Because of this the king flew into a violent rage and commanded that all the wise men of Babylon be destroyed. ¹³The decree was issued, and the wise men were about to be executed; and they looked for Daniel and his companions, to execute them. ¹⁴Then Daniel responded with prudence and discretion to Arioch, the king's chief executioner, who had gone out to execute the wise men of Babylon; ¹⁵he asked Arioch, the royal official, "Why is the decree of the king so urgent?" Arioch then explained the matter to Daniel. ¹⁶So Daniel went in and requested that the king give him time and he would tell the king the interpretation.

God Reveals Nebuchadnezzar's Dream

17 Then Daniel went to his home and informed his companions, Hananiah, Mishael, and Azariah, ¹⁸and told them to seek mercy from the God of heaven concerning this mystery, so that Daniel and his companions with the rest of the wise men of Babylon might not perish. ¹⁹Then the mystery was revealed to Daniel in a vision of the night, and Daniel blessed the God of heaven.

20　Daniel said:
"Blessed be the name of God from age
　　to age,
　　for wisdom and power are his.
21　He changes times and seasons,
　　deposes kings and sets up kings;
　he gives wisdom to the wise
　　and knowledge to those who have
　　　understanding.
22　He reveals deep and hidden things;
　　he knows what is in the darkness,
　　and light dwells with him.
23　To you, O God of my ancestors,
　　I give thanks and praise,
　for you have given me wisdom and
　　power,
　　and have now revealed to me what we
　　　asked of you,
　　for you have revealed to us what the
　　　king ordered."

Daniel Interprets the Dream

24 Therefore Daniel went to Arioch, whom the king had appointed to destroy the wise men of Babylon, and said to him, "Do not destroy the wise men of Babylon; bring me in before the king, and I will give the king the interpretation."

25 Then Arioch quickly brought Daniel before the king and said to him: "I have found among the exiles from Judah a man who can tell the king the interpretation." ²⁶The king said to Daniel, whose name was Belteshazzar, "Are you able to tell me the dream that I have seen and its interpretation?" ²⁷Daniel answered the king, "No wise men, enchanters, magicians, or diviners can show to the king the mystery that the king is asking, ²⁸but there is a God in heaven who reveals mysteries, and he has disclosed to King Nebuchadnezzar what will happen at the end of days. Your dream and the visions of your head as you lay in bed were these: ²⁹To you, O king, as you lay in bed, came thoughts of what would be hereafter, and the revealer of mysteries disclosed to you what is to be. ³⁰But as for me, this mystery has not

been revealed to me because of any wisdom that I have more than any other living being, but in order that the interpretation may be known to the king and that you may understand the thoughts of your mind.

31 "You were looking, O king, and lo! there was a great statue. This statue was huge, its brilliance extraordinary; it was standing before you, and its appearance was frightening. 32The head of that statue was of fine gold, its chest and arms of silver, its middle and thighs of bronze, 33its legs of iron, its feet partly of iron and partly of clay. 34As you looked on, a stone was cut out, not by human hands, and it struck the statue on its feet of iron and clay and broke them in pieces. 35Then the iron, the clay, the bronze, the silver, and the gold, were all broken in pieces and became like the chaff of the summer threshing floors; and the wind carried them away, so that not a trace of them could be found. But the stone that struck the statue became a great mountain and filled the whole earth.

36 "This was the dream; now we will tell the king its interpretation. 37You, O king, the king of kings—to whom the God of heaven has given the kingdom, the power, the might, and the glory, 38into whose hand he has given human beings, wherever they live, the wild animals of the field, and the birds of the air, and whom he has established as ruler over them all—you are the head of gold. 39After you shall arise another kingdom inferior to yours, and yet a third kingdom of bronze, which shall rule over the whole earth. 40And there shall be a fourth kingdom, strong as iron; just as iron crushes and smashes everything,ᵃ it shall crush and shatter all these. 41As you saw the feet and toes partly of potter's clay and partly of iron, it shall be a divided kingdom; but some of the strength of iron shall be in it, as you saw the iron mixed with the clay. 42As the toes of the feet were part iron and part clay, so the kingdom shall be partly strong and partly brittle. 43As you saw the iron mixed with clay, so will they mix with one another in marriage,ᵇ but they will not hold together, just as iron does not mix with clay.

44And in the days of those kings the God of heaven will set up a kingdom that shall never be destroyed, nor shall this kingdom be left to another people. It shall crush all these kingdoms and bring them to an end, and it shall stand forever; 45just as you saw that a stone was cut from the mountain not by hands, and that it crushed the iron, the bronze, the clay, the silver, and the gold. The great God has informed the king what shall be hereafter. The dream is certain, and its interpretation trustworthy."

Daniel and His Friends Promoted

46 Then King Nebuchadnezzar fell on his face, worshiped Daniel, and commanded that a grain offering and incense be offered to him. 47The king said to Daniel, "Truly, your God is God of gods and Lord of kings and a revealer of mysteries, for you have been able to reveal this mystery!" 48Then the king promoted Daniel, gave him many great gifts, and made him ruler over the whole province of Babylon and chief prefect over all the wise men of Babylon. 49Daniel made a request of the king, and he appointed Shadrach, Meshach, and Abednego over the affairs of the province of Babylon. But Daniel remained at the king's court.

The Golden Image

3 King Nebuchadnezzar made a golden statue whose height was sixty cubits and whose width was six cubits; he set it up on the plain of Dura in the province of Babylon. 2Then King Nebuchadnezzar sent for the satraps, the prefects, and the governors, the counselors, the treasurers, the justices, the magistrates, and all the officials of the provinces, to assemble and come to the dedication of the statue that King Nebuchadnezzar had set up. 3So the satraps, the prefects, and the governors, the counselors, the treasurers, the justices, the magistrates, and all the officials of the provinces, assembled for the dedication of the statue that King Nebuchadnezzar had set up. When they were standing before the statue that Nebuchadnezzar had set up, 4the herald

---

ᵃ Gk Theodotion Syr Vg: Aram adds *and like iron that crushes*　　ᵇ Aram *by human seed* proclaimed aloud, "You are commanded, O peoples, nations, and languages, [5]that when you hear the sound of the horn, pipe, lyre, trigon, harp, drum, and entire musical ensemble, you are to fall down and worship the golden statue that King Nebuchadnezzar has set up. [6]Whoever does not fall down and worship shall immediately be thrown into a furnace of blazing fire." [7]Therefore, as soon as all the peoples heard the sound of the horn, pipe, lyre, trigon, harp, drum, and entire musical ensemble, all the peoples, nations, and languages fell down and worshiped the golden statue that King Nebuchadnezzar had set up.

8 Accordingly, at this time certain Chaldeans came forward and denounced the Jews. [9]They said to King Nebuchadnezzar, "O king, live forever! [10]You, O king, have made a decree, that everyone who hears the sound of the horn, pipe, lyre, trigon, harp, drum, and entire musical ensemble, shall fall down and worship the golden statue, [11]and whoever does not fall down and worship shall be thrown into a furnace of blazing fire. [12]There are certain Jews whom you have appointed over the affairs of the province of Babylon: Shadrach, Meshach, and Abednego. These pay no heed to you, O king. They do not serve your gods and they do not worship the golden statue that you have set up."

13 Then Nebuchadnezzar in furious rage commanded that Shadrach, Meshach, and Abednego be brought in; so they brought those men before the king. [14]Nebuchadnezzar said to them, "Is it true, O Shadrach, Meshach, and Abednego, that you do not serve my gods and you do not worship the golden statue that I have set up? [15]Now if you are ready when you hear the sound of the horn, pipe, lyre, trigon, harp, drum, and entire musical ensemble to fall down and worship the statue that I have made, well and good.[a] But if you do not worship, you shall immediately be thrown into a furnace of blazing fire, and who is the god that will deliver you out of my hands?"

16 Shadrach, Meshach, and Abednego answered the king, "O Nebuchadnezzar, we have no need to present a defense to you in this matter. [17]If our God whom we serve is able to deliver us from the furnace of blazing fire and out of your hand, O king, let him deliver us.[b] [18]But if not, be it known to you, O king, that we will not serve your gods and we will not worship the golden statue that you have set up."

The Fiery Furnace

19 Then Nebuchadnezzar was so filled with rage against Shadrach, Meshach, and Abednego that his face was distorted. He ordered the furnace heated up seven times more than was customary, [20]and ordered some of the strongest guards in his army to bind Shadrach, Meshach, and Abednego and to throw them into the furnace of blazing fire. [21]So the men were bound, still wearing their tunics,[c] their trousers,[c] their hats, and their other garments, and they were thrown into the furnace of blazing fire. [22]Because the king's command was urgent and the furnace was so overheated, the raging flames killed the men who lifted Shadrach, Meshach, and Abednego. [23]But the three men, Shadrach, Meshach, and Abednego, fell down, bound, into the furnace of blazing fire.

24 Then King Nebuchadnezzar was astonished and rose up quickly. He said to his counselors, "Was it not three men that we threw bound into the fire?" They answered the king, "True, O king." [25]He replied, "But I see four men unbound, walking in the middle of the fire, and they are not hurt; and the fourth has the appearance of a god."[d] [26]Nebuchadnezzar then approached the door of the furnace of blazing fire and said, "Shadrach, Meshach, and Abednego, servants of the Most High God, come out! Come here!" So Shadrach, Meshach, and Abednego came out from the fire. [27]And the satraps, the prefects, the governors, and the king's counselors gathered together and saw that the fire had not had any power over the bodies of those men; the hair of their heads was not singed, their tunics[c] were not

---

a Aram lacks *well and good*   *b* Or *If our God whom we serve is able to deliver us, he will deliver us from the furnace of blazing fire and out of your hand, O king.*   *c* Meaning of Aram word uncertain   *d* Aram *a son of the gods* harmed, and not even the smell of fire came from them. 28Nebuchadnezzar said, "Blessed be the God of Shadrach, Meshach, and Abednego, who has sent his angel and delivered his servants who trusted in him. They disobeyed the king's command and yielded up their bodies rather than serve and worship any god except their own God. 29Therefore I make a decree: Any people, nation, or language that utters blasphemy against the God of Shadrach, Meshach, and Abednego shall be torn limb from limb, and their houses laid in ruins; for there is no other god who is able to deliver in this way." 30Then the king promoted Shadrach, Meshach, and Abednego in the province of Babylon.

Nebuchadnezzar's Second Dream

4 *a* King Nebuchadnezzar to all peoples, nations, and languages that live throughout the earth: May you have abundant prosperity! 2The signs and wonders that the Most High God has worked for me I am pleased to recount.

3   How great are his signs,
        how mighty his wonders!
    His kingdom is an everlasting kingdom,
        and his sovereignty is from generation
            to generation.

4 *b* I, Nebuchadnezzar, was living at ease in my home and prospering in my palace. 5I saw a dream that frightened me; my fantasies in bed and the visions of my head terrified me. 6So I made a decree that all the wise men of Babylon should be brought before me, in order that they might tell me the interpretation of the dream. 7Then the magicians, the enchanters, the Chaldeans, and the diviners came in, and I told them the dream, but they could not tell me its interpretation. 8At last Daniel came in before me—he who was named Belteshazzar after the name of my god, and who is endowed with a spirit of the holy gods *c*—and I told him the dream: 9"O Belteshazzar, chief of the magicians, I know that you are endowed with a spirit of the holy gods *c* and that no mystery is

too difficult for you. Hear *d* the dream that I saw; tell me its interpretation.

10 *e* Upon my bed this is what I saw;
        there was a tree at the center of the
            earth,
        and its height was great.
11   The tree grew great and strong,
        its top reached to heaven,
        and it was visible to the ends of the
            whole earth.
12   Its foliage was beautiful,
        its fruit abundant,
        and it provided food for all.
    The animals of the field found shade
        under it,
        the birds of the air nested in its
            branches,
        and from it all living beings were fed.

13 "I continued looking, in the visions of my head as I lay in bed, and there was a holy watcher, coming down from heaven. 14He cried aloud and said:

    'Cut down the tree and chop off its
        branches,
        strip off its foliage and scatter its fruit.
    Let the animals flee from beneath it
        and the birds from its branches.
15   But leave its stump and roots in the
            ground,
        with a band of iron and bronze,
        in the tender grass of the field.
    Let him be bathed with the dew of
            heaven,
        and let his lot be with the animals of
            the field
        in the grass of the earth.
16   Let his mind be changed from that of a
            human,
        and let the mind of an animal be
            given to him.
        And let seven times pass over him.
17   The sentence is rendered by decree of
            the watchers,
        the decision is given by order of the
            holy ones,

in order that all who live may know
    that the Most High is sovereign over
        the kingdom of mortals;
he gives it to whom he will
    and sets over it the lowliest of human
        beings.'

18 "This is the dream that I, King Nebuchadnezzar, saw. Now you, Belteshazzar, declare the interpretation, since all the wise men of my kingdom are unable to tell me the interpretation. You are able, however, for you are endowed with a spirit of the holy gods."[a]

Daniel Interprets the Second Dream

19 Then Daniel, who was called Belteshazzar, was severely distressed for a while. His thoughts terrified him. The king said, "Belteshazzar, do not let the dream or the interpretation terrify you." Belteshazzar answered, "My lord, may the dream be for those who hate you, and its interpretation for your enemies! 20The tree that you saw, which grew great and strong, so that its top reached to heaven and was visible to the end of the whole earth, 21whose foliage was beautiful and its fruit abundant, and which provided food for all, under which animals of the field lived, and in whose branches the birds of the air had nests— 22it is you, O king! You have grown great and strong. Your greatness has increased and reaches to heaven, and your sovereignty to the ends of the earth. 23And whereas the king saw a holy watcher coming down from heaven and saying, 'Cut down the tree and destroy it, but leave its stump and roots in the ground, with a band of iron and bronze, in the grass of the field; and let him be bathed with the dew of heaven, and let his lot be with the animals of the field, until seven times pass over him'— 24this is the interpretation, O king, and it is a decree of the Most High that has come upon my lord the king: 25You shall be driven away from human society, and your dwelling shall be with the wild animals. You shall be made to eat grass like oxen, you shall be bathed with the

dew of heaven, and seven times shall pass over you, until you have learned that the Most High has sovereignty over the kingdom of mortals, and gives it to whom he will. 26As it was commanded to leave the stump and roots of the tree, your kingdom shall be re-established for you from the time that you learn that Heaven is sovereign. 27Therefore, O king, may my counsel be acceptable to you: atone for[b] your sins with righteousness, and your iniquities with mercy to the oppressed, so that your prosperity may be prolonged."

Nebuchadnezzar's Humiliation

28 All this came upon King Nebuchadnezzar. 29At the end of twelve months he was walking on the roof of the royal palace of Babylon, 30and the king said, "Is this not magnificent Babylon, which I have built as a royal capital by my mighty power and for my glorious majesty?" 31While the words were still in the king's mouth, a voice came from heaven: "O King Nebuchadnezzar, to you it is declared: The kingdom has departed from you! 32You shall be driven away from human society, and your dwelling shall be with the animals of the field. You shall be made to eat grass like oxen, and seven times shall pass over you, until you have learned that the Most High has sovereignty over the kingdom of mortals and gives it to whom he will." 33Immediately the sentence was fulfilled against Nebuchadnezzar. He was driven away from human society, ate grass like oxen, and his body was bathed with the dew of heaven, until his hair grew as long as eagles' feathers and his nails became like birds' claws.

Nebuchadnezzar Praises God

34 When that period was over, I, Nebuchadnezzar, lifted my eyes to heaven, and my reason returned to me.

I blessed the Most High,
    and praised and honored the one who
        lives forever.
For his sovereignty is an everlasting
    sovereignty,

---

a Or *a holy, divine spirit*   b Aram *break off*

and his kingdom endures from
> generation to generation.

35 All the inhabitants of the earth are
> accounted as nothing,
> and he does what he wills with the
> host of heaven
> and the inhabitants of the earth.
> There is no one who can stay his hand
> or say to him, "What are you doing?"

36 At that time my reason returned to me; and my majesty and splendor were restored to me for the glory of my kingdom. My counselors and my lords sought me out, I was re-established over my kingdom, and still more greatness was added to me. 37 Now I, Nebuchadnezzar, praise and extol and honor the King of heaven,

> for all his works are truth,
> and his ways are justice;
> and he is able to bring low
> those who walk in pride.

Belshazzar's Feast

5 King Belshazzar made a great festival for a thousand of his lords, and he was drinking wine in the presence of the thousand.

2 Under the influence of the wine, Belshazzar commanded that they bring in the vessels of gold and silver that his father Nebuchadnezzar had taken out of the temple in Jerusalem, so that the king and his lords, his wives, and his concubines might drink from them. 3 So they brought in the vessels of gold and silver[a] that had been taken out of the temple, the house of God in Jerusalem, and the king and his lords, his wives, and his concubines drank from them. 4 They drank the wine and praised the gods of gold and silver, bronze, iron, wood, and stone.

The Writing on the Wall

5 Immediately the fingers of a human hand appeared and began writing on the plaster of the wall of the royal palace, next to the lampstand. The king was watching the hand as it wrote. 6 Then the king's face turned pale, and his thoughts terrified him. His limbs gave way, and his knees knocked together. 7 The king cried aloud to bring in the enchanters, the Chaldeans, and the diviners; and the king said to the wise men of Babylon, "Whoever can read this writing and tell me its interpretation shall be clothed in purple, have a chain of gold around his neck, and rank third in the kingdom." 8 Then all the king's wise men came in, but they could not read the writing or tell the king the interpretation. 9 Then King Belshazzar became greatly terrified and his face turned pale, and his lords were perplexed.

10 The queen, when she heard the discussion of the king and his lords, came into the banqueting hall. The queen said, "O king, live forever! Do not let your thoughts terrify you or your face grow pale. 11 There is a man in your kingdom who is endowed with a spirit of the holy gods.[b] In the days of your father he was found to have enlightenment, understanding, and wisdom like the wisdom of the gods. Your father, King Nebuchadnezzar, made him chief of the magicians, enchanters, Chaldeans, and diviners,[c] 12 because an excellent spirit, knowledge, and understanding to interpret dreams, explain riddles, and solve problems were found in this Daniel, whom the king named Belteshazzar. Now let Daniel be called, and he will give the interpretation."

The Writing on the Wall Interpreted

13 Then Daniel was brought in before the king. The king said to Daniel, "So you are Daniel, one of the exiles of Judah, whom my father the king brought from Judah? 14 I have heard of you that a spirit of the gods[d] is in you, and that enlightenment, understanding, and excellent wisdom are found in you. 15 Now the wise men, the enchanters, have been brought in before me to read this writing and tell me its interpretation, but they were not able to give the interpretation of the matter. 16 But I have heard that you can give interpretations and solve problems. Now if you are able to read the writing and tell me its interpretation, you shall be clothed in pur-

---

a Theodotion Vg: Aram lacks *and silver*   b Or *a holy, divine spirit*   c Aram adds *the king your father*   d Or *a divine spirit* ple, have a chain of gold around your neck, and rank third in the kingdom."

17 Then Daniel answered in the presence of the king, "Let your gifts be for yourself, or give your rewards to someone else! Nevertheless I will read the writing to the king and let him know the interpretation. 18 O king, the Most High God gave your father Nebuchadnezzar kingship, greatness, glory, and majesty. 19 And because of the greatness that he gave him, all peoples, nations, and languages trembled and feared before him. He killed those he wanted to kill, kept alive those he wanted to keep alive, honored those he wanted to honor, and degraded those he wanted to degrade. 20 But when his heart was lifted up and his spirit was hardened so that he acted proudly, he was deposed from his kingly throne, and his glory was stripped from him. 21 He was driven from human society, and his mind was made like that of an animal. His dwelling was with the wild asses, he was fed grass like oxen, and his body was bathed with the dew of heaven, until he learned that the Most High God has sovereignty over the kingdom of mortals, and sets over it whomever he will. 22 And you, Belshazzar his son, have not humbled your heart, even though you knew all this! 23 You have exalted yourself against the Lord of heaven! The vessels of his temple have been brought in before you, and you and your lords, your wives and your concubines have been drinking wine from them. You have praised the gods of silver and gold, of bronze, iron, wood, and stone, which do not see or hear or know; but the God in whose power is your very breath, and to whom belong all your ways, you have not honored.

24 "So from his presence the hand was sent and this writing was inscribed. 25 And this is the writing that was inscribed: MENE, MENE, TEKEL, and PARSIN. 26 This is the interpretation of the matter: MENE, God has numbered the days of*a* your kingdom and brought it to an end; 27 TEKEL, you have been weighed on the scales and found wanting; 28 PERES,*b* your kingdom is divided and given to the Medes and Persians."

29 Then Belshazzar gave the command, and Daniel was clothed in purple, a chain of gold was put around his neck, and a proclamation was made concerning him that he should rank third in the kingdom.

30 That very night Belshazzar, the Chaldean king, was killed. 31 *c* And Darius the Mede received the kingdom, being about sixty-two years old.

The Plot against Daniel

6 It pleased Darius to set over the kingdom one hundred twenty satraps, stationed throughout the whole kingdom, 2 and over them three presidents, including Daniel; to these the satraps gave account, so that the king might suffer no loss. 3 Soon Daniel distinguished himself above all the other presidents and satraps because an excellent spirit was in him, and the king planned to appoint him over the whole kingdom. 4 So the presidents and the satraps tried to find grounds for complaint against Daniel in connection with the kingdom. But they could find no grounds for complaint or any corruption, because he was faithful, and no negligence or corruption could be found in him. 5 The men said, "We shall not find any ground for complaint against this Daniel unless we find it in connection with the law of his God."

6 So the presidents and satraps conspired and came to the king and said to him, "O King Darius, live forever! 7 All the presidents of the kingdom, the prefects and the satraps, the counselors and the governors are agreed that the king should establish an ordinance and enforce an interdict, that whoever prays to anyone, divine or human, for thirty days, except to you, O king, shall be thrown into a den of lions. 8 Now, O king, establish the interdict and sign the document, so that it cannot be changed, according to the law of the Medes and the Persians, which cannot be revoked." 9 Therefore King Darius signed the document and interdict.

---

a Aram lacks *the days of*   *b* The singular of *Parsin*   *c* Ch 6.1 in Aram

Daniel in the Lions' Den

10 Although Daniel knew that the document had been signed, he continued to go to his house, which had windows in its upper room open toward Jerusalem, and to get down on his knees three times a day to pray to his God and praise him, just as he had done previously. [11] The conspirators came and found Daniel praying and seeking mercy before his God. [12] Then they approached the king and said concerning the interdict, "O king! Did you not sign an interdict, that anyone who prays to anyone, divine or human, within thirty days except to you, O king, shall be thrown into a den of lions?" The king answered, "The thing stands fast, according to the law of the Medes and Persians, which cannot be revoked." [13] Then they responded to the king, "Daniel, one of the exiles from Judah, pays no attention to you, O king, or to the interdict you have signed, but he is saying his prayers three times a day."

14 When the king heard the charge, he was very much distressed. He was determined to save Daniel, and until the sun went down he made every effort to rescue him. [15] Then the conspirators came to the king and said to him, "Know, O king, that it is a law of the Medes and Persians that no interdict or ordinance that the king establishes can be changed."

16 Then the king gave the command, and Daniel was brought and thrown into the den of lions. The king said to Daniel, "May your God, whom you faithfully serve, deliver you!" [17] A stone was brought and laid on the mouth of the den, and the king sealed it with his own signet and with the signet of his lords, so that nothing might be changed concerning Daniel. [18] Then the king went to his palace and spent the night fasting; no food was brought to him, and sleep fled from him.

Daniel Saved from the Lions

19 Then, at break of day, the king got up and hurried to the den of lions. [20] When he came near the den where Daniel was, he cried out anxiously to Daniel, "O Daniel, servant of the living God, has your God whom you faithfully serve been able to deliver you from the lions?" [21] Daniel then said to the king, "O king, live forever! [22] My God sent his angel and shut the lions' mouths so that they would not hurt me, because I was found blameless before him; and also before you, O king, I have done no wrong." [23] Then the king was exceedingly glad and commanded that Daniel be taken up out of the den. So Daniel was taken up out of the den, and no kind of harm was found on him, because he had trusted in his God. [24] The king gave a command, and those who had accused Daniel were brought and thrown into the den of lions—they, their children, and their wives. Before they reached the bottom of the den the lions overpowered them and broke all their bones in pieces.

25 Then King Darius wrote to all peoples and nations of every language throughout the whole world: "May you have abundant prosperity! [26] I make a decree, that in all my royal dominion people should tremble and fear before the God of Daniel:

For he is the living God,
        enduring forever.
His kingdom shall never be destroyed,
        and his dominion has no end.
27 He delivers and rescues,
        he works signs and wonders in heaven
            and on earth;
    for he has saved Daniel
        from the power of the lions."

[28] So this Daniel prospered during the reign of Darius and the reign of Cyrus the Persian.

Visions of the Four Beasts

7 In the first year of King Belshazzar of Babylon, Daniel had a dream and visions of his head as he lay in bed. Then he wrote down the dream: *a* [2] I, *b* Daniel, saw in my vision by night the four winds of heaven stirring up the great sea, [3] and four great beasts came up out of the sea, different from one another. [4] The first was like a lion and had eagles' wings.

a Q Ms Theodotion: MT adds *the beginning of the words; he said*   *b* Theodotion: Aram *Daniel answered and said, I*

Then, as I watched, its wings were plucked off, and it was lifted up from the ground and made to stand on two feet like a human being; and a human mind was given to it. 5Another beast appeared, a second one, that looked like a bear. It was raised up on one side, had three tusks*a* in its mouth among its teeth and was told, "Arise, devour many bodies!" 6After this, as I watched, another appeared, like a leopard. The beast had four wings of a bird on its back and four heads; and dominion was given to it. 7After this I saw in the visions by night a fourth beast, terrifying and dreadful and exceedingly strong. It had great iron teeth and was devouring, breaking in pieces, and stamping what was left with its feet. It was different from all the beasts that preceded it, and it had ten horns. 8I was considering the horns, when another horn appeared, a little one coming up among them; to make room for it, three of the earlier horns were plucked up by the roots. There were eyes like human eyes in this horn, and a mouth speaking arrogantly.

Judgment before the Ancient One

9   As I watched,
      thrones were set in place,
         and an Ancient One*b* took his throne,
      his clothing was white as snow,
         and the hair of his head like pure
            wool;
      his throne was fiery flames,
         and its wheels were burning fire.
10   A stream of fire issued
         and flowed out from his presence.
      A thousand thousands served him,
         and ten thousand times ten thousand
            stood attending him.
      The court sat in judgment,
         and the books were opened.
11I watched then because of the noise of the arrogant words that the horn was speaking. And as I watched, the beast was put to death, and its body destroyed and given over to be burned with fire. 12As for the rest of the beasts, their dominion was taken away, but their lives

were prolonged for a season and a time. 13As I watched in the night visions,

      I saw one like a human being*c*
         coming with the clouds of heaven.
      And he came to the Ancient One*b*
         and was presented before him.
14   To him was given dominion
         and glory and kingship,
      that all peoples, nations, and languages
         should serve him.
      His dominion is an everlasting dominion
         that shall not pass away,
      and his kingship is one
         that shall never be destroyed.

Daniel's Visions Interpreted

15 As for me, Daniel, my spirit was troubled within me,*d* and the visions of my head terrified me. 16I approached one of the attendants to ask him the truth concerning all this. So he said that he would disclose to me the interpretation of the matter: 17"As for these four great beasts, four kings shall arise out of the earth. 18But the holy ones of the Most High shall receive the kingdom and possess the kingdom forever—forever and ever."

19 Then I desired to know the truth concerning the fourth beast, which was different from all the rest, exceedingly terrifying, with its teeth of iron and claws of bronze, and which devoured and broke in pieces, and stamped what was left with its feet; 20and concerning the ten horns that were on its head, and concerning the other horn, which came up and to make room for which three of them fell out—the horn that had eyes and a mouth that spoke arrogantly, and that seemed greater than the others. 21As I looked, this horn made war with the holy ones and was prevailing over them, 22until the Ancient One*b* came; then judgment was given for the holy ones of the Most High, and the time arrived when the holy ones gained possession of the kingdom.

23 This is what he said: "As for the fourth beast,
      there shall be a fourth kingdom on earth

a Or *ribs*   *b* Aram *an Ancient of Days*   *c* Aram *one like a son of man*   *d* Aram *troubled in its sheath*

that shall be different from all the
other kingdoms;
it shall devour the whole earth,
and trample it down, and break it to
pieces.
24 As for the ten horns,
out of this kingdom ten kings shall arise,
and another shall arise after them.
This one shall be different from the
former ones,
and shall put down three kings.
25 He shall speak words against the Most
High,
shall wear out the holy ones of the
Most High,
and shall attempt to change the sacred
seasons and the law;
and they shall be given into his power
for a time, two times,*a* and half a time.
26 Then the court shall sit in judgment,
and his dominion shall be taken away,
to be consumed and totally destroyed.
27 The kingship and dominion
and the greatness of the kingdoms
under the whole heaven
shall be given to the people of the
holy ones of the Most High;
their kingdom shall be an everlasting
kingdom,
and all dominions shall serve and obey
them."

28 Here the account ends. As for me, Daniel, my thoughts greatly terrified me, and my face turned pale; but I kept the matter in my mind.

Vision of a Ram and a Goat

8 In the third year of the reign of King Belshazzar a vision appeared to me, Daniel, after the one that had appeared to me at first. ²In the vision I was looking and saw myself in Susa the capital, in the province of Elam,*b* and I was by the river Ulai.*c* ³I looked up and saw a ram standing beside the river.*d* It had two horns. Both horns were long, but one was longer than the other, and the longer one came up second. ⁴I saw the ram charging westward and northward and southward. All beasts were powerless to withstand it, and no one could rescue from its power; it did as it pleased and became strong.

5 As I was watching, a male goat appeared from the west, coming across the face of the whole earth without touching the ground. The goat had a horn*e* between its eyes. ⁶It came toward the ram with the two horns that I had seen standing beside the river,*d* and it ran at it with savage force. ⁷I saw it approaching the ram. It was enraged against it and struck the ram, breaking its two horns. The ram did not have power to withstand it; it threw the ram down to the ground and trampled upon it, and there was no one who could rescue the ram from its power. ⁸Then the male goat grew exceedingly great; but at the height of its power, the great horn was broken, and in its place there came up four prominent horns toward the four winds of heaven.

9 Out of one of them came another*f* horn, a little one, which grew exceedingly great toward the south, toward the east, and toward the beautiful land. ¹⁰It grew as high as the host of heaven. It threw down to the earth some of the host and some of the stars, and trampled on them. ¹¹Even against the prince of the host it acted arrogantly; it took the regular burnt offering away from him and overthrew the place of his sanctuary. ¹²Because of wickedness, the host was given over to it together with the regular burnt offering;*g* it cast truth to the ground, and kept prospering in what it did. ¹³Then I heard a holy one speaking, and another holy one said to the one that spoke, "For how long is this vision concerning the regular burnt offering, the transgression that makes desolate, and the giving over of the sanctuary and host to be trampled?"*g* ¹⁴And he answered him,*b* "For two thousand three hundred evenings and mornings; then the sanctuary shall be restored to its rightful state."

---

a Aram *a time, times*   *b* Gk Theodotion: MT Q Ms repeat *in the vision I was looking*   *c* Or *the Ulai Gate*   *d* Or *gate*
e Theodotion: Gk *one horn*; Heb *a horn of vision*   *f* Cn Compare 7.8: Heb *one*   *g* Meaning of Heb uncertain
b Gk Theodotion Syr Vg: Heb *me*

Gabriel Interprets the Vision

15 When I, Daniel, had seen the vision, I tried to understand it. Then someone appeared standing before me, having the appearance of a man, 16and I heard a human voice by the Ulai, calling, "Gabriel, help this man understand the vision." 17So he came near where I stood; and when he came, I became frightened and fell prostrate. But he said to me, "Understand, O mortal,*a* that the vision is for the time of the end."

18 As he was speaking to me, I fell into a trance, face to the ground; then he touched me and set me on my feet. 19He said, "Listen, and I will tell you what will take place later in the period of wrath; for it refers to the appointed time of the end. 20As for the ram that you saw with the two horns, these are the kings of Media and Persia. 21The male goat*b* is the king of Greece, and the great horn between its eyes is the first king. 22As for the horn that was broken, in place of which four others arose, four kingdoms shall arise from his*c* nation, but not with his power.

23　At the end of their rule,
　　when the transgressions have reached
　　　their full measure,
　　a king of bold countenance shall arise,
　　　skilled in intrigue.
24　He shall grow strong in power,*d*
　　　shall cause fearful destruction,
　　　and shall succeed in what he does.
　　He shall destroy the powerful
　　　and the people of the holy ones.
25　By his cunning
　　　he shall make deceit prosper under his
　　　　hand,
　　and in his own mind he shall be great.
　　Without warning he shall destroy many
　　　and shall even rise up against the
　　　　Prince of princes.
　　But he shall be broken, and not by
　　　human hands.
26The vision of the evenings and the mornings that has been told is true. As for you, seal up the vision, for it refers to many days from now."

27 So I, Daniel, was overcome and lay sick for some days; then I arose and went about the king's business. But I was dismayed by the vision and did not understand it.

Daniel's Prayer for the People

9 In the first year of Darius son of Ahasuerus, by birth a Mede, who became king over the realm of the Chaldeans— 2in the first year of his reign, I, Daniel, perceived in the books the number of years that, according to the word of the LORD to the prophet Jeremiah, must be fulfilled for the devastation of Jerusalem, namely, seventy years.

3 Then I turned to the Lord God, to seek an answer by prayer and supplication with fasting and sackcloth and ashes. 4I prayed to the LORD my God and made confession, saying,

"Ah, Lord, great and awesome God, keeping covenant and steadfast love with those who love you and keep your commandments, 5we have sinned and done wrong, acted wickedly and rebelled, turning aside from your commandments and ordinances. 6We have not listened to your servants the prophets, who spoke in your name to our kings, our princes, and our ancestors, and to all the people of the land.

7 "Righteousness is on your side, O Lord, but open shame, as at this day, falls on us, the people of Judah, the inhabitants of Jerusalem, and all Israel, those who are near and those who are far away, in all the lands to which you have driven them, because of the treachery that they have committed against you. 8Open shame, O LORD, falls on us, our kings, our officials, and our ancestors, because we have sinned against you. 9To the Lord our God belong mercy and forgiveness, for we have rebelled against him, 10and have not obeyed the voice of the LORD our God by following his laws, which he set before us by his servants the prophets.

11 "All Israel has transgressed your law and turned aside, refusing to obey your voice. So the curse and the oath written in the law of Moses,

a Heb *son of man*　　*b* Or *shaggy male goat*　　*c* Gk Theodotion Vg: Heb *the*　　*d* Theodotion and one Gk Ms: Heb repeats (from 8.22) *but not with his power* the servant of God, have been poured out upon us, because we have sinned against you. 12He has confirmed his words, which he spoke against us and against our rulers, by bringing upon us a calamity so great that what has been done against Jerusalem has never before been done under the whole heaven. 13Just as it is written in the law of Moses, all this calamity has come upon us. We did not entreat the favor of the LORD our God, turning from our iniquities and reflecting on his*a* fidelity. 14So the LORD kept watch over this calamity until he brought it upon us. Indeed, the LORD our God is right in all that he has done; for we have disobeyed his voice.

15 "And now, O Lord our God, who brought your people out of the land of Egypt with a mighty hand and made your name renowned even to this day—we have sinned, we have done wickedly. 16O Lord, in view of all your righteous acts, let your anger and wrath, we pray, turn away from your city Jerusalem, your holy mountain; because of our sins and the iniquities of our ancestors, Jerusalem and your people have become a disgrace among all our neighbors. 17Now therefore, O our God, listen to the prayer of your servant and to his supplication, and for your own sake, Lord,*b* let your face shine upon your desolated sanctuary. 18Incline your ear, O my God, and hear. Open your eyes and look at our desolation and the city that bears your name. We do not present our supplication before you on the ground of our righteousness, but on the ground of your great mercies. 19O Lord, hear; O Lord, forgive; O Lord, listen and act and do not delay! For your own sake, O my God, because your city and your people bear your name!"

The Seventy Weeks

20 While I was speaking, and was praying and confessing my sin and the sin of my people Israel, and presenting my supplication before the LORD my God on behalf of the holy mountain of my God— 21while I was speaking in prayer, the man Gabriel, whom I had seen before in a vision, came to me in swift flight at the time of the evening sacrifice. 22He came*c* and said to me, "Daniel, I have now come out to give you wisdom and understanding. 23At the beginning of your supplications a word went out, and I have come to declare it, for you are greatly beloved. So consider the word and understand the vision:

24 "Seventy weeks are decreed for your people and your holy city: to finish the transgression, to put an end to sin, and to atone for iniquity, to bring in everlasting righteousness, to seal both vision and prophet, and to anoint a most holy place.*d* 25Know therefore and understand: from the time that the word went out to restore and rebuild Jerusalem until the time of an anointed prince, there shall be seven weeks; and for sixty-two weeks it shall be built again with streets and moat, but in a troubled time. 26After the sixty-two weeks, an anointed one shall be cut off and shall have nothing, and the troops of the prince who is to come shall destroy the city and the sanctuary. Its*e* end shall come with a flood, and to the end there shall be war. Desolations are decreed. 27He shall make a strong covenant with many for one week, and for half of the week he shall make sacrifice and offering cease; and in their place*f* shall be an abomination that desolates, until the decreed end is poured out upon the desolator."

Conflict of Nations and Heavenly Powers

10 In the third year of King Cyrus of Persia a word was revealed to Daniel, who was named Belteshazzar. The word was true, and it concerned a great conflict. He understood the word, having received understanding in the vision.

2 At that time I, Daniel, had been mourning for three weeks. 3I had eaten no rich food, no meat or wine had entered my mouth, and I had not anointed myself at all, for the full three weeks. 4On the twenty-fourth day of the first month, as I was standing on the bank of the great river (that is, the Tigris), 5I looked up and saw a man clothed in linen, with a belt of

---

a Heb *your*   *b* Theodotion Vg Compare Syr: Heb *for the Lord's sake*   *c* Gk Syr: Heb *He made to understand*
d Or *thing* or *one*   *e* Or *His*   *f* Cn: Meaning of Heb uncertain

gold from Uphaz around his waist. 6His body was like beryl, his face like lightning, his eyes like flaming torches, his arms and legs like the gleam of burnished bronze, and the sound of his words like the roar of a multitude. 7I, Daniel, alone saw the vision; the people who were with me did not see the vision, though a great trembling fell upon them, and they fled and hid themselves. 8So I was left alone to see this great vision. My strength left me, and my complexion grew deathly pale, and I retained no strength. 9Then I heard the sound of his words; and when I heard the sound of his words, I fell into a trance, face to the ground.

10 But then a hand touched me and roused me to my hands and knees. 11He said to me, "Daniel, greatly beloved, pay attention to the words that I am going to speak to you. Stand on your feet, for I have now been sent to you." So while he was speaking this word to me, I stood up trembling. 12He said to me, "Do not fear, Daniel, for from the first day that you set your mind to gain understanding and to humble yourself before your God, your words have been heard, and I have come because of your words. 13But the prince of the kingdom of Persia opposed me twenty-one days. So Michael, one of the chief princes, came to help me, and I left him there with the prince of the kingdom of Persia,*a* 14and have come to help you understand what is to happen to your people at the end of days. For there is a further vision for those days."

15 While he was speaking these words to me, I turned my face toward the ground and was speechless. 16Then one in human form touched my lips, and I opened my mouth to speak, and said to the one who stood before me, "My lord, because of the vision such pains have come upon me that I retain no strength. 17How can my lord's servant talk with my lord? For I am shaking,*b* no strength remains in me, and no breath is left in me."

18 Again one in human form touched me and strengthened me. 19He said, "Do not fear, greatly beloved, you are safe. Be strong and courageous!" When he spoke to me, I was strengthened and said, "Let my lord speak, for you have strengthened me." 20Then he said, "Do you know why I have come to you? Now I must return to fight against the prince of Persia, and when I am through with him, the prince of Greece will come. 21But I am to tell you what is inscribed in the book of truth. There is no one with me who contends against

11 these princes except Michael, your prince. 1As for me, in the first year of Darius the Mede, I stood up to support and strengthen him.

2 "Now I will announce the truth to you. Three more kings shall arise in Persia. The fourth shall be far richer than all of them, and when he has become strong through his riches, he shall stir up all against the kingdom of Greece. 3Then a warrior king shall arise, who shall rule with great dominion and take action as he pleases. 4And while still rising in power, his kingdom shall be broken and divided toward the four winds of heaven, but not to his posterity, nor according to the dominion with which he ruled; for his kingdom shall be uprooted and go to others besides these.

5 "Then the king of the south shall grow strong, but one of his officers shall grow stronger than he and shall rule a realm greater than his own realm. 6After some years they shall make an alliance, and the daughter of the king of the south shall come to the king of the north to ratify the agreement. But she shall not retain her power, and his offspring shall not endure. She shall be given up, she and her attendants and her child and the one who supported her.

"In those times 7a branch from her roots shall rise up in his place. He shall come against the army and enter the fortress of the king of the north, and he shall take action against them and prevail. 8Even their gods, with their idols and with their precious vessels of silver and gold, he shall carry off to Egypt as spoils of war. For some years he shall refrain from attacking the king of the north; 9then the latter

---

a Gk Theodotion: Heb *I was left there with the kings of Persia*   *b* Gk: Heb *from now* shall invade the realm of the king of the south, but will return to his own land.

10 "His sons shall wage war and assemble a multitude of great forces, which shall advance like a flood and pass through, and again shall carry the war as far as his fortress. 11Moved with rage, the king of the south shall go out and do battle against the king of the north, who shall muster a great multitude, which shall, however, be defeated by his enemy. 12When the multitude has been carried off, his heart shall be exalted, and he shall overthrow tens of thousands, but he shall not prevail. 13For the king of the north shall again raise a multitude, larger than the former, and after some years *a* he shall advance with a great army and abundant supplies.

14 "In those times many shall rise against the king of the south. The lawless among your own people shall lift themselves up in order to fulfill the vision, but they shall fail. 15Then the king of the north shall come and throw up siegeworks, and take a well-fortified city. And the forces of the south shall not stand, not even his picked troops, for there shall be no strength to resist. 16But he who comes against him shall take the actions he pleases, and no one shall withstand him. He shall take a position in the beautiful land, and all of it shall be in his power. 17He shall set his mind to come with the strength of his whole kingdom, and he shall bring terms of peace *b* and perform them. In order to destroy the kingdom, *c* he shall give him a woman in marriage; but it shall not succeed or be to his advantage. 18Afterward he shall turn to the coastlands, and shall capture many. But a commander shall put an end to his insolence; indeed, *d* he shall turn his insolence back upon him. 19Then he shall turn back toward the fortresses of his own land, but he shall stumble and fall, and shall not be found.

20 "Then shall arise in his place one who shall send an official for the glory of the kingdom; but within a few days he shall be broken, though not in anger or in battle. 21In his place shall arise a contemptible person on whom royal majesty had not been conferred; he shall come in without warning and obtain the kingdom through intrigue. 22Armies shall be utterly swept away and broken before him, and the prince of the covenant as well. 23And after an alliance is made with him, he shall act deceitfully and become strong with a small party. 24Without warning he shall come into the richest parts *e* of the province and do what none of his predecessors had ever done, lavishing plunder, spoil, and wealth on them. He shall devise plans against strongholds, but only for a time. 25He shall stir up his power and determination against the king of the south with a great army, and the king of the south shall wage war with a much greater and stronger army. But he shall not succeed, for plots shall be devised against him 26by those who eat of the royal rations. They shall break him, his army shall be swept away, and many shall fall slain. 27The two kings, their minds bent on evil, shall sit at one table and exchange lies. But it shall not succeed, for there remains an end at the time appointed. 28He shall return to his land with great wealth, but his heart shall be set against the holy covenant. He shall work his will, and return to his own land.

29 "At the time appointed he shall return and come into the south, but this time it shall not be as it was before. 30For ships of Kittim shall come against him, and he shall lose heart and withdraw. He shall be enraged and take action against the holy covenant. He shall turn back and pay heed to those who forsake the holy covenant. 31Forces sent by him shall occupy and profane the temple and fortress. They shall abolish the regular burnt offering and set up the abomination that makes desolate. 32He shall seduce with intrigue those who violate the covenant; but the people who are loyal to their God shall stand firm and take action. 33The wise among the people shall give understanding to many; for some days, however, they shall fall by sword and flame, and suffer captivity and plunder. 34When they fall victim, they shall receive a little help, and many shall

---

a Heb *and at the end of the times years*   *b* Gk: Heb *kingdom, and upright ones with him*   *c* Heb *it*   *d* Meaning of Heb uncertain   *e* Or *among the richest men* join them insincerely. 35Some of the wise shall fall, so that they may be refined, purified, and cleansed,*a* until the time of the end, for there is still an interval until the time appointed.

36 "The king shall act as he pleases. He shall exalt himself and consider himself greater than any god, and shall speak horrendous things against the God of gods. He shall prosper until the period of wrath is completed, for what is determined shall be done. 37He shall pay no respect to the gods of his ancestors, or to the one beloved by women; he shall pay no respect to any other god, for he shall consider himself greater than all. 38He shall honor the god of fortresses instead of these; a god whom his ancestors did not know he shall honor with gold and silver, with precious stones and costly gifts. 39He shall deal with the strongest fortresses by the help of a foreign god. Those who acknowledge him he shall make more wealthy, and shall appoint them as rulers over many, and shall distribute the land for a price.

The Time of the End

40 "At the time of the end the king of the south shall attack him. But the king of the north shall rush upon him like a whirlwind, with chariots and horsemen, and with many ships. He shall advance against countries and pass through like a flood. 41He shall come into the beautiful land, and tens of thousands shall fall victim, but Edom and Moab and the main part of the Ammonites shall escape from his power. 42He shall stretch out his hand against the countries, and the land of Egypt shall not escape. 43He shall become ruler of the treasures of gold and of silver, and all the riches of Egypt; and the Libyans and the Ethiopians*b* shall follow in his train. 44But reports from the east and the north shall alarm him, and he shall go out with great fury to bring ruin and complete destruction to many. 45He shall pitch his palatial tents between the sea and the beautiful holy mountain. Yet he shall come to his end, with no one to help him.

The Resurrection of the Dead

12 "At that time Michael, the great prince, the protector of your people, shall arise. There shall be a time of anguish, such as has never occurred since nations first came into existence. But at that time your people shall be delivered, everyone who is found written in the book. 2Many of those who sleep in the dust of the earth*c* shall awake, some to everlasting life, and some to shame and everlasting contempt. 3Those who are wise shall shine like the brightness of the sky,*d* and those who lead many to righteousness, like the stars forever and ever. 4But you, Daniel, keep the words secret and the book sealed until the time of the end. Many shall be running back and forth, and evil*e* shall increase."

5 Then I, Daniel, looked, and two others appeared, one standing on this bank of the stream and one on the other. 6One of them said to the man clothed in linen, who was upstream, "How long shall it be until the end of these wonders?" 7The man clothed in linen, who was upstream, raised his right hand and his left hand toward heaven. And I heard him swear by the one who lives forever that it would be for a time, two times, and half a time,*f* and that when the shattering of the power of the holy people comes to an end, all these things would be accomplished. 8I heard but could not understand; so I said, "My lord, what shall be the outcome of these things?" 9He said, "Go your way, Daniel, for the words are to remain secret and sealed until the time of the end. 10Many shall be purified, cleansed, and refined, but the wicked shall continue to act wickedly. None of the wicked shall understand, but those who are wise shall understand. 11From the time that the regular burnt offering is taken away and the abomination that desolates is set up, there shall be one thousand two hundred ninety days. 12Happy are those who persevere and attain the thousand three hundred thirty-five days. 13But you, go your way,*g* and rest; you shall rise for your reward at the end of the days."

---

a Heb *made them white*   *b* Or *Nubians*; Heb *Cushites*   *c* Or *the land of dust*   *d* Or *dome*   *e* Cn Compare Gk: Heb *knowledge*   *f* Heb *a time, times, and a half*   *g* Gk Theodotion: Heb adds *to the end*

HOSEA

1 The word of the LORD that came to Hosea son of Beeri, in the days of Kings Uzziah, Jotham, Ahaz, and Hezekiah of Judah, and in the days of King Jeroboam son of Joash of Israel.

The Family of Hosea

2 When the LORD first spoke through Hosea, the LORD said to Hosea, "Go, take for yourself a wife of whoredom and have children of whoredom, for the land commits great whoredom by forsaking the LORD." ³So he went and took Gomer daughter of Diblaim, and she conceived and bore him a son.

4 And the LORD said to him, "Name him Jezreel;ᵃ for in a little while I will punish the house of Jehu for the blood of Jezreel, and I will put an end to the kingdom of the house of Israel. ⁵On that day I will break the bow of Israel in the valley of Jezreel."

6 She conceived again and bore a daughter. Then the LORD said to him, "Name her Lo-ruhamah,ᵇ for I will no longer have pity on the house of Israel or forgive them. ⁷But I will have pity on the house of Judah, and I will save them by the LORD their God; I will not save them by bow, or by sword, or by war, or by horses, or by horsemen."

8 When she had weaned Lo-ruhamah, she conceived and bore a son. ⁹Then the LORD said, "Name him Lo-ammi,ᶜ for you are not my people and I am not your God."ᵈ

The Restoration of Israel

10ᵉ Yet the number of the people of Israel shall be like the sand of the sea, which can be neither measured nor numbered; and in the place where it was said to them, "You are not my people," it shall be said to them, "Children of the living God." ¹¹The people of Judah and the people of Israel shall be gathered together, and they shall appoint for themselves one head; and they shall take possession ofᶠ the land, for great shall be the day of Jezreel.

2 ᵍSay to your brother,ʰ Ammi,ⁱ and to your sister,ʲ Ruhamah.ᵏ

Israel's Infidelity, Punishment, and Redemption

2 Plead with your mother, plead—
 for she is not my wife,
 and I am not her husband—
that she put away her whoring from her face,
 and her adultery from between her breasts,

3 or I will strip her naked
 and expose her as in the day she was born,
and make her like a wilderness,
 and turn her into a parched land,
 and kill her with thirst.

4 Upon her children also I will have no pity,
 because they are children of whoredom.

5 For their mother has played the whore;
 she who conceived them has acted shamefully.
For she said, "I will go after my lovers;
 they give me my bread and my water,
 my wool and my flax, my oil and my drink."

6 Therefore I will hedge up herˡ way with thorns;
 and I will build a wall against her,
 so that she cannot find her paths.

7 She shall pursue her lovers,
 but not overtake them;
and she shall seek them,
 but shall not find them.
Then she shall say, "I will go
 and return to my first husband,
 for it was better with me then than now."

8 She did not know

---

a That is *God sows* *b* That is *Not pitied* *c* That is *Not my people* *d* Heb *I am not yours* *e* Ch 2.1 in Heb
f Heb *rise up from* *g* Ch 2.3 in Heb *h* Gk: Heb *brothers* *i* That is *My people* *j* Gk Vg: Heb *sisters*
k That is *Pitied* *l* Gk Syr: Heb *your*

that it was I who gave her
the grain, the wine, and the oil,
and who lavished upon her silver
and gold that they used for Baal.

9 Therefore I will take back
my grain in its time,
and my wine in its season;
and I will take away my wool and my
flax,
which were to cover her nakedness.

10 Now I will uncover her shame
in the sight of her lovers,
and no one shall rescue her out of my
hand.

11 I will put an end to all her mirth,
her festivals, her new moons, her
sabbaths,
and all her appointed festivals.

12 I will lay waste her vines and her fig
trees,
of which she said,
"These are my pay,
which my lovers have given me."
I will make them a forest,
and the wild animals shall devour
them.

13 I will punish her for the festival days of
the Baals,
when she offered incense to them
and decked herself with her ring and
jewelry,
and went after her lovers,
and forgot me, says the LORD.

14 Therefore, I will now allure her,
and bring her into the wilderness,
and speak tenderly to her.

15 From there I will give her her vineyards,
and make the Valley of Achor a door
of hope.
There she shall respond as in the days of
her youth,
as at the time when she came out of
the land of Egypt.

16 On that day, says the LORD, you will call me,
"My husband," and no longer will you call me,

"My Baal."[a] 17 For I will remove the names of
the Baals from her mouth, and they shall be
mentioned by name no more. 18 I will make
for you[b] a covenant on that day with the wild
animals, the birds of the air, and the creeping
things of the ground; and I will abolish[c] the
bow, the sword, and war from the land; and I
will make you lie down in safety. 19 And I will
take you for my wife forever; I will take you for
my wife in righteousness and in justice, in steadfast love, and in mercy. 20 I will take you for my
wife in faithfulness; and you shall know the
LORD.

21 On that day I will answer, says the LORD,
I will answer the heavens
and they shall answer the earth;

22 and the earth shall answer the grain, the
wine, and the oil,
and they shall answer Jezreel;[d]

23 and I will sow him[e] for myself in the
land.
And I will have pity on Lo-ruhamah,[f]
and I will say to Lo-ammi,[g] "You are
my people";
and he shall say, "You are my God."

Further Assurances of God's Redeeming Love

3 The LORD said to me again, "Go, love a
woman who has a lover and is an adulteress, just as the LORD loves the people of Israel, though they turn to other gods and love
raisin cakes." 2 So I bought her for fifteen
shekels of silver and a homer of barley and a
measure of wine.[h] 3 And I said to her, "You
must remain as mine for many days; you shall
not play the whore, you shall not have intercourse with a man, nor I with you." 4 For the Israelites shall remain many days without king or
prince, without sacrifice or pillar, without
ephod or teraphim. 5 Afterward the Israelites
shall return and seek the LORD their God, and
David their king; they shall come in awe to the
LORD and to his goodness in the latter days.

a That is, "My master"   b Heb them   c Heb break   d That is God sows   e Cn: Heb her   f That is Not pitied
g That is Not my people   h Gk: Heb a homer of barley and a lethech of barley

God Accuses Israel

4 Hear the word of the LORD, O people
  of Israel;
 for the LORD has an indictment
  against the inhabitants of the
  land.
There is no faithfulness or loyalty,
 and no knowledge of God in the land.
2 Swearing, lying, and murder,
 and stealing and adultery break out;
 bloodshed follows bloodshed.
3 Therefore the land mourns,
 and all who live in it languish;
together with the wild animals
 and the birds of the air,
 even the fish of the sea are perishing.

4 Yet let no one contend,
 and let none accuse,
 for with you is my contention,
 O priest.*a*
5 You shall stumble by day;
 the prophet also shall stumble with
  you by night,
 and I will destroy your mother.
6 My people are destroyed for lack of
  knowledge;
 because you have rejected knowledge,
 I reject you from being a priest to me.
And since you have forgotten the law of
  your God,
 I also will forget your children.

7 The more they increased,
 the more they sinned against me;
 they changed*b* their glory into shame.
8 They feed on the sin of my people;
 they are greedy for their iniquity.
9 And it shall be like people, like priest;
 I will punish them for their ways,
 and repay them for their deeds.
10 They shall eat, but not be satisfied;
 they shall play the whore, but not
  multiply;
 because they have forsaken the LORD
 to devote themselves to 11whoredom.

The Idolatry of Israel

Wine and new wine
 take away the understanding.
12 My people consult a piece of wood,
 and their divining rod gives them
  oracles.
For a spirit of whoredom has led them
  astray,
 and they have played the whore,
  forsaking their God.
13 They sacrifice on the tops of the
  mountains,
 and make offerings upon the hills,
under oak, poplar, and terebinth,
 because their shade is good.

Therefore your daughters play the
  whore,
 and your daughters-in-law commit
  adultery.
14 I will not punish your daughters when
  they play the whore,
 nor your daughters-in-law when they
  commit adultery;
for the men themselves go aside with
  whores,
 and sacrifice with temple prostitutes;
thus a people without understanding
  comes to ruin.

15 Though you play the whore, O Israel,
 do not let Judah become guilty.
Do not enter into Gilgal,
 or go up to Beth-aven,
 and do not swear, "As the LORD lives."
16 Like a stubborn heifer,
 Israel is stubborn;
can the LORD now feed them
 like a lamb in a broad pasture?

17 Ephraim is joined to idols—
 let him alone.
18 When their drinking is ended, they
  indulge in sexual orgies;
 they love lewdness more than their
  glory.*c*

---

a Cn: Meaning of Heb uncertain *b* Ancient Heb tradition: MT *I will change* *c* Cn Compare Gk: Meaning of
Heb uncertain

19 A wind has wrapped them*a* in its wings,
and they shall be ashamed because of
their altars.*b*

Impending Judgment on Israel and Judah

5 Hear this, O priests!
Give heed, O house of Israel!
Listen, O house of the king!
For the judgment pertains to you;
for you have been a snare at Mizpah,
and a net spread upon Tabor,
2 and a pit dug deep in Shittim;*c*
but I will punish all of them.

3 I know Ephraim,
and Israel is not hidden from me;
for now, O Ephraim, you have played
the whore;
Israel is defiled.
4 Their deeds do not permit them
to return to their God.
For the spirit of whoredom is within
them,
and they do not know the LORD.

5 Israel's pride testifies against him;
Ephraim*d* stumbles in his guilt;
Judah also stumbles with them.
6 With their flocks and herds they shall go
to seek the LORD,
but they will not find him;
he has withdrawn from them.
7 They have dealt faithlessly with the
LORD;
for they have borne illegitimate
children.
Now the new moon shall devour
them along with their fields.

8 Blow the horn in Gibeah,
the trumpet in Ramah.
Sound the alarm at Beth-aven;
look behind you, Benjamin!
9 Ephraim shall become a desolation
in the day of punishment;
among the tribes of Israel

I declare what is sure.
10 The princes of Judah have become
like those who remove the landmark;
on them I will pour out
my wrath like water.
11 Ephraim is oppressed, crushed in
judgment,
because he was determined to go after
vanity.*e*
12 Therefore I am like maggots to
Ephraim,
and like rottenness to the house of
Judah.
13 When Ephraim saw his sickness,
and Judah his wound,
then Ephraim went to Assyria,
and sent to the great king.*f*
But he is not able to cure you
or heal your wound.
14 For I will be like a lion to Ephraim,
and like a young lion to the house of
Judah.
I myself will tear and go away;
I will carry off, and no one shall
rescue.
15 I will return again to my place
until they acknowledge their guilt and
seek my face.
In their distress they will beg my
favor:

A Call to Repentance

6 "Come, let us return to the LORD;
for it is he who has torn, and he will
heal us;
he has struck down, and he will bind
us up.
2 After two days he will revive us;
on the third day he will raise us up,
that we may live before him.
3 Let us know, let us press on to know the
LORD;
his appearing is as sure as the dawn;
he will come to us like the showers,
like the spring rains that water the
earth."

---

a Heb *her*   *b* Gk Syr: Heb *sacrifices*   *c* Cn: Meaning of Heb uncertain   *d* Heb *Israel and Ephraim*
e Gk: Meaning of Heb uncertain   *f* Cn: Heb *to a king who will contend*

Impenitence of Israel and Judah

4 What shall I do with you, O Ephraim?
   What shall I do with you, O Judah?
   Your love is like a morning cloud,
     like the dew that goes away early.
5 Therefore I have hewn them by the
     prophets,
   I have killed them by the words of my
     mouth,
   and my*a* judgment goes forth as the
     light.
6 For I desire steadfast love and not
     sacrifice,
   the knowledge of God rather than
     burnt offerings.

7 But at*b* Adam they transgressed the
     covenant;
   there they dealt faithlessly with me.
8 Gilead is a city of evildoers,
     tracked with blood.
9 As robbers lie in wait*c* for someone,
     so the priests are banded together;*d*
   they murder on the road to Shechem,
     they commit a monstrous crime.
10 In the house of Israel I have seen a
     horrible thing;
   Ephraim's whoredom is there, Israel is
     defiled.

11 For you also, O Judah, a harvest is
     appointed.

   When I would restore the fortunes of
     my people,

7 1 when I would heal Israel,
     the corruption of Ephraim is
       revealed,
     and the wicked deeds of Samaria;
   for they deal falsely,
     the thief breaks in,
     and the bandits raid outside.
2 But they do not consider
     that I remember all their wickedness.
   Now their deeds surround them,
     they are before my face.

3 By their wickedness they make the king
     glad,
   and the officials by their treachery.
4 They are all adulterers;
     they are like a heated oven,
   whose baker does not need to stir the
     fire,
   from the kneading of the dough until
     it is leavened.
5 On the day of our king the officials
     became sick with the heat of wine;
   he stretched out his hand with
     mockers.
6 For they are kindled*e* like an oven, their
     heart burns within them;
   all night their anger smolders;
   in the morning it blazes like a flaming
     fire.
7 All of them are hot as an oven,
     and they devour their rulers.
   All their kings have fallen;
     none of them calls upon me.

8 Ephraim mixes himself with the
     peoples;
   Ephraim is a cake not turned.
9 Foreigners devour his strength,
     but he does not know it;
   gray hairs are sprinkled upon him,
     but he does not know it.
10 Israel's pride testifies against*f* him;
     yet they do not return to the Lord
       their God,
     or seek him, for all this.

Futile Reliance on the Nations

11 Ephraim has become like a dove,
     silly and without sense;
   they call upon Egypt, they go to
     Assyria.
12 As they go, I will cast my net over them;
   I will bring them down like birds of
     the air;
   I will discipline them according to the
     report made to their assembly.*g*

a Gk Syr: Heb *your* *b* Cn: Heb *like* *c* Cn: Meaning of Heb uncertain *d* Syr: Heb *are a company* *e* Gk Syr:
Heb *brought near* *f* Or *humbles* *g* Meaning of Heb uncertain

13 Woe to them, for they have strayed from
        me!
    Destruction to them, for they have
        rebelled against me!
    I would redeem them,
        but they speak lies against me.

14 They do not cry to me from the heart,
        but they wail upon their beds;
    they gash themselves for grain and wine;
        they rebel against me.
15 It was I who trained and strengthened
        their arms,
        yet they plot evil against me.
16 They turn to that which does not profit;*a*
        they have become like a defective
            bow;
    their officials shall fall by the sword
        because of the rage of their tongue.
    So much for their babbling in the land of
        Egypt.

Israel's Apostasy

8 Set the trumpet to your lips!
    One like a vulture*b* is over the house
        of the LORD,
    because they have broken my covenant,
        and transgressed my law.
2 Israel cries to me,
    "My God, we—Israel—know you!"
3 Israel has spurned the good;
        the enemy shall pursue him.

4 They made kings, but not through me;
        they set up princes, but without my
            knowledge.
    With their silver and gold they made
        idols
        for their own destruction.
5 Your calf is rejected, O Samaria.
    My anger burns against them.
    How long will they be incapable of
        innocence?
6   For it is from Israel,
    an artisan made it;
        it is not God.

The calf of Samaria
    shall be broken to pieces.*c*

7 For they sow the wind,
    and they shall reap the whirlwind.
The standing grain has no heads,
    it shall yield no meal;
if it were to yield,
    foreigners would devour it.
8 Israel is swallowed up;
    now they are among the nations
    as a useless vessel.
9 For they have gone up to Assyria,
    a wild ass wandering alone;
    Ephraim has bargained for lovers.
10 Though they bargain with the nations,
    I will now gather them up.
They shall soon writhe
    under the burden of kings and
        princes.

11 When Ephraim multiplied altars to
        expiate sin,
    they became to him altars for sinning.
12 Though I write for him the multitude of
        my instructions,
    they are regarded as a strange thing.
13 Though they offer choice sacrifices,*a*
        though they eat flesh,
    the LORD does not accept them.
Now he will remember their iniquity,
    and punish their sins;
    they shall return to Egypt.
14 Israel has forgotten his Maker,
    and built palaces;
and Judah has multiplied fortified cities;
    but I will send a fire upon his cities,
    and it shall devour his strongholds.

Punishment for Israel's Sin

9 Do not rejoice, O Israel!
    Do not exult*d* as other nations do;
for you have played the whore, departing
        from your God.
    You have loved a prostitute's pay
        on all threshing floors.

---

a Cn: Meaning of Heb uncertain   *b* Meaning of Heb uncertain   *c* Or *shall go up in flames*   *d* Gk: Heb *To
exultation*

2 Threshing floor and wine vat shall not
 feed them,
 and the new wine shall fail them.
3 They shall not remain in the land of the
 LORD;
 but Ephraim shall return to Egypt,
 and in Assyria they shall eat unclean
  food.

4 They shall not pour drink offerings of
 wine to the LORD,
 and their sacrifices shall not please him.
Such sacrifices shall be like mourners'
 bread;
 all who eat of it shall be defiled;
for their bread shall be for their hunger
 only;
 it shall not come to the house of the
 LORD.

5 What will you do on the day of
 appointed festival,
 and on the day of the festival of the
 LORD?
6 For even if they escape destruction,
 Egypt shall gather them,
 Memphis shall bury them.
Nettles shall possess their precious
 things of silver;*a*
 thorns shall be in their tents.

7 The days of punishment have come,
 the days of recompense have come;
 Israel cries,*b*
"The prophet is a fool,
 the man of the spirit is mad!"
Because of your great iniquity,
 your hostility is great.
8 The prophet is a sentinel for my God
 over Ephraim,
 yet a fowler's snare is on all his ways,
 and hostility in the house of his God.
9 They have deeply corrupted themselves
 as in the days of Gibeah;
he will remember their iniquity,
 he will punish their sins.

10 Like grapes in the wilderness,
 I found Israel.
Like the first fruit on the fig tree,
 in its first season,
 I saw your ancestors.
But they came to Baal-peor,
 and consecrated themselves to a thing
  of shame,
 and became detestable like the thing
  they loved.
11 Ephraim's glory shall fly away like a
 bird—
 no birth, no pregnancy, no
  conception!
12 Even if they bring up children,
 I will bereave them until no one is left.
Woe to them indeed
 when I depart from them!
13 Once I saw Ephraim as a young palm
 planted in a lovely meadow,*a*
 but now Ephraim must lead out his
  children for slaughter.
14 Give them, O LORD—
 what will you give?
Give them a miscarrying womb
 and dry breasts.

15 Every evil of theirs began at Gilgal;
 there I came to hate them.
Because of the wickedness of their
 deeds
 I will drive them out of my house.
I will love them no more;
 all their officials are rebels.

16 Ephraim is stricken,
 their root is dried up,
 they shall bear no fruit.
Even though they give birth,
 I will kill the cherished offspring of
  their womb.
17 Because they have not listened to him,
 my God will reject them;
 they shall become wanderers among
  the nations.

a Meaning of Heb uncertain *b* Cn Compare Gk: Heb *shall know*

Israel's Sin and Captivity

10 Israel is a luxuriant vine
     that yields its fruit.
   The more his fruit increased
     the more altars he built;
   as his country improved,
     he improved his pillars.
2 Their heart is false;
     now they must bear their guilt.
   The LORD*a* will break down their altars,
     and destroy their pillars.

3 For now they will say:
     "We have no king,
   for we do not fear the LORD,
     and a king—what could he do for
       us?"
4 They utter mere words;
     with empty oaths they make
       covenants;
   so litigation springs up like poisonous
     weeds
   in the furrows of the field.
5 The inhabitants of Samaria tremble
     for the calf*b* of Beth-aven.
   Its people shall mourn for it,
     and its idolatrous priests shall wail*c*
       over it,
       over its glory that has departed from
         it.
6 The thing itself shall be carried to
     Assyria
   as tribute to the great king.*d*
   Ephraim shall be put to shame,
     and Israel shall be ashamed of his idol.*e*

7 Samaria's king shall perish
     like a chip on the face of the waters.
8 The high places of Aven, the sin of
     Israel,
   shall be destroyed.
   Thorn and thistle shall grow up
     on their altars.
   They shall say to the mountains, Cover
     us,
   and to the hills, Fall on us.

9 Since the days of Gibeah you have
     sinned, O Israel;
   there they have continued.
   Shall not war overtake them in
     Gibeah?
10 I will come*f* against the wayward people
     to punish them;
   and nations shall be gathered against
     them
   when they are punished*g* for their
     double iniquity.

11 Ephraim was a trained heifer
     that loved to thresh,
   and I spared her fair neck;
   but I will make Ephraim break the
     ground;
   Judah must plow;
   Jacob must harrow for himself.
12 Sow for yourselves righteousness;
     reap steadfast love;
   break up your fallow ground;
   for it is time to seek the LORD,
     that he may come and rain
       righteousness upon you.

13 You have plowed wickedness,
     you have reaped injustice,
     you have eaten the fruit of lies.
   Because you have trusted in your power
     and in the multitude of your warriors,
14 therefore the tumult of war shall rise
     against your people,
   and all your fortresses shall be
     destroyed,
   as Shalman destroyed Beth-arbel on the
     day of battle
   when mothers were dashed in pieces
     with their children.
15 Thus it shall be done to you, O Bethel,
     because of your great wickedness.
   At dawn the king of Israel
     shall be utterly cut off.

a Heb *he*   *b* Gk Syr: Heb *calves*   *c* Cn: Heb *exult*   *d* Cn: Heb *to a king who will contend*   *e* Cn: Heb *counsel*
f Cn Compare Gk: Heb *In my desire*   *g* Gk: Heb *bound*

God's Compassion Despite Israel's Ingratitude

11 When Israel was a child, I loved him,
and out of Egypt I called my son.
2 The more I[a] called them,
the more they went from me;[b]
they kept sacrificing to the Baals,
and offering incense to idols.

3 Yet it was I who taught Ephraim to walk,
I took them up in my[c] arms;
but they did not know that I healed
them.
4 I led them with cords of human
kindness,
with bands of love.
I was to them like those
who lift infants to their cheeks.[d]
I bent down to them and fed them.

5 They shall return to the land of Egypt,
and Assyria shall be their king,
because they have refused to return to
me.
6 The sword rages in their cities,
it consumes their oracle-priests,
and devours because of their schemes.
7 My people are bent on turning away
from me.
To the Most High they call,
but he does not raise them up at all.[e]

8 How can I give you up, Ephraim?
How can I hand you over, O Israel?
How can I make you like Admah?
How can I treat you like Zeboiim?
My heart recoils within me;
my compassion grows warm and
tender.
9 I will not execute my fierce anger;
I will not again destroy Ephraim;
for I am God and no mortal,
the Holy One in your midst,
and I will not come in wrath.[e]

10 They shall go after the LORD,
who roars like a lion;

when he roars,
his children shall come trembling
from the west.
11 They shall come trembling like birds
from Egypt,
and like doves from the land of
Assyria;
and I will return them to their homes,
says the LORD.

12[f] Ephraim has surrounded me with lies,
and the house of Israel with deceit;
but Judah still walks[g] with God,
and is faithful to the Holy One.

12 Ephraim herds the wind,
and pursues the east wind all day
long;
they multiply falsehood and violence;
they make a treaty with Assyria,
and oil is carried to Egypt.

The Long History of Rebellion

2 The LORD has an indictment against
Judah,
and will punish Jacob according to his
ways,
and repay him according to his deeds.
3 In the womb he tried to supplant his
brother,
and in his manhood he strove with
God.
4 He strove with the angel and prevailed,
he wept and sought his favor;
he met him at Bethel,
and there he spoke with him.[h]
5 The LORD the God of hosts,
the LORD is his name!
6 But as for you, return to your God,
hold fast to love and justice,
and wait continually for your God.

7 A trader, in whose hands are false
balances,
he loves to oppress.
8 Ephraim has said, "Ah, I am rich,
I have gained wealth for myself;

---

a Gk: Heb *they*   *b* Gk: Heb *them*   *c* Gk Syr Vg: Heb *his*   *d* Or *who ease the yoke on their jaws*   *e* Meaning of
Heb uncertain   *f* Ch 12.1 in Heb   *g* Heb *roams* or *rules*   *h* Gk Syr: Heb *us*

in all of my gain
no offense has been found in me
that would be sin."[a]

9 I am the LORD your God
from the land of Egypt;
I will make you live in tents again,
as in the days of the appointed
festival.

10 I spoke to the prophets;
it was I who multiplied visions,
and through the prophets I will bring
destruction.

11 In Gilead[b] there is iniquity,
they shall surely come to nothing.
In Gilgal they sacrifice bulls,
so their altars shall be like stone heaps
on the furrows of the field.

12 Jacob fled to the land of Aram,
there Israel served for a wife,
and for a wife he guarded sheep.[c]

13 By a prophet the LORD brought Israel up
from Egypt,
and by a prophet he was guarded.

14 Ephraim has given bitter offense,
so his Lord will bring his crimes down
on him
and pay him back for his insults.

Relentless Judgment on Israel

13 When Ephraim spoke, there was
trembling;
he was exalted in Israel;
but he incurred guilt through Baal and
died.

2 And now they keep on sinning
and make a cast image for themselves,
idols of silver made according to their
understanding,
all of them the work of artisans.
"Sacrifice to these," they say.[d]
People are kissing calves!

3 Therefore they shall be like the morning
mist
or like the dew that goes away early,
like chaff that swirls from the threshing
floor
or like smoke from a window.

4 Yet I have been the LORD your God
ever since the land of Egypt;
you know no God but me,
and besides me there is no savior.

5 It was I who fed[e] you in the wilderness,
in the land of drought.

6 When I fed[f] them, they were satisfied;
they were satisfied, and their heart was
proud;
therefore they forgot me.

7 So I will become like a lion to them,
like a leopard I will lurk beside the
way.

8 I will fall upon them like a bear robbed
of her cubs,
and will tear open the covering of
their heart;
there I will devour them like a lion,
as a wild animal would mangle them.

9 I will destroy you, O Israel;
who can help you?[g]

10 Where now is[h] your king, that he may
save you?
Where in all your cities are your rulers,
of whom you said, ·
"Give me a king and rulers"?

11 I gave you a king in my anger,
and I took him away in my wrath.

12 Ephraim's iniquity is bound up;
his sin is kept in store.

13 The pangs of childbirth come for him,
but he is an unwise son;
for at the proper time he does not
present himself
at the mouth of the womb.

14 Shall I ransom them from the power of
Sheol?
Shall I redeem them from Death?

a Meaning of Heb uncertain   b Compare Syr: Heb Gilead   c Heb lacks sheep   d Cn Compare Gk: Heb To
these they say sacrifices of people   e Gk Syr: Heb knew   f Cn: Heb according to their pasture   g Gk Syr: Heb for in me
is your help   h Gk Syr Vg: Heb I will be

O Death, where are[a] your plagues?
O Sheol, where is[a] your destruction?
Compassion is hidden from my eyes.

15 Although he may flourish among
        rushes,[b]
    the east wind shall come, a blast from
        the LORD,
    rising from the wilderness;
and his fountain shall dry up,
    his spring shall be parched.
It shall strip his treasury
    of every precious thing.
16[c] Samaria shall bear her guilt,
    because she has rebelled against her
        God;
they shall fall by the sword,
    their little ones shall be dashed in
        pieces,
    and their pregnant women ripped
        open.

A Plea for Repentance

14 Return, O Israel, to the LORD your
        God,
    for you have stumbled because of
        your iniquity.
2 Take words with you
    and return to the LORD;
say to him,
    "Take away all guilt;
accept that which is good,
    and we will offer
    the fruit[d] of our lips.
3 Assyria shall not save us;

we will not ride upon horses;
we will say no more, 'Our God,'
    to the work of our hands.
In you the orphan finds mercy."

Assurance of Forgiveness

4 I will heal their disloyalty;
    I will love them freely,
    for my anger has turned from them.
5 I will be like the dew to Israel;
    he shall blossom like the lily,
    he shall strike root like the forests of
        Lebanon.[e]
6 His shoots shall spread out;
    his beauty shall be like the olive tree,
    and his fragrance like that of
        Lebanon.
7 They shall again live beneath my[f]
        shadow,
    they shall flourish as a garden;[g]
they shall blossom like the vine,
    their fragrance shall be like the wine
        of Lebanon.

8 O Ephraim, what have I[b] to do with
        idols?
    It is I who answer and look after you.[i]
I am like an evergreen cypress;
    your faithfulness[j] comes from me.
9 Those who are wise understand these
        things;
    those who are discerning know them.
For the ways of the LORD are right,
    and the upright walk in them,
    but transgressors stumble in them.

---

a Gk Syr: Heb *I will be*   b Or *among brothers*   c Ch 14.1 in Heb   d Gk Syr: Heb *bulls*   e Cn: Heb *like
Lebanon*   f Heb *his*   g Cn: Heb *they shall grow grain*   h Or *What more has Ephraim*   i Heb *him*   j Heb *your
fruit*

JOEL

1 The word of the LORD that came to Joel son of Pethuel:

Lament over the Ruin of the Country

2 Hear this, O elders,
　　give ear, all inhabitants of the land!
　Has such a thing happened in your days,
　　or in the days of your ancestors?
3 Tell your children of it,
　　and let your children tell their
　　　children,
　　and their children another generation.

4 What the cutting locust left,
　　the swarming locust has eaten.
　What the swarming locust left,
　　the hopping locust has eaten,
　and what the hopping locust left,
　　the destroying locust has eaten.

5 Wake up, you drunkards, and weep;
　　and wail, all you wine-drinkers,
　over the sweet wine,
　　for it is cut off from your mouth.
6 For a nation has invaded my land,
　　powerful and innumerable;
　its teeth are lions' teeth,
　　and it has the fangs of a lioness.
7 It has laid waste my vines,
　　and splintered my fig trees;
　it has stripped off their bark and
　　　thrown it down;
　　their branches have turned white.

8 Lament like a virgin dressed in
　　　sackcloth
　　for the husband of her youth.
9 The grain offering and the drink
　　　offering are cut off
　from the house of the LORD.
　The priests mourn,
　　the ministers of the LORD.
10 The fields are devastated,
　　the ground mourns;

for the grain is destroyed,
　　the wine dries up,
　　the oil fails.

11 Be dismayed, you farmers,
　　wail, you vinedressers,
　over the wheat and the barley;
　　for the crops of the field are ruined.
12 The vine withers,
　　the fig tree droops.
　Pomegranate, palm, and apple—
　　all the trees of the field are dried up;
　surely, joy withers away
　　among the people.

A Call to Repentance and Prayer

13 Put on sackcloth and lament, you
　　　priests;
　　wail, you ministers of the altar.
　Come, pass the night in sackcloth,
　　you ministers of my God!
　Grain offering and drink offering
　　are withheld from the house of your
　　　God.

14 Sanctify a fast,
　　call a solemn assembly.
　Gather the elders
　　and all the inhabitants of the land
　to the house of the LORD your God,
　　and cry out to the LORD.

15 Alas for the day!
　For the day of the LORD is near,
　　and as destruction from the
　　　Almighty[a] it comes.
16 Is not the food cut off
　　before our eyes,
　joy and gladness
　　from the house of our God?

17 The seed shrivels under the clods,[b]
　　the storehouses are desolate;
　the granaries are ruined

a Traditional rendering of Heb *Shaddai*　　*b* Meaning of Heb uncertain because the grain has failed.

18 How the animals groan!
   The herds of cattle wander about
because there is no pasture for them;
   even the flocks of sheep are dazed. *a*

19 To you, O LORD, I cry.
   For fire has devoured
      the pastures of the wilderness,
   and flames have burned
      all the trees of the field.

20 Even the wild animals cry to you
   because the watercourses are dried
      up,
   and fire has devoured
      the pastures of the wilderness.

2 Blow the trumpet in Zion;
   sound the alarm on my holy
      mountain!
Let all the inhabitants of the land
      tremble,
   for the day of the LORD is coming, it
      is near—

2 a day of darkness and gloom,
   a day of clouds and thick darkness!
Like blackness spread upon the
      mountains
   a great and powerful army comes;
their like has never been from of old,
   nor will be again after them
   in ages to come.

3 Fire devours in front of them,
   and behind them a flame burns.
Before them the land is like the garden
      of Eden,
   but after them a desolate wilderness,
   and nothing escapes them.

4 They have the appearance of horses,
   and like war-horses they charge.
5 As with the rumbling of chariots,
   they leap on the tops of the
      mountains,
   like the crackling of a flame of fire

devouring the stubble,
   like a powerful army
   drawn up for battle.

6 Before them peoples are in anguish,
   all faces grow pale. *b*
7 Like warriors they charge,
   like soldiers they scale the wall.
Each keeps to its own course,
   they do not swerve from *c* their paths.
8 They do not jostle one another,
   each keeps to its own track;
they burst through the weapons
   and are not halted.
9 They leap upon the city,
   they run upon the walls;
they climb up into the houses,
   they enter through the windows like a
      thief.

10 The earth quakes before them,
   the heavens tremble.
The sun and the moon are darkened,
   and the stars withdraw their shining.
11 The LORD utters his voice
   at the head of his army;
how vast is his host!
   Numberless are those who obey his
      command.
Truly the day of the LORD is great;
   terrible indeed—who can endure it?

12 Yet even now, says the LORD,
   return to me with all your heart,
with fasting, with weeping, and with
      mourning;
13 rend your hearts and not your
      clothing.
Return to the LORD, your God,
   for he is gracious and merciful,
slow to anger, and abounding in
      steadfast love,
   and relents from punishing.
14 Who knows whether he will not turn
      and relent,
   and leave a blessing behind him,

a Compare Gk Syr Vg: Meaning of Heb uncertain   *b* Meaning of Heb uncertain   *c* Gk Syr Vg: Heb *they do
not take a pledge along*

a grain offering and a drink offering
for the LORD, your God?

15 Blow the trumpet in Zion;
sanctify a fast;
call a solemn assembly;
16 gather the people.
Sanctify the congregation;
assemble the aged;
gather the children,
even infants at the breast.
Let the bridegroom leave his room,
and the bride her canopy.

17 Between the vestibule and the altar
let the priests, the ministers of the
LORD, weep.
Let them say, "Spare your people,
O LORD,
and do not make your heritage a
mockery,
a byword among the nations.
Why should it be said among the
peoples,
'Where is their God?' "

God's Response and Promise

18 Then the LORD became jealous for his
land,
and had pity on his people.
19 In response to his people the LORD
said:
I am sending you
grain, wine, and oil,
and you will be satisfied;
and I will no more make you
a mockery among the nations.

20 I will remove the northern army far
from you,
and drive it into a parched and
desolate land,
its front into the eastern sea,
and its rear into the western sea;
its stench and foul smell will rise up.
Surely he has done great things!

21 Do not fear, O soil;
be glad and rejoice,
for the LORD has done great things!
22 Do not fear, you animals of the field,
for the pastures of the wilderness are
green;
the tree bears its fruit,
the fig tree and vine give their full
yield.

23 O children of Zion, be glad
and rejoice in the LORD your God;
for he has given the early rain *a* for your
vindication,
he has poured down for you
abundant rain,
the early and the later rain, as before.
24 The threshing floors shall be full of
grain,
the vats shall overflow with wine and
oil.

25 I will repay you for the years
that the swarming locust has eaten,
the hopper, the destroyer, and the
cutter,
my great army, which I sent against
you.

26 You shall eat in plenty and be satisfied,
and praise the name of the LORD
your God,
who has dealt wondrously with you.
And my people shall never again be put
to shame.
27 You shall know that I am in the midst
of Israel,
and that I, the LORD, am your God
and there is no other.
And my people shall never again be put
to shame.

God's Spirit Poured Out

28 *b* Then afterward
I will pour out my spirit on all flesh;

---

a Meaning of Heb uncertain   *b* Ch 3.1 in Heb

your sons and your daughters shall
  prophesy,
  your old men shall dream dreams,
  and your young men shall see visions.
29   Even on the male and female slaves,
  in those days, I will pour out my
    spirit.

30 I will show portents in the heavens and
on the earth, blood and fire and columns of
smoke. ³¹The sun shall be turned to darkness, and the moon to blood, before the great
and terrible day of the LORD comes. ³²Then
everyone who calls on the name of the LORD
shall be saved; for in Mount Zion and in Jerusalem there shall be those who escape, as the
LORD has said, and among the survivors shall
be those whom the LORD calls.

3 ᵃ For then, in those days and at that time,
  when I restore the fortunes of Judah and
Jerusalem, ²I will gather all the nations and
bring them down to the valley of Jehoshaphat,
and I will enter into judgment with them there,
on account of my people and my heritage Israel, because they have scattered them among
the nations. They have divided my land, ³and
cast lots for my people, and traded boys for
prostitutes, and sold girls for wine, and drunk
it down.

4 What are you to me, O Tyre and Sidon,
and all the regions of Philistia? Are you paying me back for something? If you are paying
me back, I will turn your deeds back upon
your own heads swiftly and speedily. ⁵For you
have taken my silver and my gold, and have
carried my rich treasures into your temples. ᵇ
⁶You have sold the people of Judah and Jerusalem to the Greeks, removing them far from
their own border. ⁷But now I will rouse them
to leave the places to which you have sold
them, and I will turn your deeds back upon
your own heads. ⁸I will sell your sons and
your daughters into the hand of the people of
Judah, and they will sell them to the Sabeans,
to a nation far away; for the LORD has spoken.

Judgment in the Valley of Jehoshaphat

9   Proclaim this among the nations:
  Prepare war, ᶜ
    stir up the warriors.
  Let all the soldiers draw near,
    let them come up.
10   Beat your plowshares into swords,
    and your pruning hooks into spears;
    let the weakling say, "I am a warrior."

11   Come quickly, ᵈ
    all you nations all around,
    gather yourselves there.
  Bring down your warriors, O LORD.
12   Let the nations rouse themselves,
    and come up to the valley of
      Jehoshaphat;
  for there I will sit to judge
    all the neighboring nations.

13   Put in the sickle,
    for the harvest is ripe.
  Go in, tread,
    for the wine press is full.
  The vats overflow,
    for their wickedness is great.

14   Multitudes, multitudes,
    in the valley of decision!
  For the day of the LORD is near
    in the valley of decision.
15   The sun and the moon are darkened,
    and the stars withdraw their shining.

16   The LORD roars from Zion,
    and utters his voice from Jerusalem,
    and the heavens and the earth shake.
  But the LORD is a refuge for his people,
    a stronghold for the people of Israel.

The Glorious Future of Judah

17   So you shall know that I, the LORD your
      God,
    dwell in Zion, my holy mountain.
  And Jerusalem shall be holy,

---

a Ch 4.1 in Heb   *b* Or *palaces*   *c* Heb *sanctify war*   *d* Meaning of Heb uncertain

and strangers shall never again pass
    through it.

18 In that day
    the mountains shall drip sweet wine,
      the hills shall flow with milk,
    and all the stream beds of Judah
      shall flow with water;
    a fountain shall come forth from the
        house of the LORD
      and water the Wadi Shittim.

19 Egypt shall become a desolation
      and Edom a desolate wilderness,
    because of the violence done to the
        people of Judah,
      in whose land they have shed
        innocent blood.
20 But Judah shall be inhabited forever,
      and Jerusalem to all generations.
21 I will avenge their blood, and I will not
        clear the guilty,[a]
      for the LORD dwells in Zion.

---

a Gk Syr: Heb *I will hold innocent their blood that I have not held innocent*

AMOS

1 The words of Amos, who was among the
shepherds of Tekoa, which he saw concerning Israel in the days of King Uzziah of Judah and in the days of King Jeroboam son of
Joash of Israel, two years*a* before the earthquake.

Judgment on Israel's Neighbors

2And he said:

The LORD roars from Zion,
and utters his voice from Jerusalem;
the pastures of the shepherds wither,
and the top of Carmel dries up.

3 Thus says the LORD:
For three transgressions of Damascus,
and for four, I will not revoke the
punishment;*b*
because they have threshed Gilead
with threshing sledges of iron.
4 So I will send a fire on the house of
Hazael,
and it shall devour the strongholds of
Ben-hadad.
5 I will break the gate bars of Damascus,
and cut off the inhabitants from the
Valley of Aven,
and the one who holds the scepter from
Beth-eden;
and the people of Aram shall go into
exile to Kir,
says the LORD.

6 Thus says the LORD:
For three transgressions of Gaza,
and for four, I will not revoke the
punishment;*b*
because they carried into exile entire
communities,
to hand them over to Edom.
7 So I will send a fire on the wall of Gaza,
fire that shall devour its strongholds.
8 I will cut off the inhabitants from
Ashdod,

and the one who holds the scepter
from Ashkelon;
I will turn my hand against Ekron,
and the remnant of the Philistines
shall perish,
says the Lord GOD.

9 Thus says the LORD:
For three transgressions of Tyre,
and for four, I will not revoke the
punishment;*b*
because they delivered entire
communities over to Edom,
and did not remember the covenant
of kinship.
10 So I will send a fire on the wall of Tyre,
fire that shall devour its strongholds.

11 Thus says the LORD:
For three transgressions of Edom,
and for four, I will not revoke the
punishment;*b*
because he pursued his brother with the
sword
and cast off all pity;
he maintained his anger perpetually,*c*
and kept his wrath*d* forever.
12 So I will send a fire on Teman,
and it shall devour the strongholds of
Bozrah.

13 Thus says the LORD:
For three transgressions of the
Ammonites,
and for four, I will not revoke the
punishment;*b*
because they have ripped open pregnant
women in Gilead
in order to enlarge their territory.
14 So I will kindle a fire against the wall of
Rabbah,
fire that shall devour its strongholds,
with shouting on the day of battle,

---

a Or *during two years*   *b* Heb *cause it to return*   *c* Syr Vg: Heb *and his anger tore perpetually*   *d* Gk Syr Vg: Heb *and his wrath kept*

with a storm on the day of the
    whirlwind;
15 then their king shall go into exile,
    he and his officials together,
                        says the LORD.

2 Thus says the LORD:
   For three transgressions of Moab,
       and for four, I will not revoke the
           punishment;*a*
   because he burned to lime
       the bones of the king of Edom.
2 So I will send a fire on Moab,
       and it shall devour the strongholds of
           Kerioth,
   and Moab shall die amid uproar,
       amid shouting and the sound of the
           trumpet;
3 I will cut off the ruler from its midst,
       and will kill all its officials with him,
                        says the LORD.

Judgment on Judah

4 Thus says the LORD:
   For three transgressions of Judah,
       and for four, I will not revoke the
           punishment;*a*
   because they have rejected the law of the
       LORD,
       and have not kept his statutes,
   but they have been led astray by the
       same lies
   after which their ancestors walked.
5 So I will send a fire on Judah,
       and it shall devour the strongholds of
           Jerusalem.

Judgment on Israel

6 Thus says the LORD:
   For three transgressions of Israel,
       and for four, I will not revoke the
           punishment;*a*
   because they sell the righteous for silver,
       and the needy for a pair of sandals—
7 they who trample the head of the poor
       into the dust of the earth,

and push the afflicted out of the way;
   father and son go in to the same girl,
       so that my holy name is profaned;
8 they lay themselves down beside every
           altar
       on garments taken in pledge;
   and in the house of their God they drink
       wine bought with fines they imposed.

9 Yet I destroyed the Amorite before
           them,
       whose height was like the height of
           cedars,
       and who was as strong as oaks;
   I destroyed his fruit above,
       and his roots beneath.
10 Also I brought you up out of the land of
           Egypt,
       and led you forty years in the
           wilderness,
   to possess the land of the Amorite.
11 And I raised up some of your children
       to be prophets
   and some of your youths to be
       nazirites.*b*
   Is it not indeed so, O people of Israel?
                        says the LORD.

12 But you made the nazirites *b* drink wine,
       and commanded the prophets,
       saying, "You shall not prophesy."

13 So, I will press you down in your place,
       just as a cart presses down
       when it is full of sheaves.*c*
14 Flight shall perish from the swift,
       and the strong shall not retain their
           strength,
       nor shall the mighty save their lives;
15 those who handle the bow shall not
           stand,
       and those who are swift of foot shall
           not save themselves,
   nor shall those who ride horses save
       their lives;

---

a Heb *cause it to return*   *b* That is, *those separated* or *those consecrated*   *c* Meaning of Heb uncertain

16 and those who are stout of heart among
　　　　the mighty
　　　shall flee away naked in that day,
　　　　　　　　says the LORD.

Israel's Guilt and Punishment

3 Hear this word that the LORD has spoken
　against you, O people of Israel, against the
whole family that I brought up out of the land
of Egypt:
2 You only have I known
　　　of all the families of the earth;
　　　therefore I will punish you
　　　　for all your iniquities.

3 Do two walk together
　　　unless they have made an
　　　　appointment?
4 Does a lion roar in the forest,
　　　when it has no prey?
　　　Does a young lion cry out from its den,
　　　　if it has caught nothing?
5 Does a bird fall into a snare on the earth,
　　　when there is no trap for it?
　　　Does a snare spring up from the ground,
　　　　when it has taken nothing?
6 Is a trumpet blown in a city,
　　　and the people are not afraid?
　　　Does disaster befall a city,
　　　　unless the LORD has done it?
7 Surely the Lord GOD does nothing,
　　　without revealing his secret
　　　to his servants the prophets.
8 The lion has roared;
　　　who will not fear?
　　　The Lord GOD has spoken;
　　　who can but prophesy?

9 Proclaim to the strongholds in Ashdod,
　　　and to the strongholds in the land of
　　　　Egypt,
　　　and say, "Assemble yourselves on
　　　　Mount*a* Samaria,
　　　and see what great tumults are
　　　　within it,

and what oppressions are in its
　　　midst."
10 They do not know how to do right, says
　　　the LORD,
　　　those who store up violence and
　　　robbery in their strongholds.
11 Therefore thus says the Lord GOD:
An adversary shall surround the land,
　　　and strip you of your defense;
　　　and your strongholds shall be
　　　　plundered.

12 Thus says the LORD: As the shepherd
rescues from the mouth of the lion two legs,
or a piece of an ear, so shall the people of Israel who live in Samaria be rescued, with the
corner of a couch and part*b* of a bed.

13 Hear, and testify against the house of
　　　Jacob,
　　　says the Lord GOD, the God of hosts:
14 On the day I punish Israel for its
　　　transgressions,
　　　I will punish the altars of Bethel,
　　and the horns of the altar shall be cut
　　　off
　　　and fall to the ground.
15 I will tear down the winter house as well
　　　as the summer house;
　　　and the houses of ivory shall perish,
　　and the great houses*c* shall come to an
　　　end,
　　　　　　　　says the LORD.

4 Hear this word, you cows of Bashan
　who are on Mount Samaria,
　who oppress the poor, who crush the
　　　needy,
　　　who say to their husbands, "Bring
　　　　something to drink!"
2 The Lord GOD has sworn by his
　　　holiness:
　　　The time is surely coming upon you,
　　when they shall take you away with
　　　hooks,
　　　even the last of you with fishhooks.

³ Through breaches in the wall you shall
         leave,
       each one straight ahead;
       and you shall be flung out into
         Harmon,^a
                   says the LORD.

⁴ Come to Bethel—and transgress;
       to Gilgal—and multiply transgression;
   bring your sacrifices every morning,
       your tithes every three days;
⁵ bring a thank offering of leavened bread,
       and proclaim freewill offerings,
         publish them;
       for so you love to do, O people of
         Israel!
              says the Lord GOD.

Israel Rejects Correction

⁶ I gave you cleanness of teeth in all your
         cities,
       and lack of bread in all your places,
   yet you did not return to me,
              says the LORD.

⁷ And I also withheld the rain from you
       when there were still three months to
         the harvest;
   I would send rain on one city,
       and send no rain on another city;
   one field would be rained upon,
       and the field on which it did not rain
         withered;
⁸ so two or three towns wandered to one
         town
       to drink water, and were not satisfied;
   yet you did not return to me,
              says the LORD.

⁹ I struck you with blight and mildew;
       I laid waste^b your gardens and your
         vineyards;
       the locust devoured your fig trees and
         your olive trees;
   yet you did not return to me,
              says the LORD.

¹⁰ I sent among you a pestilence after the
       manner of Egypt;
   I killed your young men with the
       sword;
   I carried away your horses;^c
       and I made the stench of your camp
         go up into your nostrils;
   yet you did not return to me,
              says the LORD.

¹¹ I overthrew some of you,
       as when God overthrew Sodom and
         Gomorrah,
       and you were like a brand snatched
         from the fire;
   yet you did not return to me,
              says the LORD.

¹² Therefore thus I will do to you, O Israel;
   because I will do this to you,
   prepare to meet your God, O Israel!

¹³ For lo, the one who forms the
         mountains, creates the wind,
   reveals his thoughts to mortals,
   makes the morning darkness,
       and treads on the heights of the
         earth—
       the LORD, the God of hosts, is his
         name!

A Lament for Israel's Sin

5 Hear this word that I take up over you in
    lamentation, O house of Israel:
² Fallen, no more to rise,
       is maiden Israel;
   forsaken on her land,
       with no one to raise her up.

³ For thus says the Lord GOD:
   The city that marched out a thousand
       shall have a hundred left,
   and that which marched out a hundred
       shall have ten left.^d

---

^a Meaning of Heb uncertain   ^b Cn: Heb *the multitude of the house of Israel*   ^c Heb *with the captivity of your horses*   ^d Heb adds *to*

4   For thus says the LORD to the house of
          Israel:
      Seek me and live;
5   but do not seek Bethel,
      and do not enter into Gilgal
          or cross over to Beer-sheba;
      for Gilgal shall surely go into exile,
          and Bethel shall come to nothing.

6   Seek the LORD and live,
          or he will break out against the house
              of Joseph like fire,
      and it will devour Bethel, with no one
              to quench it.
7   Ah, you that turn justice to wormwood,
          and bring righteousness to the
              ground!

8   The one who made the Pleiades and
              Orion,
          and turns deep darkness into the
              morning,
          and darkens the day into night,
      who calls for the waters of the sea,
          and pours them out on the surface of
              the earth,
      the LORD is his name,
9   who makes destruction flash out against
              the strong,
          so that destruction comes upon the
              fortress.

10   They hate the one who reproves in the
              gate,
          and they abhor the one who speaks
              the truth.
11   Therefore because you trample on the
              poor
          and take from them levies of grain,
      you have built houses of hewn stone,
          but you shall not live in them;
      you have planted pleasant vineyards,
          but you shall not drink their wine.
12   For I know how many are your
              transgressions,
          and how great are your sins—
      you who afflict the righteous, who take a
              bribe,

      and push aside the needy in the gate.
13   Therefore the prudent will keep silent in
              such a time;
          for it is an evil time.

14   Seek good and not evil,
          that you may live;
      and so the LORD, the God of hosts, will
              be with you,
          just as you have said.
15   Hate evil and love good,
          and establish justice in the gate;
      it may be that the LORD, the God of
              hosts,
          will be gracious to the remnant of
              Joseph.

16   Therefore thus says the LORD, the God
          of hosts, the Lord:
      In all the squares there shall be wailing;
          and in all the streets they shall say,
              "Alas! alas!"
      They shall call the farmers to mourning,
          and those skilled in lamentation, to
              wailing;
17   in all the vineyards there shall be wailing,
          for I will pass through the midst of
              you,
                                      says the LORD.

The Day of the LORD a Dark Day
18   Alas for you who desire the day of the
          LORD!
      Why do you want the day of the
          LORD?
      It is darkness, not light;
19   as if someone fled from a lion,
          and was met by a bear;
      or went into the house and rested a hand
              against the wall,
          and was bitten by a snake.
20   Is not the day of the LORD darkness, not
              light,
          and gloom with no brightness in it?

21   I hate, I despise your festivals,
          and I take no delight in your solemn
              assemblies.

22 Even though you offer me your burnt
         offerings and grain offerings,
      I will not accept them;
      and the offerings of well-being of your
         fatted animals
      I will not look upon.
23 Take away from me the noise of your
         songs;
      I will not listen to the melody of your
         harps.
24 But let justice roll down like waters,
      and righteousness like an ever-flowing
         stream.

25 Did you bring to me sacrifices and offerings the forty years in the wilderness,
O house of Israel? 26 You shall take up Sakkuth
your king, and Kaiwan your star-god, your images,*a* which you made for yourselves; 27 therefore I will take you into exile beyond Damascus, says the LORD, whose name is the God of
hosts.

Complacent Self-Indulgence Will Be Punished

6 Alas for those who are at ease in Zion,
      and for those who feel secure on
         Mount Samaria,
      the notables of the first of the nations,
         to whom the house of Israel resorts!
2 Cross over to Calneh, and see;
      from there go to Hamath the great;
      then go down to Gath of the
         Philistines.
      Are you better*b* than these kingdoms?
         Or is your*c* territory greater than their*d*
            territory,
3 O you that put far away the evil day,
      and bring near a reign of violence?

4 Alas for those who lie on beds of ivory,
      and lounge on their couches,
   and eat lambs from the flock,
      and calves from the stall;
5 who sing idle songs to the sound of the
         harp,

      and like David improvise on
         instruments of music;
6 who drink wine from bowls,
      and anoint themselves with the finest
         oils,
      but are not grieved over the ruin of
         Joseph!
7 Therefore they shall now be the first to
         go into exile,
      and the revelry of the loungers shall
         pass away.

8 The Lord GOD has sworn by himself
      (says the LORD, the God of hosts):
   I abhor the pride of Jacob
      and hate his strongholds;
      and I will deliver up the city and all
         that is in it.

9 If ten people remain in one house, they
shall die. 10 And if a relative, one who burns the
dead,*e* shall take up the body to bring it out of
the house, and shall say to someone in the innermost parts of the house, "Is anyone else
with you?" the answer will come, "No." Then
the relative*f* shall say, "Hush! We must not
mention the name of the LORD."

11 See, the LORD commands,
      and the great house shall be shattered
         to bits,
      and the little house to pieces.
12 Do horses run on rocks?
      Does one plow the sea with oxen?*g*
   But you have turned justice into poison
      and the fruit of righteousness into
         wormwood—
13 you who rejoice in Lo-debar,*h*
      who say, "Have we not by our own
         strength
      taken Karnaim*i* for ourselves?"
14 Indeed, I am raising up against you a
         nation,
      O house of Israel, says the LORD, the
         God of hosts,

---

a Heb *your images, your star-god*   *b* Or *Are they better*   *c* Heb *their*   *d* Heb *your*   *e* Or *who makes a burning for him*
f Heb *he*   *g* Or *Does one plow them with oxen*   *h* Or *in a thing of nothingness*   *i* Or *horns*

and they shall oppress you from Lebo-
hamath
to the Wadi Arabah.

Locusts, Fire, and a Plumb Line

7 This is what the Lord GOD showed me: he was forming locusts at the time the latter growth began to sprout (it was the latter growth after the king's mowings). 2When they had finished eating the grass of the land, I said,
"O Lord GOD, forgive, I beg you!
How can Jacob stand?
He is so small!"
3 The LORD relented concerning this;
"It shall not be," said the LORD.

4 This is what the Lord GOD showed me: the Lord GOD was calling for a shower of fire,ᵃ and it devoured the great deep and was eating up the land. 5Then I said,
"O Lord GOD, cease, I beg you!
How can Jacob stand?
He is so small!"
6 The LORD relented concerning this;
"This also shall not be," said the Lord
GOD.

7 This is what he showed me: the Lord was standing beside a wall built with a plumb line, with a plumb line in his hand. 8And the LORD said to me, "Amos, what do you see?" And I said, "A plumb line." Then the Lord said,
"See, I am setting a plumb line
in the midst of my people Israel;
I will never again pass them by;
9 the high places of Isaac shall be made
desolate,
and the sanctuaries of Israel shall be
laid waste,
and I will rise against the house of
Jeroboam with the sword."

Amaziah Complains to the King

10 Then Amaziah, the priest of Bethel, sent to King Jeroboam of Israel, saying, "Amos has conspired against you in the very center of the house of Israel; the land is not able to bear all his words. 11For thus Amos has said,
'Jeroboam shall die by the sword,
and Israel must go into exile
away from his land.'"

12And Amaziah said to Amos, "O seer, go, flee away to the land of Judah, earn your bread there, and prophesy there; 13but never again prophesy at Bethel, for it is the king's sanctuary, and it is a temple of the kingdom."

14 Then Amos answered Amaziah, "I amᵇ no prophet, nor a prophet's son; but I amᵇ a herdsman, and a dresser of sycamore trees, 15and the LORD took me from following the flock, and the LORD said to me, 'Go, prophesy to my people Israel.'
16 "Now therefore hear the word of the
LORD.
You say, 'Do not prophesy against Israel,
and do not preach against the house
of Isaac.'
17 Therefore thus says the LORD:
'Your wife shall become a prostitute in
the city,
and your sons and your daughters
shall fall by the sword,
and your land shall be parceled out by
line;
you yourself shall die in an unclean land,
and Israel shall surely go into exile
away from its land.'"

The Basket of Fruit

8 This is what the Lord GOD showed me— a basket of summer fruit.ᶜ 2He said, "Amos, what do you see?" And I said, "A basket of summer fruit."ᶜ Then the LORD said to me,
"The endᵈ has come upon my people
Israel;
I will never again pass them by.
3 The songs of the templeᵉ shall become
wailings in that day,"
                              says the Lord GOD;
"the dead bodies shall be many,
cast out in every place. Be silent!"

---

a Or *for a judgment by fire*   *b* Or *was*   *c* Heb *qayits*   *d* Heb *qets*   *e* Or *palace*

4 Hear this, you that trample on the needy,
  and bring to ruin the poor of the land,
5 saying, "When will the new moon be
        over
  so that we may sell grain;
  and the sabbath,
    so that we may offer wheat for sale?
  We will make the ephah small and the
        shekel great,
    and practice deceit with false balances,
6 buying the poor for silver
    and the needy for a pair of sandals,
    and selling the sweepings of the
        wheat."

7 The LORD has sworn by the pride of
        Jacob:
  Surely I will never forget any of their
        deeds.
8 Shall not the land tremble on this
        account,
    and everyone mourn who lives in it,
  and all of it rise like the Nile,
    and be tossed about and sink again,
        like the Nile of Egypt?

9 On that day, says the Lord GOD,
    I will make the sun go down at noon,
    and darken the earth in broad daylight.
10 I will turn your feasts into mourning,
    and all your songs into lamentation;
  I will bring sackcloth on all loins,
    and baldness on every head;
  I will make it like the mourning for an
        only son,
    and the end of it like a bitter day.

11 The time is surely coming, says the Lord
        GOD,
    when I will send a famine on the land;
  not a famine of bread, or a thirst for
        water,
    but of hearing the words of the
        LORD.
12 They shall wander from sea to sea,
    and from north to east;

they shall run to and fro, seeking the
        word of the LORD,
  but they shall not find it.

13 In that day the beautiful young women
        and the young men
    shall faint for thirst.
14 Those who swear by Ashimah of
        Samaria,
  and say, "As your god lives, O Dan,"
  and, "As the way of Beer-sheba lives"—
    they shall fall, and never rise again.

The Destruction of Israel

9 I saw the LORD standing beside[a] the altar,
    and he said:
  Strike the capitals until the thresholds
        shake,
    and shatter them on the heads of all
        the people;[b]
  and those who are left I will kill with the
        sword;
    not one of them shall flee away,
    not one of them shall escape.

2 Though they dig into Sheol,
    from there shall my hand take them;
  though they climb up to heaven,
    from there I will bring them down.
3 Though they hide themselves on the top
        of Carmel,
    from there I will search out and take
        them;
  and though they hide from my sight at
        the bottom of the sea,
    there I will command the sea-serpent,
        and it shall bite them.
4 And though they go into captivity in
        front of their enemies,
    there I will command the sword, and
        it shall kill them;
  and I will fix my eyes on them
    for harm and not for good.

5 The Lord, GOD of hosts,
  he who touches the earth and it melts,

a Or on   b Heb all of them

and all who live in it mourn,
and all of it rises like the Nile,
and sinks again, like the Nile of
Egypt;

6 who builds his upper chambers in the
heavens,
and founds his vault upon the earth;
who calls for the waters of the sea,
and pours them out upon the surface
of the earth—
the LORD is his name.

7 Are you not like the Ethiopians*a* to me,
O people of Israel? says the LORD.
Did I not bring Israel up from the land
of Egypt,
and the Philistines from Caphtor and
the Arameans from Kir?

8 The eyes of the Lord GOD are upon the
sinful kingdom,
and I will destroy it from the face of
the earth
—except that I will not utterly destroy
the house of Jacob,
says the LORD.

9 For lo, I will command,
and shake the house of Israel among
all the nations
as one shakes with a sieve,
but no pebble shall fall to the ground.

10 All the sinners of my people shall die by
the sword,
who say, "Evil shall not overtake or
meet us."

The Restoration of David's Kingdom

11 On that day I will raise up
the booth of David that is fallen,
and repair its*b* breaches,
and raise up its*c* ruins,
and rebuild it as in the days of old;

12 in order that they may possess the
remnant of Edom
and all the nations who are called by
my name,
says the LORD who does this.

13 The time is surely coming, says the
LORD,
when the one who plows shall
overtake the one who reaps,
and the treader of grapes the one who
sows the seed;
the mountains shall drip sweet wine,
and all the hills shall flow with it.

14 I will restore the fortunes of my people
Israel,
and they shall rebuild the ruined cities
and inhabit them;
they shall plant vineyards and drink their
wine,
and they shall make gardens and eat
their fruit.

15 I will plant them upon their land,
and they shall never again be plucked
up
out of the land that I have given
them,
says the LORD your God.

---

a Or *Nubians;* Heb *Cushites*   *b* Gk: Heb *their*   *c* Gk: Heb *his*

OBADIAH

Proud Edom Will Be Brought Low

1 The vision of Obadiah.

Thus says the Lord GOD concerning
  Edom:
We have heard a report from the LORD,
  and a messenger has been sent among
    the nations:
"Rise up! Let us rise against it for battle!"
2 I will surely make you least among the
      nations;
  you shall be utterly despised.
3 Your proud heart has deceived you,
  you that live in the clefts of the rock,*a*
    whose dwelling is in the heights.
  You say in your heart,
    "Who will bring me down to the
      ground?"
4 Though you soar aloft like the eagle,
    though your nest is set among the
      stars,
    from there I will bring you down, says
      the LORD.

Pillage and Slaughter Will Repay
Edom's Cruelty

5 If thieves came to you,
    if plunderers by night
    —how you have been destroyed!—
    would they not steal only what they
      wanted?
  If grape-gatherers came to you,
    would they not leave gleanings?
6 How Esau has been pillaged,
    his treasures searched out!
7 All your allies have deceived you,
    they have driven you to the border;
  your confederates have prevailed against
    you;
    those who ate*b* your bread have set a
      trap for you—
    there is no understanding of it.
8 On that day, says the LORD,
    I will destroy the wise out of Edom,

and understanding out of Mount
  Esau.
9 Your warriors shall be shattered,
    O Teman,
  so that everyone from Mount Esau
    will be cut off.

Edom Mistreated His Brother

10 For the slaughter and violence done to
      your brother Jacob,
    shame shall cover you,
    and you shall be cut off forever.
11 On the day that you stood aside,
    on the day that strangers carried off
      his wealth,
  and foreigners entered his gates
    and cast lots for Jerusalem,
    you too were like one of them.
12 But you should not have gloated*c* over*d*
      your brother
    on the day of his misfortune;
  you should not have rejoiced over the
    people of Judah
    on the day of their ruin;
  you should not have boasted
    on the day of distress.
13 You should not have entered the gate of
      my people
    on the day of their calamity;
  you should not have joined in the
      gloating over Judah's*e* disaster
    on the day of his calamity;
  you should not have looted his goods
    on the day of his calamity.
14 You should not have stood at the
      crossings
    to cut off his fugitives;
  you should not have handed over his
      survivors
    on the day of distress.

15 For the day of the LORD is near against
    all the nations.

---

a Or *clefts of Sela*   *b* Cn: Heb lacks *those who ate*   *c* Heb *But do not gloat* (and similarly through verse 14)
d Heb *on the day of*   *e* Heb *his*

As you have done, it shall be done to
    you;
    your deeds shall return on your own
      head.
16 For as you have drunk on my holy
    mountain,
all the nations around you shall drink;
    they shall drink and gulp down,*a*
    and shall be as though they had never
      been.

Israel's Final Triumph

17 But on Mount Zion there shall be those
      that escape,
    and it shall be holy;
and the house of Jacob shall take
      possession of those who
      dispossessed them.
18 The house of Jacob shall be a fire,
    the house of Joseph a flame,
    and the house of Esau stubble;
they shall burn them and consume them,

and there shall be no survivor of the
    house of Esau;
      for the LORD has spoken.
19 Those of the Negeb shall possess
    Mount Esau,
    and those of the Shephelah the land
      of the Philistines;
they shall possess the land of Ephraim
      and the land of Samaria,
    and Benjamin shall possess Gilead.
20 The exiles of the Israelites who are in
    Halah*b*
    shall possess*c* Phoenicia as far as
      Zarephath;
and the exiles of Jerusalem who are in
    Sepharad
    shall possess the towns of the Negeb.
21 Those who have been saved*d* shall go up
    to Mount Zion
    to rule Mount Esau;
    and the kingdom shall be the LORD's.

---

a Meaning of Heb uncertain   *b* Cn: Heb *in this army*   *c* Cn: Meaning of Heb uncertain   *d* Or *Saviors*

JONAH

Jonah Tries to Run Away from God

1 Now the word of the LORD came to Jonah son of Amittai, saying, 2"Go at once to Nineveh, that great city, and cry out against it; for their wickedness has come up before me." 3But Jonah set out to flee to Tarshish from the presence of the LORD. He went down to Joppa and found a ship going to Tarshish; so he paid his fare and went on board, to go with them to Tarshish, away from the presence of the LORD.

4 But the LORD hurled a great wind upon the sea, and such a mighty storm came upon the sea that the ship threatened to break up. 5Then the mariners were afraid, and each cried to his god. They threw the cargo that was in the ship into the sea, to lighten it for them. Jonah, meanwhile, had gone down into the hold of the ship and had lain down, and was fast asleep. 6The captain came and said to him, "What are you doing sound asleep? Get up, call on your god! Perhaps the god will spare us a thought so that we do not perish."

7 The sailors*a* said to one another, "Come, let us cast lots, so that we may know on whose account this calamity has come upon us." So they cast lots, and the lot fell on Jonah. 8Then they said to him, "Tell us why this calamity has come upon us. What is your occupation? Where do you come from? What is your country? And of what people are you?" 9"I am a Hebrew," he replied. "I worship the LORD, the God of heaven, who made the sea and the dry land." 10Then the men were even more afraid, and said to him, "What is this that you have done!" For the men knew that he was fleeing from the presence of the LORD, because he had told them so.

11 Then they said to him, "What shall we do to you, that the sea may quiet down for us?" For the sea was growing more and more tempestuous. 12He said to them, "Pick me up and throw me into the sea; then the sea will quiet down for you; for I know it is because of me

that this great storm has come upon you." 13Nevertheless the men rowed hard to bring the ship back to land, but they could not, for the sea grew more and more stormy against them. 14Then they cried out to the LORD, "Please, O LORD, we pray, do not let us perish on account of this man's life. Do not make us guilty of innocent blood; for you, O LORD, have done as it pleased you." 15So they picked Jonah up and threw him into the sea; and the sea ceased from its raging. 16Then the men feared the LORD even more, and they offered a sacrifice to the LORD and made vows.

17*b* But the LORD provided a large fish to swallow up Jonah; and Jonah was in the belly of the fish three days and three nights.

A Psalm of Thanksgiving

2 Then Jonah prayed to the LORD his God from the belly of the fish, 2saying,

"I called to the LORD out of my distress,
    and he answered me;
out of the belly of Sheol I cried,
    and you heard my voice.
3 You cast me into the deep,
    into the heart of the seas,
    and the flood surrounded me;
all your waves and your billows
    passed over me.
4 Then I said, 'I am driven away
    from your sight;
how*c* shall I look again
    upon your holy temple?'
5 The waters closed in over me;
    the deep surrounded me;
weeds were wrapped around my head
6   at the roots of the mountains.
I went down to the land
    whose bars closed upon me forever;
yet you brought up my life from the Pit,
    O LORD my God.
7 As my life was ebbing away,
    I remembered the LORD;
and my prayer came to you,

---

a Heb *They*   *b* Ch 2.1 in Heb   *c* Theodotion: Heb *surely*

into your holy temple.
8 Those who worship vain idols
    forsake their true loyalty.
9 But I with the voice of thanksgiving
    will sacrifice to you;
    what I have vowed I will pay.
        Deliverance belongs to the LORD!"
10Then the LORD spoke to the fish, and it
spewed Jonah out upon the dry land.

Conversion of Nineveh

3 The word of the LORD came to Jonah a
  second time, saying, 2"Get up, go to Nineveh, that great city, and proclaim to it the
message that I tell you." 3So Jonah set out and
went to Nineveh, according to the word of
the LORD. Now Nineveh was an exceedingly
large city, a three days' walk across. 4Jonah began to go into the city, going a day's walk. And
he cried out, "Forty days more, and Nineveh
shall be overthrown!" 5And the people of Nineveh believed God; they proclaimed a fast, and
everyone, great and small, put on sackcloth.

6 When the news reached the king of Nineveh, he rose from his throne, removed his
robe, covered himself with sackcloth, and sat
in ashes. 7Then he had a proclamation made in
Nineveh: "By the decree of the king and his
nobles: No human being or animal, no herd or
flock, shall taste anything. They shall not feed,
nor shall they drink water. 8Human beings and
animals shall be covered with sackcloth, and
they shall cry mightily to God. All shall turn
from their evil ways and from the violence that
is in their hands. 9Who knows? God may relent
and change his mind; he may turn from his
fierce anger, so that we do not perish."

10 When God saw what they did, how they
turned from their evil ways, God changed his
mind about the calamity that he had said he
would bring upon them; and he did not do it.

Jonah's Anger

4 But this was very displeasing to Jonah,
  and he became angry. 2He prayed to the
LORD and said, "O LORD! Is not this what I said
while I was still in my own country? That is why
I fled to Tarshish at the beginning; for I knew
that you are a gracious God and merciful, slow
to anger, and abounding in steadfast love, and
ready to relent from punishing. 3And now,
O LORD, please take my life from me, for it is
better for me to die than to live." 4And the
LORD said, "Is it right for you to be angry?"
5Then Jonah went out of the city and sat down
east of the city, and made a booth for himself
there. He sat under it in the shade, waiting to
see what would become of the city.

6 The LORD God appointed a bush,*a* and
made it come up over Jonah, to give shade
over his head, to save him from his discomfort;
so Jonah was very happy about the bush. 7But
when dawn came up the next day, God appointed a worm that attacked the bush, so that
it withered. 8When the sun rose, God prepared
a sultry east wind, and the sun beat down on
the head of Jonah so that he was faint and
asked that he might die. He said, "It is better for
me to die than to live."

Jonah Is Reproved

9 But God said to Jonah, "Is it right for you
to be angry about the bush?" And he said,
"Yes, angry enough to die." 10Then the LORD
said, "You are concerned about the bush, for
which you did not labor and which you did not
grow; it came into being in a night and perished
in a night. 11And should I not be concerned
about Nineveh, that great city, in which there
are more than a hundred and twenty thousand
persons who do not know their right hand
from their left, and also many animals?"

---

a Heb *qiqayon*, possibly *the castor bean plant*

MICAH

1 The word of the LORD that came to Micah of Moresheth in the days of Kings Jotham, Ahaz, and Hezekiah of Judah, which he saw concerning Samaria and Jerusalem.

Judgment Pronounced against Samaria

2 Hear, you peoples, all of you;
    listen, O earth, and all that is in it;
and let the Lord GOD be a witness
    against you,
        the Lord from his holy temple.
3 For lo, the LORD is coming out of his
        place,
    and will come down and tread upon
        the high places of the earth.
4 Then the mountains will melt under him
    and the valleys will burst open,
like wax near the fire,
    like waters poured down a steep place.
5 All this is for the transgression of Jacob
    and for the sins of the house of
        Israel.
What is the transgression of Jacob?
    Is it not Samaria?
And what is the high place *a* of Judah?
    Is it not Jerusalem?
6 Therefore I will make Samaria a heap in
        the open country,
    a place for planting vineyards.
I will pour down her stones into the
        valley,
    and uncover her foundations.
7 All her images shall be beaten to pieces,
    all her wages shall be burned with fire,
    and all her idols I will lay waste;
for as the wages of a prostitute she
        gathered them,
    and as the wages of a prostitute they
        shall again be used.

The Doom of the Cities of Judah

8 For this I will lament and wail;
    I will go barefoot and naked;
I will make lamentation like the jackals,
    and mourning like the ostriches.
9 For her wound *b* is incurable.
    It has come to Judah;
it has reached to the gate of my people,
    to Jerusalem.

10 Tell it not in Gath,
    weep not at all;
in Beth-leaphrah
    roll yourselves in the dust.
11 Pass on your way,
    inhabitants of Shaphir,
    in nakedness and shame;
the inhabitants of Zaanan
    do not come forth;
Beth-ezel is wailing
    and shall remove its support from
        you.
12 For the inhabitants of Maroth
    wait anxiously for good,
yet disaster has come down from the
        LORD
    to the gate of Jerusalem.
13 Harness the steeds to the chariots,
    inhabitants of Lachish;
it was the beginning of sin
    to daughter Zion,
for in you were found
    the transgressions of Israel.
14 Therefore you shall give parting gifts
    to Moresheth-gath;
the houses of Achzib shall be a
        deception
    to the kings of Israel.
15 I will again bring a conqueror upon you,
    inhabitants of Mareshah;
the glory of Israel
    shall come to Adullam.
16 Make yourselves bald and cut off your
        hair
    for your pampered children;
make yourselves as bald as the eagle,
    for they have gone from you into
        exile.

a Heb *what are the high places*   *b* Gk Syr Vg: Heb *wounds*

Social Evils Denounced

2 Alas for those who devise wickedness
        and evil deeds*a* on their beds!
    When the morning dawns, they perform
        it,
        because it is in their power.
2   They covet fields, and seize them;
        houses, and take them away;
    they oppress householder and house,
        people and their inheritance.
3   Therefore thus says the LORD:
    Now, I am devising against this family an
        evil
        from which you cannot remove your
            necks;
    and you shall not walk haughtily,
        for it will be an evil time.
4   On that day they shall take up a taunt
            song against you,
        and wail with bitter lamentation,
    and say, "We are utterly ruined;
        the LORD*b* alters the inheritance of
            my people;
    how he removes it from me!
        Among our captors*c* he parcels out
            our fields."
5   Therefore you will have no one to cast
            the line by lot
        in the assembly of the LORD.

6   "Do not preach"—thus they preach—
        "one should not preach of such
            things;
        disgrace will not overtake us."
7   Should this be said, O house of Jacob?
        Is the LORD's patience exhausted?
        Are these his doings?
    Do not my words do good
        to one who walks uprightly?
8   But you rise up against my people*d* as an
            enemy;
        you strip the robe from the peaceful,*e*
    from those who pass by trustingly
        with no thought of war.
9   The women of my people you drive out
        from their pleasant houses;

from their young children you take away
        my glory forever.
10 Arise and go;
        for this is no place to rest,
    because of uncleanness that destroys
        with a grievous destruction.*f*
11 If someone were to go about uttering
            empty falsehoods,
        saying, "I will preach to you of wine
            and strong drink,"
        such a one would be the preacher for
            this people!

A Promise for the Remnant of Israel

12 I will surely gather all of you, O Jacob,
        I will gather the survivors of Israel;
    I will set them together
        like sheep in a fold,
    like a flock in its pasture;
        it will resound with people.
13 The one who breaks out will go up
            before them;
        they will break through and pass the
            gate,
        going out by it.
    Their king will pass on before them,
        the LORD at their head.

Wicked Rulers and Prophets

3 And I said:
    Listen, you heads of Jacob
        and rulers of the house of Israel!
    Should you not know justice?—
2   you who hate the good and love the
            evil,
    who tear the skin off my people,*g*
        and the flesh off their bones;
3   who eat the flesh of my people,
        flay their skin off them,
    break their bones in pieces,
        and chop them up like meat*h* in a
            kettle,
        like flesh in a caldron.

4   Then they will cry to the LORD,
        but he will not answer them;

---

a Cn: Heb *work evil*   *b* Heb *he*   *c* Cn: Heb *the rebellious*   *d* Cn: Heb *But yesterday my people rose*   *e* Cn: Heb
from before a garment   *f* Meaning of Heb uncertain   *g* Heb *from them*   *h* Gk: Heb *as*

he will hide his face from them at that
time,
because they have acted wickedly.

5 Thus says the LORD concerning the
prophets
who lead my people astray,
who cry "Peace"
when they have something to eat,
but declare war against those
who put nothing into their mouths.
6 Therefore it shall be night to you,
without vision,
and darkness to you, without
revelation.
The sun shall go down upon the
prophets,
and the day shall be black over them;
7 the seers shall be disgraced,
and the diviners put to shame;
they shall all cover their lips,
for there is no answer from God.
8 But as for me, I am filled with power,
with the spirit of the LORD,
and with justice and might,
to declare to Jacob his transgression
and to Israel his sin.

9 Hear this, you rulers of the house of
Jacob
and chiefs of the house of Israel,
who abhor justice
and pervert all equity,
10 who build Zion with blood
and Jerusalem with wrong!
11 Its rulers give judgment for a bribe,
its priests teach for a price,
its prophets give oracles for money;
yet they lean upon the LORD and say,
"Surely the LORD is with us!
No harm shall come upon us."
12 Therefore because of you
Zion shall be plowed as a field;
Jerusalem shall become a heap of ruins,
and the mountain of the house a
wooded height.

Peace and Security through Obedience

4 In days to come
the mountain of the LORD's house
shall be established as the highest of the
mountains,
and shall be raised up above the hills.
Peoples shall stream to it,
2 and many nations shall come and say:
"Come, let us go up to the mountain of
the LORD,
to the house of the God of Jacob;
that he may teach us his ways
and that we may walk in his paths."
For out of Zion shall go forth
instruction,
and the word of the LORD from
Jerusalem.
3 He shall judge between many peoples,
and shall arbitrate between strong
nations far away;
they shall beat their swords into
plowshares,
and their spears into pruning hooks;
nation shall not lift up sword against
nation,
neither shall they learn war any more;
4 but they shall all sit under their own
vines and under their own fig
trees,
and no one shall make them afraid;
for the mouth of the LORD of hosts
has spoken.

5 For all the peoples walk,
each in the name of its god,
but we will walk in the name of the
LORD our God
forever and ever.

Restoration Promised after Exile

6 In that day, says the LORD,
I will assemble the lame
and gather those who have been driven
away,
and those whom I have afflicted.
7 The lame I will make the remnant,
and those who were cast off, a strong
nation;

and the LORD will reign over them in
    Mount Zion
now and forevermore.

8 And you, O tower of the flock,
    hill of daughter Zion,
to you it shall come,
    the former dominion shall come,
    the sovereignty of daughter Jerusalem.

9 Now why do you cry aloud?
    Is there no king in you?
Has your counselor perished,
    that pangs have seized you like a
    woman in labor?
10 Writhe and groan,*a* O daughter Zion,
    like a woman in labor;
for now you shall go forth from the city
    and camp in the open country;
    you shall go to Babylon.
There you shall be rescued,
    there the LORD will redeem you
    from the hands of your enemies.

11 Now many nations
    are assembled against you,
saying, "Let her be profaned,
    and let our eyes gaze upon Zion."
12 But they do not know
    the thoughts of the LORD;
they do not understand his plan,
    that he has gathered them as sheaves
    to the threshing floor.
13 Arise and thresh,
    O daughter Zion,
for I will make your horn iron
    and your hoofs bronze;
you shall beat in pieces many peoples,
    and shall*b* devote their gain to the
    LORD,
    their wealth to the Lord of the whole
    earth.

5 *c* Now you are walled around with a
    wall;*d*
    siege is laid against us;

with a rod they strike the ruler of Israel
    upon the cheek.

The Ruler from Bethlehem

2*e* But you, O Bethlehem of Ephrathah,
    who are one of the little clans of
    Judah,
from you shall come forth for me
    one who is to rule in Israel,
whose origin is from of old,
    from ancient days.
3 Therefore he shall give them up until the
    time
    when she who is in labor has brought
    forth;
then the rest of his kindred shall return
    to the people of Israel.
4 And he shall stand and feed his flock in
    the strength of the LORD,
    in the majesty of the name of the
    LORD his God.
And they shall live secure, for now he
    shall be great
    to the ends of the earth;
5 and he shall be the one of peace.

If the Assyrians come into our land
    and tread upon our soil,*f*
we will raise against them seven
    shepherds
    and eight installed as rulers.
6 They shall rule the land of Assyria with
    the sword,
    and the land of Nimrod with the
    drawn sword;*g*
they*h* shall rescue us from the Assyrians
    if they come into our land
    or tread within our border.

The Future Role of the Remnant

7 Then the remnant of Jacob,
    surrounded by many peoples,
shall be like dew from the LORD,
    like showers on the grass,
which do not depend upon people
    or wait for any mortal.

---

a Meaning of Heb uncertain   *b* Gk Syr Tg: Heb *and I will*   *c* Ch 4.14 in Heb   *d* Cn Compare Gk: Meaning
of Heb uncertain   *e* Ch 5.1 in Heb   *f* Gk: Heb *in our palaces*   *g* Cn: Heb *in its entrances*   *h* Heb *he*

8 And among the nations the remnant of
     Jacob,
     surrounded by many peoples,
     shall be like a lion among the animals of
         the forest,
         like a young lion among the flocks of
         sheep,
     which, when it goes through, treads
         down
         and tears in pieces, with no one to
         deliver.
9 Your hand shall be lifted up over your
     adversaries,
     and all your enemies shall be cut off.

10 In that day, says the LORD,
     I will cut off your horses from among
         you
     and will destroy your chariots;
11 and I will cut off the cities of your land
     and throw down all your strongholds;
12 and I will cut off sorceries from your
     hand,
     and you shall have no more
         soothsayers;
13 and I will cut off your images
     and your pillars from among you,
     and you shall bow down no more
     to the work of your hands;
14 and I will uproot your sacred poles[a]
     from among you
     and destroy your towns.
15 And in anger and wrath I will execute
     vengeance
     on the nations that did not obey.

God Challenges Israel

6 Hear what the LORD says:
     Rise, plead your case before the
         mountains,
     and let the hills hear your voice.
2 Hear, you mountains, the controversy of
         the LORD,
     and you enduring foundations of the
         earth;

for the LORD has a controversy with his
     people,
     and he will contend with Israel.

3 "O my people, what have I done to you?
     In what have I wearied you? Answer
         me!
4 For I brought you up from the land of
     Egypt,
     and redeemed you from the house of
         slavery;
     and I sent before you Moses,
     Aaron, and Miriam.
5 O my people, remember now what King
     Balak of Moab devised,
     what Balaam son of Beor answered
         him,
     and what happened from Shittim to
         Gilgal,
     that you may know the saving acts of
         the LORD."

What God Requires

6 "With what shall I come before the
     LORD,
     and bow myself before God on high?
     Shall I come before him with burnt
         offerings,
     with calves a year old?
7 Will the LORD be pleased with thousands
     of rams,
     with ten thousands of rivers of oil?
     Shall I give my firstborn for my
         transgression,
     the fruit of my body for the sin of my
         soul?"
8 He has told you, O mortal, what is good;
     and what does the LORD require of
         you
     but to do justice, and to love kindness,
     and to walk humbly with your God?

Cheating and Violence to Be Punished

9 The voice of the LORD cries to the city
     (it is sound wisdom to fear your
         name):

---

a Heb *Asherim*

Hear, O tribe and assembly of the city![a]

10 Can I forget[b] the treasures of
    wickedness in the house of the
    wicked,
  and the scant measure that is
    accursed?
11 Can I tolerate wicked scales
  and a bag of dishonest weights?
12 Your[c] wealthy are full of violence;
  your[d] inhabitants speak lies,
  with tongues of deceit in their
    mouths.
13 Therefore I have begun[e] to strike you
    down,
  making you desolate because of your
    sins.
14 You shall eat, but not be satisfied,
  and there shall be a gnawing hunger
    within you;
  you shall put away, but not save,
  and what you save, I will hand over to
    the sword.
15 You shall sow, but not reap;
  you shall tread olives, but not anoint
    yourselves with oil;
  you shall tread grapes, but not drink
    wine.
16 For you have kept the statutes of Omri[f]
  and all the works of the house of
    Ahab,
  and you have followed their counsels.
  Therefore I will make you a desolation,
    and your[g] inhabitants an object
    of hissing;
  so you shall bear the scorn of my
    people.

The Total Corruption of the People

7 Woe is me! For I have become like one
    who,
  after the summer fruit has been
    gathered,
  after the vintage has been gleaned,
  finds no cluster to eat;

  there is no first-ripe fig for which I
    hunger.
2 The faithful have disappeared from the
    land,
  and there is no one left who is
    upright;
  they all lie in wait for blood,
  and they hunt each other with nets.
3 Their hands are skilled to do evil;
  the official and the judge ask for a
    bribe,
  and the powerful dictate what they
    desire;
  thus they pervert justice.[b]
4 The best of them is like a brier,
  the most upright of them a thorn
    hedge.
  The day of their[i] sentinels, of their[i]
    punishment, has come;
  now their confusion is at hand.
5 Put no trust in a friend,
  have no confidence in a loved one;
  guard the doors of your mouth
  from her who lies in your embrace;
6 for the son treats the father with
    contempt,
  the daughter rises up against her
    mother,
  the daughter-in-law against her mother-
    in-law;
  your enemies are members of your
    own household.
7 But as for me, I will look to the LORD,
  I will wait for the God of my
    salvation;
  my God will hear me.

Penitence and Trust in God

8 Do not rejoice over me, O my enemy;
  when I fall, I shall rise;
  when I sit in darkness,
  the LORD will be a light to me.
9 I must bear the indignation of the LORD,
  because I have sinned against him,
  until he takes my side

---

a Cn Compare Gk: Heb *tribe, and who has appointed it yet?*   b Cn: Meaning of Heb uncertain   c Heb *Whose*
d Heb *whose*   e Gk Syr Vg: Heb *have made sick*   f Gk Syr Vg Tg: Heb *the statutes of Omri are kept*   g Heb *its*
h Cn: Heb *they weave it*   i Heb *your*

and executes judgment for me.
He will bring me out to the light;
  I shall see his vindication.
10 Then my enemy will see,
    and shame will cover her who said to
      me,
    "Where is the LORD your God?"
  My eyes will see her downfall;*a*
    now she will be trodden down
    like the mire of the streets.

A Prophecy of Restoration

11 A day for the building of your walls!
    In that day the boundary shall be far
      extended.
12 In that day they will come to you
    from Assyria to*b* Egypt,
  and from Egypt to the River,
    from sea to sea and from mountain to
      mountain.
13 But the earth will be desolate
    because of its inhabitants,
    for the fruit of their doings.

14 Shepherd your people with your staff,
    the flock that belongs to you,
  which lives alone in a forest
    in the midst of a garden land;
  let them feed in Bashan and Gilead
    as in the days of old.
15 As in the days when you came out of the
      land of Egypt,

show us*c* marvelous things.
16 The nations shall see and be ashamed
    of all their might;
  they shall lay their hands on their
      mouths;
    their ears shall be deaf;
17 they shall lick dust like a snake,
    like the crawling things of the earth;
  they shall come trembling out of their
      fortresses;
    they shall turn in dread to the LORD
      our God,
    and they shall stand in fear of you.

God's Compassion and Steadfast Love

18 Who is a God like you, pardoning
      iniquity
    and passing over the transgression
    of the remnant of your*d* possession?
  He does not retain his anger forever,
    because he delights in showing
      clemency.
19 He will again have compassion upon us;
    he will tread our iniquities under foot.
  You will cast all our*e* sins
    into the depths of the sea.
20 You will show faithfulness to Jacob
    and unswerving loyalty to Abraham,
  as you have sworn to our ancestors
    from the days of old.

---

a Heb lacks *downfall*   *b* One Ms: MT *Assyria and cities of*   *c* Cn: Heb *I will show him*   *d* Heb *his*   *e* Gk Syr Vg
Tg: Heb *their*

NAHUM

1 An oracle concerning Nineveh. The book of the vision of Nahum of Elkosh.

The Consuming Wrath of God

2 A jealous and avenging God is the LORD,
    the LORD is avenging and wrathful;
the LORD takes vengeance on his
    adversaries
and rages against his enemies.
3 The LORD is slow to anger but great in
    power,
    and the LORD will by no means clear
      the guilty.

His way is in whirlwind and storm,
    and the clouds are the dust of his feet.
4 He rebukes the sea and makes it dry,
    and he dries up all the rivers;
Bashan and Carmel wither,
    and the bloom of Lebanon fades.
5 The mountains quake before him,
    and the hills melt;
the earth heaves before him,
    the world and all who live in it.

6 Who can stand before his indignation?
    Who can endure the heat of his
      anger?
His wrath is poured out like fire,
    and by him the rocks are broken in
      pieces.
7 The LORD is good,
    a stronghold in a day of trouble;
he protects those who take refuge in
    him,
8   even in a rushing flood.
He will make a full end of his
    adversaries,^a
    and will pursue his enemies into
      darkness.
9 Why do you plot against the LORD?
    He will make an end;
    no adversary will rise up twice.
10 Like thorns they are entangled,

like drunkards they are drunk;
    they are consumed like dry straw.
11 From you one has gone out
    who plots evil against the LORD,
    one who counsels wickedness.

Good News for Judah

12 Thus says the LORD,
"Though they are at full strength and
    many,^b
    they will be cut off and pass away.
Though I have afflicted you,
    I will afflict you no more.
13 And now I will break off his yoke from
    you
    and snap the bonds that bind you."

14 The LORD has commanded concerning
    you:
"Your name shall be perpetuated no
    longer;
from the house of your gods I will cut
    off
    the carved image and the cast image.
I will make your grave, for you are
    worthless."

15^c Look! On the mountains the feet of one
    who brings good tidings,
    who proclaims peace!
Celebrate your festivals, O Judah,
    fulfill your vows,
for never again shall the wicked invade
    you;
    they are utterly cut off.

The Destruction of the Wicked City

2 A shatterer^d has come up against you.
    Guard the ramparts;
    watch the road;
gird your loins;
    collect all your strength.

---

a Gk: Heb *of her place*   *b* Meaning of Heb uncertain   *c* Ch 2.1 in Heb   *d* Cn: Heb *scatterer*

2 (For the LORD is restoring the majesty of
      Jacob,
   as well as the majesty of Israel,
though ravagers have ravaged them
   and ruined their branches.)

3 The shields of his warriors are red;
      his soldiers are clothed in crimson.
   The metal on the chariots flashes
      on the day when he musters them;
   the chargers*a* prance.
4 The chariots race madly through the
         streets,
      they rush to and fro through the
         squares;
   their appearance is like torches,
      they dart like lightning.
5 He calls his officers;
      they stumble as they come forward;
   they hasten to the wall,
      and the mantelet*b* is set up.
6 The river gates are opened,
      the palace trembles.
7 It is decreed*b* that the city*c* be exiled,
      its slave women led away,
   moaning like doves
      and beating their breasts.
8 Nineveh is like a pool
      whose waters*d* run away.
   "Halt! Halt!"—
      but no one turns back.
9 "Plunder the silver,
      plunder the gold!
   There is no end of treasure!
      An abundance of every precious
         thing!"

10 Devastation, desolation, and destruction!
      Hearts faint and knees tremble,
   all loins quake,
      all faces grow pale!
11 What became of the lions' den,
      the cave*e* of the young lions,
   where the lion goes,
      and the lion's cubs, with no one to
         disturb them?

12 The lion has torn enough for his whelps
      and strangled prey for his lionesses;
   he has filled his caves with prey
      and his dens with torn flesh.

13 See, I am against you, says the LORD of
hosts, and I will burn your*f* chariots in smoke,
and the sword shall devour your young lions;
I will cut off your prey from the earth, and the
voice of your messengers shall be heard no
more.

Ruin Imminent and Inevitable

3 Ah! City of bloodshed,
      utterly deceitful, full of booty—
      no end to the plunder!
2 The crack of whip and rumble of wheel,
      galloping horse and bounding chariot!
3 Horsemen charging,
      flashing sword and glittering spear,
   piles of dead,
      heaps of corpses,
   dead bodies without end—
      they stumble over the bodies!
4 Because of the countless debaucheries
         of the prostitute,
      gracefully alluring, mistress of sorcery,
   who enslaves*g* nations through her
         debaucheries,
      and peoples through her sorcery,
5 I am against you,
      says the LORD of hosts,
   and will lift up your skirts over your
         face;
   and I will let nations look on your
         nakedness
      and kingdoms on your shame.
6 I will throw filth at you
      and treat you with contempt,
      and make you a spectacle.
7 Then all who see you will shrink from
         you and say,
   "Nineveh is devastated; who will
         bemoan her?"
      Where shall I seek comforters for
         you?

---

a Cn Compare Gk Syr: Heb *cypresses*   *b* Meaning of Heb uncertain   *c* Heb *it*   *d* Cn Compare Gk: Heb
a pool, from the days that she has become, and they   *e* Cn: Heb *pasture*   *f* Heb *her*   *g* Heb *sells*

8 Are you better than Thebes[a]
    that sat by the Nile,
with water around her,
    her rampart a sea,
    water her wall?
9 Ethiopia[b] was her strength,
    Egypt too, and that without limit;
    Put and the Libyans were her[c] helpers.

10 Yet she became an exile,
    she went into captivity;
even her infants were dashed in pieces
    at the head of every street;
lots were cast for her nobles,
    all her dignitaries were bound in
        fetters.
11 You also will be drunken,
    you will go into hiding;[d]
you will seek
    a refuge from the enemy.
12 All your fortresses are like fig trees
    with first-ripe figs—
if shaken they fall
    into the mouth of the eater.
13 Look at your troops:
    they are women in your midst.
The gates of your land
    are wide open to your foes;
    fire has devoured the bars of your
        gates.

14 Draw water for the siege,
    strengthen your forts;

trample the clay,
    tread the mortar,
    take hold of the brick mold!
15 There the fire will devour you,
    the sword will cut you off.
    It will devour you like the locust.

Multiply yourselves like the locust,
    multiply like the grasshopper!
16 You increased your merchants
    more than the stars of the heavens.
    The locust sheds its skin and flies
        away.
17 Your guards are like grasshoppers,
    your scribes like swarms[d] of locusts
settling on the fences
    on a cold day—
when the sun rises, they fly away;
    no one knows where they have gone.

18 Your shepherds are asleep,
    O king of Assyria;
    your nobles slumber.
Your people are scattered on the
        mountains
    with no one to gather them.
19 There is no assuaging your hurt,
    your wound is mortal.
All who hear the news about you
    clap their hands over you.
For who has ever escaped
    your endless cruelty?

---

a Heb No-amon   b Or Nubia; Heb Cush   c Gk: Heb your   d Meaning of Heb uncertain

HABAKKUK

1 The oracle that the prophet Habakkuk saw.

The Prophet's Complaint

2 O LORD, how long shall I cry for help,
  and you will not listen?
  Or cry to you "Violence!"
  and you will not save?
3 Why do you make me see wrongdoing
  and look at trouble?
  Destruction and violence are before me;
  strife and contention arise.
4 So the law becomes slack
  and justice never prevails.
  The wicked surround the righteous—
  therefore judgment comes forth
  perverted.

5 Look at the nations, and see!
  Be astonished! Be astounded!
  For a work is being done in your days
  that you would not believe if you were
  told.
6 For I am rousing the Chaldeans,
  that fierce and impetuous nation,
  who march through the breadth of the
  earth
  to seize dwellings not their own.
7 Dread and fearsome are they;
  their justice and dignity proceed from
  themselves.
8 Their horses are swifter than leopards,
  more menacing than wolves at dusk;
  their horses charge.
  Their horsemen come from far away;
  they fly like an eagle swift to devour.
9 They all come for violence,
  with faces pressing*a* forward;
  they gather captives like sand.
10 At kings they scoff,
  and of rulers they make sport.
  They laugh at every fortress,
  and heap up earth to take it.
11 Then they sweep by like the wind;

they transgress and become guilty;
  their own might is their god!

12 Are you not from of old,
  O LORD my God, my Holy One?
  You*b* shall not die.
  O LORD, you have marked them for
  judgment;
  and you, O Rock, have established
  them for punishment.
13 Your eyes are too pure to behold evil,
  and you cannot look on wrongdoing;
  why do you look on the treacherous,
  and are silent when the wicked swallow
  those more righteous than they?
14 You have made people like the fish of
  the sea,
  like crawling things that have no ruler.

15 The enemy*c* brings all of them up with a
  hook;
  he drags them out with his net,
  he gathers them in his seine;
  so he rejoices and exults.
16 Therefore he sacrifices to his net
  and makes offerings to his seine;
  for by them his portion is lavish,
  and his food is rich.
17 Is he then to keep on emptying his net,
  and destroying nations without mercy?

God's Reply to the Prophet's Complaint

2 I will stand at my watchpost,
  and station myself on the rampart;
  I will keep watch to see what he will say
  to me,
  and what he*d* will answer concerning
  my complaint.
2 Then the LORD answered me and said:
  Write the vision;
  make it plain on tablets,
  so that a runner may read it.
3 For there is still a vision for the
  appointed time;

---

a Meaning of Heb uncertain   *b* Ancient Heb tradition: MT *We*   *c* Heb *He*   *d* Syr: Heb *I*

it speaks of the end, and does not lie.
If it seems to tarry, wait for it;
   it will surely come, it will not delay.
4 Look at the proud!
   Their spirit is not right in them,
   but the righteous live by their faith.ᵃ
5 Moreover, wealthᵇ is treacherous;
   the arrogant do not endure.
They open their throats wide as Sheol;
   like Death they never have enough.
They gather all nations for themselves,
   and collect all peoples as their own.

The Woes of the Wicked

6 Shall not everyone taunt such people and,
with mocking riddles, say about them,
   "Alas for you who heap up what is not
      your own!"
   How long will you load yourselves
      with goods taken in pledge?
7 Will not your own creditors suddenly rise,
   and those who make you tremble
      wake up?
   Then you will be booty for them.
8 Because you have plundered many
      nations,
   all that survive of the peoples shall
      plunder you—
because of human bloodshed, and
      violence to the earth,
   to cities and all who live in them.

9 "Alas for you who get evil gain for your
      house,
   setting your nest on high
   to be safe from the reach of harm!"
10 You have devised shame for your house
   by cutting off many peoples;
   you have forfeited your life.
11 The very stones will cry out from the
      wall,
   and the plasterᶜ will respond from the
      woodwork.

12 "Alas for you who build a town by
      bloodshed,

and found a city on iniquity!"
13 Is it not from the Lᴏʀᴅ of hosts
   that peoples labor only to feed the
      flames,
   and nations weary themselves for
      nothing?
14 But the earth will be filled
   with the knowledge of the glory of
      the Lᴏʀᴅ,
   as the waters cover the sea.

15 "Alas for you who make your neighbors
      drink,
   pouring out your wrathᵈ until they are
      drunk,
   in order to gaze on their nakedness!"
16 You will be sated with contempt instead
      of glory.
   Drink, you yourself, and stagger!ᵉ
The cup in the Lᴏʀᴅ's right hand
   will come around to you,
   and shame will come upon your glory!
17 For the violence done to Lebanon will
      overwhelm you;
   the destruction of the animals will
      terrify you—ᶠ
because of human bloodshed and
      violence to the earth,
   to cities and all who live in them.

18 What use is an idol
   once its maker has shaped it—
   a cast image, a teacher of lies?
For its maker trusts in what has been
      made,
   though the product is only an idol that
      cannot speak!
19 Alas for you who say to the wood,
      "Wake up!"
   to silent stone, "Rouse yourself!"
   Can it teach?
See, it is gold and silver plated,
   and there is no breath in it at all.

20 But the Lᴏʀᴅ is in his holy temple;
   let all the earth keep silence before him!

a Or *faithfulness*   *b* Other Heb Mss read *wine*   *c* Or *beam*   *d* Or *poison*   *e* Q Ms Gk: MT *be uncircumcised*
f Gk Syr: Meaning of Heb uncertain

3 A prayer of the prophet Habakkuk according to Shigionoth.

The Prophet's Prayer

2 O LORD, I have heard of your renown,
and I stand in awe, O LORD, of your
work.
In our own time revive it;
in our own time make it known;
in wrath may you remember mercy.
3 God came from Teman,
the Holy One from Mount Paran.
                         Selah
His glory covered the heavens,
and the earth was full of his praise.
4 The brightness was like the sun;
rays came forth from his hand,
where his power lay hidden.
5 Before him went pestilence,
and plague followed close behind.
6 He stopped and shook the earth;
he looked and made the nations
tremble.
The eternal mountains were shattered;
along his ancient pathways
the everlasting hills sank low.
7 I saw the tents of Cushan under
affliction;
the tent-curtains of the land of
Midian trembled.
8 Was your wrath against the rivers,*a*
O LORD?
Or your anger against the rivers,*a*
or your rage against the sea,*b*
when you drove your horses,
your chariots to victory?
9 You brandished your naked bow,
sated*c* were the arrows at your
command.*d*
                         Selah
You split the earth with rivers.
10 The mountains saw you, and writhed;
a torrent of water swept by;
the deep gave forth its voice.
The sun*e* raised high its hands;
11 the moon*f* stood still in its exalted place,

at the light of your arrows speeding
by,
at the gleam of your flashing spear.
12 In fury you trod the earth,
in anger you trampled nations.
13 You came forth to save your people,
to save your anointed.
You crushed the head of the wicked
house,
laying it bare from foundation to
roof.*d*
                         Selah
14 You pierced with their*g* own arrows the
head*h* of his warriors,*i*
who came like a whirlwind to scatter
us,*j*
gloating as if ready to devour the poor
who were in hiding.
15 You trampled the sea with your horses,
churning the mighty waters.

16 I hear, and I tremble within;
my lips quiver at the sound.
Rottenness enters into my bones,
and my steps tremble*k* beneath me.
I wait quietly for the day of calamity
to come upon the people who attack
us.

Trust and Joy in the Midst of Trouble

17 Though the fig tree does not blossom,
and no fruit is on the vines;
though the produce of the olive fails,
and the fields yield no food;
though the flock is cut off from the fold,
and there is no herd in the stalls,
18 yet I will rejoice in the LORD;
I will exult in the God of my
salvation.
19 GOD, the Lord, is my strength;
he makes my feet like the feet of a
deer,
and makes me tread upon the heights.*l*

To the leader: with stringed*m*
instruments.

---

a Or *against River*   *b* Or *against Sea*   *c* Cn: Heb *oaths*   *d* Meaning of Heb uncertain   *e* Heb *It*   *f* Heb *sun, moon*   *g* Heb *his*   *h* Or *leader*   *i* Vg Compare Gk Syr: Meaning of Heb uncertain   *j* Heb *me*   *k* Cn Compare Gk: Meaning of Heb uncertain   *l* Heb *my heights*   *m* Heb *my stringed*

ZEPHANIAH

1 The word of the LORD that came to Zephaniah son of Cushi son of Gedaliah son of Amariah son of Hezekiah, in the days of King Josiah son of Amon of Judah.

The Coming Judgment on Judah

2 I will utterly sweep away everything
    from the face of the earth, says the
        LORD.
3 I will sweep away humans and animals;
    I will sweep away the birds of the air
    and the fish of the sea.
  I will make the wicked stumble. *a*
  I will cut off humanity
    from the face of the earth, says the
        LORD.
4 I will stretch out my hand against Judah,
    and against all the inhabitants of
        Jerusalem;
  and I will cut off from this place every
        remnant of Baal
    and the name of the idolatrous
        priests; *b*
5 those who bow down on the roofs
    to the host of the heavens;
  those who bow down and swear to the
        LORD,
    but also swear by Milcom; *c*
6 those who have turned back from
    following the LORD,
  who have not sought the LORD or
    inquired of him.

7 Be silent before the Lord GOD!
    For the day of the LORD is at hand;
  the LORD has prepared a sacrifice,
    he has consecrated his guests.
8 And on the day of the LORD's sacrifice
  I will punish the officials and the king's
        sons
    and all who dress themselves in
        foreign attire.
9 On that day I will punish
    all who leap over the threshold,
who fill their master's house
    with violence and fraud.

10 On that day, says the LORD,
    a cry will be heard from the Fish Gate,
  a wail from the Second Quarter,
    a loud crash from the hills.
11 The inhabitants of the Mortar wail,
    for all the traders have perished;
  all who weigh out silver are cut off.
12 At that time I will search Jerusalem with
        lamps,
    and I will punish the people
  who rest complacently *d* on their dregs,
    those who say in their hearts,
  "The LORD will not do good,
    nor will he do harm."
13 Their wealth shall be plundered,
    and their houses laid waste.
  Though they build houses,
    they shall not inhabit them;
  though they plant vineyards,
    they shall not drink wine from them.

The Great Day of the LORD

14 The great day of the LORD is near,
    near and hastening fast;
  the sound of the day of the LORD is
        bitter,
    the warrior cries aloud there.
15 That day will be a day of wrath,
    a day of distress and anguish,
  a day of ruin and devastation,
    a day of darkness and gloom,
  a day of clouds and thick darkness,
16   a day of trumpet blast and battle cry
against the fortified cities
    and against the lofty battlements.

17 I will bring such distress upon people
    that they shall walk like the blind;
  because they have sinned against the
        LORD,
    their blood shall be poured out like dust,

---

a Cn: Heb *sea, and those who cause the wicked to stumble*   *b* Compare Gk: Heb *the idolatrous priests with the priests*
c Gk Mss Syr Vg: Heb *Malcam* (or, *their king*)   *d* Heb *who thicken*

and their flesh like dung.

18 Neither their silver nor their gold
  will be able to save them
    on the day of the LORD's wrath;
in the fire of his passion
    the whole earth shall be consumed;
for a full, a terrible end
    he will make of all the inhabitants of
      the earth.

Judgment on Israel's Enemies

2 Gather together, gather,
  O shameless nation,
2 before you are driven away
    like the drifting chaff,*a*
before there comes upon you
    the fierce anger of the LORD,
before there comes upon you
    the day of the LORD's wrath.
3 Seek the LORD, all you humble of the
      land,
    who do his commands;
seek righteousness, seek humility;
    perhaps you may be hidden
    on the day of the LORD's wrath.
4 For Gaza shall be deserted,
    and Ashkelon shall become a
      desolation;
Ashdod's people shall be driven out at
      noon,
    and Ekron shall be uprooted.

5 Ah, inhabitants of the seacoast,
    you nation of the Cherethites!
The word of the LORD is against you,
    O Canaan, land of the Philistines;
    and I will destroy you until no
      inhabitant is left.
6 And you, O seacoast, shall be pastures,
    meadows for shepherds
    and folds for flocks.
7 The seacoast shall become the
      possession
    of the remnant of the house of
      Judah,
    on which they shall pasture,

and in the houses of Ashkelon
    they shall lie down at evening.
For the LORD their God will be mindful
      of them
    and restore their fortunes.

8 I have heard the taunts of Moab
    and the revilings of the Ammonites,
how they have taunted my people
    and made boasts against their
      territory.
9 Therefore, as I live, says the LORD of
      hosts,
    the God of Israel,
Moab shall become like Sodom
    and the Ammonites like Gomorrah,
a land possessed by nettles and salt pits,
    and a waste forever.
The remnant of my people shall plunder
      them,
    and the survivors of my nation shall
      possess them.
10 This shall be their lot in return for their
      pride,
    because they scoffed and boasted
    against the people of the LORD of
      hosts.
11 The LORD will be terrible against them;
    he will shrivel all the gods of the earth,
and to him shall bow down,
    each in its place,
    all the coasts and islands of the
      nations.

12 You also, O Ethiopians,*b*
    shall be killed by my sword.

13 And he will stretch out his hand against
      the north,
    and destroy Assyria;
and he will make Nineveh a desolation,
    a dry waste like the desert.
14 Herds shall lie down in it,
    every wild animal;*c*
the desert owl*d* and the screech owl*d*
    shall lodge on its capitals;

---

a Cn Compare Gk Syr: Heb *before a decree is born; like chaff a day has passed away*   *b* Or *Nubians*; Heb *Cushites*
c Tg Compare Gk: Heb *nation*   *d* Meaning of Heb uncertain

the owl^a shall hoot at the window,
    the raven^b croak on the threshold;
    for its cedar work will be laid bare.

15 Is this the exultant city
    that lived secure,
that said to itself,
    "I am, and there is no one else"?
What a desolation it has become,
    a lair for wild animals!
Everyone who passes by it
    hisses and shakes the fist.

The Wickedness of Jerusalem

3 Ah, soiled, defiled,
    oppressing city!
2 It has listened to no voice;
    it has accepted no correction.
It has not trusted in the LORD;
    it has not drawn near to its God.

3 The officials within it
    are roaring lions;
its judges are evening wolves
    that leave nothing until the morning.
4 Its prophets are reckless,
    faithless persons;
its priests have profaned what is sacred,
    they have done violence to the law.
5 The LORD within it is righteous;
    he does no wrong.
Every morning he renders his judgment,
    each dawn without fail;
    but the unjust knows no shame.

6 I have cut off nations;
    their battlements are in ruins;
I have laid waste their streets
    so that no one walks in them;
their cities have been made desolate,
    without people, without inhabitants.
7 I said, "Surely the city^c will fear me,
    it will accept correction;
it will not lose sight^d
    of all that I have brought upon it."
But they were the more eager
    to make all their deeds corrupt.

Punishment and Conversion of the Nations

8 Therefore wait for me, says the LORD,
    for the day when I arise as a witness.
For my decision is to gather nations,
    to assemble kingdoms,
to pour out upon them my indignation,
    all the heat of my anger;
for in the fire of my passion
    all the earth shall be consumed.

9 At that time I will change the speech of
    the peoples
    to a pure speech,
that all of them may call on the name of
    the LORD
    and serve him with one accord.
10 From beyond the rivers of Ethiopia^e
    my suppliants, my scattered ones,
    shall bring my offering.

11 On that day you shall not be put to
    shame
because of all the deeds by which you
    have rebelled against me;
for then I will remove from your midst
    your proudly exultant ones,
and you shall no longer be haughty
    in my holy mountain.
12 For I will leave in the midst of you
    a people humble and lowly.
They shall seek refuge in the name of
    the LORD—
13   the remnant of Israel;
they shall do no wrong
    and utter no lies,
nor shall a deceitful tongue
    be found in their mouths.
Then they will pasture and lie down,
    and no one shall make them afraid.

A Song of Joy

14 Sing aloud, O daughter Zion;
    shout, O Israel!
Rejoice and exult with all your heart,
    O daughter Jerusalem!

---

a Cn: Heb *a voice*   b Gk Vg: Heb *desolation*   c Heb *it*   d Gk Syr: Heb *its dwelling will not be cut off*
e Or *Nubia*; Heb *Cush*

15 The LORD has taken away the judgments
          against you,
      he has turned away your enemies.
    The king of Israel, the LORD, is in your
          midst;
      you shall fear disaster no more.
16 On that day it shall be said to
          Jerusalem:
    Do not fear, O Zion;
      do not let your hands grow weak.
17 The LORD, your God, is in your midst,
      a warrior who gives victory;
    he will rejoice over you with gladness,
      he will renew you*a* in his love;
    he will exult over you with loud singing
18 as on a day of festival.*b*

    I will remove disaster from you,*c*
      so that you will not bear reproach for
          it.
19 I will deal with all your oppressors
      at that time.
    And I will save the lame
      and gather the outcast,
    and I will change their shame into praise
      and renown in all the earth.
20 At that time I will bring you home,
      at the time when I gather you;
    for I will make you renowned and
          praised
      among all the peoples of the earth,
    when I restore your fortunes
      before your eyes, says the LORD.

---

a Gk Syr: Heb *he will be silent*   *b* Gk Syr: Meaning of Heb uncertain   *c* Cn: Heb *I will remove from you; they were*

HAGGAI

The Command to Rebuild the Temple

1 In the second year of King Darius, in the sixth month, on the first day of the month, the word of the LORD came by the prophet Haggai to Zerubbabel son of Shealtiel, governor of Judah, and to Joshua son of Jehozadak, the high priest: ²Thus says the LORD of hosts: These people say the time has not yet come to rebuild the LORD's house. ³Then the word of the LORD came by the prophet Haggai, saying: ⁴Is it a time for you yourselves to live in your paneled houses, while this house lies in ruins? ⁵Now therefore thus says the LORD of hosts: Consider how you have fared. ⁶You have sown much, and harvested little; you eat, but you never have enough; you drink, but you never have your fill; you clothe yourselves, but no one is warm; and you that earn wages earn wages to put them into a bag with holes.

7 Thus says the LORD of hosts: Consider how you have fared. ⁸Go up to the hills and bring wood and build the house, so that I may take pleasure in it and be honored, says the LORD. ⁹You have looked for much, and, lo, it came to little; and when you brought it home, I blew it away. Why? says the LORD of hosts. Because my house lies in ruins, while all of you hurry off to your own houses. ¹⁰Therefore the heavens above you have withheld the dew, and the earth has withheld its produce. ¹¹And I have called for a drought on the land and the hills, on the grain, the new wine, the oil, on what the soil produces, on human beings and animals, and on all their labors.

12 Then Zerubbabel son of Shealtiel, and Joshua son of Jehozadak, the high priest, with all the remnant of the people, obeyed the voice of the LORD their God, and the words of the prophet Haggai, as the LORD their God had sent him; and the people feared the LORD. ¹³Then Haggai, the messenger of the LORD, spoke to the people with the LORD's message, saying, I am with you, says the LORD. ¹⁴And the LORD stirred up the spirit of Zerubbabel son of Shealtiel, governor of Judah, and the spirit of Joshua son of Jehozadak, the high priest, and the spirit of all the remnant of the people; and they came and worked on the house of the LORD of hosts, their God, ¹⁵on the twenty-fourth day of the month, in the sixth month.

The Future Glory of the Temple

2 In the second year of King Darius, ¹in the seventh month, on the twenty-first day of the month, the word of the LORD came by the prophet Haggai, saying: ²Speak now to Zerubbabel son of Shealtiel, governor of Judah, and to Joshua son of Jehozadak, the high priest, and to the remnant of the people, and say, ³Who is left among you that saw this house in its former glory? How does it look to you now? Is it not in your sight as nothing? ⁴Yet now take courage, O Zerubbabel, says the LORD; take courage, O Joshua, son of Jehozadak, the high priest; take courage, all you people of the land, says the LORD; work, for I am with you, says the LORD of hosts, ⁵according to the promise that I made you when you came out of Egypt. My spirit abides among you; do not fear. ⁶For thus says the LORD of hosts: Once again, in a little while, I will shake the heavens and the earth and the sea and the dry land; ⁷and I will shake all the nations, so that the treasure of all nations shall come, and I will fill this house with splendor, says the LORD of hosts. ⁸The silver is mine, and the gold is mine, says the LORD of hosts. ⁹The latter splendor of this house shall be greater than the former, says the LORD of hosts; and in this place I will give prosperity, says the LORD of hosts.

A Rebuke and a Promise

10 On the twenty-fourth day of the ninth month, in the second year of Darius, the word of the LORD came by the prophet Haggai, saying: ¹¹Thus says the LORD of hosts: Ask the priests for a ruling: ¹²If one carries consecrated meat in the fold of one's garment, and with the fold touches bread, or stew, or wine, or oil, or any kind of food, does it become holy? The priests answered, "No." ¹³Then Haggai said, "If one who is unclean by contact with a

dead body touches any of these, does it become unclean?" The priests answered, "Yes, it becomes unclean." ¹⁴Haggai then said, So is it with this people, and with this nation before me, says the LORD; and so with every work of their hands; and what they offer there is unclean. ¹⁵But now, consider what will come to pass from this day on. Before a stone was placed upon a stone in the LORD's temple, ¹⁶how did you fare?ᵃ When one came to a heap of twenty measures, there were but ten; when one came to the wine vat to draw fifty measures, there were but twenty. ¹⁷I struck you and all the products of your toil with blight and mildew and hail; yet you did not return to me, says the LORD. ¹⁸Consider from this day on, from the twenty-fourth day of the ninth month. Since the day that the foundation of the LORD's temple was laid, consider: ¹⁹Is there

any seed left in the barn? Do the vine, the fig tree, the pomegranate, and the olive tree still yield nothing? From this day on I will bless you.

God's Promise to Zerubbabel

20 The word of the LORD came a second time to Haggai on the twenty-fourth day of the month: ²¹Speak to Zerubbabel, governor of Judah, saying, I am about to shake the heavens and the earth, ²²and to overthrow the throne of kingdoms; I am about to destroy the strength of the kingdoms of the nations, and overthrow the chariots and their riders; and the horses and their riders shall fall, every one by the sword of a comrade. ²³On that day, says the LORD of hosts, I will take you, O Zerubbabel my servant, son of Shealtiel, says the LORD, and make you like a signet ring; for I have chosen you, says the LORD of hosts.

a Gk: Heb *since they were*

ZECHARIAH

Israel Urged to Repent

1 In the eighth month, in the second year of Darius, the word of the LORD came to the prophet Zechariah son of Berechiah son of Iddo, saying: [2]The LORD was very angry with your ancestors. [3]Therefore say to them, Thus says the LORD of hosts: Return to me, says the LORD of hosts, and I will return to you, says the LORD of hosts. [4]Do not be like your ancestors, to whom the former prophets proclaimed, "Thus says the LORD of hosts, Return from your evil ways and from your evil deeds." But they did not hear or heed me, says the LORD. [5]Your ancestors, where are they? And the prophets, do they live forever? [6]But my words and my statutes, which I commanded my servants the prophets, did they not overtake your ancestors? So they repented and said, "The LORD of hosts has dealt with us according to our ways and deeds, just as he planned to do."

First Vision: The Horsemen

[7] On the twenty-fourth day of the eleventh month, the month of Shebat, in the second year of Darius, the word of the LORD came to the prophet Zechariah son of Berechiah son of Iddo; and Zechariah[a] said, [8]In the night I saw a man riding on a red horse! He was standing among the myrtle trees in the glen; and behind him were red, sorrel, and white horses. [9]Then I said, "What are these, my lord?" The angel who talked with me said to me, "I will show you what they are." [10]So the man who was standing among the myrtle trees answered, "They are those whom the LORD has sent to patrol the earth." [11]Then they spoke to the angel of the LORD who was standing among the myrtle trees, "We have patrolled the earth, and lo, the whole earth remains at peace." [12]Then the angel of the LORD said, "O LORD of hosts, how long will you withhold mercy from Jerusalem and the cities of Judah, with which you have been angry these seventy years?" [13]Then the LORD replied with gracious and comfort-ing words to the angel who talked with me. [14]So the angel who talked with me said to me, Proclaim this message: Thus says the LORD of hosts; I am very jealous for Jerusalem and for Zion. [15]And I am extremely angry with the nations that are at ease; for while I was only a little angry, they made the disaster worse. [16]Therefore, thus says the LORD, I have returned to Jerusalem with compassion; my house shall be built in it, says the LORD of hosts, and the measuring line shall be stretched out over Jerusalem. [17]Proclaim further: Thus says the LORD of hosts: My cities shall again overflow with prosperity; the LORD will again comfort Zion and again choose Jerusalem.

Second Vision: The Horns and the Smiths

[18][b] And I looked up and saw four horns. [19]I asked the angel who talked with me, "What are these?" And he answered me, "These are the horns that have scattered Judah, Israel, and Jerusalem." [20]Then the LORD showed me four blacksmiths. [21]And I asked, "What are they coming to do?" He answered, "These are the horns that scattered Judah, so that no head could be raised; but these have come to terrify them, to strike down the horns of the nations that lifted up their horns against the land of Judah to scatter its people."[c]

Third Vision: The Man with a Measuring Line

2 [d] I looked up and saw a man with a measuring line in his hand. [2]Then I asked, "Where are you going?" He answered me, "To measure Jerusalem, to see what is its width and what is its length." [3]Then the angel who talked with me came forward, and another angel came forward to meet him, [4]and said to him, "Run, say to that young man: Jerusalem shall be inhabited like villages without walls, because of the multitude of people and animals in it. [5]For I will be a wall of fire all around it, says the LORD, and I will be the glory within it."

---

a Heb *and he*   *b* Ch 2.1 in Heb   *c* Heb *it*   *d* Ch 2.5 in Heb

Interlude: An Appeal to the Exiles

6 Up, up! Flee from the land of the north, says the LORD; for I have spread you abroad like the four winds of heaven, says the LORD. 7Up! Escape to Zion, you that live with daughter Babylon. 8For thus said the LORD of hosts (after his glory*a* sent me) regarding the nations that plundered you: Truly, one who touches you touches the apple of my eye.*b* 9See now, I am going to raise*c* my hand against them, and they shall become plunder for their own slaves. Then you will know that the LORD of hosts has sent me. 10Sing and rejoice, O daughter Zion! For lo, I will come and dwell in your midst, says the LORD. 11Many nations shall join themselves to the LORD on that day, and shall be my people; and I will dwell in your midst. And you shall know that the LORD of hosts has sent me to you. 12The LORD will inherit Judah as his portion in the holy land, and will again choose Jerusalem.

13 Be silent, all people, before the LORD; for he has roused himself from his holy dwelling.

Fourth Vision: Joshua and Satan

3 Then he showed me the high priest Joshua standing before the angel of the LORD, and Satan*d* standing at his right hand to accuse him. 2And the LORD said to Satan,*d* "The LORD rebuke you, O Satan!*d* The LORD who has chosen Jerusalem rebuke you! Is not this man a brand plucked from the fire?" 3Now Joshua was dressed with filthy clothes as he stood before the angel. 4The angel said to those who were standing before him, "Take off his filthy clothes." And to him he said, "See, I have taken your guilt away from you, and I will clothe you with festal apparel." 5And I said, "Let them put a clean turban on his head." So they put a clean turban on his head and clothed him with the apparel; and the angel of the LORD was standing by.

6 Then the angel of the LORD assured Joshua, saying 7"Thus says the LORD of hosts: If you will walk in my ways and keep my requirements, then you shall rule my house and have

charge of my courts, and I will give you the right of access among those who are standing here. 8Now listen, Joshua, high priest, you and your colleagues who sit before you! For they are an omen of things to come: I am going to bring my servant the Branch. 9For on the stone that I have set before Joshua, on a single stone with seven facets, I will engrave its inscription, says the LORD of hosts, and I will remove the guilt of this land in a single day. 10On that day, says the LORD of hosts, you shall invite each other to come under your vine and fig tree."

Fifth Vision: The Lampstand and Olive Trees

4 The angel who talked with me came again, and wakened me, as one is wakened from sleep. 2He said to me, "What do you see?" And I said, "I see a lampstand all of gold, with a bowl on the top of it; there are seven lamps on it, with seven lips on each of the lamps that are on the top of it. 3And by it there are two olive trees, one on the right of the bowl and the other on its left." 4I said to the angel who talked with me, "What are these, my lord?" 5Then the angel who talked with me answered me, "Do you not know what these are?" I said, "No, my lord." 6He said to me, "This is the word of the LORD to Zerubbabel: Not by might, nor by power, but by my spirit, says the LORD of hosts. 7What are you, O great mountain? Before Zerubbabel you shall become a plain; and he shall bring out the top stone amid shouts of 'Grace, grace to it!'"

8 Moreover the word of the LORD came to me, saying, 9"The hands of Zerubbabel have laid the foundation of this house; his hands shall also complete it. Then you will know that the LORD of hosts has sent me to you. 10For whoever has despised the day of small things shall rejoice, and shall see the plummet in the hand of Zerubbabel.

"These seven are the eyes of the LORD, which range through the whole earth." 11Then I said to him, "What are these two olive trees on the right and the left of the lampstand?" 12And a second time I said to him, "What are

---

a Cn: Heb *after glory he*   *b* Heb *his eye*   *c* Or *wave*   *d* Or *the Accuser*; Heb *the Adversary* these two branches of the olive trees, which pour out the oil*a* through the two golden pipes?" [13]He said to me, "Do you not know what these are?" I said, "No, my lord." [14]Then he said, "These are the two anointed ones who stand by the Lord of the whole earth."

Sixth Vision: The Flying Scroll

5 Again I looked up and saw a flying scroll. [2]And he said to me, "What do you see?" I answered, "I see a flying scroll; its length is twenty cubits, and its width ten cubits." [3]Then he said to me, "This is the curse that goes out over the face of the whole land; for everyone who steals shall be cut off according to the writing on one side, and everyone who swears falsely*b* shall be cut off according to the writing on the other side. [4]I have sent it out, says the LORD of hosts, and it shall enter the house of the thief, and the house of anyone who swears falsely by my name; and it shall abide in that house and consume it, both timber and stones."

Seventh Vision: The Woman in a Basket

5 Then the angel who talked with me came forward and said to me, "Look up and see what this is that is coming out." [6]I said, "What is it?" He said, "This is a basket*c* coming out." And he said, "This is their iniquity*d* in all the land." [7]Then a leaden cover was lifted, and there was a woman sitting in the basket![8]And he said, "This is Wickedness." So he thrust her back into the basket,*c* and pressed the leaden weight down on its mouth. [9]Then I looked up and saw two women coming forward. The wind was in their wings; they had wings like the wings of a stork, and they lifted up the basket*c* between earth and sky. [10]Then I said to the angel who talked with me, "Where are they taking the basket?"*c* [11]He said to me, "To the land of Shinar, to build a house for it; and when this is prepared, they will set the basket*c* down there on its base."

Eighth Vision: Four Chariots

6 And again I looked up and saw four chariots coming out from between two mountains—mountains of bronze. [2]The first chariot had red horses, the second chariot black horses, [3]the third chariot white horses, and the fourth chariot dappled gray*e* horses. [4]Then I said to the angel who talked with me, "What are these, my lord?" [5]The angel answered me, "These are the four winds*f* of heaven going out, after presenting themselves before the Lord of all the earth. [6]The chariot with the black horses goes toward the north country, the white ones go toward the west country,*g* and the dappled ones go toward the south country." [7]When the steeds came out, they were impatient to get off and patrol the earth. And he said, "Go, patrol the earth." So they patrolled the earth. [8]Then he cried out to me, "Lo, those who go toward the north country have set my spirit at rest in the north country."

The Coronation of the Branch

9 The word of the LORD came to me: [10]Collect silver and gold*b* from the exiles—from Heldai, Tobijah, and Jedaiah—who have arrived from Babylon; and go the same day to the house of Josiah son of Zephaniah. [11]Take the silver and gold and make a crown,*i* and set it on the head of the high priest Joshua son of Jehozadak; [12]say to him: Thus says the LORD of hosts: Here is a man whose name is Branch: for he shall branch out in his place, and he shall build the temple of the LORD. [13]It is he that shall build the temple of the LORD; he shall bear royal honor, and shall sit upon his throne and rule. There shall be a priest by his throne, with peaceful understanding between the two of them. [14]And the crown*j* shall be in the care of Heldai,*k* Tobijah, Jedaiah, and Josiah*l* son of Zephaniah, as a memorial in the temple of the LORD.

15 Those who are far off shall come and help to build the temple of the LORD; and you shall know that the LORD of hosts has sent me

a Cn: Heb *gold*   *b* The word *falsely* added from verse 4   *e* Compare Gk: Meaning of Heb uncertain   *f* Or *spirits* Heb lacks *silver and gold*   *i* Gk Mss Syr Tg: Heb *crowns* *Helem*   *l* Syr Compare verse 10: Heb *Hen*

c Heb *ephah*   *d* Gk Compare Syr: Heb *their eye* *g* Cn: Heb *go after them*   *h* Cn Compare verse 11: *j* Gk Syr: Heb *crowns*   *k* Syr Compare verse 10: Heb to you. This will happen if you diligently obey the voice of the LORD your God.

Hypocritical Fasting Condemned

7 In the fourth year of King Darius, the word of the LORD came to Zechariah on the fourth day of the ninth month, which is Chislev. ²Now the people of Bethel had sent Sharezer and Regem-melech and their men, to entreat the favor of the LORD, ³and to ask the priests of the house of the LORD of hosts and the prophets, "Should I mourn and practice abstinence in the fifth month, as I have done for so many years?" ⁴Then the word of the LORD of hosts came to me: ⁵Say to all the people of the land and the priests: When you fasted and lamented in the fifth month and in the seventh, for these seventy years, was it for me that you fasted? ⁶And when you eat and when you drink, do you not eat and drink only for yourselves? ⁷Were not these the words that the LORD proclaimed by the former prophets, when Jerusalem was inhabited and in prosperity, along with the towns around it, and when the Negeb and the Shephelah were inhabited?

Punishment for Rejecting God's Demands

8 The word of the LORD came to Zechariah, saying: ⁹Thus says the LORD of hosts: Render true judgments, show kindness and mercy to one another; ¹⁰do not oppress the widow, the orphan, the alien, or the poor; and do not devise evil in your hearts against one another. ¹¹But they refused to listen, and turned a stubborn shoulder, and stopped their ears in order not to hear. ¹²They made their hearts adamant in order not to hear the law and the words that the LORD of hosts had sent by his spirit through the former prophets. Therefore great wrath came from the LORD of hosts. ¹³Just as, when I *a* called, they would not hear, so, when they called, I would not hear, says the LORD of hosts, ¹⁴and I scattered them with a whirlwind among all the nations that they had not known. Thus the land they left was desolate, so that no one went to and fro, and a pleasant land was made desolate.

God's Promises to Zion

8 The word of the LORD of hosts came to me, saying: ²Thus says the LORD of hosts: I am jealous for Zion with great jealousy, and I am jealous for her with great wrath. ³Thus says the LORD: I will return to Zion, and will dwell in the midst of Jerusalem; Jerusalem shall be called the faithful city, and the mountain of the LORD of hosts shall be called the holy mountain. ⁴Thus says the LORD of hosts: Old men and old women shall again sit in the streets of Jerusalem, each with staff in hand because of their great age. ⁵And the streets of the city shall be full of boys and girls playing in its streets. ⁶Thus says the LORD of hosts: Even though it seems impossible to the remnant of this people in these days, should it also seem impossible to me, says the LORD of hosts? ⁷Thus says the LORD of hosts: I will save my people from the east country and from the west country; ⁸and I will bring them to live in Jerusalem. They shall be my people and I will be their God, in faithfulness and in righteousness.

9 Thus says the LORD of hosts: Let your hands be strong—you that have recently been hearing these words from the mouths of the prophets who were present when the foundation was laid for the rebuilding of the temple, the house of the LORD of hosts. ¹⁰For before those days there were no wages for people or for animals, nor was there any safety from the foe for those who went out or came in, and I set them all against one another. ¹¹But now I will not deal with the remnant of this people as in the former days, says the LORD of hosts. ¹²For there shall be a sowing of peace; the vine shall yield its fruit, the ground shall give its produce, and the skies shall give their dew; and I will cause the remnant of this people to possess all these things. ¹³Just as you have been a cursing among the nations, O house of Judah and house of Israel, so I will save you and you shall be a blessing. Do not be afraid, but let your hands be strong.

14 For thus says the LORD of hosts: Just as I purposed to bring disaster upon you, when

a Heb *he*

your ancestors provoked me to wrath, and I did not relent, says the LORD of hosts, 15so again I have purposed in these days to do good to Jerusalem and to the house of Judah; do not be afraid. 16These are the things that you shall do: Speak the truth to one another, render in your gates judgments that are true and make for peace, 17do not devise evil in your hearts against one another, and love no false oath; for all these are things that I hate, says the LORD.

Joyful Fasting

18 The word of the LORD of hosts came to me, saying: 19Thus says the LORD of hosts: The fast of the fourth month, and the fast of the fifth, and the fast of the seventh, and the fast of the tenth, shall be seasons of joy and gladness, and cheerful festivals for the house of Judah: therefore love truth and peace.

Many Peoples Drawn to Jerusalem

20 Thus says the LORD of hosts: Peoples shall yet come, the inhabitants of many cities; 21the inhabitants of one city shall go to another, saying, "Come, let us go to entreat the favor of the LORD, and to seek the LORD of hosts; I myself am going." 22Many peoples and strong nations shall come to seek the LORD of hosts in Jerusalem, and to entreat the favor of the LORD. 23Thus says the LORD of hosts: In those days ten men from nations of every language shall take hold of a Jew, grasping his garment and saying, "Let us go with you, for we have heard that God is with you."

Judgment on Israel's Enemies

9   An Oracle.

The word of the LORD is against the
        land of Hadrach
    and will rest upon Damascus.
For to the LORD belongs the capital*a* of
        Aram,*b*
    as do all the tribes of Israel;
2   Hamath also, which borders on it,

Tyre and Sidon, though they are very
        wise.
3   Tyre has built itself a rampart,
        and heaped up silver like dust,
        and gold like the dirt of the streets.
4   But now, the Lord will strip it of its
            possessions
        and hurl its wealth into the sea,
        and it shall be devoured by fire.

5   Ashkelon shall see it and be afraid;
        Gaza too, and shall writhe in anguish;
        Ekron also, because its hopes are
            withered.
    The king shall perish from Gaza;
        Ashkelon shall be uninhabited;
6   a mongrel people shall settle in Ashdod,
        and I will make an end of the pride of
            Philistia.
7   I will take away its blood from its mouth,
        and its abominations from between its
            teeth;
    it too shall be a remnant for our God;
        it shall be like a clan in Judah,
        and Ekron shall be like the Jebusites.
8   Then I will encamp at my house as a
            guard,
        so that no one shall march to and fro;
    no oppressor shall again overrun them,
        for now I have seen with my own eyes.

The Coming Ruler of God's People

9   Rejoice greatly, O daughter Zion!
        Shout aloud, O daughter Jerusalem!
    Lo, your king comes to you;
        triumphant and victorious is he,
    humble and riding on a donkey,
        on a colt, the foal of a donkey.
10 He*c* will cut off the chariot from Ephraim
        and the war-horse from Jerusalem;
    and the battle bow shall be cut off,
        and he shall command peace to the
            nations;
    his dominion shall be from sea to sea,
        and from the River to the ends of the
            earth.

a Heb *eye*   *b* Cn: Heb *of Adam* (or *of humankind*)   *c* Gk: Heb *I*

11 As for you also, because of the blood of
      my covenant with you,
   I will set your prisoners free from the
      waterless pit.
12 Return to your stronghold, O prisoners
      of hope;
   today I declare that I will restore to
      you double.
13 For I have bent Judah as my bow;
   I have made Ephraim its arrow.
   I will arouse your sons, O Zion,
      against your sons, O Greece,
   and wield you like a warrior's sword.

14 Then the LORD will appear over them,
      and his arrow go forth like lightning;
   the Lord GOD will sound the trumpet
   and march forth in the whirlwinds of
      the south.
15 The LORD of hosts will protect them,
   and they shall devour and tread down
      the slingers;[a]
   they shall drink their blood[b] like wine,
   and be full like a bowl,
      drenched like the corners of the altar.

16 On that day the LORD their God will
      save them
   for they are the flock of his people;
   for like the jewels of a crown
      they shall shine on his land.
17 For what goodness and beauty are his!
   Grain shall make the young men
      flourish,
   and new wine the young women.

Restoration of Judah and Israel

10 Ask rain from the LORD
   in the season of the spring rain,
   from the LORD who makes the storm
      clouds,
   who gives showers of rain to you,[c]
   the vegetation in the field to everyone.
2 For the teraphim[d] utter nonsense,
   and the diviners see lies;
   the dreamers tell false dreams,

and give empty consolation.
   Therefore the people wander like sheep;
      they suffer for lack of a shepherd.

3 My anger is hot against the shepherds,
      and I will punish the leaders;[e]
   for the LORD of hosts cares for his
      flock, the house of Judah,
   and will make them like his proud
      war-horse.
4 Out of them shall come the cornerstone,
      out of them the tent peg,
   out of them the battle bow,
      out of them every commander.
5 Together they shall be like warriors in
      battle,
   trampling the foe in the mud of the
      streets;
   they shall fight, for the LORD is with
      them,
   and they shall put to shame the riders
      on horses.

6 I will strengthen the house of Judah,
      and I will save the house of Joseph.
   I will bring them back because I have
      compassion on them,
   and they shall be as though I had not
      rejected them;
   for I am the LORD their God and I
      will answer them.
7 Then the people of Ephraim shall
      become like warriors,
   and their hearts shall be glad as with
      wine.
   Their children shall see it and rejoice,
      their hearts shall exult in the LORD.

8 I will signal for them and gather them in,
      for I have redeemed them,
   and they shall be as numerous as they
      were before.
9 Though I scattered them among the
      nations,
   yet in far countries they shall
      remember me,

---

a Cn: Heb the slingstones   b Gk: Heb shall drink   c Heb them   d Or household gods   e Or male goats

and they shall rear their children and
    return.
10 I will bring them home from the land of
        Egypt,
    and gather them from Assyria;
    I will bring them to the land of Gilead
        and to Lebanon,
    until there is no room for them.
11 They*a* shall pass through the sea of
        distress,
    and the waves of the sea shall be
        struck down,
    and all the depths of the Nile dried
        up.
    The pride of Assyria shall be laid low,
    and the scepter of Egypt shall depart.
12 I will make them strong in the LORD,
    and they shall walk in his name,
                                says the LORD.

11

    Open your doors, O Lebanon,
        so that fire may devour your cedars!
2   Wail, O cypress, for the cedar has fallen,
        for the glorious trees are ruined!
    Wail, oaks of Bashan,
        for the thick forest has been felled!
3   Listen, the wail of the shepherds,
        for their glory is despoiled!
    Listen, the roar of the lions,
        for the thickets of the Jordan are
            destroyed!

Two Kinds of Shepherds

4 Thus said the LORD my God: Be a shepherd of the flock doomed to slaughter. 5Those
who buy them kill them and go unpunished;
and those who sell them say, "Blessed be the
LORD, for I have become rich"; and their own
shepherds have no pity on them. 6For I will no
longer have pity on the inhabitants of the earth,
says the LORD. I will cause them, every one, to
fall each into the hand of a neighbor, and each
into the hand of the king; and they shall devastate the earth, and I will deliver no one from
their hand.

7 So, on behalf of the sheep merchants, I
became the shepherd of the flock doomed to
slaughter. I took two staffs; one I named Favor,
the other I named Unity, and I tended the
sheep. 8In one month I disposed of the three
shepherds, for I had become impatient with
them, and they also detested me. 9So I said, "I
will not be your shepherd. What is to die, let it
die; what is to be destroyed, let it be destroyed;
and let those that are left devour the flesh of
one another!" 10I took my staff Favor and
broke it, annulling the covenant that I had
made with all the peoples. 11So it was annulled
on that day, and the sheep merchants, who
were watching me, knew that it was the word
of the LORD. 12I then said to them, "If it seems
right to you, give me my wages; but if not,
keep them." So they weighed out as my wages
thirty shekels of silver. 13Then the LORD said
to me, "Throw it into the treasury"*b*—this
lordly price at which I was valued by them. So
I took the thirty shekels of silver and threw
them into the treasury*b* in the house of the
LORD. 14Then I broke my second staff Unity,
annulling the family ties between Judah and
Israel.

15 Then the LORD said to me: Take once
more the implements of a worthless shepherd.
16For I am now raising up in the land a shepherd who does not care for the perishing, or
seek the wandering,*c* or heal the maimed, or
nourish the healthy,*d* but devours the flesh of
the fat ones, tearing off even their hoofs.
17 Oh, my worthless shepherd,
        who deserts the flock!
    May the sword strike his arm
        and his right eye!
    Let his arm be completely withered,
        his right eye utterly blinded!

Jerusalem's Victory

12

                An Oracle.

The word of the LORD concerning Israel:
Thus says the LORD, who stretched out the
heavens and founded the earth and formed the
human spirit within: 2See, I am about to make

---

a Gk: Heb *He*   *b* Syr: Heb *it to the potter*   *c* Syr Compare Gk Vg: Heb *the youth*   *d* Meaning of Heb uncertain

Jerusalem a cup of reeling for all the surrounding peoples; it will be against Judah also in the siege against Jerusalem. ³On that day I will make Jerusalem a heavy stone for all the peoples; all who lift it shall grievously hurt themselves. And all the nations of the earth shall come together against it. ⁴On that day, says the LORD, I will strike every horse with panic, and its rider with madness. But on the house of Judah I will keep a watchful eye, when I strike every horse of the peoples with blindness. ⁵Then the clans of Judah shall say to themselves, "The inhabitants of Jerusalem have strength through the LORD of hosts, their God."

6 On that day I will make the clans of Judah like a blazing pot on a pile of wood, like a flaming torch among sheaves; and they shall devour to the right and to the left all the surrounding peoples, while Jerusalem shall again be inhabited in its place, in Jerusalem.

7 And the LORD will give victory to the tents of Judah first, that the glory of the house of David and the glory of the inhabitants of Jerusalem may not be exalted over that of Judah. ⁸On that day the LORD will shield the inhabitants of Jerusalem so that the feeblest among them on that day shall be like David, and the house of David shall be like God, like the angel of the LORD, at their head. ⁹And on that day I will seek to destroy all the nations that come against Jerusalem.

Mourning for the Pierced One

10 And I will pour out a spirit of compassion and supplication on the house of David and the inhabitants of Jerusalem, so that, when they look on the one*a* whom they have pierced, they shall mourn for him, as one mourns for an only child, and weep bitterly over him, as one weeps over a firstborn. ¹¹On that day the mourning in Jerusalem will be as great as the mourning for Hadad-rimmon in the plain of Megiddo. ¹²The land shall mourn, each family by itself; the family of the house of David by itself, and their wives by themselves; the family of the house of Nathan by itself, and their

wives by themselves; ¹³the family of the house of Levi by itself, and their wives by themselves; the family of the Shimeites by itself, and their wives by themselves; ¹⁴and all the families that are left, each by itself, and their wives by themselves.

13 On that day a fountain shall be opened for the house of David and the inhabitants of Jerusalem, to cleanse them from sin and impurity.

Idolatry Cut Off

2 On that day, says the LORD of hosts, I will cut off the names of the idols from the land, so that they shall be remembered no more; and also I will remove from the land the prophets and the unclean spirit. ³And if any prophets appear again, their fathers and mothers who bore them will say to them, "You shall not live, for you speak lies in the name of the LORD"; and their fathers and their mothers who bore them shall pierce them through when they prophesy. ⁴On that day the prophets will be ashamed, every one, of their visions when they prophesy; they will not put on a hairy mantle in order to deceive, ⁵but each of them will say, "I am no prophet, I am a tiller of the soil; for the land has been my possession*b* since my youth." ⁶And if anyone asks them, "What are these wounds on your chest?"*c* the answer will be "The wounds I received in the house of my friends."

The Shepherd Struck, the Flock Scattered

7 "Awake, O sword, against my shepherd,
  against the man who is my associate,"
      says the LORD of hosts.
  Strike the shepherd, that the sheep may
      be scattered;
  I will turn my hand against the little
      ones.
8 In the whole land, says the LORD,
  two-thirds shall be cut off and perish,
  and one-third shall be left alive.
9 And I will put this third into the fire,
  refine them as one refines silver,
  and test them as gold is tested.

a Heb *on me*   *b* Cn: Heb *for humankind has caused me to possess*   *c* Heb *wounds between your hands*

They will call on my name,
and I will answer them.
I will say, "They are my people";
and they will say, "The LORD is our
God."

Future Warfare and Final Victory

14 See, a day is coming for the LORD,
when the plunder taken from you will
be divided in your midst. 2For I will gather all
the nations against Jerusalem to battle, and the
city shall be taken and the houses looted and
the women raped; half the city shall go into exile, but the rest of the people shall not be cut
off from the city. 3Then the LORD will go forth
and fight against those nations as when he
fights on a day of battle. 4On that day his feet
shall stand on the Mount of Olives, which lies
before Jerusalem on the east; and the Mount of
Olives shall be split in two from east to west by
a very wide valley; so that one half of the
Mount shall withdraw northward, and the other half southward. 5And you shall flee by the
valley of the LORD's mountain,*a* for the valley
between the mountains shall reach to Azal;*b*
and you shall flee as you fled from the earthquake in the days of King Uzziah of Judah.
Then the LORD my God will come, and all the
holy ones with him.

6 On that day there shall not be*c* either cold
or frost.*d* 7And there shall be continuous day (it
is known to the LORD), not day and not night,
for at evening time there shall be light.

8 On that day living waters shall flow out
from Jerusalem, half of them to the eastern sea
and half of them to the western sea; it shall
continue in summer as in winter.

9 And the LORD will become king over all
the earth; on that day the LORD will be one and
his name one.

10 The whole land shall be turned into a
plain from Geba to Rimmon south of Jerusalem. But Jerusalem shall remain aloft on its
site from the Gate of Benjamin to the place of
the former gate, to the Corner Gate, and from
the Tower of Hananel to the king's wine
presses. 11And it shall be inhabited, for never
again shall it be doomed to destruction; Jerusalem shall abide in security.

12 This shall be the plague with which the
LORD will strike all the peoples that wage war
against Jerusalem: their flesh shall rot while
they are still on their feet; their eyes shall rot in
their sockets, and their tongues shall rot in
their mouths. 13On that day a great panic from
the LORD shall fall on them, so that each will
seize the hand of a neighbor, and the hand of
the one will be raised against the hand of the
other; 14even Judah will fight at Jerusalem. And
the wealth of all the surrounding nations shall
be collected—gold, silver, and garments in
great abundance. 15And a plague like this plague
shall fall on the horses, the mules, the camels,
the donkeys, and whatever animals may be in
those camps.

16 Then all who survive of the nations
that have come against Jerusalem shall go up
year after year to worship the King, the LORD
of hosts, and to keep the festival of booths.*e*
17If any of the families of the earth do not go
up to Jerusalem to worship the King, the LORD
of hosts, there will be no rain upon them.
18And if the family of Egypt do not go up and
present themselves, then on them shall*f* come
the plague that the LORD inflicts on the nations
that do not go up to keep the festival of
booths.*e* 19Such shall be the punishment of
Egypt and the punishment of all the nations
that do not go up to keep the festival of
booths.*e*

20 On that day there shall be inscribed on
the bells of the horses, "Holy to the LORD."
And the cooking pots in the house of the
LORD shall be as holy as*g* the bowls in front of
the altar; 21and every cooking pot in Jerusalem
and Judah shall be sacred to the LORD of hosts,
so that all who sacrifice may come and use
them to boil the flesh of the sacrifice. And
there shall no longer be traders*h* in the house
of the LORD of hosts on that day.

---

a Heb *my mountains*   *b* Meaning of Heb uncertain   *c* Cn: Heb *there shall not be light*   *d* Compare Gk Syr Vg
Tg: Meaning of Heb uncertain   *e* Or *tabernacles*; Heb *succoth*   *f* Gk Syr: Heb *shall not*   *g* Heb *shall be like*
h Or *Canaanites*

MALACHI

1 An oracle. The word of the LORD to Israel by Malachi.*a*

Israel Preferred to Edom

2 I have loved you, says the LORD. But you say, "How have you loved us?" Is not Esau Jacob's brother? says the LORD. Yet I have loved Jacob ³but I have hated Esau; I have made his hill country a desolation and his heritage a desert for jackals. ⁴If Edom says, "We are shattered but we will rebuild the ruins," the LORD of hosts says: They may build, but I will tear down, until they are called the wicked country, the people with whom the LORD is angry forever. ⁵Your own eyes shall see this, and you shall say, "Great is the LORD beyond the borders of Israel!"

Corruption of the Priesthood

6 A son honors his father, and servants their master. If then I am a father, where is the honor due me? And if I am a master, where is the respect due me? says the LORD of hosts to you, O priests, who despise my name. You say, "How have we despised your name?" ⁷By offering polluted food on my altar. And you say, "How have we polluted it?"*b* By thinking that the LORD's table may be despised. ⁸When you offer blind animals in sacrifice, is that not wrong? And when you offer those that are lame or sick, is that not wrong? Try presenting that to your governor; will he be pleased with you or show you favor? says the LORD of hosts. ⁹And now implore the favor of God, that he may be gracious to us. The fault is yours. Will he show favor to any of you? says the LORD of hosts. ¹⁰Oh, that someone among you would shut the temple*c* doors, so that you would not kindle fire on my altar in vain! I have no pleasure in you, says the LORD of hosts, and I will not accept an offering from your hands. ¹¹For from the rising of the sun to its setting my name is great among the nations, and in every place incense is offered to my name, and a pure offering; for my name is great among the nations, says the LORD of hosts. ¹²But you profane it when you say that the Lord's table is polluted, and the food for it*d* may be despised. ¹³"What a weariness this is," you say, and you sniff at me,*e* says the LORD of hosts. You bring what has been taken by violence or is lame or sick, and this you bring as your offering! Shall I accept that from your hand? says the LORD. ¹⁴Cursed be the cheat who has a male in the flock and vows to give it, and yet sacrifices to the Lord what is blemished; for I am a great King, says the LORD of hosts, and my name is reverenced among the nations.

2 And now, O priests, this command is for you. ²If you will not listen, if you will not lay it to heart to give glory to my name, says the LORD of hosts, then I will send the curse on you and I will curse your blessings; indeed I have already cursed them,*f* because you do not lay it to heart. ³I will rebuke your offspring, and spread dung on your faces, the dung of your offerings, and I will put you out of my presence.*g*

4 Know, then, that I have sent this command to you, that my covenant with Levi may hold, says the LORD of hosts. ⁵My covenant with him was a covenant of life and well-being, which I gave him; this called for reverence, and he revered me and stood in awe of my name. ⁶True instruction was in his mouth, and no wrong was found on his lips. He walked with me in integrity and uprightness, and he turned many from iniquity. ⁷For the lips of a priest should guard knowledge, and people should seek instruction from his mouth, for he is the messenger of the LORD of hosts. ⁸But you have turned aside from the way; you have caused many to stumble by your instruction; you have corrupted the covenant of Levi, says the LORD of hosts, ⁹and so I make you despised and abased before all the people, inasmuch as you have not kept my ways but have shown partiality in your instruction.

---

a Or *by my messenger*   *b* Gk: Heb *you*   *c* Heb lacks *temple*   *d* Compare Syr Tg: Heb *its fruit, its food*
e Another reading is *at it*   *f* Heb *it*   *g* Cn Compare Gk Syr: Heb *and he shall bear you to it*

The Covenant Profaned by Judah

10 Have we not all one father? Has not one God created us? Why then are we faithless to one another, profaning the covenant of our ancestors? [11]Judah has been faithless, and abomination has been committed in Israel and in Jerusalem; for Judah has profaned the sanctuary of the LORD, which he loves, and has married the daughter of a foreign god. [12]May the LORD cut off from the tents of Jacob anyone who does this—any to witness[a] or answer, or to bring an offering to the LORD of hosts.

13 And this you do as well: You cover the LORD's altar with tears, with weeping and groaning because he no longer regards the offering or accepts it with favor at your hand. [14]You ask, "Why does he not?" Because the LORD was a witness between you and the wife of your youth, to whom you have been faithless, though she is your companion and your wife by covenant. [15]Did not one God make her?[b] Both flesh and spirit are his.[c] And what does the one God[d] desire? Godly offspring. So look to yourselves, and do not let anyone be faithless to the wife of his youth. [16]For I hate[e] divorce, says the LORD, the God of Israel, and covering one's garment with violence, says the LORD of hosts. So take heed to yourselves and do not be faithless.

17 You have wearied the LORD with your words. Yet you say, "How have we wearied him?" By saying, "All who do evil are good in the sight of the LORD, and he delights in them." Or by asking, "Where is the God of justice?"

The Coming Messenger

3 See, I am sending my messenger to prepare the way before me, and the Lord whom you seek will suddenly come to his temple. The messenger of the covenant in whom you delight—indeed, he is coming, says the LORD of hosts. [2]But who can endure the day of his coming, and who can stand when he appears?

For he is like a refiner's fire and like fullers' soap; [3]he will sit as a refiner and purifier of silver, and he will purify the descendants of Levi and refine them like gold and silver, until they present offerings to the LORD in righteousness.[f] [4]Then the offering of Judah and Jerusalem will be pleasing to the LORD as in the days of old and as in former years.

5 Then I will draw near to you for judgment; I will be swift to bear witness against the sorcerers, against the adulterers, against those who swear falsely, against those who oppress the hired workers in their wages, the widow and the orphan, against those who thrust aside the alien, and do not fear me, says the LORD of hosts.

6 For I the LORD do not change; therefore you, O children of Jacob, have not perished. [7]Ever since the days of your ancestors you have turned aside from my statutes and have not kept them. Return to me, and I will return to you, says the LORD of hosts. But you say, "How shall we return?"

Do Not Rob God

8 Will anyone rob God? Yet you are robbing me! But you say, "How are we robbing you?" In your tithes and offerings! [9]You are cursed with a curse, for you are robbing me— the whole nation of you! [10]Bring the full tithe into the storehouse, so that there may be food in my house, and thus put me to the test, says the LORD of hosts; see if I will not open the windows of heaven for you and pour down for you an overflowing blessing. [11]I will rebuke the locust[g] for you, so that it will not destroy the produce of your soil; and your vine in the field shall not be barren, says the LORD of hosts. [12]Then all nations will count you happy, for you will be a land of delight, says the LORD of hosts.

13 You have spoken harsh words against me, says the LORD. Yet you say, "How have we spoken against you?" [14]You have said, "It is vain to serve God. What do we profit by keeping his command or by going about as mourners before the LORD of hosts? [15]Now we count

a Cn Compare Gk: Heb *arouse*   b Or *Has he not made one?*   c Cn: Heb *and a remnant of spirit was his*   d Heb *he*
e Cn: Heb *he hates*   f Or *right offerings to the LORD*   g Heb *devourer*

the arrogant happy; evildoers not only prosper, but when they put God to the test they escape."

The Reward of the Faithful

16 Then those who revered the LORD spoke with one another. The LORD took note and listened, and a book of remembrance was written before him of those who revered the LORD and thought on his name. 17They shall be mine, says the LORD of hosts, my special possession on the day when I act, and I will spare them as parents spare their children who serve them. 18Then once more you shall see the difference between the righteous and the wicked, between one who serves God and one who does not serve him.

The Great Day of the LORD

4 *a* See, the day is coming, burning like an oven, when all the arrogant and all evil-doers will be stubble; the day that comes shall burn them up, says the LORD of hosts, so that it will leave them neither root nor branch. 2But for you who revere my name the sun of righteousness shall rise, with healing in its wings. You shall go out leaping like calves from the stall. 3And you shall tread down the wicked, for they will be ashes under the soles of your feet, on the day when I act, says the LORD of hosts.

4 Remember the teaching of my servant Moses, the statutes and ordinances that I commanded him at Horeb for all Israel.

5 Lo, I will send you the prophet Elijah before the great and terrible day of the LORD comes. 6He will turn the hearts of parents to their children and the hearts of children to their parents, so that I will not come and strike the land with a curse. *b*

---

a Ch 4.1-6 are Ch 3.19-24 in Heb   *b* Or *a ban of utter destruction*

The
New Testament

THE GOSPEL ACCORDING TO
MATTHEW

The Genealogy of Jesus the Messiah

1 An account of the genealogy*a* of Jesus the Messiah,*b* the son of David, the son of Abraham.

2 Abraham was the father of Isaac, and Isaac the father of Jacob, and Jacob the father of Judah and his brothers, 3and Judah the father of Perez and Zerah by Tamar, and Perez the father of Hezron, and Hezron the father of Aram, 4and Aram the father of Aminadab, and Aminadab the father of Nahshon, and Nahshon the father of Salmon, 5and Salmon the father of Boaz by Rahab, and Boaz the father of Obed by Ruth, and Obed the father of Jesse, 6and Jesse the father of King David.

And David was the father of Solomon by the wife of Uriah, 7and Solomon the father of Rehoboam, and Rehoboam the father of Abijah, and Abijah the father of Asaph,*c* 8and Asaph*c* the father of Jehoshaphat, and Jehoshaphat the father of Joram, and Joram the father of Uzziah, 9and Uzziah the father of Jotham, and Jotham the father of Ahaz, and Ahaz the father of Hezekiah, 10and Hezekiah the father of Manasseh, and Manasseh the father of Amos,*d* and Amos*d* the father of Josiah, 11and Josiah the father of Jechoniah and his brothers, at the time of the deportation to Babylon.

12 And after the deportation to Babylon: Jechoniah was the father of Salathiel, and Salathiel the father of Zerubbabel, 13and Zerubbabel the father of Abiud, and Abiud the father of Eliakim, and Eliakim the father of Azor, 14and Azor the father of Zadok, and Zadok the father of Achim, and Achim the father of Eliud, 15and Eliud the father of Eleazar, and Eleazar the father of Matthan, and Matthan the father of Jacob, 16and Jacob the father of Joseph the husband of Mary, of whom Jesus was born, who is called the Messiah.*e*

17 So all the generations from Abraham to David are fourteen generations; and from David to the deportation to Babylon, fourteen generations; and from the deportation to Babylon to the Messiah,*e* fourteen generations.

The Birth of Jesus the Messiah

18 Now the birth of Jesus the Messiah*b* took place in this way. When his mother Mary had been engaged to Joseph, but before they lived together, she was found to be with child from the Holy Spirit. 19Her husband Joseph, being a righteous man and unwilling to expose her to public disgrace, planned to dismiss her quietly. 20But just when he had resolved to do this, an angel of the Lord appeared to him in a dream and said, "Joseph, son of David, do not be afraid to take Mary as your wife, for the child conceived in her is from the Holy Spirit. 21She will bear a son, and you are to name him Jesus, for he will save his people from their sins." 22All this took place to fulfill what had been spoken by the Lord through the prophet:

23 "Look, the virgin shall conceive and
　　bear a son,
　and they shall name him
　　Emmanuel,"

which means, "God is with us." 24When Joseph awoke from sleep, he did as the angel of the Lord commanded him; he took her as his wife, 25but had no marital relations with her until she had borne a son;*f* and he named him Jesus.

The Visit of the Wise Men

2 In the time of King Herod, after Jesus was born in Bethlehem of Judea, wise men*g* from the East came to Jerusalem, 2asking, "Where is the child who has been born king of the Jews? For we observed his star at its rising,*h* and have come to pay him

---

a Or *birth*　　*b* Or *Jesus Christ*　　*c* Other ancient authorities read *Asa*　　*d* Other ancient authorities read *Amon*　　*e* Or *the Christ*　　*f* Other ancient authorities read *her firstborn son*　　*g* Or *astrologers;* Gk *magi*　　*h* Or *in the East* homage." ³When King Herod heard this, he was frightened, and all Jerusalem with him; ⁴and calling together all the chief priests and scribes of the people, he inquired of them where the Messiah*a* was to be born. ⁵They told him, "In Bethlehem of Judea; for so it has been written by the prophet:

6   'And you, Bethlehem, in the land of
        Judah,
    are by no means least among the
        rulers of Judah;
    for from you shall come a ruler
        who is to shepherd*b* my people
        Israel.' "

7 Then Herod secretly called for the wise men*c* and learned from them the exact time when the star had appeared. ⁸Then he sent them to Bethlehem, saying, "Go and search diligently for the child; and when you have found him, bring me word so that I may also go and pay him homage." ⁹When they had heard the king, they set out; and there, ahead of them, went the star that they had seen at its rising,*d* until it stopped over the place where the child was. ¹⁰When they saw that the star had stopped,*e* they were overwhelmed with joy. ¹¹On entering the house, they saw the child with Mary his mother; and they knelt down and paid him homage. Then, opening their treasure chests, they offered him gifts of gold, frankincense, and myrrh. ¹²And having been warned in a dream not to return to Herod, they left for their own country by another road.

The Escape to Egypt

13 Now after they had left, an angel of the Lord appeared to Joseph in a dream and said, "Get up, take the child and his mother, and flee to Egypt, and remain there until I tell you; for Herod is about to search for the child, to destroy him." ¹⁴Then Joseph*f* got up, took the child and his mother by night, and went to Egypt, ¹⁵and remained there until the death of Herod. This was to fulfill what had been spoken by the Lord through the prophet, "Out of Egypt I have called my son."

The Massacre of the Infants

16 When Herod saw that he had been tricked by the wise men,*c* he was infuriated, and he sent and killed all the children in and around Bethlehem who were two years old or under, according to the time that he had learned from the wise men.*c* ¹⁷Then was fulfilled what had been spoken through the prophet Jeremiah:

18   "A voice was heard in Ramah,
        wailing and loud lamentation,
    Rachel weeping for her children;
        she refused to be consoled, because
        they are no more."

The Return from Egypt

19 When Herod died, an angel of the Lord suddenly appeared in a dream to Joseph in Egypt and said, ²⁰"Get up, take the child and his mother, and go to the land of Israel, for those who were seeking the child's life are dead." ²¹Then Joseph*f* got up, took the child and his mother, and went to the land of Israel. ²²But when he heard that Archelaus was ruling over Judea in place of his father Herod, he was afraid to go there. And after being warned in a dream, he went away to the district of Galilee. ²³There he made his home in a town called Nazareth, so that what had been spoken through the prophets might be fulfilled, "He will be called a Nazorean."

The Proclamation of John the Baptist

3 In those days John the Baptist appeared in the wilderness of Judea, proclaiming, ²"Repent, for the kingdom of heaven has come near."*g* ³This is the one of whom the prophet Isaiah spoke when he said,

    "The voice of one crying out in the
        wilderness:
    'Prepare the way of the Lord,
        make his paths straight.' "

⁴Now John wore clothing of camel's hair

a Or *the Christ*   *b* Or *rule*   *c* Or *astrologers;* Gk *magi*   *d* Or *in the East*   *e* Gk *saw the star*   *f* Gk *he*   *g* Or *is at hand* with a leather belt around his waist, and his food was locusts and wild honey. ⁵Then the people of Jerusalem and all Judea were going out to him, and all the region along the Jordan, ⁶and they were baptized by him in the river Jordan, confessing their sins.

7 But when he saw many Pharisees and Sadducees coming for baptism, he said to them, "You brood of vipers! Who warned you to flee from the wrath to come? ⁸Bear fruit worthy of repentance. ⁹Do not presume to say to yourselves, 'We have Abraham as our ancestor'; for I tell you, God is able from these stones to raise up children to Abraham. ¹⁰Even now the ax is lying at the root of the trees; every tree therefore that does not bear good fruit is cut down and thrown into the fire.

11 "I baptize you with*a* water for repentance, but one who is more powerful than I is coming after me; I am not worthy to carry his sandals. He will baptize you with*a* the Holy Spirit and fire. ¹²His winnowing fork is in his hand, and he will clear his threshing floor and will gather his wheat into the granary; but the chaff he will burn with unquenchable fire."

The Baptism of Jesus

13 Then Jesus came from Galilee to John at the Jordan, to be baptized by him. ¹⁴John would have prevented him, saying, "I need to be baptized by you, and do you come to me?" ¹⁵But Jesus answered him, "Let it be so now; for it is proper for us in this way to fulfill all righteousness." Then he consented. ¹⁶And when Jesus had been baptized, just as he came up from the water, suddenly the heavens were opened to him and he saw the Spirit of God descending like a dove and alighting on him. ¹⁷And a voice from heaven said, "This is my Son, the Beloved,*b* with whom I am well pleased."

The Temptation of Jesus

4 Then Jesus was led up by the Spirit into the wilderness to be tempted by the devil. ²He fasted forty days and forty nights, and afterwards he was famished. ³The tempter came and said to him, "If you are the Son of God, command these stones to become loaves of bread." ⁴But he answered, "It is written,

'One does not live by bread alone,
   but by every word that comes from
     the mouth of God.' "

5 Then the devil took him to the holy city and placed him on the pinnacle of the temple, ⁶saying to him, "If you are the Son of God, throw yourself down; for it is written,

'He will command his angels
   concerning you,'
and 'On their hands they will bear
   you up,
so that you will not dash your foot
   against a stone.' "

⁷Jesus said to him, "Again it is written, 'Do not put the Lord your God to the test.' "

8 Again, the devil took him to a very high mountain and showed him all the kingdoms of the world and their splendor; ⁹and he said to him, "All these I will give you, if you will fall down and worship me." ¹⁰Jesus said to him, "Away with you, Satan! for it is written,

'Worship the Lord your God,
   and serve only him.' "

¹¹Then the devil left him, and suddenly angels came and waited on him.

Jesus Begins His Ministry in Galilee

12 Now when Jesus*c* heard that John had been arrested, he withdrew to Galilee. ¹³He left Nazareth and made his home in Capernaum by the sea, in the territory of Zebulun and Naphtali, ¹⁴so that what had been spoken through the prophet Isaiah might be fulfilled:

15 "Land of Zebulun, land of Naphtali,

---

a Or *in*   *b* Or *my beloved Son*   *c* Gk *he*

on the road by the sea, across the
Jordan, Galilee of the
Gentiles—
16   the people who sat in darkness
have seen a great light,
and for those who sat in the region and
shadow of death
light has dawned."

17From that time Jesus began to proclaim, "Repent, for the kingdom of heaven has come near."ᵃ

Jesus Calls the First Disciples

18   As he walked by the Sea of Galilee, he saw two brothers, Simon, who is called Peter, and Andrew his brother, casting a net into the sea—for they were fishermen. 19And he said to them, "Follow me, and I will make you fish for people." 20Immediately they left their nets and followed him. 21As he went from there, he saw two other brothers, James son of Zebedee and his brother John, in the boat with their father Zebedee, mending their nets, and he called them. 22Immediately they left the boat and their father, and followed him.

Jesus Ministers to Crowds of People

23   Jesusᵇ went throughout Galilee, teaching in their synagogues and proclaiming the good newsᶜ of the kingdom and curing every disease and every sickness among the people. 24So his fame spread throughout all Syria, and they brought to him all the sick, those who were afflicted with various diseases and pains, demoniacs, epileptics, and paralytics, and he cured them. 25And great crowds followed him from Galilee, the Decapolis, Jerusalem, Judea, and from beyond the Jordan.

The Beatitudes

5   When Jesusᵈ saw the crowds, he went up the mountain; and after he sat down, his disciples came to him. 2Then he began to speak, and taught them, saying:

3   "Blessed are the poor in spirit, for theirs is the kingdom of heaven.

4   "Blessed are those who mourn, for they will be comforted.

5   "Blessed are the meek, for they will inherit the earth.

6   "Blessed are those who hunger and thirst for righteousness, for they will be filled.

7   "Blessed are the merciful, for they will receive mercy.

8   "Blessed are the pure in heart, for they will see God.

9   "Blessed are the peacemakers, for they will be called children of God.

10   "Blessed are those who are persecuted for righteousness' sake, for theirs is the kingdom of heaven.

11   "Blessed are you when people revile you and persecute you and utter all kinds of evil against you falselyᵉ on my account. 12Rejoice and be glad, for your reward is great in heaven, for in the same way they persecuted the prophets who were before you.

Salt and Light

13   "You are the salt of the earth; but if salt has lost its taste, how can its saltiness be restored? It is no longer good for anything, but is thrown out and trampled under foot.

14   "You are the light of the world. A city built on a hill cannot be hid. 15No one after lighting a lamp puts it under the bushel basket, but on the lampstand, and it gives light to all in the house. 16In the same way, let your light shine before others, so that they may see your good works and give glory to your Father in heaven.

The Law and the Prophets

17   "Do not think that I have come to abolish the law or the prophets; I have come not to abolish but to fulfill. 18For truly I tell you, until heaven and earth pass away, not one letter,ᶠ not one stroke of a letter, will pass from the law until all is accomplished. 19Therefore, whoever breaksᵍ one of the least of these commandments, and teaches others to do the same, will be called least in

---

a Or *is at hand*   b Gk *He*   c Gk *gospel*   d Gk *he*   e Other ancient authorities lack *falsely*   f Gk *one iota*
g Or *annuls*

the kingdom of heaven; but whoever does them and teaches them will be called great in the kingdom of heaven. 20For I tell you, unless your righteousness exceeds that of the scribes and Pharisees, you will never enter the kingdom of heaven.

Concerning Anger

21 "You have heard that it was said to those of ancient times, 'You shall not murder'; and 'whoever murders shall be liable to judgment.' 22But I say to you that if you are angry with a brother or sister,*a* you will be liable to judgment; and if you insult*b* a brother or sister,*c* you will be liable to the council; and if you say, 'You fool,' you will be liable to the hell*d* of fire. 23So when you are offering your gift at the altar, if you remember that your brother or sister*e* has something against you, 24leave your gift there before the altar and go; first be reconciled to your brother or sister,*e* and then come and offer your gift. 25Come to terms quickly with your accuser while you are on the way to court*f* with him, or your accuser may hand you over to the judge, and the judge to the guard, and you will be thrown into prison. 26Truly I tell you, you will never get out until you have paid the last penny.

Concerning Adultery

27 "You have heard that it was said, 'You shall not commit adultery.' 28But I say to you that everyone who looks at a woman with lust has already committed adultery with her in his heart. 29If your right eye causes you to sin, tear it out and throw it away; it is better for you to lose one of your members than for your whole body to be thrown into hell.*d* 30And if your right hand causes you to sin, cut it off and throw it away; it is better for you to lose one of your members than for your whole body to go into hell.*d*

Concerning Divorce

31 "It was also said, 'Whoever divorces his wife, let him give her a certificate of divorce.'

32But I say to you that anyone who divorces his wife, except on the ground of unchastity, causes her to commit adultery; and whoever marries a divorced woman commits adultery.

Concerning Oaths

33 "Again, you have heard that it was said to those of ancient times, 'You shall not swear falsely, but carry out the vows you have made to the Lord.' 34But I say to you, Do not swear at all, either by heaven, for it is the throne of God, 35or by the earth, for it is his footstool, or by Jerusalem, for it is the city of the great King. 36And do not swear by your head, for you cannot make one hair white or black. 37Let your word be 'Yes, Yes' or 'No, No'; anything more than this comes from the evil one.*g*

Concerning Retaliation

38 "You have heard that it was said, 'An eye for an eye and a tooth for a tooth.' 39But I say to you, Do not resist an evildoer. But if anyone strikes you on the right cheek, turn the other also; 40and if anyone wants to sue you and take your coat, give your cloak as well; 41and if anyone forces you to go one mile, go also the second mile. 42Give to everyone who begs from you, and do not refuse anyone who wants to borrow from you.

Love for Enemies

43 "You have heard that it was said, 'You shall love your neighbor and hate your enemy.' 44But I say to you, Love your enemies and pray for those who persecute you, 45so that you may be children of your Father in heaven; for he makes his sun rise on the evil and on the good, and sends rain on the righteous and on the unrighteous. 46For if you love those who love you, what reward do you have? Do not even the tax collectors do the same? 47And if you greet only your brothers and sisters,*h* what more are you doing than others? Do not even the Gentiles do the

a Gk *a brother*; other ancient authorities add *without cause*   *b* Gk *say Raca to* (an obscure term of abuse)   *c* Gk *a brother*   *d* Gk *Gehenna*   *e* Gk *your brother*   *f* Gk lacks *to court*   *g* Or *evil*   *h* Gk *your brothers* same? [48]Be perfect, therefore, as your heavenly Father is perfect.

Concerning Almsgiving

6 "Beware of practicing your piety before others in order to be seen by them; for then you have no reward from your Father in heaven.

2 "So whenever you give alms, do not sound a trumpet before you, as the hypocrites do in the synagogues and in the streets, so that they may be praised by others. Truly I tell you, they have received their reward. [3]But when you give alms, do not let your left hand know what your right hand is doing, [4]so that your alms may be done in secret; and your Father who sees in secret will reward you.[a]

Concerning Prayer

5 "And whenever you pray, do not be like the hypocrites; for they love to stand and pray in the synagogues and at the street corners, so that they may be seen by others. Truly I tell you, they have received their reward. [6]But whenever you pray, go into your room and shut the door and pray to your Father who is in secret; and your Father who sees in secret will reward you.[a]

7 "When you are praying, do not heap up empty phrases as the Gentiles do; for they think that they will be heard because of their many words. [8]Do not be like them, for your Father knows what you need before you ask him.

9 "Pray then in this way:
  Our Father in heaven,
    hallowed be your name.
10   Your kingdom come.
    Your will be done,
      on earth as it is in heaven.
11   Give us this day our daily bread.[b]
12   And forgive us our debts,
    as we also have forgiven our
      debtors.

13   And do not bring us to the time of
      trial,[c]
    but rescue us from the evil one.[d]
[14]For if you forgive others their trespasses, your heavenly Father will also forgive you; [15]but if you do not forgive others, neither will your Father forgive your trespasses.

Concerning Fasting

16 "And whenever you fast, do not look dismal, like the hypocrites, for they disfigure their faces so as to show others that they are fasting. Truly I tell you, they have received their reward. [17]But when you fast, put oil on your head and wash your face, [18]so that your fasting may be seen not by others but by your Father who is in secret; and your Father who sees in secret will reward you.[a]

Concerning Treasures

19 "Do not store up for yourselves treasures on earth, where moth and rust[e] consume and where thieves break in and steal; [20]but store up for yourselves treasures in heaven, where neither moth nor rust[e] consumes and where thieves do not break in and steal. [21]For where your treasure is, there your heart will be also.

The Sound Eye

22 "The eye is the lamp of the body. So, if your eye is healthy, your whole body will be full of light; [23]but if your eye is unhealthy, your whole body will be full of darkness. If then the light in you is darkness, how great is the darkness!

Serving Two Masters

24 "No one can serve two masters; for a slave will either hate the one and love the other, or be devoted to the one and despise the other. You cannot serve God and wealth.[f]

Do Not Worry

25 "Therefore I tell you, do not worry

---

a Other ancient authorities add openly   b Or our bread for tomorrow   c Or us into temptation   d Or from evil.
Other ancient authorities add, in some form, For the kingdom and the power and the glory are yours forever. Amen.
e Gk eating   f Gk mammon

about your life, what you will eat or what you will drink,*a* or about your body, what you will wear. Is not life more than food, and the body more than clothing? 26Look at the birds of the air; they neither sow nor reap nor gather into barns, and yet your heavenly Father feeds them. Are you not of more value than they? 27And can any of you by worrying add a single hour to your span of life?*b* 28And why do you worry about clothing? Consider the lilies of the field, how they grow; they neither toil nor spin, 29yet I tell you, even Solomon in all his glory was not clothed like one of these. 30But if God so clothes the grass of the field, which is alive today and tomorrow is thrown into the oven, will he not much more clothe you—you of little faith? 31Therefore do not worry, saying, 'What will we eat?' or 'What will we drink?' or 'What will we wear?' 32For it is the Gentiles who strive for all these things; and indeed your heavenly Father knows that you need all these things. 33But strive first for the kingdom of God*c* and his*d* righteousness, and all these things will be given to you as well.

34 "So do not worry about tomorrow, for tomorrow will bring worries of its own. Today's trouble is enough for today.

Judging Others

7 "Do not judge, so that you may not be judged. 2For with the judgment you make you will be judged, and the measure you give will be the measure you get. 3Why do you see the speck in your neighbor's*e* eye, but do not notice the log in your own eye? 4Or how can you say to your neighbor,*f* 'Let me take the speck out of your eye,' while the log is in your own eye? 5You hypocrite, first take the log out of your own eye, and then you will see clearly to take the speck out of your neighbor's*e* eye.

Profaning the Holy

6 "Do not give what is holy to dogs; and do not throw your pearls before swine, or they will trample them under foot and turn and maul you.

Ask, Search, Knock

7 "Ask, and it will be given you; search, and you will find; knock, and the door will be opened for you. 8For everyone who asks receives, and everyone who searches finds, and for everyone who knocks, the door will be opened. 9Is there anyone among you who, if your child asks for bread, will give a stone? 10Or if the child asks for a fish, will give a snake? 11If you then, who are evil, know how to give good gifts to your children, how much more will your Father in heaven give good things to those who ask him!

The Golden Rule

12 "In everything do to others as you would have them do to you; for this is the law and the prophets.

The Narrow Gate

13 "Enter through the narrow gate; for the gate is wide and the road is easy*g* that leads to destruction, and there are many who take it. 14For the gate is narrow and the road is hard that leads to life, and there are few who find it.

A Tree and Its Fruit

15 "Beware of false prophets, who come to you in sheep's clothing but inwardly are ravenous wolves. 16You will know them by their fruits. Are grapes gathered from thorns, or figs from thistles? 17In the same way, every good tree bears good fruit, but the bad tree bears bad fruit. 18A good tree cannot bear bad fruit, nor can a bad tree good fruit. 19Every tree that does not bear good fruit is cut down and thrown into the fire. 20Thus you will know them by their fruits.

a Other ancient authorities lack *or what you will drink*   *b* Or *add one cubit to your height*   *c* Other ancient authorities lack *of God*   *d* Or *its*   *e* Gk *brother's*   *f* Gk *brother*   *g* Other ancient authorities read *for the road is wide and easy*

Concerning Self-Deception

21 "Not everyone who says to me, 'Lord, Lord,' will enter the kingdom of heaven, but only the one who does the will of my Father in heaven. 22On that day many will say to me, 'Lord, Lord, did we not prophesy in your name, and cast out demons in your name, and do many deeds of power in your name?' 23Then I will declare to them, 'I never knew you; go away from me, you evildoers.'

Hearers and Doers

24 "Everyone then who hears these words of mine and acts on them will be like a wise man who built his house on rock. 25The rain fell, the floods came, and the winds blew and beat on that house, but it did not fall, because it had been founded on rock. 26And everyone who hears these words of mine and does not act on them will be like a foolish man who built his house on sand. 27The rain fell, and the floods came, and the winds blew and beat against that house, and it fell—and great was its fall!"

28 Now when Jesus had finished saying these things, the crowds were astounded at his teaching, 29for he taught them as one having authority, and not as their scribes.

Jesus Cleanses a Leper

8 When Jesus*a* had come down from the mountain, great crowds followed him; 2and there was a leper*b* who came to him and knelt before him, saying, "Lord, if you choose, you can make me clean." 3He stretched out his hand and touched him, saying, "I do choose. Be made clean!" Immediately his leprosy*b* was cleansed. 4Then Jesus said to him, "See that you say nothing to anyone; but go, show yourself to the priest, and offer the gift that Moses commanded, as a testimony to them."

Jesus Heals a Centurion's Servant

5 When he entered Capernaum, a centurion came to him, appealing to him 6and say-ing, "Lord, my servant is lying at home paralyzed, in terrible distress." 7And he said to him, "I will come and cure him." 8The centurion answered, "Lord, I am not worthy to have you come under my roof; but only speak the word, and my servant will be healed. 9For I also am a man under authority, with soldiers under me; and I say to one, 'Go,' and he goes, and to another, 'Come,' and he comes, and to my slave, 'Do this,' and the slave does it." 10When Jesus heard him, he was amazed and said to those who followed him, "Truly I tell you, in no one*c* in Israel have I found such faith. 11I tell you, many will come from east and west and will eat with Abraham and Isaac and Jacob in the kingdom of heaven, 12while the heirs of the kingdom will be thrown into the outer darkness, where there will be weeping and gnashing of teeth." 13And to the centurion Jesus said, "Go; let it be done for you according to your faith." And the servant was healed in that hour.

Jesus Heals Many at Peter's House

14 When Jesus entered Peter's house, he saw his mother-in-law lying in bed with a fever; 15he touched her hand, and the fever left her, and she got up and began to serve him. 16That evening they brought to him many who were possessed with demons; and he cast out the spirits with a word, and cured all who were sick. 17This was to fulfill what had been spoken through the prophet Isaiah, "He took our infirmities and bore our diseases."

Would-Be Followers of Jesus

18 Now when Jesus saw great crowds around him, he gave orders to go over to the other side. 19A scribe then approached and said, "Teacher, I will follow you wherever you go." 20And Jesus said to him, "Foxes have holes, and birds of the air have nests; but the Son of Man has nowhere to lay his head." 21Another of his disciples said to him, "Lord, first let me go and bury my father."

---

a Gk *he*   *b* The terms *leper* and *leprosy* can refer to several diseases   *c* Other ancient authorities read *Truly I tell you, not even*

²²But Jesus said to him, "Follow me, and let the dead bury their own dead."

Jesus Stills the Storm

23 And when he got into the boat, his disciples followed him. ²⁴A windstorm arose on the sea, so great that the boat was being swamped by the waves; but he was asleep. ²⁵And they went and woke him up, saying, "Lord, save us! We are perishing!" ²⁶And he said to them, "Why are you afraid, you of little faith?" Then he got up and rebuked the winds and the sea; and there was a dead calm. ²⁷They were amazed, saying, "What sort of man is this, that even the winds and the sea obey him?"

Jesus Heals the Gadarene Demoniacs

28 When he came to the other side, to the country of the Gadarenes,ᵃ two demoniacs coming out of the tombs met him. They were so fierce that no one could pass that way. ²⁹Suddenly they shouted, "What have you to do with us, Son of God? Have you come here to torment us before the time?" ³⁰Now a large herd of swine was feeding at some distance from them. ³¹The demons begged him, "If you cast us out, send us into the herd of swine." ³²And he said to them, "Go!" So they came out and entered the swine; and suddenly, the whole herd rushed down the steep bank into the sea and perished in the water. ³³The swineherds ran off, and on going into the town, they told the whole story about what had happened to the demoniacs. ³⁴Then the whole town came out to meet Jesus; and when they saw him, they begged him to leave their neighborhood.

9 ¹And after getting into a boat he crossed the sea and came to his own town.

Jesus Heals a Paralytic

2 And just then some people were carrying a paralyzed man lying on a bed. When Jesus saw their faith, he said to the paralytic, "Take heart, son; your sins are forgiven."

³Then some of the scribes said to themselves, "This man is blaspheming." ⁴But Jesus, perceiving their thoughts, said, "Why do you think evil in your hearts? ⁵For which is easier, to say, 'Your sins are forgiven,' or to say, 'Stand up and walk'? ⁶But so that you may know that the Son of Man has authority on earth to forgive sins"—he then said to the paralytic—"Stand up, take your bed and go to your home." ⁷And he stood up and went to his home. ⁸When the crowds saw it, they were filled with awe, and they glorified God, who had given such authority to human beings.

The Call of Matthew

9 As Jesus was walking along, he saw a man called Matthew sitting at the tax booth; and he said to him, "Follow me." And he got up and followed him.

10 And as he sat at dinnerᵇ in the house, many tax collectors and sinners came and were sittingᶜ with him and his disciples. ¹¹When the Pharisees saw this, they said to his disciples, "Why does your teacher eat with tax collectors and sinners?" ¹²But when he heard this, he said, "Those who are well have no need of a physician, but those who are sick. ¹³Go and learn what this means, 'I desire mercy, not sacrifice.' For I have come to call not the righteous but sinners."

The Question about Fasting

14 Then the disciples of John came to him, saying, "Why do we and the Pharisees fast often,ᵈ but your disciples do not fast?" ¹⁵And Jesus said to them, "The wedding guests cannot mourn as long as the bridegroom is with them, can they? The days will come when the bridegroom is taken away from them, and then they will fast. ¹⁶No one sews a piece of unshrunk cloth on an old cloak, for the patch pulls away from the cloak, and a worse tear is made. ¹⁷Neither is new wine put into old wineskins; otherwise, the skins burst, and the wine is spilled, and the

---

a Other ancient authorities read *Gergesenes*; others, *Gerasenes*   b Gk *reclined*   c Gk *were reclining*   d Other ancient authorities lack *often* skins are destroyed; but new wine is put into fresh wineskins, and so both are preserved."

A Girl Restored to Life and a Woman Healed

18 While he was saying these things to them, suddenly a leader of the synagogue[a] came in and knelt before him, saying, "My daughter has just died; but come and lay your hand on her, and she will live." 19And Jesus got up and followed him, with his disciples. 20Then suddenly a woman who had been suffering from hemorrhages for twelve years came up behind him and touched the fringe of his cloak, 21for she said to herself, "If I only touch his cloak, I will be made well." 22Jesus turned, and seeing her he said, "Take heart, daughter; your faith has made you well." And instantly the woman was made well. 23When Jesus came to the leader's house and saw the flute players and the crowd making a commotion, 24he said, "Go away; for the girl is not dead but sleeping." And they laughed at him. 25But when the crowd had been put outside, he went in and took her by the hand, and the girl got up. 26And the report of this spread throughout that district.

Jesus Heals Two Blind Men

27 As Jesus went on from there, two blind men followed him, crying loudly, "Have mercy on us, Son of David!" 28When he entered the house, the blind men came to him; and Jesus said to them, "Do you believe that I am able to do this?" They said to him, "Yes, Lord." 29Then he touched their eyes and said, "According to your faith let it be done to you." 30And their eyes were opened. Then Jesus sternly ordered them, "See that no one knows of this." 31But they went away and spread the news about him throughout that district.

Jesus Heals One Who Was Mute

32 After they had gone away, a demoniac who was mute was brought to him. 33And when the demon had been cast out, the one who had been mute spoke; and the crowds were amazed and said, "Never has anything like this been seen in Israel." 34But the Pharisees said, "By the ruler of the demons he casts out the demons."[b]

The Harvest Is Great, the Laborers Few

35 Then Jesus went about all the cities and villages, teaching in their synagogues, and proclaiming the good news of the kingdom, and curing every disease and every sickness. 36When he saw the crowds, he had compassion for them, because they were harassed and helpless, like sheep without a shepherd. 37Then he said to his disciples, "The harvest is plentiful, but the laborers are few; 38therefore ask the Lord of the harvest to send out laborers into his harvest."

The Twelve Apostles

10 Then Jesus[c] summoned his twelve disciples and gave them authority over unclean spirits, to cast them out, and to cure every disease and every sickness. 2These are the names of the twelve apostles: first, Simon, also known as Peter, and his brother Andrew; James son of Zebedee, and his brother John; 3Philip and Bartholomew; Thomas and Matthew the tax collector; James son of Alphaeus, and Thaddaeus;[d] 4Simon the Cananaean, and Judas Iscariot, the one who betrayed him.

The Mission of the Twelve

5 These twelve Jesus sent out with the following instructions: "Go nowhere among the Gentiles, and enter no town of the Samaritans, 6but go rather to the lost sheep of the house of Israel. 7As you go, proclaim the good news, 'The kingdom of heaven has come near.'[e] 8Cure the sick, raise the dead, cleanse the lepers,[f] cast out demons. You received without payment; give without payment. 9Take no gold, or silver, or copper in your belts, 10no bag for your journey, or two tunics, or sandals, or a staff; for laborers de-

---

a Gk lacks of the synagogue   b Other ancient authorities lack this verse   c Gk he   d Other ancient authorities read Lebbaeus, or Lebbaeus called Thaddaeus   e Or is at hand   f The terms leper and leprosy can refer to several diseases serve their food. 11Whatever town or village you enter, find out who in it is worthy, and stay there until you leave. 12As you enter the house, greet it. 13If the house is worthy, let your peace come upon it; but if it is not worthy, let your peace return to you. 14If anyone will not welcome you or listen to your words, shake off the dust from your feet as you leave that house or town. 15Truly I tell you, it will be more tolerable for the land of Sodom and Gomorrah on the day of judgment than for that town.

Coming Persecutions

16 "See, I am sending you out like sheep into the midst of wolves; so be wise as serpents and innocent as doves. 17Beware of them, for they will hand you over to councils and flog you in their synagogues; 18and you will be dragged before governors and kings because of me, as a testimony to them and the Gentiles. 19When they hand you over, do not worry about how you are to speak or what you are to say; for what you are to say will be given to you at that time; 20for it is not you who speak, but the Spirit of your Father speaking through you. 21Brother will betray brother to death, and a father his child, and children will rise against parents and have them put to death; 22and you will be hated by all because of my name. But the one who endures to the end will be saved. 23When they persecute you in one town, flee to the next; for truly I tell you, you will not have gone through all the towns of Israel before the Son of Man comes.

24 "A disciple is not above the teacher, nor a slave above the master; 25it is enough for the disciple to be like the teacher, and the slave like the master. If they have called the master of the house Beelzebul, how much more will they malign those of his household!

Whom to Fear

26 "So have no fear of them; for nothing is covered up that will not be uncovered, and nothing secret that will not become known. 27What I say to you in the dark, tell in the light; and what you hear whispered, proclaim from the housetops. 28Do not fear those who kill the body but cannot kill the soul; rather fear him who can destroy both soul and body in hell.*a* 29Are not two sparrows sold for a penny? Yet not one of them will fall to the ground apart from your Father. 30And even the hairs of your head are all counted. 31So do not be afraid; you are of more value than many sparrows.

32 "Everyone therefore who acknowledges me before others, I also will acknowledge before my Father in heaven; 33but whoever denies me before others, I also will deny before my Father in heaven.

Not Peace, but a Sword

34 "Do not think that I have come to bring peace to the earth; I have not come to bring peace, but a sword.

35   For I have come to set a man against
       his father,
     and a daughter against her mother,
     and a daughter-in-law against her
       mother-in-law;
36   and one's foes will be members of
       one's own household.

37Whoever loves father or mother more than me is not worthy of me; and whoever loves son or daughter more than me is not worthy of me; 38and whoever does not take up the cross and follow me is not worthy of me. 39Those who find their life will lose it, and those who lose their life for my sake will find it.

Rewards

40 "Whoever welcomes you welcomes me, and whoever welcomes me welcomes the one who sent me. 41Whoever welcomes a prophet in the name of a prophet will receive a prophet's reward; and whoever welcomes a righteous person in the name of a righteous person will receive the reward of

a Gk *Gehenna*

the righteous; 42and whoever gives even a cup of cold water to one of these little ones in the name of a disciple—truly I tell you, none of these will lose their reward."

11 Now when Jesus had finished instructing his twelve disciples, he went on from there to teach and proclaim his message in their cities.

Messengers from John the Baptist

2 When John heard in prison what the Messiah*a* was doing, he sent word by his*b* disciples *3*and said to him, "Are you the one who is to come, or are we to wait for another?" *4*Jesus answered them, "Go and tell John what you hear and see: *5*the blind receive their sight, the lame walk, the lepers*c* are cleansed, the deaf hear, the dead are raised, and the poor have good news brought to them. *6*And blessed is anyone who takes no offense at me."

Jesus Praises John the Baptist

7 As they went away, Jesus began to speak to the crowds about John: "What did you go out into the wilderness to look at? A reed shaken by the wind? *8*What then did you go out to see? Someone*d* dressed in soft robes? Look, those who wear soft robes are in royal palaces. *9*What then did you go out to see? A prophet?*e* Yes, I tell you, and more than a prophet. *10*This is the one about whom it is written,

'See, I am sending my messenger ahead
        of you,
    who will prepare your way before
        you.'

*11*Truly I tell you, among those born of women no one has arisen greater than John the Baptist; yet the least in the kingdom of heaven is greater than he. *12*From the days of John the Baptist until now the kingdom of heaven has suffered violence,*f* and the violent

take it by force. *13*For all the prophets and the law prophesied until John came; *14*and if you are willing to accept it, he is Elijah who is to come. *15*Let anyone with ears*g* listen!

16 "But to what will I compare this generation? It is like children sitting in the marketplaces and calling to one another,

17   'We played the flute for you, and you
            did not dance;
        we wailed, and you did not mourn.'

*18*For John came neither eating nor drinking, and they say, 'He has a demon'; *19*the Son of Man came eating and drinking, and they say, 'Look, a glutton and a drunkard, a friend of tax collectors and sinners!' Yet wisdom is vindicated by her deeds."*b*

Woes to Unrepentant Cities

20 Then he began to reproach the cities in which most of his deeds of power had been done, because they did not repent. *21*"Woe to you, Chorazin! Woe to you, Bethsaida! For if the deeds of power done in you had been done in Tyre and Sidon, they would have repented long ago in sackcloth and ashes. *22*But I tell you, on the day of judgment it will be more tolerable for Tyre and Sidon than for you. *23*And you, Capernaum,

    will you be exalted to heaven?
        No, you will be brought down to
            Hades.

For if the deeds of power done in you had been done in Sodom, it would have remained until this day. *24*But I tell you that on the day of judgment it will be more tolerable for the land of Sodom than for you."

Jesus Thanks His Father

25 At that time Jesus said, "I thank*i* you, Father, Lord of heaven and earth, because you have hidden these things from the wise and the intelligent and have revealed them to infants; *26*yes, Father, for such was your gracious will.*j* *27*All things have been handed

---

a Or *the Christ*   *b* Other ancient authorities read *two of his*   *c* The terms *leper* and *leprosy* can refer to several diseases   *d* Or *Why then did you go out? To see someone*   *e* Other ancient authorities read *Why then did you go out? To see a prophet?*   *f* Or *has been coming violently*   *g* Other ancient authorities add *to hear*   *h* Other ancient authorities read *children*   *i* Or *praise*   *j* Or *for so it was well-pleasing in your sight* over to me by my Father; and no one knows the Son except the Father, and no one knows the Father except the Son and anyone to whom the Son chooses to reveal him.

28 "Come to me, all you that are weary and are carrying heavy burdens, and I will give you rest. 29Take my yoke upon you, and learn from me; for I am gentle and humble in heart, and you will find rest for your souls. 30For my yoke is easy, and my burden is light."

Plucking Grain on the Sabbath

12 At that time Jesus went through the grainfields on the sabbath; his disciples were hungry, and they began to pluck heads of grain and to eat. 2When the Pharisees saw it, they said to him, "Look, your disciples are doing what is not lawful to do on the sabbath." 3He said to them, "Have you not read what David did when he and his companions were hungry? 4He entered the house of God and ate the bread of the Presence, which it was not lawful for him or his companions to eat, but only for the priests. 5Or have you not read in the law that on the sabbath the priests in the temple break the sabbath and yet are guiltless? 6I tell you, something greater than the temple is here. 7But if you had known what this means, 'I desire mercy and not sacrifice,' you would not have condemned the guiltless. 8For the Son of Man is lord of the sabbath."

The Man with a Withered Hand

9 He left that place and entered their synagogue; 10a man was there with a withered hand, and they asked him, "Is it lawful to cure on the sabbath?" so that they might accuse him. 11He said to them, "Suppose one of you has only one sheep and it falls into a pit on the sabbath; will you not lay hold of it and lift it out? 12How much more valuable is a human being than a sheep! So it is lawful to do good on the sabbath." 13Then he said to the man, "Stretch out your hand." He stretched it out, and it was restored, as sound

as the other. 14But the Pharisees went out and conspired against him, how to destroy him.

God's Chosen Servant

15 When Jesus became aware of this, he departed. Many crowds a followed him, and he cured all of them, 16and he ordered them not to make him known. 17This was to fulfill what had been spoken through the prophet Isaiah:

18 "Here is my servant, whom I have
　　　chosen,
　　my beloved, with whom my soul is
　　　　well pleased.
　I will put my Spirit upon him,
　　and he will proclaim justice to the
　　　Gentiles.
19 He will not wrangle or cry aloud,
　　nor will anyone hear his voice in the
　　　streets.
20 He will not break a bruised reed
　　or quench a smoldering wick
　until he brings justice to victory.
21 　And in his name the Gentiles will
　　　hope."

Jesus and Beelzebul

22 Then they brought to him a demoniac who was blind and mute; and he cured him, so that the one who had been mute could speak and see. 23All the crowds were amazed and said, "Can this be the Son of David?" 24But when the Pharisees heard it, they said, "It is only by Beelzebul, the ruler of the demons, that this fellow casts out the demons." 25He knew what they were thinking and said to them, "Every kingdom divided against itself is laid waste, and no city or house divided against itself will stand. 26If Satan casts out Satan, he is divided against himself; how then will his kingdom stand? 27If I cast out demons by Beelzebul, by whom do your own exorcists b cast them out? Therefore they will be your judges. 28But if it is by the Spirit of God that I cast out demons, then the kingdom of God has come to you.

a Other ancient authorities lack *crowds*　　b Gk *sons*

²⁹Or how can one enter a strong man's house and plunder his property, without first tying up the strong man? Then indeed the house can be plundered. ³⁰Whoever is not with me is against me, and whoever does not gather with me scatters. ³¹Therefore I tell you, people will be forgiven for every sin and blasphemy, but blasphemy against the Spirit will not be forgiven. ³²Whoever speaks a word against the Son of Man will be forgiven, but whoever speaks against the Holy Spirit will not be forgiven, either in this age or in the age to come.

A Tree and Its Fruit

33 "Either make the tree good, and its fruit good; or make the tree bad, and its fruit bad; for the tree is known by its fruit. ³⁴You brood of vipers! How can you speak good things, when you are evil? For out of the abundance of the heart the mouth speaks. ³⁵The good person brings good things out of a good treasure, and the evil person brings evil things out of an evil treasure. ³⁶I tell you, on the day of judgment you will have to give an account for every careless word you utter; ³⁷for by your words you will be justified, and by your words you will be condemned."

The Sign of Jonah

38 Then some of the scribes and Pharisees said to him, "Teacher, we wish to see a sign from you." ³⁹But he answered them, "An evil and adulterous generation asks for a sign, but no sign will be given to it except the sign of the prophet Jonah. ⁴⁰For just as Jonah was three days and three nights in the belly of the sea monster, so for three days and three nights the Son of Man will be in the heart of the earth. ⁴¹The people of Nineveh will rise up at the judgment with this generation and condemn it, because they repented at the proclamation of Jonah, and see, something greater than Jonah is here! ⁴²The queen of the South will rise up at the judgment with this generation and condemn it, because she came from the ends of the earth to listen to the wisdom of Solomon, and see, something greater than Solomon is here!

The Return of the Unclean Spirit

43 "When the unclean spirit has gone out of a person, it wanders through waterless regions looking for a resting place, but it finds none. ⁴⁴Then it says, 'I will return to my house from which I came.' When it comes, it finds it empty, swept, and put in order. ⁴⁵Then it goes and brings along seven other spirits more evil than itself, and they enter and live there; and the last state of that person is worse than the first. So will it be also with this evil generation."

The True Kindred of Jesus

46 While he was still speaking to the crowds, his mother and his brothers were standing outside, wanting to speak to him. ⁴⁷Someone told him, "Look, your mother and your brothers are standing outside, wanting to speak to you." ᵃ ⁴⁸But to the one who had told him this, Jesus ᵇ replied, "Who is my mother, and who are my brothers?" ⁴⁹And pointing to his disciples, he said, "Here are my mother and my brothers! ⁵⁰For whoever does the will of my Father in heaven is my brother and sister and mother."

The Parable of the Sower

13 That same day Jesus went out of the house and sat beside the sea. ²Such great crowds gathered around him that he got into a boat and sat there, while the whole crowd stood on the beach. ³And he told them many things in parables, saying: "Listen! A sower went out to sow. ⁴And as he sowed, some seeds fell on the path, and the birds came and ate them up. ⁵Other seeds fell on rocky ground, where they did not have much soil, and they sprang up quickly, since they had no depth of soil. ⁶But when the sun rose, they were scorched; and since they had no root, they withered away. ⁷Other seeds

---

a Other ancient authorities lack verse 47   *b* Gk *he* fell among thorns, and the thorns grew up and choked them. 8Other seeds fell on good soil and brought forth grain, some a hundredfold, some sixty, some thirty. 9Let anyone with ears *a* listen!"

The Purpose of the Parables

10 Then the disciples came and asked him, "Why do you speak to them in parables?" 11He answered, "To you it has been given to know the secrets *b* of the kingdom of heaven, but to them it has not been given. 12For to those who have, more will be given, and they will have an abundance; but from those who have nothing, even what they have will be taken away. 13The reason I speak to them in parables is that 'seeing they do not perceive, and hearing they do not listen, nor do they understand.' 14With them indeed is fulfilled the prophecy of Isaiah that says:

'You will indeed listen, but never understand,
    and you will indeed look, but never perceive.
15   For this people's heart has grown dull,
    and their ears are hard of hearing,
      and they have shut their eyes;
    so that they might not look with their eyes,
    and listen with their ears,
  and understand with their heart and turn—
    and I would heal them.'

16But blessed are your eyes, for they see, and your ears, for they hear. 17Truly I tell you, many prophets and righteous people longed to see what you see, but did not see it, and to hear what you hear, but did not hear it.

The Parable of the Sower Explained

18 "Hear then the parable of the sower. 19When anyone hears the word of the kingdom and does not understand it, the evil one comes and snatches away what is sown in the heart; this is what was sown on the path. 20As for what was sown on rocky ground, this is the one who hears the word and immediately receives it with joy; 21yet such a person has no root, but endures only for a while, and when trouble or persecution arises on account of the word, that person immediately falls away. *c* 22As for what was sown among thorns, this is the one who hears the word, but the cares of the world and the lure of wealth choke the word, and it yields nothing. 23But as for what was sown on good soil, this is the one who hears the word and understands it, who indeed bears fruit and yields, in one case a hundredfold, in another sixty, and in another thirty."

The Parable of Weeds among the Wheat

24 He put before them another parable: "The kingdom of heaven may be compared to someone who sowed good seed in his field; 25but while everybody was asleep, an enemy came and sowed weeds among the wheat, and then went away. 26So when the plants came up and bore grain, then the weeds appeared as well. 27And the slaves of the householder came and said to him, 'Master, did you not sow good seed in your field? Where, then, did these weeds come from?' 28He answered, 'An enemy has done this.' The slaves said to him, 'Then do you want us to go and gather them?' 29But he replied, 'No; for in gathering the weeds you would uproot the wheat along with them. 30Let both of them grow together until the harvest; and at harvest time I will tell the reapers, Collect the weeds first and bind them in bundles to be burned, but gather the wheat into my barn.' "

The Parable of the Mustard Seed

31 He put before them another parable: "The kingdom of heaven is like a mustard seed that someone took and sowed in his field; 32it is the smallest of all the seeds, but when it has grown it is the greatest of shrubs and becomes a tree, so that the birds of the air come and make nests in its branches."

---

a Other ancient authorities add *to hear*   *b* Or *mysteries*   *c* Gk *stumbles*

The Parable of the Yeast

33 He told them another parable: "The kingdom of heaven is like yeast that a woman took and mixed in with*a* three measures of flour until all of it was leavened."

The Use of Parables

34 Jesus told the crowds all these things in parables; without a parable he told them nothing. 35This was to fulfill what had been spoken through the prophet:*b*

"I will open my mouth to speak in
      parables;
   I will proclaim what has been hidden
      from the foundation of the
      world."*c*

Jesus Explains the Parable of the Weeds

36 Then he left the crowds and went into the house. And his disciples approached him, saying, "Explain to us the parable of the weeds of the field." 37He answered, "The one who sows the good seed is the Son of Man; 38the field is the world, and the good seed are the children of the kingdom; the weeds are the children of the evil one, 39and the enemy who sowed them is the devil; the harvest is the end of the age, and the reapers are angels. 40Just as the weeds are collected and burned up with fire, so will it be at the end of the age. 41The Son of Man will send his angels, and they will collect out of his kingdom all causes of sin and all evildoers, 42and they will throw them into the furnace of fire, where there will be weeping and gnashing of teeth. 43Then the righteous will shine like the sun in the kingdom of their Father. Let anyone with ears*d* listen!

Three Parables

44 "The kingdom of heaven is like treasure hidden in a field, which someone found and hid; then in his joy he goes and sells all that he has and buys that field.

45 "Again, the kingdom of heaven is like a merchant in search of fine pearls; 46on finding one pearl of great value, he went and sold all that he had and bought it.

47 "Again, the kingdom of heaven is like a net that was thrown into the sea and caught fish of every kind; 48when it was full, they drew it ashore, sat down, and put the good into baskets but threw out the bad. 49So it will be at the end of the age. The angels will come out and separate the evil from the righteous 50and throw them into the furnace of fire, where there will be weeping and gnashing of teeth.

Treasures New and Old

51 "Have you understood all this?" They answered, "Yes." 52And he said to them, "Therefore every scribe who has been trained for the kingdom of heaven is like the master of a household who brings out of his treasure what is new and what is old." 53When Jesus had finished these parables, he left that place.

The Rejection of Jesus at Nazareth

54 He came to his hometown and began to teach the people*e* in their synagogue, so that they were astounded and said, "Where did this man get this wisdom and these deeds of power? 55Is not this the carpenter's son? Is not his mother called Mary? And are not his brothers James and Joseph and Simon and Judas? 56And are not all his sisters with us? Where then did this man get all this?" 57And they took offense at him. But Jesus said to them, "Prophets are not without honor except in their own country and in their own house." 58And he did not do many deeds of power there, because of their unbelief.

The Death of John the Baptist

14 At that time Herod the ruler*f* heard reports about Jesus; 2and he said to his servants, "This is John the Baptist; he has been raised from the dead, and for this reason these powers are at work in him." 3For Herod had arrested John, bound him,

---

a Gk *hid in*   *b* Other ancient authorities read *the prophet Isaiah*   *c* Other ancient authorities lack *of the world*
d Other ancient authorities add *to hear*   *e* Gk *them*   *f* Gk *tetrarch*

and put him in prison on account of Herodias, his brother Philip's wife,*a* *4*because John had been telling him, "It is not lawful for you to have her." *5*Though Herod*b* wanted to put him to death, he feared the crowd, because they regarded him as a prophet. *6*But when Herod's birthday came, the daughter of Herodias danced before the company, and she pleased Herod *7*so much that he promised on oath to grant her whatever she might ask. *8*Prompted by her mother, she said, "Give me the head of John the Baptist here on a platter." *9*The king was grieved, yet out of regard for his oaths and for the guests, he commanded it to be given; *10*he sent and had John beheaded in the prison. *11*The head was brought on a platter and given to the girl, who brought it to her mother. *12*His disciples came and took the body and buried it; then they went and told Jesus.

Feeding the Five Thousand

13 Now when Jesus heard this, he withdrew from there in a boat to a deserted place by himself. But when the crowds heard it, they followed him on foot from the towns. *14*When he went ashore, he saw a great crowd; and he had compassion for them and cured their sick. *15*When it was evening, the disciples came to him and said, "This is a deserted place, and the hour is now late; send the crowds away so that they may go into the villages and buy food for themselves." *16*Jesus said to them, "They need not go away; you give them something to eat." *17*They replied, "We have nothing here but five loaves and two fish." *18*And he said, "Bring them here to me." *19*Then he ordered the crowds to sit down on the grass. Taking the five loaves and the two fish, he looked up to heaven, and blessed and broke the loaves, and gave them to the disciples, and the disciples gave them to the crowds. *20*And all ate and were filled; and they took up what was left over of the broken pieces, twelve baskets full. *21*And

those who ate were about five thousand men, besides women and children.

Jesus Walks on the Water

22 Immediately he made the disciples get into the boat and go on ahead to the other side, while he dismissed the crowds. *23*And after he had dismissed the crowds, he went up the mountain by himself to pray. When evening came, he was there alone, *24*but by this time the boat, battered by the waves, was far from the land,*c* for the wind was against them. *25*And early in the morning he came walking toward them on the sea. *26*But when the disciples saw him walking on the sea, they were terrified, saying, "It is a ghost!" And they cried out in fear. *27*But immediately Jesus spoke to them and said, "Take heart, it is I; do not be afraid."

28 Peter answered him, "Lord, if it is you, command me to come to you on the water." *29*He said, "Come." So Peter got out of the boat, started walking on the water, and came toward Jesus. *30*But when he noticed the strong wind,*d* he became frightened, and beginning to sink, he cried out, "Lord, save me!" *31*Jesus immediately reached out his hand and caught him, saying to him, "You of little faith, why did you doubt?" *32*When they got into the boat, the wind ceased. *33*And those in the boat worshiped him, saying, "Truly you are the Son of God."

Jesus Heals the Sick in Gennesaret

34 When they had crossed over, they came to land at Gennesaret. *35*After the people of that place recognized him, they sent word throughout the region and brought all who were sick to him, *36*and begged him that they might touch even the fringe of his cloak; and all who touched it were healed.

The Tradition of the Elders

15 Then Pharisees and scribes came to Jesus from Jerusalem and said, *2*"Why do your disciples break the tradition

---

a Other ancient authorities read *his brother's wife*   *b* Gk *he*   *c* Other ancient authorities read *was out on the sea*
d Other ancient authorities read *the wind*

of the elders? For they do not wash their hands before they eat." ³He answered them, "And why do you break the commandment of God for the sake of your tradition? ⁴For God said,ᵃ 'Honor your father and your mother,' and, 'Whoever speaks evil of father or mother must surely die.' ⁵But you say that whoever tells father or mother, 'Whatever support you might have had from me is given to God,'ᵇ then that person need not honor the father.ᶜ ⁶So, for the sake of your tradition, you make void the wordᵈ of God. ⁷You hypocrites! Isaiah prophesied rightly about you when he said:

8 'This people honors me with their lips,
       but their hearts are far from me;
9 in vain do they worship me,
       teaching human precepts as
          doctrines.' "

Things That Defile

10 Then he called the crowd to him and said to them, "Listen and understand: ¹¹it is not what goes into the mouth that defiles a person, but it is what comes out of the mouth that defiles." ¹²Then the disciples approached and said to him, "Do you know that the Pharisees took offense when they heard what you said?" ¹³He answered, "Every plant that my heavenly Father has not planted will be uprooted. ¹⁴Let them alone; they are blind guides of the blind.ᵉ And if one blind person guides another, both will fall into a pit." ¹⁵But Peter said to him, "Explain this parable to us." ¹⁶Then he said, "Are you also still without understanding? ¹⁷Do you not see that whatever goes into the mouth enters the stomach, and goes out into the sewer? ¹⁸But what comes out of the mouth proceeds from the heart, and this is what defiles. ¹⁹For out of the heart come evil intentions, murder, adultery, fornication, theft, false witness, slander. ²⁰These are what defile a person, but to eat with unwashed hands does not defile."

The Canaanite Woman's Faith

21 Jesus left that place and went away to the district of Tyre and Sidon. ²²Just then a Canaanite woman from that region came out and started shouting, "Have mercy on me, Lord, Son of David; my daughter is tormented by a demon." ²³But he did not answer her at all. And his disciples came and urged him, saying, "Send her away, for she keeps shouting after us." ²⁴He answered, "I was sent only to the lost sheep of the house of Israel." ²⁵But she came and knelt before him, saying, "Lord, help me." ²⁶He answered, "It is not fair to take the children's food and throw it to the dogs." ²⁷She said, "Yes, Lord, yet even the dogs eat the crumbs that fall from their masters' table." ²⁸Then Jesus answered her, "Woman, great is your faith! Let it be done for you as you wish." And her daughter was healed instantly.

Jesus Cures Many People

29 After Jesus had left that place, he passed along the Sea of Galilee, and he went up the mountain, where he sat down. ³⁰Great crowds came to him, bringing with them the lame, the maimed, the blind, the mute, and many others. They put them at his feet, and he cured them, ³¹so that the crowd was amazed when they saw the mute speaking, the maimed whole, the lame walking, and the blind seeing. And they praised the God of Israel.

Feeding the Four Thousand

32 Then Jesus called his disciples to him and said, "I have compassion for the crowd, because they have been with me now for three days and have nothing to eat; and I do not want to send them away hungry, for they might faint on the way." ³³The disciples said to him, "Where are we to get enough bread in the desert to feed so great a crowd?" ³⁴Jesus asked them, "How many loaves have you?" They said, "Seven, and a few small fish." ³⁵Then ordering the crowd to sit down

---

a Other ancient authorities read *commanded, saying*   *b* Or *is an offering*   *c* Other ancient authorities add *or the mother*   *d* Other ancient authorities read *law* ; others, *commandment*   *e* Other ancient authorities lack *of the blind* on the ground, 36he took the seven loaves and the fish; and after giving thanks he broke them and gave them to the disciples, and the disciples gave them to the crowds. 37And all of them ate and were filled; and they took up the broken pieces left over, seven baskets full. 38Those who had eaten were four thousand men, besides women and children. 39After sending away the crowds, he got into the boat and went to the region of Magadan.ᵃ

The Demand for a Sign

16 The Pharisees and Sadducees came, and to test Jesusᵇ they asked him to show them a sign from heaven. 2He answered them, "When it is evening, you say, 'It will be fair weather, for the sky is red.' 3And in the morning, 'It will be stormy today, for the sky is red and threatening.' You know how to interpret the appearance of the sky, but you cannot interpret the signs of the times.ᶜ 4An evil and adulterous generation asks for a sign, but no sign will be given to it except the sign of Jonah." Then he left them and went away.

The Yeast of the Pharisees and Sadducees

5 When the disciples reached the other side, they had forgotten to bring any bread. 6Jesus said to them, "Watch out, and beware of the yeast of the Pharisees and Sadducees." 7They said to one another, "It is because we have brought no bread." 8And becoming aware of it, Jesus said, "You of little faith, why are you talking about having no bread? 9Do you still not perceive? Do you not remember the five loaves for the five thousand, and how many baskets you gathered? 10Or the seven loaves for the four thousand, and how many baskets you gathered? 11How could you fail to perceive that I was not speaking about bread? Beware of the yeast of the Pharisees and Sadducees!" 12Then they understood that he had not told them to beware of the yeast of bread, but of the teaching of the Pharisees and Sadducees.

Peter's Declaration about Jesus

13 Now when Jesus came into the district of Caesarea Philippi, he asked his disciples, "Who do people say that the Son of Man is?" 14And they said, "Some say John the Baptist, but others Elijah, and still others Jeremiah or one of the prophets." 15He said to them, "But who do you say that I am?" 16Simon Peter answered, "You are the Messiah,ᵈ the Son of the living God." 17And Jesus answered him, "Blessed are you, Simon son of Jonah! For flesh and blood has not revealed this to you, but my Father in heaven. 18And I tell you, you are Peter,ᵉ and on this rockᶠ I will build my church, and the gates of Hades will not prevail against it. 19I will give you the keys of the kingdom of heaven, and whatever you bind on earth will be bound in heaven, and whatever you loose on earth will be loosed in heaven." 20Then he sternly ordered the disciples not to tell anyone that he wasᵍ the Messiah.ᵈ

Jesus Foretells His Death and Resurrection

21 From that time on, Jesus began to show his disciples that he must go to Jerusalem and undergo great suffering at the hands of the elders and chief priests and scribes, and be killed, and on the third day be raised. 22And Peter took him aside and began to rebuke him, saying, "God forbid it, Lord! This must never happen to you." 23But he turned and said to Peter, "Get behind me, Satan! You are a stumbling block to me; for you are setting your mind not on divine things but on human things."

The Cross and Self-Denial

24 Then Jesus told his disciples, "If any want to become my followers, let them deny themselves and take up their cross and follow me. 25For those who want to save their life will lose it, and those who lose their life for my sake will find it. 26For what will it profit them if they gain the whole world but forfeit

---

a Other ancient authorities read *Magdala* or *Magdalan*   *b* Gk *him*   *c* Other ancient authorities lack *2When it is . . . of the times*   *d* Or *the Christ*   *e* Gk *Petros*   *f* Gk *petra*   *g* Other ancient authorities add *Jesus* their life? Or what will they give in return for their life?

27 "For the Son of Man is to come with his angels in the glory of his Father, and then he will repay everyone for what has been done. 28Truly I tell you, there are some standing here who will not taste death before they see the Son of Man coming in his kingdom."

The Transfiguration

17 Six days later, Jesus took with him Peter and James and his brother John and led them up a high mountain, by themselves. 2And he was transfigured before them, and his face shone like the sun, and his clothes became dazzling white. 3Suddenly there appeared to them Moses and Elijah, talking with him. 4Then Peter said to Jesus, "Lord, it is good for us to be here; if you wish, I *a* will make three dwellings *b* here, one for you, one for Moses, and one for Elijah." 5While he was still speaking, suddenly a bright cloud overshadowed them, and from the cloud a voice said, "This is my Son, the Beloved; *c* with him I am well pleased; listen to him!" 6When the disciples heard this, they fell to the ground and were overcome by fear. 7But Jesus came and touched them, saying, "Get up and do not be afraid." 8And when they looked up, they saw no one except Jesus himself alone.

9 As they were coming down the mountain, Jesus ordered them, "Tell no one about the vision until after the Son of Man has been raised from the dead." 10And the disciples asked him, "Why, then, do the scribes say that Elijah must come first?" 11He replied, "Elijah is indeed coming and will restore all things; 12but I tell you that Elijah has already come, and they did not recognize him, but they did to him whatever they pleased. So also the Son of Man is about to suffer at their hands." 13Then the disciples understood that he was speaking to them about John the Baptist.

Jesus Cures a Boy with a Demon

14 When they came to the crowd, a man came to him, knelt before him, 15and said, "Lord, have mercy on my son, for he is an epileptic and he suffers terribly; he often falls into the fire and often into the water. 16And I brought him to your disciples, but they could not cure him." 17Jesus answered, "You faithless and perverse generation, how much longer must I be with you? How much longer must I put up with you? Bring him here to me." 18And Jesus rebuked the demon, *d* and it *e* came out of him, and the boy was cured instantly. 19Then the disciples came to Jesus privately and said, "Why could we not cast it out?" 20He said to them, "Because of your little faith. For truly I tell you, if you have faith the size of a *f* mustard seed, you will say to this mountain, 'Move from here to there,' and it will move; and nothing will be impossible for you." *g*

Jesus Again Foretells His Death and Resurrection

22 As they were gathering *h* in Galilee, Jesus said to them, "The Son of Man is going to be betrayed into human hands, 23and they will kill him, and on the third day he will be raised." And they were greatly distressed.

Jesus and the Temple Tax

24 When they reached Capernaum, the collectors of the temple tax *i* came to Peter and said, "Does your teacher not pay the temple tax?" *i* 25He said, "Yes, he does." And when he came home, Jesus spoke of it first, asking, "What do you think, Simon? From whom do kings of the earth take toll or tribute? From their children or from others?" 26When Peter *j* said, "From others," Jesus said to him, "Then the children are free. 27However, so that we do not give offense to them, go to the sea and cast a hook; take the first fish that comes up; and when you open its mouth, you will find a coin; *k* take that and give it to them for you and me."

---

a Other ancient authorities read *we*   *b* Or *tents*   *c* Or *my beloved Son*   *d* Gk *it* or *him*   *e* Gk *the demon*
f Gk *faith as a grain of*   *g* Other ancient authorities add verse 21, *But this kind does not come out except by prayer and fasting*   *h* Other ancient authorities read *living*   *i* Gk *didrachma*   *j* Gk *he*   *k* Gk *stater*; the stater was worth two didrachmas

True Greatness

18 At that time the disciples came to Jesus and asked, "Who is the greatest in the kingdom of heaven?" 2He called a child, whom he put among them, 3and said, "Truly I tell you, unless you change and become like children, you will never enter the kingdom of heaven. 4Whoever becomes humble like this child is the greatest in the kingdom of heaven. 5Whoever welcomes one such child in my name welcomes me.

Temptations to Sin

6 "If any of you put a stumbling block before one of these little ones who believe in me, it would be better for you if a great millstone were fastened around your neck and you were drowned in the depth of the sea. 7Woe to the world because of stumbling blocks! Occasions for stumbling are bound to come, but woe to the one by whom the stumbling block comes!

8 "If your hand or your foot causes you to stumble, cut it off and throw it away; it is better for you to enter life maimed or lame than to have two hands or two feet and to be thrown into the eternal fire. 9And if your eye causes you to stumble, tear it out and throw it away; it is better for you to enter life with one eye than to have two eyes and to be thrown into the hell*a* of fire.

The Parable of the Lost Sheep

10 "Take care that you do not despise one of these little ones; for, I tell you, in heaven their angels continually see the face of my Father in heaven.*b* 12What do you think? If a shepherd has a hundred sheep, and one of them has gone astray, does he not leave the ninety-nine on the mountains and go in search of the one that went astray? 13And if he finds it, truly I tell you, he rejoices over it more than over the ninety-nine that never went astray. 14So it is not the will of your*c* Fa-

ther in heaven that one of these little ones should be lost.

Reproving Another Who Sins

15 "If another member of the church*d* sins against you,*e* go and point out the fault when the two of you are alone. If the member listens to you, you have regained that one.*f* 16But if you are not listened to, take one or two others along with you, so that every word may be confirmed by the evidence of two or three witnesses. 17If the member refuses to listen to them, tell it to the church; and if the offender refuses to listen even to the church, let such a one be to you as a Gentile and a tax collector. 18Truly I tell you, whatever you bind on earth will be bound in heaven, and whatever you loose on earth will be loosed in heaven. 19Again, truly I tell you, if two of you agree on earth about anything you ask, it will be done for you by my Father in heaven. 20For where two or three are gathered in my name, I am there among them."

Forgiveness

21 Then Peter came and said to him, "Lord, if another member of the church*g* sins against me, how often should I forgive? As many as seven times?" 22Jesus said to him, "Not seven times, but, I tell you, seventy-seven*h* times.

The Parable of the Unforgiving Servant

23 "For this reason the kingdom of heaven may be compared to a king who wished to settle accounts with his slaves. 24When he began the reckoning, one who owed him ten thousand talents*i* was brought to him; 25and, as he could not pay, his lord ordered him to be sold, together with his wife and children and all his possessions, and payment to be made. 26So the slave fell on his knees before him, saying, 'Have patience with me, and I will pay you everything.' 27And out of pity for him, the lord of that slave released him and

---

a Gk *Gehenna*   *b* Other ancient authorities add verse 11, *For the Son of Man came to save the lost*   *c* Other ancient authorities read *my*   *d* Gk *If your brother*   *e* Other ancient authorities lack *against you*   *f* Gk *the brother*   *g* Gk *if my brother*   *h* Or *seventy times seven*   *i* A talent was worth more than fifteen years' wages of a laborer forgave him the debt. 28But that same slave, as he went out, came upon one of his fellow slaves who owed him a hundred denarii;*a* and seizing him by the throat, he said, 'Pay what you owe.' 29Then his fellow slave fell down and pleaded with him, 'Have patience with me, and I will pay you.' 30But he refused; then he went and threw him into prison until he would pay the debt. 31When his fellow slaves saw what had happened, they were greatly distressed, and they went and reported to their lord all that had taken place. 32Then his lord summoned him and said to him, 'You wicked slave! I forgave you all that debt because you pleaded with me. 33Should you not have had mercy on your fellow slave, as I had mercy on you?' 34And in anger his lord handed him over to be tortured until he would pay his entire debt. 35So my heavenly Father will also do to every one of you, if you do not forgive your brother or sister*b* from your heart."

Teaching about Divorce

19 When Jesus had finished saying these things, he left Galilee and went to the region of Judea beyond the Jordan. 2Large crowds followed him, and he cured them there.

3 Some Pharisees came to him, and to test him they asked, "Is it lawful for a man to divorce his wife for any cause?" 4He answered, "Have you not read that the one who made them at the beginning 'made them male and female,' 5and said, 'For this reason a man shall leave his father and mother and be joined to his wife, and the two shall become one flesh'? 6So they are no longer two, but one flesh. Therefore what God has joined together, let no one separate." 7They said to him, "Why then did Moses command us to give a certificate of dismissal and to divorce her?" 8He said to them, "It was because you were so hard-hearted that Moses allowed you to divorce your wives, but from the beginning it was not so. 9And I say to you, whoever divorces his wife, except for unchastity, and marries another commits adultery."*c*

10 His disciples said to him, "If such is the case of a man with his wife, it is better not to marry." 11But he said to them, "Not everyone can accept this teaching, but only those to whom it is given. 12For there are eunuchs who have been so from birth, and there are eunuchs who have been made eunuchs by others, and there are eunuchs who have made themselves eunuchs for the sake of the kingdom of heaven. Let anyone accept this who can."

Jesus Blesses Little Children

13 Then little children were being brought to him in order that he might lay his hands on them and pray. The disciples spoke sternly to those who brought them; 14but Jesus said, "Let the little children come to me, and do not stop them; for it is to such as these that the kingdom of heaven belongs." 15And he laid his hands on them and went on his way.

The Rich Young Man

16 Then someone came to him and said, "Teacher, what good deed must I do to have eternal life?" 17And he said to him, "Why do you ask me about what is good? There is only one who is good. If you wish to enter into life, keep the commandments." 18He said to him, "Which ones?" And Jesus said, "You shall not murder; You shall not commit adultery; You shall not steal; You shall not bear false witness; 19Honor your father and mother; also, You shall love your neighbor as yourself." 20The young man said to him, "I have kept all these;*d* what do I still lack?" 21Jesus said to him, "If you wish to be perfect, go, sell your possessions, and give the money*e* to the poor, and you will have treasure in heaven; then come, follow me." 22When the young man heard this word, he

---

a The denarius was the usual day's wage for a laborer   *b* Gk *brother*   *c* Other ancient authorities read *except on the ground of unchastity, causes her to commit adultery*; others add at the end of the verse *and he who marries a divorced woman commits adultery*   *d* Other ancient authorities add *from my youth*   *e* Gk *lacks the money* went away grieving, for he had many possessions.

23 Then Jesus said to his disciples, "Truly I tell you, it will be hard for a rich person to enter the kingdom of heaven. 24Again I tell you, it is easier for a camel to go through the eye of a needle than for someone who is rich to enter the kingdom of God." 25When the disciples heard this, they were greatly astounded and said, "Then who can be saved?" 26But Jesus looked at them and said, "For mortals it is impossible, but for God all things are possible."

27 Then Peter said in reply, "Look, we have left everything and followed you. What then will we have?" 28Jesus said to them, "Truly I tell you, at the renewal of all things, when the Son of Man is seated on the throne of his glory, you who have followed me will also sit on twelve thrones, judging the twelve tribes of Israel. 29And everyone who has left houses or brothers or sisters or father or mother or children or fields, for my name's sake, will receive a hundredfold,*a* and will inherit eternal life. 30But many who are first will be last, and the last will be first.

The Laborers in the Vineyard

20 "For the kingdom of heaven is like a landowner who went out early in the morning to hire laborers for his vineyard. 2After agreeing with the laborers for the usual daily wage,*b* he sent them into his vineyard. 3When he went out about nine o'clock, he saw others standing idle in the marketplace; 4and he said to them, 'You also go into the vineyard, and I will pay you whatever is right.' So they went. 5When he went out again about noon and about three o'clock, he did the same. 6And about five o'clock he went out and found others standing around; and he said to them, 'Why are you standing here idle all day?' 7They said to him, 'Because no one has hired us.' He said to them, 'You also go into the vineyard.' 8When evening came, the owner of the vine-

yard said to his manager, 'Call the laborers and give them their pay, beginning with the last and then going to the first.' 9When those hired about five o'clock came, each of them received the usual daily wage.*b* 10Now when the first came, they thought they would receive more; but each of them also received the usual daily wage.*b* 11And when they received it, they grumbled against the landowner, 12saying, 'These last worked only one hour, and you have made them equal to us who have borne the burden of the day and the scorching heat.' 13But he replied to one of them, 'Friend, I am doing you no wrong; did you not agree with me for the usual daily wage?*b* 14Take what belongs to you and go; I choose to give to this last the same as I give to you. 15Am I not allowed to do what I choose with what belongs to me? Or are you envious because I am generous?'*c* 16So the last will be first, and the first will be last."*d*

A Third Time Jesus Foretells His Death and Resurrection

17 While Jesus was going up to Jerusalem, he took the twelve disciples aside by themselves, and said to them on the way, 18"See, we are going up to Jerusalem, and the Son of Man will be handed over to the chief priests and scribes, and they will condemn him to death; 19then they will hand him over to the Gentiles to be mocked and flogged and crucified; and on the third day he will be raised."

The Request of the Mother of James and John

20 Then the mother of the sons of Zebedee came to him with her sons, and kneeling before him, she asked a favor of him. 21And he said to her, "What do you want?" She said to him, "Declare that these two sons of mine will sit, one at your right hand and one at your left, in your kingdom." 22But Jesus answered, "You do not know what you are asking. Are you able to drink the cup that I am about to drink?"*e* They said to him,

---

a Other ancient authorities read *manifold*　　*b* Gk *a denarius*　　*c* Gk *is your eye evil because I am good?*　　*d* Other ancient authorities add *for many are called but few are chosen*　　*e* Other ancient authorities add *or to be baptized with the baptism that I am baptized with?*

"We are able." ²³He said to them, "You will indeed drink my cup, but to sit at my right hand and at my left, this is not mine to grant, but it is for those for whom it has been prepared by my Father."

24 When the ten heard it, they were angry with the two brothers. ²⁵But Jesus called them to him and said, "You know that the rulers of the Gentiles lord it over them, and their great ones are tyrants over them. ²⁶It will not be so among you; but whoever wishes to be great among you must be your servant, ²⁷and whoever wishes to be first among you must be your slave; ²⁸just as the Son of Man came not to be served but to serve, and to give his life a ransom for many."

Jesus Heals Two Blind Men

29 As they were leaving Jericho, a large crowd followed him. ³⁰There were two blind men sitting by the roadside. When they heard that Jesus was passing by, they shouted, "Lord,ᵃ have mercy on us, Son of David!" ³¹The crowd sternly ordered them to be quiet; but they shouted even more loudly, "Have mercy on us, Lord, Son of David!" ³²Jesus stood still and called them, saying, "What do you want me to do for you?" ³³They said to him, "Lord, let our eyes be opened." ³⁴Moved with compassion, Jesus touched their eyes. Immediately they regained their sight and followed him.

Jesus' Triumphal Entry into Jerusalem

21 When they had come near Jerusalem and had reached Bethphage, at the Mount of Olives, Jesus sent two disciples, ²saying to them, "Go into the village ahead of you, and immediately you will find a donkey tied, and a colt with her; untie them and bring them to me. ³If anyone says anything to you, just say this, 'The Lord needs them.' And he will send them immediately.ᵇ" ⁴This took place to fulfill what had been spoken through the prophet, saying,

5   "Tell the daughter of Zion,

Look, your king is coming to you,
    humble, and mounted on a donkey,
        and on a colt, the foal of a
            donkey."

⁶The disciples went and did as Jesus had directed them; ⁷they brought the donkey and the colt, and put their cloaks on them, and he sat on them. ⁸A very large crowdᶜ spread their cloaks on the road, and others cut branches from the trees and spread them on the road. ⁹The crowds that went ahead of him and that followed were shouting,

"Hosanna to the Son of David!
Blessed is the one who comes in the
    name of the Lord!
Hosanna in the highest heaven!"

¹⁰When he entered Jerusalem, the whole city was in turmoil, asking, "Who is this?" ¹¹The crowds were saying, "This is the prophet Jesus from Nazareth in Galilee."

Jesus Cleanses the Temple

12 Then Jesus entered the templeᵈ and drove out all who were selling and buying in the temple, and he overturned the tables of the money changers and the seats of those who sold doves. ¹³He said to them, "It is written,

'My house shall be called a house of
    prayer';
    but you are making it a den of
        robbers."

14 The blind and the lame came to him in the temple, and he cured them. ¹⁵But when the chief priests and the scribes saw the amazing things that he did, and heardᵉ the children crying out in the temple, "Hosanna to the Son of David," they became angry ¹⁶and said to him, "Do you hear what these are saying?" Jesus said to them, "Yes; have you never read,

'Out of the mouths of infants and
    nursing babies
you have prepared praise for
    yourself'?"

ᵃ Other ancient authorities lack *Lord*   ᵇ Or *The Lord needs them and will send them back immediately.'*   ᶜ Or *Most of the crowd*   ᵈ Other ancient authorities add *of God*   ᵉ Gk lacks *heard*

17He left them, went out of the city to Bethany, and spent the night there.

Jesus Curses the Fig Tree

18 In the morning, when he returned to the city, he was hungry. 19And seeing a fig tree by the side of the road, he went to it and found nothing at all on it but leaves. Then he said to it, "May no fruit ever come from you again!" And the fig tree withered at once. 20When the disciples saw it, they were amazed, saying, "How did the fig tree wither at once?" 21Jesus answered them, "Truly I tell you, if you have faith and do not doubt, not only will you do what has been done to the fig tree, but even if you say to this mountain, 'Be lifted up and thrown into the sea,' it will be done. 22Whatever you ask for in prayer with faith, you will receive."

The Authority of Jesus Questioned

23 When he entered the temple, the chief priests and the elders of the people came to him as he was teaching, and said, "By what authority are you doing these things, and who gave you this authority?" 24Jesus said to them, "I will also ask you one question; if you tell me the answer, then I will also tell you by what authority I do these things. 25Did the baptism of John come from heaven, or was it of human origin?" And they argued with one another, "If we say, 'From heaven,' he will say to us, 'Why then did you not believe him?' 26But if we say, 'Of human origin,' we are afraid of the crowd; for all regard John as a prophet." 27So they answered Jesus, "We do not know." And he said to them, "Neither will I tell you by what authority I am doing these things.

The Parable of the Two Sons

28 "What do you think? A man had two sons; he went to the first and said, 'Son, go and work in the vineyard today.' 29He answered, 'I will not'; but later he changed his mind and went. 30The father*a* went to the second and said the same; and he answered, 'I go, sir'; but he did not go. 31Which of the two did the will of his father?" They said, "The first." Jesus said to them, "Truly I tell you, the tax collectors and the prostitutes are going into the kingdom of God ahead of you. 32For John came to you in the way of righteousness and you did not believe him, but the tax collectors and the prostitutes believed him; and even after you saw it, you did not change your minds and believe him.

The Parable of the Wicked Tenants

33 "Listen to another parable. There was a landowner who planted a vineyard, put a fence around it, dug a wine press in it, and built a watchtower. Then he leased it to tenants and went to another country. 34When the harvest time had come, he sent his slaves to the tenants to collect his produce. 35But the tenants seized his slaves and beat one, killed another, and stoned another. 36Again he sent other slaves, more than the first; and they treated them in the same way. 37Finally he sent his son to them, saying, 'They will respect my son.' 38But when the tenants saw the son, they said to themselves, 'This is the heir; come, let us kill him and get his inheritance.' 39So they seized him, threw him out of the vineyard, and killed him. 40Now when the owner of the vineyard comes, what will he do to those tenants?" 41They said to him, "He will put those wretches to a miserable death, and lease the vineyard to other tenants who will give him the produce at the harvest time."

42 Jesus said to them, "Have you never read in the scriptures:

'The stone that the builders rejected
    has become the cornerstone;*b*
this was the Lord's doing,
    and it is amazing in our eyes'?
43Therefore I tell you, the kingdom of God will be taken away from you and given to a people that produces the fruits of the kingdom.*c* 44The one who falls on this stone will be broken to pieces; and it will crush anyone on whom it falls."*d*

---

a Gk He   *b* Or *keystone*   *c* Gk *the fruits of it*   *d* Other ancient authorities lack verse 44

45 When the chief priests and the Pharisees heard his parables, they realized that he was speaking about them. 46They wanted to arrest him, but they feared the crowds, because they regarded him as a prophet.

The Parable of the Wedding Banquet

22 Once more Jesus spoke to them in parables, saying: 2"The kingdom of heaven may be compared to a king who gave a wedding banquet for his son. 3He sent his slaves to call those who had been invited to the wedding banquet, but they would not come. 4Again he sent other slaves, saying, 'Tell those who have been invited: Look, I have prepared my dinner, my oxen and my fat calves have been slaughtered, and everything is ready; come to the wedding banquet.' 5But they made light of it and went away, one to his farm, another to his business, 6while the rest seized his slaves, mistreated them, and killed them. 7The king was enraged. He sent his troops, destroyed those murderers, and burned their city. 8Then he said to his slaves, 'The wedding is ready, but those invited were not worthy. 9Go therefore into the main streets, and invite everyone you find to the wedding banquet.' 10Those slaves went out into the streets and gathered all whom they found, both good and bad; so the wedding hall was filled with guests.

11 "But when the king came in to see the guests, he noticed a man there who was not wearing a wedding robe, 12and he said to him, 'Friend, how did you get in here without a wedding robe?' And he was speechless. 13Then the king said to the attendants, 'Bind him hand and foot, and throw him into the outer darkness, where there will be weeping and gnashing of teeth.' 14For many are called, but few are chosen."

The Question about Paying Taxes

15 Then the Pharisees went and plotted to entrap him in what he said. 16So they sent their disciples to him, along with the Herodians, saying, "Teacher, we know that you are sincere, and teach the way of God in accordance with truth, and show deference to no one; for you do not regard people with partiality. 17Tell us, then, what you think. Is it lawful to pay taxes to the emperor, or not?" 18But Jesus, aware of their malice, said, "Why are you putting me to the test, you hypocrites? 19Show me the coin used for the tax." And they brought him a denarius. 20Then he said to them, "Whose head is this, and whose title?" 21They answered, "The emperor's." Then he said to them, "Give therefore to the emperor the things that are the emperor's, and to God the things that are God's." 22When they heard this, they were amazed; and they left him and went away.

The Question about the Resurrection

23 The same day some Sadducees came to him, saying there is no resurrection;*a* and they asked him a question, saying, 24"Teacher, Moses said, 'If a man dies childless, his brother shall marry the widow, and raise up children for his brother.' 25Now there were seven brothers among us; the first married, and died childless, leaving the widow to his brother. 26The second did the same, so also the third, down to the seventh. 27Last of all, the woman herself died. 28In the resurrection, then, whose wife of the seven will she be? For all of them had married her."

29 Jesus answered them, "You are wrong, because you know neither the scriptures nor the power of God. 30For in the resurrection they neither marry nor are given in marriage, but are like angels*b* in heaven. 31And as for the resurrection of the dead, have you not read what was said to you by God, 32'I am the God of Abraham, the God of Isaac, and the God of Jacob'? He is God not of the dead, but of the living." 33And when the crowd heard it, they were astounded at his teaching.

The Greatest Commandment

34 When the Pharisees heard that he had

---

a Other ancient authorities read *who say that there is no resurrection*   *b* Other ancient authorities add *of God* silenced the Sadducees, they gathered together, 35and one of them, a lawyer, asked him a question to test him. 36"Teacher, which commandment in the law is the greatest?" 37He said to him, " 'You shall love the Lord your God with all your heart, and with all your soul, and with all your mind.' 38This is the greatest and first commandment. 39And a second is like it: 'You shall love your neighbor as yourself.' 40On these two commandments hang all the law and the prophets."

The Question about David's Son

41 Now while the Pharisees were gathered together, Jesus asked them this question: 42"What do you think of the Messiah?ᵃ Whose son is he?" They said to him, "The son of David." 43He said to them, "How is it then that David by the Spiritᵇ calls him Lord, saying,

44 'The Lord said to my Lord,
　"Sit at my right hand,
　　until I put your enemies under your
　　　feet" '?

45If David thus calls him Lord, how can he be his son?" 46No one was able to give him an answer, nor from that day did anyone dare to ask him any more questions.

Jesus Denounces Scribes and Pharisees

23 Then Jesus said to the crowds and to his disciples, 2"The scribes and the Pharisees sit on Moses' seat; 3therefore, do whatever they teach you and follow it; but do not do as they do, for they do not practice what they teach. 4They tie up heavy burdens, hard to bear,ᶜ and lay them on the shoulders of others; but they themselves are unwilling to lift a finger to move them. 5They do all their deeds to be seen by others; for they make their phylacteries broad and their fringes long. 6They love to have the place of honor at banquets and the best seats in the synagogues, 7and to be greeted with respect in the marketplaces, and to have people call them rabbi. 8But you are not to be called rabbi, for you have one teacher, and you are all students.ᵈ 9And call no one your father on earth, for you have one Father—the one in heaven. 10Nor are you to be called instructors, for you have one instructor, the Messiah.ᵉ 11The greatest among you will be your servant. 12All who exalt themselves will be humbled, and all who humble themselves will be exalted.

13 "But woe to you, scribes and Pharisees, hypocrites! For you lock people out of the kingdom of heaven. For you do not go in yourselves, and when others are going in, you stop them.ᶠ 15Woe to you, scribes and Pharisees, hypocrites! For you cross sea and land to make a single convert, and you make the new convert twice as much a child of hellᵍ as yourselves.

16 "Woe to you, blind guides, who say, 'Whoever swears by the sanctuary is bound by nothing, but whoever swears by the gold of the sanctuary is bound by the oath.' 17You blind fools! For which is greater, the gold or the sanctuary that has made the gold sacred? 18And you say, 'Whoever swears by the altar is bound by nothing, but whoever swears by the gift that is on the altar is bound by the oath.' 19How blind you are! For which is greater, the gift or the altar that makes the gift sacred? 20So whoever swears by the altar, swears by it and by everything on it; 21and whoever swears by the sanctuary, swears by it and by the one who dwells in it; 22and whoever swears by heaven, swears by the throne of God and by the one who is seated upon it.

23 "Woe to you, scribes and Pharisees, hypocrites! For you tithe mint, dill, and cummin, and have neglected the weightier matters of the law: justice and mercy and faith. It is these you ought to have practiced without ne-

---

ᵃ Or Christ　ᵇ Gk in spirit　ᶜ Other ancient authorities lack hard to bear　ᵈ Gk brothers　ᵉ Or the Christ
ᶠ Other authorities add here (or after verse 12) verse 14, Woe to you, scribes and Pharisees, hypocrites! For you devour widows' houses and for the sake of appearance you make long prayers; therefore you will receive the greater condemnation
ᵍ Gk Gehenna

glecting the others. 24You blind guides! You strain out a gnat but swallow a camel!

25 "Woe to you, scribes and Pharisees, hypocrites! For you clean the outside of the cup and of the plate, but inside they are full of greed and self-indulgence. 26You blind Pharisee! First clean the inside of the cup,*a* so that the outside also may become clean.

27 "Woe to you, scribes and Pharisees, hypocrites! For you are like whitewashed tombs, which on the outside look beautiful, but inside they are full of the bones of the dead and of all kinds of filth. 28So you also on the outside look righteous to others, but inside you are full of hypocrisy and lawlessness.

29 "Woe to you, scribes and Pharisees, hypocrites! For you build the tombs of the prophets and decorate the graves of the righteous, 30and you say, 'If we had lived in the days of our ancestors, we would not have taken part with them in shedding the blood of the prophets.' 31Thus you testify against yourselves that you are descendants of those who murdered the prophets. 32Fill up, then, the measure of your ancestors. 33You snakes, you brood of vipers! How can you escape being sentenced to hell?*b* 34Therefore I send you prophets, sages, and scribes, some of whom you will kill and crucify, and some you will flog in your synagogues and pursue from town to town, 35so that upon you may come all the righteous blood shed on earth, from the blood of righteous Abel to the blood of Zechariah son of Barachiah, whom you murdered between the sanctuary and the altar. 36Truly I tell you, all this will come upon this generation.

The Lament over Jerusalem

37 "Jerusalem, Jerusalem, the city that kills the prophets and stones those who are sent to it! How often have I desired to gather your children together as a hen gathers her brood under her wings, and you were not willing! 38See, your house is left to you,

desolate.*c* 39For I tell you, you will not see me again until you say, 'Blessed is the one who comes in the name of the Lord.' "

The Destruction of the Temple Foretold

24 As Jesus came out of the temple and was going away, his disciples came to point out to him the buildings of the temple. 2Then he asked them, "You see all these, do you not? Truly I tell you, not one stone will be left here upon another; all will be thrown down."

Signs of the End of the Age

3 When he was sitting on the Mount of Olives, the disciples came to him privately, saying, "Tell us, when will this be, and what will be the sign of your coming and of the end of the age?" 4Jesus answered them, "Beware that no one leads you astray. 5For many will come in my name, saying, 'I am the Messiah!'*d* and they will lead many astray. 6And you will hear of wars and rumors of wars; see that you are not alarmed; for this must take place, but the end is not yet. 7For nation will rise against nation, and kingdom against kingdom, and there will be famines*e* and earthquakes in various places: 8all this is but the beginning of the birth pangs.

Persecutions Foretold

9 "Then they will hand you over to be tortured and will put you to death, and you will be hated by all nations because of my name. 10Then many will fall away,*f* and they will betray one another and hate one another. 11And many false prophets will arise and lead many astray. 12And because of the increase of lawlessness, the love of many will grow cold. 13But the one who endures to the end will be saved. 14And this good news*g* of the kingdom will be proclaimed throughout the world, as a testimony to all the nations; and then the end will come.

---

a Other ancient authorities add *and of the plate*   *b* Gk *Gehenna*   *c* Other ancient authorities lack *desolate*   *d* Or *the Christ*   *e* Other ancient authorities add *and pestilences*   *f* Or *stumble*   *g* Or *gospel*

The Desolating Sacrilege

15 "So when you see the desolating sacrilege standing in the holy place, as was spoken of by the prophet Daniel (let the reader understand), [16]then those in Judea must flee to the mountains; [17]the one on the housetop must not go down to take what is in the house; [18]the one in the field must not turn back to get a coat. [19]Woe to those who are pregnant and to those who are nursing infants in those days! [20]Pray that your flight may not be in winter or on a sabbath. [21]For at that time there will be great suffering, such as has not been from the beginning of the world until now, no, and never will be. [22]And if those days had not been cut short, no one would be saved; but for the sake of the elect those days will be cut short. [23]Then if anyone says to you, 'Look! Here is the Messiah!'[a] or 'There he is!'—do not believe it. [24]For false messiahs[b] and false prophets will appear and produce great signs and omens, to lead astray, if possible, even the elect. [25]Take note, I have told you beforehand. [26]So, if they say to you, 'Look! He is in the wilderness,' do not go out. If they say, 'Look! He is in the inner rooms,' do not believe it. [27]For as the lightning comes from the east and flashes as far as the west, so will be the coming of the Son of Man. [28]Wherever the corpse is, there the vultures will gather.

The Coming of the Son of Man

29 "Immediately after the suffering of those days

the sun will be darkened,
    and the moon will not give its light;
  the stars will fall from heaven,
    and the powers of heaven will be
        shaken.

[30]Then the sign of the Son of Man will appear in heaven, and then all the tribes of the earth will mourn, and they will see 'the Son of Man coming on the clouds of heaven' with power and great glory. [31]And he will send out his angels with a loud trumpet call, and they will gather his elect from the four winds, from one end of heaven to the other.

The Lesson of the Fig Tree

32 "From the fig tree learn its lesson: as soon as its branch becomes tender and puts forth its leaves, you know that summer is near. [33]So also, when you see all these things, you know that he[c] is near, at the very gates. [34]Truly I tell you, this generation will not pass away until all these things have taken place. [35]Heaven and earth will pass away, but my words will not pass away.

The Necessity for Watchfulness

36 "But about that day and hour no one knows, neither the angels of heaven, nor the Son,[d] but only the Father. [37]For as the days of Noah were, so will be the coming of the Son of Man. [38]For as in those days before the flood they were eating and drinking, marrying and giving in marriage, until the day Noah entered the ark, [39]and they knew nothing until the flood came and swept them all away, so too will be the coming of the Son of Man. [40]Then two will be in the field; one will be taken and one will be left. [41]Two women will be grinding meal together; one will be taken and one will be left. [42]Keep awake therefore, for you do not know on what day[e] your Lord is coming. [43]But understand this: if the owner of the house had known in what part of the night the thief was coming, he would have stayed awake and would not have let his house be broken into. [44]Therefore you also must be ready, for the Son of Man is coming at an unexpected hour.

The Faithful or the Unfaithful Slave

45 "Who then is the faithful and wise slave, whom his master has put in charge of his household, to give the other slaves[f] their allowance of food at the proper time? [46]Blessed is that slave whom his master will find at work when he arrives. [47]Truly I tell you, he will put that one in charge of all his

a Or *the Christ*   *b* Or *christs*   *c* Or *it*   *d* Other ancient authorities lack *nor the Son*   *e* Other ancient authorities read *at what hour*   *f* Gk *to give them* possessions. [48]But if that wicked slave says to himself, 'My master is delayed,' [49]and he begins to beat his fellow slaves, and eats and drinks with drunkards, [50]the master of that slave will come on a day when he does not expect him and at an hour that he does not know. [51]He will cut him in pieces[a] and put him with the hypocrites, where there will be weeping and gnashing of teeth.

The Parable of the Ten Bridesmaids

25 "Then the kingdom of heaven will be like this. Ten bridesmaids[b] took their lamps and went to meet the bridegroom.[c] [2]Five of them were foolish, and five were wise. [3]When the foolish took their lamps, they took no oil with them; [4]but the wise took flasks of oil with their lamps. [5]As the bridegroom was delayed, all of them became drowsy and slept. [6]But at midnight there was a shout, 'Look! Here is the bridegroom! Come out to meet him.' [7]Then all those bridesmaids[b] got up and trimmed their lamps. [8]The foolish said to the wise, 'Give us some of your oil, for our lamps are going out.' [9]But the wise replied, 'No! there will not be enough for you and for us; you had better go to the dealers and buy some for yourselves.' [10]And while they went to buy it, the bridegroom came, and those who were ready went with him into the wedding banquet; and the door was shut. [11]Later the other bridesmaids[b] came also, saying, 'Lord, lord, open to us.' [12]But he replied, 'Truly I tell you, I do not know you.' [13]Keep awake therefore, for you know neither the day nor the hour.[d]

The Parable of the Talents

14 "For it is as if a man, going on a journey, summoned his slaves and entrusted his property to them; [15]to one he gave five talents,[e] to another two, to another one, to each according to his ability. Then he went away. [16]The one who had received the five talents went off at once and traded with them, and made five more talents. [17]In the same way, the one who had the two talents made two more talents. [18]But the one who had received the one talent went off and dug a hole in the ground and hid his master's money. [19]After a long time the master of those slaves came and settled accounts with them. [20]Then the one who had received the five talents came forward, bringing five more talents, saying, 'Master, you handed over to me five talents; see, I have made five more talents.' [21]His master said to him, 'Well done, good and trustworthy slave; you have been trustworthy in a few things, I will put you in charge of many things; enter into the joy of your master.' [22]And the one with the two talents also came forward, saying, 'Master, you handed over to me two talents; see, I have made two more talents.' [23]His master said to him, 'Well done, good and trustworthy slave; you have been trustworthy in a few things, I will put you in charge of many things; enter into the joy of your master.' [24]Then the one who had received the one talent also came forward, saying, 'Master, I knew that you were a harsh man, reaping where you did not sow, and gathering where you did not scatter seed; [25]so I was afraid, and I went and hid your talent in the ground. Here you have what is yours.' [26]But his master replied, 'You wicked and lazy slave! You knew, did you, that I reap where I did not sow, and gather where I did not scatter? [27]Then you ought to have invested my money with the bankers, and on my return I would have received what was my own with interest. [28]So take the talent from him, and give it to the one with the ten talents. [29]For to all those who have, more will be given, and they will have an abundance; but from those who have nothing, even what they have will be taken away. [30]As for this worthless slave, throw him into the outer darkness, where there will be weeping and gnashing of teeth.'

The Judgment of the Nations

31 "When the Son of Man comes in his glory, and all the angels with him, then he will

---

a Or *cut him off*   b Gk *virgins*   c Other ancient authorities add *and the bride*   d Other ancient authorities add *in which the Son of Man is coming*   e A talent was worth more than fifteen years' wages of a laborer sit on the throne of his glory. 32All the nations will be gathered before him, and he will separate people one from another as a shepherd separates the sheep from the goats, 33and he will put the sheep at his right hand and the goats at the left. 34Then the king will say to those at his right hand, 'Come, you that are blessed by my Father, inherit the kingdom prepared for you from the foundation of the world; 35for I was hungry and you gave me food, I was thirsty and you gave me something to drink, I was a stranger and you welcomed me, 36I was naked and you gave me clothing, I was sick and you took care of me, I was in prison and you visited me.' 37Then the righteous will answer him, 'Lord, when was it that we saw you hungry and gave you food, or thirsty and gave you something to drink? 38And when was it that we saw you a stranger and welcomed you, or naked and gave you clothing? 39And when was it that we saw you sick or in prison and visited you?' 40And the king will answer them, 'Truly I tell you, just as you did it to one of the least of these who are members of my family,*a* you did it to me.' 41Then he will say to those at his left hand, 'You that are accursed, depart from me into the eternal fire prepared for the devil and his angels; 42for I was hungry and you gave me no food, I was thirsty and you gave me nothing to drink, 43I was a stranger and you did not welcome me, naked and you did not give me clothing, sick and in prison and you did not visit me.' 44Then they also will answer, 'Lord, when was it that we saw you hungry or thirsty or a stranger or naked or sick or in prison, and did not take care of you?' 45Then he will answer them, 'Truly I tell you, just as you did not do it to one of the least of these, you did not do it to me.' 46And these will go away into eternal punishment, but the righteous into eternal life."

The Plot to Kill Jesus

26 When Jesus had finished saying all these things, he said to his disciples,

2"You know that after two days the Passover is coming, and the Son of Man will be handed over to be crucified."

3 Then the chief priests and the elders of the people gathered in the palace of the high priest, who was called Caiaphas, 4and they conspired to arrest Jesus by stealth and kill him. 5But they said, "Not during the festival, or there may be a riot among the people."

The Anointing at Bethany

6 Now while Jesus was at Bethany in the house of Simon the leper,*b* 7a woman came to him with an alabaster jar of very costly ointment, and she poured it on his head as he sat at the table. 8But when the disciples saw it, they were angry and said, "Why this waste? 9For this ointment could have been sold for a large sum, and the money given to the poor." 10But Jesus, aware of this, said to them, "Why do you trouble the woman? She has performed a good service for me. 11For you always have the poor with you, but you will not always have me. 12By pouring this ointment on my body she has prepared me for burial. 13Truly I tell you, wherever this good news*c* is proclaimed in the whole world, what she has done will be told in remembrance of her."

Judas Agrees to Betray Jesus

14 Then one of the twelve, who was called Judas Iscariot, went to the chief priests 15and said, "What will you give me if I betray him to you?" They paid him thirty pieces of silver. 16And from that moment he began to look for an opportunity to betray him.

The Passover with the Disciples

17 On the first day of Unleavened Bread the disciples came to Jesus, saying, "Where do you want us to make the preparations for you to eat the Passover?" 18He said, "Go into the city to a certain man, and say to him, 'The Teacher says, My time is near; I will keep the Passover at your house with my dis-

---

a Gk these my brothers   *b* The terms *leper* and *leprosy* can refer to several diseases   *c* Or *gospel* ciples.'" ¹⁹So the disciples did as Jesus had directed them, and they prepared the Passover meal.

20 When it was evening, he took his place with the twelve;^a ²¹and while they were eating, he said, "Truly I tell you, one of you will betray me." ²²And they became greatly distressed and began to say to him one after another, "Surely not I, Lord?" ²³He answered, "The one who has dipped his hand into the bowl with me will betray me. ²⁴The Son of Man goes as it is written of him, but woe to that one by whom the Son of Man is betrayed! It would have been better for that one not to have been born." ²⁵Judas, who betrayed him, said, "Surely not I, Rabbi?" He replied, "You have said so."

The Institution of the Lord's Supper

26 While they were eating, Jesus took a loaf of bread, and after blessing it he broke it, gave it to the disciples, and said, "Take, eat; this is my body." ²⁷Then he took a cup, and after giving thanks he gave it to them, saying, "Drink from it, all of you; ²⁸for this is my blood of the^b covenant, which is poured out for many for the forgiveness of sins. ²⁹I tell you, I will never again drink of this fruit of the vine until that day when I drink it new with you in my Father's kingdom."

30 When they had sung the hymn, they went out to the Mount of Olives.

Peter's Denial Foretold

31 Then Jesus said to them, "You will all become deserters because of me this night; for it is written,

'I will strike the shepherd,
    and the sheep of the flock will be
        scattered.'

³²But after I am raised up, I will go ahead of you to Galilee." ³³Peter said to him, "Though all become deserters because of you, I will never desert you." ³⁴Jesus said to him, "Truly I tell you, this very night, before the cock crows, you will deny me three times." ³⁵Peter

said to him, "Even though I must die with you, I will not deny you." And so said all the disciples.

Jesus Prays in Gethsemane

36 Then Jesus went with them to a place called Gethsemane; and he said to his disciples, "Sit here while I go over there and pray." ³⁷He took with him Peter and the two sons of Zebedee, and began to be grieved and agitated. ³⁸Then he said to them, "I am deeply grieved, even to death; remain here, and stay awake with me." ³⁹And going a little farther, he threw himself on the ground and prayed, "My Father, if it is possible, let this cup pass from me; yet not what I want but what you want." ⁴⁰Then he came to the disciples and found them sleeping; and he said to Peter, "So, could you not stay awake with me one hour? ⁴¹Stay awake and pray that you may not come into the time of trial;^c the spirit indeed is willing, but the flesh is weak." ⁴²Again he went away for the second time and prayed, "My Father, if this cannot pass unless I drink it, your will be done." ⁴³Again he came and found them sleeping, for their eyes were heavy. ⁴⁴So leaving them again, he went away and prayed for the third time, saying the same words. ⁴⁵Then he came to the disciples and said to them, "Are you still sleeping and taking your rest? See, the hour is at hand, and the Son of Man is betrayed into the hands of sinners. ⁴⁶Get up, let us be going. See, my betrayer is at hand."

The Betrayal and Arrest of Jesus

47 While he was still speaking, Judas, one of the twelve, arrived; with him was a large crowd with swords and clubs, from the chief priests and the elders of the people. ⁴⁸Now the betrayer had given them a sign, saying, "The one I will kiss is the man; arrest him." ⁴⁹At once he came up to Jesus and said, "Greetings, Rabbi!" and kissed him. ⁵⁰Jesus said to him, "Friend, do what you are here to do." Then they came and laid hands on Jesus

---

a Other ancient authorities add *disciples*   *b* Other ancient authorities add *new*   *c* Or *into temptation* and arrested him. 51Suddenly, one of those with Jesus put his hand on his sword, drew it, and struck the slave of the high priest, cutting off his ear. 52Then Jesus said to him, "Put your sword back into its place; for all who take the sword will perish by the sword. 53Do you think that I cannot appeal to my Father, and he will at once send me more than twelve legions of angels? 54But how then would the scriptures be fulfilled, which say it must happen in this way?" 55At that hour Jesus said to the crowds, "Have you come out with swords and clubs to arrest me as though I were a bandit? Day after day I sat in the temple teaching, and you did not arrest me. 56But all this has taken place, so that the scriptures of the prophets may be fulfilled." Then all the disciples deserted him and fled.

Jesus before the High Priest

57 Those who had arrested Jesus took him to Caiaphas the high priest, in whose house the scribes and the elders had gathered. 58But Peter was following him at a distance, as far as the courtyard of the high priest; and going inside, he sat with the guards in order to see how this would end. 59Now the chief priests and the whole council were looking for false testimony against Jesus so that they might put him to death, 60but they found none, though many false witnesses came forward. At last two came forward 61and said, "This fellow said, 'I am able to destroy the temple of God and to build it in three days.'" 62The high priest stood up and said, "Have you no answer? What is it that they testify against you?" 63But Jesus was silent. Then the high priest said to him, "I put you under oath before the living God, tell us if you are the Messiah,*a* the Son of God." 64Jesus said to him, "You have said so. But I tell you,

From now on you will see the Son of
    Man
  seated at the right hand of Power

and coming on the clouds of
    heaven."
65Then the high priest tore his clothes and said, "He has blasphemed! Why do we still need witnesses? You have now heard his blasphemy. 66What is your verdict?" They answered, "He deserves death." 67Then they spat in his face and struck him; and some slapped him, 68saying, "Prophesy to us, you Messiah!*a* Who is it that struck you?"

Peter's Denial of Jesus

69 Now Peter was sitting outside in the courtyard. A servant-girl came to him and said, "You also were with Jesus the Galilean." 70But he denied it before all of them, saying, "I do not know what you are talking about." 71When he went out to the porch, another servant-girl saw him, and she said to the bystanders, "This man was with Jesus of Nazareth."*b* 72Again he denied it with an oath, "I do not know the man." 73After a little while the bystanders came up and said to Peter, "Certainly you are also one of them, for your accent betrays you." 74Then he began to curse, and he swore an oath, "I do not know the man!" At that moment the cock crowed. 75Then Peter remembered what Jesus had said: "Before the cock crows, you will deny me three times." And he went out and wept bitterly.

Jesus Brought before Pilate

27 When morning came, all the chief priests and the elders of the people conferred together against Jesus in order to bring about his death. 2They bound him, led him away, and handed him over to Pilate the governor.

The Suicide of Judas

3 When Judas, his betrayer, saw that Jesus*c* was condemned, he repented and brought back the thirty pieces of silver to the chief priests and the elders. 4He said, "I have sinned by betraying innocent*d* blood." But

a Or *Christ*   *b* Gk *the Nazorean*   *c* Gk *he*   *d* Other ancient authorities read *righteous* they said, "What is that to us? See to it your-self." [5]Throwing down the pieces of silver in the temple, he departed; and he went and hanged himself. [6]But the chief priests, taking the pieces of silver, said, "It is not lawful to put them into the treasury, since they are blood money." [7]After conferring together, they used them to buy the potter's field as a place to bury foreigners. [8]For this reason that field has been called the Field of Blood to this day. [9]Then was fulfilled what had been spoken through the prophet Jeremiah,[a] "And they took[b] the thirty pieces of silver, the price of the one on whom a price had been set,[c] on whom some of the people of Israel had set a price, [10]and they gave[d] them for the potter's field, as the Lord commanded me."

Pilate Questions Jesus

11 Now Jesus stood before the governor; and the governor asked him, "Are you the King of the Jews?" Jesus said, "You say so." [12]But when he was accused by the chief priests and elders, he did not answer. [13]Then Pilate said to him, "Do you not hear how many accusations they make against you?" [14]But he gave him no answer, not even to a single charge, so that the governor was great-ly amazed.

Barabbas or Jesus?

15 Now at the festival the governor was accustomed to release a prisoner for the crowd, anyone whom they wanted. [16]At that time they had a notorious prisoner, called Jesus[e] Barabbas. [17]So after they had gath-ered, Pilate said to them, "Whom do you want me to release for you, Jesus[e] Barabbas or Jesus who is called the Messiah?"[f] [18]For he realized that it was out of jealousy that they had handed him over. [19]While he was sitting on the judgment seat, his wife sent word to him, "Have nothing to do with that innocent man, for today I have suffered a great deal be-cause of a dream about him." [20]Now the

chief priests and the elders persuaded the crowds to ask for Barabbas and to have Jesus killed. [21]The governor again said to them, "Which of the two do you want me to release for you?" And they said, "Barabbas." [22]Pilate said to them, "Then what should I do with Jesus who is called the Messiah?"[f] All of them said, "Let him be crucified!" [23]Then he asked, "Why, what evil has he done?" But they shouted all the more, "Let him be cru-cified!"

Pilate Hands Jesus over to Be Crucified

24 So when Pilate saw that he could do nothing, but rather that a riot was beginning, he took some water and washed his hands be-fore the crowd, saying, "I am innocent of this man's blood;[g] see to it yourselves." [25]Then the people as a whole answered, "His blood be on us and on our children!" [26]So he released Barabbas for them; and after flog-ging Jesus, he handed him over to be cruci-fied.

The Soldiers Mock Jesus

27 Then the soldiers of the governor took Jesus into the governor's headquarters,[h] and they gathered the whole cohort around him. [28]They stripped him and put a scarlet robe on him, [29]and after twisting some thorns into a crown, they put it on his head. They put a reed in his right hand and knelt before him and mocked him, saying, "Hail, King of the Jews!" [30]They spat on him, and took the reed and struck him on the head. [31]After mocking him, they stripped him of the robe and put his own clothes on him. Then they led him away to crucify him.

The Crucifixion of Jesus

32 As they went out, they came upon a man from Cyrene named Simon; they com-pelled this man to carry his cross. [33]And when they came to a place called Golgotha (which means Place of a Skull), [34]they offered

a Other ancient authorities read *Zechariah* or *Isaiah*   b Or *I took*   c Or *the price of the precious One*   d Other ancient authorities read *I gave*   e Other ancient authorities lack *Jesus*   f Or *the Christ*   g Other ancient authorities read *this righteous blood*, or *this righteous man's blood*   h Gk *the praetorium* him wine to drink, mixed with gall; but when he tasted it, he would not drink it. 35And when they had crucified him, they divided his clothes among themselves by casting lots;*a* 36then they sat down there and kept watch over him. 37Over his head they put the charge against him, which read, "This is Jesus, the King of the Jews."

38 Then two bandits were crucified with him, one on his right and one on his left. 39Those who passed by derided *b* him, shaking their heads 40and saying, "You who would destroy the temple and build it in three days, save yourself! If you are the Son of God, come down from the cross." 41In the same way the chief priests also, along with the scribes and elders, were mocking him, saying, 42"He saved others; he cannot save himself.*c* He is the King of Israel; let him come down from the cross now, and we will believe in him. 43He trusts in God; let God deliver him now, if he wants to; for he said, 'I am God's Son.'" 44The bandits who were crucified with him also taunted him in the same way.

The Death of Jesus

45 From noon on, darkness came over the whole land*d* until three in the afternoon. 46And about three o'clock Jesus cried with a loud voice, "Eli, Eli, lema sabachthani?" that is, "My God, my God, why have you forsaken me?" 47When some of the bystanders heard it, they said, "This man is calling for Elijah." 48At once one of them ran and got a sponge, filled it with sour wine, put it on a stick, and gave it to him to drink. 49But the others said, "Wait, let us see whether Elijah will come to save him."*e* 50Then Jesus cried again with a loud voice and breathed his last.*f* 51At that moment the curtain of the temple was torn in two, from top to bottom. The earth shook, and the rocks were split. 52The tombs also were opened, and many bodies of the saints who had fallen asleep were raised.

53After his resurrection they came out of the tombs and entered the holy city and appeared to many. 54Now when the centurion and those with him, who were keeping watch over Jesus, saw the earthquake and what took place, they were terrified and said, "Truly this man was God's Son!"*g*

55 Many women were also there, looking on from a distance; they had followed Jesus from Galilee and had provided for him. 56Among them were Mary Magdalene, and Mary the mother of James and Joseph, and the mother of the sons of Zebedee.

The Burial of Jesus

57 When it was evening, there came a rich man from Arimathea, named Joseph, who was also a disciple of Jesus. 58He went to Pilate and asked for the body of Jesus; then Pilate ordered it to be given to him. 59So Joseph took the body and wrapped it in a clean linen cloth 60and laid it in his own new tomb, which he had hewn in the rock. He then rolled a great stone to the door of the tomb and went away. 61Mary Magdalene and the other Mary were there, sitting opposite the tomb.

The Guard at the Tomb

62 The next day, that is, after the day of Preparation, the chief priests and the Pharisees gathered before Pilate 63and said, "Sir, we remember what that impostor said while he was still alive, 'After three days I will rise again.' 64Therefore command the tomb to be made secure until the third day; otherwise his disciples may go and steal him away, and tell the people, 'He has been raised from the dead,' and the last deception would be worse than the first." 65Pilate said to them, "You have a guard*h* of soldiers; go, make it as secure as you can."*i* 66So they went with the guard and made the tomb secure by sealing the stone.

---

a Other ancient authorities add *in order that what had been spoken through the prophet might be fulfilled, "They divided my clothes among themselves, and for my clothing they cast lots."* *b* Or *blasphemed* *c* Or *is he unable to save himself?* *d* Or *earth* *e* Other ancient authorities add *And another took a spear and pierced his side, and out came water and blood* *f* Or *gave up his spirit* *g* Or *a son of God* *h* Or *Take a guard* *i* Gk *you know how*

The Resurrection of Jesus

28 After the sabbath, as the first day of the week was dawning, Mary Magdalene and the other Mary went to see the tomb. 2And suddenly there was a great earthquake; for an angel of the Lord, descending from heaven, came and rolled back the stone and sat on it. 3His appearance was like lightning, and his clothing white as snow. 4For fear of him the guards shook and became like dead men. 5But the angel said to the women, "Do not be afraid; I know that you are looking for Jesus who was crucified. 6He is not here; for he has been raised, as he said. Come, see the place where he*a* lay. 7Then go quickly and tell his disciples, 'He has been raised from the dead,*b* and indeed he is going ahead of you to Galilee; there you will see him.' This is my message for you." 8So they left the tomb quickly with fear and great joy, and ran to tell his disciples. 9Suddenly Jesus met them and said, "Greetings!" And they came to him, took hold of his feet, and worshiped him. 10Then Jesus said to them, "Do not be afraid; go and tell my brothers to go to Galilee; there they will see me."

The Report of the Guard

11 While they were going, some of the guard went into the city and told the chief priests everything that had happened. 12After the priests*c* had assembled with the elders, they devised a plan to give a large sum of money to the soldiers, 13telling them, "You must say, 'His disciples came by night and stole him away while we were asleep.' 14If this comes to the governor's ears, we will satisfy him and keep you out of trouble." 15So they took the money and did as they were directed. And this story is still told among the Jews to this day.

The Commissioning of the Disciples

16 Now the eleven disciples went to Galilee, to the mountain to which Jesus had directed them. 17When they saw him, they worshiped him; but some doubted. 18And Jesus came and said to them, "All authority in heaven and on earth has been given to me. 19Go therefore and make disciples of all nations, baptizing them in the name of the Father and of the Son and of the Holy Spirit, 20and teaching them to obey everything that I have commanded you. And remember, I am with you always, to the end of the age."*d*

---

a Other ancient authorities read *the Lord*   *b* Other ancient authorities lack *from the dead*   *c* Gk *they*   *d* Other ancient authorities add *Amen*

THE GOSPEL ACCORDING TO
MARK

The Proclamation of John the Baptist

1 The beginning of the good news*a* of Jesus Christ, the Son of God.*b*

2 As it is written in the prophet Isaiah,*c*
"See, I am sending my messenger
   ahead of you,*d*
who will prepare your way;
3 the voice of one crying out in the
   wilderness:
'Prepare the way of the Lord,
   make his paths straight,' "

4John the baptizer appeared*e* in the wilderness, proclaiming a baptism of repentance for the forgiveness of sins. 5And people from the whole Judean countryside and all the people of Jerusalem were going out to him, and were baptized by him in the river Jordan, confessing their sins. 6Now John was clothed with camel's hair, with a leather belt around his waist, and he ate locusts and wild honey. 7He proclaimed, "The one who is more powerful than I is coming after me; I am not worthy to stoop down and untie the thong of his sandals. 8I have baptized you with*f* water; but he will baptize you with*f* the Holy Spirit."

The Baptism of Jesus

9 In those days Jesus came from Nazareth of Galilee and was baptized by John in the Jordan. 10And just as he was coming up out of the water, he saw the heavens torn apart and the Spirit descending like a dove on him. 11And a voice came from heaven, "You are my Son, the Beloved;*g* with you I am well pleased."

The Temptation of Jesus

12 And the Spirit immediately drove him out into the wilderness. 13He was in the wilderness forty days, tempted by Satan; and he was with the wild beasts; and the angels waited on him.

The Beginning of the Galilean Ministry

14 Now after John was arrested, Jesus came to Galilee, proclaiming the good news*a* of God,*b* 15and saying, "The time is fulfilled, and the kingdom of God has come near;*i* repent, and believe in the good news."*a*

Jesus Calls the First Disciples

16 As Jesus passed along the Sea of Galilee, he saw Simon and his brother Andrew casting a net into the sea—for they were fishermen. 17And Jesus said to them, "Follow me and I will make you fish for people." 18And immediately they left their nets and followed him. 19As he went a little farther, he saw James son of Zebedee and his brother John, who were in their boat mending the nets. 20Immediately he called them; and they left their father Zebedee in the boat with the hired men, and followed him.

The Man with an Unclean Spirit

21 They went to Capernaum; and when the sabbath came, he entered the synagogue and taught. 22They were astounded at his teaching, for he taught them as one having authority, and not as the scribes. 23Just then there was in their synagogue a man with an unclean spirit, 24and he cried out, "What have you to do with us, Jesus of Nazareth? Have you come to destroy us? I know who you are, the Holy One of God." 25But Jesus rebuked him, saying, "Be silent, and come out of him!" 26And the unclean spirit, convulsing him and crying with a loud voice, came out of him. 27They were all amazed, and they kept on asking one another, "What is this? A new teaching—with authority! He*j* commands even the unclean spirits, and they obey him." 28At once his fame began to spread throughout the surrounding region of Galilee.

---

a Or *gospel*   *b* Other ancient authorities lack *the Son of God*   *c* Other ancient authorities read *in the prophets*
d Gk *before your face*   *e* Other ancient authorities read *John was baptizing*   *f* Or *in*   *g* Or *my beloved Son*
h Other ancient authorities read *of the kingdom*   *i* Or *is at hand*   *j* Or *A new teaching! With authority he*

Jesus Heals Many at Simon's House

29 As soon as they*a* left the synagogue, they entered the house of Simon and Andrew, with James and John. 30Now Simon's mother-in-law was in bed with a fever, and they told him about her at once. 31He came and took her by the hand and lifted her up. Then the fever left her, and she began to serve them.

32 That evening, at sunset, they brought to him all who were sick or possessed with demons. 33And the whole city was gathered around the door. 34And he cured many who were sick with various diseases, and cast out many demons; and he would not permit the demons to speak, because they knew him.

A Preaching Tour in Galilee

35 In the morning, while it was still very dark, he got up and went out to a deserted place, and there he prayed. 36And Simon and his companions hunted for him. 37When they found him, they said to him, "Everyone is searching for you." 38He answered, "Let us go on to the neighboring towns, so that I may proclaim the message there also; for that is what I came out to do." 39And he went throughout Galilee, proclaiming the message in their synagogues and casting out demons.

Jesus Cleanses a Leper

40 A leper*b* came to him begging him, and kneeling*c* he said to him, "If you choose, you can make me clean." 41Moved with pity,*d* Jesus*e* stretched out his hand and touched him, and said to him, "I do choose. Be made clean!" 42Immediately the leprosy*b* left him, and he was made clean. 43After sternly warning him he sent him away at once, 44saying to him, "See that you say nothing to anyone; but go, show yourself to the priest, and offer for your cleansing what Moses commanded, as a testimony to them." 45But he went out and began to proclaim it freely, and to spread the word, so that Jesus*e* could no longer go into

a town openly, but stayed out in the country; and people came to him from every quarter.

Jesus Heals a Paralytic

2 When he returned to Capernaum after some days, it was reported that he was at home. 2So many gathered around that there was no longer room for them, not even in front of the door; and he was speaking the word to them. 3Then some people*f* came, bringing to him a paralyzed man, carried by four of them. 4And when they could not bring him to Jesus because of the crowd, they removed the roof above him; and after having dug through it, they let down the mat on which the paralytic lay. 5When Jesus saw their faith, he said to the paralytic, "Son, your sins are forgiven." 6Now some of the scribes were sitting there, questioning in their hearts, 7"Why does this fellow speak in this way? It is blasphemy! Who can forgive sins but God alone?" 8At once Jesus perceived in his spirit that they were discussing these questions among themselves; and he said to them, "Why do you raise such questions in your hearts? 9Which is easier, to say to the paralytic, 'Your sins are forgiven,' or to say, 'Stand up and take your mat and walk'? 10But so that you may know that the Son of Man has authority on earth to forgive sins"—he said to the paralytic— 11"I say to you, stand up, take your mat and go to your home." 12And he stood up, and immediately took the mat and went out before all of them; so that they were all amazed and glorified God, saying, "We have never seen anything like this!"

Jesus Calls Levi

13 Jesus*g* went out again beside the sea; the whole crowd gathered around him, and he taught them. 14As he was walking along, he saw Levi son of Alphaeus sitting at the tax booth, and he said to him, "Follow me." And he got up and followed him.

15 And as he sat at dinner*h* in Levi's*i*

---

a Other ancient authorities read *he*   *b* The terms *leper* and *leprosy* can refer to several diseases   *c* Other ancient authorities lack *kneeling*   *d* Other ancient authorities read *anger*   *e* Gk *he*   *f* Gk *they*   *g* Gk *He*
h Gk *reclined*   *i* Gk *his*

house, many tax collectors and sinners were also sitting*a* with Jesus and his disciples—for there were many who followed him. 16When the scribes of*b* the Pharisees saw that he was eating with sinners and tax collectors, they said to his disciples, "Why does he eat*c* with tax collectors and sinners?" 17When Jesus heard this, he said to them, "Those who are well have no need of a physician, but those who are sick; I have come to call not the righteous but sinners."

The Question about Fasting

18 Now John's disciples and the Pharisees were fasting; and people*d* came and said to him, "Why do John's disciples and the disciples of the Pharisees fast, but your disciples do not fast?" 19Jesus said to them, "The wedding guests cannot fast while the bridegroom is with them, can they? As long as they have the bridegroom with them, they cannot fast. 20The days will come when the bridegroom is taken away from them, and then they will fast on that day.

21 "No one sews a piece of unshrunk cloth on an old cloak; otherwise, the patch pulls away from it, the new from the old, and a worse tear is made. 22And no one puts new wine into old wineskins; otherwise, the wine will burst the skins, and the wine is lost, and so are the skins; but one puts new wine into fresh wineskins."*e*

Pronouncement about the Sabbath

23 One sabbath he was going through the grainfields; and as they made their way his disciples began to pluck heads of grain. 24The Pharisees said to him, "Look, why are they doing what is not lawful on the sabbath?" 25And he said to them, "Have you never read what David did when he and his companions were hungry and in need of food? 26He entered the house of God, when Abiathar was high priest, and ate the bread of the Presence, which it is not lawful for any but the priests

to eat, and he gave some to his companions." 27Then he said to them, "The sabbath was made for humankind, and not humankind for the sabbath; 28so the Son of Man is lord even of the sabbath."

The Man with a Withered Hand

3 Again he entered the synagogue, and a man was there who had a withered hand. 2They watched him to see whether he would cure him on the sabbath, so that they might accuse him. 3And he said to the man who had the withered hand, "Come forward." 4Then he said to them, "Is it lawful to do good or to do harm on the sabbath, to save life or to kill?" But they were silent. 5He looked around at them with anger; he was grieved at their hardness of heart and said to the man, "Stretch out your hand." He stretched it out, and his hand was restored. 6The Pharisees went out and immediately conspired with the Herodians against him, how to destroy him.

A Multitude at the Seaside

7 Jesus departed with his disciples to the sea, and a great multitude from Galilee followed him; 8hearing all that he was doing, they came to him in great numbers from Judea, Jerusalem, Idumea, beyond the Jordan, and the region around Tyre and Sidon. 9He told his disciples to have a boat ready for him because of the crowd, so that they would not crush him; 10for he had cured many, so that all who had diseases pressed upon him to touch him. 11Whenever the unclean spirits saw him, they fell down before him and shouted, "You are the Son of God!" 12But he sternly ordered them not to make him known.

Jesus Appoints the Twelve

13 He went up the mountain and called to him those whom he wanted, and they came to him. 14And he appointed twelve, whom he also named apostles,*f* to be with him, and to be sent out to proclaim the message, 15and to

---

a Gk *reclining*   *b* Other ancient authorities read *and*   *c* Other ancient authorities add *and drink*   *d* Gk *they*
e Other ancient authorities lack *but one puts new wine into fresh wineskins*   *f* Other ancient authorities lack *whom he also named apostles*

have authority to cast out demons. 16So he appointed the twelve:*a* Simon (to whom he gave the name Peter); 17James son of Zebedee and John the brother of James (to whom he gave the name Boanerges, that is, Sons of Thunder); 18and Andrew, and Philip, and Bartholomew, and Matthew, and Thomas, and James son of Alphaeus, and Thaddaeus, and Simon the Cananaean, 19and Judas Iscariot, who betrayed him.

Jesus and Beelzebul

Then he went home; 20and the crowd came together again, so that they could not even eat. 21When his family heard it, they went out to restrain him, for people were saying, "He has gone out of his mind." 22And the scribes who came down from Jerusalem said, "He has Beelzebul, and by the ruler of the demons he casts out demons." 23And he called them to him, and spoke to them in parables, "How can Satan cast out Satan? 24If a kingdom is divided against itself, that kingdom cannot stand. 25And if a house is divided against itself, that house will not be able to stand. 26And if Satan has risen up against himself and is divided, he cannot stand, but his end has come. 27But no one can enter a strong man's house and plunder his property without first tying up the strong man; then indeed the house can be plundered.

28 "Truly I tell you, people will be forgiven for their sins and whatever blasphemies they utter; 29but whoever blasphemes against the Holy Spirit can never have forgiveness, but is guilty of an eternal sin"— 30for they had said, "He has an unclean spirit."

The True Kindred of Jesus

31 Then his mother and his brothers came; and standing outside, they sent to him and called him. 32A crowd was sitting around him; and they said to him, "Your mother and your brothers and sisters*b* are outside, asking for you." 33And he replied, "Who are my mother and my brothers?" 34And looking at those who sat around him, he said, "Here are my mother and my brothers! 35Whoever does the will of God is my brother and sister and mother."

The Parable of the Sower

4 Again he began to teach beside the sea. Such a very large crowd gathered around him that he got into a boat on the sea and sat there, while the whole crowd was beside the sea on the land. 2He began to teach them many things in parables, and in his teaching he said to them: 3"Listen! A sower went out to sow. 4And as he sowed, some seed fell on the path, and the birds came and ate it up. 5Other seed fell on rocky ground, where it did not have much soil, and it sprang up quickly, since it had no depth of soil. 6And when the sun rose, it was scorched; and since it had no root, it withered away. 7Other seed fell among thorns, and the thorns grew up and choked it, and it yielded no grain. 8Other seed fell into good soil and brought forth grain, growing up and increasing and yielding thirty and sixty and a hundredfold." 9And he said, "Let anyone with ears to hear listen!"

The Purpose of the Parables

10 When he was alone, those who were around him along with the twelve asked him about the parables. 11And he said to them, "To you has been given the secret*c* of the kingdom of God, but for those outside, everything comes in parables; 12in order that

'they may indeed look, but not perceive,
    and may indeed listen, but not
        understand;
so that they may not turn again and be
    forgiven.' "

13 And he said to them, "Do you not understand this parable? Then how will you understand all the parables? 14The sower sows the word. 15These are the ones on the path where the word is sown: when they hear, Satan immediately comes and takes away the word that is sown in them. 16And

---

a Other ancient authorities lack *So he appointed the twelve*
b Other ancient authorities lack *and sisters*
c Or *mystery*

these are the ones sown on rocky ground: when they hear the word, they immediately receive it with joy. [17]But they have no root, and endure only for a while; then, when trouble or persecution arises on account of the word, immediately they fall away.[a] [18]And others are those sown among the thorns: these are the ones who hear the word, [19]but the cares of the world, and the lure of wealth, and the desire for other things come in and choke the word, and it yields nothing. [20]And these are the ones sown on the good soil: they hear the word and accept it and bear fruit, thirty and sixty and a hundredfold."

A Lamp under a Bushel Basket

21　He said to them, "Is a lamp brought in to be put under the bushel basket, or under the bed, and not on the lampstand? [22]For there is nothing hidden, except to be disclosed; nor is anything secret, except to come to light. [23]Let anyone with ears to hear listen!" [24]And he said to them, "Pay attention to what you hear; the measure you give will be the measure you get, and still more will be given you. [25]For to those who have, more will be given; and from those who have nothing, even what they have will be taken away."

The Parable of the Growing Seed

26　He also said, "The kingdom of God is as if someone would scatter seed on the ground, [27]and would sleep and rise night and day, and the seed would sprout and grow, he does not know how. [28]The earth produces of itself, first the stalk, then the head, then the full grain in the head. [29]But when the grain is ripe, at once he goes in with his sickle, because the harvest has come."

The Parable of the Mustard Seed

30　He also said, "With what can we compare the kingdom of God, or what parable will we use for it? [31]It is like a mustard seed, which, when sown upon the ground, is the smallest of all the seeds on earth; [32]yet when it is sown it grows up and becomes the greatest of all shrubs, and puts forth large branches, so that the birds of the air can make nests in its shade."

The Use of Parables

33　With many such parables he spoke the word to them, as they were able to hear it; [34]he did not speak to them except in parables, but he explained everything in private to his disciples.

Jesus Stills a Storm

35　On that day, when evening had come, he said to them, "Let us go across to the other side." [36]And leaving the crowd behind, they took him with them in the boat, just as he was. Other boats were with him. [37]A great windstorm arose, and the waves beat into the boat, so that the boat was already being swamped. [38]But he was in the stern, asleep on the cushion; and they woke him up and said to him, "Teacher, do you not care that we are perishing?" [39]He woke up and rebuked the wind, and said to the sea, "Peace! Be still!" Then the wind ceased, and there was a dead calm. [40]He said to them, "Why are you afraid? Have you still no faith?" [41]And they were filled with great awe and said to one another, "Who then is this, that even the wind and the sea obey him?"

Jesus Heals the Gerasene Demoniac

5　They came to the other side of the sea, to the country of the Gerasenes.[b] [2]And when he had stepped out of the boat, immediately a man out of the tombs with an unclean spirit met him. [3]He lived among the tombs; and no one could restrain him any more, even with a chain; [4]for he had often been restrained with shackles and chains, but the chains he wrenched apart, and the shackles he broke in pieces; and no one had the strength to subdue him. [5]Night and day among the tombs and on the mountains he was always howling and bruising himself with

---

a Or stumble　b Other ancient authorities read Gergesenes; others, Gadarenes stones. [6]When he saw Jesus from a distance, he ran and bowed down before him; [7]and he shouted at the top of his voice, "What have you to do with me, Jesus, Son of the Most High God? I adjure you by God, do not torment me." [8]For he had said to him, "Come out of the man, you unclean spirit!" [9]Then Jesus[a] asked him, "What is your name?" He replied, "My name is Legion; for we are many." [10]He begged him earnestly not to send them out of the country. [11]Now there on the hillside a great herd of swine was feeding; [12]and the unclean spirits[b] begged him, "Send us into the swine; let us enter them." [13]So he gave them permission. And the unclean spirits came out and entered the swine; and the herd, numbering about two thousand, rushed down the steep bank into the sea, and were drowned in the sea.

14 The swineherds ran off and told it in the city and in the country. Then people came to see what it was that had happened. [15]They came to Jesus and saw the demoniac sitting there, clothed and in his right mind, the very man who had had the legion; and they were afraid. [16]Those who had seen what had happened to the demoniac and to the swine reported it. [17]Then they began to beg Jesus[c] to leave their neighborhood. [18]As he was getting into the boat, the man who had been possessed by demons begged him that he might be with him. [19]But Jesus[a] refused, and said to him, "Go home to your friends, and tell them how much the Lord has done for you, and what mercy he has shown you." [20]And he went away and began to proclaim in the Decapolis how much Jesus had done for him; and everyone was amazed.

A Girl Restored to Life and a Woman Healed

21 When Jesus had crossed again in the boat[d] to the other side, a great crowd gathered around him; and he was by the sea. [22]Then one of the leaders of the synagogue named Jairus came and, when he saw him, fell at his feet [23]and begged him repeatedly, "My little daughter is at the point of death. Come and lay your hands on her, so that she may be made well, and live." [24]So he went with him.

And a large crowd followed him and pressed in on him. [25]Now there was a woman who had been suffering from hemorrhages for twelve years. [26]She had endured much under many physicians, and had spent all that she had; and she was no better, but rather grew worse. [27]She had heard about Jesus, and came up behind him in the crowd and touched his cloak, [28]for she said, "If I but touch his clothes, I will be made well." [29]Immediately her hemorrhage stopped; and she felt in her body that she was healed of her disease. [30]Immediately aware that power had gone forth from him, Jesus turned about in the crowd and said, "Who touched my clothes?" [31]And his disciples said to him, "You see the crowd pressing in on you; how can you say, 'Who touched me?' " [32]He looked all around to see who had done it. [33]But the woman, knowing what had happened to her, came in fear and trembling, fell down before him, and told him the whole truth. [34]He said to her, "Daughter, your faith has made you well; go in peace, and be healed of your disease."

35 While he was still speaking, some people came from the leader's house to say, "Your daughter is dead. Why trouble the teacher any further?" [36]But overhearing[e] what they said, Jesus said to the leader of the synagogue, "Do not fear, only believe." [37]He allowed no one to follow him except Peter, James, and John, the brother of James. [38]When they came to the house of the leader of the synagogue, he saw a commotion, people weeping and wailing loudly. [39]When he had entered, he said to them, "Why do you make a commotion and weep? The child is not dead but sleeping." [40]And they laughed at him. Then he put them all outside, and took the child's father and mother and those who were with him, and went in where the child was. [41]He took her by the hand and said to

---

a Gk he　　b Gk they　　c Gk him　　d Other ancient authorities lack in the boat　　e Or ignoring; other ancient authorities read hearing her, "Talitha cum," which means, "Little girl, get up!" 42And immediately the girl got up and began to walk about (she was twelve years of age). At this they were overcome with amazement. 43He strictly ordered them that no one should know this, and told them to give her something to eat.

The Rejection of Jesus at Nazareth

6 He left that place and came to his hometown, and his disciples followed him. 2On the sabbath he began to teach in the synagogue, and many who heard him were astounded. They said, "Where did this man get all this? What is this wisdom that has been given to him? What deeds of power are being done by his hands! 3Is not this the carpenter, the son of Mary*a* and brother of James and Joses and Judas and Simon, and are not his sisters here with us?" And they took offense*b* at him. 4Then Jesus said to them, "Prophets are not without honor, except in their hometown, and among their own kin, and in their own house." 5And he could do no deed of power there, except that he laid his hands on a few sick people and cured them. 6And he was amazed at their unbelief.

The Mission of the Twelve

Then he went about among the villages teaching. 7He called the twelve and began to send them out two by two, and gave them authority over the unclean spirits. 8He ordered them to take nothing for their journey except a staff; no bread, no bag, no money in their belts; 9but to wear sandals and not to put on two tunics. 10He said to them, "Wherever you enter a house, stay there until you leave the place. 11If any place will not welcome you and they refuse to hear you, as you leave, shake off the dust that is on your feet as a testimony against them." 12So they went out and proclaimed that all should repent. 13They cast out many demons, and anointed with oil many who were sick and cured them.

The Death of John the Baptist

14 King Herod heard of it, for Jesus'*c* name had become known. Some were*d* saying, "John the baptizer has been raised from the dead; and for this reason these powers are at work in him." 15But others said, "It is Elijah." And others said, "It is a prophet, like one of the prophets of old." 16But when Herod heard of it, he said, "John, whom I beheaded, has been raised."

17 For Herod himself had sent men who arrested John, bound him, and put him in prison on account of Herodias, his brother Philip's wife, because Herod*e* had married her. 18For John had been telling Herod, "It is not lawful for you to have your brother's wife." 19And Herodias had a grudge against him, and wanted to kill him. But she could not, 20for Herod feared John, knowing that he was a righteous and holy man, and he protected him. When he heard him, he was greatly perplexed;*f* and yet he liked to listen to him. 21But an opportunity came when Herod on his birthday gave a banquet for his courtiers and officers and for the leaders of Galilee. 22When his daughter Herodias*g* came in and danced, she pleased Herod and his guests; and the king said to the girl, "Ask me for whatever you wish, and I will give it." 23And he solemnly swore to her, "Whatever you ask me, I will give you, even half of my kingdom." 24She went out and said to her mother, "What should I ask for?" She replied, "The head of John the baptizer." 25Immediately she rushed back to the king and requested, "I want you to give me at once the head of John the Baptist on a platter." 26The king was deeply grieved; yet out of regard for his oaths and for the guests, he did not want to refuse her. 27Immediately the king sent a soldier of the guard with orders to bring John's*c* head. He went and beheaded him in the prison, 28brought his head on a platter, and gave it to the girl. Then the girl gave it to her mother. 29When his disciples heard about it, they came and took his body, and laid it in a tomb.

a Other ancient authorities read *son of the carpenter and of Mary*   *b* Or *stumbled*   *c* Gk *his*   *d* Other ancient authorities read *He was*   *e* Gk *he*   *f* Other ancient authorities read *he did many things*   *g* Other ancient authorities read *the daughter of Herodias herself*

Feeding the Five Thousand

30 The apostles gathered around Jesus, and told him all that they had done and taught. ³¹He said to them, "Come away to a deserted place all by yourselves and rest a while." For many were coming and going, and they had no leisure even to eat. ³²And they went away in the boat to a deserted place by themselves. ³³Now many saw them going and recognized them, and they hurried there on foot from all the towns and arrived ahead of them. ³⁴As he went ashore, he saw a great crowd; and he had compassion for them, because they were like sheep without a shepherd; and he began to teach them many things. ³⁵When it grew late, his disciples came to him and said, "This is a deserted place, and the hour is now very late; ³⁶send them away so that they may go into the surrounding country and villages and buy something for themselves to eat." ³⁷But he answered them, "You give them something to eat." They said to him, "Are we to go and buy two hundred denarii*a* worth of bread, and give it to them to eat?" ³⁸And he said to them, "How many loaves have you? Go and see." When they had found out, they said, "Five, and two fish." ³⁹Then he ordered them to get all the people to sit down in groups on the green grass. ⁴⁰So they sat down in groups of hundreds and of fifties. ⁴¹Taking the five loaves and the two fish, he looked up to heaven, and blessed and broke the loaves, and gave them to his disciples to set before the people; and he divided the two fish among them all. ⁴²And all ate and were filled; ⁴³and they took up twelve baskets full of broken pieces and of the fish. ⁴⁴Those who had eaten the loaves numbered five thousand men.

Jesus Walks on the Water

45 Immediately he made his disciples get into the boat and go on ahead to the other side, to Bethsaida, while he dismissed the crowd. ⁴⁶After saying farewell to them, he went up on the mountain to pray.

47 When evening came, the boat was out on the sea, and he was alone on the land. ⁴⁸When he saw that they were straining at the oars against an adverse wind, he came towards them early in the morning, walking on the sea. He intended to pass them by. ⁴⁹But when they saw him walking on the sea, they thought it was a ghost and cried out; ⁵⁰for they all saw him and were terrified. But immediately he spoke to them and said, "Take heart, it is I; do not be afraid." ⁵¹Then he got into the boat with them and the wind ceased. And they were utterly astounded, ⁵²for they did not understand about the loaves, but their hearts were hardened.

Healing the Sick in Gennesaret

53 When they had crossed over, they came to land at Gennesaret and moored the boat. ⁵⁴When they got out of the boat, people at once recognized him, ⁵⁵and rushed about that whole region and began to bring the sick on mats to wherever they heard he was. ⁵⁶And wherever he went, into villages or cities or farms, they laid the sick in the marketplaces, and begged him that they might touch even the fringe of his cloak; and all who touched it were healed.

The Tradition of the Elders

7 Now when the Pharisees and some of the scribes who had come from Jerusalem gathered around him, ²they noticed that some of his disciples were eating with defiled hands, that is, without washing them. ³(For the Pharisees, and all the Jews, do not eat unless they thoroughly wash their hands,*b* thus observing the tradition of the elders; ⁴and they do not eat anything from the market unless they wash it;*c* and there are also many other traditions that they observe, the washing of cups, pots, and bronze kettles.*d*) ⁵So the Pharisees and the scribes asked him, "Why do your disciples not live*e* according to the tradition of the elders, but eat with defiled

---

a The denarius was the usual day's wage for a laborer　*b* Meaning of Gk uncertain　*c* Other ancient authorities read *and when they come from the marketplace, they do not eat unless they purify themselves*　*d* Other ancient authorities add *and beds*　*e* Gk *walk* hands?" [6]He said to them, "Isaiah prophesied rightly about you hypocrites, as it is written,

'This people honors me with their lips,
     but their hearts are far from me;
[7] in vain do they worship me,
     teaching human precepts as
         doctrines.'

[8]You abandon the commandment of God and hold to human tradition."

[9] Then he said to them, "You have a fine way of rejecting the commandment of God in order to keep your tradition! [10]For Moses said, 'Honor your father and your mother'; and, 'Whoever speaks evil of father or mother must surely die.' [11]But you say that if anyone tells father or mother, 'Whatever support you might have had from me is Corban' (that is, an offering to God[a])— [12]then you no longer permit doing anything for a father or mother, [13]thus making void the word of God through your tradition that you have handed on. And you do many things like this."

[14] Then he called the crowd again and said to them, "Listen to me, all of you, and understand: [15]there is nothing outside a person that by going in can defile, but the things that come out are what defile."[b]

[17] When he had left the crowd and entered the house, his disciples asked him about the parable. [18]He said to them, "Then do you also fail to understand? Do you not see that whatever goes into a person from outside cannot defile, [19]since it enters, not the heart but the stomach, and goes out into the sewer?" (Thus he declared all foods clean.) [20]And he said, "It is what comes out of a person that defiles. [21]For it is from within, from the human heart, that evil intentions come: fornication, theft, murder, [22]adultery, avarice, wickedness, deceit, licentiousness, envy, slander, pride, folly. [23]All these evil things come from within, and they defile a person."

The Syrophoenician Woman's Faith

24 From there he set out and went away to the region of Tyre.[c] He entered a house

and did not want anyone to know he was there. Yet he could not escape notice, [25]but a woman whose little daughter had an unclean spirit immediately heard about him, and she came and bowed down at his feet. [26]Now the woman was a Gentile, of Syrophoenician origin. She begged him to cast the demon out of her daughter. [27]He said to her, "Let the children be fed first, for it is not fair to take the children's food and throw it to the dogs." [28]But she answered him, "Sir,[d] even the dogs under the table eat the children's crumbs." [29]Then he said to her, "For saying that, you may go—the demon has left your daughter." [30]So she went home, found the child lying on the bed, and the demon gone.

Jesus Cures a Deaf Man

31 Then he returned from the region of Tyre, and went by way of Sidon towards the Sea of Galilee, in the region of the Decapolis. [32]They brought to him a deaf man who had an impediment in his speech; and they begged him to lay his hand on him. [33]He took him aside in private, away from the crowd, and put his fingers into his ears, and he spat and touched his tongue. [34]Then looking up to heaven, he sighed and said to him, "Ephphatha," that is, "Be opened." [35]And immediately his ears were opened, his tongue was released, and he spoke plainly. [36]Then Jesus[i] ordered them to tell no one; but the more he ordered them, the more zealously they proclaimed it. [37]They were astounded beyond measure, saying, "He has done everything well; he even makes the deaf to hear and the mute to speak."

Feeding the Four Thousand

8 In those days when there was again a great crowd without anything to eat, he called his disciples and said to them, [2]"I have compassion for the crowd, because they have been with me now for three days and have nothing to eat. [3]If I send them away hungry

---

a Gk lacks *to God*   b Other ancient authorities add verse 16, *"Let anyone with ears to hear listen"*   c Other ancient authorities add *and Sidon*   d Or *Lord*; other ancient authorities prefix *Yes*   i Gk *he* to their homes, they will faint on the way—and some of them have come from a great distance." [4]His disciples replied, "How can one feed these people with bread here in the desert?" [5]He asked them, "How many loaves do you have?" They said, "Seven." [6]Then he ordered the crowd to sit down on the ground; and he took the seven loaves, and after giving thanks he broke them and gave them to his disciples to distribute; and they distributed them to the crowd. [7]They had also a few small fish; and after blessing them, he ordered that these too should be distributed. [8]They ate and were filled; and they took up the broken pieces left over, seven baskets full. [9]Now there were about four thousand people. And he sent them away. [10]And immediately he got into the boat with his disciples and went to the district of Dalmanutha.[a]

The Demand for a Sign

11 The Pharisees came and began to argue with him, asking him for a sign from heaven, to test him. [12]And he sighed deeply in his spirit and said, "Why does this generation ask for a sign? Truly I tell you, no sign will be given to this generation." [13]And he left them, and getting into the boat again, he went across to the other side.

The Yeast of the Pharisees and of Herod

14 Now the disciples[b] had forgotten to bring any bread; and they had only one loaf with them in the boat. [15]And he cautioned them, saying, "Watch out—beware of the yeast of the Pharisees and the yeast of Herod."[c] [16]They said to one another, "It is because we have no bread." [17]And becoming aware of it, Jesus said to them, "Why are you talking about having no bread? Do you still not perceive or understand? Are your hearts hardened? [18]Do you have eyes, and fail to see? Do you have ears, and fail to hear? And do you not remember? [19]When I broke the five loaves for the five thousand, how many baskets full of broken pieces did you collect?" They said

to him, "Twelve." [20]"And the seven for the four thousand, how many baskets full of broken pieces did you collect?" And they said to him, "Seven." [21]Then he said to them, "Do you not yet understand?"

Jesus Cures a Blind Man at Bethsaida

22 They came to Bethsaida. Some people[d] brought a blind man to him and begged him to touch him. [23]He took the blind man by the hand and led him out of the village; and when he had put saliva on his eyes and laid his hands on him, he asked him, "Can you see anything?" [24]And the man[e] looked up and said, "I can see people, but they look like trees, walking." [25]Then Jesus[e] laid his hands on his eyes again; and he looked intently and his sight was restored, and he saw everything clearly. [26]Then he sent him away to his home, saying, "Do not even go into the village."[f]

Peter's Declaration about Jesus

27 Jesus went on with his disciples to the villages of Caesarea Philippi; and on the way he asked his disciples, "Who do people say that I am?" [28]And they answered him, "John the Baptist; and others, Elijah; and still others, one of the prophets." [29]He asked them, "But who do you say that I am?" Peter answered him, "You are the Messiah."[g] [30]And he sternly ordered them not to tell anyone about him.

Jesus Foretells His Death and Resurrection

31 Then he began to teach them that the Son of Man must undergo great suffering, and be rejected by the elders, the chief priests, and the scribes, and be killed, and after three days rise again. [32]He said all this quite openly. And Peter took him aside and began to rebuke him. [33]But turning and looking at his disciples, he rebuked Peter and said, "Get behind me, Satan! For you are setting your mind not on divine things but on human things."

34 He called the crowd with his disciples, and said to them, "If any want to become my

---

a Other ancient authorities read *Mageda* or *Magdala*   b Gk *they*   c Other ancient authorities read *the Herodians*
d Gk *They*   e Gk *he*   f Other ancient authorities add *or tell anyone in the village*   g Or *the Christ*

followers, let them deny themselves and take up their cross and follow me. 35For those who want to save their life will lose it, and those who lose their life for my sake, and for the sake of the gospel,*a* will save it. 36For what will it profit them to gain the whole world and forfeit their life? 37Indeed, what can they give in return for their life? 38Those who are ashamed of me and of my words *b* in this adulterous and sinful generation, of them the Son of Man will also be ashamed when he comes in the glory of his Father with the holy angels." 1And he said to them, "Truly I tell you, there are some standing here who will not taste death until they see that the kingdom of God has come with *c* power."

The Transfiguration

2 Six days later, Jesus took with him Peter and James and John, and led them up a high mountain apart, by themselves. And he was transfigured before them, 3and his clothes became dazzling white, such as no one *d* on earth could bleach them. 4And there appeared to them Elijah with Moses, who were talking with Jesus. 5Then Peter said to Jesus, "Rabbi, it is good for us to be here; let us make three dwellings,*e* one for you, one for Moses, and one for Elijah." 6He did not know what to say, for they were terrified. 7Then a cloud overshadowed them, and from the cloud there came a voice, "This is my Son, the Beloved;*f* listen to him!" 8Suddenly when they looked around, they saw no one with them any more, but only Jesus.

The Coming of Elijah

9 As they were coming down the mountain, he ordered them to tell no one about what they had seen, until after the Son of Man had risen from the dead. 10So they kept the matter to themselves, questioning what this rising from the dead could mean. 11Then they asked him, "Why do the scribes say that Elijah must come first?" 12He said to them, "Elijah is indeed coming first to restore all things. How then is it written about the Son of Man, that he is to go through many sufferings and be treated with contempt? 13But I tell you that Elijah has come, and they did to him whatever they pleased, as it is written about him."

The Healing of a Boy with a Spirit

14 When they came to the disciples, they saw a great crowd around them, and some scribes arguing with them. 15When the whole crowd saw him, they were immediately overcome with awe, and they ran forward to greet him. 16He asked them, "What are you arguing about with them?" 17Someone from the crowd answered him, "Teacher, I brought you my son; he has a spirit that makes him unable to speak; 18and whenever it seizes him, it dashes him down; and he foams and grinds his teeth and becomes rigid; and I asked your disciples to cast it out, but they could not do so." 19He answered them, "You faithless generation, how much longer must I be among you? How much longer must I put up with you? Bring him to me." 20And they brought the boy *g* to him. When the spirit saw him, immediately it convulsed the boy,*g* and he fell on the ground and rolled about, foaming at the mouth. 21Jesus *h* asked the father, "How long has this been happening to him?" And he said, "From childhood. 22It has often cast him into the fire and into the water, to destroy him; but if you are able to do anything, have pity on us and help us." 23Jesus said to him, "If you are able!—All things can be done for the one who believes." 24Immediately the father of the child cried out,*i* "I believe; help my unbelief!" 25When Jesus saw that a crowd came running together, he rebuked the unclean spirit, saying to it, "You spirit that keeps this boy from speaking and hearing, I command you, come out of him, and never enter him again!" 26After crying out and convulsing

him terribly, it came out, and the boy was like a corpse, so that most of them said, "He is dead." 27But Jesus took him by the hand and lifted him up, and he was able to stand. 28When he had entered the house, his disciples asked him privately, "Why could we not cast it out?" 29He said to them, "This kind can come out only through prayer." *a*

Jesus Again Foretells His Death and Resurrection

30 They went on from there and passed through Galilee. He did not want anyone to know it; 31for he was teaching his disciples, saying to them, "The Son of Man is to be betrayed into human hands, and they will kill him, and three days after being killed, he will rise again." 32But they did not understand what he was saying and were afraid to ask him.

Who Is the Greatest?

33 Then they came to Capernaum; and when he was in the house he asked them, "What were you arguing about on the way?" 34But they were silent, for on the way they had argued with one another who was the greatest. 35He sat down, called the twelve, and said to them, "Whoever wants to be first must be last of all and servant of all." 36Then he took a little child and put it among them; and taking it in his arms, he said to them, 37"Whoever welcomes one such child in my name welcomes me, and whoever welcomes me welcomes not me but the one who sent me."

Another Exorcist

38 John said to him, "Teacher, we saw someone *b* casting out demons in your name, and we tried to stop him, because he was not following us." 39But Jesus said, "Do not stop him; for no one who does a deed of power in my name will be able soon afterward to speak evil of me. 40Whoever is not against

us is for us. 41For truly I tell you, whoever gives you a cup of water to drink because you bear the name of Christ will by no means lose the reward.

Temptations to Sin

42 "If any of you put a stumbling block before one of these little ones who believe in me, *c* it would be better for you if a great millstone were hung around your neck and you were thrown into the sea. 43If your hand causes you to stumble, cut it off; it is better for you to enter life maimed than to have two hands and to go to hell, *d* to the unquenchable fire. *e* 45And if your foot causes you to stumble, cut it off; it is better for you to enter life lame than to have two feet and to be thrown into hell. *d, e* 47And if your eye causes you to stumble, tear it out; it is better for you to enter the kingdom of God with one eye than to have two eyes and to be thrown into hell, *d* 48where their worm never dies, and the fire is never quenched.

49 "For everyone will be salted with fire. *e* 50Salt is good; but if salt has lost its saltiness, how can you season it? *f* Have salt in yourselves, and be at peace with one another."

Teaching about Divorce

10 He left that place and went to the region of Judea and *g* beyond the Jordan. And crowds again gathered around him; and, as was his custom, he again taught them.

2 Some Pharisees came, and to test him they asked, "Is it lawful for a man to divorce his wife?" 3He answered them, "What did Moses command you?" 4They said, "Moses allowed a man to write a certificate of dismissal and to divorce her." 5But Jesus said to them, "Because of your hardness of heart he wrote this commandment for you. 6But from the beginning of creation, 'God made them male and female.' 7'For this reason a man shall leave his father and mother and be

---

a Other ancient authorities add *and fasting*   *b* Other ancient authorities add *who does not follow us*   *c* Other ancient authorities lack *in me*   *d* Gk *Gehenna*   *e* Verses 44 and 46 (which are identical with verse 48) are lacking in the best ancient authorities   *e* Other ancient authorities either add or substitute *and every sacrifice will be salted with salt*   *f* Or *how can you restore its saltiness?*   *g* Other ancient authorities lack *and* joined to his wife,*a* 8and the two shall become one flesh.' So they are no longer two, but one flesh. 9Therefore what God has joined together, let no one separate."

10 Then in the house the disciples asked him again about this matter. 11He said to them, "Whoever divorces his wife and marries another commits adultery against her; 12and if she divorces her husband and marries another, she commits adultery."

Jesus Blesses Little Children

13 People were bringing little children to him in order that he might touch them; and the disciples spoke sternly to them. 14But when Jesus saw this, he was indignant and said to them, "Let the little children come to me; do not stop them; for it is to such as these that the kingdom of God belongs. 15Truly I tell you, whoever does not receive the kingdom of God as a little child will never enter it." 16And he took them up in his arms, laid his hands on them, and blessed them.

The Rich Man

17 As he was setting out on a journey, a man ran up and knelt before him, and asked him, "Good Teacher, what must I do to inherit eternal life?" 18Jesus said to him, "Why do you call me good? No one is good but God alone. 19You know the commandments: 'You shall not murder; You shall not commit adultery; You shall not steal; You shall not bear false witness; You shall not defraud; Honor your father and mother.' " 20He said to him, "Teacher, I have kept all these since my youth." 21Jesus, looking at him, loved him and said, "You lack one thing; go, sell what you own, and give the money*b* to the poor, and you will have treasure in heaven; then come, follow me." 22When he heard this, he was shocked and went away grieving, for he had many possessions.

23 Then Jesus looked around and said to his disciples, "How hard it will be for those who have wealth to enter the kingdom of God!" 24And the disciples were perplexed at these words. But Jesus said to them again, "Children, how hard it is*c* to enter the kingdom of God! 25It is easier for a camel to go through the eye of a needle than for someone who is rich to enter the kingdom of God." 26They were greatly astounded and said to one another,*d* "Then who can be saved?" 27Jesus looked at them and said, "For mortals it is impossible, but not for God; for God all things are possible."

28 Peter began to say to him, "Look, we have left everything and followed you." 29Jesus said, "Truly I tell you, there is no one who has left house or brothers or sisters or mother or father or children or fields, for my sake and for the sake of the good news,*e* 30who will not receive a hundredfold now in this age—houses, brothers and sisters, mothers and children, and fields, with persecutions—and in the age to come eternal life. 31But many who are first will be last, and the last will be first."

A Third Time Jesus Foretells His Death and Resurrection

32 They were on the road, going up to Jerusalem, and Jesus was walking ahead of them; they were amazed, and those who followed were afraid. He took the twelve aside again and began to tell them what was to happen to him, 33saying, "See, we are going up to Jerusalem, and the Son of Man will be handed over to the chief priests and the scribes, and they will condemn him to death; then they will hand him over to the Gentiles; 34they will mock him, and spit upon him, and flog him, and kill him; and after three days he will rise again."

The Request of James and John

35 James and John, the sons of Zebedee, came forward to him and said to him, "Teacher, we want you to do for us whatever we ask of you." 36And he said to them, "What is it you want me to do for you?"

---

a Other ancient authorities lack *and be joined to his wife*   *b* Gk lacks *the money*   *c* Other ancient authorities add *for those who trust in riches*   *d* Other ancient authorities read *to him*   *e* Or *gospel*

37And they said to him, "Grant us to sit, one at your right hand and one at your left, in your glory." 38But Jesus said to them, "You do not know what you are asking. Are you able to drink the cup that I drink, or be baptized with the baptism that I am baptized with?" 39They replied, "We are able." Then Jesus said to them, "The cup that I drink you will drink; and with the baptism with which I am baptized, you will be baptized; 40but to sit at my right hand or at my left is not mine to grant, but it is for those for whom it has been prepared."

41 When the ten heard this, they began to be angry with James and John. 42So Jesus called them and said to them, "You know that among the Gentiles those whom they recognize as their rulers lord it over them, and their great ones are tyrants over them. 43But it is not so among you; but whoever wishes to become great among you must be your servant, 44and whoever wishes to be first among you must be slave of all. 45For the Son of Man came not to be served but to serve, and to give his life a ransom for many."

The Healing of Blind Bartimaeus

46 They came to Jericho. As he and his disciples and a large crowd were leaving Jericho, Bartimaeus son of Timaeus, a blind beggar, was sitting by the roadside. 47When he heard that it was Jesus of Nazareth, he began to shout out and say, "Jesus, Son of David, have mercy on me!" 48Many sternly ordered him to be quiet, but he cried out even more loudly, "Son of David, have mercy on me!" 49Jesus stood still and said, "Call him here." And they called the blind man, saying to him, "Take heart; get up, he is calling you." 50So throwing off his cloak, he sprang up and came to Jesus. 51Then Jesus said to him, "What do you want me to do for you?" The blind man said to him, "My teacher,a let me see again." 52Jesus said to him, "Go; your faith has made you well." Immediately he regained his sight and followed him on the way.

a Aramaic Rabbouni

Jesus' Triumphal Entry into Jerusalem

11 When they were approaching Jerusalem, at Bethphage and Bethany, near the Mount of Olives, he sent two of his disciples 2and said to them, "Go into the village ahead of you, and immediately as you enter it, you will find tied there a colt that has never been ridden; untie it and bring it. 3If anyone says to you, 'Why are you doing this?' just say this, 'The Lord needs it and will send it back here immediately.' " 4They went away and found a colt tied near a door, outside in the street. As they were untying it, 5some of the bystanders said to them, "What are you doing, untying the colt?" 6They told them what Jesus had said; and they allowed them to take it. 7Then they brought the colt to Jesus and threw their cloaks on it; and he sat on it. 8Many people spread their cloaks on the road, and others spread leafy branches that they had cut in the fields. 9Then those who went ahead and those who followed were shouting,

"Hosanna!
Blessed is the one who comes in the name of the Lord!
10 Blessed is the coming kingdom of our ancestor David!
Hosanna in the highest heaven!"

11 Then he entered Jerusalem and went into the temple; and when he had looked around at everything, as it was already late, he went out to Bethany with the twelve.

Jesus Curses the Fig Tree

12 On the following day, when they came from Bethany, he was hungry. 13Seeing in the distance a fig tree in leaf, he went to see whether perhaps he would find anything on it. When he came to it, he found nothing but leaves, for it was not the season for figs. 14He said to it, "May no one ever eat fruit from you again." And his disciples heard it.

Jesus Cleanses the Temple

15 Then they came to Jerusalem. And he entered the temple and began to drive out

those who were selling and those who were buying in the temple, and he overturned the tables of the money changers and the seats of those who sold doves; ¹⁶and he would not allow anyone to carry anything through the temple. ¹⁷He was teaching and saying, "Is it not written,

'My house shall be called a house of
     prayer for all the nations'?
But you have made it a den of
     robbers."

¹⁸And when the chief priests and the scribes heard it, they kept looking for a way to kill him; for they were afraid of him, because the whole crowd was spellbound by his teaching. ¹⁹And when evening came, Jesus and his disciples *a* went out of the city.

The Lesson from the Withered Fig Tree

20 In the morning as they passed by, they saw the fig tree withered away to its roots. ²¹Then Peter remembered and said to him, "Rabbi, look! The fig tree that you cursed has withered." ²²Jesus answered them, "Have *b* faith in God. ²³Truly I tell you, if you say to this mountain, 'Be taken up and thrown into the sea,' and if you do not doubt in your heart, but believe that what you say will come to pass, it will be done for you. ²⁴So I tell you, whatever you ask for in prayer, believe that you have received *c* it, and it will be yours.

25 "Whenever you stand praying, forgive, if you have anything against anyone; so that your Father in heaven may also forgive you your trespasses." *d*

Jesus' Authority Is Questioned

27 Again they came to Jerusalem. As he was walking in the temple, the chief priests, the scribes, and the elders came to him ²⁸and said, "By what authority are you doing these things? Who gave you this authority to do them?" ²⁹Jesus said to them, "I will ask you one question; answer me, and I will tell you by what authority I do these things. ³⁰Did the

baptism of John come from heaven, or was it of human origin? Answer me." ³¹They argued with one another, "If we say, 'From heaven,' he will say, 'Why then did you not believe him?' ³²But shall we say, 'Of human origin'?"—they were afraid of the crowd, for all regarded John as truly a prophet. ³³So they answered Jesus, "We do not know." And Jesus said to them, "Neither will I tell you by what authority I am doing these things."

The Parable of the Wicked Tenants

12 Then he began to speak to them in parables. "A man planted a vineyard, put a fence around it, dug a pit for the wine press, and built a watchtower; then he leased it to tenants and went to another country. ²When the season came, he sent a slave to the tenants to collect from them his share of the produce of the vineyard. ³But they seized him, and beat him, and sent him away empty-handed. ⁴And again he sent another slave to them; this one they beat over the head and insulted. ⁵Then he sent another, and that one they killed. And so it was with many others; some they beat, and others they killed. ⁶He had still one other, a beloved son. Finally he sent him to them, saying, 'They will respect my son.' ⁷But those tenants said to one another, 'This is the heir; come, let us kill him, and the inheritance will be ours.' ⁸So they seized him, killed him, and threw him out of the vineyard. ⁹What then will the owner of the vineyard do? He will come and destroy the tenants and give the vineyard to others. ¹⁰Have you not read this scripture:

'The stone that the builders rejected
     has become the cornerstone; *e*
¹¹ this was the Lord's doing,
     and it is amazing in our eyes'?"

12 When they realized that he had told this parable against them, they wanted to arrest him, but they feared the crowd. So they left him and went away.

---

a Gk *they*: other ancient authorities read *he*   *b* Other ancient authorities read "*If you have*"   *c* Other ancient authorities read *are receiving*   *d* Other ancient authorities add verse 26, "*But if you do not forgive, neither will your Father in heaven forgive your trespasses.*"   *e* Or *keystone*

The Question about Paying Taxes

13 Then they sent to him some Pharisees and some Herodians to trap him in what he said. [14]And they came and said to him, "Teacher, we know that you are sincere, and show deference to no one; for you do not regard people with partiality, but teach the way of God in accordance with truth. Is it lawful to pay taxes to the emperor, or not? [15]Should we pay them, or should we not?" But knowing their hypocrisy, he said to them, "Why are you putting me to the test? Bring me a denarius and let me see it." [16]And they brought one. Then he said to them, "Whose head is this, and whose title?" They answered, "The emperor's." [17]Jesus said to them, "Give to the emperor the things that are the emperor's, and to God the things that are God's." And they were utterly amazed at him.

The Question about the Resurrection

18 Some Sadducees, who say there is no resurrection, came to him and asked him a question, saying, [19]"Teacher, Moses wrote for us that if a man's brother dies, leaving a wife but no child, the man[a] shall marry the widow and raise up children for his brother. [20]There were seven brothers; the first married and, when he died, left no children; [21]and the second married the widow[b] and died, leaving no children; and the third likewise; [22]none of the seven left children. Last of all the woman herself died. [23]In the resurrection[c] whose wife will she be? For the seven had married her."

24 Jesus said to them, "Is not this the reason you are wrong, that you know neither the scriptures nor the power of God? [25]For when they rise from the dead, they neither marry nor are given in marriage, but are like angels in heaven. [26]And as for the dead being raised, have you not read in the book of Moses, in the story about the bush, how God said to him, 'I am the God of Abraham, the God of Isaac, and the God of Jacob'? [27]He is God not of the dead, but of the living; you are quite wrong."

The First Commandment

28 One of the scribes came near and heard them disputing with one another, and seeing that he answered them well, he asked him, "Which commandment is the first of all?" [29]Jesus answered, "The first is, 'Hear, O Israel: the Lord our God, the Lord is one; [30]you shall love the Lord your God with all your heart, and with all your soul, and with all your mind, and with all your strength.' [31]The second is this, 'You shall love your neighbor as yourself.' There is no other commandment greater than these." [32]Then the scribe said to him, "You are right, Teacher; you have truly said that 'he is one, and besides him there is no other'; [33]and 'to love him with all the heart, and with all the understanding, and with all the strength,' and 'to love one's neighbor as oneself,'—this is much more important than all whole burnt offerings and sacrifices." [34]When Jesus saw that he answered wisely, he said to him, "You are not far from the kingdom of God." After that no one dared to ask him any question.

The Question about David's Son

35 While Jesus was teaching in the temple, he said, "How can the scribes say that the Messiah[d] is the son of David? [36]David himself, by the Holy Spirit, declared,

'The Lord said to my Lord,
    "Sit at my right hand,
        until I put your enemies under your
            feet." '

[37]David himself calls him Lord; so how can he be his son?" And the large crowd was listening to him with delight.

Jesus Denounces the Scribes

38 As he taught, he said, "Beware of the scribes, who like to walk around in long robes, and to be greeted with respect in the marketplaces, [39]and to have the best seats in the synagogues and places of honor at banquets! [40]They devour widows' houses and for the sake of appearance say long prayers. They will receive the greater condemnation."

---

a Gk *his brother*   b Gk *her*   c Other ancient authorities add *when they rise*   d Or *the Christ*

The Widow's Offering

41 He sat down opposite the treasury, and watched the crowd putting money into the treasury. Many rich people put in large sums. 42A poor widow came and put in two small copper coins, which are worth a penny. 43Then he called his disciples and said to them, "Truly I tell you, this poor widow has put in more than all those who are contributing to the treasury. 44For all of them have contributed out of their abundance; but she out of her poverty has put in everything she had, all she had to live on."

The Destruction of the Temple Foretold

13 As he came out of the temple, one of his disciples said to him, "Look, Teacher, what large stones and what large buildings!" 2Then Jesus asked him, "Do you see these great buildings? Not one stone will be left here upon another; all will be thrown down."

3 When he was sitting on the Mount of Olives opposite the temple, Peter, James, John, and Andrew asked him privately, 4"Tell us, when will this be, and what will be the sign that all these things are about to be accomplished?" 5Then Jesus began to say to them, "Beware that no one leads you astray. 6Many will come in my name and say, 'I am he!'*a* and they will lead many astray. 7When you hear of wars and rumors of wars, do not be alarmed; this must take place, but the end is still to come. 8For nation will rise against nation, and kingdom against kingdom; there will be earthquakes in various places; there will be famines. This is but the beginning of the birth pangs.

Persecution Foretold

9 "As for yourselves, beware; for they will hand you over to councils; and you will be beaten in synagogues; and you will stand before governors and kings because of me, as a testimony to them. 10And the good news*b* must first be proclaimed to all nations. 11When they bring you to trial and hand you over, do not worry beforehand about what you are to say; but say whatever is given you at that time, for it is not you who speak, but the Holy Spirit. 12Brother will betray brother to death, and a father his child, and children will rise against parents and have them put to death; 13and you will be hated by all because of my name. But the one who endures to the end will be saved.

The Desolating Sacrilege

14 "But when you see the desolating sacrilege set up where it ought not to be (let the reader understand), then those in Judea must flee to the mountains; 15the one on the housetop must not go down or enter the house to take anything away; 16the one in the field must not turn back to get a coat. 17Woe to those who are pregnant and to those who are nursing infants in those days! 18Pray that it may not be in winter. 19For in those days there will be suffering, such as has not been from the beginning of the creation that God created until now, no, and never will be. 20And if the Lord had not cut short those days, no one would be saved; but for the sake of the elect, whom he chose, he has cut short those days. 21And if anyone says to you at that time, 'Look! Here is the Messiah!'*c* or 'Look! There he is!'—do not believe it. 22False messiahs*d* and false prophets will appear and produce signs and omens, to lead astray, if possible, the elect. 23But be alert; I have already told you everything.

The Coming of the Son of Man

24 "But in those days, after that suffering,
the sun will be darkened,
and the moon will not give its light,
25 and the stars will be falling from heaven,
and the powers in the heavens will
be shaken.

26Then they will see 'the Son of Man coming in clouds' with great power and glory. 27Then he will send out the angels, and gather his elect from the four winds, from the ends of the earth to the ends of heaven.

a Gk I am   *b* Gk gospel   *c* Or the Christ   *d* Or christs

The Lesson of the Fig Tree

28 "From the fig tree learn its lesson: as soon as its branch becomes tender and puts forth its leaves, you know that summer is near. ²⁹So also, when you see these things taking place, you know that he*ᵃ* is near, at the very gates. ³⁰Truly I tell you, this generation will not pass away until all these things have taken place. ³¹Heaven and earth will pass away, but my words will not pass away.

The Necessity for Watchfulness

32 "But about that day or hour no one knows, neither the angels in heaven, nor the Son, but only the Father. ³³Beware, keep alert;*ᵇ* for you do not know when the time will come. ³⁴It is like a man going on a journey, when he leaves home and puts his slaves in charge, each with his work, and commands the doorkeeper to be on the watch. ³⁵Therefore, keep awake—for you do not know when the master of the house will come, in the evening, or at midnight, or at cockcrow, or at dawn, ³⁶or else he may find you asleep when he comes suddenly. ³⁷And what I say to you I say to all: Keep awake."

The Plot to Kill Jesus

14 It was two days before the Passover and the festival of Unleavened Bread. The chief priests and the scribes were looking for a way to arrest Jesus*ᶜ* by stealth and kill him; ²for they said, "Not during the festival, or there may be a riot among the people."

The Anointing at Bethany

3 While he was at Bethany in the house of Simon the leper,*ᵈ* as he sat at the table, a woman came with an alabaster jar of very costly ointment of nard, and she broke open the jar and poured the ointment on his head. ⁴But some were there who said to one another in anger, "Why was the ointment wasted in this way? ⁵For this ointment could have been sold for more than three hundred denarii,*ᵉ* and the money given to the poor."

And they scolded her. ⁶But Jesus said, "Let her alone; why do you trouble her? She has performed a good service for me. ⁷For you always have the poor with you, and you can show kindness to them whenever you wish; but you will not always have me. ⁸She has done what she could; she has anointed my body beforehand for its burial. ⁹Truly I tell you, wherever the good news*ᶠ* is proclaimed in the whole world, what she has done will be told in remembrance of her."

Judas Agrees to Betray Jesus

10 Then Judas Iscariot, who was one of the twelve, went to the chief priests in order to betray him to them. ¹¹When they heard it, they were greatly pleased, and promised to give him money. So he began to look for an opportunity to betray him.

The Passover with the Disciples

12 On the first day of Unleavened Bread, when the Passover lamb is sacrificed, his disciples said to him, "Where do you want us to go and make the preparations for you to eat the Passover?" ¹³So he sent two of his disciples, saying to them, "Go into the city, and a man carrying a jar of water will meet you; follow him, ¹⁴and wherever he enters, say to the owner of the house, 'The Teacher asks, Where is my guest room where I may eat the Passover with my disciples?' ¹⁵He will show you a large room upstairs, furnished and ready. Make preparations for us there." ¹⁶So the disciples set out and went to the city, and found everything as he had told them; and they prepared the Passover meal.

17 When it was evening, he came with the twelve. ¹⁸And when they had taken their places and were eating, Jesus said, "Truly I tell you, one of you will betray me, one who is eating with me." ¹⁹They began to be distressed and to say to him one after another, "Surely, not I?" ²⁰He said to them, "It is one of the twelve, one who is dipping bread*ᵍ*

into the bowl*a* with me. 21For the Son of Man goes as it is written of him, but woe to that one by whom the Son of Man is betrayed! It would have been better for that one not to have been born."

The Institution of the Lord's Supper

22 While they were eating, he took a loaf of bread, and after blessing it he broke it, gave it to them, and said, "Take; this is my body." 23Then he took a cup, and after giving thanks he gave it to them, and all of them drank from it. 24He said to them, "This is my blood of the *b* covenant, which is poured out for many. 25Truly I tell you, I will never again drink of the fruit of the vine until that day when I drink it new in the kingdom of God."

Peter's Denial Foretold

26 When they had sung the hymn, they went out to the Mount of Olives. 27And Jesus said to them, "You will all become deserters; for it is written,

'I will strike the shepherd,
　and the sheep will be scattered.'

28But after I am raised up, I will go before you to Galilee." 29Peter said to him, "Even though all become deserters, I will not." 30Jesus said to him, "Truly I tell you, this day, this very night, before the cock crows twice, you will deny me three times." 31But he said vehemently, "Even though I must die with you, I will not deny you." And all of them said the same.

Jesus Prays in Gethsemane

32 They went to a place called Gethsemane; and he said to his disciples, "Sit here while I pray." 33He took with him Peter and James and John, and began to be distressed and agitated. 34And he said to them, "I am deeply grieved, even to death; remain here, and keep awake." 35And going a little farther, he threw himself on the ground and prayed that, if it were possible, the hour might pass from him. 36He said, "Abba,*c* Father, for you all things are possible; remove this cup from

me; yet, not what I want, but what you want." 37He came and found them sleeping; and he said to Peter, "Simon, are you asleep? Could you not keep awake one hour? 38Keep awake and pray that you may not come into the time of trial;*d* the spirit indeed is willing, but the flesh is weak." 39And again he went away and prayed, saying the same words. 40And once more he came and found them sleeping, for their eyes were very heavy; and they did not know what to say to him. 41He came a third time and said to them, "Are you still sleeping and taking your rest? Enough! The hour has come; the Son of Man is betrayed into the hands of sinners. 42Get up, let us be going. See, my betrayer is at hand."

The Betrayal and Arrest of Jesus

43 Immediately, while he was still speaking, Judas, one of the twelve, arrived; and with him there was a crowd with swords and clubs, from the chief priests, the scribes, and the elders. 44Now the betrayer had given them a sign, saying, "The one I will kiss is the man; arrest him and lead him away under guard." 45So when he came, he went up to him at once and said, "Rabbi!" and kissed him. 46Then they laid hands on him and arrested him. 47But one of those who stood near drew his sword and struck the slave of the high priest, cutting off his ear. 48Then Jesus said to them, "Have you come out with swords and clubs to arrest me as though I were a bandit? 49Day after day I was with you in the temple teaching, and you did not arrest me. But let the scriptures be fulfilled." 50All of them deserted him and fled.

51 A certain young man was following him, wearing nothing but a linen cloth. They caught hold of him, 52but he left the linen cloth and ran off naked.

Jesus before the Council

53 They took Jesus to the high priest; and all the chief priests, the elders, and the scribes were assembled. 54Peter had followed him

---

a Other ancient authorities read *same bowl*　　*b* Other ancient authorities add *new*　　*c* Aramaic for *Father*
d Or *into temptation*

at a distance, right into the courtyard of the high priest; and he was sitting with the guards, warming himself at the fire. 55Now the chief priests and the whole council were looking for testimony against Jesus to put him to death; but they found none. 56For many gave false testimony against him, and their testimony did not agree. 57Some stood up and gave false testimony against him, saying, 58"We heard him say, 'I will destroy this temple that is made with hands, and in three days I will build another, not made with hands.' " 59But even on this point their testimony did not agree. 60Then the high priest stood up before them and asked Jesus, "Have you no answer? What is it that they testify against you?" 61But he was silent and did not answer. Again the high priest asked him, "Are you the Messiah,*a* the Son of the Blessed One?" 62Jesus said, "I am; and

'you will see the Son of Man
   seated at the right hand of the Power,'
and 'coming with the clouds of
   heaven.' "

63Then the high priest tore his clothes and said, "Why do we still need witnesses? 64You have heard his blasphemy! What is your decision?" All of them condemned him as deserving death. 65Some began to spit on him, to blindfold him, and to strike him, saying to him, "Prophesy!" The guards also took him over and beat him.

Peter Denies Jesus

66 While Peter was below in the courtyard, one of the servant-girls of the high priest came by. 67When she saw Peter warming himself, she stared at him and said, "You also were with Jesus, the man from Nazareth." 68But he denied it, saying, "I do not know or understand what you are talking about." And he went out into the forecourt.*b* Then the cock crowed.*c* 69And the servant-girl, on seeing him, began again to say to the bystanders, "This man is one of them." 70But again he denied it. Then after a little while the bystanders again said to Peter, "Certainly you are one of them; for you are a Galilean." 71But he began to curse, and he swore an oath, "I do not know this man you are talking about." 72At that moment the cock crowed for the second time. Then Peter remembered that Jesus had said to him, "Before the cock crows twice, you will deny me three times." And he broke down and wept.

Jesus before Pilate

15 As soon as it was morning, the chief priests held a consultation with the elders and scribes and the whole council. They bound Jesus, led him away, and handed him over to Pilate. 2Pilate asked him, "Are you the King of the Jews?" He answered him, "You say so." 3Then the chief priests accused him of many things. 4Pilate asked him again, "Have you no answer? See how many charges they bring against you." 5But Jesus made no further reply, so that Pilate was amazed.

Pilate Hands Jesus over to Be Crucified

6 Now at the festival he used to release a prisoner for them, anyone for whom they asked. 7Now a man called Barabbas was in prison with the rebels who had committed murder during the insurrection. 8So the crowd came and began to ask Pilate to do for them according to his custom. 9Then he answered them, "Do you want me to release for you the King of the Jews?" 10For he realized that it was out of jealousy that the chief priests had handed him over. 11But the chief priests stirred up the crowd to have him release Barabbas for them instead. 12Pilate spoke to them again, "Then what do you wish me to do*d* with the man you call*e* the King of the Jews?" 13They shouted back, "Crucify him!" 14Pilate asked them, "Why, what evil has he done?" But they shouted all the more, "Crucify him!" 15So Pilate, wishing to satisfy the crowd, released Barabbas for them; and after flogging Jesus, he handed him over to be crucified.

---

a Or *the Christ*   *b* Or *gateway*   *c* Other ancient authorities lack *Then the cock crowed*   *d* Other ancient
authorities read *what should I do*   *e* Other ancient authorities lack *the man you call*

The Soldiers Mock Jesus

16 Then the soldiers led him into the courtyard of the palace (that is, the governor's headquarters*ᵃ*); and they called together the whole cohort. 17And they clothed him in a purple cloak; and after twisting some thorns into a crown, they put it on him. 18And they began saluting him, "Hail, King of the Jews!" 19They struck his head with a reed, spat upon him, and knelt down in homage to him. 20After mocking him, they stripped him of the purple cloak and put his own clothes on him. Then they led him out to crucify him.

The Crucifixion of Jesus

21 They compelled a passer-by, who was coming in from the country, to carry his cross; it was Simon of Cyrene, the father of Alexander and Rufus. 22Then they brought Jesus*ᵇ* to the place called Golgotha (which means the place of a skull). 23And they offered him wine mixed with myrrh; but he did not take it. 24And they crucified him, and divided his clothes among them, casting lots to decide what each should take.

25 It was nine o'clock in the morning when they crucified him. 26The inscription of the charge against him read, "The King of the Jews." 27And with him they crucified two bandits, one on his right and one on his left.*ᶜ* 29Those who passed by derided*ᵈ* him, shaking their heads and saying, "Aha! You who would destroy the temple and build it in three days, 30save yourself, and come down from the cross!" 31In the same way the chief priests, along with the scribes, were also mocking him among themselves and saying, "He saved others; he cannot save himself. 32Let the Messiah,*ᵉ* the King of Israel, come down from the cross now, so that we may see and believe." Those who were crucified with him also taunted him.

The Death of Jesus

33 When it was noon, darkness came over the whole land*ᶠ* until three in the afternoon. 34At three o'clock Jesus cried out with a loud voice, "Eloi, Eloi, lema sabachthani?" which means, "My God, my God, why have you forsaken me?"*ᵍ* 35When some of the bystanders heard it, they said, "Listen, he is calling for Elijah." 36And someone ran, filled a sponge with sour wine, put it on a stick, and gave it to him to drink, saying, "Wait, let us see whether Elijah will come to take him down." 37Then Jesus gave a loud cry and breathed his last. 38And the curtain of the temple was torn in two, from top to bottom. 39Now when the centurion, who stood facing him, saw that in this way he*ʰ* breathed his last, he said, "Truly this man was God's Son!"*ⁱ*

40 There were also women looking on from a distance; among them were Mary Magdalene, and Mary the mother of James the younger and of Joses, and Salome. 41These used to follow him and provided for him when he was in Galilee; and there were many other women who had come up with him to Jerusalem.

The Burial of Jesus

42 When evening had come, and since it was the day of Preparation, that is, the day before the sabbath, 43Joseph of Arimathea, a respected member of the council, who was also himself waiting expectantly for the kingdom of God, went boldly to Pilate and asked for the body of Jesus. 44Then Pilate wondered if he were already dead; and summoning the centurion, he asked him whether he had been dead for some time. 45When he learned from the centurion that he was dead, he granted the body to Joseph. 46Then Joseph*ʲ* bought a linen cloth, and taking down the body,*ᵏ* wrapped it in the linen cloth, and laid it in a tomb that had been hewn out of the rock. He then rolled a stone against the door of the tomb. 47Mary Magdalene and Mary the mother of Joses saw where the body*ᵏ* was laid.

a Gk *the praetorium*   b Gk *him*   c Other ancient authorities add verse 28, *And the scripture was fulfilled that says, "And he was counted among the lawless."*   d Or *blasphemed*   e Or *the Christ*   f Or *earth*   g Other ancient authorities read *made me a reproach*   h Other ancient authorities add *cried out and*   i Or *a son of God*   j Gk *he*   k Gk *it*

The Resurrection of Jesus

16 When the sabbath was over, Mary Magdalene, and Mary the mother of James, and Salome bought spices, so that they might go and anoint him. 2And very early on the first day of the week, when the sun had risen, they went to the tomb. 3They had been saying to one another, "Who will roll away the stone for us from the entrance to the tomb?" 4When they looked up, they saw that the stone, which was very large, had already been rolled back. 5As they entered the tomb, they saw a young man, dressed in a white robe, sitting on the right side; and they were alarmed. 6But he said to them, "Do not be alarmed; you are looking for Jesus of Nazareth, who was crucified. He has been raised; he is not here. Look, there is the place they laid him. 7But go, tell his disciples and Peter that he is going ahead of you to Galilee; there you will see him, just as he told you." 8So they went out and fled from the tomb, for terror and amazement had seized them; and they said nothing to anyone, for they were afraid. *a*

THE SHORTER ENDING OF MARK

⟦And all that had been commanded them they told briefly to those around Peter. And afterward Jesus himself sent out through them, from east to west, the sacred and imperishable proclamation of eternal salvation. *b*⟧

THE LONGER ENDING OF MARK

Jesus Appears to Mary Magdalene

9 ⟦Now after he rose early on the first day of the week, he appeared first to Mary Magdalene, from whom he had cast out seven demons. 10She went out and told those who had been with him, while they were mourning and weeping. 11But when they heard that he was alive and had been seen by her, they would not believe it.

Jesus Appears to Two Disciples

12 After this he appeared in another form to two of them, as they were walking into the country. 13And they went back and told the rest, but they did not believe them.

Jesus Commissions the Disciples

14 Later he appeared to the eleven themselves as they were sitting at the table; and he upbraided them for their lack of faith and stubbornness, because they had not believed those who saw him after he had risen. *c* 15And he said to them, "Go into all the world and proclaim the good news *d* to the whole creation. 16The one who believes and is baptized will be saved; but the one who does not believe will be condemned. 17And these signs will accompany those who believe: by using my name they will cast out demons; they will speak in new tongues; 18they will pick up snakes in their hands, *e* and if they drink any deadly thing, it will not hurt them; they will lay their hands on the sick, and they will recover."

The Ascension of Jesus

19 So then the Lord Jesus, after he had spoken to them, was taken up into heaven and sat down at the right hand of God. 20And they went out and proclaimed the good news everywhere, while the Lord worked with them and confirmed the message by the signs that accompanied it. *b*⟧

---

a Some of the most ancient authorities bring the book to a close at the end of verse 8. One authority concludes the book with the shorter ending; others include the shorter ending and then continue with verses 9-20. In most authorities verses 9-20 follow immediately after verse 8, though in some of these authorities the passage is marked as being doubtful.   *b* Other ancient authorities add *Amen*   *c* Other ancient authorities add, in whole or in part, *And they excused themselves, saying, "This age of lawlessness and unbelief is under Satan, who does not allow the truth and power of God to prevail over the unclean things of the spirits. Therefore reveal your righteousness now"—thus they spoke to Christ. And Christ replied to them, "The term of years of Satan's power has been fulfilled, but other terrible things draw near. And for those who have sinned I was handed over to death, that they may return to the truth and sin no more, that they may inherit the spiritual and imperishable glory of righteousness that is in heaven."*   *d* Or *gospel*   *e* Other ancient authorities lack *in their hands*

THE GOSPEL ACCORDING TO
LUKE

Dedication to Theophilus

1 Since many have undertaken to set down an orderly account of the events that have been fulfilled among us, ²just as they were handed on to us by those who from the beginning were eyewitnesses and servants of the word, ³I too decided, after investigating everything carefully from the very first,*a* to write an orderly account for you, most excellent Theophilus, ⁴so that you may know the truth concerning the things about which you have been instructed.

The Birth of John the Baptist Foretold

5 In the days of King Herod of Judea, there was a priest named Zechariah, who belonged to the priestly order of Abijah. His wife was a descendant of Aaron, and her name was Elizabeth. ⁶Both of them were righteous before God, living blamelessly according to all the commandments and regulations of the Lord. ⁷But they had no children, because Elizabeth was barren, and both were getting on in years.

8 Once when he was serving as priest before God and his section was on duty, ⁹he was chosen by lot, according to the custom of the priesthood, to enter the sanctuary of the Lord and offer incense. ¹⁰Now at the time of the incense offering, the whole assembly of the people was praying outside. ¹¹Then there appeared to him an angel of the Lord, standing at the right side of the altar of incense. ¹²When Zechariah saw him, he was terrified; and fear overwhelmed him. ¹³But the angel said to him, "Do not be afraid, Zechariah, for your prayer has been heard. Your wife Elizabeth will bear you a son, and you will name him John. ¹⁴You will have joy and gladness, and many will rejoice at his birth, ¹⁵for he will be great in the sight of the Lord. He must never drink wine or strong drink; even before his birth he will be filled with the Holy Spirit. ¹⁶He will turn many of the people of Is-rael to the Lord their God. ¹⁷With the spirit and power of Elijah he will go before him, to turn the hearts of parents to their children, and the disobedient to the wisdom of the righteous, to make ready a people prepared for the Lord." ¹⁸Zechariah said to the angel, "How will I know that this is so? For I am an old man, and my wife is getting on in years." ¹⁹The angel replied, "I am Gabriel. I stand in the presence of God, and I have been sent to speak to you and to bring you this good news. ²⁰But now, because you did not believe my words, which will be fulfilled in their time, you will become mute, unable to speak, until the day these things occur."

21 Meanwhile the people were waiting for Zechariah, and wondered at his delay in the sanctuary. ²²When he did come out, he could not speak to them, and they realized that he had seen a vision in the sanctuary. He kept motioning to them and remained unable to speak. ²³When his time of service was ended, he went to his home.

24 After those days his wife Elizabeth conceived, and for five months she remained in seclusion. She said, ²⁵"This is what the Lord has done for me when he looked favorably on me and took away the disgrace I have endured among my people."

The Birth of Jesus Foretold

26 In the sixth month the angel Gabriel was sent by God to a town in Galilee called Nazareth, ²⁷to a virgin engaged to a man whose name was Joseph, of the house of David. The virgin's name was Mary. ²⁸And he came to her and said, "Greetings, favored one! The Lord is with you."*b* ²⁹But she was much perplexed by his words and pondered what sort of greeting this might be. ³⁰The angel said to her, "Do not be afraid, Mary, for you have found favor with God. ³¹And now, you will conceive in your womb and bear a son, and you will name him Jesus. ³²He will

a Or *for a long time*   *b* Other ancient authorities add *Blessed are you among women* be great, and will be called the Son of the Most High, and the Lord God will give to him the throne of his ancestor David. ³³He will reign over the house of Jacob forever, and of his kingdom there will be no end." ³⁴Mary said to the angel, "How can this be, since I am a virgin?"*a* ³⁵The angel said to her, "The Holy Spirit will come upon you, and the power of the Most High will overshadow you; therefore the child to be born*b* will be holy; he will be called Son of God. ³⁶And now, your relative Elizabeth in her old age has also conceived a son; and this is the sixth month for her who was said to be barren. ³⁷For nothing will be impossible with God." ³⁸Then Mary said, "Here am I, the servant of the Lord; let it be with me according to your word." Then the angel departed from her.

Mary Visits Elizabeth

39 In those days Mary set out and went with haste to a Judean town in the hill country, ⁴⁰where she entered the house of Zechariah and greeted Elizabeth. ⁴¹When Elizabeth heard Mary's greeting, the child leaped in her womb. And Elizabeth was filled with the Holy Spirit ⁴²and exclaimed with a loud cry, "Blessed are you among women, and blessed is the fruit of your womb. ⁴³And why has this happened to me, that the mother of my Lord comes to me? ⁴⁴For as soon as I heard the sound of your greeting, the child in my womb leaped for joy. ⁴⁵And blessed is she who believed that there would be*c* a fulfillment of what was spoken to her by the Lord."

Mary's Song of Praise

46 And Mary*d* said,
"My soul magnifies the Lord,
47   and my spirit rejoices in God my
          Savior,
48   for he has looked with favor on the
          lowliness of his servant.

Surely, from now on all generations
          will call me blessed;
49   for the Mighty One has done great
          things for me,
       and holy is his name.
50   His mercy is for those who fear him
       from generation to generation.
51   He has shown strength with his arm;
       he has scattered the proud in the
          thoughts of their hearts.
52   He has brought down the powerful
          from their thrones,
       and lifted up the lowly;
53   he has filled the hungry with good
          things,
       and sent the rich away empty.
54   He has helped his servant Israel,
       in remembrance of his mercy,
55   according to the promise he made to
          our ancestors,
       to Abraham and to his descendants
          forever."

56 And Mary remained with her about three months and then returned to her home.

The Birth of John the Baptist

57 Now the time came for Elizabeth to give birth, and she bore a son. ⁵⁸Her neighbors and relatives heard that the Lord had shown his great mercy to her, and they rejoiced with her.

59 On the eighth day they came to circumcise the child, and they were going to name him Zechariah after his father. ⁶⁰But his mother said, "No; he is to be called John." ⁶¹They said to her, "None of your relatives has this name." ⁶²Then they began motioning to his father to find out what name he wanted to give him. ⁶³He asked for a writing tablet and wrote, "His name is John." And all of them were amazed. ⁶⁴Immediately his mouth was opened and his tongue freed, and he began to speak, praising God. ⁶⁵Fear came over all their neighbors, and all these things were talked about throughout the entire hill country of Judea. ⁶⁶All who heard them pon-

---

a Gk *I do not know a man*   *b* Other ancient authorities add *of you*   *c* Or *believed, for there will be*   *d* Other ancient authorities read *Elizabeth* dered them and said, "What then will this child become?" For, indeed, the hand of the Lord was with him.

Zechariah's Prophecy

67 Then his father Zechariah was filled with the Holy Spirit and spoke this prophecy:

68   "Blessed be the Lord God of Israel,
        for he has looked favorably on his
            people and redeemed them.
69   He has raised up a mighty savior[a] for
            us
        in the house of his servant David,
70   as he spoke through the mouth of his
            holy prophets from of old,
71   that we would be saved from our
            enemies and from the hand of
            all who hate us.
72   Thus he has shown the mercy
            promised to our ancestors,
        and has remembered his holy
            covenant,
73   the oath that he swore to our ancestor
            Abraham,
        to grant us 74that we, being rescued
            from the hands of our enemies,
        might serve him without fear, 75in
            holiness and righteousness
        before him all our days.
76   And you, child, will be called the
            prophet of the Most High;
        for you will go before the Lord to
            prepare his ways,
77   to give knowledge of salvation to his
            people
        by the forgiveness of their sins.
78   By the tender mercy of our God,
        the dawn from on high will break
            upon[b] us,
79   to give light to those who sit in
            darkness and in the shadow of
            death,
        to guide our feet into the way of
            peace."
80 The child grew and became strong in

spirit, and he was in the wilderness until the day he appeared publicly to Israel.

The Birth of Jesus

2 In those days a decree went out from Emperor Augustus that all the world should be registered. 2This was the first registration and was taken while Quirinius was governor of Syria. 3All went to their own towns to be registered. 4Joseph also went from the town of Nazareth in Galilee to Judea, to the city of David called Bethlehem, because he was descended from the house and family of David. 5He went to be registered with Mary, to whom he was engaged and who was expecting a child. 6While they were there, the time came for her to deliver her child. 7And she gave birth to her firstborn son and wrapped him in bands of cloth, and laid him in a manger, because there was no place for them in the inn.

The Shepherds and the Angels

8 In that region there were shepherds living in the fields, keeping watch over their flock by night. 9Then an angel of the Lord stood before them, and the glory of the Lord shone around them, and they were terrified. 10But the angel said to them, "Do not be afraid; for see—I am bringing you good news of great joy for all the people: 11to you is born this day in the city of David a Savior, who is the Messiah,[c] the Lord. 12This will be a sign for you: you will find a child wrapped in bands of cloth and lying in a manger." 13And suddenly there was with the angel a multitude of the heavenly host,[d] praising God and saying,

14   "Glory to God in the highest heaven,
        and on earth peace among those
            whom he favors!"[e]

15 When the angels had left them and gone into heaven, the shepherds said to one another, "Let us go now to Bethlehem and see this thing that has taken place, which the Lord has made known to us." 16So they went with haste

---

a Gk a horn of salvation   b Other ancient authorities read has broken upon   c Or the Christ   d Gk army
e Other ancient authorities read peace, goodwill among people

and found Mary and Joseph, and the child lying in the manger. [17]When they saw this, they made known what had been told them about this child; [18]and all who heard it were amazed at what the shepherds told them. [19]But Mary treasured all these words and pondered them in her heart. [20]The shepherds returned, glorifying and praising God for all they had heard and seen, as it had been told them.

Jesus Is Named

21 After eight days had passed, it was time to circumcise the child; and he was called Jesus, the name given by the angel before he was conceived in the womb.

Jesus Is Presented in the Temple

22 When the time came for their purification according to the law of Moses, they brought him up to Jerusalem to present him to the Lord [23](as it is written in the law of the Lord, "Every firstborn male shall be designated as holy to the Lord"), [24]and they offered a sacrifice according to what is stated in the law of the Lord, "a pair of turtledoves or two young pigeons."

25 Now there was a man in Jerusalem whose name was Simeon;[a] this man was righteous and devout, looking forward to the consolation of Israel, and the Holy Spirit rested on him. [26]It had been revealed to him by the Holy Spirit that he would not see death before he had seen the Lord's Messiah.[b] [27]Guided by the Spirit, Simeon[c] came into the temple; and when the parents brought in the child Jesus, to do for him what was customary under the law, [28]Simeon[d] took him in his arms and praised God, saying,

29   "Master, now you are dismissing your
            servant[e] in peace,
         according to your word;
30   for my eyes have seen your salvation,
31   which you have prepared in the
            presence of all peoples,
32   a light for revelation to the Gentiles
         and for glory to your people Israel."

33 And the child's father and mother were amazed at what was being said about him. [34]Then Simeon[a] blessed them and said to his mother Mary, "This child is destined for the falling and the rising of many in Israel, and to be a sign that will be opposed [35]so that the inner thoughts of many will be revealed—and a sword will pierce your own soul too."

36 There was also a prophet, Anna[f] the daughter of Phanuel, of the tribe of Asher. She was of a great age, having lived with her husband seven years after her marriage, [37]then as a widow to the age of eighty-four. She never left the temple but worshiped there with fasting and prayer night and day. [38]At that moment she came, and began to praise God and to speak about the child[g] to all who were looking for the redemption of Jerusalem.

The Return to Nazareth

39 When they had finished everything required by the law of the Lord, they returned to Galilee, to their own town of Nazareth. [40]The child grew and became strong, filled with wisdom; and the favor of God was upon him.

The Boy Jesus in the Temple

41 Now every year his parents went to Jerusalem for the festival of the Passover. [42]And when he was twelve years old, they went up as usual for the festival. [43]When the festival was ended and they started to return, the boy Jesus stayed behind in Jerusalem, but his parents did not know it. [44]Assuming that he was in the group of travelers, they went a day's journey. Then they started to look for him among their relatives and friends. [45]When they did not find him, they returned to Jerusalem to search for him. [46]After three days they found him in the temple, sitting among the teachers, listening to them and asking them questions. [47]And all who heard him were amazed at his understanding and

---

a Gk *Symeon*   *b* Or *the Lord's Christ*   *c* Gk *In the Spirit, he*   *d* Gk *he*   *e* Gk *slave*   *f* Gk *Hanna*   *g* Gk *him* his answers. 48When his parents*a* saw him they were astonished; and his mother said to him, "Child, why have you treated us like this? Look, your father and I have been searching for you in great anxiety." 49He said to them, "Why were you searching for me? Did you not know that I must be in my Father's house?"*b* 50But they did not understand what he said to them. 51Then he went down with them and came to Nazareth, and was obedient to them. His mother treasured all these things in her heart.

52 And Jesus increased in wisdom and in years,*c* and in divine and human favor.

The Proclamation of John the Baptist

3 In the fifteenth year of the reign of Emperor Tiberius, when Pontius Pilate was governor of Judea, and Herod was ruler*d* of Galilee, and his brother Philip ruler*d* of the region of Ituraea and Trachonitis, and Lysanias ruler*d* of Abilene, 2during the high priesthood of Annas and Caiaphas, the word of God came to John son of Zechariah in the wilderness. 3He went into all the region around the Jordan, proclaiming a baptism of repentance for the forgiveness of sins, 4as it is written in the book of the words of the prophet Isaiah,

"The voice of one crying out in the wilderness:
'Prepare the way of the Lord,
    make his paths straight.
5 Every valley shall be filled,
    and every mountain and hill shall be
        made low,
and the crooked shall be made straight,
    and the rough ways made smooth;
6 and all flesh shall see the salvation of
        God.' "

7 John said to the crowds that came out to be baptized by him, "You brood of vipers! Who warned you to flee from the wrath to come? 8Bear fruits worthy of repentance. Do not begin to say to yourselves, 'We have Abraham as our ancestor'; for I tell you, God

is able from these stones to raise up children to Abraham. 9Even now the ax is lying at the root of the trees; every tree therefore that does not bear good fruit is cut down and thrown into the fire."

10 And the crowds asked him, "What then should we do?" 11In reply he said to them, "Whoever has two coats must share with anyone who has none; and whoever has food must do likewise." 12Even tax collectors came to be baptized, and they asked him, "Teacher, what should we do?" 13He said to them, "Collect no more than the amount prescribed for you." 14Soldiers also asked him, "And we, what should we do?" He said to them, "Do not extort money from anyone by threats or false accusation, and be satisfied with your wages."

15 As the people were filled with expectation, and all were questioning in their hearts concerning John, whether he might be the Messiah,*e* 16John answered all of them by saying, "I baptize you with water; but one who is more powerful than I is coming; I am not worthy to untie the thong of his sandals. He will baptize you with*f* the Holy Spirit and fire. 17His winnowing fork is in his hand, to clear his threshing floor and to gather the wheat into his granary; but the chaff he will burn with unquenchable fire."

18 So, with many other exhortations, he proclaimed the good news to the people. 19But Herod the ruler,*f* who had been rebuked by him because of Herodias, his brother's wife, and because of all the evil things that Herod had done, 20added to them all by shutting up John in prison.

The Baptism of Jesus

21 Now when all the people were baptized, and when Jesus also had been baptized and was praying, the heaven was opened, 22and the Holy Spirit descended upon him in bodily form like a dove. And a voice came from heaven, "You are my Son, the Beloved;*g* with you I am well pleased."*h*

---

a Gk *they*   *b* Or *be about my Father's interests?*   *c* Or *in stature*   *d* Gk *tetrarch*   *e* Or *the Christ*   *f* Or *in*
g Or *my beloved Son*   *h* Other ancient authorities read *You are my Son, today I have begotten you*

The Ancestors of Jesus

23 Jesus was about thirty years old when he began his work. He was the son (as was thought) of Joseph son of Heli, 24son of Matthat, son of Levi, son of Melchi, son of Jannai, son of Joseph, 25son of Mattathias, son of Amos, son of Nahum, son of Esli, son of Naggai, 26son of Maath, son of Mattathias, son of Semein, son of Josech, son of Joda, 27son of Joanan, son of Rhesa, son of Zerubbabel, son of Shealtiel,*a* son of Neri, 28son of Melchi, son of Addi, son of Cosam, son of Elmadam, son of Er, 29son of Joshua, son of Eliezer, son of Jorim, son of Matthat, son of Levi, 30son of Simeon, son of Judah, son of Joseph, son of Jonam, son of Eliakim, 31son of Melea, son of Menna, son of Mattatha, son of Nathan, son of David, 32son of Jesse, son of Obed, son of Boaz, son of Sala,*b* son of Nahshon, 33son of Amminadab, son of Admin, son of Arni,*c* son of Hezron, son of Perez, son of Judah, 34son of Jacob, son of Isaac, son of Abraham, son of Terah, son of Nahor, 35son of Serug, son of Reu, son of Peleg, son of Eber, son of Shelah, 36son of Cainan, son of Arphaxad, son of Shem, son of Noah, son of Lamech, 37son of Methuselah, son of Enoch, son of Jared, son of Mahalaleel, son of Cainan, 38son of Enos, son of Seth, son of Adam, son of God.

The Temptation of Jesus

4 Jesus, full of the Holy Spirit, returned from the Jordan and was led by the Spirit in the wilderness, 2where for forty days he was tempted by the devil. He ate nothing at all during those days, and when they were over, he was famished. 3The devil said to him, "If you are the Son of God, command this stone to become a loaf of bread." 4Jesus answered him, "It is written, 'One does not live by bread alone.' "

5 Then the devil*d* led him up and showed him in an instant all the kingdoms of the world. 6And the devil*d* said to him, "To you

I will give their glory and all this authority; for it has been given over to me, and I give it to anyone I please. 7If you, then, will worship me, it will all be yours." 8Jesus answered him, "It is written,

'Worship the Lord your God,
    and serve only him.' "

9 Then the devil*d* took him to Jerusalem, and placed him on the pinnacle of the temple, saying to him, "If you are the Son of God, throw yourself down from here, 10for it is written,

'He will command his angels
        concerning you,
    to protect you,'

11and

'On their hands they will bear you up,
    so that you will not dash your foot
        against a stone.' "

12Jesus answered him, "It is said, 'Do not put the Lord your God to the test.' " 13When the devil had finished every test, he departed from him until an opportune time.

The Beginning of the Galilean Ministry

14 Then Jesus, filled with the power of the Spirit, returned to Galilee, and a report about him spread through all the surrounding country. 15He began to teach in their synagogues and was praised by everyone.

The Rejection of Jesus at Nazareth

16 When he came to Nazareth, where he had been brought up, he went to the synagogue on the sabbath day, as was his custom. He stood up to read, 17and the scroll of the prophet Isaiah was given to him. He unrolled the scroll and found the place where it was written:

18   "The Spirit of the Lord is upon me,
        because he has anointed me
            to bring good news to the poor.
        He has sent me to proclaim release to
            the captives
        and recovery of sight to the blind,
            to let the oppressed go free,

a Gk *Salathiel*   *b* Other ancient authorities read *Salmon Aram*; others vary widely   *d* Gk *he*   *c* Other ancient authorities read *Amminadab, son of*

19   to proclaim the year of the Lord's
          favor."
20 And he rolled up the scroll, gave it back to
the attendant, and sat down. The eyes of all
in the synagogue were fixed on him. 21 Then
he began to say to them, "Today this scripture
has been fulfilled in your hearing." 22 All spoke
well of him and were amazed at the gracious
words that came from his mouth. They said,
"Is not this Joseph's son?" 23 He said to them,
"Doubtless you will quote to me this proverb,
'Doctor, cure yourself!' And you will say, 'Do
here also in your hometown the things that
we have heard you did at Capernaum.' "
24 And he said, "Truly I tell you, no prophet
is accepted in the prophet's hometown. 25 But
the truth is, there were many widows in Israel
in the time of Elijah, when the heaven was
shut up three years and six months, and there
was a severe famine over all the land; 26 yet
Elijah was sent to none of them except to a
widow at Zarephath in Sidon. 27 There were
also many lepers *a* in Israel in the time of the
prophet Elisha, and none of them was
cleansed except Naaman the Syrian." 28 When
they heard this, all in the synagogue were
filled with rage. 29 They got up, drove him
out of the town, and led him to the brow of
the hill on which their town was built, so
that they might hurl him off the cliff. 30 But
he passed through the midst of them and
went on his way.

The Man with an Unclean Spirit

31   He went down to Capernaum, a city in
Galilee, and was teaching them on the sabbath. 32 They were astounded at his teaching,
because he spoke with authority. 33 In the
synagogue there was a man who had the spirit of an unclean demon, and he cried out
with a loud voice, 34 "Let us alone! What have
you to do with us, Jesus of Nazareth? Have
you come to destroy us? I know who you are,
the Holy One of God." 35 But Jesus rebuked
him, saying, "Be silent, and come out of
him!" When the demon had thrown him

down before them, he came out of him without having done him any harm. 36 They were
all amazed and kept saying to one another,
"What kind of utterance is this? For with
authority and power he commands the unclean spirits, and out they come!" 37 And a report about him began to reach every place in
the region.

Healings at Simon's House

38   After leaving the synagogue he entered
Simon's house. Now Simon's mother-in-law
was suffering from a high fever, and they
asked him about her. 39 Then he stood over
her and rebuked the fever, and it left her.
Immediately she got up and began to serve
them.

40   As the sun was setting, all those who
had any who were sick with various kinds of
diseases brought them to him; and he laid his
hands on each of them and cured them.
41 Demons also came out of many, shouting,
"You are the Son of God!" But he rebuked
them and would not allow them to speak, because they knew that he was the Messiah. *b*

Jesus Preaches in the Synagogues

42   At daybreak he departed and went into
a deserted place. And the crowds were looking for him; and when they reached him,
they wanted to prevent him from leaving
them. 43 But he said to them, "I must proclaim
the good news of the kingdom of God to the
other cities also; for I was sent for this purpose." 44 So he continued proclaiming the
message in the synagogues of Judea. *c*

Jesus Calls the First Disciples

5 Once while Jesus *d* was standing beside
   the lake of Gennesaret, and the crowd
was pressing in on him to hear the word of
God, 2 he saw two boats there at the shore of
the lake; the fishermen had gone out of them
and were washing their nets. 3 He got into
one of the boats, the one belonging to Simon,
and asked him to put out a little way from the

---

a The terms *leper* and *leprosy* can refer to several diseases   *b* Or *the Christ*   *c* Other ancient authorities read
Galilee   *d* Gk *he*

shore. Then he sat down and taught the crowds from the boat. 4When he had finished speaking, he said to Simon, "Put out into the deep water and let down your nets for a catch." 5Simon answered, "Master, we have worked all night long but have caught nothing. Yet if you say so, I will let down the nets." 6When they had done this, they caught so many fish that their nets were beginning to break. 7So they signaled their partners in the other boat to come and help them. And they came and filled both boats, so that they began to sink. 8But when Simon Peter saw it, he fell down at Jesus' knees, saying, "Go away from me, Lord, for I am a sinful man!" 9For he and all who were with him were amazed at the catch of fish that they had taken; 10and so also were James and John, sons of Zebedee, who were partners with Simon. Then Jesus said to Simon, "Do not be afraid; from now on you will be catching people." 11When they had brought their boats to shore, they left everything and followed him.

Jesus Cleanses a Leper

12 Once, when he was in one of the cities, there was a man covered with leprosy.*a* When he saw Jesus, he bowed with his face to the ground and begged him, "Lord, if you choose, you can make me clean." 13Then Jesus*b* stretched out his hand, touched him, and said, "I do choose. Be made clean." Immediately the leprosy*a* left him. 14And he ordered him to tell no one. "Go," he said, "and show yourself to the priest, and, as Moses commanded, make an offering for your cleansing, for a testimony to them." 15But now more than ever the word about Jesus*c* spread abroad; many crowds would gather to hear him and to be cured of their diseases. 16But he would withdraw to deserted places and pray.

Jesus Heals a Paralytic

17 One day, while he was teaching, Pharisees and teachers of the law were sitting near by (they had come from every village of Galilee and Judea and from Jerusalem); and the power of the Lord was with him to heal.*d* 18Just then some men came, carrying a paralyzed man on a bed. They were trying to bring him in and lay him before Jesus;*e* 19but finding no way to bring him in because of the crowd, they went up on the roof and let him down with his bed through the tiles into the middle of the crowd*e* in front of Jesus. 20When he saw their faith, he said, "Friend,*f* your sins are forgiven you." 21Then the scribes and the Pharisees began to question, "Who is this who is speaking blasphemies? Who can forgive sins but God alone?" 22When Jesus perceived their questionings, he answered them, "Why do you raise such questions in your hearts? 23Which is easier, to say, 'Your sins are forgiven you,' or to say, 'Stand up and walk'? 24But so that you may know that the Son of Man has authority on earth to forgive sins"—he said to the one who was paralyzed—"I say to you, stand up and take your bed and go to your home." 25Immediately he stood up before them, took what he had been lying on, and went to his home, glorifying God. 26Amazement seized all of them, and they glorified God and were filled with awe, saying, "We have seen strange things today."

Jesus Calls Levi

27 After this he went out and saw a tax collector named Levi, sitting at the tax booth; and he said to him, "Follow me." 28And he got up, left everything, and followed him.

29 Then Levi gave a great banquet for him in his house; and there was a large crowd of tax collectors and others sitting at the table*g* with them. 30The Pharisees and their scribes were complaining to his disciples, saying, "Why do you eat and drink with tax collectors and sinners?" 31Jesus answered, "Those who are well have no need of a physician, but those who are sick; 32I have come to call not the righteous but sinners to repentance."

---

a The terms *leper* and *leprosy* can refer to several diseases   *b* Gk *he*   *c* Gk *him*   *d* Other ancient authorities read *was present to heal them*   *e* Gk *into the midst*   *f* Gk *Man*   *g* Gk *reclining*

The Question about Fasting

33 Then they said to him, "John's disciples, like the disciples of the Pharisees, frequently fast and pray, but your disciples eat and drink." 34Jesus said to them, "You cannot make wedding guests fast while the bridegroom is with them, can you? 35The days will come when the bridegroom will be taken away from them, and then they will fast in those days." 36He also told them a parable: "No one tears a piece from a new garment and sews it on an old garment; otherwise the new will be torn, and the piece from the new will not match the old. 37And no one puts new wine into old wineskins; otherwise the new wine will burst the skins and will be spilled, and the skins will be destroyed. 38But new wine must be put into fresh wineskins. 39And no one after drinking old wine desires new wine, but says, 'The old is good.' "*a*

The Question about the Sabbath

6 One sabbath*b* while Jesus*c* was going through the grainfields, his disciples plucked some heads of grain, rubbed them in their hands, and ate them. 2But some of the Pharisees said, "Why are you doing what is not lawful*d* on the sabbath?" 3Jesus answered, "Have you not read what David did when he and his companions were hungry? 4He entered the house of God and took and ate the bread of the Presence, which it is not lawful for any but the priests to eat, and gave some to his companions?" 5Then he said to them, "The Son of Man is lord of the sabbath."

The Man with a Withered Hand

6 On another sabbath he entered the synagogue and taught, and there was a man there whose right hand was withered. 7The scribes and the Pharisees watched him to see whether he would cure on the sabbath, so that they might find an accusation against him. 8Even though he knew what they were thinking, he said to the man who had the withered hand,

"Come and stand here." He got up and stood there. 9Then Jesus said to them, "I ask you, is it lawful to do good or to do harm on the sabbath, to save life or to destroy it?" 10After looking around at all of them, he said to him, "Stretch out your hand." He did so, and his hand was restored. 11But they were filled with fury and discussed with one another what they might do to Jesus.

Jesus Chooses the Twelve Apostles

12 Now during those days he went out to the mountain to pray; and he spent the night in prayer to God. 13And when day came, he called his disciples and chose twelve of them, whom he also named apostles: 14Simon, whom he named Peter, and his brother Andrew, and James, and John, and Philip, and Bartholomew, 15and Matthew, and Thomas, and James son of Alphaeus, and Simon, who was called the Zealot, 16and Judas son of James, and Judas Iscariot, who became a traitor.

Jesus Teaches and Heals

17 He came down with them and stood on a level place, with a great crowd of his disciples and a great multitude of people from all Judea, Jerusalem, and the coast of Tyre and Sidon. 18They had come to hear him and to be healed of their diseases; and those who were troubled with unclean spirits were cured. 19And all in the crowd were trying to touch him, for power came out from him and healed all of them.

Blessings and Woes

20 Then he looked up at his disciples and said:

"Blessed are you who are poor,
    for yours is the kingdom of God.
21 "Blessed are you who are hungry now,
    for you will be filled.

"Blessed are you who weep now,
    for you will laugh.
22 "Blessed are you when people hate

---

a Other ancient authorities read *better*; others lack verse 39   *b* Other ancient authorities read *On the second first sabbath*   *c* Gk *he*   *d* Other ancient authorities add *to do* you, and when they exclude you, revile you, and defame you*a* on account of the Son of Man. 23Rejoice in that day and leap for joy, for surely your reward is great in heaven; for that is what their ancestors did to the prophets.

24   "But woe to you who are rich,
            for you have received your
                consolation.
25   "Woe to you who are full now,
            for you will be hungry.
      "Woe to you who are laughing now,
            for you will mourn and weep.

26 "Woe to you when all speak well of you, for that is what their ancestors did to the false prophets.

Love for Enemies

27 "But I say to you that listen, Love your enemies, do good to those who hate you, 28bless those who curse you, pray for those who abuse you. 29If anyone strikes you on the cheek, offer the other also; and from anyone who takes away your coat do not withhold even your shirt. 30Give to everyone who begs from you; and if anyone takes away your goods, do not ask for them again. 31Do to others as you would have them do to you.

32 "If you love those who love you, what credit is that to you? For even sinners love those who love them. 33If you do good to those who do good to you, what credit is that to you? For even sinners do the same. 34If you lend to those from whom you hope to receive, what credit is that to you? Even sinners lend to sinners, to receive as much again. 35But love your enemies, do good, and lend, expecting nothing in return.*b* Your reward will be great, and you will be children of the Most High; for he is kind to the ungrateful and the wicked. 36Be merciful, just as your Father is merciful.

Judging Others

37 "Do not judge, and you will not be judged; do not condemn, and you will not be condemned. Forgive, and you will be forgiv-

en; 38give, and it will be given to you. A good measure, pressed down, shaken together, running over, will be put into your lap; for the measure you give will be the measure you get back."

39 He also told them a parable: "Can a blind person guide a blind person? Will not both fall into a pit? 40A disciple is not above the teacher, but everyone who is fully qualified will be like the teacher. 41Why do you see the speck in your neighbor's*c* eye, but do not notice the log in your own eye? 42Or how can you say to your neighbor,*d* 'Friend,*d* let me take out the speck in your eye,' when you yourself do not see the log in your own eye? You hypocrite, first take the log out of your own eye, and then you will see clearly to take the speck out of your neighbor's*c* eye.

A Tree and Its Fruit

43 "No good tree bears bad fruit, nor again does a bad tree bear good fruit; 44for each tree is known by its own fruit. Figs are not gathered from thorns, nor are grapes picked from a bramble bush. 45The good person out of the good treasure of the heart produces good, and the evil person out of evil treasure produces evil; for it is out of the abundance of the heart that the mouth speaks.

The Two Foundations

46 "Why do you call me 'Lord, Lord,' and do not do what I tell you? 47I will show you what someone is like who comes to me, hears my words, and acts on them. 48That one is like a man building a house, who dug deeply and laid the foundation on rock; when a flood arose, the river burst against that house but could not shake it, because it had been well built.*e* 49But the one who hears and does not act is like a man who built a house on the ground without a foundation. When the river burst against it, immediately it fell, and great was the ruin of that house."

---

a Gk *cast out your name as evil*   *b* Other ancient authorities read *despairing of no one*   *c* Gk *brother's*   *d* Gk *brother*
e Other ancient authorities read *founded upon the rock*

Jesus Heals a Centurion's Servant

7 After Jesus[a] had finished all his sayings in the hearing of the people, he entered Capernaum. 2A centurion there had a slave whom he valued highly, and who was ill and close to death. 3When he heard about Jesus, he sent some Jewish elders to him, asking him to come and heal his slave. 4When they came to Jesus, they appealed to him earnestly, saying, "He is worthy of having you do this for him, 5for he loves our people, and it is he who built our synagogue for us." 6And Jesus went with them, but when he was not far from the house, the centurion sent friends to say to him, "Lord, do not trouble yourself, for I am not worthy to have you come under my roof; 7therefore I did not presume to come to you. But only speak the word, and let my servant be healed. 8For I also am a man set under authority, with soldiers under me; and I say to one, 'Go,' and he goes, and to another, 'Come,' and he comes, and to my slave, 'Do this,' and the slave does it." 9When Jesus heard this he was amazed at him, and turning to the crowd that followed him, he said, "I tell you, not even in Israel have I found such faith." 10When those who had been sent returned to the house, they found the slave in good health.

Jesus Raises the Widow's Son at Nain

11 Soon afterwards[b] he went to a town called Nain, and his disciples and a large crowd went with him. 12As he approached the gate of the town, a man who had died was being carried out. He was his mother's only son, and she was a widow; and with her was a large crowd from the town. 13When the Lord saw her, he had compassion for her and said to her, "Do not weep." 14Then he came forward and touched the bier, and the bearers stood still. And he said, "Young man, I say to you, rise!" 15The dead man sat up and began to speak, and Jesus[a] gave him to his mother. 16Fear seized all of them; and they glorified God, saying, "A great prophet has

risen among us!" and "God has looked favorably on his people!" 17This word about him spread throughout Judea and all the surrounding country.

Messengers from John the Baptist

18 The disciples of John reported all these things to him. So John summoned two of his disciples 19and sent them to the Lord to ask, "Are you the one who is to come, or are we to wait for another?" 20When the men had come to him, they said, "John the Baptist has sent us to you to ask, 'Are you the one who is to come, or are we to wait for another?'" 21Jesus[c] had just then cured many people of diseases, plagues, and evil spirits, and had given sight to many who were blind. 22And he answered them, "Go and tell John what you have seen and heard: the blind receive their sight, the lame walk, the lepers[d] are cleansed, the deaf hear, the dead are raised, the poor have good news brought to them. 23And blessed is anyone who takes no offense at me."

24 When John's messengers had gone, Jesus[a] began to speak to the crowds about John:[e] "What did you go out into the wilderness to look at? A reed shaken by the wind? 25What then did you go out to see? Someone[f] dressed in soft robes? Look, those who put on fine clothing and live in luxury are in royal palaces. 26What then did you go out to see? A prophet? Yes, I tell you, and more than a prophet. 27This is the one about whom it is written,

'See, I am sending my messenger ahead
    of you,
  who will prepare your way before
    you.'

28I tell you, among those born of women no one is greater than John; yet the least in the kingdom of God is greater than he." 29(And all the people who heard this, including the tax collectors, acknowledged the justice of God,[g] because they had been baptized with John's baptism. 30But by refusing

---

a Gk *he*   *b* Other ancient authorities read *Next day*   *c* Gk *He*   *d* The terms *leper* and *leprosy* can refer to several diseases   *e* Gk *him*   *f* Or *Why then did you go out? To see someone*   *g* Or *praised God* to be baptized by him, the Pharisees and the lawyers rejected God's purpose for themselves.)

31 "To what then will I compare the people of this generation, and what are they like? 32They are like children sitting in the marketplace and calling to one another,

'We played the flute for you, and you
    did not dance;
we wailed, and you did not weep.'

33For John the Baptist has come eating no bread and drinking no wine, and you say, 'He has a demon'; 34the Son of Man has come eating and drinking, and you say, 'Look, a glutton and a drunkard, a friend of tax collectors and sinners!' 35Nevertheless, wisdom is vindicated by all her children."

A Sinful Woman Forgiven

36 One of the Pharisees asked Jesus*a* to eat with him, and he went into the Pharisee's house and took his place at the table. 37And a woman in the city, who was a sinner, having learned that he was eating in the Pharisee's house, brought an alabaster jar of ointment. 38She stood behind him at his feet, weeping, and began to bathe his feet with her tears and to dry them with her hair. Then she continued kissing his feet and anointing them with the ointment. 39Now when the Pharisee who had invited him saw it, he said to himself, "If this man were a prophet, he would have known who and what kind of woman this is who is touching him—that she is a sinner." 40Jesus spoke up and said to him, "Simon, I have something to say to you." "Teacher," he replied, "speak." 41"A certain creditor had two debtors; one owed five hundred denarii,*b* and the other fifty. 42When they could not pay, he canceled the debts for both of them. Now which of them will love him more?" 43Simon answered, "I suppose the one for whom he canceled the greater debt." And Jesus*c* said to him, "You have judged rightly." 44Then turning toward the woman, he said to Simon, "Do you see this

woman? I entered your house; you gave me no water for my feet, but she has bathed my feet with her tears and dried them with her hair. 45You gave me no kiss, but from the time I came in she has not stopped kissing my feet. 46You did not anoint my head with oil, but she has anointed my feet with ointment. 47Therefore, I tell you, her sins, which were many, have been forgiven; hence she has shown great love. But the one to whom little is forgiven, loves little." 48Then he said to her, "Your sins are forgiven." 49But those who were at the table with him began to say among themselves, "Who is this who even forgives sins?" 50And he said to the woman, "Your faith has saved you; go in peace."

Some Women Accompany Jesus

8 Soon afterwards he went on through cities and villages, proclaiming and bringing the good news of the kingdom of God. The twelve were with him, 2as well as some women who had been cured of evil spirits and infirmities: Mary, called Magdalene, from whom seven demons had gone out, 3and Joanna, the wife of Herod's steward Chuza, and Susanna, and many others, who provided for them*d* out of their resources.

The Parable of the Sower

4 When a great crowd gathered and people from town after town came to him, he said in a parable: 5"A sower went out to sow his seed; and as he sowed, some fell on the path and was trampled on, and the birds of the air ate it up. 6Some fell on the rock; and as it grew up, it withered for lack of moisture. 7Some fell among thorns, and the thorns grew with it and choked it. 8Some fell into good soil, and when it grew, it produced a hundredfold." As he said this, he called out, "Let anyone with ears to hear listen!"

The Purpose of the Parables

9 Then his disciples asked him what this parable meant. 10He said, "To you it has been

a Gk *him*   *b* The denarius was the usual day's wage for a laborer   *c* Gk *he*   *d* Other ancient authorities read *him* given to know the secrets*a* of the kingdom of God; but to others I speak*b* in parables, so that

'looking they may not perceive,
and listening they may not
understand.'

The Parable of the Sower Explained

11 "Now the parable is this: The seed is the word of God. 12The ones on the path are those who have heard; then the devil comes and takes away the word from their hearts, so that they may not believe and be saved. 13The ones on the rock are those who, when they hear the word, receive it with joy. But these have no root; they believe only for a while and in a time of testing fall away. 14As for what fell among the thorns, these are the ones who hear; but as they go on their way, they are choked by the cares and riches and pleasures of life, and their fruit does not mature. 15But as for that in the good soil, these are the ones who, when they hear the word, hold it fast in an honest and good heart, and bear fruit with patient endurance.

A Lamp under a Jar

16 "No one after lighting a lamp hides it under a jar, or puts it under a bed, but puts it on a lampstand, so that those who enter may see the light. 17For nothing is hidden that will not be disclosed, nor is anything secret that will not become known and come to light. 18Then pay attention to how you listen; for to those who have, more will be given; and from those who do not have, even what they seem to have will be taken away."

The True Kindred of Jesus

19 Then his mother and his brothers came to him, but they could not reach him because of the crowd. 20And he was told, "Your mother and your brothers are standing outside, wanting to see you." 21But he said to them, "My mother and my brothers are those who hear the word of God and do it."

Jesus Calms a Storm

22 One day he got into a boat with his disciples, and he said to them, "Let us go across to the other side of the lake." So they put out, 23and while they were sailing he fell asleep. A windstorm swept down on the lake, and the boat was filling with water, and they were in danger. 24They went to him and woke him up, shouting, "Master, Master, we are perishing!" And he woke up and rebuked the wind and the raging waves; they ceased, and there was a calm. 25He said to them, "Where is your faith?" They were afraid and amazed, and said to one another, "Who then is this, that he commands even the winds and the water, and they obey him?"

Jesus Heals the Gerasene Demoniac

26 Then they arrived at the country of the Gerasenes,*c* which is opposite Galilee. 27As he stepped out on land, a man of the city who had demons met him. For a long time he had worn*d* no clothes, and he did not live in a house but in the tombs. 28When he saw Jesus, he fell down before him and shouted at the top of his voice, "What have you to do with me, Jesus, Son of the Most High God? I beg you, do not torment me"— 29for Jesus*e* had commanded the unclean spirit to come out of the man. (For many times it had seized him; he was kept under guard and bound with chains and shackles, but he would break the bonds and be driven by the demon into the wilds.) 30Jesus then asked him, "What is your name?" He said, "Legion"; for many demons had entered him. 31They begged him not to order them to go back into the abyss.

32 Now there on the hillside a large herd of swine was feeding; and the demons*f* begged Jesus*g* to let them enter these. So he gave them permission. 33Then the demons came out of the man and entered the swine, and the herd rushed down the steep bank into the lake and was drowned.

---

a Or *mysteries*   *b* Gk lacks *I speak*   *c* Other ancient authorities read *Gadarenes*; others, *Gergesenes*   *d* Other ancient authorities read *a man of the city who had had demons for a long time met him. He wore*   *e* Gk *he*   *f* Gk *they*   *g* Gk *him*

34 When the swineherds saw what had happened, they ran off and told it in the city and in the country. 35Then people came out to see what had happened, and when they came to Jesus, they found the man from whom the demons had gone sitting at the feet of Jesus, clothed and in his right mind. And they were afraid. 36Those who had seen it told them how the one who had been possessed by demons had been healed. 37Then all the people of the surrounding country of the Gerasenes*a* asked Jesus*b* to leave them; for they were seized with great fear. So he got into the boat and returned. 38The man from whom the demons had gone begged that he might be with him; but Jesus*c* sent him away, saying, 39"Return to your home, and declare how much God has done for you." So he went away, proclaiming throughout the city how much Jesus had done for him.

A Girl Restored to Life and a Woman Healed

40 Now when Jesus returned, the crowd welcomed him, for they were all waiting for him. 41Just then there came a man named Jairus, a leader of the synagogue. He fell at Jesus' feet and begged him to come to his house, 42for he had an only daughter, about twelve years old, who was dying.

As he went, the crowds pressed in on him. 43Now there was a woman who had been suffering from hemorrhages for twelve years; and though she had spent all she had on physicians,*d* no one could cure her. 44She came up behind him and touched the fringe of his clothes, and immediately her hemorrhage stopped. 45Then Jesus asked, "Who touched me?" When all denied it, Peter*e* said, "Master, the crowds surround you and press in on you." 46But Jesus said, "Someone touched me; for I noticed that power had gone out from me." 47When the woman saw that she could not remain hidden, she came trembling; and falling down before him, she declared in the presence of all the people

why she had touched him, and how she had been immediately healed. 48He said to her, "Daughter, your faith has made you well; go in peace."

49 While he was still speaking, someone came from the leader's house to say, "Your daughter is dead; do not trouble the teacher any longer." 50When Jesus heard this, he replied, "Do not fear. Only believe, and she will be saved." 51When he came to the house, he did not allow anyone to enter with him, except Peter, John, and James, and the child's father and mother. 52They were all weeping and wailing for her; but he said, "Do not weep; for she is not dead but sleeping." 53And they laughed at him, knowing that she was dead. 54But he took her by the hand and called out, "Child, get up!" 55Her spirit returned, and she got up at once. Then he directed them to give her something to eat. 56Her parents were astounded; but he ordered them to tell no one what had happened.

The Mission of the Twelve

9 Then Jesus*c* called the twelve together and gave them power and authority over all demons and to cure diseases, 2and he sent them out to proclaim the kingdom of God and to heal. 3He said to them, "Take nothing for your journey, no staff, nor bag, nor bread, nor money—not even an extra tunic. 4Whatever house you enter, stay there, and leave from there. 5Wherever they do not welcome you, as you are leaving that town shake the dust off your feet as a testimony against them." 6They departed and went through the villages, bringing the good news and curing diseases everywhere.

Herod's Perplexity

7 Now Herod the ruler*f* heard about all that had taken place, and he was perplexed, because it was said by some that John had been raised from the dead, 8by some that

---

a Other ancient authorities read *Gadarenes*; others, *Gergesenes*   *b* Gk *him*   *c* Gk *he*   *d* Other ancient authorities lack *and though she had spent all she had on physicians*   *e* Other ancient authorities add *and those who were with him*   *f* Gk *tetrarch*

Elijah had appeared, and by others that one of the ancient prophets had arisen. 9Herod said, "John I beheaded; but who is this about whom I hear such things?" And he tried to see him.

Feeding the Five Thousand

10 On their return the apostles told Jesus*a* all they had done. He took them with him and withdrew privately to a city called Bethsaida. 11When the crowds found out about it, they followed him; and he welcomed them, and spoke to them about the kingdom of God, and healed those who needed to be cured.

12 The day was drawing to a close, and the twelve came to him and said, "Send the crowd away, so that they may go into the surrounding villages and countryside, to lodge and get provisions; for we are here in a deserted place." 13But he said to them, "You give them something to eat." They said, "We have no more than five loaves and two fish—unless we are to go and buy food for all these people." 14For there were about five thousand men. And he said to his disciples, "Make them sit down in groups of about fifty each." 15They did so and made them all sit down. 16And taking the five loaves and the two fish, he looked up to heaven, and blessed and broke them, and gave them to the disciples to set before the crowd. 17And all ate and were filled. What was left over was gathered up, twelve baskets of broken pieces.

Peter's Declaration about Jesus

18 Once when Jesus*b* was praying alone, with only the disciples near him, he asked them, "Who do the crowds say that I am?" 19They answered, "John the Baptist; but others, Elijah; and still others, that one of the ancient prophets has arisen." 20He said to them, "But who do you say that I am?" Peter answered, "The Messiah*c* of God."

Jesus Foretells His Death and Resurrection

21 He sternly ordered and commanded them not to tell anyone, 22saying, "The Son of Man must undergo great suffering, and be rejected by the elders, chief priests, and scribes, and be killed, and on the third day be raised."

23 Then he said to them all, "If any want to become my followers, let them deny themselves and take up their cross daily and follow me. 24For those who want to save their life will lose it, and those who lose their life for my sake will save it. 25What does it profit them if they gain the whole world, but lose or forfeit themselves? 26Those who are ashamed of me and of my words, of them the Son of Man will be ashamed when he comes in his glory and the glory of the Father and of the holy angels. 27But truly I tell you, there are some standing here who will not taste death before they see the kingdom of God."

The Transfiguration

28 Now about eight days after these sayings Jesus*b* took with him Peter and John and James, and went up on the mountain to pray. 29And while he was praying, the appearance of his face changed, and his clothes became dazzling white. 30Suddenly they saw two men, Moses and Elijah, talking to him. 31They appeared in glory and were speaking of his departure, which he was about to accomplish at Jerusalem. 32Now Peter and his companions were weighed down with sleep; but since they had stayed awake,*d* they saw his glory and the two men who stood with him. 33Just as they were leaving him, Peter said to Jesus, "Master, it is good for us to be here; let us make three dwellings,*e* one for you, one for Moses, and one for Elijah"—not knowing what he said. 34While he was saying this, a cloud came and overshadowed them; and they were terrified as they entered the cloud. 35Then from the cloud came a voice that said, "This is my Son, my Chosen;*f* listen to

---

a Gk *him*   *b* Gk *he*   *c* Or *The Christ*   *d* Or *but when they were fully awake*   *e* Or *tents*   *f* Other ancient authorities read *my Beloved* him!" ³⁶When the voice had spoken, Jesus was found alone. And they kept silent and in those days told no one any of the things they had seen.

Jesus Heals a Boy with a Demon

37 On the next day, when they had come down from the mountain, a great crowd met him. ³⁸Just then a man from the crowd shouted, "Teacher, I beg you to look at my son; he is my only child. ³⁹Suddenly a spirit seizes him, and all at once he*ᵃ* shrieks. It convulses him until he foams at the mouth; it mauls him and will scarcely leave him. ⁴⁰I begged your disciples to cast it out, but they could not." ⁴¹Jesus answered, "You faithless and perverse generation, how much longer must I be with you and bear with you? Bring your son here." ⁴²While he was coming, the demon dashed him to the ground in convulsions. But Jesus rebuked the unclean spirit, healed the boy, and gave him back to his father. ⁴³And all were astounded at the greatness of God.

Jesus Again Foretells His Death

While everyone was amazed at all that he was doing, he said to his disciples, ⁴⁴"Let these words sink into your ears: The Son of Man is going to be betrayed into human hands." ⁴⁵But they did not understand this saying; its meaning was concealed from them, so that they could not perceive it. And they were afraid to ask him about this saying.

True Greatness

46 An argument arose among them as to which one of them was the greatest. ⁴⁷But Jesus, aware of their inner thoughts, took a little child and put it by his side, ⁴⁸and said to them, "Whoever welcomes this child in my name welcomes me, and whoever welcomes me welcomes the one who sent me; for the least among all of you is the greatest."

Another Exorcist

49 John answered, "Master, we saw someone casting out demons in your name, and we tried to stop him, because he does not follow with us." ⁵⁰But Jesus said to him, "Do not stop him; for whoever is not against you is for you."

A Samaritan Village Refuses to Receive Jesus

51 When the days drew near for him to be taken up, he set his face to go to Jerusalem. ⁵²And he sent messengers ahead of him. On their way they entered a village of the Samaritans to make ready for him; ⁵³but they did not receive him, because his face was set toward Jerusalem. ⁵⁴When his disciples James and John saw it, they said, "Lord, do you want us to command fire to come down from heaven and consume them?"*ᵇ* ⁵⁵But he turned and rebuked them. ⁵⁶Then*ᶜ* they went on to another village.

Would-Be Followers of Jesus

57 As they were going along the road, someone said to him, "I will follow you wherever you go." ⁵⁸And Jesus said to him, "Foxes have holes, and birds of the air have nests; but the Son of Man has nowhere to lay his head." ⁵⁹To another he said, "Follow me." But he said, "Lord, first let me go and bury my father." ⁶⁰But Jesus*ᵈ* said to him, "Let the dead bury their own dead; but as for you, go and proclaim the kingdom of God." ⁶¹Another said, "I will follow you, Lord; but let me first say farewell to those at my home." ⁶²Jesus said to him, "No one who puts a hand to the plow and looks back is fit for the kingdom of God."

The Mission of the Seventy

10 After this the Lord appointed seventy*ᵉ* others and sent them on ahead of him in pairs to every town and place where he himself intended to go. ²He said to them, "The harvest is plentiful, but the laborers

---

a Or *it*   *b* Other ancient authorities add *as Elijah did*   *c* Other ancient authorities read *rebuked them, and said,*
"You do not know what spirit you are of, ⁵⁶*for the Son of Man has not come to destroy the lives of human beings but to save them."*
Then   *d* Gk *he*   *e* Other ancient authorities read *seventy-two*

are few; therefore ask the Lord of the harvest to send out laborers into his harvest. [3]Go on your way. See, I am sending you out like lambs into the midst of wolves. [4]Carry no purse, no bag, no sandals; and greet no one on the road. [5]Whatever house you enter, first say, 'Peace to this house!' [6]And if anyone is there who shares in peace, your peace will rest on that person; but if not, it will return to you. [7]Remain in the same house, eating and drinking whatever they provide, for the laborer deserves to be paid. Do not move about from house to house. [8]Whenever you enter a town and its people welcome you, eat what is set before you; [9]cure the sick who are there, and say to them, 'The kingdom of God has come near to you.'[a] [10]But whenever you enter a town and they do not welcome you, go out into its streets and say, [11]'Even the dust of your town that clings to our feet, we wipe off in protest against you. Yet know this: the kingdom of God has come near.'[b] [12]I tell you, on that day it will be more tolerable for Sodom than for that town.

Woes to Unrepentant Cities

13 "Woe to you, Chorazin! Woe to you, Bethsaida! For if the deeds of power done in you had been done in Tyre and Sidon, they would have repented long ago, sitting in sackcloth and ashes. [14]But at the judgment it will be more tolerable for Tyre and Sidon than for you. [15]And you, Capernaum,

will you be exalted to heaven?

No, you will be brought down to Hades.

16 "Whoever listens to you listens to me, and whoever rejects you rejects me, and whoever rejects me rejects the one who sent me."

The Return of the Seventy

17 The seventy[c] returned with joy, saying, "Lord, in your name even the demons submit to us!" [18]He said to them, "I watched Satan fall from heaven like a flash of lightning. [19]See, I have given you authority to tread on snakes and scorpions, and over all the power of the enemy; and nothing will hurt you. [20]Nevertheless, do not rejoice at this, that the spirits submit to you, but rejoice that your names are written in heaven."

Jesus Rejoices

21 At that same hour Jesus[d] rejoiced in the Holy Spirit[e] and said, "I thank[f] you, Father, Lord of heaven and earth, because you have hidden these things from the wise and the intelligent and have revealed them to infants; yes, Father, for such was your gracious will.[g] [22]All things have been handed over to me by my Father; and no one knows who the Son is except the Father, or who the Father is except the Son and anyone to whom the Son chooses to reveal him."

23 Then turning to the disciples, Jesus[d] said to them privately, "Blessed are the eyes that see what you see! [24]For I tell you that many prophets and kings desired to see what you see, but did not see it, and to hear what you hear, but did not hear it."

The Parable of the Good Samaritan

25 Just then a lawyer stood up to test Jesus.[h] "Teacher," he said, "what must I do to inherit eternal life?" [26]He said to him, "What is written in the law? What do you read there?" [27]He answered, "You shall love the Lord your God with all your heart, and with all your soul, and with all your strength, and with all your mind; and your neighbor as yourself." [28]And he said to him, "You have given the right answer; do this, and you will live."

29 But wanting to justify himself, he asked Jesus, "And who is my neighbor?" [30]Jesus replied, "A man was going down from Jerusalem to Jericho, and fell into the hands of robbers, who stripped him, beat him, and went away, leaving him half dead. [31]Now by chance a priest was going down that road; and when he saw him, he passed by on the other side. [32]So likewise a Levite, when he came

---

a Or is at hand for you   b Or is at hand   c Other ancient authorities read seventy-two   d Gk he   e Other authorities read in the spirit   f Or praise   g Or for so it was well-pleasing in your sight   h Gk him to the place and saw him, passed by on the other side. ³³But a Samaritan while traveling came near him; and when he saw him, he was moved with pity. ³⁴He went to him and bandaged his wounds, having poured oil and wine on them. Then he put him on his own animal, brought him to an inn, and took care of him. ³⁵The next day he took out two denarii,*a* gave them to the innkeeper, and said, 'Take care of him; and when I come back, I will repay you whatever more you spend.' ³⁶Which of these three, do you think, was a neighbor to the man who fell into the hands of the robbers?" ³⁷He said, "The one who showed him mercy." Jesus said to him, "Go and do likewise."

Jesus Visits Martha and Mary

38 Now as they went on their way, he entered a certain village, where a woman named Martha welcomed him into her home. ³⁹She had a sister named Mary, who sat at the Lord's feet and listened to what he was saying. ⁴⁰But Martha was distracted by her many tasks; so she came to him and asked, "Lord, do you not care that my sister has left me to do all the work by myself? Tell her then to help me." ⁴¹But the Lord answered her, "Martha, Martha, you are worried and distracted by many things; ⁴²there is need of only one thing.*b* Mary has chosen the better part, which will not be taken away from her."

The Lord's Prayer

11 He was praying in a certain place, and after he had finished, one of his disciples said to him, "Lord, teach us to pray, as John taught his disciples." ²He said to them, "When you pray, say:

Father,*c* hallowed be your name.
  Your kingdom come.*d*
3   Give us each day our daily bread.*e*
4   And forgive us our sins,

for we ourselves forgive everyone indebted to us.
And do not bring us to the time of trial."*f*

Perseverance in Prayer

5 And he said to them, "Suppose one of you has a friend, and you go to him at midnight and say to him, 'Friend, lend me three loaves of bread; ⁶for a friend of mine has arrived, and I have nothing to set before him.' ⁷And he answers from within, 'Do not bother me; the door has already been locked, and my children are with me in bed; I cannot get up and give you anything.' ⁸I tell you, even though he will not get up and give him anything because he is his friend, at least because of his persistence he will get up and give him whatever he needs.

9 "So I say to you, Ask, and it will be given you; search, and you will find; knock, and the door will be opened for you. ¹⁰For everyone who asks receives, and everyone who searches finds, and for everyone who knocks, the door will be opened. ¹¹Is there anyone among you who, if your child asks for*g* a fish, will give a snake instead of a fish? ¹²Or if the child asks for an egg, will give a scorpion? ¹³If you then, who are evil, know how to give good gifts to your children, how much more will the heavenly Father give the Holy Spirit*h* to those who ask him!"

Jesus and Beelzebul

14 Now he was casting out a demon that was mute; when the demon had gone out, the one who had been mute spoke, and the crowds were amazed. ¹⁵But some of them said, "He casts out demons by Beelzebul, the ruler of the demons." ¹⁶Others, to test him, kept demanding from him a sign from heaven. ¹⁷But he knew what they were thinking and said to them, "Every kingdom di-

---

a The denarius was the usual day's wage for a laborer   *b* Other ancient authorities read *few things are necessary, or only one*   *c* Other ancient authorities read *Our Father in heaven*   *d* A few ancient authorities read *Your Holy Spirit come upon us and cleanse us.* Other ancient authorities add *Your will be done, on earth as in heaven*   *e* Or *our bread for tomorrow*   *f* Or *us into temptation.* Other ancient authorities add *but rescue us from the evil one* (or *from evil*)   *g* Other ancient authorities add *bread, will give a stone; or if your child asks for*   *h* Other ancient authorities read *the Father give the Holy Spirit from heaven* vided against itself becomes a desert, and house falls on house. [18]If Satan also is divided against himself, how will his kingdom stand? —for you say that I cast out the demons by Beelzebul. [19]Now if I cast out the demons by Beelzebul, by whom do your exorcists[a] cast them out? Therefore they will be your judges. [20]But if it is by the finger of God that I cast out the demons, then the kingdom of God has come to you. [21]When a strong man, fully armed, guards his castle, his property is safe. [22]But when one stronger than he attacks him and overpowers him, he takes away his armor in which he trusted and divides his plunder. [23]Whoever is not with me is against me, and whoever does not gather with me scatters.

The Return of the Unclean Spirit

24 "When the unclean spirit has gone out of a person, it wanders through waterless regions looking for a resting place, but not finding any, it says, 'I will return to my house from which I came.' [25]When it comes, it finds it swept and put in order. [26]Then it goes and brings seven other spirits more evil than itself, and they enter and live there; and the last state of that person is worse than the first."

True Blessedness

27 While he was saying this, a woman in the crowd raised her voice and said to him, "Blessed is the womb that bore you and the breasts that nursed you!" [28]But he said, "Blessed rather are those who hear the word of God and obey it!"

The Sign of Jonah

29 When the crowds were increasing, he began to say, "This generation is an evil generation; it asks for a sign, but no sign will be given to it except the sign of Jonah. [30]For just as Jonah became a sign to the people of Nineveh, so the Son of Man will be to this generation. [31]The queen of the South will rise at the judgment with the people of this gener-

ation and condemn them, because she came from the ends of the earth to listen to the wisdom of Solomon, and see, something greater than Solomon is here! [32]The people of Nineveh will rise up at the judgment with this generation and condemn it, because they repented at the proclamation of Jonah, and see, something greater than Jonah is here!

The Light of the Body

33 "No one after lighting a lamp puts it in a cellar,[b] but on the lampstand so that those who enter may see the light. [34]Your eye is the lamp of your body. If your eye is healthy, your whole body is full of light; but if it is not healthy, your body is full of darkness. [35]Therefore consider whether the light in you is not darkness. [36]If then your whole body is full of light, with no part of it in darkness, it will be as full of light as when a lamp gives you light with its rays."

Jesus Denounces Pharisees and Lawyers

37 While he was speaking, a Pharisee invited him to dine with him; so he went in and took his place at the table. [38]The Pharisee was amazed to see that he did not first wash before dinner. [39]Then the Lord said to him, "Now you Pharisees clean the outside of the cup and of the dish, but inside you are full of greed and wickedness. [40]You fools! Did not the one who made the outside make the inside also? [41]So give for alms those things that are within; and see, everything will be clean for you.

42 "But woe to you Pharisees! For you tithe mint and rue and herbs of all kinds, and neglect justice and the love of God; it is these you ought to have practiced, without neglecting the others. [43]Woe to you Pharisees! For you love to have the seat of honor in the synagogues and to be greeted with respect in the marketplaces. [44]Woe to you! For you are like unmarked graves, and people walk over them without realizing it."

45 One of the lawyers answered him,

a Gk sons   b Other ancient authorities add or under the bushel basket

"Teacher, when you say these things, you insult us too." 46And he said, "Woe also to you lawyers! For you load people with burdens hard to bear, and you yourselves do not lift a finger to ease them. 47Woe to you! For you build the tombs of the prophets whom your ancestors killed. 48So you are witnesses and approve of the deeds of your ancestors; for they killed them, and you build their tombs. 49Therefore also the Wisdom of God said, 'I will send them prophets and apostles, some of whom they will kill and persecute,' 50so that this generation may be charged with the blood of all the prophets shed since the foundation of the world, 51from the blood of Abel to the blood of Zechariah, who perished between the altar and the sanctuary. Yes, I tell you, it will be charged against this generation. 52Woe to you lawyers! For you have taken away the key of knowledge; you did not enter yourselves, and you hindered those who were entering."

53 When he went outside, the scribes and the Pharisees began to be very hostile toward him and to cross-examine him about many things, 54lying in wait for him, to catch him in something he might say.

A Warning against Hypocrisy

12 Meanwhile, when the crowd gathered by the thousands, so that they trampled on one another, he began to speak first to his disciples, "Beware of the yeast of the Pharisees, that is, their hypocrisy. 2Nothing is covered up that will not be uncovered, and nothing secret that will not become known. 3Therefore whatever you have said in the dark will be heard in the light, and what you have whispered behind closed doors will be proclaimed from the housetops.

Exhortation to Fearless Confession

4 "I tell you, my friends, do not fear those who kill the body, and after that can do nothing more. 5But I will warn you whom to fear: fear him who, after he has killed, has authority*a* to cast into hell. *b* Yes, I tell you, fear him! 6Are not five sparrows sold for two pennies? Yet not one of them is forgotten in God's sight. 7But even the hairs of your head are all counted. Do not be afraid; you are of more value than many sparrows.

8 "And I tell you, everyone who acknowledges me before others, the Son of Man also will acknowledge before the angels of God; 9but whoever denies me before others will be denied before the angels of God. 10And everyone who speaks a word against the Son of Man will be forgiven; but whoever blasphemes against the Holy Spirit will not be forgiven. 11When they bring you before the synagogues, the rulers, and the authorities, do not worry about how*c* you are to defend yourselves or what you are to say; 12for the Holy Spirit will teach you at that very hour what you ought to say."

The Parable of the Rich Fool

13 Someone in the crowd said to him, "Teacher, tell my brother to divide the family inheritance with me." 14But he said to him, "Friend, who set me to be a judge or arbitrator over you?" 15And he said to them, "Take care! Be on your guard against all kinds of greed; for one's life does not consist in the abundance of possessions." 16Then he told them a parable: "The land of a rich man produced abundantly. 17And he thought to himself, 'What should I do, for I have no place to store my crops?' 18Then he said, 'I will do this: I will pull down my barns and build larger ones, and there I will store all my grain and my goods. 19And I will say to my soul, Soul, you have ample goods laid up for many years; relax, eat, drink, be merry.' 20But God said to him, 'You fool! This very night your life is being demanded of you. And the things you have prepared, whose will they be?' 21So it is with those who store up treasures for themselves but are not rich toward God."

---

a Or *power*   *b* Gk *Gehenna*   *c* Other ancient authorities add *or what*

Do Not Worry

22 He said to his disciples, "Therefore I tell you, do not worry about your life, what you will eat, or about your body, what you will wear. 23For life is more than food, and the body more than clothing. 24Consider the ravens: they neither sow nor reap, they have neither storehouse nor barn, and yet God feeds them. Of how much more value are you than the birds! 25And can any of you by worrying add a single hour to your span of life?[a] 26If then you are not able to do so small a thing as that, why do you worry about the rest? 27Consider the lilies, how they grow: they neither toil nor spin;[b] yet I tell you, even Solomon in all his glory was not clothed like one of these. 28But if God so clothes the grass of the field, which is alive today and tomorrow is thrown into the oven, how much more will he clothe you—you of little faith! 29And do not keep striving for what you are to eat and what you are to drink, and do not keep worrying. 30For it is the nations of the world that strive after all these things, and your Father knows that you need them. 31Instead, strive for his[c] kingdom, and these things will be given to you as well.

32 "Do not be afraid, little flock, for it is your Father's good pleasure to give you the kingdom. 33Sell your possessions, and give alms. Make purses for yourselves that do not wear out, an unfailing treasure in heaven, where no thief comes near and no moth destroys. 34For where your treasure is, there your heart will be also.

Watchful Slaves

35 "Be dressed for action and have your lamps lit; 36be like those who are waiting for their master to return from the wedding banquet, so that they may open the door for him as soon as he comes and knocks. 37Blessed are those slaves whom the master finds alert when he comes; truly I tell you, he will fasten his belt and have them sit down to eat, and he will come and serve them. 38If he comes during the middle of the night, or near dawn, and finds them so, blessed are those slaves.

39 "But know this: if the owner of the house had known at what hour the thief was coming, he[d] would not have let his house be broken into. 40You also must be ready, for the Son of Man is coming at an unexpected hour."

The Faithful or the Unfaithful Slave

41 Peter said, "Lord, are you telling this parable for us or for everyone?" 42And the Lord said, "Who then is the faithful and prudent manager whom his master will put in charge of his slaves, to give them their allowance of food at the proper time? 43Blessed is that slave whom his master will find at work when he arrives. 44Truly I tell you, he will put that one in charge of all his possessions. 45But if that slave says to himself, 'My master is delayed in coming,' and if he begins to beat the other slaves, men and women, and to eat and drink and get drunk, 46the master of that slave will come on a day when he does not expect him and at an hour that he does not know, and will cut him in pieces,[e] and put him with the unfaithful. 47That slave who knew what his master wanted, but did not prepare himself or do what was wanted, will receive a severe beating. 48But the one who did not know and did what deserved a beating will receive a light beating. From everyone to whom much has been given, much will be required; and from the one to whom much has been entrusted, even more will be demanded.

Jesus the Cause of Division

49 "I came to bring fire to the earth, and how I wish it were already kindled! 50I have a baptism with which to be baptized, and what stress I am under until it is completed! 51Do you think that I have come to bring peace to the earth? No, I tell you, but rather division! 52From now on five in one house-

---

a Or add a cubit to your stature   b Other ancient authorities read Consider the lilies; they neither spin nor weave
c Other ancient authorities read God's   d Other ancient authorities add would have watched and   e Or cut him off

hold will be divided, three against two and two against three; [53]they will be divided:

> father against son
>> and son against father,
> mother against daughter
>> and daughter against mother,
> mother-in-law against her daughter-in-law
>> and daughter-in-law against mother-in-law."

Interpreting the Time

54 He also said to the crowds, "When you see a cloud rising in the west, you immediately say, 'It is going to rain'; and so it happens. [55]And when you see the south blowing, you say, 'There will be scorching heat'; and it happens. [56]You hypocrites! You know how to interpret the appearance of earth and sky, but why do you not know how to interpret the present time?

Settling with Your Opponent

57 "And why do you not judge for yourselves what is right? [58]Thus, when you go with your accuser before a magistrate, on the way make an effort to settle the case,[a] or you may be dragged before the judge, and the judge hand you over to the officer, and the officer throw you in prison. [59]I tell you, you will never get out until you have paid the very last penny."

Repent or Perish

13 At that very time there were some present who told him about the Galileans whose blood Pilate had mingled with their sacrifices. [2]He asked them, "Do you think that because these Galileans suffered in this way they were worse sinners than all other Galileans? [3]No, I tell you; but unless you repent, you will all perish as they did. [4]Or those eighteen who were killed when the tower of Siloam fell on them—do you think that they were worse offenders than all the others living in Jerusalem? [5]No, I tell you; but unless you repent, you will all perish just as they did."

The Parable of the Barren Fig Tree

6 Then he told this parable: "A man had a fig tree planted in his vineyard; and he came looking for fruit on it and found none. [7]So he said to the gardener, 'See here! For three years I have come looking for fruit on this fig tree, and still I find none. Cut it down! Why should it be wasting the soil?' [8]He replied, 'Sir, let it alone for one more year, until I dig around it and put manure on it. [9]If it bears fruit next year, well and good; but if not, you can cut it down.' "

Jesus Heals a Crippled Woman

10 Now he was teaching in one of the synagogues on the sabbath. [11]And just then there appeared a woman with a spirit that had crippled her for eighteen years. She was bent over and was quite unable to stand up straight. [12]When Jesus saw her, he called her over and said, "Woman, you are set free from your ailment." [13]When he laid his hands on her, immediately she stood up straight and began praising God. [14]But the leader of the synagogue, indignant because Jesus had cured on the sabbath, kept saying to the crowd, "There are six days on which work ought to be done; come on those days and be cured, and not on the sabbath day." [15]But the Lord answered him and said, "You hypocrites! Does not each of you on the sabbath untie his ox or his donkey from the manger, and lead it away to give it water? [16]And ought not this woman, a daughter of Abraham whom Satan bound for eighteen long years, be set free from this bondage on the sabbath day?" [17]When he said this, all his opponents were put to shame; and the entire crowd was rejoicing at all the wonderful things that he was doing.

The Parable of the Mustard Seed

18 He said therefore, "What is the kingdom of God like? And to what should I

---

a Gk *settle with him*

compare it? ¹⁹It is like a mustard seed that someone took and sowed in the garden; it grew and became a tree, and the birds of the air made nests in its branches."

The Parable of the Yeast

20 And again he said, "To what should I compare the kingdom of God? ²¹It is like yeast that a woman took and mixed in with*a* three measures of flour until all of it was leavened."

The Narrow Door

22 Jesus*b* went through one town and village after another, teaching as he made his way to Jerusalem. ²³Someone asked him, "Lord, will only a few be saved?" He said to them, ²⁴"Strive to enter through the narrow door; for many, I tell you, will try to enter and will not be able. ²⁵When once the owner of the house has got up and shut the door, and you begin to stand outside and to knock at the door, saying, 'Lord, open to us,' then in reply he will say to you, 'I do not know where you come from.' ²⁶Then you will begin to say, 'We ate and drank with you, and you taught in our streets.' ²⁷But he will say, 'I do not know where you come from; go away from me, all you evildoers!' ²⁸There will be weeping and gnashing of teeth when you see Abraham and Isaac and Jacob and all the prophets in the kingdom of God, and you yourselves thrown out. ²⁹Then people will come from east and west, from north and south, and will eat in the kingdom of God. ³⁰Indeed, some are last who will be first, and some are first who will be last."

The Lament over Jerusalem

31 At that very hour some Pharisees came and said to him, "Get away from here, for Herod wants to kill you." ³²He said to them, "Go and tell that fox for me,*c* 'Listen, I am casting out demons and performing cures today and tomorrow, and on the third day I finish my work. ³³Yet today, tomorrow, and the next day I must be on my way, because it is impossible for a prophet to be killed outside of Jerusalem.' ³⁴Jerusalem, Jerusalem, the city that kills the prophets and stones those who are sent to it! How often have I desired to gather your children together as a hen gathers her brood under her wings, and you were not willing! ³⁵See, your house is left to you. And I tell you, you will not see me until the time comes when*d* you say, 'Blessed is the one who comes in the name of the Lord.'"

Jesus Heals the Man with Dropsy

14 On one occasion when Jesus*e* was going to the house of a leader of the Pharisees to eat a meal on the sabbath, they were watching him closely. ²Just then, in front of him, there was a man who had dropsy. ³And Jesus asked the lawyers and Pharisees, "Is it lawful to cure people on the sabbath, or not?" ⁴But they were silent. So Jesus*e* took him and healed him, and sent him away. ⁵Then he said to them, "If one of you has a child*f* or an ox that has fallen into a well, will you not immediately pull it out on a sabbath day?" ⁶And they could not reply to this.

Humility and Hospitality

7 When he noticed how the guests chose the places of honor, he told them a parable. ⁸"When you are invited by someone to a wedding banquet, do not sit down at the place of honor, in case someone more distinguished than you has been invited by your host; ⁹and the host who invited both of you may come and say to you, 'Give this person your place,' and then in disgrace you would start to take the lowest place. ¹⁰But when you are invited, go and sit down at the lowest place, so that when your host comes, he may say to you, 'Friend, move up higher'; then you will be honored in the presence of all who sit at the table with you. ¹¹For all who exalt themselves will be humbled, and

---

a Gk *hid in*　　*b* Gk *He*　　*c* Gk lacks *for me*　　*d* Other ancient authorities lack *the time comes when*　　*e* Gk *he*
f Other ancient authorities read *a donkey*

those who humble themselves will be exalted."

12 He said also to the one who had invited him, "When you give a luncheon or a dinner, do not invite your friends or your brothers or your relatives or rich neighbors, in case they may invite you in return, and you would be repaid. 13But when you give a banquet, invite the poor, the crippled, the lame, and the blind. 14And you will be blessed, because they cannot repay you, for you will be repaid at the resurrection of the righteous."

The Parable of the Great Dinner

15 One of the dinner guests, on hearing this, said to him, "Blessed is anyone who will eat bread in the kingdom of God!" 16Then Jesus*a* said to him, "Someone gave a great dinner and invited many. 17At the time for the dinner he sent his slave to say to those who had been invited, 'Come; for everything is ready now.' 18But they all alike began to make excuses. The first said to him, 'I have bought a piece of land, and I must go out and see it; please accept my regrets.' 19Another said, 'I have bought five yoke of oxen, and I am going to try them out; please accept my regrets.' 20Another said, 'I have just been married, and therefore I cannot come.' 21So the slave returned and reported this to his master. Then the owner of the house became angry and said to his slave, 'Go out at once into the streets and lanes of the town and bring in the poor, the crippled, the blind, and the lame.' 22And the slave said, 'Sir, what you ordered has been done, and there is still room.' 23Then the master said to the slave, 'Go out into the roads and lanes, and compel people to come in, so that my house may be filled. 24For I tell you,*b* none of those who were invited will taste my dinner.' "

The Cost of Discipleship

25 Now large crowds were traveling with him; and he turned and said to them,

26"Whoever comes to me and does not hate father and mother, wife and children, brothers and sisters, yes, and even life itself, cannot be my disciple. 27Whoever does not carry the cross and follow me cannot be my disciple. 28For which of you, intending to build a tower, does not first sit down and estimate the cost, to see whether he has enough to complete it? 29Otherwise, when he has laid a foundation and is not able to finish, all who see it will begin to ridicule him, 30saying, 'This fellow began to build and was not able to finish.' 31Or what king, going out to wage war against another king, will not sit down first and consider whether he is able with ten thousand to oppose the one who comes against him with twenty thousand? 32If he cannot, then, while the other is still far away, he sends a delegation and asks for the terms of peace. 33So therefore, none of you can become my disciple if you do not give up all your possessions.

About Salt

34 "Salt is good; but if salt has lost its taste, how can its saltiness be restored?*c* 35It is fit neither for the soil nor for the manure pile; they throw it away. Let anyone with ears to hear listen!"

The Parable of the Lost Sheep

15 Now all the tax collectors and sinners were coming near to listen to him. 2And the Pharisees and the scribes were grumbling and saying, "This fellow welcomes sinners and eats with them."

3 So he told them this parable: 4"Which one of you, having a hundred sheep and losing one of them, does not leave the ninety-nine in the wilderness and go after the one that is lost until he finds it? 5When he has found it, he lays it on his shoulders and rejoices. 6And when he comes home, he calls together his friends and neighbors, saying to them, 'Rejoice with me, for I have found my sheep that was lost.' 7Just so, I tell you, there

---

a Gk *he*   *b* The Greek word for *you* here is plural   *c* Or *how can it be used for seasoning?*

will be more joy in heaven over one sinner who repents than over ninety-nine righteous persons who need no repentance.

The Parable of the Lost Coin

8 "Or what woman having ten silver coins,*a* if she loses one of them, does not light a lamp, sweep the house, and search carefully until she finds it? 9When she has found it, she calls together her friends and neighbors, saying, 'Rejoice with me, for I have found the coin that I had lost.' 10Just so, I tell you, there is joy in the presence of the angels of God over one sinner who repents."

The Parable of the Prodigal and His Brother

11 Then Jesus*b* said, "There was a man who had two sons. 12The younger of them said to his father, 'Father, give me the share of the property that will belong to me.' So he divided his property between them. 13A few days later the younger son gathered all he had and traveled to a distant country, and there he squandered his property in dissolute living. 14When he had spent everything, a severe famine took place throughout that country, and he began to be in need. 15So he went and hired himself out to one of the citizens of that country, who sent him to his fields to feed the pigs. 16He would gladly have filled himself with*c* the pods that the pigs were eating; and no one gave him anything. 17But when he came to himself he said, 'How many of my father's hired hands have bread enough and to spare, but here I am dying of hunger! 18I will get up and go to my father, and I will say to him, "Father, I have sinned against heaven and before you; 19I am no longer worthy to be called your son; treat me like one of your hired hands." ' 20So he set off and went to his father. But while he was still far off, his father saw him and was filled with compassion; he ran and put his arms around him and kissed him. 21Then the son said to him, 'Father, I have sinned against heaven and before you; I am no longer worthy to be

called your son.'*d* 22But the father said to his slaves, 'Quickly, bring out a robe—the best one—and put it on him; put a ring on his finger and sandals on his feet. 23And get the fatted calf and kill it, and let us eat and celebrate; 24for this son of mine was dead and is alive again; he was lost and is found!' And they began to celebrate.

25 "Now his elder son was in the field; and when he came and approached the house, he heard music and dancing. 26He called one of the slaves and asked what was going on. 27He replied, 'Your brother has come, and your father has killed the fatted calf, because he has got him back safe and sound.' 28Then he became angry and refused to go in. His father came out and began to plead with him. 29But he answered his father, 'Listen! For all these years I have been working like a slave for you, and I have never disobeyed your command; yet you have never given me even a young goat so that I might celebrate with my friends. 30But when this son of yours came back, who has devoured your property with prostitutes, you killed the fatted calf for him!' 31Then the father*b* said to him, 'Son, you are always with me, and all that is mine is yours. 32But we had to celebrate and rejoice, because this brother of yours was dead and has come to life; he was lost and has been found.' "

The Parable of the Dishonest Manager

16 Then Jesus*b* said to the disciples, "There was a rich man who had a manager, and charges were brought to him that this man was squandering his property. 2So he summoned him and said to him, 'What is this that I hear about you? Give me an accounting of your management, because you cannot be my manager any longer.' 3Then the manager said to himself, 'What will I do, now that my master is taking the position away from me? I am not strong enough to dig, and I am ashamed to beg. 4I have decided what to do so that, when I am dismissed

---

a Gk *drachmas*, each worth about a day's wage for a laborer   *b* Gk *he*   *c* Other ancient authorities read *filled his stomach with*   *d* Other ancient authorities add *Treat me like one of your hired servants* as manager, people may welcome me into their homes.' ⁵So, summoning his master's debtors one by one, he asked the first, 'How much do you owe my master?' ⁶He answered, 'A hundred jugs of olive oil.' He said to him, 'Take your bill, sit down quickly, and make it fifty.' ⁷Then he asked another, 'And how much do you owe?' He replied, 'A hundred containers of wheat.' He said to him, 'Take your bill and make it eighty.' ⁸And his master commended the dishonest manager because he had acted shrewdly; for the children of this age are more shrewd in dealing with their own generation than are the children of light. ⁹And I tell you, make friends for yourselves by means of dishonest wealth*a* so that when it is gone, they may welcome you into the eternal homes. *b*

10 "Whoever is faithful in a very little is faithful also in much; and whoever is dishonest in a very little is dishonest also in much. ¹¹If then you have not been faithful with the dishonest wealth,*a* who will entrust to you the true riches? ¹²And if you have not been faithful with what belongs to another, who will give you what is your own? ¹³No slave can serve two masters; for a slave will either hate the one and love the other, or be devoted to the one and despise the other. You cannot serve God and wealth."*a*

The Law and the Kingdom of God

14 The Pharisees, who were lovers of money, heard all this, and they ridiculed him. ¹⁵So he said to them, "You are those who justify yourselves in the sight of others; but God knows your hearts; for what is prized by human beings is an abomination in the sight of God.

16 "The law and the prophets were in effect until John came; since then the good news of the kingdom of God is proclaimed, and everyone tries to enter it by force.*c* ¹⁷But it is easier for heaven and earth to pass away, than for one stroke of a letter in the law to be dropped.

18 "Anyone who divorces his wife and marries another commits adultery, and whoever marries a woman divorced from her husband commits adultery.

The Rich Man and Lazarus

19 "There was a rich man who was dressed in purple and fine linen and who feasted sumptuously every day. ²⁰And at his gate lay a poor man named Lazarus, covered with sores, ²¹who longed to satisfy his hunger with what fell from the rich man's table; even the dogs would come and lick his sores. ²²The poor man died and was carried away by the angels to be with Abraham.*d* The rich man also died and was buried. ²³In Hades, where he was being tormented, he looked up and saw Abraham far away with Lazarus by his side.*e* ²⁴He called out, 'Father Abraham, have mercy on me, and send Lazarus to dip the tip of his finger in water and cool my tongue; for I am in agony in these flames.' ²⁵But Abraham said, 'Child, remember that during your lifetime you received your good things, and Lazarus in like manner evil things; but now he is comforted here, and you are in agony. ²⁶Besides all this, between you and us a great chasm has been fixed, so that those who might want to pass from here to you cannot do so, and no one can cross from there to us.' ²⁷He said, 'Then, father, I beg you to send him to my father's house— ²⁸for I have five brothers—that he may warn them, so that they will not also come into this place of torment.' ²⁹Abraham replied, 'They have Moses and the prophets; they should listen to them.' ³⁰He said, 'No, father Abraham; but if someone goes to them from the dead, they will repent.' ³¹He said to him, 'If they do not listen to Moses and the prophets, neither will they be convinced even if someone rises from the dead.' "

Some Sayings of Jesus

17 Jesus*f* said to his disciples, "Occasions for stumbling are bound to

---

a Gk *mammon*   *b* Gk *tents*   *c* Or *everyone is strongly urged to enter it*   *d* Gk *to Abraham's bosom*   *e* Gk *in his bosom*
f Gk *He*

come, but woe to anyone by whom they come! [2]It would be better for you if a millstone were hung around your neck and you were thrown into the sea than for you to cause one of these little ones to stumble. [3]Be on your guard! If another disciple[a] sins, you must rebuke the offender, and if there is repentance, you must forgive. [4]And if the same person sins against you seven times a day, and turns back to you seven times and says, 'I repent,' you must forgive."

5 The apostles said to the Lord, "Increase our faith!" [6]The Lord replied, "If you had faith the size of a[b] mustard seed, you could say to this mulberry tree, 'Be uprooted and planted in the sea,' and it would obey you.

7 "Who among you would say to your slave who has just come in from plowing or tending sheep in the field, 'Come here at once and take your place at the table'? [8]Would you not rather say to him, 'Prepare supper for me, put on your apron and serve me while I eat and drink; later you may eat and drink'? [9]Do you thank the slave for doing what was commanded? [10]So you also, when you have done all that you were ordered to do, say, 'We are worthless slaves; we have done only what we ought to have done!' "

Jesus Cleanses Ten Lepers

11 On the way to Jerusalem Jesus[c] was going through the region between Samaria and Galilee. [12]As he entered a village, ten lepers[d] approached him. Keeping their distance, [13]they called out, saying, "Jesus, Master, have mercy on us!" [14]When he saw them, he said to them, "Go and show yourselves to the priests." And as they went, they were made clean. [15]Then one of them, when he saw that he was healed, turned back, praising God with a loud voice. [16]He prostrated himself at Jesus'[e] feet and thanked him. And he was a Samaritan. [17]Then Jesus asked, "Were not ten made clean? But the other nine, where are they? [18]Was none of them found to return

and give praise to God except this foreigner?" [19]Then he said to him, "Get up and go on your way; your faith has made you well."

The Coming of the Kingdom

20 Once Jesus[c] was asked by the Pharisees when the kingdom of God was coming, and he answered, "The kingdom of God is not coming with things that can be observed; [21]nor will they say, 'Look, here it is!' or 'There it is!' For, in fact, the kingdom of God is among[f] you."

22 Then he said to the disciples, "The days are coming when you will long to see one of the days of the Son of Man, and you will not see it. [23]They will say to you, 'Look there!' or 'Look here!' Do not go, do not set off in pursuit. [24]For as the lightning flashes and lights up the sky from one side to the other, so will the Son of Man be in his day.[g] [25]But first he must endure much suffering and be rejected by this generation. [26]Just as it was in the days of Noah, so too it will be in the days of the Son of Man. [27]They were eating and drinking, and marrying and being given in marriage, until the day Noah entered the ark, and the flood came and destroyed all of them. [28]Likewise, just as it was in the days of Lot: they were eating and drinking, buying and selling, planting and building, [29]but on the day that Lot left Sodom, it rained fire and sulfur from heaven and destroyed all of them [30]—it will be like that on the day that the Son of Man is revealed. [31]On that day, anyone on the housetop who has belongings in the house must not come down to take them away; and likewise anyone in the field must not turn back. [32]Remember Lot's wife. [33]Those who try to make their life secure will lose it, but those who lose their life will keep it. [34]I tell you, on that night there will be two in one bed; one will be taken and the other left. [35]There will be two women grinding meal together; one will be taken and the other left."[h] [37]Then they asked

---

a Gk *your brother*   b Gk *faith as a grain of*   c Gk *he*   d The terms *leper* and *leprosy* can refer to several diseases
e Gk *his*   f Or *within*   g Other ancient authorities lack *in his day*   h Other ancient authorities add verse 36,
"Two will be in the field; one will be taken and the other left."

him, "Where, Lord?" He said to them, "Where the corpse is, there the vultures will gather."

The Parable of the Widow and the Unjust Judge

18 Then Jesus*a* told them a parable about their need to pray always and not to lose heart. 2He said, "In a certain city there was a judge who neither feared God nor had respect for people. 3In that city there was a widow who kept coming to him and saying, 'Grant me justice against my opponent.' 4For a while he refused; but later he said to himself, 'Though I have no fear of God and no respect for anyone, 5yet because this widow keeps bothering me, I will grant her justice, so that she may not wear me out by continually coming.' "*b* 6And the Lord said, "Listen to what the unjust judge says. 7And will not God grant justice to his chosen ones who cry to him day and night? Will he delay long in helping them? 8I tell you, he will quickly grant justice to them. And yet, when the Son of Man comes, will he find faith on earth?"

The Parable of the Pharisee and the Tax Collector

9 He also told this parable to some who trusted in themselves that they were righteous and regarded others with contempt: 10"Two men went up to the temple to pray, one a Pharisee and the other a tax collector. 11The Pharisee, standing by himself, was praying thus, 'God, I thank you that I am not like other people: thieves, rogues, adulterers, or even like this tax collector. 12I fast twice a week; I give a tenth of all my income.' 13But the tax collector, standing far off, would not even look up to heaven, but was beating his breast and saying, 'God, be merciful to me, a sinner!' 14I tell you, this man went down to his home justified rather than the other; for all who exalt themselves will be humbled, but all who humble themselves will be exalted."

Jesus Blesses Little Children

15 People were bringing even infants to him that he might touch them; and when the disciples saw it, they sternly ordered them not to do it. 16But Jesus called for them and said, "Let the little children come to me, and do not stop them; for it is to such as these that the kingdom of God belongs. 17Truly I tell you, whoever does not receive the kingdom of God as a little child will never enter it."

The Rich Ruler

18 A certain ruler asked him, "Good Teacher, what must I do to inherit eternal life?" 19Jesus said to him, "Why do you call me good? No one is good but God alone. 20You know the commandments: 'You shall not commit adultery; You shall not murder; You shall not steal; You shall not bear false witness; Honor your father and mother.' " 21He replied, "I have kept all these since my youth." 22When Jesus heard this, he said to him, "There is still one thing lacking. Sell all that you own and distribute the money*c* to the poor, and you will have treasure in heaven; then come, follow me." 23But when he heard this, he became sad; for he was very rich. 24Jesus looked at him and said, "How hard it is for those who have wealth to enter the kingdom of God! 25Indeed, it is easier for a camel to go through the eye of a needle than for someone who is rich to enter the kingdom of God."

26 Those who heard it said, "Then who can be saved?" 27He replied, "What is impossible for mortals is possible for God."

28 Then Peter said, "Look, we have left our homes and followed you." 29And he said to them, "Truly I tell you, there is no one who has left house or wife or brothers or parents or children, for the sake of the kingdom of God, 30who will not get back very much more in this age, and in the age to come eternal life."

---

a Gk *he*   *b* Or *so that she may not finally come and slap me in the face*   *c* Gk lacks *the money*

A Third Time Jesus Foretells His Death and Resurrection

31 Then he took the twelve aside and said to them, "See, we are going up to Jerusalem, and everything that is written about the Son of Man by the prophets will be accomplished. 32For he will be handed over to the Gentiles; and he will be mocked and insulted and spat upon. 33After they have flogged him, they will kill him, and on the third day he will rise again." 34But they understood nothing about all these things; in fact, what he said was hidden from them, and they did not grasp what was said.

Jesus Heals a Blind Beggar Near Jericho

35 As he approached Jericho, a blind man was sitting by the roadside begging. 36When he heard a crowd going by, he asked what was happening. 37They told him, "Jesus of Nazareth*a* is passing by." 38Then he shouted, "Jesus, Son of David, have mercy on me!" 39Those who were in front sternly ordered him to be quiet; but he shouted even more loudly, "Son of David, have mercy on me!" 40Jesus stood still and ordered the man to be brought to him; and when he came near, he asked him, 41"What do you want me to do for you?" He said, "Lord, let me see again." 42Jesus said to him, "Receive your sight; your faith has saved you." 43Immediately he regained his sight and followed him, glorifying God; and all the people, when they saw it, praised God.

Jesus and Zacchaeus

19 He entered Jericho and was passing through it. 2A man was there named Zacchaeus; he was a chief tax collector and was rich. 3He was trying to see who Jesus was, but on account of the crowd he could not, because he was short in stature. 4So he ran ahead and climbed a sycamore tree to see him, because he was going to pass that way. 5When Jesus came to the place, he looked up and said to him, "Zacchaeus, hurry and come down; for I must stay at your house today." 6So he hurried down and was happy to welcome him. 7All who saw it began to grumble and said, "He has gone to be the guest of one who is a sinner." 8Zacchaeus stood there and said to the Lord, "Look, half of my possessions, Lord, I will give to the poor; and if I have defrauded anyone of anything, I will pay back four times as much." 9Then Jesus said to him, "Today salvation has come to this house, because he too is a son of Abraham. 10For the Son of Man came to seek out and to save the lost."

The Parable of the Ten Pounds

11 As they were listening to this, he went on to tell a parable, because he was near Jerusalem, and because they supposed that the kingdom of God was to appear immediately. 12So he said, "A nobleman went to a distant country to get royal power for himself and then return. 13He summoned ten of his slaves, and gave them ten pounds,*b* and said to them, 'Do business with these until I come back.' 14But the citizens of his country hated him and sent a delegation after him, saying, 'We do not want this man to rule over us.' 15When he returned, having received royal power, he ordered these slaves, to whom he had given the money, to be summoned so that he might find out what they had gained by trading. 16The first came forward and said, 'Lord, your pound has made ten more pounds.' 17He said to him, 'Well done, good slave! Because you have been trustworthy in a very small thing, take charge of ten cities.' 18Then the second came, saying, 'Lord, your pound has made five pounds.' 19He said to him, 'And you, rule over five cities.' 20Then the other came, saying, 'Lord, here is your pound. I wrapped it up in a piece of cloth, 21for I was afraid of you, because you are a harsh man; you take what you did not deposit, and reap what you did not sow.' 22He said to him, 'I will judge you by your own words, you wicked slave! You knew, did you,

a Gk *the Nazorean*   *b* The mina, rendered here by *pound,* was about three months' wages for a laborer that I was a harsh man, taking what I did not deposit and reaping what I did not sow? 23Why then did you not put my money into the bank? Then when I returned, I could have collected it with interest.' 24He said to the bystanders, 'Take the pound from him and give it to the one who has ten pounds.' 25(And they said to him, 'Lord, he has ten pounds!') 26'I tell you, to all those who have, more will be given; but from those who have nothing, even what they have will be taken away. 27But as for these enemies of mine who did not want me to be king over them—bring them here and slaughter them in my presence.' "

Jesus' Triumphal Entry into Jerusalem

28 After he had said this, he went on ahead, going up to Jerusalem.

29 When he had come near Bethphage and Bethany, at the place called the Mount of Olives, he sent two of the disciples, 30saying, "Go into the village ahead of you, and as you enter it you will find tied there a colt that has never been ridden. Untie it and bring it here. 31If anyone asks you, 'Why are you untying it?' just say this, 'The Lord needs it.' " 32So those who were sent departed and found it as he had told them. 33As they were untying the colt, its owners asked them, "Why are you untying the colt?" 34They said, "The Lord needs it." 35Then they brought it to Jesus; and after throwing their cloaks on the colt, they set Jesus on it. 36As he rode along, people kept spreading their cloaks on the road. 37As he was now approaching the path down from the Mount of Olives, the whole multitude of the disciples began to praise God joyfully with a loud voice for all the deeds of power that they had seen, 38saying,

"Blessed is the king
　　who comes in the name of the Lord!
Peace in heaven,
　　and glory in the highest heaven!"

39Some of the Pharisees in the crowd said to him, "Teacher, order your disciples to stop."

40He answered, "I tell you, if these were silent, the stones would shout out."

Jesus Weeps over Jerusalem

41 As he came near and saw the city, he wept over it, 42saying, "If you, even you, had only recognized on this day the things that make for peace! But now they are hidden from your eyes. 43Indeed, the days will come upon you, when your enemies will set up ramparts around you and surround you, and hem you in on every side. 44They will crush you to the ground, you and your children within you, and they will not leave within you one stone upon another; because you did not recognize the time of your visitation from God." a

Jesus Cleanses the Temple

45 Then he entered the temple and began to drive out those who were selling things there; 46and he said, "It is written,

'My house shall be a house of prayer';
　　but you have made it a den of
　　　　robbers."

47 Every day he was teaching in the temple. The chief priests, the scribes, and the leaders of the people kept looking for a way to kill him; 48but they did not find anything they could do, for all the people were spellbound by what they heard.

The Authority of Jesus Questioned

20 One day, as he was teaching the people in the temple and telling the good news, the chief priests and the scribes came with the elders 2and said to him, "Tell us, by what authority are you doing these things? Who is it who gave you this authority?" 3He answered them, "I will also ask you a question, and you tell me: 4Did the baptism of John come from heaven, or was it of human origin?" 5They discussed it with one another, saying, "If we say, 'From heaven,' he will say, 'Why did you not believe him?' 6But if we say, 'Of human origin,' all the people

a Gk lacks from God

will stone us; for they are convinced that John was a prophet." 7So they answered that they did not know where it came from. 8Then Jesus said to them, "Neither will I tell you by what authority I am doing these things."

The Parable of the Wicked Tenants

9 He began to tell the people this parable: "A man planted a vineyard, and leased it to tenants, and went to another country for a long time. 10When the season came, he sent a slave to the tenants in order that they might give him his share of the produce of the vineyard; but the tenants beat him and sent him away empty-handed. 11Next he sent another slave; that one also they beat and insulted and sent away empty-handed. 12And he sent still a third; this one also they wounded and threw out. 13Then the owner of the vineyard said, 'What shall I do? I will send my beloved son; perhaps they will respect him.' 14But when the tenants saw him, they discussed it among themselves and said, 'This is the heir; let us kill him so that the inheritance may be ours.' 15So they threw him out of the vineyard and killed him. What then will the owner of the vineyard do to them? 16He will come and destroy those tenants and give the vineyard to others." When they heard this, they said, "Heaven forbid!" 17But he looked at them and said, "What then does this text mean:

'The stone that the builders rejected
    has become the cornerstone'?*a*

18Everyone who falls on that stone will be broken to pieces; and it will crush anyone on whom it falls." 19When the scribes and chief priests realized that he had told this parable against them, they wanted to lay hands on him at that very hour, but they feared the people.

The Question about Paying Taxes

20 So they watched him and sent spies who pretended to be honest, in order to trap him by what he said, so as to hand him over

to the jurisdiction and authority of the governor. 21So they asked him, "Teacher, we know that you are right in what you say and teach, and you show deference to no one, but teach the way of God in accordance with truth. 22Is it lawful for us to pay taxes to the emperor, or not?" 23But he perceived their craftiness and said to them, 24"Show me a denarius. Whose head and whose title does it bear?" They said, "The emperor's." 25He said to them, "Then give to the emperor the things that are the emperor's, and to God the things that are God's." 26And they were not able in the presence of the people to trap him by what he said; and being amazed by his answer, they became silent.

The Question about the Resurrection

27 Some Sadducees, those who say there is no resurrection, came to him 28and asked him a question, "Teacher, Moses wrote for us that if a man's brother dies, leaving a wife but no children, the man *b* shall marry the widow and raise up children for his brother. 29Now there were seven brothers; the first married, and died childless; 30then the second 31and the third married her, and so in the same way all seven died childless. 32Finally the woman also died. 33In the resurrection, therefore, whose wife will the woman be? For the seven had married her."

34 Jesus said to them, "Those who belong to this age marry and are given in marriage; 35but those who are considered worthy of a place in that age and in the resurrection from the dead neither marry nor are given in marriage. 36Indeed they cannot die anymore, because they are like angels and are children of God, being children of the resurrection. 37And the fact that the dead are raised Moses himself showed, in the story about the bush, where he speaks of the Lord as the God of Abraham, the God of Isaac, and the God of Jacob. 38Now he is God not of the dead, but of the living; for to him all of them are alive." 39Then some of the scribes

a Or *keystone*   *b* Gk *his brother*

answered, "Teacher, you have spoken well." [40]For they no longer dared to ask him another question.

The Question about David's Son

41 Then he said to them, "How can they say that the Messiah[a] is David's son? [42]For David himself says in the book of Psalms,

'The Lord said to my Lord,
"Sit at my right hand,
43   until I make your enemies your
                    footstool." '

[44]David thus calls him Lord; so how can he be his son?"

Jesus Denounces the Scribes

45 In the hearing of all the people he said to the[b] disciples, [46]"Beware of the scribes, who like to walk around in long robes, and love to be greeted with respect in the marketplaces, and to have the best seats in the synagogues and places of honor at banquets. [47]They devour widows' houses and for the sake of appearance say long prayers. They will receive the greater condemnation."

The Widow's Offering

21 He looked up and saw rich people putting their gifts into the treasury; [2]he also saw a poor widow put in two small copper coins. [3]He said, "Truly I tell you, this poor widow has put in more than all of them; [4]for all of them have contributed out of their abundance, but she out of her poverty has put in all she had to live on."

The Destruction of the Temple Foretold

5 When some were speaking about the temple, how it was adorned with beautiful stones and gifts dedicated to God, he said, [6]"As for these things that you see, the days will come when not one stone will be left upon another; all will be thrown down."

Signs and Persecutions

7 They asked him, "Teacher, when will

this be, and what will be the sign that this is about to take place?" [8]And he said, "Beware that you are not led astray; for many will come in my name and say, 'I am he!'[c] and, 'The time is near!'[d] Do not go after them.

9 "When you hear of wars and insurrections, do not be terrified; for these things must take place first, but the end will not follow immediately." [10]Then he said to them, "Nation will rise against nation, and kingdom against kingdom; [11]there will be great earthquakes, and in various places famines and plagues; and there will be dreadful portents and great signs from heaven.

12 "But before all this occurs, they will arrest you and persecute you; they will hand you over to synagogues and prisons, and you will be brought before kings and governors because of my name. [13]This will give you an opportunity to testify. [14]So make up your minds not to prepare your defense in advance; [15]for I will give you words[e] and a wisdom that none of your opponents will be able to withstand or contradict. [16]You will be betrayed even by parents and brothers, by relatives and friends; and they will put some of you to death. [17]You will be hated by all because of my name. [18]But not a hair of your head will perish. [19]By your endurance you will gain your souls.

The Destruction of Jerusalem Foretold

20 "When you see Jerusalem surrounded by armies, then know that its desolation has come near.[f] [21]Then those in Judea must flee to the mountains, and those inside the city must leave it, and those out in the country must not enter it; [22]for these are days of vengeance, as a fulfillment of all that is written. [23]Woe to those who are pregnant and to those who are nursing infants in those days! For there will be great distress on the earth and wrath against this people; [24]they will fall by the edge of the sword and be taken away as captives among all nations; and Jerusalem

will be trampled on by the Gentiles, until the times of the Gentiles are fulfilled.

The Coming of the Son of Man

25 "There will be signs in the sun, the moon, and the stars, and on the earth distress among nations confused by the roaring of the sea and the waves. 26People will faint from fear and foreboding of what is coming upon the world, for the powers of the heavens will be shaken. 27Then they will see 'the Son of Man coming in a cloud' with power and great glory. 28Now when these things begin to take place, stand up and raise your heads, because your redemption is drawing near."

The Lesson of the Fig Tree

29 Then he told them a parable: "Look at the fig tree and all the trees; 30as soon as they sprout leaves you can see for yourselves and know that summer is already near. 31So also, when you see these things taking place, you know that the kingdom of God is near. 32Truly I tell you, this generation will not pass away until all things have taken place. 33Heaven and earth will pass away, but my words will not pass away.

Exhortation to Watch

34 "Be on guard so that your hearts are not weighed down with dissipation and drunkenness and the worries of this life, and that day does not catch you unexpectedly, 35like a trap. For it will come upon all who live on the face of the whole earth. 36Be alert at all times, praying that you may have the strength to escape all these things that will take place, and to stand before the Son of Man."

37 Every day he was teaching in the temple, and at night he would go out and spend the night on the Mount of Olives, as it was called. 38And all the people would get up early in the morning to listen to him in the temple.

The Plot to Kill Jesus

22 Now the festival of Unleavened Bread, which is called the Passover, was near. 2The chief priests and the scribes were looking for a way to put Jesus*a* to death, for they were afraid of the people.

3 Then Satan entered into Judas called Iscariot, who was one of the twelve; 4he went away and conferred with the chief priests and officers of the temple police about how he might betray him to them. 5They were greatly pleased and agreed to give him money. 6So he consented and began to look for an opportunity to betray him to them when no crowd was present.

The Preparation of the Passover

7 Then came the day of Unleavened Bread, on which the Passover lamb had to be sacrificed. 8So Jesus*b* sent Peter and John, saying, "Go and prepare the Passover meal for us that we may eat it." 9They asked him, "Where do you want us to make preparations for it?" 10"Listen," he said to them, "when you have entered the city, a man carrying a jar of water will meet you; follow him into the house he enters 11and say to the owner of the house, 'The teacher asks you, "Where is the guest room, where I may eat the Passover with my disciples?" ' 12He will show you a large room upstairs, already furnished. Make preparations for us there." 13So they went and found everything as he had told them; and they prepared the Passover meal.

The Institution of the Lord's Supper

14 When the hour came, he took his place at the table, and the apostles with him. 15He said to them, "I have eagerly desired to eat this Passover with you before I suffer; 16for I tell you, I will not eat it*c* until it is fulfilled in the kingdom of God." 17Then he took a cup, and after giving thanks he said, "Take this and divide it among yourselves; 18for I tell you that from now on I will not drink of the

---

a Gk *him*   *b* Gk *he*   *c* Other ancient authorities read *never eat it again* fruit of the vine until the kingdom of God comes." [19]Then he took a loaf of bread, and when he had given thanks, he broke it and gave it to them, saying, "This is my body, which is given for you. Do this in remembrance of me." [20]And he did the same with the cup after supper, saying, "This cup that is poured out for you is the new covenant in my blood.[a] [21]But see, the one who betrays me is with me, and his hand is on the table. [22]For the Son of Man is going as it has been determined, but woe to that one by whom he is betrayed!" [23]Then they began to ask one another which one of them it could be who would do this.

The Dispute about Greatness

[24] A dispute also arose among them as to which one of them was to be regarded as the greatest. [25]But he said to them, "The kings of the Gentiles lord it over them; and those in authority over them are called benefactors. [26]But not so with you; rather the greatest among you must become like the youngest, and the leader like one who serves. [27]For who is greater, the one who is at the table or the one who serves? Is it not the one at the table? But I am among you as one who serves.

[28] "You are those who have stood by me in my trials; [29]and I confer on you, just as my Father has conferred on me, a kingdom, [30]so that you may eat and drink at my table in my kingdom, and you will sit on thrones judging the twelve tribes of Israel.

Jesus Predicts Peter's Denial

[31] "Simon, Simon, listen! Satan has demanded[b] to sift all of you like wheat, [32]but I have prayed for you that your own faith may not fail; and you, when once you have turned back, strengthen your brothers." [33]And he said to him, "Lord, I am ready to go with you to prison and to death!" [34]Jesus[c] said, "I tell you, Peter, the cock will not crow this day, un-

til you have denied three times that you know me."

Purse, Bag, and Sword

[35] He said to them, "When I sent you out without a purse, bag, or sandals, did you lack anything?" They said, "No, not a thing." [36]He said to them, "But now, the one who has a purse must take it, and likewise a bag. And the one who has no sword must sell his cloak and buy one. [37]For I tell you, this scripture must be fulfilled in me, 'And he was counted among the lawless'; and indeed what is written about me is being fulfilled." [38]They said, "Lord, look, here are two swords." He replied, "It is enough."

Jesus Prays on the Mount of Olives

[39] He came out and went, as was his custom, to the Mount of Olives; and the disciples followed him. [40]When he reached the place, he said to them, "Pray that you may not come into the time of trial."[d] [41]Then he withdrew from them about a stone's throw, knelt down, and prayed, [42]"Father, if you are willing, remove this cup from me; yet, not my will but yours be done." [[[43]Then an angel from heaven appeared to him and gave him strength. [44]In his anguish he prayed more earnestly, and his sweat became like great drops of blood falling down on the ground.]][e] [45]When he got up from prayer, he came to the disciples and found them sleeping because of grief, [46]and he said to them, "Why are you sleeping? Get up and pray that you may not come into the time of trial."[d]

The Betrayal and Arrest of Jesus

[47] While he was still speaking, suddenly a crowd came, and the one called Judas, one of the twelve, was leading them. He approached Jesus to kiss him; [48]but Jesus said to him, "Judas, is it with a kiss that you are betraying the Son of Man?" [49]When those who were around him saw what was coming, they asked, "Lord, should we strike with the

a Other ancient authorities lack, in whole or in part, verses 19b-20 (*which is given . . . in my blood*)   *b* Or *has obtained permission*   *c* Gk *He*   *d* Or *into temptation*   *e* Other ancient authorities lack verses 43 and 44 sword?" 50Then one of them struck the slave of the high priest and cut off his right ear. 51But Jesus said, "No more of this!" And he touched his ear and healed him. 52Then Jesus said to the chief priests, the officers of the temple police, and the elders who had come for him, "Have you come out with swords and clubs as if I were a bandit? 53When I was with you day after day in the temple, you did not lay hands on me. But this is your hour, and the power of darkness!"

Peter Denies Jesus

54 Then they seized him and led him away, bringing him into the high priest's house. But Peter was following at a distance. 55When they had kindled a fire in the middle of the courtyard and sat down together, Peter sat among them. 56Then a servant-girl, seeing him in the firelight, stared at him and said, "This man also was with him." 57But he denied it, saying, "Woman, I do not know him." 58A little later someone else, on seeing him, said, "You also are one of them." But Peter said, "Man, I am not!" 59Then about an hour later still another kept insisting, "Surely this man also was with him; for he is a Galilean." 60But Peter said, "Man, I do not know what you are talking about!" At that moment, while he was still speaking, the cock crowed. 61The Lord turned and looked at Peter. Then Peter remembered the word of the Lord, how he had said to him, "Before the cock crows today, you will deny me three times." 62And he went out and wept bitterly.

The Mocking and Beating of Jesus

63 Now the men who were holding Jesus began to mock him and beat him; 64they also blindfolded him and kept asking him, "Prophesy! Who is it that struck you?" 65They kept heaping many other insults on him.

Jesus before the Council

66 When day came, the assembly of the elders of the people, both chief priests and scribes, gathered together, and they brought him to their council. 67They said, "If you are the Messiah,ᵃ tell us." He replied, "If I tell you, you will not believe; 68and if I question you, you will not answer. 69But from now on the Son of Man will be seated at the right hand of the power of God." 70All of them asked, "Are you, then, the Son of God?" He said to them, "You say that I am." 71Then they said, "What further testimony do we need? We have heard it ourselves from his own lips!"

Jesus before Pilate

23 Then the assembly rose as a body and brought Jesusᵇ before Pilate. 2They began to accuse him, saying, "We found this man perverting our nation, forbidding us to pay taxes to the emperor, and saying that he himself is the Messiah, a king."ᶜ 3Then Pilate asked him, "Are you the king of the Jews?" He answered, "You say so." 4Then Pilate said to the chief priests and the crowds, "I find no basis for an accusation against this man." 5But they were insistent and said, "He stirs up the people by teaching throughout all Judea, from Galilee where he began even to this place."

Jesus before Herod

6 When Pilate heard this, he asked whether the man was a Galilean. 7And when he learned that he was under Herod's jurisdiction, he sent him off to Herod, who was himself in Jerusalem at that time. 8When Herod saw Jesus, he was very glad, for he had been wanting to see him for a long time, because he had heard about him and was hoping to see him perform some sign. 9He questioned him at some length, but Jesusᵈ gave him no answer. 10The chief priests and the scribes stood by, vehemently accusing him. 11Even Herod with his soldiers treated him with contempt and mocked him; then he put an elegant robe on him, and sent him back to Pilate. 12That same day Herod and Pilate be-

a Or *the Christ*   *b* Gk *him*   *c* Or *is an anointed king*   *d* Gk *he* came friends with each other; before this they had been enemies.

Jesus Sentenced to Death

13 Pilate then called together the chief priests, the leaders, and the people, 14and said to them, "You brought me this man as one who was perverting the people; and here I have examined him in your presence and have not found this man guilty of any of your charges against him. 15Neither has Herod, for he sent him back to us. Indeed, he has done nothing to deserve death. 16I will therefore have him flogged and release him." *a*

18 Then they all shouted out together, "Away with this fellow! Release Barabbas for us!" 19(This was a man who had been put in prison for an insurrection that had taken place in the city, and for murder.) 20Pilate, wanting to release Jesus, addressed them again; 21but they kept shouting, "Crucify, crucify him!" 22A third time he said to them, "Why, what evil has he done? I have found in him no ground for the sentence of death; I will therefore have him flogged and then release him." 23But they kept urgently demanding with loud shouts that he should be crucified; and their voices prevailed. 24So Pilate gave his verdict that their demand should be granted. 25He released the man they asked for, the one who had been put in prison for insurrection and murder, and he handed Jesus over as they wished.

The Crucifixion of Jesus

26 As they led him away, they seized a man, Simon of Cyrene, who was coming from the country, and they laid the cross on him, and made him carry it behind Jesus. 27A great number of the people followed him, and among them were women who were beating their breasts and wailing for him. 28But Jesus turned to them and said, "Daughters of Jerusalem, do not weep for me, but weep for yourselves and for your children. 29For the days are surely coming when they will say, 'Blessed are the barren, and the wombs that never bore, and the breasts that never nursed.' 30Then they will begin to say to the mountains, 'Fall on us'; and to the hills, 'Cover us.' 31For if they do this when the wood is green, what will happen when it is dry?"

32 Two others also, who were criminals, were led away to be put to death with him. 33When they came to the place that is called The Skull, they crucified Jesus *b* there with the criminals, one on his right and one on his left. ⟦ 34Then Jesus said, "Father, forgive them; for they do not know what they are doing."⟧ *c* And they cast lots to divide his clothing. 35And the people stood by, watching; but the leaders scoffed at him, saying, "He saved others; let him save himself if he is the Messiah *d* of God, his chosen one!" 36The soldiers also mocked him, coming up and offering him sour wine, 37and saying, "If you are the King of the Jews, save yourself!" 38There was also an inscription over him, *e* "This is the King of the Jews."

39 One of the criminals who were hanged there kept deriding *f* him and saying, "Are you not the Messiah? *d* Save yourself and us!" 40But the other rebuked him, saying, "Do you not fear God, since you are under the same sentence of condemnation? 41And we indeed have been condemned justly, for we are getting what we deserve for our deeds, but this man has done nothing wrong." 42Then he said, "Jesus, remember me when you come into *g* your kingdom." 43He replied, "Truly I tell you, today you will be with me in Paradise."

The Death of Jesus

44 It was now about noon, and darkness came over the whole land *h* until three in the afternoon, 45while the sun's light failed; *i* and

a Here, or after verse 19, other ancient authorities add verse 17, *Now he was obliged to release someone for them at the festival*   *b* Gk *him*   *c* Other ancient authorities lack the sentence *Then Jesus . . . what they are doing*   *d* Or *the Christ*
e Other ancient authorities add *written in Greek and Latin and Hebrew* (that is, *Aramaic*)   *f* Or *blaspheming*   *g* Other ancient authorities read *in*   *h* Or *earth*   *i* Or *the sun was eclipsed*. Other ancient authorities read *the sun was darkened*

the curtain of the temple was torn in two. ⁴⁶Then Jesus, crying with a loud voice, said, "Father, into your hands I commend my spirit." Having said this, he breathed his last. ⁴⁷When the centurion saw what had taken place, he praised God and said, "Certainly this man was innocent."ᵃ ⁴⁸And when all the crowds who had gathered there for this spectacle saw what had taken place, they returned home, beating their breasts. ⁴⁹But all his acquaintances, including the women who had followed him from Galilee, stood at a distance, watching these things.

The Burial of Jesus

50 Now there was a good and righteous man named Joseph, who, though a member of the council, ⁵¹had not agreed to their plan and action. He came from the Jewish town of Arimathea, and he was waiting expectantly for the kingdom of God. ⁵²This man went to Pilate and asked for the body of Jesus. ⁵³Then he took it down, wrapped it in a linen cloth, and laid it in a rock-hewn tomb where no one had ever been laid. ⁵⁴It was the day of Preparation, and the sabbath was beginning.ᵇ ⁵⁵The women who had come with him from Galilee followed, and they saw the tomb and how his body was laid. ⁵⁶Then they returned, and prepared spices and ointments.

On the sabbath they rested according to the commandment.

The Resurrection of Jesus

24 But on the first day of the week, at early dawn, they came to the tomb, taking the spices that they had prepared. ²They found the stone rolled away from the tomb, ³but when they went in, they did not find the body.ᶜ ⁴While they were perplexed about this, suddenly two men in dazzling clothes stood beside them. ⁵The womenᵈ were terrified and bowed their faces to the ground, but the menᵉ said to them, "Why do you look for the living among the dead? He is not here, but has risen.ᶠ ⁶Remember how he told you, while he was still in Galilee, ⁷that the Son of Man must be handed over to sinners, and be crucified, and on the third day rise again." ⁸Then they remembered his words, ⁹and returning from the tomb, they told all this to the eleven and to all the rest. ¹⁰Now it was Mary Magdalene, Joanna, Mary the mother of James, and the other women with them who told this to the apostles. ¹¹But these words seemed to them an idle tale, and they did not believe them. ¹²But Peter got up and ran to the tomb; stooping and looking in, he saw the linen cloths by themselves; then he went home, amazed at what had happened.ᵍ

The Walk to Emmaus

13 Now on that same day two of them were going to a village called Emmaus, about seven milesʰ from Jerusalem, ¹⁴and talking with each other about all these things that had happened. ¹⁵While they were talking and discussing, Jesus himself came near and went with them, ¹⁶but their eyes were kept from recognizing him. ¹⁷And he said to them, "What are you discussing with each other while you walk along?" They stood still, looking sad.ⁱ ¹⁸Then one of them, whose name was Cleopas, answered him, "Are you the only stranger in Jerusalem who does not know the things that have taken place there in these days?" ¹⁹He asked them, "What things?" They replied, "The things about Jesus of Nazareth,ʲ who was a prophet mighty in deed and word before God and all the people, ²⁰and how our chief priests and leaders handed him over to be condemned to death and crucified him. ²¹But we had hoped that he was the one to redeem Israel.ᵏ Yes, and besides all this, it is now the third day since these things took place. ²²Moreover, some women of our group astounded us. They were at the tomb early this morning,

a Or righteous   b Gk was dawning   c Other ancient authorities add of the Lord Jesus   d Gk They   e Gk but they
f Other ancient authorities lack He is not here, but has risen
stadia; other ancient authorities read a hundred sixty stadia   i Other ancient authorities read walk along, looking sad?"
g Other ancient authorities lack verse 12   h Gk sixty
j Other ancient authorities read Jesus the Nazorean   k Or to set Israel free

23and when they did not find his body there, they came back and told us that they had indeed seen a vision of angels who said that he was alive. 24Some of those who were with us went to the tomb and found it just as the women had said; but they did not see him." 25Then he said to them, "Oh, how foolish you are, and how slow of heart to believe all that the prophets have declared! 26Was it not necessary that the Messiah*a* should suffer these things and then enter into his glory?" 27Then beginning with Moses and all the prophets, he interpreted to them the things about himself in all the scriptures.

28 As they came near the village to which they were going, he walked ahead as if he were going on. 29But they urged him strongly, saying, "Stay with us, because it is almost evening and the day is now nearly over." So he went in to stay with them. 30When he was at the table with them, he took bread, blessed and broke it, and gave it to them. 31Then their eyes were opened, and they recognized him; and he vanished from their sight. 32They said to each other, "Were not our hearts burning within us*b* while he was talking to us on the road, while he was opening the scriptures to us?" 33That same hour they got up and returned to Jerusalem; and they found the eleven and their companions gathered together. 34They were saying, "The Lord has risen indeed, and he has appeared to Simon!" 35Then they told what had happened on the road, and how he had been made known to them in the breaking of the bread.

Jesus Appears to His Disciples

36 While they were talking about this, Jesus himself stood among them and said to them, "Peace be with you."*c* 37They were startled and terrified, and thought that they were seeing a ghost. 38He said to them, "Why are you frightened, and why do doubts arise in your hearts? 39Look at my hands and my feet; see that it is I myself. Touch me and see; for a ghost does not have flesh and bones as you see that I have." 40And when he had said this, he showed them his hands and his feet.*d* 41While in their joy they were disbelieving and still wondering, he said to them, "Have you anything here to eat?" 42They gave him a piece of broiled fish, 43and he took it and ate in their presence.

44 Then he said to them, "These are my words that I spoke to you while I was still with you—that everything written about me in the law of Moses, the prophets, and the psalms must be fulfilled." 45Then he opened their minds to understand the scriptures, 46and he said to them, "Thus it is written, that the Messiah*a* is to suffer and to rise from the dead on the third day, 47and that repentance and forgiveness of sins is to be proclaimed in his name to all nations, beginning from Jerusalem. 48You are witnesses*e* of these things. 49And see, I am sending upon you what my Father promised; so stay here in the city until you have been clothed with power from on high."

The Ascension of Jesus

50 Then he led them out as far as Bethany, and, lifting up his hands, he blessed them. 51While he was blessing them, he withdrew from them and was carried up into heaven.*f* 52And they worshiped him, and*g* returned to Jerusalem with great joy; 53and they were continually in the temple blessing God. *h*

---

a Or *the Christ*   *b* Other ancient authorities lack *within us* *"Peace be with you."*   *d* Other ancient authorities lack verse 40   *c* Other ancient authorities lack *and said to them,* *e* Or *nations. Beginning from Jerusalem* 48*you are witnesses*   *f* Other ancient authorities lack *and was carried up into heaven*   *g* Other ancient authorities lack *worshiped him, and*   *h* Other ancient authorities add *Amen*

THE GOSPEL ACCORDING TO
JOHN

The Word Became Flesh

1 In the beginning was the Word, and the Word was with God, and the Word was God. 2He was in the beginning with God. 3All things came into being through him, and without him not one thing came into being. What has come into being 4in him was life, *a* and the life was the light of all people. 5The light shines in the darkness, and the darkness did not overcome it.

6 There was a man sent from God, whose name was John. 7He came as a witness to testify to the light, so that all might believe through him. 8He himself was not the light, but he came to testify to the light. 9The true light, which enlightens everyone, was coming into the world. *b*

10 He was in the world, and the world came into being through him; yet the world did not know him. 11He came to what was his own, *c* and his own people did not accept him. 12But to all who received him, who believed in his name, he gave power to become children of God, 13who were born, not of blood or of the will of the flesh or of the will of man, but of God.

14 And the Word became flesh and lived among us, and we have seen his glory, the glory as of a father's only son, *d* full of grace and truth. 15(John testified to him and cried out, "This was he of whom I said, 'He who comes after me ranks ahead of me because he was before me.' ") 16From his fullness we have all received, grace upon grace. 17The law indeed was given through Moses; grace and truth came through Jesus Christ. 18No one has ever seen God. It is God the only Son, *e* who is close to the Father's heart, *f* who has made him known.

The Testimony of John the Baptist

19 This is the testimony given by John when the Jews sent priests and Levites from Jerusalem to ask him, "Who are you?" 20He confessed and did not deny it, but confessed, "I am not the Messiah." *g* 21And they asked him, "What then? Are you Elijah?" He said, "I am not." "Are you the prophet?" He answered, "No." 22Then they said to him, "Who are you? Let us have an answer for those who sent us. What do you say about yourself?" 23He said,

"I am the voice of one crying out in
the wilderness,
'Make straight the way of the Lord,'"
as the prophet Isaiah said.

24 Now they had been sent from the Pharisees. 25They asked him, "Why then are you baptizing if you are neither the Messiah, *g* nor Elijah, nor the prophet?" 26John answered them, "I baptize with water. Among you stands one whom you do not know, 27the one who is coming after me; I am not worthy to untie the thong of his sandal." 28This took place in Bethany across the Jordan where John was baptizing.

The Lamb of God

29 The next day he saw Jesus coming toward him and declared, "Here is the Lamb of God who takes away the sin of the world! 30This is he of whom I said, 'After me comes a man who ranks ahead of me because he was before me.' 31I myself did not know him; but I came baptizing with water for this reason, that he might be revealed to Israel." 32And John testified, "I saw the Spirit descending from heaven like a dove, and it remained on him. 33I myself did not know him, but the one who sent me to baptize with water said to me, 'He on whom you see the Spirit descend and remain is the one who baptizes with the Holy Spirit.' 34And I myself have seen and have testified that this is the Son of God." *b*

---

a Or *3through him. And without him not one thing came into being that has come into being.* *4In him was life*   *b* Or *He was the true light that enlightens everyone coming into the world*   *c* Or *to his own home*   *d* Or *the Father's only Son*   *e* Other ancient authorities read *It is an only Son, God,* or *It is the only Son*   *f* Gk *bosom*   *g* Or *the Christ*   *h* Other ancient authorities read *is God's chosen one*

The First Disciples of Jesus

35 The next day John again was standing with two of his disciples, [36]and as he watched Jesus walk by, he exclaimed, "Look, here is the Lamb of God!" [37]The two disciples heard him say this, and they followed Jesus. [38]When Jesus turned and saw them following, he said to them, "What are you looking for?" They said to him, "Rabbi" (which translated means Teacher), "where are you staying?" [39]He said to them, "Come and see." They came and saw where he was staying, and they remained with him that day. It was about four o'clock in the afternoon. [40]One of the two who heard John speak and followed him was Andrew, Simon Peter's brother. [41]He first found his brother Simon and said to him, "We have found the Messiah" (which is translated Anointed[a]). [42]He brought Simon[b] to Jesus, who looked at him and said, "You are Simon son of John. You are to be called Cephas" (which is translated Peter[c]).

Jesus Calls Philip and Nathanael

43 The next day Jesus decided to go to Galilee. He found Philip and said to him, "Follow me." [44]Now Philip was from Bethsaida, the city of Andrew and Peter. [45]Philip found Nathanael and said to him, "We have found him about whom Moses in the law and also the prophets wrote, Jesus son of Joseph from Nazareth." [46]Nathanael said to him, "Can anything good come out of Nazareth?" Philip said to him, "Come and see." [47]When Jesus saw Nathanael coming toward him, he said of him, "Here is truly an Israelite in whom there is no deceit!" [48]Nathanael asked him, "Where did you get to know me?" Jesus answered, "I saw you under the fig tree before Philip called you." [49]Nathanael replied, "Rabbi, you are the Son of God! You are the King of Israel!" [50]Jesus answered, "Do you believe because I told you that I saw you under the fig tree? You will see greater things than these." [51]And he said to him, "Very truly, I tell you,[d] you will see heaven opened and the angels of God ascending and descending upon the Son of Man."

The Wedding at Cana

2 On the third day there was a wedding in Cana of Galilee, and the mother of Jesus was there. [2]Jesus and his disciples had also been invited to the wedding. [3]When the wine gave out, the mother of Jesus said to him, "They have no wine." [4]And Jesus said to her, "Woman, what concern is that to you and to me? My hour has not yet come." [5]His mother said to the servants, "Do whatever he tells you." [6]Now standing there were six stone water jars for the Jewish rites of purification, each holding twenty or thirty gallons. [7]Jesus said to them, "Fill the jars with water." And they filled them up to the brim. [8]He said to them, "Now draw some out, and take it to the chief steward." So they took it. [9]When the steward tasted the water that had become wine, and did not know where it came from (though the servants who had drawn the water knew), the steward called the bridegroom [10]and said to him, "Everyone serves the good wine first, and then the inferior wine after the guests have become drunk. But you have kept the good wine until now." [11]Jesus did this, the first of his signs, in Cana of Galilee, and revealed his glory; and his disciples believed in him.

12 After this he went down to Capernaum with his mother, his brothers, and his disciples; and they remained there a few days.

Jesus Cleanses the Temple

13 The Passover of the Jews was near, and Jesus went up to Jerusalem. [14]In the temple he found people selling cattle, sheep, and doves, and the money changers seated at their tables. [15]Making a whip of cords, he drove all of them out of the temple, both the sheep and the cattle. He also poured out the coins of the money changers and overturned their tables. [16]He told those who were selling the doves, "Take these things out of here!

---

a Or Christ   b Gk him   c From the word for rock in Aramaic (kepha) and Greek (petra), respectively   d Both instances of the Greek word for you in this verse are plural

Stop making my Father's house a market-place!" [17]His disciples remembered that it was written, "Zeal for your house will consume me." [18]The Jews then said to him, "What sign can you show us for doing this?" [19]Jesus answered them, "Destroy this temple, and in three days I will raise it up." [20]The Jews then said, "This temple has been under construction for forty-six years, and will you raise it up in three days?" [21]But he was speaking of the temple of his body. [22]After he was raised from the dead, his disciples remembered that he had said this; and they believed the scripture and the word that Jesus had spoken.

23 When he was in Jerusalem during the Passover festival, many believed in his name because they saw the signs that he was doing. [24]But Jesus on his part would not entrust himself to them, because he knew all people [25]and needed no one to testify about anyone; for he himself knew what was in everyone.

Nicodemus Visits Jesus

3 Now there was a Pharisee named Nicodemus, a leader of the Jews. [2]He came to Jesus[a] by night and said to him, "Rabbi, we know that you are a teacher who has come from God; for no one can do these signs that you do apart from the presence of God." [3]Jesus answered him, "Very truly, I tell you, no one can see the kingdom of God without being born from above."[b] [4]Nicodemus said to him, "How can anyone be born after having grown old? Can one enter a second time into the mother's womb and be born?" [5]Jesus answered, "Very truly, I tell you, no one can enter the kingdom of God without being born of water and Spirit. [6]What is born of the flesh is flesh, and what is born of the Spirit is spirit.[c] [7]Do not be astonished that I said to you, 'You[d] must be born from above.'[e] [8]The wind[c] blows where it chooses, and you hear the sound of it, but you do not know where it comes from or where it goes. So it

is with everyone who is born of the Spirit." [9]Nicodemus said to him, "How can these things be?" [10]Jesus answered him, "Are you a teacher of Israel, and yet you do not understand these things?

11 "Very truly, I tell you, we speak of what we know and testify to what we have seen; yet you[f] do not receive our testimony. [12]If I have told you about earthly things and you do not believe, how can you believe if I tell you about heavenly things? [13]No one has ascended into heaven except the one who descended from heaven, the Son of Man.[g] [14]And just as Moses lifted up the serpent in the wilderness, so must the Son of Man be lifted up, [15]that whoever believes in him may have eternal life.[b]

16 "For God so loved the world that he gave his only Son, so that everyone who believes in him may not perish but may have eternal life.

17 "Indeed, God did not send the Son into the world to condemn the world, but in order that the world might be saved through him. [18]Those who believe in him are not condemned; but those who do not believe are condemned already, because they have not believed in the name of the only Son of God. [19]And this is the judgment, that the light has come into the world, and people loved darkness rather than light because their deeds were evil. [20]For all who do evil hate the light and do not come to the light, so that their deeds may not be exposed. [21]But those who do what is true come to the light, so that it may be clearly seen that their deeds have been done in God."[b]

Jesus and John the Baptist

22 After this Jesus and his disciples went into the Judean countryside, and he spent some time there with them and baptized. [23]John also was baptizing at Aenon near Salim because water was abundant there; and people kept coming and were being baptized

---

a Gk *him*   b Or *born anew*   c The same Greek word means both *wind* and *spirit*   d The Greek word for *you* here is plural   e Or *anew*   f The Greek word for *you* here and in verse 12 is plural   g Other ancient authorities add *who is in heaven*   b Some interpreters hold that the quotation concludes with verse 15

24—John, of course, had not yet been thrown into prison.

25 Now a discussion about purification arose between John's disciples and a Jew.*ᵃ* 26They came to John and said to him, "Rabbi, the one who was with you across the Jordan, to whom you testified, here he is baptizing, and all are going to him." 27John answered, "No one can receive anything except what has been given from heaven. 28You yourselves are my witnesses that I said, 'I am not the Messiah,*ᵇ* but I have been sent ahead of him.' 29He who has the bride is the bridegroom. The friend of the bridegroom, who stands and hears him, rejoices greatly at the bridegroom's voice. For this reason my joy has been fulfilled. 30He must increase, but I must decrease."*ᶜ*

The One Who Comes from Heaven

31 The one who comes from above is above all; the one who is of the earth belongs to the earth and speaks about earthly things. The one who comes from heaven is above all. 32He testifies to what he has seen and heard, yet no one accepts his testimony. 33Whoever has accepted his testimony has certified*ᵈ* this, that God is true. 34He whom God has sent speaks the words of God, for he gives the Spirit without measure. 35The Father loves the Son and has placed all things in his hands. 36Whoever believes in the Son has eternal life; whoever disobeys the Son will not see life, but must endure God's wrath.

Jesus and the Woman of Samaria

4 Now when Jesus*ᵉ* learned that the Pharisees had heard, "Jesus is making and baptizing more disciples than John" 2—although it was not Jesus himself but his disciples who baptized— 3he left Judea and started back to Galilee. 4But he had to go through Samaria. 5So he came to a Samaritan city called Sychar, near the plot of ground that Jacob had given to his son Joseph. 6Ja-

cob's well was there, and Jesus, tired out by his journey, was sitting by the well. It was about noon.

7 A Samaritan woman came to draw water, and Jesus said to her, "Give me a drink." 8(His disciples had gone to the city to buy food.) 9The Samaritan woman said to him, "How is it that you, a Jew, ask a drink of me, a woman of Samaria?" (Jews do not share things in common with Samaritans.)*ᶠ* 10Jesus answered her, "If you knew the gift of God, and who it is that is saying to you, 'Give me a drink,' you would have asked him, and he would have given you living water." 11The woman said to him, "Sir, you have no bucket, and the well is deep. Where do you get that living water? 12Are you greater than our ancestor Jacob, who gave us the well, and with his sons and his flocks drank from it?" 13Jesus said to her, "Everyone who drinks of this water will be thirsty again, 14but those who drink of the water that I will give them will never be thirsty. The water that I will give will become in them a spring of water gushing up to eternal life." 15The woman said to him, "Sir, give me this water, so that I may never be thirsty or have to keep coming here to draw water."

16 Jesus said to her, "Go, call your husband, and come back." 17The woman answered him, "I have no husband." Jesus said to her, "You are right in saying, 'I have no husband'; 18for you have had five husbands, and the one you have now is not your husband. What you have said is true!" 19The woman said to him, "Sir, I see that you are a prophet. 20Our ancestors worshiped on this mountain, but you*ᵍ* say that the place where people must worship is in Jerusalem." 21Jesus said to her, "Woman, believe me, the hour is coming when you will worship the Father neither on this mountain nor in Jerusalem. 22You worship what you do not know; we worship what we know, for salvation is from the Jews. 23But the hour is coming, and is

---

ᵃ Other ancient authorities read *the Jews* 　*ᵇ* Or *the Christ* 　*ᶜ* Some interpreters hold that the quotation continues through verse 36 　*ᵈ* Gk *set a seal to* 　*ᵉ* Other ancient authorities read *the Lord* 　*ᶠ* Other ancient authorities lack this sentence 　*ᵍ* The Greek word for *you* here and in verses 21 and 22 is plural now here, when the true worshipers will worship the Father in spirit and truth, for the Father seeks such as these to worship him. ²⁴God is spirit, and those who worship him must worship in spirit and truth." ²⁵The woman said to him, "I know that Messiah is coming" (who is called Christ). "When he comes, he will proclaim all things to us." ²⁶Jesus said to her, "I am he,ᵃ the one who is speaking to you."

27 Just then his disciples came. They were astonished that he was speaking with a woman, but no one said, "What do you want?" or, "Why are you speaking with her?" ²⁸Then the woman left her water jar and went back to the city. She said to the people, ²⁹"Come and see a man who told me everything I have ever done! He cannot be the Messiah,ᵇ can he?" ³⁰They left the city and were on their way to him.

31 Meanwhile the disciples were urging him, "Rabbi, eat something." ³²But he said to them, "I have food to eat that you do not know about." ³³So the disciples said to one another, "Surely no one has brought him something to eat?" ³⁴Jesus said to them, "My food is to do the will of him who sent me and to complete his work. ³⁵Do you not say, 'Four months more, then comes the harvest'? But I tell you, look around you, and see how the fields are ripe for harvesting. ³⁶The reaper is already receivingᶜ wages and is gathering fruit for eternal life, so that sower and reaper may rejoice together. ³⁷For here the saying holds true, 'One sows and another reaps.' ³⁸I sent you to reap that for which you did not labor. Others have labored, and you have entered into their labor."

39 Many Samaritans from that city believed in him because of the woman's testimony, "He told me everything I have ever done." ⁴⁰So when the Samaritans came to him, they asked him to stay with them; and he stayed there two days. ⁴¹And many more believed because of his word. ⁴²They said to

the woman, "It is no longer because of what you said that we believe, for we have heard for ourselves, and we know that this is truly the Savior of the world."

Jesus Returns to Galilee

43 When the two days were over, he went from that place to Galilee ⁴⁴(for Jesus himself had testified that a prophet has no honor in the prophet's own country). ⁴⁵When he came to Galilee, the Galileans welcomed him, since they had seen all that he had done in Jerusalem at the festival; for they too had gone to the festival.

Jesus Heals an Official's Son

46 Then he came again to Cana in Galilee where he had changed the water into wine. Now there was a royal official whose son lay ill in Capernaum. ⁴⁷When he heard that Jesus had come from Judea to Galilee, he went and begged him to come down and heal his son, for he was at the point of death. ⁴⁸Then Jesus said to him, "Unless youᵈ see signs and wonders you will not believe." ⁴⁹The official said to him, "Sir, come down before my little boy dies." ⁵⁰Jesus said to him, "Go; your son will live." The man believed the word that Jesus spoke to him and started on his way. ⁵¹As he was going down, his slaves met him and told him that his child was alive. ⁵²So he asked them the hour when he began to recover, and they said to him, "Yesterday at one in the afternoon the fever left him." ⁵³The father realized that this was the hour when Jesus had said to him, "Your son will live." So he himself believed, along with his whole household. ⁵⁴Now this was the second sign that Jesus did after coming from Judea to Galilee.

Jesus Heals on the Sabbath

5 After this there was a festival of the Jews, and Jesus went up to Jerusalem.

2 Now in Jerusalem by the Sheep Gate there is a pool, called in Hebrewᵉ Beth-zatha,ᶠ

ᵃ Gk I am   ᵇ Or the Christ   ᶜ Or ³⁵. . . the fields are already ripe for harvesting. ³⁶The reaper is receiving   ᵈ Both instances of the Greek word for you in this verse are plural   ᵉ That is, Aramaic   ᶠ Other ancient authorities read Bethesda, others Bethsaida which has five porticoes. 3In these lay many invalids—blind, lame, and paralyzed. *a* 5One man was there who had been ill for thirty-eight years. 6When Jesus saw him lying there and knew that he had been there a long time, he said to him, "Do you want to be made well?" 7The sick man answered him, "Sir, I have no one to put me into the pool when the water is stirred up; and while I am making my way, someone else steps down ahead of me." 8Jesus said to him, "Stand up, take your mat and walk." 9At once the man was made well, and he took up his mat and began to walk.

Now that day was a sabbath. 10So the Jews said to the man who had been cured, "It is the sabbath; it is not lawful for you to carry your mat." 11But he answered them, "The man who made me well said to me, 'Take up your mat and walk.' " 12They asked him, "Who is the man who said to you, 'Take it up and walk'?" 13Now the man who had been healed did not know who it was, for Jesus had disappeared in *b* the crowd that was there. 14Later Jesus found him in the temple and said to him, "See, you have been made well! Do not sin any more, so that nothing worse happens to you." 15The man went away and told the Jews that it was Jesus who had made him well. 16Therefore the Jews started persecuting Jesus, because he was doing such things on the sabbath. 17But Jesus answered them, "My Father is still working, and I also am working." 18For this reason the Jews were seeking all the more to kill him, because he was not only breaking the sabbath, but was also calling God his own Father, thereby making himself equal to God.

The Authority of the Son

19 Jesus said to them, "Very truly, I tell you, the Son can do nothing on his own, but only what he sees the Father doing; for whatever the Father *c* does, the Son does likewise. 20The Father loves the Son and shows him all that he himself is doing; and he will show him

greater works than these, so that you will be astonished. 21Indeed, just as the Father raises the dead and gives them life, so also the Son gives life to whomever he wishes. 22The Father judges no one but has given all judgment to the Son, 23so that all may honor the Son just as they honor the Father. Anyone who does not honor the Son does not honor the Father who sent him. 24Very truly, I tell you, anyone who hears my word and believes him who sent me has eternal life, and does not come under judgment, but has passed from death to life.

25 "Very truly, I tell you, the hour is coming, and is now here, when the dead will hear the voice of the Son of God, and those who hear will live. 26For just as the Father has life in himself, so he has granted the Son also to have life in himself; 27and he has given him authority to execute judgment, because he is the Son of Man. 28Do not be astonished at this; for the hour is coming when all who are in their graves will hear his voice 29and will come out—those who have done good, to the resurrection of life, and those who have done evil, to the resurrection of condemnation.

Witnesses to Jesus

30 "I can do nothing on my own. As I hear, I judge; and my judgment is just, because I seek to do not my own will but the will of him who sent me.

31 "If I testify about myself, my testimony is not true. 32There is another who testifies on my behalf, and I know that his testimony to me is true. 33You sent messengers to John, and he testified to the truth. 34Not that I accept such human testimony, but I say these things so that you may be saved. 35He was a burning and shining lamp, and you were willing to rejoice for a while in his light. 36But I have a testimony greater than John's. The works that the Father has given me to complete, the very works that I am doing, testify on my behalf that the Father has sent me.

---

a Other ancient authorities add, wholly or in part, *waiting for the stirring of the water; 4for an angel of the Lord went down at certain seasons into the pool, and stirred up the water; whoever stepped in first after the stirring of the water was made well from whatever disease that person had.*　　*b* Or *had left because of*　　*c* Gk *that one*

37And the Father who sent me has himself testified on my behalf. You have never heard his voice or seen his form, 38and you do not have his word abiding in you, because you do not believe him whom he has sent.

39 "You search the scriptures because you think that in them you have eternal life; and it is they that testify on my behalf. 40Yet you refuse to come to me to have life. 41I do not accept glory from human beings. 42But I know that you do not have the love of God in*a* you. 43I have come in my Father's name, and you do not accept me; if another comes in his own name, you will accept him. 44How can you believe when you accept glory from one another and do not seek the glory that comes from the one who alone is God? 45Do not think that I will accuse you before the Father; your accuser is Moses, on whom you have set your hope. 46If you believed Moses, you would believe me, for he wrote about me. 47But if you do not believe what he wrote, how will you believe what I say?"

Feeding the Five Thousand

6 After this Jesus went to the other side of the Sea of Galilee, also called the Sea of Tiberias.*b* 2A large crowd kept following him, because they saw the signs that he was doing for the sick. 3Jesus went up the mountain and sat down there with his disciples. 4Now the Passover, the festival of the Jews, was near. 5When he looked up and saw a large crowd coming toward him, Jesus said to Philip, "Where are we to buy bread for these people to eat?" 6He said this to test him, for he himself knew what he was going to do. 7Philip answered him, "Six months' wages*c* would not buy enough bread for each of them to get a little." 8One of his disciples, Andrew, Simon Peter's brother, said to him, 9"There is a boy here who has five barley loaves and two fish. But what are they among so many people?" 10Jesus said, "Make the people sit down." Now there was a great deal

of grass in the place; so they*d* sat down, about five thousand in all. 11Then Jesus took the loaves, and when he had given thanks, he distributed them to those who were seated; so also the fish, as much as they wanted. 12When they were satisfied, he told his disciples, "Gather up the fragments left over, so that nothing may be lost." 13So they gathered them up, and from the fragments of the five barley loaves, left by those who had eaten, they filled twelve baskets. 14When the people saw the sign that he had done, they began to say, "This is indeed the prophet who is to come into the world."

15 When Jesus realized that they were about to come and take him by force to make him king, he withdrew again to the mountain by himself.

Jesus Walks on the Water

16 When evening came, his disciples went down to the sea, 17got into a boat, and started across the sea to Capernaum. It was now dark, and Jesus had not yet come to them. 18The sea became rough because a strong wind was blowing. 19When they had rowed about three or four miles,*e* they saw Jesus walking on the sea and coming near the boat, and they were terrified. 20But he said to them, "It is I;*f* do not be afraid." 21Then they wanted to take him into the boat, and immediately the boat reached the land toward which they were going.

The Bread from Heaven

22 The next day the crowd that had stayed on the other side of the sea saw that there had been only one boat there. They also saw that Jesus had not got into the boat with his disciples, but that his disciples had gone away alone. 23Then some boats from Tiberias came near the place where they had eaten the bread after the Lord had given thanks.*g* 24So when the crowd saw that neither Jesus nor his disciples were there, they themselves got into the

a Or *among*   *b* Gk *of Galilee of Tiberias*   *c* Gk *Two hundred denarii;* the denarius was the usual day's wage for a laborer   *d* Gk *the men*   *e* Gk *about twenty-five or thirty stadia*   *f* Gk *I am*   *g* Other ancient authorities lack *after the Lord had given thanks* boats and went to Capernaum looking for Jesus.

25 When they found him on the other side of the sea, they said to him, "Rabbi, when did you come here?" 26Jesus answered them, "Very truly, I tell you, you are looking for me, not because you saw signs, but because you ate your fill of the loaves. 27Do not work for the food that perishes, but for the food that endures for eternal life, which the Son of Man will give you. For it is on him that God the Father has set his seal." 28Then they said to him, "What must we do to perform the works of God?" 29Jesus answered them, "This is the work of God, that you believe in him whom he has sent." 30So they said to him, "What sign are you going to give us then, so that we may see it and believe you? What work are you performing? 31Our ancestors ate the manna in the wilderness; as it is written, 'He gave them bread from heaven to eat.'" 32Then Jesus said to them, "Very truly, I tell you, it was not Moses who gave you the bread from heaven, but it is my Father who gives you the true bread from heaven. 33For the bread of God is that which*a* comes down from heaven and gives life to the world." 34They said to him, "Sir, give us this bread always."

35 Jesus said to them, "I am the bread of life. Whoever comes to me will never be hungry, and whoever believes in me will never be thirsty. 36But I said to you that you have seen me and yet do not believe. 37Everything that the Father gives me will come to me, and anyone who comes to me I will never drive away; 38for I have come down from heaven, not to do my own will, but the will of him who sent me. 39And this is the will of him who sent me, that I should lose nothing of all that he has given me, but raise it up on the last day. 40This is indeed the will of my Father, that all who see the Son and believe in him may have eternal life; and I will raise them up on the last day."

41 Then the Jews began to complain about him because he said, "I am the bread that came down from heaven." 42They were saying, "Is not this Jesus, the son of Joseph, whose father and mother we know? How can he now say, 'I have come down from heaven'?" 43Jesus answered them, "Do not complain among yourselves. 44No one can come to me unless drawn by the Father who sent me; and I will raise that person up on the last day. 45It is written in the prophets, 'And they shall all be taught by God.' Everyone who has heard and learned from the Father comes to me. 46Not that anyone has seen the Father except the one who is from God; he has seen the Father. 47Very truly, I tell you, whoever believes has eternal life. 48I am the bread of life. 49Your ancestors ate the manna in the wilderness, and they died. 50This is the bread that comes down from heaven, so that one may eat of it and not die. 51I am the living bread that came down from heaven. Whoever eats of this bread will live forever; and the bread that I will give for the life of the world is my flesh."

52 The Jews then disputed among themselves, saying, "How can this man give us his flesh to eat?" 53So Jesus said to them, "Very truly, I tell you, unless you eat the flesh of the Son of Man and drink his blood, you have no life in you. 54Those who eat my flesh and drink my blood have eternal life, and I will raise them up on the last day; 55for my flesh is true food and my blood is true drink. 56Those who eat my flesh and drink my blood abide in me, and I in them. 57Just as the living Father sent me, and I live because of the Father, so whoever eats me will live because of me. 58This is the bread that came down from heaven, not like that which your ancestors ate, and they died. But the one who eats this bread will live forever." 59He said these things while he was teaching in the synagogue at Capernaum.

The Words of Eternal Life

60 When many of his disciples heard it, they said, "This teaching is difficult; who can

a Or *he who*

accept it?" 61But Jesus, being aware that his disciples were complaining about it, said to them, "Does this offend you? 62Then what if you were to see the Son of Man ascending to where he was before? 63It is the spirit that gives life; the flesh is useless. The words that I have spoken to you are spirit and life. 64But among you there are some who do not believe." For Jesus knew from the first who were the ones that did not believe, and who was the one that would betray him. 65And he said, "For this reason I have told you that no one can come to me unless it is granted by the Father."

66 Because of this many of his disciples turned back and no longer went about with him. 67So Jesus asked the twelve, "Do you also wish to go away?" 68Simon Peter answered him, "Lord, to whom can we go? You have the words of eternal life. 69We have come to believe and know that you are the Holy One of God."a 70Jesus answered them, "Did I not choose you, the twelve? Yet one of you is a devil." 71He was speaking of Judas son of Simon Iscariot,b for he, though one of the twelve, was going to betray him.

The Unbelief of Jesus' Brothers

7 After this Jesus went about in Galilee. He did not wishc to go about in Judea because the Jews were looking for an opportunity to kill him. 2Now the Jewish festival of Boothsd was near. 3So his brothers said to him, "Leave here and go to Judea so that your disciples also may see the works you are doing; 4for no one who wantse to be widely known acts in secret. If you do these things, show yourself to the world." 5(For not even his brothers believed in him.) 6Jesus said to them, "My time has not yet come, but your time is always here. 7The world cannot hate you, but it hates me because I testify against it that its works are evil. 8Go to the festival yourselves. I am notf going to this fes-

tival, for my time has not yet fully come." 9After saying this, he remained in Galilee.

Jesus at the Festival of Booths

10 But after his brothers had gone to the festival, then he also went, not publicly but as it wereg in secret. 11The Jews were looking for him at the festival and saying, "Where is he?" 12And there was considerable complaining about him among the crowds. While some were saying, "He is a good man," others were saying, "No, he is deceiving the crowd." 13Yet no one would speak openly about him for fear of the Jews.

14 About the middle of the festival Jesus went up into the temple and began to teach. 15The Jews were astonished at it, saying, "How does this man have such learning,b when he has never been taught?" 16Then Jesus answered them, "My teaching is not mine but his who sent me. 17Anyone who resolves to do the will of God will know whether the teaching is from God or whether I am speaking on my own. 18Those who speak on their own seek their own glory; but the one who seeks the glory of him who sent him is true, and there is nothing false in him.

19 "Did not Moses give you the law? Yet none of you keeps the law. Why are you looking for an opportunity to kill me?" 20The crowd answered, "You have a demon! Who is trying to kill you?" 21Jesus answered them, "I performed one work, and all of you are astonished. 22Moses gave you circumcision (it is, of course, not from Moses, but from the patriarchs), and you circumcise a man on the sabbath. 23If a man receives circumcision on the sabbath in order that the law of Moses may not be broken, are you angry with me because I healed a man's whole body on the sabbath? 24Do not judge by appearances, but judge with right judgment."

a Other ancient authorities read the Christ, the Son of the living God   b Other ancient authorities read Judas Iscariot son of Simon; others, Judas son of Simon from Karyot (Kerioth)   c Other ancient authorities read was not at liberty   d Or Tabernacles   e Other ancient authorities read wants it   f Other ancient authorities add yet   g Other ancient authorities lack as it were   h Or this man know his letters

Is This the Christ?

25 Now some of the people of Jerusalem were saying, "Is not this the man whom they are trying to kill? 26And here he is, speaking openly, but they say nothing to him! Can it be that the authorities really know that this is the Messiah?ᵃ 27Yet we know where this man is from; but when the Messiahᵃ comes, no one will know where he is from." 28Then Jesus cried out as he was teaching in the temple, "You know me, and you know where I am from. I have not come on my own. But the one who sent me is true, and you do not know him. 29I know him, because I am from him, and he sent me." 30Then they tried to arrest him, but no one laid hands on him, because his hour had not yet come. 31Yet many in the crowd believed in him and were saying, "When the Messiahᵃ comes, will he do more signs than this man has done?"ᵇ

Officers Are Sent to Arrest Jesus

32 The Pharisees heard the crowd muttering such things about him, and the chief priests and Pharisees sent temple police to arrest him. 33Jesus then said, "I will be with you a little while longer, and then I am going to him who sent me. 34You will search for me, but you will not find me; and where I am, you cannot come." 35The Jews said to one another, "Where does this man intend to go that we will not find him? Does he intend to go to the Dispersion among the Greeks and teach the Greeks? 36What does he mean by saying, 'You will search for me and you will not find me' and 'Where I am, you cannot come'?"

Rivers of Living Water

37 On the last day of the festival, the great day, while Jesus was standing there, he cried out, "Let anyone who is thirsty come to me, 38and let the one who believes in me drink. Asᶜ the scripture has said, 'Out of the believer's heartᵈ shall flow rivers of living water.'" 39Now he said this about the Spirit, which believers in him were to receive; for as yet there was no Spirit,ᵉ because Jesus was not yet glorified.

Division among the People

40 When they heard these words, some in the crowd said, "This is really the prophet." 41Others said, "This is the Messiah."ᵃ But some asked, "Surely the Messiahᵃ does not come from Galilee, does he? 42Has not the scripture said that the Messiahᵃ is descended from David and comes from Bethlehem, the village where David lived?" 43So there was a division in the crowd because of him. 44Some of them wanted to arrest him, but no one laid hands on him.

The Unbelief of Those in Authority

45 Then the temple police went back to the chief priests and Pharisees, who asked them, "Why did you not arrest him?" 46The police answered, "Never has anyone spoken like this!" 47Then the Pharisees replied, "Surely you have not been deceived too, have you? 48Has any one of the authorities or of the Pharisees believed in him? 49But this crowd, which does not know the law—they are accursed." 50Nicodemus, who had gone to Jesusᶠ before, and who was one of them, asked, 51"Our law does not judge people without first giving them a hearing to find out what they are doing, does it?" 52They replied, "Surely you are not also from Galilee, are you? Search and you will see that no prophet is to arise from Galilee."

The Woman Caught in Adultery

8 ‖ 53Then each of them went home, 1while Jesus went to the Mount of Olives. 2Early in the morning he came again to the temple. All the people came to him and he sat down and began to teach them. 3The scribes and the Pharisees brought a woman who had been caught in adultery; and mak-

---

ᵃ Or *the Christ*   ᵇ Other ancient authorities read *is doing*   ᶜ Or *come to me and drink.* 38*The one who believes in me, as*
ᵈ Gk *out of his belly*   ᵉ Other ancient authorities read *for as yet the Spirit* (others, *Holy Spirit*) *had not been given*
ᶠ Gk *him*

ing her stand before all of them, ⁴they said to him, "Teacher, this woman was caught in the very act of committing adultery. ⁵Now in the law Moses commanded us to stone such women. Now what do you say?" ⁶They said this to test him, so that they might have some charge to bring against him. Jesus bent down and wrote with his finger on the ground. ⁷When they kept on questioning him, he straightened up and said to them, "Let anyone among you who is without sin be the first to throw a stone at her." ⁸And once again he bent down and wrote on the ground.ᵃ ⁹When they heard it, they went away, one by one, beginning with the elders; and Jesus was left alone with the woman standing before him. ¹⁰Jesus straightened up and said to her, "Woman, where are they? Has no one condemned you?" ¹¹She said, "No one, sir."ᵇ And Jesus said, "Neither do I condemn you. Go your way, and from now on do not sin again."]ᶜ

Jesus the Light of the World

12 Again Jesus spoke to them, saying, "I am the light of the world. Whoever follows me will never walk in darkness but will have the light of life." ¹³Then the Pharisees said to him, "You are testifying on your own behalf; your testimony is not valid." ¹⁴Jesus answered, "Even if I testify on my own behalf, my testimony is valid because I know where I have come from and where I am going, but you do not know where I come from or where I am going. ¹⁵You judge by human standards;ᵈ I judge no one. ¹⁶Yet even if I do judge, my judgment is valid; for it is not I alone who judge, but I and the Fatherᵉ who sent me. ¹⁷In your law it is written that the testimony of two witnesses is valid. ¹⁸I testify on my own behalf, and the Father who sent me testifies on my behalf." ¹⁹Then they said to him, "Where is your Father?" Jesus answered, "You know neither me nor my Father. If you

knew me, you would know my Father also." ²⁰He spoke these words while he was teaching in the treasury of the temple, but no one arrested him, because his hour had not yet come.

Jesus Foretells His Death

21 Again he said to them, "I am going away, and you will search for me, but you will die in your sin. Where I am going, you cannot come." ²²Then the Jews said, "Is he going to kill himself? Is that what he means by saying, 'Where I am going, you cannot come'?" ²³He said to them, "You are from below, I am from above; you are of this world, I am not of this world. ²⁴I told you that you would die in your sins, for you will die in your sins unless you believe that I am he."ᶠ ²⁵They said to him, "Who are you?" Jesus said to them, "Why do I speak to you at all?ᵍ ²⁶I have much to say about you and much to condemn; but the one who sent me is true, and I declare to the world what I have heard from him." ²⁷They did not understand that he was speaking to them about the Father. ²⁸So Jesus said, "When you have lifted up the Son of Man, then you will realize that I am he,ᶠ and that I do nothing on my own, but I speak these things as the Father instructed me. ²⁹And the one who sent me is with me; he has not left me alone, for I always do what is pleasing to him." ³⁰As he was saying these things, many believed in him.

True Disciples

31 Then Jesus said to the Jews who had believed in him, "If you continue in my word, you are truly my disciples; ³²and you will know the truth, and the truth will make you free." ³³They answered him, "We are descendants of Abraham and have never been slaves to anyone. What do you mean by saying, 'You will be made free'?"

34 Jesus answered them, "Very truly, I tell

ᵃ Other ancient authorities add *the sins of each of them*   ᵇ Or *Lord*   ᶜ The most ancient authorities lack 7.53— 8.11; other authorities add the passage here or after 7.36 or after 21.25 or after Luke 21.38, with variations of text; some mark the passage as doubtful.   ᵈ Gk *according to the flesh*   ᵉ Other ancient authorities read *he*   ᶠ Gk *I am* ᵍ Or *What I have told you from the beginning* you, everyone who commits sin is a slave to sin. 35The slave does not have a permanent place in the household; the son has a place there forever. 36So if the Son makes you free, you will be free indeed. 37I know that you are descendants of Abraham; yet you look for an opportunity to kill me, because there is no place in you for my word. 38I declare what I have seen in the Father's presence; as for you, you should do what you have heard from the Father."a

Jesus and Abraham

39 They answered him, "Abraham is our father." Jesus said to them, "If you were Abraham's children, you would be doingb what Abraham did, 40but now you are trying to kill me, a man who has told you the truth that I heard from God. This is not what Abraham did. 41You are indeed doing what your father does." They said to him, "We are not illegitimate children; we have one father, God himself." 42Jesus said to them, "If God were your Father, you would love me, for I came from God and now I am here. I did not come on my own, but he sent me. 43Why do you not understand what I say? It is because you cannot accept my word. 44You are from your father the devil, and you choose to do your father's desires. He was a murderer from the beginning and does not stand in the truth, because there is no truth in him. When he lies, he speaks according to his own nature, for he is a liar and the father of lies. 45But because I tell the truth, you do not believe me. 46Which of you convicts me of sin? If I tell the truth, why do you not believe me? 47Whoever is from God hears the words of God. The reason you do not hear them is that you are not from God."

48 The Jews answered him, "Are we not right in saying that you are a Samaritan and have a demon?" 49Jesus answered, "I do not have a demon; but I honor my Father, and you dishonor me. 50Yet I do not seek my own glory; there is one who seeks it and he is the judge. 51Very truly, I tell you, whoever keeps my word will never see death." 52The Jews said to him, "Now we know that you have a demon. Abraham died, and so did the prophets; yet you say, 'Whoever keeps my word will never taste death.' 53Are you greater than our father Abraham, who died? The prophets also died. Who do you claim to be?" 54Jesus answered, "If I glorify myself, my glory is nothing. It is my Father who glorifies me, he of whom you say, 'He is our God,' 55though you do not know him. But I know him; if I would say that I do not know him, I would be a liar like you. But I do know him and I keep his word. 56Your ancestor Abraham rejoiced that he would see my day; he saw it and was glad." 57Then the Jews said to him, "You are not yet fifty years old, and have you seen Abraham?"c 58Jesus said to them, "Very truly, I tell you, before Abraham was, I am." 59So they picked up stones to throw at him, but Jesus hid himself and went out of the temple.

A Man Born Blind Receives Sight

9 As he walked along, he saw a man blind from birth. 2His disciples asked him, "Rabbi, who sinned, this man or his parents, that he was born blind?" 3Jesus answered, "Neither this man nor his parents sinned; he was born blind so that God's works might be revealed in him. 4Wed must work the works of him who sent mee while it is day; night is coming when no one can work. 5As long as I am in the world, I am the light of the world." 6When he had said this, he spat on the ground and made mud with the saliva and spread the mud on the man's eyes, 7saying to him, "Go, wash in the pool of Siloam" (which means Sent). Then he went and washed and came back able to see. 8The neighbors and those who had seen him before as a beggar began to ask, "Is this not the man who used to sit and beg?" 9Some were

---

a Other ancient authorities read *you do what you have heard from your father*   b Other ancient authorities read *If you are Abraham's children, then do*   c Other ancient authorities read *has Abraham seen you?*   d Other ancient authorities read *I*   e Other ancient authorities read *us* saying, "It is he." Others were saying, "No, but it is someone like him." He kept saying, "I am the man." ¹⁰But they kept asking him, "Then how were your eyes opened?" ¹¹He answered, "The man called Jesus made mud, spread it on my eyes, and said to me, 'Go to Siloam and wash.' Then I went and washed and received my sight." ¹²They said to him, "Where is he?" He said, "I do not know."

The Pharisees Investigate the Healing

13 They brought to the Pharisees the man who had formerly been blind. ¹⁴Now it was a sabbath day when Jesus made the mud and opened his eyes. ¹⁵Then the Pharisees also began to ask him how he had received his sight. He said to them, "He put mud on my eyes. Then I washed, and now I see." ¹⁶Some of the Pharisees said, "This man is not from God, for he does not observe the sabbath." But others said, "How can a man who is a sinner perform such signs?" And they were divided. ¹⁷So they said again to the blind man, "What do you say about him? It was your eyes he opened." He said, "He is a prophet."

18 The Jews did not believe that he had been blind and had received his sight until they called the parents of the man who had received his sight ¹⁹and asked them, "Is this your son, who you say was born blind? How then does he now see?" ²⁰His parents answered, "We know that this is our son, and that he was born blind; ²¹but we do not know how it is that now he sees, nor do we know who opened his eyes. Ask him; he is of age. He will speak for himself." ²²His parents said this because they were afraid of the Jews; for the Jews had already agreed that anyone who confessed Jesus*a* to be the Messiah*b* would be put out of the synagogue. ²³Therefore his parents said, "He is of age; ask him."

24 So for the second time they called the man who had been blind, and they said to him, "Give glory to God! We know that this man is a sinner." ²⁵He answered, "I do not know whether he is a sinner. One thing I do know, that though I was blind, now I see." ²⁶They said to him, "What did he do to you? How did he open your eyes?" ²⁷He answered them, "I have told you already, and you would not listen. Why do you want to hear it again? Do you also want to become his disciples?" ²⁸Then they reviled him, saying, "You are his disciple, but we are disciples of Moses. ²⁹We know that God has spoken to Moses, but as for this man, we do not know where he comes from." ³⁰The man answered, "Here is an astonishing thing! You do not know where he comes from, and yet he opened my eyes. ³¹We know that God does not listen to sinners, but he does listen to one who worships him and obeys his will. ³²Never since the world began has it been heard that anyone opened the eyes of a person born blind. ³³If this man were not from God, he could do nothing." ³⁴They answered him, "You were born entirely in sins, and are you trying to teach us?" And they drove him out.

Spiritual Blindness

35 Jesus heard that they had driven him out, and when he found him, he said, "Do you believe in the Son of Man?"*c* ³⁶He answered, "And who is he, sir?*d* Tell me, so that I may believe in him." ³⁷Jesus said to him, "You have seen him, and the one speaking with you is he." ³⁸He said, "Lord,*d* I believe." And he worshiped him. ³⁹Jesus said, "I came into this world for judgment so that those who do not see may see, and those who do see may become blind." ⁴⁰Some of the Pharisees near him heard this and said to him, "Surely we are not blind, are we?" ⁴¹Jesus said to them, "If you were blind, you would not have sin. But now that you say, 'We see,' your sin remains.

Jesus the Good Shepherd

10 "Very truly, I tell you, anyone who does not enter the sheepfold by the gate but climbs in by another way is a thief

---

a Gk *him*   *b* Or *the Christ*   *c* Other ancient authorities read *the Son of God*   *d* *Sir* and *Lord* translate the same Greek word and a bandit. ²The one who enters by the gate is the shepherd of the sheep. ³The gatekeeper opens the gate for him, and the sheep hear his voice. He calls his own sheep by name and leads them out. ⁴When he has brought out all his own, he goes ahead of them, and the sheep follow him because they know his voice. ⁵They will not follow a stranger, but they will run from him because they do not know the voice of strangers." ⁶Jesus used this figure of speech with them, but they did not understand what he was saying to them.

7 So again Jesus said to them, "Very truly, I tell you, I am the gate for the sheep. ⁸All who came before me are thieves and bandits; but the sheep did not listen to them. ⁹I am the gate. Whoever enters by me will be saved, and will come in and go out and find pasture. ¹⁰The thief comes only to steal and kill and destroy. I came that they may have life, and have it abundantly.

11 "I am the good shepherd. The good shepherd lays down his life for the sheep. ¹²The hired hand, who is not the shepherd and does not own the sheep, sees the wolf coming and leaves the sheep and runs away— and the wolf snatches them and scatters them. ¹³The hired hand runs away because a hired hand does not care for the sheep. ¹⁴I am the good shepherd. I know my own and my own know me, ¹⁵just as the Father knows me and I know the Father. And I lay down my life for the sheep. ¹⁶I have other sheep that do not belong to this fold. I must bring them also, and they will listen to my voice. So there will be one flock, one shepherd. ¹⁷For this reason the Father loves me, because I lay down my life in order to take it up again. ¹⁸No one takes ᵃ it from me, but I lay it down of my own accord. I have power to lay it down, and I have power to take it up again. I have received this command from my Father."

19 Again the Jews were divided because of these words. ²⁰Many of them were saying, "He has a demon and is out of his mind. Why listen to him?" ²¹Others were saying, "These are not the words of one who has a demon. Can a demon open the eyes of the blind?"

Jesus Is Rejected by the Jews

22 At that time the festival of the Dedication took place in Jerusalem. It was winter, ²³and Jesus was walking in the temple, in the portico of Solomon. ²⁴So the Jews gathered around him and said to him, "How long will you keep us in suspense? If you are the Messiah, ᵇ tell us plainly." ²⁵Jesus answered, "I have told you, and you do not believe. The works that I do in my Father's name testify to me; ²⁶but you do not believe, because you do not belong to my sheep. ²⁷My sheep hear my voice. I know them, and they follow me. ²⁸I give them eternal life, and they will never perish. No one will snatch them out of my hand. ²⁹What my Father has given me is greater than all else, and no one can snatch it out of the Father's hand. ᶜ ³⁰The Father and I are one."

31 The Jews took up stones again to stone him. ³²Jesus replied, "I have shown you many good works from the Father. For which of these are you going to stone me?" ³³The Jews answered, "It is not for a good work that we are going to stone you, but for blasphemy, because you, though only a human being, are making yourself God." ³⁴Jesus answered, "Is it not written in your law, ᵈ 'I said, you are gods'? ³⁵If those to whom the word of God came were called 'gods'—and the scripture cannot be annulled— ³⁶can you say that the one whom the Father has sanctified and sent into the world is blaspheming because I said, 'I am God's Son'? ³⁷If I am not doing the works of my Father, then do not believe me. ³⁸But if I do them, even though you do not believe me, believe the works, so that you may know and understand ᵉ that the Father is

---

ᵃ Other ancient authorities read *has taken*   ᵇ Or *the Christ*   ᶜ Other ancient authorities read *My Father who has given them to me is greater than all, and no one can snatch them out of the Father's hand*   ᵈ Other ancient authorities read *in the law*   ᵉ Other ancient authorities lack *and understand*; others read *and believe* in me and I am in the Father." ³⁹Then they tried to arrest him again, but he escaped from their hands.

40 He went away again across the Jordan to the place where John had been baptizing earlier, and he remained there. ⁴¹Many came to him, and they were saying, "John performed no sign, but everything that John said about this man was true." ⁴²And many believed in him there.

The Death of Lazarus

11 Now a certain man was ill, Lazarus of Bethany, the village of Mary and her sister Martha. ²Mary was the one who anointed the Lord with perfume and wiped his feet with her hair; her brother Lazarus was ill. ³So the sisters sent a message to Jesus, *ᵃ* "Lord, he whom you love is ill." ⁴But when Jesus heard it, he said, "This illness does not lead to death; rather it is for God's glory, so that the Son of God may be glorified through it." ⁵Accordingly, though Jesus loved Martha and her sister and Lazarus, ⁶after having heard that Lazarus *ᵇ* was ill, he stayed two days longer in the place where he was.

7 Then after this he said to the disciples, "Let us go to Judea again." ⁸The disciples said to him, "Rabbi, the Jews were just now trying to stone you, and are you going there again?" ⁹Jesus answered, "Are there not twelve hours of daylight? Those who walk during the day do not stumble, because they see the light of this world. ¹⁰But those who walk at night stumble, because the light is not in them." ¹¹After saying this, he told them, "Our friend Lazarus has fallen asleep, but I am going there to awaken him." ¹²The disciples said to him, "Lord, if he has fallen asleep, he will be all right." ¹³Jesus, however, had been speaking about his death, but they thought that he was referring merely to sleep. ¹⁴Then Jesus told them plainly, "Lazarus is dead. ¹⁵For your sake I am glad I was not there, so that you may believe. But let us go to him." ¹⁶Thomas, who was called the Twin, *ᶜ* said to his fellow disciples, "Let us also go, that we may die with him."

Jesus the Resurrection and the Life

17 When Jesus arrived, he found that Lazarus *ᵇ* had already been in the tomb four days. ¹⁸Now Bethany was near Jerusalem, some two miles *ᵈ* away, ¹⁹and many of the Jews had come to Martha and Mary to console them about their brother. ²⁰When Martha heard that Jesus was coming, she went and met him, while Mary stayed at home. ²¹Martha said to Jesus, "Lord, if you had been here, my brother would not have died. ²²But even now I know that God will give you whatever you ask of him." ²³Jesus said to her, "Your brother will rise again." ²⁴Martha said to him, "I know that he will rise again in the resurrection on the last day." ²⁵Jesus said to her, "I am the resurrection and the life. *ᵉ* Those who believe in me, even though they die, will live, ²⁶and everyone who lives and believes in me will never die. Do you believe this?" ²⁷She said to him, "Yes, Lord, I believe that you are the Messiah, *ᶠ* the Son of God, the one coming into the world."

Jesus Weeps

28 When she had said this, she went back and called her sister Mary, and told her privately, "The Teacher is here and is calling for you." ²⁹And when she heard it, she got up quickly and went to him. ³⁰Now Jesus had not yet come to the village, but was still at the place where Martha had met him. ³¹The Jews who were with her in the house, consoling her, saw Mary get up quickly and go out. They followed her because they thought that she was going to the tomb to weep there. ³²When Mary came where Jesus was and saw him, she knelt at his feet and said to him, "Lord, if you had been here, my brother would not have died." ³³When Jesus saw her weeping, and the Jews who came with her also weeping, he was greatly disturbed in spirit and deeply moved. ³⁴He said, "Where

---

ᵃ Gk *him* 　 *ᵇ* Gk *he* 　 *ᶜ* Gk *Didymus* 　 *ᵈ* Gk *fifteen stadia* 　 *ᵉ* Other ancient authorities lack *and the life*
ᶠ Or *the Christ*

have you laid him?" They said to him, "Lord, come and see." 35Jesus began to weep. 36So the Jews said, "See how he loved him!" 37But some of them said, "Could not he who opened the eyes of the blind man have kept this man from dying?"

Jesus Raises Lazarus to Life

38 Then Jesus, again greatly disturbed, came to the tomb. It was a cave, and a stone was lying against it. 39Jesus said, "Take away the stone." Martha, the sister of the dead man, said to him, "Lord, already there is a stench because he has been dead four days." 40Jesus said to her, "Did I not tell you that if you believed, you would see the glory of God?" 41So they took away the stone. And Jesus looked upward and said, "Father, I thank you for having heard me. 42I knew that you always hear me, but I have said this for the sake of the crowd standing here, so that they may believe that you sent me." 43When he had said this, he cried with a loud voice, "Lazarus, come out!" 44The dead man came out, his hands and feet bound with strips of cloth, and his face wrapped in a cloth. Jesus said to them, "Unbind him, and let him go."

The Plot to Kill Jesus

45 Many of the Jews therefore, who had come with Mary and had seen what Jesus did, believed in him. 46But some of them went to the Pharisees and told them what he had done. 47So the chief priests and the Pharisees called a meeting of the council, and said, "What are we to do? This man is performing many signs. 48If we let him go on like this, everyone will believe in him, and the Romans will come and destroy both our holy place*a* and our nation." 49But one of them, Caiaphas, who was high priest that year, said to them, "You know nothing at all! 50You do not understand that it is better for you to have one man die for the people than to have the whole nation destroyed." 51He did not say this on his own, but being high priest that

year he prophesied that Jesus was about to die for the nation, 52and not for the nation only, but to gather into one the dispersed children of God. 53So from that day on they planned to put him to death.

54 Jesus therefore no longer walked about openly among the Jews, but went from there to a town called Ephraim in the region near the wilderness; and he remained there with the disciples.

55 Now the Passover of the Jews was near, and many went up from the country to Jerusalem before the Passover to purify themselves. 56They were looking for Jesus and were asking one another as they stood in the temple, "What do you think? Surely he will not come to the festival, will he?" 57Now the chief priests and the Pharisees had given orders that anyone who knew where Jesus*b* was should let them know, so that they might arrest him.

Mary Anoints Jesus

12 Six days before the Passover Jesus came to Bethany, the home of Lazarus, whom he had raised from the dead. 2There they gave a dinner for him. Martha served, and Lazarus was one of those at the table with him. 3Mary took a pound of costly perfume made of pure nard, anointed Jesus' feet, and wiped them*c* with her hair. The house was filled with the fragrance of the perfume. 4But Judas Iscariot, one of his disciples (the one who was about to betray him), said, 5"Why was this perfume not sold for three hundred denarii*d* and the money given to the poor?" 6(He said this not because he cared about the poor, but because he was a thief; he kept the common purse and used to steal what was put into it.) 7Jesus said, "Leave her alone. She bought it*e* so that she might keep it for the day of my burial. 8You always have the poor with you, but you do not always have me."

---

a Or *our temple*; Greek *our place*   *b* Gk *he*   *c* Gk *his feet*   *d* Three hundred denarii would be nearly a year's
wages for a laborer   *e* Gk lacks *She bought it*

The Plot to Kill Lazarus

9 When the great crowd of the Jews learned that he was there, they came not only because of Jesus but also to see Lazarus, whom he had raised from the dead. 10So the chief priests planned to put Lazarus to death as well, 11since it was on account of him that many of the Jews were deserting and were believing in Jesus.

Jesus' Triumphal Entry into Jerusalem

12 The next day the great crowd that had come to the festival heard that Jesus was coming to Jerusalem. 13So they took branches of palm trees and went out to meet him, shouting,

"Hosanna!
Blessed is the one who comes in the
    name of the Lord—
the King of Israel!"

14Jesus found a young donkey and sat on it; as it is written:

15 "Do not be afraid, daughter of Zion.
Look, your king is coming,
    sitting on a donkey's colt!"

16His disciples did not understand these things at first; but when Jesus was glorified, then they remembered that these things had been written of him and had been done to him. 17So the crowd that had been with him when he called Lazarus out of the tomb and raised him from the dead continued to testify.*a* 18It was also because they heard that he had performed this sign that the crowd went to meet him. 19The Pharisees then said to one another, "You see, you can do nothing. Look, the world has gone after him!"

Some Greeks Wish to See Jesus

20 Now among those who went up to worship at the festival were some Greeks. 21They came to Philip, who was from Bethsaida in Galilee, and said to him, "Sir, we wish to see Jesus." 22Philip went and told Andrew; then Andrew and Philip went and told Jesus. 23Jesus answered them, "The hour has come for the Son of Man to be glorified. 24Very truly, I tell you, unless a grain of wheat falls into the earth and dies, it remains just a single grain; but if it dies, it bears much fruit. 25Those who love their life lose it, and those who hate their life in this world will keep it for eternal life. 26Whoever serves me must follow me, and where I am, there will my servant be also. Whoever serves me, the Father will honor.

Jesus Speaks about His Death

27 "Now my soul is troubled. And what should I say—'Father, save me from this hour'? No, it is for this reason that I have come to this hour. 28Father, glorify your name." Then a voice came from heaven, "I have glorified it, and I will glorify it again." 29The crowd standing there heard it and said that it was thunder. Others said, "An angel has spoken to him." 30Jesus answered, "This voice has come for your sake, not for mine. 31Now is the judgment of this world; now the ruler of this world will be driven out. 32And I, when I am lifted up from the earth, will draw all people *b* to myself." 33He said this to indicate the kind of death he was to die. 34The crowd answered him, "We have heard from the law that the Messiah *c* remains forever. How can you say that the Son of Man must be lifted up? Who is this Son of Man?" 35Jesus said to them, "The light is with you for a little longer. Walk while you have the light, so that the darkness may not overtake you. If you walk in the darkness, you do not know where you are going. 36While you have the light, believe in the light, so that you may become children of light."

The Unbelief of the People

After Jesus had said this, he departed and hid from them. 37Although he had performed so many signs in their presence, they did not believe in him. 38This was to fulfill the word spoken by the prophet Isaiah:

"Lord, who has believed our message,

---

a Other ancient authorities read *with him began to testify that he had called . . . from the dead*   *b* Other ancient authorities read *all things*   *c* Or *the Christ*

and to whom has the arm of the
　　Lord been revealed?"
39 And so they could not believe, because Isaiah also said,
40 　"He has blinded their eyes
　　and hardened their heart,
　　so that they might not look with their
　　　eyes,
　　and understand with their heart and
　　　turn—
　　and I would heal them."

41 Isaiah said this because*a* he saw his glory and spoke about him. 42 Nevertheless many, even of the authorities, believed in him. But because of the Pharisees they did not confess it, for fear that they would be put out of the synagogue; 43 for they loved human glory more than the glory that comes from God.

Summary of Jesus' Teaching

44 　Then Jesus cried aloud: "Whoever believes in me believes not in me but in him who sent me. 45 And whoever sees me sees him who sent me. 46 I have come as light into the world, so that everyone who believes in me should not remain in the darkness. 47 I do not judge anyone who hears my words and does not keep them, for I came not to judge the world, but to save the world. 48 The one who rejects me and does not receive my word has a judge; on the last day the word that I have spoken will serve as judge, 49 for I have not spoken on my own, but the Father who sent me has himself given me a commandment about what to say and what to speak. 50 And I know that his commandment is eternal life. What I speak, therefore, I speak just as the Father has told me."

Jesus Washes the Disciples' Feet

13 Now before the festival of the Passover, Jesus knew that his hour had come to depart from this world and go to the Father. Having loved his own who were in the world, he loved them to the end.

2 The devil had already put it into the heart of Judas son of Simon Iscariot to betray him. And during supper 3 Jesus, knowing that the Father had given all things into his hands, and that he had come from God and was going to God, 4 got up from the table,*b* took off his outer robe, and tied a towel around himself. 5 Then he poured water into a basin and began to wash the disciples' feet and to wipe them with the towel that was tied around him. 6 He came to Simon Peter, who said to him, "Lord, are you going to wash my feet?" 7 Jesus answered, "You do not know now what I am doing, but later you will understand." 8 Peter said to him, "You will never wash my feet." Jesus answered, "Unless I wash you, you have no share with me." 9 Simon Peter said to him, "Lord, not my feet only but also my hands and my head!" 10 Jesus said to him, "One who has bathed does not need to wash, except for the feet,*c* but is entirely clean. And you*d* are clean, though not all of you." 11 For he knew who was to betray him; for this reason he said, "Not all of you are clean."

12 　After he had washed their feet, had put on his robe, and had returned to the table, he said to them, "Do you know what I have done to you? 13 You call me Teacher and Lord—and you are right, for that is what I am. 14 So if I, your Lord and Teacher, have washed your feet, you also ought to wash one another's feet. 15 For I have set you an example, that you also should do as I have done to you. 16 Very truly, I tell you, servants*e* are not greater than their master, nor are messengers greater than the one who sent them. 17 If you know these things, you are blessed if you do them. 18 I am not speaking of all of you; I know whom I have chosen. But it is to fulfill the scripture, 'The one who ate my bread*f* has lifted his heel against me.' 19 I tell you this now, before it occurs, so that when it does occur, you may believe that I am he.*g* 20 Very truly, I tell you, whoever receives one

---

a Other ancient witnesses read *when*　　*b* Gk *from supper*
d The Greek word for *you* here is plural　　*e* Gk *slaves*
g Gk *I am*

c Other ancient authorities lack *except for the feet*
f Other ancient authorities read *ate bread with me*

whom I send receives me; and whoever receives me receives him who sent me."

Jesus Foretells His Betrayal

21 After saying this Jesus was troubled in spirit, and declared, "Very truly, I tell you, one of you will betray me." 22The disciples looked at one another, uncertain of whom he was speaking. 23One of his disciples—the one whom Jesus loved—was reclining next to him; 24Simon Peter therefore motioned to him to ask Jesus of whom he was speaking. 25So while reclining next to Jesus, he asked him, "Lord, who is it?" 26Jesus answered, "It is the one to whom I give this piece of bread when I have dipped it in the dish." *a* So when he had dipped the piece of bread, he gave it to Judas son of Simon Iscariot. *b* 27After he received the piece of bread, *c* Satan entered into him. Jesus said to him, "Do quickly what you are going to do." 28Now no one at the table knew why he said this to him. 29Some thought that, because Judas had the common purse, Jesus was telling him, "Buy what we need for the festival"; or, that he should give something to the poor. 30So, after receiving the piece of bread, he immediately went out. And it was night.

The New Commandment

31 When he had gone out, Jesus said, "Now the Son of Man has been glorified, and God has been glorified in him. 32If God has been glorified in him, *d* God will also glorify him in himself and will glorify him at once. 33Little children, I am with you only a little longer. You will look for me; and as I said to the Jews so now I say to you, 'Where I am going, you cannot come.' 34I give you a new commandment, that you love one another. Just as I have loved you, you also should love one another. 35By this everyone will know

that you are my disciples, if you have love for one another."

Jesus Foretells Peter's Denial

36 Simon Peter said to him, "Lord, where are you going?" Jesus answered, "Where I am going, you cannot follow me now; but you will follow afterward." 37Peter said to him, "Lord, why can I not follow you now? I will lay down my life for you." 38Jesus answered, "Will you lay down your life for me? Very truly, I tell you, before the cock crows, you will have denied me three times.

Jesus the Way to the Father

14 "Do not let your hearts be troubled. Believe *e* in God, believe also in me. 2In my Father's house there are many dwelling places. If it were not so, would I have told you that I go to prepare a place for you? *f* 3And if I go and prepare a place for you, I will come again and will take you to myself, so that where I am, there you may be also. 4And you know the way to the place where I am going." *g* 5Thomas said to him, "Lord, we do not know where you are going. How can we know the way?" 6Jesus said to him, "I am the way, and the truth, and the life. No one comes to the Father except through me. 7If you know me, you will know *h* my Father also. From now on you do know him and have seen him."

8 Philip said to him, "Lord, show us the Father, and we will be satisfied." 9Jesus said to him, "Have I been with you all this time, Philip, and you still do not know me? Whoever has seen me has seen the Father. How can you say, 'Show us the Father'? 10Do you not believe that I am in the Father and the Father is in me? The words that I say to you I do not speak on my own; but the Father who dwells in me does his works. 11Believe me that I am in the Father and the Father is in me; but

---

a Gk *dipped it*   *b* Other ancient authorities read *Judas Iscariot son of Simon*; others, *Judas son of Simon from Karyot* (Kerioth)   *c* Gk *After the piece of bread*   *d* Other ancient authorities lack *If God has been glorified in him*   *e* Or *You believe*   *f* Or *If it were not so, I would have told you; for I go to prepare a place for you*   *g* Other ancient authorities read *Where I am going you know, and the way you know*   *h* Other ancient authorities read *If you had known me, you would have known* if you do not, then believe me because of the works themselves. [12]Very truly, I tell you, the one who believes in me will also do the works that I do and, in fact, will do greater works than these, because I am going to the Father. [13]I will do whatever you ask in my name, so that the Father may be glorified in the Son. [14]If in my name you ask me[a] for anything, I will do it.

The Promise of the Holy Spirit

15 "If you love me, you will keep[b] my commandments. [16]And I will ask the Father, and he will give you another Advocate,[c] to be with you forever. [17]This is the Spirit of truth, whom the world cannot receive, because it neither sees him nor knows him. You know him, because he abides with you, and he will be in[d] you.

18 "I will not leave you orphaned; I am coming to you. [19]In a little while the world will no longer see me, but you will see me; because I live, you also will live. [20]On that day you will know that I am in my Father, and you in me, and I in you. [21]They who have my commandments and keep them are those who love me; and those who love me will be loved by my Father, and I will love them and reveal myself to them." [22]Judas (not Iscariot) said to him, "Lord, how is it that you will reveal yourself to us, and not to the world?" [23]Jesus answered him, "Those who love me will keep my word, and my Father will love them, and we will come to them and make our home with them. [24]Whoever does not love me does not keep my words; and the word that you hear is not mine, but is from the Father who sent me.

25 "I have said these things to you while I am still with you. [26]But the Advocate,[c] the Holy Spirit, whom the Father will send in my name, will teach you everything, and remind you of all that I have said to you. [27]Peace I leave with you; my peace I give to you. I do not give to you as the world gives. Do not let your hearts be troubled, and do not let them be afraid. [28]You heard me say to you, 'I am going away, and I am coming to you.' If you loved me, you would rejoice that I am going to the Father, because the Father is greater than I. [29]And now I have told you this before it occurs, so that when it does occur, you may believe. [30]I will no longer talk much with you, for the ruler of this world is coming. He has no power over me; [31]but I do as the Father has commanded me, so that the world may know that I love the Father. Rise, let us be on our way.

Jesus the True Vine

15 "I am the true vine, and my Father is the vinegrower. [2]He removes every branch in me that bears no fruit. Every branch that bears fruit he prunes[e] to make it bear more fruit. [3]You have already been cleansed[e] by the word that I have spoken to you. [4]Abide in me as I abide in you. Just as the branch cannot bear fruit by itself unless it abides in the vine, neither can you unless you abide in me. [5]I am the vine, you are the branches. Those who abide in me and I in them bear much fruit, because apart from me you can do nothing. [6]Whoever does not abide in me is thrown away like a branch and withers; such branches are gathered, thrown into the fire, and burned. [7]If you abide in me, and my words abide in you, ask for whatever you wish, and it will be done for you. [8]My Father is glorified by this, that you bear much fruit and become[f] my disciples. [9]As the Father has loved me, so I have loved you; abide in my love. [10]If you keep my commandments, you will abide in my love, just as I have kept my Father's commandments and abide in his love. [11]I have said these things to you so that my joy may be in you, and that your joy may be complete.

12 "This is my commandment, that you love one another as I have loved you. [13]No one has greater love than this, to lay down one's life for one's friends. [14]You are my friends if you do what I command you. [15]I do not call you

---

a Other ancient authorities lack *me*　　*b* Other ancient authorities read *me, keep*　　*c* Or *Helper*　　*d* Or *among*
e The same Greek root refers to pruning and cleansing　　*f* Or *be*

servants*a* any longer, because the servant*b* does not know what the master is doing; but I have called you friends, because I have made known to you everything that I have heard from my Father. 16You did not choose me but I chose you. And I appointed you to go and bear fruit, fruit that will last, so that the Father will give you whatever you ask him in my name. 17I am giving you these commands so that you may love one another.

The World's Hatred

18 "If the world hates you, be aware that it hated me before it hated you. 19If you belonged to the world,*c* the world would love you as its own. Because you do not belong to the world, but I have chosen you out of the world—therefore the world hates you. 20Remember the word that I said to you, 'Servants*d* are not greater than their master.' If they persecuted me, they will persecute you; if they kept my word, they will keep yours also. 21But they will do all these things to you on account of my name, because they do not know him who sent me. 22If I had not come and spoken to them, they would not have sin; but now they have no excuse for their sin. 23Whoever hates me hates my Father also. 24If I had not done among them the works that no one else did, they would not have sin. But now they have seen and hated both me and my Father. 25It was to fulfill the word that is written in their law, 'They hated me without a cause.'

26 "When the Advocate*e* comes, whom I will send to you from the Father, the Spirit of truth who comes from the Father, he will testify on my behalf. 27You also are to testify because you have been with me from the beginning.

16 "I have said these things to you to keep you from stumbling. 2They will put you out of the synagogues. Indeed, an hour is coming when those who kill you will think that by doing so they are offering worship to God. 3And they will do this because they have not known the Father or me. 4But I have said these things to you so that when their hour comes you may remember that I told you about them.

The Work of the Spirit

"I did not say these things to you from the beginning, because I was with you. 5But now I am going to him who sent me; yet none of you asks me, 'Where are you going?' 6But because I have said these things to you, sorrow has filled your hearts. 7Nevertheless I tell you the truth: it is to your advantage that I go away, for if I do not go away, the Advocate*e* will not come to you; but if I go, I will send him to you. 8And when he comes, he will prove the world wrong about*f* sin and righteousness and judgment: 9about sin, because they do not believe in me; 10about righteousness, because I am going to the Father and you will see me no longer; 11about judgment, because the ruler of this world has been condemned.

12 "I still have many things to say to you, but you cannot bear them now. 13When the Spirit of truth comes, he will guide you into all the truth; for he will not speak on his own, but will speak whatever he hears, and he will declare to you the things that are to come. 14He will glorify me, because he will take what is mine and declare it to you. 15All that the Father has is mine. For this reason I said that he will take what is mine and declare it to you.

Sorrow Will Turn into Joy

16 "A little while, and you will no longer see me, and again a little while, and you will see me." 17Then some of his disciples said to one another, "What does he mean by saying to us, 'A little while, and you will no longer see me, and again a little while, and you will see me'; and 'Because I am going to the Father'?" 18They said, "What does he mean by this 'a little while'? We do not know what he is talking about." 19Jesus knew that they wanted

to ask him, so he said to them, "Are you discussing among yourselves what I meant when I said, 'A little while, and you will no longer see me, and again a little while, and you will see me'? 20Very truly, I tell you, you will weep and mourn, but the world will rejoice; you will have pain, but your pain will turn into joy. 21When a woman is in labor, she has pain, because her hour has come. But when her child is born, she no longer remembers the anguish because of the joy of having brought a human being into the world. 22So you have pain now; but I will see you again, and your hearts will rejoice, and no one will take your joy from you. 23On that day you will ask nothing of me. *a* Very truly, I tell you, if you ask anything of the Father in my name, he will give it to you. *b* 24Until now you have not asked for anything in my name. Ask and you will receive, so that your joy may be complete.

Peace for the Disciples

25 "I have said these things to you in figures of speech. The hour is coming when I will no longer speak to you in figures, but will tell you plainly of the Father. 26On that day you will ask in my name. I do not say to you that I will ask the Father on your behalf; 27for the Father himself loves you, because you have loved me and have believed that I came from God. *c* 28I came from the Father and have come into the world; again, I am leaving the world and am going to the Father."

29 His disciples said, "Yes, now you are speaking plainly, not in any figure of speech! 30Now we know that you know all things, and do not need to have anyone question you; by this we believe that you came from God." 31Jesus answered them, "Do you now believe? 32The hour is coming, indeed it has come, when you will be scattered, each one to his home, and you will leave me alone. Yet I am not alone because the Father is with me. 33I have said this to you, so that in me you may have peace. In the world you face per-

secution. But take courage; I have conquered the world!"

Jesus Prays for His Disciples

17 After Jesus had spoken these words, he looked up to heaven and said, "Father, the hour has come; glorify your Son so that the Son may glorify you, 2since you have given him authority over all people, *d* to give eternal life to all whom you have given him. 3And this is eternal life, that they may know you, the only true God, and Jesus Christ whom you have sent. 4I glorified you on earth by finishing the work that you gave me to do. 5So now, Father, glorify me in your own presence with the glory that I had in your presence before the world existed.

6 "I have made your name known to those whom you gave me from the world. They were yours, and you gave them to me, and they have kept your word. 7Now they know that everything you have given me is from you; 8for the words that you gave to me I have given to them, and they have received them and know in truth that I came from you; and they have believed that you sent me. 9I am asking on their behalf; I am not asking on behalf of the world, but on behalf of those whom you gave me, because they are yours. 10All mine are yours, and yours are mine; and I have been glorified in them. 11And now I am no longer in the world, but they are in the world, and I am coming to you. Holy Father, protect them in your name that you have given me, so that they may be one, as we are one. 12While I was with them, I protected them in your name that *e* you have given me. I guarded them, and not one of them was lost except the one destined to be lost, *f* so that the scripture might be fulfilled. 13But now I am coming to you, and I speak these things in the world so that they may have my joy made complete in themselves. *g* 14I have given them your word, and the world has hated them because they do not belong

a Or *will ask me no question*   *b* Other ancient authorities read *Father, he will give it to you in my name*   *c* Other ancient authorities read *the Father*   *d* Gk *flesh*   *e* Other ancient authorities read *protected in your name those whom*   *f* Gk *except the son of destruction*   *g* Or *among themselves* to the world, just as I do not belong to the world. 15I am not asking you to take them out of the world, but I ask you to protect them from the evil one.*a* 16They do not belong to the world, just as I do not belong to the world. 17Sanctify them in the truth; your word is truth. 18As you have sent me into the world, so I have sent them into the world. 19And for their sakes I sanctify myself, so that they also may be sanctified in truth.

20 "I ask not only on behalf of these, but also on behalf of those who will believe in me through their word, 21that they may all be one. As you, Father, are in me and I am in you, may they also be in us,*b* so that the world may believe that you have sent me. 22The glory that you have given me I have given them, so that they may be one, as we are one, 23I in them and you in me, that they may become completely one, so that the world may know that you have sent me and have loved them even as you have loved me. 24Father, I desire that those also, whom you have given me, may be with me where I am, to see my glory, which you have given me because you loved me before the foundation of the world.

25 "Righteous Father, the world does not know you, but I know you; and these know that you have sent me. 26I made your name known to them, and I will make it known, so that the love with which you have loved me may be in them, and I in them."

The Betrayal and Arrest of Jesus

18 After Jesus had spoken these words, he went out with his disciples across the Kidron valley to a place where there was a garden, which he and his disciples entered. 2Now Judas, who betrayed him, also knew the place, because Jesus often met there with his disciples. 3So Judas brought a detachment of soldiers together with police from the chief priests and the Pharisees, and they came there with lanterns and torches and weapons. 4Then Jesus, knowing all that was to happen

to him, came forward and asked them, "Whom are you looking for?" 5They answered, "Jesus of Nazareth."*c* Jesus replied, "I am he."*d* Judas, who betrayed him, was standing with them. 6When Jesus*e* said to them, "I am he,"*d* they stepped back and fell to the ground. 7Again he asked them, "Whom are you looking for?" And they said, "Jesus of Nazareth."*c* 8Jesus answered, "I told you that I am he.*d* So if you are looking for me, let these men go." 9This was to fulfill the word that he had spoken, "I did not lose a single one of those whom you gave me." 10Then Simon Peter, who had a sword, drew it, struck the high priest's slave, and cut off his right ear. The slave's name was Malchus. 11Jesus said to Peter, "Put your sword back into its sheath. Am I not to drink the cup that the Father has given me?"

Jesus before the High Priest

12 So the soldiers, their officer, and the Jewish police arrested Jesus and bound him. 13First they took him to Annas, who was the father-in-law of Caiaphas, the high priest that year. 14Caiaphas was the one who had advised the Jews that it was better to have one person die for the people.

Peter Denies Jesus

15 Simon Peter and another disciple followed Jesus. Since that disciple was known to the high priest, he went with Jesus into the courtyard of the high priest, 16but Peter was standing outside at the gate. So the other disciple, who was known to the high priest, went out, spoke to the woman who guarded the gate, and brought Peter in. 17The woman said to Peter, "You are not also one of this man's disciples, are you?" He said, "I am not." 18Now the slaves and the police had made a charcoal fire because it was cold, and they were standing around it and warming themselves. Peter also was standing with them and warming himself.

a Or *from evil*   *b* Other ancient authorities read *be one in us*   *c* Gk *the Nazorean*   *d* Gk *I am*   *e* Gk *he*

The High Priest Questions Jesus

19 Then the high priest questioned Jesus about his disciples and about his teaching. 20Jesus answered, "I have spoken openly to the world; I have always taught in synagogues and in the temple, where all the Jews come together. I have said nothing in secret. 21Why do you ask me? Ask those who heard what I said to them; they know what I said." 22When he had said this, one of the police standing nearby struck Jesus on the face, saying, "Is that how you answer the high priest?" 23Jesus answered, "If I have spoken wrongly, testify to the wrong. But if I have spoken rightly, why do you strike me?" 24Then Annas sent him bound to Caiaphas the high priest.

Peter Denies Jesus Again

25 Now Simon Peter was standing and warming himself. They asked him, "You are not also one of his disciples, are you?" He denied it and said, "I am not." 26One of the slaves of the high priest, a relative of the man whose ear Peter had cut off, asked, "Did I not see you in the garden with him?" 27Again Peter denied it, and at that moment the cock crowed.

Jesus before Pilate

28 Then they took Jesus from Caiaphas to Pilate's headquarters.*a* It was early in the morning. They themselves did not enter the headquarters,*a* so as to avoid ritual defilement and to be able to eat the Passover. 29So Pilate went out to them and said, "What accusation do you bring against this man?" 30They answered, "If this man were not a criminal, we would not have handed him over to you." 31Pilate said to them, "Take him yourselves and judge him according to your law." The Jews replied, "We are not permitted to put anyone to death." 32(This was to fulfill what Jesus had said when he indicated the kind of death he was to die.)

33 Then Pilate entered the headquarters*a* again, summoned Jesus, and asked him, "Are you the King of the Jews?" 34Jesus answered, "Do you ask this on your own, or did others tell you about me?" 35Pilate replied, "I am not a Jew, am I? Your own nation and the chief priests have handed you over to me. What have you done?" 36Jesus answered, "My kingdom is not from this world. If my kingdom were from this world, my followers would be fighting to keep me from being handed over to the Jews. But as it is, my kingdom is not from here." 37Pilate asked him, "So you are a king?" Jesus answered, "You say that I am a king. For this I was born, and for this I came into the world, to testify to the truth. Everyone who belongs to the truth listens to my voice." 38Pilate asked him, "What is truth?"

Jesus Sentenced to Death

After he had said this, he went out to the Jews again and told them, "I find no case against him. 39But you have a custom that I release someone for you at the Passover. Do you want me to release for you the King of the Jews?" 40They shouted in reply, "Not this man, but Barabbas!" Now Barabbas was a bandit.

19 Then Pilate took Jesus and had him flogged. 2And the soldiers wove a crown of thorns and put it on his head, and they dressed him in a purple robe. 3They kept coming up to him, saying, "Hail, King of the Jews!" and striking him on the face. 4Pilate went out again and said to them, "Look, I am bringing him out to you to let you know that I find no case against him." 5So Jesus came out, wearing the crown of thorns and the purple robe. Pilate said to them, "Here is the man!" 6When the chief priests and the police saw him, they shouted, "Crucify him! Crucify him!" Pilate said to them, "Take him yourselves and crucify him; I find no case against him." 7The Jews answered him, "We have a law, and according to that law he ought to die because he has claimed to be the Son of God."

8 Now when Pilate heard this, he was

a Gk *the praetorium*

more afraid than ever. [9]He entered his headquarters[a] again and asked Jesus, "Where are you from?" But Jesus gave him no answer. [10]Pilate therefore said to him, "Do you refuse to speak to me? Do you not know that I have power to release you, and power to crucify you?" [11]Jesus answered him, "You would have no power over me unless it had been given you from above; therefore the one who handed me over to you is guilty of a greater sin." [12]From then on Pilate tried to release him, but the Jews cried out, "If you release this man, you are no friend of the emperor. Everyone who claims to be a king sets himself against the emperor."

13 When Pilate heard these words, he brought Jesus outside and sat[b] on the judge's bench at a place called The Stone Pavement, or in Hebrew[c] Gabbatha. [14]Now it was the day of Preparation for the Passover; and it was about noon. He said to the Jews, "Here is your King!" [15]They cried out, "Away with him! Away with him! Crucify him!" Pilate asked them, "Shall I crucify your King?" The chief priests answered, "We have no king but the emperor." [16]Then he handed him over to them to be crucified.

The Crucifixion of Jesus

So they took Jesus; [17]and carrying the cross by himself, he went out to what is called The Place of the Skull, which in Hebrew[c] is called Golgotha. [18]There they crucified him, and with him two others, one on either side, with Jesus between them. [19]Pilate also had an inscription written and put on the cross. It read, "Jesus of Nazareth,[d] the King of the Jews." [20]Many of the Jews read this inscription, because the place where Jesus was crucified was near the city; and it was written in Hebrew,[c] in Latin, and in Greek. [21]Then the chief priests of the Jews said to Pilate, "Do not write, 'The King of the Jews,' but, 'This man said, I am King of the Jews.' " [22]Pilate answered, "What I have written I have written." [23]When the soldiers had crucified Jesus,

they took his clothes and divided them into four parts, one for each soldier. They also took his tunic; now the tunic was seamless, woven in one piece from the top. [24]So they said to one another, "Let us not tear it, but cast lots for it to see who will get it." This was to fulfill what the scripture says,

"They divided my clothes among
　　themselves,
　　and for my clothing they cast lots."
[25]And that is what the soldiers did.

Meanwhile, standing near the cross of Jesus were his mother, and his mother's sister, Mary the wife of Clopas, and Mary Magdalene. [26]When Jesus saw his mother and the disciple whom he loved standing beside her, he said to his mother, "Woman, here is your son." [27]Then he said to the disciple, "Here is your mother." And from that hour the disciple took her into his own home.

28 After this, when Jesus knew that all was now finished, he said (in order to fulfill the scripture), "I am thirsty." [29]A jar full of sour wine was standing there. So they put a sponge full of the wine on a branch of hyssop and held it to his mouth. [30]When Jesus had received the wine, he said, "It is finished." Then he bowed his head and gave up his spirit.

Jesus' Side Is Pierced

31 Since it was the day of Preparation, the Jews did not want the bodies left on the cross during the sabbath, especially because that sabbath was a day of great solemnity. So they asked Pilate to have the legs of the crucified men broken and the bodies removed. [32]Then the soldiers came and broke the legs of the first and of the other who had been crucified with him. [33]But when they came to Jesus and saw that he was already dead, they did not break his legs. [34]Instead, one of the soldiers pierced his side with a spear, and at once blood and water came out. [35](He who saw this has testified so that you also may believe. His testimony is true, and he knows[e]

---

a Gk *the praetorium*　　*b* Or *seated him*　　*c* That is, *Aramaic*　　*d* Gk *the Nazorean*　　*e* Or *there is one who knows* that he tells the truth.) ³⁶These things occurred so that the scripture might be fulfilled, "None of his bones shall be broken." ³⁷And again another passage of scripture says, "They will look on the one whom they have pierced."

The Burial of Jesus

38 After these things, Joseph of Arimathea, who was a disciple of Jesus, though a secret one because of his fear of the Jews, asked Pilate to let him take away the body of Jesus. Pilate gave him permission; so he came and removed his body. ³⁹Nicodemus, who had at first come to Jesus by night, also came, bringing a mixture of myrrh and aloes, weighing about a hundred pounds. ⁴⁰They took the body of Jesus and wrapped it with the spices in linen cloths, according to the burial custom of the Jews. ⁴¹Now there was a garden in the place where he was crucified, and in the garden there was a new tomb in which no one had ever been laid. ⁴²And so, because it was the Jewish day of Preparation, and the tomb was nearby, they laid Jesus there.

The Resurrection of Jesus

20 Early on the first day of the week, while it was still dark, Mary Magdalene came to the tomb and saw that the stone had been removed from the tomb. ²So she ran and went to Simon Peter and the other disciple, the one whom Jesus loved, and said to them, "They have taken the Lord out of the tomb, and we do not know where they have laid him." ³Then Peter and the other disciple set out and went toward the tomb. ⁴The two were running together, but the other disciple outran Peter and reached the tomb first. ⁵He bent down to look in and saw the linen wrappings lying there, but he did not go in. ⁶Then Simon Peter came, following him, and went into the tomb. He saw the linen wrappings lying there, ⁷and the cloth that had been on Jesus' head, not lying with the linen

wrappings but rolled up in a place by itself. ⁸Then the other disciple, who reached the tomb first, also went in, and he saw and believed; ⁹for as yet they did not understand the scripture, that he must rise from the dead. ¹⁰Then the disciples returned to their homes.

Jesus Appears to Mary Magdalene

11 But Mary stood weeping outside the tomb. As she wept, she bent over to look ᵃ into the tomb; ¹²and she saw two angels in white, sitting where the body of Jesus had been lying, one at the head and the other at the feet. ¹³They said to her, "Woman, why are you weeping?" She said to them, "They have taken away my Lord, and I do not know where they have laid him." ¹⁴When she had said this, she turned around and saw Jesus standing there, but she did not know that it was Jesus. ¹⁵Jesus said to her, "Woman, why are you weeping? Whom are you looking for?" Supposing him to be the gardener, she said to him, "Sir, if you have carried him away, tell me where you have laid him, and I will take him away." ¹⁶Jesus said to her, "Mary!" She turned and said to him in Hebrew, ᵇ "Rabbouni!" (which means Teacher). ¹⁷Jesus said to her, "Do not hold on to me, because I have not yet ascended to the Father. But go to my brothers and say to them, 'I am ascending to my Father and your Father, to my God and your God.'" ¹⁸Mary Magdalene went and announced to the disciples, "I have seen the Lord"; and she told them that he had said these things to her.

Jesus Appears to the Disciples

19 When it was evening on that day, the first day of the week, and the doors of the house where the disciples had met were locked for fear of the Jews, Jesus came and stood among them and said, "Peace be with you." ²⁰After he said this, he showed them his hands and his side. Then the disciples rejoiced when they saw the Lord. ²¹Jesus said to them again, "Peace be with you. As the Fa-

ther has sent me, so I send you." 22When he had said this, he breathed on them and said to them, "Receive the Holy Spirit. 23If you forgive the sins of any, they are forgiven them; if you retain the sins of any, they are retained."

Jesus and Thomas

24 But Thomas (who was called the Twin*a*), one of the twelve, was not with them when Jesus came. 25So the other disciples told him, "We have seen the Lord." But he said to them, "Unless I see the mark of the nails in his hands, and put my finger in the mark of the nails and my hand in his side, I will not believe."

26 A week later his disciples were again in the house, and Thomas was with them. Although the doors were shut, Jesus came and stood among them and said, "Peace be with you." 27Then he said to Thomas, "Put your finger here and see my hands. Reach out your hand and put it in my side. Do not doubt but believe." 28Thomas answered him, "My Lord and my God!" 29Jesus said to him, "Have you believed because you have seen me? Blessed are those who have not seen and yet have come to believe."

The Purpose of This Book

30 Now Jesus did many other signs in the presence of his disciples, which are not written in this book. 31But these are written so that you may come to believe*b* that Jesus is the Messiah,*c* the Son of God, and that through believing you may have life in his name.

Jesus Appears to Seven Disciples

21 After these things Jesus showed himself again to the disciples by the Sea of Tiberias; and he showed himself in this way. 2Gathered there together were Simon Peter, Thomas called the Twin,*a* Nathanael of Cana in Galilee, the sons of Zebedee, and two others of his disciples. 3Simon Peter said to them, "I am going fishing." They said to him, "We will go with you." They went out and got into the boat, but that night they caught nothing.

4 Just after daybreak, Jesus stood on the beach; but the disciples did not know that it was Jesus. 5Jesus said to them, "Children, you have no fish, have you?" They answered him, "No." 6He said to them, "Cast the net to the right side of the boat, and you will find some." So they cast it, and now they were not able to haul it in because there were so many fish. 7That disciple whom Jesus loved said to Peter, "It is the Lord!" When Simon Peter heard that it was the Lord, he put on some clothes, for he was naked, and jumped into the sea. 8But the other disciples came in the boat, dragging the net full of fish, for they were not far from the land, only about a hundred yards*d* off.

9 When they had gone ashore, they saw a charcoal fire there, with fish on it, and bread. 10Jesus said to them, "Bring some of the fish that you have just caught." 11So Simon Peter went aboard and hauled the net ashore, full of large fish, a hundred fifty-three of them; and though there were so many, the net was not torn. 12Jesus said to them, "Come and have breakfast." Now none of the disciples dared to ask him, "Who are you?" because they knew it was the Lord. 13Jesus came and took the bread and gave it to them, and did the same with the fish. 14This was now the third time that Jesus appeared to the disciples after he was raised from the dead.

Jesus and Peter

15 When they had finished breakfast, Jesus said to Simon Peter, "Simon son of John, do you love me more than these?" He said to him, "Yes, Lord; you know that I love you." Jesus said to him, "Feed my lambs." 16A second time he said to him, "Simon son of John, do you love me?" He said to him, "Yes, Lord; you know that I love you." Jesus said to him, "Tend my sheep." 17He said to him

---

a Gk *Didymus*   *b* Other ancient authorities read *may continue to believe*   *c* Or *the Christ*   *d* Gk *two hundred cubits* the third time, "Simon son of John, do you love me?" Peter felt hurt because he said to him the third time, "Do you love me?" And he said to him, "Lord, you know everything; you know that I love you." Jesus said to him, "Feed my sheep. 18Very truly, I tell you, when you were younger, you used to fasten your own belt and to go wherever you wished. But when you grow old, you will stretch out your hands, and someone else will fasten a belt around you and take you where you do not wish to go." 19(He said this to indicate the kind of death by which he would glorify God.) After this he said to him, "Follow me."

Jesus and the Beloved Disciple

20 Peter turned and saw the disciple whom Jesus loved following them; he was the one who had reclined next to Jesus at the supper and had said, "Lord, who is it that is going to betray you?" 21When Peter saw him, he said to Jesus, "Lord, what about him?" 22Jesus said to him, "If it is my will that he remain until I come, what is that to you? Follow me!" 23So the rumor spread in the community*a* that this disciple would not die. Yet Jesus did not say to him that he would not die, but, "If it is my will that he remain until I come, what is that to you?"*b*

24 This is the disciple who is testifying to these things and has written them, and we know that his testimony is true. 25But there are also many other things that Jesus did; if every one of them were written down, I suppose that the world itself could not contain the books that would be written.

---

a Gk *among the brothers*   *b* Other ancient authorities lack *what is that to you*

THE ACTS
OF THE APOSTLES

The Promise of the Holy Spirit

1 In the first book, Theophilus, I wrote about all that Jesus did and taught from the beginning 2until the day when he was taken up to heaven, after giving instructions through the Holy Spirit to the apostles whom he had chosen. 3After his suffering he presented himself alive to them by many convincing proofs, appearing to them during forty days and speaking about the kingdom of God. 4While staying*a* with them, he ordered them not to leave Jerusalem, but to wait there for the promise of the Father. "This," he said, "is what you have heard from me; 5for John baptized with water, but you will be baptized with*b* the Holy Spirit not many days from now."

The Ascension of Jesus

6 So when they had come together, they asked him, "Lord, is this the time when you will restore the kingdom to Israel?" 7He replied, "It is not for you to know the times or periods that the Father has set by his own authority. 8But you will receive power when the Holy Spirit has come upon you; and you will be my witnesses in Jerusalem, in all Judea and Samaria, and to the ends of the earth." 9When he had said this, as they were watching, he was lifted up, and a cloud took him out of their sight. 10While he was going and they were gazing up toward heaven, suddenly two men in white robes stood by them. 11They said, "Men of Galilee, why do you stand looking up toward heaven? This Jesus, who has been taken up from you into heaven, will come in the same way as you saw him go into heaven."

Matthias Chosen to Replace Judas

12 Then they returned to Jerusalem from the mount called Olivet, which is near Jerusalem, a sabbath day's journey away. 13When they had entered the city, they went to the room upstairs where they were staying, Peter, and John, and James, and Andrew, Philip and Thomas, Bartholomew and Matthew, James son of Alphaeus, and Simon the Zealot, and Judas son of*c* James. 14All these were constantly devoting themselves to prayer, together with certain women, including Mary the mother of Jesus, as well as his brothers.

15 In those days Peter stood up among the believers*d* (together the crowd numbered about one hundred twenty persons) and said, 16"Friends,*e* the scripture had to be fulfilled, which the Holy Spirit through David foretold concerning Judas, who became a guide for those who arrested Jesus— 17for he was numbered among us and was allotted his share in this ministry." 18(Now this man acquired a field with the reward of his wickedness; and falling headlong,*f* he burst open in the middle and all his bowels gushed out. 19This became known to all the residents of Jerusalem, so that the field was called in their language Hakeldama, that is, Field of Blood.) 20"For it is written in the book of Psalms,

'Let his homestead become desolate,
    and let there be no one to live in it';

and

'Let another take his position of
        overseer.'

21So one of the men who have accompanied us during all the time that the Lord Jesus went in and out among us, 22beginning from the baptism of John until the day when he was taken up from us—one of these must become a witness with us to his resurrection." 23So they proposed two, Joseph called Barsabbas, who was also known as Justus, and Matthias. 24Then they prayed and said, "Lord, you know everyone's heart. Show us which one of these two you have chosen 25to take the place*g* in this ministry and apostleship from which Judas turned aside to go to his own place." 26And they cast lots for them,

a Or eating   b Or by   c Or the brother of   d Gk brothers   e Gk Men, brothers   f Or swelling up   g Other ancient authorities read the share and the lot fell on Matthias; and he was added to the eleven apostles.

The Coming of the Holy Spirit

2 When the day of Pentecost had come, they were all together in one place. 2And suddenly from heaven there came a sound like the rush of a violent wind, and it filled the entire house where they were sitting. 3Divided tongues, as of fire, appeared among them, and a tongue rested on each of them. 4All of them were filled with the Holy Spirit and began to speak in other languages, as the Spirit gave them ability.

5 Now there were devout Jews from every nation under heaven living in Jerusalem. 6And at this sound the crowd gathered and was bewildered, because each one heard them speaking in the native language of each. 7Amazed and astonished, they asked, "Are not all these who are speaking Galileans? 8And how is it that we hear, each of us, in our own native language? 9Parthians, Medes, Elamites, and residents of Mesopotamia, Judea and Cappadocia, Pontus and Asia, 10Phrygia and Pamphylia, Egypt and the parts of Libya belonging to Cyrene, and visitors from Rome, both Jews and proselytes, 11Cretans and Arabs—in our own languages we hear them speaking about God's deeds of power." 12All were amazed and perplexed, saying to one another, "What does this mean?" 13But others sneered and said, "They are filled with new wine."

Peter Addresses the Crowd

14 But Peter, standing with the eleven, raised his voice and addressed them, "Men of Judea and all who live in Jerusalem, let this be known to you, and listen to what I say. 15Indeed, these are not drunk, as you suppose, for it is only nine o'clock in the morning. 16No, this is what was spoken through the prophet Joel:

17 'In the last days it will be, God declares,

that I will pour out my Spirit upon all flesh,
and your sons and your daughters shall prophesy,
and your young men shall see visions, and your old men shall dream dreams.
18 Even upon my slaves, both men and women,
in those days I will pour out my Spirit;
and they shall prophesy.
19 And I will show portents in the heaven above
and signs on the earth below, blood, and fire, and smoky mist.
20 The sun shall be turned to darkness and the moon to blood,
before the coming of the Lord's great and glorious day.
21 Then everyone who calls on the name of the Lord shall be saved.'

22 "You that are Israelites,[a] listen to what I have to say: Jesus of Nazareth,[b] a man attested to you by God with deeds of power, wonders, and signs that God did through him among you, as you yourselves know— 23this man, handed over to you according to the definite plan and foreknowledge of God, you crucified and killed by the hands of those outside the law. 24But God raised him up, having freed him from death,[c] because it was impossible for him to be held in its power. 25For David says concerning him,

'I saw the Lord always before me, for he is at my right hand so that I will not be shaken;
26 therefore my heart was glad, and my tongue rejoiced;
moreover my flesh will live in hope.
27 For you will not abandon my soul to Hades,
or let your Holy One experience corruption.
28 You have made known to me the ways of life;

---

a Gk *Men, Israelites*   *b* Gk *the Nazorean*   *c* Gk *the pains of death*

you will make me full of gladness
with your presence.'

29 "Fellow Israelites,*a* I may say to you confidently of our ancestor David that he both died and was buried, and his tomb is with us to this day. 30Since he was a prophet, he knew that God had sworn with an oath to him that he would put one of his descendants on his throne. 31Foreseeing this, David*b* spoke of the resurrection of the Messiah,*c* saying,

'He was not abandoned to Hades,
    nor did his flesh experience
        corruption.'

32This Jesus God raised up, and of that all of us are witnesses. 33Being therefore exalted at*d* the right hand of God, and having received from the Father the promise of the Holy Spirit, he has poured out this that you both see and hear. 34For David did not ascend into the heavens, but he himself says,

'The Lord said to my Lord,
"Sit at my right hand,
35   until I make your enemies your
        footstool." '

36Therefore let the entire house of Israel know with certainty that God has made him both Lord and Messiah,*e* this Jesus whom you crucified."

The First Converts

37 Now when they heard this, they were cut to the heart and said to Peter and to the other apostles, "Brothers,*a* what should we do?" 38Peter said to them, "Repent, and be baptized every one of you in the name of Jesus Christ so that your sins may be forgiven; and you will receive the gift of the Holy Spirit. 39For the promise is for you, for your children, and for all who are far away, everyone whom the Lord our God calls to him." 40And he testified with many other arguments and exhorted them, saying, "Save yourselves from this corrupt generation." 41So those who welcomed his message were baptized, and that day about three thousand persons were added. 42They devoted themselves to the apostles' teaching and fellowship, to the breaking of bread and the prayers.

Life among the Believers

43 Awe came upon everyone, because many wonders and signs were being done by the apostles. 44All who believed were together and had all things in common; 45they would sell their possessions and goods and distribute the proceeds*f* to all, as any had need. 46Day by day, as they spent much time together in the temple, they broke bread at home*g* and ate their food with glad and generous*h* hearts, 47praising God and having the goodwill of all the people. And day by day the Lord added to their number those who were being saved.

Peter Heals a Crippled Beggar

3 One day Peter and John were going up to the temple at the hour of prayer, at three o'clock in the afternoon. 2And a man lame from birth was being carried in. People would lay him daily at the gate of the temple called the Beautiful Gate so that he could ask for alms from those entering the temple. 3When he saw Peter and John about to go into the temple, he asked them for alms. 4Peter looked intently at him, as did John, and said, "Look at us." 5And he fixed his attention on them, expecting to receive something from them. 6But Peter said, "I have no silver or gold, but what I have I give you; in the name of Jesus Christ of Nazareth,*i* stand up and walk." 7And he took him by the right hand and raised him up; and immediately his feet and ankles were made strong. 8Jumping up, he stood and began to walk, and he entered the temple with them, walking and leaping and praising God. 9All the people saw him walking and praising God, 10and they recognized him as the one who used to sit and ask for alms at the Beautiful Gate of the temple; and they were filled with wonder and amazement at what had happened to him.

a Gk Men, brothers   *b* Gk he   *c* Or the Christ   *d* Or by   *e* Or Christ   *f* Gk them   *g* Or from house to house
h Or sincere   *i* Gk the Nazorean

Peter Speaks in Solomon's Portico

11 While he clung to Peter and John, all the people ran together to them in the portico called Solomon's Portico, utterly astonished. 12When Peter saw it, he addressed the people, "You Israelites,[a] why do you wonder at this, or why do you stare at us, as though by our own power or piety we had made him walk? 13The God of Abraham, the God of Isaac, and the God of Jacob, the God of our ancestors has glorified his servant[b] Jesus, whom you handed over and rejected in the presence of Pilate, though he had decided to release him. 14But you rejected the Holy and Righteous One and asked to have a murderer given to you, 15and you killed the Author of life, whom God raised from the dead. To this we are witnesses. 16And by faith in his name, his name itself has made this man strong, whom you see and know; and the faith that is through Jesus[c] has given him this perfect health in the presence of all of you.

17 "And now, friends,[d] I know that you acted in ignorance, as did also your rulers. 18In this way God fulfilled what he had foretold through all the prophets, that his Messiah[e] would suffer. 19Repent therefore, and turn to God so that your sins may be wiped out, 20so that times of refreshing may come from the presence of the Lord, and that he may send the Messiah[f] appointed for you, that is, Jesus, 21who must remain in heaven until the time of universal restoration that God announced long ago through his holy prophets. 22Moses said, 'The Lord your God will raise up for you from your own people[d] a prophet like me. You must listen to whatever he tells you. 23And it will be that everyone who does not listen to that prophet will be utterly rooted out of the people.' 24And all the prophets, as many as have spoken, from Samuel and those after him, also predicted these days. 25You are the descendants of the prophets and of the covenant that God gave to your ancestors, saying to Abraham, 'And in your descendants all the families of the earth shall be blessed.' 26When God raised up his servant,[b] he sent him first to you, to bless you by turning each of you from your wicked ways."

Peter and John before the Council

4 While Peter and John[g] were speaking to the people, the priests, the captain of the temple, and the Sadducees came to them, 2much annoyed because they were teaching the people and proclaiming that in Jesus there is the resurrection of the dead. 3So they arrested them and put them in custody until the next day, for it was already evening. 4But many of those who heard the word believed; and they numbered about five thousand.

5 The next day their rulers, elders, and scribes assembled in Jerusalem, 6with Annas the high priest, Caiaphas, John,[h] and Alexander, and all who were of the high-priestly family. 7When they had made the prisoners[i] stand in their midst, they inquired, "By what power or by what name did you do this?" 8Then Peter, filled with the Holy Spirit, said to them, "Rulers of the people and elders, 9if we are questioned today because of a good deed done to someone who was sick and are asked how this man has been healed, 10let it be known to all of you, and to all the people of Israel, that this man is standing before you in good health by the name of Jesus Christ of Nazareth,[j] whom you crucified, whom God raised from the dead. 11This Jesus[k] is

'the stone that was rejected by you, the builders;
    it has become the cornerstone.'[l]

12There is salvation in no one else, for there is no other name under heaven given among mortals by which we must be saved."

13 Now when they saw the boldness of Peter and John and realized that they were uneducated and ordinary men, they were amazed and recognized them as companions of Jesus. 14When they saw the man who had been cured standing beside them, they had

---

a Gk Men, Israelites   b Or child   c Gk him   d Gk brothers   e Or his Christ   f Or the Christ   g Gk While they   h Other ancient authorities read Jonathan   i Gk them   j Gk the Nazorean   k Gk This   l Or keystone nothing to say in opposition. [15]So they ordered them to leave the council while they discussed the matter with one another. [16]They said, "What will we do with them? For it is obvious to all who live in Jerusalem that a notable sign has been done through them; we cannot deny it. [17]But to keep it from spreading further among the people, let us warn them to speak no more to anyone in this name." [18]So they called them and ordered them not to speak or teach at all in the name of Jesus. [19]But Peter and John answered them, "Whether it is right in God's sight to listen to you rather than to God, you must judge; [20]for we cannot keep from speaking about what we have seen and heard." [21]After threatening them again, they let them go, finding no way to punish them because of the people, for all of them praised God for what had happened. [22]For the man on whom this sign of healing had been performed was more than forty years old.

The Believers Pray for Boldness

23 After they were released, they went to their friends[a] and reported what the chief priests and the elders had said to them. [24]When they heard it, they raised their voices together to God and said, "Sovereign Lord, who made the heaven and the earth, the sea, and everything in them, [25]it is you who said by the Holy Spirit through our ancestor David, your servant:[b]

'Why did the Gentiles rage,
   and the peoples imagine vain things?
26   The kings of the earth took their
       stand,
   and the rulers have gathered
      together
     against the Lord and against his
      Messiah.'[c]

[27]For in this city, in fact, both Herod and Pontius Pilate, with the Gentiles and the peoples of Israel, gathered together against your holy servant[b] Jesus, whom you anointed, [28]to do whatever your hand and your plan had predestined to take place. [29]And now, Lord, look at their threats, and grant to your servants[d] to speak your word with all boldness, [30]while you stretch out your hand to heal, and signs and wonders are performed through the name of your holy servant[b] Jesus." [31]When they had prayed, the place in which they were gathered together was shaken; and they were all filled with the Holy Spirit and spoke the word of God with boldness.

The Believers Share Their Possessions

32 Now the whole group of those who believed were of one heart and soul, and no one claimed private ownership of any possessions, but everything they owned was held in common. [33]With great power the apostles gave their testimony to the resurrection of the Lord Jesus, and great grace was upon them all. [34]There was not a needy person among them, for as many as owned lands or houses sold them and brought the proceeds of what was sold. [35]They laid it at the apostles' feet, and it was distributed to each as any had need. [36]There was a Levite, a native of Cyprus, Joseph, to whom the apostles gave the name Barnabas (which means "son of encouragement"). [37]He sold a field that belonged to him, then brought the money, and laid it at the apostles' feet.

Ananias and Sapphira

5 But a man named Ananias, with the consent of his wife Sapphira, sold a piece of property; [2]with his wife's knowledge, he kept back some of the proceeds, and brought only a part and laid it at the apostles' feet. [3]"Ananias," Peter asked, "why has Satan filled your heart to lie to the Holy Spirit and to keep back part of the proceeds of the land? [4]While it remained unsold, did it not remain your own? And after it was sold, were not the proceeds at your disposal? How is it that you have contrived this deed in your heart? You did not lie to us[e] but to God!" [5]Now when Ananias heard these words, he fell down and

---

a Gk *their own*   b Or *child*   c Or *his Christ*   d Gk *slaves*   e Gk *to men* died. And great fear seized all who heard of it. [6]The young men came and wrapped up his body,[a] then carried him out and buried him.

7 After an interval of about three hours his wife came in, not knowing what had happened. [8]Peter said to her, "Tell me whether you and your husband sold the land for such and such a price." And she said, "Yes, that was the price." [9]Then Peter said to her, "How is it that you have agreed together to put the Spirit of the Lord to the test? Look, the feet of those who have buried your husband are at the door, and they will carry you out." [10]Immediately she fell down at his feet and died. When the young men came in they found her dead, so they carried her out and buried her beside her husband. [11]And great fear seized the whole church and all who heard of these things.

The Apostles Heal Many

12 Now many signs and wonders were done among the people through the apostles. And they were all together in Solomon's Portico. [13]None of the rest dared to join them, but the people held them in high esteem. [14]Yet more than ever believers were added to the Lord, great numbers of both men and women, [15]so that they even carried out the sick into the streets, and laid them on cots and mats, in order that Peter's shadow might fall on some of them as he came by. [16]A great number of people would also gather from the towns around Jerusalem, bringing the sick and those tormented by unclean spirits, and they were all cured.

The Apostles Are Persecuted

17 Then the high priest took action; he and all who were with him (that is, the sect of the Sadducees), being filled with jealousy, [18]arrested the apostles and put them in the public prison. [19]But during the night an angel of the Lord opened the prison doors, brought them out, and said, [20]"Go, stand in the temple and tell the people the whole message about this life." [21]When they heard this, they entered the temple at daybreak and went on with their teaching.

When the high priest and those with him arrived, they called together the council and the whole body of the elders of Israel, and sent to the prison to have them brought. [22]But when the temple police went there, they did not find them in the prison; so they returned and reported, [23]"We found the prison securely locked and the guards standing at the doors, but when we opened them, we found no one inside." [24]Now when the captain of the temple and the chief priests heard these words, they were perplexed about them, wondering what might be going on. [25]Then someone arrived and announced, "Look, the men whom you put in prison are standing in the temple and teaching the people!" [26]Then the captain went with the temple police and brought them, but without violence, for they were afraid of being stoned by the people.

27 When they had brought them, they had them stand before the council. The high priest questioned them, [28]saying, "We gave you strict orders not to teach in this name,[b] yet here you have filled Jerusalem with your teaching and you are determined to bring this man's blood on us." [29]But Peter and the apostles answered, "We must obey God rather than any human authority.[c] [30]The God of our ancestors raised up Jesus, whom you had killed by hanging him on a tree. [31]God exalted him at his right hand as Leader and Savior that he might give repentance to Israel and forgiveness of sins. [32]And we are witnesses to these things, and so is the Holy Spirit whom God has given to those who obey him."

33 When they heard this, they were enraged and wanted to kill them. [34]But a Pharisee in the council named Gamaliel, a teacher of the law, respected by all the people, stood up and ordered the men to be put outside for a short time. [35]Then he said to them, "Fellow

---

a Meaning of Gk uncertain   *b* Other ancient authorities read *Did we not give you strict orders not to teach in this name?*
c Gk *than men*

Israelites,^a consider carefully what you propose to do to these men. ³⁶For some time ago Theudas rose up, claiming to be somebody, and a number of men, about four hundred, joined him; but he was killed, and all who followed him were dispersed and disappeared. ³⁷After him Judas the Galilean rose up at the time of the census and got people to follow him; he also perished, and all who followed him were scattered. ³⁸So in the present case, I tell you, keep away from these men and let them alone; because if this plan or this undertaking is of human origin, it will fail; ³⁹but if it is of God, you will not be able to overthrow them—in that case you may even be found fighting against God!"

They were convinced by him, ⁴⁰and when they had called in the apostles, they had them flogged. Then they ordered them not to speak in the name of Jesus, and let them go. ⁴¹As they left the council, they rejoiced that they were considered worthy to suffer dishonor for the sake of the name. ⁴²And every day in the temple and at home^b they did not cease to teach and proclaim Jesus as the Messiah.^c

Seven Chosen to Serve

6 Now during those days, when the disciples were increasing in number, the Hellenists complained against the Hebrews because their widows were being neglected in the daily distribution of food. ²And the twelve called together the whole community of the disciples and said, "It is not right that we should neglect the word of God in order to wait on tables.^d ³Therefore, friends,^e select from among yourselves seven men of good standing, full of the Spirit and of wisdom, whom we may appoint to this task, ⁴while we, for our part, will devote ourselves to prayer and to serving the word." ⁵What they said pleased the whole community, and they chose Stephen, a man full of faith and the Holy Spirit, together with Philip, Prochorus, Nicanor, Timon, Parmenas, and Nicolaus, a

proselyte of Antioch. ⁶They had these men stand before the apostles, who prayed and laid their hands on them.

7 The word of God continued to spread; the number of the disciples increased greatly in Jerusalem, and a great many of the priests became obedient to the faith.

The Arrest of Stephen

8 Stephen, full of grace and power, did great wonders and signs among the people. ⁹Then some of those who belonged to the synagogue of the Freedmen (as it was called), Cyrenians, Alexandrians, and others of those from Cilicia and Asia, stood up and argued with Stephen. ¹⁰But they could not withstand the wisdom and the Spirit^f with which he spoke. ¹¹Then they secretly instigated some men to say, "We have heard him speak blasphemous words against Moses and God." ¹²They stirred up the people as well as the elders and the scribes; then they suddenly confronted him, seized him, and brought him before the council. ¹³They set up false witnesses who said, "This man never stops saying things against this holy place and the law; ¹⁴for we have heard him say that this Jesus of Nazareth^g will destroy this place and will change the customs that Moses handed on to us." ¹⁵And all who sat in the council looked intently at him, and they saw that his face was like the face of an angel.

Stephen's Speech to the Council

7 Then the high priest asked him, "Are these things so?" ²And Stephen replied: "Brothers^b and fathers, listen to me. The God of glory appeared to our ancestor Abraham when he was in Mesopotamia, before he lived in Haran, ³and said to him, 'Leave your country and your relatives and go to the land that I will show you.' ⁴Then he left the country of the Chaldeans and settled in Haran. After his father died, God had him move from there to this country in which you are now living. ⁵He did not give him any of it as a her-

---

a Gk Men, Israelites   b Or from house to house   c Or the Christ   d Or keep accounts   e Gk brothers   f Or spirit
g Gk the Nazorean   h Gk Men, brothers

itage, not even a foot's length, but promised to give it to him as his possession and to his descendants after him, even though he had no child. [6]And God spoke in these terms, that his descendants would be resident aliens in a country belonging to others, who would enslave them and mistreat them during four hundred years. [7]But I will judge the nation that they serve,' said God, 'and after that they shall come out and worship me in this place.' [8]Then he gave him the covenant of circumcision. And so Abraham[a] became the father of Isaac and circumcised him on the eighth day; and Isaac became the father of Jacob, and Jacob of the twelve patriarchs.

[9] "The patriarchs, jealous of Joseph, sold him into Egypt; but God was with him, [10]and rescued him from all his afflictions, and enabled him to win favor and to show wisdom when he stood before Pharaoh, king of Egypt, who appointed him ruler over Egypt and over all his household. [11]Now there came a famine throughout Egypt and Canaan, and great suffering, and our ancestors could find no food. [12]But when Jacob heard that there was grain in Egypt, he sent our ancestors there on their first visit. [13]On the second visit Joseph made himself known to his brothers, and Joseph's family became known to Pharaoh. [14]Then Joseph sent and invited his father Jacob and all his relatives to come to him, seventy-five in all; [15]so Jacob went down to Egypt. He himself died there as well as our ancestors, [16]and their bodies[b] were brought back to Shechem and laid in the tomb that Abraham had bought for a sum of silver from the sons of Hamor in Shechem.

[17] "But as the time drew near for the fulfillment of the promise that God had made to Abraham, our people in Egypt increased and multiplied [18]until another king who had not known Joseph ruled over Egypt. [19]He dealt craftily with our race and forced our ancestors to abandon their infants so that they would die. [20]At this time Moses was born, and he was beautiful before God. For three months he was brought up in his father's house; [21]and when he was abandoned, Pharaoh's daughter adopted him and brought him up as her own son. [22]So Moses was instructed in all the wisdom of the Egyptians and was powerful in his words and deeds.

[23] "When he was forty years old, it came into his heart to visit his relatives, the Israelites.[c] [24]When he saw one of them being wronged, he defended the oppressed man and avenged him by striking down the Egyptian. [25]He supposed that his kinsfolk would understand that God through him was rescuing them, but they did not understand. [26]The next day he came to some of them as they were quarreling and tried to reconcile them, saying, 'Men, you are brothers; why do you wrong each other?' [27]But the man who was wronging his neighbor pushed Moses[d] aside, saying, 'Who made you a ruler and a judge over us? [28]Do you want to kill me as you killed the Egyptian yesterday?' [29]When he heard this, Moses fled and became a resident alien in the land of Midian. There he became the father of two sons.

[30] "Now when forty years had passed, an angel appeared to him in the wilderness of Mount Sinai, in the flame of a burning bush. [31]When Moses saw it, he was amazed at the sight; and as he approached to look, there came the voice of the Lord: [32]'I am the God of your ancestors, the God of Abraham, Isaac, and Jacob.' Moses began to tremble and did not dare to look. [33]Then the Lord said to him, 'Take off the sandals from your feet, for the place where you are standing is holy ground. [34]I have surely seen the mistreatment of my people who are in Egypt and have heard their groaning, and I have come down to rescue them. Come now, I will send you to Egypt.'

[35] "It was this Moses whom they rejected when they said, 'Who made you a ruler and a judge?' and whom God now sent as both ruler and liberator through the angel who appeared to him in the bush. [36]He led

a Gk *he*   *b* Gk *they*   *c* Gk *his brothers, the sons of Israel*   *d* Gk *him* them out, having performed wonders and signs in Egypt, at the Red Sea, and in the wilderness for forty years. 37This is the Moses who said to the Israelites, 'God will raise up a prophet for you from your own people*a* as he raised me up.' 38He is the one who was in the congregation in the wilderness with the angel who spoke to him at Mount Sinai, and with our ancestors; and he received living oracles to give to us. 39Our ancestors were unwilling to obey him; instead, they pushed him aside, and in their hearts they turned back to Egypt, 40saying to Aaron, 'Make gods for us who will lead the way for us; as for this Moses who led us out from the land of Egypt, we do not know what has happened to him.' 41At that time they made a calf, offered a sacrifice to the idol, and reveled in the works of their hands. 42But God turned away from them and handed them over to worship the host of heaven, as it is written in the book of the prophets:

'Did you offer to me slain victims and
        sacrifices
    forty years in the wilderness,
        O house of Israel?
43 No; you took along the tent of
            Moloch,
        and the star of your god Rephan,
            the images that you made to
                worship;
    so I will remove you beyond Babylon.'

44 "Our ancestors had the tent of testimony in the wilderness, as God*b* directed when he spoke to Moses, ordering him to make it according to the pattern he had seen. 45Our ancestors in turn brought it in with Joshua when they dispossessed the nations that God drove out before our ancestors. And it was there until the time of David, 46who found favor with God and asked that he might find a dwelling place for the house of Jacob.*c* 47But it was Solomon who built a house for him. 48Yet the Most High does not dwell in houses made with human hands;*d* as the prophet says,

49   'Heaven is my throne,
        and the earth is my footstool.
    What kind of house will you build for
            me, says the Lord,
        or what is the place of my rest?
50   Did not my hand make all these
            things?'

51 "You stiff-necked people, uncircumcised in heart and ears, you are forever opposing the Holy Spirit, just as your ancestors used to do. 52Which of the prophets did your ancestors not persecute? They killed those who foretold the coming of the Righteous One, and now you have become his betrayers and murderers. 53You are the ones that received the law as ordained by angels, and yet you have not kept it."

The Stoning of Stephen

54 When they heard these things, they became enraged and ground their teeth at Stephen.*e* 55But filled with the Holy Spirit, he gazed into heaven and saw the glory of God and Jesus standing at the right hand of God. 56"Look," he said, "I see the heavens opened and the Son of Man standing at the right hand of God!" 57But they covered their ears, and with a loud shout all rushed together against him. 58Then they dragged him out of the city and began to stone him; and the witnesses laid their coats at the feet of a young man named Saul. 59While they were stoning Stephen, he prayed, "Lord Jesus, receive my spirit." 60Then he knelt down and cried out in a loud voice, "Lord, do not hold this sin against them." When he had said this, he died.*f* 8 1And Saul approved of their killing him.

Saul Persecutes the Church

That day a severe persecution began against the church in Jerusalem, and all except the apostles were scattered throughout the countryside of Judea and Samaria. 2Devout men buried Stephen and made loud lamentation over him. 3But Saul was ravaging the church by entering house after house; drag-

---

a Gk *your brothers*   *b* Gk *he*   *c* Other ancient authorities read *for the God of Jacob*   *d* Gk *with hands*   *e* Gk *him*
f Gk *fell asleep*

ging off both men and women, he committed them to prison.

Philip Preaches in Samaria

4 Now those who were scattered went from place to place, proclaiming the word. [5]Philip went down to the city[a] of Samaria and proclaimed the Messiah[b] to them. [6]The crowds with one accord listened eagerly to what was said by Philip, hearing and seeing the signs that he did, [7]for unclean spirits, crying with loud shrieks, came out of many who were possessed; and many others who were paralyzed or lame were cured. [8]So there was great joy in that city.

9 Now a certain man named Simon had previously practiced magic in the city and amazed the people of Samaria, saying that he was someone great. [10]All of them, from the least to the greatest, listened to him eagerly, saying, "This man is the power of God that is called Great." [11]And they listened eagerly to him because for a long time he had amazed them with his magic. [12]But when they believed Philip, who was proclaiming the good news about the kingdom of God and the name of Jesus Christ, they were baptized, both men and women. [13]Even Simon himself believed. After being baptized, he stayed constantly with Philip and was amazed when he saw the signs and great miracles that took place.

14 Now when the apostles at Jerusalem heard that Samaria had accepted the word of God, they sent Peter and John to them. [15]The two went down and prayed for them that they might receive the Holy Spirit [16](for as yet the Spirit had not come[c] upon any of them; they had only been baptized in the name of the Lord Jesus). [17]Then Peter and John[d] laid their hands on them, and they received the Holy Spirit. [18]Now when Simon saw that the Spirit was given through the laying on of the apostles' hands, he offered them money, [19]saying, "Give me also this power so that anyone on whom I lay my hands may receive

the Holy Spirit." [20]But Peter said to him, "May your silver perish with you, because you thought you could obtain God's gift with money! [21]You have no part or share in this, for your heart is not right before God. [22]Repent therefore of this wickedness of yours, and pray to the Lord that, if possible, the intent of your heart may be forgiven you. [23]For I see that you are in the gall of bitterness and the chains of wickedness." [24]Simon answered, "Pray for me to the Lord, that nothing of what you[e] have said may happen to me."

25 Now after Peter and John[f] had testified and spoken the word of the Lord, they returned to Jerusalem, proclaiming the good news to many villages of the Samaritans.

Philip and the Ethiopian Eunuch

26 Then an angel of the Lord said to Philip, "Get up and go toward the south[g] to the road that goes down from Jerusalem to Gaza." (This is a wilderness road.) [27]So he got up and went. Now there was an Ethiopian eunuch, a court official of the Candace, queen of the Ethiopians, in charge of her entire treasury. He had come to Jerusalem to worship [28]and was returning home; seated in his chariot, he was reading the prophet Isaiah. [29]Then the Spirit said to Philip, "Go over to this chariot and join it." [30]So Philip ran up to it and heard him reading the prophet Isaiah. He asked, "Do you understand what you are reading?" [31]He replied, "How can I, unless someone guides me?" And he invited Philip to get in and sit beside him. [32]Now the passage of the scripture that he was reading was this:

"Like a sheep he was led to the
        slaughter,
    and like a lamb silent before its
        shearer,
    so he does not open his mouth.
[33] In his humiliation justice was denied
        him.
    Who can describe his generation?

a Other ancient authorities read a city   b Or the Christ   c Gk fallen   d Gk they   e The Greek word for you and the verb pray are plural   f Gk after they   g Or go at noon

For his life is taken away from the earth."

³⁴The eunuch asked Philip, "About whom, may I ask you, does the prophet say this, about himself or about someone else?" ³⁵Then Philip began to speak, and starting with this scripture, he proclaimed to him the good news about Jesus. ³⁶As they were going along the road, they came to some water; and the eunuch said, "Look, here is water! What is to prevent me from being baptized?"*a* ³⁸He commanded the chariot to stop, and both of them, Philip and the eunuch, went down into the water, and Philip*b* baptized him. ³⁹When they came up out of the water, the Spirit of the Lord snatched Philip away; the eunuch saw him no more, and went on his way rejoicing. ⁴⁰But Philip found himself at Azotus, and as he was passing through the region, he proclaimed the good news to all the towns until he came to Caesarea.

The Conversion of Saul

9 Meanwhile Saul, still breathing threats and murder against the disciples of the Lord, went to the high priest ²and asked him for letters to the synagogues at Damascus, so that if he found any who belonged to the Way, men or women, he might bring them bound to Jerusalem. ³Now as he was going along and approaching Damascus, suddenly a light from heaven flashed around him. ⁴He fell to the ground and heard a voice saying to him, "Saul, Saul, why do you persecute me?" ⁵He asked, "Who are you, Lord?" The reply came, "I am Jesus, whom you are persecuting. ⁶But get up and enter the city, and you will be told what you are to do." ⁷The men who were traveling with him stood speechless because they heard the voice but saw no one. ⁸Saul got up from the ground, and though his eyes were open, he could see nothing; so they led him by the hand and brought him into Damascus. ⁹For three days he was without sight, and neither ate nor drank.

10 Now there was a disciple in Damascus named Ananias. The Lord said to him in a vision, "Ananias." He answered, "Here I am, Lord." ¹¹The Lord said to him, "Get up and go to the street called Straight, and at the house of Judas look for a man of Tarsus named Saul. At this moment he is praying, ¹²and he has seen in a vision*c* a man named Ananias come in and lay his hands on him so that he might regain his sight." ¹³But Ananias answered, "Lord, I have heard from many about this man, how much evil he has done to your saints in Jerusalem; ¹⁴and here he has authority from the chief priests to bind all who invoke your name." ¹⁵But the Lord said to him, "Go, for he is an instrument whom I have chosen to bring my name before Gentiles and kings and before the people of Israel; ¹⁶I myself will show him how much he must suffer for the sake of my name." ¹⁷So Ananias went and entered the house. He laid his hands on Saul*d* and said, "Brother Saul, the Lord Jesus, who appeared to you on your way here, has sent me so that you may regain your sight and be filled with the Holy Spirit." ¹⁸And immediately something like scales fell from his eyes, and his sight was restored. Then he got up and was baptized, ¹⁹and after taking some food, he regained his strength.

Saul Preaches in Damascus

For several days he was with the disciples in Damascus, ²⁰and immediately he began to proclaim Jesus in the synagogues, saying, "He is the Son of God." ²¹All who heard him were amazed and said, "Is not this the man who made havoc in Jerusalem among those who invoked this name? And has he not come here for the purpose of bringing them bound before the chief priests?" ²²Saul became increasingly more powerful and confounded the Jews who lived in Damascus by proving that Jesus*e* was the Messiah.*f*

---

a Other ancient authorities add all or most of verse 37, *And Philip said, "If you believe with all your heart, you may." And he replied, "I believe that Jesus Christ is the Son of God."*   *b* Gk *he*   *c* Other ancient authorities lack *in a vision*   *d* Gk *him*   *e* Gk *that this*   *f* Or *the Christ*

Saul Escapes from the Jews

23 After some time had passed, the Jews plotted to kill him, 24but their plot became known to Saul. They were watching the gates day and night so that they might kill him; 25but his disciples took him by night and let him down through an opening in the wall,*a* lowering him in a basket.

Saul in Jerusalem

26 When he had come to Jerusalem, he attempted to join the disciples; and they were all afraid of him, for they did not believe that he was a disciple. 27But Barnabas took him, brought him to the apostles, and described for them how on the road he had seen the Lord, who had spoken to him, and how in Damascus he had spoken boldly in the name of Jesus. 28So he went in and out among them in Jerusalem, speaking boldly in the name of the Lord. 29He spoke and argued with the Hellenists; but they were attempting to kill him. 30When the believers*b* learned of it, they brought him down to Caesarea and sent him off to Tarsus.

31 Meanwhile the church throughout Judea, Galilee, and Samaria had peace and was built up. Living in the fear of the Lord and in the comfort of the Holy Spirit, it increased in numbers.

The Healing of Aeneas

32 Now as Peter went here and there among all the believers,*c* he came down also to the saints living in Lydda. 33There he found a man named Aeneas, who had been bedridden for eight years, for he was paralyzed. 34Peter said to him, "Aeneas, Jesus Christ heals you; get up and make your bed!" And immediately he got up. 35And all the residents of Lydda and Sharon saw him and turned to the Lord.

Peter in Lydda and Joppa

36 Now in Joppa there was a disciple whose name was Tabitha, which in Greek is Dorcas.*d* She was devoted to good works and acts of charity. 37At that time she became ill and died. When they had washed her, they laid her in a room upstairs. 38Since Lydda was near Joppa, the disciples, who heard that Peter was there, sent two men to him with the request, "Please come to us without delay." 39So Peter got up and went with them; and when he arrived, they took him to the room upstairs. All the widows stood beside him, weeping and showing tunics and other clothing that Dorcas had made while she was with them. 40Peter put all of them outside, and then he knelt down and prayed. He turned to the body and said, "Tabitha, get up." Then she opened her eyes, and seeing Peter, she sat up. 41He gave her his hand and helped her up. Then calling the saints and widows, he showed her to be alive. 42This became known throughout Joppa, and many believed in the Lord. 43Meanwhile he stayed in Joppa for some time with a certain Simon, a tanner.

Peter and Cornelius

10 In Caesarea there was a man named Cornelius, a centurion of the Italian Cohort, as it was called. 2He was a devout man who feared God with all his household; he gave alms generously to the people and prayed constantly to God. 3One afternoon at about three o'clock he had a vision in which he clearly saw an angel of God coming in and saying to him, "Cornelius." 4He stared at him in terror and said, "What is it, Lord?" He answered, "Your prayers and your alms have ascended as a memorial before God. 5Now send men to Joppa for a certain Simon who is called Peter; 6he is lodging with Simon, a tanner, whose house is by the seaside." 7When the angel who spoke to him had left, he called two of his slaves and a devout soldier from the ranks of those who served him, 8and after telling them everything, he sent them to Joppa.

9 About noon the next day, as they were on their journey and approaching the city,

---

a Gk *through the wall*   *b* Gk *brothers*   *c* Gk *all of them*   *d* The name Tabitha in Aramaic and the name Dorcas
in Greek mean *a gazelle*

Peter went up on the roof to pray. 10He became hungry and wanted something to eat; and while it was being prepared, he fell into a trance. 11He saw the heaven opened and something like a large sheet coming down, being lowered to the ground by its four corners. 12In it were all kinds of four-footed creatures and reptiles and birds of the air. 13Then he heard a voice saying, "Get up, Peter; kill and eat." 14But Peter said, "By no means, Lord; for I have never eaten anything that is profane or unclean." 15The voice said to him again, a second time, "What God has made clean, you must not call profane." 16This happened three times, and the thing was suddenly taken up to heaven.

17 Now while Peter was greatly puzzled about what to make of the vision that he had seen, suddenly the men sent by Cornelius appeared. They were asking for Simon's house and were standing by the gate. 18They called out to ask whether Simon, who was called Peter, was staying there. 19While Peter was still thinking about the vision, the Spirit said to him, "Look, three*a* men are searching for you. 20Now get up, go down, and go with them without hesitation; for I have sent them." 21So Peter went down to the men and said, "I am the one you are looking for; what is the reason for your coming?" 22They answered, "Cornelius, a centurion, an upright and God-fearing man, who is well spoken of by the whole Jewish nation, was directed by a holy angel to send for you to come to his house and to hear what you have to say." 23So Peter*b* invited them in and gave them lodging.

The next day he got up and went with them, and some of the believers*c* from Joppa accompanied him. 24The following day they came to Caesarea. Cornelius was expecting them and had called together his relatives and close friends. 25On Peter's arrival Cornelius met him, and falling at his feet, worshiped him. 26But Peter made him get up, saying, "Stand up; I am only a mortal."

27And as he talked with him, he went in and found that many had assembled; 28and he said to them, "You yourselves know that it is unlawful for a Jew to associate with or to visit a Gentile; but God has shown me that I should not call anyone profane or unclean. 29So when I was sent for, I came without objection. Now may I ask why you sent for me?"

30 Cornelius replied, "Four days ago at this very hour, at three o'clock, I was praying in my house when suddenly a man in dazzling clothes stood before me. 31He said, 'Cornelius, your prayer has been heard and your alms have been remembered before God. 32Send therefore to Joppa and ask for Simon, who is called Peter; he is staying in the home of Simon, a tanner, by the sea.' 33Therefore I sent for you immediately, and you have been kind enough to come. So now all of us are here in the presence of God to listen to all that the Lord has commanded you to say."

Gentiles Hear the Good News

34 Then Peter began to speak to them: "I truly understand that God shows no partiality, 35but in every nation anyone who fears him and does what is right is acceptable to him. 36You know the message he sent to the people of Israel, preaching peace by Jesus Christ—he is Lord of all. 37That message spread throughout Judea, beginning in Galilee after the baptism that John announced: 38how God anointed Jesus of Nazareth with the Holy Spirit and with power; how he went about doing good and healing all who were oppressed by the devil, for God was with him. 39We are witnesses to all that he did both in Judea and in Jerusalem. They put him to death by hanging him on a tree; 40but God raised him on the third day and allowed him to appear, 41not to all the people but to us who were chosen by God as witnesses, and who ate and drank with him after he rose from the dead. 42He commanded us to preach to the people and to testify that he is

a One ancient authority reads *two*; others lack the word   *b* Gk *he*   *c* Gk *brothers* the one ordained by God as judge of the living and the dead. 43All the prophets testify about him that everyone who believes in him receives forgiveness of sins through his name."

Gentiles Receive the Holy Spirit

44 While Peter was still speaking, the Holy Spirit fell upon all who heard the word. 45The circumcised believers who had come with Peter were astounded that the gift of the Holy Spirit had been poured out even on the Gentiles, 46for they heard them speaking in tongues and extolling God. Then Peter said, 47"Can anyone withhold the water for baptizing these people who have received the Holy Spirit just as we have?" 48So he ordered them to be baptized in the name of Jesus Christ. Then they invited him to stay for several days.

Peter's Report to the Church at Jerusalem

11 Now the apostles and the believers*a* who were in Judea heard that the Gentiles had also accepted the word of God. 2So when Peter went up to Jerusalem, the circumcised believers*b* criticized him, 3saying, "Why did you go to uncircumcised men and eat with them?" 4Then Peter began to explain it to them, step by step, saying, 5"I was in the city of Joppa praying, and in a trance I saw a vision. There was something like a large sheet coming down from heaven, being lowered by its four corners; and it came close to me. 6As I looked at it closely I saw four-footed animals, beasts of prey, reptiles, and birds of the air. 7I also heard a voice saying to me, 'Get up, Peter; kill and eat.' 8But I replied, 'By no means, Lord; for nothing profane or unclean has ever entered my mouth.' 9But a second time the voice answered from heaven, 'What God has made clean, you must not call profane.' 10This happened three times; then everything was pulled up again to heaven. 11At that very moment three men, sent to me from Caesarea, arrived at the house where we

were. 12The Spirit told me to go with them and not to make a distinction between them and us.*c* These six brothers also accompanied me, and we entered the man's house. 13He told us how he had seen the angel standing in his house and saying, 'Send to Joppa and bring Simon, who is called Peter; 14he will give you a message by which you and your entire household will be saved.' 15And as I began to speak, the Holy Spirit fell upon them just as it had upon us at the beginning. 16And I remembered the word of the Lord, how he had said, 'John baptized with water, but you will be baptized with the Holy Spirit.' 17If then God gave them the same gift that he gave us when we believed in the Lord Jesus Christ, who was I that I could hinder God?" 18When they heard this, they were silenced. And they praised God, saying, "Then God has given even to the Gentiles the repentance that leads to life."

The Church in Antioch

19 Now those who were scattered because of the persecution that took place over Stephen traveled as far as Phoenicia, Cyprus, and Antioch, and they spoke the word to no one except Jews. 20But among them were some men of Cyprus and Cyrene who, on coming to Antioch, spoke to the Hellenists*d* also, proclaiming the Lord Jesus. 21The hand of the Lord was with them, and a great number became believers and turned to the Lord. 22News of this came to the ears of the church in Jerusalem, and they sent Barnabas to Antioch. 23When he came and saw the grace of God, he rejoiced, and he exhorted them all to remain faithful to the Lord with steadfast devotion; 24for he was a good man, full of the Holy Spirit and of faith. And a great many people were brought to the Lord. 25Then Barnabas went to Tarsus to look for Saul, 26and when he had found him, he brought him to Antioch. So it was that for an entire year they met with*e* the church and taught a great many people, and it was in

---

a Gk *brothers*   *b* Gk lacks *believers*   *c* Or *not to hesitate guests of*   *d* Other ancient authorities read *Greeks*   *e* Or *were*

Antioch that the disciples were first called "Christians."

27 At that time prophets came down from Jerusalem to Antioch. 28One of them named Agabus stood up and predicted by the Spirit that there would be a severe famine over all the world; and this took place during the reign of Claudius. 29The disciples determined that according to their ability, each would send relief to the believers*a* living in Judea; 30this they did, sending it to the elders by Barnabas and Saul.

James Killed and Peter Imprisoned

12 About that time King Herod laid violent hands upon some who belonged to the church. 2He had James, the brother of John, killed with the sword. 3After he saw that it pleased the Jews, he proceeded to arrest Peter also. (This was during the festival of Unleavened Bread.) 4When he had seized him, he put him in prison and handed him over to four squads of soldiers to guard him, intending to bring him out to the people after the Passover. 5While Peter was kept in prison, the church prayed fervently to God for him.

Peter Delivered from Prison

6 The very night before Herod was going to bring him out, Peter, bound with two chains, was sleeping between two soldiers, while guards in front of the door were keeping watch over the prison. 7Suddenly an angel of the Lord appeared and a light shone in the cell. He tapped Peter on the side and woke him, saying, "Get up quickly." And the chains fell off his wrists. 8The angel said to him, "Fasten your belt and put on your sandals." He did so. Then he said to him, "Wrap your cloak around you and follow me." 9Peter*b* went out and followed him; he did not realize that what was happening with the angel's help was real; he thought he was seeing a vision. 10After they had passed the first and the second guard, they came before the iron gate

leading into the city. It opened for them of its own accord, and they went outside and walked along a lane, when suddenly the angel left him. 11Then Peter came to himself and said, "Now I am sure that the Lord has sent his angel and rescued me from the hands of Herod and from all that the Jewish people were expecting."

12 As soon as he realized this, he went to the house of Mary, the mother of John whose other name was Mark, where many had gathered and were praying. 13When he knocked at the outer gate, a maid named Rhoda came to answer. 14On recognizing Peter's voice, she was so overjoyed that, instead of opening the gate, she ran in and announced that Peter was standing at the gate. 15They said to her, "You are out of your mind!" But she insisted that it was so. They said, "It is his angel." 16Meanwhile Peter continued knocking; and when they opened the gate, they saw him and were amazed. 17He motioned to them with his hand to be silent, and described for them how the Lord had brought him out of the prison. And he added, "Tell this to James and to the believers."*a* Then he left and went to another place.

18 When morning came, there was no small commotion among the soldiers over what had become of Peter. 19When Herod had searched for him and could not find him, he examined the guards and ordered them to be put to death. Then he went down from Judea to Caesarea and stayed there.

The Death of Herod

20 Now Herod*c* was angry with the people of Tyre and Sidon. So they came to him in a body; and after winning over Blastus, the king's chamberlain, they asked for a reconciliation, because their country depended on the king's country for food. 21On an appointed day Herod put on his royal robes, took his seat on the platform, and delivered a public address to them. 22The people kept shouting, "The voice of a god, and not of a

a Gk brothers   *b* Gk He   *c* Gk he

mortal!" 23And immediately, because he had not given the glory to God, an angel of the Lord struck him down, and he was eaten by worms and died.

24 But the word of God continued to advance and gain adherents. 25Then after completing their mission Barnabas and Saul returned to*a* Jerusalem and brought with them John, whose other name was Mark.

Barnabas and Saul Commissioned

13 Now in the church at Antioch there were prophets and teachers: Barnabas, Simeon who was called Niger, Lucius of Cyrene, Manaen a member of the court of Herod the ruler,*b* and Saul. 2While they were worshiping the Lord and fasting, the Holy Spirit said, "Set apart for me Barnabas and Saul for the work to which I have called them." 3Then after fasting and praying they laid their hands on them and sent them off.

The Apostles Preach in Cyprus

4 So, being sent out by the Holy Spirit, they went down to Seleucia; and from there they sailed to Cyprus. 5When they arrived at Salamis, they proclaimed the word of God in the synagogues of the Jews. And they had John also to assist them. 6When they had gone through the whole island as far as Paphos, they met a certain magician, a Jewish false prophet, named Bar-Jesus. 7He was with the proconsul, Sergius Paulus, an intelligent man, who summoned Barnabas and Saul and wanted to hear the word of God. 8But the magician Elymas (for that is the translation of his name) opposed them and tried to turn the proconsul away from the faith. 9But Saul, also known as Paul, filled with the Holy Spirit, looked intently at him 10and said, "You son of the devil, you enemy of all righteousness, full of all deceit and villainy, will you not stop making crooked the straight paths of the Lord? 11And now listen—the hand of the Lord is against you, and you will be blind for a while, unable to see the sun." Immedi-

ately mist and darkness came over him, and he went about groping for someone to lead him by the hand. 12When the proconsul saw what had happened, he believed, for he was astonished at the teaching about the Lord.

Paul and Barnabas in Antioch of Pisidia

13 Then Paul and his companions set sail from Paphos and came to Perga in Pamphylia. John, however, left them and returned to Jerusalem; 14but they went on from Perga and came to Antioch in Pisidia. And on the sabbath day they went into the synagogue and sat down. 15After the reading of the law and the prophets, the officials of the synagogue sent them a message, saying, "Brothers, if you have any word of exhortation for the people, give it." 16So Paul stood up and with a gesture began to speak:

"You Israelites,*c* and others who fear God, listen. 17The God of this people Israel chose our ancestors and made the people great during their stay in the land of Egypt, and with uplifted arm he led them out of it. 18For about forty years he put up with*d* them in the wilderness. 19After he had destroyed seven nations in the land of Canaan, he gave them their land as an inheritance 20for about four hundred fifty years. After that he gave them judges until the time of the prophet Samuel. 21Then they asked for a king; and God gave them Saul son of Kish, a man of the tribe of Benjamin, who reigned for forty years. 22When he had removed him, he made David their king. In his testimony about him he said, 'I have found David, son of Jesse, to be a man after my heart, who will carry out all my wishes.' 23Of this man's posterity God has brought to Israel a Savior, Jesus, as he promised; 24before his coming John had already proclaimed a baptism of repentance to all the people of Israel. 25And as John was finishing his work, he said, 'What do you suppose that I am? I am not he. No, but one is coming after me; I am not worthy to untie the thong of the sandals*e* on his feet.'

---

a Other ancient authorities read *from*   *b* Gk *tetrarch*   *c* Gk *Men, Israelites*   *d* Other ancient authorities read *cared for*   *e* Gk *untie the sandals*

26 "My brothers, you descendants of Abraham's family, and others who fear God, to us[a] the message of this salvation has been sent. 27Because the residents of Jerusalem and their leaders did not recognize him or understand the words of the prophets that are read every sabbath, they fulfilled those words by condemning him. 28Even though they found no cause for a sentence of death, they asked Pilate to have him killed. 29When they had carried out everything that was written about him, they took him down from the tree and laid him in a tomb. 30But God raised him from the dead; 31and for many days he appeared to those who came up with him from Galilee to Jerusalem, and they are now his witnesses to the people. 32And we bring you the good news that what God promised to our ancestors 33he has fulfilled for us, their children, by raising Jesus; as also it is written in the second psalm,

'You are my Son;
    today I have begotten you.'

34As to his raising him from the dead, no more to return to corruption, he has spoken in this way,

'I will give you the holy promises made
    to David.'

35Therefore he has also said in another psalm,

'You will not let your Holy One
    experience corruption.'

36For David, after he had served the purpose of God in his own generation, died,[b] was laid beside his ancestors, and experienced corruption; 37but he whom God raised up experienced no corruption. 38Let it be known to you therefore, my brothers, that through this man forgiveness of sins is proclaimed to you; 39by this Jesus[c] everyone who believes is set free from all those sins[d] from which you could not be freed by the law of Moses. 40Beware, therefore, that what the prophets said does not happen to you:

41 'Look, you scoffers!
    Be amazed and perish,
    for in your days I am doing a work,

a work that you will never believe,
    even if someone tells you.' "

42 As Paul and Barnabas[e] were going out, the people urged them to speak about these things again the next sabbath. 43When the meeting of the synagogue broke up, many Jews and devout converts to Judaism followed Paul and Barnabas, who spoke to them and urged them to continue in the grace of God.

44 The next sabbath almost the whole city gathered to hear the word of the Lord.[f] 45But when the Jews saw the crowds, they were filled with jealousy; and blaspheming, they contradicted what was spoken by Paul. 46Then both Paul and Barnabas spoke out boldly, saying, "It was necessary that the word of God should be spoken first to you. Since you reject it and judge yourselves to be unworthy of eternal life, we are now turning to the Gentiles. 47For so the Lord has commanded us, saying,

'I have set you to be a light for the
    Gentiles,
    so that you may bring salvation to
        the ends of the earth.' "

48 When the Gentiles heard this, they were glad and praised the word of the Lord; and as many as had been destined for eternal life became believers. 49Thus the word of the Lord spread throughout the region. 50But the Jews incited the devout women of high standing and the leading men of the city, and stirred up persecution against Paul and Barnabas, and drove them out of their region. 51So they shook the dust off their feet in protest against them, and went to Iconium. 52And the disciples were filled with joy and with the Holy Spirit.

Paul and Barnabas in Iconium

14 The same thing occurred in Iconium, where Paul and Barnabas[e] went into the Jewish synagogue and spoke in such a way that a great number of both Jews and Greeks became believers. 2But the unbelieving Jews

a Other ancient authorities read you   b Gk fell asleep   c Gk this   d Gk all   e Gk they   f Other ancient authorities read God stirred up the Gentiles and poisoned their minds against the brothers. [3]So they remained for a long time, speaking boldly for the Lord, who testified to the word of his grace by granting signs and wonders to be done through them. [4]But the residents of the city were divided; some sided with the Jews, and some with the apostles. [5]And when an attempt was made by both Gentiles and Jews, with their rulers, to mistreat them and to stone them, [6]the apostles[a] learned of it and fled to Lystra and Derbe, cities of Lycaonia, and to the surrounding country; [7]and there they continued proclaiming the good news.

Paul and Barnabas in Lystra and Derbe

[8] In Lystra there was a man sitting who could not use his feet and had never walked, for he had been crippled from birth. [9]He listened to Paul as he was speaking. And Paul, looking at him intently and seeing that he had faith to be healed, [10]said in a loud voice, "Stand upright on your feet." And the man[b] sprang up and began to walk. [11]When the crowds saw what Paul had done, they shouted in the Lycaonian language, "The gods have come down to us in human form!" [12]Barnabas they called Zeus, and Paul they called Hermes, because he was the chief speaker. [13]The priest of Zeus, whose temple was just outside the city,[c] brought oxen and garlands to the gates; he and the crowds wanted to offer sacrifice. [14]When the apostles Barnabas and Paul heard of it, they tore their clothes and rushed out into the crowd, shouting, [15]"Friends,[d] why are you doing this? We are mortals just like you, and we bring you good news, that you should turn from these worthless things to the living God, who made the heaven and the earth and the sea and all that is in them. [16]In past generations he allowed all the nations to follow their own ways; [17]yet he has not left himself without a witness in doing good—giving you rains from heaven and fruitful seasons, and filling you with food and your hearts with joy." [18]Even

with these words, they scarcely restrained the crowds from offering sacrifice to them.

[19] But Jews came there from Antioch and Iconium and won over the crowds. Then they stoned Paul and dragged him out of the city, supposing that he was dead. [20]But when the disciples surrounded him, he got up and went into the city. The next day he went on with Barnabas to Derbe.

The Return to Antioch in Syria

[21] After they had proclaimed the good news to that city and had made many disciples, they returned to Lystra, then on to Iconium and Antioch. [22]There they strengthened the souls of the disciples and encouraged them to continue in the faith, saying, "It is through many persecutions that we must enter the kingdom of God." [23]And after they had appointed elders for them in each church, with prayer and fasting they entrusted them to the Lord in whom they had come to believe.

[24] Then they passed through Pisidia and came to Pamphylia. [25]When they had spoken the word in Perga, they went down to Attalia. [26]From there they sailed back to Antioch, where they had been commended to the grace of God for the work[e] that they had completed. [27]When they arrived, they called the church together and related all that God had done with them, and how he had opened a door of faith for the Gentiles. [28]And they stayed there with the disciples for some time.

The Council at Jerusalem

15 Then certain individuals came down from Judea and were teaching the brothers, "Unless you are circumcised according to the custom of Moses, you cannot be saved." [2]And after Paul and Barnabas had no small dissension and debate with them, Paul and Barnabas and some of the others were appointed to go up to Jerusalem to discuss this question with the apostles and the elders. [3]So they were sent on their way by the

a Gk *they*   *b* Gk *he*   *c* Or *The priest of Zeus-Outside-the-City*   *d* Gk *Men*   *e* Or *committed in the grace of God to the work* church, and as they passed through both Phoenicia and Samaria, they reported the conversion of the Gentiles, and brought great joy to all the believers. *a* 4When they came to Jerusalem, they were welcomed by the church and the apostles and the elders, and they reported all that God had done with them. 5But some believers who belonged to the sect of the Pharisees stood up and said, "It is necessary for them to be circumcised and ordered to keep the law of Moses."

6 The apostles and the elders met together to consider this matter. 7After there had been much debate, Peter stood up and said to them, "My brothers,*b* you know that in the early days God made a choice among you, that I should be the one through whom the Gentiles would hear the message of the good news and become believers. 8And God, who knows the human heart, testified to them by giving them the Holy Spirit, just as he did to us; 9and in cleansing their hearts by faith he has made no distinction between them and us. 10Now therefore why are you putting God to the test by placing on the neck of the disciples a yoke that neither our ancestors nor we have been able to bear? 11On the contrary, we believe that we will be saved through the grace of the Lord Jesus, just as they will."

12 The whole assembly kept silence, and listened to Barnabas and Paul as they told of all the signs and wonders that God had done through them among the Gentiles. 13After they finished speaking, James replied, "My brothers,*b* listen to me. 14Simeon has related how God first looked favorably on the Gentiles, to take from among them a people for his name. 15This agrees with the words of the prophets, as it is written,

16 'After this I will return,
    and I will rebuild the dwelling of
        David, which has fallen;
    from its ruins I will rebuild it,
        and I will set it up,

17   so that all other peoples may seek the
      Lord—
    even all the Gentiles over whom my
      name has been called.
    Thus says the Lord, who has been
      making these things 18known
      from long ago.'*c*

19Therefore I have reached the decision that we should not trouble those Gentiles who are turning to God, 20but we should write to them to abstain only from things polluted by idols and from fornication and from whatever has been strangled*d* and from blood. 21For in every city, for generations past, Moses has had those who proclaim him, for he has been read aloud every sabbath in the synagogues."

The Council's Letter to Gentile Believers

22 Then the apostles and the elders, with the consent of the whole church, decided to choose men from among their members*e* and to send them to Antioch with Paul and Barnabas. They sent Judas called Barsabbas, and Silas, leaders among the brothers, 23with the following letter: "The brothers, both the apostles and the elders, to the believers*a* of Gentile origin in Antioch and Syria and Cilicia, greetings. 24Since we have heard that certain persons who have gone out from us, though with no instructions from us, have said things to disturb you and have unsettled your minds,*f* 25we have decided unanimously to choose representatives*g* and send them to you, along with our beloved Barnabas and Paul, 26who have risked their lives for the sake of our Lord Jesus Christ. 27We have therefore sent Judas and Silas, who themselves will tell you the same things by word of mouth. 28For it has seemed good to the Holy Spirit and to us to impose on you no further burden than these essentials: 29that you abstain from what has been sacrificed to idols and from blood and from what is strangled*h*

---

a Gk *brothers*   *b* Gk *Men, brothers*   *c* Other ancient authorities read *things.* *18Known to God from of old are all his works.'*   *d* Other ancient authorities lack *and from whatever has been strangled*   *e* Gk *from among them*   *f* Other ancient authorities add *saying, 'You must be circumcised and keep the law,'*   *g* Gk *men*   *h* Other ancient authorities lack *and from what is strangled* and from fornication. If you keep yourselves from these, you will do well. Farewell."

30 So they were sent off and went down to Antioch. When they gathered the congregation together, they delivered the letter. [31]When its members*a* read it, they rejoiced at the exhortation. [32]Judas and Silas, who were themselves prophets, said much to encourage and strengthen the believers.*b* [33]After they had been there for some time, they were sent off in peace by the believers*b* to those who had sent them.*c* [35]But Paul and Barnabas remained in Antioch, and there, with many others, they taught and proclaimed the word of the Lord.

Paul and Barnabas Separate

36 After some days Paul said to Barnabas, "Come, let us return and visit the believers*b* in every city where we proclaimed the word of the Lord and see how they are doing." [37]Barnabas wanted to take with them John called Mark. [38]But Paul decided not to take with them one who had deserted them in Pamphylia and had not accompanied them in the work. [39]The disagreement became so sharp that they parted company; Barnabas took Mark with him and sailed away to Cyprus. [40]But Paul chose Silas and set out, the believers*b* commending him to the grace of the Lord. [41]He went through Syria and Cilicia, strengthening the churches.

Timothy Joins Paul and Silas

16 Paul*d* went on also to Derbe and to Lystra, where there was a disciple named Timothy, the son of a Jewish woman who was a believer; but his father was a Greek. [2]He was well spoken of by the believers*b* in Lystra and Iconium. [3]Paul wanted Timothy to accompany him; and he took him and had him circumcised because of the Jews who were in those places, for they all knew that his father was a Greek. [4]As they went from town to town, they delivered to them for observance the decisions that had

been reached by the apostles and elders who were in Jerusalem. [5]So the churches were strengthened in the faith and increased in numbers daily.

Paul's Vision of the Man of Macedonia

6 They went through the region of Phrygia and Galatia, having been forbidden by the Holy Spirit to speak the word in Asia. [7]When they had come opposite Mysia, they attempted to go into Bithynia, but the Spirit of Jesus did not allow them; [8]so, passing by Mysia, they went down to Troas. [9]During the night Paul had a vision: there stood a man of Macedonia pleading with him and saying, "Come over to Macedonia and help us." [10]When he had seen the vision, we immediately tried to cross over to Macedonia, being convinced that God had called us to proclaim the good news to them.

The Conversion of Lydia

11 We set sail from Troas and took a straight course to Samothrace, the following day to Neapolis, [12]and from there to Philippi, which is a leading city of the district*e* of Macedonia and a Roman colony. We remained in this city for some days. [13]On the sabbath day we went outside the gate by the river, where we supposed there was a place of prayer; and we sat down and spoke to the women who had gathered there. [14]A certain woman named Lydia, a worshiper of God, was listening to us; she was from the city of Thyatira and a dealer in purple cloth. The Lord opened her heart to listen eagerly to what was said by Paul. [15]When she and her household were baptized, she urged us, saying, "If you have judged me to be faithful to the Lord, come and stay at my home." And she prevailed upon us.

Paul and Silas in Prison

16 One day, as we were going to the place of prayer, we met a slave-girl who had a spirit of divination and brought her owners a

---

a Gk *When they*   *b* Gk *brothers*   *c* Other ancient authorities add verse 34, *But it seemed good to Silas to remain there*
d Gk *He*   *e* Other authorities read *a city of the first district*

great deal of money by fortune-telling. [17]While she followed Paul and us, she would cry out, "These men are slaves of the Most High God, who proclaim to you*a* a way of salvation." [18]She kept doing this for many days. But Paul, very much annoyed, turned and said to the spirit, "I order you in the name of Jesus Christ to come out of her." And it came out that very hour.

19 But when her owners saw that their hope of making money was gone, they seized Paul and Silas and dragged them into the marketplace before the authorities. [20]When they had brought them before the magistrates, they said, "These men are disturbing our city; they are Jews [21]and are advocating customs that are not lawful for us as Romans to adopt or observe." [22]The crowd joined in attacking them, and the magistrates had them stripped of their clothing and ordered them to be beaten with rods. [23]After they had given them a severe flogging, they threw them into prison and ordered the jailer to keep them securely. [24]Following these instructions, he put them in the innermost cell and fastened their feet in the stocks.

25 About midnight Paul and Silas were praying and singing hymns to God, and the prisoners were listening to them. [26]Suddenly there was an earthquake, so violent that the foundations of the prison were shaken; and immediately all the doors were opened and everyone's chains were unfastened. [27]When the jailer woke up and saw the prison doors wide open, he drew his sword and was about to kill himself, since he supposed that the prisoners had escaped. [28]But Paul shouted in a loud voice, "Do not harm yourself, for we are all here." [29]The jailer*b* called for lights, and rushing in, he fell down trembling before Paul and Silas. [30]Then he brought them outside and said, "Sirs, what must I do to be saved?" [31]They answered, "Believe on the Lord Jesus, and you will be saved, you and your household." [32]They spoke the word of the Lord*c* to him and to all who were in his house. [33]At the same hour of the night he took them and washed their wounds; then he and his entire family were baptized without delay. [34]He brought them up into the house and set food before them; and he and his entire household rejoiced that he had become a believer in God.

35 When morning came, the magistrates sent the police, saying, "Let those men go." [36]And the jailer reported the message to Paul, saying, "The magistrates sent word to let you go; therefore come out now and go in peace." [37]But Paul replied, "They have beaten us in public, uncondemned, men who are Roman citizens, and have thrown us into prison; and now are they going to discharge us in secret? Certainly not! Let them come and take us out themselves." [38]The police reported these words to the magistrates, and they were afraid when they heard that they were Roman citizens; [39]so they came and apologized to them. And they took them out and asked them to leave the city. [40]After leaving the prison they went to Lydia's home; and when they had seen and encouraged the brothers and sisters*d* there, they departed.

The Uproar in Thessalonica

17 After Paul and Silas*e* had passed through Amphipolis and Apollonia, they came to Thessalonica, where there was a synagogue of the Jews. [2]And Paul went in, as was his custom, and on three sabbath days argued with them from the scriptures, [3]explaining and proving that it was necessary for the Messiah*f* to suffer and to rise from the dead, and saying, "This is the Messiah,*f* Jesus whom I am proclaiming to you." [4]Some of them were persuaded and joined Paul and Silas, as did a great many of the devout Greeks and not a few of the leading women. [5]But the Jews became jealous, and with the help of some ruffians in the marketplaces they formed a mob and set the city in an uproar. While they were searching for Paul and Silas to bring them out to the assembly, they

---

a Other ancient authorities read *to us*   *b* Gk He   *c* Other ancient authorities read *word of God*   *d* Gk *brothers*
e Gk *they*   *f* Or *the Christ*

attacked Jason's house. 6When they could not find them, they dragged Jason and some believers*a* before the city authorities,*b* shouting, "These people who have been turning the world upside down have come here also, 7and Jason has entertained them as guests. They are all acting contrary to the decrees of the emperor, saying that there is another king named Jesus." 8The people and the city officials were disturbed when they heard this, 9and after they had taken bail from Jason and the others, they let them go.

Paul and Silas in Beroea

10 That very night the believers*a* sent Paul and Silas off to Beroea; and when they arrived, they went to the Jewish synagogue. 11These Jews were more receptive than those in Thessalonica, for they welcomed the message very eagerly and examined the scriptures every day to see whether these things were so. 12Many of them therefore believed, including not a few Greek women and men of high standing. 13But when the Jews of Thessalonica learned that the word of God had been proclaimed by Paul in Beroea as well, they came there too, to stir up and incite the crowds. 14Then the believers*a* immediately sent Paul away to the coast, but Silas and Timothy remained behind. 15Those who conducted Paul brought him as far as Athens; and after receiving instructions to have Silas and Timothy join him as soon as possible, they left him.

Paul in Athens

16 While Paul was waiting for them in Athens, he was deeply distressed to see that the city was full of idols. 17So he argued in the synagogue with the Jews and the devout persons, and also in the marketplace*c* every day with those who happened to be there. 18Also some Epicurean and Stoic philosophers debated with him. Some said, "What does this babbler want to say?" Others said, "He seems to be a proclaimer of foreign divinities."

(This was because he was telling the good news about Jesus and the resurrection.) 19So they took him and brought him to the Areopagus and asked him, "May we know what this new teaching is that you are presenting? 20It sounds rather strange to us, so we would like to know what it means." 21Now all the Athenians and the foreigners living there would spend their time in nothing but telling or hearing something new.

22 Then Paul stood in front of the Areopagus and said, "Athenians, I see how extremely religious you are in every way. 23For as I went through the city and looked carefully at the objects of your worship, I found among them an altar with the inscription, 'To an unknown god.' What therefore you worship as unknown, this I proclaim to you. 24The God who made the world and everything in it, he who is Lord of heaven and earth, does not live in shrines made by human hands, 25nor is he served by human hands, as though he needed anything, since he himself gives to all mortals life and breath and all things. 26From one ancestor*d* he made all nations to inhabit the whole earth, and he allotted the times of their existence and the boundaries of the places where they would live, 27so that they would search for God*e* and perhaps grope for him and find him— though indeed he is not far from each one of us. 28For 'In him we live and move and have our being'; as even some of your own poets have said,

'For we too are his offspring.'

29Since we are God's offspring, we ought not to think that the deity is like gold, or silver, or stone, an image formed by the art and imagination of mortals. 30While God has overlooked the times of human ignorance, now he commands all people everywhere to repent, 31because he has fixed a day on which he will have the world judged in righteousness by a man whom he has appointed, and of this he has given assurance to all by raising him from the dead."

32 When they heard of the resurrection of the dead, some scoffed; but others said, "We will hear you again about this." 33At that point Paul left them. 34But some of them joined him and became believers, including Dionysius the Areopagite and a woman named Damaris, and others with them.

Paul in Corinth

18 After this Paul*a* left Athens and went to Corinth. 2There he found a Jew named Aquila, a native of Pontus, who had recently come from Italy with his wife Priscilla, because Claudius had ordered all Jews to leave Rome. Paul*b* went to see them, 3and, because he was of the same trade, he stayed with them, and they worked together—by trade they were tentmakers. 4Every sabbath he would argue in the synagogue and would try to convince Jews and Greeks.

5 When Silas and Timothy arrived from Macedonia, Paul was occupied with proclaiming the word,*c* testifying to the Jews that the Messiah*d* was Jesus. 6When they opposed and reviled him, in protest he shook the dust from his clothes*e* and said to them, "Your blood be on your own heads! I am innocent. From now on I will go to the Gentiles." 7Then he left the synagogue*f* and went to the house of a man named Titius*g* Justus, a worshiper of God; his house was next door to the synagogue. 8Crispus, the official of the synagogue, became a believer in the Lord, together with all his household; and many of the Corinthians who heard Paul became believers and were baptized. 9One night the Lord said to Paul in a vision, "Do not be afraid, but speak and do not be silent; 10for I am with you, and no one will lay a hand on you to harm you, for there are many in this city who are my people." 11He stayed there a year and six months, teaching the word of God among them.

12 But when Gallio was proconsul of Achaia, the Jews made a united attack on Paul and brought him before the tribunal. 13They said, "This man is persuading people to worship God in ways that are contrary to the law." 14Just as Paul was about to speak, Gallio said to the Jews, "If it were a matter of crime or serious villainy, I would be justified in accepting the complaint of you Jews; 15but since it is a matter of questions about words and names and your own law, see to it yourselves; I do not wish to be a judge of these matters." 16And he dismissed them from the tribunal. 17Then all of them*b* seized Sosthenes, the official of the synagogue, and beat him in front of the tribunal. But Gallio paid no attention to any of these things.

Paul's Return to Antioch

18 After staying there for a considerable time, Paul said farewell to the believers*i* and sailed for Syria, accompanied by Priscilla and Aquila. At Cenchreae he had his hair cut, for he was under a vow. 19When they reached Ephesus, he left them there, but first he himself went into the synagogue and had a discussion with the Jews. 20When they asked him to stay longer, he declined; 21but on taking leave of them, he said, "I*j* will return to you, if God wills." Then he set sail from Ephesus.

22 When he had landed at Caesarea, he went up to Jerusalem*k* and greeted the church, and then went down to Antioch. 23After spending some time there he departed and went from place to place through the region of Galatia*l* and Phrygia, strengthening all the disciples.

Ministry of Apollos

24 Now there came to Ephesus a Jew named Apollos, a native of Alexandria. He was an eloquent man, well-versed in the scriptures. 25He had been instructed in the Way of the Lord; and he spoke with burning enthu-

a Gk *he*　*b* Gk *He*　*c* Gk *with the word*　*d* Or *the Christ*　*e* Gk *reviled him, he shook out his clothes*　*f* Gk *left there*　*g* Other ancient authorities read *Titus*　*h* Other ancient authorities read *all the Greeks*　*i* Gk *brothers*　*j* Other ancient authorities read *I must at all costs keep the approaching festival in Jerusalem, but I*　*k* Gk *went up*　*l* Gk *the Galatian region* siasm and taught accurately the things concerning Jesus, though he knew only the baptism of John. ²⁶He began to speak boldly in the synagogue; but when Priscilla and Aquila heard him, they took him aside and explained the Way of God to him more accurately. ²⁷And when he wished to cross over to Achaia, the believers*ᵃ* encouraged him and wrote to the disciples to welcome him. On his arrival he greatly helped those who through grace had become believers, ²⁸for he powerfully refuted the Jews in public, showing by the scriptures that the Messiah*ᵇ* is Jesus.

Paul in Ephesus

19 While Apollos was in Corinth, Paul passed through the interior regions and came to Ephesus, where he found some disciples. ²He said to them, "Did you receive the Holy Spirit when you became believers?" They replied, "No, we have not even heard that there is a Holy Spirit." ³Then he said, "Into what then were you baptized?" They answered, "Into John's baptism." ⁴Paul said, "John baptized with the baptism of repentance, telling the people to believe in the one who was to come after him, that is, in Jesus." ⁵On hearing this, they were baptized in the name of the Lord Jesus. ⁶When Paul had laid his hands on them, the Holy Spirit came upon them, and they spoke in tongues and prophesied— ⁷altogether there were about twelve of them.

8 He entered the synagogue and for three months spoke out boldly, and argued persuasively about the kingdom of God. ⁹When some stubbornly refused to believe and spoke evil of the Way before the congregation, he left them, taking the disciples with him, and argued daily in the lecture hall of Tyrannus.*ᶜ* ¹⁰This continued for two years, so that all the residents of Asia, both Jews and Greeks, heard the word of the Lord.

The Sons of Sceva

11 God did extraordinary miracles through Paul, ¹²so that when the handkerchiefs or aprons that had touched his skin were brought to the sick, their diseases left them, and the evil spirits came out of them. ¹³Then some itinerant Jewish exorcists tried to use the name of the Lord Jesus over those who had evil spirits, saying, "I adjure you by the Jesus whom Paul proclaims." ¹⁴Seven sons of a Jewish high priest named Sceva were doing this. ¹⁵But the evil spirit said to them in reply, "Jesus I know, and Paul I know; but who are you?" ¹⁶Then the man with the evil spirit leaped on them, mastered them all, and so overpowered them that they fled out of the house naked and wounded. ¹⁷When this became known to all residents of Ephesus, both Jews and Greeks, everyone was awestruck; and the name of the Lord Jesus was praised. ¹⁸Also many of those who became believers confessed and disclosed their practices. ¹⁹A number of those who practiced magic collected their books and burned them publicly; when the value of these books*ᵈ* was calculated, it was found to come to fifty thousand silver coins. ²⁰So the word of the Lord grew mightily and prevailed.

The Riot in Ephesus

21 Now after these things had been accomplished, Paul resolved in the Spirit to go through Macedonia and Achaia, and then to go on to Jerusalem. He said, "After I have gone there, I must also see Rome." ²²So he sent two of his helpers, Timothy and Erastus, to Macedonia, while he himself stayed for some time longer in Asia.

23 About that time no little disturbance broke out concerning the Way. ²⁴A man named Demetrius, a silversmith who made silver shrines of Artemis, brought no little business to the artisans. ²⁵These he gathered together, with the workers of the same trade, and said, "Men, you know that we get our wealth from this business. ²⁶You also see and hear that not only in Ephesus but in almost

---

a Gk *brothers*   *b* Or *the Christ*   *c* Other ancient authorities read *of a certain Tyrannus, from eleven o'clock in the morning to four in the afternoon*   *d* Gk *them* the whole of Asia this Paul has persuaded and drawn away a considerable number of people by saying that gods made with hands are not gods. 27And there is danger not only that this trade of ours may come into disrepute but also that the temple of the great goddess Artemis will be scorned, and she will be deprived of her majesty that brought all Asia and the world to worship her."

28 When they heard this, they were enraged and shouted, "Great is Artemis of the Ephesians!" 29The city was filled with the confusion; and people*a* rushed together to the theater, dragging with them Gaius and Aristarchus, Macedonians who were Paul's travel companions. 30Paul wished to go into the crowd, but the disciples would not let him; 31even some officials of the province of Asia,*b* who were friendly to him, sent him a message urging him not to venture into the theater. 32Meanwhile, some were shouting one thing, some another; for the assembly was in confusion, and most of them did not know why they had come together. 33Some of the crowd gave instructions to Alexander, whom the Jews had pushed forward. And Alexander motioned for silence and tried to make a defense before the people. 34But when they recognized that he was a Jew, for about two hours all of them shouted in unison, "Great is Artemis of the Ephesians!" 35But when the town clerk had quieted the crowd, he said, "Citizens of Ephesus, who is there that does not know that the city of the Ephesians is the temple keeper of the great Artemis and of the statue that fell from heaven?*c* 36Since these things cannot be denied, you ought to be quiet and do nothing rash. 37You have brought these men here who are neither temple robbers nor blasphemers of our*d* goddess. 38If therefore Demetrius and the artisans with him have a complaint against anyone, the courts are open, and there are proconsuls; let them bring charges there against one another. 39If there is anything further*e* you want to know, it must be settled in the regular assembly. 40For we are in danger of being charged with rioting today, since there is no cause that we can give to justify this commotion." 41When he had said this, he dismissed the assembly.

Paul Goes to Macedonia and Greece

20 After the uproar had ceased, Paul sent for the disciples; and after encouraging them and saying farewell, he left for Macedonia. 2When he had gone through those regions and had given the believers*f* much encouragement, he came to Greece, 3where he stayed for three months. He was about to set sail for Syria when a plot was made against him by the Jews, and so he decided to return through Macedonia. 4He was accompanied by Sopater son of Pyrrhus from Beroea, by Aristarchus and Secundus from Thessalonica, by Gaius from Derbe, and by Timothy, as well as by Tychicus and Trophimus from Asia. 5They went ahead and were waiting for us in Troas; 6but we sailed from Philippi after the days of Unleavened Bread, and in five days we joined them in Troas, where we stayed for seven days.

Paul's Farewell Visit to Troas

7 On the first day of the week, when we met to break bread, Paul was holding a discussion with them; since he intended to leave the next day, he continued speaking until midnight. 8There were many lamps in the room upstairs where we were meeting. 9A young man named Eutychus, who was sitting in the window, began to sink off into a deep sleep while Paul talked still longer. Overcome by sleep, he fell to the ground three floors below and was picked up dead. 10But Paul went down, and bending over him took him in his arms, and said, "Do not be alarmed, for his life is in him." 11Then Paul went upstairs, and after he had broken bread and eaten, he continued to converse with them until dawn; then he left. 12Meanwhile they had taken the boy away alive and were not a little comforted.

a Gk *they*   *b* Gk *some of the Asiarchs*   *c* Meaning of Gk uncertain   *d* Other ancient authorities read *your*
e Other ancient authorities read *about other matters*   *f* Gk *given them*

The Voyage from Troas to Miletus

13 We went ahead to the ship and set sail for Assos, intending to take Paul on board there; for he had made this arrangement, intending to go by land himself. 14When he met us in Assos, we took him on board and went to Mitylene. 15We sailed from there, and on the following day we arrived opposite Chios. The next day we touched at Samos, and*a* the day after that we came to Miletus. 16For Paul had decided to sail past Ephesus, so that he might not have to spend time in Asia; he was eager to be in Jerusalem, if possible, on the day of Pentecost.

Paul Speaks to the Ephesian Elders

17 From Miletus he sent a message to Ephesus, asking the elders of the church to meet him. 18When they came to him, he said to them:

"You yourselves know how I lived among you the entire time from the first day that I set foot in Asia, 19serving the Lord with all humility and with tears, enduring the trials that came to me through the plots of the Jews. 20I did not shrink from doing anything helpful, proclaiming the message to you and teaching you publicly and from house to house, 21as I testified to both Jews and Greeks about repentance toward God and faith toward our Lord Jesus. 22And now, as a captive to the Spirit,*b* I am on my way to Jerusalem, not knowing what will happen to me there, 23except that the Holy Spirit testifies to me in every city that imprisonment and persecutions are waiting for me. 24But I do not count my life of any value to myself, if only I may finish my course and the ministry that I received from the Lord Jesus, to testify to the good news of God's grace.

25 "And now I know that none of you, among whom I have gone about proclaiming the kingdom, will ever see my face again. 26Therefore I declare to you this day that I am not responsible for the blood of any of you,

27for I did not shrink from declaring to you the whole purpose of God. 28Keep watch over yourselves and over all the flock, of which the Holy Spirit has made you overseers, to shepherd the church of God*c* that he obtained with the blood of his own Son.*d* 29I know that after I have gone, savage wolves will come in among you, not sparing the flock. 30Some even from your own group will come distorting the truth in order to entice the disciples to follow them. 31Therefore be alert, remembering that for three years I did not cease night or day to warn everyone with tears. 32And now I commend you to God and to the message of his grace, a message that is able to build you up and to give you the inheritance among all who are sanctified. 33I coveted no one's silver or gold or clothing. 34You know for yourselves that I worked with my own hands to support myself and my companions. 35In all this I have given you an example that by such work we must support the weak, remembering the words of the Lord Jesus, for he himself said, 'It is more blessed to give than to receive.' "

36 When he had finished speaking, he knelt down with them all and prayed. 37There was much weeping among them all; they embraced Paul and kissed him, 38grieving especially because of what he had said, that they would not see him again. Then they brought him to the ship.

Paul's Journey to Jerusalem

21 When we had parted from them and set sail, we came by a straight course to Cos, and the next day to Rhodes, and from there to Patara.*e* 2When we found a ship bound for Phoenicia, we went on board and set sail. 3We came in sight of Cyprus; and leaving it on our left, we sailed to Syria and landed at Tyre, because the ship was to unload its cargo there. 4We looked up the disciples and stayed there for seven days. Through the Spirit they told Paul not to go

a Other ancient authorities add *after remaining at Trogyllium*   *b* Or *And now, bound in the spirit*   *c* Other ancient authorities read *of the Lord*   *d* Or *with his own blood*; Gk *with the blood of his Own*   *e* Other ancient authorities add *and Myra* on to Jerusalem. 5When our days there were ended, we left and proceeded on our journey; and all of them, with wives and children, escorted us outside the city. There we knelt down on the beach and prayed 6and said farewell to one another. Then we went on board the ship, and they returned home.

7 When we had finished*a* the voyage from Tyre, we arrived at Ptolemais; and we greeted the believers*b* and stayed with them for one day. 8The next day we left and came to Caesarea; and we went into the house of Philip the evangelist, one of the seven, and stayed with him. 9He had four unmarried daughters*c* who had the gift of prophecy. 10While we were staying there for several days, a prophet named Agabus came down from Judea. 11He came to us and took Paul's belt, bound his own feet and hands with it, and said, "Thus says the Holy Spirit, 'This is the way the Jews in Jerusalem will bind the man who owns this belt and will hand him over to the Gentiles.' " 12When we heard this, we and the people there urged him not to go up to Jerusalem. 13Then Paul answered, "What are you doing, weeping and breaking my heart? For I am ready not only to be bound but even to die in Jerusalem for the name of the Lord Jesus." 14Since he would not be persuaded, we remained silent except to say, "The Lord's will be done."

15 After these days we got ready and started to go up to Jerusalem. 16Some of the disciples from Caesarea also came along and brought us to the house of Mnason of Cyprus, an early disciple, with whom we were to stay.

Paul Visits James at Jerusalem

17 When we arrived in Jerusalem, the brothers welcomed us warmly. 18The next day Paul went with us to visit James; and all the elders were present. 19After greeting them, he related one by one the things that God had done among the Gentiles through his ministry. 20When they heard it, they praised God. Then they said to him, "You see, brother, how many thousands of believers there are among the Jews, and they are all zealous for the law. 21They have been told about you that you teach all the Jews living among the Gentiles to forsake Moses, and that you tell them not to circumcise their children or observe the customs. 22What then is to be done? They will certainly hear that you have come. 23So do what we tell you. We have four men who are under a vow. 24Join these men, go through the rite of purification with them, and pay for the shaving of their heads. Thus all will know that there is nothing in what they have been told about you, but that you yourself observe and guard the law. 25But as for the Gentiles who have become believers, we have sent a letter with our judgment that they should abstain from what has been sacrificed to idols and from blood and from what is strangled*d* and from fornication." 26Then Paul took the men, and the next day, having purified himself, he entered the temple with them, making public the completion of the days of purification when the sacrifice would be made for each of them.

Paul Arrested in the Temple

27 When the seven days were almost completed, the Jews from Asia, who had seen him in the temple, stirred up the whole crowd. They seized him, 28shouting, "Fellow Israelites, help! This is the man who is teaching everyone everywhere against our people, our law, and this place; more than that, he has actually brought Greeks into the temple and has defiled this holy place." 29For they had previously seen Trophimus the Ephesian with him in the city, and they supposed that Paul had brought him into the temple. 30Then all the city was aroused, and the people rushed together. They seized Paul and dragged him out of the temple, and immediately the doors were shut. 31While they were trying to kill him, word came to the tribune of the cohort

---

a Or *continued*   *b* Gk *brothers*   *c* Gk *four daughters, virgins,*   *d* Other ancient authorities lack *and from what is strangled* that all Jerusalem was in an uproar. ³²Immediately he took soldiers and centurions and ran down to them. When they saw the tribune and the soldiers, they stopped beating Paul. ³³Then the tribune came, arrested him, and ordered him to be bound with two chains; he inquired who he was and what he had done. ³⁴Some in the crowd shouted one thing, some another; and as he could not learn the facts because of the uproar, he ordered him to be brought into the barracks. ³⁵When Paul[a] came to the steps, the violence of the mob was so great that he had to be carried by the soldiers. ³⁶The crowd that followed kept shouting, "Away with him!"

Paul Defends Himself

37 Just as Paul was about to be brought into the barracks, he said to the tribune, "May I say something to you?" The tribune[b] replied, "Do you know Greek? ³⁸Then you are not the Egyptian who recently stirred up a revolt and led the four thousand assassins out into the wilderness?" ³⁹Paul replied, "I am a Jew, from Tarsus in Cilicia, a citizen of an important city; I beg you, let me speak to the people." ⁴⁰When he had given him permission, Paul stood on the steps and motioned to the people for silence; and when there was a great hush, he addressed them in the Hebrew[c] language, saying:

22 "Brothers and fathers, listen to the defense that I now make before you."

2 When they heard him addressing them in Hebrew,[c] they became even more quiet. Then he said:

3 "I am a Jew, born in Tarsus in Cilicia, but brought up in this city at the feet of Gamaliel, educated strictly according to our ancestral law, being zealous for God, just as all of you are today. ⁴I persecuted this Way up to the point of death by binding both men and women and putting them in prison, ⁵as the high priest and the whole council of elders can testify about me. From them I also received letters to the brothers in Damascus, and I went there in order to bind those who were there and to bring them back to Jerusalem for punishment.

Paul Tells of His Conversion

6 "While I was on my way and approaching Damascus, about noon a great light from heaven suddenly shone about me. ⁷I fell to the ground and heard a voice saying to me, 'Saul, Saul, why are you persecuting me?' ⁸I answered, 'Who are you, Lord?' Then he said to me, 'I am Jesus of Nazareth[d] whom you are persecuting.' ⁹Now those who were with me saw the light but did not hear the voice of the one who was speaking to me. ¹⁰I asked, 'What am I to do, Lord?' The Lord said to me, 'Get up and go to Damascus; there you will be told everything that has been assigned to you to do.' ¹¹Since I could not see because of the brightness of that light, those who were with me took my hand and led me to Damascus.

12 "A certain Ananias, who was a devout man according to the law and well spoken of by all the Jews living there, ¹³came to me; and standing beside me, he said, 'Brother Saul, regain your sight!' In that very hour I regained my sight and saw him. ¹⁴Then he said, 'The God of our ancestors has chosen you to know his will, to see the Righteous One and to hear his own voice; ¹⁵for you will be his witness to all the world of what you have seen and heard. ¹⁶And now why do you delay? Get up, be baptized, and have your sins washed away, calling on his name.'

Paul Sent to the Gentiles

17 "After I had returned to Jerusalem and while I was praying in the temple, I fell into a trance ¹⁸and saw Jesus[e] saying to me, 'Hurry and get out of Jerusalem quickly, because they will not accept your testimony about me.' ¹⁹And I said, 'Lord, they themselves know that in every synagogue I imprisoned and beat those who believed in you. ²⁰And while the blood of your witness Stephen was

---

a Gk *he*   *b* Gk *He*   *c* That is, *Aramaic*   *d* Gk *the Nazorean*   *e* Gk *him* shed, I myself was standing by, approving and keeping the coats of those who killed him.' ²¹Then he said to me, 'Go, for I will send you far away to the Gentiles.' "

Paul and the Roman Tribune

22 Up to this point they listened to him, but then they shouted, "Away with such a fellow from the earth! For he should not be allowed to live." ²³And while they were shouting, throwing off their cloaks, and tossing dust into the air, ²⁴the tribune directed that he was to be brought into the barracks, and ordered him to be examined by flogging, to find out the reason for this outcry against him. ²⁵But when they had tied him up with thongs,^a Paul said to the centurion who was standing by, "Is it legal for you to flog a Roman citizen who is uncondemned?" ²⁶When the centurion heard that, he went to the tribune and said to him, "What are you about to do? This man is a Roman citizen." ²⁷The tribune came and asked Paul,^b "Tell me, are you a Roman citizen?" And he said, "Yes." ²⁸The tribune answered, "It cost me a large sum of money to get my citizenship." Paul said, "But I was born a citizen." ²⁹Immediately those who were about to examine him drew back from him; and the tribune also was afraid, for he realized that Paul was a Roman citizen and that he had bound him.

Paul before the Council

30 Since he wanted to find out what Paul^c was being accused of by the Jews, the next day he released him and ordered the chief priests and the entire council to meet. He brought Paul down and had him stand before them.

23 While Paul was looking intently at the council he said, "Brothers,^d up to this day I have lived my life with a clear conscience before God." ²Then the high priest Ananias ordered those standing near him to strike him on the mouth. ³At this Paul said to him, "God will strike you, you whitewashed

wall! Are you sitting there to judge me according to the law, and yet in violation of the law you order me to be struck?" ⁴Those standing nearby said, "Do you dare to insult God's high priest?" ⁵And Paul said, "I did not realize, brothers, that he was high priest; for it is written, 'You shall not speak evil of a leader of your people.' "

6 When Paul noticed that some were Sadducees and others were Pharisees, he called out in the council, "Brothers, I am a Pharisee, a son of Pharisees. I am on trial concerning the hope of the resurrection^e of the dead." ⁷When he said this, a dissension began between the Pharisees and the Sadducees, and the assembly was divided. ⁸(The Sadducees say that there is no resurrection, or angel, or spirit; but the Pharisees acknowledge all three.) ⁹Then a great clamor arose, and certain scribes of the Pharisees' group stood up and contended, "We find nothing wrong with this man. What if a spirit or an angel has spoken to him?" ¹⁰When the dissension became violent, the tribune, fearing that they would tear Paul to pieces, ordered the soldiers to go down, take him by force, and bring him into the barracks.

11 That night the Lord stood near him and said, "Keep up your courage! For just as you have testified for me in Jerusalem, so you must bear witness also in Rome."

The Plot to Kill Paul

12 In the morning the Jews joined in a conspiracy and bound themselves by an oath neither to eat nor drink until they had killed Paul. ¹³There were more than forty who joined in this conspiracy. ¹⁴They went to the chief priests and elders and said, "We have strictly bound ourselves by an oath to taste no food until we have killed Paul. ¹⁵Now then, you and the council must notify the tribune to bring him down to you, on the pretext that you want to make a more thorough examination of his case. And we are ready to do away with him before he arrives."

---

^a Or *up for the lashes*　^b Gk *him*　^c Gk *he*　^d Gk *Men, brothers*　^e Gk *concerning hope and resurrection*

16 Now the son of Paul's sister heard about the ambush; so he went and gained entrance to the barracks and told Paul. 17Paul called one of the centurions and said, "Take this young man to the tribune, for he has something to report to him." 18So he took him, brought him to the tribune, and said, "The prisoner Paul called me and asked me to bring this young man to you; he has something to tell you." 19The tribune took him by the hand, drew him aside privately, and asked, "What is it that you have to report to me?" 20He answered, "The Jews have agreed to ask you to bring Paul down to the council tomorrow, as though they were going to inquire more thoroughly into his case. 21But do not be persuaded by them, for more than forty of their men are lying in ambush for him. They have bound themselves by an oath neither to eat nor drink until they kill him. They are ready now and are waiting for your consent." 22So the tribune dismissed the young man, ordering him, "Tell no one that you have informed me of this."

Paul Sent to Felix the Governor

23 Then he summoned two of the centurions and said, "Get ready to leave by nine o'clock tonight for Caesarea with two hundred soldiers, seventy horsemen, and two hundred spearmen. 24Also provide mounts for Paul to ride, and take him safely to Felix the governor." 25He wrote a letter to this effect:

26 "Claudius Lysias to his Excellency the governor Felix, greetings. 27This man was seized by the Jews and was about to be killed by them, but when I had learned that he was a Roman citizen, I came with the guard and rescued him. 28Since I wanted to know the charge for which they accused him, I had him brought to their council. 29I found that he was accused concerning questions of their law, but was charged with nothing deserving death or imprisonment. 30When I was informed that there would be a plot against the man, I sent him to you at once, ordering his accusers also to state before you what they have against him. *a*"

31 So the soldiers, according to their instructions, took Paul and brought him during the night to Antipatris. 32The next day they let the horsemen go on with him, while they returned to the barracks. 33When they came to Caesarea and delivered the letter to the governor, they presented Paul also before him. 34On reading the letter, he asked what province he belonged to, and when he learned that he was from Cilicia, 35he said, "I will give you a hearing when your accusers arrive." Then he ordered that he be kept under guard in Herod's headquarters. *b*

Paul before Felix at Caesarea

24 Five days later the high priest Ananias came down with some elders and an attorney, a certain Tertullus, and they reported their case against Paul to the governor. 2When Paul *c* had been summoned, Tertullus began to accuse him, saying:

"Your Excellency, *d* because of you we have long enjoyed peace, and reforms have been made for this people because of your foresight. 3We welcome this in every way and everywhere with utmost gratitude. 4But, to detain you no further, I beg you to hear us briefly with your customary graciousness. 5We have, in fact, found this man a pestilent fellow, an agitator among all the Jews throughout the world, and a ringleader of the sect of the Nazarenes. *e* 6He even tried to profane the temple, and so we seized him. *f* 8By examining him yourself you will be able to learn from him concerning everything of which we accuse him."

9 The Jews also joined in the charge by asserting that all this was true.

---

a Other ancient authorities add *Farewell*   *b* Gk *praetorium*   *c* Gk *he*   *d* Gk lacks *Your Excellency*
e Gk *Nazoreans*   *f* Other ancient authorities add *and we would have judged him according to our law.* 7*But the chief captain Lysias came and with great violence took him out of our hands,* 8*commanding his accusers to come before you.*

Paul's Defense before Felix

10 When the governor motioned to him to speak, Paul replied:

"I cheerfully make my defense, knowing that for many years you have been a judge over this nation. 11As you can find out, it is not more than twelve days since I went up to worship in Jerusalem. 12They did not find me disputing with anyone in the temple or stirring up a crowd either in the synagogues or throughout the city. 13Neither can they prove to you the charge that they now bring against me. 14But this I admit to you, that according to the Way, which they call a sect, I worship the God of our ancestors, believing everything laid down according to the law or written in the prophets. 15I have a hope in God—a hope that they themselves also accept—that there will be a resurrection of both*a* the righteous and the unrighteous. 16Therefore I do my best always to have a clear conscience toward God and all people. 17Now after some years I came to bring alms to my nation and to offer sacrifices. 18While I was doing this, they found me in the temple, completing the rite of purification, without any crowd or disturbance. 19But there were some Jews from Asia—they ought to be here before you to make an accusation, if they have anything against me. 20Or let these men here tell what crime they had found when I stood before the council, 21unless it was this one sentence that I called out while standing before them, 'It is about the resurrection of the dead that I am on trial before you today.' "

22 But Felix, who was rather well informed about the Way, adjourned the hearing with the comment, "When Lysias the tribune comes down, I will decide your case." 23Then he ordered the centurion to keep him in custody, but to let him have some liberty and not to prevent any of his friends from taking care of his needs.

Paul Held in Custody

24 Some days later when Felix came with his wife Drusilla, who was Jewish, he sent for Paul and heard him speak concerning faith in Christ Jesus. 25And as he discussed justice, self-control, and the coming judgment, Felix became frightened and said, "Go away for the present; when I have an opportunity, I will send for you." 26At the same time he hoped that money would be given him by Paul, and for that reason he used to send for him very often and converse with him.

27 After two years had passed, Felix was succeeded by Porcius Festus; and since he wanted to grant the Jews a favor, Felix left Paul in prison.

Paul Appeals to the Emperor

25 Three days after Festus had arrived in the province, he went up from Caesarea to Jerusalem 2where the chief priests and the leaders of the Jews gave him a report against Paul. They appealed to him 3and requested, as a favor to them against Paul,*b* to have him transferred to Jerusalem. They were, in fact, planning an ambush to kill him along the way. 4Festus replied that Paul was being kept at Caesarea, and that he himself intended to go there shortly. 5"So," he said, "let those of you who have the authority come down with me, and if there is anything wrong about the man, let them accuse him."

6 After he had stayed among them not more than eight or ten days, he went down to Caesarea; the next day he took his seat on the tribunal and ordered Paul to be brought. 7When he arrived, the Jews who had gone down from Jerusalem surrounded him, bringing many serious charges against him, which they could not prove. 8Paul said in his defense, "I have in no way committed an offense against the law of the Jews, or against the temple, or against the emperor." 9But Festus, wishing to do the Jews a favor, asked Paul, "Do you wish to go up to Jerusalem and be tried there before me on these charges?"

a Other ancient authorities read *of the dead, both of*   *b* Gk *him*

[10]Paul said, "I am appealing to the emperor's tribunal; this is where I should be tried. I have done no wrong to the Jews, as you very well know. [11]Now if I am in the wrong and have committed something for which I deserve to die, I am not trying to escape death; but if there is nothing to their charges against me, no one can turn me over to them. I appeal to the emperor." [12]Then Festus, after he had conferred with his council, replied, "You have appealed to the emperor; to the emperor you will go."

Festus Consults King Agrippa

13 After several days had passed, King Agrippa and Bernice arrived at Caesarea to welcome Festus. [14]Since they were staying there several days, Festus laid Paul's case before the king, saying, "There is a man here who was left in prison by Felix. [15]When I was in Jerusalem, the chief priests and the elders of the Jews informed me about him and asked for a sentence against him. [16]I told them that it was not the custom of the Romans to hand over anyone before the accused had met the accusers face to face and had been given an opportunity to make a defense against the charge. [17]So when they met here, I lost no time, but on the next day took my seat on the tribunal and ordered the man to be brought. [18]When the accusers stood up, they did not charge him with any of the crimes[a] that I was expecting. [19]Instead they had certain points of disagreement with him about their own religion and about a certain Jesus, who had died, but whom Paul asserted to be alive. [20]Since I was at a loss how to investigate these questions, I asked whether he wished to go to Jerusalem and be tried there on these charges.[b] [21]But when Paul had appealed to be kept in custody for the decision of his Imperial Majesty, I ordered him to be held until I could send him to the emperor." [22]Agrippa said to Festus, "I would like to hear the man myself." "Tomorrow," he said, "you will hear him."

Paul Brought before Agrippa

23 So on the next day Agrippa and Bernice came with great pomp, and they entered the audience hall with the military tribunes and the prominent men of the city. Then Festus gave the order and Paul was brought in. [24]And Festus said, "King Agrippa and all here present with us, you see this man about whom the whole Jewish community petitioned me, both in Jerusalem and here, shouting that he ought not to live any longer. [25]But I found that he had done nothing deserving death; and when he appealed to his Imperial Majesty, I decided to send him. [26]But I have nothing definite to write to our sovereign about him. Therefore I have brought him before all of you, and especially before you, King Agrippa, so that, after we have examined him, I may have something to write— [27]for it seems to me unreasonable to send a prisoner without indicating the charges against him."

Paul Defends Himself before Agrippa

26 Agrippa said to Paul, "You have permission to speak for yourself." Then Paul stretched out his hand and began to defend himself:

2 "I consider myself fortunate that it is before you, King Agrippa, I am to make my defense today against all the accusations of the Jews, [3]because you are especially familiar with all the customs and controversies of the Jews; therefore I beg of you to listen to me patiently.

4 "All the Jews know my way of life from my youth, a life spent from the beginning among my own people and in Jerusalem. [5]They have known for a long time, if they are willing to testify, that I have belonged to the strictest sect of our religion and lived as a Pharisee. [6]And now I stand here on trial on account of my hope in the promise made by God to our ancestors, [7]a promise that our twelve tribes hope to attain, as they earnestly worship day and night. It is for this hope,

---

a Other ancient authorities read *with anything*   *b* Gk *on them* your Excellency,ᵃ that I am accused by Jews! ⁸Why is it thought incredible by any of you that God raises the dead?

9 "Indeed, I myself was convinced that I ought to do many things against the name of Jesus of Nazareth.ᵇ ¹⁰And that is what I did in Jerusalem; with authority received from the chief priests, I not only locked up many of the saints in prison, but I also cast my vote against them when they were being condemned to death. ¹¹By punishing them often in all the synagogues I tried to force them to blaspheme; and since I was so furiously enraged at them, I pursued them even to foreign cities.

Paul Tells of His Conversion

12 "With this in mind, I was traveling to Damascus with the authority and commission of the chief priests, ¹³when at midday along the road, your Excellency,ᵃ I saw a light from heaven, brighter than the sun, shining around me and my companions. ¹⁴When we had all fallen to the ground, I heard a voice saying to me in the Hebrewᶜ language, 'Saul, Saul, why are you persecuting me? It hurts you to kick against the goads.' ¹⁵I asked, 'Who are you, Lord?' The Lord answered, 'I am Jesus whom you are persecuting. ¹⁶But get up and stand on your feet; for I have appeared to you for this purpose, to appoint you to serve and testify to the things in which you have seen meᵈ and to those in which I will appear to you. ¹⁷I will rescue you from your people and from the Gentiles—to whom I am sending you ¹⁸to open their eyes so that they may turn from darkness to light and from the power of Satan to God, so that they may receive forgiveness of sins and a place among those who are sanctified by faith in me.'

Paul Tells of His Preaching

19 "After that, King Agrippa, I was not disobedient to the heavenly vision, ²⁰but declared first to those in Damascus, then in Jerusalem and throughout the countryside of Judea, and also to the Gentiles, that they should repent and turn to God and do deeds consistent with repentance. ²¹For this reason the Jews seized me in the temple and tried to kill me. ²²To this day I have had help from God, and so I stand here, testifying to both small and great, saying nothing but what the prophets and Moses said would take place: ²³that the Messiahᵉ must suffer, and that, by being the first to rise from the dead, he would proclaim light both to our people and to the Gentiles."

Paul Appeals to Agrippa to Believe

24 While he was making this defense, Festus exclaimed, "You are out of your mind, Paul! Too much learning is driving you insane!" ²⁵But Paul said, "I am not out of my mind, most excellent Festus, but I am speaking the sober truth. ²⁶Indeed the king knows about these things, and to him I speak freely; for I am certain that none of these things has escaped his notice, for this was not done in a corner. ²⁷King Agrippa, do you believe the prophets? I know that you believe." ²⁸Agrippa said to Paul, "Are you so quickly persuading me to become a Christian?"ᶠ ²⁹Paul replied, "Whether quickly or not, I pray to God that not only you but also all who are listening to me today might become such as I am—except for these chains."

30 Then the king got up, and with him the governor and Bernice and those who had been seated with them; ³¹and as they were leaving, they said to one another, "This man is doing nothing to deserve death or imprisonment." ³²Agrippa said to Festus, "This man could have been set free if he had not appealed to the emperor."

Paul Sails for Rome

27 When it was decided that we were to sail for Italy, they transferred Paul and some other prisoners to a centurion of the Augustan Cohort, named Julius. ²Embarking on a ship of Adramyttium that was

---

ᵃ Gk O king   ᵇ Gk the Nazorean   ᶜ That is, Aramaic   ᵈ Other ancient authorities read the things that you have
seen   ᵉ Or the Christ   ᶠ Or Quickly you will persuade me to play the Christian

about to set sail to the ports along the coast of Asia, we put to sea, accompanied by Aristarchus, a Macedonian from Thessalonica. [3]The next day we put in at Sidon; and Julius treated Paul kindly, and allowed him to go to his friends to be cared for. [4]Putting out to sea from there, we sailed under the lee of Cyprus, because the winds were against us. [5]After we had sailed across the sea that is off Cilicia and Pamphylia, we came to Myra in Lycia. [6]There the centurion found an Alexandrian ship bound for Italy and put us on board. [7]We sailed slowly for a number of days and arrived with difficulty off Cnidus, and as the wind was against us, we sailed under the lee of Crete off Salmone. [8]Sailing past it with difficulty, we came to a place called Fair Havens, near the city of Lasea.

9 Since much time had been lost and sailing was now dangerous, because even the Fast had already gone by, Paul advised them, [10]saying, "Sirs, I can see that the voyage will be with danger and much heavy loss, not only of the cargo and the ship, but also of our lives." [11]But the centurion paid more attention to the pilot and to the owner of the ship than to what Paul said. [12]Since the harbor was not suitable for spending the winter, the majority was in favor of putting to sea from there, on the chance that somehow they could reach Phoenix, where they could spend the winter. It was a harbor of Crete, facing southwest and northwest.

The Storm at Sea

13 When a moderate south wind began to blow, they thought they could achieve their purpose; so they weighed anchor and began to sail past Crete, close to the shore. [14]But soon a violent wind, called the northeaster, rushed down from Crete.[a] [15]Since the ship was caught and could not be turned head-on into the wind, we gave way to it and were driven. [16]By running under the lee of a small island called Cauda[b] we were scarcely able to get the ship's boat under control. [17]After

hoisting it up they took measures[c] to undergird the ship; then, fearing that they would run on the Syrtis, they lowered the sea anchor and so were driven. [18]We were being pounded by the storm so violently that on the next day they began to throw the cargo overboard, [19]and on the third day with their own hands they threw the ship's tackle overboard. [20]When neither sun nor stars appeared for many days, and no small tempest raged, all hope of our being saved was at last abandoned.

21 Since they had been without food for a long time, Paul then stood up among them and said, "Men, you should have listened to me and not have set sail from Crete and thereby avoided this damage and loss. [22]I urge you now to keep up your courage, for there will be no loss of life among you, but only of the ship. [23]For last night there stood by me an angel of the God to whom I belong and whom I worship, [24]and he said, 'Do not be afraid, Paul; you must stand before the emperor; and indeed, God has granted safety to all those who are sailing with you.' [25]So keep up your courage, men, for I have faith in God that it will be exactly as I have been told. [26]But we will have to run aground on some island."

27 When the fourteenth night had come, as we were drifting across the sea of Adria, about midnight the sailors suspected that they were nearing land. [28]So they took soundings and found twenty fathoms; a little farther on they took soundings again and found fifteen fathoms. [29]Fearing that we might run on the rocks, they let down four anchors from the stern and prayed for day to come. [30]But when the sailors tried to escape from the ship and had lowered the boat into the sea, on the pretext of putting out anchors from the bow, [31]Paul said to the centurion and the soldiers, "Unless these men stay in the ship, you cannot be saved." [32]Then the soldiers cut away the ropes of the boat and set it adrift.

33 Just before daybreak, Paul urged all of

a Gk *it*   b Other ancient authorities read *Clauda*   c Gk *helps* them to take some food, saying, "Today is the fourteenth day that you have been in suspense and remaining without food, having eaten nothing. [34]Therefore I urge you to take some food, for it will help you survive; for none of you will lose a hair from your heads." [35]After he had said this, he took bread; and giving thanks to God in the presence of all, he broke it and began to eat. [36]Then all of them were encouraged and took food for themselves. [37](We were in all two hundred seventy-six[a] persons in the ship.) [38]After they had satisfied their hunger, they lightened the ship by throwing the wheat into the sea.

The Shipwreck

39 In the morning they did not recognize the land, but they noticed a bay with a beach, on which they planned to run the ship ashore, if they could. [40]So they cast off the anchors and left them in the sea. At the same time they loosened the ropes that tied the steering-oars; then hoisting the foresail to the wind, they made for the beach. [41]But striking a reef,[b] they ran the ship aground; the bow stuck and remained immovable, but the stern was being broken up by the force of the waves. [42]The soldiers' plan was to kill the prisoners, so that none might swim away and escape; [43]but the centurion, wishing to save Paul, kept them from carrying out their plan. He ordered those who could swim to jump overboard first and make for the land, [44]and the rest to follow, some on planks and others on pieces of the ship. And so it was that all were brought safely to land.

Paul on the Island of Malta

28 After we had reached safety, we then learned that the island was called Malta. [2]The natives showed us unusual kindness. Since it had begun to rain and was cold, they kindled a fire and welcomed all of us around it. [3]Paul had gathered a bundle of brushwood and was putting it on the fire, when a viper, driven out by the heat, fastened itself

on his hand. [4]When the natives saw the creature hanging from his hand, they said to one another, "This man must be a murderer; though he has escaped from the sea, justice has not allowed him to live." [5]He, however, shook off the creature into the fire and suffered no harm. [6]They were expecting him to swell up or drop dead, but after they had waited a long time and saw that nothing unusual had happened to him, they changed their minds and began to say that he was a god.

7 Now in the neighborhood of that place were lands belonging to the leading man of the island, named Publius, who received us and entertained us hospitably for three days. [8]It so happened that the father of Publius lay sick in bed with fever and dysentery. Paul visited him and cured him by praying and putting his hands on him. [9]After this happened, the rest of the people on the island who had diseases also came and were cured. [10]They bestowed many honors on us, and when we were about to sail, they put on board all the provisions we needed.

Paul Arrives at Rome

11 Three months later we set sail on a ship that had wintered at the island, an Alexandrian ship with the Twin Brothers as its figurehead. [12]We put in at Syracuse and stayed there for three days; [13]then we weighed anchor and came to Rhegium. After one day there a south wind sprang up, and on the second day we came to Puteoli. [14]There we found believers[c] and were invited to stay with them for seven days. And so we came to Rome. [15]The believers[c] from there, when they heard of us, came as far as the Forum of Appius and Three Taverns to meet us. On seeing them, Paul thanked God and took courage.

16 When we came into Rome, Paul was allowed to live by himself, with the soldier who was guarding him.

---

a Other ancient authorities read *seventy-six*; others, *about seventy-six*   b Gk *place of two seas*   c Gk *brothers*

Paul and Jewish Leaders in Rome

17 Three days later he called together the local leaders of the Jews. When they had assembled, he said to them, "Brothers, though I had done nothing against our people or the customs of our ancestors, yet I was arrested in Jerusalem and handed over to the Romans. 18When they had examined me, the Romans*a* wanted to release me, because there was no reason for the death penalty in my case. 19But when the Jews objected, I was compelled to appeal to the emperor—even though I had no charge to bring against my nation. 20For this reason therefore I have asked to see you and speak with you,*b* since it is for the sake of the hope of Israel that I am bound with this chain." 21They replied, "We have received no letters from Judea about you, and none of the brothers coming here has reported or spoken anything evil about you. 22But we would like to hear from you what you think, for with regard to this sect we know that everywhere it is spoken against."

Paul Preaches in Rome

23 After they had set a day to meet with him, they came to him at his lodgings in great numbers. From morning until evening he explained the matter to them, testifying to the kingdom of God and trying to convince them about Jesus both from the law of Moses and from the prophets. 24Some were convinced by what he had said, while others refused to believe. 25So they disagreed with each other; and as they were leaving, Paul made one further statement: "The Holy Spirit was right in saying to your ancestors through the prophet Isaiah,

26   'Go to this people and say,
        You will indeed listen, but never
            understand,
        and you will indeed look, but never
            perceive.
27   For this people's heart has grown dull,
        and their ears are hard of hearing,
            and they have shut their eyes;
        so that they might not look with
            their eyes,
        and listen with their ears,
        and understand with their heart and
            turn—
        and I would heal them.'

28Let it be known to you then that this salvation of God has been sent to the Gentiles; they will listen."*c*

30 He lived there two whole years at his own expense*d* and welcomed all who came to him, 31proclaiming the kingdom of God and teaching about the Lord Jesus Christ with all boldness and without hindrance.

---

a Gk *they*   *b* Or *I have asked you to see me and speak with me*   *c* Other ancient authorities add verse 29, *And when he had said these words, the Jews departed, arguing vigorously among themselves*   *d* Or *in his own hired dwelling*

THE LETTER OF PAUL TO THE
ROMANS

Salutation

1 Paul, a servant*a* of Jesus Christ, called to be an apostle, set apart for the gospel of God, 2which he promised beforehand through his prophets in the holy scriptures, 3the gospel concerning his Son, who was descended from David according to the flesh 4and was declared to be Son of God with power according to the spirit*b* of holiness by resurrection from the dead, Jesus Christ our Lord, 5through whom we have received grace and apostleship to bring about the obedience of faith among all the Gentiles for the sake of his name, 6including yourselves who are called to belong to Jesus Christ,

7 To all God's beloved in Rome, who are called to be saints:

Grace to you and peace from God our Father and the Lord Jesus Christ.

Prayer of Thanksgiving

8 First, I thank my God through Jesus Christ for all of you, because your faith is proclaimed throughout the world. 9For God, whom I serve with my spirit by announcing the gospel*c* of his Son, is my witness that without ceasing I remember you always in my prayers, 10asking that by God's will I may somehow at last succeed in coming to you. 11For I am longing to see you so that I may share with you some spiritual gift to strengthen you— 12or rather so that we may be mutually encouraged by each other's faith, both yours and mine. 13I want you to know, brothers and sisters,*d* that I have often intended to come to you (but thus far have been prevented), in order that I may reap some harvest among you as I have among the rest of the Gentiles. 14I am a debtor both to Greeks and to barbarians, both to the wise and to the foolish 15—hence my eagerness to proclaim the gospel to you also who are in Rome.

The Power of the Gospel

16 For I am not ashamed of the gospel; it is the power of God for salvation to everyone who has faith, to the Jew first and also to the Greek. 17For in it the righteousness of God is revealed through faith for faith; as it is written, "The one who is righteous will live by faith."*e*

The Guilt of Humankind

18 For the wrath of God is revealed from heaven against all ungodliness and wickedness of those who by their wickedness suppress the truth. 19For what can be known about God is plain to them, because God has shown it to them. 20Ever since the creation of the world his eternal power and divine nature, invisible though they are, have been understood and seen through the things he has made. So they are without excuse; 21for though they knew God, they did not honor him as God or give thanks to him, but they became futile in their thinking, and their senseless minds were darkened. 22Claiming to be wise, they became fools; 23and they exchanged the glory of the immortal God for images resembling a mortal human being or birds or four-footed animals or reptiles.

24 Therefore God gave them up in the lusts of their hearts to impurity, to the degrading of their bodies among themselves, 25because they exchanged the truth about God for a lie and worshiped and served the creature rather than the Creator, who is blessed forever! Amen.

26 For this reason God gave them up to degrading passions. Their women exchanged natural intercourse for unnatural, 27and in the same way also the men, giving up natural intercourse with women, were consumed with passion for one another. Men committed shameless acts with men and received in their own persons the due penalty for their error.

28 And since they did not see fit to acknowledge God, God gave them up to a debased mind and to things that should not be done. 29They were filled with every kind of wickedness, evil, covetousness, malice. Full of envy, murder, strife, deceit, craftiness, they are gossips, 30slanderers, God-haters,*a* insolent, haughty, boastful, inventors of evil, rebellious toward parents, 31foolish, faithless, heartless, ruthless. 32They know God's decree, that those who practice such things deserve to die—yet they not only do them but even applaud others who practice them.

The Righteous Judgment of God

2 Therefore you have no excuse, whoever you are, when you judge others; for in passing judgment on another you condemn yourself, because you, the judge, are doing the very same things. 2You say,*b* "We know that God's judgment on those who do such things is in accordance with truth." 3Do you imagine, whoever you are, that when you judge those who do such things and yet do them yourself, you will escape the judgment of God? 4Or do you despise the riches of his kindness and forbearance and patience? Do you not realize that God's kindness is meant to lead you to repentance? 5But by your hard and impenitent heart you are storing up wrath for yourself on the day of wrath, when God's righteous judgment will be revealed. 6For he will repay according to each one's deeds: 7to those who by patiently doing good seek for glory and honor and immortality, he will give eternal life; 8while for those who are self-seeking and who obey not the truth but wickedness, there will be wrath and fury. 9There will be anguish and distress for everyone who does evil, the Jew first and also the Greek, 10but glory and honor and peace for everyone who does good, the Jew first and also the Greek. 11For God shows no partiality.

12 All who have sinned apart from the law will also perish apart from the law, and all who have sinned under the law will be judged by the law. 13For it is not the hearers of the law who are righteous in God's sight, but the doers of the law who will be justified. 14When Gentiles, who do not possess the law, do instinctively what the law requires, these, though not having the law, are a law to themselves. 15They show that what the law requires is written on their hearts, to which their own conscience also bears witness; and their conflicting thoughts will accuse or perhaps excuse them 16on the day when, according to my gospel, God, through Jesus Christ, will judge the secret thoughts of all.

The Jews and the Law

17 But if you call yourself a Jew and rely on the law and boast of your relation to God 18and know his will and determine what is best because you are instructed in the law, 19and if you are sure that you are a guide to the blind, a light to those who are in darkness, 20a corrector of the foolish, a teacher of children, having in the law the embodiment of knowledge and truth, 21you, then, that teach others, will you not teach yourself? While you preach against stealing, do you steal? 22You that forbid adultery, do you commit adultery? You that abhor idols, do you rob temples? 23You that boast in the law, do you dishonor God by breaking the law? 24For, as it is written, "The name of God is blasphemed among the Gentiles because of you."

25 Circumcision indeed is of value if you obey the law; but if you break the law, your circumcision has become uncircumcision. 26So, if those who are uncircumcised keep the requirements of the law, will not their uncircumcision be regarded as circumcision? 27Then those who are physically uncircumcised but keep the law will condemn you that have the written code and circumcision but break the law. 28For a person is not a Jew who is one outwardly, nor is true circumcision something external and physical. 29Rather, a person is a Jew who is one inwardly, and real

---

a Or *God-hated*   *b* Gk lacks *You say*

circumcision is a matter of the heart—it is spiritual and not literal. Such a person receives praise not from others but from God.

3 Then what advantage has the Jew? Or what is the value of circumcision? [2]Much, in every way. For in the first place the Jews[a] were entrusted with the oracles of God. [3]What if some were unfaithful? Will their faithlessness nullify the faithfulness of God? [4]By no means! Although everyone is a liar, let God be proved true, as it is written,

"So that you may be justified in your words,
    and prevail in your judging."[b]

[5]But if our injustice serves to confirm the justice of God, what should we say? That God is unjust to inflict wrath on us? (I speak in a human way.) [6]By no means! For then how could God judge the world? [7]But if through my falsehood God's truthfulness abounds to his glory, why am I still being condemned as a sinner? [8]And why not say (as some people slander us by saying that we say), "Let us do evil so that good may come"? Their condemnation is deserved!

None Is Righteous

[9]What then? Are we any better off?[c] No, not at all; for we have already charged that all, both Jews and Greeks, are under the power of sin, [10]as it is written:

"There is no one who is righteous, not even one;
[11]   there is no one who has understanding,
        there is no one who seeks God.
[12] All have turned aside, together they have become worthless;
        there is no one who shows kindness, there is not even one."
[13] "Their throats are opened graves;
        they use their tongues to deceive."
    "The venom of vipers is under their lips."
[14]   "Their mouths are full of cursing and bitterness."
[15] "Their feet are swift to shed blood;
[16]   ruin and misery are in their paths,
[17]   and the way of peace they have not known."
[18]   "There is no fear of God before their eyes."

[19]Now we know that whatever the law says, it speaks to those who are under the law, so that every mouth may be silenced, and the whole world may be held accountable to God. [20]For "no human being will be justified in his sight" by deeds prescribed by the law, for through the law comes the knowledge of sin.

Righteousness through Faith

[21]But now, apart from law, the righteousness of God has been disclosed, and is attested by the law and the prophets, [22]the righteousness of God through faith in Jesus Christ[d] for all who believe. For there is no distinction, [23]since all have sinned and fall short of the glory of God; [24]they are now justified by his grace as a gift, through the redemption that is in Christ Jesus, [25]whom God put forward as a sacrifice of atonement[e] by his blood, effective through faith. He did this to show his righteousness, because in his divine forbearance he had passed over the sins previously committed; [26]it was to prove at the present time that he himself is righteous and that he justifies the one who has faith in Jesus.[f]

[27]Then what becomes of boasting? It is excluded. By what law? By that of works? No, but by the law of faith. [28]For we hold that a person is justified by faith apart from works prescribed by the law. [29]Or is God the God of Jews only? Is he not the God of Gentiles also? Yes, of Gentiles also, [30]since God is one; and he will justify the circumcised on the ground of faith and the uncircumcised through that same faith. [31]Do we then overthrow the law by this faith? By no means! On the contrary, we uphold the law.

The Example of Abraham

4 What then are we to say was gained by[a] Abraham, our ancestor according to the flesh? [2]For if Abraham was justified by works, he has something to boast about, but not before God. [3]For what does the scripture say? "Abraham believed God, and it was reckoned to him as righteousness." [4]Now to one who works, wages are not reckoned as a gift but as something due. [5]But to one who without works trusts him who justifies the ungodly, such faith is reckoned as righteousness. [6]So also David speaks of the blessedness of those to whom God reckons righteousness apart from works:

[7]   "Blessed are those whose iniquities are
            forgiven,
        and whose sins are covered;
[8]   blessed is the one against whom the
            Lord will not reckon sin."

[9] Is this blessedness, then, pronounced only on the circumcised, or also on the uncircumcised? We say, "Faith was reckoned to Abraham as righteousness." [10]How then was it reckoned to him? Was it before or after he had been circumcised? It was not after, but before he was circumcised. [11]He received the sign of circumcision as a seal of the righteousness that he had by faith while he was still uncircumcised. The purpose was to make him the ancestor of all who believe without being circumcised and who thus have righteousness reckoned to them, [12]and likewise the ancestor of the circumcised who are not only circumcised but who also follow the example of the faith that our ancestor Abraham had before he was circumcised.

God's Promise Realized through Faith

[13] For the promise that he would inherit the world did not come to Abraham or to his descendants through the law but through the righteousness of faith. [14]If it is the adherents of the law who are to be the heirs, faith is null and the promise is void. [15]For the law brings wrath; but where there is no law, neither is there violation.

[16] For this reason it depends on faith, in order that the promise may rest on grace and be guaranteed to all his descendants, not only to the adherents of the law but also to those who share the faith of Abraham (for he is the father of all of us, [17]as it is written, "I have made you the father of many nations")—in the presence of the God in whom he believed, who gives life to the dead and calls into existence the things that do not exist. [18]Hoping against hope, he believed that he would become "the father of many nations," according to what was said, "So numerous shall your descendants be." [19]He did not weaken in faith when he considered his own body, which was already[b] as good as dead (for he was about a hundred years old), or when he considered the barrenness of Sarah's womb. [20]No distrust made him waver concerning the promise of God, but he grew strong in his faith as he gave glory to God, [21]being fully convinced that God was able to do what he had promised. [22]Therefore his faith[c] "was reckoned to him as righteousness." [23]Now the words, "it was reckoned to him," were written not for his sake alone, [24]but for ours also. It will be reckoned to us who believe in him who raised Jesus our Lord from the dead, [25]who was handed over to death for our trespasses and was raised for our justification.

Results of Justification

5 Therefore, since we are justified by faith, we[d] have peace with God through our Lord Jesus Christ, [2]through whom we have obtained access[e] to this grace in which we stand; and we[f] boast in our hope of sharing the glory of God. [3]And not only that, but we[f] also boast in our sufferings, knowing that suffering produces endurance, [4]and endurance produces character, and character produces hope, [5]and hope does not disappoint us, because God's love has been poured

---

a Other ancient authorities read *say about*   *b* Other ancient authorities lack *already*   *c* Gk *Therefore it*   *d* Other ancient authorities read *let us*   *e* Other ancient authorities add *by faith*   *f* Or *let us* into our hearts through the Holy Spirit that has been given to us.

6 For while we were still weak, at the right time Christ died for the ungodly. [7]Indeed, rarely will anyone die for a righteous person—though perhaps for a good person someone might actually dare to die. [8]But God proves his love for us in that while we still were sinners Christ died for us. [9]Much more surely then, now that we have been justified by his blood, will we be saved through him from the wrath of God.[a] [10]For if while we were enemies, we were reconciled to God through the death of his Son, much more surely, having been reconciled, will we be saved by his life. [11]But more than that, we even boast in God through our Lord Jesus Christ, through whom we have now received reconciliation.

Adam and Christ

12 Therefore, just as sin came into the world through one man, and death came through sin, and so death spread to all because all have sinned— [13]sin was indeed in the world before the law, but sin is not reckoned when there is no law. [14]Yet death exercised dominion from Adam to Moses, even over those whose sins were not like the transgression of Adam, who is a type of the one who was to come.

15 But the free gift is not like the trespass. For if the many died through the one man's trespass, much more surely have the grace of God and the free gift in the grace of the one man, Jesus Christ, abounded for the many. [16]And the free gift is not like the effect of the one man's sin. For the judgment following one trespass brought condemnation, but the free gift following many trespasses brings justification. [17]If, because of the one man's trespass, death exercised dominion through that one, much more surely will those who receive the abundance of grace and the free gift of righteousness exercise dominion in life through the one man, Jesus Christ.

18 Therefore just as one man's trespass led to condemnation for all, so one man's act of righteousness leads to justification and life for all. [19]For just as by the one man's disobedience the many were made sinners, so by the one man's obedience the many will be made righteous. [20]But law came in, with the result that the trespass multiplied; but where sin increased, grace abounded all the more, [21]so that, just as sin exercised dominion in death, so grace might also exercise dominion through justification[b] leading to eternal life through Jesus Christ our Lord.

Dying and Rising with Christ

6 What then are we to say? Should we continue in sin in order that grace may abound? [2]By no means! How can we who died to sin go on living in it? [3]Do you not know that all of us who have been baptized into Christ Jesus were baptized into his death? [4]Therefore we have been buried with him by baptism into death, so that, just as Christ was raised from the dead by the glory of the Father, so we too might walk in newness of life.

5 For if we have been united with him in a death like his, we will certainly be united with him in a resurrection like his. [6]We know that our old self was crucified with him so that the body of sin might be destroyed, and we might no longer be enslaved to sin. [7]For whoever has died is freed from sin. [8]But if we have died with Christ, we believe that we will also live with him. [9]We know that Christ, being raised from the dead, will never die again; death no longer has dominion over him. [10]The death he died, he died to sin, once for all; but the life he lives, he lives to God. [11]So you also must consider yourselves dead to sin and alive to God in Christ Jesus.

12 Therefore, do not let sin exercise dominion in your mortal bodies, to make you obey their passions. [13]No longer present your members to sin as instruments[c] of wickedness, but present yourselves to God as those

---

a Gk *the wrath*   *b* Or *righteousness*   *c* Or *weapons* who have been brought from death to life, and present your members to God as instruments[a] of righteousness. ¹⁴For sin will have no dominion over you, since you are not under law but under grace.

Slaves of Righteousness

15 What then? Should we sin because we are not under law but under grace? By no means! ¹⁶Do you not know that if you present yourselves to anyone as obedient slaves, you are slaves of the one whom you obey, either of sin, which leads to death, or of obedience, which leads to righteousness? ¹⁷But thanks be to God that you, having once been slaves of sin, have become obedient from the heart to the form of teaching to which you were entrusted, ¹⁸and that you, having been set free from sin, have become slaves of righteousness. ¹⁹I am speaking in human terms because of your natural limitations.[b] For just as you once presented your members as slaves to impurity and to greater and greater iniquity, so now present your members as slaves to righteousness for sanctification.

20 When you were slaves of sin, you were free in regard to righteousness. ²¹So what advantage did you then get from the things of which you now are ashamed? The end of those things is death. ²²But now that you have been freed from sin and enslaved to God, the advantage you get is sanctification. The end is eternal life. ²³For the wages of sin is death, but the free gift of God is eternal life in Christ Jesus our Lord.

An Analogy from Marriage

7 Do you not know, brothers and sisters[c]—for I am speaking to those who know the law—that the law is binding on a person only during that person's lifetime? ²Thus a married woman is bound by the law to her husband as long as he lives; but if her husband dies, she is discharged from the law concerning the husband. ³Accordingly, she will be called an adulteress if she lives with another man while her husband is alive. But if her husband dies, she is free from that law, and if she marries another man, she is not an adulteress.

4 In the same way, my friends,[c] you have died to the law through the body of Christ, so that you may belong to another, to him who has been raised from the dead in order that we may bear fruit for God. ⁵While we were living in the flesh, our sinful passions, aroused by the law, were at work in our members to bear fruit for death. ⁶But now we are discharged from the law, dead to that which held us captive, so that we are slaves not under the old written code but in the new life of the Spirit.

The Law and Sin

7 What then should we say? That the law is sin? By no means! Yet, if it had not been for the law, I would not have known sin. I would not have known what it is to covet if the law had not said, "You shall not covet." ⁸But sin, seizing an opportunity in the commandment, produced in me all kinds of covetousness. Apart from the law sin lies dead. ⁹I was once alive apart from the law, but when the commandment came, sin revived ¹⁰and I died, and the very commandment that promised life proved to be death to me. ¹¹For sin, seizing an opportunity in the commandment, deceived me and through it killed me. ¹²So the law is holy, and the commandment is holy and just and good.

13 Did what is good, then, bring death to me? By no means! It was sin, working death in me through what is good, in order that sin might be shown to be sin, and through the commandment might become sinful beyond measure.

The Inner Conflict

14 For we know that the law is spiritual; but I am of the flesh, sold into slavery under sin.[d] ¹⁵I do not understand my own actions.

---

a Or weapons   b Gk the weakness of your flesh   c Gk brothers   d Gk sold under sin

For I do not do what I want, but I do the very thing I hate. ¹⁶Now if I do what I do not want, I agree that the law is good. ¹⁷But in fact it is no longer I that do it, but sin that dwells within me. ¹⁸For I know that nothing good dwells within me, that is, in my flesh. I can will what is right, but I cannot do it. ¹⁹For I do not do the good I want, but the evil I do not want is what I do. ²⁰Now if I do what I do not want, it is no longer I that do it, but sin that dwells within me.

21 So I find it to be a law that when I want to do what is good, evil lies close at hand. ²²For I delight in the law of God in my inmost self, ²³but I see in my members another law at war with the law of my mind, making me captive to the law of sin that dwells in my members. ²⁴Wretched man that I am! Who will rescue me from this body of death? ²⁵Thanks be to God through Jesus Christ our Lord!

So then, with my mind I am a slave to the law of God, but with my flesh I am a slave to the law of sin.

Life in the Spirit

8 There is therefore now no condemnation for those who are in Christ Jesus. ²For the law of the Spirit*a* of life in Christ Jesus has set you*b* free from the law of sin and of death. ³For God has done what the law, weakened by the flesh, could not do: by sending his own Son in the likeness of sinful flesh, and to deal with sin,*c* he condemned sin in the flesh, ⁴so that the just requirement of the law might be fulfilled in us, who walk not according to the flesh but according to the Spirit.*a* ⁵For those who live according to the flesh set their minds on the things of the flesh, but those who live according to the Spirit*a* set their minds on the things of the Spirit.*a* ⁶To set the mind on the flesh is death, but to set the mind on the Spirit*a* is life and peace. ⁷For this reason the mind that is set on

the flesh is hostile to God; it does not submit to God's law—indeed it cannot, ⁸and those who are in the flesh cannot please God.

9 But you are not in the flesh; you are in the Spirit,*a* since the Spirit of God dwells in you. Anyone who does not have the Spirit of Christ does not belong to him. ¹⁰But if Christ is in you, though the body is dead because of sin, the Spirit*a* is life because of righteousness. ¹¹If the Spirit of him who raised Jesus from the dead dwells in you, he who raised Christ*d* from the dead will give life to your mortal bodies also through*e* his Spirit that dwells in you.

12 So then, brothers and sisters,*f* we are debtors, not to the flesh, to live according to the flesh— ¹³for if you live according to the flesh, you will die; but if by the Spirit you put to death the deeds of the body, you will live. ¹⁴For all who are led by the Spirit of God are children of God. ¹⁵For you did not receive a spirit of slavery to fall back into fear, but you have received a spirit of adoption. When we cry, "Abba!*g* Father!" ¹⁶it is that very Spirit bearing witness*h* with our spirit that we are children of God, ¹⁷and if children, then heirs, heirs of God and joint heirs with Christ—if, in fact, we suffer with him so that we may also be glorified with him.

Future Glory

18 I consider that the sufferings of this present time are not worth comparing with the glory about to be revealed to us. ¹⁹For the creation waits with eager longing for the revealing of the children of God; ²⁰for the creation was subjected to futility, not of its own will but by the will of the one who subjected it, in hope ²¹that the creation itself will be set free from its bondage to decay and will obtain the freedom of the glory of the children of God. ²²We know that the whole creation has been groaning in labor pains until now; ²³and not only the creation, but we

a Or *spirit*　　*b* Here the Greek word *you* is singular number; other ancient authorities read *me* or *us*　　*c* Or *and as a sin offering*　　*d* Other ancient authorities read *the Christ* or *Christ Jesus* or *Jesus Christ*　　*e* Other ancient authorities read *on account of*　　*f* Gk *brothers*　　*g* Aramaic for *Father*　　*h* Or ¹⁵*a spirit of adoption, by which we cry, "Abba! Father!"*　　¹⁶*The Spirit itself bears witness* ourselves, who have the first fruits of the Spirit, groan inwardly while we wait for adoption, the redemption of our bodies. 24For in*a* hope we were saved. Now hope that is seen is not hope. For who hopes *b* for what is seen? 25But if we hope for what we do not see, we wait for it with patience.

26 Likewise the Spirit helps us in our weakness; for we do not know how to pray as we ought, but that very Spirit intercedes*c* with sighs too deep for words. 27And God, *d* who searches the heart, knows what is the mind of the Spirit, because the Spirit*e* intercedes for the saints according to the will of God.*f*

28 We know that all things work together for good*g* for those who love God, who are called according to his purpose. 29For those whom he foreknew he also predestined to be conformed to the image of his Son, in order that he might be the firstborn within a large family. *h* 30And those whom he predestined he also called; and those whom he called he also justified; and those whom he justified he also glorified.

God's Love in Christ Jesus

31 What then are we to say about these things? If God is for us, who is against us? 32He who did not withhold his own Son, but gave him up for all of us, will he not with him also give us everything else? 33Who will bring any charge against God's elect? It is God who justifies. 34Who is to condemn? It is Christ Jesus, who died, yes, who was raised, who is at the right hand of God, who indeed intercedes for us.*i* 35Who will separate us from the love of Christ? Will hardship, or distress, or persecution, or famine, or nakedness, or peril, or sword? 36As it is written,

"For your sake we are being killed all
    day long;
we are accounted as sheep to be
    slaughtered."

37No, in all these things we are more than conquerors through him who loved us. 38For I am convinced that neither death, nor life, nor angels, nor rulers, nor things present, nor things to come, nor powers, 39nor height, nor depth, nor anything else in all creation, will be able to separate us from the love of God in Christ Jesus our Lord.

God's Election of Israel

9 I am speaking the truth in Christ—I am not lying; my conscience confirms it by the Holy Spirit— 2I have great sorrow and unceasing anguish in my heart. 3For I could wish that I myself were accursed and cut off from Christ for the sake of my own people,*j* my kindred according to the flesh. 4They are Israelites, and to them belong the adoption, the glory, the covenants, the giving of the law, the worship, and the promises; 5to them belong the patriarchs, and from them, according to the flesh, comes the Messiah,*k* who is over all, God blessed forever.*l* Amen.

6 It is not as though the word of God had failed. For not all Israelites truly belong to Israel, 7and not all of Abraham's children are his true descendants; but "It is through Isaac that descendants shall be named for you." 8This means that it is not the children of the flesh who are the children of God, but the children of the promise are counted as descendants. 9For this is what the promise said, "About this time I will return and Sarah shall have a son." 10Nor is that all; something similar happened to Rebecca when she had conceived children by one husband, our ancestor Isaac. 11Even before they had been born or had done anything good or bad (so that God's purpose of election might continue, 12not by works but by his call) she was told, "The elder shall serve the younger." 13As it is written,

"I have loved Jacob,
    but I have hated Esau."

a Or *by*   *b* Other ancient authorities read *awaits*   *c* Other ancient authorities add *for us*   *d* Gk *the one*
e Gk *he* or *it*   *f* Gk *according to God*   *g* Other ancient authorities read *God makes all things work together for good*, or *in all things God works for good*   *h* Gk *among many brothers*   *i* Or *Is it Christ Jesus . . . for us?*   *j* Gk *my brothers*
k Or *the Christ*   *l* Or *Messiah, who is God over all, blessed forever*, or *Messiah. May he who is God over all be blessed forever*

14 What then are we to say? Is there injustice on God's part? By no means! 15For he says to Moses,

> "I will have mercy on whom I have
>   mercy,
> and I will have compassion on
>   whom I have compassion."

16So it depends not on human will or exertion, but on God who shows mercy. 17For the scripture says to Pharaoh, "I have raised you up for the very purpose of showing my power in you, so that my name may be proclaimed in all the earth." 18So then he has mercy on whomever he chooses, and he hardens the heart of whomever he chooses.

God's Wrath and Mercy

19 You will say to me then, "Why then does he still find fault? For who can resist his will?" 20But who indeed are you, a human being, to argue with God? Will what is molded say to the one who molds it, "Why have you made me like this?" 21Has the potter no right over the clay, to make out of the same lump one object for special use and another for ordinary use? 22What if God, desiring to show his wrath and to make known his power, has endured with much patience the objects of wrath that are made for destruction; 23and what if he has done so in order to make known the riches of his glory for the objects of mercy, which he has prepared beforehand for glory— 24including us whom he has called, not from the Jews only but also from the Gentiles? 25As indeed he says in Hosea,

> "Those who were not my people I will
>   call 'my people,'
> and her who was not beloved I will
>   call 'beloved.' "

26   "And in the very place where it was
>   said to them, 'You are not my
>   people,'
>   there they shall be called children of
>   the living God."

27   And Isaiah cries out concerning Israel, "Though the number of the children of Israel were like the sand of the sea, only a remnant of them will be saved; 28for the Lord will execute his sentence on the earth quickly and decisively."ᵃ 29And as Isaiah predicted,

> "If the Lord of hosts had not left
>   survivorsᵇ to us,
> we would have fared like Sodom
> and been made like Gomorrah."

Israel's Unbelief

30 What then are we to say? Gentiles, who did not strive for righteousness, have attained it, that is, righteousness through faith; 31but Israel, who did strive for the righteousness that is based on the law, did not succeed in fulfilling that law. 32Why not? Because they did not strive for it on the basis of faith, but as if it were based on works. They have stumbled over the stumbling stone, 33as it is written,

> "See, I am laying in Zion a stone that
>   will make people stumble, a
>   rock that will make them fall,
> and whoever believes in himᶜ will
>   not be put to shame."

10 Brothers and sisters,ᵈ my heart's desire and prayer to God for them is that they may be saved. 2I can testify that they have a zeal for God, but it is not enlightened. 3For, being ignorant of the righteousness that comes from God, and seeking to establish their own, they have not submitted to God's righteousness. 4For Christ is the end of the law so that there may be righteousness for everyone who believes.

Salvation Is for All

5 Moses writes concerning the righteousness that comes from the law, that "the person who does these things will live by them." 6But the righteousness that comes from faith says, "Do not say in your heart, 'Who will ascend into heaven?' " (that is, to bring Christ down) 7"or 'Who will descend

---

ᵃ Other ancient authorities read *for he will finish his work and cut it short in righteousness, because the Lord will make the sentence shortened on the earth*   ᵇ Or *descendants*; Gk *seed*   ᶜ Or *trusts in it*   ᵈ Gk *Brothers* into the abyss?' " (that is, to bring Christ up from the dead). 8But what does it say?

"The word is near you,
　on your lips and in your heart"

(that is, the word of faith that we proclaim); 9because*a* if you confess with your lips that Jesus is Lord and believe in your heart that God raised him from the dead, you will be saved. 10For one believes with the heart and so is justified, and one confesses with the mouth and so is saved. 11The scripture says, "No one who believes in him will be put to shame." 12For there is no distinction between Jew and Greek; the same Lord is Lord of all and is generous to all who call on him. 13For, "Everyone who calls on the name of the Lord shall be saved."

14 But how are they to call on one in whom they have not believed? And how are they to believe in one of whom they have never heard? And how are they to hear without someone to proclaim him? 15And how are they to proclaim him unless they are sent? As it is written, "How beautiful are the feet of those who bring good news!" 16But not all have obeyed the good news;*b* for Isaiah says, "Lord, who has believed our message?" 17So faith comes from what is heard, and what is heard comes through the word of Christ.*c*

18 But I ask, have they not heard? Indeed they have; for

"Their voice has gone out to all the
　earth,
　and their words to the ends of the
　world."

19Again I ask, did Israel not understand? First Moses says,

"I will make you jealous of those who
　are not a nation;
　with a foolish nation I will make you
　angry."

20Then Isaiah is so bold as to say,

"I have been found by those who did
　not seek me;

I have shown myself to those who
　did not ask for me."

21But of Israel he says, "All day long I have held out my hands to a disobedient and contrary people."

Israel's Rejection Is Not Final

11 I ask, then, has God rejected his people? By no means! I myself am an Israelite, a descendant of Abraham, a member of the tribe of Benjamin. 2God has not rejected his people whom he foreknew. Do you not know what the scripture says of Elijah, how he pleads with God against Israel? 3"Lord, they have killed your prophets, they have demolished your altars; I alone am left, and they are seeking my life." 4But what is the divine reply to him? "I have kept for myself seven thousand who have not bowed the knee to Baal." 5So too at the present time there is a remnant, chosen by grace. 6But if it is by grace, it is no longer on the basis of works, otherwise grace would no longer be grace.*d*

7 What then? Israel failed to obtain what it was seeking. The elect obtained it, but the rest were hardened, 8as it is written,

"God gave them a sluggish spirit,
　eyes that would not see
　and ears that would not hear,
　down to this very day."

9And David says,

"Let their table become a snare and a
　trap,
　a stumbling block and a retribution
　for them;
10　let their eyes be darkened so that they
　cannot see,
　and keep their backs forever bent."

The Salvation of the Gentiles

11 So I ask, have they stumbled so as to fall? By no means! But through their stumbling*e* salvation has come to the Gentiles, so as to make Israel*f* jealous. 12Now if their stumbling*e* means riches for the world, and if

a Or *namely, that*　*b* Or *gospel*　*c* Or *about Christ*; other ancient authorities read *of God*　*d* Other ancient authorities add *But if it is by works, it is no longer on the basis of grace, otherwise work would no longer be work*　*e* Gk *transgression*　*f* Gk *them* their defeat means riches for Gentiles, how much more will their full inclusion mean!

13 Now I am speaking to you Gentiles. Inasmuch then as I am an apostle to the Gentiles, I glorify my ministry [14] in order to make my own people[a] jealous, and thus save some of them. [15] For if their rejection is the reconciliation of the world, what will their acceptance be but life from the dead! [16] If the part of the dough offered as first fruits is holy, then the whole batch is holy; and if the root is holy, then the branches also are holy.

17 But if some of the branches were broken off, and you, a wild olive shoot, were grafted in their place to share the rich root[b] of the olive tree, [18] do not boast over the branches. If you do boast, remember that it is not you that support the root, but the root that supports you. [19] You will say, "Branches were broken off so that I might be grafted in." [20] That is true. They were broken off because of their unbelief, but you stand only through faith. So do not become proud, but stand in awe. [21] For if God did not spare the natural branches, perhaps he will not spare you.[c] [22] Note then the kindness and the severity of God: severity toward those who have fallen, but God's kindness toward you, provided you continue in his kindness; otherwise you also will be cut off. [23] And even those of Israel,[d] if they do not persist in unbelief, will be grafted in, for God has the power to graft them in again. [24] For if you have been cut from what is by nature a wild olive tree and grafted, contrary to nature, into a cultivated olive tree, how much more will these natural branches be grafted back into their own olive tree.

All Israel Will Be Saved

25 So that you may not claim to be wiser than you are, brothers and sisters,[e] I want you to understand this mystery: a hardening has come upon part of Israel, until the full number of the Gentiles has come in. [26] And so all Israel will be saved; as it is written,

"Out of Zion will come the Deliverer;
    he will banish ungodliness from
        Jacob."
[27] "And this is my covenant with them,
    when I take away their sins."

[28] As regards the gospel they are enemies of God[f] for your sake; but as regards election they are beloved, for the sake of their ancestors; [29] for the gifts and the calling of God are irrevocable. [30] Just as you were once disobedient to God but have now received mercy because of their disobedience, [31] so they have now been disobedient in order that, by the mercy shown to you, they too may now[g] receive mercy. [32] For God has imprisoned all in disobedience so that he may be merciful to all.

33 O the depth of the riches and wisdom and knowledge of God! How unsearchable are his judgments and how inscrutable his ways!
[34] "For who has known the mind of the
    Lord?
    Or who has been his counselor?"
[35] "Or who has given a gift to him,
    to receive a gift in return?"
[36] For from him and through him and to him are all things. To him be the glory forever. Amen.

The New Life in Christ

12 I appeal to you therefore, brothers and sisters,[e] by the mercies of God, to present your bodies as a living sacrifice, holy and acceptable to God, which is your spiritual[b] worship. [2] Do not be conformed to this world,[i] but be transformed by the renewing of your minds, so that you may discern what is the will of God—what is good and acceptable and perfect.[j]

3 For by the grace given to me I say to everyone among you not to think of yourself more highly than you ought to think, but to

think with sober judgment, each according to the measure of faith that God has assigned. [4]For as in one body we have many members, and not all the members have the same function, [5]so we, who are many, are one body in Christ, and individually we are members one of another. [6]We have gifts that differ according to the grace given to us: prophecy, in proportion to faith; [7]ministry, in ministering; the teacher, in teaching; [8]the exhorter, in exhortation; the giver, in generosity; the leader, in diligence; the compassionate, in cheerfulness.

Marks of the True Christian

9 Let love be genuine; hate what is evil, hold fast to what is good; [10]love one another with mutual affection; outdo one another in showing honor. [11]Do not lag in zeal, be ardent in spirit, serve the Lord.[a] [12]Rejoice in hope, be patient in suffering, persevere in prayer. [13]Contribute to the needs of the saints; extend hospitality to strangers.

14 Bless those who persecute you; bless and do not curse them. [15]Rejoice with those who rejoice, weep with those who weep. [16]Live in harmony with one another; do not be haughty, but associate with the lowly;[b] do not claim to be wiser than you are. [17]Do not repay anyone evil for evil, but take thought for what is noble in the sight of all. [18]If it is possible, so far as it depends on you, live peaceably with all. [19]Beloved, never avenge yourselves, but leave room for the wrath of God;[c] for it is written, "Vengeance is mine, I will repay, says the Lord." [20]No, "if your enemies are hungry, feed them; if they are thirsty, give them something to drink; for by doing this you will heap burning coals on their heads." [21]Do not be overcome by evil, but overcome evil with good.

Being Subject to Authorities

13 Let every person be subject to the governing authorities; for there is no authority except from God, and those authorities that exist have been instituted by God. [2]Therefore whoever resists authority resists what God has appointed, and those who resist will incur judgment. [3]For rulers are not a terror to good conduct, but to bad. Do you wish to have no fear of the authority? Then do what is good, and you will receive its approval; [4]for it is God's servant for your good. But if you do what is wrong, you should be afraid, for the authority[d] does not bear the sword in vain! It is the servant of God to execute wrath on the wrongdoer. [5]Therefore one must be subject, not only because of wrath but also because of conscience. [6]For the same reason you also pay taxes, for the authorities are God's servants, busy with this very thing. [7]Pay to all what is due them—taxes to whom taxes are due, revenue to whom revenue is due, respect to whom respect is due, honor to whom honor is due.

Love for One Another

8 Owe no one anything, except to love one another; for the one who loves another has fulfilled the law. [9]The commandments, "You shall not commit adultery; You shall not murder; You shall not steal; You shall not covet"; and any other commandment, are summed up in this word, "Love your neighbor as yourself." [10]Love does no wrong to a neighbor; therefore, love is the fulfilling of the law.

An Urgent Appeal

11 Besides this, you know what time it is, how it is now the moment for you to wake from sleep. For salvation is nearer to us now than when we became believers; [12]the night is far gone, the day is near. Let us then lay aside the works of darkness and put on the armor of light; [13]let us live honorably as in the day, not in reveling and drunkenness, not in debauchery and licentiousness, not in quarreling and jealousy. [14]Instead, put on the Lord Jesus Christ, and make no provision for the flesh, to gratify its desires.

a Other ancient authorities read *serve the opportune time*   *b* Or *give yourselves to humble tasks*   *c* Gk *the wrath*
d Gk *it*

Do Not Judge Another

14 Welcome those who are weak in faith,*a* but not for the purpose of quarreling over opinions. 2Some believe in eating anything, while the weak eat only vegetables. 3Those who eat must not despise those who abstain, and those who abstain must not pass judgment on those who eat; for God has welcomed them. 4Who are you to pass judgment on servants of another? It is before their own lord that they stand or fall. And they will be upheld, for the Lord*b* is able to make them stand.

5 Some judge one day to be better than another, while others judge all days to be alike. Let all be fully convinced in their own minds. 6Those who observe the day, observe it in honor of the Lord. Also those who eat, eat in honor of the Lord, since they give thanks to God; while those who abstain, abstain in honor of the Lord and give thanks to God.

7 We do not live to ourselves, and we do not die to ourselves. 8If we live, we live to the Lord, and if we die, we die to the Lord; so then, whether we live or whether we die, we are the Lord's. 9For to this end Christ died and lived again, so that he might be Lord of both the dead and the living.

10 Why do you pass judgment on your brother or sister?*c* Or you, why do you despise your brother or sister?*c* For we will all stand before the judgment seat of God.*d* 11For it is written,

"As I live, says the Lord, every knee
        shall bow to me,
    and every tongue shall give praise to*e*
        God."

12So then, each of us will be accountable to God.*f*

Do Not Make Another Stumble

13 Let us therefore no longer pass judgment on one another, but resolve instead never to put a stumbling block or hindrance in the way of another.*g* 14I know and am persuaded in the Lord Jesus that nothing is unclean in itself; but it is unclean for anyone who thinks it unclean. 15If your brother or sister*c* is being injured by what you eat, you are no longer walking in love. Do not let what you eat cause the ruin of one for whom Christ died. 16So do not let your good be spoken of as evil. 17For the kingdom of God is not food and drink but righteousness and peace and joy in the Holy Spirit. 18The one who thus serves Christ is acceptable to God and has human approval. 19Let us then pursue what makes for peace and for mutual upbuilding. 20Do not, for the sake of food, destroy the work of God. Everything is indeed clean, but it is wrong for you to make others fall by what you eat; 21it is good not to eat meat or drink wine or do anything that makes your brother or sister*c* stumble. *h* 22The faith that you have, have as your own conviction before God. Blessed are those who have no reason to condemn themselves because of what they approve. 23But those who have doubts are condemned if they eat, because they do not act from faith;*i* for whatever does not proceed from faith*i* is sin.*j*

Please Others, Not Yourselves

15 We who are strong ought to put up with the failings of the weak, and not to please ourselves. 2Each of us must please our neighbor for the good purpose of building up the neighbor. 3For Christ did not please himself; but, as it is written, "The insults of those who insult you have fallen on me." 4For whatever was written in former days was written for our instruction, so that by steadfastness and by the encouragement of the scriptures we might have hope. 5May the God of steadfastness and encouragement grant you to live in harmony with one another, in accordance with Christ Jesus, 6so that together you may with one voice glori-

a Or *conviction*   *b* Other ancient authorities read *for God or Christ*   *c* Gk *brother*   *d* Other ancient authorities read *of Christ*   *e* Or *confess*   *f* Other ancient authorities lack *to God*   *g* Gk *of a brother*   *h* Other ancient authorities add *or be upset or be weakened*   *i* Or *conviction*   *j* Other authorities, some ancient, add here 16.25-27

fy the God and Father of our Lord Jesus
Christ.

The Gospel for Jews and Gentiles Alike

7 Welcome one another, therefore, just
as Christ has welcomed you, for the glory of
God. [8]For I tell you that Christ has become
a servant of the circumcised on behalf of the
truth of God in order that he might confirm
the promises given to the patriarchs, [9]and in
order that the Gentiles might glorify God
for his mercy. As it is written,

"Therefore I will confess[a] you among
the Gentiles,
and sing praises to your name";
[10]and again he says,

"Rejoice, O Gentiles, with his people";
[11]and again,

"Praise the Lord, all you Gentiles,
and let all the peoples praise him";
[12]and again Isaiah says,

"The root of Jesse shall come,
the one who rises to rule the
Gentiles;
in him the Gentiles shall hope."
[13]May the God of hope fill you with all joy and
peace in believing, so that you may abound in
hope by the power of the Holy Spirit.

Paul's Reason for Writing So Boldly

14 I myself feel confident about you, my
brothers and sisters,[b] that you yourselves are
full of goodness, filled with all knowledge,
and able to instruct one another. [15]Never-
theless on some points I have written to you
rather boldly by way of reminder, because of
the grace given me by God [16]to be a minister of Christ Jesus to the Gentiles in the
priestly service of the gospel of God, so
that the offering of the Gentiles may be acceptable, sanctified by the Holy Spirit. [17]In
Christ Jesus, then, I have reason to boast of
my work for God. [18]For I will not venture to
speak of anything except what Christ has
accomplished[c] through me to win obedience

from the Gentiles, by word and deed, [19]by the
power of signs and wonders, by the power of
the Spirit of God,[d] so that from Jerusalem
and as far around as Illyricum I have fully
proclaimed the good news[e] of Christ. [20]Thus
I make it my ambition to proclaim the good
news,[e] not where Christ has already been
named, so that I do not build on someone
else's foundation, [21]but as it is written,

"Those who have never been told of
him shall see,
and those who have never heard of
him shall understand."

Paul's Plan to Visit Rome

22 This is the reason that I have so often
been hindered from coming to you. [23]But
now, with no further place for me in these regions, I desire, as I have for many years, to
come to you [24]when I go to Spain. For I do
hope to see you on my journey and to be sent
on by you, once I have enjoyed your company for a little while. [25]At present, however, I
am going to Jerusalem in a ministry to the
saints; [26]for Macedonia and Achaia have been
pleased to share their resources with the poor
among the saints at Jerusalem. [27]They were
pleased to do this, and indeed they owe it to
them; for if the Gentiles have come to share
in their spiritual blessings, they ought also to
be of service to them in material things. [28]So,
when I have completed this, and have delivered to them what has been collected,[f] I will
set out by way of you to Spain; [29]and I know
that when I come to you, I will come in the
fullness of the blessing[g] of Christ.

30 I appeal to you, brothers and sisters,[b] by
our Lord Jesus Christ and by the love of the
Spirit, to join me in earnest prayer to God on
my behalf, [31]that I may be rescued from the
unbelievers in Judea, and that my ministry[h] to
Jerusalem may be acceptable to the saints,
[32]so that by God's will I may come to you with
joy and be refreshed in your company. [33]The
God of peace be with all of you.[i] Amen.

a Or thank   b Gk brothers   c Gk speak of those things that Christ has not accomplished   d Other ancient authorities
read of the Spirit or of the Holy Spirit   e Or gospel   f Gk have sealed to them this fruit   g Other ancient authorities
add of the gospel   h Other ancient authorities read my bringing of a gift   i One ancient authority adds 16.25-27 here

Personal Greetings

16 I commend to you our sister Phoebe, a deacon[a] of the church at Cenchreae, [2]so that you may welcome her in the Lord as is fitting for the saints, and help her in whatever she may require from you, for she has been a benefactor of many and of myself as well.

3 Greet Prisca and Aquila, who work with me in Christ Jesus, [4]and who risked their necks for my life, to whom not only I give thanks, but also all the churches of the Gentiles. [5]Greet also the church in their house. Greet my beloved Epaenetus, who was the first convert[b] in Asia for Christ. [6]Greet Mary, who has worked very hard among you. [7]Greet Andronicus and Junia,[c] my relatives[d] who were in prison with me; they are prominent among the apostles, and they were in Christ before I was. [8]Greet Ampliatus, my beloved in the Lord. [9]Greet Urbanus, our co-worker in Christ, and my beloved Stachys. [10]Greet Apelles, who is approved in Christ. Greet those who belong to the family of Aristobulus. [11]Greet my relative[e] Herodion. Greet those in the Lord who belong to the family of Narcissus. [12]Greet those workers in the Lord, Tryphaena and Tryphosa. Greet the beloved Persis, who has worked hard in the Lord. [13]Greet Rufus, chosen in the Lord; and greet his mother—a mother to me also. [14]Greet Asyncritus, Phlegon, Hermes, Patrobas, Hermas, and the brothers and sisters[f] who are with them. [15]Greet Philologus, Julia, Nereus and his sister, and Olympas, and all the saints who are with them. [16]Greet one another with a holy kiss. All the churches of Christ greet you.

Final Instructions

17 I urge you, brothers and sisters,[f] to keep an eye on those who cause dissensions and offenses, in opposition to the teaching that you have learned; avoid them. [18]For such people do not serve our Lord Christ, but their own appetites,[g] and by smooth talk and flattery they deceive the hearts of the simpleminded. [19]For while your obedience is known to all, so that I rejoice over you, I want you to be wise in what is good and guileless in what is evil. [20]The God of peace will shortly crush Satan under your feet. The grace of our Lord Jesus Christ be with you.[e]

21 Timothy, my co-worker, greets you; so do Lucius and Jason and Sosipater, my relatives.[b]

22 I Tertius, the writer of this letter, greet you in the Lord.[i]

23 Gaius, who is host to me and to the whole church, greets you. Erastus, the city treasurer, and our brother Quartus, greet you.[j]

Final Doxology

25 Now to God[k] who is able to strengthen you according to my gospel and the proclamation of Jesus Christ, according to the revelation of the mystery that was kept secret for long ages [26]but is now disclosed, and through the prophetic writings is made known to all the Gentiles, according to the command of the eternal God, to bring about the obedience of faith— [27]to the only wise God, through Jesus Christ, to whom[l] be the glory forever! Amen.[m]

---

a Or *minister*   b Gk *first fruits*   c Or *Junias*; other ancient authorities read *Julia*   d Or *compatriots*   e Or *compatriot*   f Gk *brothers*   g Gk *their own belly*   h Other ancient authorities lack this sentence   i Or *I Tertius, writing this letter in the Lord, greet you*   j Other ancient authorities add verse 24, *The grace of our Lord Jesus Christ be with all of you. Amen.*   k Gk *the one*   l Other ancient authorities lack *to whom*. The verse then reads, *to the only wise God be the glory through Jesus Christ forever. Amen.*   m Other ancient authorities lack 16.25-27 or include it after 14.23 or 15.33; others put verse 24 after verse 27

THE FIRST LETTER OF PAUL TO THE
CORINTHIANS

Salutation

1 Paul, called to be an apostle of Christ Jesus by the will of God, and our brother Sosthenes,

2 To the church of God that is in Corinth, to those who are sanctified in Christ Jesus, called to be saints, together with all those who in every place call on the name of our Lord Jesus Christ, both their Lord*a* and ours:

3 Grace to you and peace from God our Father and the Lord Jesus Christ.

4 I give thanks to my*b* God always for you because of the grace of God that has been given you in Christ Jesus, 5for in every way you have been enriched in him, in speech and knowledge of every kind— 6just as the testimony of*c* Christ has been strengthened among you— 7so that you are not lacking in any spiritual gift as you wait for the revealing of our Lord Jesus Christ. 8He will also strengthen you to the end, so that you may be blameless on the day of our Lord Jesus Christ. 9God is faithful; by him you were called into the fellowship of his Son, Jesus Christ our Lord.

Divisions in the Church

10 Now I appeal to you, brothers and sisters,*d* by the name of our Lord Jesus Christ, that all of you be in agreement and that there be no divisions among you, but that you be united in the same mind and the same purpose. 11For it has been reported to me by Chloe's people that there are quarrels among you, my brothers and sisters.*e* 12What I mean is that each of you says, "I belong to Paul," or "I belong to Apollos," or "I belong to Cephas," or "I belong to Christ." 13Has Christ been divided? Was Paul crucified for you? Or were you baptized in the name of Paul? 14I thank God*f* that I baptized none of you except Crispus and Gaius, 15so that no one can say that you were baptized in my name. 16(I

did baptize also the household of Stephanas; beyond that, I do not know whether I baptized anyone else.) 17For Christ did not send me to baptize but to proclaim the gospel, and not with eloquent wisdom, so that the cross of Christ might not be emptied of its power.

Christ the Power and Wisdom of God

18 For the message about the cross is foolishness to those who are perishing, but to us who are being saved it is the power of God. 19For it is written,

"I will destroy the wisdom of the wise,
and the discernment of the
discerning I will thwart."

20Where is the one who is wise? Where is the scribe? Where is the debater of this age? Has not God made foolish the wisdom of the world? 21For since, in the wisdom of God, the world did not know God through wisdom, God decided, through the foolishness of our proclamation, to save those who believe. 22For Jews demand signs and Greeks desire wisdom, 23but we proclaim Christ crucified, a stumbling block to Jews and foolishness to Gentiles, 24but to those who are the called, both Jews and Greeks, Christ the power of God and the wisdom of God. 25For God's foolishness is wiser than human wisdom, and God's weakness is stronger than human strength.

26 Consider your own call, brothers and sisters:*d* not many of you were wise by human standards,*g* not many were powerful, not many were of noble birth. 27But God chose what is foolish in the world to shame the wise; God chose what is weak in the world to shame the strong; 28God chose what is low and despised in the world, things that are not, to reduce to nothing things that are, 29so that no one*h* might boast in the presence of God. 30He is the source of your life in Christ Jesus, who became for us wisdom from God, and righteousness and sanctification and re-

---

a Gk *theirs*   *b* Other ancient authorities lack *my*   *c* Or *to*   *d* Gk *brothers*   *e* Gk *my brothers*   *f* Other ancient authorities read *I am thankful*   *g* Gk *according to the flesh*   *h* Gk *no flesh* demption, 31in order that, as it is written, "Let the one who boasts, boast in[a] the Lord."

Proclaiming Christ Crucified

2 When I came to you, brothers and sisters,[b] I did not come proclaiming the mystery[c] of God to you in lofty words or wisdom. 2For I decided to know nothing among you except Jesus Christ, and him crucified. 3And I came to you in weakness and in fear and in much trembling. 4My speech and my proclamation were not with plausible words of wisdom,[d] but with a demonstration of the Spirit and of power, 5so that your faith might rest not on human wisdom but on the power of God.

The True Wisdom of God

6 Yet among the mature we do speak wisdom, though it is not a wisdom of this age or of the rulers of this age, who are doomed to perish. 7But we speak God's wisdom, secret and hidden, which God decreed before the ages for our glory. 8None of the rulers of this age understood this; for if they had, they would not have crucified the Lord of glory. 9But, as it is written,

"What no eye has seen, nor ear heard,
nor the human heart conceived,
what God has prepared for those who
love him"—

10these things God has revealed to us through the Spirit; for the Spirit searches everything, even the depths of God. 11For what human being knows what is truly human except the human spirit that is within? So also no one comprehends what is truly God's except the Spirit of God. 12Now we have received not the spirit of the world, but the Spirit that is from God, so that we may understand the gifts bestowed on us by God. 13And we speak of these things in words not taught by human wisdom but taught by the Spirit, interpreting spiritual things to those who are spiritual.[e]

14 Those who are unspiritual[f] do not re-

ceive the gifts of God's Spirit, for they are foolishness to them, and they are unable to understand them because they are spiritually discerned. 15Those who are spiritual discern all things, and they are themselves subject to no one else's scrutiny.

16 "For who has known the mind of the
Lord
so as to instruct him?"

But we have the mind of Christ.

On Divisions in the Corinthian Church

3 And so, brothers and sisters,[b] I could not speak to you as spiritual people, but rather as people of the flesh, as infants in Christ. 2I fed you with milk, not solid food, for you were not ready for solid food. Even now you are still not ready, 3for you are still of the flesh. For as long as there is jealousy and quarreling among you, are you not of the flesh, and behaving according to human inclinations? 4For when one says, "I belong to Paul," and another, "I belong to Apollos," are you not merely human?

5 What then is Apollos? What is Paul? Servants through whom you came to believe, as the Lord assigned to each. 6I planted, Apollos watered, but God gave the growth. 7So neither the one who plants nor the one who waters is anything, but only God who gives the growth. 8The one who plants and the one who waters have a common purpose, and each will receive wages according to the labor of each. 9For we are God's servants, working together; you are God's field, God's building.

10 According to the grace of God given to me, like a skilled master builder I laid a foundation, and someone else is building on it. Each builder must choose with care how to build on it. 11For no one can lay any foundation other than the one that has been laid; that foundation is Jesus Christ. 12Now if anyone builds on the foundation with gold, silver, precious stones, wood, hay, straw— 13the

---

a Or *of*   *b* Gk *brothers*   *c* Other ancient authorities read *testimony*   *d* Other ancient authorities read *the persuasiveness of wisdom*   *e* Or *interpreting spiritual things in spiritual language*, or *comparing spiritual things with spiritual*   *f* Or *natural* work of each builder will become visible, for the Day will disclose it, because it will be revealed with fire, and the fire will test what sort of work each has done. [14]If what has been built on the foundation survives, the builder will receive a reward. [15]If the work is burned up, the builder will suffer loss; the builder will be saved, but only as through fire.

16 Do you not know that you are God's temple and that God's Spirit dwells in you?[a] [17]If anyone destroys God's temple, God will destroy that person. For God's temple is holy, and you are that temple.

18 Do not deceive yourselves. If you think that you are wise in this age, you should become fools so that you may become wise. [19]For the wisdom of this world is foolishness with God. For it is written,

"He catches the wise in their
        craftiness,"

[20]and again,

"The Lord knows the thoughts of the
        wise,
    that they are futile."

[21]So let no one boast about human leaders. For all things are yours, [22]whether Paul or Apollos or Cephas or the world or life or death or the present or the future—all belong to you, [23]and you belong to Christ, and Christ belongs to God.

The Ministry of the Apostles

4 Think of us in this way, as servants of Christ and stewards of God's mysteries. [2]Moreover, it is required of stewards that they be found trustworthy. [3]But with me it is a very small thing that I should be judged by you or by any human court. I do not even judge myself. [4]I am not aware of anything against myself, but I am not thereby acquitted. It is the Lord who judges me. [5]Therefore do not pronounce judgment before the time, before the Lord comes, who will bring to light the things now hidden in darkness and will disclose the purposes of the heart. Then

each one will receive commendation from God.

6 I have applied all this to Apollos and myself for your benefit, brothers and sisters,[b] so that you may learn through us the meaning of the saying, "Nothing beyond what is written," so that none of you will be puffed up in favor of one against another. [7]For who sees anything different in you?[c] What do you have that you did not receive? And if you received it, why do you boast as if it were not a gift?

8 Already you have all you want! Already you have become rich! Quite apart from us you have become kings! Indeed, I wish that you had become kings, so that we might be kings with you! [9]For I think that God has exhibited us apostles as last of all, as though sentenced to death, because we have become a spectacle to the world, to angels and to mortals. [10]We are fools for the sake of Christ, but you are wise in Christ. We are weak, but you are strong. You are held in honor, but we in disrepute. [11]To the present hour we are hungry and thirsty, we are poorly clothed and beaten and homeless, [12]and we grow weary from the work of our own hands. When reviled, we bless; when persecuted, we endure; [13]when slandered, we speak kindly. We have become like the rubbish of the world, the dregs of all things, to this very day.

Fatherly Admonition

14 I am not writing this to make you ashamed, but to admonish you as my beloved children. [15]For though you might have ten thousand guardians in Christ, you do not have many fathers. Indeed, in Christ Jesus I became your father through the gospel. [16]I appeal to you, then, be imitators of me. [17]For this reason I sent[d] you Timothy, who is my beloved and faithful child in the Lord, to remind you of my ways in Christ Jesus, as I teach them everywhere in every church. [18]But some of you, thinking that I am not coming to you, have become arrogant. [19]But I will

---

a In verses 16 and 17 the Greek word for *you* is plural   *b* Gk *brothers*   *c* Or *Who makes you different from another?*
d Or *am sending*

come to you soon, if the Lord wills, and I will find out not the talk of these arrogant people but their power. 20For the kingdom of God depends not on talk but on power. 21What would you prefer? Am I to come to you with a stick, or with love in a spirit of gentleness?

Sexual Immorality Defiles the Church

5 It is actually reported that there is sexual immorality among you, and of a kind that is not found even among pagans; for a man is living with his father's wife. 2And you are arrogant! Should you not rather have mourned, so that he who has done this would have been removed from among you?

3 For though absent in body, I am present in spirit; and as if present I have already pronounced judgment 4in the name of the Lord Jesus on the man who has done such a thing.*a* When you are assembled, and my spirit is present with the power of our Lord Jesus, 5you are to hand this man over to Satan for the destruction of the flesh, so that his spirit may be saved in the day of the Lord.*b*

6 Your boasting is not a good thing. Do you not know that a little yeast leavens the whole batch of dough? 7Clean out the old yeast so that you may be a new batch, as you really are unleavened. For our paschal lamb, Christ, has been sacrificed. 8Therefore, let us celebrate the festival, not with the old yeast, the yeast of malice and evil, but with the unleavened bread of sincerity and truth.

Sexual Immorality Must Be Judged

9 I wrote to you in my letter not to associate with sexually immoral persons— 10not at all meaning the immoral of this world, or the greedy and robbers, or idolaters, since you would then need to go out of the world. 11But now I am writing to you not to associate with anyone who bears the name of brother or sister*c* who is sexually immoral or greedy, or is an idolater, reviler, drunkard, or robber. Do not even eat with such a one.

12For what have I to do with judging those outside? Is it not those who are inside that you are to judge? 13God will judge those outside. "Drive out the wicked person from among you."

Lawsuits among Believers

6 When any of you has a grievance against another, do you dare to take it to court before the unrighteous, instead of taking it before the saints? 2Do you not know that the saints will judge the world? And if the world is to be judged by you, are you incompetent to try trivial cases? 3Do you not know that we are to judge angels—to say nothing of ordinary matters? 4If you have ordinary cases, then, do you appoint as judges those who have no standing in the church? 5I say this to your shame. Can it be that there is no one among you wise enough to decide between one believer*c* and another, 6but a believer*c* goes to court against a believer*c*—and before unbelievers at that?

7 In fact, to have lawsuits at all with one another is already a defeat for you. Why not rather be wronged? Why not rather be defrauded? 8But you yourselves wrong and defraud—and believers*d* at that.

9 Do you not know that wrongdoers will not inherit the kingdom of God? Do not be deceived! Fornicators, idolaters, adulterers, male prostitutes, sodomites, 10thieves, the greedy, drunkards, revilers, robbers—none of these will inherit the kingdom of God. 11And this is what some of you used to be. But you were washed, you were sanctified, you were justified in the name of the Lord Jesus Christ and in the Spirit of our God.

Glorify God in Body and Spirit

12 "All things are lawful for me," but not all things are beneficial. "All things are lawful for me," but I will not be dominated by anything. 13"Food is meant for the stomach and the stomach for food,"*e* and God will destroy both one and the other. The body is

---

a Or *on the man who has done such a thing in the name of the Lord Jesus*   *b* Other ancient authorities add *Jesus*   *c* Gk *brother*   *d* Gk *brothers*   *e* The quotation may extend to the word *other* meant not for fornication but for the Lord, and the Lord for the body. 14And God raised the Lord and will also raise us by his power. 15Do you not know that your bodies are members of Christ? Should I therefore take the members of Christ and make them members of a prostitute? Never! 16Do you not know that whoever is united to a prostitute becomes one body with her? For it is said, "The two shall be one flesh." 17But anyone united to the Lord becomes one spirit with him. 18Shun fornication! Every sin that a person commits is outside the body; but the fornicator sins against the body itself. 19Or do you not know that your body is a temple*a* of the Holy Spirit within you, which you have from God, and that you are not your own? 20For you were bought with a price; therefore glorify God in your body.

Directions concerning Marriage

7 Now concerning the matters about which you wrote: "It is well for a man not to touch a woman." 2But because of cases of sexual immorality, each man should have his own wife and each woman her own husband. 3The husband should give to his wife her conjugal rights, and likewise the wife to her husband. 4For the wife does not have authority over her own body, but the husband does; likewise the husband does not have authority over his own body, but the wife does. 5Do not deprive one another except perhaps by agreement for a set time, to devote yourselves to prayer, and then come together again, so that Satan may not tempt you because of your lack of self-control. 6This I say by way of concession, not of command. 7I wish that all were as I myself am. But each has a particular gift from God, one having one kind and another a different kind.

8 To the unmarried and the widows I say that it is well for them to remain unmarried as I am. 9But if they are not practicing self-control, they should marry. For it is better to marry than to be aflame with passion.

10 To the married I give this command—not I but the Lord—that the wife should not separate from her husband 11(but if she does separate, let her remain unmarried or else be reconciled to her husband), and that the husband should not divorce his wife.

12 To the rest I say—I and not the Lord—that if any believer*b* has a wife who is an unbeliever, and she consents to live with him, he should not divorce her. 13And if any woman has a husband who is an unbeliever, and he consents to live with her, she should not divorce him. 14For the unbelieving husband is made holy through his wife, and the unbelieving wife is made holy through her husband. Otherwise, your children would be unclean, but as it is, they are holy. 15But if the unbelieving partner separates, let it be so; in such a case the brother or sister is not bound. It is to peace that God has called you.*c* 16Wife, for all you know, you might save your husband. Husband, for all you know, you might save your wife.

The Life That the Lord Has Assigned

17 However that may be, let each of you lead the life that the Lord has assigned, to which God called you. This is my rule in all the churches. 18Was anyone at the time of his call already circumcised? Let him not seek to remove the marks of circumcision. Was anyone at the time of his call uncircumcised? Let him not seek circumcision. 19Circumcision is nothing, and uncircumcision is nothing; but obeying the commandments of God is everything. 20Let each of you remain in the condition in which you were called.

21 Were you a slave when called? Do not be concerned about it. Even if you can gain your freedom, make use of your present condition now more than ever.*d* 22For whoever was called in the Lord as a slave is a freed person belonging to the Lord, just as whoever was free when called is a slave of Christ. 23You were bought with a price; do not become slaves of human masters. 24In whatever

---

a Or *sanctuary*   *b* Gk *brother*   *c* Other ancient authorities read *us*   *d* Or *avail yourself of the opportunity* condition you were called, brothers and sisters,*a* there remain with God.

The Unmarried and the Widows

25 Now concerning virgins, I have no command of the Lord, but I give my opinion as one who by the Lord's mercy is trustworthy. [26]I think that, in view of the impending*b* crisis, it is well for you to remain as you are. [27]Are you bound to a wife? Do not seek to be free. Are you free from a wife? Do not seek a wife. [28]But if you marry, you do not sin, and if a virgin marries, she does not sin. Yet those who marry will experience distress in this life,*c* and I would spare you that. [29]I mean, brothers and sisters,*a* the appointed time has grown short; from now on, let even those who have wives be as though they had none, [30]and those who mourn as though they were not mourning, and those who rejoice as though they were not rejoicing, and those who buy as though they had no possessions, [31]and those who deal with the world as though they had no dealings with it. For the present form of this world is passing away.

32 I want you to be free from anxieties. The unmarried man is anxious about the affairs of the Lord, how to please the Lord; [33]but the married man is anxious about the affairs of the world, how to please his wife, [34]and his interests are divided. And the unmarried woman and the virgin are anxious about the affairs of the Lord, so that they may be holy in body and spirit; but the married woman is anxious about the affairs of the world, how to please her husband. [35]I say this for your own benefit, not to put any restraint upon you, but to promote good order and unhindered devotion to the Lord.

36 If anyone thinks that he is not behaving properly toward his fiancée,*d* if his passions are strong, and so it has to be, let them marry as he wishes; it is no sin. Let them marry. [37]But if someone stands firm in his resolve, being under no necessity but having his own desire under control, and has determined in his own mind to keep her as his fiancée,*d* he will do well. [38]So then, he who marries his fiancée*d* does well; and he who refrains from marriage will do better.

39 A wife is bound as long as her husband lives. But if the husband dies,*e* she is free to marry anyone she wishes, only in the Lord. [40]But in my judgment she is more blessed if she remains as she is. And I think that I too have the Spirit of God.

Food Offered to Idols

8 Now concerning food sacrificed to idols: we know that "all of us possess knowledge." Knowledge puffs up, but love builds up. [2]Anyone who claims to know something does not yet have the necessary knowledge; [3]but anyone who loves God is known by him.

4 Hence, as to the eating of food offered to idols, we know that "no idol in the world really exists," and that "there is no God but one." [5]Indeed, even though there may be so-called gods in heaven or on earth—as in fact there are many gods and many lords— [6]yet for us there is one God, the Father, from whom are all things and for whom we exist, and one Lord, Jesus Christ, through whom are all things and through whom we exist.

7 It is not everyone, however, who has this knowledge. Since some have become so accustomed to idols until now, they still think of the food they eat as food offered to an idol; and their conscience, being weak, is defiled. [8]"Food will not bring us close to God."*f* We are no worse off if we do not eat, and no better off if we do. [9]But take care that this liberty of yours does not somehow become a stumbling block to the weak. [10]For if others see you, who possess knowledge, eating in the temple of an idol, might not, since their conscience is weak, be encouraged to the point of eating food sacrificed to idols? [11]So by your knowledge those weak believers for whom Christ died are destroyed.*g*

---

a Gk *brothers*   *b* Or *present*   *c* Gk *in the flesh*   *d* Gk *virgin*   *e* Gk *falls asleep*   *f* The quotation may extend to the end of the verse   *g* Gk *the weak brother . . . is destroyed*

12But when you thus sin against members of your family,*a* and wound their conscience when it is weak, you sin against Christ. 13Therefore, if food is a cause of their falling,*b* I will never eat meat, so that I may not cause one of them*c* to fall.

The Rights of an Apostle

9 Am I not free? Am I not an apostle? Have I not seen Jesus our Lord? Are you not my work in the Lord? 2If I am not an apostle to others, at least I am to you; for you are the seal of my apostleship in the Lord.

3 This is my defense to those who would examine me. 4Do we not have the right to our food and drink? 5Do we not have the right to be accompanied by a believing wife,*d* as do the other apostles and the brothers of the Lord and Cephas? 6Or is it only Barnabas and I who have no right to refrain from working for a living? 7Who at any time pays the expenses for doing military service? Who plants a vineyard and does not eat any of its fruit? Or who tends a flock and does not get any of its milk?

8 Do I say this on human authority? Does not the law also say the same? 9For it is written in the law of Moses, "You shall not muzzle an ox while it is treading out the grain." Is it for oxen that God is concerned? 10Or does he not speak entirely for our sake? It was indeed written for our sake, for whoever plows should plow in hope and whoever threshes should thresh in hope of a share in the crop. 11If we have sown spiritual good among you, is it too much if we reap your material benefits? 12If others share this rightful claim on you, do not we still more?

Nevertheless, we have not made use of this right, but we endure anything rather than put an obstacle in the way of the gospel of Christ. 13Do you not know that those who are employed in the temple service get their food from the temple, and those who serve at the altar share in what is sacrificed on the altar? 14In the same way, the Lord commanded that those who proclaim the gospel should get their living by the gospel.

15 But I have made no use of any of these rights, nor am I writing this so that they may be applied in my case. Indeed, I would rather die than that—no one will deprive me of my ground for boasting! 16If I proclaim the gospel, this gives me no ground for boasting, for an obligation is laid on me, and woe to me if I do not proclaim the gospel! 17For if I do this of my own will, I have a reward; but if not of my own will, I am entrusted with a commission. 18What then is my reward? Just this: that in my proclamation I may make the gospel free of charge, so as not to make full use of my rights in the gospel.

19 For though I am free with respect to all, I have made myself a slave to all, so that I might win more of them. 20To the Jews I became as a Jew, in order to win Jews. To those under the law I became as one under the law (though I myself am not under the law) so that I might win those under the law. 21To those outside the law I became as one outside the law (though I am not free from God's law but am under Christ's law) so that I might win those outside the law. 22To the weak I became weak, so that I might win the weak. I have become all things to all people, that I might by all means save some. 23I do it all for the sake of the gospel, so that I may share in its blessings.

24 Do you not know that in a race the runners all compete, but only one receives the prize? Run in such a way that you may win it. 25Athletes exercise self-control in all things; they do it to receive a perishable wreath, but we an imperishable one. 26So I do not run aimlessly, nor do I box as though beating the air; 27but I punish my body and enslave it, so that after proclaiming to others I myself should not be disqualified.

a Gk *against the brothers*   *b* Gk *my brother's falling*   *c* Gk *cause my brother*   *d* Gk *a sister as wife*

Warnings from Israel's History

10 I do not want you to be unaware, brothers and sisters,[a] that our ancestors were all under the cloud, and all passed through the sea, [2]and all were baptized into Moses in the cloud and in the sea, [3]and all ate the same spiritual food, [4]and all drank the same spiritual drink. For they drank from the spiritual rock that followed them, and the rock was Christ. [5]Nevertheless, God was not pleased with most of them, and they were struck down in the wilderness.

6 Now these things occurred as examples for us, so that we might not desire evil as they did. [7]Do not become idolaters as some of them did; as it is written, "The people sat down to eat and drink, and they rose up to play." [8]We must not indulge in sexual immorality as some of them did, and twenty-three thousand fell in a single day. [9]We must not put Christ[b] to the test, as some of them did, and were destroyed by serpents. [10]And do not complain as some of them did, and were destroyed by the destroyer. [11]These things happened to them to serve as an example, and they were written down to instruct us, on whom the ends of the ages have come. [12]So if you think you are standing, watch out that you do not fall. [13]No testing has overtaken you that is not common to everyone. God is faithful, and he will not let you be tested beyond your strength, but with the testing he will also provide the way out so that you may be able to endure it.

14 Therefore, my dear friends,[c] flee from the worship of idols. [15]I speak as to sensible people; judge for yourselves what I say. [16]The cup of blessing that we bless, is it not a sharing in the blood of Christ? The bread that we break, is it not a sharing in the body of Christ? [17]Because there is one bread, we who are many are one body, for we all partake of the one bread. [18]Consider the people of Israel;[d] are not those who eat the sacrifices partners in the altar? [19]What do I imply then? That food sacrificed to idols is anything, or

that an idol is anything? [20]No, I imply that what pagans sacrifice, they sacrifice to demons and not to God. I do not want you to be partners with demons. [21]You cannot drink the cup of the Lord and the cup of demons. You cannot partake of the table of the Lord and the table of demons. [22]Or are we provoking the Lord to jealousy? Are we stronger than he?

Do All to the Glory of God

23 "All things are lawful," but not all things are beneficial. "All things are lawful," but not all things build up. [24]Do not seek your own advantage, but that of the other. [25]Eat whatever is sold in the meat market without raising any question on the ground of conscience, [26]for "the earth and its fullness are the Lord's." [27]If an unbeliever invites you to a meal and you are disposed to go, eat whatever is set before you without raising any question on the ground of conscience. [28]But if someone says to you, "This has been offered in sacrifice," then do not eat it, out of consideration for the one who informed you, and for the sake of conscience— [29]I mean the other's conscience, not your own. For why should my liberty be subject to the judgment of someone else's conscience? [30]If I partake with thankfulness, why should I be denounced because of that for which I give thanks?

31 So, whether you eat or drink, or whatever you do, do everything for the glory of God. [32]Give no offense to Jews or to Greeks or to the church of God, [33]just as I try to please everyone in everything I do, not seeking my own advantage, but that of many, so **11** that they may be saved. [1]Be imitators of me, as I am of Christ.

Head Coverings

2 I commend you because you remember me in everything and maintain the traditions just as I handed them on to you. [3]But I want you to understand that Christ is the head of

a Gk *brothers*   *b* Other ancient authorities read *the Lord*   *c* Gk *my beloved*   *d* Gk *Israel according to the flesh* every man, and the husband[a] is the head of his wife,[b] and God is the head of Christ. 4Any man who prays or prophesies with something on his head disgraces his head, 5but any woman who prays or prophesies with her head unveiled disgraces her head— it is one and the same thing as having her head shaved. 6For if a woman will not veil herself, then she should cut off her hair; but if it is disgraceful for a woman to have her hair cut off or to be shaved, she should wear a veil. 7For a man ought not to have his head veiled, since he is the image and reflection[c] of God; but woman is the reflection[c] of man. 8Indeed, man was not made from woman, but woman from man. 9Neither was man created for the sake of woman, but woman for the sake of man. 10For this reason a woman ought to have a symbol of[d] authority on her head,[e] because of the angels. 11Nevertheless, in the Lord woman is not independent of man or man independent of woman. 12For just as woman came from man, so man comes through woman; but all things come from God. 13Judge for yourselves: is it proper for a woman to pray to God with her head unveiled? 14Does not nature itself teach you that if a man wears long hair, it is degrading to him, 15but if a woman has long hair, it is her glory? For her hair is given to her for a covering. 16But if anyone is disposed to be contentious—we have no such custom, nor do the churches of God.

Abuses at the Lord's Supper

17 Now in the following instructions I do not commend you, because when you come together it is not for the better but for the worse. 18For, to begin with, when you come together as a church, I hear that there are divisions among you; and to some extent I believe it. 19Indeed, there have to be factions among you, for only so will it become clear who among you are genuine. 20When you come together, it is not really to eat the Lord's supper. 21For when the time comes to eat, each of you goes ahead with your own supper, and one goes hungry and another becomes drunk. 22What! Do you not have homes to eat and drink in? Or do you show contempt for the church of God and humiliate those who have nothing? What should I say to you? Should I commend you? In this matter I do not commend you!

The Institution of the Lord's Supper

23 For I received from the Lord what I also handed on to you, that the Lord Jesus on the night when he was betrayed took a loaf of bread, 24and when he had given thanks, he broke it and said, "This is my body that is for[f] you. Do this in remembrance of me." 25In the same way he took the cup also, after supper, saying, "This cup is the new covenant in my blood. Do this, as often as you drink it, in remembrance of me." 26For as often as you eat this bread and drink the cup, you proclaim the Lord's death until he comes.

Partaking of the Supper Unworthily

27 Whoever, therefore, eats the bread or drinks the cup of the Lord in an unworthy manner will be answerable for the body and blood of the Lord. 28Examine yourselves, and only then eat of the bread and drink of the cup. 29For all who eat and drink[g] without discerning the body,[h] eat and drink judgment against themselves. 30For this reason many of you are weak and ill, and some have died.[i] 31But if we judged ourselves, we would not be judged. 32But when we are judged by the Lord, we are disciplined[j] so that we may not be condemned along with the world.

33 So then, my brothers and sisters,[k] when you come together to eat, wait for one another. 34If you are hungry, eat at home, so that when you come together, it will not be

a The same Greek word means *man* or *husband*   b Or *head of the woman*   c Or *glory*   d Gk lacks *a symbol of*
e Or *have freedom of choice regarding her head*   f Other ancient authorities read *is broken for*   g Other ancient
authorities add *in an unworthy manner,*   h Other ancient authorities read *the Lord's body*   i Gk *fallen asleep*
j Or *When we are judged, we are being disciplined by the Lord*   k Gk *brothers*

for your condemnation. About the other things I will give instructions when I come.

Spiritual Gifts

12 Now concerning spiritual gifts,*a* brothers and sisters,*b* I do not want you to be uninformed. 2You know that when you were pagans, you were enticed and led astray to idols that could not speak. 3Therefore I want you to understand that no one speaking by the Spirit of God ever says "Let Jesus be cursed!" and no one can say "Jesus is Lord" except by the Holy Spirit.

4 Now there are varieties of gifts, but the same Spirit; 5and there are varieties of services, but the same Lord; 6and there are varieties of activities, but it is the same God who activates all of them in everyone. 7To each is given the manifestation of the Spirit for the common good. 8To one is given through the Spirit the utterance of wisdom, and to another the utterance of knowledge according to the same Spirit, 9to another faith by the same Spirit, to another gifts of healing by the one Spirit, 10to another the working of miracles, to another prophecy, to another the discernment of spirits, to another various kinds of tongues, to another the interpretation of tongues. 11All these are activated by one and the same Spirit, who allots to each one individually just as the Spirit chooses.

One Body with Many Members

12 For just as the body is one and has many members, and all the members of the body, though many, are one body, so it is with Christ. 13For in the one Spirit we were all baptized into one body—Jews or Greeks, slaves or free—and we were all made to drink of one Spirit.

14 Indeed, the body does not consist of one member but of many. 15If the foot would say, "Because I am not a hand, I do not belong to the body," that would not make it any less a part of the body. 16And if the ear

would say, "Because I am not an eye, I do not belong to the body," that would not make it any less a part of the body. 17If the whole body were an eye, where would the hearing be? If the whole body were hearing, where would the sense of smell be? 18But as it is, God arranged the members in the body, each one of them, as he chose. 19If all were a single member, where would the body be? 20As it is, there are many members, yet one body. 21The eye cannot say to the hand, "I have no need of you," nor again the head to the feet, "I have no need of you." 22On the contrary, the members of the body that seem to be weaker are indispensable, 23and those members of the body that we think less honorable we clothe with greater honor, and our less respectable members are treated with greater respect; 24whereas our more respectable members do not need this. But God has so arranged the body, giving the greater honor to the inferior member, 25that there may be no dissension within the body, but the members may have the same care for one another. 26If one member suffers, all suffer together with it; if one member is honored, all rejoice together with it.

27 Now you are the body of Christ and individually members of it. 28And God has appointed in the church first apostles, second prophets, third teachers; then deeds of power, then gifts of healing, forms of assistance, forms of leadership, various kinds of tongues. 29Are all apostles? Are all prophets? Are all teachers? Do all work miracles? 30Do all possess gifts of healing? Do all speak in tongues? Do all interpret? 31But strive for the greater gifts. And I will show you a still more excellent way.

The Gift of Love

13 If I speak in the tongues of mortals and of angels, but do not have love, I am a noisy gong or a clanging cymbal. 2And if I have prophetic powers, and understand all mysteries and all knowledge, and if I have

a Or *spiritual persons*   *b* Gk *brothers*

all faith, so as to remove mountains, but do not have love, I am nothing. [3]If I give away all my possessions, and if I hand over my body so that I may boast,[a] but do not have love, I gain nothing.

4 Love is patient; love is kind; love is not envious or boastful or arrogant [5]or rude. It does not insist on its own way; it is not irritable or resentful; [6]it does not rejoice in wrongdoing, but rejoices in the truth. [7]It bears all things, believes all things, hopes all things, endures all things.

8 Love never ends. But as for prophecies, they will come to an end; as for tongues, they will cease; as for knowledge, it will come to an end. [9]For we know only in part, and we prophesy only in part; [10]but when the complete comes, the partial will come to an end. [11]When I was a child, I spoke like a child, I thought like a child, I reasoned like a child; when I became an adult, I put an end to childish ways. [12]For now we see in a mirror, dimly,[b] but then we will see face to face. Now I know only in part; then I will know fully, even as I have been fully known. [13]And now faith, hope, and love abide, these three; and the greatest of these is love.

Gifts of Prophecy and Tongues

14 Pursue love and strive for the spiritual gifts, and especially that you may prophesy. [2]For those who speak in a tongue do not speak to other people but to God; for nobody understands them, since they are speaking mysteries in the Spirit. [3]On the other hand, those who prophesy speak to other people for their upbuilding and encouragement and consolation. [4]Those who speak in a tongue build up themselves, but those who prophesy build up the church. [5]Now I would like all of you to speak in tongues, but even more to prophesy. One who prophesies is greater than one who speaks in tongues, unless someone interprets, so that the church may be built up.

6 Now, brothers and sisters,[c] if I come to you speaking in tongues, how will I benefit you unless I speak to you in some revelation or knowledge or prophecy or teaching? [7]It is the same way with lifeless instruments that produce sound, such as the flute or the harp. If they do not give distinct notes, how will anyone know what is being played? [8]And if the bugle gives an indistinct sound, who will get ready for battle? [9]So with yourselves; if in a tongue you utter speech that is not intelligible, how will anyone know what is being said? For you will be speaking into the air. [10]There are doubtless many different kinds of sounds in the world, and nothing is without sound. [11]If then I do not know the meaning of a sound, I will be a foreigner to the speaker and the speaker a foreigner to me. [12]So with yourselves; since you are eager for spiritual gifts, strive to excel in them for building up the church.

13 Therefore, one who speaks in a tongue should pray for the power to interpret. [14]For if I pray in a tongue, my spirit prays but my mind is unproductive. [15]What should I do then? I will pray with the spirit, but I will pray with the mind also; I will sing praise with the spirit, but I will sing praise with the mind also. [16]Otherwise, if you say a blessing with the spirit, how can anyone in the position of an outsider say the "Amen" to your thanksgiving, since the outsider does not know what you are saying? [17]For you may give thanks well enough, but the other person is not built up. [18]I thank God that I speak in tongues more than all of you; [19]nevertheless, in church I would rather speak five words with my mind, in order to instruct others also, than ten thousand words in a tongue.

20 Brothers and sisters,[c] do not be children in your thinking; rather, be infants in evil, but in thinking be adults. [21]In the law it is written,

> "By people of strange tongues
>   and by the lips of foreigners
> I will speak to this people;
>   yet even then they will not listen to
>   me,"

---

a Other ancient authorities read *body to be burned*   b Gk *in a riddle*   c Gk *brothers* says the Lord. 22Tongues, then, are a sign not for believers but for unbelievers, while prophecy is not for unbelievers but for believers. 23If, therefore, the whole church comes together and all speak in tongues, and outsiders or unbelievers enter, will they not say that you are out of your mind? 24But if all prophesy, an unbeliever or outsider who enters is reproved by all and called to account by all. 25After the secrets of the unbeliever's heart are disclosed, that person will bow down before God and worship him, declaring, "God is really among you."

Orderly Worship

26 What should be done then, my friends?*a* When you come together, each one has a hymn, a lesson, a revelation, a tongue, or an interpretation. Let all things be done for building up. 27If anyone speaks in a tongue, let there be only two or at most three, and each in turn; and let one interpret. 28But if there is no one to interpret, let them be silent in church and speak to themselves and to God. 29Let two or three prophets speak, and let the others weigh what is said. 30If a revelation is made to someone else sitting nearby, let the first person be silent. 31For you can all prophesy one by one, so that all may learn and all be encouraged. 32And the spirits of prophets are subject to the prophets, 33for God is a God not of disorder but of peace.

(As in all the churches of the saints, 34women should be silent in the churches. For they are not permitted to speak, but should be subordinate, as the law also says. 35If there is anything they desire to know, let them ask their husbands at home. For it is shameful for a woman to speak in church.*b* 36Or did the word of God originate with you? Or are you the only ones it has reached?)

37 Anyone who claims to be a prophet, or to have spiritual powers, must acknowledge that what I am writing to you is a command of the Lord. 38Anyone who does not recognize this is not to be recognized. 39So, my friends,*c* be eager to prophesy, and do not forbid speaking in tongues; 40but all things should be done decently and in order.

The Resurrection of Christ

15 Now I would remind you, brothers and sisters,*a* of the good news*d* that I proclaimed to you, which you in turn received, in which also you stand, 2through which also you are being saved, if you hold firmly to the message that I proclaimed to you—unless you have come to believe in vain.

3 For I handed on to you as of first importance what I in turn had received: that Christ died for our sins in accordance with the scriptures, 4and that he was buried, and that he was raised on the third day in accordance with the scriptures, 5and that he appeared to Cephas, then to the twelve. 6Then he appeared to more than five hundred brothers and sisters*a* at one time, most of whom are still alive, though some have died.*e* 7Then he appeared to James, then to all the apostles. 8Last of all, as to one untimely born, he appeared also to me. 9For I am the least of the apostles, unfit to be called an apostle, because I persecuted the church of God. 10But by the grace of God I am what I am, and his grace toward me has not been in vain. On the contrary, I worked harder than any of them—though it was not I, but the grace of God that is with me. 11Whether then it was I or they, so we proclaim and so you have come to believe.

The Resurrection of the Dead

12 Now if Christ is proclaimed as raised from the dead, how can some of you say there is no resurrection of the dead? 13If there is no resurrection of the dead, then Christ has not been raised; 14and if Christ has not been raised, then our proclamation has been in vain and your faith has been in vain. 15We are even found to be misrepresenting God, because we testified of God that he

---

a Gk *brothers*   *b* Other ancient authorities put verses 34-35 after verse 40   *c* Gk *my brothers*   *d* Or *gospel*
e Gk *fallen asleep*

raised Christ—whom he did not raise if it is true that the dead are not raised. ¹⁶For if the dead are not raised, then Christ has not been raised. ¹⁷If Christ has not been raised, your faith is futile and you are still in your sins. ¹⁸Then those also who have died*a* in Christ have perished. ¹⁹If for this life only we have hoped in Christ, we are of all people most to be pitied.

20 But in fact Christ has been raised from the dead, the first fruits of those who have died.*a* ²¹For since death came through a human being, the resurrection of the dead has also come through a human being; ²²for as all die in Adam, so all will be made alive in Christ. ²³But each in his own order: Christ the first fruits, then at his coming those who belong to Christ. ²⁴Then comes the end,*b* when he hands over the kingdom to God the Father, after he has destroyed every ruler and every authority and power. ²⁵For he must reign until he has put all his enemies under his feet. ²⁶The last enemy to be destroyed is death. ²⁷For "God*c* has put all things in subjection under his feet." But when it says, "All things are put in subjection," it is plain that this does not include the one who put all things in subjection under him. ²⁸When all things are subjected to him, then the Son himself will also be subjected to the one who put all things in subjection under him, so that God may be all in all.

29 Otherwise, what will those people do who receive baptism on behalf of the dead? If the dead are not raised at all, why are people baptized on their behalf?

30 And why are we putting ourselves in danger every hour? ³¹I die every day! That is as certain, brothers and sisters,*d* as my boasting of you—a boast that I make in Christ Jesus our Lord. ³²If with merely human hopes I fought with wild animals at Ephesus, what would I have gained by it? If the dead are not raised,

"Let us eat and drink,
for tomorrow we die."

³³Do not be deceived:

"Bad company ruins good morals."

³⁴Come to a sober and right mind, and sin no more; for some people have no knowledge of God. I say this to your shame.

The Resurrection Body

35 But someone will ask, "How are the dead raised? With what kind of body do they come?" ³⁶Fool! What you sow does not come to life unless it dies. ³⁷And as for what you sow, you do not sow the body that is to be, but a bare seed, perhaps of wheat or of some other grain. ³⁸But God gives it a body as he has chosen, and to each kind of seed its own body. ³⁹Not all flesh is alike, but there is one flesh for human beings, another for animals, another for birds, and another for fish. ⁴⁰There are both heavenly bodies and earthly bodies, but the glory of the heavenly is one thing, and that of the earthly is another. ⁴¹There is one glory of the sun, and another glory of the moon, and another glory of the stars; indeed, star differs from star in glory.

42 So it is with the resurrection of the dead. What is sown is perishable, what is raised is imperishable. ⁴³It is sown in dishonor, it is raised in glory. It is sown in weakness, it is raised in power. ⁴⁴It is sown a physical body, it is raised a spiritual body. If there is a physical body, there is also a spiritual body. ⁴⁵Thus it is written, "The first man, Adam, became a living being"; the last Adam became a life-giving spirit. ⁴⁶But it is not the spiritual that is first, but the physical, and then the spiritual. ⁴⁷The first man was from the earth, a man of dust; the second man is*e* from heaven. ⁴⁸As was the man of dust, so are those who are of the dust; and as is the man of heaven, so are those who are of heaven. ⁴⁹Just as we have borne the image of the man of dust, we will*f* also bear the image of the man of heaven.

50 What I am saying, brothers and sisters,*d* is this: flesh and blood cannot inherit

a Gk *fallen asleep*   *b* Or *Then come the rest*   *c* Gk *he*   *d* Gk *brothers*   *e* Other ancient authorities add *the Lord*
f Other ancient authorities read *let us*

the kingdom of God, nor does the perishable inherit the imperishable. [51]Listen, I will tell you a mystery! We will not all die,[a] but we will all be changed, [52]in a moment, in the twinkling of an eye, at the last trumpet. For the trumpet will sound, and the dead will be raised imperishable, and we will be changed. [53]For this perishable body must put on imperishability, and this mortal body must put on immortality. [54]When this perishable body puts on imperishability, and this mortal body puts on immortality, then the saying that is written will be fulfilled:

"Death has been swallowed up in
    victory."
[55] "Where, O death, is your victory?
    Where, O death, is your sting?"

[56]The sting of death is sin, and the power of sin is the law. [57]But thanks be to God, who gives us the victory through our Lord Jesus Christ.

[58] Therefore, my beloved,[b] be steadfast, immovable, always excelling in the work of the Lord, because you know that in the Lord your labor is not in vain.

The Collection for the Saints

16 Now concerning the collection for the saints: you should follow the directions I gave to the churches of Galatia. [2]On the first day of every week, each of you is to put aside and save whatever extra you earn, so that collections need not be taken when I come. [3]And when I arrive, I will send any whom you approve with letters to take your gift to Jerusalem. [4]If it seems advisable that I should go also, they will accompany me.

Plans for Travel

[5] I will visit you after passing through Macedonia—for I intend to pass through Macedonia— [6]and perhaps I will stay with you or even spend the winter, so that you may send me on my way, wherever I go. [7]I do not want to see you now just in passing, for I

hope to spend some time with you, if the Lord permits. [8]But I will stay in Ephesus until Pentecost, [9]for a wide door for effective work has opened to me, and there are many adversaries.

[10] If Timothy comes, see that he has nothing to fear among you, for he is doing the work of the Lord just as I am; [11]therefore let no one despise him. Send him on his way in peace, so that he may come to me; for I am expecting him with the brothers.

[12] Now concerning our brother Apollos, I strongly urged him to visit you with the other brothers, but he was not at all willing[c] to come now. He will come when he has the opportunity.

Final Messages and Greetings

[13] Keep alert, stand firm in your faith, be courageous, be strong. [14]Let all that you do be done in love.

[15] Now, brothers and sisters,[d] you know that members of the household of Stephanas were the first converts in Achaia, and they have devoted themselves to the service of the saints; [16]I urge you to put yourselves at the service of such people, and of everyone who works and toils with them. [17]I rejoice at the coming of Stephanas and Fortunatus and Achaicus, because they have made up for your absence; [18]for they refreshed my spirit as well as yours. So give recognition to such persons.

[19] The churches of Asia send greetings. Aquila and Prisca, together with the church in their house, greet you warmly in the Lord. [20]All the brothers and sisters[d] send greetings. Greet one another with a holy kiss.

[21] I, Paul, write this greeting with my own hand. [22]Let anyone be accursed who has no love for the Lord. Our Lord, come![e] [23]The grace of the Lord Jesus be with you. [24]My love be with all of you in Christ Jesus.[f]

---

a Gk *fall asleep*   b Gk *beloved brothers*   c Or *it was not at all God's will for him*   d Gk *brothers*   e Gk *Marana tha.*
These Aramaic words can also be read *Maran atha,* meaning *Our Lord has come*   f Other ancient authorities add
Amen

THE SECOND LETTER OF PAUL TO THE
CORINTHIANS

Salutation

1 Paul, an apostle of Christ Jesus by the will of God, and Timothy our brother,

To the church of God that is in Corinth, including all the saints throughout Achaia:

2 Grace to you and peace from God our Father and the Lord Jesus Christ.

Paul's Thanksgiving after Affliction

3 Blessed be the God and Father of our Lord Jesus Christ, the Father of mercies and the God of all consolation, 4who consoles us in all our affliction, so that we may be able to console those who are in any affliction with the consolation with which we ourselves are consoled by God. 5For just as the sufferings of Christ are abundant for us, so also our consolation is abundant through Christ. 6If we are being afflicted, it is for your consolation and salvation; if we are being consoled, it is for your consolation, which you experience when you patiently endure the same sufferings that we are also suffering. 7Our hope for you is unshaken; for we know that as you share in our sufferings, so also you share in our consolation.

8 We do not want you to be unaware, brothers and sisters,a of the affliction we experienced in Asia; for we were so utterly, unbearably crushed that we despaired of life itself. 9Indeed, we felt that we had received the sentence of death so that we would rely not on ourselves but on God who raises the dead. 10He who rescued us from so deadly a peril will continue to rescue us; on him we have set our hope that he will rescue us again, 11as you also join in helping us by your prayers, so that many will give thanks on ourb behalf for the blessing granted us through the prayers of many.

The Postponement of Paul's Visit

12 Indeed, this is our boast, the testimony of our conscience: we have behaved in the world with franknessc and godly sincerity, not by earthly wisdom but by the grace of God—and all the more toward you. 13For we write you nothing other than what you can read and also understand; I hope you will understand until the end— 14as you have already understood us in part—that on the day of the Lord Jesus we are your boast even as you are our boast.

15 Since I was sure of this, I wanted to come to you first, so that you might have a double favor;d 16I wanted to visit you on my way to Macedonia, and to come back to you from Macedonia and have you send me on to Judea. 17Was I vacillating when I wanted to do this? Do I make my plans according to ordinary human standards,e ready to say "Yes, yes" and "No, no" at the same time? 18As surely as God is faithful, our word to you has not been "Yes and No." 19For the Son of God, Jesus Christ, whom we proclaimed among you, Silvanus and Timothy and I, was not "Yes and No"; but in him it is always "Yes." 20For in him every one of God's promises is a "Yes." For this reason it is through him that we say the "Amen," to the glory of God. 21But it is God who establishes us with you in Christ and has anointed us, 22by putting his seal on us and giving us his Spirit in our hearts as a first installment.

23 But I call on God as witness against me: it was to spare you that I did not come again to Corinth. 24I do not mean to imply that we lord it over your faith; rather, we are workers with you for your joy, because you

2 stand firm in the faith. 1So I made up my mind not to make you another painful visit. 2For if I cause you pain, who is there to make me glad but the one whom I have pained? 3And I wrote as I did, so that when I came, I might not suffer pain from those who should have made me rejoice; for I am confident about all of you, that my joy would

be the joy of all of you. [4]For I wrote you out of much distress and anguish of heart and with many tears, not to cause you pain, but to let you know the abundant love that I have for you.

Forgiveness for the Offender

5 But if anyone has caused pain, he has caused it not to me, but to some extent—not to exaggerate it—to all of you. [6]This punishment by the majority is enough for such a person; [7]so now instead you should forgive and console him, so that he may not be overwhelmed by excessive sorrow. [8]So I urge you to reaffirm your love for him. [9]I wrote for this reason: to test you and to know whether you are obedient in everything. [10]Anyone whom you forgive, I also forgive. What I have forgiven, if I have forgiven anything, has been for your sake in the presence of Christ. [11]And we do this so that we may not be outwitted by Satan; for we are not ignorant of his designs.

Paul's Anxiety in Troas

12 When I came to Troas to proclaim the good news of Christ, a door was opened for me in the Lord; [13]but my mind could not rest because I did not find my brother Titus there. So I said farewell to them and went on to Macedonia.

14 But thanks be to God, who in Christ always leads us in triumphal procession, and through us spreads in every place the fragrance that comes from knowing him. [15]For we are the aroma of Christ to God among those who are being saved and among those who are perishing; [16]to the one a fragrance from death to death, to the other a fragrance from life to life. Who is sufficient for these things? [17]For we are not peddlers of God's word like so many;[a] but in Christ we speak as persons of sincerity, as persons sent from God and standing in his presence.

Ministers of the New Covenant

3 Are we beginning to commend ourselves again? Surely we do not need, as some do, letters of recommendation to you or from you, do we? [2]You yourselves are our letter, written on our[b] hearts, to be known and read by all; [3]and you show that you are a letter of Christ, prepared by us, written not with ink but with the Spirit of the living God, not on tablets of stone but on tablets of human hearts.

4 Such is the confidence that we have through Christ toward God. [5]Not that we are competent of ourselves to claim anything as coming from us; our competence is from God, [6]who has made us competent to be ministers of a new covenant, not of letter but of spirit; for the letter kills, but the Spirit gives life.

7 Now if the ministry of death, chiseled in letters on stone tablets,[c] came in glory so that the people of Israel could not gaze at Moses' face because of the glory of his face, a glory now set aside, [8]how much more will the ministry of the Spirit come in glory? [9]For if there was glory in the ministry of condemnation, much more does the ministry of justification abound in glory! [10]Indeed, what once had glory has lost its glory because of the greater glory; [11]for if what was set aside came through glory, much more has the permanent come in glory!

12 Since, then, we have such a hope, we act with great boldness, [13]not like Moses, who put a veil over his face to keep the people of Israel from gazing at the end of the glory that[d] was being set aside. [14]But their minds were hardened. Indeed, to this very day, when they hear the reading of the old covenant, that same veil is still there, since only in Christ is it set aside. [15]Indeed, to this very day whenever Moses is read, a veil lies over their minds; [16]but when one turns to the Lord, the veil is removed. [17]Now the Lord is the Spirit, and where the Spirit of the Lord is, there is freedom. [18]And all of us, with un-

---

a Other ancient authorities read *like the others*　　*b* Other ancient authorities read *your*　　*c* Gk *on stones*　　*d* Gk *of what* veiled faces, seeing the glory of the Lord as though reflected in a mirror, are being transformed into the same image from one degree of glory to another; for this comes from the Lord, the Spirit.

Treasure in Clay Jars

4 Therefore, since it is by God's mercy that we are engaged in this ministry, we do not lose heart. 2We have renounced the shameful things that one hides; we refuse to practice cunning or to falsify God's word; but by the open statement of the truth we commend ourselves to the conscience of everyone in the sight of God. 3And even if our gospel is veiled, it is veiled to those who are perishing. 4In their case the god of this world has blinded the minds of the unbelievers, to keep them from seeing the light of the gospel of the glory of Christ, who is the image of God. 5For we do not proclaim ourselves; we proclaim Jesus Christ as Lord and ourselves as your slaves for Jesus' sake. 6For it is the God who said, "Let light shine out of darkness," who has shone in our hearts to give the light of the knowledge of the glory of God in the face of Jesus Christ.

7 But we have this treasure in clay jars, so that it may be made clear that this extraordinary power belongs to God and does not come from us. 8We are afflicted in every way, but not crushed; perplexed, but not driven to despair; 9persecuted, but not forsaken; struck down, but not destroyed; 10always carrying in the body the death of Jesus, so that the life of Jesus may also be made visible in our bodies. 11For while we live, we are always being given up to death for Jesus' sake, so that the life of Jesus may be made visible in our mortal flesh. 12So death is at work in us, but life in you.

13 But just as we have the same spirit of faith that is in accordance with scripture—"I believed, and so I spoke"—we also believe, and so we speak, 14because we know that the one who raised the Lord Jesus will raise us also with Jesus, and will bring us with you into his presence. 15Yes, everything is for your sake, so that grace, as it extends to more and more people, may increase thanksgiving, to the glory of God.

Living by Faith

16 So we do not lose heart. Even though our outer nature is wasting away, our inner nature is being renewed day by day. 17For this slight momentary affliction is preparing us for an eternal weight of glory beyond all measure, 18because we look not at what can be seen but at what cannot be seen; for what can be seen is temporary, but what cannot be seen is eternal.

5 For we know that if the earthly tent we live in is destroyed, we have a building from God, a house not made with hands, eternal in the heavens. 2For in this tent we groan, longing to be clothed with our heavenly dwelling— 3if indeed, when we have taken it off*a* we will not be found naked. 4For while we are still in this tent, we groan under our burden, because we wish not to be unclothed but to be further clothed, so that what is mortal may be swallowed up by life. 5He who has prepared us for this very thing is God, who has given us the Spirit as a guarantee.

6 So we are always confident; even though we know that while we are at home in the body we are away from the Lord— 7for we walk by faith, not by sight. 8Yes, we do have confidence, and we would rather be away from the body and at home with the Lord. 9So whether we are at home or away, we make it our aim to please him. 10For all of us must appear before the judgment seat of Christ, so that each may receive recompense for what has been done in the body, whether good or evil.

The Ministry of Reconciliation

11 Therefore, knowing the fear of the Lord, we try to persuade others; but we our-

---

a Other ancient authorities read *put it on*

selves are well known to God, and I hope that we are also well known to your consciences. 12We are not commending ourselves to you again, but giving you an opportunity to boast about us, so that you may be able to answer those who boast in outward appearance and not in the heart. 13For if we are beside ourselves, it is for God; if we are in our right mind, it is for you. 14For the love of Christ urges us on, because we are convinced that one has died for all; therefore all have died. 15And he died for all, so that those who live might live no longer for themselves, but for him who died and was raised for them.

16 From now on, therefore, we regard no one from a human point of view;*a* even though we once knew Christ from a human point of view,*a* we know him no longer in that way. 17So if anyone is in Christ, there is a new creation: everything old has passed away; see, everything has become new! 18All this is from God, who reconciled us to himself through Christ, and has given us the ministry of reconciliation; 19that is, in Christ God was reconciling the world to himself,*b* not counting their trespasses against them, and entrusting the message of reconciliation to us. 20So we are ambassadors for Christ, since God is making his appeal through us; we entreat you on behalf of Christ, be reconciled to God. 21For our sake he made him to be sin who knew no sin, so that in him we might become the righteousness of God.

6 As we work together with him,*c* we urge you also not to accept the grace of God in vain. 2For he says,

"At an acceptable time I have listened
	to you,
	and on a day of salvation I have
		helped you."

See, now is the acceptable time; see, now is the day of salvation! 3We are putting no obstacle in anyone's way, so that no fault may be found with our ministry, 4but as servants of God we have commended ourselves in every way: through great endurance, in afflictions, hard-

ships, calamities, 5beatings, imprisonments, riots, labors, sleepless nights, hunger; 6by purity, knowledge, patience, kindness, holiness of spirit, genuine love, 7truthful speech, and the power of God; with the weapons of righteousness for the right hand and for the left; 8in honor and dishonor, in ill repute and good repute. We are treated as impostors, and yet are true; 9as unknown, and yet are well known; as dying, and see—we are alive; as punished, and yet not killed; 10as sorrowful, yet always rejoicing; as poor, yet making many rich; as having nothing, and yet possessing everything.

11 We have spoken frankly to you Corinthians; our heart is wide open to you. 12There is no restriction in our affections, but only in yours. 13In return—I speak as to children—open wide your hearts also.

The Temple of the Living God

14 Do not be mismatched with unbelievers. For what partnership is there between righteousness and lawlessness? Or what fellowship is there between light and darkness? 15What agreement does Christ have with Beliar? Or what does a believer share with an unbeliever? 16What agreement has the temple of God with idols? For we*d* are the temple of the living God; as God said,

"I will live in them and walk among
	them,
	and I will be their God,
	and they shall be my people.
17	Therefore come out from them,
	and be separate from them, says the
		Lord,
	and touch nothing unclean;
	then I will welcome you,
18	and I will be your father,
	and you shall be my sons and
		daughters,
	says the Lord Almighty."

7 Since we have these promises, beloved, let us cleanse ourselves from every defilement of body and of spirit, making holiness perfect in the fear of God.

---

a Gk *according to the flesh*   *b* Or *God was in Christ reconciling the world to himself*   *c* Gk *As we work together*   *d* Other ancient authorities read *you*

Paul's Joy at the Church's Repentance

2 Make room in your hearts[a] for us; we have wronged no one, we have corrupted no one, we have taken advantage of no one. [3]I do not say this to condemn you, for I said before that you are in our hearts, to die together and to live together. [4]I often boast about you; I have great pride in you; I am filled with consolation; I am overjoyed in all our affliction.

5 For even when we came into Macedonia, our bodies had no rest, but we were afflicted in every way—disputes without and fears within. [6]But God, who consoles the downcast, consoled us by the arrival of Titus, [7]and not only by his coming, but also by the consolation with which he was consoled about you, as he told us of your longing, your mourning, your zeal for me, so that I rejoiced still more. [8]For even if I made you sorry with my letter, I do not regret it (though I did regret it, for I see that I grieved you with that letter, though only briefly). [9]Now I rejoice, not because you were grieved, but because your grief led to repentance; for you felt a godly grief, so that you were not harmed in any way by us. [10]For godly grief produces a repentance that leads to salvation and brings no regret, but worldly grief produces death. [11]For see what earnestness this godly grief has produced in you, what eagerness to clear yourselves, what indignation, what alarm, what longing, what zeal, what punishment! At every point you have proved yourselves guiltless in the matter. [12]So although I wrote to you, it was not on account of the one who did the wrong, nor on account of the one who was wronged, but in order that your zeal for us might be made known to you before God. [13]In this we find comfort.

In addition to our own consolation, we rejoiced still more at the joy of Titus, because his mind has been set at rest by all of you. [14]For if I have been somewhat boastful about you to him, I was not disgraced; but just as everything we said to you was true, so our boasting to Titus has proved true as well. [15]And his heart goes out all the more to you, as he remembers the obedience of all of you, and how you welcomed him with fear and trembling. [16]I rejoice, because I have complete confidence in you.

Encouragement to Be Generous

8 We want you to know, brothers and sisters,[b] about the grace of God that has been granted to the churches of Macedonia; [2]for during a severe ordeal of affliction, their abundant joy and their extreme poverty have overflowed in a wealth of generosity on their part. [3]For, as I can testify, they voluntarily gave according to their means, and even beyond their means, [4]begging us earnestly for the privilege[c] of sharing in this ministry to the saints— [5]and this, not merely as we expected; they gave themselves first to the Lord and, by the will of God, to us, [6]so that we might urge Titus that, as he had already made a beginning, so he should also complete this generous undertaking[d] among you. [7]Now as you excel in everything—in faith, in speech, in knowledge, in utmost eagerness, and in our love for you[e]—so we want you to excel also in this generous undertaking.[d]

8 I do not say this as a command, but I am testing the genuineness of your love against the earnestness of others. [9]For you know the generous act[f] of our Lord Jesus Christ, that though he was rich, yet for your sakes he became poor, so that by his poverty you might become rich. [10]And in this matter I am giving my advice: it is appropriate for you who began last year not only to do something but even to desire to do something— [11]now finish doing it, so that your eagerness may be matched by completing it according to your means. [12]For if the eagerness is there, the gift is acceptable according to what one has—not according to what one does not have. [13]I do not mean that there should be relief for others and pressure on you, but it is a question of a fair balance between [14]your present

---

a Gk lacks *in your hearts*   b Gk *brothers*   c Gk *grace*   d Gk *this grace*   e Other ancient authorities read *your love for us*   f Gk *the grace* abundance and their need, so that their abundance may be for your need, in order that there may be a fair balance. [15]As it is written,

"The one who had much did not have
  too much,
and the one who had little did not
  have too little."

Commendation of Titus

16 But thanks be to God who put in the heart of Titus the same eagerness for you that I myself have. [17]For he not only accepted our appeal, but since he is more eager than ever, he is going to you of his own accord. [18]With him we are sending the brother who is famous among all the churches for his proclaiming the good news;[a] [19]and not only that, but he has also been appointed by the churches to travel with us while we are administering this generous undertaking[b] for the glory of the Lord himself[c] and to show our goodwill. [20]We intend that no one should blame us about this generous gift that we are administering, [21]for we intend to do what is right not only in the Lord's sight but also in the sight of others. [22]And with them we are sending our brother whom we have often tested and found eager in many matters, but who is now more eager than ever because of his great confidence in you. [23]As for Titus, he is my partner and co-worker in your service; as for our brothers, they are messengers[d] of the churches, the glory of Christ. [24]Therefore openly before the churches, show them the proof of your love and of our reason for boasting about you.

The Collection for Christians at Jerusalem

9 Now it is not necessary for me to write you about the ministry to the saints, [2]for I know your eagerness, which is the subject of my boasting about you to the people of Macedonia, saying that Achaia has been ready since last year; and your zeal has stirred up most of them. [3]But I am sending the brothers in order that our boasting about you may

not prove to have been empty in this case, so that you may be ready, as I said you would be; [4]otherwise, if some Macedonians come with me and find that you are not ready, we would be humiliated—to say nothing of you—in this undertaking.[e] [5]So I thought it necessary to urge the brothers to go on ahead to you, and arrange in advance for this bountiful gift that you have promised, so that it may be ready as a voluntary gift and not as an extortion.

6 The point is this: the one who sows sparingly will also reap sparingly, and the one who sows bountifully will also reap bountifully. [7]Each of you must give as you have made up your mind, not reluctantly or under compulsion, for God loves a cheerful giver. [8]And God is able to provide you with every blessing in abundance, so that by always having enough of everything, you may share abundantly in every good work. [9]As it is written,

"He scatters abroad, he gives to the
  poor;
his righteousness[f] endures forever."

[10]He who supplies seed to the sower and bread for food will supply and multiply your seed for sowing and increase the harvest of your righteousness.[f] [11]You will be enriched in every way for your great generosity, which will produce thanksgiving to God through us; [12]for the rendering of this ministry not only supplies the needs of the saints but also overflows with many thanksgivings to God. [13]Through the testing of this ministry you glorify God by your obedience to the confession of the gospel of Christ and by the generosity of your sharing with them and with all others, [14]while they long for you and pray for you because of the surpassing grace of God that he has given you. [15]Thanks be to God for his indescribable gift!

Paul Defends His Ministry

10 I myself, Paul, appeal to you by the meekness and gentleness of Christ—

---

a Or the gospel   b Gk this grace   c Other ancient authorities lack himself   d Gk apostles   e Other ancient authorities add of boasting   f Or benevolence

I who am humble when face to face with you, but bold toward you when I am away!— 2I ask that when I am present I need not show boldness by daring to oppose those who think we are acting according to human standards.*a* 3Indeed, we live as human beings,*b* but we do not wage war according to human standards;*a* 4for the weapons of our warfare are not merely human,*c* but they have divine power to destroy strongholds. We destroy arguments 5and every proud obstacle raised up against the knowledge of God, and we take every thought captive to obey Christ. 6We are ready to punish every disobedience when your obedience is complete.

7 Look at what is before your eyes. If you are confident that you belong to Christ, remind yourself of this, that just as you belong to Christ, so also do we. 8Now, even if I boast a little too much of our authority, which the Lord gave for building you up and not for tearing you down, I will not be ashamed of it. 9I do not want to seem as though I am trying to frighten you with my letters. 10For they say, "His letters are weighty and strong, but his bodily presence is weak, and his speech contemptible." 11Let such people understand that what we say by letter when absent, we will also do when present.

12 We do not dare to classify or compare ourselves with some of those who commend themselves. But when they measure themselves by one another, and compare themselves with one another, they do not show good sense. 13We, however, will not boast beyond limits, but will keep within the field that God has assigned to us, to reach out even as far as you. 14For we were not overstepping our limits when we reached you; we were the first to come all the way to you with the good news*d* of Christ. 15We do not boast beyond limits, that is, in the labors of others; but our hope is that, as your faith increases, our sphere of action among you may be greatly enlarged, 16so that we may proclaim the good news*d* in lands beyond you, without

boasting of work already done in someone else's sphere of action. 17"Let the one who boasts, boast in the Lord." 18For it is not those who commend themselves that are approved, but those whom the Lord commends.

Paul and the False Apostles

11 I wish you would bear with me in a little foolishness. Do bear with me! 2I feel a divine jealousy for you, for I promised you in marriage to one husband, to present you as a chaste virgin to Christ. 3But I am afraid that as the serpent deceived Eve by its cunning, your thoughts will be led astray from a sincere and pure*e* devotion to Christ. 4For if someone comes and proclaims another Jesus than the one we proclaimed, or if you receive a different spirit from the one you received, or a different gospel from the one you accepted, you submit to it readily enough. 5I think that I am not in the least inferior to these super-apostles. 6I may be untrained in speech, but not in knowledge; certainly in every way and in all things we have made this evident to you.

7 Did I commit a sin by humbling myself so that you might be exalted, because I proclaimed God's good news*f* to you free of charge? 8I robbed other churches by accepting support from them in order to serve you. 9And when I was with you and was in need, I did not burden anyone, for my needs were supplied by the friends*g* who came from Macedonia. So I refrained and will continue to refrain from burdening you in any way. 10As the truth of Christ is in me, this boast of mine will not be silenced in the regions of Achaia. 11And why? Because I do not love you? God knows I do!

12 And what I do I will also continue to do, in order to deny an opportunity to those who want an opportunity to be recognized as our equals in what they boast about. 13For such boasters are false apostles, deceitful workers, disguising themselves as apostles of

---

a Gk *according to the flesh*   *b* Gk *in the flesh*   *c* Gk *fleshly*   *d* Or *the gospel*   *e* Other ancient authorities lack *and pure*   *f* Gk *the gospel of God*   *g* Gk *brothers*

Christ. ¹⁴And no wonder! Even Satan disguises himself as an angel of light. ¹⁵So it is not strange if his ministers also disguise themselves as ministers of righteousness. Their end will match their deeds.

Paul's Sufferings as an Apostle

16 I repeat, let no one think that I am a fool; but if you do, then accept me as a fool, so that I too may boast a little. ¹⁷What I am saying in regard to this boastful confidence, I am saying not with the Lord's authority, but as a fool; ¹⁸since many boast according to human standards,ᵃ I will also boast. ¹⁹For you gladly put up with fools, being wise yourselves! ²⁰For you put up with it when someone makes slaves of you, or preys upon you, or takes advantage of you, or puts on airs, or gives you a slap in the face. ²¹To my shame, I must say, we were too weak for that!

But whatever anyone dares to boast of— I am speaking as a fool—I also dare to boast of that. ²²Are they Hebrews? So am I. Are they Israelites? So am I. Are they descendants of Abraham? So am I. ²³Are they ministers of Christ? I am talking like a madman—I am a better one: with far greater labors, far more imprisonments, with countless floggings, and often near death. ²⁴Five times I have received from the Jews the forty lashes minus one. ²⁵Three times I was beaten with rods. Once I received a stoning. Three times I was shipwrecked; for a night and a day I was adrift at sea; ²⁶on frequent journeys, in danger from rivers, danger from bandits, danger from my own people, danger from Gentiles, danger in the city, danger in the wilderness, danger at sea, danger from false brothers and sisters;ᵇ ²⁷in toil and hardship, through many a sleepless night, hungry and thirsty, often without food, cold and naked. ²⁸And, besides other things, I am under daily pressure because of my anxiety for all the churches. ²⁹Who is weak, and I am not weak? Who is made to stumble, and I am not indignant?

30 If I must boast, I will boast of the things that show my weakness. ³¹The God and Father of the Lord Jesus (blessed be he forever!) knows that I do not lie. ³²In Damascus, the governorᶜ under King Aretas guarded the city of Damascus in order toᵈ seize me, ³³but I was let down in a basket through a window in the wall,ᵉ and escaped from his hands.

Paul's Visions and Revelations

12 It is necessary to boast; nothing is to be gained by it, but I will go on to visions and revelations of the Lord. ²I know a person in Christ who fourteen years ago was caught up to the third heaven—whether in the body or out of the body I do not know; God knows. ³And I know that such a person—whether in the body or out of the body I do not know; God knows— ⁴was caught up into Paradise and heard things that are not to be told, that no mortal is permitted to repeat. ⁵On behalf of such a one I will boast, but on my own behalf I will not boast, except of my weaknesses. ⁶But if I wish to boast, I will not be a fool, for I will be speaking the truth. But I refrain from it, so that no one may think better of me than what is seen in me or heard from me, ⁷even considering the exceptional character of the revelations. Therefore, to keepᶠ me from being too elated, a thorn was given me in the flesh, a messenger of Satan to torment me, to keep me from being too elated.ᵍ ⁸Three times I appealed to the Lord about this, that it would leave me, ⁹but he said to me, "My grace is sufficient for you, for powerʰ is made perfect in weakness." So, I will boast all the more gladly of my weaknesses, so that the power of Christ may dwell in me. ¹⁰Therefore I am content with weaknesses, insults, hardships, persecutions, and calamities for the sake of

---

a Gk *according to the flesh*   b Gk *brothers*   c Gk *ethnarch*   d Other ancient authorities read *and wanted to*
e Gk *through the wall*   f Other ancient authorities read *To keep*   g Other ancient authorities lack *to keep me from being too elated*   h Other ancient authorities read *my power*

Christ; for whenever I am weak, then I am strong.

Paul's Concern for the Corinthian Church

11 I have been a fool! You forced me to it. Indeed you should have been the ones commending me, for I am not at all inferior to these super-apostles, even though I am nothing. 12The signs of a true apostle were performed among you with utmost patience, signs and wonders and mighty works. 13How have you been worse off than the other churches, except that I myself did not burden you? Forgive me this wrong!

14 Here I am, ready to come to you this third time. And I will not be a burden, because I do not want what is yours but you; for children ought not to lay up for their parents, but parents for their children. 15I will most gladly spend and be spent for you. If I love you more, am I to be loved less? 16Let it be assumed that I did not burden you. Nevertheless (you say) since I was crafty, I took you in by deceit. 17Did I take advantage of you through any of those whom I sent to you? 18I urged Titus to go, and sent the brother with him. Titus did not take advantage of you, did he? Did we not conduct ourselves with the same spirit? Did we not take the same steps?

19 Have you been thinking all along that we have been defending ourselves before you? We are speaking in Christ before God. Everything we do, beloved, is for the sake of building you up. 20For I fear that when I come, I may find you not as I wish, and that you may find me not as you wish; I fear that there may perhaps be quarreling, jealousy, anger, selfishness, slander, gossip, conceit, and disorder. 21I fear that when I come again, my God may humble me before you, and that I may have to mourn over many who previously sinned and have not repented of the impurity, sexual immorality, and licentiousness that they have practiced.

Further Warning

13 This is the third time I am coming to you. "Any charge must be sustained by the evidence of two or three witnesses." 2I warned those who sinned previously and all the others, and I warn them now while absent, as I did when present on my second visit, that if I come again, I will not be lenient— 3since you desire proof that Christ is speaking in me. He is not weak in dealing with you, but is powerful in you. 4For he was crucified in weakness, but lives by the power of God. For we are weak in him,*a* but in dealing with you we will live with him by the power of God.

5 Examine yourselves to see whether you are living in the faith. Test yourselves. Do you not realize that Jesus Christ is in you?— unless, indeed, you fail to meet the test! 6I hope you will find out that we have not failed. 7But we pray to God that you may not do anything wrong—not that we may appear to have met the test, but that you may do what is right, though we may seem to have failed. 8For we cannot do anything against the truth, but only for the truth. 9For we rejoice when we are weak and you are strong. This is what we pray for, that you may become perfect. 10So I write these things while I am away from you, so that when I come, I may not have to be severe in using the authority that the Lord has given me for building up and not for tearing down.

Final Greetings and Benediction

11 Finally, brothers and sisters,*b* farewell.*c* Put things in order, listen to my appeal,*d* agree with one another, live in peace; and the God of love and peace will be with you. 12Greet one another with a holy kiss. All the saints greet you.

13 The grace of the Lord Jesus Christ, the love of God, and the communion of*e* the Holy Spirit be with all of you.

a Other ancient authorities read *with him*   *b* Gk *brothers*   *c* Or *rejoice*   *d* Or *encourage one another*   *e* Or *and the sharing in*

THE LETTER OF PAUL TO THE
GALATIANS

Salutation

1 Paul an apostle—sent neither by human commission nor from human authorities, but through Jesus Christ and God the Father, who raised him from the dead— 2and all the members of God's family*a* who are with me,

To the churches of Galatia:

3 Grace to you and peace from God our Father and the Lord Jesus Christ, 4who gave himself for our sins to set us free from the present evil age, according to the will of our God and Father, 5to whom be the glory forever and ever. Amen.

There Is No Other Gospel

6 I am astonished that you are so quickly deserting the one who called you in the grace of Christ and are turning to a different gospel— 7not that there is another gospel, but there are some who are confusing you and want to pervert the gospel of Christ. 8But even if we or an angel*b* from heaven should proclaim to you a gospel contrary to what we proclaimed to you, let that one be accursed! 9As we have said before, so now I repeat, if anyone proclaims to you a gospel contrary to what you received, let that one be accursed!

10 Am I now seeking human approval, or God's approval? Or am I trying to please people? If I were still pleasing people, I would not be a servant*c* of Christ.

Paul's Vindication of His Apostleship

11 For I want you to know, brothers and sisters,*d* that the gospel that was proclaimed by me is not of human origin; 12for I did not receive it from a human source, nor was I taught it, but I received it through a revelation of Jesus Christ. 13 You have heard, no doubt, of my earlier life in Judaism. I was violently persecuting the church of God and was trying to de-

stroy it. 14I advanced in Judaism beyond many among my people of the same age, for I was far more zealous for the traditions of my ancestors. 15But when God, who had set me apart before I was born and called me through his grace, was pleased 16to reveal his Son to me,*e* so that I might proclaim him among the Gentiles, I did not confer with any human being, 17nor did I go up to Jerusalem to those who were already apostles before me, but I went away at once into Arabia, and afterwards I returned to Damascus.

18 Then after three years I did go up to Jerusalem to visit Cephas and stayed with him fifteen days; 19but I did not see any other apostle except James the Lord's brother. 20In what I am writing to you, before God, I do not lie! 21Then I went into the regions of Syria and Cilicia, 22and I was still unknown by sight to the churches of Judea that are in Christ; 23they only heard it said, "The one who formerly was persecuting us is now proclaiming the faith he once tried to destroy." 24And they glorified God because of me.

Paul and the Other Apostles

2 Then after fourteen years I went up again to Jerusalem with Barnabas, taking Titus along with me. 2I went up in response to a revelation. Then I laid before them (though only in a private meeting with the acknowledged leaders) the gospel that I proclaim among the Gentiles, in order to make sure that I was not running, or had not run, in vain. 3But even Titus, who was with me, was not compelled to be circumcised, though he was a Greek. 4But because of false believers*f* secretly brought in, who slipped in to spy on the freedom we have in Christ Jesus, so that they might enslave us— 5we did not submit to them even for a moment, so that the truth of the gospel might always remain with you. 6And from those who were supposed to be acknowledged leaders (what they

a Gk all the brothers   *b* Or a messenger   *c* Gk slave   *d* Gk brothers   *e* Gk in me   *f* Gk false brothers actually were makes no difference to me; God shows no partiality)—those leaders contributed nothing to me. 7On the contrary, when they saw that I had been entrusted with the gospel for the uncircumcised, just as Peter had been entrusted with the gospel for the circumcised 8(for he who worked through Peter making him an apostle to the circumcised also worked through me in sending me to the Gentiles), 9and when James and Cephas and John, who were acknowledged pillars, recognized the grace that had been given to me, they gave to Barnabas and me the right hand of fellowship, agreeing that we should go to the Gentiles and they to the circumcised. 10They asked only one thing, that we remember the poor, which was actually what I was*a* eager to do.

Paul Rebukes Peter at Antioch

11 But when Cephas came to Antioch, I opposed him to his face, because he stood self-condemned; 12for until certain people came from James, he used to eat with the Gentiles. But after they came, he drew back and kept himself separate for fear of the circumcision faction. 13And the other Jews joined him in this hypocrisy, so that even Barnabas was led astray by their hypocrisy. 14But when I saw that they were not acting consistently with the truth of the gospel, I said to Cephas before them all, "If you, though a Jew, live like a Gentile and not like a Jew, how can you compel the Gentiles to live like Jews?"*b*

Jews and Gentiles Are Saved by Faith

15 We ourselves are Jews by birth and not Gentile sinners; 16yet we know that a person is justified*c* not by the works of the law but through faith in Jesus Christ.*d* And we have come to believe in Christ Jesus, so that we might be justified by faith in Christ,*e* and not by doing the works of the law, because no one will be justified by the works of the law.

17But if, in our effort to be justified in Christ, we ourselves have been found to be sinners, is Christ then a servant of sin? Certainly not! 18But if I build up again the very things that I once tore down, then I demonstrate that I am a transgressor. 19For through the law I died to the law, so that I might live to God. I have been crucified with Christ; 20and it is no longer I who live, but it is Christ who lives in me. And the life I now live in the flesh I live by faith in the Son of God,*f* who loved me and gave himself for me. 21I do not nullify the grace of God; for if justification*g* comes through the law, then Christ died for nothing.

Law or Faith

3 You foolish Galatians! Who has bewitched you? It was before your eyes that Jesus Christ was publicly exhibited as crucified! 2The only thing I want to learn from you is this: Did you receive the Spirit by doing the works of the law or by believing what you heard? 3Are you so foolish? Having started with the Spirit, are you now ending with the flesh? 4Did you experience so much for nothing?—if it really was for nothing. 5Well then, does God*h* supply you with the Spirit and work miracles among you by your doing the works of the law, or by your believing what you heard?

6 Just as Abraham "believed God, and it was reckoned to him as righteousness," 7so, you see, those who believe are the descendants of Abraham. 8And the scripture, foreseeing that God would justify the Gentiles by faith, declared the gospel beforehand to Abraham, saying, "All the Gentiles shall be blessed in you." 9For this reason, those who believe are blessed with Abraham who believed.

10 For all who rely on the works of the law are under a curse; for it is written, "Cursed is everyone who does not observe and obey all the things written in the book of

---

a Or *had been*   *b* Some interpreters hold that the quotation extends into the following paragraph   *c* Or *reckoned as righteous;* and so elsewhere   *d* Or *the faith of Jesus Christ*   *e* Or *the faith of Christ*   *f* Or *by the faith of the Son of God*   *g* Or *righteousness*   *h* Gk *he* the law." 11Now it is evident that no one is justified before God by the law; for "The one who is righteous will live by faith."*a* 12But the law does not rest on faith; on the contrary, "Whoever does the works of the law*b* will live by them." 13Christ redeemed us from the curse of the law by becoming a curse for us—for it is written, "Cursed is everyone who hangs on a tree"— 14in order that in Christ Jesus the blessing of Abraham might come to the Gentiles, so that we might receive the promise of the Spirit through faith.

The Promise to Abraham

15 Brothers and sisters,*c* I give an example from daily life: once a person's will*d* has been ratified, no one adds to it or annuls it. 16Now the promises were made to Abraham and to his offspring;*e* it does not say, "And to offsprings,"*f* as of many; but it says, "And to your offspring,"*e* that is, to one person, who is Christ. 17My point is this: the law, which came four hundred thirty years later, does not annul a covenant previously ratified by God, so as to nullify the promise. 18For if the inheritance comes from the law, it no longer comes from the promise; but God granted it to Abraham through the promise.

The Purpose of the Law

19 Why then the law? It was added because of transgressions, until the offspring*e* would come to whom the promise had been made; and it was ordained through angels by a mediator. 20Now a mediator involves more than one party; but God is one.

21 Is the law then opposed to the promises of God? Certainly not! For if a law had been given that could make alive, then righteousness would indeed come through the law. 22But the scripture has imprisoned all things under the power of sin, so that what was promised through faith in Jesus Christ*g* might be given to those who believe.

23 Now before faith came, we were imprisoned and guarded under the law until faith would be revealed. 24Therefore the law was our disciplinarian until Christ came, so that we might be justified by faith. 25But now that faith has come, we are no longer subject to a disciplinarian, 26for in Christ Jesus you are all children of God through faith. 27As many of you as were baptized into Christ have clothed yourselves with Christ. 28There is no longer Jew or Greek, there is no longer slave or free, there is no longer male and female; for all of you are one in Christ Jesus. 29And if you belong to Christ, then you are Abraham's offspring,*e* heirs according to the promise.

4 My point is this: heirs, as long as they are minors, are no better than slaves, though they are the owners of all the property; 2but they remain under guardians and trustees until the date set by the father. 3So with us; while we were minors, we were enslaved to the elemental spirits*h* of the world. 4But when the fullness of time had come, God sent his Son, born of a woman, born under the law, 5in order to redeem those who were under the law, so that we might receive adoption as children. 6And because you are children, God has sent the Spirit of his Son into our*i* hearts, crying, "Abba!*j* Father!" 7So you are no longer a slave but a child, and if a child then also an heir, through God.*k*

Paul Reproves the Galatians

8 Formerly, when you did not know God, you were enslaved to beings that by nature are not gods. 9Now, however, that you have come to know God, or rather to be known by God, how can you turn back again to the weak and beggarly elemental spirits?*l* How can you want to be enslaved to them again? 10You are observing special days, and months, and seasons, and years. 11I am afraid that my work for you may have been wasted.

---

a Or *The one who is righteous through faith will live*   *b* Gk *does them*   *c* Gk *Brothers*   *d* Or *covenant* (as in verse 17)   *e* Gk *seed*   *f* Gk *seeds*   *g* Or *through the faith of Jesus Christ*   *h* Or *the rudiments*   *i* Other ancient authorities read *your*   *j* Aramaic for *Father*   *k* Other ancient authorities read *an heir of God through Christ*   *l* Or *beggarly rudiments*

12 Friends,[a] I beg you, become as I am, for I also have become as you are. You have done me no wrong. 13You know that it was because of a physical infirmity that I first announced the gospel to you; 14though my condition put you to the test, you did not scorn or despise me, but welcomed me as an angel of God, as Christ Jesus. 15What has become of the goodwill you felt? For I testify that, had it been possible, you would have torn out your eyes and given them to me. 16Have I now become your enemy by telling you the truth? 17They make much of you, but for no good purpose; they want to exclude you, so that you may make much of them. 18It is good to be made much of for a good purpose at all times, and not only when I am present with you. 19My little children, for whom I am again in the pain of childbirth until Christ is formed in you, 20I wish I were present with you now and could change my tone, for I am perplexed about you.

The Allegory of Hagar and Sarah

21 Tell me, you who desire to be subject to the law, will you not listen to the law? 22For it is written that Abraham had two sons, one by a slave woman and the other by a free woman. 23One, the child of the slave, was born according to the flesh; the other, the child of the free woman, was born through the promise. 24Now this is an allegory: these women are two covenants. One woman, in fact, is Hagar, from Mount Sinai, bearing children for slavery. 25Now Hagar is Mount Sinai in Arabia[b] and corresponds to the present Jerusalem, for she is in slavery with her children. 26But the other woman corresponds to the Jerusalem above; she is free, and she is our mother. 27For it is written,

"Rejoice, you childless one, you who
    bear no children,
    burst into song and shout, you who
        endure no birth pangs;
    for the children of the desolate woman
        are more numerous

than the children of the one who is
        married."

28Now you,[c] my friends,[d] are children of the promise, like Isaac. 29But just as at that time the child who was born according to the flesh persecuted the child who was born according to the Spirit, so it is now also. 30But what does the scripture say? "Drive out the slave and her child; for the child of the slave will not share the inheritance with the child of the free woman." 31So then, friends,[d] we are children, not of the slave but of the free

5 woman. 1For freedom Christ has set us free. Stand firm, therefore, and do not submit again to a yoke of slavery.

The Nature of Christian Freedom

2 Listen! I, Paul, am telling you that if you let yourselves be circumcised, Christ will be of no benefit to you. 3Once again I testify to every man who lets himself be circumcised that he is obliged to obey the entire law. 4You who want to be justified by the law have cut yourselves off from Christ; you have fallen away from grace. 5For through the Spirit, by faith, we eagerly wait for the hope of righteousness. 6For in Christ Jesus neither circumcision nor uncircumcision counts for anything; the only thing that counts is faith working[e] through love.

7 You were running well; who prevented you from obeying the truth? 8Such persuasion does not come from the one who calls you. 9A little yeast leavens the whole batch of dough. 10I am confident about you in the Lord that you will not think otherwise. But whoever it is that is confusing you will pay the penalty. 11But my friends,[d] why am I still being persecuted if I am still preaching circumcision? In that case the offense of the cross has been removed. 12I wish those who unsettle you would castrate themselves!

13 For you were called to freedom, brothers and sisters;[d] only do not use your freedom as an opportunity for self-indulgence,[f] but through love become slaves to one another.

---

a Gk Brothers   b Other ancient authorities read For Sinai is a mountain in Arabia   c Other ancient authorities read we   d Gk brothers   e Or made effective   f Gk the flesh

14For the whole law is summed up in a single commandment, "You shall love your neighbor as yourself." 15If, however, you bite and devour one another, take care that you are not consumed by one another.

The Works of the Flesh

16 Live by the Spirit, I say, and do not gratify the desires of the flesh. 17For what the flesh desires is opposed to the Spirit, and what the Spirit desires is opposed to the flesh; for these are opposed to each other, to prevent you from doing what you want. 18But if you are led by the Spirit, you are not subject to the law. 19Now the works of the flesh are obvious: fornication, impurity, licentiousness, 20idolatry, sorcery, enmities, strife, jealousy, anger, quarrels, dissensions, factions, 21envy,*a* drunkenness, carousing, and things like these. I am warning you, as I warned you before: those who do such things will not inherit the kingdom of God.

The Fruit of the Spirit

22 By contrast, the fruit of the Spirit is love, joy, peace, patience, kindness, generosity, faithfulness, 23gentleness, and self-control. There is no law against such things. 24And those who belong to Christ Jesus have crucified the flesh with its passions and desires. 25If we live by the Spirit, let us also be guided by the Spirit. 26Let us not become conceited, competing against one another, envying one another.

Bear One Another's Burdens

6 My friends,*b* if anyone is detected in a transgression, you who have received the Spirit should restore such a one in a spirit of gentleness. Take care that you yourselves are not tempted. 2Bear one another's burdens, and in this way you will fulfill*c* the law of Christ. 3For if those who are nothing

think they are something, they deceive themselves. 4All must test their own work; then that work, rather than their neighbor's work, will become a cause for pride. 5For all must carry their own loads.

6 Those who are taught the word must share in all good things with their teacher.

7 Do not be deceived; God is not mocked, for you reap whatever you sow. 8If you sow to your own flesh, you will reap corruption from the flesh; but if you sow to the Spirit, you will reap eternal life from the Spirit. 9So let us not grow weary in doing what is right, for we will reap at harvest time, if we do not give up. 10So then, whenever we have an opportunity, let us work for the good of all, and especially for those of the family of faith.

Final Admonitions and Benediction

11 See what large letters I make when I am writing in my own hand! 12It is those who want to make a good showing in the flesh that try to compel you to be circumcised—only that they may not be persecuted for the cross of Christ. 13Even the circumcised do not themselves obey the law, but they want you to be circumcised so that they may boast about your flesh. 14May I never boast of anything except the cross of our Lord Jesus Christ, by which*d* the world has been crucified to me, and I to the world. 15For*e* neither circumcision nor uncircumcision is anything; but a new creation is everything! 16As for those who will follow this rule—peace be upon them, and mercy, and upon the Israel of God.

17 From now on, let no one make trouble for me; for I carry the marks of Jesus branded on my body.

18 May the grace of our Lord Jesus Christ be with your spirit, brothers and sisters.*f* Amen.

---

a Other ancient authorities add *murder*   *b* Gk *Brothers*   *c* Other ancient authorities read *in this way fulfill*
d Or *through whom*   *e* Other ancient authorities add *in Christ Jesus*   *f* Gk *brothers*

THE LETTER OF PAUL TO THE
EPHESIANS

Salutation

1 Paul, an apostle of Christ Jesus by the will of God,

To the saints who are in Ephesus and are faithful[a] in Christ Jesus:

2 Grace to you and peace from God our Father and the Lord Jesus Christ.

Spiritual Blessings in Christ

3 Blessed be the God and Father of our Lord Jesus Christ, who has blessed us in Christ with every spiritual blessing in the heavenly places, 4just as he chose us in Christ[b] before the foundation of the world to be holy and blameless before him in love. 5He destined us for adoption as his children through Jesus Christ, according to the good pleasure of his will, 6to the praise of his glorious grace that he freely bestowed on us in the Beloved. 7In him we have redemption through his blood, the forgiveness of our trespasses, according to the riches of his grace 8that he lavished on us. With all wisdom and insight 9he has made known to us the mystery of his will, according to his good pleasure that he set forth in Christ, 10as a plan for the fullness of time, to gather up all things in him, things in heaven and things on earth. 11In Christ we have also obtained an inheritance,[c] having been destined according to the purpose of him who accomplishes all things according to his counsel and will, 12so that we, who were the first to set our hope on Christ, might live for the praise of his glory. 13In him you also, when you had heard the word of truth, the gospel of your salvation, and had believed in him, were marked with the seal of the promised Holy Spirit; 14this[d] is the pledge of our inheritance toward redemption as God's own people, to the praise of his glory.

Paul's Prayer

15 I have heard of your faith in the Lord Jesus and your love[e] toward all the saints, and for this reason 16I do not cease to give thanks for you as I remember you in my prayers. 17I pray that the God of our Lord Jesus Christ, the Father of glory, may give you a spirit of wisdom and revelation as you come to know him, 18so that, with the eyes of your heart enlightened, you may know what is the hope to which he has called you, what are the riches of his glorious inheritance among the saints, 19and what is the immeasurable greatness of his power for us who believe, according to the working of his great power. 20God[f] put this power to work in Christ when he raised him from the dead and seated him at his right hand in the heavenly places, 21far above all rule and authority and power and dominion, and above every name that is named, not only in this age but also in the age to come. 22And he has put all things under his feet and has made him the head over all things for the church, 23which is his body, the fullness of him who fills all in all.

From Death to Life

2 You were dead through the trespasses and sins 2in which you once lived, following the course of this world, following the ruler of the power of the air, the spirit that is now at work among those who are disobedient. 3All of us once lived among them in the passions of our flesh, following the desires of flesh and senses, and we were by nature children of wrath, like everyone else. 4But God, who is rich in mercy, out of the great love with which he loved us 5even when we were dead through our trespasses, made us alive together with Christ[g]—by grace you have been saved— 6and raised us up with him and seated us with him in the heavenly

---

a Other ancient authorities lack *in Ephesus*, reading *saints who are also faithful*   b Gk *in him*   c Or *been made a heritage*   d Other ancient authorities read *who*   e Other ancient authorities lack *and your love*   f Gk *He*
g Other ancient authorities read *in Christ*

places in Christ Jesus, 7so that in the ages to come he might show the immeasurable riches of his grace in kindness toward us in Christ Jesus. 8For by grace you have been saved through faith, and this is not your own doing; it is the gift of God— 9not the result of works, so that no one may boast. 10For we are what he has made us, created in Christ Jesus for good works, which God prepared beforehand to be our way of life.

One in Christ

11 So then, remember that at one time you Gentiles by birth,*a* called "the uncircumcision" by those who are called "the circumcision"—a physical circumcision made in the flesh by human hands— 12remember that you were at that time without Christ, being aliens from the commonwealth of Israel, and strangers to the covenants of promise, having no hope and without God in the world. 13But now in Christ Jesus you who once were far off have been brought near by the blood of Christ. 14For he is our peace; in his flesh he has made both groups into one and has broken down the dividing wall, that is, the hostility between us. 15He has abolished the law with its commandments and ordinances, that he might create in himself one new humanity in place of the two, thus making peace, 16and might reconcile both groups to God in one body*b* through the cross, thus putting to death that hostility through it.*c* 17So he came and proclaimed peace to you who were far off and peace to those who were near; 18for through him both of us have access in one Spirit to the Father. 19So then you are no longer strangers and aliens, but you are citizens with the saints and also members of the household of God, 20built upon the foundation of the apostles and prophets, with Christ Jesus himself as the cornerstone.*d* 21In him the whole structure is joined together and grows into a holy temple in the Lord; 22in whom you also are built together spiritually*e* into a dwelling place for God.

Paul's Ministry to the Gentiles

3 This is the reason that I Paul am a prisoner for*f* Christ Jesus for the sake of you Gentiles— 2for surely you have already heard of the commission of God's grace that was given me for you, 3and how the mystery was made known to me by revelation, as I wrote above in a few words, 4a reading of which will enable you to perceive my understanding of the mystery of Christ. 5In former generations this mystery*g* was not made known to humankind, as it has now been revealed to his holy apostles and prophets by the Spirit: 6that is, the Gentiles have become fellow heirs, members of the same body, and sharers in the promise in Christ Jesus through the gospel.

7 Of this gospel I have become a servant according to the gift of God's grace that was given me by the working of his power. 8Although I am the very least of all the saints, this grace was given to me to bring to the Gentiles the news of the boundless riches of Christ, 9and to make everyone see*h* what is the plan of the mystery hidden for ages in*i* God who created all things; 10so that through the church the wisdom of God in its rich variety might now be made known to*i* the rulers and authorities in the heavenly places. 11This was in accordance with the eternal purpose that he has carried out in Christ Jesus our Lord, 12in whom we have access to God in boldness and confidence through faith in him.*j* 13I pray therefore that you*k* may not lose heart over my sufferings for you; they are your glory.

Prayer for the Readers

14 For this reason I bow my knees before the Father,*l* 15from whom every family*m* in heaven and on earth takes its name. 16I pray that, according to the riches of his glory, he may grant that you may be strengthened in

---

a Gk *in the flesh*   *b* Or *reconcile both of us in one body for God*   *c* Or *in him,* or *in himself*   *d* Or *keystone*   *e* Gk *in the Spirit*   *f* Or *of*   *g* Gk *it*   *h* Other ancient authorities read *to bring to light*   *i* Or *by*   *j* Or *the faith of him*   *k* Or *I*   *l* Other ancient authorities add *of our Lord Jesus Christ*   *m* Gk *fatherhood* your inner being with power through his Spirit, [17]and that Christ may dwell in your hearts through faith, as you are being rooted and grounded in love. [18]I pray that you may have the power to comprehend, with all the saints, what is the breadth and length and height and depth, [19]and to know the love of Christ that surpasses knowledge, so that you may be filled with all the fullness of God.

20 Now to him who by the power at work within us is able to accomplish abundantly far more than all we can ask or imagine, [21]to him be glory in the church and in Christ Jesus to all generations, forever and ever. Amen.

Unity in the Body of Christ

4 I therefore, the prisoner in the Lord, beg you to lead a life worthy of the calling to which you have been called, [2]with all humility and gentleness, with patience, bearing with one another in love, [3]making every effort to maintain the unity of the Spirit in the bond of peace. [4]There is one body and one Spirit, just as you were called to the one hope of your calling, [5]one Lord, one faith, one baptism, [6]one God and Father of all, who is above all and through all and in all.

7 But each of us was given grace according to the measure of Christ's gift. [8]Therefore it is said,

> "When he ascended on high he made
> captivity itself a captive;
> he gave gifts to his people."

[9](When it says, "He ascended," what does it mean but that he had also descended[a] into the lower parts of the earth? [10]He who descended is the same one who ascended far above all the heavens, so that he might fill all things.) [11]The gifts he gave were that some would be apostles, some prophets, some evangelists, some pastors and teachers, [12]to equip the saints for the work of ministry, for building up the body of Christ, [13]until all of us come to the unity of the faith and of the knowledge of the Son of God, to maturity,

to the measure of the full stature of Christ. [14]We must no longer be children, tossed to and fro and blown about by every wind of doctrine, by people's trickery, by their craftiness in deceitful scheming. [15]But speaking the truth in love, we must grow up in every way into him who is the head, into Christ, [16]from whom the whole body, joined and knit together by every ligament with which it is equipped, as each part is working properly, promotes the body's growth in building itself up in love.

The Old Life and the New

17 Now this I affirm and insist on in the Lord: you must no longer live as the Gentiles live, in the futility of their minds. [18]They are darkened in their understanding, alienated from the life of God because of their ignorance and hardness of heart. [19]They have lost all sensitivity and have abandoned themselves to licentiousness, greedy to practice every kind of impurity. [20]That is not the way you learned Christ! [21]For surely you have heard about him and were taught in him, as truth is in Jesus. [22]You were taught to put away your former way of life, your old self, corrupt and deluded by its lusts, [23]and to be renewed in the spirit of your minds, [24]and to clothe yourselves with the new self, created according to the likeness of God in true righteousness and holiness.

Rules for the New Life

25 So then, putting away falsehood, let all of us speak the truth to our neighbors, for we are members of one another. [26]Be angry but do not sin; do not let the sun go down on your anger, [27]and do not make room for the devil. [28]Thieves must give up stealing; rather let them labor and work honestly with their own hands, so as to have something to share with the needy. [29]Let no evil talk come out of your mouths, but only what is useful for building up,[b] as there is need, so that your words may give grace to those who hear.

a Other ancient authorities add *first*   b Other ancient authorities read *building up faith*

30And do not grieve the Holy Spirit of God, with which you were marked with a seal for the day of redemption. 31Put away from you all bitterness and wrath and anger and wrangling and slander, together with all malice, 32and be kind to one another, tenderhearted, forgiving one another, as God in Christ has forgiven you.*a* 1Therefore be imitators of God, as beloved children, 2and live in love, as Christ loved us*b* and gave himself up for us, a fragrant offering and sacrifice to God.

Renounce Pagan Ways

3 But fornication and impurity of any kind, or greed, must not even be mentioned among you, as is proper among saints. 4Entirely out of place is obscene, silly, and vulgar talk; but instead, let there be thanksgiving. 5Be sure of this, that no fornicator or impure person, or one who is greedy (that is, an idolater), has any inheritance in the kingdom of Christ and of God.

6 Let no one deceive you with empty words, for because of these things the wrath of God comes on those who are disobedient. 7Therefore do not be associated with them. 8For once you were darkness, but now in the Lord you are light. Live as children of light— 9for the fruit of the light is found in all that is good and right and true. 10Try to find out what is pleasing to the Lord. 11Take no part in the unfruitful works of darkness, but instead expose them. 12For it is shameful even to mention what such people do secretly; 13but everything exposed by the light becomes visible, 14for everything that becomes visible is light. Therefore it says,

"Sleeper, awake!
Rise from the dead,
and Christ will shine on you."

15 Be careful then how you live, not as unwise people but as wise, 16making the most of the time, because the days are evil. 17So do not be foolish, but understand what the will of the Lord is. 18Do not get drunk with wine,

for that is debauchery; but be filled with the Spirit, 19as you sing psalms and hymns and spiritual songs among yourselves, singing and making melody to the Lord in your hearts, 20giving thanks to God the Father at all times and for everything in the name of our Lord Jesus Christ.

The Christian Household

21 Be subject to one another out of reverence for Christ. 22 Wives, be subject to your husbands as you are to the Lord. 23For the husband is the head of the wife just as Christ is the head of the church, the body of which he is the Savior. 24Just as the church is subject to Christ, so also wives ought to be, in everything, to their husbands.

25 Husbands, love your wives, just as Christ loved the church and gave himself up for her, 26in order to make her holy by cleansing her with the washing of water by the word, 27so as to present the church to himself in splendor, without a spot or wrinkle or anything of the kind—yes, so that she may be holy and without blemish. 28In the same way, husbands should love their wives as they do their own bodies. He who loves his wife loves himself. 29For no one ever hates his own body, but he nourishes and tenderly cares for it, just as Christ does for the church, 30because we are members of his body.*c* 31"For this reason a man will leave his father and mother and be joined to his wife, and the two will become one flesh." 32This is a great mystery, and I am applying it to Christ and the church. 33Each of you, however, should love his wife as himself, and a wife should respect her husband.

Children and Parents

6 Children, obey your parents in the Lord,*d* for this is right. 2"Honor your father and mother"—this is the first commandment with a promise: 3"so that it may be well with you and you may live long on the earth."

---

a Other ancient authorities read *us*   *b* Other ancient authorities read *you*   *c* Other ancient authorities add *of his flesh and of his bones*   *d* Other ancient authorities lack *in the Lord*

4 And, fathers, do not provoke your children to anger, but bring them up in the discipline and instruction of the Lord.

Slaves and Masters

5 Slaves, obey your earthly masters with fear and trembling, in singleness of heart, as you obey Christ; [6]not only while being watched, and in order to please them, but as slaves of Christ, doing the will of God from the heart. [7]Render service with enthusiasm, as to the Lord and not to men and women, [8]knowing that whatever good we do, we will receive the same again from the Lord, whether we are slaves or free.

9 And, masters, do the same to them. Stop threatening them, for you know that both of you have the same Master in heaven, and with him there is no partiality.

The Whole Armor of God

10 Finally, be strong in the Lord and in the strength of his power. [11]Put on the whole armor of God, so that you may be able to stand against the wiles of the devil. [12]For our[a] struggle is not against enemies of blood and flesh, but against the rulers, against the authorities, against the cosmic powers of this present darkness, against the spiritual forces of evil in the heavenly places. [13]Therefore take up the whole armor of God, so that you may be able to withstand on that evil day, and having done everything, to stand firm.

[14]Stand therefore, and fasten the belt of truth around your waist, and put on the breastplate of righteousness. [15]As shoes for your feet put on whatever will make you ready to proclaim the gospel of peace. [16]With all of these,[b] take the shield of faith, with which you will be able to quench all the flaming arrows of the evil one. [17]Take the helmet of salvation, and the sword of the Spirit, which is the word of God.

18 Pray in the Spirit at all times in every prayer and supplication. To that end keep alert and always persevere in supplication for all the saints. [19]Pray also for me, so that when I speak, a message may be given to me to make known with boldness the mystery of the gospel,[c] [20]for which I am an ambassador in chains. Pray that I may declare it boldly, as I must speak.

Personal Matters and Benediction

21 So that you also may know how I am and what I am doing, Tychicus will tell you everything. He is a dear brother and a faithful minister in the Lord. [22]I am sending him to you for this very purpose, to let you know how we are, and to encourage your hearts.

23 Peace be to the whole community,[d] and love with faith, from God the Father and the Lord Jesus Christ. [24]Grace be with all who have an undying love for our Lord Jesus Christ.[e]

---

a Other ancient authorities read *your*   *b* Or *In all circumstances*   *c* Other ancient authorities lack *of the gospel*
d Gk *to the brothers*   *e* Other ancient authorities add *Amen*

THE LETTER OF PAUL TO THE
PHILIPPIANS

Salutation

1 Paul and Timothy, servants*a* of Christ Jesus,

To all the saints in Christ Jesus who are in Philippi, with the bishops*b* and deacons:*c*

2 Grace to you and peace from God our Father and the Lord Jesus Christ.

Paul's Prayer for the Philippians

3 I thank my God every time I remember you, 4constantly praying with joy in every one of my prayers for all of you, 5because of your sharing in the gospel from the first day until now. 6I am confident of this, that the one who began a good work among you will bring it to completion by the day of Jesus Christ. 7It is right for me to think this way about all of you, because you hold me in your heart,*d* for all of you share in God's grace*e* with me, both in my imprisonment and in the defense and confirmation of the gospel. 8For God is my witness, how I long for all of you with the compassion of Christ Jesus. 9And this is my prayer, that your love may overflow more and more with knowledge and full insight 10to help you to determine what is best, so that in the day of Christ you may be pure and blameless, 11having produced the harvest of righteousness that comes through Jesus Christ for the glory and praise of God.

Paul's Present Circumstances

12 I want you to know, beloved,*f* that what has happened to me has actually helped to spread the gospel, 13so that it has become known throughout the whole imperial guard*g* and to everyone else that my imprisonment is for Christ; 14and most of the brothers and sisters,*f* having been made confident in the Lord by my imprisonment, dare to speak the word*h* with greater boldness and without fear.

15 Some proclaim Christ from envy and rivalry, but others from goodwill. 16These proclaim Christ out of love, knowing that I have been put here for the defense of the gospel; 17the others proclaim Christ out of selfish ambition, not sincerely but intending to increase my suffering in my imprisonment. 18What does it matter? Just this, that Christ is proclaimed in every way, whether out of false motives or true; and in that I rejoice.

Yes, and I will continue to rejoice, 19for I know that through your prayers and the help of the Spirit of Jesus Christ this will turn out for my deliverance. 20It is my eager expectation and hope that I will not be put to shame in any way, but that by my speaking with all boldness, Christ will be exalted now as always in my body, whether by life or by death. 21For to me, living is Christ and dying is gain. 22If I am to live in the flesh, that means fruitful labor for me; and I do not know which I prefer. 23I am hard pressed between the two: my desire is to depart and be with Christ, for that is far better; 24but to remain in the flesh is more necessary for you. 25Since I am convinced of this, I know that I will remain and continue with all of you for your progress and joy in faith, 26so that I may share abundantly in your boasting in Christ Jesus when I come to you again.

27 Only, live your life in a manner worthy of the gospel of Christ, so that, whether I come and see you or am absent and hear about you, I will know that you are standing firm in one spirit, striving side by side with one mind for the faith of the gospel, 28and are in no way intimidated by your opponents. For them this is evidence of their destruction, but of your salvation. And this is God's doing. 29For he has graciously granted you the privilege not only of believing in Christ, but of suffering for him as well— 30since you are having the same struggle that you saw I had and now hear that I still have.

---

a Gk *slaves*   *b* Or *overseers*   *c* Or *overseers and helpers*   *d* Or *because I hold you in my heart*   *e* Gk *in grace*
f Gk *brothers*   *g* Gk *whole praetorium*   *h* Other ancient authorities read *word of God*

Imitating Christ's Humility

2 If then there is any encouragement in Christ, any consolation from love, any sharing in the Spirit, any compassion and sympathy, 2make my joy complete: be of the same mind, having the same love, being in full accord and of one mind. 3Do nothing from selfish ambition or conceit, but in humility regard others as better than yourselves. 4Let each of you look not to your own interests, but to the interests of others. 5Let the same mind be in you that was *a* in Christ Jesus,

6 who, though he was in the form of
       God,
    did not regard equality with God
       as something to be exploited,
7 but emptied himself,
       taking the form of a slave,
       being born in human likeness.
    And being found in human form,
8   he humbled himself
       and became obedient to the point of
          death—
       even death on a cross.

9 Therefore God also highly exalted him
       and gave him the name
       that is above every name,
10   so that at the name of Jesus
       every knee should bend,
       in heaven and on earth and under
          the earth,
11   and every tongue should confess
       that Jesus Christ is Lord,
       to the glory of God the Father.

Shining as Lights in the World

12 Therefore, my beloved, just as you have always obeyed me, not only in my presence, but much more now in my absence, work out your own salvation with fear and trembling; 13for it is God who is at work in you, enabling you both to will and to work for his good pleasure.

14 Do all things without murmuring and arguing, 15so that you may be blameless and innocent, children of God without blemish in the midst of a crooked and perverse generation, in which you shine like stars in the world. 16It is by your holding fast to the word of life that I can boast on the day of Christ that I did not run in vain or labor in vain. 17But even if I am being poured out as a libation over the sacrifice and the offering of your faith, I am glad and rejoice with all of you— 18and in the same way you also must be glad and rejoice with me.

Timothy and Epaphroditus

19 I hope in the Lord Jesus to send Timothy to you soon, so that I may be cheered by news of you. 20I have no one like him who will be genuinely concerned for your welfare. 21All of them are seeking their own interests, not those of Jesus Christ. 22But Timothy's *b* worth you know, how like a son with a father he has served with me in the work of the gospel. 23I hope therefore to send him as soon as I see how things go with me; 24and I trust in the Lord that I will also come soon.

25 Still, I think it necessary to send to you Epaphroditus—my brother and coworker and fellow soldier, your messenger*c* and minister to my need; 26for he has been longing for*d* all of you, and has been distressed because you heard that he was ill. 27He was indeed so ill that he nearly died. But God had mercy on him, and not only on him but on me also, so that I would not have one sorrow after another. 28I am the more eager to send him, therefore, in order that you may rejoice at seeing him again, and that I may be less anxious. 29Welcome him then in the Lord with all joy, and honor such people, 30because he came close to death for the work of Christ,*e* risking his life to make up for those services that you could not give me.

3 Finally, my brothers and sisters,*f* rejoice*g* in the Lord.

---

a Or *that you have*   *b* Gk *his*   *c* Gk *apostle*   *d* Other ancient authorities read *longing to see*   *e* Other ancient authorities read *of the Lord*   *f* Gk *my brothers*   *g* Or *farewell*

Breaking with the Past

To write the same things to you is not troublesome to me, and for you it is a safe-guard.

2 Beware of the dogs, beware of the evil workers, beware of those who mutilate the flesh!*a* 3For it is we who are the circumcision, who worship in the Spirit of God*b* and boast in Christ Jesus and have no confidence in the flesh— 4even though I, too, have reason for confidence in the flesh.

If anyone else has reason to be confident in the flesh, I have more: 5circumcised on the eighth day, a member of the people of Israel, of the tribe of Benjamin, a Hebrew born of Hebrews; as to the law, a Pharisee; 6as to zeal, a persecutor of the church; as to righteousness under the law, blameless.

7 Yet whatever gains I had, these I have come to regard as loss because of Christ. 8More than that, I regard everything as loss because of the surpassing value of knowing Christ Jesus my Lord. For his sake I have suffered the loss of all things, and I regard them as rubbish, in order that I may gain Christ 9and be found in him, not having a righteousness of my own that comes from the law, but one that comes through faith in Christ,*c* the righteousness from God based on faith. 10I want to know Christ*d* and the power of his resurrection and the sharing of his sufferings by becoming like him in his death, 11if somehow I may attain the resurrection from the dead.

Pressing toward the Goal

12 Not that I have already obtained this or have already reached the goal;*e* but I press on to make it my own, because Christ Jesus has made me his own. 13Beloved,*f* I do not consider that I have made it my own;*g* but this one thing I do: forgetting what lies behind and straining forward to what lies ahead, 14I press on toward the goal for the prize of the heav-

enly*b* call of God in Christ Jesus. 15Let those of us then who are mature be of the same mind; and if you think differently about anything, this too God will reveal to you. 16Only let us hold fast to what we have attained.

17 Brothers and sisters,*f* join in imitating me, and observe those who live according to the example you have in us. 18For many live as enemies of the cross of Christ; I have often told you of them, and now I tell you even with tears. 19Their end is destruction; their god is the belly; and their glory is in their shame; their minds are set on earthly things. 20But our citizenship*i* is in heaven, and it is from there that we are expecting a Savior, the Lord Jesus Christ. 21He will transform the body of our humiliation*j* that it may be conformed to the body of his glory,*k* by the power that also enables him to make all things subject to himself. 4 1Therefore, my brothers and sisters,*l* whom I love and long for, my joy and crown, stand firm in the Lord in this way, my beloved.

Exhortations

2 I urge Euodia and I urge Syntyche to be of the same mind in the Lord. 3Yes, and I ask you also, my loyal companion,*m* help these women, for they have struggled beside me in the work of the gospel, together with Clement and the rest of my co-workers, whose names are in the book of life.

4 Rejoice*n* in the Lord always; again I will say, Rejoice. *n* 5Let your gentleness be known to everyone. The Lord is near. 6Do not worry about anything, but in everything by prayer and supplication with thanksgiving let your requests be made known to God. 7And the peace of God, which surpasses all understanding, will guard your hearts and your minds in Christ Jesus.

8 Finally, beloved,*o* whatever is true, whatever is honorable, whatever is just, whatever

a Gk *the mutilation*   *b* Other ancient authorities read *worship God in spirit*   *c* Or *through the faith of Christ*
d Gk *him*   *e* Or *have already been made perfect*   *f* Gk *Brothers*   *g* Other ancient authorities read *my own yet*
h Gk *upward*   *i* Or *commonwealth*   *j* Or *our humble bodies*   *k* Or *his glorious body*   *l* Gk *my brothers*   *m* Or *loyal Syzygus*   *n* Or *Farewell*   *o* Gk *brothers*

is pure, whatever is pleasing, whatever is commendable, if there is any excellence and if there is anything worthy of praise, think about[a] these things. [9]Keep on doing the things that you have learned and received and heard and seen in me, and the God of peace will be with you.

Acknowledgment of the Philippians' Gift

10 I rejoice[b] in the Lord greatly that now at last you have revived your concern for me; indeed, you were concerned for me, but had no opportunity to show it.[c] [11]Not that I am referring to being in need; for I have learned to be content with whatever I have. [12]I know what it is to have little, and I know what it is to have plenty. In any and all circumstances I have learned the secret of being well-fed and of going hungry, of having plenty and of being in need. [13]I can do all things through him who strengthens me. [14]In any case, it was kind of you to share my distress.

15 You Philippians indeed know that in the early days of the gospel, when I left Macedonia, no church shared with me in the matter of giving and receiving, except you alone. [16]For even when I was in Thessalonica, you sent me help for my needs more than once. [17]Not that I seek the gift, but I seek the profit that accumulates to your account. [18]I have been paid in full and have more than enough; I am fully satisfied, now that I have received from Epaphroditus the gifts you sent, a fragrant offering, a sacrifice acceptable and pleasing to God. [19]And my God will fully satisfy every need of yours according to his riches in glory in Christ Jesus. [20]To our God and Father be glory forever and ever. Amen.

Final Greetings and Benediction

21 Greet every saint in Christ Jesus. The friends[d] who are with me greet you. [22]All the saints greet you, especially those of the emperor's household.

23 The grace of the Lord Jesus Christ be with your spirit.[e]

---

a Gk *take account of*   *b* Gk *I rejoiced*   *c* Gk lacks *to show it*   *d* Gk *brothers*   *e* Other ancient authorities add *Amen*

THE LETTER OF PAUL TO THE
COLOSSIANS

Salutation

1 Paul, an apostle of Christ Jesus by the will of God, and Timothy our brother,

2 To the saints and faithful brothers and sisters*a* in Christ in Colossae:

Grace to you and peace from God our Father.

Paul Thanks God for the Colossians

3 In our prayers for you we always thank God, the Father of our Lord Jesus Christ, 4for we have heard of your faith in Christ Jesus and of the love that you have for all the saints, 5because of the hope laid up for you in heaven. You have heard of this hope before in the word of the truth, the gospel 6that has come to you. Just as it is bearing fruit and growing in the whole world, so it has been bearing fruit among yourselves from the day you heard it and truly comprehended the grace of God. 7This you learned from Epaphras, our beloved fellow servant.*b* He is a faithful minister of Christ on your*c* behalf, 8and he has made known to us your love in the Spirit.

9 For this reason, since the day we heard it, we have not ceased praying for you and asking that you may be filled with the knowledge of God's*d* will in all spiritual wisdom and understanding, 10so that you may lead lives worthy of the Lord, fully pleasing to him, as you bear fruit in every good work and as you grow in the knowledge of God. 11May you be made strong with all the strength that comes from his glorious power, and may you be prepared to endure everything with patience, while joyfully 12giving thanks to the Father, who has enabled*e* you*f* to share in the inheritance of the saints in the light. 13He has rescued us from the power of darkness and transferred us into the kingdom of his beloved Son, 14in whom we have redemption, the forgiveness of sins.*g*

The Supremacy of Christ

15 He is the image of the invisible God, the firstborn of all creation; 16for in*h* him all things in heaven and on earth were created, things visible and invisible, whether thrones or dominions or rulers or powers—all things have been created through him and for him. 17He himself is before all things, and in*h* him all things hold together. 18He is the head of the body, the church; he is the beginning, the firstborn from the dead, so that he might come to have first place in everything. 19For in him all the fullness of God was pleased to dwell, 20and through him God was pleased to reconcile to himself all things, whether on earth or in heaven, by making peace through the blood of his cross.

21 And you who were once estranged and hostile in mind, doing evil deeds, 22he has now reconciled*i* in his fleshly body*j* through death, so as to present you holy and blameless and irreproachable before him— 23provided that you continue securely established and steadfast in the faith, without shifting from the hope promised by the gospel that you heard, which has been proclaimed to every creature under heaven. I, Paul, became a servant of this gospel.

Paul's Interest in the Colossians

24 I am now rejoicing in my sufferings for your sake, and in my flesh I am completing what is lacking in Christ's afflictions for the sake of his body, that is, the church. 25I became its servant according to God's commission that was given to me for you, to make the word of God fully known, 26the mystery that has been hidden throughout the ages and generations but has now been revealed to his saints. 27To them God chose to make known how great among the Gentiles are the riches of the glory of this mystery,

---

a Gk *brothers*   *b* Gk *slave*   *c* Other ancient authorities read *our*   *d* Gk *his*   *e* Other ancient authorities read *called*   *f* Other ancient authorities read *us*   *g* Other ancient authorities add *through his blood*   *h* Or *by*   *i* Other ancient authorities read *you have now been reconciled*   *j* Gk *in the body of his flesh* which is Christ in you, the hope of glory. 28It is he whom we proclaim, warning everyone and teaching everyone in all wisdom, so that we may present everyone mature in Christ. 29For this I toil and struggle with all the energy that he powerfully inspires within me.

2 For I want you to know how much I am struggling for you, and for those in Laodicea, and for all who have not seen me face to face. 2I want their hearts to be encouraged and united in love, so that they may have all the riches of assured understanding and have the knowledge of God's mystery, that is, Christ himself,a 3in whom are hidden all the treasures of wisdom and knowledge. 4I am saying this so that no one may deceive you with plausible arguments. 5For though I am absent in body, yet I am with you in spirit, and I rejoice to see your morale and the firmness of your faith in Christ.

Fullness of Life in Christ

6 As you therefore have received Christ Jesus the Lord, continue to live your livesb in him, 7rooted and built up in him and established in the faith, just as you were taught, abounding in thanksgiving.

8 See to it that no one takes you captive through philosophy and empty deceit, according to human tradition, according to the elemental spirits of the universe,c and not according to Christ. 9For in him the whole fullness of deity dwells bodily, 10and you have come to fullness in him, who is the head of every ruler and authority. 11In him also you were circumcised with a spiritual circumcision,d by putting off the body of the flesh in the circumcision of Christ; 12when you were buried with him in baptism, you were also raised with him through faith in the power of God, who raised him from the dead. 13And when you were dead in trespasses and the uncircumcision of your flesh, Gode made youf alive together with him, when he forgave us all our trespasses, 14erasing the record that stood against us with its legal demands. He set this aside, nailing it to the cross. 15He disarmedg the rulers and authorities and made a public example of them, triumphing over them in it.

16 Therefore do not let anyone condemn you in matters of food and drink or of observing festivals, new moons, or sabbaths. 17These are only a shadow of what is to come, but the substance belongs to Christ. 18Do not let anyone disqualify you, insisting on self-abasement and worship of angels, dwellingh on visions,i puffed up without cause by a human way of thinking,j 19and not holding fast to the head, from whom the whole body, nourished and held together by its ligaments and sinews, grows with a growth that is from God.

Warnings against False Teachers

20 If with Christ you died to the elemental spirits of the universe,c why do you live as if you still belonged to the world? Why do you submit to regulations, 21"Do not handle, Do not taste, Do not touch"? 22All these regulations refer to things that perish with use; they are simply human commands and teachings. 23These have indeed an appearance of wisdom in promoting self-imposed piety, humility, and severe treatment of the body, but they are of no value in checking self-indulgence.k

The New Life in Christ

3 So if you have been raised with Christ, seek the things that are above, where Christ is, seated at the right hand of God. 2Set your minds on things that are above, not on things that are on earth, 3for you have died, and your life is hidden with Christ in

---

a Other ancient authorities read of the mystery of God, both of the Father and of Christ   b Gk to walk   c Or the rudiments of the world   d Gk a circumcision made without hands   e Gk he   f Other ancient authorities read made us; others, made   g Or divested himself of   h Other ancient authorities read not dwelling   i Meaning of Gk uncertain   j Gk by the mind of his flesh   k Or are of no value, serving only to indulge the flesh

God. ⁴When Christ who is your*ᵃ* life is revealed, then you also will be revealed with him in glory.

5 Put to death, therefore, whatever in you is earthly: fornication, impurity, passion, evil desire, and greed (which is idolatry). ⁶On account of these the wrath of God is coming on those who are disobedient.*ᵇ* ⁷These are the ways you also once followed, when you were living that life.*ᶜ* ⁸But now you must get rid of all such things—anger, wrath, malice, slander, and abusive*ᵈ* language from your mouth. ⁹Do not lie to one another, seeing that you have stripped off the old self with its practices ¹⁰and have clothed yourselves with the new self, which is being renewed in knowledge according to the image of its creator. ¹¹In that renewal*ᵉ* there is no longer Greek and Jew, circumcised and uncircumcised, barbarian, Scythian, slave and free; but Christ is all and in all!

12 As God's chosen ones, holy and beloved, clothe yourselves with compassion, kindness, humility, meekness, and patience. ¹³Bear with one another and, if anyone has a complaint against another, forgive each other; just as the Lord*ᶠ* has forgiven you, so you also must forgive. ¹⁴Above all, clothe yourselves with love, which binds everything together in perfect harmony. ¹⁵And let the peace of Christ rule in your hearts, to which indeed you were called in the one body. And be thankful. ¹⁶Let the word of Christ*ᵍ* dwell in you richly; teach and admonish one another in all wisdom; and with gratitude in your hearts sing psalms, hymns, and spiritual songs to God.*ʰ* ¹⁷And whatever you do, in word or deed, do everything in the name of the Lord Jesus, giving thanks to God the Father through him.

Rules for Christian Households

18 Wives, be subject to your husbands, as is fitting in the Lord. ¹⁹Husbands, love your wives and never treat them harshly.

20 Children, obey your parents in everything, for this is your acceptable duty in the Lord. ²¹Fathers, do not provoke your children, or they may lose heart. ²²Slaves, obey your earthly masters*ⁱ* in everything, not only while being watched and in order to please them, but wholeheartedly, fearing the Lord.*ⁱ* ²³Whatever your task, put yourselves into it, as done for the Lord and not for your masters,*ʲ* ²⁴since you know that from the Lord you will receive the inheritance as your reward; you serve*ᵏ* the Lord Christ. ²⁵For the wrongdoer will be paid back for whatever wrong has been done, and there is no partiality.

4 ¹Masters, treat your slaves justly and fairly, for you know that you also have a Master in heaven.

Further Instructions

2 Devote yourselves to prayer, keeping alert in it with thanksgiving. ³At the same time pray for us as well that God will open to us a door for the word, that we may declare the mystery of Christ, for which I am in prison, ⁴so that I may reveal it clearly, as I should.

5 Conduct yourselves wisely toward outsiders, making the most of the time.*ˡ* ⁶Let your speech always be gracious, seasoned with salt, so that you may know how you ought to answer everyone.

Final Greetings and Benediction

7 Tychicus will tell you all the news about me; he is a beloved brother, a faithful minister, and a fellow servant*ᵐ* in the Lord. ⁸I have sent him to you for this very purpose, so that you may know how we are*ⁿ* and that he may encourage your hearts; ⁹he is coming with Onesimus, the faithful and beloved

a Other authorities read *our*   *b* Other ancient authorities lack *on those who are disobedient* (Gk *the children of disobedience*)   *c* Or *living among such people*   *d* Or *filthy*   *e* Gk *its creator,* ¹¹*where*   *f* Other ancient authorities read *just as Christ*   *g* Other ancient authorities read *of God,* or *of the Lord*   *h* Other ancient authorities read *to the Lord*   *i* In Greek the same word is used for *master* and *Lord*   *j* Gk *not for men*   *k* Or *you are slaves of,* or *be slaves of*   *l* Or *opportunity*   *m* Gk *slave*   *n* Other authorities read *that I may know how you are* brother, who is one of you. They will tell you about everything here.

10 Aristarchus my fellow prisoner greets you, as does Mark the cousin of Barnabas, concerning whom you have received instructions—if he comes to you, welcome him. [11]And Jesus who is called Justus greets you. These are the only ones of the circumcision among my co-workers for the kingdom of God, and they have been a comfort to me. [12]Epaphras, who is one of you, a servant[a] of Christ Jesus, greets you. He is always wrestling in his prayers on your behalf, so that you may stand mature and fully assured in everything that God wills. [13]For I testify for him

that he has worked hard for you and for those in Laodicea and in Hierapolis. [14]Luke, the beloved physician, and Demas greet you. [15]Give my greetings to the brothers and sisters[b] in Laodicea, and to Nympha and the church in her house. [16]And when this letter has been read among you, have it read also in the church of the Laodiceans; and see that you read also the letter from Laodicea. [17]And say to Archippus, "See that you complete the task that you have received in the Lord."

18 I, Paul, write this greeting with my own hand. Remember my chains. Grace be with you.[c]

---

a Gk *slave*   *b* Gk *brothers*   *c* Other ancient authorities add *Amen*

THE FIRST LETTER OF PAUL TO THE
THESSALONIANS

Salutation

1 Paul, Silvanus, and Timothy,
To the church of the Thessalonians in
God the Father and the Lord Jesus Christ:
Grace to you and peace.

The Thessalonians' Faith and Example

2 We always give thanks to God for all of
you and mention you in our prayers, constantly ³remembering before our God and
Father your work of faith and labor of love
and steadfastness of hope in our Lord Jesus
Christ. ⁴For we know, brothers and sisters*ᵃ*
beloved by God, that he has chosen you,
⁵because our message of the gospel came to
you not in word only, but also in power and
in the Holy Spirit and with full conviction;
just as you know what kind of persons we
proved to be among you for your sake. ⁶And
you became imitators of us and of the Lord,
for in spite of persecution you received the
word with joy inspired by the Holy Spirit,
⁷so that you became an example to all the believers in Macedonia and in Achaia. ⁸For the
word of the Lord has sounded forth from
you not only in Macedonia and Achaia, but
in every place your faith in God has become
known, so that we have no need to speak
about it. ⁹For the people of those regions*ᵇ* report about us what kind of welcome we had
among you, and how you turned to God
from idols, to serve a living and true God,
¹⁰and to wait for his Son from heaven, whom
he raised from the dead—Jesus, who rescues
us from the wrath that is coming.

Paul's Ministry in Thessalonica

2 You yourselves know, brothers and sisters,*ᵃ* that our coming to you was not in
vain, ²but though we had already suffered
and been shamefully mistreated at Philippi, as
you know, we had courage in our God to
declare to you the gospel of God in spite of
great opposition. ³For our appeal does not

spring from deceit or impure motives or trickery, ⁴but just as we have been approved by
God to be entrusted with the message of
the gospel, even so we speak, not to please
mortals, but to please God who tests our
hearts. ⁵As you know and as God is our witness, we never came with words of flattery or
with a pretext for greed; ⁶nor did we seek
praise from mortals, whether from you or
from others, ⁷though we might have made
demands as apostles of Christ. But we were
gentle*ᶜ* among you, like a nurse tenderly caring for her own children. ⁸So deeply do we
care for you that we are determined to share
with you not only the gospel of God but
also our own selves, because you have become very dear to us.

9 You remember our labor and toil, brothers and sisters;*ᵃ* we worked night and day, so
that we might not burden any of you while
we proclaimed to you the gospel of God.
¹⁰You are witnesses, and God also, how pure,
upright, and blameless our conduct was toward you believers. ¹¹As you know, we dealt
with each one of you like a father with his
children, ¹²urging and encouraging you and
pleading that you lead a life worthy of God,
who calls you into his own kingdom and
glory.

13 We also constantly give thanks to God
for this, that when you received the word of
God that you heard from us, you accepted it
not as a human word but as what it really is,
God's word, which is also at work in you believers. ¹⁴For you, brothers and sisters,*ᵃ* became imitators of the churches of God in
Christ Jesus that are in Judea, for you suffered
the same things from your own compatriots
as they did from the Jews, ¹⁵who killed both
the Lord Jesus and the prophets,*ᵈ* and drove
us out; they displease God and oppose everyone ¹⁶by hindering us from speaking to the
Gentiles so that they may be saved. Thus
they have constantly been filling up the mea-

a Gk *brothers*   *b* Gk *For they*   *c* Other ancient authorities read *infants*   *d* Other ancient authorities read *their
own prophets*

sure of their sins; but God's wrath has overtaken them at last. *a*

Paul's Desire to Visit the Thessalonians Again

17 As for us, brothers and sisters, *b* when, for a short time, we were made orphans by being separated from you—in person, not in heart—we longed with great eagerness to see you face to face. ¹⁸For we wanted to come to you—certainly I, Paul, wanted to again and again—but Satan blocked our way. ¹⁹For what is our hope or joy or crown of boasting before our Lord Jesus at his coming? Is it not you? ²⁰Yes, you are our glory and joy!

3 Therefore when we could bear it no longer, we decided to be left alone in Athens; ²and we sent Timothy, our brother and co-worker for God in proclaiming *c* the gospel of Christ, to strengthen and encourage you for the sake of your faith, ³so that no one would be shaken by these persecutions. Indeed, you yourselves know that this is what we are destined for. ⁴In fact, when we were with you, we told you beforehand that we were to suffer persecution; so it turned out, as you know. ⁵For this reason, when I could bear it no longer, I sent to find out about your faith; I was afraid that somehow the tempter had tempted you and that our labor had been in vain.

Timothy's Encouraging Report

6 But Timothy has just now come to us from you, and has brought us the good news of your faith and love. He has told us also that you always remember us kindly and long to see us—just as we long to see you. ⁷For this reason, brothers and sisters, *b* during all our distress and persecution we have been encouraged about you through your faith. ⁸For we now live, if you continue to stand firm in the Lord. ⁹How can we thank God enough for you in return for all the joy that we feel before our God because of you? ¹⁰Night and day we pray most earnestly that we may see you face to face and restore whatever is lacking in your faith.

11 Now may our God and Father himself and our Lord Jesus direct our way to you. ¹²And may the Lord make you increase and abound in love for one another and for all, just as we abound in love for you. ¹³And may he so strengthen your hearts in holiness that you may be blameless before our God and Father at the coming of our Lord Jesus with all his saints.

A Life Pleasing to God

4 Finally, brothers and sisters, *b* we ask and urge you in the Lord Jesus that, as you learned from us how you ought to live and to please God (as, in fact, you are doing), you should do so more and more. ²For you know what instructions we gave you through the Lord Jesus. ³For this is the will of God, your sanctification: that you abstain from fornication; ⁴that each one of you know how to control your own body *d* in holiness and honor, ⁵not with lustful passion, like the Gentiles who do not know God; ⁶that no one wrong or exploit a brother or sister *e* in this matter, because the Lord is an avenger in all these things, just as we have already told you beforehand and solemnly warned you. ⁷For God did not call us to impurity but in holiness. ⁸Therefore whoever rejects this rejects not human authority but God, who also gives his Holy Spirit to you.

9 Now concerning love of the brothers and sisters, *b* you do not need to have anyone write to you, for you yourselves have been taught by God to love one another; ¹⁰and indeed you do love all the brothers and sisters *b* throughout Macedonia. But we urge you, beloved, *b* to do so more and more, ¹¹to aspire to live quietly, to mind your own affairs, and to work with your hands, as we directed you, ¹²so that you may behave properly toward outsiders and be dependent on no one.

---

a Or *completely* or *forever*   *b* Gk *brothers*   *c* Gk lacks *proclaiming*   *d* Or *how to take a wife for himself*   *e* Gk *brother*

The Coming of the Lord

13 But we do not want you to be uninformed, brothers and sisters,*a* about those who have died,*b* so that you may not grieve as others do who have no hope. [14]For since we believe that Jesus died and rose again, even so, through Jesus, God will bring with him those who have died.*b* [15]For this we declare to you by the word of the Lord, that we who are alive, who are left until the coming of the Lord, will by no means precede those who have died.*b* [16]For the Lord himself, with a cry of command, with the archangel's call and with the sound of God's trumpet, will descend from heaven, and the dead in Christ will rise first. [17]Then we who are alive, who are left, will be caught up in the clouds together with them to meet the Lord in the air; and so we will be with the Lord forever. [18]Therefore encourage one another with these words.

5 Now concerning the times and the seasons, brothers and sisters,*a* you do not need to have anything written to you. [2]For you yourselves know very well that the day of the Lord will come like a thief in the night. [3]When they say, "There is peace and security," then sudden destruction will come upon them, as labor pains come upon a pregnant woman, and there will be no escape! [4]But you, beloved,*a* are not in darkness, for that day to surprise you like a thief; [5]for you are all children of light and children of the day; we are not of the night or of darkness. [6]So then let us not fall asleep as others do, but let us keep awake and be sober; [7]for those who sleep sleep at night, and those who are drunk get drunk at night. [8]But since we belong to the day, let us be sober, and put on the breastplate of faith and love, and for a helmet the hope of salvation. [9]For God has destined us not for wrath but for obtaining salvation through our Lord Jesus Christ, [10]who died for us, so that whether we are awake or asleep we may live with him. [11]Therefore encourage one another and build up each other, as indeed you are doing.

Final Exhortations, Greetings, and Benediction

12 But we appeal to you, brothers and sisters,*a* to respect those who labor among you, and have charge of you in the Lord and admonish you; [13]esteem them very highly in love because of their work. Be at peace among yourselves. [14]And we urge you, beloved,*a* to admonish the idlers, encourage the fainthearted, help the weak, be patient with all of them. [15]See that none of you repays evil for evil, but always seek to do good to one another and to all. [16]Rejoice always, [17]pray without ceasing, [18]give thanks in all circumstances; for this is the will of God in Christ Jesus for you. [19]Do not quench the Spirit. [20]Do not despise the words of prophets,*c* [21]but test everything; hold fast to what is good; [22]abstain from every form of evil.

23 May the God of peace himself sanctify you entirely; and may your spirit and soul and body be kept sound*d* and blameless at the coming of our Lord Jesus Christ. [24]The one who calls you is faithful, and he will do this.

25 Beloved,*e* pray for us.

26 Greet all the brothers and sisters*a* with a holy kiss. [27]I solemnly command you by the Lord that this letter be read to all of them.*f*

28 The grace of our Lord Jesus Christ be with you.*g*

---

a Gk *brothers*   *b* Gk *fallen asleep*   *c* Gk *despise prophecies*   *d* Or *complete*   *e* Gk *Brothers*   *f* Gk *to all the brothers*
g Other ancient authorities add *Amen*

THE SECOND LETTER OF PAUL TO THE
THESSALONIANS

Salutation

1 Paul, Silvanus, and Timothy,

To the church of the Thessalonians in God our Father and the Lord Jesus Christ:

2 Grace to you and peace from God our*a* Father and the Lord Jesus Christ.

Thanksgiving

3 We must always give thanks to God for you, brothers and sisters,*b* as is right, because your faith is growing abundantly, and the love of every one of you for one another is increasing. 4Therefore we ourselves boast of you among the churches of God for your steadfastness and faith during all your persecutions and the afflictions that you are enduring.

The Judgment at Christ's Coming

5 This is evidence of the righteous judgment of God, and is intended to make you worthy of the kingdom of God, for which you are also suffering. 6For it is indeed just of God to repay with affliction those who afflict you, 7and to give relief to the afflicted as well as to us, when the Lord Jesus is revealed from heaven with his mighty angels 8in flaming fire, inflicting vengeance on those who do not know God and on those who do not obey the gospel of our Lord Jesus. 9These will suffer the punishment of eternal destruction, separated from the presence of the Lord and from the glory of his might, 10when he comes to be glorified by his saints and to be marveled at on that day among all who have believed, because our testimony to you was believed. 11To this end we always pray for you, asking that our God will make you worthy of his call and will fulfill by his power every good resolve and work of faith, 12so that the name of our Lord Jesus may be glorified in you, and you in him, according to the grace of our God and the Lord Jesus Christ.

The Man of Lawlessness

2 As to the coming of our Lord Jesus Christ and our being gathered together to him, we beg you, brothers and sisters,*b* 2not to be quickly shaken in mind or alarmed, either by spirit or by word or by letter, as though from us, to the effect that the day of the Lord is already here. 3Let no one deceive you in any way; for that day will not come unless the rebellion comes first and the lawless one*c* is revealed, the one destined for destruction.*d* 4He opposes and exalts himself above every so-called god or object of worship, so that he takes his seat in the temple of God, declaring himself to be God. 5Do you not remember that I told you these things when I was still with you? 6And you know what is now restraining him, so that he may be revealed when his time comes. 7For the mystery of lawlessness is already at work, but only until the one who now restrains it is removed. 8And then the lawless one will be revealed, whom the Lord Jesus*e* will destroy*f* with the breath of his mouth, annihilating him by the manifestation of his coming. 9The coming of the lawless one is apparent in the working of Satan, who uses all power, signs, lying wonders, 10and every kind of wicked deception for those who are perishing, because they refused to love the truth and so be saved. 11For this reason God sends them a powerful delusion, leading them to believe what is false, 12so that all who have not believed the truth but took pleasure in unrighteousness will be condemned.

Chosen for Salvation

13 But we must always give thanks to God for you, brothers and sisters*b* beloved by the Lord, because God chose you as the first

a Other ancient authorities read *the* *b* Gk *brothers* *c* Gk *the man of lawlessness*; other ancient authorities read *the man of sin* *d* Gk *the son of destruction* *e* Other ancient authorities lack *Jesus* *f* Other ancient authorities read *consume* fruits*a* for salvation through sanctification by the Spirit and through belief in the truth. [14]For this purpose he called you through our proclamation of the good news,*b* so that you may obtain the glory of our Lord Jesus Christ. [15]So then, brothers and sisters,*c* stand firm and hold fast to the traditions that you were taught by us, either by word of mouth or by our letter.

16 Now may our Lord Jesus Christ himself and God our Father, who loved us and through grace gave us eternal comfort and good hope, [17]comfort your hearts and strengthen them in every good work and word.

Request for Prayer

3 Finally, brothers and sisters,*c* pray for us, so that the word of the Lord may spread rapidly and be glorified everywhere, just as it is among you, [2]and that we may be rescued from wicked and evil people; for not all have faith. [3]But the Lord is faithful; he will strengthen you and guard you from the evil one.*d* [4]And we have confidence in the Lord concerning you, that you are doing and will go on doing the things that we command. [5]May the Lord direct your hearts to the love of God and to the steadfastness of Christ.

Warning against Idleness

6 Now we command you, beloved,*e* in the name of our Lord Jesus Christ, to keep away from believers who are*e* living in idle-

ness and not according to the tradition that they*f* received from us. [7]For you yourselves know how you ought to imitate us; we were not idle when we were with you, [8]and we did not eat anyone's bread without paying for it; but with toil and labor we worked night and day, so that we might not burden any of you. [9]This was not because we do not have that right, but in order to give you an example to imitate. [10]For even when we were with you, we gave you this command: Anyone unwilling to work should not eat. [11]For we hear that some of you are living in idleness, mere busybodies, not doing any work. [12]Now such persons we command and exhort in the Lord Jesus Christ to do their work quietly and to earn their own living. [13]Brothers and sisters,*g* do not be weary in doing what is right.

14 Take note of those who do not obey what we say in this letter; have nothing to do with them, so that they may be ashamed. [15]Do not regard them as enemies, but warn them as believers.*h*

Final Greetings and Benediction

16 Now may the Lord of peace himself give you peace at all times in all ways. The Lord be with all of you.

17 I, Paul, write this greeting with my own hand. This is the mark in every letter of mine; it is the way I write. [18]The grace of our Lord Jesus Christ be with all of you.*i*

---

a Other ancient authorities read *from the beginning*   *b* Or *through our gospel*   *c* Gk *brothers*   *d* Or *from evil*
e Gk *from every brother who is*   *f* Other ancient authorities read *you*   *g* Gk *Brothers*   *h* Gk *a brother*   *i* Other ancient authorities add *Amen*

THE FIRST LETTER OF PAUL TO
TIMOTHY

Salutation

1 Paul, an apostle of Christ Jesus by the command of God our Savior and of Christ Jesus our hope,

2 To Timothy, my loyal child in the faith:

Grace, mercy, and peace from God the Father and Christ Jesus our Lord.

Warning against False Teachers

3 I urge you, as I did when I was on my way to Macedonia, to remain in Ephesus so that you may instruct certain people not to teach any different doctrine, 4and not to occupy themselves with myths and endless genealogies that promote speculations rather than the divine training*a* that is known by faith. 5But the aim of such instruction is love that comes from a pure heart, a good conscience, and sincere faith. 6Some people have deviated from these and turned to meaningless talk, 7desiring to be teachers of the law, without understanding either what they are saying or the things about which they make assertions.

8 Now we know that the law is good, if one uses it legitimately. 9This means understanding that the law is laid down not for the innocent but for the lawless and disobedient, for the godless and sinful, for the unholy and profane, for those who kill their father or mother, for murderers, 10fornicators, sodomites, slave traders, liars, perjurers, and whatever else is contrary to the sound teaching 11that conforms to the glorious gospel of the blessed God, which he entrusted to me.

Gratitude for Mercy

12 I am grateful to Christ Jesus our Lord, who has strengthened me, because he judged me faithful and appointed me to his service, 13even though I was formerly a blasphemer, a persecutor, and a man of violence. But I received mercy because I had acted ignorantly in unbelief, 14and the grace of our Lord over-

flowed for me with the faith and love that are in Christ Jesus. 15The saying is sure and worthy of full acceptance, that Christ Jesus came into the world to save sinners—of whom I am the foremost. 16But for that very reason I received mercy, so that in me, as the foremost, Jesus Christ might display the utmost patience, making me an example to those who would come to believe in him for eternal life. 17To the King of the ages, immortal, invisible, the only God, be honor and glory forever and ever.*b* Amen.

18 I am giving you these instructions, Timothy, my child, in accordance with the prophecies made earlier about you, so that by following them you may fight the good fight, 19having faith and a good conscience. By rejecting conscience, certain persons have suffered shipwreck in the faith; 20among them are Hymenaeus and Alexander, whom I have turned over to Satan, so that they may learn not to blaspheme.

Instructions concerning Prayer

2 First of all, then, I urge that supplications, prayers, intercessions, and thanksgivings be made for everyone, 2for kings and all who are in high positions, so that we may lead a quiet and peaceable life in all godliness and dignity. 3This is right and is acceptable in the sight of God our Savior, 4who desires everyone to be saved and to come to the knowledge of the truth. 5For

there is one God;
there is also one mediator between
God and humankind,
Christ Jesus, himself human,
6 who gave himself a ransom for all

—this was attested at the right time. 7For this I was appointed a herald and an apostle (I am telling the truth,*c* I am not lying), a teacher of the Gentiles in faith and truth.

8 I desire, then, that in every place the men should pray, lifting up holy hands with-

---

a Or *plan*   *b* Gk *to the ages of the ages*   *c* Other ancient authorities add *in Christ* out anger or argument; ⁹also that the women should dress themselves modestly and decently in suitable clothing, not with their hair braided, or with gold, pearls, or expensive clothes, ¹⁰but with good works, as is proper for women who profess reverence for God. ¹¹Let a woman *a* learn in silence with full submission. ¹²I permit no woman *a* to teach or to have authority over a man; *b* she is to keep silent. ¹³For Adam was formed first, then Eve; ¹⁴and Adam was not deceived, but the woman was deceived and became a transgressor. ¹⁵Yet she will be saved through childbearing, provided they continue in faith and love and holiness, with modesty.

Qualifications of Bishops

3 The saying is sure: *c* whoever aspires to the office of bishop *d* desires a noble task. ²Now a bishop *e* must be above reproach, married only once, *f* temperate, sensible, respectable, hospitable, an apt teacher, ³not a drunkard, not violent but gentle, not quarrelsome, and not a lover of money. ⁴He must manage his own household well, keeping his children submissive and respectful in every way— ⁵for if someone does not know how to manage his own household, how can he take care of God's church? ⁶He must not be a recent convert, or he may be puffed up with conceit and fall into the condemnation of the devil. ⁷Moreover, he must be well thought of by outsiders, so that he may not fall into disgrace and the snare of the devil.

Qualifications of Deacons

8 Deacons likewise must be serious, not double-tongued, not indulging in much wine, not greedy for money; ⁹they must hold fast to the mystery of the faith with a clear conscience. ¹⁰And let them first be tested; then, if they prove themselves blameless, let them serve as deacons. ¹¹Women *g* likewise must be serious, not slanderers, but temperate, faith-ful in all things. ¹²Let deacons be married only once, *b* and let them manage their children and their households well; ¹³for those who serve well as deacons gain a good standing for themselves and great boldness in the faith that is in Christ Jesus.

The Mystery of Our Religion

14 I hope to come to you soon, but I am writing these instructions to you so that, ¹⁵if I am delayed, you may know how one ought to behave in the household of God, which is the church of the living God, the pillar and bulwark of the truth. ¹⁶Without any doubt, the mystery of our religion is great:

He *i* was revealed in flesh,
    vindicated *j* in spirit, *k*
      seen by angels,
  proclaimed among Gentiles,
    believed in throughout the world,
      taken up in glory.

False Asceticism

4 Now the Spirit expressly says that in later *l* times some will renounce the faith by paying attention to deceitful spirits and teachings of demons, ²through the hypocrisy of liars whose consciences are seared with a hot iron. ³They forbid marriage and demand abstinence from foods, which God created to be received with thanksgiving by those who believe and know the truth. ⁴For everything created by God is good, and nothing is to be rejected, provided it is received with thanksgiving; ⁵for it is sanctified by God's word and by prayer.

A Good Minister of Jesus Christ

6 If you put these instructions before the brothers and sisters, *m* you will be a good servant *n* of Christ Jesus, nourished on the words of the faith and of the sound teaching that you have followed. ⁷Have nothing to do with profane myths and old wives' tales. Train

a Or *wife* *b* Or *her husband* *c* Some interpreters place these words at the end of the previous paragraph. Other ancient authorities read *The saying is commonly accepted* *d* Or *overseer* *e* Or *an overseer* *f* Gk *the husband of one wife* *g* Or *Their wives*, or *Women deacons* *h* Gk *be husbands of one wife* *i* Gk *Who*; other ancient authorities read *God*; others, *Which* *j* Or *justified* *k* Or *by the Spirit* *l* Or *the last* *m* Gk *brothers* *n* Or *deacon* yourself in godliness, 8for, while physical training is of some value, godliness is valuable in every way, holding promise for both the present life and the life to come. 9The saying is sure and worthy of full acceptance. 10For to this end we toil and struggle,*a* because we have our hope set on the living God, who is the Savior of all people, especially of those who believe.

11 These are the things you must insist on and teach. 12Let no one despise your youth, but set the believers an example in speech and conduct, in love, in faith, in purity. 13Until I arrive, give attention to the public reading of scripture,*b* to exhorting, to teaching. 14Do not neglect the gift that is in you, which was given to you through prophecy with the laying on of hands by the council of elders.*c* 15Put these things into practice, devote yourself to them, so that all may see your progress. 16Pay close attention to yourself and to your teaching; continue in these things, for in doing this you will save both yourself and your hearers.

Duties toward Believers

5 Do not speak harshly to an older man,*d* but speak to him as to a father, to younger men as brothers, 2to older women as mothers, to younger women as sisters—with absolute purity.

3 Honor widows who are really widows. 4If a widow has children or grandchildren, they should first learn their religious duty to their own family and make some repayment to their parents; for this is pleasing in God's sight. 5The real widow, left alone, has set her hope on God and continues in supplications and prayers night and day; 6but the widow*e* who lives for pleasure is dead even while she lives. 7Give these commands as well, so that they may be above reproach. 8And whoever does not provide for relatives, and especially for family members, has denied the faith and is worse than an unbeliever.

9 Let a widow be put on the list if she is not less than sixty years old and has been married only once;*f* 10she must be well attested for her good works, as one who has brought up children, shown hospitality, washed the saints' feet, helped the afflicted, and devoted herself to doing good in every way. 11But refuse to put younger widows on the list; for when their sensual desires alienate them from Christ, they want to marry, 12and so they incur condemnation for having violated their first pledge. 13Besides that, they learn to be idle, gadding about from house to house; and they are not merely idle, but also gossips and busybodies, saying what they should not say. 14So I would have younger widows marry, bear children, and manage their households, so as to give the adversary no occasion to revile us. 15For some have already turned away to follow Satan. 16If any believing woman*g* has relatives who are really widows, let her assist them; let the church not be burdened, so that it can assist those who are real widows.

17 Let the elders who rule well be considered worthy of double honor,*h* especially those who labor in preaching and teaching; 18for the scripture says, "You shall not muzzle an ox while it is treading out the grain," and, "The laborer deserves to be paid." 19Never accept any accusation against an elder except on the evidence of two or three witnesses. 20As for those who persist in sin, rebuke them in the presence of all, so that the rest also may stand in fear. 21In the presence of God and of Christ Jesus and of the elect angels, I warn you to keep these instructions without prejudice, doing nothing on the basis of partiality. 22Do not ordain*i* anyone hastily, and do not participate in the sins of others; keep yourself pure.

23 No longer drink only water, but take a little wine for the sake of your stomach and your frequent ailments.

24 The sins of some people are conspic-

---

a Other ancient authorities read *suffer reproach*   *b* Gk *to the reading*   *c* Gk *by the presbytery*   *d* Or *an elder*, or *a presbyter*   *e* Gk *she*   *f* Gk *the wife of one husband*   *g* Other ancient authorities read *believing man or woman*; others, *believing man*   *h* Or *compensation*   *i* Gk *Do not lay hands on* uous and precede them to judgment, while the sins of others follow them there. ²⁵So also good works are conspicuous; and even when they are not, they cannot remain hidden.

6 Let all who are under the yoke of slavery regard their masters as worthy of all honor, so that the name of God and the teaching may not be blasphemed. ²Those who have believing masters must not be disrespectful to them on the ground that they are members of the church;*a* rather they must serve them all the more, since those who benefit by their service are believers and beloved.*b*

False Teaching and True Riches

Teach and urge these duties. ³Whoever teaches otherwise and does not agree with the sound words of our Lord Jesus Christ and the teaching that is in accordance with godliness, ⁴is conceited, understanding nothing, and has a morbid craving for controversy and for disputes about words. From these come envy, dissension, slander, base suspicions, ⁵and wrangling among those who are depraved in mind and bereft of the truth, imagining that godliness is a means of gain.*c* ⁶Of course, there is great gain in godliness combined with contentment; ⁷for we brought nothing into the world, so that*d* we can take nothing out of it; ⁸but if we have food and clothing, we will be content with these. ⁹But those who want to be rich fall into temptation and are trapped by many senseless and harmful desires that plunge people into ruin and destruction. ¹⁰For the love of money is a root of all kinds of evil, and in their eagerness to be rich some have wandered away from the faith and pierced themselves with many pains.

The Good Fight of Faith

11 But as for you, man of God, shun all this; pursue righteousness, godliness, faith, love, endurance, gentleness. ¹²Fight the good fight of the faith; take hold of the eternal life, to which you were called and for which you made*e* the good confession in the presence of many witnesses. ¹³In the presence of God, who gives life to all things, and of Christ Jesus, who in his testimony before Pontius Pilate made the good confession, I charge you ¹⁴to keep the commandment without spot or blame until the manifestation of our Lord Jesus Christ, ¹⁵which he will bring about at the right time—he who is the blessed and only Sovereign, the King of kings and Lord of lords. ¹⁶It is he alone who has immortality and dwells in unapproachable light, whom no one has ever seen or can see; to him be honor and eternal dominion. Amen.

17 As for those who in the present age are rich, command them not to be haughty, or to set their hopes on the uncertainty of riches, but rather on God who richly provides us with everything for our enjoyment. ¹⁸They are to do good, to be rich in good works, generous, and ready to share, ¹⁹thus storing up for themselves the treasure of a good foundation for the future, so that they may take hold of the life that really is life.

Personal Instructions and Benediction

20 Timothy, guard what has been entrusted to you. Avoid the profane chatter and contradictions of what is falsely called knowledge; ²¹by professing it some have missed the mark as regards the faith.

Grace be with you.*f*

---

a Gk *are brothers*   *b* Or *since they are believers and beloved, who devote themselves to good deeds*   *c* Other ancient authorities add *Withdraw yourself from such people*   *d* Other ancient authorities read *world—it is certain that*   *e* Gk *confessed*   *f* The Greek word for *you* here is plural; in other ancient authorities it is singular. Other ancient authorities add *Amen*

THE SECOND LETTER OF PAUL TO
TIMOTHY

Salutation

1 Paul, an apostle of Christ Jesus by the will of God, for the sake of the promise of life that is in Christ Jesus,

2 To Timothy, my beloved child:

Grace, mercy, and peace from God the Father and Christ Jesus our Lord.

Thanksgiving and Encouragement

3 I am grateful to God—whom I worship with a clear conscience, as my ancestors did—when I remember you constantly in my prayers night and day. 4Recalling your tears, I long to see you so that I may be filled with joy. 5I am reminded of your sincere faith, a faith that lived first in your grandmother Lois and your mother Eunice and now, I am sure, lives in you. 6For this reason I remind you to rekindle the gift of God that is within you through the laying on of my hands; 7for God did not give us a spirit of cowardice, but rather a spirit of power and of love and of self-discipline.

8 Do not be ashamed, then, of the testimony about our Lord or of me his prisoner, but join with me in suffering for the gospel, relying on the power of God, 9who saved us and called us with a holy calling, not according to our works but according to his own purpose and grace. This grace was given to us in Christ Jesus before the ages began, 10but it has now been revealed through the appearing of our Savior Christ Jesus, who abolished death and brought life and immortality to light through the gospel. 11For this gospel I was appointed a herald and an apostle and a teacher,*a* 12and for this reason I suffer as I do. But I am not ashamed, for I know the one in whom I have put my trust, and I am sure that he is able to guard until that day what I have entrusted to him.*b* 13Hold to the standard of sound teaching that you have heard from me, in the faith and love that are in Christ Jesus. 14Guard the good treasure en-trusted to you, with the help of the Holy Spirit living in us.

15 You are aware that all who are in Asia have turned away from me, including Phygelus and Hermogenes. 16May the Lord grant mercy to the household of Onesiphorus, because he often refreshed me and was not ashamed of my chain; 17when he arrived in Rome, he eagerly*c* searched for me and found me 18—may the Lord grant that he will find mercy from the Lord on that day! And you know very well how much service he rendered in Ephesus.

A Good Soldier of Christ Jesus

2 You then, my child, be strong in the grace that is in Christ Jesus; 2and what you have heard from me through many witnesses entrust to faithful people who will be able to teach others as well. 3Share in suffering like a good soldier of Christ Jesus. 4No one serving in the army gets entangled in everyday affairs; the soldier's aim is to please the enlisting officer. 5And in the case of an athlete, no one is crowned without competing according to the rules. 6It is the farmer who does the work who ought to have the first share of the crops. 7Think over what I say, for the Lord will give you understanding in all things.

8 Remember Jesus Christ, raised from the dead, a descendant of David—that is my gospel, 9for which I suffer hardship, even to the point of being chained like a criminal. But the word of God is not chained. 10Therefore I endure everything for the sake of the elect, so that they may also obtain the salvation that is in Christ Jesus, with eternal glory. 11The saying is sure:

If we have died with him, we will also
    live with him;
12 if we endure, we will also reign with
    him;
if we deny him, he will also deny us;

---

13   if we are faithless, he remains
> faithful—
> for he cannot deny himself.

A Worker Approved by God

14 Remind them of this, and warn them before God[a] that they are to avoid wrangling over words, which does no good but only ruins those who are listening. 15Do your best to present yourself to God as one approved by him, a worker who has no need to be ashamed, rightly explaining the word of truth. 16Avoid profane chatter, for it will lead people into more and more impiety, 17and their talk will spread like gangrene. Among them are Hymenaeus and Philetus, 18who have swerved from the truth by claiming that the resurrection has already taken place. They are upsetting the faith of some. 19But God's firm foundation stands, bearing this inscription: "The Lord knows those who are his," and, "Let everyone who calls on the name of the Lord turn away from wickedness."

20 In a large house there are utensils not only of gold and silver but also of wood and clay, some for special use, some for ordinary. 21All who cleanse themselves of the things I have mentioned[b] will become special utensils, dedicated and useful to the owner of the house, ready for every good work. 22Shun youthful passions and pursue righteousness, faith, love, and peace, along with those who call on the Lord from a pure heart. 23Have nothing to do with stupid and senseless controversies; you know that they breed quarrels. 24And the Lord's servant[c] must not be quarrelsome but kindly to everyone, an apt teacher, patient, 25correcting opponents with gentleness. God may perhaps grant that they will repent and come to know the truth, 26and that they may escape from the snare of the devil, having been held captive by him to do his will.[d]

Godlessness in the Last Days

3 You must understand this, that in the last days distressing times will come. 2For people will be lovers of themselves, lovers of money, boasters, arrogant, abusive, disobedient to their parents, ungrateful, unholy, 3inhuman, implacable, slanderers, profligates, brutes, haters of good, 4treacherous, reckless, swollen with conceit, lovers of pleasure rather than lovers of God, 5holding to the outward form of godliness but denying its power. Avoid them! 6For among them are those who make their way into households and captivate silly women, overwhelmed by their sins and swayed by all kinds of desires, 7who are always being instructed and can never arrive at a knowledge of the truth. 8As Jannes and Jambres opposed Moses, so these people, of corrupt mind and counterfeit faith, also oppose the truth. 9But they will not make much progress, because, as in the case of those two men,[e] their folly will become plain to everyone.

Paul's Charge to Timothy

10 Now you have observed my teaching, my conduct, my aim in life, my faith, my patience, my love, my steadfastness, 11my persecutions, and my suffering the things that happened to me in Antioch, Iconium, and Lystra. What persecutions I endured! Yet the Lord rescued me from all of them. 12Indeed, all who want to live a godly life in Christ Jesus will be persecuted. 13But wicked people and impostors will go from bad to worse, deceiving others and being deceived. 14But as for you, continue in what you have learned and firmly believed, knowing from whom you learned it, 15and how from childhood you have known the sacred writings that are able to instruct you for salvation through faith in Christ Jesus. 16All scripture is inspired by God and is[f] useful for teaching, for reproof, for correction, and for training in righteousness, 17so that everyone who belongs to

---

a Other ancient authorities read *the Lord*   b Gk *of these things*   c Gk *slave*   d Or *by him, to do his* (that is, God's) *will*   e Gk lacks *two men*   f Or *Every scripture inspired by God is also*

God may be proficient, equipped for every good work.

4 In the presence of God and of Christ Jesus, who is to judge the living and the dead, and in view of his appearing and his kingdom, I solemnly urge you: ²proclaim the message; be persistent whether the time is favorable or unfavorable; convince, rebuke, and encourage, with the utmost patience in teaching. ³For the time is coming when people will not put up with sound doctrine, but having itching ears, they will accumulate for themselves teachers to suit their own desires, ⁴and will turn away from listening to the truth and wander away to myths. ⁵As for you, always be sober, endure suffering, do the work of an evangelist, carry out your ministry fully.

6 As for me, I am already being poured out as a libation, and the time of my departure has come. ⁷I have fought the good fight, I have finished the race, I have kept the faith. ⁸From now on there is reserved for me the crown of righteousness, which the Lord, the righteous judge, will give me on that day, and not only to me but also to all who have longed for his appearing.

Personal Instructions

9 Do your best to come to me soon, ¹⁰for Demas, in love with this present world, has deserted me and gone to Thessalonica; Crescens has gone to Galatia,ᵃ Titus to Dalmatia. ¹¹Only Luke is with me. Get Mark and bring him with you, for he is useful in my ministry. ¹²I have sent Tychicus to Ephesus. ¹³When you come, bring the cloak that I left with Carpus at Troas, also the books, and above all the parchments. ¹⁴Alexander the coppersmith did me great harm; the Lord will pay him back for his deeds. ¹⁵You also must beware of him, for he strongly opposed our message.

16 At my first defense no one came to my support, but all deserted me. May it not be counted against them! ¹⁷But the Lord stood by me and gave me strength, so that through me the message might be fully proclaimed and all the Gentiles might hear it. So I was rescued from the lion's mouth. ¹⁸The Lord will rescue me from every evil attack and save me for his heavenly kingdom. To him be the glory forever and ever. Amen.

Final Greetings and Benediction

19 Greet Prisca and Aquila, and the household of Onesiphorus. ²⁰Erastus remained in Corinth; Trophimus I left ill in Miletus. ²¹Do your best to come before winter. Eubulus sends greetings to you, as do Pudens and Linus and Claudia and all the brothers and sisters.ᵇ

22 The Lord be with your spirit. Grace be with you.ᶜ

ᵃ Other ancient authorities read *Gaul*   ᵇ Gk *all the brothers*   ᶜ The Greek word for *you* here is plural. Other ancient authorities add *Amen*

THE LETTER OF PAUL TO
TITUS

Salutation

1 Paul, a servant[a] of God and an apostle of Jesus Christ, for the sake of the faith of God's elect and the knowledge of the truth that is in accordance with godliness, [2]in the hope of eternal life that God, who never lies, promised before the ages began— [3]in due time he revealed his word through the proclamation with which I have been entrusted by the command of God our Savior,

4 To Titus, my loyal child in the faith we share:

Grace[b] and peace from God the Father and Christ Jesus our Savior.

Titus in Crete

5 I left you behind in Crete for this reason, so that you should put in order what remained to be done, and should appoint elders in every town, as I directed you: [6]someone who is blameless, married only once,[c] whose children are believers, not accused of debauchery and not rebellious. [7]For a bishop,[d] as God's steward, must be blameless; he must not be arrogant or quick-tempered or addicted to wine or violent or greedy for gain; [8]but he must be hospitable, a lover of goodness, prudent, upright, devout, and self-controlled. [9]He must have a firm grasp of the word that is trustworthy in accordance with the teaching, so that he may be able both to preach with sound doctrine and to refute those who contradict it.

10 There are also many rebellious people, idle talkers and deceivers, especially those of the circumcision; [11]they must be silenced, since they are upsetting whole families by teaching for sordid gain what it is not right to teach. [12]It was one of them, their very own prophet, who said,

"Cretans are always liars, vicious
       brutes, lazy gluttons."

[13]That testimony is true. For this reason rebuke them sharply, so that they may become sound in the faith, [14]not paying attention to Jewish myths or to commandments of those who reject the truth. [15]To the pure all things are pure, but to the corrupt and unbelieving nothing is pure. Their very minds and consciences are corrupted. [16]They profess to know God, but they deny him by their actions. They are detestable, disobedient, unfit for any good work.

Teach Sound Doctrine

2 But as for you, teach what is consistent with sound doctrine. [2]Tell the older men to be temperate, serious, prudent, and sound in faith, in love, and in endurance.

3 Likewise, tell the older women to be reverent in behavior, not to be slanderers or slaves to drink; they are to teach what is good, [4]so that they may encourage the young women to love their husbands, to love their children, [5]to be self-controlled, chaste, good managers of the household, kind, being submissive to their husbands, so that the word of God may not be discredited.

6 Likewise, urge the younger men to be self-controlled. [7]Show yourself in all respects a model of good works, and in your teaching show integrity, gravity, [8]and sound speech that cannot be censured; then any opponent will be put to shame, having nothing evil to say of us.

9 Tell slaves to be submissive to their masters and to give satisfaction in every respect; they are not to talk back, [10]not to pilfer, but to show complete and perfect fidelity, so that in everything they may be an ornament to the doctrine of God our Savior.

11 For the grace of God has appeared, bringing salvation to all,[e] [12]training us to renounce impiety and worldly passions, and in the present age to live lives that are self-controlled, upright, and godly, [13]while we wait for the blessed hope and the manifestation of the glory of our great God and Savior,[f] Jesus

---

a Gk slave   b Other ancient authorities read *Grace, mercy,*   c Gk *husband of one wife*   d Or *an overseer*
e Or *has appeared to all, bringing salvation*   f Or *of the great God and our Savior*

Christ. [14]He it is who gave himself for us that he might redeem us from all iniquity and purify for himself a people of his own who are zealous for good deeds.

15 Declare these things; exhort and reprove with all authority.[a] Let no one look down on you.

Maintain Good Deeds

3 Remind them to be subject to rulers and authorities, to be obedient, to be ready for every good work, [2]to speak evil of no one, to avoid quarreling, to be gentle, and to show every courtesy to everyone. [3]For we ourselves were once foolish, disobedient, led astray, slaves to various passions and pleasures, passing our days in malice and envy, despicable, hating one another. [4]But when the goodness and loving kindness of God our Savior appeared, [5]he saved us, not because of any works of righteousness that we had done, but according to his mercy, through the water[b] of rebirth and renewal by the Holy Spirit. [6]This Spirit he poured out on us richly through Jesus Christ our Savior, [7]so that, having been justified by his grace, we might become heirs according to the hope of eternal life. [8]The saying is sure.

I desire that you insist on these things, so that those who have come to believe in God may be careful to devote themselves to good works; these things are excellent and profitable to everyone. [9]But avoid stupid controversies, genealogies, dissensions, and quarrels about the law, for they are unprofitable and worthless. [10]After a first and second admonition, have nothing more to do with anyone who causes divisions, [11]since you know that such a person is perverted and sinful, being self-condemned.

Final Messages and Benediction

12 When I send Artemas to you, or Tychicus, do your best to come to me at Nicopolis, for I have decided to spend the winter there. [13]Make every effort to send Zenas the lawyer and Apollos on their way, and see that they lack nothing. [14]And let people learn to devote themselves to good works in order to meet urgent needs, so that they may not be unproductive.

15 All who are with me send greetings to you. Greet those who love us in the faith. Grace be with all of you.[c]

---

a Gk commandment   b Gk washing   c Other ancient authorities add Amen

THE LETTER OF PAUL TO
PHILEMON

Salutation

1 Paul, a prisoner of Christ Jesus, and Timothy our brother,*a*

To Philemon our dear friend and co-worker, 2to Apphia our sister,*b* to Archippus our fellow soldier, and to the church in your house:

3 Grace to you and peace from God our Father and the Lord Jesus Christ.

Philemon's Love and Faith

4 When I remember you*c* in my prayers, I always thank my God 5because I hear of your love for all the saints and your faith toward the Lord Jesus. 6I pray that the sharing of your faith may become effective when you perceive all the good that we*d* may do for Christ. 7I have indeed received much joy and encouragement from your love, because the hearts of the saints have been refreshed through you, my brother.

Paul's Plea for Onesimus

8 For this reason, though I am bold enough in Christ to command you to do your duty, 9yet I would rather appeal to you on the basis of love—and I, Paul, do this as an old man, and now also as a prisoner of Christ Jesus.*e* 10I am appealing to you for my child, Onesimus, whose father I have become during my imprisonment. 11Formerly he was useless to you, but now he is indeed useful*f* both to you and to me. 12I am sending him, that is, my own heart, back to you.

13I wanted to keep him with me, so that he might be of service to me in your place during my imprisonment for the gospel; 14but I preferred to do nothing without your consent, in order that your good deed might be voluntary and not something forced. 15Perhaps this is the reason he was separated from you for a while, so that you might have him back forever, 16no longer as a slave but more than a slave, a beloved brother—especially to me but how much more to you, both in the flesh and in the Lord.

17 So if you consider me your partner, welcome him as you would welcome me. 18If he has wronged you in any way, or owes you anything, charge that to my account. 19I, Paul, am writing this with my own hand: I will repay it. I say nothing about your owing me even your own self. 20Yes, brother, let me have this benefit from you in the Lord! Refresh my heart in Christ. 21Confident of your obedience, I am writing to you, knowing that you will do even more than I say.

22 One thing more—prepare a guest room for me, for I am hoping through your prayers to be restored to you.

Final Greetings and Benediction

23 Epaphras, my fellow prisoner in Christ Jesus, sends greetings to you,*g* 24and so do Mark, Aristarchus, Demas, and Luke, my fellow workers.

25 The grace of the Lord Jesus Christ be with your spirit.*h*

---

a Gk *the brother*   *b* Gk *the sister*   *c* From verse 4 through verse 21, *you* is singular   *d* Other ancient authorities read *you* (plural)   *e* Or *as an ambassador of Christ Jesus, and now also his prisoner*   *f* The name Onesimus means *useful* or (compare verse 20) *beneficial*   *g* Here *you* is singular   *h* Other ancient authorities add *Amen*

THE LETTER TO THE
HEBREWS

God Has Spoken by His Son

1 Long ago God spoke to our ancestors in many and various ways by the prophets, ²but in these last days he has spoken to us by a Son,ᵃ whom he appointed heir of all things, through whom he also created the worlds. ³He is the reflection of God's glory and the exact imprint of God's very being, and he sustainsᵇ all things by his powerful word. When he had made purification for sins, he sat down at the right hand of the Majesty on high, ⁴having become as much superior to angels as the name he has inherited is more excellent than theirs.

The Son Is Superior to Angels

5 For to which of the angels did God ever say,

"You are my Son;
today I have begotten you"?

Or again,

"I will be his Father,
and he will be my Son"?

⁶And again, when he brings the firstborn into the world, he says,

"Let all God's angels worship him."

⁷Of the angels he says,

"He makes his angels winds,
and his servants flames of fire."

⁸But of the Son he says,

"Your throne, O God, isᶜ forever and
ever,
and the righteous scepter is the
scepter of yourᵈ kingdom.
9 You have loved righteousness and
hated wickedness;
therefore God, your God, has anointed
you
with the oil of gladness beyond your
companions."

¹⁰And,

"In the beginning, Lord, you founded
the earth,
and the heavens are the work of
your hands;
11 they will perish, but you remain;
they will all wear out like clothing;
12 like a cloak you will roll them up,
and like clothingᵉ they will be
changed.
But you are the same,
and your years will never end."

¹³But to which of the angels has he ever said,

"Sit at my right hand
until I make your enemies a
footstool for your feet"?

¹⁴Are not all angelsᶠ spirits in the divine service, sent to serve for the sake of those who are to inherit salvation?

Warning to Pay Attention

2 Therefore we must pay greater attention to what we have heard, so that we do not drift away from it. ²For if the message declared through angels was valid, and every transgression or disobedience received a just penalty, ³how can we escape if we neglect so great a salvation? It was declared at first through the Lord, and it was attested to us by those who heard him, ⁴while God added his testimony by signs and wonders and various miracles, and by gifts of the Holy Spirit, distributed according to his will.

Exaltation through Abasement

5 Now Godᵍ did not subject the coming world, about which we are speaking, to angels. ⁶But someone has testified somewhere,

"What are human beings that you are
mindful of them,ʰ
or mortals, that you care for them?ⁱ
7 You have made them for a little while
lowerʲ than the angels;

---

a Or the Son   b Or bears along   c Or God is your throne
authorities lack like clothing   f Gk all of them   g Gk he
the son of man that you care for him? In the Hebrew of Psalm 8.4-6 both man and son of man refer to all humankind
j Or them only a little lower

d Other ancient authorities read his   e Other ancient
h Gk What is man that you are mindful of him?   i Gk or

you have crowned them with glory
and honor,*a*
8 subjecting all things under their
feet."

Now in subjecting all things to them, God*b*
left nothing outside their control. As it is,
we do not yet see everything in subjection to
them, 9but we do see Jesus, who for a little
while was made lower*c* than the angels, now
crowned with glory and honor because of the
suffering of death, so that by the grace of
God*d* he might taste death for everyone.

10 It was fitting that God,*b* for whom
and through whom all things exist, in bringing many children to glory, should make the
pioneer of their salvation perfect through
sufferings. 11For the one who sanctifies and
those who are sanctified all have one Father.*e*
For this reason Jesus*b* is not ashamed to call
them brothers and sisters,*f* 12saying,

"I will proclaim your name to my
brothers and sisters,*f*
in the midst of the congregation I
will praise you."

13And again,

"I will put my trust in him."

And again,

"Here am I and the children whom
God has given me."

14 Since, therefore, the children share
flesh and blood, he himself likewise shared
the same things, so that through death he
might destroy the one who has the power of
death, that is, the devil, 15and free those who
all their lives were held in slavery by the fear
of death. 16For it is clear that he did not
come to help angels, but the descendants of
Abraham. 17Therefore he had to become like
his brothers and sisters*f* in every respect, so
that he might be a merciful and faithful high
priest in the service of God, to make a sacrifice of atonement for the sins of the people. 18Because he himself was tested by what
he suffered, he is able to help those who are
being tested.

Moses a Servant, Christ a Son

3 Therefore, brothers and sisters,*f* holy
partners in a heavenly calling, consider
that Jesus, the apostle and high priest of our
confession, 2was faithful to the one who appointed him, just as Moses also "was faithful
in all*g* God's*b* house." 3Yet Jesus*i* is worthy of
more glory than Moses, just as the builder of
a house has more honor than the house itself.
4(For every house is built by someone, but the
builder of all things is God.) 5Now Moses
was faithful in all God's*b* house as a servant,
to testify to the things that would be spoken
later. 6Christ, however, was faithful over
God's*b* house as a son, and we are his house
if we hold firm*j* the confidence and the pride
that belong to hope.

Warning against Unbelief

7 Therefore, as the Holy Spirit says,
"Today, if you hear his voice,
8 do not harden your hearts as in the
rebellion,
as on the day of testing in the
wilderness,
9 where your ancestors put me to the
test,
though they had seen my works 10for
forty years.
Therefore I was angry with that
generation,
and I said, 'They always go astray in
their hearts,
and they have not known my ways.'
11 As in my anger I swore,
'They will not enter my rest.' "

12Take care, brothers and sisters,*f* that none
of you may have an evil, unbelieving heart
that turns away from the living God. 13But
exhort one another every day, as long as it is
called "today," so that none of you may be
hardened by the deceitfulness of sin. 14For we
have become partners of Christ, if only we
hold our first confidence firm to the end.
15As it is said,

---

a Other ancient authorities add *and set them over the works of your hands*   *b* Gk *he*   *c* Or *who was made a little lower*
d Other ancient authorities read *apart from God*   *e* Gk *are all of one*   *f* Gk *brothers*   *g* Other ancient authorities
lack *all*   *h* Gk *his*   *i* Gk *this one*   *j* Other ancient authorities add *to the end*

"Today, if you hear his voice,
  do not harden your hearts as in the
    rebellion."

16Now who were they who heard and yet were rebellious? Was it not all those who left Egypt under the leadership of Moses? 17But with whom was he angry forty years? Was it not those who sinned, whose bodies fell in the wilderness? 18And to whom did he swear that they would not enter his rest, if not to those who were disobedient? 19So we see that they were unable to enter because of unbelief.

The Rest That God Promised

4 Therefore, while the promise of entering his rest is still open, let us take care that none of you should seem to have failed to reach it. 2For indeed the good news came to us just as to them; but the message they heard did not benefit them, because they were not united by faith with those who listened.ᵃ 3For we who have believed enter that rest, just as Godᵇ has said,

"As in my anger I swore,
  'They shall not enter my rest,' "

though his works were finished at the foundation of the world. 4For in one place it speaks about the seventh day as follows, "And God rested on the seventh day from all his works." 5And again in this place it says, "They shall not enter my rest." 6Since therefore it remains open for some to enter it, and those who formerly received the good news failed to enter because of disobedience, 7again he sets a certain day—"today"—saying through David much later, in the words already quoted,

"Today, if you hear his voice,
  do not harden your hearts."

8For if Joshua had given them rest, Godᵇ would not speak later about another day. 9So then, a sabbath rest still remains for the people of God; 10for those who enter God's rest also cease from their labors as God did from his. 11Let us therefore make every effort to enter that rest, so that no one may fall through such disobedience as theirs.

12 Indeed, the word of God is living and active, sharper than any two-edged sword, piercing until it divides soul from spirit, joints from marrow; it is able to judge the thoughts and intentions of the heart. 13And before him no creature is hidden, but all are naked and laid bare to the eyes of the one to whom we must render an account.

Jesus the Great High Priest

14 Since, then, we have a great high priest who has passed through the heavens, Jesus, the Son of God, let us hold fast to our confession. 15For we do not have a high priest who is unable to sympathize with our weaknesses, but we have one who in every respect has been testedᶜ as we are, yet without sin. 16Let us therefore approach the throne of grace with boldness, so that we may receive mercy and find grace to help in time of need.

5 Every high priest chosen from among mortals is put in charge of things pertaining to God on their behalf, to offer gifts and sacrifices for sins. 2He is able to deal gently with the ignorant and wayward, since he himself is subject to weakness; 3and because of this he must offer sacrifice for his own sins as well as for those of the people. 4And one does not presume to take this honor, but takes it only when called by God, just as Aaron was.

5 So also Christ did not glorify himself in becoming a high priest, but was appointed by the one who said to him,

"You are my Son,
  today I have begotten you";

6as he says also in another place,

"You are a priest forever,
  according to the order of
    Melchizedek."

7 In the days of his flesh, Jesusᵇ offered up prayers and supplications, with loud cries and tears, to the one who was able to save him from death, and he was heard because of

---

a Other ancient authorities read *it did not meet with faith in those who listened*   *b* Gk *he*   *c* Or *tempted* his reverent submission. 8Although he was a Son, he learned obedience through what he suffered; 9and having been made perfect, he became the source of eternal salvation for all who obey him, 10having been designated by God a high priest according to the order of Melchizedek.

Warning against Falling Away

11 About this*a* we have much to say that is hard to explain, since you have become dull in understanding. 12For though by this time you ought to be teachers, you need someone to teach you again the basic elements of the oracles of God. You need milk, not solid food; 13for everyone who lives on milk, being still an infant, is unskilled in the word of righteousness. 14But solid food is for the mature, for those whose faculties have been trained by practice to distinguish good from evil.

The Peril of Falling Away

6 Therefore let us go on toward perfection,*b* leaving behind the basic teaching about Christ, and not laying again the foundation: repentance from dead works and faith toward God, 2instruction about baptisms, laying on of hands, resurrection of the dead, and eternal judgment. 3And we will do*c* this, if God permits. 4For it is impossible to restore again to repentance those who have once been enlightened, and have tasted the heavenly gift, and have shared in the Holy Spirit, 5and have tasted the goodness of the word of God and the powers of the age to come, 6and then have fallen away, since on their own they are crucifying again the Son of God and are holding him up to contempt. 7Ground that drinks up the rain falling on it repeatedly, and that produces a crop useful to those for whom it is cultivated, receives a blessing from God. 8But if it produces thorns and thistles, it is worthless and on the verge of being cursed; its end is to be burned over.

9 Even though we speak in this way, beloved, we are confident of better things in your case, things that belong to salvation. 10For God is not unjust; he will not overlook your work and the love that you showed for his sake*d* in serving the saints, as you still do. 11And we want each one of you to show the same diligence so as to realize the full assurance of hope to the very end, 12so that you may not become sluggish, but imitators of those who through faith and patience inherit the promises.

The Certainty of God's Promise

13 When God made a promise to Abraham, because he had no one greater by whom to swear, he swore by himself, 14saying, "I will surely bless you and multiply you." 15And thus Abraham,*e* having patiently endured, obtained the promise. 16Human beings, of course, swear by someone greater than themselves, and an oath given as confirmation puts an end to all dispute. 17In the same way, when God desired to show even more clearly to the heirs of the promise the unchangeable character of his purpose, he guaranteed it by an oath, 18so that through two unchangeable things, in which it is impossible that God would prove false, we who have taken refuge might be strongly encouraged to seize the hope set before us. 19We have this hope, a sure and steadfast anchor of the soul, a hope that enters the inner shrine behind the curtain, 20where Jesus, a forerunner on our behalf, has entered, having become a high priest forever according to the order of Melchizedek.

The Priestly Order of Melchizedek

7 This "King Melchizedek of Salem, priest of the Most High God, met Abraham as he was returning from defeating the kings and blessed him"; 2and to him Abraham apportioned "one-tenth of everything." His name, in the first place, means "king of righteousness"; next he is also king of Salem, that is, "king of peace." 3Without father, without

a Or *him*   *b* Or *toward maturity*   *c* Other ancient authorities read *let us do*   *d* Gk *for his name*   *e* Gk *he* mother, without genealogy, having neither beginning of days nor end of life, but resembling the Son of God, he remains a priest forever.

4 See how great he is! Even[a] Abraham the patriarch gave him a tenth of the spoils. [5]And those descendants of Levi who receive the priestly office have a commandment in the law to collect tithes[b] from the people, that is, from their kindred,[c] though these also are descended from Abraham. [6]But this man, who does not belong to their ancestry, collected tithes[b] from Abraham and blessed him who had received the promises. [7]It is beyond dispute that the inferior is blessed by the superior. [8]In the one case, tithes are received by those who are mortal; in the other, by one of whom it is testified that he lives. [9]One might even say that Levi himself, who receives tithes, paid tithes through Abraham, [10]for he was still in the loins of his ancestor when Melchizedek met him.

Another Priest, Like Melchizedek

11 Now if perfection had been attainable through the levitical priesthood—for the people received the law under this priesthood—what further need would there have been to speak of another priest arising according to the order of Melchizedek, rather than one according to the order of Aaron? [12]For when there is a change in the priesthood, there is necessarily a change in the law as well. [13]Now the one of whom these things are spoken belonged to another tribe, from which no one has ever served at the altar. [14]For it is evident that our Lord was descended from Judah, and in connection with that tribe Moses said nothing about priests.

15 It is even more obvious when another priest arises, resembling Melchizedek, [16]one who has become a priest, not through a legal requirement concerning physical descent, but through the power of an indestructible life. [17]For it is attested of him,

"You are a priest forever,

according to the order of
    Melchizedek."

[18]There is, on the one hand, the abrogation of an earlier commandment because it was weak and ineffectual [19](for the law made nothing perfect); there is, on the other hand, the introduction of a better hope, through which we approach God.

20 This was confirmed with an oath; for others who became priests took their office without an oath, [21]but this one became a priest with an oath, because of the one who said to him,

"The Lord has sworn
    and will not change his mind,
'You are a priest forever' "—

[22]accordingly Jesus has also become the guarantee of a better covenant.

23 Furthermore, the former priests were many in number, because they were prevented by death from continuing in office; [24]but he holds his priesthood permanently, because he continues forever. [25]Consequently he is able for all time to save[d] those who approach God through him, since he always lives to make intercession for them.

26 For it was fitting that we should have such a high priest, holy, blameless, undefiled, separated from sinners, and exalted above the heavens. [27]Unlike the other[e] high priests, he has no need to offer sacrifices day after day, first for his own sins, and then for those of the people; this he did once for all when he offered himself. [28]For the law appoints as high priests those who are subject to weakness, but the word of the oath, which came later than the law, appoints a Son who has been made perfect forever.

Mediator of a Better Covenant

8 Now the main point in what we are saying is this: we have such a high priest, one who is seated at the right hand of the throne of the Majesty in the heavens, [2]a minister in the sanctuary and the true tent[f] that the Lord, and not any mortal, has set up.

---

a Other ancient authorities lack *Even*   b Or *a tenth*   c Gk *brothers*   d Or *able to save completely*   e Gk lacks *other*   f Or *tabernacle*

³For every high priest is appointed to offer gifts and sacrifices; hence it is necessary for this priest also to have something to offer. ⁴Now if he were on earth, he would not be a priest at all, since there are priests who offer gifts according to the law. ⁵They offer worship in a sanctuary that is a sketch and shadow of the heavenly one; for Moses, when he was about to erect the tent,ᵃ was warned, "See that you make everything according to the pattern that was shown you on the mountain." ⁶But Jesusᵇ has now obtained a more excellent ministry, and to that degree he is the mediator of a better covenant, which has been enacted through better promises. ⁷For if that first covenant had been faultless, there would have been no need to look for a second one.

8 Godᶜ finds fault with them when he says:

"The days are surely coming, says the
   Lord,
      when I will establish a new covenant
         with the house of Israel
      and with the house of Judah;
9   not like the covenant that I made with
         their ancestors,
      on the day when I took them by the
         hand to lead them out of the
         land of Egypt;
   for they did not continue in my
      covenant,
   and so I had no concern for them,
      says the Lord.
10   This is the covenant that I will make
         with the house of Israel
      after those days, says the Lord:
   I will put my laws in their minds,
      and write them on their hearts,
   and I will be their God,
      and they shall be my people.
11   And they shall not teach one another
      or say to each other, 'Know the
         Lord,'
      for they shall all know me,

from the least of them to the
   greatest.
12   For I will be merciful toward their
      iniquities,
   and I will remember their sins no
      more."

¹³In speaking of "a new covenant," he has made the first one obsolete. And what is obsolete and growing old will soon disappear.

The Earthly and the Heavenly Sanctuaries

9 Now even the first covenant had regulations for worship and an earthly sanctuary. ²For a tentᵃ was constructed, the first one, in which were the lampstand, the table, and the bread of the Presence;ᵈ this is called the Holy Place. ³Behind the second curtain was a tentᵃ called the Holy of Holies. ⁴In it stood the golden altar of incense and the ark of the covenant overlaid on all sides with gold, in which there were a golden urn holding the manna, and Aaron's rod that budded, and the tablets of the covenant; ⁵above it were the cherubim of glory overshadowing the mercy seat.ᵉ Of these things we cannot speak now in detail.

6 Such preparations having been made, the priests go continually into the first tentᵃ to carry out their ritual duties; ⁷but only the high priest goes into the second, and he but once a year, and not without taking the blood that he offers for himself and for the sins committed unintentionally by the people. ⁸By this the Holy Spirit indicates that the way into the sanctuary has not yet been disclosed as long as the first tentᵃ is still standing. ⁹This is a symbolᶠ of the present time, during which gifts and sacrifices are offered that cannot perfect the conscience of the worshiper, ¹⁰but deal only with food and drink and various baptisms, regulations for the body imposed until the time comes to set things right.

11 But when Christ came as a high priest of the good things that have come,ᵍ then through the greater and perfectʰ tentᵃ (not made with hands, that is, not of this cre-

a Or tabernacle   b Gk he   c Gk He   d Gk the presentation of the loaves   e Or the place of atonement
f Gk parable   g Other ancient authorities read good things to come   h Gk more perfect

ation), [12]he entered once for all into the Holy Place, not with the blood of goats and calves, but with his own blood, thus obtaining eternal redemption. [13]For if the blood of goats and bulls, with the sprinkling of the ashes of a heifer, sanctifies those who have been defiled so that their flesh is purified, [14]how much more will the blood of Christ, who through the eternal Spirit[a] offered himself without blemish to God, purify our[b] conscience from dead works to worship the living God!

15 For this reason he is the mediator of a new covenant, so that those who are called may receive the promised eternal inheritance, because a death has occurred that redeems them from the transgressions under the first covenant.[c] [16]Where a will[c] is involved, the death of the one who made it must be established. [17]For a will[c] takes effect only at death, since it is not in force as long as the one who made it is alive. [18]Hence not even the first covenant was inaugurated without blood. [19]For when every commandment had been told to all the people by Moses in accordance with the law, he took the blood of calves and goats,[d] with water and scarlet wool and hyssop, and sprinkled both the scroll itself and all the people, [20]saying, "This is the blood of the covenant that God has ordained for you." [21]And in the same way he sprinkled with the blood both the tent[e] and all the vessels used in worship. [22]Indeed, under the law almost everything is purified with blood, and without the shedding of blood there is no forgiveness of sins.

Christ's Sacrifice Takes Away Sin

23 Thus it was necessary for the sketches of the heavenly things to be purified with these rites, but the heavenly things themselves need better sacrifices than these. [24]For Christ did not enter a sanctuary made by human hands, a mere copy of the true one, but

he entered into heaven itself, now to appear in the presence of God on our behalf. [25]Nor was it to offer himself again and again, as the high priest enters the Holy Place year after year with blood that is not his own; [26]for then he would have had to suffer again and again since the foundation of the world. But as it is, he has appeared once for all at the end of the age to remove sin by the sacrifice of himself. [27]And just as it is appointed for mortals to die once, and after that the judgment, [28]so Christ, having been offered once to bear the sins of many, will appear a second time, not to deal with sin, but to save those who are eagerly waiting for him.

Christ's Sacrifice Once for All

10 Since the law has only a shadow of the good things to come and not the true form of these realities, it[f] can never, by the same sacrifices that are continually offered year after year, make perfect those who approach. [2]Otherwise, would they not have ceased being offered, since the worshipers, cleansed once for all, would no longer have any consciousness of sin? [3]But in these sacrifices there is a reminder of sin year after year. [4]For it is impossible for the blood of bulls and goats to take away sins. [5]Consequently, when Christ[g] came into the world, he said,

> "Sacrifices and offerings you have not desired,
>   but a body you have prepared for me;
> [6] in burnt offerings and sin offerings you have taken no pleasure.
> [7] Then I said, 'See, God, I have come to do your will, O God'
>   (in the scroll of the book[b] it is written of me)."

[8]When he said above, "You have neither desired nor taken pleasure in sacrifices and offerings and burnt offerings and sin offer-

---

a Other ancient authorities read *Holy Spirit*   b Other ancient authorities read *your*   c The Greek word used here means both *covenant* and *will*   d Other ancient authorities lack *and goats*   e Or *tabernacle*   f Other ancient authorities read *they*   g Gk *he*   h Meaning of Gk uncertain ings" (these are offered according to the law), [9]then he added, "See, I have come to do your will." He abolishes the first in order to establish the second. [10]And it is by God's will[a] that we have been sanctified through the offering of the body of Jesus Christ once for all.

11 And every priest stands day after day at his service, offering again and again the same sacrifices that can never take away sins. [12]But when Christ[b] had offered for all time a single sacrifice for sins, "he sat down at the right hand of God," [13]and since then has been waiting "until his enemies would be made a footstool for his feet." [14]For by a single offering he has perfected for all time those who are sanctified. [15]And the Holy Spirit also testifies to us, for after saying,

16 "This is the covenant that I will make
　　　　　with them
　　after those days, says the Lord:
　I will put my laws in their hearts,
　　and I will write them on their
　　　　　minds,"
[17]he also adds,
　"I will remember[c] their sins and their
　　　　lawless deeds no more."
[18]Where there is forgiveness of these, there is no longer any offering for sin.

A Call to Persevere

19 Therefore, my friends,[d] since we have confidence to enter the sanctuary by the blood of Jesus, [20]by the new and living way that he opened for us through the curtain (that is, through his flesh), [21]and since we have a great priest over the house of God, [22]let us approach with a true heart in full assurance of faith, with our hearts sprinkled clean from an evil conscience and our bodies washed with pure water. [23]Let us hold fast to the confession of our hope without wavering, for he who has promised is faithful. [24]And let us consider how to provoke one another to love and good deeds, [25]not neglecting to meet together, as is the habit of some, but encouraging one another, and all the more as you see the Day approaching.

26 For if we willfully persist in sin after having received the knowledge of the truth, there no longer remains a sacrifice for sins, [27]but a fearful prospect of judgment, and a fury of fire that will consume the adversaries. [28]Anyone who has violated the law of Moses dies without mercy "on the testimony of two or three witnesses." [29]How much worse punishment do you think will be deserved by those who have spurned the Son of God, profaned the blood of the covenant by which they were sanctified, and outraged the Spirit of grace? [30]For we know the one who said, "Vengeance is mine, I will repay." And again, "The Lord will judge his people." [31]It is a fearful thing to fall into the hands of the living God.

32 But recall those earlier days when, after you had been enlightened, you endured a hard struggle with sufferings, [33]sometimes being publicly exposed to abuse and persecution, and sometimes being partners with those so treated. [34]For you had compassion for those who were in prison, and you cheerfully accepted the plundering of your possessions, knowing that you yourselves possessed something better and more lasting. [35]Do not, therefore, abandon that confidence of yours; it brings a great reward. [36]For you need endurance, so that when you have done the will of God, you may receive what was promised. [37]For yet
　"in a very little while,
　　the one who is coming will come
　　　　and will not delay;
38 　but my righteous one will live by faith.
　My soul takes no pleasure in anyone
　　　　who shrinks back."
[39]But we are not among those who shrink back and so are lost, but among those who have faith and so are saved.

---

a Gk *by that will*　　*b* Gk *this one*　　*c* Gk *on their minds and I will remember*　　*d* Gk *Therefore, brothers*

The Meaning of Faith

11 Now faith is the assurance of things hoped for, the conviction of things not seen. 2Indeed, by faith[a] our ancestors received approval. 3By faith we understand that the worlds were prepared by the word of God, so that what is seen was made from things that are not visible.[b]

The Examples of Abel, Enoch, and Noah

4 By faith Abel offered to God a more acceptable[c] sacrifice than Cain's. Through this he received approval as righteous, God himself giving approval to his gifts; he died, but through his faith[d] he still speaks. 5By faith Enoch was taken so that he did not experience death; and "he was not found, because God had taken him." For it was attested before he was taken away that "he had pleased God." 6And without faith it is impossible to please God, for whoever would approach him must believe that he exists and that he rewards those who seek him. 7By faith Noah, warned by God about events as yet unseen, respected the warning and built an ark to save his household; by this he condemned the world and became an heir to the righteousness that is in accordance with faith.

The Faith of Abraham

8 By faith Abraham obeyed when he was called to set out for a place that he was to receive as an inheritance; and he set out, not knowing where he was going. 9By faith he stayed for a time in the land he had been promised, as in a foreign land, living in tents, as did Isaac and Jacob, who were heirs with him of the same promise. 10For he looked forward to the city that has foundations, whose architect and builder is God. 11By faith he received power of procreation, even though he was too old—and Sarah herself was barren—because he considered him faithful who had promised.[e] 12Therefore from one person, and this one as good as dead, descendants were born, "as many as the stars of heaven and as the innumerable grains of sand by the seashore."

13 All of these died in faith without having received the promises, but from a distance they saw and greeted them. They confessed that they were strangers and foreigners on the earth, 14for people who speak in this way make it clear that they are seeking a homeland. 15If they had been thinking of the land that they had left behind, they would have had opportunity to return. 16But as it is, they desire a better country, that is, a heavenly one. Therefore God is not ashamed to be called their God; indeed, he has prepared a city for them.

17 By faith Abraham, when put to the test, offered up Isaac. He who had received the promises was ready to offer up his only son, 18of whom he had been told, "It is through Isaac that descendants shall be named for you." 19He considered the fact that God is able even to raise someone from the dead—and figuratively speaking, he did receive him back. 20By faith Isaac invoked blessings for the future on Jacob and Esau. 21By faith Jacob, when dying, blessed each of the sons of Joseph, "bowing in worship over the top of his staff." 22By faith Joseph, at the end of his life, made mention of the exodus of the Israelites and gave instructions about his burial.[f]

The Faith of Moses

23 By faith Moses was hidden by his parents for three months after his birth, because they saw that the child was beautiful; and they were not afraid of the king's edict.[g] 24By faith Moses, when he was grown up, refused to be called a son of Pharaoh's daughter, 25choosing rather to share ill-treatment with the people of God than to enjoy the fleeting pleasures of sin. 26He considered abuse suffered for the Christ[h] to be greater wealth

---

a Gk *by this*   b Or *was not made out of visible things*   c Gk *greater*   d Gk *through it*   e Or *By faith Sarah herself, though barren, received power to conceive, even when she was too old, because she considered him faithful who had promised.*   f Gk *his bones*   g Other ancient authorities add *By faith Moses, when he was grown up, killed the Egyptian, because he observed the humiliation of his people* (Gk *brothers*)   h Or *the Messiah* than the treasures of Egypt, for he was looking ahead to the reward. 27By faith he left Egypt, unafraid of the king's anger; for he persevered as though*a* he saw him who is invisible. 28By faith he kept the Passover and the sprinkling of blood, so that the destroyer of the firstborn would not touch the firstborn of Israel.*b*

The Faith of Other Israelite Heroes

29 By faith the people passed through the Red Sea as if it were dry land, but when the Egyptians attempted to do so they were drowned. 30By faith the walls of Jericho fell after they had been encircled for seven days. 31By faith Rahab the prostitute did not perish with those who were disobedient,*c* because she had received the spies in peace.

32 And what more should I say? For time would fail me to tell of Gideon, Barak, Samson, Jephthah, of David and Samuel and the prophets— 33who through faith conquered kingdoms, administered justice, obtained promises, shut the mouths of lions, 34quenched raging fire, escaped the edge of the sword, won strength out of weakness, became mighty in war, put foreign armies to flight. 35Women received their dead by resurrection. Others were tortured, refusing to accept release, in order to obtain a better resurrection. 36Others suffered mocking and flogging, and even chains and imprisonment. 37They were stoned to death, they were sawn in two,*d* they were killed by the sword; they went about in skins of sheep and goats, destitute, persecuted, tormented— 38of whom the world was not worthy. They wandered in deserts and mountains, and in caves and holes in the ground.

39 Yet all these, though they were commended for their faith, did not receive what was promised, 40since God had provided something better so that they would not, apart from us, be made perfect.

The Example of Jesus

12 Therefore, since we are surrounded by so great a cloud of witnesses, let us also lay aside every weight and the sin that clings so closely,*e* and let us run with perseverance the race that is set before us, 2looking to Jesus the pioneer and perfecter of our faith, who for the sake of*f* the joy that was set before him endured the cross, disregarding its shame, and has taken his seat at the right hand of the throne of God.

3 Consider him who endured such hostility against himself from sinners,*g* so that you may not grow weary or lose heart. 4In your struggle against sin you have not yet resisted to the point of shedding your blood. 5And you have forgotten the exhortation that addresses you as children—

> "My child, do not regard lightly the
> discipline of the Lord,
> or lose heart when you are punished
> by him;
> 6 for the Lord disciplines those whom he
> loves,
> and chastises every child whom he
> accepts."

7Endure trials for the sake of discipline. God is treating you as children; for what child is there whom a parent does not discipline? 8If you do not have that discipline in which all children share, then you are illegitimate and not his children. 9Moreover, we had human parents to discipline us, and we respected them. Should we not be even more willing to be subject to the Father of spirits and live? 10For they disciplined us for a short time as seemed best to them, but he disciplines us for our good, in order that we may share his holiness. 11Now, discipline always seems painful rather than pleasant at the time, but later it yields the peaceful fruit of righteousness to those who have been trained by it.

12 Therefore lift your drooping hands and strengthen your weak knees, 13and make straight paths for your feet, so that what is

---

a Or *because*   *b* Gk *would not touch them*   *c* Or *unbelieving*   *d* Other ancient authorities add *they were tempted*   *e* Other ancient authorities read *sin that easily distracts*   *f* Or *who instead of*   *g* Other ancient authorities read *such hostility from sinners against themselves* lame may not be put out of joint, but rather be healed.

Warnings against Rejecting God's Grace

14 Pursue peace with everyone, and the holiness without which no one will see the Lord. 15See to it that no one fails to obtain the grace of God; that no root of bitterness springs up and causes trouble, and through it many become defiled. 16See to it that no one becomes like Esau, an immoral and godless person, who sold his birthright for a single meal. 17You know that later, when he wanted to inherit the blessing, he was rejected, for he found no chance to repent,*a* even though he sought the blessing*b* with tears.

18 You have not come to something*c* that can be touched, a blazing fire, and darkness, and gloom, and a tempest, 19and the sound of a trumpet, and a voice whose words made the hearers beg that not another word be spoken to them. 20(For they could not endure the order that was given, "If even an animal touches the mountain, it shall be stoned to death." 21Indeed, so terrifying was the sight that Moses said, "I tremble with fear.") 22But you have come to Mount Zion and to the city of the living God, the heavenly Jerusalem, and to innumerable angels in festal gathering, 23and to the assembly*d* of the firstborn who are enrolled in heaven, and to God the judge of all, and to the spirits of the righteous made perfect, 24and to Jesus, the mediator of a new covenant, and to the sprinkled blood that speaks a better word than the blood of Abel.

25 See that you do not refuse the one who is speaking; for if they did not escape when they refused the one who warned them on earth, how much less will we escape if we reject the one who warns from heaven! 26At that time his voice shook the earth; but now he has promised, "Yet once more I will shake not only the earth but also the heaven." 27This phrase, "Yet once more," indicates the removal of what is shaken—that is, cre-

ated things—so that what cannot be shaken may remain. 28Therefore, since we are receiving a kingdom that cannot be shaken, let us give thanks, by which we offer to God an acceptable worship with reverence and awe; 29for indeed our God is a consuming fire.

Service Well-Pleasing to God

13 Let mutual love continue. 2Do not neglect to show hospitality to strangers, for by doing that some have entertained angels without knowing it. 3Remember those who are in prison, as though you were in prison with them; those who are being tortured, as though you yourselves were being tortured.*e* 4Let marriage be held in honor by all, and let the marriage bed be kept undefiled; for God will judge fornicators and adulterers. 5Keep your lives free from the love of money, and be content with what you have; for he has said, "I will never leave you or forsake you." 6So we can say with confidence,

"The Lord is my helper;
   I will not be afraid.
What can anyone do to me?"

7 Remember your leaders, those who spoke the word of God to you; consider the outcome of their way of life, and imitate their faith. 8Jesus Christ is the same yesterday and today and forever. 9Do not be carried away by all kinds of strange teachings; for it is well for the heart to be strengthened by grace, not by regulations about food,*f* which have not benefited those who observe them. 10We have an altar from which those who officiate in the tent*g* have no right to eat. 11For the bodies of those animals whose blood is brought into the sanctuary by the high priest as a sacrifice for sin are burned outside the camp. 12Therefore Jesus also suffered outside the city gate in order to sanctify the people by his own blood. 13Let us then go to him outside the camp and bear the abuse he endured. 14For here we have no lasting city, but we are looking for the city that is to come.

---

a Or *no chance to change his father's mind*   *b* Gk *it*   *c* Other ancient authorities read *a mountain*   *d* Or *angels, and to the festal gathering* 23*and assembly*   *e* Gk *were in the body*   *f* Gk *not by foods*   *g* Or *tabernacle*

15Through him, then, let us continually offer a sacrifice of praise to God, that is, the fruit of lips that confess his name. 16Do not neglect to do good and to share what you have, for such sacrifices are pleasing to God.

17 Obey your leaders and submit to them, for they are keeping watch over your souls and will give an account. Let them do this with joy and not with sighing—for that would be harmful to you.

18 Pray for us; we are sure that we have a clear conscience, desiring to act honorably in all things. 19I urge you all the more to do this, so that I may be restored to you very soon.

Benediction

20 Now may the God of peace, who brought back from the dead our Lord Jesus, the great shepherd of the sheep, by the blood of the eternal covenant, 21make you complete in everything good so that you may do his will, working among us *a* that which is pleasing in his sight, through Jesus Christ, to whom be the glory forever and ever. Amen.

Final Exhortation and Greetings

22 I appeal to you, brothers and sisters, *b* bear with my word of exhortation, for I have written to you briefly. 23I want you to know that our brother Timothy has been set free; and if he comes in time, he will be with me when I see you. 24Greet all your leaders and all the saints. Those from Italy send you greetings. 25Grace be with all of you. *c*

a Other ancient authorities read *you*   *b* Gk *brothers*   *c* Other ancient authorities add *Amen*

THE LETTER OF
JAMES

Salutation

1 James, a servant[a] of God and of the
Lord Jesus Christ,
To the twelve tribes in the Dispersion:
Greetings.

Faith and Wisdom

2 My brothers and sisters,[b] whenever you
face trials of any kind, consider it nothing but
joy, 3because you know that the testing of
your faith produces endurance; 4and let endurance have its full effect, so that you may
be mature and complete, lacking in nothing.

5 If any of you is lacking in wisdom, ask
God, who gives to all generously and un-
grudgingly, and it will be given you. 6But ask
in faith, never doubting, for the one who
doubts is like a wave of the sea, driven and
tossed by the wind; 7, 8for the doubter, being
double-minded and unstable in every way,
must not expect to receive anything from
the Lord.

Poverty and Riches

9 Let the believer[c] who is lowly boast in
being raised up, 10and the rich in being
brought low, because the rich will disappear
like a flower in the field. 11For the sun rises
with its scorching heat and withers the field;
its flower falls, and its beauty perishes. It is the
same way with the rich; in the midst of a
busy life, they will wither away.

Trial and Temptation

12 Blessed is anyone who endures temptation. Such a one has stood the test and will
receive the crown of life that the Lord[d] has
promised to those who love him. 13No one,
when tempted, should say, "I am being tempted by God"; for God cannot be tempted by
evil and he himself tempts no one. 14But one
is tempted by one's own desire, being lured
and enticed by it; 15then, when that desire

has conceived, it gives birth to sin, and that
sin, when it is fully grown, gives birth to death.
16Do not be deceived, my beloved.[e]

17 Every generous act of giving, with
every perfect gift, is from above, coming
down from the Father of lights, with whom
there is no variation or shadow due to
change.[f] 18In fulfillment of his own purpose
he gave us birth by the word of truth, so that
we would become a kind of first fruits of his
creatures.

Hearing and Doing the Word

19 You must understand this, my be-
loved:[e] let everyone be quick to listen, slow to
speak, slow to anger; 20for your anger does
not produce God's righteousness. 21There-
fore rid yourselves of all sordidness and rank
growth of wickedness, and welcome with
meekness the implanted word that has the
power to save your souls.

22 But be doers of the word, and not
merely hearers who deceive themselves. 23For
if any are hearers of the word and not doers,
they are like those who look at themselves[g] in
a mirror; 24for they look at themselves and,
on going away, immediately forget what they
were like. 25But those who look into the perfect law, the law of liberty, and persevere,
being not hearers who forget but doers who
act—they will be blessed in their doing.

26 If any think they are religious, and do
not bridle their tongues but deceive their
hearts, their religion is worthless. 27Religion
that is pure and undefiled before God, the Father, is this: to care for orphans and widows
in their distress, and to keep oneself un-
stained by the world.

Warning against Partiality

2 My brothers and sisters,[b] do you with
your acts of favoritism really believe in
our glorious Lord Jesus Christ?[i] 2For if a

---

a Gk slave   b Gk brothers   c Gk brother   d Gk he; other ancient authorities read God   e Gk my beloved brothers
f Other ancient authorities read variation due to a shadow of turning   g Gk at the face of his birth   h Gk My brothers
i Or hold the faith of our glorious Lord Jesus Christ without acts of favoritism

person with gold rings and in fine clothes comes into your assembly, and if a poor person in dirty clothes also comes in, ³and if you take notice of the one wearing the fine clothes and say, "Have a seat here, please," while to the one who is poor you say, "Stand there," or, "Sit at my feet,"ᵃ ⁴have you not made distinctions among yourselves, and become judges with evil thoughts? ⁵Listen, my beloved brothers and sisters.ᵇ Has not God chosen the poor in the world to be rich in faith and to be heirs of the kingdom that he has promised to those who love him? ⁶But you have dishonored the poor. Is it not the rich who oppress you? Is it not they who drag you into court? ⁷Is it not they who blaspheme the excellent name that was invoked over you?

8 You do well if you really fulfill the royal law according to the scripture, "You shall love your neighbor as yourself." ⁹But if you show partiality, you commit sin and are convicted by the law as transgressors. ¹⁰For whoever keeps the whole law but fails in one point has become accountable for all of it. ¹¹For the one who said, "You shall not commit adultery," also said, "You shall not murder." Now if you do not commit adultery but if you murder, you have become a transgressor of the law. ¹²So speak and so act as those who are to be judged by the law of liberty. ¹³For judgment will be without mercy to anyone who has shown no mercy; mercy triumphs over judgment.

Faith without Works Is Dead

14 What good is it, my brothers and sisters,ᵇ if you say you have faith but do not have works? Can faith save you? ¹⁵If a brother or sister is naked and lacks daily food, ¹⁶and one of you says to them, "Go in peace; keep warm and eat your fill," and yet you do not supply their bodily needs, what is the good of that? ¹⁷So faith by itself, if it has no works, is dead.

18 But someone will say, "You have faith

and I have works." Show me your faith apart from your works, and I by my works will show you my faith. ¹⁹You believe that God is one; you do well. Even the demons believe—and shudder. ²⁰Do you want to be shown, you senseless person, that faith apart from works is barren? ²¹Was not our ancestor Abraham justified by works when he offered his son Isaac on the altar? ²²You see that faith was active along with his works, and faith was brought to completion by the works. ²³Thus the scripture was fulfilled that says, "Abraham believed God, and it was reckoned to him as righteousness," and he was called the friend of God. ²⁴You see that a person is justified by works and not by faith alone. ²⁵Likewise, was not Rahab the prostitute also justified by works when she welcomed the messengers and sent them out by another road? ²⁶For just as the body without the spirit is dead, so faith without works is also dead.

Taming the Tongue

3 Not many of you should become teachers, my brothers and sisters,ᵇ for you know that we who teach will be judged with greater strictness. ²For all of us make many mistakes. Anyone who makes no mistakes in speaking is perfect, able to keep the whole body in check with a bridle. ³If we put bits into the mouths of horses to make them obey us, we guide their whole bodies. ⁴Or look at ships: though they are so large that it takes strong winds to drive them, yet they are guided by a very small rudder wherever the will of the pilot directs. ⁵So also the tongue is a small member, yet it boasts of great exploits.

How great a forest is set ablaze by a small fire! ⁶And the tongue is a fire. The tongue is placed among our members as a world of iniquity; it stains the whole body, sets on fire the cycle of nature,ᶜ and is itself set on fire by hell.ᵈ ⁷For every species of beast and bird, of reptile and sea creature, can be tamed and

a Gk *Sit under my footstool*   *b* Gk *brothers*   *c* Or *wheel of birth*   *d* Gk *Gehenna* has been tamed by the human species, [8]but no one can tame the tongue—a restless evil, full of deadly poison. [9]With it we bless the Lord and Father, and with it we curse those who are made in the likeness of God. [10]From the same mouth come blessing and cursing. My brothers and sisters,[a] this ought not to be so. [11]Does a spring pour forth from the same opening both fresh and brackish water? [12]Can a fig tree, my brothers and sisters,[b] yield olives, or a grapevine figs? No more can salt water yield fresh.

Two Kinds of Wisdom

13 Who is wise and understanding among you? Show by your good life that your works are done with gentleness born of wisdom. [14]But if you have bitter envy and selfish ambition in your hearts, do not be boastful and false to the truth. [15]Such wisdom does not come down from above, but is earthly, unspiritual, devilish. [16]For where there is envy and selfish ambition, there will also be disorder and wickedness of every kind. [17]But the wisdom from above is first pure, then peaceable, gentle, willing to yield, full of mercy and good fruits, without a trace of partiality or hypocrisy. [18]And a harvest of righteousness is sown in peace for[c] those who make peace.

Friendship with the World

4 Those conflicts and disputes among you, where do they come from? Do they not come from your cravings that are at war within you? [2]You want something and do not have it; so you commit murder. And you covet[d] something and cannot obtain it; so you engage in disputes and conflicts. You do not have, because you do not ask. [3]You ask and do not receive, because you ask wrongly, in order to spend what you get on your pleasures. [4]Adulterers! Do you not know that friendship with the world is enmity with God? Therefore whoever wishes to be a friend of the world becomes an enemy of God. [5]Or do you suppose that it is for nothing that the scripture says, "God[e] yearns jealously for the spirit that he has made to dwell in us"? [6]But he gives all the more grace; therefore it says,

"God opposes the proud,
    but gives grace to the humble."

[7]Submit yourselves therefore to God. Resist the devil, and he will flee from you. [8]Draw near to God, and he will draw near to you. Cleanse your hands, you sinners, and purify your hearts, you double-minded. [9]Lament and mourn and weep. Let your laughter be turned into mourning and your joy into dejection. [10]Humble yourselves before the Lord, and he will exalt you.

Warning against Judging Another

11 Do not speak evil against one another, brothers and sisters.[f] Whoever speaks evil against another or judges another, speaks evil against the law and judges the law; but if you judge the law, you are not a doer of the law but a judge. [12]There is one lawgiver and judge who is able to save and to destroy. So who, then, are you to judge your neighbor?

Boasting about Tomorrow

13 Come now, you who say, "Today or tomorrow we will go to such and such a town and spend a year there, doing business and making money." [14]Yet you do not even know what tomorrow will bring. What is your life? For you are a mist that appears for a little while and then vanishes. [15]Instead you ought to say, "If the Lord wishes, we will live and do this or that." [16]As it is, you boast in your arrogance; all such boasting is evil. [17]Anyone, then, who knows the right thing to do and fails to do it, commits sin.

Warning to Rich Oppressors

5 Come now, you rich people, weep and wail for the miseries that are coming to you. [2]Your riches have rotted, and your clothes are moth-eaten. [3]Your gold and silver

---

a Gk My brothers   b Gk my brothers   c Or by   d Or you murder and you covet   e Gk He   f Gk brothers have rusted, and their rust will be evidence against you, and it will eat your flesh like fire. You have laid up treasure*a* for the last days. ⁴Listen! The wages of the laborers who mowed your fields, which you kept back by fraud, cry out, and the cries of the harvesters have reached the ears of the Lord of hosts. ⁵You have lived on the earth in luxury and in pleasure; you have fattened your hearts in a day of slaughter. ⁶You have condemned and murdered the righteous one, who does not resist you.

Patience in Suffering

7 Be patient, therefore, beloved,*b* until the coming of the Lord. The farmer waits for the precious crop from the earth, being patient with it until it receives the early and the late rains. ⁸You also must be patient. Strengthen your hearts, for the coming of the Lord is near.*c* ⁹Beloved,*d* do not grumble against one another, so that you may not be judged. See, the Judge is standing at the doors! ¹⁰As an example of suffering and patience, beloved,*b* take the prophets who spoke in the name of the Lord. ¹¹Indeed we call blessed those who showed endurance. You have heard of the endurance of Job, and you have seen the purpose of the Lord, how the Lord is compassionate and merciful.

12 Above all, my beloved,*b* do not swear, either by heaven or by earth or by any other oath, but let your "Yes" be yes and your "No" be no, so that you may not fall under condemnation.

The Prayer of Faith

13 Are any among you suffering? They should pray. Are any cheerful? They should sing songs of praise. ¹⁴Are any among you sick? They should call for the elders of the church and have them pray over them, anointing them with oil in the name of the Lord. ¹⁵The prayer of faith will save the sick, and the Lord will raise them up; and anyone who has committed sins will be forgiven. ¹⁶Therefore confess your sins to one another, and pray for one another, so that you may be healed. The prayer of the righteous is powerful and effective. ¹⁷Elijah was a human being like us, and he prayed fervently that it might not rain, and for three years and six months it did not rain on the earth. ¹⁸Then he prayed again, and the heaven gave rain and the earth yielded its harvest.

19 My brothers and sisters,*e* if anyone among you wanders from the truth and is brought back by another, ²⁰you should know that whoever brings back a sinner from wandering will save the sinner's*f* soul from death and will cover a multitude of sins.

---

a Or *will eat your flesh, since you have stored up fire*   *b* Gk *brothers*   *c* Or *is at hand*   *d* Gk *Brothers*   *e* Gk *My brothers*   *f* Gk *his*

THE FIRST LETTER OF
PETER

Salutation

1 Peter, an apostle of Jesus Christ,
To the exiles of the Dispersion in Pontus, Galatia, Cappadocia, Asia, and Bithynia, 2who have been chosen and destined by God the Father and sanctified by the Spirit to be obedient to Jesus Christ and to be sprinkled with his blood:

May grace and peace be yours in abundance.

A Living Hope

3 Blessed be the God and Father of our Lord Jesus Christ! By his great mercy he has given us a new birth into a living hope through the resurrection of Jesus Christ from the dead, 4and into an inheritance that is imperishable, undefiled, and unfading, kept in heaven for you, 5who are being protected by the power of God through faith for a salvation ready to be revealed in the last time. 6In this you rejoice,*a* even if now for a little while you have had to suffer various trials, 7so that the genuineness of your faith—being more precious than gold that, though perishable, is tested by fire—may be found to result in praise and glory and honor when Jesus Christ is revealed. 8Although you have not seen*b* him, you love him; and even though you do not see him now, you believe in him and rejoice with an indescribable and glorious joy, 9for you are receiving the outcome of your faith, the salvation of your souls.

10 Concerning this salvation, the prophets who prophesied of the grace that was to be yours made careful search and inquiry, 11inquiring about the person or time that the Spirit of Christ within them indicated when it testified in advance to the sufferings destined for Christ and the subsequent glory. 12It was revealed to them that they were serving not themselves but you, in regard to the things that have now been announced to you through those who brought you good news by the Holy Spirit sent from heaven—things into which angels long to look!

A Call to Holy Living

13 Therefore prepare your minds for action;*c* discipline yourselves; set all your hope on the grace that Jesus Christ will bring you when he is revealed. 14Like obedient children, do not be conformed to the desires that you formerly had in ignorance. 15Instead, as he who called you is holy, be holy yourselves in all your conduct; 16for it is written, "You shall be holy, for I am holy."

17 If you invoke as Father the one who judges all people impartially according to their deeds, live in reverent fear during the time of your exile. 18You know that you were ransomed from the futile ways inherited from your ancestors, not with perishable things like silver or gold, 19but with the precious blood of Christ, like that of a lamb without defect or blemish. 20He was destined before the foundation of the world, but was revealed at the end of the ages for your sake. 21Through him you have come to trust in God, who raised him from the dead and gave him glory, so that your faith and hope are set on God.

22 Now that you have purified your souls by your obedience to the truth*d* so that you have genuine mutual love, love one another deeply*e* from the heart.*f* 23You have been born anew, not of perishable but of imperishable seed, through the living and enduring word of God.*g* 24For

"All flesh is like grass
and all its glory like the flower of
grass.
The grass withers,
and the flower falls,
25 but the word of the Lord endures
forever."

That word is the good news that was announced to you.

---

a Or *Rejoice in this*   *b* Other ancient authorities read *known*   *c* Gk *gird up the loins of your mind*   *d* Other ancient authorities add *through the Spirit*   *e* Or *constantly*   *f* Other ancient authorities read *a pure heart*   *g* Or *through the word of the living and enduring God*

The Living Stone and a Chosen People

2 Rid yourselves, therefore, of all malice, and all guile, insincerity, envy, and all slander. ²Like newborn infants, long for the pure, spiritual milk, so that by it you may grow into salvation— ³if indeed you have tasted that the Lord is good.

4 Come to him, a living stone, though rejected by mortals yet chosen and precious in God's sight, and ⁵like living stones, let yourselves be built *ᵃ* into a spiritual house, to be a holy priesthood, to offer spiritual sacrifices acceptable to God through Jesus Christ. ⁶For it stands in scripture:

> "See, I am laying in Zion a stone,
>   a cornerstone chosen and precious;
> and whoever believes in him *ᵇ* will not
>   be put to shame."

⁷To you then who believe, he is precious; but for those who do not believe,

> "The stone that the builders rejected
>   has become the very head of the
>   corner,"

⁸and

> "A stone that makes them stumble,
>   and a rock that makes them fall."

They stumble because they disobey the word, as they were destined to do.

9 But you are a chosen race, a royal priesthood, a holy nation, God's own people, *ᶜ* in order that you may proclaim the mighty acts of him who called you out of darkness into his marvelous light.

10   Once you were not a people,
>   but now you are God's people;
> once you had not received mercy,
>   but now you have received mercy.

Live as Servants of God

11 Beloved, I urge you as aliens and exiles to abstain from the desires of the flesh that wage war against the soul. ¹²Conduct yourselves honorably among the Gentiles, so that, though they malign you as evildoers, they may see your honorable deeds and glorify God when he comes to judge. *ᵈ*

13 For the Lord's sake accept the authority of every human institution, *ᵉ* whether of the emperor as supreme, ¹⁴or of governors, as sent by him to punish those who do wrong and to praise those who do right. ¹⁵For it is God's will that by doing right you should silence the ignorance of the foolish. ¹⁶As servants *ᶠ* of God, live as free people, yet do not use your freedom as a pretext for evil. ¹⁷Honor everyone. Love the family of believers. *ᵍ* Fear God. Honor the emperor.

The Example of Christ's Suffering

18 Slaves, accept the authority of your masters with all deference, not only those who are kind and gentle but also those who are harsh. ¹⁹For it is a credit to you if, being aware of God, you endure pain while suffering unjustly. ²⁰If you endure when you are beaten for doing wrong, what credit is that? But if you endure when you do right and suffer for it, you have God's approval. ²¹For to this you have been called, because Christ also suffered for you, leaving you an example, so that you should follow in his steps.

22   "He committed no sin,
>   and no deceit was found in his
>   mouth."

²³When he was abused, he did not return abuse; when he suffered, he did not threaten; but he entrusted himself to the one who judges justly. ²⁴He himself bore our sins in his body on the cross, *ʰ* so that, free from sins, we might live for righteousness; by his wounds *ⁱ* you have been healed. ²⁵For you were going astray like sheep, but now you have returned to the shepherd and guardian of your souls.

Wives and Husbands

3 Wives, in the same way, accept the authority of your husbands, so that, even if some of them do not obey the word, they may be won over without a word by their

---

a Or *you yourselves are being built*   *b* Or *it*   *c* Gk *a people for his possession*   *d* Gk *God on the day of visitation*
e Or *every institution ordained for human beings*   *f* Gk *slaves*   *g* Gk *Love the brotherhood*   *h* Or *carried up our sins in his body to the tree*   *i* Gk *bruise*

wives' conduct, 2when they see the purity and reverence of your lives. 3Do not adorn yourselves outwardly by braiding your hair, and by wearing gold ornaments or fine clothing; 4rather, let your adornment be the inner self with the lasting beauty of a gentle and quiet spirit, which is very precious in God's sight. 5It was in this way long ago that the holy women who hoped in God used to adorn themselves by accepting the authority of their husbands. 6Thus Sarah obeyed Abraham and called him lord. You have become her daughters as long as you do what is good and never let fears alarm you.

7 Husbands, in the same way, show consideration for your wives in your life together, paying honor to the woman as the weaker sex,*a* since they too are also heirs of the gracious gift of life—so that nothing may hinder your prayers.

Suffering for Doing Right

8 Finally, all of you, have unity of spirit, sympathy, love for one another, a tender heart, and a humble mind. 9Do not repay evil for evil or abuse for abuse; but, on the contrary, repay with a blessing. It is for this that you were called—that you might inherit a blessing. 10For

"Those who desire life
　　and desire to see good days,
　let them keep their tongues from evil
　　and their lips from speaking deceit;
11　let them turn away from evil and do
　　　good;
　　let them seek peace and pursue it.
12　For the eyes of the Lord are on the
　　　righteous,
　　and his ears are open to their prayer.
　But the face of the Lord is against
　　　those who do evil."

13 Now who will harm you if you are eager to do what is good? 14But even if you do suffer for doing what is right, you are blessed. Do not fear what they fear,*b* and do not be intimidated, 15but in your hearts sanctify Christ as Lord. Always be ready to make your defense to anyone who demands from you an accounting for the hope that is in you; 16yet do it with gentleness and reverence.*c* Keep your conscience clear, so that, when you are maligned, those who abuse you for your good conduct in Christ may be put to shame. 17For it is better to suffer for doing good, if suffering should be God's will, than to suffer for doing evil. 18For Christ also suffered*d* for sins once for all, the righteous for the unrighteous, in order to bring you*e* to God. He was put to death in the flesh, but made alive in the spirit, 19in which also he went and made a proclamation to the spirits in prison, 20who in former times did not obey, when God waited patiently in the days of Noah, during the building of the ark, in which a few, that is, eight persons, were saved through water. 21And baptism, which this prefigured, now saves you—not as a removal of dirt from the body, but as an appeal to God for*f* a good conscience, through the resurrection of Jesus Christ, 22who has gone into heaven and is at the right hand of God, with angels, authorities, and powers made subject to him.

Good Stewards of God's Grace

4 Since therefore Christ suffered in the flesh,*g* arm yourselves also with the same intention (for whoever has suffered in the flesh has finished with sin), 2so as to live for the rest of your earthly life*h* no longer by human desires but by the will of God. 3You have already spent enough time in doing what the Gentiles like to do, living in licentiousness, passions, drunkenness, revels, carousing, and lawless idolatry. 4They are surprised that you no longer join them in the same excesses of dissipation, and so they blaspheme.*i* 5But they will have to give an accounting to him who stands ready to judge the living and the dead. 6For this is the reason the gospel was proclaimed even to the dead, so that, though

---

a Gk *vessel*　　*b* Gk *their fear*　　*c* Or *respect*　　*d* Other ancient authorities read *died*　　*e* Other ancient authorities read *us*　　*f* Or *a pledge to God from*　　*g* Other ancient authorities add *for us*; others, *for you*　　*h* Gk *rest of the time in the flesh*　　*i* Or *they malign you* they had been judged in the flesh as everyone is judged, they might live in the spirit as God does.

7 The end of all things is near;*a* therefore be serious and discipline yourselves for the sake of your prayers. 8Above all, maintain constant love for one another, for love covers a multitude of sins. 9Be hospitable to one another without complaining. 10Like good stewards of the manifold grace of God, serve one another with whatever gift each of you has received. 11Whoever speaks must do so as one speaking the very words of God; whoever serves must do so with the strength that God supplies, so that God may be glorified in all things through Jesus Christ. To him belong the glory and the power forever and ever. Amen.

Suffering as a Christian

12 Beloved, do not be surprised at the fiery ordeal that is taking place among you to test you, as though something strange were happening to you. 13But rejoice insofar as you are sharing Christ's sufferings, so that you may also be glad and shout for joy when his glory is revealed. 14If you are reviled for the name of Christ, you are blessed, because the spirit of glory,*b* which is the Spirit of God, is resting on you.*c* 15But let none of you suffer as a murderer, a thief, a criminal, or even as a mischief maker. 16Yet if any of you suffers as a Christian, do not consider it a disgrace, but glorify God because you bear this name. 17For the time has come for judgment to begin with the household of God; if it begins with us, what will be the end for those who do not obey the gospel of God? 18And

"If it is hard for the righteous to be saved,
    what will become of the ungodly
        and the sinners?"

19Therefore, let those suffering in accordance with God's will entrust themselves to a faithful Creator, while continuing to do good.

Tending the Flock of God

5 Now as an elder myself and a witness of the sufferings of Christ, as well as one who shares in the glory to be revealed, I exhort the elders among you 2to tend the flock of God that is in your charge, exercising the oversight,*d* not under compulsion but willingly, as God would have you do it*e*—not for sordid gain but eagerly. 3Do not lord it over those in your charge, but be examples to the flock. 4And when the chief shepherd appears, you will win the crown of glory that never fades away. 5In the same way, you who are younger must accept the authority of the elders.*f* And all of you must clothe yourselves with humility in your dealings with one another, for

"God opposes the proud,
    but gives grace to the humble."

6 Humble yourselves therefore under the mighty hand of God, so that he may exalt you in due time. 7Cast all your anxiety on him, because he cares for you. 8Discipline yourselves, keep alert.*g* Like a roaring lion your adversary the devil prowls around, looking for someone to devour. 9Resist him, steadfast in your faith, for you know that your brothers and sisters*h* in all the world are undergoing the same kinds of suffering. 10And after you have suffered for a little while, the God of all grace, who has called you to his eternal glory in Christ, will himself restore, support, strengthen, and establish you. 11To him be the power forever and ever. Amen.

Final Greetings and Benediction

12 Through Silvanus, whom I consider a faithful brother, I have written this short letter to encourage you and to testify that this is the true grace of God. Stand fast in it. 13Your sister church*i* in Babylon, chosen together with you, sends you greetings; and so does my son Mark. 14Greet one another with a kiss of love.

Peace to all of you who are in Christ.*j*

---

a Or *is at hand*   *b* Other ancient authorities add *and of power*   *c* Other ancient authorities add *On their part he is blasphemed, but on your part he is glorified*   *d* Other ancient authorities lack *exercising the oversight*   *e* Other ancient authorities lack *as God would have you do it*   *f* Or *of those who are older*   *g* Or *be vigilant*   *h* Gk *your brotherhood*   *i* Gk *She who is*   *j* Other ancient authorities add *Amen*

THE SECOND LETTER OF
PETER

Salutation

1 Simeon*a* Peter, a servant*b* and apostle
of Jesus Christ,

To those who have received a faith as precious as ours through the righteousness of
our God and Savior Jesus Christ:*c*

2 May grace and peace be yours in abundance in the knowledge of God and of Jesus
our Lord.

The Christian's Call and Election

3 His divine power has given us everything needed for life and godliness, through
the knowledge of him who called us by*d* his
own glory and goodness. 4Thus he has given us, through these things, his precious and
very great promises, so that through them
you may escape from the corruption that is
in the world because of lust, and may become
participants of the divine nature. 5For this
very reason, you must make every effort to
support your faith with goodness, and goodness with knowledge, 6and knowledge with
self-control, and self-control with endurance,
and endurance with godliness, 7and godliness with mutual*e* affection, and mutual*e* affection with love. 8For if these things are
yours and are increasing among you, they
keep you from being ineffective and unfruitful in the knowledge of our Lord Jesus
Christ. 9For anyone who lacks these things is
short-sighted and blind, and is forgetful of
the cleansing of past sins. 10Therefore, brothers and sisters,*f* be all the more eager to confirm your call and election, for if you do this,
you will never stumble. 11For in this way, entry into the eternal kingdom of our Lord
and Savior Jesus Christ will be richly provided for you.

12 Therefore I intend to keep on reminding you of these things, though you
know them already and are established in the
truth that has come to you. 13I think it right,
as long as I am in this body,*g* to refresh your
memory, 14since I know that my death*h* will
come soon, as indeed our Lord Jesus Christ
has made clear to me. 15And I will make
every effort so that after my departure you
may be able at any time to recall these things.

Eyewitnesses of Christ's Glory

16 For we did not follow cleverly devised
myths when we made known to you the power and coming of our Lord Jesus Christ, but
we had been eyewitnesses of his majesty.
17For he received honor and glory from God
the Father when that voice was conveyed to
him by the Majestic Glory, saying, "This is my
Son, my Beloved,*i* with whom I am well
pleased." 18We ourselves heard this voice
come from heaven, while we were with him
on the holy mountain.

19 So we have the prophetic message
more fully confirmed. You will do well to be
attentive to this as to a lamp shining in a
dark place, until the day dawns and the morning star rises in your hearts. 20First of all you
must understand this, that no prophecy of
scripture is a matter of one's own interpretation, 21because no prophecy ever came by
human will, but men and women moved by
the Holy Spirit spoke from God.*j*

False Prophets and Their Punishment

2 But false prophets also arose among the
people, just as there will be false teachers among you, who will secretly bring in destructive opinions. They will even deny the
Master who bought them—bringing swift
destruction on themselves. 2Even so, many
will follow their licentious ways, and because
of these teachers*k* the way of truth will be
maligned. 3And in their greed they will exploit
you with deceptive words. Their condemna-

a Other ancient authorities read *Simon*   *b* Gk *slave*   *c* Or *of our God and the Savior Jesus Christ*   *d* Other
ancient authorities read *through*   *e* Gk *brotherly*   *f* Gk *brothers*   *g* Gk *tent*   *h* Gk *the putting off of my tent*
i Other ancient authorities read *my beloved Son*   *j* Other ancient authorities read *but moved by the Holy Spirit saints of
God spoke*   *k* Gk *because of them*

tion, pronounced against them long ago, has not been idle, and their destruction is not asleep.

4 For if God did not spare the angels when they sinned, but cast them into hell*a* and committed them to chains*b* of deepest darkness to be kept until the judgment; 5and if he did not spare the ancient world, even though he saved Noah, a herald of righteousness, with seven others, when he brought a flood on a world of the ungodly; 6and if by turning the cities of Sodom and Gomorrah to ashes he condemned them to extinction*c* and made them an example of what is coming to the ungodly;*d* 7and if he rescued Lot, a righteous man greatly distressed by the licentiousness of the lawless 8(for that righteous man, living among them day after day, was tormented in his righteous soul by their lawless deeds that he saw and heard), 9then the Lord knows how to rescue the godly from trial, and to keep the unrighteous under punishment until the day of judgment 10—especially those who indulge their flesh in depraved lust, and who despise authority.

Bold and willful, they are not afraid to slander the glorious ones,*e* 11whereas angels, though greater in might and power, do not bring against them a slanderous judgment from the Lord.*f* 12These people, however, are like irrational animals, mere creatures of instinct, born to be caught and killed. They slander what they do not understand, and when those creatures are destroyed,*g* they also will be destroyed, 13suffering*h* the penalty for doing wrong. They count it a pleasure to revel in the daytime. They are blots and blemishes, reveling in their dissipation*i* while they feast with you. 14They have eyes full of adultery, insatiable for sin. They entice unsteady souls. They have hearts trained in greed. Accursed children! 15They have left

the straight road and have gone astray, following the road of Balaam son of Bosor,*j* who loved the wages of doing wrong, 16but was rebuked for his own transgression; a speechless donkey spoke with a human voice and restrained the prophet's madness.

17 These are waterless springs and mists driven by a storm; for them the deepest darkness has been reserved. 18For they speak bombastic nonsense, and with licentious desires of the flesh they entice people who have just*k* escaped from those who live in error. 19They promise them freedom, but they themselves are slaves of corruption; for people are slaves to whatever masters them. 20For if, after they have escaped the defilements of the world through the knowledge of our Lord and Savior Jesus Christ, they are again entangled in them and overpowered, the last state has become worse for them than the first. 21For it would have been better for them never to have known the way of righteousness than, after knowing it, to turn back from the holy commandment that was passed on to them. 22It has happened to them according to the true proverb,

"The dog turns back to its own vomit,"

and,

"The sow is washed only to wallow in the mud."

The Promise of the Lord's Coming

3 This is now, beloved, the second letter I am writing to you; in them I am trying to arouse your sincere intention by reminding you 2that you should remember the words spoken in the past by the holy prophets, and the commandment of the Lord and Savior spoken through your apostles. 3First of all you must understand this, that in the last days scoffers will come, scoffing and indulging their own lusts 4and saying, "Where is the promise of his coming? For ever since

---

a Gk *Tartaros*　　*b* Other ancient authorities read *pits*　　*c* Other ancient authorities lack *to extinction*　　*d* Other ancient authorities read *an example to those who were to be ungodly*　　*e* Or *angels*; Gk *glories*　　*f* Other ancient authorities read *before the Lord*; others lack the phrase　　*g* Gk *in their destruction*　　*h* Other ancient authorities read *receiving*　　*i* Other ancient authorities read *love-feasts*　　*j* Other ancient authorities read *Beor*　　*k* Other ancient authorities read *actually* our ancestors died,*a* all things continue as they were from the beginning of creation!" 5They deliberately ignore this fact, that by the word of God heavens existed long ago and an earth was formed out of water and by means of water, 6through which the world of that time was deluged with water and perished. 7But by the same word the present heavens and earth have been reserved for fire, being kept until the day of judgment and destruction of the godless.

8 But do not ignore this one fact, beloved, that with the Lord one day is like a thousand years, and a thousand years are like one day. 9The Lord is not slow about his promise, as some think of slowness, but is patient with you,*b* not wanting any to perish, but all to come to repentance. 10But the day of the Lord will come like a thief, and then the heavens will pass away with a loud noise, and the elements will be dissolved with fire, and the earth and everything that is done on it will be disclosed.*c*

11 Since all these things are to be dissolved in this way, what sort of persons ought you to be in leading lives of holiness and godliness, 12waiting for and hastening*d* the coming of the day of God, because of which the heavens will be set ablaze and dissolved, and the elements will melt with fire? 13But, in accordance with his promise, we wait for new heavens and a new earth, where righteousness is at home.

Final Exhortation and Doxology

14 Therefore, beloved, while you are waiting for these things, strive to be found by him at peace, without spot or blemish; 15and regard the patience of our Lord as salvation. So also our beloved brother Paul wrote to you according to the wisdom given him, 16speaking of this as he does in all his letters. There are some things in them hard to understand, which the ignorant and unstable twist to their own destruction, as they do the other scriptures. 17You therefore, beloved, since you are forewarned, beware that you are not carried away with the error of the lawless and lose your own stability. 18But grow in the grace and knowledge of our Lord and Savior Jesus Christ. To him be the glory both now and to the day of eternity. Amen.*e*

---

a Gk *our fathers fell asleep*   *b* Other ancient authorities read *on your account*   *c* Other ancient authorities read *will be burned up*   *d* Or *earnestly desiring*   *e* Other ancient authorities lack *Amen*

THE FIRST LETTER OF
JOHN

The Word of Life

1 We declare to you what was from the beginning, what we have heard, what we have seen with our eyes, what we have looked at and touched with our hands, concerning the word of life— 2this life was revealed, and we have seen it and testify to it, and declare to you the eternal life that was with the Father and was revealed to us— 3we declare to you what we have seen and heard so that you also may have fellowship with us; and truly our fellowship is with the Father and with his Son Jesus Christ. 4We are writing these things so that our*a* joy may be complete.

God Is Light

5 This is the message we have heard from him and proclaim to you, that God is light and in him there is no darkness at all. 6If we say that we have fellowship with him while we are walking in darkness, we lie and do not do what is true; 7but if we walk in the light as he himself is in the light, we have fellowship with one another, and the blood of Jesus his Son cleanses us from all sin. 8If we say that we have no sin, we deceive ourselves, and the truth is not in us. 9If we confess our sins, he who is faithful and just will forgive us our sins and cleanse us from all unrighteousness. 10If we say that we have not sinned, we make him a liar, and his word is not in us.

Christ Our Advocate

2 My little children, I am writing these things to you so that you may not sin. But if anyone does sin, we have an advocate with the Father, Jesus Christ the righteous; 2and he is the atoning sacrifice for our sins, and not for ours only but also for the sins of the whole world.

3 Now by this we may be sure that we know him, if we obey his commandments. 4Whoever says, "I have come to know him," but does not obey his commandments, is a liar, and in such a person the truth does not exist; 5but whoever obeys his word, truly in this person the love of God has reached perfection. By this we may be sure that we are in him: 6whoever says, "I abide in him," ought to walk just as he walked.

A New Commandment

7 Beloved, I am writing you no new commandment, but an old commandment that you have had from the beginning; the old commandment is the word that you have heard. 8Yet I am writing you a new commandment that is true in him and in you, because*b* the darkness is passing away and the true light is already shining. 9Whoever says, "I am in the light," while hating a brother or sister,*c* is still in the darkness. 10Whoever loves a brother or sister*d* lives in the light, and in such a person*e* there is no cause for stumbling. 11But whoever hates another believer*f* is in the darkness, walks in the darkness, and does not know the way to go, because the darkness has brought on blindness.

12 I am writing to you, little children,
    because your sins are forgiven on
      account of his name.
13 I am writing to you, fathers,
    because you know him who is from
      the beginning.
I am writing to you, young people,
    because you have conquered the evil
      one.
14 I write to you, children,
    because you know the Father.
I write to you, fathers,
    because you know him who is from
      the beginning.
I write to you, young people,
    because you are strong
    and the word of God abides in you,
      and you have overcome the evil
      one.

15 Do not love the world or the things in

---

a Other ancient authorities read *your*   *b* Or *that*   *c* Gk *hating a brother*   *d* Gk *loves a brother*   *e* Or *in it*
f Gk *hates a brother*

the world. The love of the Father is not in those who love the world; [16]for all that is in the world—the desire of the flesh, the desire of the eyes, the pride in riches—comes not from the Father but from the world. [17]And the world and its desire*a* are passing away, but those who do the will of God live forever.

Warning against Antichrists

18 Children, it is the last hour! As you have heard that antichrist is coming, so now many antichrists have come. From this we know that it is the last hour. [19]They went out from us, but they did not belong to us; for if they had belonged to us, they would have remained with us. But by going out they made it plain that none of them belongs to us. [20]But you have been anointed by the Holy One, and all of you have knowledge.*b* [21]I write to you, not because you do not know the truth, but because you know it, and you know that no lie comes from the truth. [22]Who is the liar but the one who denies that Jesus is the Christ?*c* This is the antichrist, the one who denies the Father and the Son. [23]No one who denies the Son has the Father; everyone who confesses the Son has the Father also. [24]Let what you heard from the beginning abide in you. If what you heard from the beginning abides in you, then you will abide in the Son and in the Father. [25]And this is what he has promised us,*d* eternal life.

26 I write these things to you concerning those who would deceive you. [27]As for you, the anointing that you received from him abides in you, and so you do not need anyone to teach you. But as his anointing teaches you about all things, and is true and is not a lie, and just as it has taught you, abide in him.*e*

28 And now, little children, abide in him, so that when he is revealed we may have confidence and not be put to shame before him at his coming.

Children of God

29 If you know that he is righteous, you may be sure that everyone who does right has been born of him. [1]See what love the Father has given us, that we should be called children of God; and that is what we are. The reason the world does not know us is that it did not know him. [2]Beloved, we are God's children now; what we will be has not yet been revealed. What we do know is this: when he*e* is revealed, we will be like him, for we will see him as he is. [3]And all who have this hope in him purify themselves, just as he is pure.

4 Everyone who commits sin is guilty of lawlessness; sin is lawlessness. [5]You know that he was revealed to take away sins, and in him there is no sin. [6]No one who abides in him sins; no one who sins has either seen him or known him. [7]Little children, let no one deceive you. Everyone who does what is right is righteous, just as he is righteous. [8]Everyone who commits sin is a child of the devil; for the devil has been sinning from the beginning. The Son of God was revealed for this purpose, to destroy the works of the devil. [9]Those who have been born of God do not sin, because God's seed abides in them;*f* they cannot sin, because they have been born of God. [10]The children of God and the children of the devil are revealed in this way: all who do not do what is right are not from God, nor are those who do not love their brothers and sisters.*g*

Love One Another

11 For this is the message you have heard from the beginning, that we should love one another. [12]We must not be like Cain who was from the evil one and murdered his brother. And why did he murder him? Because his own deeds were evil and his brother's righteous. [13]Do not be astonished, brothers and sisters,*h* that the world hates you. [14]We know that we have passed from death to life because we love one another. Whoever does not

---

a Or *the desire for it*   *b* Other ancient authorities read *you know all things*   *c* Or *the Messiah*   *d* Other ancient authorities read *you*   *e* Or *it*   *f* Or *because the children of God abide in him*   *g* Gk *his brother*   *h* Gk *brothers* love abides in death. 15All who hate a brother or sister*a* are murderers, and you know that murderers do not have eternal life abiding in them. 16We know love by this, that he laid down his life for us—and we ought to lay down our lives for one another. 17How does God's love abide in anyone who has the world's goods and sees a brother or sister*b* in need and yet refuses help?

18 Little children, let us love, not in word or speech, but in truth and action. 19And by this we will know that we are from the truth and will reassure our hearts before him 20whenever our hearts condemn us; for God is greater than our hearts, and he knows everything. 21Beloved, if our hearts do not condemn us, we have boldness before God; 22and we receive from him whatever we ask, because we obey his commandments and do what pleases him.

23 And this is his commandment, that we should believe in the name of his Son Jesus Christ and love one another, just as he has commanded us. 24All who obey his commandments abide in him, and he abides in them. And by this we know that he abides in us, by the Spirit that he has given us.

Testing the Spirits

4 Beloved, do not believe every spirit, but test the spirits to see whether they are from God; for many false prophets have gone out into the world. 2By this you know the Spirit of God: every spirit that confesses that Jesus Christ has come in the flesh is from God, 3and every spirit that does not confess Jesus*c* is not from God. And this is the spirit of the antichrist, of which you have heard that it is coming; and now it is already in the world. 4Little children, you are from God, and have conquered them; for the one who is in you is greater than the one who is in the world. 5They are from the world; therefore what they say is from the world, and the world listens to them. 6We are from God. Whoever knows God listens to us, and who-

ever is not from God does not listen to us. From this we know the spirit of truth and the spirit of error.

God Is Love

7 Beloved, let us love one another, because love is from God; everyone who loves is born of God and knows God. 8Whoever does not love does not know God, for God is love. 9God's love was revealed among us in this way: God sent his only Son into the world so that we might live through him. 10In this is love, not that we loved God but that he loved us and sent his Son to be the atoning sacrifice for our sins. 11Beloved, since God loved us so much, we also ought to love one another. 12No one has ever seen God; if we love one another, God lives in us, and his love is perfected in us.

13 By this we know that we abide in him and he in us, because he has given us of his Spirit. 14And we have seen and do testify that the Father has sent his Son as the Savior of the world. 15God abides in those who confess that Jesus is the Son of God, and they abide in God. 16So we have known and believe the love that God has for us.

God is love, and those who abide in love abide in God, and God abides in them. 17Love has been perfected among us in this: that we may have boldness on the day of judgment, because as he is, so are we in this world. 18There is no fear in love, but perfect love casts out fear; for fear has to do with punishment, and whoever fears has not reached perfection in love. 19We love*d* because he first loved us. 20Those who say, "I love God," and hate their brothers or sisters,*e* are liars; for those who do not love a brother or sister*b* whom they have seen, cannot love God whom they have not seen. 21The commandment we have from him is this: those who love God must love their brothers and sisters*e* also.

---

a Gk *his brother*   *b* Gk *brother*   *c* Other ancient authorities read *does away with Jesus* (Gk *dissolves Jesus*)   *d* Other ancient authorities add *him*; others add *God*   *e* Gk *brothers*

Faith Conquers the World

5 Everyone who believes that Jesus is the Christ[a] has been born of God, and everyone who loves the parent loves the child. 2By this we know that we love the children of God, when we love God and obey his commandments. 3For the love of God is this, that we obey his commandments. And his commandments are not burdensome, 4for whatever is born of God conquers the world. And this is the victory that conquers the world, our faith. 5Who is it that conquers the world but the one who believes that Jesus is the Son of God?

Testimony concerning the Son of God

6 This is the one who came by water and blood, Jesus Christ, not with the water only but with the water and the blood. And the Spirit is the one that testifies, for the Spirit is the truth. 7There are three that testify:[b] 8the Spirit and the water and the blood, and these three agree. 9If we receive human testimony, the testimony of God is greater; for this is the testimony of God that he has testified to his Son. 10Those who believe in the Son of God have the testimony in their hearts. Those who do not believe in God[c] have made him a liar by not believing in the testimony that God has given concerning his Son. 11And this is the testimony: God gave us eternal life, and this life is in his Son. 12Whoever has the Son has life; whoever does not have the Son of God does not have life.

Epilogue

13 I write these things to you who believe in the name of the Son of God, so that you may know that you have eternal life.

14 And this is the boldness we have in him, that if we ask anything according to his will, he hears us. 15And if we know that he hears us in whatever we ask, we know that we have obtained the requests made of him. 16If you see your brother or sister[d] committing what is not a mortal sin, you will ask, and God[e] will give life to such a one—to those whose sin is not mortal. There is sin that is mortal; I do not say that you should pray about that. 17All wrongdoing is sin, but there is sin that is not mortal.

18 We know that those who are born of God do not sin, but the one who was born of God protects them, and the evil one does not touch them. 19We know that we are God's children, and that the whole world lies under the power of the evil one. 20And we know that the Son of God has come and has given us understanding so that we may know him who is true;[f] and we are in him who is true, in his Son Jesus Christ. He is the true God and eternal life.

21 Little children, keep yourselves from idols.[g]

---

a Or the Messiah   b A few other authorities read (with variations) 7There are three that testify in heaven, the Father, the Word, and the Holy Spirit, and these three are one. 8And there are three that testify on earth: c Other ancient authorities read in the Son   d Gk your brother   e Gk he   f Other ancient authorities read know the true God   g Other ancient authorities add Amen

THE SECOND LETTER OF
JOHN

Salutation

1 The elder to the elect lady and her children, whom I love in the truth, and not only I but also all who know the truth, 2because of the truth that abides in us and will be with us forever:

3 Grace, mercy, and peace will be with us from God the Father and from *a* Jesus Christ, the Father's Son, in truth and love.

Truth and Love

4 I was overjoyed to find some of your children walking in the truth, just as we have been commanded by the Father. 5But now, dear lady, I ask you, not as though I were writing you a new commandment, but one we have had from the beginning, let us love one another. 6And this is love, that we walk according to his commandments; this is the commandment just as you have heard it from the beginning—you must walk in it.

7 Many deceivers have gone out into the world, those who do not confess that Jesus Christ has come in the flesh; any such person is the deceiver and the antichrist! 8Be on your guard, so that you do not lose what we *b* have worked for, but may receive a full reward. 9Everyone who does not abide in the teaching of Christ, but goes beyond it, does not have God; whoever abides in the teaching has both the Father and the Son. 10Do not receive into the house or welcome anyone who comes to you and does not bring this teaching; 11for to welcome is to participate in the evil deeds of such a person.

Final Greetings

12 Although I have much to write to you, I would rather not use paper and ink; instead I hope to come to you and talk with you face to face, so that our joy may be complete.

13 The children of your elect sister send you their greetings. *c*

---

a Other ancient authorities add *the Lord*   *b* Other ancient authorities read *you*   *c* Other ancient authorities add *Amen*

THE THIRD LETTER OF
JOHN

Salutation

1 The elder to the beloved Gaius, whom I love in truth.

Gaius Commended for His Hospitality

2 Beloved, I pray that all may go well with you and that you may be in good health, just as it is well with your soul. 3I was overjoyed when some of the friends*a* arrived and testified to your faithfulness to the truth, namely how you walk in the truth. 4I have no greater joy than this, to hear that my children are walking in the truth.

5 Beloved, you do faithfully whatever you do for the friends,*a* even though they are strangers to you; 6they have testified to your love before the church. You will do well to send them on in a manner worthy of God; 7for they began their journey for the sake of Christ,*b* accepting no support from non-believers.*c* 8Therefore we ought to support such people, so that we may become co-workers with the truth.

Diotrephes and Demetrius

9 I have written something to the church; but Diotrephes, who likes to put himself first, does not acknowledge our authority. 10So if I come, I will call attention to what he is doing in spreading false charges against us. And not content with those charges, he refuses to welcome the friends,*a* and even prevents those who want to do so and expels them from the church.

11 Beloved, do not imitate what is evil but imitate what is good. Whoever does good is from God; whoever does evil has not seen God. 12Everyone has testified favorably about Demetrius, and so has the truth itself. We also testify for him,*d* and you know that our testimony is true.

Final Greetings

13 I have much to write to you, but I would rather not write with pen and ink; 14instead I hope to see you soon, and we will talk together face to face.

15 Peace to you. The friends send you their greetings. Greet the friends there, each by name.

a Gk *brothers*   *b* Gk *for the sake of the name*   *c* Gk *the Gentiles*   *d* Gk lacks *for him*

THE LETTER OF
JUDE

Salutation

1 Jude,[a] a servant[b] of Jesus Christ and brother of James,

To those who are called, who are beloved[c] in[d] God the Father and kept safe for[d] Jesus Christ:

2 May mercy, peace, and love be yours in abundance.

Occasion of the Letter

3 Beloved, while eagerly preparing to write to you about the salvation we share, I find it necessary to write and appeal to you to contend for the faith that was once for all entrusted to the saints. [4]For certain intruders have stolen in among you, people who long ago were designated for this condemnation as ungodly, who pervert the grace of our God into licentiousness and deny our only Master and Lord, Jesus Christ.[e]

Judgment on False Teachers

5 Now I desire to remind you, though you are fully informed, that the Lord, who once for all saved[f] a people out of the land of Egypt, afterward destroyed those who did not believe. [6]And the angels who did not keep their own position, but left their proper dwelling, he has kept in eternal chains in deepest darkness for the judgment of the great day. [7]Likewise, Sodom and Gomorrah and the surrounding cities, which, in the same manner as they, indulged in sexual immorality and pursued unnatural lust,[g] serve as an example by undergoing a punishment of eternal fire.

8 Yet in the same way these dreamers also defile the flesh, reject authority, and slander the glorious ones.[h] [9]But when the archangel Michael contended with the devil and disputed about the body of Moses, he did not dare to bring a condemnation of slander[i]

against him, but said, "The Lord rebuke you!" [10]But these people slander whatever they do not understand, and they are destroyed by those things that, like irrational animals, they know by instinct. [11]Woe to them! For they go the way of Cain, and abandon themselves to Balaam's error for the sake of gain, and perish in Korah's rebellion. [12]These are blemishes[j] on your love-feasts, while they feast with you without fear, feeding themselves.[k] They are waterless clouds carried along by the winds; autumn trees without fruit, twice dead, uprooted; [13]wild waves of the sea, casting up the foam of their own shame; wandering stars, for whom the deepest darkness has been reserved forever.

14 It was also about these that Enoch, in the seventh generation from Adam, prophesied, saying, "See, the Lord is coming[l] with ten thousands of his holy ones, [15]to execute judgment on all, and to convict everyone of all the deeds of ungodliness that they have committed in such an ungodly way, and of all the harsh things that ungodly sinners have spoken against him." [16]These are grumblers and malcontents; they indulge their own lusts; they are bombastic in speech, flattering people to their own advantage.

Warnings and Exhortations

17 But you, beloved, must remember the predictions of the apostles of our Lord Jesus Christ; [18]for they said to you, "In the last time there will be scoffers, indulging their own ungodly lusts." [19]It is these worldly people, devoid of the Spirit, who are causing divisions. [20]But you, beloved, build yourselves up on your most holy faith; pray in the Holy Spirit; [21]keep yourselves in the love of God; look forward to the mercy of our Lord Jesus Christ that leads to[m] eternal life. [22]And have mercy on some who are wavering; [23]save

---

a Gk Judas   b Gk slave   c Other ancient authorities read sanctified   d Or by   e Or the only Master and our Lord Jesus Christ   f Other ancient authorities read though you were once for all fully informed, that Jesus (or Joshua) who saved   g Gk went after other flesh   h Or angels; Gk glories   i Or condemnation for blasphemy   j Or reefs   k Or without fear. They are shepherds who care only for themselves   l Gk came   m Gk Christ to others by snatching them out of the fire; and have mercy on still others with fear, hating even the tunic defiled by their bodies. [a]

Benediction

24 Now to him who is able to keep you from falling, and to make you stand without blemish in the presence of his glory with rejoicing, 25 to the only God our Savior, through Jesus Christ our Lord, be glory, majesty, power, and authority, before all time and now and forever. Amen.

---

a Gk *by the flesh*. The Greek text of verses 22-23 is uncertain at several points

THE REVELATION
TO JOHN

Introduction and Salutation

1 The revelation of Jesus Christ, which God gave him to show his servants[a] what must soon take place; he made[b] it known by sending his angel to his servant[c] John, [2]who testified to the word of God and to the testimony of Jesus Christ, even to all that he saw.

3 Blessed is the one who reads aloud the words of the prophecy, and blessed are those who hear and who keep what is written in it; for the time is near.

4 John to the seven churches that are in Asia:

Grace to you and peace from him who is and who was and who is to come, and from the seven spirits who are before his throne, [5]and from Jesus Christ, the faithful witness, the firstborn of the dead, and the ruler of the kings of the earth.

To him who loves us and freed[d] us from our sins by his blood, [6]and made[b] us to be a kingdom, priests serving[e] his God and Father, to him be glory and dominion forever and ever. Amen.

7   Look! He is coming with the clouds;
        every eye will see him,
    even those who pierced him;
        and on his account all the tribes of
            the earth will wail.
So it is to be. Amen.

8 "I am the Alpha and the Omega," says the Lord God, who is and who was and who is to come, the Almighty.

A Vision of Christ

9 I, John, your brother who share with you in Jesus the persecution and the kingdom and the patient endurance, was on the island called Patmos because of the word of God and the testimony of Jesus.[f] [10]I was in the spirit[g] on the Lord's day, and I heard behind me a loud voice like a trumpet [11]saying, "Write in a book what you see and send it to the seven churches, to Ephesus, to Smyrna, to Pergamum, to Thyatira, to Sardis, to Philadelphia, and to Laodicea."

12 Then I turned to see whose voice it was that spoke to me, and on turning I saw seven golden lampstands, [13]and in the midst of the lampstands I saw one like the Son of Man, clothed with a long robe and with a golden sash across his chest. [14]His head and his hair were white as white wool, white as snow; his eyes were like a flame of fire, [15]his feet were like burnished bronze, refined as in a furnace, and his voice was like the sound of many waters. [16]In his right hand he held seven stars, and from his mouth came a sharp, two-edged sword, and his face was like the sun shining with full force.

17 When I saw him, I fell at his feet as though dead. But he placed his right hand on me, saying, "Do not be afraid; I am the first and the last, [18]and the living one. I was dead, and see, I am alive forever and ever; and I have the keys of Death and of Hades. [19]Now write what you have seen, what is, and what is to take place after this. [20]As for the mystery of the seven stars that you saw in my right hand, and the seven golden lampstands: the seven stars are the angels of the seven churches, and the seven lampstands are the seven churches.

The Message to Ephesus

2 "To the angel of the church in Ephesus write: These are the words of him who holds the seven stars in his right hand, who walks among the seven golden lampstands:

2 "I know your works, your toil and your patient endurance. I know that you cannot tolerate evildoers; you have tested those who claim to be apostles but are not, and have found them to be false. [3]I also know that you are enduring patiently and bearing up for the sake of my name, and that you have

---

a Gk *slaves*   *b* Gk *and he made*   *c* Gk *slave*   *d* Other ancient authorities read *washed*   *e* Gk *priests to*
f Or *testimony to Jesus*   *g* Or *in the Spirit*

not grown weary. 4But I have this against you, that you have abandoned the love you had at first. 5Remember then from what you have fallen; repent, and do the works you did at first. If not, I will come to you and remove your lampstand from its place, unless you repent. 6Yet this is to your credit: you hate the works of the Nicolaitans, which I also hate. 7Let anyone who has an ear listen to what the Spirit is saying to the churches. To everyone who conquers, I will give permission to eat from the tree of life that is in the paradise of God.

The Message to Smyrna

8 "And to the angel of the church in Smyrna write: These are the words of the first and the last, who was dead and came to life:

9 "I know your affliction and your poverty, even though you are rich. I know the slander on the part of those who say that they are Jews and are not, but are a synagogue of Satan. 10Do not fear what you are about to suffer. Beware, the devil is about to throw some of you into prison so that you may be tested, and for ten days you will have affliction. Be faithful until death, and I will give you the crown of life. 11Let anyone who has an ear listen to what the Spirit is saying to the churches. Whoever conquers will not be harmed by the second death.

The Message to Pergamum

12 "And to the angel of the church in Pergamum write: These are the words of him who has the sharp two-edged sword:

13 "I know where you are living, where Satan's throne is. Yet you are holding fast to my name, and you did not deny your faith in me*a* even in the days of Antipas my witness, my faithful one, who was killed among you, where Satan lives. 14But I have a few things against you: you have some there who hold to the teaching of Balaam, who taught Balak to put a stumbling block before the people of Israel, so that they would eat food sacrificed

to idols and practice fornication. 15So you also have some who hold to the teaching of the Nicolaitans. 16Repent then. If not, I will come to you soon and make war against them with the sword of my mouth. 17Let anyone who has an ear listen to what the Spirit is saying to the churches. To everyone who conquers I will give some of the hidden manna, and I will give a white stone, and on the white stone is written a new name that no one knows except the one who receives it.

The Message to Thyatira

18 "And to the angel of the church in Thyatira write: These are the words of the Son of God, who has eyes like a flame of fire, and whose feet are like burnished bronze:

19 "I know your works—your love, faith, service, and patient endurance. I know that your last works are greater than the first. 20But I have this against you: you tolerate that woman Jezebel, who calls herself a prophet and is teaching and beguiling my servants*b* to practice fornication and to eat food sacrificed to idols. 21I gave her time to repent, but she refuses to repent of her fornication. 22Beware, I am throwing her on a bed, and those who commit adultery with her I am throwing into great distress, unless they repent of her doings; 23and I will strike her children dead. And all the churches will know that I am the one who searches minds and hearts, and I will give to each of you as your works deserve. 24But to the rest of you in Thyatira, who do not hold this teaching, who have not learned what some call 'the deep things of Satan,' to you I say, I do not lay on you any other burden; 25only hold fast to what you have until I come. 26To everyone who conquers and continues to do my works to the end,

I will give authority over the nations;
27   to rule*c* them with an iron rod,
    as when clay pots are shattered—
28even as I also received authority from my Father. To the one who conquers I will also

---

a Or *deny my faith*   *b* Gk *slaves*   *c* Or *to shepherd* give the morning star. ²⁹Let anyone who has an ear listen to what the Spirit is saying to the churches.

The Message to Sardis

3 "And to the angel of the church in Sardis write: These are the words of him who has the seven spirits of God and the seven stars:

"I know your works; you have a name of being alive, but you are dead. ²Wake up, and strengthen what remains and is on the point of death, for I have not found your works perfect in the sight of my God. ³Remember then what you received and heard; obey it, and repent. If you do not wake up, I will come like a thief, and you will not know at what hour I will come to you. ⁴Yet you have still a few persons in Sardis who have not soiled their clothes; they will walk with me, dressed in white, for they are worthy. ⁵If you conquer, you will be clothed like them in white robes, and I will not blot your name out of the book of life; I will confess your name before my Father and before his angels. ⁶Let anyone who has an ear listen to what the Spirit is saying to the churches.

The Message to Philadelphia

7 "And to the angel of the church in Philadelphia write:

These are the words of the holy one,
    the true one,
  who has the key of David,
  who opens and no one will shut,
    who shuts and no one opens:

8 "I know your works. Look, I have set before you an open door, which no one is able to shut. I know that you have but little power, and yet you have kept my word and have not denied my name. ⁹I will make those of the synagogue of Satan who say that they are Jews and are not, but are lying—I will make them come and bow down before your feet, and they will learn that I have loved you. ¹⁰Because you have kept my word of pa-

tient endurance, I will keep you from the hour of trial that is coming on the whole world to test the inhabitants of the earth. ¹¹I am coming soon; hold fast to what you have, so that no one may seize your crown. ¹²If you conquer, I will make you a pillar in the temple of my God; you will never go out of it. I will write on you the name of my God, and the name of the city of my God, the new Jerusalem that comes down from my God out of heaven, and my own new name. ¹³Let anyone who has an ear listen to what the Spirit is saying to the churches.

The Message to Laodicea

14 "And to the angel of the church in Laodicea write: The words of the Amen, the faithful and true witness, the origin*ᵃ* of God's creation:

15 "I know your works; you are neither cold nor hot. I wish that you were either cold or hot. ¹⁶So, because you are lukewarm, and neither cold nor hot, I am about to spit you out of my mouth. ¹⁷For you say, 'I am rich, I have prospered, and I need nothing.' You do not realize that you are wretched, pitiable, poor, blind, and naked. ¹⁸Therefore I counsel you to buy from me gold refined by fire so that you may be rich; and white robes to clothe you and to keep the shame of your nakedness from being seen; and salve to anoint your eyes so that you may see. ¹⁹I reprove and discipline those whom I love. Be earnest, therefore, and repent. ²⁰Listen! I am standing at the door, knocking; if you hear my voice and open the door, I will come in to you and eat with you, and you with me. ²¹To the one who conquers I will give a place with me on my throne, just as I myself conquered and sat down with my Father on his throne. ²²Let anyone who has an ear listen to what the Spirit is saying to the churches."

The Heavenly Worship

4 After this I looked, and there in heaven a door stood open! And the first voice,

---

a Or *beginning*

which I had heard speaking to me like a trumpet, said, "Come up here, and I will show you what must take place after this." ²At once I was in the spirit,ᵃ and there in heaven stood a throne, with one seated on the throne! ³And the one seated there looks like jasper and carnelian, and around the throne is a rainbow that looks like an emerald. ⁴Around the throne are twenty-four thrones, and seated on the thrones are twenty-four elders, dressed in white robes, with golden crowns on their heads. ⁵Coming from the throne are flashes of lightning, and rumblings and peals of thunder, and in front of the throne burn seven flaming torches, which are the seven spirits of God; ⁶and in front of the throne there is something like a sea of glass, like crystal.

Around the throne, and on each side of the throne, are four living creatures, full of eyes in front and behind: ⁷the first living creature like a lion, the second living creature like an ox, the third living creature with a face like a human face, and the fourth living creature like a flying eagle. ⁸And the four living creatures, each of them with six wings, are full of eyes all around and inside. Day and night without ceasing they sing,

"Holy, holy, holy,
the Lord God the Almighty,
who was and is and is to come."

⁹And whenever the living creatures give glory and honor and thanks to the one who is seated on the throne, who lives forever and ever, ¹⁰the twenty-four elders fall before the one who is seated on the throne and worship the one who lives forever and ever; they cast their crowns before the throne, singing,

11 "You are worthy, our Lord and God,
to receive glory and honor and
power,
for you created all things,
and by your will they existed and
were created."

The Scroll and the Lamb

5 Then I saw in the right hand of the one seated on the throne a scroll written on the inside and on the back, sealedᵇ with seven seals; ²and I saw a mighty angel proclaiming with a loud voice, "Who is worthy to open the scroll and break its seals?" ³And no one in heaven or on earth or under the earth was able to open the scroll or to look into it. ⁴And I began to weep bitterly because no one was found worthy to open the scroll or to look into it. ⁵Then one of the elders said to me, "Do not weep. See, the Lion of the tribe of Judah, the Root of David, has conquered, so that he can open the scroll and its seven seals."

6 Then I saw between the throne and the four living creatures and among the elders a Lamb standing as if it had been slaughtered, having seven horns and seven eyes, which are the seven spirits of God sent out into all the earth. ⁷He went and took the scroll from the right hand of the one who was seated on the throne. ⁸When he had taken the scroll, the four living creatures and the twenty-four elders fell before the Lamb, each holding a harp and golden bowls full of incense, which are the prayers of the saints. ⁹They sing a new song:

"You are worthy to take the scroll
and to open its seals,
for you were slaughtered and by your
blood you ransomed for God
saints fromᶜ every tribe and language
and people and nation;
10 you have made them to be a kingdom
and priests servingᵈ our God,
and they will reign on earth."

11 Then I looked, and I heard the voice of many angels surrounding the throne and the living creatures and the elders; they numbered myriads of myriads and thousands of thousands, ¹²singing with full voice,

"Worthy is the Lamb that was
slaughtered

ᵃ Or *in the Spirit*   ᵇ Or *written on the inside, and sealed on the back*   ᶜ Gk *ransomed for God from*   ᵈ Gk *priests to*

to receive power and wealth and
  wisdom and might
and honor and glory and blessing!"

13Then I heard every creature in heaven and on earth and under the earth and in the sea, and all that is in them, singing,

"To the one seated on the throne and
  to the Lamb
be blessing and honor and glory and
  might
forever and ever!"

14And the four living creatures said, "Amen!" And the elders fell down and worshiped.

The Seven Seals

6 Then I saw the Lamb open one of the seven seals, and I heard one of the four living creatures call out, as with a voice of thunder, "Come!" *a* 2I looked, and there was a white horse! Its rider had a bow; a crown was given to him, and he came out conquering and to conquer.

3 When he opened the second seal, I heard the second living creature call out, "Come!" *a* 4And out came *b* another horse, bright red; its rider was permitted to take peace from the earth, so that people would slaughter one another; and he was given a great sword.

5 When he opened the third seal, I heard the third living creature call out, "Come!" *a* I looked, and there was a black horse! Its rider held a pair of scales in his hand, 6and I heard what seemed to be a voice in the midst of the four living creatures saying, "A quart of wheat for a day's pay, *c* and three quarts of barley for a day's pay, *c* but do not damage the olive oil and the wine!"

7 When he opened the fourth seal, I heard the voice of the fourth living creature call out, "Come!" *a* 8I looked and there was a pale green horse! Its rider's name was Death, and Hades followed with him; they were given authority over a fourth of the earth, to kill with sword, famine, and pestilence, and by the wild animals of the earth.

9 When he opened the fifth seal, I saw under the altar the souls of those who had been slaughtered for the word of God and for the testimony they had given; 10they cried out with a loud voice, "Sovereign Lord, holy and true, how long will it be before you judge and avenge our blood on the inhabitants of the earth?" 11They were each given a white robe and told to rest a little longer, until the number would be complete both of their fellow servants *d* and of their brothers and sisters, *e* who were soon to be killed as they themselves had been killed.

12 When he opened the sixth seal, I looked, and there came a great earthquake; the sun became black as sackcloth, the full moon became like blood, 13and the stars of the sky fell to the earth as the fig tree drops its winter fruit when shaken by a gale. 14The sky vanished like a scroll rolling itself up, and every mountain and island was removed from its place. 15Then the kings of the earth and the magnates and the generals and the rich and the powerful, and everyone, slave and free, hid in the caves and among the rocks of the mountains, 16calling to the mountains and rocks, "Fall on us and hide us from the face of the one seated on the throne and from the wrath of the Lamb; 17for the great day of their wrath has come, and who is able to stand?"

The 144,000 of Israel Sealed

7 After this I saw four angels standing at the four corners of the earth, holding back the four winds of the earth so that no wind could blow on earth or sea or against any tree. 2I saw another angel ascending from the rising of the sun, having the seal of the living God, and he called with a loud voice to the four angels who had been given power to damage earth and sea, 3saying, "Do not damage the earth or the sea or the trees, until we have marked the servants *d* of our God with a seal on their foreheads."

4 And I heard the number of those who

---

a Or "Go!"   *b* Or *went*   *c* Gk *a denarius*   *d* Gk *slaves*   *e* Gk *brothers* were sealed, one hundred forty-four thousand, sealed out of every tribe of the people of Israel:

5 From the tribe of Judah twelve thousand sealed,

from the tribe of Reuben twelve thousand,

from the tribe of Gad twelve thousand,

6 from the tribe of Asher twelve thousand,

from the tribe of Naphtali twelve thousand,

from the tribe of Manasseh twelve thousand,

7 from the tribe of Simeon twelve thousand,

from the tribe of Levi twelve thousand,

from the tribe of Issachar twelve thousand,

8 from the tribe of Zebulun twelve thousand,

from the tribe of Joseph twelve thousand,

from the tribe of Benjamin twelve thousand sealed.

The Multitude from Every Nation

9 After this I looked, and there was a great multitude that no one could count, from every nation, from all tribes and peoples and languages, standing before the throne and before the Lamb, robed in white, with palm branches in their hands. 10They cried out in a loud voice, saying,

"Salvation belongs to our God who is
        seated on the throne, and to the
        Lamb!"

11And all the angels stood around the throne and around the elders and the four living creatures, and they fell on their faces before the throne and worshiped God, 12singing,

"Amen! Blessing and glory and wisdom
    and thanksgiving and honor
    and power and might
    be to our God forever and ever!
        Amen."

13 Then one of the elders addressed me, saying, "Who are these, robed in white, and where have they come from?" 14I said to him, "Sir, you are the one that knows." Then he said to me, "These are they who have come out of the great ordeal; they have washed their robes and made them white in the blood of the Lamb.

15 For this reason they are before the
        throne of God,
    and worship him day and night
        within his temple,
    and the one who is seated on the
        throne will shelter them.

16 They will hunger no more, and thirst
        no more;
    the sun will not strike them,
    nor any scorching heat;

17 for the Lamb at the center of the
        throne will be their shepherd,
    and he will guide them to springs of
        the water of life,
    and God will wipe away every tear
        from their eyes."

The Seventh Seal and the Golden Censer

8 When the Lamb opened the seventh seal, there was silence in heaven for about half an hour. 2And I saw the seven angels who stand before God, and seven trumpets were given to them.

3 Another angel with a golden censer came and stood at the altar; he was given a great quantity of incense to offer with the prayers of all the saints on the golden altar that is before the throne. 4And the smoke of the incense, with the prayers of the saints, rose before God from the hand of the angel. 5Then the angel took the censer and filled it with fire from the altar and threw it on the earth; and there were peals of thunder, rumblings, flashes of lightning, and an earthquake.

The Seven Trumpets

6 Now the seven angels who had the seven trumpets made ready to blow them.

7 The first angel blew his trumpet, and there came hail and fire, mixed with blood, and they were hurled to the earth; and a third

of the earth was burned up, and a third of the trees were burned up, and all green grass was burned up.

8 The second angel blew his trumpet, and something like a great mountain, burning with fire, was thrown into the sea. 9A third of the sea became blood, a third of the living creatures in the sea died, and a third of the ships were destroyed.

10 The third angel blew his trumpet, and a great star fell from heaven, blazing like a torch, and it fell on a third of the rivers and on the springs of water. 11The name of the star is Wormwood. A third of the waters became wormwood, and many died from the water, because it was made bitter.

12 The fourth angel blew his trumpet, and a third of the sun was struck, and a third of the moon, and a third of the stars, so that a third of their light was darkened; a third of the day was kept from shining, and likewise the night.

13 Then I looked, and I heard an eagle crying with a loud voice as it flew in midheaven, "Woe, woe, woe to the inhabitants of the earth, at the blasts of the other trumpets that the three angels are about to blow!"

9 And the fifth angel blew his trumpet, and I saw a star that had fallen from heaven to earth, and he was given the key to the shaft of the bottomless pit; 2he opened the shaft of the bottomless pit, and from the shaft rose smoke like the smoke of a great furnace, and the sun and the air were darkened with the smoke from the shaft. 3Then from the smoke came locusts on the earth, and they were given authority like the authority of scorpions of the earth. 4They were told not to damage the grass of the earth or any green growth or any tree, but only those people who do not have the seal of God on their foreheads. 5They were allowed to torture them for five months, but not to kill them, and their torture was like the torture of a scorpion when it stings someone. 6And in those days people will seek death but

will not find it; they will long to die, but death will flee from them.

7 In appearance the locusts were like horses equipped for battle. On their heads were what looked like crowns of gold; their faces were like human faces, 8their hair like women's hair, and their teeth like lions' teeth; 9they had scales like iron breastplates, and the noise of their wings was like the noise of many chariots with horses rushing into battle. 10They have tails like scorpions, with stingers, and in their tails is their power to harm people for five months. 11They have as king over them the angel of the bottomless pit; his name in Hebrew is Abaddon,*a* and in Greek he is called Apollyon.*b*

12 The first woe has passed. There are still two woes to come.

13 Then the sixth angel blew his trumpet, and I heard a voice from the four*c* horns of the golden altar before God, 14saying to the sixth angel who had the trumpet, "Release the four angels who are bound at the great river Euphrates." 15So the four angels were released, who had been held ready for the hour, the day, the month, and the year, to kill a third of humankind. 16The number of the troops of cavalry was two hundred million; I heard their number. 17And this was how I saw the horses in my vision: the riders wore breastplates the color of fire and of sapphire*d* and of sulfur; the heads of the horses were like lions' heads, and fire and smoke and sulfur came out of their mouths. 18By these three plagues a third of humankind was killed, by the fire and smoke and sulfur coming out of their mouths. 19For the power of the horses is in their mouths and in their tails; their tails are like serpents, having heads; and with them they inflict harm.

20 The rest of humankind, who were not killed by these plagues, did not repent of the works of their hands or give up worshiping demons and idols of gold and silver and bronze and stone and wood, which cannot see or hear or walk. 21And they did not repent

---

a That is, *Destruction*   *b* That is, *Destroyer*   *c* Other ancient authorities lack *four*   *d* Gk *hyacinth* of their murders or their sorceries or their fornication or their thefts.

The Angel with the Little Scroll

10 And I saw another mighty angel coming down from heaven, wrapped in a cloud, with a rainbow over his head; his face was like the sun, and his legs like pillars of fire. ²He held a little scroll open in his hand. Setting his right foot on the sea and his left foot on the land, ³he gave a great shout, like a lion roaring. And when he shouted, the seven thunders sounded. ⁴And when the seven thunders had sounded, I was about to write, but I heard a voice from heaven saying, "Seal up what the seven thunders have said, and do not write it down." ⁵Then the angel whom I saw standing on the sea and the land raised his right hand to heaven

6   and swore by him who lives forever and ever,

who created heaven and what is in it, the earth and what is in it, and the sea and what is in it: "There will be no more delay, ⁷but in the days when the seventh angel is to blow his trumpet, the mystery of God will be fulfilled, as he announced to his servants*a* the prophets."

8 Then the voice that I had heard from heaven spoke to me again, saying, "Go, take the scroll that is open in the hand of the angel who is standing on the sea and on the land." ⁹So I went to the angel and told him to give me the little scroll; and he said to me, "Take it, and eat; it will be bitter to your stomach, but sweet as honey in your mouth." ¹⁰So I took the little scroll from the hand of the angel and ate it; it was sweet as honey in my mouth, but when I had eaten it, my stomach was made bitter.

11 Then they said to me, "You must prophesy again about many peoples and nations and languages and kings."

The Two Witnesses

11 Then I was given a measuring rod like a staff, and I was told, "Come and measure the temple of God and the altar and those who worship there, ²but do not measure the court outside the temple; leave that out, for it is given over to the nations, and they will trample over the holy city for forty-two months. ³And I will grant my two witnesses authority to prophesy for one thousand two hundred sixty days, wearing sackcloth."

4 These are the two olive trees and the two lampstands that stand before the Lord of the earth. ⁵And if anyone wants to harm them, fire pours from their mouth and consumes their foes; anyone who wants to harm them must be killed in this manner. ⁶They have authority to shut the sky, so that no rain may fall during the days of their prophesying, and they have authority over the waters to turn them into blood, and to strike the earth with every kind of plague, as often as they desire.

7 When they have finished their testimony, the beast that comes up from the bottomless pit will make war on them and conquer them and kill them, ⁸and their dead bodies will lie in the street of the great city that is prophetically*b* called Sodom and Egypt, where also their Lord was crucified. ⁹For three and a half days members of the peoples and tribes and languages and nations will gaze at their dead bodies and refuse to let them be placed in a tomb; ¹⁰and the inhabitants of the earth will gloat over them and celebrate and exchange presents, because these two prophets had been a torment to the inhabitants of the earth.

11 But after the three and a half days, the breath*c* of life from God entered them, and they stood on their feet, and those who saw them were terrified. ¹²Then they*d* heard a loud voice from heaven saying to them, "Come up here!" And they went up to heaven in a cloud while their enemies watched

a Gk *slaves*   *b* Or *allegorically*; Gk *spiritually*   *c* Or *the spirit*   *d* Other ancient authorities read *I* them. ¹³At that moment there was a great earthquake, and a tenth of the city fell; seven thousand people were killed in the earthquake, and the rest were terrified and gave glory to the God of heaven.

14 The second woe has passed. The third woe is coming very soon.

The Seventh Trumpet

15 Then the seventh angel blew his trumpet, and there were loud voices in heaven, saying,

> "The kingdom of the world has
>   become the kingdom of our
>   Lord
>   and of his Messiah,[a]
> and he will reign forever and ever."

16 Then the twenty-four elders who sit on their thrones before God fell on their faces and worshiped God, ¹⁷singing,

> "We give you thanks, Lord God
>   Almighty,
> who are and who were,
> for you have taken your great power
>   and begun to reign.
> 18 The nations raged,
>   but your wrath has come,
>   and the time for judging the dead,
>   for rewarding your servants,[b] the
>   prophets
>   and saints and all who fear your
>   name,
>   both small and great,
>   and for destroying those who destroy
>   the earth."

19 Then God's temple in heaven was opened, and the ark of his covenant was seen within his temple; and there were flashes of lightning, rumblings, peals of thunder, an earthquake, and heavy hail.

The Woman and the Dragon

12 A great portent appeared in heaven: a woman clothed with the sun, with the moon under her feet, and on her head a crown of twelve stars. ²She was pregnant

and was crying out in birth pangs, in the agony of giving birth. ³Then another portent appeared in heaven: a great red dragon, with seven heads and ten horns, and seven diadems on his heads. ⁴His tail swept down a third of the stars of heaven and threw them to the earth. Then the dragon stood before the woman who was about to bear a child, so that he might devour her child as soon as it was born. ⁵And she gave birth to a son, a male child, who is to rule[c] all the nations with a rod of iron. But her child was snatched away and taken to God and to his throne; ⁶and the woman fled into the wilderness, where she has a place prepared by God, so that there she can be nourished for one thousand two hundred sixty days.

Michael Defeats the Dragon

7 And war broke out in heaven; Michael and his angels fought against the dragon. The dragon and his angels fought back, ⁸but they were defeated, and there was no longer any place for them in heaven. ⁹The great dragon was thrown down, that ancient serpent, who is called the Devil and Satan, the deceiver of the whole world—he was thrown down to the earth, and his angels were thrown down with him.

10 Then I heard a loud voice in heaven, proclaiming,

> "Now have come the salvation and the
>   power
> and the kingdom of our God
> and the authority of his Messiah,[a]
> for the accuser of our comrades[d] has
>   been thrown down,
> who accuses them day and night
>   before our God.
> 11 But they have conquered him by the
>   blood of the Lamb
> and by the word of their testimony,
> for they did not cling to life even in the
>   face of death.
> 12 Rejoice then, you heavens
>   and those who dwell in them!

---

a Gk Christ   b Gk slaves   c Or to shepherd   d Gk brothers

But woe to the earth and the sea,
  for the devil has come down to
    you
  with great wrath,
    because he knows that his time is
      short!"

The Dragon Fights Again on Earth

13 So when the dragon saw that he had been thrown down to the earth, he pursued[a] the woman who had given birth to the male child. [14]But the woman was given the two wings of the great eagle, so that she could fly from the serpent into the wilderness, to her place where she is nourished for a time, and times, and half a time. [15]Then from his mouth the serpent poured water like a river after the woman, to sweep her away with the flood. [16]But the earth came to the help of the woman; it opened its mouth and swallowed the river that the dragon had poured from his mouth. [17]Then the dragon was angry with the woman, and went off to make war on the rest of her children, those who keep the commandments of God and hold the testimony of Jesus.

The First Beast

18 Then the dragon[b] took his stand on the

13 sand of the seashore. [1]And I saw a beast rising out of the sea, having ten horns and seven heads; and on its horns were ten diadems, and on its heads were blasphemous names. [2]And the beast that I saw was like a leopard, its feet were like a bear's, and its mouth was like a lion's mouth. And the dragon gave it his power and his throne and great authority. [3]One of its heads seemed to have received a death-blow, but its mortal wound[c] had been healed. In amazement the whole earth followed the beast. [4]They worshiped the dragon, for he had given his authority to the beast, and they worshiped the beast, saying, "Who is like the beast, and who can fight against it?"

5 The beast was given a mouth uttering haughty and blasphemous words, and it was allowed to exercise authority for forty-two months. [6]It opened its mouth to utter blasphemies against God, blaspheming his name and his dwelling, that is, those who dwell in heaven. [7]Also it was allowed to make war on the saints and to conquer them.[d] It was given authority over every tribe and people and language and nation, [8]and all the inhabitants of the earth will worship it, everyone whose name has not been written from the foundation of the world in the book of life of the Lamb that was slaughtered.[e]

9 Let anyone who has an ear listen:
10   If you are to be taken captive,
      into captivity you go;
  if you kill with the sword,
      with the sword you must be
        killed.

Here is a call for the endurance and faith of the saints.

The Second Beast

11 Then I saw another beast that rose out of the earth; it had two horns like a lamb and it spoke like a dragon. [12]It exercises all the authority of the first beast on its behalf, and it makes the earth and its inhabitants worship the first beast, whose mortal wound[f] had been healed. [13]It performs great signs, even making fire come down from heaven to earth in the sight of all; [14]and by the signs that it is allowed to perform on behalf of the beast, it deceives the inhabitants of earth, telling them to make an image for the beast that had been wounded by the sword[g] and yet lived; [15]and it was allowed to give breath[h] to the image of the beast so that the image of the beast could even speak and cause those who would not worship the image of the beast to be killed. [16]Also it causes all, both small and great, both rich and poor, both free and slave, to be marked on the right hand or the forehead, [17]so that no one can buy or sell who

a Or persecuted   b Gk Then he; other ancient authorities read Then I stood   c Gk the plague of its death   d Other ancient authorities lack this sentence   e Or written in the book of life of the Lamb that was slaughtered from the foundation of the world   f Gk whose plague of its death   g Or that had received the plague of the sword   h Or spirit does not have the mark, that is, the name of the beast or the number of its name. [18]This calls for wisdom: let anyone with understanding calculate the number of the beast, for it is the number of a person. Its number is six hundred sixty-six. [a]

The Lamb and the 144,000

14 Then I looked, and there was the Lamb, standing on Mount Zion! And with him were one hundred forty-four thousand who had his name and his Father's name written on their foreheads. [2]And I heard a voice from heaven like the sound of many waters and like the sound of loud thunder; the voice I heard was like the sound of harpists playing on their harps, [3]and they sing a new song before the throne and before the four living creatures and before the elders. No one could learn that song except the one hundred forty-four thousand who have been redeemed from the earth. [4]It is these who have not defiled themselves with women, for they are virgins; these follow the Lamb wherever he goes. They have been redeemed from humankind as first fruits for God and the Lamb, [5]and in their mouth no lie was found; they are blameless.

The Messages of the Three Angels

6 Then I saw another angel flying in midheaven, with an eternal gospel to proclaim to those who live[b] on the earth—to every nation and tribe and language and people. [7]He said in a loud voice, "Fear God and give him glory, for the hour of his judgment has come; and worship him who made heaven and earth, the sea and the springs of water."

8 Then another angel, a second, followed, saying, "Fallen, fallen is Babylon the great! She has made all nations drink of the wine of the wrath of her fornication."

9 Then another angel, a third, followed them, crying with a loud voice, "Those who worship the beast and its image, and receive a mark on their foreheads or on their hands, [10]they will also drink the wine of God's wrath, poured unmixed into the cup of his anger, and they will be tormented with fire and sulfur in the presence of the holy angels and in the presence of the Lamb. [11]And the smoke of their torment goes up forever and ever. There is no rest day or night for those who worship the beast and its image and for anyone who receives the mark of its name."

12 Here is a call for the endurance of the saints, those who keep the commandments of God and hold fast to the faith of[c] Jesus.

13 And I heard a voice from heaven saying, "Write this: Blessed are the dead who from now on die in the Lord." "Yes," says the Spirit, "they will rest from their labors, for their deeds follow them."

Reaping the Earth's Harvest

14 Then I looked, and there was a white cloud, and seated on the cloud was one like the Son of Man, with a golden crown on his head, and a sharp sickle in his hand! [15]Another angel came out of the temple, calling with a loud voice to the one who sat on the cloud, "Use your sickle and reap, for the hour to reap has come, because the harvest of the earth is fully ripe." [16]So the one who sat on the cloud swung his sickle over the earth, and the earth was reaped.

17 Then another angel came out of the temple in heaven, and he too had a sharp sickle. [18]Then another angel came out from the altar, the angel who has authority over fire, and he called with a loud voice to him who had the sharp sickle, "Use your sharp sickle and gather the clusters of the vine of the earth, for its grapes are ripe." [19]So the angel swung his sickle over the earth and gathered the vintage of the earth, and he threw it into the great wine press of the wrath of God. [20]And the wine press was trodden outside the city, and blood flowed from the wine press, as high as a horse's bridle, for a distance of about two hundred miles. [d]

---

a Other ancient authorities read *six hundred sixteen*   b Gk *sit*   c Or *to their faith in*   d Gk *one thousand six hundred stadia*

The Angels with the Seven Last Plagues

15 Then I saw another portent in heaven, great and amazing: seven angels with seven plagues, which are the last, for with them the wrath of God is ended.

2 And I saw what appeared to be a sea of glass mixed with fire, and those who had conquered the beast and its image and the number of its name, standing beside the sea of glass with harps of God in their hands. 3And they sing the song of Moses, the servant*a* of God, and the song of the Lamb:

> "Great and amazing are your deeds,
>   Lord God the Almighty!
> Just and true are your ways,
>   King of the nations!*b*
> 4   Lord, who will not fear
>   and glorify your name?
> For you alone are holy.
>   All nations will come
>   and worship before you,
> for your judgments have been
>   revealed."

5 After this I looked, and the temple of the tent*c* of witness in heaven was opened, 6and out of the temple came the seven angels with the seven plagues, robed in pure bright linen,*d* with golden sashes across their chests. 7Then one of the four living creatures gave the seven angels seven golden bowls full of the wrath of God, who lives forever and ever; 8and the temple was filled with smoke from the glory of God and from his power, and no one could enter the temple until the seven plagues of the seven angels were ended.

The Bowls of God's Wrath

16 Then I heard a loud voice from the temple telling the seven angels, "Go and pour out on the earth the seven bowls of the wrath of God."

2 So the first angel went and poured his bowl on the earth, and a foul and painful sore came on those who had the mark of the beast and who worshiped its image.

3 The second angel poured his bowl into the sea, and it became like the blood of a corpse, and every living thing in the sea died.

4 The third angel poured his bowl into the rivers and the springs of water, and they became blood. 5And I heard the angel of the waters say,

> "You are just, O Holy One, who are
>   and were,
>   for you have judged these things;
> 6   because they shed the blood of saints
>   and prophets,
>   you have given them blood to drink.
> It is what they deserve!"

7And I heard the altar respond,

> "Yes, O Lord God, the Almighty,
>   your judgments are true and just!"

8 The fourth angel poured his bowl on the sun, and it was allowed to scorch people with fire; 9they were scorched by the fierce heat, but they cursed the name of God, who had authority over these plagues, and they did not repent and give him glory.

10 The fifth angel poured his bowl on the throne of the beast, and its kingdom was plunged into darkness; people gnawed their tongues in agony, 11and cursed the God of heaven because of their pains and sores, and they did not repent of their deeds.

12 The sixth angel poured his bowl on the great river Euphrates, and its water was dried up in order to prepare the way for the kings from the east. 13And I saw three foul spirits like frogs coming from the mouth of the dragon, from the mouth of the beast, and from the mouth of the false prophet. 14These are demonic spirits, performing signs, who go abroad to the kings of the whole world, to assemble them for battle on the great day of God the Almighty. 15("See, I am coming like a thief! Blessed is the one who stays awake and is clothed,*e* not going about naked and exposed to shame.") 16And they assembled

---

a Gk *slave*   *b* Other ancient authorities read *the ages*   *c* Or *tabernacle*   *d* Other ancient authorities read *stone*
e Gk *and keeps his robes*

them at the place that in Hebrew is called Harmagedon.

17 The seventh angel poured his bowl into the air, and a loud voice came out of the temple, from the throne, saying, "It is done!" 18And there came flashes of lightning, rumblings, peals of thunder, and a violent earthquake, such as had not occurred since people were upon the earth, so violent was that earthquake. 19The great city was split into three parts, and the cities of the nations fell. God remembered great Babylon and gave her the wine-cup of the fury of his wrath. 20And every island fled away, and no mountains were to be found; 21and huge hailstones, each weighing about a hundred pounds,ᵃ dropped from heaven on people, until they cursed God for the plague of the hail, so fearful was that plague.

The Great Whore and the Beast

17 Then one of the seven angels who had the seven bowls came and said to me, "Come, I will show you the judgment of the great whore who is seated on many waters, 2with whom the kings of the earth have committed fornication, and with the wine of whose fornication the inhabitants of the earth have become drunk." 3So he carried me away in the spiritᵇ into a wilderness, and I saw a woman sitting on a scarlet beast that was full of blasphemous names, and it had seven heads and ten horns. 4The woman was clothed in purple and scarlet, and adorned with gold and jewels and pearls, holding in her hand a golden cup full of abominations and the impurities of her fornication; 5and on her forehead was written a name, a mystery: "Babylon the great, mother of whores and of earth's abominations." 6And I saw that the woman was drunk with the blood of the saints and the blood of the witnesses to Jesus.

When I saw her, I was greatly amazed. 7But the angel said to me, "Why are you so amazed? I will tell you the mystery of the woman, and of the beast with seven heads

and ten horns that carries her. 8The beast that you saw was, and is not, and is about to ascend from the bottomless pit and go to destruction. And the inhabitants of the earth, whose names have not been written in the book of life from the foundation of the world, will be amazed when they see the beast, because it was and is not and is to come.

9 "This calls for a mind that has wisdom: the seven heads are seven mountains on which the woman is seated; also, they are seven kings, 10of whom five have fallen, one is living, and the other has not yet come; and when he comes, he must remain only a little while. 11As for the beast that was and is not, it is an eighth but it belongs to the seven, and it goes to destruction. 12And the ten horns that you saw are ten kings who have not yet received a kingdom, but they are to receive authority as kings for one hour, together with the beast. 13These are united in yielding their power and authority to the beast; 14they will make war on the Lamb, and the Lamb will conquer them, for he is Lord of lords and King of kings, and those with him are called and chosen and faithful."

15 And he said to me, "The waters that you saw, where the whore is seated, are peoples and multitudes and nations and languages. 16And the ten horns that you saw, they and the beast will hate the whore; they will make her desolate and naked; they will devour her flesh and burn her up with fire. 17For God has put it into their hearts to carry out his purpose by agreeing to give their kingdom to the beast, until the words of God will be fulfilled. 18The woman you saw is the great city that rules over the kings of the earth."

The Fall of Babylon

18 After this I saw another angel coming down from heaven, having great authority; and the earth was made bright with

ᵃ Gk weighing about a talent   ᵇ Or in the Spirit

his splendor. ²He called out with a mighty voice,

"Fallen, fallen is Babylon the great!
  It has become a dwelling place of demons,
a haunt of every foul spirit,
  a haunt of every foul bird,
  a haunt of every foul and hateful beast.ᵃ
3   For all the nations have drunkᵇ
  of the wine of the wrath of her fornication,
and the kings of the earth have committed fornication with her,
  and the merchants of the earth have grown rich from the powerᶜ of her luxury."

4 Then I heard another voice from heaven saying,

"Come out of her, my people,
  so that you do not take part in her sins,
and so that you do not share in her plagues;
5   for her sins are heaped high as heaven,
  and God has remembered her iniquities.
6   Render to her as she herself has rendered,
  and repay her double for her deeds;
  mix a double draught for her in the cup she mixed.
7   As she glorified herself and lived luxuriously,
  so give her a like measure of torment and grief.
Since in her heart she says,
  'I rule as a queen;
I am no widow,
  and I will never see grief,'
8   therefore her plagues will come in a single day—
  pestilence and mourning and famine—
and she will be burned with fire;

for mighty is the Lord God who judges her."

9 And the kings of the earth, who committed fornication and lived in luxury with her, will weep and wail over her when they see the smoke of her burning; ¹⁰they will stand far off, in fear of her torment, and say,

"Alas, alas, the great city,
  Babylon, the mighty city!
For in one hour your judgment has come."

11 And the merchants of the earth weep and mourn for her, since no one buys their cargo anymore, ¹²cargo of gold, silver, jewels and pearls, fine linen, purple, silk and scarlet, all kinds of scented wood, all articles of ivory, all articles of costly wood, bronze, iron, and marble, ¹³cinnamon, spice, incense, myrrh, frankincense, wine, olive oil, choice flour and wheat, cattle and sheep, horses and chariots, slaves—and human lives.ᵈ
14   "The fruit for which your soul longed
  has gone from you,
and all your dainties and your splendor
  are lost to you,
  never to be found again!"

¹⁵The merchants of these wares, who gained wealth from her, will stand far off, in fear of her torment, weeping and mourning aloud,
16   "Alas, alas, the great city,
  clothed in fine linen,
    in purple and scarlet,
  adorned with gold,
    with jewels, and with pearls!
17   For in one hour all this wealth has been laid waste!"

And all shipmasters and seafarers, sailors and all whose trade is on the sea, stood far off ¹⁸and cried out as they saw the smoke of her burning,

"What city was like the great city?"

¹⁹And they threw dust on their heads, as they wept and mourned, crying out,

"Alas, alas, the great city,
  where all who had ships at sea

ᵃ Other ancient authorities lack the words *a haunt of every foul beast* and attach the words *and hateful* to the previous line so as to read *a haunt of every foul and hateful bird*   ᵇ Other ancient authorities read *She has made all nations drink*   ᶜ Or *resources*   ᵈ Or *chariots, and human bodies and souls*

grew rich by her wealth!
For in one hour she has been laid
waste."

20 Rejoice over her, O heaven, you saints and apostles and prophets! For God has given judgment for you against her.

21 Then a mighty angel took up a stone like a great millstone and threw it into the sea, saying,

"With such violence Babylon the great
city
will be thrown down,
and will be found no more;
22 and the sound of harpists and
minstrels and of flutists and
trumpeters
will be heard in you no more;
and an artisan of any trade
will be found in you no more;
and the sound of the millstone
will be heard in you no more;
23 and the light of a lamp
will shine in you no more;
and the voice of bridegroom and bride
will be heard in you no more;
for your merchants were the magnates
of the earth,
and all nations were deceived by
your sorcery.
24 And in you*a* was found the blood of
prophets and of saints,
and of all who have been
slaughtered on earth."

The Rejoicing in Heaven

19 After this I heard what seemed to be the loud voice of a great multitude in heaven, saying,

"Hallelujah!
Salvation and glory and power to our
God,
2 for his judgments are true and just;
he has judged the great whore
who corrupted the earth with her
fornication,

and he has avenged on her the blood
of his servants."*b*
3 Once more they said,
"Hallelujah!
The smoke goes up from her forever
and ever."

4 And the twenty-four elders and the four living creatures fell down and worshiped God who is seated on the throne, saying,
"Amen. Hallelujah!"

5 And from the throne came a voice saying,
"Praise our God,
all you his servants,*b*
and all who fear him,
small and great."
6 Then I heard what seemed to be the voice of a great multitude, like the sound of many waters and like the sound of mighty thunderpeals, crying out,
"Hallelujah!
For the Lord our God
the Almighty reigns.
7 Let us rejoice and exult
and give him the glory,
for the marriage of the Lamb has
come,
and his bride has made herself
ready;
8 to her it has been granted to be clothed
with fine linen, bright and pure"—
for the fine linen is the righteous deeds of the saints.

9 And the angel said*c* to me, "Write this: Blessed are those who are invited to the marriage supper of the Lamb." And he said to me, "These are true words of God." 10 Then I fell down at his feet to worship him, but he said to me, "You must not do that! I am a fellow servant*d* with you and your comrades*e* who hold the testimony of Jesus.*f* Worship God! For the testimony of Jesus*f* is the spirit of prophecy."

The Rider on the White Horse

11 Then I saw heaven opened, and there

---

a Gk *her*   *b* Gk *slaves*   *c* Gk *he said*   *d* Gk *slave*   *e* Gk *brothers*   *f* Or *to Jesus* was a white horse! Its rider is called Faithful and True, and in righteousness he judges and makes war. 12His eyes are like a flame of fire, and on his head are many diadems; and he has a name inscribed that no one knows but himself. 13He is clothed in a robe dipped in*a* blood, and his name is called The Word of God. 14And the armies of heaven, wearing fine linen, white and pure, were following him on white horses. 15From his mouth comes a sharp sword with which to strike down the nations, and he will rule*b* them with a rod of iron; he will tread the wine press of the fury of the wrath of God the Almighty. 16On his robe and on his thigh he has a name inscribed, "King of kings and Lord of lords."

The Beast and Its Armies Defeated

17 Then I saw an angel standing in the sun, and with a loud voice he called to all the birds that fly in midheaven, "Come, gather for the great supper of God, 18to eat the flesh of kings, the flesh of captains, the flesh of the mighty, the flesh of horses and their riders—flesh of all, both free and slave, both small and great." 19Then I saw the beast and the kings of the earth with their armies gathered to make war against the rider on the horse and against his army. 20And the beast was captured, and with it the false prophet who had performed in its presence the signs by which he deceived those who had received the mark of the beast and those who worshiped its image. These two were thrown alive into the lake of fire that burns with sulfur. 21And the rest were killed by the sword of the rider on the horse, the sword that came from his mouth; and all the birds were gorged with their flesh.

The Thousand Years

20 Then I saw an angel coming down from heaven, holding in his hand the key to the bottomless pit and a great chain. 2He seized the dragon, that ancient serpent, who is the Devil and Satan, and bound him for a thousand years, 3and threw him into the pit, and locked and sealed it over him, so that he would deceive the nations no more, until the thousand years were ended. After that he must be let out for a little while.

4 Then I saw thrones, and those seated on them were given authority to judge. I also saw the souls of those who had been beheaded for their testimony to Jesus*c* and for the word of God. They had not worshiped the beast or its image and had not received its mark on their foreheads or their hands. They came to life and reigned with Christ a thousand years. 5(The rest of the dead did not come to life until the thousand years were ended.) This is the first resurrection. 6Blessed and holy are those who share in the first resurrection. Over these the second death has no power, but they will be priests of God and of Christ, and they will reign with him a thousand years.

Satan's Doom

7 When the thousand years are ended, Satan will be released from his prison 8and will come out to deceive the nations at the four corners of the earth, Gog and Magog, in order to gather them for battle; they are as numerous as the sands of the sea. 9They marched up over the breadth of the earth and surrounded the camp of the saints and the beloved city. And fire came down from heaven*d* and consumed them. 10And the devil who had deceived them was thrown into the lake of fire and sulfur, where the beast and the false prophet were, and they will be tormented day and night forever and ever.

The Dead Are Judged

11 Then I saw a great white throne and the one who sat on it; the earth and the heaven fled from his presence, and no place was found for them. 12And I saw the dead, great and small, standing before the throne, and books were opened. Also another book was

---

a Other ancient authorities read *sprinkled with*   *b* Or *will shepherd*   *c* Or *for the testimony of Jesus*   *d* Other ancient authorities read *from God, out of heaven,* or *out of heaven from God* opened, the book of life. And the dead were judged according to their works, as recorded in the books. 13And the sea gave up the dead that were in it, Death and Hades gave up the dead that were in them, and all were judged according to what they had done. 14Then Death and Hades were thrown into the lake of fire. This is the second death, the lake of fire; 15and anyone whose name was not found written in the book of life was thrown into the lake of fire.

The New Heaven and the New Earth

21 Then I saw a new heaven and a new earth; for the first heaven and the first earth had passed away, and the sea was no more. 2And I saw the holy city, the new Jerusalem, coming down out of heaven from God, prepared as a bride adorned for her husband. 3And I heard a loud voice from the throne saying,

"See, the home*a* of God is among
        mortals.
He will dwell*b* with them;
they will be his peoples,*c*
and God himself will be with them;*d*
4   he will wipe every tear from their eyes.
Death will be no more;
mourning and crying and pain will be
        no more,
for the first things have passed away."

5 And the one who was seated on the throne said, "See, I am making all things new." Also he said, "Write this, for these words are trustworthy and true." 6Then he said to me, "It is done! I am the Alpha and the Omega, the beginning and the end. To the thirsty I will give water as a gift from the spring of the water of life. 7Those who conquer will inherit these things, and I will be their God and they will be my children. 8But as for the cowardly, the faithless,*e* the polluted, the murderers, the fornicators, the sorcerers, the idolaters, and all liars, their place will be in the lake that burns with fire and sulfur, which is the second death."

Vision of the New Jerusalem

9 Then one of the seven angels who had the seven bowls full of the seven last plagues came and said to me, "Come, I will show you the bride, the wife of the Lamb." 10And in the spirit*f* he carried me away to a great, high mountain and showed me the holy city Jerusalem coming down out of heaven from God. 11It has the glory of God and a radiance like a very rare jewel, like jasper, clear as crystal. 12It has a great, high wall with twelve gates, and at the gates twelve angels, and on the gates are inscribed the names of the twelve tribes of the Israelites; 13on the east three gates, on the north three gates, on the south three gates, and on the west three gates. 14And the wall of the city has twelve foundations, and on them are the twelve names of the twelve apostles of the Lamb.

15 The angel*g* who talked to me had a measuring rod of gold to measure the city and its gates and walls. 16The city lies foursquare, its length the same as its width; and he measured the city with his rod, fifteen hundred miles;*b* its length and width and height are equal. 17He also measured its wall, one hundred forty-four cubits*i* by human measurement, which the angel was using. 18The wall is built of jasper, while the city is pure gold, clear as glass. 19The foundations of the wall of the city are adorned with every jewel; the first was jasper, the second sapphire, the third agate, the fourth emerald, 20the fifth onyx, the sixth carnelian, the seventh chrysolite, the eighth beryl, the ninth topaz, the tenth chrysoprase, the eleventh jacinth, the twelfth amethyst. 21And the twelve gates are twelve pearls, each of the gates is a single pearl, and the street of the city is pure gold, transparent as glass.

22 I saw no temple in the city, for its temple is the Lord God the Almighty and the

---

a Gk *the tabernacle*   *b* Gk *will tabernacle*   *c* Other ancient authorities read *people*   *d* Other ancient authorities add *and be their God*   *e* Or *the unbelieving*   *f* Or *in the Spirit*   *g* Gk *He*   *h* Gk *twelve thousand stadia*   *i* That is, almost seventy-five yards

Lamb. 23And the city has no need of sun or moon to shine on it, for the glory of God is its light, and its lamp is the Lamb. 24The nations will walk by its light, and the kings of the earth will bring their glory into it. 25Its gates will never be shut by day—and there will be no night there. 26People will bring into it the glory and the honor of the nations. 27But nothing unclean will enter it, nor anyone who practices abomination or falsehood, but only those who are written in the Lamb's book of life.

The River of Life

22 Then the angel*a* showed me the river of the water of life, bright as crystal, flowing from the throne of God and of the Lamb 2through the middle of the street of the city. On either side of the river is the tree of life*b* with its twelve kinds of fruit, producing its fruit each month; and the leaves of the tree are for the healing of the nations. 3Nothing accursed will be found there any more. But the throne of God and of the Lamb will be in it, and his servants*c* will worship him; 4they will see his face, and his name will be on their foreheads. 5And there will be no more night; they need no light of lamp or sun, for the Lord God will be their light, and they will reign forever and ever.

6 And he said to me, "These words are trustworthy and true, for the Lord, the God of the spirits of the prophets, has sent his angel to show his servants*c* what must soon take place."

7 "See, I am coming soon! Blessed is the one who keeps the words of the prophecy of this book."

Epilogue and Benediction

8 I, John, am the one who heard and saw these things. And when I heard and saw them, I fell down to worship at the feet of the angel who showed them to me; 9but he said to me, "You must not do that! I am a fellow servant*d* with you and your comrades*e* the prophets, and with those who keep the words of this book. Worship God!"

10 And he said to me, "Do not seal up the words of the prophecy of this book, for the time is near. 11Let the evildoer still do evil, and the filthy still be filthy, and the righteous still do right, and the holy still be holy."

12 "See, I am coming soon; my reward is with me, to repay according to everyone's work. 13I am the Alpha and the Omega, the first and the last, the beginning and the end."

14 Blessed are those who wash their robes,*f* so that they will have the right to the tree of life and may enter the city by the gates. 15Outside are the dogs and sorcerers and fornicators and murderers and idolaters, and everyone who loves and practices falsehood.

16 "It is I, Jesus, who sent my angel to you with this testimony for the churches. I am the root and the descendant of David, the bright morning star."

17 The Spirit and the bride say, "Come."
And let everyone who hears say,
"Come."
And let everyone who is thirsty come.
Let anyone who wishes take the water
of life as a gift.

18 I warn everyone who hears the words of the prophecy of this book: if anyone adds to them, God will add to that person the plagues described in this book; 19if anyone takes away from the words of the book of this prophecy, God will take away that person's share in the tree of life and in the holy city, which are described in this book.

20 The one who testifies to these things says, "Surely I am coming soon."
Amen. Come, Lord Jesus!

21 The grace of the Lord Jesus be with all the saints. Amen.*g*

a Gk *he*   b Or *the Lamb*. 2*In the middle of the street of the city, and on either side of the river, is the tree of life*   c Gk *slaves*
d Gk *slave*   e Gk *brothers*   f Other ancient authorities read *do his commandments*   g Other ancient authorities
lack *all*; others lack *the saints*; others lack *Amen*

The Green Bible Trail Guide

The Green Bible Trail Guide leads you through a selection of Bible passages touching on six green themes that appear throughout the biblical narrative. Each theme includes several passages that speak to specific ideas about God's connection to all of creation. As you read, you will find a God who not only breathed life into creation, but did so with the intention that creation would be a reflection of God and a connection to God. Both are evident in the earth's continuing creativity, in its goodness, and in its power to sustain itself in an endless cycle of life, death, and rebirth.

You can use this guide for your own personal study, or you might gather a group of friends and work through these readings together. However you use the readings, feel free to create your own schedule. You might find yourself wanting to spend several days or even weeks meditating on a reading. You might find that some themes intrigue you more than others. The goal isn't to memorize every passage discussed or rethink every nuance of a scripture. It's to move you into a deeper, fuller sense of God's connection to and with creation.

At the end of each theme, you will find a section called "Walking the Trail." In it are suggested activities to help you explore the theme in more practical ways. Think of them as a jumping-off point—you can use these activities or think of your own. You can also do the activities on your own or with a group. Use them in whatever way seems most helpful to you. No matter which activities you use, keep in mind that all this reading and studying is only worth doing if it inspires you to act. The biblical narrative was never meant to stand still in time. It is meant to motivate us to continue living out the story of God's work in the world.

Theme 1: And It Was Good

God made all things and declared them good. God continues to show love and care for creation throughout human history and for all eternity.

1. Genesis 1:1–31; 2:1–4

At the beginning of the biblical narrative God creates the heavens and the earth. God sweeps over the void and brings about light and life, declaring it "very good."

- What does the creation story in these passages tell us about God's intentions for the earth?
- How does God relate to the world God creates? What does that suggest about how we are to relate to the rest of creation?
- God declares all of creation to be "very good." Why do you think we have gotten away from that sense of creation as "good" and therefore worth saving?

2. Genesis 9:8–17

The story of Noah includes the promise of an everlasting covenant between God and all of creation.

- God repeats several times that this covenant of protection and presence involves every living creature. Was it a surprise to you that God's covenant extends beyond human beings? What does this tell you about God's view of creation?
- How are human beings a part of the fullness of this covenant? How can we be part of the protection God offers to other living creatures? Also look at Genesis 2:15.

3. Psalm 24:1–2

The psalmist declares that the earth—and all that is in it—belongs to God.

- We don't always think about the whole earth as belonging to God. How could this understanding of creation change the way we interact with the rest of the natural world?
- How might this sense of God's ownership of the earth impact the way we think about God's involvement and investment in creation?
- The psalmist—David—uses this language of ownership as a way of praising God's power and supremacy. He encourages his listeners to praise God as well. How does this image of God as the one who made all that we see inspire praise or worship in you?

4. Job 38–39

God's response to Job and his friends is perhaps the most striking example of God asserting God's relationship with creation as both its creator and provider. The long list of questions points to God's intimate connection with all of creation.

- There's a sense of God's anger and frustration with Job's friends as God asks the series of rhetorical questions in these chapters. But there's also a sense of God's deep involvement with all that God created. What do these words tell you about God's relationship with creation?
- These verses are filled with poetic expressions of God's care for creation. Which verses resonate with you the most? How could this sense of God's constant interaction with creation inform your "green" ethic?

5. Psalm 104

Psalm 104 is filled with beautiful images of God's care and provision for the natural world: mountains that hold back the flood waters, springs and grasslands that rise up to feed the animals, even wine and oil for human pleasure.

- We often think about the ways God provides for us, but how does this psalm change the way you think about God's provision for all of creation?
- There is tremendous joy and life in these verses. What does that tell us about the psalmist's perspective on creation? How can that inform our perspective on the natural world?
- How does this passage hearken back to God's covenant with "every living creature" in Genesis 9:8–17?

Walking the Trail

Take a walk during your favorite time of the day. Look around you and notice all the "good" you see in creation.

Find a stone, feather, leaf, or some other item from nature that you can bring home. Put it somewhere in your home as a reminder that God created all things and declared them good.

Theme 2: Finding God

God is present in and through creation. This means we can better understand the character of God by seeing how God interacts with all of creation. The more we know of God, the more we grow in our love for and connection to God and what God has created.

1. Exodus 3:1–6

In the story of Moses, God literally speaks through creation in the form of a burning bush. The Exodus account offers several pictures of God's presence embodied in nature. Bitter water becomes sweet and food appears on the ground each morning as signs of God's sustenance for the Israelites (15:25; 16:15). Moses is able to bring water out of a rock at God's command so that the people will not go thirsty (17:6). And an angel of God appears to the Israelites as pillars of cloud and light—a visible guide and a constant protector for them (14:19–20).

- The presence of God is clear to the Israelites, but they continue to question God's protection and care. What signs of God's presence have you seen in nature today? How could your awareness of these signs strengthen your trust in God?
- In the Exodus story, God meets the basic needs of the people—food, water, protection—through the land, fire, air, and water. What connections do you see between God's use of these natural elements and the Genesis account of creation in which God brings the water and land into being?
- How does God's presence in nature underscore the covenant relationship between God and the Israelites?

2. Psalm 147

The psalmist makes no distinction between God's action among humans and God's activity in other parts of the natural world. God's presence is evident in the whole of creation, not just in humanity.

- In this psalm, God's presence in the natural rhythms of the seasons is a reason for praise and thanksgiving. Snow, rain, wind, even hail are reminders of God's continued presence and activity in the world. Look out your window. What does today's weather suggest to you about God's connection to the earth?
- Verses 10–11 provide an interesting perspective on creation. Although God is present in creation, the psalmist suggests that this presence is intended to draw humanity closer to God. What does that tell you about God's connection to you?
- There is a sense of justice in this passage—God gathering the outcasts, God healing the brokenhearted, God lifting up the downtrodden—that might seem out of place in this otherwise "creation-oriented" psalm. Why would David include issues of justice with declarations of praise for God's presence in the natural world?

3. John 1:1–5

John 1:1–5 takes us back to the beginning of the biblical narrative—the creation story. John's words tell of Jesus being invested and involved in the very beginnings of life. Jesus, then, becomes a living symbol of the infusion of God in creation. Jesus, who was both God and human being, is the Creator and the created. The two cannot be separated.

- How was Jesus present in and through creation? How does this impact the way you think about the creation story?
- What implications does this picture of the unity of God and Jesus in creation—and therefore throughout human history—have for your understanding of the Old Testament?
- John makes a point of starting his Gospel with this idea that Jesus was connected to God from the beginning. Why would that be important to John and his readers? Why is it important for us?

4. Colossians 1:15–20

Paul takes John's picture of Jesus as part of the creation narrative even further, explaining that Jesus isn't just an observer in God's relationship with the world, but the culmination of that relationship. Jesus is the living, breathing story of God's intimate presence in and for all of creation.

- In Jesus, we can know our Creator—he is the image of God. We can see God's clearest intentions for creation in Jesus—the fullness of God dwelt in him. And in Jesus we find our own connection with God—he reconciled all things. How does this sense of Jesus as the image and fulfillment of God's presence—the ultimate connection between the Creator and the created—influence your thinking about the rest of the natural world?
- When Jesus wanted to feel connected to God, he often went to places where he was surrounded by the natural elements—the desert, the mountains, the garden—rather than the temple or a synagogue. What does this say about where we find God's presence?
- Paul says that in Jesus, God reconciled all things to himself. What does that mean to you? How might that change your understanding of your connection to other parts of creation?

5. Acts 17:24–28

The apostle Paul is talking to a Greek audience, explaining that the God he is talking about isn't like their mythological gods. This God doesn't live apart from people, but rather in and among them. Paul's God isn't remote and unknowable, but close and intimately connected with all of creation, through all of creation.

- Paul says God does not live in "shrines made by human hands." Where is Paul suggesting God *does* live?
- Paul also says that God is not far from us. What might Paul mean by that statement? How does creation help you search for and even find God?
- How do Paul's words impact your sense of who God is and where God is?

Walking the Trail

Go outside tonight and look at the stars. Or sit by a body of water tomorrow afternoon. Or simply lie on your back in your yard one morning and look at the clouds. What do these natural elements tell you about God?

Find a place outside where you feel close and connected to God. Make a point of returning to this place whenever you need reminding of God's presence in your life.

Theme 3: Connected to Creation

Humanity is part of all creation. We are meant to live in an interconnected, interdependent relationship with God and the whole of creation, acting as stewards of creation. And as we care for the earth, the earth cares for us.

1. Genesis 2:4–25

There are actually two creation accounts in the first two chapters of Genesis. The first is a bit more poetic, the second more concise. But both are very clear that human beings were created to be the caretakers of the earth and to live in harmony with everything else God made.

- In Genesis 1:26–30, God declares that human beings will be made in the image of God, so that they can care for the earth. How has this passage on dominion been misunderstood? What would it look like to care for the earth in the "image of God"?
- God doesn't give human beings any other role in creation but the stewardship of the earth—"to till it and keep it." Why is this a significant part of the conversation about Christians and the environment?
- This stewardship role is important enough that it is mentioned several times in the creation narrative. It seems to be an essential part of what God intended for us as human beings. How might becoming better stewards of the earth help us connect with our humanity in deeper ways? How might it help us connect with God?

2. Exodus 23:10–13

Because of the interdependence between humanity and creation, a time of rest doesn't just benefit humanity; it benefits the earth as well. In this passage, God commands that farmland be left fallow every seventh year.

- Why is this rhythm of Sabbath important for the earth? Why does God command a Sabbath rest for all of creation? How does this pattern of work and rest benefit humanity, animals, and land?
- The implication here is that sometimes stewardship means pulling back from our work and letting creation just be. How might this ethic impact the way you care for the earth?
- What might a season of fallow look like in your life? What parts of your world would benefit from the rest and recovery that a season of fallow or a Sabbath would provide?

3. Leviticus 26:3–26

An Old Testament description of the consequences of disobedience can be pretty harsh to read (it gets better if you read through to the end of the chapter), but it makes a clear point: God is serious about human beings living the lives we were created to live, lives of peace and connection with God. But when we step away from that life, when we step away from God, there are severe consequences. In this passage, those consequences involve the earth.

- The interdependence with the earth for which we were created is jeopardized when we reject God's commandments. That interdependence is so vital that to lose it is the worst punishment of all. In what ways has this warning from God become reality? Why is this broken connection with the earth particularly devastating?
- Think about your daily life for a moment. Where do you see this broken relationship playing out?
- It's easy to make God the bad guy in this passage. But in spite of God's clear anger, the blame for all of this destruction falls on the people who break God's commandments. How can we actively restore our broken connection with the earth and with God?

4. Revelation 11:15–19

John's record of his vivid dream includes many kinds of imagery. The biblical story begins with God creating human beings to care for the earth. And here the story ends with God's judgment upon those who actively participate in the destruction of the earth.

- How does this passage fit together with what you've read so far about God's relationship with creation?
- What kinds of human activity might be included in "destroying the earth"?
- Why might it make sense that the final judgment in John's dream includes this piece about the destruction of the earth? What does it tell you about the connection between human beings and the rest of creation?

5. Psalm 65

Acting as a lovely counterbalance to the Leviticus passage, Psalm 65 points to the ways God's provision for humanity can be seen as a sign of God's forgiveness. And that provision, that forgiveness, is found in the natural world.

- David is suggesting that the connection between humanity and God can be measured by the natural world—flowing water and a full harvest are signs that we are living in harmony with God. How does the state of the world today reflect the state of humanity's connection with God?
- There's a temptation to read this passage as a supernatural explanation of natural disasters such as drought or famine—that they happen because God makes them happen. How does your understanding of the interdependence between human beings and the earth change your sense of what this passage is saying?
- Considering that we were created to live in harmony with the whole of creation, how do you see human beings fitting into David's picture of the bounty and provision God offers in nature?

Walking the Trail

For the next two days, keep track of your environmental footprint. Write down how long your shower lasts. Notice when you turn on a light, and see if you remember to turn it off. Pay attention to the times when you jump in your car instead of using other forms of transportation. This isn't an exercise in guilt, but in awareness. Our connection to the rest of creation means we are to be mindful of how our presence impacts other parts of creation—for good and for ill.

Plant something—a seed, a tree, a whole garden. Even if you can only manage to get a little grass seed growing in a small pot, it nourishes the soul to help living things grow.

Theme 4: Creation Care as Justice

Caring for creation is an act of social justice. Because humanity is part of creation, and because we are designed for interdependence with the whole of creation, caring for creation means caring for humanity. Caring for humanity, in turn, demands protecting and restoring creation.

1. Micah 6:1–8

Micah's prophetic words pull listeners back to the covenant God made with the nation of Israel. But there's a twist in his message. God's part of the covenant is mercy and care and redemption. The human part is to live as people of justice, kindness, and humility.

- Micah juxtaposes the Israelites' assumptions about what obedience looks like—burnt offerings, blood sacrifices—with justice, kindness, and humility. Which kind of obedience is more difficult?
- The requirements for justice, kindness, and humility are all relational. They demand that we connect with other human beings in particular ways. How does this fit with what you know about the interdependence of all of creation?
- The concept of justice can be very broad. How do you see it fitting into conversations about creation care? How do kindness and humility fit in these conversations?

2. Isaiah 58:10–12

Justice is a major theme throughout Isaiah. In this passage, Isaiah makes a clear connection between justice and renewal. When we care for the poor, when we feed the hungry and work to end oppression, we bring blessings to the world.

- Isaiah's description of the blessings that come when we care for others sounds a bit like John's words in the book of Revelation—never-ending springs of water, ruins rebuilt, streets restored. What does that parallel language tell you about the importance of acts of justice?
- In what ways do acts of justice restore and renew? How do they "raise up the foundations of many generations"? And what does that have to do with caring for creation?
- Think about some concrete examples of ways in which caring for the poor demands we also care for the earth. For instance, how does the lack of clean water create pockets of poverty in the world? How might our efforts to clean up the earth's water help the poor?

3. 2 Corinthians 5:14–21

The call of all Christians is to love one another. Christ frees us from our prejudices and tendency to see the worst in others, so that we can care for each other the way God cares for us. (See John 13:34 for Jesus' commandment that we love one another.)

- What assumptions do you make that hold you back from acts of justice and mercy?
- How can the idea that we are all part of God's creation help you overcome those assumptions?
- How might caring for creation be seen as an act of love for our fellow human beings? How does this tie into the ministry of reconciliation?

4. Luke 10:25–37

The parable of the Good Samaritan, one of the most well known in the Bible, is not one you'd expect to find in a conversation about creation care. On the surface, it has nothing to do with creation. Yet if humanity is part of God's creation, and if we are intended to be the caretakers of creation, then it's essential that we understand the full reach of God's command that we love one another.

- Jesus says that showing mercy to all people—even our enemies—is the way to eternal life. How can we show mercy to those who are "enemies" of the environment and enemies of humanity?
- Jesus gives unexpected answers to the lawyer's questions about the law of God (10:27–28). How does Jesus' response make sense in light of the interconnectedness of all creation?
- Those listening to Jesus' response would have thought of Samaritans as the scum of the earth. Yet the Samaritan is the one living out the command of God to show love and mercy. What does this suggest to you about power and justice?

5. Matthew 25:31–46

Matthew 25:31–46 is perhaps the passage in which Jesus is the clearest about what it means to live as the people of God. Justice, kindness, humility, mercy, compassion—they are all part of what it means to be human. The result of ignoring this call is eternal punishment. To ignore the poor, the oppressed, the hungry is to ignore God.

- Jesus calls the poor and imprisoned members of his family. How does this sense of family underscore the idea that we are all connected to one another?
- Jesus talks about hunger, sickness, loneliness, and imprisonment as problems that Christians are called to address. How can you begin to show mercy to people in those situations right now?

• The solutions for the problem Jesus talks about are not difficult—feed the hungry, clothe the naked, welcome the stranger. Why do we find it so hard to do simple acts of justice? How are these acts related to creation care?

Walking the Trail

Think about a group of people who make you feel out of your comfort zone. The homeless? Prisoners? The aging or dying? Commit to spending one hour this month volunteering with an organization that helps that group of people. Sometimes justice starts small.

Chose one international news story from today's news and follow it for the rest of the week. What issues of justice are involved in this story? How can you connect to this story in a tangible way?

Theme 5: The Full Impact of Sin

Creation is harmed by human sin. Because our sin disconnects us from God, it distorts our relationship with God's creation as well. The result is a world out of sync with itself.

1. Genesis 3:14–19

The consequences of Adam and Eve's disobedience ripple through all of creation. The serpent is cursed to move on its belly—the ultimate humiliation—and eat from the dust. The relationship between humans and animals is broken—"I will put enmity between you and the woman." The man and woman are cursed with lives of pain and fruitless harvests. The earth itself is cursed. The harmony God embedded in creation is distorted by human sin.

• In what ways do you see the disharmony created by human sin playing out in the environment?
• When natural disasters strike, people often wonder why God would allow such destruction. How does this passage impact the way you think about that question?
• What is our role in restoring the harmony God intended for creation?

2. Hosea 4:1–3

The theme that all of creation is damaged by human sin runs through many of the prophetic books of the Bible. In Hosea, the land "mourns" and "languishes" because of humanity's failure to keep the covenant with God. In Jeremiah 4:18–28, we see a dramatic picture of a barren, wasted earth brought about by humanity's rebellion. And in Isaiah 24:4–13, God lays waste to the earth as a form of judgment. These environmental consequences of human sin point back to the interdependence between humans and the whole of creation. Our greatest punishment is to be cut off from the provisions of the earth. When we stop caring for the earth, the earth is unable to care for us.

- The connections between human beings and the rest of creation come up over and over in the Bible. How do passages like these from the prophets point to that connection?
- Undoubtedly, some among those who heard these words thought they were over-the-top warnings of disaster that would never come. How do these passages compare to the warnings about the environment we hear today?
- In some ways, the earth is the innocent victim of human sin. But if we are dependent on the earth, its destruction ultimately impacts us the most. How can we start thinking of environmental issues as human issues?

3. Ezekiel 34:17–22

In other places in the Old Testament, the damage to the environment is the indirect result of human sin. In Ezekiel's metaphor we are held accountable for our intentional destruction of God's creation—destruction that includes our mistreatment of other people.

- In what ways do we tread on the "grass" of other people and cultures? How does our treading impact the global environment?
- The image of the pushing and butting sheep calls to mind a kind of bullying. How can we keep from being environmental bullies?
- How does this passage tie in to the passages about justice as an element of caring for creation?

4. Numbers 35:33–34

Because God is present in creation, the damage we do to the earth damages God's home as well as our own. When we neglect or abuse the rest of creation, we have abused the very dwelling place of God.

- How might the idea that the earth is God's home as well as our own help us be more mindful of our connection to the environment?
- The pollution in this passage is the blood shed in violence. Why would the author use the term "pollution" for an act of violence?

5. Romans 8:18–25

All of the dreadful prophecies and dire warnings of the Old Testament find their resolution in the New Testament, as Jesus comes to reconcile all of creation to himself and to God. And because all of creation was impacted by human sin, all of creation is part of Christ's redemptive work on the cross as well. Paul writes of the whole of creation "groaning in labor pains" as it waits for the hope of the resurrection.

- How does creation "groan"? What do you see happening today that might be described as the groaning of the earth?
- We don't typically think about the redemption of the earth. But with what you know about the interconnectedness of all creation, why does it make sense to include the earth in our thoughts about redemption?
- There is tremendous hope in this passage. How does the hope found here help you reframe the despair found in the previous passages on this theme?

Walking the Trail

Make a change—any change—in your environmental impact. Change your light-bulbs, walk to the coffee shop, turn down your thermostat, recycle your newspaper, start a compost bin. You can find more suggestions at www.deepgreenconversations.org.

Take another walk and look for signs of creation in decline. What role have human beings had in that decline? What role can you play in reversing that decline?

Theme 6: The New Earth

The earth and everything in it is included in God's plan of redemption. Creation does not pass away, but is restored and renewed as part of the new heaven and the new earth of God's kingdom.

1. Isaiah 11:1–9

Isaiah's beautiful picture of the kingdom of God is filled with images of restoration, including the restoration of the interdependence and harmony God intended for creation. Animals that have become enemies will once again live in peace with one another. Human beings will no longer fear dangerous animals, because those animals no longer have the capacity to destroy life. The whole earth will be redeemed and returned to the way God made it to be.

This theme comes up repeatedly in Isaiah. In Isaiah 35:1–10, Isaiah says that the deserts will blossom and water will pour through the wilderness. In Isaiah 55:12–13, the mountains and fields rejoice in the redemption of the world. There is a sense of lush provision and well-being.

- As you read through these passages, what images strike you? What do those images suggest to you about God's intentions for creation?

- Christians believe the kingdom of God, so beautifully described in Isaiah 11:19, was ushered in with Jesus (see also Colossians 1:20). That means Isaiah's prophetic words are meant to describe the life we are to be working toward. Since we are redeemed in Christ, how can we be part of the redemption of the earth as well?

2. Isaiah 65:17–25

Isaiah makes it clear that the new earth of God's kingdom is not a replacement for the old earth, but a restoration of this one. This is a significant difference when it comes to conversations about creation care. There are Christians who struggle with "green" ideas because they believe this earth will pass away one day. But Isaiah makes a very different point.

- If the "new earth" is this world restored, what are the implications for the bigger conversation about Christians and creation care?
- How might you talk about this idea with a Christian who is wrestling with green ideology?
- What parallels do you see between Isaiah's description of the "new earth" and the Genesis creation narrative?

3. Joel 2:18–27

Joel's prophetic words speak to the restoration of all of creation. God's grace and mercy are on display as the trees bloom, the animals are fed, and the harvest is plentiful.

- In this passage, God shows grace and compassion to humanity through the restoration of the rest of creation. How is the restoration of other parts of creation an essential piece of the restoration of humanity? Can we be truly restored and redeemed without a restored earth?
- How might a passage like this have special resonance for those of us who live with hunger or poverty or war?
- What does this passage tell you about God's love and care for creation?

4. Revelation 21:1–5

John's vision of the new heaven and the new earth sounds much like the prophetic visions of Isaiah and Joel. That's no coincidence. The redemption of all of creation includes the restoration of all creation. So in John's vision of the kingdom of God, God is dwelling with us, living among us in a restored connection. It is the garden as it was intended to be.

- What parallels do you see between Isaiah's words and John's words? What do those similarities tell you about the importance of a restored creation?

- This passage hints at the end of suffering and hardship. What role would a healed earth play in the end of human suffering?
- How do the healed connections within creation contribute to both Isaiah's prophecies and John's vision? How can we be part of healing the earth?

5. Revelation 22:1–5

"Nothing accursed will be found there any more" (22:3). The hope at the heart of that statement is what has fueled Christianity for centuries—the hope for redemption, for healing, for renewal. And in John's picture of the kingdom of God that's exactly what we have. Creation is once again restored to its original design. The Tree of Life sustains the nations, and there is no more darkness. This is the kingdom of God. This is what God intended from the beginning. Our calling as the people of God has always been to care for all that God created. When we do, we are truly living as kingdom people.

- John's vision of the water of life and the Tree of Life is a clear picture of the interdependence that's built in to creation. The water nourishes the tree, the tree nourishes the nations. How might the nations—human beings—nourish the earth to keep the cycle going?
- What will it look like for you to live as a redeemed, healed, and renewed part of creation?
- As you look back over all of the themes, how have your ideas about creation care changed?

Walking the Trail

Gather six small stones from your neighborhood to make a stone cairn or memorial. Ancient peoples—including the Israelites—used piles of stone to mark meaningful events (see Genesis 31:44–53; Joshua 4:1–9, 20–24). Put your stones near your bed or your favorite chair. Use them as a reminder of the themes you've been studying. You can even use them like prayer beads, holding them as you connect with God through prayer and meditation.

Where Do You Go from Here?

A Resource Guide

C are for creation is where we turn our words into deeds. At the most basic level, this means we are called to use our resources wisely and to make sure that we do not consume more than we need. The apostle James tells us that "faith without works is…dead" (2:26). We cannot have a theology of responsible care for creation without actions that are integrated with that theology.

Included in this section are ideas to help you take some beginning steps toward caring for creation.

Actions for Individuals and Families

General

1. Engage in prayer and Bible study on a regular basis, so that you are better able to fulfill the commandments to love God and love what God loves. Ask God for spiritual contentment, the cure for overconsumption, so you can better care for God's creation.
2. During family devotion time, discuss Jesus as creator and owner, humanity's relationship to the rest of creation, how the rest of creation is harmed by humanity's sin, and God's future kingdom.
3. Continue to study and reflect on what the Bible says about caring for all of God's creation. Learn about current environmental problems. Pray for wisdom and guidance on what to do.
4. Let your voice be heard by governmental officials.

Oceans Emphasis

1. Eat fish that comes from sustainable fisheries (for suggestions, see www. environmentaldefense.org/seafood/bestpicks.cfm).

2. If you buy meat, ask whether the meat comes from livestock fed with fish-meal. Seek out meats (including chicken) fed on an all-vegetable diet. Consider vegetarian alternatives, which cause less pollution.

3. Poor land-use choices and developmental planning cause water pollution, which harms God's oceans. Support more environmentally friendly land-development plans in your community, and seek to live where open land has not been displaced. Support actions to stop suburban sprawl.

4. Agricultural runoff into streams (and subsequently into oceans) is a major source of water pollution. Consider buying local organic food that is sustainably grown and does not put pressure on threatened species or habitats.

5. Do not pollute—recycle used oil—and do not litter (plastic bags and six-pack rings easily end up in oceans, where they suffocate and entangle fish, sea turtles, birds, and other creatures).

6. Reconsider taking a cruise. Cruise ships dump tons of waste directly into the open oceans, where there are no national laws prohibiting the practice.

7. Plant trees, and encourage tree planting in your community, especially near streams. Nurture and care for the trees.

8. Pollution from our fuel-dependent transportation choices harms oceans, destroying fish habitat and coral reefs. It also causes global warming, which disrupts the oceans' hydrogeologic cycle and threatens the existence of oceanic and terrestrial species. Choose the least polluting, most fuel-efficient means of personal transportation in order to reduce your transportation pollution. When possible, bike, walk, or use public transportation. For more suggestions, see www.whatwouldjesusdrive.org.

9. Pray and act for the conservation of the earth's oceans and have faith that God will answer your prayers and honor your faithfulness to his will.

10. Tell your elected officials that you want government policies that support clean waters and ocean health.

Health

1. Cut down on air pollution by using public transportation, driving less, and using fuel-efficient vehicles. Make your home more energy efficient; select electricity produced by green power if it is available in your area. Buy products with the EPA's Energy Star label, and practice the three Rs—reduce, reuse, recycle.

2. Choose to use fewer chemicals in your home and on your lawn. Don't use pesticides if you don't have to—look for alternatives. For cleaning agents, use water, soap, white vinegar, baking soda, borax, and hydrogen peroxide (for suggestions, visit www.thegreenguide.com).

3. Ask your pediatric health-care provider to take an environmental health history to assess environmental conditions that may prevent your children from reaching optimum health. Have your children's blood lead levels tested, especially if they spend time in a house built before 1960.

4. Vary children's diets as much as possible while giving them plenty of fruits and vegetables. Consider buying organic foods if available.

5. Tell your elected officials that you want government policies to protect children's health from toxic chemicals and other environmental hazards. .

Endangered Creatures

1. Pray for endangered creatures during your daily family prayer time, including the ones in your own neighborhood and yard. Pray that God guides you and your family in your actions to care for other creatures as God intends. You can pray for threatened plants and animals by name by finding them in the International Conservation Union's Global Species Assessment Photo Gallery at www.iucnredlist.org/info/gallery2004.html.

2. Speak out on policies that affect endangered species.

3. Do not purchase anything made from endangered species or their parts (e.g., ivory, crocodile skin, corals).

4. Practice sufficiency and contentment in all your purchasing decisions. Buy only what you need, seek out products that do not contain hazardous materials, and buy products with minimal packaging. Recycle all materials—including computers—as much as possible, so they do not end up polluting lands and waters where creatures live.

5. Pollute less. Pollution is a leading cause of species extinction. See other tips at www.healthyfamiliesnow.org.

Land Conservation

1. Make personal choices that conserve land and do not contribute to suburban sprawl. Live near your work and in a place that allows use of public transportation, biking, or walking; live in redeveloped space or infill as opposed to new subdivisions built on former farmland or open space.

2. Be active in local politics and zoning debates, where critical land-use decisions affecting habitat are made.

3. Practice sufficiency and contentment in your land use and housing choices by seeking a dwelling and lot no larger than what you need.

4. Be active in public policies that support land conservation.

5. Learn more about your "neighbors downstream," those people who are affected by your land-use decisions. For example, pesticides used on your lawn can end up in the water supply of fishermen downstream who depend on clean water for their livelihood.

6. Support your local land-conservation organization.

How to Be a Deep Green Family

1. **Give Thanks:** Thank God for God's beautiful creation, and ask for help to care for it.

2. **Go Deep:** Read what God's Word says about caring for creation and the people who depend on it.

3. **Recycle:** Everyone in the family can help. Recycle paper, cans, bottles, jars, batteries, chemicals, paint. Find out what you can recycle at your curbside, and for everything else, go to www.earth911.org.

4. **Get Out:** Spend at least an hour a day outside. Turn off the TV, computer, and video games and encourage your kids to have more "green time" than "screen time." For ideas about what to do once you're outside, go to www.deepconversation.org.

5. **Save Energy:** Turn off lights when leaving a room, buy Energy Star appliances, and turn the thermostat down in winter and up in summer. Use your ceiling fans. Find out more energy-saving tips at www.powerisinyourhands.org/resources/residential_tips.pdf.

6. **Do a Home Energy Audit:** Let the kids help do a home energy audit based on your last twelve months of utility bills. Then get recommendations on how to make your home more energy efficient at www.energystar.gov/yardstick or www.energystar.gov/homeadvisor.

7. **Garden for Wildlife:** Invite creation into your yard by creating a backyard wildlife habitat. Suggestions for plants and garden plans that attract butterflies and birds to your yard can be found at www.abnativeplants.com.

8. **Combine Trips:** Poll the family before heading out in the car to see how trips can be combined. Keep a list of all your errands in one place, and don't leave until you have several you can do in one trip.

9. **Light the Way to a New Energy Future:** Use compact fluorescent lamps instead of incandescent lamps and save real money, while reducing pollution from power plants. Recycle your old lamps rather than throw them away; go to www.lamprecycle.org to find out how.

10. **Measure Your Ecological Footprint:** Size up the impact your activities and consumption habits have by taking the quiz at www.conservation.org/EcoFootprint.

Action Ideas for Churches

1. Help your church hold a "Creation Sunday" worship service. (Visit www.creationcare.org for more information.)

2. Become a "sister congregation" with a church in a community where toxic waste or pollution threatens the health of the church members. Take their youth on an annual outdoor adventure. This works especially well when church youth groups are involved.

3. Hold a "Creation Celebration" and invite your community, campus, or congregation to enjoy the outdoors with you.

4. Start a Bible study on what the Bible says about the environment. Consider inviting people outside of the church.

5. Set up a booth at a local environmental fair or Earth Day event, or plan one for your church.

6. Get your church to conduct an energy audit and implement improvements.

7. Adopt a local stream, park, or roadway for cleanup, monitoring, or restoration.

8. Identify an important environmental issue and visit or write letters to local, state, or national leaders about it.

9. Start a "Creation Club" for kids in your church. This works well even in inner-city neighborhoods.

10. Start a library of goods to share in your church. Some churches have experimented with toy libraries or tool libraries. Such ministries help us to live more simply and thereby reduce the pressures of our materialism on creation.

11. Volunteer in a city, state, or national park. With good advance planning, rangers, park personnel, or foresters can put your church group to work.

12. Hold a public prayer event with emphasis on creation care, restoration, and stewardship.

13. Plant trees, shrubs, and perennials in places where shade and beauty are needed at your church.

14. Organize a church or community garden and encourage gardeners to donate some of the harvest to local homeless shelters and soup kitchens.

50 Practical Tips to Get Started

1. Turn off the faucet while brushing teeth or shaving.
2. Turn the thermostat up three degrees (in summer) and down three degrees (in winter). In the spring and fall, open the windows as often as possible.
3. Wash dishes by hand in a dishpan and only run the dishwasher with a full load. Do not use heat for the drying cycle.
4. Wash clothes in the coolest water possible.
5. Turn off lights, TV, music, and digital entertainment when leaving the room for any length of time.
6. Take a day of rest—no shopping, no work, no driving—once a week.
7. Recycle everything possible; don't buy overpackaged items.
8. Donate a box of books to the library twice a year.
9. Hand-wash clothes instead of dry cleaning them whenever possible.
10. Clean out closets and donate clothes not worn in the past year.
11. Memorize one Bible verse about God's love for creation, such as Psalm 24:1: "The earth is the LORD's and all that is in it."
12. Install low-flow showerheads. Take showers instead of baths (they use less water).
13. Replace incandescent with compact fluorescent bulbs.
14. Clean or replace air filters throughout the house.
15. Disconnect the ice machine in your freezer, especially if you have two or more.
16. Unplug the TV and other electronic equipment when not in use or put them on a switched power strip.
17. Donate old cell phones, computers, and printers to a good cause or recycle them.
18. Plant deciduous trees along the south side of the house to save on cooling costs.
19. When replacing appliances, purchase the most efficient (Energy Star), with the lowest yearly energy costs.
20. Ask your local utility to conduct an energy audit on your home and/or business and then heed the advice.
21. Visit the grocery only once each week. Combine trips. Carpool.
22. Air-dry laundry whenever possible.
23. Avoid fast-food restaurants; pack a picnic lunch when traveling.
24. Replace church lightbulbs with compact fluorescents. Recycle church bulletins.
25. Caulk and weather-strip around windows and doors to plug air leaks.

26. Stock up on handkerchiefs, cloth shopping bags, and cloth napkins, and kick the paper habit.

27. Wait a month before buying something you "need"; when you do make purchases, buy quality items that will last for many years.

28. Save unwanted catalogs and ask to be taken off their mailing lists.

29. Set up a "share board" at church or organize a clothing exchange.

30. Give away or sell anything and everything that is cluttering your life. Donate the proceeds to charity.

31. Instead of a birthday gift or funeral flowers, send a donation to charity or plant a tree or shrub in the person's honor.

32. When replacing a car, consider one that gets great mileage and has low emissions. Suggest the same for your church, school, business, and city.

33. Organize a paint swap at church or the recycling center; combine unused portions of paint and use as a primer.

34. Organize a church-based public prayer event with emphasis on creation care and stewardship.

35. Start a study group on what the Bible says about caring for creation.

36. Hang thick or insulated curtains. Close them during the day in summer; close at night in winter.

37. Ask your children to "pare down" their toys periodically; give those gently used items to local charities or nonprofit groups.

38. Stay closer to home on your next family trip; stay home on one holiday when you usually travel.

39. Avoid the use of pesticides and chemicals on your lawn and garden.

40. Pray for people whose forests and habitats have been destroyed by our material desires; ask God to help you become a better steward of his resources.

41. Spend at least ten minutes in nature "being still and knowing God" (Psalm 46:10).

42. Cut back on soft drinks by substituting tap water at least once a day.

43. Avoid covering radiators and vents with furniture or curtains; program thermostats to come on thirty minutes before you wake up or come home.

44. Plant a vegetable or herb garden.

45. Insulate your attic with a minimum of ten inches of insulation; insulate your hot-water heater if it's an older model.

46. Write or call your city, county, or state representatives and ask them to consider conducting an energy audit in their offices; do the same at school and work.

47. Insulate your hot-water pipes; it's easy—just clip on the foam insulation.

48. Turn down the temperature on your hot-water heater to the lowest setting.

49. Cut food before cooking; put the lid on pans; cook outside in summer.

50. Follow Grandmother's advice: "Use it up, wear it out, make it do, or do without."

From www.servegodsavetheplanet.org. Used with permission.

Organizations and Web Sites

Denominational Environmental Programs

Baptist
Southern Baptist Environment and Climate Initiative
www.baptistcreationcare.org

Catholic
The Catholic Coalition on Climate Change
www.catholicsandclimatechange.org/

Catholic Conservation Center
www.conservation.catholic.org/background.htm

Catholic Fund for Overseas Development (CAFOD)
www.cafod.org

National Catholic Rural Life Conference
www.ncrlc.com/

National Conference of Catholic Bishops/Renewing the Earth
www.nccbuscc.org

United States Conference of Catholic Bishops Environmental Justice Program
www.nccbuscc.org/sdwp/ejp/

Christian Church/Disciples of Christ
Disciples Home Missions
www.homelandministries.org/publicwitness/environment.htm

Church of Christ
United Church of Christ
www.uccecoaction.org/

Episcopal

The Episcopal Church
www.episcopalchurch.org/1829_ENG_HTM.htm

The Episcopal Ecological Network
www.eenonline.org

Lutheran

The Evangelical Lutheran Church in America
http://archive.elca.org/advocacy/environment/index.html

Lutheran Earthkeeping Network of the Synods (LENS)
www.webofcreation.org/LENS/synods.html

Mennonite/Brethren

Church of the Brethren
www.brethren.org/genbd/witness/CareforCreation.htm

Mennonite Central Committee—Care for Creation
www.mcc.org/careforcreation/

Mennonite Creation Care Network
www.mennocreationcare.org/

Methodist

United Methodist Board of Church and Society
www.umc-gbcs.org

United Methodist Women Green Team
http://gbgm-umc.org/umw/green_team.cfm

Nazarene

Nazarene Compassionate Ministries
www.ncm.org/ed_ad_environment.aspx

Orthodox

Greek Orthodox Church in America
www.goarch.org/en/ourfaith/environment/

The Orthodox Fellowship of the Transfiguration
www.Orth-Transfiguration.org

Presbyterian
Presbyterian Church USA
www.pcusa.org/environment/
Presbyterian Conservation Corps
www.presbyterianconservationcorps.org/

Presbyterians for Restoring Creation
www.prcweb.org/

Quaker
Quaker Earthcare Witness
www.quakerearthcare.org

Reformed
Reformed Church in America
www.rca.org/NETCOMMUNITY/Page.aspx?&pid=1518&srcid=1542%20

United Church of Christ
United Church of Christ EcoAction
www.uccecoaction.org/

Vineyard
Vineyard Christian Fellowship—Boise
www.letstendthegarden.org

Denominational Statements and Activities

Catholic
Environmental Justice Work in the Catholic Church and Community
www.nrpe.org/statements/catholic_intro01.htm

Mainline Protestant
Environmental Engagement in Mainline Protestant Denominations
www.nrpe.org/statements/mainline_intro01.htm

Evangelical

Creation Care in the Evangelical Community
www.nrpe.org/statements/evangelical_intro01.htm

Faith-Based Environmental Organizations

A Rocha

An international conservation organization working to care for God's world with a focus on science and research, practical conservation, and environmental education
www.arocha.org

American Scientific Affiliation

A fellowship of Christians in science who share a common fidelity to the Word of God and a commitment to integrity in the practice of science
www.asa3.org

The Association for Religion, Ecology, and Society

An association that helps individuals and groups with a religious perspective find resources for practicing a more green lifestyle while joining others who have become conscious of their environmental impact
www.arecology.org/

AuSable Environmental Institute

An evangelical Christian academic institute devoted to stewardship through academic programs and resources
www.ausable.org

Blood:Water Mission

An organization founded by Jars of Clay that exists to promote clean blood and clean water efforts in Africa, tangibly reducing the impact of the HIV/AIDS pandemic while addressing the underlying issues of poverty, injustice, and oppression
www.bloodwatermission.org

Center of Concern

A Catholic organization working in collaboration with ecumenical and interfaith networks to bring a prophetic voice for social and economic justice to a global context
www.coc.org

Christian Ecology Link
A multidenominational U.K. Christian organization for people concerned about the environment
www.christian-ecology.org.uk/

Christians for the Mountains
An initiative to summon Christians to act responsibly and protect God's creation, with the first objective of ending mountaintop removal extraction
www.christiansforthemountains.org

Creation Care for Pastors
A bridge-building effort between top environmental scientists and evangelicals to protect creation
www.creationcareforpastors.com/

Creation Care Study Program
A premier study-abroad program for Christian college students, connecting Christian faith with the most complex, urgent global issues
www.creationcsp.org/

Crown Point Farm and Education Center
A community that demonstrates the practical applications of ecology and connects spirituality, social justice, and environmental protection
www.crownpt.org/

Earth Care
An organization that exists to promote creation stewardship within the Christian community, raising environmental awareness and encouraging participation in church and community
www.earthcareonline.org/

Earth Ministry
An organization that inspires and mobilizes the Christian community to play a leadership role in building a just and sustainable future
www.earthministry.org/

Eco-Justice Ministries

An ecumenical agency that helps churches answer the call to care for all of God's creation and develop ministries that are faithful, relevant, and effective in working toward social justice and environmental sustainability
www.eco-justice.org

Educational Concerns for Hunger Organization (ECHO)

An interdenominational Christian organization that assists a global network of missionaries and development workers serving agricultural workers in 180 countries
www.echonet.org

Environmental Partnerships

Urban and suburban congregations and communities that help achieve environmental justice and stewardship
www.environmentalpartnerships.org/

European Christian Environmental Network

A conference of European churches that addresses the relationship to nature and the environment from the perspective of Christian theology
www.ecen.org/

Evangelical Climate Initiative

A group of more than eighty-five evangelical leaders who are encouraging action by all Americans to make life changes necessary to help solve the global warming crisis
www.christiansandclimate.org

Evangelical Environmental Network

An organization that seeks to educate, inspire, and mobilize Christians in their effort to care for God's creation, to be faithful stewards of God's provision, and to advocate for actions and policies that honor God and protect the environment
www.creationcare.org

Floresta

A Christian nonprofit organization working to reverse deforestation and poverty in the world through community development, innovative agriculture and forestry, microenterprise, and discipleship
www.floresta.org/

Forum on Religion and Ecology

An international multireligious project recognizing that religions need to be in dialogue with other disciplines (i.e., science, ethics, economics) in seeking comprehensive solutions to both global and local environmental problems
www.religionandecology.org

Franciscan Earth Literacy Center

An environmental education center and demonstration facility designed to promote the appreciation of nature and encourage sustainable living practices
www.earthliteracy.org

GreenFaith

An organization that inspires, educates, and mobilizes people from diverse religious backgrounds to deepen their relationship with the sacred in nature and to take action for the earth
www.greenfaith.org/

Healing Waters

An organization that works to reduce water-related illness and death in developing countries by building self-sustaining projects that make safe drinking water accessible to the poor and empower local churches to bring physical, social, and spiritual healing to their communities
www.healingwatersintl.org

Healthy Families, Healthy Environment

An initiative that helps families enrich their physical and spiritual health and protect their loved ones from environmental health threats
www.healthyfamiliesnow.org/

The Humane Society of the United States

The nation's largest animal protection organization, through its Animals & Religion program, engages religious communities with critical animal welfare issues based on longstanding traditions of compassion, mercy, and caring for creation.
www.humanesociety.org/religion

Indigenous Peoples' Restoration Network

A network that develops and uses the tools of ecological restoration to enhance the survival of indigenous peoples and their cultures
www.ser.org/iprn/default.asp

Interfaith Coalition on Energy
A coalition that guides congregations to use less energy, to purchase energy at a lower cost, and to practice environmental stewardship
www.interfaithenergy.com

Interfaith Power and Light
A ministry devoted to deepening the connection between ecology and faith, specifically mobilizing a national religious response to global warming while promoting renewable energy, energy efficiency, and conservation
www.theregenerationproject.org/

National Council of Churches of Christ Eco-Justice Program
An organization cooperating with the NCC Eco-Justice Working Group to provide an opportunity for the national bodies of member Protestant and Orthodox denominations to work together to protect and restore God's creation
www.nccecojustice.org

National Religious Partnership for the Environment
An association of independent faith groups—the U.S. Conference of Catholic Bishops, the National Council of Churches U.S.A., the Coalition on the Environment and Jewish Life, and the Evangelical Environmental Network—that offers a universal effort to protect humankind's common home and well-being on earth
www.nrpe.org/

Network Alliance of Congregations Caring for the Earth
An ecumenical organization that encourages the many strands of Christian tradition in the work of healing the damaged earth out of a common concern and love for God's creation
www.nacce.org/

Religious Campaign for Forest Conservation
A coalition of Christian and Jewish denominations and organizations that promotes an end to the cutting of old-growth forests and commercial logging on public lands
www.ecostewards.org/rcfc.htm

Restoring Eden

A parachurch ministry dedicated to encouraging faithful stewardship of the natural world as a biblical, moral, and wise value, while advocating for natural habitats, wild species, and indigenous subsistence cultures
www.restoringeden.org/

Sierra Club

With 1.3 million members and supporters, the nation's oldest, largest and most influential grassroots environmental organization actively partners with diverse communities of faith to explore, enjoy, and protect the planet.
www.sierraclub.org/partnerships/faith/

Target Earth

A Christian nonprofit organization working to serve both the poor and the earth, focusing on service projects, conservation programs, resources, and awareness of spiritual and cultural links to creation care and poverty
www.targetearth.org

Tearfund

A Christian relief and development agency working with a global network of local churches to help eradicate poverty
www.tearfund.org/

Web of Creation

An environmental Web site for faith-based communities, connecting people with ideas, resources, and strategies for doing eco-justice
www.webofcreation.org/

World Vision

A Christian humanitarian organization dedicated to working with children, families, and their communities worldwide to reach their full potential by tackling the causes of poverty and injustice
www.worldvision.org

The Green Subject Index

Proverbs 12:10   The righteous know the needs of their animals
Proverbs 30:26, 28   Wisdom of the badgers and the lizard
Ecclesiastes 3:19   The fates of humans and animals are the same
Ecclesiastes 3:20   Both humans and animals turn to dust at death
Isaiah 1:11   God does not delight in the blood of bulls, lambs or goats
Isaiah 7:24-25   The hills will become a place where cattle graze
Isaiah 11:6-8   The wolf shall lie down with the lamb
Isaiah 13:20-22   The animals in the time of Babylon's judgment
Isaiah 30:6   An oracle concerning the animals of the Negev
Isaiah 34:13-15   The animals described in No Kingdom
Isaiah 43:20   The wild animals will honor God
Isaiah 65:25   The wolf and the lamb shall feed together
Isaiah 66:3   Who kills an ox, will be like killing a person
Jeremiah 7:20   God's anger will pour on people, animals and trees
Jeremiah 8:7   The animals know God's law, but not the people
Jeremiah 8:17   God let snakes loose among the people
Jeremiah 9:10   The birds and animals have fled
Jeremiah 12:4   The animals are gone because of human sin
Jeremiah 15:3-4   Four destroyers: sword, dogs, birds and animals
Ezekiel 14:21   Four judgments: sword, famine, animals, pests
Ezekiel 29:5   God said, "I give you as food to the animals"
Ezekiel 32:13   God will destroy all of the livestock of Egypt
Ezekiel 34:17   God will judge between the sheep and the goats
Ezekiel 34:25   God will banish wild animals from the land
Ezekiel 34:26   God will shower blessings on the animals
Ezekiel 38:19-20   Fish, birds and animals will quake at the Lord's coming
Ezekiel 39:4   Birds of prey and wild animals will devour you
Ezekiel 39:17   Speak to the birds and wild animals
Daniel 2:37-38   The king rules over the birds, animals and all
Daniel 6:21-22   God shut the mouth of the lions
Hosea 2:18-20   A covenant with animals
Hosea 4:3   The land mourns, the animals and birds too
Joel 1:17-18   The grain has failed, the animals groan
Zephaniah 1:3   God will sweep away people, animals, birds and fish
Zechariah 9:9b   The king is humble and rides on a donkey
Matthew 8:30-32   Jesus sent the demons into the herd of swine
John 18:27   The cock crowed at the moment of Peter's denial
Acts 10:12-15   Peter's vision of the edibility of all animals
Acts 11:4-9   Peter recalls his vision of animals as food
Revelation 5:13   Every creature in heaven and earth sings to God

BEASTS

Genesis 1:24-25   The creation of all the land animals
Genesis 8:17   Bring two of every creature into the ark
Leviticus 11:46-47   The law of the beasts and the fowl
Deuteronomy 25:4   Do not muzzle the ox that treads grain
Job 40:15   God made Behemoth
Job 41:1-34   Can you draw out Leviathan with a fishhook?
Psalm 74:14   You crushed the head of Leviathan
Psalm 104:25-26   God formed Leviathan to sport in the sea
Isaiah 27:1   The Lord will kill Leviathan, that twisting serpent
Ezekiel 5:17   For their sin God sent famine, beasts and destruction
Mark 1:13   Jesus was in the wilderness with the beasts
James 3:7   Every bird, beast or reptile species can be tamed
Revelation 5:13   Every creature in heaven and earth sings to God

BEAUTY

1 Chronicles 16:29-30   Worship the Lord in holy splendor
Psalm 27:4   I will seek the beauty of the Lord
Psalm 50:2   God shines forth from Zion, perfection of beauty
Psalm 96:9   Worship the Lord in holy splendor

Isaiah 28:5   In that day the Lord will be a diadem of beauty
Isaiah 52:7   How beautiful upon the mountains

BIRDS

Genesis 1:20-21   The Fifth Day: creation of the birds
Genesis 2:20   Adam names all of the birds
Genesis 6:18-20   Noah brings all the birds into the ark
Genesis 9:2   The animals and birds will now fear you
Leviticus 1:14   Choose pigeons or turtle doves in burnt offerings
Leviticus 11:46-47   The law of the beasts and the fowl
Deuteronomy 4:16   Do not make an idol of any animal or bird
Deuteronomy 14:11   All of the clean birds, you may eat
Deuteronomy 14:12-18   List of the unclean birds that you may not eat
Deuteronomy 22:6-7   Do not take both the hen and her eggs
Job 38:41   Who provides for the raven?
Job 39:26-27   Does the hawk soar by your human wisdom?
Psalm 50:11   I know all the birds of the air, says the Lord
Psalm 84:3   Even the sparrow finds a home, the swallow a nest
Psalm 104:12   By the streams the birds have their habitation
Psalm 104:17   The stork has its home in the fir trees
Isaiah 34:11   The owl, hawk and raven enter the Kingdom
Jeremiah 4:25   All the birds of the air had fled
Jeremiah 9:10   The birds and the animals have fled
Jeremiah 12:4   The birds are gone because of human sin
Jeremiah 15:3   Four destroyers: sword, dogs, birds and animals
Ezekiel 29:5   I give you as food to the animals and birds
Ezekiel 38:19-20   Fish, birds and animals will quake at the Lord's coming
Ezekiel 39:4   Birds of prey and wild animals will devour you
Ezekiel 39:17   Speak to the birds and wild animals
Daniel 2:37-38   The king rules over the birds, animals and all
Hosea 4:3   The land mourns, the animals and birds too
Zephaniah 1:3   I will sweep away the people, animals and birds
Matthew 6:26-27   Look at the birds, they neither sow nor reap
Matthew 10:29-30   God's awareness of every sparrow
Matthew 26:34   Jesus predicts Peter's denial before the cock crows
Matthew 26:74   At Peter's denial, the cock crowed
Mark 14:30   Jesus predicts Peter's denial before the cock crows
Mark 14:72   At Peter's denial, the cock crowed
Luke 12:6-7   Sparrows are not forgotten in God's sight
Luke 12:24   Consider the ravens, how God feeds them
Luke 22:34   Jesus predicts Peter's denial before the cock crows
Luke 22:60-61   At Peter's denial, the cock crowed
John 13:38   Jesus predicts Peter's denial before the cock crows
John 18:27   At Peter's denial, the cock crowed
1 Corinthians 15:39   One flesh for humans, another for birds and fish
James 3:7   Every bird, beast or reptile species can be tamed
Revelation 5:13   Every creature in heaven and earth sings to God

BLESS/ BLESSING

Genesis 1:22   God blessed the animals: be fruitful and multiply
Genesis 1:28   God blessed the first humans
Genesis 2:3   God blessed the seventh day and rested in it
Genesis 5:2   God blessed humankind
Leviticus 27:22-23   The blessing/consecration of the fields to the Lord
Numbers 6:24   God's blesses the people
Deuteronomy 2:7   God has blessed you through the wilderness
Deuteronomy 8:10   Bless the Lord for the good land
Deuteronomy 28:4   Many blessings flow from obedience to the Lord
Deuteronomy 33:13-16   The many blessings of the Lord in Joseph's land
Psalm 103:22   Bless the Lord in the places of his dominion
Proverbs 28:20   The faithful abound with blessings

Isaiah 41:18-20   The blessings of God for the poor and needy
Isaiah 65:16   When you bless the land, bless also the Lord
Ezekiel 34:26   God will shower blessings on the animals
Haggai 2:19   The Lord blesses his people
Acts 3:25   All the families of the earth shall be blessed
Acts 20:35   It is more blessed to give than to receive
2 Corinthians 9:8   God is able to provide you with every blessing

CARING FOR YOUR NEIGHBOR

Deuteronomy 14:28-29   Share tithe with widows and orphans
2 Kings 4:42-44   First fruits feed the hungry
Jeremiah 22:3   Do no wrong to the alien, orphan, widow
Ezekiel 34:2-4   Should not shepherds feed the sheep?
Proverbs 31:8   Speak out for those who cannot speak
Matthew 5:44   Love your enemies
Matthew 22:37-39   Love your neighbor as yourself
Matthew 25:37-46   Just as you did it to one of the least of these
John 13:34   Love one another
Luke 6:31   Do to others as you would have them do to you
Luke 6:35-36   Love your enemies
Romans 13:9   Love your neighbor as yourself
Romans 15:5-6   God grant you to live in harmony with each other
1 Corinthians 10:23-24   Don't seek your own advantage
1 Corinthians 12:12-14, 24b-26   We are many members of one body
Galatians 6:2   Bear one another's burdens
Philippians 2:4   Look not to your own interests
Colossians 3:13-14   Love binds all together in perfect harmony
1 Peter 3:8   Have a unity of spirit and love for one another
1 John 3:17-18   Sees a brother or sister in need and does not help
1 John 4:7-8   Let us love one another

CITY

Genesis 11:8-9   Lord confused the language of all the earth in the first city
Leviticus 26:25   Disobedience brings pestilence to your cities
Numbers 35:1-3   Land outside the city is for the animals
Psalm 127:1   Unless the Lord guards the city, they guard in vain
Isaiah 14:21b   Let them never cover the world with cities
Isaiah 24:10   The city of chaos is broken down
Isaiah 24:12-13   Desolation in the city and on all the earth
Isaiah 32:14   Prediction that the populated city will be deserted
Isaiah 61:4   The spirit of the Lord will repair the ruined cities
Ezekiel 7:23b   Land is full of crimes; city is full of violence
Ezekiel 26:19   When God lays waste to the city
Habbakuk 2:17   Violence to the earth and to the cities
Zechariah 1:17   God's cities shall overflow with prosperity
Revelation 21:2   I saw the holy city, coming down out of heaven
Revelation 21:10   On a high mountain he showed me the holy city
Revelation 21:27   Nothing unclean will enter the holy city

CLOUD

Genesis 9:14   God will bring clouds over the earth
Exodus 24:16   The Lord called to Moses out of a cloud
Exodus 40:34-38   The cloud of the Lord was on the tabernacle
Deuteronomy 5:22   The Lord speaks from the mountain in a cloud
1 Kings 8:10-11   A cloud filled the house of the Lord
2 Chronicles 5:13-14   A cloud filled the house of the Lord
Nehemiah 9:12   The Lord led them with a pillar of cloud by day
Job 36:29   Can anyone understand the clouds?
Job 37:15-17   Do you know the balancings of the clouds?
Job 38:34, 37   Who has the wisdom to number the clouds?
Psalm 36:5   God's faithfulness extends to the clouds

Psalm 78:14   He led them with a cloud and a fiery light
Psalm 97:2   Clouds are all around God
Psalm 104:3   God makes the cloud his chariot
Psalm 135:7   The Lord makes the clouds rise
Ecclesiastes 11:3   When clouds are full, they empty rain on earth
Isaiah 4:5   A cloud by day and a fire by night
Isaiah 19:1   The Lord is riding on a swift cloud
Ezekiel 10:3-4   A cloud filled the inner court
Ezekiel 32:7   God will cover the sun with a cloud
Matthew 17:5   From a cloud, the Lord spoke
Mark 9:7   A cloud overshadowed them and a voice spoke
Luke 21:27   The Son of Man coming in a cloud with power and glory
Acts 1:9   A cloud took Jesus out of their sight
Revelation 1:7   Look! The Lord is coming with the clouds
Revelation 14:14   Seated on a cloud was one like the Son of Man

COMMUNITY

Deuteronomy 15:7-8   Within your community, care for needy neighbors in the land
Matthew 22:37-39   You shall love your neighbor as yourself
Romans 15:5-6   God grant you to live in harmony with each other
1 Corinthians 1:10   All of you be in agreement and without division
1 Corinthians 12:12-14, 24b-26   We are many members of one body
Ephesians 4:25   We are members of one another
Colossians 3:13-14   Love binds all together in perfect harmony
1 Thessalonians 5:13b   Be at peace among yourselves
1 Peter 2:17   Love the family of believers. Honor everyone
1 Peter 3:8   Have a unity of spirit and love for one another

COVENANT

Genesis 9:1-3, 8-13   The covenant between God and creation
Genesis 9:15-17   The rainbow as a sign of God's covenant
Genesis 15:18-19   God's land covenant with Abraham and descendants
Exodus 19:3-5   Keeping God's covenant for the earth is God's
Exodus 34:10   A covenant to do marvels in the earth
Deuteronomy 29:22-25   The land is destroyed when they abandoned the covenant
Joshua 23:16   If you transgress the covenant, you will perish from the good land
1 Chronicles 16:15-18   Remember God's covenant of land for 1,000 generations
Isaiah 24:5   The earth is polluted for they broke the covenant
Isaiah 49:8   The Lord gave a covenant to establish the land
Isaiah 59:21   The Lord's covenant is that God's spirit is upon the people
Jeremiah 22:7-9   God will cut down choicest cedars when you abandon the covenant
Jeremiah 33:25   God's covenant with day and night and the earth
Ezekiel 34:25   God will make a covenant of peace and banish wild animals
Hosea 2:18   A covenant with animals
Malachi 2:5   God's covenant is a covenant of life and well being
Matthew 26:27-28   Jesus' blood of the covenant
Mark 14:24   Jesus' blood of the covenant
Luke 22:20   The new covenant in Jesus' blood
Acts 3:25   Of your descendants all the families of the earth shall be blessed
Romans 11:27   "This is my covenant: I will take away their sins"
Hebrews 7:22   Jesus is the guarantor of a better covenant
Hebrews 8:10   The design of the new covenant
Hebrews 9:15   Christ is the mediator of a new covenant
Hebrews 10:16   This is the covenant I will make, says the Lord

CREATION

Genesis 1:1   In the beginning God created the heavens and the earth
Genesis 1:3   Creation of light

Genesis 1:4-5   From the beginning, creation is good
Genesis 1:6   Creation of the "firmament"
Genesis 1:7-8   Creation of the sky
Genesis 1:9-10   Creation of land
Genesis 1:11-13   The earth brings forth grass and seeds
Genesis 1:14-19   Creation of sun, moon and stars
Genesis 1:20-21   Creation of the birds and sea creatures
Genesis 1:22   The commission to animals to be fruitful
Genesis 1:24-25   Creation of land animals
Genesis 1:26   Creation of the first human in God's image
Genesis 1:27   God creates humans as both male and female
Genesis 1:28   The charge to exercise dominion within creation
Genesis 1:31   All of creation is called "very good"
Genesis 2:1   The heavens and earth are completed
Genesis 2:2   On the seventh day, God's creation is finished
Genesis 2:3   God takes his rest in creation
Genesis 2:4   The second story of creation
Genesis 2:7   God formed man from the dust of the ground
Genesis 2:8   God planted a garden in Eden
Genesis 2:15   God charges humans with keeping creation
Genesis 8:21-22   The stability of creation
Genesis 9:1-3   The covenant between God and creation
Psalm 19:1-2   Creation reflects the Creator
Psalm 29:3-9   The voice of the Lord in creation
Psalm 77:16-19   Creation responds to God
Psalm 78:47-51   The wrath of God manifests through creation
Psalm 98:4-9   All creation praises the Lord
Proverbs 8:22-31   Wisdom's role in creation
Ezekiel 36:28-30   God restores people and creation
Joel 2:1   God's wrath is reflected in the creation
Habbakuk 3:8-12   Creation responds to its Creator
Mark 10:6   At creation, God made them male and female
Mark 16:15   Proclaim the good news to the whole creation
Romans 1:20   Since the creation of the world
Romans 8:19-23   Creation awaits its redemption
Romans 8:38-39   Nothing in creation can separate us from God's love
Galatians 6:15   Circumcision is nothing, a new creation is everything
Colossians 1:15-17   Christ is the firstborn of all creation
Hebrews 11:3   Worlds were prepared by word of God
Revelation 4:11   By God's will all created things were created and exist

CREATOR

Genesis 1:1   In the beginning God is the Creator
Genesis 1:3   God creates light
Genesis 1:6   God creates the "firmament"
Genesis 1:7-8   God creates the sky
Genesis 1:9-10   God creates land
Genesis 1:14-19   God creates sun, moon and stars
Genesis 1:20-21   God creates birds and sea creatures
Genesis 1:24-25   God creates land animals
Genesis 1:26   God creates the first human
Genesis 2:7   The Lord forms the human from the dust
Genesis 2:8   God plants a garden in Eden
Deuteronomy 4:32   God created humans on the earth
Nehemiah 9:6   God made and gives life to heaven and earth
Job 9:5-10   God spread out the heavens and the stars
Psalm 19:1   The firmament declares God's handiwork
Psalm 77:16-19   Creation responds to the Creator
Ecclesiastes 12:1-2   Remember your Creator in the days of your youth
Isaiah 40:28   The Lord is the Creator of the ends of the earth
Isaiah 45:18   God created the heavens and formed the earth

Jeremiah 5:22   God placed the sand as a boundary for the sea
Jeremiah 10:12   God made the earth by power and wisdom
Jeremiah 10:16   The Lord formed all things
Jeremiah 27:5   God made the earth
Jeremiah 31:22   The Lord has created a new thing on earth
Jeremiah 32:17   God made the heavens and the earth
Malachi 2:10   One God has created us
John 1:1-3   All things came into being through him
Romans 1:20   God's power is revealed thru what he has made
Romans 1:24-25   They served the creature rather than the Creator
1 Corinthians 8:6   From God the Father are all things
Ephesians 3:9   God created all things
Colossians 1:16   In Christ, all things were created
1 Timothy 4:4   Everything created by God is good
Hebrews 1:10   In the beginning the Lord founded the earth
Revelation 4:11   God created all things
Revelation 10:5-6   Who created the earth

CREATURES

Genesis 1:30   God provides seeds and herbs for all creatures
Genesis 2:19   Adam names the creatures
Leviticus 11:41-43   Do not eat the creeping creatures
Deuteronomy 14:20   You may eat any clean winged creature
Psalm 104:24   The earth is full of God's creatures
Acts 10:12-15   Peter's vision of the edibility of all creatures
Colossians 1:23   The gospel has been proclaimed to every creature
Hebrews 4:13   No creature is hidden from God's sight

CURSE

Genesis 3:17   Cursed is the ground because of your disobedience
Genesis 4:10-13   God's curse on Cain causes enmity with the ground
Deuteronomy 28:15-19   Disobedience brings a curse upon the land
Deuteronomy 28:30-37   List of social disasters because of disobedience
Proverbs 3:33   The Lord's curse is on the house of the wicked
Jeremiah 17:5-6   Cursed shall live in parched places
Jeremiah 23:10   Because of the curse, the land mourns
Zechariah 5:3   The curse that hangs over the land
Malachi 3:8-10   Will you rob God? You are cursed for not tithing
Malachi 4:5-6   Elijah returns to protect the earth from a curse
Galatians 3:13   Christ redeemed us from the curse of the law

DEFILE

Leviticus 11:43   You shall not defile yourself by eating certain animals
Leviticus 18:25-27   The land was defiled through the sins of the nations
Numbers 35:34   You shall not defile the land where you live
Isaiah 14:20   You who destroy the land will be cast out
Isaiah 24:3   The earth shall be laid waste and despoiled
Isaiah 24:12-13   Desolation in the city and on all the earth
Jeremiah 2:7   You have defiled my land [says the Lord]
Jeremiah 9:10   Weep for the mountains, they are laid waste
Jeremiah 9:12   Why is the land ruined and wilderness laid waste?
Jeremiah 12:4   Animals are gone because of human sin
Ezekiel 36:17   When Israel lived on its own soil, they defiled it
Mark 7:20-23   Evil thoughts defile a person
2 Peter 2:20   After they escaped the defilements of the world

DESERT

1 Kings 17:2-4   Elijah obeys God and goes into the desert
Psalm 78:17   They sinned against the Most High in the desert
Psalm 78:40   How often they grieved God in the desert
Psalm 106:14   They put God to the test in the desert

Isaiah 48:21   They did not thirst in the desert
Isaiah 50:2   God makes the rivers into a desert
Matthew 14:15-20   Jesus feeds the crowds in the desert
Matthew 15:32-38   Jesus feeds the crowds in the desert
Mark 6:35-44   Jesus feeds the people in the desert
Mark 8:4-10   Jesus feeds a great crowd in the desert
Luke 9:12-17   Jesus feeds a crowd in the desert

DESOLATION

Isaiah 24:11-13   Desolation in the city and on all the earth
Isaiah 64:10   Jerusalem has become a desolation
Jeremiah 4:27   The whole land shall be a desolation
Jeremiah 12:11   The land is made desolate
Jeremiah 44:22   Because of your evil, the land became desolate
Ezekiel 6:14   God said, "I will make the land desolate and waste"
Ezekiel 30:12   God said, "I shall bring desolation to the land"
Ezekiel 33:23-29   God will make the land desolate because of their abominations
Ezekiel 35:7   God will make Mount Seir a waste and desolation
Hosea 13:15   Rebellion brings desolation to the land
Joel 3:19   Egypt will become a desolation
Micah 7:13   The earth will be desolate for the peoples' sin
Zechariah 7:14b   A pleasant land was made desolate
Luke 21:20   Desolation of Jerusalem foretold
Acts 1:20   Let his homestead become desolate

DISOBEDIENCE

Genesis 3:17   Cursed is the ground for your disobedience
Leviticus 26:14-22   Disobedience causes the trees to be unfruitful
Leviticus 26:25   Disobedience brings pestilence to your cities
Leviticus 26:32   Disobedience brings devastation to the land
Numbers 14:27-33   Complainers shall wander in the wilderness
Numbers 20:12   Disobedience leads to loss of land
Deuteronomy 4:25-26   You will perish from the land if you worship idols
Deuteronomy 6:13-15   Do not forget God or you bring your destruction
Deuteronomy 11:16-17   Disobedience brings the loss of fruitfulness
Deuteronomy 28:15-46, 49-52, 58-59   Warnings against disobedience
Deuteronomy 29:23-25   Abandon the covenant, God will destroy the land
1 Kings 9:6-9   If you turn away, God will cut Israel off from the land
Job 24:2-4   The behavior of the wicked on the land
Isaiah 14:20   You who destroy the land will be cast out
Jeremiah 2:14-17   Israel's land made waste for forsaking the Lord
Jeremiah 9:12-14   Land is ruined when forsaken God's law
Jeremiah 44:22   Because of your evil, the land became desolate
Ezekiel 14:13-14   If a land sins by faithlessness, God will send famine
Ezekiel 33:26-29   God will make the land a desolation for their abominations
Ezekiel 36:17-19   When they defiled the soil, God poured out his wrath
Micah 7:13   The land is desolate for the peoples' sin
Zechariah 7:12-14   They would not hear, so the land was desolate
Galatians 6:7-8   Do not be deceived: you reap what you sow
Revelation 11:18   God will destroy those who destroy the earth

DOMINION

Genesis 1:26   The first human is given dominion over creation
Genesis 1:28   The first humans are given dominion over the rest of creation
Psalm 8:5-8   God gave humans dominion over his works
Psalm 22:28   Dominion belongs to the Lord
Psalm 72:8   God has dominion from sea to sea
Psalm 103:22   Bless the Lord in the places of his dominion
Psalm 145:13   The Lord's dominion endures forever
Ezekiel 30:18   God will break the dominion of Egypt
Daniel 6:26   God's dominion has no end

Daniel 7:14   To him was given dominion and glory and kingship
Zechariah 3:7   Walk in my ways and you will rule in my house
Zechariah 9:10   The king's dominion is from sea to sea
Matthew 20:25-28   Jesus teaches about dominion
Luke 22:24-27   Jesus teaches about dominion
Romans 5:14   Death exercised dominion from Adam to Abraham
Romans 5:17   Death exercised dominion thru one man's sin
Romans 5:21   Grace might exercise dominion unto eternal life
Romans 6:14   For sin will have no dominion over you
Ephesians 1:20-21   Christ is above all rule, authority and dominion
1 Timothy 6:16   To the Lord be honor and eternal dominion
Hebrews 2:7-9   God subjected all things under their feet
Revelation 1:5b-6   Glory and dominion to Jesus now and forever

DROUGHT

Deuteronomy 11:16-17   Disobedience brings drought to the land
Deuteronomy 28:22-23   Droughts are a form of the Lord's punishment
2 Chronicles 6:26-27   There is no rain because they have sinned
Job 12:15   The Lord is the master of the rains and droughts
Jeremiah 14:3-6   The word of the Lord concerning the drought
Haggai 1:11   God brings drought upon the land

DUST

Genesis 2:7   The Lord forms Adam from the dust of the earth
Genesis 3:19   People come from dust and return to dust
Psalm 103:14   God knows that we are made of dust
Psalm 104:29   When God takes away their breath, they return to dust
Ecclesiastes 3:20   All are from dust, and all turn to dust again

EARTH

Judgment on the Earth → See JUDGMENT
Pollution in the Earth → See POLLUTION
Genesis 1:10   God called the dry land Earth
Genesis 1:11-12   The earth brings forth grass and vegetation
Genesis 2:4   The generations of the heavens and the earth
Genesis 2:6   The face of the earth is watered
Genesis 2:7   The Lord forms Adam from the dust of the earth
Genesis 3:23   Adam's duty was to till the earth
Genesis 6:5-7   God's decision to purge the earth
Genesis 9:7   Abound on the earth and multiply in it
Genesis 11:9   The Lord scatters people across the earth
Exodus 19:5   All the earth is God's
Exodus 34:10   A covenant to do marvels in the earth
Deuteronomy 4:32   God created humans on the earth
Deuteronomy 4:36   From heaven his voice, on earth his fire
Deuteronomy 5:8   Make no idol from anything on earth or heaven
1 Kings 8:27   Will God dwell on the earth?
1 Chronicles 16:14   The Lord's judgments are in all the earth
1 Chronicles 29:15   Our days on earth are like a shadow
2 Chronicles 6:18   Will God reside with mortals on earth?
2 Chronicles 16:9   The eyes of the Lord range throughout the entire earth
Job 5:6   Misery does not come from the earth
Job 5:10   God gives rain on the earth
Job 8:9   Our days on earth are but a shadow
Job 9:24   The earth is given over to the wicked
Job 11:7-9   The deep mysteries of God and earth
Job 19:25   My redeemer will stand upon the earth
Job 26:7   God hangs the earth upon nothing
Job 28:5-6   Out of the earth comes bread and stones
Job 37:3   God's lightning to the corners of the earth
Psalm 8:1, 9   O Lord, your name is majestic in all the earth

THE EARTH BELONGS TO GOD   Exodus 9:29,
Deuteronomy 4:39, 10:14; Joshua 2:11, 3:11; 1 Chronicles 29:11,
Job 28:23-27, 34:13; Psalms 24:1, 89:11, 95:4; Isaiah 54:5, 66:1;
Acts 7:49, 1 Corinthians 10:26

THE EARTH PRAISES GOD   1 Chronicles 16:23, 16:31;
Psalms 66:4, 68:32, 69:34, 96:1, 96:11, 97:1, 100:1;
Isaiah 42:10, 49:13; Habbakuk 3:3; Revelation 5:13

FAMINE

Genesis 12:10   A famine comes over the land
Genesis 41:47-49, 53-57   Make provision for famine in times of plenty
1 Kings 8:37-40   When there is famine or plague
2 Chronicles 6:28-31   If there is famine in the land or blight or plague
2 Chronicles 20:9   If disaster, pestilence or famine comes upon us
Psalm 37:18-19   The Lord provides for the blameless in famine
Jeremiah 14:11-12   The Lord said, I do not hear them but by famine I
consume them
Ezekiel 5:15-17   For your sin God will send famine, beasts and destruction
Ezekiel 14:12-13   If a land sins by faithlessness, God will send famine
Ezekiel 14:21   Four judgments: sword, famine, animals, pests
Amos 8:11   God will send a famine of hearing the Lord's words
Matthew 24:7-8   There will be famines and earthquakes
Acts 7:11   A famine in which our ancestors found no food
Acts 11:28   One predicted a severe famine over the world

FARM/ FARMER

1 Kings 21:1-24   The vineyard of Naboth the Jezreelite
Isaiah 28:24-26   Do farmers plow their fields continually?
Isaiah 30:23-24   The Lord will give rain for the seed you sow
Isaiah 61:5   Foreigners will farm your land and dress its vines
Jeremiah 12:13   They have sown wheat and reaped thorns
Joel 1:11   Farmers, be dismayed, the crops are ruined

FIELD

Genesis 3:18   You shall eat the plants of the field
Leviticus 23:22   Do not harvest the corners of the field
Leviticus 27:17-24   If you consecrate to the Lord a field
Deuteronomy 14:22   Tithe the increase of seed from the field
Deuteronomy 28:15-16   Disobedience brings a curse upon the field
1 Chronicles 16:32   Let the seas roar, let the fields exult
Nehemiah 5:11   Restore their fields, vineyards and orchards
Isaiah 5:8   You who join field to field until there is room for no one
Isaiah 16:10   Joy and gladness are gone from the fruitful field
Isaiah 28:24-25   Do those who plow for sowing plow continually?
Isaiah 32:15   Until the wilderness becomes a fruitful field
Isaiah 55:12   The trees of the field shall clap their hands
Jeremiah 7:20   God's anger will pour on people, animals and fields
Ezekiel 34:14   God will feed his sheep on good pasture
Ezekiel 34:18   Must you tread down the rest of your pasture?
Joel 1:10-11   The fields are devastated, the grain is destroyed
Joel 2:22   The pastures grow green, the trees bear fruit
Micah 2:2   Woe to them that covet fields and houses
Matthew 6:28-29   Consider the lilies of the field, how they grow
John 4:35   See how the fields are ripe for harvesting

FIRE

Deuteronomy 4:33   God speaks on earth through the fire
Deuteronomy 4:36   On earth God showed you his great fire
Deuteronomy 5:4   The Lord spoke at the mountain out of the fire
Deuteronomy 5:22-24   The Lord spoke from the mountain out of the fire
Deuteronomy 5:26   The voice of God out of the fire
1 Kings 18:23-25, 38-39   Elijah's victory by fire

1 Kings 19:12   The Lord was not in the fire
2 Chronicles 7:1   Fire came down and consumed the burnt offering
Nehemiah 9:12   God led them by a pillar of fire by night
Psalm 78:14   God led them with a cloud and a fiery light
Psalm 97:3   Fire goes before God and consumes his enemies
Psalm 104:4   God makes the fire and flame his minister
Isaiah 4:5   A cloud by day and a fire by night
Isaiah 66:16   By fire will the Lord execute judgment
Ezekiel 20:46-47   Say to the forest, God will kindle a fire in you
Ezekiel 30:8   They shall know I am Lord when I set fire to Egypt
Joel 1:19-20   Fire has burned the trees, devoured the wilderness
Acts 7:30   An angel appeared in the fire of a burning bush
2 Peter 3:7   The present earth has been reserved for fire
2 Peter 3:10   The earth and all on it will be disclosed (by fire)
Revelation 8:5   Fire from the altar of God is thrown on the earth
Revelation 8:7   Fire was hurled to the earth
Revelation 19:20b   The beast was thrown into the lake of fire
Revelation 20:14b-15   Names not in the Book of Life go to the lake of fire
Revelation 21:8   The faithless and polluted will go to the lake of fire

FISH

Genesis 1:20   Let the waters bring forth living creatures
Genesis 9:2   The animals and fish will now fear you
Leviticus 11:9   The edible fish
Deuteronomy 14:9   Criteria for fish that you may eat
Deuteronomy 14:10   Fish that are unclean to eat
Job 12:8   Fish teach us about the Lord
Psalm 8:8   Fish are placed under human authority
Isaiah 19:7-8   Those who fish in the Nile will mourn
Ezekiel 38:19-20   Fish, birds and animals will quake at the Lord's coming
Ezekiel 47:7-11   Trees make for clean water and fish in the river
Jonah 1:17   The Lord provided a large fish to swallow Jonah
Jonah 2:1   Jonah prays from within the belly of the fish
Jonah 2:10   The Lord spoke to the fish
Matthew 14:17-21   Jesus feeds the 5,000 with bread and two fish
Matthew 15:34-36   Jesus feeds the 4,000 with bread and fish
Mark 6:38-43   Jesus feeds the 5,000 with bread and two fish
Mark 8:5-8   Jesus feeds the 4,000 with bread and fish
Luke 5:4-9   Jesus tells Simon to drop his net and catch fish
Luke 9:13-17   Jesus feeds the 5,000 with bread and fish
John 6:9-14   Jesus feeds the 5,000 with bread and two fish
John 21:5-6   Jesus tells them to fish on the right side of the boat
1 Corinthians 15:38-39   One flesh for humans, another for birds and fish

FLOWERS

Song of Solomon 2:12   When flowers appear on earth, time of singing
has come
Isaiah 40:7   When the breath of the Lord blows, the flower fades
Isaiah 40:8   The flower fades, but the word of our God endures forever
Matthew 6:28   Consider the lilies of the field, how they grow

FOOD

Genesis 1:29   Seed bearing trees given to humans for food
Genesis 2:9   God made food pleasing to the eye
Genesis 2:16-17   First humans were given all but one tree for nourishment
Genesis 3:18   You shall eat the plants of the field
Leviticus 7:1-6   Prohibitions in the eating of meat
Leviticus 7:22-27   Prohibition of eating certain meats
Leviticus 11:1-3   The clean animals which can be eaten
Leviticus 11:4-8   List of the unclean animals
Leviticus 11:9   The edible fish
Leviticus 11:10-19   Animals which may not be eaten

Deuteronomy 24:19-21　Leave some of the harvest for the poor
Deuteronomy 28:38-39　Locusts and worms will eat your harvest
2 Chronicles 31:5　Israel gave first fruits of grain, wine, oil, honey
Jeremiah 2:2　In a land not sown
Joel 3:13　Put in the sickle for the harvest is ripe
Amos 9:13-15　A bountiful harvest lies ahead

HOLY

Exodus 3:5　Remove your sandals, you are on holy ground
Exodus 20:8　Remember the sabbath and keep it holy
Leviticus 11:44　Be holy—don't defile yourselves with creatures of the earth
Leviticus 19:1-3　You shall be holy—keep God's sabbaths
Joshua 5:15　Remove your sandals, this place is holy
Psalm 24:3　Who shall stand in his holy place?
Zechariah 8:3　The Lord's mountain is called the holy mountain
Acts 7:33　Take off your sandals, you are on holy ground
1 Corinthians 3:17　God's temple is holy and you are that temple
Revelation 21:2　I saw the holy city, coming down out of heaven
Revelation 21:10　From a high mountain he showed me the holy city

HOME

Leviticus 27:14-15　Blessings on home and fields
Isaiah 5:8　You who join house to house until there is room for no one
Ezekiel 28:26　Israel shall live safely and build houses
Acts 7:48　The Most High does not dwell in human houses
Revelation 21:3　See, the home of God is among mortals

HUMANS

Genesis 1:26　Humankind is created in the image of God
Genesis 1:27　God created humans as both male and female
Genesis 2:7　The Lord formed man from the dust of ground
Genesis 2:8　God put man in the garden
Genesis 2:15　A charge to humans to till and keep creation
Genesis 2:21-22　The formation of woman
Genesis 3:1-7　Human disobedience in the garden
Genesis 3:17-19　Cursed is the ground because of human disobedience
Genesis 3:22-23　Adam and Eve are expelled from the garden
Genesis 9:6b　God made humankind in his own image
Genesis 11:9　The Lord scatters people across the earth
Deuteronomy 4:32　God created humans on the earth
Job 7:17　What are human beings?
Job 8:9　Our days on earth are but a shadow
Job 9:2-3　A comparison between God and mortals
Job 35:10-11　God teaches humans more than the animals
Psalm 8:4　What are humans that you are mindful of them?
Psalm 8:6-8　You gave humans dominion over your works
Psalm 115:16　The earth God has given to humans
Psalm 144:3-4　What are humans that you regard them?
Ecclesiastes 6:1-7　An evil lies heavy upon humankind
Romans 14:7-8　We do not live for ourselves, but for the Lord
1 Corinthians 2:11　What human knows what is truly human
1 Corinthians 3:16　You are God's temple and God's Spirit dwells in you
1 Corinthians 12:14　We are many members of one body
Galatians 1:11　The gospel is not of human origin
Philippians 2:5-8　Christ was born in human likeness
Hebrews 2:6-8　What are humans that you are mindful of them?
Hebrews 2:17-18　Jesus became like his fellow humans in all ways

INSECTS

Exodus 8:16-17　The third plague: the attack of the gnats
Leviticus 11:20-23　Edible and inedible insects

Deuteronomy 14:19　Winged insects are unclean and shall not be eaten
2 Chronicles 6:28-31　If there is famine, or locusts or caterpillars
Psalm 78:45　He sent swarms of flies which devoured them
Psalm 78:46　God gave their crops to the caterpillars
Psalm 105:31, 34-35　God spoke and there came swarms of flies and locusts
Proverbs 6:6-8　Go to the ants, consider their ways and be wise
Proverbs 30:24-25　The ants are a people without strength
Proverbs 30:27　The locusts are exceedingly wise
Isaiah 7:18-19　The Lord shall gather the insects
Amos 4:9　The locusts devoured your figs and olive trees
Amos 7:1-2　The Lord forms grasshoppers to eat the grass
Malachi 3:11　God will rebuke the locust so your soil will bear produce
Revelation 9:3-4　From the smoke came locusts upon earth

JUDGE / JUDGMENT

1 Chronicles 16:14　The Lord's judgments are in all the earth
Psalm 9:8　The Lord judges the world with righteousness
Psalm 58:11　Surely there is a God who judges on the earth
Psalm 82:8　Rise up, O God, judge the earth
Proverbs 31:9　Speak out, judge wisely, and defend the poor
Isaiah 3:14　The Lord enters into judgment with the princes
Isaiah 11:3-5　The Lord shall judge the earth
Isaiah 14:20　You who destroy the land will be cast out
Isaiah 18:3-6　When the trumpet blows, all will be left for birds
Isaiah 26:9　When God's judgments are in earth, people learn
Isaiah 26:21　The Lord comes to punish the inhabitants of earth
Isaiah 66:16　By fire will the Lord execute judgment on all flesh
Jeremiah 21:14　God wil kindle a fire in its forest
Ezekiel 7:27　People of the land shall tremble—God will judge them
Ezekiel 30:19　God will execute acts of judgment on Egypt
Ezekiel 34:17　God will judge between the sheep and the goats
Ezekiel 34:22　God will judge between sheep and sheep
Joel 3:2　God will judge the nations; they have divided God's land
Nahum 2:13　The judgments of the Lord in the earth
Zechariah 7:9-10　Render true judgments, show kindness, mercy
Matthew 7:1-2　Judge not, and you will not be judged
Luke 6:37　Do not judge and you will not be judged
John 12:31-32　Now is the judgment of this world
John 12:47　Jesus came not to judge the world but to save the world
Acts 17:30-31　There is a day for the judgment of the world
Romans 2:1　You have no excuse when you judge others
Romans 9:28　The Lord brings his sentence upon earth quickly
Romans 14:13　Let us not pass judgment on one another
1 Corinthians 4:5　Do not pronounce judgment before the time
1 Corinthians 5:13　God will judge those on the outside
1 Corinthians 6:2a　The saints will judge the world
1 Corinthians 11:32　When we are judged by the Lord, we are disciplined
2 Corinthians 5:10　All of us must appear before judgment seat of Christ
2 Thessalonians 1:5　This is evidence of the judgment of God
Hebrews 4:12　God's word judges the thoughts of the heart
1 Peter 1:17　God judges people according to their deeds
1 Peter 4:17　Judgment begins with the household of God
2 Peter 2:4-9　Lord keeps the unrighteous under punishment
Revelation 19:1-2　He judged the whore who corrupted the earth
Revelation 20:12　The dead are judged according to their works

JUSTICE

Deuteronomy 10:17-19　God executes justice over all
Deuteronomy 16:19-20　Pursue justice so you may live in the land
Job 34:12-13　The Almighty will not pervert justice
Psalm 37:28　The Lord loves justice

Luke 21:25 Signs will appear in the sun, moon and stars
Revelation 21:23 The city has no need for sun or moon

MOUNTAIN

Exodus 19:3-5 The Lord called to Moses from the mountain
Exodus 19:11 The Lord will come down upon the mountain
Exodus 19:17 People gathered to meet God at the foot of the mountain
Exodus 19:20 The Lord spoke to Moses at the top of the mountain
Exodus 19:23 Set limits around the mountain and keep it holy
Exodus 20:18 The Lord speaks to his people from the mountain
Exodus 34:2 The Lord calls Moses to the top of Mt. Sinai
Deuteronomy 5:4 The Lord spoke with you at the mountain
Deuteronomy 5:22-23 The Lord spoke from the mountain
Deuteronomy 27:4-8 Build an altar of unhewn stones on the mountain
Deuteronomy 32:49 The Lord calls Moses to the mountain top
Deuteronomy 34:1 Moses is called by God to the top of Mount Pisgah
1 Kings 19:11 Stand on the mountain before the Lord
1 Kings 20:28 The Lord is a god of the hills, not the valleys
Psalm 48:1-2 God's holy mountain is the joy of the earth
Psalm 65:6 God's strength established the mountains
Psalm 72:3 May the mountains yield prosperity for the people
Psalm 74:2b Remember Mount Zion where you came to dwell
Psalm 76:4 God is more majestic than the mountains
Psalm 80:10 The mountains were covered by mighty cedars
Psalm 90:2 Before the mountains were, you are God
Psalm 95:4 The mountains are God's
Psalm 97:5 Mountains melt like wax before the Lord
Psalm 99:9 Extol the Lord, worship at his holy mountain
Psalm 104:18 The high mountains are for the wild goats
Isaiah 5:25 The mountains quaked at the anger of the Lord
Isaiah 7:24-25 The hills will become a place where cattle graze
Isaiah 25:10 The Lord's hand will rest on this mountain
Isaiah 27:13 Worship the Lord on the holy mountain at Jerusalem
Isaiah 37:24 They have gone to the mountains and cut cedars
Isaiah 40:4 Every mountain and hill shall be made low
Isaiah 44:23 Break forth into singing, O mountains
Isaiah 49:11 God will turn mountains into a road
Isaiah 52:7 How beautiful upon the mountains
Isaiah 55:12 The mountains and hills shall burst into song
Isaiah 64:1 The mountains would quake at your presence
Jeremiah 9:10 Weep for the mountains, they are laid waste
Ezekiel 6:2-3 What the Lord God says to the mountains
Ezekiel 35:7 God will make Mount Seir a waste and desolation
Ezekiel 36:1 Prophesy to the mountains of Israel
Ezekiel 36:8 Mountains of Israel: yield your fruit to God's people
Joel 3:18 In that day the mountains shall drip sweet wine
Amos 4:13 He who formed mountains reveals his thoughts
Micah 1:4 The mountains melt at God's presence
Micah 6:1-2 Let the mountains hear your voice
Nahum 1:5 The mountains quake before the Lord
Nahum 1:15 On the mountains the feet of the one who brings tidings
Haggai 1:11 God brings drought upon the hills
Matthew 4:8 On a high mountain Jesus saw the world's kingdoms
Matthew 14:23 Jesus went up the mountain to pray alone
Matthew 15:29-31 On a mountain Jesus cures the sick
Matthew 17:1-8 Jesus is transfigured on a mountain
Mark 3:13-14 He went to a mountain and appointed twelve apostles
Mark 6:46 Jesus went up to the mountain to pray
Mark 9:2 Jesus is transfigured on a high mountain
Luke 3:5 Every valley will be filled, every mountain made low
Luke 6:12, 9:28 Jesus went out to a mountain to pray

John 6:3 Jesus went up the mountain and sat with disciples
John 6:15 Jesus withdrew to the mountain by himself
Revelation 6:14 I saw every mountain was moved from its place
Revelation 16:20 Every island disappears, the mountains are gone

NATION

Deuteronomy 8:19-20 Do not forget God or your nation will perish
Deuteronomy 9:5 Wickedness causes a nation to fall
Deuteronomy 15:6 Lend to many nations, but do not borrow
Psalm 2:8 God will make the nations your heritage
Psalm 22:28 The Lord rules over the nations
Psalm 33:12 Happy is the nation whose God is the Lord
Psalm 67:4 God guides the nations upon the earth
Proverbs 11:14 Where there is no guidance, a nation falls
Isaiah 2:4 God shall judge between the nations
Isaiah 19:2 God will stir up city against city, nation against nation
Isaiah 40:15 Even nations are like a drop from a bucket
Ezekiel 37:22 God will make them one nation in the land
Matthew 24:7-8 Nation will rise against nation
Matthew 28:19 Make disciples of all nations
Mark 13:8 Nation will rise against nation
Luke 12:30 The nations of the world seek after these things
Luke 21:10 Nation will rise against nation
Acts 17:26 From one ancestor God populated all nations
1 Peter 2:9 You are chosen race, a holy nation, God's people
Revelation 15:4 All the nations will come and worship God
Revelation 21:24 The nations will walk by the city's light
Revelation 22:2b The Tree's leaves are for the healing of nations

NEW EARTH/NEW CREATION

Isaiah 35:1-2, 6 The return of the redeemed to Zion
Isaiah 65:17-25; 66:22 God will create new heavens and a new earth
Romans 8:19-23 The creation waits with eager longing
2 Corinthians 5:17 If anyone is in Christ, that person is a new creation
Galatians 6:15 A new creation is everything
2 Peter 3:13 We await new heavens and a new earth
Revelation 21:1-8 Then I saw a new heaven and a new earth

OBEDIENCE

Exodus 19:5 All the earth is God's—you shall be obedient
Leviticus 25:18-19 Obedience to God brings fruitfulness to land
Leviticus 26:3-6, 9 Obedience brings God's blessing
Numbers 18:13 The fruits of the land go to the obedient (clean)
Deuteronomy 4:5-6 Heed the statutes in the land
Deuteronomy 5:16 Honor your parents that it may go well with you in the land
Deuteronomy 5:31 Fulfill the commands of God in the land
Deuteronomy 5:33 If you obey, you will live long in the land
Deuteronomy 6:1-3 Obey the Lord in the land
Deuteronomy 6:18 Do what is right to maintain the good land
Deuteronomy 7:12-13 Heed God's law and the land will prosper
Deuteronomy 8:1-2 Recall the lessons of obedience in the wilderness
Deuteronomy 11:8-10 Keep the law of God and land will flourish
Deuteronomy 11:13-15 As you occupy the land, observe God's statutes
Deuteronomy 12:1 Observe God's statutes in the land
Deuteronomy 16:19-20 Pursue justice and you will live fruitfully
Deuteronomy 18:9-13 Do not allow occult practices in the Lord's land
Deuteronomy 19:8-10 Love God and the Lord will increase your land
Deuteronomy 28:1, 9-12 Obedience to the Lord brings abundance
Deuteronomy 30:8-10, 16 When you obey, the Lord will make you fruitful in the land
Psalm 37:29 The righteous inherit the land and live in it forever

Psalm 85:10-13   Love, faithfulness, peace bring harmony to land
Proverbs 2:21-22   The upright will abide in the land
Isaiah 1:19   If you are obedient, you will eat of the good land
Mark 1:27   Even the unclean spirits obey Jesus
Acts 5:29   We must obey God rather than human authority
1 Corinthians 7:19   Obeying the commandments of God is everything
2 Corinthians 9:13   You glorify God by your obedience
Philippians 2:7-8   Jesus was obedient unto death
Hebrews 5:8-9   Jesus learned obedience through what he suffered
1 Peter 1:22   You purified your souls by obedience to the truth
1 John 2:3   We know him if we obey his commandments
1 John 3:24   All who obey his commandments abide in him

PEACE

Psalm 85:10-12   Love, faithfulness, peace bring harmony to land
Isaiah 32:18   God's people will abide in a peaceful habitation
Isaiah 57:21   There is no peace for the wicked, says the Lord
Isaiah 59:8   They do not know the way of peace
Jeremiah 14:13   I will give you true peace in this place
Jeremiah 16:5   God took away peace from this place
Ezekiel 34:25   God will make a covenant of peace with them
Zechariah 1:11   The whole earth remained at peace
Luke 2:14   On earth, peace and goodwill among people
Luke 10:5-6   Whatever house you enter, say 'Peace to this house'
Luke 24:36   Jesus stood and said, Peace be with you
John 14:27   Jesus said, Peace I leave with you, my peace I give to you
John 20:19-23   Jesus said, Peace be with you
John 20:26   Jesus comes again and says, Peace be with you
Romans 12:18   As far as you are able, live peaceably with all
1 Corinthians 7:15b   God has called you to peace
1 Corinthians 14:33   God is not a god of disorder but of peace
2 Corinthians 13:11   Live in peace, and peace will be with you
Galatians 5:22-23   The fruit of the spirit is love, joy, peace, patience
Ephesians 2:17   Jesus came and proclaimed peace to you
Philippians 4:7   The peace of God will guard your hearts and minds
1 Thessalonians 5:13b   Be at peace among yourselves
Hebrews 12:14   Pursue peace with everyone and holiness
Revelation 6:4   I saw a red horse take peace from the earth

PEOPLE

Genesis 11:9   The Lord scattered people across the earth
Exodus 3:7-8   God came down to deliver his people into a good land
Deuteronomy 26:15   Invocation to bless the people and the land
Joshua 1:6   Put the people in possession of the land
2 Samuel 7:8-9   The Lord has been with the people
2 Chronicles 21:12-14   A great plague on your people
Ezra 9:10-12   A land unclean from the pollution of the people
Job 12:24   God causes people to wander in wilderness
Psalm 72:3   May the mountains yield prosperity for the people
Psalm 95:7   We are the people of God's pasture
Psalm 105:24   The Lord made his people very fruitful
Psalm 148:11-14   All peoples, praise the name of the Lord
Isaiah 8:19-22   Misled people see only distress on the earth
Isaiah 26:9   When God's judgments are in earth, people learn
Isaiah 26:10   If favor is shown to the wicked, they do not learn
Isaiah 32:18   God's people will dwell in peace and security
Isaiah 40:6-8   All people are as grass, like a flower in the field
Isaiah 42:5   The Lord gives breath to the people on earth
Isaiah 45:12   God made the earth and humankind upon it
Isaiah 49:19-20   You will be too crowded for your inhabitants
Isaiah 60:21   Your people shall possess the land forever

Isaiah 65:22   God's peoples' days shall be like the days of a tree
Jeremiah 6:19   Hear, O earth, I will bring disaster on this people
Jeremiah 8:6-7   The creatures know God's law, but not people
Jeremiah 8:19   Harken to the cry of poor people in the land
Ezekiel 20:34-35   God will bring you into wilderness of the peoples
Ezekiel 33:30-32   My people hear your words, but they do not obey
Ezekiel 36:20   The people of Israel were forced from their land
Ezekiel 36:28-31   God will restore people and creation together
Ezekiel 43:7   God will reside among the people of Israel forever
Hosea 4:1   Indictment against the inhabitants of the land
Habbakuk 1:14   You have made people like fish of the sea
Matthew 10:30-31   You are more valuable than many sparrows
Mark 1:17   Jesus said, I will make you fish for people
Luke 2:14   On earth, peace and goodwill among people
John 3:19   But people loved darkness rather than light
Acts 10:34-35   Anyone who fears God and does what is right is acceptable
Acts 17:25   The Lord gives all mortals life and breath
Acts 18:10   Many in this city are my people, said the Lord
Acts 26:23   Jesus would proclaim light to our people
Hebrews 4:9   A sabbath rest remains for God's people
1 Peter 2:9-10   You are chosen race, a holy nation, God's people
Revelation 3:10   A trial is coming to the whole earth to test people
Revelation 21:3   See, the home of God is among people

PLACES

Deuteronomy 12:10-11   The place the Lord will choose to dwell
Joshua 5:15   Remove your sandals, this place is holy
Jeremiah 33:12   This place of waste shall again be pasture
Ezekiel 26:20   A place in the land of the living
Ezekiel 37:27   God's dwelling place shall be with them
Matthew 14:13   Jesus withdrew by himself to a deserted place
Mark 1:35   Jesus went out to a deserted place
Mark 6:31-32   Come away to a deserted place and rest awhile
Luke 4:42   Jesus departed and went to a deserted place
Luke 5:16   Jesus withdrew to a deserted place to pray
Acts 7:33   The place where you are standing is holy ground

PLAGUE

Exodus 7:16   The first plague: water turned to blood
Exodus 8:1-6   The second plague: frogs
Exodus 8:16   The third plague: gnats
Exodus 8:20-24   The fourth plague: flies
Exodus 9:1-6   The fifth plague: livestock diseased
Exodus 9:8-10   The sixth plague: boils
Exodus 9:13-16   God will send all plagues upon Pharaoh
Exodus 9:18-19, 22-26   The seventh plague: thunder and hail
Exodus 10:4-5, 12-15   The eighth plague: locusts
Exodus 10:21-22   The ninth plague: darkness
Exodus 11:4-5; 12:29   The final plague: every firstborn will die
2 Samuel 24:15   The Lord sends a pestilence upon Israel
2 Samuel 24:25   The Lord averts the plague on Israel
1 Kings 8:37-40   When there is famine or plague
1 Chronicles 21:11-17   A choice of pestilence or devastation
2 Chronicles 6:28   If there is famine in the land or blight or plague
Psalm 105:36   God struck down the firstborn in the plague
Psalm 106:29-30   They provoked the Lord and a plague broke out
Zechariah 14:12   A plague will strike all the people
Luke 21:11   There will be famines and plagues
Revelation 6:8   A green horse brings pestilence and death to earth
Revelation 15:1   I saw seven angels with seven plagues
Revelation 16:1   Seven angels pour seven plagues upon the earth

Revelation 16:21   People cursed God for the plague of hail stones

PLANTS

Genesis 1:11-12   The creation of plants and vegetation
Genesis 3:18   You shall eat the plants of the field
Exodus 3:2-4   God speaks to Moses out of a burning bush
Job 12:8   Ask the plants and they will teach you
Joel 1:7   Locusts have devastated my vines and figs
Amos 4:9   The Lord laid waste your gardens
Luke 12:27-28   Consider the lilies, how they grow
Acts 7:30   An angel appeared in the flame of a burning bush

POLLUTION

Numbers 35:33-34   You shall not pollute the land
2 Kings 2:19-22   Elisha heals the polluted waters with salt
Ezra 9:10-12   A land unclean from the pollution of the people
Isaiah 24:5   The earth is polluted for they broke the covenant
Jeremiah 3:1   Such a land would be greatly polluted
Jeremiah 3:2   You have polluted the land with your wickedness
Jeremiah 3:9   Israel polluted the land
Jeremiah 4:20   Disaster upon disaster, the land is laid waste
Jeremiah 4:27   The whole land shall be a desolation
Jeremiah 12:11   The land is made desolate, but its pain is not felt
Jeremiah 16:18   They have polluted my land with abominations
Jeremiah 18:15-16   When you forget God, you make the land a horror
Malachi 1:6-7   You have offered polluted bread on the Lord's altar

POOR

Exodus 23:11   Let your land rest so poor may eat
Leviticus 19:10   You shall leave some for the poor
Deuteronomy 15:11   Open your hand to the poor in your land
Deuteronomy 24:19-21   Leave some of the harvest for the poor
2 Kings 4:42-44   First fruits feed the hungry
Psalm 72:12-13   He delivers the poor
Psalm 82:3-4   Maintain the right of the lowly
Psalm 140:12   The Lord executes justice for the poor
Psalm 146:7   Who gives food to the hungry
Proverbs 14:31   Those who oppress the poor
Proverbs 19:17   Whoever is kind to the poor lends to the Lord
Proverbs 29:7   The righteous know the rights of the poor
Proverbs 31:9   Defend the rights of the poor
Isaiah 3:15   What do you mean by grinding the face of the poor?
Isaiah 41:18-20   The blessings of God for the poor and needy
Isaiah 58:7-9   Bring the homeless poor into your house
Jeremiah 8:19   Harken to the cry of poor people in the land
Ezekiel 22:29-31   The people in the land oppressed the poor
Amos 2:7-9   God destroyed their fruit for they trampled the poor
Amos 8:4   If you trample on the needy and bring to ruin the poor of the land
Matthew 19:21   Give the money to the poor
Matthew 25:40   Just as you did it to one of the least of these
Mark 12:41-44   The poor widow gave two coins to the temple
Luke 4:18   Jesus came to bring good news to the poor
Luke 12:33   Sell your possessions and give alms
2 Corinthians 9:8-9   God gives to the poor
Galatians 2:10   They asked that I remember the poor
James 2:5-6a   You have dishonored the poor
1 John 3:17-18   A brother or sister in need and does not help

POWER

Job 26:7-14   God's power over the world
Ecclesiastes 8:8   No one has power to restrain the wind

Isaiah 40:29   The Lord gives power to the faint
Jeremiah 10:12; 27:5   God made the earth by his power and wisdom
Matthew 24:29   The powers of heaven will be shaken
Matthew 24:30   Son of Man will come with power
Luke 9:1   Jesus gave them power and authority over diseases
Luke 21:27   The Son of Man will come with power
John 1:12-13   To those who received him, he gave power
Acts 2:22   Jesus, a man attested to by God, by power
Romans 1:20   God's power is revealed thru what He has made
2 Corinthians 4:7   This extraordinary power belongs to God, not us
2 Corinthians 12:9   I boast of weakness that Christ's power dwell in me
Ephesians 1:20   God put his power to work in Christ
Ephesians 3:20   To him whose power is at work within us be glory
Philippians 3:21   Christ's power makes all things subject to him
Hebrews 1:3   The Son sustains all things by his powerful word
2 Peter 1:3   God's divine power gives us everything needed for life
Revelation 4:11   Our Lord is worthy to receive glory and power

PRAYER

Exodus 8:8-13   Pharaoh asks for prayer about the plague of frogs
Exodus 8:28-31   Pharaoh asks for prayer about the plague of flies
Exodus 9:28-29, 33   Pharaoh asks for prayer about the seventh plague
Exodus 10:17-19   Pharaoh asks for prayer about the eighth plague
Numbers 21:6-7   Prayer for the deliverance from snakes
2 Samuel 1:21   David's prayer for no rain to fall on Mt. Gilboa
1 Kings 8:37-40   Prayer if there is famine in the land
2 Kings 20:5   Prayer for the healing of the body
Matthew 14:23   Jesus went up the mountain to pray alone
Luke 5:16   Jesus withdrew to a deserted place to pray
Luke 6:12   Jesus went out to a mountain to pray
Luke 9:28-29   Jesus went up on the mountain to pray
Luke 11:1   Lord, teach us to pray
James 5:17-18   Pray for rain and also the ending of rain

PROPERTY

Deuteronomy 4:1   Possess the land according to God's command
Deuteronomy 5:21   Do not desire your neighbor's property
Deuteronomy 9:23   Occupy the land that God has given you
Deuteronomy 10:11   The Lord said, occupy the land
Deuteronomy 19:14   You may not remove neighbor's landmark
Joshua 1:6   Put the people in possession of the land
1 Chronicles 28:8   Possess the land and leave it for an inheritance
Luke 12:44   God will put that one [steward] over his possessions

RAIN

Genesis 2:5   God makes plants before the first rain
Genesis 8:1-5   The flood rains cease
Leviticus 26:3-4   Obedience brings the rain in its season
Deuteronomy 11:13-15   Obedience brings rains and green hills
Deuteronomy 28:24   The Lord will change the rain into powder
1 Kings 8:35-36   When there is no rain because of sin
1 Kings 18:1   God will send rain on the earth
2 Chronicles 6:26-27   When there is no rain because they have sinned
Job 36:27-28   God draws up the waters and distills it in rain
Job 38:28-30   Has the rain a father?
Psalm 104:13   God waters the mountains
Psalm 148:8   God prepares rain for the earth
Isaiah 30:23   The Lord will give rain for the seed you sow
Jeremiah 5:24   The Lord gives rain in its season
Joel 2:23   Rejoice in the Lord for he pours down rain
Amos 4:7-8   God withheld the rain for three months

Zechariah 10:1   The Lord gives showers of rain
Acts 14:16-17   God provides rain, fruitful seasons and food

RENEW / RESTORE

Psalm 104:30   The Lord renews the face of the ground
Isaiah 35:5-7   The renewal of the earth and the creatures
Ezekiel 36:28-30   God restores people and creation together
Ezekiel 36:33-36   As people are restored, the land is also restored
Acts 3:19-21   Until the time of universal restoration
Romans 8:22-23   The whole creation awaits its renewal
2 Corinthians 5:17   If anyone is in Christ, that person is a new creation
Philippians 3:21   Christ will transform our humble bodies
Revelation 21:5a   See I am making all things new

RIVER

Genesis 2:10   A river flows out of Eden to water the garden
Exodus 7:17-19   Polluted river was a plague of Egypt
Psalm 65:9   The river of God is full of water
Psalm 74:15   God cut openings for springs and torrents
Psalm 104:12   By the streams the birds have their habitation
Isaiah 19:5-8   The waters of the Nile will be dried up
Isaiah 33:21   A place of broad rivers and streams
Isaiah 50:2   By God's rebuke, he makes the rivers a desert
Ezekiel 29:8-9   The river in Egypt is mine, says the Lord
Ezekiel 47:7-9   Trees make for clean water and fish in the river
Joel 1:19-20   The wild animals cry because the streams are dry
Nahum 1:4   The Lord rebukes the sea and dries the rivers
Revelation 22:1   The angel showed me the river of the water of life

SABBATH

Genesis 2:2-3   God blessed the seventh day and sanctifies it
Exodus 20:8-11   Remember the sabbath and keep it holy
Exodus 23:10-12   Let the land rest and your oxen and donkey too
Exodus 31:12-17   Declaration of the sabbath
Exodus 34:21   On the seventh day you shall rest
Exodus 35:2   Have a holy sabbath of rest to the Lord
Leviticus 19:3   The Lord said, "Keep my sabbaths"
Leviticus 23:3   The sabbath is a day of rest
Leviticus 25:2-7   A sabbath year for the land
Leviticus 25:8-12   You shall count off seven weeks/sabbaths
Leviticus 26:43   The land shall enjoy its sabbath years
Deuteronomy 5:12-14   Keep holy the sabbath; do no work on that day
Nehemiah 13:15-18, 22   Profaning the sabbath
Isaiah 56:2   Happy is the one who keeps the sabbath
Isaiah 56:6-7   To God's holy mountain God will bring the sabbath keepers
Isaiah 58:13-14   Refrain from trampling the sabbath
Jeremiah 17:21, 24-27   Do not bear a burden on the sabbath
Ezekiel 20:12   God gave them sabbaths as a sign
Matthew 12:9-12   Jesus teaches about doing good on the sabbath
Mark 2:23-27   The Son of Man is Lord even of the sabbath
Mark 3:4   Jesus teaches about the sabbath
Luke 6:1-5   The Son of Man is lord of the sabbath
Luke 6:6-10   Jesus teaches about doing good on the sabbath
Luke 14:3-5   Jesus teaches about the sabbath
John 5:9-19   Jesus heals the crippled man on the sabbath
Colossians 2:16   No condemnation over food and drink or sabbaths
Hebrews 4:9   A sabbath rest remains for God's people

SEAS

Genesis 1:9-10   The Third Day: the waters become the seas
1 Chronicles 16:32   Let the seas roar, let the fields exult

Job 38:8-11   Who shut in the sea with doors?
Psalm 24:2   God has founded the earth on the seas
Psalm 66:6   God turned the sea into dry land
Psalm 74:13   God divided the sea by his might
Psalm 78:13   God divided the sea and made the waters stand
Psalm 89:9   God rules the raging of the sea
Psalm 95:4-5   The mountains and seas are formed by God's hand
Psalm 104:25-26   In wisdom, God made the sea
Ecclesiastes 1:7   All streams run to the sea, but the sea is not full
Jeremiah 5:22   God placed the sand as a boundary for the sea
Jonah 1:9   The Lord made the sea and the land
Nahum 1:4   The Lord rebukes the sea and dries the rivers
Matthew 8:26-27   Jesus rebuked the wind and sea and calm returned
Mark 4:39-41   Even the wind and the sea obey Jesus
Mark 6:48-51   Jesus walks on the rough sea
Luke 8:24-25   Jesus commands the winds and the water
John 6:18-19   Jesus walks on the rough sea
Acts 4:24   The Lord made heaven and earth and the seas
Revelation 7:2-3   God's angel said, Damage not the earth or seas
Revelation 8:8   A mountain, burning with fire, falls into the sea
Revelation 8:9   A third of all the living creatures in the sea died
Revelation 12:12   The heavens rejoice, but woe to earth and seas

SEASONS

Genesis 8:22   Cold and heat, summer and winter will not cease
Psalm 74:17   God made summer and winter
Psalm 104:19   God made the moon to mark the seasons
Ecclesiastes 3:1   For every thing, there is a season and a time
Jeremiah 5:24   God gives the rain in its season
Zechariah 10:1   Ask rain from the Lord in the season of spring
Acts 14:16-17   God provides rain, fruitful seasons and food

SEEDS

Genesis 1:11-12   The earth brings forth grass and seeds
Genesis 1:29   God provides seeds and herbs as sustenance
Deuteronomy 14:22   Tithe of all the yield of your seed
Deuteronomy 22:9   Plant one type of seed at a time, no mixing
Isaiah 30:23   The Lord will give rain for the seed you sow
Jeremiah 12:13   They have sown wheat and reaped thorns
2 Corinthians 9:10   He supplies seed to the sower and bread for food

SKY

Genesis 1:7-8   God created and named the sky
Deuteronomy 4:19   When you look to the sky, do not worship the creation
Job 37:18   Can you, like God, spread out the skies?
Psalm 78:23   God commanded the skies above
Isaiah 45:8   Let the skies rain down righteousness
Revelation 6:14   The sky vanished like a scroll rolled up

SOIL

Ezekiel 34:27   You will enjoy security on your own soil
Ezekiel 36:17   When Israel lived on its own soil, they defiled it
Ezekiel 37:14   God will set you on your soil
Joel 2:21   O soil, rejoice and be glad for the Lord
Malachi 3:11-12   God will rebuke the locust so your soil will bear produce

STARS

Genesis 1:14-18   The 4th Day: creation of sun, moon and stars
Deuteronomy 4:19   Worship not the sun, moon or stars
Job 9:7-9   Who seals up the stars?
Job 38:31   Can you bind the chains of the Pleiades?

Psalm 136:9   The moon and stars to rule over the night
Psalm 147:4   The Lord determines the number of stars
Psalm 148:3   Praise God sun and moon and shining stars
Isaiah 13:9-10   In the day of the Lord, the stars will not give light
Jeremiah 31:35   The sun for day; the moon and stars for night
Joel 2:10   The sun and moon are darkened, the stars too
Amos 5:8-9   The maker of the Pleiades turns darkness to light
Matthew 2:9-10   A star in the heavens went ahead of them
Matthew 24:29   After those days the stars will fall from heaven
Mark 13:24-25   Tribulations of the sun, moon and stars
Luke 21:25   Signs will appear in the sun, moon and stars
1 Corinthians 15:41   A glory of the sun, another of the moon and stars
Revelation 8:10-11   A great star fell from heaven
Revelation 9:1   A star had fallen from heaven to earth

STEWARDS/ STEWARDSHIP

Genesis 1:26, 28   The origin of stewardship
Genesis 2:15   God put man in the garden to till and keep it
Ezekiel 34:1-5   Failure of the shepherds to care for sheep
Matthew 24:45-46   Who is the faithful and wise slave [steward]?
Mark 9:35   Be last of all and servant of all
Mark 10:45   Son of Man came to serve
Luke 12:42-44   Who then is the faithful and prudent manager [steward]?
Luke 16:10-11   Whoever is faithful in little is faithful in much
1 Corinthians 4:1   We are stewards of the mysteries of God

STONES

Genesis 2:11-12   The land contains minerals and precious stones
Exodus 20:25   Build an altar of unhewn stone for the Lord
Numbers 20:8-11   Moses told to command the rock to yield water
Deuteronomy 16:21   Do not build a stone pillar for worship
Deuteronomy 27:2-4, 8   Write on the stones the words of God's law
Deuteronomy 27:5-7   Build an altar of unhewn stones on the mountain
Joshua 4:2-7   The Lord commands a twelve stone memorial
Joshua 24:27   This stone shall be a witness
Psalm 78:15-16   God made streams come out of rocks
Acts 17:29   God is not like gold, silver or stone

STORM

Exodus 9:18-19, 22-26   The seventh plague: thunder and hail
Job 36:30-33   God scatters his lightning around him
Job 37:15   Do you know how God causes the lightning?
Job 38:1; 40:6   God answers Job out of a whirlwind
Job 38:35   Can you send forth lightning?
Nahum 1:3   God's way is in whirlwind and storm
Matthew 8:24-27   Jesus rebuked the wind and sea and calm returned
Mark 4:37-40   Jesus stills a storm
Luke 8:22-25   Jesus calms the wind and storm on the lake

SUN

Genesis 1:14-18   The creation of the sun, moon and stars
Deuteronomy 4:19   Worship not the sun, moon or stars
Psalm 50:1   From sun rise to setting, God summons the earth
Psalm 136:8   Give thanks to God, who gives the sun
Psalm 148:3   Praise God, sun and moon and shining stars
Ecclesiastes 1:5   The way of the sun
Isaiah 24:23   The sun will be ashamed
Joel 2:10   The sun and moon are darkened, the stars too
Matthew 5:45   God makes his sun on the good and the evil
Matthew 24:29   After those days the sun will be darkened
Mark 13:24   After that suffering, the sun will be darkened

Luke 21:25   Signs will appear in the sun, moon and stars
Luke 23:45   The sun's light failed at the death of Jesus
1 Corinthians 15:41   A glory of the sun, another of the moon and stars
Revelation 21:23   The city has no need for sun or moon

TITHING

Exodus 34:26   Give to God the first fruits of your ground
Leviticus 23:10   The first fruits are for the Lord
Leviticus 27:30   The tithe of the land belongs to the Lord
Deuteronomy 12:17   You may not eat the tithe of your grain
Deuteronomy 14:22   Tithe the increase of seed from the field
Deuteronomy 14:23   Tithe to learn to fear the Lord
Deuteronomy 14:28-29   Share your tithe with widows and orphans
Deuteronomy 26:1-2   The first fruits belong to the Lord
2 Kings 4:42-44   The first fruits of barley and grain feed the hungry
2 Chronicles 31:5   Israel gave first fruits as a tithe
Nehemiah 10:35   The first fruits are for the Lord's House
Proverbs 3:9   Honor the Lord with the first fruits of produce
Malachi 3:10   Bring the full tithe into the storehouse

TREES

Genesis 1:11-12; 2:9   The creation of trees
Genesis 2:17   Man told not to eat from the tree
Genesis 3:22   Access to the tree of life restricted
Leviticus 19:23-25   No eating fruit from trees under three years
Leviticus 26:20   Disobedience causes the trees to be unfruitful
Deuteronomy 8:7-8   The Lord will bring you to a good land with trees
Deuteronomy 20:19-20   Even in war, do not destroy the food trees
Deuteronomy 24:20   Do not strip what is left on your trees
1 Chronicles 16:33   The trees of the forest sing for joy
Job 14:7-9   Hope for a cut tree that it will sprout again
Psalm 96:12   All the trees of the forest sing for joy
Psalm 104:16   The trees of the Lord are watered abundantly
Psalm 104:17   The stork has his home in the fir trees
Psalm 105:33   God struck their vines and fig trees
Psalm 148:9   Fruit trees and cedars praise the Lord
Isaiah 41:19   God will put cedars and acacia, myrtle and pine in wilderness
Isaiah 55:12   The trees of the field shall clap their hands
Isaiah 55:13   The cypress tree shall replace the thorn
Jeremiah 7:20   God's anger will pour on people, animals and trees
Ezekiel 34:27   The trees will yield their fruit
Ezekiel 47:12   The leaves of the trees are for healing
Joel 1:12   The trees dry up and with them joy withers away
Joel 1:19   Fire has burned the trees, the streams are dry
Joel 2:22   The pastures grow green, the trees bear fruit
Amos 4:9   The locusts devoured trees because of disobedience
Habakkuk 3:17-18   Though trees fail to fruit I will rejoice in the Lord
Acts 5:30   Jesus whom you hung on a tree
Acts 10:39   They put Jesus to death by hanging on a tree
Acts 13:29   They took him down from the tree
Galatians 3:13   Cursed is everyone who hangs on a tree
1 Peter 2:24   Christ bore our sins upon a cross (lit. tree)
Revelation 2:7   To all who conquer, you may eat of the tree of life
Revelation 7:1   No wind could blow on earth or against any tree
Revelation 7:2-3   God's angel said, Damage not the earth or trees
Revelation 8:7   A third of the earth and its trees were burned up
Revelation 9:4   The "locusts" may not damage grass or any tree
Revelation 11:4   Two olive trees stand before the Lord of earth
Revelation 22:2   The tree of life has twelve kinds of fruit
Revelation 22:14   The blessed have the right to the Tree of Life

VINEYARD

Exodus 22:5   If a vineyard is harmed, restitution shall be made
Leviticus 19:10   Do not strip your vineyard bare
Deuteronomy 22:9   Do not sow a vineyard with diverse seeds
Isaiah 65:21   In the new creation they shall plant vineyards and eat the fruit
Jeremiah 31:5   Plant vineyards and enjoy the fruit
Ezekiel 28:26   Israel shall live safely and plant vineyards
Amos 4:9   God laid waste to your gardens and vineyards

WATER

Genesis 1:9-10   The creation of water and Seas
Numbers 20:7-8   Moses commanded to bring water out of the rock
Deuteronomy 8:7   A good land with flowing streams
Judges 15:18-19   God brings forth water from a hollow place
2 Kings 2:19-22   Elisha heals the polluted waters with salt
2 Kings 3:16-20   The pools shall be filled with water to drink
Job 12:15   God controls the waters
Job 36:27-28   God draws up the waters and distills it in rain
Psalm 65:9-10   God visits the earth and waters it
Psalm 77:16   When the waters saw God they were afraid
Psalm 78:13   God divided the sea and made the waters stand
Psalm 105:41   God opened the rock and water gushed out
Psalm 136:6   Thanks to God who spread out the earth on the waters
Isaiah 30:25   From every hill brooks will run with water
Isaiah 40:12   Who has measured the waters?
Isaiah 44:3-4   God will pour water on the thirsty ground
Ezekiel 32:14   God will make their waters clear
Ezekiel 34:18   When you drink of clean water
Ezekiel 47:8-9   Everything will live where the river goes
Matthew 3:16-17   Jesus was baptized in the water
Matthew 14:25-28   Jesus walked on the water
Mark 1:10   Jesus was baptized in the water
Mark 6:48-51   Jesus walked on the water
Luke 8:25   Even the winds and water obey Jesus
John 6:19   Jesus walked on water
Titus 3:5   Through the water of rebirth and renewal
2 Peter 3:5-6   The earth was formed out of water
Revelation 8:11   The waters became bitter with "wormwood"

WILDERNESS

Exodus 5:1-3   Sought permission to worship God in the wilderness
Exodus 7:16   God told Moses to worship him in the wilderness
Exodus 8:27-28   Sacrifices to God in the wilderness
Numbers 14:32-33   God said they shall wander in the wilderness
Numbers 26:65   God said they shall die in the wilderness
Numbers 32:13   God made them wander in the wilderness
Deuteronomy 8:2   Recall the lessons of obedience in the wilderness
Deuteronomy 8:15-16   God led and fed his people in the wilderness
Nehemiah 9:20-21   Sustenance and guidance in the wilderness
Psalm 65:12   The pastures of the wilderness overflow
Psalm 78:40   How often they rebelled in the wilderness
Isaiah 32:16   Justice will dwell in the wilderness
Isaiah 35:1   The wilderness and the dry land rejoice
Isaiah 40:3   In the wilderness prepare the way of the Lord
Jeremiah 9:10   Weep for the wild places, they are laid waste
Jeremiah 31:2   The people found grace in the wilderness
Hosea 13:5   God fed them in the wilderness
Amos 2:10   God led them for forty years in the wilderness
Matthew 4:1   Jesus tempted in the wilderness
Mark 1:2-3   The voice of one crying in the wilderness
Mark 1:12-13   Jesus tempted in the wilderness

Luke 3:4   The voice of one crying in the wilderness
Luke 4:1-2   Jesus tempted in the wilderness
John 1:23   I am the voice of one crying in the wilderness
1 Corinthians 10:5   God struck them down in the wilderness
Hebrews 3:8   The day of testing in the wilderness

WIND

Exodus 10:13   God brought the wind in the 8th plague
Exodus 14:21   The Lord drove the sea back by the wind
Numbers 11:31   Wind went out from the Lord
Job 38:1   The Lord answered Job out of the whirlwind
Job 38:24   What is the way to the place where the wind is scattered
Psalm 11:6   A scorching wind for the wicked
Psalm 104:4   The winds are God's messengers
Proverbs 11:29   Those who trouble their households inherit wind
Ecclesiastes 1:6   The way of the wind
Jeremiah 51:1   God will stir up a destructive wind
Jonah 1:4   The Lord hurled a great wind upon the sea
Nahum 1:3   The Lord's way is in whirlwind and storm
Matthew 8:26-27   Jesus rebuked the wind and sea and calm returned
Matthew 14:32-33   Jesus calms the winds
Mark 4:37-41   Jesus rebuked the wind and sea and calm returned
Luke 8:22-25   Jesus calms the wind and storm on the lake
Revelation 7:1   No wind could blow on earth or against any tree

WISDOM

Psalm 104:24   In wisdom God made creation
Proverbs 3:19-20   The Lord founded the earth in wisdom
Proverbs 8:22-23, 29-30   Wisdom's part in creation
Jeremiah 10:12   God made the earth by his power and wisdom
Jeremiah 51:15   God established the world by his wisdom
Revelation 5:12   Worthy is the Lamb to receive power, wisdom, glory

WORK/WORKS

Genesis 2:5   There was no human to till (work) the ground
Leviticus 23:3   Do no work on the sabbath
Deuteronomy 5:13-14   Keep holy the sabbath; do no work on that day
Deuteronomy 15:10   Have charity and the Lord will bless your work
Job 37:14   Stop and consider the wondrous works of God
Psalm 8:3   When I look at your heavens, the work of your fingers
Psalm 8:6-8   God gave humans dominion over his works
Psalm 46:8   Come, behold the works of the Lord
Psalm 77:12   I will meditate on the works of the Lord
Psalm 92:5   How great are your works, O Lord
Psalm 96:1-3   Declare the Lord's glory and marvelous works
Psalm 102:25   The heavens are the work of the Lord
Psalm 104:31   May the Lord rejoice in his works
Psalm 105:5   Remember the wonderful works of the Lord
Psalm 107:15   Thank the Lord for his wonderful works
Psalm 111:7   God's works are faithful and just
Psalm 119:27   I will meditate on God's wondrous works
Psalm 139:14   Wonderful are God's works
Psalm 145:5   I will meditate on your wondrous works
Psalm 145:10   All God's works give thanks
Proverbs 8:22   God created wisdom at the beginning of his work
Ecclesiastes 11:5   The mystery of God's work in the world
Habbakuk 3:2   O Lord, I stand in awe of your work
John 5:36   The works that I do testify on my behalf
John 17:4   Jesus glorified God on earth by finishing the work
Hebrews 1:10   The heavens are the work of God's hands
Hebrews 4:3   God's works were done at the world's founding

Hebrews 4:10   Those in God's rest cease from their own works
Revelation 15:3   Great and amazing are your deeds (works)

WORLD

1 Samuel 2:8   God has set the world on the pillars of the earth
Psalm 9:8   The Lord judges the world with righteousness
Psalm 19:4   Their words go to the end of the world
Psalm 33:8   Let the inhabitants of the world stand in awe
Psalm 50:12   The world and all that is in it is God's
Psalm 89:11   The earth is God's, the world and all that is in it
Psalm 93:1   The Lord established the world, it shall not move
Psalm 96:10   The world is firmly established, it shall not move
Isaiah 13:11   The world will be punished for its evil
Isaiah 24:4   The world languishes and withers
Jeremiah 51:15   God established the world by his wisdom
Matthew 5:14   You are the light of the world
Mark 8:36   Seek not to gain the whole world
Mark 16:15   He said to them, "Go into all the world..."
Luke 9:25   What does it profit if they gain the whole world?
John 1:9   The true light was coming into the world
John 1:10   God was in the world
John 1:29   The Lamb of God takes away the sin of the world
John 3:16   For God so loved the world
John 3:17   Jesus did not come to condemn the world
John 3:19   The light has come into the world
John 4:42   This is truly the Savior of the world
John 6:14   This is the prophet who has come into the world
John 6:33   The bread of God gives life to the world
John 8:12   Jesus said, I am the light of the world
John 8:23   Jesus said, I am not of this world
John 9:5   Jesus said, I am the light of the world
John 9:39   Jesus said, I came into this world for judgment
John 12:31   Now is the judgment of this world
John 12:46   Jesus came as light into the world
John 12:47   Jesus came to save the world

John 15:19   If you belong to the world, the world would love you
John 16:8   He will prove the world wrong about sin
John 16:28   Jesus came from the Father and came into the world
John 16:33   Take courage, I have conquered the world
John 17:5   The glory that I had before the world existed
John 17:6   Those whom you gave me from the world
John 17:11   Now I am no longer in the world, but they are
John 17:18   As you sent me into the world, so I sent them
John 17:24   You loved me before the foundation of the world
John 17:25   The world does not know you, but I know you
John 18:20   Jesus spoke openly to the world
John 18:36   Jesus said, My kingdom is not of this world
John 18:37   Jesus came into the world to testify to the truth
Acts 17:24   God made the world and everything in it
Acts 17:30-31   There is a day for the judgment of the world
Acts 22:14-15   You shall be a witness to all the world
Romans 1:20a   Since the creation of the world
Romans 3:19   The whole world—accountable to God
Romans 5:12-13   As sin came into the world by one man
1 Corinthians 7:31b   The present form of the world is passing away
2 Corinthians 5:18-19   God in Christ is reconciling the world to himself
Ephesians 1:3-4   God chose Christ before the foundation of the world
1 Timothy 1:15   Christ Jesus came into the world to save sinners
Hebrews 1:1-2   The Son of God created the worlds
Hebrews 2:5   The world to come is not subject to angels
Hebrews 4:3   God's works were done at the world's founding
Hebrews 10:5   When Christ came into the world
1 Peter 1:20   Christ was foreordained before the world began
2 Peter 2:5   God brought a flood on a world of the ungodly
1 John 2:1b-2   Jesus Christ atones for the whole world's sins
1 John 2:17   The world is passing away
1 John 4:9   God sent his son into the world
Revelation 3:10   A trial is coming to the whole world to test people
Revelation 11:15   The world has become the kingdom of our Lord

Concordance

A

ABANDON → ABANDONED
Dt 4:31 will neither **a** you nor destroy you;
2Ch 15: 2 but if you **a** him, he will **a** you.
Ac 2:27 For you will not **a** my soul to Hades

ABANDONED → ABANDON
Dt 29:25 they **a** the covenant of the LORD,
Isa 54: 7 For a brief moment I **a** you,
Sir 49: 4 for they **a** the law of the Most High;

ABBA
Mk 14:36 "**A**, Father, for you all things are possible;
Ro 8:15 When we cry, "**A**! Father!"
Gal 4: 6 into our hearts, crying, "**A**! Father!"

ABIDE
Ge 6: 3 My spirit shall not **a** in mortals forever,
Ps 91: 1 **a** in the shadow of the Almighty,
Jn 15: 4 **A** in me as I **a** in you.
1Co 13:13 faith, hope, and love **a**, these three;
1Jn 2:28 And now, little children, **a** in him,
Wis 3: 9 the faithful will **a** with him in love,

ABILITY → ABLE
Mt 25:15 to each according to his **a**.
Ac 2: 4 as the Spirit gave them **a**.

ABLE → ABILITY
Da 3:17 God whom we serve is **a** to deliver
Mk 10:38 you **a** to drink the cup that I drink,
Ro 14: 4 the Lord is **a** to make them stand.
2Co 9: 8 God is **a** to provide you with every
Eph 6:11 **a** to stand against the wiles of the devil.
Heb 2:18 **a** to help those who are being tested.
    7:25 he is **a** for all time to save
Jdt 11:18 of them will be **a** to withstand you.

ABOLISH → ABOLISHED
Da 11:31 shall **a** the regular burnt offering
Mt 5:17 I have come not to **a** but to fulfill.

ABOLISHED → ABOLISH
Eph 2:15 **a** the law with its commandments
2Ti 1:10 who **a** death and brought life

ABOMINABLE → ABOMINATION
2Ch 28: 3 the **a** practices of the nations
Eze 7:20 they made their **a** images,
1Mc 1:48 to make themselves **a** by everything

ABOMINATION → ABOMINABLE
Pr 6:16 seven that are an **a** to him:
Da 9:27 shall be an **a** that desolates,
Sir 1:25 but godliness is an **a** to a sinner.
1Mc 6: 7 that they had torn down the **a** that

ABOUND → ABOUNDED, ABOUNDING
Dt 28:11 LORD will make you **a** in prosperity,
Ro 6: 1 in sin in order that grace may **a**?

ABOUNDED → ABOUND
Ro 5:20 sin increased, grace **a** all the more,

ABOUNDING → ABOUND
Ex 34: 6 **a** in steadfast love and faithfulness,
Ps 86: 5 **a** in steadfast love to all who call
Joel 2:13 to anger, and **a** in steadfast love,
Jnh 4: 2 to anger, and **a** in steadfast love,

ABUNDANCE → ABUNDANTLY
Lk 12:15 one's life does not consist in the **a**
2Co 9: 8 provide you with every blessing in **a**

ABUNDANTLY → ABUNDANCE
Jn 10:10 that they may have life, and have it **a**.

ACCEPT → ACCEPTABLE
Jn 1:11 his own people did not **a** him.

ACCEPTABLE → ACCEPT
Ps 19:14 meditation of my heart be **a** to you,
    51:17 sacrifice **a** to God is a broken spirit;
Ro 12: 1 a living sacrifice, holy and **a** to God,

ACCOUNT → ACCOUNTABLE
Mt 12:36 judgment you will have to give an **a**
Heb 4:13 to whom we must render an **a**.

ACCOUNTABLE → ACCOUNT
Ro 14:12 each of us will be **a** to God.

ACCURSED → CURSE
Ro 9: 3 I could wish that I myself were **a**
Rev 22: 3 Nothing **a** will be found there any

ACCUSATION → ACCUSE
Lk 23: 4 no basis for an **a** against this man."

ACCUSE → ACCUSATION, ACCUSER
Ps 103: 9 He will not always **a**,
Zec 3: 1 Satan standing at his right hand to **a**
Mt 12:10 so that they might **a** him.

ACCUSER → ACCUSE
Rev 12:10 the **a** of our comrades has been thrown

ACKNOWLEDGE
Dt 4:35 would **a** that the LORD is God;
Pr 3: 6 In all your ways **a** him,
Mt 10:32 I also will **a** before my Father in

ACTIVE
Heb 4:12 the word of God is living and **a**,

ADD → ADDED
Dt 4: 2 You must neither **a** anything
Pr 30: 6 Do not **a** to his words, or else
Lk 12:25 by worrying **a** a single hour to your

ADDED → ADD
Ecc 3:14 nothing can be **a** to it, nor anything
Sir 42:21 Nothing can be **a** or taken away,

ADOPTION
Ro 8:23 groan inwardly while we wait for **a**,
Gal 4: 5 that we might receive **a** as children.

ADORNMENT
Pr   3:22 for your soul and a for your neck.
1Pe   3: 4 let your a be the inner self with the

ADULTERERS → ADULTERY
Jer   23:10 For the land is full of a;
1Co   6: 9 idolaters, **a,** male prostitutes,

ADULTERESS → ADULTERY
Lev 20:10 the a shall be put to death.
Pr   2:16 from the a with her smooth words,

ADULTERY → ADULTERERS, ADULTERESS
Ex   20:14 You shall not commit a.
Jer   3: 9 committing a with stone and tree.
Mt   5:28 committed a with her in his heart.
Lk   16:18 and marries another commits a,
Jn   8: 3 ;a woman who had been caught in a;*f*

ADVANTAGE
Ecc   7:12 a of knowledge is that wisdom gives
1Co 10:24 Do not seek your own a, but that of

ADVERSARY
1Pe   5: 8 roaring lion your a the devil prowls

ADVICE
Ps   1: 1 do not follow the a of the wicked,
Pr   8:14 I have good a and sound wisdom;
Tob   4:18 Seek a from every wise person
Sir 37:11 pay no attention to any a they give.

ADVOCATE
Jn   14:26 But the **A,** the Holy Spirit,
     15:26 the **A** comes, whom I will send
1Jn   2: 1 we have an a with the Father,

AFFLICT → AFFLICTED, AFFLICTION, AFFLICTIONS, AFFLICTS
2Sa   7:10 evildoers shall a them no more,
La   3:33 for he does not willingly a
2Th   1: 6 repay with affliction those who a

AFFLICTED → AFFLICT
Na   1:12 Though I have a you, I will afflict
2Co   4: 8 are a in every way, but not crushed;

AFFLICTION → AFFLICT
Ps   25:18 Consider my a and my trouble,
La   1: 9 "O LORD, look at my a,
2Co   4:17 this slight momentary a is preparing

AFFLICTIONS → AFFLICT
Ps   34:19 Many are the a of the righteous,

AFFLICTS → AFFLICT
Tob 13: 2 For he a, and he shows mercy;

AFRAID → FEAR
Ex   3: 6 for he was a to look at God.
Lev 26: 6 and no one shall make you a;
Dt   20: 3 Do not lose heart, or be a,
Ps   3: 6 I am not a of ten thousands
     27: 1 of whom shall I be a?
Isa 12: 2 I will trust, and will not be a,
Mt   28:10 Jesus said to them, "Do not be a;
Lk   12:32 "Do not be a, little flock,
Heb 13: 6 Lord is my helper; I will not be a.

AGE → AGES
Mt   28:20 with you always, to the end of the **a."**

AGES → AGE
Col   1:26 has been hidden throughout the a
1Ti   1:17 To the King of the a, immortal,

AGREE
Mt   18:19 if two of you a on earth about
Mk   14:56 and their testimony did not a.

AIR
Eph   2: 2 the ruler of the power of the a,
1Th   4:17 to meet the Lord in the a;

ALERT
Lk   12:37 slaves whom the master finds a
1Co 16:13 Keep a, stand firm in your faith,
Eph   6:18 keep a and always persevere
1Pe   5: 8 Discipline yourselves, keep a.

ALIEN → ALIENS
Ex   2:22 an a residing in a foreign land."
Lev 19:34 you shall love the a as yourself,
Dt   24:17 You shall not deprive a resident a

ALIENS → ALIEN
Eph   2:19 you are no longer strangers and a,
1Pe   2:11 I urge you as a and exiles to abstain
1Mc   2: 7 the sanctuary given over to a?

ALIVE → LIVE
Ac   1: 3 suffering he presented himself a
Ro   6:11 dead to sin and a to God
Eph   2: 5 made us a together with Christ—
1Th   4:17 Then we who are a, who are left,
Rev   1:18 I am a forever and ever;
     19:20 were thrown a into the lake of fire

ALMIGHTY → MIGHT
Ge   17: 1 "I am God **A;** walk before me,
Ps   91: 1 who abide in the shadow of the **A,**
Rev   1: 8 who was and who is to come, the **A.**
     21:22 its temple is the Lord God the **A**
Bar   3: 1 O Lord **A,** God of Israel,
Man   1: 1 O Lord **A,** God of our ancestors,

ALMS
Mt   6: 2 "So whenever you give **a,**
Tob 12: 8 better to give a than to lay up gold.
Sir   7:10 do not neglect to give a.

ALONE
Ge   2:18 not good that the man should be a;
Dt   6: 4 The LORD is our God, the LORD a.
Mk   2: 7 Who can forgive sins but God a?"
     10:18 No one is good but God a.

ALPHA
Rev   1: 8 "I am the **A** and the Omega,"
     22:13 I am the **A** and the Omega,

ALTAR
Ex   27: 1 shall make the a of acacia wood,
     30: 1 an a on which to offer incense;
Heb 13:10 We have an a from which those
Rev   6: 9 I saw under the a the souls of those
1Mc   1:54 a desolating sacrilege on the a of
      4:47 built a new a like the former one.

ALWAYS
Mt   28:20 And remember, I am with you a,
Php   4: 4 Rejoice in the Lord a; again I will

AMAZED → AMAZING
Mt   8:27 a, saying, "What sort of man is this,
Mk   6: 6 And he was a at their unbelief.
Ac   2: 7 **A** and astonished, they asked,

AMAZING → AMAZED
Mk   12:11 and it is a in our eyes'?"
Rev 15: 3 "Great and a are your deeds,

AMBASSADORS
2Co   5:20 So we are a for Christ,

AMBITION
Php   2: 3 Do nothing from selfish a or conceit
Jas   3:14 envy and selfish a in your hearts,

AMEN
Dt   27:15 people shall respond, saying, **"A!"**
2Co   1:20 through him that we say the **"A,"**
Rev   3:14 The words of the **A,** the faithful and

ANCESTORS
Ex   3:13 'The God of your a has sent me to
Dt   4:31 not forget the covenant with your a
La   5: 7 Our a sinned; they are no more,
Ac   5:30 The God of our a raised up Jesus,
Heb   1: 1 Long ago God spoke to our a in

ANCHOR
Heb   6:19 a sure and steadfast a of the soul,

ANCIENT
Da   7: 9 and an **A** One took his throne,
Mic   5: 2 origin is from of old, from a days.
Rev 20: 2 He seized the dragon, that a serpent,

ANGEL → ANGELS, ARCHANGEL, ARCHANGEL'S
Ex   3: 2 the a of the LORD appeared to him
     23:20 going to send an a in front of you,
Ps   34: 7 The a of the LORD encamps
Isa 37:36 the a of the LORD set out and
Da   3:28 who has sent his a and delivered
      6:22 God sent his a and shut the lions'
Mt   1:20 an a of the Lord appeared to him in
Lk   1:26 In the sixth month the a Gabriel
Ac   5:19 during the night an a of the Lord
     23: 8 say that there is no resurrection, or a,
2Co 11:14 Satan disguises himself as an a of light.
Tob   5: 4 the a Raphael standing in front of
Sir 48:21 and his a wiped them out.
LtJ   6: 7 For my a is with you,
Aza   1:26 But the a of the Lord came down
Sus   1:59 a of God is waiting with his sword
Bel   1:34 the a of the Lord said to Habakkuk,
1Mc   7:41 your a went out and struck
2Es   2:44 Then I asked an a, "Who are these,

ANGELS → ANGEL
Ge   28:12 a of God were ascending and
Ps 103:20 Bless the LORD, O you his a,
Mk   12:25 but are like a in heaven.
Jn   1:51 the a of God ascending and
Ro   8:38 that neither death, nor life, nor a,
1Co   6: 2 do not know that we are to judge a—
Heb   2: 7 for a little while lower than the a;
2Pe   2: 4 not spare the a when they sinned,
Rev   1:20 stars are the a of the seven churches,
     21:12 and at the gates twelve a,
Tob 11:14 and blessed be all his holy a.

ANGER → ANGRY

Ex 34: 6 merciful and gracious, slow to **a,**
Jdg   2:12 they provoked the Lord to **a.**
1Ki 16:13 God of Israel to **a** with their idols.
Ps   30: 5 For his **a** is but for a moment;
Pr 12:16 Fools show their **a** at once,
Joel 2:13 slow to **a,** and abounding in
Jnh   4: 2 slow to **a,** and abounding in
Mk   3: 5 He looked around at them with **a;**
Eph 4:26 not let the sun go down on your **a,**
Jas   1:19 slow to speak, slow to **a;**
Sir   5: 4 for the Lord is slow to **a.**

ANGRY → ANGER

Jer   3:12 I will not be **a** forever.
Mt   5:22 that if you are **a** with a brother

ANGUISH

Isa 53:11 Out of his **a** he shall see light;
Da 12: 1 There shall be a time of **a,**
Zep 1:15 a day of distress and **a,**

ANIMAL → ANIMALS

Ge   2:19 God formed every **a** of the field

ANIMALS → ANIMAL

Ge   3:14 cursed are you among all **a**
Ps 36: 6 save humans and **a** alike, O Lord.

ANOINT → ANOINTED, ANOINTING

Ex 30:30 You shall **a** Aaron and his sons,
1Sa 15: 1 "The Lord sent me to **a** you king
Ps 23: 5 you **a** my head with oil; my cup
Da   9:24 and to **a** a most holy place.

ANOINTED → ANOINT

1Ch 16:22 "Do not touch my **a** ones;
Ps   2: 2 against the Lord and his **a,**
Isa 61: 1 because the Lord has **a** me;
Da   9:26 an **a** one shall be cut off and
Lk   4:18 he has **a** me to bring good news to
Jn   1:41 Messiah" (which is translated **A).**

ANOINTING → ANOINT

Ex 30:25 it shall be a holy **a** oil.
Jas   5:14 **a** them with oil in the name of the Lord
1Jn 2:27 as his **a** teaches you about all things,

ANOTHER

Isa 48:11 My glory I will not give to **a.**
Jn 14:16 and he will give you **a** Advocate,
Gal 1: 7 not that there is **a** gospel,

ANSWER

Pr 15: 1 A soft **a** turns away wrath,
Isa 65:24 Before they call I will **a,**
Lk 23: 9 but Jesus gave him no **a.**

ANT

Pr   6: 6 Go to the **a,** you lazybones;

ANTICHRIST

1Jn 2:18 As you have heard that **a** is coming,
       2:22 the **a,** the one who denies the Father
       4: 3 And this is the spirit of the **a,**
2Jn 1: 7 person is the deceiver and the **a!**

ANXIETIES → ANXIETY

1Co 7:32 I want you to be free from **a.**

ANXIETY → ANXIETIES

Ecc 11:10 Banish **a** from your mind,
1Pe 5: 7 Cast all your **a** on him, because he

ANYTHING

Ge 18:14 Is **a** too wonderful for the Lord?
Jer 32:27 is **a** too hard for me?
Mt 18:19 if two of you agree on earth about **a**
Jn 16:23 if you ask **a** of the Father in my name,

APART

Jn 15: 5 **a** from me you can do nothing.
Jas   2:20 that faith **a** from works is barren?

APOSTASIES → APOSTASY

Jer   2:19 and your **a** will convict you.
Eze 37:23 I will save them from all the **a**

APOSTASY → APOSTASIES

1Mc 2:15 officers who were enforcing the **a**

APOSTLE → APOSTLES

Ro 11:13 as I am an **a** to the Gentiles,
1Co 9: 1 Am I not an **a?**
2Co 12:12 signs of a true **a** were performed
Heb 3: 1 **a** and high priest of our confession,

APOSTLES → APOSTLE

Mt 10: 2 the names of the twelve **a:**
Ac   2:43 and signs were being done by the **a.**
1Co 12:28 has appointed in the church first **a,**
Eph 2:20 foundation of the **a** and prophets,
       4:11 he gave some that some would be **a,**
Rev 21:14 are the twelve names of the twelve **a**

APPEAR → APPEARANCE, APPEARANCES, APPEARED, APPEARING

Mt 24:30 the sign of the Son of Man will **a** in
Mk 13:22 messiahs and false prophets will **a**

APPEARANCE → APPEAR

1Sa 16: 7 not look on his **a** or on the height
2Co 5:12 those who boast in outward **a**
Jdt 11:23 You are not only beautiful in **a,**
AdE 2: 7 The girl was beautiful in **a.**

APPEARANCES → APPEAR

Jn   7:24 not judge by **a,** but judge with right

APPEARED → APPEAR

Jn 21:14 that Jesus **a** to the disciples after he
1Co 15: 5 he **a** to Cephas, then to the twelve.
Heb 9:26 **a** once for all at the end of the age

APPEARING → APPEAR

Ac   1: 3 **a** to them during forty days and
2Ti 4: 8 to all who have longed for his **a.**

APPETITES

Ro 16:18 our Lord Christ, but their own **a,**
Sir 18:30 base desires, but restrain your **a.**

APPOINTED → APPOINT

Mk 3:16 So he **a** the twelve: Simon (to whom
Ac   3:20 that he may send the Messiah **a** for
Heb 1: 2 whom he **a** heir of all things,
       9:27 as it is **a** for mortals to die once,

APPROACH

Heb 4:16 **a** the throne of grace with boldness,
     11: 6 whoever would **a** him must believe

APPROVAL → APPROVED

Gal 1:10 I now seeking human **a,** or God's **a?**
Heb 11: 2 by faith our ancestors received **a.**

APPROVED → APPROVAL

1Th 2: 4 but just as we have been **a** by God
2Ti 2:15 to present yourself to God as one **a**

ARARAT

Ge   8: 4 ark came to rest on the mountains of **A.**

ARCHANGEL → ANGEL

Jude 1: 9 **a** Michael contended with the devil
2Es 4:36 the **a** Jeremiel answered and said,

ARCHANGEL'S → ANGEL

1Th 4:16 a call and with the sound of God's

ARCHITECT

Heb 11:10 whose **a** and builder is God.

AREOPAGUS

Ac 17:22 Then Paul stood in front of the **A**

ARGUE → ARGUMENTS

Isa 1:18 let us **a** it out, says the Lord:
Ac 18: 4 Every sabbath he would **a** in the
Ro 9:20 a human being, to **a** with God?

ARGUMENTS → ARGUE

2Co 10: 4 destroy strongholds. We destroy **a**
Col 2: 4 may deceive you with plausible **a.**

ARISE → RISE

Isa 60: 1 **A,** shine; for your light has come,
Mt 24:11 false prophets will **a** and lead many
1Mc 14:41 until a trustworthy prophet should **a,**

ARK

Ge   6:14 Make yourself an **a** of cypress wood
Ex 25:10 shall make an **a** of acacia wood;
1Sa 4:11 The **a** of God was captured;
Rev 11:19 the **a** of his covenant was seen
2Mc 2: 4 that the tent and the **a** should follow
2Es 10:22 the **a** of our covenant has been

ARM → ARMOR, ARMS, ARMY

Ex   6: 6 redeem you with an outstretched **a**
Dt   7:19 mighty hand and the outstretched **a**
2Ch 32: 8 With him is an **a** of flesh;
Ps 98: 1 his holy **a** have gotten him victory.
Isa 53: 1 the **a** of the Lord been revealed?
Jn 12:38 the **a** of the Lord been revealed?"

ARMOR → ARM

Ro 13:12 and put on the **a** of light;
Eph 6:11 Put on the whole **a** of God,
Wis 5:17 will take his zeal as his whole **a,**

ARMS → ARM

Hos 11: 3 I took them up in my **a;**
Mk 10:16 And he took them up in his **a,**

ARMY → ARM

Jos 5:14 as commander of the **a** of the Lord
Ps 27: 3 Though an **a** encamp against me,
     33:16 A king is not saved by his great **a;**
Rev 19:19 rider on the horse and against his **a.**

AROMA

2Co 2:15 For we are the **a** of Christ to God

ARRESTED
Mt 26:50 and laid hands on Jesus and **a** him.
Ac   5:18 **a** the apostles and put them in the

ARROGANCE → ARROGANT
Pr   8:13 Pride and **a** and the way of evil
Eze 7:24 put an end to the **a** of the strong,
Jdt 9:10 their **a** by the hand of a woman.
Sir 10: 7 **A** is hateful to the Lord and to
1Mc 1:24 much blood, and spoke with great **a**.

ARROGANT → ARROGANCE
Ps 73: 3 For I was envious of the **a**;
1Co 13: 4 love is not envious or boastful or **a**

ARROW
Ps 64: 7 But God will shoot his **a** at them;
Isa 49: 2 he made me a polished **a**,

ASCEND → ASCENDED
Ps 139: 8 If I **a** to heaven, you are there;
Isa 14:13 in your heart, "I will **a** to heaven;
Ro 10: 6 'Who will **a** into heaven?'"
2Es 4: 8 neither did I ever **a** into heaven."

ASCENDED → ASCEND
2Ki 2:11 Elijah **a** in a whirlwind into heaven.
Jn   3:13 No one has **a** into heaven except

ASHAMED → SHAME
Ge 2:25 were both naked, and were not **a**.
Mk 8:38 who are **a** of me and of my words
Ro 1:16 For I am not **a** of the gospel;
2Ti 2:15 a worker who has no need to be **a**,
Heb 2:11 Jesus is not **a** to call them brothers
     11:16 God is not **a** to be called their God;

ASHES
Ge 18:27 I who am but dust and **a**.
Est 4: 1 and put on sackcloth and **a**,
Job 42: 6 and repent in dust and **a**."
Jnh 3: 6 himself with sackcloth, and sat in **a**.
Mt 11:21 long ago in sackcloth and **a**.
Jdt 4:11 the temple and put **a** on their heads
Sir 17:32 but all human beings are dust and **a**.

ASK
Isa 65: 1 sought out by those who did not **a**,
Mt 6: 8 knows what you need before you **a**
    7: 7 **"A**, and it will be given you;
Jn 16:24 **A** and you will receive,
Jas 4: 3 You **a** and do not receive, because
1Jn 5:14 we **a** anything according to his will,

ASLEEP → SLEEP
Jnh 1: 5 had lain down, and was fast **a**.
Mt 8:24 by the waves; but he was **a**.
1Th 5: 6 So then let us not fall **a** as others do,

ASSIGNED
Ro 12: 3 the measure of faith that God has **a**.
1Co 3: 5 as the Lord **a** to each.
     7:17 lead the life that the Lord has **a**,

ASSURANCE
Dt 28:66 in dread, with no **a** of your life.
Heb 6:11 so as to realize the full **a** of hope
    11: 1 faith is the **a** of things hoped for,

ASTONISHED
Isa 52:14 there were many who were **a** at him
Lk 2:48 his parents saw him they were **a**;

ASTRAY → STRAY
Dt 30:17 are led **a** to bow down to other gods
Isa 53: 6 All we like sheep have gone **a**;
Jer 50: 6 their shepherds have led them **a**,
Mt 18:12 go in search of the one that went **a**?
1Pe 2:25 For you were going **a** like sheep,

ATE → EAT
Ge 3: 6 she took of its fruit and **a**;
Ex 16:35 The Israelites **a** manna forty years,
Ps 78:25 Mortals **a** of the bread of angels;
Mt 14:20 And all **a** and were filled;
    15:37 And all of them **a** and were filled;

ATHLETE → ATHLETES
2Ti 2: 5 And in the case of an **a**,

ATHLETES → ATHLETE
1Co 9:25 **A** exercise self-control in all

ATONE → ATONEMENT
Da 9:24 an end to sin, and to **a** for iniquity,
Sir 3: 3 who honor their father **a** for sins,

ATONED → ATONEMENT
Pr 16: 6 and faithfulness iniquity is **a** for,

ATONEMENT → ATONE, ATONED, ATONING
Ex 29:36 a bull as a sin offering for **a**.
    30:10 Aaron shall perform the rite of **a**
    32:30 perhaps I can make **a** for your sin."
Lev 23:28 for it is a day of **a**,
Ro 3:25 God put forward as a sacrifice of **a**
Heb 2:17 to make a sacrifice of **a** for the sins

ATONING → ATONEMENT
1Jn 2: 2 and he is the **a** sacrifice for our sins,
    4:10 sent his Son to be the **a** sacrifice for
Sir 28: 5 will make an **a** sacrifice for his sins?

ATTENTION
Heb 2: 1 greater **a** to what we have heard,

AUTHOR
Ac 3:15 and you killed the **A** of life,
Wis 13: 3 for the **a** of beauty created them.

AUTHORITIES → AUTHORITY
Ro 13: 1 be subject to the governing **a**;
Col 2:15 He disarmed the rulers and **a** and

AUTHORITY → AUTHORITIES
Pr 29: 2 When the righteous are in **a**,
Mk 1:27 A new teaching—with **a**!
Lk 5:24 Son of Man has **a** on earth to forgive
Ac 5:29 obey God rather than any human **a**.
Ro 13: 1 for there is no **a** except from God,
1Co 11:10 woman ought to have a symbol of **a**
Col 2:10 who is the head of every ruler and **a**,
1Ti 2:12 no woman to teach or to have **a** over
Rev 12:10 and the **a** of his Messiah,
    20: 4 on them were given **a** to judge.

AVENGE → VENGEANCE
Dt 32:43 he will **a** the blood of his children,
Ro 12:19 Beloved, never **a** yourselves,
Rev 6:10 and **a** our blood on the inhabitants
1Mc 2:67 **a** the wrong done to your people.

AVENGER → VENGEANCE
Nu 35:12 shall be for you a refuge from the **a**,
Ps 8: 2 to silence the enemy and the **a**.

AVENGING → VENGEANCE
Na 1: 2 A jealous and **a** God is the LORD,

AWAKE
Da 12: 2 in the dust of the earth shall **a**,
Mk 14:37 Could you not keep **a** one hour?
Eph 5:14 "Sleeper, **a**! Rise from the dead,
1Th 5: 6 but let us keep **a** and be sober;
Rev 16:15 Blessed is the one who stays **a** and

AWE → AWESOME
Ps 119:161 my heart stands in **a** of your words.
Isa 29:23 will stand in **a** of the God of Israel.
Mt 9: 8 saw it, they were filled with **a**,
Ac 2:43 **A** came upon everyone, because
Ro 11:20 do not become proud, but stand in **a**.

AWESOME → AWE
Ex 15:11 majestic in holiness, in splendor,
Dt 10:17 the great God, mighty and **a**,
Ne 1: 5 and **a** God who keeps covenant
Ps 47: 2 For the LORD, the Most High, is **a**,
Da 9: 4 saying, "Ah, Lord, great and **a** God,
Sir 43:29 **A** is the Lord and very great,

B

BAAL
Jdg 2:13 and worshiped **B** and the Astartes.
1Ki 18:25 Elijah said to the prophets of **B**,
Jer 2: 8 the prophets prophesied by **B**,
Ro 11: 4 not bowed the knee to **B**."

BABEL → BABYLON
Ge 11: 9 Therefore it was called **B**,

BABES
Ps 8: 2 Out of the mouths of **b** and infants
Isa 3: 4 and **b** shall rule over them.

BABYLON → BABEL
2Ki 24:15 into captivity from Jerusalem to **B**.
Ps 137: 1 By the rivers of **B**—there we sat
Isa 14: 4 this taunt against the king of **B**:
    21: 9 he responded, "Fallen, fallen is **B**;
Jer 25:11 serve the king of **B** seventy years.
1Pe 5:13 Your sister church in **B**, chosen
Rev 14: 8 "Fallen, fallen is **B** the great!
Bel 1:36 he set him down in **B**,

BACKSLIDING
Jer 8: 5 people turned away in perpetual **b**?

BAD
Mt 7:17 but the **b** tree bears **b** fruit.
1Co 15:33 **"B** company ruins good morals."

BALM
Jer 8:22 Is there no **b** in Gilead?

BANISH
Ecc 11:10 **B** anxiety from your mind,
Ro 11:26 he will **b** ungodliness from Jacob."

BANNER
Ex 17:15 and called it, The LORD is my **b**.

BAPTISM → BAPTIZE
Mk 1: 4 proclaiming a **b** of repentance for
    10:38 be baptized with the **b** that I am
Lk 20: 4 the **b** of John come from heaven,

1Th 4: 6 the Lord is an **a** in all these things,

Ac 18:25 though he knew only the **b** of John.
   19: 3 They answered, "Into John's **b."**
Ro 4: 4 buried with him by **b** into death,
1Co 15:29 receive **b** on behalf of the dead?
Eph 4: 5 one Lord, one faith, one **b,**
Col 2:12 when you were buried with him in **b,**
1Pe 3:21 **b,** which this prefigured, now saves

BAPTISMS → BAPTIZE
Heb 6: 2 about **b,** laying on of hands,

BAPTIST → BAPTIZE
Mt 3: 1 In those days John the **B** appeared
  11:11 has arisen greater than John the **B;**
  14: 8 the head of John the **B** here on a

BAPTIZE → BAPTISM, BAPTISMS,
   BAPTIST, BAPTIZED, BAPTIZING
Mt 3:11 "I **b** you with water for repentance;
Lk 3:16 He will **b** you with the Holy Spirit
1Co 1:17 For Christ did not send me to **b** but

BAPTIZED → BAPTIZE
Mt 3:13 to John at the Jordan, to be **b**
Ac 1: 5 John **b** with water, but you will be **b**
    with the Holy
  2:38 "Repent, and be **b** every one of you
Ro 6: 3 **b** into Christ Jesus were **b** into his
1Co 10: 2 all were **b** into Moses in the cloud
  12:13 one Spirit we were all **b** into one

BAPTIZING → BAPTIZE
Mt 28:19 **b** them in the name of the Father
Jn 4: 1 "Jesus is making and **b** more

BARN → BARNS
Lk 12:24 they have neither storehouse nor **b,**

BARNS → BARN
Dt 28: 8 the blessing upon you in your **b,**
Ps 144:13 May our **b** be filled, with produce
Lk 12:18 pull down my **b** and build larger

BARREN
Ge 11:30 Now Sarai was **b;** she had no child.
Ex 23:26 No one shall miscarry or be **b** in
1Sa 2: 5 The **b** has borne seven, but she who
Ps 113: 9 He gives the **b** woman a home,
Isa 54: 1 Sing, O **b** one who did not bear;
Lk 1: 7 because Elizabeth was **b,**
Heb 11:11 too old—and Sarah herself was **b**—

BASIN
Ex 30:18 You shall make a bronze **b** with a
1Ki 7:30 four corners were supports for a **b.**
Jn 13: 5 **b** and began to wash the disciples'

BASKET
Mt 5:15 a lamp puts it under the bushel **b,**
Ac 9:25 in the wall, lowering him in a **b.**

BATTLE
Ps 24: 8 and mighty, the LORD, mighty in **b.**
Ecc 9:11 nor the **b** to the strong, nor bread to
Rev 16:14 them for **b** on the great day of God
  20: 8 Magog, in order to gather them for **b;**
1Mc 3:19 the army that victory in **b** depends,

BEAR → BEARS, BIRTH,
   BIRTHRIGHT, BORE, BORN,
   CHILDBEARING, FIRSTBORN
Ge 4:13 punishment is greater than I can **b!**
Isa 7:14 is with child and shall **b** a son,

Mt 1:23 virgin shall conceive and **b** a son,
  7:18 A good tree cannot **b** bad fruit.
Lk 11:46 load people with burdens hard to **b,**
Jn 15: 2 he prunes to make it **b** more fruit.
Gal 6: 2 **B** one another's burdens,
Col 3:13 **B** with one another and,
Heb 9:28 offered once to **b** the sins of many,
Rev 12: 4 woman who was about to **b** a child,

BEARS → BEAR
Ps 68:19 Blessed be the Lord, who daily **b** us
1Co 13: 7 It **b** all things, believes all things,

BEAST → BEASTS
Rev 11: 7 **b** that comes up from the bottomless
    pit
  13:18 calculate the number of the **b,**
  16: 2 who had the mark of the **b**
  19:20 who had received the mark of the **b**

BEASTS → BEAST
Da 7: 3 four great **b** came up out of the sea,

BEAT → BEATEN
Isa 2: 4 shall **b** their swords into plowshares,
Joel 3:10 **B** your plowshares into swords,
Lk 22:63 began to mock him and **b** him;

BEATEN → BEAT
2Co 11:25 Three times I was **b** with rods.
1Pe 2:20 If you endure when you are **b** for

BEAUTIFUL → BEAUTY
Ge 12:11 you are a woman **b** in appearance;
1Sa 25: 3 The woman was clever and **b,**
Est 2: 7 the girl was fair and **b,**
Job 42:15 no women so **b** as Job's daughters;
SS 1: 5 I am black and **b,** O daughters of
Isa 4: 2 the branch of the LORD shall be **b**
  52: 7 How **b** upon the mountains are the
Ac 3: 2 the temple called the **B** Gate so that
Ro 10:15 are the feet of those who bring
Tob 6:12 girl is sensible, brave, and very **b,**
Jdt 8: 7 She was **b** in appearance,
Wis 7:29 She is more **b** than the sun,
Sir 25: 1 and they are **b** in the sight of God
Sus 1: 2 very **b** woman and one who feared

BEAUTY → BEAUTIFUL
Ps 27: 4 to behold the **b** of the LORD,
Pr 31:30 Charm is deceitful, and **b** is vain,
1Pe 3: 4 with the lasting **b** of a gentle
Jdt 16: 9 her **b** captivated his mind,
Wis 13: 3 for the author of **b** created them.
Sir 9: 8 not gaze at **b** belonging to another;
Sus 1:56 **b** has beguiled you and lust has
1Mc 2:12 And see, our holy place, our **b,**

BEGGAR → BEGS
Mk 10:46 son of Timaeus, a blind **b,**
Jn 9: 8 who had seen him before as a **b**

BEGINNING
Ge 1: 1 In the **b** when God created the
Ps 111:10 fear of the LORD is the **b** of wisdom;
Pr 1: 7 The fear of the LORD is the **b** of
  8:22 The LORD created me at the **b** of his
Isa 40:21 Has it not been told you from the **b?**
Mt 24: 8 this is but the **b** of the birth pangs.
Jn 1: 1 In the **b** was the Word,
1Jn 1: 1 declare to you what was from the **b,**
2Jn 1: 6 as you have heard it from the **b**—

Rev 21: 6 and the Omega, the **b** and the end.
Sir 1:14 To fear the Lord is the **b** of wisdom;

BEGOTTEN
Ps 2: 7 You are my son; today I have **b** you.
Ac 13:33 are my Son; today I have **b** you.'
Heb 1: 5 are my Son; today I have **b** you"?
2Es 6:58 have called your firstborn, only **b,**

BEGS → BEG
Lk 6:30 Give to everyone who **b** from you;

BEHEADED → HEAD
Lk 9: 9 Herod said, "John I **b;**
Rev 20: 4 the souls of those who had been **b**

BEHEMOTH
Job 40:15 "Look at **B,** which I made just as I
2Es 6:49 the one you called **B** and the name

BELIEF → BELIEVE
2Th 2:13 the Spirit and through **b** in the truth.

BELIEVE → BELIEF, BELIEVED,
   BELIEVER, BELIEVERS, BELIEVES
Nu 14:11 long will they refuse to **b** in me,
2Ki 17:14 not **b** in the LORD their God.
Ps 119:66 for I **b** in your commandments.
Mt 18: 6 one of these little ones who **b** in me,
  24:23 or 'There he is!'—do not **b** it.
Mk 1:15 repent, and **b** in the good news."
  9:24 "I **b;** help my unbelief!"
Lk 24:25 how slow of heart to **b** all that the
Jn 1: 7 so that all might **b** through him.
  3:18 who **b** in him are not condemned;
  5:46 believed Moses, you would **b** me,
  6:29 you **b** in him whom he has sent."
  14: 1 **B** in God, **b** also in me.
  17:20 will **b** in me through their word,
  20:29 not seen and yet have come to **b."**
Ac 16:31 answered, "**B** on the Lord Jesus,
  28:24 while others refused to **b.**
Ro 3:22 faith in Jesus Christ for all who **b.**
  10: 9 **b** in your heart that God raised him
Gal 3: 9 this reason, those who **b** are blessed
1Th 4:14 For since we **b** that Jesus died and
Heb 11: 6 would approach him must **b**
Jas 2:19 Even the demons **b**—and shudder.
1Pe 1: 8 you do not see him now, you **b**
1Jn 4: 1 Beloved, do not **b** every spirit,
Jude 1: 5 destroyed those who did not **b.**
Sir 19:15 so do not **b** everything you hear.

BELIEVED → BELIEVE
Ge 15: 6 And he **b** the LORD;
Ex 14:31 **b** in the LORD and in his
Isa 53: 1 Who has **b** what we have heard?
Jn 1:12 received him, who **b** in his name,
  12:38 "Lord, who has **b** our message,
Ac 2:44 All who **b** were together and had
Ro 4: 3 "Abraham **b** God, and it was
2Co 4:13 "I **b,** and so I spoke"—
Gal 3: 6 Just as Abraham "**b** God,
1Ti 3:16 **b** in throughout the world, taken up
Heb 4: 3 For we who have **b** enter that rest,
Jas 2:23 that says, "Abraham **b** God,
1Mc 2:59 had done, he **b** firmly in God.
  2:59 and were saved from the flame.

BELIEVER → BELIEVE
1Co 7:12 **b** has a wife who is an unbeliever,
2Co 6:15 Or what does a **b** share with an

BELIEVERS → BELIEVE
Gal 2: 4 because of false **b** secretly brought
2Th 3: 6 keep away from those who are living in
1Pe 2: 17 Love the family of **b.**

BELIEVES → BELIEVE
Jn 3: 15 whoever **b** in him may have eternal
11: 26 everyone who lives and **b** in me
Ro 10: 10 **b** with the heart and so is justified,
1Co 13: 7 It bears all things, **b** all things,

BELLY
Ge 3: 14 upon your **b** you shall go,
Jnh 1: 17 and Jonah was in the **b** of the fish
Mt 12: 40 three days and three nights in the **b**

BELOVED → LOVE
SS 2: 16 My **b** is mine and I am his;
Mt 3: 17 heaven said, "This is my Son, the **B,**
12: 18 my **b,** with whom my soul is well
17: 5 "This is my Son, the **B;**
Col 3: 12 As God's chosen ones, holy and **b,**
Rev 20: 9 camp of the saints and the **b** city.

BEND → BENT
Php 2: 10 name of Jesus every knee should **b,**
Man 1: 11 And now I **b** the knee of my heart,

BENEFICIAL → BENEFIT
1Co 6: 12 but not all things are **b.**
10: 23 lawful," but not all things are **b.**

BENEFIT → BENEFICIAL, BENEFITS
Gal 5: 2 Christ will be of no **b** to you.
Phm 1: 20 have this **b** from you in the Lord!
Heb 4: 2 message they heard did not **b** them,

BENEFITS → BENEFIT
Ps 103: 2 and do not forget all his **b**—
1Co 9: 11 if we reap your material **b?**

BENT → BEND
Hos 11: 4 I **b** down to them and fed them.
Jn 8: 6 Jesus **b** down and wrote with his *f*

BEST → GOOD
Dt 33: 21 He chose the **b** for himself,
Mk 12: 39 the **b** seats in the synagogues and
2Ti 2: 15 your **b** to present yourself to God

BETHANY
Mt 26: 6 Jesus was at **B** in the house of
Jn 11: 1 a certain man was ill, Lazarus of **B,**

BETHLEHEM
1Sa 17: 12 David was the son of an Ephrathite
B
Mic 5: 2 But you, O **B** of Ephrathah,
Mt 2: 1 after Jesus was born in **B** of Judea,
Lk 2: 15 "Let us go now to **B** and see this

BETRAY → BETRAYED
Mt 10: 21 Brother will **b** brother to death,
Mk 14: 11 to look for an opportunity to **b** him.
Jn 13: 11 For he knew who was to **b** him;

BETRAYED → BETRAY
Lk 21: 16 You will be **b** even by parents and
1Co 11: 23 Jesus on the night when he was **b**

BETTER → GOOD
1Sa 15: 22 Surely, to obey is **b** than sacrifice,

Ps 63: 3 your steadfast love is **b** than life,
Pr 15: 16 **B** is a little with the fear of
Ecc 2: 24 There is nothing **b** for mortals than
SS 1: 2 For your love is **b** than wine,
Mt 5: 29 it is **b** for you to lose one of your
Mk 14: 21 It would have been **b** for that one
Jn 11: 50 **b** for you to have one man die for
Php 1: 23 be with Christ, for that is far **b;**
2: 3 in humility regard others as **b** than
Heb 7: 22 the guarantee of a **b** covenant.
9: 23 need **b** sacrifices than these.
Tob 12: 8 A little with righteousness is **b** than
Sir 40: 26 the fear of the Lord is **b** than either.

BIND → BINDS
Dt 6: 8 **B** them as a sign on your hand,
Pr 6: 21 **B** them upon your heart always;
Isa 61: 1 to **b** up the brokenhearted,
Mt 16: 19 whatever you **b** on earth will be

BINDS → BIND
Job 5: 18 For he wounds, but he **b** up;
Col 3: 14 **b** everything together in perfect

BIRD → BIRDS
Ge 1: 21 and every winged **b** of every kind.
Lev 20: 25 the unclean **b** and the clean;

BIRDS → BIRD
Ge 7: 3 and seven pairs of the **b** of the air
Ps 50: 11 I know all the **b** of the air,
Mt 6: 26 Look at the **b** of the air;

BIRTH → BEAR
Dt 32: 18 you forgot the God who gave you **b.**
Ps 22: 10 On you I was cast from my **b,**
Mt 24: 8 is but the beginning of the **b** pangs.
Jas 1: 18 he gave us **b** by the word of truth,
1Pe 1: 3 given us a new **b** into a living hope

BIRTHRIGHT → BEAR, RIGHT
Ge 25: 34 Thus Esau despised his **b.**
Heb 12: 16 who sold his **b** for a single meal.

BISHOP
1Ti 3: 1 whoever aspires to the office of **b**
Tit 1: 7 For a **b,** as God's steward, must be

BITE
Gal 5: 15 If, however, you **b** and devour one
Sir 21: 2 if you approach sin, it will **b** you.

BITTER → BITTERNESS
Ex 1: 14 made their lives **b** with hard service
12: 8 with unleavened bread and **b** herbs.
Rev 8: 11 the water, because it was made **b.**

BITTERNESS → BITTER
Pr 14: 10 The heart knows its own **b,**
Ro 3: 14 mouths are full of cursing and **b."**
Eph 4: 31 Put away from you all **b** and wrath

BLACK
SS 1: 5 I am **b** and beautiful, O daughters
Zec 6: 2 the second chariot **b** horses,
Mt 5: 36 cannot make one hair white or **b.**
Rev 6: 5 I looked, and there was a **b** horse!

BLAMELESS
2Sa 22: 26 with the **b** you show yourself **b;**
Ps 37: 18 The LORD knows the days of the **b,**
Pr 11: 20 but those of **b** ways are his delight.
Eph -1: 4 holy and **b** before him in love.

Php 2: 15 so that you may be **b** and innocent,
1Th 5: 23 and **b** at the coming of our Lord
Tit 1: 7 bishop, as God's steward, must be **b**
Heb 7: 26 **b,** undefiled, separated from sinners,
Rev 14: 5 mouth no lie was found; they are **b.**
1Mc 4: 42 chose **b** priests devoted to the law;

BLASPHEME → BLASPHEMED, BLASPHEMER, BLASPHEMES, BLASPHEMIES, BLASPHEMOUS
Ac 26: 11 I tried to force them to **b;**
1Ti 1: 20 so that they may learn not to **b.**

BLASPHEMED → BLASPHEME
Eze 20: 27 In this again your ancestors **b** me,
Mt 26: 65 tore his clothes and said, "He has **b!**

BLASPHEMER → BLASPHEME
1Ti 1: 13 even though I was formerly a **b,**
Sir 3: 16 forsakes a father is like a **b,**

BLASPHEMES → BLASPHEME
Lev 24: 16 One who **b** the name of the LORD
Lk 12: 10 whoever **b** against the Holy Spirit

BLASPHEMIES → BLASPHEME
Mk 3: 28 their sins and whatever **b** they utter;
Rev 13: 6 its mouth to utter **b** against God,
1Mc 2: 6 He saw the **b** being committed in

BLASPHEMOUS → BLASPHEME
Ac 6: 11 "We have heard him speak **b** words
Rev 13: 1 and on its heads were **b** names.

BLEMISH
Ex 12: 5 Your lamb shall be without **b,**
Lev 22: 20 not offer anything that has a **b,**
Eph 5: 27 that she may be holy and without **b.**
Heb 9: 14 offered himself without **b** to God,
1Pe 1: 19 that of a lamb without defect or **b.**
Jude 1: 24 to make you stand without **b** in the

BLESS → BLESSED, BLESSING, BLESSINGS
Ge 12: 2 I will **b** you, and make your name
22: 17 I will indeed **b** you, and I will make
26: 3 I will be with you, and will **b** you;
Ex 20: 24 I will come to you and **b** you.
Nu 6: 24 The LORD **b** you and keep you;
23: 20 See, I received a command to **b;**
Dt 7: 13 he will love you, **b** you,
30: 16 the LORD your God will **b** you
1Ch 29: 20 "**B** the LORD your God."
Ps 5: 12 For you **b** the righteous, O LORD;
34: 1 I will **b** the LORD at all times;
103: 1 **B** the LORD, O my soul,
Hag 2: 19 From this day on I will **b** you.
Lk 6: 28 **b** those who curse you, pray
Ro 12: 14 **B** those who persecute you;
1Co 4: 12 When reviled, we **b;**
Jas 3: 9 With it we **b** the Lord and Father,
Tob 4: 19 At all times **b** the Lord God,
Sir 32: 13 But above all **b** your Maker,

BLESSED → BLESS
Ge 1: 22 God **b** them, saying, "Be fruitful
2: 3 So God **b** the seventh day and
14: 19 He **b** him and said, "**B** be Abram
Nu 24: 9 **B** is everyone who blesses you,
Job 1: 21 **b** be the name of the LORD."
Ps 118: 26 **B** is the one who comes in the name
Isa 30: 18 **b** are all those who wait for him.

Jer 17: 7 **B** are those who trust in the LORD,
Mt   5: 3 "**B** are the poor in spirit,
Mk 10:16 laid his hands on them, and **b** them.
Lk   1:42 "**B** are you among women,
      6:20 "**B** are you who are poor,
Jn 12:13 **B** is the one who comes in the name
    20:29 **B** are those who have not seen and
Ac 20:35 It is more **b** to give than to receive.
Gal   3: 8 "All the Gentiles shall be **b** in you."
Eph   1: 3 who has **b** us in Christ
1Pe 3:14 for doing what is right, you are **b**.
Rev 22: 7 **B** is the one who keeps the words of
Tob 8:15 she prayed and said, "**B** are you,
Jdt 13:17 one accord, "**B** are you our God,
Aza 1: 3 "**B** are you, O Lord, God of our
Sus 1:60 raised a great shout and **b** God,

BLESSING → BLESS
Ge 12: 2 so that you will be a **b**.
   22:18 the nations of the earth gain **b** for
Dt 11:26 before you today a **b** and a curse:
    23: 5 your God turned the curse into a **b**
Ne 13: 2 our God turned the curse into a **b**.
Eze 34:26 they will be showers of **b**.
Mk 14:22 bread, and after **b** it he broke it,
Lk 24:51 While he was **b** them, he withdrew
1Co 10:16 The cup of **b** that we bless,
Gal   3:14 in Christ Jesus the **b** of Abraham
Eph   1: 3 every spiritual **b** in the heavenly
Rev 5:12 might and honor and glory and **b**!"
     7:12 **B** and glory and wisdom and
Tob 8:15 you, O God, with every pure **b**;
Sir 34:20 he gives health and life and **b**.

BLESSINGS → BLESS
Dt 28: 2 all these **b** shall come upon you
Jos   8:34 the words of the law, **b** and curses,
Mal   2: 2 and I will curse your **b**;
Ro 15:27 come to share in their spiritual **b**,

BLIND → BLINDED, BLINDNESS
Ex   4:11 mute or deaf, seeing or **b**?
Ps 146: 8 the LORD opens the eyes of the **b**.
Isa 35: 5 the eyes of the **b** shall be opened,
Mt 11: 5 **b** receive their sight, the lame walk,
Lk   6:39 "Can a **b** person guide a **b** person?
Jn   9:25 though I was **b**, now I see."
Ro   2:19 sure that you are a guide to the **b**,
Tob 2:10 until I became completely **b**.
LtJ 6:37 They cannot restore sight to the **b**;

BLINDED → BLIND
Jn 12:40 "He has **b** their eyes and hardened
2Co 4: 4 has **b** the minds of the unbelievers,

BLINDNESS → BLIND
Dt 28:28 will afflict you with madness, **b**,
1Jn 2:11 the darkness has brought on **b**.

BLOCK → BLOCKS
Eze 14: 7 their iniquity as a stumbling **b**
Mt 16:23 You are a stumbling **b** to me;
Ro 11: 9 a stumbling **b** and a retribution for
1Co 1:23 stumbling **b** to Jews and foolishness
Sir 31: 7 It is a stumbling **b** to those who are

BLOCKS → BLOCK
Jer 6:21 before this people stumbling **b**
Mt 18: 7 the world because of stumbling **b**!

BLOOD → BLOODSHED
Ge   9: 6 sheds the **b** of a human, by a human
         shall that person's **b** be shed;
Ex   7:17 and it shall be turned to **b**.
   12:13 when I see the **b**, I will pass over
    24: 8 the **b** of the covenant that the LORD
Lev 17:11 it is the **b** that makes atonement.
Nu 35:33 for **b** pollutes the land,
Ps 72:14 and precious is their **b** in his sight.
Isa 1:11 I do not delight in the **b** of bulls,
Eze 33: 4 **b** shall be upon their own heads.
Joel 2:30 **b** and fire and columns of smoke.
Mt 27: 8 field has been called the Field of **B**
Mk 14:24 "This is my **b** of the covenant,
Lk 22:44 sweat became like great drops of b**f**
Jn   1:13 who were born, not of **b**
    6:53 of the Son of Man and drink his **b**,
   19:34 and at once **b** and water came out.
Ac   2:20 to darkness and the moon to **b**,
Ro   5: 9 that we have been justified by his **b**,
1Co 11:25 cup is the new covenant in my **b**.
Eph   1: 7 we have redemption through his **b**,
Heb 9:12 the **b** of goats and calves, but with his
         own **b**,
    9:22 without the shedding of **b** there is no
1Jn 5: 6 the one who came by water and **b**,
Rev 6:12 the full moon became like **b**,
    8: 9 A third of the sea became **b**,
   12:11 conquered him by the **b** of the Lamb

BLOODSHED → BLOOD, SHED
Isa 5: 7 he expected justice, but saw **b**;
Eze 35: 6 you did not hate **b**, **b** shall pursue
Hab 2: 8 because of human **b**, and violence

BLOT
Ge   6: 7 "I will **b** out from the earth
Ex 32:32 **b** me out of the book that you have
Ps 51: 1 mercy **b** out my transgressions.
Rev 3: 5 not **b** your name out of the book of

BOAST → BOASTERS, BOASTING
Ps 34: 2 My soul makes its **b** in the LORD;
Pr 27: 1 Do not **b** about tomorrow,
Jer   9:24 but let those who **b** b in this,
Ro   2:23 You that **b** in the law,
1Co 1:31 the one who boasts, **b** in the Lord."
2Co 11:30 If I must **b**, I will **b** of the things that
Gal   6:14 never **b** of anything except the cross
Eph 2: 9 of works, so that no one may **b**.
Sir 25: 6 and their **b** is the fear of the Lord.

BOASTERS → BOAST
2Co 11:13 For such **b** are false apostles,
2Ti   3: 2 **b**, arrogant, abusive, disobedient to

BOASTING → BOAST
1Co 5: 6 Your **b** is not a good thing.
1Th 2:19 or crown of **b** before our Lord Jesus

BODIES → BODY
Ro 12: 1 present your **b** as a living sacrifice,
1Co 6:15 that your **b** are members of Christ?
Heb 10:22 and our **b** washed with pure water.

BODILY → BODY
Lk   3:22 upon him in **b** form like a dove.
Col 2: 9 the whole fullness of deity dwells **b**,

BODY → BODIES, BODILY
Mic 6: 7 fruit of my **b** for the sin of my soul?

Mt   6:22 "The eye is the lamp of the **b**.
Mk 14:22 and said, "Take; this is my **b**."
Lk 12: 4 do not fear those who kill the **b**,
Jn   2:21 speaking of the temple of his **b**.
1Co 15:44 It is sown a physical **b**, it is raised a
         spiritual **b**.
2Co 5: 8 from the **b** and at home with the
         Lord.
Eph 4: 4 There is one **b** and one Spirit,

BOLD → BOLDNESS
Dt 31: 6 Be strong and **b**; have no fear
Pr 28: 1 the righteous are as **b** as a lion.

BOLDNESS → BOLD
Eph 3:12 whom we have access to God in **b**
Heb 4:16 approach the throne of grace with **b**,
1Jn 4:17 may have **b** on the day of judgment,

BONE → BONES
Ge 2:23 "This at last is **b** of my bones and
Eze 37: 7 came together, **b** to its **b**.

BONES → BONE
Ex 12:46 you shall not break any of its **b**.
Ps 34:20 He keeps all their **b**; not one of
Jn 19:36 "None of his **b** shall be broken."

BOOK → BOOKS
Ex 17:14 "Write this as a reminder in a **b** and
Dt 31:24 writing down in a **b** the words of
Jos   1: 8 This **b** of the law shall not depart
Ps 69:28 be blotted out of the **b** of the living;
Rev 1:11 "Write in a **b** what you see and
   21:27 who are written in the Lamb's **b**
1Mc 1:57 possessing the **b** of the covenant,

BOOKS → BOOK
Ecc 12:12 Of making many **b** there is no end,
Da   7:10 in judgment, and the **b** were opened.
Jn 21:25 world itself could not contain the **b**
1Mc 1:56 The **b** of the law that they found
2Es 14:44 ninety-four **b** were written.

BOOTHS
Lev 23:34 the festival of **b** to the LORD.
Ezr 3: 4 kept the festival of **b**, as prescribed,
Zec 14:16 and to keep the festival of **b**.

BORE → BEAR
Isa 53:12 yet he **b** the sin of many,
Mt   8:17 our infirmities and **b** our diseases."
1Pe 2:24 He himself **b** our sins in his body

BORN → BEAR
Ecc 3: 2 a time to be **b**, and a time to die;
Isa 9: 6 For a child has been **b** for us,
    66: 8 Shall a land be **b** in one day?
Lk   2:11 is **b** this day in the city of David
Jn   3: 7 'You must be **b** from above.'
1Pe 1:23 You have been **b** anew,
1Jn 4: 7 everyone who loves is **b** of God

BORROW → BORROWER
Dt 28:12 to many nations, but you will not **b**.
Ps 37:21 The wicked **b**, and do not pay back,
Mt   5:42 anyone who wants to **b** from you.

BORROWER → BORROW
Pr 22: 7 the **b** is the slave of the lender.

BOUGHT → BUY
1Co 6:20 For you were **b** with a price;

2Pe 2: 1 even deny the Master who b them—

BOW → RAINBOW

Ge 9:13 I have set my **b** in the clouds,
Ex 20: 5 You shall not **b** down to them or
Ps 95: 6 O come, let us worship and **b** down,
Isa 45:23 "To me every knee shall **b**,
Ro 14:11 every knee shall **b** to me,

BOWLS

Rev 16: 1 the seven **b** of the wrath of God."

BRANCH → BRANCHES

Isa 4: 2 On that day the **b** of the LORD shall
11: 1 and a **b** shall grow out of his roots.
Jer 23: 5 raise up for David a righteous **B**,
Zec 3: 8 going to bring my servant the **B.**
Jn 15: 2 every **b** in me that bears no fruit.

BRANCHES → BRANCH

Ro 11:21 if God did not spare the natural **b**,

BREAD

Ge 3:19 sweat of your face you shall eat **b**
Ex 12: 8 with unleavened **b** and bitter herbs.
25:30 set the **b** of the Presence on the table
Dt 8: 3 that one does not live by **b** alone,
Ecc 11: 1 Send out your **b** upon the waters,
Mt 6:11 Give us this day our daily **b.**
Lk 4: 4 'One does not live by **b** alone.'"
Jn 6:35 said to them, "I am the **b** of life.
1Co 11:26 For as often as you eat this **b** and
Wis 16:20 from heaven with **b** ready to eat,
Sir 15: 3 will feed him with the **b** of learning,

BREAK → BREAKING, BROKEN, BROKENHEARTED

Mt 6:19 where thieves **b** in and steal;
Jn 19:33 they did not **b** his legs.

BREASTPIECE → BREASTPLATE

Ex 28:15 You shall make a **b** of judgment,

BREASTPLATE → BREASTPIECE

Isa 59:17 He put on righteousness like a **b**,
Eph 6:14 and put on the **b** of righteousness.
Wis 5:18 he will put on righteousness as a **b**,

BREATH

Ge 2: 7 into his nostrils the **b** of life;
6:17 all flesh in which is the **b** of life;
Job 7: 7 "Remember that my life is a **b**;
Ecc 12: 7 the **b** returns to God who gave it.
2Th 2: 8 will destroy with the **b** of his mouth,

BRIBE

Dt 16:19 for a **b** blinds the eyes of the wise
Pr 6:35 and refuses a **b** no matter how great.

BRIDE → BRIDEGROOM

Isa 62: 5 the bridegroom rejoices over the **b**,
Rev 21: 9 the **b**, the wife of the Lamb."

BRIDEGROOM → BRIDE

Mt 9:15 as long as the **b** is with them,
Jn 3:29 He who has the bride is the **b.**

BRIGHT

Mt 17: 5 suddenly a **b** cloud overshadowed
Rev 15: 6 robed in pure **b** linen,
22:16 of David, the **b** morning star."

BROKE → BREAK

Ex 32:19 tablets from his hands and **b** them
2Ch 36:19 **b** down the wall of Jerusalem,
Jer 31:32 a covenant that they **b,**
Mt 14:19 and blessed and **b** the loaves,
1Co 11:24 he **b** it and said, "This is my body
1Mc 3: 5 and pursued those who **b** the law;

BROKEN → BREAK

Ne 1: 3 the wall of Jerusalem is **b** down,
Ps 51:17 acceptable to God is a **b** spirit;
Mt 15:37 they took up the **b** pieces left over,
Lk 20:18 who falls on that stone will be **b**
Ro 11:20 were **b** off because of their unbelief.

BROKENHEARTED → BREAK, HEART

Ps 147: 3 He heals the **b**, and binds up their
Isa 61: 1 the oppressed, to bind up the **b**,

BRONZE

Nu 21: 9 look at the serpent of **b** and live.
Dt 28:23 The sky over your head shall be **b**,
Da 10: 6 legs like the gleam of burnished **b**,
Rev 1:15 his feet were like burnished **b**,

BROTHER → BROTHER'S, BROTHERS

Ge 4: 8 Cain rose up against his **b** Abel,
Mt 5:24 first be reconciled to your **b** or
10:21 **B** will betray **b** to death,

BROTHER'S → BROTHER

Dt 25: 7 has no desire to marry his **b** widow,
Mk 6:18 lawful for you to have your **b** wife."

BROTHERS → BROTHER

Ge 9:25 lowest of slaves shall he be to his **b.**
37:11 So his **b** were jealous of him,
Mk 3:33 "Who are my mother and my **b?**"
Lk 22:32 turned back, strengthen your **b.**"
Heb 2:11 not ashamed to call them **b** and

BUILD → BUILDER, BUILDERS, BUILDING, BUILDS, BUILT, REBUILD

Ge 11: 4 "Come, let us **b** ourselves a city,
Ps 127: 1 those who **b** it labor in vain.
Mt 16:18 and on this rock I will **b** my church,
27:40 destroy the temple and **b** it in three
1Co 3:10 must choose with care how to **b**
10:23 are lawful," but not all things **b** up.

BUILDER → BUILD

Heb 3: 4 but the **b** of all things is God.)
11:10 whose architect and **b** is God.

BUILDERS → BUILD

Ps 118:22 The stone that the **b** rejected has
Mk 12:10 'The stone that the **b** rejected has
1Pe 2: 7 'The stone that the **b** rejected has

BUILDING → BUILD

1Co 3: 9 you are God's field, God's **b.**
2Co 5: 1 we have a **b** from God,
Eph 4:12 for **b** up the body of Christ,

BUILDS → BUILD

Ps 127: 1 Unless the LORD **b** the house,
Pr 14: 1 The wise woman **b** her house,
1Co 8: 1 Knowledge puffs up, but love **b** up.

BUILT → BUILD

1Ki 6:14 Solomon **b** the house, and finished
Ne 7: 1 the wall had been **b** and I had set up
Pr 9: 1 Wisdom has **b** her house,
Da 9:25 sixty-two weeks it shall be **b** again
Eph 2:20 **b** upon the foundation of the
Tob 13:16 Jerusalem will be **b** as his house for
1Mc 4:47 **b** a new altar like the former one.

BULL → BULLS

Ps 50: 9 will not accept a **b** from your house,

BULLS → BULL

Ps 22:12 **b** encircle me, strong **b** of Bashan'
Isa 1:11 I do not delight in the blood of **b**,
Heb 10: 4 it is impossible for the blood of **b**

BURDEN → BURDENS, BURDENSOME

Ps 55:22 Cast your **b** on the LORD,
Mt 11:30 my yoke is easy, and my **b** is light.

BURDENS → BURDEN

Ex 6: 6 free you from the **b** of the Egyptians
Lk 11:46 you load people with **b** hard to bear,
Gal 6: 2 Bear one another's **b**, and

BURDENSOME → BURDEN

1Jn 5: 3 And his commandments are not **b**,

BURIED → BURY

Ro 6: 4 have been **b** with him by baptism
1Co 15: 4 he was **b**, and that he was raised on

BURN → BURNED, BURNT

Ex 21:25 **b** for **b**, wound for wound,
Mal 4: 1 the day that comes shall **b** them up,
Lk 3:17 but the chaff he will **b** with

BURNED → BURN

Ex 3: 3 and see why the bush is not **b** up."
Jn 15: 6 thrown into the fire, and **b.**
1Co 3:15 If the work is **b** up, the builder

BURNT → BURN

Ex 40: 6 You shall set the altar of **b** offering
Lev 1: 3 If the offering is a **b** offering from
1Sa 15:22 LORD as great delight in **b** offerings
Ps 51:16 if I were to give a **b** offering,
Da 8:11 it took the regular **b** offering away
Hos 6: 6 the knowledge of God rather than **b**
Mic 6: 6 Shall I come before him with **b**
Mk 12:33 more important than all whole **b**
1Mc 1:45 to forbid **b** offerings and sacrifices
4:56 and joyfully offered **b** offerings;

BURY → BURIED

Lk 9:60 "Let the dead **b** their own dead;

BUSH

Ex 3: 2 he looked, and the **b** was blazing,
Jnh 4: 6 the LORD God appointed a **b**,

C

CALAMITIES → CALAMITY

1Sa 10:19 who saves you from all your **c** and
2Co 6: 4 in afflictions, hardships, **c**,
12:10 and **c** for the sake of Christ;

CALAMITY → CALAMITIES

Da 9:13 all this **c** has come upon us.
Hab 3:16 wait quietly for the day of **c** to come

CALF
Ex 32: 4 and cast an image of a c;
Lk 15:23 And get the fatted c and kill it,

CALL → CALLED, CALLING
1Ch 16: 8 to the LORD, c on his name,
Ps 61: 2 From the end of the earth I c to you,
Pr   8: 1 Does not wisdom c, and does
Isa 65:24 Before they c I will answer,
Mt   9:13 to c not the righteous but sinners."
Lk   6:46 "Why do you c me 'Lord, Lord,'
Jn 15:15 I do not c you servants any longer,
Php 3:14 goal for the prize of the heavenly c

CALLED → CALL
2Sa 22: 7 In my distress I c upon the LORD;
Isa 43: 1 I have c you by name, you are mine.
1Co 7:15 It is to peace that God has c you.
Eph 1:18 the hope to which he has c you,
1Jn 3: 1 that we should be c children of God;

CALLING → CALL
Ro 11:29 and the c of God are irrevocable.
Eph 4: 1 lead a life worthy of the c to which

CAMEL
Mt 23:24 strain out a gnat but swallow a c!
Mk 10:25 c to go through the eye of a needle

CANAAN
Ge   9:25 "Cursed be C; lowest of slaves
Nu 13: 2 "Send men to spy out the land of C,
1Ch 16:18 "To you I will give the land of C

CAPTIVE → CAPTIVITY
2Ki 15:29 he carried the people c to Assyria.
   24:16 king of Babylon brought c to
Ro   7:23 making me c to the law of sin
Eph 4: 8 he made captivity itself a c;

CAPTIVITY → CAPTIVE
Dt 28:41 for they shall go into c.
Ezr 8:35 those who had come from c,

CARE → CAREFUL, CARES, CARING
Ps   8: 4 mortals that you c for them?
Heb 2: 6 or mortals, that you c for them?
Jas 1:27 to c for orphans and widows in

CAREFUL → CARE
Dt   4:23 So be c not to forget the covenant
Jos 1: 8 you may be c to act in accordance
Eph 5:15 Be c then how you live,

CARES → CARE
1Pe 5: 7 on him, because he c for you.

CARPENTER'S
Mt 13:55 Is not this the c son?

CASE
Isa 41:21 Set forth your c, says the LORD;
Lk 12:58 make an effort to settle the c,
Jn 18:38 "I find no c against him.

CAST
Ex 34:17 You shall not make c idols.
Ps 22:18 and for my clothing they c lots.
   55:22 C your burden on the LORD,
Mk   3:23 "How can Satan c out Satan?
Jn 19:24 and for my clothing they c lots."
1Pe 5: 7 C all your anxiety on him,

CATTLE
Ge   1:25 and the c of every kind,
Ps 50:10 the c on a thousand hills.

CELEBRATE
Lev 23:37 shall c as times of holy convocation,
1Co 5: 8 Therefore, let us c the festival,

CENSER
Lev 10: 1 Nadab and Abihu, each took his c,
Eze 8:11 Each had his c in his hand,
Rev 8: 3 Another angel with a golden c came

CENTURION
Mt   8: 5 he entered Capernaum, a c came to
Lk 23:47 the c saw what had taken place,
Ac 10: 1 a man named Cornelius, a c

CERTIFICATE
Dt 24: 1 so he writes her a c of divorce,
Mt   5:31 let him give her a c of divorce.'
Mk 10: 4 a man to write a c of dismissal

CHAFF
Ps   1: 4 like c that the wind drives away.
Lk   3:17 c he will burn with unquenchable

CHAINS
Eph 6:20 for which I am an ambassador in c.
Heb 11:36 and even c and imprisonment.
2Pe 2: 4 them to c of deepest darkness

CHANGE → CHANGERS
Ex 32:12 c your mind and do not bring
Nu 23:19 a mortal, that he should c his mind.
1Sa 15:29 will not recant or c his mind;
Jer 18: 8 I will c my mind about the disaster
Jas 1:17 is no variation or shadow due to c.

CHANGERS → CHANGE
Mk 11:15 overturned the tables of the money c
Jn   2:15 poured out the coins of the money c

CHARGE
Mt 25:21 I will put you in c of many things;
Mk 15:26 The inscription of the c against him
Ro   8:33 will bring any c against God's elect?
1Co 9:18 I may make the gospel free of c,

CHARM
Pr 31:30 C is deceitful, and beauty is vain,
Sir 7:19 for her c is worth more than gold.
   26:15 A modest wife adds c to c,

CHASTISEMENT → CHASTISES
La   4: 6 the c of my people has been greater
Sir 16:12 Great as his mercy, so also is his c;

CHASTISES → CHASTISEMENT
Heb 12: 6 and c every child whom he accepts.

CHEEK
Ps   3: 7 you strike all my enemies on the c;
Mt   5:39 if anyone strikes you on the right c,

CHEERFUL
Pr 15:13 A glad heart makes a c countenance,
   17:22 A c heart is a good medicine,
2Co 9: 7 for God loves a c giver.
Jas 5:13 Are any c? They should sing songs

CHERUB → CHERUBIM
2Ch 3:11 touched the wing of the other c;

CHERUBIM → CHERUB
Ge   3:24 the garden of Eden he placed the c,
Ex 25:18 You shall make two c of gold;
Ps 80: 1 You who are enthroned upon the c,
Heb 9: 5 the c of glory overshadowing the

CHIEF
Ps 118:22 has become the c cornerstone.
Mk 15: 3 the c priests accused him of many
1Pe 5: 4 And when the c shepherd appears,

CHILD → CHILDBEARING, CHILDREN
Isa 11: 6 and a little c shall lead them.
   49:15 Can a woman forget her nursing c,
Hos 11: 1 When Israel was a c, I loved him,
Mt   1:18 with c from the Holy Spirit.
Mk 10:15 the kingdom of God as a little c
Lk   2:12 you will find a c wrapped in bands
1Co 13:11 When I was a c, I spoke like a c,
Rev 12: 4 that he might devour her c as soon

CHILDBEARING → CHILD, BEAR
Ge   3:16 greatly increase your pangs in c;
1Ti 2:15 Yet she will be saved through c,

CHILDREN → CHILD
Pr 22: 6 Train c in the right way, and when
Mt   3: 9 stones to raise up c to Abraham.
Lk 18:16 "Let the little c come to me,
Jn   1:12 he gave power to become c of God,
Ro   8:14 by the Spirit of God are c of God.
Eph 6: 4 do not provoke your c to anger,
Heb 12: 7 God is treating you as c;
1Jn 3:10 The c of God and the c of the devil

CHOOSE → CHOOSES, CHOSE, CHOSEN
Dt 30:19 C life so that you and your
Jos 24:15 c this day whom you will serve,
Jn 15:16 You did not c me but I chose you.

CHOOSES → CHOOSE
Ro   9:18 he has mercy on whomever he c,

CHOSE → CHOOSE
Mk 13:20 for the sake of the elect, whom he c,
1Co 1:27 God c what is foolish in the world

CHOSEN → CHOOSE
Isa 42: 1 my servant, whom I uphold, my c,
Mt 22:14 For many are called, but few are c."
Ro 11: 5 there is a remnant, c by grace.
1Pe 2: 6 a cornerstone c and precious;
   2: 9 are a c race, a royal priesthood,

CHRIST → CHRISTIAN, CHRISTIANS, JESUS, MESSIAH
Jn   4:25 Messiah is coming" (who is called C).
Ro   5: 6 right time C died for the ungodly.
   8:35 will separate us from the love of C?
1Co 1:23 but we proclaim C crucified,
   3:11 that foundation is Jesus C.
   11: 1 Be imitators of me, as I am of C.
Gal 5: 1 For freedom C has set us free.
Eph 4:15 into him who is the head, into C,
Php 1:21 to me, living is C and dying is gain.
   2:11 should confess that Jesus C is Lord,

Col 1: 27 **C** in you, the hope of glory.
Rev 20: 4 reigned with **C** a thousand years.

CHRISTIAN → CHRIST
Ac 26: 28 persuading me to become a **C?"**
1Pe 4: 16 Yet if any of you suffers as a **C,**

CHRISTIANS → CHRIST
Ac 11: 26 the disciples were first called **"C."**

CHURCH
Mt 16: 18 on this rock I will build my **c,**
Ac 8: 1 persecution began against the **c**
1Co 12: 28 appointed in the **c** first apostles,
14: 4 those who prophesy build up the **c.**
Col 1: 18 He is the head of the body, the **c;**

CIRCUMCISE → CIRCUMCISED,
CIRCUMCISION
Ge 17: 11 shall **c** the flesh of your foreskins,
Dt 10: 16 **C,** then, the foreskin of your heart,
Lk 1: 59 the eighth day they came to **c** the
Jn 7: 22 and you **c** a man on the sabbath.

CIRCUMCISED → CIRCUMCISE
Ge 17: 10 Every male among you shall be **c.**
Gal 6: 13 **c** do not themselves obey the law,
Col 2: 11 also you were **c** with a spiritual
1Mc 1: 60 the women who had their children **c,**

CIRCUMCISION → CIRCUMCISE
Ro 2: 29 real is a matter of the heart—
Gal 5: 6 For in Christ Jesus neither **c**

CITIES → CITY
Jos 20: 2 'Appoint the **c** of refuge,'
Rev 16: 19 and the **c** of the nations fell.

CITIZENSHIP
Php 3: 20 But our **c** is in heaven,

CITY → CITIES
1Ch 11: 7 it was called the **c** of David.
Ps 127: 1 Unless the Lord guards the **c,**
Mt 5: 14 A **c** built on a hill cannot be hid.
Heb 12: 22 Zion and to the **c** of the living God,
Rev 21: 2 I saw the holy **c,** the new Jerusalem,

CLAY
Isa 45: 9 Does the **c** say to the one who
Jer 18: 6 Just like the **c** in the potter's hand,
Ro 9: 21 Has the potter no right over the **c,**
2Co 4: 7 But we have this treasure in **c** jars,

CLEAN → CLEANSE, CLEANSING
Ge 7: 2 seven pairs of all **c** animals,
Lev 10: 10 and between the unclean and the **c;**
Ps 51: 7 with hyssop, and I shall be **c;**
Mk 7: 19 (Thus he declared all foods **c.)**
Heb 10: 22 with our hearts sprinkled from

CLEANSE → CLEAN
Ps 51: 2 and **c** me from my sin.
1Jn 1: 9 **c** us from all unrighteousness.
Sir 38: 10 and **c** your heart from all sin.

CLEANSING → CLEAN
Eph 5: 26 by **c** her with the washing of water
2Pe 1: 9 is forgetful of the **c** of past sins.

CLOTH
Isa 64: 6 righteous deeds are like a filthy **c.**
Lk 2: 7 and wrapped him in bands of **c,**

CLOTHE → CLOTHED, CLOTHING
Col 3: 14 Above all, **c** yourselves with love,
1Pe 5: 5 you must **c** yourselves with humility

CLOTHED → CLOTHE
2Co 5: 2 longing to be **c** with our heavenly
Gal 3: 27 have **c** yourselves with Christ.
Rev 12: 1 a woman **c** with the sun,

CLOTHING → CLOTHE
Ps 22: 18 and for my **c** they cast lots.
Mt 25: 36 I was naked and you gave me **c,**
Jn 19: 24 and for my **c** they cast lots."

CLOUD → CLOUDS
Ex 13: 21 went in front of them in a pillar of **c**
Mk 9: 7 Then a **c** overshadowed them,
Lk 21: 27 'the Son of Man coming in a **c'**
Heb 12: 1 by so great a **c** of witnesses,
Rev 14: 14 on the **c** was one like the Son of
Man,

CLOUDS → CLOUD
Ge 9: 13 I have set my bow in the **c,**
Da 7: 13 being coming with the **c** of heaven.
Mt 24: 30 'the Son of Man coming on the **c** of
1Th 4: 17 be caught up in the **c** together with
Rev 1: 7 He is coming with the **c;**
2Es 13: 3 this man flew with the **c** of heaven;

COIN
Mt 17: 27 open its mouth, you will find a **c;**
22: 19 Show me the **c** used for the tax."
Lk 15: 9 I have found the **c** that I had lost.'

COLLECTOR → COLLECTORS
Mt 10: 3 Thomas and Matthew the tax **c;**
Lk 18: 10 one a Pharisee and the other a tax **c.**
19: 2 he was a chief tax **c** and was rich.

COLLECTORS → COLLECTOR
Mt 5: 46 Do not even the tax **c** do the same?
11: 19 a friend of tax **c** and sinners!'

COLT
Ge 49: 11 his donkey's **c** to the choice vine,
Zec 9: 9 and riding on a donkey, on a **c,**
Jn 12: 15 coming, sitting on a donkey's **c!"**

COME → COMES, COMING
Mt 6: 10 Your kingdom **c.** Your will be done,
Lk 7: 20 'Are you the one who is to **c,**
1Co 16: 22 Our Lord, **c!**
Rev 1: 4 who is and who was and who is to **c,**
22: 20 Amen. **C,** Lord Jesus!

COMES → COME
Ps 118: 26 who **c** in the name of the Lord.
Lk 19: 38 "Blessed is the king who **c** in the
Jn 14: 6 No one **c** to the Father except
through

COMFORT → COMFORTED,
COMFORTS
Ps 23: 4 your rod and your staff—they **c** me.
Isa 40: 1 **C,** O **c** my people, says your God.

COMFORTED → COMFORT
Ps 86: 17 Lord, have helped me and **c** me.
Isa 49: 13 For the Lord has **c** his people,
Mt 5: 4 those who mourn, for they will be **c.**

COMFORTS → COMFORT
Isa 66: 13 As a mother **c** her child, so I will

COMING → COME
Mal 3: 2 But who can endure the day of his **c,**
Heb 10: 37 is **c** will come and will not delay;
2Pe 3: 4 "Where is the promise of his **c?**
Rev 22: 20 "Surely I am **c** soon."

COMMAND → COMMANDED,
COMMANDING,
COMMANDMENT,
COMMANDMENTS
Ex 34: 11 Observe what I **c** you today.
Jdg 2: 2 But you have not obeyed my **c.**

COMMANDED → COMMAND
Mt 28: 20 to obey everything that I have **c** you.
Jn 14: 31 but I do as the Father has **c** me,

COMMANDING → COMMAND
Dt 4: 40 **c** you today for your own well-being
30: 11 **c** you today is not too hard for you,

COMMANDMENT → COMMAND
Dt 6: 1 Now this is the **c**—the statutes
Ps 19: 8 **c** of the Lord is clear,
Mt 22: 38 This is the greatest and first **c.**
Ro 7: 12 and the **c** is holy and just and good.
Gal 5: 14 law is summed up in a single **c,**
1Jn 3: 23 this is his **c,** that we should believe

COMMANDMENTS → COMMAND
Ex 20: 6 those who love me and keep my **c.**
Dt 4: 13 to observe, that is, the ten **c;**
Ps 119: 66 for I believe in your **c.**
Pr 10: 8 The wise of heart will heed **c,**
Ecc 12: 13 Fear God, and keep his **c;**
Mt 22: 40 On these two **c** hang all the law and
Jn 14: 15 If you love me, you will keep my **c.**
1Co 7: 19 obeying the **c** of God is everything.
1Jn 5: 3 And his **c** are not burdensome.
Rev 14: 12 those who keep the **c** of God and
Sir 1: 26 If you desire wisdom, keep the **c,**
1Mc 2: 19 and have chosen to obey his **c,**

COMMON
Lev 10: 10 between the holy and the **c,**
Eze 22: 26 between the holy and the **c,**
Ac 2: 44 and had all things in **c;**

COMMUNION
2Co 13: 13 the **c** of the Holy Spirit be with

COMPANY
1Co 15: 33 "Bad **c** ruins good morals."

COMPASSION → COMPASSIONATE
Dt 32: 36 will vindicate his people, have **c**
Ps 103: 13 As a father has **c** for his children,
Hos 11: 8 my **c** grows warm and tender.
Mt 14: 14 had **c** for them and cured their sick.
Ro 9: 15 I will have **c** on whom I have **c."**
Col 3: 12 clothe yourselves with **c,** kindness,
Sir 18: 13 the **c** of the Lord is for every living

COMPASSIONATE → COMPASSION
Ex 22: 27 I will listen, for I am **c.**
Jas 5: 11 how the Lord is **c** and merciful.
Sir 2: 11 For the Lord is **c** and merciful;

COMPLAIN → COMPLAINING, COMPLAINT
Nu 14:27 shall this wicked congregation c
Jer 2:29 Why do you c against me?
1Co 10:10 And do not c as some of them did,

COMPLAINING → COMPLAIN
Ex 16:7 heard your c against the Lord.
1Pe 4:9 hospitable to one another without c.

COMPLAINT → COMPLAIN
Ps 142:2 I pour out my c before him;
Hab 2:1 he will answer concerning my c.
Col 3:13 if anyone has a c against another,

COMPLETE → COMPLETED
Jn 4:34 him who sent me and to c his work.
Rev 6:11 until the number would be c

COMPLETED → COMPLETE
Jer 25:12 Then after seventy years are c,
Da 11:36 until the period of wrath is c,

CONCEIT → CONCEITED
Php 2:3 nothing from selfish ambition or cs
1Ti 3:6 may be puffed up with c and fall
Sir 3:24 For their c has led many astray,

CONCEITED → CONCEIT
Gal 5:26 Let us not become c, competing
1Ti 6:4 is c, understanding nothing,

CONCEIVE
Mt 1:23 the virgin shall c and bear a son,
Lk 1:31 you will c in your womb and bear

CONDEMN → CONDEMNATION, CONDEMNED
Lk 11:31 of this generation and c them,
Jn 3:17 not send the Son into the world to c
Ro 8:34 Who is to c?
1Jn 3:21 Beloved, if our hearts do not c us,

CONDEMNATION → CONDEMN
Mk 12:40 They will receive the greater c."
Ro 5:18 one man's trespass led to c for all,
1Ti 3:6 fall into the c of the devil.
Jas 5:12 so that you may not fall under c.

CONDEMNED → CONDEMN
Mt 12:37 and by your words you will be c."
Lk 24:20 handed him over to be c to death
Jn 3:18 Those who believe in him are not c;
    16:11 the ruler of this world has been c.
1Co 11:32 disciplined so that we may not be c

CONDUCT
1Pe 1:15 be holy yourselves in all your c;
Tob 4:14 and discipline yourself in all your c.
Sir 37:17 The mind is the root of all c;

CONFESS → CONFESSES, CONFESSION
Lev 5:5 you shall c the sin that you have
Ps 38:18 c my iniquity; I am sorry for my sin.
Php 2:11 should c that Jesus Christ is Lord,
1Jn 1:9 If we c our sins, he who is faithful
Rev 3:5 will c your name before my Father
Sir 4:26 Do not be ashamed to c your sins,

CONFESSES → CONFESS
Ro 10:10 c with the mouth and so is saved.
1Jn 2:23 who c the Son has the Father also.

CONFESSION → CONFESS
Da 9:4 to the Lord my God and made c,
1Ti 6:12 for which you made the good c in
Heb 4:14 let us hold fast to our c.

CONFIDENCE
Ps 118:8 Lord than to put c in mortals.
Php 3:3 and have no c in the flesh—
Heb 10:19 we have c to enter the sanctuary

CONFORMED
Ro 8:29 predestined to be c to the image of
    12:2 Do not be c to this world,
Php 3:21 may be c to the body of his glory,
1Pe 1:14 do not be c to the desires that you

CONFUSE
Ge 11:7 go down, and c their language there,

CONGREGATION
Ps 1:5 nor sinners in the c of the righteous;
Heb 2:12 the midst of the c I will praise you."

CONQUER → CONQUERED, CONQUERORS, CONQUERS
Rev 17:14 and the Lamb will c them,
    21:7 who c will inherit these things,

CONQUERED → CONQUER
Jn 16:33 take courage; I have c the world!"
Heb 11:33 who through faith c kingdoms,
1Jn 2:13 because you have c the evil one.
Rev 15:2 who had c the beast and its image

CONQUERORS → CONQUER
Ro 8:37 all these things we are more than c

CONQUERS → CONQUER
1Jn 5:4 victory that c the world, our faith.
Rev 2:7 To everyone who c, I will give

CONSCIENCE
Ro 2:15 their own c also bears witness;
1Co 8:7 and their c, being weak, is defiled.
1Ti 1:5 a good c, and sincere faith.
Heb 9:14 purify our c from dead works to
1Pe 3:21 as an appeal to God for a good c,

CONSIDER
1Sa 12:24 for c what great things he has done
Ps 107:43 and c the steadfast love of the Lord.
Lk 12:27 C the lilies, how they grow:

CONSOLATION
Lk 2:25 looking forward to the c of Israel,
2Co 1:3 of mercies and the God of all c,

CONSPIRED
Da 6:6 So the presidents and satraps c
Mt 26:4 they c to arrest Jesus by stealth

CONSUME → CONSUMED, CONSUMING
Ex 32:12 c them from the face of the earth'?
Nu 16:21 so that I may c them in a moment.
Mt 6:19 where moth and rust c and where
Jn 2:17 "Zeal for your house will c me."

CONSUMED → CONSUME
Ex 3:2 bush was blazing, yet it was not c.
Ps 69:9 zeal for your house that has c me;
Zep 3:8 all the earth shall be c.
Gal 5:15 that you are not c by one another.

CONSUMING → CONSUME
Heb 12:29 for indeed our God is a c fire.

CONTEMPT
Da 12:2 some to shame and everlasting c.
Mk 9:12 sufferings and be treated with c?
Heb 6:6 and are holding him up to c.

CONTENT → CONTENTMENT
2Co 12:10 Therefore I am c with weaknesses,
Php 4:11 learned to be c with whatever I have
Heb 13:5 and be c with what you have;
Sir 29:23 Be c with little or much,

CONTENTMENT → CONTENT
1Ti 6:6 gain in godliness combined with c;

CONTRITE
Ps 51:17 broken and c heart, O God, you
Isa 57:15 who are c and humble in spirit,

CONVERT
Mt 23:15 sea and land to make a single c,
1Ti 3:6 He must not be a recent c,

CONVICT → CONVICTION
Dt 19:15 to c a person of any crime
Jude 1:15 to c everyone of all the deeds of

CONVICTION → CONVICT
Heb 11:1 the c of things not seen.

CONVINCE → CONVINCED, CONVINCING
Ac 28:23 and trying to c them about Jesus
2Ti 4:2 c, rebuke, and encourage,

CONVINCED → CONVINCE
Lk 16:31 neither will they be c even if
Ro 8:38 For I am c that neither death, nor
2Co 5:14 we are c that one has died for all;

CONVINCING → CONVINCE
Ac 1:3 to them by many c proofs,

COPPER
Mk 12:42 and put in two small c coins,

CORNERSTONE → STONE
Ps 118:22 rejected has become the chief c.
Isa 28:16 a tested stone, a precious c, a sure
Zec 10:4 Out of them shall come the c,
Lk 20:17 builders rejected has become the c'?
Eph 2:20 with Christ Jesus himself as the c.
1Pe 2:6 laying in Zion a stone, a c chosen

CORRECT → CORRECTING, CORRECTION
Ps 141:5 let the faithful c me.
Sir 42:8 Do not be ashamed to c the stupid

CORRECTING → CORRECT
2Ti 2:25 c opponents with gentleness.

CORRECTION → CORRECT
Jer 5:3 but they refused to take c.
2Ti 3:16 c, and for training in righteousness,

CORRUPT → CORRUPTION
Ge 6:11 Now the earth was c in God's sight,
Ac 2:40 yourselves from this c generation."
Eph 4:22 your old self, c and deluded

CORRUPTION → CORRUPT
Ac   2:31 nor did his flesh experience c.'
2Pe   1: 4 you may escape from the c

COST
1Ch 21:24 burnt offerings that c me nothing."
Lk 14:28 not first sit down and estimate the c,

COUNCIL → COUNCILS
Jer 23:18 who has stood in the c of the LORD
Mt 26:59 the whole c were looking for false

COUNCILS → COUNCIL
Mk 13: 9 for they will hand you over to c;

COUNSEL → COUNSELOR,
COUNSELORS
Ps   2: 2 and the rulers take c together,
      33:11 The c of the LORD stands forever,
Isa 28:29 he is wonderful in c, and excellent

COUNSELOR → COUNSEL
Isa   9: 6 and he is named Wonderful C,
Ro 11:34 Or who has been his c?"
Sir 42:21 and he needs no one to be his c.

COUNSELORS → COUNSEL
Pr 11:14 in an abundance of c there is safety.
      24: 6 in abundance of c there is victory.

COUNTENANCE
Nu   6:26 the LORD lift up his c upon you,
Ps 89:15 O LORD, in the light of your c;
Pr 15:13 A glad heart makes a cheerful c,

COURAGE → COURAGEOUS
1Ch 22:13 Be strong and of good c.
Jn 16:33 But take c; I have conquered

COURAGEOUS → COURAGE
Jos   1: 6 Be strong and c; for you shall put
Da 10:19 Be strong and c!"
1Co 16:13 stand firm in your faith, be c,
1Mc 2:64 be c and grow strong in the law.

COURT → COURTS
Ex 27: 9 shall make the c of the tabernacle.
Pr 25: 8 do not hastily bring into c;
Mt   5:25 while you are on the way to c
1Co   6: 6 believer goes to c against a believer

COURTS → COURT
Ps 84:10 in your c is better than a thousand
      96: 8 an offering, and come into his c.

COVENANT → COVENANTS
Ge   6:18 But I will establish my c with you;
      9: 9 I am establishing my c with you
      15:18 the LORD made a c with Abram,
Ex 19: 5 you obey my voice and keep my c,
      24: 7 Then he took the book of the c,
      40: 3 put in it the ark of the c,
Jdg   2: 1 'I will never break my c with you.
1Ki   8:23 keeping c and steadfast love
Ps 105: 8 He is mindful of his c forever,
Isa 61: 8 I will make an everlasting c with
Jer 31:31 when I will make a new c with
Eze 16:60 establish with you an everlasting c.
Mal   3: 1 The messenger of the c in whom
Lk 22:20 is the new c in my blood.
1Co 11:25 "This cup is the new c in my blood,
2Co 3: 6 be ministers of a new c, not of letter

Heb 7:22 become the guarantee of a better c.
      12:24 the mediator of a new c,
Rev 11:19 the ark of his c was seen within his
Jdt   9:13 planned cruel things against your c,
Sir 28: 7 remember the c of the Most High,
1Mc 1:15 and abandoned the holy c.
2Es 3:15 You made an everlasting c with

COVENANTS → COVENANT
Ro   9: 4 the adoption, the glory, the c,
Gal   4:24 an allegory: these women are two c.

COVET
Ex 20:17 shall not c your neighbor's house;
Ro   7: 7 had not said, "You shall not c."
Jas   4: 2 you c something and cannot obtain

CRAFTINESS → CRAFTY
Ro   1:29 of envy, murder, strife, deceit, c,
1Co 3:19 "He catches the wise in their c,"

CRAFTY → CRAFTINESS
Ge   3: 1 serpent was more c than any other

CRAVING
Nu 11: 4 rabble among them had a strong c;
Ps 78:30 But before they had satisfied their c,

CREATE → CREATED, CREATION,
CREATOR
Ps 51:10 C in me a clean heart, O God,
Isa 65:17 to c new heavens and a new earth;
Eph 2:15 c in himself one new humanity

CREATED → CREATE
Ge   1: 1 In the beginning when God c the
      1:27 So God c humankind in his image,
Dt 32: 6 Is not he your father, who c you,
Pr   8:22 The LORD c me at the beginning
Mal 2:10 Has not one God c us?
1Co 11: 9 Neither was man c for the sake of
Eph 2:10 c in Christ Jesus for good works,
Col   1:16 all things have been c through him
1Ti   4: 4 For everything c by God is good,
Rev 4:11 you c all things, and by your will
Jdt 13:18 who c the heavens and the earth,
Wis 2:23 for God c us for incorruption,
Sir   1: 4 Wisdom was c before all other

CREATION → CREATE
Ge   2: 3 all the work that he had done in c.
Mk 10: 6 But from the beginning of c,
Ro   8:19 the c waits with eager longing for
2Co 5:17 anyone is in Christ, there is a new c:
Col   1:15 invisible God, the firstborn of all c;

CREATOR → CREATE
Ecc 12: 1 Remember your c in the days of
Ro   1:25 served the creature rather than the C
1Pe 4:19 to a faithful C,

CREATURE → CREATURES
Ge   2:19 the man called every living c,

CREATURES → CREATURE
Lev 11: 2 these are the c that you may eat.
Ps 104:24 the earth is full of your c.

CRIED → CRY
Ps 22: 5 To you they c, and were saved;
Mt 27:46 Jesus c with a loud voice,

CRIMINAL → CRIMINALS
Jn 18:30 "If this man were not a c,
2Ti   2: 9 the point of being chained like a c.
1Pe 4:15 suffer as a murderer, a thief, a c,

CRIMINALS → CRIMINAL
Lk 23:32 Two others also, who were c,

CROOKED
Dt 32: 5 a perverse and c generation.
Ps 18:26 the c you show yourself perverse.
Ecc 1:15 What is c cannot be made straight,
Lk   3: 5 and the c shall be made straight,

CROSS
Dt 31: 3 your God himself will c over before
Mk 15:30 and come down from the c!"
Lk 14:27 the c and follow me cannot be my
1Co 1:18 the c is foolishness to those who are
Gal   6:14 never boast of anything except the c
Php 2: 8 of death—even death on a c.
Col   1:20 peace through the blood of his c.
Heb 12: 2 was set before him endured the c,

CROW
Lk 22:34 the cock will not c this day,

CROWD → CROWDS
Mk   8: 2 "I have compassion for the c,
      14:43 a c with swords and clubs,

CROWDS → CROWD
Mt   7:28 c were astounded at his teaching,

CROWN → CROWNED, CROWNS
Lev 8: 9 the golden ornament, the holy c,
Jn 19: 2 soldiers wove a c of thorns and put
Php 4: 1 my joy and c, stand firm in the Lord
2Ti   4: 8 there is reserved for me the c
1Pe 5: 4 the c of glory that never fades away.
Rev 6: 2 Its rider had a bow; a c was given
      14:14 with a golden c on his head,

CROWNED → CROWN
Ps   8: 5 and c them with glory and honor.
2Ti   2: 5 no one is c without competing
Heb 2: 9 now c with glory and honor

CROWNS → CROWN
Rev 4:10 they cast their c before the throne,

CRUCIFIED → CRUCIFY
Mt 27:22 All of them said, "Let him be c!"
Lk 24: 7 c, and on the third day rise again."
Ac   4:10 whom you c, whom God raised
Ro   6: 6 We know that our old self was c
1Co 1:23 but we proclaim Christ c,
Gal   2:19 I have been c with Christ;

CRUCIFY → CRUCIFIED,
CRUCIFYING
Lk 23:21 they kept shouting, "C, c him!"
Jn 19:15 asked them, "Shall I c your King?"

CRUCIFYING → CRUCIFY
Heb 6: 6 they are c again the Son of God

CRUSH
Mt 21:44 it will c anyone on whom it falls."
Ro 16:20 will shortly c Satan under your feet.

CRY → CRIED, CRYING
Pr 130: 1 Out of the depths I c to you,

Hab　1:　2　how long shall I c for help,
Mk　15:37　Then Jesus gave a loud c

CRYING → CRY
Mk　1:　3　the voice of one c out in the
Rev　21:　4　c and pain will be no more,

CUP
Ps　23:　5　my head with oil; my c overflows.
Mt　26:39　if it is possible, let this c pass
Mk　10:38　you able to drink the c that I drink,
Lk　22:17　he took a c, and after giving thanks
1Co　11:25　c is the new covenant in my blood.
Rev　14:10　unmixed into the c of his anger,

CURED
Mt　8:16　and c all who were sick.
Ac　5:16　and they were all c.

CURSE → ACCURSED, CURSED, CURSES
Ge　8:21　"I will never again c the ground
　　12:　3　the one who curses you I will c;
Job　2:　9　C God, and die."
Ps　109:28　Let them c, but you will bless.
Mal　4:　6　come and strike the land with a c.
Mk　14:71　he began to c, and he swore an oath,
Lk　6:28　bless those who c you, pray
Ro　12:14　bless and do not c them.
Gal　3:13　redeemed us from the c of the law by
　　　　becoming a c for us—
Sir　4:　5　and give no one reason to c you;

CURSED → CURSE
Ge　3:17　c is the ground because of you;
　　27:29　C be everyone who curses you,
Nu　23:　8　can I curse whom God has not c?
Mk　11:21　fig tree that you c has withered."
Gal　3:10　"C is everyone who does not
Rev　16:　9　but they c the name of God,

CURSES → CURSE
Lev　24:15　who c God shall bear the sin.

CURTAIN
Ex　26:31　You shall make a c of blue, purple,
2Ch　3:14　And Solomon made the c of blue
Lk　23:45　the c of the temple was torn in two.
Heb　10:20　that he opened for us through the c

CUT
Ge　9:11　never again shall all flesh be c off
Ps　37:　9　For the wicked shall be c off,
Isa　53:　8　c off from the land of the living,
Mt　3:10　does not bear good fruit is c down
Mk　9:43　hand causes you to stumble, c it off;
Ro　11:22　otherwise you also will be c off.

D

DAILY → DAY
Mt　6:11　Give us this day our d bread.
Lk　9:23　take up their cross d and follow me.

DANCE → DANCED
Ps　150:　4　Praise him with tambourine and d;
Ecc　3:　4　a time to mourn, and a time to d;
Lk　7:32　the flute for you, and you did not d;

DANCED → DANCE
2Sa　6:14　David d before the LORD with all
Mt　14:　6　the daughter of Herodias d before

DARK → DARKEST, DARKNESS
Ps　139:12　even the darkness is not d to you;
Lk　12:　3　whatever you have said in the d will
2Pe　1:19　as to a lamp shining in a d place,

DARKEST → DARK
Ps　23:　4　though I walk through the d valley,

DARKNESS → DARK
Ge　1:　2　the earth was a formless void and d
Ex　10:22　was dense d in all the land of Egypt
Isa　9:　2　walked in d have seen a great light;
Joel　2:31　The sun shall be turned to d,
Mt　4:16　who sat in d have seen a great light,
Jn　1:　5　light shines in the d, and the d did
　　　　not
Col　1:13　from the power of d and transferred
1Jn　1:　5　God is light and in him there is no d

DAUGHTER → DAUGHTERS
Mic　7:　6　the d rises up against her mother,
Lk　12:53　against d and d against mother,

DAUGHTERS → DAUGHTER
Ge　6:　4　of God went in to the d of humans,
Joel　2:28　sons and your d shall prophesy,
Ac　2:17　sons and your d shall prophesy,
2Co　6:18　and you shall be my sons and d,

DAWN → DAWNS
Isa　14:12　from heaven, O Day Star, son of D!
Hos　6:　3　his appearing is as sure as the d;

DAWNS → DAWN
Ps　97:11　Light d for the righteous,
2Pe　1:19　until the day d and the morning star

DAY → DAILY, DAYS
Ge　1:　5　God called the light D, and
Ex　13:21　of them in a pillar of cloud by d,
　　20:　8　Remember the sabbath d, and keep
Ps　1:　2　his law they meditate d and night.
　　118:24　is the d that the LORD has made;
Joel　1:15　For the d of the LORD is near,
Zec　14:　1　See, a d is coming for the LORD,
Mal　3:　2　who can endure the d of his coming,
Mt　25:13　you know neither the d nor the hour.
Lk　11:　3　Give us each d our daily bread.
　　24:46　to rise from the dead on the third d,
Jn　6:40　I will raise them up on the last d."
Ro　14:　5　Some judge one d to be better than
1Th　5:　2　very well that the d of the Lord
2Pe　3:　8　one d is like a thousand years,
　　3:10　d of the Lord will come like a thief,
1Jn　4:17　have boldness on the d of judgment,
Rev　16:14　for battle on the great d of God

DAYS → DAY
Ge　1:14　and for seasons and for d and years,
Ex　24:18　on the mountain for forty d and
1Ki　8:　9　that food forty d and forty nights
Ps　90:10　The d of our life are seventy years,
Eph　5:16　of the time, because the d are evil.
2Ti　3:　1　in the last d distressing times will
1Mc　4:56　dedication of the altar for eight d,
2Es　14:42　They sat forty d; they wrote

DEACON → DEACONS
Ro　16:　1　a d of the church at Cenchreae,

DEACONS → DEACON
1Ti　3:　8　D likewise must be serious, not

DEAD → DEATH, DIE, DIED, DYING
Mt　8:22　and let the d bury their own d."
Mk　12:27　God not of the d, but of the living;
Lk　24:　5　look for the living among the d?
Ro　6:11　must consider yourselves d to sin
Eph　2:　1　You were d through the trespasses
Rev　1:　5　witness, the firstborn of the d,
　　20:12　And the d were judged according to

DEAF
Ex　4:11　Who makes them mute or d,
Isa　29:18　On that day the d shall hear the
Lk　7:22　the lepers are cleansed, the d hear,

DEATH → DEAD
Dt　30:19　that I have set before you life and d,
Isa　25:　7　he will swallow up d forever.
Hos　13:14　O D, where are your plagues?
Lk　1:79　in darkness and in the shadow of d,
Jn　5:24　but has passed from d to life.
Ro　6:23　For the wages of sin is d,
1Co　15:55　"Where, O d, is your victory?
Heb　2:14　through d he might destroy the one
　　　　who has the power of d,
1Jn　3:14　that we have passed from d to life
Rev　1:18　I have the keys of D and of Hades.
　　20:14　D and Hades were thrown into the
　　　　lake
　　21:　4　D will be no more;
Sir　15:17　Before each person are life and d,

DEBTS
Mt　6:12　And forgive us our d, as we

DECEIT → DECEITFUL, DECEIVE
Dt　32:　4　a faithful God, without d,
Isa　53:　9　and there was no d in his mouth.
Ro　1:29　Full of envy, murder, strife, d,
1Pe　2:22　and no d was found in his mouth."

DECEITFUL → DECEIT
1Ti　4:　1　by paying attention to d spirits

DECEIVE → DECEIT
Eph　5:　6　Let no one d you with empty words,
1Jn　1:　8　that we have no sin, we d ourselves,
Rev　20:　8　to d the nations at the four corners

DECREES
Dt　6:　2　and keep all his d and his
Ps　19:　7　the d of the LORD are sure,
　　119:　2　Happy are those who keep his d,

DEDICATION
2Ch　7:　9　the d of the altar seven days and
Ezr　6:16　the d of this house of God with joy.
1Mc　4:56　the d of the altar for eight days,

DEED → DEEDS
Ecc　12:14　will bring every d into judgment,
Mt　19:16　good d must I do to have eternal life
Col　3:17　And whatever you do, in word or d,

DEEDS → DEED
Jer　50:29　Repay her according to her d;
Lk　23:41　getting what we deserve for our d,
Ro　2:　6　repay according to each one's d:
Rev　15:　3　"Great and amazing are your d,
　　19:　8　is the righteous d of the saints.

DEEP → DEPTH, DEPTHS
Ge　1:　2　darkness covered the face of the d,

7:11 the fountains of the great **d** burst
Ro 8:26 with sighs too **d** for words.

DEFEND
Ps 72: 4 May he **d** the cause of the poor of
Pr 31: 9 **d** the rights of the poor and needy.
Jdt 5:21 for their Lord and God will **d** them,

DEFILE
Lev 11:43 you shall not **d** yourselves
Nu 35:34 You shall not **d** the land
Mk 7:15 things that come out are what **d.**"

DEITY
Col 2: 9 whole fullness of **d** dwells bodily,

DELAY
Dt 7:10 He does not **d** but repays
Ps 70: 5 my deliverer; O LORD, do not **d!**
Heb 10:37 will come and will not **d;**

DELIGHT
1Sa 15:22 "Has the LORD as great **d** in burnt
Ps 1: 2 their **d** is in the law of the LORD,
    40: 8 I **d** to do your will, O my God;
Pr 8:30 I was daily his **d,** rejoicing before
Ro 7:22 For I **d** in the law of God in my
Sir 1:27 fidelity and humility are his **d.**

DELIVER → DELIVERANCE,
    DELIVERER, DELIVERS
Ex 3: 8 to **d** them from the Egyptians,
Da 3:17 able to **d** us from the furnace
    6:20 able to **d** you from the lions?"
Mt 27:43 let God **d** him now,

DELIVERANCE → DELIVER
Ex 14:13 and see the **d** that the LORD will
Ps 3: 8 **D** belongs to the LORD;
Php 1:19 this will turn out for my **d.**
Jdt 8:17 while we wait for his **d,**

DELIVERER → DELIVER
Ps 140: 7 O LORD, my Lord, my strong **d,**
Ro 11:26 "Out of Zion will come the **D;**

DEMON → DEMONIACS,
    DEMONIC, DEMONS
Mt 11:18 and they say, 'He has a **d';**
    17:18 Jesus rebuked the **d,** and it came out
Jn 8:48 you are a Samaritan and have a **d?"**
  10:21 not the words of one who has a **d.**
Tob 3: 8 the wicked Asmodeus had killed
    6: 8 of a man or woman afflicted by a **d**

DEMONIACS → DEMON
Mt 4:24 **d,** epileptics, and paralytics, and he
    8:28 two **d** coming out of the tombs met

DEMONIC → DEMON
Rev 16:14 These are **d** spirits, performing signs

DEMONS → DEMON
Dt 32:17 They sacrificed to **d,** not God,
Lk 11:18 that I cast out the **d** by Beelzebul.
1Co 10:20 not want you to be partners with **d.**
1Ti 4: 1 deceitful spirits and teachings of **d,**
Jas 2:19 Even the **d** believe—and shudder.
Rev 9:20 their hands or give up worshiping **d**
Bar 4: 7 by sacrificing to **d** and not

DEN
Jer 7:11 a **d** of robbers in your sight?

Da 6: 7 shall be thrown into a **d** of lions.
Mk 11:17 you have made it a **d** of robbers."

DENARIUS
Mk 12:15 Bring me a **d** and let me see it."

DENIED → DENY
Mt 26:70 But he **d** it before all of them,
1Ti 5: 8 has **d** the faith and is worse than
Rev 3: 8 my word and have not **d** my name.

DENIES → DENY
Lk 12: 9 but whoever **d** me before others
1Jn 2:22 liar but the one who **d** that Jesus

DENY → DENIED, DENIES
Mt 16:24 let them **d** themselves and take up
2Ti 2:12 if we **d** him, he will also **d** us;
2Pe 2: 1 **d** the Master who bought them—

DEPRAVED → DEPRAVITY
1Ti 6: 5 among those who are **d** in mind
2Pe 2:10 who indulge their flesh in **d** lust,

DEPRAVITY → DEPRAVED
Lev 20:14 that there may be no **d** among you.

DEPTH → DEEP
Mt 13: 5 since they had no **d** of soil.
Ro 11:33 O the **d** of the riches and wisdom
Eph 3:18 and length and height and **d,**

DEPTHS → DEEP
Ps 130: 1 Out of the **d** I cry to you;
1Co 2:10 even the **d** of God.

DESCENDANTS
Ge 15:18 saying, "To your **d** I give this land,
Dt 4:37 he chose their **d** after them.
Isa 44: 3 I will pour my spirit upon your **d,**
Ro 9: 7 Abraham's children are his true **d;**
Gal 3: 7 who believe are the **d** of Abraham.

DESERT
Ps 106:14 and put God to the test in the **d;**
Isa 40: 3 make straight in the **d** a highway
Mk 8: 4 with bread here in the **d?"**

DESERVE
Pr 14:14 and the good, what their deeds **d.**
Lk 23:15 he has done nothing to **d** death.
Ac 26:31 man is doing nothing to **d** death
Rev 2:23 give to each of you as your works **d.**

DESIRE → DESIRES
Ge 3:16 your **d** shall be for your husband,
Ps 20: 4 May he grant you your heart's **d,**
Hos 6: 6 I **d** steadfast love and not sacrifice,
Mt 9:13 learn what this means, 'I **d** mercy,
1Jn 2:16 the **d** of the flesh, the **d** of the eyes,

DESIRES → DESIRE
1Ti 2: 4 who **d** everyone to be saved
2Ti 4: 3 teachers to suit their own **d,**
Sir 18:30 Do not follow your base **d,**

DESOLATE → DESOLATES
Da 11:31 the abomination that makes **d.**
1Mc 1:39 sanctuary became **d** like a desert;

DESOLATES → DESOLATE
Da 9:27 shall be an abomination that **d,**

DESPISE → DESPISED
Job 5:17 not **d** the discipline of the Almighty.
Pr 1: 7 fools **d** wisdom and instruction.
Lk 16:13 devoted to the one and **d** the other.

DESPISED → DESPISE
Isa 53: 3 He was **d** and rejected by others;
1Co 1:28 God chose what is low and **d** in the

DESTINED
Eph 1: 5 He **d** us for adoption as his children
1Th 5: 9 For God has **d** us not for wrath but
1Pe 1:11 to the sufferings **d** for Christ

DESTROY → DESTROYED,
    DESTRUCTION
Ge 6:13 to **d** them along with the earth.
Mt 10:28 rather fear him who can **d** both soul
Jn 10:10 comes only to steal and kill and **d.**
Jas 4:12 who is able to save and to **d.**
1Jn 3: 8 to **d** the works of the devil.

DESTROYED → DESTROY
Da 6:26 His kingdom shall never be **d,**
1Co 15:26 The last enemy to be **d** is death.

DESTRUCTION → DESTROY
Pr 16:18 Pride goes before **d,** and a haughty
Mt 7:13 and the road is easy that leads to **d,**

DEVIL
Mt 4: 1 wilderness to be tempted by the **d.**
Lk 8:12 **d** comes and takes away the word
Jn 8:44 You are from your father the **d,**
Eph 4:27 and do not make room for the **d.**
    6:11 to stand against the wiles of the **d.**
1Ti 3: 6 fall into the condemnation of the **d,**
Heb 2:14 the power of death, that is, the **d,**
Jas 4: 7 Resist the **d,** and he will flee from
1Pe 5: 8 lion your adversary the **d** prowls
1Jn 3: 8 to destroy the works of the **d.**
Jude 1: 9 Michael contended with the **d**
Rev 12: 9 who is called the **D** and Satan,
    20: 2 that ancient serpent, who is the **D**

DIE → DEAD
Ge 2:17 eat of it you shall **d.**"
    3: 4 to the woman, "You will not **d;**
Ru 1:17 Where you **d,** I will **d**—
Ecc 3: 2 a time to be born, and a time to **d;**
Isa 22:13 eat and drink, for tomorrow we **d.**"
Jer 31:30 But all shall **d** for their own sins;
Mt 26:35 "Even though I must **d** with you,
Jn 11:26 and believes in me will never **d.**
Ro 14: 8 if we **d,** we **d** to the Lord;
1Co 15:32 eat and drink, for tomorrow we **d.**"
Heb 9:27 appointed for mortals to **d** once,

DIED → DEAD
Ro 5: 6 right time Christ **d** for the ungodly.
1Co 15: 3 Christ **d** for our sins in accordance
Gal 2:19 the law I **d** to the law,

DIFFERENT
2Co 11: 4 or a **d** gospel from the one you
Gal 1: 6 and are turning to a **d** gospel—

DISAPPOINT
Ro 5: 5 and hope does not **d** us,

DISCIPLE → DISCIPLES
Mt 10:24 "A **d** is not above the teacher,

Lk 14:26 even life itself, cannot be my **d**.

DISCIPLES → DISCIPLE
Mt 26:56 all the **d** deserted him and fled.
28:19 therefore and make **d** of all nations,
Lk 6:13 he called his **d** and chose twelve of
Jn 8:31 in my word, you are truly my **d**;
Ac 11:26 the **d** were first called "Christians."

DISCIPLINE → DISCIPLINED
Job 5:17 not despise the **d** of the Almighty.
Ps 94:12 Happy are those whom you **d**,
Eph 6:4 in the **d** and instruction of the Lord.
Heb 12:5 not regard lightly the **d** of the Lord,
Sir 1:27 fear of the Lord is wisdom and **d**,

DISCIPLINED → DISCIPLINE
1Co 11:32 **d** so that we may not be condemned
Wis 3:5 Having been **d** a little, they will

DISEASE → DISEASES
Mt 4:23 of the kingdom and curing every **d**
9:35 curing every **d** and every sickness.

DISEASES → DISEASE
Ex 15:26 **d** that I brought upon the Egyptians;
Ps 103:3 your iniquity, who heals all your **d**,
Isa 53:4 our infirmities and carried our **d**;
Mt 8:17 took our infirmities and bore our **d**."

DISMAYED
Dt 1:21 do not fear or be **d**."
Jos 1:9 do not be frightened or **d**,

DISOBEDIENT → DISOBEY
Ne 9:26 they were **d** and rebelled
Ro 10:21 I have held out my hands to a **d**
Tit 3:3 ourselves were once foolish, **d**,

DISOBEY → DISOBEDIENT
Lev 26:27 But if, despite this, you **d** me,
1Pe 2:8 stumble because they **d** the word,
Sir 1:28 Do not **d** the fear of the Lord;

DISTINCTION → DISTINCTIONS
Ex 8:23 I will make a **d** between my people
Lev 11:47 make a **d** between the unclean and
Eze 22:26 have made no **d** between the holy

DISTINCTIONS → DISTINCTION
Jas 2:4 you not made **d** among yourselves,

DISTRESS → DISTRESSED
2Sa 22:7 In my **d** I called upon the Lord;
Ps 81:7 In **d** you called, and I rescued you;
Lk 21:23 For there will be great **d** on the earth
Ro 8:35 Will hardship, or **d**, or persecution,
Sir 2:11 and saves in time of **d**.

DISTRESSED → DISTRESS
La 1:20 See, O Lord, how **d** I am;

DISTRIBUTED
Ac 4:35 it was **d** to each as any had need.
Heb 2:4 gifts of the Holy Spirit, **d** according

DIVIDED
Lev 11:3 Any animal that has **d** hoofs
Ps 136:13 who **d** the Red Sea in two,
Lk 11:18 If Satan also is **d** against himself,

DIVINE
Ro 1:20 his eternal power and **d** nature,

2Pe 1:4 become participants of the **d** nature.

DIVORCE → DIVORCED
Dt 24:1 so he writes her a certificate of **d**,
Isa 50:1 Where is your mother's bill of **d**
Jer 8:3 sent her away with a decree of **d**;
Mal 2:16 For I hate **d**, says the Lord,
Mt 5:31 let him give her a certificate of **d**.'
19:3 a man to **d** his wife for any cause?"
1Co 7:11 the husband should not **d** his wife.
Sir 7:26 Do not **d** her;

DIVORCED → DIVORCE
Lev 21:7 neither shall they marry a woman **d**
Mt 5:32 whoever marries a **d** woman

DOCTOR
Lk 4:23 this proverb, '**D**, cure yourself!'

DOCTRINE → DOCTRINES
Eph 4:14 blown about by every wind of **d**,
1Ti 1:3 not to teach any different **d**,
2Ti 4:3 people will not put up with sound **d**,
Tit 1:9 able both to preach with sound **d**

DOCTRINES → DOCTRINE
Mk 7:7 teaching human precepts as **d**.'

DOERS
Jas 1:22 But be **d** of the word,

DOGS
Mt 7:6 "Do not give what is holy to **d**;

DOMINION
Ge 1:26 and let them have **d** over
Ps 22:28 For **d** belongs to the Lord.
Da 7:14 His **d** is an everlasting **d**
Rev 1:6 to him be glory and **d** forever

DONKEY
Zec 9:9 humble and riding on a **d**,
Mt 21:5 humble, and mounted on a **d**,

DOOR → DOORPOSTS
Mt 7:7 knock, and the **d** will be opened
Lk 13:24 Strive to enter through the narrow **d**
Rev 3:20 I am standing at the **d**, knocking;

DOORPOSTS → DOOR
Ex 12:7 the blood and put it on the two **d**

DOUBT → DOUBTED, DOUBTING
Mt 14:31 of little faith, why did you **d**?"
Jn 20:27 Do not **d** but believe."

DOUBTED → DOUBT
Mt 28:17 they worshiped him; but some **d**.

DOUBTING → DOUBT
Jas 1:6 But ask in faith, never **d**,

DOVE
Ge 8:8 Then he sent out the **d** from him,
Mk 1:10 Spirit descending like a **d** on him.

DRAGON
Isa 27:1 and he will kill the **d** that
Rev 12:3 a great red **d**, with seven heads and
20:2 seized the **d**, that ancient serpent,
Bel 1:23 in that place there was a great **d**,

DRANK → DRINK
Ex 24:11 beheld God, and they ate and **d**.

Mk 14:23 and all of them **d** from it.
1Co 10:4 all **d** the same spiritual drink.

DRAW
Jas 4:8 **D** near to God, and he will **d** near

DREAM → DREAMS
Joel 2:28 your old men shall **d** dreams,
Ac 2:17 and your old men shall **d** dreams.

DREAMS → DREAM
Nu 12:6 I speak to them in **d**.
Sir 34:7 For **d** have deceived many,

DRIED → DRY
Ge 8:13 the waters were **d** up from the earth;
Jos 5:1 had **d** up the waters of the Jordan
Isa 51:10 Was it not you who **d** up the sea,

DRINK → DRANK, DRUNK, DRUNKARD, DRUNKENNESS
Ex 32:6 the people sat down to eat and **d**,
Ecc 9:7 and **d** your wine with a merry heart;
Isa 22:13 eat and **d**, for tomorrow we die."
Mt 20:22 to **d** the cup that I am about to **d**?"
Jn 18:11 not to **d** the cup that the Father has
Ro 14:17 kingdom of God is not food and **d**
1Co 12:13 we were all made to **d** of one Spirit.
Rev 14:10 also **d** the wine of God's wrath,

DRUNK → DRINK
Jn 2:10 after the guests have become **d**.
Ac 2:15 these are not **d**, as you suppose,
Eph 5:18 Do not get **d** with wine,
Jdt 13:2 on his bed, for he was dead **d**.

DRUNKARD → DRINK
Mt 11:19 they say, 'Look, a glutton and a **d**,
1Co 5:11 is an idolater, reviler, **d**, or robber.
1Ti 3:3 not a **d**, not violent but gentle,

DRUNKENNESS → DRINK
Gal 5:21 **d**, carousing, and things like these.
Tob 4:15 to excess or let **d** go with you

DRY → DRIED
Ge 1:9 and let the **d** land appear."
Ex 14:16 may go into the sea on **d** ground.
Eze 37:4 **d** bones, hear the word of the Lord.

DUST
Ge 2:7 Lord God formed man from the **d**
1Sa 2:8 He raises up the poor from the **d**;
Ps 103:14 he remembers that we are **d**.
Ecc 3:20 from the **d**, and all turn to **d** again.
Mt 10:14 shake off the **d** from your feet
1Co 15:47 man was from the earth, a man of **d**;

DWELL → DWELLING, DWELLS
Ex 25:8 so that I may **d** among them.
1Ki 8:27 But will God indeed **d** on the earth?
Ps 23:6 and I shall **d** in the house of
Eph 3:17 that Christ may **d** in your hearts
Col 1:19 fullness of God was pleased to **d**,
Rev 21:3 He will **d** with them as their God;

DWELLING → DWELL
Ps 90:1 our **d** place in all generations.
Jn 14:2 my Father's house there are many **d**
2Co 5:2 to be clothed with our heavenly **d**—
Eph 2:22 spiritually into a **d** place for God.

DWELLS → DWELL

Jn 14:10 but the Father who **d** in me
Ro 7:17 but sin that **d** within me.
1Co 3:16 and that God's Spirit **d** in you?
Col 2: 9 whole fullness of deity **d** bodily,

E

EAGLES

Isa 40:31 shall mount up with wings like **e**,

EAR

Isa 64: 4 has heard, no **e** has perceived,
Lk 22:51 he touched his **e** and healed him.
1Co 2: 9 "What no eye has seen, nor **e** heard,

EARTH

Ge 1: 1 God created the heavens and the **e**,
    6:11 the **e** was corrupt in God's sight,
Isa 6: 3 the whole **e** is full of his glory."
    65:17 to create new heavens and a new **e**;
Mt 5: 5 meek, for they will inherit the **e**.
    24:35 Heaven and **e** will pass away,
2Pe 3:13 wait for new heavens and a new **e**,
Rev 21: 1 I saw a new heaven and a new **e**;
Sir 40:11 All that is of **e** returns to **e**,

EAST

Ge 2: 8 planted a garden in Eden, in the **e**;
Ps 103:12 as far as the **e** is from the west,
Mt 2: 1 wise men from the **E** came to

EASY

Mt 11:30 For my yoke is **e**, and my burden is

EAT → ATE, EATS

Ge 2:16 freely **e** of every tree of the garden;
Lev 11: 4 you shall not **e** the following:
Mt 26:26 to the disciples, and said, "Take, **e**;
Ac 10:13 "Get up, Peter; kill and **e**."
1Co 10:31 whether you **e** or drink, or whatever
Rev 3:20 I will come in to you and **e** with you

EATS → EAT

Jn 6:51 **e** of this bread will live forever;
1Co 11:27 **e** the bread or drinks the cup of the

EDEN

Ge 2: 8 a garden in **E**, in the east;

EGYPT

Ge 47:27 Israel settled in the land of **E**,
Hos 11: 1 and out of **E** I called my son.
Mt 2:15 "Out of **E** I have called my son."
Rev 11: 8 prophetically called Sodom and **E**,

ELDER → ELDERS

1Ti 5:19 any accusation against an **e** except
1Pe 5: 1 as an **e** myself and a witness of the

ELDERS → ELDER

Ex 24: 1 and seventy of the **e** of Israel,
Mt 27:12 accused by the chief priests and **e**,
Mk 7: 3 thus observing the tradition of the **e**;
1Ti 5:17 the **e** who rule well be considered
Jas 5:14 **e** of the church and have them pray
1Pe 5: 5 must accept the authority of the **e**.
Rev 4: 4 on the thrones are twenty-four **e**,
Sus 1:61 they took action against the two **e**,

ELECT → ELECTION

Mt 24:22 sake of the **e** those days will be cut

Mk 13:22 to lead astray, if possible, the **e**.
Wis 4:15 grace and mercy are with his **ee**
2Es 16:73 Then the tested quality of my **e**

ELECTION → ELECT

Ro 9:11 God's purpose of **e** might continue,
2Pe 1:10 eager to confirm your call and **e**,

ELEVEN

Mt 28:16 Now the **e** disciples went to Galilee,
Ac 1:26 and he was added to the **e** apostles.

EMMANUEL → IMMANUEL

Mt 1:23 and they shall name him **E**,"

ENCOURAGE →
    ENCOURAGEMENT

1Th 4:18 **e** one another with these words.
1Pe 5:12 written this short letter to **e** you

ENCOURAGEMENT →
    ENCOURAGE

Ro 15: 5 God of steadfastness and **e** grant
Php 2: 1 If then there is any **e** in Christ,

END

Ge 6:13 determined to make an **e** of all flesh,
Pr 14:12 but its **e** is the way to death.
Ecc 12:12 making many books there is no **e**,
Mt 24:13 But the one who endures to the **e**
    28:20 always, to the **e** of the age."
Ro 10: 4 For Christ is the **e** of the law so
Rev 22:13 the beginning and the **e**."

ENDURANCE → ENDURE

Ro 5: 3 knowing that suffering produces **e**,
1Ti 6:11 godliness, faith, love, **e**,
Heb 10:36 For you need **e**, so that when you
Jas 1: 3 the testing of your faith produces **e**;
2Pe 1: 6 and self-control with **e**,

ENDURE → ENDURANCE,
    ENDURED, ENDURES

Mal 3: 2 who can **e** the day of his coming,
1Co 10:13 so that you may be able to **e** it.
2Ti 2:12 if we **e**, we will also reign with him;

ENDURED → ENDURE

Heb 12: 2 that was set before him he **e** the cross,

ENDURES → ENDURE

1Co 13: 7 hopes all things, **e** all things.
1Pe 1:25 but the word of the Lord **e** forever."
Sir 40:17 and almsgiving **e** forever.
Bar 4: 1 the law that **e** forever.

ENEMIES → ENEMY

Mt 5:44 But I say to you, Love your **e** and
Ro 5:10 For if while we were **e**,

ENEMY → ENEMIES, ENMITY

Mt 13:39 the **e** who sowed them is the devil;
1Co 15:26 The last **e** to be destroyed is death.

ENGAGED

Mt 1:18 mother Mary had been **e** to Joseph,

ENJOYMENT

Ecc 8:15 So I commend **e**, for there is nothing
1Ti 6:17 with everything for our **e**.

ENLIGHTENED → LIGHT

Ro 10: 2 a zeal for God, but it is not **e**.

Eph 1:18 with the eyes of your heart **e**,
Heb 6: 4 those who have once been **e**,

ENLIGHTENS → LIGHT

Jn 1: 9 The true light, which **e** everyone,

ENMITY → ENEMY

Ge 3:15 put **e** between you and the woman,
Jas 4: 4 with the world is **e** with God?

ENTER → ENTRY

Mt 7:13 "**E** through the narrow gate,
Mk 10:15 as a little child will never **e** it."
Jn 3: 5 no one can **e** the kingdom of God
Rev 21:27 But nothing unclean will **e** it,

ENTRUSTED → TRUST

Lk 12:48 the one to whom much has been **e**,
2Ti 1:12 guard until that day what I have **e**
Jude 1: 3 the faith that was once for all **e**

ENVY

Pr 23:17 Do not let your heart **e** sinners,
Mk 7:22 deceit, licentiousness, **e**, slander,
Ro 1:29 Full of **e**, murder, strife, deceit,

EPHOD

Ex 28: 6 They shall make the **e** of gold,

EQUAL → EQUALITY

Isa 40:25 you compare me, or who is my **e**?
    46: 5 will you liken me and make me **e**,
Jn 5:18 thereby making himself **e** to God.

EQUALITY → EQUAL

Php 2: 6 not regard **e** with God as something

ERROR

Lev 5:18 for the **e** that you committed
Ro 1:27 the due penalty for their **e**.
1Jn 4: 6 of truth and the spirit of **e**.

ESTABLISH → ESTABLISHED

Eze 16:60 **e** with you an everlasting covenant.
Heb 8: 8 when I will **e** a new covenant with

ESTABLISHED → ESTABLISH

2Sa 7:16 your throne shall be **e** forever.
Ps 89: 2 your steadfast love is **e** forever;
    103:19 The Lord has **e** his throne in the

ETERNAL → ETERNITY

Mt 25:46 but the righteous into **e** life."
Mk 10:17 what must I do to inherit **e** life?"
Jn 3:16 may not perish but may have **e** life.
Ro 6:23 is **e** life through Jesus Christ our Lord.
2Co 4:17 an **e** weight of glory beyond all
Heb 5: 9 the source of **e** salvation for all who
1Jn 5:13 may know that you have **e** life.

ETERNITY → ETERNAL

Isa 57:15 high and lofty one who inhabits **e**,
2Pe 3:18 glory both now and to the day of **e**.
Wis 2:23 made us in the image of his own **e**,
Sir 42:21 he is from all **e** one and the same.

EUNUCH

Ac 8:27 Now there was an Ethiopian **e**,

EVANGELIST → EVANGELISTS

2Ti 4: 5 do the work of an **e**, carry out your

EVANGELISTS → EVANGELIST
Eph   4:11   some e, some pastors and teachers,

EVERLASTING → LAST
Ge   9:16   remember the e covenant between
Ps   90: 2   from e to e you are God.
Isa   9: 6   E Father, Prince of Peace.
Jer   31: 3   I have loved you with an e love;
Da   4: 3   His kingdom is an e kingdom,

EVIL
Ge   2: 9   tree of the knowledge of good and e.
Jdg   2:11   Then the Israelites did what was e
Ps   23: 4   the darkest valley, I fear no e;
Pr   8:13   fear of the LORD is hatred of e,
Mt   6:13   but rescue us from the e one.
     12:35   e person brings e things out of an e
Lk   11:13   who are e, know how to give good
Jn   17:15   to protect them from the e one.
Ro   12:17   Do not repay anyone e for e,
Eph   5:16   of the time, because the days are e.
1Ti   6:10   of money is a root of all kinds of e,
1Jn   5:18   and the e one does not touch them.
2Jn   1:11   to welcome is to participate in the e
3Jn   1:11   do not imitate what is e but imitate
Tob 12: 7   Do good and e will not overtake

EXALT → EXALTED
Lk   14:11   who e themselves will be humbled,
Jas   4:10   before the Lord, and he will e you.

EXALTED → EXALT
Ps   57: 5   Be e, O God, above the heavens.
Php   2: 9   highly e him and gave him the name

EXAMPLES
1Co 10: 6   these things occurred as e for us,
1Pe   5: 3   but be e to the flock.

EXCELLENCE → EXCELLENT
Php   4: 8   if there is any e and if there is

EXCELLENT → EXCELLENCE
Isa   28:29   in counsel, and e in wisdom.
1Co 12:31   I will show you a still more e way.
Heb   1: 4   the name he has inherited is more e

EXCUSE
Jn   15:22   they have no e for their sin.
Ro   1:20   So they are without e;

EXHORT
Tit   2:15   e and reprove with all authority.
Heb   3:13   But e one another every day,

EXILE
2Ki 25:11   carried into e the rest of the people
Ezr   6:21   of Israel who had returned from e,

EYE → EYES, EYEWITNESSES
Ex   21:24   e for e, tooth for tooth,
Ps   17: 8   Guard me as the apple of the e;
Mt   5:29   If your right e causes you to sin,
     5:38   An e for an e and a tooth for
     7: 3   see the speck in your neighbor's e,
Mk 10:25   to go through the e of a needle
1Co 15:52   in the twinkling of an e, at the last
Rev   1: 7   the clouds; every e will see him,

EYES → EYE
Ge   3: 7   Then the e of both were opened,
Ps 121: 1   I lift up my e to the hills—

Pr   3: 7   Do not be wise in your own e;
Mt   9:30   And their e were opened.
Eph   1:18   with the e of your heart enlightened,
1Pe   3:12   e of the Lord are on the righteous,
1Jn   2:16   of the flesh, the desire of the e,
Rev 21: 4   he will wipe every tear from their e.

EYEWITNESSES → EYE, WITNESS
Lk   1: 2   who from the beginning were e
2Pe   1:16   but we had been e of his majesty.

F

FACE
Ge   32:30   "For I have seen God f to f,
Nu   6:25   LORD make his f to shine upon
     12: 8   With him I speak f to f—
Ps   4: 6   Let the light of your f shine on us,
Isa   54: 8   wrath for a moment I hid my f
Eze 39:29   I will never again hide my f from
Lk   9:29   the appearance of his f changed,

FADE → FADES
Ps   37: 2   for they will soon f like the grass,
Isa   64: 6   We all f like a leaf,

FADES → FADE
Isa   40: 7   The grass withers, the flower f,
1Pe   5: 4   crown of glory that never f away.

FAINT
Ps 142: 3   When my spirit is f, you know
Isa   40:31   they shall walk and not f.

FAITH → FAITHFUL, FAITHFULNESS
Isa   7: 9   If you do not stand firm in f,
Hab   2: 4   but the righteous live by their f.
Mt   17:20   have f the size of a mustard seed,
Ac   3:16   and the f that is through Jesus
Ro   3:28   that a person is justified by f apart
1Co 13:13   And now f, hope, and love abide,
Eph   4: 5   one Lord, one f, one baptism,
Heb 11: 1   f is the assurance of things hoped
Jas   2:17   f by itself, if it has no works,
1Jn   5: 4   that conquers the world, our f.
Rev   2:13   and you did not deny your f in me

FAITHFUL → FAITH
Dt   32: 4   A f God, without deceit, just and
Ps   4: 3   LORD has set apart the f for
Mt   24:45   "Who then is the f and wise slave,
1Th   5:24   The one who calls you is f,
Heb 10:23   for he who has promised is f.
1Jn   1: 9   f and just will forgive us our sins
Rev 19:11   Its rider is called F and True,
Wis   3: 9   the f will abide with him in love,
Sir   4:16   If they remain f, they will inherit

FAITHFULNESS → FAITH
Ex   34: 6   abounding in steadfast love and f,
Jos   24:14   and serve him in sincerity and in f;
Isa   11: 5   and f the belt around his loins.
La   3:23   new every morning; great is your f.
Gal   5:22   patience, kindness, generosity, f,

FALL → FELL
Pr   16:18   and a haughty spirit before a f.
Ro   9:33   a rock that will make them f,
1Co 10:12   watch out that you do not f.
Sir   28:23   Those who forsake the Lord will f

FALSE
Dt   5:20   Neither shall you bear f witness
Mk   13:22   F messiahs and f prophets will
Heb   6:18   impossible that God would prove f,
2Pe   2: 1   there will be f teachers among you,
Rev 20:10   where the beast and the f prophet
LtJ   6: 8   but they are f and cannot speak.

FAMILY
Pr   6:19   and one who sows discord in a f.
Gal   6:10   especially for those of the f of faith.
Eph   3:15   from whom every f in heaven and
1Pe   2:17   Love the f of believers.

FAST
Isa   58: 5   Is such the f that I choose,
Mt   6:16   "And whenever you f,

FATHER → FATHER'S
Ge   2:24   a man leaves his f and his mother
Ex   20:12   Honor your f and your mother,
Ps   89:26   cry to me, 'You are my F, my God,
Isa   9: 6   Mighty God, Everlasting F, Prince
Mt   6: 9   Our F in heaven, hallowed be your
     28:19   the name of the F and of the Son and
Jn   5:18   but was also calling God his own F,
     14: 6   comes to the F except through me.
Gal   4: 6   into our hearts, crying, "Abba! F!"
Rev   3: 5   confess your name before my F
Wis   2:16   and boasts that God is his F,
Sir   3: 3   who honor their f atone for sins,

FATHER'S → FATHER
Lk   2:49   that I must be in my F house?"
Jn   1:14   the glory as of a f only son,
     14: 2   F house there are many dwelling

FAVOR
Ps   30: 5   his f is for a lifetime.
Isa   49: 8   In a time of f I have answered you,
Lk   4:19   proclaim the year of the Lord's f."

FEAR → AFRAID
Dt   6:13   The LORD your God you shall f;
Ps   19: 9   the f of the LORD is pure,
     23: 4   the darkest valley, I fear no evil;
Pr   1: 7   f of the LORD is the beginning
Ecc 12:13   F God, and keep his commandments
Mt   10:28   rather f him who can destroy both
Mk   5:36   "Do not f, only believe."
1Pe   3:14   Do not f what they f,
1Jn   4:18   but perfect love casts out f;
Rev 14: 7   "F God and give him glory,
Sir   1:11   The f of the Lord is glory

FEET
Ps 119:105   Your word is a lamp to my f
Lk   24:39   Look at my hands and my f;
Jn   13: 5   and began to wash the disciples' f
1Co 15:25   put all his enemies under his f.

FELLOWSHIP
Ac   2:42   to the apostles' teaching and f,
2Co   6:14   Or what f is there between light and
1Jn   1: 3   and truly our f is with the Father

FEMALE
Ge   1:27   male and f he created them.
Mk   10: 6   'God made them male and f.'
Gal   3:28   there is no longer male and f;

FESTIVAL → FESTIVALS
Ex 23:14 in the year you shall hold a f for me.
1Co 5: 8 Therefore, let us celebrate the f,

FESTIVALS → FESTIVAL
Lev 23: 2 the appointed f of the LORD
Ne 10:33 the new moons, the appointed f,
Col 2:16 of food and drink or of observing f,

FEW
Mt 22:14 many are called, but f are chosen."
Lk 13:23 "Lord, will only a f be saved?"

FIG
Ge 3: 7 and they sewed f leaves together
Hab 3:17 Though the f tree does not blossom,
Mt 24:32 "From the f tree learn its lesson:

FILL → FILLED, FULL, FULLNESS
Ge 1:28 and the earth and subdue it;
Jer 23:24 Do I not f heaven and earth?
Eph 4:10 so that he might f all things.)

FILLED → FILL
Lk 1:15 walke be f with the Holy Spirit.
Ac 2: 4 were f with the Holy Spirit and
Eph 5:18 but be f with the Spirit,

FIND
Dt 4:29 you will f him if you search after
Jer 29:13 you search for me, you will f me;
Mt 16:25 lose their life for my sake will f it.

FINISHED
Ge 2: 2 on the seventh day God f the work
Jn 19:30 the wine, he said, "It is f."
Sir 38: 8 God's works will never be f;

FIRE → FIERY
Ex 13:21 and in a pillar of f by night,
Da 3:25 walking in the middle of the f,
Mal 3: 2 For he is like a refiner's f and like
Mt 3:11 baptize you with the Holy Spirit
        and f.
Mk 9:43 to go to hell, to the unquenchable f.
Ac 2: 3 Divided tongues, as of f, appeared
Heb 12:29 indeed our God is a consuming f.
Rev 20:14 the second death, the lake of f;
Sir 7:17 punishment of the ungodly is f

FIRST → FIRSTBORN
Ge 1: 5 and there was morning, the f day.
Pr 8:22 the f of his acts of long ago.
Isa 41: 4 I, the LORD, am f,
Mt 6:33 But strive f for the kingdom of God
Mk 10:31 But many who are f will be last, and
        the last will be f."
1Th 4:16 the dead in Christ will rise f.
1Jn 4:19 We love because he f loved us.
Rev 1:17 I am the f and the last,
     20: 5 This is the f resurrection.
     21: 1 the f heaven and the f earth

FIRSTBORN → BEAR, FIRST
Ex 4:22 Thus says the LORD: Israel is my f
Ps 78:51 He struck all the f in Egypt,
Zec 12:10 as one weeps over a f.
Lk 2: 7 And she gave birth to her f son and
Col 1:15 invisible God, the f of all creation;
Rev 1: 5 faithful witness, the f of the dead,
Sir 36:17 whom you have named your f,
2Es 6:58 whom you have called your f,

FISH
Jnh 2: 1 his God from the belly of the f,
Jn 6: 9 has five barley loaves and two f.

FLESH
Ge 2:23 of my bones and f of my f;
    2:24 and they become one f.
Eze 36:26 of stone and give you a heart of f.
Mt 16:17 For f and blood has not revealed this
    26:41 but the f is weak."
Jn 1:14 the Word became f and lived among
    3: 6 What is born of the f is f,
Ro 8: 4 to the f but according to the Spirit.
2Co 12: 7 a thorn was given me in the f,
Gal 5:19 Now the works of the f are obvious:
1Pe 1:24 "All f is like grass and all its glory
1Jn 4: 2 that Jesus Christ has come in the f

FLOOD
Ge 7: 7 the ark to escape the waters of the f.
2Pe 2: 5 a f on a world of the ungodly;
Sir 40:10 and on their account the f came.

FLOWING
Ex 3: 8 a land f with milk and honey,
Jos 5: 6 a land f with milk and honey.

FOLLOW → FOLLOWED
1Ki 18:21 If the LORD is God, f him;
Lk 9:23 take up their cross daily and f me.

FOLLOWED → FOLLOW
Mk 1:18 they left their nets and f him.
Rev 13: 3 the whole earth f the beast.

FOOD
Ge 1:30 I have given every green plant for f.
Ps 136:25 who gives f to all flesh,
Jn 6:55 for my flesh is true f and my blood
1Co 8: 8 "F will not bring us close to God."
1Mc 1:63 to die rather than to be defiled by f

FOOL → FOOLISH, FOOLISHNESS,
        FOOLS
Pr 15: 5 A f despises a parent's instruction,

FOOLISH → FOOL
Mt 7:26 like a f man who built his house
1Co 1:20 Has not God made f the wisdom of
Tit 3: 3 For we ourselves were once f,

FOOLISHNESS → FOOL
1Co 1:18 cross is f to those who are perishing,
    3:19 wisdom of this world is f with God.

FOOLS → FOOL
Ps 14: 1 F say in their hearts, "There is no
            God."
Pr 1: 7 f despise wisdom and instruction.
Ro 1:22 Claiming to be wise, they became f;
1Co 4:10 We are f for the sake of Christ,

FOREHEADS
Eze 9: 4 and put a mark on the f of those
Rev 7: 3 of our God with a seal on their f."
     20: 4 not received its mark on their f

FOREKNEW → KNOW
Ro 8:29 whom he f he also predestined to
    11: 2 not rejected his people whom he f.

FOREVER
Ge 3:22 the tree of life, and eat, and live f"

    6: 3 spirit shall not abide in mortals f,
Ex 3:15 This is my name f, and this my title
Ps 110: 4 "You are a priest f according to the
Ecc 3:14 that whatever God does endures f;
Isa 40: 8 the word of our God will stand f.
Jn 6:51 eats of this bread will live f;
    14:16 another Advocate, to be with you f.
Heb 13: 8 the same yesterday and today and f.
Rev 11:15 and he will reign f and ever."
Wis 5:15 But the righteous live f,

FORGET
Dt 4:23 So be careful not to f the covenant
Isa 49:15 these may f, yet I will not f you.

FORGIVE → FORGAVE, FORGIVEN,
        FORGIVENESS, FORGIVING
Ne 9:17 But you are a God ready to f,
Mt 6:12 And f us our debts, as we
Lk 5:24 has authority on earth to f sins"—
1Jn 1: 9 is faithful and just will f us our sins
Sir 5: 6 he will f the multitude of my sins,"
Man 1:13 f me, O Lord, f me!

FORGIVEN → FORGIVE
Ps 32: 1 are those whose transgression is f,
Mt 6:12 as we also have f our debtors.
    12:31 against the Spirit will not be f.
Ro 4: 7 are those whose iniquities are f,
Eph 4:32 as God in Christ has f you.

FORGIVENESS → FORGIVE
Mk 1: 4 a baptism of repentance for the f
Col 1:14 we have redemption, the f of sins.

FORGIVING → FORGIVE
Ex 34: 7 f iniquity and transgression and sin,
Eph 4:32 f one another, as God in Christ has

FORMED → FORMLESS
Ge 2: 7 LORD God f man from the dust
Ps 139:13 you who f my inward parts;

FORMLESS → FORMED
Ge 1: 2 the earth was a f void and darkness
Wis 11:17 created the world out of f matter,

FORSAKE → FORSAKEN
Dt 31: 6 he will not fail you or f you."
Jos 1: 5 I will not fail you or f you.
Heb 13: 5 "I will never leave you or f you."

FORSAKEN → FORSAKE
Ps 22: 1 my God, why have you f me?
Mt 27:46 my God, why have you f me?"
2Co 4: 9 persecuted, but not f;

FORTRESS
2Sa 22: 2 The LORD is my rock, my f,
Ps 71: 3 for you are my rock and my f.

FORTY
Ge 7: 4 rain on the earth for f days and f
Nu 14:34 f days, for every day a year,
1Ki 19: 8 f days and f nights to Horeb
Jnh 3: 4 And he cried out, "F days more,
Mt 4: 2 He fasted f days and f nights,
Heb 3:17 with whom was he angry f years?
2Es 14:42 They sat f days; they wrote

FOUNDATION → FOUNDATIONS
Isa 28:16 See, I am laying in Zion a f stone,
1Co 3:11 that f is Jesus Christ.

Eph 2: 20 built upon the **f** of the apostles

G

FOUNDATIONS → FOUNDATION
Heb 11: 10 looked forward to the city that has **f**,
Rev 21: 14 the wall of the city has twelve **f**,

FRANKINCENSE → INCENSE
Isa 60: 6 They shall bring gold and **f**,
Mt 2: 11 gifts of gold, **f**, and myrrh.

FREE
Jn 8: 32 and the truth will make you **f.**"
Ro 6: 23 the **f** gift of God is eternal life
Gal 3: 28 there is no longer slave or **f**,

FRIEND → FRIENDS
Pr 18: 24 but a true **f** sticks closer than
Mt 11: 19 a **f** of tax collectors and sinners!'
Jas 2: 23 and he was called the **f** of God.
Sir 7: 18 Do not exchange a **f** for money,

FRIENDS → FRIEND
Jn 15: 13 to lay down one's life for one's **f**.

FRUIT → FRUITFUL, FRUITLESS, FRUITS
Ge 3: 6 she took of its **f** and ate;
Lk 6: 44 each tree is known by its own **f**.
Jn 15: 2 branch that bears **f** he prunes to make it bear more **f**.
Rev 22: 2 tree of life with its twelve kinds of **f**,

FRUITFUL → FRUIT
Ge 9: 1 said to them, "Be **f** and multiply,

FRUITS → FRUIT
Ro 8: 23 who have the first **f** of the Spirit,
1Co 15: 23 in his own order: Christ the first **f**,
Rev 14: 4 as first **f** for God and the Lamb,

FULFILL → FULFILLED, FULFILLING
Mt 5: 17 I have come not to abolish but to **f**.

FULFILLED → FULFILL
Mk 1: 15 "The time is **f**, and the kingdom
Lk 24: 44 prophets, and the psalms must be **f.**"
Ro 8: 4 requirement of the law might be **f**

FULFILLING → FULFILL
Ro 13: 10 love is the **f** of the law.

FULL → FILL
Isa 6: 3 the whole earth is **f** of his glory."
Jn 1: 14 **f** of grace and truth.
Sir 42: 16 work of the Lord is **f** of his glory.

FULLNESS → FILL
Jn 1: 16 From his **f** we have all received,
1Co 10: 26 "the earth and its **f** are the Lord's."
Gal 4: 4 But when the **f** of time had come,
Eph 3: 19 may be filled with all the **f** of God.
Col 1: 19 in him all the **f** of God was pleased

FURNACE
Da 3: 6 be thrown into a **f** of blazing fire."
Aza 1: 26 of the Lord came down into the **f**

FUTURE
Pr 24: 20 for the evil have no **f**;
Jer 31: 17 hope for your **f**, says the LORD:
1Co 3: 22 or death or the present or the **f—**

GAIN
Lk 9: 25 if they **g** the whole world,
Php 1: 21 living is Christ and dying is **g**.

GALILEE
Isa 9: 1 beyond the Jordan, **G** of the nations.
Mt 4: 15 across the Jordan, **G** of the Gentiles
Jn 7: 41 the Messiah does not come from **G**,

GARDEN
Ge 2: 8 LORD God planted a **g** in Eden,
Jn 19: 41 and in the **g** there was a new tomb

GATE → GATES
Mt 7: 13 "Enter through the narrow **g**;
Jn 10: 7 I am the **g** for the sheep.

GATES → GATE
Mt 16: 18 and the **g** of Hades will not prevail
Rev 21: 21 And the twelve **g** are twelve pearls,

GATHERED
Mt 18: 20 two or three are **g** in my name,

GENERATION
Ex 20: 6 steadfast love to the thousandth **g**
Da 4: 34 his kingdom endures from **g** to **g**.
Mt 12: 39 evil and adulterous **g** asks for a sign,
Lk 21: 32 this **g** will not pass away

GENEROSITY
Gal 5: 22 joy, peace, patience, kindness, **g**,

GENTILE → GENTILES
Mt 18: 17 as a **G** and a tax collector.
Gal 2: 14 live like a **G** and not like a Jew,
1Mc 1: 14 according to **G** custom,

GENTILES → GENTILE
Ro 3: 29 Is he not the God of **G** also?
Tob 1: 11 from eating the food of the **G**.
1Mc 1: 11 and make a covenant with the **G**
2Es 4: 23 Israel has been given over to the **G**

GENTLENESS
Gal 5: 23 **g**, and self-control.
Php 4: 5 Let your **g** be known to everyone.
1Ti 6: 11 godliness, faith, love, endurance, **g**.

GETHSEMANE
Mk 14: 32 They went to a place called **G**;

GHOST
Mt 14: 26 were terrified, saying, "It is a **g!**"
Lk 24: 39 for a **g** does not have flesh and

GIFT → GIFTS
Ecc 5: 19 this is the **g** of God.
Jn 4: 10 "If you knew the **g** of God,
Ac 2: 38 will receive the **g** of the Holy Spirit.
Ro 6: 23 but the free **g** of God is eternal life
1Co 7: 7 each has a particular **g** from God,
Jas 1: 17 with every perfect **g**, is from above,
Rev 21: 6 the thirsty I will give water as a **g**

GIFTS → GIFT
Mt 2: 11 offered him **g** of gold, frankincense,
1Co 12: 1 Now concerning spiritual **g**,

GIVE → GIVEN, GIVER
Mt 6: 11 **G** us this day our daily bread.

Mk 10: 45 to **g** his life a ransom for many."
Jn 10: 28 I **g** them eternal life, and they will
Ac 20: 35 more blessed to **g** than to receive.'"

GIVEN → GIVE
Mt 7: 7 "Ask, and it will be **g** you;
Lk 22: 19 "This is my body, which is **g** for
Ro 5: 5 Holy Spirit that has been **g** to us.
Sir 35: 12 Give to the Most High as he has **g**

GIVER → GIVE
2Co 9: 7 for God loves a cheerful **g**.

GLADNESS
Ps 100: 2 Worship the LORD with **g**;
Pr 10: 28 The hope of the righteous ends in **g**,
Isa 16: 10 Joy and **g** are taken away from the
Zep 3: 17 he will rejoice over you with **g**,
Heb 1: 9 has anointed you with the oil of **g**

GLORIFIED → GLORY
Jn 13: 31 "Now the Son of Man has been **g**,
Ac 3: 13 has **g** his servant Jesus,
Ro 8: 30 those whom he justified he also **g**.

GLORIFY → GLORY
Ps 86: 12 and I will **g** your name forever.
Jn 17: 1 **g** your Son so that the Son may **g** you,
1Co 6: 20 therefore **g** God in your body.
Sir 43: 30 **G** the Lord and exalt him as much

GLORY → GLORIFIED, GLORIFY
Ex 33: 18 Moses said, "Show me your **g**,
1Sa 4: 21 "The **g** has departed from Israel,"
Ps 8: 5 crowned them with **g** and honor.
Isa 6: 3 the whole earth is full of his **g**."
Mt 25: 31 the Son of Man comes in his **g**,
Lk 2: 14 "**G** to God in the highest heaven,
Jn 1: 14 and we have seen his **g**,
Ro 3: 23 sinned and fall short of the **g** of God;
1Co 10: 31 do everything for the **g** of God.
2Co 4: 17 for an eternal weight of **g** beyond
Heb 1: 3 reflection of God's **g** and the exact
Rev 4: 11 to receive **g** and honor and power,
21: 23 for the **g** of God is its light,
Sir 1: 11 The fear of the Lord is **g** and
Bar 5: 4 "Righteous Peace, Godly **G**."
1Mc 1: 40 dishonor now grew as great as her **g**

GNASHING
Mt 8: 12 will be weeping and **g** of teeth."
25: 30 will be weeping and **g** of teeth.'

GOAT → GOATS
Lev 16: 9 Aaron shall present the **g** on which

GOATS → GOAT
Mt 25: 32 separates the sheep from the **g**,

GOD → GOD'S, GODLINESS, GODLY, GODS
Ge 1: 1 In the beginning when **G** created
1: 27 So **G** created humankind in his image,
6: 2 sons of **G** saw that they were fair;
Ex 34: 6 a **G** merciful and gracious, slow to
Nu 23: 19 **G** is not a human being,
Dt 6: 5 love the LORD your **G** with all
1Ki 8: 27 will **G** indeed dwell on the earth?
2Ch 2: 5 for our **G** is greater than other gods.
Ps 19: 1 heavens are telling the glory of **G**;

22: 1 My **G**, my **G**, why have you forsaken
46: 10 "Be still, and know that I am **G**!
53: 1 Fools say in their hearts, "There is no **G**."
Ecc 12: 13 Fear **G**, and keep his
Isa 9: 6 Wonderful Counselor, Mighty **G**,
44: 6 besides me there is no **g**.
Jer 10: 10 But the Lord is the true **G**;
Mt 1: 23 which means, "**G** is with us."
6: 24 You cannot serve **G** and wealth.
Mk 1: 1 news of Jesus Christ, the Son of **G**.
2: 7 Who can forgive sins but **G** alone?"
Lk 2: 14 "Glory to **G** in the highest heaven,
18: 19 No one is good but **G** alone.
22: 70 "Are you, then, the Son of **G**?"
Jn 1: 1 was with **G**, and the Word was **G**.
1: 18 It is **G** the only Son,
3: 16 So loved the world that he gave his
5: 18 calling **G** his own Father, thereby making himself equal to **G**
Ac 5: 29 "We must obey **G** rather than any
Ro 6: 23 gift of **G** is eternal life in Christ
2Co 4: 4 Christ, who is the image of **G**.
Eph 4: 6 one **G** and Father of all,
Php 2: 6 though he was in the form of **G**,
Col 1: 19 fullness of **G** was pleased to dwell,
1Jn 4: 16 **G** is love, and those who abide
Rev 4: 8 "Holy, holy, holy, the Lord **G**
Tob 4: 19 At all times bless the Lord **G**,
Sir 32: 14 seeks **G** will accept his discipline,
Bar 4: 8 You forgot the everlasting **G**,
Bel 1: 4 But Daniel worshiped his own **G**.
Man 1: 1 Lord Almighty, **G** of our ancestors,
2Es 16: 67 Indeed, **G** is the judge; fear him!

GOD'S → GOD
Mt 27: 43 for he said, 'I am **G** Son.'"
27: 54 "Truly this man was **G** Son!"

GODLINESS → GOD
1Ti 4: 7 Train yourself in **g**,
2Pe 1: 3 everything needed for life and **g**,
Wis 10: 12 **g** is more powerful than anything

GODLY → GOD
2Co 7: 10 For **g** grief produces a repentance
2Pe 2: 9 how to rescue the **g** from trial,
Sir 37: 12 But associate with a **g** person
Bar 5: 4 "Righteous Peace, **G** Glory."

GODS → GOD
Ex 20: 3 you shall have no other **g** before me.
1Co 8: 5 so-called **g** in heaven or on earth—

GOLD
Ps 119: 127 love your commandments more than **g**,
1Pe 1: 7 being more precious than **g** that,
Rev 21: 21 and the street of the city is pure **g**,
Tob 12: 8 better to give alms than to lay up **g**.
Sir 31: 5 who loves **g** will not be justified;

GOLGOTHA
Mt 27: 33 **G** (which means Place of a Skull),

GOMORRAH
Ge 19: 24 Lord rained on Sodom and **G** sulfur
Jude 1: 7 Sodom and **G** and the surrounding

GOOD → BEST, BETTER, GOODNESS
Ge 1: 31 and indeed, it was very **g**.

2: 9 tree of the knowledge of **g** and evil.
2Ch 7: 3 "For he is **g**, for his steadfast love
Ps 34: 8 taste and see that the Lord is **g**;
Isa 52: 7 who brings **g** news, who announces
Mt 5: 45 his sun rise on the evil and on the **g**,
Mk 10: 18 No one is **g** but God alone.
Jn 10: 11 "I am the **g** shepherd.
Ro 12: 21 but overcome evil with **g**.
Eph 2: 10 created in Christ Jesus for **g** works,
Tob 4: 9 laying up a **g** treasure for yourself
Aza 1: 67 to the Lord, for he is **g**,

GOODNESS → GOOD
Ps 23: 6 Surely **g** and mercy shall follow me
Heb 6: 5 tasted the **g** of the word of God and
2Pe 1: 5 support your faith with **g**,

GOSPEL
Mk 8: 35 and for the sake of the **g**,
Ro 1: 16 For I am not ashamed of the **g**;
Gal 1: 6 and are turning to a different **g**—
Php 1: 27 life in a manner worthy of the **g**
Rev 14: 6 an eternal **g** to proclaim to those

GRACE → GRACIOUS
Jn 1: 14 father's only son, full of **g** and truth.
1: 16 we have all received, **g** upon **g**.
Ac 15: 11 that we will be saved through the **g**
Ro 3: 24 are now justified by his **g** as a gift,
11: 6 otherwise **g** would no longer be **g**.
2Co 12: 9 "My **g** is sufficient for you,
Eph 2: 5 by **g** you have been saved—
Heb 4: 16 approach the throne of **g** with
Jas 4: 6 But he gives all the more **g**;
Wis 3: 9 **g** and mercy are upon his holy ones,
2Es 2: 32 and my **g** will not fail."

GRACIOUS → GRACE
Ex 34: 6 the Lord, a God merciful and **g**,
Nu 6: 25 to shine upon you, and be **g** to you;
Ps 116: 5 **G** is the Lord, and righteous;

GREAT → GREATER, GREATEST
Ge 1: 16 God made the two **g** lights—
12: 2 I will make of you a **g** nation,
Dt 10: 17 the **g** God, mighty and awesome,
La 3: 23 **g** is your faithfulness.
Mt 4: 16 sat in darkness have seen a **g** light,
20: 26 whoever wishes to be **g** among you
Heb 2: 3 if we neglect so **g** a salvation?
13: 20 the **g** shepherd of the sheep,
Rev 12: 9 The **g** dragon was thrown down,
20: 11 I saw a **g** white throne and the one
Jdt 16: 13 O Lord, you are **g** and glorious,
Sir 17: 29 How **g** is the mercy of the Lord,

GREATER → GREAT
Ex 18: 11 that the Lord is **g** than all gods,
Mk 12: 31 no other commandment **g** than these
Jn 14: 12 in fact, will do **g** works than these,
15: 13 No one has **g** love than this,

GREATEST → GREAT
Mt 22: 38 the **g** and first commandment.
Lk 9: 48 the least among all of you is the **g**."
1Co 13: 13 and the **g** of these is love.

GREEK
Jn 19: 20 in Hebrew, in Latin, and in **G**.
Ro 1: 16 to the Jew first and also to the **G**.
Gal 3: 28 There is no longer Jew or **G**,

GRIEF → GRIEVE, GRIEVED
2Co 7: 9 your **g** led to repentance;

GRIEVE → GRIEF
Eph 4: 30 do not **g** the Holy Spirit of God,
1Th 4: 13 not **g** as others do who have no hope

GRIEVED → GRIEF
Isa 63: 10 they rebelled and **g** his holy spirit;

GROUND
Ge 2: 7 formed man from the dust of the **g**,
Isa 53: 2 and like a root out of dry **g**;
Mt 13: 5 Other seeds fell on rocky **g**,
Sir 33: 10 All human beings come from the **g**,

GROW
Col 1: 10 as you **g** in the knowledge of God.
2Pe 3: 18 But **g** in the grace and knowledge of

GUARANTEE → GUARANTEED
2Co 5: 5 who has given us the Spirit as a **g**.
Heb 7: 22 Jesus has also become the **g** of a

GUARANTEED → GUARANTEE
Ro 4: 16 promise may rest on grace and be **g**
Heb 6: 17 he **g** it by an oath,

GUIDE
Ps 48: 14 He will be our **g** forever.
Isa 58: 11 The Lord will **g** you continually,
Lk 6: 39 Can a blind person **g** a blind person?
Jn 16: 13 he will **g** you into all the truth;

GUILT → GUILTY
Ps 32: 5 and you forgave the **g** of my sin.
Hos 14: 2 say to him, "Take away all **g**;
Zec 3: 9 I will remove the **g** of this land

GUILTY → GUILT
Ex 23: 7 for I will not acquit the **g**.
Nu 14: 18 but by no means clearing the **g**,
Mk 3: 29 but is **g** of an eternal sin"—
Sus 1: 53 the innocent and acquitting the **g**,

H

HADES
Mt 16: 18 and the gates of **H** will not prevail
Ac 2: 27 not abandon my soul to **H**,
Rev 1: 18 I have the keys of Death and of **H**.
20: 14 **H** were thrown into the lake of fire.
Sir 21: 10 but at its end is the pit of **H**.

HALLOWED
Ge 2: 3 blessed the seventh day and **h** it,
Mt 6: 9 Father in heaven, **h** be your name.

HAND → HANDS
Ex 15: 6 Your right **h**, O Lord, glorious
Dt 19: 21 tooth for tooth, **h** for **h**,
Ps 110: 1 says to my lord, "Sit at my right **h**
Mk 9: 43 If your **h** causes you to stumble, cut
Lk 20: 42 said to my Lord, "Sit at my right **h**,
Heb 10: 12 "he sat down at the right **h** of God,"
Rev 5: 1 saw in the right **h** of the one seated

HANDS → HAND
Ps 24: 4 who have clean **h** and pure hearts,
Lk 23: 46 into your **h** I commend my spirit."
24: 40 he showed them his **h** and his feet.
Jn 3: 35 has placed all things in his **h**.
Ac 8: 18 the laying on of the apostles' **h**,

Heb 6: 2 laying on of **h**, resurrection of the

HARD → HARDENED
Jer 32:17 Nothing is too **h** for you.
Mt 7:14 the road is **h** that leads to life,
       19:23 **h** for a rich person to enter the

HARDENED → HARD
Ex 10:20 But the LORD **h** Pharaoh's heart,
Mk 8:17 Are your hearts **h?**
2Co 3:14 But their minds were **h.**

HARVEST → HARVESTING
Ge 8:22 the earth endures, seedtime and **h,**
Mt 13:39 **h** is the end of the age, and the
Rev 14:15 the **h** of the earth is fully ripe."

HARVESTING → HARVEST
Jn 4:35 see how the fields are ripe for **h.**

HATE → HATES, HATING
Ps 97:10 The LORD loves those who **h** evil;
Ecc 3: 8 a time to love, and a time to **h;**
Am 5:15 **H** evil and love good, and establish
Mt 5:43 your neighbor and **h** your enemy.'
Lk 6:27 do good to those who **h** you,

HATES → HATE
Pr 6:16 six things that the LORD **h,**
Sir 15:13 The Lord **h** all abominations;

HEAD
Mt 8:20 of Man has nowhere to lay his **h."**
Mk 6:28 brought his **h** on a platter,
Eph 1:22 has made him the **h** over all things

HEAL → HEALED, HEALING,
   HEALS, HEALTH
Dt 32:39 and I make alive; I wound and I **h;**
Ecc 3: 3 a time to kill, and a time to **h;**
Jn 12:40 and turn—and I would **h** them."

HEALED → HEAL
Isa 53: 5 and by his bruises we are **h.**
Jas 5:16 one another, so that you may be **h.**
1Pe 2:24 by his wounds you have been **h.**

HEALING → HEAL
Eze 47:12 for food, and their leaves for **h."**
Mal 4: 2 shall rise, with **h** in its wings.
1Co 12: 9 another gifts of **h** by the one Spirit,
Rev 22: 2 leaves of the tree are for the **h** of

HEALS → HEAL
Ex 15:26 for I am the LORD who **h** you."
Ps 103: 3 iniquity, who **h** all your diseases,
Wis 16:12 your word, O Lord, that **h** all people

HEALTH → HEAL
3Jn 1: 2 and that you may be in good **h,**

HEAR → HEARERS, HEARS
Dt 6: 4 **H,** O Israel: The LORD is our God,
Mk 12:29 answered, "The first is, 'H, O Israel:
Lk 7:22 the lepers are cleansed, the deaf **h,**
Heb 3: 7 says, "Today, if you **h** his voice,
Sir 5:11 Be quick to **h,** but deliberate in

HEARERS → HEAR
Ro 2:13 For it is not the **h** of the law who
Jas 1:22 merely **h** who deceive themselves.

HEARS → HEAR
Ps 69:33 For the LORD **h** the needy,
Pr 15:29 but he **h** the prayer of the righteous.
Mt 7:24 then who **h** these words of mine
1Jn 5:14 according to his will, he **h** us.

HEART → BROKENHEARTED,
   HEARTS
Dt 6: 5 the LORD your God with all your **h,**
       30:14 in your mouth and in your **h** for you
Jos 22: 5 all your **h** and with all your soul."
1Sa 16: 7 but the LORD looks on the **h."**
Ps 51:10 Create in me a clean **h,** O God,
Pr 3: 5 Trust in the LORD with all your **h,**
Jer 9:26 of Israel is uncircumcised in **h.**
Eze 36:26 A new **h** I will give you,
Mt 5: 8 "Blessed are the pure in **h,** for they
Mk 12:30 the Lord your God with all your **h,**
Ro 2:29 circumcision is a matter of the **h—**
Sir 1:12 The fear of the Lord delights the **h,**
Aza 1:16 Yet with a contrite **h** and
Man 1:11 And now I bend the knee of my **h,**

HEARTS → HEART
Jer 31:33 and I will write it on their **h;**
Jn 14: 1 "Do not let your **h** be troubled.
Ro 2:15 law requires is written on their **h,**
Eph 3:17 Christ may dwell in your **h** through
Col 3:15 the peace of Christ rule in your **h,**
Heb 10:16 I will put my laws in their **h,**
1Jn 3:20 for God is greater than our **h,**
Rev 2:23 the one who searches minds and **h,**

HEAVEN → HEAVENLY, HEAVENS
Dt 30:12 "Who will go up to **h** for us,
Ecc 3: 1 and a time for every matter under **h:**
Mt 6: 9 Father in **h,** hallowed be your name.
       24:35 **H** and earth will pass away,
       26:64 and coming on the clouds of **h."**
Mk 10:21 and you will have treasure in **h;**
Lk 24:51 and was carried up into **h.**
Ro 10: 6 'Who will ascend into **h?'"**
Php 3:20 But our citizenship is in **h,**
1Th 1:10 to wait for his Son from **h,**
Heb 9:24 but he entered into **h** itself,
Rev 21: 1 I saw a new **h** and a new earth;

HEAVENLY → HEAVEN
Mt 5:48 as your **h** Father is perfect.
Eph 1: 3 spiritual blessing in the **h** places,
Heb 3: 1 holy partners in a **h** calling,

HEAVENS → HEAVEN
Ge 1: 1 when God created the **h** and
Isa 65:17 to create new **h** and a new earth;
Heb 4:14 priest who has passed through the **h,**
2Pe 3:10 the **h** will pass away with a loud

HEIR → HEIRS
Gal 4: 7 then also an **h,** through God.
Heb 1: 2 whom he appointed **h** of all things,

HEIRS → HEIR
Ro 8:17 **h** of God and joint **h** with Christ—
Eph 3: 6 the Gentiles have become fellow **h,**
1Pe 3: 7 also **h** of the gracious gift of life—

HELL
Mt 10:28 both soul and body in **h.**
Mk 9:43 to have two hands and to go to **h,**
2Pe 2: 4 cast them into **h** and committed

HELP → HELPER, HELPS
Ps 46: 1 a very present **h** in trouble.
Mk 9:24 "I believe; **h** my unbelief!"
Heb 2:18 able to **h** those who are being tested.
Sir 2: 6 Trust in him, and he will **h** you;

HELPER → HELP
Ge 2:18 will make him a **h** as his partner."
Ps 30:10 O LORD, be my **h!"**
Heb 13: 6 Lord is my **h;** I will not be afraid.
Tob 8: 6 Eve as a **h** and support.

HELPS → HELP
Ps 37:40 The LORD **h** them and rescues
Ro 8:26 the Spirit **h** us in our weakness;

HIDDEN → HIDE
Mt 13:44 is like treasure **h** in a field,
Mk 4:22 nothing **h,** except to be disclosed;
Col 3: 3 your life is **h** with Christ in God.
Rev 2:17 the **h** manna, and I will give a white

HIDE → HIDDEN
Dt 31:17 I will forsake them and **h** my face
Ps 13: 1 How long will you **h** your face
       17: 8 **h** me in the shadow of your wings,

HIGH → HIGHEST
Ps 91: 1 live in the shelter of the Most **H,**
Mk 5: 7 Jesus, Son of the Most **H** God?
Eph 4: 8 "When he ascended on **h** he made
Heb 2:17 a merciful and faithful **h** priest
       7:26 that we should have such a **h** priest,

HIGHEST → HIGH
1Ki 8:27 the **h** heaven cannot contain you,
Mt 21: 9 Hosanna in the **h** heaven!"
Lk 2:14 "Glory to God in the **h** heaven,

HOLINESS → HOLY
Ro 1: 4 according to the spirit of **h** by
2Co 6: 6 **h** of spirit, genuine love,
1Ti 2:15 continue in faith and love and **h,**
Heb 12:14 **h** without which no one will see

HOLY → HOLINESS
Ex 20: 8 the sabbath day, and keep it **h.**
       26:33 the **h** place from the most **h.**
Lev 11:44 and be **h,** for I am **h.**
1Sa 2: 2 "There is no **H** One like the LORD,
Isa 6: 3 **"H, h, h** is the LORD of hosts;
Mt 1:18 to be with child from the **H** Spirit.
       3:11 baptize you with the **H** Spirit and
Mk 1:24 who you are, the **H** One of God."
       3:29 against the **H** Spirit can never have
Lk 3:22 the **H** Spirit descended upon him in
Jn 14:26 But the Advocate, the **H** Spirit,
Ac 2: 4 were filled with the **H** Spirit and
Ro 12: 1 living sacrifice, **h** and acceptable
Eph 4:30 do not grieve the **H** Spirit of God,
Heb 6: 4 and have shared in the **H** Spirit,
1Pe 1:16 "You shall be **h,** for I am **h."**
1Jn 2:20 have been anointed by the **H** One,
Jude 1:14 with ten thousands of his **h** ones,
Rev 4: 8 **H, h, h,** the Lord God the Almighty
       21: 2 I saw the **h** city, the new Jerusalem,
Wis 4:15 he watches over his **h** ones.
1Mc 1:15 and abandoned the **h** covenant.
2Es 14:22 send the **h** spirit into me,

HOMETOWN
Mk 6: 4 not without honor, except in their **h,**

HONEY
Ex 3: 8 a land flowing with milk and **h,**
Mt 3: 4 and his food was locusts and wild **h.**

HONOR
Dt 5:16 **H** your father and your mother,
Ps 8: 5 and crowned them with glory and **h.**
Mt 15: 4 For God said, '**H** your father and
Ro 13: 7 **h** to whom **h** is due.
Eph 6: 2 "**H** your father and mother"—
Rev 4:11 to receive glory and **h** and power,

HOPE → HOPES
La 3:21 and therefore I have **h:**
1Co 13:13 And now faith, **h,** and love abide,
Col 1:27 Christ in you, the **h** of glory.
1Jn 3: 3 all who have this **h** in him purify
Sir 34:15 their **h** is in him who saves them.
Sus 1:60 who saves those who **h** in him.

HOPES → HOPE
1Co 13: 7 believes all things, **h** all things,

HOSANNA
Mk 11:10 **H** in the highest heaven!"
Jn 12:13 went out to meet him, shouting, "**H!**

HOSPITABLE → HOSPITALITY
1Ti 3: 2 temperate, sensible, respectable, **h,**
Tit 1: 8 but he must be **h,** a lover
1Pe 4: 9 Be **h** to one another without

HOSPITALITY → HOSPITABLE
Ro 12:13 of the saints; extend **h** to strangers.
1Ti 5:10 has brought up children, shown **h;**
Heb 13: 2 not neglect to show **h** to strangers,

HOSTS
Ps 46: 7 The LORD of **h** is with us;
Isa 48: 2 the LORD of **h** is his name.

HOUR
Mt 24:36 about that day and **h** no one knows,
Jn 2: 4 My **h** has not yet come."
17: 1 "Father, the **h** has come;
Rev 3:10 I will keep you from the **h** of trial
14: 7 for the **h** of his judgment has come;

HOUSE → HOUSEHOLD, STOREHOUSE
Ex 20:17 shall not covet your neighbor's **h;**
1Ch 22: 1 "Here shall be the **h** of the LORD
Ezr 1: 5 rebuild the **h** of the LORD in
Ps 69: 9 zeal for your **h** that has consumed
Mt 7:24 like a wise man who built his **h**
Jn 2:17 "Zeal for your **h** will consume me."
14: 2 In my Father's **h** there are many
1Pe 2: 5 be built into a spiritual **h,**

HOUSEHOLD → HOUSE
Jos 24:15 my **h,** we will serve the LORD."

HUMAN → HUMANKIND
Ps 8: 4 are **h** beings that you are mindful
Mt 15: 9 teaching **h** precepts as doctrines.'"
Ac 5:29 obey God rather than any **h**
Php 2: 7 being born in **h** likeness.
Jdt 8:16 for God is not like a **h** being,

HUMANKIND → HUMAN
Ge 1:26 "Let us make **h** in our image,
1Ti 2: 5 one mediator between God and **h,**

HUMBLE → HUMBLED, HUMBLY, HUMILITY
Ps 25: 9 He leads the **h** in what is right,
Isa 57:15 to revive the spirit of the **h,**
Mt 11:29 for I am gentle and **h** in heart,
Jas 4:10 **H** yourselves before the Lord,
Sir 3:20 but by the **h** he is glorified.

HUMBLED → HUMBLE
Lk 14:11 all who exalt themselves will be **h,**
Php 2: 8 he **h** himself and became obedient

HUMBLY → HUMBLE
Mic 6: 8 and to walk **h** with your God?

HUMILITY → HUMBLE
Pr 15:33 and **h** goes before honor.
Zep 2: 3 seek righteousness, seek **h;**
Php 2: 3 in **h** regard others as better than
Sir 1:27 fidelity and **h** are his delight.

HUNGER → HUNGRY
Mt 5: 6 "Blessed are those who **h** and thirst
Rev 7:16 will **h** no more, and thirst no more;

HUNGRY → HUNGER
Ps 146: 7 who gives food to the **h.**
Jn 6:35 comes to me will never be **h,**
Ro 12:20 "if your enemies are **h,** feed them;

HUSBAND → HUSBANDS
Isa 54: 5 For your Maker is your **h,**
Eph 5:23 **h** is the head of the wife just as
Rev 21: 2 as a bride adorned for her **h,**
Sir 26: 1 Happy is the **h** of a good wife;

HUSBANDS → HUSBAND
Eph 5:25 **H,** love your wives, just as Christ
Col 3:18 Wives, be subject to your **h,**
1Pe 3: 7 **H,** in the same way, show

I

IDOL → IDOLS
Ex 20: 4 shall not make for yourself an **i,**
Isa 40:19 An **i?**—A workman casts it,
1Co 10:19 or that an **i** is anything?

IDOLS → IDOL
Ex 34:17 You shall not make cast **i.**
1Co 8: 1 concerning food sacrificed to **i:**
1Mc 1:43 they sacrificed to **i** and profaned the

IMAGE
Ge 1:26 "Let us make humankind in our **i,**
1Co 15:49 the **i** of the man of heaven.
Col 1:15 He is the **i** of the invisible God,
Rev 20: 4 not worshiped the beast or its **i**
Sir 17: 3 and made them in his own **i.**

IMMANUEL → EMMANUEL
Isa 7:14 bear a son, and shall name him **I.**

IMMORAL → IMMORALITY
1Co 5: 9 not to associate with sexually **i**
Heb 12:16 an **i** and godless person,

IMMORALITY → IMMORAL
2Co 12:21 sexual **i,** and licentiousness
Jude 1: 7 indulged in sexual **i** and pursued
Sir 41:17 Be ashamed of sexual **i,**

IMMORTAL → IMMORTALITY
Ro 1:23 the glory of the **i** God for images
1Ti 1:17 the King of the ages, **i,** invisible,

IMMORTALITY → IMMORTAL
1Co 15:53 and this mortal body must put on **i.**
1Ti 6:16 It is he alone who has **i** and dwells

IMPOSSIBLE
Mt 17:20 and nothing will be **i** for you."
Mk 10:27 "For mortals it is **i,** but not for God;
Heb 11: 6 without faith it is **i** to please God,

INCENSE → FRANKINCENSE
Ex 25: 6 anointing oil and for the fragrant **i,**

INFANTS
Ps 8: 2 Out of the mouths of babes and **i**
Mt 21:16 'Out of the mouths of **i** and nursing
1Co 14:20 **i** in evil, but in thinking be adults.

INHERIT → INHERITANCE
Ps 37:11 But the meek shall **i** the land,
Lk 10:25 "what must I do to **i** eternal life?"
1Co 6: 9 wrongdoers will not **i** the kingdom
Heb 1:14 sake of those who are to **i** salvation?

INHERITANCE → INHERIT
Eph 1:11 In Christ we have also obtained an **i,**
Heb 9:15 the promised eternal **i,**

INIQUITY
Ex 34: 7 forgiving **i** and transgression and
Ps 103: 3 who forgives all your **i,**
Isa 53: 6 has laid on him the **i** of us all.
Tit 2:14 that he might redeem us from all **i**

INN
Lk 2: 7 no place for them in the **i.**

INNOCENT
Pr 6:17 and hands that shed **i** blood,
Mt 27:24 "I am **i** of this man's blood;

INSPIRED
Ex 35:34 And he has **i** him to teach,
2Ti 3:16 All scripture is **i** by God and is

INSTRUCT → INSTRUCTED, INSTRUCTION, INSTRUCTOR
Dt 17:10 observing everything they **i** you.
Ne 9:20 You gave your good spirit to **i** them,

INSTRUCTED → INSTRUCT
Isa 40:13 or as his counselor has **i** him?
Jn 8:28 these things as the Father **i** me.

INSTRUCTION → INSTRUCT
Pr 8:10 Take my **i** instead of silver,
Ro 15: 4 in former days was written for our **i,**
1Ti 1: 5 But the aim of such **i** is love
Sir 51:26 and let your souls receive **i;**

INSTRUCTOR → INSTRUCT
Mt 23:10 for you have one **i,** the Messiah.

INTERCEDES → INTERCESSION
Ro 8:26 Spirit **i** with sighs too deep for

INTERCESSION → INTERCEDES
1Sa 2:25 against the LORD, who can make **i?**"
Isa 53:12 and made **i** for the transgressors.
Heb 7:25 he always lives to make **i** for them.

INTERPRET → INTERPRETATION, INTERPRETATIONS

Mt 16: 3 cannot i the signs of the times.
1Co 12: 30 Do all speak in tongues? Do all i?

INTERPRETATION → INTERPRET

1Co 12: 10 to another the i of tongues.

INTERPRETATIONS → INTERPRET

Ge 40: 8 to them, "Do not i belong to God?

INVISIBLE

Col 1: 15 He is the image of the i God,
1Ti 1: 17 To the King of the ages, immortal, i,

ISRAEL → JACOB

Ge 49: 28 All these are the twelve tribes of I,
Ex 28: 11 with the names of the sons of I,
Nu 24: 17 and a scepter shall rise out of I;
Dt   6: 4 Hear, O I: The LORD is our God,
Jer 31: 31 a new covenant with the house of I
Mt   2: 6 who is to shepherd my people I.'"
Mk 12: 29 answered, "The first is, 'Hear, O I:
Ac   1: 6 you will restore the kingdom to I?"
Heb 8: 8 a new covenant with the house of I
Rev 7: 4 out of every tribe of the people of I:
Sir 17: 17 but I is the Lord's own portion.

J

JACOB → ISRAEL

Ps 135: 4 the LORD has chosen J for himself,
Mic 7: 20 You will show faithfulness to J
Ro   9: 13 "I have loved J,
1Mc 1: 28 house of J was clothed with shame.

JARS

2Co 4: 7 But we have this treasure in clay j,

JEALOUS

Ex 34: 14 whose name is J, is a j God).
Dt   4: 24 God is a devouring fire, a j God.
Ro 10: 19 "I will make you j of those

JERUSALEM

2Sa 5: 5 and at J he reigned over all Israel
2Ki 25: 10 broke down the walls around J.
Ezr 2: 1 they returned to J and Judah,
Ne   2: 17 Come, let us rebuild the wall of J,
Isa 40: 2 Speak tenderly to J,
La   1: 8 J sinned grievously, so she has
Da   9: 25 went out to restore and rebuild J
Mt 23: 37 "J, J, the city that kills the prophets
Gal 4: 25 corresponds to the present J,
Heb 12: 22 of the living God, the heavenly J,
Rev 21: 2 And I saw the holy city, the new J,
1Mc 1: 29 and he came to J with a large force.

JESUS → CHRIST

    LIFE: Genealogy (Mt 1:1–17; Lk 3:21–37). Birth announced (Mt 1:18–25; Lk 1:26–45). Birth (Mt 2:1–12; Lk 2:1–40). Escape to Egypt (Mt 2:13–23). As a boy in the temple (Lk 2:41–52). Baptism (Mt 3:13–17; Mk 1:9–11; Lk 3:21–22; Jn 1:32–34). Temptation (Mt 4:1–11; Mk 1:12–13; Lk 4:1–13). Ministry in Galilee (Mt 4:12–18:35; Mk 1:14–9:50; Lk 4:14–13:9; Jn 1:35–2:11; 4; 6), Transfiguration (Mt 17:1–8; Mk 9:2–8; Lk 9:28–36), on the way to Jerusalem (Mt 19–20; Mk 10; Lk 13:10–19:27), in Jerusalem (Mt 21–25; Mk 11–13; Lk 19:28–21:38; Jn 2:12–3:36; 5; 7–12). Last supper (Mt 26:17–35;

Mk 14:12–31; Lk 22:1–38; Jn 13–17). Arrest and trial (Mt 26:36–27:31; Mk 14:43–15:20; Lk 22:39–23:25; Jn 18:1–19:16). Crucifixion (Mt 27:32–66; Mk 15:21–47; Lk 23:26–55; Jn 19:28–42). Resurrection and appearances (Mt 28; Mk 16; Lk 24; Jn 20–21; Ac 1:1–11; 7:56; 9:3–6; 1Co 15:1–8; Rev 1:1–20).

    MIRACLES. *Healings:* official's son (Jn 4:43–54), demoniac in Capernaum (Mk 1:23–26; Lk 4:33–35), Peter's mother-in-law (Mt 8:14–17; Mk 1:29–31; Lk 4:38–39), leper (Mt 8:2–4; Mk 1:40–45; Lk 5:12–16), paralytic (Mt 9:1–8; Mk 2:1–12; Lk 5:17–26), cripple (Jn 5:1–9), shriveled hand (Mt 12:10–13; Mk 3:1–5; Lk 6:6–11), centurion's servant (Mt 8:5–13; Lk 7:1–10), widow's son raised (Lk 7:11–17), demoniac (Mt 12:22–23; Lk 11:14), Gadarene demoniacs (Mt 8:28–34; Mk 5:1–20; Lk 8:26–39), woman's bleeding and Jairus' daughter (Mt 9:18–26; Mk 5:21–43; Lk 8:40–56), blind man (Mt 9:27–31), mute man (Mt 9:32–33), Canaanite woman's daughter (Mt 15:21–28; Mk 7:24–30), deaf man (Mk 7:31–37), blind man (Mk 8:22–26), demoniac boy (Mt 17:14–18; Mk 9:14–29; Lk 9:37–43), ten lepers (Lk 17:11–19), man born blind (Jn 9:1–7), Lazarus raised (Jn 11), crippled woman (Lk 13:11–17), man with dropsy (Lk 14:1–6), two blind men (Mt 20:29–34; Mk 10:46–52; Lk 18:35–43), Malchus' ear (Lk 22:50–51). *Other Miracles:* water to wine (Jn 2:1–11), catch of fish (Lk 5:1–11), storm stilled (Mt 8:23–27; Mk 4:37–41; Lk 8:22–25), 5,000 fed (Mt 14:15–21; Mk 6:35–44; Lk 9:10–17; Jn 6:1–14), walking on water (Mt 14:25–33; Mk 6:48–52; Jn 6:15–21), 4,000 fed (Mt 15:32–39; Mk 8:1–9), money from fish (Mt 17:24–27), fig tree cursed (Mt 21:18–22; Mk 11:12–14), catch of fish (Jn 21:1–14).

    MAJOR TEACHING: Sermon on the Mount (Mt 5–7; Lk 6:17–49), to Nicodemus (Jn 3), to Samaritan woman (Jn 4), Bread of Life (Jn 6:22–59), at Feast of Tabernacles (Jn 7–8), woes to Pharisees (Mt 23; Lk 11:37–54), Good Shepherd (Jn 10:1–18), Olivet Discourse (Mt 24–25; Mk 13; Lk 21:5–36), Upper Room Discourse (Jn 13–16).

    PARABLES: Sower (Mt 13:3–23; Mk 4:3–25; Lk 8:5–18), seed's growth (Mk 4:26–29), wheat and weeds (Mt 13:24–30, 36–43), mustard seed (Mt 13:31–32; Mk 4:30–32), yeast (Mt 13:33; Lk 13:20–21), hidden treasure (Mt 13:44), valuable pearl (Mt 13:45–46), net (Mt 13:47–51), house owner (Mt 13:52), good Samaritan (Lk 10:25–37), unmerciful servant (Mt 18:15–35), lost sheep (Mt 18:10–14; Lk 15:4–7), lost coin (Lk 15:8–10), prodigal son (Lk 15:11–32), dishonest manager (Lk 16:1–13), rich man and Lazarus (Lk 16:19–31), persistent widow (Lk 18:1–8), Pharisee and tax collector (Lk 18:9–14), payment of workers (Mt 20:1–16), tenants and the vineyard (Mt 21:28–46; Mt 12:1–12; Lk 20:9–19), wedding banquet (Mt 22:1–14), faithful servant (Mt 24:45–51), ten virgins (Mt 25:1–13), talents (Mt 25:1–30; Lk 19:12–27).

    DISCIPLES see APOSTLES. Call (Jn 1:35–51; Mt 4:18–22; 9:9; Mk 1:16–20; 2:13–14; Lk 5:1–11, 27–28). Named Apostles (Mk 3:13–19; Lk 6:12–16). Twelve sent out (Mt 10; Mk 6:7–11; Lk 9:1–5). Seventy sent out (Lk 10:1–24). Defection of (Jn 6:60–71; Mt 26:56;

Mk 14:50–52). Final commission (Mt 28:16–20; Jn 21:15–23; Ac 1:3–8).

Ac   9: 5 "I am J, whom you are persecuting.
1Co 8: 6 and one Lord, J Christ,
Php 2: 10 name of J every knee should bend,
2Th 2: 1 the coming of our Lord J Christ
1Ti 1: 15 J came into the world to save
Heb 12: 2 to J the pioneer and perfecter of our
      13: 8 J Christ is the same yesterday and
1Jn 1: 7 the blood of J his Son cleanses us
Rev 1: 1 The revelation of J Christ,
      22: 20 Amen. Come, Lord J!

JEW → JEWS

Ro   1: 16 to the J first and also to the Greek.
      2: 29 a person is a J who is one inwardly,
Col 3: 11 there is no longer Greek and J,

JEWEL → JEWELS

Rev 21: 19 of the city are adorned with every j;

JEWELS → JEWEL

Pr   3: 15 She is more precious than j,
Isa 54: 12 your gates of j, and all your wall
Rev 17: 4 adorned with gold and j and pearls,

JEWS → JEW

Est 3: 13 to kill, and to annihilate all J,
Mt   2: 2 who has been born king of the J?
      27: 11 "Are you the King of the J?"
Ro   3: 29 Or is God the God of J only?

JOINED

Mt 19: 6 what God has j together, let no one
Eph 2: 21 the whole structure is j together

JORDAN

Ge 13: 10 the plain of the J was well watered
Nu 34: 12 the boundary shall go down to the J,
Mt   3: 6 were baptized by him in the river J,

JOY

Ne   8: 10 the j of the LORD is your strength."
Job 20: 5 j of the godless is but for a moment?
Ps 51: 12 Restore to me the j of your salvation
Pr 21: 15 When justice is done, it is a j to the
Isa 35: 10 everlasting j shall be upon their
La   2: 15 of beauty, the j of all the earth?"
Lk   1: 44 the child in my womb leaped for j.
      2: 10 bringing you good news of great j
Ro 14: 17 but righteousness and peace and j in
Gal 5: 22 the fruit of the Spirit is love, j,
Heb 12: 2 j that was set before him endured
Jas   1: 2 consider it nothing but j,
Tob 13: 17 Jerusalem will sing hymns of j,
Bar 5: 9 For God will lead Israel with j,

JUBILEE

Lev 25: 10 It shall be a j for you:
Nu 36: 4 when the j of the Israelites comes,

JUDEA

Mt   2: 1 Jesus was born in Bethlehem of J,
Lk   3: 1 Pontius Pilate was governor of J,
Ac   1: 8 my witnesses in Jerusalem, in all J

JUDGE → JUDGED, JUDGES, JUDGMENT, JUDGMENTS

1Sa 2: 10 LORD will j the ends of the earth;
Ps 96: 13 for he is coming to j the earth.
Eze 34: 17 I shall j between sheep and sheep,
Lk   6: 37 not j, and you will not be judged;

Jn 7:24 Do not j by appearances,
Ro 3: 6 then how could God j the world?
1Co 6: 2 that the saints will j the world?
2Ti 4: 1 who is to j the living and the dead,
Rev 20: 4 on them were given authority to j.
Sir 35:15 for the Lord is the j,

JUDGED → JUDGE
1Co 11:31 if we j ourselves, we would not be j.
Rev 20:12 dead were j according to their works

JUDGES → JUDGE
Jdg 2:16 Then the Lord raised up j,
Lk 11:19 Therefore they will be your j.
Sir 16:12 j a person according to one's deeds.

JUDGMENT → JUDGE
Ex 6: 6 arm and with mighty acts of j.
Ps 1: 5 wicked will not stand in the j,
Ecc 12:14 God will bring every deed into j,
Jer 25:31 he is entering into j with all flesh,
Da 7:22 j was given for the holy ones of the
Ro 14:10 we will all stand before the j seat of
2Co 5:10 all of us must appear before the j
Heb 9:27 to die once, and after that the j,
Jas 2:13 mercy triumphs over j.
1Jn 4:17 may have boldness on the day of j,
Rev 18:10 For in one hour your j has come."
Wis 12:12 Or will resist your j?
Sir 18:20 Before j comes, examine yourself;
2Es 7:70 the things that pertain to the j.

JUDGMENTS → JUDGE
Ps 119:75 Lord, that your j are right,
Ro 11:33 How unsearchable are his j and
Rev 19: 2 for his j are true and just;

**JUST → JUSTICE, JUSTIFICATION,
     JUSTIFIED, JUSTIFY**
Ge 18:25 Judge of all the earth do what is j?"
1Jn 1: 9 he who is faithful and j will forgive
Rev 15: 3 J and true are your ways, King of
Tob 3: 2 O Lord, and all your deeds are j;
Sir 18: 2 the Lord alone is j.

JUSTICE → JUST
Ex 23: 6 not pervert the j due to your poor
Ps 33: 5 He loves righteousness and j;
Isa 30:18 For the Lord is a God of j;
Jer 9:24 I act with steadfast love, j,
Hos 12: 6 to your God, hold fast to love and j,
Am 5:24 But let j roll down like waters,
Lk 11:42 and neglect j and the love of God;

JUSTIFICATION → JUST
Ro 4:25 trespasses and was raised for our j.
2Co 3: 9 more does the ministry of j abound
Gal 2:21 for if j comes through the law,

JUSTIFIED → JUST
Mt 12:37 for by your words you will be j,
Ro 5: 1 Therefore, since we are j by faith,
     10:10 believes with the heart and so is j,
Gal 2:16 that we might be j by faith in Christ,
Jas 2:24 is j by works and not by faith alone.

K

KEEP → KEEPER
Ge 17: 9 for you, you shall k my covenant,
Ex 19: 5 obey my voice and k my covenant,
Nu 6:24 The Lord bless you and k you;

Dt 5:10 love me and k my commandments.
Ne 1: 5 love him and k his commandments;
Pr 7: 2 k my commandments and live,
Ecc 3: 6 time to k, and a time to throw away;
     12:13 Fear God, and k his commandments
Lk 17:33 those who lose their life will k it.

KEEPER → KEEP
Ge 4: 9 am I my brother's k?"
Ps 121: 5 The Lord is your k;

KEY → KEYS
Rev 3: 7 true one, who has the k of David,

KEYS → KEY
Mt 16:19 you the k of the kingdom of heaven,
Rev 1:18 I have the k of Death and of Hades.

KILL → KILLED, KILLS
Ecc 3: 3 a time to k, and a time to heal;
Mt 10:28 not fear those who k the body but
          cannot k the soul;
Mk 14: 1 to arrest Jesus by stealth and k him;

KILLED → KILL
Mk 9:31 after being k, he will rise again."
Ac 3:15 and you k the Author of life,

KILLS → KILL
2Co 3: 6 the letter k, but the Spirit gives life.

KIND → KINDNESS
1Co 13: 4 Love is patient; love is k;
Eph 4:32 and be k to one another,

KINDNESS → KIND
Pr 31:26 teaching of k is on her tongue.
Ro 2: 4 k is meant to lead you to repentance
Gal 5:22 joy, peace, patience, k, generosity,

KING → KINGDOM, KINGS
2Sa 2: 4 there they anointed David k over
Ps 2: 6 set my k on Zion, my holy hill."
     10:16 The Lord is k forever and ever;
Isa 6: 5 have seen the K, the Lord of hosts!
Mt 2: 2 who has been born k of the Jews?
     27:37 "This is Jesus, the K of the Jews."
1Ti 1:17 To the K of the ages, immortal,
Rev 19:16 "K of kings and Lord of lords."
Tob 10:13 Lord of heaven and earth, K over all
Jdt 9:12 K of all your creation,

KINGDOM → KING
Ex 19: 6 you shall be for me a priestly k and
2Sa 7:12 and I will establish his k.
Ps 145:13 Your k is an everlasting k,
Mt 4:17 "Repent, for the k of heaven has
     5: 3 for theirs is the k of heaven.
     6:10 Your k come. Your will be done,
Mk 10:24 how hard it is to enter the k of God!
Lk 17:21 in fact, the k of God is among you."
Jn 18:36 "My k is not from this world.
Ro 14:17 the k of God is not food and drink
1Co 6: 9 wrongdoers will not inherit the k
1Th 2:12 calls you into his own k and glory.
Heb 12:28 receiving a k that cannot be shaken,
Rev 11:15 world has become the k of our Lord
Wis 10:10 she showed him the k of God,

KINGS → KING
Ps 2: 2 The k of the earth set themselves,
Isa 52:15 k shall shut their mouths because of

Ac 4:26 The k of the earth took their stand,
1Ti 6:15 the King of k and Lord of lords.
Rev 19:16 "King of k and Lord of lords."

KISS
Ps 2:12 k his feet, or he will be angry,
SS 1: 2 Let him k me with the kisses of his
Mt 26:48 "The one I will k is the man; arrest
2Co 13:12 Greet one another with a holy k.

KNEE → KNEES
Isa 45:23 "To me every k shall bow,
Ro 14:11 says the Lord, every k shall bow to
Php 2:10 at the name of Jesus every k should

KNEES → KNEE
1Ki 19:18 the k that have not bowed to Baal,
Eph 3:14 I bow my k before the Father,

KNOCK → KNOCKING
Lk 11: 9 k, and the door will be opened for

KNOCKING → KNOCK
Rev 3:20 I am standing at the door, k;

**KNOW → FOREKNEW,
     KNOWLEDGE, KNOWN, KNOWS**
Job 19:25 For I k that my Redeemer lives,
Ps 46:10 "Be still, and k that I am God!
Jer 31:34 "K the Lord," for they shall all k
Mt 6: 3 left hand k what your right hand is
     22:34 denied three times that you k me."
Jn 10:14 I k my own and my own k me,
1Co 13:12 I k only in part; then I will k fully,
Heb 8:11 'K the Lord,' for they shall all k me,
1Jn 2: 4 Whoever says, "I have come to k
Rev 3: 3 not k at what hour I will come to

KNOWLEDGE → KNOW
Ge 2: 9 the tree of the k of good and evil.
Pr 1: 7 of the Lord is the beginning of k;
1Co 8: 1 k puffs up, but love builds up.
Eph 3:19 the love of Christ that surpasses k,
Col 2: 3 the treasures of wisdom and k.
1Jn 2:20 and all of you have k.
Sir 3:25 without k there is no wisdom.

KNOWN → KNOW
Ps 139: 1 you have searched me and k me.
Lk 6:44 for each tree is k by its own fruit.

KNOWS → KNOW
Ps 94:11 The Lord k our thoughts,
Mt 6: 8 your Father k what you need before
     24:36 about that day and hour no one k,
Sir 42:18 Most High k all that may be known;

L

LABOR
Ex 20: 9 Six days you shall l and do all your

LADDER
Ge 28:12 there was a l set up on the earth,

LAID → LAY
Isa 53: 6 the Lord has l on him the iniquity
Mk 16: 6 Look, there is the place they l him.
1Jn 3:16 that he l down his life for us—

LAKE
Rev 19:20 were thrown alive into the l of fire
     20:14 This is the second death, the l of fire

LAMB

Ge 22: 8 "God himself will provide the l for
Ex 12:21 and slaughter the passover l.
Isa 53: 7 like a l that is led to the slaughter,
Mk 14:12 when the Passover l is sacrificed,
Jn   1:29 L of God who takes away the sin of
1Co 5: 7 For our paschal l, Christ, has been
1Pe 1:19 like that of a l without defect or
Rev 5:12 the L that was slaughtered to
    21:23 and its lamp is the L.

LAME

Isa 35: 6 then the l shall leap like a deer,
Zep 3:19 And I will save the l and gather the
Mt 11: 5 the l walk, the lepers are cleansed,

LAMP → LAMPS, LAMPSTAND, LAMPSTANDS

Ps 119:105 Your word is a l to my feet and a
Mt   5:15 lighting a l puts it under the bushel

LAMPS → LAMP

Ex 25:37 You shall make the seven l for it;

LAMPSTAND → LAMP

Ex 25:31 You shall make a l of pure gold.
1Mc 4:50 and lit the lamps on the l,

LAMPSTANDS → LAMP

Rev 1:20 the seven l are the seven churches.

LAND

Ge   1:10 God called the dry l Earth,
Ex   3: 8 a l flowing with milk and honey,
Nu 13: 2 to spy out the l of Canaan,
Jos 11:23 So Joshua took the whole l,
2Ki 17: 5 the king of Assyria invaded all the l
    25:21 So Judah went into exile out of its l.
2Ch 7:14 will forgive their sin and heal their l.
Ps 37:11 But the meek shall inherit the l,

LANGUAGE

Ge 11: 9 LORD confused the l of all the earth;

LAST → EVERLASTING

Isa 44: 6 I am the first and I am the l;
Mt 19:30 first will be l, and the l will be first.
Heb 1: 2 l days he has spoken to us by a Son,
Rev 1:17 I am the first and the l,

LAUGH

Ecc 3: 4 a time to weep, and a time to l;
Lk   6:21 you who weep now, for you will l.

LAW → LAWFUL

Dt   1: 5 Moses undertook to expound this l
    31: 9 Then Moses wrote down this l,
Jos 1: 8 book of the l shall not depart out of
Ps   1: 2 their delight is in the l of the LORD,
    119:97 Oh, how I love your l!
Jer 31:33 I will put my l within them,
Mt   5:17 come to abolish the l or the prophets
Lk 24:44 written about me in the l of Moses,
Ro   6:14 you are not under l but under grace.
    10: 4 For Christ is the end of the l so that
Heb 10: 1 Since the l has only a shadow of the
Jas   2:10 For whoever keeps the whole l but
1Mc 2:48 They rescued the l from the hands

LAWFUL → LAW

1Co 6:12 "All things are l for me,"
    10:23 "All things are l," but

LAY → LAID

Mt 28: 6 Come, see the place where he l.
Jn 10:15 I l down my life for the sheep.

LEAD → LEADS

Isa 11: 6 and a little child shall l them.

LEADS → LEAD

Ps 23: 2 he l me beside still waters;

LEAST

Mt   2: 6 are by no means l among the rulers
     5:19 called l in the kingdom of heaven;
Lk   9:48 l among all of you is the greatest."

LEAVE → LEFT

Mk 10: 7 this reason a man shall l his father
Heb 13: 5 said, "I will never l you or forsake

LEAVEN

Ex 12:15 on the first day you shall remove l

LEAVES

Ge   3: 7 and they sewed fig l together
Eze 47:12 and their l for healing."
Rev 22: 2 l of the tree are for the healing of

LEFT → LEAVE

Mt   6: 3 your l hand know what your right
Lk 17:34 one will be taken and the other l.

LEGS

Jn 19:33 they did not break his l.

LEPER → LEPROUS

Mt   8: 2 and there was a l who came to him
    26: 6 in the house of Simon the l,

LEPERS → LEPROUS

Lk   7:22 the lame walk, the l are cleansed,

LEPROUS → LEPER, LEPERS

Ex   4: 6 he took it out, his hand was l,
Nu 12:10 Miriam had become l,

LETTER

Mt   5:18 not one l, not one stroke of a l,
2Co 3: 6 the l kills, but the Spirit gives life.

LEVIATHAN

Job 41: 1 you draw out L with a fishhook,
Ps 74:14 You crushed the heads of L;
2Es 6:49 and the name of the other L.

LEVITES → LEVITICAL

Nu   1:53 L shall camp around the tabernacle
Jos 14: 4 no portion was given to the L in the
Ne   8: 9 L who taught the people said to all

LEVITICAL → LEVITES

Heb 7:11 attainable through the l priesthood

LIAR → LIE

Pr 19:22 and it is better to be poor than a l.
Jn   8:44 for he is a l and the father of lies.

LIE → LIAR, LYING

Nu 23:19 that he should l, or a mortal,
Ps   23: 2 makes me l down in green pastures;
1Jn 2:21 know that no l comes from the truth.

LIFE → LIVE

Ge   2: 7 into his nostrils the breath of l;
     2: 9 the tree of l also in the midst of the

Ge   9: 5 require a reckoning for human l.
Ex 21:23 then you shall give l for l,
Dt 30:19 Choose l so that you and your
Isa 53:10 you make his l an offering for sin,
Da 12: 2 shall awake, some to everlasting l,
Mt   7:14 and the road is hard that leads to l,
    10:39 Those who find their l will lose it,
    20:28 to give his l a ransom for many."
Jn   1: 4 in him was l, and the l was the light
     3:15 believes in him may have eternal l.
     6:35 said to them, "I am the bread of l.
    11:25 "I am the resurrection and the l.
    14: 6 "I am the way, and the truth, and
Ac   3:15 and you killed the Author of l,
Ro   5:21 eternal l through Jesus Christ our
2Co 3: 6 the letter kills, but the Spirit gives l.
Php 4: 3 whose names are in the book of l.
1Jn 5:20 He is the true God and eternal l.
Rev 2: 8 who was dead and came to l:
    20: 4 came to l and reigned with Christ
    20:12 book was opened, the book of l.
    22: 2 the tree of l with its twelve kinds
Sir 4:12 Whoever loves her loves l,
2Es 8:52 the tree of l is planted,

LIGHT → ENLIGHTENED, ENLIGHTENS, LIGHTS

Ge   1: 3 "Let there be l"; and there was l.
Isa 9: 2 in darkness have seen a great l;
    60: 1 Arise, shine; for your l has come,
Mt   4:16 in darkness have seen a great l,
     5:14 "You are the l of the world.
Jn   1: 9 true l, which enlightens everyone,
     8:12 saying, "I am the l of the world.
Ro 13:12 and put on the armor of l;
2Co 11:14 Satan disguises himself as an angel
        of l.
Rev 22: 5 for the Lord God will be their l,

LIGHTS → LIGHT

Ge   1:16 God made the two great l—
Jas 1:17 coming down from the Father of l,

LIKENESS

Ge   1:26 in our image, according to our l;
Ro   8: 3 his own Son in the l of sinful flesh,
Php 2: 7 of a slave, being born in human l.

LION → LIONS

Isa 11: 7 the l shall eat straw like the ox.
Rev 5: 5 See, the L of the tribe of Judah,

LIONS → LION

Da   6:20 able to deliver you from the l?"

LISTEN

Ex 23:22 But if you l attentively to his voice
2Ki 17:40 They would not l, however,
Mk   9: 7 my Son, the Beloved; l to him!"
Lk 16:31 'If they do not l to Moses and the
Jas 1:19 be quick to l, slow to speak,
Sir 11: 8 Do not answer before you l,

LIVE → ALIVE, LIFE, LIVES, LIVING

Ge   3:22 and eat, and l forever"—
Ex 33:20 for no one shall see me and l."
Lev 18: 5 by doing so one shall l:
Dt   8: 3 one does not l by bread alone,
Hab 2: 4 but the righteous l by their faith.
Mt   4: 4 'One does not l by bread alone,

Jn 11:25 even though they die, will l,
Ro 14: 8 If we l, we l to the Lord,
2Co 5:15 those who I might I no longer for
Wis 5:15 But the righteous I forever,
Sir 34:14 those who fear the Lord will I,

LIVES → LIVE
Job 19:25 For I know that my Redeemer l,
Ro 6:10 but the life he l, he l to God.
Rev 15: 7 of God, who l forever and ever,
Tob 13: 1 "Blessed be God who I forever,

LIVING → LIVE
Ge 2: 7 and the man became a l being.
Dt 5:26 the voice of the l God speaking out
Jer 2:13 forsaken me, the fountain of l water,
Zec 14: 8 that day l waters shall flow out from
Mt 16:16 the Messiah, the Son of the l God."
Jn 4:10 he would have given you l water."
6:51 I am the l bread that came down
Ro 12: 1 present your bodies as a l sacrifice,
Heb 4:12 the word of God is l and active,

LOAVES
Mk 6:41 Taking the five l and the two fish,
8: 6 and he took the seven l,

LOCUSTS
Ex 10: 4 I will bring l into your country.
Mt 3: 4 and his food was l and wild honey.
Rev 9: 3 from the smoke came l on the earth,

LONG
Ex 20:12 that your days may be l in the land
Ps 13: 1 How l, O Lord?
Rev 6:10 how l will it be before you judge

LORD → LORD'S, LORDS
Dt 10:17 God is God of gods and L of lords,
Ps 110: 1 The LORD says to my l,
Mt 7:22 many will say to me, 'L, L,
Mk 1: 3 'Prepare the way of the L,
12:29 the L our God, the L is one;
Lk 2:11 who is the Messiah, the L.
Jn 13:13 You call me Teacher and L—
20:28 "My L and my God!"
Ac 2:34 The L said to my L, "Sit at my
Ro 4:24 in him who raised Jesus our L
10:12 the same L is L of all and
1Co 8: 6 and one L, Jesus Christ,
2Co 3:17 Now the L is the Spirit,
Eph 4: 5 one L, one faith, one baptism,
Php 2:11 that Jesus Christ is L, to the glory
1Pe 3:15 in your hearts sanctify Christ as L.
Rev 4: 8 "Holy, holy, holy, the L God
19:16 "King of kings and L of lords."
22:20 Amen. Come, L Jesus!
Jdt 6:19 L God of heaven, see their
Wis 8: 3 and the L of all loves her.
Sir 1: 1 All wisdom is from the L,
Aza 1:35 Bless the L, all you works of the L;
Sus 1: 2 and one who feared the L.

†LORD → †LORD'S
Ge 2: 7 L God formed man from the dust of
13: 4 Abram called on the name of the L.
18:14 Is anything too wonderful for the L?
Ex 15: 3 The L is a warrior; the L is his name.
34: 6 and proclaimed, "The L, the L,
Lev 19: 2 for I the L your God am holy.
Nu 6:24 The L bless you and keep you;

Dt 6: 4 The L is our God, the L alone.
Jos 24:15 my household, we will serve the L."
1Sa 2: 2 "There is no Holy One like the L,
Ne 8:10 the joy of the L is your strength."
Job 1:21 the L gave, and the L has taken
Ps 1: 2 their delight is in the law of the L,
10:16 The L is king forever and ever;
23: 1 The L is my shepherd, I shall not
33:12 Happy is the nation whose God is the L
110: 1 The L says to my lord,
150: 6 that breathes praise the L!
Pr 1: 7 fear of the L is the beginning of
3: 5 Trust in the L with all your heart,
Isa 6: 3 "Holy, holy, holy is the L of hosts;
53: 6 the L has laid on him the iniquity
Jer 31:34 "Know the L," for they shall all
La 3:25 The L is good to those who wait for
Eze 37: 4 O dry bones, hear the word of the L.
48:35 time on shall be, The L is There.
Hos 14: 1 Return, O Israel, to the L your God,
Joel 1:15 For the day of the L is near,
Am 5: 6 Seek the L and live,
Ob 1:15 the day of the L is near against all
Na 1: 3 The L is slow to anger but great in
Zep 1:14 The great day of the L is near,
Zec 14: 9 the L will be one and his name one.
Mal 4: 5 and terrible day of the L comes.

LORD'S → LORD
Mk 12:11 was the L doing, and it is amazing
Lk 4:19 to proclaim the year of the L favor."
Ro 14: 8 or whether we die, we are the L.
1Co 10:26 the earth and its fullness are the L."

†LORD'S → †LORD
Dt 32: 9 the L own portion was his people,
Isa 59: 1 the L hand is not too short to save,
Ob 1:21 and the kingdom shall be the L.

LORDS → LORD
Dt 10:17 God is God of gods and Lord of l,
Rev 19:16 "King of kings and Lord of l."

LOSS → LOST
Php 3: 8 I regard everything as l because of
Sir 32:24 who trusts the Lord will not suffer l.

LOST → LOSS
Ps 119:176 I have gone astray like a l sheep;
Lk 15: 6 I have found my sheep that was l.'
19:10 came to seek out and to save the l."

LOTS → LOT, 2
Ps 22:18 and for my clothing they cast l.
Mt 27:35 among themselves by casting l;

LOVE → BELOVED, LOVED, LOVES
Ex 20: 6 but showing steadfast l to the
34: 6 and abounding in steadfast l and
Lev 19:18 shall l your neighbor as yourself:
Dt 6: 5 You shall l the LORD your God
2Ch 6:42 Remember your steadfast l
Ne 1: 5 steadfast l with those who him
Ps 18: 1 I l you, O LORD, my strength.
86: 5 abounding in steadfast l to all who
119:97 Oh, how I l your law!
136: 1 for his steadfast l endures forever.
Pr 8:17 I l those who l me,
Ecc 3: 8 a time to l, and a time to hate;
SS 1: 2 For your l is better than wine,

Isa 54: 8 but with everlasting l I will have
La 3:22 steadfast l of the LORD never ceases,
Hos 11: 4 of human kindness, with bands of l.
Joel 2:13 and abounding in steadfast l,
Jnh 4: 2 and abounding in steadfast l,
Mt 5:44 L your enemies and pray
6:24 either hate the one and l the other,
Mk 12:31 shall l your neighbor as yourself.'
Lk 6:32 For even sinners l those who l them.
10:27 "You shall l the Lord your God
Jn 12:25 Those who l their life lose it,
13:34 new commandment, that you l one
14:15 "If you l me, you will keep my
15:13 No one has greater l than this,
Ro 5: 8 But God proves his l for us in that
12: 9 Let l be genuine; hate what is evil,
1Co 8: 1 Knowledge puffs up, but l builds up.
13: 4 L is patient; l is kind;
13:13 and the greatest of these is l.
Gal 5:22 the fruit of the Spirit is l, joy,
Eph 3:19 l of Christ that surpasses knowledge
5:25 Husbands, l your wives,
1Ti 6:10 For the l of money is a root of all
Heb 10:24 provoke one another to l and good
13: 5 your lives free from the l of money,
2Pe 1: 7 and mutual affection with l.
1Jn 2:15 not the world or the things in the
3: 1 See what l the Father has given us,
5: 3 For the l of God is this,
2Jn 1: 6 And this is l, that we walk according
Jude 1:21 keep yourselves in the l of God;
Rev 2: 4 abandoned the l you had at first.
Sir 2:15 and those who l him keep his ways.
7:30 With all your might l your Maker,
Bel 1:38 have not forsaken those who l you."
1Mc 4:33 with the sword of those who l you,

LOVED → LOVE
Jer 31: 3 have l you with an everlasting love;
Jn 3:16 God so l the world that he gave his
15: 9 the Father has l me, so I have l you;
15:12 love one another as I have l you.
1Jn 4:19 We love because he first l us.

LOVES → LOVE
Pr 3:12 the LORD reproves the one he l,
17:17 A friend l at all times,
Lk 7:47 to whom little is forgiven, l little."
Ro 13: 8 who l another has fulfilled the law.
Eph 5:28 He who l his wife l himself.
Heb 12: 6 Lord disciplines those whom he l,
Rev 1: 5 who l us and freed us from our sins
Wis 8: 3 and the Lord of all l her.
Sir 4:12 Whoever l her l life,

LOWER → LOWLY
Ps 8: 5 have made them a little l than God,
Heb 2: 7 made them for a little while l than

LOWLY → LOWER
Pr 16:19 It is better to be of a l spirit
Ro 12:16 but associate with the l;
Jdt 9:11 But you are the God of the l,

LOYALTY
Dt 7: 9 God who maintains covenant l
Ru 3:10 this last instance of your l
Ps 101: 1 I will sing of l and of justice;
Hos 4: 1 There is no faithfulness or l,

LUKEWARM
Rev 3:16 because you are **l**, and neither cold

LUST → LUSTS
Mt 5:28 looks at a woman with **l** has already
2Pe 1: 4 that is in the world because of **l**,

LUSTS → LUST
Ro 1:24 gave them up in the **l** of their hearts

LYING → LIE
Pr 6:17 a **l** tongue, and hands that shed
Wis 1:11 and a **l** mouth destroys the soul.

M

MADE → MAKE
Ge 1:31 God saw everything that he had **m**,
2:22 he **m** into a woman and brought her
6: 6 was sorry that he had **m** humankind
15:18 the LORD **m** a covenant with Abram,
Ex 20:11 For in six days the LORD **m** heaven
Ps 8: 5 have **m** them a little lower than God
118:24 This is the day that the LORD has **m**;
139:14 I am fearfully and wonderfully **m**.
Ac 2:36 that God has **m** him both Lord and
Eph 2: 5 **m** us alive together with Christ—
Sir 43:33 For the Lord has **m** all things,

MAGDALENE
Mt 27:56 Among them were Mary **M**,

MAJESTIC → MAJESTY
Ex 15:11 Who is like you, **m** in holiness,
Ps 8: 1 how **m** is your name in all the earth!

MAJESTY → MAJESTIC
1Ch 29:11 the glory, the victory, and the **m**;
Ps 93: 1 The LORD is king, he is robed in **m**;
2Pe 1:16 we had been eyewitnesses of his **m**.

MAKE → MADE, MAKER
Ge 1:26 "Let us **m** humankind in our image,
2:18 will **m** him a helper as his partner."
Ex 20: 4 You shall not **m** for yourself an idol,
Nu 6:25 LORD **m** his face to shine upon you,
Mt 28:19 and **m** disciples of all nations,

MAKER → MAKE
Ge 14:19 Most High, **m** of heaven and
Ps 95: 6 kneel before the LORD, our **M!**
Isa 54: 5 For your **M** is your husband,
Sir 7:30 With all your might love your **M**,

MALE
Ge 1:27 **m** and female he created them.
Lev 20:13 If a man lies with a **m** as with a
Rev 12: 5 she gave birth to a son, a **m** child,

MAN
Ge 2: 7 LORD God formed **m** from the dust
2:18 not good that the **m** should be alone;
Mt 9: 6 Son of **M** has authority on earth to
Lk 6: 5 The Son of **M** is lord of the sabbath.
Jn 9:35 "Do you believe in the Son of **M?**"
1Co 11: 3 that Christ is the head of every **m**,
Rev 1:13 I saw one like the Son of **M**,

MANGER
Lk 2:12 in bands of cloth and lying in a **m**."

MANNA
Ex 16:31 The house of Israel called it **m**;

Jn 6:49 ate the **m** in the wilderness,
Rev 2:17 I will give some of the hidden **m**,

MANY
Mt 22:14 **m** are called, but few are chosen."
Mk 10:45 and to give his life a ransom for **m**."
Ro 12: 5 who are **m**, are one body in Christ,

MARK
Ge 4:15 And the LORD put a **m** on Cain,
Eze 9: 6 but touch no one who has the **m**.
Rev 19:20 who had received the **m** of the beast

MARRIAGE → MARRIED, MARRIES
Mt 22:30 are given in **m**, but are like angels
Heb 13: 4 Let **m** be held in honor by all,
Rev 19: 7 for the **m** of the Lamb has come,

MARRIED → MARRIAGE
1Ti 3: 2 be above reproach, **m** only once,
Tit 1: 6 **m** only once, whose children are

MARRIES → MARRIAGE
Mk 10:11 and **m** another commits adultery
Ro 7: 3 if she **m** another man, she is not an
1Co 7:28 and if a virgin **m**, she does not sin.

MASTER → MASTERS, TASKMASTERS
Mal 1: 6 if I am a **m**, where is the respect due
Jn 15:20 Servants are not greater than their **m**
2Pe 2: 1 deny the **M** who bought them—

MASTERS → MASTER
Mt 6:24 "No one can serve two **m**;

MEDIATOR
Gal 3:19 ordained through angels by a **m**.
1Ti 2: 5 **m** between God and humankind,
Heb 8: 6 he is the **m** of a better covenant,

MEDITATE → MEDITATION
Jos 1: 8 you shall **m** on it day and night,
Ps 1: 2 on his law they **m** day and night.
Wis 12:22 we may **m** upon your goodness,
Sir 6:37 and **m** at all times on his

MEDITATION → MEDITATE
Ps 19:14 of my mouth and the **m** of my heart
119:97 It is my **m** all day long.

MEEK → MEEKNESS
Ps 37:11 But the **m** shall inherit the land,
Mt 5: 5 "Blessed are the **m**, for they will

MEEKNESS → MEEK
Col 3:12 kindness, humility, **m**, and patience.
Jas 1:21 with **m** the implanted word

MEETING
Ex 27:21 In the tent of **m**, outside the curtain
40:34 the cloud covered the tent of **m**,

MELCHIZEDEK
Ge 14:18 King **M** of Salem brought out bread
Ps 110: 4 forever according to the order of **M**."
Heb 7: 1 This "King **M** of Salem, priest of

MEMBERS
Ro 7:23 I see in my **m** another law at war
1Co 6:15 that your bodies are **m** of Christ?
12:18 God arranged the **m** in the body,

MERCIES → MERCY
La 3:22 his **m** never come to an end;
2Co 1: 3 the Father of **m** and the God of all

MERCIFUL → MERCY
Dt 4:31 the LORD your God is a **m** God,
Ps 111: 4 the LORD is gracious and **m**.
Jer 3:12 not look on you in anger, for I am **m**
Mt 5: 7 "Blessed are the **m**, for they will
Lk 6:36 Be **m**, just as your Father is **m**.
Sir 2:11 the Lord is compassionate and **m**;

MERCY → MERCIES, MERCIFUL
Ex 25:17 make a seat of pure gold;
1Ch 21:13 of the LORD, for his **m** is very great;
Hab 3: 2 in wrath may you remember **m**.
Mt 9:13 learn what this means, 'I desire **m**,
23:23 of the law: justice and **m** and faith.
Ro 9:15 "I will have **m** on whom I have **m**,
Eph 2: 4 But God, who is rich in **m**,
Jas 2:13 **m** triumphs over judgment.
Sir 2:17 for equal to his majesty is his **m**,

MESSENGER → MESSAGE
Mt 11:10 I am sending my **m** ahead of you,
2Co 12: 7 a **m** of Satan to torment me,

MESSIAH → CHRIST, MESSIAHS
Mt 16:16 Peter answered, "You are the **M**,
Lk 2:11 a Savior, who is the **M**, the Lord.
Ac 2:36 God has made him both Lord and **M**
Ro 9: 5 according to the flesh, comes the **M**,
Rev 11:15 kingdom of our Lord and of his **M**,
2Es 7:28 For my son the **M** shall be revealed

MESSIAHS → MESSIAH
Mk 13:22 False **m** and false prophets will

MIDWIVES
Ex 1:17 But the **m** feared God; they did not

MIGHT → ALMIGHTY, MIGHTY
2Ch 20: 6 In your hand are power and **m**,
Zec 4: 6 **m**, nor by power, but by my spirit,
Sir 7:30 With all your **m** love your Maker,

MIGHTY → MIGHT
Ge 49:24 by the hands of the **M** One of Jacob,
Ex 6: 1 by a **m** hand he will let them go;
Ps 99: 4 **M** King, lover of justice, you have
Isa 9: 6 Wonderful Counselor, **M** God,
Rev 18: 8 for **m** is the Lord God who judges

MILE
Mt 5:41 one **m**, go also the second **m**.

MILK
Ex 3: 8 a land flowing with **m** and honey,
Heb 5:12 You need **m**, not solid food;

MILLSTONE → STONE
Lk 17: 2 better for you if a **m** were hung

MIND → MINDFUL
Nu 23:19 mortal, that he should change his **m**.
Jnh 3: 9 God may relent and change his **m**;
Mt 22:37 all your soul, and with all your **m**.'
1Co 2:16 who has known the **m** of the Lord
Php 2: 5 same **m** be in you that was in Christ
Heb 7:21 sworn and will not change his **m**,
Sir 37:17 The **m** is the root of all conduct;

MINDFUL → MIND
Ps 8: 4 beings that you are **m** of them,
Heb 2: 6 beings that you are **m** of them,

MINISTERS → MINISTRY
2Co 3: 6 to be **m** of a new covenant,
  11:15 if his **m** also disguise themselves
    as **m**

MINISTRY → MINISTERS
2Co 5:18 has given us the **m** of reconciliation;
Eph 4:12 equip the saints for the work of **m**,
Heb 8: 6 now obtained a more excellent **m**,

MIRACLES → See also JESUS:
  MIRACLES
Ps 78:11 and the **m** that he had shown them.
Ac 19:11 did extraordinary **m** through Paul,
1Co 12:29 Are all teachers? Do all work **m?**
Heb 2: 4 signs and wonders and various **m,**

MOCKED → MOCK
Gal 6: 7 God is not **m,** for you reap

MOMENT → MOMENTARY
Ps 30: 5 For his anger is but for a **m;**
Isa 54: 7 For a brief **m** I abandoned you,
1Co 15:52 in a **m,** in the twinkling of an eye,

MOMENTARY → MOMENT
2Co 4:17 this slight **m** affliction is preparing

MONEY
Mk 11:15 the tables of the **m** changers
1Ti 6:10 love of **m** is a root of all kinds
Heb 13: 5 your lives free from the love of **m,**

MOON → MOONS
Joel 2:31 to darkness, and the **m** to blood,
Ac 2:20 to darkness and the **m** to blood,
Rev 6:12 the full **m** became like blood,
  21:23 no need of sun or **m** to shine on it,

MOONS → MOON
2Ch 8:13 the new **m,** and the three annual
Col 2:16 or of observing festivals, new **m,**

MORALS
1Co 15:33 "Bad company ruins good **m."**

MORNING
Ge 1: 5 and there was **m,** the first day.
Ps 30: 5 but joy comes with the **m.**
La 3:23 every **m;** great is your faithfulness.
Lk 24:22 They were at the tomb early this **m,**
2Pe 1:19 the day dawns and the **m** star rises
Rev 22:16 of David, the bright **m** star."

MOST
Ge 14:18 he was priest of God **M** High.
Ex 26:33 the holy place from the **m** holy.
Ps 91: 1 live in the shelter of the **M** High,
Mk 5: 7 Jesus, Son of the **M** High God?

MOTH
Ps 39:11 consuming like a **m** what is dear to
Mt 6:19 where **m** and rust consume and

MOTHER
Ge 2:24 a man leaves his father and his **m**
  3:20 because she was the **m** of all living.
Ex 20:12 Honor your father and your **m,**
Isa 66:13 As a **m** comforts her child, so I will

Mt 10:37 loves father or **m** more than me is
Jn 19:27 to the disciple, "Here is your **m."**
Eph 5:31 a man will leave his father and **m**
Rev 17: 5 **m** of whores and of earth's
Tob 4: 3 Honor your **m** and do not abandon
Sir 3: 6 who honor their **m** obey the Lord;

MOUNT → MOUNTAIN,
  MOUNTAINS
Ex 19:20 the LORD descended upon **M** Sinai,
Ps 78:68 **M** Zion, which he loves.
Mk 13: 3 he was sitting on the **M** of Olives
Rev 14: 1 the Lamb, standing on **M** Zion!

MOUNTAIN → MOUNT
Isa 2: 2 the **m** of the LORD's house shall
Mt 4: 8 a very high **m** and showed him all
  17:20 you will say to this **m,** 'Move from

MOUNTAINS → MOUNT
1Co 13: 2 have all faith, so as to remove **m,**

MOURN → MOURNFUL,
  MOURNING
Ecc 3: 4 a time to **m,** and a time to dance;
Mt 5: 4 "Blessed are those who **m,**
Sir 7:34 but **m** with those who **m.**

MOURNING → MOURN
Rev 21: 4 **m** and crying and pain will be no

MOUTH
Dt 8: 3 that comes from the **m** of the LORD.
Ps 19:14 Let the words of my **m** and
Mt 4: 4 every word that comes from the **m**
Rev 19:15 From his **m** comes a sharp sword
Sir 28:25 and a bolt for your **m.**

MULTIPLY
Ge 1:28 to them, "Be fruitful and **m,**
  9: 7 And you, be fruitful and **m,**
Dt 6: 3 that you may **m** greatly in a land

MULTITUDE
Jas 5:20 and will cover a **m** of sins.
1Pe 4: 8 for love covers a **m** of sins.

MURDER → MURDERER
Ex 20:13 You shall not **m.**
Hos 4: 2 lying, and **m,** and stealing and
Mt 5:21 of ancient times, 'You shall not **m';**

MURDERER → MURDER
Nu 35:16 the **m** shall be put to death.
Jn 8:44 He was a **m** from the beginning

MUSTARD
Mt 17:20 have faith the size of a **m** seed,
Mk 4:31 It is like a **m** seed, which,

MYRRH
Mt 2:11 gifts of gold, frankincense, and **m.**
Mk 15:23 offered him wine mixed with **m;**

MYSTERY
Da 2:19 **m** was revealed to Daniel in a vision
Ro 11:25 I want you to understand this **m:**
1Co 15:51 Listen, I will tell you a **m!**
Eph 3: 4 my understanding of the **m** of Christ
1Ti 3: 9 must hold fast to the **m** of the faith
Rev 17: 5 a name, a **m:** "Babylon the great,

N

NAILING → NAILS
Col 2:14 He set this aside, **n** it to the cross.

NAILS → NAILING
Jn 20:25 put my finger in the mark of the **n**

NAKED
Ge 2:25 the man and his wife were both **n,**
Job 1:21 "**N** I came from my mother's womb,
    and **n** shall

NAME → NAMES
Ge 2:19 every living creature, that was its **n.**
  4:26 people began to invoke the **n** of
Ex 3:15 my **n** forever, and this my title
  20: 7 wrongful use of the **n** of the LORD
Ps 9:10 know your **n** put their trust in you,
Pr 18:10 The **n** of the LORD is a strong tower;
Isa 42: 8 I am the LORD, that is my **n;**
Eze 20: 9 But I acted for the sake of my **n,**
Joel 2:32 on the **n** of the LORD shall be saved;
Mt 1:21 a son, and you are to **n** him Jesus,
  6: 9 Father in heaven, hallowed be your **n.**
  28:19 baptizing them in the **n** of the Father
Jn 1:12 received him, who believed in his **n,**
  20:31 believing you may have life in his **n.**
Ac 4:12 for there is no other **n** under heaven
Php 2: 9 gave him the **n** that is above every **n**
Rev 13:17 **n** of the beast or the number of its **n.**
  19:13 his **n** is called The Word of God.
Sir 2:17 and equal to his **n** are his works.

NAMES → NAME
Mt 10: 2 are the **n** of the twelve apostles:
Rev 21:14 the twelve **n** of the twelve apostles

NARROW
Lk 13:24 "Strive to enter through the **n** door;

NATION → NATIONS
Ge 12: 2 I will make of you a great **n,** and
Ex 32:10 and of you I will make a great **n."**
Isa 66: 8 a **n** be delivered in one moment?
1Pe 2: 9 a holy **n,** God's own people,

NATIONS → NATION
Ge 18:18 the **n** of the earth shall be blessed in
Am 9:12 and all the **n** who are called
Mt 28:19 and make disciples of all **n,**
Mk 11:17 a house of prayer for all the **n'?**
Ro 4:18 become "the father of many **n,"**
Rev 22: 2 the tree are for the healing of the **n.**

NAZARETH
Mt 2:23 made his home in a town called **N,**
Jn 1:46 Can anything good come out of **N?**
  19:19 "Jesus of **N,** the King of the Jews."

NAZIRITE
Nu 6: 2 make a special vow, the vow of a **n,**
Jdg 13: 5 boy shall be a **n** to God from birth.

NEAR
Dt 30:14 No, the word is very **n** to you;
Isa 55: 6 call upon him while he is **n;**
Lk 10: 9 'The kingdom of God has come **n**
Jas 4: 8 Draw **n** to God, and he will draw **n** to

NEED → NEEDY
Mt 6: 8 for your Father knows what you **n**

Heb 4:16 and find grace to help in time of **n**.

NEEDLE
Lk 18:25 a camel to go through the eye of a **n**

NEEDY → NEED
1Sa 2: 8 he lifts the **n** from the ash heap,
Ps 113: 7 and lifts the **n** from the ash heap,

NEIGHBOR
Lev 19:18 shall love your **n** as yourself:
Dt 5:20 bear false witness against your **n**.
Mt 19:19 You shall love your **n** as yourself."

NEVER
La 3:22 steadfast love of the LORD **n** ceases,
1Co 13: 8 Love **n** ends. But as for prophecies,
Heb 13: 5 he has said, "I will **n** leave you or

NEW
Ecc 1: 9 there is nothing **n** under the sun.
Isa 65:17 create **n** heavens and a **n** earth;
Jer 31:31 I will make a **n** covenant with the
La 3:23 they are **n** every morning;
Eze 36:26 A **n** heart I will give you,
Mt 9:17 is **n** wine put into old wineskins;
Lk 22:20 is the **n** covenant in my blood.
Jn 13:34 I give you a **n** commandment,
2Co 3: 6 to be ministers of a **n** covenant,
Heb 8: 8 when I will establish a **n** covenant
2Pe 3:13 we wait for **n** heavens and a **n** earth,
Rev 21: 1 I saw a **n** heaven and a **n** earth;
     21: 5 "See, I am making all things **n**."

NEWS
Isa 52: 7 who brings good **n**, who announces
Mt 11: 5 the poor have good **n** brought to
Mk 1:15 repent, and believe in the good **n**."

NIGHT → NIGHTS
Ge 1: 5 and the darkness he called **N**.
1Th 5: 2 Lord will come like a thief in the **n**.
Rev 22: 5 And there will be no more **n**;

NIGHTS → NIGHT
Ge 7:12 on the earth forty days and forty **n**.
Jnh 1:17 of the fish three days and three **n**.
Mt 4: 2 He fasted forty days and forty **n**,
     12:40 for three days and three **n** the Son

NOISE
Ps 66: 1 Make a joyful **n** to God, all the earth
2Pe 3:10 will pass away with a loud **n**,

NOTHING
Ecc 1: 9 there is **n** new under the sun.
Jer 32:17 **N** is too hard for you.
Mt 17:20 and **n** will be impossible for you."
Jn 15: 5 apart from me you can do **n**.

NUMBER
Rev 13:18 Its **n** is six hundred sixty-six.

O

OATH
Dt 7: 8 and kept the **o** that he swore to your
Heb 7:20 This was confirmed with an **o**;

OBEDIENCE → OBEY
Ro 5:19 so by the one man's **o** the many will
Heb 5: 8 learned **o** through what he suffered;

OBEDIENT → OBEY
Php 2: 8 and became **o** to the point of death

OBEY → OBEDIENCE, OBEDIENT
Ex 19: 5 if you **o** my voice and keep my
Dt 12:28 Be careful to **o** all these words that
Mt 28:20 **o** everything that I have commanded
Ac 5:29 "We must **o** God rather than any
Eph 6: 1 Children, **o** your parents in the Lord,
1Jn 5: 3 love of God is this, that we **o** his

OFFENSE
Mk 6: 3 And they took **o** at him.
Gal 5:11 **o** of the cross has been removed.

OFFERING → OFFERINGS
Ge 4: 4 LORD had regard for Abel and his **o**,
Ps 40: 6 Sacrifice and **o** you do not desire,
Da 11:31 shall abolish the regular burnt **o**
Eph 5: 2 a fragrant **o** and sacrifice to God.
Heb 10:14 For by a single **o** he has perfected
1Mc 4:44 what to do about the altar of burnt **o**,

OFFERINGS → OFFERING
Hos 6: 6 of God rather than burnt **o**.
Mk 12:33 important than all whole burnt **o**
1Mc 1:45 to forbid burnt **o** and sacrifices

OIL
Ex 25: 6 **o** for the lamps, spices for the
          anointing **o**
Ps 23: 5 you anoint my head with **o**;
Jas 5:14 anointing them with **o** in the name

OLD
Mk 2:22 puts new wine into **o** wineskins;
Eph 4:22 your **o** self, corrupt and deluded by

OLIVE → OLIVES
Zec 4: 3 And by it there are two **o** trees,
Ro 11:17 and you, a wild **o** shoot,
Rev 11: 4 two **o** trees and the two lampstands

OLIVES → OLIVE
Zec 14: 4 Mount of **O** shall be split in two
Mt 24: 3 he was sitting on the Mount of **O**,

OMEGA
Rev 1: 8 "I am the Alpha and the **O**,"

ONCE → ONE
Ro 6:10 he died, he died to sin, **o** for all;
Heb 7:27 this he did **o** for all when he offered
     9:27 it is appointed for mortals to die **o**,

ONE → FIRST, ONCE
Ge 2:24 and they become **o** flesh.
Zec 14: 9 the Lord will be **o** and his name **o**.
Mk 12:29 the Lord our God, the Lord is **o**;
Jn 10:30 The Father and I are **o**."
1Co 12:13 For in the **o** Spirit we were all
          baptized
Eph 4: 5 **o** Lord, **o** faith, **o** baptism,

ONLY
Jn 1:14 the glory as of a father's **o** son,
     3:16 that he gave his **o** Son,
1Ti 1:17 the **o** God, be honor and glory
1Jn 4: 9 God sent his **o** Son into the world so

OPPRESSED
Ps 146: 7 who executes justice for the **o**;
Isa 53: 7 He was **o**, and he was afflicted,

Jdt 9:11 God of the lowly, helper of the **o**,

ORACLES
Ro 3: 2 entrusted with the **o** of God.

ORDAIN
Ex 29: 9 shall then **o** Aaron and his sons.
1Ti 5:22 Do not **o** anyone hastily,

ORPHAN → ORPHANED, ORPHANS
Ex 22:22 You shall not abuse any widow or **o**.
Hos 14: 3 In you the **o** finds mercy."

ORPHANED → ORPHAN
Jn 14:18 will not leave you **o**; I am coming

ORPHANS → ORPHAN
Jas 1:27 to care for **o** and widows in their
Sir 4:10 Be a father to **o**, and be like a

OUTSTRETCHED
Ex 6: 6 I will redeem you with an **o** arm
Ps 136:12 an **o** arm, for his steadfast love
Jer 27: 5 by my great power and my **o** arm

OVERCOME
Jn 1: 5 and the darkness did not **o** it.
Ro 12:21 Do not be **o** by evil, but **o** evil with
1Jn 2:14 and you have **o** the evil one.

OVERSHADOW → OVERSHADOWED
Lk 1:35 power of the Most High will **o** you;

OVERSHADOWED → OVERSHADOW
Lk 9:34 a cloud came and **o** them;

OWE
Mt 18:28 he said, 'Pay what you **o**.'
Ro 13: 8 **O** no one anything, except to love

P

PAIN
Ge 3:16 in **p** you shall bring forth children,
Rev 21: 4 and crying and **p** will be no more,

PALM
Jn 12:13 So they took branches of **p** trees
Rev 7: 9 robed in white, with **p** branches in

PARABLE → PARABLES
Ps 78: 2 I will open my mouth in a **p**;

PARABLES → PARABLE; See also JESUS: PARABLES
Mt 13:35 I will open my mouth to speak in **p**;
Sir 39: 2 penetrates the subtleties of **p**;

PARADISE
Lk 23:43 today you will be with me in **P**."
2Co 12: 4 was caught up into **P** and heard
Rev 2: 7 tree of life that is in the **p** of God.
2Es 8:52 for you that **p** is opened,

PARALYTIC → PARALYZED
Mt 9: 2 saw their faith, he said to the **p**,

PARALYZED → PARALYTIC
Jn 5: 3 many invalids—blind, lame, and **p**.
Ac 8: 7 who were **p** or lame were cured.

PARCHMENTS
2Ti 4:13 also the books, and above all the **p**.

PARDON
Ex 34: 9 **p** our iniquity and our sin,
Isa 55: 7 our God, for he will abundantly **p**.

PARENTS
Eph 6: 1 Children, obey your **p** in the Lord,

PARTIALITY
Dt 16:19 distort justice; you must not show **p**;
Pr 24:23 **P** in judging is not good.
Ro 2:11 For God shows no **p**.
Jas 3:17 without a trace of **p** or hypocrisy.
Sir 35:15 and with him there is no **p**.

PARTNERS
1Co 10:20 not want you to be **p** with demons.
Heb 3: 1 holy **p** in a heavenly calling,

PASS → PASSED, PASSING
Ex 12:13 when I see the blood, I will **p** over
33:19 make all my goodness **p** before you,
Am 5:17 I will **p** through the midst of you,
Mt 24:35 Heaven and earth will **p** away, but my
words will not **p**
2Pe 3:10 then the heavens will **p** away

PASSED → PASS
Ex 12:27 he **p** over the houses of the Israelites
2Co 5:17 everything old has **p** away;
Rev 21: 4 for the first things have **p** away."

PASSING → PASS
1Co 7:31 present form of this world is **p** away
1Jn 2:17 the world and its desire are **p** away,

PASSIONS
Gal 5:24 have crucified the flesh with its **p**
2Ti 2:22 Shun youthful **p** and pursue

PASSOVER
Ex 12:11 It is the **p** of the LORD.
Dt 16: 1 the month of Abib by keeping the **p**
Mk 14:12 when the **P** lamb is sacrificed,

PASTORS
Eph 4:11 evangelists, some **p** and teachers,

PASTURES
Ps 23: 2 He makes me lie down in green **p**;

PATH → PATHS
Ps 119:105 lamp to my feet and a light to my **p**.

PATHS → PATH
Mt 3: 3 of the Lord, make his **p** straight."'
Heb 12:13 and make straight **p** for your feet,

PATIENCE → PATIENT
Mic 2: 7 Is the LORD's **p** exhausted?
Ro 2: 4 his kindness and forbearance and **p**?
Gal 5:22 fruit of the Spirit is love, joy, peace, **p**,
2Pe 3:15 regard the **p** of our Lord as salvation

PATIENT → PATIENCE
1Co 13: 4 Love is **p**; love is kind;

PEACE → PEACEMAKERS
Ps 122: 6 Pray for the **p** of Jerusalem:
Isa 57:19 **P, p**, to the far and the near,
Jer 6:14 saying, **"P, p,"** when there is no **p**.

Mic 5: 5 and he shall be the one of **p**.
Lk 2:14 on earth **p** among those whom he
Jn 14:27 **P** I leave with you; my **p** I give
1Co 14:33 is a God not of disorder but of **p**,
Gal 5:22 the fruit of the Spirit is love, joy, **p**,
Php 4: 7 the **p** of God, which surpasses all

PEACEMAKERS → PEACE
Mt 5: 9 "Blessed are the **p**, for they will be

PEARLS
Mt 7: 6 do not throw your **p** before swine,

PENTECOST
Ac 2: 1 When the day of **P** had come,

PEOPLE
Ex 5: 1 the God of Israel, 'Let my **p** go,
Dt 4:20 a **p** of his very own possession,
Ru 1:16 your **p** shall be my **p**,
Ps 29:11 the LORD bless his **p** with peace!
Isa 40: 1 Comfort, O comfort my **p**, says
Mt 1:21 he will save his **p** from their sins."
Heb 8:10 their God, and they shall be my **p**.
1Pe 2: 9 a holy nation, God's own **p**,

PERFECT → PERFECTER, PERFECTION
2Sa 22:31 This God—his way is **p**;
Ps 19: 7 The law of the LORD is **p**, reviving
Mt 5:48 Be **p**, therefore, as your heavenly
Father is **p**.
Ro 12: 2 what is good and acceptable and **p**.
Heb 7:19 (for the law made nothing **p**);
1Jn 4:18 in love, but **p** love casts out fear;

PERFECTER → PERFECT
Heb 12: 2 Jesus the pioneer and **p** of our faith,

PERFECTION → PERFECT
Heb 6: 1 Therefore let us go on toward **p**,
1Jn 2: 5 the love of God has reached **p**.

PERISH → PERISHABLE
Est 4:16 and if I **p**, I **p**."
Ps 1: 6 but the way of the wicked will **p**.
Jn 3:16 who believes in him may not **p**
2Pe 3: 9 with you, not wanting any to **p**,

PERISHABLE → PERISH
1Co 9:25 they do it to receive a **p** wreath,
15:42 What is sown is **p**, what is raised is
1Pe 1:23 not of **p** but of imperishable seed,

PERSECUTE → PERSECUTED, PERSECUTION
Mt 5:44 and pray for those who **p** you,
Ac 9: 4 "Saul, Saul, why do you **p** me?"
Ro 12:14 Bless those who **p** you; bless

PERSECUTED → PERSECUTE
2Co 4: 9 **p**, but not forsaken; struck down,
2Ti 3:12 godly life in Christ Jesus will be **p**.

PERSECUTION → PERSECUTE
Mt 13:21 or **p** arises on account of the word,
Ro 8:35 Will hardship, or distress, or **p**, or
Heb 10:33 publicly exposed to abuse and **p**,

PERSEVERANCE → PERSEVERE
Heb 12: 1 let us run with **p** the race that is set

PERSEVERE → PERSEVERANCE
Da 12:12 Happy are those who **p**
Ro 12:12 be patient in suffering, **p** in prayer.

PHARAOH → PHARAOH'S
Ex 14:17 I will gain glory for myself over **P**

PHARAOH'S → PHARAOH
Ex 7: 3 But I will harden **P** heart,
Heb 11:24 refused to be called a son of **P**

PHARISEE → PHARISEES
Lk 11:37 a **P** invited him to dine with him;
Jn 3: 1 a **P** named Nicodemus,
Ac 5:34 a **P** in the council named Gamaliel,
Php 3: 5 as to the law, a **P**;

PHARISEES → PHARISEE
Mt 5:20 that of the scribes and **P**,
16: 6 beware of the yeast of the **P** and
23:13 "But woe to you, scribes and **P**,

PHILISTINE → PHILISTINES
1Sa 17:37 save me from the hand of this **P**."
Pm 151: 6 I went out to meet the **P**,

PHILISTINES → PHILISTINE
1Sa 5: 1 the **P** captured the ark of God,
Am 1: 8 the remnant of the **P** shall perish,

PIERCED
Zec 12:10 look on the one whom they have **p**,
Jn 19:37 look on the one whom they have **p**."
Rev 1: 7 even those who **p** him;

PIG
Dt 14: 8 the **p**, because it divides the hoof

PILLAR
Ge 19:26 and she became a **p** of salt.
Ex 13:21 and in a **p** of fire by night,

PIONEER
Heb 2:10 make the **p** of their salvation perfect
12: 2 Jesus the **p** and perfecter of our faith

PIT
Rev 20: 3 into the **p**, and locked and sealed it
Sir 21:10 but at its end is the **p** of Hades.

PLACE
Jn 14: 3 And if I go and prepare a **p** for you,

PLAGUE → PLAGUES
Zec 14:12 the **p** with which the LORD will
Rev 11: 6 strike the earth with every kind of **p**,

PLAGUES → PLAGUE
Hos 13:14 O Death, where are your **p**?
Rev 15: 1 seven angels with seven **p**, which

PLANT
Ge 1:29 I have given you every **p** yielding
Ecc 3: 2 time to **p**, and a time to pluck up

PLEASE → PLEASED, PLEASES, PLEASING
Ro 8: 8 who are in the flesh cannot **p** God.
15: 3 For Christ did not **p** himself;
Heb 11: without faith it is impossible to **p**
God,
Sir 2:16 Those who fear the Lord seek to **p**

PLEASED → PLEASE

Mic 6: 7 Will the LORD be **p** with thousands
Mt 3:17 Beloved, with whom I am well **p."**
Col 1:19 the fullness of God was **p** to dwell,

PLEASES → PLEASE

1Jn 3:22 commandments and do what **p** him.

PLEASING → PLEASE

Ps 104:34 May my meditation be **p** to him,
Eph 5:10 to find out what is **p** to the Lord.
Php 4:18 a sacrifice acceptable and **p** to God.

PLOT

Ps 2: 1 and the peoples **p** in vain?
Na 1: 9 Why do you **p** against the LORD?

PLOWSHARES

Isa 2: 4 they shall beat their swords into **p**,
Joel 3:10 Beat your **p** into swords, and your

POLLUTED → POLLUTES

Ac 15:20 from things **p** by idols and from
Rev 21: 8 the cowardly, the faithless, the **p**,

POLLUTES → POLLUTED

Nu 35:33 blood **p** the land, and no expiation

POOR → POVERTY

Ex 23: 6 not pervert the justice due to your **p**
1Sa 2: 8 He raises up the **p** from the dust;
Ps 113: 7 He raises the **p** from the dust,
Mt 5: 3 "Blessed are the **p** in spirit,
Mk 10:21 own, and give the money to the **p**,
  12:42 **p** widow came and put in two small
2Co 6:10 as **p**, yet making many rich;
  8: 9 yet for your sakes he became **p**,
Jas 2: 5 Has not God chosen the **p** in the

PORTION

Dt 32: 9 the LORD's own **p** was his people,
La 3:24 "The LORD is my **p**," says my soul,
Sir 17:17 Israel is the Lord's own **p**.

POSSESSED → POSSESSION

Mt 8:16 many who were **p** with demons;

POSSESSION → POSSESSED, POSSESSIONS

Ex 19: 5 treasured **p** out of all the peoples.
Ps 2: 8 and the ends of the earth your **p**.

POSSESSIONS → POSSESSION

Lk 12:15 not consist in the abundance of **p."**
1Co 13: 3 If I give away all my **p**,

POSSIBLE

Mt 19:26 but for God all things are **p."**
  26:39 if it is **p**, let this cup pass from me;

POTTER

Isa 64: 8 we are the clay, and you are our **p**;
Ro 9:21 Has the **p** no right over the clay,
Sir 33:13 Like clay in the hand of the **p**,

POUR → POURED

Isa 44: 3 I will **p** my spirit upon your
Eze 39:29 I **p** out my spirit upon the house of
Joel 2:28 I will **p** out my spirit on all flesh;
Ac 2:17 I will **p** out my Spirit upon all flesh,

POURED → POUR

Mt 26:28 is **p** out for many for the forgiveness

Ac 2:33 he has **p** out this that you both see
Tit 3: 6 This Spirit he **p** out on us richly

POVERTY → POOR

Mk 12:44 out of her **p** has put in everything
2Co 8: 9 by his **p** you might become rich.

POWER → POWERFUL, POWERS

1Ch 29:11 O LORD, are the greatness, the **p**,
Isa 40:29 He gives **p** to the faint,
Zec 4: 6 by might, nor by **p**, but by my spirit,
Mt 22:29 the scriptures nor the **p** of God.
Mk 13:26 coming in clouds' with great **p** and
1Co 1:17 might not be emptied of its **p**.
Eph 1:19 the immeasurable greatness of his **p**
Php 3:10 Christ and the **p** of his resurrection
2Pe 1: 3 divine **p** has given us everything
Rev 19: 1 and glory and **p** to our God,
  20: 6 these the second death has no **p**,
Jdt 9:14 the God of all **p** and might,
Sir 39:18 and none can limit his saving **p**.

POWERFUL → POWER

Mk 1: 7 one who is more **p** than I is coming

POWERS → POWER

Ro 8:38 present, nor things to come, nor **p**,
Eph 6:12 against the cosmic **p** of this present

PRACTICE → PRACTICES

Mt 23: 3 for they do not **p** what they teach.
Sir 50:29 For if they put them into **p**,

PRACTICES → PRACTICE

Ex 23:24 or worship them, or follow their **p**,
Col 3: 9 stripped off the old self with its **p**

PRAISE

Ex 15: 2 this is my God, and I will **p** him,
Dt 10:21 He is your **p**; he is your God,
Ps 150: 6 that breathes the **p** the LORD!
Pr 27: 2 Let another **p** you, and not your own
  31:31 let her works **p** her in the city gates.
Mt 21:16 nursing babies you have prepared **p**
Rev 19: 5 **"P** our God, all you his servants,
Tob 12: 6 Bless and sing **p** to his name.

PRAY → PRAYED, PRAYER, PRAYERS

2Ch 7:14 humble themselves, **p**, seek my face
Ps 122: 6 **P** for the peace of Jerusalem:
Mt 5:44 and **p** for those who persecute you,
  6: 5 you **p**, do not be like the hypocrites;
Lk 11: 1 teach us to **p**, as John taught his
Ro 8:26 do not know how to **p** as we ought,
1Th 5:17 **p** without ceasing,
Sir 37:15 But above all **p** to the Most High

PRAYED → PRAY

Mk 1:35 to a deserted place, and there he **p**.
  14:35 threw himself on the ground and **p**

PRAYER → PRAY

Pr 15:29 but he hears the **p** of the righteous.
Isa 56: 7 house shall be called a house of **p**
Mt 21:13 house shall be called a house of **p'**;
Mk 11:24 I tell you, whatever you ask for in **p**,
Ro 12:12 patient in suffering, persevere in **p**.
Jas 5:16 The **p** of the righteous is powerful

PRAYERS → PRAY

Heb 5: 7 Jesus offered up **p** and supplications
Rev 5: 8 which are the **p** of the saints.

PREACH → PREACHING

Tit 1: 9 able both to **p** with sound doctrine

PREACHING → PREACH

1Ti 5:17 those who labor in **p** and teaching;

PRECEPTS → PRECEPT

Ps 19: 8 the **p** of the LORD are right,
Mt 15: 9 teaching human **p** as doctrines.'"

PRECIOUS

Ps 72:14 and **p** is their blood in his sight.
Pr 3:15 She is more **p** than jewels.
Isa 28:16 a tested stone, a **p** cornerstone,
1Pe 1:19 but with the **p** blood of Christ,
  2: 6 a cornerstone chosen and **p**;
2Pe 1: 1 received a faith as **p** as ours

PREDESTINED

Ro 8:30 those whom he **p** he also called;

PREDICTION → PREDICTIONS

Isa 44:26 and fulfills the **p** of his messengers;

PREDICTIONS → PREDICT

Jude 1:17 the **p** of the apostles of our Lord

PREPARE

Ps 23: 5 You **p** a table before me in the
Mt 3: 3 **'P** the way of the Lord, make his
Jn 14: 2 I have told you that I go to **p** a place

PRESENCE → PRESENT

Ex 25:30 the bread of the **P** on the table
Ps 51:11 Do not cast me away from your **p**,
  139: 7 Or where can I flee from your **p?**
Jn 17: 5 with the glory that I had in your **p**

PRESENT → PRESENCE

Ro 6:13 but **p** yourselves to God as
1Co 3:22 or death or the **p** or the future—
Eph 5:27 **p** the church to himself in splendor,
2Ti 2:15 **p** yourself to God as one approved

PRICE

Mt 27: 9 the one on whom a **p** had been set,
1Co 6:20 For you were bought with a **p**;

PRIDE → PROUD

Ps 20: 7 our **p** is in the name of the LORD
Pr 16:18 **P** goes before destruction,
Mk 7:22 licentiousness, envy, slander, **p**,
1Jn 2:16 the desire of the eyes, the **p** in riches
Sir 10:13 For the beginning of **p** is sin,

PRIEST → PRIESTHOOD, PRIESTS

Ge 14:18 he was **p** of God Most High.
Ps 110: 4 "You are a **p** forever according to
Mk 14:63 Then the high **p** tore his clothes and
Heb 3: 1 apostle and high **p** of our confession
  7: 3 the Son of God, he remains a **p**

PRIESTHOOD → PRIEST

Ex 29: 9 the **p** shall be theirs by a perpetual
Heb 7:24 but he holds his **p** permanently,
1Pe 2: 5 a holy **p**, to offer spiritual sacrifices

PRIESTS → PRIEST

Ex 28: 1 the Israelites, to serve me as **p**—
Mk 15: 3 the chief **p** accused him of many
Heb 7:27 Unlike the other high **p**, he has no
Rev 20: 6 they will be **p** of God and of Christ,

PRINCE → PRINCES
Isa   9: 6 Everlasting Father, **P** of Peace.
Eze 37: 25 David shall be their **p** forever.

PRINCES → PRINCE
1Sa   2: 8 to make them sit with **p** and inherit
Da   8: 25 even rise up against the Prince of **p.**

PRISONER → PRISONERS
Mk 15: 6 at the festival he used to release a **p**
Eph   3: 1 that I Paul am a **p** for Christ Jesus

PRISONERS → PRISONER
Ps 146: 7 The LORD sets the **p** free;
Isa 61: 1 to the captives, and release to the **p;**

PRIZE
1Co   9: 24 but only one receives the **p?**
Php   3: 14 the **p** of the heavenly call of God in

PROMISE → PROMISED, PROMISES
Ps 105: 42 For he remembered his holy **p,**
Eph   2: 12 and strangers to the covenants of **p,**
2Pe   3: 9 The Lord is not slow about his **p,**

PROMISED → PROMISE
Dt   1: 11 and bless you, as he has **p** you!
Ac 13: 23 to Israel a Savior, Jesus, as he **p;**
Eph   1: 13 with the seal of the **p** Holy Spirit;
Heb 10: 23 for he who has **p** is faithful.

PROMISES → PROMISE
Jos 21: 45 the good **p** that the LORD had made
2Co   1: 20 every one of God's **p** is a "Yes."

PROOFS → PROVE
Ac   1: 3 to them by many convincing **p,**

PROPHECIES → PROPHESY
1Co 13: 8 as for **p,** they will come to an end;

PROPHECY → PROPHESY
Ac 21: 9 daughters who had the gift of **p.**
1Co 12: 10 to another **p,** to another
2Pe   1: 20 that no **p** of scripture is a matter

**PROPHESY → PROPHECIES,
PROPHECY, PROPHET, PROPHETS**
Joel   2: 28 sons and your daughters shall **p,**
Mt   7: 22 Lord, did we not **p** in your name,
1Co 13: 9 only in part, and we **p** only in part;
Rev 11: 3 my two witnesses authority to **p**

PROPHET → PROPHESY
Dt 18: 18 a **p** like you from among their own
Mal   4: 5 the **p** Elijah before the great and
Lk   4: 24 no **p** is accepted in the prophet's
Rev 16: 13 and from the mouth of the false **p.**
1Mc   4: 46 until a **p** should come to tell what

PROPHETS → PROPHESY
Nu 11: 29 that all the LORD's people were **p,**
Mt   5: 17 come to abolish the law or the **p;**
22: 40 hang all the law and the **p."**
1Co 12: 28 the church first apostles, second **p,**
Eph   2: 20 the foundation of the apostles and **p,**
4: 11 some **p,** some evangelists,
Rev 11: 10 these two **p** had been a torment to
18: 20 you saints and apostles and **p!**
1Mc   9: 27 that **p** ceased to appear among them.

PROSPER → PROSPERITY
Ps   1: 3 In all that they do, they **p.**

PROSPERITY → PROSPER
Dt 30: 15 have set before you today life and **p,**

PROSTITUTE → PROSTITUTES
Jos   2: 1 a **p** whose name was Rahab,
1Co   6: 15 and make them members of a **p?**
Heb 11: 31 By faith Rahab the **p** did not perish

PROSTITUTES → PROSTITUTE
Mt 21: 31 the **p** are going into the kingdom of
Sir   9: 6 Do not give yourself to **p,**

PROUD → PRIDE
Ps 94: 2 give to the **p** what they deserve!
Pr 21: 4 Haughty eyes and a **p** heart—
Jas   4: 6 God opposes the **p,** but gives grace

PROVERBS
Pr   1: 1 The **p** of Solomon son of David,
Ecc 12: 9 and studying and arranging many **p.**
Sir 39: 3 seeks out the hidden meanings of **p**

PROVOKE → PROVOKED
Jer 25: 6 not **p** me to anger with the work of
Heb 10: 24 how to **p** one another to love

PROVOKED → PROVOKE
Ps 78: 41 and **p** the Holy One of Israel.

PRUNES
Jn 15: 2 he **p** to make it bear more fruit.

PSALMS
Lk 24: 44 and the **p** must be fulfilled."
Eph   5: 19 you sing **p** and hymns and spiritual

PUFFS
1Co   8: 1 Knowledge **p** up, but love builds up.

**PUNISH → PUNISHING,
PUNISHMENT**
Ex 32: 34 I will **p** them for their sin."
1Pe   2: 14 by him to **p** those who do wrong

PUNISHING → PUNISH
Dt   5: 9 **p** children for the iniquity of parents
Joel   2: 13 in steadfast love, and relents from **p.**

PUNISHMENT → PUNISH
Isa 53: 5 was the **p** that made us whole,
Mt 25: 46 these will go away into eternal **p,**
1Jn   4: 18 for fear has to do with **p,**

PURE → PURIFICATION, PURIFIED
2Sa 22: 27 with the **p** you show yourself **p,**
Ps 19: 9 the fear of the LORD is **p,** enduring
Hab   1: 13 Your eyes are too **p** to behold evil,
Mt   5: 8 "Blessed are the **p** in heart, for they
Php   4: 8 whatever is **p,** whatever is pleasing,
Tit   1: 15 To the **p** all things are **p,**
1Jn   3: 3 purify themselves, just as he is **p.**

PURIFICATION → PURE
Heb   1: 3 When he had made **p** for sins,

PURIFIED → PURE
1Pe   1: 22 **p** your souls by your obedience to

PURPLE
Ex 25: 4 **p,** and crimson yarns and fine linen,
Mk 15: 17 And they clothed him in a **p** cloak;

PURPOSE
Isa 46: 10 saying, "My **p** shall stand,
Ro   8: 28 who are called according to his **p.**
2Ti   1: 9 works but according to his own **p**

Q

QUAILS
Ex 16: 13 In the evening **q** came up
Nu 11: 31 and it brought **q** from the sea and

QUARRELED
Ex 17: 7 the Israelites **q** and tested the LORD,
Nu 20: 3 The people **q** with Moses and said,

QUEEN
1Ki 10: 1 the **q** of Sheba heard of the fame of
Rev 18: 7 in her heart she says, 'I rule as a **q;**

QUIET
1Ti   2: 2 **q** and peaceable life in all godliness
1Pe   3: 4 beauty of a gentle and **q** spirit,

R

RABBI
Jn   1: 38 **"R"** (which translated means
Teacher),

RACE
Ecc   9: 11 the sun the **r** is not to the swift,
1Co   9: 24 that in a **r** the runners all compete,
Heb 12: 1 let us run with perseverance the **r**
1Pe   2: 9 But you are a chosen **r,** a royal

RAIN → RAINBOW
Ge   7: 4 For in seven days I will send **r** on
Isa 45: 8 let the skies **r** down righteousness;
Mt   5: 45 sends **r** on the righteous and on the
Rev 11: 6 so that no **r** may fall during the days

RAINBOW → BOW
Rev   4: 3 the throne is a **r** that looks like an

RAISE → RISE
Jn   2: 19 and in three days I will **r** it up."
2Co   4: 14 who raised the Lord Jesus will **r** us

RAISED → RISE
Mt 17: 23 and on the third day he will be **r."**
Ac   2: 24 God **r** him up, having freed him
Ro   4: 25 and was **r** for our justification.
1Co 15: 4 **r** on the third day in accordance

RANSOM
Ps 49: 8 For the **r** of life is costly, and can
Mt 20: 28 and to give his life a **r** for many."
1Ti   2: 6 who gave himself a **r** for all

REAP
Gal   6: 7 for you **r** whatever you sow.
Rev 14: 15 for the hour to **r** has come,

REBUILD → BUILD
Ezr   1: 3 and **r** the house of the LORD,
Ne   2: 17 let us **r** the wall of Jerusalem,
Da   9: 25 went out to restore and **r** Jerusalem
Ac 15: 16 and I will **r** the dwelling of David,

REBUKE
Pr 27: 5 Better is open **r** than hidden love.
Zec   3: 2 said to Satan, "The LORD **r** you,
Mk   8: 32 Peter took him aside and began to **r**

2Ti   4:   2   convince, r, and encourage,

RECEIVE
Jn   16:24   Ask and you will r, so that your joy
Ac   2:38   you will r the gift of the Holy Spirit.
      20:35   'It is more blessed to give than to r.'
Rev   4:11   to r glory and honor and power,

RECKONED
Ge   15:   6   LORD r it to him as righteousness.
Ro   4:   3   it was r to him as righteousness."

RECONCILIATION
Ro   5:11   whom we have now received r.
2Co   5:18   and has given us the ministry of r;

REDEEM → REDEEMER, REDEMPTION
Ex   6:   6   I will r you with an outstretched
Gal   4:   5   to r those who were under the law,

REDEEMER → REDEEM
Job   19:25   For I know that my R lives,
Ps   19:14   O LORD, my rock and my r.

REDEMPTION → REDEEM
Lk   21:28   because your r is drawing near."
Eph   1:   7   In him we have r through his blood,
Heb   9:12   own blood, thus obtaining eternal r.

REFINE
Jer   9:   7   I will now r and test them,
Zec   13:   9   r them as one refines silver,

REFLECTED → REFLECTION
2Co   3:18   though r in a mirror,

REFLECTION → REFLECTED
1Co   11:   7   since he is the image and r of God;
Heb   1:   3   He is the r of God's glory

REFUGE
Nu   35:11   select cities to be cities of r for you,
Ps   2:12   Happy are all who take r in him.

REGULATIONS
Col   2:20   Why do you submit to r,
Heb   9:10   r for the body imposed until the

REIGN
Ex   15:18   The LORD will r forever and ever."
Ps   146:10   The LORD will r forever,
1Co   15:25   r until he has put all his enemies
2Ti   2:12   we will also r with him;
Rev   11:15   and he will r forever and ever."
      22:   5   and they will r forever and ever.

REJECTED
Ps   118:22   The stone that the builders r
Isa   53:   3   He was despised and r by others;
Mt   21:42   'The stone that the builders r

REJOICE
Ps   118:24   let us r and be glad in it.
Zep   3:17   he will r over you with gladness,
Php   4:   4   R in the Lord always; again I will say, R.

RELENT → RELENTED
Eze   24:14   I will not spare, I will not r.
Joel   2:14   whether he will not turn and r,
Jnh   3:   9   God may r and change his mind;

RELENTED → RELENT
1Ch   21:15   LORD took note and r concerning
Jer   4:28   I have not r nor will I turn back.

REMEMBER → REMEMBRANCE
Ge   9:15   I will r my covenant that is between
Ex   20:   8   R the sabbath day, and keep it holy.
Dt   8:18   But r the LORD your God,
2Ti   2:   8   R Jesus Christ, raised from the dead
Heb   8:12   and I will r their sins no more."
Sir   23:18   The Most High will not r sins."

REMEMBRANCE → REMEMBER
Lk   22:19   Do this in r of me."

REMNANT
Isa   10:21   A r will return, the r of Jacob,
Jer   50:20   will pardon the r that I have spared.
Ro   9:27   only a r of them will be saved;

RENEW → RENEWAL, RENEWED, RENEWING
Isa   40:31   the LORD shall r their strength,
La   5:21   r our days as of old—

RENEWAL → RENEW
Mt   19:28   I tell you, at the r of all things,

RENEWED → RENEW
2Co   4:16   inner nature is being r day by day.
Eph   4:23   to be r in the spirit of your minds,

RENEWING → RENEW
Ro   12:   2   transformed by the r of your minds,

REPENT → REPENTANCE
Mt   3:   2   "R, for the kingdom of heaven has
Ac   2:38   "R, and be baptized every one of
Sir   18:21   and when you have sinned, r.

REPENTANCE → REPENT
Mk   1:   4   a baptism of r for the forgiveness
Lk   3:   8   Bear fruits worthy of r.
Ro   2:   4   kindness is meant to lead you to r?
2Co   7:10   r that leads to salvation and brings
2Pe   3:   9   any to perish, but all to come to r.

REPROVE
Pr   19:25   r the intelligent, and they will gain
Tit   2:15   exhort and r with all authority.
Rev   3:19   r and discipline those whom I love.

REQUIRE
Dt   10:12   does the LORD your God r of you?
Mic   6:   8   the LORD r of you but to do justice,

RESCUE → RESCUED
Mt   6:13   but r us from the evil one.
2Pe   2:   9   the Lord knows how to r the godly

RESCUED → RESCUE
Col   1:13   has r us from the power of darkness
Sir   51:12   and r me in time of trouble.

RESIST
Mt   5:39   I say to you, Do not r an evildoer.
Ro   9:19   For who can r his will?"
Jas   4:   7   R the devil, and he will flee from

REST → RESTED
Ex   31:15   seventh day is a sabbath of solemn r
Ps   95:11   swore, "They shall not enter my r."
Mt   11:28   and I will give you r.

RESTED → REST
Ge   2:   2   he r on the seventh day from all the
Ex   20:11   all that is in them, but r the seventh

RESURRECTION
Mt   22:30   For in the r they neither marry nor
Mk   12:18   Sadducees, who say there is no r,
Jn   11:25   said to her, "I am the r and the life.
1Co   15:12   you say there is no r of the dead?
Php   3:10   know Christ and the power of his r
Rev   20:   5   This is the first r.
2Es   2:23   will give you the first place in my r.

RETURN
Ge   3:19   you are dust, and to dust you shall r.
Mal   3:   7   R to me, and I will r to you,

REVEAL → REVEALED, REVELATION
Mt   11:27   to whom the Son chooses to r him.

REVEALED → REVEAL
Isa   40:   5   the glory of the LORD shall be r,
Mt   16:17   flesh and blood has not r this to you
Lk   17:30   on the day that the Son of Man is r.
Ro   1:17   in it the righteousness of God is r

REVELATION → REVEAL
1Co   14:   6   some r or knowledge or prophecy
Eph   3:   3   was made known to me by r,

REVERE → REVERENCE
Jos   24:14   "Now therefore r the LORD,
Mal   4:   2   But for you who r my name the sun
Tob   4:   5   "R the Lord all your days,

REVERENCE → REVERE
Eph   5:21   subject to one another out of r for

REVILE → REVILED
Ex   22:28   You shall not r God, or curse
Mt   5:11   people r you and persecute you

REVILED → REVILE
1Co   4:12   When r, we bless;
1Pe   4:14   If you are r for the name of Christ,

REWARD
Ps   19:11   in keeping them there is great r.
Isa   40:10   r is with him, and his recompense
Mt   6:   5   I tell you, they have received their r.
Lk   6:23   for surely your r is great in heaven;
Rev   22:12   I am coming soon; my r is with me,

RIB
Ge   2:22   r that the LORD God had taken from

RICH → RICHES
Mt   19:23   hard for a r person to enter the
2Co   8:   9   by his poverty you might become r.
Eph   2:   4   But God, who is r in mercy,

RICHES → RICH
Lk   8:14   they are choked by the cares and r
Ro   11:33   O the depth of the r and wisdom
1Jn   2:16   the desire of the eyes, the pride in r
Sir   13:24   R are good if they are free from sin;

RIGHT → BIRTHRIGHT
Ex   15:   6   Your r hand, O LORD, glorious in
Dt   6:18   Do what is r and good in the sight

Heb   4:10   those who enter God's r also cease

Ps 110: 1 says to my lord, "Sit at my **r** hand
Pr 14:12 a way that seems **r** to a person,
Ac 2:34 said to my Lord, "Sit at my **r** hand,
Heb 1:13 "Sit at my **r** hand until I make your

RIGHTEOUS → RIGHTEOUSNESS

Ps 11: 7 For the LORD is **r**; he loves **r** deeds;
Jer 23: 5 I will raise up for David a **r** Branch,
Eze 3:20 if the **r** turn from their righteousness
Hab 2: 4 but the **r** live by their faith.
Mt 5:45 rain on the **r** and on the unrighteous.
Mk 2:17 come to call not the **r** but sinners."
Ro 1:17 one who is **r** will live by faith."
Heb 10:38 but my **r** one will live by faith.
1Jn 2: 1 with the Father, Jesus Christ the **r**;
Rev 19: 8 the fine linen is the **r** deeds of the
Wis 5:15 **r** live forever, and their reward
Sir 35:22 and does justice for the **r**,

RIGHTEOUSNESS → RIGHTEOUS

Ge 15: 6 the LORD reckoned it to him as **r**.
Isa 11: 5 **R** shall be the belt around his waist,
Jer 23: 6 be called: "The LORD is our **r**."
Da 9:24 to bring in everlasting **r**,
Hos 10:12 Sow for yourselves **r**; reap steadfast
Mt 5: 6 those who hunger and thirst for **r**,
Jn 16: 8 about sin and **r** and judgment;
Ro 5:18 act of **r** leads to justification
Gal 3: 6 and it was reckoned to him as **r**,"
Eph 6:14 and put on the breastplate of **r**.
2Pe 3:13 heavens and a new earth, where **r**

RIPE

Jn 4:35 how the fields are **r** for harvesting.
Rev 14:15 the harvest of the earth is fully **r**."

RISE → ARISE, RAISE, RAISED, ROSE

Da 12:13 shall **r** for your reward at the end of
Mal 4: 2 the sun of righteousness shall **r**,
Mt 27:63 'After three days I will **r** again.'
1Th 4:16 and the dead in Christ will **r** first.

ROAD

Mt 7:13 and the **r** is easy that leads to

ROBBERS

Jer 7:11 become a den of **r** in your sight?
Mt 21:13 but you are making it a den of **r**."

ROBE

Ex 28: 4 a breastpiece, an ephod, a **r**,
Jn 19: 5 crown of thorns and the purple **r**.
Rev 6:11 They were each given a white **r** and
19:13 He is clothed in a **r** dipped in blood,

ROCK

Ex 17: 6 Strike the **r**, and water will come
Nu 20: 8 you shall bring water out of the **r**
1Sa 2: 2 there is no **R** like our God.
Mt 16:18 and on this **r** I will build my church,
Mk 15:46 that had been hewn out of the **r**.
1Pe 2: 8 and a **r** that makes them fall."

ROD

Ps 2: 9 shall break them with a **r** of iron,
23: 4 your **r** and your staff—they comfort
Pr 13:24 who spare the **r** hate their children,
Rev 2:27 to rule them with an iron **r**,

ROLL

Mk 16: 3 "Who will **r** away the stone for us

ROOT

Isa 11:10 On that day the **r** of Jesse
53: 2 and like a **r** out of dry ground;
Ro 15:12 "The **r** of Jesse shall come,
1Ti 6:10 For the love of money is a **r** of all
Rev 5: 5 the tribe of Judah, the **R** of David,

ROSE → RISE

SS 2: 1 I am a **r** of Sharon, a lily
1Th 4:14 believe that Jesus died and **r** again,

RULE

Eph 1:21 far above all **r** and authority and
Col 3:15 the peace of Christ **r** in your hearts,

RUMORS

Mt 24: 6 you will hear of wars and **r** of wars;

RUN

Isa 40:31 they shall **r** and not be weary,
Heb 12: 1 let us **r** with perseverance the race

RUST

Mt 6:19 where moth and **r** consume
LtJ 6:12 cannot save themselves from **r**

S

SABBATH

Ex 20: 8 Remember the **s** day, and keep it holy.
Mk 2:28 Son of Man is lord even of the **s**."
1Mc 1:43 to idols and profaned the **s**.

SACRIFICE → SACRIFICED

Ex 12:27 'It is the passover **s** to the LORD,
1Sa 15:22 Surely, to obey is better than **s**,
Ps 40: 6 **S** and offering you do not desire,
Da 9:27 he shall make a **s** and offering cease;
Hos 6: 6 For I desire steadfast love and not **s**,
Mt 9:13 this means, 'I desire mercy, not **s**.'
Ro 3:25 put forward as a **s** of atonement
Heb 13:15 let us continually offer a **s** of praise
1Jn 2: 2 and he is the atoning **s** for our sins,

SACRIFICED → SACRIFICE

1Co 5: 7 our paschal lamb, Christ, has been **s**.
8: 1 Now concerning food **s** to idols:

SADDUCEES

Mt 16: 6 the yeast of the Pharisees and **S**."
Mk 12:18 **S**, who say there is no resurrection,

SAFE → SAFETY

Ps 37:28 righteous shall be kept **s** forever,
Pr 18:10 the righteous run into it and are **s**.

SAFETY → SAFE

Dt 12:10 around so that you live in **s**,
Eze 34:28 they shall live in **s**,

SAINTS

Ps 31:23 Love the LORD, all you his **s**.
Ro 8:27 the Spirit intercedes for the **s**
1Co 6: 2 that the **s** will judge the world?
Eph 4:12 equip the **s** for the work of ministry,
Rev 5: 9 by your blood you ransomed for
God **s**

SALT

Ge 19:26 back, and she became a pillar of **s**.
Mt 5:13 "You are the **s** of the earth;

SALVATION → SAVE

Ex 15: 2 and he has become my **s**;
Ps 27: 1 The LORD is my light and my **s**;
Isa 52: 7 brings good news, who announces **s**,
Lk 3: 6 all flesh shall see the **s** of God.'"
Ac 4:12 There is **s** in no one else,
Php 2:12 work out your own **s** with fear
Heb 2: 3 escape if we neglect so great a **s**?
2Pe 3:15 regard the patience of our Lord as **s**.
Bar 4:29 everlasting joy with your **s**.

SAMARITAN

Lk 10:33 But a **S** while traveling came near
Jn 4: 7 A **S** woman came to draw water,

SANCTIFICATION → SANCTIFY

Ro 6:19 as slaves to righteousness for **s**.
1Th 4: 3 For this is the will of God, your **s**:

SANCTIFIED → SANCTIFY

Jn 17:19 so that they also may be **s** in truth.
1Co 6:11 But you were washed, you were **s**,

SANCTIFY → SANCTIFICATION, SANCTIFIED

Lev 11:44 **s** yourselves therefore, and be holy,
Heb 13:12 to **s** the people by his own blood.

SANCTUARY

Ex 25: 8 And have them make me a **s**,
1Ch 22:19 build the **s** of the LORD God
Heb 9:24 Christ did not enter a **s** made by
1Mc 1:21 He arrogantly entered the **s**

SAND

Mt 7:26 foolish man who built his house on **s**.

SAT → SIT

Heb 10:12 "he **s** down at the right hand of God,
Rev 3:21 and **s** down with my Father

SATAN

1Ch 21: 1 **S** stood up against Israel,
Job 1: 6 and **S** also came among them.
Zec 3: 2 "The LORD rebuke you, O **S**!
Mt 4:10 Jesus said to him, "Away with you, **S**!
16:23 said to Peter, "Get behind me, **S**!
2Co 11:14 **S** disguises himself as an angel of
light.
Rev 12: 9 who is called the Devil and **S**,
20: 7 **S** will be released from his prison

SAVE → SALVATION, SAVED, SAVIOR

Isa 59: 1 LORD's hand is not too short to **s**,
Jer 15:20 for I am with you to **s** you
Mt 1:21 he will **s** his people from their sins."
16:25 who want to **s** their life will lose it,
Lk 19:10 came to seek out and to **s** the lost."

SAVED → SAVE

Isa 45:22 Turn to me and be **s**,
Joel 2:32 on the name of the LORD shall be **s**;
Mt 10:22 who endures to the end will be **s**.
Mk 15:31 He **s** others; he cannot save himself.
Ro 10:13 on the name of the Lord shall be **s**."
Eph 2: 8 For by grace you have been **s**

SAVIOR → SAVE

Isa 49:26 know that I am the LORD your **S**,
Hos 13: 4 and besides me there is no **s**.
1Ti 4:10 who is the **S** of all people,

Tit   2:13 of the glory of our great God and **S,**
2Pe   3:18 knowledge of our Lord and **S** Jesus

SCARLET
Isa   1:18 your sins are like **s,** they shall be
Mt   27:28 stripped him and put a **s** robe on him

SCEPTER
Ge   49:10 The **s** shall not depart from Judah,.
Nu   24:17 and a **s** shall rise out of Israel;

SCRIBES
Mt   7:29 having authority, and not as their **s.**
    23:13 "But woe to you, **s** and Pharisees,

SCRIPTURE → SCRIPTURES
Lk   4:21 "Today this **s** has been fulfilled in
Jn   10:35 and the **s** cannot be annulled—
1Ti   4:13 attention to the public reading of **s,**
2Ti   3:16 All **s** is inspired by God and is useful

SCRIPTURES → SCRIPTURE
Mt   22:29 know neither the **s** nor the power
Lk   24:45 their minds to understand the **s,**
Jn   5:39 "You search the **s** because you think

SEA
Ps   95: 5 The **s** is his, for he made it,
Mic   7:19 all our sins into the depths of the **s.**
Rev   4: 6 there is something like a **s** of glass,
    21: 1 and the **s** was no more.

SEAL
2Co   1:22 by putting his **s** on us and giving us
Eph   1:13 the **s** of the promised Holy Spirit;
Rev   7: 3 our God with a **s** on their foreheads.

SEASON → SEASONS
Ps   1: 3 which yield their fruit in its **s,**
Ecc   3: 1 For everything there is a **s,**

SEASONS → SEASON
1Th   5: 1 Now concerning the times and the **s,**

SEAT
Ex   25:17 make a mercy **s** of pure gold;
Ro   14:10 stand before the judgment **s** of God.
2Co   5:10 must appear before the judgment **s**

SECRET
Dt   29:29 The **s** things belong to the LORD
Ro   2:16 will judge the **s** thoughts of all.

SEE → SEEN, SEES, SIGHT
Ex   33:20 for no one shall **s** me and live."
Jn   9:25 that though I was blind, now I **s."**
Rev   1: 7 the clouds; every eye will **s** him,

SEED → SEEDS, SEEDTIME
Mt   17:20 have faith the size of a mustard **s,**

SEEDS → SEED
Mt   13: 8 Other **s** fell on good soil
Mk   4:31 the smallest of all the **s** on earth;

SEEK
1Ch   28: 9 If you **s** him, he will be found by
Ps   34:10 those who **s** the LORD lack no good
Isa   55: 6 **S** the LORD while he may be found,
Lk   19:10 came to **s** out and to save
Heb   11: 6 that he rewards those who **s** him.
Sir   2:16 who fear the Lord **s** to please him,

SEEN → SEE
Jn   1:18 No one has ever **s** God.
    14: 9 Whoever has **s** me has **s** the Father.

SELF-CONTROL
2Pe   1: 6 with **s,** and **s** with endurance,

SEPARATE
Mt   19: 6 joined together, let no one **s."**
Ro   8:35 will **s** us from the love of Christ?

SERPENT
Ge   3: 1 the **s** was more crafty than any other
2Co   11: 3 the **s** deceived Eve by its cunning,
Rev   20: 2 He seized the dragon, that ancient **s,**

SERVANT
Isa   42: 1 Here is my **s,** whom I uphold,
    53:11 my **s,** shall make many righteous,
Zec   3: 8 going to bring my **s** the Branch.
Lk   1:38 "Here am I, the **s** of the Lord;
Ac   3:13 has glorified his **s** Jesus,
Heb   3: 5 faithful in all God's house as a **s,**

SERVE
Jos   24:15 my household, we will **s** the LORD."
1Sa   12:20 but **s** the LORD with all your heart;
Mt   6:24 You cannot **s** God and wealth.
Mk   10:45 Son of Man came not to be served
    but to **s,**
1Pe   4:10 **s** one another with whatever gift

SEVEN → SEVENTH
Ge   7: 2 with you **s** pairs of all clean animals,
Ex   25:37 You shall make the **s** lamps for it;
Jos   6: 4 march around the city **s** times,
Da   9:25 prince, there shall be **s** weeks;
Mt   18:22 "Not **s** times, but, I tell you, seventy-
    seven
Rev   1:12 turning I saw **s** golden lampstands,
    5: 1 and on the back, sealed with **s** seals;
    8: 2 I saw the **s** angels who stand before
    12: 3 a great red dragon, with **s** heads and
    15: 1 **s** angels with **s** plagues,

SEVENTH → SEVEN
Ge   2: 2 on the **s** day God finished the work
Ex   20:10 the **s** day is a sabbath to the LORD
Heb   4: 4 God rested on the **s** day from all his

SEVENTY → SEVENTY-SEVEN
Da   9:24 **S** weeks are decreed for your people

SEVENTY-SEVEN → SEVENTY
Mt   18:22 "Not seven times, but, I tell you, **s**

SHADOW
Ps   17: 8 hide me in the **s** of your wings,
    91: 1 who abide in the **s** of the Almighty,

SHAME → ASHAMED
Da   12: 2 some to **s** and everlasting contempt.
1Co   1:27 foolish in the world to **s** the wise;
Heb   12: 2 endured the cross, disregarding its **s,**
1Jn   2:28 be put to **s** before him at his coming.

SHARE
Col   1:12 to **s** in the inheritance of the saints
Heb   12:10 in order that we may **s** his holiness.
Jude   1: 3 to you about the salvation we **s,**

SHARPENS → SHARPER
Pr   27:17 Iron **s** iron, and one person **s**

SHARPER → SHARPENS
Heb   4:12 **s** than any two-edged sword,

SHED
Ge   9: 6 shall that person's blood be **s;**
Rev   16: 6 **s** the blood of saints and prophets,

SHEEP
Isa   53: 6 All we like **s** have gone astray;
Mt   9:36 like **s** without a shepherd.
Jn   10: 7 I am the gate for the **s.**
    10:15 And I lay down my life for the **s.**
Heb   13:20 the great shepherd of the **s,**
1Pe   2:25 For you were going astray like **s,**

SHEOL
Ps   139: 8 if I make my bed in **S,** you are there.
Hos   13:14 O **S,** where is your destruction?

SHEPHERD → SHEPHERDS
Ps   23: 1 The LORD is my **s,** I shall not want.
Isa   40:11 He will feed his flock like a **s;**
Mt   2: 6 ruler who is to **s** my people Israel.'"
Jn   10:11 "I am the good **s.**
Heb   13:20 the great **s** of the sheep,
1Pe   5: 4 And when the chief **s** appears,

SHEPHERDS → SHEPHERD
Lk   2: 8 there were **s** living in the fields,

SHIELD
Eph   6:16 With all of these, take the **s** of faith,

SHINE → SHINES
Nu   6:25 LORD make his face to **s** upon you,
Ps   4: 6 light of your face **s** on us, O LORD!"
Da   12: 3 Those who are wise shall **s** like the
Mt   5:16 let your light **s** before others,

SHINES → SHINE
Jn   1: 5 The light **s** in the darkness,

SHORT
Ro   3:23 sinned and fall **s** of the glory of God;

SHOW → SHOWED
Ex   33:18 Moses said, "**S** me your glory,
Ps   85: 7 **S** us your steadfast love, O LORD,
Jn   14: 8 said to him, "Lord, **s** us the Father,
1Co   12:31 will **s** you a still more excellent way

SHOWED → SHOW
Jn   20:20 he **s** them his hands and his side.

SICK → SICKNESS
Mt   8:16 and cured all who were **s.**
Jas   5:14 Are any among you **s?**

SICKNESS → SICK
Ex   23:25 I will take **s** away from among you.
Mt   4:23 and curing every disease and every **s**

SIDE
Jn   19:34 soldiers pierced his **s** with a spear,

SIGHT → SEE
Mt   11: 5 blind receive their **s,** the lame walk,
2Co   5: 7 for we walk by faith, not by **s.**

SIGN → SIGNS
Mt   24: 3 the **s** of your coming and of the end
Mk   8:12 does this generation ask for a **s?**

SIGNS → SIGN
Ge 1:14 be for **s** and for seasons and for days
Mt 16: 3 cannot interpret the **s** of the times.
Jn 20:30 Jesus did many other **s** in the
1Co 1:22 Jews demand **s** and Greeks desire
Rev 16:14 demonic spirits, performing **s**,

SILENT
Isa 53: 7 a sheep that before its shearers is **s**,
Mk 14:61 But he was **s** and did not answer.

SILVER
Mt 26:15 They paid him thirty pieces of **s**.
Ac 3: 6 But Peter said, "I have no **s** or gold,

SIN → SINNED, SINNER, SINNERS, SINS
Nu 32:23 and be sure your **s** will find you out.
2Ch 7:14 forgive their **s** and heal their land.
Ps 119:11 so that I may not **s** against you.
Isa 53:12 yet he bore the **s** of many,
Mt 5:29 If your right eye causes you to **s**,
Jn 1:29 who takes away the **s** of the world!
Ro 6:23 For the wages of **s** is death,
Heb 4:15 tested as we are, yet without **s**.
1Jn 1: 7 Jesus his Son cleanses us from all **s**.
Tob 12:10 but those who commit **s**
Wis 10:13 but delivered him from **s**.
Sir 3:30 so almsgiving atones for **s**.

SINAI
Ex 19:20 the LORD descended upon Mount **S**,

SING → SONG, SONGS, SUNG
Ps 47: 6 **S** praises to God, **s** praises;
1Co 14:15 I will **s** praise with the spirit,
Col 3:16 gratitude in your hearts **s** psalms,
Rev 5: 9 They **s** a new song:
Jdt 16:13 I will **s** to my God a new song:
Aza 1:35 **s** praise to him and highly exalt him

SINNED → SIN
Ps 51: 4 Against you, you alone, have I **s**,
La 5: 7 Our ancestors **s**; they are no more,
Ro 3:23 all have **s** and fall short of the glory
1Jn 1:10 If we say that we have not **s**,
Sir 18:21 and when you have **s**, repent.

SINNER → SIN
Lk 15: 7 over one **s** who repents than
Jas 5:20 that whoever brings back a **s**

SINNERS → SIN
Pr 23:17 Do not let your heart envy **s**,
Ro 5: 8 we still were **s** Christ died for us.
1Ti 1:15 Jesus came into the world to save **s**

SINS → SIN
1Sa 2:25 if someone **s** against the LORD,
Eze 18: 4 only the person who **s** that shall die.
Mt 6:14 forgive us our **s**, for we ourselves"—
Lk 11: 4 forgive us our **s**, for we ourselves
Ac 3:19 to God so that your **s** may be wiped
1Co 15: 3 Christ died for our **s** in accordance
Heb 9:28 offered once to bear the **s** of many,
1Jn 1: 9 If we confess our **s**, he who is faithful
Rev 1: 5 loves us and freed us from our **s**
Sir 2:11 he forgives **s** and saves

SISTER
Pr 7: 4 Say to wisdom, "You are my **s**,"

Mk 3:35 the will of God is my brother and **s**

SIT → SAT
Ps 110: 1 says to my lord, "**S** at my right hand
Mt 20:23 to **s** at my right hand and at my left,
Heb 1:13 "**S** at my right hand until I make

SIX
Ex 20: 9 **S** days you shall labor and do all
Pr 6:16 are **s** things that the LORD hates,

SKULL
Mt 27:33 Golgotha (which means Place of a **S**)

SLANDER → SLANDERED
Ps 15: 3 who do not **s** with their tongue,
Pr 10:18 and whoever utters **s** is a fool.
Mt 15:19 fornication, theft, false witness, **s**,
1Pe 2: 1 all guile, insincerity, envy, and all **s**.

SLANDERED → SLANDER
1Co 4:13 when **s**, we speak kindly.

SLAUGHTER
Isa 53: 7 like a lamb that is led to the **s**,
Ac 8:32 "Like a sheep he was led to the **s**,

SLAVE → SLAVERY
Mk 10:44 first among you must be **s** of all.
Jn 8:34 who commits sin is a **s** to sin.
Gal 3:28 there is no longer **s** or free,

SLAVERY → SLAVE
Gal 5: 1 do not submit again to a yoke of **s**.

SLEEP → ASLEEP, SLEEPER, SLEEPING
Ps 121: 4 keeps Israel will neither slumber nor **s**.
Da 12: 2 Many of those who **s** in the dust of

SLEEPER → SLEEP
Eph 5:14 "**S**, awake! Rise from the dead,

SLEEPING → SLEEP
Mt 9:24 for the girl is not dead but **s**."
 26:40 to the disciples and found them **s**;

SLING
1Sa 17:50 over the Philistine with a **s** and a stone,

SLOW → SLOWNESS
Ex 34: 6 merciful and gracious, **s** to anger,
2Pe 3: 9 The Lord is not **s** about his promise,
Sir 5: 4 for the Lord is **s** to anger.

SLOWNESS → SLOW
2Pe 3: 9 think of **s**, but is patient with you,

SNOW
Ps 51: 7 and I shall be whiter than **s**.
Isa 1:18 sins are like scarlet, they shall be like **s**;
Da 7: 9 his clothing was white as **s**,
Rev 1:14 as white wool, white as **s**;

SOBER
1Th 5: 6 but let us keep awake and be **s**
2Ti 4: 5 always be **s**, endure suffering,

SODOM
Ge 19:24 rained on **S** and Gomorrah sulfur
Lk 10:12 it will be more tolerable for **S** than

Rev 11: 8 city that is prophetically called **S**

SOLDIERS
Mt 28:12 give a large sum of money to the **s**,
Jn 19:23 When the **s** had crucified Jesus,

SON → SONS
Ex 4:23 now I will kill your firstborn **s**.'"
2Sa 7:14 and he shall be a **s** to me.
Ps 2: 7 He said to me, "You are my **s**;
Isa 7:14 is with child and shall bear a **s**,
Mt 1:23 virgin shall conceive and bear a **s**,
  3:17 from heaven said, "This is my **S**,
 16:16 the Messiah, the **S** of the living God."
Mk 10:45 **S** of Man came not to be served but to
Lk 1:35 he will be called **S** of God.
Jn 3:16 loved the world that he gave his only **S**,
1Th 1:10 to wait for his **S** from heaven,
Heb 1: 2 last days he has spoken to us by a **S**,
1Jn 4: 9 God sent his only **S** into the world
Rev 12: 5 she gave birth to a **s**, a male child,
 14:14 the cloud was one like the **S** of Man,
Sir 4:10 be like a **s** of the Most High,
2Es 13:32 then my **S** will be revealed,

SONG → SING
Ps 40: 3 He put a new **s** in my mouth,
Rev 5: 9 They sing a new **s**: "You are worthy
 15: 3 and the **s** of the Lamb:

SONGS → SING
Col 3:16 hymns, and spiritual **s** to God.

SONS → SON
Ac 2:17 **s** and your daughters shall prophesy,
2Co 6:18 you shall be my **s** and daughters,

SOON
Rev 22:20 says, "Surely I am coming **s**."

SOUL → SOULS
Dt 6: 5 all your **s**, and with all your might.
Jos 22: 5 all your heart and with all your **s**."
Mt 10:28 fear him who can destroy both **s** and
Heb 4:12 piercing until it divides **s** from spirit
Jas 5:20 will save the sinner's **s** from death
3Jn 1: 2 just as it is well with your **s**.
Sir 7:29 With all your **s** fear the Lord,

SOULS → SOUL
Jer 6:16 walk in it, and find rest for your **s**.
Mt 11:29 and you will find rest for your **s**.

SOWS
Jn 4:37 'One **s** and another reaps.'
2Co 9: 6 who **s** sparingly will also reap

SPARROWS
Lk 12: 7 you are of more value than many **s**.

SPEAK → SPEAKING
Ecc 3: 7 time to keep silence, and a time to **s**;
Mt 13:13 The reason I **s** to them in parables is
Ac 2: 4 began to **s** in other languages,
1Co 12:30 Do all **s** in tongues?

SPEAKING → SPEAK
1Co 14:39 and do not forbid **s** in tongues;
Eph 4:15 But **s** the truth in love,

SPEAR → SPEARS

Jn 19:34 the soldiers pierced his side with a s,

SPIES → SPY

Nu 13:32 we have gone through as s
Jos 2:1 two men secretly from Shittim as s,

SPIRIT → SPIRITS, SPIRITUAL

Ge 6:3 My s shall not abide in mortals forever,
Nu 11:25 s rested upon them, they prophesied.
Ps 31:5 Into your hand I commit my s;
51:17 acceptable to God is a broken s;
Isa 42:1 I have put my s upon him;
Eze 36:26 and a new s I will put within you;
Joel 2:28 I will pour out my s on all flesh;
Mt 1:18 to be with child from the Holy S.
5:3 "Blessed are the poor in s,
26:41 the s indeed is willing, but the flesh
Mk 1:8 will baptize you with the Holy S."
Jn 3:5 without being born of water and S.
4:24 God is s, and those who worship him must worship in s and truth."
14:26 But the Advocate, the Holy S,
Ac 2:4 of them were filled with the Holy S
Ro 8:26 the S helps us in our weakness,
1Co 12:4 are varieties of gifts, but the same S;
2Co 3:6 the letter kills, but the S gives life.
Gal 5:22 the fruit of the S is love, joy, peace,
Eph 1:13 the seal of the promised Holy S;
5:18 but be filled with the S,
1Th 5:19 Do not quench the S.
Heb 4:12 piercing until it divides soul from s,
1Jn 4:1 Beloved, do not believe every s,

SPIRITS → SPIRIT

Lk 4:36 power he commands the unclean s,
Rev 1:4 seven s who are before his throne,

SPIRITUAL → SPIRIT

1Co 2:13 interpreting s things to those who are s.
12:1 Now concerning s gifts,
14:1 Pursue love and strive for the s gifts,
Eph 1:3 every s blessing in the heavenly
1Pe 2:5 yourselves be built into a s house,

SPIT

Mk 14:65 began to s on him, to blindfold him,
Rev 3:16 am about to s you out of my mouth.

SPY → SPIES

Nu 13:2 man to s out the land of Canaan,
Jos 6:25 whom Joshua sent to s out Jericho.

STAFF

Ex 4:4 and it became a s in his hand—
Nu 17:6 the s of Aaron was among theirs.
Ps 23:4 your rod and your s—they comfort me.

STAND → STANDING

Ex 14:13 "Do not be afraid, s firm,
Job 19:25 at the last he will s upon the earth;
Ps 1:5 wicked will not s in the judgment,
Mt 12:25 house divided against itself will s.
Ro 14:10 all s before the judgment seat of God.

STANDING → STAND

1Co 10:12 So if you think you are s,
Rev 3:20 I am s at the door, knocking;

STAR → STARS

Nu 24:17 a s shall come out of Jacob,
Isa 14:12 are fallen from heaven, O Day S,
Mt 2:2 For we observed his s at its rising,
2Pe 1:19 day dawns and the morning s rises
Rev 9:1 I saw a s that had fallen from heaven
22:16 of David, the bright morning s."

STARS → STAR

Ge 1:16 to rule the night—and the s.
Job 38:7 when the morning s sang together
Rev 1:16 In his right hand he held seven s,

STATUE

Da 2:31 there was a great s.

STATUTE → STATUTES

Lev 16:29 This shall be a s to you forever:
Nu 19:21 It shall be a perpetual s for them.

STATUTES → STATUTE

Ge 26:5 commandments, my s, and my laws.
Dt 4:1 give heed to the s and ordinances
Ne 9:13 good s and commandments,
Ps 119:8 I will observe your s;

STEADFAST

Heb 6:19 a sure and s anchor of the soul,
1Pe 5:9 Resist him, s in your faith,

STEAL

Ex 20:15 You shall not s.
Mt 6:19 and where thieves break in and s;

STILL

Ps 46:10 "Be s, and know that I am God!
Mk 4:39 said to the sea, "Peace! Be s!"

STING

1Co 15:55 Where, O death, is your s?"

STONE → CORNERSTONE, MILLSTONE, STONED, STONES

Ex 31:18 tablets of s, written with the finger of
1Sa 17:50 the Philistine with a sling and a s,
Ps 118:22 The s that the builders rejected has
Isa 28:16 in Zion a foundation, a tested s,
Eze 36:26 from your body the heart of s
Mt 4:6 will not dash your foot against a s.'"
Mk 12:10 'The s that the builders rejected has
16:3 "Who will roll away the s for us
Ro 9:32 have stumbled over the stumbling s,
2Co 3:3 not on tablets of s but on tablets

STONED → STONE

Ac 14:19 Then they s Paul and dragged him
Heb 11:37 s to death, they were sawn in two,

STONES → STONE

Mt 3:9 God is able from these s to raise
Lk 19:40 were silent, the s would shout out."
1Co 3:12 precious s, wood, hay, straw—
1Pe 2:5 like living s, let yourselves be built

STRAIGHT

Pr 3:6 and he will make s your paths.
Isa 40:3 s in the desert a highway for our God.
Mt 3:3 way of the Lord, make his paths s.'"
Ac 9:11 Get up and go to the street called S,

STRANGER → STRANGERS

Dt 10:19 You shall also love the s,
Mt 25:35 I was a s and you welcomed me,

STRANGERS → STRANGER

Ro 12:13 extend hospitality to s.
Heb 11:13 They confessed that they were s

STREAMS

Ps 1:3 like trees planted by s of water,
42:1 As a deer longs for flowing s,

STRENGTH → STRONG

Ex 15:2 The LORD is my s and my might,
1Ch 16:11 Seek the LORD and his s,
Ne 8:10 for the joy of the LORD is your s."
Ps 46:1 God is our refuge and s,
Isa 40:31 for the LORD shall renew their s,
Mk 12:30 all your mind, and with all your s.'
Jdt 9:11 your s does not depend on numbers,
1Mc 3:19 but s comes from Heaven.

STRENGTHEN → STRONG

Ps 119:28 s me according to your word.
Heb 12:12 hands and s your weak knees,

STRENGTHENS → STRONG

Php 4:13 do all things through him who s me.

STRIFE

Pr 23:29 Who has sorrow? Who has s?
Ro 1:29 Full of envy, murder, s, deceit,
Gal 5:20 enmities, s, jealousy, anger,

STRIKE

Ge 3:15 he will s your head, and you will s
Ex 17:6 S the rock, and water will come out
Mk 14:27 'I will s the shepherd, and the sheep

STRONG → STRENGTH, STRENGTHEN, STRENGTHENS, STRONGHOLD

Dt 31:6 Be s and bold; have no fear
Jos 1:6 Be s and courageous; for you shall
Ecc 9:11 nor the battle to the s, nor bread to
Ro 15:1 We who are s ought to put up with
1Co 1:27 in the world to shame the s;
2Co 12:10 whenever I am weak, then I am s.
Eph 6:10 be s in the Lord and in the strength

STRONGHOLD → STRONG

Ps 9:9 The LORD is a s for the oppressed,
Na 1:7 a s in a day of trouble;

STUDY

Ezr 7:10 Ezra had set his heart to s the law
Ecc 12:12 much s is a weariness of the flesh.

STUMBLE → STUMBLING

Mt 18:9 And if your eye causes you to s,
Ro 9:33 a stone that will make people s,

STUMBLING → STUMBLE

Mt 16:23 You are a s block to me;
Ro 11:9 a block and a retribution for them;
1Co 8:9 not somehow become a s block to

SUBDUE

Ge 1:28 and fill the earth and s it;

SUBJECT

Ro 13:1 be s to the governing authorities;
Eph 5:21 s to one another out of reverence

SUBMISSION → SUBMIT
1Ti 2:11 a woman learn in silence with full **s.**
Heb 5: 7 was heard because of his reverent **s.**

SUBMISSIVE → SUBMIT
1Ti 3: 4 keeping his children **s** and respectful
Tit 2: 5 kind, being **s** to their husbands,

SUBMIT → SUBMISSION, SUBMISSIVE
Heb 13:17 Obey your leaders and **s** to them,

SUCCEED → SUCCESSFUL
Pr 15:22 but with many advisers they **s.**
Ecc 10:10 but wisdom helps one to **s.**

SUCCESSFUL → SUCCEED
Jos 1: 7 that you may be **s** wherever you go.

SUDDENLY
Mal 3: 1 Lord whom you seek will **s** come to
Mk 13:36 find you asleep when he comes **s.**

SUFFER → SUFFERED, SUFFERING, SUFFERINGS
Lk 22:15 this Passover with you before I **s;**
24:46 the Messiah is to **s** and to rise from
Heb 9:26 then he would have had to **s** again

SUFFERED → SUFFER
1Pe 2:21 because Christ also **s** for you,

SUFFERING → SUFFER
Isa 53: 3 a man of **s** and acquainted with
Mk 8:31 Son of Man must undergo great **s,**

SUFFERINGS → SUFFER
Ro 8:18 the **s** of this present time are not

SUFFICIENT
2Co 12: 9 "My grace is **s** for you,

SULFUR
Ge 19:24 rained on Sodom and Gomorrah **s**
Ps 11: 6 he will rain coals of fire and **s;**
Rev 21: 8 in the lake that burns with fire and **s,**

SUN
Jos 10:13 And the **s** stood still,
Ecc 1: 9 there is nothing new under the **s.**
Mt 5:45 he makes his **s** rise on the evil and
Rev 22: 5 they need no light of lamp or **s,**

SUPPER
Lk 22:20 he did the same with the cup after **s,**
Rev 19: 9 to the marriage **s** of the Lamb."

SUPPLICATION → SUPPLICATIONS
Eph 6:18 at all times in every prayer and **s.**

SUPPLICATIONS → SUPPLICATION
1Ti 2: 1 then, I urge that **s,** prayers,
Heb 5: 7 Jesus offered up prayers and **s,**

SURPASSES
Eph 3:19 the love of Christ that **s** knowledge,
Php 4: 7 the peace of God, which **s** all

SUSTAINS
Ps 3: 5 for the LORD **s** me.
Heb 1: 3 he **s** all things by his powerful word.

SWALLOW → SWALLOWED
Jnh 1:17 provided a large fish to **s** up Jonah;

Mt 23:24 You strain out a gnat but **s** a camel!

SWALLOWED → SWALLOW
1Co 15:54 "Death has been **s** up in victory."

SWEAR
Dt 10:20 and by his name you shall **s.**
Ps 24: 4 and do not **s** deceitfully.
Mt 5:34 Do not **s** at all, either by heaven,

SWEAT
Ge 3:19 By the **s** of your face you shall eat
Lk 22:44 ₁**s** became like great drops of blood*f*

SWINE
Mt 7: 6 do not throw your pearls before **s,**
1Mc 1:47 sacrifice **s** and other unclean animals,

SWORD → SWORDS
Ge 3:24 and a **s** flaming and turning to guard
Mt 10:34 not come to bring peace, but a **s.**
Eph 6:17 the **s** of the Spirit, which is the word
Heb 4:12 sharper than any two-edged **s,**
Rev 1:16 mouth came a sharp, two-edged **s,**
Sir 21: 3 All lawlessness is like a two-edged **s**

SWORDS → SWORD
Isa 2: 4 shall beat their **s** into plowshares,
Joel 3:10 Beat your plowshares into **s,**

SYMPATHIZE → SYMPATHY
Heb 4:15 unable to **s** with our weaknesses,

SYMPATHY → SYMPATHIZE
Php 2: 1 any compassion and **s,**
1Pe 3: 8 all of you, have unity of spirit, **s,**

SYNAGOGUE → SYNAGOGUES
Lk 4:16 he went to the **s** on the sabbath day,
Ac 18:26 He began to speak boldly in the **s;**

SYNAGOGUES → SYNAGOGUE
Mt 4:23 teaching in their **s** and proclaiming
Jn 18:20 always taught in **s** and in the temple,

T

TABERNACLE
Ex 25: 9 concerning the pattern of the **t**
40:34 the glory of the LORD filled the **t.**
1Ch 6:48 for all the service of the **t** of the house

TABLE → TABLES
Ex 25:23 You shall make a **t** of acacia wood,
Ps 23: 5 a **t** before me in the presence of my

TABLES → TABLE
Mk 11:15 overturned the **t** of the money changers

TABLETS
Ex 31:18 gave him the two **t** of the covenant,
2Co 3: 3 not on **t** of stone but on **t** of human hearts.

TALENT
Mt 25:25 and hid your **t** in the ground.

TAX → TAXES
Mt 11:19 a friend of **t** collectors and sinners!'
Lk 18:10 Pharisee and the other a **t** collector.

TAXES → TAX
Mt 22:17 Is it lawful to pay **t** to the emperor,
Ro 13: 7 **t** to whom **t** are due,

TEACH → TEACHER, TEACHERS, TEACHING
Dt 6: 1 to **t** you to observe in the land that
Jer 31:34 No longer shall they **t** one another,
Col 3:16 **t** and admonish one another in all
1Jn 2:27 so you do not need anyone to **t** you.

TEACHER → TEACH
Ecc 1: 1 words of the **T,** the son of David,
Jn 1:38 "Rabbi" (which translated means **T)**

TEACHERS → TEACH
Ps 119:99 more understanding than all my **t,**
1Co 12:28 second prophets, third **t;**
Eph 4:11 evangelists, some pastors and **t,**
Jas 3: 1 Not many of you should become **t,**

TEACHING → TEACH
Mk 1:27 A new **t**—with authority!

TEAR
Rev 7:17 God will wipe away every **t** from

TEETH → TOOTH
Mt 8:12 will be weeping and gnashing of **t."**

TEMPLE
2Ch 2:12 who will build a **t** for the LORD,
Mt 4: 5 placed him on the pinnacle of the **t,**
12: 6 something greater than the **t** is here.
1Co 3:16 you are God's **t** and God's Spirit
Eph 2:21 and grows into a holy **t** in the Lord;
Rev 21:22 its **t** is the Lord God the Almighty and
1Mc 4:48 sanctuary and the interior of the **t,**

TEMPTATION → TEMPTED
1Ti 6: 9 who want to be rich into **t** and
Jas 1:12 Blessed is anyone who endures **t.**

TEMPTED → TEMPTATION
Mk 1:13 wilderness forty days, **t** by Satan;
Gal 6: 1 care that you yourselves are not **t.**

TEN
Ex 34:28 the covenant, the **t** commandments.

TENT
Ex 27:21 the **t** of meeting, outside the curtain
2Co 5: 1 the earthly **t** we live in, is destroyed,

TEST → TESTED, TESTING
Dt 6:16 put the LORD your God to the **t,**
Lk 4:12 not put the Lord your God to the **t.'**
10:25 then a lawyer stood up to **t** Jesus.
2Co 13: 5 indeed, you fail to meet the **t!**
1Jn 4: 1 **t** the spirits to see whether they are
Sir 37:27 My child, **t** yourself while you live;

TESTED → TEST
Ge 22: 1 After these things God **t** Abraham.
Ps 78:41 They **t** God again and again,
Heb 4:15 been **t** as we are, yet without sin.

TESTIMONY
Mk 14:59 on this point their **t** did not agree.
Rev 1: 9 the word of God and the **t** of Jesus.

TESTING → TEST
1Co 10:13 No t has overtaken you that is not
Jas 1: 3 t of your faith produces endurance;

THANK → THANKS,
  THANKSGIVING
2Ch 29:31 bring sacrifices and t offerings to
Ps 52: 9 I will t you forever,
Sir 35: 4 gives alms sacrifices a t offering.

THANKS → THANK
1Co 11:24 and when he had given t,

THANKSGIVING → THANK
Ps 50:14 Offer to God a sacrifice of t,
Php 4: 6 with t let your requests be made
            known
Rev 7:12 glory and wisdom and t and honor

THIEF → THIEVES
Ex 22: 1 The t shall make restitution,
Jn 10:10 The t comes only to steal and kill
1Th 5: 2 day of the Lord will come like a t in
Rev 16:15 ("See, I am coming like a t!

THIEVES → THIEF
Mt 6:19 and where t break in and steal;

THINK → THOUGHTS
Ro 12: 3 not to t of yourself more highly than
1Co 10:12 So if you t you are standing,

THIRD → THREE
Mt 26:44 and prayed for the t time,
Lk 18:33 and on the t day he will rise again."

THIRST → THIRSTY
Mt 5: 6 who hunger and t for righteousness,
Rev 7:16 will hunger no more, and t no more;

THIRSTY → THIRST
Mt 25:35 I was t and you gave me something
Jn 6:35 believes in me will never be t.
Rev 22:17 And let everyone who is t come.

THORN → THORNS
2Co 12: 7 a t was given me in the flesh,

THORNS → THORN
Jn 19: 2 the soldiers wove a crown of t and

THOUGHTS → THINK
Isa 55: 8 For my t are not your t,
1Co 3:20 "The Lord knows the t of the wise,
Heb 4:12 judge the t and intentions of the
            heart.

THOUSAND
Ps 90: 4 t years in your sight are like yesterday
2Pe 3: 8 one day is like a t years, and a t years
Rev 20: 4 and reigned with Christ a t years.

THREE → THIRD
Mt 18:20 two or t are gathered in my name,
      26:34 you will deny me t times."
Mk 8:31 be killed, and after t days rise again.
2Co 12: 8 T times I appealed to the Lord
1Jn 5: 7 There are t that testify:

THRONE
Ps 45: 6 Your t, O God, endures forever
Isa 6: 1 I saw the Lord sitting on a t, high
Mt 19:28 the Son of Man is seated on the t

Heb 4:16 approach the t of grace with
            boldness,
Rev 4:10 they cast their crowns before the t,
      20:11 I saw a great white t and the one

THUMMIM
Ex 28:30 you shall put the Urim and the T,

THUNDER
Ex 9:23 and the LORD sent t and hail,
Rev 4: 5 and rumblings and peals of t,

TIME → TIMES
Est 4:14 dignity for just such a t as this."
Ecc 3: 1 a t for every matter under heaven:
Da 7:25 for a t, two times, and half a t.
Ro 5: 6 the right t Christ died for the ungodly.
2Co 6: 2 See, now is the acceptable t;
Gal 4: 4 when the fullness of t had come,
Rev 12:14 for a t, and times, and half a t.

TIMES → TIME
Mt 16: 3 cannot interpret the signs of the t.
      18:22 seven t, but, I tell you, seventy-
            seven t.
Mk 14:30 you will deny me three t."
Sir 20:12 but pay for it seven t over.

TITHE
Dt 12:17 the t of your grain, your wine, and
Mal 3:10 Bring the full t into the storehouse,

TODAY
Ps 2: 7 my son; t I have begotten you.
Heb 1: 5 my Son; t I have begotten you"?
      13: 8 Christ is the same yesterday and t

TOMB
Mk 15:46 laid it in a t that had been hewn out
Lk 24: 2 the stone rolled away from the t,

TOMORROW
Mt 6:34 "So do not worry about t,
Jas 4:14 do not even know what t will bring.

TONGUE → TONGUES
Isa 45:23 shall bow, every t shall swear."
Php 2:11 every t should confess that Jesus
            Christ

TONGUES → TONGUE
Ac 2: 3 Divided t, as of fire, appeared
1Co 12:10 t, to another the interpretation of t.

TOOTH → TEETH
Ex 21:24 t for t, hand for hand, foot for foot,
Mt 5:38 'An eye for an eye and a t for a t.'

TOWER
Ge 11: 4 and a t with its top in the heavens,
Pr 18:10 The name of the LORD is a strong t;

TRADITION
Mt 15: 2 disciples break the t of the elders?
Col 2: 8 empty deceit, according to human t,

TRAIN → TRAINING
Pr 22: 6 T children in the right way, and
1Ti 4: 7 T yourself in godliness,

TRAINING → TRAIN
1Ti 4: 8 while physical t is of some value,
2Ti 3:16 and for t in righteousness,

TRAITOR
Lk 6:16 and Judas Iscariot, who became a t.

TRANSFIGURED
Mt 17: 2 And he was t before them,

TRANSFORM → TRANSFORMED
Php 3:21 will t the body of our humiliation

TRANSFORMED → TRANSFORM
Ro 12: 2 be t by the renewing of your minds,
2Co 3:18 are being t into the same image

TRANSGRESSION →
  TRANSGRESSIONS
Ex 23:21 for he will not pardon your t;
Da 9:24 to finish the t, to put an end to sin,

TRANSGRESSIONS →
  TRANSGRESSION
Ps 103:12 so far he removes our t from us.
Isa 53: 5 But he was wounded for our t,

TREASURE → TREASURES
Mt 6:21 where your t is, there your heart
2Co 4: 7 But we have this t in clay jars,
2Ti 1:14 Guard the good t entrusted to you,

TREASURES → TREASURE
Col 2: 3 are hidden all the t of wisdom

TREE
Ge 3:24 to guard the way to the t of life.
Mt 12:33 for the t is known by its fruit.
Rev 22: 2 the t of life with its twelve kinds

TREMBLING
Ps 2:11 Serve the LORD with fear, with t
Php 2:12 your own salvation with fear and t;

TRESPASS → TRESPASSES
Ro 5:15 But the free gift is not like the t.

TRESPASSES → TRESPASS
Mt 6:14 For if you forgive others their t,
2Co 5:19 not counting their t against them,

TRIAL → TRIALS
Lk 11: 4 do not bring us to the time of t."
2Pe 2: 9 knows how to rescue the godly
            from t,
Rev 3:10 I will keep you from the hour of t

TRIALS → TRIAL
Jas 1: 2 whenever you face t of any kind,
1Pe 1: 6 you have had to suffer various t,

TRIBES
Ge 49:28 All these are the twelve t of Israel,
Ex 24: 4 to the twelve t of Israel.
Mt 19:28 judging the twelve t of Israel.
Rev 21:12 inscribed the names of the twelve t

TRIUMPHAL → TRIUMPHS
2Co 2:14 Christ always leads us in t procession.

TRIUMPHS → TRIUMPHAL
Jas 2:13 mercy t over judgment.

TROUBLE → TROUBLED
Ps 9: 9 a stronghold in times of t.
Pr 11: 8 The righteous are delivered from t,
Isa 33: 2 our salvation in the time of t.

Mt   6:34 Today's **t** is enough for today.

TROUBLED → TROUBLE

Jn 14: 1 "Do not let your hearts be **t**.

TRUE → TRUTH

Ps 119:151 and all your commandments are **t**.
Jn   1: 9 The **t** light, which enlightens
1Jn 5:20 He is the **t** God and eternal life.
Rev 3:14 the Amen, the faithful and **t** witness,
     19:11 Its rider is called Faithful and **T,**

TRUMPET

1Co 15:52 twinkling of an eye, at the last **t**.
1Th 4:16 and with the sound of God's **t,**

TRUST → ENTRUSTED, TRUSTED, TRUSTWORTHY

Ps 37: 3 **T** in the LORD, and do good;
Pr   3: 5 **T** in the LORD with all your heart,
Sir 2: 6 **T** in him, and he will help you;

TRUSTED → TRUST

Da   3:28 delivered his servants who **t** in him.
     6:23 because he had **t** in his God.
Sus 1:35 for her heart **t** in the Lord.

TRUSTWORTHY → TRUST

Ps 111: 7 and just; all his precepts are **t**.
Rev 22: 6 "These words are **t** and true,
1Mc 14:41 until a **t** prophet should arise,

TRUTH → TRUE

Pr 23:23 Buy **t,** and do not sell it;
Jn   1:17 grace and **t** came through Jesus Christ.
     4:23 worship the Father in spirit and **t,**
     8:32 and the **t** will make you free."
     14: 6 "I am the way, and the **t,** and the life.
     14:17 This is the Spirit of **t,**
Eph 4:15 But speaking the **t** in love,
2Ti 2:15 rightly explaining the word of **t**.
Tob 3: 2 all your ways are mercy and **t;**

TURNED → TURN

Isa 53: 6 we have all **t** to our own way,
Ro   3:12 All have **t** aside, together they have

TWELVE

Ge 49:28 All these are the **t** tribes of Israel,
Mt 10: 1 Jesus summoned his **t** disciples
Lk   9:17 **t** baskets of broken pieces.
Rev 21:12 inscribed the names of the **t** tribes
     22: 2 tree of life with its **t** kinds of fruit,

TWINKLING

1Co 15:52 in the **t** of an eye, at the last trumpet

TWO → TWICE, TWO-EDGED

Ge   1:16 God made the **t** great lights—
     6:19 bring **t** of every kind into the ark,
Ex 31:18 the **t** tablets of the covenant,
Dt 17: 6 of **t** or three witnesses the death
Mt   6:24 "No one can serve **t** masters;
     19: 5 and the **t** shall become one flesh'?

TWO-EDGED → TWO

Heb 4:12 sharper than any **t** sword,
Rev 1:16 his mouth came a sharp, **t** sword,

U

UNBELIEF → UNBELIEVER, UNBELIEVERS

Mk   6: 6 And he was amazed at their **u**.
     9:24 cried out, "I believe; help my **u!**"

UNBELIEVER → UNBELIEF

1Co 10:27 If an **u** invites you to a meal and
2Co 6:15 does a believer share with an **u?**

UNBELIEVERS → UNBELIEF

2Co 6:14 Do not be mismatched with **u**.
2Es 15: 4 all **u** shall die in their unbelief.

UNCIRCUMCISED → UNCIRCUMCISION

Ac   7:51 people, **u** in heart and ears,
Ro   4:11 he had by faith while he was still **u**.
Col 3:11 circumcised and **u,** barbarian,

UNCIRCUMCISION → UNCIRCUMCISED

1Co 7:19 Circumcision is nothing, and **u** is
Gal 5: 6 neither circumcision nor **u** counts

UNCLEAN → UNCLEANNESS

Lev 5: 2 when any of you touch any **u** thing
Isa 52:11 Touch no **u** thing;
Mk   3:11 Whenever the **u** spirits saw him,
Rev 21:27 But nothing **u** will enter it,

UNDERSTAND → UNDERSTANDING

Lk 24:45 opened their minds to **u** the scriptures,
Eph 5:17 but **u** what the will of the Lord is.

UNDERSTANDING → UNDERSTAND

Ex 36: 1 has given skill and **u** to know how
Pr   2: 6 from his mouth come knowledge and **u**
Lk   2:47 heard him were amazed at his **u**
Php 4: 7 peace of God, which surpasses all **u,**

UNGODLY

Ro   5: 6 the right time Christ died for the **u**.
2Pe 2: 6 example of what is coming to the **u;**

UNITY

Ps 133: 1 when kindred live together in **u!**
Eph 4: 3 to maintain the **u** of the Spirit

UNJUST

Ro   3: 5 That God is **u** to inflict wrath on us?
Heb 6:10 For God is not **u;** he will

UNLEAVENED

Ex 12:17 shall observe the festival of **u** bread,
Mt 26:17 first day of **U** Bread the disciples

UNRIGHTEOUS → UNRIGHTEOUSNESS

Mt   5:45 rain on the righteous and on the **u**.
2Pe 2: 9 **u** under punishment until the day

UNRIGHTEOUSNESS → UNRIGHTEOUS

Ps 92:15 and there is no **u** in him.
1Jn 1: 9 and cleanse us from all **u**.

URIM

Ex 28:30 of judgment you shall put the **U**

USEFUL

2Ti 3:16 scripture is inspired by God and is **u**

V

VAIN → VANITY

Ps   2: 1 and the peoples plot in **v?**
Mt 15: 9 in **v** do they worship me,
Php 2:16 that I did not run in **v** or labor in **v**.

VALLEY

Ps 23: 4 through the darkest **v,** I fear no evil;

VANITY → VAIN

Ecc 1: 2 **v** of vanities! All is **v**.

VEIL

Ex 34:33 he put a **v** on his face;
2Co 3:15 a **v** lies over their minds;

VENGEANCE → AVENGE, AVENGER, AVENGING

Ps 94: 1 O LORD, you God of **v,**
Isa 34: 8 For the LORD has a day of **v,**
Na   1: 2 the LORD takes **v** on his adversaries

VICTORY

Pr 21:31 but the **v** belongs to the LORD.
1Co 15:54 Death has been swallowed up in **v**."

VINE → VINEYARD

Jn 15: 1 "I am the true **v,** and my Father is

VINEYARD → VINE

Isa 5: 1 had a **v** on a very fertile hill.
Mt 21:33 a landowner who planted a **v,**

VIOLENCE

Ge   6:11 and the earth was filled with **v**.
Isa 53: 9 although he had done no **v,**
Hab 2:17 because of human bloodshed and **v**

VIRGIN

Mt   1:23 the **v** shall conceive and bear a son,
Lk   1:34 "How can this be, since I am a **v?**"

VISION → VISIONS

Isa 22: 1 oracle concerning the valley of **v**.
Da   8:26 As for you, seal up the **v,**

VISIONS → VISION

Nu 12: 6 make myself known to them in **v;**
Eze 1: 1 were opened, and I saw **v** of God.
Da   1:17 Daniel also had insight into all **v**
Joel 2:28 and your young men shall see **v**.
Ac   2:17 and your young men shall see **v,**

VOICE

Heb 3: 7 says, "Today, if you hear his **v,**
Rev 3:20 if you hear my **v** and open the door,

VOID

Ge   1: 2 the earth was a formless **v**

VOW

Ecc 5: 4 Fulfill what you **v**.
Sir 18:23 Before making a **v,** prepare yourself

W

WAGES
Ro   6:23 For the **w** of sin is death,

WAIT
Ps   27:14 **W** for the LORD; be strong,
1Th   1:10 to **w** for his Son from heaven,
Sir   2: 7 fear the Lord, **w** for his mercy;

WALK
Dt   10:12 to **w** in all his ways, to love him,
Ps   23: 4 I **w** through the darkest valley,
Isa   40:31 they shall **w** and not faint.
2Co   5: 7 for we **w** by faith, not by sight.

WALL
Jos   6:20 shout, and the **w** fell down flat;
Ne   2:17 let us rebuild the **w** of Jerusalem,
Eph   2:14 has broken down the dividing **w**,

WANT
Ps   23: 1 LORD is my shepherd, I shall not **w**.

WAR → WARRIOR, WARS
Ecc   3: 8 a time for **w**, and a time for peace.

WARRIOR → WAR
Ex   15: 3 LORD is a **w**; the LORD

WARS → WAR
Mt   24: 6 you will hear of **w** and rumors of **w**;

WASH
Ps   51: 7 **w** me, and I shall be whiter than
             snow.
Jn   13: 5 and began to **w** the disciples' feet

WATER → WATERS
Jer   2:13 the fountain of living **w**,
Eze   36:25 I will sprinkle clean **w** upon you,
Mk   1: 8 I have baptized you with **w**;
Jn   2: 9 tasted the **w** that had become wine,
             3: 5 without being born of **w** and Spirit.
             4:10 he would have given you living **w**."
1Jn   5: 6 the one who came by **w** and blood,
Rev   22: 1 showed me the river of the **w** of life,

WATERS → WATER
Ge   7: 7 the ark to escape the **w** of the flood.
Isa   55: 1 who thirsts, come to the **w**;

WAY → WAYS
Ps   1: 6 watches over the **w** of the righteous,
Pr   22: 6 Train children in the right **w**,
Mt   3: 3 'Prepare the **w** of the Lord,
Jn   14: 6 "I am the **w**, and the truth, and the
             life.
1Co   12:31 show you a still more excellent **w**.
Heb   10:20 the new and living **w** that he opened

WAYS → WAY
Dt   10:12 to walk in all his **w**, to love him,
Sir   2:15 who love him keep his **w**.

WEAK → WEAKNESS, WEAKNESSES
Mt   26:41 indeed is willing, but the flesh is **w**."
1Co   1:27 God chose what is **w** in the world
2Co   12:10 whenever I am **w**, then I am strong.

WEAKNESS → WEAK
Ro   8:26 the Spirit helps us in our **w**;

WEAKNESSES → WEAK
Heb   4:15 to sympathize with our **w**,

WEALTH
Rev   5:12 receive power and **w** and wisdom
Sir   5: 1 Do not rely on your **w**,

WEARY
Isa   40:31 they shall run and not be **w**,
Heb   12: 3 you may not grow **w** or lose heart.

WEDDING
Jn   2: 1 there was a **w** in Cana of Galilee,

WEEKS
Ex   34:22 You shall observe the festival of **w**,
Lev   23:15 you shall count off seven **w**;

WEEP → WEEPING
Ecc   3: 4 a time to **w**, and a time to laugh;
Ro   12:15 **w** with those who **w**.

WEEPING → WEEP
Ps   30: 5 **W** may linger for the night,
Mt   8:12 will be **w** and gnashing of teeth."

WELL
Dt   6: 3 so that it may go **w** with you,
Mt   3:17 with whom I am **w** pleased."
             17: 5 I am **w** pleased; listen to him!"
2Pe   1:17 with whom I am **w** pleased."

WICKED → WICKEDNESS
Ps   1: 5 the **w** will not stand in the judgment,
Isa   48:22 no peace," says the LORD, "for
             the **w**."
Eze   18:23 any pleasure in the death of the **w**,

WICKEDNESS → WICKED
Ps   45: 7 you love righteousness and hate **w**.
Lk   11:39 inside you are full of greed and **w**.

WIDOW → WIDOWS
Ex   22:22 shall not abuse any **w** or orphan.
Ps   146: 9 he upholds the orphan and the **w**,
1Ti   5: 4 If a **w** has children or grandchildren,

WIDOWS → WIDOW
1Ti   5: 3 Honor **w** who are really **w**.
Jas   1:27 to care for orphans and **w** in their

WIFE → WIVES
Ge   2:24 and his mother and clings to his **w**,
Ex   20:17 shall not covet your neighbor's **w**,
Pr   18:22 who finds a **w** finds a good thing,
Mt   5:32 that anyone who divorces his **w**,
Eph   5:28 He who loves **w** loves himself.
Rev   21: 9 the bride, the **w** of the Lamb."
Tob   8: 6 his **w** Eve as a helper and support.
Sir   26: 3 A good **w** is a great blessing;

WILDERNESS
Isa   40: 3 the **w** prepare the way of the LORD,
Mt   3: 3 voice of one crying out in the **w**:

WILL → WILLING
Ps   40: 8 I delight to do your **w**, O my God;
Mt   6:10 Your **w** be done, on earth as it is in
Lk   22:42 yet, not my **w** but yours be done."
Jn   4:34 "My food is to do the **w** of him who
Eph   6: 6 doing the **w** of God from the heart.
1Jo   5:14 if we ask anything according to his **w**,

WILLING → WILL
Mt   26:41 spirit indeed is **w**, but the flesh is
             weak.
Lk   22:42 if you are **w**, remove this cup from

WIND
Ecc   1:14 all is vanity and a chasing after **w**.
Jn   3: 8 The **w** blows where it chooses,
Ac   2: 2 a sound like the rush of a violent **w**,

WINE
Mt   9:17 is new **w** put into old wineskins;
Jn   2: 9 tasted the water that had become **w**,
Eph   5:18 Do not get drunk with **w**, for that is

WINGS
Ex   19: 4 and how I bore you on eagles' **w**,
Ps   17: 8 hide me in the shadow of your **w**,
Mal   4: 2 shall rise, with healing in its **w**.
Lk   13:34 hen gathers her brood under her **w**,

WIPE
Isa   25: 8 GOD will **w** away the tears from all
Rev   21: 4 he will **w** every tear from their eyes.

WISDOM → WISE
1Ki   4:29 God gave Solomon very great **w**,
Pr   1:20 **W** cries out in the street;
             9:10 fear of the LORD is the beginning
                   of **w**,
Jer   9:23 Do not let the wise boast in their **w**,
Mt   13:54 this man get this **w** and these deeds
Lk   2:52 Jesus increased in **w** and in years,
Ro   11:33 the depth of the riches and of **w** and
1Co   1:19 "I will destroy the **w** of the wise,
Col   2: 3 whom are hidden all the treasures
                   of **w**
Jas   3:17 But the **w** from above is first pure,
Rev   5:12 wealth and **w** and might and honor
Wis   6:12 **W** is radiant and unfading,
Sir   1: 1 All **w** is from the Lord,
             24: 1 THE PRAISE OF **W**

WISE → WISDOM
Ps   19: 7 are sure, making **w** the simple;
Pr   3: 7 Do not be **w** in your own eyes;
Da   12: 3 are **w** shall shine like the brightness
1Co   1:26 not many of you were **w** by human
Eph   5:15 not as unwise people but as **w**;

WITHER → WITHERS
Ps   1: 3 and their leaves do not **w**.
Eze   47:12 Their leaves will not **w** nor their

WITHERS → WITHER
Jn   15: 6 is thrown away like a branch and **w**;
1Pe   1:24 The grass **w**, and the flower falls,

WITNESS → EYEWITNESSES,
             WITNESSES
Dt   19:15 single **w** shall not suffice to convict
Rev   1: 5 faithful **w**, the firstborn of the dead,

WITNESSES → WITNESS
Mt   26:60 though many false **w** came forward.
Heb   12: 1 surrounded by so great a cloud of **w**,
Rev   11: 3 my two **w** authority to prophesy

WIVES → WIFE
Eph   5:22 **W**, be subject to your husbands as
1Pe   3: 1 **W**, in the same way, accept the

WOMAN → WOMEN
Ge   2:22 he made into a **w** and brought her to
      3:15 enmity between you and the **w**,
Ps 113: 9 He gives the barren a **w** a home,
Pr 11:16 A gracious **w** gets honor,
    31:30 **w** who fears the LORD is to be
          praised.
Rev 12: 1 a **w** clothed with the sun,
Jdt 16: 5 foiled them by the hand of a **w**.

WOMEN → WOMAN
Lk   1:42 "Blessed are you among **w**,
   23:55 **w** who had come with him from
1Pe 3: 5 that the holy **w** who hoped in God

WONDERFUL → WONDERS
Ge 18:14 Is anything too **w** for the LORD?
Isa 9: 6 named **W** Counselor, Mighty God,

WONDERS → WONDERFUL
Ex 3:20 and strike Egypt with all my **w** that
Ps 136: 4 who alone does great **w**,
Jn   4:48 signs and **w** you will not believe."
2Th 2: 9 who uses all power, signs, lying **w**,

WORD → BYWORD, WORDS
Dt 30:14 No, the **w** is very near to you;
Ps 119:105 Your **w** is a lamp to my feet and
Pr 30: 5 Every **w** of God proves true;
Isa 40: 8 the **w** of our God will stand forever.
Jn   1: 1 In the beginning was the **W**, and
          the **W** was with God, and the **W** was
          God.
     1:14 the **W** became flesh and lived among
2Ti 2:15 rightly explaining the **w** of truth.
Jas 1:22 But be doers of the **w**,
Rev 19:13 his name is called The **W** of God.

WORDS → WORD
Ex 20: 1 Then God spoke all these **w**:
Dt 11:18 put these **w** of mine in your heart
Mt 24:35 but my **w** will not pass away.

WORK → WORKS
Ge 2: 2 the seventh day God finished the **w**
Ex 20:10 you shall not do any **w**—
Php 2:12 **w** out your own salvation with fear
2Ti 3:17 equipped for every good **w**.

WORKS → WORK
Gal 2:16 and not by doing the **w** of the law,
    5:19 the **w** of the flesh are obvious:
Eph 2: 9 not the result of **w**, so that no one
          may
1Ti 6:18 to do good, to be rich in good **w**,

WORLD
Mt 5:14 "You are the light of the **w**.
   16:26 gain the whole **w** but forfeit their life?

Jn   1:10 yet the **w** did not know him.
    3:16 loved the **w** that he gave his only Son,
    8:12 saying, "I am the light of the **w**.
1Jn 2:15 not love the **w** or the things in the **w**.
Rev 11:15 kingdom of the **w** has become the

WORRY
Mt 6:25 do not **w** about your life,
   10:19 not **w** about how you are to speak

WORSHIP
Ex 20: 5 not bow down to them or **w** them;
Ps 100: 2 **W** the LORD with gladness;
Mt 4: 9 if you will fall down and **w** me."
Jn   4:24 who **w** him must **w** in spirit and
          truth."
Ro 12: 1 which is your spiritual **w**.

WORTHY
2Sa 22: 4 LORD, who is **w** to be praised;
Eph 4: 1 to lead a life **w** of the calling
Rev 4:11 "You are **w**, our Lord and God,
    5:12 **W** is the Lamb that was slaughtered

WOUNDS
1Pe 2:24 by his **w** you have been healed.

WRAPPED
Mk 15:46 the body, **w** it in the linen cloth,
Lk   2: 7 **w** him in bands of cloth,

WRATH
Nu 16:46 For **w** has gone out from the LORD;
Ps   2: 5 Then he will speak to them in his **w**,
Pr 15: 1 A soft answer turns away **w**,
Zep 1:15 That day will be a day of **w**,
Mt 3: 7 you to flee from the **w** to come?
Ro 1:18 **w** of God is revealed from heaven
1Th 1:10 rescues us from the **w** that is coming
Rev 6:17 the great day of their **w** has come,
Sir 16:11 For mercy and **w** are with the Lord;

WRITE → WRITING, WRITTEN, WROTE
Ex 34:27 LORD said to Moses: **W** these words;
Dt 6: 9 **w** them on the doorposts of your
          house
Pr 7: 3 **w** them on the tablet of your heart.
Jer 31:33 and I will **w** it on their hearts;
Heb 8:10 and **w** them on their hearts,

WRITING → WRITE
Ex 32:16 and the **w** was the **w** of God,
2Es 14:24 prepare for yourself many **w** tablets,

WRITTEN → WRITE
Lk 24:44 everything **w** about me in the law
Jn 21:25 if every one of them were **w** down,
Rev 21:27 are **w** in the Lamb's book of life.

2Es 14:44 forty days, ninety-four books were **w**.

WRONG → WRONGED
Lk 23:41 but this man has done nothing **w**."
Ac 23: 9 "We find nothing **w** with this man.

WRONGED → WRONG
1Co 6: 7 Why not rather be **w**?

WROTE → WRITE
Ex 24: 4 And Moses **w** down all the words

Y

YEAR → YEARS
Ex 23:14 Three times in the **y** you shall hold a
Heb 10: 1 continually offered **y** after **y**,

YEARS → YEAR
Ps 90: 4 For a thousand **y** in your sight are like
Jer 25:12 Then after seventy **y** are completed,
Da 9: 2 of Jerusalem, namely, seventy **y**.
2Pe 3: 8 the Lord one day is like a thousand **y**,
Rev 20: 2 and bound him for a thousand **y**,

YEAST
Mt 16: 6 beware of the **y** of the Pharisees and
Gal 5: 9 A little **y** leavens the whole batch of

YESTERDAY
Heb 13: 8 Jesus Christ is the same **y** and today

YOKE
Mt 11:30 my **y** is easy, and my burden is light."

YOUTH → YOUNG
Ecc 12: 1 Remember your creator in the days
          of your **y**,

Z

ZEAL
Ps 69: 9 **z** for your house that has consumed
          me
Jn   2:17 "**Z** for your house will consume me.
Ro 10: 2 testify that they have a **z** for God,
1Mc 2:26 Thus he burned with **z** for the law;

ZION
2Sa 5: 7 David took the stronghold of **Z**,
Ps   2: 6 I have set my king on **Z**, my holy hill.
Isa 28:16 I am laying in **Z** a foundation stone,
Mic 4: 2 For out of **Z** shall go forth
          instruction,
Zec 9: 9 Rejoice greatly, O daughter **Z**!
Mt 21: 5 "Tell the daughter of **Z**,
Ro 11:26 "Out of **Z** will come the Deliverer;
1Pe 2: 6 "See, I am laying in **Z** a stone,
Rev 14: 1 the Lamb, standing on Mount **Z**!